Dictionary of Moral Theology

DICTIONARY OF
MORAL THEOLOGY

COMPILED UNDER THE DIRECTION OF

FRANCESCO CARDINAL ROBERTI
Prefect of the Supreme Tribunal of the Apostolic Signature

EDITED UNDER THE DIRECTION OF

MONSIGNOR PIETRO PALAZZINI
Secretary of the Sacred Congregation of the Council

*Translated from the Second Italian Edition
Under the Direction of*

HENRY J. YANNONE, S.T.L.

LONDON
BURNS & OATES
PUBLISHERS TO THE HOLY SEE

This is a translation of the second edition of
Dizionario di Teologia Morale published in 1957
by Editrice Studium, Rome, Italy.

Nihil obstat: EDWARD A. CERNY, S.S., S.T.D.
Censor Librorum

Imprimatur: LAWRENCE J. SHEHAN, D.D.
Archbishop of Baltimore

April 15, 1962

FIRST ENGLISH EDITION

List of Contributors

Bar. — MSGR. VITTORIO BARTOCCETTI, Secretary of the Supreme Tribunal of the Apostolic Signature, former Professor of Missiology, Pontifical *Athenaeum de Propaganda Fide*, Rome.

Baro. — PROF. AUGUSTO BARONI, University Professor, President of the Superior Council of the Society of St. Vincent de Paul, Bologna.

Bau. — STEFANO BAUSANI, Commerce specialist, Rome.

Ben. — FR. LUDOVICO BENDER, O. P., Professor of Canon Law, Pontifical *Athenaeum Angelicum*, Rome.

Bic. — MSGR. GIUSEPPE BICCHIERAI, Pres. of *Caritas Ambrosiana*, Milan.

Bog. — PROF. ANTONIO BOGGIANO-PICO, Italian Senator, former Professor of Constitutional Law, University of Genoa, Genoa, Italy.

Boga. — PROF. ELEUTERIO BOGANELLI, Prof. of Psychotechnique, University of Rome; of Pastoral Medicine, *Pont. Institutum Pastorale*, *Pont. Univ. Lateranense*, Rome.

Bos. — FR. AURELIO BOSCHINI, Central Vice-Asst. of Christian Associations of Italian Workers (A.C. L.I.), Rome.

Boz. — FR. GIUSEPPE BOZZETTI, I. C., former Superior General of the Institute of Charity (*Rosminiani*). (†)

Bu. — FR. ANNIBALE BUGNINI, C.M. Professor of Liturgy, *Pont. Univ. Lateranense*, and *Athenaeum Urbanianum de Propaganda Fide*, and *Pont. Institutum De Musica Sacra*, Rome.

Cig. — DOM BERNARDO CIGNITTI, O.S.B., Abbot of S. Maria di Finalpia, Savona, Italy.

Cip. — DR. PIO CIPROTTI, Professor of Ecclesiastical Law, the University of Camerino, Professor of Comparative Law and Ecclesiastical Italian Law, *Pont. Univ. Lateranense*, Rome.

Cr. — FR. CAMILLO CRIVELLI, S.J., Associate Editor of *La Civiltà Cattolica*, Rome. (†)

Dal. — MSGR. VIRGILIO DALPIAZ, former Promoter of Justice, the S. C. of Holy Office; Professor, *Pont. Institutum Utriusque Iuris*, Rome.(†)

Dam. — FR. CORNELIUS DAMEN, C.SS.R., former Professor of Moral Theology, *Pont. Athenaeum Urbanum de Propaganda Fide*, Rome. (†)

De A. — MSGR. SERAFINO DE ANGELIS, former secretary of S. Apostolic Penitentiary, Rome.

Deg. - Fr. Elio Degano, C.M., Former Professor of Dogmatic Theology, St. Vincent de Paul Seminary, Turin.

Fab. - Fr. Cornelio Fabro, C.P.S., Professor of Philosophy, *Pontificale Athenaeum Urbanum de Propaganda Fide.*

Fel. - Msgr. Pericle Felici, General Secretary of the Pontifical Preparatory Commission of the Ecumenical Council (Vatican II).

Fra. - Fr. Zeffirino Franz, O.F.M., Professor of Moral Theology, *Pont. Athenaeum Antonianum,* Rome.

Gal. - Msgr. Albino Galletto, Secretary of Pontifical Commission for Movies, Radio and Television, Rome.

Gio. - Hon. Dr. Igino Giordani, Writer, Rome.

Gol. - Dr. Silvio Golzio, Professor of Statistics, the University of Turin, Italy.

Gra. - Msgr. Giuseppe Graneris, Promoter of Justice, the S. C. of Holy Office; Professor, *Pont. Institutum Utriusque Iuris,* Rome.

Lam. - Msgr. Ferdinando Lambruschini, Professor of Moral Theology, *Pont. Univ. Lateranense,* Rome.

Lat. - Msgr. Ugo Lattanzi, Professor of Fundamental Theology, *Pont. Univ. Lateranense,* Rome.

Led. - Fr. Adolph Ledwolorz, O.F.M., Prefect of Studies, *Pont. Athenaeum Antonianum,* Rome.

Loc. - Enrico Locatello, Publicist, Rome.

Mai. - Dr. Serafino Majerotto, Doctor of Economic Sciences, Rome.

Man. - Dom Gregory Manise, O.S.B., Professor of Dogmatic Theology, Affligen Abbey, Hekelgem, Belgium.

Mand. - Fr. Giulio Mandelli, I.M.C., *Aiutante di Studio,* S. C. of Religious, Rome.

M.d.G.- Fr. Mauro da Grizzana, O.F.M. Cap., General Procurator of the Capuchin Friars.

Mon. - Msgr. Giuseppe Monti, former Professor, *Pont. Univ. Lateranense,* Rome.

Oli. - Fr. Olivario Oliger, O.F.M., former Professor, *Pont. Univ. Lateranense* and *Antonianum,* Rome. (†)

Opp. - Dom Philip Oppenheim, O.S.B., former Professor, Pontifical *Univ. Lateranense* and *de Propaganda Fide,* and St. Anselm International Institute, Rome. (†)

Pal. - Msgr. Pietro Palazzini, Secretary of the Sacred Congregation of the Council.

Pa.g. - Msgr. Giuseppe Palazzini, Prelate Auditor of the Sacred Roman Rota.

Pas. - Msgr. Giuseppe Pasquazi, Prelate Auditor of the S. R. Rota, former Professor of International Law, *Pont. Institutum Utriusque Iuris,* Rome.

Pav. - Msgr. Pietro Pavan, Vice-President Permanent Committee Italian Catholic Social Weeks, Professor of Sociology, Pontifical *Institutum Utriusque Iuris* and Pontifical Gregorian University, Rome.

Per. - Fr. Boniface Perovic, O.F.M., Commissary of Croatian Friars Minor in Argentina, former Professor, *Athenaeum Antonianum*, *Ingenieros* (Buenos Aires).

Pio. - Msgr. Antonio Piolanti, Rector, *Pont. Univ. Lateranense* and Professor of Dogmatic Theology, *Pont. Athenaeum Urbanum de Propaganda Fide*, Rome.

Pug. - D. Agostino Pugliese, S.D.B., Professor of Canon Law, *Pont. Athenaeum Salesianum*, Turin.

Riz. - Dr. Carlo Rizzo, Clinical Professor of Neuropsychology, University of Rome, Italy.

Rob. - Francesco Cardinal Roberti, former Secretary of the Sacred Congregation of the Council and Dean of the Pontifical *Institutum Utriusque Iuris*, Rome; presently Prefect of the Supreme Tribunal of the Apostolic Signature.

Ses. - Msgr. Giovanni Sessolo, Secretary of the S. Apostolic Penitentiary, Rome.

Sir. - Fr. Giuseppe Sirna, O.F.M., Conv., Professor of Moral Theology, House of Studies of Minor Friars Conventual, Rome.

Spa. - Reverend Francesco Spadafora, Professor of Biblical Sciences, *S. Alessio Falconieri Collete*, Rome.

Sti. - Fr. Daniel Stiernon, A. A., Professor of Oriental Theology, *Pont. Athenaeum Lateranense* and *de Propaganda Fide*, Rome.

Tar. - Fr. Igino Tarocchi, O.F.M., former Professor of Moral Theology, Archdiocesan Seminary, Florence.

Toc. - Fr. Pietro Tocanel, Dean of Canon Law, *Pont. Institutum Utriusque Juris*, Rome.

Tur. - Reverend Nichola Turchi, Professor of History of Religions, University of Rome, Rome. (†)

Urb. - Giovanni Cardinal Urbani, Patriarch of Venice, Italy.

Ven. - Msgr. Carlo Veneziani, former *Aiutante di Studio* of the S. Congergation of Council, Rome.

Ver. - Msgr. Bartolomeo Verzeroli, former Professor of Psychology, *Pont. Univ. Lateranense*, Rome.

Vio. - Msgr. Giacomo Violardo, Undersecretary of the Tribunal of Apostolic Signature; Professor of Canon Law, *Pont. Institutum Utriusque Iuris*, Rome.

Zac. - Fr. Zaccaria Da S. Mauro, Professor of Canon Law, International College *S. Lorenzo da Brindisi*, Rome.

Zol. - Prof. Eugenio Zolli, former Professor of Hebrew and Comparative Semitic Languages, University of Rome, Rome, Italy. (†)

Preface

> I am convinced that it [Catholic moral law] is the only sacred
> and reasonable norm, both as a whole and in its every part; that
> all corruption derives either from its transgression, or from
> ignorance, or from a wrong interpretation of it.
> . . . [It is] the morality everyone would like to see practiced
> by his neighbor; which, if followed by all, would lead to the
> highest degree of perfection and happiness attainable on this
> earth . . .
>
> A. MANZONI, Observations on Catholic
> Moral Doctrine, Preface and Chapter III

TOWARD the end of the Second World War, as the vast majority of the people looked with dismay upon the enormous physical destruction caused by the war, zealous souls were contemplating the equally enormous moral havoc wrought by that same war. In fact, the hardships that people had faced, the state of utter want in which they had often found themselves, the harsh war restrictions, often enforced beyond reason or, at least, beyond ordinary human endurance, the diminished respect for civil authority and the inadequacy of the means of its enforcement, the spirit of rebellion caused by harsh and long suffering—all appeared to have weakened moral restraint and almost made any transgression lawful.

Thus, the burning passions aroused by the horrors of the bloodiest war in human memory and the onslaught of absurd ideologies appeared to threaten the collapse of the entire world of traditional ethical concepts. One solitary voice, that of the Supreme Pontiff, was raised above the fray to remind men of this truth: that the principles of the eternal moral law cannot be transgressed with impunity, and that apostasy from God gives rise to social problems which, as they become increasingly acute, explode from time to time into wars between single nations, or between entire continents.

It was in this disrupted atmosphere that a sizable group of professional men, members of Catholic Action, aware of the absolute need to recall their fellowmen to an observance of the moral law and desirous of making their modest contribution to this enormous task, in a spirit of dutiful submission to the authority of the Church, launched a project: the compilation of this Dictionary, in which modern, educated Catholics might find an up-to-date, practical, and effective moral guide. The excellent Synopsis rerum moralium et iuris pontificii alphabetico ordine digesta by the late Benedetto Oietti, S.J. (1862–1932), which was first published in Rome in 1899, with its subsequent numerous reprints, was the only work available in this field, but this was written in Latin and is now hard to obtain. Hence the need for a modern encyclopedia, which, written in modern language, would offer a useful clarification of ideas, a new method of presentation and a fresh approach to ageless questions or basic issues.

Thus, the distinguished Editrice Studium, which had done so well in similar types of work, was asked to assume the task of publishing this *Dictionary of Moral Theology*, through which Christians would find Christian orientation for their lives and safe guidance in their moral conduct. Asked to encourage the new undertaking, ultimately we were prevailed upon to assume direction of it, despite our taxing responsibilities in other fields.

We requested the originators of this project to submit an outline of the principal questions which might be of significance or of particular value for the guidance of Catholics. The result was that the first long list of subjects was thus compiled, ranging from unconsciousness to conscience, from cybernetics to conditional reflex, from blood groups to constitutional immorality, from conversion to God to financial conversion, from black market to just wage, etc. Philosophers, jurists, sociologists, physicians, economists, politicians, technicians, administrators, and students of the most diverse disciplines submitted questions and discussions revolving around the most diversified fields. This complex array, to be sure, required much careful examination, a considerable amount of research, and more than ordinary work in organization and coordination. Furthermore, it required that all new developments be checked against the Church's teachings, that exaggerations of one extreme or the other be avoided, that the rights of the individual be duly harmonized with those of the community, that the requirements of liberty and justice be properly safeguarded, and that the most delicate subjects be treated with all due propriety and balance.

According to the plans of the promoters of the project, the Dictionary was not to be a reproduction, in alphabetical order, of chapters and sections of a treatise of moral theology; but the principles contained in the latter, properly examined and wisely developed according to traditional doctrine, were to be clearly condensed and, naturally, served as the doctrinal basis of every new discussion. Moreover, to serve a useful purpose, a work of this type ought to be so broad in its scope as to encompass the many practical fields of human activity, especially the newer and not yet fully explored fields of psychology and medicine, sociology and international relations, with the hope that under the light of the eternal moral principles they might be directed to the welfare of mankind.

In order to carry out this complex plan, the cooperation of technical experts and the participation of a large number of collaborators was obviously needed. But the most difficult task was to find individuals who possessed the necessary technical knowledge and, at the same time, professed sound moral principles. To give unity to so varied and vast a project, several guiding norms were adopted in the compilation of this work. For besides a summation of the general Catholic moral doctrine, it also contains a presentation of the relationship and applications of moral doctrine to all fields of human endeavor: to the spiritual life of the individual and the family; to social, economic and political life; to education and professional orientation; to vocational, industrial, agricultural and professional activities; to business and finance, trades and professions, industry and labor. The aim of this work could not be limited to merely explaining the precepts to be observed, but it was to illumine man's entire moral life. Hence, it required that ascetical and liturgical subjects be also included.

In the search for a deeper analysis of the individual human acts (in view of the intimate connection between body and soul), it became necessary to conduct an accurate analysis of the fundamental principles, psychological and physiological, normal and abnormal, underlying those very acts. Then, too, since a Catholic is a member of the mystical body of Christ and lives and operates in the Church, it was deemed proper to offer adequate knowledge concerning the constitution and the authority of the various organs of the ecclesiastical hierarchy. Hence arose the necessity of adequate information concerning canonical as well as civil law, national and international law. In order properly to understand and evaluate the various situations with which the human conscience may be faced, it was deemed necessary, in some cases, to have certain general or specific medical, economic, and financial notions precede the discussion of situations in which basic natural principles are involved. This, of course, caused an expansion of its areas of concern to provide the reader with as wide a fundamental view as possible of the matter under discussion. A clear, concise and orderly presentation was requested of our collaborators; a presentation free of the encumbrance of superfluous disputes and conducted according to a strictly scientific method, both by a constant reference to principles and by a rational application of the same. The collaborators were requested to espouse no novel or unusual ideas but to present the ordinary doctrine with all possible clarity, and to offer other opinions with the greatest sense of objectivity. Sufficient liberty was allowed in determining the latitude in the treatment of certain subjects, particularly if new or of a technical nature. It is possible that greater formal uniformity might have been attained by placing more stringent limitations upon our collaborators, but this, it was feared, might have caused adverse results upon the scientific worth and practical usefulness of the work itself. A certain freedom was also allowed with regard to the grouping together or the separating of topics whenever the subject matter or clearness of presentation demanded it. Here, too, it seemed proper to favor substance over external form. But, whenever a topic deserved to be treated under different aspects, there was no hesitation in allowing different collaborators to do so, thereby contributing to a clearer and more exhaustive treatment of the subject. Thus, for instance, *simulation* and *dissimulation* were treated separately, in view of their ethico-juridical and psychopathological aspects.

In the systematic preparation of this work, as well as in the presentation of each topic, we have adhered religiously to instructions received from the Supreme Pontiff, Pope Pius XII of venerable memory. It must be considered particularly good fortune that its compilation was undertaken at a time when the late Pontiff, in a most unprecedented and intensive series of allocutions, exhortations, and messages, expounded and illustrated with truly exceptional richness and profoundness of doctrine, all the most difficult moral problems of our day.

Without mentioning the Code of the Oriental Church, nor the new canonical dispositions for the Latin Church, the most important of which concerns the Eucharistic fast,[1] nor even the illustration of Christian virtues on the occasion of the canonization of new saints and centennial celebrations,[2] we must note that from the very beginning of his pontificate, the late Pope Pius XII proclaimed the absolute necessity of *Divine Law* as the basis of all human institutions[3] and condemned the principle which makes utilitarianism the basis and rule of law,[4] as well as every form of juridical positivism.[5]

The universe shows forth the existence of God.[6] God is the Lawgiver, and men are brothers at the school of God.[7] God, therefore, is the basis of individual and social life;[8] on Him is based the immutability of moral law.[9] Hence, systems of individual morality or of situation ethics are to be rejected.[10] The ten commandments are the foundation of the moral order, and their observance requires war against sin,[11] and the elimination of hatred and egoism. This can be attained by training Christian conscience in a spirit of faith and sacrifice.[12]

In order to bring about a renewal of Christian life, firmness of *faith* is

[1] Constitution *Christus Dominus*, on the State of Perfection (Jan. 8, 1953: AAS 45, 15–24); the Constitution *Sedes Sapientiae* (May 30, 1956: AAS 48, 354–365); the Instruction of S.C. of Religious (March 25, 1956: AAS 48, 512–526).

[2] Exhortation on the occasion of the celebrations in honor of St. Francis of Assisi and St. Catherine of Siena (AAS 32, 181–188); Encycl. *Fulgens radiatur*, March 21, 1947, on the occasion of the XIV centennial of the death of St. Benedict (AAS 39, 137–155); the Encycl. *Doctor mellifluus*, May 24, 1952 (AAS 45, 369–384), on the VIII centennial of the death of St. Bernard; the Apostolic Letter *Quamquam*, July 25, 1954 (AAS 46, 513–517), on the XVI centennial of the birth of St. Augustine; the Epistle *Magna cum iucunditate*, July 31, 1955 (AAS 47, 548–551), on the IV centennial of the death of St. Ignatius of Loyola; the Epistle *Quo asperioribus*, Oct. 4, 1955 (AAS 47, 714–716), on the V centennial of the death of St. John Capistran; the Epistle *Hadriatici maris*, Dec. 24, 1955 (AAS 48, 77–80), on the V centennial of the death of St. Lawrence Justinian; the Epistle *Quandoquidem*, Jan. 19, 1956, on the VII anniversary of the death of St. Peter Nolasco (AAS 48, 80–81); the Epistle *Grato Animo*, Feb. 11, 1956, on the V centennial of the death of St. Rita Cascia (AAS 48, 267–268); the Epistle *Sexto decimo*, May 31, 1956, on the XVI centennial of the death of St. Anthony (AAS 48, 567–568); Radio Message of July 31, 1956, on the IV centennial of the death of St. Ignatius of Loyola (AAS 48, 617–622).

[3] Christmas Radio Message of 1939 (AAS 32, 10–11).

[4] Christmas Radio Message of 1940 (AAS 33, 12–13).

[5] At the inauguration of the juridical year of the Sacred Roman Rota, November 13, 1949 (AAS 41, 604–608).

[6] Address to the Academy of Sciences, Nov. 30, 1941 (AAS 33, 504–512).

[7] Address to the Academy of Sciences, Nov. 22, 1952 (AAS 44, 31–43); Address to International Astronomical Congress, Sept. 7, 1952 (AAS 44, 732–739).

[8] Christmas Radio Message of 1942 (AAS 35, 9–24).

[9] On Christian Conscience, March 23, 1952 (AAS 44, 270–278).

[10] To the women delegates of the Congress of the *Fédération Mondiale des Jeunesses Féminines Catholiques*, April 18, 1952 (AAS 44, 413–418); Instruction of the S.C. of the Holy Office, Feb. 2, 1956 (AAS 49, 144–145).

[11] Address to Lenten Preachers, March 13, 1943 (AAS 35, 105–116).

[12] Christmas Radio Message of 1940 (AAS 33, 12–13); Address to the *Fédération Mondiale des Jeunesses Féminines Catholiques*, April 18, 1952 (AAS 44, 413–418).

needed;[13] with fervor the Supreme Pontiff called pagans, unbelievers, and dissidents to the unity of faith.[14] Faith impels the practice of charity toward the indigent;[15] and charity possesses an irresistible force and a marvelous fecundity.[16]

The sources of supernatural life are the sacraments,[17] the Holy Sacrifice of the Mass,[18] and prayer.[19]

There is the obligation of providing for priestly vocations,[20] native clergy,[21] holiness of the priestly life,[22] the intellectual and pastoral formation of priests, adapted to the needs of our modern era,[23] an increase of cultural[24] and spiritual development among religious[25] so that the Christian way of life might flourish in a vital interior life and zealous external works.[26]

There exists the need for profound religious instruction,[27] a living participation in the sacred liturgy,[28] and provident care for sacred and religious music.[29]

The dignity, development and perfection of the human person[30] and the inviolability of the human person are principles repeatedly asserted by the late Holy Father.[31] Man is a psychological, social and transcendent unity;[32] he must

[13] Address to Women of Catholic Action on the 40th anniversary of foundation, July 14, 1949 (AAS 41, 421–425).

[14] Christmas Radio Message of 1950 (AAS 42, 121–133); Encycl. Ad Sinarum gentem, October 7, 1946 (AAS 54, 513–517).

[15] Allocution, April 4, 1946 (AAS 38, 165–169); Radio Message, February 15, 1956 (AAS 48, 141–143).

[16] Address to the Delegates of the Congress of the Conferences of St. Vincent de Paul, April 17, 1952 (AAS 44, 468–473).

[17] To the Lenten Preachers, March 13, 1943 (AAS 35, 105–116); Instructions to the Lenten Preachers, 1945 (AAS 37, 33–43).

[18] Address to the Lenten Preachers, March 23, 1949 (AAS 41, 182–187).

[19] Allocution, Nov. 2, 1941 (AAS 33, 496–502); Encycl. Ingruentium malorum, de Mariali Rosario, Sept. 15, 1941 (AAS 43, 577–582); Allocution to the Apostleship of Prayer, Sept. 27, 1956 (AAS 48, 674–677).

[20] Epistle De vocationibus sacerdotalibus, April 23, 1947 (AAS 39, 285–289).

[21] Exhortation to native clergy, June 28, 1948 (AAS 40, 374–376).

[22] Allocution Menti Nostrae, Sept. 23, 1950 (AAS 42, 657–702).

[23] At the foundation of the College of S. Eugenio in Rome, April 11, 1949 (AAS 41, 165–167); Address to Priests, Aug. 6, 1952 (AAS 44, 773–775); New Constitution of the Pontifical Theological Academy of Rome, Magistra veritatis, June 5, 1956 (AAS 48, 493–496); Radio Message of September 14, 1956 (AAS 48, 699–711).

[24] Nihil Ecclesiae, on the Institute entitled Regina Mundi, Feb. 11, 1956 (AAS 48, 189–192).

[25] Apostolic Constitution Sedes Sapientiae, May 31, 1956 (AAS 48, 354–365); Epistle Novimus Religiosorum, de perfectione religiosa ac sacerdotali et apostolatu provehendis, Sept. 20, 1956 (AAS 48, 662–665).

[26] Address to the Lenten Preachers, March 8, 1952 (AAS 42, 816–828).

[27] Address to the participants of the International Catechetical Congress, Oct. 14, 1950 (AAS 42, 816–826).

[28] Encyclical Mediator Dei, on the Sacred Liturgy, Nov. 20, 1947 (AAS 39, 521–595). Address to the International Congress of the Pastoral Liturgy, Sept. 22, 1956 (AAS 48, 711–725).

[29] Encyclical Musicae sacrae, Dec. 25, 1955 (AAS 48, 5–25).

[30] Christmas Radio Message of 1942 (AAS 35, 9–24).

[31] Address to the Delegates to Congress of Catholic Union of Obstetricians and Midwives, Oct. 29, 1951 (AAS 43, 831–854).

[32] Address to the Delegates to the International Congress of Psychotherapy and Psychology, April 13, 1953 (AAS 45, 278–286).

be defended against all forms of depersonalization[33] and any technical concept of human life.[34]

Marriage and the Family: The validity of the bond of marriage and its indissolubility;[35] the protection of the family,[36] and particularly large families,[37] maternity,[38] holy virginity,[39] artificial insemination,[40] marriage processes,[41] were all subjects which he repeatedly discussed and explained in his teaching.

The subject of *education* was treated in all its aspects by the Pope: criteria of a sound education for youth;[42] training of character, mind, and heart;[43] special care for the poor, orphaned, and abandoned children;[44] plain and professional instruction of adults;[45] the relation between physical and moral education;[46] amusement media, including movies[47] and television.[48] Parents,[49] teachers of every level,[50] particularly the university level,[51] teaching sisters,[52] Scout leaders,[53,54] girls' guides[55]—all were instructed and exhorted to discharge their

[33] Christmas Radio Message of 1952 (AAS 45, 33–46).

[34] Christmas Radio Message of 1953 (AAS 46, 5–16).

[35] Address at the Opening of the Juridical Year of the Sacred Roman Rota, 1941 (AAS 33, 421–426).

[36] Address to the Delegates to the International Union for the Protection of the Family, Sept. 20, 1949 (AAS 41, 551–554).

[37] Address to the Delegates to the Congress for the Family Front, Nov. 26, 1951 (AAS 43, 855–860).

[38] Address to Participants to Congress on Maternity, Nov. 12, 1942 (AAS 34, 370–371).

[39] Encyclical Letter *De sacra virginitate*, March 25, 1954 (AAS 46, 161–191).

[40] Address to Participants in International Congress of Catholic Physicians, Sept. 29, 1949 (AAS 41, 557–561).

[41] Address to Delegates to the XVI Italian Congress on Urology, Oct. 8, 1953 (AAS 45, 673–679).

[42] Message to Delegates to Congress on Education, Oct. 6, 1948 (AAS 40, 465–468); to the Priests Dedicated to the Study of *de recta iuvenum institutione*, Sept. 9, 1953 (AAS 45, 607–611); to the Congress of Malines on Catholic Education, Aug. 24, 1955 (AAS 47, 607–608); Allocution to the Italian Education Association, Oct. 24, 1955 (AAS 45, 780–782); Allocution to the Teachers of *Katholischen Erziehergemeinschaft in Bayern*, Dec. 31, 1956 (AAS 49, 63–65).

[43] Address to Teaching Women, Oct. 26, 1941 (AAS 33, 450–458).

[44] Encyclical *Quemadmodum*, July 13, 1945 (AAS 38, 5–14).

[45] To the Teachers and Pupils of Italian Elementary Schools, March 18, 1953 (AAS 45, 230–238).

[46] *De ratione sport et educationis physicae quoad religionem et regulam morum*, Nov. 8, 1952 (AAS 44, 868–876); Address to the Italian Sport Center, Oct. 9, 1955 (AAS 47, 725–733).

[47] Statute of the Pontifical Commission on Cinema, Dec. 16, 1954 (AAS 46, 783–784); Address to Congresses on Cinema, June 21, 1955 (AAS 47, 501–512); Oct. 28, 1955 (AAS 47, 818–829).

[48] On Television, June 16, 1954 (AAS 46, 18–24).

[49] Address to Mothers concerning the Education of Children, Oct. 26, 1941 (AAS 33, 450–458).

[50] To Representatives of the *Union Catholique de l'enseignement public de France*, March 26, 1951 (AAS 43, 209–213); to the Catholic Union of Intermediate School Teachers, Jan. 5, 1954 (AAS 54, 50–54).

[51] Address to the Academic Senate of *Studium Urbis*, June 5, 1952 (AAS 44, 381–386).

[52] To Religious School Teachers, Sept. 13, 1951 (AAS 43, 738–744).

[53] Address to the 1st International Congress of Boy Scouts, June 6, 1952 (AAS 44, 338–350); to Canadian Catholic Boy Scouts, July 28, 1955 (AAS 47, 604–605).

[54] Address to International Congress of Catholic Guides, Aug. 26, 1955 (AAS 47, 601–604).

important missions with a full measure of responsibility.

Since the practice of every virtue requires sacrifice, Pius XII entolled its necessity and value;[56] he asked those who suffer to offer their suffering for the success of the Holy Year[57] and the Marian Year.[58] *Catholic Action* and its organization were a frequent topic of papal pronouncements.[59] Men were exhorted to engage in responsible, illuminating, vivifying, unifying, and obedient action in the practice of domestic virtues, professional integrity, and the defense of public morality.[60] The young were urged to fight until victory is achieved over atheism, materialism, and social diseases.[61] Women were asked to practice with firmness of faith the apostolate best suited to their state in life.[62]

They were encouraged to promote sound political and social laws, particularly in the defense of the family and moral education of the youth;[63] to present courage, warmth and docility.[64] Young women were exhorted to protect their virtue and dignity from the many perils to which they are exposed in modern society, and to acquire a Christian education.[65] Professional people were reminded to protect their faith by sound doctrine and the practice of virtue.[66] Regarding the *social question*, the Supreme Pontiff proclaimed the necessity of reducing the exceedingly striking economic differences existing in different parts of the world and to make the attainment of a satisfactory way of life possible for everyone.[67] He taught the proper use of material goods,[68] upheld the rights of labor[69] but insisted, at the same time, on the duties of the Christian

---

[55] Address to Delegates for the care of girls, Dec. 30, 1953 (AAS 46, 44–49).

[56] Address for the Day of Sacrifice, Nov. 2, 1941 (AAS 33, 496–502); Nov. 18, 1951 (AAS 43, 860–862).

[57] Allocution, Nov. 21, 1949 (AAS 41, 610–614).

[58] *Dies pro infirmis*, Feb. 14, 1954 (AAS 46, 95–99).

[59] Exhortation *I felici sviluppi*, Jan. 25, 1950 (AAS 42, 247–250); Address to the Delegates of Catholic Action, April 3, 1951 (AAS 43, 375–379); Address to International Congress of Catholic Lay Apostolate, Oct. 14, 1951 (AAS 43, 784–793); Address to the Delegates of Marian Congregations, Sept. 8, 1954 (AAS 46, 529–532); to the Franciscan Third Order, July 1, 1956 (AAS 48, 573–577).

[60] Address to the men of Catholic Action on the Thirtieth Anniversary of its Foundation, Oct. 12, 1952 (AAS 44, 830–835); Sept. 20, 1942 (AAS 34, 282–293); Address to the Council of the International Federation of Catholic Men, Dec. 8, 1956 (AAS 49, 25–27).

[61] To the Youth of Catholic Action, Sept. 12, 1948 (AAS 40, 409–414).

[62] To the women of *Rinascita Cristiana*, Jan. 22, 1947 (AAS 39, 58–63); to the Delegates of International Union of Women of Catholic Action, Sept. 11, 1947 (AAS 39, 480–488).

[63] Address on the occasion of the Fortieth Anniversary of Foundation of the Association of Women of Catholic Action, July 24, 1949 (AAS 41, 415–421); to the Delegates of the Association of Women of Catholic Action, April 24, 1952 (AAS 44, 830–835).

[64] To Catholic Women of Italy on the dedication of *Domus Mariae*, Dec. 8, 1954 (AAS 46, 768–772).

[65] To Young Women, Sept. 4, 1940 (AAS 32, 362–372); Oct. 6, 1940 (AAS 32, 409–416); May 22, 1941 (AAS 33, 184–191); July 26, 1955 (AAS 47, 551–553); Oct. 2, 1955 (AAS 47, 721–725); April 3, 1956 (AAS 48, 272–277).

[66] To Professional Men, April 20, 1951 (AAS 33, 155–164).

[67] Christmas Message of 1940 (AAS 33, 12–13); to the Delegates of the International Labor Organization, November 10, 1954 (AAS 46, 714–718); Allocution to members of International Congress of Economists, Sept. 9, 1956 (AAS 48, 670–672).

[68] Message on the Fiftieth Anniversary of the Encyclical *Rerum Novarum*, June 1, 1941 (AAS 33, 195–205).

[69] Christmas Message of 1942 (AAS 35, 9–24); to Christian Associations of Italian

worker;[70] he suggested appropriate social reforms, the effective prevention of labor accidents[71] and the sound development of a true Christian brotherhood as taught by the Church.[72] He underscored the inadequate development of world economy and the despair of those who had failed to attain an adequate enjoyment of material goods.[73] He also concerned himself with industrial management[74] and the problems related to the proper feeding of humanity.[75]

Particularly did the Supreme Pontiff direct his interest toward young Christian workers, the hope of future society,[76] and to young working women, by underscoring their position in relation to the family and public life and to the Church.[77] He stressed their domestic, social, and political obligations as well as the necessity of safeguarding their dignity and the sanctity of the home.[78] To agricultural workers, he emphasized the necessity of safeguarding religious life on the farm and bettering the conditions of rural life as a whole.[79] Nor did he neglect speaking of specific categories of workers, such as flower growers and domestic help.[80] Finally, the Supreme Pontiff urged the study of social problems from the standpoint of Christian principles and promoted the establishment of institutions dedicated to that specific purpose.[81]

Directing his authoritative words to the representatives of the professions, the Supreme Pontiff offered to the *jurists* wise criteria for the constitution of a national[82] and international[83] penal law. He also spoke on the function of penalty[84] and offered sound norms for the establishment of a criminal police

---

Workers (ACLI), June 29, 1940 (AAS 32, 331–337); to the Workers convened on the day of labor, May 1, 1953 (AAS 45, 290–293); Letter to International Congress of Christian Labor Movements, May 8, 1955 (AAS 47, 390–392); Letter to the Bishop of Passau on the Centennial of the *Kolping* Society, May 19, 1955 (AAS 47, 452–454).

[70] To Christian Associations of Italian Workers (ACLI), March 11, 1945 (AAS 37, 68–72); May 1, 1955 (AAS 47, 402–407); May 1, 1956 (AAS 48, 287–292).

[71] Address to Members of World Congress on Prevention of Industrial Accidents, April 3, 1955 (AAS 47, 272–275).

[72] Radio Message to Spanish Workers, March 11, 1951 (AAS 43, 213–216).

[73] Christmas Message of 1943 (AAS 36, 11–24); Christmas Message of 1955 (AAS 48, 26–41).

[74] Allocution to International Congress of Industries, Oct. 6, 1956 (AAS 48, 798–801).

[75] Address to the Eighth Congress of Food and Agriculture Organization (FAO), Nov. 10, 1956 (AAS 48, 53–57).

[76] To the *Jeunesse Ouvrière Catholique*, Sept. 3, 1950 (AAS 42, 639–642).

[77] To Women Members of ACLI, Aug. 15, 1945 (AAS 37, 212–216).

[78] To the Women Delegates of ACLI, Oct. 21, 1945 (AAS 37, 284–295).

[79] To Farm-owners, Nov. 11, 1946 (AAS 38, 432–437); May 18, 1955 (AAS 47, 497–500); April 11, 1956 (AAS 48, 277–282); to International Congress for the Improvement of Rural Life, July 2, 1951 (AAS 43, 554–557).

[80] To Rose Growers, May 10, 1955 (AAS 47, 495–496); to Servants, June 3, 1956 (AAS 48, 499–503).

[81] Letter on the Occasion of the Sixth Congress of Social Studies, Aug. 30, 1956 (AAS 48, 616–617); Letter to the Institute of Social Science at the Pontifical Gregorian University, June 29, 1956 (AAS 48, 589); Letter to the *Pontificale Athenaeum Angelicum*, Nov. 25, 1956 (AAS 48, 637).

[82] To the National Congress of Catholic Jurists, Feb. 5, 1954 (AAS 47, 72–85).

[83] To Participants in the VII International Congress of Penal Law, Oct. 3, 1953 (AAS 45, 743–744).

[84] To the National Congress of Italian Jurists, Dec. 5, 1955 (AAS 47, 601–771).

force.[85] He established guiding norms between the civil and the ecclesiastical judiciary system, underscoring the particular characteristics of the latter[86] and analyzing the delicate position of a judge faced with the application of an unjust law.[87] He spoke of the moral certitude required in issuing a sentence[88] and of the elements required for acquiring such certitude;[89] of the unity of action and the spiritual purpose for the conduct of a canonical process of marriage, as well as of the duties of judges, parties, defender of the bond, promoter of justice, advocates, witnesses, experts, etc.[90]

Scholars in every field were reminded of the great responsibilities arising from learning, cautioning them against theories at variance with the purity of the Catholic doctrine,[91] and praising honest scientific work of research[92] in extolling the profound humility of the great scholars.[93]

Pope Pius XII addressed university professors,[94] philosophers,[95] historians,[96] astronomers,[97] experts in geodetics and geophysics,[98] physicians,[99] eugenists,[100] obstetricians and gynecologists,[101] hystopathologists,[102] ophthalmologists,[103] microbiologists,[104] urologists,[105] military physicians,[106] pharmacists,[107] midwives,[108]

[85] To International Congress of Criminal Investigators, Oct. 15, 1954 (AAS 46, 598–605).
[86] On the opening of the judiciary year of the S. R. Rota, 1946 (AAS 38, 391–397).
[87] To Italian Catholic Jurists, Nov. 6, 1949 (AAS 41, 597–604).
[88] On the opening of the judiciary year of the S. R. Rota, 1941 (AAS 33, 421–426).
[89] On the opening of the judiciary year of the S. R. Rota, 1942 (AAS 34, 338–343).
[90] On the opening of the judiciary year of the S. R. Rota, 1943 (AAS 36, 281–290); to the Twenty-sixth Italian Urological Congress, Oct. 3, 1953 (AAS 45, 673–679).
[91] Encycl. *Humani Generis*, Aug. 21, 1950 (AAS 42, 561–578).
[92] To Participants of International Congress of Philosophy, Nov. 21, 1946 (AAS 38, 426–430); Sept. 25, 1949 (AAS 41, 555–556).
[93] To the Academy of Sciences, Feb. 8, 1948 (AAS 40, 75–85); April 24, 1955 (AAS 47, 394–401).
[94] Address to teachers and students of the University of France, April 10, 1950 (AAS 42, 395–397); to French University Teachers, Sept. 21, 1950 (AAS 42, 735–738); to Catholic Professors of Germany, April 13, 1955 (AAS 47, 390–392); of Austria, June 3, 1956 (AAS 48, 498–499).
[95] Address to members of IV Thomistic Congress, Sept. 11, 1955 (AAS 47, 483–491).
[96] Address to members of X Congress of Historical Sciences, Sept. 7, 1955 (AAS 47, 672–686); to International Congress of Archeology, History and History of Art, March 9, 1956 (AAS 48, 210–216).
[97] To International Congress of Astronomy, Sept. 7, 1952 (AAS 44, 732–739); to the VII Congress of International Federation of Astronautics, Sept. 20, 1956 (AAS 48, 790–793).
[98] To Congress of Geodesy and Geophysics, Sept. 24, 1954 (AAS 46, 580–584).
[99] To members of International Congress of Catholic Physicians, Sept. 29, 1949 (AAS 41, 557–561); Sept. 17, 1954 (AAS 46, 577–580); Sept. 30, 1954 (AAS 46, 587–598); April 7, 1955 (AAS 47, 275–282); May 8, 1956 (AAS 48, 454–459); Sept. 11, 1956 (AAS 48, 677–686).
[100] To Participants in International Symposium of Genetic Medicine, Sept. 7, 1953 (AAS 45, 596–607).
[101] To Teachers of Obstetrics and Gynecology, Jan. 8, 1956 (AAS 48, 82–93).
[102] To members of Hystopathological International Congress, Sept. 13, 1952 (AAS 44, 779–789).
[103] To members of Latin Congress of Ophthalmology, June 12, 1953 (AAS 45, 418–422).
[104] To Members of International Congress of Microbiology, Sept. 13, 1953 (AAS 45, 666–671).
[105] To Members of XXVII Congress of Italian Urological Society, Oct. 8, 1953 (AAS 45, 673–679).

nurses,[109] sanitary assistants;[110] he spoke on poliomyelitis,[111] on cancer and tumoral chemiotherapy,[112] on the protection and social integration of lepers,[113] on human fertility and sterility,[114] to the donors of corneas;[115] he dealt with radiotelegraphy and radio broadcasting;[116] he addressed journalists,[117] publishers,[118] railroad workers,[119] technical foundry associations,[120] the National Association of the *Granatieri* of Sardinia.[121]

The *Constitution of the Church,* as the Mystical Body of Christ, was abundantly illustrated,[122] and so was, too, the Christian concept of the *State.*[123]

The Pope also spoke on the characteristics of true democracy and of the qualities required in the leaders of democracies; he spoke against absolutism[124] and of the duties of public administrators,[125] and outlined the duties and rights of the priest in public life.[126] In the matter of international relations, the Holy Father upheld the right to life and independence for all nations, particularly the rights of ethnical minorities.[127] He laid down basic principles for the establishment of a new international order,[128] underscoring the absolute necessity

---

[106] To Members of XVI Congress of Military Medicine, Oct. 19, 1953 (AAS 45, 744–754).

[107] Members of International Congress of History of Pharmaceutics, Sept. 11, 1954 (AAS 46, 536–540).

[108] To Members of Congress of Catholic Union of Midwives, Oct. 29, 1951 (AAS 43, 835–854).

[109] To the Nurses of Rome, May 21, 1952 (AAS 44, 531); to the Personnel of the Hospitals of Naples, Nov. 11, 1955 (AAS 47, 829–833).

[110] To Italian Congress of Nurses and Sanitary Assistants, Oct. 1, 1953 (AAS 45, 725–729).

[111] To Members of International Congress of Poliomyelitis, Sept. 11, 1954 (AAS 46, 533–536).

[112] Allocution to Participants to Congress of International Union against Cancer, Aug. 19, 1956 (AAS 48, 666–670); and to members of Congress of Chemiotherapy of Tumors, Oct. 6, 1956 (AAS 48, 793–797).

[113] To Members of International Congress for the Protection and Integration of Lepers, April 16, 1956 (AAS 48, 282–286).

[114] To Universal Congress on Human Fertility and Sterility, May 18, 1956 (AAS 48, 467–474).

[115] To Members of Medical Congress of Association of Donors of Cornea, May 14, 1956 (AAS 48, 459–467).

[116] On the LX Anniversary of Radiotelegraphy, Oct. 11, 1955 (AAS 47, 733–736); to the European Congress of Radiobroadcasting, Oct. 21, 1955 (AAS 47, 775–780).

[117] To Catholic Journalists, Feb. 17, 1950 (AAS 42, 251–257); to Convention of Society of Foreign Correspondents, May 13, 1953 (AAS 45, 399–402).

[118] To the Congress of Catholic Publishers, Nov. 7, 1954 (AAS 46, 712–714).

[119] Allocution to Railroad Workers of the Roman Circumscription, June 26, 1955 (AAS 47, 512–516).

[120] To Congress of Technical Associations of the Foundry, Sept. 29, 1954 (AAS 46, 584–587).

[121] To the National Association of *Granatieri di Sardegna,* Nov. 6, 1956 (AAS 48, 50–53).

[122] Enc. *Mystici Corporis Christi,* June 29, 1943 (AAS 35, 193–248).

[123] Christmas Message, 1942 (AAS 35, 9–24).

[124] Christmas Message, 1944 (AAS 37, 10–24).

[125] To International Congress of Mayors, Sept. 30, 1955 (AAS 47, 716–720); to functionaries of Ministry of the Interior, Sept. 20, 1955 (AAS 47, 833–837).

[126] To Lenten Preachers, March 16, 1946 (AAS 38, 182–189).

[127] Christmas Message, 1939 (AAS 32, 10–11).

[128] Christmas Message, 1940 (AAS 33, 12–13).

that this be based on moral principles;[129] he also outlined the characteristics of the new international organization[130] or world federation,[131] and stated the duties and responsibilities of Catholics in international life.[132]

Finally, the Supreme Pontiff insisted unremittingly on the subject of a true, just, and lasting peace among nations—a subject which has the nations of the world and their leaders so deeply perplexed.

He spoke of the basic principles for such peace and of the international institutions capable of defending it.[133] He insisted on the necessity of taking into account, both in the national and international order, the human person, the dignity of the family, the rights of labor, the protection of the juridical order and the Christian concept of the State.[134]

Peace must be based on the unity of mankind and on a society of peoples, and there must be organs adequate for its guarantee.[135] Christian civilization must be preserved, and an economic and social order corresponding to it must be created.[136] The work of peace carried on by the Church and the Holy See[137] must be respected and not obstructed. Pope Pius XII exhorted the rulers of peoples to remove international tension and bring about true justice among all nations, united in a common effort to seek divine aid for the attainment of peaceful conditions of life among all peoples.[138] He also showed a very great concern for captive and persecuted nations[139] and the tragic events in Hungary.[140]

The vastness and doctrinal profoundness of the papal teachings constitute the primary and most solid basis on which this work was built.

However, it would be presumptuous for anyone to think that all possible conclusions and all practical applications were ably draw from them so as to exhaust the entire field of the countless moral situations with which human conscience might be faced. Our only hope is that this work may be a humble contribution in this extraordinarily vast, complex, and difficult field.

---

[129] Christmas Message, 1941 (AAS 34, 10–21).

[130] Christmas Message, 1952 (AAS 45, 33–46).

[131] Congress of *Mouvement universel pour une Confédération mondiale*, April 6, 1951 (AAS 43, 278–280).

[132] Participants in International Congress *De officio catholicorum quoad vitam internationalem*, July 23, 1952 (AAS 44, 626–627).

[133] Christmas Message, 1939 (AAS 32, 10–11); Christmas Message, 1949 (AAS 42, 5–15).

[134] Christmas Message, 1942 (AAS 35, 9–24); Christmas Message, 1956 (AAS 49, 5–22).

[135] Christmas Message, 1945 (AAS 38, 10–24); to American-European Congress, Sept. 18, 1955 (AAS 47, 691–694).

[136] At the beginning of the fifth year of the war, Sept. 1, 1944 (AAS 36, 349); Letter to Cardinal Wyszynski and the Polish Hierarchy, Dec. 8, 1955 (AAS 47, 73–77); on the Occasion of the *Katholikentag* of German Catholics, Sept. 2, 1956 (AAS 48, 622–627).

[137] Christmas Message, 1946 (AAS 39, 15–25); Christmas Message, 1952 (AAS 44, 5–16).

[138] Christmas Message, 1947 (AAS 20, 7–17); to the Center for Studies for Peaceful Conditions of life, Oct. 13, 1955 (AAS 47, 764–775).

[139] Apostolic Epistle *Dum maerenti animo*, June 29, 1956 (AAS 48, 549–554).

[140] Epistle *Luctuosissimi eventus*, Oct. 26, 1956 (AAS 48, 741–744); Letter *Laetamur admodum*, Nov. 1, 1956 (AAS 48, 745–748); Encyclical *Datis nuperrime*, Nov. 5, 1956 (AAS 48, 748–749); Radio messages, Oct. 7, 1956 (AAS 48, 762–778); Nov. 10, 1956 (AAS 48, 787–789).

We are happy to express our gratitude to Monsignor Giovanni Sessolo, Substitute of the Sacred Apostolic Penitentiary, who was generous with his help in the initial phase of this work, and to Monsignor Pietro Palazzini, who successively assumed the task of editorial secretary.

We are also grateful to those readers who have taken time out to offer helpful suggestions directed to improving this edition.

We shall be no less grateful to those who, in the future, shall offer us the benefit of their wise counsel, aware as we are of the fact that this work is undoubtedly susceptible of greater improvement, not only because such is the nature of every human undertaking, but also because modern life is such as to offer, almost daily, new occasions for the application of moral principles.

Francesco Cardinal Roberti

Introduction

I am the way, the truth and the life.
John 14:6

I. DEFINITION OF MORAL THEOLOGY*

Moral theology is the science that deals with human actions considered in their relationship to their supernatural end. Since it is a theological science, its roots are in faith and in the knowledge and study of God; thus it is always fundamentally subordinate to the latter. Insofar as it is ethics, it is the science dealing with what human actions *should* be, that is, in terms of their relationship to norms, which are supposed to regulate them.

1. In the ontological order, we must make a distinction between two human ends, one in the natural order and the other in the supernatural order (even though, in the course of history, these orders have never existed as separate and distinct states of man). Moral theology deals with the latter, leaving the former domain to ethics.

The terms *ethics* and *moral theology*, taken in themselves, refer to the same areas, but custom has led us to restrict ethics to the natural, philosophical study of morality and to use the term *moral theology* as the supernatural, theological study of good and evil.

In contrast to ethics, moral theology considers man as he really is and has been in the course of history: elevated, fallen, and redeemed. It traces man's life with the aid of a light that is much more powerful than any natural light: the supernatural light of Revelation, which is the source of the knowledge that is proper to faith.

2. Moral theology can be defined as the theological science, based on the principles of Revelation, which directs human activity toward God, man's supernatural end; or, more briefly, as the science of Christian living or Christian moral activity.

Like dogmatic theology, moral theology does not rest content with proposing the data of Revelation, but rather takes these as its principle and criterion of truth in arriving at moral knowledge; it then gathers the conclusions that reason, enlightened by faith, can deduce from them; finally, it organizes these conclusions into a complex system of truths that serve as norms for human activity on the supernatural level.

Hence, the manner in which it knows and treats its object fully justifies classifying it as a science and ranking it among the speculative activities of man.

The fact, however, that it deals with the moral activity of man puts it in the category of practical sciences; as in all practical sciences, we must make a dis-

---

* A. Lanza-P. Palazzini, *Teologia morale generale*, Studium, Rome, 1952.

tinction between a theoretical part, that studies remote and fundamental principles, and a practical part, that deals with immediate principles and concrete norms for moral activity.

3. The *material object* of moral theology comprises all actions that proceed from man's rational knowledge and free will, that is, all human activity in the proper sense of the term, insofar as it is ordained to God; its *formal object* consists in the data of Revelation insofar as they constitute the principles from which moral theology scientifically draws conclusions and subsequently organizes these conclusions into a system.

4. The *extensiveness* of its material object ties moral theology in with every human action; in fact, it rules over the whole of life and its regulations govern all activity. It directs all of our external acts and internal thoughts; it pervades public and private life; it plays its role in the most varied forms of activity, such as politics, economics, health, and welfare.

Taken in this sense, moral theology has a much wider extension than is usually attributed to it in the schools. It is the basic rule governing the harmonious development of any human being and the guide for all that he does.

II. WHAT THIS BOOK PRESUPPOSES

There are two basic notions that moral theology takes for granted: one pertains to the logical order, the order of knowledge; the other is ontological or metaphysical. The first concerns the ability of human reason to know truth; the second has reference to the search for the ultimate explanation of reality: man, the world, God.

1. In the order of knowledge, moral theology, like every other science, takes it for granted that the human mind is capable of knowing truth. We must admit a real distinction between the subject which does the knowing and the object which is known, and grant that the former has the ability to reach the latter (conformity of thought to reality, objective validity of knowledge). Sometimes the search for truth may be very demanding and involve difficulties (different opinions), and we can not exclude the possibility that there will be errors, and, more often, a vision of the truth that is only partial.

In order to recall these principles, we have included certain topics in the Dictionary which bring the validity of human knowledge into sharper focus: *materialism, positivism, idealism, existentialism,* etc.

2. In the *ontological* order, moral theology presupposes a knowledge of the nature of man, the external world, and God.

3. Man is made up of body and soul. The soul is the substantial form of the body, and the body in turn gives the soul its distinctive, individuating characteristics. Man, as a rational individual, is a person.

Though the soul is spiritual, its activities are conditioned by the body, since its vegetative and sensitive faculties are exercised through organs of the body. This explains why we find such close connections between psychological states and biological conditions, and why the latter exercise an influence on man's spiritual conduct.

But the soul is not reducible to matter, for it also acts independently of the body. As a matter of fact, man retains his identity despite the changes that take place in his body, for the material elements are unified by the soul. Thus, man's spiritual nature makes him capable of knowing himself, loving himself, directing himself towards an end and choosing the means to reach it, and of feeling responsibility for good and for evil.

From the soul's superiority over matter, we deduce its immortality.

The following entries in the Dictionary have special reference to the nature of man: *body, soul, human person, personality, liberty,* etc.

4. The *external world* does not have within it the sufficient reason for its own existence. Cosmology shows this and we will soon have occasion to repeat it when we speak of the existence of God.

5. *God* is the third reality to be demonstrated. As a matter of fact, moral theology takes it for granted that we have already established that there is a personal God, who is transcendent, the Creator of the universe, and a wise and providential Lawgiver in dealing with His creatures.

The proof for the existence of God is based on the principle of causality, which sets forth that whenever a thing does not have the reason for its being or its manner of being within itself, then that reason must be sought outside of it.

The metaphysical proof for the existence of God is drawn from the nature, perfection, and order of the universe. As is generally known, St. Thomas proposes five ways of proving the existence of God.[1]

The first way is based on motion (*motus*), that is, on the *becoming* of things; it may be stated in this form: Everything in the world is in a state of *becoming*, that is, all things begin to exist, then change, and pass away. Now, *becoming* cannot be a sufficient reason for itself. So we must find a cause for this *becoming*. To say that the things that come later depend on what went before serves only to push the problem back a little farther. So we must admit a First Cause, which is immutable—God (*Primum Movens quod a nullo movetur*).

The second and third ways are closely connected to the first; they may be stated in this fashion: Many things begin to exist, and since of themselves they could not originate from nothing, we must admit that they have a first efficient cause. Again, many things pass out of existence; so it is possible for them to exist or not to exist. Yet anything that might not exist exists by virtue of some cause other than itself, that is, it derives its existence from God.

The fourth way is based on the greater or lesser perfection of things. This supposes absolute perfection, for if things had the reason for their own being within themselves, then they would all be perfect.

The fifth way is based on the order of the universe. The purposefulness of beings that have no knowledge and the way in which they move toward definite ends point to a transcendent intelligence, God.

The existence of God is also affirmed by our consciences. We are all aware of a desire for happiness. And we feel happy, at least in part, when we have

---

[1] *Summa Theol.*, I, q.2, a.3.

carried out our duty, even though it may have involved sacrifice on our part. On the other hand, we experience some kind of internal rebuke when we have failed in our duty. So conscience tells us that we must do good and avoid evil. And since this obligation is general, absolute, and constant, despite the differences and the changing moods and circumstances of men, the only explanation for it is that God has inscribed a law in our consciences.

This truth is dealt with in particular in the Dictionary under *conscience, natural law, independent morality,* etc. But this whole volume, if it does anything, confirms the validity of the moral law that we feel within us.

Our conclusion receives added confirmation from its acceptance by the overwhelming majority of men, and especially the greatest of them, who have believed in God.

It is an easy step from the proof that God, the supreme and most perfect Being, exists to a demonstration of the fact that there is only one God. The history of religions shows that primitive people admit only one God. Polytheism is a later degeneration.

Atheists deny the existence of God. Pantheists deny His personal, transcendent nature. Deists deny His providence.

It is generally held that, in the face of the evidence furnished by the proofs for the existence of God, there is no such thing as a theoretical atheist, that is, one who has found or developed a real proof for His denial. But there are agnostics, who believe that it is not possible to reach any certain conclusions about the existence of God, and indifferentists, who refuse to face the problem. And there are also many practical atheists, who live as if God did not exist. The militant atheists, the so-called godless, are really anti-religious, for if they are so concerned with fighting against God, then they presuppose His existence.

Pantheists (whether materialistic or idealistic) start out with a monistic principle that reduces everything to unity; but they confuse the Infinite with the finite, multiple, changeable and limited beings with the absolute, immutable, Supreme Being. Men, who are supposedly the loftiest expressions of this whole organism, feel an inner conscience rebelling against this, for we are aware of our smallness and our limitations and of the fact that we are definite individuals with personalities of our own.

Deists admit that there is a God, but they suppose that He keeps far from man; thus they exalt the powers of nature to the point of claiming that it is capable of taking care of itself, without any involvement of the supernatural. Thus they refuse to recognize the limitations and the dependence of created things, and the Divinity fades away almost to the point of denial.

6. The *creation* and *conservation* of the universe are two other truths that are presupposed by this book.

Once we have proved the existence of God and established that He is distinct from the world, then, since the world and men do not have the sufficient reason for their existence within themselves, and God alone is the infinite and non-participated Being, we must admit that the whole substance of the universe has been produced, that is, created, by God.

If God has created man, He certainly had some purpose in mind in doing so; and the purpose can only be to achieve His own external glory (see Glory of God), by giving man, an intelligent creature, the power and the opportunity of knowing Him and loving Him and in this way obtaining his own happiness.

God, who has created men and things for a purpose, cannot fail to care for them, by making all that they need to stay in existence and to reach their goal (providence). God governs material things through physical laws and free beings through moral laws.

Once the nature of man and of the world has been clarified and God's existence has been demonstrated, the problem of the relationships between God and man arises—this is the problem of religion, and it is treated under this title.

7. Geographical and historical studies have shown that religion is a universal, constant and spontaneous phenomenon among human beings, as the results of prehistoric and ethnological research have proven.

There are, on the other hand, many different forms of it. On the basis of content, religions may be classified as fetishism, the veneration of objects made by man; animism, devotion to souls which have gone on to enjoy divine honors; totemism, a social order made up of different classes of people organized on the basis of a relationship with certain animal or vegetable types: totem; magic, a distortion of science and philosophy; naturalism, the veneration of a divine element in natural phenomena; polytheism, a splitting up of the divinity; pantheism, a monistic conception of the universe that may be materialistic or idealistic; monotheism, belief in a unique, transcendent God.

If the criterion used is an ethnic one, religions may be classified as follows: besides the primitive ones that have survived here and there in Africa, America and Oceania, we have Confucianism and Taoism (China and Indo-China), Hinduism or Brahmanism and Jainism (India), Lamaism (Tibet), Shintoism (Japan), Buddhism (China, Indo-China, Japan). All of these are religions with a national basis, except for Buddhism, which stretches beyond political frontiers; all are polytheistic, even if they draw strength and support from some kind of moralizing (Confucianism) or philosophizing (Taoism) or from atheistic or agnostic asceticism (Buddhism). (It is truly humiliating for men to realize that a great part of the human race has not yet succeeded in seeing how absurd polytheism really is.) Finally, the monotheistic religions, aside from Christianity, are Judaism and Islamism (distortions of the Old and the New Testament respectively). Islamism arose in Asia but it has spread far and wide in Africa as well; the Jews are scattered throughout the world; Christianity is professed in Europe and America and, to some extent, everywhere. A number of schismatical groups have broken away from the Catholic Church; the principal ones are the so-called Orthodox Church and Protestantism.

Today the science of religions (hierognosis) studies various religious groups and compares them from the historical, philosophical and theological points of view. If such study is to yield real results, it must pay attention to God, the Supreme, most perfect Being, and to human nature, which aspires to truth, goodness, and happiness. In the case of each religion, it must deal with its origins, the coherence of its doctrine, and the holiness of its founder; the facts must be submitted to a severe criticism, differences noted, similarities explained, and religion set apart from science and politics. More attention must be paid to internal spirit than to external forms. Last of all, this study must take into account the natural law which God has engraved on the consciences of men, the primitive revelation that was shared by all mankind, and the influence exercised by the true religion. Such a study ought to lead to absolute certainty about which religion is true.

Although we take it for granted that this study has already been completed, this work does make mention of all the principal religious groups in existence today and offers a brief criticism of each, for comparison makes it unmistakably clear how superior Christianity is, and points out the deviations, failures, and defects that can be observed in other Christian groups when they are compared with Catholicism.

8. Thus, the *Catholic religion*, which we presuppose to have been proven as the true religion by critical examination, becomes the object of our study. The doctrine it proposes was revealed by God.

Revelation may be *natural* or *supernatural*. Natural revelation takes place when God speaks to us through nature and our consciences. A revelation may be supernatural either in its form or in its substance; in the first, natural truth is made known to us in a supernatural way; the second provides us with a truth that man would be completely incapable of attaining on his own. Since God has created our intellects, there is nothing to prevent Him from speaking to them or to stop man from listening to His words, although he may not always succeed in understanding them completely (mysteries). In fact, revelation is necessary to mankind, because, though man does succeed in knowing the basic natural truths and has the physical power to know *all* of them, in practice it is morally impossible for all men to succeed in knowing all natural truths, without some error. The reason for this is the presence of subjective difficulties and external obstacles. When it is a question of knowing truths of the supernatural order, then divine revelation is absolutely necessary. Hence, without revelation, man would not have a sure guide for directing his life.

Christian revelation encompasses the sum total of truths and norms that God gave to man in the Old and the New Testament. The purpose of the former was a preparation for the coming of Jesus Christ; the latter is directed toward the actual realization of the kingdom of Christ. The doctrines that have been revealed are contained in Sacred Scripture and Tradition, as proposed by the Church. Their truth is solidly demonstrated by an intrinsic completeness and perfection and confirmed by the miracles and prophecies of Jesus Christ, particularly His Resurrection and the Messianic prophecies fulfilled in Him. Some prophecies are still being fulfilled in our days: those dealing with the spiritual progeny of Abraham, that is, the mass of believers who were to be as numerous as the *stars in the heavens*[2] and the *sands of the sea;*[3] the never-ending struggles that the Church must endure: "*If they have persecuted me, they will persecute you as well*";[4] the divine assistance that was promised to the Church: "*The*

[2] Gen. 15:5.   [3] Gen. 22:17.   [4] John 15:20.

powers of hell will not prevail against her";[5] "I am with you all days, even until the end of the world."[6] And since the Sovereign Pontiff, Pius XII, has solemnly proclaimed the Queenship of Mary,[7] how could we help but take special note of the wonderful way in which the prophecy which the Blessed Virgin made in her humility has been verified to the letter: "Beatam me dicent omnes generationes:[8] all peoples will call me blessed"?

All of these proofs offer clear-cut evidence that the Catholic religion is the true one.

9. Theology is the science dealing with God and His relations with men insofar as they have been made known through divine revelation.

Theology is divided into two great branches: dogmatic theology and moral theology. A dogma is a truth revealed by God and proposed as such by the Church. As a matter of fact, both dogmatic and moral theology study truths which have been revealed by God, but their content is different, since they have different purposes.

Dogmatic theology studies revealed truths in order to gain a deeper knowledge of them and to illustrate them in the speculative order. Hence it treats of God's existence, His essence, and His attributes; it penetrates into the inner life of God, who is One in nature and Three in persons, and it contemplates their intimate relationship; it studies the creation of the world and of man, the latter's fall and his redemption through the Incarnation of the Son of God, who assumed human nature to redeem men from sin through His passion; it explains how the fruits of the Redemption are applied to men by means of grace that is granted us through the holy sacraments, which accompany man from the cradle to the grave, and especially through the Holy Eucharist, which unites us to Christ and serves as a pledge of our future resurrection; it points up the communion of the saints and contemplates the eternal life that will follow upon the judgment, when the beatific vision of God will be enjoyed by those who will have merited it, along with the angels and the saints, especially Mary, Most Holy Queen of heaven and earth, co-redemptrix of the human race and mediatrix of divine graces. The Christian prepares for this life of glory here in this world through the life of grace. He is guided in his efforts and struggles in this direction by the Church, the visible society of Christians on earth, to whom Jesus Christ has entrusted the mission of guiding all men to eternal happiness, under the authority of His Vicar, the Roman Pontiff, the successor of St. Peter, to whom Jesus Christ Himself entrusted the power of governing it.

Moral theology, on the other hand, directs human activity in the practical order, in the light of revealed truth. Its aim is to regulate our lives and our actions according to the dictates of right reason and faith, in a manner that will conform to the will of God.

10. *Moral theology* is the specific object of this volume; for questions of

---

[5] Matt. 16:18.
[6] Matt. 28:20. [7] Enc. Ad Coelis Reginam, Oct. 11, 1954 (AAS 46, 625–640).
[8] Luke 1:48.

dogmatic theology, we refer the reader to treatises dealing with that branch of theology.

III. WHAT THIS BOOK CONTAINS

The aim of this book is to present, not just moral theology in the ordinary sense of the term, but rather each and every aspect of practical theology that can help to enlighten the reader on how a person is supposed to act in any of the various circumstances and situations of life, not only from the point of view of his relationship to his own conscience and to God, but also with regard to his relationship to civil society and the Church with its hierarchical organization and community life of prayer and action.

The volume offers accurate and up-to-date information on each topic; an extensive and systematic bibliography has been put at the end of the volume.

Moreover, at the beginning of the work, we have given a brief account of the history of Catholic moral theology; outstanding moralists, like St. Thomas, St. Antoninus, Suarez, St. Alphonsus, and D'Annibale, are given special consideration.

1. Concerning a more detailed examination of the content of the Dictionary, first of all, the reader will find in it a summary of all the material that is generally found in the treatises and manuals of moral theology: moral principles, virtues, commandments and sacraments. Furthermore, he will find that the ordinary teaching is presented in a way that will bring him without delay to practical conclusions that are certain or at least more probable, since they are always deduced from the principles by the use of the scientific method. Hence, this work is quite different from a work of casuistry; this will be obvious to anyone who refers to the article dealing with this topic.

2. But the most original part of this work consists in the analysis of various human actions to furnish a deeper knowledge from both the psychological and the physical points of view; the integration of moral principles with the helpful data furnished by other sciences; finally, the application of moral principles to the manifold concrete situations of life.

3. Thus, with the help of philosophy and experimental psychology, the soul and its faculties have been explained under the following topics: soul, cognitive faculties, intellect, will, liberty; and the principal psychical functions have been treated under: sensation, perception, formation of ideas, concept, judgment, reasoning, subconscious, unconscious, etc.

4. An even greater contribution toward clarification of particular moral situations has been made by the medical sciences, especially constitutional medicine, psychiatry, and psychopathology. As a matter of fact, because of the intimate union that exists between the soul and the body, it is important, in making an accurate judgment of the morality of an action, to recall the findings furnished by other sciences, e.g., anthropology, criminal anthropology, endocrinology, geriatrics, preventive medicine, accident-prevention, obstetrics, pathology, applied psychology, psychotherapy, sexology, traumatology; it is also important to know how certain organs operate, e.g., the hypophysis, gonads, subrenal glands,

thyroid; to give some consideration to certain types of activity: *cenesthesis, cybernetics, cerebral functions*; to take into account certain phenomena, such as *hallucination, hypnotism, suggestion, sleep-walking, telepathy*, etc.

Of major importance, from the point of view of morality, are morbid conditions, e.g., *mental disturbance, brain-disease, cretinism, epilepsy, hysteria*, so-called *constitutional immorality, psychosis, psychoneurosis, schizophrenia*, etc. Nor can one afford to neglect lesser forms, such as *anxiety, hostility, apathy, phobia, hypochondria, melancholy*.

5. Certain topics are directed to the defense and perfection of the human person: *education, personality, personalization* and *depersonalization, child-care, public school, vocation, religious vocation, vocation to the priesthood*, etc.

6. This work does not limit itself to describing the things that have to be avoided, such as *sin, lukewarmness, imperfection*, or even to pointing up certain defects of character, like *instability, timidity*, etc., but it tries to use ascetics to guide the Christian in the practice of all the virtues. So the Dictionary treats of *asceticism*, the theological virtues of *faith, hope* and *charity*, and the moral virtues of *prudence, justice, fortitude* and *temperance*, as well as many other virtues that are in a sense offspring of more fundamental ones and generated by them, for instance, *clemency, fidelity, fervor, trust, parsimony, joy, loyalty, long-suffering, magnificence, meekness, munificence, recollection, resignation, sobriety, urbanity, zeal*; it carries through to the point where man is raised to the heights of the *heroic act of charity*, and gets him used to living in the *presence of God*, in *union with God*.

7. Man is subject to the authority of the Church, to which Jesus Christ has given the broadest powers to carry on His work of teaching, sanctifying, and ruling.[9] By virtue of these powers, the Church can issue commands and prohibitions and establish sanctions against those who violate them. The Church's power of jurisdiction is directed either toward regulating man's conduct with regard to God (internal forum) or toward governing men's conduct toward each other (external forum). The rules which the Church has established for settling bilateral conflicts—that is, present or future clashes of interests between individuals—is a juridical norm in the strict sense of the term (ecclesiastical law). The whole body of laws of the Church makes up the canonical system, which is an original, primary, juridical system, independent of all human power because of the powers that have been directly conferred on the Church by God. Canon Law regulates the conduct of the faithful and establishes the organs through which the Church's power of jurisdiction is exercised.

The principal organs that exercise the Church's power of jurisdiction in its central government are explained under the following topics: *Pontiff, Holy See, Vatican City, Cardinals, Conclave, Roman Congregations, Apostolic Penitentiary, Rota, Apostolic Signature, Apostolic Chancery, Datary, Apostolic Chamber, Secretariate of State, Papal Legate*; those who exercise jurisdiction in the local government are described under *Primate, Patriarch, Archbishop, Bishop, Vicar Apostolic, Vicar General, Chapter, Vicar Forane, Pastor, Curate*, etc.

[9] Matt. 16:18–19.

On the other hand, the regulating of the activity of subjects is taken up under topics which deal with the conditions of clerics, such as *cleric, excardination;* topics which refer to the religious life, such as *rules and constitutions, religious, secularization,* or to pious societies, such as *confraternity, pious association,* or to the *sacraments,* especially *matrimony,* or to ecclesiastical goods, such as *benefice, chaplaincy, patronage* (*right of*).

Court procedures are treated under *canonical judicial system, beatification, promoter of the faith, promoter of justice, defender of the bond, consistorial and Rota advocate, procurator of the Sacred Apostolic Palaces,* etc.

The sources from which the knowledge of Canon Law is derived, are taken up under *Acta Apostolicae Sedis, Code of Canon Law, Corpus juris canonici.*

8. Since man is also subject to civil authority, he is obliged to obey the laws which it legitimately makes. Hence *civil law* offers another large area for the application of moral theology. It is a serious mistake to separate law and morality (juridical positivism). The relationship between law and morality should not be one of separation, but only one of distinction and subordination. As a matter of fact, every regulation established by law has two aspects, one that is juridical in the strict sense insofar as it regulates the relationships of justice between men, and another that is more properly moral, which governs the subject's conduct with regard to his own perfection.

The rules of natural law which deal with obligations in justice comprise part of the general moral law and regulate a man's external relationships to other men and his internal behavior in its relationship to his own conscience and to God. The purpose and reason for positive law is to specify or determine natural law. Thus, in regulating the relationships between human beings, it may never contradict the norm of the moral law. Sometimes positive laws do depart from this norm; then we are obviously faced with the serious question of whether or not the individual who is subject to such a law has a moral obligation in conscience to observe it.

This volume treats not only the basic concepts of *law, natural law, positive divine law, civil law, unjust law, merely penal law,* but it also endeavors constantly to clarify the moral aspect of various civil obligations, i.e., whether they bind in conscience or not.

9. When it takes up the matter of the professions, occupations, and services to which men devote their efforts, our volume may be said to be at its best. Moral theology is the science of life, and often the success or failure of our lives is bound up with the activity which we have chosen as the immediate aim of our existence. Questions of choosing a profession with prudence, prayer and counsel, or taking pains to find and assume the role for which God has fitted and destined us through natural gifts and external circumstances, or preparing ourselves for this role with a real sense of responsibility, so that we can take fullest advantage of the talents that the Lord has given us, or carrying it out with the competence and the attention that are demanded by the seriousness of our position—all of these are problems that are moral in the finest sense of the word. All one has to do is think of the serious responsibility assumed by a person who ventures into a life that was not meant for him, or by someone who

disregards his own lack of preparation and uses devious means to get into a position where he does not belong, or by the man who is careless, ignorant, or unprincipled in carrying out his office. One can easily see what enormous harm any one of these people can do to public or private good. They will owe a debt to society that they may never be able to repay, and they will have assumed a responsibility in God's eyes that may well cost them their eternal salvation.

In modern life, technical progress has multiplied professions: the net result of our complex economic, social, and political organization depends on how well its individual parts function. The mechanism works well, when all of its wheels turn just as they should. Any role a man carries out is noble in God's sight if it is carried out faithfully.

This volume offers and deals with *preparation for professional life* and with the *principal professions*.

The profession of *doctor* is treated in general under the topics *medical morality* and the closely connected term *pharmaceutical morality*. Special articles are devoted to the crimes of *abortion, feticide, genocide*, and to the serious questions connected with *human experimentation, eugenics, euthanasia, artificial insemination, narcotherapy, psychoanalysis, human selectivity, truth-serum, sterilization*, etc.

The following professionals are also taken up: *artist, architect, lawyer, tax-collector, judge, salaried worker, businessman, engineer, manager, tutor, interpreter, teacher, magistrate, government official, military officer, accountant, critic, editor, mayor, inn keeper, salesman or field-representative, watchman, domestic, photographer, tailor, printer*, etc.

10. *Economics* is probably the area where the sharpest moral disputes are being carried on today. And this will cause no surprise if one recalls that modern economic science has come into being outside the Church, and hence has been reluctant to accept any direction from it.

The true notions of common good, property, and its limits; the function of capital and salary in its various forms; division of profits in business enterprises; determining what is superfluous, cases of extreme necessity, female employment, supply and demand, monopolies, the rights and duties of administrators and of brokers and stockholders, boards of trustees or governors, prices, etc., undoubtedly give rise to moral questions that are serious, delicate, and difficult.

There are many articles in this work dealing with the following: *economic autonomy, firm, bank, common good, balance sheet, boycott, burse* (exchange), *currency-exchange, capital, capitalism, coalition, collectivism, Communism, contraband, corporatism, credit, depression, concentration of wealth, economic crisis, cooperative, deficit, supply and demand, finance, investing, industrialism, inflation, interest, latifundium* (large estates), *labor, liberalism, free trade, raw materials, stocks and bonds, fee, weights and measures, just price, price controls, production, agrarian question, income, trade, strike, discount, lock-out, socialization, corporation, speculation, stability and stabilization, superfluous income, letters of credit, economic utilitarianism*, etc.

11. The *social* field, which is intimately bound up with the area of economics, presents problems which are just as serious from the moral point of view. Un-

fortunately, inhuman living conditions, inadequate living quarters with both sexes crowded into the same room, insufficient earnings, means of transportation, working conditions, recreational activities often serve as occasions of sin. The domestic institution, which is truly the germ-cell of society, must be given new strength and stability as a religious and moral, economic and juridical unit; harmony must be fostered between the various social classes; the State must be based on Christian principles and the relationships between nations must be guided by Catholic doctrine.

Aside from those already mentioned, the following articles deal with questions that are most pointedly social in nature: housing, begging, cohabitation, civilization, demography, emigration, pauperism, proletariat, social question, urbanization, etc.

Linked to these are those articles that deal with recreational activities: movies, radio, dangerous sports, vaudeville; and those that have to do with social services: news agency, press, telephone, social diseases, etc.

12. In the political field, we might point out the following articles: conservatism, demagoguery, diplomacy, government, imperialism, Machiavellism, political party, paternalism, politics, proportional representation, resistance to abuse of power, reform-movement, revolution, tyranny, totalitarianism, vote, etc., and, with regard to international relations: international arbitration, international treaty, war, economic war, cold war, United Nations Organization, peace, etc.

13. The collection of topics having to do with morality would not be complete, if we failed to speak of the means that the Lord has taught us to use in asking for the graces that we need to carry out our moral duties faithfully —namely, prayer.

Thus, the reader will find in this work articles dealing with mental prayer or meditation, vocal prayer, and ejaculations. A brief account is given of the more common prayers, such as the Our Father, the Hail Mary, and the Glory be to the Father, the Angelus, the De profundis, the Hail Holy Queen; the hymns more frequently used, such as the Pange Lingua, the Veni Creator; the canticles Benedictus and Magnificat; the sequences Dies Irae, Lauda Sion and Stabat Mater. Besides the Mass, certain other rites are explained: adoration of the Blessed Sacrament, Benediction of the Blessed Sacrament, Forty-Hours; and some pious practices: retreats and missions, special devotions for various months, pilgrimages; devotions to our Guardian Angels and the dead; sacramentals, like holy water, indulgences and the Holy Year or Jubilee Year.

To complete this liturgical information, mention is made of sacred objects, such as holy oils, relics, sacred vestments, sacred vessels, chalice, bells, candles, medals, and of sacred books, such as the Breviary, the Missal, the Ritual, the Pontificale, as well as sacred chant. Finally, sacred places are treated: church, oratory; and sacred seasons, such as Advent, Christmas, Easter, Pentecost, rogation days, all of which are coordinated by the Church calendar.

IV. THE AIM OF THIS BOOK

The purpose of this Dictionary is to give a complete picture of the ethical and supernatural evaluation of life. Moral theology rules over all human activity and it alone can bring this activity to a full development. The most serious objections to religion do not come from speculation, but rather from moral habits. There are many who would be willing to believe if the Creed did not involve the ten commandments as well. Difficulties of a theoretical nature are raised in order to justify or hide conditions of a practical nature. Man acts according to what he thinks, but he ends by thinking according to the way he acts.

Saint Augustine inveighed against the men of his time who were totally unconcerned about the fact that public life was corrupt: all that interested them was that the State be in a sound condition—rich, victorious, and tranquil. The rest, they said, did not matter. What was important was for each man to be able to increase his wealth and to keep those who were weak in subjection. No severe discipline was to be imposed; impure actions were not to be prohibited. Punishment should be meted out for any harm done to somebody else's vineyard but not for any damage inflicted on one's own innocence of life. Anyone who expressed dissatisfaction with this kind of happiness was to be considered as a public enemy, and the people were free to exile, depose, or kill him.[10]

The Bishops of the United States of America recalled these words of St. Augustine and applied them to our times in their 1951 Conference,[11] when they pointed out how our society is also menaced by two great dangers, barbarians from without and moral decadence—the product of a refined materialism—from within. So we have reason to fear that our society may fall just as the Roman Empire fell.

Today, too, dissatisfaction on the part of individuals, the break-up of families, the appalling state of society, open and hidden dishonesty, domestic and international disturbances, present evils and grave concern for the future—all are reducible to one major moral question.

It is impossible to attain the happiness to which the Lord has destined us without observing the law He has established. The will of God is the rule for all things. What is in conformity with the law of God leads man to his true goal; what is not becomes an obstacle to his final purpose.

It is impossible to have a morality that is not based on universal, unchangeable laws: a *self-made morality* is inadmissible, as is an individual morality which will change with the circumstances (*Situationsethik, morale de situation*), as this work points out. We cannot devote our lives simply to our own pleasure and interests, as *hedonism* and *pragmatism* suggest. Positive law, economics, and politics cannot be cut off from morality on the grounds that "business is business" and "religion should be kept out of politics."

---

[10] "Nullo modo curant pessimam ac flagitiosissimam esse rempublicam. Tantum stet, tantum floreat copiis referta, victoriis gloriosa, vel, quod est felicius, pace secura sit. Et quid ad nos? Immo id ad nos magis pertinet, si divitias quisque augeat semper, quae cotidianis effusionibus suppetant, per quas sibi etiam infirmiores subdat quisque potentior. . . . Non dura jubeantur, non prohibeantur impura. Quid alienae vineae potius quam quid suae vitae noceat, legibus advertatur. . . . Ille sit publicus inimicus, cui haec felicitas displicet; quisquis eam mutare aut auferre temptaverit, eum libera multitudo avertat ab auribus, evertat e sedibus, auferat e viventibus. . . ." (St. Augustine, *De civitate Dei*, Bk. 2, ch. 20: P. L. 41, 65).

[11] National Catholic Welfare Conference, News Service, Nov. 14–16, 1951.

Our whole being and all of our actions are subject to God; and so, individual life, family life, educational as well as professional life, business transactions and civic life are all subject to the will of God. Education must offer a clear teaching on right and wrong, according to the law of the Lord. In economics, men's working-conditions, their type of work, and the pay they receive are all subject to the moral law.

In politics, a deep sense of moral responsibility is demanded of both the elector and the elected official if the dignity of public life is to survive and bring about real progress.

The saintly Pontiff Pius X, while still a Cardinal, said: "Jesus Christ is King and Supreme King; and He must be honored as King. His thought must be in our minds; His moral law in our actions; His charity in all institutions; His justice in laws; His action in history; His worship in religion; His life in our lives."[12] And when he had become Pope he stated. "*Instaurare omnia in Christo* (Eph. 1:10). This is our program . . . to point up and to confirm . . . both natural and supernatural truths . . . to consolidate the principles of dependence, of authority, of justice, of equity that today are being trodden down, to guide all men according to the norms of morality, even in the area of social affairs and politics: and by *all*, we mean both those who obey and those who give orders."[13]

The specific aim of this book is to contribute, at least in a modest way, toward making the law of the Lord known, so that it may be better observed. "*Haec est vita aeterna: ut cognoscant te solum Deum verum et quem misisti, Jesum Christum.*"[14]

A description of just how unhappy the life of someone who ignores the law of God and puts all of his trust in human wisdom can really be is found in the Apostolic Letter written by the Supreme Pontiff, Pius XII, on the sixteenth centenary of the birth of St. Augustine (Nov. 13, 354).[15]

With a tone of sadness, the Pontiff adopts as his own the words of the Holy Doctor, who felt the most profound pity for those who are taken up with the ephemeral brilliance of meaningless doctrines and put all of their trust in human words and wisdom and look for nothing else. He had this to say of them: "Unhappy is the man who knows all things and yet remains ignorant of You, my Lord God; and blessed is he who knows You, even if he knows nothing else. Someone who knows You and all other things is no happier for knowing them; he is happy only because of You, if he knows You and glorifies You as God, is grateful to you and does not get lost in his own thoughts."[16]

---

[12] Acts of the Nineteenth Eucharistic Congress at Venice, 1898.

[13] Acta Pii X, vol. I, p. 56.

[14] John 17:3.

[15] Apostolic Letter Quamquam, July 25, 1954 (AAS 46, 513–517).

[16] *Summa erga eos miseratione commotus qui inanis doctrinae evanidis fulgoribus capti, humanae tantum sapientiae verbis fidem adiungunt, et nihil aliud quaerunt, haec habet: infelix homo, qui scit omnia, te autem nescit, Domine Deus meus; beatus vero qui te scit, etiamsi omnia alia nescit. Qui vero et te et illa novit, non propter illa beatior, sed propter te solum beatus est, si cognoscens te sicut Deum glorificat, et gratias agat, et non evanescat in cogitationibus suis.*" (St. Aug. Confess., Bk. 5, ch. 4: P. L. 32, 708).

Brief Summary of the History of Moral Theology

In the course of the centuries, moral theology has gradually become an autonomous science, separate from the other theological disciplines.

The first writings on Christian moral doctrine were for the most part ascetical works containing brief rules for the daily life of Christians and exhortations to the practice of virtue. The *First Letter of St. Clement to the Corinthians*, the *Didache* or *Doctrine of the Twelve Apostles*, the *Pastor Hermae* (Shepherd of Hermas) are examples of works of this type. The first to present a scientific treatment of moral theology in writing were Clement of Alexandria, Tertullian, Cyprian, Basil, and Gregory of Nyssa. They dealt with individual problems of Christian conduct; their chief aim was to defend Christian principles against pagan doctrines. Worthy of special note in this period are St. Ambrose, who contrasted Christian moral doctrine and Stoic morality in his work *De officiis ministrorum*, and especially St. Augustine. Because Augustine was a great theologian, philosopher, and psychologist, one finds in his writings a deep knowledge of the supernatural elements of Christian morality combined with an excellent understanding of the human heart and daily life. Obviously, such writings exercised a great influence on all later developments.

In the period immediately following, Gregory the Great, whose writings were rather of a pastoral nature, was particularly effective in offering a clear teaching on moral practice (*praxis moralis*) and on the laws of the Church.

Private confession, which came into use more and more at the beginning of the Middle Ages, produced a need for a new type of moral literature in so-called penitential books (*libri poenitentiales*); they had no scientific bent or leanings; they were merely intended to be helpful in pastoral practice, since they contained lists of various sins along with appropriate penances. Because of their practical usefulness, they were adopted quickly as the moral books of the clergy; examples of these books are the penitentials of St. Columban and Rhabanus Maurus.

The scientific treatment of moral teaching in the Middle Ages was closely bound up with the theology of that period; thus it developed in discussions of moral questions within the framework of the new *Summae Sententiarum* (Hugh of St. Victor, Peter Abelard, Peter Lombard) and in individual monographs, especially the *tractatus de virtutibus et vitiis* (Alcuin, Hincmar, Ratherius of Verona).

Even in the golden period of Scholasticism, moral theology was always treated in connection with theology in general, in the commentaries on the *Books of Sentences* of Peter Lombard which were written by the great theologians (Albert the Great, Alexander of Hales, Bonaventure, Thomas Aquinas, Scotus), and in the *Summae theologicae*, which treated theological problems more systematically and attached a greater importance to speculative problems and methods. The most important of these is the *Summa* of St. Thomas, the second part of which includes the best-known system of Christian moral doctrine.

The many writings of a mystical and ascetical nature which appeared at this time had no influence on scientific moral works.

The new work of the mendicant friars in the area of pastoral care, which sprang up suddenly in the thirteenth century, during the period when Scholastic theology reached its peak, necessarily led to the rise of a literature that was intended solely for the practical ministry of pastoral care; these were the *Summae confessariorum*, in which confessors found all that they needed in a condensed form. Here we have the beginnings of casuistical theology. The best-known works are: the *Summa* of St. Raymond of Peñafort, and the *Summae Astesana, Angelica, Silverstrina*. After this, as dogmatic theology could continue peacefully along its ancient paths, despite the new tasks which it had to face, moral theology was faced with many disturbing problems at the dawn of the modern era.

People had gained a knowledge not only of the ethics of the Greeks but also of their moral corruption; the simple, medieval concept of life and the world faded, and new relationships were arising between individuals and nations as a result of commerce and communications.This called for a reconsideration and reorganization of moral, juridical, and social duties. Voluminous treatises *de justitia et jure* were composed. It was the period of new impetus in moral theology which reached its apex soon after the Council of Trent, in the persons of Francisco de Victoria, the two Sotos, the two Lugos, Lessius, Suarez, Vasquez and Bartolomeo de Medina.

During this period, moral theology detached itself more and more from dogmatic theology. Previously, theological works had been written as commentaries on the *Sentences* or on the *Summa;* now books of moral theology were written along the order of the ten commandments. The practical side for confessors received more concern and was directed more and more toward a casuistical moral theology.

A period of decadence began in the middle of the seventeenth century, a kind of weariness with speculative theology; it was aggravated by the destructive influence of secular philosophy and a splitting up of theology in many schools. It was a time when moral theologians were to waste much of their energy on disputes over moral systems and to create an immense polemical literature that had nothing at all to do with theology in the true and proper sense of the term. This was the period when casuistry blossomed forth in a harmful manner, and problems were solved on the basis of different moral systems, which often led to solutions that were diametrically opposed, until the Church stepped in to condemn the two extremes of laxism and rigorism; a sound middle way was then finally found, under the guidance of St. Alphonsus. From that time on, moral theology tended more and more in the direction of casuistry, and the latter has retained the place of honor down to quite recent times, although there have been some isolated instances and examples of genuine, theological efforts.

The best-known moralists of the casuistical type are: Amort, Sanchez, Laymann, Busenbaum, St. Alphonsus, Reiffenstuel, Sporer, Elbel. The best-known representatives of the speculative-theological current are: Stapf, Stattler, Oberrauch, Sailer, Hirscher.

Even today, both methods are in use; each has its own justification and its own specific advantages. Casuists, like Gury, Scavini, D'Annibale, Marc, Lehmkuhl, Äertnys, Bucceroni, Ballerini-Palmieri, Cöpfert, Noldin, Vermeersch, Prümmer, Raus, Damen, Ojetti and Jorio have collected vast canonical and pastoral material in their manuals, which offer a wonderful preparation for the practical care of souls.

The representatives of the other trend who are best known are: Linsenmann, Simar, Müller-Seipel, Ruland, Tillmann, Koch, Schindler, Mausbach-Tischleder and Schilling. They seek a deeper knowledge of moral theology from the dogmatic and biblical points of view, defending and explaining it in the face of modern moral problems. At the moment, moral theology is being kept busy with modern problems posed by medicine, sociology, psychology, and international affairs. (Fra.)

Table of Contents

Dictionary of Moral Theology

ABANDONMENT (to God). The act or spirit of self-abandonment to God consists in complete conformity to the will of God in everything that flows from love and sacrifice. It is a high degree of the spiritual life; but if it is not well understood, it may lend itself to abuses.

The more ancient writers of ascetical theology called it *resignation* (cf. *Imitation of Christ*, III, 15, 17, 37; IV, 8).

The act or virtue of self-abandonment to God is based on the doctrine of the will of God and the will of man, which is a basic principle of Christian perfection. By conformity to the Divine Will man becomes united directly and intimately with Him who is the source of all perfection. In fact, by submitting his will—queen of all his faculties— to God, all other faculties of man are thereby placed at the service of God. Hence, it can be said that the degree of one's perfection depends on the degree of conformity of his will to the Divine Will. This conformity may consist in doing: (a) that which God has expressly indicated; and (b) that which pleases God, as shown through providential circumstances.

That which God has expressly indicated includes the following: (1) the Commandments of God and of the Church; (2) the counsels; (3) the inspirations of grace; (4) the constitutions and the rules in the case of religious men and women and religious communities in general. Obedience to the expressed will of God is the ordinary means by which perfection is achieved.

Doing what pleases God is based on the principle that nothing happens without the will or the permission of God, and that God, being infinitely wise and good, wills or permits only those things

that are for the good of souls, even though we may fail to see it. This type of conformity consists in submitting in everything to the will of God, in the joyful or the sad events willed or simply permitted by God for the greater good of man, particularly his eternal salvation. In this type of conformity there are distinguished three degrees of virtue corresponding to the three degrees of Christian perfection: (1) incipient, by which one moved by holy fear simply bears his cross (*see* Resignation); (2) proficient, by which one moved by hope bears his cross with a certain joy; (3) perfect, by which one consumed with love embraces his cross with eagerness. Anything whatsoever willed by God, particularly those things which are more especially pleasing to Him, may be the object of self-abandonment to God. Also in the incipient degree there is an inchoative form of the virtue of self-abandonment in God. This, however, is more manifest in those who have attained a perfect self-abandonment to God and who, guided by love and a desire for God's glory, welcome their crosses, desire them, embrace them with earnestness, not because they are desirable in themselves, but because they are a means by which they shall prove their love for God. They may go so far as to experience overflowing joy in the midst of their tribulation (St. Francis de Sales, *Theotimus*, 1, IX, c. 15). This last degree is called holy abandonment, and is present in the highest degrees of mysticism. As an habitual state very few souls attain it, not because God refuses such graces, but because very few correspond to them.

Conformity to the Divine Will causes a *holy indifference* to all other things except the service of God. In the conviction that God is everything and man is nothing (of himself), the soul wills nothing else but God and God's glory, being indifferent to everything else. This is genuine indifference, not a stoical insensibility, because the individual retains his inclination to things that are pleasing; nor is it a lack of concern or of prudence in the management of things temporal and human. As a matter of fact, the latter could be a matter of strict obligation.

Self-abandonment to God does not mean absolute passivity and inertia in prayer or in one's spiritual struggle; nor is it acceptance of one's own sins before their actual commission, nor acceptance of one's own damnation, nor absolute indifference regarding the virtues and one's own perfection. These are all exaggerated forms of self-abandonment to God (*see* Quietism).

A holy self-abandonment and submission to the will of God gives rise in the individual to a profound peace, for he knows well that nothing will happen to him that is not useful to his sanctification (Rom. 8:28); in fact, it will lead him to an intimate friendship with God. *Pal.*

ABBESS. Generally speaking, an abbess holds a position in a monastery of nuns similar to that of an abbot in a monastery of men.

An abbess is considered a person constituted in authority; in fact, she is *ex officio* administrator of ecclesiastical matters and enjoys a position of authority. With respect to her monastery and its dependencies, however, an abbess has only administrative and domestic authority; she possesses no legislative or judicial authority. Hence, she has no real and proper jurisdiction. According to the classic expression of theologians and canonists, the authority of an abbess in similar to that of a mother, or of a *pater familias*, so to speak. With respect to the bishop, however, she has at times a passive exemption, at least insofar as things of a material nature are concerned. With regard to her subjects, an abbess does enjoy a spiritual authority, that is, authority to direct, to cor-

rect, and to give commands, but the latter must remain within the limits set by the rule and the vow of obedience. The power of inflicting penalties does not go beyond disciplinary penalties. The power of directing is not to be understood in any way as a strictly spiritual jurisdiction, but only as concerning those measures which help toward a better observance of religious life by the individual member as well as by the community as a whole. Thus an abbess cannot bar a nun from the reception of the sacraments, nor can she hear confessions, nor distribute Holy Communion, nor apply canonical censures, nor reserve cases nor bless with a liturgical blessing the members of her community, nor bless sacred things, *etc.*

These things are mentioned because there have been some very rare cases of abbesses who, in certain periods of history, did arrogate to themselves powers which are proper to a true ecclesiastical jurisdiction. But these were cases of absurd usurpations which were quickly checked, or cases having a semblance of ecclesiastical jurisdiction interpreted in a very broad sense. *Pal.*

ABBOT. From *ab*, a root of the Semitic languages, meaning father. The abbot is the major superior who rules over a monastery or a *sui juris* house of monks or canons regular, with powers of jurisdiction and dominion, at least partially independent from other superiors.

In Egypt and in the East in general all elderly monks were called abbots by their own disciples; all religious were called abbots by the laity. Superiors of monasteries were commonly given the name of *hegumen* (which means head, leader) or *archimandrite*, signifying head of the flock. On the other hand, in the West the title of abbot was used exclusively to designate superiors, particularly the superiors of Benedictine monasteries or of monastic groups patterned after the *Rule* of St. Benedict. Later it was also used to indicate the superior of Canons Regular and corresponding branches of the female Orders (*see* Abbess).

In chapter two of the *Rule* of St. Benedict, the abbot is ideally the continuator of the paternal authority exercised by the Roman *paterfamilias*, with every right and duty over those who, having taken the vow of stability, place themselves under his direction in pursuit of evangelical perfection. Originally, every abbot was independent and had full powers; it was only with the rise of monasticism, a necessary development to be sure, that the creation of confederate abbeys subject to a general abbot came into being.

In the present legislation, the term *abbot* used without further specification always indicates the major superior (*q.v.*), although his authority may be limited by other abbots superior to him. The office of abbot is held for life. Tenure for life, however, is not enjoyed by an abbess (Can. 505–506).

The names and the distinction between commendatory abbot (clerical or lay), regular and secular abbots, and abbots *nullius* have a great juridical importance in Canon Law.

First of all, it should be noted that in the course of time many abbeys, for a great variety of reasons, suffered from a lack of monks and were therefore taken over by secular priests. This gave rise to the distinction, obtaining even today, between secular and regular abbots, depending on whether an abbey consisted of or belonged to secular priests or religious. The feudal system gave rise to the Commenda and therefore to commendatory abbots, secular priests or even laymen who enjoyed the revenues of an abbey commended to their charge in recognition of good works practiced in behalf of the Church or the monastic order. Abbots are of two kinds: "abbots *de regimine*" (ruling abbots) if they possess all effective rights in point of fact, and "abbots titular" if they merely have the title without power of government. Among the ruling abbots the Code mentions (a) the abbot primate, who presides over the federation of black Benedictines, according to a brief of Leo XIII, July 12, 1893; (b) the abbot who is the superior of a monastic congregation, presiding over a federation of several monasteries, and enjoying different titles and powers according to the various religious institutes, such as abbot president, abbot general, *etc.*; (c) the abbot of a monastery or a house *sui juris*, who, though belonging to a congregation, presides over his monastery or house *sui juris* and always enjoys, at least partially, the rights attributed by the Code to major superiors (C. 501). In some monastic religious organizations there is also the abbot visitor, who exercises a certain authority over a province or monastic territory.

A special category of abbots is that of *abbots nullius* (of no diocese), *i.e.*, abbots who have the same authority as local ordinaries over a territory set apart from every other diocese, and yet considered in everything similar to a diocese (Can. 319–327).

Abbots regular with the power of government must within three months receive the blessing from the local bishop, after which they enjoy all the privileges and rights proper to them. Of these, the most important are: the rights of using episcopal insignia, of celebrating pontifical functions, of conferring minor orders to their subjects, *etc.* (Can. 625). Man.

ABDICATION. Abdication is a formal act of voluntary renunciation of a high office, a throne, a princely dignity, and, much more rarely, the supreme pontificate. The abdication of a throne or a princely dignity is generally understood to be irrevocable. Abdication in no way implies a change in the order of succession or any future influence with regard to the office relinquished.

The abdication procedure is established by each individual constitution, which generally requires that the act of abdication be in writing and in a proper form.

Abdication of the Roman Pontiff: Abdication is not mentioned in Canon Law. The abdication of Pope Celestine V in the fourteenth century gave rise to a dispute on whether the pope could relinquish his office. Today no one denies the pope this right, and he alone can determine the procedure of abdication.

Royal and imperial abdications: The following are the more notable abdications of all times: Diocletian (A. D. 305); Charles V (1556), Napoleon I (1814); Wilhelm II of Germany (1918); Edward VIII, king of England (1936); Victor Emmanuel III, king of Italy (1946), Farouk, king of Egypt (1951).

The abdication by a prince, king or emperor may, at times, be a matter of grave obligation if required by the common good; by the same token, it could be a matter of grave obligation to resist abdication if imposed by external force, lest it become an act of treason or weakness. In all cases, the person faced with the question of abdication must be guided by consideration of the common good, rather than by his own individual advantages.

ABDUCTION (delict and sin). Abduction means violently depriving a person of liberty, for lust or with a view to contracting marriage with that person. The privation of liberty can consist either in the removal of the person from one place to another or the forced detention of the person in the place of her residence or in a place where she came freely. The violence can be either physical or moral (grave threats, deceit, *etc.*); it can be directed against the person abducted or, in the case of a minor, against those under whose custody she happens to be (parents, tutors), so that even the free consent of the minor does not do away with the malice of this sin. If for lustful purposes, the object of abduction can be any person, male or female. The scholastic term abduction approximates rather closely the modern term of rape (*q.v.*) (*Summa Theologiae,* II–II, q. 154, a. 7).

MORALITY. The particular malice of abduction is the violation of one's right to personal liberty, or, in the case of consenting minors, of the rights of their parents or tutors. If perpetrated for licentious purposes it is a species of lust and in common with rape (except in cases of consent) is a violation of the rightful use of one's own generative faculty (intentionally, if the abducted subsequently consents to the libidinous act).

In the case of the seduction of a minor who voluntarily follows her abductor, there is still a violation of the right of parents or tutors.

ABDUCTION (impediment of). The impediment of abduction is covered by Canon 1074: "Between the abductor and the woman abducted with a view to marriage there can be no marriage as long as the abducted person is in the abductor's power." Par. 2: "If the abducted woman, having been separated from the abductor and restored to a place of safety, consents to have him for a husband, the impediment ceases." Par. 3: "Insofar as the nullity of marriage is concerned there is no difference between abduction and the forced detention of a woman by a man who detains her with a view of marriage, in the place where she resides or came of her own accord."

Although the impediment is similar to that of force and fear, and for this reason the codes of civil law generally do not deal with it, yet it differs in that marriage is null until such time as she is restored to a place of safety—even if she would freely consent to marry him. In reality it represents a disqualification of the abducted woman to give a valid consent until such time as she is set free; the consent of an abducted woman is always a forced consent. Under the present discipline, therefore, the eventual marriage of an abducted woman, even if she would freely consent to marry her abductor, is null until it is contracted again according to the form established by the Council of Trent. Abduction should not, however, be confused with consensual elopement.

The impediment underwent various interpretations in ancient times, before it was definitely established by the Council of Trent. The Code has brought certain modifications to it, particularly by making it similar to forced detention.

Abductors incur canonical penalties (Can. 2353) and penal sanctions envisioned by all penal Codes. *Bar.*

ABILITY. *See* Inability.

ABJURATION. In a broad sense, abjuration is any retraction, renunciation, or repudiation of an idea, person, or thing made in the presence, and often upon request, of another person. In a theologico-canonical sense it is the renunciation or repudiation, under oath, of an apostasy, heresy, or schism made either in an internal or the external forum. In its strictest meaning, it is the renunciation under oath made in the external forum, according to a formula prescribed by the Church as a preliminary of a convert's profession of faith prior to the reception of baptism.

In the early centuries of the Church, in the history of ecclesiastical penal law, and especially in the practice of the tribunals of the Inquisition, numerous examples are found of abjuration made by penitents before becoming reconciled with the Church. The tribunals of the Inquisition demanded abjuration not only of formal heretics, but also of those suspected of heresy. Thus, according to the gravity of the crime, the offender was required to make the *abjuratio de formali, de levi, de vehementi, de violento.* Nowadays, the abjuration is required by the Code of Canon Law (Can. 2314, par. 2) in cases of reconciliation of apostates, heretics, and schismatics with the Church; it is still the practice of the Sacred Penitentiary to demand it *in an internal forum,* with definite formalities, from members of the Masonic sect and similar associations before their reconciliation with the Church (cf. Cappello, *De Censuris,* n. 302). The abjuration is not required of children below the age of puberty (Sacred Congregation of the Holy Office, March 8, 1882, *Coll. de Prop. Fid.* 2, n. 1566); such children do not even incur the corresponding penalty of excommunication (Can. 2314, par. 1; Can. 2230); those, however, who were born and raised in an heretical or schismatic

sect, even though in good faith, are required to make the abjuration, because good faith is not presumed (Can. 2200, par. 2).

The ritual for the abjuration to be made in the external forum is found in the *Pontificale Romanum* (p. 3, *Ordo ad reconciliandum apostatem, schismaticum vel haereticum*). In the case of those born in a non-Catholic sect, the Sacred Congregation of the Holy Office, in the Instruction of July 20, 1559 (*Collect. de Prop. Fide,* 2, n. 1178) established a special formula consisting of a profession of faith under oath, preceded by a brief declaration on the part of the abjurer, whereby he acknowledges that outside the Catholic Church there is no salvation. The abjurer then proceeds: ". . . against which faith I regret that I have gravely erred, having held and believed doctrines contrary to her teaching." The abjurer is then absolved from the penalty of excommunication (conditionally, if there be doubt that he may have contracted it), and a penance is imposed upon him. The Italian translation is found in the "*Collectanea*" referred to above; the French, English and German translations are found in the *Addenda* of the Roman Ritual. For the Orientals the Sacred Congregation of the Holy Office, in 1890 (no day or month indicated), approved a special formula, in which the errors of the Eastern Faith are expressly rejected (*Collect. de Prop. Fide,* 2, n. 1490, *notula* III, p. 126).

Formulae of abjuration were approved by the Holy Office in 1936, 1925, and 1933 respectively for Protestants, Eastern Orthodox and Russians. For the various texts see Ch. Quenet, *Cérémonies de l'abjuration d'un hérétique ou d'un schismatique,* Paris, 1936. The motive which inspired the formulation and approval of the more recent texts stems from a definite desire to emphasize the positive aspect of the profession of faith rather than the negative aspect of repudiation and execration. To this effect, in 1945, the Holy Office approved a shorter form for England, to be used at the discretion of the bishops. This same form was also extended to France in 1946. (*See* Y. Congar, "Abjuration," in *Catholicisme Hier, Aujourd'hui, Demain,* I, 38–40.) The abjuration must be made before the bishop or a person delegated by him, in the presence of a notary and some witnesses, but it is not necessary that it be made publicly (Sacred Congregation of the Holy Office, March 28, 1900, *Collect. de Prop. Fide,* 2, n. 2079). For the internal form the confessor may obtain from the Sacred Penitentiary the faculty to absolve heretics (except those who deliberately disseminated errors among the faithful) from excommunication and other penalties, and to receive their abjuration privately; he may also obtain the faculty to absolve from excommunication members of a Masonic sect or similar organizations, provided that they withdraw from and renounce the condemned society, as stated above.

Abjuration in an external form is required by the Church as reparation for the scandal given by the heretic or schismatic person, and as a guarantee of the sincerity of his conversion; it is required in an internal form as a guarantee for the confessor of the sincerity of the person's conversion and as a bond of perseverance for the new convert. (*See also* Heresy, Schism.) *Dam.*

ABLUTION. *See* Holy Water, Baptism, Mass.

ABOMINATION. *See* Blasphemy, Imprecation.

ABORTION. DEFINITION. Abortion is the expulsion from the mother's womb of a living fetus which is incapable of surviving outside the womb. It differs from embryotomy, which is the killing of the fetus while still in the womb. The essence of abortion consists in a deliberate separation of the fetus from the mother's body. Thus, if the fetus' natural and necessary tie to its mother's womb has already been broken, its expulsion from the womb is not abortion in the moral sense.

Abortion is: (a) natural, if caused by a condition beyond one's control; (b) artificial, if caused by human intervention; (c) therapeutic (*q.v.*) if performed by a person authorized to practice medicine; (d) criminal, if performed by a person not authorized to practice medicine; (e) direct, if the expulsion of the fetus is directly intended for any reason; (f) indirect, if the expulsion occurs as an unavoidable result of another necessary act. Thus, a deliberate expulsion of the fetus or the interruption of pregnancy is always direct abortion. Indirect abortion is an act resulting from accidental circumstances unintended and uncaused by the agent which brings about, as an accidental and secondary effect, the expulsion of the fetus.

HISTORY. Abortion, even therapeutic abortion performed for the purpose of saving a mother's life, was known and practiced by Greek and Roman pagan physicians, such as Hippocrates and Asclepiades. In the first and second centuries A.D., abortion had become a social scourge. The Christian writers Athenagoras (*Leg. pro Christianis,* 35), Minucius Felix (*Octavius,* 30), Tertullian (*Apologeticum,* 9) condemned any type of abortion as being prohibited by the divine precept: "Thou shalt not kill." By the preaching of her moral doctrine and the application of ecclesiastical penalties the Church almost succeeded in extirpating the vice of abortion. The doctrine of therapeutic abortion seemed to have been eliminated altogether by Christianized medicine; only one of the Apologists had come out in its favor (Tertullian, *De anima,* 25). But the resurgence of paganism in the wake of humanism raised the problem once again for the canonists and moralists of the fifteenth century. The problem of abortion became a burning question, so to speak, in the nineteenth century. The battle, bitter at times, lasted but a few decades. Toward the end of that century the Holy Office decided against the lawfulness of any direct abortion. Pope Pius XI solemnly promulgated this doctrine to the whole world in his encyclical *Casti Connubii* (1930).

MORALITY. Direct abortion is a grave sin and an intrinsically evil act because: (a) it is a special case of homicide and is hence prohibited by the fifth commandment; (b) tradition and Church doctrine condemn it; (c) the fetus is a human being, an intellectual creature, distinct from the mother. It is, therefore, an individual possessing natural rights, including the right to life. One who expels the fetus from the uterus deprives it of the necessary condition for life, just as one who closes the throat passage of a man places him in the condition of being unable to breathe. It is a violation of the right to life; hence, no case of direct abortion can ever be justified.

It may be objected that extreme necessity makes many things lawful. Many things, yes, but not all: there are inalienable rights which cannot be taken away, and one of these is the right to life. Human lives cannot be compared to material goods useful to all, for every individual possesses life as a constitutive part of his own person. It may be argued that if the fetus were aware of the circumstances he would certainly agree to save the life of his own mother by renouncing his own right to life; the consent of the fetus is hence prudently presumed. The answer is that no man has the power to renounce his right to life, because no one has the right to dispose of his own life (see Suicide). Even one's express consent would be invalid and would have no effect whatsoever; hence the so-called presumed consent, in the case of the fetus, is clearly insufficient to justify abortion. It may be objected that the fetus is an unjust aggressor and that the mother has a right to defend herself. The answer is that the fetus has done nothing unlawful for which it might possibly be considered an unjust aggressor. It may be objected further that it is better for one individual to lose his life rather than two, and it is morally proper to choose the lesser evil. The answer is that this is not a matter of choosing between the killing of one or of two, but of choosing between the killing of one and the failure to prevent the death of either one. The first is a moral evil; the second is not, if the only means of preventing death is a sinful act. The first—the moral evil—is the greater evil. Besides, the fact that one gains an immediate advantage by transgressing the law in no way proves that the law itself—an absolutely prohibitive law—is not to the advantage of humanity as a whole. The existence of an absolute prohibition is the only way of saving the greatest number of mothers, and it might even save them all. There are non-Christian or atheistic doctors who, after long experience, have acknowledged that the Catholic doctrine is the best method of saving the greatest number of mothers. Any wise person will admit the truth of Cicero's words: "Nothing is useful, if it does not conform with morality; not because that which is useful is moral, but because that which is moral is also useful" (*Ethics*, c.30).

CHURCH DOCTRINE. It is erroneous to say that the Church teaches that the life of the child has priority over, or is more important than, the life of the mother. The Church teaches that both are equally important and that, therefore, it is not permissible to kill one in order to save the other. To kill the fetus in order to save the mother is a sinful act, as it is sinful to kill the mother in order to save the child.

PROFESSIONAL OBLIGATION. It is often stated that the physician is sometimes required by professional obligation to perform an abortion in order to save the life of the mother. This is an error based on a false concept of professional obligation. The physician acts in the name of his patient; hence, by virtue of his contract, he has no right or obligation to perform an act that is forbidden to every man, to every patient, to every mother — namely, the direct killing of an innocent person.

ECCLESIASTICAL PENALTIES. Anyone (the mother included) who directly procures an abortion incurs excommunication; absolution is reserved to the bishop (C. 2350, par. 1). Although, strictly speaking, not a penalty, it is well to note that a procured, direct abortion also causes an irregularity *ex delicto* (C. 985, par. 4).

INDIRECTLY CAUSED ABORTION. Such an abortion is in itself illicit, but may become licit, if there is a proportionate reason, *e.g.*, the necessity of saving the mother's life provided that the death of the fetus is not caused by a direct action.

CAUSING THE DANGER OF ABORTION. If this is done with the hope and intention of causing the expulsion of the fetus, it is always gravely sinful. If done without this evil intention, it is more or less sinful, depending on whether the reason is more or less proportionate to the gravity of the danger.

CIVIL LAW AND LEGAL MEDICINE. Some modern civil codes follow a course which is somewhat different from canonical legislation. According to them, abortion as the interruption of pregnancy within the period between 180 and 265 days is called "premature delivery," and that between 265 and 275 days is said to be "precocious delivery."

Interruption of pregnancy is not always accompanied by actual expulsion (a necessary requirement for abortion in the canonical sense) of the fetus (abortive delivery); in fact, the dead fetus may remain in the uterine cavity for several months, even beyond the period of normal gestation. Such cases are referred to as *internal* abortion or *missed* abortion. If the interruption occurred within the first months of pregnancy and was not followed by an abortive delivery, it may sometimes happen that the dead ovum becomes completely reabsorbed by the surrounding tissues.

Some medical authors subdivide abortion into "embryonic" and "fetal," depending on whether the interruption of pregnancy occurs before or after the sixtieth day of gestation, since during the first two months the ovum, not having yet attained human form, is properly called an embryo (and is not yet a fetus). All students of medicine characterize abortion as either *spontaneous* or *induced,* the latter being subdivided into *therapeutic, eugenic* and

criminal (cf. above for divisions made by canonists and moralists).

Spontaneous abortion is truly and properly a morbid phenomenon brought about by the most diverse causes: constitutional, infectious, toxic, traumatic, *etc.* Among such causes, which are also distinguished as ovulary and maternal, external and internal, *etc.*, the most frequent and important is syphilis, of paternal or maternal origin; however, toxic causes (hetero-intoxications such as saturnism, tobaccoism, alcoholism, auto-intoxications of renal origin, *etc.*), traumatic causes (especially when repeatedly occurring in the vicinity of the pregnant uterus, such as surgical injuries, repeated coition, and the like) and social causes (the sum total of multiform pathogenic factors caused by the rhythm of civilization, factors which slowly contribute to the breakdown of the constitutional defense of the race), are not to be underestimated.

In view of their limited ethical value, we shall omit any detailed discussion of all the possible causes of spontaneous abortion, their mechanism, treatment, *etc.* We shall simply note here that, as Scremin says, in the case of uterine hypoplasia, the prevision of spontaneous abortion (neither intended nor desired) does not make the use of the marriage act unlawful; on the contrary, it well may serve as a means of clearing up the morbid condition.

Concerning induced abortion, it must be stated that, besides being a crime, the suppressing of an innocent life involves the danger of death for the mother (according to Maygrier, the rate of maternal mortality in induced abortion is well over 100 times greater than in spontaneous abortion) and also the danger—ethically and biologically no less serious—of permanently damaging the genital regions of the woman, which may well give rise to complications and grave disturbances in future pregnancies.

It is most deplorable to observe that the practice of abortion is constantly on the increase, independently of forms of government, ethnical origin, and economic conditions of the various peoples.

In all probability, this increase is due to the subversion of ethical values, the undermining of religious principles and the prevalence of egoistic and hedonistic instincts, characteristic of large segments of the population of the civilized world spiritually and materially shaken by two global wars within the span of thirty years.

Mention has already been made that the pontiffs have repeatedly raised their voices against abortion practices. Authoritative physicians and hygienists have also sounded a note of alarm over the grave threat levelled against the future of civilization.

REMEDIES. In view of the increasing prevalence of such perverse practices, it is imperative that remedial measures be taken, e.g., strongly reminding young couples of their moral duties, advocating severer legal penalties against the practice of abortion, and improving the economic conditions of larger families. *Riz.*

ABORTION, THERAPEUTIC. As stated in the article on "abortion," therapeutic abortion is a sub-species of induced abortion. We may add that, morally, it is its most dangerous sub-species, because, while criminal and eugenic abortion are directly repugnant to the conscience of honest men, therapeutic abortion, that is, abortion artificially induced (in the face of a grave and not otherwise avoidable danger for the life of the mother), "has some semblance of good, insofar as it is intended (in theory) to safeguard the life of the mother" (Scremin).

The cases in which therapeutic abortion is claimed in some circles as necessary may be divided into *major* and *minor*. Roughly, the major cases today may be reduced to the following four: (1) *pernicious vomiting:* when all remedies used appear to have been in vain and the patient appears unable to tolerate as little as a sip of water and develops a cachetic condition; treatments of a neuro-vegetative and psychotherapeutic nature are very effective; (2) *serious nephropathy*, when it fails to respond to medical treatment; (3) *pul-monary tuberculosis*, of a particularly serious nature; (4) *cardiopathic disturbances*. Thanks to the progress of modern medicine and improved surgical techniques, the dangers connected with the more serious cases are gradually diminishing. Their number, of course, increases if one adds the so-called minor conditions in which the main consideration is not the saving of the mother's life but a very general concern lest continuation of pregnancy will in some way impair the health of the mother; or the conditions of phobia, or fear of a eugenic or a social nature, or apprehensions of overly timid, impressionable, preoccupied and fundamentally egoistic spouses, and the like.

Catholic moral teaching makes no distinction between major and minor conditions; it simply and unequivocally states that therapeutic abortion, like all other types of induced abortion, is immoral. The Catholic moral doctrine flows directly from the divine precept, "Thou shalt not kill"—a precept recalled also by Pope Pius XI in his famous encyclical *Casti Connubii* (*De matrimonio christiano*), in which therapeutic abortion is condemned as *direct killing of an innocent person*. And indeed, as Scremin declares, the embryo (and, in its successive stage of development, the fetus) is "innocent," not only because incapable of intending any harm to the mother, but also because its presence in the mother's womb is the result of a deliberate act on the part of the parents for which the fetus bears no responsibility whatsoever.

Therapeutic abortion is forbidden by Catholic moral teaching even in the case where the condition of the fetus is such that it cannot survive outside the womb. This prohibition is based on the fact that such certainty is always relative and also on the principle that no one has the right to shorten the life of another person who, because of some grave illness, appears certainly destined to lose it within a short time (*see* Euthanasia).

The position of the Church in the matter of therapeutic abortion finds most ample justification in objective statistics, which show that (still quoting from Scremin) "the rigid application of the ethical norm, on the whole, saves the greater number of lives; therapeutic abortion, again on the whole, sacrifices the greater number of lives." In fact, in the cases of pulmonary tuberculosis and grave cardiac diseases (which are the more common reasons for performing therapeutic abortion), interruption of pregnancy saves barely 5% or more of the mothers, but is responsible for a total sacrifice of fetal lives. This one fact alone is sufficient to justify the rigid dictates of Catholic moral doctrine. Furthermore, if all obstetricians accepted the Church's position that the procuring of abortion is forbidden under all circumstances whatsoever, they certainly would make a greater effort toward putting into effect a larger number of hygienic measures and therapeutic treatments, which would certainly result in a sharp decline in the number of fatalities and perhaps in their complete elimination.

In treating an expectant mother, the Catholic doctor has but one duty, namely, to seek to bring the pregnancy to a successful end by every curative means possible, firmly resolved never to resort to any type of abortion.

Convinced of the validity of this principle, the obstetrician shall draw from the recesses of his conscience the necessary strength to reject the theory favoring therapeutic abortion on the ground that in certain cases it represents "the easier solution" (as Misch Gasper quoted by Scremin charges). He will also reject the attitude of those who, by an oversimplification of the various factors involved, decide against the life of what they call "an unknown intruder" in order to alleviate the suffering of a pregnant mother, or those who acquiesce in the natural urge to "do something" for a pregnant woman in a dangerous condition.

Not even in those cases, rare in practice, in which the obstetrician might be inclined to feel that a particular abortion, though contrary to his Catholic conscience, would seem to be medically necessary, is he allowed to resort to interruption of pregnancy. It shall be his duty to adopt all possible curative means to save the mother's life, protecting at the same time the unborn child's right to life.

In a case where the patient or a relative or the family physician were to insist on the necessity of therapeutic abortion, the obstetrician shall withdraw from the case; nor is he permitted to offer technical advice or collaborate in any other way. The physician shall confine himself to explaining the immoral and dangerous nature of any such measure; he shall endeavor to improve the condition of the woman's health and urge confidence that the pregnancy will be brought to a successful end.

In some cases, especially in cases of pernicious vomiting, which seem to be connected with a more or less unconscious aversion of the mother against pregnancy, the physician could resort, as a psychotherapeutic measure, to a simulated abortion. Such simulation is morally licit, provided that the patient does not regard therapeutic abortion as sinful, that there be no scandal and that the patient, upon recovery, be told the facts, including the disclosure that abortion was not necessary.

INDIRECT ABORTION. Indirect abortion is somewhat similar to, but not identical with, therapeutic abortion. Abortion is called indirect when the death of the fetus (or its expulsion at a nonviable stage) follows as the result of a medical treatment or surgical operation upon a pregnant patient, and there is no relation of cause and effect between pregnancy and the condition operated on; in other words, the same operation might be performed on a non-pregnant woman if the same therapeutic conditions were present.

Indirect abortion is morally licit, because the doctor does not directly kill the child to save the mother as in the case of therapeutic abortion, but simply gives medical or surgical assistance to the mother, even though he foresees the certain death of the child. The case, to use an example well-known to moralists, is comparable to that of an individual who, unjustly attacked by a pregnant woman, kills her in self-defense with the consequent death of the innocent fetus. In such a case the man is not guilty of the death of the fetus because its death was in no way intended, nor was the killing of the woman the direct cause of the death of the fetus.

It goes without saying that, while it is quite licit for a physician to treat a pregnant woman who is seriously ill, even though he foresees that abortion will follow, nevertheless he must do all that lies within his power to prevent this eventuality from occurring. *Riz.*

ABROGATION. Abrogation is the cessation of a law by virtue of a more recent one. Abrogation may occur only in reference to positive laws, not to natural laws. A subsequent law may abrogate the former law by explicit declaration, in which case it is clear that the former law is abolished either in its entirety or in part, depending on the wording used in the abrogating law. At other times abrogation is only implicit, in the sense that whatever in the former law is found to be incompatible with the more recent law is abolished, even though the latter does not state that the former law is abolished. This form of abrogation may also be total or partial, depending on whether the incompatibility extends to the entire subject matter of the pre–existing law or only to a part thereof. A third form of abrogation, also implicit, occurs when the more recent law regulates the entire subject matter already regulated by the preceding law. This form of abrogation is always total. The very fact that the new law intends to legislate *ex novo* on the entire subject matter, giving it a new aspect, reveals the intention to abolish the old law, even though it does not expressly say so. Since abrogation is a juridical effect of the new law, it does not become operative until the new law goes into force; hence, until that time, the preceding law is still in force.

Sometimes the terms *obrogation* and *derogation* (*q.v.*), as distinguished from abrogation, are employed. The term *obrogation* is used in the two cases of implicit abrogation, especially when the incompatibility of the two contrasting laws does not reach the point of contradiction; *derogation,* on the other hand, is used in the case of a partial abrogation of a law or even of a total abrogation thereof, but having a limited effect, namely, restricted to a part of society to which the law applies. This terminology, however, is not constant among authors; in fact, it is not found in modern codes of law. *Gra.*

ABSENCE, ABSENTEEISM. Besides its common meaning of non-presence, the word absence has a special connotation in juridical terminology.

In its ordinary meaning, absence has a moral import, especially in the following instances: (a) when it denotes non-presence or lack of participation in an activity that one is bound to attend (*e.g.,* deliberations or other meetings, judicial hearings, religious functions, *etc.*); (b) when it constitutes a violation of the law of residence within a specified territory, which certain individuals, by virtue of their office or for other reasons are bound to observe (*see* Benefice, Beneficiary, Pastor); (c) when it relates to the duty of employees in general who are expected to report to their places of work at specified hours.

In its special meaning absence refers to the case of a legally missing person, *i.e.,* one who has disappeared from his last place of residence or domicile and whose whereabouts are unknown. The case of missing persons is covered by civil law, which establishes norms designed to safeguard and regulate all family and property interests of the missing person, as well as those of the spouse and legal heirs, if any (especially in case of prolonged absence with presumption of death). The status of legal absence ceases with the return of the missing person, or with evidence of his whereabouts, or of his death. Almost all civil codes admit the possibility of declaring, after a certain lapse of time, the presumed death of a missing person (*see*

Presumed Death, Presumption of Death); they also contain special norms governing cases where a person, legally presumed dead, is later found to be alive, or where the death of a missing person occurs after he was legally declared to be presumed dead. *Cip. See also* Beneficiary, Choir, Residence.

ABSOLUTION. The freeing or loosing from accusation, imputation, sin, and penalty is called absolution. Absolution may be sacramental and non-sacramental.

Sacramental absolution consists in the words whereby a duly authorized priest grants, in the name of God, the forgiveness of sins or offenses against God to one who is sincerely sorry for them, confesses them, and accepts the penance he is given to do. To be effective, these words, which constitute the form of the sacrament of penance (*see* Penance), presuppose three acts on the part of the penitent: contrition, confession, and the will to make satisfaction. The essential words of the form are: "*Ego te absolvo a peccatis tuis in nomine Patris, et Filii, et Spiritus Sancti*"—"I absolve you from your sins in the name of the Father and of the Son and of the Holy Ghost" (Roman Ritual, tit. IV, c. 2, n. 2).

Sacramental absolution is imparted to each penitent following accusation of his sins. When, however, there is imminent danger of death, or when there is no time or opportunity for making a confession (*e.g.*, in the event of shipwreck or air raid in wartime), absolution may be imparted collectively to all who manifest repentance for their sins by some visible sign, *e.g.*, the striking of the breast. Such collective absolution is truly sacramental. When the danger is over, however, each person has the obligation to confess, both as to species and number, all the grave sins already remitted through collective absolution (Sacred Consistorial Congregation, December 8, 1939; AAS 31 [1939], 712; Sacred Apostolic Penitentiary, December 10, 1940; AAS 32 [1940], 571).

The Roman Ritual (*q.v.*) prescribes that sacramental absolution be preceded by absolution from ecclesiastical censures, and followed by the prayer by which the confessor implores that the passion of Our Lord Jesus Christ, the merits of the Blessed Virgin and of all the saints, and all the good works performed and the adversities borne by the penitent may be a title for him for the remission of his sins, increase of grace, and the reward of eternal life. For a good reason this prayer may be omitted, without affecting the validity of absolution.

NON-SACRAMENTAL ABSOLUTION is also called general absolution. An example is the blessing imparted by the pope, either personally or through a delegate, to all the faithful in danger of death (because of illness, old age, or any other cause), with a plenary indulgence which may be gained only at the very moment of death (Can. 468, par. 2); this blessing may not be repeated during the same illness or danger. Any priest assisting the sick and the dying has the faculty to give the apostolic blessing, which is usually imparted immediately after the administration of the last rites (*see* Papal Blessing). To gain the plenary indulgence attached to the apostolic blessing, in addition to the state of grace and the intention of gaining the indulgence, the following conditions are required: confession and Communion, if possible; resignation to the will of God, acceptance of death as a penalty for one's sins and of the sufferings accompanying death as coming from the hand of God; the oral invocation, or if this be impossible, at least with the mind and heart, of the Holy Name of Jesus, and the act of contrition and of charity (Benedict XIV, bull *Pia Mater*, April 5, 1747).

The blessing, with a plenary indulgence attached, imparted by special permission of the Holy See to members (including tertiaries and oblates) of certain religious orders on specified days is also called general absolution. The conditions for gaining the indulgence are: confession, Communion, intention to gain the indulgence, and an oral prayer for the intention of the Pope (one Our Father, Hail Mary and Glory be to the

Father will suffice (AAS, 25 [1933], 446). Man.

ABSOLUTISM.

In a literal sense, absolutism signifies that form of government in which the executive power is free (*absolutus*) from all restrictions or controls, absorbing into itself also the legislative and judiciary powers. It was through such a method that monarchism sought to become established in the national states which arose in Europe at the close of the medieval era. The aim of absolutism was to suppress the political power of the feudal lords and to eliminate the limitations which the assemblies of the three influential social classes—the clergy, the nobility, and the smaller land-owners and bourgeoisie (called in France the "third estate")—endeavored to impose upon the activities of a bureaucracy created by and directly dependent upon the king.

The absolutism that had failed in England was successful in France, where the kings' efforts to destroy political feudalism and to unify the nation met with favor among the bourgeoisie and the people. Absolutism reached its highest expression with King Louis XIV, who proclaimed: "*L'Etat c'est moi*," "I am the State." The same doctrine prevailed also in the rest of Europe, at the beginning of the modern era. It would be a mistake, however, to believe that this kind of absolutism eliminated completely all limitations on the king's power. To begin with, in those days monarchies maintained a religious character consisting of the rite of consecration of the kings, who in matters of religion and conscience were subject to the moral law of the Gospel and to the authority of the Church. Moreover, there were certain institutions, such as the French Parliament (a judiciary body), which were still able to exercise a measure of control over certain official acts of the king. Finally, ancient local customs and class privileges were potent factors in placing real and effective restrictions on the theoretically limitless authority of the crown. All these restrictive influences acted to ward off despotism, that is, a power so constituted as to be free of all controls. This type of power is in itself immoral, whether it be in the hands of one individual or a class or any group of people. Royal absolutism enjoyed the support of the populace until the period prior to the French revolution of 1789, and through the action of a bureaucracy, which gradually perfected itself both culturally and technically, it performed a beneficent historical function in behalf of modern civilization. But the reaction against it, which asserted itself in the seventeenth century in England, spread in the following century to France and exploded into a revolution. Our age is characterized by a real or presumed consciousness of political maturity in all social classes which enables them to participate in the government of their country through elected representatives (democracy).

It may not be superfluous, if only for the interpretation of history, to raise the question of how an absolute government may rise and lawfully continue in power. The answer must be found in the tacit consent of the people who would recognize as opportune and beneficial for the common good, in view of particular circumstances, that the supreme power be left in the hands of one man. The ruler (whatever his previous conduct) finds himself *de facto* invested with sovereign power. By assuming the reins of government he automatically accepts certain obligations toward the people, and he acquires also the right to rule, so long as he fulfills his obligations toward the people and so long as the conditions which made the establishment of an absolute government a necessity continue. However, the citizens do not lose their right—one of the natural rights of the human person—to participate in the national government in a manner corresponding to existing historical conditions. The minimum of such participation is always present in the right to resist abuse of power. A further imperishable and inalienable right is that of gradually acquiring a greater measure of participation in government, as the people grow in their maturity and ability to carry out such participation, and in their consciousness of such ability (this depends largely on economic, cultural, and spiritual circumstances). The presence of the two requirements—that of the absolute ruler in possession of the historical, positive, and legitimately acquired right of sovereignty, and that of the people in possession of their natural right to participate in the government according to their recently matured capacity—gives rise to problems of a rather practical nature. These two rights require a realistic evaluation of certain facts. On the part of the people, the fact to be ascertained is whether their maturity for participation in government is real or merely illusory. On the part of the ruler, the fact to be ascertained is whether, from the standpoint of the common welfare, there still exists the need for concentration of power in his hands. Because of a different realistic evaluation of these two facts, there developed among Catholics in the past century a twofold attitude in the face of internal political changes so typical of the age. Some Catholics remained in favor of absolutism, others advocated new and liberal institutions. As long as these differences continued, the followers of both attitudes were justifiable in conscience. But once the historical crisis was solved, there was no other course but to recognize and accept whatever form of government corresponded more closely to the actual needs of the times. *Boz.*

ABSTINENCE AND CONTINENCE.

Abstinence, even according to its etymological meaning, is the practice of abstaining from something, particularly certain types of food and drink, and from sexual intercourse. This practice, which is based mainly on religious motives, has been known by practically all peoples from remotest antiquity.

The practice of abstention from certain foods was based in some cases on the fact that a sacred character was attributed to an animal or (less frequently) to a plant, by virtue of which it was forbidden to kill or even to eat that particular animal; in other cases it

stemmed from ideas related to the transmigration of souls; in still other cases it was based on the belief that a certain animal was impure because possessed by the devil or because considered sacred by rival peoples, *etc.* In all probability, at least in some instances, the prohibition of certain foods had a hygienic basis, as is obvious in the prohibition of fermented and intoxicating beverages. No such prohibitions exist among Christians with the exception of abstinence from eating flesh-meat on the "days of abstinence" (Fridays and a few other days) and penance (*see* Fast and Abstinence).

Sexual abstinence (*continence* or *chastity*), not as a moral virtue, but as restricted to certain persons, times, and places, is very common even among peoples of lower civilizations. Such continence is the effect of ideas surrounding the sex act, considered wicked and nefarious if practiced, *e.g.*, between kinsmen or between persons of different tribes, or before or during certain events, such as a hunting trip, a war, religious festivals, *etc.* Among peoples of higher civilizations, absolute or relative continence is often recommended or prescribed as a duty. But only in Christianity is chastity (*q.v.*) regarded as a moral, rational virtue. This virtue extends not only to the control of external acts, but also of appetites, desires, and impure thoughts, the constant elimination of which constitutes an indispensable condition of abstinence as a virtue. Absolute continence (not commanded, but counseled by the Gospel) excludes, for reasons of greater moral perfection, all and any gratification whatever of the sexual instinct. By relative continence is meant the sexual act restricted to the married state and performed in accordance with the dictates of man's nature.

The objections commonly raised against sexual abstinence are the following: (1) it is impossible to observe it; (2) it is harmful to one's health. It is a popular misconception that men, unlike women, are incapable of practicing sexual abstinence. This preconceived notion is based on the allegation that a high percentage of men abandon themselves to the satisfaction of sexual desire rather frequently, which they try to justify on the ground that it is a widespread practice. It is a fact that many keep themselves chaste either because of a correct moral persuasion or because of fear of disease. This chastity, like any other abstinence, is easier to practice for anyone who has never contracted the habit of impure acts; as a matter of fact, the longer the abstinence from the sin of impurity, the less difficult the practice of purity, especially when practiced according to the dictates of Christian morality, *i.e.*, carefully avoiding all occasions of sin and promptly banishing from one's mind unchaste thoughts and desires. This fact, ascertainable in the personal experience of each individual, proves the great wisdom of the religious norms which (apart from their profound ethical value) constitute the best method for attaining and preserving the state of chastity, without undue hardship and almost without a struggle. As for the popular misconception that sexual continence is damaging to health, this has long since been exploded by numerous histological, biological, clinical, and neuropsychiatric studies which have shown that in man, as in the animal, sexual abstinence produces no harmful effects upon the physiological activity of the gonads or upon the physical health of the individual, or even upon his nervous and mental equilibrium.

Thus, it is a known fact that, when seminal emission ceases, spermate-genesis slows down and may even become arrested through a compensatory mechanism inhibiting the activity of the testicular parenchyma, and that upon resumption of copulation, it is readily and promptly re-established. It is also to be kept in mind that the periodical occurrence of nocturnal pollutions in man constitutes an automatic and physiological regulation of gonadic activity. There is no proof that any neuropsychical disorder, psychoneurosis, or psychosis is the result of sexual abstinence. Some few modern scholars hold the opposite view, simply because they have observed such disturbances in subjects who, either be-

cause of fear of disease or for reasons other than spiritual, practiced continence from the physical standpoint, but resorted to indulgence in sexual fancies. We, on the other hand, here refer to that form of continence which is adopted voluntarily as a moral principle and is accompanied by a sane and wholesome rule of life, which excludes all indulgence in unchaste thoughts and imagery. Finally it is to be noted that many individuals are led to practice sexual abstinence by some phobia, obsession, or other psychoneurotic condition; in such cases it is quite clear that continence is an effect, not a cause of the psychosis.

It may be useful to mention (particularly for the benefit of doctors) that opotherapeutic remedies (use of extracts of animal organs, hormonal therapy) are very often found to be beneficial in treating psychoneurotic disturbances considered as effects of sexual abstinence. In such cases, timely treatment—a combination of psychotherapy and rational physical therapy—will help to restore the psychosomatic health of the individual, or at least reduce his anxieties and other psychoneurotic disorders, with no need at all to discontinue (much less to advise discontinuance) of the practice of chastity.

Sexual abstinence, then, is neither harmful nor impossible; and even the aforementioned disturbances, essentially functional in character, may be effectively treated, with no need to interrupt or discontinue the practice of continence. On the other hand, it is a well-known fact that in individuals suffering from psychoneurosis with a sexual basis, the discontinuance of continence often leads to other obsessions and further psychical disorders caused by remorse, fear, *etc.* Hence, even for this reason (not to mention the risk of possible contagion) the interruption or discontinuance of continence as a therapeutic measure is always blameworthy, and not merely from the standpoint of Catholic morality. It is well that all this be firmly understood by doctors and others who are frequently consulted concerning such matters, so as to be able always to prescribe, with a firm and enlightened conscience, sound and wholesome measures conforming to both moral and medical norms.

Absolute continence (*see above*), dictated by motives of Christian perfection, is for this very reason the privilege of a minority. The practice of such continence, as already noted, becomes progressively easier as the individual continues to avoid every occasion of sin and to banish unchaste thoughts and desires in his efforts toward acquiring inner purity. Concerning relative continence of young unmarried people (who some day will marry and raise a wholesome family), it, too, can be facilitated by a fundamental chastity of mind; such premarital continence, far from contributing to impotency or psychoneurosis, is an effective means of insuring the development of a well-balanced psychophysical personality. According to the eminent clinician, Marañon, such continence is "a eugenic principle of primary importance." *Riz.*

ABSTINENCE AND FASTING.

In a theological sense and as a moral virtue, abstinence is a habit which inclines the will, according to the inspirations of right reason and faith, to a moderate use of food, particularly flesh meat, as a means of fostering one's spiritual life; in this sense, abstinence is a part of the cardinal virtue of temperance. (*q.v.*).

The material object of the virtue of abstinence consists in the use of food or in acts directed to self-preservation. The moderate use of food and drink, as prompted by right reason and faith, constitutes the formal object of the virtue, while its formal motive is the particular character that shines forth in the practice of said moderation.

Vices opposed to abstinence are, in one extreme, insensibility or excessive abstention from food and drink and, on the other, gluttony or the immoderate use of food. Gluttony may be committed in a variety of ways—by gorging oneself, by eating greedily and selfishly, by inordinate enjoyment of food, by outeating others for a reason other than excessive desire for pleasure.

Owing to a general attitude of aversion for any form of physical mortification, the prescriptions concerning fast and abstinence are regarded as unreasonable and ridiculous by those who fail to understand the spirit and motives behind such laws. In Scripture and tradition fasting and abstinence are represented as voluntary privations, designed to strengthen and preserve the various faculties or powers of the individual. Religion, mindful of man's deep-rooted tendency to evil and of the need to provide suitable remedies against this tendency, prescribes abstinence as a necessary aid in the struggle against the law of the flesh. Moreover, abstinence is prescribed as a means of atonement for the numerous lapses into which even the best of men fall because of human frailty. Abstinence is also prescribed for reasons of charity and justice, in the sense that the privations and mortifications of the faithful serve to help in the spiritual needs of others.

As already noted, these prescriptions, regarded in every age as necessary to man's spiritual welfare, date back to the earliest days of history. Thus, the law of abstinence from certain foods is found in the Old Testament as well as in the New. In ancient times the faithful abstained, on certain days of the year, not only from meat, but also from wine and oil. The practice of fasting and abstinence preceded the precept. In fact, the Church was compelled to intervene against certain false and objectionable practices of abstinence, such as those advocated by the Manichaeans and Catharists. Thus, according to the prescriptions of the *Apostolic Canons* (*circa* A.D. 400), punishment and excommunication (with the penalty of deposition for clerics) were inflicted upon those who for a wrong motive abstained from marriage, meat, and wine (*non propter exercitationem, sed propter detestationem*).

The discipline regarding fasting and abstinence is contained in Canons 1250–54 of the Code of Canon Law. The law of abstinence forbids the use of flesh meat and of soup or gravy made from meat, but not the use of eggs, milk, and milk products, nor the use of condiments of any kind, even though made from the fat of animals (Can. 1250). The law of fasting imposes certain restrictions concerning the amount of food one is permitted to take.

According to St. Thomas, the prohibition of meat is justified by the necessity of repressing bodily concupiscence, which is more readily and particularly stimulated by feeding upon the flesh of warm-blooded land animals, whose flesh is better suited to the needs of the human body. In determining the exact species of animals that could or could not be eaten on days of abstinence, popular opinion exercised considerable influence. Permission to use eggs, milk products, and condiments made from animal fats is but the conclusion, made into a general law, of a long and continued practice, sanctioned by repeated concessions and particular indults. The provisions of Canon Law concerning fasting and abstinence were recently modified through the use of special faculties granted by the Holy See on November 16, 1955.

The law of abstinence is binding on all who have completed their seventh year of age (Can. 1254, par. 1), provided that they have attained the use of reason, which is usually presumed at this age (Can. 12). Abstinence may be *complete* or *partial*. Complete abstinence is to be observed on all Fridays, Ash Wednesday, the vigils of the Immaculate Conception and Christmas. On days of complete abstinence meat and soup or gravy made from meat may not be used at all. Partial abstinence is to be observed on Ember Wednesdays and Saturdays and on the Vigil of Pentecost. On days of partial abstinence meat and soup or gravy made from meat may be taken only once a day, at the principal meal, the time of which is left to the discretion of each individual.

Everyone over twenty-one and under fifty-nine years of age is also bound to observe the law of fast. The days of fast are the weekdays of Lent (including Holy Saturday, until midnight), Ember days and the vigils of Pentecost, the Immaculate Conception, and Christmas. On days of fast only one full meal is permitted. Two other meatless meals, sufficient to maintain strength, may be taken according to each one's needs; but together they should not equal another full meal. On a day of fast, meat may be taken at the principal meal, except on Fridays, Ash Wednesday, and the vigils of the Immaculate Conception and Christmas. Eating between meals is not permitted; but liquids, including milk, coffee, tea, and fruit juices, are allowed.

When a holy day of obligation occurs on a day of fast or of abstinence, the law does not apply. Sometimes, too, local Ordinaries grant a dispensation when civil holidays occur on such days. When health or ability to work would be seriously affected, the law of fast and abstinence does not oblige. *Pal-Yan.*

ABULIA. *See* Will, psychology and pathology of.

ABUSE, of the sacraments. *See* Sacraments.

ABUSE OF POWER. Abuse of power (in Canon Law more properly called abuse of authority or of office) takes place whenever an individual, transgressing the limits of his proper competence (or neglecting to fulfill the inherent duties proper to his office or authority), commits an improper act. In order to understand precisely the abuse of power it is necessary to use as a starting-point the concepts relative to office and authority (*see* Superior). The sum total of attributions which a person in office (or in authority) has the right and duty to exercise, marks off the positive and negative limits of that person's authority and, therefore, constitutes that person's competence.

Starting from the premise that abuse of power always gives rise to a penal offense (Can. 2404), we shall note that Canon Law considers the matter of abuse of power under three aspects: (a) as a specific crime connected with specific criminal activities (*e.g.,* in cases of abuse of ecclesiastical authority: Can. 2405–2414, as also in cases of abuses against the legitimate observance of ecclesiastical discipline: Can. 274, n. 4; 336, par. 2, *etc.*); (b) as a specific aggravating circumstance (as in crimes enumerated in Can. 2373, n. 2; 2390, par. 2; 2399); (c) as an ordinary aggravating circumstance (Can. 2207, n. 2) relative to any offense (*e.g.*, if an individual were to take advantage of his authority or office to commit any of the offenses enumerated in Canons 2320, 2326, 2328, 2345–2346, 2360–2362, 2392, *etc.*).

In general, modern civil codes consider abuse of authority or of office under the same aspects as Canon Law. The basis of their penal dispositions is beyond dispute, namely, a specific malice is present if a given criminal activity is performed by a public official or by one who is invested with authority. This fact also gives rise to a more serious diminution of social safety; hence, the application of specific penal dispositions. *Vio.*

ACCELERATION OF BIRTH. *See* Delivery, Premature.

ACCELERATION OF DEATH. Acceleration of death is the same as the shortening of life. The first expression is used when death is already close at hand; the second, when death is still more or less remote.

Nowadays the direct killing of a person who is soon to die, even without any outside intervention, is called acceleration of death. This is a misuse of terms and tends to cause a certain confusion. If the killing of a person who is soon to die can be called "hastening of death," then the killing of a healthy and youthful person can also be called acceleration of death. The difference between the two cases is purely accidental. In the first instance life is shortened by a matter of days; in the second instance by many years—and there is no way of telling precisely how many. In a certain sense every killing is an acceleration of death. If, therefore, one can hardly speak of acceleration of death in the second case, one cannot properly speak of it in

the first case either. Direct killing (including euthanasia) is not acceleration of death but homicide or suicide. Calling it acceleration of death only serves to conceal the true nature of the act. Acceleration or hastening of death indicates an act that is distinct from homicide and suicide. It is an action or manner of acting that does not of itself cause death, but which exercises such a harmful and weakening effect on the human body as to result in a gradual depletion of its natural powers, and in eventual death, *e.g.*, working continually in an unhealthy environment, drinking alcoholic beverages to excess, performing excessive penances, *etc.*

One who does things with the intention of hastening his own death always commits a sin. Given reasons of grave necessity or of great usefulness, however, one may licitly perform an act or lead a life that will certainly or most probably hasten death or which will shorten his life. However, the more rapid the hastening of death, the more serious must also be the reasons for its justification. *Ben.*

ACCEPTANCE OF PERSONS. *See* Favoritism.

ACCESSION. Accession is an addition to property by growth, increase, or labor. It is also a manner of acquiring ownership of a thing which becomes united with another object that is possessed by another person. It may also be the joining together of two things, forming something new in the process. As regards law and morality, no particular problem arises if the things joined together belong to the same owner, or if different owners take care of the things united by virtue of a stipulated agreement. On the contrary, if two or more things belonging to different owners are joined together without mutual consent, then dominion over the new thing is determined according to the principle of equity, already in force in civil law, *viz.*, if the two things can be separated, then the separation must be effected, and each thing reverts to its respective owner; if separation is impossible, then the accessory object becomes part of the principal object (*accessorium sequitur principale*), unless the accessory object is of such economic value as to exceed, in the common estimation, the value of the principal object. In any case, the owner benefiting from the accession must make suitable payment to the original owner of the accessory object (suitable payment is determined by the amount of the addition acquired—*id quo factus est ditior*); on the other hand, if the accession is acquired in bad faith, the indemnification is determined according to the loss suffered by the innocent party (*quantum domini interest*).

Immovable goods may acquire accessory increment through the industry of man or through the mere action of nature. Examples of industrial or artificial accession are: building, planting, or sowing on another person's soil; in these instances the classic principle obtains that the increment belongs to the owner of the soil: *Quidquid plantatur, seritur vel inaedificatur, totum solo cedit, radices si tamen egit.* The landowner, however, must reimburse the owner of the material for any expense incurred in the act of building, planting, sowing, *etc.* In the event that the owner of the material did the building, planting, or sowing in bad faith, he may be obliged, according to some positive laws, to remove the material from the landlord's property at his own expense, provided that the request for the removal thereof shall have been made within the time and in accordance with the conditions specified by law.

If the owner of the incremented land, the user of the materials, and the owner of the materials are three different persons, then the owner of the materials may reclaim them, after the user of the materials has removed them from the landlord's property, and provided that the removal can be effected without great damage either to the materials or to the land. The right of reclaiming these materials, however, is not admissible, according to some positive laws, after the expiration of six months from the day that the owner of the materials was apprised of their incorporation into another's land. If no request is made for the removal of the materials from the land or if the materials cannot be separated, then the user of the materials and the landowner, if he be in bad faith, are obliged to indemnify the owner to the full amount of the value of the materials. The owner of the materials may demand indemnification even from a landowner in good faith, who, however, is obliged to pay his own share only, and not the share of the user of the materials. Furthermore, the owner of the materials may seek compensation for damages both from the person who may have used the materials without permission and from the landowner who, in bad faith, may have authorized their use.

Natural accession or accession through natural forces alone is verified in the case of *alluvion, avulsion* and formation of a *new island.* By alluvion is meant the land-to-land accretion that occurs gradually and imperceptibly on properties along the banks of rivers or streams. If such accretions of land come about perceptibly and suddenly, as by an inundation or a current, then they are referred to as avulsion. Both in the case of alluvion and avulsion the landowner becomes proprietor of the portion of land added to his property: in the case of avulsion, however, suitable payment in proportion to the increased value of the property brought by the added land must be made to the original owner, at least according to some positive laws. If a river or stream forms a new bed in place of the old, it belongs to the owners of the land bordering the two banks; the respective owners may effect a division from the limits of their property to the center of the bed. If, instead of forming a new bed, a river or stream becomes gradually disjoined from one of the banks and carries soil away with it, the washed-away soil belongs to the owner of the land where it settles; and the original owner cannot put in any claim for his lost land, since the whole occurrence was an act of nature (*natura enim contingit*).

The accession of movable goods may come about by *union, specification, confusion* and *commixture*.

In accession by *union* the different objects, although forming one unit, remain substantially distinct, as in the union of metals, the union of embroidery, painting, or writing and the materials on which they are executed. At any rate, if the different objects cannot be separated without grave damage, then the owner of the principal object becomes owner of the accessory object, unless the accessory object is of such value as to be considered itself the principal object (as, *e.g.*, a painting in reference to the canvas upon which it is executed); in which case, the owner of the accessory article may either claim ownership of the whole thing or separate his object therefrom, even though this cannot be done without loss to the other owner. In every case, however, the owner who has been deprived of his object must be suitably reimbursed, according to the principles already posited at the outset. If it cannot be established which of the two objects is the principal one, each owner retains ownership of his own object.

Accession by *specification* occurs when one thing is transformed into another, when one species has been transformed into another species, so that one may say that a new thing or a new species has been formed: it is, in other words, the accession of a new form to pre-existing matter. If an individual employs a thing belonging to another to form something new, he acquires ownership thereof, with the obligation, however, of compensating the owner of the original thing for his loss, unless the value of the original thing notably exceeds that of the newly-formed one, in which case the exact opposite holds true.

Accession by *confusion* is the commingling of different liquids; accession by *commixture* is the union of solids. If such a union, either of liquids or of solids, gives rise to a new species, the principles of accession by specification are to be

followed; if the union does not give rise to a new species and the separation of the component elements cannot be effected without notable damage, then the whole commixture becomes common property, each owner receiving a portion commensurate to his original contribution. But if one of the commingled things can be regarded as the principal thing, then the principles laid down for accession by union are to be followed. *Fel.*

ACCESSORY. *See* Accession.

ACCIDENT. By accident is meant any *sudden mishap,* unforeseeable or involuntary, resulting in injury and impairment. By injury is meant any anatomical alteration. By impairment is understood the effect caused by the alteration upon the function of this or that organ.

Accidents may be of two kinds: (1) *labor accidents or liabilities:* (2) *extra-professional accidents.* In all civilized countries labor accidents are covered by obligatory forms of insurance. Such is not generally the case with regard to extra-professional accidents, which are often covered by voluntary forms of insurance. The insurance company estimates the damage not on the basis of the injury but of the impairment, for it is this which effects the individual's usefulness, particularly his ability to work.

Labor accidents are indemnified if they are brought about by a cause outside the will of the individual and take place in connection with his work. The cause need not necessarily be mechanical; it is sufficient that it be a cause related to a task, and productive of an injury that is not altogether superficial. In fact, *professional disease* (*q.v.*) is not a labor accident because the violence of the cause is lacking. As for the connection with work and the event, the accident must happen while actually at work, or during the phases preparatory to the work (*in itinere*), or in other contingencies connected with the work.

Various conditions are required in order that extra-professional accidents may be indemnified. These are usually specified in the insurance policies or in the contracts of work. In these there may be supplementary clauses which vary according to the insurance company, which can extend or restrict the concept of accidents (*e.g.*, exclusion of accidents caused by inebriation, imprudence, disregard of laws and regulations). As to the cause, it must be proven that the injury was produced exclusively by the accident. The smaller the number of exclusions, the higher the cost of the premium.

Employers are generally obliged by law or feel inclined for reasons of self-protection to carry liability insurance. (A great variety of legislation exists in this field, and for details concerning these the reader should consult the laws and the customs of each individual country.—Editor's note.) *Par.*

ACCIDENTS (Eucharistic). *See* Eucharist.

ACCOMPLICE (in sin). By this term is meant participation in or, to be more correct theologically, cooperation (*q.v.*) in another's sin.

A penitent is not required to disclose (in fact, normally he must withhold) the name of his accomplice in sin. Hence, the confessor must guard against seeking the name of the penitent's accomplice (Can. 888, par. 2). The confessor may only demand, and at times for the common good must demand— even under penalty of denying absolution—that the penitent denounce his or her accomplice to the proper superior outside confession. He may also inquire concerning any proximate circumstances necessary for the integrity of the confession, even though he may accidentally learn thereby the identity of the accomplice. But any deliberate inquiry, direct or indirect, into the name of the penitent's accomplice (formal inquiry) constitutes a grave sin and an abuse of the confessional.

A confessor who may have had the misfortune of performing external impure acts with another is forbidden to ab-solve his accomplice from such sins, even if committed prior to his becoming a priest. In such cases, absolution of one's own accomplice is illicit and invalid for lack of jurisdiction (Can. 884); and this obtains, whether the absolution be formally and genuinely imparted or whether it is only feigned.

In order to incur the sin of complicity or to be truly considered an accomplice, the following conditions must be present: (a) the act committed must be a mortal sin, both materially and formally; (b) it must be a grave sin for both, *i.e.*, the sinful action must involve formal complicity, which is clearly present not only when both partners actively and willingly engage in the impure action, but also when one of the participants, though remaining passive, manifests consent by failure to offer proper or sufficient resistance; (c) the sin must be an external act against the sixth commandment, for only external sin admits of complicity; (d) the sin must be certain; (e) the sin must be one not yet directly remitted.

A confessor who absolves or pretends to absolve his accomplice in a sin of impurity automatically incurs excommunication reserved in a most special manner (*specialissimo modo*) to the Apostolic See (Can. 2367, par. 1). The excommunication is not incurred, however, if the priest merely hears the confession of his accomplice without imparting or pretending to impart absolution, although this, too, is forbidden. The priest accomplice does not escape the censure by inducing the penitent, either directly or indirectly, to omit mention of the sin of complicity and then proceeding to impart or feign absolution.

Thus, except in danger of death or in cases of very urgent necessity, absolution of one's own accomplice is always invalid and illicit. In danger of death, the absolution is always valid, though not always licit. To be both valid and licit the following conditions must be present: (a) no other priest, even one lacking jurisdiction to hear confessions, is present or available; (b) another priest cannot be called without danger of grave infamy or public scandal.

A priest under censure for absolving or attempting to absolve his accomplice may not himself obtain absolution from a confessor having general or special faculties to absolve from papal censures; but a very special faculty is required (Can. 2253, n. 3). Nevertheless, in danger of death (Can. 2252) and in other very urgent cases (Can. 2254, n. 3), any ordinary priest may absolve from this censure, with the duty, however, of imposing upon the penitent priest the obligation of recurring within a month to the Sacred Penitentiary under penalty of relapsing into the censure (*sub poena reincidentiae*).

The object of such ecclesiastical legislation, which dates back to Benedict XIV (Const. *Sacramentum poenitentiae* of June 1, 1741) is to avoid the danger of: (a) seduction; (b) relapse into the same sin; (c) abuse of the confessional. Certainly it would be highly improper and unbecoming for a judge in the sacred tribunal to pass sentence on his own crime. *Pal.*

ACCUSATION (because of solicitation in confession). *See* Denunciation, Solicitation.

ACCUSATION (in criminal causes). *See* Denunciation, Attorney, Promoter of Justice.

ACCUSATION (in matrimonial causes). *See* Denunciation.

ACCUSATION OF SINS. *See* Confession.

ACCUSER. *See* Plaintiff, Process.

ACOLYTE. *See* Holy Orders.

ACROBATICS. The word *acrobatics* is derived from two Greek terms: *akro,* meaning aloft, and *bainein,* meaning to go, or walk. Originally, the term was applied to a funambulist or ropewalker; later it was extended to mean the act of entertaining the public with impressive but dangerous gymnastic performances of any kind whatsoever.

Acrobatics comes in for moral consideration insofar as the acrobat exposes himself to the danger of death or of serious bodily harm (*see* Danger of death). In forming a judgment concerning the possibility of danger, the acrobat may take into account his acquired skill or ability, which makes him certain of the absence of any serious danger. He is obliged to take all possible steps to remove any danger, during practice sessions as well as during the actual performance. To invite danger, or not to take the proper measures for avoiding danger, merely to satisfy the public craving for sensationalism is not in accord with moral principles. Acrobatics is subject to the same moral norms which forbid the exposing of oneself to the danger of death or injury, without a cause proportionate to the danger. Attendance at acrobatic performances is not sinful, unless one is certain that the performance is against morality: such certainty is not easily attainable, because the spectator does not know the nature of the act nor the acrobat's skill. To attend such performances out of mere craving for sensationalism is, however, reprehensible and unwholesome. *Ben.*

ACT, HUMAN. An act is called human if man is its master. Mastery here refers to that psychological dominion or control which man exercises in determining himself to act; hence a human act may also be defined as one which proceeds from man by virtue of his free determination.

All those actions which, though physically posited by man, are nevertheless withdrawn from the psychological dominion of the subject, such as the act of an insane person or an act performed during the state of sleep, are excluded from the category of human acts. Such acts, in the technical language of moral theologians, are properly styled acts of man, not human acts. An act of man, or a non-human act (in the sense defined), escapes all ethical evaluation; hence, only human acts constitute the proper object of moral science. The individual's dominion over his actions is directly proportionate to the degree of knowledge and freedom which he enjoys.

The distinction between external and internal human acts is universally known. The former possess an aspect that renders them perceptible, even if not actually perceived, to an observer other than the performing subject, such as a gesture of the hand; the latter take place within the subject and remain enclosed within himself, such as the act of meditation, a movement of the spirit, *etc.* It is to be carefully noted that it is quite possible to have human acts that are merely internal, but it is impossible to have human acts that are merely external, for the main and simple reason that if an act is devoid of every internal element (of knowledge and will), it is no longer a human act.

Another well-known distinction is that of good and evil acts, depending on their conformity or non-conformity to the moral norm. In the abstract, *i.e.*, in a purely objective consideration, one may think of a number of acts which have no relation to the moral law and which, therefore, are indifferent; but in the concrete, *i.e.*, considering the act as related to the acting subject, the common opinion denies the existence of indifferent acts, maintaining that every true human act must be either good or bad.

From the theological standpoint human acts are divided into natural and supernatural, depending on whether they are performed only by our own natural powers or under the influence of divine grace.

A heroic act is one attended by very serious obstacles and difficulties, the performance of which requires exceptional will power on the part of the subject, such as the exposing of oneself to grave and imminent danger of death. *See also* Circumstances of the human act, Object of human act. *Gra.*

ACT, HUMAN (end of). The end of an act is that toward which the act tends.

An act may tend toward different ends. The ends, which are disposed either on the same or on different planes, may be direct or indirect, proximate or remote (both to a greater or lesser degree), intermediate or ultimate. These terms require no explanation. Here it need only be noted that, objectively speaking, the ultimate end of every human act—indeed of every man and of the entire universe —is one alone, *i.e.*, God, to be glorified and to be attained in eternal life. A plurality of ultimate ends is possible only because of human ignorance and perversion.

Less simple but more appropriate to moral doctrine is the distinction between an intrinsic and extrinsic end. The intrinsic end is that to which the act tends by its very nature; hence, it is the objective end, inseparable from the act itself. It is also called the end of the act or work (*finis operis*) and is the necessary effect of the act. The extrinsic end is that to which the act is directed by the acting subject (*finis operantis*); hence, it is the subjective end, separable from the act itself. Thus, the intrinsic end of study is to learn, but the extrinsic end may differ and vary from one individual to another, *e.g.*, vainglory, gain, deceit, *etc.*

The end toward which they tend exercises a considerable influence over the morality of our actions. There is no difficulty arising from the isolated consideration of the intrinsic and the extrinsic end; for it is quite clear that the former, entering as it does into the objective constitution of the act itself, weighs also upon the conscience of the subject performing the act. Likewise, it is quite clear that the extrinsic end, in determining the will to act, communicates its own moral quality to the act. Difficulties arise from the encounter of the two ends (intrinsic and extrinsic) and from the different relations in which they become involved. To clarify the issue, it is helpful to keep three distinct hypotheses in mind: the coincidence of the intrinsic and extrinsic ends, their concordance, their discordance.

When the subjective and objective ends fully coincide with each other, the distinction of the two ends remains purely conceptual. In this case there arises no problem or difficulty, for the subject simply makes, in a reflective way, the morality of the intrinsic end his own.

When the subjective and objective ends are in agreement, at least regarding the general quality of good or evil, then the moral aspects of the two ends merge in the conscience and in the responsibility of the subject, with the edge for the end, usually the subjective, which exercises the greater influence over the determining faculty.

When the two ends are at such variance with each other that one is good and the other evil, the greatest difficulties arise concerning the moral evaluation of the act. In this case, if the objective end (intrinsic, inseparable) is evil, the act cannot be justified by any subjective end (extrinsic, inseparable) — a conclusion necessarily flowing from the principle that evil may never justify illicit means. If, however, the objective end is good but the subjective end is evil, then the malice of this end can nullify or diminish the goodness accruing to the action from the objective end; the goodness is nullified or destroyed when the subjective end is morally evil, or when it is the exclusive motive of the act; it is diminished when the subjective end is not gravely evil and is not the sole motive of the act. *Gra.*

ACT, HUMAN (object of). Moral theologians ordinarily distinguish three elements in a human act: the object, the end, and the circumstances. This distinction appears somewhat empirical, since it is not so easy to assign exact limits to each element. Regarding the first element, it is to be noted that, in a wide but proper sense, the object of a human act includes everything that is set before the will as the matter or object of its act; thus, this object would also contain the end and the circumstances of the act. Moral theologians, however, preferring to restrict its meaning, designate as the object of the human act only that which constitutes its central nucleus, prescinding from its more concrete elements, end, and circum-

stances. The physical object, however, must be distinguished from the moral. The physical object is the nucleus of the act considered in its reality—psychological, economic, *etc.*; the moral object is the nucleus of the act considered in its ethical value—that is, it is the first element whereby the physical act is transferred into the moral field and is rendered subject to moral evaluation. Thus, the physical object of the act of insulting someone is the *fact of speaking* or saying something; the moral object is the uttering of *injuries*. In the object as thus defined, moral theologians see the first source of the morality of our actions; and justifiably so, for common sense teaches that, in order to pronounce a judgment on a man's moral behavior, one must first find out what he has done—that is, one must inquire into the object of his acts.

Certain objects are moral (*good or bad*) in themselves; hence, the actions whereby they are performed are always and necessarily either good or bad, provided that the actions are executed in a human way. As a result, certain objects and actions are intrinsically moral or immoral, *e.g.*, to praise the Lord is insically good; to blaspheme Him is intrinsically evil.

There are certain other objects which do not necessarily or intrinsically bear any moral connotation. These are called *indifferent*, and include all objects which we have called physical, *e.g.*, talking, reading, writing, walking, *etc.* Such objects are, in themselves, devoid of intrinsic morality, but they may acquire a moral connotation from an extrinsic source, *e.g.*, from a command or a prohibition. Some authors also hold that morality may here arise from the circumstances, as, for example, speaking obscenely, reading irreligious books, *etc.* This, however, is incorrect, for, morally speaking, obscenity of speech and the irreligious character of certain reading do not constitute the circumstances, but are the first moral element of the act of which they are the object; their presence marks the transfer of the act from the physical into the moral order. *Gra.*

ACT, JURIDICAL. Any fact possessing some sort of legal relevance, particularly any fact producing a legal effect, such as the institution, extinction, or modification of a legal relationship, is called a juridical fact in a broad sense.

In a strict sense, however, a *juridical fact* ordinarily designates an effect that is not directly dependent upon man's will (*e.g.*, the birth or death of an individual, the passage or lapse of time, *etc.*); whereas a juridical act usually applies to an effect brought about by man's will, an essential element for the verification of juridical effects.

Among the various kinds of juridical acts the more important ones are: (a) *licit* and *illicit*, depending on whether they are legally permitted (sometimes even commanded) or forbidden; (b) *unilateral, bilateral,* and *complex.* This second classification refers to the number of persons participating in an act and to the manner of participation therein. Thus, a *unilateral* act is that involving the activity of but one individual (*e.g.*, making a will, acknowledging paternity of an illegitimate child), or even of several subjects acting in one and the same direction (*e.g.*, the collective renunciation of a right by several possessors of that right); a *bilateral* act is one involving two or more individuals acting in opposite but convergent directions (*e.g.*, the stipulation of a contract); lastly, a *complex* juridical act is one which, besides the action of the principals, calls for the consent, approval, confirmation, attestation, *etc.*, of a third party or parties, either public or private (*e.g.*, the notarizing of a document, legal witnesses at a marriage ceremony, *etc.*).

The general category of juridical act, especially in private law, has for a long time included a more restricted distinction of acts, designated as juridical or legal transactions, for which there has been formulated a body of general principles applicable to all types of similar acts and constituting a *general doctrine of legal transactions.*

By legal transaction is ordinarily understood a juridical act consisting in a direct manifestation of intention or will to produce a juridical effect. Hence, the essential requisites of every legal transaction are: (a) *will* or intention of the subject or subjects; (b) their *competence* (natural or legal), for the will-factor alone has no effect before the law, unless it emanates from a competent subject; (c) *external manifestation,* without which the internal will has no legal force or value. Moreover, other essential requisites are established by the law for each type of legal transaction, while still other requisites may be imposed by private will.

The lack of any one of these essential requisites, as also the illegality of the transaction, renders the act *null* and *void*—that is to say, the transaction is not recognized by law as having any juridical effects; similarly, when the external manifestation does not coincide with the internal will, or when the external manifestation is executed in a manner or form other than that prescribed by law, the act or transaction is considered to be null and void. In these matters, however, the law has enacted dispositions for the protection of the innocent parties. On the other hand, the legal transaction is not rendered null and void by the lack of minor and unimportant requisites, nor even by the simple irregularity of essential requisites, but it does become voidable—that is to say, the party or parties concerned are given the legal right to contest the validity of the transaction (normally the decision of nullity or voidance must be handed down by a judge). Among the factors more commonly inducing voidable transactions are the so-called defects of will, such as grave fear, substantial error, willful deceit, *etc.* In such instances, the will factor is present, but is rendered defective by the above-mentioned irregularities.

Finally, we must consider the *pendency* of a legal transaction. A legal transaction is said to be pending when its existence and effects are prevented from realization because of the lack of some requisite, which, however, may still be realized. The most common instance of this type of transaction is found in a case where the principal parties make their will dependent upon a future contingency (condition), the verification or non-verification of which will determine the existence of the legal transaction (in this case the condition is called suspensive) or its cessation (resolutory condition). *Cip.*

ACT OF CHARITY. *See* Charity, Prayer.

ACT OF FAITH. *See* Faith, Prayer.

ACT OF HOPE. *See* Hope, Prayer.

ACT OF SORROW. *See* Contrition, Prayer.

ACTA APOSTOLICAE SEDIS (ACTS OF THE APOSTOLIC SEE). The A.A.S. is the official organ of the Holy See and of Vatican City. Its language is Latin. It was instituted by Pope Pius X by the Constitution *Promulgandi*, on September 28, 1908, and began its publication on January 1, 1909. Its editorial and administrative standings were clearly defined by appropriate regulations, published on January 5, 1910. The text of the Code of Canon Law was published in the June 28, 1917, issue of A.A.S.

Today, as provided in Can. 9 of the C.I.C., all the laws issued by the Holy See are published in A.A.S. unless an exceptional method of promulgation is used. These laws become binding three months from the date appearing on the issue of the periodical containing the law, unless the very nature of the law demands its immediate enforcement, or a different time is expressly indicated.

The publication is issued periodically and assembled into annual volumes. Besides the publication of laws, it contains citations of the Roman Tribunals, appointments, and the schedule of papal audiences granted to chiefs of states and their representatives. Since 1929, a *Supplement of Laws and Dispositions for the Government of Vatican City* is published in the Italian language. *Pal.*

ACTA SANCTAE SEDIS (ACTS OF THE HOLY SEE). The *Acta Sanctae*

Sedis is the periodical that preceded and paved the way for the Holy See's official publication *Acta Apostolicae Sedis* (A.A.S.).

At the private initiative of the Reverend Pietro Avanzini, founder and first director, the *Acta Sanctae Sedis* made its initial appearance in Rome in 1865 under a somewhat different title, *Acta ex iis discerpta quae apud S. Sedem geruntur;* this was changed to *Acta Sanctae Sedis* in 1870. It ceased publication in 1908, when the official organ of the Holy See, *Acta Apostolicae Sedis* (*q.v.*), was established. During the period of its existence forty-one volumes were published, including the indices published every ten years, and the general index published in 1909 by C. Pecorari. The publication contained the acts of the supreme pontiff and the various congregations, some commentary on the documents, and a few articles. The *Acta Sanctae Sedis* was a private publication until May 23, 1904, when a special rescript of the Sacred Congregation for the Propagation of the Faith declared it to be the authentic and official organ for the future acts of the Holy See. *Pal.*

ACTION, CATHOLIC. Catholic Action is the participation and collaboration of the Catholic laity in the apostolate of the hierarchy (Pope Pius XI).

The earliest Catholic actionists were the laity of apostolic times, whose main task consisted in disposing souls for the reception of the Gospel, in providing for the maintenance and defense of the apostles against the insidiousness of false brethren, and in assisting the faithful in their material and spiritual needs. Such collaboration, more or less extensive, was continued in Christian communities, and assumed various forms according to the needs of the times. Thus, in the different ages there came into being the Orders of Christian Knighthood, the *Misericordia* (mercy) Fraternities (institutions of charitable and merciful works), the Franciscan and Dominican Third Orders, the Art and Trade Guilds, the *Montes Pietatis* (charitable establishments of credit that loaned money at low rates of interest, especially designed for the protection of the poor against usurers), the Confraternities of Christian Doctrine, *etc.*

The Protestant revolt and, later, the French Revolution, made it even more imperative for the Catholic laity to take an active part in the defense and extension of the Church. The Lutheran attempt to overthrow the hierarchy, placing the Church at the mercy of rulers and peasants, was met with a surging tide of the faithful generously lending their cooperation in the spiritual revival of Christianity (such as the Company of Divine Love at Rome) and in the work of providential Catholic reform. As a reaction against the rationalistic, atheistic, and Jacobin spirit of the French Revolution, which dissolved the guilds and suppressed religious institutes and schools, there arose here and there, almost simultaneously, new organizations of Catholic laity: in France, the *Ligue Catholique pour la défense de l'Eglise*; in Belgium, the *Union Catholique*; in Germany, the *Katholischer Verein*; in England, *The Catholic Union*, in Spain, the *Asociaci de catolicos*; in Italy, the *Associazione cattolica per la libertà della Chiesa*. Almost at the same time there arose movements of a social character, which received the stamp of approval in the encyclical *Rerum Novarum* of Pope Leo XIII (1891). Naturally enough, these various movements and organizations were not lacking in uncertainties, conflicts, and deviations of thought; but the healthy current continued in the midst of the stormy vicissitudes that made urgent an ever-growing need for organized lay activity in the social and political spheres of life, not only for the defense of the religious and moral values of the Catholic faith, but especially to bridge, between the Church and the world, the chasm which had been created by the various sects and by liberalism, materialism, capitalism, socialism, *etc.*

After the tragic experience of the First World War, Pope Pius XI, the Pope of Catholic Action, with far-reaching insight into the exigencies of the times, reemphasized the collaboration of the laity (on the parochial and diocesan level) in the ecclesiastical order. Pope Pius XII, continuing in the footsteps of his predecessor, developed the doctrinal content of Catholic Action and contributed to the elaboration of its organizational technique. Throughout the nations of the world Catholic organizations are constantly increasing and developing under the watchful care of the bishops. This vast movement, embracing various and variable institutions according to different places and people, by its very nature transcends national borders. Catholic Action expands into international organizations, such as the *Conférences des Présidents*, while the Holy See promotes the constitution of *Actio catholica* (1940) and of the *Permanent Committee for World Congresses of the Lay Apostolate* (1952).

Catholic Action, therefore, is the principal organization of militant Catholics under the strictest direction of the hierarchy; it is officially representative of the lay apostolate. As an instrument at the service of the hierarchy and as an extension of its arm, it is by its very nature subject to the direction of its ecclesiastical superiors. By reason of this dependence, the title of Catholic Action may also rightfully (*pleno jure*) apply to the *Marian Congregations* (Pius XII, *Bis saeculari*, September 27, 1948). By divine election and personal mandate, the apostolate belongs in a full and total sense to the apostles chosen by Christ. From the apostles it was transmitted, through lawful succession, to the bishops in communion with the Roman pontiff. By virtue of their sacred ordination, priests become the *cooperators with the hierarchy in the sacred ministry*, while the laity, by reason of their incorporation in the Mystical Body of Christ, are called upon to lend their active collaboration to the coming and extension of the Kingdom of God in the world. Although God does not grant to all men the qualities and abilities proper to a specific apostolic vocation, nevertheless the apostolate binds all the faithful, as a *duty* connected with their personal *mission in life*, to an active participation in, and courageous profession of, the Faith. "For we are the good odor of Christ unto God, in them that perish" (2 Cor. 2:15).

In accordance with the particular exigencies of our era, the apostolate is organized into multiple institutions, all more or less dependent upon the ecclesiastical authority. Among these, Catholic Action, which has the same end as that of the Church itself—the salvation of souls—is especially and directly subordinated to the hierarchy and to its supreme head, the Roman pontiff.

Besides this general end, which is the salvation of souls, Catholic Action also has intermediate ends, *i.e.*, the religious, moral, and social formation of its members united to an integral Christian life; the training of consciences in their apostolic duty and mission, according to circumstances of time and place; the work of defense and promotion of Christian principles, and the practice of a singular devotion and absolute obedience to the Vicar of Christ. Although Catholic Action is not specifically mentioned in the Code of Canon Law, its juridical position in the Church and in the dioceses is clearly stated in papal pronouncements, in the dispositions of the episcopate (national and provincial councils; diocesan synods) and in several concordats (Italy, 1929; Germany, 1933; Austria, 1934). While the ecclesiastical authority always retains the high direction of Catholic Action, the lay directors have their proper and responsible executive functions, with priests appointed to render spiritual and moral assistance (Pius XII, October 11, 1946). Catholic Action is not designed to be a politically partisan force. Nevertheless, Catholic citizens united in political associations, even as members of Catholic Action, may, and are even urged, to take part in public life, particularly in those spheres which are of vital interest to religion (Pius XII, October 14, 1951).

Catholic Action may assume different forms, according to the various countries in which it is found. In the Latin countries, France and Belgium excepted, it is modeled after the pattern of the Church: parochial and diocesan, with national organs or centers of coordination, communication, and direction. In other countries, professional associations of a national type are preferred. Almost everywhere one finds other organizations having the form and the aims of the apostolate: Catholic *associations*, either directly dependent on or simply coordinated with Catholic Action; Catholic *institutions* of education, propaganda, assistance, credit, *etc.*; Catholic-inspired *movements and organizations* having a mutual relation to and cooperating with Catholic action. Urb.

ACTION, JUDICIARY (licitness of). *See* Defendant.

ACTOR. Actors are persons taking part in public, artistic performances of a dramatic, lyrical, choreographic, or musical nature or other form of entertainment according to a pre-established program. The theatre or stage has been a notable feature of every civilization from remotest antiquity. In every age one finds professional entertainers dedicated to elevating the higher natural sentiments of the masses. Generally speaking, entertainers have enjoyed a high degree of respectability and full freedom. Unfortunately this freedom led to a degrading of the theater (especially among the Romans) into vulgar and bloody spectacles. As a result, actors in general came to be regarded as individuals engaged in infamous activities (cf. D. 3, 2, 1. *Infamia notatura . . . qui artis ludicrae pronunciandive causa in scaenam prodierit*). This situation justified the attitude of the early Church as being opposed to theatrical spectacles and circus games. But in the Middle Ages the Church satisfied the people's craving for the theater through the staging of religious and educational representations (Miracle Plays, Mysteries), held inside and outside the churches. In view of this, the fundamental attitude of the Church toward the theatrical art and its related forms could hardly be called negative, much less today when the theatre and its related forms have attained a high level of cultural importance.

The juridical status of an actor remains a disputed question among legal minds. Since the actor's services are rather occasional or intermittent, it is not clearly determined whether he is to be considered as one engaged in a professional activity or in a form of employment. According to one legal opinion, the actor's is a special kind (*sui generis*) of contract which places him in a class all by himself; another opinion regards the actor's contract as one whereby he lends or sells his services (*locatio operis*), though with the benefit of a contract; finally, a third opinion considers the actor simply as a workingman (*locatio operarum*). The problem certainly has a juridical value with regard to its practical effects, inasmuch as a definite solution of the actor's juridical status would determine the applicability of the principles of collective bargaining, unemployment insurance, social security, *etc.*

The actor is usually hired through a contract in which the rights and obligations of both parties (actor and employer) are set forth, so that the actor cannot demand, nor the employer force upon him, roles not specified in the contract.

The studio director (film, theatre, television) has the discretionary right of distributing the parts among the players, unless the contract calls for specific parts to be given to specific players. If the contract merely states that the actor is to be engaged for "important roles," he is presumably held to accept any part offered by the director, provided it is not a "bit" part.

All actors, even veteran and famous ones, are held to attendance at rehearsals. When one party terminates his contractual relations upon expiration of the term or even before (except in case of necessary duration), the other party has no right to indemnification, nor must advance notice of termination be given. If, however, the terms of the contract necessarily bind for a certain period of time and one party withdraws before the expiration of that period, the injured party may claim indemnity. In no case, however, may compensation ex-

ceed the maximum profit that would have been received during the entire duration of the contract's performance; moreover, settlement of damages is to be made in proportion to the importance of the actor's role.

As a man, the actor, even when appearing before the public, is entitled to all the rights accorded other citizens, such as respect, protection, *etc.*

Besides the legal prescriptions and the natural obligation arising from contractual relations, the actor is also bound by strictly moral obligations flowing from divine and ecclesiastical laws. A Catholic actor may not engage in any theatrical performance that is contrary to or not in accordance with moral teachings. Truly artistic representations must provide mental uplift, relaxation, and honest pleasure for the viewer. Actors, therefore, who engage in performances that notably offend against public order and good morals are guilty of sin. Objectionable and offensive are all those shows which tend to condone or extol crime and vice or are designed to arouse class hatred and prejudice; those which insult, even by allusion, the sacred person of the supreme pontiff or the head of a state and government institutions, or foster disrespect for the law among the masses, or attack patriotism or religious sentiments, imperil international relations; likewise, all those which attack the dignity and prestige of public authority, the private life of individuals, or the fundamental principles of the family as an institution. If the performances are obscene or indecent by reason of place, manner of dress, or object, it is unlawful for any Catholic player to take part therein; and whoever would do so would render himself unworthy of sacramental absolution, for in such instances even material cooperation is forbidden. *Tar.*

ACTS, PONTIFICAL. DEFINITION. Acts issued by the pope personally in his exercise of the government of the Church are called pontifical acts. They are to be distinguished from acts of the Holy See, which comprise acts of the Sacred Congregations, the Tribunals and

Offices of the Holy See (cf. Can. 7). Pontifical acts are also to be distinguished from acts of an ecumenical council and from acts of the supreme pontiff as temporal sovereign of the State of Vatican City.

Pontifical acts may be written or oral (such as allocutions, radio discourses, etc.). Our exclusive concern here is with written pontifical acts, which constitute the largest number.

WRITTEN PONTIFICAL ACTS. The name popularly given to a large number of pontifical documents is that of *bull*. Properly speaking, however, this term does not refer to the documents themselves, but to the lead seal with which papal documents are authenticated. In the papal chancery the term *bull* was never officially employed (the official title for such documents being *Apostolicae sub plumbo litterae*); as already noted, it was only through popular designation that the name was given to the documents themselves. In the Middle Ages it was already customary to refer to *bulls, bullae maiores* and *bullae minores* according to the degree of importance of each pontifical document and depending on whether they were authenticated with a lead seal, with a wax seal (briefs), or with no seal at all (supplications, autograph letters, *motu proprio*).

The names officially given to written pontifical acts vary according to the *form* (the criterion of distinction employed by students of diplomacy) or according to their *contents* (the criterion employed by canonists). During the course of time these names have undergone changes; certain forms of papal acts were discarded and new ones were introduced.

In order to give a description of the forms and relative actual content of written pontifical acts, we shall examine first the papal documents according to the diplomatic criterion, then according to the criterion used by canonists. To follow a certain norm of distinction corresponding more closely to the *diplomatic criteria*, it will be useful, in examining the development of pontifical acts, to distinguish the documents into the following classifications: letters *sub plumbo*

(Apostolic letters bearing a lead seal), *briefs* (bearing a wax seal), *supplications, autograph letters, motu proprio* (without a seal).

LETTERS SUB PLUMBO. These are Apostolic letters authenticated with the lead seal and popularly called bulls. They begin with the name of the pope, followed by the title *episcopus servus servorum Dei* (bishop, servant of the servants of God)—a title used by the popes since the time of St. Gregory the Great (590–604). Until the tenth century these letters were written on papyrus; in the first half of the eleventh century this was superseded by parchment, which, since the latter half of the eleventh century, has remained the exclusive material on which such documents are written.

Always in Latin, these letters were written in Roman curial script until the twelfth century, in diplomatic minuscule in the twelfth through the fourteenth centuries, in cursive Gothic in the fifteenth century, and in the sixteenth through the nineteenth centuries a type of Gothic known as *scrittura bollatica* was used. Letters *sub plumbo* may be subdivided into two main classes: privileges and letters.

Privileges. For a long period of time the most solemn form of pontifical document was used for privileges. It first appeared at the end of the eighth century, developed during the tenth through the eleventh centuries, and disappeared in the fourteenth century. It was the form of document employed for privileges or concessions of a perpetual character, and derived its name from the fact that the document frequently contained the granting of certain rights and immunity to churches and monasteries. The characteristic features of the document were: the clause *in perpetuum* or some other equivalent phrase; the salutatory formula of the pope, *bene valete*, appearing either in large characters or in monogram, at the end of the document; the *roto* or wheel, the signature of the pope and the cardinals, the formula of dating, the minatory clauses and the signatures of the notary and the chancellor.

Not all these characteristics are found in all privileges, nor are these the only ones; one must take note of the period in which the document was composed. Generally speaking, after Nicholas II (1059–1061), many of the formulas used in the drafting of privileges became standard and are always encountered therein, e.g., the manner of dating (place, day, month, dominical year, year of pontificate and year of establishment). Moreover, not all privileges were equally important; the less important ones were called *lesser privileges* (*privilegia minora*), *simple privileges*, or even *indulgences* (*indulgentiae*). These constitute an intermediate form between the documents drafted with formal solemnity and the letters. They are not letters, because in content and in their external form they approximate the privileges. The first examples date back to Paschal II (1099–1118).

Letters. Letters have always constituted the largest number of pontifical documents. Following the custom used by the ancient Romans in their epistolary composition, the earliest papal letters bore an autograph signature of the pope in the form of a salutation or farewell (*e.g., Deus te incolumen custodiat, carissime fili*), but no original document prior to the eleventh century is extant.

Three original letters of Alexander II and two of Gregory VII, belonging to the period between the middle of the eleventh century and the first half of the twelfth, are still in existence. At the beginning of the second half of the twelfth century, letters begin to increase in number, becoming ever more numerous thereafter, with the expansion of Curial affairs.

A characteristic feature of papal letters is the simplicity of form in which they are drafted. In the course of time, two categories of letters evolved: (a) one for transmission of orders; (b) the other for concession of privileges and favors.

Along with the old system of attaching the seal with a silk thread (as in the case of privileges), a new method was introduced of attaching it with laces of hemp. Thus, there are letters *cum filo serico*, following the ancient tradition, and letters *cum filo canapis*.

Letters may be classified according to the nature of their content, method of transmission, and the external characteristics or form.

(a) According to the nature of their content, the following classification obtains: *de provisione praelatorum, de prebendis vacantibus, de prebendis vacaturis, de officio tabellionatus, etc.* Besides this specific classification, there is another (from the twelfth century on) based on the general content: *litterae gratiosae,* or letters of a gracious character, in which the lead seal is attached with silk thread, as in the case of privileges; and executory letters (*mandata* or *litterae exsecutoriae*), having the seal attached with laces of hemp.

(b) According to method of transmission on the part of the Chancery, the following classification obtains: (1) *simple* or *common letters*, which could be delivered directly by the chancellor and notaries, with precise forms already approved by the pope; (2) *litterae legendae* (letters to be read), which, because they contained concessions of favors, or dealt with exceptional matters, always had to be read to the pope. This distinction of letters is found in a formulary of the thirteenth and fourteenth centuries. Moreover, it is known that toward the end of the thirteenth century, the beginning of the *legendae* was written in small instead of capital letters, to distinguish the *legendae* from the common letters; (3) *litterae de Curia* or *curiales* (Curial letters). These make their appearance from the time of Innocent IV (1244) and are so designated both on their original copies and on their files. These were filed in a special register. *De Curia* means that these letters were issued in the interest of the Curia and, hence, were exempt from all taxes or fees; (4) *litterae secretae et patentes* (secret and open letters): certain letters were delivered open, others closed, e.g., secured with the threads or laces and the lead seal.

(c) According to their external characteristics, letters were distinguished, as already noted, into those cum filo serico (gratiosae) and those cum filo canapis (exsecutoriae).

In the thirteenth century there arose a new classification of letters (solemn), which in the introductory protocol contained the clause of perpetuity ad perpetuam rei memoriam, or some other equivalent phrase. To this category belong the so-called consistorial letters (litterae consistoriales), which in a certain sense are similar to the old privileges, insofar as external form is concerned. Bearing the signatures of pope and cardinals, they were variously called privilegia apostolica, praeceptum, etc. Still another form of letters sub plumbo were the consistorial notes (cedulae).

Turning to the criterion of distinction employed by canonists, papal letters are classified as follows:

(a) Dogmatic letters (epistulae dogmaticae), which dealt with questions of faith. Famous among them is the one sent by Leo the Great to the patriarch Flavian concerning the two natures in Christ (June 13, 419).

(b) Exhortatory or monitory letters (litterae hortatoriae seu monitorae) which were letters of admonition but without any legislative content (cf. First Epistle of St. Clement to the Corinthians) at the end of the first century.

(c) Preceptive letters (litterae praeceptoriae, later called also auctoritates). These were letters in which the pontiff manifested his will as legislator. Later they became known as decretals (litterae decretales), providing abundant material for the canonical collections. There were also the so-called authentic collections, as the Decretals of Gregory IX (1235).

(d) Letters of peace (epistulae pacis), letters sent by the pope to the bishops as proof of communion in the one faith (cf. St. Leo, Epist. III, c.1: PL 54, 1185).

(e) Synodal letters (epistulae synodicae or synodales), letters containing a profession of faith as proof of communion of doctrine between the Eastern and Western Church. This practice was observed under Pelagius I (cf. letters of Anastasius II and Pelagius I: Jaffé-Wattenbach, 746 (377), 938 (618).

(f) Clerical letters (litterae clericae— also called Catholic), a type of circular letter sent to all the faithful. These, however, were not exclusively papal and, according to the nature of content, they were variously styled: declaratory, indicative, paschal (declarativae, indicativae, paschales, etc.).

AUTOGRAPH LETTERS, SUPPLICATIONS, MOTU PROPRIO. These are documents which also belong to the category of letters.

(a) Autograph letters. Introduced in the sixteenth century, this type of letter is largely employed for the disposition of administrative matters. Autograph letters are devoid of all chancery and secretariate formalities, but bear the signature of the pope. They are still in use today, though only on rare occasions.

(b) Supplications. Letters of supplication were petitions addressed to the supreme pontiff, who replied by letters of concession. Supplications were presented under three forms: (1) as a simple petition; (2) as a petition with the formula motu proprio, i.e., with the request that the pontifical document be drafted as a motu proprio; (3) as a petition with the formula sola signatura (signature only), signifying (from the time of Martin V, 1417–1431) that the favor was granted even without transmission of the document, but by the mere signature on it.

(c) Motu Proprio. Motu proprio were and are (for they are still in use) papal letters drawn up on the pope's own accord or under his command and characterized by the use of the phrase motu proprio. Originating in the fifteenth century, the earliest forms of motu proprio were dated in the same manner as bulls (year of pontificate, day, month). But since the time of Leo X, they have been dated according to the modern method.

Written on paper, these documents bear the name of the pope and begin with the words motu proprio. The autograph signature of the pope was expressed with the formula *Placet motu proprio,* followed by the first letter of his baptismal name. In modern times, the word *placet* is lacking, and the pope's name as the reigning pontiff is used. The *motu proprio* bears no seal and lacks other formalities.

BRIEFS. Briefs also belong to the category of letters, but differ from the other two classes mentioned above insofar as they bear a wax seal. Originally, they were letters, but closed and transmitted *sub anulo piscatoris, i.e.,* sealed with the fisherman's ring bearing the image of St. Peter, fishing in the sea.

The first pope to employ this manner of sealing letters seems to have been Clement IV (1265–1268), but the earliest brief thus far known is that of Boniface IX (October 17, 1390). The name *brief* derives from the fact that such letters were *brevi manu* or *brevi via.* In its external form, the brief was distinguished from the letters *sub plumbo* by its seal, by a thinner parchment and by its script (cursive Gothic in the fourteenth-fifteenth centuries, cursive humanistic in the fifteenth-sixteenth centuries and, until 1878, cursive Roman, practically undecipherable by ordinary readers). Today, the common Latin script is used. Briefs are not signed by the pope, except in extraordinary cases. Briefs of some moment bear the signature of the Cardinal Secretary of State, while others carry the signature of the Chancellor of Briefs. Briefs are drafted, revised and sent by the Chancery of Apostolic Briefs (formerly by apostolic secretaries), the third Section of the Secretariate of State, even in the case of documents pertaining to other departments.

PRESENT-DAY CLASSIFICATION. In cataloguing modern papal documents, their content and juridical value should be taken into consideration.

(a) *Encyclical letters (litterae encyclicae).* These are addressed to bishops of the whole world (*Ad venerabiles fratres Patriarchas, Primates, Archiepiscopos, Episcopos aliosque locorum Ordinarios pacem et communionem cum Apostolica Sede habentes*) or of a particular region, giving general directives in various fields: in matters of faith, morals, customs, cult, *etc.* They open and close with the name of the pope as the reigning pontiff, *e.g., Pii Pp. XII, Litterae encyclicae . . . ; Pius Pp. XII, Venerabiles fratres salutem et apostolicam benedictionem.*

(b) *Apostolic constitutions (constitutiones apostolicae).* Issued upon the pope's own initiative, these letters deal with matters of dogma, discipline, *etc.* They begin with the words *Constitutio apostolica,* an enunciation of the subject matter and the name of the pope, followed by the formula *episcopus servus servorum Dei . . . ad perpetuam rei memoriam.* If dealing with dogmatic constitutions, they are signed by the pope alone, as *Bishop of the Catholic Church (Catholicae Ecclesiae episcopus);* in other cases, they are signed by the Cardinal Datarius and Prefect of the respective Congregation, and by the prothonotaries. This is the form generally used in cases of dogmatic definitions (cf. *Munificentissimus Deus* of Pope Pius XII, November 1, 1950, by which the dogma of the Assumption of the Blessed Virgin into heaven was defined).

(c) *Encyclical epistles (epistulae encyclicae).* These are like encyclical letters, both in the introductory protocol and in the concluding eschatocol, except that they are less formal and the word *letter* is replaced with *epistle.* These are generally employed in giving directives for a particular region. Hence, this type of document lends itself much more readily to the use of the vernacular.

(d) *Apostolic exhortation (adhortatio apostolica).* This is in the nature of an encyclical letter, but less important, insofar as it is not addressed to the entire world, but to certain categories of the faithful. It opens with the name of the pope, the title and content of the document and with a repetition of the pope's name, following which the persons to whom the exhortation is directed are addressed in the vocative case (*e.g., S.Smi D.N. Joannis divina Providentia Papae XIII, adhortatio ad clerum pacem et communionem cum apostolica sede habentem — de sacerdotalis vitae sanctitate promovenda — Joannes Pp. XXIII . . . Venerabiles fratres ac dilecti filii salutem et apostolicam benedictionem).* It bears the name of the pope as the reigning pontiff.

(e) *Decretals (litterae decretales).* These are letters relating to some particular matter and, especially today, are used for proclaiming the canonization of saints. They begin with the name of the pope, followed by the title *episcopus servus servorum Dei* and the clause of perpetuity, *ad perpetuam rei memoriam.* With the name of the pope, as *Catholicae Ecclesiae episcopus,* there are also the signatures of the cardinals present in the Curia (last of all the Cardinal Chancellor and the Prefect of the respective Congregation), and the signatures of two apostolic prothonotaries. Finally, there are the signatures of a clerk of the Apostolic Chancery, of the sealer (*plumbator*), of an apostolic secretary and of the archivist.

(f) *Apostolic letters (litterae apostolicae).* These letters are usually issued to announce new foundations, appointments, *etc.,* such as the erection of a new nunciature, a new basilica, the naming of patron saints, the proclamation of new Blesseds, the bestowal of reserved benefices. They open with the name of the pope as reigning pontiff, followed by the clause *ad perpetuam rei memoriam,* and are signed by the palace cardinals (Secretary of State or Cardinal Datarius).

(g) *Epistles (epistulae).* These are letters of appointment (*e.g.,* of legates), congratulatory messages to cardinals, bishops, superiors of religious orders, *etc.,* upon the occasion of the silver or golden anniversary of their priesthood, episcopate, or cardinalate, centennial anniversaries of religious orders, *etc.* They open with the vocative form of address, *Dilecte Fili noster* (for cardinal), *Venerabilis frater* (for bishop), *Dilecte fili* or *Dilecta filia* (for others) *salutem et apostolicam benedictionem.* They bear the signature of the pope (*e.g., Joannes Pp. XXIII*).

(h) *Motu proprio.* Cf. above.

(i) *Briefs.* Cf. above. These are used for prelatial appointments, for the bestowal of honors and titles, for the departure of cardinals and legates to Eucharistic congresses, for greetings and felicitations to sovereigns and heads of states, for concessions of indults and privileges, *etc.*

(j) *Autograph letters.* Cf. above. They open and close with the name of the pope and, in general, have the form of a common letter (cf. *e.g., AAS,* 22 (1930), 89, 93). *Pal.*

ADMINISTRATION, or ADMINISTRATIVE COUNCIL. See Stock Market, Corporation.

ADMINISTRATION (CONTROLLED). See Bankruptcy.

ADMINISTRATION (PUBLIC). See Administration, Civil Official, Military Official.

ADMONITION (*Monitio, monitum*). The remedial measure of admonition, already known in the canonical legislation of the early Church, was, in due course of time, broadened as to concept and scope. In fact, present-day canon law contains various kinds of admonition.

In the first place, admonition (*monitio*) is a penal remedy (*q.v.*), *i.e.,* a preventive measure against a violation. According to Canon 2307, it is usually employed: (a) when a person is in the proximate occasion of committing a violation; (b) when, after careful investigation, a person falls under grave suspicion of having committed a violation, which, however, cannot be sufficiently proven (Can. 1946, par. 2, n. 2). Such admonition is not exactly a canonical penalty in the strict sense of the term, for, according to Canon 2233, a penalty can only be inflicted when there is certain proof that the violation was committed. However, admonition may be considered a penalty in a broad sense, since it implies a certain loss of reputation and bears a relationship to the idea of violation. The purpose of admonition is to prevent the suspected person from committing a violation and incurring the consequent penalty. Admonitions may be given both to clerical and lay persons. The only authority empowered to give admonitions is the Ordinary, who may do so either personally or through a confidential delegate. The Vicar General may not issue an admonition unless he received a special mandate (Can. 2220, par. 2). A pastor or others may give admonitions, but these have no canonical force.

The admonition may be either public or secret. Public admonition may be given either orally (in the presence of a notary or two witnesses) or in writing (*i.e.*, by letter). When given orally, the admonition is to be recorded in documentary form, signed by the admonished person and by the notary or two witnesses, and is to be kept in the archives. A written admonition must be made in duplicate copy, one of which is to be safely delivered to the party concerned and the other, together with proof that the letter of admonition was duly received, to be kept in the archives.

No specific formalities are prescribed for the issuing of a secret admonition, although some authors hold that it should be done in the same manner as for a public admonition, with the proviso that notary and witness be sworn to secrecy. At any rate, some documentary evidence must be kept in the archives even in the case of a secret admonition (Can. 2309, par. 5). Today a secret admonition is usually regarded as canonical admonition, although some authors, dealing with this subject in conjunction with the Institution of the Sacred Congregation of Bishops and Regulars, on June 11, 1880 (GASPARRI, *Fontes*, IV, n. 2005), tend to classify it as paternal. It is left to the prudent judgment of the Ordinary whether an admonition is to be public or secret. In point of fact, even a public admonition may be kept secret, a policy which is recommended in the majority of cases. Both public and secret admonitions may be given repeatedly (Can. 2309, par. 6) with the adjunct of penances (Can. 2313, par. 2).

While the penal remedy of admoni-

tion is primarily intended as a preventive measure against a crime, the Code of Canon Law also speaks of admonitions issued after the commission of a crime. Such are: (a) the admonitions to be imparted by the competent ecclesiastical authorities (in observance of Can. 2233, par. 2; 2242, par. 2), before the penalty of a censure is inflicted; (b) the two admonitions by the major superiors of exempt clerical religious to a member with perpetual vows, before instituting a trial for dismissal (Can. 656 ff.), (c) the admonitions by the Ordinary to a cleric who neglected or violated the duties of his state, before instituting a canonical process (Can. 2168, 2176, 2182).

In all these instances, therefore, the commission of a crime must be certain (Can. 658; 2233, par. 2) or, at least, presupposed (Can. 2168, 2176, 2182). Such admonitions are neither a penal remedy in the sense of Canon 2306, nor a penalty properly so-called, but are to be considered as preparatory to the legal imposition of penalty; it is advisable, therefore, that each admonition contain a reminder or threat of the corresponding penalty.

The admonitions preceding the canonical process of dismissal of a religious cleric who violated the duties of his state are to be given in the form of penal admonitions (Can. 659–661, 2143); and although this penal form is not canonically prescribed for the admonition preceding the imposition of a censure, it is suggested or at least recommended by common teaching.

Besides admonition as a penal remedy and admonition following the crime, mention is also made of paternal admonition. This form is distinguished from canonical admonition in that it lacks any direct consequences and may be imparted by a person not invested with jurisdictional authority. It is either a simple exhortation to do something, *e.g.*, the bishop's paternal admonition to a pastor to resign his parish rather than be removed (Can. 2158, 2160, 2166), or an efficacious exhortation to an individual to amend himself, such as the admonition to a religious with temporary vows, before proceeding to his dismissal for lack of religious spirit (Can. 647, par. 2). Paternal admonition is to be imparted also in the case of suspension *ex informata conscientia*, inflicted by the Ordinary (Can. 2192). Finally, the term "paternal admonitions" is commonly applied to exhortations, recommendations, and warnings made by prefects and spiritual directors in guiding and instructing clerics in the religious life (Can. 588, par. 1). *Led.*

ADOPTION. Adoption is a practice which had its origin in Roman law, and consists in the voluntary taking of a child of other parents as one's own. The procedure and the effects to which adoption gives rise have varied considerably according to times and places. For these the reader must consult the legislation of each individual country.

The moral obligations between the adopting persons and the adopted run along the same line as the obligations between parents and children. In general, the civil laws which govern this institution are to be considered as binding in conscience, including those which forbid adoption as a protective measure for the family.

Particular moral problems may arise from imprudence in arranging adoption hastily and from possible claims on the part of the natural parent or parents of the adopted. In this regard it is improper for them, after the child has been properly reared, to claim the restitution of the child or even to bribe the adopting parents by capitalizing (strictly for gain) on the affection which ties them to the adopted child.

The relationship of adoption comes in for consideration by the Church in connection with the subject of marriage, insofar as adoption might give rise to a matrimonial impediment. In view of the diverse legislation in different countries regarding the matter of adoption, and especially in view of the fact that the degree of relationship arising from legal adoption is not the same in all countries, the Church, up until the year 1918, re-garded legal adoption as an impediment to marriage whenever the civil law followed the Roman law in the matter of adoption. The reason for this procedure was to avoid making legal adoption a matrimonial impediment even in regions where the relationship arising between adopter and adoptee was rather tenuous. However, since in practice this procedure occasioned quite a number of doubts, the new Code changed the norm to read (Can. 1059 & 1080): "Whenever the civil law of the country establishes adoption as an impediment to marriage, the Church also considers adoption a canonical impediment." Thus, marrying under such circumstances may make the marriage null (diriment impediment) or not (impedient impediment), depending on whether the civil law has established such an effect or not. In Italy, for instance, persons forbidden to marry by civil law because of the impediment of adoption also incur the impediment for a religious marriage; it is doubtful, however, whether this is a case of a diriment impediment or only an impeding impediment (although the majority of authors maintain that it is diriment), since the civil law does not permit the validity of the marriage to be impugned after six months have passed from the date of its celebration. It goes without saying, of course, that despite the Church's acceptance of the established norms of the civil law, the Church alone may grant a dispensation for the contracting of a religious marriage when the impediment of legal adoption exists. *Cip.*

(No state in the U.S.A. recognizes any impediment arising from legal adoption.)

ADORATION. In its theological meaning adoration is an act of worship (*see* Cult). It signifies the formal acknowledgment of God as our Supreme Lord, and our absolute dependence upon Him. Adoration may be (a) internal, or (b) external. It is internal if it proceeds from the mind; it is external when the formal acknowledgment of God's supremacy is manifested by physical gestures of respect. Since the internal or mental element is the very soul of external adoration, the latter has no meaning except insofar as it flows from and expresses the former. Every act of external worship of God constitutes an act of adoration, but in the strictest sense of the term adoration consists in a sacrifice, *i.e.*, the manifestation of one's sentiments of submission and the offering to God of something tangible as a formal acknowledgment of His supreme dominion. Adoration may be expressed in various ways: by prostration, genuflection, bowing of the body, *etc.* It is to be noted, however, that these gestures are not by their very nature acts of worship; they become such only through the intention of the person performing them or by a declaration of the Church. In the Latin rite gestures having the value of worship are: prostration, genuflection (on one or two knees), inclination of the body, and profound inclination of the head, provided that they are performed in the presence of living persons. The ancient form of adoration, namely, kissing one's hand and then waving it in the direction of the venerated object, has fallen into complete disuse, except in certain regions where it still remains a popular gesture of veneration.

Adoration is reserved exclusively to God; hence, it may be offered only to the Blessed Trinity, to the single Divine Persons, to Christ Our Lord, also under the sacramental species (Can. 1255, par. 1). Adoration befits also the Most Holy Humanity of Our Lord substantially united to His Divinity, and to the single parts of His Humanity (the Sacred Heart). To relics of the Holy Cross and all other relics recalling the Saviour, to His images, to those of the Blessed Trinity, and to the Crucifix a relative adoration is due, insofar as it is directed to the Person they represent.

Adoration is the expression of one of the most profound relations between intelligent creatures and their Creator. Adoration, therefore, fulfills the most intimate need of man's nature and, next to the acts of the three theological virtues, it is man's greatest perfecting act. Its absolute necessity flows from that fact. (This necessity is treated at greater

length under Cult and Religion). The cult of adoration finds its fulfillment in public worship, the most perfect expression of which is the liturgy, which in turn culminates in sacrifice. The one true sacrifice is that of the Cross, renewed in the Holy Mass (*q.v.*). Hence the necessity on the part of all members of the Church to participate in the sacrifice of the Mass.

Sins against the duty of adoring God are: (a) refusal to adore God (*see* Irreligion), and (b) adoration of persons or objects other than God (*see* Idolatry). The extreme gravity of such sins is obvious. *Pal.*

ADORATION, EUCHARISTIC. Adoration in the strict sense is the act of worship reserved to God. Eucharistic adoration is based on the doctrine of the real presence of Jesus Christ under the Eucharistic species. The perennial presence of Jesus in the sacrament of His love calls for a perennial manifestation of praise and love for Him by Christians.

This devout practice is very dear to Eucharistic souls and highly recommended by the Catholic Church. Despite practical difficulties involved in perpetual, especially nocturnal, adoration (*laus perennis*), Catholics have always endeavored to implement the adoration of the Holy Eucharist by frequent exposition of the Blessed Sacrament and by periodical and successive cycles of adoration by the faithful: the Holy Hour, Forty Hours, and the like.

In the early Christian era the Holy Eucharist was not preserved except for the purpose of administration to the sick. The Eucharistic adoration was limited to certain moments of the Mass or to the Communion of the sick. Beginning with the thirteenth century, however, one finds here and there the devout practice of a true exposition of the Eucharistic species for purposes of adoration. In France King Louis VII (after his victory over the Albigensians) requested that the veiled Blessed Sacrament be exposed in the Chapel of the Holy Cross in Avignon as an act of thanksgiving. In Spain, at Lugo, the perpetual adoration in reparation of the Priscillian heresy was instituted. But Italy is the cradle of a regular and perpetual Eucharistic adoration. In 1527, at Milan, the Society of the Holy Sepulchre inaugurated the practice of the Forty Hours to be held at various times of the year. The devotion during the thirteenth century was commonly held on the last three days of Holy Week, as a Vigil at the Holy Sepulchre. At the close of the seventeenth century there arose various Congregations and Archconfraternities dedicated to the practice of perpetual adoration for the purpose of making reparation for offenses committed against Christ, especially against the Blessed Sacrament. Among these is the organization instituted at Rome (and within a few years extended to all parts of the world) of perpetual adoration among Catholic nations, whose object is to offer reparation to God for the outrages committed against Him. Each of the Catholic nations is represented in Rome, and on a specific date the faithful of a particular nation are to visit a church where the Forty Hours are being held; elsewhere the faithful visit a church of their own choice to pray for the intentions of the organization. Thus, the altars of the Eucharistic Christ are constantly surrounded by chosen souls to represent innumerable other souls who are unmindful of the great love that the Son of God has for them.

Among the various forms of Eucharistic adoration are the visits to the Blessed Sacrament, as observed in convents and seminaries before or after dinner, daily adoration, and perpetual adoration. A more solemn form is that of the Forty Hours (q.v.). See also Eucharistic Benediction. Pal.

ADORO TE DEVOTE. The *Adoro Te Devote* is a Eucharistic prayer and hymn found in the Roman Missal among the prayers to be recited after Mass. Its meter is medieval, based upon the word accent: that is, it is made up of six-foot lines, arranged according to accent, in couplet rhyme; it consists of seven stanzas of four verses each. The first and last stanzas taken together form a Eucharistic motet. The hymn is set to Gregorian melody; it is harmonious, at once simple and profound, and is a true masterpiece.

The prayer has been preserved in about thirty manuscripts, of which three belong to the fourteenth century and all the others to the fifteenth and sixteenth centuries. All the manuscripts, with the exception of six which say nothing about its author (the most ancient is the Cod. Koslterneobutgense of *circa* 1350, containing an edition of 1323), attribute it to St. Thomas Aquinas (*q.v.*). Wilmart (*Auteurs spirituels et textes devots du Moyen-Age*, Paris, 1932, pp. 361–414) has opposed the traditional thesis for reasons which are not completely convincing. He points out the fact that the manuscripts date back to 1323, whereas St. Thomas died in 1274; that the circumstances noted in many codices, according to which St. Thomas composed this prayer before receiving Viaticum, are in conflict with the narration of the Saint's biographer, William of Tocco (*Vita*, X, 59); that there is a marked difference between the simplicity and lyricism of this composition and the office of the Feast of Corpus Christi. The uncertain value of these arguments, however, justifies the upholding of the traditional thesis.

The composition is a hymn of adoration, praise, and prayer to the Eucharistic Mystery and it is commonly recited or sung at Eucharistic functions. *Pal.*

ADRENAL. *See* Endocrinology.

ADULATION. Adulation, in a strict sense, is servile flattery, or an obsequious and fulsome praising of another for the sake of obtaining a favor. It may be expressed by words or deeds.

In itself, adulation is a venial sin. It could, however, become mortal if one were to praise a gravely sinful act of another person; or if one strove to obtain something that cannot be granted without a serious violation, or if adulation causes notable harm to the flattered person, who because of such practices would be induced to sin gravely. *Man.*

ADULATOR. *See* Cooperator in the sin of another.

ADULT. *See* Age.

ADULTERY. Adultery is voluntary sexual intercourse by a married man with someone other than his wife or by a married woman with someone other than her husband. Also, an act of infidelity, by carnal intercourse, to the bond of marriage—either one's own, or that of another person or that of both. The first two instances constitute simple adultery; the latter is a case of double adultery. Adultery may be perfect or imperfect: perfect, if there is coition; imperfect, if it is an incomplete act or a solitary act or an act against nature committed with one's own spouse. It may be occasional or habitually indulged in with the same person, in which case it is called adulterous concubinage (*q.v.*), and the two are called concubines or lovers in the worst sense of the word.

Perfect adultery is a species of lust according to nature, distinct from simple fornication. To the malice of this sin (*see* Fornication) there is added a sin against justice (the right of one's own spouse or the spouse of another) and, according to some, also a sin against religion (in cases where the marriage is a sacrament). Adultery, therefore, is a crime against the threefold good of marriage (*bonum prolis, fidei, sacramenti: Casti Connubii*, Dec. 31, 1930). This special malice is in no way diminished when adultery is committed with the consent of one's spouse: the right of the other spouse is not an absolute right that can be disposed of at one's own wish, but one that is inseparably connected with the matrimonial state, so that, although a spouse may renounce the use of his right, he cannot renounce the right itself nor the use thereof in favor of a third party. Furthermore, consent of one's spouse does not remove the offense against piety and religion (see prop. 50, condemned by Innocent XI, Decr. S.C.S. Off., March 4, 1697, D.B. 1200).

Adultery is a very grave sin and is, as such, condemned in Sacred Scripture (Eccl. 23:35–39; I Cor. 6:9). Adultery committed by a wife is more serious than that committed by a husband, because it may cause sterility (especially if committed with several men) in the woman or it may create the danger of introducing an illegitimate child into the family.

Besides establishing various ecclesiastical penalties for the public crime of adultery, Canon Law (Can. 2357, par. 2; 2359, par. 2) gives the innocent party the right to refuse, even permanently, all cohabitation with the guilty party (personal separation); this right, however, is forfeited if the injured party shall have been the cause of the crime, or if he consented to it or condoned it or, finally, committed the same crime (Can. 1129). If adultery is committed with a mutual promise of future marriage, or if it is accompanied by an attempt on the life of one of the spouses, these circumstances give rise to a matrimonial impediment (Can. 1075). If, as a result of the adulterous relationship, an illegitimate offspring is introduced into the family, the two accomplices (the aggressor only in a case of rape) are obliged to make reparation to the innocent spouse and to the other children of the family, if any. *Dam.*

ADVENT. In its original meaning, advent signifies coming, arrival, entry. Following the example of the solemn entrance of Roman emperors into the city, the Church celebrates the coming of the Incarnate Christ, the Supreme King, into His city, that is, the world. Besides commemorating the historical birth of Christ, Advent refers to another twofold coming of the Redeemer: His coming into our souls through grace and His coming at the end of time for the final judgment of mankind.

Whereas Advent originally referred only to Christ's birth, gradually it came to be applied to the period of preparation preceding and leading up to that event; thus, for many centuries Advent has come to signify that period of the year during which the Church requires the faithful to prepare for the anniversary of Christ's birth. This period also marks the beginning of the liturgical or ecclesiastical year. As such, Advent symbolizes the pre-Messianic times, during which the chosen people of God awaited their liberation by Christ the Saviour. It also represents the mysterious action of grace forming our souls in the image and likeness of the awaited Christ and uniting us to Him as living members of the Mystical Body, of which He is the head. Finally, Advent is a symbol of the centuries preceding the majestic coming of the Son of God to judge the living and the dead.

The season of Advent, therefore, ought to arouse in us (a) interior and exterior recollection: "it arouses within us the consciousness of the wretched sins we have committed; and it urges us to restrain our desires by voluntary mortification of the body and to recollect ourselves through pious meditation, so that we may be moved by the desire of returning to God, Who alone by His grace can free us from the stain of our sins and from the evil consequences resulting from them" (Pius XII, Encyclical *Mediator Dei*, November 20, 1947). Thus, in divine worship during Advent passages are read from Isaias, some referring to St. John the Baptist and others from St. Paul, in which penance and spiritual renewal is persistently inculcated. (b) Ardent anticipation and great joy for the coming of the Lord, Redeemer and Saviour, whose glorious reign is colorfully and vividly described in numerous lessons, antiphons, and responsories. The anticipation or desire is especially evident in the great antiphons beginning with O, recited on the last seven days of Advent. (c) Devotion to Mary, to whom homage is rendered through a daily antiphon, the Station at St. Mary Major, with the Gospel of the Ember Days and, in many regions, by the daily offering of a solemn and privileged Mass, the *Missa aurea*, attended by a large number of the faithful.

The observance of Advent as a preparatory season to Christmas originated between the fourth and fifth centuries. The form of its liturgical celebration seems to have been established by St. Gregory the Great. Its introduction as a preparatory period leading up to the anniversary of the birth of Christ followed the fixing of the date of Christmas. The practice of exhorting the faithful to prepare themselves for the feast of the Nativity was already known in the fifth century. Perpetuus, Bishop of Tours, about the year 480, ordered that a fast be observed three times weekly, between the feast of St. Martin (November 11) and the Nativity; this was confirmed by the Council of Macon (583), which further decreed that Mass was to be celebrated according to the Lenten rite. From France, the observance of Advent was introduced into England (St. Bede), Italy, and many other countries in which the custom of fast and abstinence—not in force originally—was observed quite extensively until the promulgation of the Code of Canon Law. The Ambrosian and Oriental rites retain, even today, an Advent of six weeks, while the Sacramentary of St. Gregory the Great prescribes five weeks. Since the ninth or tenth centuries, the Roman liturgy has observed only four weeks of Advent, beginning with the Sunday closest to the feast of St. Andrew (November 30).

The weekdays of Advent are privileged and are, therefore, commemorated daily in the Mass and the Divine Office. With the exception of the third Sunday (*Gaudete* Sunday), the use of the organ is prohibited. The *Gloria* at Mass is omitted, as well as the *Alleluia* on ferial days. The solemnization of marriage (Nuptial Mass and blessing) is forbidden during this season. At solemn Mass the deacon and subdeacon (with the exception of *Gaudete* Sunday) wear folded chasubles, instead of the usual dalmatic and tunic, which are symbols of joy. The feast of the Immaculate Conception of Mary (December 8) is celebrated as a prelude to the feast of the Nativity. *Opp.*

ADVERTENCE. The act of the mind perceiving an object. Related to human acts, it is awareness of what one is doing. It is one of the indispensable prerequisites for the morality of an act, because an act posited without advertence is automatic and unconscious—that is, not a human act—and as such is not subject to any moral evaluation (*see* Attention).

Advertence admits of many degrees, with regard to both intensity and clarity. It may be present, though in a very small degree, even when it may seem to be entirely lacking. Many times an individual is said to have acted inadvertently, whereas in reality he acted without attention but not without some degree of advertence. The difference lies in the fact that attention requires an active effort on the part of the subject toward the object; while for advertence it is sufficient merely that the object act in some way upon the individual, who is not unconscious (*see* Perception).

Actions performed habitually are frequently performed without attention, but very rarely without advertence. The same may be said concerning actions performed in a state of somnolence, semi-intoxication, grave emotional disturbance, *etc.* Such acts are generally accompanied by some degree of advertence. *Gra.*

ADVERTISEMENT. *See* Publicity.

ADVOCATE (ATTORNEY, LAW-YER). Definition. In general, an advocate (in secular courts called attorney, lawyer, counselor-at-law, barrister) is one who by his counsel and other professional services assists his client at a trial. He differs from a legal consultant or adviser, who merely gives advice and renders services while remaining at home or at the office; he also differs from a procurator (proxy), who takes the place of the party himself and acts in the latter's name and interests. Ulpianus thus described the function of an advocate or lawyer: "*desiderium suum vel amici sui apud eum qui jurisdictioni praeest exponere, vel alterius desiderio contradicere*" (D. 3, I, 1, 2).

An advocate or attorney accompanies his client in court and remains at his side for the entire duration of the trial, ready at all times to steer his client through the intricate phases of legal procedure.

By his knowledge and technical skill he helps his client in the normal development of the trial by means of a written or oral juridical defense. The office of an advocate or lawyer is indeed a very noble one; both Church and State, in an effort to prevent abuses and keep the legal profession on a high level, have always accorded special attention to it.

Historical Notes. The forensic art, which at one time flourished in Rome, was almost brought to extinction by the barbaric invasions, with their ruthless disregard of the imposing juridical structure of the invaded empire. In the twelfth century, a renewed study of the Roman tradition brought about a revival of the legal profession, which, however, soon lapsed into practices of cavil, intrigue, and dilatory discourses at trials. Gradually there arose in various regions legal advisers and illustrious orators who, following the classical tradition, were to hold high the reputation of jurisprudence. Modern law restored to the profession the high esteem it had enjoyed in the past, and defined its tasks, harmonizing and directing its efforts toward bringing jurisprudence more in line with the ideal administration of justice.

Civil and Canonical procedure. Civil procedure varies to a considerable degree from one country to another. The canonical system follows the traditional procedure substantially contained in Canons 1655–1666, integrated by interpretative details of the Pontifical Commission for the interpretation of the Code of Canon Law and of the Sacred Congregation of the Sacraments.

Professional practice. The function of an advocate or attorney is to plead the cause of one of the principals at a trial. It is his duty to counsel and advise his client, arrange for the court appearance, draw up a written defense to the case with his own signature attached and that of the procurator (proxy), discuss the case orally in court and, generally, develop the conduct of the defense according to the requirements of the trial.

In civil cases before tribunals and courts of appeals, the party may, if he so wishes, avail himself of the services of an attorney, but in cases where a proxy is required the intervention of a procurator to represent a third party is obligatory. In commercial and business cases it is greatly recommended that the party be represented by an attorney because of the specialized nature of the field. Before the higher courts, representation and defense are combined in one and the same attorney, who must be duly qualified to practice before such courts.

In a criminal trial the accused must always be represented by an advocate or defense attorney.

Canon 1655 of the Code of Canon Law prescribes one or more advocates for criminal trials and for civil trials involving the rights of minors or those affecting the public welfare. In all other cases, the party may plead and defend his own case; however, if the judge deems it necessary, he may order the party to select one or substitute the one chosen by the party or even appoint one on his own authority.

It is a matter of common experience that the involved and intricate aspects of legal procedure are much more readily and easily expedited by retaining the services of an able and competent advocate. In ordinary cases, the party either selects his advocate or one is assigned to him by the judge. An exception is made in matrimonial cases for the party upholding the validity of the marriage; he is represented by the defender of the bond, whose duty it is, by virtue of his office, always to uphold the marriage bond, since marriage enjoys the favor of the law (*gaudet favore juris:* Can. 1014).

The appointment of an advocate by the judge, however, does not exempt the party from appearing personally in court, whenever the law or the judge demand it (Can. 1647). Furthermore, even a person who has no right to attack a marriage (Can. 1970–1972) may select an advocate to defend him before the tribunal. The advocate's function is that of counseling his client, conducting the defense at the trial, and generally cooperating with the administration of justice. Naturally, an advocate is not a public official,

since he does not play a direct part in the actuation of jurisdictional power; but his office, as the exercise of a professional activity undertaken upon request of the client, has the character of a necessary public service. From this standpoint, advocates or lawyers were characterized by the ancients as doctors and priests practicing in the social field.

RELATIONS BETWEEN ADVOCATE AND CLIENT. The relation between attorney and client, based on the confidence of the latter in the former, is of a contractual nature (the hiring and rendering of intellectual services). The attorney's services at the trial are made lawful by the client's mandate or authorization. Once he has taken the case, the attorney is obliged to handle it faithfully and diligently, employing all his technical knowledge and skill toward a successful conduct of the case, independently of the eventual outcome of the trial. The attorney is not held responsible for the loss of a suit, but only for the willful and culpable violation of his professional duties.

REQUISITES. The title of advocate or attorney rightfully belongs only to one who has duly passed the State Bar examination or has been admitted to the Bar; no one may practice law without being a member of the State Bar Association. To qualify as a member, it is not sufficient merely to possess a law degree; it is also necessary to meet certain other requirements regarding moral, professional, and political conduct and to show positive proof of one's eligibility for the practice of law.

In Canon Law the personal requisites of an advocate are: (a) that he profess the Roman Catholic religion; (b) that he be over twenty-one years of age; (c) that he be a person of good repute, professional integrity, and a practicing Catholic; (d) that he have the doctorate degree in Canon Law and that, if possible, he shall have served an apprenticeship of three years in the offices of the Tribunal of the Sacred Roman Rota or in the office of an experienced lawyer. One who possesses such qualifications may proceed to apply for membership as a practicing lawyer in an ecclesiastical court. (No lay lawyer is admitted to practice in ecclesiastical tribunals in the U.S.A.)

BODIES EXERCISING CONTROL OVER THE LEGAL PROFESSION. In civil law, the competent state authorities and the Bar Association pass upon the fitness of an applicant for membership in the legal profession and law practice; in the ecclesiastical law the competent authority is the local Ordinary.

The above authorities exercise their jurisdiction over advocates or lawyers in the following manner: (a) by approving applicants seeking admission to the Bar, either enrolling them as permanent members or granting them, as the occasion arises, the necessary authorization to defend a case; (b) by expelling members for grave reasons; (c) by punishing members who are judged guilty of unethical practices.

Moreover, according to Canon Law, the president of a judicial body, after consulting with other members of the same body, may (a) assign an advocate officially to represent a party who, because of poverty or other reasons, is not represented by legal counsel (in case of poverty, the officially assigned advocate is expected to conduct the client's defense free of charge and appropriate penalties are provided for those who refuse); (b) substitute, in certain cases, or add another advocate to the one already chosen by the party. The entire council of judges must be called upon to render the decision to expel or suspend an unworthy advocate during the course of a trial.

In general, advocates do not acquire a real right to plead unless they are on the appropriate list of court advocates. In such a case, they would have a jurisdictional right (*jus ad rem*), which, upon commission by the client, is immediately converted into an actual right (*jus in re*) to plead the case.

The commission by the client is a form of mandate, *i.e.*, a written declaration with date and client's signature affixed, authorizing the advocate to handle the defense of a specific case. The declaration must be authenticated and kept in the official acts of the trial.

RIGHTS AND OBLIGATIONS OF THE ADVOCATE. The advocate has a right to a fee for his services and to be reimbursed for all expenses incurred in the course of the trial; and he has the right to be recognized as defender both by the parties and the judge.

The advocate or lawyer has the obligation to fulfill the task assigned to him faithfully and diligently, without violating the mandate of his client, and is further bound to professional secrecy. Such obligations are assumed under oath. Moreover, the advocate may not accept gifts or presents that might cause him to betray his office; his professional integrity will require that he should not undertake the defense of causes that are clearly dishonest or bad from the very outset; and his rectitude will prompt him to indicate beforehand to his client the probable outcome of the law suit. Furthermore, within the limits of his possibilities, he is obliged to defend poor clients without charge.

There are three agreements that the advocate or lawyer must absolutely refrain from making with his client: an agreement to buy the lawsuit (*litis redemptio*), an agreement for an immoderate fee in case of victory (*pactum de palmario*), and an agreement for a share of the thing in litigation (*pactum de quota litis*). According to Canon Law, if such agreements are made, they are invalid and are punishable with suitable and appropriate penalties. In addition, all such agreements, as well as the defense of false causes, are forbidden by professional ethics.

ADVOCATES IN HISTORY. In the Middle Ages the term advocate or lawyer was used to designate the official through whom the feudal lord of a territory exercised his jurisdiction over the inhabitants or tenants of the territory, who enjoyed the privilege of exemption from taxes, tributes and service (military, court, *etc.*).

The land possessions of churches and monasteries enjoyed immunity from the jurisdiction of civil authority. Charles the Great prescribed an advocate for each diocese and abbey; and if the land possessions extended into another district or county, additional lawyers were assigned. Thus, there arose a lucrative legal profession, which, however, was little coveted or sought after by the nobility. Soon the profession came upon difficult and trying times; and in the twelfth century it fell into disrepute.

After the era of Constantine, there emerged a new ecclesiastical functionary, appointed by the emperor upon proposal of the bishop, i.e., advocatus Ecclesiae (advocate of the Church), who was charged with the duty of representing the Church and ecclesiastics in temporal affairs before secular courts and authorities, and with other important duties, such as the defense of the poor, the widows and the orphans. With changing times, these functionaries ceased to exist, giving way to civil advocates or lawyers.

Worthy of mention is the *Association of Advocates of St. Peter,* instituted under Pius IX and consisting of famous lawyers known for their staunch defense of religion and the rights of the Church. Ecclesiastical dignitaries and worthy laymen may become honorary members of this association. *Pub.*

ADVOCATE, CONSISTORIAL AND ROTAL.

Consistorial advocates apparently trace their origin to the seven defenders of the City established by both Popes Innocent I (402–417) and Gregory the Great (598). Their disciplinary code was established by Benedict XII in his Constitution *Decens et necessarium* of October 26, 1340, which was completed in 1741 by Sixtus IV, who raised their number to twelve. Their exclusive task of defending consistorial causes was enhanced by numerous and important privileges, such as that of directing the University of Rome. But when, following the establishment and consolidation of the pontifical tribunals, causes were no longer handled in the consistory, there remained no other duties for consistorial advocates but those of requesting the pallium for metropolitans, archbishops and such bishops as

enjoy that privilege, and of pleading in processes of beatification and canonization. As a vestige of the ancient discipline, they are still today regarded as the proper and original advocates of the Sacred Roman Rota.

According to Articles 13–14 of the law issued by the State of Vatican City on June 7, 1929, and according to the motu proprio *Al fine* of September 21, 1932, it is the duty of consistorial advocates to represent and defend those accused of crime and also to exercise the function of State's Attorney before the tribunals of Vatican State. Moreover, the Sacred Congregation of the Sacraments, in an instruction dated August 15, 1936 (Art. 48, par. 4), grants them the right to plead matrimonial causes before any ecclesiastical tribunal, without any need of obtaining previous permission of the Ordinary.

Finally, to the college of consistorial advocates belongs the right to sit in, with the privilege of consultative vote, on disciplinary proceedings handled by rotal advocates (Norms of the Sacred Roman Rota, June 29, 1934, art. 57).

The title or degree of rotal advocate is obtained after three years of apprenticeship in the *School* of the Sacred Roman Rota, directed by a Prelate Auditor under the authority and supervision of the Dean of the Rota (Decree *Nihil antiquius*, June 8, 1945).

Rotal advocates also are authorized to plead matrimonial causes before any ecclesiastical tribunal, without previous approval of the local Ordinary. This is in obvious regard for the dignity of the Sacred Roman Rota and in official recognition that mere membership in the Roman Rota is sufficient proof of the juridical competence of an advocate.

While consistorial and rotal advocates have the right to plead matrimonial causes before any diocesan court without formal approval of the local Ordinary, it would be erroneous to infer from this that they may simply appear before any diocesan court without seeking any permission whatever, even though the bishop may not ordinarily refuse such permission. The bishop's approval, however, does not consist merely in an investigation of the juridical competence and authenticity of the advocate's degrees, but it includes an inquiry into the numerous qualifications required in such advocates. The Ordinary, of course, shall always recognize, as a matter of principle, the right of consistorial and rotal advocates to plead cases in his diocesan tribunal; but in point of fact, when any such advocate presents himself to a diocesan tribunal, the bishop has the right to check the advocate's documents and conduct and, upon proven grave reasons, he may refuse him the exercise of this right. *Pug.*

ADVOCATE (DEVIL'S). *See* Promoter of the Faith.

AFFABILITY. Affability is approachability and readiness to talk in a person conversed with or addressed. It is also a marked pleasantness of manners with all, those who live with us as well as those with whom we come into social contacts. Since man is by nature a social being, the virture of affability is an obligation.

One may sin against the virtue of affability (a) by excess or (b) by defect. By excess, if one strives to please others more than he should. This sin may be committed by words; that is, praising an action that does not merit praise, or by praising it more than it deserves; or again, it may be committed by deed. Flattery or adulation (*q.v.*) may be employed for the sole purpose of pleasing others, or with some other selfish end in view. Of itself, adulation is only a venial sin. However, circumstances may make it mortal, as when one praises a gravely sinful action; or if one seeks to obtain a favor that cannot be granted without grave sin; or if flattery even unintentionally causes a notable harm to another, inducing him to sin gravely. One may sin against the virtue of affability by defect, that is, by disagreeable manners, particularly by harsh words, or by contradicting the words or deeds of another for no good reason. Of itself, this defect is a venial sin. However, it may become mortal, as when,

because of its frequency, it makes life difficult or very unpleasant for others. At times, this defect is a symptom of sickness; in this case moral responsibility diminishes almost totally.

AFFAIRS, EXTRAORDINARY ECCLESIASTICAL (SACRED CONGREGATION OF). *See* Roman Congregations.

AFFECTIVITY, EMOTIVITY. DEFINITION. The faculty of perceiving pleasure and pain is called affectivity. It is also called "sensibility," and it constitutes the most intimate part of the psychic activity of an individual which contains the motives of his behavior. Were it not for this emotional reaction which gives a note of personal interest to the phenomena unfolding around us, making them pleasant or unpleasant, we would have no motive for emerging from a passive and completely sterile state of contemplation. If we were entirely indifferent to sensations, these would be inactive and hence thoroughly useless.

The intellective faculty enables us to understand the outward reality by mirroring, through a series of representations, the innumerable aspects of this reality; the affective faculty relays these aspects to our consciousness for whatever they are worth to us, that is, for the pleasure they give to us or the pain they cause. Affectivity, therefore, enters into and colors all the various manifestations of thought which it transforms, modifies, debases, or elevates, as the case may be, by influencing the will.

AFFECTIVE POLARITIES. Besides the tonalities of pleasure and pain, are there within us other affective tonalities or polarities? According to Wundt, the complexity of our affective life cannot be reduced merely to the two tonalities of pleasure and pain; there are four others. which, like those of pleasure or pain, may be classified in pairs of opposite value, namely, excitement-depression, tension-relaxation. All sentiments, according to the German psychologist, contain elements of these three pairs of affective polarities, in a greater or lesser degree. Thus, *e.g.*, certain types of pain are accompanied by a feeling of excitation (anger); other types are accompanied by a feeling of tension (anguish, distress); and still other types are accompanied by a feeling of depression (discomfort).

However, these three classes of affective polarity do not have the same meaning and value. In fact, while the tone—pleasant or unpleasant—of a sensation is an integral part of the sensation itself, the feelings of excitement or depression are a secondary effect of this sensitive process achieved by its transmission from the sensory to the motor system (in other words, these feelings are not identified with the sensation, but are the result thereof). The feeling of tension results, as a kinesthopathic manifestation (*see* Kinesthesis), from the impact of the initial affective experience upon muscular and visceral innervation, and, as the state of excitement builds up without finding an outlet, the tension increases. Finally, the feeling of relaxation sets in either through cessation of the affective stimulus that determined the painful tension or through the inhibiting influence of the pleasant sensations accompanying the full satisfaction of a need; in other words, the painful, kinesthopathic sensations which caused the feeling of tension are substituted by pleasant sensations of physiological kinesthesis.

Wherefore, there exist only two fundamental affective polarities, and these are pleasure-pain (or, in more general terms, pleasant-unpleasant).

EMOTIONS. Our psychical life flows habitually between a moderate fluctuating of the affective tonality toward the pleasant and the unpleasant. There are, however, moments when this tonality, exceeding its habitual limits, gives rise to a more or less profound agitation of our whole being. In such instances, we speak of *emotions*. These, then, may be defined as particularly outstanding experiences of one's affective life, causing psychological and organic changes, and manifesting themselves as characteristic and particular expressions. Anger, fear,

excitement are examples of such emotions.

According to their greater or lesser intensity, emotions are divided into two categories: *shock emotions* and *sentiment emotions*. Emotions of shock are usually accompanied by modifications in breathing and in the pulse rate, in secretions, mimicry (facial expressions), *etc.* In this connection, many students of psychology wonder whether the above organic manifestations or bodily changes are to be considered merely effects or symptoms of the emotion, or are an integral part of it, or perhaps its cause. The answers are many and varied. We shall mention here, as the more comprehensive and acceptable, the so-called "circular theory" formulated by S. De Sanctis. According to this theory, the emotional cycle is made up of the following phases: (1) stimulus and perception; (2) conscious cerebral activity and awareness of the affective or personal value of the perception (*primary emotion*); (3) reflex somatic processes set into motion by the diencephelon; (4) return of these reflex processes, as new stimuli, into the consciousness; (5) complete emotional state, or *real emotion*.

LAUGHTER AND TEARS. In dealing with affectivity and emotions, one cannot overlook such characteristic emotive reactions as laughing and crying, whose phenomenological aspects are obscure and whose mechanisms are a cause for debate.

Laughter may be described as a clamorous emotive reaction characterized by changes in breathing, facial expressions, vasomotor activities. In its more pronounced form it is characterized by a convulsive shaking of the whole body which may lead to tears, involuntary urination (especially in women, due to relatively weaker sphincters), abdominal pains brought about by irregular contractions of the diaphragm, and the thumping of the latter on the underlying viscera. Occurring much more readily in children than in adults, and more readily in women than in men, laughter is nevertheless subject to restraint and even inhibition as a result of education and self-control. This accounts for the different reaction from one individual to another even though the cause of the laughter is the same, such as a particular joke, an embarrassing situation involving a third person, a comedy bit, *etc.*

Crying is also a reflex phenomenon caused by emotive stimuli and expressed through the well-known respiratory, lachrymal, and vasomotor activities, as well as by facial expressions, *etc.* As with laughter, children and women are much more frequently given to tears; and, like laughter, tears may be inhibited, up to a certain point, through education and self-control.

Laughter and tears, therefore, are phenomenologically different reactions in response to emotive stimuli of a different type (*viz.,* pleasant stimuli in the case of laughter, and painful stimuli in the case of tears). The mimico-emotive centers of the diencephalon, when stimulated by a pleasant or painful object, release a series of reflex processes culminating in the familiar manifestations of laughter or tears. These manifestations are safety valves for the affective tone of the individual. They are useful outlets, followed by a return of a person's humor to its normal physiological level; hence, they represent helpful factors in maintaining one's psychical balance. In other words, a stimulus which, because of its abnormality, originally threatened to upset the affective tone of the individual, either in the direction of excitement or of depression, is now rendered innocuous because of its discharge through laughter or tears.

There is a sound scientific basis, therefore, for the popular saying that "silent" suffering (pent-up emotion) is the worst kind of suffering: in effect, a flow of tears brings relief and restoration, thus safeguarding the mental equilibrium of the sufferer. As a matter of fact, the relative proneness to tears and other emotive outlets of the female sex is, according to many modern students of psychology, one of the main reasons why women are less subject than men to gastroduodenal ulcers and cardio-vascular diseases, which are today one of the principal causes of mortality among men. In view of this, a reassessment of the pedagogic value of the inhibition of crying and, in general, of any other outlet of the affective life in the young, would seem quite in order, by reason of the biological benefits resulting from intense emotive reactions and the release of inhibiting controls in behalf of the psychosomatic well-being of the individual.

PASSIONS. Passions (from the Greek *paskein*—to undergo, to suffer), in modern terminology (*see* Passions), are those habitual and predominant sentiments of an individual's behavior which become the distinctive mark of his personality. They are largely rooted in the fundamental biological instincts of self-preservation and self-protection; whence such egotistical passions as avarice, ambition, envy, hatred, jealousy, *etc.* Other passions instead are fostered by sentiments of a higher ethical character, and assume the altruistic form of love, abnegation, and the like.

At any rate, the spirit is always subject to the influence of one's affective tendency. To the will, under the guiding influence of instruction, education and religion, belong the task and distinction of combating the egoistic passions, either by uprooting them or by sublimating them into sentiments of a higher moral nature. In judging the imputability of a given passional act, it is necessary to ascertain whether the rise of passion was antecedent to or consequent to the act of the will (*see* Passions).

PATHOLOGY. The pathology of the affective tendency may be considered under two different aspects: (a) the morbid change of the affective tone; (b) the morbid effects exercised by emotions upon the organism.

For excessive variations of affectivity (hyperemotivity), *see* Dysthemia, Mania, Melancholy. Here it shall be noted that there also exists an opposite psychopathological picture of affectivity, characterized by hypoemotivity, or affective indifference toward the impressions of the outside world, that is by apathy (*q.v.*), tied to a limitation or slowing down of the ideative processes observed in certain phrenasthenics, in progressive paralytics and demented seniles, or in the condition of intellectual torpor induced by toxic states and cerebral compressions. Quite different is the condition of *athymia* in schizophrenics, which strikes at the higher ethical sentiments and, at the same time, silences the more elementary instincts (this condition is treated at greater length under the entry for Schizophrenia). Finally, there is a pathological condition called *catathymia*. This refers to the profound transformations which psychical conditions can undergo when influenced by affective factors which are thus capable of falsifying thought, the recall of past events, the association of ideas, etc. (*See also* Pathology of memory.) In this connection, it is helpful to bear in mind that the mentality of certain primitives, oligophrenics, hysterics, delirious persons is enormously more catathymic than that of normal subjects; and this must be taken into account in judging the manner of thinking and the behavior of such individuals.

Lastly, concerning any harmful influence of emotions upon the organism, it is to be noted that such an influence is exerted through repercussions in the vegetative-endocrine system which as a result becomes more or less gravely disturbed for a long time. Such pathological effects sometimes give rise to special morbid conditions (*e.g.*, emotional hyperthyroidism, neurosis, and psychosis caused by fright, *etc.*), or, as is more often the case, they aggravate a psychoneurosis already in progress. On the other hand, it is a well-known fact that psychoneurotics are more than others susceptible to disturbances of the affective sphere. Proof of the deleterious effects of emotional traumata on the entire organism is provided by the frequency with which psychoneurotic or somatic conditions (such as angina pectoris, diabetes, *etc.*) are noted in individuals engaged in professions involving great risk or responsibility. *Riz.*

AFFILIATION. In general, affiliation is the adopting or the receiving of one into a family as a son; or the fixing of the paternity of an illegitimate child. In legal history this term has been employed with various meanings; in Canon Law it was used, until recent times, to indicate the act of aggregating or attaching a religious to a house or province, or to designate the aggregation of a third order to its respective first order. In the Oriental Church, especially the Byzantine Church, the term is frequently used to indicate the affiliation of the founder (benefactor) of a monastery or of several lay persons to a monastery, in order that they may share in the spiritual benefits accruing from the good works of the monks.

In some modern civil codes affiliation refers to a civil status that is intermediate between adoption and guardianship, wherein a person assumes the care of a minor, who has not yet completed eighteen years of age, and the responsibility of attending to his maintenance, education, and eventual administration of goods. (The minor may be either a child of unknown parentage or a natural child, whose father is unknown and whose mother is unable to provide for his upbringing, or a child from a welfare agency or a child who has been materially or morally abandoned.) Through the process of affiliation the affiliator acquires the inherent rights of paternal authority over the affiliated; and upon the affiliator's request the affiliated may assume his surname, or, if the affiliated is either a legitimate child or a natural child whose father is known, he shall add the name of the affiliator to his own. Generally affiliation does not give rise to any rights of inheritance. (In the French Civil Code, however, the affiliated can inherit from the affiliator property which the latter acquired by his own industry, but not property which he inherited.)

In civil codes which recognize affiliation, marriage is forbidden between affiliator and the affiliated, the spouse and the heirs thereof, between the affiliated of one and the same person; between the affiliated and the children or spouse of the affiliator. A marriage contracted without dispensation in violation of the prohibiting law is subject to annulment, provided that the marriage is attacked within six months from its date of celebration. (In the U.S.A. affiliation does not exist as an intermediate civil status between adoption and guardianship.)

AFFINITY (Impediment of). According to Canon 97 of the Code of Canon Law, affinity is, just as in modern civil codes, a personal bond arising from marriage whether consummated or not. This is a distinct departure from the old discipline according to which the relationship of affinity arose from carnal intercourse, whether licit or illicit. Affinity is contracted only between the husband and blood relatives of the wife, and between the wife and blood relatives of the husband. Therefore, no relationship of affinity exists between blood relatives of the husband and blood relatives of the wife, since affinity does not beget affinity (*affinitas non parit affinitatem*). This explains why no dispensation is required for a marriage of two sisters of one family to two brothers of another family.

The relationship of affinity is computed according to line and degree, in the same manner as for consanguinity (*q.v.*), so that affinity exists in the direct line and in the collateral line with their respective degrees. Accordingly, the blood relations of the husband are related by affinity to his wife in the same line and the same degree as they are related to him by consanguinity, and vice versa. In other words, there are as many degrees of affinity on one side as there are degrees of consanguinity on the other. Thus, those related to the husband in the direct line of affinity are, in the first degree, his mother-in-law and his stepdaughters; in the second degree his mother-in-law's mother and his stepdaughters' daughters, according to ascending or descending line. The case is exactly reversed for the wife.

Those related to a husband in the collateral line of affinity are, in the first degree, his sisters-in-law; in the second degree—touching the first—his aunts and nieces; in the second degree, his wife's first cousins. Again the case is exactly reversed for the wife.

As long as both marriage partners are alive, affinity remains a sort of quasi-relationship; upon the death of one of them, it becomes an impediment, which bars marriage between the widowed party and the blood relatives of the deceased spouse. According to Canon 1077, marriage between those related by affinity is invalid in all degrees in the direct line, up to the second degree inclusive of the collateral line.

For the impediment of affinity in the direct line no dispensation is granted. In the collateral line, affinity in the first degree and affinity in the second degree touching the first are major impediments; affinity in the second degree is a minor impediment; in this case the dispensation is always valid, even if the reasons alleged are false (Can. 1042). Affinity is multiple, whenever the consanguinity from which it derives is in itself multiple, even when marriage is successively contracted with two blood relatives of a deceased spouse.

Before the Code of Canon Law, since the fact of illicit carnal intercourse frequently gave rise to the impediment of affinity, there often was a conflict between the internal and the external forum. In other words, a marriage which appeared externally valid could in reality be null because of a secret affinity existing between the two parties. This occasioned a complex form of casuistry, freely practiced by pre-Code moralists. There also existed a kind of supervenient affinity (*affinitas superveniens*), resulting from carnal relations between husband and sister-in-law or between wife and brother-in-law. With the adoption by the Code of Canon Law of the Roman concept of the civil codes, all this has been eliminated with great benefit to the faithful. *Bar.*

AGE. Age is the whole time of a being's existence; it is also the span of years into which human life is divided. Four periods are commonly distinguished in the life of man: infancy or childhood, puberty, maturity or adulthood, old age.

Two stages are included in the period of childhood: pre-moral—before the age of seven, and moral—from the age of seven to the age of puberty. In the first stage there is a gradual appearance of those elements which later serve to form the moral life, such as awareness of order, commands, penalties, the end intended in one's own activities. All these things bring to the child a certain sense of responsibility and a certain distinction between good and evil. The motives for action in this stage are, however, essentially hedonistic and egoistic. The second stage, on the other hand, witnesses notable progress. A sense of obligation becomes apparent, though deriving more from external pressure (parents, teachers, *etc.*) than from one's own reflections. Characteristic of this age is docility on the one hand and mutability on the other.

Puberty has a twofold aspect, physical and psychological. The physiological changes in the body that characterize this period occur in females about the age of 14–19; in males about the age of 14–16. They can take place before or after this time depending on the difference of races, regions, *etc.* The changes in the psychological order often begin earlier and last longer than those in the physical; in fact, they are somewhat influenced by the latter. The more characteristic changes are: affirmation of one's own independence against authority, more confidence in oneself, a greater spirit of generosity, a desire for perfection in the moral and spiritual life, an attraction to the opposite sex which is stronger in men than in women. Sufficient consideration must be given to these factors especially in the field of education and in making judgments on the morality of acts.

Maturity is the age in which a man possesses the fullness of his physical and mental capabilities. Consequently, in this period there are no special factors, from the point of view of age, which would serve to increase or diminish imputability.

Old age is the time in which one can benefit from past experience, but in which there is a gradual deterioration of the body and often a weakening of one's moral and spiritual strength. Before women reach old age, they pass through a period called the "change of life" (menopause) in which they become infecund. In this process, besides physical changes, women undergo certain moral and spiritual changes.

In law, age is considered as a natural cause affecting a person's juridical capacity and his capacity for actions. Juridical capacity is acquired by every human being at birth (certain rights, however, are recognized even for the child not yet born), but it can be limited by law. The capacity for action, on the other hand, is ordinarily acquired with the attainment of the age of majority. Canon Law distinguishes infancy up to the age of seven completed years (Can. 88, par. 3), minority up to the completion of twenty-one years, and majority from twenty-one years and up (Can. 88). In the various bodies of law and also in Canon Law, the child, as a general rule, is not considered responsible before the age of seven (Can. 88, par. 3; Can. 2201, par. 1). Thus, in the external forum, there can be no penal imputability below the age of seven. It is different in the internal forum, where judgment is based on objective reality.

Minor age generally lessens imputability, especially when one approaches the age of infancy (Can. 2204). It is only proper that in such cases the gravity of the imputation is entrusted to the judgment of the judge. The Code of Canon Law, however, admonishes that those who have not attained puberty (both sexes below the age of fourteen) ought to be punished with medicinal-educational penalties rather than with censures or other vindictive penalties. Thus, in certain advanced countries, special tribunals have been set up to deal exclusively with the correction of juveniles. The tendency today is toward using methods adapted more to the prevention of crime than to punishment for it.

Those who have reached the age of puberty and induce minors to commit a crime or participate in their delict, do not merit any lessening of imputability (Can. 2230).

The diminution of imputability for minors is based only on a presumption of law (Can. 2204: *nisi aliud constet*). For this reason nothing prevents the judge from deciding on full imputability even in a case of one who has not reached the age of majority. It is not infrequent for this to occur, especially in the years proximate to the age of majority and among people who mature rapidly. Besides, the ability to distinguish between good and evil actions is acquired much sooner than the ability to judge civil acts in which full capacity is not considered possible until the age of majority.

Unless mental illness is present, old age of itself does not necessarily imply any lessening of imputability. At most it might be considered a factor warranting diminution of the penalty. In the ecclesiastical forum, however, this would be rather unlikely, since for the most part the penalties are spiritual.

Thus, age is a factor which can cause a diminution of personal imputability and, hence, be an advantage for the perpetrator of any crime. If the delicts are numerous, the relative age must be taken into account for each individual crime. In a continued and permanent delict, the acts committed in the time of irresponsibility must be disregarded, while in order to evaluate the responsibility of acts committed during minor age, the element of minority must be considered. Similar considerations must guide us in evaluating acts from the purely moral point of view. *Pal.*

AGE, CANONICAL. Canonical age is considered particularly in regard to the candidate for the sacrament of Holy Orders. Various orders require in candidates the attainment of a determined age, known as the canonical age.

In the old law, in order to receive tonsure it was sufficient to have attained the use of reason, that is, seven years of age. The present legislation prescribes no definite age for tonsure. However, it cannot be received before one has begun theological studies (Can. 976, par. 1). The same applies to the minor orders.

The Council of Trent prescribed the age of twenty-two years for the subdiaconate, twenty-three years for the diaconate and twenty-five years for the priesthood. It must be noted, however, that according to this legislation it was sufficient in the case of each of the orders that the prescribed year should have begun. The present Code of Canon Law prescribes twenty-one completed years for the subdiaconate, twenty-two completed years for the diaconate, twenty-four completed years for the priesthood (Can. 975).

The Third Lateran Council prescribed the age of thirty years for the episcopacy. The Council of Trent repeated and confirmed this canon of the Lateran Council. It was not enough, however, that the thirtieth year should have begun. This prescription was incorporated in the Code of Canon Law (Can. 331, par. 1, n. 2).

The computation of age is made according to the civil year, beginning with the date of birth. One who has received orders prior to the canonical age fraudulently, that is, in bad faith, is *ipso facto* suspended from the exercise of the order received (Can. 2374). The old law also contained penalties for the ordaining minister.

The right to dispense with regard to canonical age belongs exclusively to the Holy See. Unless there is a very serious and urgent cause, the Holy See, generally speaking, never grants a dispensation concerning age for the subdiaconate, grants it rarely for the diaconate, more frequently for the priesthood (however, not beyond a year and a half).

Included among the various faculties which the Holy See usually grants to Ordinaries is that of dispensing from a year of the canonical age, but only for the priesthood.

Less properly do we speak of canonical age for some of the other sacraments such as confirmation (*q.v.*), communion (*q.v.*), marriage (*see* Age, Impediment of). *Pal.*

AGE (IMPEDIMENT OF). The Code of Canon Law (Can. 1067) prescribes that a marriage is null if entered by a male who has not completed sixteen years of age or by a female who has not completed fourteen years of age. These limits are absolute, that is, the impediment binds even though spouses below the stated ages are known to possess the necessary mental discretion and maturity.

Before the Code was promulgated, however, marriage contracted earlier than the present canonical age was valid if in fact sexual maturity existed (*si malitia supplebat aetatem*). The canonical impediment of age adds two years to the presumed age of puberty of the two sexes.

As a general rule, the various civil codes impose even higher age requirements out of concern for the success of the marriage and the welfare of offspring. The Church encourages the observance of laws and customs of various regions regarding the age of spouses.

Dispensation from this impediment is rare and difficult to obtain. It is granted only in very serious cases, but never below the age of puberty (respectively 14 and 12) for obvious reasons. *Bar.*

AGENCIES OF INFORMATION. *See* News Agencies.

AGENITALISM. *See* Gonads.

AGENT OF EXCHANGE. *See* Exchange.

AGGRAVATING CIRCUMSTANCES. *See* Circumstances of Human Act.

AGGRESSOR. *See* Self-defense, Legitimate.

AGIO (PREMIUM). *See* Exchange.

AGIOTAGE. *See* Stock Market, Exchange.

AGNUS DEI. The *Agnus Dei*, which is regarded as a sacramental, is the name given to certain oval-shaped medallions of white wax, bearing a figure of the Paschal Lamb on one side and that of a saint or of some special religious event on the other. Around the figure of the Lamb there appears the inscription *Ecce Agnus Dei* [whence its name] *qui tollit peccata mundi* ("Behold the Lamb of God, who takes away the sins of the world").

The oldest known examples of the *Agnus Dei* are traced back to the times of Gregory IX (1227–1241) and John XXII (1316–1334). Most probably they originated in Rome earlier than the ninth century (an *Ordo Romanus* makes specific mention of them). Formerly, the blessing of the medallions which, as today, was reserved to the pope, took place at the Lateran on Holy Saturday. The privilege of preparing them was given to the Cistercian monks of a monastery in Rome.

The blessing, as already noted, is reserved to the pope, who performs this ceremony in his coronation year and every seventh year thereafter, during the octave of Easter. Nevertheless, the medallions are also blessed upon other special occasions, and when their supply has run out.

The medallions, thus blessed, become sacramentals and objects of devotion for the faithful, recalling to mind the fact of our Redemption in and through Christ. *Pal.*

AGONY, DYING. As the very etymology of the term indicates (*agonia*—struggle), agony refers to the last struggle of the living body against death. The state of consciousness of a person in agony is much reduced and often suppressed, although there are cases in which perfect lucidity is retained to the very end. The facial features are drawn, the lips dry, the forehead bedewed with cold sweat; the extremities are ice-cold; respiration is irregular, the pulse almost imperceptible, the body temperature habitually low (even if previously there was a high fever). The individual in his agony often lies in bed silent and still, but at times he is seized with delirium, at other times he will emit a hoarse groan, perhaps involuntary, or perhaps an expression of inner suffering.

The sum total of these various phenomena—which become increasingly accentuated up until death—represents the progressive weakening of the individual's vital functions. The duration of agony is variable: it is very brief in some cases (traumatism, acute infection, poisoning, *etc.*), and rather long in others (chronic heart disease, malignancy, *etc.*).

A person in the state of agony is to be treated and cared for lovingly and intelligently until the point of death; and the possibility of a turn for the better is to be kept in mind at all times.

Because the sense of hearing is the last to become extinguished, those around a dying person, especially the doctor, should carefully avoid expressions of hopelessness; they should strive to maintain an attitude of hopefulness and serenity, avoiding, however, an attitude of false confidence designed to make the patient unaware of the gravity of his condition.

In the case of a dying heretic, it is not always advisable to disturb his subjective good faith, especially when there is doubt that a disclosure of the facts concerning his religion would lead to his generous acceptance of the true faith.

The physician shall strive to alleviate the frequent and painful sufferings of the dying individual by administering suitable analgesics (*see also* Euthanasia); however, care must be exercised not to administer them in such dosage as to suppress all consciousness. In fact, every effort must be made to keep the dying person conscious, vigilant, and alive, enabling him to continue and even increase his struggle against death, and to avoid any interference with the mysterious relations between his conscience and God in his last moments of life, particularly in the case of an impenitent sinner. As long as the sinner maintains his consciousness, there is always the possibility, up to the very end, that he may elicit an act of contrition leading to his eternal salvation. Only when the patient has already been reconciled with his God will it be permissible to employ measures

to alleviate pain, even though one foresees that such measures may lead to the suppression of consciousness. It is perfectly clear that the administration of analgesics must exclude any acceleration of death. The same procedure is valid, by way of analogy, in the case of an individual condemned to capital punishment, if, after having been reconciled with God, he expresses the wish that his consciousness be extinguished before the moment of execution. Although conscious acceptance of the death penalty in expiation for one's crime is preferable, the doctor may, in this instance, licitly employ means of suppressing consciousness. *Riz.*

AGREEMENT, PREVENTIVE. *See* Bankruptcy.

AID. *See* Cooperation.

AIR-SICKNESS (aeroneurosis). *See* Medicine, Aviation.

ALB. *See* Sacred Vestments.

ALCOHOLIC HALLUCINOSIS. *See* Alcoholism.

ALCOHOLISM. DEFINITION. Alcoholism consists in the excessive use of alcoholic beverages. As a problem it goes back to the times in human history when fermented drinks were first prepared. In view of the disastrous consequences of excessive drinking upon the drinker, his family, and the community in general, the problem of alcoholism has always been a matter of grave concern to society, nor has such concern ceased today.

EXTENT OF ALCOHOLISM. Alcoholism is more prevalent among the laboring class and the so-called mundane circles, although the use of liquor is on a definite and alarming upswing everywhere. Witness the ever-growing popularity of cocktail lounges and parties, the cocktail hour, *etc.* "Unfortunately, the holiday season is not the only time of year that alcohol becomes a medical problem. Alcoholism now stands as our No. 4 health problem—next to cancer, heart diseases and mental illness" (Dr. Jonas Rappeport, *Current Medical Digest*, December 1958).

While alcoholism is admittedly a fundamental cause of many physical and psychical illnesses, the fact remains that individual factors and conditions play an important part in the extent of its damaging effects. It is a known fact that individuals differ in their ability to resist the influence of drinking companions or the temptation to seek an uplift or escape in intoxication, which is the main factor behind the repeated lapses of the incorrigible or heavy drinker. Hence alcoholism, and particularly alcoholic psychosis, is apt to manifest itself much more readily in the so-called "constitutional psychoneurotics," that is, the naturally hypobulic individuals, overly susceptible to suggestion and with a low tolerance for physical and moral suffering. It is also a fact that individuals differ in their degree of toleration for liquor, although the true reason is not clearly known; it is known, however, that the organism of inveterate and hard drinkers excretes ingested alcohol much more rapidly than is the case with initial drinkers: which accounts for the fact that acute intoxication in the latter type lasts longer and is more serious.

PATHOLOGICAL EFFECTS. The harmful effects of excessive drinking are due to the fact that the ingested alcohol circulates wholly unaltered for several hours in the blood stream; in fact, it is found in various amounts in the brain, medulla, liver, kidneys, gonads, in the various secretions (saliva, milk, urine, sweat) and in exhaled air. It has been estimated (Grehant) that 15% of ingested alcohol is *eliminated* through the kidneys, the skin and lungs, while 85% remains to be oxidized in the organism.

All the organs and tissues of the body of a chronic alcoholic become more or less seriously affected or injured, especially the liver, which undergoes the fatal and well-known cirrhotic process; the heart, which becomes hypertrophied; the stomach, which is affected by a condition of chronic gastritis; the blood vessels or arteries, whose walls become sclerotized;

the nervous system, which becomes subject to an irritative and more often to a degenerative process eventually leading to grave neuropsychic disorders. Alcohol produces its most harmful effects on the nervous system, leaving more lasting effects there than in other organs.

Also to be noted is the relationship of alcohol to the sexual processes. Alcohol is known to affect and injure the genital glands, and, in a pregnant woman, it is capable of invading, through the placenta, the fetus. As already noted above, lactation and respiration are two of the processes whereby alcohol is eliminated. Mention might here be made of the reprehensible habit on the part of drinking parents to "make their children taste" wine or liquor at a tender age. All these circumstances bear out the statistical findings which show that sterility, abortion, a high rate of infant mortality and, finally, delicate, deformed, phrenasthenic and criminal offspring are particularly prevalent among alcoholic parents.

Lastly it is to be noted that alcoholism is indirectly responsible for many other types of diseases and ills, as the relaxing of moral restraint and the stimulation of man's lower impulses increases the tendency toward all sorts of debauchery and gives rise to venereal diseases; it weakens organic resistance and makes the organism susceptible to infectious diseases, particularly tuberculosis: whence the aphorism of the famous clinician Landouzy, who referred to alcoholism as the bed of tuberculosis: *"L'alcool est le lit de la tuberculose."* Also, the toxicity of alcohol is increased by its combined action with other poisonous substances, such as lead and carbon disulphide, thus paving the way for all sorts of "occupational toxichoses" which strike at the health of a vast number of workers and laborers. Add to these disastrous effects the staggering number of traffic fatalities caused by intoxicated drivers.

ALCOHOLIC PSYCHOSES. In considering the effects of alcoholism, it will be useful to review briefly the alcoholic psychoses, *i.e.*, the various mental disorders that are exclusively or mainly caused by excessive drinking. We shall review only the principal forms. (Dr. Jonas Rappeport, again, in the *Current Medical Digest*, divides alcoholism into four stages: (1) Acute Inebriation; (2) Acute Tremulousness; (3) Acute Alcoholic Hallucinosis, (4) Delirium Tremens.)

Because it is well known, it may be superfluous to dwell on acute alcoholic intoxication, which is the common ordinary form of drunkenness. It will be more enlightening to single out a less common variety, *viz.,* pathological intoxication. In predisposed, psychoneurotic or definitely psychopathic individuals this form of intoxication gives rise to uncontrollable fits of rage, to impulses of incendiarism or homicide, to the vilest types of actions, which are often performed in a truly "crepuscular state" of mind. When the effects of alcohol have worn off, the individual usually remembers nothing at all of the whole episode.

Simple "chronic" alcoholism, which is found in the great majority of inveterate drinkers, is characterized by a progressive weakening of all psychical functions and, if the drinking habit is not checked in time, it may fatally develop into a demential condition. The psychical manifestations of chronic alcoholism are: excessive distraction and talkativeness, mental torpor, hypobulia, dullness of power of judgment, abnormal moodiness and, above all, a weakening and perversion of the moral sense. The neurological manifestations are sudden tremors, unsteady gait, and lack of coordination of the voluntary movements.

In the course of chronic alcoholism there may appear an acute psychosis characterized by confusion, tremor, and hallucinations. This psychosis is called *delirium tremens* and is often precipitated by infective diseases, shocks, overexhaustion (and even by sudden withdrawal of alcohol). In this state or condition, which is more frequent among drinkers of liquor than among drinkers of wine, the individual experiences the sudden appearance of typical "zooscopic visual hallucinations" (*see* Hallucination) accompanied at times by visions of flames, by insulting voices and all other sorts of hallucinations which tend to terrorize the patient and cause him to have incoherent deliriums, or to give way to gestures of extreme violence and even suicide. At other times the mood is one of calm; consciousness becomes obfuscated, though not excessively so; the tremors increase in intensity. After a few days, if the patient does not lapse into hyperthymia or become a victim of collapse, the syndrome ceases and there follows a deep and prolonged slumber. Upon awakening, the patient is aware of a state of prostration and a certain tendency to hallucinatory phenomena; at times the crisis merges into a chronic hallucinosis or into one of Korsakoff's syndromes.

The "alcoholic hallucinosis" also endures for a few days, but it is differentiated from *delirium tremens,* in that it is characterized by an almost perfect lucidity of consciousness and by the prevalence of auditory hallucinations (insulting or threatening voices) which implant in the mind of the patient fantastic ideas of persecution.

A much stronger delirium than this is the "delirium of jealousy" in alcoholics. This jealousy complex is acquired gradually and is often occasioned by the wife's apparent repugnance to submit to a brutal and perhaps now impotent husband. The most trifling incidents of daily conjugal life tend to increase and foment this delirium of jealousy. Finally, the alcoholic begins to suspect his wife's fidelity, makes all sorts of absurd accusations, quarrels with her, subjects her to brutal treatment, and may even end up committing uxoricide.

The various delirious manifestations in alcoholics, especially the delirium of jealousy, are characterized by the so-called "alcoholic paranoia," which continues more or less chronically even after the withdrawal of alcohol, and it seems to occur in drinkers having a paranoiac predisposition (*see* Paranoia).

"Korsakoff's psychosis or syndrome" is principally characterized by a serious impairment of the memory, causing the individual to forget recent facts and occurrences; the mnemonic lapses are filled in with false reminiscences and with more or less fictitious and fantastic inventions. Serious disorientations set in as a result of this condition. The mood is, on the whole, serene and even somewhat euphoric. Frequently, symptoms of polyneuritis are associated with this type of psychosis.

"Alcoholic pseudo-paralysis" has a close clinical resemblance to progressive paralysis (hence its name). It is distinguished from the latter by the negative results of biological tests designed to ascertain the lues, and by its rapid regression with mere withdrawal of alcoholic beverages.

SOCIAL ASPECTS. The many and serious evil effects that alcoholism inflicts upon the drinker, his environment, and even upon his descendants have always been a cause of major concern to governments, which have, as already noted, considered and adopted preventive and restrictive measures in an attempt to curb a real social plague.

The best prophylaxis for alcoholism consists: (a) in an intense program designed to instruct and educate the public concerning the evils of excessive drinking; (b) in a rigid ban on all alcoholic beverages in schools and educational institutions. Such a ban will serve the purpose of preventing children from becoming accustomed even to the slightest amount of alcohol, and it will prove to parents that abstemious children grow into healthier specimens, both somatically and psychically, than drinking children; (c) in providing healthier and more comfortable homes for the laboring classes, so that they will prefer their homes to the taverns; (d) in promoting after-work social, recreational, and athletic activities in order to give members of poorer classes opportunities to engage in useful and educational pursuits, instead of seeking their recreation and relaxation in drinking establishments, and to withdraw the young from social environments where the use of alcoholic beverages is all too common. Another important prophylactic method (resulting from recent studies of R. J. Williams, a vitaminologist) consists in improving man's nutrition, for it has been proved

experimentally that, in general, a nutritional deficiency gives rise to an increased craving for alcohol.

In itself, the treatment of alcoholics is not too arduous a process. It consists especially in the withdrawal of alcoholic beverages (today rendered somewhat easier and more acceptable by the use of intravenous injections of small doses of alcohol, by electric-shock treatments [see Shock therapy] and by sleep therapy) and the use of a rich diet of B^1, and PP vitamins, in the use of preventive drugs, designed especially to safeguard liver function. In 1948 a new drug called "antabus" was developed for chronic alcoholism; it is completely innocuous and of unquestioned effectiveness if employed in the proper manner.

The frequent crimes committed under the influence of alcohol are not "in themselves" liable to penal sanction, if the criminal action was the result of a real condition (even if temporary) of mental illness, with consequent suppression of intellectual and volitional functions. But from the standpoint of the moral law, the individual is considered guilty for having abandoned himself to excessive drinking in the first place, especially if he is aware of the fact, by reason of previous personal experience, that excessive drinking will deprive him of the use of his reasoning power (imputability in cause). Here, however, account must be taken of psychoneurotic predispositions found to be present in many alcoholics, for such factors lessen somewhat the degree of guilt and the imputability of an immoderate drinker. A similar extenuating circumstance may exist also in the case of an individual who takes to drinking because of some serious crisis or calamity occurring in his life. In a word, each case must be judged on its own merits, and after a fair examination of the circumstances that led to excessive drinking. For questions of a strickly moral nature, see Intoxication. *Riz.*

ALIENATION. *See* Loss.

ALIENATION, MENTAL. *See* Psychosis.

ALLELUIA. *Alleluia* is a Hebrew religious acclamation (*Hallelu* — hail or praise; *Jash,* an abbreviation of Jahweh —God; hence, praise God) adopted by Christian liturgy.

The expression is found in the last two books of the Psalter, at the beginning and the end of the psalms (cf. Psalms 106, 113, 135, 146, *etc.*). St. Augustine refers to these as alleluiatic psalms. At times, the expression had the value of a small doxology (Psalm 117, 116); at other times, it was a purely liturgical adjunct. Later it assumed the character of festive acclaim (Tob. 13: 22; Apoc. 19:1–6).

As a liturgical expression, it is found as early as the second century. At the time of St. Augustine it had become a popular refrain of the faithful (cf. Sidonius Apollinaris, Ep. 10). At first, the Roman liturgy adopted the *Alleluia* for the feast and octave of Easter and then extended it to the entire Paschal season up to Pentecost (under Pope Damasus, 363–384). Later, it was introduced into all the Masses, excepting the Lenten season and Mass and Office for the Dead (at the time of Gregory the Great, d. 604).

At present, the Church uses the *Alleluia* during all the seasons of the liturgical year (*q.v.*), with the exception of the penitential season of Lent and the Mass and Office for the Dead. The spirit of exaltation during Paschaltide is characterized by the frequency with which the *Alleluia* occurs. *Pal.*

ALLUVION. *See* Accession.

ALMA REDEMPTORIS MATER. *See* Angelus Domini.

ALMSGIVING. DEFINITION AND DESCRIPTION. Almsgiving is the act by which a person, out of love of God, gives material assistance to a neighbor in need. Almsgiving denotes properly the *act* of giving. The *thing* given, money or food, is called an alms in a secondary sense, as the object of the act of giving.

Almsgiving is an act of charity toward one's neighbor motivated by mercy, which is a readiness of the will to relieve the need of another. Almsgiving, therefore, is a work of mercy even though it is not enumerated among the seven corporal works of mercy.

The words "out of love of God" express the motive which makes almsgiving an act of *Christian* or *supernatural* charity. This motive does not exclude the presence of other personal motives such as satisfaction for sins, petition for a favor from God, *etc.* It does, however, exclude evil motives. One who gives to the poor out of evil motives is not giving alms. Occasionally, spiritual assistance given to a neighbor in need is improperly called spiritual almsgiving. We say improperly because almsgiving is more properly used to indicate material assistance, while spiritual assistance comes under the spiritual works of mercy.

OBLIGATION. Almsgiving is not only a good and meritorious act and therefore a matter of counsel, but in certain circumstances it is also a matter of obligation by virtue of the law of charity toward one's neighbor. A man cannot say that he loves his neighbor if he fails to help others through works of charity when he can easily do so. Sacred Scripture admonishes us: "And if a brother or sister is naked and in want of daily food, and you say to them: 'Go in peace, be warmed and filled,' yet you do not give them what is necessary for the body, what does it profit?" (that is, to one who acts in this manner). And also, "What will it profit . . . if a man says he has faith, but does not have works" (James 2:14–15).

In order that almsgiving may become a matter of obligation, certain definite conditions must be verified on the part of both the giver and the receiver. Insofar as the receiver is concerned, it is required that he truly be in want. Since there are and always will be poor people in the world, this condition for the obligation of almsgiving will always be present. Insofar as the giver is concerned, the required condition is that he possess superfluous goods. By superfluous goods are meant those material means not essential to an individual in order that he might live in a manner suitable to the state of life which is his by birth, vocation, personal choice, *etc.* Every man can licitly use his possessions in order to live in accordance with his social status. This would include, for example, the support of his family and the education of his children in order that they might maintain the same social status. It should also include the commendable practice of hospitality, generosity, and munificence in promoting science, art, culture, and the like. There is no absolute norm for determining what constitutes the necessities of a particular person's state in life. It can happen that of two persons in the same social status and condition one will require more than the other. Yet the former will not be living beyond his status, nor will the latter be deprived of his necessities. All of this, however, does not affect the principle that one cannot possess more than is required and is useful for living in a manner proper to his state in life. In cases where there is a superabundance, we have a situation in which goods can no longer be of beneficial service. The only other alternative is that they will serve useless purposes (or perhaps evil ones). This would constitute a wasteful abuse of goods. Those goods could be very beneficial to the poor who lack the things which are necessary for them to live in accordance with their state in life (often very modest). The goods of the world were created by God to provide for the necessities of life and to serve for the benefit of all men. It would, therefore, be contrary to the divine plan to have one man dissipate the God-given goods of which another man is greatly in need. As long as there are people in need of the necessities of life, God does not desire, in fact He forbids, that persons keep for themselves goods for which they have no beneficial use at present or of which they reasonably foresee that they cannot make good use in the future.

This divine will (commandment) is contained in the very nature of material goods inasmuch as they were created to serve the needs of all men. Therefore, it is a commandment (and not solely a counsel) to give one's surplus as alms to the poor and to those in want. The teaching is simple and clear. The fact that a man owns property or goods does not mean that he has the right to dissipate such goods or to squander them on himself and his family, and only after this must he, then, give to others. Besides rights, owners also have obligations. The right and privilege of an owner mean that he is able to use possessions for himself and for his family before all others. He also has the right (and the duty) to regulate an orderly distribution of his goods.

RECIPIENTS OF ALMSGIVING. Generally speaking, it may be said that there are two classes of people in need: (1) the ever-present number of those in *ordinary* need, and (2) the smaller number of those who find themselves in *extreme necessity*. The latter are not an ever-present problem. They are special cases which arise because of unusual circumstances. A person who finds himself in such dire straits that only immediate assistance could save him from death, or from serious danger of death, or from grave harm, such as the loss of a limb or permanent or prolonged state of bad health would come under the second category. Now, supposing that I have a surplus of goods, am I obliged to aid this particular poor person? The answer is in the affirmative if I know that he is in grave or extreme necessity and there is no one else to provide for him adequately. In fact, in such a case I am obliged to give even the things proper to my state of life, if I can give them without causing grave harm to myself. In other words, the obligation of charity toward my neighbor demands that in such cases I give even the goods that are of beneficial use to me, or which are not truly necessary for my own life. In less particularized cases, I may be at freedom to aid this or that particular person or institution. However, in giving alms, a good Christian shall not limit himself merely to that which is strictly obligatory, but he will also practice almsgiving and perform good works to earn greater supernatural merit, and to obtain pardon for his sins and God's grace. The Holy Spirit insistently counsels the giving of alms. Even in the Old Testament, *e.g.*, in the Book of Tobias, the practice of almsgiving is urgently counseled. Frequent references to it are made by Christ, who set the example for us (John 13: 29). Giving to one's brothers suffering adversity will always be an exalted manifestation of the Christian spirit. The Divine Master said: "By this shall all men know that you are my disciples, if you love one another." It is a mistake, advocated especially by materialistic socialism, to make the care of the poor an obligation of the state rather than of the individual. Such a policy, of course, is very convenient, but certainly not in conformity with the Christian spirit. Such a program tends to indicate the failure of socialism in inculcating in its adherents the spirit of fraternal charity, a practice which is proper to Christians. Assuredly, the state has duties toward the poor. But its activities cannot and must not stifle the activity of private and personal charity, for the poor would become victims of such a system and serfs of the state. (*See also* Avarice, Charity, Works of Mercy, Surplus.) *Ben.*

ALPHONSUS M. DE' LIGUORI (SAINT).

St. Alphonsus is the greatest of the moralists and the father of modern moral theology (*q.v.*).

LIFE. Alphonsus was born of noble Neapolitan parents at Maranella, near Naples, on September 27, 1696. At the early age of sixteen he was admitted to the bar and soon met with great success. Fearful of having possibly committed some injustice in the practice of his profession, he found the road to conversion in the loss of a famous lawsuit in which he was leading counsel. In truth, his well-ordered, Christian life did not stand in need of conversion in the real and proper sense of the word, but he retired from the legal profession (1723) in order to pursue a safer way of life. Alphonsus decided to enter the ecclesiastical state, and in 1726, after three years of preparation, he was ordained a priest at the age of thirty.

Even before becoming a priest, he had joined the Association of Diocesan Missionaries of Naples (called the "Neapolitan Propaganda"). As a priest, his labors were expended mainly in behalf of foreign missions, to which he was practically ready to go when Divine Providence directed his steps toward Scala. Here he came upon some monasteries whose spiritual needs he immediately recognized; he also came into contact with some religious women, through whose instrumentality God called him to his life's work. These religious women, originally organized by Father Falcoja, of the Congregation of Pious Workers, found a pillar of strength in the saint. He drew up a rule for them, and became the founder of the Congregation of the Redemptoristines (1731).

By divine inspiration Alphonsus also founded a society of missioners, whose apostolate was particularly dedicated to rural areas, the Congregation of the Most Holy Redeemer (1732). Both Congregations were soon approved by Pope Benedict XIV: the Redemptorists in 1749 and the Redemptoristines in 1750. St. Alphonsus dedicated himself to the preaching of missions to the people. At the same time he applied himself to the task of imparting to his missioners the knowledge necessary for their ministry. And for this he relied principally on moral science.

One of his first aims was to take a stand on the question concerning a doubt of conscience—a stand that was to uphold the golden mean between the two extreme views (rigorists and laxists) dividing the theological world of his time. As a youth he had instructors who had belonged to the rigorist school; but the sacred ministry and his contact with the faithful convinced him of the dangers connected with such extreme views. Thus, while strongly interested in a general reform within the Church and opposed to moral laxity, he sought above all to uproot the widespread rigorism. His was a middle-of-the-road position, one that came easily to him because he was free of all scholastic prejudice; this middle view stemmed less from his mind than from his saintliness. He felt that rigorism or tutiorism was a sort of long arm of encroaching Jansenism, which viewed everything in the light of sin and its disastrous consequences, thus creating a gloomy and despairing religiosity. St. Alphonsus was not unmindful of sin, but, contrary to the Jansenist position, he made the law of sin subordinate to the law of love. If, therefore, he opposed rigorism or tutiorism, certainly it was not because he wished to sacrifice it on the altar of a misunderstood condescension, but because he saw in such a moral tendency a sort of fashion of the times, a fleeting and precarious trend that could be damaging to souls.

The decisive victory due to his tireless labors obtained over Jansenism and all its consequences must be numbered among his other extraordinary achievements. To a Redeemer fashioned by the Jansenists as if defeated in His work of salvation, St. Alphonsus opposed a Redeemer whose redemptive efficacy is overflowing. *Copiosa apud Eum redemptio* became the motto of his Congregation. Because he opposed the prevailing trend, St. Alphonsus became the target of many enemies, not only from the Jansenist camp, but even from among those who believed themselves to be defending the orthodox views of the Church. To all these he responded calmly and firmly with many articles, which served better to crystallize his thinking, and he later summarized them in his *Moral Theology*. At the same time St. Alphonsus also concerned himself with the practical application of his thinking to the ministry: whence the treatises of pastoral theology which complete his theological work. From this time on, the practical questions receive even more emphasis in his work.

In 1762, despite his protest, he was named Bishop of St. Agatha of the Goths, a small diocese in the vicinity of Naples. He occupied that see for thirteen years (1762–1775) and was a model of pastoral solicitude. Despite the pressing duties of his episcopal office, he managed during this period to write the greater part of his apologetic and theological

works. He made frequent attacks against Jansenism, and also against Gallicanism, which at that time was often found joining forces with Jansenism. In 1770, because of illness, he submitted his resignation from the episcopal see, but Pope Clement XIV refused to accept it; however, in 1775, Pius VI acceded to his request. Alphonsus nevertheless continued as Major Superior of his Congregation, to which he dedicated his last years, sorely tried by afflictions and trials which served to complete the purification of his soul. Denounced to Rome by a superior of his Congregation as supporting the King of Naples against the Pope, Alphonsus saw the houses in Naples, including the general headquarters at Nocera, cut off from the Institute (1781). He died at Pagini on August 1, 1787. The cause of his beatification and canonization was introduced in Rome, in 1796. He was beatified in 1816, and canonized in 1839.

WORKS. (A) Dogmatic and Apologetic: *The Truths of the Faith* (1767); *The Triumph of the Church*, a history of heresies, in three volumes (1772); *A Defense of the Supreme Authority of the Roman Pontiff* (1768), against Febronius; *The Admirable Conduct of Divine Providence in the Work of man's salvation, effected by Jesus Christ,* (1746). (B) Moral and Pastoral: In 1748 St. Alphonsus published with comments a work of moral theology, written by a theologian of moderate views: the *Medulla*, of Busembaum, S.J. (d. 1668); the copious annotations show the forceful originality of the disciple. Out of this work there arose the *Theologia Moralis* in two volumes, which is the theological masterpiece of the holy Doctor (vol. I, 1753; vol. II, 1755). This work, the fruit of immense labor, constitutes a vast encyclopedia of all moral questions. At the same time St. Alphonsus contributed a special *Dissertation* (1749) to the discussion of the question of probabilism, already defended as a moral system in the first editions of his *Theologia Moralis*. Later, however, upon revising the monograph in 1762, the author, while still opposing probabilism, exposes in his own terms the theory of equiprobabilism, which became his definitive system. This system, however, did not enter the *Theologia Moralis* until the sixth edition (1767) and continued to appear in the three subsequent editions published by himself or during his life (9th edition, 1785). The *Pratis Confessarii: An Instruction for Confessors as to How to Hear Confessions Well* was written in Italian in 1748, and was later translated into Latin. In 1757 it was incorporated in the *Medulla*. The *Homo Apostolicus* was written in Latin in 1759, and, two years later, it appeared in Italian in three volumes. The *Instruction to the Faithful on the Ten Commandments* was written in Italian in 1767 and translated into Latin in 1768. It is a brief and popular treatise concerning the more common topics of Christian doctrine to be imparted to the faithful. (C) Ascetical and Mystical: *Preparation for Death* (1758); *The Great Means of Prayer* (1759): the work was designed to offer guidance and direction in questions concerning grace; *The Practice of Loving Jesus Christ* (1768): it is the principal ascetical work of the saint; *Visits to the Blessed Sacrament and to the Blessed Virgin:* it is the most popular work of St. Alphonsus (1745–1748); *Novena to the Sacred Heart of Jesus* (1758), which contributed to the growth of the new devotion, and which was received favorably in Rome; *The Glories of Mary* (1750): the first great work of the saint, it shows clearly the place that the Blessed Virgin occupied in his devotion and is a reply to the *Well-Ordered Devotion* of Muratori; *A Succinct Exercise of Perfection* (1743): St. Alphonsus reduces all the spiritual doctrine drawn from St. Teresa to two fundamental points: (1) detachment from creatures and union with God through love, (2) meditation and prayer; *The True Spouse of Jesus Christ* (1760): a book for nuns which is a true masterpiece; the author pursues the same theme as in the preceding work. (D) Sermons: The *Selva* (or *"Raccolta"*) (1760), which met with enormous success; it is a basic work in its field.

To assist the priest in his work of sanctification through prayer, St. Alphonsus also wrote the following pamphlets: *The Hasty Celebration of the Mass and Recitation of the Office* (1760); *Considerations and Affections for Thanksgiving* (1761); *The Ceremonies of the Holy Mass* (1769); a translation of the Psalms and Canticles (1774).

The above list of his works is not complete; they number 129 in all, besides the revisions. St. Alphonsus carried on a voluminous correspondence, all related to the various phases of his activities. His work is one of lasting value.

St. Alphonsus, who had almost single-handedly waged a struggle against rigorism, must have rejoiced indeed when, after his death, the Church recognized his authority in matters of moral theology. During the process of his beatification the Holy See conducted an official investigation of his writings, and in the final decree (May 18, 1803) it was declared that nothing had been found deserving of censure (*nihil in eis censura dignum repertum fuit*). In the following years a controversy continued between the disciples of the new *Beatus* and the advocates of the more rigid systems, who alleged that his position was dangerous to the welfare of souls. In 1831, during the pontificate of Gregory XVI, Cardinal de Rohan-Chabot, Archbishop of Besançon, proposed to the Sacred Penitentiary two questions relative to the authority of St. Alphonsus: (a) May a professor of moral theology with safe conscience (*tuta conscientia*) follow the opinions of St. Alphonsus in the course of his teaching? (b) Is a confessor to be reprehended for following, in the exercise of the sacrament of Penance, the opinions of St. Alphonsus without examining the reasons on which they are based, simply because the Holy See has declared that there was nothing to be censured in his works? The reply was affirmative to the first question and negative to the second. The second reply was particularly important, because the probabilists of that time did not cease to rebuke confessors who followed the opinions of St. Alphonsus in the administration of the sacrament of Penance.

The authority of Blessed Alphonsus was thus fully upheld; it was confirmed in 1839 at the time of his canonization, and in 1871 when he was proclaimed Doctor of the Church, and again more recently (April 26, 1959) when he was proposed as heavenly patron of confessors and moralists.

The mind of the Church has been mainly to approve the spirit of the holy Doctor, who sought constantly to follow the evangelical doctrine, by avoiding laxism on the one hand and rigorism on the other. His authority in moral theology is unique: His opinions are safe and may be safely followed, but no one is obliged to adopt them; his system has not received any positive approbation. Only the views of probabilists and rigorists, who persisted in holding Alphonsus under suspicion, have been definitely cast aside.

The approbation given by the Church to the holy Doctor served to bring about, in the course of the nineteenth century, a return to a more indulgent moral theory, as also a reappraisal of probabilism in its various forms and aspects. St. Alphonsus, therefore, represents a decisive turning point in the history of moral theology concerning the conduct of life and Christian piety. *Pal.*

ALPINISM. *See* Sports (Dangerous).

ALTAR. HISTORY. The altar is as ancient as worship itself. It may be correctly stated that altars were in existence before temples were erected; in fact, the origin of the altar coincides with the early beginnings of the history of mankind (cf. Schmidt, *History of Comparative Religions*).

The first sacrificial offerings were made on small mounds, usually heaps of stone or earth erected above the ground. According to some authors, the "altar" is derived from the combination of two words: *alta-ara* or *alta-res*. According to a more critical and scientific theory, the origin of the word is derived from *altum*, the supine form of *alere;*

hence, altar signifies a special table, destined for burnt sacrifices, or as mystical nourishment, offered to the Deity or deities. This practice prevailed also during the pre-Christian era. Later, the Church Fathers called the altar *mensa*, or table, with such qualifying adjectives as sacred, mystical, spiritual, celestial.

Originally, Christian altars were made in many forms and of a large variety of materials according to the needs of worship, the circumstances of time and place, and the prevailing symbolic thought. As to its form, one finds round, oblong, rectangular, and quadrangular altars; as to material, the original Christian altars were made of wood, silver, and, finally, of stone. Sometimes the altar consisted of three marble slabs, one of which constituted the *mensa* or table, placed horizontally on the other two, which were set vertically in the ground. At other times, the *mensa* or table rested on small columns, anywhere from one to five in number.

The location of the altar in the early churches was arranged in such a way as to be best suited for the Eucharistic banquet, and the center of Christian worship at all liturgical assemblies. Raised above floor level and completely separated from everything else, the altar was erected along the longitudinal axis of the main nave, between the apse and the *schola cantorum*. The erection of the altar against the wall of the apse, which caused priests and sacred ministers to have their backs turned to the faithful, was an exceptional occurrence in the early days. But with the increasing number of priests in monasteries it became a normal practice to have other altars erected along the walls in order to facilitate the frequent and often simultaneous celebration of the Mass.

The veneration of the holy martyrs, who joined their sufferings with the sacrifice of Christ, suggested the practice of celebrating the Holy Mass over their remains, in accordance with verses 9–11 of Chapter IV of the Apocalypse. When the entire bodies of holy martyrs were unavailable, their relics were used; thus, in a certain sense, the table of every altar was transformed into a small and mystical cemetery. This practice continues even today. Just as in the Old Law the altar was a symbol of the presence and majesty of God, so in the Catholic Church it is a symbol of Christ; thus, the altar is, in a sense, the heart of a church, ordinarily embellished with precious ornaments and artistic decorations.

KINDS OF ALTARS. In the Christian liturgical concept, the altar is the upper stone table, considerably raised above floor level, upon which the Eucharistic Sacrifice is offered to God. From the standpoint of its structure and consecration, the Church recognizes two kinds of altars: (a) permanent or immovable, and (b) portable or movable. The permanent altar is firmly attached to the support on which it rests (Can. 1197, par. 1, n. 1) so as to form one whole piece with it. The table itself must consist of a single slab of natural stone. And while the support may be of artifical stone, the columns on which the table rests must be of natural stone. The hole, or *loculum* (*sepulcrum*), containing the relics of the saints, is situated in the center of the table itself, and must always be the same as that of the Church (Can. 1201). The portable or movable altar also consists of a solid piece of natural stone sufficiently hard to resist fracture (called the "sacred stone," Can. 1197, 1, 2) and sufficiently large to allow the hosts and the chalice to be set on it (Can. 1198, par. 3). This too, must have a hole in the center for the relics of at least one holy martyr. This hole must have a stone cover or lid, firmly fastened with cement (blessed for this purpose) and marked with the seal bearing the insignia of the Ordinary or other consecrating bishop. The "sacred stone" is placed on the level surface of the stone or wooden table, which, by extension, is also called altar. The portable altar may also have, although it is not obligatory, its titular saint; this title may not be changed without permission of the Ordinary (Can. 1201, par. 3).

From the standpoint of dignity, the liturgy of the Catholic Church distinguishes three kinds of altars: (a) the main altar, (b) minor altars, and (c) papal altar.

MAIN ALTAR AND MINOR ALTARS. This distinction was introduced when the practice arose of erecting in a church several altars for the convenience of priests celebrating Mass daily. The central and principal altar of the church is called "the main altar" and also "choral altar," while the others are referred to as "minor" altars. If the church is consecrated, the main altar, which must always be permanent or immovable, must also be consecrated (Can. 1197, par. 2).

PAPAL ALTARS. These are the altars of major basilicas, upon which only the Supreme Pontiff may celebrate the Holy Sacrifice of the Mass; no one else is allowed to do so without a special indult (Can. 823, par. 3). An altar, whether main, minor, or papal, may be made "privileged"; this means that the privilege of gaining a plenary indulgence in behalf of the person or persons for whom Mass is offered has been attached to it. The privilege may be personal, local, or a combination of both, depending on whether the celebrating priest himself has such a privilege or it is attached to the altar alone or to both. The fact that an altar is privileged must be clearly and visibly indicated by the inscription "*altare privilegiatum*," also the conditions for the use of the privilege (Can. 918). On All Souls' Day (November 2) and during the Forty Hours' Devotion all altars become privileged altars (Can. 917). To gain the plenary indulgence attached to a privileged altar, it is not necessary that the Mass offered for a departed soul or souls be celebrated by the priest wearing black vestments (Sacred Congregation of the Holy Office, Feb. 20, 1913).

CONSECRATION AND DESECRATION. The altar, whether permanent or portable, must be exclusively reserved for divine services, especially for the celebration of Holy Mass; hence the consecration of every altar is a solemn rite, in which the following ceremonies are performed: washing of the altar with Gregorian water (water mixed with blessed salt, ashes, and wine); anointing of the altar with the oil of catechumens and holy chrism; placing and sealing in it of the relics of the martyrs. The bishop alone is the ordinary minister for the consecration of altars. Portable altars may be consecrated by any Catholic bishop, except for particular privileges; but the consecration of immovable altars is reserved to the local Ordinary, in whose territory the altar to be consecrated is located, even if it be in a place belonging to exempt religious (Can. 1155).

Both immovable and portable altars may lose their consecration for any of the following reasons: (a) a fracture considered notable either because of the extent of the break itself or of its proximity to the anointed section; (b) removal of the sacred relics from the hole or *loculum,* or removal or fracture of the cover of the *loculum,* except in cases where the bishop removed the cover in order to fasten it more securely, or to replace it, or even merely to inspect the relics; (c) separation of the table from its support, even if it be done momentarily, in the case of a permanent altar; in this case, however, the Ordinary may delegate any priest to consecrate it anew with the short form as prescribed by the Holy See (Can. 1197, 1202; cf. AAS 12 [1920], p. 449). Desecration of the church does not entail desecration of the altars in it, or vice versa (Can. 1200, par. 4).

It is always forbidden to put the altar to any profane use. It is also forbidden to bury bodies under the altar. Bodies which may be lawfully interred in a church must be buried at least one meter (39.37 inches) away from the altar (Can. 1202, par. 2).

LITURGICAL PRESCRIPTIONS. The liturgical prescriptions of the Church require certain ornamental furnishings in keeping with the beauty of the altar and the dignity of divine services. (a) The altar must not rest directly upon the floor level or ground level, but upon an elevated platform, called the *predella,* of the same length and width as the altar and having enough space in front to permit the celebrant to genuflect without danger of extending his foot over the edge (Sacred Congregation of Rites, *Decr. auth.,* n. 1265). The steps leading to the upper platform or *predella* of the main altar should be uneven in number. (b) A cross with the body of the crucified Christ must be placed in a central and prominent position over the altar, rising high above the candlesticks (Cf. *Caeremoniale Episcoporum,* I, XIII, 11), and it should be large enough to be seen easily by the celebrant and the faithful (Sacred Congregation of Rites, *Decr. auth.,* nn. 1270 ad 1, 2622 ad 7). The altar crucifix may be omitted if there is a painting or sculpture of the Crucifixion on the wall behind the altar (Sacred Congregation of Rites, *Decr. auth.,* n. 1270). (c) Six candlesticks must be placed on the main altar and on the altar of the Blessed Sacrament, but on the other altar or altars, at least two must be used (*Caeremoniale Episcoporum,* I, XIII, 11 and 16). For a Low Mass not celebrated by a bishop, only two candles must be lighted (Sacred Congregation of Rites, *Decr. auth.,* nn. 441, 567, 1125, 1131 ad 21). For other Masses, more than two candles may be lighted (Sacred Congregation of Rites, *Decr. auth.,* nn. 3059 ad 9, 3065, 3697 ad 7); in fact, for a High Mass (*Missa Cantata*), four candles are to be lighted (Sacred Congregation of Rites, *Decr. auth.,* n. 3029 ad 7), and six are to be used for a Solemn Mass (Sacred Congregation of Rites, *Decr. auth.,* n. 4054 ad 2). (d) The table of a permanent altar must be covered by a waxed linen cloth (cere-cloth), and over this are placed three other cloths of white linen or hemp (*Caeremoniale Episcoporum,* I, XIII, II; Sacred Congregation of Rites, *Decr. auth.,* n. 2600), one of which, usually the top one, must extend to the platform or *predella* on both sides (Sacred Congregation of Rites, *Decr. auth.,* n. 4029 ad 1). The altar cloths, before being used, must be blessed (*Roman Ritual,* VIII, 21). *See also* Church (the house of God), Mass (Holy), Oratory. *Tar.*

ALTRUISM. *See* Charity.

AMBITION. *See* Self-love, Pride.

AMEN. The word *Amen* (from the Hebrew *amen*) is an ancient form of acclamation, expressing a fundamental idea of certainty and truth. Hence it signifies *yes, so it is, that is right.*

The Scriptures make frequent use of the word (Deut. 27:15–26; Num. 5:22; I Paral. 16:36; Nehem. 5:13, 8:6, *etc.*). It occurs, among other passages, in the final doxologies of the first four books of Psalms (cf. Ps. 40 [41], 71 [72], 88 [89], *etc.*). Typical is the use Jesus made of the word *Amen* as an assertive formula: "*Amen, amen, I say unto you . . . .* " (Matt. 5:26; John 3:3; 5:11; 13:28; 21:18, *etc.*).

Amen was introduced in Christian liturgy by the Apostles (cf. I Cor. 15:16; Tit. 3:15; Apoc. 1:6; 5:13) and is then encountered in early Christian literature (I *Apol.* 65, 67, *etc.*). It was chanted at the most important moments of the sacrificial action as a profession of Eucharistic faith (cf. *Constitutiones Apostolorum*, 8, 13, *etc.*). Even today it is frequently employed in the responses of the Mass, at the end of doxologies, at the end of prayers, as a conclusive formula in the Creeds, *etc.*, and it is translated in most languages as *So be it.* It expresses the consensus of the faithful in the liturgical act. *Pal.*

AMENTIA. Amentia generally refers to subnormal development of the mind, with particular reference to intellectual capacities. Its synonyms are: feeblemindedness, mental deficiency, hypophrenia, oligophrenia, and oligergasia. The term implies intellectual incapacity prevalent from birth or from the early months of life. Dementia (*q.v.*) has a wider meaning, and is used to designate disorder in the intellectual, ideational, and emotional spheres. When the term dementia is used, there is ordinarily the implication that the individual at one time possessed healthy and relatively intact mental faculties, from which he subsequently regressed. Amentia, on the other hand, carries the inference that the intellectual defects have been in evidence since birth or a short time thereafter.

Some authors use the term *amentia* as a diagnosis for acute hallucinatory confusion with a toxic-infective-exhaustive etiology. Such a use of the word, originating in the Viennese school, has not been generally accepted in the United States. (Cf. Hinsie and Shatzky, *Psychiatric Dictionary*, New York, 1956, p. 25.)

At this point it should be noted that the term *amentia* as employed by canonists does not correspond with the definition given by psychiatrists and psychologists. An atttempt to bring the canonical terminology up to date in this matter, so as to eliminate all equivocation and lack of uniformity in expression, would be highly desirable.

The forms of amentia are many: acquired, congenital, deprivative, developmental, eclampsic, exhaustive, hydrocephalic, infective, inflammatory, isolational, microcephalic, mongolian, sclerotic, syphilitic, traumatic, *etc.*, for the definition of which see Hinsie and Shatzky, *Psychiatric Dictionary*, New York, 1956, pp. 25–26.

As to the treatment of these forms of amentia, its effectiveness is in relation to the severity of the form in each individual case.

From a moral standpoint, those affected by any form of amentia are responsible according to the degree of mental capacity, which is generally congenitally or almost congenitally defective. *H.J.Y.*

AMERICANISM. Americanism is a term used to describe a tendency based on aspirations and maxims in which the natural and active virtues are considered more suitable to modern man than the supernatural and passive virtues (mortification, penance, obedience, *etc.*). A controversy about this tendency, allegedly prevalent in America (whence the name Americanism), broke out in Europe after the publication of the French translation of the life of Father Hecker written by Father Walter Elliott, an American Paulist, and particularly with regard to the Introduction contributed to the French edition of the work by Abbé Felix Klein. These errors regarding man's conduct, and others concerning the faith and apologetics, were condemned by Pope Leo XIII in the apostolic letter *Testem Benevolentiae*, dated January 22, 1899, and addressed to James Cardinal Gibbons of Baltimore.

It is true that, in a very poor actualization of Christian life, very often those virtues which are improperly called natural and active virtues are neglected; but it is also true that every virtue is eminently active, and that whenever nature is aided by grace, it never becomes weaker and less productive, but stronger and more fruitful. Furthermore, through grace man is so conditioned as to be capable of attaining eternal life. *Pal.*

AMICE. *See* Sacred Vestments.

AMNESIA. *See* Memory.

AMPULLAE. *See* Vessels, Sacred.

AMPUTATION. *See* Mutilation.

AMUSEMENTS. Amusements are in themselves morally licit, and they can also be necessary. Since man, in the exercise of his spiritual faculties, also uses his physical faculties, which are limited by nature, so, too, his spiritual capacities are limited. Man's spirit cannot go on indefinitely without tiring. Hence, he has need to restore his spiritual energy through appropriate rest. While the body usually finds rest in abstaining from physical exercise, the mind, which, in a state of wakefulness cannot stop all its functions, finds its rest in diverting its attention to other pleasant activities different from those which constitute its habitual occupation. Amusements, therefore, are a part of those activities through which man must strive to attain perfection. Their use constitutes a special aspect of this system and is governed by a special virtue called eutrapelia (a subjective part of modesty taken in a broad sense; *see* Modesty), which regulates the use of amusements according to the norms of right reason.

There are two principles which set the norms and the restrictions with regard to the enjoyment of amusements: (a) amusements are not an end in themselves, but are essentially directed to the attainment of a higher end, a more efficient functioning of the human spirit; (b) like any other human act, amusements are subject to the moral law and must not offend against Christian virtues. Hence, the limits of amusements are not determined by the capacity or the desire for enjoyment, but by the necessity for honest recreation in proportion to a person's need. Whoever goes beyond such limits appears to seek amusements for amusements' sake; and he who deliberately neglects taking a proper measure of recreation fails in his obligation to keep his capacity for work at the proper level of efficiency (*see also* Dissipation); (c) amusements must be of such a nature and proportion as to promote rather than interfere with one's habitual work, nor must they be detrimental to one's physical, mental, and moral capacities. They must be of such a nature and extent as to conform to the subjective circumstances of a man's occupational life, and never debase the dignity of man. They must in no way offend against other moral norms (religion, purity, honesty, charity, *etc.*), nor must they constitute an occasion of sin or scandal either for oneself or others. For the application of these norms to some specific amusements, *see* Dances, Motion Pictures, Physical Culture, Games, Theater, Variety. *Dam.*

ANALGESICS. Analgesics refers to medications or drugs administered to suppress or, at least, alleviate pain. Technically, analgesics are distinct from hypnotics and anesthetics, though in practice the terms are employed indiscriminately. In point of fact, hypnotics are soporifics, or sleep-inducing drugs, while anesthetics suppress not only pain but all other sensations as well. It is to be noted, however, that one and the same drug may be analgesic, anesthetic, or hypnotic, depending on the dosage used and on the method of administration.

Pain, whatever its source, may be checked by analgesic action: (a) upon the ends of the sensory nerves; (b) upon the nerves themselves; (c) upon the nerve centers. In other words, analgesics may be used to prevent the pain from rising, or from being transmitted or from being perceived.

Very important because of their frequent occurrence are neuralgias which arise from irritative lesions of the sensory nerves. Relief from such pain is obtained by the use of "local analgesia" (either through administration of cocaine and other substitutes, injected or applied locally, or by physical therapy, such as hot or cold applications on the affected area), or through "general analgesia." The latter, also called "internal," is administered either orally, or by way of the rectum (clysters or suppositories), or by hypodermic injection (morphine is the quickest and safest of analgesics but must be used sparingly, as it may lead to morphinism and morphinomania), or, finally, by intravenous injection.

Alleviation of pain, which, according to the Hippocratic motto, is looked upon as a divine mission (*divinum opus est sedare dolorem*), has always been and will continue to be one of the main goals of physicians. This aim is achieved quite effectively through administration of analgesics and the recently developed tranquilizing drugs. But while pain prevention will always remain a laudable and worthy practice, the doctor must always exercise much wisdom and caution in prescribing and administering analgesics.

It is the physician's duty to guard against excessive use of analgesics, for their constant and habitual use may easily lead to chronic poisoning (such drugs tend to lower the natural resistance of the patient, thereby actually aggravating his condition). Particularly must the physician guard against the patient's becoming so addicted to these drugs as to crave increasingly larger doses and perhaps reach a point where he can no longer do without them; such addiction

is definitely detrimental to the body. Moreover, a point that the doctor might well consider is the causal connection between pain and illness. Not only illness, but pain also requires study and interpretation; often the analysis of pain can shed some light on the source, nature, and type of the illness causing the pain. Thus, the indiscriminate use of pain-killers and pain-removers might very well interfere with the doctor's efforts to attain an exact diagnosis and, consequently, with his proper handling of the case at hand.

Another very important point from the standpoint of Catholic moral doctrine is the administration of analgesics to dying persons. Their use in such cases is not systematically forbidden, as some maintain who insist that everything be done to keep the person's consciousness alert and clear to the very end. Their use is definitely permitted when the dying person is experiencing severe pain. In fact, since severe pain usually disturbs the psyche of the patient, it must be suppressed or controlled, without, of course, eliminating the person's consciousness or reducing it to an excessive degree. Before administering analgesia, a Catholic doctor must endeavor to assess the intensity of the pain and also the spiritual condition of the patient lest more harm than good result from analgesic administrations. (*See also* Agony, Euthanasia.) *Riz.*

ANARCHY. Anarchy in general stands for revolt against all authority, government, and juridical coercion. Its aim is to attain absolute autonomy of the individual, without any coercion by the state or any other organization. Instead of law it advocates free reins and free contract; in place of juridical norms it follows "conventional rule." Only that which the individual considers to be good, according to his reasonable and just judgment, must be considered as having value. Anarchy proposes to give man a very wide range of personal liberty. Anarchy may be encountered in every field — moral, intellectual, economic, international, *etc.* Today the term usually refers to political anarchy, signifying lack of government.

A. Gide states that the doctrine of anarchism is a combination of the tenets of liberalism, which attacks the state, extolling free initiative, free contract, *etc.*, and the socialistic doctrine which attacks the principle of private property and the practice of exploitation. But anarchy surpasses individualism, because it rejects government interferences not only in the economic field, but in all sectors of life. It differs from socialism, which subordinates individual freedom to a social order characterized and restricted by coercive organization. Anarchy also differs from bolshevism, because it proposes a society without a government, whereas bolshevism is a proletarian dictatorship, even though theoretically it envisages an eventual terrestrial paradise without a State. The anarchist doctrine, therefore, may be considered a limitless exaltation of the right of the individual, aiming at the development of the personality without coercion of any kind. Its formula is "Neither God nor master." Each man is an exemplar of humanity. Anarchy does not seek the triumph of egoism, but of humanity. The fundamental basis of all morality is "human respect" (Bakunin). The individual becomes free because of the freedom of others; "freedom is not an isolating factor . . . but one of union" (Bakunin). Any authority by one individual over another is a lessening of his humanity.

Since all authority is centered in the state, every attack must be made against it in order to suppress it, for the state is "the summation of all denials of individual liberties," or better, "the flagrant negation of humanity" (Bakunin). Government is a corruptive agent, even when it orders something good. The form of government is unimportant; hence, the only true revolution is the destruction of the very principle of authority.

Private property, which the state is supposedly obliged to protect, is nothing but organized exploitation which in turn is "the power and right to live on the work of others." The economic philosophy of anarchy has two tendencies: (a) the individualistic tendency, based on free private property stripped of the powerful character it now enjoys in the economic capitalistic system, and the elimination of money and interest as means of accomplishing its aim; (b) the communist or federalist tendency, aiming at a community of goods within small autonomous groups. It proposes small voluntary associations instead of large controlling groups; in other words, federalism instead of centralism. Still in the matter of freedom, anarchy favors free associations and is opposed to marriage, which is but a form of oppression and tyranny. The only authority to be respected is that of science, whose laws man obeys, not because they are imposed upon him, but because they are acknowledged by him.

Despite such exaltation of the individual and rejection of authority, anarchy recognizes the existence of society as an extension of the individual; in fact, man without it would not truly be man. Anarchy, therefore, is not a war of people against people but a federation of free associations, born of man's social instinct. In this new order work loses its burdensome and repugnant character and becomes attractive, all life becoming more gay, just, and happy. But to attain this goal, revolution, *i.e.*, violence, is necessary. In the Statutes of the International Alliance of Anarchists we read the following: "We want a universal, social, philosophical, economic and political revolution, so that of the present actual order . . . there may remain no stone upon a stone."

Concerning their philosophy of life, anarchists naturally deny all religion, setting themselves up as freethinkers.

A refutation of anarchy is superfluous. No order can ever rise out of anarchy, for order presupposes some form of subordination. Anarchy proceeds from untenable assumptions and is replete with contradictions and absurdities in its application. Man is not absolutely good and entirely free from passions. Since everyone is both law and end unto himself, community life is inconceivable. In reality, complete anarchy does not exist.

At most, it may exist for a few days during the transition from one form of government to another. But any prolongation of this transitional period will necessarily affect the spiritual and material well-being of the people, provoking a violent reaction in the form of authoritarianism and dictatorship.

As a philosophy, anarchy is as old as the world itself, since there have always been men dissatisfied with authority. It is found among the Greek philosophers. Among modern philosophers, its first traces are found in Godwin, toward the end of the eighteenth century. Proudhon is generally regarded as the father of anarchy, while M. Stirner is looked upon as the theoretician of individualistic anarchy. In more recent times, political anarchy, combined with Russian nihilism, has exercised a great influence. Bakunin and Kropotkin developed anarchist doctrine into a real system. Its influence has been varied in various countries: almost nil in the United States, England, and the German countries, but considerable in the Latin countries, Italy, and Spain (the Ferrero movement); in France, Elysée Reclus and Jean Grave are regarded as the most noted anarchists. In Russia anarchy manifested itself first as nihilism, later as bolshevism. *Per.*

ANARTHRIA. See Aphasia.

ANATOCISM. See Interest, Loan.

ANESTHESIA. See Anesthetics.

ANESTHETICS. Anesthetics refers to drugs which eliminate sensibility. Insensibility may be obtained either in a limited part of the body only or throughout the entire organism. If limited to one part, it is referred to as "local anesthesia," which is usually achieved by freezing completely the sensory nerve of the part (with ether or chloride of ethyl), or by local injection of substances which, like cocaine, paralyze the nerve endings. If not limited ("general anesthesia"), the state of insensibility extending to the entire body is necessarily accompanied by relaxation of the muscular apparatus and loss of consciousness.

General anesthesia is frequently used in the last stage of delivery and, much more generally, in surgery, where the relaxation of the muscular apparatus offers a favorable condition for the performance of the operation or several operations. The use of anesthetization has not only a humanitarian value for making patients insensible to pain during the performance of operations (pain which sometimes caused sudden death), but it has contributed to major advances in the surgical field by enabling surgeons to perform exploratory, lengthy and complicated operations, which would have been impossible on a conscious, suffering and tense patient, apt to make a sudden and fatal movement at any time.

Naturally, general anesthesia is not completely free of danger. In fact, some of the methods of administration (particularly, inhalation of chlorophorm or of ether or of special vapors and, most recently, intravenous injection of anesthetics) may occasionally cause death by asphyxia or cardiac paralysis. Hence, it is always advisable that the patient be in the state of grace before anesthesia is administered.

Anesthesia to allay labor pains, even in cases of easy and natural delivery, is lawful, but is not to be too easily indulged in because of the possibility, though remote, that the life and the health of the child may be affected by it. Modern obstetricians resort, with excellent results, to local anesthesia, which, while it alleviates the more severe pains, safeguards completely the health of the child.

Subspecies of local anesthesia more frequently employed are: regional anesthesia, spinal anesthesia (produced by the injection of anesthetic into the spinal subarachnoidal space), epidural anesthesia, paravertebral, *etc. See also* Surgery. *Riz.*

ANGEL, GUARDIAN. The doctrine concerning guardian angels is based on Sacred Scripture. According to the Bible, the "Angel of the Lord" (Ex. 14:19; 23:

20–23) protected the chosen people; and according to Ps. 90:9 ff., the angels were given charge over the souls of the just. Hence the psalmist exhorts the pious man not to fear, for no evil shall touch him nor shall any scourge come near his dwelling. "The Lord Himself hath given His angels charge over thee, to keep thee in all thy ways. In their hands they shall bear thee up, lest thou dash thy foot against a stone. Thou shalt walk upon the asp and the basilisk; and thou shalt trample under foot the lion and the dragon." St. Paul (Heb. 1:14) calls the angels "ministering spirits, sent for them who shall receive the inheritance of salvation." The angels rejoice over the conversion of sinners (Luke 15:10), watch over little ones (Matt. 18:10) and accompany the departed to the divine throne (Luke 16:22).

This doctrine, adopted by the Church, as is obvious from its liturgical prayers, culminated in the institution of the feast in honor of the guardian angels, on October 2. The feast, which at first was introduced only in certain regions (*e.g.*, Spain, Portugal) at the request of Ferdinand II of Austria, was made of obligation by Paul V in all the regions of the empire (September 27, 1608) and was extended to the whole Church by Clement X (September 13, 1670). In view of the fact that belief in angels as our appointed guardians is well founded in the Bible, it must be considered as a truth of Catholic faith proposed to us by the ordinary magisterium of the Church. Attempts made to bring about a more precise statement of this truth have given rise to divergencies in ecclesiastical tradition. That each person has his own individual guardian angel is already affirmed by the *Shepherd of Hermas*, generally regarded as the official record of faith as practiced in the second century. In the 6th *Mandatum*, II, 1–3, the author characterizes the "angel of justice, who assists man," as a "sensitive, modest, gentle and calm angel," who speaks only of "justice, chastity, sanctity, temperance, and of every just work and honest virtue."

That everyone has his own guardian angel is also clearly affirmed by St. John Chrysostom and St. Jerome. The same assertion is most clearly and distinctly made by Honorius of Autun (d. 1151) (*Elucidarium* 2, 31): ". . . . . every soul, at the moment it is infused into the body, is entrusted to an angel"; later this same thesis is adopted by St. Albert the Great (*Summa Theologiae*, II, q. 36) and by St. Thomas (*Summa Theologiae*, I, q. 113), who teach that the guardian angel never abandons the person entrusted to his care.

According to modern authors, a guardian angel is assigned to Christians at the time of baptism. The Church has never issued any dogmatic definition concerning the designation or appointment of guardian angels; nevertheless, it is a matter so firmly based on Scripture, so consistently interpreted by the Church Fathers and so universally believed, that to deny it would constitute, according to Suárez, grave temerity and a quasi-error (*De Angelis*, VI, 17, 8: *"non sine ingenti temeritate ac fere errore"*). The manner in which the guardian angels carry out their ministry is reflected in the illustrious titles that ecclesiastical tradition has bestowed upon them: the guardian angel is protector, tutor, custodian, guardian, advocate, companion, peaceful assistant, and teacher.

Man should have a corresponding cult of veneration toward guardian angels as required by their position in the sight of God, by the grace with which they have been endowed, and the great work that they perform in our behalf. The formulary of the Office in the Breviary and the formulary of the Mass in the Missal contain a model prayer and a safe doctrine on which the veneration of guardian angels may be based. *Opp.*

ANGELUS. The *Angelus* is an anthem consisting of three short phrases revolving around the mystery of the Incarnation. At the end of each phrase the Hail Mary is recited, with two concluding versicles and an oration.

In its brevity and simplicity, the *Angelus* possesses the grandeur of a three-part poem: (a) the announcement of the angel to Mary that she is predestined to become the Mother of the Word; (b) the humble Virgin gives her consent; (c) the Word becomes incarnate and dwells among us.

In reciting the *Angelus*, it is customary to add three *Glorias* to the Most Blessed Trinity in thanksgiving for the singular gifts and privileges bestowed upon the Blessed Virgin Mary; this, however, is a pious practice entirely distinct and separable from the *Angelus* itself. The official *Raccolta* of the Sacred Apostolic Penitentiary places the recitation of the three *Glorias* among the "pious exercises" in honor of the Most Holy Trinity, while the *Angelus* is listed among the "prayers" in honor of our Lady. *Enchiridion Indulgentiarum*, nn. 47 and 331).

The *Angelus* is recited three times a day: morning, noon, and evening, at the sound of the bell. The evening *Angelus* seems to date back to the thirteenth century, when the custom arose of ringing the bell about half an hour before sunset and of reciting three Hail Marys during the tolling of the bell. This was called the *Ave Maria* hour. The morning and midday *Angelus* were introduced at a later date, and they, too, were given the name of *Ave Maria* hour. But the evening hour and the tolling of the bell are characteristically called the *Ave Maria* hour. In the sixteenth century the name *Ave Maria* hour was supplanted by the name *Angelus*, which prevails even to the present day; thus we say: "It is the hour of the *Angelus*"; "the *Angelus* is ringing." The addition of the three *Glorias* dates back to 1815, during the pontificate of Pius VII.

During paschal time, the antiphon *Regina Coeli* is substituted (in accord with a decree of Pope Benedict XIV in 1742) for the *Angelus*. The former extols the Resurrection of Jesus and His Mother's rejoicing in the triumph of her Son. Like the *Angelus*, the *Regina Coeli* is also followed by two versicles and an oration.

Of the four closing antiphons in honor of the Blessed Lady (called "closing" because they are recited at the conclusion of the Divine Office), the *Regina Coeli* is the most ancient. The other three antiphons are: *Alma Redemptoris Mater; Ave, Regina Coelorum; Salve, Regina*.

The *Regina Coeli* is certainly to be dated before the eleventh century; pious tradition places its composition at the beginning of the pontificate of St. Gregory the Great (d. 604). A legend has it that during an imploratory procession for the cessation of a pestilence, upon arrival of the cortege at the bridge in front of the Tomb of Hadrian, a heavenly choir of angels greeted the blessed image of the Mother of God, which was being carried in procession, and chanted, "*Regina Coeli, laetare; alleluia; Quia quem meruisti portare, alleluia; Resurrexit, sicut dixit, alleluia.*" Having heard the angelic chorus, St. Gregory supposedly adopted this magnificent Marian hymn, completing it with his own invocation "*Ora pro nobis Deum, alleluia.*"

Anyone reciting the *Angelus* or the *Regina Coeli* (depending on the season) in the morning, noon, and evening may gain the following indulgences: (a) ten years for each recitation; (b) a plenary indulgence, under the usual conditions, if the prayer is recited every day for an entire month. The same indulgence may be gained by those who, in place of the *Angelus* or *Regina Coeli*, recite five Hail Marys at those same hours. Finally, those reciting, at the above-stated hours, three *Glorias* to the Most Blessed Trinity, in thanksgiving for the singular gifts and privileges bestowed upon the Blessed Virgin, may gain: (a) a 500-days' indulgence for each recitation; (b) a plenary indulgence, under the usual conditions, if the three *Glorias* are recited daily for a whole month. *Ses.*

ANGER. Anger is a strong passion or emotion of displeasure and usually antagonism, excited by a sense of injury or insult. A distinction must be made between passionate anger, that is, the urge of the sensitive appetite to react, and non-passionate anger, that is, the tendency of the will to inflict a punishment.

It is possible and even permissible to excite a reasonable desire accompanied by moderated anger in order to inflict a punishment. Our Lord Himself was filled with righteous anger against the venders who had used His Father's house (John 2:13) for commerce. Non-passionate anger is permissible only if it tends to punish those who deserve punishment (that is, an intelligent human being who deliberately misbehaved) according to their guilt and to the order demanded by justice, with the sole aim of re-establishing the equilibrium and correcting the erring person. Should one of these conditions be wanting, there is a sinful excess, often accompanied by hatred and a desire for revenge. Inordinate anger is gravely or lightly sinful according to the degree of harm which is intended by it and the motive which caused it.

Passionate anger is not immoderate, if the reaction is directed only against the guilty party, and if its vehemence is in proportion to the object and the circumstances; also if it is such as not to blind one's reason, or to place him in danger of overstepping the proper limits in inflicting a just punishment. As long as passionate anger is independent of one's will, it is not a sin. We are obliged, however, to repress the passionate impulse of anger as soon as it arises if it is inordinate in its object, or to moderate it if it is too impetuous. Failure to repress or moderate this impulse is in itself a venial sin; however, if the impulse places one in the danger of committing a mortal sin, he will become guilty of a serious sin if he omits repressing the impulse when he is clearly aware of the danger. To consent to an immoderate passion of anger, venting it by words or deeds on guiltless persons, animals or things, is at least a venial sin; it is also a venial sin if vented on a guilty party but in an exaggerated manner. The sin may become serious if the words used are very offensive, or are such as to cause a serious evil, or if one

places himself in the grave danger of committing such excesses.

No means must be neglected in an effort to master anger, because anger, more than any other passion, blinds one's reason and leads to grave moral disorders. Without neglecting the physical means, should there be any, the moral means must be particularly used, such as consideration of the meekness of Christ and the saints, recourse to prayer, thinking before acting. One must make every effort to react immediately against any immoderate impulse of anger and strive earnestly never to speak or act under its influence. *Man.*

ANGUISH. *See* Affectivity.

ANIMALS. *See* Animals, Fishing, Hunting, Damage, Occupation.

ANIMALS (Protection of). England deserves the credit for the founding of the first society for the protection of animals, in 1824; thereafter, similar associations were gradually organized in practically every country.

Sanctions against those who mistreat or beat domestic animals, specialized methods and techniques for bringing about a quick and painless slaying of dangerous animals and those destined to be used for food, conferences and lectures aimed at instilling, especially in children, a regard for animals have made a real contribution toward a greater refinement in human behavior. They have also diminished the revolting spectacle of cruel treatment inflicted on dumb and helpless beasts by individuals unmindful of the moral teaching of the Church, or at least of the gentle teachings of St. Francis of Assisi, the loving patron of all of God's creatures.

People of Latin mentality, however, find it difficult at times to understand the excessive concern for animals as exercised in some countries, where one finds hospitals, clinics, ambulance service, and even cemeteries for animals. Such concern does appear somewhat excessive, especially if one considers that in these same countries there is frequently a lack of hospital space and other health facilities for the treatment of humans.

A subject much more widely discussed and debatable is the agitation for the protection of animals against the practice of vivisection. The term *vivisection* is not taken here literally as meaning the dissection of a living creature, or a bloody operation performed on a living being, but as meaning any biological experiment performed on animals (operations, germ injection, study of pharmacological or physical agents, *etc.*).

Vivisection has been practiced in every age, with constant efforts made to reduce the animal's suffering to the minimum in the course of experimentation. Today, thanks to general and local anesthesia, asepsis, the hygienic conditions of animal enclosures, *etc.*, these aims have been universally attained. Catholic moral doctrine, acknowledging the great and important discoveries that medical science owes to vivisection, is not opposed to its practice, so long as it contributes (either as speculative research or as a teaching technique) to the advance of science. In fact, all this is in accord with the plan of God, Who created animals for the service of man.

In some countries the societies for the protection of animals have succeeded in securing strict legal controls on the practice of vivisection. The result is that researchers are obliged (as in England) to ask authorization in each case for practicing vivisection; moreover, they are required to submit illustrated plans of the experiment to legal authorities who, lacking sufficient knowledge of the ideas of the experimenter, often deny permission. Many times the experimenter is compelled to operate secretly, running the risk of being haled into court. Such legal restrictions constitute a definite obstacle to the progress of physiopathology, whose principal means of study and research lies in the practice of vivisection: "Nam," as Willis fittingly observed in the seventeenth century, "*aut hac via, scilicet per vulnera et mortes, per anatomiam, et quasi caesareo partu, in lucem prodibit veritas, aut semper latebit.*"

Moreover, such restrictive measures against vivisection represent a reversal of values and the hierarchical order of creatures as arranged by the Creator, Who made man king of creation, and hence proprietor and user of all lower beings. *Riz.*

Zoophilists often lose sight of the end for which animals, irrational creatures, were created by God, *viz.*, the service of and use by man. In fact, Catholic moral doctrine teaches that animals have no rights on the part of man; man, however, must treat them well and not abuse them, since they are creatures of God. To mistreat animals is sinful, though not easily a grave sin, because it renders man hard, cruel, and insensitive to the suffering of his neighbor. But not every action that causes animals to suffer is mistreatment. It is an act of cruelty to abuse an animal, or to make it suffer for no reason whatsoever. If we suffer for our own good, *a fortiori* animals can suffer for man's own good. It goes without saying that to inflict suffering upon animals without a proportionate reason or to delight in their sufferings, or to cause them to suffer merely for our pleasure is reprehensible and cruel. Hence it is necessary to educate people, particularly children, to acquire the habit of treating animals kindly and even to have a certain regard and reverence for them as creatures of God. Certainly Sacred Scripture recommends this (Prov. 12:10; Ex. 29:19); and certainly the saints, particularly St. Francis of Assisi, have always been kind and gentle to animals. *Ben.*

ANISOGAMY. *See* Sexology.

ANNIVERSARY. *See* Funeral Mass.

ANONYMOUS LETTER. *See* Letter (anonymous).

ANTHROPOLOGY. Etymologically, anthropology is "the science of man." In its biological meaning it is the science that studies man in relation to his zoological species, inquiring into his physical and psychical characteristics, so as to trace the orgin of the human races and to discover in the racial differences the reason for the diverse forms of life.

A science with exceedingly vast horizons, anthropology utilizes and elaborates notions from the most widely dissimilar disciplines, such as anatomy, physiology, psychology, archeology, philology, etc. In fact, it comprises *anthropometry* or *morphometry*, or, to use a more modern term, *somatology* (which deals with the metric study of the external forms of the human body), *osteology* (with particular reference to researches on the brain, or *craniology*), *ethnology* (study of the races and of the migrations of peoples), *paleoanthropology* (which, together with prehistoric archeology, studies human fossils and man-made utensils), *anthroposociology* (the study of relations between the bearers of given anthropological characteristics and the social groups to which they belong), *heredoanthropology* (study concerning heredity of somatic and psychic characteristics, etc.).

Despite the vast number of studies, measurements, and reports made by anthropologists within the last century (anthropology as an autonomous science goes back to 1839 with the establishment of the Ethnologic Society in Paris), the aims of this science are still far short of their attainment; in fact, it may be asserted, with Sera, that its very basis, the knowledge of human types, is still none too solid. Anthropology has, however, made findings of notable value and interest.

By way of example, we shall mention the work of research in somotology which has, in the last century, revealed the progressive increase in size of the body, apparently caused by a gradual modification of hormonal troporegulatory mechanisms. Moral Theology, of course, looks with interest to further developments in the field of anthropology from which it hopes to trace its own historical evolution, and an evaluation of the perennial influence of the immutable principles of the Ten Commandments upon the various races. *Riz.*

ANTHROPOLOGY (CRIMINAL). Criminal anthropology is the scientific study of crime and criminals. It is an important branch of general anthropology, and has a special relationship to morals. Criminal anthropology employs the same naturalistic method (especially the "somatological" method (*see* Anthropology) that general anthropology employs in studying normal individuals. Another name for this science and one more widely used, is *criminology*.

As a science, criminal anthropology had its beginnings in 1876, when an Italian professor named Cesare Lombroso published the first edition of his famous work *L'uomo delinquente* (*The Criminal Man*) in which he describes the physical anomalies, anatomical and functional, of man, and correlates them to the deviations in his conduct. His conclusion was that psychosomatic anomalies are found in criminals in greater number and in more serious forms than in individuals of normal behavior.

This conclusion is acceptable in certain cases but it may not be generalized without falling into error: many criminals are found to be structurally eurythmic, with no degenerative traces or other peculiar anomalies; on the other hand, a number of individuals of sound moral behavior manifest characteristics and deviations that are generally regarded as attributes of criminality. In their initial and understandable enthusiasm over the first findings, the more rabid advocates of criminal anthropology were led to overestimate the importance of the individual "organic terrain" as a criminological element, while minimizing other elements which might be summed up in the term "environment."

Such anthropologists made the mistake of overlooking the effectiveness of control exercised by inhibitory powers, that is, of free will, in which they as materialists did not believe. The Lombrosian dogma of the "born criminal," fatally drawn to crime as a result of constitutional deviations, lost much ground as later studies showed that any alleged equation between a criminal act and certain biodegenerative predispositions was untenable. In so delicate a matter any generalization or *a priorism* is unscientific.

The existence of the "criminal type" or the "born criminal" is contradicted daily by the successful efforts of those who, following the example of St. John Bosco, Father Flanagan, and other great apostles of charity, dedicate their lives to the training and rehabilitation of abandoned youths, thereby transforming potential criminals into useful and honest citizens. With Di Tullio and other modern criminal anthropologists, it must be stated that, while it is true that criminals are often "individuals who are the least endowed with right thinking, free will, and spiritual forces," and, therefore, easy victims of their instincts and bad influence, there nevertheless remains a wide area in which the physician, the educator, and the priest can perform a notable work of rehabilitation.

In the enthusiasm of the initial work of research, criminologists believed they found far too many anomalies and disfunctions in criminals which they quickly labelled as characteristic symptoms of criminality. More recent and calmer investigation has greatly reduced the abundant classification of such symptoms. Lack of space prevents us from listing even those symptoms that are most certain and universally acknowledged. We shall mention only one of them because of its ethical implications, namely, the "diffused tegumentary hypoalgesia" (called also Lombroso's symptom), or dullness of the sense of pain encountered in a great number of criminals, particularly those given to crimes of violence, who also show a notable lack of moral sensibility. It does not seem unreasonable to think that because of a low degree of advertence to their own pain, such criminals show little ability to fathom the pain of others, or to have "compassion" on others.

Criminal anthropology has undoubtedly produced very notable effects upon penal sciences and correctional systems in all civilized countries. It has provided a valid and rational incentive for a more humane treatment of criminals by society.

Today, these principles are clearly established: (a) criminals, generally speaking, bear varying responsibilities for their crimes; (b) society has a right to repress criminality and to defend itself against criminals. Modern penal legislations aim at gradating the treatment of criminals according to the character and tendencies of the criminal. The attention of the judge, formerly almost exclusively directed at punishing the crime, has gradually turned to the treatment of the criminal himself. In penal institutions of all sorts there is a constantly growing tendency to establish psychiatric wards where the inmate is studied, even anthropologically (in his structural and functional manifestations), with the aim of adapting the penal treatment to the special character of the criminal and of finding and applying methods which will have the best therapeutic and remedial effects.

The fact is that criminal anthropology has lost much of its initial rigidity: the possibility of moral rehabilitation for the criminal is clearly admitted today; as a matter of fact, very much is made of it in gradating the penalty and in varying the type of punishment. This, of course, is a just acknowledgment and vindication of the spiritual powers of rehabilitation and amendment with which man is endowed and which the theory of the "born criminal," constitutionally incorrigible, apparently denied.

In conclusion, though many of the Lombrosian ideas have been greatly modified, and although some of Lombroso's conclusions are acceptable in part, it should nevertheless be pointed out that a Catholic may not hold, defend, or accept criminal anthropology understood as a science based on naturalistic evolutionism; nor may he hold, defend, or accept the tenets of the positivistic school of penal law taken as a practical application of the former. It is contrary to Christian teaching to deny free will, the aid of divine grace, and the consequent moral responsibility of the individual. It is also contrary to

Christian teaching to hold that society must be guided only by the criterion of the dangerousness of the criminal. In a recent interview (*Annali Ravasini*: May 15, 1956), B. Di Tullio, dealing with the thorny problem of "criminality in backward areas," emphasized the importance of environmental factors broadly taken (poverty, promiscuity, analphabetism, lack of education, geographic and social isolation, extreme primitiviness, *etc.*) as being responsible for the rising and perpetuation of banditry and other sad criminological conditions. He also pointed to improved economic conditions, increased mental hygiene, social welfare, and general education as effective means for the prevention of criminality. *Riz.*

ANTHROPOMETRY. *See* Anthropology.

ANTHROPOSOCIOLOGY. *See* Anthropology.

ANTICLERICALISM. Attempts have been made to give this term an innocent connotation by making it signify opposition to alleged threats and abuses by the clergy in its influence over the consciences of people. In other words, the term is used to indicate a reaction against an alleged improper and egoistical meddling of a particular class in the social life of others and against the common good. A reaction against any type of abuse, within due limits, is certainly lawful; but a reaction may not be legitimately transformed into a general and permanent hostility against a class as a whole simply because of abuses perpetrated at one time or another by a few individuals.

Historical anticlericalism, a term coined in modern France together with its opposite, clericalism, denotes a mentality as well as a political and cultural movement designed to combat every influence of the Church and, hence, of the Catholic religion, on education and the moral life of nations. Its aim was to eliminate positive religion and supplant it with a natural religion of vague theism

(or deism) or, as happened in the latter half of the nineteenth century, with scientific atheism. "*Le cléricalisme, voilà l'ennemi!*" was the cry launched by Gambetta, one of the founders of the Third Republic, established in France after the debacle of 1870; and anticlericalism, as a political directive, succeeded in dechristianizing the schools, expelling religious orders, violating and, finally, repudiating the Concordat, expropriating ecclesiastical property, *etc.* In countries outside France, anticlericalism met with varying degrees of success. In Italy, where the Holy See was beset by difficulties arising from the Roman Question, anticlericalism took full advantage of existing conditions. In view of the constitution of the Church as willed and defined by Christ Himself, a true and sincere Catholic cannot possibly adhere to any form of anticlericalism, either theoretical or practical, as an habitual state of mind. The function of the hierarchy and the clergy in the teaching of evangelical doctrine, in the direction of souls, in the administration of the sacraments, in the spiritual government of the society of faithful, implies a continual contact between the laity and the clergy, a constant cooperation that excludes any and every organized hostility. *Boz.*

ANTI-MACHIAVELISM. *See* Machiavelism.

ANTIPATHY (Aversion, Prejudice). Antipathy is an instinctive feeling of aversion for one's neighbor. This aversion may arise from a large variety of causes.

Feelings of aversion which arise independently of the will are not in themselves sinful; but if they become inordinate by reason of their object, or if they constitute an occasion of sin, man has the obligation, under penalty of sin, to repress and remove them (*see* Passion, Human Act). Thus, any instinctive aversion against one's neighbor, or a neighbor's possession or asset, is an inordinate feeling because man bears the image of God in him and was made to partake of divine nature. Only the evil in him may be an object of aversion.

It is a known fact that indeliberate feelings of aversion for one's neighbor that are not checked and corrected by reason, under the guidance of faith, often lead to sin, even grave, against charity and justice. Antipathy must be checked. Neglect or failure to do so is, in itself, only a venial sin but it may become gravely sinful if the indeliberate feeling were to constitute a grave danger of sinning mortally. A sin becomes subjectively grave if full and deliberate consent of the will is given. One must not be guided by antipathy in his dealings with his neighbor.

One who has a feeling of aversion for a person should strive to be amiable and helpful to him and, above all, should pray for him; such acts have a tendency to reduce and even dispel the inordinate passion. It is also necessary to refrain from any scrutiny of the conduct and defects of others, unless one is required, as teacher or superior, to observe and study the behavior of his subjects. In dealing with our neighbor we must be guided, not by antipathy, but by love. *Man.*

ANTIPHONARY. See Liturgical Books.

ANTISEMITISM. See Judaism.

ANTONINUS (ST.) of Florence. LIFE. Moral theologian, Dominican reformer, and Archbishop of Florence, St. Antoninus was born at Florence, in March, 1389, and died at Montughi on April 2, 1459.

Baptized Anthony, the saint was called by the diminutive and more affectionate form of Antoninus because of his frail constitution and small stature. As a youth, in pursuance of an hereditary predilection, Antoninus dedicated himself to juridical studies. Later, stirred and influenced by the preaching of Blessed John Dominic, he applied for admission into the Dominican Order and received the habit in 1405. From the very beginning of his priestly life he supported Dominic's program of religious reform.

It was the period of the great Western Schism (1378–1418). John Dominici, who was already Archbishop of Ragusa and a Cardinal, and Antoninus remained loyal to Gregory XII, but in order to escape the intimidations of the Florentine Republic, they were forced to seek refuge in Umbria, where Antoninus was ordained to the priesthood in 1413. In 1414 he was appointed Vicar of the Convent of Foligno. Since the election of Pope Martin V by the Council of Constance (November 11, 1417) brought about a distinct change in the general religious situation, Antoninus returned to Tuscany, where he became prior of the convent of Cortona (1418–1421) and, subsequently, of the convents of Fiesole (1421) and of Santa Maria Sopra Minerva in Rome (1430). He was appointed auditor of the Rota by Pope Eugene IV, who was elected Supreme Pontiff in the conclave held at the Minerva, and on May 28, 1437, Antoninus was invested with the dignity of Vicar General of the Observants of central and southern Italy.

Besides his work of reform, Antoninus engaged in the task of erecting and developing the new convent of St. Mark in Florence, designed by the architect Michelozzo Michelozzi and beautifully frescoed by Fra Angelico. The convent, built with the munificent aid of Cosimo de'Medici, through the initiative and efforts of Antoninus, became a famous center of studies as well as a focus of Christian life for Florentine society. In 1439 Antoninus of Florence was made prior of the convent. With the codices of the Niccoli family he formed the first nucleus of the convent's library, which also became the first public library of Europe (1443). In 1442 he secured for his religious community the administration of St. Mark's parish and the task of preaching the Gospel through the entire region of Tuscany.

Neither friend nor foe of the Medici, since he was not a partisan of any faction, Antoninus devoted himself with true evangelical spirit to the work of saving souls and alleviating the lot of the poor and the unfortunate. Despite his objections, he was appointed Archbishop of Florence in 1445, and consecrated in the Church of St. Dominic at Fiesole, on March 12. With the same ardent zeal that had characterized his labors of religious reform in his Order, he threw himself into the important and apostolic work of transforming and elevating the sorry moral conditions of the times.

Though engaged in manifold activities, Antoninus found time to write long and precious letters of spiritual direction to pious women of the Florentine nobility, well aware of the immense good that could be accomplished through the good example of such influential ladies. He became famous for his very prudent and impartial decisions which earned him the name "Antoninus, the counsellor," by which he was commonly called.

Antoninus was present at the consistory held in Rome in 1447, in which the conflict between the pope and the elector princes of Germany was solved by the promulgation of the "Concordats of the Princes." A few days after this peaceful solution, on February 23, he was called to assist the dying Pope Eugene IV. Antoninus headed the diplomatic missions of the Florentine Republic to Nicholas V, Callistus III, and Pius II. In 1458 he publicly defended the Florentine constitution against the Medici party.

His death occurred on May 2, 1459, and his body, honored by the presence of Pope Pius II, then residing in Florence, and surrounded by a crowd of devout people, was interred in St. Mark's according to the wish expressed in his will. Less than a century later, on May 31, 1523, the feast of the Holy Trinity, Antoninus was canonized by Pope Adrian VI.

WORKS. Outstanding not only as a reformer, but also as a learned theologian and writer, St. Antoninus is known in the history of moral theology as the first who treated this subject separately. He wrote voluminous works and short treatises in Latin and in Italian. His principal works are the *Summa moralis*, and a companion volume called *Chronicae* (also called *Summa historialis*) in two sections, one moral and the other historical. Today they are considered as separate works.

(a) *Summa Moralis*. Simple in form, it contains a wealth of theologico-moral matter and the best part of the saint's intellectual effort, a truly imperishable and crowning glory of his teaching. Completed in 1454, it had twenty editions (from 1477 to 1740) and exercised considerable influence.

(b) *Chronicae*. This work, completed between 1440–1459, is divided into three parts, twenty-four titles and paragraphs, and contains compilations of persons and events. It is primarily of historical value as the author writes of events of his own age (Nuremberg edition, 1484).

(c) *Confessionale*. Under the general title *Confessionale* are grouped three little books concerning confession, written partly in Latin and partly in Italian and addressed both to the faithful and the clergy. They have no fixed title, and sometimes appear under the headings *Omnis mortalium cura, Defecerunt, Curam illius habe,* at other times as *Specchio di coscienza* ("Mirror of Conscience"), *Summula confessionalis* ("A Compendium of the Confessional"), *Medicina dell'anima* ("Medicine of the Soul"), etc.

The *Defecerunt* is written in Latin and in the printed editions it appears under the following titles besides those already mentioned: *Summa confessionis, Summa confessionalis, Summula confessionum, Confessorum refugium;* the *Confessionale* has had the widest circulation. It was translated into Italian under the title *Interrogatorio sopra le confessioni,* and also into Spanish.

The *Omnis mortalium cura* and the *Curam illius habe* were written in Italian.

(d) *De ornatu mulierum,* concerning the beautifying devices of women, was first written in 1437 and later inserted in Part II of the *Summa.*

(e) *De excommunicationibus* (Venice, 1474) was inserted in Part III of the *Summa*.

(f) *Trialogus super enarratione evangelica de duobus discipulis euntibus in Emmaus* (of uncertain date, cf. Florence edition, 1480): it is a commentary on the Messianic prophecies.

(g) *Responsiones ad LXIX quaesita fratris Dominici de Chatalonia*: These are replies to moral and juridical questions of a confrere (cf. Venice edition, 1497) written toward the end of the pontificate of Pope Eugene IV (about 1440).

(h) *Unedited works* (Florence, Biblioteca Nazionale-Magliabecchiana-Conv. supp. A. 8, 1750: *Quadragesimale Convertimini*; Bibl. Ricciardiana, cod. 308: outlines of sermons).

(i) *Opera a ben vivere* (an ascetical work; cf. 1923 edition).

(j) *24 Spiritual and Familiar Letters* (ed. Corsetto, Florence 1859). Among the spurious works are: *Flos florum, Adnotationes de donatione Constantini,* etc.

The major credit for the advancement of moral theology in the fourteenth and fifteenth centuries, a period characterized both by inactivity and renewal, belongs to St. Antoninus. Through the efforts of the saintly and learned Dominican, moral theology was separated for the first time from dogmatic theology, and was treated as an independent and complete subject in its principles and practical applications. After having deepened and enriched his grasp of the moral science through constant study and application, Antoninus conceived the vast project of compiling and editing the whole of moral doctrine in one separate body. In pursuance of so tremendous a task, he was animated by a great spirit of charity and by the deep conviction that a developed and separate moral science was indispensable.

Above all, St. Antoninus excels among the authors of the *Summae confessorum* (compendia for confessors). The *Summae confessorum* written by Raymond of Penafort (d. 1275) were being constantly augmented and enriched with doctrine, with the result that, having lost their practical usefulness and facility, they were read and consulted by only a few. It was necessary, therefore, to restore to the *Confessionalia* the simplicity and immediate practicability of their original forms, so that all might readily avail themselves of the moral doctrine contained therein. This was precisely the result attained by the saintly Archbishop of Florence in writing his *Confessionale*, which met with a truly extraordinary success.

St. Antoninus is more widely famous for his *Summa moralis*, because he brought into this work a remarkable harmony between the Scholastic and positive methods and a more complete treatment from the practical side of moral theology, virutes proper to a treatise of moral theology. *Pal.*

ANXIETY. Anxiety is an emotional phenomenon, or a painful disturbance of one's affective life frequently associated with depressive states, though it may also occur distinct from them. It is also defined as a painful uneasiness of mind over a possible or imagined ill. Anxiety manifests itself externally as a disturbing feeling of uneasiness and restlessness, characterized by increased breathing and intermittent deep sighs, abnormal rapidity of cardiac action (tachycardia), a feeling of distress and pressure around the heart (precordial anxiety), and a sense of oppression in the epigastric region—all symptomatic of a morbid condition of orthosympathetic erethism (excessive nervous irritability). The state of anxiety is usually accompanied by loss of appetite, insomnia, muscular hypotonicity, and a general sense of asthenia.

In normal individuals this disturbance is slight and of brief duration. It is due to grave preoccupations and emotional conflicts that cannot be brought to their resolutory phases. Sometimes a crisis of anxiety in normal individuals, in whom anxiety is a transitory phenomenon, appears to be without cause. In such cases the disturbance is, according to psychoanalysts, to be considered the expression of an emotional conflict, and denotes inability of the ego to control the aggressive impulses; or, rather, it indicates a dysphoric resonance of one's subjective sensation, even though vague, and of a sudden and transitory neurovegetative disequilibrium.

As already noted, anxiety is of much more frequent occurrence in depressive states, such as melancholia (*q.v.*). In these cases the emotional tension built up in anticipation of a vague and impending evil which weighs heavily upon the mind of the confused and psychologically disturbed patient is discharged into ceaseless motor actions (twisting of fingers, endless pacing of the floor, *etc.*); at this point the individual's restlessness may erupt into acts of self-violence, frequently leading to suicide (melancholia of anxiety and melancholic seizure).

Violent and apparently unmotivated crises of anxiety may also occur in other morbid conditions, such as epilepsy and schizophrenia; their cause is probably to be sought in a neurovegetative disorder. But in psychasthenics the frequent episodes of anxiety are most likely connected with the conditions of uneasiness, discouragement, and persecution which they feel as a result of obsessive ideas, of which the patients are unable to rid themselves.

An exact and early diagnosis and treatment of anxiety is very important owing to the fact that it may precipitate and protract the most varied organic disfunctions. Opium, ergotamine, ultraviolet rays, electroshock, sleep, and psychotherapy are useful aids in the treatment of anxiety states. But preparations with a strychnine base (employed in treating asthenia) are to be absolutely avoided because they are conducive to anxiety.

From the ethical standpoint, the mental distrubance accompanying a crisis of anxiety diminishes imputability, though it very seldom removes all responsibility. In judging the morality of acts performed during a state of anxiety, this is the general criterion to be followed, with due consideration for each individual case. *Riz.*

APATHY. Apathy may be defined as want of feeling or lack of emotion. In ancient philosophical language, the term was used to indicate a condition characterized by freedom from, or superiority to, disturbing emotions; in modern medico-psychiatric terminology, it designates a condition of sluggishness and affective insensibility. In normal individuals apathy may indicate an individual characteristic similar to indolence, or a torpid and sluggish personality.

In its acute form, apathy is always a psychopathological state usually present in conditions such as anemia, toxicosis, tumors, presenile decline, and in certain forms of dementia praecox which cause a serious dulling of sensibility and a general mental torpor. Such cases are characterized by lack of initiative and interest in one's surroundings, by cessation of attachment to friends and family, and, sometimes, by loss of the sense of shame, self-pride, and even of the will to live. All mimetic and psychoreactive expressions cease at the same time, and even the somatic mechanism of emotion stops functioning. In the more acute forms of apathy, the pulse and respiration rate or the vasomotor capacity (spontaneous and faithful indicators of all emotional experiences) remain unmodified and unaffected by painful stimuli or in the presence of threats, offense, *etc.*, though the patient is fully aware of their meaning. All affective life is completely extinguished, and the neurovegetative system is in a constant state of hypotonicity.

From the ethical and nosological point of view apathy is clearly distinct from the characteristic indifference manifested by the psychodegenerate (the criminal, delinquent and the like) toward his victim and, in general, toward his crime, although psychologically there exists a certain relationship between the two phenomena. Indeed, in apathy—and not in immorality—there is a more or less complete indifference toward both good and evil, so that the apathetic individual is incapable of committing any blameworthy action, since he is unable to carry out—due to lack of affective-emotional drives—any voluntary act whatever. It could, therefore, be said that in the psychodegenerate there is something more (the tendency to commit a crime) and something less (a normality or quasi-normality as regards his other somatic and psychical activities) than we find in in the apthetic, who, as a result of his disturbance, is in a completely static condition.

In the last analysis, therefore, the apathetic individual, in the specific sense indicated above, is to be considered an "abnormal" individual and, generally speaking, is not punishable for his acts. Since he is a gravely ill person (for in these ethical considerations our concern is only with the more serious forms of this disturbance, which always have a definite pathological substratum), the apathetic, like the mentally disturbed person, is often to be considered irresponsible.

For the moral evaluation of an individual possessing a so-called apathetic temperament, see Character. *Riz.*

APHASIA. Aphasia is a partial or total loss of the ability to understand spoken words or to speak, without, however, involving impairment or alteration of the organs of hearing or speech (conditions resulting from impairment of such organs are called deafness, cophosis, or respectively, aphonia, mutism).

Classical authors usually distinguish two major types of aphasia: (a) *Sensory aphasia*, consisting in the partial or total loss of the ability to understand the meaning of spoken words, so that the individual, who is unaware of his own disturbing condition, is in a position similar to that of a person listening to a foreign tongue which he does not understand. Sensory aphasia is believed to be caused by organic damage to the brain, specifically to that particular part of the brain called the "verbo-acoustical center of Wernicke," which, in right-handed persons, is roughly situated in the posterior part of the temporal lobe of the left hemisphere. Sensory aphasia is always accompanied by a more or less accentuated degree of *alexia* (inability to read), *agraphia* (loss of ability to write), *acalculia* (inability to compute numbers),

amusia (inability to recognize a piece of music previously known). Moreover, the ordinary language of an individual undergoes paraphasic alterations, that is, distortions and misuse of words previously easy and familiar to him. (b) *Motor aphasia* (inability to express oneself) consists in the loss of ability to speak, a loss that may be more or less serious or complete. When the person who is plainly aware of his condition becomes irritated by this inability to speak or even when he is affected by other emotional causes, he is able correctly to pronounce many single words (without being able to put them together), such as "yes" and "no," swear words, and always the same phrases. Motor aphasia is believed to be due to an injury of the so-called "projection area of Broca," situated, in right-handed persons, in the lower posterior portion of the frontal lobe of the left hemisphere.

No form of aphasia is believed to be caused by intellectual deficiencies, which are rather the effect of a general deterioration that usually follows serious aphasiac disturbances. Psychologically, aphasia indicates a more or less localized disturbance of memory in regard to verbal images.

According to P. Marie (1906), the following observations regarding aphasia are worthy of note: (a) *Anarthria* is a very rare disease, characterized by a person's inability to speak (or to speak only in a very distorted manner); the condition is due to a brain injury, and the part of the brain injured is, in right-handed persons, usually the inner portion of the left hemisphere. The individual, however, perfectly understands spoken or written words, and there is in him no manifestation of psychic disturbance; his "internal language" remains intact, and the injury is "extrapsychic." (b) *Sensory aphasia* (see above) is not due to loss of verbo-acoustical images, but to a disturbance of the mental activity and to a real and true mental decline. (c) *Motor aphasia* is a combined form of anarthric and sensory aphasia, brought about by a notable brain injury, both in the cortical area of Wernicke and in the subcortical area; it shows, also, an element of dementia.

More recent research shows that all aphasiacs (except pure anarthrics) manifest more or less notable deficiency characteristics regarding spatial, symbolic, and categorical thought: such deficiencies and disorders, in the more serious cases, render the patient incapable not only of constructive thought but also of employing correctly the ideas of space and time. In an aphasiac psyche, therefore, there is a fundamental deficiency which affects not only the person's speech but also the greater part of his mental activities. It is to be further noted that in aphasiacs the more highly developed phases of speech are always more seriously affected than the lower and automatic phases; the reason is that the higher activities in the integrating hierarchy of faculties possess a more complex and fragile organization and, as a result, are less resistant to the dissolutive factors of the aphasiac process—all of which is in perfect accord with the general law governing psychical functionality, according to which the higher mental processes and the more recent mental acquisitions are the first to be affected by conditions of deterioration.

On the basis of such modern psychopathological findings, it is both proper and prudent to regard aphasiacs as more or less immature as to their ability to understand and to will, depending on the seriousness of their condition. In other words, they may rightfully be included in the category of semi-responsible persons. Anarthrics, instead, retain their complete moral responsibility. Generally speaking, aphasiacs are totally irresponsible for their vulgar expressions and for any blasphemies that they may automatically utter in their vain attempt to express themselves. *Riz.*

APHONIA. *See* Aphasia.

APHRODISIACS. The term *aphrodisiac* (derived from Aphrodite, the Greek goddess of love) comprises a variety of substances, vastly different both as to their content and to their activity, and all possessing the one common feature of exercising a stimulating influence (real or hypothetical) on the mechanical functions of the reproductive processes.

Among the more widely known and important aphrodisiacs may be mentioned especially the following: (a) the powder of *cantharides* (a preparation of dried and powdered beetles, especially the blister beetle or Spanish fly). Its active ingredient is cantharadin; the action of this drug against impotency is reflex, starting with an irritation of the urethral mucus produced by the drug at the time of its elimination; its use is very dangerous, since the dosage required for the production of the aphrodisiac effect is just slightly less than the amount that causes injury to the kidney (haemorrhagic nephritis), through which the cantharadin must pass in order to be eliminated. (b) *Strychnine* (an alkaloid of *nux vomica*), whose action consists in increasing the receptiveness of the spinal nervous centers to reflex stimulations and in quickening the sensitive-sensorial processes, capable of heightening, psychically, libidinous experience. (c) *Yohimbine* (an alkaloid obtained from the bark of a tropical African tree, called yohimbe), which causes vasodilation of the genitals, thereby increasing excitability of the medullary center of erection and bringing about its quickening and heightening. (d) *Alcohol, morphine, cocaine, Indian hemp.* Because of their tendency to reduce all cortical inhibition, these diverse types of drugs may be considered as very important aphrodisiacs. (e) *Gonadal hormones* either in the form of extracts or, more effectively, as transplanted secretions.

The physician is not permitted to suggest the use of aphrodisiacs for the purpose of making extramarital coitus possible, easier, nor more frequent, because such suggestions or advice indicate approval of sexual intercourse outside of wedlock, an act which is intrinsically evil. When, however, definite circumstances require it, the physician may prudently advise to married persons the employment of such drugs, provided that the physical pleasure connected with their use is simply a means and does not become an end in itself. Thus, in the case of a spouse with low virility or of a husband whose sexual activity, due to age or illness, is on a notable decline, the administration of some aphrodisiacal drug by the physician may not only be licit but also advisable. However, in view of the dangers inherent in the indiscriminate use of such drugs, their administration must always be guarded and cautious. In this connection, it is to be added that aphrodisiacs which more properly come under the category of stupefacients (q.v.), such as cocaine, morphine, etc., must be strictly forbidden, because their manifold effects may prove physically dangerous to the user, and morally disastrous; for obvious reasons it is also advisable to prescribe the use of cantharides.

The safest course is to prescribe a hormonal treatment with a base of pituitary extracts of the anterior lobe (the "motor of sexual function") and testicular (or ovarian in the female) extracts, accompanined by physical therapy and hydrotherapeutic and psychotherapeutic treatments, eventually followed by a guarded administration of yohimbine. *Riz.*

APOSTASY. In a general sense apostasy is the voluntary withdrawal from a previous condition or state. In ecclesiastical terminology it refers to the unlawful withdrawal of an individual either from the clerical state (*apostasia ab ordine*) or from the religious state. More technically, it is the definite and unlawful withdrawal of a religious with perpetual vows from his religious organization (*apostasia a religione*, Can. 644). But in its more commonly accepted meaning, apostasy indicates abandonment of the faith. According to the Code of Canon Law (Can. 1325, par. 2), it is the act whereby a baptized person abandons the Christian faith entirely. Unlike heresy (*q.v.*), apostasy is the rejection, not merely of some particular dogma, but of the entire deposit of revelation, and the apostate either embraces a non-Christian religion or remains without any religion whatever.

Apostasy in the proper sense, *i.e.*, apostasy from the faith, is a most serious sin against faith and religion, with the aggravating circumstance of infidelity to the vows of baptism. Whether a material apostasy, *i.e.*, one carried out in good faith, may be possible (as in the case of heresy, infidelity, or schism) remains a disputed question. The Vatican Council (Sess. 3, c. 3 *de fide* and Can. 6) declared that God grants to all believers the grace of perseverance in the faith, for God does not abandon man until man abandons Him; consequently, the changing of faith by a Catholic can never be justified. Some theologians interpret this text to mean that there can never be *objectively* a just cause for giving up the Catholic religion, but the Council did not exclude the possibility of a *subjectively* just cause, as, *e.g.*, in the case of a person who erroneously but in good faith believes that the Catholic Church is not the true Church. The majority of theologians, however, do not admit this explanation, and maintain that it is impossible for any Catholic, after having freely and consciously embraced the faith, to give it up without committing mortal sin, at least in cause. The sin may be directly against faith or indirectly so, as when one exposes himself to the danger of apostasy by reading anti-Catholic literature, associating with anti-religious companions, giving in to sins of impurity, pride, etc., with the result that he draws himself away from the grace and the help of God, which is necessary and indispensable for overcoming difficulties and doubts against the faith.

Obviously, defection from the Catholic faith and the breaking of ties with the Church do not release the apostate from his subjection to the Church—a bond which he contracted upon the reception of baptism. The Church considers and treats apostates as rebellious children, and inflicts upon them the same penalties as upon heretics, especially the penalty of excommunication reserved to the Holy See (Can. 2314);

hence, concerning the means of grace (*see* Heresy) the juridical position of apostates and heretics is similar. Moreover, if the apostasy is public, the apostate is also denied ecclesiastical burial (Can. 1240, par. 1). *Dam.*

APOSTLE. *See* Apostolate.

APOSTOLATE. *Apostle* (Greek, *apostolein*—to send forth; hence, one sent) is the title given by Jesus Christ to His twelve collaborators whom He personally chose and sent forth to preach (Matt. 4:18–22; 9:9–13; *etc.*) and to whom He entrusted the propagation and instrumental application of His redemptive mission. The number, which was reminiscent of the twelve tribes of Israel, constituted a proper designation of the chosen group, *the Twelve.* Judas apostatized, but Matthias took his place. Their names are consecrated forever in the history of evangelical preaching, of sanctity, and of Christian piety: Peter, James, John, Andrew, James the Less, Philip, Bartholomew, Simon, Jude Thaddeus, Matthew, Thomas, Judas Iscariot, later replaced by Matthias, For abandoning all things and following Him (Matt. 19:27, 29), they were given by Christ a participation in His judicial function. Strictly speaking, the mission of the twelve Apostles began with the Resurrection of Jesus, of which they became the authentic witnesses. At first they were messengers to the Jews; they later became missionaries to the world.

An apostle is intended for an apostolate. The apostolate established by Jesus Christ had a universal and, by virtue of the apostolic succession, a perpetual character. In the doctrinal field, the Apostles were charged with transmitting the teaching of the Master, and with presiding over the government of the faithful by dogmatic and disciplinary prescriptions. To be sent forth by Christ was and still is the fundamental element of the apostolate.

The Apostles were given a twofold office: (a) extraordinary, by which they were to continue the work of Jesus in laying the foundation of the Church upon its cornerstone, which is Christ himself; (b) ordinary, namely the hierarchical authority within the Church. The former was to end with their death; the latter to be transmitted to their successors. According to its strict and etymological meaning, however, the apostolate is the religious and supernatural power, conferred by Jesus upon the Twelve, to go forth to all parts of the earth to preach the evangelical law and the Christian faith. In a wider, but proper and real sense, an apostolate is the work by which one consecrates himself entirely to the propagation of religious, moral, and even civil truths.

Within the Church there exists a twofold official apostolate, which entails the faculty, and also the obligation, to teach the truths of faith with supernatural authority: (a) the apostolate of administering the sacraments canonically in order to communicate grace to souls; (b) the apostolate of directing one's flock, promoting and inculcating the observance of divine law among the faithful, prescribing positive laws and norms according to the circumstances of time and place, exorcising, with legitimate authority, Satan and other evil spirits, *etc.* Such an apostolate is either inherited by legitimate Apostolic succession, as in the case of the pope for the universal Church and the bishops for their respective territories (Can. 1327); or is received by direct derivation, from the pope or from the bishops, as in the case of all others who are duly authorized by the pontiff or the bishops. In the present Code such authorization is restricted to the clergy, and more properly to priest and deacons (Can. 1328, 1342).

There is another apostolate which might be termed semi-official, and it is that which is exercised by the laity, organized in particular associations which, under the direct control of the Church, assist the clergy in reaching all levels of society and in dealing with all social conditions. Such an apostolate is known as Catholic Action, which, in its various forms, organizes elements of all age levels and social conditions (*see*

Catholic Action). This type of apostolate is not new but has been carried out for centuries by Marian Congregations, Third Orders, Pious Unions, Sodalities and the like which, as repeatedly stated by Pope Pius XII, carry out a true apostolate of Catholic Action.

Besides the official and semi-official apostolate, there is also one engaged in by individual persons who, moved by the love of Christ, labor for the spreading of His Kingdom through the ordinary method of family and social contacts. (*See* Laity and Hierarchy).

Forms of apostolate partaking of the character of all three types mentioned above, insofar as they are organized under the direction of the Church and are carried out by the laity, are: the Apostleship of Prayer, Apostolate of the Press, Apostolate of the Sea, Apostolate of Workers, Apostolate of Children, Apostolate of Immigrants, of Lay Retreats, *etc.*

The organization of the lay apostolate on an international level was discussed at the first International Congress of the Lay Apostolate, held in Rome, October 8–14, 1951. (*Cf.* Discourse of His Holiness Pius XII to members of the Congress in *Osservatore Romano*, October 15–16, 1951.) *M. d. G.*

APOSTOLATE OF THE CATHOLIC PRESS. *See* Press.

APOSTOLATE OF THE LAITY. *See* Apostolate, Catholic Action, Laity and the Hierarchy.

APOSTOLATE OF THE SICK. *See* Apostolate, Nurse.

APPARITIONS. *See* Visions and Apparitions.

APPEAL. *See* Sentence.

APPEAL FROM ABUSE. *See* Pontiff (Supreme).

APPEAL TO AN ECUMENICAL COUNCIL. *See* Pontiff (Supreme).

APPETITE, CONCUPISCIBLE AND IRASCIBLE. For moralists appetite signifies a tendency or inclination. Appetite may be (a) natural, (b) sensitive, and (c) rational. Natural appetite is the tendency of one thing toward another, without any element of knowledge, as iron is drawn to a magnet; sensitive appetite is that which moves an animal being (hence, also man) toward an object perceived by the senses; rational appetite, or will, is the tendency toward an object, consequent to intellectual cognition and appreciation.

The present discussion centers solely on sense appetite, which may be concupiscible and irascible. Sense appetite is called concupiscible insofar as the animal being through this tendency seeks its own good (the agreeable or pleasurable) and avoids whatever the senses present as harmful (pain). Sense appetite is called irascible insofar as through this tendency the animal being is confronted with obstacles in the pursuit of the good or in avoiding evil.

In the animal these tendencies are not subject to rational control and, hence, are incapable of any ethical evaluation; in man, however, these same tendencies do admit of ethical appraisal inasmuch as and to the extent to which they are subject to the control of reason and the command of the will. The phrase "to the extent to which" is used deliberately, for even in man the animal powers enjoy a relative independence and spontaneity; for this reason the ancients were wont to say that intellect and will exercise over these tendencies a political, but not a despotic, influence. Such independence is greater in the child, because of the slow and gradual development of the higher faculties; is greater in individuals addicted to certain stimulants, due to the difficulty of controlling automatic reactions; and is greater in all persons at the first moment in which the object is sensibly apprehended, due to the great rapidity of the senses in responding to external stimuli.

Sense appetite is good or bad according to the nature of the stimulating object. Generally speaking, if the object is sinful, the element of subjective responsibility is greater in the adult than in the child; and it is graver in the second moment than in the first.

Sense appetite is directed toward indefinite objects. In the concupiscible sphere the main objects of the appetite are food and sex; in the irascible sphere, dangers of death are usually said to constitute its main object. The concupiscible appetite is regulated by the virtue of temperance, the irascible by the virtue of fortitude. *Gra.*

APPLICATION OF COGNITIVE FACULTIES. *See* Intellect, Will.

APPLICATION OF HOLY MASS. The intention of the celebrant to apply the ministerial fruit of the Mass for a particular person or for a specific purpose is called application of the Mass. The celebrant alone may make the application, and the Church has condemned the doctrine set forth at the Synod of Pistoia, which denied that the priest has the power to distribute the fruits of the Holy Sacrifice (Denz., n. 1530).

The following conditions are required for a valid application: (a) a true intention on the part of the celebrant, either actual or virtual, to apply the ministerial fruit; (b) the celebrant must have this intention before Mass, or at least before the consecration of the two species, for the essence of the Mass consists in the consecration of the species; the application made between the consecration of the bread and that of the wine is probably valid; (c) the celebrant must determine the person for whom or the purpose for which he intends to apply the fruit of the Mass; the purpose, however, may be determined by another person, in which case it suffices to apply according to the intention of that person; (d) when the application is obligatory, the celebrant may not divide the ministerial fruit by assigning either the propitiatory or satisfactory effects to other intentions; in this case the fruit divides itself, if the person is incapable of receiving all the fruit, in the same manner as when Mass is applied for

several persons; if, however, the application is gratuitous, the celebrant may divide the ministerial fruit, applying the impetratory effects for one person and the satisfactory effects for another.

The ministerial fruit of the Mass may be applied for all those who are capable of receiving any part thereof, hence, for all the living and for all the souls in Purgatory, unless there be some special ecclesiastical prohibition (Can. 809). Thus, according to Canon Law, Mass may not be applied publicly for excommunicates *vitandi* or for those who were denied ecclesiastical burial. The celebrant may apply Mass privately for heretics, schismatics, and other excommunicates, as also for the conversion of excommunicates *vitandi* and of infidels (Can. 2262, par. 2). Mass may not be applied for canonized saints, except in their honor or to obtain their intercession. Mass may never be said for the damned (when their status is known with certainty) nor for unbaptized children who died before attaining the use of reason. In the case of baptized infants who died before reaching the use of reason, Mass may be offered as an act of worship and thanksgiving, and perhaps also as an act of impetration to God that we may receive divine graces through their intercession.

A priest may be obliged to apply the fruits of the Mass by the command of his Superior, by reason of a promise, vow, office, or benefice, and by reason of a stipend received or of alms offered by the faithful. *Toc.*

APPROPRIATION OF BOOKS. *See* Forbidden Books.

APPROPRIATION, UNDUE. Undue appropriation is committed when an individual, to secure an unjust profit either for himself or for others, appropriates for himself another person's money or goods, which are entrusted to him under some title or other. Upon action by the injured owner, undue appropriation is punishable with imprisonment and fine. In the moral order it constitutes theft (*q.v.*) in the true and proper sense of the word.

If undue appropriation is made of things possessed under the title of necessary deposit, the penalty is increased. In such a case there is an official proceeding, especially when the embezzlement occurs in conjunction with abuse of authority, office, domestic relations, cohabitation, hospitality, etc. *Fel.*

APTITUDE. *See* Psychotechnology.

ARBITER. *See* Arbitration.

ARBITRATION. Arbitration is a juridical procedure whereby the contending parties in a dispute, in order to avoid a judicial hearing, agree to submit their case for review and settlement to one or more persons, called arbiters or arbitrators, depending on whether the question is solved according to the provisions of the law (*ad normam juris*) or according to some principle of equity (*de bono et aequo*).

In civil law arbitration proceedings are usually dealt with by statute of the individual states. In Canon Law, excommunicated and infamous persons, after a condemnatory or declaratory sentence, may not exercise the office of arbiters; nor may lay persons act as such in ecclesiastical causes; members of a religious organization may act as arbiters only with permission of their own superiors (Can. 1931).

Once they have accepted the office committed to them, the arbiters must follow not only the norms of Canon Law, but also the rules of civil law in the area where the arbitration procedure is permitted (Can. 1930, 1926). According to Canons 1930 and 1927, arbitration may not be exercised in criminal cases, in civil cases involving the dissolution of the marital bond, in civil cases involving a benefice, when the litigation centers on the title of the benefice, unless the competent authority agrees to the arbitration, and, finally, in spiritual matters, whenever there is a question of payment by temporal goods. However, in the case of a dispute over temporal ecclesiastical goods or goods which, though annexed to spiritual things, may nevertheless be considered as separate, arbitration may be validly exercised. If the contending parties are unable to agree on an amicable settlement and are unwilling to submit the matter to arbitration, there is no course left but to institute a formal trial according to due process of law (Can. 1932). *Fel.*

ARBITRATION, INTERNATIONAL. The procedure adopted by two states or international authorities involved in dispute, usually after failure of direct negotiations, is called international arbitration. Arbitration is, in fact, nothing but a mandate conferred, by mutual agreement of the litigant powers, upon one or more persons to define judicially and according to the norms of common and special laws controversies between two or more States. It is a form of compromise between litigant powers who thus agree to select an arbitrator and to accept the consequent judgment and arbitral award.

Traces of international arbitration are found among nearly all ancient peoples. The Achaean League and Amphictyonic Council were, in substance, international tribunals of arbitration. So, too, the Universities of Law of the Middle Ages at times assumed the role of international courts. In the sixteenth century, due to the changing international relations, the policy of international arbitration suffered a setback—a situation that was to endure until the second half of the nineteenth century. However, during these three centuries authors could be found (such as Bentham) who upheld the necessity of international agreements for the securing of lasting peace, while at the same time the instrumentality of world tradition brought into existence particular treaties, such as that negotiated by England and the United States in 1794. In the second half of the nineteenth century international arbitration was once more resorted to as an instrument for the peaceful solution of international disputes. According to La Fontaine, eight arbitrations were held between 1821 and 1840; twenty between 1841 and 1860; forty from 1861 to 1880; ninety from 1881 to 1890. In the following years recourse to an International Tribunal became even more frequent. This was due to an increase of international disputes and to the fear that, if such conflicts were not resolved amicably, they would erupt, as they frequently have, into open warfare. With the sphere of international relations becoming increasingly wider and more complex, and with the constant development of newer and more destructive means of warfare, there is a growing desire on the part of world leaders to avoid the risk of a war.

Following the proposal of the International Juridical Institute of Brussels (1875) that the various sovereign States make a concerted effort to draw up a suitable plan for the solution of international disputes, and following the exhortation of Pope Leo XIII, who acted as arbitrator in the settlement of a highly important dispute, the stage was set for the two peace conferences at the Hague (1899 and 1907), which led to the establishment of the Tribunal of the Hague or Permanent Court of Arbitration. The formulation of statutory and procedural norms was elaborated and completed in subsequent conferences. Pope Benedict XV, on August 1, 1917, solemnly reminded the warring nations and peoples that international arbitration is the best method for establishing and preserving international peace, provided that the conflicting States show a minimum of good will. Since 1880, permanent treaties of arbitration were included between nations, by which they bound themselves to resolve their disputes by peaceful methods. After the failure of the League of Nations, which had created the Permanent Court of International Justice at the Hague, and following the Second World War, the United Nations was organized for the peaceful settlement of disputes. The world may not benefit too much from such an international body, but it should not demand too much of it either.

International arbitration is not the same as the real judgment issuing from public power, for it derives its authority from the private will and mutual agreement of litigant nations; nor is it the same as mediation, which is carried out outside the sphere of established law and of itself has no binding force.

Permanent Court of Arbitration at the Hague is composed of a group of jurists of proven integrity and learning appointed by the signatory powers, each submitting four delegates, whose names are placed on the list of Court judges. In the event of dispute between States, a particular tribunal of arbitration is chosen from among the Court judges; each litigant State selects two judges (arbiters), only one of whom may be a citizen of the selecting state; the four chosen judges then proceed to select a fifth to act as President of the Tribunal. Their decisions, arrived at by majority vote, are binding on the interested parties, so long as they do not exceed the matter under dispute.

The Permanent Tribunal of International Justice is a body of fifteen independent judges appointed by particular international organizations, upon designation by member nations of the League of Nations, with no regard to nationality. The function of this Court is to judge disputes between states either in solemn or summary fashion: in solemn form, the bench consists of eleven ordinary judges, plus one or two others who may be citizens of the interested states; in summary form, it consists of three judges. Moreover, every three years the Court forms two different judicial boards consisting of five judges for the review of labor disputes and disputes of traffic and communications.

In 1907 the republics of Central America also established an International Tribunal of Arbitration, with headquarters at San Jose, Costa Rica.

International arbitration may be conveniently used in disputes of an economic, commercial, or strictly juridical order but, generally speaking, it is ineffective in questions involving the honor, dignity, independence, and sovereignty of the States. States involved in dispute may request as arbitrator a head of state, a group of jurists or even a noted internationalist or politician.

Men are made to understand one another. All men, whatever their race, nationality, or government, ought to be united in charity, above all political differences and beyond all barriers. All men are children of God, hence worthy of respect, understanding, and love. States, which are entities made up of individuals, ought likewise to observe the law of charity in their efforts to understand the mutual interests of the family of nations. *Pug.*

ARCHBISHOP. According to Canon 272, an archbishop is a prelate, invested with episcopal dignity, presiding over an ecclesiastical province: in this sense, archbishop is equivalent to metropolitan. However, some bishops are immediately subject to the Holy See and titular bishops are sometimes honored with the title of archbishop *(honoris causa).*

The archiepiscopal or metropolitan dignity is attached to an episcopal see which the supreme pontiff has so constituted; and the metropolitan has in his own archdiocese the same obligations and rights every bishop has in his diocese (Can. 273). Within three months following his consecration or, if already consecrated, of his canonical appointment in the Consistory, the archbishop is obliged to request the pallium, which signifies archiepiscopal or metropolitan power (Can. 275). Before the imposition of the pallium, the archbishop, unless authorized by special apostolic indult, may not licitly perform any act of metropolitan jurisdiction nor any episcopal function in which the use of the pallium is liturgically prescribed (Can. 276). The metropolitan may wear the pallium in all churches (even exempt) of his province during solemn Mass, on days so designated in the Roman Pontifical or by a particular privilege. Should the metropolitan lose his pallium or should he be transferred to another metropolitan see, he must obtain a new pallium; all the pallia received by a metropolitan during his lifetime are to be buried with him; they may not be loaned, donated, or bequeathed to anyone (Can. 277–279).

The metropolitan has under his jurisdiction a certain number of suffragan *(q.v.)* bishops: the limits of this jurisdiction are accurately defined in Canon 274. An archbishop precedes all bishops; however, a bishop within his own diocese precedes an archbishop who is not a metropolitan. *Fal.*

ARCHCONFRATERNITY. See Confraternity.

ARCHITECT. The word architect, *architectus,* is derived from the Greek *archi,* meaning chief, and *tecton,* meaning carpenter or builder. Etymologically, therefore, the term signifies master builder or chief artificer. In general, an architect is one skilled in architecture or in the art of construction; one who draws up plans and designs of a building, supervises the works, directs the activities of the various workers engaged in the project. More properly, an architect is one who undertakes the construction of buildings, according to designs drawn up by himself. Since the types of constructions vary, the architect's field of activity also varies accordingly; thus, an architect may be civil, military, maritime, *etc.*

As an expert in the art of building, the architect undertakes, at a fixed fee or on a percentage basis, to draw up the plans of a contemplated project, to superintend and direct the execution of the work, to check the contractor's estimates and sometimes even to select the contractor. No individual is allowed to act as an architect without having attained a certificate or diploma from a school of engineering.

The architect is morally bound to observe all stipulations regarding time, materials, labor costs, *etc.*, as indicated in the contract, whether negotiated with a public organization or a private person. As a result of such a contract, he is forbidden to violate intentionally the rights of others (*e.g.*, the opening of bids and the awarding of contracts); by the same token, he is bound to direct the work and conduct himself in such fashion as to prevent all damages and dangers (both personal and material) which are known to result from certain positive or negative attitudes, referred to by classical jurists and moralists as *culpa in vigilando* and *culpa in eligendo*. Professional ineptitude and technical ignorance constitute a grave fault on the part of the architect, and he is seriously bound to make restitution for any damage caused. Finally, a Catholic architect is not permitted to cooperate in the construction of buildings that will be used openly against the faith and the moral teachings of the Gospel. *Tar.*

ARCHIVES. Every ecclesiastical Curia must have a safe and suitable place for the proper keeping of all records. Besides the general archives, the bishop shall have also a special place for secret documents (Can. 375–379) or secret archives.

In the archives are to be kept all acts and writings pertaining to diocesan affairs; they shall be locked, and only the chancellor of the Curia shall have a key to them (Can. 372, par. 1; 377, par. 2). No one may have access to these files without permission either of the bishop or the vicar-general or the chancellor (Can. 377, par. 1). Permission of the bishop is required to remove any document from the archives: in such a case the individual must leave with the chancellor a signed receipt for the removed document, which must be returned within three days, unless, for grave reasons, a longer period shall have been granted (Can. 378).

In the general archives are to be kept authentic copies of all the following: archival inventory of each chapter, parish, confraternity or pious place within the diocese; parochial books; inventory of the movable and immovable goods of each church, benefice, pious place or pious cause; all legal documents. A catalogue or index of the general archives, with protocol number, shall be made regularly. The catalogue should be brought up to date each year, within the first two months, classifying all the documents of the past year. But it is recommended that the files be kept up to date constantly (Can. 375–376).

In the secret diocesan archives are to be kept all acts of documents which, either by their very nature or by prescription of the Code, must remain secret (Can. 379, par. 1). A catalogue of such acts shall be drawn up, and it is the duty of the bishop each year to remove and burn all acts and document of trials for bad behavior, in instances where the defendant has since died or ten years have elapsed since the sentence; in this last instance, however, a brief summary of the case and the text of the final sentence is to be kept on file (*ibid.*, par. 2).

The secret archives, which are to be kept separate from the general archives, must be locked with two keys, one to be kept by the bishop (or administrator apostolic) and the other by the vicar-general or, in his absence, by the chancellor (*ibid.*, par. 3). Special canonical norms (Can. 379, par. 4; 381) indicate in whose possession the keys must remain during the vacancy of the see or during the time that the bishop may be hindered from exercising his jurisdiction. The concern of the legislator is that in no case shall the keys remain in the hands of only one person. Only the bishop (or apostolic administrator) has the right to consult, without any witness (*nemine adstante*), the secret archives. If the diocese becomes vacant and no apostolic administrator is appointed, the secret archives are to be sealed with the seal of the Curia. The first dignitary of the cathedral chapter or the senior consultor may consult the secret archives only in case of urgent necessity, and he must do so in the presence of two canons or consultors. The latter must see to it that no documents are removed from the archives, and they must remain present during the whole time of the consultation of the documents (Can. 382). When the new bishop arrives, the vicar-capitular or diocesan administrator must give him the reason that caused him to open the archives. *Fel.*

ARISTOCRACY. *See* Society.

ARMAMENTS. *See* War.

ARMISTICE. An armistice is an agreement of political and military character, whereby hostilities between powers are immediately, but only temporarily, halted. It is a sort of truce of arms proclaimed by mutual agreement between military chiefs, with the intervention of diplomatic representatives from both sides. Different from a true and proper armistice is the occasional suspension of arms for a well-defined purpose (*e.g.*, to bury the dead), ordinarily affecting only one specific battle area. Both are agreements which do not bring about cessation of war, but merely suspension of hostilities for a specified period of time.

An armistice suspends not only all acts of hostility on both sides, but also all operational movements that the enemy might have wanted or could have prevented, if a truce had not been declared; *e.g.*, during the period of armistice, it is not allowed to bring arms or soldiers into a besieged fortress or area, to repair breakthroughs made by the enemy, *etc.*, for all such operations would alter the conditions of fact obtaining at the moment the truce was declared. Each belligerent is free within his own territory to continue with preparations of arms and soldiers; in fact, the enemy is incapable of preventing such preparations, even during actual combat. An armistice does not suspend, however, application of the laws of war, unless it shall be so stated by particular dispositions. Generally, the terms of the armistice explain in detail the limitations placed on the activities of both sides. Any military officer, invested with command, is liable to punishment if he should prolong hostilities after having received official notice of an armistice.

An armistice goes into effect at the moment it is signed, unless otherwise agreed upon. But the actual cessation of hostilities cannot take place unless an official communication is sent to all military officers. Such a communication, according to international agreement, is both obligatory and necessary.

As part of its apostolic mission of peace in the world, the Church has always endeavored to prevent, through diplomatic measures, the outbreak of armed conflicts and to bring about the cessation of wars already begun. In medieval society the Church, with its "Truce of God," had succeeded in limiting hostilities between armies to only three days a week and in eliminating them altogether during certain holy seasons. In the great and small conflicts of our own day, the ceaseless efforts of the Roman pontiffs for restoration of peace and harmony in the world are well known to all. *Pug.*

ARMS. *See* War.

ART (morality of). The problem of art and morality is strictly connected with the particular philosophy of life of each individual; thus, its solution varies according to each one's philosophy. Aesthetics underscores the profound purifying or purgative virtue of art, which excludes automatically any offense against the moral conscience.

In the metaphysicians' view, art is the actuation of the beautiful, which of itself leads to God. The moralists, on the other hand, underscore the moral exigency of art. The premise that immorality is not in the things or objects themselves, but in the manner of representing or of portraying them is drawn from the Christian conception of life; it is against this background that the two terms *art* and *morality* must be viewed in order to bring about a harmony between the requirements of the moral law and those of art. Art is neither religion nor science, nor politics, nor morals; it has a distinct field of its own, *viz.*, the production of beauty. It does not teach directly, nor is it even concerned with truth, anchored as it is in the realm of creative phantasy. But despite this, it does not cease to be a human activity, one which represents and interprets life. It follows that, since art is human, it must necessarily be worthy of man and, hence, moral. Certainly the artist is capable of knowing and perceiving both good and evil in life and portrays both. The whole world of nature, of history, and of life can become and is the field of his representations. But the question arises as to whether the false and the ugly, deformity and moral turpitude are susceptible of aesthetic representation, that is, capable of inspiring a work of art. Granted that they are, a further question arises, namely, whether the artist and others are permitted to produce, distribute, and even promote the circulation of such works of art, and to advertise them for everyone to see, hear, or read about.

Unquestionably the role of art is to portray not only the good and the beautiful, but also evil and sin, which unfortunately make up such a large part of life. But if evil and sin must be portrayed, it is only to point to the triumph of goodness. Evil must be so dominated by the force of good that any aspect of evil is lost in the overwhelming radiance of good.

Art is an activity productive of beauty, which, to be complete, must possess integrity, proportion, and clarity. If one of these attributes is lacking, the harmony of the beautiful and, hence, the value of the artistic work, is thereby reduced. To be sure, art practiced independently of moral and social standards may be productive of the highest form of passionate expression; but it will then always be inferior art, as it is false and lacking in spiritual expression.

Moreover, the aim of art is to give joy, and genuine art is that which produces the highest form of enjoyment. Like all forms of enjoyment and pleasure, the enjoyment of art cannot be genuine and legitimate unless it is brought into harmony with man's nature. Art designed merely to arouse the joy of the senses in a way that does not subordinate them to reason affords but a false pleasure, a false good.

Hence, the well-known formula "art for art's sake," which implies that art is a pure technique, in and by itself, standing apart from the rest of the world, independent of all human events and institutions, is to be rejected as devoid of all meaning. It would be equivalent to wanting the realization of art apart from the artist. Every work of art is necessarily a projection of the artist's creative imagination, a part of his own being, of life and reality as relived subjectively by him; consequently, every work of art necessarily mirrors that artist's own conception of life. On the other hand, the extreme view which regards art as essentially immoral because it appeals to the senses and excites emotions that are intrinsically evil is to be likewise rejected.

It is true that art does not aim directly at portraying goodness but beauty, and that its immediate end is to please, not to lead to sanctity. It is also true that there is nothing intrinsically evil about enjoyment as such (including the enjoyment of art, which is one of its highest forms), and that it is meant to satisfy a natural need for relaxation and mental diversion. Thus, the relaxation afforded by art is, in itself, like a shining light that reflects its beneficent rays on the health and work of man. The fact that art has during the course of the ages contributed to the cause of evil and that it has been the source of depravity in no way proves that art is immoral in itself; at best, it proves that in the field of art, as in every other sphere of human endeavor, there will always be individuals ready to direct actions, objectively good or indifferent, to evil purposes. That which debases art, therefore, is the intention with which it is practiced. The author's intention is always reflected to some extent in the work of art and, through it, becomes communicable to the mind of the viewer. If the intention of the artist is evil, the work itself becomes contaminated and perverted from the true end of all things beautiful, which is universal harmony.

No matter how subtle and expert one may be in abstracting form from substance, there is no doubt concerning the reciprocal action or influence of art upon the sentiments, and of sentiments upon art. From this the moral responsibility of the artist, who is bound to observe the laws of morality in his works of art as well as in the implements he uses (models, *etc.*), stands out clearly. It is to be noted, however, that a potential danger of perversion may be entirely absent from a work of art and that it may be simply the effect of the morbid tendencies of the viewer.

The problem of the nude in art is to be solved according to those same criteria. Certainly no Christian can go so far as to say that nudity in art is never obscene, nor will he repudiate it *a priori* as immoral. The Christian view has never regarded the naked body in itself as unchaste, but rightfully and realistically insists on the great dangers involved in its representation. Wherefore, nudity in art becomes acceptable to a Christian only when it is justified by some higher reason, even if purely aesthetic, and on condition that the representation does not constitute a danger of sin. It is, therefore, ludicrous to assert that the Christian measures the morality of a figure or statue by the length of its drapery and that to remove the drapery is to render the statue highly unchaste. There are undraped statues and paintings which no one could reasonably consider unchaste; on the other hand, there are draped statues that are highly immoral, because the evil intent of the author is noticeable in almost every detail.

It is only natural that one and the same object or artistic creation may produce different reactions in different viewers. After all, the so-called aesthetic sense is the result of a certain attitude and artistic maturity, which in certain viewers may be lacking altogether, while in others it may exist in a varying degree. All this is to be taken into consideration in planning and staging art exhibits to which the public is admitted.

The environment may also influence and determine the sensitive reactions of the viewers. A statue placed in a museum acquires, even to the eyes of an unin-itiate, a certain artistic meaning; the same statue placed in a public square may easily be subject to the most vulgar interpretation. All these circumstances are connected with the ethical aspects of art, and they are to be taken into account by the artist himself, by custodians and exhibitors and viewers of art, for every man, no matter what his activity or endeavor, is bound to observe the law of God. *Pal.*

ARTICULUM MORTIS. *See* Danger of Death.

ARTISAN, CRAFTSMAN. *See* Industrialism, Labor.

ASCETICAL AND MORAL THEOLOGY. In a broad sense, ascetical theology is part of moral theology, inasmuch as its aim is, like that of moral theology, to direct human actions to the attainment of man's ultimate, supernatural end. However, not all authors are in agreement as to the relationship between ascetical and moral theology and the respective limits of each science.

Some authors (Génicot, Tanquerey, Hürth) hold that the object of moral theology is the necessary good, while that of ascetical theology is perfection and that which is better. Others, instead, rightly observe that when it is said that the good is the object of moral theology, we must understand this to mean the good in all its extension, including the better and the perfect; hence, this form of moral minimization is opposed, even when done simply for the purpose of delimiting the field of each discipline. For this reason, A. Vermeersch holds that ascetical and even mystical theology are to be considered rather as technical disciplines subsidiary to moral theology, more as arts than sciences, inasmuch as they do not limit themselves to defining the good and the better, but study the ways by which the good and the better are to be attained. However, Father Vermeersch does maintain that in practice it is quite proper to assign to ascetical theology a larger range, that is, as encompassing not only the means by which to attain perfection but also the virtues and perfection as such. J. Maritain distinguishes practical sciences into those which are speculatively practical and practically practical, the former dealing with human acts in their conceptual and abstract value, the latter, instead, with human acts in their concrete determination, without attempting to regulate each individual action, which is an area proper to the virtue of prudence. Thus, moral theology would be considered a speculatively practical science, whereas ascetical, or, more generally, spiritual theology, a practically practical science. Though we are not utterly opposed to the distinction proposed by J. Maritain, it seems to us that such a distinction does not solve the problem because in moral theology there can also be a theoretical and a practical part without in any way reducing the latter (the practical part) to spiritual theology. According to J. De Guibert, moral theology is the science of the good, while ascetical theology is the science of perfection and of spiritual progress. Our only objection against this theory is that, admittedly, perfection as such enters into the concept and the field of the good, which the thesis of De Guibert seems to overlook.

From an analysis of the above opinions, it seems that the points that must be maintained can be reduced to the following four: (a) moral theology, condered in its widest acceptance and in its determination as a particular discipline, is the science of moral good in the supernatural order in all its extent and, therefore, even with regard to the better and the perfect; any limitation drawn from the various degrees of the good, besides being arbitrary, seems to be in contrast with the function of moral theology, which is to evaluate and regulate the entire activity of man; (b) ascetical theology, on the other hand, is the science of moral progress as such and, therefore, of its nature, laws, and the ways and means of attaining it; nor can one say that ascetical theology concerns itself only with the better and the perfect, because it is its concern also to study the transition of a soul from the state of sin to that of grace, and the subsequent development of spiritual life. This observation is strengthened by the constant increase and furtherance of the study of ascetical theology; (c) since ascetical theology concerns itself with progress in its principles, it is not simply an art but must be considered as a true practical science, subsidiary to moral theology, inasmuch as it draws from the latter concepts and principles relative to the good in all its extension; (d) in ascetical theology, as well as in all other practical sciences, one can distinguish a theoretical as well as a practical part; that is, even in ascetical theology one can find Maritain's distinction of a science speculatively practical and practically practical. *Pal.*

ASCETICISM. The term *asceticism* is derived from the Greek word *askesis,* which among other things indicated strenuous exercises undertaken to improve one's physical, intellectual, and moral dexterity. Since Christian perfection, which St. Paul compares to the arduous training of the athlete in strengthening his powers of endurance so as to gain victory (I Cor. 9:24 ff.), cannot be attained without sacrifice or effort, it was only natural that the term *asceticism* should be adopted by Christian writers to signify the efforts made by a Christian toward attaining spiritual perfection. Among the first to employ the term in this sense were Clement of Alexandria and Origen; after them its use became common in Christian literature.

It is quite clear that asceticism is not an occasional renunciation but a constant and generous training exercise. First and foremost, Christian asceticism involves practices tending to eliminate all obstacles to spiritual progress, such as depriving oneself of legitimate pleasures and satisfactions and practicing acts contrary to love of self and to desires for self-enjoyment. Such mortifications, usually called negative asceticism, are not in themselves sufficient; one must practice positive asceticism, which involves acts directly aiming at advancement in supernatural life. In this regard, it is helpful to note that mortification not only removes obstacles, but also strengthens the energies of man's soul, directing him to ever greater achievements, so that asceticism, understood in the Christian sense, is always possessed of a constructive aspect and content.

The ascetical practices of a Christian are not an end in themselves, but are only indispensable means for man, as a child of God, to protect and develop all that is noblest and highest in him. It is important always to keep this in mind, in order to avoid a certain naturalism, a vain complacency in what one does, or even the danger of much severity toward self and others. If the Christian loses sight of the real purpose of asceticism, he easily runs the risk of making the mistake of setting his attention on secondary things, neglecting the sacrifices by which he can more effectively tear down the great obstacles to his union with God, i.e., self-love and pride.

Asceticism has certain limits which normally one must not exceed. Thus, one may not adopt ascetical forms or practices damaging to health or beyond one's physical powers. Today, however, there is perhaps greater danger of falling into the opposite error of minimizing the necessity of mortification and self-denial.

Although mortification occupies an important role in Christian asceticism, it is in no way designed to inspire pessimism. The true Christian is well aware that all things created by God are good in themselves, but he also realizes that the order in man's nature was upset by original sin and that, as a result, man has a strong proclivity toward material things and pleasures; hence, the true Christian sees the absolute necessity for renunciation, detachment, and mortification.

Finally, Christian asceticism is not a mere negation of life, nor does it mean that we must flee life as something odious and vile. On the contrary, the true ascetic, because of the impact of the supernatural element in his life, is able to do more useful and important work in society, as is proven by the activities of the great ascetics.

From the interpretation of Christian asceticism just given, it follows that the ascetical program to be adopted by this or that individual will partly depend upon the personal temperament of the individual himself. The ascetical practices of a strong and vigorous person will differ from those of a weak and lazy person; the sensual man has need of a different form of asceticism from that of the choleric individual. Moreover, asceticism admits of the gradual simplification and transformation of the supernatural life, in which, as time goes on, the influence of the love of God and the gifts of the Holy Ghost is felt more and more. As to the form and extent of ascetical practices, it is a wise rule to place oneself under the guidance of an experienced spiritual director. It is also most helpful, even for lay persons, to read a good treatise on ascetical theology. Such reading will serve to keep alive the desire for perfection; it will impart a certain knowledge concerning the nature of Christian life and the helpful aids to perfection; it will facilitate spiritual direction, giving a clearer understanding of those things which should be discussed in confession and in spiritual direction, and of how better to profit by the advice and counsels of the director; finally, it may even take the place of spiritual direction, in the event that a director could not be had or only rarely so. Among the better manuals of ascetical theology the following may be mentioned: A. Tanquerey, *The Spiritual Life*, and Garrigou-Lagrange, *The Three Ages of the Interior Life*. Man.

ASH WEDNESDAY. *See* Lent.

ASPERGILLUM. *See* Vessels, Sacred.

ASSERTORY OATH. *See* Oath.

ASSISTANCE (public and private). Private assistance, usually called charity, in a more precise sense is the sum total of charitable works directed to the alleviation of indigence and the suppression of its cause. Public assistance is the sum total of services and agencies organized for the relief and assistance to needy persons, orphans, infants, under-privileged and abandoned children, the sick, the mentally ill, the aged. The function of public assistance, with its method of organization, is to supplement the insufficiency of private assistance. Both public and private assistance were introduced and developed almost exclusively by the Church on the strength of the new order inaugurated by Christ Himself. To the Church, therefore, and the monastic orders and institutions the world owes the foundation of hospitals, leprosaria, asylums, *etc.* It was only in the sixteenth century, but more so in the eighteenth, that public authority began to show interest in extending assistance to the needy.

Assistance finds its true inspiration in a constitutive element of human nature called altruism. Love is a force that moves toward others; it is a movement of expansiveness and of giving. In the life of a Christian soul, altruism is supernaturalized and becomes the virtue of charity. Assistance, of course, may also be motivated by other factors, such as vanity, self-interest, and other egoistical motives. For some, the reason for bettering the economic conditions of the people may be to avoid unrest, strife, and political crises. For others, assistance may be an occasion for mere pastime. While it cannot be denied that even actions prompted by selfish motives may contribute to the relief of suffering humanity, yet such motives are responsible for the many prejudices against charity which should be the sole animating spirit behind all forms of assistance.

For a Christian living the life of grace, charity is an element that goes together with his supernatural life. This is proven by the great number of persons dedicated to works of charity, both in the religious and lay state. Charity is not limited to supernatural good, but it extends also to material well-being, to the health and prosperity of the individual, the family and society. Christ gave ample proof of this through His miracles and teachings.

In the final judgment one's moral worth will rest essentially on charity; the parable of the Good Samaritan is permeated with the sweet essence of charity. The Apostles and the Church taught and practiced charity so consistently that it became the distinguishing mark of Christians.

The forms of assistance are manifold. According to St. Paul charity is ingenious, but its more common forms consist in providing (a) relief for the poor; (b) shelter or housing for the homeless, a highly effective form of aid; (c) employment, a highly recommended form of charity; (d) hospital and medical care for the sick, the abandoned, the aged. The best form of assistance of course, is that which combines material aid with moral comfort.

Today, the principal motive for assistance is no longer the precept of charity, nor the philanthropic ideas characteristic of the eighteenth century, but the less noble, though quite effective, concept which proclaims the interdependence of all as members of one and the same social body. Common law bases the giving of public aid on the prinicple that it must be furnished by the community principally by the family, or the municipality. Many cases and forms of relief however, cannot be handled on the city or county or municipal level, principally because of limited resources. Such cases require state or federal intervention (mental hospitals, foundling institutes *etc.*, are often state institutions). The principal forms of public aid are: (a) provisional assistance for children whose parents are hospitalized, imprisoned *etc.*; (b) permanent aid for abandoned children; (c) medical aid for sick persons without financial resources; (d) aid for the mentally ill, the aged, the incurable (e) aid for expectant mothers, especially if unwed. During and after the last war many relief agencies were established for the needy and destitute victims of the war. Examples of the latter are: The Pontifical Relief Commission, the United Nations Relief and Rehabilitation Administration (UNRRA), the Bishops Relief Fund, *etc.*, which distributed and still distribute articles of food, clothing, and medicine to thousands of war victims, refugees, displaced persons, *etc.*

The state or government, whose end is the common good, has the duty to alleviate poverty and want. Public assistance, however, is not intended to substitute or eliminate private assistance, for the state cannot prevent anyone from performing charity. Generally speaking, the state is expected to provide relief measures for social ills, while private aid is intended to relieve individual need. Both forms of relief have their advantages and defects. Public aid, while having more resources at its disposal, is also more formal, cold, and impersonal. Private assistance is more discreet, effective, sympathetic, both on the part of the donor and of the receiver. At all events, public and private assistance are not to interfere with each other, but integrate their work on behalf of the needy. *Per.*

ASSOCIATION (right of). The right of association or organization refers to man's prerogative of joining his efforts with those of others for the purpose of attaining, in a systematic and consistent manner, a common, licit and honest end. The right of association is a legitimate expression of the human personality. Man is a social being with a tendency to satisfy all his fundamental needs within the sphere of two indispensable societies: the family and the state. But this natural tendency impels man to seek progress and development in all spheres of activity; hence, there is a large variety of associations. The right of association is a natural right which belongs to each individual, but sometimes the state may contest such a right. The doctrine governing the relations between the state and its citizens rests on two seemingly contrary principles: (a) every society, including the state, exists only for the good of the individual; (b) the individual is subject to society; his particular good is subordinated to the welfare of the community, with each individual subject to civil authority. The first of these principles finds its basis in the nature of man. Each man, and only

man (not society), is created to the image and likeness of God; he is a distinct personality and is immortal. Society is merely a means toward the ultimate end, and a means can never be higher than the end. As a social being, man is not self-sufficient, but has a natural need for others. Hence, society is a necessary means by which man may attain his own perfection and end.

Against certain sociological exaggerations, we state that man has an absolute, personal destiny and that society is a necessary means for the attainment of man's end. Man's rights derive from nature. Nevertheless, living in society as he does, man must logically respect the inevitable conditions which flow from the life of a community. Order demands that the individual welfare be subordinated to the welfare of the community, but only in matters deemed necessary for the realization of the end of society. Thus understood, the apparent contradiction between the two aforementioned principles disappears: men unite, submit to social authority, and collaborate for the public welfare so as to perfect themselves and prepare for the universal and final order of eternity.

The right of association is prior to any concept of a state. It is prior to the state itself, which owes its origin to this very right. It is the source of every higher form of civilization. Actually, in the current constitutions of all progressive states the right of association, though perhaps not everywhere safeguarded, is definitely established as a fundamental right. Consequently, the state is not the absolute sovereign over the citizens' right of association. The state may not suppress or restrict this right, but undoubtedly it has the power to regulate its exercise, so as to avoid abuses, prevent organizations detrimental to the common good, and promote useful associations. In point of fact, any organization may contain elements contrary to the interests of others. Thus, for instance, economic associations are also group interests. Despite assertions concerning the "natural" harmony of the interests of all, experience shows that the aims and interests of organizations are frequently in conflict with public interest, monopolies, *etc.;* hence, the need for regulations and restrictions on the part of the state.

Man's life unfolds within a number of societies, some of them necessary, others free. (a) The necessary and indispensable societies are: the family, civil society, and the Church. The family, the primary cell and model of every community, is that within which man receives life and education. The rights of the family extend to all essential aims of the family (*q.v.*). The state must respect the principle of the supplementary function of social activity. Individuals do not lose their individuality with its respective duties and rights by associating with others or by being citizens of the state. It is an inalienable right of every citizen to belong to the Church, to profess his religion, to teach and propagate religious truths. (b) The free associations are professional, social, political, national, scientific, artistic, athletic, economic, religious, *etc.* Of special importance are political associations or parties, because of their great influence in forming public opinion, professional organizations for the promotion of socio-economic life (right of coalition), and religious associations of religious formation. Free associations having a legitimate purpose possess natural rights. Associations are free and lawful if they (a) favor the common good; (b) are not opposed, directly or indirectly, intentionally or accidentally, to the well-being of the state and the family. *Per.*

ASSOCIATIONS, PIOUS.

Book II, part III, title XVIII of the Code of Canon Law deals with associations of the faithful. Traces of pious associations are found in the earliest days of the Church. The first Christian community residing at Jerusalem in Apostolic days constitutes a wonderful example of such associations. During the era of persecutions the Christians were compelled as a measure of defense to organize themselves into a juridical personality. Thus, there arose among them corporations of grave-diggers (*collegia fossorum*), charged with the task of burying the dead. In the East, about the fourth century, there appeared in Constantinople certain associations (*asceteria*) organized for the purpose of caring for burials, while at the same time there arose in Athens the *Parabolani*, a brotherhood whose members took care of the sick. In the West during the Carolingian age, unions of both clergy and laity were formed, later called guilds (*Gildoniae* or *Gildae*), whose main concern was the performing of religious works. But more definite and direct traces of present-day confraternities are found in the associations of prayer formed during the course of the sixth century, called *fraternitates, societates* (fraternities, societies), *consortia, societates fraternae* (sodalities, fraternal societies). The aim of such organizations was to provide their members, both in this life and especially after death, with spiritual benefits by prayers, Masses, and works of mercy. Similar associations were organized among the clergy of the same city or of the same diocese. A marble inscription in the Church of St. Cosmas and Damian in Rome refers to one such association in which certain priests had pledged themselves to celebrate forty Masses and engage in pious works for the souls of their departed brethren. This association was continued during the entire Middle Ages and it rose to such importance that it exercised, according to some, a certain jurisdiction over the Roman clergy. According to Armellini, traces of this association exist even in our day. In the ninth and tenth centuries there appeared the so-called *confratiae—associations* which very closely resemble, and hence may be regarded as the direct precursors of, our present-day confraternities. Such associations were, for many centuries, recognized both by the Church and the civil authority; their juridical status was questioned and threatened by the royalists of the seventeenth and eighteenth centuries.

Associations of the faithful are governed by certain general norms, among which are to be noted the following: (a) They must be erected or at least approved by the competent ecclesiastical authority. (b) They are not to take names which savor of levity or unbecoming novelty, or names of a devotion not approved by the Holy See (Can. 688); preferably, they are to be named after the various attributes of God, the mysteries of the Christian religion, the feasts of our Lord or the Blessed Virgin, or the saints, or finally, the pious works of the society itself (Can. 710). (c) The statutes of all such associations must be approved either by the Holy See or by the local Ordinary (Can. 689, par. 1). (d) More than one society having the same title and aim may not be organized in the same place (village, town, city), except by special indult or by disposition of the law. In the larger cities, however, it can be done with due permission of the local Ordinary. (Can. 711, par. 1). (e) Non-Catholics and public sinners in general (see below) may not be validly accepted for membership into pious associations (Can. 693, par. 1). (f) Only those who are fully competent and willingly request it may be accepted as members. (g) No legitimately enrolled member may be dismissed from the association, unless it be done for a just reason and in accordance with the statutes (Can. 696).

Pious associations of the faithful are divided into: *Third Orders secular* (see Third Order), *Confraternities* (see Confraternity) and *Sodalities* or *pious unions* (see Pious Union). *De A.*

According to Canon Law, the purpose of pious associations is to promote personal sanctification among the members (see Third Order), to promote works of piety and charity (see Pious Union), to increase public worship (see Confraternity), and to foster Catholic teachings in the individual, the family, and society (see Catholic Action).

No pious association is recognized in the Church unless erected or at least approved by the competent ecclesiastical authority. The right to erect religious associations is canonically vested in the Roman Pontiff and in the local Ordinaries. Neither the vicar general of a diocese nor the vicar capitular of a vacant see may, of themselves, give approval for the erection of associations (Can. 686, par. 4). Once established and approved by the Church, a pious association acquires the right of a legal person (Can. 687); nevertheless, it always remains under the jurisdiction and vigilance of the local Ordinary (Can. 690), not only in regard to the administration of temporal goods, such as funds, offerings, donations, *etc.*, an account of which must be rendered annually, but also in regard to the appointment of the director or chaplain (Can. 698), and to matters pertaining to piety and worship.

Every pious association must bear a sacred name; names that are contrary to the Faith or of unbecoming novelty, or names of a devotion not approved by the Holy See, are forbidden (Can. 688). Each association shall have its statutes approved by the Holy See or by the local Ordinary (Can. 689); nor may these statutes be modified or amended without the approval of competent authority. Every legitimately erected association has the right to hold meetings and to elect its own officers after the manner laid down in Canon Law or in their approved statutes. Admission or enrollment in a pious association is to be without charge (Can. 695), and must be conducted in accordance with its statutes (Can. 692).

To be validly enrolled in a pious association one must belong to the Catholic Church, must not be a member of a condemned sect, must be free of all public ecclesiastical censure, and not be a public sinner (Can. 693). Public sinners are those who lead openly scandalous lives, such as living in concubinage, constantly blaspheming, habitually violating the precepts of the Church.

To enjoy the rights, privileges, indulgences, and other spiritual favors of a pious association it is necessary and sufficient that a person has been validly received according to the proper statutes of the association and that he has not been legitimately expelled therefrom. According to common law, enrollment in a pious association does not entail the obligation to continue permanently as a member; hence, a member may withdraw from the association any time he wishes; the organization, in turn, has a right, upon good reason, to terminate his membership. Any ecclesiastical association may, for grave reasons, be suppressed by the local Ordinary. However, associations erected by the Apostolic See may be suppressed only by the Holy See (Can. 699). *Tar.*

ASSOCIATION WITH NON-CATHOLICS.

Association of Catholics with non-Catholics may exist either in civil matters or in religious matters or functions.

Association with non-Catholics in *civil affairs* is permitted so long as it does not constitute a danger to one's faith. Because of a danger to the faith, a Catholic may be forbidden to work for those not of the Catholic faith, to join certain societies or attend non-Catholic schools. Since debates and discussions on religious subjects with non-Catholics are fraught with many dangers, especially if they are public, they are forbidden without permission of the Holy See, or in urgent cases, of the local Ordinary (Can. 1325). According to a decision of the Holy See on June 5, 1948, this prohibition holds particularly for the so-called "Ecumenical" Congresses. Disputes or discussions that arise from circumstances and only casually, *e.g.*, with a travelling companion or at work or at social gatherings, are not forbidden. Neither are lectures or "Evidence Guild Talks" forbidden even though it is understood that any one present may heckle and raise objections. It is forbidden to participate in assemblies, unions, lectures and societies whose aim is the uniting of all Christians. The promotion of such projects is also forbidden (AAS 19–278).

Participation in *religious worship* takes place (a) when a Catholic takes part in non-Catholic services or functions, or (b) when he permits non-Catholics to participate in Catholic services. Participation of Catholics in non-Catholic services may mean that Catholics actually take part in the religious worship of non-Catholics

(active participation), or that they are only passively present at such religious functions (passive participation). *Active* participation of Catholics in non-Catholic services is entirely forbidden (Can. 1258). The natural law forbids participation in services that are heretical. If the service is one that heretics have in common with Catholics, even though no scandal were to come from such participation, it is at least forbidden by Church law. Therefore, it is forbidden to ask a heretic to baptize, or to be a sponsor for a non-Catholic (even by proxy). In general, it is unlawful to be best man or bridesmaid at a marriage performed by a non-Catholic minister, to receive Holy Communion from the hands of a schismatic priest. Some authors hold that in America it is considered only a sign of friendship to be selected as best man or bridesmaid at a non-Catholic wedding, not as officially witnessing the marriage contract. In danger of death it is lawful to ask a non-Catholic to administer a sacrament, provided that there is no Catholic present who can do so, and that no scandal is given. So, too, it is lawful, with the required dispensation for a mixed marriage, to allow a non-Catholic partner to administer the sacrament of matrimony to oneself and vice versa, but never before a non-Catholic minister. It is forbidden to sing, play the organ or other instrument at the religious services of non-Catholics. But it is not forbidden to pray or sing privately with heretics if the prayers or songs are not heretical and no scandal is given.

Whoever acts contrary to the prescriptions of Canon 1258 and takes part in non-Catholic services is suspected of heresy (Can. 2316).

Passive attendance at non-Catholic services is allowed for a good reason, *e.g.*, due to one's position or for politeness, provided that the danger of perversion is precluded (Can. 1258). Passive assistance implies that no part is taken in praying, singing, *etc.* Under these restrictions, it is permissible to attend a heretical baptism, marriage, or funeral service conducted in a non-Catholic church. It is sometimes lawful to attend a non-Catholic service through mere curiosity, if the sect has long been established in the area. A servant may also accompany his or her employers to a non-Catholic service if asked to do so. Soldiers and prisoners may attend such services if commanded to do so for the sake of order, but not *in odium fidei*. Attending the sermons of non-Catholic ministers may often be forbidden because of scandal or danger to the faith; this prohibition holds true also for listening to such sermons on the radio, especially if done often.

A Catholic may not assist at the attempted marriage of a Catholic before a non-Catholic minister since this would imply a contempt for the Church's regulation and would be a source of scandal. One doing so, however, would not be "cooperating" in a manner by which he would incur the excommunication mentioned in Canon 2231. Concerning the sin of cooperation by Catholics in non-Catholic worship, the following may be stated: A servant may accompany his master to a Protestant service if doing so will not be interpreted as membership in the sect; to sing or pray in non-Catholic services is wrong because it is a participation in an illicit form of worship. Sisters in a hospital may not summon a non-Catholic minister for a non-Catholic dying patient to assist him in death. For a very serious reason (*e.g.*, public) they may inform the minister that a patient desires to see him. It seems lawful for them even to prepare a little table for the minister's use in religious ministrations. An architect may design churches for Protestants and synagogues for Jews for some very good reason: a lesser reason justifies the ordinary laborer's work on such buildings. In both cases, however, the supposition is that the heresy has long been practiced unmolested in that particular locality. It is lawful to sell pews, tables, carpets, lights, *etc.*, to non-Catholics for their churches (if otherwise one would lose the profit); a greater reason is required to sell works of art to non-Catholic churches since these serve to enhance their divine serv-

ices and induce others to join the sect or remain in it. Catholic congressmen and other lawmakers may vote public funds for the erection of a Protestant church if it be in the interest of religious harmony. So, too, may private individuals for the sake of public peace among religious bodies attend bazaars, concerts, purchase chances, *etc.*, in benefits conducted by Protestants for the building of a church, if the Protestants have extended the same courtesy to Catholics. Ringing of bells in non-Catholic churches, and giving notice of their services in the newspapers is looked upon by many authors as merely indicating the time of their services, and can be justified for any relatively grave reason.

Concerning donations for the building and maintenance of non-Catholic schools and orphanages, this is the principle to be followed: since the main purpose of such institutions is instruction and the exercise of charity, one may contribute money toward such projects in mixed localities, provided that no scandal result therefrom and the institutions will not be used for proselytizing.

Participation of non-Catholics in Catholic worship may also be active and passive. Active participation of non-Catholics in Catholic services is forbidden insofar as it would give the impression that there is no essential difference between the Catholic and non-Catholic faiths or inasmuch as it promotes indifferentism. Protestants may not be sponsors at a Catholic baptism. Insofar as they belong to a sect they cannot perform this office validly (Can. 756). For a grave reason and if no scandal is given, they may, with the permission of the Ordinary, be witnesses at a Catholic marriage. Concerning the administration of the sacraments to dying non-Catholics who are in good faith, this is the general rule: heretics and schismatics who are in danger of death may be absolved conditionally if they are in good faith and cannot be convinced of their error. Scandal must always be avoided as far as possible. The same rule applies to an unconscious non-Catholic. The priest attending a dying non-Catholic should try to induce him to make an act of perfect contrition, after trying to awaken in him sentiments of faith, hope, and charity. Absolution is given him without his noticing it. Passive attendance of non-Catholics at Catholic services is allowed, and non-Catholics may be invited to hear sermons.

Non-Catholics may not be given sacramentals publicly. Thus, blessed candles on the Feast of Purification, ashes on Ash Wednesday, and palms on Palm Sunday may not be given to them. It is not forbidden to give them holy water, blessed medals, or to bless them privately so that non-Catholics may receive the light of faith as well as health of body (Can. 1149). They may not carry candles in liturgical functions, alternate at choir prayers, or participate in liturgical singing. For special reasons the Holy Office has allowed schismatic girls to sing with Catholic girls at liturgical functions. If no Catholic organist is available, a non-Catholic may play the organ for a time, provided that scandal is removed. A priest may not act as minister and accompany the corpse of a heretic to the grave. For a good reason and apart from scandal he may accompany the corpse as a private person and lead some prayers at the graveside. H.J.Y.

ASSOCIATIVE ATAXIA. *See* Schizophrenia.

ASSOCIATIVE SPHERES. *See* Cerebral Function.

ASTROLOGY. Astrology (from the Greek word *astrologia*) is the study or science of the stars. Until the first centuries of Christianity the term was employed indiscriminately to signify both astronomy and the art of discovering the various influences of the stars on the earth and its inhabitants. Gradually, the second meaning prevailed and, to avoid all ambiguity, the term *judiciary astrology* was adopted, meaning thereby the science of astral influence and related norms for the prediction of events and the discovery of man's fate, by the study of "judgments" made by heavenly bodies concerning things here below.

Astrology originated in Babylonia (or Chaldea), where professional astrologers were priests who engaged in developing and perfecting their understanding of celestial phenomena, and who formulated astrological predictions on the basis of their excellent astronomical and meteorological observations.

In the sixth and seventh centuries B.C., the teachings and practice of astrology spread among the Persians, Indians and Chinese. Subsequently, it also spread among the Greeks, who brought it to Rome at the time of the Punic Wars through their slaves. Because of their versatility in the practice of this Mesopotamian art, the Greek slaves were called Chaldeans. Although their art was generally crude and rudimentary, it made a profound impression on the simple minds of the plebeian element, gradually gaining the favor of the aristocracy and, eventually, of many of the emperors.

The pagan Roman priests (who practiced their own form of divination by examining the entrails of animals as well as the rising smoke from the altar on which the victims were sacrificed as burnt offerings) vigorously opposed the rival astrologers. As a result of this and with the decline of the empire, the study and practice of astrology underwent a gradual and steady deterioration. About the eighth century A.D., however, with the increasing influence of Arabic learning and the subsequent spread of Islamic culture throughout Europe, the science of astrology took on renewed vigor. In fact, Arabic scholars, zealous propagators of Greco-Oriental culture in the West and experts in both astronomy and astrology, had worked out a system whereby astrology was intimately incorporated into the other disciplines, with the result that astrology was favorably adopted by Western students along with algebra, medicine, and other branches of Arabic teachings. Indeed, astrology, which had even been taught in several European universities, between the years 1200-1600 (Cecco d'Ascoli, condemned at Florence in 1327 for astrological heresy, had occupied the chair of astrology at Bologna), was for many centuries cultivated by many scholars of note, including Marsilius Ficino, Kepler, and Galileo.

In the eighteenth century, with the introduction and acceptance of the experimental method, astrology fell into a rapid decline; and, despite isolated attempts at revival by certain "followers of the occult sciences," it may be safely stated that as the art or science of drawing a horoscope (*q.v.*), astrology became practically extinct. Popular, instead, is that which could be described as the smokescreen of charlatans who, without any skill and without any scientific pretence, avail themselves of some astrological symbols and a few phrases with which they deceive their patrons, mostly women, who turn to them for the purpose of knowing the outcome of some personal adventure or entanglement.

For the technical workings of astrology, *see* Horoscope; for its ethicoreligious implications, *see* Divination. Here it shall be briefly noted that, even from a scientific standpoint, judiciary astrology has no reason to exist; in other words, neither astrological fatalism, which maintains that every human action is definitely and strictly linked to the variable position of the stars, nor the theory holding that the stars simply determine the character and tendencies of the individual without exerting any particular and definite influence on the exercise of their free will, has any scientific basis.

It will suffice to point out that the complicated calculations of classical astrology were based on the particular position, at the moment of a person's birth, of the seven "planets" (the moon, Mercury, Venus, the sun, Mars, Jupiter, and Saturn) in relation to the constellations of the Zodiac; whereas the modern discovery of two other planets (Uranus, in 1781, and Neptune in 1846) has introduced a veritable confusion or disarrangement in the old astrological schemes. Nor shall we omit mentioning the errors committed by astrologists by their neglect of the precession of the equinoxes; an element which has eliminated the coincidence between the constellations of the Zodiac and the months of the year. Thus, in view of these and other very sound scientific reasons, the astronomer Keiny stated that if ancient humanity had possessed modern astronomical knowledge, no astrology would have ever arisen.

Moreover, mention might be made of the fact that the destinies and vicissitudes of twins are frequently found to differ considerably in actual life; also, of other individuals having the same birthday and born in the same locality—all of which is contrary to astrological norms and predictions, according to which twins, as well as others having similar birthdays, should have similar destinies or, at least, similar tendencies and inclinations. *Riz.*

ASTUTENESS. *See* Fraud, Deception, Prudence.

ASYLUM (Right of). The word *asylum* is derived from the Greek *asylon* meaning a place offering immunity from violence or from forcible seizure. The right of asylum (or of sanctuary) orginates in the respect and reverence due to churches and holy places. Asylum was a privilege enjoyed by debtors and criminals seeking refuge in a church from which they could not be forcibly taken without committing sacrilege or violating the sacred place. Even the ancient Greek and Roman temples, altars, statues of the gods and sacred forests were regarded as places of safety and asylum. The altar of the ancient Jewish temple constituted a refuge for those who had committed involuntary or unpremeditated murder. The right of asylum in the churches is an ecclesiastical institution, arising from the spirit of clemency and charity as embodied in the Church.

The reason by which the privilege of asylum is attached to sacred places is a matter of controversy. It would seem that the privilege is of divine right, insofar as the fundamental basis of the right of asylum is the respect and reverence due to sacred places. This concept, of course, excludes any violation of such places, even in the case of criminals seeking refuge therein. But insofar as the privilege of asylum sanctions the impunity of criminals and insofar as it was subject, in the course of history, to many variations regarding place, crime, and person, it is of ecclesiastical law, with the approval and the sanction of civil law.

Following the triumph of Christianity, from the fourth century on, the right of asylum was exercised in a rather broad manner. Limited at first only to the church itself, it was later extended to about fifty feet from the church doors, then gradually to the cloister and to the residences of cardinals, bishops, princes, and ambassadors, thus extending even into the lay sphere. Such exaggerated extension of the right of asylum inevitably led to many abuses and public disorders. As a result, the right of sanctuary became in time subject to numerous restrictions and limitations, even in pontifical institutions. In many regions, as in Italy (Siccardi Law, April 9, 1850), the right was, for various reasons and also through concordats, abolished in point of fact. We say "in point of fact," because authors continue to teach that the right as such exists and that all are bound to respect it.

Despite the fact that a contrary custom may abolish the right of asylum in regard to the human norms therein involved, the position of the Holy See is that such a right can never be abolished altogether. The Decree of the Holy Office, December 22, 1880, established that the law of asylum, at least in substance, should be observed in those regions where, for some time, it had fallen into disregard. In pre-code Canon Law the constitution *Apostolicae Sedis* threatened with excommunication reserved to the Holy See all those who dared to violate the right of ecclesiastical asylum or ordered others to do so. This excommunication was abrogated by the present Code.

Canon 1179 states: "The church enjoys the right of asylum, so that any fugitive from justice fleeing into it may not, except in case of urgent necessity, be taken out of it without permission of the Ordinary or at least of the rector of the church." The present Code, therefore, admits the right of asylum, but in a very mitigated form. In point of fact, all persons may be taken from the church, the one formality being that permission of the proper ecclesiastical authority be obtained. This canon has been the basis of several concordats, in which this very mitigated form of the right of asylum is sustained even today. Thus, the Lateran Treaty, under article 9, requires, except in cases of necessity, permission of the Ordinary, or at least of the rector of the church, for the extradition of a supposed criminal. Urgent necessity is present when, before permission is obtained, the criminal may escape or where the rector is not available for the required permission; no distinction is made concerning the type of crime. *Pal.*

ASYLUM, INSANE. *See* Hospital; Psychiatry; Psychosis.

ASYMBOLIA. *See* Cerebral Function.

ATHEISM. Atheism is the denial of the existence of God; and since God is the basis of the metaphysical postulate of the moral order, atheism also implies a denial of morality. To deny God is to deny the first cause and ultimate end of the moral order, hence, also the obligation to conform our conduct to the moral law (*see* Morality, Independent). Besides being a metaphysical postulate, the necessary relation between God and moral order is also an historical fact, for one of the functions most universally attributed to God (or to the gods) is that of watching over and sanctioning the observance of the moral precepts.

Moral theologians are concerned not so much with the metaphysical and historical aspects of the problem as with its psychological aspect, that is, whether, in practice, atheism is the cause or effect of immorality. They do not believe that this problem can be given a solution that would apply with certainty in all concrete cases, *i.e.*, a solution that would fit every individual person, much less to every human act. However, it is the common teaching of moralists that habitual observance of all moral duties is very difficult if not practically impossible for an atheist, and that immorality is one of the more common factors contributing to atheism. This teaching is based on the observation that the motives which prompt man to conform his conduct to the moral precepts are many; hence, even if an individual should lack the religious or theistic motive, he may eventually experience the effectiveness of other motives. But since the religious motive is one of the more effective ones as to its intensity, and one of the clearest from the standpoint of its universality, the atheist is exposed to the danger of lacking a sufficient motive to sustain him in the fulfillment of the more serious and more difficult ethical duties. Concerning atheism as an effect of immorality, it is to be noted that, while the existence of God is a definite truth, it does not possess, in relation to our weak intellect, such a degree of evidence as to exclude every practical possibility of denial. Moreover, the existence of God is one of those truths having necessary practical consequences, so that its acceptance or denial is largely influenced either by an honest or by a perverted will. *Gra.*

ATHYMIA. *See* Affectivity.

ATOMIC WARFARE. The problem concerning the morality of bombing non-military objectives has been made more difficult by the discovery of the atomic bomb. Heretofore in a just war the bombing of certain objectives was permissible if it meant eliminating enemy communications and resources (seaports, airports, railway stations, war plants, and other means contributing to the conduct of the war). But "blanket" or indiscriminate bombings for the purpose of destroying the morale of civilian populations was considered improper, insofar as civilian populations would thus become the main target of the bombing. Today, however, because of the enormous radius and effectiveness of the destructive power of modern atomic and nuclear weapons, the traditional distinction between direct and indirect results of bombing (and between combatant and non-combatant) is no longer valid. In fact, the devastating effects of atomic warfare are more comparable to gas warfare. All of which gives rise to the question as to whether the use of atomic weapons is intrinsically inhuman.

Even if the answer to the question of the intrinsic inhumanity of the use of atomic weapons were in the negative, there still remains the fatal danger of abuse of such devastating weapons. Specifically the problem is this: against which objectives may such weapons be employed? The problem is aggravated by the highly industrialized character of modern city areas and by increased civilian participation in the preparation and conduct of a war.

Under modern conditions of warfare the entire civilian population of a whole area could be destroyed by one atomic bomb aimed at destroying a single war plant. The disproportion in the results attained is all too glaring. Could one, for instance, justify the bombing of Detroit on the plea that the main and direct target is the industrial plant of the Ford Company? A realistic assessment of the facts in such an instance rules out the validity of such a distinction. Where ordinary bombs are used, there is always the possibility that non-combatants (even those close to the bombed area) may escape their devastating effects; and this has been true in many instances. But in the case of atomic bombing such possibility of escape is excluded, even for those at distances far removed from the center of the bombing. Hence, the use of atomic weapons should be restricted even more than that of ordinary bombs, and should be limited to exclusively and specifically military objectives.

In view of the general attitude of military leaders, to allow the use of atomic weapons could, at least in some cases, mean placing into the hands of one-sided and even unscrupulous men instruments of destruction capable of threatening the very existence of civilization. With feverish efforts being made on all sides to increase the stockpiles of atomic and nuclear weapons, and to develop their destructive potential, it is only natural and inevitable that in a future war these weapons would be used by both sides. One shudders even to think of the consequences. The logic of war would seem to be as follows: if the atomic bomb is the only means of defense for a country in the event of unjust attack, who is to prevent that country from using it when the unjust attack does actually occur? If it is truly a case of legitimate self-defense, why exclude beforehand the use of atomic weapons for the unjustly attacked nation? Of course, theoretically, all will promise and guarantee not to unleash atomic bombs except under certain conditions and within certain limits; but in practice events have a way of shaping their own course, and often a war reaches a point where anything goes, fair or foul. Thus, the only sane, moral and humane approach to this matter is to establish a system whereby all conflicts between nations are referred to a higher tribunal with effective power recognized by all countries of the world. The discovery of atomic weapons may still be a providential thing, in that it may open the eyes of world leaders everywhere to the absolute need, on the part of all, of excluding war as a method of solving differences or conflicts. Catholic thought on the subject of atomic weapons favors an international agreement that would ban any military use for all times (cf. Pius XII: Radio messages, Easter 1954 and 1955). *Boz.*

ATTENTION. DEFINITION. Attention is the direct focusing of the mind on a specific object. It is an act of the cognitive faculty, distinct from intention, which is an act of the will. It admits of various degrees depending on the intensity with which the mind is focused on the object. At its lowest point attention is confused with simple advertence; at its maximal point it may be called con-

centration. Lack of attention is called distraction.

MORAL VALUE. Attention is one of the requisites for the proper performance of religious acts such as prayer, the administration and reception of the sacraments, *etc.* To judge the value of acts performed without attention or in a state of distraction, it is necessary to distinguish the different aspects of the acts themselves. For the validity of the act (whenever the question can be raised) attention is not required; hence a sacrament may be validly administered and received even by an individual lacking the proper attention; the obligation to recite a given prayer is satisfied even if recited with distraction. To judge the propriety of acts performed distractedly, and the extent of imputability as a result of the accompanying distractions, one must take into account the degree of willfulness connected with the distractions. In order to estimate the moral and religious worth of the act, the concepts regarding merit, impetration, and internal fervor must be considered separately: merit and impetration may, in a limited measure, coexist with distraction; but actual fervor does not. *Gra.*

ANALYSIS OF THE ATTENTIVE PROCESS. Of the many representations which constitute the field of perception or "field of consciousness" only one (or a few) enter the "focus of consciousness" through which it acquires clarity and distinction.

While it is true that at every single moment the conscious individual adverts, in a more or less confused manner, to a variety of sensations, perceptions, images, ideas (the field of consciousness), yet these phenomena do not all possess equal intensity and vividness, nor do they follow each other with equal rapidity; some emerge into the spotlight of consciousness for a few lingering moments, others pass by hurriedly and indistinctly, almost ignored by the mind. In other words, there are always many representations competing for the individual's attention, but only one succeeds in catching the mind's eye. To borrow a term from the field of physical optics, this selectivity of one representation over the others is described as "entering or being brought into the focus of consciousness," which is precisely the function of attention.

TYPES OF ATTENTION. Attention may be *spontaneous* or involuntary, and *reflective* or voluntary. Spontaneous attention is initiated by the presence, within the perceptive field, of certain objects which stimulate or interest individual tendencies (*e.g.*, a person, walking along the street, is suddenly attracted by the sight of some object which so interests him as to arrest and divert the the course of his thoughts, while other stimuli leave him indifferent). This form of attention is mainly affective in character and requires no voluntary effort; in fact, it is so effortless that many times we have to call upon an act of the will to arrest it. Reflective attention always requires a more or less considerable effort. This kind of attention is initiated by the effort of the individual himself rather than by the attractiveness of the object, although the greater or lesser interest that the object arouses in the individual does favor the attentive process which is thereby intensified and prolonged.

Attention is also *internal* (rational, mental), if directed toward a representative content, and *external*, if directed toward a perceptive content. The latter may be subdivided into *sensorial* (visual, auditory, gustatory, *etc.*) and *motor*: this type of attention is manifested as a special state of expectancy or attitude of readiness for action or as a mental anticipation of a forthcoming action (as in the case of the athlete waiting for the "go" signal); it is characterized by an increased muscular tension, particularly in those muscles required for the particular action so that the response may be quick and effective. This type of attention may be called *expectant* attention, which is always conspicuously noticeable, but of brief duration; on the contrary, *distributed* attention (such as manifested by persons watching a performance or contest) is less intense, but much more lasting. To the latter, one

may also oppose *concentrated* attention, whose effectiveness or results bear a direct relation to the degree of concentration.

These various distinctions have a characteristically Scholastic savor. In reality, attention is one total process, in which the sensorimotor and mental components exist and function concomitantly, although each time at different levels; so, too, the spontaneous and voluntary phases are found to be concurrent and almost alternating in every attentive process. Moreover, as repeatedly demonstrated by experimental psychology, attention is constantly subject to notable oscillations and fluctuations, insofar as these concern the duration as well as the clarity and intensity of its process.

PATHOLOGY OF ATTENTION: The process of attention may be disturbed by different factors. It has already been established that in normal persons attention becomes sharper by reason of a conspicuous interest, while fatigue and disinterest dull it and weaken it. In this connection, it will not be amiss to note a fact too often overlooked by teachers and speakers: *i.e.*, that "attentional duration" (period of sustained interest) is not too long; it oscillates to about ten minutes in infants, twenty in children, twenty-five in adolescents, and thirty-five in individuals over eighteen years of age. It is further to be noted that "distracted" and "inattentive" are not exactly synonymous terms; the inattentive individual, perhaps because annoyed or tired, does not pay attention to anything, whereas the distracted person directs his attention to some other object of interest, to the neglect of everything else. Intense emotions—again in normal individuals—tend to increase or heighten attention, but at the same time also to circumscribe it, by polarizing attention to a particular set of ideas, thus obstructing it from becoming fixed on other ideas.

The most serious distrubances of the attentive process are caused by mental diseases. In cases of arrested or retarded mental development (phrenasthenia), and in cases of organic mental disorder, attention is very weak and inconstant. The greatest loss of attentive ability is observed in the confusional states, in which the patient's mind, due to the cessation of or a notable reduction of the powers of association and of integration of the various associations, is more or less completely detached from the outside world.

In other forms of mental illnesses, and in certain paranoidal syndromes, attention becomes noticeably sharp, especially during interrogations and other particular situations; this is due to the patient's diffidence, which renders him excessively vigilant and suspicious.

Neurasthenics and, in general, many psychoneurotics are found to complain of excessive weakening or loss of attention, whereas in reality they are merely suffering from distractibility due to polarization of the attentive power toward a particular set of ideas which constitute the morbid nucleus of all their interests.

Finally, in hysteria, an excessive and persistent reduction of the field of consciousness may be observed; as a result, the patient for a long period focuses his mind on a single sensory or representative nucleus and, consequently, is unable to advert to any other stimulus. This peculiar behavior of the attentive faculty explains, for the most part, the various types of insensibility and other functional disorders which characterize the hysterical syndrome.

Disturbances of attention hardly ever occur as isolated manifestations, but they constitute an element, at times even a fundamental element, of various psychopathic syndromes; hence, the ethical problems involved in disturbances of attention are better treated when dealing with the various syndromes with which these disturbances are connected.

MORALITY. Here it might be noted that, from a pedagogical standpoint, the attentive process in general needs disciplining, while spontaneous attention, in particular, needs at times to be mortified. Concerning spontaneous or passive attention, it will be helpful to bear in mind that when the attention is directed to images, objects, or ideas of a sinful content, it already constitutes, as a rule, an element of sin and may even give rise to graver sins; this is not so, however, when the attention remains within the limits or sphere of an *actus primus*, solicitously inhibited by the will. Neither is there any question of guilt in those cases of psychoneurosis (*see* Psychasthenia) in which the patient is involuntarily—sometimes even after painful resistance—drawn by a nucleus of obsessive ideas to polarize or center his attention on lewd, indecent, sacrilegious images or representations. The combined efforts of a prudent confessor and a wise physician may help to settle the grave disturbances of conscience in such individuals and may also help to cure, or at least to reduce, the morbid symptoms (*see also* Psychotherapy). *Riz.*

ATTITUDES (SEX). Some questionable attitudes concerning sex revolve around the following points: (a) continence is impossible; (b) continence is injurious to health; (c) sex instruction to youth is beneficial; (d) sex is everything.

Concerning the alleged impossibility of continence and physical and psychological evil effects to the individual who practices continence, we refer the reader to the article on Abstinence and Continence. It is a fact that numerous young persons keep themselves chaste without damage either to health or working efficiency, and without harmful repercussions on future marriage. On the contrary, a premature decline of vital energies, with resulting impotency and serious marital difficulties and psychosomatic disturbances, are often due to a lustful and libertine life; the danger of venereal diseases which inevitably spread from wife to husband or *vice versa*, affect fertility and the well-being of their offspring.

Concerning the advisability of the so-called *sex education*, see the article under the same title.

Finally, with respect to the modern concept of pan-sexualism, according to which humanity is believed to be always and only—or at least prevalently—guided by sex in its many manifestations and sublimations, it is clear that such pansexualism is more the result of doctrinaire preconceptions than of proven realities, despite a kind of scientific seal of approval of Freud and various other scientists. The irrationality of efforts to reduce to sex and sexuality all human manifestations, ideals, plans and actions characterizing man's life, appears in clearer focus as days go by.

The misconceived equality of the sexes, according to which no difference exists between man and woman insofar as life, activity, work, customs, and the like, are concerned, is becoming increasingly more widespread.

Such equality is purely utopian, for it has no biological basis and only tends to give a woman a dangerous economic and social freedom; in fact, after having attained such benefits, she is forever solicitous in extolling the virtues of her belonging to the weaker sex and her special conditions as mother or as pregnant woman.

Christian morality, proud of having given woman a hiterto unknown dignity and prestige, cannot but reprove the modern equalitarian spirit that deforms the female personality and deeply threatens domestic life, in defiance of biological laws. These laws, among other things, teach that the man has the responsibility of providing for and protecting the family while the woman shall attend to the rearing of offspring.

Anatomy shows that everything is different between the organism of man and that of woman, skeletal dimensions, weight and muscular development, endocrine glandular pleiads, and intellective-affective sphere. Psychology, in turn, points out the profound functional differences existing in the various systems and apparatus of the two sexes; hence, among others, the quantitative differences concerning capacity and resistance for work.

Modern scholars in the field of heredity warn that the woman (not the man) transmits to her offspring the good qualities as well as the defects proper to her race, and that she is the real preserver

and disseminator of the health of the family stock to which she belongs. *Riz.*

ATTORNEY. *See* Advocate.

ATTRITION. *See* Contrition.

AUCTION SALE. An auction may be defined as a public sale of goods by the method of bidding, with each object or article going to the highest bidder. If the auction is arranged by free consent of the owner or the seller, it is said to be voluntary; if it is imposed by law or by decree of a judge or public authority, it is called judiciary or compulsory.

In auctions the owner or seller may not substitute an article of a lower price for the one placed on sale, nor run up the price by inserting fictitious bidders among the buyers. In the case of a forced auction, however, the seller himself may be a bidder or even request his friends to bid for him in order to prevent the article or goods from being sold at a ludicrous price. On the other hand, a buyer or bidder may not resort to violence, fraud, or bribe to hinder others from bidding; he may, however, ask other buyers to refrain from bidding, or even make an agreement with them to this effect. In fact, moralists hold that, if the buyer's intent is to redress an unjust vexation, he may even offer money to other buyers, so that they may desist from bidding. Finally, the person conducting the auction sale, *i.e.*, the auctioneer, may not favor one bidder over another nor may he conduct the sale in any manner detrimental to the owner or to the seller. *Fel.*

AUDACITY. Audacity is an unusual effort to attain a very difficult goal, good or bad. There is a daring that remains within the proper limits of moderation; but there is also an excessive form that leads to exposing oneself to danger to a greater degree than is necessary, or in circumstances or at times where one should not do so. Such inordinate daring, also called *temerity*, stems from the fact that one does not fear what he ought to fear, or does not fear enough, or does not fear when and where he should. This lack of fear may be due to pride, inconsideration, levity of character, or even to undervaluation of one's life.

Moderate audacity is not reprehensible but rather praiseworthy if the end in view is good; however, if the end in view is evil, then it becomes sinful, and the degree of culpability depends on the nature of the end intended. Inordinate audacity, even though the end in view be good, is a sin by excess against the virtue of fortitude; it is a mortal sin if it constitutes, either for oneself or for others, a grave danger of committing a serious evil that by reason of justice or charity should be avoided, or if it causes such an evil absolutely. Inordinate audacity with an evil end in view is sinful by reason of its very object and by reason of its immoderation. *Man.*

AUDITOR. *See* Judge.

AURA (Epileptic). *See* Epilepsy.

AUTARCHY. In a sense, autarchy is the economic policy which aims at insuring the absolute self-sufficiency of a country, thereby eliminating all need for international trade. Thus defined, the system of autarchy may still be found among some primitive tribes, but as a deliberate act of a political system it cannot exist, because international trade and exchange are necessary postulates of modern civilization, which, by reason of many material and spiritual factors, is essentially supranational.

As a political act in actual practice, autarchy pursues merely a relative autonomy, that is, an autonomy whose limits are designated more by politico-military than technico-economic factors. Its aim is, not to eliminate all international trade, but simply to exclude the importation of basic food products, primary materials essential for civil industry or military preparedness, so as to give the nation a greater degree of political autonomy. Hence the autarchic system may be considered as an alternative pursued by great continental countries (without waterway outlets) as against the policies pursued for a long time by the great world powers. This variation, needless to say, is better suited to the needs of an historical period that no longer exists. A modern war would involve the engagement of such enormous and diversified energies that no country could presume to rely on its own strength and resources alone. For this reason autarchy is no longer possible within the sphere of a single State, but necessarily requires a group or bloc of States, and it is precisely within this vaster orbit of nations that autarchy tends to manifest itself today.

Entirely different from autarchy, though employing similar methods, is economic nationalism, which in its most recent manifestations is characterized by a political tendency to develop and exploit the entire resources of a country, so as to insure the full use of all national resources and labor power. The aim of economic nationalism is essentially economic (the increase of national and per capita revenue), while the goal of autarchy is essentially political (the increase of politico-military autonomy).

It has been suggested that autarchy might be a means of giving capitalism a moral conscience. It is true that the myth of autarchy, in its drive to promote national interest, limits the speed of gain and profit and directs all efforts toward a higher goal than mere individual satisfaction. But in the process it leads to an opposite derailment of spirit that is very damaging to the human person, to social progress and international harmony. Autarchy is inspired by nationalism and by a psychosis of insecurity on the international level; it is a solution dictated by discouragement, quasi-despair and impotence, opening the way to all sorts of disasters and leading to inevitable deterioration of civilization and international amity. *Maj.*

AUTHORITY. Definition. Legal or rightful power to act or to command is called authority. It also indicates the organ entrusted with power, or a person, a board or a commission, having jurisdiction in a particular field or exercising a public function.

NECESSITY OF AUTHORITY. A multiplicity of functions and activities, a converging of efforts toward the same general goal requires the formulation of a program of coordination and execution. In the construction of a house, the architect prepares the design, the builder attends to the carrying out of the plan, and the workers do the actual work of building the house under the supervision of the architect and the building contractor. Thus, too, when a society is organized, there must be an individual or a group invested with the power to see that certain plans are carried out.

Authority is a unifying and binding principle in the life of society; unifying, because there is no other way for individuals to merge their efforts; binding, because society must rest on the obligation of all its members to obey.

RIGHTS OF THOSE IN AUTHORITY. Perfect societies, that is, societies which are supreme and independent in themselves, whose aim is the common good, which in some respects is the universal good, have a right to demand of their members all that is morally necessary for the full and integral attainment of their end, by direct or indirect means. Now, in order that these societies may fully attain their end, they must have, above all, the following rights: (a) to choose the means necessary for the attainment of their end; (b) to enforce the use of such means; (c) to punish those who refuse to comply. Hence, the triple power— legislative, administrative, and judiciary. To these rights there correspond equivalent duties. There are two perfect societies, the Church and the State. (Concerning the Church, see Church and Hierarchy.)

THE AUTHORITY OF THE STATE. As no society can exist without a governing authority, so too, civil society cannot exist without such an authority. Unlike the case of the Church, God has not commanded one specific form for the exercise of authority in civil society; but as in every order that is inseparable from the natural condition of humanity, the exercise of authority is from God. For, since civil society is of divine institution, it is clear that even civil authority, without which civil society cannot exist, is of divine institution. "There is no power except from God." Hence, sovereignty does not reside in the people, nor are the people its source. People can only transmit it from one person to another or from one institution to another, through appropriate means or systems. Once the people have designated or elected their leaders, these receive their power from God and exercise it in His name. This conception of Greek origin has been revived in modern times by the natural-rightists and elaborated by the promoters of the social contract theory and of the people's sovereignty.

AUTHORITY AND DEMOCRACY. According to natural law every citizen has the right to participate in the government, at least by opposing any abuse of power. From this minimum degree one can rise to higher degrees of participation in the government. Democracy (q.v.) is the form of government which aims at extending this participation to the maximum degree. Today, however, a form of democracy in which the entire citizenry itself exercises the direct power of government (q.v.), as was done in ancient Athens, is no longer possible. Thus, we ordinarily have the indirect or representative form of democracy, in which the people are governed through representatives elected by them. This makes parties and elections indispensable elements in the selection of leaders. Theoretically, the least citizen, be he a farmhand or a worker, may hope to become prime minister or head of a nation, since no law forbids it, although in reality he participates in the government of his country indirectly, that is, by selecting his own representatives through the exercise of the right to vote (q.v.).

AUTHORITY OF THE STATE AND IN THE STATE. Public authority cannot and must not be exercised arbitrarily but according to the norms of the natural and constitutional laws. The subjective authority of the person in whom the power is vested is based on the objective authority established by the natural law and approved by custom or by law. The impersonal and abstract authority of the law becomes concrete in the administrative act, in the ordinance, in the sentence; that is, in the various acts through which the executive and judicial organs of the state (local governments) apply the law to political, social, and economic activities. The state must be neither weak, nor dictatorial, but strongly defend and protect its citizens. Absolutistic acts as well as criminal acquiescence must be avoided. Authority must be respected as the foundation of social life. The state must proceed with caution, lest it invade the rights of its citizens, and it must avoid any evil act even under the pretext of the public good. The exercise of authority must be such that no citizen will feel offended when authority is justly administered. As a matter of fact, limitations must be set to the leniency of the political power toward criminals, particularly when the condoning of their crimes would have the effect of jeopardizing security or would mean their eventual return to crime. But with due respect for the authority, and with all the necessary protection on the part of the state, the citizens must be able to move as they like, without interference by the civil power or by other citizens, provided that their movements do not offend against the rights of others or the common good.

As Pope Pius XI stated in his Encylical Letter *Quadragesimo Anno*, the natural aim of every intervention by authority is to help the members of the social body. It must not only restrain abuses, occasionally fill certain needs, but direct, organize, coordinate, stimulate, harmonize and take the initiative in all these things as circumstances suggest or necessity demands. This is the meaning of the words "to promote and guarantee" the common good. The exercise of authority, particularly in its coercive form, becomes unnecessary and even harmful, when, without it, individuals and intermediate groups attend suffi-

ciently to the needs of the common good.

Authority exercised in an arbitrary manner deserves no respect; as a matter of fact, in certain specific circumstances, which must be very carefully analyzed, it may even justify resistance on the part of the citizens (*see* Resistance to unjust power, Tyranny).

AUTHORITY AND CITIZENS. Every citizen has an obligation to exercise conscientiously his political responsibilities, among which is that of voting for the election of members of the government as well as in any referendum by which approval or rejection of a law is directly decided. Abstention from voting (*see* Political vote) is a cause of grave harm to the common good and amounts to an anti-social act. Consequently, it constitutes a sin, if done without a just and grave motive; its gravity, of course, depends on the problems at hand and on the political conditions of the moment. Furthermore, a citizen must also take an active part in public life by free and public criticism of the actions of government, either through the press (which must be free for all political criticisms) or by means of public assemblies. These criticisms, which must always be of a constructive nature, exercise at times a decisive influence upon legislative and other governmental deliberations. Other duties of legal justice of the citizen toward the state may be summed up in his duties of piety, fidelity, and obedience. The duty of fidelity is violated by the crime of lese majesty (which is, first of all, a *sin* of lese majesty), by sedition against the lawful authority, espionage, sabotage, *etc.* Obedience of unjust laws is violated by any transgression committed against such laws. *Pal.*

AUTHORIZATION. See Faculty.

AUTHORS, RIGHTS OF. In a broad sense, the term *author* applies not only to one who writes a book, but also to one who discovers or invents something, one who produces a painting, a sculpture, a piece of music, *etc.* Thus understood, an author possesses special rights over the products of his skill or genius inasmuch as he is the natural owner of his products.

The rights of authors may extend to any work of human ingenuity or inventiveness, whether scientific, literary, artistic, or didactic. In fact, all productions of a creative nature in the sphere of science, literature, music, figurative arts, architecture, theater and cinema, radio and television, whatever the method or form of expression, may come under the rights of authors. Thus, one speaks of intellectual property, of literary, artistic, or scientific property, *etc*. Regarding inventions of an industrial nature, the more applicable term is *patent* or *inventor's* rights.

The determining factor of the rights of authors is neither the value nor the scope of the production, but the concrete, palpable form in which it is cast, rendering it capable of mechanical reproduction or multiplication. In matters of literary property, even the title of the work comes under reserved copyright, unless it be a common or general title. Moreover, the author has the rights over all translated versions. However, the rights of authors do admit of certain exceptions. Thus, it is permissible to reproduce in newspapers and periodicals a report of any political or administrative lecture, and even small parts of a book, provided that the author's name is indicated.

In these matters the various nations have achieved, through a number of international agreements, a remarkable legislative uniformity. The principal agreements concerning the protection of literary works, musical productions, and industrial inventions are as follows: Berne (September 9, 1886); Brussels (December 12, 1901); Berlin (November 13, 1908); Washington (April 12, 1913); The Hague (January 10 and December 29, 1927); Rome (June 2, 1928); London (1933), *etc*.

Of the author's rights over the fruit of their creativeness, some are moral, others financial. The primary moral right of an author is recognition of authorship of his work—an imperishable and inal-ienable right recognized also by positive law. Another moral right is that of preventing reproduction or multiplication of the work. Ownership right to one's portrait or photograph is included among these rights. The financial rights reserved to authors consist of profits and royalties accruing from publication and sales of the work. The moral rights of authorship are permanent, whereas the financial are limited to a certain time. In positive law, the duration of copyright is not everywhere the same; according to some codes, it ceases fifty years after the author's death or, if the work is anonymous, fifty years after the first edition. In the United States copyrights extend for a period of twenty-eight years, renewable once for a similar period if application for renewal is made within one year prior to the expiration date. Patents on designs extend for periods of three and one half, seven, and fourteen years; on devices, processes, compounds, plants, and the like for a period of fourteen years.

According to some moral theologians (Vermeersch, Marrès, *etc*.), the primary moral right, *i.e.*, recognition of authorship, is based on natural law; whereas the secondary moral rights and the financial rights derive their moral force from positive law, for an idea cannot be copyrighted. Other moral theologians (Balerini, *etc*.) hold that all authorship rights, both moral and financial, flow from the law of nature. According to this opinion, an author has the rights to his book not only for the first edition, but also for subsequent editions over a certain period of time (until the legal time of copyright has expired), for otherwise the owner would be deprived of the fruits of his labor. Still other moralists (Genicot–Salsman), limiting themselves mainly to the consideration of literary property, introduce various distinctions: (a) to reprint or reproduce a work without permission of the author within a period immediately following its first publication would be forbidden by natural law; (b) to reproduce new editions, translations, *etc*., of a work at a somewhat later period (when the first edition has been sold out) would be lawful, because then any damage to the author would no longer be grave.

In practice, it is commonly held that the dispositions of the civil law on the subject of copyright, insofar as they determine the natural law and protect the author from loss, are binding in conscience, with the exception of some sanctions of the fiscal law. Society has the right to determine the rights concerning *non-material property*, as well as patrimonial property. *Pal.*

AUTOMATISM. Automatism refers to the mechanical and almost totally unconscious execution of certain habitual acts. Each one of these acts (dressing, walking, writing, bicycle riding, *etc.*) had to be learned through a more or less slow training process. In the beginning and through its early stages, the act required deliberate and attentive effort on our part, but by constant repetition it was gradually perfected to the point of automatic execution, in view of a tendency of the nervous processes toward coordinations by the simplest method. Indeed, the automatic act, by which one jumps from the first step of a series of mental operations to the last, is much briefer and thriftier than the original mental process, which led to the voluntary act through the conscious evocation of remembrances preserved in the mind in the form of motor images.

Besides such *motor automatisms*, there also exists a whole series of *intellectual* and *moral* automatisms, called *psychological automatisms*. Instances of intellectual automatisms are one's manner of speaking, style of writing, aesthetic attitudes, manner of working and doing things, *etc.* Moral automatisms are our ethical strivings and practices, which often enable us to combat with comparative ease, and almost instinctively, tendencies and passions formerly involving a great struggle on our part.

All such automatisms, in a certain sense, render our daily life of thought and action somewhat mechanical; and at first sight they seem to have a detrimental and impoverishing effect on our psychical life, rendering it excessively stereotyped. But the fact of the matter is that they are highly useful, in that they enable us to conserve precious energies that may be employed for further pursuits and higher achievements. In fact, it may well be said that, were it not for this quasi-mechanization of habitual acts, thoughts, and sentiments, we would be compelled daily to repeat, for each act, the entire cycle of mental operations we had to go through during the learning period; and, as a result, we would make little headway along the path of scientific, artistic, and ethical progress.

However, while automatism apparently acts outside the sphere of conscious attention, it does not escape its control altogether, as our almost daily experience well proves; if in the execution of certain habitual movements we should suddenly make a false step or commit a lapse of any kind, conscious control immediately enters into play and prevents us from falling or making a mistake. In this connection, Father Gemelli writes, "The automatic activity of physical life is automatic only insofar as and to the extent that consciousness permits it to be so."

Thus far the discussion has centered on physiological automatisms present in the life of every normal individual. We shall now review briefly the principal pathological automatisms, as expressions of an anomalous condition (such as hypnotic automatisms) or of a decidely morbid state (such as somnambulism [*q.v.*] and the automatisms of psychopaths).

In hypnotic suggestion (and, to a lesser degree, in suggestion during the waking state, as also in certain cases of accentuated autosuggestion), every reaction or response of the patient is automatic due to the dissociation and notable restriction of consciousness brought about by the suggested action. This leads to a dimming of voluntary activity, while the lower activities, mechanized and divested of all rational and critical processes, continue. In epilepsy and hysteria there may even be prolonged excesses of automatisms, during which the patient behaves in a manner that is apparently normal, but without the participation of voluntary deliberation and judgment, so that the actions are executed mechanically and instinctively, without any motivation; and the patient, upon regaining consciousness, has absolutely no recollection of his deeds, or, if he has, it is but fragmentary and uncertain. Thus, when the subject returns to a normal state, he is the first to express amazement upon being told of his deeds or (if during the crisis he may have strayed from home) upon finding himself in strange and unknown surroundings. Even in these instances there has occurred—as a result of cerebral disturbance—an episode of complete physical dissociation, with concomitant restriction of the sphere of consciousness.

In schizophrenia, particularly in its advanced stages, the action of the patient is frequently automatized, although usually he is aware of and remembers the externalization of his automatisms. Such automatisms are *echolalia* (stereotyped repetition of the same question), *echopraxia* (imitation of other's gestures), automatic obedience to verbal commands, even though the suggested actions are meaningless, humiliating, *etc.*; the patient may even execute automatisms that are dangerous to himself and others, in obedience to an "imperative hallucination," suggesting the most bizarre and outlandish deeds. The cause of all this is the liberation of the motor automatism from all influence of voluntary, personal movements, as a result of the dissociation which prevails in the psyche of such patients and which gives rise to the most diversified stimuli, no longer held in check by any effective inhibition. As the schizophrenic gets older, the process of automatization becomes stronger and more extensive, suppressing or rendering useless every remaining psychical capacity.

At the bottom of the various pathological automatisms there is, therefore, always a psycho-dissociative process,

which, in turn, is brought about by a lack of will power, temporary or permanent, imposed or spontaneous.

As already noted, every pathological automatism is involuntary and, hence, not subject to ethical sanction of any kind. The patient must be considered not responsible for any criminal action that he may commit while under the sway of such an attack. In the case of normal individuals, however, the ethico-penal problem of automatized actions cannot be posited, for an automatic criminal action is inconceivable in persons of sound mind. If a normal person were to commit a crime or a seriously incorrect deed in the course of an automatized action, his consciousness (as already noted at the outset) would immediately step in and prevent its execution.

When the mind becomes totally preoccupied with the preparation of a project, or the development of a certain problem and the like, the automatisms of the individual's remaining activity become stronger, since every attentive, affective, and voluntary faculty becomes concentrated on that one preoccupation of the mind; this is a well-known fact and is verified in the lives of great thinkers. But even in such instances there can only be useless actions, annoying oversights, and eccentric modes of behavior, which are not only beyond moral censure, but are the expression of a marvelous and exceptional power of speculative abstraction. Thus, the peculiarities, eccentricities, and famous distractions of Ampère and other great men may well evoke laughter or even ridicule, but they can never be an object of moral reproach. *Riz.*

AUTOPSY. Autopsy, a term of Greek origin (*autos*, self, *optos*, view), along with its less common synonym, "necropsy," refers to the inspection and partial dissection of a body by an expert to ascertain, from the condition of the various organs and tissues of the corpse, the cause of a person's death.

An autopsy is performed either for clinical or for medico–legal purposes. In both instances it is perfectly lawful even if done immediately after death (unless there are legal dispositions to the contrary). An autopsy must always be performed with due respect and reverence for the body, the soul's habitat in life, destined to final resurrection. It is even permissible during life to provide for a post-mortem anatomical dissection of one's own body, as did the youthful St. Francis de Sales.

The ancients confined their anatomical researches to animal carcasses. The first systematic autopsies were performed in Italy at the beginning of the thirteenth century. The Church was never opposed to the study of human anatomy or pathological anatomy carried out by means of lawful cadaveric dissections.

The aim of clinical autopsy is to check a diagnosis made while the individual was alive or to ascertain the cause of a sudden death. Such a procedure is found to be highly useful both to medical students and experienced doctors, who benefit a great deal by autopsies of their own deceased patients, in order to check their diagnoses through anatomico-pathological findings. In fact, the advance of medical science depends to a large extent upon such post-mortem anatomical inspections carefully checked against previously made diagnoses.

While necroscopic investigations are admittedly of great value and importance, they may not be performed against the wishes of the deceased or contrary to the express will of the relatives of the deceased unless the investigations are demanded by grave reasons affecting the common good. In such a case, the necroscopic investigation must be limited to those sections of the corpse whose examination is thought to offer a solution to the apparent problem. Doctors, instructors and public authorities should educate the public concerning the value of autopsies so as to dissipate the widespread prejudices against them.

A medico–legal autopsy is that which is ordered by judicial authority, irrespective of the will or the wishes of the deceased, or his relatives. Such an autopsy is very helpful, particularly in cases of accidental death, in order to determine the real responsibility of a third party, in cases where the death resulted from a crime. The physician has both a legal and moral obligation to perform the autopsy with all the diligence and care demanded by such an act and to make a full report of his examinaton to the lawful authority. *Riz.*

AUTOSUGGESTION. *See* Suggestion.

AUXILIARY. *See* Coadjutor, Bishop.

AVARICE. In its strict sense, avarice consists in holding on to, instead of making opportune use of, money or material things purchasable therewith, or in using them reluctantly. Such tenacity is rooted in an excessive attachment to money and possessions as things loved in themselves or for purely selfish reasons—an attachment that often leads to an immoderate desire for money and to greed *i.e.*, a constant seeking to increase one's riches. The inordinate love of money and greed are also called avarice in theological language.

Avarice is a most serious obstacle to spiritual progress; in fact, the excessive love of money leads to many anxieties and preoccupations which totally absorb man's mind and make him a slave to earthly things (Matt. 6:24). Avarice also leads to many other vices and for this reason it is considered one of the capital sins: thus, because of his reluctance to spend money, the avaricious person fails in his duty of charity toward the needy, violates his obligations of justice and even deprives himself and his family of necessities.

In itself, avarice is only venially sinful; however, it becomes mortally sinful (a) when, a person is disposed to commit even a mortal sin in order to acquire or hold on to material possessions; (b) when, because of excessive attachment to possessions, a person seriously violates his duty of justice or charity; (c) when a person uses gravely unlawful means to acquire money or other material goods.

Avarice is not a defect generally found

among the young, who, still carefree, are not concerned with thoughts of holding on to their possessions. Rather, it is a defect which manifests itself in persons of advanced age, when people are seized with the fear of not having enough financial resources to see them through their old age—or with fear of eventual illness or inability to work. Avarice is a defect of which it is difficult to convince ourselves, since it frequently assumes the guise of prudent concern for the future. For this reason, it is not easy to rid oneself of this vice. The best remedies against avarice are (a) the development of a deep conviction, based on religion and faith, that riches are not an end in themselves, but merely a means to provide for the present and future needs of oneself and one's dependents, and to alleviate our neighbor's needs; (b) the constant thought that death will one day separate us from all earthly things (Matt. 6:19 ff.); (c) a great confidence in divine Providence; (d) the generous practice of almsgiving and charity. *Man.*

AVE, MARIS STELLA (HAIL, THOU STAR OF THE SEA). The *Ave, Maris Stella* is a medieval Marian hymn which is recited at Vespers of the ordinary Office of the Blessed Virgin, in processions and other Marian devotions. It abounds in affections intermingled with recollections of the most orthodox Marian theology; it ends with a Trinitarian doxology. Perhaps it was its affective tone that irritated the Jansenists, who criticized it bitterly and changed some of its verses. Its frequent occurrence in the Little Office of the Blessed Virgin made it a very popular hymn in the Middle Ages.

An unrhymed, accentual hymn of medieval composition, it consists of six strophes (besides the doxology) of four lines each. The hymn dates back to the ninth century, and is found in manuscript 95 of St. Gall, who lived in that century. No doubt the hymn was imitated, and some of its concepts borrowed, by the author of the *Alma Redemptoris Mater* (see *Angelus Domini*). Among those mentioned as authors of the *Ave, Maris Stella* are St. Venantius Fortunatus and St. Bernard, but neither is correct; the authorship of St. Venantius is not supported by the facts; as to St. Bernard, he could not possibly have been the author, because the composition antedates him.

AVE, REGINA COELORUM. *See* Angelus Domini, Breviary.

AVULSION. *See* Accession.

AZOOSPERMIA. *See* Sterility.

B

BABY. *See* Age.

BAD FAITH. *See* Possession in bad faith.

BALANCE OF DEBTS OR PAYMENTS. *See* Exchange.

BALANCE SHEET. DEFINITION. The balance sheet is a tabulated statement of both the assets and liabilities of a particular enterprise at a given date. It is usually accompanied by a profit and loss statement, giving a summarized account of the financial and economic condition of the business at a specified date.

The balance sheet generally differs from a simple financial report, which may be compiled at any time. As a rule, the balance sheet is prepared at the close (or beginning) of a fiscal period. It merely contains the totals of the accounts (which result after all necessary revaluations, corrections, and adjustments have been made) and, in conjunction with the profit and loss statement, it discloses the net worth of the business property.

The balance sheet may serve to perform various functions. It is a *property report*, if it sets forth the total credits and debits for the purpose of determining the net worth (i.e., the difference between the positive and negative side of the sheet) of the business property; it is a *financial report*, if it sets forth the total receipts and expenditures for the purpose of determining the profit or loss resulting from the business operations; it is an *accrual report* if it records foreseeable receipts and expenditures for the purpose of establishing a surplus or a deficit.

FINANCIAL STATEMENT. With regard to public organizations the financial statement or statement of income depends upon the content and nature of the budget. In the statement, the income on the positive side and the disbursements on the negative side must be presented with the same classification and distinctions as in the anticipated budget. There are two accounting methods in use for the recording of income and outlay: the *cash* and the *accrual* methods. The cash method recognizes only income actually received and expenses actually paid out; the accrual method records also accounts receivable and accounts payable. Whatever the method used, it must be the same in the balance sheet as in the statement of income.

The financial balance sheet gives the profit or loss account of the business (*see* Deficit).

LEGAL DISPOSITIONS. Existing legal norms and special dispositions governing the preparation of balance sheets and financial reports have come about as a result of the practice, prevalent among industrial and commercial organizations, of compiling statements which do not truly reflect the actual financial or economic status of the business. Some of the reasons for altering balance figures are lawful, others unlawful.

Through a fairly accurate valuation of business operations in relation to time and market conditions, one may, *e.g.*, lay aside *secret* and *hidden* reserves (other than the legal and open reserves appearing in the statements: *see* Reserves). If such reserves are set aside in moderation and for the purpose of covering contingent future losses or for equalizing dividends, the practice is lawful and may even constitute a prudent measure. If, however, such reserves are set aside for the purpose of depriving stockholders of a legitimate part of their dividends, the

118

practice is obviously unlawful (see Undue Appropriation, Stealing).

If, in the preparation of a financial statement, fraud is employed to the detriment of tax laws, a moral judgment thereof is to be made according to the norms governing the payment of taxes (see Tax).

Absolutely unlawful are all deceitful and fraudulent alterations of items or totals (see Fraud) for dishonest purposes of personal gain, involving damage or injury to associates or third parties. *Bau.*

BALLERINI, ANTHONY, S.J. One of the foremost moral theologians of the past century.

LIFE. Born on October 10, 1805, at Medicina (Bologna), he died in Rome on November 27, 1881. A professor at the Pontifical Gregorian University, he first taught ecclesiastical history and later (from 1856) moral theology. In this latter field he is known for his extensive collaboration in liberating moral theology from excessive empiricism and raising it to a science of speculative inquiry. He also endeavored to consolidate the theory of probabilism.

WORKS. His better known works are: the opuscule *De morali systemate S. Alphonsi M. de Ligorio* (Rome, 1863); research notes on the *Compendium Theologiae Moralis* of Gury (Rome, 1866); and his principal work: *Opus theologicum morale in Busembaum medullam,* completed by the Rev. D. Palmieri (7 vols.; Prato, 1889–1893). This last work, despite its excessively casuistic tone, exercised considerable influence and was extensively used in the well-known moral textbook by Father Génicot (cf. E. Génicot-J.Salsman, *Institutiones theologiae moralis,* 16th ed., Brussels, 1946). *Pal.*

BALSAM. See Confirmation.

BANK. ORIGIN. The word *bank,* from the Italian *banco,* literally means bench, table, counter.

In ancient times there were no institutions or establishments comparable to modern banks. These arose and developed imperceptibly out of the growing needs of commerce, exchange, and credit activities. In the course of time, the temple treasury and the royal treasury, administered by scribes or royal functionaries, began to accept, with or without charge, the private deposit of goods useful for commerce. Such operations gradually led to the establishment of private banks, which invested funds in industrial, commercial, and maritime enterprises, and in extending loans to private individuals, as well as to governments, at variable rates of interest depending upon the maturity of the loan and the risk involved. Toward the fourteenth century there already existed a monopoly of exchange exercised by local groups of specialized individuals. This led to greater public confidence and, consequently, to increased deposits of private savings. To insure such deposits against possible failure or bankruptcy, public banks were established about the sixteenth century, thereby giving new and greater impetus to domestic and foreign trade.

FUNCTION AND PURPOSE. The chief function of banks consists in the extension of credit. This transaction was formerly conducted by private individuals but it has become, over the years, the exclusive service of banks. The reason is quite obvious. The vast and complex undertakings of modern industry require large capital outlays which very few individuals can afford. Only organized groups, corporations, trusts, and the like, can obtain loans of large size.

Originally the bank was an intermediary institution chiefly concerned with facilitating payments through exchange and transfer of funds to other banks of other cities and countries. In due time it also became a medium of credit activities. Today the original function is of secondary importance. As a credit institution, the bank's function is for deposits and loans. That is to say, through the deposits of clients the bank accumulates money or creates funds that are loaned to borrowers or invested in various enterprises. Through this system, the bank acquires obligations in relation to its depositors (*viz.*, of meeting their demands for withdrawal), while on the other hand it acquires rights in relation to its borrowers (of demanding payment on loans according to date of maturity). In other words, using the same money, the bank is both debtor and creditor, according as it performs the passive or active functions of credit.

Proper and regular bank service increases public confidence, increases the incentive for private savings, and serves to improve social conditions by a multiplicity of credit operations. The main social function of the bank consists in promoting the circulation of money and credit. It protects the private savings of its depositors by wise and well-organized investments which individual investors could not carry out by themselves.

MORAL JUDGMENT. For the protection of the public against loss and financial ruin, some measure of government control over banking institutions (with due regard, however, to freedom of operation) appears not only useful but even necessary. It is immoral to attempt or to cause a bank failure to reap gains at the expense of its depositors. Failures (*q.v.*) of this sort are a severe blow to the prestige of the banking industry looked upon as the protector of the people's savings. The modern banking system is a powerful force for progress and, as such, beneficial to society as a whole. *Bau.*

BANK CHECK. As defined by the Federal Reserve Board of Governors, a check is "draft or order upon a bank or banking house, purporting to be drawn upon a deposit of funds, for the payment at all events of a certain sum of money to the order of a certain person therein named, or to him or his order, or to a bearer, and payable on demand." The primary purpose of a check is to effect a financial transaction between two or more parties. A bank will not honor a check under the following conditions: (a) when the drawer has issued a stop-payment order; (b) when there is some irregularity or informality, *e.g.*, insufficient funds, forgery, post-dating, *etc.*; (c) upon receipt of a garnishee order; (d) upon

notice of the drawer's death; (e) upon notice of bankruptcy of the drawer, in which case the funds are held for the trustee or awaiting court order.

Should a bank honor a check in violation of these conditions, the bank may be held liable for any loss resulting from this action. A bank acts as agent for the depositor in the payment of funds, and as such is required to exercise caution and prudence in the disbursement of these funds. There are instances, however, when in spite of exercising caution and prudence, a bank will honor a check that should not have been honored. In this event, each case is weighed on its individual merits and, if it can be proved that the drawer of the check was guilty of contributory negligence, the drawer may then be forced to sustain any resulting loss himself.

The ordinary use of bank checks is in itself licit and to be recommended. In a case of fraud, the morality of the transaction is to be judged on the basis of the type of fraud perpetrated (forgery, usury, illegality, *etc.*). Thus, in the case of a forged bank check, who is to suffer the damages? Excluding the case where the bank is judged at fault, the bank must be compensated for all damages, even though the depositor suffers a loss through no fault of his own, in precisely the same way that an agent carrying out an order must be compensated for all damages incurred, even though unforeseen. *Bau-Rowe.*

BANKRUPTCY. From a juridical standpoint, bankruptcy is a state of insolvency so declared by a court of law. This action, which presupposes that the debtor is not in a position to satisfy all his creditors, provides for a just and equitable settlement of his debts while preventing a further dwindling of his possessions or assets.

The debtor has very definite obligations to fulfill both before and after bankruptcy, some stemming from the natural law, others from positive law.

If all creditors cannot be properly satisfied, the following prescriptions must be observed: (a) prescriptions of the natural law: (1) The lawful owner must be given the property under consideration (all objects loaned, rented, found, *etc.*) if it still exists *in re* and has not passed into possession of the creditor; (2) creditors who have a mortgage are to be paid next, in order of time, that is, first mortgage first, then second mortgage, and so on; (3) ultimately, all other creditors may be paid. These may be paid on a *pro rata* basis as far as funds allow; creditors whose claim is of longer standing may be paid in full. Later creditors may be paid before earlier ones if they are poor or if their claim is supported by a court action.

A debtor who cannot satisfy all his creditors becomes guilty of injustice if he disposes of his property or assets in favor of his children or if he deeds his possessions over to his wife, except the case in which she herself is one of the creditors or if he transfers to her only that which is necessary for her to live reasonably according to her social circumstances.

(b) Prescriptions of the positive law: Besides the prescription of the natural law, a debtor must also observe the prescriptions of the positive law, particularly in cases of bankruptcy which are binding in conscience. Thus, the National Bankruptcy Act stipulates that privileged creditors must be paid even before those who have mortgages. Accordingly, court costs, burial expenses, doctor and hospital bills, and servant wages must be paid first. Furthermore, all payments made within three months prior to the declaration of bankruptcy are considered invalid.

Before bankruptcy is declared, the debtor may, on his own initiative, settle with his creditors. Settlement may be made by renunciation or voluntary settlement between creditor and debtor, or by remission or condonation, total or partial, by the Holy See in cases in which church property is involved.

When bankruptcy is declared, the debtor's possessions or entire assets become subject to the provisions of the positive law, which are binding in conscience as long as they do not conflict with the provisions of the natural law. Thus, for instance, the natural law permits an insolvent person to retain what is considered necessary and proper for a moderate living for himself and his family and to establish a small business. The same applies to the debtor's widow and children. An insolvent person is incapable of making valid donations and is not allowed to contract further debts.

After bankruptcy, a debtor is still bound in conscience to pay his debts in full should he later become affluent or come into possession of wealth. Discharge from such an obligation may only come about by voluntary renunciation, condonation, or remission by the creditors.

The prevailing juridical opinion in U. S. law favors complete condonation by the creditors in the case of a *bona fide* bankruptcy. This is based on the view that debts are contracted under the implied condition that they will cease in case of *bona fide* bankruptcy, as indicated by the words "forever discharged from all debts and claims." This, however, does not necessarily apply to the internal forum, although the law (applicable in all the States and territories of the U.S.A.) that "a discharge in bankruptcy shall release a bankrupt from all his provable debts," is considered as sufficient proof for the very probable opinion that a declaration of bankruptcy liquidates a *bona fide* bankrupt's debts also in conscience.

In voluntary and malicious bankruptcy a bankrupt is bound in conscience to make restitution by reason of unjust damage done to his creditors even before any other cause. *H.J. Y.*

BANNS (of marriage). The public announcements or proclamations of an intended marriage are called banns. The purpose of the banns is to inform the faithful of a forthcoming marriage that they may disclose to competent authorities impediments which would prevent the ecclesiastical officials from permitting the marriage to take place (Can. 1022). The banns have been prescribed by canon law since late middle ages. They must be published although it is certain that there is no impediment. Besides the names and addresses of the parties, announcement is made also of any dispensation from a public impediment granted by the ecclesiastical authorities.

The banns of marriage must be announced in the parish churches of the contracting parties. If a party has lived in another place for six months after the age of puberty, the pastor is required to refer the matter to his Ordinary who will make a judgment as to whether the banns shall be announced in that place and proof gathered with respect to the free state of the party. If there is any suspicion that an impediment has been contracted, the pastor shall refer the case to his Ordinary, even though the party has been living less than six months in another place. Furthermore, the Ordinary shall not permit the marriage to be celebrated until all suspicion is removed (Can. 1023, par. 2–3).

The proper diocesan authority of the contracting parties can for legitimate reasons dispense with the banns (Can. 1028).

If another pastor has published the banns, he must notify the pastor who is to assist at the marriage of the outcome of the proclamations by a written statement (Can. 1029).

The banns are generally announced at the principal Mass on three successive Sundays or holydays of obligation (Can. 1024), or by posting them at the door of the church if the local Ordinary permits this method. All the faithful are bound to report either to the pastor or the local Ordinary any impediment of which they may have knowledge before the marriage takes place. The publication of the banns is omitted in marriages contracted with a dispensation from the impediment of disparity of cult or mixed religion, unless the Ordinary deems it proper. In this case, however, no mention shall be made of the religion of the non-Catholic party (Can. 1026).

Particular care must be taken with respect to assisting at the marriage of *vagi*. Vagi are those who have no domicile or quasi-domicile (*q.v.*), understood in a canonical sense (Can. 1032).

BAPTISM. *Nature.* Baptism is the sacrament of spiritual regeneration and the means by which a person acquires membership in the Church. The essential elements of Baptism are: (a) ablution or washing with water; (b) the words: "I baptize thee in the name of the Father and of the Son and of the Holy Ghost." For a valid reception true water must be used (Council of Trent, sess. VII, *de baptismo*, c. 2; Denz. 858; Can. 737, par. 1); for lawful reception clean water is required and, in solemn Baptism, water blessed for that specific purpose (*See* Holy Water). Not only must the water directly touch the skin of the candidate, but it must also flow, so that there will be a real ablution. The water must be poured on the head; if applied to some other part of the body, the Baptism would be of doubtful validity and would necessitate conditional repetition. The sacramental words must be pronounced while the water is being poured. In the early ages the form of Baptism usually employed was that of immersion; today the method of infusion commonly prevails. The Roman Ritual (tit. II, ch. 2, n. 19) prescribes a triple infusion in the form of a cross. The validity of Baptism by aspersion remains generally doubtful.

NECESSITY AND SUBJECT OF BAPTISM. Baptism of water is absolutely necessary (as an indispensable means) for the attainment of salvation. In cases of physical or moral impossibility, it may be substituted by baptism of desire or of blood. Such absolute necessity gives rise to serious obligations. Parents are gravely obliged to have their newborn infants brought to the baptismal font as soon as possible (Can. 770). And wherever the Ordinary has specified the period of time within which baptism is to be conferred on newborn infants, it is not permissible to go beyond this period without just reason.

In danger of death, however, baptism is to be administered without delay. If the danger of death should exist even before birth, *e. g.*, due to a difficult delivery, it is permissible and even obligatory to baptize the infant in the uterus, managing, as best as possible, to pour the water on the head, while at the same time pronouncing the sacramental words. If some other limb emerges and danger of death is imminent, conditional baptism is to be conferred upon that limb (Can. 746, par. 3). Since, however, there is always doubt concerning the validity of baptism conferred upon an infant in the uterus or upon a part of the body other than the head, the practical obligation remains of repeating the baptism conditionally if the child is born alive. The condition to be attached is: "If thou art not yet baptized."

In the case of abortion (and miscarriage), whether spontaneous or induced, there is a grave obligation to have the embryo or fetus baptized conditionally ("if thou art capable") and without delay (Can. 747), unless it is absolutely certain that death has already occurred.

In case a mother dies during pregnancy, there is a grave obligation of charity to have the fetus extracted, without delay, and baptized—absolutely if it is certainly alive, conditionally if there is doubt (Can. 746, par. 4). This obligation ceases only when there is certainty that the fetus is already dead—a certainty not to be too easily presumed, especially if the pregnancy is several months advanced. Both the relatives and the physician have a serious responsibility in this matter. If there is any doubt as to whether the fetus is alive, it must be baptized conditionally ("if thou art alive . . .").

Also to be baptized are all monstrous and abnormally shaped forms of the fetus (Can. 748). When the monstrous fetus appears as the union of two individuals, baptism is to be conferred on both. In doubt as to whether the monstrous form represents one or two human beings, baptism is to be conferred absolutely upon the head, conditionally upon the principal member of that which seems to constitute another human being, with the condition expressed with the words. "If thou art capable." As for exposed or abandoned infants, they are, likewise, to be baptized conditionally, unless it is definitely ascertained that they have already been baptized (Can. 749).

A non-baptized adult lacking knowledge and consent, provided that there be reasonable presumption that he has had at least an implicit intention of receiving baptism, is to be baptized conditionally (Can. 752, par. 3).

MINISTER OF BAPTISM. The ordinary minister of solemn baptism is any priest (Can. 738), but its administration is reserved to the pastor or to any other priest acting with permission of the pastor or of the local Ordinary. This permission may be legitimately presumed in a case of necessity.

The extraordinary minister of solemn baptism is the deacon, who, however, may use his power only upon permission of the pastor or local Ordinary, both of whom may grant permission for any reasonable cause; and when necessity urges, this permission is legitimately presumed (Can. 741).

Ordinarily, baptism is to be administered in solemn form (can. 755, par. 1). Solemn baptism is that conferred with all the rites and ceremonies prescribed by the Roman Ritual (tit. II, ch. 1–4), which provides two distinct types of ceremonies, one for infants, another for adults. If these ritual ceremonies are omitted, baptism is called "private" (Can. 737, 2). When they are omitted because of danger of death or for any other reason, they are to be supplied in church as soon as possible except in the case of conditional baptism of converts from heretical sects (Can. 759, par. 2, 3). The baptism of adults, when conveniently possible, should be administered by the Ordinary with particular solemnity (Can. 744), while the baptized adult is urged to receive Communion immediately following baptism (Can. 753, par. 2).

When in danger of death and when a sacred minister is not available, private baptism may be validly and licitly administered by any lay person (Can. 742). Everyone, therefore, ought to be instructed and prepared to confer baptism properly, especially physicians, obstetricians, and nurses (Can. 743).

BAPTISM OF NON-CATHOLICS. The baptizing of infants having two Catholic parents, or at least one, presents no difficulty; neither does the baptizing of adults who give their consent either knowingly or at least presumptively, if unconscious. All these, in seeking voluntary admittance into the Church of God, automatically come under the jurisdiction of the Church. Since baptized heretics and schismatics are in principle subject to the Church, they also could be required to present their children for baptism in the true Church. But the Church does not insist, due to lack of assurance concerning the Catholic upbringing of such children. As regards pagans, the Church, with due respect for the natural rights of parents over their children, ordains that only in danger of death may a child of pagan parents be baptized against the will of the parents (Can. 750, par. 1).

Outside the danger of death, a child of pagan parents may be baptized, with due guarantees for its Catholic upbringing, only: (a) if the parents or guardians, or at least one of them, consent; (b) if there are no parents or guardians, or if they have lost the right to the custody of the child, or if they cannot in any way exercise that right (Can. 750, par. 2). These norms are to be prudently observed even in reference to children whose parents are heretics, schismatics, or apostates (Can. 751). Upon attaining the use of reason, such children may and ought to be baptized even against the will of their parents, provided that they express the desire to receive baptism, are sufficiently instructed in the Catholic faith, and give sufficient assurance of their intention to lead a Catholic life.

RITE—NAME—REGISTRATION OF BAPTIZED PERSONS. A child must be baptized according to the rite of its parents, Latin or Oriental. If the parents belong to different rites, the baptism is to be conferred according to the father's rite, unless a contrary ruling has been made by special law. If only one parent is Catholic, the child must be baptized in the Catholic rite (Can. 756, par. 3). (For baptism of the insane, *see* Insanity.)

A person is to be given a Christian name in baptism (Can. 761) and should be assigned, if possible, at least one sponsor (*q.v.*), with whom the baptized person contracts a bond of spiritual relationship (*q.v.*).

The name of the baptized person, together with the names of the parents, sponsors, and minister of baptism, as also the place and date of baptism, must be entered in the baptismal register (*Liber baptizatorum*) without delay (Can. 777). If private baptism was administered by one other than the proper parish priest, or if solemn baptism was conferred outside the person's parish, the record is to be sent to the proper pastor, who shall make an entry of it in the parochial register (Can. 778). Baptismal records are looked upon as public documents in the Church.

When a record does not appear in the parochial register, proof of baptism may be sufficiently established by one thoroughly reliable witness or by the sworn testimony of the baptized person himself (if baptized in adult age), provided that the rights of a third party are not prejudiced thereby (Can. 779).

PLACE OF BAPTISM. The proper and ordinary place for solemn baptism is the baptistry in a church or public oratory (Can. 773). Every parish church should have a baptismal font, and the local Ordinary may permit or even demand, for the people's convenience, that a baptismal font be placed in some other church or oratory within the parish limits (Can. 774).

For the purpose of avoiding inconvenience or danger to a child, solemn baptism may even be administered in churches or public oratories without a baptistry, but not in private homes, except in cases where the candidate for baptism is an heir to the throne, or the child of a head of state, or other extraordinary cases permitted by the Bishop (Can. 775–776).

EFFECTS OF BAPTISM. The immediate effect of baptism is the imprinting upon the soul of an indelible seal or character, whereby the baptized person becomes united with Christ, consecrated to His service, and incorporated into the Church as a member subject to her jurisdiction.

The baptized person is thus enabled to participate in Christian worship and to receive fruitfully the other sacraments. Other effects of baptism are: the remission of original sin and also, in the case of an adult, the remission of all actual sin; the remission of all punishment, eternal and temporal, due to actual sin; the bestowal of sanctifying grace, together with the infusion of the supernatural virtues and gifts of the Holy Ghost (*q.v.*), and especially the conferring of a right to the actual graces necessary for leading a Christian life; a special and permanent capacity or strength to believe and practice the Faith. Baptism, therefore, effects a truly spiritual regeneration and opens the door to heaven. It does not, on the other hand, remove the inclination to sin. This is not detrimental, however, to anyone offering courageous resistance; in fact, it is beneficial, in that an opportunity is provided for the gaining of much merit (Council of Trent, sess. V, ch. 5; Denz. 792). Neither does baptism take away the consequences of original sin, such as suffering, illness, and death, for in order to become united with the triumphant and glorious Christ, the Christian must first conform to the suffering Christ (Rom. 8:17). In an adult receiving baptism, the remission of grievous sins and the infusion of grace presuppose at least imperfect contrition for the sins committed, accompanied by a firm purpose of amendment. If such disposition is lacking, the baptized adult receives indeed the baptismal character, but he does not receive the principal effects of the sacrament until all obstacles are removed. The same must be said concerning venial sins and temporal punishment due to them: before these can be remitted through baptism, an act of imperfect contrition is required.

PRACTICAL CONCLUSION. Every Christian must be constantly aware of the great dignity received through baptism, and show at every moment his gratitude to God for such an important gift. *Man.*

BAPTISMAL WATER. *See* Holy Water, Baptism.

BAPTISTERY (also Baptistry). *See* Baptism.

BARTER. *See* Exchange.

BASEDOW'S DISEASE. *See* Thyroid.

BASHFULNESS. Bashfulness implies a natural tendency to a sense of shame. This tendency often is accompanied by blushing, downcasting eyes, and the like. In a very broad sense, it implies reluctance to divulge secrets, particularly of a more personal nature. In a stricter sense it implies fear of contempt or shame (*verecundia* of scholastics) arising from things considered embarrassing. This fear may stem from an exaggerated concern about the opinions of others, prescinding from the value of the act, or, more often, from one's own erroneous judgment according to which blameless or laudable things or actions are considered embarrassing or debasing. With respect to immoral actions bashfulness, though not a virtue in itself, is a good disposition that favors the acquisition and preservation of virtue, inasmuch as it restrains a person from committing immoral actions, or after committing them, it convinces him more readily of their inordinate nature (Eccl. 41:21, 25).

Bashfulness assumes a special meaning and value in the field of sex, where it finds more characteristic application, since violations generally assume a graver evil. Sexual impulses, in fact, are less submissive to the rule of reason than other human functions (S. Theol., II–II, q. 151, a. 4); and the disorder produced in this field is perhaps one of the more debasing and evident effects of original sin (Gen. 3:7). By reason of this disorder, bashfulness extends not only to those acts that are contrary to the proper order in sexual life, but also to anything that is related to sexual life. Thus, sexual bashfulness includes not only fear of blame for a morally evil act, but also shame for less noble situations and things of life. It involves a tendency to remove from the view of others the more intimate secrets of the human person and human life (marital life). This sense of shame for every sexual act and object is a spontaneous tendency of nature, arising at the same time as concupiscence, which constitutes one of the strongest restraints against inordinate passions. The development and the manner in which it manifests itself differ according to places and time, but experience teaches that it is never completely absent (*see also*, Nudism, Nudity, Clothes).

Though bashfulness is not a product of social life, its function may be increased or decreased through education, habits, example, and the like. In view of its great value for public and private morality, bashfulness should be cultivated by a positive education, for the lack of it, particularly in view of bad example and man's tendency to evil, will lead to a loss of this important asset and, eventually, the virtue of purity (*see also*, Education, sexual). *Dam.*

BASILICA. *See* Church.

BASIOTRIPSY. *See* Feticide.

BATHS–BATHING. The word *bath* (from the Latin *balneum, balneae* and from the Greek *balaneion*) indicates the complete or partial immersion of the body in water and all such practices as exposing the body to vapor, sand, mud, sun, *etc.* The word is also used to denote establishments, places, or receptacles designed for bathing purposes, *e.g.*, bathhouse, bathroom, bathtub, public bath. At one time the word *balnea* was also used to signify a prison dungeon or pit.

Our immediate concern here is with the forms of bathing more commonly in vogue today, such as sun-bathing, bathing at the beach, *etc.* The subject is singularly vast in scope and development.

HISTORY. So fundamental and instinctive is the need for bathing that the historical origin of the practice is not really known. In the early days of the Roman empire there was great reserve and circumspection in the matter of promiscuous bathing, even among men only. Much more so was this the case

in Greece, where bathing was considered a sign of excessive effeminacy. Appearing naked in public was an act of irreligion (cf. Cicero, *De Off.* I, 35; *De Orat.* II, 55). According to Valerius Maximus, so great was the reserve practiced in such matters that it was looked upon as indecent for a man to bathe with his son, once the latter was beyond the age of puberty, or with his son-in-law. With the increase of wealth, however, all sense of shame vanished, and public and promiscuous bathing flourished both in Athens and Rome. Veritable resorts of luxury and pleasure, the public baths eventually became the scene of all sorts of refined debauchery.

The public baths were banned by Emperor Hadrian (A.D. 117–138) and again by Marcus Aurelius (A.D. 161–180). Alexander Severus (222–234), in an effort to curb the further spread of decadence and corruption, forbade the opening in Rome of mixed baths for men and women (*balnea mixta*).

In view of such widespread degeneracy, therefore, it is little wonder that certain philosophers and sages denounced the public baths and that the Fathers of the Church warned the faithful that the baths were a means to perdition. In the year 320 the Council of Laodicea expressly condemned the practice of promiscuous bathing (*lavacra mixta*). St. Ambrose, on the positive side, extolled the ancient Roman tradition of modesty (cf. *De Off.* I, 18; *PL* 16, 51).

The Church has been called the enemy of hygiene, and the accusation has been made that her reason for condemning some forms of bathing is that she regards the body and its culture as an incentive to sin. Such charges simply have no foundation in fact. If the Fathers and the Councils were somewhat severe in their condemnation of bathing, the reason is obviously to be sought in the excesses and abuses prevalent in the public baths. Rightly did St. Gregory observe that a bath taken merely for purposes of sensuality and indulgence was not permitted, but one taken for bodily necessity was permissible even on Sunday.

VARIETIES OF BATH. The bath may be (a) *common* or ordinary, if taken for cleanliness, hygiene, comfort, and relaxation; (b) *therapeutic*, if taken for curative or healing purposes. Again, the bath is said to be *simple*, if taken in natural water at variable temperature; or *medicated*, when taken in water containing medicinal preparations or substances.

ETHICO-CHRISTIAN PRINCIPLES. Physical health is one of the most prized possessions of man, and upon its preservation largely depends the fullness and value of life. Care of the body is a moral duty and entails the use of all the means necessary for preserving bodily health. Physical cleanliness is both a duty and a virtue, the basis of which is to be found in the Christian concept of the body. According to this view, the body, as the temple of the Holy Ghost, is to be regarded with reverence and respect. The body should be the mirror of the soul. Bodily cleanliness, therefore, is not merely a matter of etiquette, education, and regard for others, but it is also and mainly an expression of regard for one's own person and, as such, constitutes a Christian duty. Although the fifth commandment is expressed in a negative form, it clearly has a positive content or value, which consists in the duty of preserving one's life, hence in caring for bodily health. Quite obviously, this calls for the observance of hygiene not only in eating habits, but also in matters of personal cleanliness, as a useful and sometimes necessary means for the preservation of life.

From the foregoing the following ethical principles arise: (a) for a Christian, hygiene and, therefore, bathing, are not an end in themselves, but merely a means for attaining his ultimate end; (b) in view of man's natural inclination to evil, because of original and personal sin, bodily cleanliness must be regulated by the virtue of temperance, both infused and acquired; (c) the needs of natural and supernatural life must complement each other and must be attended to according to circumstances of time, place, and personal requirements. According to Christian ethics, therefore, bodily cleanliness is: (1) ethically and naturally good; (2) under certain conditions necessary, or at least proper and lawful; it becomes a virtuous thing if governed by temperance and other virtues such as modesty, propriety, and dignity.

In the ethico-Christian concept the human body is considered as the work and property of God; man is merely its custodian. As such, the Christian is bound to love and take care of his body not only naturally, but also supernaturally, avoiding whatever may be detrimental to his physical and spiritual health. In these matters one should be careful not to be influenced by false ascetical notions regarding mortification. Care of the body and mortification of the body are not to be considered as mutually exclusive or incompatible. The axiom *mens sana in corpore sano,* "a sound mind in a sound body," holds true even for Christian asceticism.

MORAL PRINCIPLES. Private baths for purposes of bodily cleanliness are not only lawful but good. Sun bathing, sea bathing, Turkish baths, *etc.*, are even more so if prescribed by a physician or when found to be helpful for reasons of recreation, relaxation, and, especially, physical well-being. The fact that temptations may arise on such occasions does not make bathing unlawful except for the individual who willfully consents to these temptations.

Public bathing is lawful if done for a good reason, and according to the principles of modesty and decency. Excessive exposure of the body, *e.g.,* the use of scanty costumes on beaches and at pools, is certainly an occasion of sin and, therefore, to be avoided.

He is guilty of sin, even mortal, who: (a) goes bathing with an evil purpose in mind; (b) foresees that serious scandal will arise as a result of his bathing; (c) neglects or violates other personal obligations (*e.g.,* parental duties, priestly duties, *etc.*).

Modern nudism (*q.v.*) is idolatry of the body—a cult in which the body is made an end in itself, instead of being subordinated to the dominion of the spirit. It is an expression of the sexual tendencies of a highly corrupt and list-less society, as well as an anti-aesthetic and anti-social movement; it leads to the destruction of the natural and time-honored virtues of modesty and personal dignity. Far from being a universal pan-acea for all ills and diseases, sun bathing and sea bathing, as advocated by nudists, are rather a manifestation of psycho-logical morbidities.

CIVIL LEGISLATION. In some countries, thermal or hydrotherapeutic establish-ments may not be operated without authorization of the civil authorities, who grant permission only after having con-sulted with provincial or regional health councils. In many countries and cities ordinances prescribe the observance of decency and propriety in public places, but in practice these measures are in-terpreted with great elasticity.

The only way to raise the moral stand-ards of conduct at public baths and beaches is through re-education of the Christian conscience toward a high re-gard for the human body and the time-honored virtues of modesty, self-respect, and personal dignity. *Tar.*

BEATIFICATION and CANONIZA-TION. Beatification and canonization are not to be interpreted as a jurisdic-tional act on the after-life, but simply as a valid decision for members of the Church militant; they are not to be con-strued as a promotion to glory (*promotio ad gloriam*), but as a promotion to ven-eration or cult (*promotio ad cultum*). Neither are they to be viewed as a servile imitation of the ancient pagan rite of apotheosis, for the Church does not attempt to deify the saints, but merely affirms and declares in solemn manner that God rewards and glorifies man's virtues in the hereafter. Proposing the saints as models of Christian life, she merely urges the faithful to imitate their examples and to have recourse to their intercession.

Beatification is a preparatory act whereby permission is accorded for the public veneration, usually restricted as to place and time, of a servant of God under the title of blessed. Canonization

is a solemn and definitive act of an ecumenical council or, more frequently, of the Roman Pontiff, who authorita-tively and infallibly declares that a certain beatified person is in heaven and is, therefore, worthy to be venerated by Christians as a saint.

HISTORY. The terms *beatification* and *canonization* are of relatively recent origin (twelfth century). At one time it was customary to speak of the vindication of saints or martyrs (*Sanctorum vel Marty-rum vindicatio*), a function which until the twelfth century was reserved to the bishops of the respective dioceses. The bishop, after mature investigation, simply declared which martyrs (later on, con-fessors also) were to be accorded public veneration. This accounts for the distinc-tion between vindicated and non-vindi-cated martyrs. Well known is the incident of a certain noble lady, Lucilla, who was reprehended by the Archdeacon of Car-thage for having dared publicly to kiss, before Holy Communion, the bones of one not officially recognized as a martyr. In due time the popes found it necessary to restrict the episcopal prerogative of authorizing public veneration of persons who had led saintly lives. This right was first reserved to the Holy See by Alex-ander III, in 1170, and definitely con-firmed by Urban VIII, who in 1634 issued a Bull reserving to the Holy See exclusively not only the immemorial right of canonization, but also that of beatification.

BEATIFICATION PROCEDURE. Today a distinction is made between formal and equivalent beatification. Formal beatifi-cation is based on a lengthy and detailed series of proceedings which are outlined in the Code of Canon Law. Initially, they are conducted under the authority of the local Ordinary, subsequently fol-lowed by the apostolic processes con-ducted by the Sacred Congregation of Rites, which is charged with the prepara-tion of the solemn pontifical declaration. The procedure consists in a judiciary process concerning the alleged practice to an heroic degree of Christian virtues by the servant of God, or his martyrdom suffered for love of God, as a result of hatred for the Christian Faith or in defense of a particular Christian virtue, also concerning the miracles wrought by God after the candidate's death and attributed to his intercession.

Equivalent beatification occurs when a servant of God has been the object of veneration from remote time, and the fame of his heroic virtues and miraculous intercession has been definitely established. In such a case, the Pope, omitting the judicial process and ceremonies, simply declares the servant of God blessed and worthy of public veneration.

VALUE OF THE DECLARATION. The declaration of beatification is not definitive, infallible, or irrevocable; it does not make the veneration of the blessed binding on the universal Church. The declaration may be said to have the character of an indult (q.v.). It is, however, rash for one to hold that the Church has really erred in a specific declaration of beatification.

CANONIZATION PROCEDURE. Canonization, on the other hand, is a definitive, infallible, and irrevocable act. Always preceded by beatification, canonization is based on the fact that the additional miracles required after beatification (two after formal, three after equivalent beatification) were actually wrought by God through the intercession of the blessed. The declaration of canonization is issued in the form of a decretal letter signed by the Pope and all the Cardinals present. On such a solemn occasion the Pope himself signs as Bishop of the Catholic Church.

SOLEMNITIES. Since 1662 the solemnities of beatification and canonization have taken place in the basilica of St. Peter. The beatification ceremonies are conducted in the presence of the Cardinals and the consultors of the Sacred Congregation of Rites. After the reading of the brief of beatification, a painting or image of the new blessed is unveiled. The Te Deum is then sung, and also the collect or prayer in honor of the blessed; this is followed by a triple incensation of the image of the blessed, and by High Mass. At the hour of Vespers of the same day, the Holy Father comes to the basilica to venerate the new blessed. The canonization ceremonies are conducted entirely in the presence of the Pope. Pug.

BEATITUDE. Beatitude or happiness may be considered objectively and subjectively. Objective beatitude (objective ultimate end) is the object capable of satisfying fully every need of the intellectual being, i.e., of giving this being its ultimate perfection. Subjective beatitude (subjective or formal ultimate end) consists in the full perfection of the intellectual being, in such manner as to leave nothing further to be desired or to be attained.

Several ancient pagan philosophers (Plato, Aristotle, etc.) stated long ago that only contemplation of God or assimilation with Him can make man perfect. Other philosophers held that man has no other or higher end but to contribute to the progress of the universe (Pantheists), or to the progress of human culture (Schleiermacher, Wundt), or to the increase of the material prosperity of the collectivity (Marxists). Others place man's happiness in the possession of earthly goods, in the pleasure of the senses and of the spirit (Materialists, Hedonists), or in the practice of virtue (Stoics, Kant). Pessimists are content with a negative end which presumably consists in the liberation from all misery through the extinction of self-awareness.

SOLUTION OF QUESTION. From the very nature of our spiritual faculties, whose object is unlimited being and unlimited good, it follows that only an infinite Being, God, can fully satisfy our every need and fulfill our every desire; every other finite good, however noble and grand, necessarily leaves within us a void that cannot be filled. Moreover, it is a well-known fact that material goods, honors and pleasures, even spiritual, do not render man fully happy. Man's complete perfection, or subjective happiness, may be found only in an intimate and endless union with the infinite God. This union can be attained through knowledge and love and is accompanied by the highest degree of joy.

In the purely natural order (which was possible, though it never existed) man could not have known God except through created things (hence analogously), and could not have loved Him except with a purely natural love.

In the supernatural order (the only effective order) man is called to an intuitive vision of God, *i.e.*, to an immediate, face-to-face vision (I Cor. 13: 12; I John 3:2; Benedict XII, Denz. n. 530; Council of Florence, Denz. n. 693). The endless vision and supernatural love of God, accompanied with ineffable joy, makes man perfectly happy, even in the state of separation of soul and body. On the day of final judgment, however, the body, endowed with special attributes, shall be reunited with the soul and shall participate in its happiness.

Perfect happiness is reserved to the future life. In this world there can only be imperfect happiness, that consists principally of the knowledge and love of God, but which at the same time requires good physical health, the material means necessary for such good health, and the aid and companionship of others. *Man.*

BEATITUDES (THE). The beatitudes are those virtuous acts or works especially recommended by our Lord in the Sermon on the Mount. These works or virtues are called beatitudes, because those who practice them (a) are called by Jesus blessed; (b) are given a certain foretaste of heavenly beatitude.

St. Luke (6:20 ff.) relates only the beatitudes which Jesus Christ, after descending from the mountain, proposed to the multitudes; four in number, they are directly opposed to the apparent goods sought after by many. St. Matthew (5:1 ff.) instead relates the beatitudes which the Lord proposed on the mount to His disciples, who were better disposed to accept them than the multitudes. They are eight in number; some of them refer more directly to the state of perfection.

The first three beatitudes aim at checking and extirpating from men's hearts all those things which more easily lead them to sin and which are an impediment to their union with God.

Blessed are the poor in spirit, for theirs is the kingdom of heaven. The desire and possession of created goods constitute a serious obstacle to the attainment of perfection; hence, the Lord inculcates interior detachment from material things, and also from some immaterial goods, such as one's talents and knowledge, the esteem and affection of others.

Blessed are the meek, for they shall inherit the earth. Man, esteeming himself superior to others, is easily inclined to be harsh with them. Christ recommends meekness—not a servile meekness stemming from natural timidity or fear, but one which is motivated by a profound humility and a sincere love of God and neighbor—a meekness that is perfectly reconcilable with strong will power and character.

Blessed are they who mourn, for they shall be comforted. Seeking after earthly pleasures, even legitimate ones, tends to act as a drag on human nature. The Lord calls blessed those who undergo physical or moral suffering without complaining, murmuring, or rebelling; those who deprive themselves of legitimate pleasures; those who do penance for their sins and the sins of others.

The following two beatitudes deal more directly with the positive aspects of the spiritual life.

Blessed are they who hunger and thirst after justice, for they shall be satisfied. The word *justice* here signifies whatever gives glory to God. Jesus extols those who, besides always conforming to the divine law, are constantly desirous, even in the midst of trials and tribulations, of glorifying God and seeing Him glorified by others.

Blessed are the merciful, for they shall obtain mercy. Perfection is unattainable without the practice of the spiritual and corporal works of mercy. The Divine Saviour here praises those who practice such works.

The following two beatitudes are proposed by the Lord as virtues disposing the soul in a special manner toward contemplation of God and of things divine.

Blessed are the pure of heart, for they shall see God. Purity of heart may signify freedom from sin, rectitude of intention, detachment from created things. In a strict sense, it is interpreted as freedom from every sensual attachment to creatures. Such freedom, together with the protective virtue of chastity, disposes the soul in a very particular way to an intimate relation with God, and is especially recommended by Jesus.

Blessed are the peacemakers, for they shall be called the children of God. With these words, Jesus proclaims blessed those who do not live in feverish agitation but preserve tranquillity of spirit, even in the midst of sufferings and difficulties, and those who forgive, sincerely and promptly, all wrongs received.

The concluding beatitude promised by the Master serves, in a certain sense, to ratify the preceding seven: *Blessed are they who suffer persecution for justice's sake, for theirs is the kingdom of heaven.* Fulfillment of duty and fidelity to the Lord is often made an object of ridicule and vituperation on the part of wicked and irreligious persons. Christ, therefore, has a special word of praise and the promise of heavenly reward for those who are made to suffer because of their good deeds and loyalty to His teaching.

The practice of the virtuous acts suggested by all the beatitudes is necessary for attaining perfection. Such practice requires special enlightenment and inspiration by the Holy Spirit. In view of this, as St. Augustine notes, the evangelical beatitudes are closely connected with the Gifts of the Holy Ghost (*q.v.*). Man.

BEAUTY CONTESTS. Beauty contests are public exhibitions in which female participants, by a display of their physical attributes, compete for the title of the most beautiful girl of a particular region, city or country, or even of the world.

Such contests are of Anglo-Saxon origin, but they have today spread into many parts of the world.

The decision is rendered by a committee of men and women, who submit the candidates to a series of unbecoming, measurement-tests. On the day of the contest, the scantily-clad candidates parade before the judges, in full view of the public. The circumstances and the methods employed are often scandalous, despite the pretext that a fair and favorable decision cannot be rendered without visual inspection of the physical attributes of the candidates. The winner of the contest, generally, holds the title for the duration of a year.

Until the present, beauty contests have been limited to female participants, although an occasional attempt has also been made to stage them among men.

MORAL JUDGMENT. First of all, beauty contests are wholly unfair and meaningless. The winner is supposed to be the most beautiful girl of a particular region, *e.g.*, Miss Greene County, Miss New York City, Miss America, Miss Paris, *etc.* Quite obviously, a title of this nature cannot be fairly awarded, unless all the young women of the particular region or country represented took part in the actual contest. In practice, however, only a limited number of women are selected for the competition, while the methods of selecting this limited number and the eventual winner are not entirely devoid of prejudice, favoritism, influence and the like. Under such circumstances, it is difficult to see how the winner has any right to the title and how she can possibly be crowned as the best specimen of physical beauty in a region.

Moreover, beauty contests tend to place exaggerated emphasis on the physical attributes of woman. To be sure, physical beauty is a gift of God; but the feminine personality is constituted by other intellectual and moral qualities which are as important as physical endowments and even more so.

Beauty contests are surrounded by other evils and dangers that are even more serious.

The Christian attitude toward beauty contests is that they are to be avoided because they are an offense against modesty (*q.v.*) and a cause of scandal (*q.v.*).

Modesty, as a virtue directed to the preservation and safeguarding of personal integrity against all evil and corrupt influences, was recognized even by the pagans. For this reason maidens were excluded by the Greeks from participation in the Olympic games. For the Christian man and for the Christian woman, the duty of modesty acquires special significance, for the Christian knows that the body is the temple of the Holy Ghost, and that the law of sin weighs upon the body. This imposes an obligation to practice constant and prudent vigilance.

Participation in a beauty contest encourages and emboldens a girl, so that she acquires the habit of appearing in public in various degrees of exposure, spurred on by flattery, vanity, and envy.

Not to be overlooked are some of the scandalous activities following the contest. At the reception hall the "queen" is madly feted, adulated, and surrounded by a host of reporters and photographers, who snap her picture from all angles and in every pose. Her semi-nude photograph is flashed on television screens and in the newspapers for the rest of the world to see, with a detailed account of her physical charms and dimensions. The papers speak of an "electrifying" and "super-charged" atmosphere in the presence of the queen. This is a sad euphemism and a sorry commentary on the moral conscience of the day.

RESPONSIBILITY OF PARENTS AND AUTHORITIES. From the foregoing it is easy to conclude that we are here confronted with a whole series of sins of immodesty in an active and passive sense, with a scandalous spectacle, a proximate occasion of many sins against chastity, charity, humility, etc.

Quite obviously, the responsibility must be shared by a number of people: (a) the organizers who stage beauty contests; (b) the authorities who tolerate them; (c) the parents who encourage or permit their daughters, especially minors, to expose themselves in public; (d) the participants or contestants; (e) the spectators and viewers. For the extent of responsibility in each individual case, see: Cooperation, Immodesty, Occasionist, Danger of Sin, Scandal.

Unquestionably, licentious conduct in public is encouraged by the deplorable acquiescence of so-called respectable and decent citizens. Without this tolerance these spectacles could never be staged; hence, they cannot feel free of all blame and responsibility. It is a natural duty and right for parents to protest to the proper authorities and unequivocally demand their intervention.

The intervention of public authority is within the province of the state to guard public morals and to protect decent citizens from evil and corrupt influences. In some countries "all manifestations against good public morals" are forbidden.

The audacity of those who organize beauty contests and similar exhibitions is based on the almost certain knowledge that the public will accept and tolerate them without protest, out of human respect or other motives, and remain passive and apathetic about the staging of offensive spectacles.

People have a genuine right to demand the fostering of good, public morals in a society. Consequently, they have a right to protest all infractions and violations. If they renounce this right of protest, they fail in the exercise of duty.

In some areas beauty contests occasioned a certain reaction to temper the bold and immodest tone of such spectacles by altering the rules in such a way that the search for the "ideal" woman will take into account, not only the physical attributes, but other higher moral qualities and abilities as well. This movement is deserving of public support everywhere. *Pal.*

BEGGARY, BEGGING. The term *beggar*, in a contemptuous sense, is used to indicate one who, though able to work, resorts to begging as an occupation. Needy persons who have no relatives obligated or able to provide for them become public charges.

In many countries begging in a public place or in a place open to the public is forbidden by law, and violation of such law becomes punishable with arrest. The same applies if begging is practiced in an offensive or annoying manner, if deformity or disease is simulated, or if other fraudulent means are employed to arouse the pity of passers-by. If begging is exercised through the agency of a fourteen-year-old minor—or, at any rate, one of non-imputable age—subject to parental authority of the sender or in his custody or charge, the penalty is generally more serious. The same serious penalty is incurred by anyone who permits the practice of begging by a minor subject to his authority or custody. As for parents or guardians, some modern penal codes carry penalties including suspension of parental rights or guardianship (*see also* Almsgiving, Destitution). *Pug.*

BENEDICTION OF THE BLESSED SACRAMENT. Benediction of the Blessed Sacrament is one of the most impressive sacred functions. It consists in making the sign of the Cross over the kneeling congregation with the Sacred Host placed in a monstrance or ciborium. Aside from local customs prevailing in certain countries, Benediction of the Blessed Sacrament is usually preceded by the singing of liturgical or popular hymns, especially the *Tantum Ergo* (*q.v.*). Originally, the Eucharistic Benediction was imparted only at the conclusion of the solemn exposition of the Blessed Sacrament, but later it was often used to add solemnity to liturgical and non-liturgical services. It is also frequently employed at famous shrines in the blessing of pilgrims and the sick, as at Lourdes, Fatima, Loreto, *etc.*

Benediction of the Blessed Sacrament may be solemn or private. The former is given with the ostensorium or monstrance, previously exposed in solemn manner; the latter is given with the ciborium taken out of the tabernacle. In both solemn and private Benediction, the priest employs the humeral veil. In giving the blessing, bishops and other prelates make the sign of the Cross over the people three times, while ordinary priests make a single cross. *Pal.*

BENEDICTUS, THE. So-called from the opening word of the Latin version, the *Benedictus* is the canticle uttered by Zachary, after regaining his faculty of speech on the occasion of the birth of his son, St. John the Baptist (Luke 1: 67–79).

The authenticity of the *Benedictus* is connected with the historicity of the first part of St. Luke's Gospel, and is today beyond all doubt.

On the whole, the canticle follows the pattern of the Old Testament prophecies and at one point becomes a prophecy in its own turn, predicting the future mission of the Baptist (vv. 76–77). Sentiments of praise and thanksgiving to the Lord for beginning the work of Redemption and fulfilling His promises precede an address by Zachary to his own son (the future Baptist) describing the latter's role as the herald of salvation through the Messias—a salvation that is the work of divine mercy.

Liturgical use prescribes recitation of the *Benedictus*, preceded and followed by an antiphon, at Lauds. The canticle is also used in extra-liturgical functions as a psalmodic hymn, particularly adapted for processions, in carrying the Blessed Sacrament or Viaticum, *etc. Pal.*

BENEFACTOR. See Gratitude.

BENEFICE (ecclesiastical). An ecclesiastical benefice is a juridical entity resulting from an endowment (goods or property belonging to the entity itself), the revenues of which belong to the cleric who comes into possession of the office to which said revenues are attached (Can. 1409). Thus, it can be said that the benefice is the patrimonial element of an office. A patrimonial endowment, however, at least in its traditional form, is not necessarily attached to all offices (for example, a Curia official); nevertheless, a benefice without office is hardly conceivable, for the latter is the constitutive element of the institution known as the benefice. (Briefly, the endowment constitutes the patrimonial element of a benefice; the sacred office, to which such endowment is attached, is the spiritual element of a benefice).

To these two elements (spiritual and patrimonial) a third must be added, *i.e.,* objective perpetuity. This means that every benefice must have a stable and sufficient endowment or permanent source of income, sufficient for the beneficiary's own maintenance. This element of perpetuity flows from the very concept of benefice as a legal person (Can. 102), so that upon the death, resignation, or removal of the beneficiary, the benefice is said to remain vacant. Therefore, pensions and temporary *commenda* (the custody or use of church or monastery revenues) are not considered as benefices (Can. 1412).

The majority of sacred offices, especially those more fundamentally important to the life of the Church (episcopate, pastorate, canonicate, *etc.*), are, generally, offices with a benefice. Thus, the same norms which govern the conferring and the loss of benefices govern also the conferring and the loss of offices.

It is evident that a benefice must be instituted or erected (*erectio in titulum*) by the legitimate ecclesiastical authority (Can. 1414). Following the legitimate superior's acceptance of the patrimony or endowment and pertinent assignment of it to a sacred office, the benefice automatically (*ipso jure*) acquires the character or status of a juridical personality (Can. 99). Hence, the creation of an institution by any other authority, even though such an institution be dedicated to religious purposes or to the maintenance of clerics, may give rise to a lay chaplaincy or a pious legacy (Can. 1412), but not to a benefice.

Concerning the material goods, it is to be noted that formerly the patrimony of a benefice was to consist totally, or nearly so, of immovable goods belonging to the benefice itself, with the accruing revenue going for the support of the incumbent cleric (and also toward the satisfaction of other obligations weighing on the patrimony). According to the present Code of Canon Law, however, the endowment of a benefice may consist not only of goods or property, movable or immovable, but also of any other source of stable revenues (Can. 1410), including canonical taxes or tributes, tithes, guaranteed credits, government grants, even stole fees, offerings of the faithful, and choral distributions as well (*see* Choir). Consequently, a benefice could lack a patrimony in the sense of real goods or property, while still possessing the capacity to acquire and possess property. In fact, a benefice may be instituted or erected even without a patrimonial endowment, if the incumbent can be assured of sufficient and stable revenue.

ORIGIN OF BENEFICES. Various opinions are offered in explanation of the origin of benefices. Among these is the opinion of Stutz, who holds that the benefice arose from the relations obtaining between the owner of a private church or chapel and the priest engaged to conduct services. But the traditional explanation is that benefices date back to the sixth century, when bishops began the practice of making land grants to priests assigned to "rural churches," which, in the course of time, gained increases in endowment through voluntary offerings of the faithful, legacies, bequests, and the like. Eventually this source of income was recognized as a permanent foundation for the support of the priest. When around the tenth or eleventh century this was finally accomplished, *i.e.*, when the revenue from such endowment was permanently assigned to the incumbent cleric, the modern benefice came into being.

KINDS OF BENEFICES. Benefices assume various names according to the offices to which the revenue is attached. Thus, the cardinalitial benefice is called *title*, the episcopal *mensa* (mensal fund), the canonical (benefice of a canon) *prebend*, the pastoral *congrua*, etc. Also, depending on rank or office, benefices are divided into *major* and *minor*. But the more important division of benefices is as follows: (a) *consistorial* and *non-consistorial:* consistorial benefices are those which can be erected only by the Holy See (Can. 1414), and they are usually conferred in a consistory; all other benefices are called non-consistorial; (b) *secular* and *religious*, depending on whether they concern the secular or the religious clergy; (c) *residential* and *non-*

residential, depending on whether the incumbent is, by reason of the office, held to the law of residence or not; (d) *manual* (*temporary* or *removable*) and *perpetual* (or *irremovable*), depending on whether the benefice is conferred for a time or permanently (the temporary conferment of benefice does not affect the objective perpetuity of said benefice); (e) *curate* (*curata*) and *non-curate* (*non curata*), depending on whether the care of souls is or is not attached to the benefices (Can. 1411).

CHANGES AND CESSATION OF BENEFICE. This subject is extensively treated in Canons 1419–1430. Here we shall simply limit ourselves to noting that the perpetual character of benefices may be modified or extinguished by reason of union, transfer, division, dismemberment, conversion, and suppression, as indicated in Can. 1419 and ff. *Vio.*

BENEFICENCE, CHARITY. Beneficence is the external manifestation of charity by a series of acts directed to the public or private assistance of one's fellow man (*see* Aid, public and private). External acts of charity toward God are the object of religion. External acts of charity toward one's neighbor constitute beneficence, in the widest meaning of the term. Thus doing good to a fellow man for love of God is beneficence; so, too, is performing an act of goodness or kindness toward oneself as a creature of God, destined to be united with Him as one's supernatural end. When beneficence is directed toward the needy or the poor, it is more properly called mercy (*q.v.*).

BENEFICENCE AND THE CHURCH. The practice of charity was one of the characteristics of the early Church. The Roman matron Fabiola was the first to establish a hospital for the sick and the poor. Pammachius erected an asylum for pilgrims at Porto Romano, at the mouth of the Tiber. In the sixth century Belisarius founded at Rome a hospice for the poor. These are but a few outstanding examples of a long tradition of beneficent practices for love of God.

In the Middle Ages the papacy was greatly instrumental in extending the sphere of charitable activities, carried out professionally and systematically through the agency of the various religious orders and confraternities. The medieval Christian looked upon a beggar not only as a brother, but also as an occasion for the benefactor to gain supernatural merit and atone for his personal sins.

In the second half of the fifteenth century, however, because of conditions brought on by wars, epidemics, and public disasters, or because of a weakening of the Christian spirit caused by pagan humanism and the Reformation, the charitable activities of the Church no longer seemed adequate or sufficient. The State, therefore, stepped in and in various places began to establish a number of institutions for the needy, especially hospitals.

In Protestant countries government intervention brought about a secularization of all charitable institutes of the Church; lay personnel were substituted for ecclesiastics, and laws were enacted against begging and almsgiving (*q.v.*). In Catholic countries, alongside government intervention there flourished within the Church a revival of charitable endeavors as an aftermath of the Counter Reformation (Catholic), particularly through the efforts of the newly established religious orders such as the Theatines, Barnabites, Somaschians, Jesuits and, later, the hospitalers or infirmarians of St. Camillus de Lellis, the Daughters of Charity of St. Vincent de Paul, and others. This reorganization of charitable activities within the Church continued at a growing pace during the whole of the seventeenth century and the first half of the eighteenth century.

LAY BENEFICENCE. In the second half of that century under the influence of the new philosophy of Enlightenment the Christian and supernatural concept of beneficence began to undergo a process of, as it were, naturalization. Men were no longer prompted by faith and charity to succor the needy, but merely by enlightened reason or by the simple desire of making oneself useful to others. This led to the acknowledgment of the right of the poor to receive adequate aid, which became a cornerstone of all public assistance. The principle was immediately endorsed by French revolutionary legislation and, subsequently, by the other European governments as well. Assistance of the poor is now definitely regarded as a natural duty of the State, while the charitable activity of the Church is looked upon as merely subsidiary to it. This new concept was a reversal of the long-established concept on which the matter of beneficence had rested for many centuries. Up until this time, beneficent activities—relief agencies, charitable institutions, assistance, etc.,—had been conducted by the Church on a more or less uniform basis throughout the civilized world, in view of the universal character of the Church reflected not only in its doctrine but also in its action. From this time on, however, charitable activities assumed a variable character, shaped by the different legislation of the various countries.

Among Anglo-Saxon peoples, State intervention moved in the direction of complete and organic development owing to the fact that such States had achieved a rapid and solid national structure and also to the fact that among them there had been no spontaneous flourishing of charitable organizations as in the Latin countries. The few charitable institutions with a Catholic background existing in such countries were destroyed in the wake of the revolutionary wars of the sixteenth and seventeenth centuries.

In Catholic countries, on the other hand, the tendency prevails for a revitalization of the important tradition of charity and beneficence inspired by the Church, a revitalization particularly manifest during and after the last World War. There is a tendency to look upon the State as a coordinating, subsidizing, and controlling agency in the matter of beneficence and charitable endeavors. *Pal.*

BENEFICIARY. In Canon Law a beneficiary (*beneficiatus, beneficiarius*) is the titular of an ecclesiastical benefice. According to Canon 1409, a benefice is a juridical entity, permanently constituted or erected by the competent ecclesiastical authority, and consisting of an ecclesiastical office and of the right to the revenue accruing from the endowment attached to such office.

Thus, a beneficiary is one holding an ecclesiastical office, and having the right to the endowment connected with it. Such endowment consists either of goods belonging to the benefice itself or of salary, or a fairly stable income from voluntary offerings of the faithful, stole fees, choral distributions, and the like.

The benefice was unknown in the early days of the Church, when all diocesan property constituted one large patrimony or common fund, administered either by the bishop personally or by a priest appointed by him as administrator. Only after this common patrimony was divided into various parts could the benefice (and, hence, the beneficiary) have come into being. In fact, the origin and development of the ecclesiastical benefice remains even today a matter of considerable discussion among canonists (see Benefice).

CONFERRING OF BENEFICES. A person becomes a beneficiary through the legitimate conferring of an ecclesiastical benefice. The conferring of a benefice is said to be legitimate when it is made to a qualified person by the competent ecclesiastical authority and in the manner prescribed by canonical laws.

(a) Ecclesiastical benefices may be conferred only upon clerics (Can. 118; 153 par. 1), while *curate* benefices (those entailing the care of souls) may be conferred only to priests (Can. 154). According to Canon 451, a parish may be assigned even to a juridical person, but this is to be regarded as a special union (formerly called incorporation, *incorporatio*; see Innovation) rather than conferring in the true sense (cf. Canon 452, 471, 1425), and in such cases a specific priest must always be appointed for the actual exercise of the pastoral office. Clerics appointed to benefices whether they be benefices in general or a particular one; must possess all the qualifications required by law; on the contrary, the appointment is invalid if ome cases, voidable, or at least illicit in others (Can. 153). The conferring of a benefice upon an unwilling cleric is also invalid (Can. 1436). Secular benefices are to be assigned to secular clerics only; religious benefices to members of the respective religious organizations having title to said benefices (Can. 1442).

(b) No one may confer an ecclesiastical benefice upon himself (Can. 1437) nor obtain it from the civil authority, but only by canonical appointment by the competent ecclesiastical authority Can. 147).

The Pope has the right to confer any benefice within the Church; he also can reserve to himself the right to confer certain specific benefices, so that any appointment to these by inferior authorities is null and void (Can. 1431, 1433, 1434). Reserved to the Holy See by law (*ipso jure*) are consistorial benefices, capitular dignities, and certain other offices (Can. 1435).

Non-consistorial benefices, unless reserved to the Holy See, may be conferred by cardinals, within their respective titular churches or within their proper deaconry, and by local Ordinaries, within their own diocese or territory (Can. 432, par. 5). But the vicar-general may confer such benefices only by special mandate of the bishop, while the vicar-capitular may confer only certain specific benefices and only under the conditions established by Canon Law (Can. 1432, par. 2, and Can. 455, par. 2). If the Ordinary has failed to fill a vacant benefice within six months after having received definite notice of its vacancy, the conferring of this benefice, if it is one of free appointment, devolves upon the Holy See. If the vacancy involves a benefice subject to the right of patronage, the appointment of a beneficiary pertains to the Metropolitan (Can. 1432, par. 2; 274, par. 1; 1467), with the exception of parishes where, by reason of peculiar circumstances, the Ordinary deems it advisable to delay the appointment of a pastor beyond the canonically established period (Can. 458).

(c) The conferring of a benefice consists of two conceptually distinct acts: the selection or designation of a candidate and the actual conferring of the benefice (*collatio beneficii*). The really essential act is the conferring of the benefice, which can only be made by the competent ecclesiastical authority.

Ordinarily, both acts, i.e., the selection and the appointment of the beneficiary, are performed by one and the same competent ecclesiastical authority or superior. This is called *free appointment* (Can. 148), by which the appointee acquires a right to the benefice (*ius in re*) immediately.

In certain specific cases, however, Canon Law grants to third parties the right of proposing to the competent ecclesiastical superior the candidate for a benefice. If the candidate is qualified, the superior is bound to confer upon him the benefice. This is called a necessary appointment (*collatio necessaria*). The candidate may be proposed either through election conducted by an electoral college, in accordance with canonical norms (Can. 160–178), or by presentation (also called nomination) by anyone having the right either by virtue of an apostolic indult (*e.g.*, civil authority) or by virtue of the so-called right of patronage (Can. 1448–1471). By election or presentation, the candidate acquires only the so-called right to the benefice (*ius ad rem*); but he shall acquire the *ius in re* or right over the benefice only when the legitimate superior shall have confirmed (*confirmatio*) the elected or appointed the nominated person in office (*institutio;* Can. 148).

But if the election requires no confirmation, the elected person acquires jurisdiction over the benefice (*ius in re*) merely by his acceptance of the election (Can. 148); in other words, it amounts to a free appointment made through an electoral college. It is also a case of free appointment if the electoral college elects or postulates the appointment of a person (such election is called *postulatio*) against whom there is an impediment, because the postulated candidate does not even acquire the right to the office (*ius in rem*), and the ecclesiastical superior is free to confer the benefice or not by means of the so-called admission (*admissio*; Can. 179–182).

To have the right over a benefice (*ius in re*) does not necessarily mean that the appointed can automatically exercise his office. In order to exercise the office and to enjoy the right of the benefice, the person nominated, confirmed, and instituted must take possession of the benefice in accordance with the norms established by Canon Law (cf. Can. 240; 334; 349, par. 2; 461; 1443–1445; 1472; 2394). This is called the act of taking possession, coming into possession, corporal institution (*captio possessionis, immissio in possessionem, institutio corporalis*; Can. 1443), or investiture or installation (*installatio*).

Rights and Duties of Beneficiaries. After having taken legitimate possession of a benefice, the beneficiary enjoys all the spiritual and temporal rights attached to his benefice. These rights, however, vary according to different benefices. Concerning the temporal rights of the beneficiary, particular mention must be made of the right already indicated above, to the fruits and revenues of the benefice and to use them for his maintenance, even though he may possess other revenues from other sources. He is obliged, however, to spend the superfluous income for the benefit of the poor or in behalf of charitable causes (Can. 1473) without prejudice to the right granted to Cardinals by Canon 239, par. 1, # 19.

The beneficiary is bound to fulfill faithfully the special duties attached to his benefice and also to recite daily the canonical hours. If, without legitimate reason, he fails to satisfy this obligation, he forefeits a portion of the income in proportion to the extent of his neglect (*pro rata omissionis*), and he is bound to give that portion of the income to the church fund (*fabricae ecclesiae*) or to the diocesan seminary or to the poor (Can. 1475). Moreover, he is bound to administer diligently all goods and property of his benefice and to repair all damages suffered by the benefice because of his negligent or careless administration (Can. 1476–1479; 1483).

Loss of Benefice. Prescinding from the factor of death, a beneficiary loses possession of his benefice by the following causes (Can. 183): (a) *By renunciation* (*renuntiatio, dimissio, resignatio*). Canon law distinguishes between express and tacit resignation. To be valid and lawful, an express resignation must be made according to the norm established by Canon Law and, generally, must be accepted by the competent ecclesiastical authority (Can. 184–187; 189–191; 568; 1484–1486). In certain cases specifically enumerated by the Code (religious profession or civil marriage of the beneficiary, etc.), the benefice is considered automatically or *ipso facto* vacant by tacit resignation, with no need of any declaration whatever on the part of the beneficiary (Can. 188). (b) *Through deprivation* by the legitimate ecclesiastical authority. Such privation of office or benefice may be a penalty (generally called *privatio*), either *latae* or *ferendae sententiae, i.e.*, incurred either *ipso facto* or inflicted by the judge or superior, or by administrative procedure (*amotis,* Can. 185, or *remotis,* Can. 2147 ff.). A cleric may not be deprived of an irremovable benefice, except in cases clearly established by the Code and by regular process. In the case of a removable benefice, the deprivation may be decreed by the Ordinary for any just reason, without any prescribed form of procedure; however, for the removal of a removable pastor, special norms obtain (Can. 192; 2299, par. 1; *see also* Removability). (c) *By transfer* from one benefice to another (to be distinguished from transfer of the benefice itself; *see* Innovation), which may be effected with the consent of the beneficiary or against his will. In the former case the transfer may be effected for any reasonable cause by the superior who has the right to accept the resignation from the former benefice and to confer another upon him. When the transfer is against the will of the cleric, the same norms generally apply as in the case of deprivation of office (Can. 193). The administrative transfer (*ob bonum animarum*) of pastors i governed by special norms (Can. 2162–2167). The Ordinary may propose o suggest a transfer to an irremovable pastor, but he cannot transfer him against his will, unless he shall have obtained special faculties from the Holy See. A removable pastor, however, may be transferred even against his will, provided that the new parish is equally good and the prescribed canonical norms are observed (*see* Removability).

Canon Law also admits an exchange (*permutatio*) of benefices between two beneficiaries. This, however, requires the consent of the legitimate ecclesiastical authority and observance of the prescribed canonical norms (Can. 1487–1488). *Led.*

BENEVOLENCE. See Donation.

BENIGNITY. See Clemency.

BESTIALITY. Bestiality is sexual intercourse between a human and an animal. Incomplete venereal acts committed with animals may be reduced to this category, but only if such acts are accompanied by a special affection for, or attachment to, this particular manner of satisfying one's passions. All biological findings show that a crossbreeding between man and animal is totally negative. The ancient supposition that such breeding could result in monstrous offspring is today generally discarded.

Bestiality is an abominable sin, the most grievous of all the sins of lust against nature (*See* Lust, Sexual Perversions), because it goes beyond the human species and is opposed to the primary end of the sexual act in the crudest possible manner.

Bestiality is an unnatural sin specifically different from simple pollution (Prop. 24, condemned by Alexander VII, Decree of Sept. 24, 1665: *Denz.* 1124). In Sacred Scripture it is condemned as a most heinous crime (Exod. 22:19; Lev. 18:23; 20:15–16). *Dam.*

BET, BETTING. See Gambling.

BETROTHAL (engagement to marry). By betrothal is understood a state leading to matrimony; a steady company-keeping between a man and a woman for the purpose of preparing for eventual marriage. In a wider sense, a man and a woman who are quite interested in each other and see much of each other are often called betrothed, even though they have made no decision (*procatio*) with regard to marriage. In a stricter sense (as understood here), a betrothal is that which follows a mutual promise between a man and a women to be faithful to each other, to the exclusion of all others, and to marry in the near future. This promise is made either by a formal agreement, or implicitly (*sponsalia*). Positive ecclesiastical law recognizes only a betrothal agreement made by a written document undersigned by both parties and by either the bishop or the pastor, or by two witnesses (Can. 1017, par. 1). An analogous prescription is found also in some civil codes of various countries. In practice, however, these formalities are not followed.

The attitude of older moral theologians relative to betrothal, a little more severe and negative than that of our own times, must be viewed in the climate of the matrimonial customs of that period, in which the choice of the spouse and preparation for marriage depended more on the parents than on the future spouses themselves. This practice accounted for less need of frequent dating. In modern times it is considered suitable that the betrothed themselves personally acquire a complete knowledge of the character and of the physical, psychological, and moral qualities of the future partner in order that they may, in a practical manner, become adjusted to each other, or explore the possibility of such an adjustment.

An engagement between two baptized persons is invalid both in the external forum as well as the forum of conscience if concluded without the formalities prescribed by Canon Law; it gives rise to no obligation of justice either for contracting marriage or for repairing the damages caused by an unjustified breaking off of the engagement. Christian conscience, however, recognizes the moral obligation to keep faith to a promise. (a) Concerning a future marriage: one may not withdraw a promise without a grave and proportionate cause, such as unfaithfulness or grave crimes imputable to the other party, election of a more perfect state, considerable change in the physical, psychological, moral or financial condition or, in general, any new factor which might give rise to a serious doubt as to the success of the marriage; this condition, of course, is implicit in every betrothal. (b) Concerning hidden defects (moral or physical): each party must spontaneously disclose those defects which may make marriage harmful (to the other party or to offspring) or substantially useless, such as diseases, particularly venereal, consumption, sterility, pregnancy, heavy debts, and the like. One who is unwilling to disclose these defects is under obligation to withdraw. It is not necessary, however, to disclose defects which might only make matrimony less desirable, such as one's past sins. (c) Concerning betrothal itself: mutual fidelity is an important element. Unfaithfulness in a betrothed is looked upon as a special type of unfaithfulness.

Concerning purity, the betrothed have the same obligations as all unmarried persons. Betrothal confers no right to complete or incomplete acts of impurity (see Lust, Lewdness, Kiss). Only those actions are allowed which, according to approved Christian customs of a country, are in use among betrothed, even though they may cause involuntary pleasurable feelings. Since love-making and familiarity between a man and a woman almost naturally lead to sexual relations, betrothal easily becomes a serious occasion of sin, which must be removed by judicious precautions, such as not becoming engaged unless the possibility of marriage within a reasonably short time (about a year) is foreseen, avoiding being alone too often or too long, using supernatural aids. *Dam.*

BIBLE. See New Testament, Old Testament.

BIGAMY. Bigamy is the crime committed by one who attempts a second marriage while the bond of a previous marriage is still in force. According to Canon 2356, even when the second marriage is merely civil, the bigamist is automatically (*ipso facto*) branded with infamy, and if, disregarding the Ordinary's admonition, he continues to live in the unlawful union, he is to be punished, according to the gravity of the circumstances, with either excommunication or personal interdict.

Besides bigamy properly so-called, as described above, Canon Law mentions another type of bigamy improperly so-called, in relation to individuals wishing to receive holy orders. According to Canon 984, included among those considered irregular by defect (*ex defectu*) are "bigamists," that is to say, persons who have contracted successively two or more valid marriages (see Remarriage). This irregularity is not a condemnation of the remarriage of widowers (or widows), considered unlawful by certain ancient rigorist sects, but it simply bars from sacred orders those who, by their repeated marriages, have proved to be little inclined or capable of that perfect chastity required of ministers of the Church.

BIGAMY AND REMARRIAGE. If a married person should attempt, during the life of his or her lawful spouse, a second religious marriage, the Ordinary must declare, through the promoter of justice, the second marriage null and void; and, since in such instances the nullity of the marriage can generally be proven from certain and authentic documents, the case may be decided by summary proceedings, without the formalities of an ordinary trial (Can. 1990–1991). In some countries, Italy for instance, bigamy (both marriages must have their civil effects) is punishable with imprisonment and may lead to loss of marital rights. *Bar.*

BILATERAL. See Contract.

BILLS OF EXCHANGE. See Letter of Credit.

BINATION AND TRINATION OF HOLY MASS. Divine law does not forbid the celebration of two or more Masses on the same day. In the Oriental Church, however, the priest as a rule may not celebrate more than one Mass on the same day. On the contrary, in the Latin Church priests frequently were permitted to say two Masses, especially on Sundays and holy days. But this privilege eventually led to abuses and, as a result, Pope Innocent III established that, except on Christmas Day and cases of necessity, a priest may celebrate only one Mass on the same day (X, 3, 41, 3). For the same reasons Councils and Pope Benedict XIV enacted the following regulations: Priests are never permitted to celebrate two Masses on the same day, except for the spiritual needs of the faithful, i.e., when a considerable portion of the people would otherwise fail to satisfy their obligation of hearing Mass or when a sick person would be deprived of receiving the Viaticum (P. Gasparri, Sources of Canon Law, II, n. 365).

Canon 806 grants priests permission to trinate, i.e., to say three Masses, on Christmas Day and on All Souls' Day. Trination on any other occasion requires an Apostolic indult, which is rarely granted. Permission to binate, i.e., to say two Masses on the same day, may be obtained either from the Holy See (in which case the conditions of the indult must be observed) or from the local Ordinary, who may grant such a faculty: (a) only for Sundays and holy days of obligation (for other occasions, especially suppressed feasts, the Bishop must have special Apostolic faculties); (b) whenever a considerable number of faithful, generally about fifteen or twenty people, would go without hearing Mass; (c) only in case of real necessity of the faithful, e.g., when a pastor has charge of two parishes far removed from each other, or when the parochial church is not large enough to accommodate all the faithful at one Mass (this applies in the case of other churches as well); (d) when no other priest is available to say Mass. In case of urgent necessity, the priest may presume permission to binate, with the obligation of notifying the Bishop afterwards. A priest who presumes to binate without necessity or without canonical cause is to be suspended from celebrating Mass for a period of time to be determined by the Ordinary (Can. 2321). *Toc.*

Note: Recent papal dispositions have brought about an enlargement of the concepts of the necessity and utility for the faithful. Consequently, bishops enjoy wider faculties in the matter of granting permission for bination. Thus, today such permission may be granted for First Fridays, funerals, weddings, *etc.*

BIRETTA. Dating back to the tenth century, the biretta (*pileus, pileolus*) is a clerical headdress worn during ecclesiastical functions. Originally a kind of skull cap adhering closely to the head, it gradually developed into its present triangular or square form with three (sometimes four) ridges or peaks on the upper surface, making it easier to grasp. In the sixteenth century there was added a central tuft or tassel which, however, is not always present. Its color is black with black tuft for the ordinary clergy, black with purple tuft for domestic prelates, black with crimson tuft for prothonotaries apostolic. Bishops, abbots and prelates *nullius* wear a purple biretta (Can. 325; cf., however, Can. 625), while cardinals wear a red one.

Besides the liturgical biretta, Canon Law also recognizes a *doctoral biretta* with four peaks, the use of which is permitted to clerics or laymen with degrees. Neither laymen nor ecclesiastics, however, are allowed to wear the doctoral biretta during liturgical functions (Congregation of Sacred Rites, 2877, 3873).

The use of the biretta, which forms part of the choral garb, is regulated by special liturgical norms. As regards Holy Mass, the use of the biretta is permitted only when the celebrant and officers of a solemn Mass are seated during the singing of certain parts by the choir (this norm applies to everyone; the privilege of wearing the *pileolus*, granted by Canon 811, par. 1, to cardinals, bishops, and abbots in the celebration of Mass, refers to the skull cap only). The rubrics, however, prescribe that the biretta (or the mitre by those enjoying the privilege) be worn while going from the sacristy to the altar and vice versa.

One of the most important ceremonies in the creation of cardinals is the imposition of the cardinalitial biretta. This ceremony is performed personally by the pope, after the consistory, when the newly created cardinals are in Rome. If the creation of a cardinal takes place outside Rome, the scarlet biretta is sent by a delegate of the Holy See.

Concerning the moral value of the liturgical prescriptions relative to the biretta, see Rubrics. It should be generally kept in mind that since such rubrics may be classified as accidental, they do not oblige under grave inconvenience. On the other hand, the use of the biretta at wrong times and places in liturgical functions is an abuse that needs to be corrected. *Pal.*

BIRTH CONTROL. In a general sense, birth control means the voluntary regulation of births or of the number of children. Prescinding from the motivating reasons behind the practice and the various methods or devices employed, birth control is not in itself (*per se*) reprehensible. For it cannot be demonstrated that the divine precept to increase and multiply (Genesis 1:28) is binding on each individual or as a constant obligation. In fact, the precept is directed to the collectivity; hence, voluntary abstention from conjugal intercourse on the part of married persons, with its necessary consequence of birth limitation, cannot be said to be immoral; on the contrary, such abstention can become virtuous when inspired by motives of a higher order. Neither is the use of the so-called "rhythm method" immoral when there are serious reasons for such a practice (*see* Periodic Continence).

Birth control, however, ordinarily connotes prevention of birth by the use of a contraceptive measure; such a practice takes different names according to the different methods employed and the different principles on which it is based. It is called *onanism* (*q.v.*) from Onan

(Genesis 38:9), to whom is attribute the practice of a particular method of birth control consisting in a deliberate and sinful interruption of the sexual act It is called *Malthusianism* or, more properly, *neo-Malthusianism*, from the theor of Thomas Malthus (d. 1834), who alarmed over the supposed disproportion between population increase and the increase of food supply, argued the nee for checking or limiting births, a theor later spread by his followers without regard to the moral character of the meth ods employed (*see* Neo-Malthusianism) The operation known as *sterilizatio* (which may be therapeutic, eugenic, or punitive) is also designated as birt control.

In the present article we shall dea with birth control in general. Concernin the specific morality of the various meth ods employed, their historical back ground, and the doctrine of the Church the reader is directed to the respectiv articles on Onanism, Sterilization, Abor tion, Castration, Contraceptives, *etc.*

HISTORY. Although birth control ca be traced back to the beginnings of th human race, its development as a genera and widespread movement began in th eighteenth century, when Malthus firs sounded the alarm that some day th ever-increasing population would outstri the means of subsistence. In the eco nomic sphere the fears of Malthus hav long since proved unfounded; in fac the economic crises of recent years hav been attributed to overproduction or un equal distribution, not to population in crease.

In the moral sphere, Malthus' theor (which recommended abstinence from sexual intercourse as a method of check ing population increase) was carried t deplorable extremes by Francis Place who advocated instead birth preventio or contraception, without any restrictio upon sexual relations. This policy, whic was directly opposed to the teaching of Malthus, marked the beginning of veritable social plague that has infeste our civilization, causing incalculab moral harm. Whereas prolonged sexu abstinence remains possible to but imited few possessed of exceptional will power and moral strength, the method of Places gives free reign to the most selfish form of hedonism. It is true that Places advocated artificial birth prevention only when directed by reasons of health or economic necessity, but in practice the method has been adopted by many for purely selfish reasons, as demonstrated by the fact that often it is the woman who insists on practicing birth control, and that feminism has fully endorsed the birth control movement as a necessary phase of its struggle to achieve equality of sexes, with great damage to woman's feminine character and maternal role.

Deleterious Effects. The practice of contraception is generally based on an erroneous evaluation of the world's economic necessities, on exaggerated fear of poverty and want, and on selfish allegations and concerns about physical appearance. The practice of contraception is contrary to ethico-religious principles, and is attended by effects that are gravely detrimental to the individual and society.

Induced abortion (*q.v.*) is the most criminal and anti-demographic form of birth control, a heinous crime that can only be explained by a woman's antimaternal outlook and complete lack of conscience. The crime of abortion cannot always be effectively detected by the civil law, but in the ecclesiastical sphere it is punishable by automatic excommunication reserved to the Ordinary (Can. 2350, par. 1). It also constitutes a grave danger to the physical and mental health of the woman.

The various mechanical devices used to obstruct normal conception may give rise to neuro-hormonal disturbances or chronic leukorrhea, eventually leading to sterility; they may also cause abrasions and erosions which may subsequently become a fertile ground of very dangerous tumors.

The use of acids designed to kill the spermatozoa in the long run causes corrosion of the uterine walls; and when these acids do not kill the spermatozoa, they so damage them as to cause the birth of deformed or defective offspring.

Interrupted intercourse, or contraception by withdrawal, though apparently harmless, in the long run gives rise to numerous uterine-ovarian disorders in the female, to prostatic hypertrophy in the male, and to serious psychoneurotic disturbances in both parties. Though different from interrupted intercourse, *amplexus reservatus* (reserved coitus or restrained orgasm) is not to be considered wholly unobjectionable on moral grounds (cf. Sacred Congregation of the Holy Office, Admonition of June 30, 1952); nor are those who practice it likely to escape all the physical and psychological consequences noted in connection with interrupted coition.

Sterilization (*See* Sterility) frequently gives rise to profound and complex psychoneuroses deriving from a sense of guilt, the frustration of never being able to satisfy the maternal or paternal instinct, and the like.

Whatever the method used, the practice of contraception is not only physically and psychologically harmful to those who indulge in it, but also and always a grave moral violation of the most elementary ethico-religious principles. In fact, it becomes all the more grave as those who make a regular practice of it (obstinate violators of the law of God and devoid of any trust in Divine Providence) dare speak of it without restraint or self-effacement, and even pass on to others information about their own contraceptive methods and other scandalous practices.

Remedies. In order to contain so great an evil, first of all, the Christian conscience should be re-awakened and made more aware of the grave duty to obey the commandments of God and to fear His just punishments. Nations with underpopulated areas should relax their immigration laws and open their lands to people from overcrowded countries. Adequate legislation should be enacted for the subsidizing of large families. Children are admittedly a drain on the family finances not only in infancy but all through adolescence; and as the number of children increases, the family standard of living tends to become lower. But it is also true that as the children are able to make their contribution to the family income, the standard of living of the family is susceptible of improvement and even of considerable rise.

Physicians, aware of the neuro-psycho-somatic damage which usually results from contraception, are in a very favorable position to wage an effective campaign against these practices by instructing married people concerning their effects. By their instructions they can enlighten doubtful and anxious patients and be an effective instrument in leading people back to the observance of the moral law in the matter of conjugal relations. *Riz.*

BIRTHDAY (*dies natalis*). Contrary to the common notion, a birthday, called *dies natalis* in ecclesiastical terminology, is the anniversary of the death of a saint, or in a broader sense, the day on which his feast is celebrated. Sometimes it indicates any kind of anniversary, such as the anniversary of one's ordination, baptism, of the dedication of a church, *etc.*

Exceptions to the general Christian custom of celebrating the day of the death of a person as his birthday (born to life eternal), are December 25th, on which day, since the fourth century, the Latin Church has celebrated the birth of Jesus Christ, and June 24th, the date of the birth of St. John the Baptist. These exceptions, of course, are justified by very extraordinary reasons. In the case of Christ the reasons are based on the fact that His birth was a totally exceptional one, miraculous and sinless. Similar reasons apply also to the birth of St. John the Baptist, who was sanctified in his mother's womb (Luke 1:41). *Cig.*

BISHOP. Besides the primacy of the Supreme Pontiff, the episcopate is also of divine institution in the Church. Bishops are the legitimate successors of the Apostles to whom Our Lord gave power to rule and to govern the Church under the authority of Peter (Can. 329, par. 1). Since the office of bishops is of divine law, it may not, in its essence, be suppressed by the Roman Pontiff, who nevertheless has the power to limit the extent of the jurisdiction of a bishop, the territory, and the number of individuals over whom he may preside. The individual bishoprics are, of course, institutions strictly of human law.

Bishops are *residential* or *titular*. A residential Bishop is a Prelate endowed with the fullness of the priesthood who by reason of his office possesses the power *utriusque fori*, for the government of a particular diocese in which he resides (Can. 334, par. 1). A *titular* Bishop (so called from the title of an ancient suppressed diocese) also possesses the fullness of the priesthood but he exercises no particular jurisdiction by virtue of his office (Can. 233, par. 2, 348). *Coadjutor* and *auxiliary* Bishops are chosen from among the titular Bishops. A coadjutor may or may not have the right of succession (Can. 350–354). There are also titular Archbishops, generally, Nuncios and Apostolic Delegates.

Residential Bishops, if they are dependent on a Metropolitan (*see* Archbishop) are either suffragans (Can. 274, 338, par. 4) or directly subject to the Holy See. Finally, a distinction is made between *secular Bishops* and *religious Bishops* (Can. 627–629). Religious Bishops are members of a religious order or institute; they remain bound to their religious vows within the limits compatible to their office. If they resign their posts, they are required to return to their religious house.

The right of appointing Bishops belongs solely to the Sovereign Pontiff (Can. 329, par. 2) who for their designation may grant certain privileges to the Rulers of a certain state (Can. 332, par. 1), or honor such privileges if given to them by preceding popes. These privileges are often included in concordats between governments and the Holy See. To be appointed Bishop, one must be canonically suitable, that is, a cleric endowed with excellent spiritual, moral and intellectual qualities. The judgment of his aptitude is reserved to the Holy See (Can. 331).

Bishops are announced in a consistory

their appointment is made by a Papal Bull. A newly appointed bishop must receive episcopal consecration within three months following appointment, and if an Ordinary, he must be installed in his diocese within four months (Can. 333). Upon taking canonical possession he begins to exercise his ordinary jurisdiction (Can. 334, par. 2–3).

The principal obligations of a residential Bishop are: (a) residence (*q.v.*) in the diocese (Can. 338); (b) offering of Mass for the people on established days (Can. 339); (c) *ad limina* visit (a term including various obligations of submission to the Apostolic See) to be made every five years (Can. 341, 340, 342); (d) canonical visitation of his diocese (*see* Visitation of the Diocese; Can. 343–346).

A Bishop has the title of Excellency and enjoys special prerogatives, privileges, and honors (Can. 349); among them the right of precedence in his diocese over all others, except Cardinals, Papal Legates, and his own Metropolitan. *Fel.*

BLACK MARKET. Widely used during the last war, the expression "Black Market" indicates a phenomenon common in times of economic restriction. When the total quantity of disposable goods in a community is deemed insufficient to meet the normal wants or needs of consumers, the public authorities intervene to regulate the distribution and price level of the more necessary commodities. The buying and selling of products in violation of the rationing and price laws —especially when practiced at rates far in excess of legal and normal price levels —constitutes the so-called *black market*, further aggravated by the unlawful practice of *hoarding supplies.*

The various causes leading to black market activities are: forced economic restrictions, uncertainty about the future, instability of the purchasing power of money, excessive rationing, marked disproportion between total supply of rationed goods and basic necessities of life and, finally, the factor of human selfishness, especially as manifested in the practice of depriving the community of basic necessities for the purpose of engaging in speculation or of diverting it to less serious needs. The existence and extent of black market activities in times of hardship and difficulties provide a fairly accurate index of the social conscience of a citizenry.

The repressive measures adopted by governments against black market operations bear a direct relation to the social conscience of the citizenry. When black market transactions are limited in number, they can be effectively curbed by the application of penal measures; they can also be curtailed because the public conscience itself rejects and condemns such practices.

When, however, black market activities become widespread and are practiced on a large scale, any attempt made at suppressing them becomes extremely difficult, if not impossible. In such circumstances, it is also difficult to determine the degree of immorality connected with such activities, in view of the general upheaval in social standards and relations; and black market dealings, as a common practice of the vast majority of the citizens, frequently assume the aspect of an ordinary measure of self-preservation. *Pav.*

BLASPHEMY. Blasphemy is any insulting or contumelious language uttered against the Divinity. In a strict sense, blasphemy (*blasphemia*—damaging or injurious expression) consists in the spoken word. It is quite clear, however, that mental formulation of injurious expressions against God also constitute blasphemy in the true and proper sense. Theologians also call blasphemy all insulting actions against God (such as spitting toward heaven), which may easily become sacrilegious (*see* Sacrilege) if directed against God through the misuse of things dedicated to Him (*e.g.*, spitting on a crucifix, contemptuous trampling on it). The ultimate in blasphemy is committed by the individual who, not content with uttering blasphemous words, resorts to the written or printed word.

Blasphemy may consist of expressions and actions that are variously injurious to God: (a) attributing to God something that is not befitting Him (*e.g.*, saying that God is unjust, that He is the author of sin); (b) denying Him something which is His due (*e.g.*, denying His paternal love for creatures); (c) attributing to creatures something that is exclusively God's, or worse still, attributing to His creatures greater and better qualities (*e.g.*, declaring that Satan is more powerful than God); (d) speaking contemptuously of God, ridiculing His name, scoffing at sacred persons or things, out of contempt for God or for religion; (e) uttering maledictions, imprecations, or outrages either against God or the saints.

Blasphemy may be directed against God directly or indirectly. Indirectly, if hurled primarily against persons or things dear to God, such as the saints, or creatures more prominently reflecting the grandeur and majesty of God (such as the heavens, the world, the soul, religion, *etc.*), and against sacred things, such as the sacraments, divine worship. Moreover, blasphemy may be uttered with the explicit intention of outraging or insulting God (direct or diabolical blasphemy), or it may be uttered as an outburst of passion, anger, impatience (indirect blasphemy). Finally, if the blasphemous utterance contains a denial of or an assertion against faith, it is called heretical blasphemy.

Blasphemy, whether direct or indirect, uttered with full advertence and deliberation, is always and without exception a very grievous sin. In fact, blasphemy is a violation of man's most elementary duty toward God, the duty of acknowledging the supreme sovereignty of the Creator (*see* Adoration, Worship, Religion). Consequently, blasphemy is the greatest outrage against the supreme dignity of God and an act of the greatest rebellion. At the same time, it brings the greatest degradation upon man himself, whose perfection consists precisely in his subordination to God. In essence, therefore, blasphemy is more grievous than any other violation of the Ten Commandments, even homicide — although, as St. Thomas wisely observes (*Sum. Theol.*, IIa—IIae, q. 13, art. 3, ad 1), it is less grave than homicide as to its effects, since the latter inflicts more damage upon one's neighbor than blasphemy upon God, who cannot be harmed by anyone.

It is to be noted, however, that only those expressions are to be considered blasphemous which are so intended by the one uttering them or which are so understood by their natural meaning or common acceptance of the words used. Moreover, blasphemy is imputable only when made as an assertion, not when it is merely repeated as uttered by another.

In the Old Testament blasphemy was considered a capital offense, and in the early days of the Church and throughout the Middle Ages severe penalties were meted out to blasphemers. Modern legislation is much more lenient in this regard. In present-day ecclesiastical law there is no specific penalty for blasphemy, although one may be imposed at the discretion of the local Ordinary (Can. 2323). Heretical blasphemy, however, is subject to the penalties inflicted against heretics, one of them being the penalty of *ipso facto* excommunication (Can. 2314). *Dam.*

BLENNORRHAGIA. *See* Venereal Diseases.

BLESSED. Blessed is the official title given to those who have been beatified, formally or equivalently, by the Church. Permisssion of the Holy See to venerate a Servant of God is always based on very sound reasons (*see* Beatification and Canonization). Refusal to accept a decree of beatification, obviously, would be rash and gravely sinful.

The private veneration of beatified persons, or of their images and relics (*e.g.*, kissing them, carrying them on one's person, *etc.*), is permitted to all. On the contrary, the public veneration of beatified persons is restricted to certain places or religious groups. Ordinarily, the name of a beatified person is not inserted in the martyrology, nor even in the local calendar or that of a religious order enjoying the faculty of publicly venerating the particular beatified person. Without special permission, images, statues, or paintings of such a person may neither be exposed in churches for public veneration nor placed upon altars, unless the faculty of celebrating Mass in his honor was duly granted. Again, without a special indult, the relics of a person who has been beatified may neither be exposed in churches nor carried in procession, except in those places where the Holy See has granted the faculty to say the Office and the Mass in honor of said person. Without special permission, a beatified person may not be selected as patron or titular of a church. Permission for public veneration of a beatified person granted in one place may not be extended to another place without an apostolic indult (decree of the Sacred Congregation of Rites, Sept. 27, 1659, confirmed by Alexander VII; cf. Can. 1256, 1277, 1287). *Man.*

BLESSED WATER. *See* Holy Water.

BLESSING AND CONSECRATION. In general, these two terms are used to indicate the rites whereby persons or things are set apart or dedicated in a particular manner to divine worship. If the rite is performed for the purpose of withholding a person or thing from any worldly use to be devoted exclusively or for the most part to divine service, the rite is called *consecration;* if it is performed for the purpose of making a person or a thing an instrument or bearer of divine favors, the rite is called *blessing.* The distinction between the two terms is not always maintained in liturgical or juridical texts; ordinarily, however, the difference between blessing and consecration lies in this: in the blessing a less solemn formula is employed and a lesser intimate effect and juridical value ensues from it.

Blessings and consecrations may be *common* or *reserved.* Some of the reserved blessings and consecrations are the exclusive right of the pope or of bishops (*see* Papal Blessing).

The essential elements of a blessing and consecration are: the sacred *minister,* the *matter* or object, and the *form* or the words employed. A blessing may also consist in a simple sign of the cross (*q.v.*), with or without recitation of a formula. Various examples of such blessings are found in the celebration of Holy Mass. An example of a blessing with formula attached thereto is the *blessing before and after meals,* which is of very ancient origin. Blessings and consecrations belong to the category of rites called *sacramentals.* For certain particular blessings, *see* Holy Water, Chalice, Cemetery; *also* Benediction of the Blessed Sacrament, Eucharistic Consecration. *Cig.*

BLESSING BEFORE AND AFTER MEALS. *See* Blessings, Sacramentals.

BLESSING OF HOMES. *See* Holy Water, Sacramentals.

BLESSING, PAPAL. The papal blessing is that which is solemnly imparted to the faithful on the occasion of the more important religious feasts of the year, either personally by the pope or by someone delegated by him. A plenary indulgence is attached to the blessing.

Bishops enjoy the faculty of imparting the papal blessing three times a year, twice in virtue of Canon 914, that is, on Easter Sunday and on another day of the year, and a third time in virtue of the decree of the Sacred Apostolic Penitentiary of July 20, 1942. Abbots or prelates *nullius,* vicars and prefects apostolic may give this blessing twice a year, once in virtue of Canon 914 and again in virtue of the above-mentioned decree. Likewise, most religious orders enjoy the privilege of giving the papal blessing on certain days of the year, subject, however, to the regulations of Canon 915. Moreover, this faculty may be granted, either directly by the Holy Father or by the Secretariat of State of the Sacred Penitentiary, in the name of the pope, on extraordinary occasions, such as the observance of a centenary, a silver or golden sacerdotal jubilee, a first Mass, and the like.

From the earliest days of the Church

the Roman pontiffs have usually imparted their blessing to the faithful, not only the ordinary blessing, but also the solemn one, with a plenary indulgence attached to it. The solemn blessing was given by the Holy Father personally on extraordinary occasions and on the following days: (a) Holy Thursday (after reposition of the Blessed Sacrament in the sepulchre or repository), and Easter Sunday (following solemn pontifical services) from the loggia of the Vatican Basilica (St. Peter's); (b) the feast of the Ascension, from the loggia of St. John Lateran; (c) the feast of the Assumption, from the loggia of St. Mary Major. This blessing, called *papal* or *apostolic*, and ordinarily described as a most moving and impressive ceremony, was received with great emotion by the kneeling crowds.

Among the extraordinary occasions on which the papal blessing was imparted, it suffices to mention the blessing given by Pope Clement VII on May 1, 1525, following the pontifical Mass in St. John Lateran, on the occasion of the Holy Year, and also the blessing given later from the Vatican loggia on the feast of the Holy Apostles Peter and Paul.

Since, however, only a relatively small number of faithful could come to Rome to receive the papal blessing, the Roman pontiffs on several occasions empowered others to impart this blessing in their name, while princes from remote places petitioned that the papal blessing be brought to them through their delegates. But Clement XIII, by the apostolic letter of Sept. 15, 1762, revoked every concession of this kind, decreeing that in the future, upon specific authorization of the pope, the papal blessing could be imparted once a year by the following: patriarchs, primates, archbishops and bishops (twice a year), and prelates having the privilege of wearing pontificals and jurisdiction over a certain territory. This faculty, as granted to religious orders, was left unchanged, although special regulations were issued in subsequent documents with regard to its exercise. In the present legislation, the faculty of imparting the papal blessing is regulated by the dispositions of Canons 914–915 and by a decree of the Sacred Congregation of Apostolic Penitentiary of July 20, 1942.

Besides the papal blessing, properly so called, there are also (a) the apostolic blessing or last blessing (mentioned in Can. 468, par. 2), given to persons *in articulo mortis* or in danger of death (*see* Absolution); (b) the papal blessing imparted by preachers, *in fine concionum*, that is, at the end of a Lenten or Advent course, at the end of a retreat or mission. Such a blessing is called papal or apostolic, because it is imparted in the name of the Holy Father and because it has a plenary indulgence attached to it.

Up to the time of the decree of the Sacred Apostolic Penitentiary of June 15, 1939, when the papal blessing was imparted by the Holy Father himself, the only conditions for gaining the attached plenary indulgence were physical presence and the state of grace. Following the above decree, and at the present time, physical presence is no longer required (since the blessing may also be received by radio or television), but the usual conditions for gaining any other plenary indulgence are required, namely confession, reception of Holy Communion, a visit to a Church or public oratory, and a prayer for the intention of the Holy Father.

If the papal blessing is imparted by others, the requirements for gaining the attached indulgence are the same as always, namely, physical presence and fulfillment of the usual conditions. From this it follows that if a bishop were to impart the papal blessing outside a Church, in a public square, persons receiving the blessing from adjacent windows overlooking the area could gain the indulgence, because they are considered physically present. On the other hand, nuns dwelling in an adjacent monastery would not gain the indulgence, because they are considered physically absent.

Those who go to confession and receive Holy Communion on Easter Sunday may gain the plenary indulgence attached to the papal blessing, and at the same time fulfill the Easter duty. *De A.*

BLINDNESS. Total blindness is listed among those bodily defects which constitute an irregularity, permanently barring a man from the reception of Holy Orders. Blindness constitutes an irregularity not only in a candidate to the priesthood, but also in one already ordained. Thus, a priest who contracts total blindness, or whose vision becomes so impaired as to render him unable to read the missal, is considered irregular and requires a special dispensation or faculty to celebrate Mass.

The practice of the Church (S. C. Conc. *Neapolitana*, 13 Sept. 1814, in Pampilon., 28 March 1733) is not favorable toward the granting of such a dispensation in the case of blindness or seriously impaired vision contracted before ordination, especially if the candidate is still a layman or only in minor orders. There are no recent instances of the granting of such dispensations. On the other hand, the Church readily permits a priest who has become blind to celebrate, even daily, the votive Mass of the Blessed Virgin, on condition that he celebrate in a private oratory and that he be assisted by another priest. The Church does not sanction assistance by a layman, no matter how thoroughly acquainted he may be with the rubrics of the Mass. The reason is obvious: the occasion may arise where the assistant will have to perform certain acts only permissible to a priest.

Prior to the Code of Canon Law, blindness or seriously impaired vision in the so-called canonical eye (the left eye) constituted an irregularity. Today this is no longer so, except perhaps that such a condition might be regarded as unbecoming (*ob decentiam*), a condition, however, which can easily be remedied through the fitting of a glass eye.

The dispensation of celebrating the votive Mass of the Blessed Virgin granted to a priest with impaired vision is not valid if that priest should eventually lose his sight altogether. In such a case, a further dispensation is necessary (cf. Instruct. of Sacred Cong. of Rites, Jan. 12, 1921).

The blind are exempt from all obligations of the positive law which they cannot fulfill without danger as a result of their blindness. In the field of civil law, they have all the rights and duties of other citizens.

It should be the concern of all civil authorities to promote the re-education and training of the blind, helping them to become useful members of society, and at the same time reducing the number of public charges. *M.d.G.*

BLOOD TYPES. *The transfusion of blood* (an operation by which a certain quantity of blood is taken from one individual, called *donor*, and is injected, through a vein, into the circulatory system of another) is a therapeutic treatment used intermittently since ancient times. However, in the last fifty years, the practice of blood transfusions has reached vast proportions everywhere as a result of intensive study by Landsteiner and other scholars which led to the discovery of the *serological constitution* of the blood and, therefore, to the identification of the causes of many failures and fatalities before the discovery was made.

It was observed, first of all, that certain human serums (meaning the watery portion that remains after coagulation) had the property of amassing into irregular heaps (i.e. of *agglutinating*) red corpuscles belonging to other men. This phenomenon is called *isoagglutination*; the agglutinating anti-bodies are called isoagglutinins, while the special *antigens* contained in the red corpuscles are called agglutinogens. On the theory that two agglutinogens (indicated by the letters A and B) and two isoagglutinins (anti-A and anti-B) are variously present in the blood all humans are classified into four groups from the standpoint of their blood or, as it is commonly said, four *blood types:* O (zero), A, B, AB.

A minute description of the relations between agglutinogens and isoagglutinins in each type of blood and the enumeration of the numerous subdivisions of blood types is omitted as of no great practical import to this article.

DETERMINATION OF BLOOD TYPES.

The exact determination of the type of blood of a particular individual is indispensable in the hemo-transfusion practice to avoid fatal accidents due to the agglutination of red corpuscles that are incompatible with the recipient's blood. A few drops of his blood are placed in contact with hemo-diagnostic serums containing anti-A and anti-B isoagglutinins.

If the red corpuscles gather in groups surrounded by a colorless liquid the agglutination is positive; if the corpuscles appear uniformly scattered in the liquid, which appears rose-hued, the agglutination is negative.

Once the blood type of an individual is determined, the blood transfusion is carried out according to standard procedures, carefully bearing in mind that an individual of type A blood may receive only type B or O; an individual of type AB, because he lacks iso-agglutinin, may receive blood of any type (for this reason he is called *general receiver*), while a type O individual can only receive blood of the same type; he is called *general giver* because he can give his blood to any other group.

THE "RH FACTOR." Important scientific discoveries of Landsteiner and Wiener have led to further achievements which have been of clinical value but also involve moral questions of importance.

These scholars, in 1937, inoculating female rabbits with the blood of a monkey (Macacus Rhesus), produced antibodies which caused agglutination of the red corpuscles of that type of monkey. A couple of years later, the same scholars proved that the same rabbit anti-bodies caused agglutination of the red corpuscles of certain types of human blood. The new agglutinating element, similar to the one existing in the red corpuscles of the Macacus Rhesus, was called the *RH factor*, from the first two letters of the monkey's name, and the corresponding agglutinins were called anti-RH.

Further experiments have shown that the RH factor is present in 85% of individuals of the white race, in 92% of the Negroes and in 100% of the Chinese.

Thus, human beings have been classified into two categories: RH positive (or RH plus) and RH negative (or RH minus, or simply RH).

The RH plus factor is transmitted by heredity as a dominant Mendelian character, while the RH negative character is recessive. Therefore, as genetics show, the RH negative are homozygous, while the RH plus may be either homozygous or heterozygous.

In more recent times, various RH subtypes have been discovered.

It is important to know the function of the RH factor in pathology, both for the purpose of blood transfusions and for certain serious diseases of the fetus and the new-born child.

Concerning the hemo-transfusional aspect, the RH factor is at times responsible for fatal accidents, even when the transfusion was correctly performed and the incompatibility of certain blood types described in the preceding paragraphs was taken into full account. Such accidents are due to the fact that if the blood of an RH plus individual is transfused into an RH negative individual, the latter may produce RH anti-bodies with no apparent damage at first; yet if, years later, other RH plus transfusions are made (a probable thing, since their number is very large, i.e., 85%), there will appear increasingly serious symptoms of incompatibility between the two bloods resulting in hemolytic crises of fever, hemoglobinuria, jaundice, azotemia, *etc.*

The effects of the RH factor in the pathology of pregnancy and of the new-born, is evident in a case in which the husband is an RH plus type and the wife RH negative. The possibility that in such a case the fruit of conception may be an RH plus, small quantities of fetal red corpuscles (RH plus) may enter the blood of the pregnant woman (RH negative), particularly in the last few months of pregnancy. The RH negative blood will hasten to produce anti-RH substances capable of destroying the RH plus red corpuscles; such substances, entering the fetal organism as nutritional liquids will destroy more or less rapidly and extensively red corpuscles; hence the appearance of a disease, once called erythroblastosis, but now called *hemolytic disease of the new-born* or *congenital hemolytic anemia.*

This terrible disease is characterized by a rapid and serious anemia, grave alterations of the liver and cerebral alterations (nuclear-jaundice) that may show up only at a later date, with more or less conspicuous disturbances in the somatic and psychological development of the child.

Since the production of anti-RH substances in the blood plasma of an RH negative woman is as slow and gradual as the passage of this substance into the fetus, the first child of an RH plus man and an RH negative woman usually is born free of hemolytic disease, while successive pregnancies will produce children more and more diseased and may cause the death of the fetus or abortion. After a few normal children, a number of more or less gravely diseased fetuses may follow, if in the meantime the RH negative woman received a transfusion of RH plus blood, for such a transfusion is capable of giving rise to the above-mentioned condition, that is, the production of anti-RH substances in the blood plasma of an RH negative woman. Moreover, since the RH plus father may be heterozygous some children will be RH negative, others RH plus; with the result of an apparently capricious alternation of normal and sick children.

THERAPEUTIC AND MEDICO-LEGAL CONSIDERATIONS. To combat the effects of the RH factor, physicians use two methods of treatment: preventive and curative.

As preventive measures, any blood transfusion in the case of girls and women of procreation age should be avoided unless blood type is carefully established first. If they are found to be RH negative at no time shall RH plus blood be administered to them. If it is established that the blood of a pregnant woman is RH negative, the blood of the husband should be examined, and if it is found to be the RH plus type, a periodic check of anti-RH substances in the maternal blood shall be prescribed in order to watch any possible increase, in which case timely precautions shall be taken for the protection of the coming child (*see* below).

At the present time there is only one treatment of hemolytic disease, namely, the so-called *exsanguine transfusions* (substitution of the patient's blood with an equal quantity of RH negative blood); furthermore, the mother shall not nurse her own child, for, the maternal milk also contains RH anti-bodies. Attempts made to prevent the formation of anti-RH substances in the plasma of RH negative women to check anti-bodies already formed or render them harmless, have given no effective results up to the present time.

In the medico-legal field, the study of blood types has proved extremely helpful, not only in establishing paternity (see), but also in ascertaining the real culprit in certain criminal cases, by determining, among other things, whether a blood stain belongs to the victim or to the accused. This element is often extremely important to the ends of justice.

MORAL CONSIDERATIONS. It is superfluous to state that blood transfusion is always morally lawful, just as is any other honest therapeutic aid of proven effectiveness. It is necessary, however, that the physician pay particular attention not only to the matter of blood types, but also to the RH factor.

In the obstetrical field the physician should be diligent in taking all the precautionary measures indicated in the preceding paragraph bearing in mind particularly that, as a syphilis test is always advisable in the case of a woman who has previously had spontaneous abortions, the RH factor must also be suspected as possibly responsible for similar occurrences.

Before concluding we shall dwell briefly on two important moral problems concerning the RH factor.

Among more educated people *preoccupation with the RH factor* seems to be making considerable inroads, in fact it tends to mar at times the serenity of the spouses to the point of suggesting voluntary limitation of offspring to one child to avoid unpleasant experiences. In view of this, it is advisable and dutiful that these persons be reassured of the fact that since there is a large disproportion between individuals of the RH plus and those of the RH negative types, the percentage of marriages between individuals of different blood type is very small; also, among these the risks are restricted to the few cases in which the husband is RH plus (the one possible danger to the children); that there is an additional and very notable reduction of risks due to causes generally still unknown, but which account for only 5% of the couples with different blood type (wife RH negative, husband RH plus) having children stricken with hemolytic disease; finally that such a disease usually appears in a slight form at first and only in successive pregnancies in a graver form. We must, then, conclude that in all cases the probability of having children stricken by hemolytic disease is very low. Only after the first (usually mild) occurrence one must look into the matter of taking appropriate treatments.

The second moral problem concerns the conduct of the obstetrician when he finds the characteristic agglutinins in a pregnant woman's blood or when the latter's case history is such as to give rise to a positive suspicion that the husband may be homozygous (in which case the unborn child is surely an RH plus).

The suggestion of a therapeutic abortion must be rejected since it is condemned by the moral law and devoid of any justifying reason. The attitude of non-intervention must be set aside for abstention means certain death. A cautious intervention is to be advised along the following line: the physician shall systematically check the rate of the the agglutinins in the mother's blood; by means of periodic X-rays he shall check the uterine content for the first signs of a feto-placental *anasarca* which is a sure indication of a forthcoming fetal death; at this point a premature delivery should be effected (*see* abortion) as a compromise between the increasing dangers of a hemolytic disease in evolu-

tion and the lesser risks of prematurity; this premature delivery shall be carried out at a time in which the fetus is not (at least presumably) already irreparably affected by the RH factor, and at the same time is capable of autonomous life (through with the aid of all modern facilities, such as incubator, *etc.*).

These preventive measures and a prompt recourse to the above-mentioned *exsanguine transfusions* in the case of an insurgent severe hemolytic disease make the dangers inherent in the RH factor statistically insignificant and allow the spouses to lead a matrimonial life free of the inevitable worries resulting from inexact information concerning the effects of this particular hematological factor. *Riz.*

BODY. The word *body* is taken here to mean the material and visible element which, together with the soul, constitutes the human being.

Catholic doctrine has never denied the functional reality and importance of the material element in man. On the contrary, the Church has always upheld the dignity and worth of the body against all pessimistic interpretations of matter (Gnostics, Manichaeans, Albigensians); at the same time she points out the high role and destiny assigned to the flesh in the supernatural order and in the sphere of Redemption.

The mysteries of the life of Christ, Who in the reality of his Body willed man's redemption by the sacrifice of his Flesh and Blood; the selection of a woman as his Mother and co-redemptrix of mankind; the institution of the sacraments as visible rites applied only to the body with a spiritual efficacy; the dogma of the resurrection and glorification of the bodies—give evidence of the true dignity and worth with which the human body is regarded in Christian spirituality.

Nor does such teaching contradict in any way the recurring reference by St. Paul to the conflict between the flesh and the spirit. St. Paul does not regard the physical flesh as something evil in itself; the conflict of which he speaks is between the flesh, as an expression of the old creature, and the spirit, as an expression of the new creature, regenerated and re-educated by grace (Rom. 8, 1 ff.; 12; 13; 14; II Cor. 10, 3; Gal. 5, 7, etc.).

However, one must readily acknowledge that in fallen nature flesh constitutes a stimulus and source of sin, whose consequent disorderly inclinations must be brought under control by sound discipline. To avoid any apparent contradiction between this statement which, after all, is based on ordinary daily experience, one must rightly understand the sense in which the body is said to be a source of sin. Sin, although occasioned by the flesh, always finds its formal causality in the spirit; in other words, the spirit, debasing itself, desecrates the flesh also. Moreover, not even in the line of sin can the body be granted a primacy that it does not possess in the ontological order, due to its essential inferiority and subordination to the spirit.

The ethical value of the body is necessarily derived from its ontological position in relation to the soul. Substantially united to the soul, the body shares both in the iniquity and sanctity of the soul, according as it serves as an instrument of sin or of justice. Subordinate to the soul in value and function, the body can never become an end unto itself nor can it subordinate spiritual activities to itself; on the contrary, the body remains ever subordinate to the spirit, and must be ready, if need be, to sacrifice its own inclinations and tendencies in favor of the higher order.

The duty to love and respect one's own body derives from the very nature and function of the body.

In practice, love for one's own body requires that one take reasonable care of one's health, not only because of the functional importance of the body and the necessary relation between physical and mental health, but also because of the intrinsic value of the gift of life.

The essential subordination of material values to those of a higher order, the transitory character of earthly life and its employment in a successful attainment of its ends, do not allow the care of the body or of one's health to become the main preoccupation of life. It is fully justified for the sake of a higher good or in pursuit of a higher goal to sacrifice, in a proportionate measure physical energies and even physical well being. The above considerations also justify the undertaking of certain professions or occupations that are indirectly harmful to one's physical health as well as harsh physical penances practiced by some of the saints. Thus, we are able to understand how St. Paul could, without contradiction, suggest health remedies to his disciples, while at the same time exhorting them to crucify the flesh with its vices and concupiscences (I Tim. 5, 23; Gal. 5, 24). *Pal.*

RELATIONSHIP OF SOUL AND BODY. The body-soul relationship is studied in theoretical philosophy and dogmatic theology; various theories, however, concerning these relationships enter also into the field of moral theology.

The theory of the thirteenth century that there is but one soul inhabiting all individual human bodies in the world, with all individuality and uniqueness due to the merely physical would lead to immoral conclusions for with the elimination of the fear of personal damnation, one would be free to pursue pleasure with total abandon and impunity.

Among these considerations with moral overtones would be the overestimation of the value of the body. If the body is regarded as the only adequate expression of the soul the natural conclusion is sensism or sensualism, in the fields of art, literature, philosophy and daily morals. Base animalistic instincts are given prime emphasis and usurp the value of spiritual tendencies and may go so far as to enter religion in the form of Dionysian or Bacchic excesses.

To maintain that the soul is pure spirit, united merely accidentally with the body by external or violent unity, perhaps due to sins committed in former states, is to regard the body as a prison and a cause of debasement and subjugation of the soul. This distorted view which strives to separate the body and soul from this degrading union, gives firm adherence to absurd, frightful practices found in many oriental forms of asceticism, purely negativistic and abstentionistic, pessimistic and otiose, obsessed with the suppression of the body that the soul regain freedom. These likewise lead to immorality because of the gulf created between the body and soul in order to prevent the impurities of the body from dimming the soul's splendor. Thus, the body is completely vilified, while the soul remains immaculate and pure, far above the body.

The Christian theory on the body-soul relationship is based on a more balanced doctrine. In the Christian conception, the soul is not a pure spirit, but is by nature destined to inhabit the body, neither a prison of the soul nor always a faithful reflection of the highest spiritual tendencies. As a necessary organ or instrument of the soul in the present life, the body is not to be mutilated nor destroyed. Because the body is the lower part of man, it is subject to the rational faculties of the soul; because it dangerously inclines toward satisfaction of base human tendencies, it is to be mortified; because it is destined to reunion with the soul in eternal glory, it is worthy of respect. Catholic moral doctrine, therefore, prescribes a positive asceticism with regard to the body: it aims to discipline the body but not to eliminate it; it forbids bodily mutilation, but inculcates mortification; it tends to make of the body a serviceable instrument of the soul, with a view to bringing out the best spiritual tendencies in man; it seeks to elevate and spiritualize the body, thereby preparing it for a higher spiritualization on resurrection day. In short, the Christian principle is this: as nature is not destroyed but ennobled by grace, so too, the body is not to be annihilated in favor of the soul, but must, through the soul, attain greater dignity. *Gra.*

BOLSHEVISM. *See* Communism.

BOND (IMPEDIMENT OF). From a valid marriage there arises between the married parties a bond which is of its very nature perpetual and exclusive (Can. 1110). This marriage is called *matrimonium in facto esse:* a sort of projection in time, until death, of the act performed at the moment of the marriage (*matrimonium in fieri*). In a positive sense, the bond is the direct source of all conjugal rights and duties; in a negative sense, it renders invalid any new tie by reason of the law of unity of marriage.

Before a marriage is contracted, an investigation must be conducted concerning the free status of the parties, that is, whether or not they are free from the bond of any previous valid marriage (Can. 1020), or any other impediment, unless the pastor knows from the qualifications of the parties that this investigation is unnecessary.

The bond of a ratified and consummated marriage cannot be dissolved except by the death of one of the parties (Can. 1118). A non-consummated marriage between two baptized persons (or between one baptized and the other non-baptized) is dissolved automatically by law through the religious profession of one of the married parties by papal dispensation. The bond arising from a valid and consummated marriage of two unbaptized persons can be dissolved by the application of the Pauline privilege (if one of the parties receives baptism and the other refuses to be baptized or to cohabit peacefully) or through the exercise by the pope of his vicarious authority (Petrine privilege) in favor of the faith.

Whoever attempts marriage while still bound by a previous, even if unconsummated marriage, contracts an invalid union and becomes guilty of bigamy (*see* Bigamy).

The parties to an invalid marriage may not contract a new marriage until the invalidity of their first marriage has been properly established.

The nullity of a marriage becomes effective after publication of the decree of nullity by the competent ecclesiastical authority. In a formal trial, a decision becomes executive if there are two judgments in favor of the nullity of the marriage, and no appeal is made, within ten days, by the defender of the bond (Can. 1987). In informal cases (Can. 1990–1992), that is, cases in which the impediment is clearly proved from certain and authentic documents, which cannot be contradicted, the declaration of the Ordinary suffices.

The absence or presumed death of one of the parties must be established by a decree of the Ordinary, after he has attained a moral certainty of the death of the party in question. A protracted absence of one of the parties is not of itself sufficient reason to proceed to a new marriage. A marriage declared invalid by a formal declaration never becomes irrevocably adjudged. The case may be reopened at any time if new and weighty reasons are available (Can. 1989). In order to protect the marital institution against unwarranted accusations, Benedict XIV in 1740 (const. *Dei Miseratione*) created a special official in the ecclesiastical tribunal called defender of the bond whose duty it is to uphold with every argument offered by the case the validity of marriage and the existence of the bond; he also has the duty to appeal after the first formal decision of nullity. He enjoys extensive procedural (Can. 1586 ff.) power (*see* Promotor of Justice and Defender of the Bond). *Bar.*

BOOKS, PENITENTIAL. Penitential books are extensive collections of canons in which are catalogued the various penitential works to be given to sinners, according to the nature and number of their sins. In the beginning they contained a simple enumeration of sins and corresponding mortifications, prayers, fasts and expiatory alms; later on, they were completed and integrated with other elements useful to confessors.

Although the idea of establishing a proportion between penalty and guilt had already been expressed in councils, decrees, and earlier letters, it was around the sixth century that the first chapters were compiled, by the private initiative of confessors, who had been under the influence of monastic customs, and by the German *Wergeld*. They were first used in Ireland and Scotland.

They are often attributed, without foundation, to great names, such as, Columbanus, Cummain, Theodore, although the disciples of St. Columbanus brought them to the continent.

The Penitential books contain a form of penance that differs from the ancient canonical penance; a system of private penance replaced ancient public penances.

Insular Penitential Books. (a) The most ancient of the Irish penitentials is the *Collection of Penitential Canons from the I Synod of St. Patrick* (450–456), which does not have as yet the real aspect of a penitential book. This collection is followed by the *Canones Hibernenses*, discovered by Martene, in two codices belonging to the National Library of Paris, and by the *Vinnianum Penitential* (or Finnian) of Molville (859), written in the second half of the sixth century.

(b) The British penitentials, consisting chiefly of the 16 *excerpts de libro Davidis* (around 550–600), the *Gilda Penitential* (550); the *Penitentials A and B of Columbanus* (543–615) in 42 titles, drawn up by the Saint at Bobbio and at Luxeuil, and containing the discipline of the Celtic Church.

In all these penitentials, which lack order, the sins of ecclesiastical and lay persons are listed, particularly the sins of the flesh, for which fasting by bread and water, exile, alms, fines, and the redemption of slaves are prescribed as penances.

The principle, called *de arreis*, was decreed for the first time in *Canones Hibernenses*. Thanks to this principle a long penance could be commuted into a shorter but more severe one; for instance, a year's fasting by bread and water could be reduced to three days to be spent in prayer at the tomb of a saint. At times, even a monetary offering was permitted as a substitute.

(c) Of a later date but more important are the following Penitentials: *Iudicia*, by Cummain, Abbot of the monastery of Hy in Scotland (661–662); *Iudicia*, by Theodore, so-called because (falsely) attributed to Theodore of Canterbury (668–690), including 5 particular collections (inclined very much toward laxity); the canons published by D'Achery; *canones Gregorii*, published by Kunstmann; the 214 cottonian canons; a series of the *Sangallese tripartitum*; and the *discipulus Umbrensium* in two volumes. These various collections, written in England between 690 and 740, are somewhat interrelated but the extent of such relations has not been fully established.

(d) To the above mentioned Penitentials must be added: the *Penitential* of Beda of the VIII century; the *Penitential* of Egbert (the author of which is in all probability the Archbishop of York about 732–766); the compilation of the Barberini Code, edited by Albers (Archiv. f. kat. Kirchenrecht, 81 [1901] 393–420); *the Liber de remediis peccatorum*, the confessional of Egbert.

The Penitential Books of the European Continent. At the beginning of the eighth century compilations of penitential books appear on the continent; they are from insular sources but with the addition of excerpts from canonical collections. The principal ones are:

(a) The Penitentials derived from Columbanus, that is, the *Penitential of Bobbio, of Fleury*, and of *Mersebourg*.

(b) The Penitentials derived from Cummain and Theodore, that is, the *Excarpsus Cummeani*, the *Bigotinum*, the *Remensis*, and the *Tripartita*.

Reforming councils, that of Chalon (813) and later, opposed the penitential books in which, very often, arbitrary views favoring the most lax tendencies prevailed. An order was given in Paris to search out and find them as well as others more serious and reliable. Hence the canonical collections: the *Dacheriana*, the *Penitential* of Halitgarius Bishop of Cambrai (1817–1831); the *Quadripartitus*, written after the year 800 and attributed with some hesitation to Halit-

garius; the *Penitential of Pseudo-Theodore*, compiled between 830 and 853; the *Corrector* or *Medicus* which constitute the Nineteenth book of the Decree of Burchard of Worms, written between 1003 and 1012 and very widely circulated. But by this time the fate of Penitential book was sealed. Partisans of the Gregorian reform, St. Peter Damiani, Atto of Vercelli, and others, are unanimous in their protest against the penitential books. The only penitential book contained in a Gregorian collection is the one by Anselm of Lucca in the fifteenth book of the *Decretum* of Ivo of Chartres (1094). Finally, Gratian gathered certain penitential texts in his *Decretum*.

The ancient Penitentials yield to a new literature *Summae de poenitentia* or *confessorum* and *Confessionalia*, which will give more precise rules for the administration of the sacrament of penance. *Pal.*

BOURGEOIS. Socialism is responsible for giving the term *bourgeois* a collective or class connotation, opposing it to the term *workingman: bourgeoisie* vs. *proletariat*. As defined by socialists, the bourgeois is the businessman, the capitalistic entrepreneur who exploits the laboring classes. The bourgeoisie, as a class, is made up of employers, possessors of wealth or capital and non-workers. Socialists simply call the bourgeoisie the master or dominant class, but in reality they apply the term to all groups, including workers not affiliated with socialists. Again, socialists distinguish between the bourgeois parties and the socialist party. This, however, is an erroneous distinction, because it is not based on the economic element and because the majority of workers in the world do not profess Marxist doctrine. Moreover, the bourgeoisie does not represent a uniform sociological class, as the socialists claim; on the contrary, it is made up of multiple groups, among whom there is frequently found opposition and friction, *e.g.*, between urban and rural elements, wholesalers and retailers, producers and consumers, *etc.*

Historically, the word *bourgeoisie* is encountered for the first time in the twelfth century. It had a well-defined meaning, and it designated, until the seventeenth century, those who lived in castles (Burg) and cities and who formed a group with specific privileges and duties. Thus, the bourgeois of today is entirely different from his medieval brother. Nowadays the bourgeoisie designates a social class that is much less clearly defined. Frequently, the bourgeoisie is called the middle group or middle class, but this term is far from being exact and is rather complex. As a matter of fact, today the adjective "middle" does not correspond to reality, since, juridically speaking, higher privileged classes no longer exist. In the bourgeoisie are to be found economic, social, moral, cultural, and even political characteristics. The bourgeois is referred to as one having a social status midway between the nobility and the laboring classes. In a disparaging sense, a bourgeois is one showing a tendency to live in peace and comfort, one who adheres to his own milieu and is opposed to revolutionary innovations.

Hence, the distinguishing characteristic of the present-day bourgeoisie is, more than anything else, a psychological attitude, that is, a manner of living, a point of view, a manner of reacting to things. Socialists themselves readily admit that the bourgeoisie does not constitute a uniform class with its own political and social creed, since its members are found to adhere to every different political party, even socialist. Moreover, education is no longer the exclusive mark of the bourgeois who wishes to differentiate himself from the populace. For the longest time the bourgeoisie was characterized by riches and the handling of money, because it resided in cities and was engaged in commerce and industry. And even today the desire to accumulate wealth or capital is one of the more important marks of bourgeois psychology. To identify the bourgeoisie with capitalism, however, or to make bourgeoisie synonymous with capitalistic society is more a polemic utterance than a scientific and objective fact.

Today there are many farmers and skilled workers drawing higher salaries and possessing more capital than the bourgeois, and yet they do not thereby become bourgeois. A widespread democracy could bring about a wider bourgeoisie and thus eliminate the real and proper bourgeoisie by reason of its extension. This would mean the "bourgeoisizing" of democracy. On the other hand, a system that would do away with private property, inheritance, and especially money and private savings, would mark the end of the bourgeoisie. But even in such a case, there immediately arises, as in the Soviet Union, a new class, another type of bourgeoisie, that is, a class of functionaries, since they constitute the largest representative group which no social revolution can eliminate. *Per.*

BOYCOTT. The term *boycott* came into use during the Irish land agitation of 1880 and in subsequent years. As a result of English conquest and domination (particularly under Cromwell), the Catholic people in Ireland had been dispossessed of their land rights. Captain Boycott, agent or administrator of the vast land possessions of Lord Erne, adopted such harsh and ruthless measures against the Irish tenants that these joined forces against him, refusing to gather in the crops or tend to the cattle. The result was that Captain Boycott was forced to give up his position and leave Ireland (1880). Ever since this occurrence, the word *boycott* has been used in connection with any organized movement designed to isolate a person or business from all economic relations with the rest of society. Usually the boycott is practiced by refusal to work for an employer, deal with a tradesman, and the like.

The use of boycott is justifiable only when, all other legal means of redress having failed, it remains the sole effective measure of defense against abusive or unfair practices. Moreover, before a boycott can be declared morally justifiable, there must be due proportion between the damage suffered by the boycotters and that threatened to the boycotted.

Similar to a strike and a lockout, the boycott is like a two-edged sword, capable of harming both the user and the one against whom it is used. Due consideration must be given to the *collective damage* that may ensue as a result of any violent disruption of economic activities. If the boycott is outlawed in certain countries, it is precisely because it is considered dangerous and damaging to the public interest. On the other hand, it is the duty of the State to provide sound social legislation aimed at forestalling or preventing situations that would require the use of boycott as a last resort (*ultima ratio*) in the protection of rights. Every effort should be made to promote a just and peaceable settlement of disputes. *Boz.*

BRACHYTYPE, ASTHENIC. *See* Constitution, Somatic.

BRAHMANISM. *See* Hinduism.

BRAIN, ELECTRONIC. *See* Cybernetics.

BREAD, UNLEAVENED. *See* Eucharist.

BREVIARY. The breviary is the book containing the prayers for the canonical hours to be recited daily by the duly constituted representatives of the whole Church before God, to whom they offer praise and from whom they implore graces for all the members of the Church.

From the very beginning of Christianity, along with the Sacrifice of the Mass, private and public prayer flourished in the Church. As early as Apostolic times, the faithful in their assemblies and common vigils sang hymns and psalms and read from Sacred Scripture. In due course of time this public prayer of the Church was regulated as to particulars and details, eventually becoming codified. St. Pius V, who reformed the breviary, made its use obligatory in all places where the liturgy was celebrated according to the Roman Rite, with the exception of churches and religious orders which possessed, for at least two centuries, a breviary approved by the Holy See. St. Pius X introduced a much needed revision of the breviary, distributing and arranging the psalms in such manner as to assure their entire recitation each week. In 1945 Pius XII authorized, for optional liturgical use, a new version of the Psalter from the original texts. On March 23, 1955, the Sacred Congregation of Rites issued a decree of simplification of rubrics, introducing notable modifications in the recitation of the breviary, particularly at the beginning and end of the different hours, in the *preces, etc.* (titl. IV). Even the restored liturgical Ordo of Holy Week brought some changes in the recitation of the Office prescribed for those days.

The setting of laudatory prayers, offered daily to the Lord in the name of the Church, comprises various *canonical hours,* corresponding to the different hours of the night and day: Matins with its various nocturns (the nocturnal prayer), Lauds (the prayer of dawn), Prime, Tierce, Sext, None, Vespers, and Compline. Each canonical hour consists principally of several psalms, with one or more antiphons. In addition, each *hour* contains a "little chapter" or reading from Scripture, with or without responsory or versicle, and one or more orations. At Matins the lessons, taken from Scripture and the works of the Fathers, are somewhat lengthier, and the responsories relate to the occurring feast or to the particular mystery commemorated or considered in the liturgy of the day.

Besides the prescribed norms for reciting the canonical hours, the breviary contains the Ordinary of the Divine Office for each day of the week, the Proper of the Season, the Common of Saints, the Proper of Saints, an appendix with the Little Office of Our Lady, the Office of the Dead, the seven Penitential Psalms, the Litanies of the Saints, the prayers for a departing soul, and other prayers approved by the Church. Most dioceses have obtained from the Holy See particular Offices, which constitute the "proper" of the diocese; this is also true of religious Orders, several of which have their own breviary.

In former times the breviary was the book of prayer not only for ministers of the Church but also for lay people, and it is truly deplorable that the laity of today is almost entirely unacquainted with this book. The breviary is indeed a most beautiful form of prayer. The psalms, in particular, contain vivid and expressive sentiments of divine praise and adoration, of filial fear and love, of acknowledgement and penitence, of hope for merciful pardon and for divine aid in our various needs, both individual and collective. The breviary is also an exceedingly rich source of genuine and salutary doctrine. *Man.*

BREVIARY (obligation of reciting). The daily recitation of the breviary is obligatory for all clerics in sacred orders, for those holding benefices, for members of religious orders or congregations bound by the choir obligation; it is recommended to those faithful who are able to fulfill it.

HISTORY. The obligation of choral and private recitation of the breviary was progressively and more clearly determined along with the internal and external development of the Divine Office (*see* Breviary). One can, of course, only speak of obligation in a wide sense in the first centuries of the Church. Whatever obligation was attached to the common vigils and penitential prayers of the first Christians was derived from the obligatory character of the Mass celebrated on the occasion of these assemblies of prayer. But since the obligation of attending Mass was rather elastic and variable according to local political conditions, the obligatory character of the common prayers recited before and after Mass must be regarded as equally broad and variable.

In the fourth century, the Apostolic Constitutions recommended that the bishop exhort the faithful to participate in the prayer-sessions of the morning, afternoon and evening; the same Constitutions presupposed that the clergy and bishop habitually participated in these assemblies of prayer. But it was not until the fifth century that the clergy began to practice the daily recitation of the Office in parochial churches. It was not, to be sure, the complete Office as it was known later; nevertheless a *de facto* obligation arose gradually, became established, and soon received the approbation of the Church, first by the Council of Carthage in 398, and then through the decree of Pope Gelasius in 560. These ecclesiastical dispositions, however, applied to choral recitation; nothing was yet stated as to whether clerics absent from choir would be obliged to say the Office privately.

We must come down to the eleventh century to find, along with the larger choral breviaries, smaller volumes suitable for personal recitation outside the choir; this is taken as a clear indication that there must have existed some sort of obligation of praying the breviary, privately, whenever one missed choir (Council of Treves, 1227; Fourth Lateran Council, 1215).

The strict obligation of private recitation of the breviary began only with the fifteenth century (Council of Tortosa, 1429). Canons and beneficiaries recited the Office in choir, clerics in major orders privately, religious in their monasteries.

From the sixteenth century on, the obligation of reciting the breviary was simply presupposed; all subsequent ecclesiastical legislation became concerned merely with determining and sanctioning such an obligation (Fifth Lateran Council, 1514). In 1571, St. Pius V imposed on all clerics the obligation to use the Roman breviary—an obligation that was renewed (in the Encyclical *Etsi pastoralis*) by Benedict XIV (1740–1758). But a general law establishing for the entire Church the obligation of reciting the breviary was merely among the *desiderata* of the Vatican Council, enacted only in comparatively recent times with the publication of a new Code of Canon Law.

THOSE WHO ARE OBLIGED. The obligation of reciting the Divine Office is incumbent upon (a) all clerics in major orders, even though excommunicated, suspended, or interdicted, with the exception of those who have been legitimately reduced to the lay state (Can. 213–214; 135). The obligation of saying the Office is in itself a grave one; hence anyone omitting the entire Office or a notable part thereof, such as a small hour or one nocturn, would be guilty of a grave sin. The obligation is in effect from the moment one receives the subdiaconate. (b) Beneficiaries, whether in sacred orders or not. For such individuals the obligation is not only a duty of religion, but also one of justice. Hence, if without legitimate reason a beneficiary fails to satisfy his obligation of reciting the canonical hours, he is held to restitution in proportion to the extent of his neglect (Can. 1475). Moreover, the obligation of attending choir is *personal* (*i.e.*, active participation in the psalmody is required), *local* (physical presence in choir), *temporal* (daily attendance, and not by rotation or turn: Can. 413, par. 1; 414). (c) Religious belonging to communities which have the choir obligation, according to their respective constitutions. Among these, professed members in solemn vows are bound to attend choir and, if absent for a legitimate reason, they must recite the Office privately. Novices, lay brothers, and lay sisters are in no way bound to choir attendance.

OBJECT AND CONDITIONS OF THE OBLIGATION. (a) Everyone is bound to recite the Office of the day as contained in the breviary and in accordance with a calendar approved by the Holy See. The secular clergy must use the Roman breviary, prescribed by Pius V and revised by Pius X and Pius XII. The calendar to be followed is the common one and the calendar proper to the diocese in which the cleric resides or has a residential benefice. Religious, on the other hand, must follow the calendar and breviary of their own order or congregation if they have one.

If another Office is said by mistake, the principle *officium pro officio valet* is applied; but if the Office already recited is notably shorter than the one of the day, it is better to compensate in some manner. Occasionally one may, intentionally and without sin, interchange the prescribed Office for another, provided that there be a sufficient reason (devotion, recitation with another priest, and the like). Generally, however, such commutation is not permissible, and one commits a venial or grave sin, depending on whether the substitute Office is approximately the same length as the one precribed or notably shorter. When traveling, bishops and beneficiaries must recite the Office according to the *ordo* of their own diocese. Priests, when residing for a time in another diocese, may adopt the calendar of that diocese.

(b) Since the recitation of the Office is a human act, it requires a proper intention. The question is: What kind intention? On the one hand, habitual intention is insufficient to render the recitation a human act. On the other hand, an explicit and actual intention would be rather exacting and onerous. Thus, in view of the weakness of human nature, virtual and implicit intention to pray is sufficient. Besides the intention, the Office must be recited at least with external attention, that is, attention that excludes any occupation that would hinder the mind from concentrating on prayer. According to the more common opinion, though it be desirable, neither spiritual nor literal attention is required; material attention suffices to make the recitation of the Office a true prayer.

(c) Recitation of the Office must be orderly, distinct, integral, continued. *Orderly*: the canonical hours must be recited according to the order or succession in which they appear in the breviary: Matins, Lauds, Prime, Tierce, Sext, None, Vespers, Compline; however, this order may be inverted for any good reason. *Distinct* or vocal: the words must be consciously formed by the lips, mouth or tongue, and not merely read mentally. *Integral*: the Office must be said in its entirety; it is not permissible to omit parts, skip words, make additions of any kind. *Continued* or uninterrupted: the obligation of continuity applies to each canonical hour (there must be no break between the parts of an hour). However, any good reason (charity, politeness, personal utility, and the like) suffices to interrupt the recitation at any point, or to interpose a break longer than three hours between the nocturns of Matins.

(d) The ceremonies which accompany the recitation of the Office are listed in the *Ceremoniale Episcoporum*, and their imperative tone leads theologians and liturgists to believe that they are preceptive for choir recitation, but only directive for private recitation.

(e) The obligation of reciting the Office applies to specific days, so that one may not satisfy the obligation on either the preceding or following day. The usual time within which the Office must be recited is from midnight to midnight (a natural day). The obligation may be satisfied if one recites the Office any hour of the day; however, under penalty of venial sin, one is obliged to conform to the following order: Matins and Lauds, in virtue of a privilege, may be anticipated any time after 2:00 P.M.; priests, however, should recite these hours before Mass; the Little Hours may be recited immediately after midnight; Vespers and Compline may not be recited before noon, except on weekdays during Lent. Any reasonable cause will excuse from the obligation of following this order.

(f) Choral Office, obviously, must be recited in choir, according to the order and ceremonies prescribed. Private Office may be recited in any becoming place which will not interfere with the required attention and devotion. Moreover, it may be recited in any respectful posture: kneeling, sitting, walking.

DISPENSATION FROM THE OBLIGATION OF RECITING THE OFFICE. There are three excusing causes from the obligation of the Office: (a) physical or moral impossibility, such as: lack of a breviary, illness, danger of grave injury or damage, and the like. (b) Charity toward one's neighbor, *i.e.*, an absorbing occupation that cannot be neglected without grave scandal or notable detriment to a neighbor, such as urgent and continued care of the sick, long hours of confessions, *etc.* (c) Lawful dispensation. Only the Holy

See (Sacred Congregation of the Council, Sacred Congregation of Religious, Sacred Congregation for the Propagation of the Faith, Sacred Congregation for the Oriental Church) may dispense definitively. Such dispensation is valid even if granted without cause, but it is lawful only if reasonable cause exists. The Ordinary may dispense from this obligation, but only provisionally and in particular cases, when recourse to the Holy See is difficult (Can. 81). The reasons for requesting a dispensation are: a frequently recurring cause, fear concerning moral impossibility, fear concerning grave imminent damage or injury. Finally, in any case of doubt concerning the recitation of the Office the general principles concerning doubt as indicated in moral theology may be applied.

IMPORTANCE OF RECITATION OF BREVIARY IN ASCETICAL LIFE. The importance of the Divine Office in ascetical life cannot be ignored. It should be sufficient to note that some monastic orders have made the Office the fulcrum of their entire spirituality. Indeed, the Divine Office is the prayer of the Church *par excellence*. Every aspiration of the human spirit, every sentiment of joy and sorrow, every circumstance and vicissitude of life finds in the Office the most sublime language by which one may turn to God. The mind is instructed, the heart satiated, the will strengthened; desires are placated, individual and collective needs find their most adequate expression before God. Add to all this the infinite intercessive power possessed by this prayer, precisely because it is offered in the name of the Church and in union with Christ. One can hardly refrain from calling it the ideal form of prayer, for in it are found all the objective and subjective conditions required for a perfect prayer. Humility, so necessary in prayer, is deeply and vividly impressed upon us through recitation of the psalms, whose general theme centers on the infinite grandeur of God and on our unworthiness and nothingness. Confidence inundates our heart through a knowledge and awareness that we stand in prayer before the throne of God, accompanied by the Church with her vast cohort of Saints, by the Blessed Virgin and by Christ, our mystical Head. Finally, the obligation of daily recitation practically makes the spirit and virtue of perseverance mandatory. *Pal.*

BREVILINEAR TYPE. *See* Constitution, Somatic.

BRIBE. *See* Extortion, Gratuity, Threat.

BRIEF. *See* Pontifical Acts.

BROCHETTE. *See* Sacred Vessels.

BROTHERS (and sisters). Children having the same parents are called brothers and sisters (whole brothers or sisters); those having only one parent in common are called half-brothers or sisters. To these can be added also adoptive brothers or sisters.

Between brother and sister there is a relation of consanguinity in the first degree of the collateral line by which, perhaps by divine and natural laws, certainly by Church law, marriage between them is forbidden (*see* Consanguinity). In all civil legislation one's brothers and sisters come immediately after one's children, parents and consort, or are concurrent with them, as heirs *ab intestato* (*see* Inheritance). Brothers and sisters have reciprocal duties of brotherly love; that is to say, they must help one another, at least in cases of grave necessity. *Pal.*

BRUTALITY. *See* Cruelty.

BUDDHISM. As a religion, Buddhism, like contemporary Jainism (*q.v.*), is considered a heterodox system, in that it represents a reaction against a ritualistic Brahmanic formalism based on the revelation or authority of the Veda, and is opposed to the intellectualistic framework that endeavors to justify it. In fact, Buddha rejected Brahmanic speculation and, although dependent upon it doctrinally, he denied the value of sacrifice with its intricate ritual. Moreover,

he prescinded from the caste system, the intangible cornerstone of Hindu society even to this day, and proposed to his followers a new discipline for attaining salvation, or liberation from the evil of rebirth.

As an intellectual system, Buddhism represents the ultimate term of Brahmanic speculation, which ends up in a pancosmos, since it identifies the *brahman*, or the *One* (the supreme principle or essence of the entire universe), with *atman* (the animating principle of the individual, his soul or ego). Knowledge of the identity between macrocosm and human microcosm, between universe and ego, brings redemptive liberation, that is, the suppression of every desire and disappearance of every illusion. He who fails to attain such liberating knowledge will be condemned to rebirth in the world (metempsychosis), with all its tribulations.

Buddhism pursues the same course, except for the substitution of the concept of identification of the universe with the soul, metaphysically unattainable, with the concept of the empirical reality of suffering. In fact, even for Buddhism, the cause of every evil is ignorance of the reality of suffering, which is a sad and unfortunate inheritance of life. Like Brahmanism, Buddhism also aspires to the extinction or annihilation of individual life (Nirvana), and suggests meditation and a moderate form of asceticism as a means of reaching the shores of liberation.

In propagating his concept of salvation, Buddha had an essentially practical aim: the liberation of man, that is, a liberation from the illusion which drags him through the indefinite cycle of existence (the wheel of the law), to which he is condemned by the chain (*karman*) of actions performed in a previous existence. The apostolate of Buddha had no social character; it was not meant to be a reform of Brahmanism nor the abolition of castes; instead it proceeded independently, offering to all men a philosophy of salvation which, with the development of the Buddhist movement, grew into a real and proper

ligion, and spread with local adapta-
ons beyond the confines of India.

LIFE OF BUDDHA. Buddha, whose real
ame was *Siddhartha,* was born into the
autama branch of the princely family
f Sakya, which owned some territory
ear Kapilavasthu at the foot of the
Iimalayas. His family background ac-
ounts for his names as the *Solitary of
akya Sakyamuni,* the ascetic Gautama.
Ie married at an early age and lived a
fe of ease and luxury in his father's
ourt. He had a son named Rahula.
t 29, seized with spiritual unrest, he
bandoned home and family and gave
imself to solitude, in anxious search for
way out of the iron circle of existence.
elieving he had discovered the secret
f this liberation, Buddha wandered
orth to preach his doctrine with pros-
lytizing fervor. He continued in this
ork for a period of forty years until
is death, struggling at the same time
gainst the torments of ascetic exaggera-
ions, the rival preachments of Mahavira,
ounder of Jainism, and the extremes of
naterialism. His death occurred in the
ear 480 B.C. (or 477), near Kusinara;
is body was cremated and the ashes
vere divided into eight portions for
asier distribution. The fact of such dis-
ribution is proved by the *stupa* (dome-
haped cylindrical mound) of Piprava
Nepal) and by the reliquary of Pes-
aawar. That much can be established
is certain concerning Buddha, whose
ife has been abundantly enriched by
egendary tradition.

SOURCES. The chief sources for the
tudy of Buddha's life and doctrine are
livided into three collections or baskets
Tripitaka), and are contained in docu-
nents originating in southern and north-
rn India, representing two different
chools of thought. Those of the south-
rn school are written in Pali (a dialect
kin to Sanskrit). Well-ordered and
aithfully reflecting the original teach-
ngs of Buddha, they are widely read,
specially in Ceylon, Burma, and Siam.
The documents of the northern school,
vritten in Sanskrit, are less systematic,
nore prolix and less representative of
arly Buddhistic doctrine. Outside north-

ern India, they are to be found in different versions in China, Korea, Japan,
Annam, and Tibet.

DOCTRINE. Buddhist doctrine is based
on empirical observations set forth by
previous philosophical schools, according
to which existence, with its fluctuations,
forms, and its lack of permanence, is a
misery and an evil from which one
must seek deliverance. Such an evil is
all the more grave in that existence is
not terminated at the end of one span
of life, but is prolonged, according to
the merit of our actions (the law of
karman), into an indefinite series of
successive existences. Rebirth is a fundamental postulate of Buddhism. The
only way to obtain deliverance from
rebirth is through knowledge of the four
sacred truths *intuitively* perceived and
propagated by Buddha.

The demonstration of the first truth
(the reality of suffering and misery) is
obvious, and it reflects the pessimistic
conception of life so characteristic of
Indian thought. The cause of suffering
and misery (the second truth) is to be
sought in ignorance of the four sacred
truths. This ignorance prompts man to
become attached to life when he should
flee from it, because, despite its fleeting
pleasures, it is but misery and suffering.
Extinction of suffering (the third truth)
is achieved through extinction of every
form of desire, including the desire for
one's own existence. The fourth truth
consists in pointing out the path that
leads to the extinction of suffering.
This "path to the other shore" consists
of eight avenues, namely, genuine faith,
genuine will, genuine language, genuine
memory, genuine means of subsistence,
genuine application, genuine action, genuine meditation; in substance, these
amount to honesty, wisdom, and meditation, which constitute the three basic
tenets of Buddhist ethics.

BUDDHIST MORALITY. In practice, the
good moral life consists in the observance of five great commandments, which
forbid: (a) the killing of any living
being; (b) stealing; (c) adultery; (d)
lying; (e) the drinking of intoxicating
spirits. To these five precepts the Bud-

dhist monk must also add perfect chastity and complete poverty.

The ultimate aim of Buddhist ethics is the suppression of misery, which is achieved by suppressing one's existence in Nirvana. *Nirvana* (in Pali: *nibbana*) signifies "extinguished by blowing out," or extinction of the flame of life. Nirvana is also attainable in this life (first Nirvana) by suppressing in oneself every passion and illusion; once this is accomplished the Buddhist will experience perfect spiritual rest. Complete liberation, however, is attained only after *parinirvana:* the cessation of every thought residue (*sankara*) resulting from previous existences. A new rebirth now becomes impossible, and complete extinction or second Nirvana (*parinirvana*) has been achieved.

The concept of Nirvana is closely related to the concept of the soul. For Buddhism, the soul is not an individual, spiritual, permanent substance, the subject of mental and conscious experiences, but rather a series of instantaneous sensations which arise and die down, and perennially recur. It may be compared to the flame of a nocturnal lamp, which is not the same in the first, second, and third stages of the night, but still gives the illusion of stability, because of the uninterrupted succession of moments of which it consists.

BUDDHIST MONASTIC LIFE. The desire to live more fully the teaching of Buddha led to the establishment of Buddhist monastic communities (*Samgha*). The uniting bonds of these communities, however, were moral rather than juridical, for there is no central directing organ and the monks, except in the rainy seasons, are given to a life of wandering. Adherence to a community is expressed by the formula: "I seek refuge in Buddha, in his doctrine, in his order."

Admission into a community, open to all without distinction of caste, admits of two stages: (a) renunciation (*pabbaggia*) of wordly life, a sort of novitiate; (b) arrival (*upasampada*) or admission into a community of monks, with the obligation of wearing the yellow garment, of begging for one's meals, of meditating on the teaching of Buddha and of propagating his precepts. Profession in a community does not bind for life; each member is free to return to the world at any time.

The monks engage in both regular and periodic occupations. The regular duties are: psalmodic chanting of the teachings of Buddha, study of his doctrine, and begging at the forenoon for one's daily meals. Periodic duties are: collective examination of conscience fortnightly (upon occurrence of the new and the full moon), and confession of faults committed, which are already listed in a set formula or rule (*patimokkha*) dating back, if not to Buddha himself, certainly to the beginnings of the community. Finally, every year, when the rainy season is over, the monks resume their wandering missionary life.

Alongside the communities of monks there are also communities of nuns (*bhikkuni*), which are a sort of third order, whose members are engaged principally in assisting the male communities economically.

DOCTRINAL DEVELOPMENT. The above outline corresponds to what medieval Buddhists called the *Hinayana* or *Little Vehicle*, which leads to salvation (Nirvana) through the ocean of rebirths. But this vehicle, which adhered too faithfully to the letter of the canon and was too agnostic concerning fundamental problems, did not lend itself to the development of mystical devotion; hence, it had to give way to a larger vehicle (*Mahayana*) suitable for the masses lest Buddhism become a religion of a select few. In opposition to the theological agnosticism of the Hinayana, the Mahayana form of Buddhism introduced the concept of a transcendent and permanent God in the semblance of a cosmic Buddha (*Dhyani-Buddha*), who had revealed himself (through knowledge) in the historic Buddha.

In practice, any aspirant to the dignity of Buddha must give up the idea of achieving freedom from the iron circle of existence and apply to others the merit of his sacrifice. Pious Buddhists refer to this great sacrifice as the act of *producing the thought of enlightenment:* through this selfless act the generous person hopes to become a refuge and salvation of all creatures. This altruistic spirit detains aspirants to the dignity of Buddha (*bodhisattva*) from ascending to that rank, because once a candidate enters Nirvana, every activity in behalf of others ceases as does his existence.

According to the Mahayana form of Buddhism, a Sanskrit text (known as the *Paramitasamasa* or *Compendium of Perfections*) sums up under six headings in hierarchical form the dispositions that will change an ordinary mortal into a *bodhisattva*. These virtues are: the gift of love for others, good morals, patience, ability to perform heroic acts, meditation, which increases intellectual knowledge, and, finally, gnosis, or superior knowledge, which gives value to the merits of all other perfections.

The Mahayanic current, therefore, clearly transformed the character of original Buddhism, for two reasons: (1) it does not permit its adherents exclusively to seek their personal salvation by suppression of all desire of living, but to be solicitous for the salvation of all to be attained at the cost or postponement of one's own well-being; (2) it offers, in place of the nihilistic vision of Nirvana, the vision of a place of happiness (*Sukhavati*), where Amitabba (the Buddha of contemplation, of which, according to Mahayanic speculation, the historic Buddha is a replica) reigns, together with his court of *bodhisattva.* This paradise is also accessible to any devout person who has a mystical faith (*bhakti*) in Amitabba practiced by acts of worship in his honor. This explains the importance attached to external worship, temples, statues, ceremonies, relics, prayer formulas, unknown to primitive Buddhism. All this helps to explain the amazing success enjoyed by Mahayanic Buddhism among the masses of the Asiatic continent.

STATISTICS. The number of Buddhists in the world is not exactly known. The largest concentration of them, of course, is in Asia. In 1959 there were 150,000,000 Buddhists in Asia, 165,-000 in North America, 135,000 in South America, 10,000 in Europe. A large number of them is also reported in Oceania.

CRITICAL NOTES. Upon superficial examination, Buddhist morality may appear a highly noble and elevated system, similar in some respects to the morality of the Gospel. This consideration, coupled with an attraction for novelty, has engendered in the last two centuries a sympathetic attitude toward Buddhist morality among some circles of the Western world. In Germany the system was extolled by the philosopher A. Schopenhauer, who, if not a great thinker, was certainly a great writer.

Heterodox writers to the contrary, any resemblance between evangelical and Buddhist morality is only partial, and it concerns merely certain aspects of the natural and empirical law in relation to certain ascetical precepts. In other words, the similarity between the two systems is merely one of external coincidence and only refers to certain forms or means of purification which, it is important to note, are directed to essentially different ends, and which cannot seriously be taken as an index—much less as evidence—of any Buddhist influence over Christianity.

Moreover, the basis of Buddhist doctrine is a pessimistic conception of life: every phase or form of conscious existence, from birth to death, is regarded as suffering; such universal misery stems from the desire for life and action, which can only lead, through *kamma* or *karma*, to a constant series of rebirths and continued misery. The only way to suppress suffering is by suppressing *karma* and, therefore, all desire and thus reach the supreme ideal, that is, Nirvana, in which every seed of future existence is totally destroyed and complete freedom is achieved from the chain of existences and of suffering. Such a concept of life is essentially negative in its principle, nihilistic in its end, renunciatory in its ethical doctrine and deeply egotistical in its very negativeness: "Most noble among men [it teaches] is he who cuts himself off from all social ties, from all gratitude and credulity, and has destroyed every occasion of sin and erased all hope." Sympathy itself among men is nothing but compassion, based on the universality of suffering.

Buddhism does not believe in the existence of the soul, except a material and perishable one: it holds to a mere continuity of one's own existence in the principle of life as being the seed and the mold of future existences. The truly wise man renounces even this continuity; he must not desire an heir or son, either for himself or for others.

Evangelical morality, on the contrary, is essentially positive and optimistic, with the providential and loving work of God at the beginning of life and its development (Matt. 10:19–31), and happiness at the end of life to be attained even by those leading a life of tears and persecution (Matt. 5:1–2).

A point of similarity between Buddhism and Christianity, frequently referred to by writers, is monasticism. The implication is that Christian monasticism is of Buddhist derivation. The historical orgin of Christian monasticism, however, is sufficiently well established and known to exclude with certainty any dependence upon Buddhist monasticism. Moreover, the striving for perfection in these two systems is based on an entirely different form of asceticism. Buddhist asceticism is negative and anti-psychological, leading to extinction of all desire, hence to a renunciation of all activity and life. In the Christian form of asceticism, on the other hand, the passions are not to be destroyed, but disciplined; life is a gift of God to be valued and preserved, and not negated as in the Buddhist system.

Finally, as Pius XII pointed out to the peoples of India on the occasion of the centenaries in honor of St. Thomas the Apostle and St. Francis Xavier (*Osservatore Romano*, January 1, 1953): ". . . while there may be elements of truth and good in other religions, [both elements] find their deepest meaning and perfect complement in Christ; at the same time, the Catholic faith reveals such an understanding of divine truth and such powerful means for saving, sanctifying, and uniting man to God that it is rendered infinitely superior to all other religions." *Pal.*

BUREAUCRACY. *Bureaucracy* refers to the complex system and organization of modern public administration, based on the principle of remunerative employment of functionaries and personnel. This system, originally limited in its form (in feudal states and even in absolute monarchies public offices were largely honorary), became increasingly extended, especially in the nineteenth century, with the gradual establishment of liberal forms of government based on constitutions and elected representatives. By extension, the term *bureaucracy* is applied also to private administrations having structural and functional characteristics similar to those of public administrations, *i.e.*, differentiation of departments or bureaus, routine and uniform action, regard for established precedents and formalities, tendency to refer responsibility to higher officials, and the like.

MERITS AND DEFECTS. The bureaucratic system has both its good and bad aspects. Since defects are more noticeable and apparent than its merits, it is easy to understand how the word *bureaucracy* has acquired in the public mind an indefinable connotation of disparagement.

Among its good points we shall mention the following: (a) it eliminates dilettantism and improvisation; (b) it gives a sense of awareness of the continuity of the State which is preserved even when peoples and nations undergo revolutionary and far-reaching changes; (c) it creates an official sense of duty, which serves to keep the State machinery in operation, even when political and social agitators, often seizing upon the precarious economic conditions of bureaucratic elements, seek to overthrow the democratic government from within.

Among its defects are to be enumerated the following: (a) a tendency to multiply government departments and functions, with a consequent lack of initiative and resourcefulness on the part of subordinates and other local entities; (b) a tendency to conceal or cover up instances—rare, but grave—of corruption and abuse of power among members of the bureaucratic family; (c) a slow-moving government machinery, characterized by red tape, routine and dilatory methods, often the result of unintelligent planning, inefficient distribution of assignments, overlapping of authority, and jurisdiction.

THE BUREAUCRATIC CIRCLE. The bureaucratic circle, which becomes increasingly wider with increased centralization and consolidation of government powers, naturally tends to differentiate itself from all other groups and to constitute itself as a class apart, its members adopting common interests and activities, as well as a characteristic attitude (*forma mentis*) and behavior. Bureaucrats tend to regard themselves as depositaries of the permanent technical functions of the modern State, over and above all fluctuations of government by parties.

When the bureaucratic group is not sufficiently aware of its responsibilities and functions, it risks becoming (a) an instrument of forces, outwardly beneficent, but in reality allied to ideologies and interests opposed to the State; and since these forces generally have an inner hierarchy of their own, the various government bureaus frequently find themselves insidiously stymied in the execution of their proper functions (*see* Secret Societies); (b) a more or less witting instrument of other forces, likewise allied to particular ideologies and interests and designed to interfere with the democratic processes of government, thereby paving the way for revolutionary movements, eventually leading to the formation of a totalitarian government (*see* Communism). *Pav.*

BURIAL, ECCLESIASTICAL. Ecclesiastical burial comprises transfer of the body to the proper church for the funeral, the funeral itself, and the burial of the remains.

Transfer of the body. By ordinary law, the church to which the body is to be taken for the funeral is the parish church of the deceased, unless the deceased has lawfully chosen another church (Can. 1216, par. 1). If the deceased had two parochial domiciles or quasi-domiciles (*q.v.*) the funeral should be held in the church of the parish in which he died (Can. 1216, par. 2). Those who die in the hospital, with due consideration for particular provisions, may be taken to the church of the hospital only if they acquired in it at least a quasi-domicile or the funeral procession to the parish church is too inconvenient. The burial of Cardinals, residential Bishops, residential beneficiaries, religious men and women, seminary residents and those having a family burial plot are governed by particular regulations.

Funeral. Funeral services are ordinarily conducted in the parish church by the pastor, except in the case of a definite choice of another church by the deceased, special cases indicated in the Code of Canon Law, or by local customs and lawfully approved statutes.

Burial. The provisions of the Code of Canon Law are based on the principle *ubi funus ibi tumulus*, i.e. the burial is to be made where the funeral was conducted. Therefore, after the funeral service is over, the remains must be buried, as a general rule, in the cemetery of the parish church if there is one, unless the deceased chose another church for the funeral and burial, or the deceased must be buried in the family's burial plot.

When the deceased is not buried from his own parish church, his proper pastor is to receive the parochial share of the funeral offering, unless a particular or approved customs dispose otherwise. If two or more parishes have a right to share the fee, the parochial portion is to be shared equally by the various proper pastors. There is no obligation of paying the canonical portion to the parish church of the deceased if his body could not conveniently be taken to that church (Can. 1236, par. 1).

DENIAL OF ECCLESIASTICAL BURIAL. Unbaptized persons may not receive ecclesiastical burial, with the exception of catechumens who without grave negligence died without having been baptized. Ecclesiastical burial must be accorded to all baptized persons who are not expressly barred by law. The following persons are deprived of ecclesiastical burial unless before their death they gave some signs of repentance: (a) Notorious apostates from the Christian faith, notorious followers of an heretical, schismatical, or masonic sect, or similar societies; (b) persons excommunicated or interdicted by condemnatory or declaratory sentence; (c) individuals guilty of deliberate suicide; (d) those who died in a duel or from wounds received in it; (e) those who ordered the cremation of their own bodies; (f) finally, all other public and manifest sinners (Can. 1240). In doubt concerning any of the foregoing cases, the local Ordinary must be consulted, if time permits; ecclesiastical burial shall be granted in such a manner that scandal be avoided. *Fel.*

BURSE (for chalice). *See* Sacred Vestments.

BUSINESS. Any transaction involving an exchange of goods or values executed for the purpose of gain is called business. In the world of economics generally there are four distinct phases of business: production, distribution, circulation, and consumption. Ordinarily, the activities of a business man range from the bank to the market, to the stock exchange, to a business establishment, wholesale or retail. All these activities are often governed by the well-known aphorism: "Business is business" (in French: *"Les affaires sont les affaires"*; in Italian: *"Gli affari sono affari"*). This saying is meant to convey the thought that all business dealings are to be transacted on the sole basis of one's own business interest, apart from all other considerations.

Such a criterion raised to the dignity of a universal and absolute principle is morally unacceptable. It wrongly presupposes that the business world is a sphere all its own, entirely detached from the moral law. The world of business is created by man knowingly and freely. When, therefore, he chooses to enter this field, he does not become automatically detached from moral principles or the dictates of his conscience. The observance of the moral law remains in force for him as for every other citizen. Certainly he may, and even must, in his business transactions work in his own interest; but the moral law forbids the use of illicit means, such as deception, lying, or violence, or taking advantage of the ignorance or the misfortune of others (*see* Black Market). *Pav.*

BUSINESS ENTERPRISE. A business enterprise is the organic union or combination of the factors of production, established for the purpose of producing goods and rendering services in the most economic form.

FORMS. A business organization or enterprise may be of various types: (a) *individual* or *collective*, depending on whether the business is controlled by one individual alone or by several jointly (partnership); (b) *private* or *public*, depending on whether the immediate interests pursued are of a private or public nature; (c) *agricultural, commercial, financial, industrial, etc.*, according to the nature of the commodity produced or the type of service rendered; (d) *small, medium* or *large*, according to the size of the business, although, practically speaking, it is almost impossible to draw the line between one and the other; (e) *simple* or *complex*, depending on whether the factors of production are controlled by one individual (as in the case of artisans, farmers) or by several distinct individuals (as in a factory or plant). These distinctions, as is easily understandable, do not possess an absolute value. Definitely empirical in character, one form may easily be reduced to the other. It is quite obvious, for example, that a simple business is at the same time small, individual, and almost certainly private; on the other hand, a large business might simultaneously qualify as a simple business. The modern economic structure, quite different from the medieval, is characterized by a clear preponderance of medium and large businesses in the manufacturing industries, while the small business still continues to prevail in the agricultural field.

VARIOUS ASPECTS. A business organization or enterprise, a little world in itself, presents many and varied aspects: technical, organizational, financial, fiscal, commercial, social, and hygienic. Each one of these aspects is constantly under ethical norms in every phase of business life, whether it be purchase of raw materials, productive processes, marketing and sale of products, distribution of goods; in all these phases, the pursuit of economic interests is always accompanied by demands of justice and humanity.

A business is a productive organism whose functional processes are necessarily regulated by economic laws. Basic among these is the so-called *dimensional law*, which prompts a business organization to adopt the position that would yield the maximum return. A business organization, however, is also a social union or gathering of human beings, with each individual engaged in a specific activity. In the modern economic world a business organization, especially of medium and large size, is characterized by a marked distinction between workers and management, that is, between those who occupy a dependent role and those who, either as owners or officials, direct the various departments of the business and bear the economico-juridical responsibilities. In the present economic structure the salary system still largely prevails insofar as the workers are concerned. In recent years, however, the historical evolution of labor, especially in the more progressive countries, shows a growing tendency toward giving workers a larger share of responsibility in the business itself. In other words, it appears that the worker is in the process of gaining a position of greater participation and recognition in the life of a business organization, which may well lead every business enterprise to assume the form and substance of a genuine community of workers. *Pav.*

BUSINESS MAN (entrepreneur). A person who conducts an economic activity for the purpose of producing or exchanging commodities or services is called a business man. Farmers who work their own land, craftsmen, small tradesmen, and those who conduct a business activity alone or with the help of the members of their own families, are called small business men. Those who conduct a business in which they employ the labor of others are generally called big business men. A person who owns, runs, and directs a business, and is responsible to no one except himself, is usually called an independent business man. A business man differs from the stockholder, who usually owns part of the business but does not manage it. He also differs from the manager, who runs the business but does not own it and who acts within the limits usually set for him by the board of directors, who, in turn, act in the name and in the interests of third parties. The business man, small or big, is the mind and the spirit of his enterprise. He knows all its aspects, he follows its trends, he coordinates and decides on possible developments alone or with the aid of the board. The success or failure of the business depends largely on him. The primary aim of his manifold activities is obviously the success of the business from the viewpoint of profits.

The activities of a business man are primarily economic in nature; he also, however, has many responsibilities toward those who work for him, responsibilities that in recent times have become increasingly more important. Today, the big business man must be not only a leader in production, but also and above all a leader of men. Therefore, it is his duty to study his personnel, as far as possible, in order to know them and to be able to treat them with understanding, wisdom, justice, and humanity. Today, the worker has risen to full awareness of his dignity as a human person. He no longer allows himself to be considered as a mere instrument of production. He demands to be treated on a plane of human equality, except for the inevitable hierarchical order based on ability or functions. For this reason, the business man must endeavor to establish a relationship of mutual esteem and human understanding with his employees, or he will almost inevitably fail as a producer. *See also* Industry. *Pav.*

BUYING AND SELLING. A *Contract.*

The transaction known as buying and selling is a contract whereby one party (the seller) transfers the ownership of an article or title to another (the buyer) for a considered price. On the part of the seller there is an alienation of goods, while on the part of the buyer an acquisition or purchase. The act of buying and selling is, first of all, a contract, at least in the general sense, despite the fact that many civil jurists do not consider it to be a true contract technically, on the ground that in its most developed phase the transaction of sale consists in the exchange of ownership of property for an abstract obligation of a sum of money, a process which, precisely because of the abstract element involved, is the negation of a contract (cf. Archi, *The Transfer of Ownership in Roman Law*, Padua, 1934, pp. 76 ff.).

In Roman law the act of buying and selling (*emptio-venditio*) was a consensual contract (*juris gentium*), merely giving rise to mutual obligation between the parties; it was, therefore, a two-sided relation, in which one party contracted to buy or acquire (*emere*), the other to sell for a price (*vendere* or *venum dare*). The exchange of the article for the price was effected by the *mancipatio*. Today, a sale not only gives rise to obligations between the parties, but it is principally a transfer of ownership; hence, the buyer acquires ownership of the sold articles through the very contract of sale.

ORIGIN AND ELEMENTS OF THE CONTRACT. It is not the purpose of this article to deal with the opinions of civil jurists concerning the nature of sale. It is certain, however, that buying and selling is among the earliest contracts introduced by men united in society for the purpose of exchanging useful or necessary goods according to their mutual needs. Since barter or permutation (*q.v.*), certainly the first among such contracts, is a cumbersome method of effecting exchanges (owing to the different mutual needs of buyers and sellers, the difficulty of arriving at a satisfactory quantitative balance of exchangeable goods, *etc.*), the system of money was introduced as a more convenient and equitable medium of exchange. Such transaction is termed buying and selling; it is so called because of the bilateral character of the transaction: one party agrees to pay the price, the other to surrender the article for the convened price. A sales contract is perfected by the mere consent of the parties, even though the object has not as yet been consigned nor the price paid. But to ensure the contractual effects and to consummate the act, the material consignment of the article sold and payment of the corresponding price are required. Thus, the two elements of a sales contract, *article* and *price*, must be so united that the will (as the essential element) of the contracting parties must want the transfer of ownership of the object for the corresponding price. And even if the transfer be subject to conditions or terms, the intent to execute the sale must be definitely affirmed through the actual consent of the parties. There is no need to mention the transfer of ownership, for this is implied in the will to buy and sell.

RESULTING OBLIGATIONS. A sales contract gives rise to a threefold category of obligations: (a) those extending to all particular contracts (such as the capacity to contract) and to all the different contractual appositions, such as the various possible and honest conditions; (b) those naturally deriving from an act of sale as such, even though not expressed in the contract, such as the obligation of the seller to hand over the article sold, and that of the buyer to pay the stipulated price; (c) those established by particular civil laws.

THE CONTRACTING PARTIES. Unless expressly forbidden by natural or civil law (*e.g.*, children and the insane are excluded by natural law), all may execute an act of sale. Nevertheless, for obvious reasons in the juridical and moral order, all civil codes list certain categories of persons who are forbidden to buy or sell, either directly or through an interposed person.

SPECIFIC OBLIGATIONS OF SELLER. The purpose of buying things is to possess and enjoy them; from this, there arise three obligations on the part of the seller: (a) he is bound to deliver the object sold, precisely as it was at the time of purchase and, unless otherwise agreed upon, together with all its accessories, appurtenances and fruits; he is also bound to hand over all titles and documents relative to ownership and use of the commodity sold; until actual delivery or consignment of the purchased article, it is held by the seller in the name of the buyer. (b) If ownership of the object was not transferred simultaneously with the sales transaction, the seller must see to it that the buyer receives such title of ownership. (This, in reality, occurs when one sells someone else's goods.) The seller must grant a guarantee against dispossession or eviction and against defects in the thing sold. The buyer is entitled to the undisturbed possession and enjoyment of the purchased property, which the seller is bound to protect against all claims of third parties. Any contrary arrangement is null, and the seller is liable to restitution and to reimbursement of all legitimate expenses incurred by the buyer; and if the seller was in bad faith, he is also liable to reimbursement of non-essential expenses. If the buyer, however, has made the purchase at his own risk and is aware of the danger of dispossession, the contract has an aleatory character, and no reimbursements of any kind may be claimed. (c) The seller is bound to reveal all hidden substantial defects in his product, *i.e.*, all defects affecting the substance of the thing itself or rendering the object noxious or useless to the buyer. Plainly apparent accidental defects need not be mentioned, and the buyer can only blame himself for not having detected

them, unless the seller had declared the object to be free of all defects. In cases of hidden defects, two courses of legal action are usually open to the buyer: he may either seek an annulment of contract (*invalidating action*) or for reduction of price (*revaluating action.*)

SPECIFIC OBLIGATIONS OF BUYER. The fundamental obligation of the buyer is to pay the price stipulated. But should the buyer reasonably fear that the purchased object or a part thereof may be reclaimed, he may suspend payment on the plea of unfulfilled contract (*exceptio nonadimpleti contractus*), unless the seller is ready to grant a suitable guarantee; however, if the buyer was aware of such danger at the time the sale was executed, payment may not be suspended. Payment must be made according to the terms established by the contract. Unless other stipulations are agreed upon, payment is to be made upon delivery or consignment of the commodity in question. Unless otherwise stated, the thing sold passes over to the buyer with all its fruits and risks.

DETERMINATION OF PRICE. An essential element of the sales contract is that the purchase be paid for in money. The price is intended to be equivalent to the value of the thing sold. Hence, the price is primarily determined by the common judgment or estimate of men concerning the value of the object. This estimate is based chiefly on the intrinsic value or utility of the object, but also on production cost, scarcity or availability of the object in question, *etc.* The contracting parties may, therefore, safely follow the common judgment of a given region, unless it is substantially erroneous (cf. De Lugo, *De Just., disp. 26, s. 4, n. 43*). Obviously, the common estimation of men concerning the value of an object is not something mathematically exact; hence, the common price is generally determined by the market price, based on supply and demand; and this market price is subject to variations, fluctuating between two extremes, high and low. The market price, therefore, constitutes the common or current price. If the matter of price is left to the judgment of buyers, it is termed conventional price, to distinguish it from market price. The legal price is that which is set by public authority to avoid speculation.

The general principles regarding price may be formulated as follows: (a) the legal price is to be regarded as just and is to be observed by all; (b) where no legal price has been fixed, the common price may be considered just, at least for such objects as have a market price; (c) as a rule, no commodity should be bought below the lowest nor sold above the highest price. Hence, prices should be kept within the limits of the market; to exceed these limits is to violate justice and this entails the obligation of restitution. However, at times there can be special reasons for going above or below these limits, e.g., if a merchant would have to sustain a great loss by selling at the current price, he would be justified in demanding more; similarly, if an object is exceptionally rare or especially valuable to the owner, he can demand more (*price of affection*, as theologians call it).

SALE AND MORALITY. Everyone is entitled to the fruits of his labor; hence, it is only reasonable that those engaged in business or commerce should realize a profit. But such profit must be legitimate and honest. Unfortunately, however, the business world is notorious for its unethical practices. Who can possibly enumerate all the devious methods used for purposes of financial gain? Falsifications, adulteration of products, unfair competitive practices, collusion and tacit agreements, bribery and corruption, *etc.*

There is a common conviction among men today that the business world is a sphere all its own, in which everyone must necessarily look out for his own ends. It is an arena of rugged and fierce competition, in which only the strongest survive in a dog-eat-dog struggle. Hence, the first rule for getting ahead is to distrust everyone and to take advantage of others, before they take advantage of you; it is only realistic thinking to follow the general practice. Such thinking, however, is not morally valid, and one cannot justify this outlook by saying that everyone is doing it, nor by saying that the business world involves a free-for-all struggle, with no holds barred. The dog-eat-dog method is the law of savages, not of civilized men. Right reason tells us that human conduct must always conform with the moral law; and if man listens to the dictates of his conscience, he knows that he is never permitted to take advantage of the good faith or inexperience of others, or knowingly to deceive others.

SALE OF SACRED OBJECTS. For the sale or alienation of ecclesiastical goods and of sacred things. *See* Administration of Ecclesiastical Goods and Simony. *Tar.*

C

CALENDAR, ECCLESIASTICAL.

The *ecclesiastical calendar* is a tabular register containing a list of feasts and ferial days in the ecclesiastical year (*see* Liturgical year), with indications of the Office and Mass for the day.

Since Easter is a movable feast, certain Offices and feastdays are transferred to different days, which necessitates a yearly compilation and revision of the calendar.

In early times calendars had a strictly local and particular character. Today, every diocese, religious order and congregation of men has its own calendar, which, with due local modifications, is based on the *calendar of the universal Church*. The earliest known calendar is the *Philocalion Calendar*, so called from the name of its copyist; this was a calendar of the Roman Church of the fourth century. It listed the dates of the death of the various popes and the anniversaries of the martyrs; it also indicated the place and the church where the feast was celebrated.

As a general rule, every priest must follow the calendar for the celebration of the Mass (*q.v.*) and the recitation of the Divine Office (*see* Breviary). When celebrating in another church or public oratory or in a principal semi-public oratory of a seminary, hospital, jail, etc., he must follow the calendar of the place where he celebrates. In non-principal, private, and semi-public oratories, he may follow his proper calendar. In the recitation of the breviary, the priest follows his proper calendar, wherever he goes. These prescriptions do not oblige under grave sin; a reasonable cause may excuse from their observance. *Cig.*

CALUMNY. *See* Defamation.

CANDLES.

Historical Notes. From the earliest times candles have been used in the liturgy of the Church, not only for the purpose of illumination, but also as a sign of worship and respect. The polemic delivered by St. Jerome in the sixth century condemned the heretic Vigilantius, who complained that piles of candles were lighted in church, while the sun was still shining. In reply to this criticism, the holy Doctor defended the use of candles at Mass and at the reading of the Gospel as a sign of respect for the word of Christ. The candle was already at this time the distinguishing mark of the acolyte, one of the lesser ministers of the altar. Walking in procession to the sanctuary, the pontiff was preceded by seven acolytes carrying candles.

Until the introduction of gaslight and electricity in the modern era, candles and oil lamps constituted the only means of illumination in the churches. In the fourth century, the pilgrim Etheria (Egeria or Sylvia) writes of having witnessed in the churches of Jerusalem an array of *infinite lights* produced by thousands of candles. The ancient chronicle *Liber Pontificalis* relates that Pope Adrian I donated to the Vatican Basilica a *polycandelum*, shaped in the form of a cross and capable of holding 1570 candles.

But on the altar itself candles do not appear until the middle of the twelfth century. Before this, they were placed on the floor of the sanctuary, at the sides or in front of the altar. For strictly liturgical use at the altar, candles must contain a minimum of fifty-one percent beeswax. It is known with certainty that the practice of carrying candles in processions existed in the eighth century, and the custom of blessing candles on the feast of the Purification of Our Lady (Feb. 2—*Candelora*, Candlemas) appears in the tenth century. The particular significance of candles in this function is that they are used to honor Christ, the *Light and Revelation to the world.*

Present Use of Candles in Church. For low Mass celebrated by a priest, two lighted candles are required; for a low Mass celebrated by a bishop, four are permitted. For a solemn Mass, six lighted candles are required by common practice, and seven are used for a pontifical Mass.

For private exposition of the Blessed Sacrament in a ciborium, it is required that at least six candles be lighted; for solemn Benediction, the prescribed minimum number of candles is twelve. In all these instances, candles may not be replaced by electrice lights (*see* Electricity). In case of necessity, as in wartime, the Church did relax these rules, by permitting more extensive use of electric or other types of lighting as substitutes for beeswax candles. Today, by a decree of the Sacred Congregation of Rites (Aug. 18, 1949) a minimum of four beeswax candles must be used for a high Mass and for solemn Benediction of the Blessed Sacrament; the canonically prescribed number of candles are made up with other types of lights. *Cig.*

CANNIBALISM. See Perversions, Sexual; Murder.

CANON. See Chapter.

CANONIZATION. See Beatification and Canonization.

CANONIZATION (Of Laws). This expression is used, however improperly, to indicate the acceptance or adoption of civil norms within the sphere of Church legislation, as in Canon 1529. Wherever possible, to simplify matters, the Church adopts (*canonizes*) certain civil laws. By the same token certain canonical norms are adopted by the civil codes of particular countries.

The Church tends to adopt the positive civil laws of the various countries concerning contracts and temporal matters in general, provided that the laws do not contravene divine, natural, or positive laws, except if the Church has equivalent regulations of her own. Conversely, civil law should follow or adopt, in spiritual matters, more canonical norms and related concepts than it actually does.

Concordats between Church and State, as agreements necessarily affecting matters of positive law of both parties, and all conventions and pacts between the two societies are undoubtedly an important source for the canonization of laws. At times the very nature of the matter involved requires the canonization of laws in order to create a better understanding and mutual dependence between the two legislative spheres. *Pug.*

CANON, PRIVILEGE OF. See Clergy, Privileges of.

CANOPY. See Eucharist; Sacred Vestments.

CANTATORIUM. See Liturgical Books.

CANTHARIDES. See Aphrodisiacs.

CAPACITY. In psychology, the word *capacity* designates an ability to understand, intellectual power or, simply, intelligence (*q.v.*). In criminal law and legal medicine, the term is more comprehensive; it includes volition, so that juridical or legal capacity means ability to will or to commit a specific act, joined with the ability to understand the act performed. Thus, the faculties to understand and to will form the basis of juridical capacity and of moral and criminal imputability or responsibility. Generally, in law, capacity is an ability or fitness in a physical or legal person to become the subject of a juridical relation (juridical or legal capacity) or the active or passive subject of a juridical act (capacity to act).

CRIMINAL IRRESPONSIBILITY. In modern civil codes, the following are generally regarded as criminally irresponsible: (a) minors up to fourteen years of age; (b) persons intoxicated or under the influence of narcotics, provided that the crime was committed while in a state of complete intoxication or grave stupefaction induced either accidentally or by force; (c) mentally deranged or seriously demented persons.

The following are generally considered semi-responsible: (a) minors between fourteen and eighteen years of age; (b) persons who, at the time of the crime, are in a psychopathological condition gravely reducing their intellective and volitive powers—a condition which embraces the vast intermediate area between mental sanity and positive mental derangement.

LEGAL INCAPACITY (INCOMPETENCY). In civil law, incapacity is an individual's inability or unfitness to attend to his own interests; it is similar to, though not identical with, the range of criminal irresponsibility. Moreover, legal incapacity varies depending on its reference to interdiction, last will and testament, marriage, etc. In the case of marriage, legal incompetency may arise, not only from insufficient age or psychopathic condition, but also from the so-called impediment of impotency.

Legal incompetency may co-exist with *natural capacity*, broader in meaning than legal capacity, for it includes all persons with the use of reason. What, then, of legal transactions negotiated by persons having the use of reason. What, possessing natural capacity? And what of the binding force of such transactions in the sphere of conscience? For an answer to these questions the reader is referred to the articles on Contract, Interdiction, Marriage, Legal Transaction, Testament (last will).

A conflict may also arise between canonical and civil laws in establishing legal capacity in ecclesiastical matters. In such an event, the canonical, not the civil laws, are binding in conscience (Cans. 1529; 1527, par. 2).

JURIDICAL CAPACITY AND CAPACITY TO ACT. *Juridical capacity*, in a strict sense, is ability or fitness of a person to become the subject of a juridical relation, i.e., to

have a right (power) or a duty (obligation). In order that the act may not be void by reason of incompetency on the part of the subject, it is absolutely necessary that the subject be competent, not only as agent, but also with respect to those to whom the act is directed.

Capacity to act means that a person possesses all the qualifications necessary to perform a valid act or to be the recipient of the act. Hence, legal capacity may exist without capacity to act, but not vice versa.

In Canon Law, until some time ago, baptism was held to be a necessary requisite both for juridical capacity and capacity to act. Today some authors maintain that every man (*homo viator*), including a fetus, is to be considered a person, with this distinction: one who has been baptized is a person in the Church; one who has not been baptized is a person outside the Church (Can. 87). For juridical persons, other norms obtain (*see* Person, Human). Capacity is extinguished only with death; other causes may merely reduce or diminish it. *Riz.*

CAPITAL. One of the major factors in production, *capital* is commonly defined as instrumental good or produced wealth to be used for the production of further wealth. It is distinguished from *land* because it is produced; it is likewise distinguished from *labor*, as the effect and instrument of the labor. Of its many divisions and subdivisions, we shall mention only two, fixed and working capital.

Fixed capital includes all those relatively durable goods which are capable of entering into a successive series of productions, or all those goods which, in each single service of production, undergo only a partial consumption (depreciation, obsolescence). Such are: commercial and industrial buildings, land improvements, implements of labor, machinery, utensils, equipment.

Working capital consists of goods or implements capable of only one single service, i.e., goods which in each single production undergo complete transformation and consumption. Such are the raw materials used in manufacturing industries: silk, linen, aluminum, etc. In a normally functioning economy, fixed capital and working capital coexist as factors of production in equal proportion.

The source of capital has always been a subject of wide discussion; undoubtedly, the most tenable theory today maintains that capital results from savings and investments. Of the wealth produced by men, part is consumed for living purposes and part employed for increasing their productive capacity. The portion of wealth not consumed and invested in production constitutes the capital; thus, capitalization is the sum-total of investments and other actions whereby savings are transformed into capital. Capital, at least in its embryonic form, has always existed; instruments of labor (hammer, scythe, sickle, etc.) are found in remotest antiquity. But in the last two centuries capital has attained, in contrast to labor, an exceedingly high degree of importance; hence, the modern era is rightly designated as a capitalist era.

SOCIAL PROBLEMS. *Capital* has given rise to many moral problems; of these we shall consider here only the following three:

(a) In the past century capital gained such an ascendancy over labor in regulating the productive process that labor came to be treated as an instrument of capital. Such a condition is contrary to the hierarchy of values, since labor is a source and reason for capital. Hence, capital must be placed at the service of labor, which is today precisely the objective of the human family of workers.

(b) Wealth attained through the concourse of both capital and labor, must be distributed in both spheres. The question is in what proportion. In the past, capital has frequently grabbed the lion's share. But justice demands that in the distribution of produced wealth, labor be given first consideration, for man does not live to produce, but produces to live. Hence, capitalization is justified only if it contributes to the betterment of man's living conditions.

(c) An economic system is sound only if production is proportionate to consumption. Hence, the adoption of measures, especially by the government, designed to disturb this balance, sometimes for political or aggressive reasons, is not only contrary to economic laws, but also morally wrong. *Pav.*

CAPITALISM. In its scientific aspects, *capitalism* has a variety of meanings. In the economic sense, it is defined as a system characterized by the preponderant function of capital, or a system in which capital and labor exist separately. In general, Catholic authors accept this definition. Others stress not so much an economic as a social character in the system in which the possessors of capital exercise total control even over persons, with obvious grave abuses. Under this aspect, capitalism is defined as the system of *plutocracy* or the regime of a *dictatorship of gold* (Marx). This definition, according to which a modern capitalistic system is not the separation of capital and labor, but the complete subordination of an enterprise to finance, is also used by some Catholic sociologists. Finally, the term *capitalism* is sometimes taken to indicate a certain tendency of spirit: greed for wealth or devotion to the pursuit of wealth (mammonism). Because of this variety of descriptions, the Encyclical *Quadragesimo Anno* avoids the use of the word *capitalism.*

Prescinding from all variable factors, it is possible to determine the elements which constitute the essence of capitalism. The stable factors in a capitalistic economy are: the mechanical-technical formation of capital, its employment for the organization of economy, and the personal management of capital. The variable factors are the attitude and the goal of each individual, which depend on the purpose for which the economic means and methods are employed.

Each economic system is not merely a structure or material organization but also a philosophy and a way of life: a tendency characterized by its own *spirit*. The capitalistic spirit is primarily one of enterprise, natural and necessary to man, especially in large undertakings or ventures. But it also represents a hierarchy of values, in which the economic occupy the first place, while all other values—religious, cultural, esthetic, scientific, social, domestic, national—are evaluated in relation to this. Acquisition of wealth under any form becomes the primary good and principal aim in life. The precapitalistic axiom "The standard of all things is man" (*mensura omnium rerum homo*) implies the satisfaction of man's needs; it is a sin to go beyond this measure (*in excessu hujus mensurae consistit peccatum*), as St. Thomas observes. While the spirit of the precapitalistic regime was impregnated with moderation, the capitalistic spirit tends toward unlimited gain and profit, beyond all proportion to personal needs or wants. This spirit of gain sets the pace of every activity and becomes the aim of every undertaking or enterprise. It develops into a sort of puritanical asceticism, leading the capitalist to deprive himself of rest, pleasure, and the enjoyment of life. Finally, it becomes an obsession, prompting man to produce as much as possible, in order to accumulate the largest profits. In this light, the worker comes to be regarded as a mere machine, evaluated according to productivity. Moreover, no longer producing for a specific clientele or group of consumers, as in precapitalistic days, but with an eye to world markets, the capitalist launches into a sphere of unbridled competition, a mad race for gain, dangerous risks and ventures, frequently without any sentimental, social, or moral scruples. Such inversion in the economic sphere eventually gives rise to a particular concept of the social sphere, and to a capitalistic psychological attitude. The capitalistic spirit is egocentric: it relegates the common good to second place, sometimes leading to the absurd belief that the community or State exists for no other reason than to serve the interests of the employer or industrialist. Fellow citizens are no longer regarded as equals, but as rival competitors, business connections, or simply as consumers. The emphasis is no longer on the quality of the product,

which was a matter of personal pride in the precapitalistic era, but on quantity or volume of sales.

However, within a capitalistic economy are found elements, such as technical skills and abilities, labor-saving methods, time-saving devices, etc., which, although utilized with a capitalistic attitude or spirit, in themselves have nothing whatever to do with this spirit and, hence, cannot be condemned. Initiative, inventiveness, risk, investment are indispensable elements of economic progress. Sacred Scripture abounds in passages urging man to use his talents fruitfully (Matt. 25:14–30; Luke 19:11–28), just as it contains numerous texts condemning mammonism or accumulation of wealth for its own sake (Luke 16:9; 18: 18–30; Mark 10:17–31; Matt. 19:16–30).

A capitalistic employer assumes the responsibility of producing constantly new products for the market, in keeping with the ever-increasing, changing needs of the public. To be successful, a modern businessman must be an individual of wide ability and enormous activity. He must endeavor to satisfy his customers, interpret business trends and conditions of world market, keep abreast of the times by following the socio-politico-economic conditions, keep informed about new technical developments, prices of raw materials, transportation costs, labor costs, etc. He must also know how to handle organizational problems: production, division of work, sales, publicity, etc. All this requires special ability in the employer. Despite all this, the fact remains that the capitalistic method of production has taught man to conceive and utilize all material goods as capital and that the capitalistic spirit, ignoring ethical principles, tends to apply the capitalistic scale of values to all things. However, it is also true that these errors do not form an integral part of the system, whose main purpose is to derive a maximum profit from a minimum investment of capital.

Evaluation. It is clear that a purely capitalistic spirit, which may be characterized as mammonism or dedication to the pursuit of wealth, is anti-moral, anti-social and anti-Christian. It is likewise clear that, insofar as capitalism has brought about grave abuses and injustices in the social sphere, it is irreconcilable with Christian social principles. Concerning the evaluation of the capitalistic method of production, the Encyclical *Quadragesimo Anno* states: "It is evident that this system is not to be condemned in itself." It is not in itself immoral. Hence, capitalism is not to be rejected as intrinsically evil, either in its juridical premises, such as private ownership and freedom of contract, or in its real roots, such as separation of the workers from the means of production, a separation which constitutes the basis of the wage contract. As a matter of fact, some of these premises are to be defended as fundamental to every socio-economic order. The abuses and errors connected with capitalism stem only from a distortion of such premises or principles. The task of Catholics, therefore, consists (1) in combating and overcoming the mammonistic spirit, which has to some extent made great inroads everywhere; (2) in establishing harmony between social classes for the goal of peaceful collaboration; (3) finally, in helping to restore the primacy of spiritual, cultural, and social values in private and social life. Leaving a scientific criticism or evaluation of the capitalistic method of production to expert economists, we may state that indiscriminate condemnation of capitalism is both unscientific and unrealistic; it would only serve to advance the cause of Marxism, which consists in a total rejection of capitalism "under all conditions." Papal documents on social and economic problems point out both the concrete abuses and injustices of the capitalistic system and a constructive criticism of the system. The study of these documents should enable us to contribute effectively to the reconstruction of the social and economic order of modern society. *Per.*

CARBONARI. *See* Secret Society.

CARDINAL. Cardinals are the chief associates and counselors of the supreme pontiff in the government of the universal Church. Historically, they are the successors of the twenty-five priests attached to the principal titles or churches of Rome, the seven (later fourteen) regional deans, the six palatine deacons, and the seven suburbicarian bishops.

The Sacred College of Cardinals (papal senate) was established in the year of 1150; it had a dean, who was the bishop of Ostia, and a camerlengo or chamberlain in charge of the administration of revenue. Pope Sixtus V set the number of cardinals at seventy; this group included six cardinals of the order of bishop, fifty of the order of priests, and fourteen of the order of deacons. Cardinals are members of the various Roman congregations. As royal princes of the Church they enjoy the title of *Eminence*. According to the terms of the Lateran Treaty, cardinals living in Italy are considered citizens of the Vatican State.

The creation of cardinals is reserved to the free choice of the pope, who makes the selections from among priests and bishops noted for distinguished service to the Church. The appointment of a cardinal is characterized by two phases: *selection* and *publication* of the name, which usually occur in the same secret consistory. The dignity, rights, and privileges of the cardinalate begin with the publication of the names. The pope may choose a cardinal in a consistory, but defer publication of the name until a later date; this is known as a *reservatio in pectore*. Irrespective of the time of publication of the names, seniority and precedence of the cardinals are reckoned according to the date of selection and appointment, even though the name is reserved *in petto*.

Other special ceremonies, which usually occur in the next consistory, include the imposition of the red hat, the oath of loyalty, the opening and closing of the mouth, the assignment of a titular church; but these are considered secondary. If the newly appointed cardinal is not in the curia, the red hat is sent to him by a special delegate, to whom the selected candidate must promise under oath and under the pain of nullifying the dignity of the cardinalate received that he will go personally to Rome for the other ceremonies described, unless he is legitimately impeded.

RIGHTS AND PRIVILEGES.

During the reign of the supreme pontiff, cardinals assist the pope in the government of the Church by attending consistories, by taking active part in the administrative functions of the Roman congregations, by fulfilling various papal missions and assignments. Cardinal bishops are true Ordinaries of their dioceses, with full episcopal powers. Cardinal priests and cardinal deacons, after they have taken canonical possession of their titular churches or deaconries, enjoy ordinary authority in matters pertaining to offices, benefices, discipline, and service of the church; but they have no jurisdiction over the faithful, nor may they exercise any judicial or penal power over clerics (Can. 240, par. 1–2).

Among the extensive privileges common to all cardinals are the following: (a) the right to a deliberative vote in an ecumenical council, even though they are only cardinal deacons; (b) the right to choose for themselves and members of their household a confessor, who, if he lacks jurisdiction, obtains by the fact of this choice the faculty of absolving from all sins and censures not reserved to the Holy See in a most special manner (*specialissimo modo*); (c) the right to perform pontifical functions in all churches outside of Rome (*extra Urbem*); in the city of Rome, (*in Urbe*), a cardinal priest may celebrate pontifical functions in his own titular church; a cardinal deacon in his own titular church may only assist at pontifical functions, but not celebrate, even though he possesses the sacerdotal character; (d) the right to bless and consecrate churches and altars anywhere (but not holy oils, unless the cardinal also possesses the episcopal character); (e) the right to confer first tonsure and minor orders; (f) the right to administer the sacrament of confirmation.

DUTIES. The obligations or duties of cardinals derive largely from their eminent status and function in ecclesiastical government. As chief counselors and aids to the pope, cardinals are obliged to reside at the Papal Court, and they may not leave Rome without permission of the pope. An exception, however, is made for cardinal bishops, who may visit their suburbicarian sees whenever necessary. Cardinal priests, who are local Ordinaries of non-suburbicarian dioceses, are exempt from the obligation of residence at the Papal Court; but, whenever they come to Rome, they must visit the pope and may not leave the city without papal permission.

Upon the death of the pope, the cardinals have the right and duty to elect a new supreme pontiff. During the interregnal period (*Sede vacante*), the ordinary administration of the universal Church is entrusted to the Sacred College. United in general assembly, they decide, by majority vote, upon the authentic interpretation of the laws concerning papal election, expedite matters of particular urgency, and elect a Cardinal Camerlengo and a Cardinal Grand Penitentiary, if a vacancy exists.

All other affairs of minor importance are managed by a special commission consisting of the Cardinal Camerlengo and three other cardinals, one from each order (episcopal, presbyteral, diaconal). Every three days, during the conclave, a new group of three cardinals is appointed, according to seniority.

During a vacancy of the Apostolic See (*Sede vacante*), the activity of the Sacred Congregations is almost completely suspended, except for current business only. All pressing matters are to be referred to the Sacred College.

During the interregnal period, the functions of the Secretary of State cease, while the Cardinal Grand Penitentiary continues in the normal exercise of his office. Normal operation is maintained by the office of the Cardinal Vicar of Rome. *Fel.*

CARDINAL PROTECTOR. A Cardinal Protector is appointed to promote the interests of a particular religious body or community by his counsel, patronage, and mediation. The practice originated in the early part of the thirteenth century. The first recorded instance is found in the life of St. Francis of Assisi, who, in 1220, asked Pope Honorius III, for a Cardinal Protector and received one in the person of Cardinal Ugolino Conti, (the future Pope Gregory IX). In the twelfth chapter of his Rule written in the year 1223, and in his Testament of the year 1226, St. Francis enjoined upon the ministers of the fraternity the duty of requesting the Holy See for a Cardinal Protector. Simultaneously, if not previous to this event, mention of a Cardinal Protector is found in chapter 89 of the Rule of the Hospitallers of the Holy Ghost (PL 217, 1152).

The practice was soon followed by the Hermits of St. Augustine (1243), the *Humiliati* (1246), the Trinitarians (1261), the Carmelites (1286), the Vallambrosans (1289) and certain Benedictine monasteries. Among the Dominicans, express mention of a Cardinal Protector does not occur until the year 1376. Today, with the exception of the Society of Jesus, practically all religious orders and congregations have a Cardinal Protector. Sometimes the pope himself acts in this capacity, as he does today for Dominicans and Passionists.

From the fifteenth to the eighteenth century, it was also customary for nations, kingdoms, empires, etc., to have Cardinal Protectors, whose function was to represent the religious and political interests of those sovereign states at the Vatican. The appointments, to which a remuneration was attached, were made by the respective rulers (Catholic). The French Revolution brought an end to this institution, which flourished especially in the sixteenth and seventeenth centuries.

Other types of cardinal protectorates, which, however, will not be specifically treated here, are those exercised over churches, colleges, archconfraternities, etc.

The selection of a Cardinal Protector is made by the individual religious institutes, more specifically by the respective superiors general, who, after having received indication of acceptance by a particular cardinal, submit a formal petition to the supreme pontiff. The appointment is made through an apostolic brief, which is read when the cardinal takes possession of his protectorate. Following the reading of the papal letter, the Cardinal Protector addresses a few words to the community present, after which all proceed to pay him due homage.

DUTIES. The duties of a Cardinal Protector were not always clearly delineated, but varied according to the different regulations or tenor of the pontifical document. In the Rule of St. Francis, the Cardinal Protector is described as governor, protector, and corrector, and is considered a link for closer union between the order and the Church. In the sixteenth and seventeenth centuries, Cardinal Protectors so exercised real and extensive jurisdictional power over the community and its members, that they intervened in matters of internal government. These extensive powers were greatly reduced by Pope Innocent XII through the constitution *Christi fidelium*, of February 16, 1694. This constitution was substantially embodied in the present Code of Canon Law, which rules that the Cardinal Protector does not enjoy any jurisdiction over the institute or the individual members, but his function is to promote the good of the community by his counsel and patronage (Can. 499, par. 2). A Cardinal Protector is usually delegated to preside at the general chapter assembled for the election of the superior general.

PRIVILEGES. The Cardinal Protector exercises his office without remuneration, except for small gifts offered as a token of esteem and gratitude. On the other hand, many spiritual privileges and benefits are extended to him by most religious communities, especially in the form of prayers and suffrages at his death. The constitutions of some religious institutes prescribe that, upon the death of the Cardinal Protector, a Mass be offered by each priest, the Office of the Dead be recited by the clerics, and special prayers be offered by the lay brothers. *Oli.*

CARDIOPATHIES. *See* Diseases, Social.

CARE OF SOULS (Cura Animarum). By this expression is meant the juridical and moral obligations incumbent on pastors of souls relative to the sanctification of those under their charge. The pope for the entire Church, bishops for their own respective territories (diocese) and parish priests or pastors for their respective parishes are pastors of souls, who have the care of souls upon their shoulders.

The direct and immediate exercise of the care of souls belongs primarily to the parish priest or pastor. The care of souls has both positive and negative aspects, for it is actually designed to provide the faithful with the means of sanctification and to remove dangers and obstacles from their path of salvation.

A pastor must fulfill his obligation concerning the care of souls: (a) *by knowing his flock;* that is, the number of his parishioners, their Christian way of living, the practice of their religious duties and reception of the sacraments. To this effect, a pastor shall personally visit every family in his parish. Also, he must conduct or arrange for a census and maintain an up-to-date file on all his parishioners and their problems. (b) *By correcting and admonishing errant members of the parish* (Can. 467, par. 1), i.e., those who are negligent in their Christian duties, those living in sin or in danger of sin, etc. (c) *By exercising paternal care for the poor and the suffering.* The pastor should endeavor to find out the number of needy and unfortunate individuals within his parish, making it a point to visit them, assist them with alms, seek employment for those able to work, promote charitable organizations for the relief of the poor, etc. (d) *By taking special care of the sick* (Can. 468, par. 1). The pastor is obliged to concern himself with the spiritual condition of the sick, visiting them fre-

quently, even if not requested, and especially seeing to it that they receive in time the last rites, i.e., Holy Viaticum and extreme unction. (e) *By guarding his parishioners against all dangers to faith and morals within the parish* (Can. 469). The pastor must be prepared to oppose with all the power at his command the evil effects of an unscrupulous press, of perverse organizations, of indecent and dangerous shows, etc. (f) *By promoting works of charity, faith, and devotion* (Can. 469), particularly by promoting Catholic Action, confraternities and other pious associations, religious schools or courses of religious instruction, organizations for the promotion of Catholic literature, etc.

MEANS OF PROVIDING FOR THE CARE OF SOULS. The particular means of providing for the care of souls are:

(a) *Preaching.* According to the Code: (1) The pastor has a personal and grave obligation to preach a homily to the people on Sundays and holy days of obligation (Can. 1344, par. 1); if legitimately impeded, this obligation must be satisfied through a substitute.

(2) Local Ordinaries must see to it that during Lent more frequent sermons are given in cathedral and parish churches (Can. 1346), and that pastors arrange a mission for their parishioners at least once every ten years (Can. 1349).

(3) Catechetical instruction must be provided for the people (Can. 1329). This includes: preparation of children for the sacraments of penance and confirmation (Can. 467); instruction of children for the reception of their First Holy Communion (Can. 1330); follow-up instructions for children who have already made their First Communion (Can. 1331); catechetical instructions for adults at a convenient time (Can. 1332).

(b) *Conducting divine services.* (Can. 467, par. 1). A pastor is obliged to say Mass in behalf of the people (the parish Mass) on Sundays, holydays of obligation, and other feast days. He is further obliged to conduct other prescribed liturgical functions, such as blessing candles, palms and baptismal font, on Holy Saturday or on the Vigil of Pentecost; prayers and litany on Rogation Days; customary processions; Sunday vespers; the rosary of the Blessed Virgin, the Forty Hours Devotion, etc. All such functions are to be conducted, not for financial gain, but for the glory of God and the edification of the faithful. All ceremonies of a superstitious character or contrary to the decorum of divine cult are to be eliminated.

(c) *Administration of sacraments* (Can. 467). The sacraments are to be administered not only to the faithful who are well but also to those who are sick or dying, when legitimately requested. *Per se* this is a grave and personal obligation for a pastor, especially when personally requested.

A pastor would sin gravely, if he were to place unreasonable restrictions regarding the day or hour for the reception of the sacraments, or if he were habitually to manifest displeasure or annoyance when requested to administer the sacraments. Indeed, in cases of extreme or quasi-extreme necessity, the pastor is bound, even at the risk of his own life, to administer the Sacraments which are necessary for man's salvation: baptism, penance, extreme unction. The extent of the obligation to administer the sacraments is determined by the nature, necessity, or importance of the individual sacraments. *M.d.G.*

CASE ADJUDGED (RES JUDICATA).

The term *res judicata* means that a controversy is considered irrevocably decided so that it cannot be re-tried by any court in ordinary procedure. Canon Law attaches to an adjudged case an absolute presumption (*juris et de jure*) of truth, which means that the sentence rendered is considered true and just, and cannot be directly attacked (Can. 1904, par. 1). General interest and public welfare demand that, if a case has been adequately and sufficiently tried, the litigants accept the sentence of the court as definitive. Our immediate concern here is with a case adjudged in the sphere of Canon Law.

JURIDICAL VALUE. In a judicial sentence one must distinguish the decision (dispositive or decisive) from the reasons or motives on which the decision is based. The decision of the sentence substantially establishes the position of right and wrong between the parties. This gives rise to a right to execute a sentence and to preclude further trial (Can. 1904, par. 2). Although secondary, the reasons or motives for the decision rendered may never be lacking in a judicial sentence (Can. 1873, par. 1, n. 1), except when the sentence is issued by the supreme authority. Thus, sentences issued by the pope or by the supreme tribunal of the Apostolic Signature are effective even if they do not contain the reasons for the decision rendered (Can. 1605, par. 2). The presumption of truth indicated above applies only to the dispositive part of the sentence, although by way of exception it may also apply to the reasons or motives, as in a legal flaw committed by a judge who, in drawing up his decision, extended the motivating part of the decision beyond what was required with practical effects on the sentence that followed. In this case, of course, the sentence could be attacked, although only indirectly, i.e., *querela nullitatis* or *restitutio in integrum*.

ADJUDICATION IN INTERLOCUTORY SENTENCES. Interlocutory sentences rendered in incidental cases are considered adjudged, unless the effects are nullified by subsequent proofs furnished during the proceedings. Thus, an interlocutory sentence, admitting or rejecting a certain proof, becomes an adjudged matter. But an interlocutory judgment on suspicious guilt, competency, or the parties' right to adjudication would seem to be binding on the judge issuing the sentence on the merits of the case itself.

An adjudged issue is, by way of exception, permanent and irrevocable, for it is based on the principle that an issue, already decided and considered objectively closed after the objective truth and justice has been established, is not subject to re-trial. The exception may be claimed *ex officio*, even if the interested party fails to claim it. However, since it is a reason of fact, the exception may not be claimed in the Tribunal of Signature, unless already proposed in a lower tribunal.

An issue becomes irrevocably adjudged: (a) when two uniform sentences have been rendered on the subject; (b) when a court sentence was not appealed within the specified time or, if appealed, it was not prosecuted before an appellate judge within the appointed period of time; (c) when the law grants no appeal in the case; (d) when the right of appeal is declined.

Questions concerning the status of persons, strictly speaking, do not become irrevocably adjudged, but may always be re-examined, provided that new and serious evidence can be exhibited (Can. 1903). Hence, sentences rendered in cases relating to marital separation or marital bond, ordination, and religious profession never become irrevocably adjudged. Moreover, in marriage cases the defender of the bond has, according to Canon 1897, the right to propose an appeal, even after two uniform declaratory sentences on the nullity of a marriage have been issued.

EFFICACY OF ADJUDICATION. Adjudication is valid only insofar as the object of the sentence is concerned. Hence, a new trial is ruled out if the judicial petition is the same as the previous one, concerns the same object or matter, or is between the same parties and based on the same reasons and conditions.

A sentence in a contentious case, which has become irrevocable, does not necessarily prove the existence of an offense, even if the judge may have suspended the trial with pronouncement of the sentence to follow; but it may prove the existence of a fact as the basis for a criminal trial, as it may also prove the existence and consolidation of a right stemming from a former trial, in which the sentence was considered prejudicial to the particular party. At the same time, a condemnatory sentence, which has become adjudicated, proves the existence and the effects of a crime, as in litigation concerning indemnification for damages.

ADJUDICATION IN CIVIL LAW. The concept of adjudication in civil law is substantially the same as in Canon Law. In civil law, however, the effects of an adjudged case are more absolute. This is due to the fact that most civil trials concern property matters; hence, all sentences rendered usually become adjudged issues.

An adjudged case is presumed just and generally binding in conscience. However, if an adjudged issue should serve to safeguard a state of fact that is certainly and objectively unjust, the winner may not in conscience avail himself of the benefits of the adjudication; the injured party may resort to occult compensation (q.v.). The judge, who is voluntarily responsible for such an unjust decision, is bound to make restitution for damages which may have been suffered. *Pug.*

CASE, RESERVED. See Reservation of Sin, Reservation of Censure.

CASE, URGENT. See Urgency.

CASTRATION. *Castration* is the surgical removal of the sex glands. This operation today is generally performed in the following cases: (a) in a serious pathological condition of the sex organs; (b) in particular cases of hermaphroditism; (c) for the removal of a serious pathological condition of other organs, especially in the treatment of certain psychical disorders (*therapeutic castration*).

Castration, unless restricted to the removal of just one gland, always has serious effects on the organism and personality, especially if the operation is performed prematurely before puberty. This fact has been positively ascertained by extensive clinical research and numerous experiments conducted on both humans and animals. It has been conclusively proven that the gonads, as glands of internal secretion, bear an intimate relationship with many anatomical and functional characteristics of the organism, as well as to psycho-affective and psycho-intellective manifestations of the individual. It has also been demonstrated that removal of a single testicle or of a single ovary has no appreciable effect upon fecundity, power of copulation, or psychosomatic characteristics of the individual.

Prepuberal castration produces, besides absolute impotency, a characteristic type of infantilism, in which the individual, male or female, is unable to acquire the characteristics proper to his or her sex, developing instead into a neutral or epicene type, with conspicuous anomalies of growth, metabolism, and the neuropsychical sphere. An arrested development of the penis and other sex organs occurs with a lack of beard and sparse hair growth in other parts of the body, a permanently small larynx, an infantile voice with a high pitch, permanent gigantism characterized by an excessive enlargement of the hands and feet, excessive adipose tissue, often hypertrophic and, in in the male, female characteristics and mannerisms and a decreased metabolism. In the female, menstruation ceases. The psyche of the castrated individual is generally torpid, languid, and, in the male, devoid of the characteristics of alacrity, courage, and vigor, usually found in normal subjects.

When castration is performed during puberty or in adulthood, the effects are not as grave as described above, but there is always considerable damage to the system and personality. In a castrated male the following characteristics are usually observed: increased adiposity distributed according to feminine characteristics, in regions of the breast, pelvis, buttocks, hips; diminution of hair growth; loss, within a short time, of *libido* and virile potency. The sexual act is sometimes accompanied by ejaculation of the prostatic fluid. In a castrated female the effects are as follows: cessation of menstruation; general plethora and obesity; appearance of masculine hypertrichosis (excessive growth of hair, especially on the face); abnormal pigmentation; arthritic, myalgic and neuralgic pains; nervous and psychical disorders. In both sexes there obviously results complete sterility.

MORAL ASPECTS OF CASTRATION. Castration, if performed for the purpose of removing or correcting a serious pathological condition of the gonads or other sex organs, is always morally licit. The same must be said concerning cases of hermaphroditism, in which diligent medical diagnosis indicated the necessity of removing one gonad, in order to revitalize the sexually antagonistic gonad, which, as is clearly noticeable in the psychosexual behavior of a hermaphrodite, already appeared to be clearly predominant.

Therapeutic castration, instead, is a grave matter and still unsettled, since there is no final agreement on the nature of this operation, which is bound to affect not only the internal secretion of the sexual glands, but also the external secretion expressly designed for the reproduction of the species. Admittedly, removal of the gonads, especially the testicles, with its tranquilizing effects on temperament and its restraining influence on *libido*, is indicated as a therapeutic measure in cases of sexual perversion and in instances of mental disorders of sexual origin, with obvious beneficial results for the individual and society (reduction of sex crimes). On the other hand, this operation irreparably suppresses the reproductive capacity, although, as previously noted, the power of copulation may be retained for a while. Suppression of the reproductive organs may never be intended either as an end or as a means in correcting a mental disease or preserving chastity. Thus, to deprive an individual of his reproductive faculty, even if he should give his consent, is illicit. The problem is rendered more difficult and complicated by the fact that therapeutic castration does not always achieve its aim, that is, the radical cure of sexual aberrations and mental disorders, for which it is suggested and used.

In conclusion, the recent and authoritative opinion of Scremin might here be quoted: "It cannot be definitely asserted that therapeutic castration is universally illicit, because the sexual glands possess an internal secretion distinct from the external. It is not impossible that in certain cases therapeutic castration may be indicated as the only suitable means of removing a pathological and damaging internal secretion. Hence, it cannot be denied that, with further scientific progress, some reasonable indication may be offered in which such mutilation may be justified even in the ethical field. At the present level of knowledge, therapeutic castration of sex criminals is neither theoretically nor morally justifiable."

The greatest prudence and judgment must be used in such operations, which may be allowed only in the more serious cases of psychosexual anomaly, after all other therapeutic measures have failed.

CURATIVE MEASURES. Against the grave disorders which follow castration, modern medical science possesses valid remedies, which, though ineffective in preventing sterility, are successful in combating the morphological and psychical consequences resulting from the suppression of internal secretion. Reference is here made especially to hormonal therapy, i.e., the administration (orally, parentally, or by transplantation) of sex hormones. To these may be added hormones of other glands pertaining to the genital sphere, or other effective therapeutic and psychotherapeutic measures.

In the treatment of sexual perversions and sexual psychoneuroses, in general, before resorting to therapeutic castration (doubtfully licit), it is advisable to employ, besides the numerous spiritual aids at our disposal, other curative measures of proven efficacy, such as: (a) removal of one gonad; (b) administration of epiphyseal hormones and opotherapeutic extracts of the opposite sex; (c) removal of patient to a suitable health institution, where the individual may be launched on a program of moral rehabilitation through the aid of ergotherapeutic and opotherapeutic techniques, designed to curb and re-educate instinctive impulses and to diminish or remove the disturbing influences of "sexual phantasies," which are at the bottom of all perversions. *Riz.*

CASUISTRY. *Casuistry* is a methodology common to the practical sciences in which a general principle is applied to practical and specific cases. As such the casuistic method may be applicable to any science, but the term has become primarily applied to the field of moral theology or ethics. It signifies the method of illustrating an established principle of revealed moral theology through the formulation of a question, example, or practical case which explains the concrete application of Christian doctrine to conscience and conduct. Hence, the application of general moral principles to the particular concrete cases of daily life and the discussion of moral questions with their practical solutions according to general principles is termed *casuistry* or the science of moral behavior. It resembles applied sciences insofar as it is based on principles and conclusions already solidly established by eminent theologians and moral apologetics to demonstrate that the basis of natural and supernatural morality is the revealed principles that pertain to the concept of obligations. True casuistry demonstrates the presence or lack of conformity of our actions with divine law, manifested by conscience or based on the authority of Holy Scripture and Catholic traditions.

As an applied science, casuistry is different and distinct from purely speculative moral theology. The term is, consequently, improperly and erroneously used to signify the whole series of theological works of authors and writers who treated of moral theology after the fifteenth century.

HISTORICAL NOTES. Casuistry, in fact if not in name, is as ancient as the Church itself. Aside from any reference to the Scriptures (e.g., St. Paul's epistles, wherein we find true casuistic prescriptions), it is certain that the Fathers of the Church were called upon to guide people in matters of great practical concern, such as whether it was permissible to serve in a pagan army, whether one could hide or flee in time of persecution, whether it was licit to tell a lie, etc. Thus, St. Augustine in two complete works *De mendacio* and *Contra mendacium* (PL 40, 487–518), written in a distinctly casuistic form, examines and explains the nature of a lie, and discusses such questions as whether it is permissible to tell a lie in jest or as a figure of speech, whether a good intention in such cases excuses from guilt, etc.

In the thirteenth century, casuistry was joined to the study of Canon Law and the general doctrines treated in theology, as is evidenced in the *Summa Theologiae* of Saint Thomas Aquinas.

During this period, St. Raymond of Peñafort (d. 1275), illustrious teacher and confessor of the sacrament of penance, wrote a *Summa de casibus poenitentialibus*. Divided into four books, it was compiled from the works of eminent authors for the express purpose of helping priests to solve the more difficult cases occurring in the confessional. This opened a new era in the study of theology; an era in which authors endeavored to apply moral principles to the conduct of life. Together with scholastics and canonists there arose "doctors of cases of conscience," who sought to solve practical cases, not as ecclesiastical pastors and divinely constituted doctors, but as private interpreters of the Scriptures, laws, and other subjects already explained and clarified by the Fathers. Those who treated of moral matters were called *summists*, for their works were compilations or collections of moral doctrines reflecting the various *cases* of conscience. Eventually they were given the odious name of *casuists*, to distinguish them from those who treated of canonical questions and who were called *canonists* or *decretists*.

Thus, a multitude of common opinions arose regarding matters of common or human law and the moral principles originating from natural and divine law. This gave rise to the following dictum: *Tota theologia moralis nova est: doctrina fidei repetenda est ab antiquis, doctrina vero morum ab junioribus.*

Characteristic, therefore, of this period were the *Summae casuum* and *Summae confessorum*, which, following the ancient Penitential Books (*q.v.*), set forth the rules of morality and law to be applied in the sacramental forum. Some of these *summae* were canonical with moral sections drawn from the works of theologians and jurists; some were arranged alphabetically, others systematically. These attained particular importance after the Fourth Lateran Council (1215), which prescribed annual confession to one's own pastor (*proprio sacerdoti*).

During the fourteenth and fifteenth centuries, there appeared a great number of manuals by various authors, which were called *Confessionalia* and were substitutes for the Penitential Books and *summae*. Although these manuals had a temporary usefulness for confessors, they also caused ridicule for moral theology among Protestants and some Catholics. Casuistic authors were termed *artificers of doubt*. One reason for a multiplication of these volumes was the personal attitude of many authors. Led by a sense of vanity and exhibitionism, they adhered boldly to their own opinions and used sophistry and subtlety to refute opposite theories.

During the seventeenth century, the treatment of moral theology became progressively less scientific. Authors neglected extensively the principles of Christian living, the means of acquiring and preserving virtue. Instead, they focused attention almost exclusively on the ways and means of avoiding sin. Moreover, the Jansenistic heresy and the controversy over the doctrine of probabilism led a number of authors to confine the study of moral theology to the simple issue of what was "grave or slight, forbidden or tolerated." Moral theology was reduced to little more than a skeletal catalogue of sins and cases; the term *casuistry* became odious. A few casuists were found to be actually ignorant or neglectful of Scripture, tradition, conciliar decisions, etc., as if the use of reason and ordinary common sense were the only requisites for a good moralist and confessor. Such abuse, however, in no way justifies the excessive severity of some, such as Pascal, who attacked the lax moral doctrine of certain obscure casuists. Even when moral theology seemed to be at its lowest ebb, there still emerged eminent and spiritual authors, capable of making a correct application of moral principles and precepts through the aid of a sound casuistry. Among such authors it may suffice to mention Francis Toledo (d. 1596), whose *Summa casuum conscientiae* was recommended to the clergy by St. Francis de Sales. John Azor and many others were considered by St. Alphonsus as respectable authors.

In this applied science, vast and excellent, the casuist must combine prudent judgment with an adequate knowledge of moral theology, ecclesiastic and civil law, and, in particular, local rights and privileges. He also must have a grasp of psychology and related subjects. He must rely, not on human reason alone, but on the light of divine revelation and the teaching authority of the Church, mindful of the fact that man is not the maker of the divine law, but a son who must live and act according to the precepts imprinted within his being. Hence, he must not be concerned merely with the negative aspects of morality, such as determining the nature and extent of sin and guilt, but also with positive aspects, such as inculcating virtue and spiritual life, lest he neglect the true purpose of theological science and the good of souls. *Tar.*

CATACOMBS. *See* Cemetery.

CATALEPSIS. *See* Will, pathology of.

CATALEPSY. *See* Hypnotism.

CATAPLEXY. *See* Narcolepsy, Sleep.

CATATHYMIA. *See* Affectivity, Memory.

CATATONIA. *See* Hebephrenia.

CATECHISM. *See* Doctrine, Christian.

CATECHUMEN. Almost universally in force in the first centuries of the Church, the catechumenate was a period of preparation of adult persons for baptism, with a particular system of instructions, probations, examinations, etc. Its purpose was to prepare candidates for a worthy reception of baptism and to ascertain their sincerity and fitness. When, in the course of time, infant baptism became increasingly prevalent and mass conversions to the Catholic faith declined, the catechumenate practically disappeared in the public life of the Church in Western Europe. Today, however, it is flourishing in many lands and in foreign missions, where conditions are similar to those existing in the primitive Church.

Strictly speaking, the term *catechumen* applies only to those receiving public instruction as a preparation for baptism, under the direction of approved ecclesiastical authority. But in a wide sense, with practically the same juridical and moral effects, the term is also applied to all those preparing for baptism, whether publicly or privately, under the direction of priest or catechist.

A catechumen is one who is not yet a member of the body of the Church. By eliciting an act of faith and perfect love of God, with the desire to receive baptism, he is already a member of the Church; if in the state of grace, he possesses the infused virtue of faith. A return to error at this stage would not constitute apostasy or heresy in the juridical sense, although it would constitute a serious sin against faith. A deliberate and unreasonable deferment of baptism would be a sin against the virtue of religion, harmful to the soul, since it deprives the soul of the benefits of the other sacraments and of participation in the Communion of Saints. The Church treats catechumens with particular regard and benevolence. They are granted the same blessings (Can. 1149) and exorcisms (Can. 1152) as Catholics.

If, through no fault of their own, they should die without baptism, they are granted ecclesiastical burial in the same manner as Catholics. Consequently, Mass may be offered publicly for the repose of their souls, because the Church considers them to have received a baptism of desire (Can. 1239, par. 2; *see also* Non-Catholics, Infidels). *Dam.*

CATHEDRAL. See Church.

CATHEDRATICUM. The *cathedraticum* or *synodaticum* is a moderate tax levied upon all churches, benefices, and lay confraternities under the jurisdiction of the bishop. It is paid annually to the Ordinary as a token of submission (Can. 1504). The amount is determined by the provincial council or meeting of provincial bishops, but is subject to the approval of the Sacred Congregation of the Council. If the amount has been fixed by custom, this is to be observed.

The origin of the *cathedraticum* dates back to the fifth century approximately. Gratian cites the second canon of the Council of Braga (572), and the fourth canon of the eighth Council of Toledo (663), in which a tax was imposed (C. 10, q. 3, c. 1, 8).

The Code of Canon Law acknowledges (Can. 1509) an absolute and unprescriptible right of the bishop to exact a tax, which, however, is to be uniform for all churches and benefices, without regard to size of benefice or amount of revenue.

Taxes are useful and necessary means, if other revenue are lacking, or in extraordinary circumstances, if ecclesiastical society is to attain its end. It is certain that the Church, as a perfect society, has a right to exact such contributions from the faithful, either directly or indirectly. Concerning the liceity of such taxes, canonical provisions established in this regard must be observed. To exact anything over or contrary to canonical laws is a sin against distributive justice, except for the Roman Pontiff, who is above all canonical legislation. *See also* Taxes, Ecclesiastical. *Sir.*

CAUSE, EXCUSING (Observance of the Law). An excusing cause is a circumstance in virtue of which an individual, still remaining subject to the law, is released from observance of the law in a particular case.

In order to determine whether the obligation to observe the law ceases in a particular case, one must institute a comparison, each time, between the law with its obligation deriving therefrom, and the cause or circumstance believed to be excusing.

The general norm is that *the obligation to observe a law ceases whenever its execution becomes morally impossible.* To understand this principle, the following observations are necessary:

(a) The principle does not apply in the case of negative or prohibiting natural laws, for such laws forbid actions that are intrinsically evil and never permissible, e.g., blasphemy. The principle does not apply if non-observance of the law implies contempt for authority, public harm, or scandal.

(b) Moral impossibility is a difficulty of such a nature that the performance of an obligation, while remaining physically possible, is rendered unusually burdensome.

(c) The difficulty or inconvenience must be unusually or exceptionally grave; in other words, a difficulty, no matter how grave, which is inseparable from the ordinary observance of the law is not considered to be an excusing cause.

(d) Moral impossibility admits of degrees and must be proportioned to the gravity of the law and the obligation imposed. The highest degree of moral impossibility is present when the object of an obligation has become morally illicit. In such a case, non-compliance with the law is not only permissible, but obligatory.

Moralists posit the question whether it is ever permissible to create for oneself an excusing circumstance or cause, i.e., to place oneself in a condition that would make the observance of a law morally impossible. The answer is that, generally speaking, this is not permissible without a sufficiently valid reason. And the more important the law, or the graver the obligation, the greater must also be the reason for placing oneself in an excusing circumstance.

It is to be borne in mind that these norms merely regard the matter of lawfulness in the sphere of conscience. In other words, they are moral norms, not juridical. In the juridical order other principles apply. In fact, invalidating laws apply in their full force even when their observance is morally (or physically) impossible, except in those cases which are specifically mentioned in the law itself. *Gra.*

CAUSE FOR DISPENSATION. *See* Dispensation.

CAUSE, PIOUS. *See* Foundation, Pious; Legacy, Pious.

CAUSE (voluntary in). *See* Voluntary in cause.

CAUTION. *See* Guaranty.

CELEBRATION. *See* Mass.

CELIBACY, CLERICAL. A *celibate* is one who has freely resolved to observe life-long continence by abstaining permanently from carnal pleasures. Hence, the distinguishing mark of a celibate is the virtue of chastity, which, according to St. Jerome, consists in living in the flesh but outside the flesh, as it were (*vivere in carne praeter carnem*). This virtue excludes not only libidinous acts, but also sinful thoughts or desires of the flesh.

Understood as such, celibacy is a lofty ideal and the summit of Christian perfection, which man is unable to attain through his own powers alone. For this reason, it was not commanded, but counseled or recommended by God. Hence, celibacy is a gift of God (Matt. 19:12; I Cor. 7:7). *Clerical* or *sacerdotal celibacy* is an expression used to indicate the state of chastity observed by clerics in major orders.

Clerical celibacy is a disciplinary disposition which developed gradually in the Latin Church. The Eastern Church chose to follow a different course. The state of celibacy is observed by clerics, in order that they may be left free to devote themselves to the things of God and to the service of the Church and the faithful.

This arduous and uncommon form of life is voluntarily chosen, after a period of trial and preparation. But once the first major order (subdiaconate) is received, clerical celibacy becomes a matter of obligation regulated by the law of the Church.

CANONICAL NORMS. On the premise that clerics are bound to lead a particularly holy and exemplary life (Can. 124), among the principal positive obligations, the Code of Canon Law enjoins that of absolute chastity (Cans. 132–133). By virtue of this obligation, clerics in major orders can neither validly nor licitly contract marriage and any sin committed against chastity is also a sacrilege. Clerics in minor orders, however, are not barred from contracting marriage, but, by so doing, they automatically cease to be clerics, unless the marriage is shown to have been forced upon them (*see* Order, impediment of).

Implicit in the vow of chastity is the obligation of living under such conditions that the vow can be observed. Hence, clerics are forbidden to allow women against whom suspicion might be lodged to reside in the same house. To safeguard chastity and to eliminate suspicion, only women related to the priest by natural bond or those of advanced age and of good repute are allowed to reside in rectories. It is the duty of the Ordinary to exercise vigilance in these matters and, if need be, to intervene in individual cases with timely admonitions and warnings. Contumacious clerics in this regard are to be presumed guilty of concubinage (Can. 133). According to some synodal statutes, women under the age of forty are not permitted to reside in rectories.

Again, to safeguard chastity, clerics are forbidden to attend public theatrical performances, dances, shows or other forms of entertainment, which, though in themselves legitimate, are unbecoming to the clerical state or a source of scandal to the faithful. In these matters, however, much depends on regional customs and local attitudes. As a rule, in the United States clerical attendance at respectable theatres and reputable places of amusement is not regarded by the public as improper or scandalous.

By a decree of the Sacred Congregation of the Sacraments (Dec. 27, 1930), it is now required that every candidate for the priesthood, before receiving subdiaconate, sign a sworn statement, in which he declares that he is freely embracing the state of celibacy and fully understands the obligations attached thereto.

HISTORICAL AND THEOLOGICAL QUESTIONS. Concerning the law of celibacy, some questions are still open to discussion. One is whether clerical celibacy derives from a divine precept or from a disposition of the Church. Today it is commonly agreed that: (a) though celibacy is virtually recommended in the New Testament, it does not appear to be obligatory; (b) though widely practiced among the clergy in the early centuries of the Church, there is no indication that it was compulsory. The law of celibacy began to take definite form during the fourth century, both in the East and in the West. In the East, the prohibition of marriage after ordination arose, although subdeacons, deacons, and priests were permitted to retain wives wedded before ordination. Bishops, however, were required to observe absolute chastity. This movement was finally adopted into law by the Council of Trullo, in 692.

In the Western Church, the earliest reference to absolute continence is found in Canon 33 of the Spanish Council of Elvira (between 295 and 302). A similar law, enacted by the Roman Council of 386, was confirmed in the fifth century by Pope Leo the Great and extended to the subdiaconate and higher orders. Conciliar and papal legislation gradually followed, in the midst of opposition of the anti-celibacy movements, which marked the course of the historical development of the law of clerical celibacy. In the tenth and eleventh centuries the quarrel over investitures raged; this resulted in the teaching that clerical celibacy constituted a diriment impediment to a valid matrimonial contract. The vow of celibacy was to be regarded as nullifying

any attempted marriage. This teaching was adopted into law at the Second Lateran Council, in 1139 (Can. 7). In 1180 Pope Alexander confirmed this law and extended it to clerics in major orders, beginning with subdiaconate (X, 4, 6, 1–2). This law was later reaffirmed by the Council of Trent (*Sess.* XXIX, Can. 9) and finally incorporated in the Code of Canon Law (Canons 132–133; 213–214; 1072; 2171–2181; 2358–2359; 2388).

Clerical celibacy has survived other anti-celibacy movements and crises during the course of history: during the French Revolution, another by Old Catholics, during the First World War in Czechoslovakia, and, recently, in Germany (neo-modernist program of Leipzig in 1940).

Since the Council of Trent, theologians and canonists have been divided in their opinions of the basis of clerical celibacy. According to one theory, today practically discarded, sacerdotal celibacy and the diriment impediment of sacred orders in relation to marriage are of divine law, i.e., they are based on a natural incompatibility, established by divine law, between priesthood and marriage. This theory, which, at least in the past, numbered noted authors among its supporters, gives rise to most important consequences from a juridical standpoint. The most notable effect is that, since the law of celibacy is viewed as deriving from divine law, it could never be abrogated by ecclesiastical authority; the Church would have no right to suppress clerical celibacy.

A second theory, however, maintains that clerical celibacy and the diriment impediment of sacred orders to marriage are not of divine law, but have simply been introduced by the human law of the Church (ecclesiastical law). The principal effects of this theory are: (a) Since the Church can undo her own legislation, she could certainly repeal clerical celibacy. (b) The Pope could, without difficulty, grant a dispensation from the diriment impediment of sacred orders. This theory, considered more common today, is more easily reconciled with the historical development of the law of celibacy. It permits the Roman Church to look with prudent tolerance upon the practice of the Greek Church.

Another question concerns the juridical basis for the direment impediment of sacred orders in relation to a subsequent attempted marriage. Canonists, past and present, offer a twofold explanation. According to one theory, the more common, which could be called certain (Canons 132; 1072–1073), this impediment derives from a direct and imperative disposition of the ecclesiastical law, rendering a cleric unable to contract either a valid or a licit marriage from the very moment he receives subdiaconate. A second theory, embraced by relatively few, maintains that the nullity of marriage, in this case, derives from the solemn vow of chastity, presumably made by the cleric upon receiving the major orders.

OBJECTIONS AGAINST CLERICAL CELIBACY. Objections against the law of celibacy have been voiced in all ages. They are largely based on the prejudiced view that such law cannot be observed.

Of course, the exalted state of celibacy cannot be faithfully observed through man's natural powers alone. Unaided human will is insufficient to cope with the serious temptations against chastity. It becomes necessary, therefore, to look to and ask for assistance of divine grace, which is the basis of the entire edifice of spiritual perfection. And in every age countless individuals have used precisely this combination of human will and divine grace to belie the theory that absolute continence is impossible.

Naturally, prudence dictates that, before deciding to embrace such a lofty state, an individual make a diligent study and appraisal of his whole character, taking into account his tendencies, habits, and hereditary characteristics. In some instances, the findings may be such as to dissuade the individual from entering the celibate state.

Finally, episodic instances of irregularities or abuse against celibacy cannot be cited as proof that the very institution or law is impossible. The law of celibacy finds its best apology in the fact that a celibate priesthood has for centuries been of great service and strength to the ecclesiastical hierarchy. *Pal.*

CEMETERY. A *cemetery* is a place set apart for the interment or entombment of human bodies. In the ancient era sepulchral tombs and monuments were not located in cemeteries as today, but were situated alongside the great roads outside the city walls. There also were common burial places (*sepulcreta*), but these were used only for burial of the poor. *Cemetery* in its present sense, foreign to the ancient classical language, was first employed by the early Christians, who applied the term to single graves or tombs, and, later, to a whole graveyard.

Religious sentiment, the Christian concept of life, love and respect for the dead, belief in a future life—all are closely interrelated concepts testifying to a congenital yearning in every human being for true life, in which death is not and cannot be the end of all, but the beginning of a future life.

Although Romans attached little or no value to human life, they religiously and faithfully honored their dead. According to the Laws of the Twelve Tablets, violators of sepulchres or graves were meted grave punishment. In due time, Christian cemeteries were recognized by common law as sacred and religious places (*loca sacra et religiosa*). The first Christian cemeteries were burial places, now commonly known as *catacombs* or Christian *necropolis*. Following the peace of Constantine, it became common practice to bury the dead in church courtyards or annexes and beneath the church.

Since Christian cemeteries were regarded as religious places, they were always governed by ecclesiastical laws, for the Church, as a perfect and legitimate society, was granted the inherent right to legislate in cemetery matters.

In the eighteenth century the first movements toward a laicizing of cemeteries began. Ostensibly, these movements were based on sanitary considerations, but in reality they reflected the materialistic concept of life prevalent among civil legislators. As a result, cemeteries were withdrawn from exclusive ecclesiastical jurisdiction and placed under civil control.

The Church, with the legitimate right to possess her own cemeteries (Can. 1206, par. 1), prescribes that the bodies of the faithful must be buried in places or cemeteries (Can. 1205, par. 1), blessed according to the form prescribed in the *Roman Ritual* (tit. 8, ch. 29). Every parish has the right to have its own cemetery (Can. 1208, par. 1); the same right is extended to exempt religious (Can. 1208, par. 2); legal persons, and private families (Can. 1208, par. 3).

If cemeteries are entirely under civil jurisdiction, they are to be blessed if the persons usually buried there are for the greater part Catholic. If they are used for Catholics and non-Catholics, a section of the cemetery, properly blessed, should be reserved for Catholics. If the civil authorities refuse to grant such a request, the individual graves are to be blessed at each burial service (Can. 1206).

In parochial cemeteries the faithful may, with permission of the Ordinary, erect for themselves and their families private or special mausoleums (Can. 1209, par. 1). Wherever possible, a section of the cemetery should be set apart for clerics and priests, and another section for infants (Can. 1209, par. 2; 1209, par. 3).

Besides requiring that every cemetery be blessed, suitably enclosed on all sides, and carefully guarded (Can. 1210), the Church also prescribes that there be a separate non-blessed area, reserved for the interment of those who were denied ecclesiastical burial (Can. 1212). Such persons are: (a) all unbaptized individuals, except catechumens who through no fault of their own failed to receive baptism before dying; (b) notorious apostates, schismatics, Freemasons and other members of banned sects or societies; (c) all individuals under excommunication or interdict, following a condemnatory or declaratory sentence; (d) individuals guilty of deliberate suicide; (e) individuals who requested the cremation of their bodies; (f) other public and impenitent sinners, such as concubinarians, etc. (Can. 1239–1240).

A Christian cemetery is considered violated and, therefore, must be re-blessed before further burials, in the following circumstances: (a) a crime of homicide committed there; (b) serious and sinful shedding of human blood; (c) burial of an infidel or an individual under excommunication following a condemnatory or declaratory sentence (Cans. 1207 and 1172).

Canon 1211 prescribes that neither the cemeteries themselves nor the individual tombstones contain epitaphs, inscriptions, or ornaments contrary to Christian sentiment or piety. Hence, all pagan symbols, nude statues or paintings, exaggerated or materialistic inscriptions are forbidden.

Concerning the prescriptions of the civil law with regard to cemeteries, the reader must consult the legislative enactments of each individual country.

Common practice admits of two methods of burial: *inhumation* and *tumulation* (entombment). Inhumation is simply interment or burial of the dead in graves dug in the ground. Specific civil regulations govern such matters as to depth and width of the grave, distance from adjacent graves, material of inner and outer casket, problems of exhumation, etc. As a rule, the law requires that human bodies be buried in separate graves, except in the case of a mother and infant, whose deaths resulted from delivery.

In some countries the law requires the exhumation of interred bodies after a lapse of ten years, and the remains placed in a common ossuary.

The method of tumulation is burial in tombs erected above the ground, such as vaults, niches, mausoleums, etc. This form of burial is likewise regulated by specific dispositions of the civil law. Except for the State's right of eminent domain, tombs erected above the ground remain permanently undisturbed. *Tar.*

CENESTHESIA. *Cenesthesia* (Greek, *koinos*—common; *aithesis*—feeling) is a difficult term to define in a few words; it is the general bodily feeling, a more or less confused synthesis of various internal feelings or the sensations produced by the functioning of the body organs. If this functioning is normal, under the regulatory physiological influence of neurovegetative apparatuses and not disturbed by particular states of consciousness, the cenesthetic sense is perfect; it expresses itself in a vague sensation of well-being which barely reaches the fringes of conscious life. If, instead, organic functioning undergoes pathological modification, there arises a general feeling of ill-being or discomfort which may be the first symptom of an infirmity.

CENESTHOPATHIES. The study of cenesthesia is important in psychology, for it constitutes a basic element of the emotional or affective life; cenesthetic conditions are an important factor in many forms of mental disorders.

Of particular significance are the morbid alterations of cenesthesia (cenesthopathies), occurring in a vast group of individuals who are the so-called *constitutional cenesthopaths*. Morbid alterations of the cenesthetic sense, at times attended by moral deficiencies and schizoid tendencies, occur largely in neuropaths and psychopaths of various kinds, dysphorics, epileptics, and hysterics. In all such individuals, the cenesthopathia is based on a condition, perhaps congenital, of vegetative hyperexcitability, predominantly of the orthosympathetic system; hence, it is a permanent neurovegetative dysequilibrium with preponderant orthosympatheticotonia. The coexistence of an hyperthyroidal condition is probable.

Accurate and prolonged treatment by bland sedatives, antithyroid preparations, especially ergotamine tartrate and other sympathicolytic drugs, effectively combat these cenesthopathies and offer considerable aid in the neuropsychical readjustment of this large group of individuals living in constant suffering on the fringes of normality. *Riz.*

CENESTHOPATHIA. *See* Cenesthesia.

CENSORSHIP. In the broad sense of the term, ecclesiastical *censorship* may be described as a form of supervision and vigilance over existing media of communication (press, radio, television, stage, motion pictures, etc.) which is established, not for the purpose of exercising control in any of these areas, but merely to alert the faithful against possible trends of abuse. In this sense, the function of the Legion of Decency and the National Office for Decent Literature in the U. S. A. might be termed as a form of censorship.

Strictly speaking, however, the term refers to literary censorship or censorship of books. This may be practiced in two ways: (1) by examination of the manuscript before publication (previous or preventive censorship), (2) by banning a work already published (repressive censorship), as by the Index of Forbidden Books. This is the double meaning of the classical word *censura*. Ordinarily, however, *censorship* with qualification refers to previous or preventive censorship, which is the subject of the present article.

Censorship, then, may be defined as the examination and judgment of writings, prior to their publication, by an ecclesiastical tribunal, specifically appointed for the task. It is the law of the Church that writings intended for publication are to be submitted to the proper ecclesiastical authority for previous examination and approbation. This is a purely preventive measure against spreading doctrine detrimental to faith or morals. This judgment, exclusively *negative* in character, does not express approval of the content of a book, but merely indicates that no errors against faith or morals are contained therein and that the book may, therefore, be published and read by the faithful without danger of spiritual harm.

Also subject to ecclesiastical censorship are all reproductions of sacred images, with or without prayers. Ecclesiastical approval of such reproductions means that they may be safely used by the faithful as devotional objects.

The Church strongly believes that free expression of thought is a basic human right of every individual. At the same time, she realistically recognizes that unrestrained freedom of expression easily degenerates into license and abuse, with spiritual harm to the faithful. Hence, as a good, vigilant, and kind mother and a divinely appointed guardian of the deposit of faith and morals, the Church exercises preventive censorship of books, periodicals, and other published writings (Can. 1384). As a means of safeguarding public morals and social order, the right of censorship is rooted in the nature of the Church as a supreme and independent society. For the same reason, the State has such a right, which, in fact, it does exercise in certain circumstances, as in time of war or great national danger. Nor would anyone deny the State such preventive power in these circumstances, and few would contend that this is undue restriction of freedom.

As the divinely appointed guardian of the precious heritage of faith and morals, the Church exercises ecclesiastical censorship for the following: (a) books of Sacred Scripture, and all annotated editions and commentaries on Scripture (Can. 1385, par. 1, n. 1); (b) books dealing with Sacred Scripture, moral and dogmatic theology, Church history, Canon Law, natural theology, as well as all prayer books, books and pamphlets of a devotional, catechetical, moral, ascetical and mystical nature, and, in general, all writings in any way related to religion and morals (Can. 1385, par. 1, n. 2); (c) all reproductions of sacred images, with or without prayers (Can. 1385, par. 1, n. 3).

All Catholics are required to observe the law of preventive censorship (Can. 1384, par. 1). Permission to publish books and images listed above may be granted either by the author's local Ordinary or by the Ordinary of the place where the books or images are published. When approval is denied by any of these Ordinaries, the author is required to disclose the fact of refusal in seeking permission of another Ordinary (Can. 1385, par. 2). Authors who are members of a religious institute must obtain the permission of their own major superior before requesting approval of the local Ordinary (Can. 1385, par. 3).

The right of preventive censorship is vested in bishops, who exercise it through officially appointed examiners or censors. Church law directs that in every diocese there be official censors for the examination of works intended for publication (Can. 1393, par. 1). These examiners, to be selected from among secular and religious clergy, must be mature men, known for learning, prudence, and sound judgment (Can. 1393, par. 3). Authors are not to be informed beforehand of the name of the censor assigned to examine their work (Can. 1393, par. 5). In the exercise of their office, censors shall set aside all regard for persons, and consider only the dogmas of the Church and common Catholic doctrine, as contained in the decrees of ecumenical councils, the constitutions and prescriptions of the Holy See, and in the consensus of approved authorities (Can. 1393, par. 2). The preventive judgment expressed by the censor is only concerned with doctrinal orthodoxy; in no way does it indicate agreement with or approval of theories expounded in the work. Only after the decision of the censor, to be given in writing (Can. 1393, par. 4), does the local Ordinary usually, though not necessarily, grant the *Imprimatur* (permission to publish).

Authors and editors who publish, without due permission, books of Sacred Scripture or annotations and commentaries thereon, immediately (*ipso facto*) incur non-reserved excommunication (Can. 2318, par. 2). *Tar.*

CENSURE (Doctrinal or Theological). *See* Condemned Propositions.

CENSURE (Ecclesiastical penalty). A *censure* may be defined as an ecclesiastical penalty whereby a baptized person, who is delinquent and contumacious, is deprived of certain spiritual benefits, until he repents and obtains absolution (Can. 2241, par. 1). It is, therefore, a punishment inflicted for punitive purposes. Inherent in any penalty, this *spiritual* punishment, which produces spiritual effects, proceeds from a spiritual authority and is directed to spiritual ends. It is principally a *medicinal* punishment, for the chief purpose is the spiritual emendation of the delinquent. Finally, it presupposes obstinacy or *contumacy*, i.e., formal disobedience to constituted authority.

Censures may be inflicted only on baptized persons, even if they have defected from the faith. With the exception of an interdict, they may not be visited on legal persons nor on insufficiently specified persons. This does not mean, however, that the unknown author of a certain crime is not punishable with censure. On the contrary, censures *latae sententiae* are designed to punish guilty persons, though the crime be totally occult (Cans. 2242, par. 1; 2254).

In ancient Rome, the censor or officer in charge of military registration and conscription would make an entry against the name of individuals guilty of a misdeed that was not actionable at law. The annotation remained as a black mark against the individual's character and served to bar him from promotion to any office. In the first four centuries, the Church, within its own sphere, resorted exclusively to punitive penalties against offenders. Gradually, there began an increasing application of medicinal penalties or censures. During the Middle Ages there was such extensive application of ecclesiastical penalties that the Council of Trent directed all superiors to exercise moderation and discretion in this regard, lest they frustrate the efficacy of penalties or violate the Christian principle of mercy and charity.

Since the time of Innocent III (1214), three types of ecclesiastical censure existed: *excommunication* (Can. 2257, par. 1), *interdict* (Can. 2268, par. 1) and *suspension* (Can. 2278, par. 1). Excommunication and interdict are applicable both to ecclesiastical and lay persons known to be delinquent and contumacious, until they make amends. However, there is a difference between the two penalties: excommunication affects only individual persons, wherever they may be; interdict directly affects a place or territory and only indirectly the persons, physical or legal, living therein. But if the interdict is personal, it applies to the individual wherever he goes. Suspension is applicable only to ecclesiastical persons, physical or legal.

Certain censures are *reserved*, i.e., absolution can be validly given only by a superior authority (bishop or pope); others are *non-reserved*. Moreover, certain censures are predetermined and contained in the positive law itself; others are established by the superior inflicting the penalty. Finally, some censures are incurred immediately, at the moment the crime takes place, wherever the delinquent may be; other censures are incurred through the direct and immediate intervention of the legitimate superior.

Incurring or inflicting of a censure is predicated upon commission of a crime which is external, grave and consummated, i.e., complete in its constitutive elements and species. A necessary condition for a valid infliction of censure is contumacy on the part of the delinquent, that is, contempt or disregard of the threatened penalty or formal warning. Contumacy is considered removed only if the delinquent, with true repentance of his offense, makes due reparation for damages and scandal caused or earnestly promises to do so. Only then may absolution from censure be given.

CENSURES LATAE AND FERENDAE SENTENTIAE. Certain censures are incurred or inflicted automatically upon commission of the crime, without intervention by a superior or judge. These are *ipso facto* censures or censures *latae sententiae*. Since the matter is taken care of by the law itself, the superior either does not intervene at all or, if he does, he simply declares that the author of a particular offense has incurred a specific censure. Other censures, however, are inflicted by the superior or judge, either with judicial sentence or formal precept; these are known as censures *ferendae sententiae*. Against a judicial sentence or precept of a lower superior, a delinquent has the right of appeal to a higher authority.

These clearly point to the high sense of justice and mercy in the Church. By the same token the Church inflicts punishment on unknown delinquents or those guilty of occult crime, so that no offense may go unpunished. At the same time, she is greatly concerned with providing adequate protection and means of redress against possible errors by authority.

Accumulation of Censures. Generally speaking, there are as many penalties as there are offenses (Can. 2224); hence, not only censures of different species, but of the same species, may be multiplied in one and the same offender (Can. 2244, par. 1).

Removal of Censures. Once incurred, a censure cannot be removed except through legitimate absolution (Can. 2248), though the delinquent may have already repented and made amends for damages and scandal caused. The one exception to this general rule is the infliction of a censure under a resolutory condition; if this condition is verified, it carries with it implicit absolution. In a case of accumulation of censures, a person may be absolved from one or another of several censures, but the rest remain. Since a censure is a penalty binding in the external forum, it follows that removal of a censure must be effected through absolution in the external forum. The absolution thus imparted, however, holds good for the internal or sacramental forum as well. Absolution may also be given in the internal forum, but the following points are to be noted: (a) whenever the censure is absolutely occult, absolution in the sacramental forum is, in itself, valid for the external forum; (b) whenever the censure is publicly known, the sacramentally absolved, in order to avoid scandal, must be absolved in the external forum. The superior may demand external enforcement or observance of the censure, unless granting absolution in the internal forum is proven or legitimately presumed (Can. 2241). In some censures, if the absolved person fails to follow the orders of the confessor, he relapses into the same censure from which he was absolved. For the faculties of absolving from censures, *see* Reservation of Censures. In danger of death, all reservations of censures cease, and every priest is empowered to absolve from all censures without exception, but in the sacramental forum only. In the event of recovery, the external bond remains, with an obligation of submitting to the external authority of the Church. Even in urgent cases (imminent marriage, impending trip, etc.), the Church maternally authorizes, with certain stipulations, every confessor to absolve from those censures which are incurred without intervention of the superior (censures *latae sententiae*). In such instances, the confessor is obliged to give the penitent appropriate admonitions and a suitable penance, and impose a further obligation of recourse to the superior for the proper admonitions, corrections, and penance relative to the reservation. *Pug.*

CENSURE OF BOOKS. *See* Censorship, Forbidden Books.

CENTERS, DIENCEPHALIC. Below the hemispheres and in the center of the cerebral basis, there is a small but very important nerve center, called *diencephalon*. It seems that the main centers of man's instinctive-emotive life are located in it. Pende, in fact, called it a *bridge between soul and body.*

Feelings of hunger and thirst, emotional reactions of self-defense, sexual instinct, the rhythm of vigil and sleep, the vasomotorial faculty, various metabolisms, activities of the various internal secretion glands—all are believed to depend on the regular function of the diencephalon. The diencephalon also receives the sensations of pain, heat, cold, etc. The hypophysis (*q.v.*) is also found in it. Hence, the great importance of the diencephalon for the thymopsychical equilibrium of the individual, as confirmed by recent psychosurgical findings (*q.v.*).

Notwithstanding a truly imposing number of anatomical, physiological, and clinical investigations, the more important questions concerning cerebral activity and its relations to the activities of the spirit still remain unanswered.

We can only say that, at present, it cannot be proved that a functional differentiation in the cerebral cortex corresponds to its imposing structural differentiation; that cerebral localizations concern functions above all, or that they are less precise and definite, the more complex their functions; that the physiological development of the various cerebral functions calls for a constant, harmonious collaboration of the entire nervous system, or, still better, of the whole organism, with its complex contribution of stimuli, neuro-vegetative and harmonic correlations, etc.

Quite unsolved remains the central problem of cerebral functions concerning what makes the brain feel, react, think, want. Physiology cannot answer these questions. The study of physiology has contributed a better understanding of the physical bases of the activities of the spirit, the means which it uses, the manifestations and, to a great degree, the laws by which it is governed (*see* Psyche). But an understanding of the essence of such manifestations and its connection with the body, is still unknown; as a matter of fact, it is not even known whether the psychical activity is certainly connected with a particular nervous disposition or with special cerebral formations.

Despite painstaking and keen physiological research by modern neuro-surgical scientists, no exact correlation has been established between individual cerebral mutilations and individual psychical defects. As a matter of fact, neurosurgical reports are often so disconcerting as to cast doubts upon things which physiologists had believed certain before. Thus, for instance, it has been found that pre-frontal lobotomy usually modifies the thymopsyche much more than the intellective functions of patients operated on, although it had been considered as a fact that the seat of instincts and emotions was sub-cortical and diencephalic, and that the organs producing higher psychi-

cal functions were located in the prefrontal lobes.

It must, then, be acknowledged that, although cerebral functions offer useful elements by which human behavior may be at least partially explained, they fail, however, to reveal the essence of man's spiritual faculties.

In conclusion, with Lhermitte it can be stated that, although physiologists know well the material organization of the substratum of human psychological activity, they still remain perplexed before the problem concerning the relations btween spirit and matter. *Riz.*

CEREBRAL FUNCTIONS. In superior animals and in man, the nervous functions of *relation*, that is, those activities which put the organism in relation to environment, originate from special centers staggered along the *neuraxis*, i.e., that anatomical formation, composed chiefly of nervous cells and fibers. The neuraxis comprises the *encephalon* (contained in the skull and consisting of the anterior brain, the cerebellum, and the encephalic trunk) and the *spinal marrow* (contained in the vertebral column).

Each nervous unit, which constitutes the *nervous system*, with its wonderful network of centers, bands, and peripheral nerves, is produced by *neurons*. The neuron consists of a nervous cell which has at one pole its protoplasmatic prolongation or neurite. Each neuron represents both an *anatomical* unit with contigual connections to other neurons, and a *physiological* unit, with functional properties somewhat different from those of other neurons. The nervous current spreads from the cell of a neuron to its neurite. It is transmitted by a physicochemical process to the dentrites and from these to the cell of the next neuron and so on and with a reverse flow of transmission.

The various neurons are assembled in systems or groups of units with fundamentally identical functions. Systems of *afferent* or *centripetal neurons* bring the stimuli from the periphery to the centers; systems of *efferent* or *centrifugal neurons* carry the stimuli from the centers to the periphery; systems of *association* connect the various centers in which complex specific functions are elaborated.

Furthermore, a sort of hierarchy exists in the functional importance of the various systems of neurons and the various nervous centers. Functional autonomy tends to a gradual decline in passing from the lower or medullary to the higher centers of the cerebral cortex.

THE ANTERIOR BRAIN. The anterior brain (the brain properly so-called) or *telencephalic* is chiefly composed of two cerebral hemispheres which constitute its larger part. The cerebral hemispheres, in turn, are made up of a *gray substance,* (*cortex* or *cerebral mantle*) consisting of innumerable nervous cells of different structure and distribution according to the particular cortical portion or *area,* and of a *white substance* prevalently subcortical, consisting of bands of nervous fibres which link the various cortical centers and the cortex to the underlying portions of the nervous systems.

Numerous *breaks* furrow the cerebral cortex and create a certain number of elevations called *circuits* or *circumvolutions;* wider and deeper breaks set the limits of the four major *lobes* (frontal, parietal, temporal, occipital) of which each hemisphere is constituted.

Modern cerebral studies are chiefly based on the hypothesis of a *localization* of the cortical centers for the diverse elementary activities into which the complex global function of the brain may be divided.

The origin of this theory goes back to Franz Joseph Gall (1758–1828). This German scholar held that for each psychical function there corresponds a particular cerebral localization, that is, an elevation which can be found by the inspection of the surface of the skull. This elevation will be more noticeable the more developed is the corresponding psychical function. Thus, thirty-eight elevations, generally double and two-sided, were observed on the skull-cap. Ten of them represent the instincts (genetic, dominion, etc.); twelve, the moral faculties (religious sentiment, ambition, socia-

bleness, etc.); sixteen, the intellectual faculties (orientation, recollection of persons, mathematical talent, philosophical spirit, etc.). The organs of the intellectual faculties were grouped toward the forehead; those of the moral faculties toward the upper part of the head; and the instincts toward the temples and the occiput.

F. J. Gall must be credited with having clearly understood that the brain is the organ of the intellectual and affective faculties. This notion, which was hinted at by Alcmeon of Croton in the sixth century B. C., was still obscure and debated. Furthermore, Gall perceived that the superior psychical functions are related to the frontal lobes. He also was the forerunner of those morphological and anatomicopsychological inquiries which, later, were used as a basis for pathological and criminal anthropology. A great part of his empirical doctrine fell rapidly into dispute, chiefly because Flourens, on the basis of experiments on animals, established that any lesion on any part of the cerebral hemispheres caused a more or less serious weakening of all superior nervous activities.

Later (1870), Hitzig and Fritsch proved that this alleged functional unity of the crust was unproven. Since then, due to experiments conducted by a large group of scientists, the modern theory of cortical localizations as the basis of the entire cerebral physiopathology, has steadily gained ground.

It would be impossible to report here the work of these scholars and to sum up the results obtained by them. It may suffice to point out that patient and accurate work of research by means of electric stimulation and the study of limited destruction of nervous tissues established that there are in the cortex numerous identifiable areas, each endowed with peculiar histological characteristics and each, to a certain extent, the source of unique activities. As a matter of fact, *cerebral localization* does not mean functional independence of distinct centers destined to autonomous functions, but a localization in distinct areas of mechanisms (motorial, sensitive, sensorial, etc.) whose normal physiological activity must be integrated with that of other centers.

In any function which is not plainly elementary, the intervention of the cortical centers is always required; the more complex the function, the more numerous the centers which must concur in it. In higher psychomotorial and psychosensorial activities, almost the entire cortical system is involved. Nor are functional substitutions impossible. Certain functions can be re-activated after their disappearance, following the destruction of their respective centers. Thus, in general, each cerebral center has a prevalent importance only with regard to a specific function.

DISTRIBUTION OF CEREBRAL ACTIVITY. The cortical centers of motorial activity or voluntary motility are distributed along the rear portion of the frontal lobes, called the *motorial zone*. The impulses of the voluntary movements of the opposite half of the body originate in this zone. The upper part of the motorial zone is related to the lower limb and to the trunk, the middle part is related to the superior limb, the lowest part is related to the head, in such a way that the centers of the movements of the various muscular groups are in an upside-down position in relation to the position of the corresponding muscular groups. Furthermore, the extension of the various motorial centers is not in proportion to the size but to the functional importance of the respective organs. Thus, for instance, the center of the movements of the hand is by far wider than the one required for the movements of the shoulder or the trunk. We also know that motorial cortical centers do not control the movement of each individual muscle but the activity of muscular groups with a specific synergetic function (seizing, lifting, and the like).

The sensitive cortical centers, i.e., the center of general sensitivity, are distributed in a way similar to that of the motorial centers, but, generally, are found in a somewhat posterior zone, corresponding to the most forward portion of the parietal lobes. A little further back (exactly in the inferior parietal circumvolution), there seems to be a center to which the sensibility of the higher psychological functions is related. In fact, particular disturbances have been observed in the lesions of this circumvolution (*agnosia* and *tactile asymbolia*) which cause the individual to be incapable of identifying objects by touch. To the lesions of this circumvolution are also attributed by many authors the psychological alterations of the *bodily* outline, that is, the immediate consciousness of the unity of the human body and the special tridimensional image man has of himself.

These alterations consist in a false perception of missing parts of the body (the so-called *phantom-limb* of many amputees) or in the loss of awareness concerning parts of one's body, as it happens in the case of some particular hallucinatory forms regarding one's own person.

The cortical centers of the visual function are located in the internal part of the occipital lobes. Those of hearing, smell, and taste are found in different places of the temporal lobes.

The centers related to the associative faculties, called also associative areas, are located in the so-called pre-frontal lobe, or anterior portion of the frontal lobe. The destruction of these centers (caused in man by therapeutico-surgical action) gives rise to more or less serious psychical disturbances with affective hypotension, manifestation of instincts, childish behaviour, decrease of reproductive memory, absentmindedness, disinterestedness, loss of initiative, impossibility of seeing a situation or a problem in its entirety or of foreseeing its developments, defectiveness of the volitive impulse, and other phenomena attesting to the existence, in that cortical region, of centers related, not to a single elementary function, but to superior integrating processes and to other processes of synthesis and control.

It is interesting to note that psychical disturbances arising after operations on pre-frontal lobes and consisting of modifications of one's personality, accompany neurological deficiencies characterized by an impeded motorial activity lacking the refinement and ability acquired previously by the individual. The picture may vary considerably not only on the basis of the extent and the unilaterality or bilaterality of the demolition, but also on the basis of individual factors still unknown.

It must be observed, however, that alterations of personality, always to be feared after a surgical removal of a prefrontal lobe invaded by a tumor, must not stop the surgeon's beneficent action, for, as clinical experience proves, the effects of those alterations will always be of a smaller entity than the disturbances caused by the tumor itself. The symptoms caused by the surgical intervention are (according to the neurologist Jackson) mere negative symptoms which are likely to benefit from *functional substitutions* more than from the *positive symptoms* caused by a tumor which are always quantitatively and qualitatively more serious than the *negative symptoms*.

CEREBROPATHIES (Brain Diseases).

Cerebropathies or *encephalopathies*, a related but more extensive term, are diseases of the brain, especially of the cerebral hemispheres: malformations, degenerations, vascular or traumatic lesions, etc. Depending on the age in which they occur, these diseases are distinguished into *infantile* and *adult* cerebropathies. This distinction transcends a mere chronological factor and reaches into the symptomatology and pathogenic process of various types of disease, for cerebropathies in adults are usually restricted to a particular cerebral area affected by the morbid process, and the resultant syndrome itself corresponds to the functional disturbance produced by that localized lesion. In children, instead, the injury caused by the pathological processes exercises a damaging influence on further development of the other cerebral regions; hence, a brain disease in a child is more extensive and grave than in an adult.

Today deeper diagnostic research on brain diseases is conducted by the use of artificial tests, such as encephalography, ventriculolography, arteriography, etc., and by electroencephalography. These modern methods of study are of immense practical value, for purely clinical research is merely a preliminary orientation.

Cerebropathies of Adults. Usually, the various diseases of the nervous system are differentiated, not according to the nature (traumatic, vascular, etc.), but according to the location of the injury that caused them. In other words, various nervous diseases are usually and principally characterized by the particular cerebral region destroyed or altered by the morbid process.

According to the nature of the cerebropathies in adults, they are: *vascular*, largely hemorrhagic, thrombotic or embolic; *traumatic, inflammatory*, forms of encephalitis, caused mostly by, or originating from, filtrable viruses and cerebral abscesses; *syphilitic, degenerative, atrophic*, due to precocious senescence; *tumoral.*

According to their location, the cerebropathies of adults may be characterized exclusively or prevalently as: (a) paralytic manifestations, in lesions affecting the motor centers or the initial points of the motor paths; (b) anesthetic manifestations, in injuries affecting the centers or paths of general sensibility; (c) sensorial centers or paths; (d) aphasiac or apraxic manifestations, in injury to the speech centers or ideomotor centers; (e) extrapyramidal manifestations (chorea, atethosis, spasms, syndromes of a Parkinson character, etc.), brought about by injuries to the various areas of the extrapyramidal system, etc.

Brain diseases in adults are highly complex, because they involve two or more neuronic *systems*. Thus, *hemiplegia* or paralysis of one side of the body is associated with *hemianesthesia* in hemorrhages of the particular cerebral portion called the *internal capsule*, through which motor fibers and sensory fibers run.

Infantile Cerebropathies. Infantile cerebropathies comprise forms highly differentiated by the nature, anatomico-pathological substratum, and clinical expression, but with this in common: they show up in early infancy and usually leave permanent and grave effects, for, striking a still undeveloped organ, they exercise a damaging influence on all further cerebral development.

The causes of infantile cerebropathy may be divided: (a) according to their origin, into *exogenous* and *endogenous*; (b) according to age incidence, into *prenatal, natal* and *postnatal*; (c) according to species, into *infective, toxic, traumatic*, etc. Among the most frequent and grave causes are hereditary syphilis and neurotropic viruses.

From the anatomico-pathological standpoint, brain diseases of children are divided into: malformations (anecephaly, meningocele, mircocephaly, etc.), encephalitis and meningo-encephalitis, cerebral hemorrhages, hydrocephalus, etc.

Clinically, the syndromes occurring with greatest frequency are: hemiplegia (due to encephalitic or hemorrhagic processes); Little's congenital rigidity of limbs (a tetraplegia or paraplegia due, it seems, to hypoplasia of the motor paths); certain extrapyramidal forms, convulsive seizures of an epileptic type and, especially, more or less serious lack of mental development or phrenasthenia.

These various syndromes rarely occur in an isolated manner. They usually present complex clinical forms with a predominance of one or the other of the above-mentioned symptoms, depending on the localization of the morbid process, and with an almost constant concurrence of psychiatric disturbances.

MORAL CONSIDERATIONS. A brain disease in any individual often may occasion grave juridical and moral problems concerning the moral and criminal responsibility, as well as the civil competency in last wills, testaments, marriage contracts, etc. Obviously, it is not possible that a general solution can be offered here, for final assessment depends upon accurate psychical examination of each individual. As a general rule, though, the graver is the nervous disturbance (extensive paralysis, frequent convulsive seizures, etc.), the stronger the suspicion that the psychical sphere has been affected by a cerebral lesion. This is especially so in cases of infantile cerebropathies, as indicated.

Infantile cerebropathies, especially if congenital or prenatal, are frequently the result of hereditary syphilis and indicate a lack of moral judgment and charity on the part of at least one of the parents for entering marriage under such a condition, without previous medical examination or treatments.

The pathetic plight of cerebropathic individuals should serve as a strong warning to young people contemplating marriage and desiring to have healthy offspring, and a constant reminder to abstain from all pre-marital sexual and dangerous contacts to protect the physical well-being of the other party as well as of their children. *Riz.*

CEREMONIES. Ceremonies are the external, material actions accompanying a liturgical service. These embody movements, gestures, and attitudes for the various moments of the liturgical function. The principal postures and gestures employed in the liturgy are: standing, kneeling, sitting, praying with hands joined or extended; raising the hand to bless or absolve; elevation of the Sacred Host; imposition of hands; genuflections, inclinations or bows; prostrations, incensations, striking the breast, washing the hands, presenting and receiving liturgical objects, or a liturgical kiss, etc. Some are merely of a practical nature; others interpret the words of the liturgical action; others still are strictly symbolical.

In the administration of the sacraments certain ceremonies acquire a particular or, sometimes, essential value. For example, the imposition of hands in confirmation and holy orders. At other times, ceremonies express a symbolism which cannot be omitted without detracting from the beauty of the rite, such as praying with extended hands during Holy Mass. Certain ceremonies with an historical significance possess the same normative value as rules of etiquette, except that they apply to sacred actions in the house of God.

It is forbidden during the celebration of the Mass to add ceremonies or prayers of private choice (Can. 818). Deliberately to add a genuflection or blessing is *per se* a slight sin, although it could become grave if done in functions of notable importance, to introduce a new rite, or with disedification of the faithful. *Cig.*

CERTIFICATE. A *certificate* is a written statement or document issued by a competent and trustworthy person, attesting to the truth of a fact or condition, such as a complete course of studies, freedom from disease, value of a precious object, etc.

To issue a false or falsified document can have important social implications; hence, anyone issuing a false document, either by stating a falsehood or by omitting data required by law or custom, commits a sin. It is also a sin if one releases a certificate without certainty of the facts attested to or without a preliminary investigation, inquest, medical examination, etc., required by law or contract or by the very nature of the matter itself.

To issue a false or falsified document is, in itself, a serious sin, since grave injustice is inflicted on all those who will thereby be deceived or exposed to the danger of deception and damages. If deception and damages suffered are inconsequential, the sin is only venial. This is rarely the case, since, as a rule, certificates are requested and issued for important reasons.

The obligation to professional secrecy does not forbid the release of a true, complete certificate to persons legitimately requesting it. Moreover, it is to be noted that no illicit or dishonest means may be employed for keeping a secret. *Ben.*

CERTIFICATE, MEDICAL. *See* Deontology, Medical; Medicine.

CERTIFICATE, PRENUPTIAL. *See* Marriage; Examination, Prenuptial.

CERTITUDE, CERTAINTY. Considered in a superficial manner, truth, evidence, and certainty seem to be synonymous terms, but, upon close analysis, each will be found to possess a different connotation.

The human mind may be compared to a camera photographing the world of reality. When this mental photography or representation agrees with reality, one has truth (*q.v.*), a conformity between reality and mental representation, since we are concerned with logical truth. Hence, before one may speak of possessing the truth, the intellect must reproduce things as they are in themselves. *Evidence* is the splendor, light, or clarity with which truth is presented or manifested to the mind, causing it to become convinced and to give its assent. In the presence of reality or truth, the intellect may find itself in one of these three states: (a) *uncertainty* whether to embrace the truth or not (*doubt*); (b) *partial conviction:* the intellect lends its assent, but with fear of error (*opinion*); (c) *firm convinction:* the intellect gives adherence without fear of erring (*certitude*). The last state, certitude, results from the evidence or clarity with which truth appears to the mind.

Certitude, then, presupposes two elements or conditions: *truth* and *evidence.* Without truth, there can be no adherence of the mind; without evidence, assent is possible, but fear of error always remains. Adherence to falsity, without a conscious or subjective fear of erring, does not exclude an objective fear, which is called *error* (*q.v.*). In such a case, good faith may be safeguarded, but not truth. The fact that one adheres to falsity in all sincerity does not remove objective error. Thus, a bomb, which one honestly and firmly judged to be a ball, would not eliminate the error and danger which are objectively present.

KINDS OF CERTITUDE. Truth begins in *ideas*, but formally exists only in the *judgment*. An idea, of itself, cannot be said to be either true or false, until, by a process of comparison with objective reality, a judgment of that conformity of the idea to reality is affirmed or denied. Certitude consists precisely in this: the mind clearly perceives and recognizes a conformity or correspondence between the judgment and reality, which it embraces without fear of erring. Certitude may be *metaphysical, physical,* or *moral.* *Metaphysical certitude,* based on the essence of things, involves an intrinsic necessity, so that any exception is absolutely impossible or absurd. For example, the radii of a circle are all equal; the sum of all the angles of a triangle is equal to two right angles. *Physical certitude* is based on the constancy of physical laws, any exception to which is impossible in the ordinary course of nature; in itself it is not absurd or contradictory that the Creator and Author of nature could suspend the effects of these laws by a miracle. For example, an unsupported beam will fall, unless a miracle occurs.

Moral certitude is based on a firm and rational persuasion resulting from the testimony of mankind about the existence of some contingent fact, or on laws which govern human conduct; these laws can be violated by the will of an individual, but are generally presumed to be observed. For example, we are certain that parents love their children.

Skepticism. The opposite of certitude is skepticism, which may be *absolute* or *relative.* Absolute skepticism, whose founder is Pyrrho, maintains that truth is unattainable by the human mind and that, therefore, everything is to be doubted. Relative skepticism is followed by those who reject the validity of one or another of the criteria of truth. Traditionalists contend that unaided human reason is incapable of attaining religious and moral truths and, hence, posit revelation as the ultimate criterion of truth. Positivists reduce all certitude to the verdict of the senses. All forms of skepticism find their ultimate contradiction, if from theory they pass into practice. In practice, skeptics doubt only what they choose to. The trouble with skeptics is not doubt but apathy, indifference, and hatred.

Certainty and Moral Theology. In the field of moral theology certitude is a factor of fundamental importance. Since conscience, as the proximate norm of morality, is simply the application of law to a particular case, it requires certainty as a condition for acting. To act with doubt, in which one is uncertain whether an action is good or bad, would be to declare oneself indifferent to good or evil. Cicero, prompted by common sense, illustrates this same point: *"Bene praecipiunt qui vetant quidquam agere quod dubites aequum sit an iniquum. Aequitas enim lucet ipsa per se, dubitatio cogitationem significat injuriae"* (De officiis, 1. I, ch. 9). Naturally, moral certitude is sufficient in the sphere of conscience; once such certitude is attained, there is an obligation to act in accordance. To act rightly, one must follow a *certain* conscience. Though the conscience may be *invincibly* erroneous, it is to be followed as long as it remains subjectively certain, for we are responsible for our actions only as we understand and will them. True, the action in such a case will be materially evil, but not formally, for it is willed in good faith and performed as good. If, however, error is vincible, one would be responsible *in cause* for an action performed in a state of culpable negligence concerning the knowledge of the truth and, therefore, the licit and illicit. Subjective certitude is sufficient in moral theology.

Certainty and Conscience. An uncertain or doubtful conscience may not be followed. Before acting, one is obliged to resolve his doubt in some manner: by studying the question more deeply, by seeking counsel, or by consulting moral systems (*see* Systems, Moral). These systems are to be used only in matters in which licitness or illicitness is involved. It would be erroneous to employ them in questions of validity or invalidity or in cases dealing with injustice to third persons. This rule must always be kept in mind to avoid misunderstandings and gross errors, from which writers of repute have not been immune. *Ver.*

CESSATION OF LAW. Cessation of a law exists when a law ceases, becomes extinct, or is abolished or loses its binding force for the entire community. The actual cessation of a law may occur through abrogation by the legislator, through an action of the community itself, through a cause intrinsic to the law itself.

Cessation of a law may be brought about by the community, either negatively, through non-observance of the law by allowing the law to fall into disuse, or positively, by introduction of a contrary custom. Non-use and custom exercise no force in respect to a divine law, whether natural or positive; they have force in the sphere of human laws alone; even in this case their effectiveness depends on the norms of each individual legislation.

Canon Law expressly recognizes that custom or non-use have the power to abolish or bring about cessation of an ecclesiastical law, with one exception: if the law itself by its wording forbids the introduction of a contrary custom.

A law is said to cease by extrinsic cause, if, due to changed circumstances, it loses its purpose or reason for existence. This is usually expressed by saying that the matter of the law has changed or that the intrinsic reason for the law no longer avails. This happens whenever the content of a law becomes universally unjust, immoral, physically or morally impossible, or simply useless.

It is not quite clear whether a law ceases by total and universal cessation of its extrinsic purpose, which the legislator may have intended, but did not indicate in the content of the law. It may be conceded that even in such a case the law ceases, if its content is, in itself, wholly indifferent and merely prescribed as a means of attaining an end assigned by the legislator. If this purpose no longer avails, the reason for observing the content of the law ceases, and thus the law itself ceases. If, however, the matter of the law contains an objective element of reasonableness, utility, or goodness, apparently one must hold that, even though the extrinsic and accidental end of the law no longer obtains, the law itself continues to exist in virtue of its intrinsic value or end, which certainly must have been a determining cause in the mind of the legislator. As long as this cause continues to exist, the law itself continues to bind. *Gra.*

CHALICE. The *chalice* is one of the most sacred of liturgical vessels, for it comes in direct contact with the blood of Christ in the sacrifice of the Mass. Its form has been more or less the same since medieval times. Originally the chalice may have had the form of an ordinary glass (Latin—*calix*). Today a chalice must be made of metal and the inside of the cup, at least, must be gold-plated. In the early days of the Church, chalices were made of glass, precious stone, agate, and even wood. In the early Middle Ages, chalices, in the form of a cup, had side handles (*ansae*).

No chalice may be used for liturgical purposes unless previously consecrated by one of the following: bishop, cardinal, prefect apostolic, abbot or prelate *nullius* (Cans. 1147; 239, par. 1, n. 20; 249, par. 2; 323, par. 2). Clerics are alone permitted to touch and handle consecrated chalices but, by special permission, Sisters and sacristans may do so if officially appointed to take charge of the vestments and sacred vessels. A chalice loses such consecration: (a) if it undergoes such damage or alterations that it loses its original form and is no longer fit for its purpose; (b) if used for unbecoming purposes or displayed for public sale. A chalice, however, does not lose its consecration by long use or re-plating; in fact, a priest has a grave obligation to have it replated if the gilding has worn out (Can. 1305, par. 1–2).

Rubrics prescribe that the chalice be covered with a veil (a piece of silk fabric of the same color and quality as the vestments) from the beginning of the Mass until the Offertory, and after Communion until the end of the Mass. During the other parts of the Mass the chalice is covered with the *pall*, which is a small stiff, generally square, white cloth. During the celebration of the Mass, the chalice and the host must be placed on the corporal (a square piece of fine linen or hemp spread out over the altar stone). Before pouring wine at the Offertory and after the consumption of the Sacred

Species, the chalice is cleansed with a small white cloth called *purificator.* Used purificators are usually washed first by a priest or deacon.

These norms are obligatory in themselves. *Cig.*

CHAMBER, APOSTOLIC. From the middle of the twelfth century, the administration of all property and revenue of the Holy See and Pontifical State was entrusted to the so-called *camera thesauraria* (papal treasury department), which was presided over by the *camerlengo* or chamberlain (*camerarius*).

At the time of the reorganization of the Roman Curia by Pope St. Pius X, in 1908, the Apostolic Chamber was retained, together with three other officers, properly so-called, but its character was greatly modified and its function restricted almost exclusively to the administration and care of the temporal goods and rights of the Holy See during a vacancy of the pontificate (*sede vacante*). This remains the present disposition (Can. 262). The Apostolic Constitution *Vacantis Apostolicae Sedis* (Dec. 8, 1945) defines the duties of the Cardinal Camerlengo during the vacancy of the Holy See.

Besides the Cardinal Camerlengo of the Holy Roman Church, who is in charge of the Apostolic Chamber, there are three other officials: the Vice-Chamberlain of the Holy Roman Church, the Treasurer General and the Auditor General of the Reverend Apostolic Chamber. In matters of precedence, the Vice Camerlengo follows immediately after archbishops and bishops assistant to the throne; the Auditor General and the Treasurer General come immediately after the Prince Assistant to the throne and precede all other archbishops and bishops who are not assistants to the throne. The three Chamber officials or prelates are assisted by other prelates, who constitute the College of Chamber Clerics (eight in number, according to the present ruling; cf. Constitution *Ad incrementum,* Aug. 15, 1934), and by Chamber notaries (*notarii*). *Cip.*

CHANCERY, APOSTOLIC. One of four offices, properly speaking, of the Roman Curia, the Apostolic Chancery is charged with the preparation and delivery of papal bulls concerning major benefices, the establishment of new dioceses, or affairs of major importance. These bulls are issued by order of the Sacred Consistorial Congregation, the Congregation for the Eastern Church, the Congregation for the Propagation of the Faith, or the Supreme Pontiff. *Cip.*

CHANT, SACRED. *Sacred chant* is the official music of liturgical functions. It has been employed by all religions, including Christianity, as an element inseparable from collective religious manifestations.

Chant was first used in the *psalmody,* which from the beginning was added to the Mass, the first and, for some time, the only liturgical function of the Church (*see* Breviary, Liturgical Books, Psalter). In the East, particularly Antioch and Constantinople, sacred chant attained a high degree of development. St. Ambrose, bishop of Milan, introduced it in the West (*canendi mos orientalium partium*). Its effective influence on the faithful is attested to by St. Augustine in a memorable page of his *Confessions* (bk. IX, ch. 7): "How many tears did I shed, as my heart was deeply moved by the melody of the hymns and canticles resounding in Thy Church!" The hymns are of the metrical compositions belonging to the period immediately following the first Christian era. In the East the hymns of St. Ephrem are famous, in the West those of St. Ambrose. In the beginning, psalmody was performed by a solo lector, with the congregation responding either at the end or intermittently (*responsorial psalmody*); this later developed into *antiphonal psalmody,* consisting of alternate chanting by two choirs. This custom of psalmodizing with two choirs was eventually introduced in Rome, where it attained its perfection.

GREGORIAN CHANT. For nearly a thousand years unison chant was prevalent in the churches. Later it was called

Gregorian chant from St. Gregory the Great (590–604), who reformed and codified it. With the modification of the liturgy of the Mass, which until his time was always solemn, Gregory found it necessary to reform the accompanying chant; for this purpose he instituted a *Schola Cantorum*.

Gregorian chant was transmitted by oral tradition, especially in monasteries, where it was principally cultivated, until Guido of Arezzo, a monk of Pomposa, invented musical notations in the eleventh century.

With the introduction of psalmody in the liturgy of the Mass, it was only natural that Gregorian chant should become a part of it. The ordinary parts of the Mass (*Kyrie, Gloria, Credo, Sanctus, Benedictus, Agnus Dei*) were sung by the congregation, and the changeable parts (*Introit, Gradual, Offertory, Communion*) were sung by the *Schola Cantorum*. Solo chants consisted of the *Preface* by the celebrant, the Gospel by the deacon, and the Epistle by the subdeacon.

ORGAN. The instrument considered by the Church as the most suitable for the accompaniment of chant was the organ. Already in use in the eighth century, the organ was perfected in the fourteenth and especially in the fifteenth century, when it became a solo instrument in its own right. Organ composition attained its highest point during the seventeenth and eighteen centuries: in Italy, with Frescobaldi; in Germany, with Johann Sebastian Bach; in England, with George Frederick Handel. Such development proved partly detrimental to the liturgy, which requires the organ as an accompanying instrument. The purpose of chant and music in church is not to distract, but to elevate the spirit. The introduction of other instruments proved even more detrimental.

In the ninth century attempts were made at writing musical compositions in several parts. Scotus Erigene (d. 880) speaks of two part melodies. This art was developed by the Flemish School of the fifteenth and sixteenth centuries; its greatest composer was Orlando of Lasso.

But such an artistic achievement did not enhance the decorum of religious functions, since many of the themes were borrowed from secular songs, and the singers tended toward virtuosity and dilettantism.

The Council of Trent included in its reform program sacred chant; it decreed that the bishops "ban from churches all musical compositions, whether for organ or voice, in which there is any admixture of the secular or vulgar, so that the House of God may truly appear and be called a house of worship" (*Sess.* XXII, *Decretum de observandis et evitandis in celebratione Missae*). It further commissioned Cardinals Vitellozzi and Borromeo (the future St. Charles) to reform the Pontifical *Sistine Choir*. The commission conferred the title of Composer of the Pontifical Choir and Director of St. Peter's Choir on Pier Luigi da Palestrina, who was choirmaster at St. Mary Major's Basilica and a friend of St. Philip Neri. Palestrina remained the unsurpassed master of sacred music and a source of inspiration to subsequent masters of classic polyphonic music, Tommaso Lodovico da Vittoria, Felice Anerio, Lodovico da Viadana, Francesco Suriano, Gregorio Allegri, Andrea Gabriele, etc.

The eighteenth and nineteenth centuries saw decline from this glorious tradition. Composers of sacred music became at the same time composers of new theatrical compositions introduced by melodrama; thus they brought theatrical music into the church.

Not even the great masters could escape the influence of the new musical style, though they managed to remain on a higher plane. Thus, Pergolesi's *Stabat Mater*, Mozart's *Requiem*, Beethoven's *Missa Solemnis*, Rossini's *Stabat Mater*, Verdi's *Requiem* are examples, not of ecclesiastical, but of lyrical and dramatic music. Not even Rome escaped such trends, as in Gaetano Capocci's *Vespers*.

PLAIN CHANT REFORM. During the nineteenth century, both in Germany (Munich and Ratisbon) and in Italy, a movement for restoration of ecclesiastical music to its ancient spirit and glory began. In Germany, the key figures of this reform movement were Gaspar Ett, Earl Proske, and Franz Witt; in Italy, Rev. Ambrogio Amelli, Rev. Angelo De Santi and, above all, Don Lorenzo Perosi, who became its foremost leader. When St. Pius X became pope, the Church assumed direction and control of the reform movement through a motu proprio of Nov. 22, 1903, *Inter pastoralis Officii*. This document dealt not only with sacred music, but with Gregorian chant, now restored to a primary position in liturgical functions.

Pioneers of Gregorian chant reform in France were the Benedictine monks of the abbey of Solesmes, who, by diligent study of the *codices*, were able to restore Gregorian melodies to their primitive purity.

The first *motu proprio* of St. Pius X was followed by a letter, *Quod nobis*, of Dec. 8, 1903, and by a second *motu proprio*, *Nostro motu proprio*, of April 25, 1904. These were followed by instructions and decrees of the Sacred Congregation of Rites, on Nov. 27, 1908, and March 24, 1909. In 1911, by a rescript of the Secretariate of State, July 10, 1914, the Superior School of Sacred Music was established and authorized to confer degrees. This school has been known as the *Pontifical Institute of Sacred Music* since May 24, 1931 (Apost. Constitution *Deus Scientiarum Dominus*).

The fundamental provisions of the reform were condensed in the Code of Canon Law: "Musical compositions, whether instrumental, for organ or other instruments, or vocal, in which there is any admixture of the secular or impure, must be absolutely barred from churches; and the liturgical laws regarding sacred music must be observed" (Can. 1264, par. 1).

"Religious women, when allowed by their constitutions or liturgical laws or by the local Ordinary to sing in their own church or public oratory, shall do so from a place where they cannot be seen by the people" (Can. 1264, par. 2).

Meanwhile, the paleographic study of Gregorian chant codices led to official editions of the entire liturgical repertory, which became mandatory from their date of publication: *Graduale* and *Kyriale* (1907); *Antiphonarium* (1919); *Officium defunctorum* (1927); *Officium Nativitatis Domini* (1927); *Officium Maioris Hebdomadae* (1929).

The documents of St. Pius X on sacred music were further elaborated by the apostolic constitution *Divini Cultus Sanctitatem* of Pius XI (Dec. 20, 1928); the encyclical *Mediator Dei* of Pius XII (1947); the various decrees of the Sacred Congregation of Rites, including the one which permits, with the consent of the Ordinary, the use of electronic and automatic organs (Decr. July 15, 1949; Feb. 27, 1948); finally, by the encyclical *Musicae Sacrae*, of Dec. 25, 1955, (AAS: 48 (1956), 5–25). Besides recalling the norms outlined by St. Pius X, this last encyclical encourages, along with Gregorian chant, the increased use of polyphonic chant in sacred functions and permits the playing of fine and delicate string instruments.

Popular religious singing of religious hymns by the faithful in the vernacular originated in Germany, where it existed before Luther; the latter, however, was largely responsible for its very extensive use in the Reformation liturgy.

A decree of the Sacred Congregation of Rites, January 31, 1896, permits the singing of hymns in the vernacular during low Mass and at non-liturgical services. Such singing, however, is not allowed during high or solemn Mass, at sung Vespers or *during* Benediction of the Blessed Sacrament. In his last encyclical on sacred music, Pius XII encouraged the singing of popular religious hymns as an aid rather than an obstacle to prayer. *Pal.*

CHAPEL. See Chaplain, Chaplaincy, Church, Oratory.

CHAPLAIN. A *chaplain* is one who has charge of a chapel. According to Du Cange (*Glossarium mediae et infimae latinitatis*), the term *cappellanus* comes from *cappa* or *cappella*, which was a short cloak worn by St. Martin of Tours.

This short cloak was preserved as a relic by the French kings, who carried it with them to war and enshrined it under a tent on the field. Those assigned to safeguard this relic were called *cappellani* or *custodes*. Later on, the term was also applied to clerics officiating in royal palaces in other court duties. In due course of time, other types of chaplains came into being: chaplains of the papal household, episcopal chaplains, and those assigned, not to a chapel, but to a community, as chaplains of religious institutes, pious associations, schools, hospitals, etc.

According to present-day canonical law and doctrine, there are four main categories of chaplains:

(a) *Chaplain of a religious institute.* A priest more or less permanently assigned to conduct ecclesiastical functions in a religious community of women or of brothers. For non-exempt religious institutes of men or women, the local Ordinary has the right to appoint the chaplain. For exempt religious institutes, such a right belongs to the religious superior or, in default of the latter, to the local Ordinary (Can. 529). As a rule, it is the right and duty of the chaplain to celebrate Mass, to administer the Holy Eucharist, to conduct other customary religious services and, frequently, to preach. Preaching, which may be assigned to a priest other than the chaplain, requires permission of the local Ordinary (Can. 1337). *Per se* the chaplain has no right to conduct services reserved to the pastor of the territory (Can. 462). However, for exempt religious communities or if the Ordinary has withdrawn the community from the care of a pastor (Can. 464, par. 2), the chaplain is usually authorized to exercise pastoral functions, provided that they are compatible with the norms concerning religious, e.g., administration of the last rites (Can. 514, par. 3) and the conduct of funeral services (Can. 1230, par. 5), and provided also that they are not functions reserved to another, such as the administration of the last rites to cloistered nuns, which is reserved to their ordinary confessor (Can. 514, par. 2).

(b) *Chaplain of ecclesiastical associations.* Unless an apostolic privilege expressly provides otherwise, the appointment of such chaplains pertains to the local Ordinary. For associations erected by religious in their own churches, the right of appointing chaplains belongs to the religious superior; the consent of the Ordinary is required, if the chaplain is chosen by the superior from among the secular clergy (Can. 698, par. 1). For a just reason chaplains may be removed by those who appointed them, or by their successors or higher superiors (Can. 698, par. 3). There are no general norms relative to the rights and duties of such chaplains; they are governed by the particular regulations of the individual associations. However, according to common law, one and the same priest may act as chaplain and moderator of an association (Can. 698, par. 4). Moderators and chaplains can, during their term of office, bless the habit, insignia, scapulars, etc., of the association, and invest new members therewith (Can. 698, par. 2). If the association has its own chapel or oratory, ordinarily the chaplain may conduct services therein, with rights and duties similar to those of a chaplain of a religious institute. If the association has its own church, the chaplain ordinarily acts as rector of the church, with respective rights and duties (Can. 479 ff.).

What was said of chaplains of associations will, in general, apply to chaplains appointed to serve institutions, whether ecclesiastical or not (e.g., schools, hospitals, prisons, etc.). Concerning functions reserved to the pastor, the same norms apply as those for chaplains of religious institutes.

(c) *Military Chaplain.* The juridical character of military chaplains differs somewhat from that of the other two categories. According to the Code of Canon Law, military chaplains, who are distinguished into *major* and *minor*, are governed by special regulations of the Holy See (Can. 451, par. 3). These dispositions, with the exception of particular prescriptions for different countries, are contained in the Instruction of the

Sacred Consistorial Congregation of April 23, 1951 (AAS: 43 [1951], 562–565). Frequently, military chaplains are placed under the jurisdiction of a military Ordinary endowed with quasi-episcopal powers. In such a case, chaplains are considered personal pastors appointed to minister to the spiritual needs of those in the military service and others allied with the military service, as members of their families, military police personnel, etc.

The jurisdiction of a military Ordinary and military chaplains is not exclusive; hence, quarters and other military establishments are not withdrawn from the jurisdiction of the local Ordinary or the pastors of the territories, although the jurisdiction of these latter over subjects of the military Ordinariate is exercised only in a secondary way. For judiciary jurisdiction, the military Ordinary shall select one of the tribunals of the territory, subject to approval by the Holy See.

In some countries, military chaplains are dependent on a military Vicar (*major chaplain*), who obtains his faculties from the Holy See with the power of subdelegating them to the chaplains. In other countries, military chaplains are appointed by the local Ordinary, who retains exclusive jurisdiction over them. In such instances, chaplains cannot be considered personal pastors, though they possess the juridical character and title of military chaplains. Finally, pastors also may be assigned for ordinary spiritual assistance to military personnel in their area.

By a special decree of the Sacred Consistorial Congregation, issued in 1957, a Military Vicariate was established in the United States of America, with its own curia in New York City, and with the incumbent Archbishop of New York as its military vicar. By virtue of special decree, the Archbishop of New York is charged with double jurisdiction: his own archdiocese and secular and religious priests who serve as regular military chaplains or who render their services on a temporary basis as chaplains of Veter-

ans Administration hospitals and other functions.

The military chaplains, whether minor or major, are appointed by and remain subject in every way to the military vicar; they exercise the care of souls entrusted to them, with the duties and obligations of *pastors*, in accordance with the Instruction on Military Vicars mentioned above.

(d) *Chaplain of a so-called foundation.* This chaplain becomes the titular of a foundation (*q.v.*). He differs from other chaplains in that the latter are assigned to a specific group of the faithful, while the former is assigned to a particular place with no particular reference to the people but simply to fulfill certain obligations stipulated in the charter of foundation. *Led.*

CHAPLAINCY. A *chaplaincy* consists of two elements: (a) the obligation to provide religious services (usually the celebration of Holy Mass) in a specific church or chapel or at a specific altar; (b) the corresponding right of support from the foundation or from canonical taxes, imposed upon physical or juridical persons who enjoy the benefits of the chaplaincy.

A chaplaincy is *ecclesiastical,* if it is erected by the ecclesiastical authority or belongs to a juridical ecclesiastical person; otherwise it is a *lay* chaplaincy. In the former case, all property is considered ecclesiastical; in the latter case, it is not, although it is subject to the Ordinary's supervision inasmuch as it is a property *destined for a charitable cause.* An ecclesiastical chaplaincy erected into a juridical person by the proper religious authority is a true ecclesiastic benefice (*q.v.*), subject to all the canonical prescriptions governing these. In the case of a lay chaplaincy, the titular may be either a cleric or a lay person. If a lay person, he will have the duty to engage a priest for Holy Mass and other religious services. There are no lay chaplaincies in the U. S. A. *Led.*

CHAPTER. A *chapter* is a college or body of clerics attached to a certain church and instituted for the purpose of rendering to God a more solemn worship. If attached to a cathedral church, it is a cathedral chapter and has the additional function of assisting the Ordinary in the government of the diocese, in accordance with the prescriptions of the sacred canons. A chapter, therefore, is a collegiate institute erected into a legal person (legal entity), with rights and duties distinct from those of its individual component members, who are called *canons* or *capitulars*.

A collegiate chapter is established in special churches for purely liturgical purposes. The more important collegiate chapter bears the title of *capitulum insigne*, either by apostolic privilege or by immemorial custom. Other chapters of less importance come under the category of *capitulum non insigne*.

A chapter is said to be: (a) *secular* or *regular*, depending on whether it is composed of secular or religious clergy; (b) *numbered* (closed) or *not numbered* (open), depending on whether the number of canons is fixed or not.

A chapter consists of dignitaries and canons. Although the bishop has the right to preside over the capitular body and to issue orders, he is not, strictly speaking, a member of the chapter. He is not *de gremio*. In other words, the chapter forms a body distinct from the bishop, with its own head for purely capitular matters.

The erection, reorganization, or suppression of any chapter is reserved to the Holy See.

RIGHTS AND PRIVILEGES. As a collegiate or corporate body, a chapter enjoys all the rights belonging to a legal person. Moreover, capitular members have ordinary and particular rights with corresponding duties, assigned to them by the Code of Canon Law. Among the particular duties of canons are the daily choir service, according to the prescriptions of the sacred canons, and assistance to the bishop at Solemn Mass or other pontifical functions.

If a parish is juridically (*pleno jure*) attached to a chapter, the care of souls must be entrusted to an irremovable parochial vicar (*q.v.*).

The relations between the chapter and vicar or between the chapter and the pastor, if the church is simultaneously a collegiate and parish church, are regulated by Canon 415 (Can. 391 ff.). *Fel.*

In the U. S. A. there are no Diocesan chapters, either cathedral or collegiate. Some of the tasks of the cathedral chapter are carried out by the Diocesan or Archdiocesan Board of Consultors.

CHARACTER. *Character* is defined by many as the moral nature of an individual. The term *nature* in this definition, however, is employed loosely to indicate a more or less habitual state or quality of will. This stable quality is manifested through tendencies; the will, confronted by the same set of stimuli, reacts in a more or less constant manner, by regularly seeking either some good or evil, or fluctuating between the two. *Character* may be reduced to *habit*, so that, generally speaking, one is said to reveal his character by his habitual manner of reacting to external stimulation. Character may be strong or weak. Quite commonly, *character* without qualification is used to signify will power, in which case the term becomes synonymous with *strong character*. A man of character, possessed of strong will power and not easily influenced by external factors, consistently strives to achieve certain values, aims, or goals, which he considers good under all aspects—that is, morally good—or only under a specific aspect, though not, in itself, a good. On the contrary, a man *without character*, lacking will power, allows himself to become easily upset by contradictions, difficulties, and obstacles, e.g., laziness, physical weakness, tiredness, illness. The man of character stands out over others and overcomes tendencies which are the product of passion or physical weakness.

Human character is not immutable, but liable to formation and development. The foundations of character formation are laid in the early years of childhood through the beneficent influence of parents and educators. Character development is really formation or education of the will. The aim of parents and educators should be to teach the young to acquire a strong will in the direction of good. The child must be encouraged to take an active part, according to age and other factors, in programs of character training. A widespread error among modern parents and educators is to lay relatively great stress on intellectual development, and practically almost to neglect the formation of the will, which accounts for a great lack of men of character in society today. For further treatment of the term *character*, as opposed to constitution, personality and temperament, *see* Cyclothymia, Constitution, Personality. *Ben.*

CHARACTEROLOGY. *See* Personality.

CHARACTER, SACRAMENTAL. The *sacramental character* is a spiritual reality, indelible both in this life and in the next, which places the soul in a special relationship with Christ, and confers on the faithful a special active and passive quality or power. Hence, the sacramental character is a distinctive mark or seal. It is also a title or right to sanctifying grace, without which the character is not in its connatural state, and to special actual graces necessary for the proper fulfillment of duties resulting from the character itself. It is also a safeguard of grace, since it removes or reduces the influence of the devil and draws one into the protection of the Angels and of God.

Three sacraments imprint an indelible character on the soul: baptism, confirmation, and holy orders. Because of this indelible mark, none of these sacraments may be received more than once (Council of Trent, Sess. VIII, *De sacramentis in genere*, C. 9; Denz. 852). In any doubt concerning the valid reception or administration of these sacraments, they must be repeated conditionally.

Through the baptismal character, man acquires a relationship with Christ the King: he becomes a child of God, heir of heaven, consecrated to the service of Christ and a member of His true Church. Moreover, by reason of the baptismal character, man acquires a right to participate in the public worship of the Church and to receive the other sacraments. Through the character imprinted by the sacrament of confirmation, a baptized person is molded according to Christ, Teacher of Divine Truth; he is consecrated a soldier and defender of the same truth, with power to profess and defend the faith *ex officio*; it also qualifies him for a fruitful reception of the other sacraments. Finally, through the character imprinted by the sacrament of holy orders, a baptized and confirmed person becomes united with Christ, the High Priest, a consecrated minister of Christ, qualified to offer the unbloody Sacrifice of the Mass and to dispense grace through the sacraments.

A Christian should strive to preserve within himself a constant and vivid awareness of his dedication to Christ. Ever mindful of his supernatural dignity, he must endeavor to maintain at all times a great respect for his own person and that of others. He must conduct himself always in a manner befitting a soldier of Christ and member of His Mystical Body. *Man.*

CHARITY (Love). Charity is the first and foremost of all Christian virtues, including the theological virtues, to which it belongs. Because charity is the primary, essential effect of sanctifying grace, the terms *grace* and *charity* are used interchangeably. Grace and charity are not identical, but are intimately connected as fire and heat, sun and light. Grace elevates and perfects nature and the will indirectly, by producing within the will the virtue of charity, which is the perfection of the will. Grace and charity are expressions of supernatural life, grace in the line of being and charity in the line of action. Charity causes man to love God, who loves man directly. On the strength of such reciprocal love, charity constitutes true friendship with God. In Christ's own words: "I will not now call you servants . . . but friends" (John 15:15).

OBJECT. The person loved constitutes the object of charity. The object of supernatural charity is twofold: the primary object is God Himself; the secondary object is man destined to become a child of God through grace or participation in divine life. Through charity we love all men; we love all men precisely because they are children of God. Though charity has a twofold object, it is essentially one; we either possess charity in its entirety or we lack it completely. For this reason St. John teaches that "if a man says he loves God and hates his brother, he is a liar." For this reason, too, Christ states that love of neighbor is the sign by which we shall be recognized as His disciples (John 13:35).

The love of God consists in desiring the divine good, in loving God for His own sake. This love is primarily expressed through an internal act of the will, whereby we desire and rejoice at the fact that God is infinitely good, omnipotent and loving in Himself. Thus, the first three petitions of the Lord's Prayer are sublime expressions of our love of God. Furthermore, this love is expressed by external works designed to promote the divine good, insofar as this can be attained by our activities. These include: the observance of God's commandments, a conformity to His manifest will, the promotion of His honor and glory, by making Him known and loved by others, etc.

EMINENCE. Charity, which prompts us to love God Himself and His adopted children and our fellowmen, is the most eminent of all Christian virtues. Proof of this is found in Christ's reference to the love of God and neighbor as the first and greatest commandment. This is not to say that charity enjoys a primacy of value over all other moral precepts. Its primacy is one of degree. The precept of charity is an altogether special precept, since charity is the reason and purpose for the observance of other precepts. To love God is the purpose of life. God, the highest good and ultimate end of life, can only be attained through love. It is only because we are bound to love God that we are required to observe the other commandments. In other words, if we are obliged to pray, forbidden to work on Sunday, forbidden to blaspheme, etc., it is because such precepts are necessary to preserve and increase the love of God in us. And if we are obliged to honor our parents, forbidden to kill, steal, lie, etc., it is only because such precepts are necessary to preserve and increase proper love of self and neighbor. All the other precepts depend on the commandment of charity, in the same way that the morality of the means employed in the performance of our actions depends upon our end in view. Hence, St. Paul calls charity the plenitude or fulfillment of the Law (moral). He who loves God, self, and neighbor with a *true* and *operative* love that dominates his entire activity, always performs good, because to love is to want good and nothing else. This is the profound meaning of St. Augustine's words: "Love and do whatever you will." He who wants good, because he loves and does whatever he wills, always does good.

The cause of charity is God, i.e., the Triune God or the three Divine Persons together. But the virtue of charity is especially attributed to the Holy Ghost, who is the Person of the reciprocal love between the Father and the Son. God infuses charity with sanctifying grace, which makes us His adopted children and permits us to call Him *our Father*. God also increases charity within us, once it has been infused. In children not yet possessing the use of reason, the infusion of charity is effected by God alone, without any cooperation on their part. This God accomplishes through baptism, the administration of which, however, requires human cooperation. In a person who has attained the use of reason, neither infusion nor increase of charity can take place without the subject's cooperation, the final act of which, at least, is an act of charity. We collaborate in the increase of charity by performing acts of love, by assisting at Mass, by receiving the sacraments, especially Holy Communion, by praying, by performing good and meritorious deeds in the state of grace. We collaborate in two ways: (a) by disposing ourselves toward a more fervent act of love in the erformance of the above-mentioned eeds; (b) by actually eliciting a more ervent act of love. A more fervent act f love actually increases the degree of harity, which, once acquired, abides vithin us. Mortal sin removes charity ntirely. Venial sin does not diminish harity as such, but decreases its fervor nd, as a result, hinders any increase. A Christian must not only avoid losing harity through mortal sin, but he must trive to increase the charity he already possesses, by avoiding venial sin, performing good works, frequenting the sacraments, eliciting fervent acts of love of God.

Charity toward one's neighbor prompts is, first of all, to seek the good of our ellowmen, i.e., to desire the well-being of our neighbor as our own. Love of neighbor manifests itself in external acts designed to procure, as far as lies within is, the well-being of our fellowmen. The main difference between love of God and love of neighbor consists in this, that the good or well-being of our fellowmen s more dependent on our assistance and cooperation. God is not. Charity prompts is to avoid, as much as possible, whatever may bring displeasure, sadness, suffering, or injury to our neighbor. On the positive side, it prompts us to do everything possible to render our neighbor's ife good and happy. The words "as much as possible" refer not to absolute, but moral, possibility.

Love itself must be without limitations, but the external acts of charity are necessarily subject to the limitations of our powers and means. Our power, time, and goods can only be expended to relieve a specific need of a neighbor. Moreover, since everyone is bound to ove self, it is perfectly legitimate to provide for one's own needs first. Indeed, n some instances this is a matter of duty. The rule of charity may be formulated as follows: Love God first, then yourself, lastly others; but genuinely love all three. This general rule gives rise to certain regulatory norms of a well-ordered charity: (a) never help yourself or your neighbor if that means offending God; (b) love of neighbor does not oblige one to succor the needs of another at the expense of incurring similar damage or inconvenience to self; (c) perfect charity consists in extending aid when there is no strict obligation to do so, to make sacrifices beyond the call of duty, to reduce personal needs in order to lend greater assistance to a neighbor (*see* Neighbor, Almsgiving, Enemy).

It is to be well understood, however, that assisting the needy is but a small part of the practice of love of neighbor. Many Christians do not sufficiently realize that charity must be effectively or externally practiced toward any person with whom they come into contact.

Charity must aminate all our activities and make us kind, helpful, and courteous to all: superiors, equals and subordinates; rich and poor; one's own family and strangers. Charity demands that we strive to check our own whims and to correct any defects of character or manners that make us unkind, discourteous, or unpleasant in our dealings and conversations with others.

The thought of charity to others renders life happier. The principal motive must be that, in loving our neighbor, we love Christ, who said: "That which you have done to the least of these my brethren, you have done it to me." Christ, who is present in our neighbor, expects to receive from us not only alms and other material assistance, but also courteous and kind treatment. *Ben.*

CHARLATANISM, CHARLATANRY.
Charlatanry is the sum total of evil arts practiced to deceive the good faith of others. As such, charlatanry is an illicit action, fundamentally contrary to the natural law, which forbids injury or damage to another (*alterum non laedere*). However, not every form of charlatanry is necessarily evil.

Magician. Performances or games involving prestidigitation, legerdemain, sleight of hand tricks, juggling, etc., unless attended by some evil circumstances, are of themselves morally acceptable, since they are mainly designed for the purpose of entertainment and recreation. But it is never permissible to use illicit or immoral means in any such performances, especially in games which depend on chance. In games involving personal skill or strength, the rules of natural equity must be observed, and conditions must be equal for all participants; hence, it is improper to attempt such games with minors or elderly persons.

Venders. In general, the distinguishing criterion between legitimate or illegitimate (charlatan) venders is drawn from the public conscience and ideas prevailing in the society where the vender sets up his stand or peddles his wares. In the common estimation, various wiles and artful practices resorted to by charlatan venders are regarded as innocuous, for practically everyone is prepared to deal cautiously with such individuals. Some moralists hold that such practices employed to lure the buyer are a violation of justice. We believe, with Fr. Vermeersch, S.J., that such is not the case, since there is no juridical relation between a charlatan and buyer. However, the charlatan vender would certainly be guilty of sin, if he attempted to practice complete deception or fraud, e.g., to pass off a gilded object as pure gold.

Religious charlatans. Religious charlatans attempt to reduce or destroy belief in the supernatural through the use and promotion of superstitious practices, magic formulae, witchcraft, talismans, amulets, etc. These arts not only contradict common sense and rudimentary natural science, but are also contrary to purity and sincerity of faith, for they attribute to the supernatural a purely natural phenomenon or to nature that which is beyond its powers. The faithful are forbidden either to practice or lend credence to such charlatanic activities.

He who practices charlatanry in religion sins gravely against the virtues of religion and faith, and against charity by diminishing his neighbor's belief and trust in God. Moreover, a charlatan is subject to canonical penalties (Canons 2325–2326). Civil laws also provide penalties for such offenders. *Tar.*

CHARLATANISM, MEDICAL. Medical charlatans or quack doctors are those

who publicly prate and boast of possessing bottled miracles, secret cures or remedies, magic formulae, etc. Such individuals are natural rivals of doctors, by whom they are disdained and branded as disseminators of unwarranted claims. In fact, the law itself protects the interests and dignity of the medical profession as well as the welfare of the people from unprofessional and unapproved practitioners.

Such disdain by the medical profession and such severity by the law are justified undoubtedly, especially in view of the harm that quack doctors can cause, if only by delaying proper medical attention and treatment. On the other hand, if one were to take an objective view of various aspects of this complex question, he might think that a general and absolute condemnation of every medical charlatan may be unwarranted, for it must be recognized that there have been cases in which a charlatan provided a successful remedy, where medical science had failed.

Bleuler, D'Antona, and other reputable authorities have shown that charlatans have had successful results in treating not only purely functional diseases, but several organopathies, in which, especially due to neuro-vegetative disequilibrium, the psychical factor seemed to have exercised considerable influence over the body. These scientists have reached the acceptable conclusion that such successful treatments were due to the fact that the charlatan was able to dominate the psychical forces underlying the disease in question; forces that the physician ordinarily, and unfortunately, ignores. Of course, the health of the people must be entrusted to professional men. But as long as charlatans continue to come up with successful treatments in cases where academic medicine has failed, legal and medical opposition to charlatanry becomes less understandable. After all, as D'Antona wisely observes, "the sick do not ask to be studied and treated according to the rules of codified science, but to be cured." We do not, of course, advocate a simple recognition of such practices, but we believe that medical charlatanry can be eliminated only after it is studied and investigated like other natural phenomena, without prejudice, disdain, indignation and rivalry. In this manner, it shall be possible to understand the real value of such artifices, which, if found to be genuine, could be incorporated into official medicine with obvious benefits for therapeutic progress and suffering humanity. *Riz.*

CHASTITY. *Chastity*, a subjective part of temperance, is the moral virtue which inclines man to moderate the use of and appetite for venereal delectation or sexual pleasure according to the norms of right reason. To this rational norm, which regulates the exercise of the procreative faculty within the limits of a natural purpose, one must add a Christian consideration of the dignity of the human body, elevated through baptism to be a living temple of the Holy Ghost and a member of the Mystical Body of Christ (Cor. 6:15–20). The material object of the virtue of chastity is the sexual act or sexual pleasure, properly so-called, which the virtue of chastity moderates. Modesty moderates secondary or unconsummated external acts related to venereal pleasure (*see* Modesty). Chastity implies a facility in the exercise of its acts; hence, merely to abstain from illegitimate sexual pleasure at the cost of great efforts is not chastity, but continence. Chastity is perfect and imperfect. Imperfect chastity implies abstention from the *inordinate* use of the sexual faculty, without, however, excluding its legitimate use, whether present for married persons, future for single persons, or past for the widowed. Perfect chastity implies abstention from all, even legitimate, sexual pleasure, both present and past, and accompanied by a plan, with or without a vow, of remaining chaste in the future (*see* Virginity).

Though chastity occupies a relatively low position in the hierarchy of virtues, it plays a predominant role in practical Christian life. It is this virtue which preserves man from the tyranny of concupiscence of the flesh, and those vehement passions which seriously disturb the moral functions of the higher faculties of intellect and will. Defects and vices against chastity give rise to great difficulties, and frequently make it impossible for man to lead a virtuous life based on charity (*Summa Theol.*, II–II, q. 153, art. 5; *see* Lust). Chastity perfects the individual man and at the same time benefits society. This may be indirect insofar as individual perfection is reflected on the life of society, or direct, (a) in a negative way, by rational, orderly procreation and the proper rearing and education of offspring; (b) in a positive way, by contributing to the increase of the human race, since it forbids, even in marriage, a complete sexual act not of itself apt to procure procreation. The observance of chastity is not contrary to man's nature. Complete sexual abstinence, whether during the premarital period or for one's entire life, is in no way detrimental to health, as shown by experience and proven by many experts (*see* Abstinence, Continence).

METHODS FOR SAFEGUARDING CHASTITY. All methods and aids for preserving purity may be reduced to a two-word program: *vigilance* (flight from dangerous occasions) and *action* (prayer and struggle).

Flight from dangerous occasions of sin is imperative for the cultivation of purity and modesty, the last bulwark of chastity. Among natural aids supplied by medical science, psychotherapy is generally considered effective and morally licit. It is especially recommended in the case of habitual sinners.

Specific aids to chastity are: (a) *a profound and genuine piety*; (b) spirit of *prayer*, including, above all, the practice of meditation as the most effective method of training the will; (c) *frequent reception of the sacraments of penance and Holy Communion*; (d) *examination of conscience*, especially the particular examen, as an excellent means of acquiring self-knowledge and self-control; also a spiritual retreat, whenever possible; (e) *devotion* to the Blessed Virgin, the model of purity, to the Guardian Angels, St. Aloysius Gonzaga, St. Maria Goretti, and other saints renowned for their exemplary lives of chastity; (f) *spiritual direction or guidance.*

The virtues contributing in a particular manner to the preservation of chastity are (a) *mortification,* particularly of the senses, as an effective way of preventing temptation and strengthening the will; (b) *humility;* and (c) *spiritual cheerfulness.*

Mental aids are: (a) the habit of cultivating elevated and noble thoughts; (b) the fostering of ideals (family, priesthood, religious life, apostolate); (c) the habit of cherishing fond and pure memories (mother, spouse), and of thinking frequently of the last things, the divine presence, the worth of spiritual values.

Other human aids to chastity are: (a) a sound esthetic education; (b) orderly, peaceful, and serene atmosphere in the home; (c) the cultivation of wholesome friendships; (d) flight from idleness in pursuing a hobby, engaging in games and recreation, etc.; (e) physical therapy under the direction of a reputable physician. *Dam.*

CHASUBLE. *See* Sacred Vestments.

CHILD WELFARE INSTITUTES. *See* School; Assistance.

CHILDREN. Relationship to Parents. The mutual relations between the child and parents are the objects of the virtue of piety (*q.v.*); the special bond that characterizes them excludes under some aspects elements proper to the virtue of justice because of the absence of a real equality and independence required for justice. In fact, children are in a sense a part of their parents (*aliquid patris*). Under some aspects, however, between parents and children, relations of strict justice do exist, which are all the more impelling because of the further and concurrent obligation of piety or devotion.

The duties and respective rights of parents and children, as established by the natural law, find solemn sanction in the divine-positive law expressed by the fourth commandment: *Honor thy father and thy mother.*

First of all, children owe their parents love, respect, and obedience. The obedience due to parents involves matters in which they are subject to their parents and as long as they remain subject to parental authority. Children are subject to their parents, primarily to the father, until they become of legal age.

The basis of these obligations is that children owe their life to their parents and that parents, to a certain extent, are invested with the authority of God with respect to their children. Thus, the duties of children toward their parents are seriously binding. Because of the obligation of loyal devotion toward their parents, even duties of justice become more serious insofar as sin is concerned, although, at times, because of the special bond which exists between parents and children, the latter are exempt from the obligation of restitution (*q.v.*). Of particular importance are patrimonial relations between children and parents.

Patrimonial Relations. According to the law of nature, children, even minors, insofar as they are individuals, are capable of possessing and acquiring goods, although the father has the right and duty (*ex pietate*) to administer them in the interest of his children, if the children are subject to him either because of age or incapacity to perform juridical acts.

Goods belonging to children may be of two categories: (a) goods acquired by transfer of ownership through donation, inheritance or legacy: (b) goods acquired through personal industry or by any remunerative work in general. Children possess the right of ownership over both categories of goods; parents may not claim them as their own without violating justice. Children, however, may have obligations towards their parents with respect to such goods. First of all, a child is bound in justice to repay his father, unless he should condone it as loss, for expenses incurred by the latter in feeding and educating his child. A child has a strict right *ex justitia* to such benefits only if he has nothing of his own and is unable to earn his living because he is a minor. A father who administers his child's property may in conscience repay himself from the fruits of the child's property for all expenses incurred in rearing and educating his child and in administering the latter's possessions. The child has an obligation in justice to restitution for any unjust loss or damage to his parents, if he is responsible as a cause; a son who defrauds his father or in any way is responsible as the cause of an unjust damage sins against justice; the sin is greater because of an additional violation of the virtue of piety (loyal devotion).

On the contrary, in view of the close bond which exists between children and parents, a child may, for instance, take small sums of money for lawful pastimes, food or other items, over and above the allowance which the father himself usually gives him. These appropriations do not have all the elements of theft, which is taking goods from the rightful owner who is reasonably opposed to this theft (*rationabiliter invitus*).

In view of the same close bond, the obligation of children to make restitution to their parents is less binding than that which exists between unrelated persons. If the sum taken from the parents or the damage caused to them is not excessive, and if the sum, arbitrarily squandered by the child, was not destined by the father for a definite purpose, such as the child's education, condonation may be presumed. This, obviously, exempts the child from restitution, provided that the amount is not too large.

Furthermore, the same special relation, existing between parents and children, has a bearing on determining the gravity of the matter, and, therefore, also on the obligation of restitution. This obligation must be considered less binding if the sum unjustly taken or the damage unjustly caused is more removed from that which is usually considered grave matter in ordinary theft. Following St. Alphonsus, the greater number of moral theologians generally hold that in child-parent thefts, grave matter consists of twice the amount required in the case of unrelated persons.

Children have a grave obligation (*ex pietate*) to help their needy parents, provided that they can do so without causing themselves a notable damage.

INCOME OF CHILDREN. Concerning the obligations of children toward their parents on the question of earnings, one must consider the circumstances surrounding the children's work in general and their rights and obligations within the framework of the family. (a) If a child carries on his work independently of his father, the income from such work belongs to him, although, if he is a minor, it is the father's right to administer the funds and receive from his child, *ex justitia*, adequate compensation for room and board. Moral theologians consider this an obligation of justice (Vangheluwe dissents); this is apart from a grave obligation from loyal devotion (*ex pietate*) to aid needy parents, as stated above. This obligation of justice ceases if the father allows. This condonation may easily be presumed by children of sufficiently prosperous families, but not of families that depend on the father's average salary. From this it is clear that working minors who keep their earnings may not be guilty of injustice if they pay for their room and board and refuse to turn their salary over to their parents on request, although they may be guilty of disobedience and violating the virtue of piety.

(b) If a son engages in a trade, business, etc., in his own name and for his own benefit, with means provided by his father or belonging to his father but used without the latter's knowledge, the earnings from such type of work, according to the common opinion of moral theologians, belong entirely to the son. The son, however, has the obligation to make restitution to his father for all consumed fungible goods and to compensate for the use of all non-fungible goods. Besides these obligations, he must also fulfill the obligations which arise in points treated above under (a).

(c) If a son lends his work to his father's trade or business as an employee, nothing is due him, if the profits from his work do not surpass the expenses sustained by the family for his support. Similarly, the father owes his son no compensation for services rendered by the latter, if the father accepted such services as gratuitous, and if it was reasonable for him to expect aid, either because other brothers would have given such gratuitous assistance on request, or because other persons would have done it at low cost. This is valid even in the case in which the son's services are productive of profits which exceed the expenses sustained by the family for his support. On the contrary, if the profits accruing from the son's work exceed the expenses sustained by the family for his support or if no assistance is given by other brothers in equal measure and gratis, or if such assistance was given but clear terms were agreed on between the son and the father, then the net profits, after subtracting the above expenses, belong completely to the son. Various factors play a part in determining whether or not the son has any right to the profits and the extent of such a right. Among these factors one must include the possibility of a son's renunciation to any claim, which can be easily presumed if the assistance given by the son to his father benefits the son or prepares him for an independent position. Upon the son's request, the father may not presume this renunciation of compensation, because the son previously made no claim before this for compensation.

The provisions of civil law must be considered, for these may determine and specify the natural law. Customs of the various places and times must be taken into account, for they may limit or wholly eliminate the right of a son to compensation.

If the father reimbursed himself for the expenses sustained from his son's earnings (or condoned these), the son shall be free of any obligation of justice. At best, he may have an obligation of devotion (*ex pietate*), in the event of need or want on the part of his parents.

Modern civil codes deal in a general manner with patrimonial relations and provisions, which interpret and integrate the provisions of the natural law. Thus the norms of the civil codes, with the exception of legitimate local customs to the contrary or special circumstances, are to be considered as generally binding in conscience. *Pal.*

CHIROGNOMY. See Chiromancy.

CHIROGRAPHER. See Acts, Pontifical.

CHIROMANCY (Palmistry). *Chiromancy* (etymologically, divination through the medium of the hand) may be defined as the prediction of the future through an examination and study of the hand.

An ancient art, with definite references found in the works of Aristotle, chiromancy, especially in its pretence to reveal the future, has always been the easy tool of mystifiers, magicians, and charlatans. But it is also an object of serious research, especially designed for the study of the character, tendencies, and habits of individuals. Those who today study chiromancy under this scientific aspect define it as "the experimental study of the various forms, lines, mounts or elevations and other markings of the hand."

CHIROGNOMY. *Chirognomy*, the study of the different types of hands, was initiated about a century ago by D'Arpetigny. Regarded as a branch of chiromancy, it has yielded results of more than biological import. Thus understood, chirognomy is worthy of the same respect and consideration as physiognomy and other anthropological studies whose aim is to deduce the particular inclinations and tendencies of individuals from their peculiar physical and somatic characteristics.

By observation of the habitual movements of the hand, its skeletal formation, the development of adipose tissue, the degree of coloration, warmth, and perspiration, and on the basis of empirical control in numerous experiments, a qualified and experienced observer may be able to formulate a well-founded judgment of the character and temperament of a person. Thus, to cite a few casual examples, a small and plump hand is indicative of goodness and joviality; a long, tapering hand supposedly indicates sensibility, idealism, rich imagination; broad fingers seemingly characterize active, energetic, hardworking individuals; the length of the thumb is believed to be related to volitional power, and so forth.

Clinically, the hand lends itself to the observation of various symptoms for diagnostic purposes in circulatory, nervous, and endocrine diseases.

Chiromancy Properly So-called. Chiromancy properly so-called is chiefly concerned with the lines and mounts found along the fingers and across the palm of the hand. The hand submitted for examination usually is the left hand, probably because its surface is less altered by daily activity.

The main lines of the hand generally studied—on what basis it is not known—are the following: (a) *The line of life,* starting at a point between the index and the thumb, goes around the base of the latter. The length and depth of this line are presumably related to longevity and physical robustness, while the transversed lines at the base of the wrist (wrist lines) supposedly indicate the total life span of the individual, with each line representing a span of thirty years. (b) *The line of the head* has the same starting point as the line of life and runs across the palm of the hand; the formation and development of this line are supposedly related to intelligence. (c) *The line of the heart,* roughly originating at the base of the index, running transversely across the palm and ending at the base of the middle finger, is supposedly related to the affective or emotional sphere. (d) *The line of Saturn* (destiny) runs longitudinally from the wrist to the base of the middle finger and is supposed to represent success or good fortune in life.

Among the various mounts, we shall mention: *Venus* at the base of the thumb; *Jupiter* at the base of the index finger; *Apollo* at the base of the ring finger; *Mercury* at the base of the little finger. These mounts are indicative, respectively, of a gallant and amorous disposition, of ability to command or rule, of appreciation for art and beauty, of interest in trade.

Chiromancy and Predictions. Mounts, lines and various other markings of the hand, with their numerous combinations of position and development, make up the complicated book scanned and studied by chiromancers.

If chiromantic deductions are merely intended to give a general estimate of a person's character, they may, to some extent, be regarded as worthy of consideration and acceptance. The systematic reading of countless palms could possibly be conducive to the discovery of a group of marks prevailing in certain talented individuals or indicating certain somatic or personality traits. But if they are alleged to give a precise estimate of the character of a person, or are carried to a point of excessive sublety, or, even more, credited with predicting the future, such deductions must be considered absolutely arbitrary.

It may well happen that in certain cases a clever chiromancer will succeed in making a correct prediction; but this is not necessarily due either to superhuman powers or simply to charlatanry. An experienced practitioner of chiromancy not only examines his client's hand or palm, but he also observes his features, his manner of dressing, his behavior, etc. On the basis of this general scrutiny, the chiromancer can form a judgment concerning his client's character, as a diligent and industrious person or as a lazy and dubious person. A prediction of eventual success in the former case and eventual brush with the law in the latter is fairly obvious, with great probability that this prediction will be verified.

Chiromancy and Morality. From the standpoint of Catholic morality, *chirognomy,* if seriously pursued and practiced without charlatanry, is licit. In fact, it may well be considered a branch of medicine, whose pursuit may yield useful information in the psychosomatic study of the patients.

Chiromancy properly so-called cannot be condemned, if it is restricted to honest research for the eventual discovery of symptomatic relations between chirological marks and personality traits or tendencies; these relations, however, as yet are very scarce and uncertain.

Chiromancy is morally illicit if it pretends to foretell the future, for such divinatory power is in reality false. Anyone practicing the art of chiromancy with a view to predicting the future either practices divination (*q.v.*), pretending to be in contact with occult forces, or at least commits a grave sin of injustice against clients, who are usually weak, neuropathic, susceptible to suggestion and superstition, and easily disturbed by any sort of prediction. Under this aspect chiromancy must be condemned as harmful to the individual and society. *Riz.*

CHOICE OF STATE. *See* Vocation.

CHOIR. *Choir* may mean (a) a group of singers or chanters, (b) a place in church specifically set apart for the recitation of the Divine Office, (c) the choral service itself. The present article deals with choir in this third meaning.

According to current legislation, choral service is incumbent on all cathedral and collegiate chapters, as well as some religious orders, with somewhat different prescriptions.

CHORAL SERVICE OF CHAPTERS (Can. 413 ff.). (This service does not exist in the U. S. A., although it is maintained in Canada and other countries of the Western Hemisphere.)

(a) *Nature.* The choral service consists in the daily recitation of the Divine Office in common and the celebration of the conventual Mass, or other Masses prescribed by the liturgy or by obligations arising from pious foundations. The conventual Mass must be a *Missa Cantata*, except on days when the bishop or his substitute celebrates a solemn Mass in the church or chapel of the chapter (Can. 413).

(b) *Obligation.* Every chapter has the obligation of the daily recitation of the Divine Office in choir, unless, by stipulation of the foundation or by subsequent apostolic indult, the obligation has been reduced to the daily choral recitation of part of the Divine Office or of the entire Office on certain days. Such reduction is sometimes granted by the Holy See for grave reasons. The obligation of choral recitation is incumbent on all persons holding a choir benefice in a cathedral or collegiate church, i.e., on all dignitaries, canons, and minor beneficiaries. All such capitular members are obliged to daily choir duty, including attendance at the conventual Mass, unless, by stipulation of the foundation or by apostolic indult, a rotating service is allowed. The statutes of the chapter also provide for alternate service of the conventual Mass, which is to be offered for benefactors. According to these provisions, each beneficiary is required to discharge the role of celebrant, deacon, and subdeacon. However, the dignitaries, the canon theologian, and the canon penitentiary are always dispensed from serving as deacon or subdeacon. The same applies to presbyteral canons in chapters where distinct prebends are provided for canons who are deacons and subdeacons (Can. 416).

Since choral service is the principal duty of possessors of a choir benefice, those who daily attend the choir service or are lawfully excused are entitled to their respective portion of the revenue (fruits) of the benefice (Can. 2381, n. 1). Those who daily perform choir duty are entitled to daily distributions and distributions *inter praesentes* (among those present). For those lawfully excused from choir, as enumerated in Canons 418–421, the following regulations obtain: (a) They forfeit the daily distributions, but are entitled to general income of the prebend, during a legitimate vacation (Can. 418), e.g., professors of sacred theology or Canon Law with permission of the local Ordinary (Can. 421); (b) in other cases, legitimate absentees are entitled both to the income from the prebend and the daily distributions, e.g., the canon theologian engaged in the office of preaching; the canon penitentiary hearing confessions during choir service; those who are sick or physically unable to attend choir, etc.

(Can. 420, par. 1); (c) some in other cases are entitled even to the distributions *inter praesentes*, e.g., jubilarians of the chapter, canons assisting the bishop in pontifical functions according to the prescriptions of Canon 412, par. 1.

CHORAL SERVICE OF RELIGIOUS. (Can. 610).

(a) The Code of Canon Law does not impose the obligation of choir on religious, but merely defines the extent of such obligation for those religious who are bound to choir duty by their particular constitutions or by custom. According to the teaching of canonists, religious organizations bound to choir duty are principally those orders that originated prior to the sixteenth century (monks, canons regular, mendicants and nuns of papal enclosure). There are also religious orders and congregations of later centuries, including some communities of women, bound to this obligation by particular law (cf. Pontifical Commission for the Authentic Interpretation of the Code of Canon Law, May 20, 1923, in AAS: 16 [1924], 113–114).

(b) The choir obligation of religious institutes, similar to cathedral and collegiate chapters, consists in the daily recitation in common of the Divine Office, and attendance at the conventual Mass.

(c) However, this obligation is not incumbent on all religious houses and churches, as in the case of chapters, but only on those houses with at least four resident religious (clerics or nuns with temporary or solemn vows) who are bound to choir service and not lawfully impeded, unless the particular constitutions of the institute prescribe choir duty even in houses with less than four religious. The obligation of reciting the Divine Office in choir is a grave one, binding the community directly, but only indirectly the individual religious members. In other words, it is primarily the duty of the superior to see to it that this grave obligation is fulfilled. For the individual religious members, all those bound to choir service and not lawfully impeded or excused are required to be present at the recitation of the Canonical Hours and the conventual Mass.

(d) In male religious institutes with the obligation of choir, the conventual Mass is strictly prescribed. In female religious communities bound to choir duty, including nuns of papal enclosure, the conventual Mass is prescribed only if possible (Commission for the Authentic Interpretation of Canon Law, May 20, 1923, in AAS: 16 [1924], 113–114). Unlike chapters, only one conventual Mass is prescribed (Sacred Roman Congregation, May 2, 1924, in AAS: 16 [1924], 248–249). The Code does not prescribe that the conventual Mass be a *Missa Cantata* nor that it be offered for the benefactors. Such matters are regulated by the particular constitutions of the individual religious organization. Led.

CHRISM. See Confirmation.

CHRISTMAS. HISTORICAL NOTES. Easter and Whitsunday were borrowed from ancient Judaism and given a new Christian flavor, but Christmas is a feast of strictly Christian origin. Christmas is celebrated always on the same day of the year (December 25), although the exact date of our Saviour's birth is not known. The East observes it on January 6; the West, on December 25. This indicates that the first Christian generation had learned that the Saviour was born during the winter time.

According to the *Liber Pontificalis*, Pope Telesphorus (125–136) is said to have revised the celebration of Christmas and instituted the Midnight Mass; the information, however, is not believed authentic. In fact, Christmas is not mentioned before the fourth century, although Hippolytus, in a passage not altogether certain, of his commentary on Daniel, states that our Lord was born on December 24, in the forty-second year of the reign of Augustus. Christmas, as a feastday, was unknown to Origen and Tertullian, nor is any mention made in a paschal computation for the year 243.

The *Depositio Episcoporum*, a Roman document of the year 336, mentions the celebration of Christmas as held on December 25. The *Depositio Martyrum* by Dyonysius Filocalus, written in Rome in 354, says explicitly: *VIII kal. Jan. natus Christus in Betleem Judeae*, that is, "on December 25, Christ was born in Bethlehem of Juda." The celebration introduced between 243 and 336 had its origin in the West; to be exact, in Rome. In the East, our Lord's birthday was already celebrated on Jan. 6, probably in place of the feast celebrated on that day in Alexandria, in honor of the god Aion (A. Baumstark, *Von geschichtlichen Warden der Liturgie*, Freiburg i. B., 1923, p. 27). The celebration of the feast on December 25 was perhaps arranged to oppose with a Christian feast the birthday of the unconquered sun god (*Natalis Solis invicti*), established at the time of emperor Aurelian (270–275) as a pagan festival in the empire. This feast was celebrated with much solemnity by the followers of Mitra. The choice of December 25 may have contributed the natural symbolism between the beginning of the lengthening of daylight, following the winter solstice, and the birth of the Sun of Justice.

During the third century, the celebration spread rapidly from Rome to the East. This movement coincided with the controversies stirred by Arianism, which effected an increase among Catholics of a more ardent veneration for the Son of God, consubstantial with the Father.

Recent studies by the late Cardinal Borgoncini-Duca on Daniel's prophecy confirm with surprising accuracy the theory of December 25, as the date of the Nativity; the date of the Incarnation is placed on March 30, and that of our Lord's death on April 7.

After the sixth century Christmas was characterized by the celebration of three Masses (*Liber Pontificalis*, I. 129; St. Gregory the Great, *Hom. 8 in Evang.*). Medival symbolism saw in this a reference to a triple birth of Jesus: (a) in eternity, in the bosom of the Father; (b) in time, in the womb of the Virgin Mary; and (c) in the Christian soul. Historically, the custom of the midnight Mass started in the churches of Jerusa-

lem, where Christmas was celebrated during the night, at Bethlehem, at our Lord's manger. In Rome, this Mass was celebrated in a cave which was a replica of the one in Bethlehem, as it appears from the stational inscription "*Statio ad S. Mariam Majorem et Praesepe*" (Station at the crib of St. Mary Major). The second Mass, *ad auroram*, originally had no particular relation to the Nativity, except for chants taken from the processional chants sung while the faithful went from Bethlehem to Jerusalem, after the celebration at the crypt. The Mass was celebrated in honor of St. Anastasia of Sirmio, whose feast occurred on December 25. The saint enjoyed great veneration in Constantinople, whence, at the time of the Byzantine domination, it was brought also to Rome at the church of the imperial palace on the Palatine, the present church of St. Anastasia, although Anastasia may mean *resurrection*. With the spread of the Roman sacramentary books, the celebration of the three Masses was extended to other places outside of Rome.

MYSTICAL MEANING. The celebration of the Nativity of our Lord should have the effect of leading us in spirit to the grotto of Bethlehem, and of making us aware of the necessity of a spiritual rebirth. This can only be done by a close union with the Word of God made man and by becoming partakers of His divine nature, to which man was raised (Pius XII, Encyclical *Mediator Dei*, November 20, 1947). The meaning of Christmas is clearly explained both in the epistles of the feast and in the lessons of the first nocturn of the Divine Office.

CUSTOMS. Many Christian customs exist, particularly in the northern parts of Europe. The exchanging of gifts is meant to be a reminder that the Eternal Father gave His Son as a gift to man; the Christmas tree, though of pagan origin, was quickly taken up as a symbol of Christ, the true tree of life, who by His coming brought life to the whole world; dating the more solemn papal documents on Christmas day was done to point out the feast of the Nativity as the beginning of the Christian era. *Opp.*

CHURCH BELLS. Already known and used for a variety of purposes in pre-Christian eras, bells were introduced at an early date in the liturgical life of the Church as a means of summoning the faithful to divine services. Tiny bells were used in the catacombs. By the sixth century the use of bells became a general practice in monasteries and churches. In the eighth century, Pope Stephen II donated three bells to the Vatican Basilica. Originally small in size, larger bells came gradually into use. The *Mater Gloriosa* bell of the Erfurt Cathedral in Germany (cast in 1497) weighs thirteen tons. The practice of adorning bells with dedicatory inscriptions and sacred images is an ancient one.

Church bells are customarily blessed, not only because of their relation to divine worship, but also to remove, by means of exorcisms, all the evil influences attributed to them in early times. The ancients believed that the sound of a bell was unwelcome to evil spirits (storm spirits). Any effect of bell-ringing upon a storm is today explained as a physical phenomenon. But the ancients believed that a subsiding storm was due to some magic element in the sound of the bell itself (pagan notion) or to a power acquired by the bell as a result of a blessing (Christian notion). The principal use of church bells remains that of inviting the faithful to prayer. The blessing of bells is reserved to the bishop.

In the Eastern Church, a device frequently used in place of bells to summon the faithful to worship is the *semantron*, i.e., a wooden or metal plank, which, when struck with a mallet, produces a songlike sound. From this device is derived the clapper (*crota-alus*) used on the last three days of Holy Week, which is one of the most ancient liturgical traditions.

Ecclesiastical legislation prescribes that every church should have bells for summoning the faithful to divine and other religious services (Can. 1169, par. 1). Bells must be either consecrated or blessed (Can. 1169, par. 2). The use of church bells is exclusively subject to ec-clesiastical authorities (Can. 1169, par. 3). Church bells may not be used for any purpose other than religious, except in necessity, by permission of the Ordinary, or in legitimate customs and circumstances approved by the Ordinary (Can. 1169, par. 4).

The ringing of bells, prescribed by the Ordinary for a public reason, applies also to exempt religious (Can. 612).

The bell ringer is appointed exclusively by the Rector of the Church, without prejudice, however, to legitimate customs approved by the Ordinary (Can. 1185). *Cig.*

CHURCH (Deportment in). No special form of dress is prescribed, but all are required to be properly and modestly dressed. On entering a church, men are required to remove their hats, and women to don a suitable head covering. All conversation should be discontinued before entering the church as a minimum of preparation for recollection and intimate union with God.

Upon entering the door, one dips the middle finger of the right hand into the holy-water font and blesses himself with the Sign of the Cross (*q.v.*), and pays homage to the Blessed Sacrament, either by kneeling at the altar rail for a short prayer, or in the pew which he will reach after making a simple genuflection, on one knee, in the aisle. If the Blessed Sacrament is exposed for solemn adoration, one genuflects on both knees before entering the pew.

It is not proper to exchange greetings or make introductions in church. The most that is permissible, provided that the Blessed Sacrament is not exposed, is a simple nod of the head or some other dignified but modest gesture of recognition, particularly on the occasion of a wedding ceremony, funeral, etc.

When no liturgical service is going on, one is at liberty to kneel, sit, or stand. If one drops in for a brief visit, it is more proper to maintain a kneeling posture throughout, since this is best suited for private prayer. During a protracted visit, one may pray in alternating positions. In all events, one should make every effort to be recollected and devout in the house of God, with the least possible disturbance or distraction to other praying faithful.

If one goes to a church to view and admire works of art, he should first make it a point to kneel, if the Blessed Sacrament is present, for a brief prayer. In circulating through the church, care should be exercised not to disturb any of the praying faithful, by conversing in a subdued tone, if necessary. In a word, it must always be remembered that the church is the house of God.

When a sacred function is taking place, the faithful are expected to interrupt their private devotions and join with others in common prayer.

Principal regulations concerning bodily posture:

(a) During a low Mass one should remain kneeling throughout, standing only for the reading of the two Gospels. Should this prove too difficult in individual cases, it is permissible to sit or stand for a while; but one shall kneel at least from the *Sanctus* to the end of the *Elevation* or, better, to the end of *Communion.*

The best way to assist at Holy Mass is to follow the prayers and actions of the celebrant with the aid of a missal.

(b) For a high Mass the rules of posture do not differ from those of a low Mass, except that the faithful sit during the singing of *Gloria* and *Credo* and stand during the chanting of the *Preface.* For a solemn Mass the following general rules obtain: (1) The faithful kneel: (a) during the prayers of the *Confession*, recited at the foot of the altar by the celebrant, deacon, and subdeacon; (b) from the *Sanctus* to the end of *Consecration* or in some places until the end of *Communion*; at the *Blessing* imparted by the celebrant before the *Last Gospel*. (2) The faithful sit: (a) during the incensation of the altar; during the singing of *Kyrie* and *Gloria*, the reading of the *Epistle* and verses immediately following (*Gradual, Alleluja, Tract, Sequence*), and the *Credo*; (b) from the *Offertory* until after the incensation of the choir, but the congregation rises at incensation

of the faithful by the thurifer: (c) during the chanting of the *Communion* antiphon. (3) At all other times, the faithful stand.

At a Funeral Mass the faithful, in addition to the times indicated above, also kneel during the singing of the *Collects* (prayers before the *Epistle* and after *Communion*) and from the end of *Consecration* to the *Pax Domini sit semper vobiscum* (immediately before the *Agnus Dei*).

(c) At sung Vespers, the faithful follow the movements of the celebrant.

(d) The rules for assisting at Eucharistic functions are as follows: during Mass or Vespers celebrated in the presence of the Blessed Sacrament solemnly exposed, the faithful follow the regulations given above for Mass and Vespers; at other Eucharistic functions, they are to remain kneeling throughout, if possible.

(e) During a sermon, the proper position is sitting.

Ordinarily, the use of a prayerbook will be found helpful, even necessary, in preparing for a worthy reception of the sacraments of penance and Holy Eucharist.

Concerning confession (*q.v.*), the following practices are to be avoided (a) walking into the first available confessional immediately upon entering the church, without having made the proper preparation or examination of conscience (b) sitting, kneeling, or standing too close to the confessional; (c) not reciting in church the prayer of thanksgiving after confession or the prayer assigned by the priest as a penance. Unless otherwise indicated by the confessor, the penance should be fulfilled without delay. If reception of Holy Communion follows confession immediately, it is to be highly recommended to spend the intervening time in preparation for reception of the Eucharist, without the immediate fulfillment of the penance.

Although it is permitted it receive Holy Communion outside of the time of Mass, one should attempt to receive reverently at the usual time appointed during the celebration of the Mass, in mediately after the priests's Communion. Communicants should make it a point, especially at weekday Mass, to approach the communion rail in time; it is advisable that at least one of the communicants approach the rail shortly after the *Agnus Dei.*

In going to the altar rail, one should proceed devoutly, making a simple genuflection on the right knee before kneeling at the rail. Communicants should so kneel at the rail as to form one continuous line. The priest should not be made to walk unnecessarily from one end of the rail to the other, nor should he be kept waiting without necessity.

The communion plate is placed beneath the chin either by the server or by the communicant himself, who holds it with two hands and then passes it over to the person on his left, and so on down the line, with the person at the extreme end of the rail handing it to the priest. At the moment of receiving, each communicant, with eyes downcast, raises his head a little and extends his tongue for the reception of the Sacred Particle. Shortly after receiving, each communicant, with hands joined at the breast, rises to return slowly and devoutly to his pew, where he kneels and with bowed head pauses to adore, to express his thanks, and to meditate on the great gift received. Following these moments of profound recollection, a prayerbook may be used to complete one's thanksgiving.

On days of general communion, extreme care should be exercised to avoid all unnecessary rushing and crowding. All should proceed to the altar rail in orderly fashion, leaving the passage clear for those who are returning to their pew.

Manner of Leaving Church. In leaving the church after making a private visit, one genuflects toward the Blessed Sacrament and proceeds with dignity toward the exit.

Before leaving, it is customary to bless oneself with holy water, if the font can be conveniently reached, without interfering with other people entering the church. In all events, with or without holy water, one should make the Sign of the Cross at the church door, without, however, turning to face the altar.

When assisting at a sacred function, one should not leave, without a legitimate reason, before the end of the service or before the priest has left the altar to return to the sacristy. If one must leave before the service is over, he should make his exit as quietly and unobtrusively as possible, so as not to disturb the rest of the faithful. Unless absolutely necessary, one should avoid leaving during the *Consecration* or *Communion* of the Mass, or during *Benediction* of the Most Blessed Sacrament.

Upon leaving the church, one should genuflect toward the Blessed Sacrament, as above directed, and walk out in an orderly manner. Beyond the church door, men may cover and women uncover their heads, if they so choose. *Ses.*

CHURCH, EASTERN (Sacred Congregation). *See* Roman Congregations.

CHURCH, (Edifice). In the Code of Canon Law, *church* means a sacred edifice dedicated to divine worship, especially with a view to enabling all the faithful to participate in public worship (Can. 1161).

The earliest Christian edifices of worship were the private homes of members of the Roman nobility. These kept ownership of the property before the law, since the corporate right of ownership by the Church was not recognized by the State. How these original houses of prayer, as private homes, were fitted for church uses, little or nothing is known with certainty. St. Eusebius relates that "the great number of people seeking admission into the Church and the vast multitudes turning to these houses of prayer rendered the early places of worship inadequate and made necessary the erection of vast and spacious churches everywhere (Eusebius, *Ecclesiastical History*, VIII, ch. 1). During the era of peace initiated by Constantine, the number of churches increased quite rapidly. Amid this vast growth, a particular style, called *basilica,* developed, whose main lines served as a general norm in the construction of churches during the entire Middle Ages. The Church has never made a definite pronouncement in favor of any one particular type of church structure to the exclusion of others; nor has she created a new art, in the sense of originating new architectural styles.

Always manifesting an amazing adaptability to the customs of every age in all things which are not of their nature irreconcilable with God's law and the good of souls, the Church borrowed freely from Oriental, Grecian, and Roman art to produce the triumphant art of the early Christian centuries (Grisar, *Rome at the End of the Ancient World*, I, 385).

According to the degree of dignity, churches are classified as basilicas, cathedrals, collegiate, and parochial churches:

(a) *Basilicas* are major or minor. The major basilicas in Rome are: St. John Lateran, St. Peter's at the Vatican, St. Paul's-outside-the-Walls, and St. Mary Major's. Major basilicas outside of Rome are: St. Francis and St. Mary of the Angels in Assisi, the cathedral of Anagni. A minor basilica is a title of honor, granting certain ceremonial privileges to the clergy of the church thus honored (Cathedral of the Assumption, Baltimore, Md.).

(b) A *cathedral* is the official church of a diocese, in which the local Ordinary maintains his permanent episcopal throne or *cathedra*. Cathedral churches are called patriarchal, primatial, metropolitan, or simply cathedral, depending on whether the Ordinary is a patriarch, primate, metropolitan, or simply a resident bishop.

(c) A *collegiate* church is one served by a college or chapter of canons with special privileges and the obligation of reciting the Divine Office in choir. (No collegiate church exists in the U.S.A.)

(d) A *parochial* or parish church is one charged with the care of souls, which is administered by a legitimately appointed pastor or rector.

In addition to these, some churches are dependent on a parish church, as a mission, chapel, conventual churches (attached or belonging to a religious community), *abbatial* churches (attached to an abbey).

MATERIAL CONSTRUCTION. No particular artistic norms are prescribed for the structure of a church, although the form most commonly used from the beginning is that of a rectangular, cruciform structure. Canon 1164 directs that Ordinaries, consulting with experts in ecclesiastical architecture, see to it that the traditional rules of sacred art be observed (Can. 1162, par. 1; Instruction of the Sacred Congregation of the Holy Office, 30 July, 1952: AAS, 44 [1952], 542). Liturgists are more or less generally agreed in prescribing the following norms:

(a) A church destined for public worship should be erected on a dry and, if possible, elevated site, with at least three steps leading to the entrance. The church location should be as far removed as possible from noisy and business areas, which are a hindrance to recollection.

(b) As far as possible, the walls of a sacred edifice should be separated from adjacent buildings or dwellings. It is forbidden to have a door or window of a church opening into a private home. The area below the floor or above the ceiling of a church may not be used for merely secular purposes (Can. 1164, par. 2).

(c) In designing and building a church, it is recommended that the traditional form of a rectangle be followed, with the ground plan presenting the shape of a cross.

(d) If possible, the church should be situated with the front entrance facing the west and the apse facing the east. The body of the church should be sufficiently large to accomodate not only the normal congregation, but also larger crowds for special religious celebrations.

Moreover, the church should have several doors for the safety and convenience of the faithful, and adequate space for the proper performance of the sacred functions. Every church must have a sacristy where sacred vessels, vestments, and other equipment are preserved. Also considered standard equipment in every large church is a pulpit or ambo, conveniently placed on one side of the sanctuary, not far from the altar, within open view of the entire congregation. In the body of the church, outside the sanctuary, confessionals are to be provided in conspicuous and accessible places. The floor of the sanctuary, where the main altar is located, should be elevated above the floor of the nave, so that the faithful may have a clear view of the sacred ceremonies. The chancel (choir and sanctuary) is to be separated from the nave by a railing or balustrade (altar rail or communion rail). The cantoria or choir loft (gallery or balcony for singers) and organ are generally on the north side and separated from the sanctuary. The façade of the church, even if it is to remain temporarily incomplete, should always have a cross.

CONSECRATION. The consecration of churches is first encountered under Constantine, following the era of persecutions; but it must have begun in earlier times, when the celebration of sacred functions was transferred from private homes to appropriate edifices. In the course of time, the custom arose of regularly dedicating a church to a saint, which may have given rise to the translation of relics as a permanent ceremony in the rite of consecration. The purpose of the consecration rite is to make the place exclusively sacred, withholding it from all common and profane uses.

Modern canonical legislation prescribes that cathedral churches and, insofar as conditions permit, collegiate, conventual, and parochial churches be solemnly consecrated (Can. 1165, par. 3). Only churches constructed of masonry may be consecrated; those built of wood, iron, or other metal may be blessed, but not consecrated (Can. 1165, par. 4). The consecration of churches, even those belonging to religious communities, is reserved by law to the local Ordinary (Cans. 1155–1157). For the lawfulness of the ceremony, it is required that the main altar and one of the side altars must be consecrated (Can. 1165, par. 5). The essential elements in the rite of consecration are the annointing with holy chrism of the twelve crosses on the inner walls of the church and the formula pronounced by the Bishop during the annointing (Sac. Cong. of Rites, April 12, 1614).

Churches which cannot be consecrated must at least be blessed, before divine worship may be held in them.

A blessed or consecrated church may become desecrated or violated: (a) by criminal homicide committed within the church itself; (b) serious shedding of human blood as a result of inflicted injury; (c) conversion of the church to profane and sordid purposes; (d) burial of an infidel or an excommunicate by condemnatory or declaratory sentence. It is forbidden to celebrate divine services, administer the sacraments, or bury the dead in a desecrated church, until the rite of reconciliation shall have been performed (Can. 1173). The reconciliation of a consecrated church rightfully pertains to the local Ordinary, who, however, may delegate any priest to perform the ceremony. The reconciliation of a blessed church may be performed by its rector or by any other priest with at least the presumed consent of the rector (Canons 1176–1177; 1156).

CIVIL DISPOSITIONS. Before building a church, one must obtain the written consent of the local Ordinary (Cans. 1161 ff.). No special authorization of civil authority is needed, except the usual building permit and the observance of the regulations of the State Building Code.

Requisition or occupation of churches by the civil power is regulated by the particular legislation of individual countries.

Churches are usually exempt from taxation of any sort.

As a "house of God and of prayer," a church deserves the full respect and love of the faithful. The Lord, of course, may be honored everywhere, but the church is the place especially dedicated and consecrated to divine worship. Here men are more inclined to turn their thoughts to God and to the interests of their own soul; here all social conditions and classes, fused into one, form one single people in the presence of God. Needless conversa-

tion, laughter, careless postures, and unbecoming dress in church are inconsistent with the sacred character of the house of God (*see also* Church, Deportment).
Tar.

CHURCH, ORTHODOX. *Orthodox* (Greek, *orthos*—correct, straight; *dokse* —opinion, teaching) in the theological sense is a term used to indicate purity of faith, or a practice or attitude which is in perfect accord with a doctrine of faith. Following the schisms of the ninth and eleventh centuries, the Byzantine Church assumed the name of *Orthodox Church* to emphasize its possession of the true faith. In reality, other than doctrine concerning the primacy of the Roman Pontiff, the Orthodox Church presents no dogmatic difference from the Catholic Church.

Orthodox moral theology is basically identical to Catholic moral theology. No doubt, this explains why few Catholic theologians have attempted to make a special study of it. Yet, in view of a certain originality, the moral system of the Orthodox Church is deserving of particular attention, as clearly demonstrated by Father S. Tyszkiewicz, S.J., in a recent and interesting study on Russian moralists.

GENERAL CHARACTERISTICS.

(a) *Morality and spirituality.* Intimately connected with spirituality to the point of near identity, pre-Slavic moral theology is less a science than a series of casual, light exhortations. It may be described as lay spirituality, or the application of the principles of Christian perfection to the ordinary life of the faithful, and an adaptation of monastic asceticism to persons living in the world. Quite effectively, Eastern theologians, in examining moral problems, always take into account the action of grace and Christian asceticism.

In the exposition of their moral system, pre-Slavic theologians begin with the principle, cherished by the Greek Fathers, of restoring within oneself man's resemblance to God, of renewing within oneself the image of God destroyed by sin. On the basis of this principle, to

which they constantly refer, Eastern theologians formulate general norms of morality and rules with particular applications.

This constant reference to the work of sanctification, which is the aim of all moral teaching, is not to be rejected, but recommended. Modern Catholic theologians have come to the realization that, although the distinction between morality and spirituality is necessary for didactic purposes, it actually receives too much emphasis in Catholic moral textbooks. Dublanchy seems to imply this in his article on morality, as he calls for a return to a more adequate concept of moral theology (D.T.C., vol. x, col. 2456).

(b) *Lack of systematization.* The first thing that strikes a Catholic moralist coursing through a pre-Slavic textbook, is a lack of unity and cohesion. Accustomed to the orderly and logical coordination of the textbooks of Ballerini, D'Annibale, Prummer, Genicot-Salsmans, etc., a Catholic moralist is completely unfamiliar with vague, fluid, and imprecise presentations by Orthodox authors. It is here that he learns to appreciate more fully the value of the speculative method. On the other hand, this method has always been looked upon with suspicion by dissident Eastern moralists, who follow a more or less catechetical and ascetical method, in which one finds neither logical sequence nor scholastic subtleties. Dissident theologians fondly state that a minutely regulated life is contrary to the Christian spirit. There is no need to imitate Catholic moralists, who break down or divide the divine precepts into so many small articles and comb the Scriptures and the Fathers to form a collection of particular rules of morality. A horror of *vivisection* and speculative deductions has always prevented Orthodox theologians from constructing and developing moral theology as an autonomous science with its own subject matter and its own method.

(c) *Protestant influence.* Despite this Eastern aversion, the scholastic method succeeded, in the seventeenth and subsequent centuries, in finding its way into

Eastern theological schools, especially Russian. This method was largely instrumental in clarifying a few points on the fundamental notions of conscience, moral freedom, etc., and in formulating pertinent distinctions. But a strong reaction soon set in, that interrupted this work of clarification. At the beginning of the eighteenth century, the preponderant influence of Lutheran moralists began to assert itself, reaching its culmination particularly among the so-called scientific moralists at the end of the nineteenth century. In this connection, a role of primary importance was exercised by the German Protestants Budde and Martensen, at a time when an Orthodox moral system had not yet been elaborated. This explains why in the work of the highly influential Russian moralist Ianysev (d. 1910), one finds no reference to Bulgar or Greek authors, whereas Protestant authors are abundantly quoted. It also explains why the Archimandrite Scriban, a Rumanian moralist, preferred to quote Palmer, Smith, Luthardt, Göpfert and Martensen, instead of following the expositions of Russian moralists, the least inept among Eastern Orthodox theologians. Protestant influence succeeded in drawing the attention of dissident Eastern moralists to questions of a psychological nature, and induced them to discard the strong intellectualism of the Fathers, by filling them with enthusiasm for such things as moral sense, esthetic taste, and the irrational element in morals.

(d) *Prejudices against Catholic moral theology.* Overly well-disposed toward Protestant moralists, pre-Slavic moral theologians manifest a complete distrust of Catholic moral theology. This distrust is the main reason for the lack of cohesion in treatises of Orthodox moral theology. Eastern dissidents prefer to remain in the realm of imprecision, confusion and chaos, rather than give ground to the *papists*, whom they accuse of advocating a system of juridical, fanatical, and pharisaical morality. According to Eastern dissidents, Catholic morality is simply a system of imperative ethics, based on the Roman concept of law, which destroys the spirit of freedom and happi-

ness and replaces it with servile fear. As a result, any attempt at systematization, such as the one made by Solarskij (d. 1890), has always been attacked as too scholastic and contrary to the spirit of freedom. In the East, it is too easily forgotten that, from the twelfth to the nineteenth century, Orthodox morality, especially in Russia, was strongly juridical in character and replete with canonistic and frequently onerous prescriptions. If today there exists, by way of reaction, a radical and formal contempt for the juridical element in morality, this is plainly due to the fact that for a long time the pre-Slavic people, like the Hebrews, were burdened with numerous and burdensome prescriptions. This juristic, legalistic element, so characteristic of ancient Russia and of Old Testament inspiration, is clearly reflected in Raskol's work.

But the epithet most frequently applied to Catholic morality by Orthodox polemists is that of pharisaism. Particular reference is made to the doctrine of probabilism, completely misunderstood by the Easterns from the very beginning. According to Olesnitskij, the school of probabilism teaches an immoral and degenerate morality; it affirms that the end justifies the means, that adultery for procreative purposes is morally justifiable, that sins of drunkenness need not be confessed. Archbishop Nicanor asserts that the pope, exercising his prerogative of infallibility, sanctioned the theory of probabilism to the extent of making it official Catholic doctrine. Certain religious orders, particularly the Jesuits and Redemptorists, are accused of being the promoters of this pernicious doctrine, which is, so they say, an outright negation of the natural moral law. Other religious orders, with no connection whatever to such systems, are accused of nomism, anti-nomism, neo-Pelagianism, casuistry, fanaticism, all perversions proper to Catholics.

Needless to say, such assertions are complete distortions of the truth. The only observation that might here be made is that the rigorism and pessimism of many pre-Slavic moralists have paved the way to laxism and other serious excesses.

Orthodox moralists, therefore, do not believe in the purity and sincerity of Catholic morality. According to them, it is a totally diplomatic and superficial doctrine or system, expressly designed for the political triumph of the pope. Catholic ritual is censured for its purely speculative character and dramatic effects. Interior life has no part in it; if Catholic devotion at times emerges from its cold formalism, it is only to fall into sheer emotionalism and mystical sensualism.

PARTICULAR ASPECTS.

(a) *Evident religious and moral values.* Orthodox moralists strongly insist on the veneration of images, on the use of the holy books and the works of the Fathers, on the necessity of dedicating Sundays and holydays to prayer and recollection, on the obligation of compensating for pious works by hearing Mass, if for some grave reason the obligation could not be fulfilled. The most frequently mentioned virtues to be cultivated are humility, kindness, meekness, love of silence, respect for the aged, charitable hospitality toward pilgrims or wayfarers. Moreover, the evangelical beatitudes occupy an important and central position in textbooks of pre-Slavic morality.

(b) *Doctrinal deficiencies and errors.* Relative to the sacrament of penance, Orthodox moralists are hardly ever concerned with confessional integrity. Some even go to the extent of criticizing Catholic authors for insisting on a detailed enumeration of sins by the penitent (I. Pianitskij). Frequently, they seem to ignore altogether the question of jurisdictional power and reserved sins. The duties of the confessor as a judge are barely mentioned. For some authors, the confessor merely acts as a physician. The problem of restitution is only considered and treated in summary fashion. The treatise *De Justitia* is completely lacking in the moral textbooks, and the solution of questions concerning justice is frequently left to the jurisdiction of the State. Concerning the method of dealing with the different categories of penitents, especially the scrupulous, few directions

are given. No clear distinction is ever made between valid and licit administration or reception of the sacrament of penance.

Concerning the distinction between formal and material, and mortal and venial sin, Orthodox moralists lack precision. The distinction between mortal and venial sin, generally admitted, is not based on the definition of gravity and levity of matter, but on the degree of evidence or force with which a moral act is commanded or forbidden by God.

But the most serious defect in the realm of the sacrament of penance, in which interference by civil authority (caesaropapism) is most apparent, concerns the seal of confession. Following the ecclesiastical regulation of Peter the Great, all pre-Slavic moralists, including such eminent authorities as Tikhon Zandoskij and Popov, make it mandatory for confessors to reveal to the police all information obtained through confession if it relates to national security, sovereignty, or false miracles.

The form of matrimony, according to the majority of Orthodox theologians, consists in the blessing of the priest. All authors admit at least one exception to the indissolubility of marriage: adultery automatically (*ipso facto*) dissolves a marriage.

In conclusion, it may be stated that dissident Eastern moralists reject the doctrine of the evangelical counsels and supererogatory works. They list the commandments of God differently, by making two out of the first commandment and uniting the ninth with the tenth in a prohibition of all internal sins.

Defective in presentation and the victim of Protestant infiltration, Orthodox moral theology may be said to contain appreciable elements only in the measure in which it remains faithful to the doctrine of the Fathers of the Church. *Sti.*

CHURCH, SCHISMATIC. See Schism

CHURCH (Society). The *Church* founded by Jesus Christ, is an external visible society, whose members, under hierarchical authority headed by the pope, constitute with him one visible body, tending to the same spiritual and supernatural end, i.e., sanctification of souls and their eternal happiness.

The Church, which in the Gospels is repeatedly referred to as the *kingdom, kingdom of God, kingdom of heaven,* attains the fulfilment of its spiritual and social aspects in time but has extra-temporal aims and goals. This kingdom has: (a) its own subjects, the faithful; (b) its own hierarchy, bishops, priests, ministers, and deacons; (c) its own means of social transformation, the sacraments; (d) its own specific aims, sanctification and salvation; (e) its own visible or secular history.

The primitive Christian community of Jerusalem, far from being the mystical group of Jewish enthusiasts claimed by rationalist critics, looked to the inspiration of the Holy Spirit for their sole guidance; this community was a true organization or society, with a visible head acting with full authority and vindicating his rights to govern (Acts 1:12 ff.; 6:1 ff.; 15:6 ff.). Moreover, converts, joining this original Christian community, were not abandoned to the alleged guidance of an internal enlightenment, through which they would learn all things, but were directed to obey their leaders (Acts 15:6 ff.).

A careful reading of the entire New Testament (Gospels, Acts of the Apostles, Epistles of St. Paul and the other apostles, and the Apocalypse) and the study of Christ's words and the attitude of the apostles leave no room for doubt that the Christian Church founded by Jesus Christ is not only hierarchical (e.g., John 20:21), but also monarchical, under the authority of one supreme head (Matt. 16:19). Peter and the other apostles were equal in *charismata,* or divine gifts (knowledge, tongues, miracles, etc.) but they were in no way equal in authority. Primacy was Peter's alone.

Peter was chosen supreme head of the Church by the express will of Christ, not by subsequent initiative or agreement on the part of the other apostles. He acted as a representative, not of a pastoral body, but of the Lord. His power, as that of

the members of the apostolic college, could not cease or terminate with the demise of Peter and the other apostles for the obvious reason that the Church, in its authoritative constitution, was to endure until the consummation of the world (Matt. 16:18; 28:20; John 14:16).

The bishops are the legitimate successors of the apostles in their pastoral function, with this difference that, whereas the authority of the apostles extended to all men and to all places, the bishops' authority extends only to the particular territory assigned to them by the Roman Pontiff, from whom directly (at least according to the more common theory) they receive jurisdiction.

Except for the Supreme Pontiff, the bishops are not successors of any apostle in particular, but of the apostolic body or college, whence they inherit their ordinary powers of jurisdiction. Along with an apostolic function, the role of supreme head entails permanent duration and perpetual succession. The authority of the prince of the apostles is the foundation rock of the Church: if this cornerstone crumbles, the edifice built on it by Christ Himself will also crumble.

Peter's physical person ceased to be on the day of his martyrdom, but his juridical and moral personality continues in the popes, who possess the same pastoral dignity. The Sovereign Pontiff enjoys full and supreme power of jurisdiction over the entire Church in matters of faith and morals, as well as in affairs of ecclesiastical discipline.

By virtue of his office, in all ordinary and extraordinary circumstances, the pope possesses a universal pre-eminence and enjoys a truly episcopal authority. His authority is not merely a right of vigilance and control, such as that exercised by metropolitans or patriarchs over their provinces, but a real power of government, similar to that enjoyed by every bishop in his own particular diocese.

Papal authority is direct because it is exercised directly over all the Christian communities, collectively and individually, over the entire body of pastors, collectively and individually, without requirements of any intermediate channels charged with local jurisdiction.

Actually, every diocese in the world has two pastors governing simultaneously with immediate and ordinary jurisdiction, although the bishop is subordinate to the supreme head and teacher by virtue of his primacy. Although ecclesiastical government is monarchical, and the pope is the sole head of the universal Church with all other bishops subject to him, there are elements of aristocratic and democratic rule. The aristocratic aspect is not due to a papal sovereignty divided or divisible, but because the pope, by divine institution, is directed to entrust part of his mission to the care of the bishops. It is democratic, because any members of the Church, regardless of social condition, may, if possessed of the proper qualifications, aspire to the highest ecclesiastical dignities, including the episcopacy and papacy.

THE TRUE CHURCH. Of the numerous Churches calling themselves Christian, and claiming to be established by Christ, the Catholic Church alone is the true one, because she alone possess the true notes or marks of the Church instituted by Christ: unity, holiness, catholicity, appostolicity. For a detailed explanation of these four marks and for proofs showing how they are found in the Roman Church alone, consult works of dogmatic theology.

POWER OF THE CHURCH. Instituted directly by Christ, who endowed it with hierarchical and monarchical authority until the end of the world, the Church has the task of assisting men in their sanctification through administration of the sacraments and other means capable of leading them to the attainment of eternal happiness; the Church is truly a visible society, juridically complete and perfect in its own sphere.

In continuing the work of its Divine Founder, as Teacher, Priest and King, the Church possesses a threefold power: *magisterial, ministerial, jurisdictional.* The *magisterial* power, or teaching authority, was conferred upon the Church by an express mandate of Christ, to go forth and teach all nations (Matt. 18:

18–20; Mark 16:15; *see* Cans. 1322–1323). This teaching authority is exercised by the Church both in a solemn or extraordinary magisterium and in an ordinary magisterium, through *ex cathedra* definitions, conciliar enactments, pontifical acts, the episcopacy, preaching, etc. *Ministerial* power of orders of a priest is conferred through the valid administration of the sacrament of holy orders (*q.v.*) and is directed to divine worship and the sanctification of the faithful. This power embraces primarily the administration of the sacraments (*q.v.*) and the observance of the moral precepts. *Jurisdictional* power is the authority of government (*see* Jurisdiction, Ecclesiastical). It consists in the power to regulate the acts and customs of the faithful according to the requirements of the common good (Canons 196, 218, 335, 2214). Jurisdictional authority comprises a threefold power: legislative (I Cor. 7:12), judicial (Matt. 18:15; I Cor. 4:18; I Tim. 5:19) and coercive (*see* Censure). Wherefore, the Church is a juridically complete and perfect society within its own sphere.

Like every perfect society, the Church exercises true sovereign jurisdiction within her own sphere. Thus, she enacts whatever laws are necessary for her life and development; imposes these laws on all her subjects, by virtue of a divinely acquired right; passes judgment on her subjects, whether or not their attitude is in conformity with her legislative dispositions; inflicts sanctions or penalties on those who disobey her laws.

Finally, it is the right of the Church to exercise civil power over a particular territory (*see* Vatican City), as a necessary means for a free and independent exercise of her authority. She, therefore, has the right to establish contact with all her subjects throughout the world by all means of communication; to send Nuncios and Legates (ordinary and extraordinary) to civil governments and to receive ambassadors from the various chiefs of State. Moreover, as a public authority with legislative, judicial, coercive and civil power, the Church maintains constant relations with other temporal powers, whose subjects are also and at the same time subjects of the Church.

The juridical power of the Church has been the object of attack by those who do not accept the distinction between ecclesiastical and civil society; by those who refuse to recognize the Church as a perfect society; by those who, like Marsilius of Padua and his followers, attack the Church's internal constitution and, therefore, her juridical sovereignty. But despite the denial of the validity of the arguments from Scripture and Tradition, the juridical nature of the Church is clearly manifest in the actual exercise of her spiritual power and in the actual recognition granted to her by temporal rulers. It is an undeniable fact that the Church exists and has exercised for centuries a spiritual, religious, social, and external activity. This is a fact attested to by history and by her role and position in the international sphere.

Through the agency of the Church, men from all quarters of the universe are united in a profession of one creed, an acceptance of one moral code, a participation in the same sacraments and means of sanctification, and obedience to one supreme head, the Roman Pontiff.

From the beginning of her existence, the Church has, without interruption, exercised a true public and legislative power. *The Corpus Juris Canonici* (*q.v.*), the numerous decrees of particular and ecumenical councils, and the countless laws enacted in questions of every kind offer abundant evidence of this. In exercising this public and legislative power, the Church has always considered herself a society distinct from civil authority, and has constantly claimed and vigorously defended her autonomous existence. Temporal kingdoms and empires have crumbled in the wake of revolutionary upheavals, but the Church alone, despite her many enemies, continues, strong, stable, and immutable, through twenty centuries of existence. This extraordinary and amazing phenomenon at least proves the legitimacy of her origin. The continued existence of the Church is even more remarkable, if one considers that this society embraces men of all races, countries, and times, and to each and everyone alike, rich or poor, learned or ignorant, noble or common, she proposes the same ideal of sanctification and the same spiritual means for gaining eternal happiness.

By social and religious action, legislative enactments, actual recognition by civil powers, by political, diplomatic, and other relations (historically undeniable), the Church appears before the entire world as a distinct, independent, and perfect society within her own sphere.

CHURCH AND STATE. By virtue of their separate purposes, Church and State both enjoy sovereign authority in their own respective spheres. In matters pertaining exclusively to their respective spheres, each society is supreme and independent of the other. The Church has received from her Divine Founder the authority to teach, rule, and sanctify men. Hence, whatever is sacred and religious in character that relates to the salvation of souls and the worship of God is subject to the authority of the Church. By the same token, the State enjoys perfect independence in purely civil and political affairs. This is traditional doctrine.

There is no doubt that by their specific ends the two types of society also have specific objects, spiritual in one case, material in the other. Concretely, in practice, it is difficult to determine the exact limits of their jurisdiction. In certain matters an absolute distinction is difficult. Since Church and State both have a visible and social character, both exercise public authority over the same subjects and often legislate for the same matters.

Their respective positions must then be determined by the study of the particular end of each society, religious in one, civil in the other, or by the concept of indirect authority.

Since the spiritual end of man is by nature more exalted and the only true end, for all temporal ends are but means to the spiritual end, a society entrusted with the mission of leading man to the attainment of his spiritual goal is obviously superior to the society whose purpose is to safeguard man's temporal interests. This superiority of the Church over the State and all things temporal is in no way a direct and essential subordination of the latter to the former, but simply an indirect or accidental one. Wherefore, it follows that the Church (a) possesses the right to regulate with full independence of the State all matters directly related to the religious life of the faithful, and the State should yield to ecclesiastical legislation in such matters. (b) In so-called mixed matters, in which the temporal and the spiritual are interconnected, as in matters of education, the State is expected to respect the rights of the Church and recognize her claims. (c) In doubt concerning the religious character of a social institution or movement, the right of deciding the issue belongs to the Church. This constitutes the most difficult norm of all, for it gives rise to the greatest misunderstanding and resentment among those concerned with the temporal interests and prestige of the State. Either the Church is superior to the State or her claim to existence means nothing, for either the spiritual is above the temporal or it does not exist at all. Nor is it fair for one to state that such a principle constitutes an indirect consecration of theocracy which permits the Church to usurp all sorts of authority. The fact of the matter is that from the standpoint of principles this claim is quite consistent with the specific domain of the Church. From the practical standpoint, the danger of abuses by the Church must be considered based more on fear than on fact. The actual danger lies not so much in a restoration of theocracy as in the enslavement of the Church.

These principles govern relations between the Church and State; their application is sought only in Catholic countries. In non-Catholic countries, the Church is satisfied if Catholics are allowed to live unmolested and practice their faith freely. She also seeks to obtain from the State, whenever possible, recognition as a distinct and independent society, entrusted with the religious interests of Catholics (Pius XII, Allocution to members of the 10th International Congress of Historical Sciences, Sept. 2, 1955; Allocution to members of the 6th Congress of the Association of Italian Jurists, Dec. 5, 1954). Since the actual existence of the Church is a fact, many non-Catholic States acknowledge this fact and prefer to negotiate with the Church on the juridical status of Catholics within their territory (see Concordat). Other States deem it incompatible with their sovereignty to deal with an alien power on the legal situation of their own nationals. In such a case, it is up to the Catholic citizens of the country to demand juridical recognition consonant with the exigencies of their faith.

DUTIES TOWARD THE CHURCH. The primary duty of every individual toward the Church, as the continuation of Christ's work, is the same as that owed to Christ Himself, namely, to look into the legitimacy of her claim to spiritual power and to draw the necessary inferences.

The recognition of the legitimacy of the Church's claims binds the members of this society of believers: (a) respectfully to submit to the pastoral office of the Church and those who exercise this office (pope, bishops, and priests); (b) faithfully to observe all ecclesiastical legislation; (c) to accept the juridical and coercive authority of the Church; (d) to participate in the responsibilities and labors of the apostolate. As a living member of the Church, the true Christian will seek daily to increase and strengthen this spiritual life, by endeavoring to overcome his own personal failings, and accepting generously (if unable to remedy) the human elements he finds in the Church, in individuals and institutions. *Pal.*

CIBORIUM. See Custody of the Holy Eucharist.

CINCTURE. See Sacred Vestments.

CINEMA. The *cinema* is unquestionably the most popular form of entertainment and also one of the gravest problems confronting Christian morality. In many respects it is similar to problems which arise from literature and the press, except that the influence of motion pictures on the masses is more powerful and suggestive than that of the printed word. The movie can be an instrument of good and evil. It can serve as a medium of culture and education, legitimate recreation and honest relaxation, and yet it can be a powerful stimulant of man's base passions and emotions. "There exists today no more powerful means of influencing the masses than the cinema" (Pius XI, *Vigilanti Cura,* June 29, 1936; *see also* Letter of the pro-Secretary of State for Ordinary Affairs to the President of the International Catholic Office of Cinematography, June, 1954; Letter of the President of the Pontifical Commission for Cinematography, June, 1953).

A motion picture may come into conflict with the moral law on two grounds: (a) the *theme* portrayed is evil in itself (endorsement of divorce and free love, glorification of vice and crime, ridicule or travesty on religion and public morals); (b) the *manner* of portrayal is objectionable (indecent actions, suggestive or seductive poses, provocative nudity and the like). Nevertheless, in the production of motion pictures it is permitted to have pictures for the young and pictures for adults with broader norms. A morally offensive moving picture does not cease being objectionable simply because of a few final corrective scenes of disapproval. The practical rules in the evaluation of the morality of moving pictures are, with due allowance for certain differences, the same as those established for forbidden books (Can. 1339); *see* Art, Morality of). *Per se,* an immoral motion picture constitutes a proximate occasion of sin and must be judged as such (*see* Occasionist). The classification of motion pictures by the Legion of Decency is simply a declaration that certain films are morally dangerous and constitute a proximate occasion of sin. These classifications, as such, are an exercise of the ordinary

teaching authority of the Church and do not impose any new obligations; they merely specify and underscore an already existing obligation incumbent on every individual not to expose himself rashly to the danger of sin. Naturally, such danger will be more or less proximate, and more or less grave, depending on the character and maturity of the individual. Thus, to view a morally objectionable film admits of various excusing causes. In practice, it is quite difficult to establish absolute norms for all, because individual excusing causes are admissible and the moral classification of films differs in various countries. The production of an immoral motion picture is an evil action in itself, which cannot be justified under any circumstance. Cooperation or participation in harmless roles in an immoral film is permissible for proportionately grave reasons (*see* Cooperation). Viewing an immoral film is a more or less grave sin, depending on the gravity of the danger present, the intensity of venereal excitation (*see* Lust, Chastity, Sin, Actual), the extent of influence on one's moral and religious convictions, etc. Moreover, to attend the showing of an immoral film is always a form of cooperation in evil and is frequently accompanied by an element of scandal. Immoral films involve not only chastity, but other virtues as well. Certain films may undermine religious faith and convictions, destroy respect for life and property, lessen affection for the family. It is a known fact that films glorifying passion and crime give rise to imitative tendencies, especially in the young. It is also to be noted that frequent attendance at the movies, even though the films be morally unobjectionable, may produce unwholesome physical and mental effects, such as a distorted sense of reality, day-dreaming, yearning after inaccessible luxuries and comforts, etc.

The whole problem assumes an even greater magnitude, if one considers that motion pictures hold a particular fascination for children and adolescents, many of whom attend movies several times a week. The harm that bad movies can cause to these impressionable young minds and souls should be a cause of grave concern, and parents and educators must exercise all possible influence that producers adhere scrupulously to the code of decency and morality.

CIRCUMSPECTION. See Prudence.

CIRCUMSTANCES OF A HUMAN ACT. A *circumstance* is something accessory to an act. Since a human act presents both physical and moral aspects, circumstances are distinguished into physical and moral. *Physical* circumstances are all those conditions or accessories which surround the material substance of the act, without modifying or affecting its moral character. *Moral* circumstances are conditions or factors which are added to and modify an already existing morality found in the object of the act. The object of the act is the primary source of morality; circumstances are the secondary source.

Cicero lists seven circumstances: *quis, quid, ubi, quibus auxiliis, cur, quomodo, quando. Quis* indicates the accidental qualities of the operating subject or agent (e.g., the rank, status or condition of a person); *quid* denotes the object of the act, not in its moral substance, but in its accidental forms of quantity or quality (e.g., the quantity or quality of the thing stolen); *ubi* refers to the location or place; *quibus auxiliis* indicates the means used to perform the action (e.g., defamation of character may be committed verbally or by published reports); *cur,* which constitutes the most important circumstance of all, indicates the external motive of the agent (*see* End); *quomodo* expresses the manner of execution, both subjective (e.g., degree of advertence in the agent) and objective (e.g., theft by violence, fraud, etc.); *quando* refers to the time (e.g., duration of an evil intent).

From the standpoint of their efficacy, circumstances are divided into: (a) those which do not alter the moral species of the act, but merely increase or diminish its malice within the limits of the same species (*aggravating* and *extenuating* circumstances); (b) those

which transform the moral species of the act, i.e., add a new species to the already existing morality of the act (e.g., the circumstance of vow adds to a sin of impurity a sin of sacrilege). From the explanation given, it appears that the latter factors changing the moral species of the act do not exactly correspond to the concept of circumstance. They are perhaps circumstances of the physical act. But in a strictly moral sense, one should say that such factors constitute a new object, morally distinct from the one which they physically accompany. If one insists on calling these circumstances, it would be more correct to say that these circumstances add a new moral species, but do not change it. The sacred quality or character of a stolen object does not change the species of the sin, but adds a new sin; it does not alter the species of theft, but to the sin of theft adds a sin of sacrilege.

Some authors prefer the following classification of circumstances: (a) the *moral* species of the act is altered when a new sin or malice is added; (b) circumstances may change the *theological* species of the act by converting a venial sin into a mortal sin and vice versa. For such a classification, aggravating or mitigating circumstances are a subdivision of the categories that alter the theological species of the act. *Gra.*

CITATION, SUMMONS. See Trial.

CITIZEN, CITIZENSHIP. See Subject.

CIVILIZATION. *Civilization* is often synonymous with *culture;* in reality, however, each has its own particular meaning. *Civilization* indicates a process and a state. As a *process,* it refers to the progress of people toward a higher form of social life. As a *state,* it indicates an advanced condition of social life characterized by relative progress in the arts, sciences, customs, and government. *Culture* is a peculiar aspect of civilization, with particular reference to the intellectual achievements of a certain people or a particular period of its history.

In past ages, civilization progressed at a slow pace. Modern civilization, instead, is incessantly on the march, extending to every social sphere, spreading to countries and regions which, until a short time ago, were living in primitive tranquillity. This very fact has created many serious problems in the field of medicine and agriculture, industry and commerce, but particularly in the field of morals.

In the following paragraphs we shall deal with civilization, not as it ideally should be, but as it actually is. We shall examine its advantages and disadvantages both for the individual and society, particularly from the moral point of view.

ADVANTAGES.

(a) *Promotion of culture.* A reduction of illiteracy and the increase of the media of communication (radio, moving pictures, television, etc.) enable man to keep abreast of national and international developments, scientific discoveries, the manners and mores of distant countries, etc. A widespread diffusion of culture has turned modern man into a true citizen of the world. However, a true civilization should contribute in a particular manner to man's moral and religious development.

(b) *Improvement of transportation and travel.* Modern means of transportation are daily becoming more comfortable, rapid, safer, and relatively economical. All this facilitates exchange of commodities between countries, the delivery of food and medical aid to areas stricken by disaster, famine, or other calamities. It helps people attain a better knowledge of other people's ways and customs, which, in turn, contributes to a greater reciprocal understanding. Add to all this increased opportunities of spreading religious practices in regions and territories heretofore nearly inaccessible.

(c) *Control of infectuous diseases.* Civilization has brought a general improvement in hygienic standards, offering protection not only against the epidemic onslaughts of the past, but also against many infectuous diseases which, until relatively recent times, took a heavy toll in human lives. It suffices to consider the marvelous results of *antibiotics* (see

Drugs), which have increased the average life span of human beings.

(d) *Promotion of sports.* General enthusiasm for competitive games and sports must also be considered a beneficial aspect of modern civilization, for such activities undoubtedly contribute to the physical development of the youth of a nation, and help them to release excess energy and to keep occupied and therefore out of trouble. However, sports must be practiced with moderation. Sports and games must not constitute an end in themselves, nor must they be pursued at the expense of man's spiritual development.

(e) *Improved working conditions.* Civilization has brought about social measures designed to improve the workingman's lot; shorter hours, safer conditions, more pleasant and hygienic surroundings, and other benefits. Such improvements enable the working man to carry on his activities without those dangers and physical exertion which until recently made his lot slightly better than that of a brute. More progress, however, remains to be made and such that will enable man to devote more time to his intellectual, social, and moral pursuits.

DISADVANTAGES. Against these obvious benefits of civilization, we cannot ignore the harmful effects wrought by the extremely rapid and tumultuous pace of modern civilization, Enough to mention the following:

(a) *Urbanization.* Lured by the prospect of easier work and bigger pay, as well as by hedonistic mirages of every kind, rural populations leave the tranquillity of their rural living to migrate to the city. Thus, often, the simple, inexperienced but physically fit farmer usually becomes an unskilled worker, living in squalid and over-populated conditions, easy prey of vice and disease. In view of this exodus from the country areas and the fast tempo of city life, the birthrate of some of the more civilized nations shows a sharp decline, with a corresponding rise in deathrate, prostitution and delinquency, which contribute in a considerable degree to the general biological improverishment of the white race.

To the problems of urbanization one can add, at least in some countries, the problems arising from another modern phenomenon known as *suburbanization*, which are no less disturbing.

(b) *Sterility and impotency.* Urbanization with its growing passion for excitement, amusement, and dissipation causes people to lose their reproductive vigor. Sterility and impotency are due not only to vitamin deficiencies caused by modern dietary habits, but even more to a disorderly, restless, and tense way of living. Another factor responsible for sterility and impotency is masculinization of woman; for reasons of financial gain or for a distorted concept of freedom, they entered fields of endeavor not suited to their physical potential, and often incompatible with their fundamental role of motherhood.

(c) *Increase of chronic diseases:* ulcers, tumors, arthritis, heart ailments, arteriosclerosis, etc. This increase is due partly to a lowered mortality rate from acute infection, partly to the fact that modern diagnostic methods are much more accurate than before (especially for the detection of tumors). But the rapid pace of modern living must not be discounted as somewhat responsible for an increase in the number of chronic diseases.

(d) *Increase of neuropsychical diseases.* Constant economic preoccupation, enormous increase of stimuli (especially acoustic), the need to keep up with the times in order to get ahead, emotional labors, hurried eating habits, insufficient and irregular sleep, excessive use of stimulants, tobacco, and drugs, are but some of the dangerous reefs which threaten the vigor of our intellectual life. Genil-Perrin says, "Most of modern man's activities are concentrated in the city, although the din of machines has even reached the countryside. In the city, the artisan's shop has been replaced by the giant department store, the retail shop by the big warehouse; automobiles and trucks roar constantly along, sirens shriek, the telephone rings incessantly.

One eats, works, sleeps in hurried fashion, in an atmosphere of noise, trepidation and restlessness. And our nervous systems, minds, and emotions pay the price for this new evolution." Hence the alarming increase of the mentally ill, the neurotics, the suicidals, and the like.

(e) *Threat of new and more disastrous wars.* Modern means of transportation have been so developed as to practically erase all distance, and make this a small world indeed. Indirectly, this has increased the desire for expansion on the part of the great powers, engaged in a struggle for the conquest of new markets and new sources of wealth. This struggle for expansion and domination, often camouflaged in ideological programs, is favored by the possession of so-called *secret weapons*, which may well ultimately bring about the destruction of humanity.

REMEDIES. Despite serious handicaps, modern civilization must be considered a great good for mankind. But it is necessary that all those concerned with man's future—doctors, sociologists, moralists—collaborate assiduously in making modern progress truly healthy and beneficial and work tirelessly for the reduction and complete elimination of the major causes of material suffering and spiritual harm.

Following are some of the measures required to combat the evils of modern civilization: a well-regulated immigration, permitting a more even distribution of the world's population; improvement of living and working conditions in the rural areas; the encouragement of small business, in order to stem the rush to cities; adequate housing for the poorer classes, keeping in mind that there is an element of truth in the wise aphorism: "Morality is a question of square feet" (R. Sand); social legislation designed to provide economic aid to large families; the return of woman to her natural role of mother and housewife (a move considered indispensable, even by promoters of feminism, for the biological improvement and refinement of modern society).

The Church, especially through the recent popes, has been ever solicitous in warning man against the evils of modern civilization and becoming slaves of machinery, by exhorting woman to return to her queenly position in the home, by recalling that the chief causes of social misery are to be sought in the blind egoism of individuals and wealthier nations.

All the moral and material ills of society have but one source, i.e., a lack of charity, which is the inevitable result of the neglect of the principles of the Gospel. This can only lead, as history teaches, to loss of spiritual values, moral decay, and material ruin.

It is therefore necessary that scientific progress be accompanied by progress in charity taken in the most noble and extensive meaning of the term. Only a progress based on true human solidarity and Christian charity can check and conquer individual egoism, class egoism and the egoism of nations, by eliminating unemployment, poverty, vice, and attempts made at thwarting the very source of life under the most specious pretences.

Individuals must learn to make a wise use of their time, to discipline their pleasures, and to practice honesty, faithfulness and altruism. This will enable them to acquire the balance and inner serenity necessary to proper and sane living and to enjoy the benefits of civilization. *Riz.*

CLANDESTINITY. *See* Marriage, (Form of).

CLASS-WARFARE. *See* Society, Communism.

CLAUSE. *See* Rescript, Testament.

CLAUSTROPHOBIA. *See* Psychasthenia.

CLEARING. *See* Exchange.

CLERGY (Possessions of). Temporal goods of the clergy are possessions from which clerics assigned to the ministry have to derive sustenance, according to the laws of the Church; an inherent right to possess temporal goods is essential to the attainment of the specific ends of the Church and her ministers (Canons 1495, 1496, 1409 ff.).

HISTORICAL BACKGROUND. Priests and Levites of the Old Testament did not receive portions or inheritances, but were supported by offerings and so-called tithes (Num. 18–34; Deut. 18; Jos. 14). Clerics of the primitive Church did not own any particular possessions, but all goods were held in common. (Acts 2:5–6). Later, common possessions were entrusted to cathedral or episcopal churches; the revenue thereof was used to help the poor and needy of the Christian community, for the maintenance of the bishop and the support of the clergy. In Rome the obligatory system was introduced for dividing the entire ecclesiastical revenue into four parts: for the support of the bishop, for the maintenance of the clergy, for the relief of the needy, and for repairs and general maintenance of the sacred edifices. As the number of churches increased, particularly in rural areas, foundations and offerings of the faithful to individual churches made them economically independent.

In the ninth century, the term *beneficium* (benefice) was used to denote the right of a cleric to income derived from the immovable goods of a church to which he was assigned. More properly, however, the term indicated the immovable goods themselves, as a source of income for the cleric (*see* Benefice, Ecclesiastical).

As time went on, clerics acquired personal possessions from their families and other legitimate sources, which they were allowed to retain and to administer. In such cases, they were not permitted to receive an income from church property or to hold benefices, since these were destined solely for those in need. Since certain foundations had been expressly established for the maintenance of the cleric assigned to a particular church or sacred office, the incumbent had a right to the corresponding revenue; this right has been canonized in the present Code of Canon Law (Can. 1409).

Classification of Possessions. Since the establishment of ecclesiastical property was predicated on needs of the poor, the question arose whether clerics were real proprietors of the goods acquired by reason of their office. To solve this doubt, canonists and moralists classified clerical possessions as follows:

(a) *patrimonial possessions* or personal property, acquired by the cleric from inheritance, personal donations, personal industry, etc.;

(b) *quasi-partrimonial possessions* or revenue obtained from the exercise of an ecclesiastical office and functions, stipends or recompense for work performed or services rendered;

(c) *beneficiary or ecclesiastical possessions*, revenue accruing from the ecclesiastical benefice held by the cleric (Can. 1410).

This category admits of a threefold subdivision, which clarifies the proposed doubt. Beneficiary goods are thus classified: (1) *necessary* for proper and decent sustenance, such as food, clothing, home, etc.; (2) *parsimonial*, saved or left over from necessary goods through frugal living; (3) *superfluous*, or left over from both necessary and parsimonial goods.

There is no doubt that clerics have full ownership of patrimonial and quasi-partrimonial property. Concerning revenue from beneficiary goods, clerics have the full dominion required for their suitable maintenance. A benefice is granted to a cleric simply as remuneration for service. Hence, if a cleric has both patrimonial property and beneficiary revenue, he may freely use his beneficiary revenue for his proper maintenance and save his patrimonial possessions (Cans. 1472–1475). He is, however, bound to use superfluous income for the relief of the poor or charitable causes (Can. 1473).

The holder of a benefice is not the owner thereof (*see* Benefice, Ecclesiastical); hence, he may not perform acts or contracts beyond the area of simple administration. He does not have absolute but curatorial right over the benefice; his right is subordinated to the exercise of his sacred office. In other words, a beneficiary is like a tutor or guardian who must protect the interests of his benefice.

During his tenure (*pro rata temporis*), he is entitled not only to all legal revenue, but to all natural proceeds and pending returns. The beneficiary has obligations similar to those of the usufructuary; he has no right of prescription with regard to the benefice (Cans. 1476 ff.; 1522 ff.).

In the eyes of the civil law, clerics do not constitute a special class of citizens. *Tar.*

CLERGY (Privileges of). In a broad sense, the expression *privileges of the clergy* may be used to denote the special prerogatives of the clerical state, e.g., the exclusive right to ecclesiastical jurisdiction and ecclesiastical benefices (Can. 118), the right of precedence (Can. 491), etc. According to traditional canonical doctrine, confirmed by the Code of Canon Law (bk. II, part I, sect. I, tit. 2), the expression is technically employed to indicate four specific privileges or special rights of the clerical state, aimed at protecting the dignity of the clergy (Cans. 119–122).

(a) *Privilege of the Canon* (*privilegium canonis*). By this privilege, also known as the privilege of personal inviolability, clerics are accorded special juridical protection against all personal violence or real injury: striking or wounding a cleric constitutes a sacrilege (*q.v.*) punishable by grave ecclesiastical penalties. Historically, the privilege derives its name from the Second Lateran Council (1139), "*si quis suadente diabolo*" (C. 17, 4, 29) in which the crime is punished with severe canonical penalties, including excommunication. In earlier times penalties were not as severe. In the middle of the twelfth century, due to the instigation of politico-religious agitators, such as Arnold of Brescia, excesses were committed against defenseless clergy and religious, who were forbidden to carry weapons; the Church was compelled to make stricter laws. The Second Lateran Council decreed that whoever laid malicious hands on a cleric or monk incurred *ipso facto* anathema; absolution from this excommunication was reserved, except in danger of death, to the pope, and nust be sought in person at Rome. This extraordinarily severe penalty was somewhat mitigated in subsequent legislation. According to the present Code of Canon Law (Cans. 119, 2343), penalties vary according to the dignity of the cleric attacked: persons who lay violent hands on the person of the Roman pontiff automatically incur excommunication (*latae sententiae*) reserved in a most special manner (*specialissimo modo*) to the Holy See; persons who lay violent hands on the person of a cardinal, apostolic legate, patriarch, metropolitan, or bishop automatically incur excommunication reserved in a special manner (*special modo*) to the Holy See; persons who lay violent hands on other clerics, including religious men or women, automatically incur excommunication reserved to the local Ordinary of the aggressor.

(b) *Privilege of the Forum* (*privilegium fori*). By virtue of this privilege, the clergy is exempt from the authority of secular courts. Clerics are tried, in civil and criminal matters, by the ecclesiastical tribunal, unless it shall legitimately established otherwise, either by concordat or custom. In the early Church, following the suggestion of St. Paul (I Cor. 6:1 ff.), many of the faithful requested their bishop to be a judge, not only in ecclesiastical, but in civil matters. From this practice, a true system of privileges for the clergy was gradually incorporated in Canon Law (C. II, q. 1, 43, 46–47; X, 2, 1, 8, 10, 17; X, 2, 2, 1, 2, 9, 12, 13). This system of privileges was recognized by Roman law (*Nov.* 123, c. 8 and c. 21) and, later, by Germanic law (*Synod. Francofurti,* a. 794, c. 30 and c. 39; *Authentica Friderici II, Statuimus,* a. 1220). However, after the Middle Ages, the privilege of the forum was gradually restricted and, finally, abrogated by civil authority. The Church has always defended the *privilegium fori* as a matter of principle, but in practice, frequently, has been compelled to relinquish this position, either by granting particular derogations in concordats, or by recognizing contrary customs. The Code of Canon Law (Can.

120) retains in principle the privilege of the forum; it does not permit citation of a cleric before a secular court without permission of the competent ecclesiastical authority. None of the following may be sued before secular courts without permission of the Holy See: cardinals, apostolic legates, bishops, abbots or prelates *nullius*, the supreme heads of religious organizations of pontifical right, and major officials of the Roman curia. All other clerics may not be sued in secular courts without permission of the Ordinary of the place where the case is to be tried (Can. 120, par. 1–2). If anyone, in violation of these regulations, dares to cite before a lay judge any of these officials, cardinals, apostolic legates, officials of the Roman Curia in matters pertaining to their office, or the local Ordinary, he incurs *ipso facto* (automatically) by his actions an excommunication which is reserved in a special manner (*modo speciali*) to the Holy See. If one dares to cite another bishop, abbot, prelate *nullius*, or supreme head of a religious organization of papal right, he automatically incurs excommunication, reserved simply (*simpliciter*) to the Holy See. Specific penalties are also established for other cases (Can. 2341).

(c) *Privilege of Immunity* (*privilegium immunitatis*). By immunity is meant *personal immunity*, distinguished from real and local immunity. This privilege consists in exemption of the clergy from certain civil burdens and obligations. This exemption dates to the time of Constantine the Great, who exempted ecclesiastics from certain burdens (*munera sordida*: Nov. 123, c. 5); this was also generally recognized by Germanic law. The Church sought this privilege especially in the Middle Ages (X, 3, 49, 4, 7; VI, 3, 20, 4; VI, 3, 23, 3). It was also recognized by Frederick II (*Authentica, Item Nulla*) in the year 1220. In modern times, especially after the French Revolution, the privilege was not recognized by civil authorities, but the Church has constantly held to it. The Code of Canon Law (Can. 121) establishes that clerics are exempt from military service and from all civil duties and offices incompatible with the clerical state, such as the office of judge, notary, juror, witness, etc. (Can. 139). The privilege of personal immunity is not protected by special penalties, but by general criminal law, which inflicts excommunication on those who issue laws, mandates, or decrees against the rights of the Church (Can. 2334). In certain States the question is regulated by concordats.

(d) *The Privilege of Competency* (*privilegium competentiae*). By virtue of this privilege, the clergy retains the right, in the event of attachment of property by creditors, to a sufficient income for decent maintenance, according to the prudent judgment of the ecclesiastical judge. Clerics, however, are bound to satisfy their creditors as soon as possible (Can. 122). Similar to the *beneficium competentiae* of Roman law in favor of soldiers (D., 42, 1, 6 and 18), this principle is actually based on an ecclesiastical principle, contained in several canons: a cleric may not be reduced to such a condition in life that he is forced to seek livelihood in an unworthy manner. This is probably the motivating idea behind the extensive interpretation (X, 3, 23, 3) frequently quoted as the source of this privilege. This privilege, like the preceding one, is not protected by any special penalties. Today, it is recognized in a number of nations, either by concordats or by similar civil laws relating to civil servants, including clerics.

The aforementioned privileges are enjoyed by the following: (a) clerics; (b) male or female members (including novices) of orders or congregations (Can. 614); (c) members of a society living common life without vows (Can. 680).

Those who enjoy these privileges cannot renounce them (Can. 123), because the privileges are granted to them by reason of their clerical state, as such. The privileges are lost immediately by reduction of an ecclesiastic to the lay state, by degradation, or by loss of the right to wear the ecclesiastical garb (Canons 123, 2300, 2304, 2305). Lay religious and members of religious communities without vows lose these privileges if they leave the clerical state of their own accord or by dismissal (Canons 637–640; 648; 669, par. 1). *Led.*

CLERIC. Since the third century, the term *cleric* (Greek, *kleros*—portion, lot) has been used to designate those set apart for the service of the altar, because they "are the Lord's portion or because the Lord is their lot" (St. Jerome, *Ep. 52 ad Nepot. 5*).

Men become clerics or members of the clergy by divine or ecclesiastical right in the initial ceremony of tonsure. Clerics are a special group in the Church, distinct by divine right from the laity; hence, they have special rights and duties. According to the order received, they have partial or full power of orders, which makes them eligible for the power of jurisdiction and ecclesiastical offices (Can. 118). The clerical state implies higher duties than those of ordinary faithful. Such duties may be negative and positive.

NEGATIVE DUTIES OF CLERICS.

(a) They must abstain from all things that are unbecoming to the clerical state (Can. 138): (1) they must not exercise arts unbefitting the clerical state; (2) nor take part in games of chance for money; (3) nor carry weapons, unless there is a justifying cause; (4) they must not, as a rule, engage in hunting games, particularly if accompanied by much display and publicity; (5) they must stay away from saloons or other similar places, except in necessity or other just reasons, approved by the local Ordinary.

(b) They must avoid occupations or arts which, not unbecoming in themselves, are alien to the clerical state (Can. 139). Specifically, (1) without apostolic indult, clerics must not practice medicine or surgery, except in a case of necessity; (2) they must not exercise the office of notary public, except in an ecclesiastical curia, (3) nor accept offices entailing secular jurisdiction or administration. (4) Without permission of their Ordinary, they must not act as agents concerning goods and property of lay people, nor assume secular offices with the obligation to submit an administrative account. (5) They shall not exercise the office of solicitor or attorney, except in an ecclesiastical court. In the civil court, this is permissible only in cases in which their own personal affairs are involved or the affairs of their own church. (6) They are exhorted further not to take part, not even as witnesses, in criminal cases tried in secular courts, unless compelled to do so, when it is necessary to avert grave personal damage. (7) Without permission of the Holy See, clerics are not allowed to seek or accept the offices of senator or representative in those countries where this is forbidden by the Holy See. In other countries, they shall not seek or accept these offices without permission of their own Ordinary as well as of the Ordinary of the place where the election may take place. (8) They must not attend public spectacles, such as theatrical performances, dances, and shows, unbecoming to the clergy, where their attendance might cause scandal (Can. 140). (9) They must not volunteer for military service (Can. 141, par. 1), without permission of their Ordinary, nor for the sake of discharging their service at an earlier date in those countries where there is compulsory military service for all. Clerics who contravene this disposition of the law automatically (*ipso facto*) forfeit their clerical rank (Can. 141, par. 2). (10) They are forbidden to engage either personally, or through others, in any business or trade, whether for their own benefit or that of others (Cans. 142, 2380). Violation of this law is today punishable by automatic excommunication (*latae sententiae, speciali modo reservata*) reserved in a special manner to the Holy See (AAS: 42 [1950], 330–331). (11) They are forbidden to post bail or be surety for anyone, even with their own money, without permission of their own Ordinary (Can. 137). (12) They are not permitted to wear a ring, except by right or by apostolic privilege (Can. 136, par. 2). (13) Clerics, including those without a benefice or office which requires residence, are forbidden to be absent from their diocese for a notable length of time, without at least a presumed permission of their Ordinary (Can. 143). (14) *Incardination* (*q.v.*) is a grave obligation and the source of all other obligations (Can. 11, 144). (15) Clerics are strictly forbidden to induce any person to promise by a vow, to swear or otherwise to promise with or without an oath, that they shall select their church or cemetery for funeral or burial, or change a selection already made (Can. 1227). (16) They are not allowed to act as pallbearers at the funerals of lay persons, no matter what their dignity or status; they may, however, carry the body of another cleric (Can. 1233, par. 4). (17) Secular clerics are forbidden to publish any book on secular topics, or to contribute to or publish daily papers, periodicals, pamphlets, booklets, without permission of their Ordinaries; religious must have permission of both their own major superiors and the local Ordinary (Can. 1386). (18) A cleric in major orders may not resign his benefice, and the Ordinary may not accept such renunciation, unless it is certain that the cleric has other sources from which to derive a suitable livelihood.

According to Canon 124, clerics are required to lead a particularly holy and exemplary life.

POSITIVE OBLIGATIONS.

(a) *Absolute Chastity* (Cans. 132–133; 1072; 2176–81; 2358–59; 2388). Clerics in major orders are bound by this obligation of chastity so that they can neither validly nor licitly contract marriage (in the Latin Church); by violation of this law, a cleric sins against chastity and commits a sin of sacrilege. Clerics in minor orders, on the other hand, may contract marriage, but, by so doing, they automatically cease to be clerics, unless the marriage is declared null by reason of violence or intimidation (*see* Celibacy; Orders, impediment of).

As a consequence of the obligation of chastity, clerics may not allow women under suspicion to live in their houses (*see* Celibacy).

(b) *Obedience to the Ordinary*. All clerics, particularly priests, are bound by a special duty to respect and obey their own Ordinary (Can. 127). Hence, unless there is a legitimate impediment, clerics must accept and faithfully discharge any office assigned to them by the Ordinary, as often and as long as the bishop deems it necessary for the good of the Church (Can. 128).

(c) *Common Life.* This is not an obligation in a strict sense. However, it is a laudable custom and is to be encouraged (Can. 134); moreover, wherever such custom exists, it is to be continued insofar as it is possible.

(d) *Ecclesiastical Garb.* All clerics, without exception, must wear a becoming clerical garb, in accord with approved customs of the country and relative prescriptions of the local Ordinary. They must have clerical tonsure, unless the custom of the country disallows it, and they must avoid vanity in the dressing of their hair (Can. 136).

(e) *Pursuance of Sacred Studies.* After their ordination to the priesthood, clerics must not neglect study, especially that of the sacred sciences. Canon 130 requires annual examinations following sacerdotal ordination; and Canon 131 demands the so-called clerical or diocesan conferences. In the sacred sciences they must always follow sound doctrines and opinions handed down by the Fathers and commonly accepted by the Church, and avoid all secular novelties of expression and false science (Can. 129; Encycl. *Humani generis,* August 12, 1950: AAS, 42 [1950], 561–578).

(f) *Catechetical Instruction to Children.* Priests and other clerics, unless legitimately impeded, are obliged to assist the pastor in the religious instruction of children; they may be ordered to perform this holy work by the Ordinary, even under threat of ecclesiastical penalties (Can. 1333, par. 2).

(g) *Participation* in all processions organized by the Church to which they are assigned (Can. 1294, par. 2).

(h) The cleric or religious who has received goods in trust for pious causes must notify the Ordinary, listing all movable and immovable goods with all the obligations attached thereto (Can. 1516, par. 1).

The power of orders (*see* Orders, Holy) enjoyed by a cleric is never lost, even if its exercise is forbidden or restricted. A cleric, however, may lose the juridical status and other juridical effects of holy orders for a variety of causes, among them reduction to the lay state (*q.v.*).

Concerning privileges, *see* Clergy (privileges of the).

CLERICALISM. *See* Anticlericalism.

CLIMACTERIC. *See* Gonads.

CLOISTER. *Cloister* (Latin, *clausura*—an enclosure) refers to the rigorous rule of certain religious institutes of men and women, which forbids the free egress of members from the religious house (*active cloister*) and the free entry of outsiders into a religious house (*passive cloister*). Taken in a material sense, *cloister* refers to the entire space within a convent enclosed and reserved for the exclusive use of its religious members.

Of very ancient origin, the cloister was introduced through custom more than by a general written law. Nevertheless, particular synods spoke of a monastic cloister in the active meaning of the term, i.e., in the sense of forbidding egress from the monastery, but such discipline was not uniform and general within the Church, nor were sanctions or canonical penalties for violators attached thereto. No general law of enclosure is found either in Gratian or in the *Decretals.* The first general law regarding enclosure of nuns was issued by Boniface VIII (1294–1303). In his Constitution *Periculoso* (*De Statu Regularium,* VI, 3, 16) he imposed cloister on all nuns, strictly forbidding all egress from the monastery as well as any free entry of outsiders. These prescriptive measures were later confirmed by the Council of Trent (*Sess.* XXV, c. 5, *De regul.*), in which the penalty of excommunication was added for those entering the cloister unlawfully.

The cloister of male religious, which up to the time of Pius V (1566–1572) was governed by particular laws and customs, was imposed as a general law by the same Pontiff through the Constitution *Regularium personarum* of October 24, 1566. The notable feature was the exclusion of women from convents of male regulars under penalty of excommunication. Subsequent privileges and abuses occasioned the Constitution *Regularis* (Jan. 3, 1742) of Benedict XIV, who reorganized the discipline of the cloister and increased the already existing penalties in order to discourage any abuse. General prescriptions regarding cloister are found in Canons 597–607 of the present Code. Penalties for violators of the law of enclosure are contained in Canon 2342.

The principal object of the law of enclosure is to safeguard the virtue of religious chastity and to insure the recollection and tranquillity required for religious life.

According to present ecclesiastical discipline, enclosure is either *papal* or *episcopal*. *Papal* enclosure, which carries severe penalties established by common law for its violators, must be observed in all houses of religious men and women with solemn vows. *Episcopal* enclosure, with no special penalties of the common law for violators, is to be observed in institutes of religious men and women bound by simple vows only. These two types of enclosure oblige both male and female religious, but in a different manner.

Papal enclosure, considered with particular reference to male religious, extends to the entire religious house or convent inhabited by the regular community, even if it consists of less than six members (*domus non formata*: Can. 597, par. 1). Under the law of enclosure are included orchards or gardens reserved exclusively to the religious (Can. 597, par. 2). Excluded from the enclosure are the church, sacristy and parlors, which should be near the entrance of the religious house. Women of any age, status, or condition are strictly forbidden to enter under any pretext the encloistered portions of a house of male religious. Exception to this law is made for the wives of the highest actual rulers of states and their lady attendant (Can. 598).

No person, regardless of sex, age, rank, or condition, may be admitted within the enclosure of nuns with solemn vows without permission of the Holy See. The only exceptions are: (1) The local Ordinary or the regular Superior of the nuns, in making the canonical visitation; in this case they must be accompanied by at least one cleric or religious of mature age (Can. 600, par. 1). (2) The confessor, chaplain, or any other priest, in administering the sacraments to the sick, assisting the dying (Can. 600, par. 2), or conducting funeral services. (3) Rulers of state with their wives and retinue, and cardinals (Can. 600, par. 3), accompanied by a cleric or a lay domestic. (4) Doctors, surgeons, and repairmen, with at least habitual or presumed permission of the local Ordinary (Can. 600, par. 4).

Without approval or permission of the Holy See nuns may not admit young girls within the enclosure either for teaching or any other religious purpose, such as First Communion.

Following their profession, under no pretext may the sisters go out of the cloister, even for a short time, without special permission of the Holy See, except in the following cases: (a) danger of death, or other serious peril, such as fire, war, necessary surgical operation or medical treatment; (b) to accompany a sister requiring an operation, or medical treatment; (c) any other grave necessity, such as protection of property, administrative reasons, the apostolate, and the like (Can. 601, par. 1–2; Instruction of the Sacred Congregation for Religious, March 25, 1956: AAS 48 [1956] 516 ff.).

In societies of men or women living in community life, with or without vows, the enclosure must be observed according to the dispositions of their respective constitutions, under the immediate vigilance of the local Ordinary (Cans. 604; 679, par. 2).

Violators of papal enclosure of male religious incur excommunication simply reserved to the Holy See. The excommunication is incurred not only by those admitting women or girls (even if under twelve years of age), but also by women who enter the enclosure, if they are over the age of puberty (Can. 2342, par. 2). Religious superiors must see to it that the prescriptions of their constitutions be faithfully observed concerning both the egress of their subjects from the cloister and receiving visits from outsiders (Can. 606, par. 1).

Violators of the enclosure of nuns also incur excommunication simply reserved to the Holy See. The penalty is incurred by those who enter the enclosure, by those who introduce or admit outsiders within its limits, and by the nuns who unlawfully go outside the cloister (Can. 2342, n. 1).

The local Ordinary has the right to inflict penalties and censures (Can. 603, par. 1) against violators of the enclosure of male or female institutes living in community life.

By virtue of the Apostolic Constitution *Sponsa Christi*, (Nov. 21, 1950; AAS, 43 [1951] 1 ff.), and the complementary Instructions of the Sacred Congregation for Religious (Nov. 23, 1950; AAS, 43 [1951] 37 ff.; March 25, 1956; AAS, 48 [1956] 512–526), rules concerning the enclosure of nuns underwent notable changes and relaxations, aimed at making the life of cloistered nuns better suited to present-day conditions.

It should be noted that papal enclosure may be *major* (more rigorous form) or *minor* (a more moderate form). The major papal enclosure is the one described in the Code of Canon Law and in the above-mentioned Instructions of the Sacred Congregation for Religious. It is obligatory in all monasteries of religious with solemn vows, leading a strictly contemplative life. The minor papal enclosure, obligatory in all monasteries of nuns, even those which by apostolic indult or by way of exception take only simple vows, is restricted to monasteries engaged in external activities. It may be extended also to those sisters who, leading a strictly contemplative life, profess only simple vows. In the case of minor enclosure, the convent has parts reserved exclusively to the sisters and parts set aside for external activities, i.e., accessible both to the sisters engaged in such activities and to other persons so authorized. Externs who unlawfully enter these latter sections of the convent are subject to penalties determined by the Ordinary. But if they enter the sections reserved exclusively for the sisters, they incur the penalties set forth in Canon 2342, par. 1.

Mention was made of the fact that cloistered nuns may, according to the new legislation, engage in an external apostolate without prejudice to their special form of life.

A cloistered monastery is, of itself, an independent and autonomous unit without juridical dependence on any other. The new norms, while preserving such autonomy, envision the possibility of a federation of monasteries, to be effected with papal approval, for the purpose of attaining greater moral, religious, and economic advantages for the entire community.

CLOTHES. The use of clothes is based upon three fundamental factors: (a) *hygienic* protection of the body; (b) *aesthetic* ornament; (c) *modesty* (*q.v.*). The considerations based on hygiene and aesthetics stem from man's physical and psychological constitution. The factor of decency, instead, is the result of original sin, which upset the harmony between reason and the sensitive appetite as it existed in the state of original innocence, when all clothing was superfluous (Gen. 2:25; 3:7). These factors gave rise to a vast quantitative and qualitative diversity of clothes among the various peoples, which were regulated by their different climatic conditions, their degree of civilization, and their moral sense.

Christian morals permit and prescribe a modest and reasonable way of dressing, in keeping with one's social condition, without exaggeration or negligence, and according to the requirements of hygiene and modesty (*q.v.*).

Fashion is not evil in itself. Abuses in the mode of dressing are caused either by a disregard for the purpose of dress itself or by an exaggeration of its use. In practice, a way of dressing is immoral either by reason of an inordinate end in view (immoderate pleasure, desire to attract, seduction, etc.) or because of the detrimental effects it produces, even if done unintentionally (economic, physical, and especially moral damage). With regard to the moral effects of dressing, all wearing apparel that endangers the virtue of the one who wears them or of others is objectionable. These clothes, especially feminine, either because of exaggerated exposure, transparency or fit do not conceal enough or emphasize the sexual characteristics to excite the passions. In sacred places, in religious services, or in reception of the sacraments, dresses must be unprovocative of temptation and positively modest, as is demanded by the reverence due to such places and services (I Cor. 11:5; Can. 1262, par. 2).

The sad experience of grave harm caused by immodest dressing justifies fully the complaints of pastors of souls on this point. These complaints have been voiced in every period of history by many holy and apostolic men. But in recent decades high ecclesiastical authorities have stepped into this field. Among many official pronouncements are: the address of Benedict XV to the members of the Italian Catholic Women's Union, October 21, 1919; the instruction of the Sacred Congregation of Council, *Ad Ordinarios dioecesanos: de inhonesto feminarum vestiendi more*, January 12, 1930; and the address of Pius XII to young women of Catholic Action of Rome, May 22, 1941. Among the many pastoral letters of bishops in almost every country in the world, the circular letter of the German Episcopate in 1925 deserves special attention: *Katholosche Leisätze und Weisungen zu verschiedenen modernen Sittlichkeitsfragen*, along with the commentary by Father Schroteler, S. J., *Um Sitte und Sittlichkeit*, Dusseldorf, 1926. *Dam.*

COACTION. See Violence.

COADJUTOR. In Canon Law the general term *coadjutor* applies to those who permanently assist a beneficiary in his office (Can. 1433). Coadjutorships as such are not beneficed positions (Can. 1412, n. 2). The Council of Trent (*Sess.* XXV, *De reform.*, ch. 7) abolished all but episcopal and abbatial coadjutorships (*ecclesiae cathedralis et monasterii*); the present Code of Canon Law expressly speaks only of coadjutors to bishops and pastors. However, the other forms of coadjutorships may be instituted by particular law.

EPISCOPAL COADJUTORS. The position of the episcopal coadjutor, already well-defined in the first centuries of the Christian era, evolved into a variety of forms. The so-called *chorepiscopi* were, at least in the beginning, rural bishops, who assisted the diocesan bishops, residing in the cities; these may be considered coadjutors. Furthermore, coadjutors were assigned to bishops incapacitated because of age or illness. Thus, St. Augustine served for a certain period of time as coadjutor to Valerius, bishop of Hippo. In the Middle Ages, exiled bishops or bishops expelled from their own sees (ordinarily called thereafter titular bishops) were frequently employed as coadjutors to Ordinaries of a diocese. At the beginning of the present century, canonists were wont to distinguish coadjutors into *Vicarii in pontificalibus* and *coadjutores Episcoporum* (F. X. Wernz, *Ius Decretalium*, II, p. 635 ff.; I. B. Sagnuller, *Lehrbuch des Katholischen Kirchenrechts*, I, P. 460 ff.).

Present ecclesiastical law (Cans. 350–355) distinguishes three types of episcopal coadjutors: coadjutor to the person, coadjutor to the see, and coadjutor assigned at the same time to the person and to the see. Since the time of Boniface VIII, episcopal coadjutors may be appointed only by the pope.

(a) *Coadjutor assigned to the person of a bishop incapacitated because of age or illness.* Such a coadjutor may be assigned to an Ordinary with or without right of succession upon vacancy of the see. In the former case, he is more properly called *coadjutor*; in the latter case, he is called more properly *auxiliary*. The personal powers of a coadjutor are generally established in the apostolic decree of appointment. Unless otherwise stated in the decree, the following canonical norms apply: the coadjutor assigned to an Ordinary who is entirely incapacitated has full episcopal rights and duties; in other cases, the coadjutor may exercise only such rights and duties as are committed to him by the incumbent bishop. But the latter may not delegate to others what the coadjutor could and is willing to do. The coadjutor is obliged to perform, unless legitimately impeded, all pontifical functions entrusted to him by the Ordinary. Upon vacancy of the see, the coadjutor with the right of succession automatically becomes the Ordinary, i.e., bishop of the diocese. Otherwise, the office of auxiliary bishop expires with the death or removal of the Ordinary whose personal assistant he was, unless the decree of appointment provides otherwise.

(b) *Coadjutor assigned to an episcopal see, generally because of the size of the territory.* Such a coadjutor has the right to exercise all episcopal functions within the diocesan territory, except sacred ordination. (Hence, in Germany such a bishop is called *Weihbischof.*) In other episcopal matters, he can do only whatever is committed to him either by the Holy See or by the Ordinary. Since such a coadjutor is assigned to the see or diocese, his office continues during the vacancy of the see.

All episcopal coadjutors are bound by the law of residence within the diocese.

Parochial Coadjutors. The priest who acts for a pastor who, because of old age, mental debility, incompetence, blindness, or other permanent disability, is unable to discharge his duties properly, is called a *vicar coadjutor* (Can. 475, par. 1; *see* Vicar Parochial).

Abbatial Coadjutors. As noted above, besides episcopal coadjutors, the Council of Trent admitted also abbatial coadjutors. The present Code does not expressly mention the latter type of coadjutorship, but neither does it indicate that such an office was abrogated. Thus, even on the basis of the present Code (Can. 6) it is possible to have abbatial coadjutors, for whom the same norms apply as for episcopal coadjutors (Mayer, *Benediktinisches Ordensrecht,* II [1932], p. 161).

Coadjutors to other Beneficiaries. By particular law, i.e., by apostolic indult, coadjutors may be assigned to other beneficed persons. The juridical condition or status of such coadjutors is determined by the particular law. *Led.*

COALESCENCE OF THEFTS. See Theft.

COALITION, MERGER. A *coalition* or *merger* is a term which is used to designate an economic system of industrial concentration, quite different from that of competition and more or less approximating that of monopoly. This system is effected through the establishment of coalitions or industrial syndicates or mergers.

Combinations may be effected by:

(a) *Temporary agreement.* Various firms, for the purpose of controlling the market, buy the available quantity of a particular commodity or agree to diminish the production of a certain commodity or limit its distribution or supply, all for the sake of artificially raising price. Such combinations may be effective in systems of closed market, particularly during war time.

(b) *Cartels.* Each enterprise preserves its own autonomy, but joins with others for the sake of exercising control over all or one of the following factors: quantity of production, price, respective market.

Cartels are called *pools* if a central controlling body is established to supervise the activities of the associated enterprises in the purchase of raw material, an assigned production, and sales quotas.

In a special form of cartel the separate enterprises nominally preserve autonomy but their shares and stocks are acquired and held by one and the same *holding company,* which controls and directs the business policies of the member organizations.

(c) *Trusts.* Individual business organizations are united or integrated into a new industrial organism (*board of trustees*), with each member organization losing its own juridical personality.

Combinations may be constituted of business units in the same type of industry or in complementary industries; in either case, the aim is always the same: to increase profit by diminishing the cost of production and maintaining the sales price unaltered.

Combinations are the result of competition. In the competitive business struggle, the smaller and weaker enterprises succumb, while the more energetic and efficient survive. The struggle among the survivors becomes ever more intense and costly, reaching a point where competitors are either driven to bankruptcy or forced to establish one of the above-mentioned combinations.

Combinations often give rise to grave social and moral problems. We shall mention here a few of the more important ones. First of all, they may grow to the point of assuming gigantic proportions involving the investment of enormous capital; while they create work for tens and even hundreds of thousands of employees, they are often responsible for crises of overproduction. In such cases they become so powerful that they exert extensive pressure on government authorities to favor their interests against the interests of the community. Furthermore, as already noted, the aim of combinations is to lower cost rather than to increase prices. Once they have gained control of the markets, they often seek increasingly greater profits for themselves by setting their own prices, without regard for the interests of the consumer.

Combinations are even capable of selling their wares in foreign markets at abnormally low prices, thus breaking the local market and driving local producers out of business (*dumping*). Pav.

COCAINE. See Aphrodisiacs, Drugs, Narcotics.

COCKTAILS. See Alcoholism.

CODE OF CANON LAW. *Sources of Law before the Code of Canon Law.* In the eighteenth and nineteenth centuries the general canonical (pontifical) law of the Latin Church was found in the collections belonging to the *Corpus juris canonici* (*q.v.*) and the decrees of the Council of Trent. Besides these sources, whose texts were arranged in a very unsatisfactory way, there were compilations containing the acts of the popes and the various departments of the Roman Curia, all arranged in a chronological order.

This made the study and application of Canon Law quite difficult. It was even more so because many of the texts were abrogated; some were provisions of a particular nature from which often a norm had to be drawn; quite a few of them were mere repetitions, in which gaps of various sorts were present.

In view of this situation, but especially because the civil States had begun to organize a great part of their juridical norms into codes, canonists considered the advisability of codifying the entire legislation of the Church according to modern criteria.

Preparatory Work for Codification. In studies and meetings preparatory to the First Vatican Council (1869–1870), cardinals and prelates urged various reforms concerning this or that point of ecclesiastical legislation, with frequent allusions to its codification.

Besides such doctrinal preparation, there was also legislative preparatory work. Several apostolic constitutions were issued which, while reforming current legislation on specific matters, served as partial codifications or special texts. Principal among these are: *Apostolicae Sedis,* (Pius IX, Oct. 12, 1869), *Officiorum ac munerum* (Leo XIII, Jan. 23, 1897), *Conditae a Christo* (Dec. 8, 1900).

In 1904, the preparatory work for the codification of canon law was officially begun by order of Pope St. Pius X. Bishops throughout the world were requested to make known to the pope the reforms they desired. At the same time a commission of cardinals, assisted by numerous consultors and collaborators, was charged with preparing outlines of various parts of what finally became the Codex Juris Canonici. The outlines were submitted to intense and accurate study, frequent discussions, and revisions.

In 1914 the plans thus elaborated were forwarded to the Ordinaries of the Latin Church, whose observations were carefully considered before a new and final plan was prepared and submitted to all the cardinals and prelates of the Roman Curia for their observations.

Promoter and chief architect of all this preparatory work was Peter Cardinal Gasparri.

On May 27, 1917, Pentecost Sunday, Benedict XV, through the Apostolic Constitution *Providentissima Mater* promulgated the new Code, the text of which was published in *Acta Apostolicae Sedis* (vol. IX, part II, June 28, 1917). The Code went into effect on Penecost Sunday, May 19, 1918, with the exception of a few canons which were put into force earlier.

The official title of the Code is: *Codex iuris canonici Pii X Pontificis Maximi iussu digestus, Benedicti papae XV auctoritate promulgatus.*

The Code consists of 2414 canons, plus eight documents (later nine, but presently reduced to six) containing particular norms, to which the reader is referred by the Code itself.

The Canons are grouped into five books: *Normae generales* (Can. 1–86), *De personis* (Can. 87–725), *De rebus* (Can. 726–1551), *De processibus* (Can. 1552–2194), *De delictis et poenis* (Can. 2194–2414). Canon 1099 was modified by the motu proprio *Ne temere* of August 1, 1948; similarly, Canon 2319, par. 1, n. 1, by the motu proprio *Ecclesiae bonum*, of December 25, 1953. There have also been modifications relative to the Eucharistic fast on the last three days of Holy Week (*see* Communion, Holy Mass) and those relative to the right of appeal to the Tribunal of the Sacred Rota, in derogation of Canon 1599, par. 1 (*see* Roman Rota, Sacred).

Each book is divided into parts, sections, titles, chapters, and articles; the longer Canons are divided into paragraphs and/or numbers.

Besides the official edition which appeared in the above-mentioned volume of *Acta Apostolicae Sedis*, many other unofficial editions of various format have been published under the auspices of the Holy See, which holds the copyright. All these editions contain, besides the text of the Code, the preface of Cardinal Gasparri, the text of the motu proprio establishing the Commission for the authentic interpretation of the Code, and an alphabetical index of the Code's contents. Some editions have footnotes to each Canon, designating the sources of pre-Code legislation; this, too, was the work of Cardinal Gasparri.

The codification represents a notable progress in ecclesiastical legislative technique. One need only compare the *Codex* with previous collections to note its superiority in systematic arrangement, conciseness, clarity, and relative terminological precision. These qualities, however, are not such as to exclude all room for improvement, although one will find in the Code the same elasticity and flexibility that have always characterized ecclesiastical legislation.

The Code does not ordinarily apply to the Eastern Church, nor does it regulate, except incidentally, matters pertaining to relations between Church and State.

Since 1929, work has been going on towards preparing a Code of Canon Law for the Eastern Church, similar to the one of the Latin Church. Certain parts of the future Eastern Code have already been separately published: the norms governing matrimonial matters, in the motu proprio *Crebrae allatae* of February 22, 1949; the norms regulating procedural matters, in the motu proprio *Sollicitudinem nostram* of January 6, 1950. *Cip.*

CODICILE. See Testament.

COEDUCATION. Coeducation advocates the education of boys and girls in the same classrooms, with the intent of promoting a natural and progressive adjustment between the sexes.

The coeducational system is supported by the promoters of naturalism, who claim that coeducation is conducive to healthy attitudes between the sexes and opposed to the dangers of autoerotism inherent in separate schools for each sex. Coeducation has also been praised by some Catholics who consider it as a gradual vaccination, as it were, against evil, and an incentive to refinement and emulation, similar to home life.

The Church has always voiced opposition to coeducation, which constitutes a grave danger to the purity and the proper formation of the young. This, of course, is more particularly true in certain age groups. The analogy between coeducational systems and family life is obviously a forced one, nor is it necessary to further refute that. The claim that coeducation serves as a gradual immunization against evil, is clearly an exaggerated interpretation of the principle "things to which we become accustomed do not bother us" (*ab assuetis non fit passio*). It is true that a constant contact with a natural stimulus may reduce the newness of impact, but it does not remove the reaction. Frequent exposure to a natural stimulus seldom lessens the reaction; it merely makes one accustomed to it, so that it ceases to bother one's conscience. Hence, the above principle is only partly true. The fact remains that constant association with the opposite sex constitutes a natural stimulus for the passions and presents a constant danger. And experience supports this observation.

Moreover, coeducation militates against the specific and distinct formation of the two sexes. As opportunely noted by Pope Pius XI in his encyclical *Divini Illius Magistri*, Dec. 31, 1929: These (the two sexes), in keeping with the wonderful designs of the Creator, are destined to complement each other in the family and in society, precisely because of their differences, which therefore ought to be maintained and encouraged during their years of formation, with the necessary distinction and corresponding separation, according to varying conditions and circumstances."

The position of the Church regarding this question may be summed up as follows: the system of separate schools for boys and girls must be regarded as the ideal toward which we should strive. If, because of particular circumstances, this ideal cannot be realized, proper measures should be taken to assure adequate supervision and separate instruction in pertinent areas. *Pal.*

COFFEE. See Drugs.

COHABITATION. Taken in a strict sense, *cohabitation* implies not only living together under the same roof, but in a familial way. Cohabitation gives rise to civil, moral, and canonical relations.

Cohabitation is the principal obligation of married persons (Can. 1128). Consequently, the separation of spouses, which, among other things, implies disruption of family life, either temporarily or permanently, is not allowed except for just and grave reasons. Among these are: formal adultery by one of the parties (Can. 1129); excessive cruelty, to the extent of rendering common life too difficult to bear; criminal and disreputable life, bringing dishonor and disgrace to the other spouse; threats of bodily injury or spiritual harm; heresy, schism, or apostasy (Can. 1131); refusal on the part of the husband to provide a suitable home in keeping with his means. In these and similar cases, the innocent party has a just cause for separation, for which, however, permission of the Ordinary is ordinarily required.

Cohabitation gives rise to the presumption that a marriage was consummated (Can. 1015, par. 2), so that the parties claiming otherwise must give positive and conclusive proof that, despite cohabitation, the marriage was not consummated.

COHABITATION, FRATERNAL. *Fraternal cohabitation* is a term used to signify the state of a man and woman living together under the same roof in what is characterized as a brother-sister relationship: the cohabiting parties treat each other as if they were brother and sister. Such a relationship differs from that existing between husband and wife, for the cohabiting parties exclude not only sexual relations, but all intimacies and liberties permitted to married couples. On the other hand, fraternal cohabitation is not the same as the relationship between master and maidservant.

Fraternal cohabitation, or the brother-sister relationship, is a self-imposed condition of life by persons who have entered an irregular marital union, which, because of an existing impediment, cannot be rectified or validated and which, because of very grave reasons, cannot easily be severed. Of course, if the union can be severed, even at the cost of great sacrifice (Matt. 5:29 ff.), it should be done to eliminate radically all danger of sin and scandal.

There may be at times very grave reasons for tolerating such union, if it is considered necessary. Some such reasons are: children to be reared and educated, the need for mutual assistance, the danger of scandal or loss of reputation, particularly if residents of the community commonly believe the couple are legitimately married.

Granted such grave reasons, the pseudo-married couple may: (a) pray, without presumption, that God will grant them the necessary assistance to live chastely; (b) reasonably hope, through opportune and prudent explanations, to remove all scandal among those who know of their irregular union. If the pseudo-married partners lead a truly chaste life, as brother and sister, and if all scandal has been effectively removed, they may be permitted to live fully a Christian life and even receive the sacraments. The case, of course, must be submitted to the local Ordinary, who is the only judge in the matter.

Concerning the removal of scandal, the local Ordinary has the right: (a) to prescribe the necessary measures for effective removal of scandal; (b) to decide, if and when scandal has been effectively removed, to allow the couple to go to the sacraments.

COLBERTISM. *See* Exchange.

COLLABORATION. *See* Cooperation.

COLLATERAL. *See* Guaranty.

COLLECT. The first *oration* or prayer occurring in the Mass (before the Epistle) is called a *collect*, because it served to gather, as it were, the secret aspirations of the faithful and preceded the more solemn prayer of the priest at Mass. Today the term *collect* is usually applied to the orations prescribed by the Ordinary (*oratio imperata*).

Originally, all the faithful, upon the priest's invitation to pray (*Oremus*), stood or, in penitential seasons, remained kneeling, and, with arms uplifted, prayed in silence for the intention expressed by the priest or contained in the current feastday. After this silent prayer of the faithful, those kneeling were invited to rise (*Levate*); the priest proceeded to sum up this common prayer or petition in a formula that followed a well-regulated pattern and style. Except in a few prayers of recent origin, collects are always addressed to God the Father. This practice was officially sanctioned in the Council of Hippo (393). The address to the Father, however, is never made without interposition of the sacerdotal mediation of Christ, so that the collect always concludes with the words *Per Dominum nostrum Jesum Christum* or with some other equivalent formula.

Another characteristic note of the collect is its even flow or rhythm, resembling a poetic strophe. In every collect the various phrases and words are so arranged as to give the various parts a special rhythm (*cursus*) that is slow, even, dispondaic, rapid or trispondaic. This special rhythm is obtained by a wise choice of words, distributed into certain equal and parallel parts with combinations of accented and unaccented syllables.

According to Canon 818, the celebrant is forbidden to alter or add anything to the fixed prayers of the Mass; hence, he is also forbidden to omit the collect. Omission of the collect alone, however, does not constitute *per se* a grave sin, nor is it a grave sin to omit the orations (collects) prescribed by the Ordinary. *Cig.*

COLLECTIVE BARGAINING. *See* Wage, Living; Labor.

COLLECTIVISM. This term, employed in France, England, and America, designates systems advocating collective ownership and economy. Hence, collectivism embraces all those theories and movements whose aim is the establishment of an economic order based on a more or less accentuated form of collective ownership. Collectivism finds its strictest expression in communism, with its theory of total socialization. Next follows socialism, also of Marxian inspiration, with its theory of socialization of the means of production only (*see* Socialization).

Besides economic collectivism, there is also a sociological collectivism or a *collectivistic concept of history*, as some people prefer to call it. According to this, the unfolding of events in a similar objective condition of life gives rise to a uniform way of thinking and acting among men. This is precisely the condition which bolshevists hope to achieve through their theory of classless society, characterized by a community of sentiment, mind, and will. According to this collectivistic theory, it is not the great personages or leaders who decisively influence the course of history, but the collective will and action. W. Ropke introduces a new element into it, when he describes collectivism as a social philosophy, which seeks to increase, to the fullest extent, the competency and constructive power of the State, and which, therefore, presupposes the division of men into governing and governed, leaders and subjects.

Actually, one of the factors behind the present-day social crisis is a *de facto* sociological collectivization. Man's opinions, attitudes, tastes, behavior, entertainment, education, choice of career or profession follow a common or collective pattern of mediocrity. There is a notable

lack of individual style, a marked tendency toward dilettantism and mass conglobation, a *Vermassung* lacking all individual structure and organic hierarchy.

It is the supreme duty of every man to cultivate his own personality, and not to become absorbed or lost in a mass pattern. *Per.*

COLLEGE. *See* Education.

COLLEGIATE CHURCH. *See* Church.

COLLUSION. *Collusion* is conspiracy between two or more persons for a fraudulent or deceitful purpose, e.g., testifying in court to the veracity of a statement or fact which in reality is not true. The element of conspiracy or agreement between the parties is essential to the concept of collusion.

An agreement to practice collusion is an agreement to commit perjury. If collusion is exercised in court, under oath, the collusive parties are liable to the same punishment as perjurers. The moral guilt of collusion lies in the fact that it involves fraud or deceit and is prejudicial to the case under trial. Collusion is proof that the testimony of the collusive parties is false. *Fel.*

COLONIZATION. Colonization may be studied under the ethical, juridical, political, economic, medical and historical aspects. The subject will be studied here only in its ethico-juridical aspect, for the purpose of establishing whether and on what grounds colonization conforms with the principles which must regulate the relations between peoples.

The establishment of colonies over the centuries was not always characterized by the same motives. Among some ancient peoples, like the Phoenicians and the Greeks, colonies were established exclusively, or prevalently, for the purpose of decongesting overpopulated or poor and underdeveloped territories. The establishment of colonies by the Romans followed their military conquests. In territories occupied by their legions, the Romans frequently established permanent encampments for military personnel and their families, for whom they erected public buildings, baths, tribunals, etc.

Colonization or the conquest of territories inhabited by people of lower civilization in the sixteenth century, centered, first, around the newly discovered American continent, and, later, around African and Asian territories.

A number of moralists and jurists have posed the question whether and on what grounds civil powers may resort to military conquest of territories inhabited by less civilized people, subjecting them to their political domination. The first to treat of this problem, formally and extensively, from an ethico-juridical standpoint was the Spanish Dominican theologian Francisco de Vitoria (1486–1546), who, in the fifth and sixth editions of *Relectiones theologicae* under the title *De Indis*, examined whether the Spaniards had a legitimate right to occupy the American territories discovered by Christopher Columbus.

Many other jurists and theologians, even in recent times, have dealt with this question.

Of the various titles adduced to justify colonization in the sense explained above, the right of conquest obviously is not a legitimate title, for this is merely the result of fortunate military operations. It is certain that superiority of material force does not *per se* constitute a source of legitimate political rights over any alien territory, even if inhabited by people of inferior civilization.

Neither does so-called racial superiority constitute a legitimate title, for, apart from the fact that degrees of difference are to be found also among higher civilizations, it must always be borne in mind that natural rights, including that of independence and freedom, are common to all peoples, regardless of their race and their degree of civilization.

Nor is the right of first occupancy a legitimate title, for such a right presupposes that the object or thing occupied belong to no one (*res nullius*). But the principle *res nullius* can hardly be applied to a territory inhabited by inferior peoples, who not only possess the private right of ownership, but also the right of sovereignty. For, as generally is the case, they have at least a rudimentary form of political organization of their own. Hence, such territory, even from the standpoint of public right, cannot be considered *res nullius*.

Nor does colonial conquest find its justification in the intention of a colonizing power to bring the benefits of civilization to inferior peoples. True, civilized nations have a moral duty to encourage and favor the civilization of inferior peoples, and the latter have a moral obligation of tending toward a higher culture. But it cannot be said that to this moral duty or obligation there is a corresponding right on the part of a civilized nation to impose its culture on inferior peoples by depriving them of their independence and political freedom. This general principle, however, may be susceptible to an exception in the case of uncivilized natives given to inhuman practices and heinous crimes, such as the killing of innocent people for sacrificial or cannibalistic purposes. In such a case, even armed intervention is morally justified.

In more recent times, the title of expropriation or exploitation for the public good has been advanced as justification for colonial conquest. This title would seemingly apply if an abundance of natural resources of uncivilized territories were unused by the natives and were available to outsiders. It is argued that the goods and riches of the earth exist for the benefit of mankind in general, so that, if the natives of a territory did not make use of such goods and others were prevented from using them, a right of human collectivity would be violated.

In answer to this, humanity, as an abstract entity, has no real right to demand that an uncivilized people use its riches or resources for the benefit of the human collectivity, nor does a specific civil power have a right to assume a mandate from mankind to occupy and colonize a given uncivilized territory. Moreover, by natural law the peoples of the earth are all equal, and the non-use or abuse of their own goods is not *per se* a violation of the rights of others nor does it give others the right to occupy their territory. Assuming, however, that in a concrete case the principle whereby the goods of the earth are to be distributed for the benefit of mankind is combined with the natural right of every nation to procure the goods necessary for its existence, colonial conquest might be considered as a licit act. Certain conditions, however, must be verified: (a) that the goods sought for are superfluous to the inhabitants possessing them; (b) that occupation or conquest exceeds neither territorially nor in duration the limits of the need of the occupying country. *Pas.*

COLONY. *See* Colonization.

COMEDY. *See* Theatre.

COMINFORM. *See* Communism.

COMINTERN. *See* Communism.

COMMERCE (Trade). Commerce may be defined as the productive service of intermediate exchange. This definition brings out the following facts: (1) commerce is a service, a human act; (2) it is productive, that is, it increases the usefulness of commodities and services and contributes to the attainment of their end, which is the ultimate consumption of production; (3) the specific character of the service is mediation of exchange, i.e., the intervention of a third party between buyer and seller by which the simple operation of buying and selling is broken up into a series of operations designed to facilitate the process of buying and selling. Such intermediary service, whose function is somewhat similar to that occurring in barter, does not affect any industrial transformation of commodities. In the actual fact, however, merchants often do bring about certain transformations in their products, before they sell them or arrange for their transfer in space and time.

Commerce is a natural consequence of the division of labor. All those living in an economy dominated by a division of labor must perforce exchange goods and services. Commerce, through the medium of exchange, aids and facilitates further expansion of the division of labor, and, as the market expands from the standpoint of products and clients, commerce itself becomes an increasingly specialized field. Commerce may be conducted on a small scale between small consumers and producers or on a large scale between large consumers and producers; the former constitutes *small business*, the latter *big business*.

Commerce, which is a result of a division of labor, is also an important phase thereof. It lessens in some respects the commercial risks and the immobilization of products with which producers are naturally confronted. Larger producers, however, no longer have this problem, for, unless the law forbids it, they engage in wholesale business, and at times also in retail business. This process of integration, a particular effect of the vertical concentration, operates successfully even in the strictly commercial sphere, in which the success of certain commercial devices, e.g., chain stores, is due precisely to the fusion between wholesale and retail business. *Mai.*

Medieval theologians did not look too favorably upon commerce exercised solely for profit and unlimited gain (*Summa Theol.*, II–II, q. 77, a. 4). They did not, however, consider it illicit to engage in commerce for honest reasons, such as support of one's family or providing necessary commodities for the public. As for profit, it finally became justified by moralists as a quasi-stipend, prescinding, of course, from the motives of the individual merchant.

Today, commerce is commonly regarded as a legitimate activity, as a highly useful occupation and even necessary to social life, which would be gravely endangered or at least inconvenienced by the lack of national and international exchange of commodities. Nor does the element of profit in commerce constitute any difficulty from the moral standpoint, for there is nothing to prevent the directing of profit to a legitimate end.

The moral law requires of all merchants: (a) that they observe the rules of commutative justice in all their transactions; (b) that they observe the precept of charity, incumbent upon everyone to the extent of one's means and circumstances; (c) that they subordinate the mere desire for profit to the higher end of human life (*Summa Theol.*, II–II, q. 78, a. 1–2), bearing in mind that the commercial world is not a world apart, as if standing all by itself. And since the fundamental act of commerce consists in buying and selling, it is especially necessary to observe all the rules of justice relative to the contract of sale. The principal application of justice to the contract of sale is that of just price (*q.v.*); all commodities must be sold at a price which is according to justice. However, it cannot be disputed that goods in the hands of a merchant acquire greater value because of the expense and work involved in securing and preserving them. Neither can it be disputed that for the same reasons a retailer is permitted to charge a proportionately higher price than a wholesaler.

It might here be noted that commerce is frequently the occasion of fraud, deception, and other sins against justice. But these are not so much defects of the art of commerce itself as they are vices attributable to man. Such vices may be encountered anywhere, although it is true that they seem to occur more frequently in the world of commerce.

It is precisely against such abuses that commercial laws have been enacted in all civilized countries. Designed to regulate the conduct of commerce, such laws are more or less uniform throughout the commercial world, with due allowance for local differences. Commercial laws regulate such matters as the juridical status of business owners, business permits, partnerships, account books, contracts, bankruptcy, etc.

Civil commercial laws, insofar as they create rights and duties, generally bind in conscience.

SPECULATION. In itself, there is nothing dishonest in buying and selling with an eye to future fluctuations of market.

A transaction advantageous both to oneself and to society is good speculation and a wise action, but one which requires much prudence and reflection. Wise speculation presupposes knowledge and experience concerning the trend of business, and not everyone is equipped with such knowledge; hence, it would be rash for an unqualified person to engage in speculation.

The word *speculation* (*q.v.*) is often used in a derogatory sense to signify manipulations in the stock market or dishonest business maneuvers, such as unfair competition, monopolistic tactics, black market activities, etc.

Concerning these various phases of national and international commerce, *see* Stock Exchange, Black Market, Competition (system of), Monopoly.

COMMERCE AND CANON LAW. Positive ecclesiastical legislation forbids clerics to engage in commerce. The reason is easy to understand: competition, hazards, and cares of business life are incompatible with the dignity of the clerical state. This law, which dates back to the early days of the Church, was invoked rather frequently in the fourth and eighth centuries. It was developed in many particular Councils, as shown in the Decree of Gratian (D. 86, c. 26; D. 88, c. 1, 2, 9–10; C. 1, 3, 8, etc.), and in the collections of the *Decretals*.

The prohibition was renewed by the Council of Trent (*Sess.* XXII, c. 1; *Sess.* XXIV, c. 12, *De reform.*), the Code of Canon Law (Cans. 142, 2380) and recently by the Sacred Congregation of the Council (Decree of March 12, 1950). *See also* Clerics. *Pal.*

COMMERCE, INTERNATIONAL. International commerce (foreign trade) is the interchange of commodities between countries. The basic fact underlying international trade is that, due to conditions of soil, climate, cultural differences, and other factors, the production of goods is unequally distributed in the world. In other words, the resources of various countries differ both in kind and quantity. Hence, nations use international commerce to import needed commodities and to export surplus goods. In this manner, nations can tend to those industries for which they are suited and equipped, but import other needed commodities at a cheaper price than it would be possible for them to produce at home. The business of international trade, then, rests on the relative usefulness of commodities exchanged or on the relative differences in prices thereof (Ricardian law of comparative costs).

International commerce is of *imports*, *exports* and *transit*, depending on whether commodities are acquired from abroad, sent abroad, or transported through the territory of another country. It is erroneous to think that exports always indicate excess of goods or that a nation only exports surplus commodities. The fact is that necessity, utility, or political economy might suggest otherwise.

One of the benefits brought about by an increased production through the use of machinery and employment of skilled labor, is the reduction of costs. It is to be noted that international trade depends on the economic policy of nations. Today, in many nations a tendency is noted toward increasing exports even at the cost of selling at lower prices while maintaining a constantly high price at home. The motive, of course, is to gain monopoly of certain markets or to unload on it surplus goods (*dumping*) that cannot be used at home.

Very useful to the promotion and facilitation of international trade are also international commercial stock exchanges wherein enormous amounts of merchandise are easily exchanged between persons perhaps unknown to each other and living at great distances. Commercial stock exchanges deal only in fungible goods: wheat, grain, cotton, wool, etc. Exchange of raw materials is frequently transacted by international trusts or combines, owners of mines, quarries, oil, and mineral deposits in their natural state, or processed on their original locations. *Bau.*

COMMISSION FOR THE INTER-PRETATION OF THE CODE OF

CANON LAW. *See* Interpretation of Law.

COMMIXTURE. *See* Accession.

COMMODATUM, LOAN. *See* Precarium, Loan.

COMMON GOOD. The *common good* is the good of a society; as such, it is superior to the good of the single individual. This superiority has a quantitative aspect, insofar as the common good: (a) extends to many subjects or to an area wider than the individual; (b) comprises a greater number of objects than does the individual good. However, it also possesses a qualitative aspect inasmuch as: (a) the subject or society is, in certain respects, superior to the individual; (b) social collaboration makes it possible to attain greater and higher goods than those attainable in individual life.

It is not possible to express objectively in one single formula just what constitutes the common good of every society; each society has its own common good which is determined by the nature of the society itself.

Different Evaluations. From the standpoint of its subject, the common good may be individualistic, if one regards the common good as the sum total of all the goods enjoyed by the individuals, or collective, if one considers the common good to the society itself, conceived as distinct from its component members. According to this latter view, the members of society bear the whole burden of contributing to the common good, with no claim to enjoy its advantages at all times. Christian philosophy accepts neither view, but maintains that the good of society is not to be sacrificed to the good of the individual, nor the good of the individual to society. It teaches that the common good must always resolve itself, even though indirectly, into a real good for the members of society.

This doctrine implies the duty of cooperation toward the common good even at the sacrifice, within due limits, of one's individual good. In determining these limits, the moral theologian is faced with a grave problem, for the solution of which both subjective and objective factors are to be taken into account. Among the subjective factors, of particular importance is the duty of office: a man occupying a public office and charged with protecting and safeguarding public good, is obviously required to sacrifice much more than a private citizen. Among the objective factors, the respective values of the hierarchy of goods come first in a conflict between individual and common good; the latter is to prevail, as long as these goods pertain to the same order; but if the two conflicting goods belong to a different order, then the individual good may prevail over the public good. Indeed, at times, it must, when, for instance, the material common good is opposed to the spiritual and eternal good of the individual. The second objective element to be taken into account is the quantity of the conflicting goods: a private good may be such as to justify the sacrifice of a small portion of the common good. A third element is the urgent nature of the goods themselves: a good of a lower order but of the greatest urgency may justify putting off a higher good of a less urgent nature.

Moreover, a distinction must be made between voluntary and imposed sacrifice. An individual may licitly sacrifice his personal good to a public good, when society would have no right to impose or demand such a sacrifice. *Gra.*

COMMUNICATION OF PRIVILEGES. *See* Privilege.

COMMUNION, FIRST. Dogmatic Premises. Every living and baptized person, barring any obstacle, is capable of receiving Holy Communion (Can. 853). Hence, *per se*, even baptized children below the age of discretion are to be considered capable of receiving the sacrament of the Holy Eucharist.

The possibility of giving the Holy Eucharist to children was considered by the Church from the very beginning. The early practice was to give Com-

munion to children below the age of reason. To avoid any danger of profanation, the sacrament was administered to them under the consecrated species of wine alone. Moreover, children under the age of reason were permitted to receive, not once, but frequently (St. Cyprian, *De Lapsis*, ch. 25: PL 4, 4730485; St. Augustine, *Sermo in I Tim*, 15, e. 6; *ibid.* 38, 944). This practice existed from the early days of Christianity down to the twelfth century, and it is still practiced today in the Greek Church.

In the twelfth century, for reasons unknown to us (perhaps to avoid abuses), the practice of permitting infants and children below the age of reason to receive Holy Communion was discontinued. Instead, it was decided that the Holy Eucharist was to be administered only to children who had attained the age of discretion. This was sanctioned by the Fourth Lateran Council in 1215 (*Sess.* XXI, *Denz.*, 437) and confirmed by the Council of Trent (*Sess.* XIII, *De Eucharistia*, c. 9, Denz., 890). On the strength of these deliberations, it became a general rule that all the faithful, upon attaining the age of reason, are obliged to go to confession and to receive Holy Communion at least once a year.

Inevitably, the question arose when children are said to have attained the age of discretion. Some were of the opinion that a different age requirement should be established concerning reception of Holy Communion, distinct from that required for confession, in view of the greater reverence and, therefore, greater maturity for the reception of the sacrament of Holy Eucharist. As a result of this theory, children were deprived of a powerful remedy against difficulties and temptations. This, of course, was contrary to the mind of the Council of Trent, which has defined that Holy Communion is an antidote against everyday defects and protection against mortal sin. Abuses were carried to such an extent that sometimes adolescents died without the benefit of Holy Viaticum, since they had not made their First Communion.

Actually, the Lateran Council had established the same requirement (use of reason) for both sacraments, on the obvious assumption that if a child is capable of receiving the sacrament of penance when he is able to distinguish right from wrong, so, too, he is capable of receiving Holy Communion when he is able to distinguish the Holy Eucharistic from ordinary bread. In other words, the required age for both sacraments is when a child has attained the use of reason. This was also the interpretation given by St. Thomas (*Summa Theol.*, III, q. 80, a. 9, ad 3), Vasquez (*Summa Theol.*, III, q. 80, a. 9, *dub.* 6), Ladesma (*in Summa Theol., disp.* 214, e. 4, n. 43), and St. Antoninus (*Summa moralis*, p. III, tit. 14, c. 2, 5).

The Council of Trent, the Roman Council held under Benedict XIII, and the Roman Catechism reaffirmed this conclusion, but all in vain.

It was St. Pius X who put an end to all controversies in this matter. Through the decree *Quam Singulari*, issued by the Sacred Congregation of Sacraments (Aug. 8, 1910: AAS, 2 [1910], 582, ff.), he re-affirmed the principle that in practice the age required for First Communion is that at which a child is able to distinguish the Holy Eucharistic from ordinary bread. Nor is perfect knowledge of the faith required, but only a rudimentary knowledge (*aliqua cognitio*). Hence, not the full use of reason, but only the initial use thereof is sufficient. The decree of St. Pius X further states that the practice of deferring First Communion to a more mature age is reprehensible; in fact, this practice has frequently been condemned by the Holy See.

The present legislation of the Church regarding First Communion is contained in Canon 854 of the Code of Canon Law and is based on the above-mentioned decree of St. Pius X. Present-day regulations concerning First Communion may be summarized as follows:

(a) The age of discretion, required both for confession and Communion, is that in which the initial use of reason is attained. This normally occurs around seven years of age, but may also take place earlier or later, depending on the psychological development of each individual. The obligation of receiving confession and Communion obtains from the age of reason onward.

(b) For admission to the sacraments of penance and Holy Eucharist, complete knowledge of Christian doctrine is not required, though it must be acquired later.

(c) The amount of religious knowledge required in order that a child may be suitably prepared for First Communion is the knowledge of the principal mysteries of faith and a knowledge that enables him to distinguish the Holy Eucharist from ordinary bread. Such knowledge is deemed sufficient to enable a child of seven or thereabout to receive Holy Communion with devotion.

(d) The obligation of preparing children for First Holy Communion is incumbent especially on the parents, those who take their place, on the confessor, teachers, and pastor. According to the Roman Catechism, it belongs to the father (or the one who takes his place) and to the pastor to decide whether a particular child is sufficiently prepared for admission to First Communion.

(e) Once a year, and even more often, pastors shall arrange for a general Communion of children, including those who have already made their First Communion.

(f) Those charged with the care of children should instill in them the beautiful practice of receiving Holy Communion frequently, even daily. Moreover, parents, guardians, etc., should be reminded of their serious obligation to send their children to classes of religious instruction, unless this is given to them in some other way.

St. Pius X predicted that the practice of admitting children to Holy Communion would give the Church child saints. This prediction has become a reality. *Pal.*

COMMUNION, HOLY. *Holy Communion* (Latin, *communio*—union with another) is the reception of the Body and Blood of Jesus Christ, really and substantially present under the consecrated species, offered as a sacrifice to God in Holy Mass (*q.v.*).

In instituting the Holy Eucharist (*q.v.*), our Lord Jesus Christ enjoined His followers to eat of His Body and drink of His Blood (Luke 22:19; John 6:54).

Catholics are obliged to receive Holy Communion at least once a year, during Easter time (Can. 859). If for any reason one has not made his Easter duty, as it is called, within the prescribed time, he must fulfill the obligation at the earliest possible time thereafter. It is the mind of the Church that the Easter Communion be received in one's own rite (Can. 856, par. 2) and in one's own parish church; one who makes his Easter duty elsewhere should inform his own pastor of that fact (Can. 859, par. 3). The obligation of receiving the Holy Eucharist is binding on all who have attained the use of reason (*see* First Communion). Children who have made their First Communion are bound by this precept (Can. 860). The time for fulfilling the Easter duty is between Palm Sunday and Low Sunday (Sunday after Easter); this period may be extended by the local Ordinary from the Fourth Sunday of Lent to Trinity Sunday (Can. 859, par. 2). By special concession, the period for the Easter duty in the United States extends from the First Sunday in Lent to Trinity Sunday.

The precept to receive the Holy Eucharist is gravely binding on anyone who is in danger of death (Can. 864) from whatever cause, illness, old age, accident, etc. (*see* Viaticum), and whenever Holy Communion is considered necessary to avoid serious sin.

Furthermore, since man's spiritual needs are many and reception of Holy Communion is most efficacious, the faithful should be encouraged to receive frequently and, if possible, even daily (Can. 863; Sacred Cong. of the Council, Dec. 20, 1905).

Reception of Holy Communion is also the most effective way to participate in the Holy Sacrifice of the Mass. For devotion's sake one may receive the Holy Eucharist in any rite (Can. 866, par. 1).

Concerning the manner of treating public sinners in relation to Holy Communion, *confer* Public Sinner. Occult sinners who secretly request Holy Communion shall be refused if the minister knows that they have not amended; but if they publicly approach the Eucharistic table and the priest cannot pass them by without causing scandal or defamation, they are not to be turned away (Can. 855, par. 2).

MINISTER OF HOLY COMMUNION. The priest is the ordinary minister of Holy Communion. Any priest may distribute Holy Communion during Mass or immediately before and after Mass, unless particular restrictions have been issued by the local Ordinary (Cans. 845, par. 1; 846; 869). A priest may distribute Communion outside Mass only by permission, at least presumed, of the rector of the church (Can. 846, par. 2). Each priest must administer Holy Communion according to the ceremonies of his own rite, except in cases of necessity (Can. 851). Though Holy Communion under both species was common practice until the twelfth century, there are numerous instances in the early days of the Church in which Holy Communion was received under one species alone. It is impossible to determine historically the exact time when the Church enacted the law requiring the faithful to communicate under the species of bread alone, but the disposition was already universal at the time of the Council of Constance. The reasons behind this ecclesiastical disposition were both practical (reverence toward the Blessed Sacrament) and dogmatic (refutation of the heretical theory that Christ is not entirely present under one species alone). The Council of Trent defined that the practice of administering and receiving the Holy Eucharist under one species alone is based on solid and reasonable grounds (*Sess.* XXI, *Can.* 1–2: Denz. 934–935).

The deacon is the extraordinary minister of Holy Communion, but he must have permission of the local Ordinary or the pastor. Permission may be given for a grave reason or may be legitimately presumed in case of necessity (Can.

845). Clerics below the rank of deacon and, in the absence of clerics, ordinary lay persons may administer the sacrament to themselves and to others, if necessary to protect the Holy Eucharist from profanation, fire, flood, etc.

TIME AND PLACE. Holy Communion may be administered at any time and in any place in which the celebration of the Mass is permitted, even in a private oratory, unless the local Ordinary, for good reasons, may have forbidden it in particular cases (Can. 869). On sick calls it is permitted in extraordinary cases to administer the Holy Eucharist even to non-sick persons wishing to receive Communion but unable to go to church on that day, provided that the place is decent and permission of the local Ordinary has been duly obtained (Sac. Cong. of the Sacraments, May 5, 1928). Concerning bringing the Blessed Sacrament publicly to the sick, whether in the form of Viaticum or not, confer Pastoral Functions, Viaticum.

Holy Communion may be distributed on any day during the hours in which it is permitted to celebrate Mass, unless a reasonable cause may suggest otherwise (Can. 867, par. 4; S. S. Congr. of Holy Office, March 21, 1960 and Oct. 21, 1961: AAS 52 [1960], 355–356; AAS 53 [1961], 735). Regulations concerning the last three days of Holy Week are as follows: (a) on Holy Thursday Communion may be distributed only during the evening Mass or immediately after; (b) on Good Friday it may be distributed during the solemn afternoon service; (c) on Holy Saturday it may be distributed during the solemn Easter Vigil Mass, if celebrated before midnight, or immediately after this Mass. Holy Viaticum, however, may be administered at any time of day or night (Sac. Congregation of Rites, Nov. 27, 1955).

No one may receive Communion more than once on the same day, unless the second reception is in the form of Viaticum, or it becomes necessary to safeguard the Blessed Sacrament against irreverence (Cans. 857–858).

DISPOSITIONS. For a worthy reception of Holy Communion two conditions are required and suffice: (a) *state of grace;* (b) *right intention.* One who presumes to approach the Eucharistic table while in the state of mortal sin commits a serious sacrilege. The Easter obligation is not satisfied by a sacrilegious Communion (Can. 861). A person conscious of mortal sin on his soul is required to make a sacramental confession before reception; if, however, necessity urges and confession is impossible, an act of perfect contrition may suffice (Can. 856).

The right intention demanded by the Church consists in the desire to receive the Holy Eucharist for the purpose of pleasing God, satisfying the divine precept, becoming more intimately united with Him by charity, or seeking this divine remedy for one's weaknesses and defects. On who receives merely because of an existing custom, vanity, or some other purely human motive lacks right intention and fails to attain the salutary effects of Holy Communion; he might also be guilty of grave irreverence. If, in receiving the Holy Eucharist, the right intention is accompanied by some other purely human but not seriously inordinate motive, one would not be totally deprived of the fruits of Holy Communion, but would, nevertheless, commit a venial sin of irreverence toward the Sacrament.

For a more fruitful reception of Holy Communion, one must be free from all deliberate attachment to venial sin and must approach the Eucharistic table with great faith, profound humility, heartfelt compunction, and a fervent desire to receive Christ and become more intimately united with Him. The more perfect the dispositions of the recipient, the more copious fruits will he receive from the Sacrament. Hence, the necessity and importance of making a good preparation for Holy Communion, of receiving with the greatest possible recollection, and of spending some time in fervent thanksgiving after Communion.

The new regulations concerning the Eucharistic fast require that one ordinarily be fasting from solid foods and alcoholic beverages for three hours before receiving Communion, and from non-alcoholic liquids for one hour. Water no longer breaks the fast (Pius XII, Apostolic Constitution *Christus Dominus*, Jan. 6, 1953, and the added Instruction of the Holy Office: AAS: 45 [1953], 25–51; motu proprio *Sacram Communionem*, March 19, 1957: AAS: 49 [1957], 177–178. These constitute a modification of Canon 858, par. 1).

The infirm, even if not bedridden, may take non-alcoholic beverages and real and proper medicine, whether in liquid or solid form (even though perhaps containing alcohol), anytime before Holy Communion.

The motu proprio *Sacram Communionem* exhorts those who are able to observe the old and venerable form of Eucharistic fast from midnight, out of devotion and mortification; however, this is merely a question of gaining greater merit, not a matter of obligation.

Although the text of the motu proprio is clear in itself, it will be helpful to define a few points: (a) Water is to be interpreted as that which is commonly held as such. The adjective *natural* has been eliminated, thereby removing all questions of doubt and interpretation. (b) Since the regulations governing the Eucharistic fast are clear and simple in themselves, the faithful are no longer obliged to consult the confessor for advice or permission, as formerly. (c) At evening Masses, Holy Communion may only be received during the celebration of the Mass, and immediately before or after. (d) The time for celebrating evening Mass is between 4 p.m. and 9 p.m.

The faithful approaching the Eucharistic table at an evening Mass are required to fast three hours from solid food and one hour from non-alcoholic beverages. At the principal meal it is permitted to partake moderately of such alcoholic beverages as are customarily taken with meals, except liquor; outside this principal meal, alcoholic beverages are not permitted. These new regulations regarding the Eucharistic fast abrogate all previous dispensations, but do not preclude new ones, though the need for such dispensations has greatly diminished.

EFFECTS. Holy Communion, as spiritual food of the soul, effects a union with Christ and the members of the Mystical Body of Christ. A worthy reception of Holy Communion increases the infused virtue of charity (primary effect of the Sacrament of the Altar), sanctifying grace, and the infused virtues and gifts of the Holy Ghost, which are connected with grace and charity. Communion also gives a constant right to receive, at the opportune time, special actual graces necessary for the attainment of the proper effects of the Sacrament: the restraint of excessive self-love, an increase in the love of God and neighbor, and the imitation of Christ, Priest and Victim. According to a well-founded theory, Communion produces a stable disposition capable of healing egoism, so deeply imbedded in fallen nature. Because of Christ's special concern for those who partake of His Flesh and Blood, the Holy Eucharist is an effective remedy against sin and a pledge of eternal glory. Holy Communion strengthens the soul and indirectly effects the remission of venial sins and a partial remission of the temporal punishment for sins already forgiven. The Council of Florence summarizes the effects of Holy Communion by stating that it produces a spiritual nourishment similar to the nourishment which the body receives through ordinary food and drink. In other words, Holy Communion sustains, increases, repairs and comforts (Denz. 698).

PRACTICAL COROLLARIES. The time best suited for the reception of Holy Communion, though no particular prescriptions exist in this regard, is during the Holy Sacrifice of the Mass, immediately following the priest's Communion (Pius XII, Enc. *Mediator Dei*, Nov. 20, 1947, AAS: 39 [1947], 56).

The prayers of the Mass, recited with attention and fervor, are most suitable for producing in the recipient the dispositions necessary for proper reception of the Sacred Body of Christ.

Thanksgiving after Communion ought to include fervent acts of love of God, intimate conversation with Christ, acts of self-abasement, together with a complete dedication to God's service, and a firm resolve for immediate action in this direction. The moments of thanksgiving are also most propitious for requesting the grace of intimate union with Christ, asking for the grace of perseverance, praying for special persons and intentions and for the general needs of the Church and of souls. If it is impossible for one to remain in church for at least fifteen minutes of thanksgiving, he could do this on his way to the office, school, or work. It is highly beneficial to reflect, during the course of the day, on the great gift of Holy Communion and, at the same time, renew sentiments of gratitude and of complete self-surrender to God.

If sacramental Communion is impossible, one ought to make at least a spiritual Communion, which, among other things, comprises an act of faith in the presence of the Eucharistic Christ, sorrow for sins committed, regret at being unable to receive sacramentally, and a fervent desire to become united with the Eucharistic Christ.

Holy Communion, as a sacrament, is beneficial only to the one receiving it. However, this does not exclude the possibility of offering one's Communion for other persons, living or dead. The reception of Holy Communion is a virtuous act, whose satisfactory and impetratory value may be applied to others. Moreover, the internal fervor produced by the Sacrament renders the recipient more fitting to implore the Lord for favors in behalf of others. *Man.*

COMMUNION OF SAINTS. *See* Deceased, Indulgence, Saints.

COMMUNISM. The term *communism* is used to designate several theories and movements having in common, as their specific aim, the collective ownership of the means of production, and sometimes also of consumption. Self-defined as a scientific and heretical system, communism is an advanced form of Marxism. For based on a materialistic conception of the world, Marxism aims at lead-ing the working class (proletariat) into a class warfare against capitalism in order to establish, by violent seizure of power, the new State and a perfect classless society, based on the principle of equal economic conditions for all in a dictatorship of the proletariat. The terms *socialism* and *communism* are frequently interchangeable. It is almost impossible to distinguish exactly the two concepts or theories, for the history of one is often the history of the other. According to Sombart, every social group or party is based either on power or reason or love. Socialism, as a theory of a social order based on reason, is really distinguished from communism, which aims at the establishment of a collective society based on the instinctive use of force. Some authors, however, maintain that the real distinction between the two theories lies in their different attitudes toward private property. Socialism primarily seeks to reconstruct the social order through collective ownership of the means of production, but communism would extend collectivization even to the means of consumption, although this is not necessarily true of every form of communism. Others hold that the two theories are distinguished by the different nature of the struggle each advocates. Socialism aims at total socialization by relying on the natural and necessary evolution of capitalism, but communism seeks to precipitate this evolution through violent seizure of power. In the communist view, the end of society is not the welfare of the individual but society itself; the individual good can be sacrificed to that of society. Consequently, collective ownership is for communism the technical means for the realization of the essence and end of a communistic society as a classless society, devoid of democratic freedoms. This society, based as it is on sheer materialism, is necessarily opposed to God and the human person.

COMMUNISTIC SYSTEM. The basic principle for all communistic systems is a division of property, presented as absolutely essential for the realization of ideal justice. Under this aspect communism assumes a typically redemptive and messianic character. However, all communistic systems have endeavored to take on a deeper doctrinal basis, which they have drawn either from religion, philosophy, or history. The medieval systems of the Cathari and Albigenses in northern Italy and southern France, and, later, the Patarine movement in Lombardy were of a religious nature. The systems outlined by Plato in his *Republic* and by Karl Marx were of a philosophical nature; while the various *Utopias* of Thomas More, Campanella, and others, are mainly of historical origin. Of all these systems, only the Marxian has succeeded in taking root among the masses, to the extent of becoming an international movement, supported, after the First World War, by the Soviet Union. The *Communist Manifesto* of 1848 is the Magna Carta of modern socialism. Only after the First World War did the socialist movement make a clear cut distinction between socialists and communists. Both parties are agreed that the proletariat must bring about the conversion of capitalistic economy to a communist regime, although they differ as to the means and methods of reaching this goal. The socialists advocate the process of evolution; the communists, revolution. With the establishment of the communist regime in Russia, communism became synonymous with bolshevism. Communist parties gradually arose everywhere, under instigation and direction of the Russian communist party, all forming together the *Communist International* (Third International) or *Komintern* (1915–1943). Officially abolished for propaganda purposes during the Second World War (1939–1945), this was reorganized in a more modern fashion in accord with the aims set forth in the Kominform.

THE DOCTRINE OF COMMUNISM. Communism is based on Marxist doctrine, with the many variations introduced by Lenin, Stalin, and now Khrushchev. Initially, the Russians adopted Marxism in its objective-scientific aspect, according to which socialism should be the inevitable result of the natural evolution of capitalistic economy. But since Russia was a rural country, it was necessary to establish first a capitalistic economy. As Plekhanov stated, "the entire dynamism of our social life stems from capitalism." The Russian social democrats, later to be known as *mensheviks*, consequently maintained that the socialist revolution was conditioned by the development of industrial capitalism, thus confirming the scientifico-deterministic Marxian tenet. This is the basis of the entire revolutionary struggle. Plehanov believed in a social revolution: the emancipation of the workers must depend on the workers themselves and not, as Lenin thought, on a revolutionary group, because the working class must be prepared for revolution and dictatorship. But such an interpretation and application of Marxism in Russia would have entailed a long waiting period. Thus, Lenin proceeded to prepare the revolutionary will through his small revolutionary groups. He was opposed to a literal interpretation of Marxism, maintaining that socialism could be realized in Russia apart from capitalistic evolution and without the establishment of a large working class. In fact, the bolshevik revolution in Russia was the work of a minority. In general, Russian, orthodox Marxists drew from Marxism entirely new principles, which neither Marx nor Engels would have found acceptable.

The task of Lenin and the bolshevists was to elaborate a Russian Marxism in keeping with the Russian revolutionary spirit, by tending to a total integration of their whole life. This Russian form of Marxism was to be and is a philosophy, a religion, a totalitarian concept of life. In view of the natural tendency of the Russian revolutionaries toward totalitarianism, Russian Marxism or Leninism did not adopt the scientifico-deterministic aspect of Marxism, but its messianic, religious, mythical character, under the leadership of a well-organized minority. Thus a basically materialistic movement became a proof of the power of ideas and of the will. "Lenin organized the revolution in the name of Marx, but not according to Marx" (Berdiaev). Thus, ie communist revolution, in Russia, igoslavia, Poland, Romania, Hungary, nd Czechoslovakia was accomplished in pposition to many Marxian assertions n social evolution and against the will f the overwhelming majority of the peo-le. The myth of the *mujik* people of the opulists was transformed into a myth of ie proletariat, with a sort of fusion be-ween the Russian people and the prole-ariat, between a Russian messianism nd proletarian messianism. Bolshevism more traditionalistic than is commonly elieved. It remains bound to the original istorical development of Russia. In fact, ie realization of communism in Russia as produced a *Russification* and *Orien-ilization* of Marxism.

COMMUNIST TACTICS. The Komintern, ermanently organized in Moscow dur-ig the Second World Congress, in 920, had as its purpose, according to its tatutes, waging a struggle for the anni-ilation of the international *bourgeoisie* y any means whatsoever, including rms, as well as the creation of an inter-ational Soviet Republic. The only iethod of liberating humanity from the trocities of capitalism was to be the ictatorship of the proletariat.

The Komintern was established for ie purpose of organizing and unifying ie activities of the proletariat in every ountry. The organs for accomplishing his purpose were the annual world con-resses and the executive committee, ith headquarters in Moscow. The omintern represented the Central In-rnational Communist Party. The par-ies in various countries were termed ections, and were subordinated to the entral party in Moscow. Affiliation with ie Komintern was subject to various onditions. In particular, along with the gal organization, there was to be an legal one consisting of propaganda mong soldiers, peasants, and other roups. The affiliated party was obliged o endorse every Soviet government, es-ecially in time of war. After World Var I (1914–1918), the communists elieved that the time was ripe for a vorld revolution. Revolutionary out-reaks occurred in Berlin, Munich, Buda-

pest, etc., but it was soon discovered that a mistake had been made. In the Con-gress of 1921, an attempt was made to mitigate the regolutionary tactics; social-ist workers were dissociated from their leaders and were invited to a more direct collaboration (United Front). The tac-tics of that era consisted in waging a frontal attack on capitalism, the *bour-geoisie*, governments, political parties, and everything else that was not commu-nist-inspired. Such tactics of general op-position to non-communist institutions and causes led to the suppression of communist parties in almost all Euro-pean countries. In the seventh World Congress (Moscow, 1935), a new method was inaugurated, the so-called *Popular Front*. This consisted in collabo-rating everywhere with all those who, on a democratic basis, desired to follow the leadership of communists. This was the policy of the "extended hand," even to Catholics. The word from Moscow was no longer a struggle against the *bour-geoisie*, but against Fascism. After World War II, a third phase was initiated, less ideological and not so openly imperial-istic: the so-called *progressive democracy*.

In the first phase, the leading Euro-pean communists saw the liberation of all proletarians in the world through bol-shevism, but failed to grasp that in a Russian revolution even internationalism has an autonomous and national char-acter. Gradually, Stalin eliminated all influential communists, Russian and in-ternational, who saw in bolshevism the common cause of a world proletariat. Bolshevism is a Russian revolution, and all communist parties are but sections of the Russian party, lending support to Russian imperialism. If one grants that the workers' revolution of the last cen-tury was *per se* justified, then one must be willing to admit that, following the bolshevistic evolution, communism be-came pure Russian imperialism, politi-cally, socially, and culturally. This turned bolshevism into a betrayal of the just cause of the workers. It is no longer the workers' cause they are promoting; the Russian policy toward sovietized coun-tries and the new international communist organization, called the *Kominform,* is motivated by Russian imperialistic aspirations. Even the most recent developments in Russia—repudiation of Stalinism and the cult of personality, the introduction of collective leadership and an illusory democratization of communism—are simply a change of tactics in the relentless struggle toward internal enslavement and the triumph of communism in the world. *Per.*

CONDEMNATION OF COMMUNISM. The attitude of the Church toward communism has always been one of unequivocal condemnation, as appears from the encyclicals of Pius IX (*Qui pluribus,* 1846; *Quanta cura,* 1864; and the *Syllabus,* 1864); of Leo XIII (*Rerum novarum,* 1891; *Quod apostolici muneris,* 1878); and of Pius XI (*Quadragesimo anno,* 1931; and *Divini Redemptoris,* 1937). In this last encyclical, every illusion of a possible reconciliation between communism and Christianity, entertained even by some Christians either in bad faith or out of miscalculation, was entirely dissipated. Communism was also unequivocally condemned by Pius XII in his Christmas radio messages of 1941 and 1942, and again in important documents issued in 1949–1950.

In his exhortation to the clergy, in *Menti nostrae* (1950), the Pope, addressing himself directly to the clergy, writes: "There are some who, in the face of the evil of communism, which seeks to snatch the faith from those to whom it promises material well-being, show themselves fearful and uncertain. But this Apostolic See has in recent documents clearly indicated the course to follow." These documents, issued by the Supreme Sacred Congregation of the Holy Office, are: (1) a general decree of July 1, 1949; (2) a declaration on marriage, August 11, 1949; (3) an admonition on the education of youth, July 28, 1950.

The decree of July 1, 1949 (AAS, 41 [1949], 334) declares:

(a) It is forbidden to join or support the Communist party, because communism is materialistic and anti-Christian. (b) It is forbidden to publish, dissemi-

nate, or read books, periodicals, newspapers, or leaflets which uphold communistic doctrine and practice, or to contribute articles to such organs, because this is forbidden by the law itself (Canon 1399). (c) The faithful who knowingly and willingly perform any of the aforementioned actions may not be admitted to the sacraments. (d) The faithful who profess and, worse, who defend and spread the materialistic and anti-Christian doctrine of communism become automatically (*ipso facto*) apostates from the Catholic faith, and incur excommunication reserved *speciali modo* to the Holy See (Can. 2314).

Concerning the sacrament of penance in ordinary cases the followers, supporters, or members of the Communist party, before being absolved: (a) must express sorrow for their actions and clearly manifest a firm resolve to quit the party or to cease giving it any support; (b) must consent to make reparation for scandal given to others, according to the circumstances of the case and according to the prudent judgment of the confessor. If these two conditions are met, the penitent may be absolved without further ado.

Concerning persons excommunicated as formal materialistic communists: (a) if the confessor has the required faculty he may absolve the penitent; (b) if the confessor does not have the required faculty, he may in urgent cases absolve according to Canon 2254, (par. 1), after imposing on the penitent the obligation to make recourse to the Sacred Penitentiary within a month, under penalty of relapse into the same excommunication. If such recourse is morally impossible, then, according to par. 3 of the same Canon, the confessor may absolve him according to the norms provided for excommunicated persons and after he has imposed a salutary penance.

Concerning dying persons, *see* Extreme Unction, Death.

In regard to the reception of Holy Eucharist, the following obtains: (a) if one is a publicly known communist, he may not be admitted to Holy Communion, either publicly or privately, unless he first retracts his affiliation and support to the party; (b) to one whose communist affiliation is not publicly known, Communion may be given, if he publicly approaches the Eucharistic table; but if he request for Communion is made privately, it is to be denied.

MARRIAGE OF COMMUNISTS. In view of the particular nature of marriage as a sacrament, the Holy Office has issued a special Declaration (AAS, 41 [1949], 427) concerning the marriage of communists. Besides this declaration, one must also note the decision of the Pontifical Commission for the authentic interpretation of the Code of Canon Law (July 30, 1934), which treats the members of an atheistic sect in the same manner as the members of a non-Catholic sect: "*Qui sectae atheisticae adscripti sunt vel fuerunt, habendi sunt quoad omnes juris effectus etiam in ordine ad . . . matrimonium ad instar eorum qui sectae acatholicae adhaeserunt vel adhaerent.*"

On the strength of the aforementioned documents, the following conclusions regarding marriage of communists prevail:

(1) Militant atheists, who constitute special nuclei in communist ranks, labor under the impediment of mixed religion, not because they are communists, but because they are atheists. This is based on the above-mentioned reply of the Pontifical Commission; this impediment, however, does not exist for other communists.

(2) Those who profess the anti-Christian tenets of communism are required to sign the customary guarantees which are signed by non-Catholics (*ad instar acatholicorum:* Can. 1061). The marriage is to be celebrated without sacred rites and not in the church (Cans. 1102; 1109, par. 3). The Ordinary may in certain cases modify or mitigate the law, but he may never permit the celebration of Holy Mass. The sermon generally delivered by the pastor must be in catechetical form.

(3) Those who do not profess communistic doctrine, but are members or supporters of the party, belong, in respect to marriage, under the decree of July 1, 1949; but, on the occasion of their marriage, they are to be treated as public sinners or members of a forbidden society (Cans. 1065, 1066).

(4) In any marriage case involving communists, the pastor may not perform the ceremony without first consulting the Ordinary, who may allow the marriage for a grave reason and on condition that sufficient provision is made for the Catholic education of offspring and for removal of all danger of perversion for the non-communist spouse.

Admonition of July 28, 1950. Unfortunately, there are parents who permit their children to join communist-inspired youth movements and associations. The Admonition of the Holy Office of July 28, 1950 (AAS, 42 [1950], 553), is directed precisely to such parents, reminding them of their obligation to educate their children in a Christian way. The admonition is the application of the Decree to practical cases. *Pal.*

COMMUNITY OF GOODS. See Husband and Wife, Dowry.

COMMUTATION OF VOWS. See Vow, Act of religion.

COMPANIONSHIP. Man is by nature a social being; that is, he tends to associate with others, at work, play, in large endeavors or in everyday tasks. But man's association with other men is fraught with many dangers. In fact, the Psalmist warns: "With the innocent man thou wilt be innocent and with the sincere man thou wilt be sincere: and with the perverse thou wilt act according to his perversity" (Ps. 17:26).

Example, particularly if bad, exerts tremendous influence. Hence, the need for all to exercise great care in the choice of their companions. Everyone should make it a point to select his company from among persons of good, virtuous, and Christian character, and carefully avoid all those who are in any way evil or indifferent. Every man owes this to himself, as a matter of duty. Parents, educators, guardians, and all those entrusted by God with the care of the young have the duty of exercising vigilance regarding the kind of company their charges keep. This duty primarily falls on parents and guardians. Parents must not be satisfied merely to know in a general way that their children are not exposed to evil influences; they must know exactly who their children's associates are. This, of course, requires supervision, vigilance, and control. It should not prove too difficult, if children are properly trained, particularly with regard to honesty and sincerity. Nor will such supervision be resented by the young, once they are made to realize that it is entirely for their own benefit. Parents must positively and authoritatively forbid their children from associating with bad companions. But they must, before anything else, direct them by counsel and encouragment to seek good, wholesome, and Christian companions. It is perfectly natural for a child, as for all men, to seek the company of others. But proper guidance and direction are absolutely essential in order to protect the child against the tragedies resulting from evil associations. Particular vigilance must be exercised regarding the delicate matter of purity. Evil influences can very easily lead to seduction and perversion, causing disastrous and irreparable harm. *Ben.*

COMPENSATION, OCCULT. *Occult compensation* is the act whereby one takes secretly from another something which the latter owes him; it is a secret appropriation of the goods of another to which one has a just claim, but which he cannot obtain by ordinary means. It amounts to collection of a debt by taking the law into one's own hands. Occult compensation is in itself morally illicit, because, ordinarily, the law furnishes ample means for the collection of unpaid debts. This matter of occult compensation can be replete with dangers, for it is an act of appropriation; it is extremely difficult for one to be an impartial judge in one's own case. Nevertheless, theologians recognize occult compensation as lawful under the following conditions: (a) the debt must be

due in strict justice; (b) the debt cannot be recovered by ordinary legal process without serious damage or great expense to the creditor; (c) there is no likelihood that the debt will be paid in the long run, for this would amount to being paid twice for the same debt, and the creditor would be bound to occult restitution; (d) every precaution must be taken to prevent harm to the debtor or to a third party.

In practice, servants, workmen and other employees may resort to occult compensation, provided that the foregoing conditions are present, in the following circumstances: (a) if the employer refuses to pay the wage agreed upon; (b) if the worker is clearly underpaid but agreed to the low wages simply because of compulsion by necessity; (c) if the employee is required, against his will, to do more than his normal work or to do a work which is not contemplated in the employment contract.

Likewise, merchants may resort to occult compensation if the above enumerated conditions are present: (a) if they are compelled to sell their merchandise below a just price; (b) if by mistake they sold an article for a price far beneath the established price; (c) if they cannot, without serious damage, recover in any other way payment of a debt, and the like. *Fel.*

COMPENSATION (Stipend). See Honorarium, System, Moral.

COMPENSATIONISM. *See* Moral System.

COMPETENCY (Privilege of). *See* Clergy, Privileges of.

COMPETITION (System of). The system of competition is that in which the following conditions or elements are verified: (a) the individual is at liberty to produce, buy, and sell what he sees fit, wherever and however he chooses; (b) buyers and sellers conclude contracts in full freedom; (c) the government does not intervene in determining the prices.

In the competitive system, every producer constantly strives to improve the processes of production in order to reduce production costs and at the same time increase both the quantity and quality of the product. This enables him to sell his merchandise at a lower price than his competitors. Such competitive activity benefits the consumer, who can improve his standard of living. Technical progress, reduction of costs and prices, rise in the living standard of all consumers—all are the objectives of the system of competition.

Frequently, however, producers cannot estimate accurately the market capacity and find themselves producing in excess of the demand. As a matter of fact, they often maintain a high level of production, despite a slowing down in the demand and falling prices, because of the huge investment tied up in their industrial plants, which are not easily convertible to other types of production. In reality, however, the imbalance between production and consumption will continue to increase, and eventually lead to an economic crisis.

Competition, if practiced within the sphere of honesty, is morally permissible and economically advantageous. There is nothing wrong with using the most profitable methods of production or employing techniques that bring about reduction in cost and price of a product. Such action may drive competitors out of business, but it also proves very beneficial to the consumer. Hence, a competition of this kind is fair and ethical. In fact, by his competitive action, a business man makes a positive contribution to socio-economic progress, as it is his duty to do.

However, the use of unfair methods of competition is definitely immoral, if not always illegal. Examples of unfair competitive practices are: false advertising, adulteration of products, selling below cost, and the like. These and similar practices are not only immoral, but also economically detrimental. *Pav.*

COMPOSITION, COMPROMISE.
Composition or compromise is the agreement or friendly settlement of a litigation or controversy. By making mutual concessions, the two disputants involved settle the litigation without resorting to a suit. In Canon Law, compromise is admitted and proposed by the judge in cases dealing with private affairs. In such cases, if the two disputants succeed in coming to terms, without bringing the matter to judicial trial, the agreement reached is called a *composition of the litigation.*

In settling disputes through compromise or composition, local civil laws are to be observed, unless they contravene divine or ecclesiastical law (Can. 1926). Canon Law excludes compromise or composition (a) in criminal cases; (b) in matrimonial cases involving the dissolution of marriage; (c) in matters pertaining to benefices if there is a litigation concerning the title itself to a benefice and, finally, (d) in cases involving material compensation for a spiritual good or value (Can. 1927, par. 1).

The Holy See permits composition in cases involving: (a) illegitimate possession of ecclesiastical goods; (b) goods owed to unknown creditors. In such cases, the composition consists in making restitution to some charitable cause or to the poor. Such composition is granted by the Sacred Congregation of the Council, but in occult cases it is made by the Sacred Penitentiary. The Sovereign Pontiff, as supreme administrator of all ecclesiastical goods and property, may, for the sake of the common good, condone the illicit possession of ecclesiastical goods both by civil governments and private persons.

The legal and natural institution of composition is an excellent means of settling the conscience, maintaining peace and harmony, and avoiding the expenses and hazards of a court action. However, in certain cases, specifically enumerated in the law, composition is excluded for the sake of the common good to avert social harm. In such cases, private good must give way to the common and higher good. *Sir.*

COMPROMISE, NEGOTIATION.

Compromise is a contract in which two or more persons prevent an anticipated litigation or suppress one that has already begun, by means of reciprocal concessions. The right to compromises exists in those who have the capacity of disposing of things which are the object of litigation. In a contract of compromise, there is a lawful right for the parties to affix sanctions against defaulting members or negotiators.

The effect of a compromise is termed a settlement or agreement (Can. 1928, par. 1); it has the value of an irrevocable sentence. Yet it can be nullified or rescinded in some cases by civil law.

Canonical Legislation. Canon Law strongly recommends compromise in all causes concerning private affairs (Can. 1925, par. 1). It is suggested that the judge entrust the case to another priest, who can be properly chosen from among the synodal judges, since it is not becoming to the dignity of a judge to make the proposal personally.

Canon Law commits compromise to civil legislation at the place where the compromise is made, provided that no contravention of the divine or ecclesiastical laws occurs (Can. 1926). A compromise cannot be validly made in a criminal or contentious cause; in a case involving dissolution of marriage; nor in the case of a benefice whose title itself is in question, unless the legitimate authority approves of the compromise; nor in spiritual matters if the compromise involves payment by means of temporal goods (Can. 1927, par. 1).

Furthermore, if litigation revolves around temporal ecclesiastical property or property which, though attached to spiritual things, can be dealt with apart from their spiritual aspect, the compromise is licit. But the requirements of the law, concerning alienation of ecclesiastical goods, must be observed, if the matter so demands (Can. 1927, par. 2).

Expenditures for settlement are shared equally by the disputants (Can. 1928, par. 2). *Fel.*

COMPROMISE. *See* Contract.

COMPULSORY SHARE. *See* Inheritance, Will.

CONCENTRATION. *See* Attention.

CONCENTRATION OF WEALTH.

Statistical studies on the distribution of national wealth, based on income and inheritance tax reports, reveal that a considerable portion of the national wealth is concentrated in the hands of a few. This phenomenon, encountered in almost all societies, reaches its highest point in communistic societies, where practically all productive capital belongs to the State.

CAUSES. The concentration of wealth is a phenomenon due, first of all, to historical factors, especially in economically backward societies, where the principal source of wealth consists in land property and immovable goods. Secondly, it is due to political factors and special aspects inherent in the existing economic and financial system, which allows the quick enrichment of a few. The importance of this last factor, however, is greatly reduced because of the prevailing tendency toward increased public control of economic and financial activity. Along with progressive taxation of inherited wealth and personal income, there has been an effort to obtain progressive levelling of functional wealth, which restricts the possibilities of amassing great fortunes.

ERRORS OF MARXIAN THEORY. The concentration of wealth was declared by Marx to be a dynamic law of the capitalistic process, a necessary counterpart of the law of general proletarian impoverishment. This Marxist assumption, however, has been proven false. Statistics show that, although a portion of increased wealth tends to become concentrated in the hands of a few, the remainder tends to become distributed, and concentration proceeds at an equal pace with distribution. Moreover, present tax policies and the prevailing tendency toward increased social control of economic, financial, and fiscal activities will ultimately reduce concentration of wealth in non-communistic societies.

In view of the human tendency toward egoism, the phenomenon of concentration of wealth is definitely a serious social problem. It is the duty of legislators to enact appropriate corrective measures, prompted by the consideration that an equitable distribution of wealth will tend to insure a measure of social peace. *Mai.*

CONCEPT, IDEA. *Concept* and *idea* are here treated under the same heading for a twofold reason: (a) frequently they are synonymous; (b) the difference between the two terms is more clearly brought out by contrast.

Concept may be defined as a *mental word*, the means by which the knowing subject expresses to himself an object known. The knowing subject forms the mental word by conceiving it in his mind. Concept, therefore, stresses the subjective aspect of the mental word. The term *idea*, often employed as synonymous to concept, properly signifies an *image*; hence, it stresses the objective aspect of a mental word, that which an image reflects outside of us. *Concept* and *idea*, therefore, are two terms relating to one and the same inner fact or psychological factor; the difference between them is that *concept* expresses the subjective aspect of this inner fact, and *idea* underlines the objective aspect.

The subjective orientation of a concept is clearly noticeable in the philosophical theory of conceptualism, which denies any relation between our universal concepts and reality. The objective orientation of the idea had its most impressive manifestation in the realistic idealism of Plato, who endowed ideas with real or extramental existence in a transcendent world of substantialized ideas, perfect exemplars of earthly things, that were permanently condemned to imperfection. The ethical implications of these two philisophical theories are all too clear. Conceptualism denies all objective value to practical principles, and paves the way to a sheer absence

of morality; idealism, instead, offers incentive to conform our conduct to the transcendent exemplar of perfection placed before us.

A new interpretation of the distinction between concept and idea has recently gained considerable ground in ethical sciences. It is a new interpretation, though not in an absolute sense, because it bears a certain resemblance to ancient theories; the idea still retains, as in Platonism, its distinctive character of perfection, exemplar, or essence. In the modern interpretation, *concept* and *idea* are distinguished by their comprehensive notes: a concept is more comprehensive than an idea. Concept conveys a certain indifference to notes or elements rejected by a determined, noble idea. Thus, in the *concept* of *morality*, vices are included, which, as immoral, are excluded from the sphere of the *idea* of morality. Thus, too, the concept of right includes a so-called unjust right, which is a denial of right. The concept of religion includes superstition, idoltary, etc., which are excluded from the sphere of religion as an idea. In short, *idea* expresses all the essential elements of an ethical fact, whereas *concept* merely indicates some formal characteristics thereof. *Idea* tells what the ethical ought to be; *concept* describes its imperfections, aberrations, and negations.

No particular objection can be raised to this modern distinction between concept and idea, provided that it does not cause confusion and remains a purely terminological question designed to clarify certain difficulties. *Gra.*

CONCLAVE. *Conclave* (Latin, *cum*—with; *clavis*—key), as a general term, is applied to any room, chamber, closet or hallway, that could be securely locked with a key. In the course of time, this original usage or meaning was lost. Today the word is used primarily to signify the assembly of cardinals engaged in the election of a new pope, and the meeting place for this assembly.

The dogmatic principles concerning a conclave are as follows: (a) the supreme power of jurisdiction is conferred upon the pope directly by God, not by the electors, whose action is not so much election as a designation of person; (b) all lay intrusion or intervention is unwarranted usurpation (Can. 219; Const. *Vacante Sede Apostolica,* tit. II, ch. 1, n. 27 in Appendix to the Code of Canon Law; Motu Proprio *Cum Proxime,* March 1, 1922; Const. *Vacantis Apostolicae Sedis,* Dec. 8, 1945).

Other norms for the conduct of a conclave are considered merely disciplinary prescriptions and susceptible of change according to circumstances.

In the first centuries of the Church, the method of papal election did not differ substantially from that used for episcopal elections. The election of the new pope was made by the Roman clergy together with the faithful, under the guidance of the neighboring bishops of Ostia, Albano and Porto. After the death of Constantine (337), the Christian Roman emperors and civil magistrates, and later the Ostrogoth kings, took part in the election of a new pope, often exerting a very marked influence. Naturally, this accounts for dissensions among the Roman factions at every vacancy of the Holy See (P. Albers, *Ecclesiastical History,* I, Rome 1928, p. 232 ff.). In the Roman Council of 499, Pope Symmachus (498–514) decreed that the election of a new pope should be carried out by majority vote of the clergy alone. This decree was later renewed, unfortunately in vain, in the Roman Council of 769. Ecclesiastical freedom in papal elections began to prevail with Nicholas II (1058–1061), who issued the constitution *In nomine Domini,* promulgated in the Lateran Council of 1059. Through this constitution all privileges usurped by emperors were abolished and the electoral vote was restricted to cardinals alone. The election was to be carried out in the following manner: the selection of a candidate was first to be made by the cardinal bishops, who, together with the other cardinals, proceeded to election; this was then made known to the rest of

the clergy and laity. However, a tragic period of investitures impeded the fulfillment of this decree (Albers, *op. cit.,* II. 3 ff.). It was not until the reign of Alexander III (1159–1181), that imperial privileges, together with the last vestiges of lay intervention in papal elections, were completely abolished through the constitution *Licet de vitanda,* promulgated in the Lateran Council of 1179. At this Council, the constitution of Nicholas II, *In nomine Domini,* was revised so that not only cardinal bishops, but all cardinals, regardless of order, should be summoned to elect the new pope. It was further established that the pope was to be chosen by a two-thirds majority vote of the electors present, through the ballot system (Const. *Licet de vitanda,* VI, I, 6, 3).

The practical difficulties encountered in obtaining the required two-thirds majority eventually led to the establishment of the conclave system. It was hoped that, by confirming the electors in seclusion and uncomfortable quarters, with all outside communications cut off, a quick decision would be reached, and thus shorten the vacancy period. The conclave was not a new system, but it was used for municipal elections by many medieval Italian States.

All previous constitutions and decrees concerning papal elections were abrogated by the constitution of St. Pius X (1903–1914), *Vacante Sede Apostolica,* December 25, 1904. The motu proprio of Pius XI (1922–1939), *Cum proxime,* March 1, 1922, contains the current legislation governing papal elections. Recently, some changes were made by Pope Pius XII, in the Constitution *Vacantis Apostolicae Sedis,* December 8, 1945, (AAS: 38 [1946], 65ff.).

CEREMONIAL OF THE CONCLAVE. Immediately upon the death of the pontiff, the Dean of the Sacred College notifies all the cardinals throughout the world. These convene at a solemn conclave within a secluded section of the Vatican Palace, especially prepared for the election of the new pope. The conclave may not commence earlier than fifteen, nor later than eighteen, days after the pope's death (motu proprio *Cum proxime*, n. 1). The right to elect the new pope belongs exclusively to cardinals appointed in a consistory (*Vacante Sede Apostolica*, n. 30), provided that they have entered the conclave before the final balloting (*loc. cit.*, n. 34). Cardinals under ecclesiastical censures of excommunication, interdict, or suspension enjoy the same right; deposed cardinals, however, or those who have renounced their cardinal dignity are excluded (*loc. cit.*, n. 29, 31).

Besides the cardinals, the following are admitted to the conclave: the various prelates or officers of the conclave; two conclavists or attendants, lay or ecclesiastical (in case of illness a third may be allowed); the sacristan of the Vatican Palace together with clerics (six at most) to act as masters of ceremonies; the secretary of the Sacred College; a religious as confessor; two physicians; a surgeon and a few servants (*loc. cit.*, n. 38, motu proprio *Cum proxime*). Persons related to the cardinals, either by consanguinity or affinity in the first and second degree, may not be admitted (n. 38). Except in the case of a duly verified illness, no one is permitted to leave before the conclave is ended (n. 41).

Prior to the electoral proceedings, several meetings or sessions are held at which the constitutions governing the conclave are read; then the cardinals take an oath to observe them. All are equally sworn to maintain absolute secrecy and not to hinder the election by any political veto (n. 40, 45).

The new pope may be elected in one of these three ways; (a) *quasi-inspiration*, which supposes that the cardinals, without previous agreement among themselves, as if moved by the Holy Spirit, unanimously proclaim aloud the name of the same candidate (n. 55); (b) *compromise*, which supposes that, after inconclusive action, the cardinals unanimously delegate a certain number of them (three, five, or seven) to designate the new pope, with the members of the group thus designated barred from candidacy (n. 56); (c) by *secret ballot*,

which is the method ordinarily used.

In this last form, a majority of two-thirds plus one is required for election. Voting is held twice daily, in the morning and in the evening, until the prescribed majority is obtained. If no selection is made, the ballots are burned with damp straw and voting begins anew. If the necessary majority has been obtained, the ballots are burned without the straw (nn. 57; 72–77, *Vacantis Apostolicae Sedis*).

The election becomes complete and irrevocable the moment that the chosen candidate indicates his acceptance to the Dean of the Sacred College (nn. 87–88, *Vacante Sede Apostolica*). If the pope-elect is not already a priest and bishop, he is immediately ordained and consecrated by the Dean of the Sacred College (n. 90). The coronation ceremony, which follows a few days later, is a mere liturgical solemnity that adds nought to the pope's power.

Election by any system other than the ones described above is null and void. The election, however, is not nullified by failure to observe prescriptions concerning the enclosure or seclusion of cardinals in conclave nor by any simoniacal action or agreement occurring in the course of the election (n. 79).

Any baptized layman may be elected pope; however, since 1389, only cardinals have become popes.

By virtue of article 21 of the Lateran Treaty, February 11, 1929, the Italian government is committed to guarantee full freedom and safety to cardinals coming to the conclave, and to insure the security of the conclave itself. *Tar.*

CONCORDAT. A concordat is an agreement in the form of an official treaty between the Church and a nation, for the intent purpose of regulating the affairs of common juridical interest.

Competent to make a concordat are those persons in the Church or State with supreme authority in their respective spheres, and the right to conclude formal and binding treaties. For the Church, this is the Roman Pontiff; for the State, it is the person or persons who are invested with supreme power by the constitution. However, concordats are usually negotiated by plenipotentiaries, i.e., diplomatic representatives with full powers to conduct the negotiations. It is to be noted that, whenever the constitution of a country requires the approval of its legislative bodies for the enactment of the concordat into law, the Supreme Pontiff does not sign the concordat until a reasonable assurance is secured that such approval is forthcoming; nor does he permit any exchange of ratifications until the necessary approval has actually been expressed.

Concordats may vary considerably, according to the subject of mutual interest for the two supreme societies. Particularly important in such treaties are the so-called mixed matters (*res mixtae*), i.e., matters pertaining both to the temporal and the spiritual orders, e.g., public education, marriage, etc.

In the present day, concordats do not differ in form from other international treaties (*q.v.*). Accordingly, they are negotiated by two juridically distinct phases: (a) the *signing* of the concordat in duplicate by the respective plenipotentiaries; this official act, duly prepared in documentary form, or so-called *procès verbal*, is signed in duplicate by the same plenipotentiaries; (b) *ratification* by the Supreme Pontiff and by the chief of State. A *procès verbal* of this formal ceremony is also drafted in duplicate and signed by those assigned to handle the exchange of ratification. Frequently, appended to the concordat are clauses or declarations under the general title of protocol, which define, explain, or interpret words or articles contained in the body of the treaty.

The nature of concordats still is a much discussed subject. Mention shall first be made of the legalistic or civil theory, widely prevalent among those who hold that the State is above the Church. The State cannot enter into a bilateral contract with a subordinate institution; hence, a concordat is a purely civil law which, though morally binding because of an agreement, can

be changed and revoked at will by the civil ruler, but not by the pope. This view is to be rejected.

There are two other views, however, which remain open for discussion: the *compact theory*, and the *privilege theory*. According to the *compact theory*, which seems the more tenable, a concordat is really and truly a bilateral pact, *sui generis*, which binds in justice both parties (*ex justitia commutativa*). According to the *privilege theory*, concessions made by the Church to the State are mere privileges, to which the Church is held, not in justice, but in loyal adherence to the stipulated agreement; but the State is bound to observe concordatory dispositions as particular laws issuing from the supreme spiritual power in a specific territory.

The interpretation of concordats is to be made jointly by the Church and the State. In case of conflict, the interpretation of the Church, which is, at least indirectly, superior to the State, should prevail.

Concordats are terminated under the following conditions:

(a) If observance of concordat details becomes physically or morally impossible. A distinction, however, must here be made: if the observance of all the principal articles is impossible, the concordat ceases; if only one of the principal articles or if the secondary articles become impossible, the concordat remains in force, at least insofar as the principal articles are concerned. In all other cases, any alteration or abrogation is to be made by mutual accord.

(b) If the concordatory agreement was deliberately violated by one of the contracting parties, the innocent party may suspend or rescind the concordat or demand its proper observance.

(c) If the State ceases to exist, by division into several States or by union or incorporation into another State. However, if only part of a State is united or incorporated into another State, the concordat ceases only for the united or incorporated part of the State. If a State has merely undergone a change in its form of government, the concordat may not be considered terminated.

(d) Mutual consent of the contracting parties terminates a concordat.

(e) If the agreement was fraudulently or deceptively negotiated, or if it is vitiated by substantial error, the agreement, though valid, may be rightfully voided.

(f) Finally, by prescription. *Fel.*

CONCUBINAGE. In moral theology *concubinage* is a more or less permanent state or continued practice of sexual intercourse between a man and a woman not legitimately married to each other, with or without cohabitation. If the illicit relationship or absence of marriage is a fact known only to a few persons, without danger of further disclosure, the concubinage is regarded as occult or hidden; otherwise, it is public or notorious (Can. 2197). Concubinarians, therefore, are all those living in a state of illicit, extra-marital relationship, whether covered by some sort of legality, as a purely civil marriage of persons bound by the canonical form, or none at all (Can. 1094–1099).

From the moral point of view, concubinage is equivalent to fornication, of which it is a continued form. Some theologians consider concubinage a lesser sin than prostitution or fornication, because it limits concupiscence to one specific person, constituting, therefore, a lesser violation of the natural law than promiscuity. Others, instead, regard concubinage as a more serious sin, because it supposes greater pertinacity or obstinacy. Frequently, because of the presence of certain factors which prevent the unlawful union from being rectified by legitimate marriage, concubinage takes on the added malice of adultery, incest, or sacrilege.

Canon Law, besides penalties against notorious concubinarians (Can. 2357, par. 2), considers them public sinners, to be barred from the sacraments (Can. 855, par. 1) and from ecclesiastical burial (Can. 1240, par. 1, n. 6). Public or notorious concubinage gives rise to the matrimonial impediment of public decency, which invalidates any marriage between a concubinarian and a blood-relative of the other party, in the first and second degree of the direct line (Can. 1078). *See also* Fornication. *Dam.*

CONCUPISCENCE. Employed in a very wide sense, *concupiscence* is synonymous with *passion*. At times, it is restricted to one of the numerous passions, that is, as the tendency to pleasures aroused by passion and directed to the enjoyment of the object loved and desired. Frequently it is used as a synonym for that tendency in general, although not specifically to the passions. Saint Paul in the Epistle to the Galatians (5:17) emphasizes this aspect, that the spirit has concupiscences opposed to those of the flesh. Moral theologians, as a rule, employ the term in its first two meanings. In other words, they view concupiscence either as embracing all passions, or as the passionate tendency to pleasure, especially sensitive and illicit varieties. In other words, moralists generally consider concupiscence as a tendency, inclination, or movement of the sensitive appetite, contrary to reason.

The moral problem to which concupiscence gives rise is the influence it exercises on the will or freedom, that is, the morality of human acts committed under the impulse of passion.

For the proper understanding of the problem, a distinction must be made between *antecedent* and *consequent* concupiscence. The former arises, uncaused by the will, without voluntary or unlawful cooperation on our part. The latter arises under the influence of the will and is caused by the will. In both, but particularly in consequent concupiscence, there is an increase or intensification of will-energy. In antecedent concupiscence, stirred up spontaneously and inadvertently, both freedom and responsibility are diminished. In consequent concupiscence, caused by and fostered with the consent of the will, freedom and imputability are increased.

Actions performed under the impact of an overwhelming antecedent impulse, that is, before one is able to exercise any control, are called *primo primi;* they do not admit of ethical evaluation, for there is no question of blame or imputability.

On the subject of concupiscence, ascetical moralists refer to a text of the First Epistle of St. John (2:16), in which the Apostle states that moral evil may be due to concupiscence of the flesh, concupiscence of the eyes, and pride of life. The first is a tendency to sensual pleasures; the second is a tendency to riches and luxury; the third is a tendency to glory or fame. These three forms of concupiscence may well be considered the principal source of all sins and vices in the world. *Gra.*

CONCUPISCIBLE. See Appetite, Concupiscible and Irascible.

CONDIGN MERIT. See Merit.

CONDIMENT. See Abstinence.

CONDITION. In general terms, a *condition* is a circumstance attached as an accessory clause to a declaration of will, that is, to a juridical act or transaction by which it is established that validity shall depend on the presence or verification of the stipulated circumstance.

In a more restricted and proper sense, employed in most modern codes, *condition* signifies a future, uncertain event, upon verification of which the efficacy or dissolution of a juridical transaction is made to depend by the parties of the transaction. By virtue of metonymy, even the principal declaratory clause, subordinated to the future uncertain event, is called condition.

Thus understood, a condition is an accidental element capable of modifying a juridical transaction, insofar as it may, depending on the case, nullify the act in root or void its effects.

The essential elements of a *proper* condition are as follows: (a) the condition must regard a future event which

is uncertain, but possible; (b) the apposition of a condition must proceed from the will of the principal or principals involved in the juridical transaction. If either of these requisites is lacking, the condition is said to be an *improper* one.

PROPER CONDITIONS. From the standpoint of *efficacy*, conditions are suspensive and resolutive. A condition is *suspensive* if the effects of the act remain suspended until such time as the event is actually verified (I shall give you a certain sum of money if you leave the country). It is *resolutive* if the effects of the act, already in operation, cease as soon as the event is verified (I give you this house of mine until such a time when I shall need it for myself).

From the standpoint of the cause upon which verification of the event depends, conditions are *casual* if the event depends, not on the will of the principals involved, but on some unforeseen event or on the will of a third party; *authoritative*, if verification of the event is made dependent on the will of one of the principals (e.g., if you come to my house); *mixed*, if verification of the event depends partly on the will of the subject, partly on extraneous causes (e.g., if you marry Mary). In other words, a mixed condition is partly authoritative, partly casual. If verification of the event depends solely on the will of the subject, the condition is said to be purely authoritative.

From the standpoint of *formulation*, a condition may be: (a) *positive* or *negative*, if it involves verification (if you go to Europe) or non-verification of a fact (if you do not go to Europe); (b) *express* or *tacit*, if it is expressly stated or implicitly contained in the declaratory clause, or even presupposed by a disposition of the law.

Regarding the *nature* of the event, a condition is said to be *licit* or *possible* and *impossible* or *illicit*. A condition may be physically or morally impossible. An event which cannot naturally occur is called *physically impossible* (e.g., to touch the sky with one's finger, to drink the ocean). Something which is unlawful or illegal is said to be *juridically impossible* (e.g., for a private citizen to sell the city hall). Something against morality is said to be *morally impossible* or an immoral condition (e.g., if you kill your father).

IMPROPER CONDITIONS. Improper conditions are those lacking the necessary requisite of objective pendency or uncertainty: if the objective uncertainty of the event is lacking, or the event has already been objectively verified, or is certainly unrealizable.

Past and present conditions, i.e., those regarding a past or present fact (*condiciones in praesens vel in praeteritum conlatae*) are called improper, because they exclude the quality of objective pendency or uncertainty of the event. Technically, if the event has already been verified, one cannot speak of an objectively conditioned transaction. Subjective pendency has no juridical effects.

Also considered improper is a *future necessary condition*, i.e., one regarding a future event which is necessary or certain to occur (e.g., if the sun rises tomorrow), even though there may be uncertainty regarding the time of its occurrence (*certus an, incertus quando*), unless such a condition is intended to indicate the terminus of the transaction. "If my father dies," means "when or as soon as my father dies": a terminus or limitation rather than a condition is posited. On the other hand, a *future contingent condition*, that is, one which contains real uncertainty regarding verification of the event (*incertus an*), is considered a proper condition.

Impossible conditions, whether physically, juridically, or morally impossible, are also included within the category of improper conditions.

Improper conditions are also those which change in many cases the juridical status of individuals in respect to Canon Law. All the more so is this true in the moral field, where responsibility is measured and situations are solved mainly on the basis of subjective factors, and where the intent of a person is taken into consideration even before positive norms.

For a juridical and moral evaluation of a conditional transaction, the three phases of pendency, verification, and failure of a condition must be kept in mind.

(a) *During the phase of pendency* (*condicio pendet*), if the condition is suspensive, although the act is not yet carried out, the one interested in its verification has a real right protected by the law, while the other party has the obligation to wait for the event to take place and not to hinder or minimize its actuation. Otherwise, the latter is liable to damages. In some instances, as in contracts, the condition may be considered by the law as having been fulfilled if its verification was deceitfully hindered or frustrated. If the condition is resolutive, the act immediately produces its normal effects as if no condition were attached, and the rights deriving therefrom may be legitimately exercised; but the obligation of suspending the exercise of these rights and restoring matters to their original status, if the event failed to materialize, remains.

(b) Upon *verification* of the event (*condicio exsistit*), if the condition was suspensive, the transaction becomes consummated and the relation between the parties is definitely established. If the condition was resolutive, the transaction is considered dissolved, and its effects cease. As a rule, verification of the condition has retroactive effect, so that the efficacy or non-efficacy of the juridical transaction obtains not simply from the moment the condition is verified (*ex nunc*), but also from the moment the declaration of will was made (*ex tunc*). Hence, if a suspensive condition is verified, the effects of the transaction are considered as produced from the very beginning. If a resolutive condition is verified, the transaction is considered non-existent from the beginning, and all effects produced are regarded as non-existent (Cans. 1529, 1926, 1930). An exception in Canon Law to this general principle is the suspensive condition *de futuro* attached to the matrimonial consent, whose efficacy obtains *ex nunc*, (Cans. 1081; 1092 n. 3).

(c) If the condition *fails* to materialize (*condicio deficit*), the opposite of what was stated above is true: if the non-verified condition was suspensive, the transaction is considered as never to have existed; if the unfulfilled condition was resolutive, the transaction is regarded as definitely completed.

Moreover, it is to be noted that by virtue of natural law *future impossible* conditions render the act, or contract, invalid, since the intention of the party attaching such conditions is obviously not serious. The same is true for improper and immoral conditions *de futuro*, since no one can be bound to sin. According to positive law, instead, acts or transactions *inter vivos* are invalid by the apposition of impossible and immoral conditions; in acts *mortis causa* (in view of death) or last will dispositions, such conditions, although they do not void the act itself, are regarded as not to have been placed. As a general principle of the natural and canonical laws, any condition entailing or implying the commission of sin by any of the principals involved in the transaction (*condicio nutritiva peccati*) is always unlawful.

EFFICACY OF CONDITIONS IN THE ADMINISTRATION OF THE SACRAMENTS. Generally speaking, if, in administering the sacraments, there exists an insoluble doubt concerning an essential requisite for validity (whether the matter is valid; whether a subject is conscious or living); or if, in the case of those sacraments which imprint a character, there is prudent doubt as to whether they were validly conferred or conferred at all, the minister may and sometimes must attach to the sacramental formula a condition which subordinates the new conferral of the sacrament to the existence of the necessary requirements (Can. 732, par. 2).

As a general rule, it is always permissible to confer the sacrament conditionally if there is serious danger that

the sacrament might be exposed to nullity if it were to be conferred absolutely, while outright denial of the sacrament would deprive a person of a great good.

However, the only conditions which may be licitly attached to the administration of the sacraments are suspensive conditions of the present or the past (*de praesenti vel de praeterito*), in which the pendency or uncertainty is only subjective.

Absolutely excluded, as wholly illicit, are suspensive conditions *de futuro* (except in the case of marriage). Such conditions render the sacraments null for the following reasons: (a) at the moment of placing the condition, the sacrament would remain suspended, and the minister would lack the full intention of conferring the sacrament; (b) upon verification of the condition, there would be dissociation of matter and form, the coexistence of which is absolutely essential for the validity of a sacrament (*see* Sacraments). For the same reasons, resolutive future conditions are absolutely illicit. Concerning Holy Mass, it is to be noted that the celebrant is never permitted to consecrate *positively doubtful* matter, not even under a condition *de praesenti* or *de praeterito*, because of the danger of exposing the faithful to idolatry by offering for adoration that which is not the Body and Blood of Christ.

The Code of Canon Law lists a number of cases where apposition of a condition to the sacramental formula is mandatory; for instance, in the repetition of sacraments that imprint a character (Can. 732, par. 2), in certain cases of administration of baptism (Cans. 746, par. 3–5; 747; 748; 752, par. 3) and of the sacrament of extreme unction (Cans. 941–942).

Among the sacraments, only marriage, because of its contractual nature, admits of a suspensive condition of the future (*de futuro*), within the limits designated by Canon 1092 (*see* Consent, Matrimonial).

However, the marriage contract does not admit of resolutive conditions, because these are equivalent in practice to conditions *contra substantiam*. In other words, since such conditions are directly contrary to the indissolubility of the bond, they are against the substance of marriage itself.

In rescripts of favor or of justice, issued by the ecclesiastical authority in its administrative and jurisdictional functions, there may be attached conditions which subordinate the granting of the favor to the verification of certain circumstances. Conditions attached to rescripts are considered essential to the validity of the concession only if they are conditions in the true sense of the word: if they are expressed by the conjunctions *if, provided (si, dummodo)* or some other equivalent term. By law, all rescripts are considered given with a tacit condition *"si preces veritate nitantur"* (provided the petition is truthful.) This condition certainly affects the validity of the concession (Cans. 39–40; *see* Rescript).

In establishing a benefice, the founder or patron may, with the consent of the Ordinary, append to the charter of foundation (*in limite fundationis*) conditions contrary to the common law (*contra jus commune*), provided that they are honest and not incompatible with the nature of the benefice (Can. 1417).

Conditions attached to a vote in canonical elections are illicit and considered as non-existent (Can. 169, par. 2); so are conditions contrary to the common law (*contra jus commune*) in elections by compromise (Can. 172, par. 3); conditions affecting the canonical conferring of a benefice or the use of its revenue in the case of renunciation of benefices in favor of others (Can. 1486); conditions exempting the administrators of a foundation from rendering an annual account to the local Ordinary (Can. 1492, par. 2); conditions not accepted by the Ordinary in the renunciation of a parish (Can. 2150, par. 3).

EFFICACY OF CONDITIONS IN CONTRACTS. The above principles regarding conditions are also applied by civil law, especially in the case of contracts. The dispositions of the civil law in this regard, according to Canon 1529 and within the limits designated therein, have equal force in canonical legislation and are binding in conscience. *Zac.*

CONDONATION. *Condonation* is the remission of a debt by a creditor with power and dominion over the property involved. To be valid, condonation must be completely voluntary on the part of the creditor, i.e., free of coercion, fear, deceit, or error.

Condonation is said to be: (a) *express*, if it is granted upon the debtor's petition or request; (b) *tacit* or implied, if the creditor of his own volition (*sciens et volens*) cancels his claim to payment; (c) *presumed*, if the debtor can prudently judge that the creditor on request would readily grant the desired remission of debt. Such presumption may be reasonably invoked in the case of small thefts by children, husbands, wives, servants, the poor, etc.

Equivalent to condonation is settlement, whereby a creditor, in receipt of part of the debt, waives his claim to the rest as a way of settling the matter (*see* Debt).

Condonation is to be interpreted in a restrictive sense: it may not be extended to persons or objects other than those involved or intended. It is common doctrine among moral theologians that if condonation is made because of the debtor's poverty, the debt is fully extinguished; there is no obligation of restitution, even if the debtor's financial condition should later improve. *Fel.*

CONFABULATION. *See* Memory.

CONFERRAL OF BENEFICES. *See* Beneficiary; Benefice, Ecclesiastical.

CONFESSION. In theological language, *confession* is one of the constitutive elements of the sacrament of penance (*q.v.*). It consists in telling one's sins to a duly authorized priest (*see* Confessor), for the purpose of obtaining absolution (*q.v.*).

By divine precept (Denz., 899, 917),

one is bound to confess, after diligent self-examination, all mortal sins committed after baptism which are not yet directly remitted in the sacrament of penance, i.e., not explicitly mentioned in a previous good confession (Can. 901).

A penitent is further obliged to state accurately the species and number of all mortal sins and the circumstances (Can. 901) which may change the theological species of a sin (venial sin or mortal) or may add to a sin new malice (see Circumstances of human act). If the exact number of sins cannot be remembered, an approximate estimate must be given. Should the penitent be unable to give even an approximate number, it is sufficient that he manifest the state of his soul as best he can.

By ecclesiastical law, all the faithful who have attained the age of reason are bound to confess their sins at least once a year (Can. 906) and in danger of death. But if confession proves necessary to avoid relapse into serious sin, which is not at all impossible, one is obliged to confess more frequently. One who is not in the state of grace but wishes to receive Holy Communion, must first go to confession (Can. 856). In urgent necessity of receiving communion without an opportunity for confession, one may make an act of perfect contrition and receive communion.

The nature of the sacrament of penance requires confession of sins in a simple, concise, humble, and contrite manner. Furthermore, confession must be complete.

Neither intense shame nor a long waiting line of penitents excuses one from the obligation of a complete confession. However, physical or moral impossibility, such as extreme illness, imminent danger of death, inability to find a confessor who understands one's language, would excuse from this obligation. Such obstacles dispense from material integrity, but the obligation still remains of making a full confession at the next suitable opportunity.

If a penitent cannot confess a sin or the circumstance of a sin without incurring the danger of revealing the identity of his accomplice, he is not bound to seek a confessor to whom the accomplice is unknown. If this cannot be done without grave inconvenience the penitent may and, in all probability must confess his sins, even though there be danger of indirectly revealing his accomplice. The confessor is never permitted formally or indirectly to inquire into the name of an accomplice in sin, nor is the penitent obliged to answer any such question. However, the confessor may rightfully ask questions concerning any circumstance which he may deem necessary for determining the species of a sin or for deciding an obligation to restitution.

A penitent who knowingly fails to make an integral confession of his sin commits a sacrilege and renders confession invalid and unworthy. In order to return to the state of grace, he is obliged to manifest in his next confession the sacrilege committed, all the mortal sins mentioned in the invalid confession, the sins he failed to confess, and all mortal sins committed since that time (Can. 907).

A mortal sin inadvertently omitted or forgotten in one confession, must be mentioned in the next confession. The same applies to the inadvertent omission of either the number of mortal sins or their species. If a person is in danger of death and under an obligation to rectify the integrity of a past confession, he must attend to it without delay.

Although there is no obligation to confession of venial sins, it is of great spiritual benefit for one to do so (see Penance). Sins already confessed and directly remitted in the sacrament of penance are a sufficiently valid, though not necessary, matter of confession (Can. 902). It is of great spiritual benefit for one to express renewed sorrow for a sin or sins of one's past life, through such sins have already been confessed and forgiven. In confessing venial sins it is advisable to lay particular stress on sins committed with greater frequency, ease, or deliberation, and to xplain the cause for such lapses. This helps the penitent in the practice of humility and enables the confessor to suggest more effective and salutary remedies.

Insufficient matter for confession are ins committed before baptism and anything which is not genuinely sinful, such s imperfections. Doubtful sins are doubtful matter, for which one may nly receive conditional absolution. Hence a person with nothing but doubtful sins to confess, must include one r more certain sins of the past, although lready confessed and forgiven. The socalled general confession or accusation f sins of the past life can be advantageous to a person not inclined to scrupulosity. A general confession is beneficial at certain times of one's life, uch as during a mission or annual rereat, on entering a new state of life marriage, priesthood, religious life), t the time of a jubilee, in dangerous llness. Needless to say, in a general confession one is not obliged to repeat all ins previously confessed. A scrupulous person should be dissuaded from general confessions, for such a practice will aggravate rather than improve his condition. A general confession becomes necessary if former confessions were certainly invalid or sacrilegious. *Man.*

CONFESSIONALIA. See Summas for Confessors.

CONFESSION, FREQUENT. The practice of receiving the sacrament of penance weekly or fortnightly is referred to as frequent confession. Such a practice is productive of many salutary benefits, such as the preservation and ncrease of grace, a more genuine sorrow for personal sins committed, greater assurance of forgiveness, opportunity of gaining many plenary indulgences, etc. Practically all plenary indulgences require confession as one of the necessary conditions.

Frequent confession, even without grave sins, is considered a fundamental principle in Christian ascetical life. For this reason the Code of Canon Law directs Ordinaries to see to it that the clergy receive the sacrament of penance frequently (Can. 124, par. 1).

The same directive applies to students preparing for the priesthood; these are to be provided the opportunity of confesion at least weekly. Weekly confession is also prescribed for members of religious institutes (Can. 595, par. 1, n. 3). *Pal.*

CONFESSOR. The minister of the sacrament of penance (*q.v.*) is called a *confessor*. The confessor exercises a threefold office: judge, teacher, and physician. He is a *judge*, because the sacrament of penance is judicial in character, for by his sentence he grants a penitent the remission of his sins and restores supernatural life to his soul. He is a *teacher*, assigned by the Church to instruct penitents who are ignorant of the necessary truths of faith and of the more important duties of Christian life (*Roman Ritual, tit.* IV, c. 1, n. 14). A confessor is a *physician* of souls. In his capacity as physician he is required to impart to the penitent salutary advice and admonitions, and the proper remedies for avoiding future sin and healing the wounds left on the soul by past sins (Can. 888, par. 1; *Roman Ritual, tit.* IV, c. 1, n. 18). The confessor, therefore, exercises a true spiritual paternity; he takes the place of God, who, though offended by our sins, is nevertheless infinitely merciful.

A penitent must have a deep respect for his confessor. He should be anxious to manifest his conscience to him so that he may fruitfully exercise his office. In particular, the penitent should be willing to disclose to his confessor personal problems and difficulties, the temptations encountered in performing his duties, occasions and causes of past sins, and the virtues which he finds easier to practice (*see* Direction, Spiritual). Finally, a penitent will find it most useful for his spiritual progress to have a regular confessor. *Man.*

CONFIRMATION. *Confirmation* (Latin, *confirmare*—to render stable, or firm) is the sacrament which gives to a baptized person the grace and strength to profess and defend the faith courageously. The essential elements of confirmation are: imposition of hands, anointing of the forehead with chrism by the bishop (Can. 789) and the words: *I sign you with the sign of the Cross and confirm you with the chrism of salvation, in the name of the Father and of the Son and of the Holy Ghost. Amen.* (*Roman Ritual.* III, c. 2, n. 6).

The foregoing words, in theological language, are called the *form* of the sacrament. The *remote, valid matter* of this sacrament is chrism, a mixture of olive oil and balm, specially blessed by the bishop for the purpose of confirmation. The chrism must have been blessed on the preceding Holy Thursday. Even if the sacrament is conferred by an ordinary priest, the chrism must have been blessed by a bishop (Can. 781, par. 1). The validity of confirmation administered with oil of the catechumens or oil of the sick, is doubtful.

The proximate matter of this sacrament consists in an anointing of the forehead with chrism, in the form of the Cross, simultaneous with the imposition of hands. This imposition of hands and anointing are required for the validity of the sacrament, but the extension of hands at the beginning and end of the ceremony are not required for validity. The anointing may never be performed with an instrument (Can. 781, par. 2), but by the direct use of the hand.

MINISTER. Since apostolic times, the bishop alone has been the ordinary minister of confirmation (Can. 782, par. 1); since confirmation is the perfecting or completing sacrament, it is fitting that it be conferred by one possessing the fulness of the priesthood. The power of confirming may be extended by the pope to priests without the episcopal character. In a number of Eastern rites, by virtue of a special faculty of a general nature, priests are ordinary ministers of the sacrament of confirmation. In the Latin rite, certain priests (cardinals, abbots and prelates

nullius, vicars and prefects apostolic are empowered by common law to ac minister confirmation (Can. 782, pa 3). Moreover, by a decree of Pope Piu XII, issued Sept. 14, 1946 (AAS: 3 [1946], 349 ff.), pastors were grante the faculty to confirm, within the limit of their parish, non-confirmed person in danger of death, whenever the bisho is unavailable.

RECIPIENT. The valid reception o confirmation requires that the subjec be a baptized person. Moreover, thos who have attained the age of reaso: must have at least an implicit intentio: of receiving the sacrament.

Lawful reception requires that th recipient be in the state of grace. I: addition, one who has attained the ag of discretion must be adequately in structed (Can. 786). In the Latin rite confirmation is generally conferre(shortly after one has reached the us of reason, generally in the seventh yea of age. However, for weighty and jus reasons, it may be administered at a: earlier age (Can. 788).

Although it cannot be demonstratec with certainty that everyone is oblige(to receive the sacrament of confirma tion, in practice the reception of thi sacrament may not be neglected with out committing a sin (Can. 787). I the failure to receive the sacrament i due to contempt, or causes scandal o constitutes a danger to salvation, the si: is certainly grave.

Concerning sponsors at confirmation *see* Sponsors.

RITE, TIME, AND PLACE. Solemn con firmation is to be administered by th(bishop with mitre and pastoral staff An ordinary priest conferring this sacra ment must wear at least surplice anc stole. In a private administration. fo: any good reason, the stole alone suffices Confirmation may be administered o1 any day and at any hour, but the mos appropriate time is the Pentecostal sea son (Can. 790). Although a church is the proper place for the ceremony nevertheless, for a just and reasonabl(cause, any becoming place may b(selected (Can. 791). The names of al

ersons confirmed, together with other
ertinent data, are to be duly recorded
a special confirmation book by the
astor, who must also make proper nota-
on in the baptismal register (Can.
98).

EFFECTS. The sacrament of confirma-
on produces within the soul an
ndelible character, whereby the bap-
zed person is signed and consecrated
a soldier of Christ, the Teacher of
vine Truth. Confirmation, therefore,
ads the baptized individual to a state
f supernatural maturity, by enabling
im to profess and defend the faith
ourageously and firmly. Confirmation
roduces an increase of sanctifying
race, and of the infused virtues and
even gifts of the Holy Ghost; it brings
ne Divine Persons to a firmer posses-
on of the soul. Reception of the sacrament also gives a constant right to re-
eive special strength and the actual
races required to profess the faith
ravely and staunchly, especially in times
f difficulty. In this connection, the
Christian soldier is vividly reminded of
he timorous Apostles, who, after re-
eiving on Pentecost Day the gifts of
he Holy Ghost promised by Christ
efore His Ascension, proceeded fear-
essly to preach the Gospel everywhere.
inally, confirmation also gives special
nd permanent strength against so-
alled human respect.

If the recipient of confirmation should
nknowingly lack the state of grace, the
acrament would still convey sanctify-
ng grace and the effects attached there-
o, provided that the subject have at
east imperfect contrition for his grave
ins, with a firm purpose of amendment.
Should any of these conditions be
acking, the confirmed person would be
eprived of sanctifying grace and its
ffects until this obstacle was removed
see Reviviscence of Sacraments).

All should have a high regard for the
xcellent gift received from God in the
acrament of confirmation, and always
nd everywhere show themselves firm be-
ievers not only by words, but also by
leeds. As soldiers of Christ, Christians
nave the obligation not only to practice
the faith, but also to safeguard and
defend it.

The recent decree of Pope Pius XII
empowering pastors to confirm shows
clearly the grave concern of the Church
that none of her children depart this
life without the indelible character of
Confirmation. Whenever, therefore, an
infant, even of very tender age, is in
danger of death, the local pastor should
be immediately notified, so that confirmation may be administered by the
bishop, if available, or by the pastor
himself. *Man.*

CONFISCATION. Confiscation is the
appropriation or the seizure of the
private property of a citizen for public
uses; it is a forfeiture to the State.

In Roman law, confiscation was considered a real and proper penalty, wholly
or partially inflicted on the estate of a
person guilty of a legal offense. In the
last years of the Republic and the
Empire, to encourage accusation in cases
of proscriptions and persecution, the
property of the guilty party was divided
between the accuser or witness and the
public treasury; the latter portion was
frequently transferred to the imperial
coffers.

In the period of intermediate legislation, confiscation was further practiced
as a means of extracting from the delinquent the object of crime (*corpus
delicti*) or the weapons employed in
the commission thereof. In this sense,
confiscation appears as a coercive measure or as a civil provision resulting from
a condemnatory or criminal judgment.

In canonical criminal law, confiscation is neither a penalty nor a coercive
measure. Although the Church retains
her natural right to punish guilty subjects with both spiritual and temporal
penalties (Can. 2214, par. 1), in practice she refrains from applying the
penalty of confiscation, for the sake of
avoiding the hostility of many civil
legislations, which would not recognize
such a right to the Church.

In some modern civil codes, a distinction is made between confiscation
and criminal sequestration of property.

Sequestration is the temporary seizure of property, pending some further action or proceeding in its regard. Confiscation, instead, implies definite expropriation or permanent deprivation of property rights in regard to a certain object. In some civil codes, confiscation is enacted as a measure of safeguarding property rights, in which case its character is rather administrative.

Confiscation may be *optional* or *obligatory*. *Optional* confiscation is carried out as an effect of a condemnatory sentence or conviction, and it requires that the confiscated objects be related to the offense or crime committed; it must be used in the commission of a crime or as yield or profit derived from a crime. *Obligatory* confiscation is enacted independently of any punitive sentence; it applies to objects whose manufacture, retention, use, or sale constitutes a legal offense. Such objects are legally forbidden in themselves, hence may be seized, even though they belong to a third party. They may be the prize of the crime, in which case they may be seized, unless they belong to a third party.

The Roman concept of confiscation as a real and proper penalty is also found in some modern legislations. In some countries, for instance, the penalty of confiscation may be applied against wartime deserters, expatriates who committed a serious misdeed or crime against their country of origin. In such a case, the penalty of confiscation, together with sequestration of property and loss of citizenship, constitutes a repressive measure against persons residing outside the country and outside the reach of the law.

There is no doubt of the lawfulness of criminal or administrative confiscation, since, for reasons of public order and security, it is not against the natural law to deprive a man of his freedom, or even his life. And certainly deprivation or despoliation of property is a minor penalty compared to the loss of freedom or life. Moreover, confiscation is *per se* based on criteria of justice, especially in the case of objects used

for criminal purposes. In other word for serious and valid reasons, confisc. tion of property is morally justifiabl In practice, however, the matter of con fiscation, especially if too frequentl left to the will of the judge, may lea to grave abuses.

In view of the fact that ecclesiastic property is constituted to belong t one or few juridical persons, it is le subject to the vicissitudes of divisio and partition which characterize the i heritance of personal or private estate In other words, since ecclesiastic property has greater consistency over th years, it has frequently been the objec of covetous interests on the part c governments not too friendly to th Church. Hence, in the course of th centuries, there have been frequent i stances of governmental appropriatior of ecclesiastical possessions by confisc tion, more or less disguised under th title of secularization of ecclesiastic property, abolition of the mortmai (property made permanently inalienabl through possession by the dead hand) etc.

Now, confiscation, criminal or a ministrative, of ecclesiastical propert is always a form of unjust usurpatior which is punishable by excommunic tion specially reserved (*speciali modo* to the Holy See, and, for clerics coopera ing in or consenting to such usurpatior by other special penalties (cf. Can 2345, 2346). The reason is eviden As a supreme and independent societ the Church possesses its goods an property by sovereign right, indepenc ently of the State. Hence, except b special agreement, the State can exercis no right over ecclesiastical possession not even the right of eminent domair i.e., the right to expropriate a privat property for a necessary public use Naturally, when the necessity for suc uses arises, the Church does not hesitat to cooperate, but any settlement mus be effected through appropiate agree ments. And even if the State, by virtu of a concordat, is granted the privileg of instituting criminal action against cleric guilty of a public offense, con iscation can only apply to the personal property of the cleric, never to beneficiary or strictly ecclesiastical possesions. *M. d. G.*

CONFLICT OF LAWS. By this term is meant a clash of various laws containing contrary, discordant, or divergent dispositions regarding the same matter or act. In reality, the conflict is only apparent because, objectively speaking, one of the laws will ultimately prevail over the others. Subjectively, however, the solution of the conflict is rather difficult, since one must decide which law is to prevail. In the realm of conscience, the problem amounts to this: if several laws may apply, which law is to be obeyed?

In the presence of conflicting laws, the following norms obtain: (a) the natural law takes precedence over positive laws; (b) among positive laws, the divine law prevails over human laws; (c) among human laws, the legislation of a higher or more noble society has precedence over the legislation of lower societies, whose superiority or nobility is measured by the nobility of their end and mission (the religious society is higher than any civil society); (d) among laws of the same society, laws from a higher authority prevail over those from a subordinate authority; (e) however, in legislation of the same society, a particular law prevails over a general law.

The coexistence of the last two norms (d and e) may appear inconsistent, since general laws usually stem from a higher authority, and particular laws from a subordinate authority. But this is not always so: the supreme authority may also issue particular laws regarding territory or goods; in this case, it is evident that the particular law prevails over the general. If the particular law proceeds from a subordinate authority, ordinarily precedence is given to the general law, as the higher, unless, as frequently occurs, the conflict has been previously solved through appropriate legislation.

In the moral field, prescinding from detailed instances of conflicting laws, usually presented by jurists, it is sufficient to consider one general principle. It is formulated as follows: in the presence of conflicting obligations or duties, preference must generally be given to the stricter and more urgent obligation; thus, e.g., an obligation of justice generally prevails over one of charity, unless specific circumstances suggest the contrary. *Gra.*

CONFORMITY. *See* Abandonment to God.

CONFRATERNITY. Throughout the long history of the Catholic Church, confraternities are, generally, associations of the faithful established, under the authority of the hierarchy, for one of the following purposes: fostering a more decidedly Christian life among their members, practice of works of charity, a furtherance of public worship. More specifically, confraternities are duly approved sodalities established for the purpose of promoting private and public worship (Can. 707, par. 2). Confraternities are distinguished from *pious unions*, which are associations instituted exclusively for the practice of some pious or charitable work; they are also distinguished from sodalities, which are pious unions established after the manner of an organic body (Can. 707, par. 1).

Confraternities are said to have been organized in ancient Greece, for the furtherance of the worship of particular divinities or cults (Muratori, *Antiquitates*, diss. 73). In Christian Imperial Rome fraternities existed for the practice of pious and charitable works. The first fraternities with a religious character and purpose are found in the Chapters of Charlemagne, but they did not spread until the thirteenth century. Such associations or organizations have been known over the centuries by a variety of names: guilds, brotherhoods, sodalities, congregations, companies, societies, fraternities, etc.

The associations or sodalities brought many advantages to society: the fusion of different social classes into mutual benevolent brotherhoods, the promotion of public charity and assistance, the preservation and defense of religion against hostile forces. In due course of time, these associations became so numerous that they were brought under episcopal authority and supervision by the Council of Trent (*Sess.* XXII, c. 8–10).

The first general norms applicable to the whole Church, regarding the establishment of confraternities, were enacted by Clement XIII (1592–1605) through the apostolic constitution *Quaecumque,* Dec. 7, 1604 (*Bull. Rom.,* t. 5, III, p. 85–88). Today confraternities are governed by appropriate dispositions of the Code of Canon Law (Can. 707–719).

The Church acknowledges the right of the faithful to establish associations for any laudable purpose whatever and commends those who join such associations (Can. 684). The only requirement is that these associations be approved by the Church, to whom alone is reserved the right of granting juridical recognition. Confraternities are established by a formal decree of erection obtained from the legitimate ecclesiastical authority (Cans. 687, 708). By this decree of erection confraternities are entitled to possess and administer temporal goods under the authority of the local Ordinary (Can. 691), to enact by-laws, conduct meetings, hold non-parochial functions in their own church or chapel. Each confraternity must have its own special name or title. The Confraternities of the Blessed Sacrament and of Christian Doctrine must be established in every parish, and, once legally erected, they become automatically bound to the corresponding Archconfraternities in Rome (Can. 711, par. 2). It is forbidden to have several confraternities in the same place with the same title and scope (Can. 711, par. 1), except in large cities or areas.

Confraternities should be erected only in parish churches, public, or semi-public oratories. In churches of religious women only confraternities of women may be established. For the erection of confraternities in cathedral or collegiate churches the consent of the chapter is required (Can. 712).

Confraternities may in no way interfere with the rights of the pastor in the parish church. Hence, confraternities with their own church within a parochial territory may hold therein only non-parochial functions, independently of the pastor. The right to decide questions of doubt or dispute is vested in the local Ordinary (Can. 716). A confraternity may, with the consent of the local Ordinary, be transferred from one center to another; if the confraternity is affiliated with a religious organization, the permission of the proper religious superior is required (Can. 719). Women may be enrolled in confraternities merely to gain indulgences and spiritual favors attached thereto (Can. 709, par. 2).

All members of a confraternity are expected to observe the statutes of their organization, constantly striving to lead a life in conformity with divine and ecclesiastical law. Moreover, all members should be dedicated to the furtherance of divine worship, not only through external manifestations or demonstrations, but also through genuine apostolic work, under the direction of the legitimate ecclesiastical authority. The participation of confraternity members in public processions and other sacred functions (Can. 713) with their proper garb and insignia (Can. 709) is an excellent way of promoting the apostolate of good example. It is of little value to secure a large enrollment, if the members are not imbued with zeal for the promotion of divine worship. Members who fail to observe the statutes of a confraternity or lead an indifferent or scandalous life, offer a legitimate cause for expulsion from the confraternity. Those who confine their membership to paying dues and giving material contributions to religion without ever participating in the activities and programs of the confraternity or without practicing religion in their individual, family, and social life, certainly cannot be justified before God.

Concerning the gaining of indulgences and privileges by members, the reader must consult the statutes of the respective confraternities. *Tar.*

Besides the Confraternities of the Blessed Sacrament and Christian Doctrine, which, according to canonical legislation (Can. 711, par. 2) must be erected in every parish, there is a large number of confraternities throughout the world. Some of the more notable confraternities are: of the Holy Rosary, directed by the Dominican Fathers; of the Seven Dolors, directed by the Servites; of the Holy Trinity directed by the Trinitarians; of the Infant of Prague, erected in the Carmelite church at Prague.

ARCHCONFRATERNITIES. A confraternity that possesses the right to aggregate or affiliate other associations of the same kind, with the same title and purpose, is called an *archconfraternity*. Archconfraternity status can be attained only through apostolic indult (Can. 721).

By virtue of aggregation, the affiliated association acquires all indulgences, privileges and other communicable spiritual favors directly and specifically granted by the Holy See to the affiliating body (Can. 722, par. 1).

Among the many archconfraternities, it may suffice to mention those of the Blessed Sacrament and of Christian Doctrine located in Rome. All duly erected Confraternities of the Blessed Sacrament and of Christian Doctrine throughout the world acquire automatic (*ipso iure*) affiliation with their corresponding archconfraternities in Rome (Can. 711, par. 2). *De A.*

CONFRATERNITY OF CHRISTIAN DOCTRINE. By canonical prescription (Can. 711) and by a decree of the Sacred Congregation of the Council (*Provido sane*, Jan. 12, 1935, n. 190/135), the Confraternity of Christian Doctrine must be established in every parish. As the diocesan catechetical office (*q.v.*) constitutes the organizational and directive center of religious instruction in every diocese, so the Confraternity of Christian Doctrine repre-sents the principal and most important promotional center of Christian life for the faithful of a parish.

The need for such a catechetical organization is not clearly understood by all. The chief aim of this confraternity is to assist the pastor in the work of instructing and training children, young people, and adults in a knowledge and practice of Christian doctrine. Since the parish represents the primary cell of the great Christian family, which is the Church, and since knowledge of religion constitutes a primary duty of man, it follows logically that the Confraternity of Christian Doctrine should hold a primary place in the life of every parish.

Governed by statutes approved by the local Ordinary, the Confraternity of Christian Doctrine is a parish organization normally consisting of: (a) *teachers* or *catechists*, who undertake to teach Christian doctrine to the various parish groups; (b) home visitors, whose chief work consists in seeking candidates for enrollment in religion classes, promoting attendance at such classes, making family visits, etc.; (c) *benefactors* or *helpers*, who render whatever service they can toward promoting the work of the Confraternity and making it as fruitful and effective as possible, by offering or arranging transportation to religion classes, acting as baby-sitters for adults anxious to attend inquiry classes or discussion clubs, distributing literature, etc.

The members of the Confraternity of Christian Doctrine are principally charged with assisting the clergy in the instruction and preparation of candidates for First Communion and confirmation, and with promoting and carrying out all those liturgical activities which enhance the religious life of the parish.

The Confraternity of Christian Doctrine affords every member of a parish an excellent opportunity for developing a lay apostolate, which is of fundamental importance for the preservation and promotion of the faith, especially in areas where religious vocations are inadequate for the needs.

An effective catechetical organization is a great aid in providing religious instruction for children, inquiry classes or discussion clubs for young people and adults, and in combating the damaging effects of religious ignorance in domestic and social life. Ven.

CONFUCIANISM. *Confucianism* is a name given to the ancient national religion of China, systematized by the philosopher Confucius. Strictly adhering to the ancient Chinese traditions and beliefs, Confucius divested the system of its cruder and baser elements and raised it to a higher philosophical level.

HISTORICAL BACKGROUND. The earliest phase and core of primitive Chinese religion consisted in *the worship of heaven* (T'ien), conceived under a rather material aspect. Intimately linked to the reigning dynasty and through it to the country, this god is called *Shang-ti* (ruling spirit of heaven); he is venerated as supreme ruler of the world. This celestial deity is above human strife, personal contentions, and impulsive action. His action unfolds through the general order of nature, through which he regulates the succession of meteoric and telluric phenomena according to the desires of the Chinese farmers and bureaucratic government leaders. The normal progress of national affairs is indicative of harmony between heaven and the inhabitants of the earth. Sudden calamities, disasters, and national crises are an obvious sign that harmonious relations between heaven and earth have been seriously distrubed. In such a case, the emperor or king, whose title is *Son of Heaven*, through appropriate rituals and ceremonies, establishes direct communication with the god *T'ien* (heaven), imploring him to restore order and harmony on earth. The Chinese does not fix his gaze on heaven, but on earth. His mind is not given to speculation concerning the nature of God nor to mythology, but merely seeks harmonious relations between a mysterious power above and the inhabitants of earth.

The Chinese mentality is concerned with the social aspect of religion and accepts only those elements conducive to social welfare. Hence, the Chinese people attach special value to rituals and ceremonies, since they restore harmony between heaven and earth.

Together with adoration of heaven, *ancestor worship* is another fundamental element in the simple Chinese religious structure. This consists of feasts, rituals, and sacrifices performed in honor of departed ancestors, from whom all family and civil traditions flow. The deceased relatives are believed to participate in these ceremonies along with the living members of the clan. Ancestor worship goes back to the remotest times in China. The imperial palace contained seven shrines dedicated to the religious veneration of ancestors. The ordinary people carried out this sacred ritual in a chamber or room of the family home.

After the worship of heaven and the departed ancestors come the *spirits* or *deities* of higher and lower ranks, including those assigned to preside over the phenomena of nature and various human activities. This secondary world of spirits is quite vast and gives rise to numerous magico-spiritual practices that make the Chinese religion similar to that of the nomadic Mongols in the high plains and steppes of Central Asia.

This ancient religion, without mythology, doctrine, or a special priesthood, was called *Confucianism* after the name of its chief teacher, Confucius (*Kungste*), a wise reformer of the King family, born in the feudal state of Lu, in 551 B.C.

Confucius lived in a troubled era. China was still a country of feudal States, ruled by unprincipled, unruly ministers and lords, whose political intrigues and machinations contributed to the steady dissolution of ancient Chinese traditions and beliefs. Orphaned at an early age and compelled to support himself, Confucius decided o enter public service, hoping thereby o restore a measure of political and moral order. Twice exiled, he traveled about from region to region, and became intimately acquainted with his native land. He died in 479 B.C. About the year 445 B.C., a temple was dedicated to his honor, and there soon followed other temples in the more important cities of the various provinces.

The philosophy of Confucius creates a desire to lead a life based on virtue and justice. Confucius did not intend to lead men to metaphysical speculations. His aim was merely to inculcate in individuals the desire for a life of practical virtue, a life within the reach of all ordinary humans. His conception of life is at once individualistic, social, and political. In the political sphere, he taught that the organization and activity of the State must be strictly based on the sacrosanct duties of each government member. The State cannot adopt a dualistic morality such as was widely practiced by the various States of his time in their political struggles against each other. The State may not transgress the limits of the existing order, nor escape the censure of conscience. No less than the individual, the State has a duty to promote love and justice. In an era characterized by steady dissolution of ancient institutions, Confucius, ever mindful of the classical beauty of Chinese traditions, became a militant leader in the cause of moral restoration. Teaching and traveling for forty years or more, he constantly sought to promote his plans for the restoration of a regime based on justice and love.

The position of Confucius was that of a thinker who neither intended nor felt the need to formulate and elaborate a doctrine into a complete system, despite his intimate conviction and practice thereof. The grandiose spectacle of nature led him to admire the silent eloquence of heaven. He was fully convinced that heaven had entrusted to him, as to all men, the mission of spreading the doctrine of virtue, which was completely disregarded in the political sphere of his age. According to Confucius, all things in the world are the result of the will of heaven, which controls life and death and does not follow the course of human love or hatred.

Confucius is rightly credited with having systematized the traditional religion of China. However, in his insistence that material prosperity is rigidly dependent on the observance of the prescribed rites of the official religion, he caused it to remain stagnant and unprogressive for the last two thousand years.

MORALITY. The cardinal tenets upon which Confucian and, hence, the entire traditional Chinese morality hinges, are: (1) existence of a heaven-god as giver of the cosmic law and moral law; (2) worship of ancestors as observers and perpetuators of the law in their lifetime; (3) the performance of rituals and ceremonies as a necessary means of insuring the efficacy and continuity of the law. Confucian morality may be reduced to the observance of five fundamental precepts: (1) humanity must be considered a family, with each member entitled to benevolence and respect; (2) a practice of the virtue of justice, rendering to each person his due; (3) an equanimity of spirit, accepting praise or blame with equal indifference; (4) the practice of filial piety, especially in the rites due to ancestors; (5) the practice of rectitude, sincerity, and good faith toward others. Upon the observance of these precepts depend individual, domestic, and national harmony, which insure general peace and prosperity.

NEO-CONFUCIANISM. The suppression of traditional religion by order of emperor *Shi Hwang-ti* opened the way to *Neo-Confucianism* in China. The emperor's aim was to eliminate feudal States by the destruction of Confucian customs and beliefs and thus to unify the empire. All sacred books were ordered burned or dispersed, and 406 Confucian scholars and adherents were killed. However, in the year 206 B.C. the Han dynasty restored Confucianism and gave greater importance to the personality and the teachings of Confucius, as the father of Chinese culture. This restoration, however, was opposed by Taoism (*q.v.*) and Buddhism (*q.v.*), but it ended with Confucianism accepting the cosmological theory of the former and the mahayanic psychology of the latter.

The two Tcheng brothers, in the eleventh century, may be regarded as the advance guard and founders of *Neo-Confucianism*. Its chief modern exponent was *K'ang-yu-wai* (d. 1927), who, hostile to Christianity but indoctrinated in Western philosophy, sought to present Confucius as the founder of a universal religion, by describing him as a divine emissary entrusted with the mission of lifting humanity from its misery.

The Chinese revolution of 1911, with its suppression of the worship of Heaven (1914) and the abolition of State examinations for public office, greatly reduced the privileged position of Neo-Confucianism, although the latter still continued to exert its influence in the moral life of the people, despite the infiltration of communistic doctrines. *Tur.*

CRITICAL OBSERVATIONS. For the elements which Confucianism borrowed from Buddhism and Taoism, *see* Buddhism *and* Taoism.

Properly speaking, Confucianism in itself is neither a religion nor a philosophy, but simply a set of teachings, although it must be admitted that, for the past two thousand years, these teachings have taken the place of religion and philosophy for millions of Chinese. Confucius never pretended to be a founder of religion, much less a god. As a matter of fact, at his death he proclaimed that his mission had failed. His religious thought is similar to that of the ancients who venerated a Supreme Being. The atheistic and rationalistic interpretation given to his doctrine originated in the twelfth century and may be attributed to *Chu Hsi* (1130–1200 A.D.).

In the field of ethics, like the Chinese in general, he was inclined to the practical life rather than to metaphysical speculation. Confucius set a remarkably high standard of moral conduct, going as far as attaining the concept of negative charity. Though one may see in this traces of God's primitive revelation to man, yet no one can fail to see how this primitive revelation becomes seriously deformed even in more noble spirits, as they move away from its source. Polygamy is expressly endorsed, even recommended, to insure male progeny. Certain excesses in ancestor worship, such as offering food to the spirits of the deceased, border on the ridiculous. Finally, Confucius was unable to commit himself regarding the good and evil in man.

The worship rendered to Confucius after his death was restricted to his native Lu; not until five hundred years later was it extended to the whole of China. And it was more than a thousand years before shrines or temples were erected in his honor. Whether the worship rendered to Confucius is of a religious or civil character has been a widely discussed question ever since the fifteenth century, when the Jesuit missionary Father Matteo Ricci asserted that Confucianism was not properly a religion, but a politico-literary movement, and that the cult rendered to Confucius is merely civil in character, hence permissible to Chinese who become converts to Christianity. Other missioners have thought otherwise. This question, together with that of Chinese rituals, was recently solved along lines suggested by Ricci and many pronouncements by government leaders to the effect that Confucian cult is merely civil in character (Pius XII, Dec. 8, 1939, AAS: 32 [1940], 25). *Pal.*

CONFUSION. *See* Accession, Obligation.

CONFUSION, MENTAL. *See* Amentia.

CONGREGATION, RELIGIOUS. *See* Religious Order; Religious Congregation.

CONGREGATIONS, ROMAN. The Roman or Sacred Congregations are collegiate bodies composed of a number of cardinals who assist the Supreme Pontiff in the government of the Church. The competency or jurisdiction of these Congregations is exercised in the external forum only and, as a rule, is merely administrative, although in some instances they also exercise judiciary (Sacred Congregation of the Holy Office) or legislative (Sacred Congregation of Rites) power.

Each Congregation is presided over by a cardinal-prefect or, if the Pope himself is prefect of the Congregation the Holy Office, the Consistorial Congregation and the Congregation for the Eastern Church, by a cardinal-secretary. Moreover, each Congregation is staffed by a number of major and minor officials, under the direction of a secretary, who, according to regulations for personnel of the Roman Curia (issued March 2, 1951), ranks as a major prelate with the title of *Most Reverend* and *Excellency*. The secretary is usually assisted by an under-secretary. In those Congregations where the Pope himself holds the prefecture or presidency, the secretary and under-secretary are called *assessor* and *substitute* (associate), respectively. Finally, each Congregation enjoys the services of a number of consultors who advise on matters of a certain importance.

Major matters are discussed and deliberated in a *plenary session*, attended by the cardinal-members of the Congregation. Ordinary affairs and matters of minor importance are transacted in a *congress* or meeting attended by the cardinal-prefect, the secretary and under-secretary (or, respectively, by the cardinal-secretary, assessor and substitute), with a number of minor officials and consultors also in attendance. Decisions taken in plenary session do not become effective until approved by the Pope.

No judiciary action is admitted against the dispositions and deliberations of the Congregations. However, if a party feels wronged over a decision or sentence rendered, he is granted the privilege of appealing directly to the Pope or of petitioning, except in specific instances, the Congregation itself for a re-examination of the case, particularly if the decision was handed down, not in a plenary, but a congressional session.

In the past, the number and extent of jurisdiction of the Congregations varied. Today the Congregations are eleven in number. Until 1870, some Congregations exercised jurisdiction in matters pertaining to the civil administration of the Papal States.

SACRED CONGREGATIONS IN PARTICULAR. (a) *Sacred Congregation of the Holy Office.* Instituted by Paul III in 1542 for the sake of combating and extirpating heresy. Its original title was the Holy Office of the Inquisition and Punishment of Heretics. This Congregation has undergone several reorganizations. Among other things, the extent of its jurisdiction has been considerably increased. From 1909 to 1917, it covered even matters concerning indulgences, which today come under the jurisdiction of the Sacred Penitentiary (*see* Penitentiary, Apostolic).

The present jurisdiction of this Sacred Congregation encompasses all questions relating to faith and morals; matrimonial cases involving the Pauline privilege (*q.v.*); the impediments of mixed religion and disparity of cult; examination of books and publications dangerous to faith and morals and the compilation of the Index of Forbidden Books; and matters pertaining to the Eucharistic fast of the priests. In the criminal sphere, it has jurisdiction in all crimes against the faith and the unity of the Church, and a few other crimes.

This Congregation also acts as a tribunal in matters of its own competency. All its proceedings are conducted in strictest secrecy, violation of which entails severe ecclesiastical penalties.

(b) *Sacred Consistorial Congregation.* Although of ancient origin, this Congregation was definitely established by Sixtus V, in 1588. Besides its original tasks of providing for the erection of new dioceses and preparing the agenda for consistories, it controls all matters relating to the establishment, preservation, and status of dioceses. It proposes the appointment of Ordinaries, coadjutor and auxiliary bishops, and apostolic administrators. It exercises supervision over diocesan Ordinaries in the performance and fulfillment of their duties. The competency of this Congregation in the above matters, however, does not extend to territories dependent on the Sacred Congregation for the Eastern Church or the Congregation for the Propagation of the Faith. If any of the above matters involves negotiations with civil powers, the Congregation for Extraordinary Ecclesiastical Affairs takes over.

(c) *Sacred Congregation for the Eastern Church.* This Congregation exercises jurisdiction over the clergy and faithful of the Eastern rites. It combines the powers of all congregations controlling the affairs of the Latin Church into one congregation, with the exception of the jurisdiction of the Holy Office, which is exempted. This Congregation for the Eastern Church has exclusive jurisdiction, apart from that exercised by the Holy Office, throughout the following territories: Egypt, the Sinai peninsula, Eritrea, Northern Ethiopia, Southern Albania, Bulgaria, Cyprus, Greece, Dodecanese, Iran, Iraq, State of Israel, Lebanon, Palestine, Syria, Transjordan, Turkey and Turkish Thrace.

(d) *Sacred Congregation of the Sacraments.* Instituted by St. Pius X in 1908, it concerns itself with the discipline of the seven sacraments and the celebration of Holy Mass, except in matters reserved to the Holy Office or the Sacred Congregation of Rites.

In matrimonial matters, this congregation exercises general competency, with the following exceptions: (a) marriage cases involving the Pauline privilege; the impediments of mixed religion and disparity of worship, which fall under the jurisdiction of the Holy Office; (b) certain cases involving the validity or nullity of marriages, which are not of exclusive competency of the ecclesiastical tribunals, although it exercises supervision over the tribunals themselves with regard to matrimonial trials, and has exclusive competency concerning dispensations in all cases of a *matrimonium ratum et non consummatum.*

(e) *Sacred Congregation of the Council.* This Congregation, instituted by Pius IV, in 1564, was charged with providing an authentic interpretation and application of the norms established by the Council of Trent. Today it takes care of the entire discipline of the secular clergy and Christian faithful. Its competency encompasses all matters relating to catechetical instruction and the observance of Christian precepts. It governs minor ecclesiastical benefices or offices, but matters pertaining to the conferring of benefices reserved to the Holy See come under the jurisdiction of the Apostolic Datary. Confraternities and pious associations, pious legacies, ecclesiastical goods and property, ecclesiastical taxes and tributes are under its control. It also enjoys the right of supervision over acts of particular councils, and episcopal meetings fall under its jurisdiction.

Annexed to this Congregation is an academic department designed to prepare young priests in the method of handling ecclesiastical affairs, especially those of administrative nature.

(f) *Sacred Congregation for Affairs of Religious.* This Congregation has jurisdiction over orders, religious congregations, and secular institutes, in all matters pertaining to organization, discipline, studies, goods and property, obligations, rights and privileges, except specific matters coming under the competency of the Holy Office, the Congregation of the Council, or the Congregation for the Eastern Church.

(g) *Sacred Congregation for the Propagation of the Faith.* This Congregation exercises general jurisdiction over all mission territories in which a regular ecclesiastical hierarchy is not yet established or, if established, is still in its incipient stages (as vicariates and prefectures apostolic, missions *sui juris*).

Except matters coming within the competency of the Holy Office, the Congregation of Rites, or the Congregation for the Eastern Church, and matters involving matrimonial trials, its competency in mission territories is complete. Outside mission territories, it has exclusive jurisdiction over all schools and seminaries established for the training of missionaries, and over all societies promoting the cause of the missions.

Religious in mission territories are subject to the Congregation for the Propagation of the Faith in all matters relating to missionary activity. In matters pertaining to religious life, they are subject to the Congregation for Affairs of Religious.

(h) *Sacred Congregation of Rites.* Instituted by Sixtus V in 1588, this Congregation has jurisdiction over all that pertains to the sacred rites and ceremonies of the Latin Church, relics, processes of beatification, and canonization.

(i) *Sacred Ceremonial Congregation.* Instituted by Sixtus V in 1588, it has jurisdiction over all that pertains to ceremonies in the papal chapel and palace. It also determines the matter of precedence among cardinals, prelates of the Roman Curia, and diplomatic representatives accredited to the Holy See.

(j) *Sacred Congregation for Extraordinary Ecclesiastical Affairs.* To this Congregation are entrusted all matters involving negotiations with civil governments or in any way concerning relations between the Holy See and the civil governments, such as stipulation of concordats and, in countries where such matters require dealing with government authorities, appointment of bishops, division of dioceses, etc. Other questions, especially those connected with civil law, are also occasionally referred to this Congregation by the Pope. The prefect of this Congregation is the Cardinal Secretary of State. Its offices are located in the Secretariate of State.

This Congregation was established by Pius VII, in 1814, as an extension of the Congregation *super negotiis extra-ordinariis Regni Galliarum,* instituted by Pius VI, in 1793.

(k) *Sacred Congregation of Seminaries and Universities.* Although of ancient origin, the title and functions of this Congregation were not defined until 1915. As it appears from its name, its jurisdiction extends to all ecclesiastical universities or faculties and seminaries, except those subject to the Congregation for the Propagation of the Faith or the Congregation for the Eastern Church, or those in charge of the formation of missionaries or religious. Attached to this Congregation is an office which supervises all educational institutions under ecclesiastical auspices, including those directed by religious.

(l) *Sacred Congregation of the Basilica of St. Peter.* This Congregation came into being during the reign of Julius II (1503–1513), who, in launching the reconstruction of St. Peter's Basilica, appointed a group of persons to supervise the work. Over the years, this Congregation underwent various changes, but its primary function even today remains the supervision and administration of the Vatican Basilica. Although not mentioned in the Code of Canon Law, it is listed in the Pontifical Directory (*Annuario Pontificio*) as one of the Sacred Congregations. This Congregation is composed only of cardinals, assisted by a financial secretary (*secretary-econome*) and a number of minor clerks and workers. *Cip.*

CONGRESSES (organization of). *See* Action, Catholic.

CONGRUA. *See* Benefice, ecclesiastical.

CONGRUOUS MERIT. *See* Merit.

CONJUGICIDE. *See* Crime (impediment of).

CONSANGUINITY. *Consanguinity* is the blood relationship existing among persons descending from the same stock or common ancestry. The degree of blood relationship is dependent upon the degree of proximity to the common ancestry. Consanguinity or blood relationship may result from both legitimate and natural procreation. In consanguinity the following elements are to be noted: (a) *the common root or stock*, i.e., the father or mother from whom the others descend. (b) *The line of descent*, i.e., the series of persons descending from the same stock. This line is *direct*, if one person descends from another through procreation (grandfather, father, son, grandson, great-grandson); *collateral* or *oblique*, if one person does not descend from another, but both have a common ancestor (brother and sister, first cousins, uncle and niece, or aunt and nephew, second cousins). (c) *Degree*, i.e., the degree of distance from the common ancestor, or line of descent.

In computing the degrees of collateral consanguinity, the method used in Canon Law differs from that of the civil law. Whereas Canon Law computes only one side of lineal descent, civil law reckons both sides, thereby increasing the number of degrees. Canon Law (Can. 96) takes into account the number of generations: there are as many degrees as there are generations in the same line. Thus, if two persons are equally distant from the common ancestor, they are related to each other in a degree that is called equal (first degree: brother and sister; 2nd degree: first cousins; 3rd degree: second cousins). But if the distance from the common ancestor is not the same, as in the case of uncle and niece, the degree of consanguinity between the two persons is called unequal. In the latter case, the degree is expressed by mentioning the more remote degree and adding to it the next nearest degree which it touches; thus, e.g., uncle and niece are related in the second degree touching the first.

There are also cases of multiple consanguinity: more than one common ancestor, as a person with children by a blood relative or several blood relatives. In such instances, consanguinity is multiplied with every additional common ancestor.

For genetic, social, and moral reasons, Canon and civil law considers consanguinity a marriage impediment for definite degrees of kindred relationship. According to present canonical legislation: (a) in the direct line of consanguinity, marriage is invalid between all ascending and descending blood relatives, whether legitimate or natural; (b) in the collateral line, marriage is invalid between blood relations, up to the third degree inclusively (i.e., up to and including second cousins). According to civil law legislation, second cousins are considered blood relatives within the sixth degree, and marriage between two such persons is forbidden to the third civil degree (first touching on second, according to Canon Law), that is, between uncle and niece. Concerning dispensation from the impediment of consanguinity, the following obtains: (a) cases of consanguinity in any degree of the direct line or in the first degree of the collateral line (brother and sister) are not dispensable; (b) cases of consanguinity in the second degree of the collateral line (first cousins) or in the second degree touching the first (uncle and niece, aunt and nephew) are rarely granted and only for very special reasons; (c) cases of consanguinity in the third degree of the collateral line (second cousins) are generally granted a dispensation.

Consanguinity in the third equal degree, and that in the third degree touching the second, constitute impediments of a minor degree, and a dispensation granted is valid, even if the reasons adduced are not true (Can. 1076).

Though the civil laws regarding marriage differ in different countries and in the various States of the U.S.A., most civil codes rule that marriage between relatives in any degree of the direct line and in the first degree of the collateral line (between brother and sister) is void. Most civil codes also bar marriage between uncle and niece, or aunt and nephew and, in many instances, even marriage between first cousins.

In ancient legislation, and even in

ecclesiastical law before the promulgation of the Code, the impediment of consanguinity was much more extensive. This condition still prevails in some oriental countries (China, India, etc.). *Bar.*

CONSCIENCE. *Conscience* is a judgment made by an individual concerning the morality of his actions. More precisely, conscience is a judgment of the practical reason deciding by inference from general principles the moral goodness or malice of a particular act.

This judgment of the practical intellect constitutes the immediate and proximate rule or subjective norm of moral conduct, because no objective norm or external law may be the actual norm of an act, unless the agent applies it to a concrete act. To be a valid norm of conduct, this particular application must not only follow but precede and accompany the act.

A conscience is *right* or *erroneous*, depending on whether the judgment formed agrees or disagrees with the objective norm or law. If the error of judgment may be attributed to the subject, a conscience is said to be *vincibly erroneous*; if not attributable to him, it is said to be *invincibly erroneous*. Hence, the malice of an act posited with an erroneous conscience is imputable or not, depending on whether the error is vincible or invincible.

An erroneous conscience is called *lax*, if it exaggerates the lawfulness of the act; *scrupulous*, if it tends to exaggerate the unlawfulness of the act. A *hardened* conscience is one which is habitually extremely lax in its judgments. A pharisaical conscience is one that usually applies a false criterion in making judgments on his own conduct, by frequently attaching exaggerated importance to small and minute matters, as it neglects the more serious obligations of life.

Conscience is *certain* or *doubtful* depending on the degree of assent with which a judgment is made. A *certain* conscience judges the morality of an act without prudent fear of erring. A *doubtful* conscience gives rise to a positive judgment with a prudent fear of error or simply to a negative judgment in which one does not know whether an act is lawful or unlawful.

To be a proper and valid norm of conduct, conscience must be certain and, if possible, right. Since an invincibly erroneous conscience cannot normally be corrected, the malice of an act posited by such a conscience is not morally imputable. A vincibly erroneous conscience must be corrected by diligent inquiry, study, consultation, etc. A doubtful conscience must be resolved before acting (*see* Spiritual direction, Moral systems). *Gra.*

CONSCIENCE (Freedom of). *See* Freedom of conscience.

CONSCIENCE (Training of). Conscience is susceptible of continuous improvement, no less than reason itself, of which it is a typical expression. In fact, the complex character and nature of ethical judgment, which must necessarily conform to the multifaceted character and nature of the human act, makes a training of conscience one of the most difficult of all tasks.

Not everyone receives from nature the same ability to judge correctly. Some find it comparatively easy to formulate an ethical judgment; others find it difficult to gather all the ethical aspects of a human act and to correlate these with different norms of morality. Coupled with ignorance, prejudice, habit, passion, and various other defects of the human spirit, the mind is easily influenced in judging the ethical value of a specific action from the standpoint of self-interest.

The correctness of a judgment of conscience implies exact knowledge and wise application of a law to a concrete action. The training of conscience, therefore, must be directed to fostering: (a) a diligent love of truth and the law, not as a burden, but as a pathfinder on the road of life; (b) the habit of reflecting before acting; (c) the exercise of virtue, for a more practical understanding of the hierarchy of values in life; (d) the search for and use of supernatural gifts from which Christian prudence constantly draws its nourishment.

Conscience may be habitually affected by two main weaknesses, laxism (*see* System, Moral) and scrupulosity (*see* Scruple).

A person with a lax conscience tends to minimize the immorality of certain acts and responsibility for his own actions. This habit can only be overcome by the development of a contrary habit, gradually acquired through a more diligent examination of doubts, by a more sincere love of truth and duty, a greater docility to one's confessor, and a more critical evaluation of one's own actions.

A person affected by scruples, not as a sporadic condition, but as a morbid disease of the soul, is a person obsessed by doubts in the sphere of morality. Scrupulosity shows the characteristics of an obsessive idea; that is, it has its lucid, irresistible, tormenting, and persistent moments, despite the fact that the individual himself recognizes it as unreasonable. Scrupulous persons must be encouraged to submit to appropriate psychiatric treatments. *Pal.*

CONSCIOUS. *See* Unconscious.

CONSCIOUSNESS, ALTERNATING. *See* Hysteria.

CONSCRIPTION. *See* Service, Military.

CONSECRATION. *See* Benediction and Consecration.

CONSECRATION (of altar). *See* Altar.

CONSECRATION (of church). *See* Church, Dedication.

CONSECRATION, EUCHARISTIC. The Eucharistic consecration is the essential and central act of Holy Mass (*q.v.*). By recalling the action of our Lord Jesus in instituting the Holy Eucharist on the evening before His passion and death, the priest, as minister of Christ, assertively pronounces over the bread and wine the very same words that Christ Himself uttered over the bread and wine at the end of His Last Supper: *"This is my Body. This is the chalice of my Blood, of the new and eternal testament, the mystery of faith, which shall be shed for you and for many unto the remission of sins"* (Matt. 26:26 ff.; Mark 14:22 ff.; Luke 22:19 ff.). By virtue of this consecration the entire substance (prime matter and substantial form) of bread and the entire substance of wine are changed into the Body and Blood of Christ; the accidents or species of bread and wine remain unchanged. This mysterious and miraculous change, technically called *transubstantiation,* causes Christ to be really present on the altar.

The rite of Eucharistic consecration embodies the solemn memorial of the bloody sacrifice of the Cross, which it renews, and the essence of the unbloody sacrifice of the New Law. The act of consecration is a true immolation of the Divine Victim, present on the altar, but not a bloody immolation such as that which took place on the cross. It is an unbloody and mystical immolation. Through the rite of consecration, Christ is wrapped in the appearances of destruction and death. His Blood becomes figuratively separated from His Body. The words of consecration actually cause the real presence of Christ under two distinct species: that of bread signifies the presence of His Body; that of wine signifies the presence of Christ's Blood. However, our Divine Lord, impassible and immortal since His resurrection, undergoes no change within Himself, nor any form of suffering, although His Body, Blood, Soul, and Divinity are present under both species, not by virtue of the words of consecration (*vi verborum*), but by reason of a natural concomitance (*vi concomitantiae*).

The consecration is also a sacerdotal oblation of the Divine Victim to God. When pronouncing the words of consecration, in obedience to the Lord's command: *"Do this in commemoration of me"* (Luke 22:19), the visible priest, as minister of Christ, the principal and invisible Priest, renews all that Christ did at the Last Supper. The night before He died, the Divine Savior, in His capacity as High Priest, offered to the Heavenly Father His own Body and Blood mystically separated and destined to become actually separated on the Cross, by death, in order to acknowledge God's supreme dominion and to render a worthy satisfaction to His Infinite Majesty outraged by sin.

The Eucharistic consecration is also an act which transforms Christ into spiritual food and drink for our souls. It is through the consecration that the greatest of all sacraments is performed. The sacrament of the Holy Eucharist is also called "the Sacrament of the Altar." *Man.*

CONSENT. See Contract, Sin.

CONSENT, LACK OF (Defective). *See* Consent, Matrimonial.

CONSENT, MATRIMONIAL. NECESSITY AND NATURE. Following a principle of Roman law, the Church holds that the marriage contract requires a lawfully expressed consent of two parties legally qualified to form the marriage contract. Without this consent the marriage contract cannot be effected, for marriage is a union of minds and souls, not simply of bodies. For this reason authors commonly list marriage among consensual rather than real contracts. As the basis or efficient cause of marriage, consent is so essential that it cannot be supplied by any human power. "Matrimonial consent is an act of the will whereby each of the two contracting parties gives and accepts the perpetual and exclusive right to the body for the performance of actions which of their very nature pertain to the procreation of offspring" (Can. 1081, par. 2).

The essential object of matrimonial consent is a right to the body (*jus in corpus*) for the purpose of conjugal intercourse, not the use or exercise of this right (*usus aut exercitium juris*); in fact, the latter could be excluded from the consent without affecting the essence and, therefore, the validity of the marriage contract. The transfer of the right to each other's body is perpetual and exclusive, and so obligates the parties that the indulgence by either party in acts of self-abuse or extramarital sexual relations is a violation not only of chastity, but also of justice.

DEFECTIVE CONSENT. As an act of the will, consent must be preceded by an act of the mind (*nil volitum nisi praecognitum*). Thus, a matrimonial consent may be vitiated by defective or insufficient knowledge (lack of the use of reason, ignorance, error), or by any fact which hinders a full consent of the will (simulation, force and fear, condition).

Lack of the Use of Reason. Incapable of giving the matrimonial consent are all persons lacking the use of reason, whether *actually*, such as infants, intoxicated, hypnotized, drugged persons and persons in the state of sleep, or *habitually*, as in the case of the mentally ill. In the case of monomaniacs, their ability to contract marriage is at least to be doubted, since they are regarded by modern medical authorities as incapable of full deliberation. Concerning the mentally ill who enjoy lucid intervals, some authors hold that such individuals are capable, during their lucid moments, of giving a valid consent; others deny this, and maintain that with such patients lucid intervals cannot be easily established. The same applies to idiots. The following, however, are to be considered capable of contracting marriage: (a) feeble-minded persons, if they possess sufficient understanding; (b) deaf-mutes and blind, deaf-mutes, provided that they are aware of the nature and purpose of marriage.

Ignorance. Since consent is necessarily related to the object of the marriage contract, i.e., to the nature and obligations of marriage, it is clear that one who is ignorant of this cannot give a true matrimonial consent. "The matrimonial consent cannot be validly given unless the contracting parties know at least that marriage is a permanent union between man and woman for the procreation of children" (Can. 1082, par. 1). Thus, if one enters marriage with an understanding that it is a temporary union or transient companionship, to be terminated at the will of the contracting parties, or that it is a merely scientific, social, economic, or sportive arrangement, the marriage contract is invalid. Full juridical knowledge of the effects of marriage is not required, but the contracting parties must at least know that marriage is a stable union intended for the procreation of children. Thus, if the parties are ignorant of the manner by which procreation takes place, they contract validly, provided that they know at least that procreation requires a bodily union of man and woman; otherwise, knowledge of the essential object of matrimonial consent is lacking (Can. 1081, par. 2).

In practice, the lack of the necessary knowledge concerning the essential object of the marriage contract cannot be established because the law presumes such knowledge in persons who have reached the age of puberty (Can. 1082, par. 2). Interpretative will, i.e., the allegation that one might not have married had he known the facts, avails nothing, because, as long as this act of the will was never present, it can produce no effect. A marriage believed invalid because of lack of necessary knowledge offers three possible courses of action: (a) petition for declaration of nullity; (b) validation according to the norms of Canon 1136; (c) petition for dispensation *super rato non consummato*.

Error. Error is a subjective judgment which does not conform with objective truth. Error in marriage may be of law (*error juris*) or of fact (*error facti*) depending on whether it concerns the essential properties and blessings of marriage, or the identity, qualities, or motives of the persons involved in the marriage contract. Error concerning the validity of a marriage contract may be of *law* or of *fact*. An error is said to

be *antecedent*, motivating the contract, if at the time of the exchange of consent the contracting party was so minded that, if he had known the true facts, he would have not contracted marriage.

Since the will is directed to its object as it is presented by the intellect, it is clear that error may have an effect on the will. However, not every act posited by error is null and void, but only an act which is null and void by virtue of the natural law, as defective consent, or by positive law (Can. 104).

Error of Fact. (a) Error concerning the identity of the person with whom one intends to contract marriage makes marriage null and void (Can. 1083, par. 1), since this error affects the very substance of marriage. In such a case, the marriage is rendered null and void by the natural law itself, because the consent is directed to a person entirely different from the one the contracting party intended to marry. Nor will it help to say that the contracting party might have been willing to marry the other person if the error had been discovered before; such interpretative will is purely hypothetical, hence ineffective.

(b) Generally speaking, error about a quality of the person does not invalidate the marriage, neither by the natural nor positive laws, though it was the cause of the contract (Can. 1083, par. 2). Two cases are excepted (*see below under c*). Error of quality does not invalidate the marriage by virtue of the natural law, because the required consent is truly and substantially present. Despite an error concerning a quality, the intellect presents the object to the will in an absolute manner, not conditionally; consequently, the will accepts the object absolutely. Furthermore, the substantial object of the contract, that is, the person as such, is present; hence, the contract is by virtue of the natural law valid.

It does not invalidate a marriage by virtue of the positive law, because the Church does not accept such an error as an invalidating cause in a marriage contract, not even if it can be shown that the error was caused by fraud and deception of the other party. The reason is to avoid a flood of doubts and questions that would arise concerning the validity of so many marriages, with serious public detriment to souls. Hence, if a man marries with the idea that the bride is healthy, rich, a virgin, etc., and later discovers that he was in error regarding one of these qualities, he contracts a valid marriage, though he would not have married had he known the true facts. Such an error would invalidate the marriage only if the quality in question were made an indispensable condition (*sine qua non*) of the contract; for, in that case, consent would naturally be restricted.

In marriage, which is by its very nature indissoluble, error and fraud are not grounds, as in other contracts (Cans. 103, par. 2; 104), for rescinding action; fraud, however, could be a ground for recovery of damages.

(c) Error regarding a quality of a person invalidates marriage only in two cases:

(1) If the error regarding a certain quality amounts to an error concerning the identity of the person (Can. 1083, par. 2, n. 1). This type of error may occur if the quality is a proper and distinguishing characteristic of the person one intends to marry. Thus, if a man intends to marry someone's oldest daughter, but through a skillful deception he is made to marry the second oldest daughter, he contracts invalidly, for the main and simple reason that his consent was directed to the first person, not to her substitute.

(2) If a free person contracts marriage with a person whom he believed to be free, but who, in reality, is in a condition of slavery in the proper sense (Can. 1083, par. 2, n. 2). Such nullity in favor of freedom is a purely ecclesiastical law and was established to obviate the grave difficulties arising in such marriages with respect to the exercise of conjugal rights. However, the nullity is predicated on the presence of two conditions: (a) one party must be free and the other a slave, strictly speaking; (b) the free party must be ignorant of the other's servile status. Hence, if a free person knowingly marries a slave, the contract is valid. The same is true if a slave marries a slave, whom he or she believes to be free. If a slave acquires free status through marriage, the contract is valid from the beginning. But if the slave acquires free status before the other party becomes aware of the error, the marriage is invalid, because the law makes no exception. Moreover, renewal of consent is excluded by the very fact that error continues.

Since this is a purely ecclesiastical disposition, it does not apply to infidels. Hence, if the slave party is an infidel and the free party a Christian, the marriage is certainly invalid, because the law applies directly to the Christian and only indirectly to the infidel. If, on the contrary, the free party is an infidel and the slave party a Christian, the marriage, prescinding from disparity of worship, is probably valid.

Error of Law. (a) Error concerning the very nature of marriage renders the contract invalid for obvious lack of consent.

(b) On the contrary, a simple error regarding the unity, indissolubility, or sacramental dignity of marriage, even if such error was the motivating reason or cause of the contract, does not invalidate matrimonial consent (Can. 1084). Error is simple if it remains within the realm of the mind and does not extend to the will; but if the will acts and by a positive action excludes unity or indissolubility (essential properties of marriage), the contract becomes null and void. Theoretical error concerning the essential properties of marriage does not necessarily imply the intention of excluding such properties, because ordinarily the will of the parties is to contract a valid marriage, as other people do, according to the law of Christ. This general intention, as a dominant factor, obviously prevails over particular error or private opinion. Nor is the situation altered by the fact that the error was the cause of the contract, because, since error does not alter the nature of the contract, it does not affect the will, which retains its capability of eliciting a true matrimonial consent. For this reason, marriages of infidels, heretics, and schismatics are considered valid, despite the fact that such individuals admit the dissolubility of marriage in case of adultery and reject the sacramental character of Christian marriage.

(c) Knowledge or belief of nullity of a marriage does not necessarily exclude matrimonial consent (Can. 1085). There are two instances of erroneous belief or knowledge regarding the validity of marriage: (1) one may believe that he is contracting a valid marriage, when in reality the marriage is invalid, due to an existing impediment of which he is unaware; (2) one may believe that he is contracting an invalid marriage because of a diriment impediment, while actually no such impediment is present. Not only is matrimonial consent possible in both instances, but it can never be positively excluded, not even if one attempts marriage with the certain knowledge that a diriment impediment exists. In fact, despite bad faith of an individual, who knows the marriage will be invalid because of the impediment, that person wishes to contract marriage insofar as he can, i.e., to give and accept the conjugal right. Matrimonial consent may exist independently of the fact that one knows or thinks that he is unable to contract marriage canonically. Such knowledge does not impair matrimonial consent. The marriage may be invalid for some other reason, but not for lack of consent. Evident confirmation of all this is to be found in the practice of validating certain marriages without renewal of consent (see Sanatio in radice); such, of course, is presumed to exist.

On the contrary, one who enters marriage with the intention of going through a mere ceremony or formality does not contract a valid marriage. This is a question of fact, whose solution depends on the intention of the contracting parties; once consent is given,

it is presumed to endure, even in invalid marriages, until there is certainty of its revocation (Can. 1093).

SIMULATED CONSENT. Simulation is present if one externally gives consent, but internally has no intention of contracting marriage or binding himself to fulfill the obligations which marriage entails.

(a) *Intention of not Contracting Marriage (total simulation)*. If one goes through the wedding ceremony with the intention of not contracting marriage, the marriage is invalid, because the individual's consent is here directed to an object other than marriage, e.g., lust, material interest, etc. In the external forum the presumption of the law is always against such an intention; in other words, the internal consent of the mind is always presumed to be in agreement with the words or signs employed in the marriage ceremony (Can. 1086, par. 1). Hence, it does not suffice for one merely to assert that the consent expressed at the marriage ceremony was simulated; one must furnish proof of such allegation, which, in view of the fact that consent is a purely internal act of the will, is extremely difficult to produce. However, if sufficient proof is offered, simulated consent is accepted as an invalidating cause of the marriage contract. Existence of simulation is admitted, if, besides the sworn statement of the interested party —particularly if given immediately after the marriage—the following facts are established to the satisfaction of the ecclesiastical court: (a) the manifest cause of simulation; (b) existence of antecedent, concomitant, and consequent circumstances corroborating evidence of simulation.

If a simulated marriage is already consumated and the parties are unable to furnish juridical proof of simulated consent, an insoluble conflict arises, for, while the marriage may be null and void in the internal forum, its validity is upheld in the external forum. Consequently, the parties to the putative marriage, if aware of the nullity of the marriage, may not exercise their conjugal rights, even if the ecclesiastical judge were to enjoin cohabitation on them.

If the simulator is not willing to supply the necessary consent to validating the marriage, or if validation is impossible for other reasons, he must at least indemnify the innocent party for damages unjustly sustained. Nor is there any other practical way of compensating the deceived party, especially a woman.

Also invalid is a marriage contracted jocosely, because the consent is given merely in jest.

(b) *Intention of not Binding Oneself.* If either party or both parties by a positive act of the will exclude marriage itself or all right to the conjugal act or to any essential property of marriage, the marriage contract is invalid (Can. 1086, par. 2). The reason for such a conclusion is that two positive contrary acts of the will cancel each other out. Externally to want marriage, while internally excluding it by a positive act of the will, amounts to not wanting marriage. Similarly, to pronounce words of consent externally, while positively excluding all right to the conjugal act, is not to want marriage, for the right to each other's body is of the very essence of marriage. The same is to be said of the exclusion of one of the essential properties of marriage (unity, indissolubility), for marriage cannot exist without these essential elements. However, if one excludes the sacrament but absolutely wants marriage, the contract is valid, because the sacramental character in such a case ensues from the divine will. But if the sacrament is so excluded as to be made a necessary condition for the consent ("I want marriage only if it is not a sacrament"), the contract is invalid, for in that case the proper marriage consent is lacking.

(c) *Intention of not Fulfilling the Marital Obligations.* Such an intention does not make marriage invalid because it is subsequent to marriage itself, which is already essentially established by the intention of contracting marriage and assuming its obligations. Hence, the intention of refusing the conjugal act,

of practicing birth control, of committing onanism, adultery, etc., does not render marriage invalid, because the *bona fidei et prolis* do not pertain to the essence of marriage, that is, they do not pertain to the right over the body (*jus in corpus*), but only to the use or exercise of this right; the essence of a thing is certainly not dependent upon its use or abuse. However, indissolubility (*bonum sacramenti*) admits of no distinction between assumption and fulfillment of obligation, because marriage simply cannot exist without indissolubility. Hence, to want marriage is to intend it as a perpetual contract; to intend a dissoluable marriage is to want no marriage at all.

FORCE AND FEAR. Actions performed as a result of physical violence or force that cannot be resisted are involuntary; hence null and void (Can. 103). The present discussion does not concern physical, but moral force or violence (coercion, compulsion, duress).

In Canon Law the terms *force* and *fear* are correlated to each other as cause to effect and frequently used interchangeably. Fear is *trepidation of mind regarding an impending or future evil*, which so influences the will that, to escape the impending evil, one is induced to perform an action that he would not otherwise do of his own free choice.

Fear may be induced by an external cause, either free or necessary (*ab extrinseco*), or by an internal cause (*ab intrinseco*). It may be *just* or *unjust. Just* fear exists if impending evil is rightfully and fittingly inflicted by another person: otherwise it is unjust. Fear may be *grave* or *slight*, insofar as an impending evil is grave or slight. Fear is *grave*: (a) if the impending evil is grave in itself, either *absolutely*, i.e. grave for all men (the threat of death, mutilation, exile, infamy, etc.) or *relatively*, i.e., grave for a certain individual (in view of the person's temperament, age, sex, etc.); (b) if one is convinced that the impending evil or danger is imminent and that the only way to escape it is by doing something against one's will. Absolutely grave fear is designated as *cadens in virum constantem*, i.e., capable of effecting even a courageous man. Finally, there is *reverential fear*, which implies that one is fearful of displeasing those upon whom one is dependent or to whom he owes reverence and respect, e.g., parents, guardians, superiors, etc. Reverential fear is generally regarded as a form of slight fear; but, if it is coupled with other grave circumstances (threat of disinheritance expulsion from parental dwelling, ill-treatment, excessive and prolonged anger of parents, etc.), it could become grave.

In the external forum reverential fear is presumed slight, but it may frequently become grave, especially in the case of young ladies.

A marriage contracted under the influence of force or *grave* fear is invalid if fear was unjustly inflicted by an outside agent, from which one may only be freed by choosing marriage (Can. 1087, par. 1). In order to invalidate marriage, fear must be: (a) *grave*, either absolutely or relatively, with the threat of imminent evil to the contracting party or to members of his family, relatives, etc. (b) *Inspired or inflicted from without*, by an external free agent, whether this be the other contracting party or some other person; internal fear, arising from within, does not impair the validity of a marriage, since such fear is never unjustly inflicted. (c) *Unjust*, i.e., the threatened evil must be unjust, either in itself or in its mode. Fear is unjust not only if the penalty is in no way deserved, but also if it is applied without due process of law. Hence, if the judge were to give a seducer the alternative of marrying the seduced woman or going to prison, he would be inflicting unjust fear on the culprit, because the latter is entitled to another choice, i.e., indemnifying the woman for the damages sustained. (d) Finally, fear must be so grave as to *force one into contracting marriage*, for only such fear invalidates marriage. The impending evil need not necessarily be inflicted for the express purpose of ex-

torting marriage; it suffices that the person undergoing fear be convinced that he cannot free himself from the threatened evil except by choosing marriage.

No other kind of fear, even if it be the cause of the contract, entails nullity of marriage (Can. 1087, par. 2). Hence, marriage is not invalidated by a justly inflicted fear, however grave, nor by internal fear, nor by slight fear, even if, in any one of these instances, fear may have been the sole cause of the contract.

Whether fear invalidates marriage by reason of the positive law alone or by the natural law also remains a disputed question. Other contracts, even if negotiated under fear, are valid but rescindable, whereas marriage is indissoluble. Hence, there would seem to be some basis for the theory which maintains that the invalidity of a forced marriage derives from the natural law. On the other hand, it is difficult to understand why this should not also apply to marriages in which one partner has practiced fraud and deception regarding position, wealth, health, etc., causing irreparable injustice to the other party. Wherefore, many authors regard the impediment of force and fear as an impediment of the positive or ecclesiastical law, though rooted in the natural law.

Pagan marriages are not affected by the impediment of fear, unless such an impediment is established by the civil authority. Since there is some probability that the impediment of fear may be rooted in the natural law, the validity of a pagan marriage contracted out of grave and unjust fear remains doubtful. Naturally, in individual cases the presumption is in favor of validity, aside from the Pauline privilege, dealt with in Canon 1127. However, a marriage between a baptized and a non-baptized person contracted out of fear is always invalid, whether the victim be the baptized person or the pagan: in the first case, the consent by the Christian party is invalid by Church law; in the second case, the Church declares a baptized person incapable of contracting such a marriage for the sake of safeguarding freedom.

Again, in view of the probable fact that the impediment of fear may derive from the natural law, a dispensation from this impediment is not granted by the Church; neither are marriages laboring under the impediment of fear convalidated without renewal of consent (*sanatio in radice*), unless the fear has ceased.

In this matter, the following are considered to be guilty of mortal sin (always presupposing, of course, advertence and deliberate consent of the will): (a) the person who inflicts grave and unjust fear; (b) the one who contracts marriage, knowing that the other party is under grave fear; (c) the intimidated party, who enters marriage with the intention of consummating it, while aware that the contract is null and void.

CONDITION ATTACHED TO MATRIMONIAL CONSENT. A condition (*q.v.*) is a circumstance added to an act determining the validity thereof. A condition may relate: (a) to a past event (*condicio de praeterito*); (b) to a present event (*condicio de praesenti*); (c) to a future uncertain event (*condicio de futuro contingenti*); (d) to a future necessary event (*condicio de futuro necessario*), e.g., if the sun rises tomorrow; this last type is equivalent to a condition of the present. Again, a condition is said to be *possible* or *impossible*, dependent on whether capable of verification or not. An *immoral* or sinful condition is one contrary to morals or other legislation, and, in law, equivalent to an impossible condition. If one attaches a condition relating to a future uncertain event but intends his act to be valid until the condition is fulfilled (e.g., I marry you until I find someone richer), the condition is said to be *resolutive* (i.e., it nullifies the act); other conditions are suspensive in their effect (i.e., the validity of the act is in suspense until the condition is fulfilled).

As in other forms of contract, so in marriage one may attach certain conditions, although such practice is permitted by the Church only for grave reason. Secretly attached conditions have a juridical effect: in the internal forum, always; in the external forum, only if they can be proven. A condition attached and not revoked is presumed to persevere, even if it was not expressed in the manifestation of consent. As the condition is not presumed in law but must be proven, so too, the revocation of a condition must be proven. Anyone contracting marriage conditionally, against the will or without the knowledge of the other party, *per se* sins gravely and is obliged to make compensation for damages caused.

(a) If a condition relates to a *future* event which is *necessary, impossible*, or *immoral*, though not contrary to the substance of marriage, it is to be considered as not having been made (Can. 1092, n. 1). This is a simple presumption of law; in point of fact, the validity or invalidity of the marriage depends on the intention of the contracting parties. A person claiming to have attached one of the above conditions to his matrimonial consent must furnish proof. If conclusive proof is produced, the following distinctions prevail: (1) in a necessary, future condition, the completion of the bond is suspended until the condition is verified; (2) in an impossible future condition, the marriage is invalid; (3) in an immoral future condition, the completion of the marriage bond is suspended until verification of the condition, to which, however, the parties are not bound, since no one can be obliged to do evil.

(b) If a condition concerns the future and is contrary to the substance of marriage, it renders the contract invalid (Can. 1092, n. 2). Conditions contrary to the substance of marriage are directed against one of the three blessings or fruits of marriage: offspring, conjugal fidelity, the sacrament. Thus, stipulations to exclude children, such as to avoid conception, procure abortion, commit infanticide, etc., would be conditions against the blessing of offspring (*bonum prolis*); however, a condition contrary to the moral welfare of offspring, e.g., the intention of rearing the children as atheists, would not be against *bonum prolis* in the juridical sense. Conditions excluding marital fidelity or unity by reserving the right to commit adultery, or to take other wives, would be against the blessing of conjugal fidelity (*bonum fidei*). Exclusion of indissolubility by stipulating that commission of adultery by either party will dissolve the marriage bond, would be against the blessing of the sacrament (*bonum sacramenti*). Since such conditions exclude an essential element of marriage, they nullify marriage by virtue of the natural law itself. Apart from instances of marriage, rendered invalid by reason of conditional consent, there are also cases in which the marriage bond is dissolved by a disposition of the law itself; thus, a validly contracted but non-consummated marriage is automatically dissolved by solemn religious profession and by papal dispensation (Can. 1119).

Here it is necessary to note that conditions against *bonum prolis* and *bonum fidei* frequently are not directed against the essence of marriage, but are merely intentions or resolutions not to fulfill the obligations of a validly contracted marriage. This distinction between exclusion of the obligation itself and exclusion of its fulfillment does not, however, apply in the case of *bonum sacramenti*; here, the consent is impaired at its very source. In practice, each case is to be examined separately to determine whether the attached conditions are intended to exclude the conjugal right itself, with its corresponding obligations, or merely the fulfillment of obligations already assumed.

A marriage contracted with the agreement, condition, or vow of observing perpetual chastity is probably valid. The reason is that the right to the body (*jus in corpus*) is distinct from the exercise of this right (*exercitium juris*), and, in the present case, the intention of the marriage partners is to exclude, not the conjugal right itself, but only the use thereof, even though perpetually. The opposite theory, which claims that permanent exclusion of the use of marriage amounts to exclusion of the right itself, confuses the conjugal right with the exercise thereof. A marriage contracted with the agreement of observing perpetual chastity excludes the possibility of another marriage. Moreover, the fact and the condition of marital abstinence may be revoked by mutual agreement, in which case conjugal intercourse becomes perfectly licit, as it is perfectly licit if the partners are dispensed from their vow. Even if the partners were to exercise the conjugal right without dispensation from their vow, they would be sinning against the vow, not against the virtue of chastity. Certainly valid is a marriage in which both parties give true matrimonial consent, but only one party intends or vows to observe perpetual chastity. In this case, the vow is illicit and invalid (*see* Vow); but in no way does it affect the validity of the marriage, for that which binds the partners to each other is consent, not the vow.

(c) If a condition concerns the future and is lawful, the efficacy of the consent is suspended along with the validity of the marriage (Can. 1092 n. 3), until such time as the condition shall be verified. If the condition is fulfilled, the marriage becomes immediately valid without any need for renewal of consent; if the condition is not fulfilled, the marriage remains invalid. Hence, the parties do not commit sin if they lack the state of grace at the time of the marriage contract, but they do sin if they lack the state of grace at the time the condition is verified, because at that moment the marriage becomes effective and the sacrament is performed. It matters not whether the condition was attached by both parties or one only, whether by agreement or not, whether openly or secretly. If a secretly added condition cannot be proven in the external forum, the validity of the marriage is upheld before the law, even if the condition has not been verified. The party who secretly attaches a future, lawful condition sins gravely. If, before fulfillment of the condition, one proceeds without the knowledge or against the will of the other party to contract marriage with a different person, the second marriage is valid, though illicit. Both parties are bound to wait and not to impede fulfillment of the condition; however, revocation of the condition is always valid, though illicit, if done without a just reason, and the marriage becomes immediately valid. Finally, before fulfillment of the condition, the contracting parties are not true spouses, hence they may not engage in actions which are forbidden to the unmarried.

(d) If a condition concerns the *past* or the *present*, the marriage will be valid or not, according as the object of the condition exists or not (Can. 1092, n. 4). If the condition concerning the present or the past is impossible and yet seriously made, the marriage is null. If the condition is immoral and seriously made, the marriage is valid if the condition is verified; otherwise, it is invalid. If a condition concerning the past or the present is possible and lawful, the marriage is valid from its inception, if the condition is fulfilled; otherwise, it is null from the very beginning. Hence, conjugal intercourse is not permitted until the partners are certain that the condition has been actually verified.

EXPRESSION OF CONSENT. In order to contract a valid marriage, it is necessary that the consent be expressed externally by some sensible sign which may be perceived by the other party. External manifestation of consent is required, not only because of the contractual character of marriage (*intentio mente retenta nihil in humanis contractibus operatur*), but also because of its sacramental character, which consists essentially in a visible sign. Whereas, before the Code of Canon Law, it was possible to contract marriage by letter or through a messenger, today "in order to contract marriage validly, the contracting parties must be present either in person or by proxy" (Can. 1088, par. 1). Moreover, consent must ordinarily be expressed in words, and the pastor may not permit other equivalent signs (such as nodding the head, pressing the hand, etc.), unless the contracting parties are unable to speak. *Dal.*

CONSENTIENT, CONCURRENT. *See* Cooperation in evil.

CONSERVATISM. Today the term *conservatism* has a disparaging connotation: more often than not, it is used to indicate a faulty mental attitude or excessive attachment to the past in matters of custom, laws, and government. Taken in this sense, it was applied to the Church during the last century, because of its diffident attitude toward the liberal revolution. Difficult as it may be in its practical determinations, the search for a balance between the dynamic and the static forces present in the life of any organism, including the social organism, is fully justified. The need for progress must not cause one to ignore the need to hold firmly certain fundamental principles and values, on which the very existence of man and society depends. A conservation that insists on maintaining principles, forms of life, or customs that are not truly fundamental and, though useful in the past, are no longer useful in a later period, is indeed blameworthy.

CONSERVATIVE PARTY. Perhaps only in England is there a conservative political party. Elsewhere the term is so despised that no one employs it, for fear of seeming to oppose social reforms which everyone considers essential. As a matter of fact, even British Conservatives have introduced social reforms in their program; this indicates an organic concept of conservatism and the realization that progress and development is necessary for the preservation of life and society. Conservatives on the European continent, on the contrary, have generally failed to show such adaptability, which accounts for their present disrepute in the political arena.

CONSERVATIVE CLASS. The term *conservative* is also applied to the social class of owners or proprietors, who naturally stand for the defense of property and ownership. Aligned against this group are the so-called *have-nots,* who seek greater *social justice* (*q.v.*) or more equitable distribution of wealth. True social justice must be placed above particular interests, and the legitimate rights of all classes must be properly recognized. To attain real social justice, it is necessary to rise above mere positive laws and return to the principles of natural law, which, in keeping with the changed conditions of life, allow new applications of the fundamental principles of justice, that are objective and not subordinate to the interest of any particular class. A return to these principles has given rise to a recent elaboration of social doctrine favored and promoted by the supreme authority of the Catholic Church itself. *Boz.*

CONSORTS, SPOUSES.

A man and a woman, living together in legitimate wedlock, are called *consorts* or *spouses.* In a valid marriage, the bond endures as long as both partners are alive, even though they may be legally separated from each other (Cans. 1128–1132). Consequently, neither party may, during the lifetime of the other, validly contract a new marriage (Can. 1118).

If a marriage is invalid but at least one of the parties is ignorant of the fact, they are called putative spouses; the children born of this marriage have the same rights as legitimate offspring (Cans. 1015; 114).

A valid marriage of two baptized persons creates a perpetual and exclusive bond between them and gives them the grace of the sacrament, provided that they place no obstacle in the way (Can. 1110).

From the moment the marriage contract is concluded, both partners possess equal rights and duties relative to actions proper to conjugal life (Can. 1111). The wife assumes the surname of her husband. Spouses are bound to marital fidelity and mutual assistance. As head of the family, the husband normally has the obligation to provide for the maintenance of the family.

Parents are bound by a most serious obligation to provide, to the best of their ability, for the religious, moral, physical, and intellectual training of their children and for their temporal welfare (Can. 113). (*See* Family, Piety.)

Prolonged absence or the probability of death of one of the parties is not sufficient to permit the other party to marry again; definite proof of the missing partner's death must be furnished (Can. 1069). The same applies in doubt concerning the validity of the marriage contract. Mere doubt does not dissolve the marital bond. To be freed, the nullity of the marriage must be established with certainty and by the legitimate authority (executive decree). *Bar.*

MUTUAL RIGHTS AND DUTIES IN PROPERTY. By virtue of marriage, a man and a woman join to establish a new family in which the man is the head; all other rights are equal for both spouses.

Both parties preserve, in the married state, their natural rights, including the right of ownership (*see* Property). Thus, though the husband is bound to support his wife, the latter is expected to help her husband if necessary.

Of those goods which exceed the requirements of proper maintenance of the family, husband and wife may dispose as they see fit, in accordance with the specific dispositions of civil law, if such dispositions exist.

The respective rights and duties of a married couple in property matters may be determined by pre-nuptial agreement or by the particular system of property settlement adopted at the time of marriage. A prospective bride and groom are free to choose the particular system according to which their respective property is to be administered, and to add whatever agreements they wish, provided that these do not contravene the law or general custom. The principal systems usually adopted are: *the system of community of goods,* which admits of various degrees (total, partial, simple, common administration), *the system of separation of goods; the dotal system* (*see* Dowry). If two persons contract marriage without any special agreement regarding their property, it is assumed that they have adopted the system commonly prevalent in the region.

DISPOSITIONS OF THE NATURAL LAW. According to the natural law: (a) the wife retains full dominion of goods acquired by personal industry, inheritance, donation; (b) husband and wife possess equal right of ownership over common goods; (c) if the husband's means and common funds are insufficient, the wife is bound to contribute to the family maintenance out of her own possessions. *Pal.*

CONSTELLATION. See Endocrinology.

CONSTITUENT. *See* Subject.

CONSTITUTION. *See* Rules.

CONSTITUTION, APOSTOLIC. *See* Acts, Pontifical.

CONSTITUTION, BIOTYPOLOGICAL. In a wide sense, *constitution* is the sum-total of an individual's somatic and psychological characteristics. In this sense, the term is synonymous with *personality*. But more properly speaking, the term *personality* (*q.v.*) refers to the psychological make-up, and *constitution* refers to physical make-up. This is defined as "the particular combination in an individual of the variant physical characteristics of the species" (Viola).

TYPOLOGY. The peculiar combination of certain dominant physical characteristics, presenting the specific morphological aspect and particular functional attitudes of a person, is a morphological type, or *habit*. The basic combination upon which modern typometry is based is a relation between the measurements of the trunk and those of the extremities.

The principal morphologico-constitutional types are as follows:

(a) The *normal* or *normolinear* type indicates an individual with average height, normal physique, proper proportion between trunk and extremities, an eurythmic disposition of various anatomic formations and an harmonious efficiency in the various organic functions.

(b) The *megalosplanchnic brachytype* (*brevilinear* or *pyknic*) indicates an individual of medium height with a rounded, thickset build, excessive development of the trunk and distribution of fat about the stomach, tendency to overweight; functionally, it shows a preponderance of the parasympathetic over the orthosympathetic system, of the vagomimetic, hormonal system (thymus, parathyroids, pancreas, etc.) over the sympathicomimetic, endocrine system (hypophysis, pituitary gland, thyroid, etc.), of anabolism (assimilation) over catabolism (disintegration.)

(c) The *microsplanchnic longitype* (*longilinear* or *leptosomatic*) presents an anatomical and functional picture diametrically opposed to that just described.

A different neuroendocrine orientation is found in the various constitutional types, which characterizes their vegetative function and affects the activities of life and psychological tendencies. Thus, it is commonly noted that the thin or leptosomatic type is agile, quick to act, but with a tendency to tire easily; he is also quick-thinking (*tachypsychical*), usually with a brilliant mind, but is inclined to moodiness and discouragement. The pyknic or brevilinear type, on the other hand, is usually slow, calm, and inclined to heavy work and endurance; mentally, he is brachypsychical (slow-thinking) and inclined toward a euphoric disposition.

Hormonal Influence. At this point it is well to note that, in practice, not every leptosomatic or pyknic individual conforms to the typical patterns of behavior just described; the same must be said of brachytypes. This is due to the fact that in the present article only the three more important morphological types are outlined; in reality these are more numerous. In view of the complex interplay of hormonal correlations, any excess or insufficiency in the function of one endocrine gland may cause more or less conspicuous or, at times, radical changes in the vegetative and psychical activities, thus giving rise to many morphologico - constitutional subtypes, with anatomical and functional characteristics widely different from the patterns described above.

We shall mention here, by way of example, the influence exercised by the suprarenal glands (*q.v.*) on the individual constitution. The *sthenic brachytype*, a pyknic individual, with *hyperfunction* of the suprarenal glands, is plethoric, sanguine, exceptionally strong, and inclined to violence. The *asthenic pyknic* type, with suprarenal *hypofunction*, is notably lymphatic, pale, torpid, somnolent. The leptosomatic type of the *sthenic* and *athletic* variety, with suprarenal *hyperfunction*, is full-blooded, muscular, and resistant; but the *asthenic* leptosomatic type, with suprarenal *hypofunction*, is pale, delicate, incapable of physical exertion, and frequently contracts tuberculosis.

As can be readily seen from the rapid survey given above, the subject of individual constitution is highly complex and polymorphous. This study is of great importance in the fields of medicine, psychology, psychopathology, and morality, for the constitution represents a substratum of various physiological and pathological aspects of the individual, ultimately exercising a notable influence on the human mind.

On the other hand, although consciousness constitutes the unitive and permanent center of the entire psychophysical individuality, and although its sphere is largely independent of constitutional factors, these so shape and color the personality that no study of any organ or organic function can be of real value without taking into consideration the constitutional endowment of the individual. Even infectious diseases, which until recent times were explained simply as the result of specific pathogenic germs, are today known to be intimately related to the constitution. The very symptoms of such diseases are biological reactions of the organism, which differ,

both quantitatively and qualitatively, according to the diversity of individual constitutions.

Finally, the study of biological constitution is a fundamental requisite for all research on the problem of normal and pathological psychosomatic growth. All such research, which has led to a new and dynamic branch of medicine (*auxology*), not only provides us with an integrated, reliable picture of the state of infancy, adolescence, and youth, but also contributes to the health of humanity. *Riz.*

CONSULTANT. See Cooperation.

CONSULTANT, TECHNICAL. See Deontology.

CONSULTATION, MEDICAL. A *medical consultation* consists in a meeting of two or more doctors for the purpose of diagnosis, prognosis, and treatment of the case on hand. Generally, it takes place beween the family physician and a specialist called in to check and discuss the condition and treatment of the patient.

A medical consultation may be requested by the patient, the members of his family, or by the physician in charge of the case.

In the first instance, although it seemingly indicates a diminished confidence of the patient in his physician, the latter should not only refrain from expressing any opposition, but should willingly acquiesce, bearing in mind that a well-conducted consultation is almost certain to result in an increase of his prestige with his patient. The physician should consider it as an opportunity to shed new light on the case and, perhaps, produce a more accurate diagnosis. Moreover, if, as frequently happens, the consultant is a specialist in his field, he may well suggest new and more effective drugs. Another important consideration is the psychological benefit for the patient's morale. Frequently, in chronic illness, the mere knowledge that another doctor is being called in for consultation increases the patient's hope and, perhaps, his chances of recovery.

If requested to call in a consultant, the physician in charge of the case, whose sole concern should be the recovery of the patient in his care, should check on the ability and reputation of the new doctor if one is suggested by the patient or the members of his family. Frequently members of the family, disturbed over the gravity or the length of a patient's illness, turn for advice to friends and acquaintances, who are always ready to suggest the name of a new doctor and new methods of treatment, often inferior to the methods used in the case. In such circumstances, the physician may frankly express his opinion and suggest the name of a reliable consultant professionally known to him. If the patient were to insist on calling in a consultant who is clearly incompetent, the physician will be fully justified in withdrawing from the case altogether (see Withdrawal from a Medical Case).

If the physician is asked to recommend a consultant, he is bound to select one who will best serve the interests of his patient, avoiding all motives of friendship and base opportunism. In other words, it is morally improper for a physician to recommend a consultant for purposes of: (a) showing favor to a colleague; (b) falsely enhancing one's own reputation by instructing the consultant to corroborate his own diagnosis and treatment; (c) splitting the consultation fee.

In the course of the consultation, the physician in charge of the case must show cordial cooperation and be ready to furnish the consultant with all pertinent data in his possession. The consultant, on his part, is bound to make known the full results of his examination, the diagnosis of the case and the treatment suggested. The report is to be made in a professional and gentlemanly manner, without haughtiness or criticism, so as not to subject the family physician to humiliation or other harm.

In order that the consultation may be conducted in a calm atmosphere and in the best interest of the patient, the exchange of views between the two doctors should take place privately and not in the presence of the patient or members of his family, who, however, are entitled to a full report of the findings.

If the results of the consultation should clearly indicate that the family physician has erred in his diagnosis and treatment of the case, the consultant is bound to observe the rules of professional courtesy, that is, he must report his findings and conclusions in such a manner as to avoid any humiliation for his colleague. However, in cases of gross incompetence or grave negligence, the consultant is obliged to inform the patient. In all events, the consultant shall be guided by prudent judgment and by the law of charity. *Riz.*

CONSULTORS, DIOCESAN. In dioceses where a cathedral chapter does not exist or cannot be constituted, a group of priests is appointed by the local Ordinary and, known as the board of diocesan consultors (Can. 423), performs all the duties of the cathedral chapter in assisting the bishop in the administration of the diocese. The board of diocesan consultors takes the place of the chapter as the bishop's council.

Diocesan consultors—at least six for larger dioceses, and four for smaller ones—are selected by the Ordinary from among diocesan priests known for their piety, character, learning, and prudence. Required to live either in the episcopal city or in adjacent areas, they are appointed for one or more terms of three years. If the three-year term expires during a vacancy of the see, the consultors remain in office until the new Ordinary takes possession and proceeds, within six months, to appoint new consultors or reappoint the old ones. If a consultor dies during his term of office or retires for any reason, the Ordinary shall appoint a substitute, who remains in office for the rest of the unexpired term. If a consultor dies or resigns during a vacancy of the see, the administrator of the diocese shall, with the consent of the other consultors, appoint a successor, who, however, needs the approval of the new Ordinary who takes possession of his diocese (Can. 426).

During their term of office, diocesan consultors may not be removed except for a just cause and with the consent of the other consultors (Cans. 423–428).

CONSUMPTION. *Consumption* represents the culmination or result of the entire economic process. In other words, goods are produced to be used or consumed. Although consumption is the final cause of production, it is not its efficient cause, nor do the productive factors of land, labor, and capital increase with increased consumption, which functions only as a stimulus to production. The problem of consumption, with its political and social implications, is connected not only with the problem of *production,* but also with that of *distribution, savings, and population.*

According to fears expressed by certain economists, increased consumption must sooner or later reach a point where production will be unequal to the demands of consumption or where the population will exceed its means of subsistence. In fact, Malthus formulated a pseudo-economic law which attained considerable renown because of its moral implications. Malthus stated that population tends to increase in geometric proportion, but the means of subsistence can only increase in arithmetical proportion. In other words, population tends to multiply faster than food supply. On the basis of this law, Malthus advocated the limitation of births.

The Malthusian theory has long since been disproved. Economic wealth has grown at a faster rate than population, with the aid of mechanization, which made possible a more intense cultivation of the soil and increased distribution of goods. The problem of overpopulation has been revived recently and is currently discussed under a new term: *population explosion.* In answer to the alarm sounded by pressure groups and exponents of secularism and materialistic philosophy, the Bishops of the U.S.A. issued a brilliant rebuttal in a statement released at the conclusion of their 1959 Annual Meeting in Washington, D. C.

Connected with the problem of consumption are a number of other economic factors, such as distribution of wealth, competition (*q.v.*), domestic markets, and, on the international level, imports and exports (*see* Commerce, International Commerce).

When commodities are scarce and prices are higher, consumers tend to form associations or consumer cooperatives, designed to cut prices by eliminating the presence of the middleman. Because of the obvious advantages they bring, consumer cooperatives in normal times are a means of keeping business within the bounds of moral law.

The problem of consumption has given rise in certain countries to government controls exercised over the prices of certain essential commodities and markets. Such controls tend to insure a sufficient quantity of commodities, by preventing skyrocketing prices and protecting the consumer against adulteration of products.

Another problem related to consumption is luxury (*q.v.*), which is a disproportion between the amount of work expended and the degree of individual satisfaction obtained.

Christian morality does not condemn normal savings for the future, but it does condemn excessive luxury, undue waste of wealth, inequities in the distribution of wealth caused by selfish hoarding, greed, exploitation, speculation, etc. *Bau.*

CONTAGION, CONTACT. *Contagion* or *contact* indicates a manner or way whereby certain diseases, produced by infectious agents, germs, or filtrable viruses are communicated from one person to another.

Infectious diseases may be spread:

(a) by *direct contact* with a sick or con-valescing person, or even by a healthy person who acts as the carrier or trans-mitter of an infectious agent, by com-municating it to others, thus causing them to contract the disease. (b) By *in-direct contact*, that is, the pathogenic germs are transmitted by various con-taminated objects, such as polluted water, milk, or dust particles in the air, mosquitoes, and other insects.

From the moral standpoint, the mat-ter of contagion is an important one, for the following points in particular: (a) the deliberate transmission of a contagious disease; (b) the transmission of venereal diseases.

The deliberate transmission of a con-tagious disease from one person to another, generally by indirect contact, is not a fiction of the imagination but a real fact. Moreover, it is an open secret that certain governments have in-cluded among their arms of offense, in case of war, *bacteriological warfare*, which consists in contaminating the at-mosphere and the waters of enemy territory by disseminating bacterial cul-tures with a high pathogenic potential.

The deliberate transmission of in-fectious diseases, whether perpetrated by individuals or governments, is a true crime, inspired either by a criminal mind or by the nefarious principles of total war. Perhaps any moral discussion of this subject is unnecessary in view of the obvious heinousness of such criminal acts worthy of the most unqualified con-demnation.

Transmission of contagious disease by direct contact, however, is a more subtle and difficult problem. Since trans-mission of a disease is, in such a case, wholly involuntary, generally, there is no question of moral guilt. Nevertheless, there are certain aspects of the problem which may be worthy of ethical con-sideration.

Needless to say, a person affected by any form of contagious disease has both the right and duty to seek proper medi-cal care and treatment. And it is like-wise a duty for the immediate members of his family to exercise loving and

tender care toward such a patient. Furthermore, the practice of the Chris-tian precept to visit the sick must not be neglected. This precept implies pro-viding effective and useful assistance to the sick. However, visitors must be made aware that frequently the patient seeks companionship simply to while away the time, without realizing the possible grave consequences for the visiting per-son.

In cases of epidemico-contagious dis-ease, the doctor, nurse, or other re-sponsible person, must instruct the patient on the proper hygienico-pro-phylactic measures to be taken. The patient and the members of his family must especially be warned about the possibility of direct contagion and made aware of the duty of using adequate dis-infectants and the obligation of exclud-ing all visitors and friends unless their presence is absolutely necessary.

Of greatest importance, both morally and socially, is the problem of the trans-mission of venereal diseases.

According to the dictates of Catholic moral doctrine, a person who engages in sexual relations and contacts outside legitimate marriage is automatically guilty of a violation of the sixth com-mandment of God. If such a person is knowingly the cause of a venereal in-fection, he also violates the fifth com-mandment.

Unfortunately, many individuals, com-pletely unaware of having contracted a venereal infection, continue to transmit it to others. This is especially true of women, who, due to the particular structure of their genital organs, become easily unwitting transmitters of venereal diseases.

But there are also instances in which an individual, fully aware of his ve-neral infection, deliberately transmits it to others, either out of a criminal spirit of revenge, or because of a dangerous and widespread misconception that ve-nereal disease is cured through sexual intercourse with a virgin. Such cases call for the most severe moral sanctions, particularly because of the harm in-flicted upon society and other individuals. To prevent such widespread immorality, sex education is important, but it is insufficient, unless it is accompanied by adequate religious instruction, through which a deep awareness of the divine precepts and sanctions might be properly instilled in every person. *Riz.*

CONTAGION, PSYCHICAL. This term, borrowed from the field of epidemiology, means the transmission of psychical disorders from one individual to another through suggestion, imitation, and the like. It is basically of two types, *family* and *mob* (mass) contagion. They differ both from the standpoint of their pathogenesis and the types of individuals affected.

Because of a psychological resemblance among the members of the same family, it often happens that psychical disorders affecting one member of the family are passively acquired also by the others. In other words, among the various members of a family there seems to run a thread of mutual influence or suggestion, a form of slow and spontaneous collaboration, whereby the initial disorder is gradually increased to such a status that it becomes a true and proper syndrome affecting all the members of a family circle. This occurs more frequently between elderly married individuals, whose long and continued association in the same restricted environment, with but little outside communication, makes them highly susceptible to mutual influence or suggestion.

These psychopathic conditions stem generally from paranoiac deliria or hysterical psychoses.

Another type of psychical contagion is the pathogenic condition responsible for psychopathic epidemics affecting relatively large crowds, also called *psychopathies of the masses.* Such epidemics explode in large gatherings under the drive of intense collective emotions brought on by famine, war, revolution, etc., or by strong suggestible influence of a leader, agitator, or rabble-rouser.

In such cases, the psychical contagion may be of an hysterical or paranoiac character. Hysterical contagion usually arises from hallucinatory or convulsive hysteria, gripping at first minor hysteriacs in the crowd and, then, spreading gradually even to normal persons. The suggestible influence is as great as the number of hysterically affected persons. This explains the historical epidemics of demoniacal obsession, St. Vitus' dance, and the like. These conditions are much rarer in our days of improved cultural, social and economic standards. But, despite such improved conditions, a psychical contagion is still possible under certain circumstances, which today are largely of a revolutionary character. In such occurrences, the beast in man inevitably comes to the fore, driving him to actions of unrestrained cruelty which would hardly occur apart from such deplorable circumstances.

These collective manifestations may also be caused by a paranoiac contagion promoted by an intelligent and energetic paranoiac, who, under favorable circumstances, acquires an immediate and facile ascendancy over the masses of ignorant and brutalized people, incapable of rational resistance. But not altogether rare is the case where the leaders of a crowd in revolt are overpowered by the movement itself, and the anonymous and blind collectivity becomes itself the actual leader.

A more frequent example of collective psychical contagion is the outburst of panic and terror which occasionally grips audiences assembled in public places as a result of a wild rumor, sudden shriek, or yell. At times such manifestations end in real disaster. Autosuggestion deprives the spectators of all rational powers and throws them into a state of unreasonable panic.

The modern media of communication, such as the press, radio, movies, and television, are dangerous instruments capable of throwing an entire country into a psychotic state.

Antisocial and even criminal mob manifestations are not the result of a pre-existing collective plan, as in the case of organized criminal groups, but often are spontaneous and unpremeditated. They are simply occasioned by autosuggestion, collective passion, and frenzy under the instigation of some madman or astute agitator.

More particularly, mob crimes are determined by the sudden emergence of aggressive and destructive tendencies, or instincts of hatred and vengeance. Such tendencies and instincts, germinally present in the best of individuals, in normal circumstances are effectively controlled by the will strengthened by education. But in an atmosphere of commotion, political agitation or revolutionary riot, these germinal instincts and tendencies come forth in a crowd by reason of mutual passional influences. There thus rapidly develops a peculiar collective psychosis, with a chain reaction similar to that of atomic energy, in which the emergence of latent primordial tendencies trigger the mob into committing the most savage and brutal actions—actions which would not occur under normal circumstances.

Thus, although in organized crime the deliberate merging of individual criminal tendencies gives rise to aggravating circumstances of individual dangerousness, in the mob's suggestible exaltation it is possible to have extenuating circumstances. In other words, crimes committed by such a mob are the result of blind passion or even temporary insanity, because the intellectual and volitional capacity of a rioting mob is always noticeably reduced. The fact that women are more liable to psychical contagion, by reason of their higher susceptibility to suggestible influence, seems to confirm that position.

An entirely different judgment, both morally and legally, is to be rendered in the case of those few agitators who exert their evil influence on the crowd. Such instigators or agitators, unless clearly hysteriacs or paronoiacs, must be considered as individually responsible for all atrocities and crimes committed by the mob.

A more subtle, less clamorous, but more widespread source of psychical contagion is furnished by a sensational publication of crimes in some daily or weekly papers and magazines. The steady publication of stories of crimes and passion in all their lurid details and with full pictorial illustrations seems to be the deliberate policy of certain papers, magazines, and cheap books, bent on catering systematically to the morbid and erotic tendencies of certain readers or groups of readers. Such publications and illustrations exercise an insidious and poisonous influence, especially on youthful minds.

Catholic morality and social medicine must rise and speak out against such perversions of journalistic functions which constitute a constant peril and are often the cause of irreparable harm to the spiritual welfare of the readers. *Riz.*

CONTEMPLATION. *Contemplation* is a gaze of the mind accompanied by admiration. Contemplation may be purely natural or supernatural, rooted in faith. The latter extends to all things revealed by God and has, as its principal object, God Himself. Of all creatures which come within its sphere, the Sacred Humanity of Christ occupies a prominent place.

Contemplation, rooted in faith, may be *active* (acquired) or *passive* (infused). Active or acquired contemplation is the result of our own activity aided by ordinary grace. Frequently, the gifts of the Holy Ghost, especially understanding and wisdom, exert their hidden influence in helping to fix our gaze lovingly on God. Active contemplation is also called mixed or active-passive contemplation by reason of these frequent, though latent, influences of the gifts of the Holy Ghost.

Passive or infused contemplation of God and of divine things is not the result of our own efforts, but of a special grace (operative grace), under the influence of which the mind is more passive than active. This contemplation is mystic in nature, and, sublime as it may be, according to the opinion of many theologians, is not *per se* an extraordinary grace. Hence, any soul may desire to have it and humbly ask God for it. As the soul's love of God increases, mental prayer acquires a more simple and perfect form; in other words, from discursive prayer, it gradually becomes contemplative. And if the soul is truly generous and especially profits from the purgative trials sent by God, there comes a moment when God raises that soul to the infused contemplation of the divine mysteries.

CONTEMPLATION AND ACTION. Some temperaments are more inclined to contemplation than to action, and vice versa. The lives of the saints demonstrate that the work of grace respects such tendencies. In some saints we find a life of calm contemplation predominant; in others, it is a life of apostolic action, which does not, however, exclude contemplation. Familiar examples of this type are found in the Curé of Ars, Saint Vincent de Paul, Saint John Bosco, etc. True contemplatives are men of action; their activity flows from the contemplation of the divine mysteries of faith.

The Code of Canon Law urges the clergy to cultivate in a special way the practice of daily meditation and contemplation of eternal truths (Can. 125, n. 2). Pope Pius XII earnestly stressed this same point in his apostolic exhortation to the clergy, by recalling that contemplation is to the spiritual life what bread is to the material life (AAS: 42 [1950], 672). *Man.*

CONTEST, COMPETITION. *See* Dispute, Polemic.

CONTINENCE. *See* Abstinence, Chastity.

CONTINENCE, PERIODIC (Rhythm method). *Periodic continence* is an artificial regulation of sexual life in marriage, in which husband and wife agree to refrain from sexual intercourse during periods when the conjugal act, though fully and properly performed and without positive interference or contracep-

tive measures, is not expected to result in pregnancy, because of the natural physiological process in the woman. Insofar as it implies partial *abstinence*, the purpose of the rhythm method is to avoid pregnancy; insofar as it means a partial or periodic *use* of the conjugal right, its aim is to secure the secondary ends of marriage (mutual assistance, fostering mutual love, allaying concupiscence); it thus avoids the hardships that total abstinence might bring.

HISTORICAL NOTES. The belief or theory that the period of time intervening between two menstruations is divided into fertile and sterile days dates back to very ancient times. During the latter part of the nineteenth century, a number of doctors believed that they could determine, with a considerable degree of probability, the sterile period in women. This period was reckoned in reference to the preceding menstruation, but their theory proved to be inaccurate. In some cases, it was successful; in others, it was not.

After much research, the physicians Ogino (Japanese), Knaus (Austrian) and Smulders (Dutch) proposed a new theory. Its main points may be summarized as follows: (a) The female monthly cycle comprises a period of consecutive fertile days; in other words, pregnancy may result only from sexual relations during this period; outside this period, no pregnancy may occur. (b) The beginning and end of this fertile period bear a fixed relationship of time to the *next* menstruation. The error of Capellmann and others consisted in this: they established a fixed time, the same for all women, between the fertile period and the *preceding* menstruation. This is a biological error, for menstruation is the end, not the beginning of a biological cycle. All the biological phenomena occurring in the menstrual cycle bear a natural relation to subsequent menstruation, not to the preceding one. (c) The general rule for all women is the following: sexual relations between the nineteenth and twelfth day before subsequent menstruation may result in pregnancy; on the remaining days of the cycle, normally no pregnancy will result from sexual relations. (d) Since the menstrual cycle is not the same in all women, for variation may extend from twenty-six to thirty-five days, it follows that the intervening time between the fertile period and the preceding menstruation is not the same in all cases. (e) In the same woman, the cycle tends to be constant, unless upset by physical or psychological disturbances, such as grave illness, serious emotional shock, etc.

It is possible for a woman to establish the number of intervening days between her fertile period and the preceding menstruation. This can be done by keeping an accurate record of the length of her menstrual cycle over a period of some months. Thus, in a cycle of twenty-nine days, the fertile period would be from the tenth to the seventeenth day following the previous menstruation; in a cycle of thirty days, the fertile period would be from the eleventh to the eighteenth day; in a cycle of thirty-one days, it would be from the twelfth to the nineteenth day. In other words, there are eight fertile days, including the extreme limits. The days preceding and following this fertile period represent the so-called "safe" periods of the cycle. According to competent medical authorities, a safe use of the rhythm method is impossible without the guidance of an able physician.

MORAL DOCTRINE. Periodic continence of the rhythm method presents a number of moral problems. (a) One may be the case of a spouse who uses the rhythm method against the will or serious wishes of the other spouse, either simply by refusing to have marital intercourse during the fertile periods or by unjustly extracting the partner's consent, who agrees simply to avoid greater evils or hardships, to maintain peace, etc. Such conduct is a *grave violation* of the duty to render the marital right. (b) Another case may be that of a married couple, freely and mutually agreeing to practice periodic continence. This question touches the core of the problem concerning the morality of periodic continence. The practice of periodic continence involves the use of a specific *means* to attain a specific *end*. In such a case, one may sin in two ways: either because the end is evil or because the means employed is evil. It is necessary to consider the morality of the means and the morality of the end, which is the limitation of offspring or size of the family.

The means used in partial abstinence. There is nothing evil about sexual abstinence. Married partners are not obliged to use the conjugal right, but may, by mutual accord, abstain whenever they wish. The only requirement to justify their conduct is that the end in view be good and honest. No element of sin can be found in *partial* continence, which amounts to the use of the conjugal right only at certain times of the month. Proper marital intercourse, even if there is certainty that no conception will follow, is never considered sinful. Marriage also has secondary ends, which are good and lawful. This is traditional and uncontroverted Catholic doctrine. The reply of the Holy See in 1880, that married persons could practice periodic continence with tranquillity of conscience is based on traditional doctrine. But the meaning of the reply is simply that periodic continence is not an evil; anyone employing this means does not sin, provided that the end is good.

The end of partial abstinence. The end of periodic continence is the limitation of offspring or the size of the family. Catholic moral teaching has never held that married persons have the duty of begetting the greatest possible number of children, without regard for other considerations. The procreation of children is a human activity to be regulated rationally. But Catholic doctrine has always insisted on this: the primary end of marriage and, hence, of conjugal life, is the procreation of children; not one or two children, but as many as will naturally result from normal conjugal life. The Catholic Church considers a large family to be the normal and natural effect of a normal conjugal life. A large family provides better assurance for the proper upbringing and education of children, an essential and most important part of the primary end of marriage. The burdens and sacrifices imposed upon parents by a large family are considered by Catholic moral doctrine to be ordinary burdens. From this it does not follow that it would necessarily be sinful for married people to practice periodic continence for the purpose of limiting the size of their family. For, if they have special and grave reasons to do so, their conduct is quite lawful. It would be sinful, however, to resort to periodic continence without special or serious reason, or for slight, selfish, and frivolous reasons, e.g., to escape the responsibilities and burdens of parenthood, to enjoy greater freedom in pursuit of pleasure and other selfish interests. Limitation of offspring without justifying reasons would be morally reprehensible, even if the couple were to practice absolute continence to accomplish this end. Good, virtuous Christian couples, aware of their duty to God, Church and country, do not think of limiting the number of children, unless compelled by special, abnormal and truly urgent circumstances. Such circumstances must be all the more urgent and grave, if a notable restriction or limitation of family is involved. In conclusion, the use of the rhythm method for a few months after parturition, to allow the mother a period of recovery from the burden of childbirth, is almost always morally justifiable. Use of the rhythm method for an indefinite period of time or for the rest of their married life can only be justified by grave and special reasons. Certainly, the ideal means for a justified limitation of offspring is total abstinence. But this entails spiritual dangers affecting the secondary ends of marriage (mutual assistance, fostering mutual love, allaying of concupiscence), as well as the primary end (proper upbringing and education of children). Too many people easily deceive themselves into believing that they have justifying reasons for practicing periodic continence. In order to avoid any danger of self-deception in this regard, Catholic married couples are admonished not to resort to the use of the rhythm method without first consulting a confessor, appointed by God to judge the moral aspects of their conduct.

A third moral question arises as to whether a couple may resort to the use of the rhythm method instead of total abstinence if the life or the health of the wife might be endangered by a future pregnancy. In such circumstances, they may resort to the use of the rhythm method if there is absolute certainty that no pregnancy will ensue. Such certainty, of course, cannot be had without the professional aid of a competent and responsible physician. Doctors can provide the required certainty in this case. To suggest to a couple in such circumstances the use of the rhythm method, without ascertaining the facts, is an act of grave imprudence.

The doctrine regarding the lawfulness of periodic continence was further confirmed by the teaching authority of the Church in an allocution by Pope Pius XII to the Italian Catholic Union of Obstetricians, Oct. 29, 1951 (AAS: 43 [1951], 844–845). *Ben.*

CONTRABAND. Contraband (Latin, *contra* — against; *bannum* — proclamation, edict) signifies the violation of a law forbidding the importation of a commodity or item from one country to another or from one territory to another within the same country. It always involves violation of a law or statute. Such a law may be applied to any article or object, and the purpose of the prohibition may be fiscal, economic, political, or moral. Generally, the prohibition is enacted for fiscal reasons.

Contraband may be practiced by land, sea, or air, and in times of peace or war. If practiced on the seas in wartime by neutral nations or subjects in behalf of a belligerent nation, it constitutes contraband of war; this is regulated both by international law and by particular laws of the various nations.

Contraband is unlawful. Internal or external contraband, as a violation of laws enacted by the legitimate authority, is clearly an unlawful act and, therefore, punishable. Nevertheless, a distinction is usually made between moral laws and penal or merely penal laws. The former oblige in conscience (*sub culpa*); the latter are merely penally (*sub poena*), that is, the transgressor must accept the penalty established by law if inflicted by the competent authority. The obligation to accept the penalty is a moral one, hence binding in conscience. Laws relative to contraband for evading taxes are regarded as penal or merely penal laws.

Contraband of war. This type of contraband occasions a number of questions concerning actual persons with a right to classify articles of contraband; the rights which belligerent nations may exercise in order to prevent contraband; the sanctions which may be applied against those practicing contraband; etc. It is generally recognized that a state of war imposes many restrictions on freedom of commerce, even upon neutral nations and their subjects. However, in view of the grave economic consequences resulting from such restrictions, it is clear that the prohibition of trading with belligerent powers should be limited only to war material, thus allowing neutrals as much liberty of commerce as possible. Moreover, it should be clearly defined what articles constitute contraband; and the list of articles thus classified should be made public to all neutral nations and their subjects.

In practice, the classification of articles of contraband in war is not free of difficulties. For, although there is general agreement insofar as arms and munitions are concerned, the same is not true with respect to many other items, such as ships, coal, food, money, etc., which are susceptible of military as well as civilian uses. Such items are generally placed in the category of conditional contraband.

An international agreement on this matter would be highly desirable. In the London Declaration of 1909, a tentative list of absolute war contraband items was formulated, but the declaration was not ratified by all the nations. In the absence of an international agreement, classification of contraband material is unilaterally formulated by the belligerents themselves. Since, in recent times, motivated by the prevalent concept of global or total warfare, belligerents have sought to wage economic as well as military war, the range of contraband articles has been vastly increased, to prevent or at least gradually restrict maritime commerce between neutrals and belligerent nations.

It is generally recognized that, in order to prevent the practice of contraband in time of war, belligerent states have the right of inspecting and searching the merchant ships of neutrals. This right may be exercised only on the high seas and in the territorial waters of belligerents. It is to be noted, however, that neutral nations and their subjects are not forbidden to trade across adjacent borders with belligerents, even though the transported merchandise include items considered as contraband of war (*see* Neutrality).

If the commander of a belligerent ship discovers war material on board a neutral merchant ship, he has the right to seize the ship and the contraband cargo (*see* War, Booty). *Pas.*

CONTRACT. The Latin term *contractus* in Roman Law referred not so much to the consent of the parties but to the negotiation or transaction itself, considered as the cause of the obligatory bond. The essential elements of a contract were: *negotium contractus*, which provided a *justa causa* or legal reason for the obligation as the primary, original, and causal element of the contract, and the *agreement* or *consent* of the parties, an element of later origin.

In early Roman legislation, the establishment of obligations, not from law itself, required the observance of solemn and formal procedures. Before the classical period, there were definite instances of contracts formed and recognized, independent of the use of typical and solemn requirements. Such contracts were divided into two classes: *re contrahitur* or *consistat obligatio*; from these are derived the modern terms, *real* contracts and *consensual* contracts.

Today, however, there is no longer any difference between *contract* and *agreement*, nor fixed formulae to which agreements must necessarily be reduced; there is merely the general concept of contract.

Contract is the consent of two wills about an object of common interest (*duorum vel plurium in idem placitum consensus*), or, as defined in civil jurisprudence, the agreement of two or more persons in a concurrent expression of will for the purpose of establishing or extinguishing a juridical relation concerning a property. According to modern opinion, contract belongs to the category of juridical transactions. Some moralists apply the term *quasi-contract*, in a less proper sense, to certain agreements, such as the acceptance of an office, which are true contracts, but tacit or implied. In a legal and more precise sense, *quasi-contract* (*q.v.*) is an obligation freely assumed by one party, who performs a licit act (such as picking up a lost article for another party); but this creates a further obligation, although no consent is expressed by this other party, not even a tacit one. This consent is presumed simply because it is according to equity.

DIVISION. A contract is called *in fieri* if one considers only the act of mutual consent; *in facto esse* if one considers the effects arising from a contract already concluded.

A contract is *bilateral* or *synallagmatic*, if it imposes obligations on both contracting parties (e.g., contract of sale); *unilateral*, if the obligation rests on one party only (e.g., a deposit).

A contract is called *onerous*, if it causes a burden and a benefit for both contracting parties (e.g., sale, interest loan); *gratuitous*, if one of the parties receives a benefit without a corresponding burden (e.g., a gift). From the standpoint of certainty, an onerous contract may be *commutative* or *aleatory*; in a commutative contract the object of the contract is certain with respect to a future event; in an aleatory contract the object of the contract is contingent on some future event (life insurance contracts).

With respect to the form of the contract, it may be a *solemn* or *nonsolemn* one: a solemn contract depends on a solemn formality of writing and sealing as a requirement for validity and approval, or for approval alone.

A *nude* contract is one which merely gives rise to a natural obligation in conscience; a *vested* contract is one which gives rise to legal action, because of the legal formalities it implies.

A *real* contract creates a real right; an *obligatory* contract creates an obligation only. Both are called *nominate*, if they have a particular name; if not, they are termed *innominate* (such as contracts *do ut des, do ut facias, facio ut des, facio ut facias*).

A contract may also be *preliminary* or *definitive*. In a preliminary contract the parties bind themselves to conclude a further contract (e.g., promise of sale, of hiring, etc.); all other contracts are definitive.

ELEMENTS OF CONTRACT. The elements of a contract are: *essential*, without which the contract cannot exist; *accessory* or accidental, without which the contract can exist. The latter is considered excluded from the contract, unless expressly inserted by the parties. *Natural*, if by law or custom they are considered inherent in the contract (e.g., protection of buyer against eviction).

The essential elements in every contract are: *fit or apt matter, contractual capacity* of subjects, *legitimate consent* of parties. Certain authors, instead of apt matter, prefer to speak of an object, determined by the bond or licit cause of the obligation.

Many modern authors deny the existence of cause as a distinct element in contracts, claiming that the cause of a contract is either identified with the will or consent of the parties, as in onerous contracts, or with the object, as in gratuitous contracts. They further add that the concept of cause is not univocal in all contracts. Actually, the general concept of cause is identical in all contracts, although it differs in individual contracts. Moreover, cause does not coincide with consent or object. Thus, in gratuitous contracts, the cause is not the consent but the intent to donate, from which the consent receives its specification. In onerous contracts the cause does not consist in the thing or service promised (burden), but in the bilateral or reciprocal assumption of a burden.

OBJECT OF CONTRACT. The object or matter of contract may be a thing, an action, or an omission. For matter to be considered fit, apt or lawful, the following conditions are required:

(a) The matter must be both *physically and morally possible.* No one is held to the physically impossible, and it is presumed that no one may intend to bind himself to something which is morally impossible. A moral impossibility implies that the execution of a thing is accompanied with great difficulty. A distinction must be made between objective or absolute impossibility, and relative or subjective impossibility. Absolute impossibility is a fact or event impossible for all men, either by reason of law or the very nature of the thing; it renders the contract null, although the guilty party is liable to damages. Relative impossibility does not destroy the entire value of the contract; if there are other parts capable of fulfillment, they must be carried out. If only a part of the contractual obligation is possible, this part must be observed, unless the obligation is considered indivisible by nature or by the express will of the contracting parties.

(b) The matter must be *existent in reality,* or at least in expectancy (*in spe*); even a future thing can be the object of a contract.

(c) The matter must be something rightfully belonging to the disposing party to the contract; no one can transfer ownership of a thing he does not possess. One may, however, contract for a third party. In such a case, no obligation is incurred by the third party, but the agent is bound to guarantee that the thing promised is properly delivered.

(d) The matter must be *certain and specified,* or at least capable of being determined, to prevent the contract from being illusory or fictitious. In other words, the nature of the matter contracted must somehow be determined by the parties.

(e) Finally, the matter must be *substantially honest and lawful.* No one can be obliged to perform something forbidden by the natural or positive law. Thus, it would be unlawful to transfer an inheritance not yet received.

CAUSE OF CONTRACT. Roman law always required mention of the cause or reason for the contract. This is not required by modern codes, although at times it is presumed. That a contract may be valid, the cause must be true and licit. A true cause is opposed to a false one. A putative cause is considered false, but a simulated or erroneous cause is not considered false. A licit cause is opposed to an illicit one, that is, contrary to the natural or positive laws.

A contract for a false cause is null; neither approval nor voluntary execution can render it valid. Similarly, a contract for an immoral cause is null and void by the natural and positive laws. Prior to execution of an immoral contract, neither party can be obliged to fulfill its terms. After its execution, three cases may be verified:

(A) One party carries out the immoral act, but does not receive the stipulated consideration from the other party. Here, the question arises whether there is any obligation to pay the stipulated consideration. According to some authors (Ballerini-Palmieri, Carrière), there is no such obligation, and this for two reasons: (1) the contract is null; (2) there can be no price or reward for an evil thing. Many others, however, maintain that the obligation to pay the consideration remains. This second opinion is regarded as certain by modern authors, although St. Alphonsus called both opinions probable. At any rate, different reasons or explanations are given for the second opinion. (a) The obligation remains, because, although it is true that an illicit deed deserves no price or reward, still the deed has inconvenienced one party and benefited the other (Piscetta-Gennaro). (b) The obligation remains, because there is a twofold contract involved here: the first is vitiated by reason of the immoral act; the second, an innominate contract (*do ut des*), arises upon performance or execution of the evil deed (Genicot-Salsmans, D'Annibale).

(B) Both parties hold to their part of the contract. In this case: (a) According to the natural law, if the evil deed has been committed by the one receiving the consideration, restitution must be made. (b) If, instead, the evil deed has been committed by the one paying the consideration or by both parties, the question is disputed: some say that the consideration may be retained, others that it may not.

(C) The third case is that wherein one party has paid the stipulated consideration, but the other has not executed the evil deed demanded. In this case, the common opinion is that the consideration may not be retained.

CONTRACTUAL CAPACITY OF SUBJECTS. The subjects forming a contract are called parties: the one making the proposal is known as *offerer*; the one accepting, as *offeree*. In order to contract validly, it is essential that both parties possess contractual capacity.

All persons lacking the use of reason are by natural law incapable of contracting. In civil law, ordinarily all can enter contracts, unless expressly declared legally incompetent. As a rule, the following dispositions obtain:

(a) *Minors* are deemed incapable of contracting, and any contract entered into by them can be nullified. An exception is made in employment, after

sixteen years of age, and marriage contract. Hence, the contract of a minor is not invalid, but can be annulled.

(b) Wives are as fully capable as husbands in contracts regarding paraphernalia property, but for dotal goods there are many legal restictions (*see* Married persons or Spouses).

(c) The category of *civilly dead* persons, serving life imprisonment, in Roman law, has been abolished in modern codes.

(d) Interdicted persons are declared incompetent to contract. Interdiction is criminal or legal, depending whether it is inflicted for a definite crime or as a result of a judicial sentence.

CONTRACTUAL CONSENT. To have a contract, it is necessary that two or more wills agree and consent to the same thing. However, consent is not always necessarily valid, nor does it always and immediately possess efficacy.

Contractual consent must have the following qualities:

(a) It must be internal, true, and deliberate. Hence, if a person feigns external consent without the intention of binding himself, the contract is void. If, however, the intention is actually to contract but not to fulfill the obligations implied, the contract is valid.

(b) It must be external, i.e., the consent must be externally manifested, either expressly or tacitly.

(c) It must be mutual, i.e., the two wills of the contracting parties must be morally united in agreement.

A unilateral promise is binding, but in virtue of fidelity, not of strict justice. According to some civil codes, such a promise produces effects merely in certain cases.

Can a person validly contract with himself, i.e., represent himself and another person in the same contract? The answer is in the affirmative, because, in the case cited, one and the same person represents two wills.

For defects of consent, *see* Error, Simulation, Fear, etc. For defective consent with respect to marriage, *see* Matrimonial Consent.

In the matter of contracts the Church

follows the civil law, except in those points which may be contrary to the natural law or to its own special regulations (see Ecclesiastical Goods).

CONTRACTUALISM. See Rationalism.

CONTRAVENTION, TRANSGRESSION. *Contraventions* are penal infractions or punishable offenses, involving no violation or real danger of violation of subjective, personal rights; they are transgressions of objective norms established to safeguard the juridical order. Penal violations differ from criminal offenses; a crime always implies the presence of moral guilt, both subjectively and objectively speaking. A contravention implies that a voluntary action or omission, with or without moral guilt, is liable to legal punishment. In modern civil codes, contraventions constitute a separate matter, with specific penalties or fines attached to specific violations.

In the Code of Canon Law, contraventions are not considered a separate category, because canonical legislation always takes into account the subjective element involved in an offense. Moralists frequently discuss the question of obligation to accept a penalty for transgression of the law. The solution to this question is connected with a more general question regarding penal laws, which are not directly binding in conscience but oblige acceptance of the penalty imposed for a transgression.

It is impossible to give a classification of contraventions, because these will be found to vary in different countries, as well as in different regions of the same country. Generally, it may be stated that penal laws are established for one of the following purposes: to safeguard public order and tranquillity; to protect human and animal life or private and public property; to insure the proper function of the public administration; to levy taxes for the public treasury, etc. Contraventions are violations of civic and police ordinances, public housing and health laws, traffic regulations, hunting and fishing laws, tax laws, etc.

Contraventions, as violations, are not based on the natural law or on divine positive laws. They are precautionary measures designed to avert possible evil or injury, to insure a fiscal benefit for the State, to regulate industrial and commercial competition, etc. With the exception of the latter, in which problems of commutative justice are frequently involved, contraventions do not imply any subjective moral imputability; hence, they do not impose on the subject any moral obligation to observe the prescriptions of the penal law. Naturally, if a penal transgression causes damage or injury to a fellowman, one is bound in conscience to make restitution. Finally, he who has committed a penal violation has a moral obligation to accept the penalty; otherwise, the entire social order would be subverted. *Pug.*

CONTRITION. *Contrition* (Latin, *conterere*—to grind) is a sorrow for and detestation of sin with a firm purpose of not sinning in the future (*Council of Trent, Sess.* 14, ch. 4: Denz. 897). The essence of contrition does not consist in physical sorrow, much less mere words, but of a determination of the will against personal sins as transgressions of God's law, and offenses against the majesty of God, the Author of the supernatural order. A resolution not to sin again is necessarily included.

Contrition may be *perfect* or *imperfect* (attrition). *Perfect* contrition is sorrow which springs from a pure or disinterested love of God and a desire to seek the glory of God; hence it is a detestation of and hatred for sin insofar as it deprives God of the external glory due Him. The ultimate motive of perfect contrition is God, considered as the fullness of perfection, worthy of all love, without regard for one's own well-being. *Imperfect* contrition (attrition) is sorrow and hatred for sin from a supernatural motive, inferior to perfect love (charity), such as fear of eternal or temporal punishment; the evil of sin, considered as ingratitude, disobedience, and an offense against God, the Father and Supreme Benefactor; or as an evil which deprives man of divine grace, makes him detestable in the eyes of God, or a slave of the devil.

Necessity of Contrition. Without contrition there can be no remission of sin, either venial or mortal. Contrition, at least imperfect, is necessary for the validity of the sacrament of penance (*q.v.*), for the external manifestation of contrition is an essential element of the sacrament. Perfect contrition, provided that it is accompanied by the desire or intention of confessing grave sins, effects the remission of sin. Attrition suffices to effect pardon of sins, even mortal, but only if actually joined to the sacrament of penance.

Qualities of Contrition. Contrition must be intrinsically *supernatural,* i.e., elicited with the help of actual grace, which God never denies; it must spring from a motive drawn from Revelation and known through the light of faith. In other words, the motive of contrition must be: either (a) the thought of God, as worthy of all love for His own sake, or as Author of the supernatural order and ultimate end of all things; or (b) any consideration related to God as Author of the supernatural order, such as fear of punishment or the hideousness of sin as an evil which is offensive to God. Contrition must be *general,* that is, extend to all mortal sins not yet remitted, including sins forgotten or still to be mentioned in the present confession. If one has no mortal sins to confess, it is necessary to elicit contrition for at least one of the sins already confessed. To confess a venial sin without the required contrition would in itself be at least slight irreverence. Finally, contrition must include a firm resolution (*q.v.*) not to sin again; it must exclude all intention of committing new sins. This resolve must be externally manifested in confession.

In approaching the tribunal of penance, it is important always to have intense and perfect contrition. To this end, it is highly useful in devotional confessions to single out, though not exclusively, some particular sin which one considers to be more serious or more displeasing to God. The act of contrition should be made prior to confession, but for a valid confession it suffices that it be elicited before the actual reception of absolution. *Man.*

CONTROVERSY. *See* Polemic.

CONTUMACY, CONTEMPT (of Court). *Contumacy* (Latin, *contemnere*—to contemn, despise) may be described as defiance of authority. However, it has a different meaning in canonical judical procedure, canonical criminal law, and civil jurisprudence.

In canonical procedural law, *contumacy* is a willful and obstinate disregard of an order to appear before the judge.

In primitive Roman law, a court summons was considered an act of the plaintiff, not of the judge; failure by the defendant to appear in court was held as a renunciation of the right to defend one's own interests. The plaintiff had the right to use force in order to bring a reluctant defendant before the judge. Hence, contumacy was a rare thing, because the defendant either appeared voluntarily or by force, or through others who assured the court of the defendant's appearance. Later, this procedure was replaced by another which permitted the plaintiff to take possession of the property of the accused in order to compel him to appear in court; the latter's failure to appear resulted in confiscation of property. Eventually, the practice arose in which failure to appear after the third summons was considered contempt of lawful authority and, therefore, a crime. A bill of complaint, presented by the plaintiff to the magistrate, was the instrument through which the citation was served. Contumacy or contempt of court in Canon Law is based on this Roman concept.

Canonical Procedural Law. Contumacy or contempt of court may be incurred by either the defendant or the plaintiff. The defendant becomes guilty of contumacy if he fails, without just reason, to answer a first or subsequent citation of the judge. The plaintiff becomes contumacious by failing to appear in court at the specified time. Thus understood, contumacy is construed as an obstruction of due process of law, which weakens the position of the violator and makes him liable to punishment. Contumacy, however, is not equivalent to a tacit confession of guilt; on the contrary, the contemner is given the opportunity to purge himself of contempt by appearing in court at any time before the final sentence, and by presenting his conclusions and proofs, unless it is obvious that his failure to appear before the court was designed as a deliberate obstructive tactic (Can. 1846).

Contumacy or contempt of court must be so declared; this is done by the judge upon request of the plaintiff, the promoter of justice, or the defender of the bond. But before such a declaration may be issued, it must first be ascertained that the summons was duly served and that the defendant offered no valid excuse for failure to appear in court. The judge, however, is not obliged to issue a new summons, except when, in the interests of the plaintiff or of the common good, he intends to break the obstinacy of the guilty party by threatening him with canonical penalties (Can. 1845, par. 1-2).

The defendant's persistent contumacy or absence from the court entitles the plaintiff or his representative to petition the judge to proceed with the trial on the basis of the original bill of complaint, up to the final sentence and execution (Can. 1844, pars. 1, 2). After the sentence has been given, the contumacious defendant may petition the judge for a restitution *in integrum*; namely, that the trial revert back to the point at which contumacy was declared. But this petition must be made within three months from the day he received notice of the

sentence, or even after a lapse of three months (Can. 1847), if it is one of those cases which are never irrevocably adjudged.

If the defendant puts in an appearance at the time indicated in the summons and the plaintiff is absent, the defendant may request the judge to re-summon the plaintiff. If the new summons goes unheeded or if, after answering the citation, the plaintiff fails to prosecute, the judge at the request of the defendant or the promoter of justice or the defender of the bond shall declare the plaintiff guilty of contempt (Can. 1849). Such a declaration deprives the plaintiff of the right to prosecute his case, although the promoter of justice or the defender of the bond may make the case his own and proceed with the trial, if such action is found to be necessary in the public interest (Can. 1850, par. 1-2). Thereafter, the plaintiff may appear only if summoned. The judge's declaration, charging the plaintiff with contempt, entitles the defendant to petition the court for any of the following: dismissal of the case; nullifying all legal acts excuted up to the time of the plaintiff's contempt; prosecution of the trial to a conclusion, even in the plaintiff's absence, for purposes of self-vindication (Can. 1850, par. 3).

The party guilty of contempt, whether plaintiff or defendant, shall be condemned to pay all court expenses resulting from such contempt and also to indemnify, if necessary, the other party. If both plaintiff and defendant are guilty of contempt, they are obliged to pay the expenses of the trial *in solidum*, i.e., jointly and severally, unless one party is expressly directed to pay the entire amount (Can. 1851).

Contumacy in Canonical Criminal Law. In canonical criminal law, the concept of contumacy is entirely different; here, contumacy constitues a requisite condition for incurring ecclesiastical penalties or censures (*q.v.*).

According to the Code of Canon Law, a contumacious person is one who, notwithstanding the canonical admonitions, fails to desist from or refuses to do penance for a violation or to make proper amends for the damage and scandal caused. Contumacy of an offender is implied in the deliberate violation of a law or precept to which a penalty *latae sententiae* is attached, threatened, and specified by the law itself (Can. 2242, par. 2). In canonical criminal law, therefore, contumacy is disobedience in which the delinquent manifests contempt for the ecclesiastical authority; it is a perverse and obstinate will in the violation of a canonical law, to which a sanction is attached; it is contempt for the penalty itself, which entails contempt for the authority threatening or inflicting the said penalty. Contumacy is formal if the delinquent manifests, either by word or action, contempt for the superior who threatens or inflicts a penalty; it is virtual or interpretative if an individual, aware of the threatened penalty, proceeds to commit the offense.

The contumacy required for incurring a censure must be at least interpretative, and it must be externally manifested. In the case of penalties *latae sententiae*, the necesssary admonitions are contained in the law itself. In the case of penalties *ferendae sententiae*, i.e., applied by subsequent sentence of the competent authority, the admonitions must precede the imposition of the penalty (Can. 2242, par. 1–2). A censure inflicted when the delinquent is no longer contumacious would not be valid. Prior to the Code, two or three admonitions were required. Current legislation prescribed no number, but simply states that the offender shall have been previously admonished and given sufficient time to desist from his contumacy (Cans. 2242, par. 2; 2233, par. 2). Contumacy is to be regarded as terminated if the delinquent has sincerely repented of the offense committed and has made proper amends for the damage and scandal caused, or at least has seriously promised to do so. It is the duty of the one from whom absolution is sought to determine whether repentance is sincere, satisfac-

tion adequate, and the promise serious (Can. 2242, par. 3).

Contumacy in the Dismissal of Religious. Contumacy is required for the dismissal of a religious with perpetual vows from a clerical religious organization. Contumacy here is synonymous with incorrigibility. Before proceedings for dismissal may be instituted, there must have been three offenses or one continued offense that is virtually threefold in view of repeated admonitions. The admonitions following the first and second offense must have been accompanied by a threat of expulsion. Only after the third offense, preceded by the required admonitions following the first and second offense, may the delinquent be considered contumacious or incorrigible, and proceedings for dismissal be instituted (Cans. 657, 660, 661). Such contumacy is not properly designed for the punishment of the offenses committed, which must be considered under the aspect of criminal offense; but it is established for the sole purpose of instituting trial for dismissal, which may take place even if the delinquent should repent after the third offense.

As already stated, in criminal law contumacy is synonymous with incorrigibility; hence, gravely sinful. In procedural law, contumacy is not necessarily a refusal to submit to the authority of the judge; it could also be a special procedural measure, deemed necessary to safeguard one's rights. But if the judge issues a summons to a contumacious party whose testimony is deemed necessary in the interest of truth and the public welfare, the refusal to desist from contumacy becomes an act of disobedience to the lawful authority. M. d. G.

CONTUMELY. *Contumely* is an offense against another by words, deeds, gestures, writing, and the like, which makes use of arrogant and insulting language or treatment with an intent to detract from a person's dignity.

Contumely is a sin against justice, because every man has a right to be properly treated. In Canon Law contumely is considered a crime (*see* Defamation). In civil law it is a punishable crime, only if legal action is instituted by the injured party. Contumely is a grave sin if the insulting is done with a serious intent. Not so, however, if it is done jokingly or in banter, without seriously detracting from a person's dignity. Anyone guilty of unjustly violating another's dignity, either by words or deeds, is obliged to make reparation for the offense. Reparation is made by asking pardon of the injured person or by showing him signs of respect and honor, either privately or publicly, depending on whether contumely was inflicted privately or publicly. The method of reparation is largely determined by the circumstances of the particular case.

The virtue of patience demands that a Christian be prepared to bear insults, accusations, and ridicule by his neighbor, if necessary. Thus a person so injured may not seek revenge. One may, however, defend and protect his own honor by just and charitable means, in the face of contemptuous treatment (*see* Enemy). Protection of honor is, at times, commendable and even obligatory, especially if necessary to correct the offender or if the good of a third party or community is at stake, particularly a person in authority or in high public office, as the pope, chief of state, etc. *See also* Defamation, Reputation, Honor. *Ben.*

CONVENTION. *See* Contract, Agreement.

CONVERSION, SPIRITUAL. In a general sense, *conversion* means a spiritual change or transformation leading to God. An atheist acquiring the faith, a heretic or schismatic returning to orthodoxy, a sinner or indifferentist resuming the practice of religion—all are referred to as conversions. Many are the paths leading to conversion. The mystics speak of a second and third conversion taking place in an ordinary Christian, who has already accepted the deposit of truth and practices his faith. They speak of a first conversion by which a soul is introduced into the illuminative way, and of a third conversion leading to the unitive way. In fact, every Christian ought to undergo a continuous conversion, a progressive change for the better, a constant growth in union with God.

In the ordinary sense of the term, however, a convert is one who, rejecting paganism, atheism, heresy or hostility, embraces the Catholic religion and undertakes to live by its doctrine. Conversion to the true faith may come about in a great variety of ways: through the path of reason, observation, experience or study; through extraordinary events, personal contacts, suffering, love, etc. The initial motion in the process of conversion is not the same in each case. It may be a direct call of the Lord (Paul of Tarsus); the result of reading a particular book or pamphlet; the study of the problem of evil in the world; a visit to Rome or other famous shrine; a chance contact with a Catholic priest; the stupendous fact of the growth of the Church and the continuity of the Papacy in the midst of the gravest vicissitudes of history. Such factors as the persecution endured by the Church, its charitable work, art, culture, etc., have impressed and stirred many a soul to conversion. It can be truly said that "all roads lead to Rome." But the final and decisive impetus is always provided by grace.

Without grace, one may well become intellectually convinced of the truth of the entire deposit of the Catholic faith, without ever becoming a Catholic. Grace always is the deciding factor. And the history of conversions—some gradually, others suddenly, some in early life, others at the eleventh hour, but all the result of a personal crisis—reveals the human and divine plot of God's love for man and of man's struggle to find God.

Since Christ first launched His appeal to men (*metanoeite*—convert yourselves), some of the world's most outstanding and generous men have found their way into the Church. Among these are Paul of Tarsus, Cyprian, Augustine, Francis of Assisi, Jacopone of Todi, and so on down to present-day converts. Often, it was not so much a turning away from heresy as the rejection of a contemptuous scientism, a destructive agnosticism, or an idealism or materialism bent on deicide. Noted modern converts, whose names come to mind, are Manzoni, Chateaubriand, Brentano, Newman, Benavine, Soloviev, Benson, Chesterton, Thompson, Bourget, Claudel, Maritain, Hopkins, Péguy, Psichari, Salvadori, etc.

A chapter apart is that of the conversions effected by missionaries in pagan or non-Christian lands. Greater difficulties are generally encountered in those countries where the activity of the Church is opposed by law. In some communistic countries (Russia, Romania, etc.), conversion to Catholicism is practically forbidden, which means an individual is denied the right to become a convert. For doctrinal and traditional reasons the conversion of Jews remains a rather difficult matter, although not a few embraced Catholicism during the war years under the impact of racial laws.

Indeed, some of the best Catholic literary works of our day, especially in Anglo-Saxon countries, are authored by converts, who have succeeded in brilliantly dramatizing their thrilling discovery of the true faith. Among others, Evelyn Waugh, Graham Greene, Giovanni Papini, Claudel, Jammes, Chesterton. Even socialistic and communistic materialism have contributed some eloquent witnesses to Rome: Louis Budenz, Douglas Hyde, Dorothy Day. Impressive, too, is the list of scientists and scholars, such as Alexis Carrel, Lecomte de Noüy, the Maritains, Bergson (who died with the desire for baptism), and many others.

Irrespective of their material sacrifices, all converts are unanimous in acknowledging that in the Church they found peace, dogmatic stability, and interior freedom. Conversion, then, may be considered as the happy solution of a spiritual odyssey. *Gio.*

COOPERATION. See Cooperator.

COOPERATIVES. A *cooperative* is a voluntary association of several persons who pool their resources or services, for the purpose of obtaining an economic benefit. The fundamental aim of the members of a cooperative is either to increase revenue or to reduce the price of products and services. Cooperatives may be of various types: (a) producers' cooperative, consisting of individuals who join in the production of a certain item or items; (b) consumers' cooperative, organized to promote buyers' benefit; (c) credit cooperative or union, consisting of members who benefit by certain privileges in borrowing money.

Cooperatives are also classified according to the different activities or enterprises they engage in, such as farming, banking and insurance, building or marketing cooperatives, etc.

Cooperatives produce many social and economic benefits. The following are some of the more important ones: (a) an opportunity for a small farmer to purchase all the technological equipment required by modern agricultural methods; (b) greater opportunity for small producers of any type of industry, by reason of a diminished need for hired help and a reduction of the payroll; (c) improvement of the standard of living either by increase in the revenue (producers' cooperatives) or by a lowering of the price of products (consumers' cooperatives); (d) finally, a greater sense of responsibility on the part of its members, who learn to handle administrative tasks and to subordinate individual interests to the common good.

The benefits of cooperatives are so numerous that some sociologists have stated that, once the cooperative movement takes hold, it will radically change the structure of society, even to the point of superseding or eliminating the capitalistic system. However, as experience has already demonstrated, cooperatives are more effective and advantageous within a limited sphere. It is highly improbable that they will succeed in replacing the big industrial combines of modern society.

A cooperative demands of its component members a certain amount of administrative ability, for the administration of cooperatives must depend on its own members. But they also must possess good moral qualities. Every cooperative is born and grows on the mutual trust and honesty of its members. The whole cooperative movement is intimately connected with the technical and moral evolution of the working class. *Pav.*

COOPERATORS (in evil). A *cooperator* in wrong-doing is one who does not commit an offense directly, but concurs through or with others either physically or morally in causing harm to another. Cooperation in wrong-doing may be *positive* or *negative*. It is *positive* if one orders, counsels, approves, flatters, shelters, or participates, in wrong-doing. It is called *negative* if one who has the duty of safeguarding a third person's property or right fails to restrain a violator of such rights or neglects to report him to the proper authorities.

Cooperation, both positive and negative, may be either *moral* or *physical*. *Moral positive* cooperation consists in exerting one's influence on another's will; *physical positive* cooperation consists in concurring in another's action. Failing to use one's influence when one is obliged to do so, or to prevent the violation of a third party's property or right is called *moral negative* cooperation; *physical negative* cooperation is failing, in similar circumstances, to offer resistance or to use a preventive action of some kind.

Positive cooperation, whether physical or moral, admits of a greater or lesser degree of guilt, depending on whether one concurs in a violation as principal author, inducer, or only as assistant. Thus, in an unjust business transaction, owners, managing directors, advisors or consultants who give their vote of approval, and persons employed in the execution of an unjust deal are considered as cooperating in various degrees in the commission of injustice and, therefore, are variously guilty.

As it appears from the terminology used thus far, complicity and co-responsibility (joint liability) are synonymous with cooperation in wrong-doing.

Complicity implies aid or assistance in the commission of an offense or a sin. Assistance, whether moral or material, must be such as to exert an effective influence on the execution of the act. It matters not whether assistance is direct or indirect. What does greatly matter is whether or not the offense would have been perpetrated even without the help of an accomplice. If the violation would not have been committed without such help, the accomplice is regarded as a principal in the case, since his assistance was a necessary condition for the commission of the act (Can. 2209, par. 3). If, however, the assistance of the accomplice served merely to facilitate the commission of the offense which would have been committed even without his help, the accomplice is simply regarded as an accessory element to the commission of the offense (Can. 2209, par. 4).

Co-responsibility (joint liability), strictly speaking, is present when persons conspire to commit an offense and physically concur in its execution, whether the offense be of such a nature as to require an accomplice (Can. 2209, par. 2) or not (Can. 2209, par. 1). It matters not in what manner or for what reason each individual participates in the execution of the act. Hence, if several persons have conspired to commit a murder, all are equally guilty, even though only one does the actual shooting while the others merely stand by on guard or as onlookers. In fact, after the consummation of the crime, all are equally guilty also of the preparatory acts which led to the commission of the crime.

VARIOUS MODES OF COOPERATION. The various modes of cooperation are expressed by the following terms,

"*Jussio, consilium, consensus, palpo, recursus, participans; mutus, non obstans, non manifestans.*" Of these, the first six are forms of positive cooperation, both moral (*jussio, consilium, palpo, recursus*) and physical (*consensus, participans*), while the last three (*mutus, non obstans, non manifestans*) are forms of negative cooperation.

(a) *Cooperation by command.* One is guilty of cooperation in the sin of another if he induces another to do an injury to a third person in his name or on his behalf. The one issuing the command or order is called *jubens* or *mandans.* Technically, there is a difference between the two: *jubens* implies abuse of authority; *mandans,* implies other reasons or motives. But it does not matter whether the person giving the order is in a position of authority or not; nor does it matter for what reason (fear, gain, etc.) the person executing the order (*mandatarius*) is induced in performing the evil action. It suffices that an unjust action be executed, expressly or implicitly, on the strength of an order received and in the name of the person giving the order. The *mandans* or *jubens* is principal author of the crime; the *mandatarius* or executor is secondary or instrumental cause. Hence, damages resulting from the unjust action are principally imputed to the *mandans.*

(b) *Cooperation by counsel.* This form of cooperation is present when one advises or urges another to commit an injustice. Counsel may be *doctrinal* (designed to influence the intellect) or *compulsive* (designed to influence the will). Compulsive counsel is, in turn, *vestitum* or *nudum,* depending on whether it is based on intellectual motives or not.

The advisor's role is similar to that of the *mandans,* in that he induces another to commit an evil deed; but whereas the *mandans* is principal author of the resulting damage, the advisor is ordinarily secondary cause. In fact, a person who follows the advice of another acts in his own name, but a person who carries out a command acts in the name of another. Hence, the executor of a counsel is primarily bound to make restitution, while the advisor is bound to do so only in a secondary manner.

(c) *Cooperation by consent.* This form of cooperation is present when one gives his consent or approval to an unjust action committed by another. If the consent given is not an influencing factor or effective cause of the unjust action, the person giving consent or approval is not responsible for the damage inflicted except *per accidens.* If, however, the consent given is a true cause of the unjust action, the person giving the consent (*consentiens*) is a true and effective cooperator in the damage inflicted. This form of cooperation is present either when one gives external consent to an unjust action or votes for it or culpably neglects to register a protest.

(d) *Cooperation by flattery or challenge.* This mode of cooperation is present when one, through flattery, praise, ridicule, or challenge, induces another to commit an injustice. The person employing such methods becomes a real, effective, and formal cause of the injury inflicted. It is not necessary that the adulator intend the unjust action directly; it suffices that he foresee the action as resulting from his praise or challenge. The adulator might be considered as one giving counsel or advice by flattery.

(e) *Cooperation by sheltering.* The technical term for this type of cooperation is *recursus,* which may take place by furnishing aid, shelter, or protection to a delinquent; concealing weapons, tools or stolen goods; buying or selling ill-gotten articles; issuing false documents or testimonials, etc. By these and similar practices, one aids and abets his fellowman in committing evil instead of deterring him therefrom. If a person gives protection to a delinquent, not primarily as a delinquent, but as a relative or friend, he cannot exactly be called a cooperator by sheltering; at any rate, his responsibility is greatly diminished. This form of cooperation principally applies to those who knowingly buy or sell stolen goods.

(f) *Cooperation by participation.* There are two ways of participating in another's injustice: (a) sharing in the division of the spoils or loot stolen by another (*participans in praeda*); (b) helping another in the execution of an unjust action, either by participating in the execution of the act with the principal agent and under his direction, or by supplying the principal agent with the means required to carry out his action, e.g., offering a thief the keys to a house.

As already noted, *mutus, non obstans,* and *non manifestans* are forms of negative cooperation; and they are substantially the same.

(g) *Mutus* (silent) is present when one permits injury to be done to a third person's property or right which he is bound to protect by office or contract, either by failing to speak up before the commission of the offense, or by willfully neglecting to warn the person involved.

(h) *Non obstans* (not restraining) is present when one, though bound to do so, fails to restrain a criminal.

(i) *Non manifestans* (not denouncing) is present when one, though bound to do so, neglects to report the criminal to the proper authorities.

Cases of cooperation in evil-doing may be said to be innumerable. Such problems perplexed the early Christians, and even today are often raised in mission territories and elsewhere; e.g., whether a Catholic is permitted to make images or statues intended for idolatrous worship, whether he is allowed to help in the erection of pagan temples, etc. (*S. Cong. de Propaganda Fide,* Jan. 8, 1851; Holy Office, decrees of Jan. 14, 1818; March 15, 1848; Jan. 31, 1872; March 26, 1885; July 26, 1885; July 26, 1888; June 15, 1889; Dec. 12, 1898).

Modern civil legislations have created new problems of cooperation for Catholic magistrates, lawyers, judges and political leaders, especially concerning the application of laws regarding divorce, confiscation of ecclesiastical goods, supporting non-religious schools.

The problem of cooperation in such instances takes on a different aspect in view of considerations of an economic nature, as in the case of a lawyer who may have no other way of earning his livelihood expect by the exercise of his chosen profession.

LIABILITY OF THE VARIOUS COOPERATORS. The prescriptions of Canon 2209 of the Code of Canon Law concerning cooperation in crime may serve as a guide also in the case of the various types of cooperators as listed above.

(1) Principles to be observed in cases of *positive cooperation:*

(a) The *mandans* is considered the principal author of the offense committed (Can. 2209, par. 3). Hence, he is primarily bound to make restitution for the damage inflicted in his name and as a result of the order given, unless the executor of the command clearly exceeded the instructions received. He may also be bound to make restitution for all damages suffered by the executor in the course of carrying out the command, if the latter was induced by unjust means, such as abuse of authority, threat or violence, to commit a violation.

The *mandatarius* or executor of the order is secondary and instrumental cause of the offense.

(b) A cooperator by *counsel,* after the commission of the crime, is just as liable as the actual perpetrator of the offense (Can. 2209, par. 3), inasmuch as the counsel given was the cause of the offense. If the counsel given proved ineffective, the advisor is guilty of attempted crime (Can. 2212, par. 3). If the perpetrator of the offense was already determined to commit the violation even without the aid of counsel, the advisor is less liable (Can. 2209, par. 4). If a different crime was committed, the advisor is not liable, unless this crime was in some way implied in the counsel given. The advisor is culpably responsible for all foreseeable excesses resulting from the counsel given. If the counsel given was the effective cause of the injustice committed, the advisor is bound, with the principal agent, to make restitution *in solidum* for all damages inflicted, unless the counsel was effectively revoked before the commission of the crime. He who advises another to commit a lesser evil than the latter had planned, is not bound to make restitution, unless counsel is aimed at causing damage to a specific person, who would have been spared except for the counsel given.

(c) A cooperator *by consent* is responsible for all damages caused, if the consent given was the effective cause of the unjust action committed. If consent to an unjust action is given by vote, all voting members, including those who fail to register a protest, are responsible for the damage done, and are consequently bound to make restitution *in solidum* (i.e., one for all and all for one). One who gives his consenting vote after sufficient majority has been attained is not bound to make restitution, although he is guilty of the sin of cooperation.

(d) A cooperator *by flattery*, or praise, is bound to make restitution in the same manner as a cooperator by counsel. However, mere approval of an injustice already committed does not render liable to restitution one who approves of it.

(e) One who *shelters* a thief is bound to make restitution *in solidum*, in the same manner as the principal agent or perpetrator of the crime, for such cooperation prevents the punishment and rehabilitation of the criminal, and also the possibility of restoring stolen goods to the rightful owner.

(f) One who *participates* in the commission of an injustice by sharing in the spoils or loot stolen by another is considered a possessor in bad faith. One who formally cooperates in the execution of the unjust act is bound to make restitution *in solidum* for the damage caused. The same applies in the case of one who, without sufficient reason, cooperates only materially.

(2) Principles regarding *negative cooperation*. Although everyone is bound (at least by the virtue of charity) to prevent a fellowman from committing a crime, not everyone who fails to do so is to be considered an accomplice. Thus, one who by reason of his office is bound to prevent a violation and neglects to do so, is, of course, guilty of negligence of his office, and of lack of charity toward his neighbor; but he is not necessarily a cooperator or partner in crime (Can. 2209, par. 6). Instead, if one were to neglect his duty by conspiring and cooperating with the perpetrator of wrong-doing, he would be an actual partner in crime. Persons who are bound by contract or office to prevent an offense but fail to do so, are liable to restitution *in solidum* for the damage done, provided that the crime could have been averted without grave inconvenience to themselves.

RETRACTION OF INFLUENCE. Retraction of a cooperator's influence in a crime or sin takes place when all relation of causality between cooperation and offense is removed. The manner of retracting one's influence depends on the form of cooperation involved. A cooperator's liability ceases with a complete withdrawal of his influence. If such influence is not completely removed, liability is diminished, but not entirely cancelled (Can. 2209, par. 5). If, despite the withdrawal of a cooperator's influence, the principal agent proceeds to commit the offense on his own, he alone shall be responsible (Can. 2209, par. 5). If the principal agent of his own accord desists from a crime already begun, he is free of all external imputability, except that he shall be responsible for any damage caused or scandal given by his attempted crime (Can. 2213, par. 3).

If, after having made all necessary preparations for the commission of a crime, the principal agent or one of the accomplices prevents the said crime from being consummated, the one actually preventing the crime shall be liable to attempted violation, the others to frustrated violation.

FAVOR AND RATIHABITION. (a) *Favor* may be shown to delinquents before the commission of a crime (counsel), during its execution (assistance) or after its completion (praising the accomplished violation, participating in the spoils, concealing the weapons or loot, sheltering the offender). Favor shown to a delinquent before or during the execution of a crime constitutes real cooperation; not so, however, if shown after completion of the offense. Since the crime has already been consummated, favor shown at this stage can exert no influence either on the will of the offender or on the execution of the crime. However, if aid, shelter, protection, etc., have been promised to the delinquent before the perpetration of his crime, or if the offense is such that it enjoys the benefit of continued favor, then there is true complicity (Can. 1705, par. 2). Finally, if the favor extended to a delinquent after commission of an offense constitutes a forbidden action by law, there is true imputability (Can. 2209, par. 7).

(b) *Ratihabition* is approval of another's accomplished violation without prior knowledge of the deed itself. In the present discussion, it signifies approval of an accomplished offense, without having exercised any influence whatever in its execution. *Per se*, such approval cannot be considered true cooperation, since it follows the commission of the offense. However, if the offense has a certain continuity and approval of it assists its ultimate execution, it must be considered as true cooperation. Apart from all this, approval may constitute a sin independently of other elements, as a form of sinful pleasure, scandal, and the like. *Pal.*

COOPERATUS. *See* Vicar, Parochial.

COPE. *See* Sacred Vestments.

COPHOSIS. *See* Aphasia, Deaf-mutism.

CORPORAL. *See* Chalice.

CORPORATION. *See* Foundation, Pious.

CORPORATISM. Corporatism, solemnly endorsed by the Church (*Rerum Novarum, Quadragesimo Anno*), is the theory of social reconstruction elaborated by Catholic sociologists in the second half of the past century. Corporatism was principally directed against the proletarization of the lower classes, brought about by the so-called industrial revolution, under the influence of conservative ideologies.

Motivating Factors. Catholic sociologists were led to the formulation of this theory by dialectic motives, some of a negative, others of a positive nature. Socialism, which was guided partly by positive but mainly by negative motives, aided this inasmuch as it revealed the fact that the social disorder caused by the industrial revolution was not only the effect of a lack of charity, but also of flagrant injustices. In fact, it alerted them against the evil of proletarization, which socialists considered as a necessary prelude to the revolutionary regeneration of society in general. An entirely positive attitude was taken by labor unionism, which had asserted itself in various countries by the adoption of a pragmatistic program, directed at promoting the interests of the working class, independently of any socialist influence. The revival of neo-scholastic studies and medieval historiography made a very positive contribution to the elaboration of the corporatist theory. These studies furnished a philosophical means for diagnosing the profound causes of the ills of society in a manner that was completely different from that of the socialists, and it also brought to the attention of corporatists a form of pluralistic society.

Principal Authors. Standard-bearers of the corporative movement were not those few thinkers, as Max Muller claims, who, immediately after the French Revolution, thought and wrote nostalgically of the *ancien régime*, but certain Catholic writers and thinkers who, during the second half of the last century in

Germany, France, Italy, America and elsewhere, sought to understand the reasons underlying the workers' complaints, to ascertain the legitimacy of their claims and to provide measures designed to improve their lot.

Doctrinal Premises. The fundamental premises of corporatism are, first of all, the awareness of the fact that man is constituted of a twofold element: one personal and individual, as a social being capable of a multiplicity of functions, social, authoritative and hierarchical; the other concerning the dignity of man as a human person, by which he infinitely transcends all social functions and the very institutions established for their implementation. In other words, man cannot be regarded at any time as an instrument of social functions or institutions because he is their ontological end. Another basic premise of corporatism is the dogmatic truth concerning the fact that man is radically inclined toward evil, and that he tends to debase not only his individual actions but his associative actions as well. This fact led corporatism not only to establish intermediate associations to check the actions of the individual, but also to increase these intermediate institutions or associations in order to establish a system of checks and balances, that is, of mutual controls; hence the characteristic conception of priority of the social organization over the political pluralism of both.

Specific Notes. The concrete application of the aforementioned principles, much more universal and, hence, much more realistic than socialistic principles, was studied by the corporatists with a view to solving the *social question* (*q.v.*). By this expression was meant at that time the complexity of problems created by the social transformation effected by industrialism.

The analysis of the existing historical situation, which they conducted in order to arrive at the above-mentioned solution, convinced them that: (a) irrespective of the type of organization of industrial production, there will always be employers and employees; (b)

between management and labor there exists a direct conflict of material and moral interests—the employer is tempted not only to haggle over the worker's wage but also to regard him as a pure commodity, and to forget the regard due to him as a human person; (c) in defending his rights and interests, the individual employee is much weaker than the individual employer; (d) a community of interests, traditions, aspirations and way of life creates an atmosphere of natural association between the two groups; (e) on the level of partnership between management and labor in a common work there exists a certain solidarity of interests; (f) this solidarity may constitute a basis for association. These convictions are common to all corporatists. On the basis of such convictions, they went on to promote corporative associations in order to eliminate the causes of the difficult conditions which had developed in democratic societies because of particular institutional crystallizations in the relations between employer and employee, as well as to strengthen the intrinsic weakness of the individual workers in the defense of their common interests. According to corporatists, this was the essence of the social question. They also defended more effectively the common interests of industry itself. The goal of all corporatists was to organize mixed associations consisting of both management and labor; the wiser among them recognized that the historic diffidence existing between the two categories was going to make the realization of the plan practically impossible. Thus, it was decided to begin with associations of workers on the one hand, and of employers on the other. The specific task of these respective associations was to re-establish a condition of friendship among the individual members of the organization for the purpose of constituting a united front in their dealings with the other group, for their own material and moral assistance, and, above all, for the reestablishment of an *esprit de corps.* These conditions were to give the associations not only the right of self-government within the framework of the common good, but also the right to become, in due time, and together with other associations, the structural basis for the constitution of essential political organs. This, in short, is the essence of corporatism.

Pseudocorporatism. In recent times, newly risen political movements, after giving by due process of law the name of corporatism to existing organizations, deprived them of their autonomy and made them to serve the aims of the State as organs of the same. Obviously, the new setup had nothing in common with corporatism except a name. *Mai.*

CORPSE. See Cremation, Inhumation, Interment, Burial, Funeral.

CORPUS JURIS CANONICI. The *corpus juris* (body of laws), in general, indicates a complete collection of juridical documents. Thus, the four collections of Justinian (Pandects, Code, Institutions, and Novels) constitute the body of Roman civil law (*corpus juris Romani*).

The term was adopted by Canon Law. Thus the collection attributed to Anselm (*Collectio Anselmo dicata*), complied in northern Italy about 882–886, was called *Corpus canonum*, and the Decree of Gratian was called *Corpus decretorum* and *Corpus juris canonici*. The same term was also applied to the ancient compilations, especially the collection of Gregory IX. Following the Council of Basle, it became customary to designate by the title *Corpus juris canonici* the authentic collections of Gregory IX, Boniface VIII, and Clement V, which the Council, in the matter of reservation of benefices, had distinguished from the collections *Extravagantes* and *Regulae Cancellariae.*

Subsequently, Gregory XIII, in the constitution *Cum pro munere* (July 1, 1580), for the first time added the Decree of Gratian, the Decretals of Gregory IX, the Sixth Book of Boniface VIII, the *Clementinae* collections of Clement V, the *Extravagantes* of John

XXII, and the *Extravagantes communes.* This entire collection subsequently appeared in printed editions under the title *Corpus juris canonici*, especially after the seventeenth century. Actually, after the Clementine collection, no other authentic collection was published until the Council of Trent. In this sense, the *corpus juris canonici* was said to have been closed (*clausum*) with the Clementine collection.

In chronological order, which is also the order in which the various editions appeared, the principal collections forming the *corpus juris canonici* are as follows:

(a) *The Decree of Gratian.* This work was composed about 1140 by John Gratian, a Camaldolese monk, who named it *Concordia discordantium canonum.* This is a collection of pseudo-apostolic documents; canons of councils held between the fourth and the twelfth century; papal letters, including some spurious ones, from the period of Pope Anacletus to that of Innocent II; texts of the Fathers and ecclesiastical writers; fragments of the *Corpus juris civilis*, the *Codex Theodosianus*, etc. The Gratian Decree is divided into three parts: the first part contains 101 divisions or distinctions (*distinctiones*), subdivided into canons; the second part contains thirty causes (*causae*), subdivided into questions (*quaestiones*); the third part comprises five distinctions, subdivided into canons. The Decree was never recognized by the Church as an official collection, and the documents retain their respective worth. The work, however, was of fundamental importance for Canon Law (Dante, Paradiso, X, 103–105). In the present book the *Decree* is quoted as follows: I lib.: D.I., 1; II lib.: D.I., 1; III lib.: D.I., 1 *de consecr.*

(b) *The Decretals (Decretales) of Gregory IX.* This work was prepared by St. Raymond of Peñafort, in 1230, by order of Gregory IX; the Bull *Rex pacificus* (Sept. 5, 1234) had it published as an authentic collection. This is a collection of papal decretals, some conciliar canons, texts of the Scriptures and of the Fathers, civil laws, etc. The matter is distributed in five books, subdivided into titles and chapters. The Decretals of Gregory IX are indicated in this book by the conventional letter X (abbreviation for *extra*, i.e., outside the matter contained in the Decree of Gratian), followed by the book number, the title, and the chapter. For example: X, II, 4, 2.

(c) *The Sixth Book of Boniface VIII.* This is a compilation of decretals issued after the year 1234 and appended as a sixth book to the collection of Gregory IX. It was authorized by Boniface VIII, who promulgated it through the Bull *Sacrosanctae Romanae Ecclesiae* (March 3, 1298). The work contains the canons of the I (1245) and II (1274) Councils of Lyons, papal decretals from the year 1239 to 1298, and 88 *Regulae juris* of Dino da Mugello. Though called the Sixth Book, it is itself divided into five books, subdivided into titles and chapters. In the present book it is quoted in the same manner as the Gregorian Decretals, except that the letter X is omitted at the beginning and *in VIo* is added at the end; for example: I, 6, 2, in VIo.

(d) The *Clementinae*. This is a collection of the decretals issued by Clement V. This compilation was ordered by John XXII, who promulgated it through the constitution *Quoniam nulla juris* (October 25, 1317). In the present book this work is quoted in the same manner as the *Liber Sextus*, except that *in VIo* is substituted with *in Clem.*

(e) The *Extravagantes*, i.e., extra or outside-the-authentic collections. These are decretals added to the Sixth Book or to the *Clementinae*, in the manuscripts and editions. In the first editions, they vary in number and are not always found in them. From the year 1550 on, these two unauthentic collections were regularly added: (a) the *Extravagantes of John XXII*, a collection of twenty decretals of this pope, divided into fourteen titles, subdivided into chapters; this work was compiled by Jesselin de Cassagnes in 1325; (b) the *Extravagantes communes*, a collection

of decretals belonging to the period between 1281–1478, divided into five books (of which the fourth is missing), subdivided into titles and chapters. These two collections were regarded as part of the traditional *Corpus juris canonici*.

After the above-mentioned constitution *Cum pro munere* of Gregory XIII, an official edition of the *Corpus juris canonici* was prepared in 1582, although it was never promulgated. Thereafter, it was regarded as the *Corpus juris canonici*, though not officially or legally.

Actually, the *Corpus juris canonici* was never a single collection, with all its parts having the same value. The Decretals of Gregory IX, the Sixth Book and the *Clementinae* were, up until the Code of Canon Law, regarded as authentic collections, whereas the Decree of Gratian the *Extravagantes* of John XXII, and the *Extravagantes communes* never attained the status of official collections, even though they were part of the *Corpus juris canonici*.

Various additions to the *Corpus juris canonici* were made over the years, besides the many indices compiled by Peter Guenois, a French jurist of the seventeenth century. However, these indices did not become part of the Richter-Friedberg or Leipzig edition.

The most common appendices are as follows: (1) at the end of the Decree of Gratian: (a) 47 penitential canons (*canones poenitentiales*) derived from the *Summa Aurea* of the Cardinal of Ostia; (b) 84 canons of the Apostles (*Canones Apostolorum*), taken from a translation of Gregory Hoffman, German jurist (d. 1531); (2) at the end of the *Extravagantes*: the seventh book of the Decretals (*Liber septimus Decretorum*) of Pierre Mathieu, a jurist from Lyons who collected the Decretals from the time of Sixtus IV (1471–1484) to that of Sixtus V (1583–1590), with the addition of other Decretals of the predecessors of Sixtus IV and several dispositions of the Council of Trent. This collection was never approved by the Holy See; on the contrary, it was placed on the Index in 1683. (3) Still another appendix to the *Corpus juris canonici*, consisting of the Institutions of Canon Law (*Institutiones juris canonici*), was prepared by John Paul Lancellotti (1522–1590) by order of Paul IV, but was never confirmed or approved; instead, other material, more authoritative, was inserted in the *Corpus juris canonici*.

Subsequently, the papal documents were collected in the *Bullaria* and, later, in the *Acta Gregorii XVI, Pii IX, Leonis XII,* and *Pii X.* The acts of the Council of Trent and the Vatican Council were compiled separately; so also were the collections of decisions and answers of the Sacred Congregations. Today all official acts of the Holy See are published in *Acta Apostolicae Sedis* (*q.v.*).

The *principal editions of the Corpus Juris Canonici* are as follows: the edition of John Chappuis and Vitale of Thebes (Paris, 1500, 1503); the edition prepared in Rome by order of Gregory XIII by Roman editors (Rome, 1582); the edition of Peter and Francis Pithou (Paris, 1687); that of Christopher Henry Freiesleben (Prague, 1728); that of J. Henning Bohmer (Halle, 1747), which in certain sections departs from the authentic text; the edition of Emil Richter (Leipzig, 1839); that of Emil Friedberg (Leipzig, 1879–1881), the best and the most critical edition of all.

Following the promulgation of the Code of Canon Law (1918), the *Corpus juris canonici* has only source value. *Pal.*

CORRECTION. *See* Remedies, Penal.

CORRECTION, FRATERNAL. *Fraternal correction* is a spiritual admonition or instruction designed to bring about the spiritual reform of a fallen or errant person. It is an act of charity toward one's neighbor who needs outside help to abandon a sinful state.

It is essential to fraternal correction that it be administered for the sole purpose of helping another in a spiritual difficulty, and that it be prompted by a desire to curb evil as something damaging the soul. Any other motive, though good and useful, is not fraternal correction in the proper sense of the word.

Fraternal correction is contained in the general precept of charity by which one is bound, to the extent of his ability, to aid others in all their needs, including, of course, a spiritual need. Generally speaking, one may be said to be bound to practice fraternal correction for the same reason that he is bound to give alms or material aid. In practice, however, fraternal correction is subject to certain limitations. In other words, although in the material order hardly a needy person would refuse help in time of need, many refuse spiritual help because they are not disposed to give up a life of pleasure or because they resent correction. Thus, fraternal correction frequently becomes an odious and unpleasant task for the one who makes it and disturbing to the one who receives it. For this reason, the obligation of fraternal correction is binding only on those in authority or those with a direct responsibility for the conduct of others. Among these, parents, guardians, educators, masters, superiors are included. Other persons do not normally have a grave obligation to practice fraternal correction. Fraternal correction becomes a grave obligation if the following conditions are present: (a) a certainty of another's grave spiritual need from which he apparently cannot be relieved except by such correction; (b) the correction must be made without serious harm or inconvenience to the one who makes it; (c) there is a reasonable hope of success. Consequently, one is rarely obliged to admonish or correct strangers, or to remonstrate if there is no reasonable hope that the other person will accept and pay heed to correction.

Fraternal correction is, indeed, a good and meritorious act if done charitably, kindly, and prudently. Much of course, depends on the manner in which it is done. A correction which is not humble, kind, and earnest will fail to obtain its effect. The errant must be made to feel that the person making the correction is genuinely interested only in his spiritual welfare. It is also important to wait for the proper moment to make the correction. A Christian, prompted by love of God and neighbor, will endeavor prudently to perform all the good he can in behalf of his neighbor. *Ben.*

CORRUPTION OF MINORS. By *corruption of minors* is meant any act or series of acts designed to excite, encourage, or promote moral perversion in persons who, because of their inexperience, are less capable of offering resistance to the wily arts of seduction.

In the moral order, corruption of minors is a form of cooperation in evil, especially impurity (*q.v.*). Besides sins against chastity, it constitutes a sin of scandal against charity; in certain cases it assumes an additional specific malice, as against the virtue of piety.

In canon and criminal law in various countries, the corruption of minors resulting from the commission of sex acts on minors (generally, under sixteen) or in their presence, constitutes a criminal offense.

In the commission of such acts, though the actual consent of the minor is not excluded, the legislator presumes the exercise of force. At any rate, taking advantage of the inexperience and simplicity of a person below or just beyond the age of puberty is certainly a grave moral and anti-social abuse. Legislation enacted for the protection of minors is generally based on the well-known aphorism: *Maxima debetur puero reverentia.*

Commission of the sin of corruption of minors requires that the following elements be present: (a) commission of impure acts; (b) cooperation in evil and scandal; (c) minority age of the passive subject, whether he consents or not. Corruption of minors is a crime: (a) if the victim is below the age of full experience and knowledge, which is generally under sixteen; (b) if libidinous acts are committed, whether by the corruptor on the minor or by

the minor at the instigation of the corruptor. If the latter used violence, he becomes guilty of the crime known as carnal abuse of a minor; if he seeks to obtain the consent of his victim, he becomes guilty of seduction. The corruption acquires greater gravity if the corruptor is related to the victim by a natural bond.

Corruptive acts may be committed either on the minor or in his presence. Hence, for further protection of minors, the law also punishes libidinous acts not involving bodily contact, but performed in the presence of minors with implicit corruptive influence (exposure, exhibitionism).

From the moral standpoint, any act capable of exercising a corruptive influence (immodest speech, impure book, obscene picture, etc.) suffices to constitute a sin of corruption. From a criminal standpoint, it is sometimes required that the libidinous acts be directed to sexual satisfaction.

At all events, both for the sin and crime, it is required that the libidinous act be such as to exercise a corruptive influence on the minor, arousing within him base elements of passion. The commission of one sole libidinous act suffices to constitute a sin of corruption, provided that such an act is potentially capable, at least in the mind of the one who commits it, of having a corruptive effect. In the legal and criminal field, at times a series of acts is required before one may be accused of the crime of corruption. At any rate, the act must always be external and potentially capable of exercising a corruptive influence.

The corruption of minors may be prompted by various motives: (a) satisfaction of one's passion; (b) lucrative purposes (e.g., prostitution); (c) hatred of good and virtue, more or less explicitly translated into hatred of God.

Thus, hatred of God and innocent youths has prompted in some countries certain communist-inspired youth movements and associations with the sole purpose of corrupting the youth. To parents who become accomplices by permitting their children to join such movements, is directed the grave Admonition of the Holy Office of July 28, 1950 (AAS: 42 [1950], 553).

Persons guilty of the crime of corruption of minors may incur the following penalties: (a) a lay person is automatically branded with infamy and other penalties, appropriately imposed by the Ordinary (Can. 2357, par. 1); (b) a cleric in minors orders may be discharged from the clerical state (Can. 2358); (c) a cleric in major orders may be suspended, declared infamous, deprived of office, benefice, dignity or charge, and, in more serious cases, be deposed (Can. 2359, par. 2). *Pal.*

CORSAIR. *See* Piracy.

COST OF LIVING. *See* Wages.

COST OF PRODUCTION. *See* Price.

COTTA (Surplice). *See* Sacred Vestments.

COUNCIL. Etymologically. The Latin term *concilium* derives from the verb *consulere* (to consult, deliberate) or from *considere* (to sit together, to hold a meeting) or even from *concurrere in eamdem sententiam* (to concur in the same decision). *Council* always implies the notion of a meeting or assembly of several persons for the purpose of deliberating and deciding on a specific matter or question.

In old Roman days, the formal and general assemblies of all the people were called *comitia*. The convocations of part of the people and of distinguished citizens were called *concilia* or *synodi*. In the course of time, this terminology became exclusively ecclesiastical, acquiring a particular importance in the organism of the Church, even to the present day.

Council is not synonymous with *Church*. The Church embraces all Christians in general, whereas a council is an assembly of ecclesiastical authorities only. But the council is strictly related to, and founded on, the Power of the Keys given by Christ to the apostles and their legitimate successors (Acts 25).

A more precise definition of *council* is: a lawful assembly of bishops and other prelates, summoned by one with proper authority, for the purpose of regulating matters pertaining to faith, morals, and discipline.

The Church recognizes three types of councils: (a) *ecumenical* (Cans. 222–229); (b) *plenary and provincial* (Cans. 281–292); (c) *diocesan* synods (Cans. 356–362).

Canonical Prescriptions. An *ecumenical* or general council is an assembly of all the bishops of the world, convened under the presidency of the pope or his legates, for the purpose of discussing and deciding matters pertaining to the whole Church. Its authority derives from the pope, who has the right to set the date for the assembly and to determine the topics of discussion. The pope also has the right to transfer, suspend, or dissolve a council, and to confirm all its decrees (Can. 222). The following have the right to take part in the council with a deciding vote: cardinals, patriarchs, primates, archbishops, residential and titular bishops, abbots and prelates *nullius*, the abbot primate and abbots who are superiors of monastic congregations, and, finally, the supreme heads of exempt clerical organizations of religious. Theologians and canonists invited to the council merely have a consultative vote (Can. 223). If titular bishops are called to the ecumenical council, they also have a deciding vote, unless it is otherwise stipulated in the decree of convocation.

As a rule, ecumenical or general councils are not summoned except for very grave reasons; in 1900 years only twenty such councils have been held. These reasons generally are: to institute necessary reforms, to define a truth of faith, to condemn error, to enact grave provisions demanded by the exigencies of the times. Strictly speaking, an ecumenical council is never necessary, especially after the definition of the dogma of papal infallibility in 1870

(Denz. 1832–1840), for the pope has power to decide whatever might be decided by the council under his leadership (Cans. 218–220).

An ecumenical council enjoys the prerogative of infallibility in its decrees on matters of faith and morals, inasmuch as the council is presided over and approved by the pope (Cans. 222–227; 228, par. 1). Appeal to the council against a decision of the pope is inadmissible (Can. 228, par. 2); anyone attempting such an appeal becomes suspect of heresy, automatically incurring excommunication specially reserved to the Holy See (Can. 2332). In an ecumenical council every bishop is free to vent his private views on doctrines and matters proposed for discussion, but, after the council has rendered its definitions, these must be internally and externally professed by each bishop.

A *plenary* council is one in which the bishops of several ecclesiastical provinces are assembled. It is called *national* if attended by all the bishops of a country. (Such a council is summoned by the pope or the primate.) It is called *regional* if attended by the bishops of a particular territory or region. A plenary council may not be held without authorization of the pope, (Can. 281) who presides over it through a papal legate. Besides the papal legate, the following have a right to attend a plenary council with a deciding vote: metropolitans, residential bishops, apostolic administrators of dioceses, abbots and prelates *nullius*, vicars and prefects apostolic, and vicars capitular. Members of the secular and religious clergy may also be invited to a plenary council but they have only a consultative vote (Can. 282).

Canon 283 prescribes that a *provincial* council be held in each ecclesiastical province at least once every twenty years. Such a council is called by the metropolitan bishop or, if he is legitimately impeded, by the suffragan bishop who is senior in order of appointment. Suffragan bishops of the metropolitan see and non-suffragan bishops who have chosen this see for the purposes of attending the provincial council (Can. 284) have a right to attend.

The diocesan council, properly called *synod* (*see* Diocesan Synod), is a meeting of the priests of a diocese called by the bishop to consider matters pertaining to the welfare of clergy and faithful. Among those in attendance, besides the bishop who presides over it (Can. 357), are the pastors of the city where the synod is held, at least one pastor from each deanery, and other priests whom the bishop may wish to invite (Can. 358). A diocesan synod is to be held at least every ten years (Can. 356).

Councils have always had a great importance in the Church. Generally speaking, their aim is disciplinary; they are convoked for the purpose of considering the particular needs of clergy and laity (Cans. 290; 356, par. 1). In matters of faith, conciliar definitions do not have absolute and binding value for the whole Church, unless they are specifically approved by the pope. *Tar.*

COUNCIL CHAMBER. *See* Sentence.

COUNCIL, EPISCOPAL. An *episcopal council* is the assembly of the bishops of an ecclesiastical province. Called at least every five years (Can. 292) by the metropolitan, or, in his absence, by the senior suffragan, this meeting is held either in the metropolitan city or one of the cities of the province, to discuss ways and means of promoting the welfare of souls and the cause of religion in the various dioceses, and to prepare the agenda for the next provincial council. In some countries, the episcopal meeting is held annually.

The episcopal conference must be attended by all bishops, abbots and prelates *nullius*, and archbishops with no suffragan diocese. The latter shall choose for themselves permanently (*semel pro semper*), and with the approval of the Holy See, one of the neighboring metropolitan cities for participation in the provincial council (Can. 285).

At the meeting, the bishops shall appoint the place for their next episcopal conference (Can. 292, par. 3). *Fel.*

COUNSELS. A *counsel* is an exhortation without binding force to do or say some specific thing for a particular purpose. Among deliberate actions or omissions that can be directed to God as to their ultimate end, some are a matter of duty (precepts), others are proposed only as a matter of free choice (counsels). The latter are helpful toward an easier and more secure attainment of one's ultimate end. Precepts and counsels are found in the Holy Scriptures (Matt. 19:17; I Cor. 7:25–40); their existence may also be logically demonstrated.

Our first parents were created in a state of justice. Their soul was completely subordinate to and united with God. Their senses were harmoniously subject to their higher powers of intellect and will, and all external creatures were under the full dominion of man. They were incapable, therefore, of causing him the least harm. By destroying the highest of these three harmonies, sin also disturbed the other two, with the result that the threefold harmony was replaced by a threefold disorder (John 2:16). After the fall, weakened in his will to pursue good, man tends to self-interest without much regard for God and neighbor. He thinks so highly of himself as to disregard what he really is. Man's will no longer exercises perfect dominion over his senses, and his sensitive appetite, independently of the dictates of reason or even in opposition to them, tends toward the pleasures of the senses (*concupiscence of the flesh*) and material goods (*concupiscence of the eyes*). Though salvation may be attained through created goods, provided that such goods are in conformity with the dictates of faith and reason, yet total renunciation of worldly goods makes man more inclined to apply himself to the pursuit of spiritual ends and God, as Supreme Good and man's ultimate end. For this reason, Christ, who came down on earth to reestablish the order disturbed by sin, exhorted His disciples to renounce, as much as possible, the perishable goods of the world.

EVANGELICAL COUNSELS. The principal *evangelical counsels* recommended by our Savior are three: poverty, perfect chastity, and obedience.

Poverty consists in the voluntary renunciation of the right to possess and to dispose of material goods. It checks the inordinate desire for worldly possessions; it frees man from material solicitude and eagerness to possess such goods. It increases the desire for spiritual goods and enhances man's trust in God. *Perfect chastity*, highly praised by Christ, implies the renunciation of all carnal pleasures, including the legitimate joys of married life. It tends in some manner to spiritualize the body, making it more inclined to serve the soul, to work for the material and spiritual welfare of others, and to love God more freely and generously. *Obedience*, which is the renunciation of one's own natural right to follow, within certain limits, one's own legitimate wishes, curbs the tendency to overestimate oneself, and increases faith in God.

The essence of Christian perfection does not consist in the observance of evangelical counsels. Perfection may exist even without such observance (*see* Christian Perfection). Nevertheless, the counsels are highly useful in attaining holiness much more readily and effectively. And it may be said that, in practice, perfection will not be attained unless one lives at least in spirit according to evangelical counsels. The spirit of poverty is practiced by depriving oneself of many useless and superfluous things and by making good use of one's possessions (I Tim. 6:17). The spirit of chastity is observed by moderating and restraining lawful carnal pleasures. The spirit of obedience is practiced by docile submission: (a) to one's superiors, as representatives of God; (b) to the will of God in all things; (c) to the inspirations of grace, under the guidance of a prudent spiritual director.

Persons binding themselves by public vow to the observance of evangelical counsels are called *religious* (*q.v.*). Theirs is a state of detachment from the world and total consecration to God. Lay persons not bound by vows will find a promise of obedience to their spiritual director, with his permission and for a time determined by him, a highly useful practice. Also, renunciation of all right to dispose freely of certain material possessions may be a most useful practice, which will foster that inner detachment from all created goods, whether internal (knowledge, talents, renown and esteem and affection of others, consolations, pleasures) or external (possessions, honors, offices, comforts of life). Finally, one should always strive to avoid all deliberate imperfections. *Man.*

COUNSELS, EVANGELICAL. *See* Counsel; Perfection, Christian.

COUNTRY. It is not easy to spell out the idea of one's country, but most people have a natural grasp of what it means and an awareness of the duties of patriotism. Often it is mistakenly identified with the territory of one's native land, or with the people, nation, or State to which someone belongs by birth or by adoption. All of these things have something to do with the notion of country, but none of them actually defines it. *Native land* is where a person was born, but a person may have a different country from the one in which he was born. A *people* is a specific social group living in a given territory, but you can have a people living in a foreign land without a country. *Nation* (*q.v.*) in the sense of race, involves the common origin of a people who have descended from the same ancestors. Almost the same as country, in many cases the two notions merge into the same reality. The only difference between them is as concepts; but you can have a nation without its own soil and, hence, without a country (e.g., a nomad nation), just as you can have a nation divided into many States. *State*

is a territory, a people, a juridically organized nation which has achieved its political independence. The State is a collective organism that perfects the country insofar as it can offer a definitive solution to all of the problems of life in society, but it also presupposes the country and cannot last long if it is based simply on force of arms, while the identity of the State and country is a guarantee of stability, strength, and peace.

In other words, the idea of country is a synthesis of many elements, a combination of geographical, ethnical, and political bonds, bonds of language, domestic or religious institutions, traditions, customs, and interests; it can be defined as a society midway between the family and civil society, whose purpose is to attain the good that these two cannot supply. Hence, as a natural and necessary society, it is not up to the free choice of the individual to accept, reject, or exempt himself from his obligations toward it.

DUTIES TOWARD COUNTRY. The duties toward one's country are similar to those toward one's family, for the former is an extension and a completion of the latter. The family is an imperfect society that must be completed by another larger and stronger society to assure for individuals indispensible goods of intellectual, moral, social, and economic development. The country is a mother, not just in a metaphorical sense. Hence, according to Christian moralists (*Summa Theol.*, II–II, q. 101), duties toward one's country pertain to the virtue of piety (*q.v.*), which binds us to the sources of our being, to the authors of our life and development. Piety implies obligations of love, assistance, defense against internal and external enemies of our country to a point of self-sacrifice, the summit of love, of obedience to laws, of cooperation with the religious, moral, cultural, social, and economic progress. "The natural law commands us to have a special love and be willing to sacrifice for the country where we were born and raised, even to the point that a good citizen will not be afraid to face death for his country" (Leo XIII, Enc. *Sapientiae Christianae*, January 10, 1890).

EXAGGERATED NATIONALISM. One can sin against any virtue by excess or by defect. A sin of excess of patriotism is committed by an exaggerated nationalist. *Nationalism* is a modern term with various meanings that refers to a variety of questions. There is a sound, laudable, and justifiable nationalism that inclines us to love our nation and the people with whom we have a common origin, blood, language, customs, and history. This kind of nationalism is closely related to patriotism; when country and nation form a single, undivided, social unit, the two feelings are fused in practice into a single love. But along with this reasonable and dutiful kind of nationalism, another type, egoistic and fanatical, makes one's own country an absolute good and sacrifices the universal values of law, morality, and religion to it. It regards other nations with contempt, is the cause of hatred and wars between peoples, breaks the supernatural bond that should unite us all as sons of one and the same Church, as brothers in Christ, as heirs and protectors of Christian civilization. "It is more difficult, if not impossible, for peace to endure between peoples and States, if, instead of true and genuine love of country, you have a hard and egoistic nationalism raging supreme; for it means hatred and envy in place of a mutual desire for good, suspicion and mistrust in place of brotherly trust, competition and struggle in place of harmonious cooperation, lust for power and domination in place of respect for and protection of the rights of everybody, even the weak and small" (Pius XI, Christmas Talk, December 24, 1930). "Love of country becomes the source of much evil and injustice when it goes beyond the limits of what is right and becomes an immoderate love of one's nation. Those who give in to this are forgetting that . . . all peoples are part of the great human family, bound to each other in brotherhood, and that other nations also have the right to live and to aspire to prosperity" (Pius XI, Enc. *Urbi et orbi*, December 23, 1922).

COSMOPOLITANISM. The opposite extreme of excessive nationalism is a vague cosmopolitanism; its roots are ancient and it has grown a great deal in modern times for different reasons. The Stoics had earlier denied the idea of patriotism and asserted that the whole world is our country. The French Revolution spread an anti-patriotic humanitarianism. Freemasonry was an unseen but effective agent in breaking down the idea of country. Marxist socialism preached an internationalism of the workers in behalf of a class struggle. And many materialists adopted the motto: *ubi bene, ibi patria*. Even philosophers and writers of great renown were led astray by the idea of a universal Republic or of a United States of the World that would bring a kingdom of brotherhood, justice, and peace into being among all men. "Mankind has no country" (Goethe). "I write as a citizen of the world. Long ago I gave up my country and exchanged it for the whole vast world" (Schiller). "*Country* is a combination of prejudices and of backward ideas that the whole of mankind cannot accept" (Renan). "Ethnologically speaking, the word *nation* no longer represents anything. In the future there will be only the human race; there will be only one human people" (Tolstoi).

Mankind is too large, too different, and its interests and needs too divergent for it to be ruled easily by a single government. Of course, mankind is a reality, in the sense that each State is not self-sufficient and needs the collaboration of other States for its own well-being and to promote and guarantee the good of all mankind; but these common and mutual interests can also be protected by international unions, institutions, and sanctions, regulated by law, without any need of a single hierarchical or governmental organization in the strict sense of the word. Mankind is a vaster concept than that of country, but it does not exclude it, just as the concept of country takes in that of family. "The ascending steps of society go from family to country and from country to mankind, but none of the broader types of union modifies or destroys the preceding one" (A. Conte).

In conclusion, a proper love of one's country does not exclude a love for all mankind. By the example of Jesus Christ, man is capable of loving all men while still retaining a special love for his own country. We can be patriotic within the universal brotherhood of Christ under the universal fatherhood of God. Patriotism is an important and necessary spiritual force that protects individuals and families, assures the progress and greatness of a people, and is the source of heroic sacrifices in the decisive moments of its history. *Mon.*

COUP D'ETAT. *See* Revolution.

COURTESY. *See* Charity.

CRANIOCLASTY. *See* Feticide.

CRANIOLOGY. *See* Anthropology.

CRANIOTOMY. *See* Embryotomy.

CREDO (Creed). *See* Faith, Prayer.

CREMATION. *Cremation* is the violent destruction of a human corpse by means of fire or intense heat. In practice, it is generally accompanied by a funeral rite, which, however, is not necessarily religious. A distinction must be made between cremation as a *common* or *ordinary practice* (cremation properly so-called) and that resorted to *in exceptional circumstances* (war, pestilence, epidemic) as an extraordinary measure and a necessary protection against the spread of contagion, which an ordinary burial would not provide.

A simple and crude form of cremation (funeral pyre) was practiced among certain ancient pagan peoples, such as the Pre-Canaanites who inhabited Palestine. Chaldeans, Medes, Persians, Greeks, and Romans may be said to have practiced cremation as well as inhumation, the general form of burial. Jews and Christians have always rejected cremation as totally unbecoming and repugnant to the dignity of the human body. Toward the end of the thirteenth century, certain Christian groups initiated a movement for a special form of cremation, but this was effectively thwarted by Pope Boniface VIII. At the time of the French Revolution, similar attempts were made, but without effective results. The movement launched in Italy about 1870 by Masonic and other anti-Catholic societies met with more lasting, though limited, success. This movement was definitely characterized as an anti-Christian tendency. The Masons had hoped, through their action, to destroy Christian belief in the resurrection of the body. In 1872, crematories or incinerators were constructed in Padua; later, in many other European countries, and in the United States. Civil laws, which until then had recognized only interment, were amended to include cremation as a legally acceptable practice. Despite intensive propaganda in favor of cremation, interment of the dead remains the accepted practice among the majority of peoples, including non-Christians. The number of human corpses disposed of by cremation is relatively small.

Morality. The Church is opposed to cremation, and by her supreme authority has expressly forbidden the following: (a) cremation of a human corpse; (b) formal cooperation in the act of cremation (*see* Cooperation); (c) disposition for the cremation of one's own body or that of another; (d) membership in societies advocating or promoting cremation; (e) imparting sacramental absolution to a person who, having ordered that his body be cremated after death, refuses to rescind such an order; (f) granting ecclesiastical burial to such a person upon his death

Sac. Cong. of the Holy Office, 1886; Canons 1203; 1240, par. 1, n. 5; 2339).

The Church's opposition to cremation is not based on dogma of the Catholic faith. Resurrection is no more difficult after cremation than after total natural decay of an interred body. The Catholic Church condemns cremation primarily because disposal of the human corpse by cremation runs counter to the most ancient Christian and human tradition. The custom of inhumation of the bodies, as old as man himself, is deeply rooted in the concept of man's reverence for the mortal remains of man. The Church holds it unseemly that the human body, once the living temple of the Holy Spirit and the instrument of the soul, so often sanctified by the sacraments, should, upon its demise, be consigned to flames. The method of interment not only conforms more to traditional Catholic liturgy, but also to any other funeral rite that seeks to express and inculcate in the survivors the spiritual meaning of the great mysteries surrounding death and a future life. A secondary reason for the ecclesiastical prohibition of cremation was the anti-Christian tendency displayed by the advocates and promoters of cremation.

In conclusion, the burning of a human corpse is not an intrinsically evil act, i.e., not sinful by its very nature. At the same time, it is false to assert that such a method of disposing of a human corpse is merely a matter of positive law. The Church will never alter her position regarding cremation, except of course in exceptional circumstances, as in an epidemic, when the burning of the bodies is necessary to avoid the spread of contagion. *Ben.*

CRETINISM, IMBECILITY. *Cretinism* is a disease rather common among inhabitants of mountain regions, from which it sometimes spreads, in diminishing degree, to adjacent valleys and planes. Largely prevalent in the regions of the Alps, Apennines, and Pyrenees, where it always appears in endemic form, it is also found in other parts of the world. *Endemic cretinism* is usually accompanied by an enlargement (goiter) or other serious alterations of the thyroid gland, in a state of functional deficiency. Accentuated hypothyroidism, a lack of thyroid secretion, appears to be the immediate cause of the disease.

Isolated cases may also occur among a normal population. These are referred to as cases of *sporadic cretinism*, usually caused by some morbid process impeding or gravely affecting the normal development of the thyroid gland.

In individuals affected by cretinism the following symptoms are noted in birth or early infancy: pronounced tumefaction of subcutaneous tissues, especially in the regions of face and neck (*myxedema*, which diminishes somewhat with age); thick skin, which later becomes dry, wrinkled and sallow; *nanism* or dwarfism (a thirty-year-old person might have the stature of a five-year-old child); thick lips, with mouth open and drooling and with various dental anomalies; undeveloped genitals (but not to the extent of impeding procreation); monstrous mixture of infantile and senile characteristics; low basal metabolism; general retardation of the vegetative life and of the whole organism.

Concerning psychical functions, a general retardation is noted, with considerable torpor and general insufficiency. Cretins are generally dull and apathetic, timid, lacking initiative, interested only in satisfying their elementary needs. They possess good memory and a clear sense of gratitude toward anyone extending them help or assistance. Shying away from all company, they prefer to lead a purely vegetative life within the strict family circle, thus manifesting, from the psychological standpoint also, the peculiar combination of senility and infantilism which characterizes their physical aspect. Not infrequently, deaf-mutism completes and aggravates the morbid picture.

The primary cause of endemic cretinism is still not completely known. The most that can be said is that, in regions where cretinism prevails, its endemic character is somehow attributed to particular climatic and environmental conditions.

The treatment, extraordinarily effective if begun promptly on early diagnosis, consists in daily administration of small doses of dessicated thyroid.

MORAL PROBLEMS. In comparison with other widespread serious diseases (e.g., tuberculosis, cancer, malaria), endemic cretinism has been given inadequate attention, even in those countries where the largest number of cases occurs. Cretinism is bound to affect to a considerable degree the economic and social welfare of the country. Perhaps one reason for such inadequate attention is the fact that cretins are apathetic, lacking in initiative, and resigned to their morbid condition. Another reason may be the fact that cretinism strikes the poor and rural elements of the population, far removed from more developed centers. But all this does not take away the fact that this serious problem requires intensive study and research, with the hope for a rational solution soon. The ethical, humanitarian implications of this problem are obvious enough to claim a greater interest by national and international organizations.

Another moral consideration concerns the position of cretins, often the object of ridicule rather than commiseration in their relation to human and divine laws.

Cretinism in its most serious forms is characterized by a purely vegetative life and a complete lack of psychical activity; this renders the subject penally irresponsible and civilly incapable of contracting marriage. From this standpoint, cretins are comparable to idiots or *amentes* (in the canonical sense).

In the lesser forms of the disease, ranging from definite semicretinism to proximate normality, the formulation of any judgment—moral, penal, civil or canonical—must be based on an accurate study of the mental condition and general behavior of each particular individual. Concerning the evaluation of

moral and penal responsibility, it is useful to note that, except in rare case where cretinism is accompanied by brain disease or other psychical disturbances that might give rise to perversion or compulsiveness, the commission of crime is alien to the peculiar mental formation of cretins and semicretins who are naturally inclined to timidity and simplicity. If crime is committed by such individuals, it is essentially due to an ingenuous manifestation of their natural instincts, unchecked and undirected by reason, or to an excessive reaction to the cruel taunts of tormentors. In either case, the rigors of the laws are not applicable. At most the law may impose temporary confinement in some institution where the cretin or semicretin may be given appropriate medical treatment and a measure of moral training. *Riz.*

CRIME, ATTEMPTED. See Crime.

CRIME, DELICT (*Delictum, Crimen*). The term *crime* indicates any willful act by which the right of another is violated in a manner considered by positive law as punishable by law Canon Law defines crime as "an external and morally imputable violation of the law to which at least an indeterminate canonical sanction is attached" (Can. 2195, par. 1). The elements common to every crime are: (a) a human external act (objective or material element); (b) fraud or guilt (subjective, moral, or psychological element); (c) a law or precept, the violation of which carries a penalty (juridical element). This last element, which is the application of the axiom *nullum crimen sine lege* (there is no crime unless there is a law), is accepted in Canon Law in principle, despite the fact that for safeguarding the social order in the Church, punishment is admitted for a violation if the particular gravity of the transgression or the scandal to which it gave rise may demand it (Can. 2222, par. 1).

In the civil law of some countries, any external violation of law is called crime, whether it be a criminal offense or a merely penal offense. The latter could more properly be considered a misdemeanor. In reality, there is a difference between a crime and a merely penal offense; in the former, the act, considered by the law as punishable, is necessarily predicated upon the will of the agent and necessarily connected with the violation of a specific right of another; but in a merely penal offense, this does not or may not happen. Therefore, although the material object may be identical in both, in a merely penal offense the connection with the subjective element in the agent and the specific violation of the right of another are either lacking altogether or simply defective. The other difference, established by the law itself, is based upon the severity or the lightness of the penalty.

CONSTITUTIVE ELEMENTS. The constitutive elements of crime are: (a) the *formal* element or malice, which is the basis for imputability; (b) the *material* element, that is the *corpus delicti*, the physical fact of the external violation of the law, without which one would have a moral disorder or sin, but not a crime; (c) the *juridical* element, or the existence of a criminal law or precept making a certain criminal act legally punishable. The essence of crime is consitituted by (a) malice and (b) the physical effect of an external violation in the direct or indirect damage resulting from the offense. The existence of a criminal law gives the crime a specific form, by which it can be individualized and made punishable before society. In the practical evaluation of crime, one must consider its natural elements, which are proper to any law. These are: (a) the *object*, that is, the law of society violated; (b) the *subject*, endowed with sufficient intellect and will; (c) the human external *act* or *omission*; (d) the *type* of violation; and (e) the *circumstances*, which may constitute aggravating or extenuating elements of the crime.

According to the concept prevailing today in Canon Law (not without dissent, however), the active subject of a crime can be only a physical, not a juridical, person. As a matter of fact, a baptized person (Catholic or non-Catholic) is the only subject of the Church's criminal laws. Unbaptized persons are not the Church's subjects. Furthermore, the supreme pontiff cannot be active subject of criminal law, since the penalties established by him are not applicable to him; nor are cardinals, unless they are explicity mentioned (Can. 2227, par. 2). Bishops, sovereigns and their children are not liable to certain penalties (Can. 2227).

The passive subject of crime is the person (physical or juridical) whose right is in danger of being violated or actually violated, as a result of the crime. In the Code of Canon Law, all circumstances excluding imputability are considered circumstances of a general character. *Aggravating circumstances* are: passion voluntarily and deliberately aroused or fostered (Can. 2206); the greater dignity of the person offended or committing the offense (Can. 2207, n. 1); the abuse of authority or office, for the purpose of committing a crime (Can. 2207, no. 2); and recidivism (Can. 2208). *Extenuating circumstances* are: grave fear, grave inconvenience, or a condition of necessity, if the crime consists of an act which is intrinsically evil, involves contempt of the Faith or ecclesiastical authority, or is against the good of souls (Can. 2205, par. 3); exceeding limits in repelling an aggressor or a provocation (Can. 2205, par. 4); passion, if not voluntarily aroused (Can. 2206). *Excusing circumstances* are: grave fear, necessity, or grave inconvenience, apart from the cases mentioned above (Can. 2205, par. 2); legitimate self-defense (Can. 2205, par. 4); non-deliberate passion, if it precedes or totally impedes the consent of the will (Can. 2206); an act carried out in fulfillment of an obligation imposed by law, etc. Above all, the age and mental condition of the offender may either exclude or diminish his capability of committing a crime, or, as in temporary mental disturbance, exclude or diminish imputability (*see* Amentia, Dementia, Age, Insanity, Schizophrenia, etc.; *also* Accidental cause, Excusing cause, Circumstance of the human act, Legitimate self-defense, Impossibility, Necessity, Responsibility, Fear, etc.).

GRAVITY OF CRIME. The quality of a crime is derived from the object protected by the law. This is the criterion according to which the Code of Canon Law and criminal codes classify crimes. Its gravity, instead, is the concrete entity, in a combined consideration of imputability and the damage caused.

CLASSIFICATION OF CRIMES. Crimes may be classified according to their notoriety, forum, effects, etc. (a) From the standpoint of its notoriety, a crime is *public* (*q.v.*), or *notorious* (*q.v.*), either of *law* or of *fact*, or *occult* (*q.v.*). (b) According to its forum, a crime is *ecclesiastical*, if it involves a violation of Church law; *civil*, if it involves the violation of a law of the State; *mixed*, if it involves the violation of a law of the State and of the Church. The Church usually does not punish a lay offender, if he is already punished or expected to be punished by civil authority (Cans. 1553; 1933, par. 3). (c) According to its effects, crime is *consummated*, that is, carried out, *frustrated*, or *attempted*. The prosecution of ecclesiastical crimes belongs to Church authority, which has the right to request the aid of the civil power (Can. 2198). However, today, not all States recognize the so-called doctrine of the *secular arm*. In concordat agreements, the Church expects, whenever possible, that due consideration be given by the State to such doctrine: in a *negative* sense, by protecting the clergy in the exercise of their ministry and guaranteeing the free exercise of ecclesiastical jurisdiction; or in a *positive* way, by enforcing the execution by force of law for certain criminal and disciplinary provisions, and certain sentences issued by the competent ecclesiastical authority, after the State has been properly informed.

ATTEMPTED CRIME. An attempted crime is an incomplete violation of a criminal law, or a partial execution of those actions which lead to the commission of a violation. An attempted crime, therefore, presupposes that the criminal willfully conceive the commission of a specific offense (*voluntas sceleris*); that the action be effectively initiated after adequate preparation; that the means used be suitable to the commission of the crime; that there be a voluntary or involuntary interruption in the execution of the crime. The suitability of the means must be taken, not in an absolute sense, but objectively; it does not always coincide with the adequacy or sufficiency of the means. The voluntary or involuntary interruption in the execution of the crime is a distinctive character, which differentiates the attempted from the frustrated crime (Can. 2212, par. 1–2).

To induce another, even if unsuccessfully, to commit a crime is to be guilty of attempted crime. The Code of Canon Law does not require that there be notoriety, absolutely speaking (Can. 2212, par. 3), although some criminal codes do. Imputability for an attempted crime is evidently lesser than that for a consummated crime; the penalty must naturally be in proportion to the means employed and the proximity to which the criminal has come in the commission of a crime (Cans. 2213, par. 1; 2235). In Canon Law, however, a person who of his own accord desisted after he had initiated a crime is free from all imputability, if no damage resulted and no scandal was given by the attempt (Can. 2213, par. 3). Sometimes criminal law looks upon an attempted crime as a real crime, as the attempted corruption of ecclesiastical ministers, judges, procurators, and the like (Can. 2407). In such cases the crime consists in the attempt made (Can. 2212, par. 4).

FRUSTRATED CRIME. An offender who, with the evident intention of committing a crime, institutes all those actions which objectively are considered necessary for and, by their very nature, capable of leading to the commission of a crime, is guilty of a frustrated crime (Can. 2212, par. 2), if the completion of the crime is not attained for reasons that are independent of his will. Imputability for a frustrated crime is undoubtedly greater han that of an attempted crime, because in the former the criminal intent is more evident; however, it is lesser than the imputability for a consummated crime because, in reality, the crime was not carried to completion. Penalties for a frustrated crime are left by Canon Law to the discretion of the judge (Cans. 2213, par. 2; 2235). *Pug.*

CRIME (Impediment of). The diriment or nullifying impediment of crime, after a somewhat varied history, has been adopted into law by the Church, in order to safeguard the sanctity of marriage and to protect legitimate spouses. This impediment, currently regulated by Canon 1075, presents four different forms: (a) adultery with a promise of marriage; (b) adultery with attempted marriage, even by mere civil ceremony; (c) adultery with conjugicide perpetrated by one of the adulterous parties; (d) conjugicide with mutual conspiracy or cooperation, even without adultery. Any one of these forms constitutes the impediment of crime which invalidates marriage to the accomplice in the crime.

In the two forms involving the serious crime of conjugicide, a dispensation is never granted, if the crime is public or notorious. If it is occult, a dispensation may be obtained, though rarely, with certain conditions imposed in each individual case, either by the Sacred Congregation of the Sacraments in the external forum, or by the Apostolic Penitentiary in the sacramental forum.

In the two forms involving adultery either with promise of marriage or with attempted marriage, a dispensation is not denied, since the impediment is of lesser degree.

The lesser impediment of crime is incurred if the promise of marriage or the attempted marriage is verified while one of the adulterous parties is still bound by a previous valid marriage. Hence, mere adultery, without promise of marriage or without attempted marriage, does not give rise to the impediment of crime, even though the two adulterers are living in concubinage. The adultery must be connected either with a mutual promise of marriage (whether the promise precede or follow the adultery is irrelevant, as long as it is made and accepted during one and the same legitimate marriage) or with attempted marriage, i.e., an invalid marriage ceremony, either religious or civil. Moreover, the adultery must be complete or consummated; it must be formal, i.e., both adulterers must know that at least one of them is bound by a previous valid marriage.

MULTIPLICATION. When adultery is combined both with promise of marriage and attempted marriage, there is duplication of the impediment which must be made known in applying for a dispensation. *Bar.*

CRIME (of contact). *See* Contagion, Contact.

CRIME, POLITICAL. A *political crime* is an ordinary crime inspired in its entirety or in part by political motives. It is also a crime directed against a political interest of the State or a political right of a citizen. There are two types of political crime: (1) *subjective,* if the motive that inspired it is political, the crime also is political; (2) *objective,* if the nature of the norm violated is political, the crime also will be political. A political crime may be committed by: (a) the State against a citizen; (b) a citizen against the State; (c) one citizen against another.

Crime by the State Against a Citizen. This crime is committed if the State pursues the rigid doctrine of the supremacy of the State, and does not hesitate to sacrifice all moral interest to the exigencies of a mere practical utilitarianism, with the aggravating circumstance of deceitful devices used to achieve it. Such devices are illustrated by the obvious pseudo-scientism of *The Prince* by Macchiavelli (cc. 15–18). The State's rights are invoked as a pretext to justify any cunning device employed in the elimination of innocent citizens, simply because they represent the opposition, or in a suppression of fundamental rights of the individual. Macchiavelli's doctrine attains its ultimate expression and evil culmination in Hegel's metaphysical formula, in which Reason is identified with the State, and the State becomes ultimate goal of human reason. From this premise of false and inhuman principles, flows the interminable history of political crimes stretching across all ages. The same was expressed by Caiphas in his peroration: "You know nothing at all; nor do you reflect that it is expedient for us that one man die for the people, instead of the whole nation perishing" (John 2:49–50). It re-echoes in the pages of *The Prince,* as justification of the crimes of Duke Valentino; in the pages of *Mein Kampf,* with its actualization in the gas chambers and the purges of Berlin in 1934 and 1944. It re-echoes, too, in the works of the principal exponents of communism, and attains its application in the infamous *purges* of the Katyn Forest. Catholic doctrine has always rejected these principles, and the Church has never ceased to raise its voice in condemnation of the innumerable political crimes, homicides, genocide and crimes against humanity. The distinction of a limited moral law for private life and a more general moral law for public life, devised by Mirabeau to justify certain crimes, was intended to engender confusion in the minds of the people. The moral law must be universal and absolute or it ceases to be altogether. No field of human activity is exempt from the application of St. Paul's injunction to the Romans, "And why should we not, as some calumniously accuse us of teaching, do evil that good may come from it? The condemnation of such is just" (Rom. 3:8).

Political Crime by a Citizen Against the State. The principles outlined apply to political crimes committed by one citizen against another or by a group of citizens against another group, as in the strife of parties. The common crime committed for political motives is no less detestable than a crime inspired by other motives, for, as stated above, the end, no matter how noble, does not justify the means. Thus, killing a person for political motives is no less abominable than killing him for personal or private motives. Life is always sacred. A political doctrine that teaches crime as a means of propaganda for intimidation and elimination of the

opposition, is intrinsically, in itself, evil. Those who teach such a doctrine share in the moral responsibility of the one who actually carries out the crime and are juridically culpable of the crime itself. He who teaches hatred for, and suppression of, a political opponent must be considered as culpable as he who orders the commission of the crime: he who carries out a crime does so under the influence of ideas to which he has been exposed and which he has been deliberately indoctrinated. It is effective doctrinal counsel (*see* Cooperators in evil). Thus, too, it is a positive cooperation in crime for those who print and circulate books advocating extermination of an opponent. Whoever writes, prints, or in any way promotes this philosophy is guilty of true and effective cooperation in crime and, as such, should be held accountable before the law. A hero's acclaim given to a political criminal found guilty of crime, is a justification of a political crime; those who organize or take part in such demonstrations are considered to approve the crime committed. As such, they are guilty of a grave wrong and should be punished accordingly. A State that does not have adequate laws to deal with such, is morally bound to enact them, lest it become guilty of failing to fulfill its end, the guarantee of public order and the safety of its citizens. The State is guilty of negative cooperation in crime if it fails to do all that it can to prevent the commission of crime.

Political Crime by a Private Citizen Against the State and its Representatives. It is possible to have a political crime committed by a private citizen against the State or its representatives. John Wilkes Booth, who killed President Lincoln, committed a political crime. For a sound moral judgment in this field, however, it is necessary to proceed with much prudence. This is particularly true in one who unlawfully wrests public power and then, for his own protection, enacts punitive laws of a political nature against those who criticize him as head of the State. It is clear that the violation of such laws of a purely political nature (political crime) cannot be considered a moral violation. Likewise, the violation of a law which arbitrarily limits the freedom of assembly, the press, religion, and the like, for the sake of keeping a party in power, is no longer a moral violation. For the law is totally or partially unjust and, as such, loses its binding force.

Passive resistance is always lawful and, at times, an obligation. With regard to active resistance, the following principles apply: (a) True and open rebellion and related subversive activities, directed to the overthrow of a lawful government which does not *gravely* abuse its power, are intrinsically, in themselves, wrong. (b) Active armed resistance is permissible, and, according to some theologians, obligatory, in the following cases: (1) if grave and evident injustice is present; (2) if no more effective means are available; (3) if greater evil is not created; (4) if the counsel of wise persons was obtained; (5) if it is done by honest means. On these principles is based the liceity or toleration of tyrannicide, defended by some theologians (see Resistance to unjust ruler, Revolution, Tyranny). With regard to this debated question, two principles are certain: (a) a private citizen has no right to lay his murderous hand upon a legitimate sovereign who becomes a tyrant; (b) the people, taken as a whole, that is, as a body politic, has the right to defend itself by means of active resistance against despotic government, if the oppression has reached a particular degree of intensity in which the rights of the individual and personal security are in jeopardy, and there appears to be no other way of shaking off the yoke of its tyrannical power. *Pal.*

CRIMINAL. *See* Anthropology, Criminal.

CRIMINALITY. *See* Delinquency.

CRIMINOLOGY. *See* Criminal Anthropology.

CRISIS OF ANXIETY (Anxiety Complex). *See* Anxiety.

CRISIS, DELIRIOUS. *See* Amentia, Schizophrenia.

CRISIS, ECONOMIC. The phenomena which systematically disturb economic equilibrium constitute what is currently called *economic crisis*. In ordinary language, *economic crisis* refers to the ups and downs in business. In scientific parlance, it is the economic condition which appears after statistical elaboration has sifted the data of seasonal and accidental variations.

The doctrine of economic crisis has been advanced during the last twenty years as a development of the various theories concerning the economic cycles, so that some observers have been led to believe that *economic oscillations* are essential and normal in an economy.

ECONOMIC FORECASTS. Such orientation has undoubtedly aided the work of research in economic dynamics and interpretation of economic equilibrium. Nevertheless, the thesis holding that the cyclical movement is something determined, natural, and lasting appears extravagant. Elaborators of the so-called *economic barometers* used to forecast economic trends have based their views precisely on such a thesis.

The strict interdependence of economic factors, the complexity of the processes of production and the nature of trade and exchange as practiced in the modern economic world render the variations of economic crises particularly grave, especially where the competitive system still prevails. Hence, there is acknowledged need for control measures enacted by the government, or even by individuals guided by a more complete knowledge of the economic conditions.

The limited results achieved by economic barometers, however, leave one rather skeptical about the possibility of reducing or eliminating economic oscillations by the action or control of individual operators. Government intervention, though a matter of much discussion insofar as its limits are concerned, is generally accepted. Notable among government interventions was the one of 1929–1933, in the United States.

Morally one cannot but approve any

study or research directed to a better understanding of economic dynamics. The control measures adopted by individual operators must, insofar as it is possible, always be guided by criteria of justice and charity. Government intervention is undoubtedly licit, provided that it remains within the limits of the common good (*q.v*). *Gol.*

CRITIQUE. As an act of the mind, a critique is a judgment rendered by the human mind. In actual usage, the term is restricted to critical evaluations of the products of the human mind. One thus speaks of literary, historical, and aesthetic critique. In philosophy the term has come to mean a judgment of the secondary order, an evaluation of the veracity of our judgments or a judgment of the objective value of human knowledge.

PHILOSOPHICAL CRITIQUE. The solution to the fundamental problems of philosophy and the critique of knowledge have serious repercussions in the field of moral doctrine. A negative solution to this problem is termed *skepticism*, the complete destruction of all human persuasions and ethical precepts. A positivistic solution could be termed *dogmatism*, which may be idealistic and realistic, depending on the value of human knowledge: whether restricted to ideas or extended to extramental objects.

These problems became acute, principally because of the theories of Kant and Descartes. Kant is considered the father of modern critical philosophy, which has assumed an idealist character. Kant's position regarding the role of human knowledge may be summarized as follows: neither sensitive nor intellectual knowledge brings us into contact with the reality of things. Our judgments are subjectively valid, but have no objective value whatsoever. The human mind does not represent things as they are in themselves, but as they appear to be; such a theory destroys the objectivity of human knowledge.

This doctrine seemed to effect a salvation of the moral order from destructive skepticism, for, with a rejection of the value of purely cognitive faculties, Kant was compelled to accept the sense of awareness of duty; upon this he based his belief in God, human freedom, and the immortality of the soul. His followers, however, were quick to see the contradiction: if our cognitive faculties lack objective truth in the theoretical sphere, how can they possibly assure us of certainty in the practical order? To accept a concept of knowledge or the edifice of knowledge on a consciousness of duty, an acceptance of the objectivity of the concepts of good and evil is necessary. This is to revert to the theoretical and speculative sphere. Hence, if Kant's conclusions in the *Critique of Pure Reason* are true, his conclusions in the *Critique of Practical Reason* are false. This makes a total shipwreck of ethics. *Gra.*

CROSS-BREEDING. *See* Bestiality, Experiments on Man.

CROSS (Meaning of). In a moral sense the cross signifies suffering, whether physical or moral. Faith teaches the true meaning and worth of suffering. It provides man with the necessary strength to bear up under the weight of the cross and to carry it with joy. Suffering was not a part of God's original plan, but came into the world through sin. Adam forfeited the first gifts of original justice for himself and posterity; suffering became an inevitable reality for men, and the necessary means for the expiation of sins.

Through unspeakable sufferings Christ redeemed man; there can be no communion of life with Christ nor share in His glory without a share in His passion and sufferings (Luke 9:23; 14:27; Rom. 8:17; Col. 18:24). Moreover, suffering detaches man from self and creatures and elevates his soul to God. It is also a powerful means of acquiring merit and of cooperating in the salvation of souls. Following Adam's fall, no grace is given except in virtue of the infinite merits of Christ. Nevertheless, by special condescension on the part of the Lord, man is permitted to become a cooperator in the work of redemption by uniting his good works and sufferings to those of Christ. Man's good works and sufferings draw their full value from the passion nd death of Christ and serve as titles to race in behalf of other souls.

Man has the duty to accept and bear suffering patiently, without murmuring or rebellion against God, who permits suffering for man's spiritual welfare. Many rejoice in following the path of suffering in order that they may resemble the Divine Model. Such a disposition presupposes a lively faith and total abandonment of self to Divine Providence, who disposes all things with wisdom for man's greater good.

At least once each day, we should offer up our sufferings to God and unite these with the intentions of our crucified Savior for sinners. *Man.*

CROSS, SIGN OF. According to the teachings of the New Testament and the life of Christ, the cross tells the story of man's redemption by Christ, the God-Man (Col. 1:20). For this reason the cross holds a central place in the Christian faith (I Cor. 1:17); it is also the source of all grace (Eph. 2:16). To a Christian, the cross is both a reminder and an invitation to mortify himself (Matt. 10:38; Gal. 2:19); it is to follow Christ along the road of suffering (Matt. 16:24).

In order to keep these fundamental Christian truths vividly before their minds, primitive Christians not only made reproductions of the cross but also signed themselves frequently with the sign of the cross: at the beginning of the day, on leaving and on entering the house, while dressing, at bath, at table, upon lighting lamps (Tertullian, *De corona militis*, 3, 11), and before facing martyrdom. They made the sign of the cross over the bread they ate and over the cup from which they drank (St. Cyril of Jerusalem, *Catechesis*, 22, 36). At the time of St. Augustine (*Tract. 11 in Job*), blessing oneself with the sign of the cross was regarded as an external profession of the Christian faith. By the sign of the cross, a source and cause of all grace (St. Leo the Great, *Sermon 8, De passione Domini*), all things in the Church are withdrawn from the power of the devil; everything is blessed, sanctified and consecrated, as stated in the Litany of the ordination rite: "*that is may please Thee to bless, sanctify, and consecrate this chosen one.*" By the holy cross Christ acquired a particular right over all persons and things; and the use of the sign of the cross is like a seal of that right (cf. Oppenheim, *Commentationes ad ritum baptismalem*, I, Turin-Rome 1943, p. 103–132). In medieval times, it was customary to trace a cross at the beginning of every public writing, inscription, legislation, etc. It also served as a substitute for the signature of illiterates. Frequently, it preceded the signature of ecclesiastics, as today it precedes that of cardinals, bishops, abbots, etc. The sign of the cross was also placed over house doors and city gates, walls, ovens, etc. Cruciform reliquaries, sometimes engraved with a formula for exorcism, have been handed down from antiquity. Finally, ecclesiastical documents dating back to the third century attest to the use of the sign of the cross in Eastern and Western liturgies, especially in the celebration of the Mass and in the ceremonies of baptism and sacred ordination (Chrysostom, *In Matt., homilia* 54; Augustine, *In Job, tract.* 118).

VARIOUS FORMS. The Christians of the first centuries habitually made the sign of the cross on their foreheads, and this was done with the thumb or forefinger of the right hand (Tertullian, *loc. cit.*). Soon, the sign of the cross was made also on the breast or heart (Prudentius, *Cathemer.*, 6). Gaudentius of Brescia (*De lect. evang.*) speaks of a triple sign: on the heart, lips, and forehead, which, a few centuries later, Beleth (*Explicatio divini officii*, 39) explains thus: "I am not ashamed of the Gospel (the sign of the cross is made high on the forehead), but confess it with my lips and heart." In the eighth century, Alcuin (*De Psalmorum usu:* PL 101, 468) also mentions the sign of the cross made on the lips. According to the *Ordo Romanus* (II, n. 8) of the tenth century, it was customary at the reading of the Gospel to sign oneself with the sign of the cross on the forehead and on the heart. From the twelfth century on, it became general practice to sign oneself on the forehead, lips, and heart, with the so-called small cross, which was also made over ailing parts of a sick person's body (Gregory the Great, *Dialog.*, 2, 20; Cassian, *Collat.*, 8, 18). This small cross, traced with the thumb, is employed in the anointings prescribed in the administration of certain sacraments (baptism, confirmation, extreme unction).

In the Middle Ages, it was customary to impart blessings with three fingers of the right hand, in honor of the Blessed Trinity. Only in the thirteenth century did the practice arise of blessing with all fingers extended and joined together, in such a way that the small finger is directed toward the object or the person receiving the blessing. Our present larger cross, the Latin cross, made by moving the right hand from the forehead to the breast and from the left to the right shoulder, came into general liturgical use much later, although it is occasionally mentioned in earlier periods. *Opp.*

CRUCIFIX. The crucifix is a representation of Jesus Christ on the cross. The image of the Crucified Christ should be precious to every Christian. As a representation of the sufferings and death which Christ endured for the salvation of man, it must be regarded as an object of worship, even though relative. To treat the crucifix disrespectfully is a sin against the virtue of religion.

As a profession of faith and as a manifestation of reverence and love, the crucifix should hang prominently not only in the home, but also in public places (workshop, office, classroom, courtroom, hospitals, barracks, etc.). The crucifix is also intended to be a reminder of God's presence, of the need for mortification, of the obligation to sanctify one's daily actions. It is, indeed, a commendable practice always to carry on one's person a crucifix, blessed and enriched with a plenary indulgence to be gained at the hour of death. The faithful who ardently love the Divine Savior are wont to use any opportunity, private or public, to show gratitude, reverence, and affection to the Crucified Lord and Savior of man. *Man.*

CRUELTY. *Cruelty* is a vice opposed to meekness. Meekness, also called *clemency*, inclines toward moderation of just anger and its consequent effects (just punishment or vengeance of evil); cruelty incites man to inflict upon another being (human or animal) excessive punishment, pain, or suffering, without a justifying or proportionate reason.

The malice of cruelty is manifested through a cruel act, which is sinful. Cruelty toward one's neighbor is of itself a serious sin. But, if the excesses are of small consequence, it is only a slight sin. Cruelty to animals is also a sin, though seldom a grave one. To inflict needless suffering on animals is an abuse of God's creatures. Moreover, cruelty to animals tends to harden man's heart and to render him less sensitive to human suffering (*see* Maltreatment of animals, Vivisection). *Ben.*

CRYPTESTHESIA. *See* Telepathy.

CULT, DISPARITY OF. *See* Disparity of Cult; Impediments, Matrimonial.

CULT, FALSE. *See* Superstition.

CULT, WORSHIP. According to its classic definition, *cult* is a mark of submission to another's acknowledged excellence (*nota submissionis ad agnitam excellentiam alterius*). It is not simply acknowledgement of another's excellent qualities (honor, praise), but of another's superiority shown by our dependence on him. Hence, a true act of cult is that by which the superiority of another is acknowledged by the manifestation of one's submission to him. From this it is abundantly clear that religious cult is an actuation of the virtue of religion (*q.v.*), which inclines man to acknowledge his total dependence on God, who is the Supreme Lord, the first beginning and the ultimate end of all things.

There are different kinds of cult, essentially different from each other, depending on the kind of superiority that one intends to acknowledge. *Civil* cult is directed to men who are superior to us because of our natural dependence on them (parents, superiors, governors, country). Civil cult is an act pertaining to the so-called virtue of piety (q.v.). *Religious* cult is directed to God, Supreme Lord, and to things essentially related to Him. If cult is limited solely to the natural relation of a creature to his Creator, it is designated as *natural religious* cult. If it is directed to God as Author of the supernatural order, it is called *supernatural religious* cult, in which, besides the element of servitude, there also enters the relation of sonship or heir (God is Lord and Father).

If religious cult is directed to God to render Him the honor exclusively belonging to His incommunicable superiority as Creator, it is called cult of adoration (q.v.) or *latria* (latreutic cult or worship). If it is directed to the saints because of their sanctity and role in the mystical body of Christ, it is called cult of veneration or *dulia*. A special form of cult is due to the Blessed Virgin not only because of her supereminent sanctity, but also because of the supereminent rank she holds among creatures as mother of God. This cult is called *hyperdulia*. For analogous reasons of eminent sanctity and relation to the person of Christ, a special cult is due, according to a number of theologians, to St. Joseph. This is called *protodulia*.

Cult is *absolute* if directed to the person; *relative* if directed to things (image, relics, etc.) bearing a special relation to the person honored.

Besides these essential distinctions, others refer more to the manner in which cult or worship is rendered. Thus, cult is said to be *internal* or *external*, depending on whether it is rendered through the internal faculties, especially spiritual faculties of intellect and will, or through the external faculties and the body. Again, cult may be *public*, if rendered officially in the name of the Church; or *private*, if rendered by individuals or groups not officially representing the Church, as such (Can. 1256). However, public cult may be rendered privately, without the direct intervention or participation of the Church. Thus, a priest reciting his breviary alone, or celebrating Mass with only the server present performs an act of public worship. Public cult, insofar as it concerns the administration of the sacraments or sacramentals, arranged by the Church as a series of acts of worship, is called *liturgy*; but there are also extra-liturgical forms of expressing public cult (Benediction of the Blessed Sacrament). The acts proper to internal cult are: *devotion* (q.v.), whereby the will is placed at the service of God; and *prayer* (q.v.), whereby one's mind is directed to God. Through the external acts of cult we subject to God our body (adoration) and possessions (sacrifice, offering, vow). Finally, we may honor Divine Excellence by acknowledging our dependence on God by a proper and devout use of the means He has given us for our sanctification (*see* Sacraments, Liturgy), by the use of the divine name in taking an oath (q.v.), by exorcisms (q.v.), and by praise or the outward manifestation of prayer (*see* Liturgy, Prayer).

Cult flows logically from the virtue of religion (q.v.). A particular objection, stemming principally from a hyperspiritualistic and hyperindividualistic mentality, is raised by certain groups against external and public worship. According to them, their objection is based also on a passage of St. John's Gospel (4:23), in which the Evangelist speaks only of the spiritual character of the New Law. The conduct of Christ and the practice by the primitive Church of public and external worship is ample refutation of such an objection (*see* Eucharist, Sacraments). Furthermore, public worship is a need deeply ingrained in man's nature, whose every element, sensitive, corporal, and social, is entirely dependent on God. Human nature cannot live without externally manifesting its interior sentiments. A growing liturgical movement toward external and public worship is also noted among Protestants.

It goes without saying that external worship must always be a sincere manifestation of an internal religious attitude. Furthermore, external worship, properly followed, serves admirably to generate a sincere devotion. *Pal.*

CULTURE. *See* Civilization.

CULTURE, PHYSICAL. *Physical culture* consists of physical exercises designed to keep the body physically sound, or of certain forms of activities which are intended to contribute to improving one's physical fitness. Physical culture and care of the body are concepts closely allied. *Care* of the body comprises those things considered necessary by all, in ordinary as well as special circumstances, for the preservation of life and health, for prevention and cure of diseases, for the correction of defects, etc. *Physical culture*, on the other hand, implies systematic care of the body in excess of the minimum required for maintaining normal good health. It aims at a more perfect physical development of an already sound and normal body. Forms of physical culture are sports, gymnastics, swimming, sun-bathing, and the like.

The morality of physical culture is governed by the principle that the body is an essential part of man, but only a part, not the principal part of man, for this distinction belongs to the soul. On the basis of this principle, Catholic moral teaching condemns two extreme attitudes in this matter. One was promoted by the Manichaeans, who held that physical culture is the work of the devil, and all care of the body is regarded as the handiwork of God, hence, as something good in itself. Furthermore, the soul, which is united to the body to form one single being (man), is dependent in its operations, including the more highly spiritual ones, on the physical condition of the body. The other extreme attitude regarding bodily care comprises a variety of excesses in that regard. First of all, Christian moral teaching condemns any *cult* of the body which reflects a materialistic mentality and aims at perfecting the body as if it were the *supreme* good to which all else is to be subordinated and sacrificed. Christian morality also condemns any organized physical culture which fails to take into account the natural and supernatural interests of the soul, or which affords no time or opportunity for the individual cultural and spiritual welfare of man and for supernatural values. The practice of scheduling sports activities or games which take up the greater part of Sunday, especially Sunday morning, allowing the participants little or no time to attend Mass or other religious duties, is highly objectionable. Sports and other physical exercises, if engaged in with moderation and for recreational purposes, are not forbidden on Sunday. But it must not be forgotten that Sunday is and must be the Lord's day, dedicated primarily to the welfare of the soul. It is a very serious social abuse to permit Sunday to degenerate into a day of sports and games, leaving little or no time for divine worship. A reasonable and moderate amount of physical exercise benefits even the soul, inasmuch as it fosters the development of character, competition, and a spirit of endurance. Many individuals neglect physical culture, not because they give preference to spiritual values, but because they lack courage to overcome laziness and to perform the sacrifices entailed in a proper and beneficial culture of the body.

In general, particularly in the case of youths, *indirect* forms of physical culture are preferable—that is, activities or exercises which are directed to the attainment of sound objectives, diversion, competition, prizes, etc. In some branches of sports, especially in gymnastics or calisthenics, the moral law and good common sense require that men and women perform such exercises separately; that the physical director be of the same sex as the group; and that young women refrain from engaging in public and strenuous exhibitions. Costumes worn at such performances must be in keeping with the rules of decency and Christian morality while allowing for comfort and freedom of movement. Nudism and exhibitionism are to be avoided as being in no way necessary for sports performance and as morally and spiritually harmful to performers and spectators as well. *Ben.*

CURATOR. *See* Interdict, Teacher.

CURE, TREATMENT. *See* Therapy.

CURIA. In its original meaning, the term was seemingly used to indicate a division of the Roman populace; specifically, the tenth part of a tribe. Later, it was used to signify the seat of control of the Roman senate and, eventually, the center of other Roman offices. In a similar sense, the term was employed in the various municipalities of the Empire. In the Middle Ages the term had various meanings, but it soon acquired the prevalent meaning of tribunal or totality of offices relative to the administration of justice.

In Canon Law, besides the medieval meaning of judiciary department (which has almost disappeared from the official terminology and completely from ordinary language), the term *curia* was and still is employed primarily to designate the totality of departments or organs which ordinarily assist the pope or a bishop in the exercise of his jurisdictional power and in the transaction of affairs connected therewith. There are various types of curia.

(a) ROMAN CURIA. By this is meant all the departments or organs which assist the sovereign pontiff in the government of the universal Church.

The Roman Curia consists, first of all, of the Sacred Congregations (*q.v.*), the Tribunals (Apostolic Penitentiary, Sacred Roman Rota, Apostolic Signature), and the Offices properly so-called (Apostolic Chamber, Apostolic Chancery, Apostolic Datary, Secretariat of State). All these departments or bureaus, each headed by a Cardinal Prefect or Cardinal Secretary, constitute the Holy See in the wide sense of the term (Can. 7). Moreover, the Roman Curia comprises the Pontifical Commissions, usually made up of cardinals, prelates, and experts charged with permanent or temporary responsibility for certain ecclesiastical affairs, under the personal direction of the pope. Also considered part of the Roman Curia is the administration of the property and goods of the Holy See.

Though at times included, the following are not a part of the Roman Curia: (1) the Vicarate of Rome and of Vatican City (*q.v.*), both of which correspond to a diocesan curia (*see* below), since their function is to assist the pope in matters pertaining to the diocese of Rome; (2) offices with functions related to the Vatican State but not directly connected with the Church government.

In a rudimentary form at first, but gradually becoming more complex, the Roman Curia has been in existence from the very beginning of the Church. Its present organization may be said to have originated with the Congregations of Cardinals instituted by Paul III in 1542, and especially with the constitution *Immensa* of Sixtus V (Jan. 22, 1588), by which the number and competency of the various Congregations was permanently determined. In more recent times, Pius X, through the constitution *Sapienti consilio* (June 29, 1908), brought about a significant reorganization of the Roman Curia. This reorganization, with some minor modifications, remains the same at the present time.

The term *Roman Curia*, as such, was not used before the thirteenth century, after which it came into frequent usage.

Since the various departments of the Roman Curia, with few rare exceptions, have always been in Rome, the expression *Roman Curia* (or simply *Curia*) was frequently employed to indicate the diocese or city of Rome. Instances of such usage are to be found even in the present day, when mention is made of a cardinal as a Curia cardinal (Cans. 237, par. 2; 238, par. 3); this refers to cardinals permanently residing in Rome, who may or may not have any official duty in the Roman Curia.

(b) DIOCESAN OR EPISCOPAL CURIA. The diocesan curia (chancery) consists of various administrative and judiciary offices, charged with the responsibility of the Ordinary or his representative in the government of the entire diocese. Similar to diocesan chanceries, though perhaps smaller in size, are those established in such territories as vicariates and prefectures apostolic, prelatures, or abbeys *nullius*.

The diocesan curia may be said to consist of two departments: administrative and judiciary.

The administrative department comprises: (a) *the vicar-general*, if appointed, the head of the curia, directly subject to the Ordinary; (b) the *chancellor*, who acts as archivist, and other notaries, who, if necessary, may also be laymen (Can. 372–384); (c) *synodal examiners* (*q.v.*) and *parochial consultors* (*see* Pastor). The judiciary department comprises: (a) *synodal* or *pro-synodal* judges, headed by the *officialis*, who may be assisted by one or more vice-officials (*see* Canonical judiciary organization); (b) the *promoter of justice and defender of the bond* (*see* Plaintiff, States Attorney); (c) the *notary* or *actuarius* (*see* Notary), who often is the chancellor himself; (d) *cursors* and *summoners*.

Although participating in the government of the diocese, the cathedral chapter (*see* Chapter) or the board of diocesan consultors is not a part of the diocesan curia.

(c) GENERAL CURIA. In many male religious orders, especially exempt clerical, there is a general curia, which is made up of the superior general and other religious charged with matters concerning the entire order. *Cip.*

CURIA, DIOCESAN. *See* Curia. Curia.

CURIA, ROMAN. *See* Curia.

CURIOSITY. *Curiosity,* as understood here, is meddlesomeness, or an inordinate desire for intellectual or sensitive knowledge.

In the sphere of intellectual knowledge, curiosity is manifested in many ways: by applying the mind to matters which are beyond one's capacity, or which are of no concern or benefit to one; by pursuing knowledge inopportunely, or with neglect of higher and more important duties; by seeking, without justifying cause, knowledge which may bring on temptations or place one in the danger of sinning; by reading a book too hurriedly without assimilating its content; by using improper means of gaining possession of certain information. All such instances may be described as curiosity of the mind. In the sphere of sensitive knowledge, curiosity may also be manifested in different ways: by seeking to see and hear things which are not of one's concern or which are useless and unprofitable; by seeking to see and hear things which are

likely to lead one into temptation. These and similar instances constitute curiosity of the senses. It is important to note that any application of the cognitive faculties must be accompanied by a right intention.

In itself, curiosity is but a venial sin; however, it may become a mortal sin in the following instances: (a) if it leads to a grave danger of falling into mortal sin; (b) if it causes neglect of an important duty; (c) if knowledge or information is sought through improper means; (d) if one seeks to achieve an end which is in serious conflict with the moral law.

Curiosity may be overcome by the practice of a certain degree of restraint and moderation in the exercise of one's faculties of seeing and hearing. He who seriously seeks salvation will endeavor to guard his eyes and turn a deaf ear to anything which is opposed to the Christian sense of modesty, charity, and other virtues. Considering the weaknesses of human nature and the many evil and unwholesome influences surrounding us, it is imperative that we at times curb and mortify the desire to know, see, and hear things. To succeed in this, we must discipline our cognitive faculties and train ourselves to guard and be discriminating in our attitudes, habits, and actions. In our associations with our fellowmen, we should strive to cultivate the art of directing the conversation to edifying, useful, or, at least, innocuous topics, without, however, giving the appearance of being prudish or overly serious. In our reading habits, we should be discriminating, selecting good books and wholesome literature. In studying, preference should be given to what is necessary and profitable, rather than to what is simply pleasing. Finally, even in the study and pursuit of spiritual matters, we should endeavor always to have a right and noble intention, and seek to improve our moral and spiritual life. *Man.*

CURRENCY, FORCED. *See* Economics, Finance.

CUSTODIAN, DEPOSITARY. A custodian is one entrusted with the charge of guarding and preserving an object, movable or immovable, animals or persons. Implied in such a notion is the idea of a contract of deposit: a mutual agreement between two parties regarding a certain object placed in deposit or custody. Hence, merely to place an object into a person's hands does not make him a custodian, but it is required that he consent at least tacitly.

The concept of custody does not consist, as some maintain, in the simple obligation of returning the object intact to the depositor, but primarily in guarding and preserving it; this, in turn, gives rise to the consequent obligation of returning the object to its lawful owner. Vigilance and preservation are strictly and mutually related to each other as means to end; the purpose of preservation, in substance, is to render the object available to the depositor whenever (ad nutum) he may request it.

OBLIGATIONS. The fundamental obligations of a custodian, therefore, are: (1) preservation of the deposited object, and (2) restitution upon request of the depositor. In guarding and preserving a deposited object, a custodian is gravely bound to exercise the same care that he would if the object were his own. A custodian is obliged to return a deposited object fully intact and on the day indicated; he may not damage or keep any part of it.

The obligations of a custodian, strictly speaking, are personal and are not as such binding upon his heirs. However, the heirs may be civilly responsible for the preservation and restitution of the object in custody, as well as for damages culpably caused to the depositor. A custodian has the right to examine and check beforehand the exact number and condition of the objects placed in his deposit or custody. Moreover, he is entitled to full payment of charges stipulated.

The problems which arise in connection with the function of custodian in its broad sense are manifold. (a) Soldiers appointed to guard frontiers must issue fair warning to all persons attempting to cross the border without authorization; only if such warnings goes unheeded are they permitted to fire on suspect persons. (b) Wardens of mountains, vineyards, orchards, forests, etc., are liable to all damages they could have averted but failed to, and are bound to manifest all facts and information wilfully withheld. (c) Prison wardens who advise and encourage prisoners to escape, who inflict inhuman and cruel treatment upon inmates, who fail to carry out just orders, who practice favoritism as a result of bribery or other remuneration, are liable to all damages ensuing from such culpable actions. (d) Custodians of small children, sick persons, house, flock or herd of animals, etc., are excused from the obligation of hearing Mass on Sundays and holy days, if they are unable to find a substitute to take their place. *Tar.*

CUSTODY OF THE HOLY EUCHARIST. The preservation of the Holy Eucharist consists in the reservation of the consecrated species in the tabernacle for (a) visits by the faithful (see Eucharistic Adoration); (b) distribution of Holy Communion (q.v.); (c) administration of Holy Viaticum to the dying (q.v.); (d) Eucharistic exposition and benediction (see Benediction of the Blessed Sacrament, Forty Hours).

In the early centuries of the Church, because of persecution, the Holy Eucharist was frequently kept in private homes, but this practice was later abolished to prevent a danger of profanation. In churches, the Blessed Sacrament was originally reserved in the *conditorium* (chest, or box), placed either in the sacristy, beneath the altar-table, or in a recess in the apse.

The practice of reserving the Blessed Sacrament on the altar originated in the eleventh century, at which time there arose the liturgical use of Eucharistic doves, suspended by a cord under the *tegurium* or *ciborium*. In the twelfth century the Eucharist was enshrined in a little "sacrament house" or Gothic tower placed in a recess of the wall, a short distance from the altar. The first real tabernacle was constructed and placed in the center of the main altar by G. Matteo Giberti (1495–1543), in the cathedral of Verona. There followed in the field of art a veritable iconography of tabernacles, to the point that the Popes, starting with Paul V, recommended the use of permanent tabernacles, and prescribed them as obligatory in Rome. It was not, however, until the year 1868 that the use of the tabernacle, already widespread, was made universally obligatory by a letter (Aug. 21, 1868) of the Sacred Congregation of Rites to the Bishop of Limburg, Germany.

Following the promulgation of the Code of Canon Law in 1917, reservation of the Blessed Sacrament was made obligatory in every cathedral church, in the principal church of an abbey or prelature *nullius*, and of a vicariate or prefecture apostolic, in every parochial or quasi-parochial church, and in a church attached to an exempt religious house, both of men and women (Can. 1265, par. 1, n. 1).

With permission of the local Ordinary, the Blessed Sacrament may be reserved in collegiate churches, in the principal oratory (public or semi-public) of pious or religious houses, and in the principal oratory of ecclesiastical colleges conducted by the secular clergy or by religious (Can. 1265, par. 1, n. 2).

For reservation of the Blessed Sacrament in other churches or oratories, an apostolic indult is required (Can. 1265, par. 2).

Churches wherein the Blessed Sacrament is kept must be open to the faithful for at least a few hours daily (Can. 1266). Moreover, wherever the Blessed Sacrament is reserved, the Code prescribes that there be a responsible person to guard it and that, as a rule, Mass be celebrated at least once a week (Can. 1265, par. 1).

Today, it is no longer permitted to keep the Holy Eucharist in private homes, nor in the interior of religious houses, nor within the choir or enclosure of nuns' convents (Can. 1267). It is forbidden to carry the Blessed Sacrament on one's person during a journey (Can. 1265, par. 3).

The Blessed Sacrament should be reserved habitually only in the tabernacle of one altar of the churches permitted to reserve it. Nor may the bishop dispense in this matter, except for the reason of nocturnal reservation in a more secure place (Can. 1269, par. 3). All contrary customs, even though centenary or immemorial, are abolished (Can. 1269, par 1). The normal place for reserving the Blessed Sacrament is the tabernacle of the main altar, unless another altar is more convenient and in keeping with the reverence and worship due to this great sacrament (Can. 1268, par. 2). In cathedral, collegiate, and conventual churches in which choral functions are conducted at the main altar, it is more convenient that the Blessed Sacrament be reserved at a side altar or in a side chapel.

The tabernacle should be permanent or fixed, to remove all danger of irreverence and profanation, and should be situated in the center of the altar. The practice of placing the tabernacle at the side of the altar or elsewhere may no longer be permitted.

The tabernacle should be securely closed on all sides, properly ornamented according to the liturgical laws, free of all other things except vessels containing the Blessed Sacrament, and zealously guarded so as to exclude all danger of sacrilegious profanation (Can. 1269, par 2). More detailed directions regarding methods of rendering the tabernacle safe are contained in the Instruction of the Sacred Congregation of the Sacrament of May 26, 1938 (AAS 30 [1938], 198-207).

The reverence due to the august Sacrament of the Altar requires that the tabernacle be artistically constructed. Without determining either the form or material the legislation of the Church prescribes (a) that the tabernacle have but one opening or door; (b) that the interior of the tabernacle be covered with white silk, be gold or silver plated, or at least gilded; (c) that the exterior of the tabernacle be covered with a tent-like veil or canopy. The material for the tabernacle veil is not specified; it may be of silk cotton, wool, hemp, or any other fabric. It must be white or the color prescribed by the Office of the day. A black veil is never permitted. On All Souls' Day and at Requiem functions, a violet or white veil is to be used. For exposition of the Blessed Sacrament, except when it follows immediately another function, a white veil is prescribed.

The use of the veil or canopy on any tabernacle containing the Blessed Sacrament is obligatory, even if the tabernacle is of gold, silver, or any other precious material. Nothing excuses from this obligation, except the physical or moral impossibility of obtaining such a veil or if the tabernacle is so constructed that it is impossible to veil it.

No other vessels, except ciboria and lunette containing the Blessed Sacrament, may be kept in the tabernacle. An empty ciborium, that has not yet been purified, may also be kept therein; but it is forbidden to reserve anything else in it; whether it be an empty ciborium that has been purified, holy oils, relics of the Cross or of the saints, keys, purificators, and the like.

Relics, images, flowers, etc., may be placed on either side of the tabernacle but not on top of it. No image or relics of saints may be placed before the door of the tabernacle, not even on the occasion of a saint's feast day. All contrary customs are condemned as an abuse.

According to the Code of Canon Law, the tabernacle itself must stand directly on the table of the altar and in the center. Only a small cross may be placed in the middle of the altar between the candlesticks, preferably outside the area of the tabernacle. If this cannot be conveniently done, it is permissible to place it on top of the tabernacle.

The key of the tabernacle in which the Blessed Sacrament is reserved must be most carefully guarded. This is a grave obligation of conscience on the part of the priest who has charge of the church or oratory (Can. 1269, par. 4). The key may be of gold, silver, or other metal. The obligation to guard the key of the tabernacle most diligently is a grave one, both by reason of the purpose of the law and its wording. Hence, any wilful negligence on the part of the priest responsible for the safekeeping of the key would constitute a grave sin. Moreover, such negligence is also punishable in the external forum (Constitution of the Congregation of the Sacraments). The custody of the tabernacle key is normally and *per se* committed to the rector of the church and oratory. He may either carry the key on his person, or keep it locked in the sacristy or in his room or other safe place.

Wherever the Blessed Sacrament is reserved, at least one lamp should burn continually. The lamp is to be placed somewhere in the vicinity of the altar, but not on the altar-table nor on the upper gradines of the altar. The lamp must be an olive-oil lamp; in extraordinary cases the Ordinary may permit other oils, preferably vegetable oils or beeswax. In the absence of any other kind of oil or beeswax, an electric light may be used (Decree 4334, Can. 1271). The sanctuary lamp, a richly significant symbol, serves as a sign and reminder to the faithful of the presence of the Blessed Sacrament. *Pal.*

CUSTODY OF THE HOLY LAND. *See* Holy Land.

CUSTOM, IMMEMORIAL. *See* Custom.

CUSTOM. A *custom* may be defined as an unwritten, objective law resulting from long practice in a community, at least with a tacit approval of the lawful authority. We speak here of ecclesiastical custom, which may have the force of law, if the following conditions are present: (a) the custom exists in a community, which is capable of enacting or, at least, possessing juridical norms; (b) it must result from free, public, and frequent actions of the same nature performed by its members with the intention of carrying out an obligation, and not simply for the purpose of edification, devotion, liberality, and the like; (c) it must be introduced for the common good; (d) it is legitimately prescribed, that is, it must have had the continuity demanded by law; Canon Law ordinarily requires a continuance of forty complete years (Can. 27 par. 1); (e) finally, it is approved by competent authority. Such approbation, not a requisite in civil law, is expressly required by the ecclesiastical law (Can. 25). It is sufficient that approbation be tacit; this is juridically presumed whenever the competent superior freely and knowingly refrains from opposing the custom. Besides express and tacit approbation, there is also a legal approbation, a form of express approval, which is present whenever the legislator antecedently approves by means of a law all customs that meet certain specified conditions (Can. 27).

In its extension, a custom may be *universal*, if it is followed everywhere, or *particular*, if followed in a specific territory or by certain communities of persons.

In its relation to the law, a custom may be *according to law, beyond the law*, or *against the law* (*secundum legem, praeter legem, contra legem*). From the standpoint of prescription or duration, a custom may be *ordinary* (lasting forty years), *centennial* (lasting one hundred years), *immemorial* (beyond the reach of memory, record, or tradition).

A custom *juxta legem* (in harmony with the law) represents the best interpretation of an existing statute or law (Can. 29). Before prescription, such a custom serves as a doctrinal interpretation of the law. After prescription, it is an authentic interpretation. A custom *praeter legem* (*beyond the law*), theoretically, has the force of a new law. However, in the present discipline, many matters are withdrawn from its sphere or scope (e.g., the introduction of new or additional irregularities, censures, matrimonial impediments, and the like). Finally, a custom *contra legem* (contrary to the law) abolishes entirely, or in part, an existing statute or law. A universal custom abrogates entirely, or partially, an existing universal law. A particular custom abolishes both a particular and a universal law, because a class or *genus* is abolished through the species (*generi per speciem derogatur*). Centennial and immemorial customs are removed from the scope of a law which excludes all contrary customs (Can. 27, par. 1).

Customs cease in the same manner as laws: intrinsically, if their content becomes morally illicit or publicly useless; extrinsically, by a contrary law or custom. A general law does not abolish particular customs, unless it is so specifically stated in the new law. Thus, any opposing law does not abolish centennial or immemorial customs, unless it is so specifically stated in the new law.

Similarly, a new custom abrogates an older contrary custom, if the two are absolutely irreconcilable. If this is not the case, an effort must be made to reconcile the two customs (*jura sunt amice concilianda*). Fel.

CYBERNETICS. *Cybernetics* (Greek, *kybernetes*—pilot) is a term given to a new science founded by Norbert Wiener, American mathematician and professor at M.I.T. Cybernetics studies the mechanisms which, in a pilot-like fashion, regulate or control activity and communication in machines.

By analogy to machines, certain physicists and biologists have attempted to reduce the study of all communication phenomena in organized structures to a common denominator or mathematical calculation. Thus an attempt has been made to establish a relation between machines and the nervous system, particularly the brain. This is precisely the subject of this article.

The fundamental mechanism at the basis of modern self-regulating machines, such as the electronic computer and the pilotless plane, is called *feedback*. According to certain authors, the nervous system, reduced to its most schematic functional expression, is also a sort of self-regulating machine, which, through impulses constantly going to and from the various organs and external environment, modifies the action of these organs and the entire organism, and thus contributes to maintaining the individual in the best biological condition.

Actually, man does possess a type of self-regulating machine in his vegetative nervous system, i.e., the part of the nervous system designed for the regulation of internal, vital functions, which is called the *autonomic* system. This term implies a concept of self-regulation or automatic regulation, independent of voluntary control. A clear example of how this exercises its own activity can be seen in the maintenance of the so-called *acid-base equilibrium*, which is fundamentally important to the normal functioning of man's organism. Any variation in the relation between oxydized and reduced ions, e.g., the accumulation of carbonic anhydride in the blood, stimulates a bulbar center, sending specific *impulses* to it, warning it of the disequilibrium. Thus stimulated, the bulbar center transmits stimuli to the spinal centers of the respiratory muscles, which, by accelerating their habitual movements, increase respiration and, thus, facilitate the elimination of excessive carbonic anhydride, until the bulbar center is notified that the physiological equilibrium between acid and basic valences has been restored.

A less pronounced but notable analogy with the self-regulating machine is found in the more simple processes of relational life, such as *automatic actions* (*see* Reflex) involved in our daily, habitual life. Analyzing one of these automatic acts or gestures (banishing a fly from the cheek while absorbed in reading), we notice that it involves elements of communication and control characteristic of the feedback in a self-regulating machine. As soon as the brain is warned, through afferent neurons, of the existence of a disturbing stimulus, a chain of processes is automatically set in motion to localize and evaluate the entity of said stimulus. If the stimulus, common or habitual, is a disturbing one, the brain almost automatically, without warning the higher faculties, which may be engaged in more important tasks (reading), transmits from its centers a series of impulses, which, by means of efferent neurons, stimulate the muscles into initiating the single movements, the sum total of which constitutes an act capable of routing the annoying fly. These orders are predisposed from the beginning but relayed one after another as the action is executed. It is to be further noted that, as soon as the muscles enter into action from the very beginning of the movement, they transmit *sensations* or *impulses* along the sensory paths to special centers designed to regulate the tonic muscular reflexes. By synchronizing the contraction or relaxation of the agonist and antagonist muscles of the extremity, they control the execution of the movement. At every step, therefore, of an automatic action, impulses and signals of every kind course throughout the organism. In the particular action we have been examining, the impulses are transmitted from the cheek to the cortex, from the cortex to the hand and vice versa. The sum total of impulses involved in an automatic action may be said to constitute a *feedback*, similar in many respects to that of a pilotless plane, whose course is constantly adjusted to the changing environmental conditions indicated by the instruments, according to a set of instructions previously fed into the plane.

The above-mentioned action and other rather simple automatic actions are ultimately reducible to a play of elementary reflexes, which can be analyzed to a certain point by cybernetic processes. But in no way does it follow that such an interpretation is valid in the case of psychical phenomena, which involve at least three distinct faculties: *memory*, to retain messages and other information; *associations*, to compare the new messages with those previously received and thus make them useful; *choice*, to select, among the numerous messages stored up, the one most useful in the present circumstances.

Cybernetics has endeavored to approximate or reproduce the more complex patterns of higher cerebral functions, by introducing the concept of *reactive circuits*, i.e., closed circuits in which signals or communications circulate continuously in the manner of an oscillating system with a specific rhythm. This is the system employed in modern electronic calculators or computers (also called *electronic brains*, because they perform tasks similar to those of the human brain). In order to utilize for further calculations the results of previous computations, these must be stored up for some time in the calculator, as if they were capable of memory. This is made possible precisely through the reactive circuits in which a signal (the result of an operation) circulates continuously, but always returns to the same point.

The analogy between some of these machines and certain properties of the nervous system has given rise to the boastful desire to create a mechanism capable of reproducing, along essential lines, the properties of the human brain.

Thus, in recent years the robot or *homeostat* (Ashby) and the *electronic snail* (Walter Grey) have been constructed. This latter, equipped with photoelectric cells, propulsive mechanisms, etc., moves toward the light, avoids obstacles and presents other aspects of animal behavior, which, at first sight, seem marvelous. However, such mechanisms lack variation, particularly variation of behavior encountered, when stimuli and situations *per se* indifferent become conditioned stimuli (*see* Conditioned Reflex). Of course, such mechanisms lack, above all, freedom.

Conclusions. Undoubtedly, there are in the human brain numerous and important processes, such as speech, writing, the portentous memory of certain phrenasthenics, which can be better understood with the aid of cybernetics. However, mechanical brains or similar machines are in no way comparable to the human brain. Indeed, the analogy between them and the human brain is only apparent, not only in structure, but in the nature of the output. It suffices to note that the 20,000 circuits of the most perfect computing machine occupy an enormous space when compared with the human cranium, in which there are many millions of neurons. In output, it is to be noted that the mechanical brain is limited to the logic of numbers, developed only in pre-established directions; whereas the human brain is endowed with consciousness, initiative, selection of actions, that are controlled and regulated by effective tonality. In short, the human brain possesses an almost infinite capacity for thought and progress. Hence, between the mechanical and the human brain there is an unbridgeable chasm. Mechanical brains can only put out what is put into them, as it is properly recorded by a human mind. Hence, whatever is produced by machines is always due to human ideation. Thought is completely outside the reach of mechanical contrivances, though these may be advantageously used as instruments of work.

It is to be sincerely hoped, however, that cybernetics will some day enable scientists to acquire an insight into the meanderings of the cerebral function, for a better understanding of neuro-physiological and neuro-pathological problems. *Riz.*

CYCLE, ECONOMIC. The economic life of a nation is subject from time to time to alternating phenomena of various durations. These are commonly divided into: (a) alternations of brief duration, brought about by occasional factors, such as price fluctuations due to accidental market conditions; (b) periodic alternations which resolve themselves in the course of the year, or are caused by seasonal factors; (c) alternations of a cyclic duration of an average period of four to nine years; (d) alternations lasting much longer. The latter cannot be properly studied except within the framework of economic history. Occasional fluctuations are susceptible of statistical observation, but not of a particular study. Seasonal oscillations can be statistically estimated, but economic science is little concerned with them. Cyclic alternations, instead, in view of their regularity and importance, offer the economists a challenge to find a theoretical explanation for them; they have thus become decisively a phase of economic dynamics.

So-called economic crises constitute a phase of cyclic alternations characterized by conditions of expansion and recession in economic activity; these occur with apparent regularity in industrial countries. The actual duration of this cyclic phase admits of no consensus of opinions. It is variously estimated to last anywhere from four to nine years; economists believe that in the modern world the periods of cyclic alternations have definitely become shorter.

Theories of Economic Cycles. The numerous theories offered to explain economic cycles may be classified into two categories. The first category embraces all those theories which tend to stress factors external to the economic system, from the theory of the periodic cycle of the sun spots (according to which, sun spots create metereological conditions which determine the extent and quality of crops, and thereby affect all business conditions), to the theory which explains the cycle of prosperity and depression in terms of social optimism and pessimism (psychological theory). The second category includes strictly economic theories, based on errors of predictions, intrinsic to long cycles of capitalistic production; the special potentialities which bank deposits possess in respect to such production; structural deficiencies in consumption and investments which appear with the increase of the national income; or a combination of these various elements.

In the past, economic cycles were regarded as inevitable phenomena, against which nothing could be done. More modern theories, on the contrary, are devoted to the elaboration of anti-cyclic programs, designed to shorten depressions or eliminate them altogether. Such an objective is not only morally licit, but also socially desirable. *Mai.*

CYCLE, EMOTIONAL. *See* Affectivity.

CYCLE, LITURGICAL. *See* Liturgical Year.

CYCLOTHYMIA. *Cyclothymia* (Greek, *kuklos*—circle, cycle; *thumos*—mood, spirit) is a psychiatric term, which is used to indicate a specific type or temperament characterized by light periodic changes of humor, from excited to depressed, and vice versa. Such fluctuation of moods occurs in many individuals, independently of external events or inner motives, in complete contrast to the actual environmental circumstances. Cyclothymia may be described as a lighter form of dysthymia or manic-depressive psychosis (dysthymic psychosis, circular insanity, affective psychosis). For a fuller treatment of the subject, *confer* Dysthymia, for between cyclothymia and dysthymia there is merely a difference of quantity. Many authors do not accept this distinction with a somewhat scholastic flavor, but use the two terms interchangeably.

It should here be noted that there are no recognizable boundaries between dysthymia and cyclothymia, just as there are no boundaries between fluctuations of mood occurring in cyclothymic individuals and unmotivated fluctuations occasionally experienced even by normal persons.

Apropos of the latter observation, it should be mentioned that, according to Kretschmer's theory, widely accepted in modern psychiatry, there exists a *cyclothymic temperament* (roughly corresponding to the definition given above), characterized by a ready and intense response to environment (*syntony*), by facile and vivid emotional reactions and by frequent, not always motivated, fluctuations of mood. To this, Kretschmer opposes the *schizothymic* temperament, characterized by scarce affective response to environmental circumstances, a tendency toward introspection and inner life, and stability of mood.

Cyclothymic and schizothymic elements are presumably found in all normal individuals, although in different proportions, which readily accounts for the temperamental differences existing among individuals.

Such temperamental elements and differences are to be taken into account in the moral evaluation of human actions. *Riz.*

CYCLOTHYMIC TEMPERAMENT. *See* Cyclothymia.

D

DAIRY PRODUCTS. *See* Abstinence, Fasting.

DALMATIC. *See* Sacred Vestments.

DAMAGE. According to the Roman jurist Paulus, the word *damage* is derived *ab ademptione et quasi diminutione patrimonii dicta est.* But more properly the origin of the word is to be found in these roots: *dap* (to violate), *dabh* (to destroy), *dan* (to lose). Damage "is the privation of a thing which belongs to us, caused independently of our will, and in a manner which makes the thing irretrievable" (Volfio). This notion includes any diminution of either the material or spiritual well-being or goods of an individual, as, for example, his reputation.

Civil jurists admit only two forms of damage: penal and civil. By the first, they mean that damage which is inherent in every crime punished by law; by the second, they mean that damage which is satisfied by means of a fine. Civil codes generally do not admit the fact of moral damage. The concept of damage in civil codes is specific in nature, essentially material, physical, and natural; for this theoretical definitions, nor with the civil theoretical definitions, nor with the civil-moral notion of damage, but is limited to *damnum datum* (damage inflicted) by means that are material and externally and physically noticeable. Likewise, common jurisprudence does not recognize as damage the preventing of a person from enjoying a thing to which he has a right. The ethico-moral field is much wider, since it extends to the realm of the spirit, as, for instance, to the damage resulting from bad example, prevention from the attainment of a benefit to which one has a right, etc. These are titles or damages which according to the moral law must be repaired or compensated for.

In ancient legislations, damage as a willful offense against other people's property and without personal gain for the offender was looked upon rather as a private crime and punished by a fine. Only in the more serious cases of common peril was it considered a crime in the modern sense. Modern legislation, in establishing the crime of damage, has followed different systems: some judge it on the basis of the means by which the destruction or the damage was wrought; others on the basis of the motive; others, finally, on the basis of the value of the objects destroyed or damaged. With regard to aggravating circumstances, some are common to all codes of law, others vary from one code to another. In general, however, the great majority of modern laws regard damage as a special crime characterized by a connotation of fraud and bearing upon a thing which belongs, at least partially, not to the criminal but to others. In practice, however, the connotation of damage is restricted to a terminology which implies "destroying, deteriorating or rendering unusable" a real property or other type possession belonging to another, taking the term *damage* as a synonym of a reparable damage. Thus, it is something quite distinct from the simple unfulfilled obligation; it becomes something more than that, and indicates a diminution of the patrimony of another brought about by a personal and free act. In order that damage may be such, both in its juridical and moral acceptance, it is necessary that it be caused by a free agent and not by natural causes, such as floods, lightning, etc. The essential element must be an actual diminution of possession (taken in its wide meaning) due to a cause imputable to an individual. Moreover, the fact causing the damage may be positive or negative, or, if you will, active or passive. The damage sustained may consist of a real loss or a failure to reap a gain, which in forensic language is described as *damnum emergens* or *lucrum cessans* (actual loss or failure to gain). These gains must be such as would have been obtained, were it not for the action of the criminal. Hence, civil codes speak of *damages and interests*.

OBLIGATION OF REPARATION. The basis upon which the obligation rests for the criminal to repair the damage inflicted, is the unlawfulness of the act by which he caused it. Whoever acts by virtue of a right is not responsible for any damage which may result to another from his act. If, however, the unlawfulness of the act is well established, a person is responsible for the damage caused, not only if it results from a personal action fraudulently or culpably placed, but also from his negligence or imprudence. Likewise, an individual is responsible not only for damage caused by his own action, but also (1) by the actions of persons or animals in his charge or responsibility, as in the case of a father, a teacher, a master, a guardian; or (2) by the action of animals which are in his custody, as in the case of the owner or caretaker of an animal, or of one who may be using the animal or who used it while the damaging action was taking place. In a case where the action was the result of a crime, then, besides reparation for the original damage, criminal or correctional penalties are also to be applied according to the seriousness of the crime. But if it is a queston of facts which civil law considers as "quasi-crimes," then they are punishable by fines inflicted by law-enforcing officers, since in penal legislation those actions are considered as simple transgressions of the law. On the contrary, if it is a question which does not affect the public order, then the author of the damage is only held to the reparation of the damage done.

DAMNUM EMERGENS ET LUCRUM CESSANS. Under the aspect of *damnum emer-*

gens and *lucrum cessans* it must be kept in mind that agreements (contracts, loans, etc.) oblige not only as to the terms expressed in the contract but also as to the consequences which natural equity (therefore justice taken in its strict and altruistic sense), customs, and law contribute to the obligation, according to its nature. The most important of these effects is precisely the repairing of the damage and the payment to the creditor of interest owed by the debtor. This obligation arises from justice itself. Besides the damage, therefore, the debtor must also pay the interest on account of his delay in satisfying his obligation. Thus, if failure to fulfill or delay in satisfying an obligation is caused by fraud or negligence on the part of the debtor, there arises the obligation to pay for the damage plus the interest owed to the creditor both for the loss he suffered and for the gain he failed to realize. Let it be noted, however, that in the absence of fraud, the debtor is obliged in conscience (before any judiciary action) to pay only for the damage and the interest which were foreseen, or which were foreseeable at the time of the contract. On the contrary, if failure to fulfill is due to fraud by the debtor, he must repair the real, not the hypothetical damage. On the other hand, if the delay or the total failure to fulfill is due to accident or to a cause beyond the debtor's control, the latter is not obliged to pay for the damage and the interest, on the basis of the axiom: *casum nemo praestat*, that is, no one controls accidents. (L. 23ff. *De reg. Jur.*) The title to *lucrum cessans* and *damnum emergens*, provided that it be real and true, is a morally just title to the exaction of a rate of interest on a loan greater than usual (Cf. Billuart, *De contr. diss.* IV, a.5). *Tar.*

D'ANNIBALE, CARDINAL GIUSEPPE. A moral theologian of the nineteenth century, Cardinal D'Annibale was called the Tacitus of moral theology because of his qualities of style, exposition, and language, reminiscent of the great Roman historian. Born at Borbona (Rieti), September 22, 1815, he was ordained a priest September 21, 1839. He devoted himself to the study of moral theology following his appointment in 1851 as a teacher of that subject at the Rieti Seminary. To this field he brought a background of culture in Roman and civil law, although it was only in 1852 that he obtained a doctorate in both civil and Canon Law (*in utroque iure*). Actually, he was a self-taught man. He was appointed Vicar-Capitular and then Vicar-General of the Rieti Diocese and on August 1, 1881, Titular Bishop of Caristo. In Rome he became canonist of the Sacred Penitentiary, Consultor (April 25, 1883), and then Assessor of the Holy Office and Canon of St. Peter. In the consistory of February 11, 1889, he was nominated Cardinal and shortly thereafter appointed Prefect of the Sacred Congregation of Indulgences. He died July 17, 1892, at Borbona.

Works. His first work (1873), *In Constitutionem Apostolicae Sedis Commentarii*, published at Rieti, was very well received and went through several editions. But his principal work is the *Summula Theologiae Moralis* on which he labored for twenty years. The first volume appeared in Rieti in 1874, the second in 1875, and the third in 1876. The last two editions (4th and 5th) appeared after his death. To the last one (1907–1908) a *Supplementum* was also added by Domenico Mannaioli, Bishop of Montefiascone and formerly professor of moral theology at the Roman Seminary (Rome, 1909). Unfortunately, an adaptation of the work to the Code of Canon Law and the modern codes of civil law is still desired. The condensation of the subject matter, the abundance of footnotes, and the excessive brevity of form make the reading of the work rather difficult. Often the thought of the author is clearer than the actual phrase. Thus the work would seem to be more useful to teachers than to students. But the accuracy of its conclusions, and the harmony achieved between moral theology and law, particularly in *De iustitia et iure*, have earned the *Summula* enormous authority among theologians and canonists, in the Congregations, the Tri-

bunals, the Offices, and in teaching circles. (Cf. A. Vermeersch, *Cinquant' anni di Teologia Morale,* Milan, 1930, p. 4.)

In the Rotal sentences handed down from 1909 to the present day, perhaps no theologian or canonist, including Pihring, Reiffenstuel, De Luca, and Schmalzgrueber, is more often quoted than Cardinal D'Annibale. With the exception of some positions abandoned today (a modified equiprobabilism, the lawfulness of embryotomy, etc.), even today D'Annibale is one of the most authoritative teachers in the field of moral theology. *Pal.*

DATARY (APOSTOLIC). An Italian word from late medieval Latin, *datary* is the name given to one of the four offices of the Roman Curia. It has charge over everything related to the distribution of minor benefices, except their conferral which is reserved to the Holy See. The Datary is in charge of the Cardinal Datario, who is assisted by a Substitute-Datario or by a Regent, and by several clerks.

The origin and the name of this office is derived from the custom introduced at the time of the Western Schism of entrusting a definite person (*Datario*) with the task of affixing the date on Papal Letters. The duties of the *Datario* and of the Datary were, however, eventually increased to include even the matter of granting dispensations from matrimonial impediments. Since 1908, its competence has been limited to its present sphere of activities. *Cip.*

DATIO IN SOLUTUM. See Bankruptcy.

DAUGHTER-IN-LAW. See Affinity.

DEAF-MUTISM. Deaf-mutism is a grave condition caused by congenital or prematurely (before the age of seven) acquired deafness which, in turn, causes mutism.

In approximately half the cases, deaf-mutism is almost exclusively due to deafness; wholly degenerative and hereditary in nature, it occurs as a recessive characteristic (in the Mendelian sense). These constitute the cases which are more susceptible to training. In the other half of the cases, deaf-mutism is due to cerebral lesions which cause not only deafness, but also an obvious mental deficiency, and in these instances susceptibility to training is limited or nonexistent.

When deafness is acquired after birth, in infancy, the speech faculty undergoes a more or less rapid involution to the point of disappearance. But if the auricular disturbance that caused deafness clears up, speech may also be recovered. At any rate, the acquired form of deaf-mutism is the most susceptible to education and training.

To determine deaf-mutism, it is not necessary that deafness be complete; partial deafness suffices, that is, deafness to a notable portion of the tonal scale. Thus, certain deaf-mutes are able to perceive noises and even some musical sounds, but are unable to speak.

TRAINING OF DEAF-MUTES. A deaf-mute is mute, not because of defective speech organs, but solely because of deafness. In other words, mutism is the result of deafness. This is confirmed by the fact that a pure and simple deaf-mute (that is, one not affected also by some psychical deficiency or phrenasthenia) may learn to speak through an adequate training course in which other stimuli are substituted for auditory stimuli. Visual, tactile, and mechanical stimuli are sometimes capable of arousing the activity of the speech centers.

In the works of Pliny and St. Augustine the fact is vaguely mentioned that in ancient times some attempt had been made to instruct deaf-mutes. But the credit for having laid the foundation and, to a large extent, for having solved the problem concerning the training of deaf-mutes, belongs to the Spanish Benedictine Father Ponce (1520–1584). His method consisted in writing out the words and then illustrating them by means of corresponding visual images or aids. Thus, by a patient substitution of

visual for auditory stimuli, he was able to drill his pupils in pronouncing first the single letters, then the syllables and, finally, the words. In this manner he succeeded in teaching deaf-mutes to speak. This *oral method* was later supplanted, especially in France, by the easier and faster mimetic or *manual method*, which, however, has the disadvantage, among other things, of preventing conversation between deaf-mutes and those who can hear. Fathers De l'Epée (1716–1789), Deschamps (1745–1791) and Sicard (1746–1822), who dedicated themselves entirely to the training of deaf-mutes, were recognized as the apostles of this French school, which attracted a number of philanthropists desirous of learning the method and spreading it in their own countries. Among these is to be mentioned Father Silvestri, who in 1748 opened a school for deaf-mutes in Rome. Almost simultaneously, the German S. Heilicke made extensive application of the *oral method*, which in the meantime had been developed and improved upon by another German, Ammon; from that time on, this method became the most commonly used in the training of deaf-mutes.

JURIDICAL AND MORAL QUESTIONS. According to modern legal systems deaf-mutes are generally divided into two categories insofar as penal imputability or responsibility is concerned: the first category consists of those who are not liable for their actions, because they lack the mental and volitional capacity; the second category consists of those in whom imputability is reduced, because the person's intentional and volitional capacity is greatly diminished. Obviously, the first category includes deaf-mutes who are also phrenasthenic, while the second includes ordinary deaf-mutes, who, as previously noted, may be more easily educated. The moral evaluation of the actions of deaf-mutes may be established along these same lines. It is to be noted that moral imputability is based not on presumption, but on fact.

In Canon Law deaf-mutism has a bearing on the reception of the sacraments, particularly penance and matrimony, and on the application of penal law. Concerning this aspect, deaf-mutism constitutes a diminishing or wholly excusing circumstance, according as the crime is more or less grave (Can. 2218, par. 1–2).

Concerning the sacraments, deafness may also be a cause of incapacity to receive them, if the capacity to understand or to will is lacking. In any event, baptism is always to be conferred. The sacrament of holy orders, if conferred, would be valid. If ability to sin is assumed, penance and extreme unction are to be conferred. Wherein penance is concerned, however, deafness is a cause excusing from material integrity; hence a deaf-mute may not be obliged to write out his sins (the partially deaf person, on the other hand, is obliged, generally speaking, to confess in a specially designated place). Confirmation and Communion are to be conferred if the deaf person has sufficient capacity to understand and to will.

In matrimonial matters canonists, adhering to the clinical reality of the facts, usually divide deaf-mutes into three main categories: (a) Deaf-mutes who have become such in adult age (obviously as a result of distinct lesions of speech and hearing organs, for deafness alone, especially in adults, is not enough to cause mutism), who possess the knowledge of the nature and meaning of marriage and are perfectly capable of contracting marriage. (b) Deaf-mutes from birth or from infancy who have been trained also are generally permitted to contract marriage. (c) Deaf-mutes from birth or from infancy lacking the necessary instruction: these, according to some scholars, are to be considered capable of contracting marriage, unless the contrary is proven; according to others, they are to be presumed legally incapable of marriage until otherwise proven.

In practice, each case is to be judged and decided on its own merits, so that having examined all the facts in the case, the nature of the disturbance, the natural capacity of the individual to understand and to will, it will be possible to determine whether the subject is sufficiently aware of the nature and meaning of marriage.

A deaf-mute can gain the indulgences attached to public prayer by raising his heart and mind to God and by joining the faithful assembled in prayer; for the gaining of private indulgences, mental recitation of prayer is sufficient (Can. 936). *Riz.*

DEATH. Death is the cessation of life in the body due to the separation of the soul from the body. A being not composed of body and soul cannot die, such as angels and the soul itself. This separation of the soul from the body cannot lawfully be brought about by man upon himself or another. Death, caused by acts which directly bring about such changes in the body that it is no longer suited for living, thus depriving the body of such dispositions *directly*, is termed direct murder, although death itself occurs after a period of time as a consequence of such an act.

Death may be accidental or natural, depending on the cause which produced it. Internal causes such as disease or old age produce natural death; external causes such as falls, injuries, natural disasters, or another person produce accidental death. When death is due to a free agent, whether oneself or another person, it is termed violent death, either suicide or murder.

Death may be real or apparent. An apparent death is a state in which no signs of life are present, though the person is in fact living; at times, one may be conscious of events and persons around him. Such apparent death is sometimes termed a state of intermediate death; this state admits of the possible return to life of such a person through his own natural powers of recovery or by the intervention of another through heart massages, artificial respiration, or other means. In this state of intermediate death, life is to be presumed as probable in that brief span of time from the moment in which a person is believed dead until death actually occurs with the departure of the soul from the body. Such a period of time may extend from a few moments to a length of three or more hours. There are weighty reasons for believing such a state exists, in which one is considered dead without actual death occuring, although death generally follows irrevocably.

MORAL DOCTRINE. From what is known about death in the apparent sense, a grave duty is incumbent on all persons, especially physicians, to ascertain with certainty the presence of real death before funeral arrangements are made. The following are definite signs of death: (1) signs of decay in the body; (2) steady and quick cooling of body temperature until it reaches that of room temperature; (3) verification of the absolute absence of heart beat; (4) absence of muscular contractions, ascertained with appropriate instruments; (5) cadaveric rigidity (see Thanatology). Without these positive signs an apparently dead person must be treated as living; hence anything harmful must be avoided until a positive medical diagnosis and certification is completed.

The probability of intermediate death makes licit and, at times, obligatory the conditional administration of the sacrament of penance and extreme unction, during the four or five hours immediately following the time of death. Such an administration is always licit and often a duty, as long as there is a reasonable objective possibility of life in the person. Relatives and others may cause grave spiritual harm to the sick person by failure to summon the priest because they believe death to have occurred. For that reason one should summon the priest even though death seems to have occurred. (See Acceleration of Death; Euthanasia; Last Things; Deceased; Thanatology.) Ben.

DEATH, DESIRE FOR. Although man is not permitted to dispose of his own life, he is not obliged to desire to continue living. In view of the hope for a greater good in the future life, man may desire to die. A Christian who longs for death shows by his desire to be with God a full understanding of his faith (Phil. 1:23). Because of advanced age or disability, a man, unable to work, might understandably desire to leave the world, rather than languish here and undergo the difficulties of old age. In itself this is not unlawful, although it is more meritorious to endure in a spirit of atonement all the difficulties of life with complete acceptance and abandonment to the dispositions of the Divine Will. *Pal.*

DEBATE. *See* Disputation.

DEBT. (Latin, *debitum*—due, owed.) A debt is a promise or guarantee, in justice, concerning an obligation assumed by one toward another. Debts are real, personal, contractual, and arising from crime.

In the case of real debts, that is, when the property of another is held as deposit, rent, loan, or because of theft, etc., it must be returned to its owner in its entirety, and in the condition in which the real right of the owner requires it to be. If the thing no longer exists in its individuality, but only in its equivalent, the owner does not enjoy a greater privilege over the other creditors. As to personal debts, privileged debts (judiciary, funeral, and medical expenses, salaries of domestics, etc.) have priority over other obligations. Hypothecary debts must be paid in the order in which they were recorded. Debts with onerous title have priority over those with gratuitous title. It is not proven that debts arising from crime have a preference over contractual debts. Restitution of things belonging to known owners must precede that of things belonging to dubious owners. In case of bankruptcy (*q.v.*) the order set by the law or court must be followed.

As long as a relationship exists between creditor and debtor concerning a thing to which one has a title and the other is in debt, it is forbidden to use any subterfuge to escape paying the debt (prescription requires that good faith be present during the entire period of the prescription). If the matter is light the sin is simply venial, except when the conditions in which the creditor finds himself are such as to make the matter grave or the debtor (through erroneous conscience) may consider it grave. Unjustly to postpone the payment of a debt increases the seriousness of the sin, if it results in a damage to the creditor. For the payments of debts in inflated currency, see Loan. Sir.

DECALOGUE. (Ten Commandments.) The Decalogue (Greek, deka—ten, logos—word) is a summary of ten moral precepts, proposed in very brief but pregnant formulae and found, almost in identical forms, in two places in the Bible: Exodus 20:1–17, and Deuteronomy 5:6–21. God, the Almighty gave these, inscribed by His Hand upon two stone tablets (Exod. 34:27), to Moses on Mount Sinai (Arabia) for the people of Israel. In the texts now extant, we find some variation concerning the order of some of the precepts.

The Bible speaks of two tablets but makes no mention of the exact number on each table of the Ten Commandments. There are two opinions: one, basing itself on their number, divides the commandments into five for each tablet; the other, using content as a norm, divides them into three for one one tablet and seven for the other: the first three covering the obligations toward God, the other seven covering the obligations toward one's neighbor. To this we may add also the division into four and six, because even among those who use the criterion based on content there are two schools, or traditions, according to whether they consider the precept forbidding the making of graven images and the worshipping of idols as one with the precept commanding the worship of God alone, or as two separate and distinct precepts. In the first case we would have a division of the Ten Commandments as followed by Catholics and many other Christians, ending with two distinct commandments concerning internal sins

(sins of desire). In the second case, we would have four commandments concerning man's obligations toward God, with the commandment "Honor thy father and thy mother" as the fifth, and ending with the coveting of a neighbor's wife and a neighbor's goods under one commandment. The latter form is common in many Eastern Churches and among the Calvinists in the West. Other religious groups follow the Catholic enumeration, and Catholics in turn follow St. Augustine. Thus, when a Calvinist speaks of the seventh commandment, he refers to "Thou shalt not commit adultery"; whereas Catholics and others would have in mind "Thou shalt not steal."

With the exception of the prohibition against graven images and statues, and the precept concerning the observance of the Sabbath as the Day of the Lord, the content of the Ten Commandments is a part of natural law. They repeat, inculcate, give new force to the precepts which every man knows by virtue of his natural understanding. If God had not given the Decalogue on Mount Sinai, man would still be expected to live by its commandments, in which some acts are prescribed, others are forbidden, according as they are good or bad; they are not good or bad because they are prescribed or forbidden. Their promulgation and presence in the Bible has contributed very much to the preservation of the correct and exact knowledge of these laws, so very important not only in themselves but also because they are the basis of many other moral precepts which can easily be derived from them. More or less extensive sections of the Decalogue are found in the laws of other peoples, both civilized and primitive. No people, however, had moral laws as perfect and as highly developed as the Hebrew people. The principal points in which the Decalogue excels by far the legislations of all other peoples are the following: monotheism (belief in one God), the doctrine of God's awesome majesty and boundless goodness, and the extension of moral obligations which reach down to even the most intimate and hidden acts, such as desires. Given to a chosen people, they transcend all national elements, and apply to all humanity for all times, even after the abrogation of the Hebrew religion with the advent of the New Testament. The Decalogue is not a summary of the entire natural moral law. The division of moral law along the lines of the Ten Commandments is a relatively recent and certainly very inadequate method. It produces unsatisfactory results, for it leads to placing under the various commandments elements which have but an exterior and often superficial relationship with them—for example, to treat under the fourth commandment, "Honor thy father and thy mother," the obligations of parents, or even of employers toward their employees. The Ten Commandments are undoubtedly an excellent aid in making a good examination of conscience, although it is not sufficient to examine oneself only on the Ten Commandments. To memorize the Ten Commandments in the order and according to the text found in the catechism, though not an obligation, is certainly befitting a Christian. *Ben.*

DECEASED. *The Christian Concept.* St. Paul, speaking of the deceased, *i.e.,* of those who have gone into eternity, admonishes: "Brethren, we would not have you ignorant concerning those who are asleep lest you should grieve, even as others who have no hope. For if we believe that Jesus died and rose again, so with him God will bring those also who have fallen asleep through Jesus" (1 Thess. 4:13–14). Thus, those who die to this life are living insofar as God and men are concerned. With death, the dissolution of the body is effected, but the soul of man lives on because it is immortal. In fact it cannot cease to exist because of a disintegration of parts, since the soul is a spiritual and indivisible entity, capable of living and operating independently of the body. Nor can it cease to exist because of annihilation, since the power of annihilation belongs to God alone as Creator.

Upon separation from the body, souls reach different destinations: those who die while in full possession of grace, which is the source of glory, are admitted forever into the joy of the beatific vision; those, on the other hand, who die without possessing such grace, are excluded forever from eternal happiness. Those who, while in God's grace, are yet in need of being purified (by paying the debt of temporal punishment due to sin) are detained in Purgatory, where through satisfaction they will earn admittance to the infinite joy of possessing God.

The immortality of the soul explains the cult of the dead in the course of the centuries, a cult which is found not only among the civilized but also the primitive peoples of the world. In the Christian era, from the beginning of the Church, the cult was supernaturalized by Christian teachings. Thus, besides the Divine Sacrifice, which according to Tertullian (*P. L.* 2, 99) was offered for the dead ever since the beginning of the Christian era, the funereal agapes celebrated in behalf of the dead are worth mentioning. St. Paulinus of Nola praised Senator Pammachius, who, on the occasion of the burial of Paulina his wife, had spent the money required for the useless burial rite to feed a famished crowd of indigents whom he had gathered in St. Peter's Basilica. Confirmation of this is found in the funeral epigraphy of the first centuries which reports the prayers offered beside the corpse and at the graveside of the dead by the faithful or by the priest or deacon during the celebration of the Divine Sacrifice offered for the repose of souls. Ever since those early days, the Church has ceaselessly maintained great solicitude for her children who have passed into eternity. A daily remembrance is made of them in her public and official prayer (the Divine Office) by the kindly plea to the mercy of God, "May the souls of the faithful departed through the mercy of God rest in peace." On all the altars in the world, the Divine Sacrifice is offered daily for the living and the dead. A special Memento for the dead is made following the consecration in every Mass. Since the tenth century the faithful offer special prayers throughout the month of November of every year in behalf of all departed brethren. To aid spiritually the innumerable souls of those who died during the First World War, His Holiness Benedict XV, by the Apostolic Constitution *Incruentum altaris* of August 10, 1915 (AAS 7 [1915], 401), granted to all priests the privilege of celebrating three Holy Masses on November 2nd, the day dedicated to all the faithful departed. This privilege was added to another important one, by which a plenary indulgence may be gained *toties quoties* (every time one visits a church on All Souls Day), applicable exclusively to the souls of the departed (AAS 6 [1914], 378).

RELATIONSHIP BETWEEN THE LIVING AND THE DEAD. All these proofs of motherly solicitude by the Church toward her departed children are a definite reminder that a precise duty of love toward them is incumbent on everyone. After expounding the doctrine on the existence of Purgatory, and on the effectiveness of our prayers in behalf of the souls detained therein, the Council of Trent makes an urgent appeal to the bishops to promote piously and devoutly the use of such aids as Holy Masses, prayers, alms, and other devotional practices (Session XXV). The manner in which such aids can best be applied to our departed brethren and the practical way by which people on earth can live in intimate loving communion with them is found in the consoling doctrine of the Communion of Saints, which teaches us that men, pilgrims on earth (the Church Militant), the souls in Purgatory, craving for the possession of God as their Supreme Good (the Church Suffering), and the Blessed already in the possession of the Beatific Vision of God (the Church Triumphant), all constitute one Church, that is, one body of which Jesus Christ is the Head and the faithful are the members, intimately united by the bond of charity, each having a title to the spiritual goods of the community as belonging to himself and applicable to the welfare of each (1 Cor. 12:12–26). In virtue of this community of spiritual treasure the faithful on earth are enabled to offer aid to their brethren in Purgatory and glory to the blessed in Heaven. This charity in behalf of their departed brethren is all the more incumbent on the faithful on earth as one realizes that their souls detained in Purgatory, by a decree of Divine Justice, are unable, of themselves, to alleviate their sufferings or shorten the time of their expiation, and are waiting for any possible aid which might hasten the day of their possessing God as their supreme and only joy.

This charity is most pleasing to God because God loves with a particular love these souls redeemed by the blood of Jesus Christ and sanctified by the grace of the Holy Spirit. St. Thomas Aquinas does not hesitate to state that prayer for the departed is more acceptable to God than prayer for the living, because the departed cannot help themselves while the living can (Supp. 3, q. 71, a. 5). On the other hand, the souls of those who are in Heaven, the kingdom of peace and love, glorified by the Church Militant by virtue of the sweet communion of the supernatural treasure, will not fail to present to God through the efficacy of this intimate communion in supernatural treasures, their pleas and petitions in behalf of their brethren, pilgrims on this earth. The souls in Purgatory, too, aided by their prayers, will surely pray for their benefactors once they have reached Heaven. And while they cannot gain merit for themselves while members of the Church Suffering, they can certainly intercede for others (as the majority of modern theologians believe) by virtue of the bond of charity which unites them with the Church Militant and the Church Triumphant. Among the many reasons for comfort which the remembrance of the departed raises in all human souls is the consoling truth contained in the words of the Preface of the Mass of the Dead: "For unto Thy faithful, O Lord, life is changed, not taken away: and the abode of this earthly sojourn being dissolved, an eternal dwelling is prepared in heaven." *de A.*

DECEIT. *See* Dissimulation, Simulation, Truth, Prudence, Lying.

DECLARATIONS (of the Sacred Congregations). The interpretations by the Sacred Roman Congregations of doubts concerning ecclesiastical laws are called declarations. Their value is dependent upon their form and content. They can be classified as follows:

FORMALLY PARTICULAR declarations are contained in decisions concerning particular cases, particular rescripts, and all other acts regarding particular cases. These declarations, though juridical and authentic, do not constitute a norm of general law, but they have the value of law in respect to the parties to whom they are directed. Actually, they are but applications of general laws to particular cases and are subject to the particular circumstances of each individual case. Uniform and constant declarations can, however, become a matter of real jurisprudence to be applied as common norms in similar cases.

DECLARATIONS EQUIVALENTLY GENERAL are contained in those acts issued as the result of doubts submitted by one or more persons or applying to one particular place. The answers or declarations are, however, of a general character because the doubts were proposed in a general manner. Hence, as to their form, the place to which they apply, and the persons to whom they are directed, they are of a particular nature; although insofar as their effect is concerned, they are general, because the subject they deal with is of a general nature. Therefore, even the declaration constitutes a binding norm for all. It follows, then, that this interpretation or declaration need not be promulgated if it concerns laws which are certain; but if it clarifies laws which are obscure or extends or restricts the application of a law, it must be promulgated in order to be binding upon all; otherwise they would bind only one or a few.

FORMALLY GENERAL declarations answer general doubts in a general way; the act itself is formulated in a general manner. In this case they constitute a norm which is binding upon all, following its promulgation. *Toc.*

DECREE. IN ROMAN LAW AND IN MODERN CIVIL LAW. A decree, in general, is an order issued at the conclusion of a deliberation or discussion of a particular matter. In the Roman Law, orders, commands, dispositions, and concessions issued by public authority, pontiffs, emperors, senate, presiding officers, consuls, and other magistrates who exercised direct personal jurisdiction, were called decrees as opposed to the acts issued by legislative or judiciary bodies. Thus the following were given by decree: (1) title to a property, (2) appointment of tutor, (3) restitution *"in integrum"* (total), (4) interdicts, etc. . . . Later the term *decree* was applied to sentences given by the emperor in cases reserved to him personally. In modern civil codes provisions, orders, and prescriptions issued by executive and administrative powers, such as kings, presidents, ministers, governors, and heads of municipalities are called decrees.

DECREE IN CANON LAW. All dispositions which were not laws or sentences were called decrees in earlier times. Later, all pontifical laws, as opposed to conciliar laws, were called decrees, as well as laws and disciplinary statutes of councils as opposed to canon and real laws. Finally, the term *decree* was extended to collections of canons, such as the *Decretum Gratiani.* Today, in the legislative field, all disciplinary laws of ecumenical and particular councils, decisions taken at meetings of imperfect societies, and acts, formerly called general decrees, are called decrees. In the procedural field the name *decree* is given to all orders and decisions by judges in the course of trials, which have no relation to the fundamentals of the controversy or to the causes which are incidental to it. Thus, publications of dispositions (Can. 1782), *conclusio in causa* (Can. 1860, par. 3), are announced as decrees. In the administrative field, all acts of the governing and administrative powers of the Roman Pontiff, of the SS. Congregations which often have legislative or disciplinary character, of the offices of the Roman Curia, regulations of bishops and other ecclesiastical prelates are called decrees.

VALUE. Decrees, particularly those issued by the executive and administrative powers are either particular, in which case they contain precepts, privileges, etc. . . or general, that is, they extend to the whole Church, province or diocese. In this case, they are considered as laws, statutes, or instructions. In this latter sense, but with a special importance, are the general disciplinary decrees by the Sacred Congregations with the authority of the Roman Pontiff and doctrinal decrees issued by the Holy Office. These may, at times, be confirmed in a specific or general manner by the Roman Pontiff, but they are not for this reason infallible.

DECRETUM GRATIANI. See Corpus Iuris Canonici.

DEDICATION. Dedication is the official term for the rite by which a new church, or one which has been renovated, is set aside for divine worship. It differs from a benediction or blessing in that the latter may be given by a duly authorized priest, whereas a dedication is reserved to the bishop and, as a privilege, to cardinals everywhere (*ubique terrarum*), and to abbots within the confines of their own jurisdiction. Dedication is restricted to edifices destined for public worship. Oratories are excluded. Dedication is mandatory for cathedral churches and recommended for parochial churches. A wooden church and one made of metal can be blessed but cannot be dedicated by solemn consecration. The entire legislation concerning this matter is found in the Code of Canon Law, Canons 1165–1171. See Church, Oratory, Sacred Place.

Dedication as such, aside from the natural diversity of the rite, was common in ancient Roman times. It represented the homage by city or state expressed in the offering of an edifice to the divinity. Permission for a dedication was reserved to the civil authority. This explains how, in the first Christian centuries, all dedications were undertaken at the initiative of the Christian emperors. Dedication as a rite was in ancient times extremely simple. In the case of a church which was not dedicated to the memory of a martyr, it consisted mainly in the transferral of holy relics and the celebration of the Mass on the new altar, or simply in the celebration of the Mass in the case of a memorial church. Today the dedication rite is much more complex. Many of its elements—the anointing, the writing of the alphabet and the monogram of Christ on the floor of the church—are not of Roman origin. On the contrary, ever since early times, the use of water as an exorcising element easily found its way into the dedication rite by reason of its extensive use in the Roman worship. In fact, St. Gregory considers the use of holy water in the dedication of a church as a quasi-natural preliminary rite. Hence, properly speaking, it is a preliminary, not a dedicatory rite.

The dedication is, in a way, the official birthday of a church. Hence its annual liturgical celebration is commemorated by a special Mass and office. *Cig.*

DEFAMATION (Detraction). Defamation is an unjust denigration (blackening) of one's good name. It consists of telling facts which destroy the general good name another enjoys; for example, to say that one has stolen. Defamation is committed while the victim is absent. This fact differentiates defamation from contumely. The words "unjust denigration" distinguish real defamation from damage done to one's good name by acts or words not intended to cause such damage but which may accidentally or unintentionally follow. To tell a person who perhaps does not know it a defaming fact which is *true* and publicly known is not defamation in the strict meaning of the term, since the other person's good name is already damaged. Such action, however, is ordinarily uncharitable. Much depends on the circumstances surrounding the case.

Defamation is committed in two ways: (a) by spreading defamatory things which are true but not publicly known, or (b) by telling defamatory things which are false. The former constitutes detraction, the latter is called calumny.

Defamation is a sin against justice, in itself grave. Calumny is a more serious sin than detraction because it is an injury to one's good name caused by the spreading of defamatory reports generally false. Even when the reports are true, in which case it is called detraction, defamation is by its very nature a grave sin because it deprives a person of a good to which he has a right; namely, his good name, which will remain unharmed as long as the sin committed or the improper action performed remains unknown. A good name is an asset of great value. Sacred Scripture considers it more precious than riches. Defamation could also be a venial sin, if the damage done to one's good name in a specific case is slight. The seriousness of the damage done depends on the nature of the disclosure, the dignity of the revealer (whether a person in authority, serious and prudent or light and frivolous), of the listeners (whether reserved or talkative) and of various other elements, such as the number of listeners, etc. The sin of defamation is committed with great facility and frequency, even by persons who, in other things, are rather serious and at times even scrupulous. The source of this evil which causes much resentment and damage is twofold: talkativeness and an excessive desire to report and listen to sensational stories. It seems that some men and women get a feeling of being

better persons or less wicked than others when they hear bad reports about other people. The telling of defamatory stories is a sin, and sometimes even a serious sin. Listening to them with pleasure and outward signs of joy is also sinful. Charity demands that everything that is morally possible be done in order to avoid defamation; for example, by showing displeasure, disappointment, and disapproval, according to the specific circumstance, and even correcting the defamer according to the norms of fraternal correction.

The damage caused by defamation must be repaired. However, often this is morally and even physically impossible. When the story told is false, reparation of the damage may not be difficult. The defamer is obliged to retract what he has said and circulate his retraction to the point that all who heard his false report may now hear his retraction if possible. When the story told is true, reparation is much more difficult. Nor will it do to say that the story was not true, because this would be telling a lie. Instead, he must confess to have erred in speaking of that person as he did; he must speak well of that person before those who heard his defamatory report and make allowance, insofar as it is possible, for the weakness of the person, and praise the defamed person for his other good qualities, etc. The embarrassment resulting from the obligation of making reparation should have the effect of making those persons more prudent and restrained who, with extreme frivolousness, speak evil of, and circulate defaming reports about, others. *Ben.*

DEFECT (Predominant). The word *defect* indicates, among other things, a proclivity to a specific sin resulting from a frequent repetition of the same act. Each individual is born with a predisposition to certain good acts as well as to some evil acts. If from the beginning the will offers no resistance to one's natural inclinations to evil, they soon grow stronger and become real defects. A predominant defect in a man is a proclivity whose impulse is more frequent and stronger than others, even if it is not always noticed.

The predominant defect is man's constant enemy, pursuing him and often leading him to do wrong things. This defect is all the more to be feared as it is a powerful arm used by the devil to lead man into sin. If the predominant defect is not energetically checked, it slowly blinds one's mind and leads to increasingly more frequent and graver faults.

To combat the predominant defect, one must, first of all, be aware of it. This is not an easy task, since there is nothing a man loathes more than self-knowledge. To discover one's predominant defect, one must pray and examine his conscience with regard to the faults which he more frequently commits, searching for their causes, scrutinizing his thoughts and noting whatever in others may be displeasing to him. Another way is by a frank, open manifestation of one's soul to a confessor so that he may make a thorough search and point out the predominant defect to him. Often, criticism of one's actions has the effect of throwing considerable light upon the predominant fault. Once it has been discovered, one should go to work immediately and relentlessly to uproot it, particularly through the practice of those virtues which are directly opposed to it. Constant prayer, of course, is a very effective means, coupled with a constant examination of conscience with regard to the progress made. To this effect, St. Augustine and other saints suggested that a close count be taken daily or even weekly, of the number of times one may fall into the same predominant fault so as to assess the effectiveness of one's efforts. Other effective means are frequent interior contrition and the performance of a self-imposed penance every time one falls into the particular fault he is endeavoring to uproot. It may require years of continuous effort to eradicate the predominant defect, but one must not tire. With God's grace, the most rebellious natures can be reformed, nor

is it at all wise to let down one's guard on the conviction that the battle is won. *Man.*

DEFENDANT. The defendant is the person who in a contentious judgment, civil or canonical, is summoned to appear before judicial authority for the settlement of a specific controversy. The Code of Canon Law, in treating of trials in general, employs the expression *"reus . . . conventus"* (Can. 1646). The defendant remains such from the beginning to the end of the trial, that is, from the time of the citation to the handing down of the sentence, even if in the course of the trial he shall have introduced a counter-claim of his own. He is permitted to use a measure whereby he can change his position from defendant to plaintiff; namely, the measure or plea of exception, in support of which, however, he shall furnish proofs acceptable to the court.

POSITION OF DEFENDANT IN A TRIAL. The defendant appears in court not of his own volition, but because he is summoned; hence, he is favored by the law insofar as the procedure is concerned, for he is assigned an advocate or lawyer to plead his case (Can. 1647, 1655), unless he shall choose his own in a contentious trial or plead his own cause (Can. 1655, par. 3). While not bound to directly prove his innocence, the defendant must answer the charge or accusation; if this is not proved, he has the right to be left in peace.

The defendant is party to the trial and may not exempt himself from appearing in court (Can. 1646). Parents, tutors, and guardians are required to answer for minors (Can. 1648, par. 1), under penalty of being declared guilty of contempt of court (Can. 1842); the judge may even threaten penalties to force obedience to the court (Can. 1845). Obstinate persons (i.e., those who continue to ignore the summons of the judge) leave themselves open to strong suspicion of guilt in the case at hand and all their rights may well be jeopardized.

MORAL OBLIGATIONS. The defendant

is bound to answer truthfully all questions legitimately directed to him by the judge, but he is not obliged to answer questions concerning an offense committed by himself. The telling of the truth is based on the fact that he stands before a legitimate authority while in exercise of his office, which would be nullified, if everyone were free to disobey. The reason for not being obliged to admit to his own crime is that no law can oblige one to be one's own accuser. These moral principles are also embodied in the Code of Canon Law (Can. 1743, par. 1; *cf.* also Can. 1947).

The question may be asked as to whether the defendant, as a measure of self-defense, may reveal the secret crimes of the witnesses for the purpose of destroying or discrediting their testimony. The answer is in the affirmative, as long as the defendant remains within the limits of legitimate self-defense and the charges he makes are true.

A second question concerns whether the defendant, upon conviction of an offense, must reveal the names of his accomplices. Here too the answer is in the affirmative, if the accomplices are already under suspicion and silence would cause grave harm to society.

A final question concerns whether a person found guilty, but actually innocent, may escape or actively resist arrest. Again, the answer is in the affirmative, provided that in so doing he does not wound or kill anyone. As a matter of fact, even a truly guilty party is morally permitted to escape, on the principle that it is every man's natural right to avoid an impending grave evil or danger. *Pug.*

DEFENDER OF THE BOND. See Promoter of Justice; Trial, Canonical; Marriage.

DEFERMENT. A deferment is the granting of a longer period of time than that allotted by the law or the lawful superior for the performance of a juridical act. It is conceived as an act of grace on the assumption by a legislator that a person may have been prevented from availing himself of the time allotted because of ignorance, sickness, or inability to act, according to the slogan: *ignoranti vel agere non valenti (tempus) non currit* (Can. 35). Yet it may not be an arbitrary act of the judge or the superior, but must be based on a just cause, that is, on public or private good. It can be granted at the request of both disputing parties or of only one, provided that the other be at least warned in order that he may be able to face the eventual damages caused by the deferment. Of course, a deferment must be requested and granted before the expiration of the time allotted (Can. 1634, par. 2).

Deferment has extensive application in ecclesiastical juridical procedure in which the judge receives ample discretionary powers limited only by the necessity of listening to the defendant, the promoter of justice, or the defender of the bond. Furthermore, the judge is cautioned that the trial be not prolonged by deferments. Thus: (a) judicial and conventional limits, before their lapse, may be deferred for a just cause after hearing the parties, provided that the controversy is not excessively prolonged and that this is not the reason why the deferments are requested by one of the parties (Can. 1634); (b) an automatic deferment of the judicial limits occurs in the case where they eventually fall on ferial days. In such case, they are automatically postponed to the successive non-ferial day, unless by a decree of the judge the tribunal was authorized to sit even on that day (Can. 1635); (c) a deferment may be granted to the parties to the dispute in order to give ample time (*tempus utile*) for the presentation of the evidence (Can. 1731, par. 2), the judicial certifications (Can. 1799), the allegations or defense by the advocates (Can. 1862, par. 2); to the defender of the bond to present his deductions (Can. 1969, par. 1); (d) to anyone who wishes to develop the so-called action *de nuntiatione novi operis vel damni infecti* within the two months granted to him by the law, provided that there be a just cause and the other party is duly heard (Can. 1676, par. 3).

In the case of other juridical acts a deferment may be granted for reasons of greater security in acting or greater convenience and usefulness. Thus: (a) the major superior may defer the time of probation for six more months (Can. 539, par. 2) of the novitiate (*q.v.*); also for six more months (Can. 561, par. 2) of the temporary profession of the vows but not for longer than a three-year period (Can. 674, par. 2); (b) the Ordinary may defer the time of incardination of a religious in his diocese by extending his time of trial for a second three-year period, at the end of which he will become definitely incardinated unless the Ordinary send him back to his community; (c) the local Ordinary may extend the time for the fulfillment of the Easter Duty by the faithful, but not beyond the feast of the Most Holy Trinity (Can. 859, par. 2); (d) local Ordinaries may also, if deemed helpful, extend the time granted a removable pastor requested for canonical reasons to give up his parish within a definite time (Cans. 2160, 2161); (d) the local Ordinary may also extend the time granted to an irremovable pastor requested to give up his parish if it is not certain that the latter received the request in ample time to enable him to make his defense against the accusations (Can. 2149, par. 2); (f) the president of a plenary or provincial council has power to extend the time of the meetings of the council, with this difference, however, that the president of a plenary council may do so on his own authority as a delegate of the Holy See, while the president of a provincial council needs the consent of the majority of the Fathers (Can. 288). *M.d.G.*

DEFLATION. See Inflation.

DEFLORATION (Violation of virginity). *See* Gynecology, Fornication, Virginity.

DEGRADATION. Degradation is the most severe canonical penalty for clerics guilty of grave crimes. It includes deposition, perpetual deprivation of the clerical garb, and reduction to the lay state (Can. 2305, I). It can be inflicted as a further penalty following deposition and perpetual deprivation of the ecclesiastical garb, if these prove insufficient in deterring the criminal.

From the manner in which it is inflicted, degradation may be classified as either (a) *verbal* or by edict; this obtains immediate juridical effect and is ordinarily published in the *Acta Apostolicae Sedis*; or (b) *real* and complex, which results from the judicial sentence of a tribunal consisting of five judges (Can. 1576, par, 1, no. 2) and is described in detail in the *Pontificale Romanum*.

Regarding the juridical effects produced, both verbal and real are equivalent. The degraded cleric is reduced to the lay state; he must wear lay clothes and consider himself in everything a lay person. However, properly speaking, the obligations resulting from his ordination remain, e.g., the reading of the Breviary and the vow of chastity, although a dispensation from reading the Breviary is often given.

MILITARY DEGRADATION. Penal military law contains degradation as an accessory penalty and a moral consequence of other penalties which disqualify the criminal from serving in the military service of the state in any capacity, or from holding any public office, retaining decorations, collecting pensions or claiming any benefits for services previously rendered or for any military or civil ranks obtained. *Pug.*

DEGREE OF RELATIONSHIP. See Affinity, Consanguinity.

DELECTATION (Pleasurable). *See* Pleasure, Deliberate; Sins of Thought.

DELEGATE (Apostolic). A Delegate is a prelate, ordinarily a Bishop, assigned by the Holy See to some region with ordinary delegated power (in fact, he presides by a mandate and in the name of the Supreme Pontiff) to watch over the condition of the Church and keep the Supreme Pontiff informed as to the same conditions. Some are under the jurisdiction of the Sacred Consistorial Congregation, others of the Sacred Congregation of the Propagation of the Faith (de Propaganda Fide), and others of the Sacred Congregation for the Oriental Church.

FACULTIES AND PRIVILEGES. Besides the ordinary faculties connected by right to his office, the Delegate (Apostolic) usually receives other faculties in the nature of delegated faculties. He has the title of "Excellency" and, even though he may not be a consecrated bishop, he takes precedence over all Ordinaries except Cardinals. If he is a Bishop, he can, without prior permission, bless the people in all the churches except the cathedral church, and pontificate in them, using also the throne and canopy (Can. 269). The office of the Delegate ceases when the object of his mission is accomplished, or by revocation, or by resignation accepted by the Supreme Pontiff. *See* Legates (Papal). *Fel.*

DELEGATION. *See* Jurisdiction, ecclesiastical; Marriage, form of.

DELIBATION. *See* Sentence.

DELIBERATION (Deliberative process). In a free act, a distinction must be made between the cause and the motives of volition, that is, between subjective and objective cause. The objective cause of volition is the free will itself; the basis for such freedom is its active indifference owing to the fact that the will is not determined to act except by an absolute good. The objective cause or motive for willing is not exclusively the pleasure which accompanies the act, as some modern psychologists hold, but any good known and considered by the individual as his own good. The deliberative process consists precisely in comparing the motives and in the final selection of one of them.

Ancient scholastics analyzed and described this process quite differently from modern psychologists. The difference is not always nominal or purely formal. This difference is at times concerned with the very substance and originative principle of the free act whose intrinsic and immediate principles are to be sought for at the moment the intention and deliberation are elicited by the intellect and the will respectively; whereas, in the order of execution, other elements may be added, determined, directed, and informed by the former. According to St. Thomas, the knowledge and evaluation of the good pertains to the intellect, and also the practical judgment as to the possibility of attainment and feasibility, the evaluation and concrete election of the means suited to attainment, the deliberation to will it (*imperium*) and the direction of the other faculties required in the execution of what has been deliberated upon. To the will, on the other hand, belong the enjoyment of the known good, the effective intention to attain it, the deliberation to employ the appropriate means by which to attain it, the choice, the application of the other faculties in the execution of the command and, finally, the fruition of the good attained.

Naturally, these acts, though distinct, are not separated one from the other; as a matter of fact, they integrate and condition one another, and are at times fused in the unity of the volitive and deliberative processes. *Pal.*

DELIGHT, MOROSE. *See* Pleasure, Deliberate; Sins of Thought.

DELINQUENCY (CRIMINAL). A delinquent is a criminal or one guilty of at least one crime. Delinquency is the act of the criminal or the complex of crimes relative to a specific time and place. In this second sense delinquency is the equivalent of criminality. The questions before us with particular reference to the last century are: whether the criminal is an individual different from others, possessing peculiar psychosomatic characteristics; whether crime is the result of organic, biological and environmental factors, or of factors generally so strongly affecting the criminal (the acting subject) as to nullify in him all free will (or choice) and, therefore, all imputability and responsibility; or whether, allowing for due exceptions, the crime is the product of the will freely directing itself toward evil.

The theories of Cesare Lombroso (1836–1909), according to whom the criminal is the victim of abnormal heredity, pathological or degenerative conditions, enjoyed a great popularity in the past century and the beginning of the present. By means of a series of morphological and psychiatric studies, attempts were made at diagnosing the distinctive characteristics of the criminal. At the same time, to eliminate the will as a factor from crime, the positivists of the Lombrosian school extended the concept of crime even to animals (v.g., the spider killing the fly). Other scholars held that determination towards crime was the effect of socioenvironmental factors. Another group, consisting mainly of Italian scholars (Sergi, Sighele, Ottolenghi), held that improper behavior is essentially the result of motives of a psychic order; that is to say, the criminogenous stimuli of criminal origin erupt at the surface following the antagonistic action of the counter-stimuli. This argument was subsequently developed by Freud (*See* Psychoanalysis). A recent school of thought endeavors to demonstrate an intimate correlation between temperament and organic constitution. However, in the last few years there has been a partial return, and rightly so, to the teachings of the classical school, improved on the basis of subsequent deductions, which despite exaggerations contained elements of truth. Thus, it is recognized that the cause of crime must be found in the criminal's will. This, however, does not exclude the existence of factors influencing man's free will. Due account must be taken of this in the administration of justice to reach a correct evaluation of the crime and the

relative penalty. Nor are we to rule out the fact that a crime may sometimes be the manifestation of a pathological state to which (even preponderantly) anthropological, constitutional, psychopathological, glandular causes, etc., contribute. Moreover, as judiciary statistics show, delinquency varies according to sex, age, condition in life, and education.

In the field of criminality, much importance must be given to the social conditions prevailing in a given country. In a post-war period, for instance, when a variety of factors converge together to disturb public morality and to intensify disregard for the law (marked economic unbalance with rapid gains amid the general poverty of the nation, the spread of immorality, disorientation of returnees, unemployment, political agitations, etc.), criminality always takes much more aggravated forms and proportions.

Of less import is the "penalty" factor, in that no well-defined relation seems to exist between the gravity of codified penalties (death penalty not excluded) and the reduction of crime.

TYPES OF CRIMINALS. Criminals are variously classified. Often classification reflects the various schools of thought on the subject. For the sake of general information we shall give a sample classification of criminals based on tenets of the positivistic school, but with notable reservations on our part.

(a) *Mentally ill criminal:* This is one who because of a psychic disease is totally or partially incapable of understanding or of willing; he is not liable or only partially liable to the sanctions of the law. In the more serious cases, however, provisions are made for a period of treatments in an insane asylum or a sanatorium, for therapeutic reasons as well as the protection of society against the possibility of further crimes.

(b) *Habitual criminal:* The term *habitual criminal* is one usually applied to a criminal on the basis of the number of crimes previously committed by him and of the nature of the crimes, the period of times within which he committed them, the type of life he leads, etc.

(c) *Professional criminal:* He is a sub-species of the habitual criminal. The conclusion again is made by the judge whenever, from the accumulation of circumstances, he believes that the criminal habitually makes his living in part or in its totality from earnings obtained through crimes.

(d) *Criminal by inclination* (tendency): One who reveals some peculiar inclination to crime, the cause of which is not to be found in a mental disease, but "in a particularly evil temperament of the criminal" is called a criminal by inclination. This type of criminal is reminiscent of the "born criminal" of the Lombrosian school of criminology (*See* Anthropology, criminal).

(e) *Passionate criminal:* The one who commits a crime while under the spell of an intense emotional state is known as a passionate criminal. This constitutes an extenuating circumstance if, in the judgment of a magistrate, the criminal "acted on the basis of motives of special moral and social value," or "reacted in a state of rage, caused by an unjust act committed by another person," or, perhaps, on the "incentive furnished by an aroused crowd."

(f) *Occasional criminal:* One who does not fit any of the preceding descriptions may be called an occasional criminal. The above descriptions are determined on the basis of preconceived theories endeavoring to replace the essential elements by secondary and accidental elements or circumstances in a crime. Thus, they appear to be rather theoretical, abstract and removed from the concrete reality, which, among other things, lessens the possibility of their being reduced to predetermined categories. Much more appropriately, Canon Law prefers to speak of habitual or continued crime, (Can. 1705, par. 3), of accidental cases (Can. 2203, par. 2), etc., rather than of habitual, occasional criminals, etc., taking into consideration all the subjective circumstances of the criminal. (Can. 2218, par. 1).

SOCIAL CONDITIONS AND CRIMINALITY. Individual conditions predisposing to the commission of a crime which would require a special treatment for each individual subject (endocrine-vegetative anomalies, physiological and psychological changes, multiple psycho-pathological affections), are omitted in this study. Among social causes of major import must be mentioned the toxic causes, above all, alcoholism which is a notable cause of criminality both in itself and in its hereditary consequences, addiction to cocaine and morphine, hereditary diseases, etc. The other social causes of criminality can be summed up in poverty and *psychic diseases.* Extreme poverty (hence malnutrition—a factor which acts also as an individual cause), total absence of hygienic facilities, moral and even material neglect by parents, the impossibility of attending schools, etc., constitute a notable incentive to criminality, especially among the young. Bad example from companions already given over to crime, who appear to live a more prosperous life, is responsible to a considerable degree for leading some individuals to vice and criminality.

From the preceding observations, it is clear that to combat the many causes of criminality, effective means must be provided. Such provisions must be based on the sound education of each individual, with guidance and protection supplied from infancy with opportunities for a suitable profession or trade that would assure him of a satisfactory standard of living. He should be protected against bad influences, disease, and all eventual disabilities, and given proper vocational guidance. Appropriate aids must be provided to prevent his becoming an habitual criminal if after his first crime he may (as the result of bad influence from jail companions), find it difficult or often impossible to obtain employment following his release from prison. The main needs which modern social medicine must endeavor to provide range from the prophylaxis of infectious diseases to the reasonable medical cures of the infirm, from a fight against syphilis and hereditary-syphilis to that against all types of intoxication; from sanitary conditions of the homes to those of food; from an increase in the number of infant asylums and schools for the sub-normal and handicapped to the employment of the latter in satisfactory paying jobs; from an increase in the number of clinics of mental hygiene for the prophylaxis and early treatment of psychopathic illnesses to the useful re-employment of those who have recovered from such disorders; from a rational professional orientation of the youth to an intelligent censure of publications and shows which too often offer incentive to criminality; from an increase in rehabilitation programs in behalf of occasional criminals while in jail or during their post-incarceration period to the ethical amelioration of currents of thought.

But all those provisions (which resolve themselves into an essentially materialistic program, "health, bread, and work") will fall far short of the desired objective unless they are integrated in a comprehensive ethico-religious program of education or re-education which will lead everyone, especially the unstable, the confused, and the frustrated, to the acceptance of duty and to prayer for divine grace. Empirical considerations alone will not suffice. An adequate understanding of the problem of criminality is doomed to utter failure unless there is a return to a sound philosophy and to the acceptance of revealed truths (original sin, man's elevation to a supernatural order leading to the attainment of an eternal life). These elements must be added and used as a basis for the others in order that we may understand the reasons for man's difficulty in doing good and the ease with which he can fall into evil, the causes of his internal struggle and of moral disorder, also the possibilities of man's reacting to these forces (effects of original sin) by the proper use of freedom of the will in the natural order, and through the aid of supernatural grace in the supernatural order. *Riz.*

DELIRIUM. Delirium (Lat. *delirium, deliro*—to go crooked in ploughing) is an aberration of judgment, caused by emotional disturbances due to a disease. Such aberration is characterized by its uncontrollability, as it is corrected neither by reasoning nor by actual evidence of the facts. The emotions' influence upon one's judgment is a well known fact and its exercise is present in a more or less marked degree even in normal individuals. It is not, therefore, surprising if in a person affected by a pathological condition, on account of a constitutional defect of judgment, such influence can grow to such proportions as to lead to completely false evaluations. Delirium can be considered an opinion which derives its tenacity from emotional tension rather than from an accumulation of experiences; as a matter of fact, this opinion exercises such an active influence upon experience and judgment as to strengthen the delirium. In fact, the judgment becomes so unilateral as to inveigh against anything which might uproot the delirium, overlooking the error which strengthens it. The subjective images are produced by the imagination, under the influence of passion, as images of reality, but are distorted with illusions and may cause hallucinations which strengthen the delirium. In this manner, the delirious judgments, originating in suspicion, soon assert themselves as convictions both erroneous and obstinate, and usually serve as unhindered guides to action.

DELIRIUM AND OBSESSION. Despite the fact that both obsession and delirium originate from emotional disturbance, their characteristics are usually different and contrary. Obsession is characterized by anxious doubts in the mind of the infirm person who is conscious of being sick, and its absurdity is not in regard to its substance but in the intensity of the distressing reactions to which it gives rise. Delirium, filled with errors of an absurd and paradoxical nature, is characterized by an attitude of certainty on the basis of which the patient refuses to discuss either his opinion or his mental condition. In a psychic personality, obsession is an element in a constant state of agitation, incapable of penetrating the consciousness of the individual or of exerting any positive influence upon his actions because of his strenuous resistance to it.

The delirious idea orginates from the most intimate nucleus of one's personality with which it becomes so identified as to assume despotic rule and unchallenged control of the individual.

There are cases in which the obsessive idea slips gradually into delirium, and other cases which present mixed forms very difficult to evaluate properly, as in some cases of jealousy.

CLASSIFICATION. Deliriums, following the fluctuation of emotions, can be divided into depressive, pessimistic (deliriums of ruin, persecution, guilt, damnation, etc.), and expansive, optimistic, of exultation (deliriums of vanity, of great ability for social reforms, and the like). Deliriums, which are as varied in their contents as the human spirit itself, and which revolve around the various instincts and passions of human nature, can be classified as follows: (a) Deliriums based on the instinct of preservation: (1) regarding health (euphoric, hypochondriac, transformation or negation of vital organs, of persecution); (2) regarding possessions (riches, losses, financial failures, revenge, etc.). (b) Deliriums based on sexual instincts; erotic, of impotence, jealousy, etc. (c) Deliriums based on feeling of one's worth: of greatness, of unworthiness, of ability for political and social reforms, scientific greatness, etc. (d) Deliriums based on religious sentiment: of perfection, of unworthiness, of damnation, of apostolate, etc. Commonly also, the agitated wandering which often accompanies high fever, is called delirium, but this is an improper use of the term.

ASPECTS OF DELIRIUM IN VARIOUS MENTAL DISEASES. Deliriums arise the more easily as the reasoning power of the individual becomes weaker and assume different aspects as the individual personalities vary from one another. In phrenetics they are unintelligent, incoherent and vague; in schizophrenics, they are extravagant and unrealistic; in the confused, they are chaotic, tumultuous, and most inconsistent. In paralytics, deliriums are exaggerated and often paradoxically grandiose. In senile dementia they assume great dimensions, but they very easily crumble and change because of the weakness of the memory; in manic-depressives they follow the course of their emotional crises in such a way that during the melancholy phase, depressive delirious ideas appear; while during the maniacal phase, ideas of exaltation become entrenched. The most complete and convincing form of delirious manifestations is present in paranoiacs (See Paranoia); it is called "systematized chronic delirium." In such patients, because of the gravity and the constitutional deficiency of their judgment and of their passional anomalies, delirium, strengthened by events which are constantly interpreted by them in a delirious sense, consolidates and becomes much more entrenched as a coherent system of unchangeable convictions.

The imputability in delirious patients varies according to the type of the mental illness of the patient, phrenetic, schizophrenic, paralytic, demential, etc. (See individual entries.) It is possible, however, to speak of imputability *in causa* in those cases in which the mental disease of the patient is the effect of some criminal or sinful act or acts. *Riz.*

DELIRIUM (from Jealousy). *See* Alcoholism, Paranoia.

DELIRIUM (Hypochondriac). *See* Hypochondria.

DELIRIUM (Mystical; pseudo-mystical). *See* Hallucination.

DELIRIUM (of greatness). *See* Paranoia.

DELIRIUM (of persecution). *See* Paranoia.

DELIRIUM (Oneirific). *See* Sleep.

DELIRIUM TREMENS. *See* Alcoholism.

DELIVERY. Delivery is the expulsion from the mother's womb of a fetus that is capable of living outside of it. This final phrase distinguishes birth from abortion or miscarriage. (*See* Abortion.) Delivery is accompanied by pains that are quite intense. After original sin, God designated these pains as part of the punishment imposed on woman (Gen. 3:16). Jesus spoke of these pains and used them in a beautiful comparison (John 16:21). He pointed out the transition from suffering to joy in a mother, who is first tormented by the pangs of delivery and then happy with her new child.

Delivery is *natural* or *induced*, insofar as it is the result of a natural process or the intervention of man. A delivery before the 280th day after conception is called premature.

MORAL DOCTRINE. For a time moralists discussed whether or not it was permissible to use artificial means to eliminate the ordinary pains of birth (without some special reasons). Today, after the authoritative statement of Pope Pius XII in this regard, it is clear that it is not only permitted when harm or serious danger threatens mother or child, but it is morally permissible in any case, as long as it is certain that the means used is not itself harmful. The words of God, "In pain will you bring forth your children," are not a divine commandment. Their meaning is: "These pains are a penal consequence of the sin that was committed"; in no way do they mean that it is improper to use means that are not bad in themselves to avoid these pains. The method of conditioned reflexes, now one of the most frequently used methods, contains nothing wrong in itself; as a matter of fact, it is preferable to other methods from a moral point of view, for it presents no danger to mother or child, unlike other methods based on analgesics and anesthetics. Nor does the use of this method imply acceptance of the materialistic theories of Pavlov, who invented it (cf. Pope Pius XII, Address to members of the IVth International Congress of Catholic doctors, Sept. 29, 1949, AAS, 41 (1949) 557; Address to doctors and gynecologists, January 8, 1956, AAS, 48 (1956) 82–93). But ordinarily it is better and more in keeping with the Christian ideal to bear the pains of delivery if they are not exceptionally strong with courage and a spirit of penance. This is to be advised in ordinary cases.

It is permitted to induce labor pains artificially, for a reasonable cause if it will not result in a premature delivery. If surgical and medical action (e.g., injections) involve harm or danger to the mother or child, it is permitted only for a serious reason, proportionate to the seriousness of the harm or the danger.

For the morality of premature delivery *see also* Pregnancy, Obstetrics. *Ben.*

DELIVERY, PREMATURE. The expulsion of the fetus from the mother's womb at a time when it is not yet fully mature, but nevertheless capable of staying alive outside the womb is termed premature delivery. The latter condition distinguishes prematurally induced delivery from abortion (*q.v.*). Premature delivery may be natural or artificial, depending on whether it is produced by natural causes (sickness, rupture not produced by human cause) or by a deliberate action on the part of some person.

A premature delivery may be induced to save the mother, by bringing to an end a harmful pregnancy, or to facilitate a delivery that will be impossible or very difficult if the fetus is fully developed.

MORALITY. There must be a serious reason to justify an induced premature delivery. The reason or necessity should be all the more urgent the farther the fetus is from full maturity, for it is wrong to expose a human being to the danger of death or other serious harm without a reason that is proportionate to the danger involved. If, on the basis of ordinary experience, there is no reasonable hope of keeping the fetus alive, then an induced premature delivery is never permitted; for it might be better to say that this would not be a case of premature delivery but rather of a deliberately induced abortion. Whenever premature delivery is the only way of saving the fetus, it is always licit; the slightest hope, as long as it is a reasonable one, is enough to justify it. *Ben.*

DEMAGOGY (Demagogism). Demagogism is an ancient term designating a deviation from democracy (*See* Democracy) by a people already under a free government in a free society, due to the power of influential men skilled in the art of arousing the prejudices and passions of the populace. Usually, demagoguery is short-lived; it gives way to tyranny or totalitarianism (*See* Totalitarianism). Characteristic of demagogism is the semblance of liberty it keeps and the widespread deception by which the people believe themselves to be free. Much oratory (or rather blabbering) goes on, the casting of votes is publicly done and popular sovereignty seems to be at its apex. In reality, however, those who make the final decisions, though without appearing to do so, are a few able meddlers, often of less than ordinary intelligence.

A lack of political maturity, found even among highly civilized peoples, may give rise to the type of deception on which demagogism thrives. Strangely, demagogism, in its strict sense, is a phenomenon more commonly found among people who have reached a higher degree of civilization. It is the effect of a widespread excessive desire for superfluous pleasures which become almost absolute necessities for them. (Such cravings grow out of a materialistic philosophy of life.) Thus, it is a common occurrence in our days to see many so-called proletarians put more value on refinement in dress, smoking, sports, and other superfluous amusements than on the possession of a suitable home. This lack of maturity is due

to a prevalence of emotional criteria or to attitudes based on considerations of selfish or class interests, void of a genuine and responsible appreciation of one's best interests or the common good (*See* Common good). It fails to meet the requirements of a true social justice, or to understand the necessity of public order and discipline as indispensable factors of stability for state and nation. To play on such weaknesses is demagogism. A politician who out of set purpose or out of personal weakness exploits these conditions commits a very serious sin. Unfortunately, it is a common occurrence. It is easy for a politician addressing the masses to be carried away by their emotional response and to compromise with the dictates of right reason and good judgment. It is a difficult task, indeed, to educate crowds in the direction of right thinking. The temptation to which politicians are ordinarily exposed is to accede to their demands as to an overpowering force. This fact tends to aggravate the deviations of the collective conscience, which like a spoiled child becomes more and more incapable of knowing and of seeking the common good as their true interest.

The democratic form of government demands an accomplished political maturity in which the rulers and representatives of the people show the way. Seeking after popularity prevents the politician from fulfilling that duty; hence demagogism becomes inevitable and the possibility of loss of liberty very real. How to avoid these consequences, especially in view of the voting systems prevailing in some countries, is a problem which still remains practically unsolved. *Boz.*

DEMENTIA. Dementia, an acquired psychosis, consists of a grave progressive and irreparable mental deterioration, produced by diffused destruction lesions of the cerebral cortex, which tend gradually to spread. Commonly, but incorrectly, the term *dementia* is used indiscriminately to indicate foolishness, madness, and other mental disorders.

Dementia differs from amentia, which is either a congenital state or one closely connected. From the standpoint of terminology, it is well to make it clear that when canonists speak of *dementes* they do not refer exactly to those whom psychiatrists call dementes but rather to *amentes* (*See* Amentia). In the initial forms of dementia it is possible to observe only a certain deterioration of the reasoning power of the individual and a weakening of his power of concentration and memory. Then, the intellectual power becomes increasingly weaker, and some manifestations of delirium and hallucination may appear. Finally, as the psycho-intellective weakness increases, even the volitive and emotional processes may show signs of alteration, while profound anomalies and relevant changes appear in the psychic personality, even to the point of complete disintegration.

Syphilitic infections, alcoholic intoxications, and complex degenerative alterations taking place in the brain of the aged are the basis of the more common forms of dementia which take the name of paralytic, alcoholic, and senile insanity, respectively. However, epilepsy, sclerosis in blotches and other neurological phenomena caused by extensive pathological processes upon the cerebral cape (Mantello) can also lead to serious forms of mental disorder.

In view of its fatally progressive syndrome caused by the progressiveness and irreversibility of the cerebral lesions which accompany it (except the cases of a luetic nature, which a rational treatment is often apt to check and even turn back its psychopathological progress, and some very few cases of alcoholism that can be treated by disintoxication and other modern treatments), dementia taken on the moral level allows various orders of considerations of which the two most important are the following: (a) From the standpoint of moral and penal imputability, civil responsibility, the ability to contract marriage and the like, the confirmed dement (who comes under the category of *amentes* as understood by canonists)

must be considered as totally free of responsibility, because at this point he is permanently incapable of understanding and willing. In its less advanced forms there may be a more or less pronounced degree of semi-responsibility and semi-capability, the exact evaluation of which must be made in each individual case by the confessor in the internal forum and through appropriate medical examinations by experts in the external forum. (b) Regarding the danger involved, dement persons, even when maintaining a sufficiently correct and restrained behavior, could be dangerous to themselves and to others; hence, they should be under proper supervision. In the more serious forms, or when a surveillance in the home cannot be conveniently provided, such patients should be placed in appropriate institutions. This step, which ordinarily prevents serious incidents, is recommended because, when promptly and properly treated, such patients are more apt to show notable improvement and can even be cured, with evident advantages for the patient, his family and society. The important factor, however, is that such treatments must be administered by specialists in the field and usually in hospitals properly equipped. *Riz.*

DEMENTIA (Paralytic). *See* Paralysis (Progressive).

DEMENTIA (Praecox). *See* Schizophrenia.

DEMENTIA (Senile). A slowly progressing and incurable mental deterioration which arises almost exclusively after the sixtieth year of age and is caused by an organic cerebral disorder of a degenerative type with preference for the cortex of the frontal lobes. Individuals with hereditary psychopathic tendencies are more susceptible to this type of disturbance.

In the beginning, the psychic disturbance is limited to some difficulties in the development of the analytical and synthetic mental processes and in the acquiring of new notions. Thus, to a stiffening of opinions and a weakening of their ethical tone must be assigned the well known fact that such patients become obstinate extollers of the past, unyielding, and pitifully egoistical. There follows a dimming of the memory, particularly of immediate events or of fixation, with more or less notable disorientation with regard to time, place, and persons and with "confabulations" arising from falsification of the memory and from real and true fantastic inventions to which the sick person will adhere with firm faith. Slowly but progressively all mental faculties crumble with evident repercussions on the attitude of the patient, who becomes stubborn, diffident, greedy and prone to committing incongruous acts (wills, contracts, and unsuitable marriages), of a foolish rather than a scandalous nature as is the case with other forms of dementia. The attitude of the patient is fundamentally indifferent; at times, either depressed or exalted.

Forms of episodical delirious excitement at night are not rare. In such cases, the patient, while calm during the day, experiences, at night, insomnia and uncontrollable agitations. Neurological, aphasiac, and apraxial disturbances can be associated with the phenomena described above; among such disturbances, frequent tremor is noteworthy.

ARTERIOSCLEROTIC. Arteriosclerotic dementia bears an affinity with senile dementia, with which it is often confused. Arteriosclerotic dementia is caused by cerebral arteriosclerosis and is characterized by the fact that it occurs in a less advanced age, is associated with a subjective element of sickness (while the senile insane person is convinced that he is psychologically sound), proceeds by successive jumps (as if the sick person were descending a step-ladder) and is often accompanied by other notable neurological and mental manifestations produced by localized cerebral alterations (soft spots and the like), as effects of the arteriosclerotic process.

Senile dementia is an incurable disease. Therapeutic treatments, however, need not be neglected. Besides a diligent assistance and prompt treatment of the symptoms (such as sedatives when the patient is nervous), the administration of iodine prescribed for arteriosclerotic affections is usually helpful. Moreover, in the attempt at curbing cerebral disintegration, preparations of phosphorus and glutamic acid, vitamins B, some types of hormones as well as vasodilatory drugs, prudently used to improve the flow of blood to the brain, can bring much help to the patient.

As to moral and medico-legal implications, what was said with regard to dementia in general can also be applied to senile dementia. From more strictly moral considerations, it is well to point out that the love and devotion which children normally owe to their parents demand of them even greater patience and understanding when their parents become victims of senile dementia, so as to prevent their very difficult dispositions from becoming aggravated in their declining years, while helping to temper and keep within moderate bounds their egoistic urges and many eccentricities. Prudence, of course, suggests that timely measures be taken when the patient's behavior threatens to seriously disturb order and harmony in the home by a tendency to squander family possessions, excessive display of parental authority or by making very unreasonable demands upon the members of the family and other relatives. Perhaps in no other case is the practice of charity, prudence, and even justice needed more than when dealing with persons affected by senile dementia. *Riz.*

DEMOCRACY. Democracy (Gr. *demos-krateo*, government by the people) is a form of government in which the governing heads are elected with equal right by all the citizens and in which there exists the widest individual liberty. In its general meaning, democracy is but a norm by which the social community aims at attaining its common good. In order to achieve such norm there must be honesty of ideas, freedom from bias and from disorderly passions. Democracy is not an end in itself, but a means to the attainment of a condition which conforms to the end. A democratic State is one in which all capable adult citizens have equal rights to obtain a public office, even the highest. It differs from absolute monarchy in this: that the power in a monarchy is in the hands of one person or of a group; it differs from a republic, both aristocratic (Venice) and oligarchic of one party (Nazism and Communism). In recent years mention has been made of an economic democracy in which labor relations (such as those existing between employers and employees) are changed into juridical relations between the two groups by stipulations of contracts freely entered into in a mutual understanding, as becomes free individuals working together. Everything pertaining to labor is submitted to free conciliation. Marxist socialism proposes also a social democracy, that is, a mechanical equality of the masses, which may be reached through the socializing of the means of production, of production itself, and of distribution of consumer goods. Under these conditions the function of the State is eliminated. This thesis is contrary to the natural organic evolution of society.

Democracy is (a) limited or unlimited insofar as all the citizens or only a part of them have equal right to public offices. A *limited democracy* (one limited only to intellectuals and large property owners) was installed by the French Revolution. (b) Direct or indirect. A direct democracy is one in which the people as a whole possess full power and exercise directly all governing functions. This is possible only in small social communities. Today, this is at least partially true in Switzerland. The indirect democracy (representative government) is that in which the people are governed through their legitimate representatives elected by them. Democracy can exist also in constitutional monarchies in which the power of the crown is limited (Great Britain). Indirect democracy is predicated upon the trust by the people expressed by the free election (*q.v.*), of candidates from various parties who assume, after election to office and installation in office, the responsibility of the government as representatives of the people. Parties and elections are indispensable elements of indirect democracy insofar as the people are concerned; responsibility and authority are indispensable elements insofar as the government is concerned. Once in office, the representatives must look after the national welfare, not that of the party that sponsored them. It is the majority group that governs in the parliament. Parliamentary government originated in England. In the nineteenth century, it was introduced into many other states from France.

As individualism was the premise of collectivism, so, too, a mechanical and formalistic democracy, based exclusively on the number of votes (pseudo-democracy), has given way to a triumphant super-power of the mass over the individual. Thus, even in the economic field there prevails a democratization of corporations under the form of stock companies, which end up in the concentration of the capital anonymously. Thus, too, democracy, according to the communist conception, should become a progressive democracy, that is, a dialectic democracy, which may eventually end up in imperialism and dictatorship.

EVALUATION OF DEMOCRACY. Every form of government has its advantages and its failings. The Church recognizes as good any form of government capable of fulfilling the end of the State, that is, the common good. It is necessary, therefore, that the government express the will of the people and that it set the tone to the moral values which the citizens carry into political life. Democracy rests on the principle of the natural brotherhood of all men without discrimination of classes based upon religion, race, or political philosophy. In the democratic structure this fundamental brotherhood contains certain absolute rights and liberties, such as the right to life, freedom of conscience, individual freedom, the right to have a family. Other specific civil rights are derived from these, equality before the law of all citizens, the right of every citizen to participate in the political life of the nation, the right of the people to self-determination, the right of assembly, the right of opposition to the party in power, the right of freedom of speech, the right of freedom of the press, freedom from compulsory migration and forced labor.

For a long time, people were satisfied with a monarchical form of government. When spiritual and economic life reached new developments, new obligations also arose in public life requiring greater autonomy and individual responsibility, with the tendency in classes and individuals to take the future into their own hands. Hence, since the middle of the last century, all peoples have moved toward democracy and democratic governments. For the welfare of the nation, this transition should be an organic thing, taking place gradually, for haste in making changes leads to revolution and disaster. Every form of government has its shortcomings and power is never free from abuses. It is very easy for power to be turned from a service to the people to a privilege of sway over the people and a source of gain for privileged groups, as history repeatedly proves. However, democracy, too, has its defects. A democratic government requires adequate moral and intellectual maturity. But since every citizen has the right to public office, it is obvious that abuses are likely to occur. Moreover, during electoral campaigns, the various parties are known to make promises which are beyond possibility of realization. Demagogism, therefore, is an ordinary medium by which democracy loses its genuine character. A purely formalistic and mechanical democracy generates bureaucracy, absorption of individual responsibility, oppression of minorities, plutocracy, political deviations and corruption. Democratic life rests safely on an organized community united as one in achieving a common end. *Per.*

DEMOGRAPHY. Demography (from *demos,* people, and *graphein,* to write) is a science which concerns itself with the study of human groups, particularly from the point of view of statistics both with regard to number and quality, and with regard to their continuity and consistency. It is hardly distinct from population statistics, although the latter's proper function is limited to supplying demography with material for study (*See* Statistics, applied).

On the basis of the data obtained from population statistics, demography studies the character of each individual group of human society, the laws that govern their development, their power of assimilation and elimination, their modes of living and social status, their reproductive activities, the relations between populations and the soil, the heredity of character, the phenomena of mortality, birth-rate, professional activities, the cost of living, the spread of positive religions, etc.

One of the positive results of modern demographic studies is that which concerns the possibilities of providing sufficient food for an ever-increasing population of the earth. Thus, according to recent calculations, it is estimated that, if properly developed, according to present-day methods, the earth could feed over eight billion people as compared to the two and one half billion now living on this earth. If the birth-rate increases at the present rate, it would take three centuries to reach that number. In the meantime, it is thought, science will have found ways and means of increasing the proper development of the products of the earth and of modifying in part the nutritional systems as they exist today.

Demography is a science subsidiary to politics and morality. In fact, the knowledge of the laws which regulate the flow of life among the various peoples in the world and of the relations between the different branches of (consociated life) life in society—economics, general education, morals, religion, politics, law,— enable people in governing positions and educators to conduct their activities with greater awareness of the problems before them and with more effective results. It would be a fallacy, however, to believe that such knowledge inevitably leads to sure results, for in the interior development of human nature and in the variety of relations between man and man as well as group and group, human freedom is an extremely important element which often escapes all human calculation, no matter how keen. *Pav.*

DENIGRATION. *See* Contumely, Defamation, Honor.

DENUNCIATION. It is any general declaration or proclamation related to a penal, disciplinary, or administrative censure. Denunciation may be obligatory if demanded by natural or positive law, that is, if it is intended to protect the common good; or free and spontaneous, if it stems from a personal right which can be waived by the person. The objectives of denunciation in civil and canonical laws are crimes, nullity of marriage, bad books, a new work or a feared damage, etc.

CRIMINAL DENUNCIATION is the declaration of a crime made to a superior for the purpose of obtaining satisfaction or reparation of a damage sustained or reparation of a public damage or scandal (Can. 1935, par. 1). If the denunciation is made to obtain a private satisfaction or indemnity, it is more properly called accusation. Criminal denunciation is distinct from charitable denunciation in that the latter is made in order to bring about the amendment rather than the punishment of the offender, and is made to a superior so that he may act as a father rather than as a judge; it is distinct also from canonical denunciation in that the latter is made to a superior as moderator of a community, in order that he may proceed to prevent the evil or the offense.

The obligation to denounce an offender may arise either from a law or a specific precept of a superior or even from natural law, if a danger to the faith or religion or imminent public scandal (Can. 1935, par. 2) is involved. There is an obligation to denounce a priest guilty of the delict of solicitation in con-

fession (see Can. 904), and clerics or religious who join a masonic sect or other similar societies (Can. 2336, par. 2).

The denunciation of crimes is always of a private nature. In modern legislations and in Canon Law a public denunciation of a crime, that is, criminal actions or accusations, is reserved to a public official called, in Canon Law, Promoter of Justice (Can. 1934), and in civil law, State's Attorney General or similar names. The denunciation must be made by the denouncer either in a signed document or orally to the local Ordinary, the Chancellor of the Curia, deans, etc. If the denunciation is made orally, it must be promptly put in writing and forwarded to the Ordinary. No attention is paid to anonymous letters except when they contain elements which might make the accusation probable (Can. 1942, par. 2). Moreover, the denouncer must render assistance to the superior or prosecutor in proving the crime he reported (Can. 1397). In cases of injuries or defamation, the criminal action is not instituted except on the denunciation or complaint of the injured party. However, if a cleric or religious were the agent or victim of an injury (especially if he be an ecclesiastical dignitary), the criminal action may be brought also *ex officio* (Can. 1938) since reasons of public order are involved.

DENUNCIATION OF THE PRIEST GUILTY of SOLICITATION IN CONFESSION. The denunciation of the priest guilty of the delict of solicitation in confession obtains particular importance in Canon Law. The terms of this delict are set by the Constitution *"Sacramentum Poenitentiae"* (June 1, 1741) of Benedict XIV, recalled in Canon 904, and more extensively in the Appendix to the Code of Canon Law. Canon 904 speaks of the obligation to denounce the priest, the penalties connected with such a delict, as well as those for failure by the penitent solicited to denounce it within a month. The wording of the Canon and the gravity of the penalty inflicted upon the one who fails to report the delict make it clear that it is a matter of grave obligation, and understandably so when one considers the necessity of safeguarding the sanctity of the sacrament and the spiritual welfare of the faithful exposed to serious danger by the delict of solicitation.

As a personal obligation subject to sanctions, denunciation binds only the penitent who was solicited, even if the penitent took the initiative or consented to the solicitation, nor is it required that fraternal correction precede it. The obligation to denounce the solicitor holds even if the solicited penitent cannot prove the accusation. As a moral obligation, denunciation is binding upon any person who has knowledge of the delict committed.

The denunciation is made in judicial form either to the local Ordinary or to the Holy Office (Can. 1936). If the denouncer fails to do that, the local Ordinary or the Holy Office will see to it that it is reduced to judicial form. The denunciation of a soliciting confessor must be made within a month from the commission of the delict or from the time the solicited person became aware of the obligation to denounce it. The gravity of this obligation is such that a priest must refuse absolution to the solicited person unwilling to make the denunciation, and if the latter fails to carry out such obligation within a month, he incurs *ipso facto* (automatically) excommunication *nemini reservata* (not reserved) but which no confessor or superior can absolve from until the penitent has satisfied his obligation or has made a serious promise to do so. If one falsely denounces a confessor as guilty of solicitation, he automatically incurs excommunication reserved in a special manner (*speciali modo*) to the Holy See, and he can in no case be absolved from this penalty until he has formally retracted the false denunciation, and has within the limits of his ability repaired the damages, if any, caused by his crime. Moreover, severe and lasting penances are to be imposed (Can. 2362). To protect the good name of the confessor and so that the false accuser may not escape the penalties due him for his crime, the sin of false denunciation is reserved *ratione sui* to the Apostolic See (Can. 894). This censure, which restricts the power of the confessor, is incurred even in the case of ignorance on the part of the offender.

DENUNCIATION OF THE NULLITY OF A MARRIAGE. An invalid marriage can be attacked (1) by the Promoter of Justice or (2) by the parties to the marriage— by the Promoter of Justice in the case of impediments (*see* Marriage Impediments) of their very nature and actually public; by the married parties for any public or occult impediment, provided that they themselves were not through fraud or other gravely culpable act, the direct cause of the invalidity of the marriage (Can. 1971). In such cases the married parties must be exhorted to have their marriage validated. If this is not done and the invalidity of the marriage is publicly known, and therefore a scandal, the Promoter of Justice has the right to intervene and denounce *ex officio* the marriage in question. Relatives of the married parties and other persons have no right to attack the marriage, but they can denounce its invalidity to the local Ordinary or the Promoter of Justice. As to any judiciary action, this can be entered into and pursued only by the married parties or by the Promoter of Justice (Can. 1971, par. 2).

DENUNCIATION OF PERNICIOUS BOOKS. All the faithful, especially clerics constituted in authority and well-educated persons, are bound by the virtue of charity to denounce to the local Ordinary or to the Holy See any book which they may judge to be pernicious. The representatives of the Holy See, the local Ordinaries and Rectors of Universities must by a particular obligation of justice denounce bad books, since it is their particular office to promote sound doctrine among the faithful. In denouncing a book, besides the title, intrinsic as well as extrinsic reasons must be given why it is considered bad. To this effect, local Ordinaries must set up, wherever possible, a council of vigilance consisting of a group of experienced priests whose duty it is to be vigilant concerning books circulated in the diocese. Books which on account of their content require a more accurate and profound examination or a more effective prohibition must be referred to the Holy See (Can. 1397). (*See* Forbidden Books).

DENUNCIATION OF NEW WORK OR A FEARED DAMAGE. According to Canon Law (Can. 1676, 1677) and also civil law, the denunciation of a new work or enterprise (*novi operis nunciatio*) is a judicial action by which the proprietor of or title holder to some property, fearing that he may incur damage on account of some new work or enterprise initiated by another, denounces it to the proper authority and demands that it be halted or that security be posted against a feared damage. If the judge who receives the denunciation orders suspension of the work, he must order the plaintiff to offer appropriate security against damage sustained by the other party if the court should determine that the injunction was unjustified; if the judge allows the work to proceed, he must ask that security be offered by the defendant against possible damage to the plaintiff, should the court decide that the action was justified. After these emergency provisions, the court by ordinary process defines by a definitive sentence the respective rights of the litigants.

Thus, according to Canonical (Can. 1678) as well as civil laws, one who fears grave damage to his property from a building or another thing belonging to others which threatens to collapse, has the right to request either the removal of the danger or the posting of a certain security to compensate for the damage. According to Canon Law, the party who denounces and obtains an injunction against a new enterprise has two months within which he must prove his right. This period of time may be either extended or shortened by the judge, after hearing the other party to the dispute (Can. 1676, par. 3). According to civil codes, the right to denounce a new work ends upon completion of the work or a year after its initiation. *MdG.*

DEONTOLOGY (Medical). The term *deontology* (from the Greek *deonta*, necessity, duties, and *logia*, study; therefore, a study of what one must do) entered into philosophical usage in 1834, when Bentham gave his "Science of Morality" the title "Deontology," by which he meant to describe his utilitarian doctrine of duties. Subsequently, the same term was used to indicate the treatment of a specified category of duties related to particular professions or social situations.

Thus, by medical deontology, is meant the summary of norms or duties of the physician in his relations with the law, the public, his colleagues. In a more comprehensive sense, since it reflects primarily the obligation which a physician assumes before his conscience in the exercise of his profession, the term *deontology* is the same as *professional morality* of the physician. In France, for instance, and also in some other nations, medical deontology is a separate scholastic subject. It embraces theoretical and practical questions of the greatest importance to which the full attention of all future physicians should be directed.

Based on the ancient Hippocratic Oath, whose principles turned medicine into a real mission, a number of *deontological codes* have been formulated at various times in various nations. They represent the fruit of successive experiences, based on principles of a higher order, and their aim is to supply physicians with precise norms to be followed in their professional life. The late Stefano Perrier pioneered in this field with his "Deontological Code" which he compiled in 1948 for the Medical Society of Turin.

Since deontology deals with the rights and duties of a physician, it is concerned with professional secrecy, medical examinations, the manner of examining patients, fees, mistakes, responsibilities and that deplorable habit which is making great inroads in the medical profession known as dichotomy or "fee splitting." Because of the importance of these subjects, each is being treated under its separate title. Here we shall treat of the professional formation of physicians, their duties in general, medical certificates, and other specific subjects.

PROFESSIONAL FORMATION. In all civilized nations today there is usually an organization for medical studies; in Europe these lean more toward the theoretical, in the United States, more toward the practical. These studies extend over a period of five to six years and their programs, in general, are divided in such a way as to require that the first two years be spent in the study of physics, chemistry, biological science and, primarily, anatomy. The next two years are dedicated to the study of the various branches of pathology, and the last two to clinical medicine, clinical surgery and other specialties. The examinations are also conducted along similar lines, and in almost all nations, following the successful termination of studies, a State examination is required before the new graduate may be allowed to practice medicine. Since the end of the last century, because of increased developments in the various fields of clinical medicine and diagnostic and therapeutic techniques, it has become impossible for one person to become adept in every aspect of medical science. This fact has given rise to a large variety of specializations: pediatrics, dermatology, neurology, and psychiatry, as branches of medicine, and to obstetrics, gynecology, ophthalmology, otolaryngology, etc., as branches of general surgery. Consequently, alongside the general practitioner (equipped with considerable knowledge of internal medicine and a general knowledge of some special field) there arose, in an ever increasing number, the specialists (neuropsychiatrists, oculists, phthisiologists, odontologists, etc.) to whom the general practitioner refers patients in need of special diagnostic and therapeutic assistance, or to whom the patients themselves may go for treatment of their

particular illness. A physician must undertake special postgraduate studies for a period of two years or longer, and pass an appropriate examination before he is given a license to practice in the particular field of his specialization. The professional preparation of a physician requires long and serious study supplemented by a period of practical experience (internship), acquired through the daily attendance of patients in clinics and hospitals and integrated by outstanding personal qualities, partly natural, partly acquired through self-discipline and the example of other doctors. These factors taken together constitute the moral personality of a good physician, consisting of correctness of manners, prudence, tolerance, understanding, spirit of sacrifice and, above all, charity.

SPECIALIZATION. From time to time the whole idea of the advantages and disadvantages of specialization comes under discussion; but this is purely academic, for modern progress and scientific development make specialization mandatory. It is necessary, however, to avoid the dissecting of medical science into specializations which are too limited in scope and too restricted (as sometimes happens when it is limited to the study of one function or to the use of one instrument only). Above all, the exaggeration must be avoided by which specialists often become so exclusively absorbed in pursuing their own field as to neglect the most general notions concerning the rest of medical science. In doing this they run the risk of not being able to formulate accurate diagnoses, particularly today when, with the triumph of the conception of constitutional biological uniformity (Neo-Hippocraticism—*See* Pathology), the fundamental principles concerning the various medical disciplines are also uniform. A good physician (whether he is a general practitioner or a specialist) is one who possesses sufficient basic knowledge of pathology and clinical medicine to enable him to recognize, in the interest of his patient, the necessity of conducting particular examinations or of consulting a particular specialist. He must be able to understand and properly evaluate, at least in their broad implications, the findings of the specialist so as to fit them properly within his own findings or the findings of other specialists, thus assuring a correct diagnosis and the prescription of proper treatment. With intelligent collaboration, the presence of both the general practitioner and the specialist will be fully justified and will be to the credit of the entire field of medical science.

DUTIES OF THE PHYSICIAN. These can be grouped as follows: to the community, to people, to his colleagues, and to himself. His duties toward the community consist of promptly reporting to the proper authority all cases of contagious diseases and cases having a criminal character and cases of abortion. Besides these duties of a general character, some physicians may have special duties related to specific public positions, such as public welfare officials, coroners, and the like.

With regard to the public, he must, among other duties, offer his services in case of any emergency. Prompt care may help save a life or alleviate grave suffering. In charity, a physician is obliged to make himself known when he happens to be present at the scene of an accident. Since the practice of medicine is above all a humanitarian duty, we incline toward the opinion of those who hold that the physician must give his services in any circumstance, independently of the real or presumed gravity of the condition of the patient he is called upon to attend. A physician is obliged to attend with the same loving interest any patient, regardless of race, nationality, political ideologies, social status, personal antipathies, and the like. He must respect the religious and philosophical convictions of the patient and must refrain from any moral judgment concerning the patient's past. He must be prudent and self-disciplined in examining his patients (*See* Examination, Physical), and keep professional secrecy (*See* Secret, Professional). Reasons dictated by charity oblige a physician to

make known a remedy he has discovered and from which the public at large would benefit; even if in so doing he might suffer a financial loss under the form of *lucrum cessans* (loss of gains).

A physician must deal with his colleagues according to the good norms of proper and social behavior prevailing in a civilized society. He must refrain from drawing clients away from his colleagues, or setting fees far too low; he must avoid uncharitable criticisms or any criticism of other doctors which may turn out to be detrimental to the entire medical profession. Charity and kindness toward other doctors is always a great asset to the entire profession.

The dignity and the decorum of his profession demand that the physician live in a home in which an atmosphere of morality, tranquillity, and respectability prevail. This applies in a particular manner to his wife. In this regard, observe what Hippocrates recommended twenty-three centuries ago in his Aphorisms:

If thou, O woman, wishest to be deserving of the beautiful title of a true wife of a doctor ...

Thou shalt be more virtuous than other wives, also morally better, gay and discreet.

Thou shalt not be jealous and shall have the greatest trust in thy master and spouse.

Thou shalt keep thy house in order and refrain from any curiosity concerning thy husband's patients.

Thou shalt avoid meddling in the practice of his art .... but shalt visit the unfortunate and comfort them in their suffering. . . .

Thou shalt forgive the offenses which thy husband may receive from unworthy colleagues and ungrateful patients, and when unhappy, sick or disappointed, thou shalt surround the companion of thy life with loving care and affectionate attention.

RIGHTS OF THE PHYSICIAN. The principal rights of the physician are these two: (a) to expect that his patient will follow diligently the hygienotherapeutic treatments he prescribes, if he is to assume full responsibility for the sick person; (b) to demand that, except in special cases, the family of the patient will not surreptitiously turn for aid to another doctor. These and other related points are treated under the entry "Withdrawal from Medical Case."

It may not be superfluous to add that insofar as treatments are concerned, (whether medical or, even more so, surgical), the physician has no right to use methods which are still in the experimental stage, since he has no sufficient assurance of the effectiveness of its employment by recognized physicians in well-known hospitals and other medical institutions. In the exceptional case, however, in which the patient is in a critical condition and time and place make it impossible to consult with other physicians, a doctor may rely solely on his own judgment and conscience and use a new medicine or a new surgical method, even though there may be a risk. In this case, for his own protection, he must obtain the consent of the patient's relatives. Another right of the physician is to expect a fair recompense for his services. This matter, which must be considered under the aspects of justice and also charity, is to be determined by local customs, the standing of the physician, the financial possibilities of the client, and the extent of the medical services rendered.

MEDICAL CERTIFICATES. It is within the exclusive competence of a physician to issue certification concerning the extent of the infirmity found in a patient, the treatment prescribed, the results obtained, the degree of the patient's inability to work, the extent of rest needed by a patient, etc. The only criterion by which a physician must be guided in issuing such affidavits or certificates is an honest evaluation of the case. Moral and penal laws forbid and punish quite severely the issuing of false medical certificates, even when issued simply for reasons of good will, which is a rather frequent occurrence. Certificates containing some exaggeration concerning the real condition of health of the client or the necessity of treatments are, in general, morally objectionable because in a certain sense they offend against the truth. Extenuating circumstances, however, should be taken into consideration. In view of the fact that medical certificates today are systematically underestimated by those authorities or private individuals to whom they are submitted, the deeper shades with which certificates are colored (with no financial gain in view, of course) can be considered as a legitimate corrective medium against the general underevaluation of the document.

For *pre-matrimonial certificates*, see Examination, Prenuptial.

For *deontology concerning other professions, see* each respective profession; for general subjects, *see* Professional Moral Theology. *Riz.*

DEONTOLOGY (Pharmaceutical). The professional morality of the pharmacist, also called pharmaceutical deontology involves complex and numerous aspects. The deontological problems treated here regard relations between pharmacist and doctor, pharmacist and the public, pharmacist and his colleagues. These relations always must be governed by a sense of propriety, dignity and, above all, of charity.

RELATIONS BETWEEN PHARMACIST AND DOCTORS. The reason which demands that doctors refrain from acting as pharmacists (selling, that is, to their clients sample medicines supplied by pharmaceutical houses for the purpose of study and, at times, for gratuitous administration) also demands that pharmacists refrain from acting as doctors, imparting, that is, to their clients, even if requested, opinions and therapeutic suggestions regarding the treatment of some illness. It is, indeed, an abuse for the pharmacist to give medicines simply on the claim by the caller of alleged subjective disturbances (headache, cough, constipation, etc.) affecting himself, or, worse still, some other sick member of his family. At best, this constitutes a case of improper competition with doctors. Nor is the possibility to be excluded that it may constitute a real delict in view of the danger that he may make a wrong diagnosis of the case which would cause a delay in the securing of proper medical attention with possible serious and even fatal consequences.

Another objectionable practice between pharmacist and doctor is that of the use of agents. Nor should it be considered licit to practice a mutual exchange of clients, arranged on a strictly business basis. In other words, it is unethical for a pharmacist to send patients to a specific doctor with the agreement that the doctor shall send them back to him for the medicine he will prescribe. However, if requested, the pharmacist is under moral obligation to direct a patient to the physician he honestly considers more capable or better equipped to treat this or that particular sickness. Likewise a doctor may suggest a particular pharmacist whom he considers more dependable and as carrying a better and larger supply of medicines. It is immoral for a pharmacist to suggest a particular physician to a client simply for egoistic reasons of gain while having no regard for the client's best interests.

DISHONEST PRESCRIPTIONS. The case is not infrequent when a doctor, either on account of haste or because of the impossibility of consulting a book on pharmacology, or of a lapse of memory concerning the exact name of a drug or of its chemical components, will prescribe medicines with names easier to remember and which are considered specialties and are more expensive than their normal equivalent. The pharmacist, whose right it is to check the prescription for any possible error, may out of charity substitute for the specialty type of medicine an equivalent ordinary type product, provided he does not price it as a specialty, and provided he is certain of the equivalent effectiveness and that he informs the doctor of the substitution. It is not rare, in fact, that the doctor himself, conscious of the fundamental equality of the two products, may have intentionally prescribed the specialty type medicine for psycho-

therapeutic reasons or for other motives of which he alone is responsible before his own conscience.

The prescription of narcotics directed at fostering drug-intoxication is gravely dishonest. A pharmacist who, because of the large dosage prescribed or the frequency of such prescriptions or for other reasons is certain of the unethical purposes of the prescription, is bound in conscience to refuse to supply the drug. In doubtful cases he should consult the physician, for there may be cases when the latter may feel justified in prescribing even large dosages of such drugs to alleviate the suffering in cases of inoperable cancer, or similar serious diseases.

Equally illicit is the prescription of medicines or instruments directed to the performing of abortion. If the pharmacist (who knows that there are no medicines having an exclusive abortive effect, and who also knows that in some specified cases indirect abortion is permissible) is ignorant of the true purpose of the purchase of that particular medicine or instrument, he is permitted to fill the prescription leaving all responsibility to the physician. On the contrary, if he is aware of the evil use to which the medicine will be put, he is bound in conscience to refuse outright to sell that medicine, without recourse to the untruthful excuse of not having it at the moment, since such an excuse might be taken as approval of the illicit use of the medicine. Only in urgent cases and when some probability exists as to a licit use of the medicine, may the pharmacist, even when he suspects on good ground the bad use of the instrument or the medicine prescribed by a doctor, fill the prescription, for there is room for supposing that grave complications may have arisen which are known only to the physician. In such a case, however, he should inform the client and the doctor of the possible impropriety involved and should voice his disapproval.

RELATIONS BETWEEN THE PHARMACIST AND THE PUBLIC. A frequent motive of perplexity for the conscientious pharmacist is that which revolves around the lawfulness or unlawfulness of the sale of contraceptive products. A pharmacist is not permitted to sell contraceptive products, be they instruments or chemical substances. The only exception to this rule is when the client is able to show a prescription in which it is stated that the product is not intended for contraceptive uses, but is exclusively for diagnostic and therapeutic purposes. The sale of hygienical products is lawful only when it is certain that they will be used for lawful purposes. Forbidden and punishable by law is the sale of "free samples" of medicines. Too, it is improper to sell products which have lost their effectiveness because of staleness and of specialties insufficiently controlled, or even worse, prepared with ingredients different from those indicated in their composition formula. Improper and fraudulent is the filling of a prescription with medicines of inferior quality and a quantity smaller than that prescribed by the physician.

PROFESSIONAL SECRECY. The pharmacist, like the physician whose strict collaborator he is, is bound by professional secrecy. This, according to Masino, "must be the bond of justice and charity between the pharmacist and his client." This obligation continues even after the death of the interested party, and an unauthorized disclosure of such secret constitutes a crime punishable by law, except when a just cause may require it, as in cases of infectious diseases, toxicomania, procured or consummated abortion, etc. The more common temptation to disclose a professional secret may occur when a client requests information concerning the use of some antivenereal medicine the pharmacist sold to the client's relative. The pharmacist cannot supply such information and must hide behind professional secrecy. In such cases, it may be well for him to refer the inquirer to the family doctor, if the possibility of a grave infection is suspected or if the inquirer is a parent of the patient (See Secrecy, Professional; Parents).

RELATIONS BETWEEN THE PHARMACIST AND HIS COLLEAGUES. Besides the ordinary professional relationship which normally arises between him and other pharmacists for the protection of their common rights and interests, the pharmacist must feel bound to his colleagues by relations of friendship and mutual respect in which the greater part of true pharmaceutical ethics are summed up. Thus, the pharmacist must speak and act always with prudence, justice and Christian charity and show understanding and tolerance of minor irregularities by other pharmacists. He should avoid malicious criticisms and insinuations with regard to his colleagues, a thing that often is done out of a base and misguided spirit of competition, with the obvious effect of disorienting the client and damaging the entire pharmaceutical profession. It is not by a justified or unjustified criticism of others that he will keep or increase the number of patrons, nor by underselling them or fraudulently imitating some of their products, but by improving his knowledge in the professional preparation of medicines and by treating his clients with charity, dignity, and justice.

Likewise, the pharmacist-employer must deal with his employees in a spirit of justice and charity, giving them just compensation for their work and manifesting the kindness and patience which spring from Christian principles. Nor shall he fail by his good example to impress them, particularly the young ones, with the observance of the norms of conduct outlined above, which alone can give their profession the luster and the honor which it well deserves. *Riz.*

DEPORTATION. *See* Democracy, Rights, Human; Person, Human.

DEPOSIT. To deposit is to enter into a contract by which one party accepts a thing from another with the obligation of saving it and of returning it as received. In this regard civil law determines the obligations which fundamentally flow from the very nature of the contract, considered in itself, independently of any positive juridical disposition. It can be gratuitous or onerous. Some authors, however, hold that this contract is, by its very nature, only gratuitous. This, of course, favors the depositor. Hence, if the depositary receives a compensation for the item deposited, no contract of deposit ensues but only the onerous work-contract (*locationis operae*). At any rate, all agree that in both cases the rights and duties of the depositor and the depositary are equivalent, with the exception that if the depositary charges a fee, he is obliged to keep safe the deposited item with greater diligence.

OBLIGATIONS OF THE DEPOSITARY. (a) The depositary (*see* Guaranty) must be as diligent as a good father, and use the same diligence in safeguarding a deposit as he would his own things. No greater diligence is required; so that in a general danger, he is not obliged to protect the property of the depositor before his own, unless he expressly obligated himself to that or charges a fee for safekeeping it. (b) The depositary is not permitted to use the deposit if he cannot at least legitimately presume the depositor's consent. If a gain is obtained from an unauthorized use of the deposit, the following distinction must be made: if the gain is a natural fruit of the deposit, restitution must be made; if the gain is the result of a civil or industrial use, no restitution is necessary. Thus, if the depositary, even if unauthorized, used the money deposited with him and by such investment obtained some gains, he can properly keep the gains as the fruit of his own personal industry. (c) The depositary must return the deposit upon request of the depositor unless a different agreement was made. If the depositor refuses to pay the stipulated charges, the depositary may refuse to surrender the deposit; likewise, according to some codes, in the case in which he learned that the deposit was the fruit of a crime, he is obliged to report it to the proper authorities. (d) The depositary is obliged to pay for any damage the deposit incurred while in his custody; this he can do before or after the sentence of the judge, depending on whether the damage was the result of a grave theological fault, or simply of juridical guilt. He has no obligation if the damage cannot be assigned to the depositary's responsibility, unless he expressly obligated himself to it.

OBLIGATIONS OF THE DEPOSITOR. The depositor is obliged to pay the stipulated charge for the safe-keeping of the deposit and all other compensations he agreed to make. The obligation, if any, to repay the depositary for possible loss or damage, even in this case, can be made before or after judiciary sentence, depending on whether it was a matter of juridical or simply of theological guilt.

DEPOSIT AND CONVENTIONAL SEQUESTER (SEQUESTRATION). Conventional sequestration (to be distinguished from juridical sequestration, which is ordained by the judge, Canon 1672 ff.) is also a type of deposit. It can be defined as the deposit of a controverted item by one or more persons with a third person (a trustee) who assumes the obligation to convey the deposit upon settlement of the controversy, to the person who by law is declared to be the legitimate owner. *Pal.*

DEPOSITION. Deposition is one of the gravest vindictive penalties imposed by the Church, which, while leaving intact the obligations arising from sacred orders (chastity and the Divine Office) and the clerical privileges, implies suspension from office actually held, and disqualification to obtain or discharge any other offices, dignities, benefices, pensions, or ecclesiastical positions as well as the privation of any other ecclesiastical prerogative or possession over and above those already mentioned (Can. 2303, par. 1). This includes the very title under which one was ordained, which in itself is considered an inalienable patrimony. Thus, a deposed cleric, who was ordained under the title of a benefice, is by his deposition deprived of it, although the local Ordinary shall charitably provide for him in the best possible manner so as to avoid any dishonor upon the clerical state which might result from the necessity of providing his living by begging.

Until the end of the twelfth century the term *deposition* was used interchangeably with the term *degradation*, and it described a particularly grave penalty inflicted upon clerics guilty of grave infractions of ecclesiastical laws. It deprived them of offices and ecclesiastical benefices and disqualified them for any other office including the exercise of any clerical order which they had already received. It was true penal reduction to the lay state such as occurred in the case of Origen, who was guilty of being ordained by a bishop other than his own, against the disciplinary regulations of the Church. A milder form of deposition, also very ancient, consisted of the privation of office without loss of dignity or of the clerical state; a reduction, as it were, from a higher to a lower ecclesiastical position. After the twelfth century this milder form was called *deposition*, while the more rigorous one, which entailed loss of office and ecclesiastical dignity and the complete reduction to the lay state, was called *degradation*.

The Code of Canon Law does not consider this penalty as imposed simply by the law, that is, without the intervention of the superior. As a matter of fact, as a very grave penalty, the law itself prescribes that it should not be resorted to except by the decision of a collegiate tribunal of five judges (Can. 1576, par. 1, n. 2) and only in those cases which are specifically mentioned by the law.

The Church is a society composed of human beings and therefore subject to human weaknesses. It is only natural that even among ecclesiastics there may be men who are unworthy of their calling. Once discovered, they should be effectively removed from the clerical ranks so as to prevent abuses of their dignity and powers, and to avoid scandal to the faithful. *Pug.*

DEPRIVATION OF OFFICE. *See* Removal.

DE PROFUNDIS. The 129th (130th) Psalm, the sixth of the seven Penitential Psalms, and, next to the *Miserere* (*q.v.*), the best known, particularly on account of the extensive use made of it in the liturgy for the dead, takes its name from the opening words *"de profundis,"* "out of the depths."

It is one of a special collection of canticles (from Psalms 119 to 133) called Songs of Ascent, probably because they were chanted in going up to Jerusalem (III Kings 12:28; I Mach. 4:36 ff.; Matt. 20:17 ff., *etc.*) to the Temple, on the three annual solemnities (Es. 8:8–16; Deut. 16:1–16; Luke 2:41 ff.). However, not all were composed for that occasion. The *De Profundis* seems to have reference to the time of the exile or of Nehemias. The Psalm is a prayer for forgiveness of sin. The people of Israel, in the person of the psalmist, having realized that sin is the root of all the evils which afflict them, turn to God from the abyss of sufferings, confidently asking for forgiveness. It can be divided into two parts: Part I (1–4) is a cry of repentance to a merciful and forgiving Lord; God alone can condone the debt a sinner contracts by his sin. In Part 2, (5–8) the psalmist is confident that God in his mercy will not fail to deliver him from the effects of sin, in the day of redemption.

LITURGICAL USE. The *De Profundis* is generally used in the services for the dead, not because it is in any particular way related to them but because the words are adaptable in a remarkable way to the state of the souls in purgatory on whose lips, so to speak, they are placed by the Church. *Pal.*

DERISION. *See* Contumely, Honor.

DEROGATION. A partial or total abrogation of a law, but affecting only particular groups, not the whole of society.

EFFECTS. With regards to its effects, *see* Abrogation, Law. *Gra.*

DESIRE. Desire is an act of the will tending towards an object which is absent. In psychology, mention is made, also, of a desire of the inferior faculties (sensitive appetite); but a moralist is concerned with desire only insofar as it is a voluntary act, that is, originating in the will or, at least, accepted by the will.

A desire is effectual, if it is absolute and consists of a real intent to proceed to the execution. It is ineffectual if it is conditional and inoperative, that is, if it is not a real determination but rather a velleity or sterile desire to act, so that the person deliberately refrains from carrying it out due to the absence of some condition. Obviously, the object determines the morality of desire, although there can be a great difference between effectual and ineffectual desire.

MORAL EVALUATION. The effectual desire extends, in the order of thought, to the entire morality of its object, including all the circumstances surrounding it, provided that they are adverted to by the person. Likewise, the ineffectual desire takes on the morality of its object and can extend also to that of its circumstances, but it is more likely that these are not adverted to by the person; hence they do not exercise a marked influence upon the morality of the desire. Moreover, there is excluded from the ineffectual desire, whenever the exclusion is possible, the influence by the circumstance which constitutes its main condition, that is, the reason why the person stops at the mere desire without proceeding to the intent to act. We say, "when the exclusion is possible," because this does not always happen; for instance, it is possible for me to desire an object on condition that it has no owner; but since it is impossible for blasphemy be to lawful, I cannot desire it on condition of its licitness; the condition would be absurd. It must be noted that these conditional desires in the first case (possible condition) may reveal an evil tendency of the individual and may constitute for him a more or less grave danger according to the matter with which they deal; in the second case (impossible condition) they may indicate faintness of desire. Moreover, it is necessary to bear in mind that, particularly in the matter of impurity, if pleasure in the actual disturbance of the senses accompanies the desire, no condition can excuse from imputability. Gra.

DESERTION. Desertion, in general, is the relinquishing of a thing with the intention of abandoning all claims to it or all obligations connected with it. The term *desertion* or *abandonment* is also used as synonymous with renunciation, desistance, abdication, recession, depending on the object to which it is referred.

Desertion (*derelictio*) of a property has as its effect the loss of the property itself, so that it becomes *res nullius* and is susceptible of acquisition by the first occupant. The unlawful desertion of an ecclesiastical office is a sin; in Canon Law it is considered a crime punishable with suspension *a divinis* (Can. 2399). Also, the unlawful desertion of residence or of an office to which the obligation of residence is attached, is both a sinful act and may constitute a real and proper crime (Can. 2381); it is considered, at best, as a tacit renunciation of an office by a cleric (Can. 188, n. 8).

Sinful and, at times, also criminal, is the unauthorized relinquishment of the clerical habit or the religious garb.

Among the sinful and criminal acts of desertion must be included also the arbitrary desertion or abandonment of the spouse or of the conjugal bed, which may constitute ground for a temporary or even permanent separation from the other party. See Separation of Husband and Wife. *Pal.*

DESERTION. See Military Service.

DESPAIR. In general, despair is the loss of hope in the attainment of a coveted good not yet possessed. In a theological sense, it is the act by which one loses hope of attaining eternal life, because he thinks that God cannot or will not grant him remission of his sins or give him the aids necessary for his final perseverance in grace, or because he believes that the observance of the divine precepts is simply too difficult. A distinction must be made between desperation and immoderate fear of not attaining eternal life on account of difficulties or one's own weakness. Despair must not be confused with sloth in facing difficulties.

Despair, in its technical sense, is a serious sin against hope in God, who wills the salvation of every man, and who gives every man the graces necessary for the observance of His precepts and the attainment of eternal life. In view of its motive, despair could imply also a sin against faith. It is the first of the so-called "sins against the Holy Spirit." Excessive fear of not attaining eternal life is not directly opposed to the virtue of hope but to fortitude; the sin is grave when that fear places a person in danger of desisting from the efforts necessary for the attainment of eternal life or when it causes a total cessation of such efforts, for this is despair. The same applies to sloth. Despair is a vicious sin in that it causes a spiritual paralysis with regard to efforts in doing good and overcoming difficulties.

CAUSES AND REMEDIES. The causes of despair are excessive love of material pleasures, almost habitual and unrestrained melancholy, an immoderate fear of the divine justice, too vivid a consideration of one's sins. The remedies against it are avoidance of vice and melancholy, moderate fear of divine justice, consideration of God's infinite mercy and fidelity to His promises and filial devotion to the Blessed Virgin. *Man.*

DESPOTISM. *See* Absolutism, Tyranny, Totalitarianism.

DETENTION. *See* Possession.

DETERMINISM. Determinism is any doctrine which denies man's free will on the claim that man's will does not of itself determine its volitions, but is determined by other causes. According to the source to which the necessitating determination is attributed, there are different schools of deterministic doctrines, theological, fatalistic, psychological, materialistic, astrological.

THEOLOGICAL (perhaps better called theologistic) DETERMINISM nullifies human liberty by the divine causality, stating (and correctly so) that our acts proceed from ourselves as from secondary causes, from God as primary cause; then they add (but erroneously so) that we are blind and powerless instruments in the hands of God. This doctrine is based on ignorance of the great difference between divine acts and human acts. Man could not be the cause of another man's action (much less of his volition) without violating or at least limiting his freedom, whereas God's action is outside this law. It is an error to believe that our freedom (in order to remain such) must withdraw itself from its primary cause. The contrary is true: man's freedom is so much fuller and the more secure as the divine influence is more intimately brought to bear upon it. Not only his power but also the freedom of his will is in God as in the first cause.

FATALISTIC DETERMINISM assigns the moving cause of our volitions to an obscure force (fate) which is not strictly divine (because even the gods are subject to it), nor is it of cosmic origin.

PSYCHOLOGICAL DETERMINISM holds that our will is forced by one of our other psychic faculties; hence it assumes diverse forms according to the faculty from which our determinations flow. The most common form in moral philosophy is that which is called rationalistic which holds that our will is impelled by reason and that we elect always that which our reason presents to us as the better thing. This doctrine ignores an incontestable fact, namely, that in the very act in which man's reason makes its practical judgment concerning the better thing, it is under the influence of his will. In practical life man's freedom extends beyond his actions and covers his very judgments as well.

MATERIALISTIC DETERMINISM fails to distinguish between human actions and the action of physical forces. Hence, it subjects man's actions and volitions to the laws and causes which govern the material world, namely, to a naturalistic determinism.

ASTROLOGICAL DETERMINISM holds man's will to be subject to the influence of the stars. As far as the world of culture is concerned, this has no value. From the theoretical standpoint it can be reduced to one of the preceding forms, according as the stars are considered to be material, psychic, or divine beings. *Gra.*

DETRACTION. *See* Calumny, Defamation.

DEVIL. In Sacred Scripture and in the entire Christian Tradition the devil is considered as the great antagonist of God and of good, the principle of moral evil (Wisdom 2:24); his kingdom is in perpetual conflict with the kingdom of God, constantly bent on causing the greatest possible damage to it, sowing evil everywhere, destroying the work of grace, by open or secret attack (Matt. 12:22; 13:39; 16:18; John 12:31; Apoc. 12:7-9; 13:1-7). Besides his general opposition to the kingdom of God, the devil, immutably determined toward evil as the result of his own sin (I John 3:8), seeks by particular solicitations to lead each man to evil, employing his spiritual faculties, which excel those of man. Moreover, using the triple concupiscence (I John 2:16; 5:19) and man's own corrupt nature (James 1:14), he is the principal cause of man's temptations. Man's tempter par excellence from the very beginning (Matt. 4:3-11; John 8:44), he tempts him throughout his entire life, to his last breath (Mark 4:15; Luke 22:31; I Pet. 5:8; Eph. 6:12; Council of Trent, Sess. XIV, *de Extr. Unct. proemium*). Sometimes, the devil tempts man by external means (hallucinations, apparitions, etc.). Generally, however, the devil tempts man by internal suggestions, not by directly moving the intellect or the will, but indirectly so, by acting upon the imagination and the senses. There are many cases of diabolical possession in which the devil actually takes possession of the body and the faculties of an individual, but in such cases, the sins which he might cause the person to commit (e.g., blasphemy) would not be true sins imputable to the person, except in cause. (*See* Voluntary.) Man must and can resist the insinuations of the devil and of his power through the redemptive efficacy of Christ's death. Hence, assisted by divine grace, man can by his free will overcome temptations, if he will but use the proper means placed at his disposal, such as prayer and vigilance (I Pet. 5:9; James 4:7; I John 2:14).

In view of the fact that the devil's nature and faculties are superior to those of man and are surrounded by a certain degree of mystery, he can become the object of a false cult, gravely sinful, and extremely offensive to God. This cult can be explicit and formal. It can be offered to God's great antagonist either out of hatred of God (satanism, diabolical mass), or to seek his aid in some difficulty, or even for the purpose of working false miracles (pact with the devil, explicit invocations). Often however, this cult is practiced implicitly in the sense that veneration is accorded by some individuals to a being who is practically no one else but the devil, while others pretend to do things which cannot be done except by his intervention, though they are not fully aware that such may be the case. *See* Divination. *Dam.*

DEVOTION. The word *devotion* has a variety of meanings. In its broad sense it means any religious practice toward God or a saint: in this sense, we speak of devotion to the Blessed Sacrament, to the Blessed Virgin, or to a saint. It also means recollection and attention while praying; thus one is said to pray with much or little devotion. In a stricter sense, it means dedication of oneself to the service of God, or promptness in doing something which belongs to the service of God. This dedication to God is an act of the virtue of religion by which one is inclined to give God the cult owed to Him; as a matter of fact, it constitutes the fundamental act of such cult and it can exercise an influence over the other acts which glorify God, and also upon man's outward demeanor. Devotion may be influenced by love of God. Devotion does not consist in an exaltation of one's imagination or emotions, nor in a sweet feeling or a sensitive joy experienced, at times, while praying. These sentiments, insofar as they dispose a person to prayer and to fervor in the service of God, are useful; hence, God often arouses them at the beginning of a person's spiritual life. However, frequently they are sought too eagerly and with considerable detriment to a genuine union with God. To remove such danger and to purify the soul, God, more often than not, deprives it of such joys, especially in the case of those who have made great strides in the spiritual life.

Jesus Christ gave us a perfect example of devotion by performing, out of love, at the very moment of His entry into this world, an act of absolute dedication to His Eternal Father (Ps. 39:7-9; Hebr. 10:5-10). Christians are expected to imitate this example and to renew often their total dedication to the service of God. They should also consecrate their actions to God, beginning them with the sign of the Cross, and injecting into their prayers and other acts of worship a profound devotion. *Man.*

DEVOTION (Practices of). The practices of devotion are means for the acquisition of devotion as an end. The principal Catholic devotions are directed toward the Blessed Trinity, Our Lord Jesus Christ, the Blessed Virgin Mary, St. Joseph, the angels and saints and even toward the holy souls in Purgatory. The more common practices of devotion, such as the Sign of the Cross, the Stations of the Cross, the Holy Hour, the Visit to the Blessed Sacrament, the Rosary, Processions, the First Fridays of the month, etc., enjoy the explicit or implicit approbation of the Church and the favor of directors of souls. These practices of devotion offer many benefits (indulgences, etc.) and particular graces of a spiritual and also of a material order. All of them produce

moral and social effects of the highest quality.

All abuse in this field must be avoided. Practices of devotion become objectionable when they are preferred to more fundamental acts of worship and of Christian living; when they occupy a preponderant part in the life of an individual to the point where obligations of his state in life are neglected; when their entire effectiveness is made dependent on the external act or, worse yet, upon a combination of external acts. An interior cult combined with the practice of Christian virtue is an essential condition that practices of devotion may achieve their end and avoid superstition. *Pal.*

DIACONATE (Deacon). *See* Sacred Orders.

DIATRIBE. *See* Polemics.

DICHOTOMY (Fee-splitting). The term *dichotomy* (etymologically, *di-cho-tomos*—a cutting in two) has come into common usage with professional groups to indicate an aggregate of mutually bestowed favors, reflecting upon professional morality. Here are examples: A public official directs one of his clients in need of legal counselling to a specific lawyer and the lawyer reciprocates by directing one of his own paying clients to the public official; a lawyer receives a case from the Clerk of the Court or a similar official and gives the Clerk or the favoring official a part of his fee or other gifts; a physician directs a surgical case to a surgeon and receives from the latter a certain amount of money as part of a business deal; another doctor prevails upon his client to enter a particular hospital and the hospital rewards him with a certain percentage of their revenues from the case, on a business basis.

Since, strictly speaking, no compensation may be considered honest except when obtained for services actually rendered, it is clear that the cases above mentioned cannot be considered morally justified; nor is it proper for a physician to send a patient to a particular hospital or to a particular surgeon under the conditions mentioned above, since in such practices, the patient involuntarily ends up paying more than he would if the physician had done what was his strict duty, such as giving a definite diagnosis and prescribing the most effective remedy. It is not unethical, of course, if the surgeon of the hospital chooses to give the physician part of his normal fee, being satisfied, for reasons of competition, with a smaller profit. It is absolutely objectionable and immoral for a professional man to refer cases to a colleague technically less qualified than others only because of the financial compensation or other gifts that he will receive from him; also, when a group of professional men of various professions work together to exploit certain clients indefinitely, for medical, legal, financial and other needs. Since this is done sometimes by persons of dubious professional ability, and clearly for reasons of exploitation, it is easy to see how such practices border on fraud and are strongly objectionable from the moral standpoint, particularly in view of the fact that such persons are often exempt from legal prosecution because of the general character of their work.

Outside the typical cases mentioned above, moral principles are seldom directly violated, especially when the cooperation between physician and surgeon or between doctor and hospital is motivated by real interest in the client and the love of neighbor. In a field as delicate as this, it is easy to rationalize and from egoism to seek easy gains. In practice, granting that it is difficult for a professional man to refuse dichotomic compensations, he must never solicit them, but must always abide by the moral principles which are such a great part of professional dignity.

Use of Promoters. Similar, under certain aspects, to dichotomy and equally objectionable, is the use of professional promotionalism, which consists of hiring promoters or agents to solicit clients for a physician. These promoters, who operate also in higher professional levels, engage in exalting the more or less hypothetical qualities of a certain professional man and stoop to almost any means to convince credulous clients to patronize the professional men they recommend. These practices are improper, reprehensible, and totally illicit. *Riz.*

DIES IRAE. A poetical composition of great lyrical and dramatic effect, which has inspired the greatest musical geniuses of all times and faiths. For a long time it was ascribed to Thomas of Celano, the biographer of St. Francis of Assisi; however, the discovery of a Cassinese manuscript earlier than the Celanese, places the origin of the *Dies Irae* in the seventh century.

It is a variation on the subject of the final judgment. This topic exercised a great influence on the arts of the period. It was perhaps originally composed for use on the last Sunday of Pentecost and the first of Advent. The only reference to the liturgy of the dead, of which today it is such an important and peculiar part, is contained in the last two verses, which are absent in the Cassinese manuscript and which in view of change in the rhythm, betray an addition by a later writer. It was first found in the Franciscan Missals of the thirteenth century and was introduced into the official Roman liturgy at the time of the edition of the Missal by Pius V (1570), although it was already present in the edition of 1504.

The *Dies Irae* has to be recited only at Masses for the Dead, designated as *in die obitus seu depositionis*, "the corpse being present," or for a reasonable cause also when it is not present, and in one of the three Masses said on November 2nd, either the first or the one given more solemnity. In all other Masses of the dead it is optional (Decree of the Sacred Congregation of Rites, March 23, 1955). *Cig.*

DILIGENCE. *Diligence is a gift and a virtue* that is founded on love. Diligence is the fruit of love. In general, it is a constant and solicitous care in doing something, or a particular attention in carrying out a definite assignment. Dili-

ence may be a purely natural gift which
s always an object of praise and respect;
c acquires a moral and even a supernatural value, if the motive is the glory
of God. It is opposed to negligence, that
s, habitual carelessness in one's own
duties because disliked.

CANONICAL DILIGENCE. Diligence required by the Code of Canon Law has
an external character; it does not exclude
the internal; as a matter of fact, it presupposes it. Diligence is enjoined upon
a) the person who administers or receives the sacraments, the principal
means of sanctification and salvation
Can. 731, par. 1.); (b) those who attend the sick and are to see to it that
they receive the Last Rites while still in
a state of consciousness (*sui compotes*,
Can. 944); (c) the person in charge of
the diocesan archives (Can. 375, par.
2); (d) the master of novices, with
regard to the religious formation of the
latter (Can. 562); (e) the administrators of ecclesiastical property, with
regard to the proper handling and safekeeping of all acts and documents concerning property rights (Can. 1523);
f) the trustee who is the custodian,
the caretaker, and the preserver of goods
entrusted to him as if they belonged to
him (Can. 1675, par. 2).

Diligent attendance at choral service
gives the choristers or canons the right
to the daily distributions (Can. 395, par.
3); those who fail to be present are
deprived of them. Distributions were
instituted precisely to reward those who
are diligent in attendance at choir.

CANONICAL NEGLIGENCE. Omission of
proper diligence can constitute an element of imputability in a crime (Can.
199). It can also cause a diminution of
liability with regard to a deliberate offense, *dolus* (Can. 2203), even to the
point of excusing the offender from the
penalty, except in those cases in which
the law contains the following clauses:
*praesumpserit, ausus fuerit, scienter,
studiose*, etc. (Can. 2229, par. 3, n. 2).
In the procedural part, regarding the
causes of saints, mention is made of
processiculus diligentiarum, which consists of the acts of the Bishop in the

juridical investigation conducted with
reference to the writings of a servant of
God that are to be transmitted to the
Holy See (Can. 2061). *M.d.G.*

DIMISSORIAL (Letters). According to
Canon Law, a candidate is duly ordained only by his own Bishop or by
another with his Bishop's permission expressed by the so-called *dimissorial letters* (Can. 955) (*See* Orders, Holy).
Dimissorial letters are the documents
with which a diocesan Bishop or other
competent ecclesiastical superior (Can.
957, par. 1; Can. 958) authorizes another
Bishop or a priest to ordain his own
subjects. Dimissorial letters are not to
be confused either with testimonial letters or with letters of excardination.
Whoever ordains the subject of another
Bishop or superior without dimissorial
letters of the candidate's own ecclesiastical superior incurs automatic (*ipso
facto*) suspension from the conferring of
orders for the period of one year. This
censure is reserved to the Holy See
(Can. 2373, no. 1). A man who maliciously presents himself for ordination
without dimissorial letters or with forged
letters is (*ipso facto*) automatically suspended from the order unlawfully received (Can. 2374).

Besides the Supreme Pontiff, the following superiors have power to give dimissorial letters: (a) For the secular
clergy: (1) the proper Bishop after he
has taken canonical possession of his
diocese, though he has not yet been
consecrated; (2) the Vicar General by
special mandate of his Bishop; (3) the
Vicar-capitular with the consent of the
Cathedral chapter and, except in cases
of emergency, after the episcopal see has
been vacant for one year, under penalty
of *ipso facto* suspension *a divinis*, that
is, from all acts performed in virtue of the
power of ordination. He must not give
them to those who were rejected by the
Bishop unless the obstacle was removed.
(4) Vicars and Prefects Apostolic, Abbots and prelates *nullius*, even though
not titular bishops. All these can issue
dimissorial letters as long as they retain

the power of jurisdiction in their respective territories (Can. 958).

Dimissorial letters may be sent by the above mentioned prelates to any Catholic Bishop, provided that he be of the same rite as the candidate for ordination. Otherwise, an Apostolic indult is required (Can. 960). Moreover, dimissorial letters may be sent for the conferral of tonsure and minor orders to a Cardinal (non-Bishop) (Can. 239, par. 1, no. 22) or to a Vicar or Prefect Apostolic and also to an Abbot or Prelate *nullius* (non-Bishops), who may validly confer these orders only during their tenure of office and within their own territory (Can. 957, par. 2).

(b) With regard to members of the regular clergy (religious), a distinction must be made between exempt and non-exempt religious. (1) Exempt religious cannot licitly be ordained by any Bishop without the dimissorial letters of their proper major superior. The latter may issue dimissorial letters for all orders in the case of religious with perpetual vows, but only for first tonsure and minor orders in the case of religious with temporary vows which must precede perpetual vows (Can. 574). The superior may address the dimissorial letters only to the Bishop in whose territory the religious house to which the religious is attached is located, with the exception of five special cases indicated in Canon 1006. A superior who sends the dimissorial letters to a Bishop outside the five cases mentioned in the above canon is *ipso facto* suspended from the celebration of the Mass for a month, and the Bishop who ordains such a religious is suspended from conferring orders for a year (Can. 2373, no. 4). (2) The regulations governing candidates of the secular clergy apply also to non-exempt religious, with the exception of those who enjoy special privileges. Every indult granted to superiors before the promulgation of the Code of Canon Law, to issue dimissorial letters for major orders to religious with temporary vows, is revoked (Can. 964–967). (3) Requirements which must precede dimissorials. Those who have

the right to grant dimissorial letters must be in possession of all the testimonial documents required by Canon Law (Can. 993–1000) regarding candidates for ordination, such as testimonial letters attesting to the completion of their studies, their good conduct, etc. (Can. 960, par. 1). The dimissorials may be revoked or limited by the Bishop or other ecclesiastical superior or by their successors. A dimissorial letter issued by one's bishop or superior does not become void by subsequent loss of jurisdiction by the one who gave them. (Can. 963). *Led.*

DIPLOMACY. Diplomacy is defined by many as the science and art by which relations between sovereign States are regulated. It is a science because it requires a profound knowledge of the nature of the international relations which are to be regulated; it is an art also, because special aptitudes are required of those who are called to regulate such relations.

In the sense indicated above, it can be said that there always has been a diplomacy, because there has always been a need to regulate relations between States, particularly in peace time. However, as a permanently organized science, it came into being in the last few centuries, as the result of a constant increase in the relations between the States which, besides establishing centralized offices in their own respective territories, found it necessary to send special missions, first on a temporary basis, then permanently, to other States. Permanent diplomatic legations were already in existence in the thirteenth century through the initiative of the Holy See and of the Venetian Republic. In the seventeenth century almost all States had such legations.

The importance of diplomacy is easily understood, if one takes into consideration the large number and the nature of the relations—political, juridical, economic, cultural, etc.—to be maintained and regulated between States. The condition of independent existence for many States requires that the relations existing between States be properly and diligently regulated.

The purpose of diplomacy is to maintain and increase complete harmony and peace among the peoples and to develop to the greatest possible degree justice, mutual understanding, and friendship among them. Such an end must be obtained by honest and sincere means. The sense of loyalty of diplomats must apply to their own country as well as to the State to which they are appointed. *Pas.*

DIPSOMANIA. Dipsomania is derived from the Greek word *dipse*—thirst. One of its characteristics is a sudden and imperious urge to drink alcoholic beverages to the point of drunkenness. Such an urge is possible even in individuals who are habitually abstemious. During the intervals between drinking spells, the dipsomaniac can without great effort reach a state of complete abstinence and sometimes may even feel a strong repugnance to alcohol.

The dipsomaniac drinks avidly without enjoying the taste of liquor, and often he can tolerate a very large quantity of it, without showing signs of drunkenness. At times, however, the drunkenness takes a rather abnormal form and causes grave dizziness, confusion, anguish, and some types of delirium. During the crisis, the dipsomaniac may experience lack of appetite and insomnia. Then a state of general malaise sets in, and not infrequently he has either no recollection at all of events or only vague and distorted memories.

Typical conditions of dipsomania are present in chronic epileptics and could be the only symptoms of epilepsy. Sometimes dipsomania constitutes one of those impulsive obsessions present in psychasthenia, characterized by an immoderate desire for alcoholic beverages; the individual fights it off for a time, not without a struggle, until, overwhelmed by a pathological impulse, he gives in to the obsessive idea, and obtains temporary relief from it and a passing sense of tranquillity. At other times the crisis of dipsomania could be the expression of a state of excitement indicative of dysthymia, of progressive paralysis or other types of psychosis.

Similar to dipsomania in nature and symptoms are other pathological manifestations which are more difficult to detect and which affect the nutritional, sexual, motor functions, etc. These manifestations take the names, respectively, of bulimia (or sitomania), erotomania, dromomania, and also of clastomania (impulse to break), pyromania (impulse to set fire), kleptomania (impulse to steal), etc.

Moral Observation. As appears from this summary treatment, the dipsomaniac is not a depraved or a vitiated individual, but a sick person in need of medical attention (for treatments see each individual disorder of which dipsomania is a symptom). The dipsomaniac deserves sympathy rather than condemnation. The same rule applies, of necessity, to other common forms of alcoholism caused by a frequent occurrence of dipsomaniacal crises.

Obviously those afflicted with any of the pathological manifestations listed above as neuropsychic disorders are generally exempt from moral imputability and moral penal sanctions.

In such cases, one must ascertain through accurate clinical examinations whether any such disorder may not be rather the manifestation of so-called constitutional immorality or of common delinquency, which is up to a neuropsychiatrist to determine. *Riz.*

DIRECTION (Spiritual). Spiritual direction means imparting (or receiving) concrete norms of conduct suited to the spiritual condition of the recipient. It presupposes a great degree of candor on the part of the one under direction. While confession covers only the sins committed, spiritual direction covers, besides sins and their causes, anything related to the spiritual progress of the person: the natural temperament with its favorable and unfavorable aspects, good or bad habits acquired, likes and dislikes, special difficulties, temptations and dangers, imperfections, imprudences and inconsistencies, the means used in avoiding sin, in eradicating bad inclinations and in developing good ones, etc. For those who have not chosen a state in life, there is also the question of the choice of a vocation to be discussed and, once this is settled, the means with which the calling is to be pursued.

A prudent and solid spiritual direction is very important and, in general, even necessary if one is to make spiritual progress. The ancient Fathers and the later ecclesiastical writers recommend an unlimited candidness not only as to sins, but also little faults, temptations, and special difficulties.

Leo XIII sanctioned this traditional doctrine by his Letter *"Testem benevolentiae,"* of January 22, 1899. The need of good spiritual direction is even greater in times of special temptations and difficulties.

Though not necessary, it is, however, helpful that the confessor and the spiritual director be one and the same person and that spiritual direction be given at the time of the confession of sins in the sacrament of penance. Profound respect for the spiritual director is required; the person must recognize in him the representative of Jesus. While an all-out familiarity with him is to be avoided, the penitent must place in him the greatest trust, opening to him the condition of his soul in a brief, clear and sincere manner, being careful to avoid taking a certain satisfaction in speaking of himself or to draw upon himself the interested attention of the spiritual director. The penitent must accept from the spiritual director with humility and docility all his admonitions and must put them into practice. Wherever such dispositions are lacking, spiritual direction fails to obtain its desired fruits. Once selected, a spiritual director should not be changed without good reason. *Man.*

DIRIMENT (Impediment). *See* Impediments, Matrimonial.

DISABILITY (Accidents, Liability). By *accident* is understood an unforeseen event that has caused an injury or damage whether from labor, traffic, or war.

The study of the legislative, medical, social, statistical, technico-industrial measures relative to accidents constitutes a new and important sector in the field of social and economic protection. Its importance is the result of a growing industrialization in all countries, of ever-increasing risks proper to modern living, and of small and large armed conflicts that have wrought incalculable damage on the world since the turn of the century.

It is therefore a question with which the entire civilized world should be concerned, since a host of victims of accidents weighs heavily on the economy of individual families (never sufficiently repaid) and, in some cases, on the economy of the State loaded down with expenses for the care or indemnification of victims of accidents.

If we add to these expenditures the temporary or permanent loss of *manpower* (whether the victim dies or is permanently disabled), the losses suffered by industry (every accident necessarily causes an interruption and a disturbance in the working rhythm of an establishment where work is done on assembly lines), the economic, physical and moral problems created in many families for whom the victims were the only source of income, it becomes crystal clear that these accidents have a social impact of primary importance.

This impact is even greater if one considers that a large number of labor accidents escape statistics either because they are of a minor nature or because they affect domestic workers or workers who are not insured.

It is easy to understand how, because of the *damnum emergens* (that is, the money spent to remedy the effects of an accident), every nation loses millions of dollars each year because of labor accidents.

If the number of victims of labor accidents is large, in the past ten years the number of road accidents has become even larger.

In the aftermath of the war, whether

as a result of a lowering of respect for human life (a phenomenon that unfortunately follows in the wake of all great catastrophes), or as a result of the enormous increase in mechanized means of transportation, road accidents have increased enormously.

As to the presumable causes of these accidents, an accurate research of statistics shows that a large majority are caused by the drivers because of physical incapacity or carelessness, or even more by excessive speed, too often as the result of a state of inebriation, as demonstrated by modern research in alcoholism.

MEDICAL ASSISTANCE TO ACCIDENT VICTIMS. This particular phase of assistance has become more and more definite with the spread of modern industrialization. Today the workers' right to compensation for unemployment, more particularly from labor accidents, is recognized everywhere. Medical benefits to workers have grown to what at the beginning of the century was almost a Utopian dream of a few far-seeing scholars.

The worker who has been victim of an accident has the right not only to medical and surgical care, but also to a fair compensation for the injury suffered. The exact value of this compensation requires accurate medical and legal investigation. We note further that, onerous as these provisions may be, they are now not only peacefully accepted, but they redound to the general welfare of the community as well as to the benefit of employers themselves; since "in giving and receiving, in offering and in the accepting of the offer, industry and labor must not act under the rigid aspect of the *ego* and the *alter* but under the aspect of *socius* (partner) in which the *ego* and the *alter* are firmly brought together" (Bellucci). This is also the Christian spirit.

The anatomical and functional restoration of the damage suffered by a worker because of accident is by far more important than the pecuniary indemnification, for the former is something generally more durable from which not only the individual but the entire community may benefit.

The means necessary for the treatment and care of accident victims require a complex organization which, in practice, is far from being perfect anywhere.

First aid should be given immediately after the accident by experienced physicians. On this depends the complete *restitutio ad integrum* and often the very life of the victim. In reality, due to a lack of suitable doctors or nurses on farming and industrial establishments sometimes hours go by before a victim of accident can obtain the proper medical care. The victim should be kept under proper medical care until complete physical recovery is attained. This requires a far greater number of hospital personnel, and for the more serious cases, many more hospital beds than are in existence today. Since in 50% of the cases, if not more, the victim is not in condition to resume his work after mere physical recovery, there should be suitable institutions for kinesitherapy, psychotherapy, and rehabilitation, for the complete recovery of so many accident victims, who at times are led to conclude so-called permanent settlements without careful psychosomatic treatments which in the great majority of cases are needed to bring about a truly complete recovery.

Therefore, the importance of intelligent medical assistance for accident victims is evident. And if it is true that the means to carry it out are very costly, the fact remains that the damage sustained by society from deficiencies still existing in this fundamental field of accident liabilities is much more serious.

PREVENTION OF ACCIDENTS. The social importance of the care of accident victims is undoubtedly great, but the prevention of accidents is even greater and, of course, more complicated since it requires the active collaboration of technicians, employers, doctors, and workers.

An accident is by definition unforeseeable, although it is susceptible of statistical forecasting. In other words, accidents can be studied statistically; and it is from these studies that the fundamental elements in the calculation of risks are derived as an essential premise for an intelligent prevention of them.

The unpredictability of accidents with physical injury is allied to another characteristic, namely *involuntariness*. But in this connection there is a certain relativity in the sense that the greater part (as much as 80%) of accidents occur under the influence of joint causes stemming from the so-called *human factor* which is indirectly influenced by the will. It follows that the knowledge of the intrinsic and extrinsic conditions existing as causal elements of accidents together with the human factor in an individual is important for the prevention of accidents. It permits the timely elimination of likely causes and the adoption of rules and devices suitable for the prevention of damaging effects.

A careful statistical study of the times when accidents occur has demonstrated the great importance of factors such as fatigue, environment, monotony, and, more so, a series of constitutional psychosomatic elements (quite different from real and proper nervous or mental disorders), which have a notable influence on the occurrence of accidents involving physical injury.

In this respect, undoubtedly of great ethical and social value, we may recall that ever since the beginning of systematic statistical research, it has been noted that accidents are not uniformly distributed among the workers. In every factory and working community it is easy to isolate a group of workers who have never had an accident, and a second group (known as accident-prone) who have had several and are likely to keep on having them. Minor defects and lack of coordination of the neuromuscular apparatus, lack of will power, habitual state of depression, excessive worrying (characteristic of the so-called accident prone) would seem to be the most frequent causes of this recidivity which, although involuntary, is nevertheless closely connected with the human factor.

From the standpoint of provisions for the protection of the health of the workers, if the importance of curative provisions is great, that of prevention is greater still. This is achieved not only by technicians through ingenious contrivances directed to the elimination of the element of danger coming from the machines, and by psychologists and physicians in the selection of workmen (*See* Psychotechnique), but also by the industrialists themselves in bettering their factories, improving the lighting system, reducing the noise, and other measures suitable for stimulating the laborers' interest in their work. The latter has turned out to be the principal element in the prevention of accidents, more effective than any anti-accident propaganda, including that based on the useful showing of telling films. It is an established fact that the drive against physical accidents must be based on the collaboration of the workers; hence, the necessity of enacting provisions, ranging from *anti-accident competitions* between teams or groups in the same factory, with annual prizes for those who had the least number of accidents, to a direct share in the business profits, on the basis of the worker's fidelity to his job and on profits of the business.

MORAL CONSIDERATIONS. It seems to us that the most important duties of the laborer, the employer and the authorities regarding disability from accidents are the following: (1) the workman must take care of his health. He is responsible for his own body and its efficiency as a trust given to him by God for his own good and that of the community. He must go to work physically and spiritually conditioned. This is the best guarantee against negligence, distraction, and boredom with his daily work, which are the common reasons for physical accidents. (2) The employer must place the workman in moral and material conditions that are best suited to protect him against accidents. Neither warnings written on the walls of the factory, nor propaganda posters (which no one sees after the first day) are sufficient for this purpose. It is necessary to awaken and to keep alive the collaborative enthusiasm of the workmen. (3)

School and other authorities must promote a reasonable fear against road, industrial, or domestic accidents. They must impress the young minds with the serious consequences brought about by accidents and the very easy ways of avoiding them. (4) They must encourage frequent free showings of anti-accident films. They must firmly enforce traffic discipline and provide for a methodical and really rigorous education of those responsible for public safety (engineers, pilots, drivers, etc.). (5) Once an accident has taken place, the injured person should not capitalize on the accident (even if so advised by others), nor should he refuse, out of excessive fear, to submit to treatments which, even though painful, could restore his health completely. (6) On the other hand, the financial reparation of the damage should be prompt and generous, as it is a well-known fact that lengthy judiciary processes constitute the principal reason for those traumatic psychoneuroses which prolong a state of invalidism in the injured. (7) Lastly, apropos of road accidents, let the ugly feeling so prevalent among drivers and pedestrians that the road belongs to them cease. (8) In case of accident the driver must always be ready to help the victim, even when he considers himself not responsible for the accident. Prompt help and a timely transfer of the victim to the nearest hospital may save a life or avoid a permanent injury to the victim. In conclusion, all preventive and curative provisions must always be based on the principles of justice and evangelical charity. *Riz.*

DISARMAMENT. *See* War.

DISARTRIA. *See* Paralysis, progressive.

DISCERNMENT (OF SPIRITS). *See* Gifts of the Holy Spirit.

DISCIPLINE (OF THE SACRAMENTS). *See* Congregations, Roman.

DISCOMFORT. *See* Affectivity.

DISCORD. The pagans termed discord "maleficent deity" and "pernicious fury" on account of its disastrous consequences. Discord consists in a disagreement of men's wills about a good to be willed as necessary and prescribed by charity. Discord causes a separation or division of wills and spirits among those who are supposed to be united by the bonds of charity for the same end and for the same motive. Some consider discord as hatred, which, unable to be contained, bursts into open enmity, spreading dissension among peoples.

Hate, anger, and man's perversity are the source of discord. Often, envious of other people's goodness, man tries to depreciate it in them. Ancient philosophers and poets attributed to discord (*Eris* for the Greeks) not only the wars among peoples and the strife among citizens, but also the dissensions in families and domestic disturbances, murders, snares, and intrigues. To appease it and to be spared the possible evil effects of discord, they offered sacrifices to a mythological "deity of discord."

Discord is not a divergence of opinions nor a dispersion of efforts in the realization of a common end, but properly speaking, a formal divergence of two or more wills concerning the same good to be attained in common. The attainment of this good may be optional or obligatory. The divergence of men's wills with regard to an optional good is not a sin of discord. To be sinful, there is required a divergence of two or more wills under obligation to desire the same good, for instance, peace in the family. The nature of this obligation is based on the requirement that the same means be used in the attainment of an end common to more than one person, such as love toward God or one's neighbor, or the practice of justice or some other virtue. The malice of discord is not simply in disagreeing, but in refusing to love and pursue the same necessary good which the other party accepts.

In general, discord offends against charity and is contrary to the peace and harmony which must reign among God's children. It also can offend against justice. St. Thomas says (*S. Theol.* II–II, q. 36, a. 1) that, when mutual discord destroys charity entirely, it is, of its very nature, a mortal sin. The reason is clear, for, according to St. John the Evangelist, whoever does not love his brother is dead to grace. Hence, when discord is such as to destroy the virtue of charity and thus cause division and hatred, it is a grave sin.

A diversity of opinions or feelings (provided they are not contrary to the spiritual interests of a soul) is not a sin of discord. Discord may be a sin only for one of the parties in disagreement, when one is obstinate in a matter involving injustice against God or neighbor, while the other defends his just right. For example, a son who defends his faith against the unbelief of his father, exercises a just right in discord. Discord could be a sin for both parties if both obstinately defend opinions false and contrary to charity.

In practice, the responsibility for discord often is elusive because each person believes himself on the side of truth but neither can reach the objective truth. In such cases, however, it is generally more a matter of disagreement of the mind than of the will. There is no excuse for those who simply spread discord, for, as St. Bonaventure declares, "The mouth of the devil is the mouth of the sower of discord (*Os diaboli est seminatoris discordiae os*" Sermo, 2 fer., IV post Pentecost).

They are rebuked by God Himself: "The Lord detesteth him that soweth discord among the brethren (*Qui seminat discordias inter fratres, eum detestatur Deus*" Proverbs, 6:16 and 19).

Canonists include the spreading of discord and dissension in a community among the reasons for the expulsion of a member from a religious order or congregation. (Cf. Schaefer, *De Religiosis*, Munster, 1927, n. 579, p. 593.)

DISCOURAGEMENT. As the term itself indicates, discouragement is a loss of courage or a lack of hope. In this sense it is distinguished from despair (*q.v.*), which is the abandonment of hope.

Discouragement may be the result either of a loss of faith or of faintness of heart. Nevertheless, if not prudently controlled, discouragement can gradually turn into despair. Discouragement can be overcome mainly by recalling the many graces received, by the thought of our incorporation in Christ, by a serene acceptance of trials as a means of sanctification or a sign of divine love, and by a humble acknowledgment of one's own misery. *Pal.*

DISCOVERY. *See* Possession; Finder.

DISCRIMINATION (Economic). It is a law of a free competitive market that there must be one stabilizing price. The possibility of establishing a plurality of prices is inherent in monopoly and semi-monopolies. Any deviation from the rule of one price constitutes discrimination. The price can be imposed by the buyer or seller in a monopolistic position.

In the case of the seller, monopolistic discriminations are practiced in a great variety of ways, such as apportioning the supply over a certain period of time and in different localities (this presupposes a separation of markets), or presenting the merchandise under diverse forms or styles.

A special and important type of discrimination is the one practiced by governments which, in virtue of their sovereign power, establish conditions whereby their citizens are induced to prefer certain markets over others. These conditions consist in the establishment of preferential duty, import and export licensing, trade quotas, clearing agreements or by a government-operated trading system for some or all exchangeable products in order to obtain conditions more favorable to imports, or by setting various prices for a government's product or exports. The reasons for these practices, common today, are political or monetary. Different prices in various countries for the same merchandise on the basis of parity of currencies is an obvious result of these discriminatory practices.

The morality or immorality of discrimination depends on the motive which determines it and on the limits of the practice. Good reasons justify discriminatory measures if kept within limits compatible with the common good. *Mai.*

DISCUSSION (INTER-FAITH). Discussions or debates between Catholics and heretics or other non-Catholics, if undertaken in good faith by both groups and conducted expertly and without animosity, could be productive of much good, particularly in countries of mixed religions. However, in regions where non-Catholics are particularly aggressive, such discussions, especially if public, have proved to be quite harmful to religion.

All Catholics should be ready at all times to deal with and, wherever circumstances warrant it, even repel attacks made by non-Catholics against the Catholic Faith and its institutions. On the other hand, experience shows that a debate with heretics, particularly a formal one, if undertaken by persons inadequately prepared for the task and, in an unfavorable atmosphere, is liable to cause considerable damage to the Catholic Faith. Lack of good faith in some non-Catholics, who sometimes seek propaganda effects rather than objective truth, and the aroused emotions of the hearers could well nullify the honest intent behind such debates and cause confusion among the faithful.

In view of the dangers, the Church, as guardian of revealed truth and zealous custodian of the sacred mission conferred upon her by Jesus Christ to teach the Catholic Faith, has forbidden all such debates with non-Catholics except by permission of the Holy See or, in exceptional cases, by permission of the Bishop (Can. 1325, par. 3). This prohibition was brought to the attention of the faithful once again by a *Monitum* issued by the Holy Office on June 5, 1948 (AAS., 1948, p. 257), on the occasion of Mixed Congresses intended to promote the so-called Ecumenical Movement, whose aim is a closer unity among Christians. Moreover, on December 20,

1949, the Holy Office published an "Instruction" which specified the conditions under which Catholics may be permitted to participate in such conventions (AAS. 42, 1950, p. 142). *Dam.*

DISEASES, OCCUPATIONAL. Occupational diseases and illness are the direct result of labor, accidents, or a combination of causes due to one's occupation. This variety of causes may be divided into four main categories: (1) *diseases caused by excessive work*, such as muscular strains (pulmonary emphysema, acute heart enlargement, vein ruptures) or the results of long hours of work (syndromes of neurosis, myocarditis, arterial hypertension); (2) *diseases from occupational environment* due to lighting, temperatures, pressure, noise, dampness; (3) *diseases due to materials*, such as the professional poisonings: lead poisoning among printers, miners, painters, called *saturnism; hydrargyrism* or mercurial poisoning among the miners or manufacturers of mercury, mirrors, electric bulbs, felt hats; *phosphorism* or phosphorus poisoning among workers in fertilizers or pharmaceuticals; *benzolism* or benzol poisoning among workers in rubber and explosives; *sulphacarbonism* among rubber and rayon workers; *arsenicism, stybism, manganism, chromism* among arsenic, antimonium, manganese, and chromium workers; also included are the so-called dust diseases: *silicosis, asbestosis,* and *anthracosis;* those diseases connected with handling infected matter, such as *epizootic aphta, aspergillus fungus;* due to vibrations; or radioactivity, as cancers; (4) *posture diseases,* due to the particular abnormal or prolonged posture required for certain work, such as flat feet and varicose veins among people forced to stand for long periods, or cuvatures of the spine (scoliosis) among tailors, etc.

Among occupational diseases must be considered the diseases of the mind and mental labor. Persons outside the medical profession believe mental work can be the source of nervous diseases and breakdowns; doctors hold the opposite view, provided that the mental operations involve neither excessive work nor worry. Due to the natural protective warning systems supplied by the nervous system, as fatigue, lack of alertness, and sleepiness, mental labor has ordinarily no serious effect on the nervous system. Only the failure to heed nature's warnings, the use of stimulants such as coffee and sympanina or the sacrifice of rest periods and recreational or physical exercise bring on illnesses such as neurasthenia (*q.v.*). Mental work is more harmful under worrisome conditions, particularly if it involves great responsibility or is subject to critical scrutiny, in which case emotional pressures many times cause neurotic manifestations. Furthermore, it is true that behind nervous breakdowns there is generally an organic disposition for mental sickness.

The provisional measures necessary for the control of occupational diseases are definitely threefold: prevention, cure, and insurance. The prevention of illnesses consists in the betterment of working conditions and environment. Industrial hygiene studies the effects of environment upon the health of the working man, the effects of the materials used, and the handling of machines to find the most rational method of protection against illness and accidents. It also extends in the wider sense to the worker's personal welfare as well as that of his family, physical examination, labor organizations, recreational activities, assistance to nursing mothers, children's care, housing, transportation. In this sense, complex studies must accompany a knowledge of pathology, psychotechnique, and general hygiene as well as industrial and economic theory, jurisprudence, and morality. All of these enable the first symptoms of disease to be checked, prompt diagnosis, detection and removal of the source of the very illness, as well as involve necessary interventions in the realm of legislation directed to the organization of the workman's technical, medical, and social needs.

MORAL COROLLARIES. The ethical and practical importance of occupational medicine is of great significance to a community, and the progress in this field of endeavor must go hand in hand with the profound knowledge of Christian social ethics, since the fight on illness and disease demands the wholehearted cooperation of all those who have the obligation to provide and use the proper remedies. (*See also* Accidents, Medicine.) *Riz.*

DISEASES, SOCIAL. Despite its definitely individual character, medicine pursues social aims. In fact, the origins of social medicine can be considered as lost in the night of times. Hygienic rules made by the most ancient lawmakers, both civil and religious, welfare provisions for the poor and the needy, the extensive use of sports and public baths, campaigns against contagious diseases, are early hygienico-prophylactic-remedial aspects of medicine. With the advent of Christianity, acts and provisions of a therapeutic and welfare nature increased considerably. The sick are visited and treated gratis; foundlings, orphans, old people are lovingly cared for. Practically every church and convent is turned into welfare and employment centers, open to anyone in need, offering hospitality to travelers and help to the sick. Welfare activities, previously considered an expression of charity and supported by private funds, were declared by the French Revolutionists to be a responsibility of society, to be organized and maintained by the State, on the basis of human solidarity and justice. However, shortage of funds prevented France in 1793 from carrying out its ambitious State-controlled welfare program. A few years later, State-controlled social medicine attained a partial realization in England, where it gained considerable ground by the development of a real *social legislation* under the pressure of the industrial revolution and of socialism.

At the turn of the twentieth century, the increasing need of bettering the conditions of the working classes and of protecting them against diseases, unemployment, and want gave a new impulse to the enactment of social legislation and the fostering of social medicine.

Thus studies, proposals, and projects were aimed at improving the health of the masses, by preventing or treating work-connected diseases, conducting full-scale campaigns against disease, improving all types of social benefits, such as old age and sickness benefits, assistance to pregnant women, mother-and-child care, war and labor casualties, emigrants, and mental hygiene. The modern concept and purpose of social medicine can be summed up as follows: "Social medicine looks at the physiological needs of the individual as related to social contingencies, at the sick in his relation to the collectivity, at diseases in relation to the moral and economic environments. It studies, prevents, and treats contagious diseases; it studies the social causes which give rise to and spread such diseases, and keeps them in check by applying social remedies enforced by law" (Tropeano), without overlooking the great contribution which a moral environment can make even in matters of hygiene.

PRINCIPAL SOCIAL DISEASES. Since the main goal of social medicine is the biological improvement of man, it is obvious that no branch of pathology can be excluded. Social diseases, of course, are understood to be mainly contagious diseases which are a major threat to the health of the nations. Some, such as alcoholism, blennorrhagia, cancer, heart ailments, accidents, mental diseases, narcotic addiction, syphilis and tuberculosis, concern all civilized peoples; others concern more particularly certain nations. Since alcoholism, psychopathies and psychoses, venereal diseases, narcotics and accidents are treated in separate articles, we shall confine ourselves to the following:

Cancer. Cancer, an ancient disease, derives its name from *karkinos* (crab) because it settles in the human body and in a crab-like fashion tears the tissues and spreads gradually over the whole body.

Although cancer has been the object of intensive research, it remains one of the deepest mysteries of pathology and one of the greatest concerns of social medicine. The number of victims is frightfully on the increase and the means for combating it are still inadequate. For these reasons an increasing number of doctors, biologists, chemists, physical scientists, mathematicians, bacteriologists and geneticists in concerted works of research holds high hopes for a relatively early break-through in the subject of tumors. Of the various aspects of this problem, one has bearing on social medicine. While it is true that cancer is on the increase everywhere due to the fact that the span of life has increased with larger numbers of old people (after the age of fifty a person is more apt to contract cancer), it is also true that mortality from cancer among the more civilized populations is proportionately on the decrease due principally to early diagnosis. Therefore, the most effective action against cancer consists in frequent check-ups, surgery, and the use of radium and X-ray treatments. If people are prompt in going to a physician as soon as lumps or skin eruptions appear, an early medical check-up and the use of available treatments often arrest the growth of the infection at its inception and save the life of the person.

Heart diseases. In the last quarter of a century, heart circulatory ailments have become a problem of vast social import by reason of their increase and extensive effects on the working ability of their victims. Heart ailments are causing the highest number of deaths in many countries; in Italy, in 1946, there were 97,100 heart casualties against 42,413 caused by tumors and 38,353 by tuberculosis. In the U.S.A., in 1950, 745,000 persons died of heart ailments while 705,000 died from other causes. Over nine million Americans are affected by heart ailments.

The increase in the number of heart patients is caused by the tempo of modern living, an increased span of human life, the larger number of cardio-circulatory ailments among the old, and the increase of rheumatic conditions.

Medical therapy and surgery have made great strides in the treatment and cure of heart ailments, particularly those discovered in early examination and diagnosis.

Trachoma (Greek, *trachus* — harsh, rough) is an ancient eye ailment of a contagious nature characterized by a granulous conjunctivitis which, if neglected, can cause blindness. The sad inheritance of the poorer classes in tropical countries, it thrives on lack of sanitation and poor living conditions. Four hundred million persons are believed (1954) to be affected by trachoma. A particularly grave social disease, though not a mass killer like cancer or tuberculosis, trachoma certainly interferes with ability to work of large numbers of people as well as being a vast contributing factor in causing blindness. It seems certain that trachoma is caused by an ultra-virus which is quite effectively controlled by antibiotics. Specialized clinics, located in the more affected areas, anti-trachoma prophylaxis, and greater hygienic education are actively used in fighting and preventing this dreadful disease.

Tuberculosis. Tuberculosis is a social disease par excellence because of its contagious nature, widespread occurrence and duration, and, until recent times, for its seriousness and high mortality among those affected by it.

Recent surveys tell us that in Europe at the beginning of this century deaths from tuberculosis averaged 2,400 per million persons a year; this number decreased to 1,625 in 1922, and to a low of 800 in 1939. During World War II a resurgence and high mortality was registered, but the number is again on the decrease; as a matter of fact, deaths are altogether rare, thanks principally to generally improved hygienic conditions, antibiotics, and surgery.

GENERAL REMARKS. The brief data above show the striking impact of the so-called social diseases on the life of civilized nations and, hence, the need for a more intensive effort in developing adequate and intelligent social assistance, aided, wherever conditions may require it, by appropriate legislation and carried out by hygienists, biologists, physicians and nurses effectively prepared for the handling of the tasks demanded by the needs of modern society.

This hard and long battle can best be fought not so much by medicines as by sound hygienic conditions, better housing and food, rational work, and a real crusade against want, slums, vice, ignorance, and filth.

Some countries have much to accomplish before they can attain full control of social diseases, from alcoholism to tuberculosis and mental disorders: the most dreaded causes of diseases and death. Happily in our days one sees a noble competition between State and private agencies, between financial and medical groups striving in a true Christian spirit to better mankind physically. An example of this effort is the International Union for the Hygienic Training of Peoples organized in Paris in 1951. The aims of this highly humanitarian organization deserve the support and cooperation of every citizen for an ever greater effectiveness in protecting the health and well-being of individuals and nations everywhere. *Riz.*

DISEASES, VENEREAL. Under the term *venereal disease* (from Venus, the goddess of love) are grouped the contagious infections generally contracted through sexual relations. These diseases, venereal ulcer, blennorrhagia, syphilis, and venereal lymphogranulomatosis, are also called *sexual diseases*, particularly by those scholars who distinguish syphilis from the other three infections and limit the term *venereal* to these alone.

For this reason and because of its particular impact on moral and social life, syphilis shall be treated apart from other venereal infections (*see* Syphilis).

VENEREAL ULCER. A venereal disease par excellence because there are practically no cases known to have been caused by extra-sexual contact. It is called *soft ulcer*, because of a painful, purulent ulceration, which is soft at the touch of the physician; it is found on the genitals and sometimes on the skin of other areas of the body.

This disease is caused by the streptobacillum of Ducrey (an Italian dermatol-gist who discovered it in 1889). It has a short period of incubation, ranging from one to two days. The ulcer tends to multiply and to become chronic, producing inflammation of local lymphae and lymphoglands and a tumoral condition and abscess which tends to break spontaneously.

Venereal ulcer is more common among people who neglect habitual body cleanliness, a condition which favors the development of the germ.

BLENNORRHAGIA. The oldest known venereal disease was so named in the seventeenth century because it was believed to be a mucous discharge. In earlier centuries it was called gonorrhea, "semen discharge," which prevails as a term to this day.

Between the fifteenth and nineteenth centuries the idea prevailed which considered blennorrhagia, venereal ulcer, and syphilis three aspects of the same disease, appearing under three different forms according to the areas affected. With the discovery of the gonococcus germ by Neisser, in 1879, blennorrhagia took its own separate identity, and became known as the inflammation of the mucoses caused by gonococcus.

The blennorrhagic infection generally follows sexual contact with an infected person. It can, however, be contracted by accidental infections caused by a contact with gonococcal pus deposits on the conjunctive cord of new-born children, or by linens and other objects used by infected persons.

Generally two to five days after the infectious contact, the male experiences an itch and burning feeling followed by pus emissions from his urinary organs; to these manifestations of blennorrhagic urethritis, others follow due to the extension of the gonococcal infection to the bladder and the prostate gland. Blennorrhagia is less dangerous and of shorter duration in women, who experience superficial inflammations and, at times, may suffer painful cystitis, bartholinitis, cervicitis, endometritis, salpingitis, etc.

Serious complications may arise, such as arthritis, nephropyelitis, endocarditis, peritonitis, meningitis, gonococcal septi-cemias. One must keep in mind, in view of possible relapses after years of apparent recovery, blennorrhagia may easily become chronic due to the fact that the gonococcus may nestle in the numerous ducts of the genital-urinary apparatus.

Lymphogranulomatosis, a generally benign venereal disease, is also called Nicolas-Favore disease, the names of the doctors who identified and described it in 1913. It is also called "fourth venereal disease," to distinguish it from the other venereal infections known for a long time. An infection caused by a tiny germ (filterable virus) of the virus family transmitted through sexual relation, which, generally, settles in the lymphatic vesicles; whence, the swelling of inguinal ganglions which tend to harden like fistulas and which are sometimes mistaken for tubercular adenitis.

NON-VENEREAL DISEASES OF THE GENITALIA. The skin of the genital regions may present all common skin infections. Thus, there are diseases which attack these regions, but which are not of a venereal nature. They can be thus summarized: *Tinea Cruris:* a frequently occurring dermatosis produced by a particular fungus involving portions of the inguinal, scrotal, thigh, and peri-anal regions. It presents large reddish patches, with a slight itch. Those affected frequently confuse it with intertrigo, an innocuous condition resulting from perspiration. *Herpes Progenitalis:* an acute eruption of vesicles on the mucous membrane of the external genitals. The vesicles become eroded and are accompanied by itching and a burning sensation. The affection tends to heal spontaneously; recurrence, however, is frequent. *Molluscum Contagiosum:* a small tumor, from pinhead to bean size, consisting of degenerated epithelial cells and produced by a filterable virus. *Condyloma acuminata:* small wartlike tumors, produced by a filterable virus, and therefore infectious. Because of their characteristic digitate elevations, they are also called "pointed condylomas." They are found rather frequently on the mucous membrane of the external genitals when hygienic measures are grossly neglected.

Balanitis: inflammation of the region of the glands and prepuce brought about by various germs which become implanted in the tissues. When local hygiene is neglected the germs multiply and become virulent. *Non-specific urethritis:* this is less serious but of much more frequent occurrence than gonorrheal urethritis. It may develop as follows: (a) from sexual relations; (b) as an extension of a balanitis infection; (c) from urine infected with bacilli coli, enterococcus, and other germs, each contamination coming from a focus somewhere in the body; (d) bloodbone infections from systemic diseases such as typhoid fever, septicemia, etc.; (e) the passing of a urinary calculus; (f) improper instrumentation of the urethral canal. *Phagedena* (fulminating gangrene of the genitals): frequently encountered in tropical lands and believed due to a combination of germs implanted in a simple excoriation of the genital organs. The coexistence of balanitis, chancroid, chancre and secondary infection is the usual beginning. Rapidly there develop severe local and general manifestations that quickly bring about vast mutilations as a result of necrotizing septical thromboses. Quick, energetic treatment with special sera and arsenic compounds is effective.

These and other less important diseases of the external genitals can be transmitted through sexual contacts: but as they arise independently of genesic functions, they are commonly considered as non-venereal.

PROPHYLAXIS OF VENEREAL DISEASES. The most rational and morally appropriate weapon against venereal diseases is chastity. If the whole of mankind observed the sixth commandment, venereal disease would disappear in a few years.

One must first of all insist on the observance of moral norms, a healthy education, and protection of youth. Doctors and leaders must strive to improve the hygiene of the individual, the environment and timely treatment of the diseased. It is necessary, therefore, to increase the social controls of such diseases, by better and more numerous preventive

clinics, by uprooting the false notion that venereal diseases must be kept secret, a notion absolutely harmful to the individual and the cause of the spread of the disease.

MORAL CONCLUSIONS. Venereal diseases exercise an adverse social impact upon the individual, the family and society. Blennorrhagia is the main cause of sterility. Blennorrhagia and syphilis are responsible for an appalling number of psychosomatic abnormalities of various types. Such infirmities, of course, affect also the productive and lucrative capacity of a nation, not to mention the heavy financial expenditures which the treatment of such diseases and their consequences require sometimes for generations.

The individual must be made aware of the necessity of observing the norms of morality, especially the sixth commandment. He must be made to realize that if he contracts such a disease he must promptly submit to a medical examination and abstain from all sexual contacts until such time as he is completely cured; on the contrary he shall become morally responsible for the harm caused to others. The physician will seize upon the fear engendered by venereal contagion to stress to his patients the need for a proper moral conduct; it is immoral for him to suggest the use of so-called preventives. Responsible leaders, assisted by the medical profession, shall provide the best means for the moral, economic, and hygienical betterment of their people.

DISEMBODIMENT. *See* Innovation.

DISMISSAL (From religion). Dismissal is the expulsion of a subject from a religious order or congregation for the reasons and according to the procedure established by the Code of Canon Law.

Ever since the beginning of religious life, the right and the duty existed to remove from a particular religious order the unworthy and the inept. For a long time there existed no real and proper doctrine concerning the dismissal, and the

Holy See gave to the respective religious superiors the faculty of using appropriate measures for each individual case. In 1501, by the Constitution *Cum sicut nobis*, enacted by Alexander VI, a uniform practice was established, which was more specifically implemented by his successors, Urban VIII and Innocent XII.

PRESENT LEGISLATION. The entire doctrine concerning dismissal is specifically prescribed in the Code of Canon Law as follows:

(a) The following named persons are considered *ipso facto* lawfully dismissed: (1) religious who publicly apostatize from the Catholic faith; (2) a religious, man or woman, who has run away with a person of the opposite sex; (3) religious who attempt marriage, even the so-called "civil marriage" (Can. 646). In these cases, it suffices that the major superior make a declaration of the fact in the manner prescribed by the law.

(b) Dismissal of religious in temporary vows: In the case of religious of congregations of pontifical right, the dismissal can be effected by the Superior General with the consent of his council; in the case of religious of diocesan right and religious women subject to the Ordinary, the Ordinary himself can dismiss the subject; in case of religious women subject to a male religious group, the local Ordinary and the religious superior can effect the dismissal. Both the local Ordinary and the religious superior, however, must obtain the consent of the superior or superioress of the respective subject (Can. 647).

The causes and the procedure of dismissal are not listed by the Code, but are determined by the Constitutions of each individual congregation. The reasons for dismissal must always be grave, both on the part of the religious organization and on the part of the individual. They must be made known to him or to her and ample opportunity given to answer the charges (Can. 647). The religious has the right to appeal, within ten days, to the Holy See against the decree of dismissal, and pending the appeal, the dismissal has no juridical effect (Can. 647, par. 2, no. 4). With the issuance of the decree of dismissal, if no appeal was interposed or the appeal was rejected by the Holy See, the religious of temporary vows is reduced to the lay state, even if he is a cleric in minor orders. If, instead, he is a cleric in major Orders, the obligations of the Orders remain (Can. 648).

(c) The dismissal of religious with perpetual vows in non-exempt male organizations and exempt lay organizations. This must be effected by means of an administrative process by which it is established that the religious committed three different and successive offenses against the common law or a law proper to the religious organization with full imputability. Appropriate warnings or canonical admonitions by the superiors must have followed the commission of the crimes within a sufficient space of time, and the religious must have showed his incorrigibility by making those admonitions unproductive of amendment. In organizations of Papal law, the Superior General of the organization has the right to issue the decree of dismissal after due investigation and with the consent of his council, expressed by majority vote and secretly; in congregations of diocesan law, the local Ordinary, to whom the results of the investigation are to be referred by the religious superior, will issue the decree of dismissal (Can. 649, 650). Before the decree of dismissal from an organization of Papal right may become effective, it must be confirmed by the Holy See (Can. 650, par. 2). In any case the religious must be informed of the reasons for his dismissal and be given adequate opportunity to answer the charges, which are properly transcribed and sent to the Holy See. The religious has the right to appeal within ten days (Can. 650).

(d) For the dismissal of religious women with perpetual vows, either simple or solemn, serious external causes are required together with incorrigibility proved and documented by the Superior General or major superior. As always, the religious must be informed of the reason for her dismissal and be given a chance to defend herself. All the documents relative to her defense must be transmitted to the local Ordinary in the case of a religious of diocesan congregations or to the Holy See in other cases, since it is the right of the Ordinary or of the Holy See to issue the decree of dismissal. The religious has the right to interpose, within ten days, an appropriate appeal to the Holy See against the decree of dismissal. Pending the appeal, the decree has no juridical effect (Can. 651, 652).

(e) Religious with perpetual vows in exempt clerical organizations, ordinarily shall not be dismissed except by appropriate canonical trial conducted according to regulations established by the Code of Canon Law.

(f) Canon 653 of the Code of Canon Law considers a simpler form of dismissal applicable to all religious men and women in unusual cases requiring immediate action in view of the external scandal connected with the case or of grave and imminent danger to the religious community.

In such emergencies, the major superior with the consent of his council or the local superior with his council or with the intervention of the local Ordinary, if it is impossible to refer the case to the major superior, may issue the decree of dismissal. Such decree produces immediately its juridical effects of separating the religious from his community and returning him to the lay state (Can. 653), although the case must be referred to the Holy See, whose competence alone it is to confirm the decree of dismissal already issued. In exempt religious organizations, a regular trial must be initiated following the issuance of the decree of dismissal.

Following his dismissal, the religious with perpetual vows remains bound by his vows, unless the Holy See should dispense him or the Constitutions dispose otherwise. A dismissed cleric in minor orders is reduced to the lay state (Can. 669); a cleric in major orders who has committed a crime punished with the loss of good repute (*infamia juris*), or with deposition, or with *ipso facto* dismissal (Can. 646), incurs other very grave penalties determined by the Code, according to each individual crime, such as degradation, suspension, etc. A dismissed religious who is not dispensed from his vows is always required to return to the religious community and, if he give signs of amendment, the religious organization is under obligation to take him back, although he can be subjected to an appropriate period of probation (Can. 672). *Mand.*

DISPARITY OF CULT. This impediment is present when one of the contracting parties to a marriage is a baptized Catholic or a person received into the Church from heresy or schism (even if he lapsed back into it) and the other is a non-baptized person.

In other words, this impediment is present, if one of the parties is an infidel and the other is or was, even for a very short time only, a member of the Catholic Faith. This impediment of ecclesiastical origin, introduced by custom, underwent an important change with the publication of the Code of Canon Law (May 18, 1918), for Canon Law has restricted such impediment to the Catholic only, whereas, before the Code, it applied also to a Protestant who married an unbaptized person. As a result of this change, the marriage between a Protestant and a non-baptized person is to be considered a valid union (and therefore indissoluble), while before the Code it was considered dissoluble under certain conditions (Cans. 1061, par. 2, and 1070–1071).

DISPENSATION. The dispensation from the impediment of disparity of cult is reserved to the Holy Office. The Bishops in the United States can dispense from the impediment by virtue of delegated power granted to them in their quinquennial faculties. Grave reasons are required and guarantees (*cautiones*) must be furnished by the non-baptized party that he shall not hinder the Catholic party from practicing freely the Catholic Faith, and a promise made by both parties that all the children born of their marriage shall be baptized and reared in the Catholic Faith, and that there will be no religious ceremony except the Catholic ceremony. A moral certitude that these guarantees are given in good faith is also a requirement. Particular difficulties exist in a case of marriage between a Catholic and a Jew, and even greater difficulties if the non-Catholic is Mohammedan. A dispensation from this impediment more frequently and easily is granted if it happens that a small number of Catholics live among a greater number of non-Catholics, as in mission territories. *Bar.*

DISPENSATION. Dispensation is an act by which competent authority releases a subject from the observance of a law in a particular case. The authority empowered to grant a dispensation is the law-maker or some superior authority. Sometimes, a dispensation is granted by an inferior authority, but only if delegated power is given by the ordinary competent authority. Let it be observed that a dispensation does not abrogate the law, but only suspends temporarily and often partially the observance of that law.

A licit or lawful dispensation must be predicated upon the presence of special reasons and circumstances. Indeed, this requirement is necessary for the validity of a dispensation if this is granted by an authority invested with delegated power. The necessity of just and proportionate causes is an important element for the applicant. If he resorted to deception to obtain a dispensation, that is, if the dispensation is granted on the basis of false or non-existing reasons, the dispensation is usually invalid and the applicant, who committed a sin because of the fraudulent way of obtaining it, sins also by making use of the dispensation. It must be noted that this is true even in the case in which the competent superior might dispense from the impediment without reason, if he so wills. But when this deliberate will to waive the reasons is not apparent, it must be reasonably presumed that he intends

that the dispensation be made dependent upon the existence of adequate reasons.

The necessity for a sufficient cause effects also the cessation of the dispensation, so that besides revocation by the superior, expiration of time, or completion of the case or cases for which it was granted, it also ceases when the cause for which it was given no longer exists.

No human authority can dispense from an impediment of divine law, either natural or positive. So-called pontifical dispensations from vow, oath, or a non-consummated marriage are variously interpreted by theologians; that is, either as dispensations granted by virtue of a divine delegation residing in the Pontiff or simply as authentic interpretations of divine law by the Supreme Pontiff. Whichever may be the interpretation of the papal power, all theologians teach that even the Pope, in the face of a superior law, must have just and adequate reasons not only for the licit but also the valid granting of a dispensation. *Gra.*

DISPENSATION, FROM MATRIMONIAL IMPEDIMENTS. See Impediments, Matrimonial.

DISPENSATION OBTAINED BY FALSE PRETENSES. See Dispensation, Rescript.

DISPUTATION. Disputation (contest, debate, polemical discussion) is a debate carried on either orally or in writing, publicly or privately, in which one person opposes the opinion, the doctrine, or the view of another. A controversy is not always a bad thing or a sin. If a controversy is engaged in to defend the truth (a truth of faith, a religious or moral doctrine), or a truth belonging to the field of speculative science (philosophy), or practical sciences (economy, medicine, technology, politics), it is a good and praiseworthy thing, provided that it is conducted in the proper manner.

Disputation can be sinful in two instances: (1) if conducted to oppose the truth; (2) if conducted in a manner contrary to charity and the respect due to the opponent. Disputation conducted to willfully oppose truth is almost always a grave sin, especially when directed against religious or moral truths or against branches of human knowledge important to man's life. The defender of truth who falls into the pitfall of uncharitableness or lack of respect toward his opponent seldom incurs a grave sin. Those who fight for the truth do a good thing, but their manner is not always commendable. Frequently they allow themselves to be guided by secondary motives such as love of self, vanity, interests, etc., which blind them to any truth in the opponent's point of view, and cause insults and the use of other offensive terms. Rarely, if at all, do such disputations attain any good effect; often a greater degree of animosity results from them (See Diatribe). Good polemics (public disputation in writing) is an art requiring not only great ability in the disputant but also many Christian virtues, such as, humility, patience and principally true charity toward one's opponent. The same principles apply to other forms of disputation. For debates with non-Catholics, *see* Discussion. *Ben.*

DISSECTION (of a body). *See* Autopsy.

DISSIMULATION. Dissimulation is external behavior or attitude used to conceal from others what we are really thinking, doing, etc.

Dissimulation, which differs from simulation or feigning on the basis of its intrinsic motive, is licit when there are good reasons justifying this method of withholding the truth from another person who has no right to our disclosure. This method, which is not immoral in itself, should be used but rarely and with much discretion in view of its possible adverse effects in social life. *See* Restriction, Mental; Simulation. *Ben.*

DISSIMULATION (in psychotics). Dissimulation consists in a willful concealment of some infirmity in order to obtain some advantage (enlistment in a special corps, insurance, etc.) or to avoid a feared damage. The latter motive is present in some particular mental patients who willfully dissimulate their illness in order to avoid being sent to or retained in a mental institution or other situations limiting freedom.

It is very important that dissimulation arising from mental infirmity be detected as early as possible, because delay may lead to serious consequences. In fact, dissimulation is often used for criminal purposes. This is often the direct result of a condition (*delirium*) which constitutes the fulcrum of psychosis. Accordingly, the melancholy type will try to appear cured of the depressive phases of his illness in order to execute his suicidal plan which the vigilance exercised in mental institutions makes difficult to carry out—a thing he hopes to do once he has been dismissed from the institution. Thus, too, the paranoiac with a persecution complex will conveniently use dissimulation to regain his freedom in order to execute his vindictive plan.

Like simulation, dissimulation could take on particularly clever and astute forms, and the physician must be well aware of this if he is to prevent unpleasant consequences. Since failure to recognize a dissimulator could open the way to suicidal or homicidal attempts, the psychiatrist must exercise all possible caution to avoid errors. Often the dissimulator unmasks himself either because, while intent on concealing one particular symptom, he is not careful enough to conceal other mainfestations of his disturbance, or because he is unable to continue in his deceptive tactics. Hence, when confronted with a dissimulator, the psychiatrist must proceed with great prudence, avoiding haste in declaring the subject cured. It should not be difficult through prolonged and accurate observations to establish whether the patient is really cured or is a dangerous dissimulator.

Dissimulation in a psychiatric patient is an effect of his disease, and his moral responsibility is to be judged according to the severity of his disturbance.

DISSIPATION. Dissipation is a wasteful employment of energy and time on worldly things or in aimless conversations which prevent a person from applying himself to more serious matters, particularly of God and the spirit. It must not be confused with necessary or useful engagement in work nor with honest and moderate recreation necessary to man.

Dissipation is a sin and a serious obstacle to perfection. In itself it is a venial sin, but it is a mortal sin if it renders impossible the fulfillment of one's obligations or constitutes an occasion of serious damage or of mortal sin.

Those who are compelled to live amid many distractions should bear in mind that it is extremely important to keep, insofar as it is possible, one's mind on God and to mortify one's attraction to vain things.

DISSOCIATION, MENTAL. Dissociation may be defined as a pathological process which breaks up psychological elements and functions, previously physiologically associated. It is also defined as "a separation of an idea or a desire from the main stream of consciousness, making it co-conscious." Sometimes this process appears to be the result of the destruction of or severe pain in the neurons which tie diverse cerebral centers together. At other times, it may be the result of minute and reversible lesions, or of functional disturbances without any apparent histopathological substratum whatsoever.

In normal individuals there may be, on account of intense emotions, the limitation of psychological activities to instinctive reactions, so that consciousness, thus restricted, remains impervious to any activity of experience or judgment; indeed, complete forgetfulness of an entire incident could result precisely from this dissociative isolation. In abnormal individuals these effects are more pronounced and protracted. In some attacks of epilepsy and somnambulism, for instance, because of dissociation, only the automatic psychological functions remain active, and the personality of the subject appears to be absent. Or in some cases of hysteria, in medianic trance, and in an artificially induced hypnosis, the dissociative process may cause the psychic individuality to be broken into two or more minor and different personalities, operating independently in succession or even simultaneously.

The frequent forms of *hysterical anesthesia* (in which sensibility continues but remains extraneous to the consciousness) are caused by dissociations of this type.

SCHIZOPHRENIC DISSOCIATION. The multiform symptomatology of that frequent and very grave form of psychosis which is called precisely dissociative schizophrenia must be attributed to minute and complex phenomena of mental dissociation. Some decades ago, it was called, by Kraepelin and others, *dementia precox*. Here, a true demented condition appears to be absent, but the habitual, conspicuous, and characteristic anomalies of the intellect, of the emotions and of the general behavior of such patients, seem to be caused by more or less constant and systematic obstacles which impede the proper use of the memory, distort the reasoning power or block it altogether, disjoin the normal connections between thought, emotion and action, and determine permanently that deep incoherence which renders the attitude of such patients particularly stolid.

With regard to the various moral problems in the field of dissociative affections, *see* Schizophrenia. Mental dissociation constitutes the principal psychopathological process of this disease.

DISTRIBUTION, ECONOMIC. Distribution in economy is, in a static sense, the division of property, economic goods or related matters; in a dynamic sense, it is the act of partitioning the yearly assets among all participants in production, namely, company, capital, and labor under the form of profit, interest, and wages. The social doctrine and economic principles of distribution determine the manner in which this distribution is to take place, whether money, salary, interests or profits to stockholders in dividends. According to the examples of economists, distribution is divided into *functional* and *personal* (some add *contractual*). Functional distribution seeks to establish economic laws according to which the value of a product must be divided among the participants of production (corporation, capital, labor). Personal or normative distribution deals with norms to be followed in the effective distribution of the value of the product among various economic persons (owners of capital, workers, producers).

Functional distribution, a physiocratic doctrine, first conceived of economics as an organic unity in which all co-operate toward equitable distribution of the wealth. It made the powers of nature the only source of public wealth. Since the means of production were one, this theory recognizes only personal distribution. The classical school, besides other elements of production, emphasized the productivity of labor, and on the basis of free competition endeavored to explain distribution entirely by automation and the mechanics of prices. Marshall, instead, based his theory of distribution on the law of limitation of productivity, stating that the distribution of productive factors is governed by circumstances. No element of production, beyond a certain limit, finds profit from production in which the profit of another element is greater (principle of substitution).

Normative personal distribution was a theory of Saint-Simon: "To each one according to his capacity, capacity is to be rewarded according to work." He applied this criterion of the individual to distribution.

Marxists, on the basis of the exploitation of labor, raised the principle of the "right of the worker to the full return for labor." Hence they advocate confiscation of property, complete socialization, and so forth. The entire economic life of the nation is under the control of the working class, or rather, the party, which imposes upon all, at least in theory, a uniform distribution of consumer's goods. Despite many attempts to provide good merchandise at a low price for the working people, the experiment to this time has failed.

The doctrine of the Church concerning distribution is that the right to private property is to be encouraged, "so that the number of private owners may increase as much as possible; from this a more equitable distribution of the national wealth will result" (*Rerum Novarum*). The right to private property must prevail, nor does the State have a right to prevent such a right among its citizens. Moreover, property has a social function; hence the obligation to use it according to the exigencies of the common good and to render assistance to the needy and poor, particularly with the surplus. The distribution of goods, according to the theory of private property, is established by nature itself in order that created things may better serve man with stability and order. Therefore, the theory of private property must be respected. One class of citizens must not exclude another class from participating in profits. Those err who insist on the permanence of conditions favoring them exclusively. That position of the working class is erroneous which seeks to exact the entire fruit of labor as the sole result of the work of its hands, as a vindication of its rights or alleged rights. Wages must be determined not from a unilateral point of view, but on the basis of social justice, and the needs of the workingman and his family, of the economic ability of the employer and the general prosperity, etc., so that the largest possible number of people may benefit by the fruits of production.

Among States, no less than among individuals, the solution to the problem of distribution (particularly of raw material) requires a practical approach, based on the principle of universal solidarity, capable of rising above the blind and dangerous collective egoism of nations, that are powerful by their political force, yet exasperated by problems of prestige and a spirit of reprisal.

DIVIDEND. *See* Corporation; Stock-Market.

DIVINATION. Divination is the art of knowing and declaring future events or hidden things by means of communication with occult forces. It is an act of religious nature. There is no divination if the religious element is wanting, as when one sets about the discovery of the future or the occult by a scientific deductive method, conjecture, psychological ability, or if there is any natural explanation of the method used. This explanation, however, must have a reasonable foundation, which will vary in accord with the cultural status and conditions of civilization, not the frivolous and ridiculous basis of the followers of spiritism and of other so-called occult sciences.

Communication with occult powers may be *explicit* (express) or *implicit*. It is explicit when there is an evocation of these powers for help or a petition that certain signs be given to indicate their presence or response. In the first case, an attempt is made to obtain an evocation of the dead (necromancy) or other apparitions, or it is pretended that the occult powers have taken possession of the invoker or of another person having special aptitudes such as the medium (pythonism, medianship). See Spiritualism, Medium, Metapsychology. Divination may be *natural* or *artificial*, depending on whether it proceeds from casual signs or from signs requested and obtained by the invoker. The following are forms of natural divination: astrology, chiromancy, etc., understood as a means of predicting the future; forms of artifical divination are lots, cards, ouija board, etc. Communication with occult powers is implicit (tacit) if the means employed to know the future or other occult things are inadequate and, therefore, require the intervention of said powers even though not expressly invoked.

Divination either with express or tacit invocation of occult powers is always a grave sin for the following reasons: (a) occult powers must be identified with diabolical powers because it is impossible that either God or the spiritual powers subject to God would lend themselves to frivolous practices and to the ridiculous and often irrational experimentations of divination or that they would subject themselves to any evoking human force (*See* Magic arts). Hence, their invocation, either express or tacit, is always an appeal to Satan's aid, the declared enemy of God and man. (b) It is a grave offense against God to attribute to the devil a certain knowledge of the contingent future, which, as dependent on free will, is known only to God. (c) In any case, through these arts, man exposes himself to most serious spiritual dangers: (1) even in those cases in which the precise intervention of Satan is not sought, man exposes himself to the danger of very serious sins, as indicated under (a) and (b); (2) he exposes himself to the danger of grave deception with regard to his eternal salvation and his faith by him who is the "father of lies from the beginning."

The same applies to consultations undertaken with all seriousness, because they constitute a sin of formal cooperation in the above mentioned sins. On the basis of the above explanation it is easy to understand the gravity of the prohibition by Sacred Scripture (cf. Lev. 19:26; 19:31; 20:6; 20:27; Deut. 18:10–12). It is not a grave sin, however, if the consultant and the consulted indulge in magic arts for a manifestly jocose purpose without attributing to such practices any religious meaning. The magician, fortune-teller, etc., who indulges in such arts for fraudulent reasons, is not guilty of the above mentioned serious sins, although he commits a grave sin of scandal and of injustice. Often, however, those who go to magicians and fortune-tellers are only guilty of venial sin, because they act out of simplicity or ignorance. *Pal.*

FORMS OF DIVINATION. Originally, divination was a branch of sympathetic magic. Later, its meaning changed; that is, it considered certain phenomena no longer as causes of some future effects, but as signs by which the divinity made its will known.

The numerous means and types of

divination are variously classified and distinguished. We shall follow the traditional classification, which is very extensively based on the work by M. T. Cicero, *De divinatione*. First of all, divination is *personal* or *direct* if an individual is able to reveal future or hidden things immediately and clearly, either by virtue of extraordinary ability of his own, or by virtue of a spirit by whom he is possessed. Divination which is *real* or *indirect* consists in interpreting signs already in existence. The oracles, the best known system of direct divination, were divine responses given to special priests who also supplied an interpretation of them, on the supposition that often those responses were obscure and that few were able to interpret the supposed language of the gods.

Indirect divination, which extends to the majority of divining mediums, is natural or artificial. Of the varieties of natural divination, already mentioned above, some deserve particular attention. *Astrology*, based on the observation and interpretation of celestial signs, holds that the movement of the celestial bodies and various atmospheric changes have an inevitable influence upon man's life. *Oneiromancy*, or interpretation of dreams, is a much valued art among all peoples and at all times.

Ornithomancy, an augural art in which the Romans distinguished themselves, is based principally on the observation and interpretation of flying birds.

Among the very numerous types of artificial divination, we shall mention the following:

Hydromancy. This type of divination is concerned with the observation either of the movements of an object thrown into a sacred fountain or of the movements and the meeting of various liquids (ordinarily water and oil) poured into a cup. At times, the divinator focused his eyes upon a glass full of water and then, falling into a trance, would see figures and scenes of the future forming in the water. By this method Cagliostro is supposed to have seen and predicted the horrors of the French Revolution.

Pyromancy. According to this type of divination, the forms assumed by the flames of a sacrificial fire indicated the will or counsel of the divinity in whose honor the victim was immolated.

Necromancy. This divination was practiced by observing and interpreting the phenomena connected with the decomposition of human corpses. The term *necromancy* more often is taken to mean the art of evoking the dead in order to learn from them hidden things or future events. A by-product of the necromantic art, very common in the Middle Ages, was the so-called *test of the bier*. In a case of homicide by unknown hand, the victim's body was placed in an open casket and all those suspected of the crime were requested to touch the body. If the body moved or the wound bled upon being touched by one of the suspects, this man was considered to be the responsible criminal.

It is obvious that such a test, although it led some weak or superstitious criminal to confess the crime, yet, more often than not, was a cause of grave errors arising from emotional reactions (or from evil intent) of the judges who watched the proceedings.

Cleromancy or divination by "chance" or lots, very common in ancient and medieval Italy, was practiced by the use of sticks or discs having an inscription on them (sometimes a verse from the *Aeneid* of Virgil) and suspended by a cord. The stick or disc, picked at random, contained some future prediction in the motto it carried.

Cartomancy. This more common means of divination in modern times, practiced mainly by women and by the use of playing cards, each with a particular meaning, deceives not only the uneducated but even persons of intelligence and culture. For other types of divination, *see* Magic Premonition, Rhabdomancy.

Modern science, based on the observation of facts and the objective criticism of experimental results, rejects divination in its diverse forms and manifestations because it contradicts reason and, in turn, is nullified by experience. Geminiano Montanari, illustrious astronomer, may well be considered the first representative of modern scientific scepticism in the field of divination. Referring to the noblest of the arts of divination, he wrote, in 1680, his famous work, *Astrology Convicted of Falsity*, arriving at the conclusion, based on a long and serious comparative study of events in relation to astral phenomena, that the rare coincidences must be considered as purely fortuitous. *Riz.*

DIVINING ROD. See Rhabdomancy.

DIVISION OF BENEFICES. *See* Innovation.

DIVISION OF LABOR. *See* Labor.

DIVORCE. Divorce, in general, is understood to be the faculty given by a civil magistrate to married persons to separate and enter on a new marriage. Unfortunately, following the Protestant Reformation and particularly after the French Revolution, almost all civil codes admit divorce for various reasons in the presence of specified grounds. Experience has shown that, once divorce is introduced as a remedy in special cases (life imprisonment, incurable disease of the consort, or because of adultery), it cannot be restrained. It extends and increases so that it profoundly affects the stability of the institution of marriage, the security and the peace of the home, and causes incalculable damage, particularly to the wife and the children. Divorce encourages immorality and fosters, to an extremely high degree, juvenile delinquency.

The Catholic Church has always rejected divorce, even in the case of the lawful marriage of non-baptized persons, and has always held to the doctrine that a ratified and consummated marriage of baptized persons cannot be dissolved by any human power but only by death (Can. 1118, which follows the definition of the Council of Trent, Sess. XXIV, Can. 7).

Catholic teaching does permit the separation of husband and wife even for an indefinite period of time or permanently for reasons established by the Code (Can. 1128–1932). The marriage bond, however, remains unbroken and the separated spouses are not permitted to enter on a new marriage.

There are, however, two cases in which a marriage intrinsically indissoluble becomes dissoluble under special circumstances: 1. The lawful marriage of two unbaptized persons can be dissolved by virtue of the Pauline Privilege, when one of the parties becomes a Catholic and the other refuses to live without offense to God (Can. 1120–1127). 2. The ratified marriage (sacrament) of two baptized persons, which was never consummated; this union can be dissolved either by solemn profession of one of the parties or by a dispensation of the Supreme Pontiff for good and just reasons (Can. 1119).

A declaration of nullity granted by the legitimate ecclesiastical authority must not be confused with divorce. In fact, by such declaration, the ecclesiastical authority does not dissolve any bond of marriage, for this it cannot legitimately do. But it does declare, after proper investigation and regular process, that the union in question was never a valid union because of the presence of an impediment or a defect of consent or of form.

Such declarations of nullity are something entirely different from the granting of divorce. By a divorce the attempt is made to break a valid bond, of its own nature unbreakable; whereas, by a declaration of nullity, the ecclesiastical judge acknowledges that, despite the semblance of marriage, there never existed between A. and B. a true marriage bond.

The Church has fought long and hard to eliminate divorce, which was imbedded in the marriage concept of the Romans as well as of the barbarians. After the patient efforts of many centuries, the Church, around the year 1000, succeeded in having its doctrine and practice of the indissoluble marital union accepted everywhere. But today, separated from the Church's influence, society has by and large lapsed back into the old error, while the Church's doctrine and practice continue in faithful adherence not only to Revelation but to natural law as well, protecting and safeguarding the social interests of the people, as clearly demonstrated by Popes Leo XIII and Pius XI in their respective encyclical letters, *Arcanum* and *Casti Connubii*. *Bar.*

DIVULGING OF NEWS. *See* News Agency; Press.

DOCILITY. Docility (from the Latin *docere*, to teach) is the act by which we are disposed to accept another's teaching. It is a disposition both of mind and will to follow the instructions and injunctions of another, or to be willing to accept the opinions of another and even to prefer them to one's own.

In general, docility is a part of the virtue of prudence. Prudence is the virtue which, in a proper manner and to a proper end, regulates all of man's actions. Since these actions are of a nearly unlimited variety, a man finds it quite impossible to weigh and ponder by himself each and every one of them, either because of lack of time, required knowledge, or the influence passions exercise upon the faculties which should direct him. If one is docile, he will allow others to direct him, thus benefiting by their experience and knowledge. By so doing he is said to be acting with prudence.

In a more specific and precise sense, he is docile who follows the counsels and, even more, the will of those in authority, recognizing in them an expression of the Divine Will. In this sense, docility is the same as meekness, patience, and especially obedience. Hence, against the general background of the virtue of prudence, whose function it is to direct man's actions to their proper end, the virtue of docility will be a particular form of obedience, insofar as it inclines the will to accept the directions given by the will of the superiors. *M.d.G.*

DOCTOR. *See* Deontology (Medical).

DOCTORS' FEES. *See* Honorarium.

DOCTRINE, CHRISTIAN. In the Code of Canon Law (Can. 1329–1336), the Church prescribes that religious instruction (dogma and moral) be imparted not only for children in preparation for the reception of the sacraments of penance, first Holy Communion, and confirmation, but also for adult Catholics that they may acquire a deeper knowledge of the Catholic Faith. It is the continuation of the ancient catechumenate. It consists of a regular and methodical catechetical instruction intended to refresh those principles learned at an earlier age and to broaden and solidify the content of religious truth. Far from fully achieving its goal with the termination of primary education, religious instruction and training becomes even more imperative as youth launches out into the world to face problems often involving faith and morals. In France, the continuation of religious instruction is called *"Catéchisme de persévérance"* for the simple reason that it does not stop at the elementary level, but endeavors to give adults a deeper and more mature religious training.

The term *Christian doctrine* was adopted from its analogy with the *doctrina Christiana* of the ancient Church, popularized principally by Saint Augustine (PL 34, 15–122) in a book of the same name and later by St. Peter Canisius in his Latin Catechism. It was made official by the Decree of Reform of the Council of Trent and by the Constitution of Benedict XIV (1742), *De doctrina Christiana populis tradenda.* Thus, the word *catechism* was born to designate a booklet in question and answer form, containing a summary of Christian doctrine. Despite the importance and usefulness of the book for the teaching of Christian doctrine, the fact remains that it can never replace the oral teaching which Christ Himself enjoined upon His Apostles.

"To make a new generation Christian is to strike at evil in its root and to assure the salvation of peoples" (Gerson). "Now this is eternal life," says the Lord, "that they may know thee, the only true God, and Jesus Christ, whom thou hast sent" (John 17:3). But how can the knowledge of such exalted truths be achieved without teaching? "And how are they to believe in him," asks St. Paul, "until they listen to him? And how can they listen, without a preacher to listen to?" (Rom. 10:14—Knox version). Teaching, of course, is the way chosen by God to communicate to man the knowledge of the truth. Religious instruction imparts to children and adults as well, the truths they must know to achieve eternal salvation; it exercises at the same time salutary influence upon the entire spiritual nature of man and it becomes, even in the merely natural order, the most potent means of formation and education (Cf. Enc. *Acerbo nimis*, Pope Pius X).

"As the Father hath sent me, I also send you" (John 20:21), said Jesus to His Apostles. Is there a greater mission than to be sent by God to bring His divine word of salvation to all the people? Obviously, it is the right of the Church and her ministers to teach Christian doctrine, for, to His Apostles and their successors, Jesus Christ addressed these words: "Going, therefore, teach ye all nations" (Matt. 28:19); to them alone did He promise His effective assistance till the end of time (Matt. 28:20). In this regard, the authority and responsibility of the ministers of the Church vary according to the extent of their jurisdiction.

The Roman Pontiff, Vicar of Jesus Christ and successor of St. Peter, possesses a supreme and universal authority (Can. 218). When he teaches *ex cathedra*, his word is the infallible expression of the truth, and all the faithful owe complete and entire submission to him. Immediately under the supreme authority of the Pope come the Bishops. They, too, have been established to govern the fold of Christ, each one in his own Diocese. The other ministers receive their authority from the Bishops (Can. 329). Pastors, assistant pastors, and other priests impart religious instruction by delegated power (Can. 1327). But since the number of priests is relatively small, compared to the large

number of people to be instructed, it is clear that the ministers of the Church who have received the direct mission to teach, can and must call upon zealous and well-prepared assistants who will help in discharging such an important task.

The Church has never ceased, through Councils, Doctors, and the Supreme Pontiffs down to our present Pontiff, Pope John XXIII, happily reigning, to emphasize the grave responsibility incumbent upon all those who care for souls to teach Christian doctrine—"a proper and most serious office," according to Canon 1329. Canonical sanctions are provided for those pastors found to be negligent in the discharge of this grave obligation (Cans. 2182–2185; 2382). However, such obligation does not rest alone with pastors and other priests, but it extends also to parents, who are bound by the duty of justice and piety toward their children to provide proper religious instruction in Christian doctrine. It is the positive will of the Church, and a duty of Christian charity for all who are capable to dedicate themselves to the eradication of religious ignorance and the propagation of the Catholic Faith.

Under the date of March 9, 1930, the Supreme Pontiff Pope Pius XI granted the following indulgences to those who engage in the teaching of Christian doctrine: (a) a plenary indulgence twice a month to be gained by all those lay persons who at least twice a month for the space of one half hour, or, at least twenty minutes, engage in the teaching of Christian doctrine; (b) a partial indulgence of three years (S. Penitentiary, May 26, 1949) for each time one engages in the teaching of Christian doctrine.

Prudence, piety, love of souls, and a desire for the spreading of the kingdom of God should guide the catechist in seriously preparing his instructions both as to their form and substance, so as to avoid any doctrinal inaccuracy. In the teaching of moral doctrine, it is necessary to strike a proper balance between rigorism and laxity. Considerable judgment is necessary to discern mortal sins from venial sins and to distinguish counsel from precept, in order to avoid the formation of a false or erroneous conscience. Everyone should feel the need of becoming an apostle of the truth of the Christian Faith, and not shirk the task of enlightening one's own brethren in the ways of God by using imaginary obstacles as excuses. *Tar.*

DOCTRINE, SOCIAL, CHRISTIAN.

Christian teachings concerning the origin, nature, and end of society, Christian social doctrine, were greatly enhanced by the Supreme Magisterium of the Church in the past century, primarily through the efforts of Pope Pius IX, Leo XIII, Pius XI, and Pius XII. In the contemporary age, human society has undergone radical transformations in every field, economic, political, cultural, and international which led to theories of the nature and function of society that are essentially erroneous or otherwise inadequate. Hence came the need for the Magisterium of the Church to stamp out errors, while proposing, at the same time, principles of sound doctrine under new and more richly developed formulas as norms of safe conduct in the work of social restoration.

According to Christian social doctrine, the human person is the foundation, end, and subject of social life; this basic concept characterizes social doctrine, makes it humane, and explains its ever growing importance in the regulation of social relationships, following the bankruptcy of liberal individualism and growing disappointment in collectivist experimentations. *Pav.*

DOCUMENTS (False).

Generally speaking, false documents are private instruments or writings, as deeds, notes, wills, or signatures, prepared in imitation of other things, with the intention of substituting the false for the genuine, or otherwise deceiving or defrauding by the use of the spurious article. The fabrication or counterfeiting of evidence, or the deceptive arrangement of genuine facts or things in such a way as to create an erroneous impression or false inference in the minds of those who may

observe them are false documents. Forgers of documents are liable to criminal prosecution.

Persons who forge or falsify letters, rescripts, or decrees of the Holy See or make use of them with full knowledge of the forgery, either to their own advantage or to that of others, incur severe penalties (including excommunication), even if the desired effect is not obtained (Can. 2360–2362).

DOMICILE.

In the canonical sense, domicile is the place in which one lives with the intention of remaining there permanently. Domicile presupposes the fact of actual living in a place and the intention to live there permanently. The fact easily can be ascertained, but the same cannot be said of the intention which is in a man's mind. However, the intention is presumed (such presumption is *iuris et de iure*, that is, it does not admit of direct proof to the contrary), if the actual habitation is continued for a period of ten complete years. The place in which one acquires his domicile is, according to Canon Law, the parish or quasi-parish; hence, properly speaking, domicile refers to parochial domicile, by which a person becomes a member of a parish and subject to the pastor. There is also, in an analogous sense, a diocesan domicile, by which a person becomes subject to the Bishop.

Domicile is voluntary if freely selected; necessary, if determined by law, (e.g., a wife necessarily shares the domicile of her husband, a minor that of his parents or guardian). The Code of Canon Law, also, speaks of a quasi-domicile which is acquired by residence in a place with the intention of staying there for the greater part of the year; such intention, similar to the case of domicile, is presumed if residence is actually prolonged for more than six months. Even in this case, there may be quasi-parochial domicile and a quasi-diocesan domicile. A wife shares the quasi-domicile of her husband; a minor, that of his parents; an insane person, that of his guardian; however, both wife and minor may have at the same time a voluntary quasi-domicile of their own. It must be noted, however, that as one can be said to live in various places, so too, it is possible to speak of various domiciles and quasi-domiciles, provided there exists a corresponding intention. Although all agree in recognizing the possibility of the coexistence of a domicile and a quasi-domicile, most authors deny the practical possibility that one may have several quasi-domiciles; furthermore, some do not admit of the possibility of two domiciles at the same time. In the Code of Canon Law, a person is called *incola* or resident in the place where he has a domicile, an *advena* or tenant of a quasi-domicile, and *peregrinus* or visitor while he is actually and temporarily outside the place of his domicile or quasi-domicile which he still retains. A *vagus* or wanderer has neither domicile nor quasi-domicile. *Fel.*

DOMINION. *See* Property.

DOMINIUM UTILE. *See* Usufruct.

DONATION. Donations proceed from benevolence and liberality, as the donor freely transmits to another some part of his fortune or property, or assumes another's obligation under a fully gratuitous title. The cancellation of a debt could be an act of donation. The one who donates or gives is called "donor," he who receives is called "donee." The donor may request that the donee signify his acceptance or rejection of the donation within a convenient span of time. For validity, it is sufficient, according to natural law, that a donation be accepted or received from another. Positive law, however, may require further elements, such as that it be made by a public act, etc.

Generally speaking, any object can be given as gift. Some positive laws contain a number of exceptions, particularly regarding future possessions. Anyone who possesses the power to freely dispose of his own goods can donate; positive laws, however, contain several exceptions. Concerning donations to charitable causes, the laws of the Church must be taken into consideration. *See* Foundation, Pious; Legacy, Pious.

The natural law allows gifts to any person, even to the unborn; positive laws contain certain limitations in this regard. For further details regarding civil law legislation in matters of donation, the reader may consult the civil legislations of the various countries.

The necessary conditions for a valid donation require that it be given deliberately and freely, that it can lawfully be given as a gift, that the other party accepts it and that he can properly accept. Thus, by the natural law, only those who have sufficient use of reason can donate; positive laws, however, contain several exceptions. It is necessary to distinguish a purely liberal donation, that is, one without a preceding obligation, from remuneration. Various civil legislations recognize a qualified donation and a donation *sub modo*. The latter is an obligation added to the contract which must be satisfied by the donee or recipient. A donation, properly so called, implies a *ius in re*; but the promissory donation implies a *ius in rem*. With regard to its effect, a donation is called *inter vivos* (from one person to another) if it is given immediately and irrevocably; it is called *mortis causa*, if made by means of a valid will or bequest conveying a right to the thing itself and to its future transfer.

The Code of Canon Law recognizes not only the dispositions of natural law but also those of positive legislations with few exceptions, provided these do not go counter to the natural law (Can. 1529).

Exceptions cover (1) the cases of pious causes in which the validity requires only natural and canonical ability (Can. 1513), and for which the observance of the formalities of civil law is not strictly required (Can. 1516); or (2) the inability of solemnly professed religious to accept gifts and donations except in favor of their religious order, if the order is capable of possession, or of the Holy See if the order itself is unable to accept the gift (Can. 582); or (3) the protection of the church's patrimony, insofar as the donation made to the rector is presumed to be intended for the church (Can. 1536, par. 1); the rector of himself cannot refuse it (Can. 1536, par. 2), but in the event of an illegitimate refusal by the rector, the church has the right to a *restitutio in integrum* (Can. 1536, par. 3). Ingratitude on the part of the rector does not constitute a sufficient reason for the recall of a donation made to the church (Can. 1536); (4) church rectors, prelates, etc., cannot make donations from movable goods belonging to churches entrusted to them, unless these be a just cause of remuneration, piety or Christian charity (Can. 1535); the same applies to religious superiors (Can. 537). Unlawful donations are revocable by their successors in office. *Pal.*

DOUBT. Doubt is a state of mind, which, faced with two contrary or contradictory propositions, fails to see sufficient reasons for adhering to one rather than to the other. In this proper sense, a doubt is a suspension of judgment. In a wider sense, doubt extends to other mental states in which some sort of judgment is present but mixed with uncertainties; in this latter sense, it includes suspicion and opinion. In suspicion, the mind inclines toward a proposition without presuming to adhere to it; in opinion, the mind gives its assent but with the fear of error.

Moral theologians ordinarily treat doubt under all these aspects because they affect the morality of a human act. Theologians distinguish a positive doubt and a negative doubt. In a positive doubt there is no suspension of judgment, because the reasons for each of the two opposed propositions seem to be of equal value. In a negative doubt there is a suspension of judgment, because there is not sufficient reason for adherence to one of the two opposed propositions. A further distinction is made between a practical doubt and a theoretical doubt; a practical doubt has as its immediate object the lawfulness of an act which the person is supposed

to perform in the concrete; a theoretical, also called speculative, doubt only indirectly refers to a concrete act, but directly considers another object, usually a law, or the act itself, abstractly considered.

The terms *prudent* or *imprudent doubt, founded* or *unfounded doubt, probable* or *improbable doubt* hardly need any explanation.

Jurists make a further distinction between *doubt of law* and *doubt of fact*: the former deals with the meaning, extension, existence or cessation of a law; the latter, with the existence of a fact and its circumstances to which the law must be applied.

All moral theologians agree that it is a sin to perform an action while concretely doubting its lawfulness (doubt of fact.) *See* Systems, Moral. However, if an individual finds himself in such a confusing situation as to fear that he will sin no matter which course he takes, then, theologians say that, if he must act, he does not sin, regardless of the course he takes, although he is under obligation to choose the minor evil, if he can discern it. *Gra.*

DOUBT, CONCERNING THE FAITH. *See* Heresy.

DOUBTFUL FAITH. *See* Possession in doubtful faith.

DOWRY (Religious Women). The dowry is a certain amount of money or other goods destined for the maintenance of a professed religious, which she turns over to the religious institute at the beginning of her novitiate.

On the basis of the prescriptions of the ancient Councils (II of Nicaea, 787), of Rouen (1180), and of Lateran (1179)), the Canons of Decretals (X, III, 19, 25) ordered that the reception of religious into the monasteries was to be done without any offering whatsoever. However, it was already an accepted practice, at least for more needy monasteries, to accept some gift for the expenses of the investiture and board for the duration of the trial period. Saint Thomas himself and St. Raymond of Penafort did not consider the use of such gifts as simony. Moreover, the gratuitous acceptance of postulants, especially in the late medieval period, led to conditions whereby many parents prevailed upon their daughters to enter a monastery so that the other children might receive a larger inheritance. Thus, also, for this reason, the custom arose by which all those who wished to enter a monastery were requested to give a certain sum of money. Nor were the regulations by the Sacred Congregations effective enough to abolish such practices, despite the fact that the Council of Trent renewed the ancient prescriptions regarding the gratuitous acceptance of postulants into religious life. With the rise of female congregations of simple vows, the dowry was revived along new lines and the Holy See itself undertook to place it under juridical legislation, particularly in the approbation of the constitutions of the respective congregations.

According to the Code of Canon Law (Can. 547), the dowry, properly so-called, consists of a certain sum of money or other goods which the postulant brings at the beginning of her novitiate, to the monastery or religious institute, for the maintenance of the religious herself throughout the duration of her stay. An essential requisite of the dowry is that it be set up as a permanent and fruitful capital at the disposal of the monastery or institute. Hence, a dowry is not a certain amount of money requested by some religious communities for the expenses of the period of postulancy and novitiate, or other sums of money given to a religious community without being set up as permanent capital, nor money given by or requested of parents of a candidate, which the community maintains the right to dispose of as it sees fit. Likewise, the fungible goods which the candidate brings with her at the time of her entrance into the religious community are not a dowry.

According to the Code, the dowry is compulsory only for nuns who enter a monastery; in institutes with simple vows the prescriptions of the constitutions must be followed. Wherever the dowry is a necessary requirement, a dispensation from it can be given only by the Holy See. The dowry must be given before the reception of the habit or at the beginning of the novitiate, unless a formal promise is made, valid also in a civil court, to give it to the community after the candidate's profession. The community, however, acquires absolute possession of the dowry only after the death of the religious (Can. 548); during her religious life, the community has the obligation of preserving it by administering it prudently and diligently under the supervision of the Ordinary (Can. 550) through fruitful investments; nor is the community permitted to dispose of it in any manner whatsoever (Can. 549). The purpose of the legislation concerning the dowry is the welfare of the religious, so that her maintenance may at least partially be provided for while she is in religion, or if she should leave religious life, that it may serve to give her a start in the world. For this reason, the Code prescribes that, when the religious woman leaves religious life for any reason, including dismissal, her dowry must be returned to her without accrued interest (Can. 551). *Mand.*

DREAMS. Dreams are the effect of psychic activity protracted in sleep. They usually represent an ideational anarchy in which the imagination, stimulated by affectivity and no longer inhibited by attention, critique or ethical controls, has full sway. Oneiric activity starts early in children, whose dreams are characteristically simple and always constitute a wish-fulfillment. Women are given to dreaming much more than men or, at least, they seem to recall and relate their dream experiences more readily. In aged persons oneiric activity is found to decrease along with a general diminishing of psychic vitality.

Dream representations are largely expressed in visual form; however, auditory, olfactory, and gustatory dreams occur.

Sometimes the dream is easily explainable, due to some external cutaneous stimulus (as in the noted case of Descartes, who dreamed of being wounded, only to discover upon awaking that a flea had settled on his body); or to kinesthetic impressions (e.g., the thirsty Crusaders dreamed collectively of fresh-water springs, and during the retreat from Moscow, Napoleon's famished soldiers dreamed of sumptuous banquents). More frequently, a dream seems to lack all outward explanation. Many times one is able to decipher the symbolic meaning of dream images, despite their apparent incoherence.

Although the structure of dreams is *asyntactical,* disregard for temporal and special relations and logical associations, replaced by a purely catathymic association of images (*See* Memory), nevertheless, the dream contains a latent meaning; for dreams are a symbolic transference or version of situations, ideas, and sentiments previously experienced by the dreamer. This transference or transformation of a latent idea in an obvious content but with a meaning usually obscure and difficult to decipher, is due to the subconscious psychical power within us which masks the manifest meaning of our tendencies and passions when these clash with certain principles. This power, which psychoanalysts call *censorship* (*See* Psychoanalysis), is apparently active not only during our waking hours but also in our oneiric representations, which it disguises.

The transference of the latent idea in the manifest content of the dream is usually accomplished (1) through the process of *condensation* (several different images having a different affective tone are fused into one single dream image); (2) through the process of *displacement* (one element is replaced by or substituted with another having the same affective tone—that is, the repressed object of desire, preoccupation, etc., merely appears in a substitute form); or finally, (3) through the process of *symbolization* (an abstract idea is, in the dream, transformed into a concrete image). In other words, the dream image is an unconscious and symbolic representation of a repressed idea or desire.

The psychological analysis of dreams, by unmasking the various and multiple condensations, displacements and symbolizations, may reveal the real hidden meaning of dreams and show that sometimes in dreams things are said or done which during our waking hours are properly repressed by the restraining influence of the moral sense. However, generally speaking, it is deemed inadvisable to resort to dream analysis. First of all, dream interpretation is still and often a matter of conjecture. Secondly, dream analysis would only serve to disturb certain timorous consciences or individuals given to excessive worry and preoccupation. *Riz.*

NIGHT DREAMS. These are dreams in the common and proper sense of the word. In sleep, which is by no means a passive state, the individual's sense activity is not dominated by his higher faculties (reason and will). This sense activity may be initiated by a variety of causes or agents, especially by intellectual agents outside of man. Certainly God, if He so wishes, may cause a dream, and the Scriptures testify that God has at various times delivered messages through the medium of the dream. In such instances God also provides a certainty about the divine origin of the dream. Spirits and angels in their role of divine messengers are also capable of causing dreams. The devil, too, for reasons and purposes of his own can cause dreams. If a dream originates neither from God nor from a good or evil spirit, then, it is the product of sense activity. This does not mean, however, that sense activity is not at the same time subject to the influence of other contributing factors, both internal, such as the physical condition of the body (pains, functional disturbances, disease), and external (excitation of the external sense by outside stimuli, such as the ringing of a bell, an alarm signal, etc.). Also influencing sense activity during dreams are psychical factors, such as desires, fears, past thoughts, and experiences. In short, dreams are frequently the result, at least partially, of existing factors either within or outside the dreamer. It cannot be denied that natural science, which studies the causes by their effects, is also capable of attaining the causal realities behind the dreams, such as the mental or physical condition of the dreamer, his past experiences, desires, fears, etc. Hence, not every attempt at dream interpretation is to be frowned upon; for the fact remains that a purely human science is well equipped to derive from dream analysis data that may be found useful in the treatment and healing of sick individuals, especially those afflicted with some psychical abnormality or disease (see Psychotherapy). If in certain situations dream analysis and therapy are indicated, the patient should always make sure to seek out a thoroughly reputable, serious and honest therapist, one who will not do things that are contrary to Christian moral teaching.

To use one's own dreams or those of another to gain knowledge of future things is permissible if it is certain that the dream is due to natural causes. From the knowledge of present natural causes we may reasonably draw certain conclusions regarding the future. To believe in dreams, one's own or those related by others, as foretelling future events, is a sin of superstition, unless there is sufficient evidence that the dream is of supernatural origin (a very rare case). Thus, it is not permissible to consult diviners or to lend credence to their predictions.

DAYDREAMS. These are called dreams in an improper sense. They are products of the imagination deliberately evoked by man. They are images permitted to arise and to linger in one's mind for the purpose of giving oneself the illusion of living a life different from real life and to experience whatever sensations may be connected with such an illusion. It is a sort of imaginary life that the individual creates for himself and lives through, because he finds his external life unsatisfactory. The individual seeks in the realm of fantasy what he desires in the realm of reality but is unable to attain; or perhaps the thing is not yet attainable in real life (as in the case of the young), or is no longer attainable (as in the case of the aged). Daydreams may become sinful depending on the nature of their content. To take pleasure in wrong things conjured up by the imagination (e.g., acts of revenge) constitutes a sin. But even if their content is not improper, daydreams generally represent a waste of time and energy; they weaken one's character, diminish one's strength and will to pursue the real or possible goals of life, and they prevent the individual from becoming a useful member of society. For all these reasons habitual indulgence in daydreaming may be harmful and objectionable. It is the duty of parents, teachers, and educators to prevent and to correct (in the more serious cases with the aid of a good psychiatrist) any such morbid tendency noted in children or young persons. *Ben.*

DROMOMANIA. *See* Dipsomania.

DRUG. *See* Deontology, Pharmaceutical; Medicine.

DRUGS (Pleasure-giving). Drugs are substances, such as coffee, tobacco, etc., which have little nutritive value but are used by man because they excite his nervous system and give, at the same time, some sort of pleasure to the senses, particularly of taste.

The use of pleasure-giving drugs is not in itself immoral. However, under some aspects, their use can be sinful: (a) If taken simply for pleasure and sensual satisfaction to the positive exclusion of any usefulness. They can be useful if taken to relieve tiredness or to provide the body with some necessary recreation to the end that it may be a fit instrument of the soul. (b) If taken in a measure that would be harmful to the body, either because of nicotine intoxication which the drug might cause or because of its tendency to be habit-forming. (c) When an unreasonable amount of money is spent to provide such drugs; that is, when one spends for the purchase of such drugs the money he should use for the honest maintenance of his family or for other necessary or more noble uses. *See* Narcotics. *Ben.*

DRUNKENNESS. Drunkenness may indicate a state or an act. As a state, it means a condition characterized by a temporary loss of the use of the normal mental faculties caused by the abuse of alcoholic beverages. As an act, drunkenness is the abuse of alcoholic beverages causing a temporary loss of the use of one's normal mental faculties.

The sin of drunkenness consists exactly in the *act*, for it is the act of drinking or overindulging that causes the deliberate loss of the normal mental faculties which is the effect of the sin.

As a result of the abuse of alcoholic beverages, a person may become guilty of other sins, such as damaging one's physical health, although he may never lose the use of his mental faculties (*see* Alcoholism). In this case, however, the specific sin of drunkenness is not present. Complete drunkenness, if fully deliberate, is a grave sin. This is the teaching of moral theology based on Sacred Scripture and on the general consensus. It is a grave disorder to deprive oneself of the use of the mental faculties, for reason is the very faculty that must direct man's actions in order that they may conform to God's law. Many other sins and ills may result from drunkenness. A man who is aware of this and yet willfully becomes drunk is responsible for his actions, although he is not aware of what he does while in a state of intoxication. Partial drunkenness, in which one's mental faculties are only partially disturbed or impaired, of itself, is not a grave sin, but it could become grave because of particular circumstances—if, for instance, the lack of the full use of one's mental faculties were to gravely endanger one's life or the life of others (while driving, etc.), or if it were to cause grave scandal.

Drunkenness is a detestable sin because it deprives man of the use of his mental faculties by which he stands above irrational animals. (There is a strong tendency today to regard drunkenness as a disease.—Note of the Editor.)

Once drunkenness has become a habit, it is very difficult to overcome. *Ben.*

DUEL. A contest or combat between two persons fought with deadly weapons, prearranged in order to kill or seriously injure, is called a duel. Generally, the contestants agree in advance on time, place and type of weapons, the witnesses (seconds), and other circumstances. If the arms agreed upon are not apt to cause at least grave injury, the contest is not a duel in the proper sense of the term. However, its moral character remains the same. A duel may be public or private. A public duel, no longer practiced today, was engaged in by order of public authority to decide the outcome of a war. The private duel includes also the so-called "tourney," more common in the past and not always engaged in with hostile intent. The intention which motivates the contest generally determines its morality. Contests entered to acquire dexterity in the use of certain arms are lawful, if everything is regulated in such a way as to eliminate the danger of killing or of causing injury.

Duel with the intent to kill is an act intrinsically immoral. This applies to the action of each of the participants. It is gravely sinful not only for the challenged who agrees to the duel, but also for the challenger or provoker as well. Dueling is nothing else but a remnant of barbaric customs, when the wrongs which were not righted by the intervention of public authority were left to private vengeance. It is a form of juridical and spiritual immaturity tolerated by society, not fully imbued with the spirit of the Gospel, but guided by a false concept of honor.

The malice of the duel follows from the very nature of the act, which consists of two elements: (1) the killing or serious injury to another person outside of legitimate self-defense (the alleged element of self-defense can be avoided simply by avoiding the duel); (2) exposure by the contestant to the danger of being killed or gravely wounded without sufficient reason. Moreover, he directly seeks this danger since he consents to the use by his adversary of the same deadly weapons which he himself uses. Hence, dueling, considered under this twofold aspect, is a sin against the fifth commandment, which forbids the killing or injuring of another, or the exposing of oneself to being killed or injured.

The various arguments alleged to minimize the malice which flows from the very nature of the duel are many, but all are fallacious: (a) Some hold that a duel is lawful because it is a means of defending or vindicating one's honor. Obviously, such persons overlook the fact that the defense of one's honor must be done by moral means, but the duel is in itself immoral. Furthermore, a duel is not an adequate means of defending one's honor, because killing or wounding in this case is rather the result of chance, which proves nothing. At the most, it may prove physical strength or dexterity on the part of the winner, but it will never prove his honesty or his right. (b) In some countries, the individual (officer) who fails to accept the challenge is declared a coward (infamous). Obviously, this is based on an erroneous concept of what constitutes honor or bravery.

The Church has always shown her opposition to dueling both by positive condemnation of the philosophy behind it, including the false maxims concerning man's honor, and by direct and indirect penalties incurred by those who engage in or favor it. The Council of Trent issued the most solemn condemnation against dueling, calling it "the detestable custom devised by the malice of the devil." The same condemnation was repeated by Pope Leo XIII in his Encyclical Letter *Pastoralis Officii* (1891), directed to the Bishops of Germany and Austria. Presently, according to the Code of Canon Law, those who engage in dueling incur *ipso facto*, that is, automatically, excommunication reserved to the Holy See. And if they die unrepentant while dueling or as the result of wounds received during the contest, they are denied ecclesiastical burial.

The same penalty is incurred *ipso facto* by those who challenge, and by those who accept the duel; those who promote or favor dueling; those who permit it or do not forbid it while they have the power to do so, and those who willfully witness the contest.

The brute-force contest customary in German universities (*Bestimmungsmensur*) falls directly under the canonical sanctions because it is not simply an athletic exercise, but corresponds to the classic concept of dueling, even if it stops at the first blood, that is, even when there is no intent to prolong it to the death of the adversary (*S. C. Concilii*, June 13, 1925).

In modern codes, for instance, the Italian Penal Code, dueling is forbidden and those who participate in it, contestants, or seconds and others, incur a variety of penalties ranging from fines to detention. Those who provoke it are subject to the penalty of detention (art. 400). *Ben.*

DULIA. *See* Cult.

DUMBNESS AND MUTE. *See* Aphasia; Melancholy; Deaf-mutism.

DUMPING. *See* Coalition, International Commerce.

DURATION (OF LABOR). *See* Labor.

DUTIES (OF ONE'S OWN STATE). In ordinary language, the word *duty* has the subjective connotation of a moral obligation; objectively, its connotation is that of moral law. Duty, in its purely abstract sense and without any connotation, is taken to mean the obligation to perform or to omit a certain action. In its concrete sense, it means the action one is obliged to perform or to omit. In this sense, it is said that one is faithful to duty, meaning, of course, that he does with fidelity what he is expected to do. (Obligation is the center or the hinge of the entire moral order; it is the effect of a law; that is, an obligation imposed by law.) In ordinary language expressions such as these are used: duty of office, professional duty, duty as a citizen, duty of friendship, etc. Hence, the duties of one's own state are those moral obligations relative to a particular condition (or state) of life in which he finds himself and which he is obliged to fulfill in determined circumstances.

In social life there are, of necessity, various states in which individuals may attain their earthly as well as their eternal destiny. As the human body would have no consistency nor perform its tasks if it were not that each member had its own functions and particular duties to fulfill (Cf. 1 Cor. 12:12–27), so, too, in human society there are various states and offices, special or ordinary, each having a different function directed to the welfare of society as a whole. This flows from the very nature of man and is confirmed by divine Revelation, in which we find, "The Lord hath divided them and diversified their ways" (Eccl. 33:11).

The Ten Commandments are, in substance, but obligations of nature; that is, obligations which flow from the very nature of man and apply to all, irrespective of age, place or time. Besides the Ten Commandments common to all, there are obligations which arise from one's own condition or state. These, too, are imposed by God in virtue of creation, in the sense that He created man social by nature, that is, subject to the (social) necessity of living in a state or society where there are rulers, laws, as a condition of that society or state. These duties and obligations are not found explicitly formulated in the simple and concise wording of the Ten Commandments, but they are implicitly contained in each of them, particularly in the seven last commandments, by which man's relations to his fellow man are regulated in the variety of conditions and offices in which he may find himself. The duties and obligations of the legislator differ from those of ordinary citizens: of the physician, the patient, the teacher, the pupil, the lawyer and the judge, the criminal, the priest, the religious, etc.

Whatever the state in life to which

God calls an individual, if he is to follow it in the light of Christian principles, he must first of all recognize the duties of that particular state. Each individual must learn the manner by which the commandments of God and the evangelical counsels, more closely applicable to his own particular state, are concretely carried out through his professional duties.

At no time must the Ten Commandments or the evangelical counsels be viewed outside the framework of one's own profession or state, lest they be applied erroneously. Whoever fails to see his professional duties as the duties of his own state will fail to understand what he must do in order to fulfill the duties imposed upon him by God. Any good Christian must and can attain his own sanctification in the state in which he finds himself and must not entertain illusions of a better one. Moreover, the duties of one's own state are not only for the personal good of the individual but have a social importance as well.

In the times in which we live, it is extremely important to recapture the moral values of the functions and office which man performs or will perform in his social life, and, at the same time, to stress the obligations relative to each type of social function. These duties are often forgotten because of the erroneous attitude that professional duties have no moral character or have no obligatory value. *Tar.*

DUTY. *See* Taxation.

DUTY. Duty is the norm which regulates freedom by introducing into it the maximum degree of necessity compatible with it. Duty is an obligation imposed upon a free person to use his freedom in a given manner. It is one of the basic elements of moral life. It is synonymous with obligation (moral); its transgression constitutes a sin.

In the sphere of human freedom, in certain fields there are rules that do not constitute a duty; such fields are literature, the arts, science, and the technical fields. There are, besides, three areas of human freedom in which norms are accompanied by a sense of duty. These are the moral, religious, and legal fields. However, in any field in which a duty makes itself felt, it always bears the stamp of a moral or ethical value; for every duty, if it be really such, has ethical connotations. Thus, it obliges in conscience and a voluntary violation of it is sinful. The sense of duty is one of the most marked traits characterizing man's intellectual nature and rendering him superior to brute nature; it is a mysterious force which has completely baffled both positivistic philosophies and the destructive power of the Kantian critique. All attempts made to explain the existence and origin of the sense of duty in the human conscience on the basis of materialistic, evolutionistic, and collectivistic hypotheses, have utterly failed. It may go unheeded, but it can never be altogether suppressed; quite the contrary, the greater the efforts to stifle it, the more forceful and threatening it becomes.

Moralists usually divide man's duties (taken in an objective sense) into three classes: toward God, toward oneself, and toward one's neighbor. Another classification is made into general duties and those specific or proper to the various states in life. It may be well, however, to observe that modern theologians give this distinction a connotation that is somewhat different from that which it had with earlier theologians. For the latter, the different states were, generally, the various forms and degrees of Christian perfection; whereas for modern theologians these states in life are identified with the various professions of social life. In the *Summa* of St. Thomas, the treatise on duties has a structure quite different from that found in manuals of contemporary moralists. *See* Duties of one's own state. *Gra.*

DYSTHYMIA. Etymologically, *dysthymia* means despondency, an affective disorder closely analogous to manic-depressive psychosis, and characterized by depressions associated with hypochondriasis. Some consider it as psychosis characterized by an unusual exaggeration of the individual's emotional tone (mood). For this reason Dr. Cerletti prefers to call this mental disorder hyperthymia.

Emotional tone (or affective mood) is a peculiarly subjective sensation, associated with organic functions and cenesthesia, which imprints a particular pleasant or unpleasant mood upon the consciousness of an individual. Normal individuals, when not under special influence arising from external causes or their bodily organisms or from conscience itself, are in a tranquil and indifferent mood; tranquil, because of the absence of abnormal tensions arising from the past or concerned with the future; indifferent, because of a tendency to adjust itself in its mood of pleasure or displeasure according to the emotional content. With the variations in this content, caused by events considered useful or harmful to the biological and psychological scope of the individual, the mood in normal persons varies according to the emergence of pleasant sensations of happiness (joy, good mood) or of unpleasant sensations of displeasure (sadness, bad mood). In a normal person, the characteristics regarding the intensity and duration of these variations are in proportion to the nature of the stimulus-producing factors which determine the disturbance of the mood. These disturbances, however, from the physiological standpoint, slowly subside and in a more or less short period of time disappear altogether. But the intensity and the duration of such varied reactions in the mood of the individual present considerable differences, even in normal individuals with relation to the degree of sensibility and susceptibility of influence on emotional tone (temperament). This makes it possible to have some individuals rather emotionally cold (hypothymics) and others, on the other hand, vivacious and susceptible to quick reactions. Among the latter one finds persons of quick temperamental reactivity moving equally in both directions, and persons whose temperament is habitually oriented either toward joyfulness (euphoric) or toward sadness (dysphoric).

The pathological exaggeration of the temperament could be either in the direction of gaiety and optimism (See Mania), or of sadness and pessimism (See Melancholy) or now in one direction, now in another (in this case one would speak more properly of circular psychosis or of manic-depressive psychosis), sometimes with free intervals of normality between the two dysthymic phases, and, at other times, without any intervals at all. This rarely occurs. These are the fundamental characteristics of dysthymia: *constitutionality, essentiality, curability, periodicity.*

The *constitutional* nature of dysthymic psychoses is evident from common occurrence and heredity. Dysthymia of a depressive and melancholic nature affects persons with no hereditary diseases, and is the result of conspicuous emotions, toxic forms, menopause, or advanced age. This does not belong, strictly speaking, to real dysthymic psychoses; it must be considered rather a psychogenic reaction or disturbance of the mood due to endocrine disorder (usually from genital or thyroid malfunction) or psychoses proper to the degenerative age. In a case of true dysthymia, one can notice a specific hereditary transmission and dominant characteristic. The essential characteristic of the appearance of dysthymic episodes is often evident by the absence of any event which might justify the particular emotional tone proper to the event itself.

At any rate, the pathological disturbance of the mood is always out of proportion to the eventual stimulus. Sometimes an antinomy is present between the stimulus (v.g., joyous) and the emotional reaction (melancholic).

The *curability* of individual psychological affections is certain and absolute. This could come spontaneously even after years of illness, but it can also be notably aided by modern therapeutic treatments, especially by electric shock treatment. *Periodicity*, that is, the repetition at more or less long intervals of the same manifestations (mania or peri-

odic melancholia) or by opposite manifestations, is another peculiar manifestation of this type of psychosis of which we spoke before.

It is rare that a manic individual gives way to homicide or other grave crimes, due to the fact that the mental disorder and the fundamentally euphoric humor of the patient do not allow coordinated criminal actions, and also because ordinarily such patients are promptly confined to hospitals. Crime is even more rare among hypomanics (See Mania), whose behavior is limited to a gay exuberance, unless the period of excitement is manifested in a degenerate criminal tendency. In this case, the more or less latent impulses to criminality are stimulated by the manic or hypomanic episodes. Other crimes which hypomanics can commit because of the sub-chaotic state of their conscience are much more important because of their frequency and the ethico-legal consequences involved.

Men affected by hypomania frequently tend toward crimes connected with civil responsibility; reckless commercial speculations, falsifications of public documents, all kinds of frauds, false depositions, etc. This happens primarily because these patients are easily led to presumptuousness, mythomania, hyperoptimism, and irresponsibility, since they have lost the proper estimate of their capacities.

In women affected with hypomania, there frequently appear cases of pathologically exaggerated eroticism, caused both by a neurohormonical hyperactivity and by a breakdown of censure (See Psychoanalysis). As a result of these conditions, all instinctive actions (ordinarily pushed into the subconscious, inhibited, or sublimated) rush to the fore of consciousness. Hence, exhibitionism, lewd and provocative attitudes, may develop into sexual crime. In this connection an important ethical question comes to the fore: If, in a particular case of carnal violence or other similar crime, the moral and juridical responsibility of the hypomanic patient is more or less sensibly reduced, depending on the extent of the illness (responsibility which is generally totally annulled in chronic manic forms), what will be the moral and juridical responsibility of the sane party who participated in the criminal act? There is no doubt that from the point of view of Catholic moral doctrine, any such action is a grave sin. Besides, there are aggravating circumstances, consisting in the abuse of a person who is incapable of reacting as he should. From the medico-legal standpoint, however, the seducer is often in reality an ignorant victim, and the magistrate will need the counsel of a psychiatrist to evaluate fully the personality of the seduced, to establish the true extent of the responsibility.

In the melancholic, however, crimes against one's own body are known to be relatively frequent (suicide, self-injury, etc.).

These crimes usually escape all sanction because they are committed by individuals who, on account of grave psycho-affective disturbances, have lost their capacity to properly understand or will. Since these conditions are likely to occur, the relatives of such patients should be alerted more promptly and effectively than ordinarily done. Too often relatives do consider such patients as being sick, but fail to detect the possibility that the latter may harm themselves or others, and consider them "incapable of doing harm to a fly," and very religious. Relatives must be warned insistently that any even slightly melancholic patient is always potentially suicidal and that even the most apparently tranquil patient can experience an extremely dangerous condition of *raptus* (*See* Melancholia); that, above all, the patient must be committed to an appropriate hospital for safety and for prompt and scientific treatment of his condition.

Insofar as moral responsibility is concerned, the suicide of a melancholic may at times be attributed either to the doctor's negligence in failing to warn effectively the relatives of such a possibility, or to the relatives themselves for underestimating the timely warning of the doctor. *Riz.*

E

EASTER. The English name is believed to be related to Eostre, a Teutonic goddess of the rising light of day and spring. The feast is also referred to as the Pasch (a word derived from the Greek, *pascha*, which is itself a transliteration of the Hebrew word *pesah*, which means *passage*. Pasch refers to the mysterious and prophetic passage of the Hebrews through the Red Sea, after their enslavement in Egypt. From very ancient times the Church has applied this name to its greatest liturgical feast.

Originally, some of the Churches of Asia Minor used this name to refer to the Passion of Christ *(Pascha crucifixionis)*, while the Westerners laid the main stress on the theme of the Resurrection *(Pascha resurrectionis)*. At one point in the second century the difference became so obvious that Rome sought to intervene and decide the matter. This would have been done but for the conciliatory influence of St. Polycarp, who came to Rome in his old age for this specific purpose. The words of the disciple of St. John the Apostle did not win the Pope over to his own position, but did prevent the condemnation of Christians. When the controversy continued to become more acute at the end of the second century, Pope Victor ordered a number of Councils to convene, and they decided that only the Roman usage was proper. Once again an Easterner of great fame intervened, Irenaeus of Lyons, who prevented the use of strong measures against those who disagreed.

DATE OF EASTER. After the controversy over the main meaning of Easter had been settled, a brand new one arose almost immediately about the date on which it should be celebrated. The Council of Nicea settled this controversy, by deciding in favor of the Roman and Alexandrian point of view and fixing the date in three articles: (a) Easter must always fall on a Sunday; (b) the Christian Easter must never fall on the same day as the Jewish Passover; (c) Easter must fall on the first Sunday after the 14th of Nisan. At the same time, the Patriarch of Alexandria was given the task of determining the date on which Easter should be celebrated each year and communicating it to the Church of Rome. Even then, the uncertainties did not disappear until the sixth century, when Denis the Little, using a figure based on a cycle of nineteen years, evolved a perfect scientific basis for determining the Sunday on which Easter should be celebrated.

In ancient times, the celebration of Easter began during the night between Holy Saturday and Sunday; it was marked by a long and solemn vigil, which included the baptism of neophytes; this was followed by the celebration of the Mass of the Resurrection, during which neophytes received the Holy Eucharist for the first time.

By the fourth century in Jerusalem, Easter included a celebration of eight days. In 389, the civil laws recognized the solemn festive nature of the day and put it on the same level as the feast of Christmas at Rome and Constantinople. Easter closed with the Sunday *in albis*, which was the day the neophytes put off the white baptismal garments they had received on the night of Easter.

Today, with the liturgical reform of Pope Pius XII, including the celebration of Easter in the night between Saturday and Sunday, a most beautiful part of the ancient liturgy has once again been given a place of honor and brought back to life in all its beautiful symbolism.

442

In connection with Easter, the Church has enjoined upon all the faithful the obligation of receiving the Holy Eucharist (see Communion). *Cig.*

ECCLESIASTIC. *See* Cleric.

ECONOMICS. Economics is the science that treats of the production and distribution of wealth, by considering the rational use of products, which are limited and susceptible of alternate uses in meeting unlimited human needs. The economic criterion is based on the attainment of given ends by the employment of the least possible amount of means. It must, therefore, take into consideration both the essential and existential hierarchy of ends and means.

Economics is dependent upon morality; historically, it is conditioned by the elements of place and time. It is dependent upon morals insofar as its object is a human activity. It is conditioned by time and place, insofar as the ends and means are conditioned historically. An American businessman and an American society cannot equally be compared to an Italian businessman and an Italian society. Furthermore, the Italian businessman and the Italian society of today are vastly different from the Italian businessman and the Italian society of four hundred years ago. The science of economics cannot be the same in all three cases, although the moral principles to which the science is subordinated remain unchanged.

Economics is also a social science, as is evident from man's social nature as well as from the limited availability of means and the alternate modes of use which are often the outcome of the social diversity of men. In view of this, a single businessman or a single enterprise cannot be the starting point for economics, since this would be begging the question.

Economics, finally, is a practical science inasmuch as its aim is to set down norms of guidance for heads of government in the field of economics. These determinations of the nature of economics are the final product of a long historical and doctrinal evolution in constant contrast with contemporaneous factors. *Mai.*

ECSTASY. *See* Mystic.

ECTOPIC. *See* Ectopic Fetus.

ECUMENICISM, ECUMENICAL MOVEMENT. The term *ecumenical movement* or *ecumenicism* commonly signifies the attempt by various interdenominational movements, especially among Protestants, to achieve a closer unity of Christian Churches through some form of confederation.

From a total world population of 2,500,000,000 people, Christians comprise 750,000,000. This Christian population includes 425,000,000 Roman Catholics, 176,000,000 Protestants, and 128,000,000 Orthodox Christians. According to these statistics, therefore, nearly one half of the Christian population, including all those who consider Christ as their founder, are non-Catholic. Previous attempts at union with the Greek Orthodox Church made by the Council of Lyons (1274) and by the Council of Florence (1439) proved to be ephemeral. In 1910, Protestant missionaries met at Edinburgh to work out a method of avoiding interference with one another in their missions. Charles Brent then proposed extending an invitation to all Christians to unite, and he became the protagonist of the movement at subsequent conferences in Geneva in 1920 (*Faith and Order*), Lausanne in 1927, and Edinburgh in 1937. Parallel to this was another movement inspired mainly by Soderblom, Lutheran bishop of Upsala (*Work and Life*). The two movements joined after World War II and met in an assembly at Amsterdam in August-September, 1948, where they established the World Council of Churches, with headquarters at Geneva. This was followed by a second assembly at Evanston, Illinois, in October, 1954 and a third at New Delhi (India) in 1961. Protestants gained the adherence of the Orthodox Christians whose views on the ecumenical movement were brought into the effort.

THE ECUMENICAL MOVEMENT AND THE CATHOLIC CHURCH. The position of the Catholic Church has been stated on many occasions. Recently, the anxious attempts of some Catholics to effect an agreement with non-Catholics and the force of world public opinion induced the Catholic Church to clarify in several pronouncements its position on reunion. The doctrinal position was stated chiefly in two encyclicals: *Orientalium animos* of Pope Pius XI (January 6, 1928), and *Orientales omnes Ecclesias* of Pope Pius XII (December 23, 1945). Disciplinary directives on the subject were issued mainly in the Response of June 5, 1948 and in the Instruction of the Holy Office, December 20, 1949 (*see* Discussion, Interfaith).

On the question of common activities for Church unity, the specific norms to be followed are these: discussions between Catholics and non-Catholics can be permitted by the Ordinaries in their own dioceses; competency to grant permission for inter-diocesan and international conferences is reserved to the Holy Office; it is the right and obligation of the hierarchy to exercise vigilance over such activities. (The Catholic periodical which concerns itself with the problems of Church unity is *Unitas*.) *Pal.*

EDICT. ROMAN LAW. Edicts were public pronouncements issued by magistrates who had the *ius edicendi*, in which they informed the people of their policy in matters within their competence. The most important was the edict of the praetor. Before assuming his office, the praetor notified the people of the principles according to which he intended to decide transactions coming within his jurisdiction. This edict was called *annuum* (annual), since it remained in force during the whole year of the praetor's tenure of office and could not be modified. For this reason it was also called *perpetuum* (continuous) to differentiate it from provisional edicts or ordinances of the moment, issued on the occasion of a particular incident. The succeeding praetor would issue for his year in office a new edict. It was the custom, however, for the new praetor to take over and republish the bulk of the continuous edicts of his predecessors, making only those modifications and additions which changed times and contemporary needs demanded. Thus, in the course of time, there came into existence a system of true, traditional law which was called praetorian or magisterial. Emperor Hadrian entrusted Salvius Iulianus with the task of giving to praetorian law a definitive form; he took from the praetors the authority to introduce modifications or alterations in the edict. Edicts issued by emperors, such as the Edict of Caesar or Constantine's Edict of Toleration, were general edicts, which had the force of law.

CANON LAW. The term *edict* was employed at times to designate general laws; at other times, to signify the laws of the Roman Pontiff for his temporal State. In the present law, the term is used most frequently in procedural law and designates jurisdictional acts which contain public citations. Public citation is resorted to when the parties cannot be cited personally. These edicts are displayed in public places or inserted in newspapers, particularly in the *Acta Apostolicae Sedis* (*q.v.*). The term *edict* is also used to signify the summoning of all those who may have an interest in some matter of administration or government. Thus, for example, it might designate the notification sent to those who claim the right of patronage over a certain benefice or who wish to oppose an election to office, etc. The word *edict* may also refer to announcements informing the faithful of some matter of interest to them. Finally, the term is used at times to designate general precepts issued by ecclesiastical superiors. The stability and binding force of edicts must be gathered from their nature. *Toc.*

EDITOR. See Cooperation, Forbidden Books, Press.

EDUCATION. Man is not born a perfect being. He comes into the world endowed with many faculties that wait to be developed: his individuality, his inherent propensity to knowledge, experience, adaptation to environment, etc. Education is a basic human phenomenon, insofar as it guides man's inclination toward further development. Education, therefore, is a means to a higher end, which consists in preparing man for the free and complete use of his God-given faculties and in directing these faculties towards the perfect integration and development of man. Education, consequently, is not mere professional or technical training, nor solely the teaching of scholastic and scientific notions, but it is the formation of man in accordance with his vocation. Education must see to it that the various faculties in man are developed sufficiently and with balance. Education is the gateway of man's moral entrance into society and the means by which he participates in the moral and material goods of society; through education, he also becomes a debtor to society and, in particular, the family.

EDUCATION AND THE FAMILY. The family has the natural right and duty to educate its own members. The primary and essential end of the family is the procreation of offspring. Since, up to a certain age, a child lacks the use of reason and is unable to provide for himself, the family must assume the responsibility for the intellectual and moral training of the child. Nature, after all, does not intend only the birth of the child; it intends also the growth and development of the child until he reaches the perfect state of man as man, that is, the state of virtue (*S. Theol.*, I–II, q. 100, a. 5 ad 4; II–II, q. 101, a. 1 c.). Education is not the task of an individual; it is of necessity a social endeavor. Since man must live his life in three societies, established by God—in the natural order: family and civil society; in the supernatural order: the Church—these three societies must co-operate harmoniously with each other to achieve the same end: the education of the young in preparation for life. The school can be the common meeting-ground for the

various societies cooperating in a person's education; the Church directs the child to his supernatural end; the State forms the citizen; the family readies him for manhood.

Of primary importance is the family, "instituted by God immediately, and having as its natural purpose the procreation and education of children." In any question of rights of education, the family has first claim (Pius XI, *Divini illius Magistri*, December 31, 1929: Denz. 2203). This natural right of the family, confirmed today in article twenty-six of the "Declaration of the Rights of Man" (U.N.), was elevated and perfected through the institution of the sacrament of matrimony, which raised the family to the supernatural order. Under this aspect, education no longer belongs solely to the family, which generates the child for the natural order, but it belongs also to the Church, which generates him for the supernatural life. The Church is a mother who "generates, while she educates souls in the divine life of grace through the sacraments and her teaching" (Denz. 2204). The sacred character of marriage is derived from its purpose, which is the perpetuation of a human race destined to adore, glorify, and serve God.

In view of this sacred purpose, it is incumbent upon the family to form its members so that they will be fitting subjects for the supernatural life. The family, therefore, must instill in the child knowledge and love of God and see to it that he is properly nourished in the supernatural life. Modern pedagogy has clearly shown that the method of education used in the family ought to be applied also in the schools. It consists in the freedom of self-expression, love for and cooperation with the pupil, achieved through the use of spontaneous conversation, illustrative examples, and insight into his mind, habits, etc.

TASK OF EDUCATION. The countless latent potentialities in a pupil are impelled toward the infinite, that is, toward God. Education must be at the service of man; it must recognize his position in the cosmos. The tasks of education can be summed up into the following three aspects of man: (a) As a natural being, man seeks his perfection through the development of his faculties in the objective world. This is accomplished by mutual interplay between the individual and his environment. On the one hand, man must develop his own faculties in an objective world. On the other, he must enter the world that surrounds him, and become a part of an existing civilization. The tasks of education in this sphere are inexhaustible; they span the extent of domestic, civil, economic, social, national, political, scientific, and artistic education. This natural formation of man, however, cannot remain in isolation; otherwise, it would be onesided training. By necessity, it must be fitted to the tasks of a general, human education. (b) As a moral being, man seeks his development by means of a free subjection of himself to the will of God. This subjection in education is effected through the mutual influence between spirit and matter in man. Matter and the senses must be subordinated to the soul, while the organs of the body must enable the soul to act in and with the body. This moral education of the perfect man is not something isolated, external, or independent; it must penetrate the whole soul and all its action, effected in such a way that there is no morally neutral formation, not even in those activities seemingly remote from the spiritual, such as sports or technical training. Any type of education is for man a spiritual creation. (c) In the present order of Providence, man is elevated to the supernatural life. He is called to a divine life, a life of grace. This truth must be acknowledged in the field of education, especially by Catholics. The child or the adolescent is destined to serve God through love, and to unite himself to God. The growth of this vocation is achieved through the mutual influence between nature and grace. Grace must penetrate the natural potentialities. This is, therefore, the third category of the task of general education: to prepare the soul for the action

of grace, and, at the same time, bring grace to man through the means of sensible reality. The whole social, cultural, and ethical formation would be lacking if education failed to promote and develop this tendency in man toward the supernatural.

The individualistic concept of education regards the ultimate factor in education as the mature will of the adult. The basic relationship in education is the relationship between educator and pupil. The aim is toward a conscious, deliberate and planned education of the young. The individualistic concept of education is the traditional one. The pupil, however, is not exposed merely to the influence of the educator, but also to many other elements, prominent among which are society and his surrounding environment. These forms of influence are categorized as social forms. To investigate these forms is the task of social pedagogy. In such a study, the community is considered a means, not an end.

The social concept of education considers the community as the ultimate factor in education. As a rule, the educator has before him many pupils, and the pupils have before them many educators. Both groups become members of larger communities: the educators as members of their professional, State, and Church organizations; the pupils as members of the family, etc. It becomes a serious obligation of social pedagogy to see that all these influences are coherently unified in their educational purposes. Social pedagogy, on the one hand, considers the pupil as he is found in definite social surroundings and standards of living; on the other hand, it investigates how these surroundings may be aligned and organized for educational purposes. *Per.*

EDUCATION, SEXUAL. Sexual education denotes knowledge directed at providing the young with a correct physical and moral attitude toward sex. More specifically, it signifies a form of education which seeks to introduce the very young to information on sex and its dangers, and, disregarding the aids of religion and morality, sees in this early initiation one of the principal means of preparing the young for life. The disseminators of this view claim that it is one of the most effective antidotes to sexual abuses among the young. According to them, the cause of these early sexual excesses is to be found in ignorance about sex and in a lack of training in meeting its dangers. Akin to this, is the view held by some Catholics who, though insisting on a solid religious and moral education, believe that great benefit can be derived from serious instruction on sex provided indiscriminately to pupils in their early youth. They hold that enlightenment on the true purpose and value of the sexual life could eliminate many abuses and difficulties, as it would generate, they say, a sense of responsibility and a certain idealism concerning future temptations and even prevent any element of surprise and improper information.

The Church position on this subject has been made clear on several occasions. Of particular moment are the letter of the Congregation of the Index to the Cardinal of Barcelona, on January 18, 1908 (*Periodica de religiosis institutis et personis*, 4 [1909], 165–166), and a passage from the Encyclical *Divini illius Magistri*, of December 21, 1929; finally, the decree of the Sacred Congregation of the Holy Office, of March 21, 1931. (a) These documents condemn the method of sex education, which, as a sexual pedagogy, "advocates the use of purely natural means, such as a foolhardy initiation and precautionary instruction for all indiscriminately, even in public; and worse still, by exposing them at an early age to the occasions, in order to accustom then . . . and to harden them as it were against such dangers" (Encyclical *Divini illius Magistri*: Denz. 2214). Sexual instruction privately imparted is preferable to instruction given to a group or a class; it should be given "at an opportune time by those who hold from God the commission to teach and have the grace of office," and "with all the precautions well known in traditional Christian education" (*ibid.*). (b) They insist on a

positive Christian method based on the love of virtue, hatred for sin, on prayer, the sacraments, avoidance of occasions of danger and training in modesty (*q.v.*). This position of the Church is prompted by theoretical conviction and practical experience concerning the sad effects of original sin. These show "that evil practices are the effect not so much of intellectual ignorance as weakness of will, exposed to dangerous occasions and unsupported by the means of grace" (*loc. cit.*). Catholic teaching certainly does not condemn a proper initiation into matters of sex; in fact, it considers this a normal step in education, geared, however, to the progressive development of the adolescent. Catholic teaching insists that, before all else, a sense of responsibility be instilled in the soul, strong enough to resist the onslaught of evil inducements which often accompany knowledge of sexual matters. The fact of having to face the serious dangers and inducements of present-day conditions requires that, as a lesser evil, sexual instruction be given much earlier than would otherwise be considered normal. *Dam.*

EFFECT (Culpability of). The effect of an action or its omission involves a moral problem of imputability. If an effect is directly willed by an agent, it involves imputability for that action which is always certain. The situation, however, becomes difficult and doubtful if the effect is not directly willed by the agent. In this hypothesis, the effect becomes imputable if the following three conditions are present: (1) The agent must have foreseen the effect, at least in a confused manner. On this point it is important to note the distinction between the juridical order and the moral order. An effect is frequently imputable in the juridical order, if it could have been or ought to have been foreseen, even though it was not foreseen. Moral theology, however, makes an act imputable only if the effect was actually foreseen by the agent at least in a confused manner. For example, an intoxicated person, who foresees that in the state of intoxication he will blaspheme or disturb the peace of the family, is thereby responsible for these events if he becomes intoxicated. (2) It must be within the power of the agent to omit the action or to remove the cause of such an effect. It is not only a matter of physical (absolute) necessity but of moral necessity as well, which might destroy the freedom necessary to imputability. This moral necessity might be occasioned by a proportionately grave inconvenience, which must be judged in its gravity with the foreseen effect. (3) If the agent must prevent or omit the effect because of an obligation which arises from his office, duty, justice (a contract), or charity (another, without awareness incurring the danger of death, must be warned).

Moral imputability, unlike juridical, is incurred by the agent, not after the effect is realized, but at the moment when the action or cause is posited culpably. *Gra.*

EFFECT, DOUBLE. The question of the double effect can be stated as follows: Is it licit to posit an act that is good *in se* but from which it is foreseen that two effects will follow, one good (or at least indifferent) and the other evil? The solution of moralists to the problem of the double effect is given on the basis of a subtle doctrine, difficult to understand and easily abused in its application. Caution, therefore, in the use of this principle is a necessity.

The solution given by moralists can be thus stated: It is licit to place such an act if the following three conditions are verified: (1) The agent acts with a right intention and honestly aims at achieving the good effect and not the evil one. (2) The two effects are not so interrelated, objectively, that the good effect flows from an evil act; in other words, the two effects must spring from the same action in a simultaneous way or the evil effect must follow from the good, not good from evil. The reason for this is that, in the latter case, an evil would be willed in order to obtain a good, which it is not licit to do. (3) A proportionately just reason is present for permitting the evil effect.

This last condition gives rise to many serious difficulties, since it is not always easy to determine when a proportionately just reason exists. The principal factors to be considered in the solution of each individual case are: the importance of each of the two effects respectively; also the immediacy, necessity and probability with which the effects will follow the action as from a cause. These considerations, at times, can become complicated by reason of social repercussions resulting from both the action and its effects. Such repercussions may even modify the ethical judgment. *Gra.*

EGOCENTRISM. *See* Egoism.

EGOISM. Egoism consists in thinking only of oneself and of one's own well-being. The egoist seeks self-interest and self-satisfaction without due regard for others. Egoism is a necessary consequence of self-love. In fact, the term *egoism* is often used to designate this disorderly self-love.

Egoism is sinful. It constitutes a mortal sin when it causes one to neglect a grave obligation toward God or toward one's neighbor, or when it places one in a serious danger of neglecting such an obligation.

Egoism is a serious obstacle to perfection and makes a man despicable in the eyes of others. The means to overcome egoism are those which one must use to counteract self-love (*q.v.*). One of the most effective ways of overcoming egoism is to seek the benefit and pleasure of others before one's own benefit and pleasure at all times. *Man.*

EGOISM, MEDICO - PSYCHOLOGICAL. Generally, an ordinary, normal man experiences alternating feelings of egoism and altruism. When, however, the egoistic feelings predominate exclusively, or are carried to excess and permeate all the thoughts of the individual, then we are faced with a special aspect of that morbid aberration of the ethical sense which bears the name of "compulsive immorality" (*q.v.*).

EGOCENTRISM AND EGOMANIA. In cases of hysteria (*q.v.*), epilepsy (*q.v.*), mania (*q.v.*), and in other less common types of morbidity, one encounters a particular variety of egoism, which arises from the fact that the afflicted person, incapable of adapting himself to his environment, feels that the environment should adapt itself to him and so, craving personal prominence, he strives to draw the attention and interest of others. In such cases, it would be more exact to speak of *egocentrism*—a spiritual attitude in which one's own ego is taken as the point of reference for all values and aspects of life. In order to explain more clearly the difference between normality, egocentrism, and egoism, it might be helpful to give a simple example found in the work of H. Rorschach. When a normal person gives a gift, he tries to give something that will be to the liking and taste of the one who is to receive it. The egocentric gives a gift he himself would like to receive. The egoist tries to avoid giving gifts.

Egomania, a term not too commonly used, denotes a sort of "pride of the ego" (Tedeschi), a morbid overestimation of oneself. It appears, at times, in the adolescent period and constitutes a symptom of schizophrenia or, more exactly, of hebephrenia (*q.v.*).

NARCISSISM. In psychoanalysis (*q.v.*), the term *narcissism*—derived from the myth of Narcissus—is applied to the first stage of infantile sexuality, since it is autoerotic in character. This love which the individual directs to his own person is an apparent variation of ordinary egoism.

MORAL OBSERVATIONS. When egoism, in the various forms described above, is the expression of a mental illness or of a pathological distortion of the personality, the responsibility of the person and the culpability of acts elicited under pressure of the egoism are more or less considerably diminished. The degree of diminution will depend on the psychopathological form of which the egoism itself is an expression. The diagnostic

evaluation, needless to say, is reserved to the psychiatrist. *Riz.*

EGOMANIA. *See* Egoism.

EJACULATORY PRAYERS. Ejaculatory prayers are mental or vocal prayer, consisting of invocations or lifting the heart in a call upon God or His saints. All the more efficacious, the more spontaneously and fervently they are elicited, because of their easy formulation ejaculations are a form of prayer accessible to all and convenient in all contingencies of life.

St. Augustine speaks of them in a letter to Proba: "It is said," he observes, "that our brethren in Egypt (the anchorites) pray often, but that their prayers are very brief and like arrows (*quodammodo iaculas*) directed toward heaven, as if the attention, so necessary to those who pray, is by necessity bound to diminish and die out altogether when prayers are protracted a little too much" (Ep. 129, 20: PL 33, 501; *see also* PL 38, 158; 49, 831; 73, 943).

Recourse to God through ejaculatory prayers is found to be a constant practice in the lives of the saints and strongly recommended by the masters of the spiritual life. Of St. Francis Xavier we are told that he repeated his beloved ejaculatory prayer "Most Holy Trinity!" (*O Sanctissima Trinitas!*) so often that heathens too had formed the habit of using it without quite understanding the meaning of the words (Biography by Fr. Bouhours, I, VI).

It is clear that it is not necessary to formulate ejaculatory prayers distinctly, for they may also consist of a simple elevation of the mind to God. Two rules, however, are suggested by the masters of the spiritual life: (1) avoid excess, leading to weariness of mind and eventual distaste; (2) follow the inspirations of grace, for the Holy Spirit inspires different persons in a different manner. It is also fitting to add spiritual requests to petitions for material things. The recitation of the *Angelus* (*q.v.*), for instance, indicates a desire to call to memory at least three times a day the great benefice of the Incarnation of the Word, by uniting the practice of short prayers to specific hours of the day. The ejaculatory prayers recommended are undoubtedly those recently issued and indulgenced by the Church (*see* Indulgence). In fact, according to the mind of the Roman Pontiffs who have promoted them, they are considered best suited to the needs of modern times and, filled with a profound sense of piety, lively faith, and ardent charity, they are easy and suitable expressions for any intelligence.

A list of indulgenced ejaculatory prayers may be found in the *Enchiridion indulgentiarum, Preces et pia opera,* Rome, 1950.

As regards ejaculatory prayers indulgenced by the Church and for which mere mental recitation is sufficient, *see* S. Paen., Dec. 7, 1923: AAS, 26 (1933), 35 ff. *Pal.*

ELECTION, CIVIL. Voting is a civic and moral duty, in which free citizens choose their country's legislators and rulers. Great importance, therefore, must be attached to elections, for on good or evil laws the destiny of a nation rests. The government and parliament can either greatly assist or gravely injure the Church, the clergy, the Christian family, the Catholic education of the young, public morality, ecclesiastical institutions, various public manifestations of religion, and the achievements of Christian civilization. The exercise of one's one's right to vote, therefore, is a civic and moral duty.

The gravity of this obligation varies according to circumstances. As a general norm, the obligation to vote is more grave as the religious, moral, and social interests of the nation are more seriously involved and the outcome of the voting in a particular political election is more uncertain. Failure to vote is serious matter, unless the voter is prevented from casting his ballot because of illness or grave or extreme moral harm, according to circumstances. "In the present circumstances, there is a strict obligation for men and women who have the right to vote to participate in the elections. He

who abstains, especially through indolence or cowardice, commits by this very fact a grave, mortal sin." (P. Pius XII, address to Roman pastors and Lenten preachers, March 10, 1948, in *L'Osservatore Romano,* March 11, 1948.)

VOTING ACCORDING TO ONE'S CONSCIENCE. If it is a serious duty to go to the polls, it is even a greater obligation to vote according to one's conscience for candidates who are competent and honest, motivated in their political life by Christian teachings and Christian morality. As Pope Pius XII admonished in the discourse cited above: "Everyone is obliged to vote according to the dictates of his conscience. Now, it is evident that the voice of conscience places upon every sincere Catholic the responsibility of giving his vote to those candidates or to that list of candidates who propose truly sufficient guarantees, based on Divine Law and on Christian moral principles, for the protection of the rights of God and of souls, for the real welfare of the individual, the family, and society."

Our vote places in the hands of those elected a powerful force for good or for evil; hence, we assume indirectly responsibility for their activities in the exercise of the mandate we have given. Needless to say, this responsibility of ours will be in proportion to our foreknowledge and in relation to the influence exercised by our vote. He who knowingly and effectively votes for unworthy candidates must be held responsible for cooperating in an evil action; if damage accrues to society, individuals, or the Church through the officials elected by him, he is bound to restitution in accordance with his share of the responsibility.

When in a political election there are capable Catholic candidates truly worthy of the name who are running for office, they should receive the concentrated vote of their Christian fellow citizens, for they are the only ones who can fully safeguard in parliament the interests of Christian people. They are also best qualified to bring into public life sound opinions, fervent zeal, and integrity of conscience. No one denies in principle the right of

Catholics to vote for a non-Catholic candidate when they do not share the political views of the candidate. A political objective, after all, can be conceived in a multitude of ways and attained by a variety of means. There is a limit, however, to the division of Catholics in an election campaign. And this limit is reached every time that circumstances demand the united front of all Catholic forces for the preservation of the fundamental interests which, in the last analysis, are identified with the civic and social welfare of the nation. In many countries the divided and scattered vote of Catholics has brought to the Church and to society severe and irreparable calamities. *Mon.*

ELECTION, ECCLESIASTICAL. An ecclesiastical election is the selection by ballot of a qualified person in a properly constituted assembly for a *de iure* vacant office, confirmed by the competent higher superior if such confirmation is required. Such is the election of certain bishops, abbots, prelates *nullius*, vicar capitulars, and superiors of religious orders; the Pope is elected in this manner, without confirmation of higher superiors since none exists.

According to the general norms of the Code of Canon Law (Can. 160–178), only clerics and religious with active voice may participate in the assembly of an election as electors. Lay interference, contrary to or in violation of ecclesiastical liberty, renders an election invalid. The absence of one third or more of the electors, whose presence is required for election, renders an election invalid (Can. 162, par. 3). The absence of less than one third of the qualified electors does not render the election invalid, unless within three days after they have been informed of the election the absent electors file petition that the election be set aside (Can. 162, par. 2). The nomination of the candidates for an election may be carried out by balloting or through compromise (Can. 172–173). To be duly elected, an absolute majority of the votes is necessary; however, after two inconclusive ballots, a relative ma-

jority suffices. In the event of a tie, which the chairman does not break, the election is determined by seniority in ordination, profession, or age (Can. 101, par. 1, n. 1; Can. 174). The elected official must declare his acceptance or rejection of the office, to which he has been chosen, within eight days after the election (Can. 175). For offices which do not require confirmation, the elected acquires authority (*ius in re*) immediately upon his acceptance; for offices that require confirmation, the elected individual must request this confirmation within eight days. Until he receives this confirmation, he acquires only *ius ad rem* or a right *to* the office (Can. 176, par. 2; 177, par. 1).

The failure to hold an election by an assembly within the required time, deprives that assembly of the right to elect; competent higher superiors may thereupon confer the office upon another in lieu of the proper election (Can. 178).

A true delict with consequent penal sanctions is committed by (a) those who interfere with the freedom of ecclesiastical elections (Can. 2390, par. 1); (b) by electors who solicit or welcome the interference of laymen or secular powers in elections. Furthermore, the elected person commits a delict if he consents to his election with knowledge of this interference. If this occurs, the election is invalid; the electors are deprived of the right to exercise their vote; the elected person becomes ineligible for the office or benefice in question. (c) An assembly, willingly and with knowledge electing an unworthy candidate, is deprived of the right to proceed to a new election (Can. 2391, par. 1); and (d) electors who knowingly depart from the substantial form of the election, i.e., from the proceedings prescribed for a valid election or compromise, are subject to punishment by the Ordinary according to the gravity of the fault (Can. 2391, par. 2). *Toc.*

ELECTRICITY, USE OF. The rights and obligations both of the suppliers, who produce and distribute the electricity, and the consumers, who acquire the right to make use of it, are regulated by contract. In some countries the terms of such contract are regulated by particular state laws. The cost of electricity is not an object of the contract between the parties, except indirectly, insofar as the consumer agrees to pay the common price pre-established for every unit hour (kw.). The just common cost is established after an appraisal of expenses in the installation, maintenance, and repair of the central stations and transmission network. Consideration must be given also to the right of private and associate owners of electric companies to a reasonable profit.

This contract requires a steady supply of electricity, and the voltage necessary for various uses of the consumer, whether it be lighting, motor power, or other. The monthly bill, however, is determined on the basis of the actual consumption recorded by the meter. The supplier is obliged to make restitution only if through some default he caused a damage to the consumer. If, however, he fails to supply the electricity in the proper manner, he shall be in default of his part of the contract. Failure by the company to supply electrical energy adequately is justified only if it is the result of unusual circumstances, such as lack of water due to severe drought, lack of coal for the central steam turbines, breakdown of installations caused by hurricanes, floods, strong winds, etc. On the other hand, a consumer is not permitted to interfere with the proper functioning of the meter or tamper with data recorded by the meter. Such illicit acts by the consumer are simply theft; restitution is obligatory in these cases.

The licitness of electric lights of such low voltage that the meter does not register at all is open to discussion. The public sale and the general use of such light bulbs, coupled with the knowledge of the fact by the electric companies, seems to justify the assumption that the companies have given implicit consent, which makes the use of such lights licit. Special laws govern the civil responsibilities of both producers and consumers of electricity.

ELECTRICITY IN CHURCH. The Church has always followed the policy of excluding the use of electric lights in strictly liturgical functions while it permits them for purposes of illumination, provided that theatrical effects are avoided (SRC, June 4, 1895). For special reasons, the Holy See on various occasions during the war permitted electric lights to be used as substitutes for sanctuary lamps or candles at the celebration of Mass. *M.d.G.*

ELECTROENCEPHALOGRAPHY. *See* Encephalography.

EMANCIPATION OF WOMEN. *See* Woman, Feminism.

EMBARGO. An embargo is a prohibition, or restraint, placed on ships whereby they are forbidden to enter or leave the ports or waters of another nation. It thus is a type of hostile action, which prevents the ships of a sovereign nation from returning to their home ports or those of a sovereign third nation; it may blockade the entry of these ships into the harbors of the hostile nation. Occasionally resorted to in time of peace, embargo is a measure more frequently adopted in time of war or near hostilities.

A peace-time embargo may be imposed for special reasons, such as the prevention of a foreign crew or passengers from divulging information on particular conditions or circumstances, as preparations for war, news of civil war, reports on health or economic conditions. Rarely used, such an embargo is usually of short duration. A peace-time embargo may also be employed as a means of retaliation, whereby a nation takes reciprocal action against a real or supposed violation of its sovereign rights by placing an embargo on the ships or subjects of the violating nation to obtain satisfactory redress of honor or money.

An embargo in time of war is frequently carried out when hostilities are undertaken. By such action, a nation prevents the departure of ships or citizens of the country that is now its enemy.

As a general rule, a peace-time embargo is licit for a special reason, provided there are no hostile intentions and it lasts only for the period of time strictly necessary. It would not be licit to place an embargo on ships owned by subjects of a violating nation, but not by the nation itself, as a form of reprisal. For, presumably, such subjects are not directly or indirectly responsible for the violation through their government of rights for which redress is sought. Hence, considerable damage consequent upon such an embargo is injustice upon those subjects. In general, jurists condemn the use of peace-time embargo for purposes of retaliation.

An embargo placed on ships or citizens of nations close to the state of war is illicit. Many justify such an embargo through the argument that such ships, if permitted to return to their home port or other countries, will be employed in the event of war for belligerent purposes. Such reasoning cannot justify an act which is, in reality, hostile and, therefore, prohibited as long as no state of war exists. Those ships entered the ports in good faith according to juridical norms existing in time of peace; these norms should govern all relations between the vessels and the nation in whose waters they are anchored. Once a state of war exists, it is certainly licit to place an embargo on ships belonging to the enemy nation or its subjects, provided that before the declaration of war they were permitted the opportunity of leaving the ports of anchorage. *Pas.*

EMBRACE. *See* Kiss.

EMBRYOTOMY. Embryotomy (Gr. *embryon*—fetus; *tome*—excision) is any surgical intervention on the human fetus to bring about the death of the infant. Occasioned principally by the presence of some physical abnormality in the fetus or the mother, which renders parturition impossible or at least dangerous, embryotomy is performed in such circumstances to save the life of the mother or to avoid a Caesarian section (*q.v.*).

Embryotomy is direct homicide, distinguished from other murders only inso-

far as the victim is located in a special place, the womb of the mother; this factor is completely secondary and irrelevant. The character and moral malice of homicide does not depend on the location nor age of the victim. Embryotomy is never lawful. If, however, it is absolutely certain that the fetus is already dead, the fetal body can be mutilated and excised, since such an action is no longer, in the proper sense of the word, homicidal embryotomy.

Embryotomy, as a sin, resembles direct abortion; the principles of morality applicable to direct abortions likewise apply to embryotomy (*see* Abortion).

Abortions are punished with the ecclesiastical penalty of excommunication; the same penalty, however, is not incurred in the case of embryotomy, though it is no less serious a sin. The imposition of an ecclesiastical penalty attached to a sin does not depend solely on the gravity of the sin. Other factors, such as the extensiveness of the evil, and the judgment of the legislator, enter into excommunications. (*See also* Feticide.) *Ben.*

EMIGRATION. Emigration is a collective or individual movement of people from one place to another with the intention of establishing permanent residency. A more exact term defining this displacement is *migration*. Emigration is migration considered from the viewpoint of a country from which the migration originates; immigration is a consideration of migration from the viewpoint of the country in which the displacement terminates. In modern times, this displacement has assumed particular importance in the increased movements of vast peoples due to the search for more favorable and secure conditions of employment, as well as political reasons in certain countries which lend impetus to this movement.

The first significant emigration in history took place when over-population in non-productive areas of ancient Greece promoted the shift of entire segments of the population to the Italian peninsula, where such groups established colonies

(Magna Graecia). Later, Roman emigration had more of a political character, as colonies of soldiers and administrators with their families were transferred from Rome to various territories of the Empire to set up politico-military cohesion among the different nations in the Roman Empire. History records the emigratory phenomena of the eleventh and twelfth centuries, known as the barbarian invasions. Between the twelfth and fourteenth centuries came a certain stability among the populations of Europe. With the discovery of the New World, the flow of emigrants assumed unforeseen proportions. Migratory movements since have gone in one direction, from the old European lands to the newly discovered territories: the Americas, Australia, the coasts of Africa and many islands. Fearful of a loss in national production, some countries, notably England and France, tried in vain to check the exodus of their populations by legislative provisions. The flow was too great to be stemmed by such measures. Besides, the movement was enhanced to some extent by religious strife and political rivalries. After a short period of stability, the migratory flow from European countries to the New World resumed with increased intensity in the second half of the nineteenth century.

In emigration a complexity of moral problems arises from such an uprooting of human beings from the land in which they grew physically and spiritually into an environment which is frequently strange and hostile to the religious, cultural, and social standards and life which once existed for these individuals. These aspects of life suffer severe difficulties and evils. A growing attempt to remedy these must be encouraged by a variety of measures. The Catholic Church has endeavored to assist emigrants in their religious and moral needs by providing priests from the same ethnic group (Cf. encyclical of Pope Pius XII, *Exul familia*, of August 1, 1952). Governments have shown their concern through specific agreements to assure emigrant laborers the same economic and juridical considerations as are given to natives.

International organizations are already deliberating the feasibility of a *Code for the Emigrant* which would propose on a world-wide basis uniform regulations for the migratory movements. *Pav.*

EMOTION. *See* Passion.

EMPHYTEUSIS. Emphyteusis (etymologically, meaning a graft, planting) is a juridical agreement involving land, in which a person, called the *lessee, grantee* or *holder*, consequent upon leasing property from an owner, exercises over that land the right to the use and profit from that land, perpetually or for a time, with an obligation of payment of annual rent (canon) in money or commodities and of making the required and necessary improvements. This relationship can be established through a will or through acquisition of ownership for a period of time or perpetually. The juridical nature of emphyteusis, whether based on a real right or a right of obligation, or even an intermediate, real obligation, is much disputed. The more prevalent opinion considers it a true and real right to the use of another's property (*ius in re aliena*).

Unknown to classical Roman law, emphyteusis was a creation of Greek law, which Justinian incorporated into his *Corpus Iuris*. It developed during the Middle Ages, particularly through the instrumentality of the Church, which saw in it a means of cultivating land without prejudice to canonical laws concerning the inalienability of ecclesiastical goods. Thus it assumed a role of primary importance in the agricultural economy of the past.

Emphyteusis is a creation of positive law. Positive ecclesiastical law recognizes it and incorporates the positive laws of individual nations with particular limitations as found in Canons 1529 and 1542.

RIGHTS AND DUTIES OF THE GRANTEE. Positive law gives the lessee or grantee a variety of rights which constitute an almost total dominion over the owner's property. Two fundamental obligations must be observed by the lessee with diligence: (1) he must improve the land and administer it with paternal care, (2) he must pay the lessor a periodic rent in money or products. Unlike the usufructuary, a lessee cannot demand a remission or reduction of rent because of the lack of productivity in the soil or crop losses. His obligations are of strict justice, and, in the event of failure to meet these obligations, a lessee is bound in conscience to make restitution for damages, independently of court decisions. Taxes and other obligations attached to the land are the responsibility of the lessee.

CANON LAW. By virtue of the principle established in Canon 1529, the prescriptions of civil law concerning obligations in general and contracts in particular are canonically valid, exercise force in ecclesiastical matters, and bind in conscience unless such prescriptions are contrary to divine law or Canon Law decrees otherwise. In Canon Law, emphyteusis is governed by regulatory norms both in addition to and at times in conflict with civil law. First, since emphyteusis with the power of redemption practically amounts to alienation, the contract in question cannot be agreed upon without the observance of the prescriptions in Canons 1530–1532, particularly that on the permissions required from competent authority in Canon 1533. It is furthermore strictly prescribed that a twofold clause be included in the contract of emphyteusis: (1) that in eventual conflicts, the competent authority to settle the dispute must be an ecclesiastical court; (2) that all improvements accrue to the benefit of the owner or the property as such. Suitable security must also be given as a guarantee of payment of rent and fulfillment of the other conditions (Can. 1542).

The lessee is strictly and expressly forbidden to exempt himself from the obligation of payment of annual rental without the consent of ecclesiastical superiors, according to the provisions of Canon 1532. Furthermore, an agreement must be made that, if such permission is obtained, the lessee must pay an amount sufficient to yield interest equal to the fixed rental (Can. 1542). Such a provision, although in direct conflict with the faculty of redemption found in civil codes, binds in conscience upon the lessee. To disregard the necessary permissions or to have recourse to civil courts for compulsory redemption would be a grave sin. According to Canons 120 and 2341, such a person incurs an excommunication, reserved to the Holy See in a special manner, if he summons into civil court the Ordinary of the place for such purposes; he also becomes subject to grave ecclesiastical sanctions if he summons a cleric or religious into court for these reasons, since these persons enjoy the privilege of the forum (*see* Clergy, privileges of). Moreover, he is considered excommunicated by virtue of the provisions of Canon 2346, because of his usurpation and unjust detention of ecclesiastical goods. He cannot be absolved unless he first makes restitution and reparation of the damages (Cf. S. Cong. Conc. Instructions of June 20, 1929, art. 41; May 18, 1943; May 1, 1945; December 30, 1952). *Zac.*

EMULATION. Emulation is the ambition to equal or excel another in some good, as, for example, knowledge or virtue. Emulation is not to be confused with envy (*q.v.*), which is a sadness or resentment toward the good or excellence of another as if a personal affront. Emulation differs from jealousy in that jealousy seeks to be the sole possessor of a certain good or goods, which others may licitly possess. Emulation is not morally evil if the intention is upright and the means chosen are just. *Man.*

ENCEPHALOGRAPHY. A modern, scientific method of examining cerebral activity, encephalography permits to great advantage the study of cortical dynamism without the necessity of opening the cranium or performing a direct operation on the nerve center. Electroencephalography consists in the registration and analysis of the electric phenomena appearing at the surface of the brain, consisting of oscillations from potentials, the so-called *brain waves*.

The physiologist R. Caton (1875) is

credited with having made the first observations concerning the existence of differences in electric wave patterns among the various areas of the brain in animals. Another physiologist, Nemminsky (1913), first made such observations (1929) on the human brain without opening the cranium, and established their fundamental characteristics. Subsequently, research work on the subject greatly increased; now no important centers of neurophysiology, neuropsychiatry, or neurosurgery lack electroencephalographic facilities.

In healthy adults at rest, the electroencephalographic tracing consists of a regular succession of waves averaging 10 cycles a second in frequency, with waves between 20 and 50 microvolts. These are called *alpha waves*, while *alpha rhythm* or *Berger rhythm* is the name given to the process itself. The rhythm, width, and form of the oscillations vary, according to laws, for the most part known. If the subject under examination is sleeping, doing mental work, is under sensory stimulation or the influence of drugs, is suffering from some mental illness, is affected by epilepsy, brain tumor, etc., these oscillations change and provide for research important data on normal and pathological electric brain activity. It was possible to determine, among other things, that, in physiological conditions, this activity is generally carried out according to the Berger *alpha rhythm*, regardless of the area of the brain explored. It was observed in inferior vertebrates and even in insects (Adrian), regardless of the animal examined. According to this study, each nerve cell possesses an identical rhythmic activity, which generally reacts in identical patterns under the influence of the same stimuli. In newborns the frequency in electric potential is minimal and increases slowly with growth until it reaches normal frequency of the alpha rhythm, at the age of nine or ten years. Furthermore, the brain wave frequency decreases as sleep becomes deeper. In brain tissue diseases (tumor, encephalitis, infantile cerebropathy, etc.), serious disturbances, observed in the electric activity, generally indicate a decline in the frequency of electroencephalographic potential or marked irregularities, particularly in epileptics. Normal electroencephalograms, however, are not rare even in cases of profound neuropsychical disturbances (progressive paralysis, schizophrenia, phrenasthenia, and the like).

The study of brain waves is contributing to an increasingly greater understanding not only of encephalic pathology, particularly the diagnosis of the location of disease, but also of the physiology of the brain, where enormous progress has been made due to the study of the electric brain waves. Much remains to be done, however, in the field of psychology, because of variable findings and the intrinsic difficulty of the subject. For this and other aspects, particularly ethical, of the subject, see Brain function. *Riz.*

ENCHANTMENT. *See* Witchcraft, Sorcery.

ENCYCLICAL. *See* Acts, Pontifical.

END, ULTIMATE. The ultimate end of man is the supreme good which transcends all other values and to which all secondary, temporary or intermediate ends are subordinated. The common good (*q.v.*) of civil society is, in itself, an ultimate end, not in the absolute sense, but only in a specific and limited order, as well as an intermediate end with the value of ultimate end for the temporal or terrestrial order; that is, an end to which everything material is ordained, but not the pure and simple ultimate end of man, because this is supra-temporal and supra-terrestrial.

Every end has value; the supreme end has a supreme value. The ultimate end, therefore, is the supreme good in virtue of which all other goods are desired and sought. It is ordained to no other good; on the contrary, all other goods are subordinated to it. It is, then, the good in the possession of which all longing ultimately finds repose, and from which ultimate and complete happiness flows.

EXISTENCE OF AN ULTIMATE END.

Reason demands the existence of an ultimate end. The act of the will tends necessarily to an end; that is, it is ordained to good as to an end. Moreover, it tends necessarily to an ultimate end; for if it were not so, by this very motive it would be ordained to a further end and so on, continually *ad infinitum.* As in the order of efficient causes one must of necessity arrive at a first cause, so, too, in the order of final causes, one must of necessity arrive at an ultimate end, if he is to explain intermediate ends. The end toward which I strive must be, as least in my estimation, a complete good for me. (It is not possible that I may be satisfied with an incomplete good; because, were I to be satisfied with it, at that very moment, that good would become my supreme good.)

But does this supreme good really exist? If it did not exist, every desire would have no meaning whatsoever, a state not only contrary to God's wisdom and goodness, but also to the innermost constitution of the human being. We would have, in fact, an essentially imperfect creature—an absurdity, indeed, for the creature would be lacking the very thing to which it is, by its very essence, ordained.

ULTIMATE END AND HAPPINESS. The notion of ultimate end involves two distinct elements: the desire for the perfect good and happiness which is necessary and predetermined by nature; and the desire for a good which *we believe* is the perfect good and happiness. This of course depends on the exercise of our freedom. A distinction must be made between an ultimate end and happiness itself; for happiness flows from the possession of the end and thus is called a secondary ultimate end, while the good from which it flows is called the primary ultimate end. A concrete election through our natural desire for happiness in concentrating this natural desire upon a specific object, does not depend necessarily upon our essential nature, but upon our freedom. The nature of man is to choose specific ends and the means to those ends; in animals this is impossible, since they lack the necessary intellectual knowledge of the good and of means to an end. Man, on the contrary, is distinct from the animal insofar as he elects his own ends, which will constitute his happiness.

GOD, ULTIMATE END IN THE NATURAL ORDER. Psychological analysis of the dynamism of the human mind and will reveals an immeasurable capacity for learning in human intelligence to be satisfied only by the knowledge of an infinite Being, and an intrinsic orientation of the will towards infinite Good, as its end. The infinite Being and infinite Good is God alone, as is evident simply from the notion of Supreme Being. The ultimate end of man and of his actions, therefore, is God, known and loved. God could not have placed man's perfection in any other good except Himself, for in this supposition, He would contradict the transcendental order by which all creatures are necessarily bound to Him and derive from Him.

Therefore, it also follows that God Himself, i.e., the manifestation of His glory, is the purpose of creation; hence, all creatures must be directed to God's glory as their ultimate end. Irrational creatures pursue this end necessarily; rational creatures, on the contrary, pursue it freely, that is, by their complete subjection to Him. By the fulfillment of this duty, man has the opportunity to find his own happiness, which he would seek in vain among other created goods. Limited and finite, material goods could never fill the unlimited, operative capacity of the human mind and will.

Because the end of human actions is identical with the very operations of man's intelligence and will, man's ultimate end, in a subjective sense, is the knowledge and possession of God, the perfect actuation of his faculties by supreme Truth and supreme Good. But however great man's knowledge and love of God may be, perfect realization cannot be attained in this life because of the imperfections and limitations of the material world. Necessarily, then, there must be a timeless survival of man beyond the grave, in order that his happiness may be perfect. Man reaches his ultimate end in a future life through possession, knowledge, and love of God. God is man's ultimate end as He is the ultimate end of the universe. But He is not man's beatitude in the natural order. There is no beatitude for man in the natural order.

According to John of St. Thomas, by his own ability man cannot attain perfect happiness, but only an imperfect one. This, the only happiness humanly obtainable, consists in the intellectual and moral virtues. In effect, neither in man's purely natural state, nor in this life, is perfect happiness possible of attainment, but only an imperfect one (*Cursus Theologicus*, Book V, p. II, a. 1, n. 14).

GOD, ULTIMATE END IN THE SUPERNATURAL ORDER. The true end of man is supernatural: the vision of God and beatitude surpassing all desire. In the order of grace, God wills to elevate man, inviting man to partake of His own intimate life, which is naturally incommunicable. Our search for God shall not end in an indirect knowledge of God, but an intuitive knowledge of God. We shall no longer know God as through a mirror of the material things of earth, but will see Him face to face (1 Cor. 13:12), as He really is. Between God and us there shall be neither the intermediateness of an idea, nor verbal concepts of our contemplation. No created idea can contain the Infinite; no word besides the "Word" (John 1:2) can express the Ineffable.

This supernatural knowledge shall be accompanied by a similar supernatural love, eminently necessary, absolute, and spontaneous, which nothing shall destroy or diminish. Infinite Good, contemplated as He really is, will quench our thirst for happiness and fill our power of love; our will shall be seized by His infinite attraction. We will, then, be sharers of the divine life and partakers of the knowledge and love with which God knows and loves Himself. We shall be, in a sense, deified: knowledge and love are always proportionate to the nature of the being who knows and loves.

THE ULTIMATE END AND REVELATION. The existence of this ultimate end is a matter of faith. Revelation clearly speaks of this Supreme Good. The Gospel calls it life everlasting and the kingdom of heaven, promised to man as a prize and reward for good works (Matt. 5:11), an imperishable crown (1 Cor. 9:25), the crown of justice (2 Tim. 4:8), retribution for the works of this life (2 Cor. 5:8). The purpose of life for a Christian is to strive towards perfect possession of God, and constantly develop the divine germ implanted in us by God Himself, so that the Father may be fully glorified, and in this glorification, we, His adopted children, shall find full happiness.

No human value is disowned; on the contrary, all values are elevated and energized by the supernatural end for the attainment of which these are to be employed.

SUMMARY OF THE ABOVE DOCTRINE. The positive data of Revelation and reason may be summed up in the following principles: (a) The ultimate end of man's life is the formal glorification of God. Formal glory (knowledge and praise) is distinguished from objective glory (the perfection of a thing). When viewed in the same person, glory is called internal; when looked at in others, it is called external. God could not subordinate His work to an end distinct from Himself; nor could He fail to demand of man, who is capable of it, His own formal glorification; this is in the very nature of ontological dependence of all things on God. (b) The secondary ultimate end of man is his happiness and beatitude. (c) God alone is the objective beatitude of man. By objective beatitude is meant the object whose possession makes one happy. Since God is an infinite Being and man is finite, a quantitative or qualitative equality by possession is impossible and not necessary between the object of beatitude and the subject of beatitude, but only a proportional one. (d) Formal beatitude consists in the perfect possession of God through the intellect and the will. As a pure spirit, God cannot be known and possessed except through acts of the spiritual faculties. Perfect possession is that which is suited to the capacity of man and exhausts, therefore, all his possibilities. (e) It follows that man cannot reach his ultimate end in this life, since in this life he is naturally further perfectible in knowledge and will. (f) In view of man's elevation to the supernatural order, God's possession is also supernatural.

God demands of man that he pursue on earth the perfection of love. This end, the real imperative of life, must be sought in a total, true, and uncompromising manner as the saints did—a superhuman end, not shunned in vigorous battle, which requires that the entire world be renounced insofar as this has been contaminated by evil.

NON-CHRISTIAN CONCEPTS. Theoretical views of life for some have been void of positive purpose or final end (pessimism); for others, despite their admission of an ideal, their views entail a mechanistic outlook, or a neo-romantic approach that does not admit of determination in life, or finally one that doubts of the nature of any final causality or purpose as Bergsonian followers would advocate.

A concrete solution to this problem of life has, therefore, predominantly entailed either egotistical views of exaggerated individualism or the opposite tendency to subordinate each individual to a collective or universal finality. The outcome has been either a hedonistic or utilitarian concept of destiny despite its disguises under many forms. The tendency to subordinate the destiny of the individual to a collective utilitarianism is not a sufficient or adequate means of improving upon the doctrine of hedonistic living. Utilitarianism is found as a tendency today among the hybrid forms of exaggerated nationalism, or an idealized class struggle which seems an amalgamation of individualism and universalism. This latter aspect modifies the forms of utilitarianism, by turning a former individualistic utilitarianism into collectivism. Placing class or national welfare above all other purposes and ends, it goes so far as to make it the absolute and ultimate end of all the activities of the individual. It justifies any violation of rights and liberties in the name of an arbitrary ideal, in a sense mythologically sustained, and foments rivalries and collective pride of necessity—a situation that is no less dangerous or evil than individual pride. *Pal.*

ENDOCRINOLOGY. The etymology of the word (*endo*, within; *krinein*, to secrete) aptly epitomizes the notion. Endocrinology, as a branch of biology, studies the *glands of internal secretion,* or the *endocrine glands,* which secrete the products of their chemical process, called *hormones* (*q.v.*), into the blood stream or into the lymphatic system, in contrast to those glands whose products are conveyed through excretory ducts to the surface.

Hormones are distributed throughout the entire organism by means of the circulatory system. Although their concentration in the blood is extremely minute, the significance of their effects is profound. Hormones act as regulators of nutrition, growth, and cellular metabolism. Each hormone is in various ways linked to others by laws of functional correlation. The glands of internal secretion, considered as a group, form the *endocrine* (hormonic or incretory) *system.* The endocrine glands, joined with the neuro-vegetative and neuro-sympathetic systems, constitute the apparatus which balances and regulates the forms and functions of man's psychosomatic individuality.

The following are considered today as endocrine organs: (a) the *hypophysis* or *pituitary gland* (*q.v.*), regarded, on account of its influence on the other glands of internal secretion and the neuro-vegetative system, as the master control of the neuro-hormonic life of the organism; (b) the *thyroid* (*q.v.*), important for the psychosomatic development of the individual; (c) the *parathyroid glands,* tiny endocrine glands, located behind or beside the thyroid, which produce a hormone that regulates the metabolism of calcium and phosphorous;

(d) the *adrenal glands*, indispensable for life; (e) the *pancreas*, which, along with the internal secretion produced by the *islets of Langerhans*, acts as an agent in the conversion of sugar, and produces external secretion necessary for digestion; (f) the *gonads* (*q.v.*), or sex glands (testicles, ovaries), which manufacture an external secretion for reproduction; (g) the *placenta*, which secretes a hormone active on the ovaries.

It is not clearly demonstrated but probable that the kidneys, thymus, pineal gland, carotid glomus, and certain glands of the gastro-duodenal mucose secrete special hormones.

PHYSIOLOGY AND CLINICAL ENDOCRINOLOGY. With Nicola Pende, we classify the special functions of hormones into four categories: (a) *Morpho-regulating functions.* Functions consisting mainly in the stimulation of growth, and in the differentiation and development of the various organs and tissues, are regulated by the correlated activities of two *hormonic constellations* or *groups.* One of these groups, composed of the pancreas, adrenal cortex, somatotrophic hormone of the anterior pituitary gland, and perhaps also of other homones produced by the thymus, the spleen, the liver and the lymphatic glands, favors the development of the tissues of vegetative life. The other group, made up of the thyroid, parathyroid, adrenal medulla, gonads, and pituitary hormones which stimulate the thyroid, the gonads and the adrenal medulla, favors the development of the neuro-sympathetic system. At determined periods of development in the individual, the group favoring vegetative life is predominant, with resultant increases in body-size, particularly the trunk. On the other hand, when the group favoring the neuro-sympathetic system predominates, the result is a more marked differentiation of the forms and disproportionately long limbs as compared with the trunk. In the field of morpho-regulating functions, hormonal action may be highly selective in the development of this or that apparatus. Thus, the thyroid hormones stimulate the development of the neuro-sympathetic system, as well as the apparatus of psychic life; the anterior pituitary gland, and perhaps the thymus, have a marked influence on osteogenesis; the same anterior pituitary gland is a motor-organ for the sexual function; the gonads regulate osteogenesis; the adrenal glands favor the development of the circulatory and muscular apparatus; the gonads are also chiefly responsible for the development of sexual characteristics. (b) *Chemio-regulating functions.* These consist in the diversified influence of hormones on cellular metabolism. Two groups of hormones can be distinguished: an *excito-anabolic group* (insulin, parathyroid hormones, etc.) stimulating anabolism or cellular absorption; and an *excito-catabolic group* (thyroxin, adrenalin, etc.) influencing the degenerative processes. In addition, certain hormones stimulate the consumption of sugar (insulin, cortin, etc.); others favor its increase in the blood (adrenalin, thyroxin, folliculin, etc.). Hormones increase the deposit of fats in the body (cortin, insulin, certain ovarian hormones, etc.), and aid in its consumption (hormones of the anterior pituitary gland and the genital glands). Hormones increase the concentration of water in tissues (pituitrin, insulin, etc.) or lower the concentration of water (such as thyroxin), etc. (c) *Neuro-regulating functions.* These consist in the excitation or inhibition of the activity of certain nerve areas. For example, adrenalin, thyroxin, and parathormone are selective in their stimulation of the orthosympathetic system, while cortin, the pancreatic hormones, and the thymus stimulate the parasympathetic nervous system. (d) *Psychoregulating functions.* The hormones of the thyroid, adrenal, and sexual glands have an excitatory influence on the emotional life and activate the psychic biotic; the internal secretions of the parathyroid and pituitary glands act in the opposite manner.

The wide range of application of endocrinology is apparent; its expansion affects physiopathological and clinical medicine. These branches are basically concerned with an understanding, prevention, and cure of anomalies of the somatic and psychic growth and development of individuals; with the study and treatment of morphological, constitutional anomalies; with the interpretation, prophylaxis, and therapy of morbid and sub-morbid temperaments and characters—all of which has important repercussions not only on general medicine but on social hygiene, psychiatry, and, at least indirectly, morality.

PRINCIPLES OF THERAPY. Glandular transplants, through the continuous study and identification of the functions of the individual endocrine glands and their respective hormones, have successfully been developed in the fields of therapy. This applies particularly to the treatment of the diseases caused by malfunctioning glands of internal secretion. These treatments differ depending on the gland affected and the state of the malfunction as hyperfunction or hypofunction. Consisting of diverse means, such as radiation, to bring about an inhibitory or stimulatory activity in the given gland, these treatments have been of some success in checking the excessive activity of antagonistic glands. Glandular extracts and, more frequently, hormones for the suspected malfunctioning glands are administered; at present either pure hormones or synthetically prepared chemical equivalents of multi-glandular extracts have been most used. In the opinion of expert specialists, multi-glandular extracts produce more effective results because the broader application is less likely to cause harmful secondary side-effects. This means that the deficient production of natural hormones, a condition characteristic of many endocrinopathies, has been replenished by the protracted and continuous administration of the required hormone. This has greatly assisted the development of the therapy known as implantation by graft or transplantation of the endocrine glands. The use of pure hormone tablets is practiced more commonly today.

Transplanted glands are considered autoplastic or heteroplastic; the former are derived from man, and the latter are derived from an animal. In the use of animal glands, the transplantation seems to be more effective, as the more structurally similar to man is the species of mammal from which the source material is derived. The implantation is carried out subcutaneously, or in the muscles, or the abdominal cavities. The most common and successful transplantation has been of the gonads. A commonly used method, devised some years ago by Sergei Voronoff, was the implantation of the testes of anthropoid monkeys into the scrotal cavity of men. This method produced significant results, though far short of the intended enduring rejuvenation in old or diseased persons. Transplants of thyroid, parathyroid, adrenals, and hypophysis glands for treatment of specific functional deficiencies of the endocrine glands are seldom performed. As a result, less is known about their effects. Any definite judgment in these matters requires a larger clinical experience.

MORAL COROLLARIES. The practice of performing transplantations of the glands of internal secretion raises several moral questions that warrant comment. Setting aside, for the moment, the question of transplanting gonads, grafts of the other glands are always morally licit. In the case of autoplastic intervention, transplantations are permitted as long as the surgeon leaves in the donor a section of the gland sufficient to prevent the occurrence of harmful effects that would follow from total absence of it. The same norm holds also for transplanting sexual glands, with the added observation that the operation, even if only a matter of tablets of chemically prepared pure hormones is not permitted if there is a well-founded presumption that the patient wishes to avail himself of this treatment merely or mainly to continue or resume a life of licentiousness. The autoplastic transplant of ovaries in a sterile woman with the intention of rendering procreation possible, is morally licit. In no way does this contradict the condemnation of artificial insemination (see Sterilization), effected through the use of spermatozoa not belonging to her husband. In fact, in artificial insemination, the semen introduced into the female vagina (*in vas*) is an element completely apart from the husband's body. In an autoplastic transplant of the ovary, although the woman upon whom the transplant is performed can never influence the hereditary chromosome content of the ovules of the implanted ovary, nevertheless, this gland becomes through nutrition and correlated influences of other hormones an organ of the woman who later will become a mother. Nor can we overlook the fact that artificial insemination of married women, with semen from a donor other than the husband, can very easily give rise to serious disturbances in the harmony of the family, while artificial insemination of unmarried women deprives the offspring of the material and moral support which a father usually gives a child in a normal family. From this, it is very apparent that there is a vast difference between the two phenomena in question.

The transplant of a testis is morally licit if done to strengthen or restore erections in a married man or one intending to be married and who has become impotent by reason of age. This operation, however, is not lawful in cases of eunuchs who wish to contract marriage. The reason for this is that such a marriage would be invalid, since the individual, though capable of erections, would always remain incapable of emitting that *verum semen* which alone makes the *copula perfecta* or marriage possible. *Riz.*

ENEMY. An enemy is one who is hostile to another, or who manifests by harmful acts his hostility. Those who have voluntarily injured or caused damage to another without reparation; those who hate or wish evil on another, are said to be enemies. At times we refer to those toward whom we feel antipathy or aversion for just motives as enemies; likewise, we discover that to have or to be an enemy is not always a question of our free choice.

Our enemy is our neighbor, a child of the same Heavenly Father, a brother of Christ, for whom He shed His most Precious Body and Blood in death for us.

Since man must love his neighbor and brother, he must love his enemy as well. The commandment of Our Lord could not be more clear or definite: "You have heard that it hath been said, 'Thou shalt love thy neighbor and hate thy enemy.' But I say to you, 'Love your enemies, do good to them that hate you: and pray for them that persecute you and calumniate you' " (Matt. 5:43-44).

Our clear obligation to love our enemy is not because of the fact that he is our enemy, but despite it. It does not suffice not to hate him: we are obliged to love him—that is, to wish him well. Charity, an act of the will, must be manifested externally by deeds, if the situation demands it. For this reason, the obligation to love our enemy comprises the obligation to do good to him, if one finds himself in circumstances where Christian duty dictates help and assistance to our neighbor, whoever he may be. A Christian may not exclude his enemy from that which he does for all other men: the recitation of prayers, for example, that are recited for all; works of charity wherein all benefit; courtesy and respect shown to all.

External affection toward an enemy is not mandatory, nor is any special love of obligation beyond the love that is due to all and which, as good Christians, we give to all men with whom we have no special relationship or acquaintance. The direct opposite of the precept of love is to hate one's enemy, to wish or do him evil, or to rejoice at his reverses and failures. It is not, however, contrary to our duty to love our enemy when we are happy about his difficulties or cause him harm, if this will prevent further evil and harm which we and others are suffering because of his evil and unjust actions. Nor does one violate the precept of charity who wishes that his enemy may receive a just punishment, provided that he does not wish it as an evil but as a good, that is, as a just corrective retribution or, at least, as a means whereby he, out of fear of this just retribution, shall refrain from violating our rights and those of others. In other words, revenge as such, that is, as a retribution for an evil committed against us, is forbidden.

It is not forbidden, however, to do him harm if necessary to protect oneself from actual violence (self-defense) and as a just punishment directed at discouraging others from similar violations of right and justice. The laws, forbidding a subjective criterion of justice by violence, must be respected; in such cases one should seek the aid of public authority.

Refraining from revenge, loving one's enemy, and treating him as we treat all other men are tokens of forgiveness of one's enemy. I forgive my enemy when I do not exclude him from my charity, despite the harm he has done or is still doing to me; when, outside the case of just punishment or self-defense, I treat my enemy as if he had done no harm to me. It is our duty to forgive our enemy, particularly if he is sorry for the harm caused us, and expressly indicates by words, or implicitly by actions, that he wishes to be reconciled with us. Thus, the duty to forgive includes facilitating reconciliation. Between two enemies, certainly the more guilty of the two must first seek reconciliation. But this rule does not justify a hard or an unconciliatory conduct on the part of the other, nor does it dispense him from every positive action on his part. A true Christian does not simply do that which is necessary to avoid a grave sin; he endeavors to heed the injunction of the Master, "Be therefore perfect, as your Father in heaven is perfect."

TEACHING AND EXAMPLE OF THE DIVINE MASTER. Jesus knew well how difficult it would be for man to love and pardon his enemy; hence, He spoke of this precept with great solemnity, exceptional clarity, and at every opportunity. He enjoined His followers to ask God each day to forgive us our sins, as we "forgive those who sinned against us," that is, our enemies.

It would be difficult to think of a stronger and more persistent exhortation. It is ironic to say this prayer daily and refuse to forgive one's neighbor. Who can fail to appreciate the impressive parable of the servant who asked for and obtained forgiveness from his master, but, when he himself would not forgive his friend, was severely punished (Matt. 18:23–35)? Above all, Jesus taught us by example. He loved and forgave His enemies. To Judas, who had led the soldiers into the Garden of Olives, Jesus said: "Friend . . . you betray the Son of man with a kiss?" For Peter's denials He had but love and forgiveness; while hanging on the cross, He cried out, "Father, forgive them, for they know not what they do." Christ's commandment is an invitation to follow His divine example in which we always can depend on the aid of His grace. *Ben.*

ENGINEER. The term *engineer* comes from *ingenium* in the sense of contrivance, not in the sense of talent; in its origin, it is, therefore, related to the ancient war machines called *ingenia* in early Latin history.

The duties of an engineer as well as those of an architect are generally determined and governed by appropriate regulations. Besides those duties relative and common to all labor contracts or services, he has other obligations, specifically moral, such as the preparation of plans, estimates, etc. An engineer must acquire all the technical knowledge his work requires in accredited schools and approved programs. He must possess integrity, reliability, and diligence.

In view of the grave responsibilities connected with his profession, an engineer must attend to an extensive and scrupulous preparation, both theoretical and practical, without which he risks not only failure in his field but also incalculable damage.

He must not assume any work for which he is not competent; on the contrary, he shall make himself culpably responsible for any damage caused by miscalculations on his part due to lack of knowledge. He has a grave responsibility of supervising the execution of his plans and must answer for errors of omission or commission in the exercise of his profession. These responsibilities, according to their respective personal role and competence, are shared by architects and builders. Generally speaking, a Catholic engineer is not permitted to participate in the construction of a building which he is certain will be used to foster a false religion or in works opposed to Catholic faith and morals. *Tar.*

ENJOYMENT. Moral theologians term *enjoyment* special forms of voluntary pleasure, particularly rational pleasure (i.e., of the will and not of the sensitive appetite), in an action performed by ourselves or another person.

Morality in enjoyment depends evidently on the morality of its object. Enjoyment in an evil act easily assumes all the circumstantial malice of the act, since it is a detailed recollection.

Moral theologians generally raise the question whether it is morally licit to take pleasure in an act objectively illicit but not imputable—for instance, homicide committed by a completely involuntary error. Their answer is in the negative, for enjoyment would very likely voluntarily extend to the act in its objective illicitness. They add, however, that it is not improper or illicit if the enjoyment is limited to the good effects of the illicit act, considered independently of their cause. *Gra.*

ENTHUSIASM. *See* Fervor.

ENTOMBMENT. *See* Cemetery; Burial, Ecclesiastical.

ENVY. Envy is unhappiness or discontent at the excellence, success, good fortune, or talents of another, which the envious considers a diminution of his own excellence and an injustice done to himself. Envy is not to be confused with discontent in seeing oneself without the possessions that another has, even undeservedly. Envy is not depression caused through the realization that another, by his wealth or possessions, is in a position to do harm to oneself or one's relatives. Furthermore, envy is not to be confused with emulation (*q.v.*), which is the ambition to equal or surpass another. In itself, emulation is not a defect, if the

intention and means chosen to this excellence are honest and just.

MORALITY. Envy is a sin against charity of its nature grievous (*ex genere suo*). Guilt is diminished, however, by lack of consent or the insignificance of the object envied. The most serious sin of envy occurs when one is envious of the supernatural gifts or graces which another receives for his salvation (*see* Sins against the Holy Ghost).

The source of envy is pride and self-love; frequently it is found in persons suffering from inferiority complexes (*see* Psychasthenia). Envy is likewise the cause of other evils: slander, calumny, rejoicing over the misfortunes of others, and hatred of one's neighbour. Envy destroys peace of mind, threatens health, and brings one into disfavor in the eyes of others.

Deep humility, without excluding a just self-esteem, which is useful in conquering envy, as well as a sincere and supernatural love for all men are the chief weapons in conquering the spirit of envy. *Man.*

EPACT. *See* Liturgical Year.

EPICUREANISM. *See* Hedonism.

EPIDEMIC. *See* Contagion.

EPIKEIA. *See* Equity; Prudence; Cause, Excusing.

EPILEPSY. Epilepsy is a complex and not uncommon syndrome with a variety of neurological and psychic disturbances characterized by their sudden and repeated occurrence. At times, these disturbances cannot be ascribed to any ascertainable organic disease; in such cases we speak of *essential, genuine,* or *idiopathic* epilepsy. More frequently the disturbances are due to a variety of fetal or infantile diseases, including birth traumata, cerebral tumors, meningitis, cranial encephalic lesions, intoxication, etc.: in such cases we speak of *symptomatic* epilepsy.

The best-known epileptic form is the generalized convulsive attack (the *grand mal*). This attack may or may not be preceded by a very brief preliminary phase (*aura*) in which the patient experiences unusual sensations or performs some peculiar action. The beginning of the crisis is often characterized by a loud cry with loss of consciousness, paling of the face, and seizure. All the muscles go into a state of *tonic* contraction, lasting a few seconds. After this, the second or *clonic* phase immediately follows, characterized by generalized muscular, jerking spasms, at first rapid, then gradually slower, with an emission from the mouth of foamy saliva, often bloodstained as a result of biting of the tongue. After a few minutes, the clonic spasms cease; with a complete relaxation of the muscles, a comatose state follows in which the patient lapses into deep sleep, lasting at times for several hours. Upon awakening, the patient usually will complain of violent headaches, general fatigue and will have no memory of what happened to him.

At other times, the seizure is characterized by clonic convulsions, starting always in the same muscular group, without impairment of consciousness, and often followed by paresis of the part of the body afflicted with convulsions. This is called *Jacksonian epilepsy*, from the name of the English doctor, J. H. Jackson, who made a study of it. Jacksonian epilepsy is the manifestation of a disturbance affecting Rolandic, a particular portion of the cerebral cortex, which contains the centers controlling the voluntary mobility of the opposite side.

A third epileptic manifestation bears the name, *petit mal*. The attack is characterized by *blackout spells*, that is, momentary losses of consciousness without convulsive phenomena. Generally there is no falling to the ground nor recollection of the attack. Occasionally, the momentary blackout of the mind is associated with phenomena of motor automatism, incoherent words, or actions, etc.

The so-called *epileptic equivalent* seizures are not associated with the typical, convulsive attack. Instead, they display particular manifestations such as wandering spells, abnormal sensations, temper tantrums, which at times break out into dangerous acts of violence, twilight stages during which the patient may act in a confused manner or be subject to vivid hallucinations or experience psychomotor disorientation and retardation.

Aside from seizures, some epileptics, especially those subject to frequent morbid attacks, present definite anomalies of character which make up the so-called *epileptic temperament* and give to the personality of these patients a typical "epileptic make-up." At times, the problem is due to a serious emotional instability, an abnormal *impulsiveness*, reacting violently to any opposition, or a strong *egocentric* tendency. More frequently, though, there are manifestations of a special *psychic viscosity*: the patient is very docile, acquiescent, even to the point of being annoying, irksome, demanding, slow to comprehend, pedantic. In severe and prolonged cases, in which epilepsy began in childhood, the psychic symptoms, mentioned above, become more pronounced as the intellect and ethical sense gradually become more enfeebled. The result of this process is often *epileptic dementia*.

PATHOGENESIS. The mechanism through which the epileptic attack erupts is only partly known. Various factors (cerebral lesions, endocrine malfunctions, alkaline state of the blood, anoxemia, retention of water in nerve cells, intoxication) increase cerebral excitability to the critical phase that erupts into a seizure. Epilepsy, therefore, as far as presently known, is a particular form of reaction by the nerve centers to a variety of causes.

Although epilepsy often begins in infancy or adolescence, it is rarely hereditary (about 5% of cases). The early appearance is due to the fact that traumata and infections (usual causes of the disease) are all the more damaging as they affect the brain of the fetus or of the infant. The course of the disease is most varied: some cases are characterized by almost daily seizures; in others, the interval between attacks may be of months or years. At times the attacks display always the same characteristics; at other times, seizures of the *grand mal* may alternately manifest characteristics of blackouts and psychic equivalents. Particularly important because of its gravity is the so-called *status epilepticus,* in which the convulsive fits succeed one another almost without intermission, and without regaining of consciousness during the intervals. Often such a state terminates in the death of the patient.

The treatment of epilepsy is based generally on the prolonged use of special medication and hygieno-dietetic rules. Barbiturates and sodium diphenyl-hydantoin are the preferred drugs in the treatment of the *grand mal* type; the *petit mal* seizures are usually treated with trimethyloxazolidine dione ("tridione"). At the same time, meticulous care of the intestinal functions, abstinence from alcoholic drinks, reduction in the consumption of meat and a low diet of salt and liquid intakes are basic elements of diet in reducing the number and severity of the attacks. When syphilis, toxicity, or arteriosclerosis are found to be causes of the epilepsy, treatment of these causes will be of necessity and great benefit. Finally, surgical treatment will become necessary when there is evidence of tumors, cysts, bone chips, etc. (occurring more frequently in the Jacksonian types). In some cases (brain tumors, etc.), X-ray treatment may be suitably prescribed.

In an actual attack, the best procedure to follow is to place a pillow or some other soft object under the victim's head, put a spoon or other hard item between his teeth to prevent him from biting his tongue, and loosen his neckwear to prevent possible constrictions. Attempts to revive the patient by throwing water on his face, using *ammonia,* or resorting to other stimulants should be carefully avoided as useless if not harmful. If the *status epilepticus* is evidently present, a specialist should be called without delay for the administration of appropriate therapeutic aids (barbiturate injections; possibly even suboccipital puncture, etc.).

MORAL AND JURIDICAL ASPECTS. As a general rule, in the period between convulsive attacks, the epileptic is a fully conscious and perfectly normal person, responsible for his actions. When the seizures are rather frequent, and there are manifestations of equivalent psychoses or the patient possesses the so-called "epileptic temperament," there can be not only a diminution but a total absence of moral and penal responsibility as well as of civil capacity.

The moral and medico-juridical evaluation of a given illicit or criminal action can be difficult if there have been no certain epileptic convulsions prior to the action. The reason is that there exist forms of transient epilepsy in otherwise normal individuals which manifest themselves as impulsive psychic equivalents, that can lead to the commission of sexual attacks, arson, murder, or other serious crimes with a complete lack of responsibility. One called upon to adjudicate such cases must be prudent in his judgment. He ought to request adequate investigation by medical experts and also, if possible, a sufficient period of observation in a special institution and a report of the findings of electroencephalographic studies (*see* Cerebral Waves).

Finally, it must be noted that since epilepsy is a morbid syndrome generally acquired and only rarely congenital (in the latter case, commonly the result of serious toxic infections of the parents), one ought not to advise against the marriage of epileptics. If the prospective bride is an epileptic, she ought to be informed that her affliction does not justify any recourse to "therapeutic abortions" (*q.v.*). This will give the woman sufficient opportunity to weigh the risks that her marriage will entail. *Riz.*

EPISCOPACY. *See* Orders, Holy; Bishop.

EPISTLE. *See* Mass.

EQUIPROBABILISM. *See* System, Moral.

EQUITY. The concept of equity is very difficult to define. The following are three formulas by which it is described: (1) correction of an existing law; (2) higher form of justice; (3) justice in a particular case. In order to understand these formulas, one must remember that justice, as conceived in the juridical order, tends towards uniformity and rigidity; two qualities made necessary by the exigencies of social life. At times, however, these two features of justice lead to conclusions, different in the circumstances of a concrete case from the rigid, uniform rule. In such instances, the necessity for a different norm to supplant the juridical norm in force must take into consideration all the particulars of a concrete situation. This is called the norm of equity, which corrects the existing law, actuates a higher form of justice, and adapts justice to the particular case. Since it is the task of morality, not of law, to take into consideration all the circumstances of a concrete case, it is said that equity is the removal of justice from abstract juridical theory and its restoration to concrete moral circumstances.

At times, equity is spoken of simply as a synonym for a liberal interpretation and merciful application of law—a colloquial and vague meaning of the term. In a more exact and scientific sense, as explained above, it can lead equally to greater severity or to greater clemency, depending on the case.

RELATION TO EPIKEIA. *Equity* is a word more commonly used by jurists than by moralists. The latter generally speak of *epikeia*, by which term they strive to unite the two senses of equity mentioned above, the scientific and the colloquial. Beyond the letter of the law in a benign sense, unusual circumstances of the concrete case reasonably lead to conclude that the legislator could not or would not have wished it to be included in the law. Moralists, especially of the older school, include under the name *epikeia* cases in which they see the obligation of the law ceasing *ab intrinseco* (*see* Cause, Excusing). *Gra.*

EROTOMANIA. *See* Dipsomania.

ERROR. Error may be defined as a false judgment; or belief in what is untrue.

Considered simply as a fact of intelligence, error has no ethical value. It acquires value insofar as it has either a voluntary cause or morally relevant effects, for the voluntariness of the cause extends to its effects. Thus, an error in matters of faith is not morally imputable and, hence, cannot constitute a sin, unless it is the result of culpable negligence on the part of the individual in acquiring proper religious training. Thus, too, error in the exercise of an art or profession may be morally indifferent, excusable or culpable, depending on its cause or effects. For example, the errors of a judge in giving a sentence or of a doctor in the care of the sick are to be evaluated from the moral point of view by taking into consideration the culpability of the ignorance or negligence from which such errors proceed, as well as the culpability of the consequences flowing from those errors, even if foreseen only in a confused way. In view of this, a magistrate or a doctor who does not possess at least a degree of knowledge, ordinarily required, will be morally responsible for any error committed in the exercise of his profession. Similarly, culpability will be present if their error is due to the lack of diligence in treating individual cases, since a judge or a doctor is required to use always at least an ordinary diligence, proportionate to the difficulties and the gravity of the case. Therefore, error in difficult cases surpassing one's knowledge will be culpable if recourse to the skill of another is possible yet deliberately neglected or, worse, if such help is refused. There is no doubt about the culpability of the error in such cases, for both the judge and the doctor are fully aware of the fact that their ignorance and negligence expose them to a constant danger of errors harmful to their neighbor, when by virtue of their office they are obliged to avoid them. Concerning the effects of error in contracts, *see* Contract. Concerning the effects of error in matrimonial consent, *see* Consent, Matrimonial. *Gra.*

ERROR (IN MARRIAGE). *See* Consent, Matrimonial.

ERROR OF THE PHYSICIAN.

JURIDICAL AND MORAL PRINCIPLES. Penal codes prescribe that no one can be punished for an action or omission foreseen by the law as a crime, unless it was done knowingly and voluntarily. Consequently, error committed by a doctor is beyond the realm of liability, unless he is mentally abnormal, or would knowingly harm his patients. If, on the other hand, damage is the result of grave negligence, evident lack of skill, or marked imprudence, or if, as Palmieri says, the doctor "has adopted a behavior, whether active or passive, commissive or omissive, which is manifestly inexcusable," then there is room for legal action, if only to provide adequate financial reparation in favor of the injured person or, if he died, in favor of his legitimate heirs.

On this subject, Catholic morality is much more severe toward considerations of responsibility in the conscience of a doctor in errors of negligence, imprudence, or lack of skill. Naturally, the degree of responsibility varies and due consideration must be taken of antecedents constituting imputability *in causa.* No matter how slight the injury to the sick person is, reparation binding in conscience must be made every time moral guilt is present.

The responsibility of a medical doctor or surgeon in the exercise of his profession is a serious one. Everyone will admit that an error in diagnosis can easily be made; that it can be the misfortune of any doctor to prescribe a harmful therapeutic treatment; that an accident during an operation can happen to the most outstanding surgeon. In all of this, of course, there is nothing deserving of blame, not even from a moral point of view, provided that the physician acted in perfect good faith and was not led into error by lack of ability, thoughtlessness, or negligence.

In the common case in which there occurs unjustifiable error with the participation, simultaneous or successive, of several doctors, the guilt falls on him who *de facto* attended the patient. Thus, for example, if a doctor formulates an erroneous diagnosis, and a second doctor, on the basis of such a diagnosis, prescribed the wrong treatment, and a third doctor carried out the harmful treatment on the sick person, moral responsibility may be ascribed to the first two doctors because of their incompetence, but penal responsibility is imputed to the last, since he performed the action which produced the actual damage.

To say that the treatment used was prescribed by a colleague of obviously good reputation is no excuse. A doctor is not the executor of orders like a nurse. "Every time that he [a doctor] places his hands on a sick person he acts on his own responsibility . . . If he is not convinced that the treatment prescribed by others is the proper one, he must cease giving it. If he does not desist, he must bear the consequences of his action" (Palmieri).

The old aphorism *Ars longa, vita brevis* is particularly fitting to the medical disciplines. No doctor, no matter how competent he may be, can fail to recognize the necessity of constant study in order to become more and more proficient in the difficult art of healing people. Study, caution, prudence and sagacity, therefore, are essential qualities in a doctor in order that he might properly fulfill his arduous duties. The layman, on the other hand, needs to have a mature understanding of the life, work, and sacrifice which is the lot of the majority of physicians. He must appreciate the fact that the life of a doctor is often one characterized by lack of comforts, ever-present dangers, and constant emotional tension. Particularly deplorable is the ever-increasing number of suits brought against doctors on allegations of incompetent service, when it was simply a question of an unfortunate accident. A more careful preparation on the part of doctors will lessen the number and seriousness of involuntary errors; an increased spirit of understanding on the part of the public will diminish the hatred against physicians when such unfortunate errors do occur. In this way, the bond of affection and esteem between the physician and the public will grow with mutual benefits to both (*See also* Surgery). *Riz.*

ESCAPE. *See* Prison.

ESTIMATION, ESTIMATE. *Estimation* (Lat., *aestimare*—to appraise, to evaluate) signifies the value of an object in terms of money, the price of an object, whether a movable or immovable good. An estimate, a form of contract analogous to commission, is governed by the natural and juridical forms of common contracts, with the addition of trust. Estimation is a science, or, according to some, a discipline, used to determine the value of economic goods. In practice, its field of study is limited to immovable goods. There are two kinds of estimation: *ordinary*, in buying-selling, consignments, re-consignments, damage, etc., and *cadastral*, the assessment of landed property.

Medieval documents concerning buying-selling, barter, etc., speak of *homines, boni viri, idonei, aestimatores*, especially in transactions involving minors and ecclesiastical institutions. These persons were called in to check, by evaluation of immovable property, whether or not the minor was benefiting in the transaction. Later, this practice was extended to the common business transactions and included in various codes of law.

The primary duty of those who make the estimation is to appraise the object to be bought or sold. Such persons are called *expert appraisers*, or *estimators*, also, at times, *arbiters*.

PRINCIPLES. Estimation is based on certain fundamental principles of economics. One of the basic concepts underlying the practice of estimation is the following: the same economic good may possess a variety of uses and consequent advantages. A second principle is that the judgment given by the appraiser has value for the particular market and moment to which the appraisal refers. Appraisers must be guided by these fundamental principles. Furthermore,

they must take into account whether the estimation or inventory concerns (a) liquidation or (b) measurements and inventory, or (c) hereditary property. From different kinds of estimation arise different responsibilities and obligations of conscience: for example, in the case of liquidation, if the appraiser were to take advantage of the unfortunate condition of the liquidator, he would be sinning more seriously than in ordinary cases.

OBLIGATIONS. Estimation presupposes in the appraiser a detailed, technical knowledge of the good to be evaluated, and the market taken in its broadest sense—that is, (a) the market value (quantity, quality, unity); (b) the value of transformation or use (permissive and obligatory transformation); (c) the cost value, that is, the sum total of the expenses that a contractor of average capacity would have to sustain in ordinary conditions, whether actual or potential; (d) its replacement value.

Without such knowledge, appraisers are subject to serious errors and, hence, liable to indirect responsibility for consequent damage. Appraisers must be honest men, of blameless lives and above reproach. They must possess qualities that make them immune to corruption, favoritism, or other passions. In case of inaccurate evaluation, appraisers must make good all losses. They are also liable to fraud, incompetence, and negligence. Nor may they have recourse to occult compensation.

The Code of Canon Law requires that estimation be made by approved and experienced persons in all cases of alienation of movable or immovable ecclesiastical goods (Cf. Canon 534, 1530). *Tar.*

ETHICS. Ethics is the science of moral values and duties. It is divided into *natural* or philosophical ethics and *supernatural* or theological ethics. Natural ethics is the study of the moral world and its norms in the light of human reason; theological ethics is the study of the moral world in the light of Divine Revelation (*see* Theology, Moral).

The subject matter of philosophical

ethics (practical philosophy or the philosophy of the practical) is not given the same broad scope by everyone. We shall mention two schools of thought on this question. For some, especially more ancient authors, it is a complete moral system, at times called the doctrine of the natural law, embracing general principles as well as a particularized list of moral obligations and juridical relations concerning man as man, but not specifically a Christian. Other philosophical ethicians restrict ethics to the study of general principles, that is, the principles of moral doctrine in two special ways: the doctrine of virtue and the doctrine of law. Such, of course, become no longer philosophical but simply preceptive or technical sciences. A third tendency separates law from ethics by reducing ethics to pure morality as opposed to law. This division or opposition cannot possibly be admitted. Law, as a preceptive norm of human action, must of intrinsic necessity be in conformity with other obligating norms concerning the same action. We recognize, however, that a more precise distinction between the formal characteristics of a juridical norm and those of a general ethical norm would be helpful. But in making such a distinction, one must keep in mind that it is a question only of internal distinction, not one extrinsic to ethics (*see* Norm, Moral).

The main problem of philosophical ethics is the search for the supreme norm of human acts. Its solution, of course, depends necessarily on the general principles of the individual philosophical systems. *Gra.*

ETHNOLOGY. See Anthropology.

EUCHARIST. Etymologically, the word *Eucharist* means thanksgiving, or a good favor, or the highest benefit. In theological language, *Eucharist* refers to the Sacrament of the Body and Blood of Our Lord, that is, the consecrated species of bread and wine; or the Body and Blood of Christ, present under the sacramental species; finally, the consecrated species together with the Body and Blood

of Christ. The word *Eucharist* can be used also to indicate the rite of consecration which makes Christ present under the Eucharistic veil. This rite is the solemn memorial of the bloody sacrifice on the cross, the essence of the unbloody sacrifice of the New Law, and the rite that makes the Eucharistic Christ the spiritual food and drink of our souls.

MATTER, FORM, AND MINISTER. The valid remote matter of the Eucharist is bread, made from wheat, and wine, made from grapes (Canon 814 ff.). The bread must be made from wheat, mixed with water, and baked. Bread from other cereal or mixed with milk, oil, or butter, would not be valid except when the amount of such elements is extremely small. For licit use or liceity, it is required that no other substance be mixed with the flour; that the bread be fresh; that it be unleavened and that it be round in shape (in the Latin Church) and of different size according to its intended use for the celebration of the Sacrifice of the Mass or for Communion (Canon 815, par. 1). For validity the wine must be made from ripened grapes. Regarding liceity of wine, the wine must be unadulterated, well fermented, unspoiled, and clear (Canon 815, 2).

The proximate valid matter of the Eucharist is the bread of wheat and the wine, both physically present and specified for consecration by the intention of the celebrant. Neither the bread nor the wine can be licitly consecrated under pain of mortal sin, unless each is located on a consecrated altar (an altar with an altar stone) and on the corporal.

The form of the Eucharist consists of the words of the Eucharistic consecration (*q.v.*).

The minister of consecration of the Eucharist is only a priest (*see* Mass). The minister of Communion may be a deacon (only as extraordinary minister), or, in a case of necessity, the faithful (*see* Communion). Concerning the recipient of the Eucharist, *see* Communion.

The Eucharist can well be called the epitome of faith and of all benefits granted by God to man, as well as the center of the Catholic religion; hence, the numerous descriptive names given to the Eucharist. The Sacrifice and the Sacrament of the altar should be for us the object of deepest veneration and the source of copious graces, obtained through devout assistance at Mass, frequent visits to the Blessed Sacrament and participation in the Eucharistic banquet. *Man.*

EUGENICS. Eugenics (Greek: *eugenes*—well-begotten, well-born) is the science which seeks to promote the procreation of healthy and physically perfect children for the purpose of improving the state of health of mankind. Depending on the means and the norms chosen for directly producing healthy specimens or for preventing an unhealthy child, one speaks of *positive* and *negative* eugenics. Obviously, sterilization is not a means to healthy procreation, since it removes every possibility of generation. If, nevertheless, sterilization is called a eugenic medium, it must be understood as a means of preventing unhealthy generation.

MORALITY. The Church is the strongest supporter of eugenics and eugenic activities, for it considers natural health as one of the precious gifts of the Creator. Man has an obligation to use suitable, licit means to improve his own health and that of his children. This includes eugenics. It is wrong to neglect the proper and licit means apt to promote the health of offspring. The Church and Catholic moral doctrine, however, do not approve or accept all the methods and means which in modern times are publicized and recommended as useful for eugenic purposes. The Church condemns eugenicists who, in their limited outlook, exalt eugenics as the supreme principle of action. Physical health is a great gift but it is not the only and supreme good of man. Thus, it is not sufficient that a means is useful for eugenic purposes, to be considered good under every aspect and therefore to be accepted for its practical application.

In human life there are also other values which must be considered, and man must keep these in mind even if he is a eugenicist. For this reason, the Church, favoring eugenic activities and the use of many eugenic means, condemns and prohibits the use of certain methods and eugenic means which are contrary to the law of God. The Church holds that any transgression of this law is always harmful in a broad view, though in particular cases it may appear beneficial from a limited point of view. Thus, any transgression of the law of God must be avoided. The moral law aims at safeguarding the good of man and his universal happiness. On the strength of this sound principle, the Church condemns immoral eugenic means, among which are sterilization and the absolute prohibition of marriage.

The Church urges both the civil authority and private persons to promote projects which have an effective eugenic value; the moral life of the people, including public morality; the protection of the great values contained in Christian life, in religion, in Christian marriage, in the family, in the education of children in the family, in daily, steady, energetic and fruitful work, suitable to the rational nature of man and productive of satisfaction and joy. Even under the eugenic aspect, good health is best secured in a life spent in an environment morally, mentally, and physically sound, not from a violent and unnatural suppression of the evil effects of an immoral and unwholesome life. The first and principal duty of doctors is to combat and remove, not the effects, but the causes of hereditary diseases. *Ben.*

EUNUCH. A eunuch is a man who lacks gonads (*q.v.*), by reason of natural defect, accident, surgical operation, or violent mutilation. Absence of such organs makes a man incapable of sexual union and, consequently, incapable of contracting marriage (*see* Impotency). In view of such incapacity, in ancient times Eastern monarchs used eunuchs, by birth or, as often happened, by surgical intervention, as custodians of the harem, the residence of the monarch's wives and concubines. As a result of this custom, the term *eunuch* gradually assumed a wider and secondary meaning, that of custodian or servant of the royal harem.

When Christ proclaimed His doctrine on the indissolubility of marriage, He used the term *eunuch* obviously to an audience acquainted with this Oriental custom. In reply to the Jews, Christ said: "There are eunuchs who were born so from their mother's womb; and there are eunuchs who were made so by man; and there are eunuchs who have made themselves so for the kingdom of heaven's sake." By the latter words, Christ did not mean eunuchs who made themselves so by mutilation of the body. He was referring to the principal effect of the complete renunciation of conjugal life and sexual pleasure. To make oneself a eunuch for the love of the kingdom of heaven means to renounce, by a voluntary act (perpetual vow of chastity), conjugal life and sexual pleasure for all time.

For the morality of mutilation by which a man becomes a eunuch, *see* Sterilization. *Ben.*

EUNUCHOIDISM. *See* Eunuch, Gonad.

EUTHANASIA NEGATIVE. Euthanasia (*eu*, well; *thanatos*, death) means a voluntary omission of an action through which it would be possible to preserve the life of another individual person. This omission is due, not to the difficulty, inconvenience or incapacity of the action of preserving life, but solely to the desire to end another person's life that he might be free from suffering or a hard and burdensome life in the coming years.

Negative euthanaia is illicit and sinful. It is sinful if one fails to use all the means at one's disposal to preserve life, such as a refusal to call a doctor. Negative euthanasia is sinful, because it is a violation of the obligation of preserving one's own life or that of others, because the right of life is God's alone. This obligation extends to the ordinary means of preserving life, that is, those that are not too difficult, burdensome, or severe (*see* Health of Body). This obligation does not cease even if life is painful, hard, or a burden to others. Euthanasia is a violation of the fifth commandment, since it is a form of murder.

A doctor does not sin if he fails to use the necessary means for preserving life which the patient refuses or, in the case of minors, the parents refuse. The doctor offers his services to patients; the patient is responsible for his own health. The doctor cannot intervene against the will of the patient, even if this will is manifestly sinful. The omission of an act which one cannot perform without injuring another's right is not sinful. *Ben.*

POSITIVE. The killing of old persons, deformed and weak children, as practiced among more or less barbarous nations, was a form of euthanasia. Christianity brought about the disappearance of this inhuman practice. In morality and in law, euthanasia is universally regarded as murder or suicide. Today we witness an unfortunate tendency to a return to barbarous customs by the proposal of laws which would authorize doctors to kill, without pain, sick persons who desire death, or provide for the killing, by order or permission of public authority, of persons useless to society because of disease, insanity, imbecility, old age. It would permit the killing of soldiers mutilated or seriously wounded, without hope of recovery.

We must distinguish two essentially different cases: (a) causing a peaceful death, that is, a death but without pain; (b) causing a peaceful death, not directly, but by intervening in such a way that death, the result of another cause, such as disease, insanity, imbecility, old age, etc., will occur without pain. In the first case, we have killing in the true sense of the word; not so in the second case. In other words, there is a death-causing euthanasia and a euthanasia that does not cause death. Euthanasia used without any further qualification refers to death-causing euthanasia.

MORALITY. Death-causing euthanasia is an intrinsically evil thing, suicide or murder depending on the particular case.

It is murder even if executed at the request or with the consent of the patient, since the painful condition in which the patient finds himself can be assumed to exclude freedom of will in his request. Morality is in no way altered by circumstances: the fact that the person is suffering or will not live much longer. Euthanasia is always a serious sin for the same reasons that murder (*q.v.*) and suicide (*q.v.*) are grave sins. Prescinding from the fact that one can never be certain of the absolute incurability of a disease or that error in diagnosis and prognosis is always possible, we must consider euthanasia directly contrary to the true end of medicine and the noble office of a doctor. The role of a doctor is *to heal*, that is, to save the life of a man, using, as much as possible, all available medical resources. Euthanasia, therefore, is diametrically opposed to the office and obligations of a doctor. Euthanasia, accepted in practice and not opposed by proper authority, would in addition bring serious harm to society. Men would lose confidence in doctors and not readily entrust themselves to their care, with consequent serious harm to the state of health of the people. Not even public authority is permitted to kill an innocent person. Laws which permit or impose such an action either on doctors or on others are evil laws. To obey such laws is to commit the sin of murder. Moreover, once these laws are permitted, *per absurdum*, how could one prevent great crimes? For example, relatives, anxious to receive the inheritance of a sick kin, might strive to obtain in every possible way the consent of a sick person to euthanasia or persuade or force a doctor to such an act. What a dangerous debasement of man's moral sense! For these reasons the Holy Office rightfully issued its condemnation on December 2, 1940 (AAS, 32 [1940], 553).

Euthanasia that does not cause death but only removes or lessens the pain of the dying person is not prohibited, provided that it is not used merely for the harmful effects which are often the consequence of the means applied, as in the case of narcotics. Among these effects at times are acceleration of death (*see* Acceleration of Death), permanent or temporary privation of consciousness, etc. It is never licit to use such means without the consent of the patient. A doctor sins very seriously if he deprives a person of consciousness when that person is not prepared for death, especially from the spiritual and supernatural point of view, or when the patient still has need of reconciliation with God through the reception of the sacraments. It would also be a serious sin for relatives or friends of the sick person to ask the doctor to do this. A doctor, worthy of his Christian heritage, will oppose such a manifestation of love based on a distorted intention and religious ignorance, but he must strive to properly instruct the patient as well as those taking care of him. Also in the case of persons prepared for death, it is not expedient that they be deprived of consciousness in the moments that precede death. A Christian knows that suffering and death, accepted with holy resignation to the will of God, are an excellent means of atoning for sins committed during one's life.

Christ instituted a special sacrament, extreme unction (*q.v.*), to give particular strength to die well and to bear the sufferings which accompany death. For this reason the Church wishes that prayers be offered at this moment for and with the dying person. Moreover, modern medical science possesses various pharmaceutical and surgical means of lessening the suffering of the sick without deadening their higher mental activities; such means are valid, therefore, and perfectly licit. *Ben.*

EVANGELIARIUM. *See* Liturgical Books.

EVICTION. *See* Possession in Bad Faith.

EVIL. The concept of evil in its broadest sense is one of privation. Accordingly, any negation or limitation is an evil. But this is the metaphysical concept of evil, according to which any essential limitation of a being is an essential evil or, rather, the root of possibility of its every evil. In a more ordinary and restricted sense, evil, considered in a specific being, is lack of a perfection which belongs to it, as the lack of speech in a man. In this category are included all those evils which we consider physical, such as infirmities and the like. In moral theology, *evil* is used as synonymous with *sin*. But evil can also assume a wider meaning and include anything that may impair our ethical advancement (imperfection, or cause of imperfection) though it be not sinful. Moral theologians, particularly teachers of ascetical theology, insist on the usefulness of looking upon moral evil as the only real evil, attributing to physical or metaphysical evil (and also to physical good) only the value which it acquires as a means leading to or against moral good or moral evil. *Gra.*

EVIL EYE. *See* Magic.

EXACTION. *See* Duty; Taxation.

EXAMINATION OF CONSCIENCE. Examination of conscience consists in a close scrutiny of the moral aspect of one's own acts. Before sacramental confession, self-examination is required unless physical weakness, as in the case of a seriously ill person, or imminent danger of death were to preclude the possibility of such an examination. Examination of conscience is not of obligation where its omission would constitute no danger of omitting the confession of some serious sin. This would apply, for example, to those who approach the tribunal of penance frequently, without mortal sins to confess. But even for such persons the examination of conscience is always beneficial and certainly counseled.

Examination of conscience before sacramental confession ought to be made with the same diligence used in important affairs by prudent persons. One who approaches the tribunal of penance with full awareness that the omission of the examination offers a strong possibility of omitting a mortal sin would be guilty of a grave sacrilege. No special method is prescribed for the examination of conscience. It is well to follow the order of the precepts or the virtues.

A daily examination of conscience is most beneficial in the spiritual life. In order to be able to subdue one's own defects, especially a predominate vice (*q.v.*), and advance in the practice of virtue, one must necessarily know himself well and take account of his progress as well as regression in virtue. Along with a glance at all the actions of the day, he shall use the daily examination to concentrate on a specific point for a more particular scrutiny. This scrutiny should cover not only faults but also their causes, defects that hinder progress, efforts made to eliminate these defects and to develop virtuous dispositions, and, finally, the concrete means to be used. In the particular examination one should not pass too quickly from one point to another.

Furthermore, one should examine himself often on the good that he could have done and which was neglected, even though without any fault, and also on the efforts made to live in intimate union with God (*see* Union with God). It is fitting to begin the examination with a brief prayer to implore the help of the Holy Spirit, and to terminate with an act of contrition, a concrete and firm resolution, and, finally, an act of thanksgiving to God. *Man.*

EXAMINATION, PHYSICAL. A physical examination always begins with an account by the patient or person accompanying him of the manner in which his illness started and developed; of contingent sicknesses that may have preceded it; the condition of health of his relatives; the habitual standard of living of the sick person, and everything else having proximate or remote bearing on the illness under scrutiny. Depending on circumstances, time, experience and professional habits, the physician shall allow the patient to speak freely and question him as he may see fit. In all cases he is expected to exercise great patience in the face of prolixity and digressions by the patient or his companion. Since he must ask rather personal and delicate questions, he must carefully avoid any frivolous remark and, more so, any reference to things that may be a cause of scandal to the patient or others accompanying him.

A real and proper *medical examination* should be conducted in the presence of a member of the patient's family or a friend, especially if the patient is a young woman. Excessive denudation and, above all, any act, look, or word that may offend the natural sense of modesty of the patient must be avoided.

After the diagnosis, the physician should disclose the nature of the illness if susceptible of easy cure. In cases of particularly grave, dangerous, or incurable illness, he should cautiously withhold it from the patient, but disclose the entire truth to some member of his family. Accordingly, he shall offer suggestions and prescribe treatments that are best suited for alleviating sufferings and prolonging the patient's life. It may not be out of place for the attending physician to advise one of the patient's more responsible relatives to perform the delicate task of suggesting to the sick the necessity of handling important matters such as settlement of property, a will, reception of the sacraments, and the like, on which the spiritual welfare of the patient and the economic well-being of his family may depend. By a similar suggestion, more urgent if it concerns a dying person without close relatives, the physician shall personally, and tactfully, urge the patient to settle any material or spiritual interest which needs to be settled, without, however, taking away from him all hope of a possible recovery.

It is improper for a physician to express an unfavorable prognosis or indicate in any manner in the presence of a seriously ill or dying patient that all hope is gone. Since the hearing is the last faculty to become dim, it would be a truly deplorable thing for a physician to refer to the oncoming of death within earshot of a patient who, though at the point of death, still hopes for recovery.

Aware at all times of his arduous and noble task, he shall find inspiration and comfort in the words of Pius XII, pronounced on the occasion of the Fourth Congress of the Latin Medical Union: "The sick person deserves the greatest respect because he reflects the image of God, of an incarnate and suffering God. The smallest service rendered to him is directed in reality not only to the weak and fragile man, but to the Lord of all things, who will give an eternal reward for the good done in His name to the least of His children. It is for this reason that the moral norms which the physician carries out greatly exceed the prescriptions of a professional code of honor; they rise to the nature of personal activity toward a living God. Thence, stem the very high dignity and nobility of a physician's actions; thence, too, the sacred character, as it were, of his person and his interventions."

At the bedside of his patients, or in the course of his office practice, a physician is constantly requested for counsel in matters having a strict relation to morals. Having at heart the welfare of his patients, the doctor will avoid any tendency to religious indifference. Well aware of the fact that every word is carefully heard, remembered, and followed, he shall not spare suggestions motivated by Christian ethics and, whenever the opportunity presents itself, he shall not hesitate to express sound religious ideas, or to make declarations of faith or to exhort his patients to a faithful practice of religion and good works. Every physician knows, by personal experience, that often a strong faith and trust in God, a reconciliation with an enemy, the relinquishing of a bad habit, the practice of prayer and patience, acceptance of sickness—all play an important role in restoring peace of mind and in improving the physical condition of many sick persons.

Whether a physician practices liberal medicine or some form of socialized medicine, as is the case in many parts of the world, he is bound by the same norms of morality. *Riz.*

EXAMINATION, PRENUPTIAL,

CANONICAL. Canon 1020 imposes on the pastor, who has the right to assist at the marriage, the duty of conducting a careful investigation of impediments to a licit and especially a valid marriage celebration. For this purpose the pastor must interrogate both the bride and the groom separately, to determine the presence of any impediment which would prevent them from contracting marriage; he must ask whether both, especially the woman, are giving their consent freely; finally, he must ascertain if they are sufficiently instructed in Catholic doctrine. The same canon prescribed that the Ordinary lay down particular norms for such an examination of the spouses.

In order to make such an examination more effective and uniform, the Sacred Congregation of the Sacraments on June 20, 1941, sent to all Ordinaries the instruction *Sacrosanctum* (AAS, 33 [1941], 297 ff.). In this instruction the Sacred Congregation proposed a questionnaire for the prenuptial investigation, which both spouses are to sign, after they swear by an oath that they have answered all questions truthfully. The questionnaire, thus completed, must be filed with the acts of the marriage.

In this questionnaire, each party is asked whether he is completely free from compulsion concerning the union which he is about to contract. If there is suspicion to the contrary, the pastor must make further investigations, since even the responses which the spouse makes to the interrogation might themselves be the result of force. They are asked if they understand and accept the obligations of marriage, concerning the procreation of children, conjugal fidelity and the indissolubility of the bond; if there is any condition attached to their consent. Where a spouse intends to place a condition to his consent, the priest shall consult the Ordinary and await his instructions. The aim of the instruction as well as of the canon is to make as rare as possible the celebration of marriages that would be invalid because of impediments or a defect of consent. A secondary purpose is to have more substantial evidence in nullity cases, inasmuch as one of the spouses, who has sworn to bring to the marriage a completely valid consent, might later allege in an ecclesiastical tribunal that he can prove that he did not give a valid consent. *Bar.*

MEDICAL. The aim of a prenuptial medical examination is to establish if a person is physically and mentally fit to contract marriage. It is advisable for future spouses to submit to a complete examination by a prudent doctor who will be able to determine the possible existence of malformations or diseases, suggest appropriate therapeutic aid, counsel for or against marriage. The examining physician would then issue a prenuptial certificate for the other spouse containing his conclusions. The examination would discover defects of the genital regions whose importance is not recognized at times by those who are so affected. These might prove an obstacle to the union or be grounds for nullity. It would reveal in time pelvic abnormalities which a woman ought to know about in order that she might have sufficient opportunity to reflect on the advisability of marriage, insofar as deliveries might be dystocial (Caesarian section, etc.). Early diagnosis and timely treatment could be effected in the case of contagious diseases, such as syphilis, gonorrhea, and pulmonary tuberculosis, which would seriously disturb family life with more or less serious repercussions on future offspring. Finally, a prenuptial examination would bring to light psychopathic difficulties and psychoses whose presence should be brought to the attention of the other spouse, along with accurate information on the transmissibility of the morbid disease to the children. The medical certificate could also be of help to parents of the couple in consideration of the advisability of such a marriage. The prenuptial examination, therefore, with its relative certificate has many evident advantages. Even St. Thomas More, the famous English humanist, statesman and martyr, in his well-known *Utopia*, advocated the advisability of each of the spouses submitting before marriage to a form of physical examination. The purpose of such an examination, according to More, was to dissuade from marriage the infirm and the deformed while promoting unions between healthy young people in order to procreate healthier generations.

Defenders of the so-called *negative eugenics* (*see* Selection, Natural) maintain that the human race can better itself only if the State employs repressive means to eliminate unhealthy stock (or dysgenic persons). Among the principal means proposed by this group is an obligatory prenuptial examination with medical certificates, and consequent legal prohibition of marriage for those judged to be dysgenic persons. The Church, as we shall see later, opposes such obligation and legal prohibition.

MORALITY. The common teaching of moralists denies that man has a strict obligation to submit to a prenuptial medical examination or that he has the right to demand from the other party a certificate of such an examination. The reason seems to be based on the fact that examples of unsuitability for marriage due to unknown causes are too rare to warrant even the discussion of a general obligation. Marriage is something so common that a man can carry out its obligations, at least in ordinary cases, without the need of a physician. But if one of the parties has serious and positive doubts about his own health, and the doubt involves a disease that would render his marriage illicit, without any other means of resolving the doubt, then an obligation arises to submit to a prenuptial examination and show a medical certificate to the other party. (This obligation is incumbent also on the parents of both parties before they give their consent.)

While the question of a medical certificate is not a matter of strict moral obligation, the practice has much to recommend it. As noted before, the medical certificate is a very effective safeguard against marriages which would prove harmful not only for the spouses themselves but also for the respective families and the common good. For this reason many competent moralists, doctors, and

especially eugenists are striving to promote the general practice of a prenuptial physical examination. Not all of them, however, express their views with the reserve called for by the extremely delicate nature of the subject. The advocates of prenuptial examinations can be divided into three groups. (a) Some demand a civil law imposing upon all future spouses the obligation of a physical examination by a competent doctor; if the medical report is unfavorable, the marriage is to be forbidden. (b) Others want the civil law to impose upon all the intended spouses only the obligation of obtaining and exchanging medical certificates. After this, it is left to the contracting parties or parents to decide what should be done. (c) Advocates of the third opinion do not demand any legal certificates. Theirs is a program of instructions, recommendations, etc., through which they hope to introduce on a wide scale the custom of voluntary prenuptial examinations and mutual exchange of medical certificates.

The first opinion is rejected by Catholics since the prohibition of marriage for reasons of health, especially eugenic reasons, is contrary to the natural law. A Catholic doctor, therefore, while remaining faithful to the norms of professional secrecy (*q.v.*), cannot, except within the limits of licit material cooperation (*q.v.*), conduct prenuptial health examinations nor release medical certificates demanded by the civil authorities for the purpose of forbidding marriage to dysgenic persons. The second opinion does not contain anything contrary to the law of God. However, it also is to be rejected, since the interference of the civil authority in matters so intimate and delicate cannot be accepted by the people. The law would not be observed and other social and moral harm might result. A law of that nature would cause damages that could be greater and more serious than the advantages to be gained. The third position not only seems devoid of any harmful effects but it offers the prospect of significant benefits.

In marriage, man strives for a happy family life, not only for himself but also, if he is unselfish, for the person whom he weds and the children that may come. But such happiness is based to a large extent on the state of health of all the members of the family, which, in turn, depends on the physical fitness of the spouses. From all this it follows that the purpose of a prenuptial examination and a mutual exchange of certificates is to prevent one spouse from causing harm and suffering, often cruel, to the other. The practice likewise serves to avoid harm to society and to promote human happiness even beyond the limits of strict obligation.

Eugenists, doctors, and others will be performing beneficial work if they co-operate in making the voluntary prenuptial examination more widely accepted. In order not go beyond its scope, the examination must be done by a reputable doctor who is competent, honest, and sincere. On these physicians naturally falls the obligation of making the prenuptial examination properly and of giving a certificate which contains the whole truth and nothing but the truth. This certificate is to be given to the interested party, who always reserves the right to withdraw from the marriage if he does not wish to show the other party or the other party's parents the certificate which he received. It goes without saying that the certificate ought to be obtained long before the date of the wedding. *Ben.*

EXAMINER. The term *examiner* commonly refers to a person who subjects a candidate to an examination to obtain proof of his capabilities. Included also in this definition is the notion of *judge*, insofar as the examiner must make a judgment concerning the scientific or technical ability of the candidate undergoing the examination. He who assumes the office of examiner must possess certain fundamental qualifications, such as sufficient knowledge of the matter in this particular examination, equity, and impartiality of judgment in grading the answers given by the candidate.

As *interrogator* or *investigator*, the examiner cannot and must not neglect three essential elements which are present in every examination: (a) he must take into consideration the particular psychological condition of the candidate; (b) he must diligently act as examiner and judge; (c) he must keep in mind the essential purpose of the examination, that is, whether it concerns an annual examination, or promotion to a higher position, or a diploma which will open the way to social position, etc. (*see* Judge, Justice).

As a *judge*, therefore, the examiner must possess, among other qualifications, justice and equity towards all, rectitude, disinterestedness, firmness in rejecting the unworthy, especially if it is an office concerning public or social welfare. An examiner would be guilty of sin, at times serious, and would be obliged to restitution for damages caused, if he violated justice by approving unworthy and unsuitable candidates; more so, if he were to accept bribes. For the juridical prescriptions of Canon Law, cf. Canon 130, par. 2, where it is stated that the granting of a benefice to unworthy candidates is invalid. Also cf. Canons 130, par. 1; 459; 996–997. The Council of Trent declared that examiners are to judge not only the knowledge of the candidates but also the other qualities required in them by the natural and ecclesiastical laws (Sess. VII, cap. 3, *De refor.*) *Tar.*

EXAMINER, SYNODAL. Synodal examiners are priests chosen from the diocesan and provincial clergy or, in case of necessity, from extra-diocesan clergy whose function is to conduct the examinations prescribed by the Code for conferral of parishes (Can. 389, par. 1), admission to sacred orders, granting of faculties for confessions and preaching (Can. 389, par. 2), as well as for the completion of certain processes of an administrative nature, as indicated in Canons 2147–2185 (Can. 389, par. 1). In the case of admission to sacred orders, and granting of faculties for hearing confessions and preaching, the Bishop is not obliged to use their services. Synodal examiners are appointed in the synod (*q.v.*), after their names have been pro-

EXAMPLE [479] EXCARDINATION

posed by the Bishop (Can. 385, par. 1). Their number cannot be less than four nor more than twelve (Can. 385, par. 2). Their office ceases after a period of ten years or with the convocation of a new synod (Can. 387, par. 1). The examiners appointed by the Bishop (de consilio capituli cathedralis) as substitutes for those who have died or who, for some other reason, no longer hold the office, are called pro-synodal examiners. The latter continue in office throughout the unexpired term of those whom they succeeded (Can. 387, par. 2). Also called pro-synodal examiners are those who have been appointed by the Bishop of a diocese, when no synod is held (Can. 386). A synodal examiner cannot be removed by the Bishop except for a grave and just cause, and always with the counsel of the Cathedral Chapter (Can. 388). The same person can be synodal examiner and parish consultor (q.v.) but not in the same case (Can. 390). Fel.

EXAMPLE. Man is by nature inclined to follow or imitate the conduct of his neighbor. This propensity exists to a stronger degree in persons of less strength of character without the ability to form their own conduct and decisions, such as the immature, the uneducated, or simple people. For this reason, our conduct as seen by others comes to be an example for good or evil, without our intention or awareness, automatically. The force of such example is greater, the more loved or esteemed is the person who gives it, whether because of office, or position, or vocation in life, as superiors, parents, teachers, priests, guardians, etc.

To give bad example is a sin against charity, termed *scandal*. To give good example is an act of charity toward one's neighbor. Whether it is of obligation or counsel depends upon circumstances. For those who hold a duty of educating others, it becomes of obligation. Parents, teachers, priests, and others entrusted with the care of souls cannot properly inculcate character when they fail to show good personal example. Good ex-

ample in public may be a matter of obligation, if it is known that others, because of spiritual weakness, are fearful and ashamed of doing good unless they see someone perform good deeds openly. A sincere Christian does not limit himself to good example only under obligation; a person who openly lives a Christian life can do great good for his country, Church, community, and especially for other immortal souls, if he casts aside false shame, fear of derision, insults, irreligion or indifference in others and, motivated instead with a love of God and neighbor, strives to give good example everywhere and always. *Ben.*

EXAMPLE OF THE SAINTS. See Spiritual Reading.

EXCARDINATION. Excardination is the absolute and perpetual severance of a cleric from the diocese in which he was incardinated. Excardination *per se* refers only to diocesan secular clergy. Excardination is called *formal* when the purpose of the act is the severance of the cleric from his diocese; *virtual* when the excardination of the cleric from his diocese comes as a result, for instance, of the conferral upon him of a residential benefice in another diocese (Can. 114), or of perpetual religious profession, simple or solemn (Can. 115).

Formal excardination is valid if the Bishop gives the cleric a letter of perpetual and absolute severance from his diocese in order that he may be incardinated in another diocese (Can. 112). The Vicar-General cannot give this letter without a mandate; nor can the Vicar Capitular grant this letter until a year after the vacancy of the episcopal see and with the consent of the Chapter (Can. 113). For virtual excardination the cleric requires the written consent of his own Bishop to accept a residential benefice in another diocese or the written permission of his own Bishop to leave the diocese permanently (Can. 114).

Excardination is licit if there is a just cause on the part of the Bishop (Can. 216), for example, necessity or utility for the diocese in which he is to be incardinated, the benefit to the diocese from which the cleric is being excardinated; on the part of the cleric, if there are reasons of health, studies, or the desire for religious life. In the latter case, however, the cleric in major orders must inform his Bishop (Can. 542, n. 2), who can oppose this step as long as he judges that the departure of the cleric would result in grave detriment to souls, which cannot be avoided in any other way. When the cleric passes to another diocese, his own Bishop must in conscience give a report on the life, character, and virtues of the excardinated cleric (Can. 117, n. 2). The excardination takes effect at the moment of incardination in the other diocese (Can. 116). *Toc.*

EXCEPTION. *See* Plaintiff, Trial, Tribunal, Defendant.

EXCHANGE. Exchange is the fundamental operation through which goods are mutually transferred in society, according to the criterion of equal worth, or equivalency. Originally, exchange was practiced under the form of *barter* (exchange of certain goods for other goods). The inconveniences connected with barter (principally those caused by the difficulty of finding relative needs and of establishing equivalency between interchanged goods) were eliminated when money was invented and used as a measure of value (*see* Money). Thus, from a personal factor, exchange became a social factor.

The economists of old, as far back as Aristotle, used to distinguish two kinds of value: the *value of use* (attributed to an individual's goods according to his need) and the *value of exchange* (determined by and resulting from the needs or desires of all members of society). The former could be called individual or subjective value; the latter, social or objective. The direct use of an individually produced item gives way to its exchange, only through *profit* that one may make by personally producing the same item. Sometimes the value of exchange is called *price,* but the two are not exactly

the same thing; value is an established *ratio* between two things; price is a relation in which one of the two terms is always money (good serving as measure of value).

The classic writers on economics have enunciated a formula that explains the problems concerning value, stating that value of exchange varies in a direct ratio with the demand and in inverse ratio with the supply. The defect of this formula is that it seeks to achieve mathematical precision. In practice, it is not true that a reduction to one *half* of the quantity of a certain available merchandise would result in a redoubling of the price. It is evident that if an increase of the demand causes the price to rise, the rising of the price will cause a decrease in the demand. An exact balance can never be attained; in fact, often demand and supply are independent of the quantity of goods available, but this is determined by a variety of factors (intensive production, estimate based on hope of future conditions).

Exchange as a fundamental operation for the circulation of economic goods presupposes an area of development, as well as roads and means of communication between the various areas of production, means of transportation, meeting places, called *markets* (*see* Market), brokers between producer and consumer (merchants, traders), means for their measurement (weights and measures) and, finally, *money* and credit titles.

With respect to a given territory, markets are national or foreign (international). *International exchange,* between nations and continents, involves many problems of an economic and political character (monetary problems, conventions and agreements, commercial treaties, problems of production, competition, and protection of national productions, etc.). The ratio between the value of imports and exports in a given country constitutes what is usually called *balance of trade.* Actually, a true balance of trade is never achieved. When a country's imports exceed exports, this results in an indebtedness toward another country which must be paid in gold. In a normal regime of freedom of exchange, more or less limited by conventions and agreements, the monetary factors of international exchange are reflected upon the entire economic system.

During and after the last two wars, the *clearing* system (a kind of clearing-house for trade between two countries) was adopted with the intention of eliminating the export of money and the use of gold, but the system proved detrimental to the development of international trade.

In order to ascertain whether the foreign trade of a country is in good condition or not, it is not sufficient to examine the *trade-balance* (imports and exports), but it is also necessary to check the balance of *debts and credits*. The two are not the same thing. Besides the credits arising from export and debts deriving from import, there may also be others, appropriately called invisible exports and imports. Some of these are: *freight* of exported goods, *interests* of capital employed abroad, purchases made by foreign tourists, *remittances* of emigrants, bank *commissions* for international operations, *sales* of ships, etc. Such debts or credits may well bring about a trade-balance or even a condition of exports over imports. Concerning commercial and customs policies, *see* Free Trade; Exchange, Foreign.

MORAL OBSERVATIONS. Throughout history the influence of religion has been great in the field of exchange. The temple of Delphus was the principal meeting place for tradesmen, the mint, deposit bank, and archives of debts and records. The influence exercised by Christianity has been great, for from the closed economy of the barbaric periods, in which monasteries became centers of production and exchange through pilgrimages, improvement of transportation, and a large outward movement brought about by the Crusades, Christianity brought unity to European exchanges and a resumption of intercontinental trade.

Moral theology made a considerable contribution to the development of the circulation of goods, by its application of *justice* to problems in exchange, through the doctrine of *usus proprius* and *usus communis*, and the notion of just price (*justum pretium*) (*see* Price, Just). This just price is not the result of the particular judgment of the two persons exchanging goods, but of an *aestimatio communis*. Such a norm of commutative justice was, in turn, subordinated to distributive justice, not by altering the interests of the different classes or exploiting the weaker multitudes through prices, but by respecting legal and common justice, without bringing harm to the whole society and the State by monopolistic activities or advance purchase of sale committments. By subordinating the whole economical life to lofty ethical-juridical norms, moral theology ennobled the eminently social function of exchange in such a way that an equitable distribution and use of goods resulted from it for the attainment of a higher spiritual progress. *Bau.*

EXCHANGE (FOREIGN). Foreign exchange is the mechanism by which commercial investment and other transactions between countries are settled. While foreign exchange is usually defined as comprehending all those transactions concerned with the purchase and sale of money for foreign countries, it is more accurately described as the transferral of credits or debits through their banks by individuals or corporations in one country, through credits or debits in other countries on the books of correspondent or branch banks through which transmission is arranged.

Transmission of foreign exchange may take the form of cable transfer, commercial or bankers' bills of exchange, international postal money orders, mail payments, travelers' cheques and travelers' letters of credit. While foreign exchange, not foreign money, is normally used in the settlement of international transactions, yet each foreign exchange instrument mentioned above is convertible into the currency of the country in which it is made.

Thus, foreign exchange is a method

of effecting payments in a foreign country without the actual shipment of gold, although the latter is practically the only universally acceptable medium for the settlement of balances arising among countries in their trade relationships. Gold shipments, however, are reduced to the minimum, since a nation's exports are largely offset by its imports, and vice versa. Foreign exchange, closely akin to domestic exchange, is arranged through the maintenance of reciprocal balances by banks engaging in the business. The bank of one country (U.S.A.) keeps a balance with its correspondent bank in another country (England) in the currency of the correspondent country.

Foreign exchange differs from domestic exchange in another important respect. It is impossible for an individual or corporation in the U.S.A., for instance, to settle a foreign obligation by drawing a check on a local bank in favor of a foreign seller. This is true because the check is payable only in the currency of the United States, and the credit of the individual is not sufficiently well known. Bank credit, especially of the larger institutions in the East, however, is established internationally; so that the exchange facilities of these banks must be called upon to execute transfers of credits and debits abroad.

Exchange may be accumulated, sold, or reduced. Foreign exchange rates are subject to constant fluctuation, but unless a nation is unable to settle its trade balances in gold, free and unrestricted commercial rates can fluctuate only within certain defined limits above or below the mint par of exchange. This differential or range of variation, the upper limit of which is called the "gold export point" and the lower limit the "gold import point," is determined itself by a variable, consisting of the sum of the following costs: (1) loss of interest on the gold while in ocean transit; (2) ocean freight charges; (3) marine and war insurance charges; (4) packing and unpacking charges; (5) bullion broker's profit; and (6) terminal haulage charges.

Market quotations will not rise appreciably above the mint par of exchange, since the foreign exchange banks, seeing an opportunity for profit, will sell bills of exchange against shipments of gold. Conversely, if market quotations fall too far below the mint par, these banks will buy bills of exchange and order the importation of gold. Within the normal limit imposed by the gold points as explained above, foreign exchange rates will constantly fluctuate. Such fluctuations are caused by the variations in the supply and demand of bills in the foreign exchange market. Foreign shipping is somewhat seasonal in character and, whenever exports largely exceed imports, an equally larger volume of bills is offered for sale than there are orders to buy. In absorbing the excess of bills to be purchased, rates tend to fall. Conversely, when imports exceed exports, the demand for bills is greater than the amount offered for sale, and the rates tend to rise.

This normal limitation in the fluctuation of exchange rates is predicated upon the free movement of gold among countries. If, for any reason, a nation declares an embargo upon gold exports; if the gold reserves are so depleted that it can no longer settle its trade balances in gold; if it sets up exchange control mechanisms designed to restrict the free fluctuation of exchange—then the normal limitations of rate variation are no longer valid, and market rates will be arbitrarily fixed by exchange controls. In recent decades of unsettled budgets, adverse balances of trade, loss of gold and exchange difficulties, many nations have imposed regulations to stop free trading in currencies, exchange, or bullion or to restrict such trading as to prevent or modify fluctuations in exchange. The international monetary fund is designed, among other purposes, to bring stability to exchange rates and prevent international races in currency depreciation. (From *Encyclopedia of Banking and Finance*, Glenn G. Munn (5th ed.), Cambridge, Mass., 1949.)

MORAL PROBLEMS CONCERNING EXCHANGE CONTROLS. The control of foreign exchange gives rise to delicate moral problems. Undoubtedly, such control is lawful if dictated by the common good and practiced within the limits thereof. However, the lawfulness of the methods used in exercising control do raise serious problems. Usually, control measures consist in a request to sell to the government at a fixed rate all foreign currency or other precious assets that one may possess or expect to possess; in the prohibition to export or import national currency; and in the public allocation of disposable currency for specific purposes. Such regulations, in general, seem to be also morally binding, provided that the purchase price of foreign currency is right. In a system of controlled currency, the basic price of foreign money depends upon the price of commodities constituting the object of reciprocal trade, both within and without the country, that is, on the relative purchasing power of the money estimated according to the commodities constituting the object of international trade. If the compulsory exchange rate is approximately equivalent to the price just indicated, it does not seem morally permissible to evade the obligation of selling the foreign currency at the established rate, even though one were able to obtain a higher exchange rate in clandestine markets given to speculation. On the contrary, evasion of control measures cannot be altogether condemned. *Mai.–Yan.*

EXCITABILITY. *See* Cerebral Function, Impulse, Inhibition, Hysteria, Anger.

EXCLAUSTRATION. Exclaustration (Latin, *extra*—outside; *claustrum*—cloister) is an indult granted for just causes by ecclesiastical authority to a religious, permitting him to live temporarily outside the religious institute without the obligation of the common life, and without direct dependence upon the superiors, retaining, however, the obligations of the vows and affiliation with his religious community (Can. 639).

In the old canonical terminology, instead of exclaustration, the term *temporary secularization* was used to contra-

distinguish this from permanent secularization (*q.v.*). The word *exclaustration* was used only for the permission to remain outside the religious house in the sense of Canon 606, par. 2, of the present Code. This canon states that no religious can live outside a religious house without permission of the Holy See for a period of more than six months, except by reason of studies. While perpetual profession incorporates the professed religious in a definitive and permanent manner to the religious state and to a determined religious community, obliging him to the common life (594), nevertheless, from the very beginnings of the religious life, circumstances of time and persons have required superiors to grant and, in fact, at times, to command the temporary withdrawal of a religious from the community for reasons of health, public good, harmony, etc. Such a separation was granted in each case by the superiors. No need was felt for special, uniform legislation on this matter until the seventeenth-eighteenth centuries. The widespread suppression of religious institutes in past centuries necessitated the direct intervention of the Holy See and, in this way, the present legislation gradually evolved.

PRESENT LAW. In the present Code, exclaustration can be granted only by the Holy See in cases of religious communities of pontifical right; in the case of diocesan religious organizations, such an indult may be granted by the local Ordinary (Can. 638). The causes must be grave and, in the present practice of the Holy See, exclaustration will not be granted, if the petition of the religious is not accompanied by the recommendation of the major superior or the procurator general. Exclaustration leaves the religious bound to his vows and to the other obligations of his community, but only insofar as they can be reasonably kept in his life outside the religious house. In practice, therefore, only the obligations arising from the vow of chastity remain completely unchanged. The vow of poverty, though it still binds the religious by the very nature of the vow, will have to undergo, in accordance with the dispositions of superiors, certain modifications regarding the free administration and use of goods. This includes goods ordinarily belonging to the religious himself, in the case of a professed religious with simple vows, as well as possessions ordinarily belonging to the community. The prescription of Canon 594, par. 2, remains unchanged, that is, whatever the religious will earn through his own industry belongs completely to the community. The vow of obedience remains in force; but besides his own religious superiors, the exclaustrated religious is bound by the same vow to obey the Ordinary of the place who received him. It is the present common practice of the Holy See not to grant the indult of exclaustration to religious priests before they have found a benevolent Ordinary who will accept them into his diocese, where they can celebrate Mass and exercise their priestly ministry (Can. 639). Since the exclaustrated religious remains a religious, he cannot be incardinated into any diocese. He continues to enjoy the spiritual privileges of his religious community, but he does not have either active or passive voice for the whole period of his exclaustration. Furthermore, he is not allowed to wear the habit proper to his community (Can. 639). Once the period granted has expired, the religious is bound to return to his community or else request an extension of the rescript. *Mand.*

EXCOMMUNICATION. *See* Censure, Reservation of Sins; Remedies; Penal.

EXECUTOR. *See* Rescript; Testament.

EXECUTION OF RESCRIPTS. *See* Rescript.

EXEMPTION, CANONICAL. In Canon Law, exemption (Latin, *eximere*—to remove) generally denotes a particular juridical disposition by which, through a stable privilege, a legal or physical person is withdrawn from the power of the immediate superior on whom he would ordinarily depend and is put directly under the authority of the superior who

grants the exemption. The Code of Canon Law speaks of exemption in many places, treating it both from the point of view of the individual from whose authority one is removed and from the point of view of the individual who is removed from that authority. For example, it speaks of removal from the power of the local Ordinary, the Metropolitan, or the pastor. Then, there are canons that deal with the exemption of Cardinals, Abbots *nullius*, Bishops, titulars of churches, etc.

The term *exemption*, however, is more frequently used to indicate the removal of religious communities from the authority of the local Ordinaries. Taken in this sense, exemption may be defined as the complexus of faculties or liberties granted by the Holy See to religious communities, concerning juridical relations or actions which ordinarily would fall within the competency of local Ordinaries but which, instead, by reason of the exemption, are reserved to the Holy See, or given to the internal superiors of the religious communities.

In the present Code of Canon Law, when we speak of exemption under this aspect, we consider it insofar as it is common to all religious communities, although its application to individual religious groups may vary considerably. To illustrate the minimum exemption from the local Ordinary, which every religious community enjoys today, we may mention Canon 494, which forbids the bishop to suppress a religious community; Canon 1308, which states that the Holy See is the legislator in the matter of religious public vows; Canon 501, which excludes every Ordinary from being an internal superior, etc. It could not be otherwise because of the nature of public association proper to religious bodies, as well as the establishment of religious communities in many dioceses while they maintain unity of government; and, above all, in view of the nature of the authority of religious superiors, which carries a more or less lofty degree of importance and publicness. These are the intrinsic reasons in favor of the creation of an exemption enjoyed by religious communities to varying degrees. To these, other historical reasons may be added, such as the influence of Germanic Law, the Feudal System, etc.

Religious exemption in the present-day meaning of the term, is distinguished into an exemption in the strict sense and an exemption in the broad sense. Exemption in the strict sense implies a removal of the religious community from general jurisdiction of the local Ordinary insofar as the relations between religious communities and Ordinaries are generally reserved to the Holy See or to internal superiors. This type of exemption is generally presumed. Instances in which it is restricted are expressly enumerated in the Code (Can. 501). This exemption is enjoyed by those religious communities which are called *exempt*, in the Code of Canon Law either by law, as Orders, or by special privilege, as Congregations (Can. 488, n. 2; 501, par. 1). The other type of exemption, in a broad sense, excludes only in a general way the authority of the local Ordinary in those juridical relations which have to do with internal administration. For other relations, however, the principle of subjection remains unchanged, except when the contrary is expressly stated. This applies to *non-exempt* congregations of simple vows (Can. 488, n. 2; 500, par. 1; 618, par. 1).

A full treatment of the scope of the two exemptions is impossible since many canons of the Code are involved. In broad terms, it can be stated thus: (a) Exemption in the strict sense forbids the local Ordinary from interfering in any way with persons, things, and places belonging to exempt religious communities, except when the contrary is expressly stated in specific instances, as situations dealing with the care of souls in the diocese, or in conflict over public manifestations of worship, etc. However, the actual extent of the exemption, in these exempt religious groups, varies according to the nature of the individual communities. For instance, the fact that a religious body consists of men or the fact that its members are clerics has important bearing on the extent of the exemp-

tion. It is possible to formulate the following gradation among exempt religious communities in order to have a picture of the varying degrees of positive exemption: exempt clerical orders; exempt clerical congregations; exempt orders of men; nuns, subject to the regular superiors of exempt first orders. (b) The extent of exemption in the wide sense is primarily determined on the basis of a fundamental distinction in non-exempt religious communities, namely the distinction between pontifical congregations and diocesan congregations (see Religious Congregations). In the first group, freedom from the local Ordinary in matters of internal administration is practically absolute (Can. 618, 2). Internal administration ordinarily includes the organization, government, acceptance, dismissal, and punishment of members of the religious community. Not excluded are certain external relations which arise from the fact that the religious state, as an integral canonical state, contains the character of the faithful and the cleric existing at the same time in a religious. As a result, many juridical transactions, although not belonging to internal administration in the proper sense of the term, nevertheless have been placed by the legislator within the competency of the internal superior, because of their necessary connection with the same individual religious.

On the other hand, in diocesan religious communities the principle of exemption in matters of internal administration loses its absolute value, in the sense that, though the Ordinary is not the internal superior and generally has no power of command over the members of the community, nevertheless, he cannot be denied the right of vigilance over every activity of the religious community. This is tantamount to supervision over the exercise of authority by the internal superiors. Such is the meaning of Canon 492, par. 2, stating, as it does, that diocesan congregations are completely subject to the local Ordinaries. Even among religious communities enjoying only exemption in the wide sense, the actual extent of their positive exemption depends upon the qualities already mentioned, primarily on the clerical or male character of the community. With this in mind, it is now possible to formulate the following gradation of communities enjoying exemption in the wide sense: (1) Among pontifical religious communities—clerical congregations; congregations of men; congregations of women (sisters); nuns subject to the Ordinary or to the Holy See. (2) Among diocesan congregations — clerical congregations; congregations of men; congregations of women (sisters). In these congregations, it must be added that their expansion into other dioceses has an important effect, since by its very nature the expansion will result in a decrease of authority of the individual Ordinaries in each diocese. *Mand.*

LEGAL. Authors are not consistent in the meaning which they attach to this expression. Some use it as the equivalent of *excusing cause* (*q.v.*); others, however, make a distinction, in which they consider excusing cause as the circumstance which, though suspending the obligation of observing the law, leaves us subject to it, and they reserve the term *exemption* to that circumstance which removes us from the dominion of the law. This second interpretation is more exact and, therefore, preferable. In other words, exemption is restricted to cases in which a subject removes himself from the law by transferring himself from a territory or class in which the law is in force to a territory or class in which the law does not oblige, even if it does not oblige because of a privilege.

By its very nature, exemption is valid only with regard to positive laws. The determination of its modalities is the task of jurists; to moralists belongs the duty of evaluating the licitness of the act or conduct of one who freely and willingly, for the purpose of not observing the law, manages to obtain exemption from it. It is the common opinion that such an act or conduct is not forbidden. The reason for this opinion is that the law obliges us to observe it as long as we are its subjects; but it does not oblige us to remain its subjects

in order to observe it. Nevertheless, strict law can forbid or render ineffective the transition which brings with it an exemption. If the transition is made ineffective, it is no longer a question of exemption. If it is only forbidden, the transition remains illicit even from the moral point of view, unless it is a question of a law which, because of other considerations, does not oblige in conscience. *Gra.*

EXERCISES OF PIETY. *See* Devotion; Piety.

EXHAUSTION, NERVOUS. *See* Medicine, Psychosomatic; Neurasthenia.

EXHIBITIONISM. *See* Peversion, Sexual.

EXISTENTIALISM. ETHICAL ASPECT. In a general sense, existentialism is entirely dominated by ethics insofar as existence coincides with liberty in act, and expresses precisely the demand for freedom in an individual as opposed to necessity proclaimed by various philosophical systems such as idealism, materialism, positivism, etc. Existentialism is particularly opposed to Hegelian pantheism, which affirmed a necessity in historical evolution as a product of the *world-spirit* (*Weltgeist*). In opposition to the latter, existentialism asserts the unlimited openness (*Offenheit*) of liberty and the essentially individualistic structure of the act of *choice* carried out only in the decision (*Entscheidung*) which everyone must make by himself. Thus, man's existence is not the expression of necessary relations, but is actualized always within the particular *situations* in which each man makes his act of *choice*. Concerning this situation, the decision of choice is not effected through a continuous process but by means of a *leap* (*Sprung*) in which the act of liberty becomes concrete. It opposes Hegelian freedom, which wills itself insofar as it is embodied in the totality of the State as the sole substantial ethical personality "which thinks and knows itself and does that which it knows and insofar as it knows it" (Hegel, *Grundlinien der Philosophie der Rechts*, par. 257, ed. Gans. Berlin, 1840, p. 305 ff.). Existential liberty wills itself insofar as the individual overcomes anguish in which he finds himself engulfed because of his finiteness, and by means of this decision passes into being. In every act of choice, precisely because the will of the individual remains faithful to itself and, therefore, basically chooses itself before all else in the unlimited openness of being, the individual always keeps open the possibility of choice, so that he can ever make a new beginning and a new choice. In existentialism, therefore, liberty and, with it, the complete structure of the moral act, are made to converge in the individual and, for the first time in modern philosophy, the value of the truth and the freedom actuating it is explained in the sense of an ever-open openness. No longer, according to the traditional form of systematic philosophy (especially of rationalism and idealism), is it a system based on the abstract and dialectic universal (Reason, State) enclosed in its absoluteness.

FORMS. Since existentialism represents not so much a definite philosophy as a trend of thought on the orientation of man's existence, the meaning of this existence and, hence, its ethical conception lie in the functions of such ontological perspective. As a basic classification, we can distinguish three forms of existentialism: *atheistic, neutral,* and *religious.*

(a) The most determined exponent of atheistic existentialism is Jean-Paul Sartre (b. 1906). Starting from the principle that "existence precedes essence," Sartre affirms that man "is nothing else than what he makes himself," or, in other words, that man is identified with his existence. The choice *(choix)* of man consists precisely in his receiving his own existence, which is that of "all other" men; in this sense "my" choice involves all of humanity above and beyond the notion of good and evil, since nothing is chosen except what is good, and evil cannot be chosen. (Cf. *L'exis-*

tentialisme est un humanisme, Paris, 1946, p. 25.) The point of departure of the ethics of atheistic existentialism is the famous saying of the *demons* of Dostoevski: "If there is no God, nothing is forbidden," and man remains absolute judge of himself, without encumbrances either of "laws" compelling him, or of "values" in some way justifying his behavior, or of "passions" stimulating him to action. Sartre calls this condition of man "abandonment" *(délaissement),* since man, not having been created by himself and yet being free, finds himself "condemned to being free" *(op. cit.,* p. 37). There is no "general morality" which can indicate that which ought to be done, but in the state of "abandonment to oneself" in which man finds himself, "we always choose our own being." Thus "anguish" and the consequent "desperation" constitute the ontological background of all human action, insofar as the existence of man is shown to be founded on nothing *(op. cit.,* p. 47 ff.). Sartre had planned to come out with a special work on the ethics of existence but as yet he has not fulfilled his promise (Cf. *L'être et le néant,* Paris, 1943, p. 722). At present he is still immersed in the atheism and pan-sexualism which dominate his series of romantic novels, from *Les chemins de la liberté,* and dramas, *Les Mouches, Huis Clos, Morts sans sépulture, Le Diable et le bon Dieu,* etc., to his blasphemous *Saint Genès, comédien et martyr* (Paris, 1952). Other defenders of atheistic morality are Albert Camus and Simone de Beauvoir.

(b) More moderate and restrained in the discussion of the problems of ontology is the German existentialist school, which holds that the problems of morality insert themselves time after time in the very openness of being. In relation to this openness, any sort of rigid and universal law or authority remains, of itself, outside and assumes the character of "violence" *(Gewalt).* For Karl Jaspers (b. 1883) this static nature of moral laws must give way to the "unconditionality of existence" *(Unbedingtheit der Existenz)* which remains, in itself, in its historical manifestation, not by instinct or caprice but in its tendency toward transcendence, since "without a relation to God, all morality becomes dehumanized ("*Ohne Bezug auf Gottist jede Moralitat unmenschlich*"—Cf. *Philosophische Logik*, I, Von der Wahrheit, Munich, 1947, p. 718). But in this conception, God is simply the Absolute that guarantees the actuation of the "kingdom of ends" in this world by means of "rational philosophical faith" (*philosophische Glaube*) as Kant conceived it in his *Die Religion innerhalb der Grenzen der blossen Vernunft*, (1793). In Italy, N. Abbagnano adheres to Jaspers' position of interpreting Kierkegaard's existence by means of a "return to Kant" (Cf. *Esistenzialismo positivo*, Turin, 1948, p. 33). A more cautious position is that of Martin Heidegger (b. 1889), who, at least to the present, has limited himself to the presentation of the analytics of human existence. First of all, he has strongly rejected the atheism ascribed to him by Sartre, stating that human existence or *Dasein*, insofar as presented as a *being-in-the-world (In-der-Welt-sein)*, cannot as yet meet God, nor does it deny God; therefore, there is no question of atheism (Cf. *Brief uber Humanismus*, Bern, 1947, p. 100 ff.). In reality, the problem of God has meaning only through the *presence* of God, and this is found in what Heidegger calls the dimension of the *sacred (das Heilige)*, which, however, remains closed in itself unless the openness of being is illuminated. Moreover, Heidegger states that the divinity constitutes the fourth component, along with the third component, heaven and mortals, of that which forms the *square (Geviert)* of human existence. This is represented as a "remaining before God" (Cf. *Bauen, Wohnen, Denken, Darmstadter Gesprach*, 1951, Darmstadt, 1952, p. 75 ff.; *see also* the conference *Das Ding*, published in the volume: *Gestalt u. Gedanke*, Munich, 1951, p. 128 ff.).

In this light is to be understood also Heidegger's bitter criticism of the "philosophy of values" and the existential interpretation of the expression of Nietzche (which expression, as is known,

goes back to Hegel) that "God is dead" (Cf. Nietzsche's work "*Gott ist tot*," in *Holzwege*, Frankfurt-on-Main, 1950, p. 193 ff.; *see also Brief u. Hum.*, p. 99).

(c) Existential ethics which is clearly based on Christian theism is represented above all by the founder of existentialism, the Danish Sören Kierkegaard (1813–1855). According to the latter, the "ethical stage" constitutes the intermediary sphere of conscience between the aesthetic and the religious stages. Contrary to the affirmation of Kant (categoric imperative), however, this stage does not have a proper autonomy, but is destined to resolve itself either into the aesthetic sphere or into that which is authentically religious.

(1) In fact, the Kantian principle of the *autonomy* of practical reason abolishes all law, on the assumption that the man in A (he who binds) assuredly cannot be more severe than what he is or might desire to be in B (he who is bound). Consequently, to be in earnest, it is necessary that he who binds be greater than the ego itself, that is, must be God. (Cf. *Diary 1850*, X² A 396). In order to be truly free, man must exist *vor Got*. Only God, precisely because He is omnipotent and can give completely, can also create a free nature; that is, one which is independent in its actions (*Diary 1847*, VII A 181). He who does not choose "before God," becomes the prey of finiteness, as a result of which he falls from the original anguish into sin and is abandoned to desperation.

(2) Man saves himself from desperation by *faith* (*Diary 1850*, X² A 493), which offers man *Archimedes' fulcrum*, that is, an absolute basis of salvation which is the Incarnation of Christ. In opposition to Lessing and the whole philosophy of immanence, one has to admit the *insertion of eternity into time* is Christ, who is both man and God, since He arose from the dead and ascended into Heaven. Consequently, the man with faith in Christ can insert his temporal existence into eternal truth. (For the criticism of immanence, see *Briciole di filosofia del 1844* and *Postilla con-*

clusiva non scientifica del 1846. On the Incarnation, see *L'esercizio del Cristianesimo de 1850.* On the function of faith, see *Il concetto dell'angoscia del 1844 e la Malattia mortale del 1849.*)

(3) Faith, however, can effect the insertion in the Absolute only if it becomes the "principle of acts," that is, through the *imitation (Efterfoelgelse)* of Christ. Kierkegaard derived this principle from a noted medieval opusculum and from an appreciation of Catholic asceticism and mysticism. He even found highly suitable the cult of *models,* namely, of the Virgin and of the saints (*Diary 1852,* X⁴ A 521). The so-called *theological existentialism* of Gabriel Marcel (b. 1889) also interprets Christian existence through *faith, fidelity,* and *hope,* but it has not yet clarified the contents of such theological *situations* to distinguish them from similar situations in the sphere of the immediate conscience. Nor has this theological existentialism shown concretely how such situations can be made to fit in with the Incarnation of the Word of Christ. On the contrary, the term *incarnation* is used by Marcel to indicate the condition of the human spirit "bound to the body" (Cf. *Etre et avoir,* Paris, 1935, p. 11 ff.). Closer to orthodox Christian spirituality is German Catholic existentialism, which develops the dialectics of the existentialism of Kierkegaard and ties it to the Newman-Pascal pattern (K. Adam, R. Guardini, Th. Haecker, E. Przywaera, Th. Steinbuechel), and, in the last analysis, to the difficult spirituality of St. Augustine (Cf. P. Wust, *Der Mensch u. die Philosophie,* Regensburg-Muenster, 1947, p. 28 ff., 85 ff.).

Existentialism which asserts the priority of existence over essence must also uphold immorality and anarchy. Nevertheless, it must be said on behalf of existentialism that in its original form it uprooted the foundations of illuministic and idealistic rationalism by vindicating the priority of the act of freedom of the individual in the moral structure of man. But if existentialism is to save itself from falling into a negative or purely neutral phenomenology, it must base the "pos-

sibility of freedom" on a principle which will detach it from historical indifference. This will assure it ultimate success and, in the end, enable it to rescue man from evil. *Fab.*

EXORCISM. Exorcism is a sacramental consisting in an adjuration in which the devil is either commanded to depart from a possessed person or forbidden to harm someone (*see* Devil, Obsession). The power of performing the act of exorcism is conferred in the minor order of exorcist. Nevertheless, the driving out of the devil from a possessed person may be done only by a priest who has the special and express permission of the Ordinary (Can. 1151, par. 1). Private exorcism, however, that is, the private adjuring of the devil from harming someone, may be performed by any priest, and also by a lay person; for example, by the use of the sacramentals or by invoking the name of Jesus. *Fel.*

EXORCIST. See Orders, Holy.

EXPERIMENTATION (ON MAN). Experimentations are surgical operations, injections, administration of medicines, and certain foods whose effects are unknown. These experimentations are resorted to, not because they are the best means for the welfare of a patient, but simply to increase man's knowledge and experience, particularly in the interest of medicine. Experimentation on man may be defined in a general sense as the use of the human body (there is no question here of his natural activities) in the interest of science and experience.

MORALITY. First of all, it is forbidden to perform experimentations on a person without his consent. No man has the right to do what he wants with the body of another. Even if it is certain that the experiment will not cause any harm, the act is evil because it is a violation of the natural right of another. Such a consent is not implicit in the fact that a person entrusts himself to the care of a physician, and allows him to do what he thinks useful. When a patient does this, it is understood from the very nature of the circumstances that he is limiting the permission to acts necessary or useful for his cure. The patient gives the doctor a general permission insofar as he is a doctor, that is, a man whose sole duty is to obtain the cure and welfare of his patient.

The question still remains as to whether a man can give permission to others to use his own body for their experiments and whether in such case the experimenters would be committing an evil by using such a permission. In answer to this question, we must distinquish three possibilities. (a) If it is an experiment in which there is moral certitude, which excludes the probability or serious fear of error, that no harm will come to the man, such experiment is lawful if the results will benefit humanity. (b) If it is an experiment which not only offers no benefit to the physical well-being of the person, but even presents a more or less serious danger of harmful consequences to the body, then such experiment is contrary to the moral law. The reason for the illicitness of such experiment is that it would imply that the human body and, therefore, man himself was a thing ordained for an external good; it would be tantamount to performing evil in order to achieve a good. One who performs an experiment in such circumstances does it *precisely because* he is uncertain, and it is in this uncertainty that the danger lies. Therefore, he *directly* wills a danger that will cause physical harm; this is never licit. (c) The third case concerns experiments useful not only for science in general but also for the person, as when, in the absence of certain means apt for curing or saving the patient, the doctor uses means that may produce either good or harmful results. In this case the doctor will act in accordance with the moral law, if he is guided only by interest in his patient without any concern for the utility which the experiment might have for science. If there is greater hope of saving the patient's life or of curing him with the use of the uncertain means than without them, it is lawful to use those means. *Ben.*

EXPERIMENTS ON THOSE CONDEMNED TO DEATH. Experimentation on those condemned to death is licit only if it is prompted by a very precise scientific purpose, if there is a proportionately grave motive and the experimentation is performed with the express consent of the individual. On the contrary, reasons of humanity and justice preclude such experiments. The individual, though condemned to death in expiation of a crime, does not by this fact lose his human dignity nor his right to respect from others.

If it should happen that, in an experiment authorized for just motives by the proper civil official as a commutation of the death penalty, and so understood with the consent of the individual, a particularly dreadful affliction then should result, this would in no way justify the killing of the individual. By the very fact that he subjected himself to the experiment, the criminal paid his penalty. This would hold if the individual himself requested to be put out of his misery. Instead, every means should be used to lessen his suffering and make his life as comfortable as possible (*see* Euthanasia).

EXPERIMENTS ON INFANTS AND THE DEMENTED. Since in experiments the primary consideration is the free consent of the individual, it is not licit to perform dangerous experiments on persons incapable of valid consent, such as infants and the demented. Such dangerous experiments are illicit even when the irrational individuals are afflicted with a disease that makes a normal life impossible.

EXPERIMENTS ON THE DYING. Similarly, it is illicit to perform on the dying dangerous experiments which might hasten or render more painful the person's death. Nevertheless, for proportionately grave reasons it is morally licit to perform on them harmless and painless experiments in the interest of science, such as the injection of harmless coloring substances, for the purposes of identifying in later studies on the cadaver special morphological structures or definite functional processes.

PSYCHOLOGICAL EXPERIMENTS. Another series of experiments, except for very serious reasons, may not be performed without the authorization of the individual, obtained after he has been made aware of the scope of the intended investigation and of their usual results. We refer to those investigations which, though they cause the individual no physical damage, can harm him psychologically, insofar as the individual undergoing them loses his self-control and lays bare his inclinations, feelings, and ideo-affective life. For, while it is true that the experimenter, besides a scrupulous observance of ethical and religious norms, is bound to professional secrecy, still the individual to be examined might want to refuse to undergo such experimentations as hypnotism or other methods, requiring the use of drugs which remove the checks on conscious inhibition, once he knows what the effects will be. In view of this, the experimenter has the obligation of pointing out these effects beforehand. Absolutely condemned are those experiments which, like psychoanalysis (*q.v.*), produce immoral dreams and fantasies, or, in general, disturb the conscience of the individual because of subtle, scandalous, and persistent sexual investigations.

SURRENDER OF ONE'S BODY UPON PAYMENT. It is unlawful to surrender one's own body for payment in order that it might be the object of dangerous or harmful experimentations. Equally unlawful is it for the experimenter to make such a purchase. Only when such experiments might have a reasonable purpose of great scientific or practical value can they become lawful, provided that the experiments are performed by the use of moral means. In such lawful experiments, the money offered by the scientist and accepted by the subject of the experiment assumes the value of a reasonable compensation for risks knowingly accepted for the primary purpose of a notable common good.

EXPERIMENTS ON HUMAN HYBRIDIZATION. Intrinsically unlawful are experimentations directed to the study of the effects of the crossing of man and animals, whether this is to be accomplished

naturally or through the use of artificial insemination. In the first case, an act which belongs really to the category of sexual perversions rather than to the field of biological investigations, the prohibition obviously flows from the sixth commandment of the Decalogue. In the second case, the prohibition arises from the fact that artificial insemination is intrinsically forbidden, as pointed out in the article on sterility. Not even if the experiment be performed with the use of spermatazoa procured by lawful means can it be approved by the Church, the faithful and vigorous defender of human dignity and of the clear distinction, willed by God, between man and other creatures.

AUTO-EXPERIMENTATION. Scientific achievements are obtained at times by the unselfish sacrifice of victims that are rightly pointed out as heroes to future generations. Among these outstanding benefactors, doctors hold the first place. Those doctors, for the sake of scientific progress and the welfare of the community, did not hesitate to experiment on themselves with new drugs, or the virulence of a microbe, or the effectiveness of a vaccine, etc. Catholic morality on this matter only recently (1952) restated by Pope Pius XII, admits the licitness of such experiments on oneself, as long as there is a concrete possibility of success, a justification proportionate to the risk incurred, and it is not possible to obtain the same result by less dangerous methods. *Riz.*

EXPORTATION. *See* Commerce, International.

EXPOSITION OF THE BLESSED SACRAMENT. *See* Eucharist; Benediction; Forty Hours Devotion.

EXPOSURE OF INFANTS. Etymologically, the word *exposition* (Latin, *exponere*—to put forward, to put out) indicates the act of exposing or abandoning children. Abandonment of children, in the true sense of the term, consists in rejecting them without any concern for their life; in fact, with the frequent intention of killing an infant. Abandonment of infants was practiced in the Greco-Roman world. The infant was generally carried out into remote places, unaccompanied by any precautionary measures for the child's safety, with the result that, as a rule, the infant died. Among the Greeks and Romans there was no relationship between exposed children and illegitimate children, since the absolute nature of the *patria potestas* permitted any infant to be exposed in any manner whatsoever. In the Middle Ages, the exposition of infants meant rather the action by which parents would abandon their offspring to public charity. With the creation and development of special charitable institutions, exposition became a custom of leaving an infant at appropriate hospices. Today a distinction exists between exposition and abandonment. Exposition presumes in the responsible person an intention of providing for the infant help which he himself cannot or does not wish to give. This presumed intention is manifested by the fact that ordinarily unwanted children are left in churches or in the vicinity of foundling hospitals. Abandonment, on the other hand, denotes the desertion of an infant in a manner that indicates the intention of freeing oneself of the child without any concern for its life or death.

Illegitimate and *exposed* are interchangeable terms not by natural, historical, or juridical reasons, although, generally, exposed children are illegitimate offspring. It has been said that moral decadence produces illegitimate children while misfortune produces exposed children. Such a statement does not seem to be completely true, at least as it is expressed. Both conditions are responsible for exposition of infants.

Humanitarian tendencies existed in the Roman world from the beginning of the Empire and led to some degree of organized assistance for infants in the manner permitted by the spirit of the times. These were adopted by Christianity and raised to the heights of charity, in foundling hospitals or institutions where exposed children are taken care of and reared. Since the technical notion of a foundling hospital is the same today as it was at the time of its origin, it is necessary to point out that originally it was not an organized institution, as today, where illegitimate children are taken when their parents do not wish to recognize them, but arose as a place for sheltering infants who had been abandoned either in streets or in the proximity of churches or other places. Through a period of gradual development the modern foundling home was ultimately developed. A certain Zoticus may be given credit as the pioneer of assistance to exposed children, for in a directive of the year 472 by the Emperors Artenius and Zenon to the Prefect Dioscurus, he is mentioned as first founder of orphanages. Orphanages and foundling hospitals are analogous organizations. As early as the year 787, we find in Milan the foundation charter of a foundling hospital in the true sense of the term, a place for infants born of unlawful unions. This institution, therefore, may well be considered the first foundling hospital in the West.

EXPOSITION IN MODERN LAW. Legislation in all countries considers abandonment a crime punishable according to the norms of the code of penal law. Legislative systems based on the Germanic spirit, however, recognize neither foundling hospitals nor foundlings. Behind this non-recognition is a principle aimed at protecting the rights of illegitimate children. Such legal systems, therefore, not only prescribe an investigation directed at discovering the maternity of the child but impose a denunciation of the mother. These same laws also prescribe in all cases a search for the child's father. The laws in the so-called Latin countries give foundlings a special character all their own, namely, that of children of no one. The aim of such legislations is to protect the reputation of the family; for this reason there is no obligation to recognize one's own responsibility in the procreation of an illegitimate child. In these countries, an inquiry into the maternity of the child is permitted only in certain well-defined cases;

determination of paternity is not admitted as a matter of principle.

From a moral point of view, the responsibility for an illegitimate child belongs to both parents (*q.v.*), just as in legitimate procreation, where the duties of both mother and father are on an equal plane. Nevertheless, for reasons of social order, the law may justly limit the fulfillment of those duties in regard to what is fitting or not strictly necessary, and thus sacrifice the rights of the individual for the broader rights of the family and society. This does not mean that an innocent child is being punished, for illegitimacy is not a penalty but a condition of nature. If one considers that the goods of family, such as the paternal name, wealth, and social position are not so much the exclusive property of the parents as they are goods of and for the family, then, strictly speaking, an illegitimate child has no right to them since it lacks family status, as in the case of an illegitimate child born within an already established family, or born of a man or woman already married. In the case of purely natural filiation, however, we do not hesitate to say that the bond of blood in some way takes the place of the family bond, and that, therefore, recognition and inheritance would be warranted. A restriction of the rights of an illegitimate child in comparison with a legitimate child is justified only to the extent that the essential interests of the family demand it. Beyond this, no other discrimination against the illegitimate child must be approved.

For this reason moralists affirm the obligation on the part of parents to raise the child even though illegitimate, regardless of the degree of illegitimacy. Moral theologians consider placement of a child in a foundling hospital as lawful in unusually grave cases, in questions of harm to social and family welfare (adulterine children) or to one's personal welfare or honor. However, the obligation of supporting the child to the best of one's ability remains in full force. *Pal.*

EXPROPRIATION. *See* Property; Socialization.

EXTORTION. Extortion is the act of taking anything from a person by illegal use of fear. Similar to robbery and kidnapping due to the common element of threat and violence, extortion forces an owner to do or to omit doing something against his own interests so that another may obtain a profit. In robbery, the thief, through violence or threats, takes possession of another's property physically, or resorts to violence or threats in order to insure for himself or others either the possession of the thing taken or impunity for his action. Kidnapping is the seizure of a person for the purpose of securing an unjust profit in ransom, with a promise of returning in exchange the person seized. Blackmail is a form of extortion in which a sum of money is demanded with threats to publish embarrassing documents or some other harm.

Extortion is more serious than theft and robbery because it is a lasting harm or sin. It is an aggravated robbery, which changes the moral species of the sin. The gravity of the sin is based primarily on the damage caused to the person on whom the violence was inflicted and on the amount of improper gain derived from it. On these elements must be based a criterion concerning the amount of restitution and reparation to be made. Circumstances surrounding the sin and delict, such as abuse of authority, minor age, violation of secrecy are additional elements on which the gravity of the sin can be evaluated. *See also* Gratuity. *Sir.*

EXTREME UNCTION. Extreme unction is a sacrament in which a Catholic, in danger of death from illness or injury, is anointed with consecrated oil by a priest who offers prayers from the Ritual. The essential elements of extreme unction are: (a) the anointing with olive oil, consecrated for this purpose by the Bishop or by a priest authorized by the Holy See (matter of the sacrament), and (b) the prayers said during the anointing (form) (Can. 945). In the Latin rite, the priest is obliged to anoint the various parts of the body, considered the channels of sin: eyes, ears, nostrils, mouth, hands, and feet. In imminent danger of death, however, one anointing on the forehead is sufficient. When the anointing is multiple, the priest can omit the anointing of the feet for a reasonable cause (Can. 947, par. 1). The sacramental formula is as follows: "Through this holy anointing and His most loving mercy, may the Lord forgive thee whatever faults thou hast committed through sight, hearing, etc. . . . Amen." (Roman Ritual, VI, c. 2, n. 8–9). When extreme unction is administered with one anointing alone, the words are: "Through this holy anointing may the Lord forgive thee whatever faults thou hast committed" (Can. 937).

MINISTER. As Sacred Scripture and Tradition (Epistle of St. James, 5:12–15; Council of Trent, Sess. XIV, *De extr. unct.*, Can. 1–3: Denz. 926–929) point out, the minister of extreme unction is a priest or a bishop. Of its nature, this ministration is reserved to the pastor of the place where the sick person is staying, but he can give permission to another priest; at times this permission can be reasonably presumed (Can. 938). The pastor is bound by justice to administer extreme unction or see that it is given by another priest to those who reasonably seek it within the boundaries of his parish. Other priests are bound by charity to give this sacrament, if the parish priest is not available. In exempt religious communities, the superior has the right of administration, personally or through a substitute, of the sacrament of extreme unction to novices and professed religious as well as those who reside in the house, night and day, as servants, students, invalids, or convalescents (Can. 514, par. 1). The canons in order of dignity or according to statutes have the right to administer extreme unction to the Ordinary (Can. 397, n. 3).

RECIPIENT OF EXTREME UNCTION. Extreme unction can be given only to a Catholic who has attained the use of reason and who is in danger of death by reason of illness, injury, or old age (Can. 940, par. 1), but not, however, to one who, although close to death, for example, a criminal awaiting execution, is still in good physical health. In order to receive extreme unction, it is not necessary that death be imminent or that there be little or no hope of recovery. It is sufficient that the illness be such as to cause apprehension for the life of the patient although recovery may still be probable. In doubt whether a person is really in danger of death, extreme unction may be administered conditionally (Can. 941). During the same dangerous illness, extreme unction may be administered only once (Can. 941, par. 2); it may be repeated, however, if the sick person has recovered somewhat and then relapsed into danger of death.

In addition, the recipient must have the intention, at least implicit or habitual (Can. 943), of receiving extreme unction. This intention is contained in the unretracted desire to die as a good Catholic. Of its nature, extreme unction is a sacrament of the living and, therefore, must be received in the state of grace. Should it happen, however, that the sick person cannot confess his sins, it takes the place of the sacrament of penance, provided that the sick person has at least attrition for his mortal sins (*see* Contrition) and a firm will not to sin again. Strictly speaking, there is no grave obligation to receive the sacrament of extreme unction. If, however, the sick person refuses it through contempt, or is unable to provide effectively for his own salvation in another manner, he is guilty of serious sin.

For the administration of extreme unction to the mentally ill, Sacraments.

EFFECTS. Extreme unction places a sick person in the hands of mercy throughout the duration of the danger. It gives an increase of sanctifying grace and related gifts, as well as the right to receive, as long as the danger continues, special actual graces to bear more patiently the physical sufferings and to resist temptations with greater facility. Extreme unction also gives consolation and strength to the sick, burdened by illness and the consequences of sin. In addition, it remits in whole or in part, according to the disposition of the individual, the temporal punishment due to sin already forgiven. At times, it can also restore the person's bodily health. If the recipient is not in the state of grace, but is unaware of this or unable to confess his sins, the sacrament gives, as has already been stated, sanctifying grace and the connected effects, on the condition that he has at least imperfect contrition for his mortal sins and a firm will not to sin again. If one of these conditions is lacking, the sick person remains for the time being deprived of grace and related effects. If, before the end of the danger, the obstacle (obex) is removed, the effects are produced by the virtue of the sacraments (see Sacrament; Reviviscence of Sacrament).

PRACTICAL OBSERVATIONS. Extreme unction, bestowed on the sick in due time, while they are fully conscious, is a source of great consolation and help to them. A doctor and the relatives have in this connection a very serious responsibility. Moreover, the faithful must rid himself of all unfounded fears concerning reception of a sacrament so beneficial for the soul as well as for the body. Needless to say, extreme unction cannot be administered to those already dead. Since, however, one cannot exclude the possibility of a state of latent life, which in certain cases lasts for some time after the heart and breathing have ceased, the Church, as a loving mother, permits within a short time (½ hour) after death the conditional administration of extreme unction to those who appear dead, and for a longer time (2 or 3 hours) after sudden death. In such cases, there should be no delay in summoning a priest, especially if the person still shows some sign of life. Finally, it should be emphasized that extreme unction does not remit sins, not even in cases where the sick person is unable to confess, unless he has at least imperfect contrition and a firm desire not to sin again. *Man.*

F

FACULTY. The word *faculty* may have various meanings, not only when taken in its general connotation but also as a technico-juridical term. In Canon Law, for instance, it may mean a possibility, a permission, *etc.* In a stricter juridical sense, faculty means an ordinary or delegated power to act validly or licitly from a juridical standpoint, such as the faculty of granting a dispensation, of absolving from ecclesiastical penalties, and the like. In a more strictly canonical sense, however, a faculty has no reference to ordinary power, namely that which is attached to an office (according to Can. 197, par. 1) nor to that which is given by law itself or by custom, but only to a power specifically delegated by a competent ecclesiastical superior: for instance, the power delegated to an ordinary priest to dispense from a matrimonial impediment.

Persons who enjoy ordinary jurisdiction and who are not forbidden by law to delegate others may grant such faculties; also persons enjoying a delegated jurisdiction with power of subdelegation. If this faculty is granted by them for one or more cases, specified with respect to the persons and the matter, it is called *particular*; if it is granted *in perpetuum*, or for an indefinite or a definite period of time (for instance, a *quinquennium*), or for a specified number of cases, with no reference to specified persons, it is called *habitual*.

The better known faculties are the *papal* or *apostolic faculties,* granted by the pope personally or through the Sacred Congregations. Moreover, habitual faculties are also granted to local ordinaries and major superiors of exempt clerical institutes.

Habitual faculties in Canon Law are considered as privileges *praeter ius,* beyond the law and, therefore, they are to be broadly interpreted. With the exception of two cases, namely, when the faculties are given personally to some one for a special reason (*industria personae*) or when the contrary is expressly stated, habitual faculties granted to the ordinaries by the Holy See do not cease when the jurisdiction of the ordinary ceases (at the death of the bishop or the major superior), but they pass to his successor (vicar capitular, or succeeding bishop); moreover, the faculties given to the ordinary belong also to the vicar general, and in mission lands to the so-called vicar delegate (S.C.de Prop. Fide, 8 December, 1919, in *AAS* 12 [1920] 120). The granting of a faculty also carries with it the other powers necessary for the use of the faculty; thus, in the faculty of granting dispensations there is also included the power to absolve from eventual ecclesiastical penalties. This absolution, however, has simply the effect of making valid the granting of the dispensation, but it does not eliminate the effects of the ecclesiastical penalty.

In the thirteenth century the Holy See granted certain faculties, first of all, to Apostolic Legates, and since the fourteenth century they have been granted particularly to missionaries (Dominicans, Franciscans, *etc.*). These indults, intended mainly for the many needs arising in mission territories and the so-called diaspora, were of various types; at times, they gave rise to confusion and abuses. This prompted Pope Urban VIII to establish, in 1633, a special Congregation of Cardinals whose task it was to draw up one or more precise formulae. Five formulae were thus compiled and later approved by Pope Urban VIII; in the following centuries others were added to them. In the beginning, faculties were granted through papal bulls or apostolic briefs, later, by the Holy Office and, still later, by the Sacred Congregation for the Propagation of the Faith, as well as by other Congregations.

Since the promulgation of the Code of Canon Law the apostolic faculties have again been revised. Among the faculties which the Holy See is in the habit of granting are the following: (a) Faculties by the *Sacred Congregation for the Propagation of the Faith* to ordinaries scattered in mission lands, approved in 1919 and in force since January 1, 1920. Until 1940, there were three formulae, each divided into major and minor formulae, but since January 1, 1941, there is but a single formula divided into a major formula for ordinaries with episcopal character, and a minor formula for all other ordinaries. These faculties are granted for ten years at a time and concern the administration of the sacraments, absolution from ecclesiastical penalties, *etc.* (b) *The quinquennial faculties of the Sacred Consistorial Congregation* for ordinaries subject neither to the Sacred Congregation of Propaganda Fide, nor to the Sacred Congregation for the Oriental Church. After the promulgation of the Code of Canon Law, the Congregation abrogated these faculties because they were considered included in the concessions contained in the Code itself, but upon petitions of the bishops they were introduced again, first in 1922, with distinct formulae for each Congregation, then again in 1923 (see AAS 15 [1923] 193 & 194) they were granted by the Sacred Consistorial Congregation on a single sheet, as before, but containing also the faculties ordinarily granted by the other Congregations, namely, the Holy Office, the Sacred Congregation of the Sacraments, of the Council, of Religious, of Rites and the Sacred Penitentiary Apostolic. Presently, there are four distinct formulae for these faculties, according to the various groups of countries. Furthermore, in the last decades, the Sacred Consistorial Congregation has granted special faculties to Latin America (AAS 41 [1949] 189–191). (c) *Faculties for Nuncios, Internuncios and Apostolic Delegates,* which, however, are not the same for all. (d) *Faculties of the Sacred Penitentiary* for the internal forum (the so-called *Pagella*) for ordinaries and confessors, chiefly confessors belonging to religious institutes. *Led.*

FACULTY (Authorization). Faculty is a provision, existing both in canonical and civil laws, by which the public authority increases the capacity of a subject to whom it is granted (*authorization* is the term more commonly used by the civil authority). A faculty, however, is not intended to be the source of a new right or power but rather a means by which the subject is permitted to exercise a right or power which, strictly speaking, he already possesses, but which the law permits him to exercise only in a specific case in which no serious danger is involved.

Faculty differs from dispensation (*q.v.*) inasmuch as the latter is a real and true deviation from the law, as it gives a right which the law does not recognize, removing a legal prohibition or exempting from an obligation established by the law. The distinction between faculty and dispensation is not always clear in practice, and often there is confusion even insofar as the doctrine is concerned, particularly the older doctrine.

The granting or refusal of a faculty is always left to the discretion of the authorities, who may grant or deny it depending on whether or not the act to be authorized by the faculty is considered proper and convenient.

An act which cannot be lawfully performed without a faculty is juridically unlawful if performed without having obtained the necessary faculty. Even from the moral point of view, the act is, at least objectively, almost always unlawful, except when the law which subordinates the act to the obtaining of the faculty is a merely penal law (*mere poenalis*). Whether the moral unlawfulness is serious or not depends primarily on the degree or nature of the obligation to request the faculty (the obligation varies according to the matter, but usually is serious), and also on the nature of the act performed. (*See,* for instance, what was said about retaining or reading forbidden books [*q.v.*] without due permission).

If the act subordinated to obtaining a faculty is a juridical matter, it is as a rule invalid if performed without the faculty, and the invalidity can, according to the case, assume the form of nullity or of annullability. In the first case the act remains null even if, later, the faculty is granted; in the second case, on the other hand, the faculty granted later validates the act (although by its very nature the obtaining of the faculty should precede the putting into effect of the act subordinated to it). The first possibility is more frequent in Canon Law; the second, on the other hand, is ordinary (but with a number of exceptions) in civil law. In the Code of Canon Law various acts are subject to the obtaining of a faculty: for example, the readmission into the ecclesiastical state of clerics who were demoted to the lay state (cf. Can. 212).

For other acts subject to the obtaining of a faculty *see* Property, Ecclesiastical (the administration of); Forbidden Books; Matrimony (form of); Jurisdiction, Ecclesiastical. *Cip.*

FAITH. Faith, the first of the three theological virtues and foundation of all other supernatural virtues, is, in a theological sense, the virtue by which we firmly believe the truths revealed by God, not because of intrinsic evidence, but because of God's authority proposing them through the Church (Vatican Council, Sess. 3, ch. 3). Therefore, besides the intellectual assent to truth, the concurrence of the will (*pius credulitatis affectus*) compelling the intellect to this assent for reasons other than objective evidence is an essential element of the act of faith. As an act of free will, faith belongs to the moral field (Vatican Council Sess. 3, *de fide*, can. 5).

Faith is necessary by a necessity of means; that is, without faith (even inculpably) it is absolutely impossible to work out one's eternal salvation (Heb. 11:6). This is true for all, without distinction, insofar as the habit of faith infused in the soul with sanctifying grace is concerned. The act of supernatural faith, on the other hand, is necessary for all those who have reached the age of reason, as the beginning of their salvation and foundation and root of all justification (Mark 16:16; Rom. 1:17; 3:26; Heb. 11:6; Council of Trent, Sess. 6, ch. 8; Vatican Council, Sess. 3, ch. 3). The obligation to elicit an act of faith is binding not only at the beginning of one's use of reason, but also during one's life, at least by necessity of precept. This is particularly so at the time when a more earnest practice of Christian virtue is required (as in danger of death, serious temptations, reception of the sacraments); an act of faith *in actu exercito,* that is, implied in other acts of virtue (prayer, *etc.*), is sufficient.

Faith must extend to all revealed truths, at least implicitly; that is, by an act of faith we include them all, even if not individually known. "I believe all the truths the Holy Catholic Church believes and teaches." Furthermore, by necessity of precept, every Christian is bound to know and explicitly believe at least the essential truths of Christian religion, the Apostles' Creed, the sacraments, grace, the Ten Commandments, and those which are necessary for good Christian living, such as the requirements for the proper reception of the sacraments, the principal prayers, and the like. It is debated among theologians which truths are to be known and explicitly believed by a necessity of means. It is certain that all must believe in the existence of God, author of the supernatural order, rewarder of good and avenger of evil (Heb. 11:6; 22nd proposition condemned by Innocent XI, Denz., 1172; Decree of the Holy Office, March 4, 1697); it is open to question whether or not this necessity extends to the doctrine concerning the Most Holy Trinity and the Incarnation. The negative opinion finds no small support in the great difficulty with which the holders of the opposite opinion are faced in explaining the possibility of attaining eternal salvation by those numberless heathens who, through no fault of their own, never had any knowledge of the Gospel. *Dam.*

FAITH (good, bad, dubious). See Possession in good faith; Possession in bad faith; Possession in dubious faith; Prescription.

FAITHFULNESS (Loyalty). Faithfulness implies a relationship to another. In this sense one speaks of loyalty to one's friends, work, duty; also to God, country, *etc.* In this general sense, faithfulness may apply to that which is due to another (obligatory) and that which is not due to him (non-obligatory). In a more specific sense, faithfulness is the virtue by which one is inclined to give another what is his due by reason of a promise made to him. When a given word gives rise to an obligation of strict justice, the obligation of faithfulness is contained therein as being one with it; so that if one violates a contract or bilateral agreement, the violation of justice also involves unfaithfulness.

Faithfulness and the sin of unfaithfulness appear in their proper perspective in the case in which one has an obligation arising from a given word without involving an obligation of justice. One such case is that of the so-called gratuitous promise or simple word. The promise, of course, gives rise to the obligation of being faithful to one's given word. This duty toward one's neighbor implies no obligation of justice because it does not concern a thing pertaining or due to another. What is due to him is, not the object of our gratuitous promise (a promised gift), but that we act in accordance with our given word, that we be honest, faithful. Faithfulness so understood is quite similar to veracity (*q.v.*), which is the virtue requiring us to behave according to our promises and our given word. Failure to keep a simple promise is generally a venial sin, but in some specific circumstances the sin may

also be mortal, if the consequences are such as to have caused sizeable damage to another. The earnestness by which one keeps every promise, word, and appointment, even in the little things of his daily life, amounts to faithfulness. To fall short or to be habitually negligent in this regard, or so to conduct oneself that one's neighbor can never depend on one's given word, is a real lack of kindness and respect toward him. Such a habit, which is rather general among some particular groups of people, makes social living very difficult and unpleasant, and causes great loss of time and energy. *Ben.*

FAITHLESSNESS (absence of faith). See Infidelity.

FAKIRISM. See Metapsychosis.

FALSE DENUNCIATION. See Denunciation, Forgery.

FALSEHOOD. See Lie.

FALSITY. See Forgery.

FAMILY. The family consists of a man and a woman living in a permanent matrimonial union with, generally, children as the natural fruit of such a union. The constitutive elements of the family are two: (a) absolute freedom of the spouses in making their choice; (b) permanency of the union, as required by its very nature. The primary end of the family is the procreation and education of offspring, which makes the family the fundamental condition for the physical, moral, social, and economic existence of human society; the family is the fundamental unit of society. As a natural society charged with the task of providing its members with the most important goods of life, it is not only the primary unit but also the pattern of all other societies, which it antedates. Polygamy (*q.v.*), polyandry (*q.v.*), and the like, are deviations or aberrations from normal and natural family life.

In the last few decades attempts have been made, with the aid of fervid imaginations, to reconstruct a historical evolution of the family. These have been efforts to prove that, in its origin, the family institution lacked all its essential elements. Until the beginning of the last century no sociologist had called into question the monogamous character of the family as being at the base of the evolution of society. The traditional doctrine was opposed by Bachofen (in *Das Mutterrecht*), who held to the theory that there were three stages in the evolution of the family: (a) inordinate sexual promiscuity: (b) agriculture, devised and practised by the woman, which paved the way for orderly sexual relations, and eventual assertion of the rights of the mother (matriarchate); (c) patriarchate, the last stage of the evolution of the family. With the aid of ethnological material, this theory was elaborated by Lewis H. Morgan, while Lilienfeld, Lubbock, Letourneau and others endeavored to popularize it. The theorists of socialism, Marx, Engels (*Der Ursprung der F., des Privateigentums u. der Socialismus*), Bebel (*Die Frau u. der Sozialismus*), spread it among the masses. At no time was there lacking a critical opposition to these groundless structures (C. N. Stareke, E. Westermack, E. Grosse, *etc.*); many other ethnologists (H. Spencer Tylor, Fr. Ratzl, H. Schatz, *etc.*) never accepted them.

A hard blow, however, was struck at the evolutionistic theory in the past few decades by the discovery of new, abundant, and authoritative material and also by more scrupulous investigations conducted on sound principles of historical critique. In his valuable work *Die Stellung der Pigmaeenvolker in der Entwicklungsgeschichte des Menschen* (1910), W. Schmidt proved that among Pygmies, belonging to the most ancient primitive culture, marriage is monogamous. Newer investigations by Wundt, W. H. Rivers, R. H. Lowie, Ankermann, W. Koppers, *etc.*, confirmed monogamy as the family's primary form.

Monogamy, then, together with a permanent bond between spouses, was the system prevailing among all primitive peoples. Spouses had full freedom in the choice of their mate, children were welcome and their training was the mother's duty. In successive phases of civilization, due to various causes, there appeared sexual debauchery, polygamy, and the establishment of the *patria potestas* (matriarchate is not a phase of this evolution). The Founder of Christianity restored *monogamy* and indissolubility to the family. "From the beginning it was not so" (Matt. 19:8). In the history of mankind no words have had consequences as important as these; they brought monogamy back into Western culture, and gave Christian civilization an intrinsic superiority over all other civilizations; matrimony was raised to the dignity of a sacrament; the protection of the child, before and after birth, was strengthened in a positive way.

All existing provisions for the protection of the family are Christian-inspired. All anti-Christian doctrines and attitures unfailingly become also anti-family doctrines and attitudes. All errors which stemmed from the Renaissance and the Reformation tended toward a steady breaking down of the family until the advent of Bolshevism, which treats matrimony as a mere contract, dissoluble at the simple request of one of the parties.

From a study of the comparative history of culture it is possible to conclude that the family, or domestic society, is beyond any doubt the society which antedates all other societies. The family, therefore, has rights and duties independent of the state, as pontifical documents have incessantly stated. These rights extend to all the essential ends of the family, primarily to the preservation and education of children, and also to the liberty of providing all other goods necessary for daily life. The education of children belongs to the family; the state's function is only subsidiary to that of the parents. (Cf. Pope Pius XII, Address to the National Congress of the Italian Catholic Union of High School Teachers, September 4, 1949.) State control of schools is, then, an abuse against the primary rights of the family (*see* Schools, Lay). In general, any interference by the state in the family sphere must be kept down to the minimum.

The function of the state toward the family consists in providing favorable conditions for its existence and development as a fundamental unit of society. "It is indeed wise statesmanship to protect the family institution by suitable laws through which its fundamental prerogatives are properly guaranteed" (Pius XI, Letter to the 1926 Italian Social Week). Appropriate civil laws and institutions must guarantee a just wage (*q.v.*) to the worker, or a family wage (*q.v.*) sufficient to satisfy all immediate and future needs of the family, so that mothers and young boys and girls may not be required to go to work.

Every family should be enabled to own a modest home in a healthy environment; its health should be protected by adequate hygienic provisions by greater protection against unemployment, tuberculosis, alcoholism (*q.v.*), venereal diseases (*q.v.*), etc. It is also necessary to protect the sanctity of the family against immorality, prostitution, obscene literature, the spread of divorce (*q.v.*), the practice of abortion (*q.v.*), acknowledging in an effective way the beneficent and indispensable influence of religion on matrimony and the family. Not to be overlooked is the need of assistance in the form of easy loans to young married men and women, relief from taxes in proportion to the number of children, and the official recognition of the importance of the family. In short, every possible benefit must be provided for the family, on which the future of society's cultural, political, and economic progress so largely depends. *Per.*

FAMILY ALLOWANCE. *See* Wage, Living.

FANTASY. Fantasy (from the Greek *phantasia*) as a philosophical term was first used by Aristotle to define the faculty of recreating mentally the data of sensation in the absence of the objects that had caused them. This is still the current meaning of the term. From the seventeenth century on, however, it has been used to mean also aesthetic concepts; thus according to Vico, for instance, fantasy is not only the motive of art, but of the whole first phase of human civilization; Croce identifies fantasy with pure aesthetic intuition.

In the Middle Ages the Greek term was translated *imaginatio* (imagination), but today imagination is principally a psychological term. Maintaining the distinction of meanings for the two terms, as favored by a good number of modern scholars, it may be said that fantasy is considered as the aesthetic elaboration of images, while this character is usually denied to imagination, which follows the practical elements in the reproduction or new association or creation of images. This distinction, however, is rather too fine and is not accepted by everyone. Summing up, we may define fantasy as the faculty (sensitive and internal) by which absent things are represented through their images (which are ordinarily called mental).

The images of objects and facts which constitute our experience may be presented to our mind in two distinct ways: as reminiscences of certain specific representations, or as new combinations without strict relation to reality, in which case we speak of imagination or fantasy. Between memory and imagination, however, there is no total difference of content, because the imagination always makes use of elements of our experience, *i.e.*, of reminiscences, while the memory (*q.v.*) never gives a faithful reproduction of the past, and the reminiscences which remain in it are completed by new representations which are a product of fantasy.

The imagination plays a very important role in our psychological life and there is no activity of the human mind in which it does not enter in some degree: from the extravagances of the dream to the creation of an artist, from the formulation of a hypothesis to the solution of a problem or the invention of a mechanism, the imagination is always at work. It constitutes the creative activity which prevents the human mind from becoming stagnant and the slave of habits.

In the main, imagination may present itself under the following three aspects: (a) disassociated from other psychological activities, without being controlled by censure, nor directed to a specific end (to be found in dreams and day-dreaming, which is a passive surrender to the free play of fantasy); (b) connected with and supported by other psychological activities for the purpose of attaining a specific end (as in the case of philosophical and scientific speculations); (c) directed to an end all of its own, with no reference to other ends extraneous to it (as in artistic creations).

The imagination has always played an enormous role in the minds of children and of primitive people; as a matter of fact, one of the fundamental characters in a child's mentality is the lack of a precise differentiation between memory and imagination, between reality and fancy, so that the child in his first years of life (usually until five years) is in the habit of believing as real what he has simply imagined, and he often thinks he has lived what he simply dreamed.

In the field of psychopathology, an excessively fervid imagination is generally observed in persons suffering from excitatory conditions, while the opposite is observed in oligophrenic, sluggish personalities and, generally, in cases of psychological torpor. Qualitative alterations (deformations) of the imagination are found principally in prattlers (senile insane, hystericals, etc.).

In the realm of fantasy, two main moral problems ordinarily arise. One concerns the control of a morbid imagination, the other the dependability of certain individuals having exuberant fantasies. Concerning the first problem, the use of supernatural means (prayer, the sacraments, etc.) and the diverting of the mind to other objects can be very effective remedies. But material activities (ergotherapy) and engaging and tiring physical labor (see Psychoneurosis, Psy-

chotherapy) can aid even more in acquiring control of a morbid imagination.

Concerning those with excessively prolific fantasies, one must accept always with the greatest caution and the broadest reservation accounts and testimonies given by them, especially when the topic interests them personally and contains emotional elements (see also Memory). For the training of fantasy see the following article. *Riz.*

FANTASY (training of). The knowledge of the effects which fantasy exercises on practical life, either through the senses or through the will, is of special interest to moral theologians. Each image tends to its actuation; and the more vivid and richer with particulars, the more forcefully will it tend to it. This is particularly true in cases of sexual or criminal acts, especially if fomented by a spirit of revenge. Hence, it is morally dangerous to feed the mind and entertain images of immoral or criminal scenes, while on the other hand one's moral life will greatly benefit by good and inspiring images.

These considerations are particularly important for those engaged in the education of the young and those in the entertainment industry. It is a known fact that the imagination exercises greater power on the young and the uneducated than it does on the adult and the learned. *Gra.*

F.A.O. (Food and Agriculture Organization). *See* United Nations.

FARMER, SELF-EMPLOYED. Self-employed farmers are those who directly cultivate their own land (*direct proprietors*), or those who, on their own initiative and responsibility, till land owned by another, to whom they pay annual rent (*tenant farmers*).

Self-employed farmers are considered autonomous (independent) or not, according as the acreage they cultivate is or is not sufficient to employ the services of an average farm family through the year. As a rule, autonomous or independent farmers make a modest but comfortable living, and on the whole they are law-abiding, conservative people who adhere to tradition in every sphere. On the other hand, the lot of non-autonomous farmers is frequently one of a struggling existence.

In the more advanced regions of the world during the past century, the tendency of agriculture, unlike industry, has been toward a growing number of independent farms, conducted and managed as family enterprises. This accounts for the low percentage of family disruption in the agricultural world; in fact, among farmers the opposite is frequently verified, that is, consolidation of the family, with a tendency toward preserving and developing the concept of common effort or labor. *Pav.*

FARM HAND. *See* Labor, Proletariat.

FASHION. In moral theology, fashion is considered an occasion of sin (*see* Occasionist); hence, it is not condemned outright. According to Catholic moral teaching, women are permitted, within reasonable boundaries, to dress in a manner in keeping with the times and in accord with the general customs of the place, and their condition in life. But the manner of dressing must at no time be such as to stimulate man's concupiscence. Thus, a woman is guilty of sin if she follows an immodest or altogether indecent fashion, even if only out of levity and vanity (*see* Luxury, Ornaments, Feminine).

Since the manner of dressing belongs to a secondary category of instinctive decency, one must take into consideration many circumstances of time, place, and person, when assessing which type of dress is indecent or constitutes an occasion of sin. *Fel.*

FATHER. One who has begotten a child, is a father or a male parent. In the language of all ancient peoples, the term *father* is referred not only to the person from whom one received life, but also to a teacher, doctor, protector, benefactor, and the like. In ancient times, the head of the *gens* was called *pater*

(father); the senators, i.e., the assembly of lords, originally the heads of the *gentes*, or *patricians*, were called *patres*, meaning the class of lords as opposed to plebeians. The title of father was also given to ancient divinities and to leaders in ancient legend, as *pater Aeneas*. In primitive times, when there was no other society except the family, the father was supreme (*dominus*) in his own house, the sole owner of children and domestics (slaves). His authority was not limited by civil law, but only by the natural law, by his fatherly love, and by his interest in preserving his offspring. Ancient Roman law, for example, recognized in the head of the house (*paterfamilias*) the most rigorous authority ever recorded in history, although the purely Roman concept of authority of a father excluded the idea of *dominium* over his children, who in ancient Latin were called *liberi* (free). The rights of a father in his personal relations with his children consisted principally in an unlimited right to correct and punish them, and to dispose of them as he pleased—even to the extent of transferring them to another (D. 48, 8, 2; D. 37, 12, 5).

CIVIL DISPOSITIONS. In the civil codes of all nations the obligations of a father are contained in the concept of paternal authority (*patria potestas*), understood as the sum total of the rights and duties of parents over their children, especially regarding education.

In the fulfillment of duty, a father has the power to act with respect to his children; this faculty is not subjective, but a *potestas* or authority which implies the exercise of a superior will placed at the service of a superior interest, as a right proper to *officium* or duty. In respect to the children the *patria potestas* means authority; in external circumstances there exists a right for the father, that is, a right to his office and its exercise. According to Civil Law, a father's duty towards his children embraces two specific obligations: (a) *Maintenance*. This grave duty carries a penal sanction; it is considered a crime for a father not to support his children. Support is moral and economic assistance. Lack of proper care in illness, abandonment of children, and a general lack of interest are the material element of a father's crime against his children.

(b) *Education.* This must be taken in the widest sense of the word. To guarantee the proper formation of the child, civil law obliges the father to live with his children and to watch over them. This implies the normal obligation for the father to keep the children with him. A father, who without just reason leaves the home, expels one of his children, or neglects to get them back if they left the home, is liable to the penalties of the law. Paternal authority (*patria potestas*) also gives the father the right to represent his children and to administer their possessions if they are minors.

Moral duties toward the children. Since the father is the head of the family (Ephes. 5:22–32), he holds an eminent, moral position of responsibility before the Divine Law, his conscience, and the children themselves. The duties of a father may be summed up as follows:

(a) Duties concerning the physical well-being of his children. A father must protect, and preserve life, a gift of God, which belongs to God as a right and gives glory to Him. A father must respect the essential subordination of means to end, established by God, in the material order proper to matrimony and generation. This subordination makes the use of matrimony with a deliberate exclusion of procreation sinful. Any act contrary to the purpose of marriage, as ordained by God, is always and under all circumstances unlawful. Life must be communicated in a holy manner, that is, by a well-ordered and holy life—sanctified by God's grace and by a sincere love of the family.

(b) Duties concerning the mental well-being of the children. The father must be the first teacher of his children in the practice of Christian virtue. The most beautiful exhortations and the most weighty counsels would be of little avail coming from a father whose behavior is at variance with his exhortations and counsels. It is a grave duty of a father to exercise vigilant care concerning his chil-

dren's friendships, reading matter, conversations, indecent pictures, shows, and the like.

(c) Duties to train the will, by sincere, sound, and effective means. A father's authority is doomed to failure if its exercise is wanting either by excess or by defect. . . . In the training of his children, a father must be guided by the principle of the dignity of the human person (without anger, brutality, violence), discernment, firmness, self-control, justice, and gentleness.

(d) Duties concerning grace. Since a father is the priest of the *ecclesia domestica* (domestic sanctuary), he must strive to have God with him always, in order that he may give Him to the children. A father must not forget that, primarily, the children are God's and bear His image in their souls; hence the specific obligations of religious training, prayers, good example. These obligations are summed up in the old saying: "The children dance to the rhythm of the song which their parents have sung."

Moral duties towards wife and children. Concerning the obligations of a father toward his wife and the administration of property, *see* Husband and Wife (goods of), Family.

Since the father is the head of the family, he also has duties toward servants and dependents (*See* Parent, Servant). The father, or master, must never forget that the servants have given up one of the most precious gifts, i.e., their personal liberty. This ought to prompt him to use toward them understanding, gentleness, kindness, justice, and charity. Thus, he shall (a) order them to do only what is just and honest; (b) teach them to do what they do not know; (c) bear with their faults; (d) provide for them not only adequate food and rest, but other comforts as well; (e) the father, or master, must not be too exacting—nor shall he command in a haughty manner—or, worse still, use vulgar or unbecoming language; (f) he shall trust them and insist that his children treat them with greatest respect. The master shall give his servants some free time, every day, especially on Sundays and Holy Days, making it possible for them to attend to their religious obligations. He shall supervise by advising, helping, and consoling them, especially if they are young, and impress them by his good example and honesty. (*See also,* Education, Parents, Mother, Paternal Authority, Piety, School).

FATS. See Abstinence and Fasting.

FAVORITISM. *Favoritism* is a term derived from *favor* or *grace*, taken as a proof of benevolence or protection for, and of commendation of, some particular person. The term *favoritism* is of modern origin; the concept, however, is as old as humanity itself, being the equivalent of the ancient expression *"acceptance of persons"* (cf. II Reg. 19, 7: Eccl. 20:24). By extension we call favoritism that action by which one, through devious and dishonest means, succeeds in getting into the good graces of a person (superior or subject) from whom he expects physical or moral protection. To be exact, a dishonest quest for favors becomes favoritism when the other party accedes to it. Favoritism which remains within the limits of benevolence is good and moral if the motive is lawful and honest. Unfortunately, favoritism as acceptance of persons has become an almost incurable plague in all strata of society. Favoritism may be defined as an act by which one person is preferred over another for a cause other than honest (cf. Van Espen, *Jus Eccl.,* II p., vol. 3k, ch. 1, n.1). Consequently, in its strictest juridical and moral sense, favoritism is an injustice, because of a deliberate disorder it causes in society and in human relations (cf. S. *Theol.* II–II, q. 63, a.1). Moral theologians treat the various forms of favoritism when dealing with the different kinds of cooperation.

Favoritism may be a sin, more or less serious, against distributive justice if the following two conditions are present: (a) the goods to be distributed, insofar as their distribution among the claimants is concerned, belong in some way to all of them; (b) in distributing them, consideration is given to a particular condition of the person (relationship, recommendation, gifts) rather than to justice.

Favoritism occurs more frequently in the following cases: (a) in the conferral of offices, commissions, benefices, *etc.*; (b) in the appointment of a person to an office, either civil or ecclesiastical; (c) in the distribution of burdens or tasks; (d) in the public bestowal of honors, esteem, and respect.

The Code of Canon Law contains very grave presciptions against favoritism (cf. Cann. 153, 459, 232, 267, *etc*). Some modern penal codes ordinarily consider favoritism only under the aspect of cooperation in crime, and as an unethical act. *Tar.*

FEAR. Fear is a passion, a virtue, and a gift of the Holy Ghost.

As a *passion,* fear is disturbance or anxiety created in one's mind by an impending evil which he desires to avoid. In this sense, moralists look upon it as an impediment against voluntary acts (*q.v.*).

According to the influence which an evil may exercise on one's mind, fear may be very grave, and slight. Fear is *very grave* if it inhibits the power of reasoning; it is *grave* if it so obscures one's mind and disturbs one's will that he cannot easily escape an impending grave evil; fear is *slight* if such effects are not produced to any perceptible degree.

This is the psychological scale of fear used by moralists. When these notions of fear are transferred into the juridical field, under the guise of the same words, they acquire a different meaning; fear is explained no longer from the point of view of the reality of the psychological disturbance but of the cause producing it. Accordingly, fear is called slight if the evil feared is improbable or of a trifling entity; grave, if the impending evil is such as to upset a serious and courageous man, such as death, *etc.*

This transposition of the estimative criterion reflects the external and social requirements of the juridical system. From the same juridical aspect, it has some importance in the distinction of fear according to whether it proceeds *from a cause intrinsic* to the subject, as fear of dying of natural sickness, or *from a cause* which is *extrinsic* to him, as fear of dying by assassination. Also the distinction into *just* or *unjust* fear, depending on whether the person causing the extrinsic fear is justified in so doing or not. All these considerations and distinctions do not have a direct bearing on fear considered from the psychological and moral point of view, that is, exclusively as a voluntary act which the subject places under the pressure of fear. This voluntary character is nullified by a very grave fear, diminished by a grave fear, and unaffected by a slight fear.

MORAL COROLLARIES. If an objectively sinful act is performed out of fear, its subjective imputability is non-existent under very grave fear; it is diminished by grave fear, but remains unaltered by slight fear. It is to be observed, however, that in the second hypothesis (grave fear) the juridical consideration could interfere with the moral: the gravity of the impending evil could become an excusing cause from the observance of a positive law. In such a case, the subject is free from sin, not by reason of the internal disturbance, but because of the external, grave inconvenience or hardship.

As a virtue and gift of the Holy Ghost, fear is said to be the beginning of wisdom. It may be fear of God or fear of sin; its object is either the punishment promised and inflicted by God for sin, or sin itself as an offense to God. In the first case it is called *servile* fear; in the second, *filial* fear, a salutary fear, numbered among the gifts of the Holy Ghost. Servile fear is good and virtuous but inferior to filial fear; it may become evil if it were to exclude in a positive manner all fear of offending God, which would mean continued attachment to sin. For fear concerning marriage, *see* Consent, Matrimonial. *Gra.*

FEAST DAY. *See* Sanctification of Holy Day.

FEASTS, MOVABLE. *See* Liturgical Year.

FECUNDATION. *See* Reproduction, Sterility.

FEMINISM. Feminism (from the French word *féminisme*) refers to all the theories, controversies, and debates expounded by women in behalf of woman's equality with man in the social and political fields and, implicitly, in behalf of her emancipation. Much credit for the emancipation of woman goes to Christianity, particularly insofar as her moral equality is concerned. Feminism, as understood today, however, is a typically modern phenomenon and not always of Christian inspiration.

It goes back to the French Revolution; its charter is in the *Déclaration des droits de la femme* (Declaration of Women's Rights) which Olympus de Gowegs presented before the French Constituent Assembly in 1791. In 1792 the feminist movement was also started in England with the publication of Mary Wollstonecraft's *Vindication of the Rights of the Women*, demanding equal education for all, coeducation, *etc.* In the same year a similar stand was taken by Theodore von Hippel in Germany. Today there is no field of activity—commercial, industrial, cultural, political, parliamentary—in which women are not represented. Womanhood has reached a very high degree of emancipation in the leading nations of the world, but it is not too far behind in the other nations. To promote a greater emancipation of woman and relieve her, so they say, of all burdens, attempts are being made in some countries to abolish the family altogether.

There is no denying that through this movement of emancipation certain advantages have been gained for women. But has the overall condition of woman actually improved? Many doubt it. Out of egotistical aims (economic and military strength), certain governments ignore the specific character proper to the female sex and the close coordination of the two sexes. In view of the general conditions of society, it may be that the present juridico-social position of womanhood will benefit the community; however, no attempt should be spared to restore womanhood to the dignity of its high mission as queen of domestic society (cf. Pius XII, Allocution of October 21, 1945, AAS 37 (1945), 288 ff.). *Pal.*

FERIA (ferial day). In ecclesiastical and liturgical usage ferial days are weekdays or non-feast days. In the ancient Christian calendar, the term *feria* with the addition of *secunda, tertia, quarta, quinta, sexta,* was used to indicate the days of the week purged of any pagan connotation; thus Monday was called *feria secunda,* Tuesday *feria tertia, etc.*

Dominica (dies), the day of the Lord, was called *feria prima;* the last feria (day) of the week, on the other hand, retained, even among Christians, the Hebrew name: *sabbatum,* Sabbath, from *Shabba't.* Perhaps the name feria, which properly means *feast day* or *holiday,* in the beginning was given to those days of the week on which the Eucharistic celebration was held. Such use is first found in Tertullian (*De jejun.,* 14), who speaks about *feria quarta* and *feria sexta* as of liturgical days; but it could also be considered as a literal translation of the Hebrew classification of days of the week: *prima sabbati,* which literally means the *first day after the rest* (Sabbath-rest), *secunda sabbati, etc.*

Ferial days (*dies feriati*—vacations of the court) in ecclesiastical language are days of the year on which no judicial acts may be conducted. Such days are *ordinary* (holydays of obligation and the last three days of Holy Week; Can. 1939) and *extraordinary,* that is, declared such by the lawful authority by reason of particular events (Can. 1638, par. 1). Judicial acts performed on such days are unlawful unless required by charity or the public good (Can. 1639). *Cig.*

FERVOR. Fervor consists in a keen desire to love God and, consequently, to do anything to which one is moved by love of God, even during periods of spiritual aridity and amid severest trials. An ever-increasing readiness and diligence in the fulfilment of one's duties and in doing good, a great purity of intention, an ever-increasing care in avoiding venial sins and voluntary imperfections, are integrating elements of the state of fervor.

In particular, a fervent person is very diligent in attending to the little things, which play such an important role in one's life; he endeavors to know and to do that which pleases God, even if it requires sacrifice; he is very attentive to the inspirations of grace; he dispels any trifling thought, and frequently raises his mind to God; he is prompt in his spiritual exercises; he practices internal and external mortification; he embraces and carries his cross without complaint, yes, even with joy; he examines his conscience with diligence, generously trying to overcome his defects; he strives to be an apostle by word and deed, and even more by example, prayer, and suffering.

There are many degrees of fervor; perfection, of course, requires a high degree of fervor. He who has attained perfection, in fact, is thoroughly intent on God, to whom he refuses nothing, constantly endeavoring to glorify Him in the highest possible measure.

Fervor is a source of great merit: it also gives deep peace of soul and fills the heart with joy, even amid severest trials. *Man.*

FETICIDE. Feticide, which differs from abortion (*q.v.*) is the direct killing of the fetus by means of an *embryotomical operation* performed for the purpose of effecting the delivery of a fetus not otherwise deliverable, either because of serious defects of the pelvis or of particular conditions surrounding a gemelliparous pregnancy, or because of the large size of the fetus or a part of it.

The so-called demolishing operations (called also *reducing interventions,* because they are intended to reduce the fetal size and mass) are always allowed on a dead fetus if it cannot be drawn out by an easier method, or if it would otherwise cause harm to the mother. Reduction in size of a living fetus is equivalent to feticide and is as immoral as abortion (*q.v.*). God's Commandment, "Thou shalt not kill," applies here in all its force. Catholic moral doctrine strictly forbids the killing of the child even if done to save the mother, and even if a "wait-and-see" policy would endanger the life of both the fetus and the mother.

This strict doctrine seems, at first, to be unjust; it would seem that the killing of the fetus in the case of a dilemma might be more in the line of a painful but necessary choice of the lesser of two unavoidable evils. But the fact is that the very choice of the lesser of two evils is immoral, because the direct killing of an innocent person is not permitted under any circumstances. It is indeed difficult to see why such a principle should not be valid in the case of an infant when by universal consent it is admitted in all other cases. No one would justify the action of a survivor of a shipwreck if he killed another survivor to ward off starvation.

We may add that absolute respect for the life of the yet unborn, if accepted and practiced by all and everywhere, would benefit humanity, for it would promote greater and more systematic care for pregnant women everywhere. The moral precept forbidding feticide must be credited with having stimulated the scientific progress in obstetrics which has made not only possible but far less dangerous than before obstetrical interventions directed at saving both the mother and the child. It may suffice to recall the *caesarean section* (consisting in the drawing out of the fetus through a breach opened in the abdominal and uterine walls), which, with the aid of antibiotics, has become so effective and safe as to have made any recourse to feticide technically unnecessary.

Since obstetrical knowledge is a specialized field, it should be a practical norm for the attending physician or the midwife to check a pregnant woman periodically during her pregnancy with regard to any possible anomaly of the mother or of the fetus which might hinder a normal delivery; in which case the patient should be admitted to the hospital to make certain that the birth of the child shall occur with the least possible risk for the mother. Unfortunately, it is not a rare occurrence, even today, at least in some more backward countries or regions, for a physician to be faced with the problem of feticide, either because of ignorance and negligence on the part of some people, or of deplorable environmental contingencies and attitudes, or because of some sudden adverse circumstance which would have been avoided if proper measures had been taken at an appropriate time.

Under such circumstances, irrespective of the environment or the condition of the woman in confinement, the physician, conscious of the absolute unlawfulness of the direct killing of the fetus, shall summon his scientific skill and personal experience to assure a delivery that will be safe both for the child and the mother. Only when he is certain that the fetus is no longer alive may he make recourse to an embryotomical intervention to relieve the mother without delay. On the other hand, if the mother dies first, he shall promptly effect a caesarean section (a relatively easy intervention on a corpse) if there is any probability at all that the fetus may still be alive. Furthermore, the physician shall always attend to or provide for a prompt baptism of the fetus (*See* Sacraments; Physician; Baptism).

Feticide seems to give rise to the most serious conflict between Catholic moral principles on one hand, and certain medico-doctrinal principles and medico-surgical practices on the other. In fact, while moral law unconditionally forbids embryotomy on a living fetus, some authors of books on obstetrics nevertheless suggest such an operation in certain specific cases and with due precaution, inasmuch as they consider unjustified the position whereby one must wait for the death of the fetus before intervening. By so doing, they say, the sentence is already passed on the fetus and any further delay cannot be but detrimental to the mother, whose life may be endangered by the interposed delay.

Often their position is strengthened by the attitude and even the request of the woman's relatives, who at times go as far as threatening the physician with physical damage and denunciation unless he perform embryotomy on the living fetus and remove without delay all danger of death for the expectant mother. In the face of such circumstances no one can fail to appreciate the perplexity arising in a doctor's conscience. This state of uneasiness is bound to disturb the spiritual serenity which is an indispensable premise to a proper and intelligent action by the physician (cf. Pius XII, Address to Surgeons, May 22, 1948).

In order to prevent the occurrence of such conflicts, a Catholic physician (a) shall make clear, beforehand, to the close relatives of the expectant mother that, regardless of the circumstances surrounding the delivery, he will endeavor to obtain the best possible result, by all the means at his disposal, but that he will *never have recourse to feticide*. This position by the physician will convince even the most backward and ignorant person to arrange for a periodic obstetrical examination as well as for an early admission to the hospital if a difficult delivery is feared. (b) He shall secure the collaboration of a reputable obstetrician, and with him make the necessary preparation for a caesarean section or any other operation which may be required to assure the safety of both the mother and the child. With these precautions, the Catholic physician, dedicated to the strict observance of the moral principles, will be able to carry out such principles without fear or risks to his person. No other policy would be consistent with the observance of the law of nature. *Riz.*

FETUS, ECTOPIC (tubular pregnancy). In general, an ectopic (out-of-its-place, or extra-uterine) fetus is a fetus which is not attached to the wall of the uterus as its natural place but to another part of the mother's body, such as the Fallopian tube, the ovary, or the abdominal cavity. The possiblity that such a fetus may attain a state of viability is extremely remote. In the process of growing, the ectopic fetus destroys the tissues of the organ to which it is attached, giving rise to a serious danger of rupture or hemorrhage with the possibility of death for the mother. A tubular pregnancy is generally detected from the rupture of the organ to which it is attached and the pains that accompany the rupture. In this case, the fetus has already severed its contact from the mother's body and may, therefore, be drawn out. From the moral standpoint this is considered a case of natural abortion, and any medical treatment directed at restoring the mother's health is quite in order.

The ectopic fetus raises a peculiar moral case when the fetus is discovered still intact on the occasion of another operation. Is it lawful in this case to draw it out by a so-called laparotomy? Those who might answer in the affirmative give as a reason the fact that it would inevitably die and very soon; but this reasoning is not morally sound. The precept "Thou shalt not kill" also applies to human beings who, because of natural causes, might die prematurely. The answer depends on whether or not laparotomy is direct killing. It is clear that if laparotomy is direct killing, it is immoral. The answer in the affirmative seems more logical but it is not final. The declarations of the Holy See on the subject in question do not convey certainty in the matter. Theologians, on the other hand, are not in agreement on this matter; hence, one cannot speak of a common opinion. We incline to the theory of P. Payen, who states that it is never lawful to act directly on the fetal body, whether it means damaging the body in any way or drawing it out of the fetal pouch or removing it from its place. However, when the part of the mother's organ which bears the fetus is in such a condition as to constitute a serious and *imminent* danger for the mother, then it is lawful to eliminate that part, even though inevitably the fetus may go with it and die. In this case the killing of the fetus can be considered as an indirect act. The probability of this opinion is such that it can be followed safely. *Ben.*

FETUS, HUMAN. The human fetus is a human being from the first moment of conception to its birth. The fetus is a distinct being and not a part of the mother. According to almost all modern physiologists and many theologians, the fetus is animated by a human soul from the first moment of its conception, or, according to many other theologians, from a moment which is very near the beginning of conception.

From the moment of its animation the fetus is a human being with a right to life. To kill it, even by abortion, constitutes murder (*see* Abortion, Feticide). The killing of the fetus before its animation would not constitute homicide but a grave sin very close to homicide. The fetus is capable of receiving baptism, at least conditionally. If for any cause it is prematurely expelled from the mother's womb, it must be baptized conditionally.

If a pregnant woman dies, the fetus must be drawn out of her womb surgically and baptized conditionally, if alive or probably alive (*see* Baptism). *Gen.*

FIDEICOMMISSUM (legacy, trust). *Fideicommissum* is one of the various means used for the assignment of goods to charitable causes. Today, we understood by fideicommissum a legacy left in trust to a person (physical or legal) on condition that he should give it to another person *indicated in the disposer's act.* The recipient is called *fiduciary* (trustee), and the person (physical or legal) to whom the goods are to be ultimately transferred is called legatee or heir.

This legal medium, widely used in the Middle Ages, was opposed by the modern civil codes which were influenced by the Napoleonic Code. Canon Law always defended it, and even today the Church claims exclusive jurisdiction in matters concerning donations and bequests in behalf of charitable and religious causes (Can. 1513, par. 2). A cleric or religious who receives goods in trust for pious causes shall notify the Ordinary concerning the trusteeship; as *ex officio* executor of all donations in favor of pious causes (Can. 1515, par. 1) the Ordinary will supervise the fulfillment of the pious intentions of the donor. (Can. 1516). *Vis.*

FIGHT. *See* Sports (dangerous).

FINANCE, PUBLIC. The term *finance* has three meanings: (a) To raise money necessary to organize, reorganize, or extend an enterprise, whether by sale of stocks, bonds, notes, or otherwise. (b) A general term to denote the theory and practice of monetary credit, banking, and promotion operations in the most comprehensive sense. It includes money, credit, banking, securities, investment, speculation, foreign exchange, promotion, reorganization, underwriting, brokerage trusts, *etc.* (c) Originally the term was applied to the raising of money by taxes or bond issues and the administration of revenues and expenditures by a government. This is now known as public finance.

Public finance includes the science of budgeting, the principles and administration of taxation, the expenditures of public revenues and accounting thereof. The government, in undertaking those functions necessary for promoting collective welfare, administration of the laws and courts of justice, protection afforded through the army, navy, and police system, education and extension of public works, is concerned with financial principles just as any parties would be which might administer these functions privately.

The essential elements of public finance are three: the budget, the fiscal year, the administration.

The budget is the financial statement of the estimated revenues and expenditures concerning a specific period of time. The budget means also the content of the financial statement. The compiling and presenting of the budget before the congress, council, or parliament, the debate, the approval and the actual operation of the budget are some of the most engaging acts in the life of a government or an administration.

The fiscal year is the period of time covered by the budget. It generally covers a twelve-month period. Not always, however, does it coincide with the calendar year: in the U. S. A., for instance, the public fiscal year starts on July 1st and ends on June 30th.

The fiscal year consists of all the administrative acts which constitute the financial operation for the year.

The relations between public finance and morals are many. The most important, however, is the criterion by which the government determines the manner of raising revenues considered necessary for the attainment of its ends. It is known, for instance, that in some countries, due to inefficiency in their tax systems, the taxpayers usually report lower income on the assumption that the government taxation rate is based on such a presupposition. This, of course, causes the government to raise the taxation rate to a higher level than actually required by the common good. The consequences of this practice are very harmful both to the more honest citizens, who thus have to bear a heavier burden than is fair, and to the state itself, which is compelled to put into effect hateful and complex measures weighing down on the entire community.

On the basis of the principle of the common good, all citizens are obliged to pay taxes. However, where the tax laws are only penal laws, they oblige in conscience to the entent of accepting the penalties incurred for their violation. If they are not mere penal laws, they oblige in conscience to the payment of the taxes even before a judicial sentence is issued. Thus, indirect taxes, such as duties, customs, and excise taxes are commonly held to be levied as mere penal laws; whereas direct taxes, such as personal taxes, real estate and property taxes, are probably levied by legislation which obliges in conscience prior to a judicial sentence. Customary interpretation and the intention of the lawgiver, however, would seem to render an obligation in conscience highly questionable in the United States, in which case, *post factum,* restitution would not have to be urged. It is to be noted that even though one does not sin by transgressing a purely penal law, it might readily occur that disobedience will offend against some other virtue, such as charity, or truthfulness. All citizens have a general obligation to pay their fair share of taxes. *Pav.-Yan.*

FINDER (OF LOST THINGS). Anyone finding an object that was lost is under obligation to return it to its owner. If he does not know who the owner is, he should hold on to the object, or, if this is impossible, sell it and hold on to the money until all reasonable efforts to find the owner shall have failed. In this case, he may either use the money for charitable purposes, or as other moralists maintain, keep it for himself.

No one has the right to enrich himself with another's property; *res clamat ad dominum:* an object claims its proper owner. When the value of a lost thing reaches the point of constituting grave matter, it is a serious sin to retain it without a legitimate reason; if it is light matter, then the sin is venial. If the owner cannot be found, then one may with a clear conscience follow the provisions of local laws. *Sir.*

FIRE (ARSON). Fire is a large, destructive burning caused by the combustion of flammable substances such as wood, paper, gasoline, *etc.*

A fire can be produced by a variety of causes, including spontaneous combustion. But in order to establish the moral responsibility connected with it, one must ascertain whether the fire was caused by a voluntary act. In the latter case, the responsible party is guilty before God and man and he is held responsible for the damage done to the individual and to society. Also, it is a sin for an individual to set fire to his own property for the purpose of causing damage to another person. In the case of a just war, one may set fire to his own property in order to prevent the enemy from making use of it.

If the fire is indirectly voluntary (*voluntarium in causa*), one must consider carefully whether all the conditions set by the well-known principle of the action with a double effect are fulfilled (*see* Effect, Double), in the light of which moral responsibility shall be established. Even if the author of a fire remains unknown, he is not only guilty of sin but he also must make restitution for the damage done, even though in an secret manner, if he is able to do so and to the extent to which he is able. If the fire is not *morally imputable* to a person, not even on the ground of negligence or imprudence, he is guilty neither before God nor before man.

One, however, might be compelled by an unjust sentence, or by force, to make reparation for the damage; but if this were thoroughly unjust, the victim could resort to secret compensation, provided that no greater damage result to himself or to others. *Sir.*

FIRST COMMUNION. *See* Communion, First.

FISCAL YEAR. *See* Finance.

FISH. *See* Abstinence and Fast.

FISHING. Fishing (*piscatio*) like hunting (*venatio*) and bird-catching (*aucupium*) is an exercise of a natural right directed to acquiring ownership of naturally free, aquatic animals by means of appropriation (*q.v.*). Subjectively, it is the right of appropriation through capture of animals living in natural freedom, which belong to no one (*res nullius*).

The lawfulness of this right rests on the natural law and the positive law,

since taking possession of a *res nullius* is a lawful title of ownership in the natural and positive law.

Yet this right is not absolute either on the plane of the natural law or the positive law in the sense that particular conditions of fact can arise to limit the extent and lawfulness and, in special cases, nullify that right altogether. Under this aspect, civil laws that govern fishing acquire an indicative value of particular importance.

The general, moral evaluation of fishing does not differ specifically from hunting, so that, with the exception of a few details, general principles governing the practice and morality of hunting apply also to fishing (*see* Hunting).

From its economic aspect, fishing is much more important than hunting, at least with regards to certain countries surrounded nearly everywhere by waters.

The moral evaluation of the exercise of this right depends on three factors: (1) a natural right, (2) the civil laws of each country, and (3) the common attitude or conviction prevailing in each respective locality concerning the moral obligation arising from fishing and hunting.

The Natural Law. The classic distinction, generally made with respect to hunting, between wild animals (*efferate*) and domestic animals (*mansueta*) or domesticated (*mansuefacta*), for obvious reasons does not apply to fishing. In its stead, the simple distinction between aquatic animals in their natural freedom and aquatic animals in custody serves the purpose. With this distinction, it is clear that only animals of the first category may be the object of free fishing, because they alone, as long as they live in a state of natural liberty, are properly a *res nullius* and, as such, belong by right to the first occupant. This fundamental condition is not present in the case of animals in custody, which by the general principle of natural law, cannot be the object of fishing as long as they remain in a state of forced custody.

Clearly, these are principles of a fundamental nature. For their interpretation and practical application one must consult the laws of each nation, which admit of degrees of variation.

(a) Legislation, regulating the exercise of that right, which requires possession of a license, or forbids or limits the exercise to special times, places or instruments, is in the main considered merely penal, particularly in view of a common interpretation and custom.

(b) On the contrary, regulations and legislation, whose violation involves a damage or a serious danger to the common welfare, are binding in conscience. These are: laws concerning the protection, reproduction, and maintenance of the species; laws that prohibit fishing by means of explosives, narcotics, or poison and laws that forbid the sale of fish caught by such means.

(c) Particularly binding in conscience and commutative justice, with an obligation of reparation in case of violation, are the laws directed to the protection of private property and rights acquired with onerous title; among these are laws which forbid fishing in private waters, or waters subject to exclusive rights, as a result of contracts of lease or private concession.

For an exact, ethical appraisal of the exercise of the respective rights, one must take into account not only the natural norms and directives of the positive laws concerning fishing and hunting, but also the general conviction, created by the common opinion in each respective locality, regarding the lawfulness of individual acts and the obligatory value of the laws established to regulate them. *Zac.*

FOLLICULINE. *See* Endocrinology, Gonads.

FORBIDDEN BOOKS. Since the mission of the Catholic Church is to guide people to their eternal salvation, it is her duty to point out to them the dangers of which they must beware. Now it is an undeniable fact that the press, which is a powerful instrument for great good, also can be an easy instrument of perversion. It is therefore the right and the duty of the Church, as it is also of the state, to check the promotion of books and writings whose aim it is to undermine the moral life and the foundations of both societies. A book that places obstacles in the way of truth is contrary to the nature and purpose of man's reason and the common welfare. It is an intrinsic right of the legislator to pass judgment on books or printed matter that hinder good and foster evil. Often, the reader becomes so completely overtaken by the content of a book that he speaks and acts according to the sentiments and convictions expressed in it.

The right of the Church to condemn bad books is a consequence of her right of self-preservation and self-defense. As a perfect society, the Church, as also the state, has the right and duty to protect herself and to keep away from her subjects anything which can bring them harm.

From the earliest centuries of its existence the Church has always been conscious of this right (cf. Rom. 16:17; I Tim. 6:20; Acts 19:19); in fact, the discipline forbidding bad books goes as far back as the fourth century. As time went on, especially after the invention of the printing press, a greater vigilance became necessary. The Church provides her subjects with a guide called the *Index* (see Index of Forbidden Books).

It would be wrong to think that only those books listed in the *Index* are forbidden, for the prohibition extends also to certain categories of books which, although not specifically listed by their title are nevertheless damaging to the soul in that they may cause a person to waver in the faith, or deprive a soul of the treasure of purity, or obscure the truth of faith. These books are condemned by virtue of the natural law. The scope of the natural law is, of necessity, much wider than the *Index* of forbidden books published by the Church. Therefore, to know whether or not a book is forbidden one must not be satisfied with looking at the catalogue of forbidden books, but he must see whether the book is by its very nature objectionable.

According to the Code of Canon Law (Can. 1399), books that come under the general ban, even though not listed individually are: (a) sacred books (on the Holy Scripture) published without Church approval; (b) books written by any writer whatsoever advocating heresy, schism, or attacking the very foundations of religion; (c) books whose purpose is to oppose religion and good morals; (d) religious books without the Church's approval; (e) texts and commentaries on the Holy Scriptures, books of devotion and piety, books relating new apparitions, visions, revelations, prophecies, and miracles, or suggesting new devotions not bearing the approval of the Church, *i.e.*, the *imprimatur*; (f) books attacking and deriding a dogma of the Faith, defending errors condemned by the Church, criticizing divine worship and ecclesiastical discipline, or scoffing at the ecclesiastical hierarchy and the clerical or the religious state; (g) books teaching or sanctioning any form whatsoever of superstition, witchcraft, divination, evoking of spirits, *etc.*; (h) books justifying duels, suicide, and divorce, as well as those which would have us believe that masonry and other allied sects are not harmful to the Church and society; (i) all books dealing with, describing, or teaching lust and obscenity; (j) liturgical books not in agreement with the authentic editions approved by the Holy See; (k) books containing indulgences that are false or which were outlawed or revoked by the Holy See.

None of these forbidden books may be either published, translated, read, or even kept; nor may they be praised or passed on to others (Can. 1398), but they must be destroyed if possible or held under special custody if it is necessary that they be kept. The reading of forbidden books is generally a mortal sin; the reader of books written by apostates, schismatics, or heretics in defense of their errors incurs excommunication reserved in a special manner to the Holy See (Can. 2318, par. 1). Since this pro-

hibition is a positive law aimed at preventing dangers, it is valid for everyone without distinction, even if in some particular case the danger is not concrete. Those who are required to read such books for professional reasons or study or who engage in exposing error can obtain permission (Can. 1402, 1403) from lawful ecclesiastical authority.

Permission to read forbidden books is granted by the Holy See, or in special cases by the local Ordinary. At times permission is granted with the condition "according to the judgment of one's own confessor." This is based on the very reasonable consideration that no one better than one's confessor can know the honesty of intention, the practical necessity, and the discernment of the interested person.

He who disregards the laws of the Church concerning forbidden books may, in the more serious cases, incur ecclesiastical censures, such as: (a) excommunication reserved in a special manner to the Holy See, incurred at the very moment (*ipso facto*) of the publication of books written by apostates, heretics, schismatics as well as those who defend or knowingly and without due permission read or keep these same books or other books specifically forbidden by apostolic letters; (b) non-reserved excommunication to which authors and publishers become liable at the very moment of the unauthorized publication of books of Holy Scripture, or notes and commentaries on the same (Can. 2318). *See also* Censorship of Books, Index of Forbidden Books. *Tar.*

FOREIGNER. *See* Emigration.

FORFEITS (or fallentiae). *See* Chapter.

FORGERY (FALSIFICATION). Forgery is the deceitful counterfeiting or suppression of truth for the purpose of doing harm to another. Two elements concur in forgery, alteration of truth (*immutatio veri*) and fraudulent intent to hurt another. Thus, forgery violates not only the virtue of veracity but also the virtue of justice. Forgery may be committed by words said or written and also by deeds. Forgery may be material and ideological, or conceptual. The former consists in the alteration of a written document, the latter in the improper use of a document, if by trickery, deception or false statements, a value is attributed to it which it does not possess.

Forgery is a sin inasmuch as it is a lie (*q.v.*) and a fraud (*q.v.*). Both Canon Law and civil law consider it a crime. But since forgery is one of the so-called crimes of mixed forum, Canon Law ordinarily leaves the punishment of the crime to civil courts (though it reserves the right to punish clerics), being concerned rather with some aspects of the crime of forgery peculiar to the ecclesiastical forum. For all practical purposes Canon Law concerns itself with the following: (a) *counterfeiting of sacred relics or use of false relics:* their counterfeiting is punished with excommunication reserved to the Ordinary (Can. 2326), while the selling of relics is considered a simoniacal act (Can. 1289, par. 1); (b) *falsification or fabrication of apostolic letters,* punished with excommunication reserved in a special manner to the Holy See (Can. 2360, par. 1); (c) *false statement (obreptio), or failure to mention an existing impediment (subreptio)* in the petition for a rescript (*see* Rescript); (d) *falsification of other ecclesiastical documents,* which may be punished by the judge according to the seriousness of the crime (Can. 2362) and with greater severity if the forgery is committed by the official keeper (Can. 2406, par. 1). *Pug.*

FORM OF THE SACRAMENTS. *See* Sacrament.

FORNICATION. Fornication is voluntary sexual intercourse between two unmarried persons who are free from any bond (matrimony, vow, consanguinity, etc.). In itself, fornication falls within the kind of lust (*q.v.*) classified as according to nature (*intra naturam*) i.e., opposed to acts against nature (*contra naturam*). Prostitution (*q.v.*) and concubinage (*q.v.*) are particular forms of fornication, though not specifically different from it.

Fornication is a mortal sin because it is a serious violation of a basic order established by nature for the good of offspring, of the individual himself, and of the community. The sexual act is by its very nature ordained by God not simply to physical procreation but to a procreation befitting man's rational nature, that is, a procreation in which the proper education of offspring can be duly provided for. Since an adequate education requires a stable and continued interest of both parents, it can be guaranteed only by a stable union of the parents, protected by mutual juridical rights and duties.

By keeping the satisfaction of the sexual appetite within certain rational limitations this natural order indirectly protects also the good of entire society. It also guarantees the good of the individual inasmuch as only the sexual union in matrimony preserves man's dignity and completes the personalities of man and woman in stable cohabitation.

Nor does it matter if positive means are sometimes used to correct a given situation (a stable cohabitation without marriage or adequate education for offspring), or if in some particular case the natural effect fails to follow, or is plainly impossible, as in the case of sterility; accidental factors do not affect the validity of the natural order. In Holy Scripture fornication is absolutely condemned as a grave violation of the law of God (Deut. 22:21; Job. 4:13; I Cor. 6:9; Gal. 5:19; Eph. 5:5-6). The teaching of the Church re-echoes the teaching of Revelation: cf., for instance, Error 7 of Beguards and Beguines condemned by the Council of Vienna (1311-1312) (Clem. 5, 3, 3) and Prop. 48, condemned by Innocent XI in a decree of the Sacred Congregation of the Holy Office, March 4, 1679 (Denz. 1198). *Dam.*

FORTITUDE. In a broad sense, fortitude is a steadiness or stability of the will in doing good. In a strict sense it is a particular firmness of spirit which prompts us to be strong in the face of grave obstacles encountered in the fulfillment of one's duty, or the practice, even optional, of a virtue. Fortitude is one of the gifts of the Holy Ghost (*see* Gifts of the Holy Ghost) which gives us strength in difficulties.

Fortitude moderates fear, which paralyzes efforts in behalf of a good cause, and rashness, which leads to excess in the face of difficulties and dangers.

It is proper to the strong-hearted to undertake praiseworthy projects despite the foreseeing of difficulties, working at them in the proper manner and the proper time, persevering to the very end, even in the face of increased obstacles and difficulties. This is a more difficult task than the undertaking of an arduous project in a moment of enthusiasm.

Fortitude is needed to desist from committing an unjust action or to perform an act recommended by the Lord (martyrdom); to fight for the defense of right, to exercise heroic charity; to practice religion in spite of persistent criticism, mockery, and persecution; to give up conspicuous temporal advantages rather than compromise with the dictates of one's own conscience; to follow the Lord's calling to a more perfect state of life demanding great sacrifices; to live for years in a state of spiritual aridity and to endure for a long time temptations and all kinds of trials not only without failing in one's duties, but using these difficulties to tend with increased enthusiasm toward God; to endure death rather than deny a revealed truth. Constant and perfect faithfulness to one's ordinary duties in life often demands great fortitude of spirit.

Fortitude can be acquired by the practice of distrust of self and unlimited trust in God. One must convince himself that there are goods much more precious than riches, health, reputation, esteem and affection of other people, and even life itself; these are the benefits flowing from the possession of grace, a prelude to everlasting bliss. Hence, one must be disposed to sacrifice generously the former in order that he may gain the goods that are imperishable. Before acting, one must ask himself whether the action he is about to engage in is such that it will lead him to God and to eternal happiness. If the answer is in the affirmative, he must proceed to do it. If the answer is "no," he shall abstain from doing it even if it means enduring all kinds of temporal evils. In order that one may overcome difficulties successfully, he shall endeavor to foresee them, without exaggerating them, but relying on God's help. The difficulties that are foreseen are half overcome. Finally, one must bear in mind, above all, that true love of God is the greatest source of strength (Rom. 8:38, 39; 2 Cor. 5:14); it is the love of God that makes martyrs, virgins, missionaries, and saints.

One may sin against fortitude by defect (*see* Timidity) and also, though less frequently, by excess (*see* Rashness). Concerning fortitude as a gift of the Holy Ghost, *see* Gifts of the Holy Ghost. *Man.*

FORTITUDE, Integral Parts of the virtue of. Unlike other virtues, the virtue of fortitude has no specifically different subjective parts by reason of its own special object, which consists mainly of the dangers of death. These dangers are of the same species, although they do admit a certain graduating scale, the culminating point being martyrdom (*q.v.*). From the standpoint of its primary material object (danger of death), the virtue of fortitude has only integral parts, but from the standpoint of its secondary material object (serious evils and dangers less serious than those of death), it has also potential or secondary parts.

The integral and potential parts of the virtue of fortitude have in common the firmness of spirit against dangers and the impulses of passions which is the very substance of the virtue, although they differ insofar as their primary object is concerned.

The acts of the virtue of fortitude are: (a) aggressiveness, and (b) endurance. To act with courage, two things are necessary: preparedness of heart and fearlessness in the face of danger. Thus, the first integral part of fortitude is that which leads the individual to conceive and to will great, heroic, highly praise-worthy things: this is *magnanimity* (*q.v.*). Opposed to the virtue of magna-nimity, *by defect*, is cowardliness or nig-gardliness of spirit, by which a person, because of a constant fear, refains from doing that which he is naturally capable of doing; *by excess*, is *presumption* (*q.v.*), by which a person is led to face dangers which are beyond one's strength; also *vainglory* and *ambition*, by which one is moved in a disorderly manner to seek after honor and glory (*see* Pride).

The second integral part of fortitude is constancy in pursuing something already initiated with confidence; this constitutes the virtue of *magnificence* (*q.v.*), which is a moral virtue inclining man toward doing great works. When, however, such enterprises are inspired by a false magnificence, then we have, by defect, the vices of niggardliness or stinginess, by which one fails to main-tain due proportion between the cost and the works to be undertaken, result-ing in doing small or insignificant things; by excess, the vice of *sumptuousness*, prodigality, or squandering, leading to waste and expenditures beyond reason. The second act of the virtue of forti-tude, that is, endurance, requires two integral virtues: *patience* (*q.v.*), which sustains man against discouragement in the struggle against dangers; and *per-severance* (*q.v.*), which inclines man to fight to the end without tiring and with-out becoming discouraged or surrender-ing to evil.

Opposed to the virtue of patience are, by excess, *insensibility* (*q.v.*), by which one gives no proper weight to dangers; by defect, *impatience* (*q.v.*), which causes one to run away from a difficulty because of exaggerated discouragement.

Opposed to the virtue of perse-verance are, by excess, *obstinacy*, or stubbornness, by which one strives un-reasonably toward a goal, notwithstand-ing tiredness and fatigue; by defect, *inconstancy* (*q.v.*), or weariness or weak-ness, which causes one unreasonably to interrupt a work already started simply because of the prolonged effort it re-quires. *Pal.*

FORTY HOURS. The Forty Hours de-votion consists in the solemn exposition of the Blessed Sacrament for a period of forty hours, consecutively day and night, or only during the hours of the day. According to St. Augustine (*De Trinitate*, 4, 6), Christ is believed to have remained in the sepulchre that many hours. It seems that the devotion of the Forty Hours began in Milan, Italy, in 1534. In 1558 Pope Pius IV approved the practice of this devotion for the city of Rome when he ratified the Roman Sodality for Prayer and a Happy Death, whose main objective was the monthly adoration of the Blessed Sacrament in solemn exposition.

In Rome, the devotion of the Forty Hours is conducted according to a rotat-ing system, and without interruption. This form of adoration of the Holy Eucharist became very popular in that city through the efforts of Father Joseph da Fermo, a Capuchin, St. Anthony Maria Zaccaria, founder of the Barna-bites, and St. Ignatius of Loyola. The Jesuits brought the devotion to Germany, where it assumed principally the char-acter of reparation for the sins com-mitted during the worldly celebrations ending with Mardi Gras; originally it was mainly a pious practice for peace in the Church. This intention is also maintained at the present time by the celebration of a votive Mass for peace on the second day of the devotion.

The ceremonial of the Forty Hours was provided by the *Instructio Clemen-tina* (approved by Clement VIII and published by Clement XI in 1705), which is found at the end of the third volume of *Collectio Authentica Decre-torum S. Rituum Congregationis*. In Rome the observance of the ceremonial is mandatory, while outside of Rome it is not, but its observance is required for the gaining of the indulgences con-nected with the Forty Hours devotion. *Pal.*

FORUM. DEFINITION. Etymologically the word *forum* is derived, according to some, from *"ferendo"* (that is, carrying over), because all controversies to be solved and goods to be sold were taken to the forum. The word *forum*, therefore, could mean: (a) the market place: the *forum boarium* (oxen-market), located at the foot of the Palatine Hill near the Circus of Maximus, was the place where oxen and other beasts of slaughter were sold; (b) the place where litigations were settled; (c) the power given to the judge authoritatively to decide a judicial case; (d) the territory within which the magistrate could exercise his jurisdiction over the accused. A forum, today, is a tribunal, whether ecclesiastical or civil.

HISTORY. The forum is of very ancient origin. It is known that Jews had places where they met three times a month to settle their disputes. The forum was called by the Greeks, *agora,* and the different kinds of forums were ordinarily located in the center of the city; almost all Greek cities had their forums. In Rome there were seventeen forums: fourteen of them were used as food markets and were called *fora venalia,* the others, set aside for the administration of justice, were called *fora civilia* and *iudiciaria.*

DIVISION. The forum may be (a) *ecclesiastical, civil, or mixed,* according to whether the matter to be dealt with is reserved to either the ecclesiastical or the civil authority, or is one in which two authorities are equally competent. The causes of mixed forum are either civil or criminal: criminal causes, for instance, are those which concern crimes against chastity (Can. 2357); civil causes, on the other hand, are those which revolve around contracts under oath concerning temporal matters, such as property or similar things. (b) *Competent and non-competent,* according to whether or not the accused is subject to the jurisdiction of the judge before whom he is summoned to appear; (c) *necessary,* if the trial is about a matter which by law or injunction must be conducted by a specified tribunal,

for instance, a cause concerning a benefice, which, though non-residential, is to be dealt with by the Ordinary of the place where the benefice lies (Can. 1560, n. 2); however, since the incompetency of other judges in these cases is *relative,* the judgment shall be valid (*see* Tribunal, Ecclesiastical) if by the consent of the parties the cause is handled by other courts; (d) *privileged* (*see* Clergy, Privileges of) is that which exempts clerics from lay jurisdiction (privilege of the forum), so that even for temporal matters, they may not be summoned before a lay court, at least as defendants, unless in some particular places it was lawfully arranged otherwise or permission was obtained from the competent ecclesiastical authority. It is said "at least as defendants," because it is debatable whether or not a cleric may be summoned as a witness: the affirmative opinion, however, is more probable. Dispensation from or limitation of this privilege is negotiated by concordats (*q.v.*) or by custom (*q.v.*) of at least 100 years' standing (Belgium, Holland). Permission to summon a person enjoying the privilege of the forum can be granted only by the Holy See or the local Ordinary depending on the persons involved (Can. 120). The privilege is not violated if the cleric is summoned before the mayor or the governor of the state, or the prime minister because, properly speaking, they are not judges; (e) *secular,* the civil court, before which a member of the clergy may not be summoned (Can. 2341).

The ecclesiastical forum is *internal* and *external.* The external forum concerns the government of the Church and deals with both temporal and spiritual affairs of groups or individuals as members of a society. In this tribunal the accused is absolved or condemned exclusively on the basis of the evidence. The internal forum, instead, aims directly at the sanctification of souls and deals with matters concerning the conscience of the individual. In such a tribunal the judge relies on the penitent who accuses or excuses himself (*asserenti pro se* and *contra se*), unless the contrary is evident. The internal forum may be *sacramental* or of *conscience;* the sacramental forum is concerned with sins, that is, all those matters which are dealt with in sacramental confession (*q.v.*); the forum of conscience, on the other hand, is that to which everything dealt with outside the sacrament of penance and related to the spiritual welfare of the individual is referred. The sacramental forum differs from the forum of conscience in that the former is exclusively a penitential forum while the latter is broader and more general. It is also exercised outside the sacrament of penance, for instance, in absolving from censures, in dispensing from irregularities, *etc.* Concerning the Holy See, the Sacred Apostolic Penitentiary (*q.v.*) is a tribunal of the internal forum, because its jurisdiction extends over all matters of the internal forum, including non-sacramental matters; it grants absolutions, dispensations, commutations, sanctions, condonations, only for the internal forum (Can. 258, par. 1). The other congregations and offices of the papal curia, on the other hand, have jurisdiction over all matters concerning the external forum.

WAYS OF ACQUIRING THE FORUM. According to Canon Law the (external) forum may be acquired in many ways; namely, by reason of domicile, location of the thing, contract, and crime.

(a) *Ratione domicilii* (by reason of domicile). The criterion of domicile is held as the most natural one. By reason of domicile (*q.v.*), or quasi-domicile, anyone can be sued before the local Ordinary who has jurisdiction over his subject even if he is absent from the diocese (Can. 1561). The bishop may also exercise such jurisdiction through the Ordinary of the place where the defendant may be presently living. The Ordinary of the accused, therefore, can issue a summons to be served on the accused living in another bishop's territory; and if he fails to appear he may be declared contumacious (*q.v.*). The domicile of the husband is also the domicile of his wife; the domicile of minors is that of their parents or tutors, the domicile of the mentally ill is that of their guardians. If the accused has more than one domicile or quasi-domicile, the petitioner has the right to choose the competent forum. If the defendant (*q.v.*) changes domicile during the trial, the competence of the judge who had the summons served is in no way affected. If a person has lived in Rome for a year, he may refuse to be tried before the tribunal of his own Ordinary and ask to be tried by the tribunal of Rome (Can. 1562, par. 2); such a tribunal, for a cause tried in the first instance, is that of the Vicariate of Rome, not the tribunals of the Holy See.

(b) *Ratione rei sitae* (by reason of the location of the thing around which the controversy revolves), the party may be summoned to appear before the Ordinary of the place where the thing is located (Can. 1564). In this forum, however, suit may be brought only against the thing itself; if the thing happens to be under the jurisdiction of more than one Ordinary, the right of prevention is followed.

(c) *Ratione contractus* (by reason of contract). By reason of contract, the party may be summoned to appear before the Ordinary of the place where the contract was made or must be executed (Can. 1565, par. 1). At the time the contract is made, the contracting parties are permitted to choose a place in which they can be summoned and convened, even though they may be absent from the place (Can. 1565, par. 2). The selection of the place may be made only at the time of the stipulation of the contract, that is, when the parties give their consent.

(d) *Ratione delicti* (because of an offense). The accused becomes subject to the forum of the place in which the offense was committed. If, after committing the crime, the accused left the place, the judge of that place has the right to summon him to appear before him and pronounce the sentence in his case (Can. 1566). The place of crime is the diocese in which the offense was committed; if the crime was started in a diocese and consummated in another, both dioceses are competent forums; in this case the right of prevention between the judges is to be followed (Can. 1566). The forum of the crime is only valid for criminal action arising from the crime, not for civil action, unless a civil action be proposed at the criminal trial itself, as is often the case. *de A.*

FORUM, PRIVILEGE OF THE. *See* Immunity, Ecclesiastical.

FOUNDATION, PIOUS. Evolution of the Pious Foundation, Corporation, Pious Cause. *Foundation* is a rather equivocal term, being used to mean different entities. In the doctrine of legal persons, *corporation* is diametrically opposed to *foundation.* Roman Law, in its more ancient period, knew only the corporation. Foundation, on the contrary, is linked with the first forms of social assistance established by the Church on behalf of the sick, the aged, and the needy. In the opinion of various scholars, the Church has greatly contributed to the development of the corporation form of the legal person. They hold that the legal person developed from the very structure of the Church, which is a corporation (the word *Church* in its original meaning implies that) or, more exactly, from the doctrine of the Mystical Body. Futhermore, in carrying out its precepts of charity and religion, Christianity gave life to institutions which consisted of properties under the authority of the bishop; one fourth of such properties was set aside for works of charity. The property, its purpose and administration, gave rise gradually to a new structure of legal person known as a *pious cause* (charitable institutions). The zeal of Roman noblemen, whose possessions were given to pious causes, is described by St. Jerome as a well-known fact. The pious cause was accepted in the Justinian legislation. In his code, Justinian speaks of "bequests, legacies, deeds of trust, donations, contracts," on behalf of the Church and pious causes (C. 1, 2, 23; cf. also C. 3, 45; Nov. 131, 11, 11).

When it allowed property to be turned over to charitable or religious causes, the Church not only gave life to the foundation, but opened new ways to the use of property, developing the existing Roman juridical institutions in the direction of her own necessities and juridical realizations. It may suffice to mention, for instance, that despite the fact that the law did not approve of *donation*, it became the most common way by which works of charity and religion were favored in Christianity. This, of course, caused the setting aside of many established juridical axioms of Roman law.

It can be stated that, when the activity of the Church in the field of legal persons attained its final development (and the Church property had been split into various entities), the juridical person was conceived as a *universitas personarum* (corporation) or a *universitas bonorum* (pious foundation). The basic element of a corporation was a group of physical persons, while the constitutive element of a pious foundation was a property or fund considered as a center of juridical relations; and while in the former persons were managing their own property, in the latter (at least in the case of some minor forms), persons administered a property which had been entrusted to them by the founder. But this criterion of distribution was not always followed in practice. It is to be observed, however, that gradually there developed in Canon Law such a vast array of legal persons, entities without a juridical personality, and properties and funds constituting intermediate categories, that it is difficult today to give a precise description of all of them. But these general notions may suffice in explaining the evolution of the concepts of pious cause, foundation, and corporation.

The Pious Foundation in Present-Day Canon Law. In present-day Canon Law a pious cause in its true concept, is a property destined for works of religion or charity. It includes all those non-collegiate entities which the law recognizes as subjects of rights (a benefice); also, properties devoid of a juridical personality but which adhere, in some way, to the same subjects (Can. 1491, par. 2; 1514–1517 ff.), and those properties destined for a pious end, which for any reason (*e.g.*, if the testator destined them for a non-eccesiastical physical or legal purpose) could not, strictly speaking, be made a part of ecclesiastical property, though they came under the canonical law precisely as destined to a pious cause (Can. 1513, par. 2; 1516). *Pious cause*, therefore, is a general concept which, according to the form it assumes, is called pious foundation, ecclesiastical institution, pious legacy (*q.v.*), *etc.*, but the difference beween the pious cause and the other entities is simply that which occurs between gender and species; in other words, these other forms, pious foundation, legacy, *etc.*, are types of pious cause, even though not all of them enjoy juridical personality.

The distinction between corporation and pious foundation may be considered as being similar to the distinction set down by the Code of Canon Law between a legal collegiate and non-collegiate person (Can. 99). In order to attain a more concrete idea concerning a pious foundation it is necessary to pursue the matter further.

EXTENSION OF THE CONCEPT OF PIOUS FOUNDATION. Canonists (and also civil lawyers) use *foundation, institution, pious cause, pious place, pious legacy, pious bequest, pious foundation, modal donation, spiritual benefits, Mass foundations, chaplaincy, etc.*, in a rather indiscriminate way. To set this terminology in order (because often a juridical transaction is mistaken as foundation, and a foundation is confused with other forms that are not a foundation), we incline to the opinion that pious foundation embraces a very broad concept which includes (a) *benefices;* (b) *charitable institutions* or *independent foundations;* (c) *pious foundations* or *fiduciary foundations;* (d) *pious legacies.* In these four categories are included all the above-mentioned institutions with a meaning all of their own. Regarding

category (a) *see* Benefice. Concerning the other three categories, the founder— a physical person (or persons) or a legal person who by a direct donation or by a last will and testament (*inter vivos* or *mortis causa:* Can. 1513) designates a property or part thereof for works of religion or charity (Can. 1489, par. 1; 1515, par. 1; 1410; 1500, *etc.*)—may intend one of the following: (a) to assign such a property for works of religion to be carried out by an institution to be erected for that purpose, in the sense that he makes his donation (*q.v.*) or testamentary disposition directly in favor of the juridical person with the request that it be lawfully erected, *ipso iure*, by the very acceptance of money given or left by him by the lawful ecclesiastical authority, or by a formal decree issued by the latter (Can. 100, par. 1); (b) to assign the property to an *already existing ecclesiastical* legal person with the obligation (modal disposition) to perform permanently a certain work of religion or charity with the revenues obtained from the same property; (c) to assign the said property to a physical person (lay or ecclesiastical) or to a non-ecclesiastical *legal person*, with the obligation to carry out certain religious or charitable works.

In the *first case* one would have the creation of an ecclesiastical legal person (benefice, seminary, church), but more frequently an *autonomous foundation* or *pious* institution governed by Canons 1489–1494; in the *second case* one would have a true and proper *pious foundation*, or trust (fiduciary) foundation (*see also* Legacy, Trust) governed by Canons 1544–1551; in the third case one would have a *pious legacy* or a simple *modal disposition* regulated by Canons 1513– 1517.

In the first two cases the property so transmitted by the founder will become to all effects ecclesiastical property (Can. 1425; 1499, par. 2; 1497); in the *third case* one cannot properly speak of ecclesiastical foundation or ecclesiastical property since the property was not acquired by an ecclesiastical body.

AUTONOMOUS FOUNDATION, OR EC-
CLESIASTICAL INSTITUTE. In the case
of an independent foundation, or ecclesiastical institute, the following requirements are necessary: (a) a permanent
purpose, (b) a religious purpose (Can.
100, par. 1), (c) a property sufficient
and adequate for the attainment of the
purpose, (d) approval of the competent ecclesiastical authority. Therefore,
Canon Law dictates the following rules:
(a) the Ordinary shall issue a formal
decree of erection of the pious institution only when, after diligent inquiry,
he will have found that the religious
purpose intended by the founder and a
sufficient endowment (Can. 1489) are
present; (b) in the charter of the
foundation, the pious founder shall accurately define the nature of the desired
institution, its purpose and endowment,
the employment of the revenue and
their disposition in case of extinction
of the institute (Can. 1490, 1501); (c)
the Ordinary has the right and duty to
supervise, visit, control, *etc.* (Can. 1451–
1493); (d) property so transmitted by
the founder shall become property of
the legal person thus established, and
its administration shall be conducted
according to the charter of the foundation and the Code of Canon Law (Can.
1489, par. 3); (e) the erection is presumed to have been made according
to the stipulations contained in the
charter of the foundation. For any
change concerning either the institution
or its purpose, the permission of the
Holy See shall be required, unless the
charter of the foundation disposes otherwise (Can. 1494).

It is clear that a property destined
for works of religion may be subject to
canonical laws (Can. 1513–1517) even
in the event that the competent ecclesiastical authority fails to intervene or that
the dispositions of the founder are not
accepted for any reason whatsoever. On
the contrary, the property should revert
to the founder's estate (if the purpose
is found to be non-ecclesiastical). If
the civil authority intervenes as executor
of the purpose of the foundation, a lay
foundation (some authors call it *simple*

pious foundation) might ensue, but this,
too, is subject to Canon Law (Can.
1513–1517) if it is destined for works
of religion.

PIOUS OR FIDUCIARY FOUNDATION.
This is defined in Can. 1544, par. 1,
in a manner that cannot be misunderstood: "By *pious foundations* are understood temporal goods given in any
manner to an ecclesiastical legal person
with the obligation to offer Masses or
to hold other specified ecclesiastical
functions or to perform other works
of religion or charity, perpetually or for
a long period of time in return for the
revenue from the goods."

We have here the case of a property
or fund without a juridical personality,
because it *must be given* to an already
legal person; in other words, it becomes
the latter's possession and, consequently,
ecclesiastical property (Can. 1499, par.
2). From the standpoint of procedure
by which such goods are transferred
by the donor, there arises here a modal
disposition as the result of which certain
obligations are placed upon the accepting institute.

Canon 1544, paragraph 2, states that
an unnamed bilateral contract ensues
(*do ut facias*) when the foundation was
legitimately accepted. But by this it
must not be understood that such goods
become confused with the pre-existing
legal person's property, without any obligation to preserve the goods received,
for paragraph 1 of the above-quoted
Canon, defining *pious foundation*, speaks
of given goods (*bona data*), but it adds
that the obligations must be fulfilled
with the yearly revenue (*ex redditibus
annuis*); so that, in order to have a
pious foundation it is necessary that
the capital (understood in a juridical,
not an economical sense) yield fruit and
therefore not be confused with the pre-
existing property of the accepting institute. The foundation must keep its
own individuality as a property upon
which there weighs an obligation to
carry out the purpose indicated by the
founder. Hence, it cannot be disposed
of by the accepter. As a matter of fact,
if all personal property belonging to

the legal person becomes extinct, the obligations of the foundation do not become extinct, even if the beneficiary were to die; but they are transmitted to the successor or successors of the foundation (Can. 1501). This is valid also if the legal person were suppressed by the civil authority, on whom the obligations arising from the foundation would revert. On the contrary, if the assets of the pious foundation perished through no fault of the institute that accepted them, all obligations connected with it are considered extinct.

Norms for the Establishment of a Pious Foundation. (a) It is the right of the Ordinary to prescribe the limits within which the pious foundation may be established and the manner in which the revenue from the endowment is to be distributed (Can. 1545); (b) the acceptance of the property by the Institute must be authorized in writing by the Ordinary, who must ascertain that the accepting legal person can fulfill the new obligations and that the income from the property given is fully adequate to the obligations imposed. The patron of a church has no right to interfere in the accepting or in the constituting and administration of the foundation (Can. 1546). Concerning its administration, if the goods consist of money or removable goods, these must be deposited as soon as possible in a safe place to be designated by the Ordinary until such time when they shall be profitably invested in accord with the good judgment of the Ordinary (Can. 1547). Each church must keep a record of all obligations of pious foundations. Should it prove necessary, a petition for it shall be made to the Holy See (Can. 1551).

Pious Foundation and Civil Law. Though the Church has, in general, accepted in its Law the civil laws of the individual nations with regard to contractual matters, an exception is made (Can. 1529) concerning the act by which a founder assigns his property (*actus inter vivos, donatio sub modo* or *mortis causa,* will, legacy, fiduciary donation, feoffment). Canon Law holds that such right can only be drawn from

natural and canonical laws (Can. 1513). The Church claims exclusive jurisdiction concerning donations, endowments, and bequests in favor of religion or charity (pious cause). In some countries these matters are generally settled by Concordat Agreements. *Vio.*

FOUNDLING ASYLUM (or HOSPITAL). *See* Exposure (of infants).

FRAUD. Fraud is a deception consummated against another person. From the psychological standpoint, fraud is an understandable fact in the case of one who wants to avoid a penalty or obtain an object belonging to another, or employment, or the fulfillment of a promise, *etc.*; it is considered as the only or the safest or the easiest way to obtain a specific aim. Fraud, consequently, is as ancient as man (Cain invites Abel to accompany him in order that he may kill him).

Special rules are established by Canon Law and also by the civil law of various nations for fraud committed in connection with juridical acts or rescripts. In the Decretals of Gregory IX we read: "No one must gain through fraud or artifice" (ch. 16, X, I, 3); the canonical legislation, in fact, is predicated on this principle. According to some authors, the difference between artifice and fraud consists in this: that the former is committed by deeds or by stealth; the latter, on the other hand, by untruthful words or openly.

Fraud is a sin even if in some particular instances the law may not declare invalid an act committed or a concession obtained through fraud; as a matter of fact, even if the legislator upholds the validity of the act (see, for instance, Can. 1054). The sin of fraud could be excused only if it were a matter of secret compensation or a cause having a double effect (one good, one bad), provided that all the conditions required for the licitness of such acts were present (*see* Effect, Double). *Sir.*

FREEDOM (Marital). Marital freedom is freedom from anything that might be an obstacle to a valid and licit marriage. In particular, it means freedom from matrimonial impediments and other defects that could invalidate the consent of either party, especially fear (*q.v.*) and violence (*q.v.*).

Before a marriage may be celebrated, the pastor, who by law has the right to assist at the marriage, must make certain that there is no obstacle to a valid and licit celebration (Can. 1019, par. 1). This free state is considered established if the absence of any impediment is known not from merely negative arguments or indications, but on positive, morally certain grounds supported by the proofs required by law.

On several occasions the Code of Canon Law refers to this matter as an obligation of the pastor by virtue of his office, not only on the basis of Canons 1019 and 1920, but also of Canons 1096 and 1097. The seriousness of this obligation is deduced also from three Instructions issued by the Sacred Congregation for the Discipline of the Sacraments, on March 6, 1911 (AAS, 3 [1911], 102), on July 4, 1921, (AAS, 13 [1921], 348–349), and on June 29, 1941 (AAS, 33 [1941], 297–307). Canons 1096–1097 enjoin the pastor and the local Ordinary not to give permission to another priest to assist at a marriage until all the provisions demanded by the Code for proof of the free state of the parties have been complied with (Can. 1096, par. 2). Thus, the pastor or the local Ordinary may lawfully assist at a marriage, after they have complied with all the norms laid down by the law concerning the state of freedom of the contracting parties (Can. 1097, par. 1, n. 1).

The second of the Instructions of the Sacred Congregation of the Sacraments mentioned above declares that Ordinaries should exert every effort to remind pastors that they are not permitted to assist at marriages, not even for the purpose of removing the danger of concubinage from the faithful or of avoiding the scandal of a so-called civil marriage, until they are legitimately sure of the state of freedom of the contracting parties and

have observed all of the prescriptions of law in this regard (Can. 1020; Can. 1097, par. 1, n. 1). They are also to be warned not to fail to require the contracting parties to produce baptismal certificates (Can. 1021), if they were baptized in another parish.

The means for ascertaining the free state of the parties to a marriage are these three: (a) personal interrogations by the pastor; (b) the manifestation by the parties of certain records or documents; (c) the publication of the banns (*see* Banns of Marriage).

According to Can. 1020, the investigation ought to be made by the pastor who has the right of assisting at the marriage. If the parties to the marriage belong to different parishes, then both pastors have the right and duty to conduct the investigation. On the basis of Can. 1097, par. 2, this investigation is usually conducted by the bride's pastor (*see* Bond, Impediment of). *Pal.*

FREEDOM (Moral). Freedom may be considered under several aspects, psychological, ethical, ascetical, and social. Concerning psychological freedom, *see* Will, Freedom of.

Ethical freedom is the lawfulness of an act or behavior in the face of the ethical order. We may also call ethical freedom that part of psychological freedom which is not bound by law. Thus, there can be as many kinds of (ethical) freedoms as there are (ethical) laws capable of binding psychological freedom; and since ethical laws can be reduced to two types (moral and juridical), thus, too, ethical freedom may be *moral* or *juridical*. Moral freedom concerns acts which are neither imposed nor forbidden by the moral law (indifferent acts); juridical freedom, on the other hand, concerns those acts which are neither imposed nor forbidden in a specific juridical system. These two types of freedom very often, though not always, coincide; that is, there can be acts which are morally free but juridically bound, and vice versa.

By moral freedom sometimes is meant a superior form of psychological freedom by which man, strengthening his better tendencies, is able to achieve constant victory over his lower or sinful tendencies, to the point that he shall not only be able to do good or evil (first degree of psychological freedom, or freedom of contradiction), but also to acquire a facility in doing good and the better things. This is the freedom extolled by Saint Paul as the freedom proper to the Christian who has freed himself of sin and has become the servant of justice, that is, the kind of Christian to whom virtue becomes second nature, as it were, to the point that he would be incapable of giving himself to vice.

We also speak of external freedom in a sense that could be called social; external freedom is simply absence of coercion. Thus, we call free a person who acts of his own will (whether that will is really free or necessitated), provided that he is not forced or impeded by an act of violence from another. This form of freedom is most significant in the field of positive law. From a moral point of view it almost represents only a negative criterion of evaluation, in the sense that the responsibility of the act committed or omitted through violence falls directly on the one who commits violence, and only indirectly or hypothetically on the victim, depending on whether he consented to it and in the degree in which he consented to it (*see* Violence). Concerning the existence of freedom, *see* Will. *Gra.*

FREEDOM OF THE PRESS. *See* Press.

FREEDOM OF THOUGHT, OF CONSCIENCE, OF RELIGION. Freedom of thought, of conscience, and of religion are treated together here for the simple reason that the first two (freedom of thought and freedom of conscience) are usually understood as functions of freedom of religion. In fact, the consitution of the Freethinkers, published in England by Anthony Collins in 1713, revolves around religious questions and is considered to be the manifesto of theism. In order properly to understand the meaning of each of the three above-mentioned freedoms, one must establish the terms of reference for the claimed freedom; in other words, one must indicate with respect to whom or to what freedom is claimed.

The claim that man is free with respect to truth or the moral law is obviously unacceptable; only those who, following extreme forms of individualism or philosophical anarchism, place man outside any norm that transcends him could make such a claim. If one, on the other hand, claims to be free from the impositions of others, that is, if one rejects the notion that others have the right to impose on us their own ideas, or to pry into the most intimate recesses of our consciences, or to compel us to profess a particular religion, then such freedoms can assume a reasonable meaning. One, however, must specify who the "others" are from whom he claims to be free. If they are private individuals with whom he has no ties of dependency, there can be no question as to his being completely free from them. The question, however, becomes more complex when the "others" are either educators or society itself.

Concerning educators (parents are among the principal educators), the situation varies depending on whether those who are being educated have reached the age of reason or not. Concerning those who have reached the age of reason, the educator may propose and inculcate, but not impose, specific doctrines or membership in a given religion. Concerning those who have not reached the age of reason, the educator may even impose such things upon his charges in the sense that he may teach his pupils those doctrines which he honestly believes to be true, and he may school them according to the religion to which in all good conscience he adheres. To carry the respect for freedom to the point of allowing children to grow up without any religious convictions or practices in order that they may later choose their own beliefs and religion, amounts to not educating them at all and to failing in the fulfillment of an educator's obligation.

The matter of the three freedoms becomes quite involved when considered in their relationships with the two great historical forms of society: State and Church. It is a known fact that the pre-Christian State often assumed the right to impose certain specific forms of religion, at least in their external practices of worship. It can be said that a large part of the political history of non-Christian peoples was guided by the same principle which, later in history, was summed up into the famous controversial formula *cuius regio, huius religio*. But early Christianity followed an entirely different course. In fact, the first three centuries of its history are a history of struggle and martyrdom endured to uphold the three freedoms against governmental encroachment upon the conscience of the individual.

The position of the Church, of course, is obviously different because, unlike the State, the Church's jurisdiction, by its very nature, encompasses the conscience of its subjects and doctrinal elements; hence, of necessity, she must interest herself in the conscience of the faithful and doctrines touching upon religion. But a distinction must be made between the position of those outside and those inside the Church. Those who are outside the Church cannot be forced to join the Church; in other words, they cannot be compelled either to obey the precepts of the Church or to accept her doctrine, although they are bound by virtue of the natural law honestly to search for the truth. But those who are in the Church (one becomes a member of the Church through baptism) cannot dispense themselves from the duty of obedience concerning both doctrinal principles and disciplinary precepts considered by the Church as integral parts of its organism. To deny this right to a religious society amounts to crippling the very concept of that society. One last observation must be made concerning the difficulty of finding appropriate and effective means by which to enforce compliance with obligations relative both to conscience and doctrine. Whatever these means may be, it is clear that they cannot in any way resemble those used by civil society in enforcing the observance of its laws. *Gra.*

FREE ENTERPRISE. Free enterprise is an economic system, based on individualism, which developed towards the end of the eighteenth and during the first half of the nineteenth century. Its essential points may be summed up as follows:

(a) The world of wealth is governed by a combination of absolute and universal laws similar to those existing in the field of physics and chemistry. Its primary force is egotism; hedonism is the fundamental principle according to which all its decisions are made; the greatest profit for the smallest output (economic naturalism). (b) Collective good has no specific form of its own: it resolves itself into the sum total of the advantages of the various individuals (socio-economic atomism). (c) To every economic crisis the economic world responds *automatically* with a reaction capable of restoring the equilibrium (economic automatism). (d) The State must not inject itself into the economic field. If anything, its task is to eliminate the obstacles that hinder the free expansion of production. The reason is evident: the individual is perfectly aware of his own interests and is better fitted to pursue them than the state. On the other hand, while it is true that in the economic world there are periods of recession and inflation, they can be overcome by a spontaneous play of the forces of production. Therefore, any interference by the State would merely be obstructive. This is the principal reason why the system was called free enterprise.

Adam Smith (1723–1790) is justly considered the founder or, at least, the principal planner of free enterprise. His theories are expounded in *The Wealth of Nations* (1776). The book had a very wide circulation, especially in Germany. Smith's idea had a twofold opposite development, one pessimistic, the other optimistic.

Robert Malthus (1763–1834) and David Ricardo (1772–1823) took a pessimistic course. In his book *On Population*, Robert Malthus maintains that, while riches increased in arithmetical proportion, the population instead grew in geometrical proportion; this, of course, would increase considerably the disequilibrium between the means of subsistence and the surplus population. Here was the basis for his theory on the necessity of reducing the birth rate by deferring marriage. In *Principles of Political Economy* (1817), David Ricardo states that even labor would have to submit to the cold law of demand and supply. Progress would, of necessity, continually reduce the demand for human labor; consequently, in the labor market the supply would be in continual increase, while the demand would be in decline; the price of labor would steadily go down, resulting in the most miserable living conditions for the laborer.

Smith's idea was optimistically developed by B. Say and P. Bastiat. The latter in his book *Economic Harmony* extolls very vividly the innate capacity of recovery of the economic forces and the identity between individual and collective interests.

Free enterprise contributed to the elimination from the economic world of cumbersome and anachronistic structures which had been built up through the centuries. In practice it was responsible for an enormous increase in production. However, it also contained very serious errors. The good of the collectivity is not the same as the sum total of the individual good. It has a specific nature and consistency all of its own, and in order to put it into realization it is necessary that the interest of the individual be pursued in accord with the general welfare of all. The automatism of the productive force is not effective enough. Order must also be established in the economic world and, if upset, it must be re-established by the will of free men who, in seeking private ad-

vantage, must do so in subordination to or in harmony with duty. Nor may the state simply assume the attitude of a bystander, for it has a positive responsibility; and the greater the disorder in the world of wealth, the more extensive and important is also the responsibility of the State.

From the errors of a theory of unbridled competition arose, at least partially, the exploitation of the working class by capitalism; exploitation that exploded into the ever-increasingly vigorous reactions of the social movements of the last and the present centuries. *Pav.*

FREE LOVE. *See* Sexuality.

FREE TEACHING. *See* Freedom of Thought; School, Lay.

FREE TRADE. Free trade is the theory held by economists advocating freedom in international trade or exchange, as opposed to the protectionist theory. The two theories are tied up with the historical growth of trade.

In ancient and medieval times international commerce was in the hands of seafaring people. The taxes and tolls paid by traders had a fiscal rather than a protective character. With the rise and development of the modern States (sixteenth and seventeenth centuries), there became manifest a tendency not to import, but to be self-sufficient and to accumulate money (gold and silver), to which the States attributed enormous importance. The promoters of the mercantile system (mercantilism) held to the necessity of exporting as much as possible and importing as little as possible in order to maintain a commercial balance always favorable to them (*See* Exchange). In order to promote national industry, mercantilists opposed foreign competition by custom duties which, having lost their fiscal character, became protective (protectionism, Colbertism).

Free enterprise as promoted by the English economist Adam Smith and others, was not generally practiced and was short-lived. By the end of the nineteenth century nearly all nations, with the exception of Holland, Belgium, and Denmark, turned to a more or less pronounced protectionism.

The protectionist system does not consider commerce as a form of labor and of collaboration between nations, but as a *struggle* for the existence of individual countries against foreign competition, according to the maxim, "Everyone for himself, everyone in his own country." The system of free trade, on the other hand, maintains the formula of live and let live, allowing free competition to bring about a sort of division of labor among nations in the field of production, and thus create a balance in the economic and monetary field. According to free trade advocates, protective tariffs increase the cost of living, create costly and anti-economical superstructures and bring harm to national production.

The system that reconciles the two theories is one which is based on international cooperation, that is, a system of commercial treaties (bilateral treaties between two countries, or the unification of customs among various countries). Such a system presupposes a general tariff and also protective custom tariffs, but its bilateral nature assures the exchange of certain advantages. Moreover, the stability of tariffs over a specified period encourages commercial operations and increases the spirit of solidarity, thanks to the *most favored nation clause* (by which any concession made by one country to another is extended by right to the other nations with which treaties have been established), and puts into effect the system of reciprocity.

Today, after the economic upheaval caused by the war, the tendency is for a return to the system of treaties, with obvious difficulties due to monetary and economic problems which are only partially alleviated by general agreements.

Christian social economists condemn unbridled competition in the economic sphere, nor do they favor political and economic autarchy. Inspired by the principle of human solidarity, they work toward a regulated international trade in which this principle may be fully applied. This would have the tendency to eliminate the major causes of the struggle for commercial supremacy which have been the source of many disasters for humanity. *Bau.*

FREE WILL. *See* Will, Free.

FREUD. *See* Psychoanalysis.

FRUGALITY. In a strict sense, frugality is moderation in taking food. This moderation belongs to the virtue of temperance (*q.v.*).

In order to preserve his good health and to be able to attend to his work effectively, man needs wholesome and sufficient nourishment. Each individual has the obligation to take food according to his need, the amount being dependent on each one's temperament and on the nature of the work he does. In taking food, man has the obligation not to exceed the limits of that which makes him physically and spiritually fit to do his work and to engage in those activities which will enable him to tend effectively to God, his ultimate supernatural end.

God attached a particular enjoyment to the act which is directed to the preservation of the individual; it is, therefore, lawful to enjoy the pleasure connected with the moderate taking of food. But there is a certain margin between that which is for one's need or even of a legitimate satisfaction of the sense of taste and that which is beneficial; dieticians recommend leaving the table with a feeling of lightness. It is indeed a good practice to eat a little less of the food which one likes and to eat a little of the food which one does not like. Mortification of the sense of taste is one of the most helpful means of strengthening one's will and of keeping the body subject to the spirit. In taking food, as in all other actions, man tends to it as to a thing which he desires for itself, that is, as an end.

It is not lawful to take food, even moderately, simply to satisfy the sense of taste (Innocent XI, Denz., n. 1158). All admit that it is an inordinate thing to seek after the pleasure with a positive exclusion, even if only intentional, of the primary end of the act of eating, which is man's physical and spiritual fitness. There are theologians, however, who hold that it is improper to seek after the pleasure without subordinating it, at least implicitly, to a better and a higher end (such as the nutritive action which favors the good disposition of body and soul) which is always intended by one who acts according to the dictates of reason.

A moderate use of food is susceptible of being directed to a higher end than its specific ends. To seek after such higher ends increases, from a moral point of view, the value and the merit of the act, provided that the person performing the act is in a state of grace; thus, it is better to take food to obey a divine precept, or to give glory to God, than to do it simply to feed oneself. The prayer before meals has the function of placing one's mind in the framework of Christian living and of sanctifying the act of eating which, like all others, must also be directed to the glory of God.

One may sin against frugality by excess or by defect. By excess, if one takes an excessive amount of food; the sin is grave when excessive eating hinders the fulfillment of an important duty or causes serious scandal; when it causes a notable damage to one's health, or if it constitutes a serious danger of becoming severely ill; when it leads to expenditures which are damaging to the family finances or which place one in the impossibility of paying his debts. One sins against frugality by defect if he deliberately fails to take the food he needs. The failure is a mortal sin if it constitutes a grave danger of contracting a severe infirmity, or if it makes a person unable to perform important duties. *Man.*

FRUITS. See Usufruct.

FUNCTION, LITURGICAL AND EXTRA-LITURGICAL. See Liturgy.

FUNCTION, PASTORAL. Sacred functions (from *fungi*, to conduct, to perform) are acts by which public worship is performed (*see* Liturgy). *Pastoral functions* come under the general heading of sacred functions, and are not to be confused with pastoral rights (Can. 463). In fact, pastoral functions are ecclesiastical duties or offices, while pastoral rights are faculties to which stole fees and priority privileges are attached. By virtue of Canon 462 pastoral functions are reserved to the pastor. Unless otherwise prescribed in individual cases, the following are considered to be the functions of a pastor: (a) The solemn administration of baptism. In case of necessity the pastor's permission may legitimately be presumed (Can. 738, par. 1). The supplying of ceremonies omitted in an emergency baptism is also reserved to the pastor. It is less certain whether a baptism which is to be repeated, because conferred conditionally, is reserved to the pastor. (b) The carrying of the Blessed Sacrament publicly to the sick within the parish's territory, where such custom prevails. When the pastor makes use of his right, no other priest is allowed to bring Holy Communion to the sick, not even privately. Canon 847 prescribes that Holy Communion be brought to the sick publicly, unless good reasons make private administration advisable. In the United States the Blessed Sacrament is not carried publicly to the sick. Canon 849 states that any priest may privately take Holy Communion to the sick. Whether the solemn First Holy Communion of children is a pastor's function depends on particular laws, because no determination of the matter was made in the general law. It is obvious, then, that the decrees promulgated in this regard by diocesan synods must be observed. The Easter duty is not a pastor's function, although the Code exhorts the faithful to satisfy the precept in one's own parish church, or at least that one's own pastor be informed if the obligation was satisfied elsewhere. (c) The administration of the Holy Viaticum, whether public or private, and of Extreme Unction within the limits of his parish, except in the cases stated in Canons 397, n. 3, and 514 (Can. 850). In case of necessity or, at least with the presumed permission of the pastor, any priest may administer the above-mentioned sacraments, even in a solemn manner (Can. 848).

The following cases are exceptions to the above-mentioned prerogatives of a pastor: (a) The administration of the last rites to the bishop, which is done by the cathedral church's dignitaries or canons (Can. 397, n. 3). (b) The superior of clerical institutes has the right to administer the sacraments to all persons who normally live in the religious house (Can. 514, par. 1); in monasteries of nuns the right is vested in the ordinary confessor (Can. 514, par. 2); in lay congregations the chaplain has this right (Can. 514); in the seminary, the rector. (c) Publications of sacred orders (Can. 998, par. 1) and marriages (Can. 1022 ff.); the blessing of, and assistance at, marriages (Can. 1180, 1094). (d) Funeral rites. Ordinarily the deceased person's own pastor has the right to conduct funeral rites, *i.e.*, to accompany the remains from the house to the church and from there to the cemetery, and to officiate at the burial (Can. 1216). However, if a person dies outside the limits of his own parish and the heirs do not intend to transfer the body to the parish church of the deceased, the right then passes on to the pastor of the place where the person died (Can. 1218). (e) The blessing of the houses from Easter Monday on, according to the new Paschal liturgy. (Where the old rite is still observed the blessing is given on Holy Saturday or on another day, depending on local customs.) This matter concerns the solemn blessing of houses to be given by the pastor after the manner prescribed in the Roman Ritual. (f) The blessing of the baptismal font on Holy Saturday. In cathedral churches where the chapter holds its functions, the right of blessing the baptismal font is vested in the chapter. (g) To hold public processions outside the church and to preside over them, even if they originate from other churches or from churches of religious communities, provided that they start within the limits of the parish boundaries. Members of religious communities, however, have the right to hold the Corpus Christi procession within the octave of the feast (Can. 1291), and with the permission of the rector of the principal church on the feast days of St. Mark and Corpus Christi. Religious have also the right to conduct processions around their own churches without permission of the pastor of the area. The cathedral chapter has the right to conduct processions in its own church. (h) To impart solemn benedictions outside the church. Benedictions with one minister or without lay participation are not called solemn. Thus, benedictions given in lay or religious houses are not reserved to the pastor. (i) The blessing of church furnishings which according to liturgical laws are to be blessed before being used, if they are for his parish church or for churches and oratories located in his territory (Can. 1304, n. 3) except in the following cases: (1) if the rector or the superior of churches having their own rectors claim that right for themselves; (2) in churches belonging to a clerical institute; (3) in churches of nuns subject to a religious superior; (4) in churches or oratories of charitable institutions or religious houses which the ordinary exempted from his ordinary jurisdiction (Can. 1304).

The pastor's jurisdiction cannot be subdelegated, because it is a power of order (Can. 210) for which the Code does not admit delegation or subdelegation except by explicit concession (Can. 1304, n. 3).

The blessing of new mothers (churching of women) is not reserved to the pastor by the general law; it may be so reserved, however, by a particular law. Concerning stole fees, *see* Taxes, Ecclesiastical; *see also* Pastor. *Pal.*

FUNCTION, SACRED. *See* Liturgy.

FUNERAL SERVICE. In the Catholic liturgy, by funeral services are understood the last rites as prescribed in the Roman Ritual in behalf of a departed person, and the burial of the body.

The offering of prayers for the soul of a departed person is a very ancient practice in the Church. It was obvious that the Church could not show less solicitude for the deceased than that manifested from earliest times by pagans and Jews, among whom praying for the dead was a normal ritual (II Mach. 39–46). Explicit testimonies concerning prayers for the repose (*refrigerium*) of the deceased are found as far back as the second century. The *Apologia* of Aristides, for example, speaks of a farewell service for the deceased consisting of the celebration of the Eucharist and the recitation of prayers at his tomb. The apocryphal *Acta Johannis* (C. 150) speak of the Apostle praying at the tomb of Drusiana three days after her death, where he celebrated the *breaking of the bread* (Holy Mass). At the end of the second century Tertullian refers to the celebration of the Mass for the deceased on the anniversary of their death (*oblationes pro defunctis, pro nataliciis, annua die*) as a normal practice in use at Carthage. St. Cyprian fully confirms this practice. Consequently, in the most ancient liturgical documents we find collections of formulae and special prayers, such as the *Hanc Igitur* to be inserted in the Canon (*Eucologium Serapionis* of the fourth century; the *Apostolic Constitutions* of the fourth century; the Leonine and Gelasian Sacramentary of the fifth-seventh centuries). Besides the Mass, the services for the deceased were also characterized by the *Vigilia*, or wake, at which prayers from the *commendatio animae* and psalms were recited. This vigil with the recitation of psalms is often mentioned by such writers as St. Gregory of Nazianzus in *Vita S. Macrinae sororis*, 41, and in *Vita S. Pacomii: PG* 73, 239; St. Augustine in his *Confess.*, 9, 12; St. Caesarius of Arles in his *Reg. virginum*, 70; St. Gregory of Tours in his *Historia Francorum*, VII, 1; St. Gregory the Great in his *Dial.* IV, 55, *etc.*

Of equal antiquity (c. sixth-seventh centuries) is the Office of the Dead (*Officium defunctorum*), recited on the third, seventh, and thirtieth day after death and on the anniversary day. Of relatively recent date, on the other hand, is the *absolution* service, which in its present form does not go back farther than the ninth or tenth centuries, although some parts of it are older than that period (for example, the introductory prayer, *Non intres*, is found in the Gregorian Sacramentary; the *Libera me, Domine* dates back to the ninth century). There are two formulae of absolution, one used for ordinary people, laymen and priests, found in the *Rituale Romanum*, the other, which is more solemn, is used for the pope, cardinals, bishops, and high civil officials. The latter is found in the *Liber Pontificalis*.

Today the funeral service comprises: the prayers (*De profundis* and *Miserere*) recited in the home of the deceased or where the body has been laid out and on the way to the church, the *Subvenite* upon entering the church; the Mass; the absolution; the *In Paradisum* and *Benedictus* at the cemetery or on the way with the prayers and the final *Oremus* at the moment of committal.

Besides the funeral rite *in die obitus*, there are also services for the third, seventh, and thirtieth day after death and for the anniversary. Ordinarily, these services comprise only the celebration of the Mass and the absolution over the catafalque in place of the body. At times the Mass is preceded by the recitation either of Matins or of only one nocturn from Matins and Lauds in its entirety from the Office of the Dead. Funeral services with the body present are forbidden on major solemnities of our Lord, of our Blessed Mother, of the saints and on the last three days of Holy Week. The services of the third, seventh, and thirtieth day after death and on the anniversary are forbidden on Sundays, feasts of first and second class, vigils of Christmas and Pentecost, and on the days during the octaves of Christmas, Easter, and Pentecost, on Ash Wednesday, and during Holy Week. The above rules apply only in the case of solemn services, that is, celebration of the Mass and chanting of the Office. Non-solemn or private services are permitted on many of the days excluded above.

All the faithful, after death, must be transferred to the church for the funeral service. As a general rule, the obligation is a grave one (Can. 1215). Besides the baptized, catechumens also have the right to funeral services. Catechumens are those who, through no fault of their own, died without baptism (Can. 1239). Excluded, however, are all others who have not been baptized. As a penalty, the following are denied ecclesiastical burial: baptized apostates, heretics, schismatics, those who joined a society condemned by the Church, those who died in a duel, and, finally, public sinners, unless before dying they showed some sign of repentance (Can. 1240–1241).

As a general rule, funeral services are to be held in the parish church of the deceased; if the deceased belongs to more than one parish the funeral services shall be held in the church of the parish in which he died (Can. 1216, par. 1–12). If a person died outside his parish or parishes, the funeral services should be held in the proper parish of the deceased if this can be done conveniently and if it is so desired by the relatives (Can. 1218, par. 1–3). Every faithful can choose for the funeral services a church other than his own parish church provided that it is a parish church, or a church of regulars in the strict sense of the term (not, however, of monastic nuns) or a church subject to the right of patronage (for the patrons), or a church which enjoys a special privilege in this regard (Can. 1216, par. 1; 1223, par. 2; 1224, #1; 1225).

If a cardinal dies in the city of Rome, his funeral services will be held in the church which the Holy Father shall designate; if he dies outside of Rome, services must be held in the most prominent church in the city or place of his death unless the cardinal has chosen another church for his funeral (Can. 1219, par. 1). The funeral of a residential bishop, even if he be a cardinal, shall be held in his own cathedral church; the funeral of an abbot and prelate *nullius* shall be held in the abbatial or prelatial church, as the case may be. Funerals of religious are to be held in the church of the religious house in which they resided or any other church of their institute (Can. 1221, 1224, n. 2). The above norms apply also in the case of those who die in a religious house or a college where they reside either as guest or for reasons of health or education, unless the deceased has acquired a domicile there (Can. 92), or the place is exempt from parochial jurisdiction (Can. 464, par. 2).

The pastor is bound in conscience to observe these norms (Can. 1230). The poor shall be given decent funeral and burial services absolutely free of charge. In other cases, the so-called stole fees shall be contributed in accordance with local customs and diocesan regulations. *See also* Stole Fees; Burial, Ecclesiastical. Cig.

GAIN. *See* Interest, Labor, Price, Work.

GAMBLING DEN. *See* Gaming and Gambling.

GAMING AND GAMBLING. When not indulged in as a mere pastime, gaming and gambling are contracts of playing (*contractus ludi*) in which the contestants, two or more, agree that the stakes go to the winner. In order that gambling may be morally lawful as a contract, all fraud or force must be excluded, the participants must be free to dispose of what they stake, and all must enjoy equal advantages.

In case of fraud or coercion the contract can be voided at the option of the one against whom such improper means were employed. Such a person may keep what he wins. If the cheater wins, he is bound to make restitution even if the other party does not rescind the agreement because of ignorance. He is guilty of cheating who purposely takes a position whereby he can see the cards in his opponent's hands. Generally, however, it is not considered cheating if one looks at another's cards when he holds them carelessly; or if one simulates fear in order to allure his opponent to play or bet rashly.

The gambling contract is invalid for those who gamble with money or goods over which they have no *free disposal*. The loser who cannot pay may retain the stakes if he wins, since the lack of an object makes a contract void. Thus, too, playing with one who is semi-intoxicated is an illicit operation, since such a person cannot contract validly. If the *inequality* of the players is so great that it is morally certain who will be the winner, the loser need not pay unless he knew beforehand of the superiority of his opponent. But one who is merely more experienced than the other may safely keep what he wins, even though his opponent was unaware of his superiority, unless the one who is more experienced fraudulently induces the other to play.

Gambling is not favored by the law, although betting on horse or dog races is legalized in a dozen states in the U. S. A. Some forms of gambling are criminal offenses, but usually the only penalty for private gambling is the unenforceability of the transaction in the court. In most states of the U. S. A. *lotteries* are prohibited by law. There will always be difficulty in legally defining gambling and distinguishing between acts which violate gambling laws and those which, while presenting questionable appearances, are yet not obviously to be placed in the same category (H. Jone, *Moral Theology*, 309). Canon 138 of the Code of Canon Law forbids clerics to engage in gambling.

Sports as a moderate pastime are quite legitimate; as a matter of fact, if taken as a form of recreation, they may be not only useful but even necessary, particularly for persons engaged in very taxing work and burdensome responsibilities. The ancient adage "a sound mind in a sound body" is true today as in centuries past. "To exercise the body in a healthful manner and thereby rest the mind and prepare it for new undertakings, to sharpen the senses in order to acquire a greater intensity of penetration of the intellectual faculties, to exercise the muscles and accustom them to force in order to build up character and a strong will are some of the ideas with which people should engage in sports activities." In like manner, competitive sports must be kept within proper bounds and engaged in with the understanding that they are not ends in themselves, but are means to a "perfect and balanced formation and education of the entire man, for whom sports are an aid toward the ready and joyful fulfillment of his duties, whether they be connected with his work or his family." In the words of Pope Pius XII, "Sports are a school for loyalty, courage, endurance, determination, universal brotherhood; all natural virtues, but which serve as a solid foundation for the supernatural virtues and prepare one to withstand without weakness the weight of more serious obligations."

The athlete must never lose sight of the fact that "the body does not occupy the first place in man" . . . "The primacy in the human composition does not belong to the body taken from the earth's slime, but to the spirit, to the spiritual soul."

Thus, competitive sports are legitimate when not carried to extremes and when pursued without neglect of duties and obligations of a higher order. H. J. Y.

GENITAL HERPES. *See* Diseases, Venereal.

GENOCIDE. Genocide is a new word which means destruction of a nation or a race. According to a declaration of the United Nations Assembly, genocide involves a variety of actions against an ethnical, national, or religious group: (a) extermination of all its members; (b) grave material or mental harm, as the deliberate spreading of diseases, alcoholism, *etc.*; (c) imposition of such conditions of living as to cause a total or partial physical destruction of people; (d) hindering of new births; (e) forced transfer of the children of a given group from their places of birth.

This crime has often been committed in the history of mankind. In ancient times, conquests were generally consolidated by extermination of the vanquished or by their reduction to slavery, as in the case of the Helots on the part

of the Spartans. Pharaoh had planned the destruction of the Israelites in Egypt by ordering their male children exposed. In more recent times, Cromwell devised the subjugation of the Irish Catholics whom he dispossessed almost entirely of their territory, barred them from the professions, deprived them of all political rights and some civil rights as well (such as the prohibition, applicable also to merchants, to own more than six horses, which in those days were the only means of transportation), and finally, left the peasants (the major part of the population) to the mercy of implacable agents of English landowners. This regime continued for nearly two hundred years.

In this century, the national Turkish hero, Ata-Turk, tried to annihilate the Armenians by mass deportations. Throughout Europe, Hitler directed his policy of extermination against the Jews, of whom he destroyed millions.

Genocide, properly so-called, implies the intention of proceeding systematically to the destruction of a certain people. Thus the case of the Indians in America, for instance, cannot be called genocide because, while it is true that the indigenous groups of the northern regions were decimated by the English settlers, they were spared in the areas dominated by Spain, from Mexico downward. In fact, in the English territories the survivors were allowed to live in the so-called *reservations*, and to those who desire it, the U. S. A. grants full citizenship; it even accords them a certain distinction, precisely because they are the original Americans.

A juridical position against genocide was only taken in recent times. After World War II, the United Nations concerned itself with this question in opposition to the race theory expounded by Rosenberg in his *Myth of the Twentieth Century*, and applied by Hitler with appalling cruelty. Genocide is contrary to the fundamental principles of natural law. Each man and, therefore, each race and nation, has a right to exist. Only God, as Creator of all and, consequently, as absolute master of all created things, governs this right.

Christian teaching condemns genocide not only because it is opposed to natural law and the universality of Christ's message calling all peoples to be children of God, but also because it is contrary to the plans of Divine Providence. In calling all men to contribute to the realization of the kingdom of God on earth, Divine Providence uses not only individual action, but also the activities of men as members of society. Families, nations and empires, each with its own characteristics, have a mission of their own to fulfill. In His inscrutable designs God uses even the different qualities of each race to fulfill particular functions. The destruction of a race or a nation, devised or decreed by the human mind under any pretext, even that of the common good, or for purported zeal for the glory of God, constitutes an act of intolerable pride and sacrilegious arrogance with respect to God's Wisdom, who has reserved to Himself the judgment of all peoples and nations. *Boz.*

GERIATRICS. Geriatrics refers to the modern branch of medicine concerned with the diseases of the aged. Another term, similar in meaning, though more comprehensive in scope, is *gerontology*, which is the science concerned with the scientific study of the phenomena of old age.

The fact that medicine should concern itself with the aged is not, to be sure, a novelty. What is new is rather the fact that prevention and treatment of the diseases of the aged, their hospitalization and assistance has been raised to the level of specialization. Indeed, this is not an idle fancy nor the result of a desire for innovation, but a necessity dictated by the biological progress of modern society.

In recent years, due to improved hygienic conditions everywhere and the widespread use of antibiotics, we are witnessing a real revolution in the field of population distribution from the standpoint of age, susceptibility to sickness, and mortality of the individual. The end result of these changed conditions is that while, until a few years ago, the aged represented a minority, today they are fast becoming a majority. And the irony of it all is that, despite these facts, public welfare legislation and health services continue to concentrate their widest attention on contagious diseases.

STATISTICS. A century ago 70% of deaths were the result of contagious diseases. This percentage was about 30% in 1935 and now it has become half that amount. Child mortality during the past fifty years has been reduced by two thirds, and the average span of life, meanwhile, has almost doubled by its rise to above 65 years of age. Furthermore, while, according to statistics of seventy years ago, out of 1000 new-born children only 326 reached 60 years of age, and 67 the eightieth year, now these limits are reached by 577 and 167 individuals respectively. Finally, today 10% of the population of civilized nations surpasses 65 years of age.

These data, together with the fact that the mortality rate is notably on the decline in all civilized countries, have caused the population of aged persons to increase everywhere to an unprecedented high level. Obviously, this has brought an increase in the number of diseases characteristic of old age, generally called *degenerative chronic diseases*: cardiopathies, arteriopathies, hypertension, chronic nephritis, hepatopathies, diabetes, arthritis, cancer, *etc.* A mere glance at North American statistics shows that in the last fifty years mortality due to chronic and acute diseases has had approximately the following course:

	1901	1920	1945
Chronic forms	50	60	86
Acute forms	50	40	14

Finally, from the statistical data of a large American insurance company we gather that, while in 1925 one half of all hospital admissions were for cases of acute infections and only 5% for cases of chronic diseases (typical of aged persons), in 1945 hospital admissions for acute cases were 14% while for chronic cases they were 28%.

SANITARY CONSIDERATIONS. This inversion of statistics justifies the statements by pioneers of geratrics to the effect that, to quote Luigi Ferrannini, "we are at a turning-point in the medical science dealing with old age diseases. . . . These diseases, of course, have always existed but they are not receiving all the attention that they deserve." In fact, statistics by no means cover all the cases of chronic diseases, many of which are often either ignored and neglected because of financial difficulties, or are not indicated on death certificates, which usually record only the immediate or main cause of death.

Furthermore, the problem confronting geriatrics is complicated by the fact that the diseases of the aged are practically incurable and assume peculiar characteristics with a generally deceitful beginning, a slow course and a mild symptomatology, so that often they they go unobserved; hence, the need for particularly diligent investigations for the prevention of such diseases, for protracted and patient treatments, scientific, social and clinical facilities for the prophylaxis, study, care, and treatment of old age diseases.

Such facilities, whether they be called hospitals for the aged or for the chronically ill, are greatly wanting even in the most progressive, civilized nations. Hospitals are almost exclusively used for the care of acute illnesses, and a patient is promptly discharged as soon as the disease slides into a chronic phase. Facilities for the treatments of old age diseases are positively indispensable in view of the increased possibilities for the prevention and cure of chronic infirmities. It is true that in almost every large city there are asylums, old peoples' rest homes and the like, but these praiseworthy institutions, as Ferrannini keenly observes, have as much in common with hospitals for chronic diseases of the aged as kindergartens have with children's hospitals.

GEROSURGERY. The use of "surgery for the aged" until a few years ago was limited to a few emergency cases, such as strangulated hernias, acute appendicitis, perforative or occlusive gastroenteric conditions, prostate infection, and the like. Other types of pathological surgery for the aged were shunned as too risky for those who had reached or surpassed the seventieth year of age and who, being near the limit of the human span of life, were "to be left to die in peace."

The constant increase in the span of human life has so gradually changed the general attitude that old age is no longer considered an obstacle to active surgery.

PSYCHOGERIATRICS. Contrary to common belief, senile deterioration is due more to psychological than to somatic causes, and the latter are undoubtedly enhanced by factors of a psychopathological nature. The deterioration, in fact, is to some extent the result of the frustrations of modern living, such as compulsory retirement, ineligibility for employment beyond a certain age limit, and the like. This is even more clearly brought out by the fact that the woman who, as "queen of the home," remains in her own natural environment, usually outlasts man in her usefulness to society.

Aware of having been "cast aside," the elderly person assumes necessarily a disappointed attitude which leads him to melancholy. This often occurs despite his efforts to react to such a depressing condition by resorting to one or more of the defense mechanisms indicated by M. H. Hollander: (a) *projection* (it is the world that has worsened, not the aged person that has become incapable of adjusting to it); (b) *rigidity* (the aged person refuses to adjust to conditions as a matter of principle, thus avoiding a forced admission that adjustment was made impossible by the age factor), and (c) *exploitation of the past* (as escape from actual difficulties). The understanding of such defense mechanisms is useful to the psychologist and psychiatrist in his efforts to help the individual become adjusted to old age. As a matter of fact, the main tragedy is not so much physical suffering as his being condemned to a demoralizing inertia and to an ill-tolerated dependency on others. Geriatrics can, and even must, help the aged in their desire and need to reach a sound old age "as useful citizens both to themselves and to the community."

MORAL CONSIDERATIONS. The ethical value of geriatrics and of cultural and health institutions as advocated by gerontologists is clearly established. Their aim is to prolong life and, what counts more, to wage a timely and effective fight against infirmities and diseases which make man's declining years difficult and unhappy. Their efforts are directed to a decisive increase in the productivity of society and to assuring comfort and well-being to those who contributed so many years of their existence to the welfare of society.

It is, therefore, a work of exquisite Christian charity to aid this increasingly large segment of society, alleviating by every possible means their many and often grave physical pains, thus making a rich and rewarding contribution to their spiritual serenity. *Riz.*

GERONTOLOGY. See Geriatrics.

GHETTO. See Judaism.

GIFTS OF THE HOLY SPIRIT. As man is dependent on God concerning his being, so too he is dependent on Him concerning his actions: every human action requires a motion from the First Cause. Actual graces (*see* Grace) are divine motions leading man to perform supernatural actions. There are graces that move man's spiritual faculties to perform actions which are proper to them, such as discursive or deliberate actions (common or ordinary graces); there are others which move man's spiritual faculties to act in a superior manner, that is, in a superdiscursive and superdeliberative manner (special graces); the actions corresponding to such special graces are actions of a superhuman character. God's activity in His creatures is common to the Three Divine Persons. However, the divine operations having a special resemblance to the personal attributes of one or the other of the Three Persons are attributed to that Person; hence, all of God's operations in which God's love for man shines forth in a particular manner, especially the special motions of grace, though they be not the exclusive action of the Third Person of the Blessed Trinity, are attributed to the Holy Spirit, who is God's personal Love. The special motions of grace, therefore, can rightfully be called gifts of the Holy Spirit. It is, however, the common doctrine of the Church that at the moment of man's justification (baptism), together with sanctifying grace, God gives some entities which dispose man's intellect and will to receive special motions of grace and to elicit superhuman acts corresponding to such motions. These infused entities, which are real habits distinct from infused virtues, are properly called gifts of the Holy Spirit. They render the soul, already in the state of sanctifying grace, an apt instrument of the Holy Spirit, who works in it in a superior manner. St. Gregory of Nazianzus compares the gifts of the Holy Spirit to the strings of a cithara; touched by the Divine Artist, these strings produce the most melodious sounds. These gifts are also compared to the sails of a ship blown by favorable winds that move the vessel. The encyclical letter *Divinum illud munus* (AAS 29 [1897], 654) explains fully the doctrine of the gifts of the Holy Spirit.

Man's needs are many, and multiform is the action of the Holy Spirit in man. According to traditional teaching, the gifts of the Holy Spirit are seven: *wisdom, understanding, counsel, fortitude, knowledge, piety,* and *fear of the Lord.* This enumeration is based on a text of Isaias (11:1 ff.).

By the gift of *wisdom,* the Holy Spirit enables man to understand more deeply the truths of faith and to discover their intimate meaning, their hidden treasures and sublime harmonies: no evidence is obtained of the mysteries, properly so-called, but by this gift one can understand that there is no opposition between them and rational truths, and that their apparent obscurity is the effect of a persistent inadequacy of our intelligence, too weak to gaze on divine light.

By the gift of *understanding*, the Holy Spirit enables man to understand created things in their relation to God; to see in other men the image of God and in irrational creatures the vestiges of God through which man is led to God; to find in the happy or sad events which take place in the life of individuals and nations the means through which purification and a more intimate union with God is attained; it also enables man to see with much clarity the horror of sin.

By the gift of *knowledge*, the Holy Spirit gives man a superior knowledge of God as a lovable Being, and a proper appreciation of all created things in God. This knowledge of God, though still obscure, is nevertheless far superior to the knowledge which can be obtained of God by faith alone and the naked reason; it is, in fact, an almost experimental knowledge of God, Who, producing marvelous effects in the soul (Rom. 8:16), causes in it a sense of nearness to Him as a life-giving Principle and as a Being Who is extremely amiable and infinitely superior to all other concepts. The gift of knowledge is, in a way, similar to the presence of the soul in man, which, though not seen, is nevertheless felt in his actions.

By the gift of *counsel*, the Holy Spirit suggests that which is to be done or not to be done in a specific case, thus eliminating uncertainties and perplexities which may arise in the application of general norms to particular cases.

By the gift of *piety*, the Holy Spirit causes in man's will a superhuman filial love toward God as our Father, and sentiments of fraternal love toward his neighbor, including those who may have wronged him. This love prompts man to a complete dedication to the cause of the glory of God and the good of souls.

By the gift of *fortitude*, the Holy Spirit gives to man's will the energy enabling him to undertake without hesitation, and to carry on to their ultimate ends, the most arduous tasks for God's glory and the good of souls, and also

to bear gladly, even for many years, the most severe sufferings.

By the gift of *fear of the Lord*, the Holy Spirit produces in man's soul a filial respect, that is, a reverent fear of Divine Majesty, a fear which does not interfere with an intimate union with God, our Father, but which deters man from anything which might offend God; it also prompts him to mortify his senses and all inordinate affections.

It is certain that the gifts of the Holy Spirit do not remain inoperative in the soul, although they are not equally active in everyone. Man may dispose himself to receive with greater frequency the special motions of the Holy Spirit by thinking often of God, by mortifying the love of self and his inclination to pleasure, by never deliberately resisting divine inspirations, clearly perceived (discerning of spirits), even when the sacrifices required appear difficult; by asking with humility and confidence the special motions of the Holy Spirit. *Man.*

GIGANTISM, GIANTISM. *See* Hypophysis, Pituitary.

GLORIA PATRI (Glory be to the Father). The *Gloria Patri* ("Glory be to the Father"), called also the minor doxology, is an important liturgical formula used to glorify the One and Triune God. Attributed to Pope St. Damasus, it has a very rich epigraphic and literary tradition. According to Origen (*De oratione*, 33), each prayer is to be ended with the praise to God through Christ in the Holy Spirit. The Fathers often concluded their discourses in such a manner. The ancient Oriental formula was *Gloria Patri per Filium in Spiritu Sancto* ("Glory be to the Father through the Son in the Holy Spirit"). A Syriac inscription of the year 369 was adopted in place of this formula by Flavianus, Bishop of Antiochia (c. 381), and by many monks, as one which indicated more accurately the con-substantiality of the three Divine Persons; this formula was *Gloria Patri et Filio et Spiritu Sancto* ("Glory be to the Father and to the Son and to the Holy Spirit"), and it was generally used as a characteristic formula against the Arians.

In the Mozarabic liturgy, in accordance with Psalm 28:3, and a precept of a Council of Toledo, held in 633, the formula is *Gloria et honor Patri et Filio et Spiritui Sancto* ("Glory and honor be to the Father and to the Son and to the Holy Spirit"). For centuries in the West and even now in the east, the second part of the minor doxology was simply *Nunc et semper et in saecula saeculorum* ("Is now and ever shall be world without end") after Romans 16: 27 and Hebrews 13:21. It is not exactly known when and where the addition *sicut erat in principio* ("as it was in the beginning") was introduced: it came into use in the West at the time of the Arian controversies, and only in the West has it attained a very wide use. The Second Vaison Synod (529) decreed that by reason of the Arian heresy, the formula used in Rome should also be used in Gaul. The first testimony concerning a doxological ending to the Psalms is found in Cassianus (*De instit. Coenobiorum*, 2, 8).

The Gloria Patri is said at the end of each Psalm: by this the chants of the Old Testament are given, even outwardly, a Christian flavor, and the praise contained in it is expressly addressed to the Most Holy Trinity. In accord with an ancient custom in the Church, during Passion time it is omitted in the Mass and the Responsories of the Divine Office, during the Sacred Triduum of Holy Week, and also in the Psalms of the Divine Office, Masses, and Office of the dead. *Pal.*

GLORY OF GOD. Glory, formally understood, consists in this: that the excellence of an intellectual being be known and praised. St. Augustine defines it as "a clear knowledge with praise." The basis of formal glory (called objective glory) is the excellence of an intellectual being and also the manifestation of his eminent qualities in his works.

There is in God a twofold glory: in-

ternal and external. The internal glory of God consists in the infinite knowledge God has of Himself and in the infinite love with which He loves Himself. His objective external glory, called also fundamental glory, is the manifestation of the divine attributes in His creatures and their manifold activities. The external and formal glory of God consists in this: that the intellectual creatures know God and freely tend toward Him as to their ultimate end; among the acts constituting God's formal glory, loving God above all things is the main one here on earth.

God, who because of His infinite perfections is worthy of all honor, and who in His works depends on no creature, made the world for His own external glory (Vatican Council, Denz., 1805). However, since this glory is not really distinct from the perfection of His creatures, God not only cannot be accused of being an egotist, but His work of creation is an act of supreme benevolence. Man in particular, who has the obligation of formally glorifying God in all his free actions, shall be perfect and blessed in the measure in which he shall have given God this external glory. *Man.*

GLOVES. *See* Sacred Vestments.

GLUTTONY. Gluttony consists of an excessive seeking after the pleasure connected with the use of food and drink. The right amount of food and drink may be exceeded in various ways: taking more than is useful in maintaining a good disposition of body and soul; using exceedingly exquisite food and drink or food and drink whose cost is beyond one's own state and financial circumstances; seeking after very highly seasoned dishes; taking, without reason, food or drink outside the hours of regular meals; eating or drinking with too much avidity; taking alcoholic drinks to the point of losing one's reasoning faculty (*see* Temperance).

Moreover, it is generally admitted that it is an inordinate thing to seek after the pleasure of taste in a way that the primary end of the taking of food or drink is excluded in a positive manner. There are, however, theologians who also hold that it is improper to seek after the pleasure of taste without subordinating it, even implicitly, to a higher and more honest end (the nourishing effect which favors the good disposition of body and soul), as done by those who behave in conformity with the dictates of reason.

Of itself, gluttony is a venial sin, but it may become a mortal sin (a) if one is so minded as to be ready to violate a serious precept rather than deprive himself of the pleasure of taste; (b) if one transgresses in a serious manner the Church law of fasting and abstinence; (c) if one exceeds the proper limits to the point of causing considerable damage to his health, or when such excesses give rise to a serious danger of severe illness; (d) when the intemperance is such as to cause expenditures far in excess of the family budget or if it places the intemperate in the impossibility of paying his debts; (e) when it hinders a person from fulfilling an important duty or is the cause of grave scandal; (f) when one takes such a quantity of alcoholic drink as to deprive himself totally of the power of reason, or even only partially, but with grave scandal.

Gluttony is a serious obstacle to perfection and a source of many other sins. It produces a state of mental obfuscation and euphoria; it leads to a lack of dignity in behavior, to the use of vulgar language, to the revealing of secrets which are not to be disclosed, and to damaging other peoples' names; it also weakens the will and disposes to incontinence, which is a direct effect of gluttony. *Man.*

GOD. God is the primary basis of the moral law inasmuch as He is its efficient, exemplary, and final cause. As Creator and Supreme Ruler of the entire universe, God, from all eternity, conceived the laws according to which all human actions must be performed, and impressed them in His creation. Such laws may be seen both in the ob-

jective order of things and their nature (insofar as a human mind is capable of knowing it), and in positive precepts (*see also* Law, Eternal, Natural, Divine-Positive). Thus, every law comes either directly from God or indirectly, that is, from an authority which derives its power from Him. Man tends to his ultimate end by the observance of this moral law because the moral perfection which results from it makes him similar to his Divine Exemplar and, above all, because such perfection leads him to the possession of God known and loved supernaturally in paradise. He who denies the existence of God destroys the only foundation upon which the moral law rests. This foundation cannot be replaced by any other criterion, be it based on utilitarianism, or welfare, or categoric imperatives, or the accomplished fact externally imposed by other men: ". . . there exists no authority except from God" (Rom. 13:1).

Thus, every law or precept refers ultimately to God Himself, and any violation of the moral law constitutes a rebellion against God. However, while this rebellion is indirect insofar as the largest part of the moral law is concerned (for its direct object is a created good [human life, material goods, honors, *etc.*], in respect to another part of the law), disobedience to God is direct, particularly insofar as it concerns those things of which God and the things of God are the immediate object and which determine our duties toward Him, such as adoration, cult, faith, hope, charity, *etc.* For all practical purposes, these duties are contained in the obligations arising from the three theological virtues, and the first three of the Ten Commandments of God (*see* Adoration, Blasphemy, Charity, Cult, Faith, Oath, Liturgy, Hope, Tempting God, *etc.*). *Dam.*

GOLD. Gold is a metal which because of particular properties of high value, unalterableness, physical, and economic divisibility and general estimation has been used by nearly all civilized nations as legal currency.

Essentially, however, gold is the currency used in international exchange. After the first world war this became its only function. At first, gold theoretically served as a basis for determining the value of national currency compared to a determined amount of gold, though gold was no longer in internal circulation. Hence, the primary function of gold is a juridical one.

Today various currencies are calculated in relation to the dollar, not to gold. The monetary value of gold is officially anchored to a price fixed by the dollar, in 1934. It remained unaltered, in spite of the fact that all other currencies expressed in dollars have more than doubled since 1934, through public control of monetary transaction in gold and foreign trade in gold. Along with the official gold market, free, semi-free, and clandestine gold markets have developed, where gold is traded at much higher prices. This shows that the so-called myth of gold has by no means been eliminated.

Gold as currency and standard of all values, was, in the past, recognized as helpful since production was limited by factors, to a large extent independent of the human will, which constituted a protection against monetary speculation. Today, when all monetary systems have become rigid, the principal complaint against gold is that it is oscillating in value subject to circumstances. Nevertheless, gold has a value partially independent from monetary or quasi-monetary use; thus these monetary services are greatly appreciated in times as politically disturbed as ours. In another period of great political disturbances at the beginning of the modern era, when precious metals were still the only internal currencies because of the limited development of the credit system, gold was considered the very core of wealth. This generally does not occur today, although it is probable that gold will still continue to render monetary services to mankind.

From a moral point of view, in dealing with economic problems one must recall that gold has an instrumental function; hence, it must not be allowed to absorb the attention and activity of man as if the economic well-being, of which the possession of gold is a sign, were the ultimate end of individual or social life. *Mai.*

GONADS. Gonads (from the Greek *gonos*, reproduction) are the genital glands, or glands producing the germinal elements; they are the testes or *testicles* in males, the *ovaries* in females.

The male gonad consists of two secreting tissues: (a) a tubular tissue in which the sperms are formed; these are the fecundating elements ejected with other secretions from accessory glands and constituting the external testicular secretion; and (b) a purely endocrine *interstitial tissue*, which exercises the following very important physiological actions: (1) trophomorphe-exciting action favoring the development of the sexual characteristics, even secundary and tertiary (tone of voice, distribution of hair, bodily proportions, characteristics of combativeness and aggressiveness); (2) specific stimulating action; (3) metabolic action; (4) tonic action on the nervous system (including the psychological biotone); (5) correlations with other glands of internal secretion (synergia with the prehypophysis, suprarenal glands, thyroid; antagonism with the thymus and the hypophysis).

In senility the gonads are subject to a more or less conspicuous process of degeneration, simple or fibrous atrophy, with a progressive reduction and degenerative alteration of the spermatogenesis.

The female gonad also has an external secretion (the production of the *ova*) and an internal secretion regulated by the ovulation, *i.e.*, the development and maturation of the oöphorous follicles, which, under the stimulating influence of special hormones of the prehypophysis, grow and make it possible for the ovum contained in them to be surrounded by a liquid mass, the *liquor folliculi*, containing a special hormone called *folliculine* or *extrine*. When the follicle breaks, the ovum passes through the Fallopian tube into the uterine cavity, where it is eventually fecundated. The walls of the follicle undergo notable modifications, giving rise to the formation of the so-called *corpus luteum* (lutein body) which produces a particular hormone called *lutein*. If fecundation has taken place, the lutein body becomes hypertrophied for several months and, by its hormonic secretion, protects the embryo from premature expulsion (abortion). If fecundation failed, the corpus luteum regresses within about two weeks and another oöphorous follicle matures; and so on, for about thirty-five years.

The task of the folliculine is that of governing the first phase of the menstrual cycle (two weeks), emphasizing all the somatic and psychological characteristics of femininity; the "Prolan A" hormone of the prehypophysis and the thyroid hormone act in correlation with the follicular hormone. The second phase of the cycle (the other two weeks) is governed by the lutein which inhibits the maturation of a new follicle and stimulates the phenomena relative to the maternal functions. The prehypophysial ("Prolan B") hormone, the hormone of the suprarenal crust and insulin act synergically with the hormone of the corpus luteum.

The entire female endocrinology is based physiologically on the secretion of the two above mentioned hormones; but it is necessary also to recall the existence of a viriligenic hormone secreted by the "interstitial cells of the ovarian hylo" which, under specific conditions, may favor the appearance of more or less marked masculine characteristics.

In both sexes the reproduction period goes from puberty to the climacteric: these phases of the sexual life are more definite in woman than in man.

Puberty (more precocious in girls than in boys) appears between the tenth and the sixteenth year of age. It is characterized by a gradual development of a sexual individuality coordinated with an increase and maturation of the gonads and with the final development of the whole of the sexual characteristics,

such as voice change and growth of hair in the male, development of the breasts and growth of hair and also the appearance of the menses in females. These complex manifestations, often accompanied by periodic emotional disequilibrium, well known also to moralists and educators, depend on the evolution of the various endocrine and exocrine components of the gonads. This evolution is stimulated and guided by the gonadotropic hormones of the anterior hypophysis (pituitary gland), which is the real motor of sexual life.

The latter abates more or less rapidly with the advent of the *climacteric*: this phase, which is much more noticeable in the woman on account of the cessation of the menses (menopause) appears around the fiftieth year in the female, and between fifty-five and sixty in the male (*anthropause*): it is characterized by functional depression and regression of the gonads and also by a dysfunction of the hypophysis and the thyroid. Hence, a more or less transitory endocrinal disequilibrium affecting the entire organism and giving rise to the well-known psychosomatic manifestations noticed during this delicate biological phase, such as neurovegetative disturbances, cephalalgias, virilism in the woman, adiposity, nervous crises, humor depression, *etc.* Modern clinical medicine, however, aided by endocrinology, is able to control the disorders of the climacteric with remarkable results.

This is not the place to discuss the disturbances caused by ill-formed gonads. We shall mention only that to attribute, as it is often done, to the uterus (*sic et simpliciter*) any disorder of the female sexual regions and the neuropsychological disequilibrium observed in the woman, is, to say the least, an exaggeration. The uterus is merely a kind of nest destined to receive and protect the fecundated ovum or egg-cell, up to its full development. When the egg-cell is not fecundated, the uterus undergoes periodic modifications of its mucous membrane which bring on the menses. But the ovary is the regulator of the entire female sexual activity; the ovary is, in turn, variously regulated by the other endocrine glands, chiefly the hypophysis (*q.v.*) and the thyroid (*q.v.*).

We shall recall also that the absence or removal of the gonads gives rise to a typical condition of *agenitalism* and *eunuchism*, the fundamental elements of which are dealt with in the article on "Castration." *Hypogenitalism* offers a less serious clinical condition which, on the basis of the prevalence of one or the other group of symptoms, is called feminism (in man), virilism (in woman), senilism, gigantism, amenorrhea, *etc.* *Cryptorchidism* (failure on one or both testicles to descend into the scrotum), besides being a frequent cause of male hypogenitalism, is an important phenomenon because often it is the primary cause of functional impotence (*see* Impotence). Finally, *hypergenitalism* may cause a particular case of dwarfism (hypergenital dwarfism), precocious puberty, *etc.*

For other sexual disorders having a close relation to morals, *see* Impotence and Perversion, Sexual.

GONOCHORISM. *See* Sexology.

GONORRHEA. *See* Diseases, Venereal.

GOOD, ECONOMIC. Human want constitutes the basis of all economic activity. In order to attain his ends and self-development, man is compelled to seek the necessary means from the external world around him. A *good* is whatever is regarded as apt to satisfy a need. But such goods have an economic character if, besides being useful in satisfying certain needs, they are material (moral and spiritual goods are not economic goods), external, and limited or relatively scarce (air, sunlight, *etc.*, are not economic goods).

Physiocrats made the concept of economic good synonymous with that of wealth and held that only things having an exchange value are to be considered goods. According to other economists, the concept of exchange is linked with

that of limited supply or scarcity of goods. However, there are goods which possess an economic character independently of any relation between supply and demand (*e.g.*, works of art). Marshall defined economic goods as those things which can be evaluated or measured by the common denominator of money.

Economic goods may be classified as follows: (a) material goods (wares, commodities, products) and services (labor, professional services, *etc.*); (b) consumer goods or goods of direct use (foodstuffs, clothing, *etc.*) and producer goods, also called capital or instrumental goods (capital, machines, raw material); (c) complementary goods (things which are not sufficient of themselves but must be combined with other goods in the process of production and consumption).

The diverse evaluation concerning the usefulness of goods in their relation to need gives rise to the concept of *value*. This concept, in practice, is tied to the concept of *exchange*, and to that of *price* as a result of the relation established between the goods exchanged. The usefulness of economic goods is not constant, but variable, for it depends upon their availability (supply). As the supply more closely approaches the point of exceeding the demand, the more does the value tend to decrease; and as the supply is further removed from that point, the more does the value tend to increase. "In the concept of value the idea of usefulness is always connected with the idea of quantitative limitations, which involves sacrifice" (Toniolo). This, of course, gives rise to the economic laws of the marginal usefulness of economic goods and to the consequent laws of supply and demand (*q.v.*).

The increase of economic goods (wealth) is related to increase of human needs. Modern civilization and progress are also the effect of increased human wants (improvement of standard of living). From the moral standpoint, is this good or evil? We shall answer by stating that social progress consists in limiting those wants and economic goods which tend to become an end in themselves (luxury, accumulation of riches, *etc.*), and in increasing the production of goods having a higher end. The law which constitutes the norm of economic activity, *i.e.*, the attainment of the maximum benefit with a minimum effort, is universal (valid even in the physical world) and is in no way immoral in itself; in fact, it "coincides with the concept of order, which consists precisely in the proportion between means and end, and upon which the logical, cosmic, and social equilibrium depend" (Toniolo).

GOOD, ETHICAL. Taken in its broadest and most generic sense, good is that toward which one tends (the object or end of appetite), or that which one desires, insofar as everyone desires that which he considers worthy of actuation or attainment. This is the formal concept of good, which can also be purely subjective or illusory. Objective good, on the other hand, is that which truly has within itself something that makes it desirable.

A thing or object may be desired for a variety of motives (real or apparent), all of which may be reduced to these three: useful, delectable, virtuous (moral); hence, there is a threefold division of good. A *useful* good is that which serves as a means to the attainment of some end. Such goodness is merely one of means to end, and is estimated by the value of the end to which it leads and by its effectiveness in contributing to the attainment of the end. A *delectable* or pleasurable good is that which is desired merely for the pleasure or satisfaction it affords. And since there is a wide scale of pleasures, ranging all the way from animalistic to intellectual and ethical, so also there is a correspondingly wide scale of pleasurable goods. A *virtuous* or moral good (*bonum honestum*) is that which is desired as conforming to the norm of reason. Such goodness can never be the object of the senses; hence, it cannot be known, estimated, or intended except by a rational being.

The different manner of correlating and grading these three kinds of good constitutes the basis of differentiation among the various schools and theories of moral philosophy. Thus, utilitarianism holds that the primary and fundamental good is the useful good. Hedonism gives the primacy to pleasurable good; and the more it encompasses itself within the sphere of bodily pleasures, the baser and more vulgar it becomes. Catholic moral doctrine teaches that the primary good is the moral good. The useful and the pleasurable may accompany the moral good if worthy of man as a being endowed with rational powers. Separated or dissociated from the moral good, the other two are not worthy of man's pursuit. *Gra.*

GOOD EXAMPLE. *See* Example.

GOOD FAITH. *See* Possession in Good Faith, Prescription, Restitution.

GOODNESS. Goodness is a disposition of spirit prompting man to do good to his neighbor, or to be of effective help to him in his spiritual and temporal needs. Certain individuals are naturally inclined to be pleasant, affable, kind, and helpful to others. Such a disposition may be acquired and developed through studied effort and practice, but man has, by the infused virtue of charity (*q.v.*), a disposition to treat his neighbor as himself.

Goodness toward others, whether as a disposition or an act, is highly praiseworthy from the moral standpoint; it is a part of the great and noble precept of fraternal love; this is particularly so, when lack of goodness or kindness to others might reasonably cause sadness or grief to them.

A Christian must make an honest effort to see Christ in his fellowman and treat him, by thought, word, and deed as he would treat Christ Himself, keeping in mind the words of the Lord: "*As long as you did it to one of these My least brethren, you did it to Me.*"

Any lack of kindness or goodness to others is unkindness to Christ Himself. A Christian must examine himself frequently on this subject. *Man.*

GOODS, ECCLESIASTICAL (and administration thereof). CONCEPT OF ECCLESIASTICAL GOOD. A thing is said to be an *ecclesiastical good* if it belongs to an ecclesiastical legal person (Can. 1497, par. 1; 1499, par. 2). The term "ecclesiastical good" is not as extensive as the term "Church property." In point of fact, there are goods which, while remaining the property of private individuals or non-ecclesiastical legal persons, nevertheless fall within the juridical sphere of the Church. Such are, *e.g.*, blessed or consecrated objects remaining in the possession of private individuals (Can. 1150), donations (*inter vivos*), bequests assigned (*mortis causa*) in favor of a religious or charitable cause, without becoming the property of an ecclesiastical legal person (Can. 1513–1517). Such temporal goods come under the jurisdiction and control of the Church, not because they constitute ecclesiastical goods, properly so-called, but because the end to which they are destined and the sacred character which they possess brought them into the juridical sphere of ecclesiastical authority.

Canon Law establishes norms concerning only ecclesiastical legal persons and ecclesiastical goods, insofar as these are considered as means (Can. 726) for the attainment of their supernatural end (Can. 100, par. 1; 1544, par. 1; 1496). Since, however, legal persons cannot act for themselves, it becomes necessary that specific individuals or physical persons be appointed to represent such moral entities and to administer the goods attached thereto. The two functions of representation and administration may be found combined in one and the same person (as, *e.g.*, in the case of a parochial benefice), but they may also be exercised by different subjects (as, *e.g.*, in the case of a cathedral or collegiate chapter). We shall deal here only with the administration of ecclesiastical goods.

ADMINISTRATION AND ADMINISTRATORS OF ECCLESIASTICAL GOODS. By administration is understood "the activity of a legitimate person (or college) directed to the conservation, fructification, and utilization of a specific ecclesiastical property" (*immediate administration,* cf. *Index analytico-alphabeticus of CIC,* under "*administratio*"). According to this definition, it follows that Canon Law holds to the principle whereby every administration must be exercised by direct *administrators* in the name of the owner (*nomine domini*). In other words, the individual persons appointed to a title or benefice are the actual administrators of the ecclesiastical property attached thereto, and the higher authorities may not undertake personally to conduct the ordinary administration of such property as long as the affairs are being conducted according to law, for the rights enjoyed by Ordinaries (Can. 1519, 1520, 1521, 1545, 1547, 1415, par. 2, *etc.*) or by the Sacred Congregations (Can. 248, par. 3; 250, par. 2; 251, par. 1, *etc.*) are not to be interpreted as powers of direct administration, but of jurisdiction (indirect administration). Nor is the above enunciated principle contradicted by Canon 1518, which declares the Roman Pontiff to be the supreme administrator and dispenser of all ecclesiastical goods, or by Canon 1499, par. 2, which speaks of the supreme authority of the Holy See; for here, again, these powers are to be interpreted in the sense of *jurisdictional supremacy* or *primacy,* and not of direct administration. The consequence of all this is that the property of ecclesiastical entities, though subject in certain respects to local and central ecclesiastical authority and to the supreme authority of the Holy See, may nevertheless be considered as autonomous, not only in the sense that the ecclesiastical goods belong to the entity itself, but also in the sense that the individual holding title to it is the only one authorized to exercise direct administration.

In Canon Law legal entities are expressly regarded as equivalent to minors

(Can. 100, par. 3), which accounts for an extensive system of protective measures or organs designed to guarantee the legitimate interests and subjective rights of such legal persons, including the extraordinary measure of restitution *in integrum* (full reinstatement in its previous condition, Can. 1687). Wherefore, administrators are to be regarded as trustees or custodians (Can. 1476). They may become such either by law (Can. 1476, par. 1; 1353, par. 2; 1357, par. 4, *etc.*), or by virtue of statutory dispositions (Can. 691, par. 1; 1489, par. 3, *etc.*). Furthermore, administrators may be ecclesiastics or laymen (Can. 1183; 1521, par. 2), and temporary or permanent (Can. 1521, par. 1; 1438, *etc.*).

ORDINARY AND EXTRAORDINARY ADMINISTRATION. Fundamental in this field is the distinction between ordinary and extraordinary administration. *Ordinary administration* consists of such acts as the collecting of revenue and paying of bills, the making of necessary repairs, the use and enjoyment of goods (or, as others would say, it consists of activities occurring regularly or of actions considered necessary for the normal transaction of affairs). Extraordinary administration (act of disposing) consists in the acquiring and disposing of goods other than normal revenue, in assuming obligations, in instituting legal action (or, as others would say, it consists of activities which do not occur regularly, such as making extraordinary repairs or alterations, renovations, or the alienation of goods, and the like). (Cf. P. Gasparri, *Codicis Iuris Canonici Fontes*, vol. VII, p. 348; Sacred Congregation of the Council, *Litterae Circulares*, June 20, 1929; Sacred Consistorial Congregation, *Norms*, June 30, 1934.) This distinction, though most important, has no other effect except to establish when administrators are required to seek authorization for their acts (Can. 1527, par. 1; 1530–1533) under penalty of rendering said acts null and void (Can. 1527, par. 2). The invalid act may be contested by the administrator himself, by his superior, his successors in office

and by any cleric assigned to the church sustaining the loss (Can. 1534, par. 2); the action for restitution of illegally disposed goods may be brought against any holder of them although the latter retains the right to sue the one who disposed of said goods illegally (Can. 1534, par. 1).

SYSTEM OF SUPERVISION AND INSPECTION. According to Canon Law, all ecclesiastical entities are subject to inspection by both the Holy See and the diocesan Ordinary. Inspections are ordinary (*e.g.*, Can. 344) and extraordinary (*e.g.*, the Circular Letter of June 20, 1929). Some of these inspections are exercised over the administrators themselves (Can. 1525); finally the measures of inspection may be preventive (Can. 1530) or repressive (Can. 1534), *etc.* All ecclesiastical entities and goods (Can. 1518; 1499, par. 2) are subject to the jurisdiction of the Holy See; all matters pertaining to provinces, dioceses, cathedral, collegiate chapters, and mensal fund (Can. 248, par. 2; and *Norms*, 1934) are subject to the authority of the Sacred Consistorial Congregation. The Sacred Congregation of the Council has charge over prebends, parochial benefices (and generally over all entities lower than dioceses), associations of the faithful, pious legacies, Mass foundations and stipends, pious institutions, *etc.* (Can. 250, par. 2). The Sacred Congregation of Religious has jurisdiction over the members of religious organizations and their property (Can. 251). The Sacred Congregations of Seminaries, for the Propagation of the Faith, and for the Eastern Church have charge over matters pertaining to their respective spheres. (Following ratification of the Lateran Treaty, a *diocesan administrative bureau* with headquarters in the offices of the Sacred Congregation of the Council was established, having particular jurisdiction in matters pertaining to ecclesiastical goods and property in Italy [art. 59–62 of the Circular Letter of the Sacred Congregation of the Council, June 20, 1929]).

The local Ordinary has wide powers of supervision and inspection over all ecclesiastical property within his territory, excepting the property of exempt religious organizations (Can. 1519–1522, 1525, 1528, 1541, 1545–1548, 1492, par. 1, etc.)

OBLIGATIONS OF ADMINISTRATORS. Before assuming office, administrators are required to take an oath before the local Ordinary that they will faithfully attend to all administration; moreover, they are required to take an accurate and specific inventory of all ecclesiastical goods and property, keeping it constantly up to date (Can. 1522). Their further duties are: to administer with the diligence of a good father of a family the ecclesiastical property entrusted to their care; to observe canonical and civil norms in the matter of administration; to collect diligently all revenues, using them according to the norms of foundation; to keep an accurate record of all receipts and expenditures and all other documents relative to the administration (Can. 1523). Moreover, administrators are required to pay a decent and just wage to all individuals in their employ, providing for their religious, moral, social and family needs (Can. 1524; cf. also Leo XIII, *Rerum Novarum*, May 15, 1891, and the social encyclicals of Pius XI and Pius XII). Finally, administrators must make an annual report of their administration to the local Ordinary, and also to others if so required by particular laws (Can. 1525, par. 2).

When the administrator is also the beneficiary, he is obliged, after having provided for his own maintenance, to contribute his superfluous income to the poor and to charitable causes (Can. 1473).

RESPONSIBILITIES OF ADMINISTRATORS. If the entity or benefice has sustained some damage or loss through culpable negligence of the administrator, the latter may be subject to civil prosecution (Can. 1529), or to disciplinary measures, leading to possible removal (Can. 1476, par. 2; 2147, par. 2, n. 5), and, in the case of wilful deceit or malice, even to criminal prosecution (Can. 2347).

CESSATION OF ADMINISTRATORSHIP.

The holder of a benefice or office has charge of its administration for the entire duration of the office, unless he is removed by the lawful authority (*e.g.*, Can. 2147, par. 2, n. 5). A temporary administratorship ceases upon expiration of the term (generally a three-year term). Temporary administrators are subject to removal (Can. 2346), and they may also resign with permission of the Ordinary. However, an administrator who arbitrarily abandons his administration is liable to reparation of damages (Can. 1528); a cleric in major orders shall incur ecclesiastical penalties (Can. 2399).

APPRAISAL OF CONTRACTS CONCERNING ECCLESIASTICAL GOODS. In view of the fact that at the time the Code of Canon Law was published the lira and the Swiss franc maintained parity with the gold standard, canonists have, until recently, discussed the question whether the lire and francs mentioned in Canons 534, 1532 and 1541 (see n. 3 above) are to be reckoned in gold value or according to their nominal value. The question has been resolved in a practical way by the Holy See, which has decreed as follows: where the Canons state that permission of the Holy See is required for alienation of goods exceeding the sum of 30,000 lire or francs, now read "exceeding the sum of 10,000 lire or francs in gold"; where the Canons state that permission of the Ordinary is required for transaction of goods exceeding in value the sum of 1,000 lire, now read "exceeding 1/30th of 10,000 lire in gold." Cf. Decree of the Sacred Consistorial Congregation, July 13, 1951; Decree of the Sacred Congregation of the Council, December 17, 1951; Decree of the Sacred Congregation for the Eastern Church, May 10, 1952; *AAS* 43 (1951) 602–603; 44 (1952) 44, 632. *See also* Confiscation. *Viol.*

GOODS OF CLERICS. *See* Clerics, Goods of.

GOODS, SPIRITUAL (rights of the individual over). By natural goods of the spirit one may understand, (a) man's spiritual faculties as such (intellect and will); (b) the proximate power or ability to exercise these same faculties; (c) the actual use or exercise of these faculties.

Quite obviously, the spiritual faculties as such cannot be destroyed or in any way impaired by the human will; the power or ability to exercise these faculties, however, can be destroyed or diminished, while the actual exercise of these faculties can be unjustly interfered with or impeded.

When, in practice, is injury inflicted upon these faculties? Certainly, man's right to the *actual* exercise of his spiritual faculties cannot be altogether unlimited. Limitations may arise both from the individual's own moral obligations and from the rights of other men. Thus, a child's right to exercise his faculty of reading is restricted by the parental injunction not to read certain types of literature and by his duty to obey and respect them. Outside such cases, injury is done to man's rational dignity (a) whenever his sphere of activity relative to obligatory actions is restricted; (b) whenever an attempt is made to impede his lawful actions by those having no right to do so. As to the power of exercising one's spiritual faculties or ability to act, this can neither be restricted nor taken away even temporarily, without obvious injury. And even the consent of the individual himself would, in this case, be unlawful, unless there were a justifying reason.

Applying the above principles to the sphere of *intelligence*, the following conclusions obtain: The rights of the human person are violated (a) if a man is deprived of his reasoning faculty; (b) if the exercise of knowledge is restricted by those who have no right to do so or if they do it without just reason; (c) if erroneous doctrines are imparted to those who have a strict right, with respect to a specific person, to be taught the truth, or if they are deprived of the instruction to which they have a right.

Aside from these cases, can the teaching of error constitute an injustice? Rosmini answers in the affirmative, arguing on the premise that truth ennobles man and that any attempt made at depriving him of the knowledge of truth is to deprive him of his inherent dignity. Rosmini limits his theory to necessary truth, which alone truly ennobles man. As to the knowledge of contingent things, he holds that, while truth is useful in its effects, its nobility depends on "that element of universal knowledge which is connected with it and which makes it a matter of knowledge." From this it follows that man's connatural right is violated by all those lies "which contain malicious attempts to instil into the minds erroneous principles, whether logical, moral or religious; for these are the very errors which truly disturb and diminish the adherence of man's spirit to the light of truth" (Rosmini, *Philosophy of Law,* I, 284). In fact, if one takes into account not only man's innate but also his acquired rights, then "any lie violates the right acquired by each man as a member of society."

While appreciating the Rosminian reflections, it seems that the original question must be answered in the negative—that is to say, the teaching of error, excepting to those who have a strict right to be taught the truth, does not constitute a real injustice, except perhaps in the *manner* in which error is imparted. Furthermore, the teaching of erroneous doctrines does no violence to the intellect of another since he retains the power of rejecting error. It would be an injustice, however, if, besides the right to know the truth, man also had the right to be instructed therein by others.

Man's primary right is the right to pursue his ultimate end (*see* End, Ultimate). This is the basis of all other rights of man to the employment of the means *necessary* for the attainment of the last end. Concerning the means that are merely *useful*, see the principle stated above in connection with the natural goods of the spirit. Man's right to the means useful for the attainment of salvation cannot be extended in an absolute manner to all that is lawful and permissible, for even in this field man must of necessity consider and respect the rights of others. *Pal.*

GOSSIP. *See* Defamation; Judgment, Rash.

GOVERNMENT. Generally, by government is meant the exercise of administrative powers, or a governing body; also those in whose hands public authority lies. This, of course, may be in the hands of one person (absolute monarchy, dictatorship), or of a group of individuals (constitutional king or president, executive power, parliament houses, *etc.*). Often by government is meant the executive power as exercised by the cabinet as a whole or by its individual departments. It is in this sense that it will be treated in this article.

For all practical purposes, the form of government is of secondary importance; it matters little whether a government be monarchical or republican, constitutional or parliamentary. The important thing is that there be a government. This is required by the very nature of society and by the intrinsic nature of the relations between those who live in a society.

The fact that there must be a government gives rise to a moral obligation for all citizens to respect it, even when it happens to be only a *de facto* government. In this case, of course, the respect due to it does not extend as far as that due to a government of law. A *de facto* government is in function, for instance, in time of war, or during enemy occupation. In these and similar cases the general norm is that all measures taken by a *de facto* government for the maintenance of public order and for immediate social necessities (provision, ordinary trade, *etc.*) must be complied with. A lawful government is that which derives its power from the people, by direct or indirect investiture, by systems which bear the people's implied or expressed consent. A lawful government that becomes habitually tyrannical (*see* Tyranny) ceases to be a lawful government.

According to divine law, each citizen has the right to participate in government, at least by the right to oppose the abuse of power. From this minimum degree of participation, one may rise to higher degrees. The system of government in which the realization of a maximum of participation may be attained is called *democracy* (*q.v.*). This wide participation is achieved either by bringing into government the largest possible number of citizens, or by increasing the means for a more direct participation by the citizens. True democracy demands that to such wide degrees of participation there be a corresponding awareness on the part of the citizens of the obligation incumbent upon them to seek above all the *common good* (*q.v.*) of society, and to acquire the knowledge, principally practical, that will make them capable of exercising their rights. Where such a sense of social responsibility is wanting, even the right to vote could bring harm to the common good and become an anti-social measure. Participation in government by the citizens is exercised chiefly (a) through the right to vote, by which the people designate or elect those who are to represent them in the administration of municipal, state, or federal government (*see* Elections, Civil), (b) by direct approval or rejection of a law through a *referendum*. Furthermore, the citizens participate in the government through their free criticism of government actions, either publicly, or through the press, or in free assemblies. This criticism, at times, exercises a decisive influence upon the deliberations of the lawmakers.

It must be noted that today any government must depend on technical personnel for its efficient operation. The complex array of employees constitutes the so-called *bureaucracy* (*q.v.*), which in modern times has increased to an unprecedented proportion. It is true that government employees are dependents of the state; but often, owing to their technical skill and to the fact that the continuity of official business rests in their hands, they become servant-masters and essential elements of modern administration. Their moral duty, however, is to work for the common good and as instruments of the public authority, without ever presuming (especially in the case of officials) to substitute in any way the directives of the lawmakers with their own. For all practical purposes it is not possible to have a good administration without an efficient and conscientious bureaucracy; states prospered and enjoyed the people's approval (*e.g.*, Austria, particularly at the time of Marie-Thérèse) exactly because of the use of a skilled, diligent, and well-disciplined bureaucracy as an important instrument of government.

It is the duty of any government, according to the conditions of the times, to promote the attainment of a degree of social welfare consistent with the material and spiritual resources of the nation. For this reason, the government has the right to regulate the exercise of the rights of the citizens, such as freedom of conscience, preservation and development of life and faculties, work and private ownership, juridical liberty of movement and of initiative, of association, and the like. All government measures directed at procuring a satisfactory social life must be respected by all, even if it should require the sacrifice of one's own private interests—provided, however, that while regulating the exercise, the very essence of those rights is not violated. The protection of these rights should be guaranteed by an *International Supreme Court of Justice* armed with power to veto laws, decrees, or ordinances which violate the essence of the above rights, even if issued with external legality and the unanimous approval of the parliament.

A government, culpable of such violations, even if declared to be democratic, loses at that very moment its authority, inasmuch as it sets itself against natural divine law from which it derives its very authority (*see* Revolution). Outside this hypothesis, the power of government is universal, *i.e.*, it extends without interruption to all the activities which may develop in a nation, regulating them by its juridical system, not only by a *negative* function limited exclusively to the maintenance of public order and the preventing of abuses by one citizen against another, but also by a *positive* governmental intervention as advocated in modern times in all matters concerning public services such as transportation, communications, banks, schools, houses, hygiene, and disputes between capital and labor and economy in general for the purpose of promoting greater social justice (*q.v.*).

Characteristic of modern governments is an ever-increasing tendency toward a system of *government planning* which tends to reduce private initiative to the minimum. This tendency may be questioned on two counts, namely, (a) the inviolability of the essential rights of the individual guaranteed by the natural law, and in many a state also by the positive law, and (b) the real common advantages accruing from such a system. Concerning the former, everything must be excluded that is opposed to the inviolability of the essential rights of the individual. As to the latter, the answer depends on the practical results; nor is it in itself unlawful to try it out. In a democratic form of government, of course, the majority must decide in these matters.

Any government (including a *de facto* government within the limits indicated above) has the right to defend the exercise of its function and, therefore, of suppressing even by force any individual or collective attempt made against its very existence. This is particularly true in a democratic state, which has the right and duty to prevent the action of those who try to undermine its very foundation, which is precisely the *principle* of political freedom. Such individuals have no right of organization in a democratic state. Boz.

GRACE. In current language *grace* means a quality which makes a person amiable; also benevolence inspired by amiableness, or a favor done out of benevolence, or even gratitude for such a favor. In theological language it designates a gratuitous gift of God to an intelligent creature in order to effect his sanctification and the attainment of eternal life.

Taken in a theological sense, grace may be habitual or actual.

Habitual grace is by its very nature permanent. It is uncreated and created. *Habitual uncreated* grace consists in the presence of the Divine Persons in the soul of the just; this presence can almost be experientially known and can be enjoyed by the soul; it is a true indwelling, and it makes of the just the temple of God (John 17:23; Rom. 5:5; I Cor. 3:16 ff; 6:16 ff; Eph. 1:18; 4:30; II Cor. 1:22). *Habitual created* grace, in a strict sense, is sanctifying grace, *i.e.*, a physical entity (entitative habit), infused by God into the very essence of the soul; it makes man partaker of the divine nature (II Pet. 1:14), adoptive son of God (Rom. 8:15; Gal. 4:5; I John 9:11), heir of eternal life (Rom. 8:17); it is the root of the infused virtues and of the gifts of the Holy Spirit. Sanctifying grace is infused in the very act of justification, which is compared by Christ to a regeneration (John 1:12 ff.; 3:5 ff.) and by St. Paul to a new creation (II Cor. 5:17). It is increased through good works and the proper reception of the Sacraments (Council of Trent, Denz., nn. 834, 849); it is lost through mortal sin (*ibid.*, n. 808). The indwelling of the Divine Persons is connected with the state of grace. Habitual graces, in a broader sense, are the infused virtues (*q.v.*) and the gifts of the Holy Spirit (*q.v.*), which are like a ramification of sanctifying grace. All these graces are of themselves ordained to the good of the recipient. Revelation testifies also to the existence of created habitual graces, primarily directed to the good of others; they are the gifts of tongues, of curing the sick, of prophecy, and others.

Actual grace is a grace of transient nature; it is an aid toward the achievement of eternal life. The existence of actual graces as graces merely sufficient with respect to the deliberate and supernatural act of the will are attested to by Holy Scripture, which speak of impulse (Acts 9:5), of illumination (Ps. 12:4), of attraction (Cant. 1:3; John 6:34). They are graces which dispose a person to such an act, giving him the proximate power to perform it, even though the act is not always performed; in fact, at times it is not performed because of a failure on the part of the will which has nothing to do with graces themselves. These graces assume very different forms. They may consist in an external influence exercised on the mind by God either by means of circumstances and events of their very nature apt at causing salutary thoughts and inclinations, or at keeping away non-salutary dispositions, or by means of a special and direct action upon the sensitive faculties. They may also consist of an internal motion of the intellect or of the will to perform an indeliberate act: illumination or impulse toward good, taken in a strict sense. These are called *prevenient graces*. Molina and a few others do not admit a direct influence of God on man's operative faculty, but only on its act, in which the First Cause and the creature simultaneously concur, though from different aspects. According to the Thomistic School, besides prevenient grace there is also another actual grace, which of itself effectively leads the will to a deliberate and salutary act: it consists in a new and positive influence of God, which, without taking away the freedom of willing the opposite, and without interfering in any way with the exercise of liberty, internally moves the will to direct itself toward the good with full active indifference and supernaturally. The will, though able to oppose this grace, in fact never does. The necessity of such a motion for each deliberate and supernatural act of the will is rightly deduced from the definite principle whereby no potency can become an act by itself, and from the fact that infused virtues and prevenient grace, however strong they may be, leave the will in a state of potency with respect to a deliberate and salutary act. Several texts of the sacred scriptures can be quoted in favor of this thesis. Molinists do not admit an actual grace as distinct from either prevenient grace and the grace of itself efficacious, but they hold that prevenient grace, being sufficient, becomes efficacious precisely because of the consent of the will which can also oppose it, leaving sufficient grace fruitless.

Sanctifying grace is indispensable in order that one may perform meritorious acts and attain, after death, life eternal (John 15:5; Eph. 4:15; II Council of Orange, Denz., n. 191; Council of Trent, Denz., nn. 803, 809, 842). On the strength of his own natural capacity, man is absolutely incapable of performing any act adequate to the attainment of eternal life, particularly to accept God's revealed word in the proper manner; actual grace is physically necessary for any supernatural act (John 3:27; 15:5; I Cor. 15:10; Philip. 1:6; 2:13; Council of Carthage, Denz., n. 105; II Council of Orange, Denz., nn. 179, 180, 193; Council of Trent, Denz., nn. 809, 811, 812). Actual grace is also physically necessary to an adult person in order that he may prepare himself in due manner for his justification (II Council of Orange, Denz., nn. 176, 177, 179; Council of Trent, Denz., nn. 797, 798, 813). Moreover, as a result of original sin it is morally impossible for man without the special aid (*i.e.*, graces) of God to avoid all mortal sins for a long time (Council of Carthage, Denz., no. 104, 105; Council of Trent, Denz., no. 804, 823). It is also impossible for man to avoid all venial sins; this is a privilege accorded to the blessed Virgin Mary (Council of Trent, Denz., nn. 810, 833). The consequences of original sin, nevertheless, do not take away from man the capability of doing some good simply on the strength of his natural capacities; such capability is denied by Lutherans, Baianists, and Jansenists.

Everyone has a sufficient motive for doing good, and all receive sufficient graces to avoid sin and observe the pre-cepts. But man's will can reject these graces and prevent them from becoming efficacious and, therefore, productive of good (Osee, 13:8; Denz., n. 816).

God deigned to call man to a supernatural destiny. But man must deserve it by performing actions that are intrinsically adequate to it and to sanctifying grace, which makes us partakers of the Divine Nature. Only supernatural acts performed in state of grace are man's title to the reward of eternal life. The time spent in the state of (mortal) sin is irretrievably lost for eternity. Man must convince himself of this truth as well as of the inestimable worth of actual grace and the need of actual grace for any supernatural act. He must humbly beseech God to give him the help of His grace; many graces are granted to those who humbly and trustingly ask for them. It is also very important never to oppose prevenient graces; he who rejects grace becomes unworthy of receiving further help from God. *Man.*

GRAFTS AND TRANSPLANTS. Although the two terms are used indiscriminately in pathological surgery, there is a difference between them: *graft* is the removal of a more or less large portion of tissue or of an organ from one part of the body of the same individual to another part (or in some cases from one individual to another), without any direct vascular connections; *transplant*, on the other hand, implies immediate circulatory relations maintained or established between the host and the portion of tissue or organ transplanted.

Graft (or transplant) is resorted to because of the necessity of replacing certain tissues (as in the treatment of large skin sores), or of substituting a part or an entire organ either missing from birth or almost completely atrophied.

From a biological point of view grafts and transplants may be distinguished into four groups: *autoplastic, homoplastic, alleloplastic,* and *heteroplastic,* depending on whether the donor is the same individual as the recipient, or another person of the same race, of a different race, or even of a different species. (In a certain sense, *blood transfusion* could be classified as a homoplastic transplantation).

It was recently discovered that the tissues possess the same group of factors as the blood of the organism to which they belong. Therefore in grafting, or in homoplastic transplantation, the blood type must be checked just as it is done in blood transfusions. Further studies are being made to improve the joining of grafts.

Grafts (or transplantations) are always allowed with elements removed from a corpse if they can help a sick person (Pius XII, Allocution of April 11, 1956; *see also* Surgery).

Grafting and transplantations are not permissible if practiced on human beings out of mere experimentation and without immediate therapeutic purpose, especially when very important organs are involved (as is done at times on the mentally ill or on criminals condemned to death).

Grafts and transplants, of course, are immoral if the purpose of the operation is to enable a person to indulge in a life of sin or if the surgeon honestly suspects that this is the reason. Often such operations are requested for the purpose of reactivating the functions of endocrine glands already extinct or about to become extinct. Outside these cases, it is a disputed question among theologians as to whether or when such operations are permitted on a living being; in some circumstances, the practice cannot be condemned outright. *Riz.*

GRAPHOLOGY. Graphology is the art of understanding the character of a person from the study of his handwriting. This term was first used by J. H. Michon around 1870.

The first worthwhile contribution to graphological research was the *Trattato come da una lettera missiva si conoscano la natura e qualitaà dello scrivente*, pub-

lished by the Italian philosopher, C. Baldi, in 1622. Others works followed: among them those of an Italian physician, Severino of Lavater (founder of *physiognomy*), Hocquart (who in his *L'art de juger de l'esprit et du caractère des hommes sur leur Ecriture*, published in 1812, endeavored to give graphology a scientific basis), Descuret, Henze, and Delestre. The works of these latter authors influenced Abbé J. H. Michon, who in 1875 published his classic *Système de Graphologie* and who is rightly considered the founder of graphology.

Michon's research gave rise to the work of contemporary graphologists who follow either the French school, the largest of all, headed by Crepieux-Jamin, or the German school, headed at first by W. Preyer and later by Klanges, or the English school established by Sondek.

The graphological system of Abbé Michon was based on the theory of the so-called *fixed signs*. According to this theory each peculiarity of handwriting corresponds always and only to a given peculiarity in a person's character. Thus, for instance, if the lines of a handwriting go upward, they indicate aggressiveness and ambition, while if they go downward, they are indicative of sadness and laziness; straight handwriting is a sign of egotism, the one leaning to the left is indicative of dissimulation and distrust, and so on. Michon's was a very detailed analytic study, concerning not only the single letters but also the principal parts of each letter.

The French followers of Michon, however, hold that every psychological quality shows itself through a complexity of graphic properties, and instead of minutely analyzing the peculiarities of each writing, they endeavor to bring into evidence its general characteristics grouped according to seven fundamental elements: speed (fast, slow, dynamic), pressure (firm, soft, *etc.*), form (simple, harmonious, confused, *etc.*), direction (bent-down, descending, *etc.*), dimension (small, exaggerated, *etc.*), continuity (equal, unequal, *etc.*), appearance (neat, rough, *etc.*).

The other schools disagree with the French school on several details, but all agree on the meaning of the vast majority of the elements of a handwriting. There is, therefore, a fundamental concordance among graphologists concerning the characteristics of handwriting as revealing the principal motives determining the behavior of the writer, habitually or at the time of the writing of a letter, such as love of profit, selfishness, vanity, anger, frankness, constancy, etc. Peculiar talents, memory, mathematical aptitude, artistic talent, etc., are less distinctly established. The rest presents many problems, so that for a complete graphological diagnosis, one must depend on the personal sagacity, intuition, and skill of each of those devoted to graphological pursuits. Because of this fact, graphology remains more an art than a real science.

The use of graphology in the diagnosis of mental disturbances and many other nervous diseases is well-known and it has given good results. Some psychoanalysts attach great importance to a patient's handwriting, for it seems that through it—as through many other spontaneous and semi-spontaneous acts —the unconscious side of his personality comes to the fore.

The existence of a basis of truth in the considerations inferred from the study of one's handwriting is a matter beyond doubt. As gestures and words are the expression of one's personality, and a manifestation of an individual's psychophysical ego, so, too, is one's handwriting. Future research may well suggest greater prudence in the application of conclusions obtained from graphological studies, but this must in no way be construed as rejection of the value of conclusions scientifically drawn by means of graphology.

This coincides also with the point of view of moralists concerning this subject, who caution against exaggerated predictions concerning the future free behavior of the individual as well as against trying to see too much in what may be considered as generally reasonable predictions based on circumstances and psychosomatic tendencies.

Graphological studies, whether conducted for neuropsychiatric diagnoses or for psychological study of the character or tendencies and talents of healthy persons, are, from a moral standpoint, lawful, provided that the graphologist makes an honest, prudent, and reasonable use of the results obtained from his study. *Riz.*

GRATITUDE. Gratitude or thankfulness consists in the internal acknowledgment of the value of a benefit received and of the benevolent intention of the giver; also the manifestation by words and deeds of this acknowledgment, reciprocating, on occasion, the benefit received, particularly if the benefactor is in distress.

Gratitude is a duty. The internal thankfulness must be constant; not in the sense that it must be shown at every moment, but whenever the opportunity presents itself.

One may sin against gratitude by excess (false gratitude), or by defect; by excess, if one were to reciprocate a benefit at a time or in a manner that is inopportune. The degree of culpability in a case of false gratitude depends on the gravity of the damage done to one's benefactor. One may sin against gratitude by defect (*ingratitude*), if one fails to acknowledge a gift received and the donor's benevolence; or by despising a benefit or the benefactor himself; by plainly considering as harmful a benefit received; by not showing in the proper way and in due time one's gratefulness, or, worse still, by doing something against one's own benefactor. Lack of thankfulness for a benefit or failure to show at the proper time feelings of gratitude is in itself a venial sin; but it may become a grave sin if one is able to help but fails to give his benefactor, now in serious distress, the assistance he needs. Contempt for a benefit received or for the giver's benevolence could also be a mortal sin: it is grave, if it causes serious distress to one's benefactor or if one does something truly offensive against him.

In view of the great importance of gratitude in social life, teachers and educators must concentrate their efforts on instilling this virtue in the hearts of their pupils. One, however, must not be too hasty in accusing another of ingratitude. Even in a case in which ingratitude seems evident, it is highly commendable for the benefactor not to withdraw his benefits if there is hope that the ungrateful person may mend his ways. Gratitude must be shown particularly to God and to parents. *Man.*

GRATUITY (Gift). Gratuity in the present, ordinary meaning of the word connotes a gift in money or a tip. It may be licit or illicit. It is *licit* if intended either as an allurement to customers, a simple manifestation of liberality, or a commission, established by law or specific contract and given to an agent as legitimate compensation for his part in a sales or business deal. It is *illicit* if there is the intention to corrupt. If it is given to public officials or similar persons with such an intention, it is also called a bribe. In general accepting a gratuity can be reconciled with the precepts of justice; a person, nevertheless, exposes himself to the danger of deals which may, at times, greatly hinder freedom of action or tax his conscience, as well as involve a grave danger of scandal. To determine the liceity of gratuities or gifts, one must consider each individual case and distinguish between giving and accepting them.

Gratuities to functionaries. A gratuity as a bribe is intended for the purpose of obtaining services or favors. It can be also a simple tip given to a minor official. Reprehensible as this custom may be, to give or receive tips does not constitute a moral lapse or offense.

But if in a more serious form of retribution or promised retribution, to which the public official has no right, either to induce him to perform an official act or as a compensation for an official act already performed, or, worst still, to induce him to perform acts contrary to his duties of office, it becomes a grave violation by the one who accepts this bribe because he has no title to the retribution. Nor can it be said to be a case of liberality. The degree of guilt, of course, is greater if it is a question of inducing someone to perform acts contrary to his duties of office; less grave if it is intended as compensation for an act already performed. In general, penal codes consider these criminal.

Furthermore, if a public official forces someone to give or promise these gratuities, thereby obviously abusing his functions, the guilt becomes all the more serious; in the penal code it assumes the proportions of a special crime, called extortion.

To offer a bribe involves more or less the same degree of guilt, if it is done without the necessity of protecting self-interests in jeopardy; it would be a form of contract to evil, and both contracting parties are more or less on the same level. The guilt of one offering would be lessened if he were impelled by circumstances, to make an offer or give retribution because of evil practices in existence, so that, unless he complied with these practices, he would not obtain what he legitimately desires or in equal measure or with the same facility. There is no lessening of guilt if the favor sought of the public official, either with retribution or of reward is illicit.

If public morality thrives in a climate of normalcy, there is no reason why a citizen should have to put up with such practices as mentioned above. A public official who indulges in such practices the citizen has the right to report to higher superiors or to a law enforcement agency.

Gifts to politicians, mayors, etc. We can more or less repeat what was said above. What now becomes object of barter is no longer the instrumental evasion of a given policy, but rather political influence which one places at the disposal of the client in order to by-pass certain requirements, obtain a position, receive preferential treatment or evade the law, etc. It is this political influence that is rewarded.

If, upon compensation, a public official favors an evasion of the law, he is held to restitution to the State; he is also bound to make restitution to the private citizen if a monetary compensation was involved. He is not held to this, however, if the money was spontaneously offered.

A minor official, who is ordered by his superior to rubber stamp an evasion of the law, is held to resistance in whatever way possible. He can only go along with this unjust order if, by opposing it, he should himself suffer grave harm (see Favoritism).

Gratuities (gifts) to intermediaries. If compensation to a mediator, properly so-called, is recognized by law or custom, it is perfectly licit (see Mediation). If it is compensation to a publicity agent it is still licit, provided that it remains within the limits of moderation and does not alter the value of the merchandise. If it is compensation to members of a firm or domestics for the sake of winning over a client, agent, or owner, it is licit if moderate and not intended to silence go-betweens and thus defraud the unwary client.

Commissions, demanded by buying agents or large firms for placing orders with particular wholesalers are permissible, provided that this practice is allowed by the firm or its representative and does not cause damage to the firm itself. In this case commissions can be considered integrated forms of stipend; otherwise, they are illicit.

Much less licit would be gratuities, (gifts) to members of a commission in charge of selecting projects, assigning contracts, *etc.*

All this falls under the classical heading of cooperation in sinful actions (see Cooperators). In these damage to third parties creates the obligation to compensate for the damage done.

To do away with these abuses the burdens of public morality, a gradual but energetic moulding of the professional conscience of individuals is necessary, and a greater vigilance on the part of public authorities.

GREGORIAN MASSES. *See* Masses, Gregorian.

GREGORIAN WATER. *See* Holy Water, Altar.

GUARANTY. Guaranty, in general, is an agreement by which one person promises to make another secure in the possession, continued enjoyment, or the like, of something. It is subordinated to a protected right; that is, it has an accessory character and is called into play only in a case of default or non-fulfillment of an obligation or debt.

A guaranty may be required by law or by a decision of the judge; it may also be agreed upon by the parties to an agreement or it may be given by the obliger himself or by a third person in the obliger's behalf.

A guaranty may be established by a *jus in rem* on a personal property (see Loan) or on real estate (see Mortgage) or by the constitution of obligations by which a new debtor is added to the principal debtor (see Debt) or by a down-payment or in the form of added obligation as a penal clause (a kind of penalty in case of non-performance or mere delay of performance).

The system of guaranty, which finds its broadest application in the field of property rights, is applied to the debtor in order to strengthen the creditor's rights. At times, guaranty is a burden on the debtor, as in the case of a pawn; at other times, it implies only an advantage for the creditor, with no immediate privation to others.

There are two ways of guarantying a debt, guaranty of payment, and guaranty of collection. In the first case the guarantor is in default the moment the debt is due and unpaid, while in the second the guarantor is in default only after the principal debtor has been sued, and the creditor (guarantee) has employed every expedient to enforce payment. It is a natural right for the creditor to protect himself against possible damage to his rights when mutual trust comes to an end. The natural law, however, does not determine the forms of guaranty, which are established exclusively by positive laws; and inasmuch as these complete the natural law in this matter, they are normally binding in conscience, unless they be too damaging to the debtor's right. It is the creditor's duty not to press the defense of his rights too strongly, lest he violate the virtue of charity. *Pal.*

GUILT, THEOLOGICAL. The concept of theological guilt (in the moral field) is ordinarily identified with the notion of sin (*q.v.*) as a wrongful act performed with deliberate advertence and full consent. Actually, however, guilt more properly indicates a consequence or effect of a sinful act; the latter is its cause. He who commits a sin incurs guilt at the same time that he sins. Guilt lies in the sin, it arises from the commission of sin. Man becomes guilty through sin.

Thus, the concept of theological or moral guilt lies rather in the concept of imputability-responsibility, inasmuch as the effects of a human act are charged to a free agent. This appears even more clearly when we consider the definition of moral responsibility (*q.v.*) as the charge for which one is responsible or accountable to a lawful authority. Accordingly, theological guilt implies accountability or responsibility for a sinful act, in the same manner that juridical guilt implies accountability for a violation of the law to a lawful human authority.

Theological guilt presupposes two necessary elements: (a) a norm obliging in conscience before God; (b) a free human act in violation of this norm or moral law. From this it follows that whenever knowledge of such a norm is lacking (*see* Ignorance), or whenever freedom of the will is lacking (*see* Human Act, Freedom, Passions) responsibility is lacking and so also is guilt.

Obviously, guilt implies a certain malice; nor is it necessary that one intend evil in itself. To be guilty it suffices that one have at least a confused knowledge of evil and fail to avoid it (*see* Effect, Double). Evil may never

be intended, not even for a good purpose, for a good intention cannot alter the nature of evil; hence, failing to avoid evil means becoming guilty in a theological sense. *Tar.*

GYMNASTICS. *See* Culture, Physical.

GYNECOLOGY. Gynecology is the branch of medicine dealing with the care and treatment of women in general, their diseases, hygiene, and the like. In this article we shall devote our attention only to the more important moral problems linked with gynecology.

The female genital cycle is very complex and one which affects the greatest part of a woman's biological life for nearly thirty-five years, from puberty to the climacteric, or menopause. In fact, the pituitary gland and the ovaries are directly involved in that cycle, and so also, though indirectly and in a more or less considerable degree, are the thyroid and other endocrine glands, the neuro-vegetative system with a relation (at times with moderate, at other times with very evident effects) on the thymopsyche and even the noopsyche itself. Concerning the hormonic processes and the principal changes which occur during puberty and the climateric (change of life), *see* Gonads. We shall here dwell upon the neuropsychological disturbances which often occur during that cycle and which account for (and, to a certain extent, justify) the periodic anomalies of behavior noticeable in many a woman.

To this effect we shall note that the cycle follows a normal physiological course only in about 20% of the cases; in 60% of the cases it is preceded or accompanied by minor local or general disturbances, which do not affect the normal activities and behavior of the person, while in the remaining 20% of the cases, disturbances are so relevant as to interfere with the normal activities of the woman to the point of changing, even though only temporarily, the nervous reactions and at times the psychological conditions of the individual.

Frequently such disturbances consist in very painful or migraine headaches; other times in keen, shooting pains in the hypogastric and lumbar regions. In a considerable number of cases these painful phenomena are associated with reflex disturbances (gastralgia, constipation, cardiac palpitations, *etc.*), and also with neuropsychological disturbances, such as sleeplessness, nightmares, nervous erotism, depressing or anxious manifestations, obsessions, feelings of persecution, *etc.*

The knowledge of this phenomenology and of its exact ethiopathogenetic individualization is important not only for the treatment, but also for the understanding and the moral justification of certain occasional psychological deviations of the patients. Indeed, certain women appear whimsical, unstable, and very difficult, but in effect they are sick, though only temporarily; and their moral responsibility diminishes in varying degrees, owing to the fact that the occasional unusual actions they commit under those circumstances are the result of abnormal stimuli or of excessive reactions of a strictly pathological nature.

Any surgical intervention on these organs is morally justified only if it be required by conditions resulting from malformation or other local diseases not otherwise curable. Hence, interventions which cause unjustified mutilations and sterility are not permitted in cases of mild or non-malignant conditions, or of conditions curable by the use of conservative techniques. Concerning the moral issues involved in such operations, *see* Surgery, Sterilization.

Though defloration and loss of virginity are not necessarily the same thing, because of a possible elasticity of the hymen in the first case or of an accidental injury in the second, which may have caused an apparent loss of virginity, considerable importance is given to the integrity of the hymen; hence, very appropriately Dr. Scremin writes: "It is not licit for a physician to offer advice or assistance to a woman in simulating or rebuilding the characteristics of virginity willfully and culpably lost in order that she may deceive others." A surgeon is morally justified in the rebuilding of it only if he is certain that the laceration occurred by an accident or other involuntary cause. Obviously, a gynecologist is permitted to perform incisions on the hymen if considered necessary for the performing of the conjugal act, or to treat surgically other *gynatresias*, if the husband should request the operation and the wife consents to it.

If *vaginism* (*see* Impotence) was caused by an inflamatory or a local traumatic lesion which occurred either before or after the marriage, cauterization of the lesion is usually effective and definitive. At other times the condition may be the result of incomplete defloration or a fibrous hymen which causes the conjugal act to be difficult and painful, giving rise to a defensive psychological resistance which is hardly reversible; it is proper, then, to cut off the hymen and to do whatever is deemed necessary for the removal of a cause of impotence.

Feminine frigidity, though irrelevant insofar as the nullity of marriage is concerned (*see* Impotence), often becomes a motive of disagreement and ill-humor between consorts. In such cases it is morally licit to treat it. Sometimes the treatment consists of hormones or in the elimination of various infections, or in the removal of noxious effects arising from neuro-psychological infirmities. At other times frigidity is caused by the position of the clitoris (*teleclitoridia*) or by its hyper-sensitiveness. In the former case it is lawful to correct the defect by the Halban operation; in the latter, the process of desensitization or enervation proposed by Leriche may be used; in a very severe case, the removal of the clitoris (clitoridectomy) is permitted.

These operations are also permitted in order to attain the ends of matrimony. A woman's sexual hyperesthesia (*see* Perversions, Sexual), on the contrary, may be a symptom of nervous or mental condition, or it may be caused (or at least favored to a considerable degree) by endocrine disorders or abnormal local stimuli *e.g.*, dermatosis, irritation due to fungus, *etc.* All these conditions, however, are the province of the physician, and it is logical and proper that they be treated by medical means. *Riz.*

H

HABIT (CLERICAL). The clerical habit or garb is the attire proper to clerics, lending decorum and dignity to their clerical state. The general law prescribes ecclesiastical garb, that is, different from that of lay persons, and becoming or suitable to the clerical state and condition. Leaving the matter of more detailed specifications to particular legislations of the various regions, the Code enjoins the observance of the legitimate customs of the place and provincial and diocesan statutes (Can. 146, par. 1); nor is it lawful for clerics arbitrarily to introduce innovations in this regard (Apostolic Exhortation *Menti Nostrae* of Pius XII, September 23, 1950). The clerical garb of the diocesan clergy (with the exception of the Holy Father, cardinals, and bishops) consists of a black, ankle-length cassock. This garb is prescribed for all in liturgical functions (Can. 811, par. 1). Generally, in all regions of Southern Europe, and in Central and South America, clerics must also wear the cassock outside sacred functions. In the United States the matter of clerical habit is governed by the decrees of the Third Plenary Council of Baltimore (n. 77).

The wearing of clerical garb is the exclusive right of the clergy; Canon 683 expressly forbids laymen to wear it, but permits its use to seminarians and other candidates for the priesthood, and to laymen employed in the service of a church, while working in and around the church building.

Clerics have the further obligation, enforced by canonical sanctions, of wearing the clerical garb outside sacred functions (except in those countries, as in the U.S.A., where local legislation disposes otherwise). Clerics in minor orders who, without a just cause and without permission, lay aside the ecclesiastical garb are to be admonished by the Ordinary and, if not obeyed within one month's time, are immediately (*ipso jure*) deposed from the clerical state (Can. 146, par. 5); clerics in major orders may incur penalties of various degrees, including deposition from the clerical state (Can. 2370).

As a penalty for certain well-defined offenses (Cans. 2300; 2304, par. 1; 2305), the Code commands temporary or permanent deprivation of the right to wear the clerical garb; the latter entails deprivation of clerical privileges.

In the first four centuries of Christianity clerics wore the same mode of dress as laymen; when, at a later period, the ample and majestic garments of the Romans were replaced by abbreviated barbaric costumes, it was deemed proper that clerics keep the ancient garments as more suited to their dignity. This custom gave rise to laws confirmed by various synods as early as the sixth century. Present-day legislation is, in substance, the disciplinary legislation established by the Council of Trent. *Fel.*

HABIT (CUSTOM). *Habit* means a quality of a person or his way of behaving. In moral science the quality of a person (substantive or entitative habit) has only a secondary and indirect importance, insofar as it influences a person's behavior; hence, moralists treat habit principally and directly from the standpoint of its second meaning, that is, as an operative habit, habitude, or habitual disposition.

From the moral aspect, habits may be good (virtues) or bad (vices), insofar as they conform or do not conform with human nature, that is, contribute to its perfection or to its debasement.

From the standpoint of origin, habits

are infused or acquired. Infused habits are given by God (ordinarily) with sanctifying grace; these are only good habits; they are not restricted to the theological virtues but include moral virtues as well. Acquired habits can be either good or bad; these are formed by the repetition of the same act. The more frequent the repetition, the stronger the acquired tendency; often the forming of acquired habits is favored and facilitated by natural and congenital dispositions.

A habit makes the execution of a respective act prompt, easy, and pleasurable, and consequently makes resistance to such an act increasingly difficult; habit, therefore, is one of the elements to be taken into consideration in evaluating the morality of an act. Also to be taken into account is the part which the will plays in the habit itself; in other words, a habit that is voluntarily acquired, retained, and favored makes the acts proceeding from it voluntary and free (at least in their cause, which is the habit itself) though the acts are almost mechanically executed; whereas, if the habit is not supported by the will but resisted by the individual, then the acts proceeding almost automatically from it have but the lowest degree of imputability, and perhaps none at all, if the habit was sincerely retracted. *Gra.*

HABIT (MATERIAL). *See* Habit, Religious.

HABIT (RELIGIOUS). The special attire proper to members of a religious group or organization is called a religious habit.

The first religious of the early Christian era, ascetics and anchorites, did not wear any special habit; they merely continued to wear the same garb worn in the world, or they put on, each according to his own judgment, rough penitential garments made of bristly hairs, herbs, or hides. In the fourth century, when Pachomius organized cenobitic life, he provided his followers with special garb and attached to the reception of the habit such importance that it came to be considered as a formal beginning of their religious life (Rule of St. Pacho-

mius, c. 49). The holy virgins, Tertullian testifies, as early as the third century wore "a habit consecrated to God." St. Jerome relates that these virgins had their hair cut off (*PL* 22, 1199), and the abundant literature that has come down to us from the fifth century concerning the ceremony of consecration of virgins and of their taking the veil is strongly reminiscent of the ceremonies of the present-day "profession."

With the establishment of monachism, especially by St. Basil and St. Benedict, the habit assumed greater importance, so that the wearing of the habit at the inception and during the course of monastic life became an essential practice demanded not only by monastic legislation but by legislation of the ecclesiastical councils as well. The Council of Trent reaffirmed the grave obligation of wearing the habit at all times with a penalty of excommunication for those who disregarded the law (C. 15, Sess. 25; and C. 19, Sess. 29).

According to the present code, every religious organization must have its own particular habit. Its external form must be at least slightly different from that of diocesan priests and lay persons. In recent years, the Holy See has recommended a simpler habit for all female religious institutes (cf. Pius XII, Address of December 8, 1950; Letter to Cardinal Micara, November 12, 1950; Apost. Const. *Sponsa Christi*, November 21, 1950. The Holy See requires the constitutions of each religious organization to provide an accurate description of the style, color, and material of the habit and urges simplicity and propriety. It is unlawful, after approval of the religious institute by the Holy See, to alter the habit without apostolic permission.

New religious organizations may not adopt the habit of an already established religious institute (Can. 492, par. 3). Since the habit, at least in present-day legislation, constitutes a distinctive characteristic of each religious institute, all religious must wear it inside and outside the house, unless there be grave reason or necessity to make an exception (Can. 596). Novitiate begins with the reception of the habit, which is to be worn throughout the entire canonical year (Can. 553); nevertheless, failure to carry out this prescription does not invalidate the novitiate. Postulants may wear a special garb, which must be modest and different from the habit of novices (Can. 540, par. 2). Religious who possess the indult of exclaustration (Can. 639) or secularization (Can. 640) and religious who have been dismissed (Cans. 648; 669, par. 2) are forbidden to wear the religious habit. *Man.*

HABITUAL. See Grace, Intention, Sin.

HAIL MARY. The Hail Mary is the principal prayer in honor of the Blessed Lady. It is also called the *Angelical Salutation*, because it begins with the words of greeting addressed to the Virgin by the Archangel Gabriel when he delivered the message that she had been chosen Mother of God. The prayer consists of two principal parts: (a) laudatory phrases or salutation; (b) an invocation, or petition.

The first part consists of two salutations, one spoken by the Archangel Gabriel on the day of the Annunciation, the other uttered by St. Elizabeth on the day of Mary's Visitation to her; the names *Mary* and *Jesus* were added by the Church. The words spoken by the Archangel are: "Hail, full of grace; the Lord is with thee, blessed art thou among women" (Luke 1:28). St. Elizabeth repeated the last phrase of the Archangel, "blessed art thou among women," and then added "and blessed is the fruit of thy womb" (Luke 1:42). The two salutations, with the addition of the name of Mary, are found in the Offertory prayer of the Mass for the fourth Sunday of Advent in the Antiphonary of St. Gregory the Great (d. 604); in all probability, however, the practice of combining the two salutations as a prayer to Mary dates back at least one century earlier, since the two salutations are found together in the earlier Antiochene liturgy of St. James. The name of Jesus is found in use at the end of the two salutations in the seventh

century in the East, and in the twelfth century in the West. By repeating the salutation of Gabriel to Mary, interwoven with Elizabeth's blessings, we rejoice at the singular privileges and gifts bestowed upon her by God above all other creatures, and we bless and thank God at the same time for having given us Jesus Christ through Mary.

The second part was composed in relatively recent times. The practice of adding a prayer of petition to the words of praise contained in the Gregorian Offertory seems to be of early Franciscan origin. These humble, tender, and affectionate invocations to Mary may be found frequently in varying lengths. Among them, it is worth mentioning the following, frequently used by Palestrina (d. 1594): "*Sancta Maria, Regina coeli, dulcis et pia. O Mater Dei, ora pro nobis peccatoribus, ut cum electis te videamus*" ("Holy Mary, Queen of heaven, tender and holy. O Mother of God, pray for us sinners, that we may see thee together with the elect"). The Hail Mary as we know it today is found in use sporadically toward the middle of the fifteenth century; later adoption by Pope Pius V in his edition of the Breviary (1568) brought it thereafter into general use. In the second part of the Hail Mary we ask Mary's maternal intercession on our behalf throughout our present life, but especially at the hour of our death.

The Hail Mary or parts of it occur frequently in the liturgy. The Gregorian Offertory, which uses the first part of the Hail Mary, is read not only in the Mass for the fourth Sunday of Advent, but also in other Masses in honor of Mary; the complete Hail Mary is recited three times at the end of all private Masses. Until recently (1956), the Hail Mary was recited (together with the Lord's Prayer) at the beginning and end of the Divine Office, and at the beginning of each part or hour of the Divine Office. It is a general custom to recite the Hail Mary at the end of a Confirmation ceremony with the Creed and the Lord's Prayer; in the final prayers for a dying soul, together with the Lord's Prayer; in performing exorcisms, together with the Lord's Prayer and the Creed.

The recitation of the Hail Mary is more frequent in so-called extra-liturgical devotional exercises, as the holy Rosary, and the prayers required for the gaining of a plenary indulgence (six Our Fathers, Hail Marys, and Glorias to be recited each time). *Ses.*

HALLUCINATION. The word *hallucination*, from the Latin *hallucinor*, is probably of Greek origin (*halukein*—wander in mind); the Latin term conveyed the notion of sensory images which give the appearance of external reality, although they are not caused by any external stimulus to which they seem suited. They are created by an entirely internal process caused by the mind of the individual who accepts them as real. In brief, it is purely subjective perception, to which there corresponds no external objective reality.

Hallucinations differ from the phenomenon of "illusion," which consists in a distorted or erroneous perception (*see* Perception) to which a sensory reality corresponds. Thus, for example: in the case of illusion one hears a noise and believes it to be an insult; in hallucinations, on the other hand, one hears an insulting voice, when, in fact, there is absolute silence.

Hallucinations are extremely more rare than illusions. Illusions due to false interpretation of a sensory experience may in fact occur even in normal subjects. The source of illusions may be objective or subjective: objective if due to an external cause, e.g., in a dimly lighted place it is easy to mistake one person for another; subjective, if due to internal causes, e.g., the mistaken identity of persons may be brought about by emotional tension caused by impatient waiting. Illusions are more easily produced under psychopathological conditions due to mental or emotional disturbances.

Hallucinations never occur in normal individuals, except in a state of semi-vigilance or drowsiness (*see* Dream, Sleep), in which case they are called "hypnagogic hallucinations." Hallucina-

tions in psychopathic individuals occur mainly in confusional states (*see* Alcoholism) and dissociative syndromes (*see* Schizophrenia), but they may also appear in other mental diseases.

Two factors intervene in the production of hallucination: a sensory factor (arising from irritative processes or from incongruous stimulation of the sensitive nerves or sensory centers of the cortex), and an ideo-emotional factor; these two factors determine the form, the content, and the convincing character of the hallucination. Thus, the depressed emotional tone of the melancholic shapes hallucinations (and illusions) with an afflicting and terrifying content; the morbid suspicion of the individual suffering from a persecution complex supplies the insulting and threatening content of the voices he hears. These two factors are not always present in equal proportion. In "psychical hallucinations," to be discussed later, the sensory element is present in an extremely reduced measure. On the other hand, the convincing character of the hallucination may be more or less lacking in certain types of hallucinations (also called "hallucinoses") in which the patient is fully aware of his morbid condition. Such hallucinations are usually found to occur in certain neurological syndromes brought on by irritative lesions of the brain-stem.

VARIETIES OF HALLUCINATIONS. Hallucinations (and illusions) may affect all of the senses, but they occur more frequently in the sphere of vision and hearing, since the two senses are rich in image elements. Psychoses caused by alcoholic intoxication are characterized by so-called "zooscopic visual hallucinations," in which the patient envisions himself surrounded by insects and all sorts of tiny animals. In epileptics (*see* Epilepsy), hallucinations may assume episodically a terrifying content, such as a raging fire and the like; the nature of these hallucinations is detected from their stereotyped, repetitive pattern. Of less frequent occurrence are gustatory, olfactory, and tactile hallucinations, and those of the genesial sense (the sexual areas). Characteristic of such types of hallucinations are sensations by the patient of the taste of poisonous substances; the odor of incense, flowers, or of a dead body; the sensation of blows, caresses, or unclean touches, of animals creeping around within his body or of the transformation of organs (vitrification of the heart, and the like); finally, the painful sensation of defloration, etc. But in all such instances it is extremely difficult to ascertain whether these are cases of genuine hallucinations or, perhaps, of illusions induced by local irritations and later interpreted by the patient in a delirious fashion. Certain individuals subject to chronic delirium are apt to hear their own thoughts spoken aloud by others (the so-called "sonorous repetition of thought"); in these instances the subject may convince himself that others are stealing his ideas (plagiarism). Lastly, a particular type of hallucination in which the sensory character of its content is not too clearly defined is referred to as a "psychical hallucination" or "pseudo-hallucination." In these instances the patient does not really hear commands, voices, or spoken thoughts, but nevertheless he senses something as being external to his own person, or something imposed upon him by others, and in trying to describe these experiences he uses such terms as "internal voices," "compulsory or commanded thoughts," and the like.

EFFECTS. Illusions and hallucinations affect the behavior of the patient greatly. Considered as real facts, hallucinations may drive the patient to all sorts of reactions, to acts of aggression, homicide, and suicide. The hallucinated individual who hears threatening words spoken by his supposed persecutor may react by attacking him and, in all good faith, consider this an act of legitimate self-defense. The patient who in his hallucinatory state sees himself encircled by raging fire may seek to escape by jumping from a window to his death. Any action, no matter how illogical or absurd, can find its rational justification in the mind of an individual subject to hallucinatory influences.

MORAL COROLLARIES. On the strength of the above considerations, criminal acts committed by hallucinated individuals may well be reactions that can be justified by the content and vividness of their hallucinations. Before pronouncing any judgment, therefore, it is necessary accurately to determine in each individual case whether the crime was committed under the influence of an hallucinatory process. This task should not be too difficult for a psychiatrist, to whom the confessor, with much prudence, should direct his penitent.

At times the more delicate and difficult problem is to determine whether a given phenomenon is of a supernatural origin, or perhaps the product of hallucination or illusion. We are referring to certain phenomena, such as hearing prophetic voices, experiencing heavenly apparitions and the like, which may occur in a case of so-called "mystical delirium" (actually pseudo-mystical) experienced by certain paranoiacs; to certain "diabolical possessions" (these, too, are false diabolical possessions) by which various hallucinations and kinesthetic illusions are explained even by the patient himself; or to possible "collective illusions" experienced by a group of persons who, under intense emotional reaction, claim to witness the moving about of images of saints, or the revolving of the eyes of the crucified Lord, etc., merely because they had previously heard that such "miraculous" occurrences had taken place. In this last case, judicious interpretation of the alleged phenomenon by ecclesiastical authorities can set the matter in the proper perspective. In the other cases, a thorough psychological examination of the individual is usually sufficient to reveal the existence of a pathological cause for the phenomena experienced. At all events, the principle enunciated by the Divine Master, "every tree is known by its fruit" (Luke 6:44), is always valid. In other words, the genuine character of alleged heavenly apparitions is to be judged according to the reaction and behavior of the person experiencing them; so that, if the individual who claims to have experienced heavenly apparitions is known to practice Christian virtues to an heroic degree, it will be quite likely that his experiences are brought about by the intervention of divine grace. *Riz.*

HAPPINESS. Happiness is a state of well-being wherein all of a person's needs are satisfied, a state of beatitude (*q.v.*). Full beatitude is reserved to the hereafter; it consists in the most intimate and everlasting union with God, seen face to face and loved with the soul's whole strength, and is accompanied by intense joy. There cannot be full happiness on earth. Knowledge and love of God and the exercise of virtue, however, do cause a relative happiness which, though short of perfection in one's lifetime, yet surpasses by far any other human joy.

Many vainly seek true happiness in material goods and pleasures; man's nature and aspirations are so far superior to the perishable things of earth that he never finds more than a relative happiness in them. *Man.*

HAZARD (Gambling). *See* Games.

HEBEPHRENIA. The term hebephrenia (from the Greek *hebe*: youth; and *phren*: mind) was coined by Kahlbaum about 1870 to designate a psychosis that generally develops in youths between the ages of fifteen and twenty. In its initial stage the disease is often mistaken for neurasthenia. As it progresses, there gradually appear signs of puerility, fatuity, and impassivity in behavior, depressed mental disturbances, mannerisms, negativism, impulsive outbursts and, at times, hallucinations and deliriums which come and go during the disorder. The mental disorganization usually advances rapidly to the point where the individual loses complete contact with reality. This final and very serious stage is typical, at least in appearance, of dementia and is verified in the majority of cases. The *heboid* or *heboid-phrenic syndromes* are milder types of hebephrenia, although generally of a chronic nature.

In 1874 Kahlbaum discovered another psychopathic syndrome, *catatonia*, which develops in the third decade of life. It is characterized by a sort of stupor and impassivity interrupted by sudden, impulsive action and prolonged agitations; hallucinations are very frequent; deliriums either do not occur or, if they do, they are of a transient nature.

Kahlbaum noted numerous similarities between catatonia and hebephrenia and the frequent change of one into the other. Later, Kraepelin, concentrating more on the analogies between the two syndromes, joined to them the paranoid type (in which delusions, often complicated by hallucinations, are foremost) and called all three (hebephrenic, catatonic, and paranoid) by one name, i.e., *dementia praecox*. Still later, Bleuler substituted the term *schizophrenia* for *dementia praecox*. In the article on schizophrenia the reader will find more extensive observations concerning this very important subject and its moral aspects. *Riz.*

HEDONISM. Hedonism is the doctrine of those who hold that pleasure is the sole or chief good in life and that moral duty is fulfilled in the gratification of pleasure-seeking instincts and dispositions. Hedonism is also called *Epicureanism* from the name of its more famous advocate, Epicurus.

The doctrine of hedonism is basically sensualistic and materialistic. As a result, it is concerned neither with the soul nor with virtue. At times, however, it seems to make room even for the soul by promising it superior pleasures. It even inculcates moderation, but only as a means that will guarantee a more enduring ability to enjoy pleasure. This moderation, rather than being a corrective force of the baseness of the system, is a refinement in the art of exploiting pleasure. Hedonism confuses pleasure with goodness, or rather subordinates the latter to the former. In so doing, it overturns the whole moral order and poisons the very source of morality. *Gra.*

HEDONISM, Somatic. *See* Medicine, Psychosomatic.

HEGEMONY, ECONOMIC. *See* Economics, Monopoly.

HEMP, INDIAN. *See* Aphrodisiacs.

HEREDITARY AXIS. *See* Heredity.

HEREDITARY SUCCESSION. *See* Heredity.

HEREDITY, BIOLOGICAL. In biology, heredity, or hereditary transmission, may be defined as the whole aggregate of morphological and psychical properties or characteristics derived from the parents and originally contained in that cell (fertilized egg) from which the development of a new individual has its beginning. In the nucleus of the fertilized egg are particular and well-defined threadlike corpuscles called chromosomes. Chromosomes are made up of a double band of very minute, ultramicroscopic elements called *genes*. Each of the genes has a specific function and a particular task to fulfill in the formation of a new individual. Thus, one gene—or, more accurately, one group of genes—will be responsible for the color of the eyes, another for the structure of the nose, another for a particular psychological quality, etc. Since each parent provides a complete set of genes, the fertilized egg cell contains a double set of such elements. This arrangement serves as an added guarantee of normality since both members of any pair of genes fulfill the same function. In other words, the normality of a given function is ordinarily assured if at least one of the two genes responsible for the function is normal. The development of the individual, however, is not completely subordinated to the hereditary properties explained above, for it is also influenced by environmental elements taken in the widest sense of the word (nutrition, climate, illness, education, etc.).

It is important to distinguish that which is hereditary from that which is *congenital*. By hereditary pathological conditions must be understood only those which are transmitted by the parents to the offspring in the same manner in which the characteristics of the species and of the individual are transmitted. Thus, a pathological factor is truly hereditary if it has the same material substratum upon which the factors of normal heredity depend. In short, transmission must take place through a defective pairs of genes. By congenital pathological conditions, on the other hand, must be understood those which exist at the time of birth and which derive from a serious impairment either of the sex cells before fertilization or of the product of conception during its intra-uterine development. Obviously, hereditary pathological conditions, for the most part, are also congenital, since they are already present at birth. Thus, for example, many malformations and monstrosities, albinism, daltonism, besides being hereditary, are also congenital. The so-called heredolues, instead, is only congenital. A peculiar contraction of the hands, called Dupuytren disease, is hereditary but not congenital, since it develops in adult age. Haemophilia occurs only in males and is transmitted exclusively through the female members of the same family. This disease is an example of hereditary conditions linked with sex. In the realm of mental diseases, manic-depressive frenzy also is generally hereditary; frequently, schizophrenia (*q.v.*), paranoia (*q.v.*), and compulsive immorality are also hereditary.

Degeneration (etymologically, *departure from race or kind*), according to an important theory formulated by Morel in 1857 and developed by his followers, is a strictly morbid, hereditary process which begins with an abnormality acquired by the ancestors of a family but which inevitably develops in their descendants. According to an over-simplified theory indicated by Morel as taking place in the field of psychopathology, degeneration becomes increasingly more serious with each succeeding generation, going from a simple neuropathic temperament to eccentricities, deliriums, serious anomalies of behavior, imbecility, idiocy, and finally, to monstrosities and infecundity, even to the complete extinction of the family stock. Thus, according to Morel's theory, the descendants from a stock, accidentally afflicted with toxic infections affecting the sex cells, are from birth already doomed to degeneration which they would, then, transmit in an increasingly more serious form to their own descendants. In reality, the process of degeneration is much more irregular and complex than this, for there are instances of an arrest of the disorder and even of *regeneration*. Besides, one cannot foresee the course of degeneration, nor is it possible, at least in practice, to make a clear-cut distinction between truly degenerative phenomena and pathological phenomena. What seem to be marks of degeneration often are not and it would be extremely fallacious to admit the existence of a rigid pattern between the physical and psychological symptoms of degeneration. At any rate, the concept of what constitutes degeneration and the term itself are very much under study. The present knowledge of heredity derived from the study of genes, the laws of Mendel, and other principles and concepts too well-known to bear repeating here fully justify, on the biological level, the ethico-juridical prohibition of marriage between close blood-relatives. Blood relationship ordinarily does not seem to have real pathogenic significance but it does tend to increase and often to cause the appearance of latent hereditary tendencies of the parents. Such tendencies remain concealed when the parties to a marriage are individuals who are not blood relatives.

Present-day ideas concerning the factors governing heredity justifiably lay great stress on the physical, intellectual, and moral education of the individual. Such education has a significant influence on the individual's intelligence, temperament, emotional life and ethico-social attitude. It is easy to understand that if the education of the individual is well integrated with appropriate environmental influences (taken in the broadest sense of the term), such as healthy food, hygienic home conditions, good example, etc., the physical and mental health of the individuals will benefit more, par-

ticularly if they are subjected to such conditions and treatments from early childhood and for an adequate period of time. The application of such hygienico-pedagogic methods, from the time of St. Philip Neri to St. John Bosco and to the more recent founders of "Boys' Towns," accounts for the remarkable successes attained in the work of rehabilitation of delinquent youths. *See also* Inheritance, Testament, Sterilization. *Riz.*

HEREDO - ANTHROPOLOGY. *See* Anthropology.

HERESY, HERETICS. Heresy (from the Greek *hairesis*, choice; 2 Peter 2:1) is the pertinacious error of a baptized person who, though believing in Jesus Christ, denies one or more truths proposed by the Church as revealed (Can. 1325, par. 2). According to the definition, only baptized persons are heretics in a strict sense. Nevertheless, members of sects which today no longer administer baptism validly are also called heretics, but in a wider sense. The essential element in heresy is opposition to the magisterium of the Church (both solemn and ordinary, that is, as contained in the common doctrine of the Church). A heretic does not accept the Church magisterium as the rule of faith but follows his own interpretation. One who denies a truth which he personally holds as revealed but which was not proposed by the Church as such, commits a sin against faith, but would not be guilty of heresy. A heretic is not only one who denies absolutely a revealed truth, but also one who obstinately doubts a revealed truth; that is, one who, after having recognized a truth taught by the Church as revealed, continues to doubt it. Obviously, a momentary suspension of judgment as in a case of temptation against the Faith, is not considered a doubt against the Faith.

Heresy, as well as infidelity, may be *material* (negative or privative) or *formal*. Formal heresy is the sin of those who deny or obstinately doubt a truth known by them as taught by the Church as a revealed truth. The sin of heresy is very serious, the most serious in the genre of infidelity (St. Thomas, *S. Theol.*, II–II, q. 10, a. 6). He who denies a truth connected with the Faith and infallibly taught by the Church (such as theological conclusions, dogmatic facts, canonization of saints, etc.), is not guilty of formal heresy, but commits a sin against the Faith. A doctrine taught by the Church, not as revealed or infallibly certain, but commonly to be held as true, must be accepted not only with an external, reverential assent, but also with an internal assent, even though it may not be irrevocable; to deny it pertinaciously would not be heresy but it would be an act of disobedience against the authority of the Church (P. Pius IX, Letter *Tuas libenter* to the Archbishop of Munich, December 21, 1863; Vatican Council, Sess. 3, *De fide ratione;* S.C.S. Off., Decr. *Lamentabili,* July 3, 1907, prop. 8, Can. 1324).

Material heresy on the part of those who until now belonged to the Church does not cause them to be separated from the Body of the Church. On the other hand, those who were baptized in a non-Catholic sect, but err in good faith, do not belong to the visible body of the Church although they are said to have a certain relationship with the Mystical Body of Christ by "an unconscious desire and longing." By their sin formal heretics immediately place themselves outside the Church. In addition, if the sin is external, whether public or private, it is punished with excommunication, absolution from which is reserved in a special manner to the Holy See. If, however, the case is referred to the bishop in the external forum, recourse to the Holy See is no longer necessary (Can. 2314). For heretical books, *see* Forbidden Books, Press.

Heretics in good faith, though not guilty in conscience, are treated in the external forum as excommunicates, unless their good faith is proven. No sacraments may be administered (Cans. 1149; 2260, par. 2) to heretics even if in good faith, unless they are first reconciled with the Church (Cans. 731, par. 2; 2260, par. 1). Simple assistance at Holy Mass is permitted (Can. 2259, par. 2); it is also lawful to offer Mass for them privately, provided that there be no scandal (Can. 2262, par. 2). If they die as members of a non-Catholic sect without signs of conversion, ecclesiastical burial may not be given (Can. 1240, par. 1). *See also* Non-Catholics, Blasphemy, Faith, Infidels. *Dam.*

HERMAPHRODITISM. Hermaphroditism is a permanent condition characterized by the coexistence in the same individual of the two sexes, each with its own specific genital gland containing completely matured elements. The condition takes its name from *hermaphroditos,* signifying a hybrid being, an imaginary creation of ancient Oriental poets, in which the male (*Hermes:* Mercury) and the female (*Aphrodite:* Venus) sexes were united.

Hermaphroditism is common in inferior animals, particularly worms; but in superior animals and in man, it constitutes a condition of malformation due to arrested development or distortion in the development of some of the elements characterizing the sex; this condition will cause such a deviation in the formation of the genitalia as to make doubtful the sex to which the individual belongs. To understand this phenomenon, it must be recalled that during the development of the embryo, even superior animals and man go through a phase in which both sexes are represented in a rudimentary way in the same individual. While the rudiments of one of the two sexes will remain in its embryonic state, those of the other sex gradually will evolve to the point where the proper primary and secondary sexual characteristics are formed. Occasionally an anomaly may occur in the development of the genital organs of a man so as to cause, among other things, the testicles to remain lodged in the abdomen, while the external genital organs take on a close resemblance to those of a woman. This condition, present at birth, gives rise to a doubtful and, at times, to a mistaken judgment about the sex of the individual. An individual equipped with male genital glands, but having the external appearance of a woman, constitutes an example of *male pseudo-hermaphroditism* or of *androgynism*. At other times, though more rarely, the opposite condition occurs, namely, *female pseudo-hermaphroditism* or *gynandry*, caused by anomalies in the development of the female external organs so as to make them resemble the male organs. In the latter condition, while the individual has no testicles, it does have a uterus and ovaries, which often are in a state of hypotrophy or atrophy.

It would be superfluous to speak here of the other types of hermaphroditism. It will suffice to remember that it is impossible to have in an individual the simultaneous complete development of both male and female genital glands. Much less is it possible for them to function in such a way as to permit auto-fertilization as in the inferior animals mentioned above.

We shall add, however, that there seems to exist today a decisive way (proposed by Moore in 1953) of determining the real sex in doubtful cases. It consists in the biopsy of the epidermis which is believed to yield evidence of the actual chromosomic sex of the individual, thereby permitting children with uncertain sexual characteristics (the so-called "intersexuals") to be reared according to their sex—an education which is extremely important in the psycho-sexual orientation of the adult.

HERMAPHRODITISM AND MARRIAGE. In reference to marriage, the old canonists classified hermaphrodites as follows: (a) *Perfect hermaphrodites:* those possessing at the same time (as it was believed then) the complete male and female genital organs, in such a manner as to have the full capacity to perform, according to their choice, the proper sexual acts of one or the other of the two sexes indiscriminately. These, once they had become adults, were bound to choose definitively one of the two sexes, with a sworn promise of never changing to the other, and of never making use of the organs of the other sex. Only in this way was permission given them to contract marriage validly and licitly in the sex of

their choice. (b) *Imperfect hermaphrodites:* those possessing complete and perfect organs of one sex and, in a rudimentary fashion, also an organ or more of the opposite sex. (c) *Apparent hermaphrodites:* those who only apparently, in the estimation of the ordinary person, seemed to be bisexual, while in reality they could be recognized by a medical expert as belonging to one or the other sex.

Today, as a result of physio-pathological studies, there is no longer any question of perfect hermaphrodites since they do not exist. In the light of these same scientific results, the Church admits the other types of hermaphrodites (pseudo-hermaphrodites) to marriage in their predominant sex, except the case in which impotency is certainly present even in the predominant sex. Hence, even though it be a case of hermaphroditism, the diriment impediment would only and always result *ex capite impotentiae.*

HERMAPHRODITISM AND THE PRIESTHOOD. In the case of hermaphrodites, we are dealing with individuals afflicted with morphological anomalies which sooner or later could easily be aggravated by an endocrine anomaly causing a neuro-vegetative imbalance and serious psycho-sexual disorders. For these reasons, such persons are not encouraged to go on to the priesthood nor even to the religious life. On this point, Scremin is most rigid and advises the exclusion even of those "who are afflicted with the slightest morphological anomaly." With Bon, we feel that it is possible to be less uncompromising and thus consider admission to the priesthood of individuals affected by a very slight case of androgynism as is feasible. It must be understood, however, that in these cases the most exacting examinations will have to be conducted so as to exclude the co-existence of any utero-ovarian formation, even in the hypotropic stage, for the development of such organs in later years might still be possible. The same would hold for females bearing the characteristics of the opposite sex who aspire to the religious life.

SURGICAL CORRECTION OF HERMAPH-

RODITISM. Surgical intervention for the correction of the sex of pseudo-hermaphrodites is lawful as long as the purpose of the correction is to improve the characteristics of the true sex and not further to develop the rudimentary features of the non-existent sex. In short, as Tuffier and Lapointe point out, "any operation whose aim is contrary to the real sex must be avoided at all costs." Also to be avoided is the removal of the sex glands of pseudo-hermaphrodites on the pretext that it is merely a question of organs without functional value and that the individuals are not capable of completing the sexual act. The sex glands of such individuals, while not suitable for reproduction, always contain important internal secretions. One thing is certain: no surgeon is permitted to transform a pseudo-hermaphrodite into a eunuch. If in the course of a gynecological examination or an extra-genital operation (for example, on the occasion of a herniotomy), the surgeon becomes aware of the fact that the real sex of the person is different from the apparent one, he need not inform his patient of his discovery. This silence is justified by the compensating benefits of not disturbing the person's conscience and of avoiding the overthrow by the individual of firmly established habits and tendencies. The individual's parents, however, ought to be apprised of the situation tactfully in order that they might realize the imporance of refraining from both improper sexual suggestions and from encouraging regrettable and immoral conditions.

Finally, it can happen that a surgeon, called upon to give his counsel and assistance to a married couple, discovers that he has on his hands the case of a normal individual being married to an hermaphrodite of the same sex. If the condition is unknown to both spouses, it may be left to his conscience to decide whether he should reveal the truth (which will profoundly disturb the couple) or leave the spouses in good faith by silence. If we were called upon to decide in such a case, all things being equal, we would lean toward the first solution on the general principle that truth is always to be preferred, even if painful and even if it should give rise to a request of annulment of the marriage.

THERAPY. Besides the usual, though complicated, surgical operations, hormonic therapy has shown notable curative possibilities. Hormonic treatment of male pseudo-hermaphroditism consists in a careful administration of testerone and of chorionic gonadotrophin. In female pseudo-hermaphroditism, cortisone is recommended since it has an indirect reaction against the androgens or male hormones, and fosters ovarian development. Such therapy ought to be initiated as early in life as possible and be continued for a long period of time. But the use of hormonic treatments is recommended at any age in order that everything possible be done to assist in the biological adjustment of these unfortunate individuals. *Riz.*

HERMITS. *See* Religious Order.

HEROIC ACT. *See* Human Act, Law.

HEROIC ACT OF CHARITY. The heroic act of charity is an extraordinary act of charity in behalf of the souls in Purgatory. It consists in this: a member of the Church on earth, either by a set formula or simply by an act of his will, offers to God in behalf of the souls in Purgatory all the satisfactory works which he will perform during his lifetime and all the suffrages which may accrue to him after his death (Decree *Urbis et Orbis,* December 19, 1885). This offering is an act of true charity, indeed of heroic charity, because the offerer is willing to assume undiminished pains of Purgatory in order that other souls may be released the sooner from Purgatory. The heroic act of charity, though often called a vow, is not binding under pain of sin. As a matter of fact, it is revocable at will, according to a decree of the Holy Office, February 20, 1907.

Many Christians, upon making this vow, usually deposit their satisfactory works and suffrages into the hands, as it were, of the Blessed Virgin, in order that she may distribute these favors to the souls in Purgatory according to her own merciful desire. However, this quasi-designation is not to be considered an integral part of the act itself but only an accessory devotion to be recommended to the faithful (Decree of December 19, 1885).

St. Gertrude (1256–1302) is said to have been the originator of the heroic act of charity, but the first to use it in its present form seems to have been Father Ferdinand de Morroy (died at Lima in 1646), while the practice was widely promoted by the Theatine Father Gasper Olider of Oleala and by St. Alphonsus. The heroic act of charity was canonically approved by Pope Benedict XIII (August 23, 1728). The object of the offering made through the heroic act of charity consists of satisfactory works and suffrages. Hence, the vow or offerings (1) does not include the fruit of merit that is not applicable to others; (2) does not take away the impetratory power of our prayers, so that, even after having made the vow, a person may freely pray to obtain a grace or favor either for himself or for others; so also may a priest making such a vow continue to celebrate Mass according to the intention of those who request it and offer a stipend for it; (3) includes the offering of the satisfactory part of our works, i.e., the special fruit accruing to us from our works, insofar as they are satisfactory, as well as the offering of all suffrages applicable to us after death. These fruits or merits one must surrender in order to fulfill the vow or offering; hence, anyone intending to reserve to himself indulgences granted to the living would not satisfy the vow (Decree of December 19, 1885). In other words, besides one's satisfactory works, it is necessary to offer in behalf of the souls in Purgatory not only indulgences applicable to the dead, but also those granted only to the living (Decree of November 24, 1854). Nevertheless, a priest celebrating Mass at a privileged altar must apply the indulgence attached thereto in favor of the soul for whom Mass is being offered.

Persons making the heroic act of char-ity need not fear that they thereby condemn themselves inevitably to a long term in Purgatory. Since they daily exercised charity toward the deceased, they can justly place their confidence in the divine mercy, according to the words of St. Luke (4, 38): "Give, and it shall be given to you . . . ; for with what measure you measure, it shall be measured to you." It is to be further noted that the least increase of merit must be esteemed above release from the greatest pain in Purgatory, for purgatorial suffering will one day come to an end, whereas increase of merit will render us more blessed for all eternity.

The indulgences granted to persons making such a vow are listed in the decrees of September 20, 1852, November 20, 1854, and January 26, 1932. A plenary indulgence, applicable only to the deceased, may be gained: (1) on any day of the year under the following conditions: confession, Holy Communion, a visit to a church or public oratory and prayer for the intention of the Holy Father; (2) on each Monday of the year, if one shall hear Mass for the faithful departed and observe the usual conditions. If one, besides hearing Mass on Monday, shall also receive Holy Communion, he may gain two plenary indulgences, provided that he shall twice visit a church and each time pray for the intentions of the Holy Father.

If one be legitimately impeded from receiving Holy Communion or from assisting at Mass, the Bishop may subdelegate an approved confessor to authorize commutation of these requirements for other pious works.

Finally, priests making the heroic act of charity may enjoy, on every day of the year, the personal indult of the privileged altar. *Pal.*

HEROIN. See Drugs.

HEROISM. *See* Martyrdom, Saints, Virtue.

HIERARCHY. Hierarchy, in general, means a division of powers with a subordination of rank for a specific purpose.

This concept applies to any society governed by one central authority. The term, however, is used almost exclusively in the Catholic Church. By analogy Dionysius Areopagite speaks of a celestial hierarchy based on the degree of nearness to God of the heavenly spirits.

Subjectively, the hierarchy of the Church consists of individuals organized in orderly subordination and invested with those ranks of power Christ conferred upon His Church; objectively, it consists of those very ranks of power established by Christ and by the Church. The aim of the hierarchy is to guide the faithful in the attainment of their supernatural end, (1) by sanctification and (2) by discipline.

There is in the Church a hierarchy of order and a hierarchy of jurisdiction; the former for the sanctification, the latter for the government of the faithful. The second is generally rooted in the first, although not in every conceivable case: a lawfully elected pope possesses the fullness of jurisdictional power even though he may have received no orders. The fullness of jurisdictional power is vested only in the Roman pontiff, who receives it directly from God upon his legitimate election; he shares with the bishops the power of order, which in his case has no territorial restriction, neither as to the validity, nor the licitness of its exercise (certain functions of ecclesiastical institution are reserved exclusively to him, e.g., the canonization of Saints).

By divine institution, the hierarchy of order consists of Bishops, priests and deacons (Can. 108, par. 3) who are constituted in major or sacred orders (with due reservation for subdiaconate). To meet increased liturgical necessities, and for a more convenient distribution of ministerial work, the Church added, in time, several lower orders, those of subdeacon, porter, lector, exorcist, and acolyte. The latter four, in the Latin Church, are called minor orders; subdiaconate was raised by the Church to the rank of major or sacred order. Admission into the hierarchy of order is by reception of the first tonsure (Can. 108, par. 1).

The hierarchy of jurisdiction consists of two ranks of divine institution; the Supreme Pontificate and the Episcopate subordinated to it (Can. 108, par. 3). Many other ranks were added by ecclesiastical institution according to the needs of the times. These various ranks share directly either in the supreme power or in the episcopal power. According to present-day discipline, the following share in the supreme jurisdiction: Ecumenical Councils (a gathering of the Bishops of the whole Church under the leadership of the Pope), Cardinals, Roman Congregations, Tribunals and Offices of the Roman Curia, Pontifical Legates (*Legati a latere*, Nuncios, Internuncios, Apostolic Delegates), Patriarchs, Primates, Metropolitans, Plenary and Provincial Councils, Vicars and Prefects Apostolic, other lower prelates (prelates *nullius*), and Administrators Apostolic. Exarchs, Chorepiscopi, Archimandrites do not exist any longer in the Latin Church; Patriarchs (*q.v.*) and Primates are still used but only as titles. The following share in the episcopal jurisdiction: Coadjutors and Auxiliaries of residential Bishops, the Diocesan Synod, whose function it is to convene the clergy of a Diocese under the leadership of the Bishop, the Episcopal Curia (consisting of the Vicar General (*q.v.*), the Officialis, Chancellor, and various notaries, synodal examiners, parish Consultors), the Cathedral Chapter (or Board of Diocesan Consultors where no chapter exists), the Vicar Capitular during the vacancy of the Apostolic See, rural Deans, Pastors, and Rectors of churches. There are also the hierarchies of Religious Orders or Institutes, of which many, i.e., exempt religious, are directly dependent on the Holy See.

In the Eastern Church the hierarchical organization is somewhat different with regard to those ranks which are not of divine law.

The hierarchy of order: (1) The first tonsure exists in almost every Eastern rite; the effects thereof, however, are different, particularly insofar as enrollment into the ecclesiastical state and the rights and privileges of clerics are concerned. (2) The minor orders in the Ruthenian, Rumanian, Copt, Bulgarian, Greek and Melchite Rites are only two: that of lector and of subdeacon; all others are included in these two. In the Chaldean, Syrian, Malabaric rites, the minor orders are three: that of chorister, of lector and of subdeacon; the Armenian rite has the same number of minor orders as the Latin rite. (3) The major orders are the same as in the Latin Church with the exception of subdiaconate, which in the Eastern Church is numbered among the minor orders.

In the hierarchy of jurisdiction there are no purely titular ranks, but all have jurisdictional power. The ranks are: Patriarch (of Alexandria for the Copts, of Antiochea for Syrians, Melchites, and Maronites, of Babylonia for Chaldeans, of Cilicia for Armenians), who has a true jurisdiction over all the faithful of his rite; Metropolitan, Bishop, Exarch (the latter may be either a Bishop or an ordinary priest with ordinary jurisdiction), Vicar patriarchal, Auxiliary Bishop, Chorepiscopus, Archimandrite (Abbot), protopresbyter or protopriest, and priest. M.d.G.

HINDUISM. Hinduism (also called *neo-Brahmanism*) is an outgrowth of ancient Indian religions, brought about through the efforts of the Brahmins as a means of overthrowing Buddhism and its many cumbersome reforms. This new movement required a long period of time (from the beginning of the Middle Ages to the year 1500) to become stabilized and bears the marks of those factors which contributed to its development. Principal among them are the ample concessions made to ancient religious elements which were to be won over by this device to the movement for the rejection of Buddhism. Theoretically, Hinduism kept the ideological deposit of Brahmanism, such as the unitary vision of the universe, the transmigration of souls or rebirth (*samsara*) based on the actions performed during one's lifetime (law of *karman*), the daily celebration of the domestic sacrifice, and the four castes.

It is a well-known fact that the con-quest of India by the Aryan race divided the Indians into two ethnically distinct classes or castes: Aryans and non-Aryans, with Aryans further sub-divided into secondary groups (castes), separated according to their respective activities. The priestly or Brahminical caste takes precedence over all and maneuvers to turn religious laws to its own advantage, by making their sacrifice the center of the world and Brahmin a veritable god on earth, while it claims for the sacrificial act the infallible effect of rendering ineffective any recourse to gods who are mere symbols. The *brahmana* (theological commentaries of the Veda) explain the chants and the sacrificial ritual in the mystico-theurgical sense, mentioned above, and make of Brahma, in the formula of the sacrificial prayer, the center of the sacrifice and, ultimately, of the universe.

DOCTRINE. Brahmanical speculation, so abstractly monistic, was not the kind of doctrine to satisfy the Hindu spirit, to whom the figures of traditional polytheism were always dear. Hence, a mixture of divinities, beliefs, and rites resulted. The venerable Vedic gods are made so grotesque as to become unrecognizable; the liturgy is contaminated with magic; the monistic philosophy of classic Brahmanism is so strangely and incongruously interpreted as to lead to the conception of a purely nominal triad in which the god creator, Brahm, proper to the Brahmins, is given second place and kept out of the people's devotion, whereas the god preserver, Vishnu, and the god destroyer, Shiva, become the heads of two real and truly independent religions, *Vishnuism* and *Shivaism*. Their proximity to men has given rise to the idea of a kind of transformation of superior gods into inferior ones or at times into men to a degree which responds to a monistic tendency while it is at the same time an application of the doctrine of transmigration (both so characteristic of the Indian mentality) that there is no longer a definite distinction between the two worlds. While neo-Brahmanism with intellectual tendencies loses itself in a mysticism colored with gaudily theosophical tinges, the popular brand assumes a bizarre fetish tint that gratifies the sentiments of the people with practices full of magic, bordering on delirium.

In fact, as the concept of the divinity has become degraded, so have the ways and means of communicating with it. The two classical ways suggested by Vedism and philosophical Brahmanism, action (sacrifice) and knowledge (meditation), are still open. But sacrifice has become more than ever a ceremony of gross idolatry, while meditation has become a series of the worst kind of theurgical and mystical practices leading the individual to the *moksha*, or "liberation," through the universal soul. This second method has a consecrated name of its own, *bhakti*, or devotion, and it admits five degrees that go from simple quiet or repose of the spirit to ecstatic tenderness. But this mystical union with the god turns out to be, in fact, a true erotism degenerating into obscene practices the like of which are not found except among gnostic sects. These practices are raised to a system and codified by accommodating Brahmins in handbooks of amatory art for the purpose of attracting lascivious sympathizers to their religion.

SECTS. Hinduism does not have a unitary form, but is divided into sects. The faithful, who make up two thirds of the Indian population, gather around whichever god they prefer (*ishta deva*, god of one's own choice) according to the theory of the Brahmins.

Besides Vishnu and Shiva, we must also mention Krishna, who is closely related to Vishnu, to a point that in certain sects he is one with him. The myth describes him: first, as a boy among the shepherds, taking part in their games, feasts, and love affairs (for example the passion for Radha); later, as a famous warrior. The legends of his pastoral life are filled with burning erotism, reflected in the lyric drama *Gita-Govinda*. The figure of Krishna is frequently represented in statues, pictures, and the like.

Durga, Shiva's wife, personifies the creative power (*shakti*) of the god and, as such, she receives a special veneration from her devotees (*shaktism*). These are divided into two groups: one of the *right hand*, following the normal practices of worship; the other of the *left hand*, engaging in wild rites.

Nor are deistic sects lacking. Besides the one founded by Nanak (d. 1539), whose disciples (*Sikh*) ended by forming a separate religion (*see* Sikhism), there is the Brahm Samaj, a monotheistic sect founded in 1830. This sect rejects the Veda and professes a deism that brings to mind Liberal Protestantism. There is also the Arya Samaj, also monotheistic, anti-mythological, opposed to practices of idolatry and the caste system, but hostile to Christianity. It is a close follower of the Veda, which, by a forced exegesis, it tries to bring into harmony with modern thinking.

The public worship of the Hindus is not practiced in the open, but inside temples which only the Brahmin may enter during the ceremony. The Brahmins bear the insignia of the sect to which they belong; they spend their lives reading holy books and preside mainly at the ceremonies of private worship.

MORAL VIEW. The morality of Hinduism conforms to its fundamentally monistic vision of the universe, despite the many forms and objects of worship. The absolute and eternal unity of the universal One and of the Ego, compels the individual to respect others, because an offense against one single being falls upon all; wherefore everything that favors harmony and union must be constantly pursued. In order to achieve this end, a constant control over mind, tongue, and body is necessary, for these must never be left unchecked lest they become the prey of intemperate desires that disturb the peace of the spirit.

The first thing that one observes in Hinduism is a religious syncretism or agglomeration of religious and philosophical doctrines. The trinitarian conception of divinity in Hinduism cannot be even analogically compared with the Trinity of Catholic theology. In Hinduism, the three gods have different influences; the three Persons in the Catholic dogma are equal, though distinct, and

God is One in nature, but Triune in persons. The cult of the miraculous boy Krishna is not always a source of good example to his devotees; for instance, the exaltation of the erotism of his youth. Many of the various Hindu sects imitate these examples with decidedly epicurean programs. Many aspects of its worship are ridiculous, indeed. In certain sects, the image of the miraculous boy is treated like a living child; every day it is washed, dressed, offered various kinds of food, and then placed on a throne for veneration by the faithful. Yoga itself abounds with absurd practices, such as covering the body three times a day with ashes, simulating insanity with laughter, songs and dances, or imitating the bellowing of a bull. A section of the sakata sect practices secretly wild rites in honor of the goddess Durga, which in Eastern Bengal and in Assam degenerate into complete debauchery. Magic and mysterious powers in the various sects are also attributed to ritualistic formulae. The migration of the soul, which seems to be one of the fixed canons in the Indian religions, is also recognized by Hinduism. *Pal.*

HOLY WATER FONT. See Water, Holy.

HOLY YEAR. See Jubilee.

HOMEOSTATIS. See Cybernetics.

HONESTY. See Morality.

HONOR (AND DISHONOR). Honor is the recognition of excellence in another who absolutely (God) or relatively in one or more aspects (virtue, sanctity, authority, science) excels others. This testimony may consist of words or other signs expressed in a way that the individual himself and others would recognize this excellence. To render honor to outstanding persons is an act of justice and, therefore, a good and praiseworthy act. To honor persons who are not deserving of it is called adulation (*q.v.*) or flattery. Honor is not fame merely for

the latter is the *general esteem* resulting from the excellence of a person.

Dishonor consists in acts aimed directly against a person's honor. This is done by attack, contumely, or derision. Slander, instead, consists in acts aimed at others indirectly, that is, insofar as they are directly perceived by others, as in defamation, calumny, detraction. The same act may have two aspects and double malice; e.g., when one publicly and falsely calls another an adulterer. (*See* Adulation, Contumely, Defamation, Calumny, Detraction, Slander, Lying, Falsehood.) For *honor* as recognition of the excellence of persons who are superior by reason of their dignity, *see* Respect. *Ben.*

HONORARIUM. An honorarium is the fee for professional services. Every professional man is entitled to a suitable compensation for services rendered (*see* Wage). The stipulation, collection, and payment of these fees give rise to various problems of justice and charity which are dealt with in moral theology. For questions of this nature concerning each individual profession *see* the respective entries. Here we shall deal with some particular aspects of medical fees, which seem to cause particularly complex problems.

In many countries, during normal times, a doctor's fee is indicated by a *"special scale of fees for medical and surgical services"* established by the Order of Physicians or Medical Association. The listing indicates the lowest fee which a doctor may charge for visits, consultations, injections, operations, laboratory tests, etc. No doctor may normally go below the established minimum so that a degrading of the profession or improper competition among physicians might be avoided. According to a centuries-old tradition, a physician-patient is generally treated without charge regardless of his financial condition and the renown of the treating physician. The care given to another physician should be especially solicitous, particularly in serious cases, out of a spirit of comradeship and because the conventional words of sympathy and comfort usually employed with sick people have little or no effect on a sick physician. It will be the duty of the physician-patient to show in a tangible way his gratitude to the treating colleague. Generally, a physician's parents and other close relatives are charged lower fees or no fee at all. In times of political upheavals and economic slumps, it is very difficult to follow any regulation at all, although in such circumstances medical fees generally reach a level which reflects the particular political and monetary conditions of the times. There are those who strongly advocate what is called variable fees: higher fees to rich patients, more moderate ones to poorer patients, and nothing to very poor persons. But this method is riddled with obvious difficulties, at least in some countries.

MEDICAL COMMERCIALISM. In all cases, a physician should refrain from bargaining about his fee, which must always be fair and equitable. Of course, while the doctor must avoid any kind of greedy commercialism, the patient in turn should refrain from taking advantage of the physician. The role of the doctor is as much a mission as a profession, but he has a right to live and to secure from the practice of his art the means by which he may properly meet all his own needs as well as those of his family. It is improper and usually forbidden by medical deontology to stipulate to a patient the size of a fee according to the outcome of the treatment. An old and wise aphorism says: *"The doctor's duty is to treat his patient, not to cure him,"* meaning that the doctor must use every means at his disposal to cure his patient, but that he cannot guarantee a cure, so often independent of the worth of the therapy.

It is highly immoral and altogether infamous, as Hoffman brands it, for a physician to prolong the treatment in order to reap larger profits. *Riz.*

HONORS. *See* Titles and Honors.

HORMONES. This term, created by the English physiologist Starling, indicates certain substances secreted by special cells in an organism, indispensable for the stimulation, regulation, and balance of various processes of life, such as growth, development, reproduction, nutritional metabolism, etc. To carry out these important functions, hormones must act either directly or indirectly through the neuro-vegetative system on distant organs and tissues, so as to maintain the *correlation* between the various parts of the organism and assure its harmonious psychosomatic functioning and determine the vital physiological unity of the individual. Hormones, active in the quantity of a millionth part of a gram, pass from the original cells into the circulatory system or, in the case of hormones of the posthypophysis, reach adjacent nervous formations; hence, the name *products of internal secretion* also given to such substances and the name of *endocrine glands* or *glands of internal secretion* given to cellular formations productive of hormones. Substances produced by *exorcine glands* (such as tear, saliva, kidney glands, etc.), which reach the outside by means of special excretory channels, are called products of *external secretion.*

The experimental and clinical study of the properties of hormones, of rather recent date, began about a century ago, principally by Muller, C. Bernard, and Brown Sequard. Of even more recent date is the successful work of research directed at the discovery of the chemical composition of hormones, which led to synthetic production and, consequently, therapeutic ministration of drugs with the identical structure and properties of the original. Today it is possible to know the exact properties and chemical composition of numerous hormones, many of which are produced by one and the same gland: folliculin and lutein hormones of the ovary; cortisone and desossicosterone and adrenal of the adrenal glands; gonadotrophic hormones, hormones of growth, hypertensive and uterocynethic hormones, anti-diuretic hormones, and the pigment-spreading hormones of the hypophysis. The knowledge of the complex inter-glandular, or better inter-hormonic, and neuro-hormonic correlations, and of the true nature of the various disturbances affecting the development and the metabolisms of the organism, as well as adequate therapeutic aids (from the transplantation of endocrine glands to the administration of synthetic hormones with the same effect as missing or defective ones) brings about the possibility of a return to health of many patients.

Concerning the influence of hormones on the temperament, character, and the moral acts of man, *see* Endocrinology, Gonads, Hypophysis, Adrenals, Thyroid. *Riz.*

HOROSCOPE. The word *horoscope* (Greek, *hora*—time; *skopein*—to look) denotes a study of the situation of the stars at the time of birth of an individual in order to forecast the destiny of the individual on the basis of these astronomical observations. The practice of determining a horoscope is the major objective of astrology, a most ancient practice among men. At the beginning of the Christian era, the Greeks in Alexandria practiced three types of astrological inquiries. These were subsequently developed by the Arabs and later spread by them to Europe. The first type consisted of *interrogations*, used for the little needs of everyday life, but disdained by astrologists of a higher caliber; the second consisted of *elections*, to determine the most propitious moment for carrying out a certain undertaking. The third type was called *birthday* inquiry, used to forecast the future of individuals, cities, or nations. The most complicated of all these engaged the entire ability and experience of the astrologist in the preparation of the exact wording. This investigation was based on: (a) the astronomical notions of the period, based on the knowledge of the seven *planets* (Moon, Mercury, Venus, Sun, Mars, Jupiter, Saturn) and their changing relationship between one another and between the constellations of the Zodiac; (b) the position of the ecliptic at the time of the birth of an individual whose destiny was being forecast in relation to the eastern horizon of the individual's

birthplace. The position was called *ascendant,* while the instrument used in making the astral observations was called *horoscopium* (horoscope); (c) the division of the celestial sphere into twelve immovable *houses,* through which the seven planets and various portions of the zodiacal band successively passed; (d) the precise knowledge not only of the specific qualities or *virtues,* good or bad, propitious or unpropitious of each planet, but also of the variations of these virtues according to the zodiacal sign in which the planet appeared and the *house* in which the zodiacal sign found itself as it harbored the planet at the time in which the position of the ascendant was established.

It is easy to understand, without going further into the abstruse particulars of astrology, that since the constellations of the zodiac and the seven planets had well-known and fixed series of dwellings and movements, the mere determination of the planet emerging at the time of one's birth was sufficient to reveal the entire prospectus of the celestial disposition at that specific moment. Thus, on the strength of the meanings and the virtues of the various stars and the changing of their influences according to their reciprocal positions, days of the week, and a series of other accidents, it was possible to know the destiny, though very complicated and difficult, to which the newly-born would be subject during his whole life. Alongside the fortuitous unfolding of events foreseen by astrology, most of the horoscopes fell short of realization, although the astrologists were always ready to state "that the fault was not with the science, but with those who did not know how to make the best use of it." Thus, until the beginning of the eighteenth century, the art of drawing a horoscope was in great favor.

From the moral standpoint, the principles laid down in the treatment of *Divination* may also be applied to horoscopy and, more generally, to astrology. *Riz.*

HOSPITAL. *Hospital,* of Latin derivation (*hospitalia* was the name given by the Romans to rooms for guests), replaced, around the eighth century of our era, the Greek term *xenodechon* used to indicate hospices for pilgrims. Only later did *hospital* assume its present meaning as a place for the treatment of the sick.

Although hospitals existed even in pre-Christian times, they were rare. They were either established by some wise monarch or grew out of practical needs, as the military hospitals built by the Romans. They lacked, however, the distinctive character proper to Christian hospitals built for the purpose of carrying out the works of mercy taught by Jesus. In fact, in the early times of Christianity the poor and the sick were cared for and given hospitality by bishops, deacons, and wealthy Christians. Later, with the close of the era of persecutions, real and proper hospices which were distant forerunners of present-day hospitals finally were established, where needy pilgrims were sheltered and given proper care in sickness. St. Basil and St. John Chrysostom, shortly after the Edict of Constantine, built large hospices with special sections for the care of the lepers *(leprosaria)* and homes for the sick. The two great men can be truly called the forerunners of a glorious hospital tradition which rapidly spread from the Christian East to the West, particularly through the work of St. Jerome. Through the Middle Ages, hospices and houses for the sick were built everywhere, usually in the proximity of cathedrals, because, as pious institutions, they were favored, subsidized, and protected by bishops and major deaconries. Other hospices, similar to modern hospitals, arose near the monasteries. In those centuries numerous hospitaller Orders, both military and religious, dedicated to the care of the sick, were founded; among them the Order of Jerusalem, the Teutonics, the Crosiers, the Trinitarians, and the Order of the Holy Ghost. In 1198, Innocent III ordered the erection of a two-hundred-bed hospital with facilities for feeding daily a thousand poor, which he placed in the care of the Order of the Holy Ghost, which Guy of Montpellier established a short time before in France.

The new hospital, built on the former site of a Saxon hospice, was called Santo Spirito in Sassia. The religious nurses of the Order of the Holy Ghost spread all over the Christian world. In the first centuries of the modern era, particularly through the efforts of St. John of God, in Spain, and of St. Camillus de Lellis, in Italy, who founded the Orders of the "Fatebenefratelli" and the Ministers of the Sick respectively, hospital care was greatly improved. Also medical service made great progress, to the point that, beginning with the seventeenth century, the principal hospitals became schools of medicine and surgery, the forerunners of the university hospitals.

Politico-religious revolutions in Europe from the sixteenth century on brought changes in the traditional forms of charity through the introduction of State assistance; this practice became permanent with the French Revolution and the advent of industrialism. Hospitals were transformed from purely charitable institutions to public institutions, subsidized and controlled, according to circumstances, by local or State authorities. This post-revolutionary change contributed to the suppression of numerous small but useful hospitals built in Rome and other places, by flourishing craftsmen's guilds for the benefit of their members. These intelligent and pioneering cooperative achievements disappeared nearly everywhere at the beginning of the nineteenth century, perhaps as the result of a misunderstood economic liberalism.

The medieval homes for the sick were generally modest buildings built near episcopal residences or abbeys. During the Renaissance monumental hospital buildings arose with immense halls, artistically decorated, and with beds arranged in several rows. Despite the impressiveness of architectural grandeur, hygienic conditions were not quite satisfactory, for want of sufficient ventilation and heating facilities, which often caused contagion to spread.

In the eighteenth century, first in England, then in France and other countries, hospital construction underwent a profound change. Instead of concentrating the sick in a few large wards in monumental structures, they were decentralized in separate pavilions with rooms containing only a few beds. The pavillions were flanked by large and beautiful streets. The hospitals actually looked more like parks on the outskirts of urban communities than homes for the sick.

More recently, due to economic conditions as well as technical considerations, the pavilion-type hospitals (too costly and difficult to run) have been substituted, particularly in America, by a one-building vertical structure, with a great number of stories but with small wards of only a few patients, with private and semi-private rooms, and with large facilities for administrative offices.

EMERGENCY MEDICAL SERVICE. This service in some countries consists of a group of physicians and specialists, nurses and appropriate equipment ready to give emergency service to patients who come to such centers or when called to the home of the sick. Such service is generally connected with large hospitals and is continuous, day and night. The calls are made by physicians according to pre-established turns. The emergency service provides transportation capable of taking the doctor to the patient's home in the shortest possible time with all the necessary equipment (obstetrical aids, blood transfusions, etc.), anywhere and everywhere it may be needed. Through this permanent emergency medical service, which is developing rapidly in the larger cities, independent professional doctors are relieved of numerous and inopportune demands made upon them by unknown patients. More important, the citizens are able to obtain suitable professional help at any time of day or night.

Concerning the moral aspects of this subject, it must be noted that while it is gratifying that authoritative voices are being raised for a greater increase of the scientific facilities of all hospitals, for a more efficient administrative organization, for better trained medical staffs, and other useful services, it is of primary importance that the charitable aspect of hospitals be stressed, both with respect to more extensive free or half free services for a larger number of needy or less prosperous patients, and facilities that would assure a greater degree of *respect for the human person.*

The first is principally a social and financial problem, pressing and serious, whose importance goes beyond the benefits of the individual. With the notable increase in the cost of hospital care, hospitalization has become prohibitive for anyone who does not have the benefit of some form of medical insurance (*q.v.*). With regard to respect for the human person, all experts in hospital work agree that it is on the decline and that a *"real and proper reform* of hospital practices" is urgent (Grenet). This lack of respect is felt from the very moment that the patient enters the hospital. The personal medical history of the patient often is compiled either with haste or without the discretion required, particularly when, as it often occurs, it is done in a crowded ward. The patient is often regarded simply as a number, not as a person with his own spiritual needs, internal pains, and personal privacy. And while many doctors do see to it that a rational treatment be instituted and a good diagnosis made, practically nobody bothers about the patient's personal and family worries and responsibilities.

The indiscriminate mingling of patients in the wards without regard to age or sex is often morally dangerous. Guided by the criterion of space, one often finds a young boy next to a vicious old man, or a young girl between two women of easy morals. Toilet rooms are often common to all; recreation rooms are wanting; and no circulation libraries exist. This disturbs the patient who has a claim and a right to a certain amount of personal respect. Often, the chronically ill are made to feel that they are scarcely tolerated; any pretext is good enough to send them home. This same reason leads to a curtailment of their hospital care in cases of acute illnesses. Often, as the patient's condition takes a turn for the worse, the relatives are not notified in time, nor is a timely administration of the last rites always attended to. Sometimes, the administration of the sacraments has to be carried out under very unfavorable conditions.

Undoubtedly, this whole problem has an important financial aspect. Increasing the number and capacity of hospitals, bettering the financial remuneration of doctors, giving all hospital personnel better wages would permit better selection and better results and bring the moral condition of hospitals closer to what they really should be. A greater collaboration is needed between social workers (*q.v.*) and doctors and the families of the patients, which would make for better understanding of the needs of the patient and a quicker recovery. This, of course, is not so much a question of money as it is a matter of raising the moral level of the entire administration, for treating with greater respect the psychological side of the patient costs nothing, yet it often aids the treatment and care of the physical ills of the individual. Administrators, doctors and nurses must remember that hospital care is not only therapeutic, but also *"ethico-charitable"* (Alonzo) in the widest sense of the word, and that, as a great French philanthropist well stated, "in order to help and cure human beings one must understand them, and to understand them one must love them." Only in this manner can one hope that hospitals may become once more *beacons of love*, with definite advantages also for therapy and scientific progress. *Riz.*

HOSPITAL SHIP. See Medicine, Naval.

HOST. *Host* is the name given to the bread which constitutes, together with wine, the matter of the Eucharistic Sacrifice (*see* Holy Eucharist). Today it is used in the specific sense of bread for the Eucharist, but in former times the word could be applied to sacrifice and offering synonymously, whether the sacrifice was bloody or unbloody, liquid or solid. The host is a thin wafer of unleavened bread, made by mixing flour and cold water which is then baked at very high temperatures between two hot plates. Of two sizes generally, the large

host is used by the priest celebrating the sacrifice, or for use at special exercises of worship of the Holy Eucharist (*see* Benediction, Forty Hours); and the smaller host is used for the communion of the faithful. In ancient times hosts were prepared in monasteries amid ceremonies, chants, and special psalms.

Hosts made with flour and other substances added to it are not lawful matter for the sacrament of the Eucharist; if the mixture is proportionately large, it is invalid matter or, at least, doubtful matter. For lawfulness a host must be used that is of recent baking (15 days or one month at most), clean, entire, and made in the prescribed form, which is circular in the Latin Church (Can. 1272; 815, par. 1). Grave infractions of these norms constitute serious sin, particularly if they endanger the validity of the matter and, therefore, of the Eucharistic Sacrifice. *Cig.*

HOSTILITY. See War.

HOURS (CANONICAL). See Breviary, Choir.

HUMILITY. Humility is a moral virtue by which we acknowledge that of ourselves we are nothing and can do nothing without divine aid. St. Bernard defines humility as the virtue by which man, being fully conscious of what he really is, thinks lowly of himself (*De gradibus humilitatis et superbiae*, C I, n. 2; PL, 182, 965); St. Thomas defines it as the virtue by which man, considering his limitations, holds himself as lowly as he really is (*S. Theol.*, II–II, q. 161, a. 1 ad 1). Humility is essentially an act or disposition of the will, the basis of which is an exact evaluation of oneself, without illusions or deceptions, in comparison to God. Humility grows with man's consciousness of his total dependence on God, his extreme insignificance when compared with God, his inclination to sin, and his many faults. It follows, therefore, that humility is not a debasement of man's dignity or a degradation of his qualities or aptitudes, but the acknowledgment of the true facts about himself. Humility is perfectly compatible with the use of the talents received from God and with magnanimity that leads a person to accomplish great things with God's help. Humility is also compatible with a just vindication of honor and esteem proper to the person as such, or because of an office he holds, as shown by the divine Redeemer Himself (John 18:22 ff.) and by St. Paul (Acts 16:36 ff.).

Humility inspires complete and plain truthfulness in man's relations with God. An humble man is full of reverence toward God; he submits, even in difficult things, to God's will and that of his superiors; he does not expect more than that which God gave him; when he has done his best, he will not think he has done extraordinary things from which to draw reasons for pride or self-praise, but recognizes he has simply done his duty in putting to use the graces and talents received from God.

From humility stems also a correct behavior toward one's neighbor. A humble person refrains from singling out or speaking of other persons' faults; he does not extoll himself above others, whose many qualities often are not seen and whose intentions are hidden to him as is the measure of divine grace received from God. It is quite proper for one to think that those who appear to be less good than he might in fact be better than he, if they had received as many graces from God as he did. In this light, saintly souls sincerely hold themselves the least among men. He who is humble does not try to bend others to accept his own views and will; he rejoices over the virtues and accomplishments of his neighbor; he is condescending toward all. Another effect of humility is a great modesty in one's demeanor. He who is truly humble does not seek to display his own talents and accomplishments to win praise, nor does he seek to be esteemed for virtues or talents he does not possess. He recognizes his own faults and limitations and is satisfied with what is less comfortable and pleasant; he avoids singularity, speaks with dignity and gravity, is mod-

est in his general demeanor and in all his actions. Since humility is none other than truth, it is incumbent upon all.

Sins against humility. One may sin against humility by excess or by defect. By excess one sins through pride (*q.v.*); by defect through a denial of the good qualities which one possesses, through false declarations of wrongdoing, or through debasing occupations that are damaging to talents or office. Inordinate self-debasement is, in itself, a venial sin, but it becomes a mortal sin if it causes grave damage which should be avoided by reasons of charity or justice.

Humility removes the greatest obstacle to eternal salvation in man: pride; for this reason humility is called the foundation of the spiritual life. The means by which humility may be acquired and developed are: self-examination in the light of God; meditation on the examples of the Divine Savior; immediate and swift repression of any, even involuntary, feelings of pride. *Man.*

HUNTING. Objectively, hunting is a natural human right, recognized and regulated by positive law, consisting of the acquisition of ownership over naturally free animals by appropriation. Subjectively, it is the right to kill, capture, or appropriate naturally free animals, i.e., wild beasts or beasts who have regained their former liberty, insofar as they are regarded as belonging to no one (*res nullius*). The right to hunt animals is based on the natural principles acknowledged and sanctioned by civil legislation; thereby appropriation of things belonging to no one constitutes a legitimate title of ownership. In dealing with the appropriation of animals, Roman legal exactness distinguished *aucupium* or *aucupatio* (fowling or hunting of birds and fowls of the air) from *venatio* (hunting of land animals), as well as from *piscatio* (fishing). In the moral field this distinction is a pure formality, since the normative principles are the same for all three categories. Nevertheless, modern civil legislation, generally, admits separate regulations for hunting and fishing.

MORAL EVALUATION. Three factors enter into the moral evaluation of the hunting sport: (a) the natural law, as the fundamental source of the inherent right to hunt; (b) positive civil legislation; (c) common estimation of mankind concerning the binding force of such civil legislation.

PRINCIPLES OF NATURAL LAW. The natural principles regulate the acquisition of ownership over animals and fundamentally determine the object of hunting. These principles, enunciated and interpreted by ancient Roman jurists and subsequently adopted by moralists, are today universally accepted as the basis of all hunting regulations. Since such principles regulate relations of strict justice, their violation generally gives rise, in the sphere of conscience, to the obligation of making restitution and reparation of damage.

Insofar as hunting is concerned, it is customary to divide animals into wild *(fera)*, tame *(mansuefacta)*, and domestic *(mansueta)*. (a) Wild animals are those which naturally avoid human company and have never lost their natural freedom (e.g., hare, deer, fish). (b) Tame animals are those which normally avoid man's company but are brought under his control by his skill and industry (e.g., swarms of bees, pigeons in a dove-cot, fish in a pond, rabbits). (c) Domestic animals are those which are naturally accustomed to the society of men (e.g., sheep, horses, dogs, chickens). Tamed or reclaimed animals which have reverted to their natural habitat *(efferata)* are in the same category as wild animals.

Only animals enjoying natural freedom, viz., wild animals and those which have recovered their former liberty, constitute the object of appropriation through hunting. As *res nullius*, such animals belong to their first occupant. However, if said animals are captured or held in custody by another occupant, they cease to be the object of appropriation through hunting.

Tame animals, unless they have regained their former liberty, belong to their respective owners. Such animals are said to recover their primitive freedom when they escape from their place of custody, and no longer return to their customary habitat provided by the owner, or when it becomes morally impossible for the owner to exercise complete control over them or when he has given up pursuit. The particular laws of different countries and regions provide more specific determinations in this regard.

Domestic animals, however far they may stray, can never be appropriated, but must always be restored to their original owners. Keeping such animals without making any attempt to locate their owners is undue appropriation. The principles of natural law also provide the key to the solution of the ancient and classic question regarding acquisition of ownership over an animal wounded by one hunter and seized by another. Of the noted solutions offered by Roman jurists (cf. Gaius, *Rerum cottid.*, 1. 2; D. 41, 1, 5, par. 1), moralists have unanimously adopted the one attributed to Trebatius Testa as more adequately corresponding to the criteria of justice: the hunter who wounds an animal acquires ownership over it as long as he pursues it; if another person seizes such an animal, he violates justice; if the hunter ceases to pursue his wounded game, it reverts to the category of *res nullius* and, hence, belongs to the first occupant.

CIVIL LAWS REGARDING HUNTING. The right to hunt and fish is controlled by civil laws in almost every country, which vary somewhat in different regions, because of diverse conditions. But generally a permit or license is required and a small tax imposed; moreover, there are restrictions regarding the time, place, and kind of animals that may be hunted or fished.

There is considerable disagreement among moralists concerning the nature of hunting and fishing laws, particularly concerning the extent to which they are binding in conscience and the consequent morality resulting from transgression of such laws. Old moralists commonly held that hunting and fishing laws are mere penal laws, binding in conscience only to the extent that the violator pay the penalty imposed for his transgression. Today there is a tendency among moral theologians to reconsider this position along with the entire theory concerning merely penal laws, on the ground that there is no solid reason justifying departure from the unchangeable principle whereby every just law binds in conscience fully, i.e., both as to the act of the law and the penalty affixed thereto. Despite this modern tendency, the older theory which holds hunting and fishing laws to be merely penal laws may be said to be still prevalent (Vermeersch, Genicot, Merkelbach, Iorio, etc.), and on the basis of probabilistic principles, they may be safely adopted and followed in practice, outside of certain exceptions. The defenders of this theory hold that the mind of the legislator, i.e., maintenance or promotion of the common good, is sufficiently achieved through the threat of punishment attached to the violation of the law; furthermore, the concept of mere penalty (i.e., of merely penal laws), even if objectively unfounded, is firmly rooted in the general estimation and in approved customs.

Quite obviously, the above interpretation cannot apply to game laws en bloc. In general, the following exceptions are to be made: (a) Laws expressly designed to safeguard the reproduction and preservation of the species are certainly and fully binding in conscience (Noldin, Aertyns-Damen, Prummer); such are the laws which forbid hunting out of season, in reserved areas, the killing of rare species, etc. It is obvious that in such cases the mere threat of punishment is insufficient to achieve the end intended by the legislator; moreover, men are generally convinced that such laws are really binding in conscience and not merely penal. (b) The same is to be said concerning laws designed to prevent damage to private property and cultivated land. (c) The same applies to laws established for the protection of human life, such as the laws which forbid hunting in public gardens or parks, firing at game over the highway, etc. (d) Also binding in conscience are laws designed to safeguard the exclusive right legitimately acquired over certain landed property, such as the laws which forbid trespassing or hunting

on posted grounds. However, poaching on such land does not always involve the violation of strict (commutative) justice with the consequent obligation of restitution or reparation of damage. In practice, a distinction must be made. If the concession on restricted or posted property is a merely personal or group privilege, obtained gratuitously or at a slight fee, then poaching on such land violates legal justice only, and rarely will it be of itself a grave violation. The present basis is more or less comparable to that of a monopoly, where, as is well known, third persons dealing or selling against a monopolist do not violate commutative justice (*see* Monopoly). If, on the other hand, the concession on reserved grounds is acquired by onerous title (rental, lease, or hire), poaching on such grounds constitutes a violation of commutative justice. But, in all cases, the obligation to restitution is determined, not by the value or number of animals captured, but by the extent of damage caused to the landowner for the diminished possibility of realizing a just gain from his investment.

In this connection, it is to be noted that, according to natural law, mere ownership of the land does not give an automatic right over animals straying or migrating into the confines of the property, but merely the right to exclude others from hunting or trespassing therein. Hence, game shot down or captured on another's land, which is not reserved or enclosed, belongs by right to the hunter; but the owner of the land is entitled to indemnification for damages caused to his property. If the land is so enclosed that the animals confined therein cannot possibly stray and can be captured at will by the owner himself, there is no doubt that outsiders are bound in strict justice to refrain from hunting or shooting such animals. Such animals are to be considered as domestic animals, and the hunter who clandestinely captures them is guilty of theft and bound to make restitution. This is all the more so, if the enclosure is a real game preserve.

In order to give a prudent judgment

on the morality of hunting, special consideration must be given to the general opinion concerning illegal types of hunting which are viewed with varying degrees of severity in different places. This factor is to be taken into account especially by the confessor. *Zac.*

HYGIENE. Hygiene (Greek *hygieinos*—healthful) is the branch of medicine that studies means for the prevention of illnesses. It dates back to early human civilization, but as an organic science of solid research it goes back to the second half of the last century, the period of the great discoveries on the nature of contagious diseases. To achieve its proper objectives, hygiene cannot be limited to the study of man, as such, but must extend to all external environmental circumstances having influence on man, such as water, air, soil, food, dry-goods, clothing, housing, schools, hospitals, bacteriology and protozoology, prevention and prophylaxis of epidemics, working conditions, mental hygiene, sanitary officials and departments. The development and application of the principles of hygiene are responsible for an evident decrease in the rate of illnesses and death. Suffice to think of the great number of lives saved by the use of vaccination, polio vaccine, and land reclamation.

Hygiene is practiced mainly by: (a) direct observation of facts; (b) detailed statistical study of findings from observation of phenomena of interest to medical science; (c) research. These methods are an effort to acquire complete knowledge of pathogenous causes and their behavior, with a view to establishing rational procedures in the fight against diseases. The effectiveness of these procedures is checked, both with respect to immediate effects on individuals and communities, and to long range studies conducted on large masses of people.

HYGIENE AND THE MORAL LAW. Clearly, not all the principles of hygiene have equal importance, nor, in general, are the principles of hygiene, as such, binding in conscience. In other words, the violation of a principle of hygiene does not always constitute a sin, at times

not even venial. On the other hand, the matter is not entirely a morally indifferent question. In the first place, some moral laws given by God Himself are at the same time principles of hygiene. Who is not aware that transgression of certain moral laws is not only harmful to an individual's health (venereal disease), but also to the welfare of communities and nations (i.e., alcoholism with its destructive consequences). Hence, the Holy Ghost warns that "he that sinneth in the sight of his Maker, shall fall into the hands of the physician" (Eccles. 38:15).

On the other hand, we may be bound in conscience to observe certain hygienic principles in no way related to the moral law. Compulsory hygienic norms, prescribed by the public authority for the protection of public health against a well-known danger, such as the treatment of patients suffering from a contagious disease, and the curbing and prevention of serious epidemics, may not be neglected without serious danger to our own health or our neighbor's. Man's duty to preserve his health, as a precious gift of God, and as a necessary means for effective fulfillment of other duties, makes it unlawful to expose one's health to positive harm or to serious danger, unless sufficiently important reasons justify such a line of conduct. The obligation is greater and the transgression less justifiable whenever a more important principle of hygiene is involved, because in such instances the harm risked is greater or the danger is more immediate.

HYGIENE AND SOCIAL LEGISLATION. It cannot be denied that the living conditions of great masses of mankind still leave much to be desired from the standpoint of hygiene. More diligent observance of the principles of hygiene would eliminate many causes of premature deaths, of long and painful illnesses, of serious distress to the life of many families. But it would be a mistake to think that the fault lies solely or mainly with the lower classes. It is true that there is often a lack of cooperation, indifference, willful neglect, irresponsibility; but there is also a lack of education. Great masses of people today still live under economic and social conditions that make the observance of many hygienic principles absolutely impossible, or so difficult that it cannot be demanded or expected either of individuals or families. The most pressing hygienic need of modern times is the creation of general economic or social conditions favorable to hygiene. Were governments to combat more seriously and effectively public immorality, pauperism, and social injustice, as the Church and the Supreme Pontiffs have constantly insisted, the people would heed more effectively not only the prescriptions but also the counsels of hygiene. *Ben.*

HYGIENE (Mental). Mental hygiene, a branch of general hygiene, is directed to the prevention and prophylaxis of mental diseases, to which psychiatrists have devoted special interest. Mental hygiene studies, the hereditary predispositions (*see* Heredity) of an individual, the healthy development of family life, the practice of healthy forms of sport and physical exercise, hygienic facilities for mentally deficient children, testing programs for diagnosis and treatment of mentally disturbed individuals, the education and home care of the mentally ill or those discharged from mental hospitals.

In this important work, social workers, nurses, home visiting, psychiatric social workers, and physical and mental therapists play most significant roles in the formation of a link between the home and the place of treatment, with particular emphasis upon the family of the mentally ill person. Particularly gifted with patience, kindness, tact, and a thorough knowledge of their work and environment in discharging such a difficult and meritorious mission, these workers must study the environment in which the patients live and the family conditions from which they have come. The economic, social, and hygienic conditions are most influential in a healthy development of the family.

As this brief survey shows, the field of mental hygiene is extremely broad, and barely at its primary stages of development. The physical and moral betterment of humanity, particularly the poorer and more backward, rests greatly on a satisfactory solution of the problems connected with mental hygiene. For the ethical aspect, *see* Hygiene. *Rizzo.*

HYMEN. *See* Gynecology.

HYPERADRENALISM. *See* Adrenal, Supradrenal Glands.

HYPERDULIA. *See* Cult.

HYPERESTHESIA. *See* Perversion, sexual.

HYPERGENITALISM. *See* Gonads.

HYPERPITUITARISM. *See* Hypophysis.

HYPERSOMNIA. *See* Sleep.

HYPERTHYMIA. *See* Dysthymia.

HYPERTHYROIDISM. *See* Thyroid.

HYPERTONICITY. *See* Cerebral Functions.

HYPNOTICS. *See* Anesthetics.

HYPNOTISM. The word *hypnotism* (Greek, *hypnotikos*, put to sleep), indicates the phenomenon of artificially induced sleep that is promoted by a variety of methods which stir up in the victim a suggestibility to action or thought. This phenomenon is characterized by the domination of the subject to ideas or suggestions of the hypnotist to the point of carrying out such suggestions under the state of hypnosis or later.

Hypnotic phenomena were known in ancient times, but no real study was made of them until a little over a century ago, when a Scotch doctor, J. Braid, collected in his *Neurypnology* (1843) and other publications the results of a conscientious scientific investigation of Mesmer's experiments and those of his followers (which were not free of charlatanry) on so-called *animal magnetism* (*see* Metapsychology). In his study Braid concluded that those experiments were manifestations of a subjective nature, induced by the use on the part of the operator of means capable of tiring the attention of the subject. By the simple method of having his patients concentrate on a luminous object, Dr. Braid caused in them an hypnotic sleep during which he cured various psychoneurotic conditions (nervous-tick, spasms, convulsions, etc.), with the same results obtained fifty years before by Mesmer through his theatrical methods.

Later, the famous neuropathologist, J. M. Charcot, distinguished two principal types of hypnotism: *great* hypnotism induced only and with the greatest ease in hysterical subjects (in whom it can also be spontaneous); *small* hypnotism induced in normal subjects by the power of suggestion. He held that the great hypnotism, which he studied with particular interest, had three progressive stages: *lethargy, trance, somnambulism* (*q.v.*). These views of the "Paris School" were criticized by H. Bernheim and other scholars of the "School of Nancy"; this school rejected Charcot's distinction and thesis that real hypnotism was a neuropathological phenomenon; they expressed the opinion, instead, that it was a manifestation of a suggestive nature, sometimes involuntary, which could be produced in nearly all individuals.

As the result of further research by modern scholars, these contrasting views have been largely reconciled. The majority, today, believes that hypnotism is produced by suggestion (*q.v.*) and is a particular psychological condition, fundamentally of a pathological and psychoneurotic nature, favorable to suggestion; hence, suggestion and hypnosis appear to be two poles of a single circuit, influencing one another, though in a different degree.

Concerning the reciprocal psychological relation between the hypnotist and the hypnotic-hypnotized, the key to the whole problem, Freud suggested an original interpretation based on the hypothesis that during the hypnosis the subject replaces his super Ego with the hypnotist himself, who generally awakens in him the image of his father; that the hypno-

tist, exalting this image in the subject's psyche (an image, which is at the same time model, guide, and judge of his behavior) determines at the same time the weakening or disappearance of that other image of which the super Ego is composed and concerns his sense of reality, critique. From this we have the principal characteristics of induced hypnosis: unconsciousness of the process, submission and emotional attachment of the subject to the hypnotist, a critical realization of the ideas suggested to him.

This purely psychological explanation overlooks the physiological mechanism, still unknown, of induced hypnosis. Moreover, it can hardly be applied to phenomena connected with hypnosis or similar to them, such as the trance of the medium and the manifestations which follow this condition. For this reason some believe that hypnosis is part of the phenomenology of metapsychology (*q.v.*).

HYPNOTISM IN THERAPY. The use of hypnotism in therapy is allowed "on condition," Scremin writes, "that the hypnotist knows enough about clinical physiology to avoid any dangerous mistakes." We believe that this sentence is to be interpreted as follows: before deciding to turn to hypnosis, the doctor must study carefully, on the basis of the patient's psychological condition and illness, whether hypnotic therapy will restore his health or leave him, instead, in a worse condition. While induced hypnosis can relieve and even check (usually only temporarily) many functional disturbances in psychoneurotic individuals or individuals easily subject to suggestion, it has the tendency to increase the pre-existing neurotic disposition and favors the rise of other pathological manifestations (*see* Psychotherapy, Suggestion). It must also be remembered that organic illnesses do not subside, not even temporarily, as a result of hypnotic treatments. For these reasons, we oppose the use of induced hypnosis in therapy.

Another valid reason against the use of therapeutic hypnosis is the curative effectiveness of other methods, such as *narcoanalysis, suggestion in state of wakefulness*, and *persuasion*, which have the advantage, when used with proper diligence, of being practically harmless.

Narcoanalysis consists in inducing narcosis by intravenous injection of pentothal or other barbiturates, in order that the subject might be questioned and his spontaneous utterances be analyzed during the pre-narcosis phase and the phase that follows it. This is done to free him of his morbid psychological complexes to which his psychoneurosis is anchored. As the result of this very modern method, extensively used in Anglo-American hospital units for a quick recovery of the psychoneurotics of the war, it was found that barbiturates ease anxieties, modify the normal interneuronic, cerebral hierarchies, remove inhibitions and all psychological barriers, whether deliberate or involuntary. All these factors favor a better diagnostic evaluation of the psyche of the patient by the doctor. Furthermore, promoting, as it does, the understanding and exact evaluation by the subject himself of the psychological injury, which had given rise to his psychoneurotic condition, it often removes from him, within a short time, his whole burdensome morbid condition.

In conclusion, the narcoanalysis method adds a pharmacological treatment to the psychotherapeutic action, which thus becomes more effective and helps to avoid at the same time certain difficulties proper to classic hypnosis, as embarrassing *transports* of the patient toward the doctor. Narcoanalysis has the advantage over Freud's psychoanalysis of being easier to use and broader in scope, of requiring one or a few applications, and of avoiding those too personal and searching sexual inquiries which often upset the patient and, generally, create "an erotic type atmosphere between the doctor and the patient" (Jaschke) which is morally objectionable. Concerning *suggestion while in a state of wakefulness* and *persuasion, see* Psychotherapy.

MEDICO-LEGAL AND MORAL CONSIDERATIONS. From a medico-legal standpoint, hypnotism lends itself to undoubtedly interesting moral observations. To allow oneself to be hypnotized, even if only out of curiosity or play, is damaging to one's health, because it favors, as it was pointed out before, the appearance of new psychoneurotic disturbances, or aggravates those already existing. Hypnotism is, therefore, not allowed except, we repeat, for a specific therapeutic reason; hence, all public hypnotic exhibitions should be forbidden.

It is even more gravely unlawful if one were to use hypnotism to snatch secrets from a person or perform criminal actions on him. On the first point, it is not lawful to subject persons under arrest or on trial to hypnosis in order to learn the truth, aside from the fact that such procedure offers no sure guarantee of success because of the capacity of resistance by the hypnotized individual.

The possibility that an unscrupulous hypnotist may use hypnotism to commit criminal deeds or sexual abuse upon or through the actions of his passive subject, should emphasize dangerous aspects of hypnotism. For the hypnotist there is danger, for in some cases, after giving hypnotic treatment, they have been unjustly accused by clients. To avoid improper or unpleasant experiences, the hypnotist should not engage in such therapeutic experiments without witnesses. Homicides or other serious crimes are said to have been committed under the influence of hypnotic suggestion; this, of course, is strongly contradicted by the larger number of psychiatrists.

Since the end of the last war, however, psychologists have indicated the possibility of the use of hypnotism in war. They maintain that individuals could be hypnotized, without their knowledge or consent, and be made to commit all kinds of actions of treason, espionage, or sabotage. Possible abuses should counsel the greatest caution with regard to any use of hypnotism. *Riz.*

HYPOABULIA. *See* Will, pathology of.

HYPOADRENALISM. *See* Adrenal, Suprarenal Glands.

HYPOCHONDRIA (HYPOCHON-DRIASIS). Hypochondria is a morbid anxiety about one's own health, conjuring up imaginary ailments, particularly internal (heart, lung, liver, intestines, etc.). This anxiety leads the individual to the mistaken conviction that he is suffering from a serious somatic disease, while actually his disturbance is of a psychogenic nature, purely functional or, at the most, caused by some trite cenesthopathia (*see* Cenesthesia). This mistaken conviction becomes increasingly stronger because of a continuous and vexing self-analysis. Every vegetative function is meticulously analyzed; every internal sensation is judged an unquestionable symptom of serious illness; the slightest indisposition is magnified to become unbearable. At this point *hypochondriacal delirium* sets in and becomes organized. This delirium is found in the various neuroses (*q.v.*), psychoses (*q.v.*), neurasthenia (*q.v.*), traumatic neurosis, psychasthenia (*q.v.*), and hysteria (*q.v.*). In all these forms hypochondriacal ideas are not far removed from the probable thing; but in melancholia (*q.v.*), dementia (senile, schizophrenic, paralytic, etc.), they go far afield and become grotesque; thus, the heart has become a cork, the intestines have disappeared, the brain has been ejected with the excrement, and similar absurdities. The hypochondriac is impervious to reasoning that might show how unfounded his convictions are. As a matter of fact, he uses medical articles and advertisements in the daily papers, and even his doctor's solicitude and recommendations to justify and confirm his convictions.

HYPOCHONDRIASIS OF PERSECUTION (*Paranoia*). In certain cases cenestopathic sensations produce in the patient the firm conviction that others are trying maliciously to torment or kill him by mysterious and powerful physical means. In such cases, real problems to doctors and magistrates, the patient torments the judges with repetitious denunciations and accusations and may go as far as killing the person whom he believes to be the cause of his suffering. Sometimes the person afflicted with hypochondriasis of persecution becomes convinced that the primary cause of his trouble is a surgical operation he underwent perhaps many years before: it is not rare for such a patient to think of murdering the surgeon in revenge.

It is not easy to distinguish hypochondriasis of persecution from the chronic hallucinatory delirium of physical persecution which accompanies paraphrenia (*q.v.*). Age (usually presenile), a uniform and persistent content of hallucinations, and the normality of the rest of his psychological make-up point to hypochondriasis of persecution, while the presence of some dissociative symptoms and deliriums of greatness generally characterize paraphrenic forms.

MORAL OBSERVATIONS. Moral responsibility and imputability of an individual afflicted by hypochondriasis is strictly in relation to the gravity of his hypochondriasis, particularly the psychosis of which hypochondriasis is a symptom. This must be established by the psychiatrist in each individual case. *Riz.*

HYPOCRISY. Strictly speaking, hypocrisy is simulation of a good moral quality which one does not possess, or the act by which one feigns to be or feel what he is not or does not feel in reality.

Hypocrisy is a sin because it is deception. Generally a venial sin, it can become a mortal sin by reason of the scorn of virtue, the intention, or the means used. Our Lord used harsh words in condemning hypocrisy (Matt. 23:27). Certain morbid forms of hypocrisy spur the patient to simulate to an unbelievable degree. In these cases, the moral responsibility of the individual is either greatly reduced or totally absent (*see* Hysteria, Simulation). *Man.*

HYPOESTHESIA. See Cerebral Functions.

HYPOGENITALISM. See Gonads.

HYPOMANIA. See Mania.

HYPOPHYSIS (PITUITARY GLAND). The word hypophysis (Greek, *hypo*, under; *physis*, nature) was used by Soemmering at the beginning of the nineteenth century to define a small organ, the size of a pea and weighing about half a gram, leaning towards the center of the cerebral base, enclosed and protected by a wedge-shaped bone at the base of the skull. Because of its position, it was at one time mistakenly believed that it secreted the nasal mucus (or pituita); this caused the gland to be called pituitary gland or pituitary body, particularly by French and American medical schools. Despite its small size, the pituitary gland is one of the most important of all internal secretion glands (*see* Endocrinology), because it affects by a generally stimulating action nearly all other endocrine glands and the vegetative nervous system: it is, therefore, a fundamental gland whose function of carrying on the normal biological activity of the organism cannot be substituted.

STRUCTURE AND FUNCTIONS. The diencephalo-hypophyseal theory explains the hypophysis (pituitary gland) as two parts or lobes: an anterior (epithelial or *glandular*) lobe constituting the larger portion of the organ; a posterior or *nervous* part which is the continuation of the diencephalon (vegetative brain), to which it is connected by a very small peduncle. Between the two lobes there is an *intermediate* thin layer which in human beings is only partially developed. The cells of the anterior lobe are subdivided, according to certain histological properties: *chromophobic, chromophilic, bascophilic,* and *acidophilic.* The cellular secretion of the pituitary gland enters for the most part into the bloodstream *(hemocrinia)*; the remainders flow along the peduncle into the nearby nucleii of the diencephalon or terminate in the adjacent third ventricle (*neurocrinia*). It seems that some of the nerve cells of the diencephalon produce granules of secretion with hormonic properties similar to those of the pituitary gland (*neurocrinia*).

The close relationships between the pituitary gland and the adjacent diencephalon led to observations by numerous scientists that alterations limited both to the pituitary gland and the hypothalamus (the portion of the diencephalon located under the optic thalamus near the pituitary gland) can be responsible for the same disturbances. As a result, Aschner formulated the so-called diencephalo-hypophyseal theory, widely accepted by scholars today, according to which both the pituitary and the hypothalamus participate in the neurovegetative control of the organism, and, though they consist of elements morphologically diverse, they constitute a special functional unit.

Several hormones (*q.v.*) have been extracted from the pituitary gland. Their exact number is not known because some are incompletely identified and others differ more probably by reason of the effects caused by the method used in extracting them or by the diversity of subjects on whom they have been tried. According to most authors, of approximately thirty hypophyseal hormones, the following have been clearly identified: (1) *hormone of growth*, secreted by the acidophilic cells; (2) *prolan A*, secreted by the basophilic cells, the gonadotropic hormone controlling spermatic and follicular activity; (3) *prolan B*, another gonadotropic hormone, exercising stimulating action on the interstitial tissue of the testicle and the lutein; (4) *thyrotropic hormone*, secreted by the basophilic cells, stimulating the activity of the thyroid gland; (5) *parathyrotropic hormone*, also secreted by the basophilic cells, stimulating the parathyroid glands; (6) *diabetogenic anti-insulin hormone*, inhibiting the action of insulin; (7) *corticotropic hormone*, secreted by the basophilic cells, stimulating the superadrenal cortex; (8) *prolactin*, stimulating the lactic secretion; (9–11) *hormones stimulating the metabolism*, respectively, of sugar, fats, and proteins; (12) *intermedin*, causing the expansion of cutaneous pigmentations; (13) *vasopressin*, increasing the efficiency of capillary blood-vessels; (14) *oxytocin*, acting on uterine muscles; (15) *anti-diuretic* hormone, controlling diuresis. The first eleven of the above mentioned hormones are secretions of the anterior lobe of the pituitary gland, the twelfth of the intermediate layer, and the remaining three of the posterior lobe. The secretion of these various hormones influences the activity of the adjacent hypothalamic nervous centers, which, in turn, exercise their influence on the many-sided, secreting activity of the adjacent hypothalamic nervous centers. These in turn exercise their influence on the many-sided secreting activity of the pituitary gland. This phenomenal cycle proves the diencephalo-hypophyseal theory.

PATHOLOGICAL AND CLINICAL NOTES. From the preceding notions one cannot refer exclusively to hypothalamic or hypophyseal lesion as causes of the numerous and serious infirmities which arise as the result of tumors or other pathogenic conditions affecting the diencephalo-hypophyseal region. On the other hand, the pituitary gland and the hypothalamic centers are so close to each other that any morbid process affecting one will necessarily have repercussions also on the other. Nevertheless, the majority of scholars hold, on the basis of biological observation which it is irrelevant to report here, that syndromes of the hypophyseal region, such as, agromegaly, pituitary gigantism, certain forms of dwarfism and infantilism and Cushing's disease (to mention a few) are caused prevalently by disorders of the pituitary gland; while adipose-genital dystrophy, Simmonds' disease, lipodystrophies, diabetes insipidus, involve the pituitary gland and, perhaps even more, the hypothalamus as the cause of such disturbances. This is not the place for a complete description of the various diseases. A brief summary should sufficiently illustrate the importance of these diseases from the standpoint of their ethical effects.

A morbid process, generally a tumor, stimulates excessively the acidophilic cells of the pre-hypophysis and makes them hyperplastic: a condition termed anterior *hyperpituitarism*, depending on when the disease appears, before or after the period of growth, *hypophyseal gigantism* or *acromegaly* occurs. This consists in a characteristic enlargement of the bones of the face, feet, and hands. As the skeleton becomes longer and broader, the skin becomes thicker, the viscera larger, and often, a gradual insufficiency of the gonads (*q.v.*) ensues.

The opposite happens when anterior *hypopituitarism* is caused by a functional disturbance of the acidophilous cells, which may give rise to *hypophyseal dwarfism* (small individuals, with small heads, hands and feet, but eurhythmical and well-proportioned) or *hypophyseal infantilism*, in which an insufficiency of the hormones of growth is accompanied by an insufficiency of gonadotropic hormones.

If hyperpituitarism affects the basophilic cells of the pre-hypophysis, *Cushing's disease* develops, which is accompanied by alterations of the suprarenal cortex (*see* Suprarenals) and is characterized by obesity, hypertrichosis, high blood pressure, hyperglycemia, an increase in the number of red corpuscles, the appearance of pseudo-scar lines on the trunk and at the base of the limbs; at the same time, a neuro-muscular asthenia and sexual insufficiency develop.

Froelich's disease, developing usually in infancy, is characterized by progressive obesity with arrest of growth and sexual development (adipose-genital dystrophy): the effect of an involvement in the pituitary gland and adjacent hypothalamus centers which control trophism and the genetic function. It may be produced by tumors or other injuries in the hypophyseal region. Sometimes, in so-called *belated Froelich's disease*, these pathogenic factors develop in adults; in this case, besides obesity and other metabolic disorders, more or less important manifestations of sexual regression appear. An opposite clinical picture is presented by the *hypophyseal cachexia of* Simmonds, a neuro-endocrine disease of the hypophyseal region, in which, instead of obesity, the patient grows progressively thinner.

Diabetes insipidus, a chronic disease, characterized by excessive elimination of urine (from three to twenty or more quarts a day) independent of the amount of liquid intake, is caused by a change, because of tumor or other conditions in the diencephalo-hypophyseal mechanism that controls the metabolism of water. It may be accompanied by other metabolic and growth disorders caused by the complex functional importance of the pituitary region. The importance of disturbances, related to sleep, due to a great extent to diencephalo-hypophyseal disfunction, are treated in two separate articles under *Narcolepsy* and *Sleep*.

MORAL NOTES. For many reasons a summary knowledge of the functions and disorders of the pituitary gland and its adjacent diencephalic region is extremely important to moral theologians, lawyers, judges, and teachers in general. The diencephalo-hypophyseal region is the coordinating and directing center of nearly all the functions of growth in the organism, whose efficient functioning is a fundamental requirement of the state of internal well-being that plays such an important part in conserving our psychosomatic alertness, good humor, and spiritual serenity; also, disorders in these areas are usually accompanied or followed by very grave disturbances of the genital organs and their functions.

With a lazy, apathetic, depressed, asthenic person, we must always suspect the possibility of an initial hypophyseal infirmity and consult an experienced doctor who, after a clinical examination of the patient, X-rays, and necessary biochemical tests, can either rule out or, as more frequently will be the case, confirm its presence and thus suggest a timely therapeutic treatment. In the presence of sexual disturbances, one must at once think of a diencephalo-hypophyseal disorder and proceed to check the suspicion.

Regarding persons afflicted with the above-mentioned morphological deformities, since it is not possible to establish *a priori* a degree of imputability, one should be prone to judge kindly psychological disturbances that affect the humor, the will, and the psychological attitude of the patient because of the relations between the diencephalo-hypophyseal region and the emotive-instinctive functions (*see also* Cerebral Functions).
Riz.

HYPOPITUITARISM. *See* Hypophysis.

HYPOTHALAMUS. *See* Hypophysis.

HYPOTHYROIDISM. *See* Thyroid.

HYPOTONIA. *See* Cerebral Functions.

HYSTERECTOMY. *See* Abortion.

HYSTERIA. *Hysteria* is a diagnostic term referring to a wide array of symptoms thought to stem from the psyche. According to some experts, hysteria is a psychoneurosis, common to all ages, races, sexes, intellectual and social levels, though it is found more frequently in young women. Hysteria, seemingly caused by disorders in the diencephalic centers controlling the instinctive-emotive system, offers a great diversity of symptoms which enable it to simulate any organic disorder. By others, hysteria is considered a pathogenic disorder.

Persons subject to hysteria are generally of undeveloped personalities, characterized by instinctive, hyper-emotive and changeable moods; they tend to a lack of self-control over inhibitions, to impulsive actions, and voluble dispositions; they are easily inclined to likes and dislikes, so that they become quickly depressed or excited, seem unstable in their opinions and ideas and, at times, contradictory in behavior patterns. A proneness to suggestibility renders them fit subjects to the influence of others and to hypnotic trances, particularly when their condition is based on a phrenasthenic condition. Mental automatism, psychological dissociation, and hypochondriacal ideas as well as egocentricity lead them to an excessive concentration upon themselves with further tendencies to an over-exaggeration of their qualities, faults, and ills. Furthermore, they may resort to any diverse form of lies, simulations, and false attempts at suicide as devices to draw attention to themselves. They seek always to make an impression, love theatrical display and exhibitionism and, therefore, seem unspontaneous, false, dissatisfied, envious, and malevolent.

In hysteria, temperament controls character; the instinctive-emotive-affective life rules intellectual life; a dream fantasy supplants logic and practical common sense. Often these persons possess noble, romantic, or mystical aspirations.

Gifted with high sentiment, intelligence, and education, these types develop at times exceptional artistic or social ability, probably because of the emotional exuberance characteristic of their hysterical natures. Others, however, may turn to a growing tendency to criminal or immoral activity.

In the hysterical nature, periodic psychopathic crises arise, generally manifested by confusion which is at times accompanied by hallucinations, the particular reactions linked to mental or emotional representations. Finally, amnesia may occur. Rarely do such individuals reach the state of split-personality or alternating consciousness, consisting of two alternating states of awareness and personality, each with its own ideo-affective content and behavior. A suspension of memory breaks any associative connections between the two states, which emphasizes contrasts in the attitude and behavior of the patient. These interesting manifestations, which constitute basically the periodic exaggeration of tendencies to dissociation and abnormal psychological automatism characteristic of hysterical persons, are quite different from those occurring, for example, in schizophrenics, who tend to form a split personality with homogeneous coherent nuclei and create, as it were, minor personalities, each free from intrinsic paradoxical contradictions, and endowed with a fair degree of functional ability.

MORALITY IN HYSTERICAL PERSONS. Prescinding from the behavior of patients during psychopathic crises and from borderline cases in which the hysterical mentality is distorted by morbid complexes, not really due to hysteria, the thinking and acting of these patients differs only in quantity from that of normal persons. The average individual is generally somewhat egoistic, instinctive, impulsive, emotional and suggestible, capricious and theatrical, but these tendencies are controlled by the activity of conscience and education, whereas for hysterical persons, egocentrical tendencies, contradictions, and defects are increased by more intense emotional forces and the inadequacy of their conscious processes of equilibrium, reasoning, and critique. Thus, with respect to moral responsibility, hysterical persons are comparable to the average normal human being, except that they are more prone to compromises, deviations, and falls than the average normal person. Thus the hysterical person is usually able to understand the moral responsibility of others, though he may be unable to assimilate it. He may be more inclined to point out and criticize the failings of others.

(1) The degree of imputability of hysterical persons in violations of morality or in crimes is strictly in relation to the type and degree of disturbance at the time of the crime. Thus a crime committed by a subconscious pathological personality during its splitting phase frees an individual from responsibility fully, since consciousness must be considered completely absent. Apart from these exceptional cases, hysterical persons retain a more or less notable sense of moral responsibility, the extent of which cannot be easily established, insofar as it is subject to conspicuous variations from one moment to the next in one and the same individual. The will of these patients can rarely be considered free, for generally it is dominated by the deviations of a predominant emotive and affective factor.

The judgment of faults related by hysterical persons demands prudence, for they generally tend to exaggerate or minimize misdeeds due to the distorted evaluation of their own duties, actions, and qualities. The abnormal tendency of these patients to bury in their subconscious all recollections, especially of an unpleasant nature, renders any examination of conscience extremely difficult. In other words, they usually possess erroneous consciences; for this reason, extenuating circumstances exist in their favor insofar as their faults are condemned by a confessor.

(2) Hysterical children, whose home

environment may frequently cause indirectly their illness either because of extreme severity or laxity, can be aided noticeably if they are removed from that environment and furnished with adequate and constant hygienico-therapeutic treatments, which allow them to live as much as possible in the open air, in healthy circumstances under psychosomatic treatments and suitable religious and social training.

Hysterical adults may be capable of improvement under the guidance of a doctor endowed with great patience, firm and constant, not too rigid nor sentimental, who will methodically substitute his own solid and balanced will for the weak and uncertain will of the patient. By sound advice, capable of stirring in the patient a healthy pride, by interior discipline for the repression of emotional exuberances, the necessary direction to sound moral behavior will control the tumultuous and chaotic energies of the patient.

(3) One must not overlook the dangers facing those exposed by profession to familiarity with those afflicted with hysteria. This is particularly true with the female hysterics. Adopting the greatest prudence and reserve in dealing with such individuals and remembering the facility with which many hysterics become involved in amorous inclinations, doctors will be prepared to deal with tendencies to trick and deceive and the consequent inclination to turn to scandalous gossip in retribution for a rejection of their love and affection.

(4) Yet further symptoms, such as signs, raptures, ecstasies, diabolical possessions, may arise in hysterical persons through simulation or spontaneous manifestations of their illness. It is true that these could be supernatural phenomena, but in view of the neuro-psychopathological characteristics of hysterical persons it should not be difficult to detect the real nature of the case. Such will generally indicate chronic hysteria, particularly if this conforms to the social pattern of life of the individual. The psychological mechanism inclining one to dream and relive one's own personal experiences makes it possible that these phenomena may occur in pious and religious persons, as the results of hysteria without conscious simulation. To be able to distinguish these persons from the select, genuine few who are real mystics is a difficult task, for there always exists the possibility of real holiness accompanied by true supernatural phenomena in an hysteric temperament. Extensive clinical examination and suitable therapeutic aids can, of course, help in making the proper diagnosis.

Great care must also be exercised in determining the value of certain seemingly miraculous cures and certain pseudo-resurrections which are the apex of cataleptic manifestations. Of course, it is possible that hysterics may be cured miraculously, but, because of their great suggestibility, they are favorably predisposed to successful results of psychotherapeutic treatments, not only in the vast sphere of functional disorders, but also in certain organic conditions. This, of course, is proof of the well-known fact that the psyche exercises a considerable influence on the vegetative activities and, therefore, also on the body.

(5) Concerning the relations between the sexual organs and hysteria, although there has been much exaggeration in the past; nevertheless a relationship exists which cannot be ignored. Sexual abstinence may either disclose a psychoneurosis or aggravate it. Appropriate hygienic suggestions and treatment of hormones may well help the patient.

Marriage for hysterics, generally, may be suggested as a means of checking active hysteria or preventing a recurrence, provided the future spouse is endowed with the capability of providing the sick partner with the affectionate guidance described above. But if founded suspicions exist that in the new family environment the patient will only find incomprehension and friction, marriage should be discouraged, because these circumstances may well give rise to regretful psycho-sexual disorders which can, in turn, cause regrettable harm to their domestic moral life. *Riz.*

I

IDEA. *See* Concept; Thought; Idealism.

IDEA, FIXED, DELIRIOUS, OBSESSIONAL. *See* Delirium; Obsession; Psychasthenia.

IDEALISM. *Idealism*, as a general term, designates any philosophical system that stresses the ideal world over the natural in its explanation of the universe. Hence, idealism is opposed to naturalism, materialism, positivism, and, in general, all systems in which nature is a predominant element. Today, idealistic systems stress definite monistic and actualistic explanations, insofar as they limit their theories to a subordination of nature to forms or ideas and ultimately tend to reduce nature to ideas. Ideas are stripped of all substance and are termed *spirit action,* or other designations, which are always without substance, as an agentless activity.

Idealistic systems in relation to the field of ethics are both obscure and dangerous. First of all, idealism stresses an enlargement of the boundaries of the moral order. Disavowing all distinctions between intellect and will, idealism demolishes the barriers separating theory and practice, by attributing equal dominion to the will and the intellect over life. Thought itself is action, an act, a creation, and freedom. Therefore, the whole of life is theory and, at the same time, practice or ethics.

Such quantitative extensions in the concepts of ethics, even if accepted as true and legitimate, do not adequately compensate for the qualitative distortion imposed by idealism on moral reality. A radically monistic tendency, unifying the theoretical and the practical, leads to the suppression of all other definite distinctions; it considers these, on the whole, as errors or abstractions. If these are admitted at all, it is merely in a formalistic and dialectical sense only. Among the distinctions condemned to extinction practically, are those of truth and error, evil and good, which are fundamental to the whole of ethics, and, subsequently, virtue and vice. The Stoics equalized all sins; today the idealists apply the same theory to sin and virtue. Without any distinction between the world of reality and ideas, the idealist is unable to differentiate what *is* from what *must be,* and thus, establishing the principle that all reality is rational, he proclaims with Hegel that whoever pictures the world of what *must be* as separate from that of *being*, merely surrenders to a world of illusion. What *must be* coincides exactly with what *is;* whatever happens, had to happen; whatever one does, one had to do. This is the good.

Since it is difficult for an idealist to uphold the optimism of the latter statement, he must admit evil in this world as well. He assigns to it an exclusively dialectical function. Evil is the opposite of good, just as nature is the opposite of spirit; the abstract is opposed to the concrete; non-existence, to existence; the past, dead and outdated, is the opposite of the present, in which life pulsates. Every action, good at the time and in the person who performs it, can become bad as the result of another action which transcends and condemns it. This leads one to historicism and a most disconcerting form of relativism. One loses every positive and objective criterion to distinguish between good and evil; the only criterion still possible is transcendence, which is historical contingency.

To find an element of truth in this doctrine, we must place ourselves on the psychological level which we observe. The will seeks all under the aspect of

594

good. This aspect, however, is so general that it cannot adequately guarantee to all our actions the distinction of being good in the moral sense. Furthermore, at the time of the action, we usually try to convince ourselves of the goodness of our actions; we also know that often we do this in bad faith, and our effort goes for nought. This proves that we feel a sense of disapproval of our action at the very moment in which we perform it. *Gra.*

IDEATION. Ideas are formed from immediate images or recollections in a series of processes, the principal one of which is abstraction. By abstraction we can proceed from simple images to *concepts*, namely, the knowledge of characteristics common to the various images of objects in the same species, and to ideas, which are the relations between different concepts. To think is, therefore, to discover relations.

ABERRATIONS. Pathological aberrations in the formation of ideas are many. Linked to sense knowledge, intellectual activity may undergo distortions. These distortions may become defects at birth or during the early years of life, as in *phrenasthesia*, which may bring about a more or less conspicuous deficient power of thought and idea formation. At other times, the mind may suffer disturbances and disorganization, as in the vast and heterogeneous forms of mental derangement. In other cases, the process of idea-formation is affected either by an arrest or retardation in the flow of ideas and thought, as in *melancholia*, or by a process involving conspicuous acceleration and increase in the number of ideas in the mind simultaneously, as in *mania*. At other times, the normal flow of thought is disturbed and hindered by obsessive, compulsive, or fixed images or ideas, devoid of a morbid content in themselves, but which acquire pathological characteristics insofar as they settle, so to speak, invincibly and untimely in the area of consciousness, with subsequent strong affective influences of distressing coloration, as in *phrenasthenia*. Finally, the affective state may influence the idea-formation process with a consequent alteration in value judgments, which may give rise to completely mistaken notions of reality, such as are found in delirious ideas. These can lead to serious errors in conduct. The latter type of aberration is proper to *paranoia*, but it may be found in any form of mental illness.

In some cases, normal responsibility or imputability is non-existent; in others, it is proportionate to the seriousness of the pathological aberration in idea-formation processes. *Riz.*

IDIOCY. *See* Phrenasthenia.

IDLENESS. In a strict sense, idleness is a state of inactivity of both the mental and the physical faculties. In a broader sense, it also implies occupation with futile matters, or affairs of a purely recreational nature; hence, extensive amusements, games, and reading, indulged in without any intention of improving one's physical or mental welfare, may also be called idleness. Work is the lot of every man. Those who, because of their prosperous condition, are not required to work for their living still have the duty to avoid idleness and thus remove from themselves and others all occasions of sin. Furthermore, one's obligation to make a positive contribution to the community demands of everyone responsible and productive activity. Work (*q.v.*), whether manual or intellectual, ennobles man; in fact, without it, man's life becomes sterile and futile. Those blessed by God with greater material goods or talents have the obligation to use them for their own betterment and in behalf of their neighbor. From this it can be clearly seen how idleness can constitute a grave sin. Idleness makes a person listless and incapable of profitable, serious work. It exposes him to all kinds of temptations which make the work of the devil much easier. *Man.*

IDOLATRY. *Idolatry* is offering to creatures the worship due to god (*latria*), either by paying homage to the image of a false divinity or idol which one considers as the true deity (common idolatry), or to a being believed to be the embodiment of divinity (sun, moon, emperor, etc.). Idolatry is *formal*, if joined with the sincere intention of giving to a creature the worship due to God; *material*, or simulated, if it externally feigns latria out of fear, with no deliberate intent to worship a creature. Formal idolatry is called perfect, if based on a sincere belief in the divinity of a creature; imperfect, if it proceeds from another motive, e.g., hatred of God, or the wish to obtain something from the devil.

SERIOUSNESS OF THE SIN OF IDOLATRY. In the Old and New Testament, the sin of idolatry is very severely condemned; in fact, it is considered also an intellectual aberration (cf., e.g., Exodus 20:2–5; Deut. 4:15–19; 5:6–10; Wisdom 13:14; Rom. 1:18–25; I Cor. 8:4–5; 10:14–20). Idolatry is truly a crime of lese majesty against God because by it a person gives to a creature honor due to God alone (*see* Adoration; Cult; Religion). It is however, obvious that material idolatry, lacking the interior aspect and real intention, is less serious than formal idolatry by which a person really honors a creature as God. Since in acts of public worship, the significance of the act depends on the general estimation and so-called custom, in addition to constituting a serious sin of scandal, material idolatry, by which a person really honors God, may be a grave fault against the duty of professing the faith outwardly, thereby constituting a real crime against the virtue of religion. In the objective order, in formal idolatry, the sin of incredulity is added to idolatry, insofar as another alien god is worshipped together with the true God. Regarding subjective responsibility, imperfect idolatry is generally more serious because it is a sin of sheer bad will without any extenuating circumstance in its favor, while perfect idolatry is often the result of ignorance, and material idolatry, the result of fear. *Pal.*

IGNORANCE. Ignorance is a lack of knowledge which one should possess. Moral theologians are particularly concerned with the causes and effects of ignorance. In its cause, ignorance may be considered *vincible* or *invincible*. *Invincible* ignorance is involuntary and due to an inculpable cause. For instance, we may be ignorant of facts which do not concern us, which we are not obliged to know, or which, despite our obligation to have knowledge of them, we cannot possibly know because of a lack of means or other morally invincible obstacle. On the other hand, ignorance due to willful or culpable negligence is called *vincible*. The various degrees of vincible ignorance are determined by the gravity of the negligence. Ignorance which is caused by a form of exceptional laziness or negligence is termed *crass* or *supine;* if such laziness is accompanied or replaced by malice, whereby one refuses to acquire knowledge in order to continue living as he pleases, this form of ignorace is termed *affected.*

A moral judgment concerning the consequences of ignorance is strictly related to its cause. With respect to the good effects of ignorance, these are never credited to the person who unwittingly caused them. The problem, however, does arise with respect to evil effects. On these points, moral theologians have established the following principles: (1) Any effect resulting from invincible ignorance is not voluntary and, therefore, not imputable. (2) An evil effect due to or resulting from vincible ignorance, more or less voluntary, is imputable to the individual according to the degree of vincibility, that is, of culpability, of the ignorance itself. The degree of culpability decreases but slightly in crass or supine ignorance, and not at all in affected ignorance. An immediately invincible ignorance may possibly have been overcome at a prior stage; in such cases, the resultant effect is imputable in its remote cause, that is, with respect to the original negligence, which caused the ignorance.

Ignorance, furthermore, may be of fact or of law; this distinction is of greater interest to the jurist than to the moral theologian.

That which was said about ignorance also applies to error. *Gra.*

ILL. *See* Infirm.

ILLEGITIMATE. *See* Legitimation.

ILLUMINATION. In the theological sense, illumination means an interior enlightenment of the intellect by God. It is a form of actual grace (*see* Grace). Mention is appropriate of a so-called *illumination of the dying*, which, according to certain recent theologians, refers to a beneficial crisis of conversion, alleged to occur under a special divine influence in the interval between apparent and real death. This attractive theory has not met with favor. Writers of ascetical theology also speak of an *illuminative way*, by which they describe the state of the souls progressing in virtue who, after the experiences of the purgative way, strive to imitate Jesus Christ, the Light of the world, in the positive practice of Christian virtues. *Pal.*

ILLUMINISM. *See* Individualism.

ILLUSION. *See* Hallucination.

IMAGES, OBSCENE. Obscene images, objectively considered according to the content of the picture and not the subjective dispositions of the viewer, are paintings, sculptures, photographs, etc., which (1) are deliberately intended (*ex fine operantis*) to promote indecency or created by the author with the obvious intention of simply stimulating lustful sentiments; or (2) *ordinarily* cause lustful sentiments or sensations in the majority of normal people because of the subject chosen or the manner in which it is portrayed. The judges of obscenity are not to be the authors themselves, nor individuals exceptionally hardened to such things, nor the young and inexperienced.

Obscenity refers to images depicting nudity in a provocative manner, by which, because of the setting, art, color, style, etc., a person is not able to dismiss easily from his mind images depicting obscenity. It is apparent that this admits of a variety of degrees.

To create such pictures is always sinful, since they are objectively evil. To look at such pictures, in itself, is not necessarily sinful, unless one does so with evil intentions, allows evil desires and thoughts to be fostered by these, or gives scandal to others by this action. To expose oneself to the danger of serious sin is obviously, in itself, a serious sin. *Dam.*

IMAGES, SACRED, CULT OF. *See* Cult.

IMAGINATION. *See* Fantasy, psychological nature.

IMBECILITY. *See* Phrenasthenia.

IMMIGRATION. *See* Emigration.

IMMODESTY. Immodesty is the deliberate pursuit of things which readily stimulate the sexual appetite, such as looks, touches, kisses, embraces, conversations, reading or singing. In themselves, these are not necessarily sinful; they become sinful by reason of an evil intention, or the degree of sexual pleasure aroused by their influence.

An intention, whether implicit or explicit, to arouse sexual pleasure by such actions amounts to a direct sin of lust. These activities are always gravely sinful. The influence exerted by these actions in stimulating sexual pleasure makes them gravely, venially, or not sinful at all, depending whether the influence on the passions is grave, slight, or nil.

Because of the varying degrees of influence which the parts of the human body may exert in exciting carnal pleasure, moral theologians usually distinguish them into *decent* (face, hands, feet); *less decent* (breast, back, arms, legs); and *indecent* (sex organs and adjacent parts). This distinction, of course, is theoretically valid. In practice, however, the determination of the gravity of the sin depends entirely on the pleasure that these acts really produce, insofar as it was foreseen. The possibility of such pleasure varies greatly according to the subjective circumstances of the individual and the objective circumstances of the act. Since the acts are in themselves indifferent and offend against the rules of morality only because of an inordinate intention or an inordinate effect, they are permissible if they are performed for an honest purpose, out of necessity, or if the real usefulness of such actions proportionately justifies the inordinate results which might follow; among these reasons are study, art, medicine, care of the body, etc. In practice, a right intention and an honest purpose lessen the gravity of the evil effect greatly.

These directly stimulating acts (*per se influentes*) must be distinguished from those which, for mechanical reasons, apart from the area of sex, at times produce sexual pleasure (*per accidens influentes*); for example, horseback riding, exercising, bicycle riding, bathing, and the like. Such acts do not fall in the category of sins against modesty or purity; if performed for a just cause (legitimate recreation), they are licit; if without just reason, they are, in themselves, only venial sins.

For certain specific acts of immodesty and their occasions, *see* Kiss; Obscenity; Song; Cinema; Amusements; Talk, Obscene; Reading; Nudism; Nudity; Theatre; Television; Immodesty; Impurity; Chastity. *Dam.*

IMMORALITY, COMPULSIVE. At

one time, psychiatrists and criminologists held that serious ethical failings could not exist independently of mental disturbances. As a result of this concept, certain scholars have labelled psychopathy (also called *moral insanity, congenital delinquency, instinctive perversity*) as *moral imbecility*; certain legislations—for instance, English law—consider individuals affected by such anomalies as "persons who, from the tenderest age, gave signs of some form of permanent mental deficiency, accompanied by intense inclinations to vice and crime, and upon whom punishment had little or no effect."

Experience has demonstrated that disorders can exist in the ethico-emotional sphere without noticeable anomalies of the intellect. These ethico-emotional disorders, when not accompanied by epilepsy or other psychopathological manifestations, have been called *compulsive* (or even *constitutional*) *immorality*. But this designation, as well as the preceding ones, are absolutely inaccurate and inadequate in describing the morbid forms to which they refer. In point of fact, the expression *com-*

pulsive immorality seems to exclude on principle any form of moral imputability, because it refers to a morally wrong act as an inevitable consequence of a specific constitution without any participation of free will (positive school). Now, while it is true that in the so-called compulsive immoral person, the exercise of free will can be impaired by anomalies of a psychological nature, the fact remains that ordinarily it is not completely nullified. There remains, therefore, a more or less wide margin of imputability which must be properly evaluated in each individual case.

Nevertheless, the term is still maintained and used to indicate anomalies in the ethico-emotional sphere without any appreciable disorder of the intelligence. In cases which also present intellectual disturbances, one must look for some kind of mental disorder the frequent instances of disturbances of a defective type are generally to be related to phrenasthenia (*q.v.*).

CAUSES. The causes of the ethico-characterological aberrations of the so-called compulsive immoral persons are not well known. Since the vegetative nervous system and the endocrine glands play an important part in the field of affectivity and emotions, it is quite probable that a subtle neuro-humoral disorder, probably produced by toxic-infectious conditions developed during the period of a person's growth, may be the basis of a constitutional anomaly. Also, a hereditary factor (presumably by transmission of neuro-hormonic anomalies) is of significant importance as a cause of the disease. The same must be said of the environmental factor.

SYMPTOMS. So-called compulsive immoral individuals show common psychopathological characteristics. These, according to Regis, are principally: a lack of the moral sense, which, however, seldom implies complete absence of moral evaluation; inaffectivity, inadaptability, impulsiveness, and overbearing instinctiveness. These characteristics never appear in equal measure in the various patients; this gives rise to several clinical types of compulsive immorality.

Thus, Levy-Valensi established the following distinctions: (a) the simply *instinctive*, whose instincts do not register the restraining influence of education and private and social ethics; (b) the *instinctive perverts*, whose instincts are distorted and deformed from the very beginning. Other scholars propose other distinctions.

MORAL ASPECTS. It must not be assumed that the norm of conscience is completely extinct in these people, unless they are affected by certain extreme forms of mental disorders, although it can be more or less seriously dimmed. It is principally a matter of reawakening in them, by a wise and patient training that implements the work of a psychiatrist, the norm of conscience, which makes the individual once again aware of his personal responsibilities. Left to themselves, mentally defective persons aggravate their already unstable moral balance by a repetition of errors. At any rate, in these persons the measure of imputability is in proportion to the awareness and consent of which they are capable.

MEDICO-LEGAL AND THERAPEUTIC ASPECTS. The cases of the mentally abnormal often give rise to very lively discussions in certain courts of law, where at times one finds a psychiatrist or a defense attorney following theories of criminal anthropology (*q.v.*), while the judge follows the principles of classic penal law. In other words, the former would hold to the theory that the accused is properly and really mentally ill and, as such, cannot incur the punishments of the law; yet the judge believes that he is a criminal, at least "by tendency" (*see* Delinquency) and must receive the specific punishment provided for the type of crime committed. To avoid error, one must analyze each case carefully, to ascertain whether or not the individual is suffering from a morbid form which diminishes his moral responsibility, and to what extent such responsibility was actually diminished at the time of the commission of the crime.

Bearing in mind that the so-called immoral individuals are not ordinarily insensible to the dictates of conscience or the restraints established by the law, which in fact have a greater influence on them because of the material nature of the punishment, these temperamentally abnormal people can be considered ordinary criminals in the penal forum, though with extenuating circumstances in their favor.

With regard to the penal and correctional aspects, a diligent choice of the place and method of detention is very important: the usual prisons or places of detention are often most inappropriate because of the possibility of association with lesser criminals or with more callous and inveterate types. They should, therefore, be placed in special places where they could be adequately studied and given psychotherapeutic and neuroendocrinologic treatments as well as religious and spiritual assistance. It is only by these means that one can hope to obtain useful results in the rehabilitation of these individuals by the time their detention expires. Without these aids, they will succumb again to vice and crime and will continue to be a constant danger to society.

However, therapy for these abnormal adults, often too naturalistic, has, until the present time, yielded only scanty results, whereas preventive treatment for the morally abnormal has already given promising results. One can only hope that it will be improved and used in treating the greatest possible number of abnormal children.

It should be remembered, with regard to this preventive method, that abnormality often shows up in the very first years of life. The child does not manifest the usual spontaneous affection for its parents, but is indifferent; he may sometimes give way to violent and unrestrainable fits of temper; or he may be sullen, deceitful, given to lying or stealing; almost always he vents his cruel instincts on animals or on a weaker child. He is a truant at school, inclined to wander, incorrigible, disobedient and rebellious; he may also show signs of precocious and perverted sexual instincts.

These patients must be treated in

specially equipped correctional houses, where they shall be guided with discipline but not without affectionate interest in their studies and in learning crafts. These activities should be organized as much as possible in the open, and should alternate with physical therapy. Idleness must be strictly avoided. Plentiful and healthful food, sound methods of teaching and training, capable of developing and strengthening a sense of honor and self-control and of engendering in young minds a social interest in their surroundings, will contribute effectively to the physical and spiritual vigor of these abnormal children. Specialized doctors should study each individual, accurately, from the aspects of medical history, constitutional and psychological make-up. They must use every possible means capable of correcting the physio-psychological deviations in their patients, guiding them toward occupational activities that are more suitable to their inclinations and their psychosomatic possibilities.

Religious instruction and formation must not be omitted, for it may well constitute the principal basis for the return to society of these unfortunate individuals. *Riz.*

IMMUNITY (ECCLESIASTICAL). Ecclesiastical immunity is a right by which places of worship and ecclesiastical persons or things are exempted from certain secular obligations and burdens, as well as from acts unbecoming to their religious character. In other words, this is not simply a question of suitable ethical measures, but also of juridical, natural exigencies; ultimately, ecclesiastical immunity rests on divine law, though its concrete application is made by the positive law.

ORIGIN AND EVOLUTION OF THE CONCEPT OF IMMUNITY. Originally, *munus* meant only gift; *munera* generally referred to military bonus-gifts to soldiers at the conclusion of a campaign, or reward-gifts to lawyers and jurisconsuls for their technical work and assistance. Subsequently, the term assumed the metaphoric meaning of the office itself which received reward. At the creation of municipalities there arose a distinction between citizens subject only to bearing the burdens (*munera onera*) of the public administration and those who could also compete for offices (*honores*). But since some cities were not municipalities but were considered free, that is, *immunes*, insofar as they were not subject to taxation or other obligations of a personal or economic nature, consequently, the inhabitants of the free cities were also called *immunes*, that is, free from taxes and public services. From this came the abstract term *immunity*, which indicates exemption from public duties or burdens.

Ecclesiastical immunity is of three kinds: *personal, local,* and *real*. Personal immunity exempts members of the clergy from the jurisdiction and liabilities imposed by the lay authority. Among these are exemptions of ecclesiastics from public services incompatible with the sacred nature of their ministry; the exemption from certain personal liabilities and, in some countries, from certain personal and property taxes, and other civil laws; the so-called *privilege of the forum*, which safeguards the dignity of ecclesiastics and assures them the means for a suitable existence in the case of honest insolvency (*see* Clergy, privileges of). Local immunity protects sacred places and buildings dedicated to worship from profane uses and recognizes in them the *right of asylum* (*q.v.*). Real immunity exempts, to a certain extent, ecclesiastical property from taxation commonly applied to private properties.

The concrete formulation of ecclesiastical immunities gradually developed according to the social climate of the times. Immunities are based on the decorum befitting the members of the clergy because of their sacred character and as a direct requirement of their specific status. For the same reason, this immunity extended to sacred places and property. Violation of immunity is punished by the Church with appropriate canonical penalties. The Church endeavors to obtain recognition of these immunities in her concordats with the individual States. Certain States, under the pretext of freedom and democracy, often raise obstacles against the free exercise of religion and the proper understanding of the divine mission of the Church in the world. Others are somewhat reluctant to recognize long-established immunities and ignore them altogether. Yet, in the majority of cases, immunities are of great benefit also to civil society, as, for example, in the case of the exemption of the clergy from active military service. *Pug.*

IMMUTABILITY OF LAWS. *See* Law, Natural.

IMPATIENCE. *See* Patience, virtues connected with.

IMPEDIMENT. In the sacramental system, an impediment is a circumstance which prohibits or invalidates a specific act. With regard to holy orders, an impediment is a circumstance that by the law of the Church forbids a man (not permanently, and in this it differs from irregularity) from being admitted to holy orders (e.g., military service, matrimony). *See* Irregularity and impediments. Insofar as marriage is concerned, an impediment affects the contracting parties and, by virtue of a divine or ecclesiastical law, makes them incapable of contracting a valid or lawful marriage. In marriage, an impediment may be *impeding* if it renders marriage *illicit* without invalidating it (e.g., simple vow, mixed religions, legal relationship, civil legislation regarding an impeding impediment) or *diriment*, if the marriage is thereby made also *invalid* (e.g., age, impotency, former bond, disparity of cult, sacred orders, solemn religious profession, abduction, crime, consanguinity, affinity, public honesty, spiritual relationship, and legal relationship, wherever the civil legislation considers it as a diriment impediment). *Pal.*

IMPEDIMENTS, DIRIMENT, MATRIMONIAL. Among diriment impediments, which not only prohibit matrimony but also make it invalid, are certain physical and mental defects that hold a special interest for doctors. These defects so distort an individual's personality that they make him unsuited for the attainment of the physiological, social, and moral ends of marriage and even unable to understand and to will the marriage contract. As diriment impediments belonging to the field of legal medicine, we shall study here the following: identity of sex, intellectual-volitive incapability, impotency. The first two are impediments in an improper sense, whereas impotency is a real and proper impediment.

IDENTITY OF SEX. Since the primary objective of marriage is the procreation of offspring, matrimony is possible only between two individuals of opposite sex. This aspect, all too obvious in itself, is connected with a special question concerning the capability of hermaphrodites (*see* Hermaphroditism) to wed, and consequently the validity of a marriage contracted by them. As indicated in the article on hermaphroditism (*q.v.*), perfect hermaphroditism does not exist; there are only imperfect or apparent forms of it, better described as *pseudo-hermaphroditism*. In dealing with this problem, the Church looks into its ultimate nature and essence by reducing it practically to a question of impotency (*see below*). The objective, therefore, will be to ascertain in each individual case whether the sick individual has the sexual capacity proper to the sex according to which he married or wishes to marry, as required in all normal individuals of that sex for the fulfilment of the conjugal act.

INTELLECTUAL-VOLITIVE INCAPABILITY. Another diriment impediment is psychic deficiency. It is easy to understand why a canonical marriage, both as a sacrament and contract, necessarily demands of the contracting parties two fundamental requirements concerning their natural aptitude: physiological (*capacitas corporis*) and intellectual-volitive (*capacitas animi*). The latter consists of a capability of judgment in understanding and willing the bond of marriage (*ad vinculum intelligendum et eligendum*). It requires in turn two adequately efficient faculties: intelligence or intellectual capacity (*maturitas cognitionis*) and will or volitive capacity (*maturitas libertatis*). We refer to adequately efficient faculties, not absolute integrity of psychic powers, having in mind, as Berri indicates concerning civil capacity in general, that such capacity "does not presuppose, as a condition, a complete state of psychic equilibrium, but a mental ability sufficient to enable a person to adequately assess the act he intends to perform and sufficient autonomy to make the decision."

Impediments of a psychopathological nature may be classified as follows: (a) *Chronic mental derangement (amentia habitualis)*: real and proper forms of mental derangement, acquired psychoses, and permanent, total psychic disturbances. (b) *Mental disorder (mentis exturbatio)*: mental disorders, permanent but incomplete, consisting rather of a weakness of the mental faculties (*e.g.*, psychoneurosis and idiocy). To these should be added *impaired senses (defectus sensuum)*: the lack of two or more senses, insofar as this deficiency may be accompanied by a psychic insufficiency making the individual comparable to one suffering from chronic mental derangement (*amentia habitualis*). (c) *Impotency*, described under its own particular entry. Impotency differs from sterility. Sterility, according to the Code (Can. 1068), neither prevents nor invalidates matrimony (*matrimonium nec dirimit nec impedit*). Real and proper impotency is the incapability on the part of the husband or the wife of performing the conjugal act, either because of the absence of the specific organs, their undeveloped or over-developed size, or some other specific defect which impairs their proper function and effectiveness.

CONDUCT OF THE PHYSICIAN. The doctor who is aware of a diriment impediment is morally bound to warn the patient that the marriage, if contracted, would be invalid. It is perfectly proper for a physician to use all his medical knowledge, not to conceal the impediment (which would be improper), but to try to remove the impediment, wherever it may exist. Since a physician is bound by professional secrecy, according to some moralists he may not be required to reveal the diriment impediment of which he has become aware in the practice of his profession, but he should at least advise his patient to make the impediment known to the lawful authority.

For other diriment impediments, *see* individual entries. *Riz.*

IMPEDIMENTS, MATRIMONIAL. A matrimonial impediment may be described as a circumstance affecting the contracting parties which, by virtue of a divine or ecclesiastical law, renders a person unable to contract marriage lawfully or validly. Impediments which make a marriage unlawful but not invalid are called *impeding;* those which also make marriage invalid are called *diriment.* The word *diriment* means that, if a marriage is contracted without the removal of the impediment, the marriage is null and void and the couple must separate (*dirimi*), or have the marriage validated.

According to the definition of the Council of Trent (Sess. XXIV, Can. 4) in the case of baptized persons, only the Church has the power to establish matrimonial impediments by positive law (Can. 1038, 2); consequently, only the Church can grant the necessary dispensation from impediments. This power is vested in the Supreme Pontiff. Ordinaries have power to impose only a temporary prohibition in specific cases. Civil authority can establish impediments by positive law for the non-baptized.

A diriment impediment makes a marriage invalid even if the couple do not know of its existence (Can. 16), or if only one of the contracting parties is originally affected by it, because the marriage contract cannot be valid for one party and null for the other (Can. 1036, par. 1).

Impediments may be classified according to the following categories:

(a) *Origin.* Divine *natural law*: impediments of impotency, consanguinity, at least in the first degree of the direct line, etc.; divine *positive law*: impediments of bond or ligamen, etc.; *ecclesiastical law*: impediments of age, affinity, crime, etc.; *civil law:* impediments of legal relationship or others adapted and accepted by ecclesiastical law.

(b) *Certainty.* Impediments are said to be *certain* or *doubtful.* They are doubtful either with a doubt of law (*dubium juris*), if the law is not clear in defining them and, therefore, not obligatory; or with a doubt of fact as to whether the law applies (*dubium facti.*)

(c) *Extension.* Impediments are *absolute,* if they extend to everyone without exception, as the impediments of holy orders; or *relative,* if they pertain to particular cases, such as the impediments of consanguinity, crime, etc., without dispensations.

(d) *Duration.* Impediments may be *temporal,* that is, cease in course of time, such as age, prior marriage bonds; or *perpetual,* that is, remain in force permanently (unless dispensed), such as consanguinity, affinity, crime, etc.

(e) *Notoriety.* Impediments may be *public* or *occult. Public* impediments are provable in the external forum (Can. 1037); *occult* impediments are not provable in the external forum. At times, impediments, public by nature, may be occult in fact, as consanguinity in a relationship with an illegitimate child whose parents are not publicly known. Likewise, occult impediments may become public or be subject to public knowledge later.

(f) *Dispensability.* If it is within the power of the Church to grant a dispensation, the impediment is said to be dispensable, and the Church customarily dispenses from it. This occurs when the impediments are not of divine or natural law.

(g) *Degree.* Impediments are of *major* degree, if the dispensation is valid only on the basis of the truth of the reason given; *minor,* if the dispensation is valid even though the alleged reason for seeking it is not true; among these are consanguinity in the third degree, affinity, and crime. One of *major* degree is adultery with the promise or attempt at marriage (Can. 1042). *Bar.*

IMPEDIMENTS, MATRIMONIAL (DISPENSATION FROM). A dispensation is an exemption from an ecclesiastical law granted in a specific case for a good reason (Cans. 80 and 84). Dispensations are used extensively, particularly in matters involving marriage because of the great variety of circumstances existing in the various countries, that frequently demand exceptions from the observance of the general law. Marriage is an institution subject not only to divine and natural law but also to ecclesiastical law. Impediments arising from natural or divine law cannot be dispensed, whereas impediments of purely ecclesiastical law may be dispensed. As a rule, dispensations regarding matrimonial impediments are granted by the Supreme Pontiff through the competent Sacred Congregation (principally, the Congregation of the Sacraments), or by one who has received such power from the Holy See. In emergency cases, local Ordinaries, parish priests, and confessors have extraordinary faculties to grant dispensations (Cans. 1043–1045).

No one, not even the Supreme Pontiff may dispense from impediments of divine-natural law; e.g., antecedent and perpetual impotency, an existing marriage bond, a ratified and consummated marriage, consanguinity in the direct line (father and daughter), or in the first degree of the collateral line (brother-sister). As a rule, the Pope does not dispense from an impediment arising from the priesthood or public conjugicide; very rarely and only for grave reasons is a dispensation granted from the impediments of age, sacred orders below the priesthood, or consanguinity of the second degree touching upon the first (uncle and niece). For good reasons a dispensation is granted in cases of collateral consanguinity in the second degree, or in collateral affinity in the first degree.

The reasons or motives for obtaining a dispensation are called *honest* if they do not imply the existence of guilt in the parties to a marriage; otherwise, they are called *dishonest.* Among honest reasons more frequently given are: *angustia loci:* the limitation of opportunity and, therefore, of choice due to a sparse population; super-adult age of the bride (if she has completed her 24th year of age); in the case of a widow, her relatively young age (under 40) is a good reason for dispensation; inadequacy or lack of dowry; an orphan girl; convalidation of the marriage; arrangements for the marriage already made and news of the forthcoming event already publicized; preservation of peace and harmony; well-founded hope for the conversion of one of the spouses; welfare of children bereft of one parent in the case of a second marriage. Among dishonest reasons are: concubinage to be regularized, elopement, loss of one's good name, suspicion of improper relation, danger of contracting civil marriage, legitimation of offspring, etc.

The person in need of a dispensation must submit his request to the diocesan curia (chancery office) through the parish priest. By virtue of the faculties delegated by the Holy See to the bishops, the latter may grant many dispensations for which, in times past, application had to be made to Rome. Having received the petition, the bishop or vicar general or chancellor grants the dispensation needed for the celebration of the marriage. A record of the dispensation must be properly entered in the parish marriage register. *Bar.*

IMPENITENCE. One who persists in sin, that is, in a state of separation from God, is impenitent. This persistence may be due either to neglect, as one who does not take time to rectify his state of soul; or to ill will, as one who actually refuses to repent and to make amendment of his life. Final impenitence is a refusal to repent at the last moment of one's life.

Impenitence, even temporary, if willful, is a grave sin against the Holy Spirit (*see* Sin Against the Holy Spirit).

IMPERFECTION. Imperfection is the lack of a necessary quality or totality of perfection, in which one is incomplete or defective in his nature. God alone is absolutely perfect, since He lacks nothing. The perfection of creatures is relative, that is, commensurate with their capacity. In the moral order, perfection may be either *terminal*—that is final—

which is said of the blessed in heaven, or *viable*, which is predicated of people on earth. The perfection of those living on earth (*viatores*) differs from that of the blessed in the final or terminal state. One who exercises on earth all the talents he has received is considered perfect. Talents, if properly used, tend to increase in geometric proportion.

Imperfection, therefore, consists in a lack of perfection, which one might be capable of attaining, at any given moment. It is *negative*, if it is involuntary; *positive*, if it is voluntary. Imperfection arises either from a lack of psychological perfection, as defects in deliberation, or the lack of ontological perfection, found in an action, itself inferior to another act which might have been chosen, or lacking the intensity of feeling which the act might have possessed.

At this point a question arises about the nature of imperfections and their relationship to venial sins: Are there actions which might be morally imperfect, yet not venially sinful?

NEGATIVE AND POSITIVE IMPERFECTION. Negative imperfection cannot be considered sinful, precisely because it is involuntary; in fact, it is not properly called imperfection, nor can one speak of an actual capacity for perfection if the lack of it does not depend on the will. The same point is not true with respect to *positive* imperfection. In truth, in our actions we are not always bound to choose the best; nor is it true that an objectively more perfect deed is always and necessarily more perfect for an individual. Positive imperfection occurs if one excludes an action which is better than another, from the standpoint of content and meaning, and more clearly suitable to the agent, upon the basis of a direct analysis of the action itself or a clear inspiration of the Holy Spirit. In such a case, this implies the choice between doing and omitting something, or between acceptance of what is good with refusal of what is better. Acceptance of a good must be right, but refusal of the better cannot be considered morally right. This refusal cannot be due to a reasonable motive. Neither the use of one's own freedom, given by God not only as a gift to be enjoyed but as a means to be put to good use, nor the difficulty surrounding an action (which, by supposition, can be overcome by the individual) can be considered as a reasonable motive. Furthermore, if there were a reasonable motive, the action could no longer be considered as advisable here and now for the individual to perform. Thus, the motive must, of necessity, be one of the many variations of human egoism, which, by prevailing upon the will, clearly indicates the presence of a false hierarchy of values in the mind.

How can *refusal* to choose a better action be acceptable to God and remain in conformity with the universal obligation to tend to perfection? Finally, it seems unreasonable for one to omit doing a good thing precisely and solely because it is not imposed by law or as a command. One who acts in this way simply prefers a thing which is less good than a higher good. This is contrary to the principle of right reason, which requires that man seek his end by every means suitable to him (*S. Theol.*, II–II, q. 184, a. 3). There is no limitation in man's search for his end and good; hence he does not act according to his end if he neglects a superior good solely because it is not imposed by a precept. To act without reasonable motivation is to act in a manner opposed to the purpose of human life. To perform an act incapable of reference to one's ultimate end is proper to venial sin, in which man is not separated from God, his ultimate End, but wavers from the order that must lead him to God as his ultimate End.

In conclusion, the omission of a choice of a superior good either is justified by a sound reason or not. If not justified, then it is a sin, because God wants man to act according to the reasonable side of his nature. If the omission is justified for one reason or another, then the presupposition is wrong, insofar as the superior good is not such in every aspect and, therefore, not necessarily to be preferred in that specific case.

Certain theologians have treated this matter differently (DeLugo, *Opera Venetiis*, I, *De poen.*, d.3, s. I, c.9–10; Genicot - Salsmans, *Institutiones theo-*

logiae moralis, I, 12, 112). Probably the difference of approach, rather than theory, leads to a theoretical solution without concrete consideration of each individual in specific circumstances.

Are imperfections sufficient matter for the sacrament of penance? In other words, does one who has committed only imperfections receive absolution validly? In view of the above, the answer must necessarily be in the affirmative, if it is a matter of positive imperfections, which, as we stated, involve guilt; the answer, if it concerns negative imperfections, must be in the negative. Since some authors hold that imperfections are not sins, imperfections are to be considered as doubtful matter for the valid absolution in the sacrament of penance. *Pal.*

IMPERIALISM. In a general sense, imperialism is the tendency to dominate and extend dominion over other nations. In its internal policies, imperialism is a despotic form of government, based on force; it is also a domination for political purposes, a policy striving to increase its sphere of influence and dominion.

Imperialism might be distinguished by the motives which lead to expansion, as Sombart says; thus there is political, military, ideological, economic, and sociological imperialism. Proudhon and Marx both championed an imperialism which was founded on proletarian or class struggles.

EVOLUTION. Agricultural nations tend to a peaceful life, aimed at self-sufficiency. If the myth of war, racial, economic or any form of supremacy is created, a transition occurs from a stable to a dynamic life; this leads to eventual competition, war, subjugation or domination. A war-minded nation is no longer satisfied with the mere defense of rights, but by attacks and invasions becomes a threat to the security of other people. This creates a change in values, in which the State policy becomes an end in itself; cities gain priority over rural areas, industry over agriculture, wage-earning citizens over rural population, big business over small business.

Some authorities consider the essence of imperialism in the tendency of a State to unlimited expansion, the real motive and not the result of imperialism. A typical example is found in Prussia, which succeeded throughout the years under the policies of Bismarck, William II, and Hitler in subjugating large areas of the continent of Europe.

Imperialism, as the tendency to universal power, has existed for centuries, in Persia, Macedonia, and the Roman Empire. The idea of a universal monarchy is found in *The City of God* by Saint Augustine; it also appears in the writings of Saint Thomas Aquinas and Dante. This notion became a reality in the medieval Roman Empire, since this was more the fruit of a trend toward unification than of power supremacy by force. A religious motive of a supernational character dominated this ideal.

With the gradual emancipation of the secular sword from the sacerdotal power, the State became a secular, autocratic dominion in its own right. This movement began with the Renaissance and the Reformation, with proclamations for an anarchical type of freedom for individuals as well as nations. The French Revolution promoted the reawakening of the idea of the rights of man, which were distorted by a form of exaggerated individualism, which opposed the individual to the State and the collectivity of the people. This gave birth to the nation, a form of exaggerated individualism which was embodied in the term *nationalism*. Through Napoleon these ideas spread throughout the continent.

The industrialization of the nineteenth century enabled England to attain unprecedented economic expansion, which was characterized by a conquest of numerous foreign markets and the close economic ties with colonies and dominions. England extensively expanded in Latin America, Africa, the Middle East and the Far East. Thus she enlarged the fortune of the nation with the theocratic nature of an Empire based on the Calvinistic notion which created vast sociological effects. Oliver Cromwell justified expansionist policies as an extension of the Kingdom of God on earth, as he claimed for himself the title of executor of the will of the Lord of Hosts.

The fourteen points of Woodrow Wilson re-echoed the idea of the universal mission of the Anglo-Saxons. Other countries, through the creation of a *balance of power*, sought to oppose these British economic expansions. Disraeli and Chamberlain proclaimed a federation of British colonies and thus gave birth to the Imperial Federation League of 1884, the basis of classic English imperialism. After World War I, the economic power of the United States entered into strong competition with England, and gradually saw the balance of superior force shift to America as the leading nation in the world following World War II.

MARXIST IMPERIALISM. According to Karl Marx, imperialism was a capitalistic phenomenon, from which the system of production created imperial expansion, competition, and the struggle for new markets. Lenin labelled imperialism as the monopolistic arena of capitalism. To survive, free economy expands in circles; capital must be provided new and more profitable uses. Opposed to the concept of Lenin, Kautsky described imperialism as an invasion by industrial capital for the sake of subjugating rural areas and counteracting depressions. Sombart rejects a concept of imperialism as a necessary phase in the evolution of capitalism and sees in it only the nature of a potential policy.

In supreme irony, the Marxist theory of imperialism as a necessary phase of capitalism has been contradicted by a new and more apparent determination of bolshevistic imperialism looming on the world horizon. In its motives and effects, it represents a new form of imperialism. The first phase represented an extension of influence, not economic and military, but ideological, by means of the Komintern, the national communist parties, and propaganda. The second phase, after the Second World War, no longer was satisfied with economic and ideological expansion but resorted to subjugation by power and efforts to alter or destroy culture, faith, and social orders in an attempt to create a new order and world. In this activity, it holds all means lawful, as long they actually skillfully succeed.

Thus, those who condemned imperialism in the name of a pacifist ideology have installed a new form of imperialism; those who endeavored to attribute an ethical value to imperialism have discovered that the law of force as the supreme law of nations is the negation of every sound ethical principle. *Per.*

IMPERIALISM, ECONOMIC. *See* Economy; Imperialism; Monopoly.

IMPERIALISM, MARXIST. *See* Imperialism.

IMPERIALISM, POLITICAL. *See* Imperialism.

IMPORTATION. *See* Commerce, International.

IMPOSSIBILITY. In moral theology, impossibility is a condition which excuses a person from observing a law or fulfilling an obligation. Impossibility may be *physical* or *moral*. *Physical* impossibility exists if the means required for the fulfillment of an obligation are lacking; for example, if a singer loses his voice. Moral impossibility exists if it is physically possible to perform an obligation, but the obligation involves a grave inconvenience, either for the subject acting or others connected intimately with the act.

In the juridical order, impossibility, as an extenuating cause for the non-fulfillment of an obligation, is far less easily accepted than in the field of morality. Not even physical impossibility is generally accepted as an adequate excusing cause for failure to observe invalidating or disqualifying laws. Thus, acts are generally invalid, even if the omission of the formalities required for validity is due to physical impossibility. *Gra.*

IMPOSTURE. Imposture is a deceitful action which foists upon another an article, basically worthless, as genuine, authentic, etc. It may also be the deceit which involves the false representations or identity of a person.

Imposture is sinful because it is misrepresentation and a form of deception. In itself, it is a venial sin, as long as it does not involve the violation of other virtues besides truthfulness. It can, however, become a mortal sin, if it implies a grave violation of justice, charity, or a disregard of virtue in general, or if the purpose intended or the means employed are gravely offensive. In addition to being a moral fault, it is also one of the most repulsive social failings, because it destroys mutual trust. At times, it may also be the effect of a morbid condition; in this case, of course, responsibility is reduced, and, at times, completely nonexistent (*see* Hysteria; Simulation, etc.).

IMPOTENCY (Canonical). Impotency in Canon Law is the inability or incapacity of a member of a married couple to perform the conjugal act. It may be *organic*, if it is due to anatomical defect, or *functional*, if it exists despite anatomical normality. Functional impotency is presumed to be temporary. In canonical jurisprudence, at least by a reflex principle since there is a doubt of law, the absence of internal genital organs (ovaries, uterus) in the woman is not considered to be impotency but sterility.

IMPOTENCY AS AN IMPEDIMENT. Antecedent and perpetual impotency, either on the part of the husband or the wife, whether known to the other party or not, and whether absolute or relative, invalidates marriage by the very law of nature (Can. 1068). If the impediment of impotency is doubtful, either as to fact or to law, marriage is not to be forbidden, although it is advisable that doubt be removed before the celebration of marriage (Can. 1068, par. 2). Sterility neither invalidates nor makes a marriage unlawful (Can. 1068, par. 3).

In order to prove impotency in a judicial forum, husband and wife must undergo a physical (corporal) examination by experienced physicians (usually two). If, after proper examination, there remains a positive doubt concerning the potency of the man or woman, the marriage cannot be declared null (Cans. 1976–1981).

If a marriage is declared null on the basis of impotency, the impotent party cannot marry again, except in a case of relative impotency. In the rare case in which a married person proves cure of impotency, formerly declared permanent by judges, the case must be re-opened. No dispensation can be given in a case of certain impotency (Can. 1068). Bar.

In Canon Law the sole form of impotency which is capable of invalidating a marriage is, in practice, the incapacity of a man or woman to perform the conjugal act (*impotentia coeundi*). Frigidity or sexual unresponsiveness is not a canonical impediment, although it is considered a mild form of impotency in medicine, because the primary purpose of marriage is not a sexual satisfaction dependent on responsiveness.

The inability to beget children (*impotentia generandi*) is referred to, in a general sense, as impotency but it is, in fact, distinct. This is called *sterility*, a term not adopted by all moralists.

CAUSES OF IMPOTENCY. Impotency in women, comparatively rare, is possibly due to an anatomical anomaly, which impedes the performance of the conjugal act, or to a peculiar functional disturbance known as *vaginism*. The latter, however, generally lacks the necessary requirements for a true and proper cause for invalidity of marriage. Impotency in men is more frequent. Apart from mutilations or local alterations, it may be due to any one of the psychic, nervous, hormonic, dyscrasic, toxic or other conditions that effect an inhibitory influence on the sexual act of the male. Many of these disturbances are not serious, nor do they possess the necessary characteristics to make them real and proper causes of invalidity.

In both sexes, impotency from malformations or organic lesions (instrumental) are infrequent and of negligible importance in medical or moral questions. The few thus affected easily recognize their condition, and accept this without involving others harmfully. In rare exceptions, if one should decide to marry, this is unwise and can occasion grounds for separation or annulment. A diagnosis of the disorder and medical and legal proof is generally readily available.

FUNCTIONAL IMPOTENCY. In *males*, cases of purely functional impotency are frequent; they are identified by age

factors, peculiar somatic or psychic diseases of a general nature, or exclusively neuropsychic disorders of the generative faculty, known as a *sexual psychoneurosis*. These cases interest the moralist, not merely because of their numbers, but because of diagnostic and evaluative difficulties, which favor simulation and concealment with obvious detrimental effects upon matrimonial morality.

Impotency with a psychoneurotic background is, generally, either a case of sexual neurasthenia or psychic impotency. This depends on the basic cause of the disorder, such as nervous disturbances, psychasthenia, or hysteria. These diseases with their peculiar backgrounds of development are discussed under the articles Neurasthenia, Psychasthenia, and Hysteria. It should be added that a study of the background is extremely important for diagnosis, since it is practically the only element that enables the specialist to correctly diagnose the case, whose symptoms are generally doubtful and are to be considered with the greatest reservation.

(a) *Sexual neurasthenia.* This clinical variation of neurasthenia consists of an irritable weakness of the spinal centers involved in the genetic function. Often identified by a premature ejaculation, it is intensified, because of a constitutional predisposition, by excessive local excitement, capable of producing a form of exhaustion of the above-mentioned spinal centers.

(b) *Psychic impotency.* This is always linked to a peculiar psychopathological source, generally of a psychasthenic nature; it frequently follows an incipient case of sexual neurasthenia, which becomes more complicated because of the anxious preoccupation which transforms the original form of neurasthenia into a more serious mixed form of neuropsychasthenia. Thus sexual psychoneurosis is stabilized by an inevitable, though often concealed, repercussion on the whole mental sphere.

In *women*, functional impotency is usually a painful act in conjugal relations or vaginism. If the disturbance is exclusively or primarily of a psychoneurotic nature, it is generally the result of hysteria. Other genesic female disturbances are *dyspareunia* and *frigidity* (*anaphrodisia*). These disturbances are, at times, aggravated by previous onanistic habits, sentiments of revulsion, or more common psychic fears of sexual contact, pregnancy, and real or pseudo-religious scruples.

IMPOTENCY IN MARRIAGE LEGISLATION. Sexual impotency of husband or wife can render marriage null and void. Impotency may be *absolute*, that is, extending to all other persons, or *relative*, with respect to one person, such as the spouse. Impotency, as a basic cause for nullity, is limited in Canon Law to antecedent, perpetual, and certain impotency (Can. 1068, par. 1). Medical testimony and the analysis of every element of indirect or presumed evidence combine to enable the judge to gain a moral certitude concerning the actual existence of impotency. Impotency is said to be permanent in canonical legislation, even if it could be cured by a serious surgical operation.

A physician aware of impotency is morally bound to advise the patient, as far as possible, to desist from marriage, since it would be invalid if contracted under such circumstances. Since it involves professional secrecy, the physician is not bound to make a canonical denunciation of the case.

A doubt regarding impotency in the mind of one of the contracting parties obliges that party to submit to physical examination by a reputable and experienced physician. The decision rests on his diagnosis. If the doubt remains, he may contract marriage, if he first warns the other party of the possibility, which that party accepts and then agrees to proceed with the marriage (Can. 1068, par. 2).

Marriage contracted despite doubt cannot be declared null and void. In certain impotency, the couple in good faith may be left in good faith, when serious difficulties are expected in a declaration of nullity of the marriage. In bad faith, the couple are under obligation to separate and live in perpetual continence. They must be admonished of this fact by those in authority.

SUICIDE AND SEXUAL PERVERSION. Impotency may lead to suicide, especially if the condition is the effect of psychasthenia and assumes the nature of an obsessional idea, whose destructive notion is intimately bound up with an inferiority complex. On the eve of marriage, such a condition might lead to despondency or suicide.

Impotency may also lead to exhibitionism, vampirism, and other perversions, as sexual satisfactions unavailable in normal sexual behavior.

IMPOTENCY QUOAD UXOREM. A particular form of impotency, distinct from ordinary psychic impotency, may be caused by the presence of a grave deformity or revolting disease concealed by the bride, which thereby renders the conjugal act impossible, since the man, who is normal, becomes impotent with respect to his wife because of this state. In such a case, the Church in all justice declares the marriage null and void, if the existence of impotency and the gravity or hopelessness of the disease in the woman is clearly proven. Since this is difficult in practice, the dispensation from a ratified but non-consummated marriage is more easily proven than is impotency. *Riz.*

IMPRECATION. In current theological language, *imprecation*, or *curse*, is practically synonymous with *malediction*. A curse is an expression of hatred or anger containing an invocation for harm or injury to oneself or another person or animal. Ordinarily, imprecation is confused with *blasphemy*. It should be noted, however, that imprecation or cursing is blasphemous only when it is directed against God, or people and things with a special relation to Him (*see* Blasphemy).

MORAL NOTES. Both imprecation and malediction may be a sin of superstition (*q.v.*), if one believes that a curse possesses in itself the power to cause the desired harm (magic words). At times these are aggravated by invocation of the devil. Generally, however, imprecation and malediction are considered as sins of uncharitableness or anger, inasmuch as they are contrary to Christian meekness and brotherly love. They are a serious sin, if serious harm, such as death or hellfire, is deliberately intended for oneself or a fellow being. These conditions are usually lacking when an imprecation is hurled in a fit of anger, when a person seeks to use forceful expressions to give vent to his enraged feelings. Generally, outside the possibility of scandal, it is not considered a serious sin if one curses animals.

On the other hand, an imprecation or malediction directed, even without animosity, against people to whom we owe special respect (parents, church officials) may quite likely be a grave sin (*see* Piety). Thus, too, an imprecation or malediction hurled against God, the saints, or other creatures, inasmuch as they reflect God's greatness, is always a grave sin against the virtue of religion (*see* Blasphemy). According to St. Alphonsus, maledictions hurled against the dead do not belong to this latter group, but are to be considered as simple imprecation, and in themselves venial sins. It should be noted that it is not a sin if no spiritual harm is wished on another by imprecations or maledictions, but physical harm to convert him or terminate a state of sin in which he may be involved, or serve as well-deserved punishment—as for example, in the imprecatory psalms. However, one must be careful in these cases, in view of the danger that such feelings might be prompted by hatred, grudge, and the like. *Pal.*

IMPRIMATUR. *See* Censure; Forbidden Books.

IMPRUDENCE. *See* Prudence.

IMPUBER. *See* Age.

IMPULSE. An impulse is the first natural and spontaneous reaction to a stimulus without the direct influence of the will. Impulses are: physical, especially in the sexual field (*see* Impurity), or psychic, i.e., the reaction of the sensitive appetite to an impression in the perceptive faculties from a pleasant or unpleasant object. According to an order of succession and increasing attention and will, impulses are usually distinguished into *first-primary*, without any deliberation; *second-primary*, with imperfect deliberation; and *secondary*, no longer impulses in the above-mentioned sense, but entirely voluntary.

Psychological impulses may precede, accompany, or follow the first advertence by the intellect concerning acceptance or rejection of the object of the stimulated appetite. Evil impulses, though often causing temptation, are not in themselves temptation (*q.v.*) because man, generally, is able to repress them immediately and without great difficulty, that is, without serious conflict between the will and the inordinate passion (*see* Passion).

MORAL ASPECTS. First-primary impulses are good or bad depending on the conformity of the object to the objective moral order; formally, these do not fall within the scope of morality because a human act is good or bad only insofar as it flows from the free will of man (*S. Theol.*, I–II, q. 74, a. 4). Second-primary impulses, even in serious matter, would constitute at most a venial sin. Although formally outside the moral scope, first-primary impulses are strictly related to morality as a cause, giving the first impulse to the will, which is frequently an occasion of good or bad acts, and as an effect. The remote cause of all evil is original sin, which deprived man of the preternatural gift of immunity from concupiscence (*q.v.*). Also, first-primary impulses may in a more immediate manner be the result of personal acts. As such, they are more or less voluntary in cause, in the sense that these acts either create a positive disposition of virtue or vice, from which the first-primary impulses really and readily originate, or exert a certain influence on the energy that should encourage or restrain them, particularly in sexual matters. The objects which are apt to provoke them more directly are also either sought for or avoided by these actions. *Dam.*

PHYSIOLOGICAL PREMISES. In neurophysiology, impulses are the active processes in the neurons of a stimulating or an inhibiting nature (*see* Inhibition).

In the first case, we speak of *excitation* and *stimulus*, and refer to *excitability* or *irritability* as the fundamental property of all living cells, but possessed in the highest degree by the nerve cells. This excitability reacts to changes in the external environment, called stimuli. Excitability is specific; each cell, according to its nature, reacts to the stimuli in its own characteristic way. Thus, if an electric stimulus is applied to a motor nerve, *it* will produce a muscular contraction; *if* applied to a sensitive nerve, it will produce a sensation of pain, etc. But the cell itself reacts in a specific manner, according to the nature of the stimulus. The nerve cells of the retina are excited in a specific manner by the light stimuli; those of the cochlea are excited by acoustic stimuli, etc.

NEUROPATHOLOGICAL ELEMENTS. Among the illnesses of the nervous system, some are characterized by a sluggishness of normal excitability, which at times may even disappear entirely, as in certain serious cases of medullary compression; others, more numerous, are characterized by excessive irritability. Typical of these is tetany, caused by a malfunctioning of parathyroid glands, and the very common neurasthenia (*q.v.*), one of whose principal symptoms consists in pronounced hypersensitiveness to the most varied stimuli and an excessive irritability of temperament.

IMPULSE IN PSYCHOLOGY. In current psychological language, impulse, instinct, and inclination are synonymous; however, it is helpful to distinguish one from the other. Thus, in psychology, we shall speak of *instinct* when referring to the tendency of an agent to perform acts without awareness of their purpose; of *inclination* when reference is made to a tendency accompanied by awareness of the purpose of the act.

Instinct (*see* Reflexes) are congenital and hereditary tendencies more proper to animals. By virtue of inflexible mechanisms and constant processes, they impel the animal to perform acts which are useful for its own survival as well as that of the species. In other words, they are the unchangeable, hereditary rules of a laborious, complex mechanism that guides animals in order that they may automatically take advantage of all environmental circumstances which aid in the procurement of nourishment, defense, and reproduction.

Inclinations, proper to man, are stimulated by the emotions and directed by the intelligence. They constitute superior psychological tendencies in which the will has its part. When a voluntary act is spurred by a greater intensity of sentiments, we speak of *impulse, impulsion, or impulsive act.* The appetites that more effectively stimulate impulses are the lower or sensorial sensations, such as pain, hunger, etc. Impulses are greatly enhanced by a lack of inhibiting power or power of self-control.

IMPULSE IN PSYCHIATRY. From the above it is easy to understand the reason for the frequent occurrence of impulsive acts among the mentally ill. From sudden, morbid impulses, generally without apparent reason, an action, sometimes criminal, automatically bursts forth, without opposition or remorse, even without awareness and, therefore, without subsequent recollection. Thus, we have the violent impulses of maniacs, due to psycho-motorial over-excitement; those of certain melancholics, as the sudden motorial discharge after a gradual accumulation of painful tension; of certain epileptics, in whom the impulses are the equivalent of convulsive manifestations; of the mentally confused and the schizophrenics under the impulse of hallucination, etc.

In psychasthenics, an entirely different type of impulses, that is, obsessive impulses, arise from the torment of an unrestrained idea to which the patient fears to have to submit, because he has no trust in his power of self-control. The psychasthenic is all too conscious of the impropriety or criminality of the act that has come to his mind. But while he opposes a strong resistance to it, he also develops an internal tension which becomes increasingly more troublesome, especially when it has to do with acts that are useless, ridiculous, perhaps improper but not morally wrong, until the inhibiting will gives in. The impulse is translated into an act, and the sick person experiences, for a short time, a relieving distention.

Another type of impulse, observed in

criminals, is due to an exuberance of tendencies in the lower instincts and a marked lack of inhibitory powers. These are frequently results of poor rearing and corruptive environmental influences.

MORAL COROLLARIES. True impulses belong to the field of psychiatry, for they are an expression of mental disturbance; hence, frequently, they are neither morally nor juridically imputable, for, in reality, these acts, for the most part, are performed indeliberately and involuntarily, as in the case of obsessive impulses. Where there has been neither awareness nor free will, there can be neither responsibility nor imputability. Granted, however, a minimum of freedom of choice, imputability would be proportionately small; yet it would exist. In any event, it should also be noted that, besides the responsibility of the act at the moment in which it is performed, a "responsibility in cause" (*see* Voluntary in cause) must also be taken into consideration. Under this latter aspect, mainly, acts committed by criminals and described as *by a tendency* (to indicate an absence of mental infirmity in the criminals, but an inclination toward a vicious and disorderly life) may be fully imputable to them.

Similar to the impulses of mentally ill individuals are those acts, even criminal, performed by a normal person but in the throes of a violent passion. In such cases, justice demands that the intensity of the passion experienced by the individual be taken into full account in establishing the exact degree of responsibility for the commission of a criminal act.

Finally, impulses are generally the result of an excess of emotion and a lack of inhibition. We must understand the importance of preventive education, both for improving and refining the sentiments, and, above all, for moderating and strengthening the power of self-control. *Riz.*

IMPUTABILITY. Imputability is the capability of ascribing an action or fact to a particular person as the cause or author of that act. An act performed by a person without necessary freedom implies physical imputability, which attributes an effect to its material cause. If the person performed the action as a free agent, then that person is responsible for the act by virtue of moral imputability. This is the concern of moral theologians. An *act* is imputable to a person, if he performed it with knowledge and freedom of activity in his will; a *fact* is imputable to an individual, if it is the effect of his free (*liber*) will and a deliberate act or a deliberate omission of an act, and if the effect was at least foreseen in a confused manner (*see* Voluntary in cause).

Moral imputability is predicated on freedom of the will in an agent; moral imputability increases or diminishes according to the degree of freedom of the will possessed by the agent in an act. In this regard, it should be noted that juridical imputability does not always coincide with moral imputability. Juridical imputability is more varied in its application than moral imputability, for legal imputability does not conform frequently to the outline of psychological reality, but is mainly motivated by social requirements. Thus, certain modern codes of law consider as definitely imputable an activity or action performed in the state of drunkenness. This criterion is psychologically wrong, but not unreasonable in the juridical order, since this alone effectively prevents abuses. *Gra.*

INABILITY. The absence or lack of capacity or legal qualification to validly perform certain specific acts is termed *inability;* the act declaring a person incapable is called *disqualification.* To protect the general welfare, society is at times obliged to enact laws regulating the validity of human acts and voiding them at times, despite the fact that a natural capability is present. By this restriction positive law does not violate the natural law, but regulates it in the light of specific circumstances in behalf of the general welfare, which must prevail over individual interests. We confine ourselves to inability in Canon Law.

NATURAL INABILITY. In general, inability is the lack of a capacity or legal qualification required for the performance of a juridical act, the possession of an office, benefice, or ecclesiastical dignity.

Inability, whether total or partial, is *natural,* if it is due to the lack of the requirements of the natural or divine law; for example, an incapability of performing a juridical act because of the lack of the use of reason, or the incapability of reception of the sacraments of the living because of the lack of baptism. A positive inability is determined by the positive ecclesiastical laws, such as the inability of a minor to personally exercise his rights (Can. 89), or the inability of a cleric to accept two offices which are incompatible (Can. 1439, par. 1), or the inability of a woman to exercise ecclesiastical authority.

PENAL INABILITY. A disqualification imposed by Canon Law, either on lay persons or clerics, as a punishment for a crime committed, is a penal inability. This penalty makes lay persons ineligible for specific graces or offices in a broad sense, and for academic degrees conferred by ecclesiastical authority (Can. 2291, par. 9). Clerics become ineligible for offices, benefices, honors, and ecclesiastical pensions according to Canon 2298 (par. 5). However, neither disqualified lay persons or clerics are to lose their rights previously acquired (Can. 2269, par. 2). The following disqualifications obtain effect immediately in both the internal and external forum: (1) a cleric who knowingly accepts an appointment which is invalid by virtue of interference of lay persons in the office or benefice involved (Can. 2390, par. 2); (2) a cleric who becomes infamous as the result of a crime (*infamia juris*) with respect to benefices, offices, honors, or pensions, and other lawful ecclesiastical acts (Can. 2294, par. 1); (3) a cleric who, without authorization, possesses an office, benefice, or ecclesiastical honor and exercises the rights connected with it, is disqualified for that office, benefice, honor, etc. (Can. 2394, par. 1); (4) the same applies to a cleric accepting an office or benefice that is not yet juridically vacant (*de jure*) (Can. 2395).

Moreover, certain cases require a declaration of disqualification from the superior before it comes into effect. Such cases of disqualification from offices, benefices, and ecclesiastical honors are:

clerics usurping and possessing the property and rights of the Roman Catholic Church (Cans. 2345–2346); clerics who hear the confession of a person whom they previously solicited in the confessional; a religious nun who, because of her position as a superior or one possessing authority over others, induces others to withhold the truth or facts from a canonical visitor (Can. 2413). One who is qualified by the general law can only be disqualified by the Apostolic See (Cans. 2296, par. 1; 2237, pars. 1 and 3). *Tec.*

INCAPACITY. *See* Capacity.

INCARDINATION. The Church has never approved of *vagrant* clerics, that is, clerics without a stable residence and corresponding dependence upon a particular superior. Thus, every cleric must belong either to a diocese or to a religious community (Can. 111, par 1). The canonical membership of a cleric in the clergy of a diocese is called *incardination.* Incardination by the lawful superior through a specific act is *formal,* if the act tends directly and formally to incardination; such is the incardination in writing of a member of the clergy following excardination (*q.v.*) from another diocese; incardination may be *virtual* (implied) if it is the indirect result of an act directed to another purpose, as in the case of a layman, who, by the reception of the first tonsure, becomes a member of the clergy and at the same time is incardinated into the diocese in whose service he was promoted (Can. 111, par. 2). A cleric, with permission to accept a residential benefice in another diocese, is by this very fact incardinated into this diocese (Can. 114). A religious in major orders (subdeacon, deacon, or priest) who, by virtue of perpetual religious profession, leaves his diocese, cannot exercise the duties of his major orders outside the religious organization until a bishop accepts him. The bishop may accept a secularized religious, either immediately and unconditionally, or for a probationary period of three years. If he is accepted unconditionally, the secularized religious is immediately incardinated into that diocese; otherwise, acceptance and subsequent incardination may occur during the probation period of three years. This probation, however, may be extended for another three years, at the end of which the secularized religious is automatically (*ipso facto*) incardinated into the diocese, unless he has been specifically rejected or dismissed by the bishop (Can. 641, par. 2). This is the only instance of an implicit incardination; it is termed implicit, because it is effected by the Code of Canon Law itself.

CONDITIONS. A *valid* formal incardination into another diocese requires that the cleric possess a letter of excardination from the bishop of the diocese to which he formerly belonged and a letter of perpetual and unconditional incardination into the new diocese from the bishop of that diocese (Can. 112). For a virtual incardination, the valid bestowal of a residential benefice, first tonsure, or the proper admission of the secularized cleric is sufficient. The bishop, vicar general with special mandate, or vicar capitular with the consent of the cathedral chapter, if such exists, has the power to incardinate a cleric, if the see of the diocese has been vacant for more than one year (Can. 113). In some countries, such as the United States, the diocesan administrator takes the place of the vicar-capitular, and the board of diocesan consultors takes the place of the cathedral chapter.

A licit formal incardination takes place if the diocese has need of priests; if the excardination has been lawfully executed; if the candidate's fitness is certified to by a document from his former curia; if the cleric has the intention to dedicate himself permanently to the services of the new diocese (Can. 117). The same conditions are required for a virtual incardination; these are: written approval by the bishop regarding a residential benefice in another diocese, or at least a permission in writing to leave his diocese permanently (Can. 114). *Toc.*

INCEST. Incest is the crime of cohabitation between persons related within the degrees in which marriage is prohibited by natural and positive human laws. The latter determine and perfect the extent of the former according to existing circumstances. Incest may originate from natural, spiritual, or legal relationship. (a) *Natural* relationship arises from consanguinity or natural affinity. In Canon Law (for non-Christians civil law applies), consanguinity constitutes a matrimonial impediment in every degree of the direct line, and extends to the third degree of the collateral line; affinity extends to and includes the second degree (Cans. 1076–1077). (b) *Spiritual* relationship, as a matrimonial impediment, exists between the baptized person and the minister of the sacrament of baptism, and the godfather or godmother (Can. 1079). (c) *Legal* relationship, arising from legal adoption (*q.v.*), is considered a matrimonial impediment by the Church only in those countries where it is recognized as such by civil law (Cans. 1059, 1080).

Morality. Incest is a sin of lust (*q.v.*) according to species, in which a grave sin against piety (*q.v.*) is added to the sin of fornication (*q.v.*). In Holy Scripture incest is condemned as a special sin (Lev. 18:6–18; 20:11–14; 1 Cor. 5:1–5).These are some of the reasons: (a) The children born of a union between close blood relatives are more apt to be subject to hereditary defects. (b) The reverence due to parents, either directly in their own person, or indirectly through the person most intimately bound to them by ties of blood, cannot be reconciled with sexual relation (*see also* Modesty). (c) In order to have a healthy family life, any sinful sexual element must be kept out of it; otherwise, the natural order of procreation would be subject to continuous violations.

The instinctive horror of sexual relations between closer relatives indicates the unnatural character of these acts. Spiritual incest adds to the sin against piety a sin against religion (*see* Sacrilege). It is a disputed question whether incest between direct blood relatives is a different species of sin from that between collateral blood relatives. St. Thomas and other theologians deny this because in both cases the basic reason for the prohibition is the same: consanguinity. Another point in question is the extent to which the different degrees of kinship constitute different species of incest. It is almost unanimously agreed that incest with a first degree blood relative or affinity in the direct line constitutes a particular species of incest because the blood tie is immediate, and the prohibition is invariable in the order of nature. In the other degrees, the tie is not immediate, and the impropriety of the sexual relationship is more by participation; hence, in these degrees law and custom allow certain variations. Several theologians consider incest between brother and sister as distinct from incest between other degrees of blood relation. There definitely is no difference of species in the other degrees of relationship. *Dam.*

INCONSTANCY. Inconstancy is a lack of perserverance in pursuing the desire for good. It may stem from a definite instability of character, the dread of annoyances, the necessity of repetition and effort, or from other discomforts.

Inconstancy is a sin against the virtue of perseverance and prudence. Of itself it is generally a venial sin. It can, however, become a mortal sin by reason of the importance of omitted action or effort, the seriousness of the neglect or because of other circumstances. *Man.*

INCONTINENCE. *See* Abstinence; Continence; Chastity.

INCONVENIENCE. In moral theology and law, inconvenience is a condition rendering the observance of a law or the fulfillment of a certain obligation particularly difficult for an individual. Inconvenience can be more or less grave and, in certain cases, may constitute a reasonable excuse from observance of a law, or from fulfillment of an obligation. Inconvenience admits of various degrees. Extreme inconvenience is equivalent to moral impossibility. An inconvenience is called serious, if the difficulty is serious; mediocre or slight, if the difficulty, though consistent, is not serious. Moral theologians speak of general and specific inconvenience. To judge the extent of inconvenience in general as an excusing cause from observing a law, comparison must be made each time between the law

and the obligation it imports and the seriousness of the inconvenience. Inconvenience as an excusing cause does not apply to a prohibiting law of nature, because such laws forbid acts that are intrinsically evil and, therefore, never permitted. One such case would be blasphemy. Laws of nature are binding, even in the face of danger to life, which is the greatest possible inconvenience.

The principle of inconvenience as an excusing cause is valid only for preceptive natural law, divine-positive law, or human ecclesiastical or civil law, except when their non-observance entails contempt of authority, public damage, or scandal.

Furthermore, inconvenience is a valid excusing cause, if the inconvenience is grave and concerns only an extrinsic difficulty, namely, one that is not inseparable from the ordinary execution of the law.

To estimate the value of inconvenience as a cause excusing from the fulfillment of the obligation, comparison must be made between the need of the one asking help, the hierarchies of value, the degree of inconvenience encountered, the relationship existing between the one in need and the benefactor, and the anticipated efficacy of the assistance given.

Moral theologians ordinarily divide the hierarchies of value into two classes: spiritual and material; and the needs of our neighbor belong to one of these classes. Thus the degree of need may be (a) *very serious* or *extreme* material or spiritual need, involving temporal life or eternal life, which would be lost without aid; (b) *serious*, if without assistance one would be in danger of eternal damnation or the loss of a serious temporal good other than life; (c) *slight* or *ordinary*, such as the need experienced by every sinner or one in poor economic straits.

The following conclusions may be drawn. (1) We are obliged to assist anyone in extreme spiritual need, even to the point of danger to our own life, beyond a grave inconvenience, provided that there exists a well-founded hope of success. (2) We must aid one in extreme physical need, or in serious spiritual and material need, in the face of average inconvenience, unless more weighty and particular reasons, such as close relationship, exist to demand assistance to the needy. (3) We must aid one in ordinary material or spiritual need at the expense of a slight inconvenience to the one helping his neighbor. These norms are particularly relevant in matters dealing with the administration of the sacraments and alms-giving. *Pal.*

INCORPORATION. *See* Innovation.

INCREDULITY, UNBELIEF. To withhold an act of faith or to refuse to make an inquiry about the faith when one is sufficiently exposed to revelation to query its significance is termed incredulity or unbelief. The assent of faith is subjectively binding upon everyone who achieves a rational certainty about the divine origin of the Christian religion with a certain judgment of its credulity. The essential distinction, from the aspect of knowledge of the object and motive, between the judgment of faith and the judgment of credibility, admits of the possibility of an individual refusing to make an act of belief in the Christian religion, even though he is convinced that it is revealed truth. This possibility is rare, however.

Ordinarily, lack of faith is associated with a deficient judgment of credibility; hence, culpability in a lack of faith depends on the degree of culpability in the deficient judgment of credibility.

Incredulity as a psychological problem. The rejection of revelation raises serious problems from the psychological and theological points of view. These problems may be formulated as follows: (1) In what does the rejection of revelation consist, and how can it be explained from the psychological point of view? (2) Is it possible to lose one's faith without being guilty of it?

A man may, through his own fault, fail to arrive at the knowledge of revealed truth. This is not necessarily a rejection of faith; for example, a Protestant simply due to negligence fails to embrace Catholicism. He does not reject the Christian faith; in fact, he may be habitually disposed to accept the truth as soon as it becomes evident to him. His attitude is not one of formal opposition to the authority of God, the Revealer.

Does rejection of faith necessarily consist in the fact that a man, with a knowledge of revelation, refuses to give it his assent? This has been held by some authors; absolutely speaking, it is possible, as the very nature of the act of faith indicates; but, from the psychological standpoint, it is hardly conceivable and certainly quite rare, in reality.

A true rejection of faith consists, instead, in an abhorrence of the truth. In this act a person either chooses to ignore revelation, simply because he does not want to accept it, or willfully denies its truth, despite the fact that he has acquired sufficient knowledge of it. A rather frequent case, psychologically explained by the fact that the metaphysical certitude about a religious truth in the natural order and a moral certitude about the reality of revelation and its proof, are not mere mathematical certitudes that cannot be dimmed by a truly serious doubt. Certitude in faith develops progressively in one's mind, by a process of overcoming minor doubts that may arise regarding the truths of faith. At times man's intelligence prefers to dwell on such doubts rather than to heed truths which conflict with human passions and human interests. It is true that many people become guilty of a refusal to accept the light of truth.

Faith can be lost through one's fault; incredulity, as error, may be sinful. However this difficulty may arise: if a heretic or an unbeliever may legitimately entertain doubts about religious truths and, from doubt, start on his spiritual journey to full acceptance of Christ and the Church, why cannot a Catholic entertain doubts about his faith without guilt? This parallel, if understood as the objective equalization of truth and error, must be absolutely rejected; it is unacceptable from a subjective point of view, because the gift of faith in the true Church of God is entirely different from the state of practising a false religion. This is so for two reasons, one of them logical, the other psychological.

Error cannot retain the same force as truth. Grace, which aids a man in error to come to a knowledge of truth, strengthens also the faith of those who have passed from unbelief to faith by means of grace. It can be said that God does not abandon man, but that man turns away from God.

Loss of faith is, therefore, always due to sin; frequently it is a series of violations and general compromises, which gradually pave the way to apostasy.

The solution to the problem, from the standpoint of grace as well as the power of truth, applies only to the believer, who is cognizant of his faith due to the guidance of the Church. *Pal.*

INDEMNITY. *See* Damage; Restitution.

INDEX OF FORBIDDEN BOOKS. The Index of Forbidden Books is a catalog of books condemned by the Holy See as dangerous to faith and morals. Such books may not be either read or kept without special permission (*see* Forbidden Books). As early as 1497, Innocent VIII and a few years later, in 1507, Alexander VI decreed that printers in certain provinces in Germany should submit books for publication to censorship. The bishops of those provinces were also ordered to collect condemned books in circulation and to forbid the reading or keeping of them. The Fifth Lateran Council, under Leo X, in 1513, extended a similar law to the entire Church. Consequently, in various cities, by order of the bishops, catalogs were compiled of books that should neither be read nor kept. Thus, in 1542, shortly after the invention of the printing press, Paul III appointed a commission to examine all books that could be harmful to Christians. In 1557, by order of Paul IV, a catalog was published in which all books containing moral or dogmatic errors were listed or *indexed.* This book was called the *Index.* Since then, many other editions have been published, the latest in 1948.

Extent of the Index. In this task the Church moves with great caution. No book is placed on the Index without accurate and thorough examination by men well-versed in the subject matter of the book. This examination is done with objectivity and caution. Thus, when a book is placed in the Index, there is a moral certainty that it is at least dangerous. As well as a warning, such judgment by the Church is also a prohibition enjoined on the faithful as a protection from dangers to their salvation.

The prohibition of a book is not, in itself, a personal criticism of the author, nor a judgment of the literary value of the book, but merely a practical conclusion indicating that the reading of a particular book by the faithful is believed to entail a proximate danger to their faith or morals. All books, whether by living and known authors or by unknown and dead ones, fall under the censuring authority of the Congregation of the Index, which is now part of the Sacred Congregation of the Holy Office (*see* Congregations, Roman). The task of the Congregation is, not to formulate discussions or scientific conclusions for the benefit of scholars, but to examine the book diligently to see whether it is free of moral and doctrinal errors and to prohibit its reading and possession if found to contain ideas considered dangerous to faith or morals.

Appeal against the prohibition of a book is allowed but it does not have a *suspending effect* (Can. 1395, par. 2). This means that the prohibition stands while the appeal is pending. The decrees of condemnation of books are also valid for the faithful of the Eastern Church (S. Congregation pro Ecclesia Orientali, May 26, 1928).

Obligations of the faithful. Laws concerning the Index of Forbidden Books bind in conscience; such an obligation is of its very nature grave, although admitting of light matter. As laws issued to avoid a general danger, they are binding on all, even in a particular case where no danger would seem to exist (Can. 21). Concerning the gravity of the sin in reading such books, *see* Forbidden Books.

All the faithful, especially the clergy, have the duty to report to the Ordinary or the Holy See any book which they consider dangerous. This is required particularly of legates of the Holy See, Ordinaries, and rectors of Catholic Universities (Can. 1397). Some regard the Index as a means of thought control by the Church. Nothing could be farther from the truth. The truth is that, since the Church's mission is the salvation of souls, she considers it her sacred duty to protect her children from evil, regardless of its source, at least by warning them against certain dangers into which they might stumble unawaredly, but with no less destructive consequences. It is obviously erroneous for anyone to think that to forbid the reading of bad books means to obstruct either progress or scholarship. The prohibition aims simply at obstructing evil, which leads inevitably to ruin and decay. Besides the obligation of using all the possible means to attain faith and a life of grace, man must also preserve, protect, and defend his faith and grace. Natural law requires that we avoid not only evil itself but also the proximate occasion of evil. And the reading of bad books is certainly at least an occasion of sin. Concerning the possibility of obtaining permission to read forbidden books, *see* Forbidden Books. *Tar.*

INDIFFERENT ACT, MORAL. A morally indifferent act is one which is neither good nor bad. Moral theologians dispute whether such an act is concretely possible. The question is difficult, nor is there complete agreement among authors. For the sake of clarity we shall keep the various questions separate. All moral theologians agree that certain acts, considered only in themselves or in the abstract, can be indifferent; for example, writing, walking, and the like. Thus, too, all admit the possibility that certain acts performed without deliberation may remain indifferent in concrete practice. There is a difference of opinion, however, with respect to acts deliberately performed. According to the more common doctrine, which is also that of St. Thomas, there can be no indifferent acts in the restricted and precise sense of the word. This opinion is based on the consideration that, insofar as an agent is concerned, the determining factor in placing such acts is always a certain motive or end, which removes that act

from the sphere of indifference. If the motive is in conformity with the nature of man, the act become morally good; if it is not in conformity with man's nature, it becomes a morally evil act. The opinion which taught the possibility of morally indifferent acts, even though deliberate and concrete, is attributed to Scotus.

Pursuing the problem further, moral theologians ask whether, apart from its indifference, a deliberate act is always meritorious or not. Among various answers, the most convincing one seems to be that of St. Thomas and the Thomists. According to them, an act becomes supernaturally meritorious if it is elicited under the influence of charity (*see* Merit). *Gra.*

INDIFFERENTISM, RELIGIOUS. Religious indifferentism is theoretical or practical. Theoretical religious indifferentism is a tendency to consider all religions as equal, or to proclaim religious belief as an irrelevant aspect of the righteousness and salvation of the soul. While it strives to dissociate intellectual life from practical conduct, it contradicts the most elementary principles of psychology, thereby leading to conclusions that are pedagogically erroneous. For in actual fact, religious indifferentism is one of the most destructive heresies of all time. This subjectivism tries to justify itself on the grounds of the supposed exigencies of liberty, but it ignores the rights of objective truth, as manifested by the light of both reason and revelation. It thus concludes with the proposition that religion is an entirely individual matter, to be adapted to the disposition of each individual who will fashion his own religion, or that one religion is as good as another, even though they be contradictory to each other. The hostility of indifferentism to Catholicism, above all, is explained by its aversion to a higher authority naturally enforcing a uniform adherence to one, absolute Truth as presented in the most definite and concrete way in the Catholic Church.

Practical religious indifferentism opposes more the spirit than the content of the faith. It manifests itself by neglecting the practices of religious life and the observance of the precepts of the Church. *Pal.*

INDIFFERENTISM (SCHOLASTIC).
See School, Lay.

INDISSOLUBILITY OF MARRIAGE.
Any validly contracted marriage enjoys intrinsic indissolubility by virtue of the natural and divine laws. Such a marriage may be dissolved neither by the consent of the parties to the contract nor by any other human authority. This also holds true with regard to a marriage contract not raised to the dignity of a sacrament (*Syllabus*, n. 67).

The abiding stability of marriage is conducive to the proper rearing of children and necessary for the welfare of society and of husband and wife, despite the fact that in certain particular cases it may prove burdensome for some individuals. Consequently, not even civil authority has the right to dissolve a lawful marriage, that is, a marriage between two non-baptized persons. A sacramental marriage, or marriage between two baptized persons, if consummated, can be dissolved only by death. If not consummated, a dispensation can be obtained from the Sovereign Pontiff. The same also applies in the case of a marriage between two non-baptized persons. By virtue of the Pauline privilege (*q.v.*), the marriage between two non-baptized persons may be dissolved after the baptism of one of the parties, if the other party is not willing to live together without offense to the Creator.

Effects of marriage indissolubility. The law of indissolubility gives rise to the impediment of bond (*ligamen*), by reason of which any successive marriage attempted by one bound by a former marriage is invalid. Since it is an impediment of divine law, not even the Sovereign Pontiff can dispense from this (Can. 1069, par. 1). A decree of nullity obtained through fraud or error does not dissolve the marriage bond; any future union is invalid despite the decree. No new marriage may be properly contracted unless termination of the first bond has been established legitimately and with

certainty. By reason of the indissolubility of the bond of marriage, a validly married person who attempts a new marriage commits a sin of bigamy, (*see* Bigamy). *Bar.*

INDIVIDUALISM.
This term is applied to philosophical, political and economic beliefs which are referred to as liberalism in European and papal writings, but considered in the United States as individualistic liberalism or simply individualism. Historically, it is rooted in the Renaissance, humanism, illuminism, and rationalism.

Individualism extolls the value of the individual, his individual liberty against authority, his individual activity against social activity; it may attribute to the human person qualities which it does not have (*see* Human Being). Individualism is based on the pinciples that man is sufficient unto himself (autarchy) and responsible only to himself (autonomy). One's own conscience is the only criterion of good and evil.

Individualism manifests itself mainly in religion, ethics, politics, and economics. Religious individualism rejects any definite *credo* or submission to an external religious authority, acknowledging only the autonomy of the voice of conscience. Political individualism is based on J. J. Rousseau's *Social Contract* (formal democracy). Socio-economic individualism is derived from the theory of Hobbes, who denies natural social law, and holds that man is by nature but an egotistic being. Therefore, according to individualism, the individual is the only social reality, whereas society is only a reality derived from and dependent on the free will of man. As these theories evolved, they gradually took form in everyday life, legislation, economic activities, and institutions.

INDIVIDUALISM AS A WAY OF LIFE. Individualism holds the autonomy of reason, which becomes the ultimate judge of Revelation and the doctrine of the Church. It places an unlimited faith in the power of the intellect and is inseparable from the rationalism of the seventeenth and eighteenth centuries. It rejects all that the intellect cannot grasp. Hence, it intends the secularization of public life. The State is neutral: it professes tolerance for all currents of thought and cults; it gives a maximum of liberty to science, art, literature, the theatre, economy, etc. The Church, defender of the principle of authority, is expelled from the schools and denied any competency in marriage. Individualism believes in the essential goodness of human nature and its infinite capacity for evolution, as well as in the harmony between free individuals and their interests. The greater the liberty, the greater also is progress and order. This is the road to the unlimited autonomy of economy, science, politics, etc. Individualism is, therefore, anthropocentric. It makes man the center and the ultimate end, while the free evolution of his natural faculties is considered the whole purpose of life.

INDVIDUALISM IN SOCIAL LIFE. Since the liberty of the individual is a fundamental principle of individualism, the entire social structure rests on this principle. Society is no longer an organism with its manifold internal, moral, vital relations but an automatism, a mechanism, without the common good as its end, and an aggregate of free individuals who regulate their interests on the basis of selfish motives. Another principle is that each human activity (politics, economics, science, literature, art, etc.) must be governed by its own internal laws; all outside intervention, even those arising from the norms of ethics and religion, are to be excluded. This gives rise to the separation of life from religion and of culture from the Church. These are also the principles followed by the secular State, which, as a juridical State, should be a guarantor of the freedom and security of the individual and of property; this State is ironically called by Lassalle *the night watchman* (Police State).

INDIVIDUALISM IN ECONOMIC LIFE. The principles affecting the masses more directly during the reign of individualism were the principles and activities carried on in the economic field. With the fall of the guilds, individualism declared that the welfare of society could better be attained if the autarchic and autonomous individual pursued only his own interests (*laissez faire*). Hence, freedom of production, work contracts, traffic, exchange, and the market were necessary—all regulated naturally according to free supply and demand, free production and need, profits and prices (Law of Demand and Supply).

This capitalistic form increased production to unexpected proportions with an enormous technical progress which enhanced the economic possibilities for an increased population in the world. But by the second half of the nineteenth century, individualism began to disown its own principles in the economic field with the formation of concentrations, monopolies, cartels, trusts, etc., on the labor market. As a reaction, workers' unions and syndicates of employers developed. From this competition arose a struggle for power, a real class struggle with periodical crises and economic chaos (the typical crisis of 1929). The social characteristics of individualism (de-humanization, omnipotence of money, exploitation, etc.) gave rise to bitter criticism on the part of Catholics and socialists, although the latter have not succeeded in freeing themselves from it.

EVALUATION OF INDIVIDUALISM. Individualism was a general reawakening of the middle class in reaction to political absolutism. Therefore, it was a fight for freedom, honor, the rights of the human person, restriction of governmental powers, free development of forces about to assert themselves. But freedom of the human person is not limitless. To rights there correspond respective obligations. There is no such thing as an isolated individual, because, in one way or another, his being belongs to the various social communities of the past, the present, and the future. Individualism has exaggerated the individual side of man to the detriment of the social; communism (*q.v.*) moved to the opposite extreme. All the high-sounding words of individualism have proved fallacious. Liberty and equality meant slavery for millions of human beings. The widely heralded religious tolerance (*q.v.*) turned into atrocious anticlericalism, accepting into society all types of subversive tendencies and passions, thus threatening the foundations of morality and of society itself. Individualism has clearly shown that, without spiritual help, the human being becomes a slave of material things. Proof of this is found in bolshevism, a logical and inevitable evolution of individualism. Therefore, the main error of individualism is ignorance of the mysteries of original sin and of Redemption. Contrary to Rousseau's claim, without supernatural grace man cannot be *good*. There is no liberty without obligations; there are no personal rights without social duties. More than a century ago the Church rose up against the errors of individualism, through the *Syllabus* of Pope Pius IX (1864), the encyclicals of Pope Leo XIII (especially *Libertas, Immortale Dei, Rerum novarum*), and other Catholic documents.

INDOLENCE. Indolence is a tendency to laziness or slowness in acting. It may be a morbid disposition, the effect of abulia, a lack of will power, or other illnesses, particularly of a psychic nature; but it may also be simply the result of lack of initiative or a dread of exertion. As a dread of exertion or effort, indolence is a moral fault. Insofar as it is contrary to the universal law by which all are supposed to work, the sin of indolence ordinarily is not, in itself, serious. It can, however, become serious if it leads a person to the neglect of serious obligations or becomes a mode of living. Indolence is a fertile ground for temptations and impedes serious progress toward moral perfection. *Pal.*

INDUCEMENT. *See* Cooperator (in evil).

INDULGENCE. *Historical notes.* Forms of indulgences are found in the very early days of the Church. The mitigation granted by St. Paul (2 Cor. 2:6–8) of the punishment inflicted on the incestuous Corinthian, is generally considered as an indulgence.

During the course of the centuries, the Church has exercised this power of granting indulgences, but not always in the same form. In the first centuries, indulgences appear in the form of reduction or mitigation of penalties established in the penitential canons. Later, beginning with the seventh century, we find so-called *Redemptions* and *Roman Peregrinations*, which were titles for the reduction or substitution of a penalty. Indulgences, properly so-called, appear in the eleventh century; among them, the more notable ones were connected with the Crusades. In the fifteenth century we have indulgences for the dead. This custom increased until the time of the Council of Trent, which defined the authority of the Church with respect to indulgences, explained their usefulness for the Christian people, and eliminated all abuses.

DEFINITION AND NATURE. An indulgence is defined as follows: "An indulgence is the remission before God of the temporal punishment due for sins already forgiven insofar as their guilt is concerned, which the ecclesiastical authority, drawing from the treasure of the Church, grants to the living by way of absolution, and to the dead by way of suffrage" (Can. 911, Code of Canon Law). From this definition it appears that an indulgence may be considered as complementary to the sacrament of penance. In fact, in confession the guilt is remitted and the eternal punishment that follows every grave sin is condoned, but the temporal punishment that remains after any sin whatsoever is not always, nor completely, remitted. Remission of such temporal punishment may be obtained in this life by means of expiatory works and indulgences; otherwise, due satisfaction must be made in purgatory.

The granting of an indulgence is an act of jurisdiction requiring proper authority in the one granting it, and the state of grace in the one receiving it. As long as there is mortal sin, there can be no remission of guilt. Such remission, which is operative in the external as well as the internal forum, is granted to the living by means of *absolution*, that is, the remission by an act of judicial authority which can be exercised only on one's own subjects. For the dead, instead, it is granted by way of suffrage, inasmuch as, on the basis of the dogma of the communion of saints, the Church or her individual members availing themselves of her generosity offer to God the merits of Christ and the saints in satisfaction for the debt of justice which the deceased may still owe to God (*S. Theol., Suppl.* 25, a. 2, ad 1).

Indulgences are drawn from the treasury of the Church, "a treasury of supererogation," as St. Albert the Great says, "containing the superabundant merits of the passion of Jesus Christ, of the glorious Virgin Mary, the Apostles and martyrs, and of all the saints of God, living and dead." (St. Thomas, *In IV Sent.*, D. XX, q.1, a.2). Their distribution is effected by virtue of the communion of saints, which makes possible the interchange of spiritual merits and goods among the members of the Mystical Body of Christ (1 Cor. 12:16). The power to grant indulgences belongs to the Church. This truth was defined by the Council of Trent (Sess. XXV, *Decr. de indulg.*), and is founded on the so-called "power of the keys" given by Jesus to St. Peter (Matt. 16:19) and his successors.

An indulgence may be *plenary* or *partial*. A plenary indulgence is that by which full remission is obtained for all the temporal punishment. It can be an absolutely (*totaliter*) or relatively (*relative*) plenary indulgence, according to the disposition of the individual (Can. 926). Unless the contrary is expressly stated, a plenary indulgence may be gained only once a day. When it is possible to obtain it more than once a day, it is called a plenary indulgence *toties quoties*. Famous among these is the *Portiuncula*. An indulgence is *partial* when by it a partial remission of the temporal punishment is gained. Unless the contrary is stated, it can be gained more than once a day. An indulgence may be *personal*, *real*, and *local*, depending on whether it is granted directly to certain persons or groups of persons, or is attached to the use of certain objects of devotion, or is granted for visiting certain holy places (shrines). It may also be granted in *perpetuity* or *temporarily*; that is, it may be gained at all times or only on certain particular occasions. Indulgences may ap-

ply to the *living* or only to the *dead*, or to the *living and the dead*.

The ordinary conditions required for gaining a plenary indulgence are: confession, Communion, a visit to a church or public oratory (a semi-public oratory for those who can legitimately use it), and prayer according to the intentions of the Holy Father. Confession, when required, must be made within eight days before or after the day on which the indulgence may be gained; it is required also of those who are not in mortal sin. Communion must be sacramental. The Easter Communion is valid, provided that it is not a Jubilee; Communion received as viaticum is valid. Communion must be received within nine days, from the eve of the indulgence to eight days after the day on which the indulgence may be gained (Can. 931, par. 1). The visit to a church is governed by a decree of the Sacred Apostolic Penitentiary, issued on September 20, 1933, which states that it must be accompanied by some oral and mental prayer. By disposition of Can. 934, par. 1, the prayer should be both mental and oral, but the actual choice of prayers is left to the discretion of the faithful. According to the decree of the Sacred Apostolic Penitentiary mentioned above, in oral prayer it is sufficient to recite one *Pater, Ave,* and *Gloria*. In the case of a plenary indulgence *toties quoties*, six *Paters, Aves,* and *Glorias* must be recited on each visit (ASS, 25, 1933, 446; AAS, 22, 1930, 363).

For partial indulgences, the clause "*at least with a contrite heart*" is generally added. More than a condition, this clause is to be understood as a disposition, inasmuch as the state of grace is necessary as an essential requirement for gaining any indulgence whatsoever (*Decr. auth. cit.*, n. 427).

ADVERSARIES. The forerunners of the enemies of indulgences were the Valdesians, who appeared in the thirteenth century. Their leader was condemned by the Third Lateran Council (1179), and his followers were excommunicated by Pope Lucius III (1184). But the true and direct adversaries of indulgences were the Wyclifites and the Hussites, condemned by the Council of Constance. This condemnation was issued by Pope Martin V, in the Bull *Inter cunctas*, February 22, 1418 (Mansi, XXVII, 1209, 1212; Denz., 622, 676 ff.). In the second half of the fifteenth century, there appeared in Germany two adversaries of indulgences: John Ruchrath of Wesel, and Wessel Gansfort of Groningen, and almost at the same time, Peter of Osma, in Spain, who was condemned by Pope Sixtus IV in the Bull *Licet ea*, August 9, 1478.

It was the religious strife that broke out at the beginning of the sixteenth century that marked the most violent struggle against indulgences, at the principal instigation of Martin Luther. In the beginning he seemed to be attacking the selling of indulgences, but later he attacked the indulgences themselves, calling them pious frauds invented to make money. He was condemned by Leo X in the Bull *Exsurge Domine*, June 15, 1520. Immediately after Luther, Michael Baius and Michael Molinos came out against indulgences, followed by the Jansenists, who were condemned by the Bull *Auctorem fidei*, August 28, 1794.

APOCRYPHAL INDULGENCES. Innumerable apocryphal indulgences have been circulated at different times among the Christian people down through the centuries, especially by the *quaestores* or *quaestuarii* appointed to collect the alms required for the gaining of indulgences. The Church, however, used every suitable means for checking and preventing abuses. False indulgences were condemned by several councils convened for this specific purpose. Most notable among others was the Council of Trent, which abolished the office and name of *quaestores*. It further established that, in the future, indulgences were to be granted without any compensation. Subsequently, certain Roman Congregations, especially the Sacred Congregation of the Holy Office (*see* Congregations, Roman), continued this work of supervision and vigilance against abuses. This work was later taken over by the Sacred Congregation of Indulgences, established for the purpose of eliminating abuses and apocryphal indulgences. *de* A.

INDULGENCE (PLENARY). *See* Indulgence.

INDULGENCE (PORTIUNCULA). *See* Indulgence.

INDULGENCE (TOTIES QUOTIES). *See* Indulgence.

INDULT. An *indult* is a general and rather vague term which is used to indicate any benevolent concession by authority, in which individuals or groups are exempted from the obligation to conform to a law (*see* Dispensation, Privilege). An indult may be temporary or perpetual; particular, general, or universal. *Gra.*

INDUSTRIALISM. Industrialism is characteristic of our modern economic world due to the large prevalence of machinery over other means of production. The history of the economy of the Western world is usually divided into four periods: slavery, serfdom, craftmanship, and capitalism. The first three periods extend over many centuries. Despite the various levels of productivity in each era, the greatest amount of production during that very long period was the result of sheer human labor, though man always made use of some mechanical instruments (knife, hammer, needle, plow, etc.) in connection with his work. In the present era, however, production and circulation of wealth are attained to a large extent by complex machineries run by natural forces. In the use of these, for the most part, man has only an accessory role, though he retains a directive part in the overall operation.

Early significant successes in the textile fields gave impetus to industrialization in the mining, iron, metallurgical, chemical, and transportation fields. Today industry concerns that vast area opposed to, or at least distinct from, the area of agriculture. However, as a result of enormous chemical-biological progress, the process of industrialization is being extended more and more to the field of agriculture, in farming itself and the processing of farm products. It can be said that there is no sphere of social life that is not affected by industrialization, whether it be schools, amusements, medicine, banking, or other fields of human endeavor.

DEFECTS AND MERITS. It is often said that industrialization has marked the triumph of machine over man, more than the trimuph of man over nature. Urbanization, a disintegration of craftsmanship, and salary-system in its historical sense have been and are distinctly negative socio-human aspects. Man, however, by hard struggle, is slowly regaining his former position. Larger and more vigorous labor organizations, political trends more in keeping with the times, social legislations embued with genuinely human solicitude, a progressive insertion of labor relations into the juridical order, a growing interest of the worker in the activities of the industrial plants—all are milestones in the struggle that man is waging over the machine, a struggle that can lead to full victory. The machine then becomes what it should be—a means by which man turns the forces of nature into his service, and frees himself from humiliating and hard labor, thus gaining more time in which he may attend to a greater spiritual enrichment of his being. *Pav.*

INEBRIATION. *See* Alcoholism; Dipsomania.

INFALLIBILITY, PONTIFICAL. *See* Pontiff, Supreme.

INFAMY. Infamy, the opposite of a good name, is a public disgrace or loss of reputation, incurred by a person convicted of a definite crime (*see* Reputation). The reason for infamy can be: evil public behavior, defamation, or a just punishment (*infamia juris*).

Infamy is a grave damage. Hence, there arises a moral obligation for everyone to avoid it for oneself and to refrain from bringing it upon another. (*See also* Sinner, Public; Defamation.) *Ben.*

INFAMY OF LAW AND OF FACT (*iuris et facti*). Infamy of law (*iuris*), in the Code of Canon Law, is a vindictive penalty incurred for committing certain

crimes (Can. 2293, par. 2). The ecclesiastical legislator, however, also considers the total or partial loss of reputation, that is, the respect of good and wise men, as a *de facto* condition, independent of any penalty, and attaches to it certain juridical effects. Infamy of law does not arise canonically from a conviction by a lay judge, even if the penalty is of a degrading nature, unless Canon Law expressly carries such a penalty (*see*, for example, Canon 2354, par. 2). Such sentences can, however, effect infamy of fact (*facti*). Infamy in Canon Law, therefore, is either of law or of fact (Can. 2293, par. 1).

(a) *Infamy of law* arises directly and immediately from the disposition of the law, for a crime to which, by common law, automatically (*ipso facto*), without declaratory sentence, the penalty of infamy is attached, even for an occult crime (Can. 2232, par. 1), or following a condemnatory sentence. The cases in which infamy arises automatically (*latae sententiae*) from crime, are well defined (Can. 2320; 2328; 2343, par. 1 M. 2; par. 2 M. 2; 2351, par. 2; 2354, par. 1). They include the most serious crimes, e.g., those committed against the Sacred Species (Can. 2320) or graves (Can. 2328). Those who are to be declared infamous are so indicated by the legislator; such are apostates, heretics and schismatics who, after being admonished, fail to show signs of repentance (Can. 2314, par. 1, #2) and clerics who, after receiving major orders, commit crimes against the sixth commandment (Can. 2359, par. 2).

(b) *Infamy of fact* is incurred when, either through the commission of a crime or evil conduct, one has lost his good repute with righteous and serious Catholics; the judgment as to whether infamy of fact exists in a given case, is vested in the Ordinary (Can. 2293, par. 3). In no case does infamy affect the offender's blood-relations or relatives by marriage, although (*see* Can. 2147, par. 2, #3) the loss of reputation by relatives of a parish priest who live with him could be sufficient reason for removal of the pastor from the parish itself (Can. 2293, par. 4; also Can. 987, #1).

Effects of Infamy. (a) One who has incurred infamy of law is not only irregular (Can. 984, #5) but also disqualified from receiving benefices, pensions, ecclesiastical offices and dignities; from performing legal ecclesiastical acts; from discharging any ecclesiastical right or duty; from the exercise of all sacred functions (Can. 2294, par. 1). Consequently, the reception of a benefice or office, or the performance of a legal ecclesiastical act by one who has incurred infamy of law, is invalid. Benefices or pensions previously received are not automatically lost (*ipso facto*), but only if the sentence explicitly so states (Can. 2296, par. 2). (b) Those who incur infamy of fact must be restrained from receiving holy orders (Can. 987, #7), dignities, benefices, or ecclesiastical offices and from exercising the sacred ministry or performing legal ecclesiastical acts (Can. 2294, par. 2).

The major difference between the effects of infamy of law and infamy of fact consists in this: the person incurring infamy of law cannot validly obtain ecclesiastical benefices, pensions, offices, or dignities, nor can he validly exercise the rights connected with them, nor perform a valid legal ecclesiastical act; the person incurring infamy of fact obtains ecclesiastical offices, benefices, pensions, etc., validly but illicitly.

Cessation of Infamy. Infamy of law ceases only by dispensation granted by the Holy See. Infamy of fact ceases when the Ordinary shall prudently judge that the guilty individual has regained good repute with serious and upright Catholics, particularly after a long (about three years) and practical proof of amendment (Can. 2295). *Pal.*

INFANT. *See* Age.

INFANTICIDE. Infanticide is the violent killing of an infant. It constitutes a grievous murder, inasmuch as, besides the offense against justice and charity that accompanies any murder, there is an additional violation against the virtue of compassion toward a being who has absolutely no chance of defending himself.

Canonical punishments. Direct and voluntary infanticide, like murder, is a grave sin and punished by canonical and civil laws. If infanticide is perpetrated while the infant is still in the maternal uterus, more correctly termed *feticide* or *embryotomy* (*q.v.*), many maintain that the penalties established by the sacred canons for abortion are not applicable (*see* Abortion), insofar as abortion in its real meaning is ejection of the immature fetus from a womb, and, whenever penalties are concerned, a more favorable interpretation must be given (*in poenis benignior est interpretatio facienda*). There are, on the contrary, those who apply to direct and voluntary feticide the same penalties established for abortion. Concerning the penalties of civil law, the reader can consult the legislation of the respective countries. *Fel.*

INFANTILISM. *See* Hypopituitarism; Sterilization.

INFANTS, ABANDONED. *See* Exposition of Infants.

INFERNO, HELL. *See* Last Things.

INFIDELITY, CONJUGAL. *See* Adultery.

INFIDELITY, UNFAITHFULNESS. *See* Faithfulness.

INFIDELS. An infidel is an unbaptized person. Non-baptized individuals are monotheists (Hebrews and Mohammedans), polytheists (Hindus, Buddhists, etc.), and atheists.

Moral Observations. Infidels are such (a) in a purely negative sense, that is, if, without fault of their own, they do not know the true faith; (b) in a privative sense, that is, if they do not know the true faith through their own fault; (c) in a formal sense, that is, if they have sufficient knowledge of the true faith but refuse to accept it. Since negative lack of faith is not due to personal fault, obviously it is not a sin (John 15:22; Rom. 10:14; 68 Prop. Baius, condemned by Pius V in the Bull *Ex omnibus afflictionibus,* October 1, 1567; Denz. 1068). To infidels of this category who faithfully follow the precepts of the natural law, God certainly will not deny the means of salvation, at least by inward inspirations (St. Thomas, *De verit.*, q. 14, a. 11). Privative lack of faith is not directly opposed to faith. It is a sin of omission rather than of commission, insofar as one deliberately avoids the opportunity of knowing the true faith. It is more or less serious sin, according to the degree of negligence. Formal lack of faith, which consists in a denial or a constant doubt of truths revealed by God and sufficiently known as such, is a most grave sin (Mark 16:16; John 3:18; 3:36; 12:48; 8:24; Rom. 11:20; Heb. 3:18; Apoc. 21:8). Next to open hatred of God, this is a most grievous sin.

Infidels and the Church. Infidels are not subjects of the Church, nor are they subject to canonical laws, except indirectly, that is, insofar as they enter into particular relationships with baptized persons, such as those who contract marriage with a person who is baptized (Can. 1070; 1119, etc.). Although infidels are outside of the Church, participation in her spiritual benefits is not denied to them, insofar as they are capable of receiving them. The Church prays for their conversion and invokes many blessings on them, that they may receive the light of faith and health of body (Can. 1149). Holy Mass may be offered for living infidels, privately or publicly, for their conversion as well as other reasons, provided that it does not give rise to scandal (S.C.S. Off. July 12, 1848). In the case of deceased infidels, Mass may be offered only privately (never publicly—Can. 1241), and ecclesiastical burial is not permitted (Can. 1239). (For catechumens, *see* Catechumens; *also see* Non-Catholics.) *Dam.*

INFIRM PERSONS. Moral theology deals with the infirm from various aspects.

DUTIES OF THE INFIRM. Sickness and suffering are a consequence of sin (*q.v.*). Christian faith teaches that physical suffering is a precious means of expiating personal sins and those of others, in the teaching on the communion of saints. Suffering, accepted and endured with resignation to the holy will of God, brings men into closer harmony with our Divine Lord, who voluntarily became man to suffer and to offer satisfaction to God's justice for the sins of mankind.

A grave error, quite common among the infirm, is that suffering is a sign that God does not love them. If this were correct, it would mean that God loved His own Son and the most holy Mary less than all other men: an obviously false deduction. Sickness and suffering are a proof of God's benevolence toward the sufferer. It is not only proper but also obligatory for an infirm person to seek a cure, if it be possible. The fact that one has become ill does not mean that God wants him to be ill permanently. If, however, the infirm person fails to obtain a complete cure of his infirmity, then he must accept it and ask the Lord for strength to bear it with resignation, patience, and even with joy. Faith, prayer, meditation on the Passion of Jesus, frequent reception of the sacraments of penance and Holy Eucharist are great sources of spiritual strength. To these, one must add the conviction that through his suffering he can render himself useful to society and the Church by winning for himself and others the blessings and the grace of God, which he should direct particularly toward the conversion of sinners. In many countries there are pious unions for the infirm under the name "Apostolate of the Sick." The aim of these unions is to encourage the infirm to offer their sufferings, filled with Christian patience, to God for the good of the Church and the world. This guarantees that the benefits accruing from the inevitable vicissitudes of this life well-accepted should not be in vain. This apostolate is carried out through instructions, exhortations, letters, magazines, retreats, triduums, and appropriate lectures. The Catholic Church is particularly mindful of the sick; the Missal has a votive Mass for the sick; the Ritual contains a special blessing for the ailing.

Duties Toward the Sick. In view of the words of the Divine Master: "I was sick and you visited me," etc., Christians have always considered the care of the sick as a special task of religion and Christian charity. The Church has always encouraged associations and confraternities engaged in the building and maintenance of hospitals for the care of the sick, especially the poor. Many religious congregations of men and women choose, as their principal aim, the care of the sick. (On the duties of doctors and nurses, *see* Physician, Nurse.)

All Christians, especially priests and relatives of a sick person, have duties of charity towards the sick; duties all the more pressing when the sick person is in great pain or ill for a long time. A visit, a gay conversation, a comforting and encouraging word, a good book, a little gift—all are very much appreciated by sick persons and do much to assist them. Anyone who has been ill knows well the good these works of charity do. Relatives and others responsible for the care of the sick must fulfill their duties with charity, cheerfulness, and eagerness, even when it becomes difficult because of the long duration of the sickness and of the fact that often a sick person is short of patience. Anything that might tend to give the sick person the feeling of being a burden must be scrupulously avoided. This, of course, is all but easy; hence, not only the infirm person, but also those who care for him, need all the strength that can come from faith and the frequent reception of the sacraments. Visitors frequently disturb a sick person with over-anxious and exaggerated concern over the gravity of the illness. This is a lack of charity toward the infirm. The priest, and above all the parish priest, has a special responsibility toward the sick. Sickness makes a man more apt to think of the welfare of his soul; it is often a way used by Divine Providence to save souls. The priest must take advantage of the occasion and not wait until the last moment; he must visit the sick as soon as it becomes evident that the case is serious; he must try to gain his confidence in order that his beneficial ministry may be made easier. Relatives are expected to inform the priest as soon as possible when there is an infirm person in the house.

Infirmity as a Cause Excusing from Observance of a Law. Infirmity is one of the causes excusing a person from the observance of certain Church laws. Sickness, even though it be only in the form of weakness, excuses from the laws of abstinence and fast (*q.v.*). A sick person, even though not seriously sick, is excused from attending Holy Mass on Sundays and holy days (*see* Santification of Sundays; Holy Days). The sick person, in danger of death, may receive Holy Communion every day without fasting (Can. 864, par. 2 and 3). For the faculties given to confessors in behalf of persons in danger of death, *see* Faculties, Confession, Urgent cases. *Ben.*

INFLATION. Inflation is a disproportionate and relatively sudden increase in the quantity of money or credit, or both, relative to goods available for purchase. Generally, inflation is the result of a temporary shortage of revenues in countries faced with a compelling necessity of engaging in immediate expenditures required by war conditions or other emergency. Inflation, especially if acute, shakes the entire economic structure of a country. The buying power of money decreases; the price of products and services increases. Those who live on salary or on pension and the working class suffer most, because, despite increases in salaries and pensions, they can never catch up with rising costs. Creditors also suffer damage, whereas debtors and the State are likely to benefit because the public debt loses consistency in proportion to the depreciation of currency.

Ethico-Social Consequences. The ethico-social consequences of inflation are of great importance. First of all, inflation cuts into the real value of income, thus creating an imbalance in the welfare of the people. It destroys savings invested in public stocks and bonds or entrusted to banking institutions, frequently accumulated from many years of work. Real estate and other property owners, generally, remain unaffected. Thus, economico-social contrasts are intensified: some are forced back into a state of poverty from which they emerged through great efforts; others are able to consolidate their own positions. It gives a mortal blow to the desire to save, encourages speculation, and weakens the trust in public authority. *Pav.*

INFUSED VIRTUES. See Virtue.

INGRATITUDE. See Gratitude.

INHERITANCE. According to Julian, *Hereditas nihil aliud est quam successio in universum ius quod defunctus habuerit* (D. 50, 17, 62), or more succinctly: *universum ius seu patrimonium defuncti*, that is, the entire patrimony of an ancestor is called inheritance (J. D'ANNIBALE, *Summula*, II, 5, Rome, 1908, n. 334, p. 278). In other words, inheritance comprises all the rights and obligations (goods, rights, credits, and debts) that belonged to the deceased at the time of his death, except those rights and obligations inherent in his person as such. Inheritance gives rise to an *universitas iuris* with all the consequences proper to this category. Alongside this form of universal succession, there is also a succession based on a particular title, called *legacy*. The heir represents the continuation of the personality of the deceased and takes over all the rights of the deceased (*in locum et ius*), whether he actually inherits his entire possessions or part. In Roman law, the formal designation as heir, or the reception of this qualification, gave one the right to all the goods of the deceased person. Today, instead, the right of succession (*in universum ius*) indicates the heir to whom are associated the effects indicated below. This relationship arising from universal succession (*universitas iuris*) is created by the law with a view to the ends to be achieved and the particular origin of the sum-total of the goods considered as a unit. On this concept are based all the legislations derived from the Roman law, including Canon Law—a concept which differs substantially from the Germanic law. The following consequences flow from the succession *in universum ius:* (a) Once the inheritance is accepted, the qualification of heirs is no longer lost (*semel heres, semper heres*, Ulpianus, D. 4, 4, 7, par. 10). (b) The unity of patrimony is maintained even in the case in which not one (*heres ex asse*) but more persons (*heredes ex parte*) are named to a quota (not to a part), that is, to a mathematical fraction of the whole succession, because, by reason of a certain communion of goods, the single individuals (despite the fact that they receive a quota portion of the inheritance) inherit all the active and passive relations of the deceased. It can happen, therefore, that if the other co-heirs refuse or are disqualified, the one who remains acquires also the unclaimed part, in accordance with the norms of the law of increase. There may also be a designation of an heir *ex re certa*. In such a case the indication of particular goods constitutes the inheritance when it is clear that the testator intended to assign those goods as a quota portion of the patrimony (subjective criterion). (c) There is no incompatibility between the universality of acquisition and the existence of legacies, that is, an assignment by the testator of specific things to one of the heirs or to other persons. (d) Outside the case in which an heir accepts the inheritance with the benefit of inventory, and the case in which the creditors of the deceased or the legatees request a separation of the goods, the patrimony of the heir and that of the deceased are intermingled. One must not, however, confuse the requirements of the concept of inheritance with its effects. To have been called to the universality or to a quota of the goods is what constitutes an heir; the succession to the active and passive assets is the effect. In other words, a person is not an heir because he is designated responsible also for the debts. He is responsible for the debts because he is an heir. In a succession there can be one heir or several co-heirs. There can be heirs and legatees at the same time. There may also be a legacy in favor of a co-heir.

PROXIMATE SOURCES OF INHERITANCE. An inheritance may come from two sources: from the will of a deceased (*see* Testament), or from the law (*successio ab intestato*). In some codes of law, a third source is admitted: the so-called *successional pact.* This is a contract which has for its object relations based on future successions outside the will and testament, whether the pact constitutes an heir or disposes of a future succession. Other codes of law, however, do not recognize this pact in order to provide a practical certainty of absolute revocability of the will, and to avoid the *votum captandae mortis*—that is, the desire of coming into possession of the inheritance as soon as possible, by wishing or, worse, by plotting the death of the testator. This lack of recognition applies also to the abdicative pact, which is the act whereby a living person renounces his succession.

MORAL PRINCIPLES CONCERNING THE RIGHT OF INHERITANCE. Civil laws dealing with the right of inheritance are binding in conscience as long as they are not contrary to the natural law or to Canon Law. Inheritance is legitimate title for the acquistion of property, based on the right of the owner to dispose of his goods. Such a right is justified by its beneficial effects: (a) it serves as an incentive for the owner to a careful, active, and prudent administration of his property; (b) it permits the owner to maintain a certain authority over the members of his family and to dispose of his property in their favor with a consideration of their respective needs; (c) it provides the means of support for many institutions of general welfare (scientific, charitable, etc.). If the owner fails to designate his heirs, by natural law his children have the right to inherit the property of the father. Since the family is a moral unit, before the death of a father, children share in some way in the ownership of paternal property. To deprive them of these goods would be tantamount to expropriation, for the children are a continuation of the person of the parents and, hence, of their rights. Parents, moreover, are by instinct inclined to provide for their children in the future. Such an instinct, far from being irrational, is sensible, especially since it is a most effective motive for the preservation and increase of a patrimony through wise administration. This duty of parents toward their children, to which there corresponds a right on the part of the children to the inheritance, though certainly a strict and grave duty, yet is only a moral obligation. Any legislation, that would make the State the sole heir would do so in violation of the natural law. On the other hand, since the natural law does not for the most part give detailed norms on the subject, it is the right of the public authority to deal with and regulate the right of inheritance in accordance with the principles explained above. Consequently, civil laws on this matter are binding in conscience as long as they do not conflict with the higher, though more general, principles of the natural law.

The Supreme Pontiffs in recent documents, although they did not discuss directly the question of the right of inheritance, have expressed their thoughts on the subject by dealing with the matter of safeguarding private property as well as the function and stability of the family.

"What we have said," writes Leo XIII, "in reference to a right of ownership inherent in the individual, holds true also for man as head of the family; in fact, such a right in him becomes stronger the more his personality is extended and included in the family society" (I. Giordani, *Rerum novarum: le encicliche sociali*, Rome, 1938).

Pius XI states: "The natural right both of possessing and of transmitting one's own goods through inheritance must of necessity remain intact and inviolate; the State has no right to suppress it" (AAS, 23(1931), 71).

"It is in the spirit of *Rerum novarum*," adds Pius XII, "to affirm that only the stability which is rooted in one's own land makes the family the most perfect and productive living cell of society, uniting in a marvelous way by this progressive bond the present and future generations" (Pentecost Message of 1931: AAS, 23 [1931], 157).

From this, one must conclude that the principal purpose of inheritance is to provide for the economic stability of the family. It is for this reason that inheritance comes under the natural law. Developing this concept with his usual profoundness, V. Cathrein observes: "The family, in general, has its foundation in ownership, as the tree in the ground . . . But the family can have independence and the moral quality necessary to the fulfillment of its duties only in the supposition of a right of inheritance and, above all, of the last will and testament. A family without possessions, in which there is no sort of inherited property, cannot last; on the death of the parents it will be scattered like sand before the wind. Only property, and, above all, landed property, or at least the possession of one's own house, shall keep the successive generations internally united." *Pal.*

INHIBITION. Inhibition (Latin, *inhibeo*—repress, obstruct, check) is an active process which represses the effect of a stimulus, or arrests an action about to take place or already begun. Also, it is any inner impediment to free activity, expression, or functioning; principally, any psychic activity imposing restraint upon another activity.

Physiological Considerations. In general physiology, inhibition is a slowing down or temporary arrest of the function of a living organ through the influence of external actions, or actions which are inherent in the organ itself. Inhibition differs from paralysis not only insofar as it is temporary (for the organ or system inhibited, unlike the paralyzed one, is capable of resuming its function) but also because it implies the action of an active process.

The effectiveness of inhibitory impulses, like impulses of an excitable nature (*see* Impulse), varies in intensity, according to the organ affected and the physiological condition of the organ at the time. Thus, to mention only one of the more common cases, the same stimulus that excites a muscular group (for example, the bending muscles of a limb), inhibits the opposing muscular group (stretching muscles). This is known as Sherrington's *law of reciprocal innervation.* A weak stimulus may stimulate and a strong one may inhibit the very same organ, as happens in the case of cutaneous capillaries in *dermographic tests*; an initial stimulus may have a stimulating effect, while a successive one of the same identical force may have an inhibitory effect (Bethe).

Psychological Considerations. Similarly, in the field of emotional states, a painful stimulus will excite the individual if the stimulus is light, yet depress him if the stimulus is intense or of long duration. Generally speaking, moral suffering excites or depresses according to its intensity and duration, the person, and the time in

which it occurs. Happiness, particularly if very intense, may exert a depressing or an inhibiting action. In certain cases one may weep for joy or, although less frequently, laugh under the impact of a particularly grave sorrow.

Another and more important aspect of inhibition, because of its moral effects, is found in the study of the processes of the will (*q.v.*). A volitive act may spring from an unopposed desire, simply because it is fitted to one's character, inclinations, or upbringing. At other times, it may spring from a laborious conflict of desires in which the strongest tends to prevail. In these different cases inhibition does not come into play. More frequently, in individuals with noble and fine principles, the strongest desire does not prevail, but a morally superior desire. The prevailing of the latter proves that selfish sentiments and instinctive tendencies were effectively inhibited.

Psychopathological Considerations. Both excessive and defective inhibitions are abnormal conditions. With excessive inhibition, depressive syndromes arise, as in the area of inferiority complex; with a lack of inhibition, occur syndromes of great excitability or maniacal excesses. Alteration of inhibition in the intellective-volitive area may provoke excessive inhibitions or a psychasthenic syndrome; on the other hand, a lack of inhibition may produce an instinctive temperament, as in compulsive immorality (*q.v.*). In current psychiatry, inhibition is treated by psychoanalysis, but it does not necessarily indicate a pathological condition as a symptom.

The lack or excess of inhibition and self-control are frequently partially hereditary; the first symptoms may be observed in infancy. The scrupulous, fearful, and timid; the blustering, malicious, and arrogant—both types of children are well-known to educators. The inhibited are likely to become candidates for depressive neurosis, introvertedness, and phychasthenia in adult years; the unrestrained are easily inclined to a life of criminal delinquency.

A sound education, begun early and directed to the development of self-confidence with the first group and the teaching of the value of renunciation, duty, and discipline to the second group, may normalize the inhibitory processes in these young individuals. Aided by natural (*see* Psychoneurosis) and supernatural means, they may become mentally and spiritually healthy, well-balanced persons, with great benefit to themselves and society. *Riz.*

INHUMATION. In the strict sense of the word, *inhumation* is the burial of a human corpse in the ground or burial vault of a church or monastery. The term may be applied also to the use of monuments or mausoleums above ground as burial spots. The essential difference is that inhumation applies to burial, in which natural decomposition takes place; it is, however, to be considered distinct from other methods of burial, such as burial at sea, abandonment to wild animals, or violent destruction by fire. All methods are very ancient, but inhumation is the method generally employed in various stages of history.

The Catholic Church does not sanction any other method of disposing of corpses except burial or inhumation. In periods of necessity, epidemic, or war, the Church allows the violent destruction of human bodies. The traditional method of burial was inherited from Jewish customs as the method most suited to the reverence due to the body, which was previously united to the soul and sanctified as the temple of the Holy Spirit. The body cannot be saved from corruption; but it is our duty to leave it intact with due reverence and to allow the natural processes of disintegration to take place. Violent destruction does not harm the dead, but it does hurt us as human beings, insofar as external actions do affect emotions. Under ordinary circumstances, a Catholic is obliged to inhumation of the dead, with the assistance of the clergy and the liturgical rites of the Church. These beautiful and consoling ceremonies are directed to the elevation of the human spirit to God and to the increase of faith and hope in the mourners.

If, out of a desire to aid science or for judicial purposes, an autopsy is performed, upon its completion, the body and its parts must be decently and reverently buried. The same principle applies to limbs amputated in the lifetime of an individual or to a fetus delivered prematurely or as the result of a miscarriage. *Ben.*

INITIATION (SEXUAL). Initiation, in general, consists in a series of ceremonies or rites expressing and consecrating an individual's passage from one religious or social status to another, considered almost as a new life for the individual. One may be initiated into a religious society, a secret society, or adulthood. We shall deal here with initiation into adulthood. Initiation of youth dates back to very ancient times, as it appears from the fact that it is deeply rooted among the savages of pre-agricultural civilization, such as Fiji and the Australian tribes. According to their customs, a young man who has reached the age of puberty is removed from among women and children and is introduced among men in order that he may acquire the virile dignity that will enable him to contract marriage, take part in the discussions of the elders and go to war. This initiation, therefore, is most important in the life of the individual, and a notable event in the social life of the clan or tribe. Ceremonies relative to initiation usually include three rites: *separation* from the group of children to which he belonged; *trial,* consisting of teachings, fasting, and other painful tests; *aggregation* to the company of adults. Among certain savage peoples, girls attaining the age of puberty are admitted by special initiation rites into the society of older women and the status of marriageability. Initiation of youth among primitive peoples implies in notable measure sexual initiation.

Among modern peoples, sexual initiation is no longer linked with special ceremonies but for the most part is done on an individual basis. Initiation may be *theoretical* or *practical.* Theoretical sexual initiation is dealt with under Psychoneurosis, sexual (*q.v.*), and more amply still under Education, sexual, (*q.v.*). Practical sexual initiation is usually the corrupting enterprise of adults who do not hesitate to destroy the purity of young persons. To this must be added the practice of "free love" and pre-marital experiences that is growing with appalling boldness among the younger generations.

Moral Observations. There is no moral justification whatsoever for premarital sexual initiation. It stands condemned even from a strictly medical point of view, for practical sexual initiation often leads to venereal diseases and to a dissolute life involving abortion, infanticide, hasty marriage, divorce, and bigamous living. The ethico-religious value of premarital chastity and the biological and hygienic benefits stemming from it have been strongly underscored in many Church documents, particularly those of Pius XI and Pius XII. (Cf. Pius XI, Enc. *Casti connubii*; Pius XII, *Address to Midwives,* Oct. 29, 1951.) All young men and women should be made aware of the fact that marriage with chastity of mind and body as a basic premise and beginning is a sign of high moral sense, a guarantee of domestic happiness, and an aid to the physical and mental well-being of parents and children to follow. *Riz.*

INJUNCTION (SEQUESTRATION). An injunction is the suspension of the exercise of a right. This inhibiting action consists in a person's right to seek the prohibition of the use of a contested right in view of the possible damage that its exercise may bring to himself or others. This must be requested before a judge or civil power. This action is similar to sequestration, but differs in that sequestration applies to a material object, whereas an injunction applies to the exercise of a right; the prohibition of the exercise occurs despite the claim which the possessor has to a right. In sequestration, the object is entrusted to the keeping of a third party.

An injunction may be obtained at the initiative of the interested party, if he demonstrates that he has a right to the retained article, or is threatened with damage as the result of the exercise of a right by another, unless the damage is forestalled or repaired by other means of security (Cans. 1672, 1674). An injunction may be gotten *ex officio* at the request of the promoter of justice or the defender of the bond if the public welfare demands it (Canon 1672, par. 3).

The violation of an injunction upon the exercise of a right constitutes an action which the other party may seek to nullify or rescind by judicial proceedings (Can. 1854 ff.). In marriage cases, during the period of time when an annulment is pending, the use of the marital right or the right to board and bed may be suspended by an injunction.

INJURY. Any damage or hurt, done or suffered, is called an injury; also any violation of the rights of another. In this latter sense, an injury is synonymous with injustice. Not every damaging act is necessarily an injury; for instance, to build a house on one's property which cuts off the sunlight from another's garden. The act is damaging to another individual, but, since it represents the exercise of a right, it does not constitute an injury. For the same reason, it is wrong to speak of injustice or to refer to a fetus as an unjust aggressor because it is harmful to the mother; for, if there is not an action against a just law, divine or human, there is no injury. Therefore, although the general right to a definite good stands, one is permitted to act to destroy that good, provided that the act is not opposed to the natural law, as in killing an unjust aggressor. An aggressor has a right to life, but not to the extent that a victim is not permitted to defend himself, even to the point of killing his enemy, if that is necessary. Self-defense is a principle of the natural law; thus, if, in the exercise of this right to self-defense, one damages a good to which another has a right, this is not an injury in the strict sense.

Injury may consist of a positive act: the violation of the rights of another by a positive deed; or of an omission: the failure to fulfill a required or obligatory action. This positive act may consist of stealing the possessions of someone else, retaining the stolen property of another, or the destruction of another's property. By retention, the property of another is safe in itself or in its equivalent value (the price realized from the sale of the property). By destruction, the property no longer exists. Technically speaking, the crimes are distinct, insofar as one retains another person's property, while the other concerns an unjust damage done to another's property. The distinction is very important with respect to restitution (*q.v.*).

An injury may be either *objective* or *subjective*. It is *objective* if the conduct, in fact, is opposed to the norms of the natural or positive law. Ordinarily, such an injury is also *subjective*, that is, deliberate and imputable to the person, so that he is both morally (sin) and juridically guilty (juridical offense). When the injury is merely objective, an element of accident or lack of responsibility generally absolves from guilt. But even in the case of a feared, purely objective injury, one has the right to defend himself against an unjust aggressor. Punishment, however, is predicated on the fact that any injustice committed be also subjective—that is, deliberate.

Morality. To injure another is never justified for any motive whatsoever. The rule "Injury must be avoided" admits of no exception. The first rule of the moral order, "Evil must be avoided" (*malum est vitandum*), applied to one's neighbor, is the same as to say "Injury (damage) must be avoided (*injuria est vitanda*) in our dealings with others."

Axiom. "To him who is willing or to him who consents one does no injury" is true if interpreted in its proper sense, which is not as general as the words seem to imply. It holds true if the consent is freely given and not extorted by trickery, fraud, menace, or other unjustifiable means, and also if the consenting party is capable of surrendering his right. Anyone who kills a man with his consent (for example, euthanasia with the patient's consent) commits a most grave injury (damage) and cannot justify his action by the above-mentioned axiom, because no one has the right to take his own life.

Gravity of the Sin. Damage to another is frequently a mortal sin. Under certain circumstances, however, it may be a venial sin, that is, when the harm caused to another is not serious, nor are the effects produced by the action harmful to the community. For other types of injury *see*

Contumely; Defamation; Fame; Honor.
Ben.

INJURY, PERSONAL. A personal injury is a harm done to the physical or mental well-being of oneself or another person. It differs from mutilation, for mutilation is limited to the severance of a particular organ of the body. A personal injury is grave or venial depending on the importance of the injured area or the seriousness of the damage. Grave injury may occasion or necessitate mutilation.

To judge the personal injury, it is well to recall the difference between indirect and direct damage. Indirect personal injury is one not intended or desired by the agent, but merely allowed or tolerated, as the indirect effect of an action. Thus, for example, in a legitimate self-defense if the indirect effect of an act is that the aggressor is wounded, the personal injury occurs simultaneously with another effect, which the agent intended as a right and duty. Direct personal injury is an immediate and intended result of a harmful action against another.

The lawfulness of an indirect personal injury is judged according to the general moral principle of the double effect (*q.v.*). Any direct personal injury is forbidden as an intrinsically immoral act, since no one has dominion over the body of another or himself.

CANONICAL ASPECTS. In Canon 119, the violation of the privilege protecting the life, dignity, and liberty of a cleric or religious house (Can. 2343) may be considered a type of personal injury. This real and true personal injury is a crime of "mixed" forum. A lay offender is punished by civil law; a cleric is under the jurisdiction of the Church. In modern civil codes of law, the cleric may, however, be considered as a layman, which an ecclesiastical judge should consider in establishing a penalty (Can. 2223, par. 3). A layman condemned in civil court must be excluded from legal acts in the ecclesiastical forum and from offices in the Church (Can. 2354, par. 1). A cleric has an obligation to reparation for violations of this nature as well as the further penalties of censure, penances, privation of office, benefices and dignities, or, finally, deposition. Homicide demands degradation, if it is culpable (Can. 2354, par. 2). Mutilation creates an irregularity (Can. 985). *Pug.*

INJUSTICE. *See* Justice, Injury.

IN-LAWS. *See* Affinity.

INN KEEPER AND HOTEL OPERATOR. An inn keeper or hotel keeper is one who operates an establishment providing lodging and meals for travelers, in return for a set rate. In ancient days, travelers and pilgrims were wont to find lodging in private homes. But as trade developed, private home facilities were no longer adequate to accommodate the ever-growing number of travelers. The *diversoria, cauponae,* and *stabulae* of ancient times were private lodging places, frequently operated in conjunction with taverns and eating places (*tabernae, popinae*). Over the course of the years an increasing number of lodging-houses of various types were established, but the changing times and increased social needs of modern man made the old type lodging obsolete and the construction of larger hotels a necessity. These were first erected in the vicinity of religious shrines, health-resorts, and the like. In modern times, the hotel industry has assumed such enormous proportions that it necessarily involves legal and moral aspects. The modern juridical concept of *inn keeper* and *hotel operator* is one who, by profession, provides temporary lodging for transient people or guests.

Civil Legislation. Modern civil laws concerning the hotel industry are designed to protect the public interest. The contract entered into between guest and hotel keeper is a special relationship involving the hiring and lending of services, rental of objects, deposit and other things, generally covered by particular laws. A hotel operator is required to secure a license, which generally is denied to one convicted of felony or serious crime. Besides legal obligations relative to the security of individuals and valuables, equitable rates and services, a hotel keeper is also bound by moral obligations, which stem from positive divine law as well as from ecclesiastical law. Thus: (a) A Catholic hotel (motel, lodge, etc.) operator would be guilty of grave sin and unworthy of sacramental absolution, were he formally to provide habitual and prolonged lodging to suspect couples, or sponsor or permit obscene and gravely scandalous dances, gambling, or meetings of subversive societies. (b) He would be guilty of sin if he displays immodest statues and paintings, immoral illustrations suggestive of illicit love, publications attacking religion or forbidden by the Church (cf. Canon Law, Can. 1399, n. 3, 9; 1398, 1404). (c) All hotel keepers are bound by the natural and divine law to protect the good name not only of their immediate family but also of those in their employ by refraining from exacting of them duties or services forbidden or detrimental to their spiritual welfare. They must allow the time required for the proper observance of their religious obligations. (d) An innkeeper who also provides meals may not, on his own initiative, serve Catholic guests meat or meat-soup on days of abstinence. He may, however, according to common practice, serve meat to those who request it, unless the request is clearly made out of formal contempt of religion. Generally, a hotel keeper has the right to presume that those who ask for meat on days of fast and abstinence either do not come under the law, have a dispensation, or are in good faith. The same applies to operators of food stands at railroad stations, where lunches and sandwiches are sold. (e) Moreover, an inn or hotel keeper may not serve his guests more liquor than necessary, especially if he reasonably foresees that further drinking would lead to intoxication, unless he fears that refusal might cause serious harm. In conclusion, every hotel keeper is obliged to carry out not only the dispositions provided by the law but also the moral obligations intended for the protection of the well-being, both material and spiritual, of his guests. *Tar.*

INNOCENCE (State of). The state of innocence was the primitive state in which God placed our first parents when He created them: it is also called the state of original justice. Our first parents were then raised to the supernatural order by sanctifying grace with its respective virtues and gifts. Moreover, they were given preternatural gifts, that is, certain privileges which integrated human nature (gifts of integrity), so as to purify it of all defects and make it in itself completely perfect (preternatural order). The state of innocence is an entirely gratuitous gift of God to which man had no claim. But since elevation by grace exceeds any other created, possible nature, human or angelic, the preternatural gifts were far inferior, even though God alone can produce them in us, without any right on man's part. They constituted integrity, for human nature. According to revelation, the preternatural gifts were four: a state of innocence; preservation of the body from death and pain; preservation of the soul from concupiscence; and preservation from ignorance.

Hence, there existed in the state of original justice a triple harmony: (a) the body was subject to the soul; (b) sense passions were subject to the intellect, by reason of the preternatural gift of integrity; (c) the soul was subject to and united with God by means of the supernatural gift of grace.

By virtue of this harmony, sin for our first parents was unlikely but not impossible, since they were not confirmed in grace, nor did they see God directly in His Divine Essence, as the blessed in heaven see Him.

Besides elevation by grace (q.v.), revelation speaks clearly also of the preternatural gifts of our first parents (Gen. 1 and 2). Though more explicit about the gift of preservation from death and suffering, yet there are sufficiently clear indications of the more exalted but less conspicuous privileges of immunity from concupiscence and ignorance. Thus, while the state of primitive innocence is an accepted fact, theologians are not in agreement about the essence of original justice. Setting aside the theory of St. Anselm, who distinguishes the state of innocence from grace and describes it as a natural rectitude of the will, we shall follow the doctrine of St. Thomas as the best explanation.

According to St. Thomas, (a) original justice is a gratuitous gift added to human nature by the generosity of God; (b) the material element of this justice is the gift of integrity, which brings about the subordination of the passions, particularly concupiscence; the formal element is sanctifying grace, which implies submission of the soul to God; (c) the cause and root of every submission is grace.

Loss of the state of innocence and effect of this loss. As a result of their sin, our first parents lost the state of innocence for themselves and for their posterity. The sin of our first parents in view of their state of full illumination was enormous. Furthermore, since the two lesser subordinations, that is, subordinations of the body to the soul and of the senses to the intellect, were dependent on the union of the soul with God by grace, these also ceased to exist when this union was destroyed. The Redemption wrought by Jesus Christ did not restore these subordinations to their original condition, but it supplies man with sufficient aid to keep them in check by the power of grace. *Pal.*

INNOCENT. See Judge; Murder; Homicide.

INNOVATION. The Code of Canon Law does not use the word *innovation* but, according to traditional canonical doctrine, *innovation* means any change or modification in the standing of an ecclesiastical benefice. *The present law distinguishes the following types of innovation:* (a) *union,* (b) *transfer,* (c) *division,* (d) *dismemberment,* (e) *conversion* and (f) *suppression.* (a) Union has sundry forms. It is called *extinctive union* when a new benefice is constituted out of two or more suppressed benefices, or when one or more benefices are joined to another in such a way that they lose the juridical identity they had before the union. All privileges and obligations of the suppressed benefices now belong to the new or remaining benefice. Union is called *aeque principalis,* when the joined benefices retain the juridical entity existing before the union, and neither becomes subject to the other; however, because of the union, they must be conferred on the same person. Another form is a union *minus principalis* or *per subiectionem*, when, namely, the joined benefices, while maintaining their individual juridical identity, are subordinated to one as the principal one and follow it in all its fortunes, so that by obtaining the principal benefice one automatically acquires also the subsidiary benefice or benefices (Can. 1419–1420). A particular union (*sui generis*) is the union of a benefice with a legal person who is not the subject of a benefice. In ancient times it was called *incorporatio*. The union of a parish with a monastery may be made either *ad temporalia tantum*, that is, only with regard to the income of the parish, or to all effects (*pleno iure*); in this case the parish becomes a religious benefice and is in charge of a member of a religious community (Can. 1423–1425). (b) *Transfer* consists in moving the seat of a benefice from one place to another. This is not to be confused with the transfer of the beneficiary (*see* Beneficiary). (c) *Division* is had when two or more benefices are created out of one. (d) *Dismemberment*, when a part of the territory or property of the benefice is separated from it and assigned to another benefice or to another ecclesiastical body. (e) *Conversion*, when the nature of the benefice is changed; for example, a secular benefice is converted into a religious benefice. (f) *Suppression* is the extinction of the benefice (Can. 1421). Furthermore, the *imposition of a pension*, (*see* Pensions, ecclesiastical), that is, the concession of the right to part of the revenues of a benefice made to a person other than the titular of the benefice, may also be considered as innovation (Can. 1429).

Those who are authorized to make innovations:

(a) The following innovations are reserved to the Holy See: all innovations involving consistorial benefices (Cc. 1423, par. 1; 1414; 215); extinction, union and suppression of all benefices; dismemberment of religious benefices (Can. 1422); the union of a parish with the *capitular* or *episcopal* "*mensa,*" or

with the benefices of cathedral or collegiate churches; the incorporation of a parish in a juridical person, except the bishop's right to incorporate insofar as its revenues are concerned, *ad temporalia tantum*, with a cathedral or collegiate church, a parish in whose territory this church lies (Can. 1423, par. 2; Can. 1425); any union between the benefice of one diocese with a benefice of another diocese, or between benefices, one of which is exempt or reserved to the Holy See (Can. 1424); the imposition of a pension upon a benefice, except the right of the bishop in cases established by law (Can. 1429); the conversion of curate into non-curate benefices, of religious into secular, of secular into religious (Can. 1430).

(b) With respect to other innovations, the Ordinary has the right (to mention the more practical cases) to join *aeque* or *minus principaliter* one parish with another and also a parish with a non-curate benefice; to transfer a secular parish from one place to another within the same parish (Can. 1426); to divide the parishes and dismember their territories even against the wishes of the parish priests involved and without the consent of the people (Can. 1427); to convert a simple into a curate benefice (Can. 1430, par. 2). However, the Ordinary is obliged to observe the canonical prescriptions, some of which pertain to the validity of the measure, such as the existence of a just and canonical reason for the union, transfer, division and dismemberment (Can. 1428, par. 2). In general, necessity and usefulness to the Church (Can. 1423, par. 1) are considered canonical reasons for the division and the dismemberment of a parish. The Code of Canon Law recognizes only two canonical causes: (1) grave difficulty on the part of the people to get to the parish church on account of the distance or because of boundary difficulties; (2) the large number of faithful whose spiritual welfare would not be properly cared for by the appointment of more curates (Can. 1427, par. 2). *Led.*

INQUISITION. The Inquisition was an extraordinary ecclesiastical tribunal established in the twelfth century for the defense of religion by repressive as well as preventive means. It achieved final form under the pontificate of Pope Gregory IX. It reflected the mentality of the age whereby orthodoxy of faith was considered a requirement of civil life, and heresy a public danger to be removed by the civil government in accord with the ecclesiastical authority.

PROCEDURE. The inquisitorial method, though simple and inconspicuous (summary procedure), was required to conform rigorously to the norms of a law, at that time in its infancy. In fact, popes decreed that the inquisitors should, as a matter of course, engage the services of legal experts who were required to be present at the trials and examine the acts. The accused was allowed to defend himself, although he was not permitted to have a defense attorney. This ruling was eventually changed. The names of witnesses, though kept secret from the accused (who, however, was interrogated concerning his personal enemies), were disclosed to the jurists. The accused was allowed to take his own defense and to be heard every time it was considered necessary; he was permitted to reject the judge-inquisitor and to appeal against his procedure; above all, he could appeal to the pope. The function of inquisitor was entrusted to judges selected from among honorable persons (for the most part members of religious orders, such as Dominicans and Franciscans). The unpopularity of the Inquisition is due, above all, to later writers, and to the confusion between the regular inquisition and the Spanish Inquisition.

After the final expulsion of the Moors (1492), the kings of Spain took control of the local Inquisition, despite opposition by the popes. Political preoccupations about the large number of Jews and the Moriscos (false converts) gave rise to a situation of continued and almost habitual suspicion. Obviously, it was no longer a tribunal under the control of the Church for purely religious motives. The Spanish Inquisition must be judged apart from a real ecclesiastical Inquisition. Nor is it possible to properly judge the latter outside the general framework of the times in which it arose and functioned. It should also be noted that, with the exception of Spain, the Inquisition was brief and its role rigorously governed; in several countries of Europe it never went into effect. In fact, despite his efforts, Philip II was unable to establish it in his dominions in Italy and in Flanders.

HISTORICAL JUDGMENT. From a positive point of view, it is historically certain that the Inquisition made a definite contribution to saving the unity of the Christian world during the most flourishing period of medieval civilization (1175–1200). Today there is much insistence on freedom of conscience, but the fact is overlooked that freedom of conscience cannot be understood to mean license, and that the Christian world, often incapable of staying on its proper course, must be guarded and protected against heresies, political, social or religious.

Today, naturally, other methods more in keeping with modern times are preferred. But events of the past must be judged according to the temper of the times in which they took place. Nor must one overlook the fact that exaggerations were fabricated and slanderously spread against the Inquisition by anticlerical forces of the nineteenth century. *Boz.*

INSEMINATION, ARTIFICIAL. Artificial insemination is the artificial implantation of semen in the uterine canal. *Morality.* Artificial insemination of a woman is forbidden by the natural moral law, according to which the sexual act of intercourse between husband and wife is the proper and exclusive means for the procreation of offspring. Artificial insemination practiced on an unmarried woman or on a married woman but with the semen from a man other than her husband, even with the latter's consent, is forbidden by the natural law, for the same reasons that fornication (*q.v.*) and adultery (*q.v.*) are forbidden. That artificial insemination of a married woman with her own husband's semen is against the moral law, as contrary to the natural order, was explicitly stated by Pius XII in his Allocution to the International Congress of Catholic

Physicians, Sept. 29, 1949 (AAS, 41 [1949], 557–561). Moreover, artificial insemination practised by the use of semen obtained by unnatural means, that is, by an act other than the proper act of intercourse, is a true and proper act of masturbation. The real reason for the unlawfulness of artificial insemination is in the fact that it is not the *production* of the genes that creates the relationship of paternity with its important moral and juridical consequences both for the begotten individual and society, in the generative act, that is, the human and natural act of intercourse. Strictly speaking, a child brought into existence by artificial insemination would have no father; hence, he would not be entitled to be fed, cared for, and raised by two persons. Thus, he would have no right to a very important good which God and nature assigned to him for his own benefit and that of society.

By this doctrine also is condemned the practice, recently introduced in America and England, whereby women whose husbands were away because of the war were permitted to be fecundated with the semen of other men. A popular *referendum* conducted among persons of all social ranks showed that a great number of ordinary persons by a natural instinct revolted against the wickedness and grave impropriety of such an unnatural act.

Artificial insemination improperly so-called. Another type of insemination, also called artificial, is not considered as contrary to the moral law. This consists in placing farther into the woman's uterine canal semen collected by an appropriate instrument from the vagina in which it was deposited by a normal intercourse between husband and wife. The reason for this is to facilitate fecundation in some abnormal case. Many moralists deem it lawful if the physician considers it necessary in situations where fecundation would be impossible or slightly probable because of natural defects or other abnormal circumstances. In order that such an artificial intervention may be lawful, it is necessary that the sexual act between husband and wife be possible, properly performed, at least as far as its essential elements are concerned, and

that the semen be properly placed in the vagina. *Ben.*

Decree of the Holy Office. By a decree of March 24, 1897, the Holy Office settled with a simple "No" the question whether or not artificial insemination of woman was permissible. But the spreading of such an unnatural practice, especially in America and in England—in the latter, the number of known cases seems to have passed one hundred—a firm stand by Church authority was needed once more. This came through a pronouncement of the late Pope Pius XII, as he addressed the IV International Congress of Physicians, Sept. 29, 1949 (AAS, 41 [1949] 557–561), and again in another address of May 19, 1956.

After he discussed the distinction between the two types of artificial insemination, abbreviated in the Anglo-Saxon countries into AID (Artificial Insemination by Donor) and AIH (Artificial Insemination by Husband), the Pope condemned the former as a manifest violation of the laws governing prematrimonial and conjugal continency, and as, among other things, acts of fornication, adultery, and, perhaps, of a particular kind of incest (*sui generis*). Ultimately, it gives rise to a natural paternity, if such may be called, which goes back to a stranger rather than to the lawful husband. The Pope voiced objections to the case of the lawful husband and rejected artificial insemination altogether inasmuch as its practice fails to show how the active element of fecundation can be obtained without recurring to an act which is against nature and cannot be justified by the desire, however lawful, to beget children. The Holy Father also solved the theologico-juridical questions concerning the licitness or illicitness of artificial insemination. (a) Artificial insemination, even when it obtains its effect, does not in any way make valid a marriage vitiated by impotency on the part of the man or woman; (b) consequently, it can never be accepted as a canonical fact of consummation in marriage. The act of consummation must be natural and performed with at least a minimum of human dignity and modesty, which must be preserved even in conjugal intimacy. This, however, does not exclude that nature may be assisted in overcoming certain defects and difficulties by means of what theologians call imperfect artificial insemination.

INSOLVENCY. In the abstract sense, insolvency is an impossibility of meeting an obligation or paying a debt. It is the quality or state of financial failure, or bankruptcy; this may be either judicial, if so declared in court, or extrajudiciary, if recognized as such without any legal action.

The true and actual impossibility of payment of debts does not release the debtor from the obligation; it merely permits a deferment of payment, until the debtor is able to pay his debts. Total bankruptcy is a legal institution, founded on the law of nature; it is directed to the protection of the creditors against damage, and the debtor against creditors. In bankruptcy proceedings, the debtor may not conceal his assets, but he may retain that which is necessary for his maintenance and that of his family to avoid a state of pauperism. A question arises whether judicial bankruptcy frees the debtor from further responsibility. The answer, in general, is negative. In certain places, however, the law explicitly states that he is released from further obligations, as in the United States of America (U.S. Bankruptcy Laws of July 10, 1898, and June 5, 1910). Certain theologians maintain that the debtor, who surrendered his assets, is also free from further obligations in conscience. *Tar.*

INSOMNIA. *See* Sleep.

INSPIRATION, DIVINE. Divine inspiration (Latin, *inspirare*—to blow into, infuse) is a supernatural direction and illumination of the human soul by the Holy Spirit. Divine inspiration, belonging to the order of actual graces, consists in special illuminations of the mind and impulses in the human will. Insofar as these are not necessarily noticeable, inspiration may lead to error or confusion, and, therefore, require the counsel of others in following them. Furthermore, inspiration means, more properly, a charismatic impulse prompting a man to communicate to others that which God wants to make known. If it is an oral communication, it is called a prophetical inspiration; if it is written, it is called a biblical, hagiographic inspiration.

Biblical inspiration was defined by Pope Leo XIII in the encyclical *Providentissimus Deus* (Nov. 18, 1898), as "a supernatural power by which God so moved and impelled them [the sacred writers] to write the things which He ordered and those only which they first correctly understood, then willed faithfully to write down, and finally expressed in apt words and with infallible truth" (*Enchiridion biblicum*, n. 110). This is the inspiration given by God to the prophets and the evangelists.

Ordinary divine inspirations must be accepted with humility and docility. It may be presumptuous, however, to claim to have received them, before careful examination with the help of prudent persons, particularly a confessor and spiritual director. *Pal.*

INSTIGATION. Instigation, in general, is inciting to evil. The instigation may be caused by another human being, since irrational creatures provide merely the occasion for evil without any will to provoke another, or it may be due to a superior being, called the devil, who is orientated to evil. Instigation from the devil is commonly termed *temptation*.

In a strict sense, instigation is the attempt by one or more persons or instigators to lead others on the path of moral evil, that is, sin and crime. Instigation to crime belongs to the juridical field of penal law and is condemned by moral and civil laws, with civil punishment of the instigator, even if the sin or the offense does not follow. Instigation, in fact, even without effect, is always a moral violation, for, since it implicitly promotes evil, it is a danger to society.

Instigation may be exercised in many ways, including that of simple manifestation of ideas. Law, however, usually specifies what constitutes instigation to crime, with a consideration also for publicity surrounding the instigation.

Moral and Canonical Sanctions. In

moral theology instigation is judged according to the principles of cooperation in evil (*q.v.*), the principles of charity toward one's neighbor, and the principles of justice insofar as it concerns reparation for the damage caused by the instigation.

In Canon Law instigation is involved in many canons: Canons 2316–2317 refer to heresy; Canon 2318 concerns preaching heretical theories; Canon 2331 treats of instigating disobedience to the Holy Father; Canon 2337 concerns rebellion against legitimate pastors; Canon 2351 treats of duelling; etc.

INSTIGATION IN CIVIL LAW. In civil legislation, the term *instigation* has the same meaning and effect as in Canon Law.

Instigation means to incite others to commit a violation; in other words, it is an attempt to arouse in others a criminal intent or to strengthen an already existing intent. Instigation may be exercised by words, writings, actions, and any means designed to achieve this end.

Instigation, whether direct or indirect, produces apprehension and uneasiness. For this reason, it is generally considered by the penal codes of all civilized nations as an offense against the public good. Since instigation motivates a public disturbance, independent of the commission of the crime fomented, it is often punished as a crime, in itself and in every case, regardless of the effect of the instigation upon the public or the subsequent criminal acts.

There are various kinds of instigation: to delinquency in general; to violation of law; to crimes against the State; to corruption of the public officials; to prostitution; to abortion; to suicide; to class-hatred.

The malice of the instigation belongs to the same nature or kind of sin as the violation which it incites; the gravity of the sin varies according to the influence it exerts to the violation itself. It also is an offense against charity and justice (see Cooperation in Evil). *Tar.*

INSTINCT. Instinct is a natural tendency to actions leading to the attainment of a goal, natural to the species. In its proper and strict sense, instinct belongs to animal life; in fact, in its pure state it is found only in animals, which are guided by such a force in their normal or unusual actions. In human beings, animal instinct is subordinate to the influence of rational faculties which modify and moderate the instinct. Hence, instinct in human beings is less developed than in most animals, although man is fully compensated by the possession of the power of reason, a superior guide. In a broader sense, any natural tendency that acts without reflection, even if it belongs to superior psychic faculties, is called instinct. Thus, we speak of the instinctive impulse of the will toward good, and of the intelligence toward the truth. Some theologians speak also of supernatural instincts, referring by such a term to those impulses which God's grace excites in man, to lead him in a way that could be called irresistible to the practice of virtue in an heroic degree. *Gra.*

INSTITUTES, SECULAR. Secular institutes are clerical or lay institutes in which the members, though remaining in the world, profess the evangelical counsels for the purpose of attaining Christian perfection and engaging fully in the apostolic works of religion and charity. These institutes, in existence for some time, obtained juridical status on February 2, 1947, with the publication of the Constitution *Provida Mater Ecclesia*, the motu proprio *Primo feliciter* of March, 1948, and the Instruction of the Sacred Congregation of Religious *Cum Sanctissimus* of March 19, 1948.

At the present time secular institutes are found in fifteen nations in Europe and America; more than one hundred have been approved by the Holy See.

According to the decrees mentioned, a secular institute is organized basically as follows: (a) The members take no public vows, do not live a community life. Not religious in the usual sense of the word, as members living in a community life, they are not subject to the law for ordinary religious institutes. They are governed by the apostolic constitutions and norms given by the Sacred Congregation of Religious on those constitutions, and regulations or laws for each institute as approved by lawful authority. Under all circumstances, they are and must remain *secular*, that is, strive for perfection in the world in a way of life centered on the apostolate chosen by their respective professions of life.

(b) The requirements for the erection of a secular institute are: (1) The members must consecrate themselves to God by the profession of the vows, oaths, or promises of celibacy and perfect *chastity*, *obedience* to their lawful superiors in the works of the apostolate and charity, and *poverty* by the limitations freely accepted on the use of goods, according to the norms of each organization. (2) The members must bind themselves to the institute in a stable manner (perpetual or temporal), and the institute accepts them and obliges itself to their maintenance. (3) Despite the absence of community life in the proper sense of the term, the institute must have houses for the general or regional superiors, for training and forming the new members, for retreats and other similar exercises of piety, and for the sick members or others who are without lodging or care.

(c) By virtue of their full consecration to God and the salvation of souls, by their internal government, whether of pontifical or diocesan right, these institutes of seculars are numbered among the states of perfection juridically recognized by the Church, and are accordingly under the jurisdiction of the Sacred Congregation of Religious. Missionary apostolates among certain secular institutes bring these under the jurisdiction of the Sacred Congregation for the Propagation of the Faith. Institutes lacking the necessary approval of the papal authority are classified as pious associations of the faithful and are subject to the Sacred Congregation of the Council.

(d) Local Ordinaries, but not vicar capitulars or vicar generals, with due permission (*nihil obstat*) of the Sacred Congregation, may erect secular institutes as legal persons, and these are considered of diocesan right. Those, however, which have obtained the *laudatory degree* of approval by the Holy See become institutes of pontifical right. To obtain this approval, basically the same procedure is followed as for religious institutes.

(e) Secular institutes of pontifical right are subject to the local Ordinaries in the same manner as the congregations or societies with community life; those of diocesan right are completely under the jurisdiction of the local Ordinary, who has the authority not only to watch over their internal government but also to change their constitutions.

(f) Internal government may be organized in the hierarchical form of religious congregations or societies with community life; it is, therefore, possible to have a central organization of interdiocesan, regional, or world-wide form as an organized body. Attention must be paid, however, to the nature, scope, and other elements which determine the activities carried out by the members of the institutes. No federations are excluded, whether of diocesan, regional, or national character, provided they are in keeping with and directed to fostering the Catholic character of the Church. *M.d.G.*

INSTITUTION, ECCLESIASTICAL.

An institution is a place or legal person, such as a house, hospital, or other establishment, which is constituted for works of charity, religion, social welfare, and the like.

The institution or foundation may be religious or secular, according to the purpose of its work; an institution, engaged in a religious work or for religious purposes, is called a religious or ecclesiastical institution.

A charitable institution may be ecclesiastical or secular. Institutions, established by the authority of the Church or formally approved by such authority, are called ecclesiastical institutions. These may be collegiate or non-collegiate.

A collegiate institution consists of several physical persons, united together to form an associated body, living a community life in monasteries or chapters. A non-collegiate institution is a union of materials or properties which are destined for charitable purposes. Formally constituted as a separate legal entity apart from other patrimonies, a non-collegiate stitution is said to be an ecclesiastical institution.

Non-collegiate institutions usually shelter, train, or maintain needy persons, such as orphans, aged, or mentally ill; they may also be houses in which charity, piety, and religion are publicly professed.

If ecclesiastical authorities participate in the erection or foundation of the institution, they are said to be ecclesiastical institutions.

The local Ordinary has the right to approve and erect these institutions. Since non-collegiate institutions admit of constitution as a legal or juridical person, the local Ordinary has the power of establishing them as such by a formal decree, according to Canon 100 (par. 1). As legal persons they acquire all the rights belonging to legal persons, particularly that of possession of temporal goods.

ADMINISTRATION. The administration of the property of these institutions is in the hands of the rector of each place, and is to be carried out in accordance with norms stated in the charter of foundation. The rector has the same obligations and enjoys the same rights as the administrators of other ecclesiastical properties (Can. 1489, par. 2).

The local Ordinary who formally erects the institute as ecclesiastical, as the moderator and executor of the charitable works, has broad rights and obligations with respect to these institutions, including the right and duty of visitations of these places, even though they are erected as legal persons or are exempt (Can. 1491, par. 1).

Charitable institutions, even those not constituted as legal persons, are completely subject to the jurisdiction of the local Ordinary, if they are entrusted to a religious community of diocesan right; institutes operated by religious of pontifical right are subject to the supervision of the local Ordinary in all matters pertaining to the teaching of religion, moral conduct, the exercises of piety and the administration of sacred things, despite their exempt status (Can. 1491, par. 2).

Pious institutes, by foundation, prescription, or apostolic privilege, exempt from the jurisdiction and visitation of the local Ordinary, are subject to his right to demand a financial accounting of their status, despite any custom to the contrary (Can. 1492, par. 1). Any foundation in which independence in the administration of financial matters is sought to the exclusion of the authority of the local Ordinary cannot be approved (Can. 1492, par. 2).

The Ordinary shall take care that the pious purposes of the institute are fully carried out as expressed in the charter of foundation (Can. 1493). Without the permission of the Holy See these institutions may not be suppressed, merged, or diverted to other uses than those determined by the founders, unless such provisions were made in the statutes of foundation (Can. 1494). *Pal.*

NOTE: *Pious Institutes in the U. S. A.* The civil laws of the various States in the United States provide incorporation by law by which juridical persons or bodies are created and their rights and duties defined. In view of the fact that there is no official recognition in the U. S. A. for any particular religion or Church, religious bodies, the diocese, parish, or any other ecclesiastical institute must protect themselves and their rights by means of the law of incorporation.

INSTRUCTION. See Education; Father; Piety; Schools, Lay.

INSULIN. See Endocrinology.

INSULT. See Contumely; Abuse.

INTEGRITY (of Confession). See Confession.

INTELLIGENCE. Intelligence is synonymous with intellect; it is the result of a coordinate activity of all the psychic functions of perception, memory, imagination, and thought. Ordinarily, intelligence in the narrower sense indicates a flexibility and quickness of judgment, a swift adaptability when faced with new demands and circumstances.

Man's intelligence develops during the formative period of his life, through the utilization of personal experience and knowledge. Attention and perception and other psychic functions work closely together in the development and consolidation of intellectual ability until a mature capacity for reasoning is achieved in a sound development of the powers of logic and critique, as well as a creative-inventive aptitude in particularly gifted individuals.

At a definite point in life, with the beginning of psychic senility, which varies greatly from individual to individual, thought processes lose their elasticity, become incapable of invention and new acquisition. The progress of these deteriorating processes may cause a morbid state of dementia.

The development of the intellect varies greatly in individuals, according to their natural talent, capacity, additional acquired knowledge, efforts, and the development of their critical powers and ideas. The intellectual variations depend upon the efficiency of the cerebral cortex.

Various classifications of intellectual ability have been suggested, which it seems superfluous to mention here. We note Jung's distinction into introvert and extrovert intellects. The former are more profound and creative and go through the phases of life with a remarkable capacity for interior reflection, entirely absorbed in the world of thought and invention; the latter are reproductive intellects, easily adaptable, sociable, brilliant, and the promoters of the main discoveries of the introverts.

GENIUS AND TALENT. The Romans called *genius* the divinity who, according to their mythology, accompanied man during his entire natural life, supervising his accomplishments. Those acts which appeared to be the expression of functions beyond the normal capacity of an individual were attributed to *genius*. The attribute of brilliancy, talent, cleverness was given to a high intellectual capacity which, however, did not go beyond the bounds of human capability. Hence, gradually, the denomination of *genius* was given to creative activity, particularly in the field of art.

Talent is synonymous with *genius*. Perhaps more properly, many consider talent as midway between genius and intellectual brilliancy. They prefer to speak of talent as an indication of special ability in the artistic, scientific, or even manual fields of endeavor.

MENTAL TESTS. The quantitative and qualitative evaluation of the intellect has enormous practical importance in judging the intellectual development of children, and in the selection of those who show propensity for higher education or specialized work. Such evaluations are made by means of *tests* or *mental reactives* (I.Q.'s). The best-known methods are the *Metric Scale* of Binet-Simon and the more modern test of Terman. According to these methods, the individual is submitted to tests of memory, critical ability, etc., which become increasingly more difficult and complex according to age groups, starting from three years of age. Still more recent are the *Progressive Matrices* (1938 and 1947) the *Intelligence Scales* of Wechsler Bellevue and the Wechsler Adult Intelligence Scale (1955). Other methods are employed for the testing of individual intellectual functions: the Bourdon *test* for voluntary attention; methods of repetition and recognition by memory tests; syllogism test for judgment and critical ability; the Alexander *scale* for the so-called practical intelligence.

An excellent mental test, which allows one to examine and weigh the various aspects not only of the intelligence but also of the emotional sphere and makes possible a considerable degree of observation into the deep psychology of the individual to be studied, is the *Psychodiagnostic Method* of H. Rorschach. He uses a series of ink blots which reveal a *psychogram* from an accurate study of the number and quality of the answers given by the examinee during the course of the test.

These methods contain nothing intrinsically illicit; in fact, insofar as they favor a more selective counselling to professions, they promote an ethical improvement in the living conditions. The data supplied by these methods do not have an absolute value; this and other aspects of the ethical order shall be treated under the entry Mental Tests.

INTELLIGENCE AND MORALITY. Some believe that there exists a certain antagonism between high intellectual ability and morality; that men of genius prefer to lead a rather inordinate life and possess, therefore, low ethical standards. This is an erroneous opinion. Recent studies in applied psychology have demonstrated, instead, that the more intelligent person more readily understands that goals in life must be reached through honesty rather than cheating, by acceping social obligaions rather than by trying to avoid them. "Honesty is certainly tied to intelligence" (A. E. Wiggam). The result of these inquiries of ethical value cannot fail to spur educators to a further development of the intelligence of their pupils, in the certainty that by so doing they will also train their characters and improve their morals. *Riz.*

INTEMPERANCE, MORAL. *See* Criminal Anthropology.

INTENTION. An *intention* is the motive of the will in acting to achieve some end. Intention is important to the subjective morality of the objectively indifferent acts and to the liceity of acts which produce simultaneously different moral effects (*see* Effect, Double). Intention renders an action meritorious, is essential to acts of worship, indulgences, and the administration and reception of the sacraments.

An intention may be *explicit* or *implicit*. An *explicit* intention considers an act distinctly as an end in itself; an *implicit* intention considers an act as an end, not directly in itself, but contained in attaining another end, expressly intended. The intention to hear Mass, for example, is contained in the explicit intention to sanctify the Lord's Day.

Intention may also be *actual, virtual,* or *habitual.* An *actual* intention is the end which motivates the act to which it is referred, such as the singing of a sacred hymn with the intention of glorifying God here and now. A *virtual* intention, without directly and explicitly accompanying an act, is the end for which the act is made; this might occur in the distracted singing of a hymn which initially was intended as an act glorifying God. An *habitual* intention neither accom-

panies nor causes an act, but merely precedes it. Some authors add an *interpretative* intention, which neither accompanies, causes, nor precedes the action, but is really a non-existent intention, which would exist under certain circumstances if the one placing the act were to be later asked his intention in acting.

From the moral point of view, we must strive with a constant effort to elicit proper and holy, explicit and actual intentions. However, one must avoid the danger of over-evaluating the intention at the expense of action, whereby one loses his power to act because of idle and foolish ideas. Intentions must be carried over into acts, and not become substitutes for actions.

Intention and the Sacraments. No intention is demanded of children, the insane, or semi-imbeciles, in the reception of the sacraments, when they are capable of receiving baptism, confirmation, or Holy Communion; the Church supplies the intention for them.

Adults and those endowed with the use of reason must have at least an habitual and implicit intention to receive the sacraments; at times, an interpretative or conditional intention suffices (Denz. 798 ff.; Cans. 745, 752). *Gra.*

INTENTION, RIGHT. In all actions, internal or external, man is moved to action by that which he considers simply a good, which he loves and seeks simply for what it is; that is, he intends something as an end. This intention is right, if it conforms to the requirements of the moral law.

The thing desired in itself can be considered an end, that is, not subordinated to another thing as an intermediary end. Obviously it is not permitted to seek, as an end, any good except that desired and sought in itself, insofar as it is in accord with the requirements of human nature elevated by grace, or at least destined to be elevated thus, and in accord with the requirements of reason, under the guidance of faith. These requirements, in fact, manifest the will of God. Such an end is honest and, in itself, capable of being desired for the love of God.

Since man was created by God and for

God, this Infinite Good deserves to be loved for Himself above all things. It is never permissible to put any other good before God, by excluding, even implicitly, God as the supreme End. Man must, by his actions, positively tend to God as his supreme End.

Man may intend God as his ultimate End, either explicitly or implicitly. An explicit intention seeks God actually as the supreme End by virtue of a pure act of love of God, elicited previously. Implicit intention is directed toward an end that is honest, but distinct from God, without actually subordinating this end to God or intending it to be under the influence of a prior act of love of God, with the condition, however, that this end be not preferred even implicitly to God.

Texts of Sacred Scripture (III Kings 8:38 ff.; Eccles. 21:1; 44:28; Jer. 3:12 ff. Exod. 29:19 ff.; Dan. 4:24; Zacc. 1:3; Luke 18:13; Rom. 1:21; 2:14) and the condemnations directed against the opinions of Baius and Quesnel (Denz., nn. 1016, 1025, 1035, 1038, 1399, 1405) show that there is no obligation to explicitly intend in our every action God as our ultimate End. An implicit intention is sufficient. We are nevertheless obliged to make pure acts of disinterested love of God, which are implicitly directed to God as our ultimate End and the ultimate End of everything that may be capable of reference to God.

From the moral point of view, the value and merit of our actions depends to a considerable degree on the end actually and explicitly intended, and whether or not the action is placed by one who is in the state of grace. Thus the express, formal intention to tend to God in a love that seeks Him above all things is important. Hence the usefulness of a frequent renewal of the intention to perform every act for the love of God, at least each morning, and the habit of frequent recollection during the day before acting or beginning a task one is about to perform. In this way the value and merit of actions increase despite the insignificance of the task. A fickle and unstable will demands the occasional renewal of this good intention, as it can happen that an action, begun for the love of God, may be continued under the influence of curiosity, sensuality or pride. Those in the state of grace and supernaturalized, as it were, by grace and the infused virtues, direct every non-sinful action by the virtue of charity, the queen of all virtues, to God. In each non-sinful action, the aim of those living in grace is, not a purely natural good, but a supernatural one.

On the other hand, a good action performed with more than one good intention acquires more merit and greater value. Thus, in an action that is evil by nature or circumstance, even a good intention does not remove its sinful nature. The guilt may, however, be of lesser degree than under an evil intention. Furthermore, a good action may become sinful if it is performed with an evil intention; the degree of guilt, however, depends on the nature of the motive. *Man.*

INTERCESSION. Intercession is mediation in behalf of another. It may be human or divine.

Divine intercession can only be exercised on behalf of those who are pilgrims on this earth, that is, those who have not yet reached an unchangeable state insofar as their relationship with God is concerned. Thus, the blessed in heaven, who can, of course, assume the office of intercessors, and the damned in hell are excluded. Intercession is termed *impetrative*, a prayer of petition; *expiatory*, the offering of meritorious and atoning works; or *impetrative* and *expiatory* at the same time.

Intercession in the divine order. God, who sees the needs of His children, could certainly provide for them directly, but in His divine wisdom He loves to dispense His gifts through intermediaries. Strictly speaking, the only mediator between God and His children is Jesus Christ, the God-Man: He has with God an infinite and efficacious power of intercession, because He earned every grace by strict justice (Matt. 11:27; John 14:6; Rom. 5:1; 12:24). Any other intercession must be understood as subordinate to and receiving efficacy from Christ. Hence, in the liturgy, all prayers are offered "through Christ Our Lord," High Priest between God and man (Hebr. 4:14–15), Universal Redeemer by the sacrifice of His Blood (Hebr. 9:11–28; Rom. 3, 25 ff.; Eph. 1), forever interceding in behalf of His brethren.

The doctrine approving impetrative and expiatory intercession by the living in behalf of other living persons is a dogma of faith proposed by the ordinary teaching authority of the Church and attested to by Holy Scripture (Es. 32: 11–14; Num. 14:13–20; I Sam. 7:8 ff.; Acts 7, 60; 12, 5).

Also a dogma of faith is the doctrine stating the efficacy of impetrative and expiatory intercession by the living in behalf of the souls in Purgatory (Denz. 464, 693) by means of all types of spiritual acts (Holy Masses, prayers, alms, Holy Communion, indulgences, etc.). It is common doctrine, supported by Christian practice, that the souls in Purgatory can exercise impetrative intercession in behalf of the living. However, the efficacy of their intercession cannot be compared to that of the saints.

Intercession by the saints consists of prayers by which the saints implore heavenly favors from Christ. The Blessed Virgin Mary, as the mediatrix of all graces, is most influential in our behalf, next to Christ, who is the Divine Mediator in man's behalf. Next are the angels and saints. The Council of Trent, in defense of the ancient practice of the veneration of the saints in the Church, declared that those who reject the cult of the saints, by calling it senseless, are impious (Denz. n. 984; *Professio Fidei*, n. 998). Furthermore, Trent explains the precise relationship between the Church Militant on earth, and the Church Triumphant: the saints pray for the faithful on earth; the faithful honor the saints and invoke their assistance.

We do not render to the saints the supreme cult of adoration but a subordinate cult of veneration, which is called *dulia*. We venerate them with a real cult which is based on the gifts and graces bestowed upon them by Almighty God. This cult of veneration is ultimately directed at God, who alone has made them worthy of our veneration and honor, through the gifts of the supernatural order, graces and privileges, which His goodness bestowed upon them. Any accusation of adoration of the saints is simply unjustified.

Invocation of the saints is based directly on the union of the saints with God, and their concern for the propagation of His Kingdom on earth. Therefore, the objection of Protestants against the veneration and invocation of the saints is without basis.

It is true that the Scriptures contain no specific texts concerning a cult of the saints, but there are, indeed, many traces and allusions. The Old Testament speaks with great reverence of the Patriarchs and Fathers: *"Their name liveth unto generation and generation. Let the people show forth their wisdom: and the Church declare their praise"* (Ecclus. 44:15–16). Sirach details a long series of holy persons (Ecclus. 44–50). Onias and the prophet Jeremias, both dead, are said to love their brothers left on earth and to pray for their people and the holy city (Cf. II Macc. 15:12–14). Jesus and the Apostles gave no specific instructions concerning the cult of the saints. But Jesus speaks with great veneration of Moses (Matt. 23:2 ff.; Mark 7:10; 10:3; 12:26; John 5:45–46; 7:23), of David (Matt. 22:42–43), of the three Patriarchs (Matt. 8:11; 2:32; Luke 16:22). He speaks of them as united with the living God (Matt. 22:32). The "Bosom of Abraham" is interpreted by Jesus and the people of His time as peace (Luke 16: 22). The Apostles often refer to Abraham (Rom. 4; Gal. 3; James 2:21), Noah (II Pet. 2:5), Job (James 5:11) and the saints (Hebr. 11). The Roman Catechism rightly stands on these Biblical texts (Part III, ch. 2, q. 12). Concerning the obligation to invoke the saints, *see* Saints. *Pal.*

INTERDICT. An interdict is a decree of prohibition; it may be civil or ecclesiastical.

(a) *Civil Interdict.* Originally an administrative order of the praetor, issued in virtue of his *imperium,* the interdict prevented the fulfillment of a punishment for an offense against sacred or public property or for breaches of the peace. Later, it was issued by the praetor as a remedy in various cases, particularly of disputed possession. If it commands an action, it is termed a *decree*; if it prohibits an action, it is called an *interdict*. It acquired a later meaning similar to that of an injunction in English law.

Interdicts may be restitutory, exhibitory, or prohibitory; little evidence indicates that interdicts were a form of interim injunction or summary process. In the systems of civil law in general, the interdict resembles an injunction.

(b) *Ecclesiastical Interdict*. This is a prohibition by the Pope, bishop, or other ecclesiastical superior whereby a cleric or layman is restrained from performing or attending a divine service, or from administering an office or enjoying a privilege of the Church. An ecclesiastical interdict may be *general* or *particular*, *personal* or *local*. As a personal canonical penalty, interdict goes back to the fourth century; as a local penalty, to the sixth century. It was frequently used by ecclesiastical authorities until the eleventh century. The misdeeds of Philip I forced Gregory VII to allow the French bishops to suspend divine services; the misdeeds of Boleslaus caused an interdict to be placed on the whole ecclesiastical province of Poznan. It may be imposed on a particular place where the exercise of certain sacred offices or functions is restricted. The administration of the sacraments or the exterior solemnity accompanying the administration of those sacraments considered necessary for the salvation of souls, such as baptism, penance, and Holy Viaticum may be suspended. An interdict may be personal or local (Can. 2268, par. 2); general or particular (Can. 2269); *latae sententiae* or *ferendae sententiae*—that is, either a vindicative punishment in which the penal intent is primary, or a medicinal punishment in which a remedial or medicinal intent prevails.

Effect of a Local Interdict. A local interdict may be general or particular; in the former the effects are broad and severe for a specific area (Can. 2271), and the latter is limited to one church, altar, or cemetery (Can. 2272). The cele-

bration of divine services is interrupted or restricted; all solemnizations are forbidden. In cathedral or parochial churches, however, the administration of the sacraments, preaching, funeral services, or other sacred functions, such as daily Mass, may be permitted without the solemnities of choir, organ, music, bells, etc. (Can. 2272, par. 2). Priests not under personal interdict are allowed to celebrate Mass behind locked doors, with only the server assisting (Can. 2271, par. 1). Only in danger of death are these effects suspended regarding sacraments and sacramentals, and Holy Viaticum, which must be carried to the dying person privately (Can. 2270). Consequently, under interdict, confirmation, except in danger of death, and ordination are absolutely forbidden. On the day of Christmas, Easter, Pentecost, Corpus Christi, and the Assumption, the interdict is suspended (Can. 2270, par. 2). Famous among interdicts were the roving interdict placed by Innocent II on all places to which Ludwig the Younger went, as well as that imposed by Alexander III on Cremona, Leon, and France, and those by Alexander IV on Portugal, and Gregory IX on Sicily. After the fourteenth century the effectiveness of interdict on society decreased; hence, its use became rare. However, in 1909 Pius X issued a general, local, and personal interdict on the city of Adria and its outlying districts, and, in 1913, on the town of Galatina, for assaults on the person of a bishop. There have been also more recent examples of personal interdicts following the latest condemnations of atheistic communism (1949–1953).

In ancient times the juridical effects of interdict and excommunication were not clearly distinct. An interdict usually effected a suspension of divine services and the administration of the sacraments and the closing of churches. Later, the penalties became less severe, and the administration of the necessary sacraments such as baptism, penance, and Holy Viaticum as well as preaching outside the church were permitted; divine services were permitted behind locked doors. The effects of interdict were suspended on the principal solemnities of the year, such as

Christmas, Easter, Pentecost, the Assumption, and Corpus Christi.

Nature and Kinds of Interdict. Interdict, as a canonical penalty, deprives the faithful of certain spiritual benefits and specific rights (Can. 2268, par. 1). The medicinal objective at times may prevail over the penal; hence, it compels a stubborn and obstinate offender, previously duly admonished, to make amends and suitable reparation. In cemeteries under interdict, bodies may be buried, but without the usual solemnities and ecclesiastical rites (Can. 2272, par. 2).

An interdict inflicted as a censure ceases with sacramental absolution; if imposed as a vindicative penalty, it ceases upon the fulfillment of the penalty, or by a resolutory condition, or by lawful dispensation.

Effects of a Personal Interdict. A personal interdict becomes effective directly and immediately upon promulgation and follows the individual everywhere; it may be inflicted on individuals or communities as such, or on individuals and communities at the same time (Cans. 2268, par. 2; 2269, par. 2).

An individual under personal interdict may not celebrate nor assist at divine services, although he is allowed to listen to the preaching of the word of God; nor is it necessary to expel those who assist at divine services only as bystanders. Furthermore, interdicted persons cannot exercise the ministry or any other spiritual or temporal ecclesiastical right. Lastly, they are deprived of an ecclesiastical burial; they retain, however, rights connected with the exercise of legal ecclesiastical acts and acts of jurisdiction (Can. 2275).

Communities under interdict cannot exercise spiritual rights proper to them. Innocent members, however, who are not members of the interdicted community, retain their full spiritual rights (Cans. 2274–2276).

Interdict from Entering a Church. One who violates a local interdict, by taking part in the divine services, incurs the special personal interdict "from entering a church." This personal interdict entails a prohibition from celebration or assistance at sacred functions in the church, but not in an oratory. They are deprived of ecclesiastical burial. But if, nevertheless, one attends services, he need not be expelled; if he is buried in consecrated ground, the body need not be removed (Can. 2277).

Interdicts in Present Canon Law. Few interdicts are listed in present-day Canon Law (Cans. 2328; 2329; 2338, par. 3–4; 2339–2356), and these are only against individuals. With regard to local interdicts, a wide discretion is given to local authorities. *Pug.*

INTERDICTION. Interdiction (Latin, *inter-dicere*—to prohibit, interpose) is the act of prohibiting or being prohibited in civil law by a voluntary or judicial restraint imposed upon a person with regard to his capacity to exercise a right. This frequently occurs in cases which, because of mental weaknesses or lack of age, require the appointment of a legal guardian. This prohibition is also applied to the exercise of other civil rights for various reasons.

CANON LAW. Canon Law recognizes civil law in questions of interdict, except for questions involving spiritual or judiciary matters pertaining to ecclesiastical jurisdiction. It leaves to the discretion of the local Ordinary the use of an interdict issued by civil authority, the issuance of a new decree by ecclesiastical authority, or reparation necessary for deficiencies of a civil interdict. Once civil or ecclesiastical sentence has been pronounced, the interdicted person is put under guardianship, unless, in the opinion of the Ordinary or judge, he is considered capable of acting for himself in certain matters without a guardian.

A person under interdict is incompetent in the performance of certain patrimonial or legal proceedings and activities, which relate to his position as the head of a family. Among these are contracts without the assistance of the guardian assigned by competent legal authority. When the causes which justified interdiction cease, the sentence may be revoked by the same authority which issued it.

Interdiction from public office, inflicted as a punishment after a temporary or perpetual penal sentence, deserves special attention. It deprives the interdicted individual of all political rights, public or elective offices, academic degrees or dignities, titles, decorations, honorary or lucrative rights connected with a public office and the further capacity to acquire these. Canon Law carries its own further penalties: inability (*q.v.*) and incapacity (*q.v.*). *Pug.*

INTEREST. Interest is the "price of money," or rental payment upon money, that is, a charge made to the borrower by the lender for the use of money.

With respect to the moral lawfulness of charging interest, some theories attempting to justify the reasons why a capital should produce interest are untenable. The theory of "productivity," which compares the interest on a capital to the rent of land, is acceptable only if the loaned capital is used in a productive way, that is, if it produces a benefit, as the land produces its fruits. The doctrine that considers interest as the price of time seems to be a more justifiable one.

Rate of Interest. The rate of interest is a percentage charged for the use of money. Rates of interest are determined by the demand for money. In many countries the rate of interest is fixed by law at an official rate, governed, like a minimum wage and price (*q.v.*) of merchandise, by various factors of demand and supply, capital, savings, and the degree of risk.

Loans at interest were condemned in classic antiquity (Aristotle, Cato), because it was largely practiced in abusive and cruel forms by the rich against the poor. The Fathers of the Church condemned it, as well as civil (Justinian) and Canon Law. The Koran also condemned it. The condemnation was, not of honest interest, but the practice of usury, which had become a characteristic of the times. One of the causes of the decadence and fall of the Roman Empire (Toniolo) was usury as practiced by capitalism. The Church did not stop at Aristotle's declaration concerning the sterility of money but tried to curb the monopoly of money and its exploitation, by forbidding loans at interest. A "loan for consumption," as such, did not justify charging interest; until recent times, credit and money loans could be made only if they were to be used for purposes of consumption (*q.v.*). When former canonists stated that loans were sterile, they showed a precise knowledge of the state of the economy of their days. The Lateran Council (1515) put the question in its exact perspective when it stated: "There is usury when the lender's profit is not derived from fruitful sources and does not require labor, expense, or risks on his part" (Can. 1543). Nowadays, one can say that the nature of loan contracts has completely changed. Money is borrowed for investment, and loans for consumption are rare. Mortgages have taken on a true economic aspect as a form of production. The interest itself is included in the cost of production as wages and rent are; thus it becomes part of the "cost" of the finished product. In the early days, the Church opposed the charging of interest on loans because, identified with the most monstrous usury, it tended to destroy the benefits obtained by the emancipation of serfs and slaves. Nor did such an attitude harm economic progress; in fact, it favored small companies and corporations, by recognizing man and his work as the real source of true wealth. *Bar.*

INTERMEDIN. *See* Hypophysis.

INTERNUNCIO. *See* Nuncio, Apostolic.

INTERPRETATION (of Law). Interpretation of law is sometimes necessary if a law is obscure. From the standpoint of the source of the interpretation, interpretation is *authentic, juridical, doctrinal,* or *common.* An *authentic* interpretation is given by the legislator himself, or by an organ established for this purpose, such as the Commission for the Interpretation of the Code in the Church; *judicial* interpretation is provided by a judge in issuing a definite decision; *doctrinal* interpretation is given by scholars and research; *common* interpretation results from the manner in which a law is commonly observed in society.

From the standpoint of content, interpretation may be *declaratory, extensive,* or *restrictive.* It is termed a declaratory interpretation if the law is explained without any alteration in terminology; an extensive interpretation enlarges the scope of laws; a restrictive decision limits the law. These are new laws, in fact, which do not become binding until promulgation (*q.v.*) of those clauses which require enforcement; declaratory interpretation is not subject to these requirements.

Interpretation and observance. For the moral guidance of the individual in his daily observance of the law we shall propose the following norms: (a) a law must be interpreted and observed honestly and loyally according to the proper and commonly accepted meaning of the words in which it is expressed; (b) the individual is not allowed to interpret the law with either a restrictive or extensive application or intent, and thereby enlarge the range of his own liberty; (c) an interpretation of a law which would thereby authorize or compel a person to act contrary to the moral precepts is to be rejected. *Gra.*

INTERPRETER. An interpreter acts as intermediary in conversation between two or more persons of different language capabilities. Interpreters are used particularly in international conventions and meetings, judiciary interrogations, business, the preparation of contracts, etc. The interpreter is also at times necessary in the celebration of a marriage or in confession to a priest who does not understand the language of the penitent (Can. 903). An interpreter is not obligatory in such confessions, but one may be used if it is deemed necessary or advisable for the penitent, and he so wishes. The seal of confession must be protected by guarantees that the interpreter does not see the penitent and by other devices.

The principal moral obligation of an interpreter is to faithfully fulfill his office by translating accurately without alterations in the meaning. Furthermore, an obligation of secrecy according to the intention of the person involved, or the nature of the information acquired, exists toward his duties.

An interpreter in confession is bound by the same seal of confession as the confessor himself (Cans. 889, par. 2; 2369, par. 2); hence, he may not for any reason whatsoever reveal any information learned by such duties (*see* Seal of Confession). *Ben.*

INTERSTICES. In the reception of the various holy orders, certain proper intervals of time must intervene; these intervals of time between the different sacred orders are called interstices. Intervals of time for the gradual and progressive reception of holy orders were established by the Church for the sake of testing and forming clerics or candidates for holy orders. The Church also requires that the order received must be exercised for a short time at least.

Church discipline concerning intervals has varied from the time of the early centuries in the Church. The necessity of ordaining at an appointed time in each year, and the obligation to exercise a lower order before admittance to a higher one made it necessary to exact interstices, first as custom and later as law. These rigid prescriptions of ancient times have been mitigated by Canon Law (Can. 978).

The intervals between first tonsure and ostiariate and the intervals between the individual minor orders are left to the discretion of the bishop; it is forbidden to confer first tonsure and minor orders at one time, or all four minor orders at the same time. At least one year must elapse between each major order. The bishop, if he judges it necessary or useful to the Church, may dispense from this law; without permission of the Roman Pontiff, a bishop cannot confer on the same day a minor order and sub-diaconate to the same candidate or two major orders, despite any custom to the contrary.

Between the priesthood and episcopacy a lapse of five years is prescribed (Can. 331, par. 1, n. 3).

INTESTATE. *See* Inheritance; Will; Testament.

INTOXICATION. *See* Alcoholism.

INVALID ACT. *See* Human act.

INVENTOR, INVENTION. *See* Authors, Rights of.

INVENTORY. *See* Estimate; Bankruptcy; Liquidator; Usufruct.

INVOLUNTARY. *See* Voluntary.

IRONY. Irony, a form of humor, ridicule or light sarcasm, implies the opposite of the literal sense of the words employed in speech. It is generally directed against a peculiar state or attitude of mind, a physical condition or the behavior of an individual. The figurative or ironical meaning is evident from the manner in which a statement is expressed by gesture or tone of voice. Irony may be employed seriously or in a joking sense to correct a fault, or to deride or discourage a person from pursuing an action that is good.

In the joking sense, irony is not a sin, if moderation prevails and does not inflict anguish. If these different conditions are absent, irony may be sinful; gravely so, if a grave offense is inflicted on the other, or it tends to render life extremely difficult, or incites formal disrespect for authority. In such cases it is more accurate to term this *sarcasm*, which is an irony mixed with hatred and animosity. Irony, employed for the correction of a fault or defect, is not only permissible but, at times, very useful if expressed in an appropriate manner. Irony simply for ridicule or to hinder another from carrying out good deeds is always sinful—a grave sin, if the irony is seriously harmful or is the cause of grave sins or omissions of good. Derision of God, parents, superiors, or virtue implies a particular form of moral deformity. *Man.*

IRREGULARITY AND IMPEDI-MENTS (to Holy Orders). An irregularity is a canonical impediment which permanently bars a man from holy orders. Generally it also forbids the exercise of orders already received. Irregularities may be based on defects or crime (Can. 984–985).

(1) *Irregularities from Defect.*

(a) Illegitimate offspring, whether public or occult, unless the impediment is removed by legitimation or by solemn vows.

(b) Persons afflicted with bodily deformities which would make them unable to exercise the sacred ministry in a safe or becoming manner; among these are blindness, deafness, or physical deformations.

(c) Epileptics, the mentally deranged, or diabolically possessed. If such occur after ordination, the Ordinary may permit the exercise of orders, after the individual has recovered entirely from the disorder.

(d) Persons who have been validly married twice.

(e) Persons under infamy of law (*see* Infamy of Law and Fact). This is contracted automatically (*ipso facto*) for very grave crimes: desecration of the Sacred Species (Can. 2320) or graves (Can 2328); physical violence against the Pope (Can. 343, par. 1) or a cardinal (Can. 2843, par. 2); duelling (Can. 2351); bigamy properly so-called, that is, if a person attempts a second marriage while a lawful spouse is still living; certain specific crimes of impurity (Can. 2357, par. 1); infamy incurred after a court sentence in cases of apostasy, enrollment in a non-Catholic sect (Can. 2314), or crimes of immorality (Can. 2359, par. 1).

(f) A judge who imposed a death sentence, even just.

(g) One who acted as executioner. The last two cases are considered as defects of meekness (*defectus lenitatis*).

(2) *Irregularities from Crime.* Crimes which create an irregularity are:

(a) Apostasy, heresy, and schism.

(b) Voluntary acceptance of a non-Catholic baptism.

(c) Civil marriage despite the bonds of a prior marriage, holy orders, or a religious vow.

(d) Voluntary homicide, procured abortion or cooperation in an abortion or homicide.

(e) Self-mutilation or attempted suicide.

(f) The practice of surgery or medicine, without permission, by a cleric, with the consequent death of the patient after this practice.

(g) The performance of acts reserved to clerics in major orders by persons not in these orders or while barred by some canonical penalty from performing such acts.

These violations or crimes do not cause an irregularity unless they are mortal sins committed after baptism, except for the dispositions of Canon 985, par. 2. Also, these crimes must be external acts, public or occult (Can. 986).

Impediments. The following involve simple impediments but not permanent irregularities:

(a) Children of non-Catholic parents as long as the latter remain in their condition.

(b) Married men, as long as the wife lives.

(c) Persons who hold a position of responsibility or an administration forbidden to clerics for which they must give an account.

(d) Slaves, properly so-called, before emancipation.

(e) Those subject to ordinary military service, until completion of that service.

(f) Converts to the faith, until sufficient proof of conversion is present in the judgment of the Ordinary.

(g) One guilty of infamy of fact, until he has regained his good reputation in the judgment of the Ordinary.

Ignorance of irregularities or impediments is not an excuse (Can. 988). Irregularities and impediments may increase in number according to the diversity of causes found in them, but not from repetition of one and the same cause, except the irregularity which is incurred from homicide or abortion.

Dispensation. In general, only the Holy See can dispense from irregularities and impediments, e.g., Sacred Congregation of the Sacraments, Sacred Penitentiary, Propagation of the Faith, etc. Local Ordinaries can dispense only from irregularities due to an occult crime, except homicide and abortion, or those before a judicial

forum (Can. 990, par. 1). Confessors may dispense in urgent cases for the exercise of orders already received (Can. 990, par. 2). In a petition to the Holy See for a dispensation, irregularities and impediments must be properly indicated. If they are not all indicated, a general dispensation is valid for those omitted in good faith, except irregularities reserved by Canon 990, that is, voluntary homicide and crimes brought before a court. This dispensation is invalid for crimes committed in bad faith. In the case of an irregularity incurred for voluntary homicide, the number of crimes must be clearly stated; otherwise, the eventual dispensation may be invalid (Can. 991, par. 1 and 2). A general dispensation for the reception of orders applies also to major orders, but not for the episcopate; neither can one, so dispensed, be designated a cardinal, bishop, abbot, prelate *nullius*, or a major superior in an exempt clerical religious order (Can. 991). *Bar.*

IRRELIGION. Irreligion, a vice opposed to the virtue of religion, inclines man to oppose the performance of acts of worship due to God either directly or through His sacred ministers or things (*see* Religion, Cult). In other words, irreligion is a vice dishonoring God personally or in his sacred ministers or objects. It may take the form of blasphemy (*q.v.*), tempting God (*q.v.*) or perjury (*q.v.*); these are direct violations against the honor due to God or His sacred ministers. The positive refusal to offer worship due to God is a sin of irreligion; all those who obstinately refuse to profess the true religion commit the sin of irreligion.

This theological meaning differs from current use for the term, which signifies a spiritual attitude, in theory and practice, completely disinterested in religion and religious practice from a spirit of general apathy. This attitude is more correctly designated religious indifference (*see* Indifferentism).

Irreligion is a very great sin, since it is a serious violation of moral virtue in open rebellion against God. *Pal.*

ISLAMISM. *Islamism* was the religion preached by Mohammed to the tribes of Arabia. Due to the lack of direct sources of information, little is known of the Arabian religion before the preaching of Mohammed. Information gathered by Moslem historical research on inscriptions and scattered references in Christian writings indicates that previous Arab beliefs retained characteristics proper to other Semitic religions: an animistic foundation, in which spirits (*ginn*) are attributed to sacred trees, fountains, and stones; and a naturalistic element, particularly found in worship of the sun, moon, and stars. The act of cult consisted of a bloody sacrifice, offered on special occasions, and the consecration of young male children to the divinity by a cutting of hair. This sacrifice was offered on sacred stones, as indicated by discovery of these stones in the desert.

Islamism (*islam*—abandonment in Allah) was a monotheistic reform movement against the polytheism of the Arab tribes; it was centered at Mecca, in the holy sanctuary called *Kaaba*. This sanctuary held the sacred images set in a cubic stone.

The Islamic movement was initiated by Mohammed, who possessed all the necessary qualifications for success. He was representative of the redemption of Arabia; his name (*hamada*—to glorify) signified the *glorified one*. His private life is relatively unknown, save for his marriage to Khadigia, to whom he was a faithful husband. He began his mission at a mature age. Believing himself inspired to carry out his mission, he began by proclaiming himself the executor of a superior will. Apart from ethnic elements, stemming from his race and circumstances, his preaching was based on a Christian doctrine of Monophysite and Nestorian extraction, which at the time flourished in the monasteries on the boundaries of the Arabian territory. He also borrowed from the doctrines of Judaism, prevalent in sections of Arabia.

Mohammed first preached reform to the tribe called *Corescites*; he affirmed the unity of God against the multiplicity of gods adored in the Kaaba; he called for greater charity and justice to heal the economic and social imbalance in Arabia. These Corescites, at first, ridiculed and ignored the prophet; later, as his success and fervor met with enthusiasm, they proceeded to persecute him. He fled to Iathrib, which was then called "the town of the prophet" (*Madinat al-Nabi, Medina*).

Mohammed met with success in destroying the idols of the sanctuary and engaged in subjugating those tribes beyond the borders of Arabia by conquering neighboring countries in battles at Honian, Taif, and Tebuk, which was subject to Heracleus, the Emperor of the East.

Triumph for the new movement was assured because of the coordination of an innate power within the Islamic organization, for Islam repaired the major defects of the Arab society: it established a rough but firm political organization, that was created by a strong military system; it introduced a sense of discipline, thereby turning anarchical tendencies among the Arabs to a respect for law and obedience to an executive power invested with authority beyond individual whim.

In the year 631 A.D., Mohammed made his last pilgrimage to Mecca, and died the following year at Medina, where his remains were laid to rest.

SUCCESSORS OF MOHAMMED. Since Mohammed died without male descendants, the question of a successor became a lively issue, upon which rested the fate of the Moslem movement. Four caliphs (*khalifa*—successor, vicar), who succeeded Mohammed, were extremely orthodox and patriarchical. These were Abu Bake (d. 634), Omar (d. 644), Othmann (d. 656), Ali (d. 661), who was Mohammed's son-in-law.

With the death of Ali, the era of patriarchical Islamism ended. This era was characterized by an elected succession in accordance with ancient Arab customs, a simple and austere life by the caliphs, and a certain degree of democracy.

Noawiyn, Ali's successor, who left Medina and took up residence at Damascus, turned the fortunes of Islam from religious to political ambitions. By conquest, Islamism spread to Syria, Persia, Turkestan, Egypt and the northern coast of Africa; from there it swept into Spain, where it was eradicated finally after a bitter struggle made famous in Spanish literature. It also spread into Western Asia, China, and Europe through the efforts of the Abbasids and Ottomans.

KORAN. The Koran (*Al Quran*—reading, meditation) is the main Islamic sacred book, containing the religious, moral, and social Islamic legislation. It consists of 144 chapters, divided into a number of versicles, which represent the revelations that Mohammed allegedly received from God through the angel Gabriel. The first was received at night on Mount Hira; the last in Medina. In these the prophet summarizes the maxims of his religion and exhorts his followers to remain faithful to their commitment.

The language of the Koran is the finest in the Arabic tongue, but the style, in its inspired vein, departs from the poetical language proper to the Arabs. Mohammed wished his language to differ from the poets because they spoke under the inspiration of the demons, whereas he spoke under the influence of the Holy Spirit.

Coherence is not to be expected in a book compiled chapter by chapter according to the various conditions prevailing in the Islamic community. For this reason, Arab exegetes, faced with the impossibility of reconciling the irreconcilable, have with pious ingenuity stated that in the Koran some verses, which they term *abrogating*, cancel out others, called *abrogated*, and in a third category, called *dubious*, no positive conclusions can be drawn.

Besides the holy book, the *Hadith* or tradition, which was written down after the number of followers dwindled, contained the authentic interpretations, which were said to have been provided by the companions of the prophet to new or dubious cases arising from the practice of the Moslem religion. "Companions" are all those men and women who came into contact with the prophet, and whose testimony, therefore, deals with the more particular facts of Mohammed's intimate life. The guarantee of authenticity for this tradition is given by the *isnad* (chain of testimonies), allegedly the chronological list of all persons who transmitted the tradition orally, until it was put into writing.

This whole body of doctrines, developed in the Islamic theological schools, constitutes the Sunnite confession to which the Mohammedans of European and Asiatic Turkey, Arabia, Africa, Russia, Ceylon, and the Malayan Archipelago adhere.

ISLAMIC DOCTRINE. The foundation of the Moslem doctrine is well stated in *sura* 112: "Thou shalt say: Allah is the only God, the God to whom all have recourse. He did not generate anyone nor was he generated; no one is like unto him." This dogma of rigorous unity in God, to the exclusion of any Trinity or Incarnation, which he considered polytheistic (Kor. V, 76–77), is a fulcrum of the whole Islamic doctrine. For this reason Mohammed opposed the Arab polytheism concentrated in the Kaaba. A simplicity of content was certainly the principal intellectual reason for the success of Islamism. In Mohammed's preaching, in which one finds both Christian and Jewish elements, Allah has the same attributes as the God of the Jews and the Christians: omnipotence, omniscience, justice, a creative and conserving providence. Allah communicates with mankind, not directly, but through his envoys, either invested with a special mission or as prophets, such as Abraham, Moses, Jesus, or Mohammed, the main prophet of the present time.

Some Moslem sects arose in opposition to the universalistic expansion of Caliph domination. It suffices to name the *Khangites*, who tend to a patriarchical life of a distinctly Arab tinge; the *Ismaelites*, an important branch of *Schiism*, imbued with Neo-Platonic doctrines and preaching the second appearance of Allah to mankind; the *Carmathians*, who tried to translate into practical, revolutionary form the aspirations of the Ismaelites; the *Druses*, a branch of the Carmathians, found in a few remote locales in Lebanon; the *Nospites*, representatives of the remnants of the old Syrian paganism with some Christian and Moslem elements; the *Sufites*, who express the mystic currents of Islamism and are found particularly in Persia, where the melancholy feeling of national decadence led many to embrace a more austere ideal; and *Babiism* or *Bahaiism*, which arose in the nineteenth century to elevate a religiously decadent Persian Islamism.

The Mohammedan place of prayer is the mosque (*mesgid*—kneeling place); it contains a *mihrale*, which shows the direction of Mecca, toward which each Mohammedan must face in prayer. The mosque must have a minaret or tower, which summons the faithful to ritual prayer with its bells.

There is no priesthood in Mohammedan beliefs; the *Iman* or presiding officer, in charge of the religious functions, represents the Caliph. He wears no special vestment or costume.

Moslems follow the lunar calendar. All feast days begin at night, since the Mohammedans, adopting Jewish beliefs, consider the new day to begin at sundown. Their principal feasts are seven: (1) the prophet's conception; (2) his birth; (3) his ascension; (4) the feast day of the diploma, on which the angels fixed the day of his death; (5) the destiny; (6 and 7) the nights preceding the Great and Little Bayram. The Little Bayram is a feast at the end of the fast of Ramadan; the Great Bayram is a feast at the time of the solemn pilgrimage to Mecca. Each Mohammedan celebrates this feast in his own house with a sense of spiritual union with the actual pilgrims.

MORAL DOCTRINE. The basic moral prescriptions are five in number: (1) *prayer*, which the Koran exemplifies and stresses as necessary; (2) *fasting*, or the abstention from eating, drinking, or smoking throughout the entire day during a specified period of the year (*Ramadan*), for those who have reached the age of puberty; (3) *tithing*, which is a two-fold obligation—*Zakat* or purification, corresponding roughly to the notion of a tenth part of income, and *sadaga* or a voluntary offering; (4) *pilgrimage to Mecca*, by each Mohammedan once in his life, which can be fulfilled by a substitute

if he is prevented from making a pilgrimage; (5) *holy wars*, in which one dies as a martyr and enters paradise at once, if he defends his religion.

SCHISMS. The division of the religion of Mohammed into two main sects, Sunnite and Shiite, was a natural result of the characteristics of the religion itself and due to its two main geographical centers, Medina and Mecca. Medina, the center of early followers who freely accepted the reform of the prophet, was far from Mecca, the center of those forced into conversion through the successes of the prophet. This tended to make Islamism a religious and political force, which subordinated the true religious advantages of the Moslem doctrine to the powers of each group.

The Shiites represented the Medina legitimism, which they spread throughout the East, especially in India. Some followers exist today in the Hegiaz and Egypt. They reject the Sunnah, but respect the Koran, which, however, they interpret differently. Shiites have practically deified Ali, to whose tomb they make a pilgrimage. A Shiite is not permitted to make a pilgrimage to Mecca, for Mohammed is considered an infidel. Because of its Persian characteristics, Shiism is more accessible to rationalistic influences and covers with an amiable smile of mystical toleration the deepest expressions of irreligion. Shiism continues to exist for political reasons in general.

The holy day of the week is Friday, perhaps in remembrance of the ancient cult to the planet Venus, for, on that day, the Caliph used to say his ritual prayer in the mosque.

There is no obligation to community prayer except on Friday, but, since assembly prayer is twenty-five times more valuable than individual prayer, it is always advisable to pray together. In assembly prayer, following the example of their leader in the prayer, all repeat the movements he directs.

Mohammed determined in a specific form the more vague doctrines of ancient Arabia concerning the destiny of the soul after death, by borrowing, it seems, from Christian and Hebrew sources. Mohammed was absolutely convinced of the final resurrection, when at the end of the world men will be scattered like butterflies and the mountains will fly about like locks of wool, and God will judge mankind by weighing each man's deeds on the scale of His justice. If the outcome of this judgment is favorable, the good Mohammedan will pass over the bridge of *Siath*, cross the abyss, and enter into paradise, which resembles a garden of delights of the senses and the spirit, and is located at the right hand of Allah. The infidel and evil Mohammedan will be cast down from the bridge into the abyss of hell to remain for a limited time, if he is Mohammedan, or forever, if he is not.

Today Islamism is affected by a modernistic current, both in India and Egypt. This modernism reached its heights in Turkey under Kemal Pascha (Ataturk), who suppressed the caliphate and laicized the State. It also tends to adapt Moslemism to modern requirements and seeks a return to the simple faith of earlier days, through a downgrading of subsequent theological developments, such as the *salifiyyah* and *neowahabita* movements. *Tur.*

COMMENTS. The religion of the Koran is a religion of dogma and precepts; these exist without a trace of the supernatural; the mysteries of the Trinity and Incarnation are completely denied. In its substitution of monotheism for polytheism, it was religious progress for mankind; it also supplanted Persian magic and African fetishism. It further borrowed many elements of good from Christianity, yet its incongruities, defects, and errors destroy, in the negative sense, whatever positive good Islamism might accomplish.

Islamic monotheism is too rigid; God, a despot and not a father, distributes rewards and punishment capriciously. He treats men as slaves.

The Shiites and philosophers attempted a mitigation of the fatalism of the Koran, but failed. The beatitude of the elect, instead of the state of happiness of children sharing the joy of the Father, is a liberation from slavery and a coarse appeasement of the senses, which philosophers have in vain attempted to allegorize.

The Ramadan is a parody of fasting and mortification, instead of an ascetical exercise; restrictions are limited to daytime alone. Virginity is not valued at all, but is considered an offense against nature. Conjugal chastity is shattered by polygamy and divorce. So great a liberty granted to the Moslem man brought about the degradation of the Moslem woman; the physical and intellectual torpor of the Moslem people and its conquered States was due in great part to the fatalism and sensuality of Islamic doctrines. *Pal.*

ISLANDS OF LANGHERANS. *See* Endocrinology.

ITERATION OF THE SACRAMENTS. *See* Sacraments.

J

JAINISM. The founder of Jainism was Vaddhamana, who was born at Kundaggana (Vesali) in the sixth century B.C., and was surnamed Nahavira, *the great hero,* or Jina, *the conqueror* over human passions. Jainism appears as a revolt against Brahmanic exegesis, which placed the whole Indian society in the hands of a caste system. This revolt, prepared by Upanishadic speculation, rejected the value of ritual and placed salvation in meditation. Along with contemporary Buddhism, Jainism is considered by Brahmans as an heterodox doctrine because of its rejection of the authority of the *Vedas.*

According to Jainism, there are two kinds of beings in the world, clearly opposed to one another: on one side, a multitude of irreducible, real, independent souls *(jiva);* on the other, matter *(pudgala),* conceived as capable of becoming anything at all, according to the shape given to it by the soul. The latter is impelled by an irresistible external impulse to shape matter and to develop within matter itself a certain activity called *karman,* which, depending on whether it is good or bad, determines its transition to higher or lower forms. But in order that the soul may obtain absolute independence and complete rest (through extinction), it must become free of this law of transmigration.

Like Buddhism, Jainism believes in the *three gems* through which one attains freedom: (a) refuge in Jina; (b) knowledge of the world's nature and the means of attaining knowledge; (c) true behavior, i.e., extinction of the *karman,* which leads to deliverance or *mukti* (a sort of Nirvana).

The most effective practical means is asceticism, but on this subject Jainists are divided into two schools: (a) *the digambara,* "clothed by air," that is, naked, and (b) the *aretambara,* or "dressed in white." The former are more rigorous and observant of fasting; in imitation of their master they wear no clothes, at least during their meals, and believe that it is proper to hasten death by total inaction; the latter do not follow the rigors of the *digambara.* The difference in dressing between the two schools is noticeable also in the statues of their gods.

As a philosophical system, Jainism stands midway between Brahmanic speculation and Buddhism, inasmuch as it admits with the former the absolute and unitary permanence of the *atman* and conceives matter as something permanent. It agrees with Buddhism in upholding the fleeting character of all things, whose qualities or accidents are changeable. Hence, each individual thing may be judged right in one respect, wrong in another.

Jainism has a body of sacred scriptures called *Siddhanta,* presently followed by the *Svetambara,* whose final constitution was arranged in the Council of Valabhi, held about A.D. 450. The *digambara* have a body of scriptures of their own, divided into four *Vedas.*

Currently, Jainists number about a million; they are well off and are given to trading; they occupy the Mow, the presidency of Bombay, and the Mysore. *Tur.*

Jainism is an atheistic sect. It is true that Jainists honor and worship supreme beings, but these are souls who have attained a happier condition for having done good things. The common people, however, have come to consider them as true and proper divinities to whom they offer gifts and from whom they ask favors.

Metaphysics and cosmology, which form the basis of Jainist ethics, are full of the coarsest errors, ranging from the eternity of substance (*dravya*) to a relativism of being, undetermined and in continous becoming, to a universal animism (whatever exists, from man to the infinitestimal particles of the earth, has a soul).

To the Jainists the union between soul and body in the sense of traditional Christian philosophy is not natural, but rather an imprisonment of the soul in matter, which is conceived as a chemical compound; hence, the struggle between processes of absorption and separation, until deliverance of the soul is attained. The Jainist moral precepts aim exactly at the absolute annihilation of matter, and their rigor is inhuman. The discipline imposed on the Jainists, which extends to the smallest human acts, and the fundamental concept of nonviolence (*haimsa*), by which the suppression of any form of life is forbidden, impels them to rigorous fasting even to the point of total inaction and voluntary death. It is little wonder, then, that the number of Jainists is very small, consisting of a few castes in a continuous state of regression. *Pal.*

JANSENISM. HISTORICAL BACKGROUND. Jansenism is a doctrine condemned by the Church because it contains theological principles contrary to orthodox teaching. It takes its name from the standard-bearer of this doctrine, Cornelius Jansenius, bishop of Ypres (1585–1638), whose ideas were expounded mainly in his work *Augustinus,* on which he labored for over twenty-two years. *Augustinus* was published in 1640, two years after Jansenius' death.

On August 1, 1641, the Sacred Congregation of the Index and Inquisition condemned eighteen works of Cornelius Jansenius, including the *Augustinus.* The condemnation met with fierce opposition, inasmuch as Jansenism appeared to some as a compromise between Catholicism and Protestantism, while to ultra-liberal individuals it even appeared as the best part of Catholic Reform. New condemnations, therefore, followed in the bull by Pope Urban VIII, *In eminenti,* March 6, 1642; in the constitutions *Cum occasione,* by Pope Innocent X, May 31, 1653; and *Ad sacram beati Petri Sedem,* by Pope Alexander VII, October 16, 1656. In the face of these condemnations, the monastery of Port-Royal assumed a polemic attitude similar to a schism, under the spiritual leadership of the famous abbot of St.-Cyran, DuVergier de Hauranne, and the legal leadership of Antoine Arnauld. Also involved in the controversy were Blaise Pascal (*Lettres provinciales*), and Pierre Nichole, who very soon withdrew from it.

The controversy, however, was later rekindled by Paschasius Quesnel with the publication of his *Réflexions morales* (1671), condemned by Pope Clement X (1675), and also by the pamphlet *A Case of Conscience,* in which it was stated that a respectful silence concerning Jansenius' condemned propositions was sufficient. The pamphlet also was condemned by Clement XI on February 12, 1702. Moreover, Clement XI renewed the condemnations issued by his predecessors, first in the bull *Vineam Sanctam* (Denz., 1350; because the nuns of Port-Royal rejected this bull, they were disbanded and their monastery razed to the ground in 1710), and again in the Bull *Unigenitus,* September 8, 1713, which contains and condemns 101 propositions of Quesnel, i.e., the entire theological, ascetic, and moral doctrine of Jansenism. Later on, Pope Clement XI excommunicated those who opposed the condemnation (party of the appellants) in the bull *Pastoralis officii,* 1718. In his bull *Unigenitus,* issued in 1718, Benedict XIV renewed all previous condemnations.

The centers of revolt that remained active after the various condemnations were mainly the schismatic Church of Utrecht, the movement of St. Medardus' Convulsionaries, and a few others. But Jansenism was kept alive above all by anti-Jesuit opposition, by the Gallican policies of the courts, and by the controversies on grace and the moral systems. In Italy, the controversy was kept alive in two centers: in Pavia, under the leadership of Pietro Tamburini, and the other in Pistoia, which became the experimental ground of Scipione Ricci, the promoter of the infamous synod of Pistoia (1786). Eighty-five propositions were extracted from the acts of the Synod and condemned by Pius VI in the bull *Auctorem fidei*, August 28, 1794.

MORAL DOCTRINE. The moral doctrine of Jansenism is rather obscure. Basically, it appears as a rigoristic doctrine. One of its dogmas consists in diminishing human liberty and debasing nature in order to extol the efficacy of grace. As a whole, it is based on the concept of God as a severe and exacting Lord. The fundamental part of Jansenist doctrine, which consists of the theology of grace (borrowed from Baius), was fully explained by Jansenius himself; the sacramentarian moral doctrine was rather the work of Antoine Arnauld, while disciplinary and spiritual practice was elaborated and promoted by the abbot of St.-Cyran.

In order to give even a concise summary of the moral doctrine of Jansenism, one must first necessarily recall the doctrine of grace, and then analyze the keen synthesis of the human act as proposed by Jansenius and his followers. The initial postulate in the doctrine of Jansenius is the essential distinction between the state of innocence and that of sin, and the influence which grace exercises in each of the two states; a state of pure nature is excluded as impossible. The central idea is the irreducible alternative between concupiscence and charity: man is allured by a twofold love (*delectatio victrix*—conquering delectation), one earthly, the other heavenly. Grace, which is necessary in order to do good, is necessarily efficacious. Jansenius draws a distinction between Adam's grace and that of man in the state of fallen nature; the two graces, he holds, are intrinsically different.

Adam's will was totally indifferent and freedom was the mistress of grace: after the Fall, however, there is no other liberty except to sin. In man's present state, grace dominates, not liberty. Before his sin, man could merit; now, all merits are God's. Consequently, after the Fall sufficient grace no longer exists, because it is impossible that sufficient grace may become a sin.

Jansenius, then, endeavors to prove that theologians are simply reviving the Pelagian theories. The properties of grace, for him, are: efficaciousness, omnipotence, an irresistible sweetness of attraction. It is a *victrix* (conquering) grace, because it breaks all obstacles. *Trahit sua quemque voluptas.* Good cannot be thought of, or desired, or pursued without this grace. The struggle between the two delights is at the root of all works. It is erroneous to think, as philosophers say, that man remains free during temptation. The saints are impeccable because of the *delectatio victrix* (conquering delectation). Devils do sin, because they continuously have a *victrix* delight for sin. Grace is essentially a product of charity, and virtues are but love of God (identity between grace and charity; between charity and virtues). Even the theological virtues are but forms of charity. There is no true faith without charity. Hope, too, is implicit in love, for every love tends to an absent good.

Speaking of hope, Jansenius distinguishes a twofold fear: filial and servile. Servile fear is vicious, as vicious as concupiscence. When St. Augustine and the Council of Trent speak of the licitness of servile fear, they speak of perfect contrition. Servile fear is *initium sapientiae*, but not wisdom, because it hinders the external action and moves the sinner to beg of God true love.

In the Jansenistic conception of grace there is hardly a place for free will. It is grace that gives freedom to man. Jansenius has a negative notion of free will; for him it means the absence of external slavery. An action is in our control when it proceeds from our will; whatever is voluntary is also free. A previously existing indifference is foreign to the concept of liberty. We must only distinguish between internal and external necessity; the former does not take freedom away, the latter does.

The power of doing evil is not essential to liberty. Now, the better one knows what good is, the less he is able to choose from among the various goods. Consequently, God and the blessed are free, not because they can choose freely from among various things, but because they can only do good. Neither freedom of contradiction nor of contrariness is necessary to liberty. From this there follows a conciliation between liberty and grace. Truth is neither in Thomism nor in Molinism. Thomism is right when it affirms the efficacy of grace, but this efficacious grace is none other than the act of the will. Grace does not wait for the assent of the will, but produces it. Grace and good works are synonymous. Every grace obtains its effect; and the reason why the effect does not always follow is that not all graces are equal: some are destined to produce a slight wish, others a firm deliberation, but grace is always efficacious. Sufficient grace, on the other hand, only stimulates pride; it is a monstrous grace because it never produces its effect.

If God does not always give the grace to fulfill certain precepts. He does not do so because He wants to teach us humility. When He gives grace He performs an act of mercy; when He does not give it, He does a work of justice, because a man without grace has no right to grace.

To sum up: (a) Man cannot do good because his free will is a slave of concupiscence; it is grace, therefore, that frees man from concupiscence. (b) Man must of necessity do wrong: without grace, in fact, each precept necessarily leads him to sin in every action. Without grace, not even a struggle is possible; hence the fall is inevitable. Without grace, victory itself cannot be without sin, because one fights either because of pride or of carnal fear. A struggle for virtue, as such, is the begin-

ning of pride; only charity is justice, and it gives power to do good. (c) The law impels to sin not only because it increases concupiscence but also because it causes one to act out of self-love. Mere absence of faith causes all actions of non-believers to be sinful. A non-believer is incapable of virtue, not because he is unable to accomplish a repetition of acts, for then he would have at least a beginning of virtue, but because each act of his is corrupt from the very beginning.

From the aforesaid it is clear that Jansenism (a) leads to theological fatalism; (b) debases the justice of God, inasmuch as concupiscence is made imputable to God; (c) from theological fatalism it is easy to slide into psychological determinism, and from that to destruction of liberty and, consequently, of imputability.

In the field of sacramental theology Jansenists demand too great a perfection in those who receive the sacraments in order that these may effectively sustain human weakness irresistibly tending toward evil. Only the violence of grace can stop it on its downhill sliding, because as a result of original sin human nature is maimed. No other means can be proposed except penance, for it is only through penance that one may make his predestination sure. Therein, according to Jansenist doctrine, lies the value of the Christian life. The fallacies of this doctrine of pessimism and desperation are rebutted by Molinism in dogmatic theology, and by probabilism (*q.v.*) in moral theology. *Pal.*

JEALOUSY. Jealousy is an unpleasant fear, resentment, or suspicion stemming from mistrust of another person. It is also an intolerance of rivalry, or more often the desire to be the sole possessor of a good which others too may properly possess, whether it be a financial or social status, a specific quality, popularity or the like. Fundamentally, jealousy stems from egoism and undue attachment to worldly things. It is an offense against the precept of love of neighbor; it may be gravely or lightly sinful depending on the nature of the thing of which one desires to be the exclusive possessor, and also on the damage one may cause or is disposed to cause to others in order to hinder them from attaining a good similar to the one possessed.

At times jealousy takes the form of an unpleasant suspicion of the faithfulness of husband or wife. Obviously, the protection of one's exclusive marital rights is indeed good and dutiful, but it must not be allowed to become an oppressive exaggeration for the other party to the point of inhibiting him or her from participating in normal human activities, or from honest friendships which in no way touch upon conjugal faithfulness.

In some particularly predisposed individuals jealousy often assumes serious forms. Principal among these are (a) *melancholic jealousy*, observed in depressed individuals hostile toward their own environment (*see* Melancholy): (b) *paranoic jealousy*, found in paranoic individuals (*see* Paranoia); (c) *obsessive jealousy*, which is a symptom of obsessive diathesis (*see* Obsession, Psychasthenia); (d) *jealousy stemming from alcoholic delirium*, peculiar to chronic alcoholics (*q.v.*); (e) *jealousy of morphinomaniacs*, which is, in its effects, similar to the preceding one, but stems from a different cause (*see* Medicines, Narcotics); (f) *senile jealousy*, which appears in cases of senility or pre-senility.

In view of the individual's mental state, imputability in these cases is often diminished, unless it is a self-induced condition with imputability *in causa*; in extreme forms, imputability may be altogether absent.

Many evils stem from jealousy: groundless suspicions, unnecessary preoccupation, deep discouragement, envy, and other failings against charity and even justice. Development of a generous love of God and neighbor and detachment from worldly things are good remedies against jealousy.

Concerning medical treatments of morbid forms of jealousy, *see* Paranoia, Melancholy, Psychasthenia; for forms connected with alcoholic delirium, all treatments against alcoholism (*q.v.*) are valid here too; for cases of jealousy arising from morphinomania, the treatments used against morphinism are also good for them; for senile jealousy, a treatment based on hormones could be tried. *Man.*

JESUS. *See* Sacred Heart of Jesus, New Testament.

JEWS. *See* Judaism.

JOURNALISM. Journalism is a news service which consists in reporting and interpreting events of everyday life almost as soon as they take place. This function is carried out through the printed word (daily newspapers and weeklies with wide circulations), the *broadcast* (radio news) and the *telecast* (newsreels and television reports). The main elements that go into the making of a newspaper are four: news, articles, illustrations, advertising, but all these four may be reduced essentially to news. In fact, in a true journalistic sense, articles are commentary on the news; illustrations are news with a particular appeal to the sense of sight; advertising, commercial and industrial reports are news concerning goods or services available to the people. Modern journalism operates under the following basic conditions: (a) gathering of a large *quantity* of information from all parts of the world, and rapid diffusion of same; (b) *limitation* of time allotted to the production cycle (writing and printing), which, insofar as the main part of a daily paper is concerned, is of very few hours.

The basic responsibilitiy of the press, particularly daily and weekly publications, stems from the influence it exercises on public opinion. This responsibility, however, must be evaluated within the framework of the above-mentioned conditions as the only way by which the morality of the acts of a journalist can be observed and assessed. Considered as a *social service*, journalism not only entails particular rights for those who engage in it, but it also imposes on them particular duties, whether journalism undertakes to shape public opinion (*q.v.*) or, as seems more equitable, it places itself at the service of public opinion (Pius XII, Address to Catholic Newspapermen, in *Osservatore Romano*, February 18, 1950).

The encyclical *Rerum omnium* of Pope Pius XI (*AAS*, 25 [1923] p. 49), by which St. Francis de Sales was named patron of "all those Catholics who, through the publication of newspapers and other printed matter, explain, promote, and defend Christian doctrine," contains what could be considered as a condensed code of professional morality for newspapermen. "Let them [newspapermen] study above all, with the greatest diligence, the Catholic doctrine, in order to acquire, as much as possible, a thorough knowledge of it; let them be cautious neither to fail truth, nor to dilute or dissimulate it, under the pretext of seeking to avoid offending the adversaries; let them take care of the style of their language, endeavouring to express their thoughts with wisdom and form, so that the reader shall take delight in the truth. If it be a case of defending the truth, let them so confute error and expose the dishonesty of wicked people as to make clear that in so doing they are motivated by uprightness and, above all, by charity." Though these rules are intended for Catholic journalists, they are valid in all other cases as well. For if the study of Catholic doctrine is specially necessary for the former, no newspaperman worthy of the name can properly exercise his profession without a general and particular knowledge of the religious, social, and economic doctrines of the Catholic Church or of any other large or small religious body he may be required to write about. In no country is a journalist required to possess academic degrees for the exercise of his profession. But the great variety of subjects he is called upon to deal with demands that he possess an extensive and solid cul-tural preparation for the proper exercise of his responsible profession. In some countries, however, a *professional roster* is provided for journalists who become eligible for it upon approval of their moral and cultural background.

The main duties of a journalist revolve around the truthfulness of his reports. It may be noted in passing that precise formulations concerning a journalistic deontology are still wanting. But, as in the cases of the juridical professions, and those of writers and artists, the truth the newspaperman is bound to seek after is not necessarily absolute truth; *journalistic truth* suffices, that is, rational, probable, and even partial truth, if lack of time prevents him from checking more dependable sources. Of course, if the journalist has time and the opportunity to check all the facts of a report or a doubtful statement, he is morally bound to do so. A responsible reporter must not rely on the possibility of retracting or making a later rectification, because there is no moral certainty that a retraction or rectification will reach all those who read his unchecked report; hence, he must exercise good judgment and self-restraint to the farthest possible extent. But, if a newspaperman finds himself in the alternative situation, not infrequent indeed, of presumably failing to report something which cannot be checked properly because of lack of time or the late hour of the night, or of failing in his moral duty by the publication of a report which he fears might be inaccurate, false, slanderous or scandalous, then he must let his conscience be his guide—not any conscience, but a conscience properly trained and enlightened.

A particular sense of responsibility must be displayed by journalists with regard to the respect due to the human person, the family and society, especially news or comments concerning scandalous deeds, homicide, suicide, adultery and, generally, all those events which usually stir up public opinion, as peace and war, relations between social groups, and the like. The dignity of Christian life, as a norm of civilized life, the rights of justice and love, must prevail over the rights of information and reporting; the exercise of the rights of minorities and pressure groups must give way to the rights of public authority to exact from each individual and from the community the fulfillment of obligations which are in the interest of the common good. As in the case of morality in art, the newspaperman must bear in mind that often morality and immorality are not so much in the thing itself as in the manner it is viewed and expressed; in other words, morality does not require that evil be ignored, but that it be not justified, extolled, or praised. It is not wrong to publicize evil when good can be derived from it, but it is an obligation to ignore evil when its publication amounts to its exaltation.

This applies in equal measure to all the four elements which go into the making of a newspaper; in other words, the above principle is valid as much for general news as for articles of any kind (political, literary, artistic, scientific, etc.), for illustrations and advertisements, without exception.

A field in which a newspaperman may fail not only in his moral duties but also in his obligation of charity, is that of polemics. This always must be kept on the plan of issues rather than personalities, avoiding irony and sarcasm, personal insults, or any reference to physical defects, family misfortunes, and the like. This rule applies not only to newspapermen but also to newscasters, telecasters, politicians, and debaters.

Every country has positive regulations concerning the specific activities of newspapermen, reporters, and the like. It is the duty of every newspaperman, reporter, and journalist to be thoroughly familiar with such regulations and to observe them diligently. Efforts toward an international codification of such rules are in progress in the United Nations' subcommittee on freedom of information and of the press, where the project for an "international code of honor" and an international tribunal for the crimes of the press are under study. For other matters concerning journalism, see News Agencies. *Luc.*

JOY. In a strict sense, joy is a pleasant condition caused in one's will by a thing cherished and present (spiritual joy). With this disposition of the will there is nearly always connected a feeling of pleasure in the sensitive appetite, which in a broader sense, may also be called joy (sensitive joy). Such feelings, however, may arise independently of a free act of the will and may exist without a corresponding spiritual joy. The object of joy may be an external thing, particularly a good action done by others or the well-being of a beloved person; it may also be an internal thing, especially an act of the intellect or other faculty, elicited under the impulse or with the consent of the will.

Joy does not necessarily require that the thing loved be present; its imaginary presence suffices. Thus, the object of joy may be a thing which was real in the past, of which one preserves the memory, or a thing foreseen as being realized in the future, or even a thing which never was and never will become a reality. Joy is in itself a useful thing inasmuch as it disposes a person to work with greater eagerness and diligence and to endure with greater courage the trials of life.

There are joys which are of themselves lawful, that is, whose object may be lawfully enjoyed. The more elevated the object, the nobler the joy itself; the noblest of all joys is that which has God as its object. There are also unlawful joys or pleasures, which are such because of their object, i.e., those which revolve around things which may not be lawfully loved or enjoyed. Among the joys which are lawful in themselves are those which are connected with our good actions. Of course, it is unlawful for one to enjoy the good effects of an action which is not good.

Since joy is a natural complement of other acts, the guilt from unlawful pleasures is never, primarily or exclusively, in the spiritual or sensitive joy itself; joy cannot be sinful except by participation, i.e., insofar as it is dependent on a free and inordinate act of the will with which morally it is all one thing. This act may consist either in taking pleasure in the object of joy or in an implicit or explicit failure to banish the inordinate feeling of joy which preceded the free exercise of the will. In the first case, the degree of guilt depends upon the nature of the object; in the second case, the guilt is in itself venial, but it can became mortal if failure to banish the inordinate feeling were to constitute a serious danger of committing a mortal sin. A pleasure inordinate in itself, but which preceded the free exercise of the will, cannot be formally sinful; however, as soon as one perceives the presence of such a pleasure, he is obliged to do all he can to banish it.

Even an ordinate joy or pleasure must be kept within bounds; that is, it must not be allowed to lead a person to improper behavior. Failure to check an excessive, though honest, pleasure, constitutes in itself a venial sin; but it could even be mortal if the excess were such as to cause scandal or place a person in the impossibility of fulfilling a very important duty.

In the spiritual life one must regulate well his feelings of joy and never lose self-control. In order to succeed in this, one must look at things from the viewpoint of faith and eternity. One must endeavor to preserve, amid the most painful trials, a deep and serene tranquility born of the consciousness of having fulfilled one's duty and of being in the grace of the Lord, who some day will make perfectly happy those who will have been faithful to Him. One must also endeavor to disseminate a little serenity by showing genuine signs of esteem and good-will and by helping those in need. *Man.*

JUBILEE (Holy Year). By a *jubilee* is meant a solemn plenary indulgence, with manifold privileges, proclaimed by the Roman Pontiff in particular historical circumstances.

The jubilee was one of the most singular Jewish institutions. The year following the seventh Sabbatic year (a cycle of seven years) or every fiftieth year was called the *jubilee year*, that is, year of rejoicing and of reparation. It was celebrated by three main enactments: (a) rest of the soil; (b) restoration of landed property to its original owners, who had been compelled by poverty to sell it; (c) the freeing of those Israelites who, because of poverty or otherwise, had become the slaves of their brethren. The jubliee year was promulgated by the priests on the day of the atonement (corresponding to the nineteenth day of the seventh month, *Tisri*), by the clangor of a trumpet.

By virtue of the second enactment, a very special privilege was added to those of the Sabbatic year; it consisted in the restoration to the original owners of all Levitical real estate not redeemed before that date; the loss was compensated according to a contract agreed upon. An exception was made for the real estate of walled cities not redeemed during the first year after their sale. From an economic and social standpoint the effects of this law were of the highest importance.

It is little wonder that the Catholic Church gave this name to its solemn granting of indulgences, as it does on certain historical events. After the year 1000, centennial celebrations gradually acquired something of a sacred character among the Christian peoples. At the approach of a new century the whole Christian world was on the move and pilgrims in great numbers flocked to Rome. Though the general belief of the great benefits attainable from this centennial pilgrimage had no official approval, Pope Boniface VIII (1300), nevertheless, saw in it a providential instrument for good and a sign of God's will. On the strength of this conviction, he officially established the celebration of the *Holy Year*, to extend from one Christmas to another, in order to give those who fulfilled certain specified conditions (Cf. Bull *Antiquorum habet fida relatio,* February 22, 1300) an opportunity to gain a plenary indulgence. Though the Holy Year had already attained its essential form, the term *jubilee* was not used until the year 1350, when Pope Clement VI, who had shortened the time to every fifty years, officially introduced it in the ecclesiastical terminology. His Bull *Unigenitus Dei Filius* is in a sense the *Magna Charta* of the jubilee.

Later, to adapt this dispensation to man's short span of life, the supreme pontiffs shortened the term from fifty to thirty years (by Urban VI), then to twenty-five years (by Paul II in his Bull *Ineffabilis Providentia,* April 17, 1470), as it is today.

The jubilee may be *ordinary* or *extraordinary, universal* or *particular.* An *ordinary jubilee* is one that, according to the present discipline of the Church, recurs every twenty-five years. It begins on Christmas Eve and ends on Christmas Day of the following year. The pope, generally, announces it with much solemnity on Ascension Day. This indulgence may be gained only in Rome, but the supreme pontiff customarily extends it to the entire world during the following year. An *extraordinary* jubilee is one which the supreme pontiff grants in particularly historical circumstances, as on the occasion of the fiftieth anniversary of his priestly ordination. A *universal jubilee* is that which is granted to the Catholic faithful throughout the world. A *particular* jubilee, on the other hand, is one granted for special reasons to a specific place, shrine, or ecclesiastical province.

The fundamental conditions required for the gaining of any plenary indulgence are also required for the gaining of a jubilee indulgence, i.e., confession and Holy Communion, the intention, at least virtual or implicit, to gain the indulgence, and prayers according to the intentions of the Holy Father. As special conditions for the gaining of a jubilee indulgence, one must perform certain good works during the jubilee year, such as visits to certain churches, recitation of special prayers, fasts,

alms, etc. As special privileges, broader faculties are granted to priests in the administration of the sacrament of penance for the duration of the jubilee. The particular conditions and privileges are specified in the papal bull announcing the jubilee. Indulgences for the living, with a few exceptions, are generally suspended. Sacramental confession and Holy Communion must be distinct from the annual Easter confession and Communion. Other prescribed works, such as fasting and visits to churches, may be condoned by confessors to those who are morally or physically unable to perform them, such as cloistered nuns, persons detained in prison, or the sick. The indulgence of the jubilee may also be gained more than once, provided that the conditions prescribed by the bull are fulfilled each time.

The last ordinary jubilee was proclaimed in 1950 by Pope Pius XII in the Apostolic Constitution *Jubilaeum maximum* of May 26, 1944 (AAS, 41 [1949], 258–259).

JUDAISM. The Hebrew people, also called Jews, who had once been the channel of God's revelation to man, rejected such revelation when it came to them in its fullness through Christ and the Apostles. By this rejection, the vast majority of the Jews placed themselves outside the fold of the Church, although they continued to hold on to their religious life by their own worship, beliefs, and system of morality. One finds in these an echo of the teachings of the Old Testament, but their general orientation has become anachronistic. While the Church is completely oriented toward Him who came to redeem and save, the Jews still live in a hopeful but vain expectation of His coming.

The word *abhodah,* which at one time designated the liturgical action expressed by a bloody sacrificial worship, assumed after the destruction of the temple of Jerusalem the meaning of prayer. The victim is offered as a gift to obtain reconciliation with God;

through prayer and the works of charity man offers himself. According to the Palestinian doctors, *serving God with the whole heart* (cf. Deut. 11:13) refers to prayer; a similar interpretation is also given by them to the passage in Osee (14:3), "Take away all iniquity and receive the good and we will render the calves of our lips" (Douay Version).

At dusk and throughout the night the Jewish faithful were taken with a fear of the demons; thus the teachers insisted that each evening the exodus from Egypt, that is, the protecting and saving work of God, be called to mind. This is the meaning which the doctors wished to attribute to the phylacteries worn on the arm and forehead, and to the rolls of parchment placed on door posts, considered by the Semitic Orient as the favored abode of the evil spirits.

The Jewish concept of revealed law continuously calls to mind the Legislator, the holy and transcendent God. Though not accepting the concept of hypostasis, post-biblical Judaism considers God the personification of Wisdom and of the Word (Logos, *memra*), although in a sense which is quite different from that of Christian theology. Each morning and evening, every adult male in Israel recites the *Shema* (Deut. 6:4–9; 11:13–21; Num. 15:37–41), the profession of faith in the absolute unity of God. The *Shema* is introduced and concluded with the recitation of certain blessings. After the recitation, a liturgical passage ("*It is true and certain*") is repeated, confirming the content of the main text.

The *Eighteen Benedictions* speak of God as the God of the patriarchs, and as the God who gives rain and makes the dead to rise; of God, who is holy, the giver of the interior awareness of truth and the bestower of power to differentiate good from evil; of God as the giver of the fruits of the earth; from Him the conversion of those living without faith in God is sought and the grace that all the scattered faithful may return to the Promised Land. The last benedictions contain petitions for bread and praises to the Lord.

Israel considers itself a chosen people, tied to God by means of a Covenant, or as a people especially protected by God. To Israel the Lord has entrusted a sacerdotal mission among the nations. The Messias is the king anointed by God Himself, the king who will bring salvation to Israel, and justice and salvation to the whole world.

The life of man in Israel is, of course, a combination of good works and sins, merit and blame. God will judge not only peoples as a whole, but each individual as well. The Jews recognize the principle of human frailty but not the notion of original sin. With the help of the Law, man must fight against evil, although he is in all things dependent on God. The study of the Law keeps man away from sin and opens to him the way to sanctity.

The Decalogue (The Ten Commandments) is the basis of morality, which has for the Jews a religious and legal character. The *golden rule* is: "*Do not do to another what you would not have him do to you.*" In other words, the negative aspect is emphasized over the positive. Life is considered as dedicated to the service of God out of love, not out of self-interest. Man must preserve a certain self-respect; he must ask of God pardon for his sins; he must observe the feasts, the days of fast and expiatory rites without, however, resorting to excessive ascetical practices or any desire for pain and suffering. Much is made of a pure family life based on *mutual* respect and affection; not much is made of the state of virginity. The marriage bond is dissoluble through the voluntary giving and acceptance of the *letter of dismissal* before the rabbinical tribunal. With the duty of loving God is associated also the duty of loving a co-religionist and even a stranger, mindful that "*you were strangers in the land of Egypt*" and, thus, "*you know the feelings of a stranger.*" Justice and charity must be practiced toward everyone. The value of charity lies in its goodness.

Jewish mystical doctrine does not recognize the state of ecstasy or absorption of man in God. Mystical teachings were based on the concept of the *chariot of God* described in Ezechiel and on the celestical vision of Isaias, who hears the chant of the *trisagion*; the rest amounts to interior religious life. Mystical literature revolves around the work of creation by God, around *pre-existing* man, as an expression of the *Ten Sefirot*, and the mystery of the name of God. The purpose of prayer is to create a bond of union between man and God. Love of God implies readiness to give one's life for the sanctification of God's name. Cabalistic writings, from the historical and literary points of view, are considered a product of the Middle Ages, but the constitutive elements of the doctrine as such are traced back to the beginning of Christianity. The principal work is the *Zohar* (Splendor). Hasidism, a form of pietism, represents the resurgence of cabalism in more recent times. The celebrations of the principal feasts and of the Sabbath contain a rich combination of mysticism and angelology.

More than its moral system, the worship and dogmatic doctrine of Judaism can be said to be an insult to God, because their rejection of things Christian is based on their refusal to heed the voice of God, which was heard more clearly and distinctly in the fullness of time (cf. John 1:1 ff.). As a result, the practices of Jewish worship are contrary to the virtue of religion, since they honor God with a cult which history has proved untenable. Moreover, its moral system has remained imperfect for having rejected the teachings of Christ, which alone could have completed and perfected it. *Zol.*

JUDGE. The juridical doctrine derived from classical sources fails to give an exact definition of the judge, but it describes his office, limiting his task to the application of the law to the fact at issue within the framework of the positive norms established by law. In a contentious trial the judge takes cognizance of the fact and defines it; he does not pass any judgment on the laws or on their greater or lesser applicability or justice, but after careful study he applies the laws to the fact, objectively and according to the dictates of his conscience (D. 5, 1, 15, par. 1). He must not allow himself to be misled by examples (C. 7, 45, 13) or interested witnesses (Cicero, *De Republica*, 1, 38, 59), nor be swayed by any outside influence. In the absence of positive norms applicable to the case, he is free to make recourse to the general principles of law, jurisprudence and doctrine, to juridical analogies, and outside historical research concerning the will of the legislator; he is also free in the actual application of the penalty.

Today a doctrinal tendency is noted, partially accepted by some codes, to give a judge greater liberty to make the rule to be applied to a specific case, at least when no appropriate law exists.

In the canonical system, the highest judicial power is vested in the Supreme Pontiff, who has the right to reserve to himself certain particular cases (Can. 1557, par. 1). However, he exercises his power through the Apostolic Tribunals or special Commissions. He can be judged by no one (Can. 1556).

In a diocese the natural judge is the local Ordinary (Can. 1572, par. 1), who constitutes one tribunal with his *Officialis* or diocesan judge (Can. 1573, par. 2), to whom he entrusts the ordinary exercise of the judicial power in the diocese (Can. 1578). Others are entrusted with judicial power either by appointment to an office or by delegation. Canon Law considers the office of judge as essential to the very existence of a tribunal and as the sole office to which the procedural jurisdiction is necessarily attached. According to Canon Law, cases may be tried either by a group of judges (a college) or by a simple judge.

A collegiate tribunal consists of three or five judges chosen by the Ordinary or, by exception, indicated by the law itself (Can. 1572, par. 2), from among the so-called Synodal (elected by the

Diocesan Synod upon designation of the Ordinary) or pro-Synodal judges (appointed by the Ordinary with the consent of the Chapter or the Diocesan Consultors, Can. 1574, 385–388). A collegiate tribunal acts as a body and its competence extends to judicial cases concerning the validity of sacred ordination or marriage, and criminal cases implying the imposition of heavy penalties; also all cases directly committed to it by the Ordinary (Can. 1576, pars. 1–2).

In a trial conducted by one judge, the latter can enlist the aid of two *assessores* of his own choice (from among the Synodal judges; Can. 1575), or appointed by the Ordinary (Can. 1576, par. 3), or by a positive prescription of the law.

The Apostolic Tribunals (Sacred Roman Rota [*q.v.*]) and Apostolic Signature (*q.v.*) may also judge *videntibus omnibus*, i.e., without an established number, with all judges participating.

The *Officialis*, who is a kind of Vicar General (from whom he is generally distinct; Can. 1573, par. 1), heads the Diocesan Ecclesiastical Tribunal (Can. 1573, par. 1–2); he has ordinary power to judge affairs except cases which the bishop may reserve to himself; he may be assisted by one or more *Vice-officiales* (Can. 1573, par. 3). He presides over the judging college (Can. 1577, par. 2) and directs the procedure in all cases, except where local customs or the number of cases may suggest otherwise (*see* Tribunals, Ecclesiastical). Judges may be ordinary or delegated. The Ordinary may appoint one or more auditors (priests who prepare the judicial acts) or judge *instructors*, and the *ponens* or referee (Can. 1580–1584), ordinarily from among the Synodal (or pro-Synodal) judges.

Ecclesiastical judges must be priests of unblemished character, over thirty years of age, and, if possible, doctors in Canon Law (Can. 1574, par. 2; 1573, par. 4). Upon assuming their office, they must take an oath that they will fulfill their office diligently (Can. 1621, 1622) and will maintain absolute secrecy about all things they will learn by reason of their office (Can. 1623).

Judges can be removed from office at will (*ad nutum*) by the Ordinary or by the Supreme Pontiff, and they are forbidden to accept anything from the parties, either in the form of presents or fees (Can. 1624). They may not judge cases they already judged in another phase of the trial (Can. 1571), or in which they have a personal interest (Can. 1613, par. 1).

The civil judicial system varies in a considerable manner from its ecclesiastical counterpart. Its hierarchical order is related to the importance of the judicial function exercised by the judges in individual cases. Concerning the civil judicial system, the reader must consult the system of each respective country.

The importance of the administration of justice in the State as well as in the Church requires that the judges possess sound knowledge and moral probity in order to discharge the serious tasks committed to them. Professional morality requires that they use the greatest diligence and thoroughness in conducting a trial, and the utmost prudence in the issuing of a sentence. The sentence must be based on the validity of the reasons rather than on the words of the witnesses. Though a judge must necessarily proceed within the framework of the law, he must in his eager search after the truth endeavor to form a moral conscience through the study of the judiciary acts and documents and hand down his decision accordingly.

In the face of an unjust law, a judge may not sentence the defendant to commit an immoral act nor may he give him a very severe penalty, even if this entails the loss of his post or other grave consequences. But if the act is not intrinsically evil, or the penalty is rather mild, he may apply the law, though unjust. Thus, according to moralists, it is lawful for a civil judge to carry out divorce laws, wherever these are in force, provided that the parties are aware of the fact that the effects of the divorce apply only to property and moral rights. In such a case the judge makes no pronouncement concerning the lawfulness or unlawfulness of divorce, but he merely declares that the civil law, as it stands, permits in given circumstances the dissolution of the marriage by the breaking of the purely civil bond.

If an innocent person appears convicted by the available evidence, the judge must do all in his power to arrive at the truth; if he fails in this but remains firmly convinced of the innocence of the accused, he may give him a minimum penalty, if acquittal might jeopardize his own position. If, on the basis of the proofs submitted, the judge is unable to attain the evidence or the moral certitude regarding right and wrong, he must endeavor to settle the dispute in a friendly way and favor the defendant within the limits allowed by the law.

Concerning the matter of accepting gifts from the parties to a dispute, the following moral principles apply: (a) it is improper to accept gifts and, even worse, to demand them for services to which the parties have a right; (b) it is not against justice to accept or to demand them for services rendered to which the parties have no title; (c) it is absolutely improper and sinful to accept or to demand them from the beneficiaries of an unjust sentence. Obviously, any violation of justice is to be restored by the restitution of the gift and indemnification of eventual damages (Can. 1625, par. 12). *Pug.*

JUDGMENT, DIVINE.

Divine judgment is the accounting for one's own life which every man must render after death to God, Lord and Supreme Judge, to receive reward or punishment according to his due. Judgment is twofold: particular and universal. Particular judgment (individual) will take place immediately after death; universal (final) judgment will take place at the end of the world (judgment day) after the final resurrection.

Man's reason admits the necessity of a divine sanction and, therefore, of a divine judgment concerning man's use of the gift of life. A clear reference to a particular judgment is found in St. Luke's Gospel (cf. the parable of the rich man and Lazarus). Explicit on this subject is the language of St. Paul ("it is appointed unto men once to die, and after this the judgment" [Hebr. 9:27; cf. also 2 Tim. 4:6]) and of the Fathers (cf., above all, St. Augustine). No less explicit is the magisterium of the Church (Denz. 464, 530, 693).

Christ Himself gave a lively description of the final judgment (cf. Matt. 25; also Rom. 14:10; 2 Cor. 10:2; Thess. 1–2, etc.), Universal judgment is a very important truth of faith professed in the Apostles Creed: (". . . He shall come to judge the living and the dead"). The Judge will be Christ, the God-man. *Pal.*

JURISDICTION, ECCLESIASTICAL.

Ecclesiastical jurisdiction may be defined as the authority belonging to the Church, as a perfect society, of ruling her members for the attainment of their eternal salvation. This power, which is of divine institution, includes legislative, executive, and judicial authority. Thus, while the power of orders stems from the sacrament of holy orders and is immediately directed to the sanctification of her members, the power of jurisdiction or government springs from the very nature of the Church as a supreme and perfect society that needs to be guided and governed in order fully to attain her spiritual end. Ordinarily, ecclesiastical jurisdiction can only be exercised by clerics (Can. 118).

Ecclesiastical jurisdiction has a twofold nature, and consists of an *internal* and an *external forum.* Jurisdiction of the external forum concerns the common good directly; it governs social relations, and its exercise produces juridical effects of a public nature. The jurisdiction of the internal forum aims chiefly at the good of each member; it regulates the relations between the faithful and God, and its exercise is productive of moral effects. The jurisdiction of the internal forum (or forum of conscience) is called "of the internal sacramental forum" if it can be exercised only in sacramental confession; in other circumstances it is called "of the extra-sacramental internal forum."

Jurisdiction is also *ordinary* and *delegated*. In view of its importance we shall dwell on it at greater length in the following paragraph. Jurisdiction is voluntary or contentious, depending on whether it is exercised on members who accept it and even request it or in any way bear it without opposition (the legislative power is improperly reduced to voluntary jurisdiction), or it is exercised in trials between contending parties or against reluctant persons.

Ordinary jurisdiction is that which is attached by law to an ecclesiastical office (Can. 197, par. 21). It is called proper if it is exercised in one's own name (e.g., by the Supreme Pontiff or by the Ordinary etc.) or delegated (vicarious) if it is exercised in another's name (e.g., by the Roman Congregations or by the Cardinal Vicar in the name of the Supreme Pontiff, by the Vicar General in the Bishop's name, etc.). The limits of a vicarious jurisdiction are not always well defined by law (as in the case of the jurisdictional limits of the Cardinal Vicar and his Vicegerent of Rome), but this does not destroy the fact that it is ordinary, attached as it is by law to the ecclesiastical office, despite the lack of well-defined limits.

Some of those who enjoy ordinary jurisdiction are called Ordinaries by the Code. These are the Roman Pontiff (who exercises his power either directly or through the Apostolic See, i.e., Congregations, Tribunals, and Offices), resident bishops, abbots and prelates *nullius*, with their Vicars General, Apostolic Administrators, Vicars and Prefects Apostolic (called *Ordinarii locorum* because their jurisdiction is of a territorial nature); finally, major superiors of exempt clerical Congregations, who are properly called Prelates Regular, or simply Ordinaries.

Delegated jurisdiction is that which is exercised by commission of another in his name and by his right. Clearly, delegated jurisdiction derives properly from the person (*ab homine*) rather than from the law, and is attached not to the office but to a particular person. Nevertheless, canonists also speak of a delegated jurisdiction attached to an office (in which case, however, it must be understood that the person derives his jurisdiction not from the office but has it because of his office), and of a jurisdiction delegated by the law (*a iure*). Such instances, in the discipline in force, are rare, but, according to some canonists, they are not wanting (cf. Cans. 884, 1044, 2252, 2254).

Delegated jurisdiction may be *special* if limited to a specific case, or *general* if it extends to all the cases (*ad universitatem causarum*) within a certain field.

Canon 199, paragraph 1, states that he who possesses ordinary power may delegate it totally or in part, unless the law expressly forbids it (as in the ordinary faculty of hearing confessions which is vested in the pastors). He who has a delegated power may, in turn, subdelegate it (a) either for a single act or habitually, unless the delegation was directly derived from the Apostolic See or was granted to a specified person (*industria personae*), or subdelegation was forbidden; (b) for a single act, if the delegation was given by a superior below the Supreme Pontiff for a whole series of acts (*ad universitatem causarum*); (c) in all cases in which the faculty of subdelegating was expressly granted by the delegating person (Can. 199, pars. 2, 3, 4).

A subdelegation cannot be subdelegated, but the subdelegated person may entrust a third person with the execution of some acts which are not jurisdictional (e.g., to make inquiries, etc.).

Ordinary and universally delegated jurisdiction (*ad universitatem causarum*) is to be interpreted liberally; special delegated jurisdiction, on the other hand, must be interpreted strictly. Jurisdiction, whether ordinary or delegated, is acquired, exercised, and terminated according to the provisions of the sacred canons. Concerning jurisdiction in a case of doubt or common error, *see* Jurisdiction, Supplied. Here we shall add some general criteria: (a) A jurisdiction granted without limitation or determination is meant as granted for both the internal and the external forum unless the contrary is certain from the very nature of the power (Can. 202, par. 3). (b) Acts of jurisdiction granted for the external forum must be performed in the external forum, although they may be validly exercised also in the internal forum, but not vice-versa (Can. 202, par. 1). (c) A power conferred for the internal forum may also be exercised in the extrasacramental internal forum, unless the sacramental forum be expressly required (Can. 202, par. 2). (d) The power of jurisdiction may be exercised only on one's own subjects (Can. 201, par. 1). A contentious power cannot be exercised in one's own cause or outside one's own territory. Exception is made for a judge who, having been expelled from his territory or unjustly impeded in the exercise of his jurisdiction in his territory, is permitted to exercise it in the territory of another, after having notified the local Ordinary. Non-contentious power may be exercised both in one's own favor (*in proprium commodum*) and outside one's own territory, and also on one's subjects away from his territory (cf. Can. 201, pars. 2–3). (e) Finally, if a subject applies to a higher superior, passing over a subordinate, the latter's jurisdiction is not thereby invalidated; he shall not, however, interfere in a matter submitted to the higher superior except for grave and urgent reason; in which case he shall immediately notify the superior of his action (Can. 204). *Fel.*

JURISDICTION, SUPPLIED. The supplying of jurisdiction by the Church is a provision of the law whereby jurisdiction is supplied automatically at the very moment in which it is exercised (*ad modum actus*), lest the spiritual welfare of a person suffer harm because of a lack of jurisdiction by the priest through no fault of the beneficiary. By virtue of Canon 209 the Church supplies jurisdiction for the external as well as the internal forum, (a) in a case of common error, or (b) in a positive or probable doubt, whether of law or of fact (Can. 209).

The Church supplies jurisdiction in a case of common error. The error may be due to a false conviction concerning the possession of the required jurisdiction. It is necessary, however, that this conviction arise from a positive fact which would cause the faithful reasonably to assume that the priest had the required jurisdiction. A case in point might be that of a priest who acts as a lawful pastor, while in fact he is an intruder, not validly appointed to his office either by error or because of a concealed disqualification; or the case of a priest who, acting as if he had jurisdiction, occupies the confessional or imparts absolution, when in fact he has no jurisdiction or his faculty has expired. In such cases the people (prescinding from one or another individual who might exceptionally know it) would, of course, legitimately think that such priests possessed the proper jurisdiction, and might even ask for its exercise, but would run the risk of receiving grave spiritual and also material harm unless the Church supplied the proper jurisdiction. Error about possession of jurisdiction, however, is not to be confused with ignorance concerning the required faculty.

A common error may be of fact (*facti*), or of law (*iuris*), i.e., potential. A common error of fact is present when the majority of the faithful in a given place believe that a priest has the required jurisdiction, while for some hidden reason he does not. It is called a potential common error, or error of law, when it stems or may stem from a fact which of itself is such as to lead many people into error even though in fact no one errs. The interpreters of the law are not in agreement about the error for which the Church must supply jurisdiction. Notwithstanding the opinion of some who held that it is the error of fact, today it is generally held (and such an interpretation may be called certain) that the error of law or potential error is sufficient to require that jurisdiction be supplied.

In fact, the spiritual common good is at stake not only when many together are deceived by an error, but also when many, taken individually, may fall into a dangerous error, for there is in such a case a reasonable ground for a possible error of fact. As already stated, this interpretation is held as certain. But even if one were to consider it as doubtful, by virtue of the same Canon 209, which is also applied in a positive as well as a probable doubt of law, it is certain that the Church supplies the jurisdiction in a common error both of fact and of law.

The Church also supplies jurisdiction in a case of doubt. The doubt, however, must be positive, i.e., there must be reasons justifying the belief that the jurisdiction was given. If, on the contrary, the doubt is negative, i.e., if sound motives for doubt are absent, a distinction must then be made. If the doubt exists on both sides, i.e., if there are no reasons for believing either that the jurisdiction was given or that it was not given, certainly the Church does not supply the jurisdiction, and the absolution (if the question is about confession) will be doubtfully valid, because the value of absolution depends exclusively on whether the priest *de facto* has the jurisdiction or not. Therefore, in this case, the use of a doubtful jurisdiction and the conditional absolution of the penitent is permitted only in case of grave necessity, that is, if it is likely that the penitent will remain without absolution for a long time. Properly speaking, the confessor should then warn the penitent to submit again to the power of the keys the sins confessed under such circumstances.

In a case of positive doubt, the Church supplies the necessary juridiction. In particular: (a) The Church supplies jurisdiction in a case of probable jurisdiction based on probability of law, when the doubt, really probable and serious, concerns a common question of law on which authors do not agree, and the opinion holding to the possession of jurisdiction is probable. (b) The Church supplies jurisdiction in a case of probable jurisdiction based on probability of fact, that is to say, when the positive and probable doubt revolves around a private fact. Thus, if a priest is uncertain about whether or not the time of his faculties has elapsed, or whether or not a certain sin is reserved in the diocese, or whether or not the superior granted the faculty, and if, after having reasonably examined the various circumstances, there still remains a probable reason to believe that the jurisdiction is still in force, the priest absolves the penitent validly, because, if the jurisdiction is really lacking, the Church will supply it.

A doubt must be objective and morally insoluble, for if the doubt is merely subjective, i.e., dependent upon a lack of diligent investigation which in that case can and must be conducted, the Church does not supply the jurisdiction.

These principles find their broadest application in the administration of the sacrament of penance; thus, in order to avoid possible errors or doubts, besides the power of orders, a priest must also possess the power of jurisdiction.

Until a short time ago, canonists wondered whether the principles concerning a common error and a positive and probable doubt could also be extended to the case of doubtful faculty in assisting at a marriage, or other such errors; in other words, whether a marriage celebrated before a putative pastor, held by error to be a true pastor, when by a hidden defect he had invalidly received the pastorship, was valid or not. The opinion in the affirmative is common today, and according to an authentic interpretation of March 26, 1952, it is called certain (AAS 44 [195], 497). Thus, too, his assistance at a marriage in case of positive and probable doubt, whether of law or of fact, is held valid by virtue of supplied jurisdiction.

JURY. A jury is a body of adult men and women, of good reputation from various walks of life, selected to assist in the administration of penal justice or to render a verdict according to the evidence.

Individuals who have served a penal sentence of considerable gravity or were dismissed from certain employments, and those whose physical, moral, or intellectual capacity makes them ineligible for the task, are excluded from serving on the jury. The following are exempt from serving as jurymen: public officials, clergymen, physicians, surgeons and veterinarians, attorneys, police officers and other law enforcement agents, druggists and others who have good reasons to be excused. The list of jurymen is generally prepared by the clerk of the court from the city directory, list of voters, and from lists of property owners, etc.

The jury was never accepted by canonical legislation on the ground that it is illogical that a judge should sentence a person, not according to his own judgment, but according to the judgment of other people. Nevertheless, moral theologians are concerned with the moral aspect of a juryman's duty, wherever it is exercised. Accordingly, they teach that a juryman's judgment must be formed on the basis of true, conscientious convictions; hence, he may not and must not agree to convict an individual whom he thinks to be innocent, even though all appearances are against him. Furthermore, he may, in conscience, favor a real culprit, if the latter's guilt has not been lawfully and satisfactorily proved. *Pug.*

JUSTICE. Considered as one of the four cardinal virtues, justice is the virtue by which we give each one his due. It was defined by Ulpian as the constant and perpetual inclination to give each one his due (*"constans ac perpetua voluntas ius suum cuique tribuendi"*: D. I, 1 fr. 10 pr.); *constant* because it appears as a habit and, therefore, as a virtue; *perpetual* because the recognition of each one's right is intended to extend to every case and for all times. By *right* is meant here the object of justice. Giving everyone that which belongs to him is an unchangeable element proper to the virtue of justice, for the object of other virtues, charity, for instance, is subject to changes either because of diversity of circumstances or of positive laws.

The properties of justice are three: (a) tending to another (otherness); (b) giving what is due; (c) giving all that is due until the equilibrium is restored. *Tending to another:* justice presupposes other persons and always tends to another; no one, in fact, will speak of making restitution to himself, as no one, properly speaking, can contract a debt with himself. *Giving what is due:* this presupposes a strict right on the part of another. The title giving rise to the obligation to make restitution is the fact that something is involved which belongs to another. To this obligation there corresponds a right to claim what is one's own, even by legitimate use of force. The internal attitude by which one gives (willingly or unwillingly) is of no concern here, since what does matter is the object to be given or to be exacted. Hence, the virtues of faithfulness, gratitude, and liberality have no place here. (c) *Giving all that is due until the equilibrium is restored:* all must be given to which another has a right. For this reason, if one fails to give all that he owes, justice is not complete.

The matter of this virtue is the external actions and the external things themselves, because, while the other virtues regard man as he is in himself, justice perfects man by his orderly relations toward others. Furthermore, while the object of other virtues is the attainment of a reasonably happy medium, the object of true justice is in the very thing due; in other words, the only rule of perfect justice is the right of another, and he who renders to another exactly what he owes him attains the apex of justice. In other virtues, on the other hand, their true object is detected and attained after a longer and deeper study.

Justice and equity (*q.v.*) are not the same thing, though they are not distinct virtues. Equity may be said to be a moderate application of positive law to particular instances with due consideration for natural justice and the end of the law. Too strict an application of the law is due at times to a failure to take into account other aspects and peculiar circumstances of human relations and, consequently, it turns out to be inhuman, cruel, though perfectly in accord with strict law. In this sense the Romans spoke of iniquity of the law, which the *Praetor* sought to correct by the practice of equity. This also explains the meaning of the ancient saying: *Summum ius summa iniuria.* As a supernatural virtue, justice may be said to be an operative habit, although only improperly so, inasmuch as it gives only a certain inclination and potentiality to the attainment of the supernatural good of life. Christian justice, of course, revolves around man but only insofar as he is raised to the supernatural order and, therefore, constituted in a higher dignity. This widens the scope of justice and includes in its object actions and things not only of the natural but of the supernatural order as well. Furthermore, Christian justice is integrated by charity, and the practice of the latter lessens more effectively than purely natural equity the harshness of justice.

As in other virtues, so too in the case of justice some theologians distinguished subjective, potential, and integral parts. It is not as important to explain the integral parts of the virtue of justice (to do good and avoid evil from the standpoint of what is due to others), nor is it as important to explain its potential parts (religion, piety, respect, veracity, faithfulness, gratitude, *vindicatio*, i.e., the virtue that moves us rightly to punish injustices, liberality, affability, equity). It is essential to explain its subjective parts, which distin-

guish the virtue of justice into various species, all belonging to the same genre.

Following the Pythagoreans, who must be credited with having explained the connection between equity and justice, Aristotle distinguished justice into *general* and *particular*; this division was later accepted and used by St. Thomas. *General* justice is that which directs man to seek the common good; it is called general because it may concern itself with the acts of all virtues. It is also called legal justice because it is fixed by law. *Particular* justice, on the other hand, is that which aims at private good, and is subdivided into commutative and distributive, depending on whether it regulates the mutual relationships of partners or disposes those in authority (prince, ministers, etc.) to distribute honors and burdens according to equity. Many authors, however, keeping their eyes only on the subject of a relationship, prefer the division of justice into legal, commutative, and distributive. There are others who, not too aptly, add a fourth type, namely, punitive justice, which is more properly a part of distributive justice.

(a) *Legal* justice is that which leads man to give to society what is its due for the internal good of society itself of which he is a part (*see* Common Good). The subjects of legal justice are the members of society, both the rulers (in whose case legal justice takes the name of administrative justice), and the ordinary citizens. The object of this justice is any moral act insofar as it refers to the common good. However, not all good acts performed by citizens in the interest of the common good constitute the object of legal justice, because if they are not strictly due to society, they are the object of either the virtue of piety or another virtue. Strictly speaking, the object of justice is a right, and to this right there corresponds a real obligation.

(b) *Distributive justice* is the virtue by which goods and burdens of the community are distributed with due proportion among the citizens. The goods with which this virtue is concerned are those belonging to the community as such, and the main ones are public *offices* and responsibilities, honors, rewards, help, effective protection of freedom and property. The criterion of distribution shall be adequate to the type of society and its goods, nor shall the benefit of each particular individual be the primary concern, but the common good; for this motive, the formal reason of distribution must always be sought in the good of the community.

(c) *Commutative justice* is the virtue which moves the will to give each person his own strict due, keeping the proper equilibrium between things. It has been said, and perhaps not wrongfully, that this type of justice is one in which the elements of its definition are more exactly implemented. By commutative justice, in fact, direct relationship is established to the thing which is, on the one hand, an object of obligation and, on the other, an object of right; in the other types of justice the relationship to the thing is indirect, that is, it is due because of the mutual relations between individuals. Furthermore, equality in commutative justice is not the same as in the other types of justice: in commutative justice, in fact, arithmetical equality is required (perfect equality of services, prescinding from persons); in the other types of justice a geometrical equality is maintained, namely, one based on the proportion of the whole to its parts (society and citizens). There are those, however, who maintain that commutative justice is the only true justice, and that the other types are called justice only analogically. Against this position we hold that all three, commutative, legal, and distributive, are true types of justice, because each has its proper corresponding rights.

Commutative justice is seriously binding and implies the obligation of restitution. (a) Every grave violation of commutative justice is objectively a mortal sin. In fact, commutative justice, insofar as it protects the juridical position of each individual, aims at keeping the natural independence of the human person. There is a metaphysical independence and a moral independence. The former is exemption from all subjection in those things which concern man simply as an absolute being; the latter, on the other hand, is exemption in those things which refer to man as a relative being, i.e., in his mutual relations with other men. The independence arising from the right of property is based on the fact that man is a relative being, although it is always subject to an indispensable element (moral law) for the full protection of the human person. The violation of this independence is in itself a grave violation of the right of another and of his juridical position, so that if the other elements are present, namely, grave matter and due advertence, the violation will constitute a mortal sin. (b) Violation of commutative justice calls for restitution, because he who violates commutative justice unjustly deprives another person of some good to which he has a strict right. Adequate reparation of this violation is effected only by restoring the former order of things, that is, by restoring the equilibrium in full, without taking into account the person's merits, but only the thing itself taken from another. This is the true meaning of the word *restitution* (*see* Restitution). Therefore, as long as the disequilibrium remains, the obligation to restore it also remains, and the offender is not discharged of this obligation until the disequilibrium is removed.

The other two kinds of justice are of themselves also gravely binding, but they carry no obligation to make restitution. This norm is commonly held as certain, although there are those who would also like to extend the obligation of restitution to legal and distributive justice. Obviously, these two are also gravely binding because their violation could produce a serious damage against the order in society, as it would be, for instance, if many citizens refused to pay taxes and, therefore, to contribute to the maintenance of the government. We said "of themselves" because by chance (*per accidens*) there could be cases in which, because of parvity of matter or other circumstances, the disorder might be slight; in such cases the obligation would not be grave. Nor is there any obligation to make restitution, because only he is bound to make restitution who unjustly deprives another of some good to which he has a strict and direct right. Now, a violation against distributive or legal justice is not the violation of a right belonging directly to another, but only of an indirect right.

As stated before, a direct right is that which one has directly over a thing, whereas the right of society on the property of its subjects (legal justice) or that of the subjects on society's goods (distributive justice) is an indirect right, because it is obtained through the right which society has on its individual citizens and vice versa. Since there is no strict and direct right, there is no obligation to make restitution. Thus, if the head of a department promotes a worthy person to a position over a worthier one, he violates distributive justice and, therefore, commits a sin, but he is not bound to make restitution, because he did not violate commutative justice. However, since distributive and legal justices are often connected with commutative justice, they may by accident give rise to the obligation of restitution, by reason of a contract, or damage, or because of a provision of the law, custom, etc. *Pal.*

JUSTICE IN TAXATION. Justice in taxation, as understood here, is the relation between the tax-paying citizen and the tax-imposing State. The relations of the State with its citizens, of course, are governed by distributive justice, its object being constituted by the distribution by the State of tasks and responsibilities, burdens and honors; on the other hand, the relations of the citizens with the State are governed by legal (general) justice, its object being the acts by which the citizens may contribute in some manner to the common good. Justice in taxation, taken in its broadest sense, is as much a part of distributive justice as it is of legal (general) justice, for it extends both to the tax-imposing activity of the State and to the paying of taxes by citizens. Ordinarily, however, it is considered more a subdivision of the former than of the latter.

Justice in taxation may concern the amount of taxes imposed as well as the manner in which these are assessed and collected. The amount of taxes is closely connected with the concept of the State and its ends. Thus, in a conservative conception, the ends of the State are the protection of the political community, the maintenance of public order, and the administration of justice; in the socialist conception its tasks are far broader and deeper. It is obvious that in the former conception of the State, justice in taxation does not allow but the most limited fiscal pressure, while in the latter, it allows and demands a much heavier pressure.

In the Christian conception, the end of the State is the furthering of the common good, which, of course, includes not only the essential elements contained in the other conceptions but also the constantly changeable elements resulting from conditions of time and space. Consequently, justice in taxation requires that fiscal pressure be adequate to the actual requirements of the common good. However, it must never be such as to destroy individual initiative; on the contrary, it must be itself an element of protection of and a stimulus to such initiative, supplying the State with the means with which to strengthen the relations of the community and to favor the flourishing of life in all sectors of the community.

With regard to the manner of assessing and collecting taxes, today the universally recognized fundamental requisites are: equality, progressiveness, and public character. (a) Equality. The citizens who are in the same economico-social conditions should be taxed in equal measure, according to their income. (b) Progressiveness. The citizens who are not in the same earning category should be taxed according to the degree of sacrifice they are required to make, the benefits they receive from society, and the actual ability to pay. It is only fair that those with very large incomes should pay taxes according to a progressively higher rate; in other words, the higher the income, the higher should be the taxation rate because of the greater benefits higher income groups often receive from society. The same general criterion should be used fundamentally with regard to exemptions from taxation, bearing in mind that every citizen has a right to an untaxed minimum necessary for an adequate standard of living. (c) Public character. With the adoption of a constitutional, democratic system in the organization and functioning of the modern State, it has become a rule of public morality for the government to account for and make public the collection and employment of tax moneys: this is generally attained through a discussion of municipal, State, and national budgets. *Pav.*

JUSTICE, SOCIAL. Many modern authors distinguish legal justice (*q.v.*) from social justice. Both, of course, tend to the common good; legal justice tends to the common good of a perfect society, civil or ecclesiastical, while social justice is concerned with the common good of groups and associations (imperfect societies) within the two supreme societies, State and Church. The aim of social justice is to promote the common good (*q.v.*), organizing men into free and voluntary associations, and also directing the activities of corporations and other social groups to the attainment of the common good for the welfare of all the members of society, without distinction of classes or ranks.

It is not so much a question of establishing whether or not there exists a specific obligation of social justice, particularly if one considers the use Pope Pius XI made of it in his encyclical *Quadragesimo anno* (*AAS*, 33, 177–228), by which he consecrated, as it were, that expression (already found in some medieval sources). The ques-

tion is rather to establish whether or not social justice is contained in legal justice, which governs the relations between the members and the Church or the civil State.

Some sociologists reduce social justice to one or more of the three classic types of justice. Others intend social justice to promote law and justice in the State and in human society; in this case the term embraces not only legal justice but distributive and commutative justice as well. Some others see in social justice a new aspect or function of justice binding the State even beyond the pure and simple function of statutory law for a more effective attainment of economic and social ends (Pesch, Lopez). Still others reduce social justice to legal justice, either by making it all one with the latter, insofar as it tends to give the community that which is its due in accordance with its laws (Gillet, Prummer), or on the basis of the natural and positive laws (Vermeersch, Salsmans, Merkelbach, Vangheluwe), or by making it a subspecies of legal justice, or as natural justice (Van Gestel), or as economico-social justice (Schilling, Lange). Others, finally (and they are many), consider social justice as a fourth kind of justice which either transcends the others or regulates and contemplates them, or is distinct from them, since its task is to protect either the natural rights of the social systems existing in an economico-social society, or the natural rights of the individual members of society as such, with respect to the economic goods of the earth (Gundlach, Mathis).

Two ways of thought are generally followed in determining the specific character of social justice:

(a) In the first theory the concept of social justice is formulated in this manner: All the relations of the members of society to one another, and the relations between them and society as such, are exhausted within the triple division of commutative, distributive, and legal justice, so that there is no possible way of adding a fourth type of justice. On the other hand, it would be too narrow a concept of justice if one were to look upon the members of society only as individuals. In fact, if it is true that there are societies of a lower order whose members are individuals, it is also true that there are societies of a higher order whose members are other societies. The tripartite relation of justice between individuals and between individuals and the society of which they are members is also found to exist, with due reservations and variations, on a higher level between societies having smaller societies as their members and the very societies that are members of this organism of a higher order. In the first case, the relations are called an outline of individual justice; in the second, an outline of social justice. With this in view, it is possible to see how social justice has the rights of social groups as its proper and adequate object.

(b) Another scientific presentation of the question arrives at a different concept of social justice in this manner: while particular justice has as its supreme principle "to each his due" (*"unicuique suum"*), general or social justice has as its principle "the public good must be protected" (*"bonum publicum est servandum"*). This principle is often interpreted in the following manner: a firm and durable social order must be pursued and maintained, and a common good—already crystallized as to its content, determined and stable as to its concreteness—must be kept in its stability. This interpretation is unilaterally static and needs to be completed insofar as its dynamic side is concerned. In fact, society is a living organism and, as such, is in perpetual growth or diminution, in a continuous and real, though accidental, process of stabilization and transformation. The social order of a living society, despite a certain immutability of the fixed structure of society, must be in a permanent process of development. Thus, too, despite the immutability of the concept of common good, the concrete content of the public good, that is, the concept of what must be contrib-

uted as a general requirement for the welfare of society and, therefore, also of the individual members of society, must be continually developed.

Through this consideration we attain the deepest understanding of the principle concerning the furthering of the common good (*"bonum commune est servandum"*). The meaning of *servare* (to preserve) is not only to keep what has been already established and fixed (though this conservative element must never be absent), but it also includes in its essence, a dynamic element, i.e., a perpetual, concrete tendency toward the perfecting, the rejuvenating of the social order totally in keeping with the new exigencies stemming from the growth and progress of the living organism of society. This dynamic aspect of the law and justice constitutes an essential element of the social organism, and is as important as its static aspect. This dynamic aspect of justice and of law, in opposition to the often overemphasized static aspect, is precisely intended when we speak of social justice, because all the exigencies of this justice are founded on, or tend to, the common good. Perhaps (with Father Brucculeri) we could define social justice as "the virtue which moves us to perform every virtuous act in behalf of the public interest, from which man could not exempt himself without violating the right of society to the cooperation of its members."

There are some authors who see in the natural law the obligation of promoting not only the common good of civil society and the various social classes living in it, but also the common good of all civil societies; the virtue governing these relations is called *international legal* (general) *justice*. Others prefer to reduce even this kind of justice to the three classic types, inasmuch as the tasks of international justice can be taken care of by legal, distributive, and commutative justice, if one looks upon the individual nations as legal persons ordained to the promotion of the common good of the whole family of nations. *Pal.*

K

KINDERGARTEN. *See* Scholastic Medicine.

KINDNESS. *See* Charity.

KINETOSIS (Motion sickness). *Kinetosis* (from the Greek *kinesis,* motion) refers to any disorder or disturbance caused by travel in moving vehicles; or it may be defined as any disease due to unaccustomed motions. Kinetosis is as ancient as human nomadism.

Any means of transportation (automobile, camel, elevator, train, ship, airplane, etc.) may cause kinetosis. The principal forms of this sickness are: (a) *car-sickness,* which is caused by travel in automobiles or other land vehicles (train, trolley-car, elevator, escalator, etc.); (b) *seasickness* (also called *naupathia* or *mal de mer*), which is brought on by travel in sea vessels; it is usually experienced on an ocean voyage, particularly in turbulent waters, but it may also occur on a short boat ride and in calm waters; some people, highly susceptible to the sickness, become affected immediately upon boarding a ship, even before it sets sail; (c) *air-sickness,* which is caused by travel in air vehicles (planes, funicular railways, cable-cars, ski-lifts, etc.). There are also other forms of kinetosis, e.g., the dizziness, nausea, etc., experienced on a swing, merry-go-round, revolving chair, and the like. Finally, there are some forms which are symptomatologically similar to kinetosis, but have nothing to do with the element of motion, e.g., altitude disease or mountain sickness, which is principally due to excessive rarefaction of the atmosphere, to which the organism is not accustomed.

The fundamental symptoms, common to all these forms of kinetosis, are as follows: first, the subject begins to grow pale, experiencing a vague feeling of bodily discomfort (malaise), a painful and heavy sensation in the head, a sense of constriction in the epigastric region, a general feeling of exhaustion; there then follow in order: cold perspiration, palpitations, a growing feeling of despondency (sometimes leading to apathy), nausea and, in more severe cases, vomiting.

The pathogenic mechanism of kinetosis is more complex than is commonly believed. Undoubtedly, at the bottom of the disease lies a disturbance of the labyrinthine sense, abnormally stimulated by the movements—rhythmic or irregular—of the vehicle in which one is riding. Further pathological stimulation stems from vision, due to constantly shifting relations between passenger and surrounding objects (receding scenery). (Some persons may experience a mild form of kinetosis simply by watching the film of a ship in rolling motion or by watching the shadow of a leaf stirring in the wind.) In addition, there is a notable disturbance of the neurovegetative system, stimulated in different directions by pathological reflexes of various origin. Finally, the mental condition of the subject, especially when one has had previous experience of the painful effects of motion sickness, constitutes a highly important factor. Some people, due to fear, anticipation, impressionability, etc., are already conditioned to contracting the sickness.

At one time, the remedies for motion sickness (especially for seasickness) were largely of a preventive character: the subject was told to eat plenty of solid food, to lie down in his berth as soon as he boarded the ship, to lie down on his back, with eyes shut, etc. One already in the throes of seasickness was given smelling salts or a soothing agent, with no other alternative but patiently to await the end of the trip. Today several highly effective drugs may be taken to relieve the sickness.

From a moral standpoint, the importance of the various forms of kinetosis lies in the fact that they cause a relaxation of the patient's critical and volitive powers. Thus, e.g., a person in the throes of seasickness loses his powers of self-control, becomes utterly disinterested in self and others around him and, reduced to a pitiful state of moral despondency, desires but one thing, the cessation of his suffering. When such sickness assumes a grave form, the persons affected are partially, sometimes wholly, excused for their actions. And anyone abusing such persons or taking advantage of their apathetic and abulic condition would be guilty of a moral and legal offense, in the same manner as one taking advantage of an insane person. *Riz.*

KISS, KISSING. Employed among nearly all peoples from time immemorial as a mark both of profound reverential affection and of love, the kiss must be looked upon as an external manifestation of one's affectionate, deep dedication. As such, the kiss was frequently used and is still used even in the liturgy of the Church, e.g., the reverential kiss, the kiss of peace (cf. F. Cabrol, *"Baiser,"* in *DACL*, II, 117–130). The same may be said of embrace, which consists in an affectionate encircling of another person with the arms.

As an expression of love, the kiss, as well as the embrace, becomes an object of special consideration in moral theology. In fact, kissing and embracing may enter the sexual field not only as signs of sexual love, but above all because, in view of the structure of the human body, they bear a close relation with the genital apparatus; in other words, they can very easily arouse venereal commotion. For this reason, kissing and embracing attended by circumstances not in conformity with the virtue of purity or modesty are listed by moral theologians among impure acts (*see* Impurity). Now, applying the moral norms governing such acts, it follows that: (a) a kiss or embrace is not in itself illicit, but a legitimate expression of affection; (b) they may become illicit either because of an evil intention (seduction, voluntary excitation of passion in oneself or in another, etc.; *See* Sensuality), or because of an inordinate affection, even if not directly intended (scandal, danger of consenting to sin, sexual commotion, etc.). An adequate reason would be required to justify exposing oneself to the dangers attendant upon kissing. For this reason eventual sexual commotion resulting from decent kissing or embracing is excusable if not intended and no pleasure is taken in it.

Certain special conditions, such as marriage (*q.v.*) and betrothal (*q.v.*), justify, even more particularly, the possible danger of carnal commotion attendant upon kissing and embracing. *Dam.*

KLEPTOMANIA. *Kleptomania* (from the Greek *klepto*, I steal) signifies a morbid tendency to stealing. In its more pronounced form, kleptomania is observed in certain cases of psychasthenia (*q.v.*) and consists in an irresistible impulse to commit theft. The psychasthenic kleptomaniac steals whatever happens to constitute the object of his obsessive impulse, independently of the value of the stolen object and frequently without having any actual need for it. He steals knowingly, for he is perfectly aware of committing an offense, although he is unable to rid himself of the persistent and tormenting impulse—in fact, he can find no rest until his obsessive idea is carried out. Usually, the great feeling of relief he experiences upon satisfying his obsessive desire is followed by an intense feeling of remorse which induces him to restore the stolen object or—if this appears risky—to indemnify the owner in some manner or even to dispose of the stolen article.

Kleptomania is more frequently observed in other forms of mental diseases,

Thus, it appears in phrenasthenia, especially as an expression of moral imbecility; in the first stages of senile dementia, of schizophrenia and of progressive paralysis, as a symptom of mental deterioration or of thoughtless inconsiderateness; in mania, as an expression of skillfulness, arrogance, or playfulness. In all such cases, the voices of reason and conscience are greatly stifled by the particular psychosis, so that there is little or no internal struggle between the impulsive and repulsive idea and the will.

Kleptomania is noted even more frequently in cases of hysteria, where the theft (usually limited to articles of clothing and objects of ornament) is carried out with studied ingeniousness, under the influence of an almost uncontrollable impulse, further strengthened by pronounced egocentricity. Finally, in certain cases of epilepsy, kleptomania, when not a manifestation of a patient's degenerative character, may constitute the equivalent of a convulsive crisis.

A kleptomaniac is not responsible for his act of theft committed involuntarily, or—as in the case of the psychasthenic kleptomaniac—carried out despite the resistance of a right and tormented conscience; only in the case of hysterics may one speak of semi-responsibility, and even here each case is to be considered and judged on its own merit.

An entirely different judgment is to be rendered concerning the frequent thefts of sane persons who, without necessity or motive, appropriate various objects (not always of little intrinsic value), under the specious pretext that they are not really pilfering such objects, but simply taking them as "souvenirs" of their travels, sojourn, visit, etc. Many tourists have thus attempted to justify their pilfering silverware, ash-trays, towels and the like from ships, hotels, restaurants, etc. Such conduct has little to do with kleptomania, and it is to be considered as morally reprehensible, even though in the general estimation it is regarded as innocuous pilfering.

Sometimes, especially in court, an attempt is made to classify a theft committed by a person of means as kleptomania, thereby exonerating the guilty party from legal sanction; this is but a gratuitous and blameworthy extension of the psychiatric slogan that kleptomania is a disease of the "idle rich."

Related to kleptomania, but really different from it, is the complex of those who steal rare articles (such as objects of art, stamps, books, etc.) for collection purposes. Such a tendency is relatively common among bibliophiles, philatelists, etc. In such cases, the mere sight of an item missing in his collection arouses in the collector a strong impulse to appropriate that item. And it is to be noted that apart from such objects of particular interest, the collector would scrupulously refrain from stealing the smallest thing. The stealing of articles for collection purposes may be called a sort of complex or mania, not always harmless nor morally excusable. At the same time, there may be extenuating circumstances in his favor, in that the collector may be seized by more or less hidden obsessive-impulsive tendencies, somewhat similar to those experienced by the psychasthenic kleptomaniac. *Riz.*

L

LABOR (Work). Labor in a broad sense is any effort, physical or mental, directed to the production of some object. In this sense, the term might be applied to men or to animals. Metaphorically, we also speak of work with reference to instruments or other material objects used in the production of an item. This definition transcends the nature and purpose of the item of labor, whether for relaxation or motives of economic gain.

In a restricted sense, the term *labor* is used with an economic meaning. It can be defined as the activity of man on external objects to obtain a certain economic gain. This economic advantage consists in the fact that the article produced can with an equivalent price be exchanged for another item. Thus, labor in this sense is the meaning of our present article. (Cf. Pius XI, Encyclical *Quadragesimo Anno*; AAS, 23 [1931], 195.)

PURPOSE OF LABOR. Although arduous, labor is unavoidable because of the nature of man and his necessities. It exists that we may improve created goods by adapting them to meet human needs and thus become more perfectly ordained to the end for which God created them.

In Genesis labor was assigned to man in his state of trial as a pleasure without burden (Gen. 2:15). Stripped of his preternatural qualities because of his original sin, man then discovered that the pleasurable became a burden and a punishment because physical weakness resulted in the natural state to which he was reduced (Gen. 3:19; St. John Chrysostom, *In Joan. hom.* 36, 2, PG 59, 206).

Labor did not lose its creative power; the difficulty of labor was accepted by the faithful servant of God as a humble recognition of the dominion of the Creator over him, and as an instrument of service to himself, his dear ones and society.

Nor did Christ reject labor; on the contrary, He enforced it (Matt. 10:10; 25:30; Luke 10:7-10; John 6:27). He labored at one of the hardest trades; He consecrated it; with the abundance of His grace He endowed it with merit. The example and teachings of Christ were re-echoed by the Apostles (John 21:1-7; Acts 20:30-35; II Thess. 3:7-13; I Cor. 9:7-14; Eph. 4:28; James 5:4). Hence, the true Christian performs his productive work and accepts its burdens with a supernatural spirit: as the acknowledgment of God as his Lord, and a means by which he may serve himself and others in justice and charity. (Cf. *The Papal Social Encyclicals from Pius IX to Pius XII*, edited by I. Giordani, Rome, 1948; Pius XII, *Address to a group of directors, employees of the Rome office of the Bank of Italy*, April 25, 1950). Thus, though the Book of Genesis (3:7-18) speaks of work more as a harsh necessity than a real, true precept, it is apparent that by the law of nature man has an obligation to work insofar as he comes within the precept. The principal aim of the obligation to work is the attainment of a livelihood for himself, his dependents, and society. When this cannot be achieved without work, especially insofar as the individual and his family are concerned, any failure to work would be a violation of charity toward himself and his dependents, as well as of his duties in justice. Aside from these strict requirements, there is, in itself, no grave obligation to work. The obligation to work, rarely serious, may arise from a combination of circumstances. In modern life, work has a social, moral, educational, and ascetical value, for it avoids idleness, always a danger to one's spiritual and moral life, and it provides for charity and mutual aid. Thus work can easily become a duty for man. If work is ordinarily a duty, there must be a corresponding right to work, since every duty implies a right.

WORK CONTRACT. Man as master of his own actions, both physical and spiritual, becomes by the same natural right also the master of the fruits produced by his labor. For this it is necessary that (a) he work for himself, that is, that no contract or fact exists which binds the fruits of labor to a third party; (b) that he work on an object belonging to himself or to no one.

The work contract between the employer and the employee is lawful; for since human activity belongs entirely to man himself, he can dispose of his activity as he thinks best, even by surrendering it over to another.

No objection is valid that says human labor is far broader than the requirements of the economic order. This is true, of course, if labor is considered only as a human act. However, labor can be considered solely as productive of an economic benefit; as such it can be the object of a contract or marked for suitable retribution. The liceity of such a contract, in which human labor is given in exchange for a specified salary, is approved within the limits of a just agreement by universal practice and by moral theologians. This is clearly stated in the Encyclicals *Rerum Novarum* and *Quadragesimo Anno*.

The difficulty which states that labor contracts make the laborer equal to a machine by putting him in a servile position is easily refuted. Man, as master of his acts and labor, can dispose of his services as he wishes, even by leasing his labor to another. By leasing his intellectual or physical energies and working in the services of another, he bestows on those for whom he works the fruits of his labor. He retains the right to demand a just remuneration for his labor (*see* Wage, family). The obligations arising from a contract, both for the employer and the employee who leases his services, are true obligations of justice with all the consequences of restitution and the legitimate protection of the interests of each one (*see* Strike, Lock-out).

PROTECTION OF LABOR. Such a contract is of special nature, for human labor is not ordinary merchandise but involves the dignity of the human person. Hence a labor contract must be governed by more humane laws than those which govern purely commercial things. First and foremost, work must not conflict with the duty to worship God (*see* Sanctification of Holy Days).

Aside from other considerations, labor cannot be considered merely an item for negotiations, such as capital. It involves the necessity for reasonable working hours, sufficient rest, proper protection for women and children, moral and hygienic provisions, and adequate social legislation to protect the weaker parties in labor contracts. These objectives are to be attained, not by revolution, but by the Christianization of the individual and society, which alone can effect a harmonious evolution of the social system (cf. Pius XII, Radio message, June 13, 1943, AAS, 35 [1943], 174–175).

In contemporary society, legislation and measures of protection for labor are common in State constitutions and laws. An efficient protection of labor was created also on the international plane with an elaborate series of international agreements entered into by labor organizations and corporations. The largest institution is the *International Organization of Labor*, recognized as a special institution by an appropriate agreement of the United Nations Organization (1946). *Pal.*

LABOR. *See* Proletariat, Union.

LABOR, FORCED. *See* Slavery.

LABOR, MENTAL. *See* Disease, Occupational.

LABOR, PATHOLOGY OF. *See* Disease, Occupational.

LABOR, PHYSIOLOGY OF. See Psychotechnique.

LABOR, SOCIAL. See Social Worker, Public Assistance.

LACTATION (Nursing). Lactation is the breast feeding of the newborn, whose digestive system tolerates only milk as the physiological nourishment suited for normal functioning and development. According to this form of feeding, lactation may be divided into: (a) natural lactation by the mother or wet-nurse; (b) artificial lactation by formula; (c) mixed lactation.

Breast feeding by the mother is undoubtedly the best. First, the mother's milk is best suited for the proper nutrition of her child; secondly, the period of lactation brings the mother into a more intimate relationship with her child, involving, as it does, the practice of tender, if somewhat burdensome, tasks of dedication and renunciation; thirdly, it tends to increase the child's love and respect for the one who provides not only life but also nourishment at great personal sacrifice, and protection in the early, difficult months of a tender and delicate existence.

The cause of too many hyperemotional, "difficult," and "nervous" children may well be assigned to the lack of maternal breast feeding, or to sudden and premature weaning, which should be effected gradually and cautiously at eight months.

According to Valvassori-Peroni, "Every newborn infant has a right to its mother's milk"; the mother has, therefore, a duty of nursing her own child, all fanciful ideas and whims to the contrary. These fanciful notions ordinarily stem from vanity, fear of possible "nervous exhaustion," a new pregnancy, premature menstruation, attacks of fever of short duration, development of an oligohemic or anemic condition, rhagades or fissures of the nipples, and other eventual disturbances of minor importance and easily curable. Conditions advising against maternal lactation are tuberculosis, grave psychosis or psychoneurosis, neoplasms, infections of long duration, agalactia (lack of milk secretion by mammary glands), flat nipples, or congenital malformation of the infant's mouth. Syphilis, far from advising against maternal lactation, increases the obligation, unless the mother contracts the disease in the last month of pregnancy, in which case the child, who will probably be born healthy, may easily contract the infection through breast feeding.

If, because of grave disease contracted by the mother or pathological mammary conditions, maternal lactation is impossible, it is advisable to hire, if possible, the services of a wet-nurse to breast feed the child as a substitute. Since the selection of a wet-nurse is fraught with dangers and difficulties, a method of bottle feeding or mixed lactation becomes an inevitable necessity.

This method of lactation, in the past considered harmful to the newborn, has become thoroughly satisfactory and safe due to improved hygienic formulae, the use of condensed or powdered milk scrupulously prepared and mixed with fruit juices or other vitamin substances. *Wherever possible mixed lactation* should be used.

A manifest hypogalactic condition or debilitating weakness on the part of the mother may make a method of mixed lactation preferable to bottle feeding. In mixed lactation a suitable quantity of animal milk is administered to the infant immediately after each limited breast feeding from the mother to supplement a scanty amount of maternal milk. The results of this type of lactation are similar to a purely maternal breast feeding.

Such results are an added reason for condemning the practice of many mothers, prompted largely by selfish motives, who shirk their duties of breast feeding. When a mother, for reasons of work, recurring illness, or hypogalactia cannot adequately attend to the obligation of breast-feeding, she can properly and easily fulfill her duty by mixed lactation with no harm to herself but with obvious advantages to the child. *See also* Parents, Children. *Riz.*

LAICISM. *See* Anticlericalism.

LAITY (Layman). The terms *laity, lay person,* or *layman* must be defined from a twofold viewpoint: (1) as ordinary members of the faithful; (2) in opposition to those who exercise the public ministry in the Church. In the first case the concept of layman is particularly Christian. In fact, a layman is "a member of that people who is the real Israel of God" (Gal. 6:16), "a chosen generation, a kingly priesthood, a holy nation," of whom St. Peter speaks in his first epistle (2:9). The concept of *layman* does not coincide with the concept of *secular,* for a layman, insofar as he is a member of the Mystical Body of Christ, an intrinsically holy reality in origin, constitution and destiny, partakes of this sanctity, belongs to Christ and is sacred to Him (I Cor. 3:23). In the light of the second relationship, a distinction arises between *layman* and *cleric.*

As Israel was considered according to the flesh (I Cor. 10:18) with respect to the other peoples of the earth a "kingdom of priests and a holy nation" (Ex. 19:6). There was a distinction by divine law between ordinary Israelites and Levites (Num. 18:6). Thus, too, in the Israel of God, there is a similar distinction, also by divine law, between layman and cleric. In fact, Christ chose a group of twelve men out of the crowd of disciples (Mark 3:13–15; Luke 6:12) and called them Apostles (Luke 6:13). With this title He also gave them important prerogatives and public ministries for the welfare of the Church. These public ministries are: (a) The ministry of the Word or missionary apostolate (Acts 6:4; 20:24). This is devoted to the conversion of all peoples. (b) The ministry of the mysteries or administration of the sacraments (I Cor. 4:1). (c) The pastoral ministry, exercised through the authority to teach, govern, and rule and charged with the mission of leading all Christians to a state of personal sanctity (Eph. 4:12).

Since these ministries must be exercised by the apostolic college until the end of time, as it is clearly evident from the Gospel text (Matt. 28:18–20), we deduce that the apostolic college shall exist forever in the sense that until the end of time there will be in the Church a transmission of public ministries in an unbroken line of sacred ministers, invested by divine right with such ministries. Thus the Church consists of two orders of members: a hierarchy invested by divine right with public ministries, and the laity.

The hierarchy is twofold: the hierarchy of orders and the hierarchy of jurisdiction. The former is constituted by the reception of holy orders; the latter consists in a power of jurisdiction received from a source of jurisdiction. Both hierarchies admit of ranks. The hierarchy of orders consists of three primary ranks: bishops, priests and deacons; by ecclesiastical law the minor orders of subdeacon, porter, lector, acolyte, and exorcist were added. The hierarchy of jurisdiction consists of two ranks: the supreme pontificate and the episcopacy subordinate to it (Can. 108); to these are added by ecclesiastical law other ranks above and below the episcopacy.

The distinction between laymen and clerics is not based on the investiture with a pastoral ministry but on the sacrament of holy orders (Can. 948). Consequently, a layman is a member of the Mystical Body of Christ who does not belong to the hierarchy of order in any sense.

LAITY AND MISSIONARY APOSTOLATE. The relationship of the laity to the hierarchy of jurisdiction and its dual ministry of the work and pastoral government must be understood with particular reference to the missionary apostolate in the pagan world and the pastoral ministry among Christians. The missionary apostolate of the hierarchy to the pagan world, technically speaking, is the mandate to preach the Gospel according to Christ's command: "Preach the Gospel to every creature" (Mark 16:15), like heralds and public criers (*keruksate*) for the sake of making all people Christ's disciples (*matheteusate*). This is to be continued until the end of the world (Matt. 28:20).

By this mandate, the hierarchy alone are named ambassadors of Christ to the pagan world (II Cor. 5:10). Down through the centuries the hierarchy alone receives official recognition by virtue of the miracles Christ still performs to ratify the truth of this preaching: "Yet the signs of the apostleship have been wrought among you in all patience, in signs and wonders and mighty deeds" (II Cor. 12:12). The mandate of the hierarchy, therefore, is authentic; it demands of the hearers benevolent attention, cordial adherence, and the obligation to accept the preaching as the Word of God (I Thess. 2:13). This mandate to pagan people is not exercised by virtue of jurisdiction (I Cor. 5:12), but by virtue of a *missio divina (poreuthentes . . . matheteusate*—Matt.; *poreuthentes . . . keruksate*—Mark). This mandate is endowed with a charism of infallibility as deduced from the fact that it is accompanied by signs (Mark 16:20) and that it bears an eternal sanction (Mark 16:16). With this in mind we may ask: Can the hierarchy call laymen to take part in the missionary apostolate? Are there forms of a missionary apostolate not only permitted by the hierarchy but commanded by Holy Scripture in support of the apostolate of the Word? We shall answer these questions one by one.

Luke relates that the Lord called and sent forth (*apesteilen* Luke 10:1) seventy-two disciples to prepare the way of the Lord in support of the twelve he had sent to preach the kingdom of God (*apesteilen:* Matt. 10:5). Despite a common mission, Christ conferred the title of apostle only on the twelve (Luke 6:13).

From this we argue that the seventy-two were assistants to the apostles. A lay missionary apostolate may co-exist alongside the authentic and infallible missionary apostolate entrusted to the Apostles and their successors. Thus the hierarchy has the right to reserve to itself the ministry of the Word (Acts 6:4; 20:24); by the definite example of Christ, the hierarchy possesses the right to appoint ordinary laymen to cooperate

by a special *missio canonica* with the official missionary apostolate. This special mission, however, provides neither authenticity nor infallibility on the lay missionary apostolate. In other words, the lay apostolate must always be governed by the hierarchy, to which it must remain constantly subject. Initiative in the field of the missionary apostolate under special circumstances may be permitted, for the history of the apostolic times indicates that our Lord gives evidence of His intention that in special circumstances laymen might take the initiative in a missionary apostolate among pagans. The Acts of the Apostles relate that laymen, dispersed by the persecution which killed Stephen, spread the Gospel not only to the Jews but also to the Gentiles in the city of Antioch in Syria, without any canonical mandate, as it quite clearly appears from Acts 2:19-22. We must underscore the fact that the Lord was pleased with this initiative and confirmed this apostolate by miracles (Acts 2:21). The hierarchy, however, reserved the right of supervision directly, by approving the genuine character of the preaching and by the appointment of Barnabas to take charge of the community which they had established (Acts 2:22-24).

The hierarchy had already claimed the missionary apostolate for its exclusive jurisdiction, even though an apostolate was carried out by a qualified man "full of the Holy Ghost," namely, the deacon Philip (Acts 8:12). Peter and John were sent on an official visit to give approval to the missionary apostolate among the Samaritans and to confer the sacrament of confirmation on those who had already been baptized (Acts 8:14).

Women, such as Evodia and Syntyche, worked for the Gospel and collaborated in the missionary apostolate with Clement and the other workers of St. Paul (Phil. 4:2; Rom. 13:3). We are not told whether this was done by canonical appointment or on their own initiative. The laity, therefore, does a truly deserving work worthy of being written down in the Book of Life (Phil. 4:3), when it assists the hierarchical apostolate in spreading the Gospel.

Various forms of the lay apostolate were not only permitted but advised and commanded in the Scriptures: (1) *The apostolate of prayer,* according to the precept of Christ: "Pray, therefore, the Lord of the harvest to send forth laborers into his harvest" (Luke 10:2). (2) *The apostolate of material help* (Matt. 10:42). (3) *The apostolate of defense of the faith:* "Be ready always with an answer to everyone who asks a reason for the hope that is in you" (I Peter 3:15). (4) *The individual apostolate of the word:* "Walk in wisdom as regards outsiders, making the most of your time. Let your speech, while always attractive, be seasoned with salt, that you may know how you ought to answer each one" (Col. 4:5–6). (5) *The individual apostolate of good works:* "Behave yourselves honorably among the pagans; that, whereas they slander you as evildoers, they may through observing you by reason of your good works glorify God in the day of visitation" (I Peter 2:12). (6) *Relieving the Apostles of many menial and temporal duties,* as the deacons of old did (Acts 6:2–3).

THE LAITY AND THE AUTHORITY OF THE HIERARCHY. The relationship between the laity and the hierarchy as a teaching and ruling body is logically the same as between disciple and teacher, subject and superior, in the sense that the laity must respond with obedience and discipline to the "work" organized and directed by the hierarchy for the welfare of the Church. The layman must support in every possible way the hierarchy in the internal social order. The brethren must "teach and admonish one another" (Col. 3:16), correct each other when they sin grievously (Matt. 18:15) and, as in the case related by our Lord, denounce the impenitent brother to the Church (Matt. 18:17), forgive all trespasses (Luke 17:3), pray one for another (James 5:16), give good example to all (Matt. 5:16), accept suffering for the progress of the Church (Col. 1:24), supply that which is wanting to the saints (II Cor. 9:12 ff.).

In short, the layman, as one of the brethren, must practice the various spiritual and corporal works of mercy. However, in view of the fact that in the early times of the Church even ordinary laymen were invested by our Lord with charisms related to the *teaching authority,* as prophecy (I Cor. 12:10; Rom. 12: 6) or teaching proper to catechists (I Cor. 12:8; Rom. 12:7) or *to the power of government* (I Cor. 12:28; Rom. 12:8), it can be concluded that ordinary laymen may be *called* by canonical appointment to work as auxiliaries to the hierarchy in many fields of spiritual jurisdiction (Cc. 1328 and 1333).

However, as the charismatics were to be subject to the hierarchy according to St. Paul (I Cor. 14:26–40), so, too, laymen, called by the hierarchy to work in the hierarchical apostolate collectively (Catholic Action) or individually, must be subject to the hierarchy. In the hierarchy alone rests the power of teaching and ruling in the Church of Christ. *Lat.*

LAMAISM. Lamaism or Buddhism, practiced in Tibet and Mongolia, derives it name from the monks or Lama, who, until recent times, governed the religious and political life of that area. An independent section was governed by the Dalai Lama residing in Lhassa. The Eastern section is annexed to China (Provinces of Tsinghai and Sikiang). Before Buddhist penetration, the religion of the indigenous tribes of Tibet, called Bon, possessed the animistic characteristics proper to the Mongolian populations (Schamanism). These characteristics are still noticeable despite the superimpositions of Taoism and Mahayan Buddhism.

After several centuries of gradual influence from Nepal, Mahayan Buddhism became established in Tibet in the seventh century, through the efforts of the Prince of Lhassa. He invited the monks of the Great Vehicle (Mahayana), whose religion possessed strong Tartaric aspects joined to a conglomeration of Mahayan doctrine and magical practices. Buddhism became firmly established in the country in the eighth century through the work of Padmasambhava (or Son of the Lotus).

After a period of decline due to religious persecutions by the princes, Tibetan Buddhism experienced a strong revival in the tenth century through the labors of Rin c'en bzan po, a monk imbued with Indian culture, the translator of sacred books, builder of temples, founder of a school for the development of his work under the protection of the powerful reigning princes of Western Tibet.

During the fifteenth century, Tibetan Buddhism took on a stricter hierarchical form and a political aspect under the influence of monk Tsong-Khapa (1355–1417), who founded so-called Lamaism. His successors united the temporal and spiritual powers; at Lhassa, they inaugurated a theocratic government under the rule of Dalai Lama and assisted by special counsellors, the Khampe and Lamas or abbots of the great Buddhist monasteries. Each Dalai Lama is a sacred person, insofar as the soul of Cianresi, a special *bodhisattwa* protector of Tibet, becomes incarnate in him. At one time the Dalai Lama was elected by the Lamas through a divination process; later, the Chinese government took charge of the election in the desire to control the Dalai Lama, considered by Chinese Buddhists as the head of their Church.

In another part of Tibet, government is in the hands of another Lama, who resides in Tashilumpo, and is thought to be the re-incarnation of Od-pagmed, the father of Cianresi. Apart from this monastico-theocratic reform, a few non-reformed Lamas, called Red Lamas to distinguish them from other Lamas, who wear yellow garments, are particularly dedicated to the practices of magic, witchcraft, and divination.

Ancient Indian paganism entering Tibet through the magic arts of Buddhism, created a multitude of grotesque gods and goddesses of the moon, destruction, the dead, fire, war, etc.

CULT. The cult is practiced through a number of rites and ceremonies which attest to the detailed organization of the Tibetan Church. Bells, amulets, *dorje* or "bolts of lightning" (a kind of weapon used by the priests against demons) are common. The most peculiar of all is the *Khor-lo* or praying mill (prayer-wheel), a cylinder moved on a pivot and by wheel turned by hand, water, or wind. At every turn of the wheel the faithful gains the same merit gained by one who recited the prayers printed on the cylinder.

Among the formulae written on the cylinder, thought to have great magic power, is the invocation: "*Om mani padme. Hum:* Oh jewel of the lotus flower! Amen."

The political power of the Lamas increased with the rise of the Mongolian dynasties, particularly that of Kublai Khan, whose counsellor was the abbot of the Sakta monastery. The Kublai Khan reigned over all of Tibet until, after the fall of the Mongols, Chinese political supremacy took over. This supremacy, however, was in reality nominal, because the entire socio-religious power in Tibet and Mongolia rested in the large monasteries and their very powerful Lamas. *Tur.*

CRITICAL REMARKS. Inasmuch as Lamaism is a form of Buddhism, it is subject to the criticism due to the latter (*see* Buddhism). Moreover, in order to enter Tibet, Lamaism combined with Bon, the primitive religion of Tibet, and admitted a certain number of Bon-po divinities and cosmogonic theories to its own religious doctrine; it further was altered by Iranian and centro-Asiatic influences. The result became a form of religious synchretism, a mixture of polytheism, fetichism, animism, etc. The theory of the incarnation of the great chiefs, bestowed upon the unique, Lamaistic theocracy an absolute, hierarchical continuity. However, political influences from time to time have changed the possessor of incarnation, so that its true nature appears a *terrenum inventum* (a pure invention). Lamaism, opposed to philosophical knowledge, concentrates on mystical intuition. The borderline between mysticism and magic is a vague one, frequently inadvertently crossed. Some liturgies are merely simple magic, others black magic. The technical Yoga is practiced in its most violent form. The Lamaist cult is complicated and gaudy. Their iconographical representations and rites have a pronounced sexual aspect. In villages local divinities of Bonpo origin are still worshipped; these divinities are frequently malicious with a light veneer of Lamaism. *Pal.*

LAMP. *See* Custody of the Holy Eucharist.

LAND, HOLY. The Holy Land in Holy Scripture has various names (cf. I Kings 13:19; Ezek. 7:2; Gen. 40:15; Josh. 9:3; Ruth 1:1; Matt. 2:20; Zech. 2:12; Wisd. 12:3; II Mach. 1:7). Biblical Palestine extended from Dan to Beersheba (Judg. 20:1 ff.), from the descent of Hamath to the torrent of Egypt (I Kings 8:65 ff.), that is, from Tyre to Negeb, and between the Mediterranean coast and the Jordan river. Its length is about 142 miles and its width extends from a minimum of 23 miles in the north to a maximum of about 93 miles, with a total area of about 10,000 square miles.

In the Old Testament Palestine is described as a *land* flowing with milk and honey and rich in all products (cf. Deut. 8:7). Christians called it *holy* because, as the country where Jesus Christ was born, lived, and consummated the sacrifice of His life, the Holy Land designates those localities of Palestine made famous by the particular teaching, works and miracles performed by Jesus Christ. Palestine has been an object of veneration and of great struggles in the course of the centuries. Renowned among these were the Crusades. After the Christian powers gave up their attempts to liberate the Holy Land from the hands of non-Christians, the spiritual sons of St. Francis courageously took over the protectorate of the Holy Places by opening missions among non-Christians as early as the year 1219. With the fall of Acre in 1291 at the end of the last Holy War, the Christians left Palestine with only a few Franciscan Fathers remaining at the Holy Sepulcher in charge of the holy places. Through their work, pilgrimages to the holy places continued uninterrupted during very difficult periods, and hospices were built for the comfort and protection of the pilgrims.

After the year 1291, the custody of the Holy Land took the form of a temporal power; it became a State within a State. It established the Knights of the Holy Sepulcher, authorized captains of merchant vessels to fly the flag of the Holy Land (five red crosses on a white field), had its own commissaries in the principal European cities, who not only promoted and supervised the collection of offerings for the Holy Places but also represented the Francisan Order at the courts of the ruling powers. They also protected the interests and rights of religious and faithful of the Latin rite in the lands beyond the sea.

Catholic nations vied with one another in supporting and protecting the work of the custody, appealing to the Sultan in its behalf through their ambassadors and special envoys. In addition to the Holy See, the Italian States and the rulers of Naples, Robert and Sancia in the fourteenth century, distinguished themselves in its behalf. After difficult negotiations, and the payment of large sums, they obtained for the Friars Minor the right to be in control of the Cenacle and the Holy Sepulcher and a permanent abode in the enclosure of the Shrine. The interest displayed by Genoa, Florence, and Venice was very notable and effective.

The protectorate of the Kings of Naples over the Franciscan institutions in the Holy Land was recognized by Clement VI with the bull *Nuper carissimae*, of November 21, 1342, and, later by Innocent XI, with the bull *Exponi nobis*, of April 30, 1686.

The custody of the Holy Shrines was placed by Clement VI under the jurisdiction of the guardian of Mount Sion, who was the Franciscan provincial of all of Syria. Since 1434, the appointment of that provincial has been made by the general chapter or by the minister general assisted by his council. This choice must be approved by the Holy See, since the provincial is Prefect Apostolic of the Franciscan Missions in the Orient. The government of the custody is conducted by a council whose custodian has the right to wear episcopal insignia and bear the title of *Custos of the Holy Land.* He is always an Italian. The Vicar and the Procurator are always, respectively, a Frenchman and a Spaniard; the other five members belong to other European countries.

As a Christian institution, the custody of the Holy Land organized a whole network of *Commissaries of the Holy Land,* that is, of Franciscan religious, entrusted with collecting offerings required for the maintenance of the Holy Shrines, schools and hospices for pilgrims.

The Holy See has always sought custody of the Holy Places; through the centuries this custody has been recognized and supported by the faithful. Innocent X, in a brief of September 19, 1645, ordered a collection be taken up twice a year all over the world for the needs of the Holy Land. Benedict XIV, by a brief of August 20, 1743, ordered that such collection be taken up four times a year in every church and parish. Pius VI, on July 31, 1778, again reminded everyone of the obligation in behalf of the Holy Places, which were now in a poor state of disrepair. Thus, subsequent Supreme Pontiffs, Pius IX, Leo XIII, and St. Pius X, and finally, on October 4, 1919, on the occasion of the centenary of the custody of the Holy Land, Benedict XV prescribed under obedience that Bishops, Archbishops, and other Ordinaries the world over make an appeal to the charity of the faithful in behalf of the needs of the Holy Places, in every parish church at least once a year, on Good Friday, or any other suitable day. A very moving appeal for the Holy Places was made on April 15, 1949, by Pope Pius XII, with his Encyclical *Redemptoris nostri.*

That the Holy Land might be more significant to every faithful Catholic, Pope Leo XIII, in a decree of June 26, 1894, granted to pious benefactors, in addition to the participation in all spiritual benefits of the Franciscan Fathers, and to the faithful who visit the Holy Shrines, a plenary indulgence, applicable to the departed souls, to be gained on

(a) December 25; (b) Easter Sunday; (c) at the hour of death; (d) and, for promoters, on January 1, and August 15.

PRESENT JURIDICAL CONDITION OF THE HOLY PLACES. By a resolution of the Assembly of the United Nations, of November 29, 1947, Palestine was divided between Arabs and Jews. Jerusalem was declared an international city and the Holy Shrines internationalized, including those outside Jerusalem. On December 29, 1949, the U. N. reaffirmed its intention; on April 4, 1950, the new statute for the city of Jerusalem was approved by the Trusteeship Council of the United Nations. At present the plan is opposed by both the States of Israel and Jordan.

The individual Holy Shrines disputed by Catholic and non-Catholic groups are the Holy Sepulcher, the place of the Nativity at Bethlehem, and the tomb of our Lady in the Valley of Josaphat. The Cenacle must be added to these, since it is contested by the Jews. *Tar.*

LANGUAGE, AMBIGUOUS.

Ambiguous language or equivocation is the intention by the speaker to apply a meaning to words which is different from that ordinarily intended by the use of the words. This, of course, renders the meaning of the words ambiguous and obscure. Equivocation may also be caused by the natural double meaning which a word or phrase possesses. Examples of this are found in all languages; in English, many words sound or are spelled alike, but possess two different meanings. In the use of ambiguous or equivocal language, one may have an intention of a serious nature or facetiousness.

It is a common opinion that ambiguous language is not a lie, although the positive obligation to tell the truth is not fulfilled by such language, for a mixture of language in such a way might be taken by the hearers as truth. Father Vermeersch explains that the ambiguous speaker simply intends to convey the notion that he does not wish to give an answer or the particular information sought from him. Equivocation is a form of mental restriction upon information which the speaker has a legitimate right to reserve.

LANGUAGE, EVIL. Evil language is the use in ordinary conversation of obscene or vulgar words and phrases. These are generally classified as indecent (*erotica*), lascivious (*sordida*), and vulgar (*rustica.*)

Of late, base and evil language seems to enjoy almost normal use among people who should not employ this because of their advantages of birth, education, and position. It consequently seems appropriate to study the reasons and mechanisms of a psychological or psychopathological nature responsible for the formation and use of evil language as well as the passage of this type of speech from the lower, pathological levels of society as far as the highest strata.

Studies by sociologists show that coarse and boorish language (*rustica*) is the result of amputations and mechanical deformations of words in current usage; frequently these are degradations of objects which are expressed by the new words. Thus a head becomes a pumpkin; the hand, a paw. Words of normal usage are thus disfigured and turned into vulgar language to attack, injure, or ridicule persons, things, or ideas represented by these words. At times, coarse words amount to an aggressive explosion by those on a lower level of the social strata, as a form of resentment toward the higher levels of society. They express their envy with attacks and comments bearing the marks of man's lower instincts.

Immodest words (*erotica*) must be considered as a display of man's lower instincts, which well-bred people control and turn aside; whereas vulgar people employ them at times for an otherwise unattainable sexual pleasure. It is to be noted further that obscene words occur with frequency in the language of oligophrenetics and phrenasthenics. "It has to do," wrote Sollier sixty years ago, "with a particular tendency of mind in these sick people."

The psychological reason for filthy words (*sordida verba*) is similar to that suggested for immodest words with the addition of a certain feeling of cruelty. "The predilection for that which is foul and repugnant can have hidden roots in a sense of cruelty and eroticism. Here, too, for biological reasons or adverse pressure from an unfavorable environment or other causes, individuals and masses experience frequently a surge of instinctive impulses of their lower nature which they transform into verbal explosions." These impulses generally explode for lack of adequate education and sufficient self-control. The light of sociology and psychology explains the genesis of bad language; we shall endeavor to explain the inroads into the higher, social levels of this type of language.

Coarse words have gradually had an influence because of a certain pictorial conspicuousness which leads people to forget or, at least, overlook the reasons for their rise among people of the lower strata of society. A laxity in moral customs, more proper to certain periods but from which our times are certainly not immune, strengthened the anarchical reaction of the lower instincts and indirectly fostered the growth of vulgar language in general. Such widespread use seems to be the result of war and postwar conditions, which led to the adoption of evil langauge as a reaction against the many inhibitions and serious sufferings experienced by a large section of humanity. Promiscuity of the sexes (*see* Sex), now so much in vogue, offers another incentive to use "*verba erotica et sordida,*" sexy and filthy language; such a habit is easily initiated by those who believe that in the use of words and expressions of the gutter they acquire a form of intellectual maturity.

The use of evil language by people of a lower stratum of society is explainable. With limitations one can understand the use of vulgar language by writers of comedy and novels if employed for the purpose of portraying with greater effectiveness a character of such a type.

It is not morally objectionable if "*rustica verba*" or common language and expressions are employed to a limited extent by educated persons, for a good reason, with moderation and restraint, because such words or expressions may well add, at times, greater exactness and clarity of expression to the conversation. There is no justification with regard to the use of *"verba erotica et sordida."*

Any remedy for evil language is a matter of education or rather re-education; it is necessary that he who uses bad language be firmly but charitably reprimanded every time he utters base expressions. According to the psychology *of behavior*, words are actions, because, ultimately, to say is to do—that is, to behave accordingly; hence, the obvious conclusion that vulgar language denotes a lack of personal dignity and the awareness of one's intellectual and moral standing. Those who realize the significance of this will lose no time in getting rid of a bad habit, acquired by the senseless notion of keeping up with the times through such questionable signs of distinction. Those who are unable to get rid of the habit by ordinary methods may well need the aid of a neuro-psychiatrist to treat the intellectual, affective, or moral anomalies of which vulgar language is the expression. Concerning the kind and the seriousness of the sin resulting from the use of vulgar language, *see* Talk, Obscene. *Riz.*

LANGUAGE, VULGAR. *See* Talk, Obscene; Language, Evil.

LAST THINGS. The *last things* summarize in one phrase all the events that occur at the end of life for man; these are death, judgment, heaven, or hell. The Holy Scriptures admonish men to a constant recollection of these four last things as a great bulwark against sin (Eccles. 7:40) and as thought-filled truths which spur a man toward perfection.

Death, a punishment no man can escape, may come at any time. Death separates man from all earthly possessions in a most definite manner. The state of a man's soul at the moment of death determines his eternal destiny, for at the particular judgment, following death immediately, his fate for all eternity is decided irrevocably according to the pres-

ence or lack of sanctifying grace in the soul. No thought, word, deed, or omission will be hidden from the Divine Judge. This particular judgment will be publicly confirmed at the General Judgment at the end of time (I Cor. 4:5; Heb. 9:27; Benedict XII, Constitution *Benedictus Deus*, Jan. 29, 1336: Denz. 531).

A soul which departs from this life in the state of grace, without guilt even of venial sin and without a necessity of atonement for sins already forgiven, will go immediately to heaven to enjoy the Beatific Vision of God, as He is in Himself, One in Nature, Triune in Persons; no obstacle shall prevent his vision of God, for none will exist between his intellect and God, and the soul will love God with a perfect love. The possession of God, loved above all things, and the contemplation of His infinite perfections, fully satisfy all of a man's desires and needs and fill the soul with intense joy. The degree of the vision and knowledge of God and, consequently, of happiness is proportionate to the grace possessed; all, however, are absolutely happy because they will always possess the Supreme Good and need fear no ill. The souls of the blessed enjoy the amiable company of the most sacred Humanity of Christ, the friendship of the Blessed Virgin Mary, the saints, and the angels. After the General Judgment the bodies will be reunited with the souls and endowed with special qualities to share in the beatitude of the soul. The happiness of the blessed surpasses by far any imaginable joy (John 17:24; I Cor. 2:9; I Peter 1:4; 5:4; I John 3:2; Apoc. 21 and 22).

A soul in the state of grace at death yet still burdened with venial sins or the need for atonement for sins already forgiven, will be detained in purgatory before admission into heaven, where among other grave punishments it will be deprived of God. The duration and severity of the suffering of the souls in purgatory are determined by the state of the soul at death, but may be mitigated by the prayers of the living. Purgatory is a temporary state (II Macch. 12:43 ff.; I Cor.

3:12 ff.; Council of Lyons: Denz. 464; Council of Trent: Denz. 840).

A soul which meets death in mortal sin goes straight to hell, where the soul and, following the Last General Judgment, the body will suffer unfathomable punishment. The damned is forever deprived of the vision of God and the joys connected with this vision. The state of loss of the final and Supreme Good, which he suffers through his own fault, and the state of aversion from this final end and destiny, in which he must remain for all eternity, will cause the damned unspeakable torments. To these, further torments will be added: a pain of inextinguishable fire, darkness, the company of the devils and of other damned souls (Matt. 3:12; 13:42; 18:8; 25:41 and 46; II Thess. 1:9; Apoc. 14:9 ff.; 21:8; Denz. 531). The loss of the Supreme Good is the same for all the damned; other punishments differ according to the number and gravity of the sins.

Those dying with the stain of original sin alone, as children without baptism and the use of reason, are permanently deprived of the vision of God but do not suffer pain or other punishment because of this privation; they enjoy natural knowledge of God, natural love of God above all things, and other joys in Limbo. *Man.*

LATERAN (PACTS). See Pontiff, Acts, Pontifical.

LATIFUNDIUM. *Latifundium* applies to vast land-holdings, for the most part used for cultivation or pasture. A condition peculiar to certain countries of Europe, a *latifundium* consists frequently of waterless, unhealthy and uninhabitable areas, predominantly large estates or farm areas.

The living conditions of the workers in the *latifundium*, regardless of their economico-juridical status as tenant-farmers, direct-farmers, share-farmers, permanent, hired help or seasonal help, are most wretched. In food, clothing, living quarters, and education, farm laborers in these areas represent a sorely underprivileged section of humanity.

In many countries, especially with a dense population, attempts are made to reduce the *latifundium* despite many difficulties from climatic, economic, and psychological conditions. From the moral standpoint it is a duty of all responsible leaders to work effectively and tirelessly toward the elimination of the *latifundium* wherever it is humanly possible. *Pav.*

LATRIA. *See* Cult.

LAUDATE DOMINUM. The psalm *Laudate Dominum, omnes gentes; laudate eum, omnes populi* (Praise the Lord, O ye nations; praise him, O all ye people) has been customarily sung at the close of the Eucharistic Benediction (*q.v.*); it is the shortest psalm in the Psalter (n. 116 [Hebrew 117]). A simple but important doxology by which all the nations of the earth are urged to worship the one true God, it contains a Messianic reference which prophesies the conversion of all peoples. Since there is no title in the Hebrew text, it is not known who composed it nor under what circumstances it was composed. It would seem to be a liturgical chant for the beginning or at the end of sacred ceremonies.

The psalmist calls not only Israel, the chosen people, but all peoples and nations (therefore, also pagans), to praise God because of His great mercy. The mercy and the truth of God, the grace of the Lord and His fidelity to His promises are the foundation on which our very hope of salvation rests. (Cf. Psalm 99, where the prophecy of the call of the Gentiles to the true faith is more fully developed. Also cf. Psalms 25:3; 35:6; 38:11–12.)

The *Laudate* is usually sung immediately after Eucharistic Benediction, as a song of praise to the Lord. In the Hebrew text, the psalm ended with *Alleluia* (*q.v.*); now it is followed by the *Gloria Patri*, a doxology to the Blessed Trinity. *Pal.*

LAUDA, SION, SALVATOREM. The *Lauda, Sion*, the Sequence of the Mass for the feast of *Corpus Christi*, was composed by St. Thomas Aquinas at Orvieto in 1264, on the occasion of the bull *Transiturus*. This bull by Pope Urban IV extended to the entire Church the Eucharistic feast instituted at Liege in 1246, because of the revelations to Blessed Julienne of Cornillon. St. Thomas' authorship of the Office and Mass, in which the sequence is found, was contested by Papebroch but vindicated by Natalis, whose opinion is decidedly accepted today.

The sequence, verbally similar to the hymns of Adam of St. Victor, consists of twenty-four stanzas. After a solemn exordium or invitation to praise and exultation (1–5), the rhythm swells to a rapid recollection of symbols of the Old Testament (6–8), now realities in the Holy Eucharist (9–10). Through the mystery of transubstantiation Christ becomes food for all souls (11–15), a source of spiritual life or death, according to the dispositions of those who receive the holy sacrament (16–20). A cry of admiration (*Ecce panis Angelorum*) and a tender prayer to the Divine Shepherd bring to a close this geometric composition, filled with intimate fervor.

The symmetrical structure of the *Lauda, Sion* flows from the internal logic of the thought. The rhythm rises from a conceptual directness of content to the heights of pure speculation, and resolves itself into a lyrical expression of loving imploration.

These stanzas, clear enough to form a perfect *Eucharistic creed*, are a jewel of the Catholic liturgy which well justify the title given to St. Thomas as the greatest poet of the Holy Eucharist: "*Eucharistae praeco et vates maximus*" (Pius XI, Encyc. *Studiorum ducem*, June 29, 1923, AAS 15 [1923], 320). *Pio.*

LAW. The concept of law is broad. It embraces every necessary norm for events or actions. Thus, there are many types of law, distinguished according to the forms of necessity and the methods of execution.

From the standpoint of the forms of necessity, a law may be (1) *physical*, (2) *artistic* (technical), and (3) *ethical*. Physical law is brute necessity without liberty. Artistic law is necessity in subjects, psychologically free and without obligation. Ethical law is necessity in subjects endowed with freedom, to which there is attached an obligation. We will discuss here only ethical law.

The source of *necessity* in ethical laws is either the nature of the thing or the free will of the legislator; wherefore, we have *natural* law and *positive* law. Positive law is either *divine, ecclesiastical,* or *civil,* depending on whether the legislator is God, ecclesiastical or civil legislators.

The methods of execution of a law are either voluntary or compulsory. These methods account for the distinction of ethical law into *moral* and *juridical*. The former is an internal bond of conscience; hence, it requires always the will of the subject, that is, the voluntary and free execution of the law. The second is an external bond of social compulsion; hence, it can be enforced even against the will of the subject, that is, compulsory execution. It must be kept in mind, however, that juridical law often unites with moral law, in which voluntary execution of the law can become a duty.

The essential qualities of a law, the absence of which would deprive the law of binding force, are *legitimacy, reasonableness, common good,* and *promulgation. Legitimacy* is present if the law proceeds from legitimate authority according to a specific manner, found in the constitution of each society. *Reasonableness* is demanded by the very nature of man and indicated in the content of the law. An immoral law is unreasonable; this is certain at all times. A law exacting heroism, i.e., actions superior to the ordinary capacity of the subjects, is unreasonable. The *common good* is defined by the law itself, which must serve the interests of all members of society. This interest for the common welfare must be interpreted in a higher, more noble sense, and not of purely material or immediate goods. A lack of distributive justice is an offense against this requirement of the law (*see also* Law, civil; Law, divine-positive; Law, ecclesiastical; Law, natural; Legislator; Resistance to unjust authority). For questions on the *Promulgation* of the law, *see* Promulgation. For cessation of a law, *see* Abrogation, Cessation, Exemption. For interpretation of law, *see* Interpretation, Extension. *Gra.*

LAW, CIVIL. The principal question concerning civil law for a moral theologian is the relationship and force of civil law in obligations of conscience. This is a disputed matter: some affirm an obligation in conscience for every civil law; others require the sentence of a court before this obligation arises; still others deny any obligation in conscience for civil law, if it is purely civil. The diversity of opinions arises from general doctrinal positions and the complexity of the problem. In general, civil authority has a right to enact laws binding in conscience because it represents God Himself in these matters (Rom. 13:1).

No unjust law is binding in conscience either before or after the sentence of a judge. A law is unjust (1) if it is contrary to higher law, especially the natural or divine positive law; (2) if it does not proceed from legitimate authority; (3) if it is not directed to the common welfare; (4) if it violates distributive justice. We are not permitted to obey a law commanding acts against the moral law. Yet if the law does not lead us to commit illicit acts, we may obey an unjust law; we might at times be obliged to observe such a law for reasons of general welfare above and beyond the scope of the law. Furthermore, once a law has been promulgated by competent authority, it must be considered just, until the contrary is proved. To prove a law unjust is difficult, for it must be shown to be against the common welfare or else a violation of distributive justice.

In penal laws, we must distinguish the general obligation to obedience from the hypothetical obligation to accept the penalty for transgression. The first obliges in conscience, except for the purely penal law, which, according to many moral theologians, allows the free choice of observation or payment of the penalty. The second, hypothetical obligation of submitting to a penalty, is never binding in conscience unless one is convicted of transgression.

Laws involving the right of ownership, in which a conflict with the natural law arises, may create some doubt of law; these are binding in conscience before and after the sentence of the judge as long as the law of nature is doubtful. Not all moral theologians teach that there is an obligation before the sentence of a judge.

Invalidating and disabling laws, which declare an act null or a person disqualified, do not, as a rule, oblige the person to admit the nullity of an act before the issue is settled by the decision of a judge, because civil legislation usually considers such acts not initially null and void; they may become null upon request of one of the parties before a judge. The civil legislation, however, cannot be denied the authority to annul an act even prior to the judicial sentence. If it is ascertained that this is the intent of the law, such must be admitted with the duty to conform. *Gra.*

LAW, DIVINE POSITIVE. Divine positive law is the law which comes from the legislating Will of God, above and beyond the requirements of the natural order. In other words, it is a command given by God which He could also not give without opposition to the nature of created things. God did give such laws at different periods in human history, classified as *Primitive, Mosaic,* and *Christian.* The *Primitive* period embraces laws given to the Patriarchs, from Adam to Moses; the *Mosaic* period embraces the entire span of the history of the Jews, whose laws are collected in the Old Testament; the *Christian* or New Testament period contains the laws of the Gospel.

The laws of the first two periods (Primitive and Mosaic) are considered abolished as positive laws; in fact, it would be unlawful to observe the laws of those periods which govern worship (ceremonial laws). Christian laws, of course, are primarily for Christians, but, since Christianity is a universal religion, they can be said to apply indirectly to infidels, insofar as they, too, are called into the fold of the Church. *Gra.*

LAW, ECCLESIASTICAL. Ecclesiastical law is an ordinance or law which is issued by legitimate authority of the Church. The legislators for the Church are: the Sovereign Pontiff and Ecumenical Councils for the entire Church; the bishops and local councils for their respective territories; superiors of religious institutes, according to their constitutions.

Every baptized person, even a non-Catholic, is subject to ecclesiastical laws except special cases indicated by the law itself, or introduced by legitimate custom. The obligation to observe ecclesiastical laws begins at the age of seven, except particular cases expressly mentioned in the law. Universal laws bind everywhere. Those having a domicile or a quasi-domicile in a particular territory are bound by the particular laws of their respective territories as long as they actually reside there; if they leave their territory, they are no longer bound by these laws; individuals are not bound by the laws of the place in which they enter, if they stay there as visitors without acquiring a domicile or quasi-domicile. Visitors are obliged to observe everywhere laws concerning public order. Visitors or travelers, however, are always bound by any law of the Universal Church which binds in the locality they are visiting even if it does not bind in their own territory. Moreover, though they are not, strictly speaking, bound by a particular law of the area they are visiting, yet they may be obliged to observe a law if by disregarding the law they would give scandal.

Laws issued by the Holy See are promulgated in the official organ *Acta Apostolicae Sedis* (*q.v.*) and take effect three months after publication, except those laws which by their very nature are binding immediately or laws for which a longer or shorter period of time is explicitly provided (Can. 9).

The general rule is that ecclesiastical laws are binding in conscience. Invalidating or disabling laws are not binding in doubt of law; in doubt of fact, the Ordinary may dispense from laws within his ordinary faculty of dispensation (Canons 15, 1043, 1045). Concerning the effect of ignorance on invalidating and disabling laws, *see* Ignorance. *Gra.*

LAW, ETERNAL. The eternal law, the essence of God's dominion over the world, is the ordination of all creatures to an end in accord with their natures. It is eternal, supreme, universal as creation itself for the government of the world. No one can evade it; those who disobey it are drawn into the orbit of its dispositions, for they are compelled to submit to the punishment decreed for them by a divine will. Evil itself, as it occurs among individuals, may become a particular or universal good. St. Thomas defines eternal law as "the plan of divine wisdom inasfar as it directs all acts and motions toward the end of the universe" (*Summa Theol.* I–II. q. 93, a. 1). From the standpoint of its relationship to man, the eternal law embraces (a) the hypothetical order of pure nature; (b) the order of elevated nature; (c) the order of man's fallen nature restored in Christ.

From the infinite knowledge and wisdom of God it is a reasonable and necessary conclusion that God must have a plan according to which all creatures attain their end in a manner suitable to their respective natures. Thus, man is directed to the fulfillment of the Divine Will by a norm which shines before his reason, bends his will without coercion and guides him on the road proper to him. This norm of conduct, expressed through the commanding voice of conscience under the light of reason and man's free will, is called natural law (*q.v.*).

Irrational creatures are guided by necessitating laws; those who enjoy a limited degree of liberty are guided to their end through their limited liberty. Inanimate things obey an eternal law of God expressed in the forces of nature called physical laws, while animals fulfill a divine purpose by their instinctive tendencies. God in His infinite nature contains the perfections of the whole universal order; as Intelligence, He knows it; as a creative and ruling Will, He determines its existence and nature. In Him, then, must we look for the foundation of every order. Man, in his nature, carries an imprint of the divine nature insofar as it concerns his individual and social life. As a being endowed with a rational faculty, he participates in the knowledge which God has of human nature, of its needs and congenital aims. As a being endowed with free will, he can either conform to the divine law or violate it. *Pal.*

LAW, HUMAN. *See* Law, civil; Law, ecclesiastical.

LAWS, INVALIDATING AND DISABLING. *See* Law, civil; Law, ecclesiastical.

LAW, MOSIAC. *See* Divine - positive law.

LAW, NATURAL. In the field of ethics any law which has a binding force flowing from the very nature of things prior to any knowledge or determination by a human legislator is called the natural law. The primary source of this law is God, for the natural law is the participation in the eternal law by a rational creature. The eternal law (*q.v.*) is Divine Wisdom itself guiding all creatures to their end.

Natural law manifests itself in the human conscience, where it is expressed by tendencies or dictates of nature, evaluated and regulated by right reason.

Natural law is binding in conscience as the source of every moral duty; human, positive law is binding in conscience only if it is connected with and in conformity with the natural law in the conscience.

Natural law is universal, immutable, not dispensable, and perceptible. It applies everywhere and for all men; it cannot change with the passage of time; no one can dispense from its observance; it may be understood or perceived by anyone who attains the use of reason; its observance obliges when it is perceived by a person who has the use of reason.

Difficulties against these characteristics of the natural law are based on violations of the law, sanctions given to unlawful changes of the law, and the acceptance of customs contrary to the law on a wide scale. In this regard the following observations are significant:

(a) The universality of the law is not to be confused with the universality of its observance. No one will deny transgressions of the law, but this does not alter the value or extent of the law.

(b) Changes, apparently adopted at one time or another in the law, are in fact changes of circumstances or the matter to which the law must be applied, but certainly never of laws imposing on man direct obligations toward the Creator.

(c) Certain customs, obviously contrary to natural law, although widespread and accepted among people of inferior culture, do seem to contradict the perceptible nature of the law. Reason can be greatly hindered by passions; furthermore, the perceptible natural law is not obscure in the primary precepts. Secondary precepts may involve obscurities and uncertainties, which are further illations from the primary precepts.

(d) The same distinction applies to certain dispensations granted in the area of the natural law, such as permission granted to the ancient Hebrews to practice polygamy and divorce. Such permission concerned secondary precepts of the natural law. *Gra.*

LAW, OBSERVANCE OF. A law is, by its very nature, binding. A law must be observed to the extent, at the time, and in the manner prescribed by the law itself. The observance of a law may be either juridical or spiritual. It is juridical if one observes the law in its material expression; it is spiritual if one endeavors to capture the spirit of the law in order to reach the same purpose intended by the legislator. Only a juridical observance can be imposed by human law, as such. Such observance, of course, is not the best manner of fulfilling one's duty. As a matter of fact, the welfare of the individual and, at times, the welfare of society may demand an observance more in accord with the spirit of the law, for society does not benefit merely by the external actions of its citizens. *Pal.*

LAW, PENAL. Theory of. *Purely* penal and *merely* penal law are not synonymous terms. A *purely* penal law is a law that imposes no obligation with regard to the observance or the penalty. A *merely* penal law is a law obliging one to pay a penalty if one is convicted of a violation of the law. We deal here with the latter. The theory of *merely* penal laws endeavors to explain the nature of such laws if such laws do exist.

Nearly all the authors are agreed that the origin of the theory goes back to the Prologue to the Dominican Constitution of the General Chapter of Paris, of 1236, wherein it is stated that the Dominican rules do not oblige in such a way that their transgression gives rise to guilt but merely to bear the penalty imposed (Humbert de Romanis, *De vita regulari*, vol. II, p. 45).

The formulation of the theory developed gradually by Henry of Ghent, Giovanni Andrea, Angelo da Chivasso and, above all, Alphonsus de Castro, who is credited with the well-known triple division of moral, mixed, and merely penal laws. The latter, according to di Castro, involve only an obligation to pay the penalty, for this is what the legislator intends principally. The legislator intends that the law be observed, but he does not intend observance as an obligation. Suarez gave a final touch to this enunciation of the theory by Alphonsus de Castro.

The concept of *merely* penal laws was accepted with some reluctance; today some theologians deny the possibility of such laws, for, they argue, no penalty can be imposed without a previous guilt, since penalty and guilt are correlated.

Among the majority who admit merely penal laws, there is no argument concerning the basis and the nature of these laws. In unison, mere-penalists repeat that the will of the legislator makes the law merely penal. The individual who violates such laws incurs no guilt because the legislator intended a law without obligation. Some isolated voices would make a merely penal law dependent, not on the will of the legislator, but on the nature of the matter of the law itself as irrelevant insofar as the internal forum is concerned.

Diverse Conceptions of Merely Penal Laws. In an effort to explain the nature of merely penal laws the following solutions are proposed.

(a) *The moral obligation to submit only to the penalty.* According to this theory, the merely penal law does not intend to make that which it prescribes binding; however, since the legislator desires fulfillment, he imposes a penalty in case of transgression, to induce subjects to observe the law. In any case, it is a real law, because it obliges the judge to impose the penalty and the subject to accept it without resistance. Alphonsus de Castro, Suarez and, among the modern authors, Creusen, are numbered among the defenders of this theory.

(b) *The juridical obligation concerning the moral obligation to bear the penalty.* According to this theory, the violation of a law concerns only the external forum. It is an offense for which man is held accountable only to society. But the obligation to accept the penalty binds in conscience. Among the defenders of this theory are Reiffenstuel; among the modern authors, Coronata and Janssen.

(c) *The juridical obligation concerning the precept and the penalty.* This theory is applicable to purely juridical laws, a concern of the external forum only. Some maintain that they cannot be called laws in the true sense, but orders. Among the sponsors of this theory are Cajetan (some include St. Alphonsus) and among modern authors are D'Avine, and Vermeersch in the first two editions of his moral theology.

(d) *Separate moral obligation to observe the precept or accept the penalty.* According to this theory, the merely penal law is such that the legislator wants either that it be observed or that the penalty be accepted. The peculiarity of this solution is that it makes the obligation disjunctive: to observe the precept or to accept the penalty. This theory, which had a large following in the past century, including D'Annibale and Bouquillon, seems to have been looked upon with favor also by Suarez as one of the possible solutions.

(e) *Other explanations* of the theory of merely penal laws were recently given by Voroniecki (*"De legis sic dictae poenalis obligatione,"* in *Angelicum,* 18 [1943], 379–386), who holds that the merely penal law is a law of little importance, which carries in itself the faculty of self-dispensation, with the obligation for the transgressor to submit to the penalty if discovered. Ledrus taught that merely penal religious laws should be made a part of the sphere of non-binding morality, called laws of generosity, the violation of which would not constitute a trespassing of the boundaries of morality (M. Ledrus, *"Le problème des lois purement pénales,"* in *Nouv. rev. théol.,* 59 [1932], 46 ff.). Civil laws, to the extent to which they are merely penal, are not specifically imposed for the common good; hence they give rise only to an indirect obligation of conscience not to disobey the dispositions of the constituted authority when it punishes the violation. Further explanations are also offered by Gaglio (*"La lex mere poenalis,"* in *Palestra del clero,* 102 [1931], 402 ff.). He teaches merely penal laws are only civil, not criminal, laws. Brisbois thinks that, though every just law is binding and although the law accidentally might not oblige by reason of grave inconvenience, there remains in these cases a juridical obligation to accept the penalty, since it involves the violation of a legitimately established order. Van Hove (*De legibus ecclesiasticis,* Mechliniae-Rome, 1930, p. 157 ff.) holds that the only obligation arising from merely penal laws is the recognition of the justice of the punishment and the obligation in conscience to accept it although the act commanded or forbidden is only a juridical obligation sufficient to make the penalty lawful. According to Harmignie (*"Ordonnances humaines et obligation de conscience,"* in *Revue néo-scholastique de philosophie,* 32 [1930], 276–320), merely penal laws are only counsels which cannot be imposed on the masses but which the authority equips with penalties so that the citizens may not violate them too easily.

Our opinion is that the question is not yet ripe for a solution. At present, those who flatly deny the existence of merely penal laws speak louder than others because, not finding any satisfactory solution, they insist that it is not sufficient ground to punish a person for a merely penal guilt, and still less acceptable is the fact that one be punished for no guilt at all.

Identification of Merely Penal Laws. According to those who admit merely penal laws, they are identified by the following criteria: (a) explicit declaration of the law; (b) interpretation and judgment of competent and conscientious people; (c) lack of proportion between guilt and punishment; (d) a morally indifferent matter, regulated by the law.

On the basis of these criteria, to consider a law as merely penal and violate it accordingly at this point of the controversy is not certain moral guilt except for the obligation to submit to the penalty, or if a violation is accompanied by scorn for authority, scandal, or the attempt to corrupt public officials. *Pal.*

LAW, UNJUST. *See* Resistance to unjust power.

LAWYER. *See* Advocate.

LAWYERS' FEES. *See* Honorarium.

LAXISM. *See* System, Moral.

LEAGUE OF NATIONS. *See* United Nations (U. N.).

LEASE. In general a lease is a consensual bilateral contract in which one of the contracting parties (lessor) conveys to another (lessee, or tenant) the right of use to a definite thing, work, or service, during a specified length of time, for a corresponding payment (rent, hire, freight, salary, etc.). One of the oldest forms of contract in the history of law, the lease is much in use today in a variety of modern forms.

Of fundamental importance in a lease contract is the Roman distinction of the lease *of things (locatio-conductio rerum)*, *of work (locatio-conductio operis)* and of *services (locatio-conductio operarum)*. This signifies whether the object of the contract implies the leasing or renting of a thing, or labor—that is, a specific product of labor—or a service. In any case, the essential element in any leasing contract is its binding character; however, unlike emphiteusis *(q.v.)* and usufruct *(q.v.)*, which give rise to a real right of use and enjoyment, a lease gives rise in a lessee only to a personal right or credit.

The definition given above contains a fundamental concept of the varied gamut of contracts which modern law, on the basis of a Roman tradition, has progressively developed. These contracts, whose minimum common denominator is that of lease, can no longer be contained within one contractual scheme or be treated in a manner common to all. Thus, the various agricultural contracts (rent, crop sharing arrangement, sharing of cattle or farming profits, colonizing system, etc.), rent contracts and the various concessions for the development of industrial, commercial, and agricultural enterprises are referred to as *locatio rerum* (leasing of things) and are specific types of contracts. Other distinct types of contracts have evolved from *locatio operis*, such as business enterprise, (*see* Business Enterprise), construction contract, agency, mediation *(q.v.)*, storage *(q.v.)* and mandate. The formula of *locatio operarum*, lease or rent of services, has been supplanted by or substituted with modern labor or employment contracts, which may be individual, collective, or national, and are of great importance today in the juridical as well as the social fields. Following a system adopted by civil and canonical codes in which lease is restricted to the lease of things, we must, by necessity, limit our present treatment to this aspect only and refer the reader to specific entries (business enterprises, construction contract, labor or employment contract, service, company, etc.), for other aspects of lease referring to work and services.

LEASE OR RENT OF THINGS. The lease of things is the contract by which one party binds himself to let another party enjoy a movable or immovable article for a specified period of time in exchange for a determined price. The contract may be determined to any object, movable or immovable, which the law has not declared non-negotiable. If the object is a movable thing, then we have a contract of hire or charter; if the object is immovable, then we have a sub-type of lease, as in a lease of locations for living quarters, and rural properties for cultivation purposes. This is properly called rent. Lease and rent are substantially identical terms, although rent may involve a lease whose object is the enjoyment of a productive thing. Any person capable of performing administrative acts can lease. Lease is essentially temporary.

LEASE OF ECCLESIASTICAL PROPERTY. By virtue of Canon 1529, the Code of Canon Law, in contracts and leases, recognizes the civil laws of the respective territories as valid and effective in the ecclesiastical system. (*See* Contract.) If there are dispositions of divine or canonical laws to the contrary, the above-mentioned norms and dispositions must be considered as applicable to the leasing of ecclesiastical properties, as long as due consideration is given to certain norms, partly contrary, partly adjunctive, explicitly mentioned in Canon Law. Canon Law, for instance, establishes that the lease of immovable ecclesiastical goods is normally done by public auction according to the prescription of Canon 1531, par. 2, and that explicit conditions be added in the respective contracts with regard to diligent protection of boundaries, proper cultivation of the soil, and payment of the rent. All of these must be secured by adequate guarantees (Can. 1541, par. 1). Also, according to Canon 727, par. 1, sacred articles are not negotiable (*extra commercium*). Moreover, Canon Law declares that the lease of an immovable ecclesiastical property for a period exceeding nine years or a rental above $1,000.00 a year is an act which exceeds the limits of ordinary administration and must, therefore, be authorized by ecclesiastical authorities possessing faculties extending beyond those of ordinary administrators.

In those places where concordats exist, a lease for more than nine years must also be authorized by civil authorities. With regard to the properties of a benefice, it is forbidden, without permission of the local Ordinary, to pay or collect rent more than six months in advance (Can. 1541, par. 2; Can. 1479); also, it is forbidden, without special permission of the local Ordinary, to lease immovable property of a church to the administrators of the church or to persons related to them in the first and second degree of consanguinity or affinity (Can. 1540). *Zac.*

NOTE—Concerning the rights and obligations of lessor and lessee, the rights of subletting, the termination of a lease, and the detailed and specific civil legislations concerning this subject, the reader must, of necessity, consult the codes, statutes or customs of each respective country, and the various areas of the same country. There are very few churches or ecclesiastical institutions in the U.S.A. that lease property; thus, it might have seemed proper to omit this entry altogether, but for reasons of erudition, the entry was carried over from the original work. [Editor.]

LEASE OF WORK. *See* Lease.

LECTIONARY. *See* Liturgical books.

LECTORATE. *See* Orders, Holy.

LEGACY. *See* Inheritance.

LEGACY, PIOUS. A pious legacy is a disposition of property by transfer to a physical or juridical person, entrusted with the obligation of fulfilling a religious or charitable intention (modal legacy). A religious intention places such dispositions under ecclesiastical discipline. If such dispositions become permanent by death or by an act *mortis causa,* they are properly called dispositions of a last will or dispositions of a spiritual nature (*pro anima*).

If, because of death or an act between two living persons (*actus inter vivos*), these dispositions of property are assigned to a juridical, ecclesiastical person with a perpetual or permanent obligation to fulfill definite, religious intentions with income accrued from property, this is called a pious foundation (*q.v.*). If the dispositions demand that ecclesiastical authority administer this by assigning a cleric or priest with the duty of fulfilling these obligations and of collecting the accrued income, this is termed an ecclesiastical chaplaincy (*q.v.*). If this foundation is perpetual, it is a true benefice (Can. 1409). If the above-mentioned property is allotted to a physical person (ecclesiastical or lay) or to a non-ecclesiastical legal person, we have a simple legacy or lay chaplaincy. This differs from a pious legacy only insofar as it is assumed as a transaction for a chaplaincy (Can. 1412, n. 2). It remains under the discipline of Canons 1513–1517, which govern legacies, but the property does not become ecclesiastical (Cans. 1497, par. 2; 1499). Canon Law requires that the provisions of civil law be observed in such cases (Can. 1513, par. 2). *Vio.*

LEGAL ACTION. *See* Plaintiff.

LEGATE (PAPAL). A Legate is a prelate commissioned by the Holy See to conduct certain ecclesiastical affairs in a specified locality, in the name and by a mandate of the Sovereign Pontiff. His authority is ordinary and vicarious because it is inherent to his office by law. He may receive further delegated authority. (*See* Jurisdiction.)

In our days there are generally three types of Papal Legates: *Legatus a latere,* a Cardinal commissioned to represent the Sovereign Pontiff as *alter ego* in certain affairs of major importance (*see* Cardinals); *Apostolic Nuncio* or *Internuncio* (*q.v.*) with official recognition by the civil power of a country; *Apostolic Delegate* (*q.v.*), who is not officially accredited by the civil authorities (Can. 267).

The Office of Papal Legate does not terminate with the death of the Sovereign Pontiff, unless it was to be exercised at the Pontiff's will (*ad beneplacitum Nostrum*); it may terminate upon completion of the mandate, by revocation of the mandate, or by resignation accepted by the Sovereign Pontiff (Can. 268). *Fel.*

LEGENDARIUM, LEGENDARY. *See* Liturgical books.

LEGISLATION. *See* Law, Civil; Justice, Social; Legislator; Laws, Penal; Law, Ecclesiastical.

LEGISLATOR, LAWGIVER. A legislator is a maker of laws or lawgiver. A legislator may be one individual, as an absolute monarch, or one or more assemblies, as parliamentary governments. The theory that (civil) authority resides in the people must also recognize the people as the primary legislator, and monarchs or assemblies are legislators only by delegation of the people. This doctrine, predicated on the principle that God is the ultimate source of all authority, applies only in the case of the civil authority; in the ecclesiastical society authority is inherent in a divinely established hierarchy.

The legislator is a nominal one, whose laws do not bind unless he is legitimately invested with authority by society. Consequently, a usurper has no authority to make laws; his acts are not binding as laws. For reasons of order in society, the citizens may be indirectly bound to observe them unless they prescribe unlawful acts.

When laws are enacted by an assembly, the individual members of the assembly are subject to the laws, as are all other citizens. If the laws are made by one person, it is debated whether he is subject to a law enacted by himself or his predecessor. In general, it is held (with St. Thomas) that the legislator is subject to his own laws insofar as their directive and obliging force is concerned, but not with regard to their coercive force. In other words, he is bound in conscience to observe his laws to the same extent to which his subjects are bound, yet accountable to God alone for his observance or non-observance, for he cannot apply to himself coercive measures. Since penalties are considered as compelling measures, it may be concluded that the legislator is exempt from criminal laws. The doctrinal basis of this theory is not really exact, but it expresses exactly a fact. It is generally believed, however, that the legislator is not bound directly by virtue of his own laws but by a generic law of nature which requires that he abide by the same laws imposed on his own subjects.

Since he can dispense his subjects from observing the law, he can also dispense himself, or consider himself dispensed, by virtue of the same general law of nature indicated above, if the circumstances justifying a dispensation for his subjects are also present in his own case. *Gra.*

LEGITIMATION. The Church and the State regulate, independently of each other, the legitimacy or illegitimacy of offspring and the juridical status of illegitimate children.

CANON LAW. According to Canon 1114, a legitimate child is: (a) one conceived by lawful intercourse, during a valid or putative marriage, even if born after the dissolution of the marriage, or after the marriage ceased to be putative (*see* Marriage, Putative); (b) one, although conceived out of wedlock, in intercourse with a man at the time not the husband of the mother, yet born after the father had contracted a valid and putative matrimony with the child's mother.

A child is considered illegitimate if neither conceived nor born of a valid or putative marriage or if either parent at the time of conception was bound by solemn vows or Holy Orders, although the child was conceived in matrimony. Since absolute and direct proof of the facts necessary to establish the legitimacy or illegitimacy of offspring is almost impossible, the Church has established two presumptions for both of which a proof to the contrary is admitted.

The first presumption is that a child born more than 180 days after the celebration of marriage (valid or putative) or not more than 300 days after discontinuance of conjugal life, is presumed to have been conceived by an act between the mother and her lawful husband; in other words, it is presumed to be a legitimate child (Can. 1115, par. 1). This presumption of legitimacy favors a child born 180 days after the celebration of the marriage and not over 300 days after discontinuance of conjugal life. In other words, this child is presumed to have been conceived during the marriage and by an act between the mother and her lawful husband (Can. 1115, par. 2). The second presumption is that a child born within 180 days from the celebration of the marriage is presumed neither to have been conceived during the marriage nor by an act of the husband of the mother. However, if the conception by an act of the husband of the mother can be demonstrated, the child is considered legitimate, as he comes under the case indicated above. By the same token, a child born 300 or more days after discontinuance of conjugal life is presumed to have been conceived neither during the marriage nor by an act of the husband of the mother, but he may be considered legitimate only if both of these facts are proved. When there are doubts concerning any of these facts on which the presumptions rest, as frequently occurs with foundlings, the child must be considered legitimate, even if one or both parents are unknown.

An illegitimate child is called a natural child. The strict sense of this term is applied to illegitimate children whose parents, either at the time of conception or birth, or even during pregnancy, were free of any direment impediment or other disqualification for matrimony. Other illegitimate children are called spurious. These children (*orti ex damnato coitu*) are begotten of an adulterous, sacrilegious, or incestuous union. The parents of these children, or at least one of the parents, were affected for the entire period from conception to birth by an impediment of previous marriage, Holy Orders, religious profession, or a relationship of consanguinity.

An illegitimate child may be legitimated and thus acquire a juridical status similar but not always equal in Canon Law to the status of legitimate children. Legitimation in Canon Law can be effected in the following manner: (a) If the children of a union are natural and not spurious children, and the parents enter into a putative or valid marriage subsequently. A convalidation of marriage is equivalent to the celebration of a marriage. (b) If the parents are dispensed from a diriment impediment, provided that at the time of the granting of the dispensation (Can. 1116), the child actually has been already born or conceived. (c) If the Holy See grants legitimation as a favor. For the faithful of the Latin Rite, the Sacred Congregation of the Sacraments usually handles this case.

If the marriage of the parents receives a sanation (*sanatio in radice*), illegitimate children enjoy the same status of legitimacy as they would have possessed at the period to which the sanation applies, i.e., at the beginning of the marriage, as if a valid marriage had been celebrated and a dispensation had been received at the time of the original ceremony. A radical sanation allows even a spurious child to be considered legitimate, and not merely legitimated (Can. 1138, pars. 1 and 2).

Generally in civil law, unlike canonical legislation, a state of legitimacy or illegitimacy has no effect, except with respect to domestic and patrimonial relationships between the parents and children. For details on this matter, the reader must consult the particular civil legislations.

LEGITIMISM. Legitimism is a theory which teaches the undeniable right of a legitimate king to rule by lawful descent. This right was said to come directly from God, in opposition to the French Revolution, which had proclaimed the right of the people to depose a sovereign. This concept of direct, divine investiture was first molded into a theory by King James I (1603) of the Stuart dynasty, which ruled Scotland for centuries. It compared the sovereignty of a king to the privilege bestowed by God on the family of David to be rulers of the Hebrew people. Favored on the continent during the Revolution which followed the fall of Napoleon, legitimism became widespread as a reaction among Catholics against the demagogic excesses of the Revolution.

The Thomistic doctrine maintaining that all power comes from God through the people is re-echoed in the declarations of the highest ecclesiastical authorities. It was generally accepted in the Middle Ages as most acceptable and in conformity with the natural law. Not a pure and simple acceptance by the people of popular sovereignty as understood in the French Revolution, which recognized no limitation upon a sovereign, Catholic doctrine considers even the people subordinate to the moral, natural law, which is of divine origin. This dictates obligations for the common good, the purpose of all civilized society. This norm applies to the investiture of authority and rulers as well as to altering the forms of government. In opposition to legitimists, even a situation in which these laws are observed conscientiously by a prince who rules legitimately does not provide an absolute right to power. For the legitimists, only a voluntary renunciation of power by a prince resolved any conflict, since no one could destroy his right. If deposed, he had the right to use force to regain power. The later doctrine of a constitutional king, who ruled by the will of the people, excluded this right to use force. A tendency away

from monarchism makes the question less significant today. *Boz.*

LENT. Lent is a period of forty days (*Quadragesima*) of penance and fasting in preparation for Easter. A characteristic of this season is the daily fast and abstinence, except for Sundays.

Historically, as a period of fasting and penance, Lent does not seem to have been formally established before the fourth century, for no mention of this appears in earlier writings. Introduced in Rome as a period of fast, Lent was arranged so that a week of mitigated fast followed a week of more rigorous penance. This practice seems to have prevailed in Ravenna and Turin, as it appears from the sermons of St. Peter Chrisologus and St. Maximus. Prior to the fourth century the observance of special days of fasting marked a preparation for the feast of the Resurrection of Our Lord. In the second and third centuries the practice of fasting was not general; all agreed on a fast of two days, Good Friday and Holy Saturday, which are mentioned by Tertullian (*De jejun.* 2:14). Tertullian says that this custom existed in Africa; the Apostolic Tradition of Hippolytus says that the same custom existed in Rome, and Irenaeus testifies to its practice in Gaul. Later, the fast for the entire week was introduced. The ceremony of the reconciliation of sinners on Holy Thursday may have been a decisive factor in extending the period of preparation for Easter to forty days, for it is known that the *lapsi* observed a period of fasting for forty days (St. Peter of Alexandria, 306).

CATECHETICAL INSTRUCTION IN LENT. A period of general preparation for the faithful and repentant sinners, Lent also became the time when the catechumens received a detailed instruction in the Faith in preparation for their initiation into the Christian religion by baptism on Holy Saturday. The *examinations, exorcisms, traditio symboli* and the *traditio orationis dominicae* were held during the Lenten season.

THE ASHES. Among the particular ceremonies of Lent is the *distribution of ashes* on the Wednesday preceding the first Sunday of Lent. This rite made that particular Wednesday *caput sacratissimae quadragesimae,* the beginning of the holy season of Lent.

RITES AND CEREMONIES PROPER TO LENT. One of the special Lenten rites was Lenten Stations which was the celebration of the Lenten liturgy each day in a different church in Rome; on Mondays, Wednesdays, and Fridays, later on Saturdays. These *stations* were preceded by a procession during which the Litany was chanted.

An external characteristic of the Lenten liturgy is the use of purple vestments at a low Mass; folded chasubles instead of dalmatics and a full chasuble at a solemn Mass; flowers are not used on the altar and the playing of the organ is generally discontinued. By a recent *motu proprio* of Pope John XXIII (July 25, 1960) the use of folded chasubles has been discontinued. Today, the rigorous observance of fast and abstinence common in olden days has given way to a much more mitigated form. *Cig.*

LEPROSARIUM. *See* Hospital.

LESBIANISM. *See* Sodomy; Perversion, Sexual.

LESSER EVIL (Choice of). The choice of an action as the lesser of two evils is illicit, if it is a question of two moral evils, that is, actions in themselves violations of the moral law. The reason is evident. One evil does not become right or licit simply because a greater evil could be chosen. The moral problem as to whether it is licit or obligatory to choose the lesser of two evils presupposes a non-existent dilemma in which a man would be required to choose between two sinful acts, so that if he does not choose the one, he must necessarily choose the other. Such a case is morally impossible because man can always abstain from positive action altogether, if one or the other would invariably be a sin, and if to do neither would in itself be no sin (refrain from abortion). If, by reason of circumstances, serious dam-

age were to result from this omission, e.g., the death of the mother, or mother and child, the individual would not be responsible for such consequences because no one may be held accountable for not doing something which, if done, would constitute a sin. To choose the lesser of two evils is permissible if the lesser evil is not in itself a moral evil (sin), but a purely physical evil or the omission of something good or indifferent, from which in a specific case an accidental bad effect will follow, less serious, however, than that which another course would produce. For example, of two medicines both productive of a bad effect on one's health but equally useful to the patient, the physician must choose the less damaging because it is his duty to avoid harm to his patient's health.

In a question whether it is permissible to advise a person bent on committing a sin to commit another less grave instead, as advising fornication for one intending adultery, or drunkenness instead of murder, the answer is that one may never suggest the commission of sin, not even to a person bent on committing a graver sin, because to advise a person to commit evil is the same as inducing him to commit that act. Inducing another to commit a sin is sinful. It is wrong to lead another to will or to commit a sin. A comparison of one sin to another does not take away the malice of the first. The desire to prevent a greater sin is good; but the end, though good, does not justify the means if this is not in itself permissible. It is immoral to do an evil in order to avoid a greater evil.

However, to dissuade another from part of a total evil already planned and insofar as the evildoer cannot be deterred from the complete wrong is a good deed. For instance, to suggest to a thief who wants to kill a proprietor and steal his money, to take only the money, is not advising theft but advising against murder. The theft, already decided upon, was not carried out because of advice received. The effect of the advice by its very nature was to deter the thief from the murder planned. Indeed, to deter another from evil is a good act, licit by its very nature. This is true if advice deters another from part of a sin when it is not possible to deter the other from the entire evil. The difference between counseling the lesser of two evils and advising against a part of a proposed evil act is as follows: the first case employs an act, by its very nature evil, as a means to a good end; the second case, instead, employs an act, by its very nature good, as a means to a good end.

The morality of the act is not in words as such, but in their true *intent*. This intention may be determined by circumstances. Advice is said to be opposed to a portion of the evil act, if the remaining evil is already formally or, at least, virtually decided upon as part of the whole sin which the other intends to commit. *Ben.*

LESSON. *See* Teacher, Epistle, Mass.

LETHARGY. *See* Sleep, Hypnotism, Narcolepsy.

LETTER, ANONYMOUS. An anonymous letter is a letter concealing the identity of the sender. To write an anonymous letter is in itself a morally indifferent act. It may be licit or good, if the motive behind it is good and the content of the letter does not violate justice or the charity due to the recipient or another. It is possible that the writer may have good reasons for not signing his letter.

If the conditions indicated above are not present, as frequently happens in anonymous letters, and the letter contains threats, abuses, offenses, contumely, or defamation, the act is both sinful and socially reprehensible. The gravity of the sin and its species depends on the content of the anonymous letter. The sinfulness and the content of the letter render the use of an anonymous letter a generally aggravating occasion for subsequent acts morally more serious and socially more detestable.

In canonical trials anonymous letters may be used but may not be included in the acts. They must be destroyed at the end of a trial (Can. 1645, par. 1). Though not accepted as proof, they may be useful in orientating the judges on some fact which, if proved, renders the letters valid proof. *Ben.*

LETTER, DECRETAL. *See* Acts, Pontifical.

LETTER, DIMISSORIAL. *See* Dimissorial (letters).

LETTER OF THE MARTYROLOGY. *See* Liturgical year.

LETTER (opening of). *See* Secret.

LETTER, PONTIFICAL. *See* Acts, Pontifical.

LETTER, TESTIMONIAL. *See* Novitiate, Novice.

LEUCHOTOMY. *See* Neuro-surgery, Psycho-surgery.

LEVITATION. *See* Metapsychosis.

LEWD. *See* Image, Indecent; Obscene.

LIBELLUS, SUPPLEX. *See* Process.

LIBELS (EMOTIVE). *See* Dysthymia.

LIBERALITY. Liberality in the theological sense is a spirit of generosity in the use of money or possessions for proper and worthy charity. If it involves large donations for public welfare or charitable institutions, it is termed munificence or magnificence (*q.v.*). Liberality presupposes a just appreciation of material goods and an absence of excessive attachment to them.

Liberality is a duty for all.

One may sin against liberality by excess—extravagance; by defect—avarice. *Man.*

LIBERA ME, DOMINE. *See* Funeral.

LIBER GRADUALIS. *See* Liturgical books.

LIBIDO. *See* Lust.

LIBRARIES, LENDING. Stable or mobile lending libraries have become important in recent years, as the main and sometimes only source of reading matter for many. In many countries great impetus is given to the establishment of well-supplied Catholic lending libraries, with a two-fold purpose: (1) to promote sound ideas and decent sentiments; (2) to combat the evils of the secular press, which, due to a tremendous appeal to human passions and low costs, represent an incentive to large segments of the population to patronize such publications. In view of the fact that libraries constitute a most useful medium of religious propaganda and moral preservation, the Church has an incontestable right and also a duty to exercise this type of apostolate.

Catholic library authorities, directors, and personnel have a grave responsibility concerning the type of books in their establishments. To keep on the shelves, without due permission, books forbidden either by the general law of the Code (*ipso jure*; Can. 1399) or by special decree of the Holy See, constitutes a grave sin (Can. 1398, par. 1). If such directors are not owners of the establishment and have little to say concerning the type of books placed in the library, they naturally do not incur the penalties indicated by the Code. The principles of cooperation (*q.v.*) in the sin of another may apply to those who give to others books forbidden by the Church. The lending of books written by apostates, heretics, or schismatics, expressly forbidden by Apostolic Letters, constitutes a violation punishable with excommunication incurred *ipso facto* (automatically) and reserved in a special manner to the Holy See (Can. 2318, par. 1). Permission to keep on hand and lend out forbidden books does not extend to obscene books. Finally, librarians may give out forbidden books only to those who are presumed to have permission to read them (Can. 1404). *See* Literature, Press. *Dam.*

LIFE. *See* Right to Life, Danger of Death, Body, Soul, Psychology, Physicians, Medicine.

LIFE, AFFECTIVE. *See* Affectivity.

LIFE, COMMON. *See* Cleric, Nun, Religious.

LIFE, RESPECT FOR. *See* Murder, Suicide.

LIGAMEN, IMPEDIMENT OF. *See* Bond, impediment of.

LIGHT, ELECTRIC. *See* Electricity.

LIQUID (FASTING). *See* Abstinence and Fasting.

LIQUIDATOR, LIQUIDATION. A *liquidator*, in the juridical sense, is an official appointed to legally foreclose a bankrupt company or commercial property. A liquidator may be appointed either by law (*ex lege*), by a declaration of a judge (*ex sententia judicis*), or by a decision in a meeting of the stockholders.

Liquidation is a series of ordinary and extraordinary administrative acts, carried out by a liquidator to obtain the realization, distribution, or assignment of the property and assets to those legally entitled to them.

Canon Law does not legislate the matter of liquidation, but accepts the decisions of civil law in each individual country (Can. 1529). Thus, for details concerning the various methods and rights connected to this subject, including the legal obligations and responsibilities of a liquidator, the reader should consult the legislation of each respective country.

Regarding moral questions in liquidation, the principles governing the acts of an agent apply to acts of liquidation (*see* Agent). The material abuse of a mandate by the liquidator is a juridical violation which obliges the liquidator in conscience to restitution, but only after the sentence by the judge. A formal abuse, which is theologically culpable in the liquidator due to gross negligence, abuse of power, theft, or undue appropriation in his own behalf, despite any approval by a final balance-sheet acceptable to the juridical or external forum, is binding in conscience to restitution for such damages even before a judicial decree or decision. Irregularities in the balance sheet or reports involve a crime only if committed by fraud, that is, with an intention to cause damage to others for one's own benefit.

Fraud in a financial report is present only if the evaluations in the prices are above what the moral theologians call a reasonable price, that is, based on an excessively generous criterion. Prudence requires that all excesses be avoided. The criterion of evaluation in an inventory depends on the purchase price of the new merchandise and not on the probable price for some future sale. If the current sales price is lower, then it is licit to ascertain immediately the loss to be incurred and evaluate the merchandise on the basis of a lower price. Prudence requires that the depreciation of machinery and the solvency of creditors be considered. If there is moral certitude that credits cannot be collected at nominal value or that merchandise cannot be sold at the original purchase price, the virtue of justice demands a rectification in the values. A "doctored" balance-sheet cannot always be considered real and proper fraud if it is done for a just cause, such as to avoid a lowering of the market. The prohibition against borrowing from corporation funds is based on a danger of injustice arising from the possibility that the liquidator may take advantage of his position to obtain a more advantageous loan or arbitrarily delay payments, or be tempted to turn it into undue appropriation. The prohibition against any violation of official secrecy is based on the natural law; its gravity depends on the gravity of the harm caused by the violation. *Bic.*

LITANIES. A litany (Greek *litaneia*) is a series of humble supplications and fer-

vid prayers. St. Basil used the word *litania* to indicate public supplications to implore our Lord's help and mercy (Ep. 63). As prayers of supplication, litanies are of ancient origin; they were recited by ancient pagans in their processions to the altars of the gods. Several authors speak of litanies of the Old Testament recited by the Jews in the Temple and in their homes. In the Catholic Church, an ancient Roman Ritual mentions the recitation of one hundred *Kyrie Eleison* (Lord, have mercy on us) prescribed for the procession on the vigil of the feast of the Assumption of our Lady from St. Mary Minor (now St. Frances of Rome) to the Basilica of St. Mary Major. The invocation *Kyrie Eleison* was employed by Jews, Christians and pagans. St. Augustine tells us that Latins and barbarians used it (Ep. 178). St. Gregory I is credited with the addition of *Christe Eleison* (Christ, have mercy on us); the invocations to the saints were added shortly after the time of St. Gregory, from the martyrologies attributed to St. Jerome.

LITANY OF THE SAINTS. The litany of the saints was in use in the East at the time of St. Gregory Thaumaturge. This series of invocations to the saints is called Lesser or Greater depending on recitation on the feast day of St. Mark the Evangelist (April 25), or Rogation days. According to some authors, this distinction is derived from processions held on those days. The explanation of the titles varies: a procession to major or minor churches; procession on St. Mark's day of a more solemn nature; a variety in the length of the itinerary for these processions.

A Gregorian Sacramentary tells us that the procession on the feast of St. Mark went from the Church of St. Lorenzo in Lucina, along the Via Flaminia, across Ponte Milvio and the fields of Nero, past the church of St. Valentine and a shrine on the other side of the bridge, to the Basilica of St. Peter, where Solemn Mass was celebrated, after the recitation at the entrance of the collect *Adesto, Domine.* Many believe this litany was composed and instituted by St. Gregory the Great in the year 600; this opinion is rejected by others because mention is made of it in councils prior to St. Gregory's time. Instead, it is commonly believed that the minor litany was established by St. Mamert to implore deliverance from wolves, which had infested the town with great harm to the population.

The following indulgences may be gained for the recitation of the litany of the saints: (a) partial indulgence of ten years and a plenary indulgence, if recited on the day of St. Mark's feast or during the sacred functions usually celebrated on Rogation days; (b) an indulgence of seven years, if recited on those days and apart from sacred functions; (c) five years, plenary once a month, recited on any day of the year (*Enchiridion indulgentiarum*, ed. 1952, n. 687).

THE LITANY OF LORETTO. This litany consists of a series of invocations in honor of the Blessed Virgin Mary; it is called "of Loretto" because it is chanted with great solemnity and devotion each Saturday at the Shrine of Loretto. Its authorship is unknown, but it is of ancient origin. Some hold that the Apostles composed it after the Holy Virgin's Assumption into heaven. According to more recent studies, however, the Litany of Loretto is not considered that ancient. De Santi believes it was published for the first time in an Italian manual of prayers at Loretto, in 1576; Dr. Paulus has demonstrated that it had already been published in Dillingen, in 1558, probably by St. Peter Canisius. Everything points to the belief that it was in use at Loretto at the beginning of the sixteenth century. There have been several recent additions; the last was "Queen assumed into heaven," following the definition of the dogma of the Assumption by Pope Pius XII, on November 1, 1950.

A previous indulgence of 300 days, granted by Pope Pius VII (Sept. 30, 1817) was altered to an indulgence of seven years and a plenary indulgence once a month, granted through the Sacred Apostolic Penitentiary, March 28, 1933.

LITANY OF THE MOST HOLY NAME OF JESUS. This litany was in use at the beginning of the fifteenth century; the probable authors are considered to be St. Bernardine of Siena and St. John Capestran, zealous promoters of the devotion to the Holy Name of Jesus. On various occasions the Holy See had been requested for an expressed approval, but the Sacred Congregation of Rites had always given a negative reply. However, in 1862, on the occasion of the solemn canonization of the Japanese Martyrs, several Cardinals and Bishops begged the Holy Father to choose one of many versions and attach indulgences to its recitation. Their request was favorably considered by Pope Pius IX, who granted an indulgence of 300 days to be gained in the dioceses of the Bishops who had requested the favor. The same indulgence was, later, extended to the rest of the world by Pope Leo XIII. According to a rescript of the Sacred Apostolic Penitentiary, an indulgence of seven years and a plenary indulgence once a month may be gained by those who recite this litany.

LITANY OF THE SACRED HEART. This litany in honor of the Sacred Heart of Jesus was recited for the first time in the year 1721, during a solemn procession along the roads of Marseilles, through the initiative of the Bishop of that city, the Most Reverend De Belzunce, to implore of our Lord the grace to spare Marseilles from the plague. The litany was taken from a pious book of the Venerable Anne Magdelene de Ramusat, but its principal author is believed to have been Father Croiset, S. J. It was approved on June 7, 1898, for the dioceses of Marseilles and Autun, and for the Visitation Order, but shortly afterwards, upon request of the Society of Jesus, its use was extended to the whole Church by a decree of the Sacred Congregation of Rites, issued on April 2, 1899. An indulgence of 300 days, once a day, granted by Pope Leo XIII through the above-mentioned decree of April 2, 1899, was supplanted by an indulgence of seven years, and plenary once a month, granted by the Sacred Apostolic Penitentiary through a rescript of March 10, 1933.

LITANY OF ST. JOSEPH. This litany in honor of St. Joseph, foster-father of our Divine Savior, was approved by a decree of the Sacred Congregation of Rites, issued on March 18, 1900, and an indulgence of 300 days was attached to its recitation. By a decree of the same Sacred Apostolic Penitentiary, issued March 21, 1935, a partial indulgence of five years, and a plenary indulgence once a month, was granted for its recitation.

Approval for any litany is reserved to the Sacred Congregation of Rites (Clement VIII, Const. *Sanctissimus*, Sept., 1601). For private devotion, no new litany may be put into circulation without approval of the local Ordinary (Can. 1259, par. 2). No text of the above listed litanies may be published without approval of the Ordinary (Can. 1391).

LITANY OF THE BLESSED VIR-GIN. *See* Litanies.

LITANY OF THE MOST HOLY NAME OF JESUS. *See* Litanies.

LITANY OF THE SACRED HEART. *See* Litanies.

LITANY OF THE SAINTS. *See* Litanies.

LITANY OF ST. JOSEPH. *See* Litanies.

LITERARY RIGHTS. *See* Rights of authors.

LITURGICAL BOOKS. With the exception of the texts of the Holy Scriptures for reading and singing the Psalms, in the beginning, the Apostolic Church used no particular books for liturgical services, since the liturgical formulae were under a charismatic influence. The *Didache* (10:7) and St. Justin (*Apol.*, I, 67) bear witness to this. In the third century and in some places as early as the second century, definite liturgical

formulae were written down, especially for the Eucharistic canon. Their use, however, was not obligatory; gradually a great variety of liturgical formulae were adopted, usually according to the discretion of the composer. In the fourth and fifth centuries, Councils of the Church discussed at great length this tendency and consequently required formal approval for the texts of the liturgy. This gave rise to the liturgical books.

THE SACRAMENTAL BOOKS. The earliest and most important liturgical books are the sacramentary books: Leonine, Gelasian, and Gregorian. These do not indicate the authorship by Popes Leo, Gelasius and Gregory the Great; they indicate the time of composition determined from liturgical and stylistical characteristics.

The *Leonine* is the oldest sacramentary and the most authentically Roman in inspiration and elements. It exists in only one manuscript preserved in the capitular Library of Verona, and probably dates back to the fifth–sixth centuries. The manuscript is not complete, is more a hand-book than a full volume with definite and fixed formulae.

The *Gelasian*, transmitted from France through an uncial manuscript of the seventh–eighth centuries, is definitely official, and certainly Roman in origin despite many interpolations of French origin. It dates back to the second half of the sixth century.

The *Gregorian* originally must have been a restoration of the Gelasian sacramentary, although some authorities consider them two distinct compositions from one and the same source, the *libelli Missarum*. This was written either directly by or under the influence of St. Gregory the Great. Several complete and incomplete manuscripts exist but they represent different readings of texts. As the most official of the Roman sacramentaries in common use at the time, it underwent many alterations and additions.

LECTIONARY AND EVANGELARY. In addition to books used directly by the celebrating priest or Bishop, other books were used by the assistant ministers, such as the *lectionary* and the *evangelary*, containing the lessons of the Mass in Epistles and Gospels; compiled completely from the Holy Scriptures, or composed of chosen passages suited to the feasts and liturgical days. If the beginning and the end of the passage chosen for a liturgical feast was marked on the margin or in the appendix of the text of the scripture lessons, the *lectionary* of the Epistles or of the Gospels was referred to as *capitular*.

The *lectionary*, also called *comes*, *liber comicus*, *apostolus*, included a selection of texts from the Prophets and the Apostles in use at Mass on the various feasts. Its use in Rome is certain at least from the fifth century. The most famous texts preserved are the *Capitular* of *Wurzburg* of the seventh century, of a decidedly Roman character; and the *comes of Alcuin*, of the thirteenth century, which accompanied the Gregorian-Adrian sacramentary.

The *evangelary* was a collection of Gospels taken from the Bible for liturgical use. The number of texts in which they are found is exceedingly large. The oldest capitulars of the Gospels date back to the seventh century.

The *evangelary*, the most honored book in ancient Christianity, was written in letters of gold on purple parchment, bound in gold, silver and ivory, decorated with precious stones and works of art with filigree incisions and miniatures. The *evangelarium* was carried with covered hands, placed on the altar beside the Eucharist, with a candle, and incensed in the liturgical service.

CANTATORIUM, ANTIPHONARY, LIBER GRADUALIS. The liturgical books of the chants of the Mass were called the *cantatorium*. These contained the chants or the verse of a responsory psalm after the Epistle and the Alleluia, sung by soloists on the ambo or step. From this came the name *liber gradualis* (*Graduale*). The *antiphonary* included the chants of the schola or choir, such as antiphonary chants for the introit, offertory, and communion. Often it included also the *cantatorium*. The antiphonary should be dated to the fourth or fifth

centuries, as many Popes prior to St. Gregory helped compose it. St. Gregory left us the basic part of our present *liber gradualis*.

Furthermore, the schola used an *antiphonarium officii*, which included the chants of the antiphons, hymns and psalms, intoned according to the requirements of the Divine Office. The oldest manuscripts of that antiphonary date back to the ninth–tenth centuries.

PSALTER, HOMILIARY, LEGENDARY, MARTYROLOGY. Other liturgical books used in the recitation of the office were the psalter or collection of psalms, the homiliary or collection of talks and writings of the Fathers of the Church to be read during the Nocturns (the most widely circulated text was composed by the Cassino monk, Paolo Warnefrido by order of Charles the Great in the seventh century) and the *legendary* containing the *Passiones* or *Acta Martyrum*, usually read during the Second Nocturn, as it is today. The *martyrology*, a brief summary of the lives of the martyrs and later of all the saints commemorated on certain days, was read in the *officium capituli*, after the hour of Prime.

ORDINES. Of considerable importance are the ceremonial books, called *ordines*, which define the ceremonies to be observed during the celebration of the Mass, in the administration of the sacraments, and other rubrics. The most famous belonged to the Roman Church, but frequently those of other churches, especially monastic, are useful for a proper understanding of the ceremonies. Many manuscripts containing the *ordines Romani* have been classified and critically revised recently. (*Les Ordines Romani du haut moyen age*: I. *Les manuscrits*, Louvain, 1931; II. *Les testes* (*Ordines I–XIII*), Louvain, 1948; III. *Les testes* (*Ordines XIV–XXIV*), Louvain, 1951, by M. Andrieu. The edition of 15 *ordines* by Mabillon in *Musaeum Italicum*. *Ordines* I–VI describe the Papal and Episcopal Mass; *Ordines* VII–IX relate the ceremonies of baptism and ordination; *Ordines* X–XII are a collection of ceremonies and various customs for the ecclesiastical year; *Ordines* XIII–XV contain customs relating to papal election and consecration.) The so-called *Ordo Romanus Antiquus* is among the least ancient of the *ordines*, for it is dated no earlier than the tenth century. It is not Roman.

PRESENT LITURGICAL BOOKS. The various ancient liturgical books during the course of the centuries were combined into the liturgical books in use today: the *Missal* (*q.v.*), the *Liber gradualis* for the Mass, the *Caeremoniale episcoporum*, the *Pontificale* (*q.v.*), the *Rituale* (*q.v.*) for the sacraments and the various blessings, and the *Breviary* (*q.v.*) for the divine office. The Breviary became a separate book toward the eleventh century and was circulated through the so-called *Breviaria portatilia vel de camera*, which was used by the pontifical court in the thirteenth century and approved by Innocent III. Later it was officially adopted for the first time by the Friars Minor, who published it under the title of *Breviarium secundum consuetudinem Romanae Curiae*. The monastic churches compiled their own *Breviarium* according to the Benedictine *Cursus*, which was established with great detail in the Rule of Saint Benedict. The *Breviarum* which was adopted for general use in the cathedral churches, underwent various revisions. Pius V (1568) and the Council of Trent gave the book a definitive form, which in later centuries was adapted to present use by Pius X, Pius XII, and John XXIII. Pius XII permitted the use of a new version of the Psalms, translated from the Hebrew text by the Pontifical Biblical Institute in Rome in place of the Gallican Psalter from earliest times (March 25, 1945: AAS [1945]). Pope John XXIII approved various other changes, including the shortening of Matins and the elimination of many duplications (July 25, 1960: AAS [1960]).

LITURGICAL YEAR. The liturgical year consists of a regulated order of special seasons and feasts in the Church, designed principally to commemorate important events in the life of Christ.

The Catholic Church, mindful of the needs of the community of faithful, saw fit to arrange the principal religious observances according to a definite order of time. This was done not only by following the civil arrangement of the year but also according to a calendar all of her own. According to the ecclesiastical arrangement, the liturgical year is centered on Easter (*q.v.*); its various parts are arranged according to the following: (a) the *golden number*, which indicates the day of each new moon and, consequently, the Easter date; (b) the *epact*, which indicates the moon's phase on January 1st; (c) the *Sunday letter* which serves to mark the week in the permanent calendar; (d) the *letter of the martyrology*, which refers to the moon on each day of the month; and (e) the *movable* feasts, which vary according to the date of Easter, as opposed to the *fixed feasts*, permanently set for definite days.

At one time the liturgical year began with Easter, which always depended upon the vernal equinox—the first Sunday following the 14th day of the March moon; today it begins with the Sunday following November 30 (first Sunday of Advent) and closes with the Saturday immediately preceding that Sunday.

Unlike the civil year, divided into days, months and seasons, the liturgical year is divided into weeks, linked together into special periods of time which compose the *cycles*. The most important cycle, and the first in chronological and historical formation, is the Psychal cycle, commemorating the feast of the Resurrection or Easter. This is followed by fifty festive days after Easter; the Ascension is the fortieth day after Easter. A forty-day period of preparation for Easter is called Lent; this is divided into the four Sundays of Lent, First Passion Sunday and Second Passion Sunday (formerly called Palm Sunday), which opens Holy Week, the commemoration of the Passion and Death of Christ.

A second cycle, which parallels in composition the Easter cycle, is the Nativity, commemorating the birth of Christ (Dec. 25). A period of preparation, likewise, precedes this feast; this period of four weeks, called Advent, recalls the long period of expectation of a Saviour by the Jewish race. The Nativity is followed by a period of joyful celebration, comprised of the Sunday after the Nativity, the Epiphany, and an undetermined number of Sundays after the Epiphany, which number six at the most. Next occurs a transition period before Lent, called Septuagesima (seventy days), Sexagesima (sixty days) and Quinquagesima (fifty days), based on the number of days preceding Easter.

The period of time following the feast of Pentecost constitutes a definite section called the *Season after Pentecost,* consisting of 24 Sundays, to which are added, as occasion demands, the remaining Sundays after the Epiphany. This post-Pentecostal period forms a connecting link with Advent and, hence, with the beginning of the new liturgical year. The feast of Corpus Christi, commemorating the triumph of the Eucharistic Christ, is celebrated on the second Thursday after Pentecost.

To these sublime feasts of the Lord were added other minor ones commemorating various phases of His life: the Transfiguration, the Sacred Heart, elevated to a feast of primary importance, the Holy Name of Jesus.

Along with solemnities in honor of our Lord Jesus Christ, feasts commemorating the glories of His Blessed Mother were inserted in the calendar: the Assumption, the most ancient (Aug. 15), the Immaculate Conception (Dec. 8), the Annunciation of the Incarnation of the Word (March 25), and other minor Marian feasts (the Purification, the Seven Dolors of Mary, the Immaculate Heart of Mary, the Holy Rosary, etc.).

The cult of the saints, whose intercession we know through faith to be pleasing to the Lord, also occupies a large part of the liturgical year.

On Nov. 1, one of the principal feasts of the year, the Church honors all saints in one general solemn feast, inviting everyone to look to them for inspiration to follow in their footsteps; this is known as the *Feast of All Saints* (All Saints' Day), followed on the next day by a *general commemoration of all the faithful departed* (All Souls' Day).

The feasts in honor of individual saints, which began with the practice of celebrating the birthdays of martyrs, are spread throughout the year; some have a simple commemoration; others a proper feast. The feasts of more important saints are also holydays of obligation (St. Joseph, March 19; SS. Peter and Paul, June 29), in some countries.

The *Sanctorale* or commemoration of the saints follows the civil calendar, while the *Temporale* follows the Easter cycle with movable feasts. *Pal.*

LITURGY. The word *liturgy* has several meanings. Etymologically, *liturgy* (Greek, *leitourgia,* public service) signifies a public religious rite or service. In the Church it means, primarily, the whole system of public or official worship of the Church. Public worship refers to any act performed in the name of the Church by a lawfully appointed minister and carried out according to the laws and prescriptions of the Church. The act may be performed privately or with great secrecy, as in the recitation of the Divine Office in private or the reception of the sacrament of penance in secrecy; yet these acts still are considered public. *Public* is synonymous with *official.*

Secondary meanings are derived from and linked to the primary meanings of the term *liturgy;* nevertheless, differences can only be understood from the context, which clearly indicates the true significance and meaning in a particular case. Thus, if the various acts of public worship are considered separately, we can properly speak of the liturgy of the Mass, the liturgy of the sacraments, the liturgy of Vespers, etc. Since the public worship is not everywhere performed in the same way, we speak of a Western liturgy, an Eastern liturgy, a Roman, Ambrosian, Antiochean, Alexandrian, Armenian, etc. Since public worship was carried out in different ways and at different times, we speak of ancient, medieval, and present-day liturgy. Furthermore, the acts of public worship are not always the same in every individual act, but allow for changeable prayers and variations according to the time of the year, the feast day, or the season. The variations proper to a particular time, feast, or season sometimes are termed the liturgy of the period, feast, or season. Thus we speak of the liturgy of Advent, Christmas, Epiphany, Lent, Easter, Holy Thursday, the Assumption, etc. Frequently these variations contain a spirit or a thought which predominates the considerations of the time; thus the term "to live the liturgy" or "to understand the liturgy" of a particular feast or season may be adapted to common use. Finally, public worship may entail a study of the origin, form, execution, meaning, effects and relationship of worship to other acts and notions; this becomes the definite science of the liturgy.

LITURGICAL ACTS AND FUNCTIONS. The following are acts of public worship: (a) the Holy Sacrifice of the Mass; (b) the administration of the sacraments and sacramentals, such as blessings, consecrations, processions; (c) the recitation of the Divine Office.

The principal liturgical books used in the official worship of the Church follow the classification for the various acts of public worship as follows: (a) for the Mass, a *Missal*; (b) in the administration of the sacraments and sacramentals a *Rituale* for priests and a *Pontificale* for Bishops; (c) for the recitation of the Divine Office, a *Breviary*.

Various acts of worship, although approved and governed by Church regulations to a large extent, are called extra-liturgical functions if they are not a part of the official worship of the Church. Among these are the *Via Crucis* or Stations of the Cross, the Holy Rosary, tridua of devotion, novenas, and special monthly devotions in honor of our Lord, the Blessed Virgin, or saints. These functions in their entirety and separate parts ought to be in keeping with the spirit of the liturgy which prevails in the various seasons of the year. Thus the Stations of the Cross are particularly suited for Fridays and, in particular, the Fridays of Lent and Good Friday. Devotions in honor of our Lady are particularly suited for Saturdays and her feasts. The *Miserere* is suitable for all times of penance; the *Magnificat* for feastdays dedicated to the Blessed Virgin and the novena in preparation for Christmas. Even the popular hymns in extra-liturgical functions should harmonize with feasts and liturgical seasons; for this reason it is desirable that among the well-known songs and hymns some should be more suited for feastdays and the main liturgical periods of the year.

AIMS OF LITURGY. Liturgy, like religion and worship in general, has a double object or purpose: (1) honoring God, and (2) sanctifying souls. These two objectives are so closely related that it is possible to speak of them as one and the same: to honor God by the sanctification of souls. The honor and glory of God is more particularly sought through the Divine Office; the sanctification of souls through the sacraments and sacramentals; the pursuit of both objectives is fully expressed in the Holy Sacrifice of the Mass.

PARTICIPATION IN THE LITURGY. The laity must take an active and lively part in liturgical functions, particularly Holy Mass and Vespers on holydays. Properly instructed and guided, the laity draw from their participation in the liturgical functions a solid spiritual nourishment for their piety and great assistance in living a truly Christian life. This active participation is made easier nowadays by the publication in the vernacular language of small missals, Vesper books, ritual extracts for the laity, and numerous leaflets or booklets containing the Sunday Mass and Vespers. *Ses.*

LOAN. *See* Interest; Precarium.

LOAN (Mutuum). A loan for consumption *(mutuum)* is a contract in which a person or lender lends to another (borrower) a definite amount of money or other fungible thing, and the borrower obligates himself to return in due time the equivalent of the loan both in quantity and quality. As a user of the thing borrowed, the borrower alone is liable for all damage and receives all profits derived. The duration of the loan is indicated in the contract; a default in this payment is arbitrated by a judge, who, according to some legislations, has power to decide the matter even if it was agreed that the borrower pay only *when he was able to.* If things other than money were borrowed and their return has become impossible or obviously difficult through a fault that is not imputable to the debtor, he is required to pay in value with due consideration for its use. If payment of a financial loan was arranged by installments and the borrower failed to pay even one installment, the lender has a right to demand immediate payment of the entire loan. Strictly speaking, the lender may not require remuneration for the item loaned. In the present day, for extrinsic reasons, generally verifiable, a just rate of interest may be charged for financial loans; this rate of interest is generally subject to established civil laws or customs. (The customary highest rate of interest in the United States for collateral loans is six per-cent annually.) By mutual agreement between the borrower and lender, a higher rate of interest may be approved if there exists an unusually grave risk of loss or a greater hope of large profit. To charge a higher rate of interest without the presence of these reasons is usury and, as such, is a sin against justice, which obligates the lender to make restitution to the borrower, his heirs or, if such are unknown, to the poor.

In ancient times the principle of gratuity of loans *(date mutuum, nihil inde sperantes)* prevailed. But when it was proved that the loan was useful to the borrower for a real productive profit, a moderate interest rate was allowed. Pope Benedict XIV, in the Bull *Vix Pervenit* of 1745, despite an acceptance of the concept of gratuity of loans, specified exactly when interest could be charged and what constituted usury. According to moral theology, confirmed in canonical legislation (Can. 1543), an agreement to pay more than the legal rate of interest is licit, if a just and proportionate reason permits such an agreement.

In the U.S.A. most states have statutes against usury, "taking or reserving by contract a greater compensation or rate of interest for the loan of money than the highest rate of interest allowed by law" (Clark and Marshall, *The Law of Crimes* [2nd ed.], p. 723). According to Canon Law, in those states or countries which tolerate a rate of interest against natural equity, the law cannot be followed in conscience. An exorbitant rate of interest varies with diverse local conditions. At the present time, money is in no way a dead and unproductive thing. No civilized nation of the world could prosper today without a system of loans and interest.

Some peculiar moral and juridical difficulties connected with this subject arise if modern legislations allow the nominalistic principle. The nominalistic principle may be expressed as follows: loans are to be repaid with the currency in use in the country at the time of payment; if the currency in use at the time of the reception of a loan no longer has legal value at the time of payment, payment must be made in the present legal currency irrespective of any changed value. According to this principle, resultant devaluations present a loss or damage to the creditor, as far as the nominal value of the currency is concerned. Vermeersch thought this a wrong against justice and taught that if the intrinsic value of the currency changed because of a devaluation of the gold standard or because of inflation, the borrower was obliged to repay the loan with currency of the same intrinsic value at the time of contracting for the loan. If law or jurisprudence takes a different position, one must avoid generalizations and handle each case according to its own merits, with consideration for the benefits to the borrower. This may demand the judgment of experts for an equitable solution. The same applies to the opposite case, that is, when the currency is revaluated. At any rate, it is to be hoped that in such cases positive law not remain silent, nor the precept of charity be ignored toward the victims of such fluctuations. In economic depression or crisis, principles should be applied so that the entire collectivity share the burdens of financial reverses, rather than some particular class or classes as others register all the gains.

LOBOTOMY. See Cerebral Function; Psychasthenia, Psychosurgery.

LOCALIZATION OF THE BRAIN. See Cerebral Functions.

LOCK-OUT. The opposite of a strike (*q.v.*), a lock-out is the closing of a plant by an employer (*q.v.*) over a failure to reach agreement with employees. In other words, a lock-out presupposes a controversy between employees and their employer, who withholds employment from them as a means of making them accept his terms.

Today the lawfulness of a lock-out is questioned, for it cannot be placed on the same level with a strike, since one individual suffers damage as a result of the strike, while in a lock-out, generally, a large number of employees suffer the damages. Furthermore, a strike finds a natural control in the dependence of the employees upon a wage as the only means of subsistence. It is unlikely that the employer would be compelled to abandon a lock-out because of pressing need. True, both a strike and lock-out can increase the price of commodities. Although this always damages the employees, it may be advantageous to the employer, who may even cause such increase in prices by a deliberate lock-out of his plant. Finally, a lock-out is contrary to the social function of private property as a means of production, a function considered fundamental to a nation's economy. In reply to these reasons against the lawfulness of lock-out it is generally agreed that both a strike and lock-out affect society adversely; however, it is difficult to exclude absolutely a lawful lock-out. It is possible that an employer can escape ruin only by recur-

rence to lock-out, as in a so-called *slowdown strike* by his employees. Nor does the numerical difference between employer and employees constitute a decisive factor, for it is hard to understand why a strike lawful for many cannot be equally lawful for one, who has no other possibility of protecting his own interests except by a lock-out. Moreover, there are business enterprises in which the owners are more numerous than the workers employed, as in joint stock companies. Nor does the argument drawn from a social function of private ownership have greater weight, since this argument applies to a strike, since work is not only a source of gain but also a service rendered to the community. Property has a social function inasmuch as the owner is responsible also to the community; it is certainly possible that in some cases a property could not be protected in these rights except through a lock-out.

Today, in view of a greater interdependency among various industries, more suffer the effects of a lock-out than those directly involved in a dispute. Furthermore, a lock-out offends the mass feelings more than a strike, since it is harder to accept the motives justifying a lock-out. Finally, in view of the power of trade unions in many countries with a democratic form of government, a lockout by one or more employers may constitute a serious danger to public order. This may explain why in some countries a lock-out is forbidden by law. *Pav.*

LONG-LINED TYPE. See Constitution (biotypological).

LONG-SUFFERING. Long-suffering is a virtue or quality manifested by a person in a patience and tolerance which is not over-indulgent in clemency. Long-suffering (*longanimitas*—great spirited) is a disposition of spirit that endures wrong beyond expectations.

With God, long-suffering is principally a tolerant expectancy in the face of sin; a patience dedicated by His mercy: "Neither will God have a soul to perish, but recalleth, meaning that he that is cast off should not altogether perish" (II Kings 14:14); "But thou hast mercy towards all men, because thou art all-powerful, and concealeth the sins of men for love of penance" (Wisd. 2:24); "The Lord does not delay in his promises, but for your sake is long-suffering, not wishing that any should perish but that all should turn to repentance" (II Peter 3:9).

But woe to those who abuse God's long-suffering. "Or dost thou despise the riches of his goodness and patience and long-suffering? Dost thou not know that the goodness of God is meant to lead thee to repentance? But according to thy hardness and unrepentant heart, thou dost treasure up to thyself wrath on the day of wrath and of the revelation of the just judgment of God" (Rom. 2:4–5).

With man, long-suffering means constant expectation not only of the end of his trials but the coming of blessings. Holy Scripture calls it the patience of the saints (*patientia sanctorum*): "Here is the patience of the saints, who keep the commandments of God, and the faith of Jesus" (Apoc. 14:12). They know that this world is a vale of tears, and the happiness and joy they long for intensely will be found in the next life. In the certainty of obtaining these, they patiently endure the prolongation of their exile; and if a word of lament is heard from them, it is always united with a perfect submission to the will of God. Their long-suffering rests on patient endurance of suffering and expectation of joys. As God is merciful and patient with us, so we, too, should be long-suffering and compassionate with others. Sometimes the actions of our neighbor may cause us physical or moral inconvenience. We shall be long-suffering if we bear these patiently, as a sacrifice for the love of God and as an effort to spare our neighbor embarrassment and discomfort. In the majority of cases our neighbor acts without realization of the discomfort he is causing us; any reaction on our part would be dictated by a desire for selfish satisfaction. At times, of course, a reaction on our part may be a duty if required by reasons of the public

good. A superior, for example, must not tolerate insults against his authority.

If the inordinate acts of another person do not affect us directly, our long-suffering toward that person may be productive of greater good if we wait for more propitious occasions for the correction of his faults, particularly if it may appear that a resentful reaction on our part will accomplish nothing. It is no virtue if we fail to react for fear of creating difficulties for ourselves or because the welfare of our neighbor is of no interest to us or due to the fear of displeasing our neighbor, etc. It is less commendable to omit a punishment for faults that harm the common good, particularly in the case of one whose duty it is to guard it, or even the private good, in the case of those who have the responsibility of well-being for the souls involved. *Mdg.*

LOTTERY. A lottery (German, *Lot*—chance) is an onerous contract, which is a form of aleatory contract that depends on luck. It consists of the purchase of a ticket or the posting of a sum of money for the right to a certain prize if in the drawing a number or combination is selected by chance.

To be licit, a lottery must exclude cheating in drawing the numbers or the tickets and in the payment of the stipulated prize. A fair proportion must exist between the prize, the price paid, and the probability of winning. A lottery for different charitable causes, as a means of fund-raising, with the promise of a small prize is licit if the participants agree to the conditions. In some countries, to avoid abuses, civil law forbids or limits lotteries; these laws, with few exceptions, are considered merely penal laws, that is, not directly binding in conscience nor obliging to restitution if they are violated. However, one is obliged in conscience after judicial sentence for the penalties involved in violating the law. In grave matter the sin may be grave if the conditions required for a formal sin are present. *Sir.*

LOVE. See Charity.

LOVERS. *See* Adultery, Engagement.

LOYALTY. Loyalty (Latin, *legalis*—legal), in a broad sense, means faithfulness to duty. In a more restricted sense, it means speech and action without simulation or deceit.

Loyalty is a duty. He who deceives sins against veracity (*q.v.*); he who does not keep his word sins against fidelity (*q.v.*) and justice (*q.v.*). These failings are grave faults if they cause a serious damage to another.

Loyalty is important in social life. Loyalty gains the trust and the respect of others. *Man.*

LUCRUM CESSANS. *See* Damage.

LUES. *See* Syphilis.

LUKEWARMNESS. Lukewarmness in spiritual matters is a deliberate lack of fervor in loving God, and a consequent lack of enthusiasm and solicitude for obeying the promptings of grace. Lukewarmness must not be confused with an inactive spirit due to poor health, nor with aridity, a chastisement for past faults, nor with exhaustion due to labor or trials sent by God.

The state of lukewarmness is characterized by an increasing lack of promptness in fulfilling one's duties or definite good works, as well as by an increasing negligence in avoiding imperfection and sins. The lukewarm person has no concern for the so-called little things which play an important role in spiritual life; he does not seek to know and do that which is more pleasing to God. The tepid or lukewarm person is not attentive to the inspirations of grace, but rejects them as his mind dwells on useless thoughts which give pleasant and delightful distraction; he omits exercises of devotion and seeks comfort and leisure; he avoids external and internal mortification, complains and murmurs against the crosses of daily life; he omits examination of conscience and neglects defects that soon gain dominion in his life. Tepid persons have no zeal for souls.

Lukewarmness even in its initial stage is a serious state (Apoc. 8:15 ff.). Like a consuming disease, it gradually eats away vitality and leads inevitably to death. By concessions to self-love, pride, and sensuality in little things, the weakened will yields in more important things; if the danger is not halted, grave sin will become inevitable, the return to grace more difficult, and the gradual descent leads toward the abyss. Furthermore, lukewarmness diminishes the value and merit of good deeds because they are performed without enthusiasm, and leads to the neglect of many meritorious works which one might have performed. Lack of promptness and enthusiasm in willing and performing good deeds, not of obligation, often becomes sinful because of sloth or contempt. Ultimately, lukewarmness fills the heart with bitterness.

REMEDIES. A lukewarm person desirous of reform must keep before his eyes the end for which he was created and the shortness of life; he must enliven the virtues of faith and love of God, have a great esteem of small tasks and the little things, follow generously the inspirations of grace, mortifying self at least once daily, especially in those points in which he is weaker; he must be candid with his confessor, and follow the confessor's counsels with diligence and constancy. *Man.*

LUNATIC. *See* Psychosis, Mania.

LUNETTE. *See* Vessels, Sacred.

LUST (Wantonness). Lust is an inordinate desire for and enjoyment of sexual pleasure. By *inordinate* is meant that the desire or act does not conform to the natural ends of the sexual act, namely, the procreation and education of children. Sins of lust may be classified as follows:

(a) *Internal or external.* This depends on the extent of the evil desire, whether the sins are expressed as interior thoughts and desires or carried out in external acts.

(b) *Natural or unnatural.* This distinction indicates the attainment or frustration of the natural purpose of the sexual act. Under the heading of natural lust, other lustful acts add a particular malice against justice (sins of adultery, rape, and abduction); against piety (incest); or against religion (sacrilege). Under the heading of unnatural lust are sins committed alone (masturbation); sins with others of different sex (onanism); sins with persons of the same sex (sodomy); with animals (bestiality).

(c) *Complete or incomplete.* Sins involving full sexual satisfaction are of a different species than sins in which complete sexual satisfaction is not attained.

(d) *Direct voluntary or voluntary in cause.* Direct voluntary sins are sins in which sexual gratification is purposely provoked or consented to after spontaneous or indirect provocation; voluntary-in-cause sins are the result of another action which has been freely elicited, but which does not intend the sexual gratification directly in itself but as the result of another act. Indirect lust generally coincides with immodesty (*q.v.*).

According to the teachings of Holy Scripture, direct lust is a grave (mortal) sin, for it is numbered among those sins which desecrate the human person as a Christian and prevent entrance into the kingdom of heaven (I Cor. 6:9; Gal. 5:19–21; Eph. 5:5; I Tim. 1:10; II Peter 2:19–20; Apoc. 22:15). The inordinate sexual act is contrary to a substantial social good: the proper procreation of potential human life. The pleasures intended by nature for this social good are usurped by an act contrary to this end and performed for personal satisfaction. This doctrine applies not only to complete but incomplete acts as well. Complete lust is always a grave sin; because of the danger of reaching a complete act and in itself, incomplete acts are gravely sinful, for these are essentially directed to one sole purpose by nature. In the sexual order of nature, sexual pleasure does not exist apart from the complete act but enters from the beginning into the sphere of procreation; thus one consents to a complete act virtually by consenting to incomplete sexual acts. This is the sense expressed by the Church (Decree of the Sacred Congregation of the Holy Office, March 18, 1666; Decree of the Holy Office, Feb. 11, 1661; and in the reply of May 1, 1929 in ordering the withdrawal of *Quaedam moralia,* a pamphlet by Laarakkers).

Indirectly voluntary sexual pleasure is not always a mortal sin; it may be grave or venial according to the sexual satisfaction and degree of influence exercised by the action causing it, as well as a due consideration for the reasons which may justify the provocation. If it is simply a sexual commotion from a legitimate cause, it is not sinful.

Lust is a pernicious vice for individuals and society. For the individual: (a) it is insatiable: the more one satisfies lust, the greater is the subject's subsequent desire; (b) it is one of the capital sins, for in the desire to satisfy lust many other sins are committed; (c) it renders a destructive influence on the whole character of an individual; (d) it generates spiritual blindness, inconsiderateness, rashness, and instability; (e) it causes in the will an egoistical affection and aversion against God and spiritual things; (f) it may cause damage, at times severe, to one's physical (venereal diseases, sterility, etc.) and mental health (nervousness, morbid tendencies). With regard to society, this vice, considered from its purpose (*ex fine operis*), is opposed to the natural end of the sexual act (proper procreation) and leads to other public evils such as divorce, prostitution, criminality, etc. *See also* Chastity. *Dam.*

LUSTRAL WATER. *See* Holy Water.

LUXURY. Luxury is a mode of living beyond the moderate standard of living for a normal environment, with due consideration for the time, locale, personal status, and economic general well-being of a country. The basis of luxury is primarily economic wealth, which seeks indulgence in costly food, dress, and the gratification of the appetites.

Luxury by its nature belongs to the field of morality, for the use of temporal goods must be regulated by the norms of right reason and the teaching of the Gospel. Right reason dictates that normal need and reasonable customs proper to one's state and social position must be the criterion adopted for the use of material goods; the virtue of moderation regulates the use of goods, by following the middle course between indulgence and neglect. To exceed an average standard of living in the use of articles of luxury and to spend money liberally is permissible, of course, to wealthy or socially prominent persons beyond the normal status of the average citizen. St. Thomas calls the special virtue of magnificence (q.v.) an inclination by which a man undertakes from time to time, according to financial condition, increasingly greater works of Christian charity. This applies to the areas of social life as well, for recreational or other suitable activities contribute to better living and a more humane, sounder economic standard of living for all. Luxury becomes unlawful if it deviates from the norms of right reason by going beyond the relative status of the individual and his financial position, or is based on improper motives, such as pride, vanity, sensuality, etc., or is pursued with excessive eagerness. Such is not only contrary to the virtue of moderation, but also to fraternal charity and social justice. These demand that man employ his superfluous wealth in behalf of his neighbor or the community. Despite the fact that luxury creates employment and social well-being, it is clearly responsible for creating social disorders in the minds of the poorer classes by its extreme practices. The law of the Gospel has perfected the norms of reason, not only because it urges Christian charity even when no strict obligation of the natural law to help one's neighbor exists, but also because it makes the total or partial renunciation of the comforts of life for the love of God a much greater virtue. The writings of the Fathers of the Church abound with norms for the wealthy in the use of riches. See also Moderation. Dam.

LYING. A lie is an utterance, sign or action by which one expresses the opposite of what he thinks or wills. Generally this is done to deceive others. The malice of a lie consists primarily and essentially, not in the untruth, as such, of the words spoken, but in the discordance between the words, signs or actions and what one actually thinks or knows to be the truth. Thus, if one says what he thinks and this is objectively false, he utters an untruth but not a lie; on the contrary, if one says something which he believes to be false, though in fact it is true, he speaks a lie. The intention to deceive or mislead another need not necessarily be present; without such intention a declaration that is not in conformity with one's thought may constitute a lie in the proper sense of the word. On the contrary, if an expression is openly and obviously false, i.e., if the words as spoken and generally understood do not affirm anything, but merely express a joke for the sake of amusement or diversion, it does not constitute lying. Similarly, it is no lie to employ ironical or hyperbolic expressions, manifest exaggerations or expressions commonly accepted with a connotation different from the ordinary and obvious meaning. To say, for example, "Mr. Jones is not at home" may be a polite and conventional form of saying "He cannot or does not wish to receive you" (broad mental reservation or restriction). The reason for this is always clear. Since the meaning of the conventional phrases used in certain circumstances is clear and obvious to every sensible person, it cannot be said that there is any real discrepancy between the utterance and the thought on the part of the speaker. Through daily usage or custom it is certainly possible for man to give an expression or phrase a meaning different from the one it had before.

Furthermore, it is to be noted that a lie is not a lie because another has a right to be told the truth. The matter of right does not enter the question of lie. The malice of lying consists primarily and essentially, not in the fact that an untruth is spoken to one having the right to know the truth, but in the discrepancy between what one says and thinks. On the other hand, if the matter of one's right to the truth must be taken into account, then we must say that there are instances when the inquirer does not have the right to the truth, although everyone has the right not to be deceived or misled. Thus, it is possible, at times, to withhold or conceal all or part of the truth from others without at the same time being guilty of lying. How is it possible to conceal the truth without telling a lie? The answer is through the use of ambiguous statements or broad mental reservations. Conditions which justify the use of mental reservation are: (1) if one is gravely bound by duty not to reveal the truth or secret in his possession, as a priest, doctor, lawyer, social worker, etc.; (2) if one is asked to reveal some damaging act about himself or others, e.g., if a wife should be asked by her husband whether she was ever unfaithful to him; (3) if the inquirer is rash, indiscreet, or probes purely private and personal affairs, etc.; (4) if certain conventional phrases are generally accepted and recognized by society as containing the concealment of truth. In these and similar instances the inquirer or hearer is required to exercise his good sense in interpreting the nature of the reply given to him.

According to the purpose for which they are uttered, lies may be *jocose, officious,* or *malicious.* A *jocose* lie is told merely for the sake of amusement or diversion. An *officious* lie in necessity or as an excuse (courtesy lie) is told for some personal reason, intended to ward off an injury, inconvenience, or embarrassment. A *malicious* lie is a damaging lie, injurious or harmful to another, and dictated by a desire to damage the life, property, or reputation of another, or perhaps to inflict spiritual injury.

Lying is intrinsically evil, that is, sinful by its very nature. Hence it is never lawful nor permissible, not even to attain a noble end or to avoid some evil or injury. Whatever is intrinsically evil may not be used as a means to a good end, nor can it be justified by a good or noble end. The good order of human society requires that there be truthful communication between man and man; thus, lying would be a violation of the natural order based on the nature of language as the principal means of intellectual and social intercourse. Hence, lying is a violation of the moral order. Sacred Scripture frequently condemns lying, and Christ Himself says that the devil is the father of lies (John 8:44).

Ordinarily jocose and officious lies do not exceed venial sin. Malicious or harmful lies are mortal sins, if the damage caused is grave; if the damage is slight or of small import, these are venial sins, in the same way that stealing a thing of little value would constitute a venial sin.

It is sad to observe the ease with which many supposedly good and honest people resort to telling lies, particularly officious lies. Even pious persons are frequently found to have erroneous ideas about this subject. The problem of correcting liars and teaching the right is made more difficult by the fact that among those who frequently misuse the noble faculty of speech are parents and educators. Certainly there are many parents and teachers who show displeasure when the young are given to deception and lying, and become enraged and mete out punishment to any youngster who is given to lying. But, at the same time, such adults overlook the obvious, blatant truth that it is impossible to teach truthfulness and sincerity to youngsters, when they themselves do not practice it. When adults practice constant deception in their daily affairs, and glibly lie themselves out of situations or encourage children to give false reasons and excuses to the teacher, state a false age to the ticket-agent or train-conductor, etc., then it is almost absurd to hope that these children will be sincere with their own parents. In practical matters children are extremely logical, particularly when it is to their advantage. An effective way of avoiding officious lies is to lead a thoroughly honest life. He who has nothing to fear from the truth has no need to resort to lying. *Ben.*

LYPEMANIA. *See* Melancholy.

M

MACHIAVELLIANISM. Niccolo Machiavelli (1496–1527), author and statesman, wrote the famous work *Il Principe*, concerning political problems and the creation of a strong state. Machiavelli was dedicated to the unification of Italy and the preservation of a precarious national independence. The last chapter of his volume is a famous, impassioned exhortation for the liberation of Italy. In the pursuit of this noble aim, however, he advocated the theory that rulers can resort to any treachery or deceit to retain power. Such political cunning soon became known as Machiavellianism.

In the Renaissance period, Machiavelli was extolled for his impossible ambitions rather than his doctrine. Later, in less sentimental times, he was extolled as a philosopher who discovered the autonomy of politics as a dynamic science, independent of morality. According to Machiavelli, morality and politics need not oppose nor be intermingled with each other; each possesses its own *raison d'être* and both operate on two separate levels. The criteria applied to one science do not apply to the other. Machiavellianism represents the attitude and policy of any ruler who thus constructs and develops his State from the lessons of history and human experience, independently of moral law.

Moral and spiritual values must be held in esteem, insofar as they actually affect the realities of life; such evaluation must be strictly realistic, not dictated by criteria derived from an absolute moral law or divine religion. State policies are to be motivated by other factors, not subject to moral or religious considerations, as was the case implicitly before the time of Machiavelli. Thus Machiavelli has the dubious distinction of being a philosopher who advocated a new and unfortunate political theory.

The formation of modern European States, generally monarchical at the time, dealt a fatal blow to medieval unity and the universal nature of the Christian Empire. One by one, new States claimed sovereignty and total independence. After the French Revolution, all liberal States pursued this course more strenuously, so that Machiavellianism became the philosophy of European politicians. Many rulers, like Frederick II of Prussia, were spending hours of leisure in writing against the theories of Machiavelli and, at the same time, were practicing his theory in government. Further forms of Machiavellianism developed in which national, self-centered interests, concealed under the mantle of justice, in reality perpetrated grave injustices. Thus, Machiavellianism became synonymous with the ability to hide selfish, personal ambitions, the sacrifice of everything of value to ruthless personal gains, and the pursuit of success with a complete disregard for moral considerations.

Machiavellianism is essentially an immoral theory, for, unless the moral law is accepted as absolute and universal, it is not accepted at all. The Mirabeau formula of a *small morality* for private life and a *great morality* for public life, which sought to justify the crimes of the French Revolution, was a legalistic subterfuge intended to confuse the issues. Machiavellianism conflicts with the Gospel teaching that it is not permissible to do evil that good may come of it (Rom. 3:8).

Machiavellianism, furthermore, conflicts with the true nature of the State. The purpose of the State is the common good of the citizens, which is to be attained through the recognition of the dignity of the human person and a proper ordering of values, including the moral order. A State which suppresses or ignores these values defeats its own purpose. Any injustice committed by the State to secure material gains is a violation of the dignity of its citizens, whom the State is to represent and serve. To the extent that a State knowingly pursues such activities, it acts immorally; it exposes its citizens to the risk of deprivation of its most precious good.

The realistic wisdom boasted of by the followers of Machiavelli is at best more apparent than real, for its goal is passing success. Modern European politics, the result of Machiavellianism, is but a struggle for the balance of power which produces our present unstable world. Unavoidable wars of the past brought limited damage to nations; now the destruction of civilization and humanity itself is threatened; the unstable successes of Machiavellianism may lead to an inevitable, universal, and final catastrophe. Materialistic, totalitarian Communism is a logical development of Machiavellianism. The world of today invites analysis of the illusory successes of Machiavellianism, for the distinction between reality and morality with the consequent disruption of the profound unity of the human being is a metaphysical error which may wreak its destructive effects on the life of the individual as well as the human race. *Boz.*

MACHINATION. *See* Premeditation.

MACHINES. *See* Industrialism.

MACHINES, AUTOMATIC. *See* Cybernetics.

MAGIC. According to Herodotus, the magicians were one of six tribes, probably the priestly tribe, into which the Medes were divided. In the classical world, magicians were confused with the Babylonian priests who devoted their time to natural sciences and astronomy. The Magi of St. Matthew's Gospel (11:1) seem to reflect this secondary, Babylonian tradition. Thus the term *magician* signified in the West a thaumaturge or student of magic.

Magic first comprised the doctrine or art of magicians but eventually embraced all operations performed by occult power. The work of a magician was once directed to good deeds, such as the preparation of medicine and therapies through apotropaic devices or rites and to the study of nature and its secret forces. This was termed *white magic.*

Magic intended to harm people through formulae, gestures, and various procedures or to cause injury to an enemy or his family was called *black* magic. Black magic among the Christian writers was considered an art by which contact was established with infernal spirits in a secret agreement with the intention of causing preternatural phenomena. *White magic*, instead, was used to indicate, usually in jest, the skill of an entertainer who performed amazing stunts with physical or chemical media without supernatural implications.

In the Middle Ages, magic was widely practiced; it was again revived in the period of the Renaissance with a general, renewed interest in the pagan world and customs. The eventual classification of magicians as witches or others who practiced black magic was primarily due to the engagement by magicians in scientific experimentation or the use of morbid suggestions stemming from hysterical or psychasthenic conditions. Thus eventually arose the famous witch trials concerning which much exaggeration and fiction has developed.

The Catholic Church has been accused by some modern writers of the responsibility for the cruel and unjust measures applied as late as the eighteenth century against real or alleged witchery. The fact is that the popes and bishops did relentlessly condemn black magic practices. The pontiffs condemned, likewise, inhuman sanctions by the civil authorities which were aimed at curbing magic; they strove to restrain the inhuman and illogical procedures applied in punishing magicians. The Church is also accused of accepting magic, for proof of which the accusers refer to the Bull of Innocent VIII *Summis desiderantes* (Dec. 5, 1484). It is true that this Bull seems to accept many cases and crimes of magic, but it must be noted that the pope states only that such facts were reported to him; he refrains from any doctrinal comment on their value. As a matter of fact, he strives with great zeal to safeguard the faithful against the danger of superstition.

Folklore sometimes involves popular beliefs that witches, sorcerers, and magicians are human beings who are born under peculiarly unique circumstances; they are said to possess a little tail at the back of the neck, at the base of the spine; they are reputedly capable of transforming themselves into black dogs, cats, or goats. The same risk or danger might befall one who is guilty of a grave sacrilege. Witches and sorcerers are supposed to meet on Saturday in nocturnal orgies, move about by riding brooms, and are devils in the form of goats. They are continually bent on ensnaring or harming domestic animals and children. As a protection against this witchcraft, a broom behind one's front door, a pinch of salt in the fire on Saturday, or the recitation of special exorcisms are supposedly recommended as effective by these folklore tales. These beliefs are in general common to all people and all times, but obviously are the products of fervid imaginations.

Historically, the first instance of black magic is recorded in the acts of an investigation conducted by the Egyptian court toward the end of the year 2000 B.C. It concerns a plot in which sorcery was performed on statuettes which represented rivals to be suppressed. It was customary with the ancient nations, and still remains a practice among primitive tribes in our times, to consider the religious practices of a conquered people as witchcraft, and the divinities of these people as demons of the victors.

Modern research on the customs of barbarian peoples has allowed a broad study of magical practices as the art of controlling occult forces of nature, and exploiting these for one's own benefit. Primitive people believe the magician to be a person psychologically more receptive and endowed with a highly developed nervous sensitivity. His great knowledge is thought to be a personal gift from a particular spirit who abides in him and empowers him to control other spirits and nature itself. In view of such powers, inherited from a magician-father or acquired through laborious initiation by an older magician, the magician is logically the tribal doctor, because sickness is said to originate from the evil spirits. His role also involves divination for the tribe, because the spirit, supposedly abiding in him, bestows a gift of clairvoyance. Sometimes a magician is a political chief, for his alleged communication with other spirits offers him prestige and authority over all his fellow men.

TYPES OF MAGIC. Magic is based on two postulates: (a) An individual being acts on a similar being; this principle gives rise to *imitative* or *symbolical* magic, insofar as a magical action signifies and reproduces on a miniature scale whatever is to occur in reality. This notion occasions *omeopathetic* magic, which produces an effect equal to the one represented. (b) The second principle is that one being acts on another if it is contiguous to it. Thus a *sympathetic* magic developed which was based on a connection or affinity between things. This affinity remains in the part of a whole even after separation of a whole; thus too the parts bear the same fate as the whole and vice versa. This occasions *contagious* magic, in which a power which perfoms an action on a part also affects the whole.

A typical example of imitative magic is found among the natives of Tower Strait. When they wish to bring about rain, the magician digs a hole in the ground, puts in it a stone representing man and pours on the stone juices from several plants; large fans made of leaves symbolizing the clouds, and a lighted torch representing lightning, are moved back and forth over the hole, while drums imitate the noises of thunder. The sought-for rain is expected to fall when the concoction poured on the stone undergoes changes. The use of medical herbs is frequently based on imitative magic (yellow saffron cures jaundice, etc.). Examples of contagious magic are suggested by hostile acts by the magician on the human body, such as the nails or hair, or on the attire of a certain person, or on his image. Whatever the magician performs on one part (burning, burial, piercing) will be fatal to the person to whom the part belongs. This stupid belief is the most fertile source of witchcraft and sorcery used by people against their foes or competitors.

Ethnological studies indicate the position of magic with reference to religion and science. When it is not demoniacal intervention, magic is the science of barbarian primitives, based upon sophistic associations of ideas existing primarily among a lower class of people. A magician or sorcerer in good faith knows that the rules of his art will inevitably obtain the desired effect. In this lies the analogy between the magical and the scientific concept. However, magic differs from science insofar as magic is not concerned with reviewing accomplishments or methods, cares little about improving a technical heritage acquired *ab antiquo*, and holds stubbornly to a mistaken interpretation of two basic laws of association of ideas: association by similarity in imitative magic, and association by proximity in contagious magic.

Magic and religion are interrelated among less civilized peoples with polytheistic beliefs. The mechanical rites of magic are confused with religious rituals. One finds among the more ignorant groups in civilized nations a real dependence by a subjectively fervent religion upon a mild form of magic or lucky numbers, charms, the evil eye, etc. These are called superstitions.

Magic, even if not a fraud, is a corruption of religion. Superstition is, in itself, a by-product of magic, the effect of a distortion of the true notion of God or the departure from forms of worship sanctioned by the Church.

Notwithstanding progress in science and customs, magic has not been eliminated from even the higher social circles of civilized nations. In fact, one finds remnants in a minor degree in many well-known superstitious manifestations and beliefs; it survives in the doctrine and practices of occultism (*see* Metapsychology) and it generally enrolls followers who are victims of hysteria, psychasthenia and the like.

Modern Catholic scholars agree on the subject of magic. The possibility of witchcraft or activities engineered by diabolical power is not to be discounted; against these the Church instituted exorcisms. Concrete examples of diabolical witchcraft, however, must be viewed with extreme caution because of easy credulity in this field. More often than not, stupid superstition or commonplace tricks by interested quacks can startle the less educated. All this is bound to vanish under the impact of a sound education based on true moral and religious principles. One must not overlook the fact that many cases of so-called witchcraft and sortileges may be actually linked to actions, suggestions, illusions, and false interpretation of deranged, oversensitive and timid minds. A skillful physician can ascertain the true nature of such conditions.

It is a well-established fact that in countries where cultural standards and the condition of health are much improved, cases of supposed witchcraft are almost non-existent. *Riz.*

MAGICIAN. *See* Magic.

MAGISTERIUM, ECCLESIASTICAL. The *solemn* or the ordinary magisterium of the Church is the norm of faith in truths revealed by God. The solemn magisterium consists of papal or conciliary dogmatic definitions. The ordinary magisterium is the unanimous teaching of the bishops united with the pope (Can. 1322–1323).

A dogmatic definition must be clear and certain in order to bind in faith. Consequently, a doubtful definition is practically an invalid definition. In certain cases, the teaching Church expresses doctrinal judgment without committing to a final form her whole authority. The ecclesiastical magisterium often approves or condemns a doctrine without a final judgment on the absolute truth or falsity of the doctrine. These acts of the ecclesiastical magisterium are issued by the pope, councils, and at times, with previous specific approval of the Roman pontiff, by Roman congregations and pontifical commissions, through decrees, constitutions, replies to questions, condemned propositions, etc.

The faithful are bound in conscience to assent to such acts. Their assent must be not only external but internal and sincere, because the proximate norm of certainty in matters of faith is, not the private judgment of the faithful, but the authoritative judgment of the teaching Church. The obligation to profess the faith includes the duty to accept all the decisions of the ecclesiastical magisterium. This assent to the decisions of the teaching Church binds one in relation to their merits (see Propositions, Condemned). The object of the magisterium of the Church is the proposal of all truths contained in the Word of God, written or orally handed down through tradition, or the condemnation of errors concerning these truths. Apart from official public revelation destined to all men, according to His mysterious plans, God manifests Himself by visible signs and visions or apparitions, particularly to souls who, in humility and detachment, seek a closer contact with Him and endeavor to deserve His love. Private revelations must be shown never to conflict with the public revelation in the *depositum fidei*, for private revelations merely possess relative and secondary importance in sustaining the faith of the generous believer. Such private revelations have never been imposed as a part of Catholic faith indispensable for salvation. We cannot, however, agree with certain modern theologians who seem to deny the teaching Church any right to pass judgment on private revelations. This position must be considered a theological minimism, contrary to the almost unanimous opinion of theologians.

The magisterium of the Church may intervene, though generally with great caution and in a negative manner, in questions of private revelations, by the condemnation of abuses or by cautioning against special dangers. The Church can intervene, also, in a positive manner, such as is indicated in the pronouncements of Benedict XV in the canonization Bull of St. Margaret Mary Alacoque on the revelations at Paray-le-Monial (ASS:12 [1920] 486; also Pius XII, encyc. *Haurietis Aquas*, AAS: 48 [1956] 309–353).

It is within the competency of the Church to render a formal judgment of approval or condemnation upon visions and apparitions because this is within the scope of directing all men to the attainment of their ultimate end.

This intervention may take various forms: condemnation or negative decision; an imposition of silence for the sake of diligent and extensive investigation; a negative and general approval expressed in the form of toleration; a solemn, negative approval in the proclamation of the existence of heroic virtues in a person favored with private revelations; the approval of a particular devotion related to a private revelation; the particular approval of a bishop; and, finally, the canonical approval by the Holy See, expressed in pontifical documents.

MAGISTRATE. A magistrate is a person entrusted with legal power as a public or civil official; as such, he is a judge with legal or judicial authority. The first magistrates among the Jews were appointed by Moses, who selected from among the people a few God-fearing men of known integrity, opposed by oath against deceit and avarice. To these men, Moses gave delegated authority (Exod. 18). In the Roman Republic, consuls, censors, praetors, and builders were ordinary magistrates to whom power was given to assemble the populace, modify edicts and decrees, propose legislation to the Senate, etc. The magistrate as a sacred person participates in sovereign authority according to diverse degrees, as the governor, mayor, etc. In the Middle Ages, the Waldensians, among others, maintained that a Christian was not permitted to exercise the office of magistrate because it placed upon him the necessity of sentencing others to death or inflicting penalties which were, for them, supposedly against the Christian virtues of meekness and charity. In his work *Morals of the Fathers*, Barbeyrac, a Protestant (1699), held that such views were taught by the Fathers of the Church. But St. Paul (Rom. 13:1–8) openly teaches that a ruler is God's minister, set up to avenge the crimes of others and to punish criminals. Law would be useless if there were no magistrates to enforce it.

The obligations of magistrates are to uphold the supremacy of the law by wise decisions, and to render service useful to the State and its citizens. Therefore, a magistrate should be a person possessed of nobility of heart, sound judgment, excellent discernment, and a thorough knowledge of law and jurisprudence, acquired by study and experience. As custodian of law, the magistrate cannot make arbitrary use of authority but seek the common welfare through justice, absolute unselfishness, and watchful care in detecting error and fraud. He must treat with humility and kindness those subject to his jurisdiction.

A general and remote knowledge of law is not adequate; the magistrate must possess immediate and proximate knowledge of the case in question. Consequently, a magistrate who becomes incompetent because of a lack of skill or diligence in study and thereby inflicts a damage upon another, is bound in justice to make restitution according to the degree of culpability. When a damage is caused inadvertently, the magistrate is bound to advise the injured party, if he can do so without embarrassment, to appeal his verdict to a higher court. This is an obligation in charity. In the exercise of jurisdiction, a magistrate must be guided by integrity and good conscience, free from personal favoritism, hatred or love, and independent of the influence of gifts, pressures, threats, or anything else, lest he violate divine law and become liable to reparation for the harm done. For specific ethical problems, *see* Judge.

MAGNANIMITY. Magnanimity is a quality of mind and spirit tending to nobility (*Summa Theol.*, II–II, q. 129, a. 1). Magnanimity is an integral aspect of fortitude which conquers the natural inclinations of revenge, pettiness, and meanness. Magnanimity is sometimes confused with heroism. Heroism implies superlative, transcendent courage in carrying out a superhuman, noble purpose against great odds. Magnanimity can be a natural virtue motivated by purely human motives, or a supernatural virtue based on faith and religious belief. This article refers to the supernatural virtue; as such, it is a disposition of the heart to practice great acts of virtue of exceeding worth before God. A magnanimous Christian cares little for human recognition in itself; what he cherishes most are outstanding virtues and deeds which are rightfully deemed worthy of honor. The truly magnanimous person attributes little importance to honors from men, for he values only that which he hopes to receive from God.

Magnanimity is a Christian obligation and an instinctive need, begotten and nourished by Christian faith. "You, therefore, are to be perfect, even as your heavenly Father is perfect" (Matt. 5:48) was the personal command of Christ.

As a general inclination toward nobility of spirit, magnanimity refers to every field of human endeavor, for in disregarding fleeting values, man may direct his efforts at great and outstanding deeds in any area of activity.

MAGNANIMITY AND HUMILITY. Magnanimity and humility are compatible virtues, since the desire for a high degree of holiness and great and noble sentiments are in no way indicative of a lack of humility; to undertake great and arduous enterprises for the glory of God is not a lack of humility. The magnanimous person seeks the fruit of goodness and not honor achieved; his goal is goodness and virtue. He is not overjoyed at well-merited praise; his heart is not disturbed or resentful if he receives undue blame. For this reason, calmness and serenity remain amid contumely; peace and tranquility are not lost as he comes to a state of pure indifference regarding contempt heaped upon him (*Summa Theol.*, II–II, q. 129, a. 2). Greatness in undeserved obscurity or deserved glory is a characteristic trait: the proud man is a slave to glory; the magnanimous, above it. Magnanimity does not involve pride; true Christian magnanimity demands deep Christian humility, for the magnanimous person excels in everything, including humility.

SINS AGAINST MAGNANIMITY. One sins by excess against this virtue: (a) by presumption, the disorderly desire to succeed by personal strength alone, with extreme confidence in self; (b) by an insatiable desire for recognition as such; (c) by vainglory, the excessive desire for human fame and glory. These sins are in themselves venial, but, due to peculiar circumstances or harmful consequences, they may become mortal; for example, to accept an important office with the knowledge of a physical, moral, or intellectual lack of fitness due to a spirit of vainglory. One sins by defect: (a) by acts of cowardice or pusillanimity; (b) by false humility, which seems to shun anything which appears great, different, or honor-laden.

The timid man sees difficulties in all things: he considers everything unworkable and quickly shrinks into inactivity. This defect is often the result of false humility or a strange form of pride (*Summa Theol.*, II–II, q. 183, a. 1). It may stem from a weak character, psychical or physical illness. In itself it is a venial sin, but it could become mortal if one failed to obey a grave precept, simply because of the inconvenience entailed.

MAGNETISM, ANIMAL. *See* Hypnotism, Metapsychology, Psychotherapy.

MAGNIFICAT. The *Magnificat*, a canticle recited at Vespers, is derived from the first words of the statement of the Blessed Virgin in response to the inspired salutation of Saint Elizabeth hailing Mary as the Mother of God (Luke 1:46–55).

The authenticity of the canticle is linked with the historical validity of the infancy narratives in Saint Luke's Gospel. Today this is beyond question. Harnack and Loisy at one time doubted the application of this text to the Blessed Virgin, but attributed it to Elizabeth on the basis of three codices of an ancient Latin translation of the Gospels, a Latin code of the time of Origen and Irenaeus, and other casual testimony. These documents, extremely scarce and peculiar, did not stand up in the face of the unanimous testimony of other, more reliable codices and translations, the internal arguments of the text and context, and the belief of tradition (*see* Pontif. Biblical Comm., June 26, 1912, Denz. *Enchirid. Symbol.*, 2158).

Poetical parallelism reveals the Semitic origin of the *Magnificat*, which St. Luke learned personally from the Virgin Mary. This canticle is a hymn of praise to God, who deigned to extol his humble maiden by performing prodigious things in her, whom all nations shall call blessed. God humbles the proud, the rich, and the powerful; He extols the humble and the poor. Finally, God fulfills His promises, to Abraham and his descendants. The canticle is reminiscent of Anna's canticle (I Sam. 2) as well as other psalms.

The use of the canticle is not restricted to the breviary but occurs on many occasions as a hymn of joy (Christmas novena). At Vespers, the *Magnificat* is preceded and followed by an anthem containing special liturgical significance. The recitation of the *Magnificat* is the climactic point of Vespers; significantly, at solemn Vespers the altar is incensed during the chanting of the *Magnificat*. *Pal.*

MAGNIFICENCE. The word *magnificence* conveys the idea of splendor and spectacular beauty, the fruit of a noble soul and generous heart. To struggle for a great and generous ideal under the light of reason is an integral aspect of the virtue of fortitude (q.v.). Magnificence inspires noble and beautiful creations, particularly external works, such as buildings, institutions, and charities. As such, it is a virtue befitting the wealthy and powerful.

The expression *doing great things* has a twofold meaning: (a) a common and ordinary meaning which considers the internal motivation basic to the nature of an action; in this sense, virtue of any type tends to greatness if motivated by a particularly upright motive (*see* Magnanimity); (b) a literal meaning of the term refers to outstanding external achievements, particularly in the field of arts; this is the specific object of the virtue of magnificence. Thus the virtue of magnanimity and magnificence differ. Magnificence signifies external things; magnanimity refers to internal motives.

Great and spectacular works are the proximate object of magnificence; large sums of money spent in such works are its remote object. Thus the money required to create or support such works becomes the formal object of magnificence; magnificence is itself the essential motive insofar as the person intends to perform a moral good. When such works are motivated by pride or vanity, magnificence ceases to be a virtue. If God's glory or the neighbor's well-being are the object of one's magnificent desire, such motives rise to the supernatural level and the innate love for material riches is thus properly moderated and directed.

One may sin against magnificence by excess or defect: (a) by excess, if one spends or squanders money without restraint or beyond good judgment and prudence; (b) by defect, if one spends too sparingly and below the amount required by the dignity and the importance of the project undertaken. Squandering, prodigality, avarice, and stinginess are, in themselves, venial sins, but may become grave sins under certain circumstances. For example, vain and worldly purposes, extravagant banquets, entertainments, or the spending of money owed to creditors or the poor may be seriously sinful, as well as the neglect of obligations of vows, oaths, or contracts (*Summa Theol.*, II–II, q. 134, a. 3.) *Tar.*

MAJORITY. *See* Age.

MALARIA. *See* Contagion.

MALEDICTION. *See* Curse.

MALEFACTOR, KILLING OF. *See* Punishment, Capital.

MALTHUS. *See* Birth Control; Neo-Malthusianism.

MALTREATMENT of Animals. Domestic animals may be maltreated either by physical abuse or by acts of negligence toward them. To overwork or beat an animal excessively is a positive act of abuse; to neglect or fail to provide food, drink, medicine or death in the face of extreme suffering are sinful acts of omission. Abuse or excessive cruelty is sinful, unless an extremely important reason compels it; the gravity of a sin depends on the extent of abuse and the motive for inflicting harm. The abuse of animals is also harmful to those who commit such acts, because they tend to make a person harsh, indifferent, and cruel to human beings. (*See also* Protection of Animals, Cruelty, Vivisection.) *Ben.*

MAMMON. *See* Money; Capitalism; Concentration of Wealth; Poverty.

MANDAEISM. Mandaeism, a religion followed by persons living near Baghdad, is considered the last expression of a movement which attained notable import in Eastern Mesopotamia, where it once engaged primarily in gnostic speculations. Its probable origin was, not Palestine, but in the area north of Baghdad, possibly Adiabene. Its sacred books, written in oriental Aramaic, are full of confusion and incoherencies. These books are: *Sidra, Babba,* and *Ginza* (Treasure), containing the fundamental doctrines of the sect; *Sidra of Iahya* (The Book of John) contains the teaching of the great prophet, John the Baptist; *Qobosta* is the liturgical book pertaining to funerals and baptisms.

Mandaeists call themselves *Nazarenes*

(*Nasuraiia*, *Nasoreans*). Early travellers in the area termed them *Christians of St. John* and considered them heretical Christians or Hebrews who accepted the baptism of the Precursor. The Arabs refer to them as *Mughtasilah* and *Sabeans*.

Mandaeist theology is dualistic and typically gnostic. It recognizes a Supreme Being, called Great Mana or Manda, the King of Light, the First Life; from this Being three successive worlds emanate, two of them of time, the third is the present one. The present world has been polluted by the presence of evil spirits of an astral nature (*ruha*), represented by the planets and the signs of the zodiac. Such evil effects would have been irreparable had not a divine mediator, *Manda of Haije* (*Hayyê*), the Knowledge of Life, intervened. He made salvation of souls possible by the knowledge (*manda* or *gnosis*) which he imparts to men. The way of salvation lies in freeing the soul from the body. The soul is the daughter of light, and the body is the work of darkness. On reaching the eighth zone or gnostic *ogdeade*, by an austere life and the renunciation of worldly goods, yet without the anti-matrimonial exaggerations of Manichaeanism, one has attained salvation.

Mandaeist rites are conducted before edifices called *Masken* (elevations), reserved exclusively for priests, in which are preserved the sacred vestments. The temple are facing south; the direction for prayer is northward, if outside the temples.

The priesthood consists of three orders or grades: *skanda*, or lesser ministers; *tarmidha*, or priests ordained by a ritual of sixty days of segregation and ablutions; and *ganzibra*, the supreme head or treasurer, who is similar to a bishop and elected by the priests. Presently, the only *ganzibra* for the whole sect lives in Soyukh. Women may become ministers, provided they are virgins upon entrance to the first order and provided that they marry a priest before admittance to the second order.

The basic Mandaeist rite is baptism (*masbutha*), which can be repeated at least every week by immersion or by a triple aspersion of water over the head with special invocations to Manda of Haije. The water must be stream water, and the stream from which it is taken is termed symbolically *Jordan*, in memory of the Baptist. This fact give rise to the erroneous belief that Mandaeists were of Palestinian origin as heirs to the baptismal practices of the Baptist. It is more probable that this rite for baptism was taken from the Nestorians. An anointing with oil, a meal consisting of unleavened bread (*pitha*) and water (*mambuha*), and the occasional addition of a little bit of wine completes the rite of baptism; these aspects are obviously borrowed from Christian religious practices in baptism. The bread is to be placed in the hands of the candidate for baptism and the water is poured into a cup which he himself raises to his lips.

The weekly holy day is strictly kept. The great annual holy rite, called *Pantscha*, falls on the five days between eighth and the ninth month of the year. The rite consists of three daily ablutions. The ritual vestments are white; the priests wear a stole from the shoulders to the feet, and a turban. *Tur.*

Doctrinally, Mandaeism combines Christian beliefs and gnostic dualism. The principles of light and darkness with intermediate beings, the concept of souls as particles of light imprisoned in the darkness of a body, the series of enchantments and exorcisms give evidence of deformations for anti-Christian polemical purposes. The Mandaeist conception of morality, though of a rather high level with its embodiment of some Christian ideals, does not know the beauty of all the Christian precepts and counsels. Virginity, for example, is looked down upon, as marriage is considered obligatory. *Pa.*

MANDATE. *See* Procurator; Cooperators in Evil.

MANGANISM. *See* Professional Diseases.

MANIA. In ancient times, *mania* (Greek, *mania*—madness) was synonymous with insanity. Esquirol, at the beginning of the nineteenth century, first attempted a classification of mental disorders and used the term *mania* to signify insanity in general. Later scientific classifications of insanity applied the term *mania* to several systematized deliria, such as mania of persecution (*see* Paranoia), or to certain obsessions and impulsive tendencies, among which *kleptomania* (*q.v.*) and *dipsomania* (*q.v.*) are more common. Mania still retains these meanings, although, strictly speaking, it signifies a condition of exaltation or excitement present in affective or dysthymic psychosis (*see* Dysthymia); mania may occur in a single episode or a succession of attacks interrupted by melancholic depression (*q.v.*).

At the initial point of disturbance (hypomania), the maniac is gay, talkative, optimistic, and dynamic. As long as the symptoms of his illness are contained within moderate bounds, he may present the impression that his sickness is not a psychical one. As he worsens, his behavior becomes unbearable. His gay and carefree attitude gives way to furious agitation; his loquaciousness changes into irrational talking and coprolalia; from clear thinking he slips into a dearth of ideas and mental confusion. The maniac acquires frightening facial contortions, quick mimicry, continual agitation and incoherence. He becomes disquieted, excitable, and chaotic; he prattles, insults, shouts, or sings at the top of his voice; not infrequently he goes through moods of wrath and dangerous, aggressive, quarrelsome periods, which may at times reach a frightening fury. Less frequently, the mental disorder is followed by a condition of static beatitude called *maniacal stupor*.

When not treated, maniacal disorders and episodes may end within a few weeks, but in general they last for a few months. When a complete cure, which can be expected in most cases, occurs, no debility or other psychopathological residue is found except an occasional mild delirium. The patient is wholly unable to evalute precisely the events occurring during his

mental infirmity. The prognosis for each single crisis is favorable, and modern electric or insulin shock therapies bring about a general amelioration in the patient by shortening the duration of each crisis. The prognosis is cautious, since crises may reoccur after years. (*See* Phrenosis, Dysthymia). *Riz.*

MANIPLE. *See* Sacred Vestments.

MANNERISM. *See* Schizophrenia.

MANUFACTORY. *See* Corporation.

MANUSCRIPT. *See* Author, Rights of.

MARRIAGE. Nature. Marriage is a bilateral contract (*q.v.*) by which a man and a woman give and reciprocally receive a perpetual and exclusive right to each other's body for the performance of those actions which, of their very nature, are directed to the procreation of children (Can. 1081, par. 2). Marriage is a totally unique contract, by reason of its divine origin in the very law of nature; its consent (*q.v.*), which cannot be supplied by human authority (Can. 1081, par. 1); its object and essential properties, which are beyond the free will of the contracting parties. Furthermore, the number and sex of the contracting parties, the purpose and duration of the marriage are predetermined. The purpose intends a union of bodies; the duration of the contract lasts until the death of one of the parties. The contract is strictly bilateral or individual, so that even if only one of the parties is unable to contract it, marriage is invalid for both parties (*matrimonium claudicare non potest*). It is strictly bilateral also with regard to its formal object, that is, a life in common, for both parties have the same rights and duties (1 Cor. 7:3-4).

Marriage is necessary for mankind for its preservation and propagation, but not for each individual; on the contrary, for serious reasons (impotency, sterility, sickness, etc.) some can be impeded from or advised against contracting it. However, the right to marriage is common to all and, therefore, those laws which absolutely forbid or make it impossible to anyone for any pretext whatsoever are unjust. "No human law may deprive man of the natural and primitive right to marriage or restrict in any way the primary purpose of marriage established from the beginning by God Himself: 'Increase and multiply'" (Gen. 1, 28). Virginity (q.v.) and celibacy (q.v.) for a supernatural motive elevate the soul to a higher level of Christian perfection; in fact, they have been for many centuries a crown of the clerical and religious state (Council of Trent, Sess. XXIV, Can. 10).

ENDS. The primary end of marriage is the procreation and the education of children, while the secondary end is mutual aid (Gen. 2:18) and a remedy against concupiscence (1 Cor. 7:9; C.I.C. 1013, par. 7). "The blessing of offspring, however, is not complete by the mere begetting of them, but something else must be added, namely, their proper education. For the most wise God would have failed to make sufficient provision for children that had to be born, and so for the whole human race, if He had not given to those to whom He had entrusted the power and right to beget them, also the power and the right to educate them" (Pius XI, Enc. *Casti connubii*). From the standpoint of man's temporal and eternal happiness, marriage, instituted by God Himself in the earthly Paradise, not only is licit but, in view of its divine origin and primary end, also has a sacred and religious character. For this reason, marriage can be licitly contracted for any of the ends for which it was instituted. As a matter of fact, to these intrinsic ends of the marriage contract, other honest ends can be licitly added; if contracted for a dishonest end, a marriage would be illicit but valid, provided that the essence of the contract remains intact.

Recently, some writers, among whom Dons and Krempel, have tried to give the traditional doctrine on marriage a new interpretation, by emphasizing the mutual perfection of the parties and attempting to relegate the procreative end to second place.

The confusion is primarily in the terminology used. They seem to prefer speaking of *sense* and *motive* of marriage, sometimes called proximate and immanent objective ends of marriage, as the *fruits* rather than of ends of marriage.

With subverted terminology, one can more easily achieve a subversion of ideas. The essence of married life is placed in a personal union and mutual perfection of the parties. Seeing that the diversity of the sexes is not entirely physiological but embraces the sensitive and, at least indirectly, the spiritual life, they state that man and woman are two beings born to understand and to perfect each other in a complete dedication to one another, apart from any ulterior consideration. This mutual dedication is said to reach its zenith in the marriage act.

A decree of the Holy Office (March 30, 1944) rejects this doctrine and any equalization of the intrinsic ends of marriage, as it insists on the essential subordination of the secondary ends to the primary end (AAS, 36 [1944], 103).

Pope Pius XII returned to this subject in his address to midwives, on October 29, 1951. "The truth is that the primary and intrinsic end of marriage as a natural institution by virtue of the will of the Creator is not the personal improvement of the couple, but the procreation and education of new life. The other ends, though also intended by nature, are not in the same rank as the first, much less are they superior to it. They are essentially subordinated to it. This holds true for every marriage, even if childless, just as it can be said that every eye is made to see, even though in certain abnormal cases, by reason of special internal and external conditions, it will never see" (AAS, 43 [1951], 848–849).

Sometimes an inadequacy of expression betrays concepts. If we speak of secondary or accessory ends, there must be no equivocation. Although *secondary* indicates subordination to the primary, and in this sense secondary ends of marriage are subordinate to the primary, yet in the order of execution primary and secondary ends are hierarchically ordained to the welfare of the species and of the couple. Therefore, as Pope Pius XII observes, the distinction between primary and secondary ends is not meant to be a denial or diminution of what is good and proper in personal values consequent upon marriage or its realization. Certainly not. For the procreation of new life the Creator has called human beings made of flesh and blood, endowed with minds and hearts; and He has called them to be the fathers of their posterity insofar as they are men, not purely rational beings. For this reason God has ordained the union of man and woman. All this, therefore, is good and willed by God; but it must not be divorced from the primary function of marriage" (AAS, 43 [1951], 849–858).

PROPERTIES. Unity and indissolubility are essential properties of marriage since its origin (Gen. 2:24; Cor. 6:16; Eph. 5: 28). By natural law, they are binding on all, even unbelievers. Polyandry (*q.v.*), that is, the possession by a woman of more than one husband is contrary to the unity of marriage, because it excludes the ends of marriage and is absolutely contrary to natural law; polygamy (*q.v.*), that is, plurality of wives at the same time, is assuredly contrary to natural law, but not in the same way as polyandry because it is only contrary to the secondary ends of marriage. The dissolution of the bond is opposed to the indissolubility of marriage. Ancient Hebrews and Gentiles were permitted polygamy, repudiation of spouses, and dispensations which later were suppressed by Christ. This is explained by the fact that indissolubility can be removed by a positive divine dispensation. Also, polygamy is not absolutely contrary to divine law, as polyandry is. It is clear that successive polyandry or polygamy, that is, consecutive marriages after the death of the spouse (Can. 1142), are entirely different from simultaneous polyandry or polygamy, which are forbidden by the law of nature (Can. 1142).

To the primary end and essential properties of marriage are closely related the three goods of marriage: the good of offspring (*bonum prolis*), that is, the faculty to procreate and educate children; the good of faith (*bonum fidei*), that is, the fidelity which the parties must maintain to one another; and the good of the sacrament (*bonum sacramenti*), that is, the indissolubility of the contract. These three goods are so essential to marriage that if one of the contracting parties refuses to assume these obligation he would contract marriage invalidly. If one assumes these obligations for the *bonum prolis* and the *bonum fidei* but resolves not to fulfill it, he contracts a valid marriage, because in the assumption of the obligation the substance of the contract is still safe; it would be useless, however, to make a similar distinction for the *bonum sacramenti*, because there is no marriage without indissolubility.

MARRIAGE AS A SACRAMENT. It is a dogma defined by the Council of Trent that a marriage between two baptized persons is a true sacrament (Sess. XXIV, Can. 1). The natural contract of marriage was raised to the dignity of a sacrament without changing its nature and became a supernatural contract. "Christ the Lord elevated the same matrimonial contract between baptized persons to the dignity of a sacrament" (Can. 1012, par. 1). It follows that "no valid marriage contract can exist between baptized persons without being at the same time a sacrament" (Can. 1012, par. 2). Since the contract did not change nature by its elevation to the dignity of a sacrament, and since its value is dependent not only on the natural and divine positive law but also on the ecclesiastical law, the Church has the power to legislate in matrimonial matters without in any way undermining the work of Jesus Christ.

The ministers of the sacrament of matrimony are the contracting parties themselves, because the sacrament does not differ from the contract; the priest acts as minister of the ceremonies and as a public witness. The matter and the form are constituted by the consent expressed by the contracting parties insofar as it signifies the mutual giving and accepting of each other's body (*corporum traditio et acceptatio*). It is a disputed matter whether the contracting parties sin gravely by mutually administering marriage to each other while in a state of sin. The more common sentence denies it because they are not consecrated ministers.

The marriage of unbelievers (pagans) is not a sacrament, since they are incapable of receiving a sacrament before receiving baptism. But if both parties receive baptism, their marriage, if valid, immediately becomes a sacrament. There is no sacrament if only one of the parties receives baptism while the other remains an infidel, or if a baptized person contracts marriage with an unbaptized person (see Privilege, Pauline).

DIVISION. Marriage is *valid* if it creates the bond; if it does not, it is *null* and *void* or invalid. If contracted with knowledge of an impediment affecting even only one of the contracting parties, a marriage is called *attempted*. A valid marriage between baptized persons is called *ratified*, before the conjugal act; after the conjugal act, it is called *ratified and consummated*. If coition was not completed or preceded the marriage, juridically speaking, there is no consummation. If cohabitation of the couple is proved, consummation is presumed unless there is evidence to the contrary (Can. 1015, par. 2).

A valid marriage between two unbaptized persons is called *legitimate*. An invalid marriage is called *putative*, if it was celebrated in good faith at least by one of the parties, until both parties become certain of its nullity (Can. 1015, par. 4). The marriage strictly concealed or *of conscience* is that which is celebrated without any announcement and with the obligation of keeping it secret (Can. 1104–1105). *Morganatic* marriage (German, *morgengaba* —morning gift) is that in which a noble marries a woman of inferior social condition, who, together with her children, must accept certain restrictions insofar as the titles of nobility, the rights, the privileges and property of her husband are concerned (see Marriage, Morganatic). Such is not recog-

nized by the civil legislations of many countries, but is admitted in the case of certain families by German legislation, which fixes the limits of the purely civil effects for the wife and children.

THE FAVOR OF THE LAW. Marriage generally enjoys the favor of the law (*favor juris*); that is, in doubt, whether of law or of fact, validity is upheld unless the contrary is proved (Can. 1014). This principle has only one exception: namely, if the nullity favors the faith (Can. 1127; *see also* Privilege, Pauline). *Pal.*

MARRIAGE, CIVIL. Civil marriage is the pronouncing of the matrimonial contract before a civil magistrate, official or representative. The law in this respect varies from country to country.

Compulsory Civil Ceremony. In some nations, particularly since the French Revolution and the publication of the Napoleonic Code, the civil ceremony for a marriage has become the only marriage recognized by the civil authority for all its citizens, Christians and non-Christians alike. No recognition of civil rights is granted to the religious ceremony of any type, unless there is also held a civil ceremony. Generally, in countries where a civil ceremony is mandatory by law, it must precede in the order of time any religious ceremony if there is one.

Optional Civil Ceremony. In other countries (England and the United States of America, except the State of Maryland), civil marriage is optional, in the sense that every citizen, Christian and non-Christian alike, can choose either civil marriage or religious marriage; both are recognized by the State. For a Catholic, of course, the only valid marriage is the religious ceremony according to the canonical form.

Auxiliary Civil Marriage Ceremony. In other nations, as in Italy after the Concordat of 1929 (art. 34), while the religious ceremony with full civil effects is recognized for Catholics and for persons baptized in a Protestant Church, there is also a civil marriage ceremony for the unbaptized and for baptized persons who do not wish to have a religious ceremony. Catholics, of course, who marry only in a civil ceremony, unless they have received an exceptional permission by ecclesiastical authority, are considered public sinners.

It is evident that a compulsory civil ceremony is extremely offensive to religion and the natural law, as well as repugnant to freedom of conscience, because it imposes upon believers a civil ceremony which is not a real marriage. The adverse effects on public morality are simply obvious.

A marriage by an optional civil ceremony is less reprehensible, since an auxiliary civil ceremony often represents a necessity under the present condition of society: unbaptized persons in every nation are unwilling to observe the laws of the Church. Where the civil ceremony is mandatory, the Church, to avoid greater evils, does not generally admit to the religious ceremony persons not previously married in the civil ceremony. *Bar.*

MARRIAGE, FORM OF. Strictly speaking, the free and reciprocal consent of the parties is sufficient for the natural validity of the matrimonial contract, whether such consent is expressed by words, motions, or other signs; nor is the presence of another person strictly required. For the interests of society, the positive law of the Church prescribes the observation of definite formalities for the validity of the marriage contract between two Catholics. These formalities constitute the *juridical* form of marriage as distinct from the *liturgical* form, or the rites prescribed for the marriage between two baptized persons; the omission of these rites or rubrics has no invalidating effect upon the marriage.

HISTORICAL NOTES. No form was prescribed for the validity of marriage previous to the Council of Trent; only clandestine marriages, celebrated without the presence of relatives or a priest, were severely forbidden and, therefore, unlawful because of the dangers inherent to any marriage contracted privately.

The Council of Trent (Sess. XXIV, c. 1, *De reform. matrim.*) with the decree *Tametsi* declared that all marriages, under penalty of invalidity, be contracted in the presence of one's own parish priest and two or three witnesses. This was done to prevent abuses which occured in the past.

The effect of the decree *Tametsi* was dependent on its promulgation in each individual country; this promulgation varied even from parish to parish, especially in regions with non-Catholic majorities. In view of this, marriage regulations differed in various countries with considerable confusion as a result.

This situation was to be remedied with the decree *Ne temere*, of August 2, 1907, by which the form of the Council of Trent with some modifications was extended to all Catholics and to marriages between Catholics and non-Catholics. These changes became effective on Easter Sunday, April 19, 1908.

With the promulgation of the Code of Canon Law, the provisions of the *Ne temere* ceased to be in effect. Today the form of marriage is regulated by the provisions of Canons 1094–1099 of the *Codex Juris Canonici*, which follow to a large extent the provisions of the decree *Ne temere*.

ORDINARY JURIDICAL FORM AND REQUIREMENTS FOR VALIDITY. Canon 1094 establishes that under ordinary circumstances only those marriages are valid which are contracted in the presence of the parish priest, the local Ordinary, or their delegates, and at least two witnesses, except for cases requiring the use of the extraordinary form (Can. 1098 and 1099).

Thus, three witnesses are required by the ordinary juridical form of marriage: one, a qualified witness, possesses the faculties required by the law; the other two are ordinary witnesses. A *qualified witness* is the local Ordinary or parish pastor or a priest delegated by either. Parish priests are properly called pastors, whether irremovable or movable, and those defined by Canon Law as pastors (*see* Pastor.)

The term *Ordinary* includes in this regard: the Roman Pontiff for the entire Church; a residential bishop for his own territory; an abbot, prelate *nullius* and their vicar-general for their own subjects; a vicar or prefect apostolic and those who rule in their absence over a territory, either by disposition of the law or by approved customs. Such are the vicars capitular, the pro-vicar, or the pro-prefect apostolic (Can. 198).

A priest may be delegated either by the pastor or by the local Ordinary. The latter has the right to delegate a priest even against the wishes of the pastor. A pastor who delegates a priest against the wishes of the Ordinary would do so validly but illicitly.

A *non-qualified witness* may be any person capable of witnessing a legal act. Positive law requires no particular ability except suitability in witnessing a contract such as marriage.

The witnesses must notice that the parties in a marriage contract actually do contract the marriage. Thus, if, by chance or other reason, the designated witnesses fail to hear the exchange of mutual consent, the marriage is valid provided that other persons present can testify to the exchange of the consent by both parties (AAS, 9 [1917]).

The blind, deaf, insane, intoxicated or mentally incompetent are excluded as witnesses. Finally, a simultaneous presence of the pastor or official priest-witness and the two ordinary witnesses is required. Their presence must be such that the witnesses are fully aware from all the circumstances and actions that the marriage was actually contracted.

REQUIREMENTS FOR THE QUALIFIED WITNESS. Canon 1095, par. 1, prescribes that a parish priest or the local Ordinary validly assists at marriage: (1) from the day of taking canonical possession of the benefice or office (Can. 334, par. 3; 1444, par. 1), unless he is laboring under a sentence of excommunication, interdict or suspension from his office, or is declared such; (2) within the confines of their own respective territories, at the marriage of

their own subjects and non-subjects; outside their own territories, they must have the delegation of the parish priest of the place; (3) on the condition that they request and receive the free consent of the contracting parties, that is, provided that the parties are not laboring under a state of violence or grave fear.

In view of the fact that the Church supplies jurisdiction in common error (Can. 209), a marriage is valid even if celebrated before a putative parish priest. Thus, in a case of positive or probable doubt either of law or of fact, the priest may validly assist at a marriage (*see* Jurisdiction, supplied).

In the case of delegated jurisdiction, the following conditions are required for the validity of a marriage: (a) Since jurisdiction in matrimonial matters is now strictly territorial, the delegating person may not delegate another priest to assist at a marriage outside the limits of his own territorial jurisdiction (Can. 1095, par. 2). (b) The delegated person must be a priest (Can. 1095, par. 2); it is not necessary that he be appointed as pastor of souls. The delegation must be given to a specified priest for a specified marriage (Can. 1096, par. 1); this may be done either orally, in writing, or by action, even if the delegated priest remains unknown to the delegating person. The permission may also be granted to the parties in marriage, allowing them to marry before a designated priest. There is no prohibition against delegating several specified priests, since the legislator only intended to exclude permission given to an unspecified priest. Thus, the parish priest may delegate all his assistants or all the priests who have the care of souls in the parish. Proper care must be used, lest marriage be exposed to the danger of nullity by indefiniteness in the designation of the officiating priest or qualified witness. (c) The delegation must be granted for a specific marriage (Can. 1096, par. 1) or for several specific marriages. Therefore, a delegation is invalid if given for all marriages or for those to be celebrated in the course of a week or of a month. The marriage must be specified according to the names or occupation of the contracting parties, the hour, or the place where the marriage is celebrated. A general delegation is excluded except in the case of *vice-parochi* of the parish to which they are attached (Can. 1096, par. 1). The term *vice-parochi* is not well defined in the law and may well include assistants. Thus, if a pastor intends to be absent from his parish for several days, he may not delegate an outside priest except for individual cases; instead, he must apply to the Ordinary for the proper faculties. If he intends to be absent for more than a week, he must appoint a *vicarius substitutus*, approved by the bishop, who can assist or delegate another priest to assist at marriages. (d) The delegation to assist at marriage must be given expressly, in writing or orally or by an externally equivalent sign; a tacit permission is not sufficient. Therefore, a presumed or interpretative delegation, or simple toleration is invalid, nor is approval after the marriage of any value. The delegation must be freely and deliberately given.

It is also required that the delegated person be aware of and accept the delegation at least implicitly. A priest who makes use of a delegation after it is granted but before it is communicated assists invalidly, if the delegation was requested without his knowledge.

On the other hand, if a priest assists at a marriage after he has requested authorization to do so but before such authority has been communicated to him, the marriage is considered valid, for the petitioner's request contains an implicit acceptance. Finally, it is required that the authority of the delegating priest be still in force.

JURIDICAL FORM, REQUIREMENTS FOR A LAWFUL MARRIAGE. The parish priest or the local Ordinary assists lawfully at a marriage: (a) If he is certain of the free state of the contracting parties according to the provisions of the law (Can. 1096, par. 2). (b) If he is certain of the domicile, quasi-domicile,

or one-month residence of the parties in the particular place of the marriage. (In the case of the vagrant, after ascertainment of the habitual residence of one of the contracting parties in the particular place of the marriage, they may lawfully assist at the marriage.) (c) If the domicile, quasi-domicile, or residence of a month is lacking, the official witness, priest or Ordinary, may assist if the parties have the permission of the parish priest or the local Ordinary of their domicile, quasi-domicile, or residence of one month. (For vagrants the permission of the Ordinary of the place is required.) However, grave necessity may exempt from the obligation of obtaining permission. The permission referred to here is quite distinct from the delegation mentioned hitherto, despite the fact that the Code of Canon Law uses the same term, *licentia*, in both cases.

The law provides that the marriage must be solemnized in the presence of the parish priest of the bride, unless there is a justifying motive for doing otherwise. The marriages of Catholics of mixed rites, however, unless particular legislations provide otherwise, must be solemnized in the rite and before the parish priest of the bridegroom.

The parish priest who assists at the marriage without obtaining the permission required by canonical law may not keep the fee received but must remit it to the married couple's own parish priest.

EXTRAORDINARY JURIDICAL FORM OF MARRIAGE. This form may be used if the contracting parties cannot, without serious inconvenience, obtain the services of their parish priest, or the Ordinary, or a priest delegated by them to assist at their marriage according to the norms indicated above. There are two such cases indicated in the law: (a) In danger of death, the marriage is lawful and valid if contracted before two witnesses alone. (b) Outside the danger of death, prudent foresight indicates the impossibility of observing the ordinary form for the duration of a month at least.

In both cases, if the services of another priest, even excommunicated, can be secured, he must be summoned, although a marriage contracted before two witnesses alone (Can. 1098) is equally valid under the circumstances.

Inability to have a qualified priest does not mean absolute or physical impossibility; a relative or moral impossibility is sufficient. This is verified when one cannot obtain the services of a qualified priest without serious inconvenience, which may be prudently presumed if a notable moral or temporal harm would result either to the parties or to a third person or to the public good.

However, the simple fact of the absence of the parish priest is not sufficient for a couple to contract marriage before witnesses alone. There must be a moral certainty obtained from a known fact or diligent investigation.

THOSE HELD TO THE CANONICAL FORM. All those baptized in the Catholic Church or converted from heresy or schism, even if they later apostatized, are held to the canonical form of marriage in marrying another Catholic or a baptized or non-baptized non-Catholic (Can. 1099, par. 2). If a Catholic marries a person belonging to one of the Eastern rites, which presently have a well-defined marriage form (May 2, 1949; cf. Motu Proprio *Crebrae Allatae* of February 22, 1949: AAS, 41 [1949]), a new question arises concerning which of the two forms must be preferred. While more exact provisions and specifications are expected, the answer seems to be that for the lawfulness of the marriage one must follow the form of the bridegroom's rite. Baptized and non-baptized non-Catholics are not held to canonical form in marriage (Can. 1099, par. 2; Motu Proprio of Pius XII of August 1, 1948: AAS, 40 [1948], 305).

LITURICAL FORM. Liturgical form in marriage concerns the lawfulness of a marriage, not validity. Except in necessity, the rites contained in the liturgical books, the *Roman Ritual* and the *Missal*, shall be observed in the celebration of marriage (Can. 1100).

Besides the matrimonial consent which the officiating priest elicits from the couple by a question form, the sacred rites include the joining of the hands of the bride and bridegroom, the blessing of the ring or rings (*Rituale*, tit. viii, c. 2) and the nuptial blessing, which may not be given except during the celebration of Holy Mass. The nuptial blessing is given separately; it may also be given in the sanation of a marriage after the parties have lived together for a long time.

However, the nuptial blessing is not repeated for a widow who contracts a new marriage, nor may it be given during the penitential seasons (Can. 1101, par. 1; *Ritual*, tit VII, c. 1, n. 16, 18; *Missal*, *Votive Mass for Bride and Bridegroom*). Solemn marriage is forbidden from the first Sunday of Advent until Christmas inclusive, and from Ash Wednesday until Easter Sunday inclusive. Ordinaries, however, may permit the solemn nuptial blessing during these seasons, but they must admonish the parties to refrain from excessive pomp (Can. 1108, par. 3).

A marriage may be validly celebrated anywhere, but the marriage of Catholics is to take place in the parish church, and, as a rule in the bride's own parish. The Ordinary may for a good reason permit the celebration of a marriage in a private home or in private oratories, but only in grave necessity shall he permit a marriage to take place in oratories, churches of religious houses of women, or a seminary (Can. 1109, par. 2).

Generally, mixed marriages are not contracted in church. The Ordinary may dispense from the laws concerning the place and the rite of marriage but is not to permit the celebration of Holy Mass (Can. 1109, par. 3; 1102, par. 2). (In a few dioceses in the U.S.A. (Boston, Baltimore, etc.), mixed marriages are contracted in the church, generally at the altar rail, but the parties are required to take a course of instructions on the fundamentals of Catholic doctrine. In other dioceses, (Washington), the church ceremony is optional.—Editor's note.)

All marriages are registered in marriage (*Liber matrimoniorum*) and baptismal registers (*Liber baptizatorum*), with all proper and necessary data. Every parish must have these registers. *Pal.*

MARRIAGE, INVALID. *See* Invalidity of matrimony.

MARRIAGE, JURISDICTION OF. In order to establish the competency or jurisdiction of the Church in marriages, the following distinctions must be made:

MARRIAGE OF BAPTIZED PERSONS. The marriage of baptized persons is governed by Can. 1016 of the Code of Canon Law. "The marriage of baptized persons is governed not only by divine but also by Canon Law. Civil authority has competency only concerning the purely civil effects of such marriages." Divine law, which governs marriage as a juridical institution of natural and divine positive law, is immutable even on the part of the Church, which can only interpret or declare authentically if divine law forbids or annuls a marriage (Can. 1038, par. 1).

As a contract-sacrament, the marriage of baptized persons is subject to the religious and social authority of the Church with legislative (Can. 1038, par. 2), judicial (Can. 1960), and coercive (Cans. 2319, 2375) power as a proper, exclusive, and independent right.

MARRIAGE BETWEEN A BAPTIZED AND A NON-BAPTIZED PERSON. The marriage between a baptized and a non-baptized person, though not a sacrament, is subject to the exclusive jurisdiction of the Church by reason of the baptism of one party and the strictly bilateral nature of the contract, by which a law concerning one of the contracting parties indirectly but necessarily applies also to the other (cf. Can. 1036, par. 3).

LEGITIMATE MARRIAGE. Since the Church has no jurisdiction over non-baptized persons (1 Cor. 5:12), and since the public good demands as absolutely necessary legislation complementing the natural law (indefinite in itself) to govern the marriage of the unbaptized, it is commonly admitted today that the civil authority is competent for regulating this matter. This doctrine, universally accepted until the end of the eighteenth century, was attacked by some writers in the nineteenth century, but it is still unanimously held by Canonists. Civil authority does not lack the prerequisites for this function, because the marriage of non-baptized persons is a natural contract. Such legislation, however, must be rational and conform to natural and divine laws. Canonists do not agree on whether the exercise of this power by the civil authority is a right proper to the latter or merely a transferred right. Also, it is not clear whether the individual civil codes that have legislated in this field have intended to make nullifying laws binding in conscience, prohibitive laws, or merely penal laws. Each case must be examined separately.

In the past, the Church judged, because of an intimate union of power, the purely civil effects of a marriage between baptized persons; at present, such matters can be adjudicated by an ecclesiastical court, if they are incidental or accessory to a case concerning the validity or lawfulness of marriage. If treated as a principal action, the adjudication belongs exclusively to the civil court (Can. 1961). The word *purely* of Canon 1016 limits this jurisdiction to the effects of the natural order, which are separable from the essence of marriage, such as the size of the dowry, the inheritance rights of wife and children, the civil rights and privileges of the husband, etc. Hence, civil authority has no jurisdiction over the inseparable effects of such a marriage, such as the mutual rights and duties of the couple, the legitimacy of offspring, the rights of parents over their children, and the duties of children toward their parents; still less can civil authority judge the validity or lawfulness of marriage itself. *Pal.*

MARRIAGE, MORGANATIC. A morganatic marriage is the marriage of a man with a woman of inferior social status, which is contracted with the agreement that both the woman and her children are to be excluded from hereditary property, titles, and civil dignities. The agreement is based on the so-called *Morgengaba* (gift of the morning) of the German legal code, which is a financial and property arrangement reached at the beginning of the marriage.

Ecclesiastical law regards marriage of this type as completely and fully valid and effective. The restrictions reached in this type of marriage pertain only to the civil and patrimonial effects of marriage and, if these are just, they are recognized by the Church. Morganatic marriage was formerly called *Salic* (left-hand marriage) because, according to the law of the Salians, children born of such marriages could inherit only after all the other children or descendants of a regular marriage were dead. *Bar.*

MARRIAGE OF CONSCIENCE. A marriage of conscience is a marriage contracted in secret, without banns, in the presence of the parish priest and two witnesses. Despite the strong attitude of the Church to give marriage the character of a public contract to avoid deception either by the man or the woman, yet there are cases in which the Church permits an occult marriage for exceptional or very serious reasons. Such reasons may be to avoid a secret sinful relation or illegitimacy of offspring.

Regulations concerning occult marriage were established by Benedict XIV in his Encyclical *Satis vobis*, of November 27, 1741. Canons 1104–1107 of the Code of Canon Law are largely based upon this document. The Code fails to specify the reasons for which such a marriage may be permitted but it requires a very grave and urgent reason

before the local Ordinary; the vicar general only by a mandate of the Ordinary may permit an occult marriage. Generally, it may be stated that if the spiritual welfare of the parties demands it, such a marriage may be allowed.

In permitting such a marriage, the bishop or priest who witnesses the marriage, the witnesses, and the parties are bound to maintain perpetual secrecy, unless in the future the parties consent to the publication of their marriage. This obligation ceases to bind the bisop if the secret were to give rise to scandal or the parties failed to observe the obligations assumed in the marriage.

According to Can. 379, a marriage of conscience must be recorded in a special register of marriages and baptisms and kept in the secret archives of the diocesan Curia. *Bar.*

MARRIAGE, PROXY. Proxy or power of attorney in connection with marriage is exercised when one of the contracting parties is absent, and his consent is expressed through an agent, who represents him and acts in his name (procurator). As in a mandate the power of attorney applied to a marriage is based on the relationship of confidence existing between the principal and the agent; in addition, it implies a relationship of representation. Unlike an ordinary mandate, which can be executed with the consent alone, the mandate of proxy for marriage requires also the observance of certain norms demanded by the special nature of this juridical transaction of marriage set forth in Canon 1088, par. 1, of the Code of Canon Law.

For the validity of marriage by proxy the following rules must be observed: (a) The proxy must be designated by the bride or bridegroom and must possess an appropriate mandate to contract with a specified person. (b) The mandate must be a public document; that is, it must be signed by the person giving the mandate, by the parish priest, the local Ordinary, or a priest delegated by either, or by the person exercising the mandate, with at least two witnesses. If the person giving the mandate does not know how to write, it must be so stated in the mandate itself and another witness shall be employed who shall sign the mandate; otherwise the mandate shall be void. (c) If the person giving the mandate revoked it or became mentally ill before the proxy contracted marriage in his name, the marriage is invalid, for marriage consent cannot be supplied as in other contracts. This applies even if the proxy or the other contracting party did not know about the revocation of the mandate. (d) The proxy must personally execute the mandate; every power of subdelegating to another is forbidden at the risk of nullity of the marriage (Can. 1089) even if the person giving the mandate consented to such delegation. With the fulfillment of these prescriptions, the marriage is immediately valid without later renewal of consent by the couple.

Since the celebration of a proxy marriage or a marriage through an interpreter (*q.v.*) could occasion difficulties, Can. 1091 forbids the parish priest to assist at one "unless there is a good reason, and every doubt concerning the authenticity of the mandate and the loyalty of the interpreter is excluded, and the permission of the Ordinary, if there is time, obtained."

The proxy or an interpreter is not a minister of the sacrament; therefore he contracts neither consanguinity nor affinity; he does not commit sin if he is in a state of sin at the time of the marriage contract; on the other hand, the represented party sins gravely if he contracts while in a state of sin.

As in a typical mandate, the proxy of marriage is terminated by completion of the action, by withdrawal or revocation by the one who issued the mandate, by refusal of the agent, or by the death of the person who issued the mandate or the agent.

Few countries allow marriage by proxy. Confer marriage legislation for each individual country. For proxy in general, *see* Procurator. *Pal.*

MARRIAGE, PUTATIVE. A putative marriage is an invalid marriage contracted in good faith by one of the parties at least. It is considered putative until both parties become aware of the invalidity (Can. 1015, par. 4).

The declaration of nullity of a marriage has in itself a retroactive effect; in other words, the marriage may be considered as having never taken place. The rigid application of such a principle could produce severe disturbances in a family established in error of a valid marriage. Thus, to lessen the juridical consequences of the rigid application of the above principle, particularly with reference to offspring, putative marriage was established. A clear reference to this is found in Peter Lombard (*Sentent.* IV, D. 11). Since that time, the doctrine of putative marriage has found constant application in the ecclesiastical forum for all marriages celebrated *in facie Ecclesiae*, that is, publicly contracted, with the calling of banns as prescribed by the IV Lateran Council, 1215, and the observance of the form established after the Council of Trent.

The effects of a putative marriage, limited at the outset to the legitimizing of offspring, gradually were also extended to the matrimonial relations between parents and children and between the parents themselves.

In the present law, any invalid marriage is considered putative if contracted in good faith *coram Ecclesia*, as the Pontifical Commission for authentic interpretation of the Canons of Canon Law declared on January 26, 1949; that is, any marriage contracted according to the form prescribed by Canon Law is considered valid until both parties to the marriage become certain of its nullity. According to canonical tradition, children conceived or born of such a marriage are considered legitimate, as if born of a valid marriage, provided that the parents were not forbidden to use the marriage rights at the time of conception either by reason of solemn religious profession or sacred orders (Can. 1114).

Children born of unmarried persons are legitimized by a putative marriage provided that the parents were capable of contracting marriage at the time of the conception, pregnancy, or birth (Can. 1116).

The provisions of some modern civil codes concerning putative marriage do not agree altogether with Canon Law. For details the reader must consult the marriage legislation of each individual country. *Pal.*

MARRIAGE, RATIFIED. A marriage between two baptized persons that is not consummated by a conjugal act is called a ratified marriage. Intrinsically, such marriage is indissoluble; yet it can be dissolved (1) by solemn religious profession by one of the parties, or (2) by dispensation granted by the Supreme Pontiff in virtue of his vicarial or ministerial authority, at the request of at least one of the parties, even if the other is opposed (Can. 1119). This second form of dissolution has been used with increasing frequency from the fifteenth century. Exclusive jurisdiction over the inquiry or process relative to the dispensation must be conducted by the Sacred Congregation of the Sacraments (Can. 249) for the Latin Church. The Sacred Congregation may, if it deems proper, entrust the task to the Sacred Roman Rota. The cases for Eastern rite Catholics are dealt with by the Sacred Congregation for the Eastern Churches. At times non-Consummated mixed marriages are dealt with by the Sacred Congregation of the Holy Office.

The purpose of this investigation is to ascertain: (1) the fact of non-consummation; (2) the presence of good reasons for a dispensation. It is considered a valid reason if the dispensation is believed to benefit the souls of both parties, or at least one; with freedom to contract a new, valid marriage, they shall be able to avoid incontinence. Proof of non-consummation is furnished by showing that the parties were never alone long enough after marriage to permit them to consummate the marriage; but if they did live together (Can. 1015, par. 2), then proof of non-consummation must be obtained by a deposition of the parties, confirmed by the so-called witnesses *septimae manus*, or seven reliable persons for each party who will attest to the trustworthiness of the couple. Other witnesses *ex officio*, and a physical examination of the woman by two specialists for the purpose of ascertaining virginal integrity, unless such examination is obviously useless, as in the case of a widow, are employed in this process.

The bishop to whom the petition is directed, after diligent study of the case, must request permission of the Sacred Congregation of the Sacraments to institute the necessary investigation. Once the faculty is obtained, the procedure is conducted according to the norms of the *Regulae servandae* issued by the Sacred Congregation of the Sacraments (AAS, 15 [1923], 389 ff.). The administrative process, that is, without advocates but with the intervention of the defender of the bond, gathers the evidence; the bishop prepares a *votum* in which he states the reasons in support of granting the dispensation; the defender of the bond writes his *observations*, pointing out all the doubtful elements apparent from the acts. The documents are then sent to the Sacred Congregation of the Sacraments, whose duty it is to examine the acts and to decide on the advisability of requesting the Supreme Pontiff to grant the grace of dispensation. Acting upon the report submitted by the Cardinal Prefect or the Secretary of the Congregation, the Holy Father grants or rejects the petition. The dispensation, if granted, always contains implicitly the dispensation from the impediment of *crime* in its first two forms, namely, adultery with a promise of or an attempt at marriage (Can. 1075, par. 1).

Sometimes a clause is inserted in the

dispensation by which one or the other of the parties is forbidden to contract a new marriage, as in a case with strong evidence of impotency. A request for removal of that clause may be made to the Sacred Congregation.

The dispensation, which becomes effective from the moment it is granted by the Supreme Pontiff, must be recorded in the parish marriage register. *Bar.*

MARRIAGE, USE OF. PURPOSE OF MARRIAGE. Canon 1013, paragraph 1, states: "The primary purpose of marriage is the procreation and education of offspring; the secondary purpose is to furnish mutual assistance and a remedy for concupiscence." This sacramental remedy for the sexual appetite is not an approval by the Church of a theory, formerly rejected, which holds that marriage is lawful if its primary end is the satisfaction of physical pleasure as evidenced by the sexual act, nor is it an approval of a corollary of this theory that a marriage has greater probability of success if the gratification of the sexual appetites is greater. The alleged truth of this theory is refuted by facts, for according to Beard, "unhappy marriages are those in which the partners give themselves over to excesses."

This, of course, does not minimize in any way the right of husband and wife to full enjoyment of the conjugal act nor does it make it improper for a physician to instruct them, if necessary, in order to overcome dispareunia (*see* Impotency).

Furthermore, under the guidance of the teachings of the Supreme Pontiffs, Innocent XI, Pius XI and Pius XII, it should be borne in mind that love is not libidinous sensuality and that the quest for or practice of libidinous pleasure as the exclusive end of marriage may constitute sin, whereas legitimate pleasure strengthens the love between husband and wife. Sexual pleasure constitutes one of the secondary purposes of marriage, even in a union where

children are impossible or excluded for extrinsic circumstances.

LICIT AND ILLICIT ACTS. Between husband and wife the excitation of the sexual faculties and desire without directing these to the conjugal act is illicit. Similarly, the use of means directed at the frustration of the natural completion of the conjugal act is forbidden in marriage for husband and wife (*see* Neo-Malthusianism).

A physician, when requested by patients to provide the best means or method of preventing children, should simply indicate continence, which is all the more endurable as it is more complete (*see* Abstinence and Continence).

If morally certain that the inquiry is motivated by serious reasons (health, economic, or social condition), a physician or obstetrician may explain to his patient the method of *periodic continence* (*q.v.*) called the rhythm method. It is illicit for a physician to suggest *artificial insemination* (*q.v.*); he may, however, offer suggestions or other assistance aimed at enabling potent married persons to complete the conjugal act, though with partial effectiveness.

The use of all those means offered by medicinal science against *conjugal sterility* (uterine suspension, administration of hormones, appropriate vitamins, etc.) is always lawful and, at times, a matter of obligation.

CONTINENCE. Continence is advisable at definite times in marital life. Thus, if husband or wife are not disposed to engage in the conjugal act, the other must refrain from demands out of charity. Hygienic reasons counsel abstinence during the menstrual period. Finally, a suspension of the marital relation is advisable during pregnancy. In the first few months of pregnancy, intercourse is liable to cause hemorrhages and abortions; toward the end of pregnancy, frequent intercourse may cause premature deliveries, puerperal and other infections which may endanger the health of both the fetus and the mother.

CONSANGUINITY AND AGE. Recent demographic findings have shown that the *consanguinity of husband and wife* exercises an adverse influence on off-spring. Thus, Sutter and Tabah have shown that, in 1955, the figure of 3% of babies affected by congenital abnormalities in a French population studied by them rose to 6%, 8%, and 18%, when the consanguinity of the spouses was respectively of the 6th, 5th and 4th degree. This fully justifies the provisions of the ecclesiastical and civil laws which seek to prevent marriages between relatives.

The question concerning the influence of the age of the parents upon the health of the children seems less important, for, in fact, an inquiry conducted a few years ago by a German professor, Hegnauer, on the families of three-hundred outstanding scientists and artists revealed that there was no possible evidence which might indicate that the age of the parents at the moment of the birth of those outstanding persons was an element contributing to their pre-eminence.

Recent statistics of French geneticists show that males are more frequent among the first-born infants of a marriage; it is evident also that the sex of successive children is related to the length of time in the interval between the births; the shorter the interval of time, the greater the probability of another child with the same sex as the one immediately preceding it in birth and vice versa. Biologists and gynecologists have suggested numerous methods of great variety that are allegedly capable of predicting the offspring's sex. Among these suggestions, from time to time, on the basis of alleged laboratory experiments, statistical evidence and physiopathological deduction are the more common ones, such as the performance of the conjugal act in a definite period of the menstrual cycle or the change of diet for husband or wife. None of these suggestions is apparently effective. According to Fischer, all constitute "an unjustified intrusion into the biological order that determines the growth and increase of a people." If not absolutely illicit, yet, because ineffective in results, these are not moral, in view of the fact that, if they were effective, they would disturb the numerical equilibrium between the two sexes, which is so important from the standpoint of monogamy and morality. *Riz.*

MARTYRDOM. NATURE.

A *martyr* (Greek, *martyrion*—witness) in the Church is one who gives witness or testimony to the truth of the Christian faith by the shedding of blood and physical death. Martyrdom is the supreme act of the virtue of fortitude (*q.v.*).

Three conditions are required for martyrdom. (a) *Physical death, truly suffered.* The martyr is called a perfect witness of the Christian faith, for which one should be disposed to suffer any physical hardship. The renunciation of physical life is an absolute proof of detachment from earthly things and of true love of Christ. In an absolute sense, no one can be called a martyr without suffering death for our Lord.

The second requirement is that (b) *death be inflicted out of hatred for the Christian faith.* Christian belief demands not only an internal adherence of the mind to revealed truths (*pia credulitas cordis*) but also an external profession by words and deeds. Death must be inflicted by those who hate the faith or Christian virtue. Thus, in a strict sense, those who (1) suffer death in the service of the sick, (2) for natural truths, (3) in defense of heresy, (4) or who commit suicide to preserve Christian virtue are not martyrs.

The third requirement is that (c) *death be voluntarily accepted.* If an adult is killed for the faith while asleep or without thought of martyrdom, he is probably not to be considered a real martyr in the strict sense. However, some authors teach that one who has left everything for the Lord is a martyr; thus, one is a martyr although he is killed while asleep by the enemies of religion out of hatred for the faith. The Holy Innocents, who were killed out of hatred for Christ, are considered true martyrs, because in this case the acceptance by the will was supplied by an actual grace. Investigations conducted into causes for the beatification or canonization of martyrs extend to all these elements (Can. 2020). If martyrdom is proved, there is a dispensation from all examination of the practice of heroic virtue and, at times, from complementary miracles (Can. 2116, par. 2).

EFFECTS. A sinner, whether adult or child, baptized or unbaptized, is saved through martyrdom, because in the voluntary acceptance of death for the love of God, sorrow for sin is implied. Since martyrdom is the most perfect act of charity, (1) it destroys in the victim all venial sins and temporal punishment still to be atoned for in past sins. Every martyr immediately enters heaven without the necessity of atonement for sin in purgatory. Innocent III stated the lack of necessity of prayers for a martyr for this reason. (2) Martyrdom obtains for the martyr a notable increase of grace and glory and is rewarded with a special prize in heaven, which is called a crown. This crown of the martyr is explained as a special joy (*gaudium*) by Saint Thomas, a special prize for a special victory (*In 4 Sent. Disput.*, 49, q. 5, a. 5).

Martyrdom was foretold by Jesus as a distinguishing mark of His Church (Matt. 10:16–22; Luke 21:12). The Apostles serenely faced death because of their faith in Christ (Acts 2:32; I Peter 5:1). The martyrdom of the Apostles and the early Christians is a proof of the historical reality of the Gospel and the truth of the doctrine of Jesus Christ, for they testified with their bodily death and blood to their belief and experiences. Martyrdom is a proof of the truth of the Christian faith. For the veneration of martyrs, *see* Saints; for the veneration of their relics, *see* Relics; for the martyrology, *see* Liturgical Books. *Pal.*

MARTYROLOGY. *See* Liturgical Books.

MARY, BLESSED VIRGIN. PREROGATIVES. The greatness of Mary is written on many pages of the Bible. Destined to be the Mother of God, Mary was preserved from the guilt of original sin and filled with grace from the first moment of her existence. This grace increased constantly until her death, for she never resisted the impulses of grace in the slightest way, as at every moment she gave herself to God with all the strength which she was able to bring to bear in the fulfillment of His will and in the closest contact with Jesus, the source of all merit. Thus, next to Jesus, Mary is the most perfect model of all virtues. By reason of her divine maternity, Mary came closest to the possession of divinity. Assumed into heaven, body and soul, after her death Mary reigns with her Son over all creation.

Mary is also the mother of the whole human race, redeemed by Christ. The early Fathers of the Church, throughout their writings, saw in Mary the new Eve, who was mentioned in the Book of Genesis (3:15), and who was to be closely united in the work of Redemption with the new Adam, Christ. And as the first Eve was in truth the cause of the spiritual death for all humanity, so Mary is the cause of supernatural life for the human race. Having become the Mother of Jesus in the human flesh, not only as an individual but as a Redeemer and Saviour, Mary thus became the Mother according to the spirit of all those whom Christ came to redeem.

Not only did Mary give the world all graces by giving it Jesus, author and meritorious cause of grace, but she also has merited, not by reason of strict justice (*de condigno*) but of fitness (*de congruo*), all graces merited by Christ in justice. She merited them not only by freely pronouncing her *fiat* on the day of the Incarnation and by preparing the victim for the sacrifice, but, above all, by consenting at the foot of the Cross to the immolation of her Divine Son and by suffering with Him (St. Pius X, Denz., n. 3034).

Christ, who offered Himself for all and who needed the cooperation of no creature in order to redeem the world, is the only perfect Mediator between

God and man (1 Tim. 2:5). Yet, this is no obstacle if He willed to have His mother as co-redemptrix of the human race (Denz. n. 3034, note 4). An increasingly common doctrine among theologians that, besides this universal ascending *mediation* of Mary, one must also admit a universal descending mediation, makes it extremely fitting that the graces merited by Mary in union with Jesus are not distributed without her intervention. Many theologians hold that Mary implores and obtains all graces granted to humanity. By this it is not meant that, to receive these graces, one must necessarily request them from Mary, for her intervention may occur without these requests. Theologians acknowledge a more direct and physical intervention by Mary in the distribution of graces. Mary is truly the Mediatrix of all graces; since her mediation is entirely dependent upon the mediation of Christ, it follows that Mary's mediation brings into clearer focus the value and richness of Christ's mediation.

VENERATION. The personal dignity of Mary and her role in the Redemption demand that we pay honor to her in a way that is less than that due to God, but greater than that given to the angels or saints. This honor, called hyperdulia, means a truly filial affection for Mary and an internal recognition of her excellence with due submission. We honor Mary by extolling her privileges, by acts of penance or good works in her honor, by displaying her image with lights and flowers, by entrusting our spiritual and material welfare to her special protection so that she may guard them and make them productive of eternal fruits. Some entrust to Mary the free disposal of their merits, the satisfaction and impetrative value of their good works insofar as these benefits are transferable; it is suggested that this act of holy abandonment be not made without mature reflection or without the explicit consent of one's own spiritual director. We also honor Mary by observing her feastdays: the Immaculate Conception, the Assumption into heaven, the An-

nunciation, Nativity, the feast of the Name of Mary and her Divine Maternity, and many other feasts instituted by the Church in her honor. The fervent Christian prepares himself for these feastdays by penitential and charitable works. In addition, the devotees of Mary practice special devotions in her honor during the months of May and October and on Saturdays, especially the first Saturday of each month.

Since, next to Jesus, Mary is the most perfect model of virtue, we should meditate on her as a model, for the example of her virtue should foster a life of faith and fidelity to duty and fill us with zeal for the salvation of souls. The imitation of Mary is the most dedicated homage that can be rendered in her honor.

The maternal solicitude and powerful intercession of Mary should engender in all Christians an unlimited trust in her powerful intercession in behalf of all our spiritual and material needs. To make use of this means of special devotion and appeal to her powerful intercession is an excellent form of honor to pay to our celestial Mother.

Devout children of Mary do not allow a single day to pass without reciting the chaplet of the Rosary, or meditating on the mysteries of their salvation. The Little Office of the Blessed Virgin resembles the breviary recited by priests, since it recalls many times during the day the greatness and powerful intercession of Mary.

The recitation of the *Angelus* prayer thrice daily is a form of honor to Mary, which recalls the moment at which she submitted to the will of God in accepting her role as the Mother of God. *Man.*

MASOCHISM. *See* Perversions, sexual.

MASONRY, MASONS. *See* Secret Society.

MASS. The Holy Mass, the highest act of public worship of the Church, is the series of ceremonies through which the unbloody sacrifice of the New Law is offered and re-enacted until the end of time as a memorial of the bloody sacrifice of the cross. The Mass is the means through which the fruits of the merits acquired by Jesus Christ on the cross are obtained. The essence of the sacrifice of the Mass—that is, the renewal of the acts of Christ at the time of His Last Supper with the Apostles—is contained in the consecration (q.v.) of the Mass. The Mass is a pre-eminently sacred rite practiced since the early days of the Church; it includes the bloodless offering of the Divine Victim and the oblation of Himself to God as an act of adoration, thanksgiving, atonement and petition. As conditions of time and place suggested, prayers and rites were added by competent authorities to the essential part instituted by the Lord. These additions gave rise to the various Eastern and Western rites (see Missal). In the Mass of the Latin rite, the following parts may be distinguished: (1) the preliminary part, also called Mass of the Catechumens, which extends from the prayers at the foot of the altar to the end of the Nicean Creed (Credo); (2) the sacrificial part, called Mass of the Faithful, which includes the offertory, the pre-eminently liturgical action of consecration and communion (q.v.); (3) the conclusion of the Mass.

The High Priest at the sacrifice of the Mass is Jesus Christ, who acts through His minister, the visible priest. Although the faithful are not the ministers of the Eucharistic Sacrifice, they nonetheless participate, by virtue of baptism, in the offering of the Body and Blood of Jesus Christ by the very fact of their membership in the visible body of the Church. They offer to God the sacrifical Victim through the priest who represents them at the altar in each Mass. As a matter of fact, it can be said that to a certain extent the faithful offer the Mass with the priest as they join their sentiments of adoration, thanksgiving, atonement, and supplication with the prayers of the priest to be offered to God along with the Victim

of the sacrifice (Pius XII, Encyclical Mediator Dei, November 29, 1947).

In each Mass each of the faithful is also offered to God together with Jesus Christ; that is, he is committed to a life entirely dedicated to the service of God; in fact, the offering of the Victim expresses the unconditional giving of self to God by those whose place the Victim takes on the altar. As to the matter and minister of the Eucharistic Sacrifice see Eucharist, Holy.

EFFECTS. The Holy Mass gives to God the praise and thanksgiving due to Him by the members of the Mystical Body of Christ; it appeases God, offended by sins, and obtains the application of the merits of the sacrifice of the cross: the grace of conversion for sinners, and graces for the just to practice Christian virtues, forgiveness of part of the punishment due for the sins already forgiven for the faithful on earth and those detained in purgatory. Since one of the aims of Holy Mass is the growth of the Church, it also obtains graces for those who are not yet members of God's Church. However, not everyone derives from Holy Mass the same amount of fruits or benefits (see below, "Value of the Mass").

The obligation to provide the required materials for the celebration of the sacrifice of the Mass is, in our present times, fulfilled through the making of an offering or stipend to the priest. The donor is thereby entitled to the ministerial fruits of the Mass, which the priest can dispose of in favor of others. The celebrant is entitled to a very special fruit. The universal Church draws from every Mass a so-called general fruit. From the special fruit which belongs to those who participate in the celebration of the Mass, each shares according to the degree of union with the sacrifice. This can best be attained by the use of the Sunday Missal, singing or reciting with the priest, in a loud tone of voice and in accordance with the laws of the Church, certain prayers of the Mass and the responses to the priest; also by serving at the altar, and by the collective observance of the same ritual practices. However, the most important thing of all is to arouse in oneself the sentiment of adoration, appreciation, and complete dedication of oneself to God, by binding oneself to a life of generous acceptance of adverse and painful trials, as from God, and perfect obedience to the divine law in satisfaction for sins committed. This dedication of oneself places the faithful in union with the Victim who offers himself to God, hour after hour, for God's honor and the sanctification and salvation of souls. The participation in the sacrifice has its fulfillment in the reception of Holy Communion, following the communion of the priest.

VALUE OF THE MASS. Since the High Priest of the Mass, of infinite dignity, is the Victim sacrificed and offered, the Mass gives to God a worship of praise and thanksgiving that infinitely surpasses anything which creatures, however numerous and holy, are able to offer. The Mass is sufficient to obtain from God, who is disposed to mercy by the offering of the Mass, the application of the merits of the sacrifice of the cross in a limitless measure. Under these aspects, the Mass has an infinite value. However, since man's capacity for receptiveness is limited, as is the number of those who participate in the fruits of the Mass, the efficacy of the Mass, great though it be, remains, with regard to them, limited.

Whether the Mass, applied to more persons under equal conditions, benefits each one as if it were applied to him alone is disputed. Many theologians say that the special fruit of entreaty and propitiation is not diminished for individuals by the increase of the participants. However, since the matter remains uncertain, the priest cannot satisfy, with the application of one Mass, obligations which he assumes by accepting various stipends or other onerous titles (Alexander VIII, Denz. n. 1110; Can. 825, n. 2 and 3).

APPLICATION OF THE MASS. The application of the Mass includes two general topics: (a) persons for whom the Eucharistic Sacrifice may be applied; (b) the obligation to apply the Mass by a priest. Concerning the first question *see* Application of the Mass; in answer to the second question it shall be noted that the obligation of the priest to apply a Mass may arise (a) from his office, (b) a benefice (chaplaincy), (c) or stipend received.

(a) By reason of pastoral office, bishops (Can. 339, par. 1), vicars capitular (Can. 440), abbots and prelates *nullius* (Can. 323), parish priests (Can. 466, par. 1), parochial vicars who are real administrators of a parish (Can. 451, par. 2, and 473, par. 1), and at times substitute vicars (Can. 474) must apply the Mass for the faithful entrusted to their care, on all Sundays and feastdays, even suppressed (Can. 339, par. 1). Vicars and prefects apostolic (Can. 306) and quasi-parish priests (Can. 466, par. 1) are similarly obliged on Christmas, Epiphany, Easter, Ascension, Pentecost, Corpus Christi, Immaculate Conception, Assumption, St. Joseph, the feast of the Holy Apostles Peter and Paul, and All Saints' Day (Can. 306).

The above-mentioned persons, if not hindered, must personally apply the Mass, since it is a personal obligation; if lawfully hindered, they may commission others to do so or, later on, say the Mass or have it said later, but at the earliest possible time (Can. 339, par. 4, and 466, par. 1). Finally, they must say the Mass in the parochial church, although exceptions are permitted for particular reasons (Can. 466, par. 4).

(b) The obligation of applying Holy Mass because of a benefice (Can. 1475, par. 1) generally flows from foundation statutes, to be religiously observed. From the same foundation statutes one may also learn whether the obligation is predominantly personal or real.

(c) The obligation of applying the Mass may also arise from acceptance of the stipend (*see* Mass Stipend).

The same obligation may also arise from a promise made. The promise, however, must be kept, not in justice, but in fidelity.

The obligation of applying a Mass implies the obligation of celebrating Mass. Every priest is gravely obliged to say Mass only a few times a year (Can. 805). There is, however, a general custom followed by all priests of daily celebration, which the Pope could change into law. The local Ordinaries can directly order their priests to say Mass on feastdays or holydays of obligation by reason of necessity on the part of the faithful; but they can only indirectly order them to say Mass on other days insofar as it is required by the fulfillment of a legitimately imposed office (Can. 128). Perhaps they have the right also to order them to apply the Mass; they can do so with certainty when it involves the Mass *pro populo* or bination (Sacred Congregation of Council, May 8, 1920, and November 18, 1937).

DISPOSITIONS REQUIRED FOR CELEBRATION. Certain dispositions of soul and body are needed in the minister for a licit celebration of Holy Mass.

(a) The *dispositions of soul* imply the state of grace, immunity from irregularity, censure or other penalties which forbid the exercise of sacred orders, and an appropriate remote and proximate preparation.

(b) *Physical dispositions* imply, in addition to the external propriety which such an exalted rite requires, the observance of the Eucharistic fast according to the rules set down by the Constitution *Christus Dominus* of Pius XII, and the corresponding Instruction of the Holy Office (January 6, 1953). According to these dispositions, besides water, which is permitted at all times, a priest may take something in the form of beverage, always excluding alcoholic drinks, and even something solid as medicine if he is sick or experiences serious inconvenience from the fast; outside of sickness, he may also take something in the form of beverage (excluding alcoholic drinks) one hour before Mass, in case of serious discomfort.

Serious discomfort may arise from these three specific conditions: serious debilitating work, preceding the celebration, which arises from the sacred ministry; a late hour (after 9:00 a.m.); and a long walk of at least a mile to the place of celebration.

In the case of evening Masses, the priest must fast from food and beverages usually taken at meals three hours before the Mass; from non-alcoholic beverages one hour before (*see also* Communion). The observance of this very grave ecclesiastical law does not apply in these two cases: (a) necessity of terminating the Eucharistic Sacrifice, when the priest is compelled to discontinue the Mass after the consecration; (b) special dispensation, which is within the jurisdiction of the Sacred Congregation of the Holy Office (Can. 247, par. 5).

TIME AND PLACE OF CELEBRATION. Mass may be celebrated every day except on the last three days of Holy Week. Only the priest who conducts the respective solemn function may celebrate Mass on Holy Thursday and Holy Saturday (Easter Vigil) except where privileges and customs to the contrary exist; on Good Friday a votive Mass (*de Passione Domini*) may be celebrated only when necessary for the administration of Viaticum (Can. 820).

With regard to the time of day for celebrating Mass, a priest may not begin Mass earlier than one hour before daybreak, nor later than one hour after midday (Can. 821, par. 1) except by privilege or special concession. Regular exceptions are made on (a) Christmas Eve, when a parochial Mass may start at midnight (Can. 82, par. 1), and (b) on the night between Holy Saturday and Easter Sunday (Easter Vigil).

Today, after the promulgation of the above-mentioned Constitution, local Ordinaries may allow the celebration of Holy Mass in afternoon hours, whenever special circumstances require it. By general disposition, permission may be granted on all holydays of obligation, suppressed feastdays, first Fridays of the month, solemnities observed by a large number of people apart from holydays, and on a weekday besides those named, if the spiritual welfare of a considerable number of faithful or a particular group of persons should require it.

An afternoon Mass, however, may not be started before 4:00 p.m., nor should it become a night Mass.

Mass may be celebrated in all churches and in all public and semi-public oratories (Can. 822). With permission of the Holy See (Can. 1195), Mass may be said habitually in private oratories; the local Ordinary may give permission for one or two times (Cans. 1192, 1194). In private chapels of cemeteries more than one Mass (Can. 1194) may be celebrated habitually by permission of the local Ordinary. Concerning the observance of holydays of obligation in private oratories, see Sanctification of Holydays.

Bishops or Ordinaries of exempt religious may permit the celebration of Mass in a place which is neither a church nor a chapel or even outdoors, for a reasonable and extraordinary cause (Can. 822, par. 4). Mass may be said aboard a ship, only with permission of the Holy See, obtained through the Apostolic Delegate, unless a chapel was canonically erected on the ship.

A priest may say Mass only once a day except on Christmas Day and All Souls' Day, when he is permitted to say three Masses (Can. 806, par. 1), or in cases of authorized bination and trination (see Bination, Trination).

SERVERS, AND NECESSARY FURNISHINGS. A priest must have a server to assist him at Mass and answer the prayers (Can. 813, par. 1). No girl or woman may serve Mass; however, if no male server is available, a woman may answer the prayers from outside the sanctuary (Can. 813, par. 2).

The following furnishings are required for the celebration of the Mass: *altar, chalice, paten,* and these must be consecrated by a bishop; *three altar cloths, amice, alb, cincture, maniple, stole, chasuble, corporal* and *pall,* all of which are given a special blessing; *purificator, veil, burse,* Missal, *crucifix,* two *candles, finger towel,* for which no blessing is required (*see* Sacred Vessels, Chalice, Candles, Cross, Sacred Vestments). For the rubrics of the Mass, *see* Rubrics. The small cruets for wine and water are considered accessory furnishings.

OBLIGATION OF ASSISTING AT MASS. Those who have reached the age of discretion (seven years of age) are obliged to attend Holy Mass on Sundays and holydays of obligation. This is a grave obligation. In order to satisfy the obligation, the following are required: physical presence with the intention to offer a religious act, that is, to honor God by assisting at Mass; at least some thought of God during the Mass or of things which refer to God; abstinence from anything inconsistent with the proper manner of assisting at Mass, such as sleeping, reading a secular book, turning one's attention to things that have no relation to God or to the Mass, and speaking of worldly things. The faithful must assist at the entire Mass; failure to assist at the whole Mass is seriously or lightly sinful depending on the particular part of the Mass omitted. Theologians maintain that it is a venial sin to omit the part before the Gospel or that which immediately follows Communion. If one omits a noteworthy part of the Mass, he is generally obliged to make it up by assisting at that part in another Mass, but the Consecration and Communion must be parts of the same Mass. Physical impossibility, considerable discomfort, or damage resulting to oneself or others may excuse from the obligation (*see* Sanctification of the Lord's Day).

COROLLARIES. It is beneficial to assist often at Holy Mass with a real participation in the Holy Sacrifice. If a person is unable to assist at weekday Mass, he should at least join mentally in the celebration of the Mass. With the aid of grace obtained through Holy Mass, one should endeavor to put into practice generously the offering made of oneself at the Mass and to unite the sacrifice of oneself to the sacrifice of

Christ. The practice of faith and Christian conduct offer abundant opportunities for doing this. *Man.*

MASSES, FUNDED. Funded masses are those whose alms are obtained from the revenue of pious foundations and whose number and other stipulations are specified in the foundation statutes (Can. 826, par. 3). For the meaning of pious foundation, *see* Foundation, pious.

The Ordinary has the right for parochial churches of exempt religious, and the major superior has the right for non-parochial church of exempt clerical religious, to determine the constitution of an endowment, the distribution of revenue, and the investment of capital.

Besides the book of manual Masses (*q.v.*) and a copy of the foundation agreement (*tabulae fundationis*), the rector of the church must keep a book of funded Masses. A summary of the statutes of the pious foundation shall be kept in every church (Cans. 1548, 1549, 1550).

The beneficiary, the rector of the Church, or whoever is canonically bound by the obligation of satisfying manual Masses, is accountable for the celebration of these Masses, according to the number and the terms indicated in the foundation statutes. Unless otherwise stated, the obligation is not personal but real; thus, the beneficiary may commission another priest, and must do so, if for a good reason he is unable to celebrate. On the other hand, if the obligation is personal, the beneficiary is not required to commission another, if by reason of a sickness of less than two months, a short journey, or a retreat, he is unable to say the Masses. In case of substitution, the beneficiary is not, strictly speaking, bound to give his substitute more than a regular stipend fixed by diocesan regulations (*Missae ad instar manualium*), unless different terms were specified by the founder (Can. 840, par. 2).

COMMUTATION. Unless the Ordinary was expressively given the faculty by a founder to commute or reduce the obligation, any commutation or reduction of funded Masses is reserved to the Holy See (Can. 1517, par. 1). The Ordinary can for a reasonable motive diminish other obligations (cf. Can. 1551, par. 2; AAS 14 [1922], 529). With the exception of faculties concerning autonomous legacies, contained in the quinquennial faculties, the Holy See does not generally grant the faculty of reducing the number of Masses, although it may do so in individual cases for justifiable reasons (cf. Decree of the Sacred Congregation of Council, June 30, 1949; AAS, 41 [1949], 374).

If the revenue becomes completely exhausted without fault on the part of the one who had the obligation of saying the funded Masses, he is released from such an obligation; this obligation revives if the property becomes productive again. However, for all practical purposes, the extinction of the obligation of celebrating Masses must be so decreed by the Holy See.

The stipends of funded Masses which should have been offered in the course of the year but which remained unsatisfied as of December 31, shall be turned over to the local Ordinary. *Pal.*

MASSES, GREGORIAN. A cycle of thirty Masses said on thirty successive days for the repose of a soul are called Gregorian Masses (*tricenarius gregorianus*). St. Gregory the Great is regarded as the founder of this devout practice which is considered implicitly approved by the Church.

As related by St. Gregory the Great in his *Dialogues* (1, IV, chap. 55: PL 77, 420–421), the prior Precious obtained by this practice the release from purgatory of the soul of the monk Justus. Followed at Cluny, the practice was never rejected by the Church, which condemned exaggerations connected with it (Benedict XIV, *Institutiones ecclesiasticae*, XXXIV, n. 22; Holy Office, March 17, 1934). The Sacred Congregation of Indulgences (March 15, 1884) declared a pious devotion a belief by the faithful which held that the same effect was obtained by the celebration of only one Mass at the altar of the Church of St. Gregory at the Celio as by the celebration of Gregorian Masses.

It is not necessary that all the thirty Masses be Requiem Masses, even if they be permitted by the rubrics, nor that all Masses be celebrated by the same priest. The only requirement is that the thirty Masses be celebrated on thirty consecutive days. In case of interruption due to culpable negligence, the cycle must be resumed from the beginning. In a case of interruption caused by a legitimate impediment, one may request the Sacred Congregation of the Council or the Sacred Penitentiary, through one's confessor, that the number be made up by the Sovereign Pontiff from the treasury of the Church, if the obligation has no relevance in the external forum. The series is not interrupted by circumstances attendant upon the last three days of Holy Week. *Man.*

MASSES, MANUAL. Masses said for the intention of the one who gives an offering or stipend are called manual Masses (Can. 826, par. 1). Quasi-manual Masses (*ad instar manualium*) are funded Masses given to others to be said (Can. 826, par. 2).

A priest must say one Mass for each stipend received (Can. 828, Denz. 1110). If the stipend was given for several Masses without specifying the number, the priest shall say as many Masses as their sum allows by alloting for each Mass the stipend established by diocesan regulations of the place where the donor resides, unless the donor designated otherwise. No priest may accept more Mass intentions than he can personally say within the year (Can. 835); the rule also applies to religious communities, where the superior may not accept more intentions than his dependents can say within a year (Can. 836–837), unless the donor consents to the acceptance of a greater number of Masses than the canonical rule allows. The obligation of saying the Masses

remains even if the stipend or stipends are lost.

The Mass or Masses must be said within the time explicitly or approximately indicated by the donor; if the time is left to the discretion of the priest, they must be celebrated within a relatively short time (Can. 834); in all cases, within a year. The quasi-manual Masses must be said by the last day of December of the respective year (Can. 841, par. 2).

The priest must observe not only the circumstances of time but also the other conditions stipulated by the donor. *See also* Holy Mass; Mass Stipend. *Pal.*

MASS STIPEND. A Mass stipend is an offering which a donor gives to a priest with the stipulation that the ministerial fruits of the Mass be applied for a designated person or purpose. The stipend is, not a payment for the fruits of the Mass, but a contribution for the support of the priest. Such a practice cannot be called simony since the priest has a real right to support from the faithful for whom he applies the fruits of the sacrifice. This is confirmed by the words of St. Paul (I Cor. 9:7–13), and sanctioned by Can. 824, which permits the celebrant to accept a stipend for the application of the Mass.

In the early times of the Church, all the faithful assisting at Mass offered bread and wine. Out of this the priest consecrated as much as he deemed necessary and divided the remnant between the clergy and the poor. The celebrant then applied the Mass for all the donors, all of whom generally received Holy Communion. After the seventh century, offerings diminished; instead of bread and wine, some began to donate a certain sum of money. This donation was given before or after the Mass with the intention that the Mass be applied in a special way for them. The main reason for the contribution, however, was always the support of the priest.

The stipend given and accepted gives rise to a contract between the donor and the priest. By virtue of this contract the priest must either apply the Mass for the intention specified by the donor or return the stipend. Failure on the part of the priest to do this is a violation of justice and a serious sin, since he would be depriving the donor of spiritual benefits and would be contravening the law of the Church. In order to fulfill this obligation, the priest must observe all the conditions imposed by the donor concerning time, place, type of Mass, etc. He must apply as many Masses as he has received stipends, no matter what the amount is. He may not accept the stipend if the Mass is already obligated. The priest who binates or trinates may accept a stipend for only one of the Masses, except on the feast of Christmas, when he is permitted to take a stipend for each of the three Masses he may say (Canons 825, 828, 834).

The amount of the stipend may be determined either by a decree of the local Ordinary, by a synodal statute, or by custom. In any case, all priests in the diocese are bound by the diocesan regulation. Hence, it is forbidden under pain of sin for a priest to demand a larger stipend. A larger stipend, however, may be requested by reason of some extrinsic title, e.g., for a High Mass or for a Mass to be said at a late hour or in a distant place. The priest is permitted to accept a larger stipend if freely offered by the faithful, just as he may agree to take a stipend smaller than the one established. The acceptance of a smaller stipend, however, can be prohibited by the Bishop (Can. 832). Needless to say, the priest is always bound to apply as many Masses as he has accepted stipends. *Toc.*

MASTER OF NOVICES. *See* Novice, Novitiate.

MASTURBATION. *See* Onanism.

MATERIALISM. Materialism, as a philosophical theory, explains the origin and nature of the universe solely by the existence and nature of matter. Materialism which terms matter the complete, final and basic explanation of the universe, through mechanistic or biological theories, is called *mechanism or biologism.* A materialism based on pleasure and self-interest as the only motive or guide of human behavior is called *practical materialism.* A materialism which explains all manifestations in human life, politics, law, morality, and religion from the economic organization of society is called *historical materialism;* this theory is best known today as Marxism. Any doctrine which aims at oversimplification of the facts, through the explanation of history by only one of the elements of human life, is basically false. The reality of life is more complex than that. Historical data consist in a variety of elements and factors, which progress through a complicated intricacy of actions and reactions always in activity and always in variable degrees. This exaggerated value of the economic factor, not only a philosophical and historical error, becomes a dangerous seed, which makes the so-called social question more acute and class struggle increasingly violent, after it has been introduced into the mind of the masses. All forms of materialism are immoral, for they imply or lead inevitably to a denial of God, the soul, freedom of the will, and the sense of obligation. *Gra.*

MATERIALISM, DIALECTICAL. *See* Communism, Materialism.

MATERIALISM, HISTORICAL. *See* Communism, Materialism.

MATERNITY. *Maternity* designates a woman's primary function of child-bearing, for which she is predisposed by moral, physical, and psychological qualities as well as by a special natural inclination. For, as a procreator, the mother is endowed with an intense love toward her offspring. This love, instinctive in animal life, is capable of elevation to a virtue in a woman, if she practices it rationally.

Literature and art present maternal love as the most exalted form of love for one's neighbor, which is capable of the highest degrees of heroism (*see* *Iliad*, 28, 4; Cicero, *Epist.* 9, 20, 3; and *De Oratore* 2, 227; Horace, *Carmina* 4, 5, 10, and *Epist.* 1, 18, 20 ff.). In Sacred Scripture maternal love is spoken of as a typical love (II Sam. 1:26; Eccl. 15:2); the role of maternity is called the purest, crowning joy of all sacrifice (Sol. 112:9; John 16:21). Insults against one's mother are said to call down God's curse upon the offender (Eccl. 3:18; Matt. 15:4); God Himself uses the image of a mother's love for her children to indicate His own love for mankind (Eccl. 15:2; Is. 49:15; 66:13).

In the Christian religion motherhood enjoys a dignity and respect far superior to that of other religions. Maternal love, as well as paternal and filial love, is for a Christian a share of the love of God, who planted the seed of love in human nature.

Although a mother does not share equal authority with the father, to whom she is subject, she deserves equal respect and dignity, with equal right to the obedience and affection of her children. Apart from the right to affection and respect from her children, a mother shares with the father duties and obligations of love, support, education, and training.

Special duties are imposed by nature on a mother; these extend from the time of conception to the period after parturition. These are evident from physiological changes which maternity occasions during pregnancy. These duties center on the three important phases of the child's existence: in the womb, at birth, and in the period of nursing.

With regard to the period of the child's life in the womb, much is said under the articles "Abortion" and "Embryotomy" about the crimes which a mother might commit through failure in her duties and vocation as an expectant mother. These duties demand an heroic spirit and the acceptance of the sacrifice of her own life, if necessary, to save a newborn child (*see* Childbirth, Accelerated). Further duties arise after the birth of the child, which initiate the gradual fostering of independence and growth under the assistance and guidance of the parents.

Whether the child is legitimate or illegitimate, the same biological conditions prevail for the mother. Her psychological state varies, however; a ready acceptance welcomes the legitimate child into an established order and home, whereas the illegitimate child remains apart from this, considered an intruder or an enemy, at least until its birth. Though such a psychological attitude is quite understandable, it cannot be justified, not even if the woman becomes a mother against her will or as the result of a violent assault. For this attitude is contrary to the primary duty of a mother toward her offspring: love.

In accord with the order of nature, the unwed mother ought to keep her child and give it her name. This not only aids the offspring, but frequently rehabilitates the mother (*see* Exposition of Infants). In the moral order the first principle to be borne in mind is that, once the wrong has occurred, every possible way must be found to avoid an abnormal social and legal stigma that might unduly harm the innocent child. Moreover, though the natural father and mother share equal responsibility (at times, the responsibility weighs more heavily upon the man), the mother is still by nature more intimately united to the fruit of her womb, not only until the birth of the child but thereafter. The mother should be encouraged, therefore, to accept her responsibility intelligently, and assistance should be provided when necessary. This must be the guiding principle for social workers to the extent that any help given or promised to an unwed mother should be directed to preventing any harmful action affecting herself or her child. This assistance, however, must not be viewed as an approval or condonation of her behavior.

MATERNITY, ADOPTIVE. *See* Affinity, Consanguinity.

MATINS. *See* Breviary; Choir; Divine Office.

MATTER, SACRAMENTAL. *See* Sacraments.

MATTER, SINFUL. *See* Sin.

MEANS, NECESSITY OF. *See* Necessity of Means, of Precept.

MEDAL. The use of medals is very ancient. In the ancient pagan world, Gentiles used to wear medals with an effigy of their own sovereign; in the course of the centuries, Roman Pontiffs have coined medals to commemorate particularly solemn events, as the Holy Year, the elevation to the pontifical throne, the canonization of saints.

The custom of wearing religious medals around the neck out of devotion or for protection goes back to the third century. The practice of blessing religious medals to be worn by the faithful began around 1566, at the beginning of the pontificate of St. Pius V, when sedition and plots were started in Flanders by heretics (called *Geusi* or *Gheusi*) who had made common cause with the Huguenots. In order to distinguish themselves from Catholics, they began to wear a medal around the neck. On one side of the medal was the image of their king, Philip II of Spain, with the motto *Fidèles au roi* (loyal to the King); on the other side a bag was held by two hands connected together with the words *Jusque à la besace*, in reference to the nickname of the *Geusi* or beggars, which was applied to them.

However, Duke Arescott opposed such a sect and coined another gold medal bearing the image of the Madonna with Child, which he attached to the braid of his hat. His example was followed by all true Catholics of the region. To foster devotion among the people, St. Pius V blessed such a medal and granted an indulgence to all those who wore it. This practice rapidly spread among the faithful.

In order that a medal may be blessed and indulgenced, the following requirements are prescribed: (a) It must be of durable material but not necessarily of gold, silver, bronze or other metal; it suffices that it be made of unbreakable material, such as plastic. (b) It must represent the image of a canonized saint or one mentioned in the approved martyrology. However, medals bearing on one side the image of a saint and on the other the representation of a blessed may be indulgenced, as well as medals bearing on one side the image of a saint and on the other that of an illustrious man, the supreme pontiff, or the reproduction of a shrine (*Decr. auth.*, n. 32). (c) It must be blessed with the appropriate formula and by a priest who has the necessary faculty.

The principal religious medals are the miraculous medal and the medal of St. Benedict.

(a) The *miraculous* medal, so-called because of extraordinary favors obtained through its use, originated from a vision that St. Catherine Labouré, a sister of the Daughters of Charity of St. Vincent de Paul, had in 1833. During this vision, our Lady appeared as she is represented on the medal: radiant, with her arms turned toward the earth and her open hands shining with rays, and her feet trodding upon the head of the serpent. The invocation reads: *O Mary, conceived without sin, pray for us who have recourse to thee.* On the reverse side of the medal there is the name of Mary surmounted by the cross, with the Hearts of Jesus and Mary under it, the former crowned with thorns, the latter pierced by a sword. This medal became very popular during the pontificate of Pope Gregory XVI. The Roman Pontiffs have enriched it with several indulgences;

(b) The medal of St. Benedict is twofold: *ordinary* and *jubilarian*. The ordinary was common since the sixth century but acquired its greatest popularity in the eleventh century, following the miraculous cure of the young Bruno of Egisheim-Dagsburg, who later became Pope Leo IX (1049–1054). On one side there is the image of St. Benedict holding a small cross in his hand, and on the other a larger cross with some letters having a symbolical meaning. Pope Benedict XIV enriched it with numerous indulgences (*Decr. Auth. ed. Prinziavalli*, App., p. 8). The jubilarian medal was coined in 1880 by the Abbot Ordinary of Monte Cassino, on the occasion of the fourteenth centenary of the birth of Saint Benedict. The faithful who wear this medal may gain, in addition to the indulgences granted for the ordinary medal, many others granted by the Supreme Pontiffs Pius IX and St. Pius X. *de A.*

MEDIANISM. *See* Medium.

MEDICINE. *Medicine is not only the art of curing man,* as generally defined, but also, to a large extent, a *science*. According to an ancient and wise aphorism, the duty of a physician is to treat, not necessarily to cure; in fact, a cure is primarily a gift of God; from the standpoint of secondary causes, a cure is the happy result of a series of biological events which in great part escape the power of control of the physician. Thus, medicine could be defined as the science of physical health and sickness in man, and the art of preserving the health and curing diseases.

HISTORICAL NOTES. The origins of medicine are lost in the shades of time. In fact, every attempt to soothe pain or repair damage caused by sickness, whether of known or unknown origin, comes within the range of medicine; such attempts obviously were instinctive to the first men, and thus make medicine contemporaneous with humanity. Examples of instinctive medicine abound even among animals: they disinfect wounds with saliva, lower fever by plunging into water, destroy skin parasites, pick shrewdly among many herbs proper remedies for their discomforts, etc.

In a later period, in ignorance and superstition, primitive people thought that contagious diseases were caused by mysterious or evil spirits; thus, medicine became magic in which people were concerned above all with identifying the cause of diseases and suggesting the most suitable means (amulets, etc.) to avoid or cure them with formulas and special rites. The intention was always to placate a deity or drive away an evil spirit. Present-day medicine among savages is a faithful reproduction of primitive medicine; strong remnants are found even among beliefs of popular medicine in our times, as students of so-called medical folklore will testify.

In this second stage or era of magic, the personality of the physician assumed great importance and an essential sacredness in the community because he was believed to be in contact with the deified forces of nature. This gave rise to a caste, very jealous of its functions, composed, for the most part, of individuals who handed down their magic secrets from father to son. We have many examples of this in uncivilized populations of today, among whom the bewitcher has a sacred character and transmits his art by a natural or spiritual heredity.

With the progress of civilization, a third stage developed which could be called the modern or experimental stage of medicine. Man began to know and to appreciate the use of medicinal plants and other substances found in nature. The intrinsic therapeutic value of practices initially suggested by magical arts, as baths and diets, gained recognition; the role of the physician, as a student of diseases and the physical means of treatment, gradually became detached from that of magician or miracle worker with which it had been associated before.

It would be too long to trace, even briefly, the vicissitudes and progress of medicine among the ancient civilized peoples. It suffices to recall, with Jastrow, that the progress of medicine has always occurred by leaps or sudden explosions, as it were, that blast a rigid pre-existing structure into fragments. In the wave of enthusiasm created by these discoveries, progress followed until an understandable desire for stabilization arrested the influence of innovations.

Medicine became fixed in rigid methods, different from the preceding ones but equally sterile and unproductive. This remained until a new and fortunate combination of great minds and favorable circumstances ushered in another fruitful era of discovery.

History records two great epochs in the progress of medicine. The first began around the sixth century B.C. and reached its apex with the school of Hippocrates (see Oath, Hippocratic). This school asserted for the first time that to diagnose a sickness one must observe the individual with a critical spirit, immune from preconceptions, and study the morbid symptoms with diligence. Successively, through the work of the school of Alexandria and the Greco-Roman civilization, physiology, pharmacology, and obstetrics developed until the time of Galen, after Hippocrates the most renowned physician of ancient times, who made notable contributions to medicine. His work was the basic reference book of medicine throughout the long and unproductive standstill in medicine that lasted nearly fifteen hundred years. In fact, his systematic attempt to record every phenomenon and answer every query crystallized into a doctrinal body of medical knowledge which, for all the appreciated values bestowed upon it by posterity, still hindered further progress until the period of the Renaissance.

The second period of expansion had its beginning in the sixteenth century, with a select group of scholars who attracted the flower of European intellects to the illustrious universities of that period.

RAMIFICATIONS. In recent times the rapid progress achieved by medicine, characterized by the quality and increase of technical research aimed at every possible aspect of serious illness, has made it practically impossible for the student to apply himself to the mastery of the entire field of medicine. To become an expert in every field is out of the question; thus the work of specialization is indispensable.

Omitting branches of medicine which concentrate on the study of special systems or apparatuses of the human organism, we shall mention special aspects of modern medicine directed at the safeguarding of the psychosomatic welfare of the general populace.

Special functions of contemporary medicine, with specialization and the creation of appropriate research institutes and therapeutic centers of treatment, involve the care of definite classes of individuals with special rules and therapeutic approaches. To mention a few, there is the aspect of medicine for the school, for work, military, naval, aviational, colonial, missionary, and insurance medical services. In view of their particular impact on morality and the general social welfare, these are dealt with in separate articles. Social medicine, which in a sense is a summary of all of these services, is treated quite extensively under the heading of social diseases (q.v.).

THE MODERN PHYSICIAN. The status of the physician was basically uniform until a few decades ago. In the position of mastering all the doctrine of the medical art, according to his learning and ability, he conveniently took care of every type of illness. The noble and gentle role of the family physician flourished in which gradually the doctor became the esteemed counsellor for every illness or vicissitude in the small communities in which he labored. The physician of the past was adequately versed in the branches of medicine, as hygienist, psychologist, obstetrician, internist, pediatrician, and gerontologist.

Because of the enormous progress made by medical science and the increased demands of his clientele, this type of physician is no longer in vogue today. A faint resemblance may be found in the so-called general practitioner who, endowed with particular experience in internal medicine and the possession of a general knowledge of various specializations, continues to assist his patients in various emergencies, but is ready at all times to advise specialists and hospital treatment as soon as prudence demands it.

The changed demands of medicine justify and require that the thick network of general practitioners, who remain the backbone of the medical profession, should be supported by a larger number of specialists, with further groups of physicians skilled in the fields of social medicine.

Medicine is a science and an art. As an objective and universal *science*, medicine pursues extensive research and constant study of cases in laboratories, surgical operations, and at the bedside of the ill. As an *art*, medicine involves psychological skill, by which the physician gains the confidence of a patient in carrying out prescriptions and suggestions. In addition to science and skills, a Catholic physician should always be guided by an active Christian charity, a sense of affectionate understanding, constant sacrifice, generous altruism, true and total dedication to suffering humanity, without which science is sterile and art degraded to the level of mystifying witchcraft.

This shall be attained if a physician recalls the maxim of Schleich (1859–1942), the inventor of modern local anesthesia: "If you give advice to a sick person, consider it as given to yourself. Measure your suggestions according to your own feelings. What you do not wish done on your body, do not do to the body of others. Think of yourself as in the place of the sick; only this kind of hypochondria has value."

Equipped with these altruistic intentions, joined to an adequate preparation and stable personality, the physician may be truly a follower of Christ, the supreme Physician of bodies and souls, as St. Luke so well describes Him. He shall bring luster to the noble medical art, the practice of which is a true mission, second only to that of the priest.

In the article on psychosomatic medicine, we shall treat in greater detail important ethical implications of the more recent theoretical and therapeutic developments of modern medicine. Relevant medico-moral problems, medical deontology, experiments on man, medical visits, professional secret of physicians, etc., are dealt with under other entries. *Riz.*

MEDICINE, AVIATION. Aviation medicine is a branch of medicine concerned with the selection and health of fliers and the employment of aviation to various medical services.

Following a period of growth from an individual, pioneering phase, aviation became increasingly important as a means of transportation in government and private industry. Stress has been put on the proper selection of pilots, for the cause of many air disasters is found to be in the physical or psychomatic deficiences of the pilots. The rate of accidents has been reduced with the adoption of special methods of examination and selection of pilots. Regulations for recruiting civil and military pilots have assumed a more restrictive character in recent years due to the fact that increasingly faster and more powerful aircraft are being built for flights of much greater distances and altitudes.

The selection of pilots is based on two main considerations: (1) physical and psychological fitness and (2) psychotechnical aptitudes. The first is a negative function which eliminates those who show deficiencies, weaknesses, or organic functional disorders of a type that would interfere with proper flying ability. The latter has a positive role in selecting candidates who possess the greatest aptitudes required for flying.

Consequently, the selection of pilots is the most arduous task of aviation medicine. Lesser restrictions may govern the selection of other flight personnel, yet travelling service personnel for civil aviation are to be carefully chosen with particular reference to the special tasks assigned to them.

The employment of aviation for the prompt rescue of the seriously wounded or ill was carried out in the First World War, chiefly by the French, and later in colonial areas for the prompt removal of the sick from deserted areas where slow and inadequate means of transportation exist.

During the Second World War aviation was utilized for medical purposes by the armed forces and the International Red Cross, as medical or surgical ambulances, for first aid, medical supplies, sanitation purposes, and the transfer of the wounded to military or civilian hospitals for further necessary treatments.

Among more recent applications of aviation medicine, helicopters and the use of radio, especially in collaboration with the International Radio-Medical Center, provide medical assistance to ships at sea or to the inhabitants of small islands. The health of modern aviators, subjected as they are to the limits of psychological endurance, may incur a variety of disturbances and be subject to early deterioration. The causes and treatment of these constitute a fundamental aspect of aviation medicine which we shall treat of here in its essential elements.

Excessive acceleration, great, frequent and rapid changes in altitude, the effects of noise, vibration, temperature changes and long flights according to rigid, fixed schedules without regard for weather conditions are among the numerous causes of illnesses among fliers. Such conditions not only act on the organic structure of the pilot, especially the vegetative-nervous system, but also exert a damaging influence on their general psychic well-being.

The damages inflicted on their personality and general psychological welfare will be proportionately more premature and grave according to the increased frequency of fatigue, protracted emotional tensions, or similar occupational diseases and hazards.

Any tendency to neuropsychical weaknesses should be thoroughly investigated by diligent examinations at the time of the selection of pilots, since these are frequent causes of sudden failures with possible tragic consequences for others because of aeroneuroses that exhaust the resistance of those affected.

Its growing importance has prompted us to dwell on aviation medicine at length despite the lack of particularly grave ethical problems connected with this field. Ordinary medical deontology offers solutions to general medical problems.

Although planes are the most vicious instruments of death created by mankind, they may be useful instruments of good, particularly in regions far removed from inhabited areas of the world. With the aid of medicine, aviation thus fulfills somewhat the aspirations of its pioneers, who intended the invention of the airplane to be an instrument of progress for civilization. *Riz.*

MEDICINE, COLONIAL. *Colonial medicine* is a term applied to a branch of medicine concerned with diseases found to be characteristic of or prevalent in underdeveloped lands. The name is derived from the fact that such diseases were observed and studied especially in countries colonized by white settlers. Since these lands are chiefly located in tropical or sub-tropical zones of the globe, colonial medicine is also termed *tropical pathology* or *tropical medicine*.

In describing their voyages in ancient times, explorers never failed to point out bizarre or unusual diseases observed in these remote lands, but their allusions, mingled in with geographical, ethnographic, or biological reports of every kind, contained no real clinical or scientific value.

The first scientific treaties on tropical medicine, dating from the seventeenth century, are the work of physicians and naturalists who were attracted to these lands by the need for their services or a love of research. An Englishman, named Lind, published the first treatise on tropical pathology in 1768; the others, which followed, were dominated by an essentially clinical and descriptive character. At the end of the last century, with the discovery of pathogenic microorganisms, pathological anatomy, and parasitology, colonial medicine became the object of renewed interest and scientific studies; these reached a peak in the years 1900 to 1915. Rising colonial expansion led teams of clinical specialists, pathologists, hygienists, pharmacologists, veterinarians, naturalists, serologists and others to tireless labor in laboratories throughout the tropical countries. The discovery and study of the etiological agents in diseases led to the initiation of scientific studies to cure these diseases, a development which gave rise to the great schools of tropical and colonial pathology in London, Hamburg and Paris. Special periodicals and university professorships firmly established this branch of medicine as an autonomous area of specialization.

The principal diseases with which colonial medicine is concerned are the following: diseases caused by anthropoids (myiasis, etc.), by vermin (filariasis, bilharzia, etc.), by protozoa (malaria, sleeping sickness, etc.), by spirochetes (sodoku, bronchospirochetosis, etc.), by bacteria (plague, cholera, leprosy, etc.), by ultraviruses (smallpox, etc.), by mushrooms (dermatomosis, etc.), by poisonous animals and plants, by malnutrition (beriberi, etc.), by sickness or nervous infirmities characteristic of warm countries. Colonial medicine also studies the areas of distribution, contagious character, pathogenesis, prophylaxis, and therapy of the various tropical diseases.

If medicine is the healthful art of healing, it is also the apostolate of charity par excellence, particularly in the underdeveloped areas of the world. Those who practice in distant lands among primitive peoples are looked upon by the astonished populations as representatives of the divinity. This imposes on the physician a special discipline of the senses and mind; for good example and moral uprightness can contribute effectively to the progress of these civilizations on the road to a better life, whereas the opposite lack of these qualities can cause serious harm to this progress.

One particular aspect of colonial medicine interests Catholic morality in a special manner: namely, the important services in the spiritual, cultural, and practical order which this field of science brings to the religious mission. *Riz.*

MEDICINE, LEGAL. Legal medicine is a branch of medical science which operates within the field of legal problems and question; this discipline deals with a variety of biological, medical, or surgical problems related to the development of the juridical or social questions encountered in judiciary proceedings.

Legal medicine has a twofold task: one, primarily theoretical, which consists in collaboration with the ethico-juridical system through its own medical and biological studies; the other, primarily practical, consists of the application of scientific knowledge and progress in the establishment of definite facts, aimed at shedding light on justice in various controversies; these constitute the scientific and technical aspects of an investigation.

In the thirteenth century, medicine and law were united for the first time in the development of Canon Law, the beginnings of modern medical investigations. The opinion of legal and medical experts was expressly required by an ordinance of Pope Innocent III (1209) to discover, in a particular case, which of many injuries had been the fatal one. Hugo of Lucca was authorized officially to give medico-legal opinions under oath in his capacity of what would be called today the health officer of Bologna.

In the sixteenth century, the first systematic development of legal medicine was contributed by the Sicilians D'Allessandro, Ingrassia, and Fedele.

The subjects dealt with in legal medicine are numerous and diversified. We shall mention here the principal and more important ones. (a) *Legal psychopathology*: a preliminary examination of the human personality, and extreme cases of mental disturbances insofar as they affect the ability to understand, will, and act in relation to juridical decisions. (b) *Legal traumatology*: the study of physical, chemical, and biodynamical determinisms in their various forms and consequences. (c) *Legal thanatology*: a consideration of the changes that occur in a corpse, prescinding from all inquiries concerning the cause of death. (d) *Legal necroscopy*: the techniques of judiciary autopsy and proofs directed at discovering whether an infant corpse has lived an autonomous life. This is done by a study of the changes that occur in the respiratory functions of a newborn child. (e) *Legal hematology*: the various medical and legal problems in which the expert in hematology investigates the nature of bloodstained items to identify the nature of the blood, the date of its formation as a stain, etc. This is done by a delicate, laborious investigation of a micro-crystallographic, morphological, biological, or spectroscopical order. Spermatic spots may also be subjected to investigations in particular cases before a jury. (f) *Identification*. The identification of race, sex, profession, as well as the personal identification based on the examination of physiognomy and fingerprints are frequently required in legal matters; individuals may be identified on the basis of an examination of separated limbs, skeletal remains, or dental structures.

Medicine in the useful and important role of insurance payments is treated in a separate article.

Legal medicine is also concerned with the various types of reports which the physician is required to make either voluntarily or by disposition of a competent authority. Legal medicine provides rules and methods of compiling these reports of great significance to authority. Among them are records of births, statements of deaths, abortions, deformed infants, injuries involving permanent disability for work, therapeutic treatments apt to cause sterility in women (hysterectomy, bilateral ovariotomy, sterilizing radiotherapy), infectious diseases, professional diseases, accidents, dangerous mental illnesses, chronic alcoholism, vaccinations, etc. At times medical reports requiring a specific competence for their proper ascertainment of facts may be requested of a physician by a canonical or civil magistrate or court.

The physician in legal medicine must have a high degree of professional ability, as well as ethical standards for the proper functioning of justice; diligent care must be employed in the selection of physicians particularly competent in the field in which the medical inquiry is conducted. These experts must show objectivity, exact skill and impartiality in their reports. *Riz.*

MEDICINE, MILITARY. The presence of physicians among fighting troops is of ancient origin; we find mention of them among the Egyptians in the narratives of Diodorus Siculus and Xenophon, where it is said that State-paid physicians had the responsibility of collecting the wounded in battle onto wagons. Among the Roman armies this reached greater importance, for every legion and warship had a physician of officer's rank with exemption from fighting or guard duties. Also military hospitals were set up for the wounded and prisoners of war. There is depicted on the sixth turn of the Column of Trajan a first aid station for the wounded.

The advent of Christianity brought about a change in warfare, for it ceased to be the indiscriminate extermination of individuals; furthermore, progressively more benevolent sentiments developed toward victims of conflict as hospitals and aid for the victims of war flourished. The merchants from Amalfi founded in Jerusalem a hospital dedicated to Saint John the Baptist at the time of the Crusades, where the Knights of Jerusalem had the task of aiding and treating the victims of combat.

The sixteenth century saw a new impulse given to military medicine, for, with the spread of firearms and a modernization in the art of war, the extraction of bullets, the treatment of wounds caused by explosions, as well as amputations and trepanations became new and more perfect means of saving lives.

The constitution of a proper medical military corps became a reality two centuries later. A method of recruiting medical personel was fixed, and their tasks in peace and war established; Napoleon Bonaparte, assisted by his excellent medical physicians, improved these services and established the custom of bringing ambulances and hospitals close to the field of battle, so that first aid came to the wounded instead of waiting for the wounded to be brought to it.

In peacetime, military medicine performs two main tasks: (a) it protects the health of the troops; and (b) it studies, allocates, and prepares everything necessary in the personal and technical areas for the exigencies caused by the eventual entry of a nation into war. In time of civil emergencies, like floods, earthquakes, and epidemics, the military health services are accustomed to put their resources of men and material at the disposal of the area or country faced with emergency.

In wartime, military medicine provides medical services for the maintenance of the health of combat forces, the gathering, treatment and removal from the battlefield of the wounded; it provides in thoroughly equipped field hospitals an immediate treatment of the severely wounded. This service also performs the work of sanitation to prevent the spread of contagious epidemics throughout an army. In short, it cooperates in alleviating the toll of war in the front lines and at home.

In some countries, besides the Red Cross, private organizations are sponsored to help the country in emergencies. The best known and perhaps oldest of these is the Sovereign Military Order of Malta, whose origin dates back to the Knights of Jerusalem. The emergency organization which is most effective is the National and International Red Cross. The origin of this organization is of recent date, although the centuries have witnessed many individuals (St. Camillus de Lellis, St. Vincent de Paul, Count De Stair, G. Pringle, Florence Nightingale, etc.) who never ceased in their efforts to help the victims of war. Individual efforts were not enough, so that the representatives of the twenty-six countries meeting at Geneva signed a pact on August 22, 1864, for the creation of the International Association of the Red Cross with the symbolic emblem of a red cross on a white field (reversed colors of the Swiss flag). Turkey, for religious reasons, adopted the red crescent instead of the cross symbol.

Corollaries. Considering the numerous and varied duties of the military physician for the protection of the health of the armed forces and, consequently, for the welfare of the nation, the need for notable ability, scholarly knowledge and administrative skill is obvious, since the health of an army or nation might depend on these qualities. The moral qualities of the physician stand out most clearly on the field of battle, where in the midst of dangers he serenely performs his humane work, which can be nobly compared to that of the military chaplains.

Proud of its noble mission, military medicine opposes with justice any attempt to limit the humane efforts of the physician toward an enemy. Were these attempts, openly opposed to mercy, able to succeed, they would deal a severe blow to the humanitarian and Christian principles that influenced and inspired the Geneva Convention and thus effectively mitigated the damages of recent conflicts. The determined resolution by all physicians to provide only works inspired by charity and professional duty is an indispensable requirement for the Charter of the International Organization of Medicine so that the art of healing may never be transformed into an instrument of vengeance and inhumanity. *Riz.*

MEDICINE, MISSIONARY. Medicine practiced by missionaries is not a special branch of medicine but constitutes a special application of particular relevance to this volume.

The missionary in distant, hostile, or altogether uncivilized mission lands ought to combine with the spiritual and cultural preparation necessary for the fulfillment of an arduous religious task, a definite knowledge of medical and surgical skills necessary for the preservation of his own life and the lives of the inhabitants of the area. This knowledge should not only be theoretical, but practical as well, especially on points of hygiene, medical treatment and minor surgery. Frequently the missionary must carry on an apostolate in lands where he must be his own physician.

HISTORICAL NOTES. The combination of priestly dignity and a knowledge, even profound, of medicine is not a novelty of our time. Prescinding from prehistoric times when one individual exercised the functions of priest and physician, the successful practice of medicine by members of religious orders is something for which the world owes a debt to Christianity. Toward the middle of the fourth century, St. Basil the Great instituted in Caesarea the famous Basiliades, which was the greatest inn and hospital of that time. In Basilian monasteries established in southern Italy, Basilian monks kept alive the flame of medical knowledge by their practice of medicine and their work of translation of Greek texts. A century later, in 529, St. Benedict wrote the famous rule of his monastic order; he prescribed that great attention be given to sick brothers and that their care be entrusted to a diligent monk (ch. 36). These religious, experienced in medical disciplines and aided by suitably instructed assistants, cultivated medicinal plants, prepared and distributed medicines, transcribed and commented on Roman and Greek medical codes, which handed down medical theories and experiments. Hospitals arose in the environs of monasteries for the treatment of the laity. Often the services of these monk-physicians were requested in homes. Later, in the great Benedictine monastic houses centers (studium) were formed where the religious were instructed in the medical sciences and assigned to smaller houses.

In the following centuries, when instruction in medicine became a prerogative of all the lay universities, priests and religious in general were required to abandon the direct practice of medicine; the mission lands alone saw remnants of this former custom of priests and religious acting as medical men.

Under present discipline, a cleric, especially a priest, is forbidden to practice medicine or surgery without an apostolic indult, since the role of a priest as a physician of souls is primary. This rule applies despite any honors or medical knowledge and skills acquired before entrance into the religious or priestly life (Can. 139). These provisions are based on the principle that a man should not be distracted from the primary work of his vocation.

In mission lands, the Church adopts a different attitude since medical assistance is sometimes non-existent and the practice of medicine can be truly an effective form of apostolate. As far as conditions permit, the missionaries are required to pursue medical training in some general area of medicine in medical schools and universities under Catholic auspices (Can. 1379, par. 2; Can. 1380).

In more recent times, by the encouragement of Pius XI, special missionary congregations and societies have been established whose members are all future medical missionaries equipped with degrees in medicine, dentistry, surgery, obstetrics, pharmacy, or tropical diseases. Outstanding among others is the *Society of Catholic Medical Missionaries* (a society of religious women) with its motherhouse in Philadelphia.

The usefulness of the study of medicine is self-evident. The missionary-physician is in a much better position to keep himself healthy and, therefore, to exercise his mission more effectively as well as to protect the health of his brethren. (It is estimated that missionary activity reduces the span of life of an individual on an average of fifteen years compared with fellow-countrymen who remain in their native lands.) In addition, he also brings great benefits to the natives by educating them to hygienico-prophylactic standards, by curing their sicknesses, and by notably prolonging and bettering their existence; thus he performs a great work of corporal mercy.

From this, enormous moral advantages contribute to a better and more rapid propagation of the faith, for the native who experiences personally the healing ability of the missionary will more readily believe in his apostolate and have confidence in him. In fact, medicine and religion are one with primitive peoples, for the healing of the sick is considered a divine work among them. The native witch-doctor loses ground irremediably before the medical missionary, for every hut receives him with grateful joy and children are voluntarily entrusted to him for religious instruction. The struggle against local superstitions and tabus less strenuous.

The usefulness of the medical missionary is attested by these figures: in 1948–49, Catholic missions operated 952 hospitals, 63 leprosaria and about 23,000 pharmaceutical dispensaries with an annual total of 685,000 bed-patients and 20,500,000 ambulatory treatments.

SELECTION OF MISSIONARIES. In view of the high rate of mortality among missionaries, due to abnormal climatic conditions, improper diet, unusual foods, fatigue, and privations of every kind, it is quite clear that the process of selection of missionaries from the standpoint of physical endurance is of great importance. It was stated at the Congress of Catholic Physicians held in Lisbon in 1947: "When we estimate both the number of years of evangelization lost by the missionaries who die young, and the enormous sums of money spent for the education and the training of all these valuable men whose time of service is cut short by premature death, we are confronted by staggering totals."

On the basis of these and similar consideration, the need was felt to establish a medical examination for young candidates to the missions in order to appraise their health in relation to future tasks. This procedure has been in force for some years in Belgium, France, and Holland; it is hoped that it will be pursued in every nation by all the religious institutes engaged in the training necessary for this apostolate.

MEDICINE, NAVAL. Naval medicine is a branch of medicine which is concerned with the hygiene, prophylaxis and treatment of those who travel on ships, whether as passengers or members of the crew, as well as the safeguarding of land populations from infections transmitted by seafarers. Naval medicine is divided into various specializations.

NAVAL HYGIENE. Naval hygiene is concerned with water supply, waste disposal, cleanliness, chemical disinfectants, and all other measures designed to assure the good health of seafarers. Ocean liners and large warships usually have one or more physicians assigned to them, with a number of nurses working under the physicians' supervision, in well-equipped stations wherein a multiplicity of pathological disturbances are treated, as seasickness (see kinetosis), first aid, accidents, maternity care and isolation of contagious persons, or even surgical operations of some importance are performed.

The *chief physician*, in addition to care of the sick, must supervise hygienic conditions aboard ship, as the technical advisor of the commandant in this regard. Special medical centers (I.R.M.C.—International Radio Medical Center) have existed in every civilized nation for some years, to receive from ships radio signals concerning particularly serious clinical cases and to transmit appropriate information for the best treatment of these persons. Through such practical consultations many lives have been saved. Aerial first aid centers, equipped with sea-planes and helicopters, are used to pick up from ships on the high seas and from small islands without adequate medical assistance particularly serious and urgent cases requiring special hospital care. In naval warfare there must be adequate ships for the transport home of the sick and the wounded.

MORAL CONCLUSIONS. The particular conditions in which ship physicians must practice their profession require that they be possessed of uncommon technico-scientific ability and solid morality. A ship physician, especially if alone, is the only person responsible for the health of all aboard the ship; he must always be able to face the most diversified problems of pathology without the benefit of the advice of specialists, hospital laboratories, or the like. However, the relatively short duration of modern voyages, due to the increased speed of the ships, and the possibility of consulting with specialists by radio have reduced in some measure these responsibilities, but, despite all, they still remain quite notable.

The general deontological and moral norms followed on land apply also in the navy, merchant marine, etc. For these, see **Deontology, Medical; Visiting; Secret, Professional.** *Riz.*

MEDICINE, PASTORAL. Pastoral medicine, as a branch of medicine, deals with medical questions in their relationship to moral theology. In other words, pastoral medicine is a reliable and up-to-date anatomico - physiologico - clinical guide for the theologian and confessor so that he may properly discern and judge in particular cases with a knowledge of their medical implications.

Despite ancient origins, it was not until the thirteenth century that definite attempts at codification of medical data necessary to pastoral questions were made. These questions refer particularly to medical issues concerning cases of nullity in matrimony under the title of impotency.

In the seventeenth century, works on this subject were produced by the physician Paul Zacchia and the moralist T. Sanches; in the eighteenth century, by St. Alphonsus Maria de Liguori. At the end of the last century, complete treatises on the subject of pastoral medicine were written by Von Olvers, Capellman and Antonelli.

There is no medical subject foreign to pastoral medicine, for the latter is not a branch or specialized field of medicine, but is medicine in its entirety in relation to theology. Thus the main subjects of interest to pastoral medicine are as follows: (a) sexual questions concerning eugenics, hermaphroditism, masturbation, pollution, the sexual act, sexual perversions, impotency, sterility, artificial fecundation, abortion, chastity, etc.; (b) the administration of the sacraments to individuals in particular pathological circumstances or conditions, such as the baptism of fetuses, monsters and the mentally ill, ordination or matrimony for persons afflicted with physical or psychical abnormalities, and the confessions of the mentally deranged; (c) psychological and psychopathological problems, spiritualism, hypnotism, alcoholism, narcotic addiction, truth serums, etc.; (d) thanatological questions on euthanasia, real or apparent death, suicide, murder, etc. These and other related subjects are developed with adequate explanation in numerous articles throughout this work. *Riz.*

MEDICINE, PSYCHOSOMATIC. *Psychosomatic medicine,* a term recently coined in North America, expresses an ancient medical point of view that is linked to the unitary Hippocratic tradition. It is not a special branch of medicine but a concept applicable to all branches of medicine and surgery. Despite the number of followers of the mechanistic and positivistic theories of medicine, which attribute every infirmity of body or mind to physio-chemical changes, the so-called unitary theory, by which illnesses are attributed to reciprocal and interdependent physical and psychical influences, has become more widely accepted.

Psychosomatic medicine is based on an interrelation, not only of all the physical organs of the human body, but also of the body and the mind, an aspect ignored in previous centuries. An emphasis on pathological anatomy, microscopy, and serology led scientists to limit all research to that organ which was diseased, with a consequent neglect of a consideration of the whole person who was ailing, particularly in his psychological makeup.

The advocates of psychosomatic medicine do not suggest a neglect of the body, but exercise greater attention on the mind of the ill person. They tend to study the nature and effects of the psychological and emotional well-being of the individual on his bodily welfare and functions.

Those who consult a physician may be divided into three classes: (1) the less numerous psychotics or mentally ill; (2) those affected by apparent organic diseases or ailments; (3) those who, though not mentally deranged, fail to manifest organic disorders to explain their disturbances.

This latter class consist of purely functional cases, in which the physician may confine himself to a much-abused, and at times erroneous, diagnosis of "nervous breakdown" with which he dismisses the patient with general, soothing words or with the prescription of a general tonic. Or a physician may subject the individual to long, expensive laboratory tests in the hope that they might reveal minor neurovegetative or hormonic anomalies on which to pin the patient's ailments. The physician may consider his patient an hysterical or hypochondriacal simulator and thus send the patient away with the knowledge that he will eventually turn to quack physicians.

On the contrary, approximately one-third of the clinical cases of physicians are particularly related to psychosomatic medicine. On the basis of an increasingly growing and profitable experience, vain exhortations "to be brave and not to think about the illness" or prescriptions of medicines which fix the conviction in the mind of the patient that he is seriously ill, must be supplanted by a careful and profound study of the personality and environmental factors in the life of the patient. From these areas emotional traumas may have unloosed the chaotic disturbances of which the patient complains. The physician must be able to recognize the types of psychoneurotic disturbances related to neurasthenia, hysteria, or obsessive neuroses, in order that he may effectively treat them with adequate and patient psychotherapy.

Another large group of patients may complain of illnesses which are partly due to psychological or emotional factors during periods of organic changes or disturbances. In this case, the general practitioner may be satisfied with a diagnosis that the anatomic disorders are sufficient to explain the complete, morbid state and, based on this diagnosis, subsequent treatments may fail to effect a complete cure or may fall short of expected success. On the contrary, psychosomatic medicine considers the coexistence of psychical factors, inquires into the nature and importance of their effects, and seeks to combat them with a greater improvement in these areas of the patient's well-being. Experience teaches that, if anxieties and suffering are capable of producing many organic disturbances with a consequent aggravation of these illnesses, these organopathies may in turn occasion grave fears and obsessions. In many cases, any state of illness or disease under these circumstances is complicated and aggravated; hence it must be wisely treated in its somatic as well as psychical aspect.

The second class who suffer from disturbances considered by the majority as strictly somatic is not apart from the concern of psychosomatic medicine. For psychosomatic medicine is able to detect a large number of cases in which the psychogenic factor is of capital importance in etiopathogenesis and the treatment of the morbid condition. Cases of asthma, migraines, hypertension, Basedow's contagion, diabetes mellitus, etc., are due in some cases to no less a cause than an original psychological disturbance often traceable to psychotraumas or a state of extended emotional tension. The duodenal ulcer, until a short time ago considered the result of a strictly somatic cause, is due primarily to so-called psychological factors.

PSYCHOPATHOLOGY OF PSYCHOSOMATIC SYNDROMES. It is difficult to attempt to show in a few pages the mechanisms of the various psychosomatic forms. The nature, complexity, and importance of these are progressively becoming better understood, with a consequently more effective application of therapeutic remedies. We shall attempt, nevertheless, a concise and general presentation of these syndromes in order that our conclusions might be better understood in the following paragraphs.

The concept of illness handed down by Wirchow and other eminent pathologists of the last century involved as follows: (a) cellular change, (b) anatomic lesions, (c) functional disorders. According to present-day psychosomatic medical opinions, such a division is obsolete and must be supplanted with the present analysis: (a) psycho-emotive disturbances, (b) functional disorders, (c) cellular changes, (d) anatomic lesions.

Today, significant evidence indicates that the emotions have a well-defined physiological effect; emotions, if too intense or persistent, produce chronic changes and disorders, which in turn produce irreversible cellular changes and definite anatomic lesions. These are frequently verified in subjects reared in unfavorable social environments or in individuals suffering from faulty hygienic or mental training in their early years. So-called psychotraumas produce in those predisposed to them more or less relevant disorders in the functioning of the vegetative or nervous system. Such disorders produce a localized illness in a specific organ or system, which is determined by congenital or acquired deficiencies in these organisms due to past functional disorders in a specific organ or to an apparatus caused by infantile psychoneurotic disturbances. The results of psychoanalytical studies on conditioned reflexes and an ever-increasing knowledge of the complex psychoneuro-endocrine mechanisms that govern vegetative life have brought about basic inquiries into the etiopathogenesis of psychosomatic sicknesses which have been briefly summarized in this article.

In conclusion, every sickness has its physical and psychological aspects. This means that every branch of medicine mut be considered psychosomatic. To have taken this into consideration makes useless the expression *psychosomatic medicine*, for the two concepts are implied in the single term *medicine*.

THERAPY. It is clear in treating a patient that a modern psychosomatic approach by a physician will strive to effect an adequate psychotherapy directed at rebuilding the emotional life of the patient, without failing to treat according to the best medical knowledge all the individual somatopathies detected under clinical laboratory tests and analyses.

Medical science has confirmed by its research that it is practically futile to depend on the "will power" of sick persons. The powerful forces of the subconscious exert an influence on the functioning of our physical and emotional processes, which completely escape the power of the will when it becomes upset by disturbances.

The simple reassurance that there is nothing serious is a great aid to the patient, especially when he wrongfully fears a serious illness or organic disease. These effects are usually temporary; assistance provided to the patient through the power of suggestion, either in the state of wakefulness, hypnosis or narcosis, must as a result be temporary.

A proper therapy should be geared to the effective completion of a process of rehabilitation and to the development of the emotional maturity and life of the patient. These must be accompanied by solutions to the basic conflicts that have hindered his maturity and by clear explanations of the nature of the disorders affecting the patient. In such a way, under the patient and expert guidance of the physician, the patient regains confidence in himself and serenely, without harmful exaggerations, estimates the gravity of the somatic sickness by which he may be afflicted. Egocentricity in his self-centered and unhappy illness gives way to pleasant interest in his own work and environment which is characteristic of the healthy, normal person.

In the greatest number of cases, a careful psychological investigation combined with direct persuasion and a systematic rehabilitation will be sufficient definitely to dispel the emotional substratum of his psychosomatic disorders.

HINTS OF PROPHYLAXIS. Everyone knows how much more important preventive treatment is than therapy, and how much more advantageous it is to prevent a contagious disease than to treat it after it has appeared. However, what Bauce has recently called the *prophylactic clinic* still represents little more than a utopian wish. Every physician is certainly aware, not without regret, that a great deal of the illnesses of patients could have been avoided if they had followed good hygienic rules. He is certainly aware of the fact that many other sicknesses would have been much more easily overcome if the patient had turned to a physician for treatment at the first appearance of the condition. What the same Bauce calls *somatic hedonism*, by which the individual rashly makes himself a slave of so many harmful toxicoses, such as excessive eating, alcohol, smoking, and *ancestral repulsion* of man to timely recourse to the aid of the physician, are the leading factors preventing the rational treatment of so many sicknesses.

To this very simple yet much neglected prophylaxis, which we shall call general, psychosomatic medicine adds another more specific prophylaxis aimed at the prevention in the personality of the patient, during an evolutive age, of any irregular or defective development which is so important in the etiopatho-genesis of emotional and psychoneurotic disturbances, as explained in the preceding paragraphs.

This fundamental prophylactic task belongs primarily to the mother, then to other educators of the child; the mother will effectively contribute to a balanced formation of the personality of her child by means of direct lactation, a gradual training free from impatient outbursts of nervousness and, above all, by much warm affection. Even the father and the other members of the family should collaborate in this educational undertaking by creating and conserving a serene, affectionate, and domestic climate. In fact, the child instinctively imitates his parents; he thinks, reflects, acts according to pattern of behavior in his elders. Thus he could become a victim of ruinous *psychotraumas* by growing up in a family of neurasthenic, crabbed, and quarrelsome persons.

Parents should attend to the educational work of the family by encouraging self-control in the child, promoting his capacity for adaptation to environment, avoiding sharp inhibition, but particularly by checking the beginnings of any feeling of anger, rancor, and hatred, for, as Weiss and English caution, "hatred is a harmful pathological emotion, socially and economically, to the normal functioning of the organism." Teachers and spiritual directors must complete the work.

Thus reared and trained, the child will have the greatest prospects of preserving a "normal personality" in his adult age, as an individual without neurotic disorders, free from embarrassing psychological conflicts, with a healthy attitude toward work, capable of sincerely becoming fond of someone other than himself" (E. Glower). In this manner, he will be better prepared to bear the hardships of life, to live honestly and to act always with uprightness.

MORAL COROLLARIES. Much of what has been said belongs strictly to morality, and it seems very important and commendable from the ethical standpoint that modern medicine again direct attention and care to the study of the whole human psychophysical personality and to

the best method for maintaining this in an efficient state. Modern psychosomatic orientation truly carries out the beautiful maxim of P. Sanson: "The body is possessed of the soul and the soul is possessed of the body. To take care of one, neglecting the other, is to separate deliberately that which God united together from the very beginning."

The notion according to which the family, school, and, in general, all educators must direct a maximum of attention to a formation of character in the child so that he may become a truly normal adult is not a new notion; nor is it a new or strange idea that in all sickness the mind plays a more important part than the body, nor, finally, that the physician should chiefly concern himself with treating the psycho-emotional sphere of the patients. We owe psychosomatic medicine a great debt for emphasizing these factors by promoting and fostering a deeper study of them for the purpose of achieving an effective improvement in future generations.

From a practical point of view, and without falling into the exaggeration of those who hold that psychotherapeutic methods of psychosomatic medicine are a panacea for all infirmities, we shall add that a deeper study of the personality of sick persons and the use of therapies with special care for psychological components will be a positive step in avoiding many withdrawals of unhappy psychoneurotics from productive work and society. Such a study will also be an effective aid in avoiding moral disturbances and will contribute to a more prompt and complete recovery of so many sick pesons who are, instead, subjected to interminable, useless, and often harmful treatments by the methods of common medico-surgical practice. *Riz.*

MEDICINE, SCHOLASTIC. Scholastic medicine is a branch of medical science concerned with the health of children and young people during the period of their school years.

For all practical purposes, scholastic medicine is concerned with all biological aspects of the school population, such as school hygiene, diligent prevention of contagious diseases, biological improvement, mental hygiene, and the professional orientation of the pupils, not only by selecting and encouraging the best pupils to higher education but also by directing others to trades or occupational work more suited to the capacities and tendencies of each individual.

HYGIENE AND PROPHYLAXIS. Scholastic medicine is practiced fundamentally in the hygienico-prophylactic field. Its importance is recognized in the following areas: (a) construction of schools with adequate illumination and sufficient hygienic facilities in proportion to the number of pupils; (b) in the area of equipment, with particular attention to desks' style and size, according to the subjects taught and the age of the pupils; (c) in the fight against epidemico-contagious diseases, by vaccinations; removal from school of any initial case of contagious disease, accurate proof of the cure before readmission into the school, and systematic disinfections, etc.; (d) in the subject of general medicine, dental, visual, or other care.

To achieve its aims, scholastic medicine requires particular conditions for effective functioning: the cooperation of family, teacher, medical and scholastic agencies. That the medical-school service may achieve these goals, it must adopt a biotypological study of the pupils. *Biotypology*, a term introduced by Dr. Pende, is the science that studies the different classes of individuals in the same ethnic group and determines morphological and functional temperaments distinguishing one class from another, for the purpose of discovering unhealthy tendencies or attitudes toward various forms of work activity.

Accordingly, in modern scholastic centers, a *medical report* or individual *biographical file* is compiled for each pupil. This report is so arranged as to permit the classification of students on the basis of constitutional type, health, and psychosomatic defects and imperfections. Each card includes an accurate report on the hygienic, economic, and moral conditions of the family environment in which the pupil lives, as well as past medical history of the subject, treatments received, and any other thing that can be of use for a complete medical history of the individual. On the basis of this report, it will be possible to determine, within reasonable limits, which pupils may continue in a regular school and those who need to attend a special school.

In order that this type of study, sorting, and, in some cases, rehabilitation treatment may be effective, the physician needs the collaboration not only of the teacher but also of specialized personnel, consisting principally of school nurses and counsellors (*see* Social Worker). Thus, it is necessary to get the families of the pupils to work with the school and assist opportunely with the intention of achieving a greater efficiency on the part of the pupils, as well as greater economic, biological and moral betterment of their domestic environment.

SPECIAL SCHOOLS. Experience shows many children require special training which ordinary schools are not adequately equipped to provide. The selection of "special" children and the clinical supervision to be exercised over them constitute important tasks of scholastic medicine.

Of particular importance are the *schools for psychologically abnormal* children. The three main types of such schools consist of: (1) *differential classes* for the apparently psychological abnormalities in children: repeaters, slow, lazy, peevish, inhibited and unstable children; these pupils are kept in such classes as long as the causes and effects of their difficulties continue, but they are eventually returned to ordinary schools; (2) *annexes*, or *special auxiliary classes*, permanently separated from ordinary schools and maintained for oligophrenics, i.e., those capable of receiving sufficient instruction and training by special pedagogical methods at a slower pace than that prescribed for ordinary pupils; (3) *school asylums*, called *autonomous* or *auxiliary schools*, for children who are still capable of receiving a certain amount of instruction but in no way eligible for ordinary schools nor for *special auxiliary classes* or annexes. They must have continuous moral, hygienic, and medical assistance, with the benefits of constant collaboration between the physician-pedagogist and educators and teachers, trained in appropriate orthophrenic teaching institutes. Their purpose is to utilize the modest energies of the oligophrenics, with the intention of giving, not a complete scholastic training, but preparation for employment and a role in society.

Serious phrenasthenics, psychotics or those afflicted with compulsive immorality are out of the jurisdiction of school medicine, for they belong in special institutes of assistance (see Asylum, Insane).

A particular modern branch of scholastic medicine is concerned with children of pre-school age trained and educated in the so-called kindergartens.

MORAL CONSIDERATIONS. Scholastic medicine, as a field concerning particularly delicate and important periods of physical and mental development in the individual, is for this very reason an important part of social medicine. It must be added, as Plutarch perceived nineteen centuries ago (On the Rearing of Children), that, as it is inconceivable for a farmer not to know the quality of the soil in which he must sow, so, too, it is inconceivable for an educator to ignore the psychosomatic qualities of his pupils, which vary from one individual to another according to successive phases of growth; hence, the necessity of collaboration between school physicians, clergy, and teachers. School medicine concerns itself with more than a fourth of the total population of civilized countries.

The practitioners of scholastic medicine must not only be hygienists, but must also possess good clinical, biotypological, psychological, psychiatric and moral knowledge. They must be familiar with the current problems of pedagogy and modern sociology. However, it is a serious mistake for anyone to think that such improvements can be attained by relying only on somatic and biological elements, disregarding the moral, religious, natural or supernatural elements.

While it is true that the importance of scholastic medicine is recognized in all civilized nations, and the studies in this field are everywhere pursued with in-

creased intensity, the same cannot be said as it concerns its practical realization. In fact, while there exist laws and directions concerning the activities of school physicians, the institution of differential schools, of homes for children and, in general, the development of institutes for the various categories of disabled little individuals, the practical application of such regulations is far from being satisfactorily realized. Of course, it is always a question of material means, which can be solved only with time and the generous aid of the State, which must encourage and assist effectively private initiatives in this important field.

It is to be hoped that the assistance advocated as indispensable by the participants in the First National Symposium of Scholastic Medicine, held in Rome in October, 1955, will not fail such a large section of society, in which the hopes of tomorrow lie. Riz.

MEDICINE, SOCIAL. See Medicine; Diseases, Social.

MEDICINE (SPORTS). Gymnastics should be distinguished from athletics. Gymnastics or physical education, as it is called today, is orderly activities or other exercises performed in a gymnasium; athletics or sports include games characterized by competition between teams.

Physical education must be able to offer a variety of progressive exercises "directed to a harmonious physical formation of adolescents and youths, not only for the development of muscles but other organic apparatus as well in the interest of attaining bodily robustness based on such harmony. A physician can effectively contribute to the attainment of such good results by timely checks, appropriate suggestions and a general supervision over the programs.

On the contrary, the preparation of the athlete consists in "a variety of practices, physical exercises, and special training engaged in for sheer pleasure, for reasons of competition, or for ideological or material interest" (Pende). Sports, therefore, consist in constant training for athletic competition in which an athlete gives his whole self;

the *sports physician* has the duty of eliminating as soon as he can the least suitable candidates, of helping weaker ones, and, especially, of suggesting provisions which help make athletic events generally safe.

Since athletic sports are a form of activity requiring not only special, variable and often opposite aptitudes according to the types of sports, as well as considerable work and exertion beyond the physiological capability of the individual, and in view of the intrinsic danger of certain sports and the strain to which the organism of the athlete is subjected (hence unexpected collapses; *professional deformations*, as hunchbacks among mountain climbers and cyclists, epicondylitis among tennis players; premature aging, etc.), it is easily understandable how sports must be authorized and practiced under the control of a physician so that all possible benefits may be drawn from them without allowing them to become a source of harm by reason of a blind impulse for competition or unreasonable spirit of emulation.

In view of these ends, sports physicians have the responsibility of checking the psychosomatic condition of the candidates, admitting only those who are in perfect and vigorous health, barring others from certain types of athletics, maintaining and improving the efficiency of their organisms, supervising their training and seeing to it that the athlete transforms into habits all the rules of hygiene and behavior that are best suited to him.

In recruiting and selecting athletes, the physician shall take into consideration certain fundamental qualities, such as speed, skill, *endurance*, and *muscular strength*.

The medical supervision of athletes fundamentally consists in periodic checkups and scrutiny of training to avoid frequent and unfortunate cases of *overtraining* and competitions in which greater efforts are made than the actual ability of the subject could stand. In addition, particularly dangerous types of sports, such as boxing, riding, winter sports, and automobile or motorcycle racing, require of a physician appropriate first aid services for any emergency which might arise during the respective competitions. In some countries, the physicians closely connected with sports are organized into regional and even national federations.

The modern growth of sports in its various branches, and the imposing mass of interests connected with it in newspapers, radio, television, movies, have caused sports to assume great economic, cultural and moral importance in the life of civilized nations. Consequently, medicine in sports has become a notable branch of social medicine.

Limiting ourselves to some phases of the moral aspect of the subject, in the light of the teachings of Pius XII (*see* Address to the delegates to the National Scientific Congress of Sports and Physical Education, November 8, 1952, AAS 44 [1952], 868–876), we shall recall that:

(a) The body is not the most important part of man; it must give way to the interests of the soul. (b) The training of the body is neither the sole nor the leading element of human behavior; it is to be valued, of course, but not as an indispensable element. (c) Certain forms of sports are likely to foster dangerous instincts; hence, they must be looked upon with reservation. (d) The physician of athletes can and must exercise a moral influence on environment where a thoughtlessness common to youth and, in the case of many sports, conspicuous financial gains for the athletes tend to favor a relaxation of morals. The physician who limits himself merely to insisting on the basic importance of psychosomatic hygiene, which has its foundation in the discipline of the senses and the spirit, will be of notable aid to the moral as well as physical prowess of the athlete. (e) The physician must insist on the necessity of refraining by the athletes from the widespread use of stimulating drugs before or during the contests. Although drugs provide a sensation of vigor, they are not always timely nor adequately graded. Hence a collapse which overtakes the athlete in the course of the contest, or the production of severe injury may ruin in the long run the athlete's health and career—aside from the fact that it is fraud, which, of course, makes the action more serious and objectionable from the moral standpoint, despite the fact that its widespread practice may lessen its seriousness. (f) It is likewise necessary that sports physicians continue with firmness to censure contests that are too dangerous (*see* Sports, Dangerous). In these cases, a word of frank criticism by sports physicians would be very helpful, to stress the fact that sports should be a noble and happy competition intended for the betterment of mankind and not be transformed into a source of harm. This applies not only to the athlete but also to the public, which often receives harmful effects from athletic spectacles that are not too different from those once offered in pagan amphitheatres. *Riz.*

MEDICINES. Medicines, or pharmaceutical preparations, are substances employed in the prevention, alleviation, or cure of disease. *Pharmacy* is the art of preparing and preserving medicines. *Pharmacology* is the science which studies the action exerted by medicines on the organism; *bromatology* studies the effects of medicine in general; *toxicology* studies their poisonous effects. *Pharmacopeia* is the title of an official book issued by an authority and recognized as a standard reference, in which medicines are listed with their characteristics, methods of preparation, maximum dosage, etc.

The use of medicines, based on empirical study of the effectiveness of certain plants or other basic remedies, dates back to the most ancient past, when pharmacy and medicine were practiced by the same individual. The Greek Dioscorides Pedonius, a military physician at the time of Nero, is considered the founder of pharmacology, which he discussed organically in a work of five volumes, entitled *Concerning Medical Matters* (*De Materia Medica*), written about 78 A.D. A century later, Galen wrote several treatises on the same subject. In the Middle Ages, thanks also to the Arabs, the pharmaceutical art became independent of the medical profession. At the end of the sixteenth century, druggists organized guilds, which they entrusted to the patron saints Cosmos and Damian.

Pharmacy reached its golden age at the turn of the nineteenth century with the discovery and isolation of chemical substances in that period due to the work of research by men such as C. Scheele, who prepared the malic, citric, and gallic acids, isolated uric acid, discovered molybdenum, wolfram, chlorine, etc.; F. Serturner, who first isolated the alkaloid, morphine; M. Klaproth, who discovered cerium, zirconium, and titanium, as well scientists such as Pelletier, Liebig, Mohr, etc. Large-scale preparation of medicines and the increasingly effective use of *wonder* drugs have considerably reduced the scientific activity of the pharmaceutical profession as it was practiced before. In view of the large sums of money required, medicines are generally prepared in the laboratories of universities or large producers of patent medicines.

CLASSIFICATION OF MEDICINES. Medicines may be classified in a variety of ways. According to their manufacture, they are solids, liquids or gases; according to their method of administration, they are termed gastroenteric, respiratory, skin, subcutaneous, genito-urinary, vein, depending on the part of the body which receives these drugs. According to their subsequent activity, medicines may be considered local, reflex, or general.

The most useful classification is according to their chemical composition. *Inorganic* substances include arsenic, bismuth, calcium, phosphorus, sulphur, etc. *Organic* substances are subdivided into the *fat series*, such as glycerine, formic acid, chloroform, lactose; the *aromatic series*, as phenol, saccharine, tannin, antipyrine; *alkaloids*, such as strychnine, theobromine, morphine, atropine; *glucoses*, such as strophantus, sculla, podophyllin; *essential oils* and *balsams*, such as pepsin, lipase, yeast; *serums* and *hormones*; *vitamins*, such as A and B2 (growth vitamins), B_1 (anti-beriberi vitamin), B6 and PP (anti-pellagrim), B12 (anti-anaemic), C (anti-scorbutic), D (anti-rickets), E (fecundity), K and P (anti-hemorrhagic); *sulfanamides*, such as streptozine, diazine, coliseptale, sulfones; *antibiotics*, such as penicillin, streptomycin, terramycin, etc.

According to their curative properties,

medicines are considered: *anti-elmintic* (santonine, male fern, thymal), *anti-pyretic* (phenacetin, pyramidon, quinine), *anti-rheumatic* (salicylate of sodium), *cardiac* (digitalis, caffeine, adonide, sparteine), *expectorant* (senega, aniseed, ammonia, terpene), *purgative* (sulphate of sodium, castor oil, cascara sagrada, phenolphthalein), *sedative* (bromide, opiate, barbiturate, balerian).

USE OF MEDICINES. Each *individual* has a moral obligation to keep medicines carefully guarded and, if possible, in suitably locked cabinets. Very often children swallow pills or tablets in large numbers, due to attraction for the color or sweet taste of the coating, or adults distractedly or drowsily select a bottle containing antiseptic for one containing medicines, causing internal burns or other serious injuries. Easy access to barbiturates or permanganates may be an easy temptation for a despondent member of the family to commit suicide. Hospital nursing staffs can never be sufficiently warned to keep bottles with acids or harmful substances always separate and adequately marked, because they are so often mistaken for entirely different medicines and administered to patients with serious consequences. Unfortunately, familiarity with medicines has a tendency to create a false sense of assuredness capable of causing, in a moment of distraction, the gravest and most harmful mistakes.

Neuropaths, cenesthepaths, hypochondriacs and individuals excessively concerned about their health cannot be warned strongly enough not to overindulge in the use of advertised patent medicines, generally bought without prescription. Such an abuse affects principally the pocketbook, but often it produces many disturbances by a harmful influence on gastric secretions, cardiac innervation, etc. Even the most harmless medicines should always be prescribed by a physician, for the diagnosis is supremely necessary for treatment. A correct therapeutic prescription is inconceivable if separated from an exact diagnostic judgment. In addition, the physician is the only person capable of checking the clinical effects of medicines, which can noticeably vary from case to case on the basis of constitutional factors or other elements unknown to the patient, such as reactions, toleration, habit formation, etc.

MANUFACTURE AND SALE OF MEDICINES. Pharmaceutical houses authorized to produce patent medicines cannot put a product on the market without previous registration with the Drug Administration. This registration implies a previous examination of and experimentation with the new drug in order to avoid the sale of quack medicines or medicines void of the ingredients indicated on the label or unproductive of the claimed results.

The pharmacist is obliged to check every prescription before preparing the medicine in order to avoid possible errors in quantity or chemical incompatibility. In addition, he is required by law not to use extraordinary, diluted or different medicines from those prescribed by the physician (except in the case of substitution of a genuine specialty with an equivalent *product* made within the limits and according to the methods suggested in the pharmacopeia.) *Riz.*

USE OF MEDICINES. *"The Most High hath created medicines out of the earth and a wise man will not abhor them . . . And the Most High hath given knowledge to men that he may be honored in his wonders. By these he shall cure and shall allay their pains"* (Eccl. 38:4–7).

In these few words Holy Scripture offers priceless advice regarding medicines. It points out a twofold aim in the use of medicines: to cure illness or to allay pain. The former is the primary aim; the latter, if not the result of the first, is secondary but useful, important, and good. Furthermore, the sacred text implies that the use of medicines may be binding in conscience and must be regulated and controlled by the physician.

The use of medicines without the advice or prescription of the physician is illicit, except for certain household remedies which are harmless and useful in slight indisposition. The intemperate and frequent use of common medicines could constitute a sin, if by their use one caused damage to his health. On the other hand, a person is bound to use medicines prescribed as necessary by the physician for his cure or to avoid damage to his health. Recourse to quack physicians or their diverse medicines is to be censured for two reasons: (1) it delays recourse to a proper physician, and this may be fatal; (2) medicines recommended by these quack physicians, despite an occasional, surprising cure, frequently produce other serious harmful effects and diseases which do not develop immediately.

DUTIES OF PHYSICIANS. By virtue of a contract, which is at least tacit, a physician is bound to administer and prescribe the most reliable, effective, and least expensive medicine for his patient. If no such medicine exists or if a more reliable one is more expensive, the physician must choose an appropriate one, preferring the more reliable one. If the cost is too great, he can select the best medicine from those that are less expensive. In case of doubt, he must inform the patient or relatives of the various possibilities for their decision on the expenses to be incurred. It is illicit for the physician to use untried medicine for experimental purposes, unless certainty exists that the experiment will not cause injury to the patient. Apart from possible direct damage, other factors must be considered: indirect damage caused by delay in the use of more reliable medicines, or financial damages created by the use of ineffective medicine. Experiments with obviously harmful medicines are illicit unless the person has been informed of their use and possible effects and consents to this. Dangerous experiments are never licit, not even with the patient's consent, except in a case of desperation. When the patient is near death, such experiments may be licit, if there is a reasonable, though small, hope of saving the life of the patient. The immediate motive must always be the good and health of the patient, and the sole motive of providing evidence or proof of the effectiveness of an untried medicine for the benefit of other patients or of medicine is not sufficient to justify its use. For other questions, *see* Analgesics, Anesthetics, and Narcotics. *Ben.*

MEDITATION. Meditation, as prayer, consists in the application of the mind to a religious truth with a concomitant reflection upon the practical application of this truth to daily life; this leads to resolutions and affections of the heart. Meditation must involve a true elevation of the mind and soul to God, to be true prayer. It must not, therefore, be restricted merely to mental considerations, but requires faith, love, praise, thanksgiving, petition, and contrition in union with the work of the intellect. Contrition should permeate the entire prayer, but especially the conclusion; mental reflection must be conducive to concrete, positive resolutions to serve God better.

In the beginning, the spiritual life is characterized by a prevalence of vocal prayer; as the soul progresses in spirituality, the work of the intellect tends to diminish while the affective part becomes more prevalent; gradually meditation changes into an intimacy with God as a soul contemplates with love God who dwells within it.

METHOD. It is not easy for beginners to meditate well. Many of the saints have provided instructions about methods of mental prayer, including, in more recent times, specific methods of mental prayer referred to as Ignatian, Salesian, and Sulpician. These share many points in common: a remote preparation, which is primarily a truly Christian life; a proximate preparation, which consists in placing oneself in the presence of God with a recognition of one's unworthiness and incapability of praying well, for which one must implore divine aid. The body of the meditation includes reflections upon some religious truth, with its relation to one's own soul, with subsequent pious affections aroused by these reflections; these are followed by a commitment to specific and firm resolutions for a better life. The meditation is concluded with an act of thanksgiving, a brief examination of the meditation itself, a final prayer and the selection of a thought to which the mind will return throughout the day.

Any truth apt to be conducive to the practice of virtue can be a good topic for meditation: God, His attributes and rights; man's creation and destiny to a supernatural end; sin, its cause and consequences; the passion and death of our Lord Jesus Christ as model of man's perfection; death, judgment, heaven and hell; the ways of avoiding sin, eradicating defects and practicing virtue; one's individual duties; grace and its need. The variable parts of the Mass are also suitable material for very helpful meditation.

It is impossible to suggest a method of meditation suitable for everyone, for its effectiveness depends on many circumstances. A more practical norm is the consideration of results which one derives from a definite method, together with consultation with a spiritual director. St. Ignatius suggests pausing in prayer if a particular consideration proves effective in stimulating the affective powers of the soul; for souls who have made some progress in the spiritual life, he suggests more effective methods of mental prayer and contemplation. It is not, however, particularly necessary to be concerned about the method of expressing one's affections, for the simplest method is always the best.

USEFULNESS. Meditation is a very effective means of assuring eternal salvation. St. Thérèse of the Child Jesus said that a soul who is faithful in meditating for ten minutes a day is sure of his salvation. Meditation is not merely helpful but necessary for perfection. Every person should devote at least a few moments a day to this pious exercise. There are numerous, easily obtainable books of meditation, such as the Gospels, *The Imitation of Christ,* or any life of Christ.

At times planned meditation may seem impossible, for one experiences only dryness and weariness. Such difficulty may be the result of a tepid soul or physical indisposition; it could also be a trial sent by the Lord to purify the soul and dispose it for a much more effective meditation. If the above-mentioned condition is due to a cause dependent on the will, it must be removed. In any case, these difficulties should not prompt one to omit or shorten the meditation or alter it to simple spiritual reading. Every effort

must be made to avoid distractions, to keep the attention of the mind fixed on God and to express again and again one's affection for the Lord, with a sincere intent to follow Him even to Calvary. One may grieve over dryness and the inability to pray, but such a meditation is very beneficial. Many intimate friends of God have for years lived thus united with the sorrowful life of Jesus. *Man.*

MEDIUM. A person through whose cooperation unusual phenomena are produced is called a medium. The original meaning of the word is related to a current of ideas of the so-called *spiritualistic movement,* according to which individuals endowed with special talents, such as clairvoyance, xenolossia, telekinesis, are considered as the *means* of communication between the world of the spirits and the physical world (*see* Spiritism).

Two categories of mediums are distinguished according to the phenomena presented: whether the phenomena are produced with their cooperation in the physical and sensitive, or the psychological and intellectual order; however, no particular somatic or mental characteristic allows any such classification *a priori.* In fact, we can very well say that from an anatomico-physiological or physio-pathological point of view, mediums, generally, do not seem to differ from normal individuals. Specific differentiations, however, are perceived, sometimes in a very evident manner, in neuro-psychological aspects. The personality of the medium has many analogies with that of psycho-neurotics (puerilism, narcissistic infatuations, hyperemotivity), or may even present hysterical, psychastenic and cyclothymic traits.

The special type of sleep, called *trance,* which the mediums usually employ during the manifestation of the phenomena that occur with their passive cooperation, is in many respects similar to hypnotic sleep (*see* Hypnotism). However, it is not automatically identical, for some mediums are not fit subjects of hypnotism. In addition, the *trance* is usually spontaneous, and does not require special hetero- and auto-hypnotic intuitions proper to hypnotism. For a moral evaluation of medium activity, *see* Metapsychology. *Riz.*

MEEKNESS. Meekness is the moral virtue by which one is able to restrain the passion of anger in accord with right reason; meekness permits anger only to the extent necessary and proper. Insofar as meekness indicates a quality of a person, which reflects the behavior of the humble heart (Matt. 11:29), meekness may be considered a character trait rather than a special virtue. Meekness is the mark of a true Christian (II Cor. 10:2; Eccl. 2:19).

Meekness belongs to the cardinal virtues of temperance and fortitude, inasmuch as it directly restrains the irascible part of man and controls the passion of anger, thus enabling man to moderate the desire of revenge. It acts on the irascible appetite in two ways: (a) by repressing initial impulses to anger which has no sufficient reason; (b) by controlling just anger within bounds. Thus the anger of the meek is: *just* in the infliction of a punishment upon one who, objectively speaking, deserves it; *moderate*, by keeping the expression of anger within bounds or limits required by the offense committed and the order demanded by justice; *charitable* in intention, not motivated by feelings of hatred, but by a desire for the restoration of order and the correction of the guilty person (Ps. 4:5; 36:11).

Thus understood, meekness is not a sign of a weak character or of natural goodness; meekness does not destroy the wrath or anger in man; meekness restrains and regulates anger, prevents excesses, avoids contentions and insults, whether by word or deed. The zeal of the meek is the outgrowth of charity and not of passion.

In general, meekness may be caused in an individual by a variety of motives: indolence, political interest, extreme fear, or truly Christian spiritual values. Meekness due to physical or moral indolence is found in persons who lack character and are incapable of true virtue. Political meekness may be a serious defect or sin, particularly slothfulness in the management of public affairs or justice. Christian meekness is a true moral virtue, rendering man pleasing to God and his fellow men. It is acquired by humility and moral fortitude.

One may sin against meekness by excess or defect: by excess, in an unreasonable or unnecessary anger; by defect, in the failure to act in just anger when it is necessary; this is called indolence, sloth, and the like. Serious instances of sin would include bad example or a failure to admonish one's charges. *Tar.*

MELANCHOLY. *Melancholy* (Greek, *melas*—black; *chole*—bile) is of Hippocratic origin; this term indicates a mental syndrome characterized by a morbid and persistent sadness, independent of external circumstances, with invincible pessimism, a profound sense of dejection, and a lack of confidence that paralyzes action. This syndrome was thought by the ancients to have been caused by an excess of black bile (*see* Pathology). Among the synonyms applied to melancholy are *lypemania* and *melancholia*; the latter is the more exact scientific term.

In less serious forms, melancholy does not differ from depression which occurs in an otherwise normal individual as the result of some misfortune; however, a long period of melancholy or a condition of depression lacking adequate cause may indicate the presence of a more serious disorder. In such cases, a psychical disorder or an unreasonable sadness may fill the mind with pessimism; yet this never leads to delirious interpretations. The following verses of Paul Verlaine, who personally experienced affective depressions, very effectively convey the depressing nature of this form of sadness: "This sorrow is without reason. . . . It is far the worst pain—not knowing why, without love and without hatred, my heart has so much pain."

In the more advanced stages, the disease becomes complicated with mental derangement, delirium, hallucination, and phenomena of motor inactivity. The beginning of this condition is always characterized by a tormenting and invincible insomnia, lack of appetite, and constipation. Every external impression is unpleasant to the melancholic; every idea of action involves him in complicated considerations of punishment and injury; the sick person, whose mind disconsolately rambles in a closed circle of sad ideas, complains of a deep affective dryness even toward his dearest friends, which increases his moral suffering and sense of guilt and unworthiness.

In this ground, saturated with pessimism and disconsolate anguish which overwhelms and cancels all judgments, true deliriums of guilt, misery, ruin, etc., easily grow. These deliriums are frequently sustained and fed by illusions, and at times by hallucinations. People are criticizing and accusing him of every bad action; prison awaits him and the jailer's steps are heard outside the door; the flames of hell are enfolding him; the physician is the devil who came to snatch his soul.

The intensive emotional depression affects not only the patient's ideation process but his will and movements as well. The melancholic is usually undecided, an abulic person living apart, silent, inert, incapable also of initiating the simplest actions. He does not wash, dress, or feed himself; he answers questions with delay and in a low voice, or may not reply at all (*muteness*); he may obstinately refuse food (*sitophobia*); sometimes he is affected by a total arrest of every psychomotorial activity (*melancholic stupor*). At other times, anxiety, rather paralyzing the will, determines a state of rising tension which seeks an outlet in a condition of motorial restlessness; hence, the anxiety is expressed in a monotonous stereotyped moan (*anxious melancholia*) or in a tumultuous and incessant agitation (*agitated melancholia*). Sometimes the agitation suddenly explodes after a long lethargic period into acts of extreme violence (*raptus melancholicus*) which may appear very dangerous and are performed in a semi-conscious state, when he suddenly gives in, without later recollection of the incident. During the *raptus* the patient may inflict upon himself the most serious injuries or attempt suicidal acts. Suicide may also be the premeditated effect of a desperate disgust with life; in such a case, it is prearranged with cleverness, and, if it coexists with the delirium of general ruin, it may be preceded by the slaughter of his entire family.

It is important to note that the tendency to suicide is also found in relatively light forms of melancholia which may be inherited, for, in some families, a high number of suicides can be attributed to a depressive congenital disorder.

DURATION AND TREATMENT. The melancholic syndrome may appear in any mental illness: from progressive paralysis to schizophrenia, from epilepsy to hysteria. In its typical and pure form, as such, it is a cloak of one or another form of dysthymia. If it is not properly treated, it may have a duration of one or more years; then the morbid phase ceases and the patient happily regains a condition of complete well-being, with only some fragmentary and general remembrance of his former state of illness. At times, the melancholic episode is unique, as in mania (*q.v.*); more often, several occur alternately with periods of complete psychical normalcy (*periodic melancholia*), or alternating maniacal crises with melancholic crises (*manic depressive frenzy*) are observed. Thus, the prognosis of a single depressive episode is rather favorable; a reservation is necessary in judging cases of mental illness, by reason of the likely possibility of new crises of dysthymia.

In the critical age or in old age, depressive episodes may arise in persons who formerly never showed any melancholic manifestations. The nature of these episodes differs from that of a manic-depressive frenzy with respect to the greater duration of these episodes and the prevalence of actions that indicate anxious disturbances as symptoms.

Until a few years ago, psychiatry was helpless in regard to melancholia: hot baths and sedating drugs were the only remedies in use, but their effectiveness was limited. Today, thanks to electroshock therapy, depressive episodes can be checked rather quickly without damage to the sick person and with a high percentage of favorable results. A number of new drugs are used effectively in many cases of melancholia. *Riz.*

IMPUTABILITY. For the ethical and medico-legal considerations in melancholia, *see* Dysthymia and Affectivity. We shall note only that definite causes dispose a person to melancholia, originating in hereditary and educational factors, or in other causes, called determining, such as the death of a dear friend, domestic difficulties, a very serious sin. These elements must be taken into consideration not only with regard to treatment but also imputability. Acts which are the effect of the illness itself must be considered involuntary acts and, therefore, not imputable; however, there could be imputability *in causa*, due particularly to a deliberately wrong mode of life or to a failure to act promptly at the first signs of the illness. This is to be taken into consideration in the assessment of its effects. Furthermore, objectively speaking, the desire for death from an improper motive, such as despondency, impatience in adversity, etc., is unlawful but rarely gravely sinful, because insufficient reflection or deliberation of will accompanies this act in a state of great mental depression. *Pal.*

MEMORY. The faculty by which man preserves, reproduces, and identifies his past experiences or learning is called memory. The ancients distinguished *sensitive* or organic memory from *intellectual* memory, depending on whether the object recalled was a matter of external or internal sensitive knowledge or of intellectual knowledge. Modern experimental psychology has introduced new distinctions, especially in the field of sensitive memory.

The training of the memory has a practical importance from the moral point of view. It is effected by acquiring the habit of recalling frequently those states of mind and ideas which are capable of giving incentive to good. This recall is fostered either by retaining such objects in our mind when they are spontaneously presented to it or by establishing certain associations, even artificial, between these and other states of mind that more frequently occur to us. One of the good effects of meditation (mental prayer) is this strengthening of the memory for moral good. *Gra.*

MEMORY, PATHOLOGY OF. The memory preserves the traces of impressions received and permits their reproduction and identification. The remembrance of an event is fixed by means of the attention (*q.v.*) and is proportionate to the intensity and vividness of the impression received and the frequency of repetition of that impression. Thus, emotion and will acquire an essential importance in fixing remembrances, although other constitutional factors may have preponderant values in some individuals, as is evident in the strong memories possessed by phrenasthenics.

DISORDERS OF THE MEMORY. For didactic purposes the mnemonic function is usually subdivided into elementary functions, as the memory of fixation, conservation, and evocation, each subject to its own individual disorders.

Memory of Fixation. Difficulty experienced by certain individuals in the formation of mnemonic remembrances, as well as the scarcity or extreme weakness of remembrances, frequently may be due to lack of attention, which in turn may result from fatigue, definite toxic conditions, serious emotional disturbances, acquired cerebropathies (especially senile), or a serious impairment to one's psychological development (phrenasthenia). In some phrenasthenics, however, one may find an excessive development of the memory; this is generally a condition of partial hyperamnesia, explained by some as an unusual enlargement of the individual cerebral areas, due to a mild pathological stimulus produced by a fundamental illness which gave rise to the arrest of development and a disturbance of other encephalic centers.

Retentive Memory. Particularly violent emotions, especially commotive cranial traumas, may occasion a temporary amnesia of fixation or even a complete oblivion of events over a long period following a traumatic experience, even though consciousness was promptly recovered. This disorder, named *anterograde amnesia*, is explained by a confusional post-traumatic condition which impeded the forming of mnemonic remembrances. If this state extends to a period more or less immediately preceding the moment of the trauma, it is termed *retrograde amnesia*, because the mnemonic traces, formed a little before the lesion occurred, did not become firmly fixed. A mixed and more frequent type of *retro-anterograde amnesia*, which tends to disappear in time, always leaves a well-defined and complete mnemonic void which ensued while the trauma occurred.

Apart from these morbid accidents, amnesia of retention may occur; as a matter of fact, a weakening of the memory of retention is clearly observed in all aged persons, a disorder which, according to Ribot's law, affects first the more recent events, as less stably fixed. The destructive processes of cortical parenchyma, cerebral arteriosclerosis, and other serious encephalic lesions are wont to erase the mnemonic recollections more extensively and deeply; this may happen suddenly (*amnesia ictus*), although only temporarily.

Memory of Evocation. Not only in localized cerebral lesions but also in diffused cortical processes there are collateral disorders associated with the definite destruction of certain mnemonic images. This causes amnesia to appear more extensive than it is in reality. These disorders of the memory are perceived with the greatest evidence in various demential forms, especially in senile dementia, where it is easy to observe the interesting phenomenon of *confabulation*, that is, the replacement of lost recollections with capricious, fantastic creations; in fact, the sick person tends to fill his own mnemonic void with products of his own fantasy which he firmly believes real. In addition, the chatterer, who forgets with extreme ease what he has perceived a moment before, soon forgets also his own inventions and readily contrives others. The continual variety of such tales betrays his morbid nature.

It is not altogether uncommon to observe occasional cases of amnesia of evocation in normal persons. The phe-nomenon may be caused by distraction, as with the thinker absorbed in his abstract problems; by sudden emotions, as before an assembly or a group of examiners the restraining element intervenes in the revocatory process; by auto-suggestion, as in the case of many psychoneurotics who, because of fear of amnesia, are unable, for a few moments, to recapture certain specific recollections.

Paramnesia. Besides the disorders mentioned above, which are the leading and more common disorders of the memory, others, more subtle and quantitavely more modest, are of great moral and juridical interest because they can be observed even in normal individuals and influence depositions of testimony or other circumstances which rely on mnemonic functions.

When we propose to recall to our mind in the most precise way possible images seen, events witnessed, speeches heard, mental states, emotional reactions, ideas, and judgments which previously occupied the field of our consciousness, the memory deceives us in a greater or lesser degree depending on the time elapsed, the emotional coloring of the particular event which we wish to recall, or the psychological conditions in which we find ourselves at the moment of recall.

Recollection is never a faithful copy of a past perception but always contains something new and different, because a part, though small, of the traces left by the perception is usually lost; some extraneous element is ordinarily, though unconsciously, added to the residue of past perceptions. This deformation and unintentional falsification of recollections is usually considerable in emotional and suggestible persons, such as children and psychoneurotics. In such cases, one speaks of *paramnesia*; this factor should be considered in testimony much more than is actually done. It is a known fact, and a subject of thorough study by experimental psychologists, that testimonies are often unintentionally fallacious. Sometimes this fallacy is due to a lack of attention; at other times, it is caused by the emotional condition of the person at the moment at which the event took place; often, of course, it depends also on modifications produced on the recollections by the present emotional state.

Catathymia. The transformation which psycho - intellective processes undergo under the influence of emotional elements is called *catathymia.* This catathymic influence, found above all in recollection, becomes accentuated on the occasion of testimony, particularly in a courtroom where the witness necessarily is under the effect of many emotional tensions. The tendency to catathymic transformations differs according to temperaments. There are individuals, otherwise normal, who are absolutely incapable of repeating a narration without introducing therein some subjective invention which they themselves believe as true. When this tendency reaches a high degree, it is called *fantastic pseudology,* and it occurs mainly in persons endowed with a rich fantasy, egocentric, and incapable of weighing properly the products of their imagination on the scale of critique, particularly if they themselves are the protagonist of the story. Furthermore, it is interesting to note that the individual with a tendency to pseudology, by repeating his tale, modifies and enriches it more and more with new details to the point that his embellishments and transformations change the original story into an entirely new one which the narrator himself believes true because of autosuggestion.

Feeling of Anteriority. Of a fundamentally paramnesic nature is the relatively common phenomenon of the *already seen* or *already lived* that, for brief instants, can also be found in normal individuals. It is a matter of a peculiar expression, always associated with a sense of painful uncertainty and surprise before a mysterious phenomenon which one experiences in perceiving scenes or facts observed for the first time but which seem to be the repetition of scenes or facts witnessed before. This curious *feeling of anteriority* of an event does not presumably depend on repetitions or resemblance of perceptions, but on the repetition of an emotional state previously experienced in the midst of different perceptions no longer present in the memory. The phenomenon is connected with agitation or tiredness and is found frequently in cases of neurasthenia, in conditions of slight confusion, in crises of depression, or in phases of imperfect consciousness which accompany epileptic attacks. In some individuals of delicate and visionary disposition, the phenomenon of the *already seen* can also give rise to the conviction that his present life is a repetition of a life already spent.

MORAL APPRAISAL. Similar conditions evidently modify the degree of imputability of actions which occur directly or indirectly as the effects of disorders of the memory, especially in an advanced state. Therefore, all these elements must be taken into consideration when evaluating moral guilt, testimony in trials, and penal responsibility. *Riz.*

MENACE. A menace or threat is the display of intent to inflict evil or injury on someone, by injecting the fear of a forthcoming harm or by inducing the performance of actions which are not voluntarily intended by the victim. This might, for example, involve the surrender of a sum of money, a forced marriage contract, or the threat to reveal or force the revelation of a secret. A special form of menace is extortion or protection money.

A menace is not always sinful. If the purpose of the menace is a legitimate, good act, and the display of a threat or evil intention involves no abuse, the menace is not sinful. To threaten the denunciation of a swindler to the police, unless he immediately restores unjustly obtained money, is justified.

However, menace may entail grave sin. The malice of a menace consists primarily in the menace itself, as an action intended to produce fear; secondarily, in the harmful consequences for the person against whom it is directed. Menace and extortion are evil crimes. Often it is most advisable for victims of menace to report this at once to authorities who deal with the matter competently. Many turn to public authority too late or after suffering grave injury. Extortionists rely on fear engendered in their victims for their daring. It is evident that any injuries caused to another by menace or extortion must be repaired under an obligation of restitution. *Ben.*

MENDICANCY. *See* Poverty.

MENSA EPISCOPALIS (Revenue of a Bishop). The bishop's revenue is a benefice, which is derived from a variety of ecclesiastical goods, movable and immovable; income from this belongs to the bishop or ordinary. Hence, *mensa episcopalis* is a juridical entity, recognized as such by law, and capable of possessing patrimonial goods.

The bishop is the head and administrator of the *mensa* (Canons 1653, par. 1; 1483, par. 1). During a vacancy of the bishopric, this is to be administered by a capitulary vicar or apostolic administrator, under the supervision of the Sacred Consistorial Congregation (Decree of the Sacred Consistorial Congregation, June 30, 1934).

According to Canon 1423, one may also speak of a capitular or collegiate *mensa* (par. 2); it is, however, preferable to speak of a capitular or collegiate *revenue*. *Vio.*

MENSTRUATION. *See* Gonads.

MERCANTILISM. *See* Free Exchange.

MERCY (Works of). *Mercy*, founded on compassion, differs from compassion or the feeling of sympathy insofar as mercy implements this feeling with a ready desire to render assistance—the essential element of mercy. The works of mercy are the methods or actions which express this desire.

Human nature is inclined to practice mercy. This law of mercy was obscure and unrecognized before the advent of Christianity; some pagan philosophers considered mercy a vice. Christ restored the practice of mercy to its proper and rightful role in human affairs.

Since the needs of our fellow man are corporal and spiritual, the works of assistance are also corporal and spiritual. On the basis of principles drawn from the Scriptures, Christian tradition codified those practices into a twofold group, each consisting of seven corporal works and seven spiritual works of mercy.

In St. Matthew's Gospel (25:35 ff.) are listed the ways of tending to the material needs of one's neighbor. The first four alleviate the corporal needs of primary necessity: feeding the hungry, giving drink to the thirsty, clothing the naked and sheltering the homeless; two others tend to other needs: visiting the sick and visiting the prisoners. The last corporal work of mercy, burying the dead, was taken from the book of Tobias (6:12).

Among the seven spiritual works of mercy (Luke 17:3; Rom. 12:12 ff.; Gal. 6:1 ff.; Col. 4:2; 1 Thes. 5:14 ff.; 2 Thes. 3:15; Jam. 5:19 ff.), two attend to the needs of the intellect: instructing the ignorant and counselling the doubtful; others attend to the needs which more directly touch the affective part of the soul: comforting the afflicted, admonishing the sinner, forgiving all injuries and bearing wrongs patiently. The series is concluded with a work of mercy which can and ought to be extended to all: praying for the living and the dead.

The Lord declared blessed the merciful because they shall obtain mercy with God (Matt. 5:7); He prefers mercy to sacrifice offered to God (Matt. 12:7); of the heartless He says that they gamble with divine goodness (Mark 4:24). *Man.*

MERIT. *Merit* in the broad sense signifies a work worthy of a reward or retribution; as such, it involves a relationship between the work and the one rewarding. A necessary condition of merit is that the work be within the authority of the one who performs it and be directed to the benefit of another. In fact, merit may refer to good or evil, since both are worthy of retribution; thus we speak of deserving a reward or punishment. Theologians speak of merit with reference to reward, and demerit is applied to works deserving punishment. Consequently, merit may be defined: a good work, freely performed in honor of or for the benefit of another, which is worthy of reward.

DIVISION. If one considers the relation between a meritorious work and its reward, merit is either *condign* (*de con-*

digno) or *congruous* (*de congruo*). Condign merit is a reward due to one in justice, if a just and proportionate relationship exists between the work and its reward. Congruous merit, in which no proportion exists between a work and its reward, is a reward not due in justice but granted because it is fitting or simply out of benevolence. Condign merit is merit in the proper sense; congruous merit is merit analogously speaking, *secundum quid*.

CONDITIONS. The conditions for condign merit are as follows: (a) A meritorious act must be free, because only a free act is fully ours, and no title may be acquired to a reward except from a deed truly ours. (b) The act must be morally good, because only such an act is worthy of reward; a sinful act is worthy only of punishment. (c) The act must be *supernatural*, i.e., it must proceed from grace, as the source of every beneficial act, and be based on faith, which is the root of merit. (d) The act must be *performed in the state of grace*, because a sinner is not a friend of God, and the reward promised by the Lord is given to God's friends. (e) The act must be *destined by God for a reward*, because a creature owes everything to his Creator; in fact, St. Thomas teaches that our actions have no title to merit except by a disposition of God ("*Actio nostra non habet rationem meriti nisi ex praesupposito divinae ordinationis*": *Summa Theol.*, I-II, q. 114, 1 to 3).

For congruous merit, although it is required that the meritorious act be *free*, *good*, and *supernatural*, the state of grace is not required as in *condign* merit.

POSSIBILITY OF MERIT. The possibility of merit for good works was defined by the Council of Trent (*Sess. VI, Can.* 32; cf. I Cor. 15:58). The basis of this doctrine is found in many passages of Holy Scripture: "*Your work is not in vain with the Lord.*" St. Paul calls expected reward a crown of justice (*corona justitiae*); Jesus Himself, in His Sermon on the Mount, while predicting persecutions for His disciples, also spoke of the great reward coming to them (*merces magna*, Matt. 5:12). In Holy Scripture reward is relative to the entity of the works: ". . . *The Son of Man is to*

come with his angels in the glory of his Father and then he will render to everyone according to his conduct" (Matt. 16:27).

OBJECT. (a) It is certain that man can merit neither *de condigno* nor *de congruo* first actual grace, i.e., all those aids of a supernatural order that illuminate his intellect in a transient manner and move his will to salvific acts. (b) Man in the state of grace can merit *condignly* an increase of sanctifying grace and eternal life (Council of Trent, *Sess. VI, Chap.* 16). But he can not merit final perseverance or efficacious grace, because these are gratuitous gifts of God. (c) With regard to *congruous* merit, a man in the state of grace can merit *for himself* efficacious graces and final perseverance; for others he can merit the first grace and aids to further graces. The sinner can merit the aid of grace by means of good works, e.g., prayer, fasting and almsgiving, in order that he may avoid sin and obtain justification.

It follows that, except Jesus Christ, as Head of the Mystical Body, no man can merit condignly for others because, according to the divine order, there is no proportion between his works and the sanctification of others; he can merit congruously; that is, by a holy life, he may obtain the conversion of his brethren. This, of course, is more effectively accomplished as the more intense are his love for and friendship with God, because, as the Angelic Doctor says, "it is proper that God fulfill man's will concerning the salvation of another according to the degree of friendship [with Him]." *de A.*

METABOLISM. *See* Nutrition.

METAGNOMIA. *See* Premonition.

METAPSYCHOLOGY. *Metapsychology*, in a general sense, includes all the scientific inquiries that concern the phenomena of mediums, telepathy, premonitions, and the like. These phenomena are believed to be beyond the field of normal psychology. To avoid terminology which defines metapsychology as a study of "whatever is beyond the mind," many prefer to refer to this as psychic research, despite the fact that the object of this psychological study is in no way psychic. Less properly, this psychological research may be called *occultism,* meaning the study of data which lie beyond the power of natural means of explanation. Occultism, at least in its common sense, refers to influences and theories linked to medieval magic, which originated at the close of the thirteenth century. According to such theories, many non-sensible elements or forces in the normal, empirical range of experience and consciousness are understood and controlled through a wide variety of practices, involving deep individual psychic modifications. Under this aspect, occultism is similar to magic.

HISTORICAL NOTES. Phenomena which constitute the object of metapsychology have been known since ancient times, but the scientific study of these is relatively recent, with the work of Mesmer and his followers on so-called *animal magnetism.* This consisted at first in the treatment of neuropathies by the use of magnetism, then by indirect application of magnetized water, and finally by the employment of artificial somnambulism, from which modern hypnotic and psychoanalytical methods were derived.

Other phenomena which did not fall under the general study of medicine or classic psychology became the object of that vast movement which goes under the name of *spiritualism* (*q.v.*) This is practiced by individuals who are moved partly by pseudo-religious motives, partly by a mundane and snobbish curiosity. A small number of researchers, however, undertook a scientific study of those manifestations called *psychical and metapsychical research.* Among the better known students of metapsychical phenomena were Prof. R. Hare (1856), the naturalist Wallace, the physicist Crookes (1870), A. Aksakov (1880), and the pysiologist Charles Richet (1900).

METHODOLOGY. Generally, the phenomena studied by metapsychology, take place in the presence of a certain number of persons, with the participation of special individuals called *mediums* (*see* Medium).

"Mediumistic experiences," Geley explains, "are similar to collective psychophysiological experiences, because the phenomena are the result of an unconscious collaboration between the *medium* and the *researchers.*" However, the production of such phenomena is subject to particular circumstances, such as habit and the existence of a sympathetic feeling between *medium* and spectators, and the fact that the place is scarcely illuminated or darkened completely. Generally, the work of research by metapsychological societies is conducted in laboratories equipped with modern instruments, suitable for the observation and verification of the experiments.

PHENOMENA. The phenomena of this science are mental and physical. Among the physical must be included: *moving tables* (*see* Spiritualism); *telekinesis* or the movement of objects without any apparent control; *levitation* of solid bodies and of the medium himself; *ectoplasia,* the loss from the body of the medium of a special dynamic substance, termed by Richet *ectoplasm,* which often can be photographed and to which some attribute the above-mentioned telekinetic activities; manifestations of acoustical sounds or raps; optical phenomena, such as phosphorescences, luminous globules; thermal effects, such as cold chills; chemical reactions and the introduction of objects into closed places, such as through walls.

The more important phenomena are *autoscopy* or the perception by the subject of his internal organs; *transposition of the senses,* whereby it seems that the subject senses through entirely different organs, such as sight through the ears, etc.; *personality changes* in which alterations or incarnations of deceased persons are supposedly accomplished; *clairvoyance* and *telepathy; pragmatic cryptesthesia,* a form of clairvoyance in which the subject is placed in contact with persons, places, or other objects of unknown origin but which he fully is able to describe; and finally, *xenoglossia,* in which the person who acts as the medium speaks or writes in a language that is unknown to him.

INTERPRETATION. The phenomena briefly outlined in the preceding paragraph have been the subject of the most diverse interpretations, which might be separated into one or two categories: (a) spiritualistic-occultistic hypotheses which make metapsychological phenomenology dependent upon the action of the spirits of the dead or, in some way, on the intervention of extra-human forces; (b) the hypothesis of scientific applications endeavoring to reduce these phenomena to a formula through increasingly objective efforts at research controlled by instruments, to come to an eventual naturalistic explanation.

The followers of the latter hypothesis depend on the research and investigation of normal and para-normal phenomena which they refer to as physico-chemical forces, or hyper-physical mechanism, that implies the existence of a special fourth dimension. This is defined as a particular "cerebral radiation" or a dissociative hallucinatory manifestation or a sublimating ego. However, no theory is such as to satisfy the requirements of scientific thought.

The interpretations of these categories rest on alleged interventions of disincarnated spirits, according to the spiritists; according to modern theosophists, the explanation rests on the appearance of apparent bodies of spirits with an appearance only of personality, or of lemures or other extra-human beings whose intervention would be harmful to anyone who invoked them. Recent occultists tend to teach that it is not the immortal souls of deceased persons but of residual groupings of this or that deceased person, which die after a certain period of larval existence. Even here it is simply a matter of thoroughly fanciful hypotheses.

CATHOLIC VIEW. Although the Catholic Church has never given a definition of the many and heterogeneous paranormal phenomena studied by metapsychology, yet in decrees of the Holy Office (March 30, 1898: Analecta eccl. 6[1898], 187; April 26, 1917: AAS, 268) it has consistently forbidden the faithful from engaging in magic, mediums or spiritualist practices (see also Spiritualism).

Theoretically, Catholic authors incline to a naturalistic or partly preternatural explanation; extra-human powers are more an intervention of the devil than of the spirits of the deceased, who are entirely dependent on God. God would not tolerate that their spirits be made a blind instrument of man's curiosity.

Irrespective of any theoretical explanation of the phenomena, the motive of the Church prohibition is clear, for, whether manifestations of a preternatural order or phenomena belonging to the sphere of the natural laws or plain tricks, the harm that can come to those who participate in such meetings or other activities of a magical or spiritualistic order is very serious.

In fact, even if one were to engage only in metaphychological experiments of *white magic* (see Magic) or in activities of a scientifico-naturalistic order, he would be likely to be affected by more or less serious psychoneurotic disorders, for the environmental surroundings and the individual sessions are likely to cause psychotraumatic conditions which lead to neuropsychological derangements and agitations because of their strong emotional impact.

If those manifestations are of a preternatual order, of necessity they are the result of diabolical intervention, since they are not the result of prayer to God or of other devout practices, but are promoted by individuals, indifferent, to say the least, if not directly hostile to true religion. And this acknowledgment is even more compelling in the case of those sessions at which the devil is explicitly evoked. Thus, to damage to physical health the sin of superstition, divination, or idolatry is added, inasmuch as it concerns actions and gatherings that are intentionally irreligious and sacrilegious. However, a true scientist who has sufficient reason to attend those sessions commits no sin if the motive is to investigate the nature of the spiritualistic manifestations without taking an active part in them or giving scandal by his presence.

The illicitness of a recourse to metapsychological methods for curative purposes will be discussed under spiritualism. Here we shall add that the Catholic scholar, whether lawyer, judge, or physician, may not propose nor accept the use of such methods for the purpose of solving judiciary questions. This is so not only because the aid of so-called *clairvoyants* can prove ruinous to the ends of justice but also because the nature of metapsychological phenomena is still uncertain and debatable. *Riz.*

METEOROPATHIES. Ancient writers considered morbid illnesses of a neuropsychological nature, particularly if the symptoms indicated alternating phases, to be more or less due directly to atmospheric or meteorological variations. Due to the progress made in pathological anatomy, cellular pathology, and bacteriology, that opinion is completely obsolete and continues to be held only by popular legend.

The concept of meteoropathies was reaffirmed by Lombroso in his essay on *Thought and Meteors*; further research on constitutional medicine held that atmospheric agents have a greater influence than believed in the determination of some mental and nervous diseases, as was formerly held by the ancients. Recently in Germany, Hellpach conducted inquiries into the relationship between pathology and meteorology. His monumental work appeared in English under the title *The Patient and the Weather*.

NATURE OF METEOROPATHIES. Although science may admit that the nervous system possibly gives evidence of morbid reactions under the influence of atmospheric variations, meteorological changes or seasonal climate, it is also true that the consensus of experts which would attribute these as real causes of such reactions, as well as any consensus on the pathogenesis of such states, is in fact still lacking. Some attribute such reactions to the influence of magnetic disturbances connected with solar spots; others point to barometric factors, variations of atmospheric humidity, cosmic rays, or the ionization of the air. This is all basically conjectural, although it is possible that the variety of contributing factors may include meteoropathological elements that occasion a selective sensibility in different individuals.

The consensus of scholars is not unanimous for the precise pathogenesis of meteoropathies. One opinion gaining ground advocates that meteoropathics or meteorosensitive individuals show an hepatic insufficiency associated with vagal weakness; two factors tend to accentuate the general reaction of an organism to external agents, which hinder the habitual adaptation of the individual to meteorological variations.

MORAL COROLLARIES. Prescinding from more serious but less frequent manifestations of the influence of atmospheric conditions on the mental states of individuals, such as the defense mechanism of fear in some individuals during severe storms, in which any meteorological elements, if they exist, give way to reactions caused by thunder and lightning, meteoropathies offer points for consideration in the moral order. We limit ourselves to two: one concerns *nervous* temperaments, the other, *lunatics*. In examining an individual with a *nervous* temperament, the physician should consider the possibility that he may be dealing with a meteoropathic individual. If this hypothesis proves correct, he must with appropriate words explain to the patient his condition; this might suffice to improve the morbid condition, for, with an awareness of the cause of his disorder, the patient will become calmer and endeavor to control excessive reactions. Thus he can overcome future crises more effectively with the aid of appropriate hepato-neuro-vegetative remedies.

Those close to patients must look with particular sympathy upon *lunacy* and other psychoneurotic manifestations and contribute to their cure by directing these persons to competent specialists and by cooperating fully in establishing a full and clear picture of the conditions present in the patient. An understanding of these patients is necessary, for they are not evil but ill; as a result, they seek to vent their ill-humor and nervousness on others. *Riz.*

METHOD OF MORAL THEOLOGY. *See* Theology, Moral.

METHOD, PREVENTIVE. *See* Education.

METROPOLITAN. *See* Archbishop.

MIDWIFE. The function of midwife, until fifty years ago common everywhere, is no longer so; in some countries it has been completely absorbed by the medical profession. Since it still remains an important institution in many countries, the article retains a relative value.

The midwife is a woman possessed of necessary scientific and practical knowledge to assist pregnant women at the time of delivery. Two elements make the presence of a midwife necessary: in the most simple and normal delivery, a woman has always need of help and assistance; though not indispensable, it is useful and highly desirable that this assistance be given by a person well prepared with a knowledge of hygiene and capable of looking after the mother and the child. Although a natural function, a delivery may often present difficulties and complications and an element of danger. By her training, a midwife is able to detect abnormalities and take the necessary precautions in time, personally or, in the more serious cases, by seeking the aid of a physician. For this reason, in more progressive countries, the profession of midwife can only be exercised by women who have obtained a certificate in a recognized institute.

The moral obligations of a midwife are quite similar to those of a registered nurse (*q.v.*). The midwife must know exactly how and when a child must, according to the doctrine of the Catholic Church, be baptized during the various phases of a difficult delivery, in serious danger following the delivery, or in case of abortion (*see* Baptism). In normal deliveries a midwife may exercise her profession without the direction of a doctor. In modern times, a truly Christian midwife can exercise a beneficial influence in problems regarding the limitation of a family, by instructing clients of the evil and dangers of artificial birth-control, by an effort to encourage mothers through supernatural reflections, and by helping them with kindness and charity, prompt-

ness and gentleness. Therefore, a midwife must possess high moral qualities and a great spirit of sacrifice.

JURIDICAL DUTIES. Canon Law entrusts to midwives the task of a corporal, physical examination of women in trials involving non-consummation or impotency in marriage. It lays down specific rule to be observed in this examination, which normally bind in conscience (Can. 1979, par. 2, #3; 1980; 1981). It demands that the midwife learn the form of baptism (Can. 743), and it exonerates her from the obligation of disclosing to a judge any information which might come to her in professional secrecy (Can. 1775, par. 2, #1). *Ben.*

MILITARISM. Militarism includes all philosophical or sociological currents which, in one way or another, glorify war or advocate its cosmic, biological, and moral necessity.

Opposed to these theories, based on blind, fatalistic naturalism, founded on mechanistic, biological, and monistic concepts of the universe, stands intransigent *pacifism*. For the advocates of pacifism, man's highest and loftiest ideal is peace, a peace which, however, is not based on rational and Christian philosophy. Theirs is a peace consisting of simple tranquillity as such, not a tranquillity with order.

Connected with pacifism is another philosophy called *humanitarianism*, which in its theoretical reverence for man seeks to abolish religious, political and national boundaries as the sources of continual wars, for the purpose of establishing a perpetual peace and condemning all wars as immoral. *Pal.*

MIMIC. *See* Theater, Artist.

MINISTER OF THE SACRAMENTS. *See* Sacraments.

MINISTRY. *See* Government.

MINOR. *See* Age.

MINOR EVIL. *See* Evil, Minor.

MINORITIES, NATIONAL. By *minority* is understood a foreign group established within the limits of a State. The technical term is new, although the problem goes back to the treaty of Westphalia. The problem of national minorities became grave after the First World War (1914–1918); it was further aggravated by disintegration of the national aggregate known as the Austro-Hungarian Empire, for, previously, order in a nation was considered an internal political affair; after the First World War this became a problem in international law.

The question of religious or racial minority always has been a matter of international law, which now is extended to national minorities of newly created States on the basis of the peace treaty drafted after the war. The protection of minorities by international law was based on the principle of self-determination contained in the famous Fourteen Points of Wilson. But the value of this proclaimed doctrine was short lived, for at the end of the Second World War no one spoke of minorities any longer. Instead, we were witnesses to forced removals of minorities and voluntary abandonment of the mother country.

The methods for which much blame had been laid on the Nazis were tacitly sanctioned by the peace treaties. Thus, those who belonged to minority groups were, in fact, incorporated into the State despite the fact that they were a separate, cultural group, different from the majority of the citizens in race, language, religion, and a cultural life. The question of minorities, therefore, has its roots in the natural law; it is the duty of international law to uphold the sacredness of the norms of the natural law.

A real minority group must possess the following characteristics: (a) it must represent a notable group capable of developing its own cultural life; (b) the members of the minority must enjoy the civil rights in the State in which they live; juridically speaking, aliens, as such, are not a part of the minorities of the State in which they live; (c) minorities must be different in race, language, or religion. These are objective characteristics; a subjective note is based on a voluntary declaration of a desire to be considered members of a minority.

In the peace treaty of 1918, the victorious nations resolved to protect national minorities; that was done in the peace treaties with Austria, Hungary, Bulgaria, Turkey, and in specific treaties with Poland, Czechoslovakia, Jugoslavia, Rumania and Greece. The text or the concept of these treaties was to serve as an example for other international treaties concerning the protection of minorities. The stipulations concerning the minorities as contained in the peace treaties were formulated according to a general pattern, substantially as follows: (a) the right to life, private liberty, and worship; (b) equality before the law with equal right to offices and honors; (c) free use of their own language in religious and private life, commerce, press, meetings and courts of law; (d) equal freedom to establish and administer their own social, religious, and charitable institutions; in addition, free schools and similar institutions; (e) equal treatment concerning taxation.

All these provisions were guaranteed by the League of Nations but the result was short lived. Many of these decisions of international law are none other than specific determinations of the natural law, which requires that national minorities have equal rights in common with all citizens, and that they must be permitted to preserve freely their ethnic traditions, which constitute their particular characteristics. *Per.*

MIRACLE. *See* Suggestion.

MISERERE. The word *miserere* (Latin, to have mercy) is the first word in the Latin version of psalm 50 (Heb. 51), *Miserere mei, Deus* (Have mercy on me, O God). This became the title of the psalm itself, the fourth penitential psalm. It is attributed to King David, who was stirred to repentance for his double sin of adultery and murder by the words of Nathan the prophet (II Sam. 11:2–12:16).

A careful examination of the text reveals nothing contrary to such authorship. The psalmist, sincerely repentant, requests the purification of his soul (9–11) and a complete interior renewal (12 ff.), for he acknowledges himself to be deeply corrupt (7). Then, as an example of perfect conversion, he promises to serve God with a true spiritual worship (15–19).

Profound moral truths are stated in this psalm: (a) God is offended not only by sins directed against Him, but also by those committed against one's neighbor, as in the case of David; for the moral law and the rights of man flow from God. Hence, forgiveness of God must necessarily be sought for any violation against the moral law or the rights of man. (b) There exist not only actual sins but the reality of human nature deeply corrupt and inclined to evil. (c) The knowledge and practice of a moral life must not be an external gloss but come from inner conviction. (d) God wants the internal affection of a heart sincerely dedicated to Him. More than the external and material sacrifices of animal victims, God wants the internal affections of the heart. The last two verses (20–21) were added at the time of the exile, when the psalms began to be used to deplore the sins of the whole nation.

The psalm, one of seven penitential psalms, is used in the visitation of the sick, in extreme unction, in penitential times, in the ferial office during Lent, and especially in Holy Week. It is also used in the office of the dead and at funeral services. *Pal.*

MISERY. Misery is a state in which one, lacking indispensable goods, is depressed in spirit at finding himself unable to improve his lot by his own ability. Among allegoric Roman representations of misery, a baby chained in his crib was particularly employed. This indicated that adversity strikes man from the time of his birth. Misery is not the same as *poverty*. Poverty is the lack of some goods; it can also be the deliberate detachment from all the goods of the earth in order to attain a good of a higher order, as the *poverty* of St. Francis, or the vow of *poverty* of the religious orders. Misery is a condition of extreme indigence in which one may find himself against his own will.

Misery is a problem against which man has always struggled, but which he has never been able to conquer completely. Both the State and private individuals have incessantly sought measures against the spread of misery: from the Roman laws (*lex agraria, lex annonaria, frumentaria tessera, congiaria, donativa, sportula, epulae, etc.*), which constituted a complete system of relief and assistance, to institutions of charity among the early Christians; from the *double Sabbath* and the tithes of the Old Testament to the ration system and medieval Benedictine institutions.

In the modern world the problem has become more widespread with the system of salary wages for the industrial masses— a real source of misery whenever sufficient work is lacking. An inquiry made in England at the end of the nineteenth century showed that of 1,610 families in a state of misery, forty-three per cent were suffering from a shortage of work.

It is the duty of the State to intervene to combat misery with unemployment compensation programs or other positive measures of direct and indirect assistance. Among the latter are a fair distribution of opportunities for work, State employment regulations, and an increase of public work programs. *Pav.*

MISSAL. The *Missal* is the liturgical book of texts and prayers to be used by the priest in the celebration of the Mass. A liturgical book made use of by the faithful at Mass is also referred to as a missal.

Christ determined the essential elements of Christian worship, in which the Eucharistic Sacrifice is basic, but He left to the Apostles and their successors the responsibility of further organization of worship according to the requirements of time and place. This freedom gave rise to various Eastern and Western liturgies. Among the latter, the Roman liturgy, the leading one, is celebrated in the Latin tongue.

The documents which permit us to trace the development of the Roman liturgy are chiefly: *Traditio Apostolica,* written by St. Hyppolitus in the third century, and the *Leonine, Gelasian,* and *Gregorian Sacramentaries.* St. Gregory the Great, among the Sovereign Pontiffs, contributed greatly to the development of the liturgy. Since his reign, the Roman liturgy has undergone few modifications of importance; this is particularly true with respect to the canon of the Mass, which to this day has preserved its original form as found in the *Gregorian Sacramentary.* Upon the request of many bishops, the Council of Trent reformed the Roman liturgy; St. Pius V promulgated the new *Roman Missal* in 1570, and its use was made obligatory in all areas where the liturgy is celebrated according to the Roman rite, with the exception of those churches which had employed for at least two hundred years a missal approved by the Holy See. By order of St. Pius X, important rubrical changes and additions were made, but the text of the liturgical book was left as it was. The changes introduced by Pius XII concern only the rubrics (cf. Cost. *Christus Dominus,* January 6, 1953, especially the decree of the Sacred Congregation of Rites of March 23, 1955, with Replies of June 2, 1955: AAS, 48 [1955], 218–224, 418). For the three days of Holy Week the Sacred Congregation promulgated a new *Ordo hebdomadae sanctae (ibid.,* 830).

CONTENTS. In addition to the rules or rubrics to be observed during the celebration of the Mass, the Missal contains the unchangeable parts of the Mass (prayers, with a few exceptions, said in every Mass) and also the variable parts of the Masses said during the year. The variable parts of the Mass include: Introit, Collect, Epistle, Gradual, Alleluia or Tract (Sequence), Gospel, Offertory Prayer, Secret Prayers, Communion Verse, and Post-Communion Collects. The Missal also contains the proper of each season, the commons and propers of the saints, and the votive Masses.

In recent years, the Missal has been translated into vernacular languages for the benefit of the faithful. The use of the Missal by the laity is an effective and fruitful method of participation in the offering of Mass, since it fosters greater union between the faithful and the invisible High Priest and Victim of the Sacrifice, as well as the visible priest and the other members of the Mystical Body of Christ in rendering to God the most acceptable act of worship. *Man.*

MISSIONS. *Mission* (Latin, *mittere*—to send), in its broadest meaning, refers to any commission or power given to someone for carrying out an assignment entrusted to him, as an ambassador, legate, or representative. In its strictest sense, *mission* refers to religion, chiefly the preaching of the Gospel. In a canonical sense, it indicates the ministry of preaching given by a lawful ecclesiastical superior (Can. 1328) for the propagation of the Gospel in fulfillment of the command of the Divine Master: "*Euntes, docete*" (Mark 15:16; Matt. 28:19–20). Thus, *mission* may be described as a sacred expedition directly instituted either to revive Christian fervor and convert sinners or to propagate the Catholic faith among heretics and pagans. Thus we have two kinds of missions: (a) *home* or parish missions, also called popular or sacred missions (Can. 1349, par. 1), and *foreign* missions (Can. 1349, par. 1; and 1350, par. 2), whose essential purpose is the extension of Christ's kingdom among pagans and the increase of the number of the faithful.

Parish missions, also called spiritual exercises for the laity, are an extraordinary ministry of one or more preachers, approved by the competent authority (Cans. 1328, 1337). Following a particular format, they preach the Word of God to a city, parish, or region, by a systematic explanation of the truths of faith, for the conversion of sinners and the advancement of moral and religious life among the people.

Foreign missions are foreign territories where priests are sent to introduce or consolidate the Catholic faith among non-Catholics. Generally, the work of foreign missions begins with the preaching of the Gospel and extends progressively to the full exercise of the priestly and pastoral office.

Parish missions began in the eleventh century, while the origin of foreign missions actually goes back to the Divine Master Himself. The power and office of teacher given by Jesus Christ to His Church is the dogmatic basis on which the missionary work rests. This power and office gives to the Church alone the right and duty to propagate, defend, preach, and propose Christ's revelation authoritatively to all men, independently of any human power. Mankind has the duty to accept, believe and practice this. "Go into all the world," the Divine Master ordered, "and preach the Gospel to every creature. He who believes and is baptized, shall be saved; but he who does not believe, shall be condemned" (Matt. 16: 15–16). It is the Church's duty to instruct all; no one has the right to hinder the Church from carrying out this duty, imposed by Jesus Christ Himself (cf. L. Billot, De Ecclesia Christi, Romae, 1898; Can. 1322–1323). Only the teaching Church, under the leadership of the Sovereign Pontiff (Can. 1327–1328), has the right to organize, rule, and direct the entire missionary work, by authoritatively giving a mandate to preach (Can. 1328) and by assigning and distributing in a suitable manner various fields of activity.

Prior to the Code of Canon Law, there were no general or special prescriptions binding parish priests or priests with the care of souls regarding parish missions, although they were prescribed by particular laws for certain specific times. Today, Can. 1349 prescribes that local Ordinaries see to it that such missions be held in every parish at least every ten years. The Church grants special indulgences to those attending a mission, and special faculties are also granted to the preachers of missions. In 1622, Pope Gregory XV established a special department for foreign missions, called the Congregation for the Propagation of the Faith. In 1624, Pope Urban VIII formed a seminary for young men from various nations, who were sent after ordination to mission lands to work for the extension of God's kingdom. To understand the great interest of the Church in foreign missions, read the various encyclicals and apostolic letters of the recent Sovereign Pontiffs, e.g., Maximum illud of

Benedict XV, November 30, 1919; Romanorum Pontificum of Pius XI, May 3, 1922; and Evangelii praecones of Pius XII, June 2, 1951.

Today, Catholic missions, entrusted to various institutes and religious orders, are under the jurisdiction of the Congregation for the Propagation of the Faith, whose power of government is exercised through delegates, vicars, and prefects apostolic (Can. 293–311).

The work of the missions involves a complexity of activities directed to an intensive and organized effort in propagating the effects of redemption and in bringing men to the knowledge, love, and service of God according to the will of our Lord Jesus Christ. An army mobilized in behalf of the reign of God for the salvation of souls, missionaries, catechists, doctors and other auxiliaries are fully dedicated to the apostolate of the conversion of the world to God.

While it is true that the burden of the propagation of Christ's kingdom rests in a special manner on the teaching Church, it is also true that the faithful are not exempt from all responsibility; it is their duty to cooperate in the conversion and evangelization of the world. To be a Christian implies a moral obligation to participate in the conversion of the world. This will be easily understood by the following: (a) Jesus Christ gave us the faith that we may share it with our brethren. (b) Jesus Christ died to save all; we cannot, therefore, remain indifferent to the possibility that many men may not be saved because of their ignorance of Jesus Christ. (c) Those who love Jesus Christ must do all they can in order that He may be known and loved also by others. (d) If it is a duty of charity to practice the works of mercy, it is even a greater duty to assist in the work of evangelization, because the soul is certainly worth more than the body. Therefore, the faithful cannot, without being guilty of sin, remain aloof from aiding the missionary apostolate.

There are many ways to assist: (a) By becoming a missionary, if God calls one. The missions need missionaries and people of many skills for important mission works; hence, he who is called by grace to the missionary vocation must respond generously. (b) By prayer and sacrifices for the missions. The redemption of souls is the fruit of the greatest and most heroic sacrifice ever made, the sacrifice of Jesus Christ; nothing helps more than sacrifice in making redemption of souls possible (cf. Matt. 9:37; Enc. *Maximum illud* of Benedict XV, November 30, 1919). (c) By sustaining the missionary works with material means of support for missionaries and mission institutions, such as orphanages, seminaries, and schools. (d) By subscribing to missionary publications, by making missionary action known to others, and by enrolling one's name in the works of the missionary apostolate.

Many organizations of missionary cooperation exist, and every institute and religious order with missionaries in the mission field has a third order, guild, or group of cooperators who devote themselves to raising funds and to the practice of special works of religion in behalf of the missions under the care of that institute. Among these organizations there are three outstanding ones: (1) *the Society for the Propagation of the Faith;* (2) *the Sanctuary of the Holy Childhood;* (3) *the Society of St. Peter the Apostle for Native Clergy* (cf. Apostolic Letter of Pius XI, February 28, 1926).

The spiritual benefits granted to members of such organizations are many. In addition to the numerous indulgences granted by the Church, they may gain the following benefits: (a) a great reward for their work of charity in behalf of their fellow man; (b) the grace to understand and preserve more surely their faith; (c) participation in the merits of the missionaries and the new members of God's Church. The necessity of an international protection for missions and missionaries is evident because missionaries have a right to such a protection by their own State, whose citizens they remain. The principle of freedom of conscience and the civilizing work they do demand this protection of the international personality of the Church. *Tar.*

MITER. *See* Vestments, Sacred, Rubrics.

MIXEDEMA. *See* Cretinism.

MIXED RELIGION (Impediment). Canon 1060 of the Code of Canon Law states that the Church *most stringently* prohibits the marriage of two baptized persons in which one is a Catholic and the other a member of an heretical or schismatic sect. Furthermore, if there exists a danger of perversion of faith for the Catholic party or the children, the marriage is forbidden by divine law itself. However, the impediment is not such as to invalidate the marriage. If a mixed marriage is celebrated without permission of the Ordinary, it is valid although it would be illicit, a sinful violation of the law.

The manner of obtaining a dispensation from this impediment varies from country to country, but in all cases the Church requires grave and just reasons as a basic condition.

In countries where the large majority of the population is Catholic, the Holy See, specifically the Holy Office, seldom grants such dispensation; whereas, if Catholics are in a minority, the dispensation is more easily granted by the local Ordinary, provided that a non-Catholic party gives guarantees by promises in writing that danger of perversion of the faith for the Catholic party is removed, and both parties give definite assurance that all children born of their marriage shall be baptized and reared as Catholics (Can. 1061).

In addition, the Catholic party assumes the obligation of striving as far as possible to lead the non-Catholic to the Catholic faith (Can. 1062).

FORM TO BE OBSERVED IN THE CELEBRATION. Couples of mixed marriages are forbidden to contract marriage according to a non-Catholic rite; they may appear before a non-Catholic minister only if he acts as a civil official (Can. 1063) in those places where the civil ceremony must by law precede the religious ceremony. The Catholic celebration of a mixed marriage must be without solemnity or pomp; a nuptial Mass may never be celebrated (Can. 1064). By these restrictions the Church intends to show how much she opposes such marriages, from which deplorable effects often follow, despite examples of sincere conversions of the non-Catholic party. In general, however, experience shows that good results are rather exceptions which stress the great concern of the Church with regard to mixed marriages.

He who contracts a mixed marriage without a dispensation may incur various canonical penalties, even excommunication, although the marriage would be valid. *Bar.*

MODESTY. *Modesty* admits of a variety of meanings. St. Thomas considers it a potential aspect of temperance (*q.v.*). In fact, temperance regulates and restrains the pleasure of feeling, of taste, and of the sexual act. There must be another virtue restraining other appetites, which is associated with the virtue of temperance. In a broad sense, modesty is the virtue that regulates all external and internal appetites and actions which do not offer particular difficulty. In a stricter sense, *modesty* refers only to actions and customs (*modestia morum et cultus*), which it governs according to right reason. Thus, one is induced by this virtue to a reasonable control of his actions and external customs in clothes, ornaments, etc., according to his status, with a moderation between neglect and exaggeration (*see* Luxury).

In modern language, the broader sense of the scholastic meaning of modesty is no longer used, but a more restricted and negative sense is common today. Frequently the term, in a more specific meaning, refers to actions and external customs in connection with the virtue of purity. Thus, modesty regulates one's actions and external customs with the intention of avoiding sexual commotion in oneself or others.

In this latter sense, modesty is not the same as chastity or purity, although it is frequently mistaken for these virtues. Modesty is an external protection and effect of the virtue of chastity or purity, which aims (a) to focus attention on the more noble part of man, his soul in its domination over sexual life, and (b) to prevent temptations and dangers contrary to purity. Training in the virtue of modesty is vital for the preservation of individual virtues of chastity and public morality.

In the broader sense, modesty allows of variations in customs according to particular times, places, and individual temperaments. Excess for one may not be so for another; immodest garb in one place may not be considered so in another.

Modesty has a function which is not only individual but social; its application and customs depend, not on the criterion of individual preference and judgment, but on objective social considerations and effect on social morality. *Dam.*

MOLINOS. See Quietism.

MONARCHY, ABSOLUTE. See Democracy; Government; Paternalism.

MONASTICISM. See Order, Religious.

MONEY, CURRENCY. To satisfy needs, man finds the inevitable necessity of exchanging the products of his labor for some other item. This may be done by barter or by the selection of a specific commodity as a medium of exchange for all transactions (*see* Exchange).

At different times and places the most diversified commodities were used as a medium of exchange; the more common ones always had at a particular time a greater degree of salability: regular bars of salt in Abyssinia, furs in Siberia, seashells in the Indian Ocean, oxen in Central Europe, tobacco in Virginia, etc.

With the passage of time, especially when exchanges became numerous and markets larger, precious metals, such as gold and silver, became the medium of exchange, principally because of their almost invariable inalterability, divisibility, homogeneity, easy manufacture, and easy identification by color, sound, and weight. In modern times the use of paper currency has become prevalent and universal; in fact, it can be said to constitute a specific characteristic of the economic world of our time.

Today, currency may be: (a) *metallic*, typical money or currency; its legal or nominal value corresponds to the metal's market value, with a slight increase for cost of coinage; (b) *paper currency,* either (1) *representative* or *free rate,* which, upon request of the bearer, can be converted into metallic-standard currency by the State or related issuing body, or (2) *paper notes at a compulsory rate* which are accepted for payments by force of law, but not accepted for conversion (*see* Inflation); (c) of very great importance in exchange are the *checks* issued on actual bank deposits.

Currency fulfills an intermediary function in the *exchange* of economic commodities. Secondly, it acts as a *standard* for all merchandise and values. All merchandise in relation to others has its own exchange value; such value is determined by the relation between its unit and that of other merchandise. For example, if we can purchase a pint of wine with one pound of wheat, we say that the value of exchange of the wheat in respect to the wine is one to one. However, since the value of each individual commodity cannot be easily determined by comparing one with all others, we refer all commodities to one, i.e., currency. This facilitates the regulation of prices, which are precise values expressed in money. Thirdly, currency serves as a means of accumulating wealth. Often man is in possession of commodities which cannot be preserved, for by their nature they are perishable. On the other hand, he may not wish to acquire other commodities for immediate consumption since he has no actual need of them. Thus he exchanges such commodities for money, which is not perishable and is always valuable.

Currency, too, has its price, which is ordinarily termed *purchasing power.* The price of money, like other merchandise, is subject to the law of supply and demand (*q.v.*); that is, determined by the amount of money available in a market in a unit of time and by the general demand for it. As the monetary supply increases, its value decreases and the price of products rises; if the quantity of money decreases, its value rises and the price of products goes down.

However, currency always maintains its essential character as an instrumental good in effecting exchanges of products. Now, the same money may be used for one or two or more exchanges in the same period of time. It is obvious that the greater the speed of its circulation, the smaller the volume of demand; for this reason, the value of money is inversely proportional to two elements: volume or quantity and speed of exchange on one hand, and total volume of other economic commodities on the other hand. These bring a variation in the price of money. It appears now a proven fact that in the course of time the quantity of money and exchange speed increase more than the total volume of other commodities; hence, its real price or real purchasing power is inevitably destined to decrease, although its nominal price (*see* Price) remains the same. It follows that he who lends money today finds himself in an unfavorable position with respect to the one who must pay it back tomorrow, since tomorrow the same money may show the same face value but diminished purchasing power. Furthermore, it must be observed that he who lends money is ordinarily the person who has saved it and is the lender of work. The latter lends his work valued in money (salary), while the one to whom the money is loaned is the entrepreneur; it follows that the cycle almost always works in favor of profit and to the damage of interest and salary. This, as everybody knows, has happened to a great extent in the last few years.

The nature and function of money must be taken into consideration in the moral evaluation of economic transactions between men, contracts, work, interest rates, etc. *Pav.*

MONK. *See* Order, Religious; Congregation, Religious; Religion; Religious Rules and Constitutions.

MONOPOLY. (system). A system of monopoly consists in exclusive control by one person or corporation of the supply of a commodity or service in a given market. Monopoly may be: (a) *natural,* if it involves natural productive factors, as water sources in mountain or river rights; (b) *customary,* if the ownership of a commodity or service is actually reserved to one person or a family—for example, certain special products or curative methods; (c) *legal*, if it is fixed by law, as the monopoly of mail service in U.S.A.

The distinguishing mark of a monopoly system is that a monopolized commodity or service cannot be reproduced. In a competitive system (*see* Competition), increase in the price of a commodity or service finds a restraint in the fact that others can produce the same commodity or lend the same service by offering it at a fairer price. This is not done in a monopolist system, since the monopolist is the only controller of the good or service.

The lower the price of a commodity the greater the number of potential buyers, but the number of buyers decreases inversely in proportion to increase in price. Consequently, the monopolist can control either the price or the quantity, not both simultaneously. If he increases the price, he must of necessity decrease the quantity; if he increases the quantity, he must lower the price or else the rest of the commodity would remain unsold. For this reason, the monopolist, exclusively motivated by economic interest, does not aim at selling the greatest possible quantity of the monopolized product nor obtaining the highest price; he aims, instead, at disposing of that quantity which permits him to realize the best price, that is, the largest net income (*q.v.*) on the whole.

It has been stated that the monopoly system hinders progress because the monopolist, safe from competition, has no incentive toward improving his business. It is also stated that monopoly harms the interests of the consumer because the monopolist, adjusting the price to the quantity, is naturally inclined to look after his own interest rather than the common good.

This is true; but it is also true that the monopoly system offers some positive elements in comparison with the competitive system. First of all, the monopoly system must be credited with saving considerable expenditures required by competition. Secondly, it offers a greater stability, for the monopolist can produce easily according to consumption. Thirdly, if the monopolist is a public institute, the price could be fixed at a level that would permit the largest number of consumers to acquire the commodity or avail themselves of the service. Finally, it may be observed that, if a public monopolist were to realize a benefit, that benefit could well be turned to the community. Therefore, one must not necessarily take a dim view of the monopoly system, especially if products of large consumption are involved or services which are indispensable to the normal life of society.

Even when monopoly is fair in itself, it may not exceed in its profits the limits of the highest price of the merchandise (*see* Price, Just) unless it is a State monopoly in the form of taxation. Excessive profits are all the more unjust as they are made on products of primary necessity. *Pav.*

MONSTER. *See* Baptism; Surgery; Sacraments.

MONSTRANCE. *See* Benediction, Host, Vessels, Sacred.

MONTESSORI, METHOD. *See* Education, School, Lay.

MONTHS, SACRED. *Sacred months* is a term embracing the custom of dedicating a particular month of the year to the honor of God, Jesus, the Virgin Mary, or a particular saint by special extra-liturgical devotions on each day of that month. These devotions became general practices among the faithful, particularly after the eighteenth century; many of these practices have become an integral part of the devotional life of the faithful.

These particular forms of devotion, linked to an orderly succession of days, also occur in the devotions called novenas or tridua; such practices are in no way superstitious, because the final intention, the efficacy of prayer or devotion, is not made to depend upon a time schedule but upon the exercise performed. The notion of continuous days is an aid to the orderly execution of these devotional practices and the continuity of prayer in honor of a particular saint or person.

Practically every month is marked by some particular devotion or dedication; some monthly devotions are more widely observed than others. Thus, March is dedicated to St. Joseph; May, to the honor of the Blessed Virgin; June, to the Sacred Heart of Jesus; November, to prayers for the suffering souls in purgatory. The Church has enriched these devotional practices with numerous indulgences. The monthly devotions ordinarily consist of morning or evening services. Morning services are generally linked to the celebration of Holy Mass; evening services are generally concluded with Benediction of the Blessed Sacrament, the blessing with a relic, or the recitation of the Holy Rosary. The prayers consist of a brief meditation on eternal truths or an explanation of the particular devotion. Sometimes the meditation is replaced by a sermon on the particular meaning of the devotion.

JANUARY. This month is dedicated to the Most Holy Name of Jesus. Although the devotion to the Holy Name was promoted by St. Bernard and St. Bernardine, it became a popular, general practice only in recent times. It originated with the celebration of the feast of the Circumcision of our Lord, when the Second Person of the Blessed Trinity was given the Holy Name of Jesus, as suggested to St. Joseph by divine revelation (Luke 2:21).

Indulgences. All the faithful who participate in spiritual exercises of devotion in honor of the Most Holy Name of Jesus may gain an indulgence of seven years once each day; if these devotions are practiced for a whole month, a plenary indulgence may be gained under the usual conditions. These indulgences are applicable to the souls of the deceased.

On the feast of the Holy Name, the faithful may gain a plenary indulgence, which may be offered for the deceased, if with a true spirit of penitence the faithful receive the sacraments of penance and the Holy Eucharist, visit a church, public or semi-public oratory, and pray for the intentions of the Holy Father.

MARCH. This month is dedicated to St. Joseph, the spouse of the Blessed Virgin, and the patron of the Universal Church (December 8, 1870).

Indulgences. The faithful who devoutly take part in prayers and public devotions during the month of March may gain an indulgence of seven years each day, and a plenary indulgence if they participate in the exercises for at least ten days of the month and fulfill the usual conditions of confession, communion, and prayers for the intentions of the Holy Father. Those who privately perform the same exercises are granted an indulgence of five years for each day, and a plenary indulgence for the private performance of these exercises if they are legitimately hindered from participation in public exercises.

The same indulgences may be gained by the faithful who perform these exercises of devotion from February 16 to March 19, or, in the event that they are hindered from doing so at this time, at another time for one whole month (Pius IX, April 27, 1865).

MAY. May is dedicated to honoring the Blessed Virgin Mary, the Mother of God. In the southern hemisphere, in South America, these devotional practices are held in December, the spring in those regions, for May occurs in the middle of winter.

Indulgences. The indulgences granted to the faithful who publicly participate in devotions in May are seven years' indulgence for each day and a plenary indulgence under the usual conditions of confession, Communion, and prayers for the intention of the Holy Father, if the devotional exercises are repeated for at least ten days. The faithful who practice this devotion privately may gain an indulgence of five years at each exercise and a plenary indulgence if practiced for a whole month. But this is granted only to those who are unable to participate in public acts of devotion.

JUNE. This month is dedicated to the honor of the Sacred Heart. This devotion reached its apex in the last century.

Indulgences. The faithful who devoutly and publicly perform some religious exercises in honor of the Sacred

Heart during the month of June may gain an indulgence of ten years at each exercise and a plenary indulgence if the prayers and devotional exercises are performed for at least ten days.

Those unable to attend public acts of devotion may gain the same indulgence if they perform these exercises privately for an entire month.

If the month of the Sacred Heart is solemnly celebrated with the preaching of a sermon on each day of the month, or at least for a period of eight days in special exercises in churches, public, or semi-public oratories, the following indulgences may be gained: (a) a plenary indulgence under the usual conditions by those who participate in the devotions on the closing day after attending the sermons and spiritual exercises for at least ten days; (b) an indulgence of 500 days may be gained by all those who promote the aforesaid exercises, and a plenary indulgence if the usual conditions are fulfilled—namely, confession, Communion, and a visit to a church or oratory with prayer for the intentions of the Holy Father; (c) the indult of a personal privileged altar on the closing day of the month is granted to preachers and rectors of churches or oratories where the aforesaid month was solemnly observed. The same indulgences may be gained if the celebration is transferred to another month with the permission of the Ordinary.

JULY. This month is dedicated to honoring the Most Precious Blood of Jesus, an exercise of piety which dates back to the last century and the occasion of extending the feast of the Most Precious Blood of our Lord to the whole Church (July 1).

Indulgences. The faithful who attend public exercises of devotion in honor of the Most Precious Blood may gain an indulgence of ten years for each exercise and a plenary indulgence if they are present at these exercises for at least ten days of the month of July. Confession, communion, and prayers for the intentions of the Holy Father are also required.

To those who perform exercises of devotion privately, an indulgence of seven years is granted on each day, and a plenary indulgence if the practices of a pious exercise are carried on throughout the whole month. These indulgences may be gained only by those who are legitimately hindered from participating in the public exercises of devotion, when they are held.

AUGUST. This month is dedicated to honoring the Immaculate Heart of the Blessed Virgin Mary. This devotion was extended from private to public status in the seventeenth century, until full recognition was granted in the nineteenth century. The feast was first celebrated in 1805, after which devotion in honor of the Immaculate Heart of the Blessed Virgin Mary became widespread. This devotion attained a new drive following the consecration of mankind to the Immaculate Heart of Mary (October 31 and December 8, 1942) and after the extension of the feast of the Immaculate Heart of Mary to the whole Church (March 4, 1944: AAS, 37[1945], 55 ff.). The date of the feast is August 22.

Indulgences. An indulgence of five years is granted to all those who privately or publicly offer prayers or attend devotional exercises during the month of August in honor of the Immaculate Heart of the Blessed Virgin Mary, and a plenary indulgence under the usual conditions for all those who attend the exercise throughout the whole month of August.

SEPTEMBER. This month is dedicated to the honor of the Sorrowful Virgin, the Queen of Martyrs. Devotion to the Sorrows of the Blessed Virgin Mary is remotely linked with the mystic literature of the twelfth century and to the Order of the Servites, who were its promoters. In addition to the commemoration of the Sorrows of the Blessed Virgin Mary on the Friday after Passion Sunday, they were permitted (1688) to celebrate another feast of the Seven Sorrows of the Blessed Virgin Mary in September.

The dedication of the month of September in honor of our Lady of Sorrows began to spread after Pius VII extended the September feast day to the whole Church.

Indulgences: All the faithful who, during the month of September, publicly or privately attend religious exercises in honor of the Mother of Sorrows, may gain a five years' indulgence each time and a plenary indulgence under the usual conditions, if they shall have attended the pious exercises for the entire month.

OCTOBER. This month is dedicated to the Blessed Virgin under the title of the Holy Rosary. It is connected with the devotion of the Holy Rosary (*q.v.*) but developed more recently. The victory celebration instituted by St. Pius V after the battle of Lepanto (October 7, 1571) became the feast of the Most Holy Rosary of the Blessed Virgin Mary under Gregory XIII; but Leo XIII, recalling the numerous victories obtained through the devout recitation of the Holy Rosary, and encouraged by the new center of devotion established in Pompei (Italy) through the zealous work of Bartolo Longo, prescribed the public recitation of the Holy Rosary during the month of October.

Indulgences: Those who, during the month of October, recite one decade of the Rosary either publicly or privately may gain an indulgence of seven years each day, and a plenary indulgence if, besides the usual conditions of confession, Communion, prayer for the intentions of the Pope and a visit to a church or oratory, they recite the rosary on the feast day of our Lady of the Rosary (fixed by St. Pius X on October 7) and during the eight days following. Moreover, a plenary indulgence under the usual conditions may be gained by those who recite the Rosary for ten consecutive days, even outside the octave of the feast day. A seven years' indulgence may be gained by those who, in the month of October, add to the recitation of the Holy Rosary the prayer in honor of St. Joseph: *To you, O Blessed Joseph* (Enc. *Quamquam pluries* of August 15, 1899).

In addition, Leo XIII (decree of September 21, 1899) granted a plenary indulgence to the faithful who for fifteen consecutive Saturdays (either before the feast of the Holy Rosary or at another time of the year) devoutly recite one decade of the Rosary or meditate on the mysteries of the Holy Rosary, and on one of the aforementioned Saturdays or Sundays following, go to confession and Holy Communion, and pray for the intentions of the Holy Father. The same privilege is extended to those who, being legitimately impeded on Saturdays, practice the devotion on fifteen consecutive Sundays, under the same conditions.

NOVEMBER. This month is dedicated to the souls in purgatory. The veneration of the dead, resting on the belief of the immortality of the soul and the resurrection of the body, is as ancient as the world. The date of November 2 was introduced long ago in the worship of the Church, at the time of St. Odilone (1030–1031); but the *Commemoration of the Faithful Departed* took on new vigor at the end of the pontificate of St. Pius X by virtue of the decree of June 25, 1914, and with the Bull of Benedict XV, *Incruentum* (August 10, 1915). This Bull gave the privilege of celebrating three Masses on November 2 to all priests. From that time on, the observance of the month of November has become more widespread.

Indulgences: The faithful who, in the month of November, offer prayers or other devotional exercises in behalf of the souls of the faithful departed may gain a three years' indulgence on each day of the month, and a plenary indulgence under the usual conditions, if they offer the same prayers or devotional exercises for the whole month. Those who offer them in a church or public oratory may gain a seven years' indulgence each day, and a plenary indulgence if they offer them for at least fifteen days, with confession, Holy Communion, and prayers for the intentions of the Holy Father.

The *toties quoties* indulgence, similar to the Portiuncula, is granted on the day of November 2 (St. Pius X, decree of June 25, 1914). The recitation of six *Our Fathers, Hail Marys,* and *Glorias* each time, in addition to confession, Communion and a visit to a church or oratory is required to gain this indulgence. By virtue of the decree of the Sacred Penitentiary, January 2, 1939, this *toties quoties* indulgence may also be gained on the following Sunday under the same conditions. *Pal.*

MORALITY. Morality is the relation between a human act and man's ultimate end or the norm of behavior that flows from man's ultimate end. The relation is manifested through law, especially the natural law; it binds man through the voice of conscience. Since morality is a strict relation of dependence upon the ultimate end of man, there shall be as many moral systems as there are concepts of the end of man, also called man's supreme good. The enumeration of these systems is necessarily empirical and somewhat chaotic. We shall, however, indicate three elements of reference: the three types of good, as they are traditionally classified, are the pleasurable, the useful (altruistic or egoistic, social or individual) and the honest. Hence, there will be three systems of morality: the virtuous, the utilitarian and the hedonistic. Other classifications contain systems in which the three elements may be contained in different degrees, as the morality of heroism, esthetics, asceticism, and wisdom. Some speak also of idealistic, rationalistic, and instinctive morality, but these terms are often used to indicate, not a norm of morality, but rather a way by which some acquire knowledge of morality.

According to Catholic doctrine, the ultimate end or supreme good of man is the possession of God; accordingly, the moral norm of human acts consists in their aptitude at leading man to that end. Such an aptitude cannot be created by the human will, nor is it entirely at the disposition of divine freedom, but flows necessarily from the nature of God, from man's nature, and from the nature of the acts themselves. Hence, the norm of morality contains precepts which transcend every legislative will; the acts related to them are said to contain an intrinsic morality of good or evil. Extrinsic morality, instead, is that which depends upon the free disposition of the legislator. In order to determine concretely (empirically) the morality of a human act, one must study its object, end, circumstances, and the three elements which constitute the sources of morality for each individual act. *Gra.*

MORALITY IN ART. *See* Art, morality of.

MORALITY, INDEPENDENT. Under the term *independent morality* are concealed many doctrines. These doctrines have one thing in common, a negative element: a proclaimed independence. Positive elements are matters of complete disagreement, not only about the objective identification of the burden they wish to throw off but also about the subjective attitude which they assume in its regard. From the standpoint of objective differences, morality may be *independent* from religion, from the idea of God, from metaphysics, sanction, and obligation. From the standpoint of subjective differences, morality may be *agnostic,* if its followers ignore all the above-mentioned burdens; *skeptic,* if they doubt or dare not pass judgment on the value of the burdens they reject; *dogmatic,* if they reject the ancient, revered, and demanding dogmas, for which they substitute, in revolutionary fashion, new, irreverent, and convenient dogmas. Omitting all discussion of the subjective attitudes, which would require a review of all philosophical systems from idealism to materialism, we shall analyze the objective differences affecting independent morality.

MORALITY INDEPENDENT OF CHRISTIAN MORALITY. If we were to identify in a positive way this first step, it could be called the way of natural ethics. Its doctrine can be understood in a way that is consistent with Catholic doctrine insofar as it states that man, even without the aid of divine revelation, is capable of recognizing those norms of human conduct known as natural law. Often, however, that doctrine is understood in a sense that is contrary to Catholic thought, inasmuch as it rejects any intervention of revealed religion in the world of morals; in other words, it denies that God can help man in acquiring a better knowledge of the content of the natural law and that God can add new commandments to such a law.

MORALITY INDEPENDENT OF THE IDEA OF GOD. This is the way of *atheistic* morality. Its position is more serious than the first. Perhaps it is still possible to give an acceptable meaning to this phrase on condition that two problems be kept clearly distinct: one psychological, the other metaphysical. Human psychology is so complicated that it creates positions difficult to explain. In other words, as long as we remain in the field of facts and states of conscience, we believe that it is possible for man to hold athestic theories and still have a dignified moral sense; he may deny God and still continue to hear the commanding voice of conscience; he may even endeavor to obey that rather mysterious voice. But if we go beyond the fact and inquire into the origin, meaning, and value of the commands of conscience, that is, if we pose the problem in metaphysical terms, then, we no longer find a satisfactory answer in an atheistic hypothesis. If there be no God, one no longer knows the value of the voice of conscience which imposes definite obligations on him. Then the ethical imperative drops either to the level of illusion from which the wise man will free himself, or to the level of violence against which a man, conscious of his dignity, will rebel. The metaphysical impossibility of ethics without God is a profound teaching of philosophies such as that of Kant, which refused to reach God through speculative reason, but allowed this by following the paths of practical reason.

MORALITY INDEPENDENT OF METAPHYSICS. This coincides with the preceding in the sense that its followers refuse to approach metaphysics because they fear that it will finally lead them to God. Leaving these timid persons in the atheistic enclosure, we shall concern ourselves, instead, with those who reject metaphysics for more praiseworthy motives, all reducible to a desire of giving to morals (and perhaps also to faith in God) a more solid and universally accepted basis than intricate and variable philosophical props. While admiring such noble motives, we shall note that the rejection of metaphysics is impossible because the human act carries in itself an inseparable connection with metaphysical problems. Moral doctrine and practice necessarily depend on the response given

to the eternal questions of the origin and destiny of man which envelop the entire concept of the universe and which, for this reason, are anchored in metaphysics. Until such a time as we shall have answered those questions, our ethics will remain up in the air; hence, as someone will put it, if one abandons metaphysics for fear of building on the sand, he winds up building in the clouds. A reproof of this may be seen in the weakness of all the substitutes enlisted in support of the moral structure, from physiology to sociology, and from aesthetics to solidarity.

MORALITY INDEPENDENT OF SANCTION. This independence is a form of pride, now infantile, now heroic, by which one pretends neither fear of punishments nor expectation of reward, as he alleges a fulfillment of duty for duty's sake and good for the sake of good. Catholic moral doctrine does not reject heroism, but, aware of human weakness, does not forbid the hope of reward nor fear of punishment as aids to doing good or avoiding evil. Certainly, Catholic doctrine, too, condemns a narrow, mercenary spirit interested in the extent of recompense, but at the same time it also distrusts the systematic ostentation of disinterestedness. To impose the use of crutches on one who has healthy legs is stupidity, but to forbid their use to the cripple is cruelty; and in the world of ethics there are many cripples, and even the healthy have their moments of weakness. The puritanism of the stoics and Kant is not suited to mankind.

MORALITY INDEPENDENT OF OBLIGATION. This final stage of descent into an extreme ethical puritanism, removes the sense of duty to free the conscience from every shade of compulsion. Having reached this final point, so alien to ordinary thinking, we rest our case, but not without making the following observations. First of all, fear of duty is due to a confusion between the moral and the juridical orders. In the field of law, a narrow segment of the vast ethical world, obligation is presented with those characteristics of exteriority, compulsion, and hostility which make it so hateful. Moral conscience, especially if somewhat refined, has no such experiences at all, because duty coincides with love. Secondly, the destruction of a sense of duty could have been foreseen as a necessary end of the descent through which independent morality has travelled. With the collapse of all the foundations of the structure, the entire structure itself was bound to crumble; and the ethical structure, in the philosophy of good sense, has always been in the reign of duty. Therefore it is logical that morals and duty go together. Guyan, who gave form to the latter proclamation of independence, simply made explicit what was already contained in a more or less concealed way in the preceding formulas.

To establish a truly independent moral structure there is but one true and clear method: the elimination of the first of the three aspects under which "good" has always been presented: honest, useful, and pleasurable. If we eliminate the *honest* good, then morality is restricted to a search after pleasure and economic gain. The structure, of course, will stand in complete independence of everything transcendent. But it will no longer be the ethical structure such as it has always been understood by honest persons. Instead, there will be two structures: one economic, the other sensual. The first will house people working in war plants, while the second will be crowded with revellers seeking to become intoxicated in bacchanalian orgies. This is the fatal end product of independent morality. *Gra.*

MORALITY, PROFESSIONAL. *See* Deontology, Pharmaceutical and Medical.

MORALITY, SITUATION. Situation morality or ethics is less a body of doctrine than a moral tendency, more a mental attitude than morality in the proper sense. In fact, it is not fully codified in any authentic document, although practiced in many fields under the most diverse forms. Some of its more characteristic manifestations are found in literature, through which bold and snobbish people undertake to put the law of individual morality before the laws of the Catholic Church, which they judge to be too strict. Therefore, the error consists in an attempt to substitute aims and personal feelings for objective rules and general directives concerning the many moral problems of life.

This error crudely reflects the exigencies and deficiencies of our contemporary mentality; the weakening, even in practicing Catholics, of the spirit of faith, humility, and confidence in the Church; a rationalistic spirit, especially in those who openly profess lay morality; a longing for an exaggerated emancipation and an immoderate desire for vindication. This evil is found among married couples who judge Catholic morals to be out of step with their social and individual exigencies, and above all in the existentialistic atmosphere that so deeply impregnates modern thinking.

This attitude is found in several tendencies which are seldom presented in a systematic manner. Thus, in the book by E. Michel, *Eine Anthropologie der Geschlechtsgemrinschaft* (2nd ed., Stuttgart, 1950), which was placed on the Index (Decree of the Holy Office, December 15, 1952), we find a risky application of situation morality to the problems of marriage. Thus, too, Theodore Steinbuchel, outstanding philosopher and theologian, is indicted for favoring a system of individual morality. By stressing the personal element in a given situation, he fails to place in due light the sense of law and universal principles. Steinbuchel shows the effects of a strong influence upon him of the personalistic doctrines of many non-Catholic philosophers and theologians, such as F. Ebner, M. Buber and Kierkegaard. Situation morality is a product of Protestant theology, as E. Michel frankly admits.

Catholics influenced by such tendencies very often have failed to realize adequately that the moral doctrine of Protestant scholars is strictly bound to the fundamental dogmas of their theology. This appears quite clearly in the treatises of Protestant moral doctrine by E. Brunner, and in the more recent one by H. Thielicke, and also in the large amount of literature published after 1945 on natural law and on the theological bases of law.

The problem is ancient, indeed; it is the problem of universal principles and their application to moral life, which rests on a philosophy that refuses to recognize in every human being, and in concrete situations faced by the individual, the universal structure of a unified, essential order. It rests on a philosophy which holds that it would be equally false to affirm that this essence is found in an absolutely unique manner in each individual. Consequently, in this perspective, general moral law can no longer be understood as a principle having a real value for the individual man in such a particular situation. The sophism is clear: from the fact that a general law is incapable of fully covering a concrete situation, they erroneously infer that the situation cannot in any manner come under this law.

Situation morality, carried to extremes, must not be understood as an escape from the heavy burden of moral integrity. For, though its advocates truly deny the absolute value of universal norms, some are motivated by the belief that in this manner they are better safeguarding the eminent sovereignty of God. They believe that a law which is effective without any exceptions, is an absolute power of the one absolute, God. But they fail to realize that law is absolute only in the measure in which it participates of the absolute essence of God. Under this aspect, it is, indeed, effectively absolute.

From the anthropo-theological standpoint, advocates of situation morality base the non-absolute nature of obligation on the personal character of the relationships between man and God and between man and man. We, so they say, consider law as an intermediary element between God and man, which disturbs direct collaboration of a man, striving by the effectiveness of his own free activity, to respond to the appeal from God in a suitable manner in a present situation. They simply bring out the fact that the essence of man, as much as revealed divine law, is a permanent word of God, Creator and Redeemer. Man has the duty to respond because he is not a mere person but a man, already existing and placed in the historic development of revelation.

One must not think that these tendencies of modern philosophy or Protestant ethics are simply devoid of any authentic interest. Protestant ethics is right when it interprets the "situation," and not merely an extreme-limit situation, in the way of existentialists, i.e., as a unique appeal from God to which man responds by a personal decision. In fact, by taking a position, one takes a stand in regard to God. This position constitutes a primary element with respect to a moral decision, or, rather, within such a decision.

All know that it is not only by dialectics but above all by the virtue of prudence and a right intention that one must govern his own conduct. But to claim that one's own practical doubts can be solved without any obligatory reference to common precepts and universal principles is an entirely different matter. To ignore the fact that the negative precepts of the natural law apply indistinctly to all, because by definition they are directed against intrinsically bad acts which are absolutely never permitted, is to destroy morality entirely by one single stroke.

Indeed, someone may legitimately allege good faith as a subjective excuse; we will admit that in such a case he would be only materially guilty. But this is no reason for setting up the rule that one may with impunity disinterest himself in the objective value of his own acts and deeds.

Concerning the positive precepts which, in scholastic terminology, are always binding but not in every single case (*semper at non pro semper*), it is true that at times someone could be even objectively dispensed or excused because of a serious difficulty in a particular case. But it is understood that, within the limits of physical or moral possibility, one must always conform to prescriptions affecting the common good. In fact, to place oneself, even materially, outside the objective norm of our activities, weakens the dignity of the general order and the success of a life in common, which, in turn, strongly affects the destiny of everyone. Finally, the effort to bring about an objective harmonization of our individual conduct is an indispensable tribute to the Absolute, upon whom we depend entirely; it is a sign of the respect we owe to the dignity of our specific nature.

Here one can see the grave risks of the illusions to which he is exposed who allows himself to be guided only by his immediate and personal point of view in assessing values so formidable in their consequences and in their relation to the reality surrounding them.

CONDEMNATION. The danger of this new tendency in the field of morality is evident; hence, it is no surprise that by a decree of the Holy Office, February 2, 1956, the Church condemned it (ASS, 48[1956], 144–145).

This document was preceded by at least three solemn pontifical declarations in which the error of a subjective, individualistic morality opposed to abstract traditional morality was denounced. In his radio message to Christian educators on March 23, 1952, Pius XII denounced the evil inflicted upon human conscience by those who attempt to throw off all obligations imposed by divine law, by substituting the absolute principle of their own determinations (AAS, 44 [1952], 273). On April 18 of the same year, Pius XII dedicated his entire address to the delegates of the World Federation of Catholic Young Women to the subject of situation morality, which he compared to existentialism, actualism, and ethical individualism (AAS, 44 [1952], 414). Finally on April 13, 1953, Pope Pius returned to the same subject on the occasion of the Fifth International Congress of Psychotherapy and Clinical Psychology, to underscore the danger that exists in proposing a "personalistic morality" against traditional morality, prudently too vague to conform to the exigencies of concrete man (AAS, 45 [1953], 278).

In the face of the clear-cut and logical position taken by the Church, a Catholic has only one duty, that is, obedience. Traditional morality has always given the proper importance to the *circumstances of a human act* (q.v.). Pal.

MORALITY, SOCIAL. *See* Theology, Moral.

MORALS, CHRISTIAN. *See* Theology, Moral.

MORGANATIC MARRIAGE. *See* Marriage, Morganatic.

MORIBUND. *See* Danger of Death; Examination, Medical.

MORPHINE. *See* Aphrodisiacs; Drugs, Narcotics.

MORPHOLOGY. *See* Anthropology.

MORTAL SIN. *See* Sin.

MORTIFICATION. Mortification is the voluntary abstention from pleasurable actions or the voluntary imposition upon self of actions or elements unpleasant to human nature. In acts of mortification one may forego a pleasure or undertake a supererogatory sacrifice. Mortification in sinful matters is a matter of precept, but the Christian must not limit himself to these mortifications. Man, with a nature weakened by original and personal sins, has perverse inclinations, particularly a strong tendency to pleasures (Rom. 7: 22 ff.). To fail to repress these perverse tendencies of the heart by mortification in licit pleasures is to become a slave of the passions and fall into sin gradually. Moreover, we have an obligation to offer satisfaction to God for sins committed. We cannot make amends except by patiently enduring the tribulations of life or by the denial of licit pleasures.

Christian mortification is not an end in itself but a means absolutely necessary for the avoidance of sin and the fostering of a supernatural life (John 12:25; Rom. 8:13). Based on a love for God and a hatred for sin, Christian mortification is clearly distinct from the fanaticism professed by Montanists in the early centuries of the Church or by sects of the Middle Ages.

The external senses are the primary

area for the practice of mortification, i.e., sight and hearing, taste and touch, smell and instinct; there is also a mortification of the memory, dismissing useless thoughts from the mind, repressing inordinate impulses of the heart, especially those towards pride and self-love.

There exists a hierarchical order in mortifications: interior mortifications aim more directly at the root of sin and are therefore of greater value, although the practice of external acts of mortification renders the practice of the interior acts much easier. Mortification must be accompanied with generosity and discretion, in proportion to one's strength, and in harmony with the duties and obligations of one's state in life. One must strive to accept without complaint annoyances, adversities, and sufferings which come without being sought; one must add voluntarily renunciations, practiced with regularity and perseverance. *Man.*

MOTU PROPRIO. *See* Acts, Pontifical.

MOUNTAIN SICKNESS. *See* Kinetosis, Medicine, Aviation.

MULCT. The term *mulct* means to punish by imposing a successive increase or multiplication of amounts. This concept is based on its original character as a private reparation for non-fulfillment of a debt. Often the word *amends* (med. Latin, *mendum*—reparation) is used in the same sense.

Although both terms are at times interchangeable as a general notion applied to pecuniary fines, mulct presupposes a crime and amends a lesser injustice. A fine consists of the payment of a certain sum as a penalty for positive infractions of law or regulations concerning the orderly execution of activities of a generally administrative or governmental nature. A mulct may be an accessory penalty imposed for violations of a criminal nature. In practice, no distinction is made between mulct and amends.

Canonical law considers pecuniary fines among vindictive penalties (Can. 2291, par. 2); administrative or judiciary canonical procedure make moderate use of

them in the sense of reparation. According to canonists, the local Ordinary has the right to impose a fine on a cleric for his failure to attend a conference of the clergy, his negligence in the fulfillment of the duties of an office, or a fine may imposed on one who possesses a benefice for failure to attend choir without a sufficient reason (Can. 395, par. 2). Furthermore, fines are also imposed for interference in the free and expeditious handling of affairs by an ecclesiastical tribunal (Can. 1625, par. 2; 166), the free and honest administration of ecclesiastical property (Can. 2347, par. 2), the diligent observance of rules governing the preparation, preservation, or transcription of the documents of the Curia (Can. 2406, par. 2), for arbitrary increases of ecclesiastical taxes and assessments (Can. 2408).

The imposition of canonical fines may be accompanied by other spiritual penalties. In some cases recourse to civil or secular authority may be necessary. Fines thus collected must be disposed of according to the provisions of Canon 2207 as alms or for other pious usage, unless the law dictates otherwise. Fines and taxes imposed belong to the treasury of the tribunal which imposes them for violations of canonical judicial procedure.

MUNICIPALIZATION. *See* Socialization.

MUNIFICENCE. *See* Magnificence.

MURDER. Murder is the direct and unlawful killing of another person. The killing is direct if the act, chosen as the means to the end, inflicts death of itself, and not accidentally; or if the agent intends to inflict death. To throw a man from a high window with the intent of killing is direct homicide or murder. To blow up a bridge on which a person might be killed is indirect homicide or murder.

Direct killing is unlawful except in two cases: *self-defense* against an unjust aggressor, whether as a private citizen or a soldier; *carrying out a death penalty* which is lawfully and justly inflicted.

Homicide or murder, as the direct

killing of another person, differs from suicide as the direct killing of oneself. To exclude from the definition of homicide or murder the two lawful exceptions, we may define murder as the direct killing of an innocent person, which, therefore, as stated, is always an intrinsically evil act. This definition is correct, provided that it is properly understood. For to kill a notorious, admitted criminal would be homicide, if it did not occur in one of the two exceptions above.

Homicide or murder is considered simple or qualified. A qualified homicide involves the violation of another virtue besides that of justice in the murder. Thus parricide, murder of one's father, implies a violation of the virtue of piety as well as justice; sacrilegious homicide, as in the murder of a priest or religious, involves a violation of the virtue of religion and justice.

Homicide is intrinsically evil, as stated above, and is a serious, particular form of offense against the person killed primarily, against God, and against society. The individual is deprived of his life; God is deprived of His right to dispose of human life; society is deprived of one of its members unjustly. As an intrinsically evil act, murder is never lawful, as is clearly shown from (1) Revelation (Exod. 20:13; 23:7); (2) the constant and evident tradition of the Church; (3) the unswerving, universal testimony of the consciences of all men at all times; (4) the intrinsic nature of the act of murder itself.

INTRINSIC PROOF. Every man precisely as a man, that is, as an intelligent being, is the subject of rights; among these, the right to life is one of the most important. This right to life is a right not to be taken by another. Man has this right both with respect to another individual and to the State. This can never be violated without committing a sin. As a natural right founded in nature, the right to life may never be lost. But as a positive right, it is often limited by other positive rights; so, too, a natural right may have intrinsic and natural limitations by reason of other natural rights. The fact of the natural right of self-defense and that of the death penalty imply that my right to life does not include the right not to be killed, if, by becoming an unjust aggressor or a criminal, I make it necessary for another to kill me in defense of his essential rights, or for the public authority to punish me with the death penalty in order to preserve public order. The right to life, thus limited by the very nature of right, can never be violated without committing a sin. It is also proved that in the two exceptions generally accepted, it is possible to have a killing which is not a sin, because it is not a violation of the right to life; hence, it cannot be called homicide. These two cases are enlarged upon in their respective entries, self-defense (q.v.) and capital punishment (q.v.).

Indirect killing, that is, an act from which the killing of another occurs simply because of a coincidental and unintended circumstance, or is unconsciously caused by the agent, in itself, is unlawful. It may be lawful only if it results from an act which may not be omitted, and the reason for not omitting it is so important that the good intended fully justifies the indirect effect caused by the indirect killing. *Ben.*

MUSIC. Music, as art and a medium of general entertainment, is in itself morally indifferent; its moral character depends on its purpose or use. By its nature music exercises a wonderful influence on human sentiment. For this reason, as in ancient Jewish worship, the Church makes wide use of music in her liturgy. Music may serve evil purposes as a medium of attracting large crowds to places of entertainment where the sensual nature is stimulated and passions aroused. This type of music gives rise to a moral problem of cooperation in illicit actions. As formal cooperation (q.v.) in the sins of others, such music is never permissible. As material cooperation in the sins of others, that is, in a performance not intended to induce evil actions, it may be licit under certain circumstances, for proportionately grave reasons, and provided that all scandal is removed (*see* Cooperation, Amusements, Scandal, Chants, Sacred music, Church music. *Dam.*

MUTILATION. An action by which one deprives himself or another of a bodily organ or its use is called mutilation. This mutilation may be direct or indirect. *Direct* mutilation is deliberately intended by an act of its very nature capable of causing mutilation. If the effect is not directly intended, it is called indirect mutilation, e.g., to throw a bomb against an enemy among whom some civilians will certainly become gravely maimed.

Mutilation belongs to the category of murder: the difference is that mutilation is partial destruction of an individual, whereas murder is the total destruction of the physical life of the individual. Moral law is concerned with mutilation because no man is absolute in his dominion over the body, and the violation of this principle is, of itself and by itself, forbidden. However, by virtue of the coercive nature of law, at times, mutilation is lawful and morally licit, as in the case of legitimate self-defense or as a penalty imposed by legitimate authority. Its application in a specific case may be justified if the conditions required for the use of legitimate self-defense or punishment for criminal acts are present.

Amputation of a limb or organ is lawful if performed with the consent, at least legitimately presumed, of the person involved and if the amputation would offer the best means of effecting the preservation of the life or health of the individual.

The intrinic morality of such an act is to be judged from the specific effect that the act produces on the whole man. To deprive a person of a good and useful limb is obviously an evil act. To deprive a man of a diseased limb or organ that could cause death or other serious damage is a good act; hence, it is lawful.

Apart from cases indicated above, indirect mutilation is an intrinsically evil act; for this reason it is absolutely illicit and cannot be justified for any end whatsoever. Self-mutilation is a sin against nature and society; mutilation of another is an outrageous violation of the natural right of a man to physical integrity, which he may not renounce by any form of consent. In itself, the sin of mutilation is grave, although it may be venial if the mutilation is slight. The gravity of the sin is not measured by the size of the mutilation, but by the importance of the organ involved.

Indirect mutilation is of itself an indifferent act which, because of circumstances, produces mutilation; it is lawful if the act is proportionate to the damage ensuing, or justified by circumstances. *Ben.*

MUTILATION, PENALTY OF. In earlier times, the penalty of mutilation for serious crimes was generally practiced. The laws among pagan peoples condemned a violator of the bodily integrity of another to suffer this penalty. This retaliatory penalty of "an eye for an eye and a tooth for a tooth" is found in the Mosaic Law (Exod. 21:22–25; Lev. 24: 17–20; Deut. 19:21). This penalty was practiced among the Greeks and Romans. In the Christian world the penalty of mutilation continued for a time, but today it is totally in contradiction with modern concepts of punishment, despite the fact that it is less grave than capital punishment. In fact, it finds no place in modern penal codes. *Ben.*

MUTINY. *See* Resistance to unjust power.

MUTUALITY. *See* Assistance, Compensation.

MYSTERIES OF FAITH. *See* Faith.

MYSTICISM. The term *mysticism* embraces a variety of meanings. In Catholic theology, mysticism is a superior, almost experimental, knowledge of God, who lives in a soul in the state of grace. Such knowledge is not, nor can it be, the fruit of inquiries, logical reasoning, or sense perception, but of a special movement by God, who allows the soul to feel His presence whenever and in the manner He chooses. The mysterious contact of the soul with God is not a real vision. Descriptions by mystics tend to compare this contact to an awareness of the soul, which we possess in our activity as a human person but which is not sensibly perceived. By causing wonderful effects in the soul (Rom. 8:16), God allows the soul almost to contact Him, as the Principle who gives it life and as a Being who is extremely lovable and infinitely superior to all other beings.

A fervent, super-human, or infused love of God, ordinarily united with this vivid perception of God, is also considered an aspect of mysticism. The divine movements which lead the human faculties to these acts of knowledge and love of God, are mystical graces *par excellence*.

By an extension of the term, theologians also refer to *any divine action* which renders the gifts of the Holy Ghost active. These same gifts are frequently found in more perfect souls. The entire supernatural activity of those in whom the influence of the gifts of the Holy Ghost prevails is called mysticism.

In Catholic theology, definite phenomena of a psychological, physiological, or intellectual order, not essential to mystical life but accompanying mystical union with God, are visions, ecstasies, speaking or understanding supernatural words, touches, or delightful spiritual sentiments impressed on the will, levitations, luminous radiation, fragrant emanations, prolonged abstinence, and the stigmata.

In addition to these meanings of the term *mysticism*, all firmly grounded, there exist other practices sometimes called mystical; these involve external or internal practices whereby certain religious followers or devotees endeavor to attain a special contact with God, as well as ecstatic experiences occurring to followers of these sects. These are commonly known as Neo-Platonic, Islamic, or Buddhist mystical doctrines. Further uses of the term *mystical* may be applied to any religious sentiment, doctrine, or manifestation. Finally, the word might designate any tendency to the suprasensible or a certain sentimentality prevalent in the lives of some individuals.

CHRISTIAN MYSTICISM. An authentic mysticism has flourished in Christianity from the beginning to the present time. It is wrong to attribute all mystical phenom-

ena to a form of psychoneurosis, as unbelievers, in their ignorance, might do. The moral equilibrium of the great Christian mystics and the beneficial works undertaken and successfully concluded by them would be sufficient to disprove these theories. It is equally wrong to see in mystical phenomena only a sublimation of the sexual side of human love. If the terms *spiritual marriage, divine caresses*, and the like frequently recur in the writings of the great mystics on the union with God, it is because no other terminology suitably expresses analogically the tenderness of the mystical union between the soul and God. Nor can one say that mystics are victims of autosuggestion or hallucination. The heroism which they demonstrate in the practice of virtue and their great works for the public good cannot be inspired except by a sublime reality. Nor must one confuse mysticism with sentimentality, which has nothing to do with genuine mystical phenomena; in fact, the soul is not prepared for the reception of special graces from the Lord by fostering sentimental attachment, but by subduing any sentimentality. Genuine mystical life builds on an earnest ascetical life and a generous acceptance and endurance of painful passive purifications of the senses and the spirit.

The Church has always been prompt in checking any degeneration in the mystical field. One of the most important condemnations was that directed against Quietism (*q.v.*) in 1687 (Denz. n. 1221 ff.).

CALL TO MYSTICAL LIFE. A doctrine more and more common among modern theologians, with many authoritative defenders in the Patristic and Scholastic ages, holds that mystical union with God, though a free gift among extraordinary graces, such as revelations, ecstasies, and the stigmata, is a vocation, not proximate, but remote, which God extends to all souls in the state of grace. If one will keep in mind that God is present in every soul in state of grace as an object of special knowledge and love, the mystical union of the soul with God appears as an element without which the supernatural life does not reach the fullness of its normal development in this world. Therefore, it is not improper to desire this union and to implore it humbly from the Lord.

If the number of those who actually enjoy a mystical union with God is small, it is not due to the nature of this union nor to an arbitrary limitation of favors on the part of God, but to the fact that very few persons fully correspond with grace and desire to submit without resist-ance to the painful purifications of the senses and of the spirit. Without this, man remains inordinately attached, at times in a subtle manner, to self and created things. Failure to attain a mystical union with God may also be due at times to the absence of circumstances, such as intelligence and capacity for a superior formation. These prevent a person from actually attaining a complete mystical union with God, despite his or her generous efforts. *Man.*

N

NAME, BAPTISMAL. *See* Baptism.

NAME, OF GOD. *See* Blasphemy, God.

NANISM. *See* Gonads, Hypophysis.

NARCISSISM. *See* Egoism; Perversion, sexual.

NARCOANALYSIS. *See* Hypnotism, Truth serum.

NARCOLEPSY. Narcolepsy (Greek, *narke*—torpor; *lepsia*—fit, seizure), also termed Gelineau's disease after the scientist who identified it in 1880, is a disturbance of the hypnic function, characterized by overwhelming attacks of sleep or increased tendencies to states of partial sleep (*see* Sleep). It is distinguished from lethargy, in that narcolepsy presents all the characteristics and reversibility proper to true physiological sleep. Narcoleptics, despite adequate sleep at night, at certain times and circumstances, are overtaken by the overwhelming desire for sleep, silence, darkness, heat, and boredom, which they can only resist with great effort. Paroxysms which range from a few minutes to one or two hours may recur several times a day, whether the individual is actively engaged in work or physical tasks. The immediate causes very frequently vary with the individuals. The patient will emerge from the hypnic attack spontaneously or by the normal means used to arouse a person from ordinary rest. He will then present all the characteristics of a person fully awake, fully rested and satisfied, only to become victim after a span of time, sometimes brief, to a new attack.

CATALEPSY. The second phenomenon accompanying an attack of narcolepsy is a particular behavior displayed under stress of emotional conditions of an upsetting nature. This behavior, called catalepsy, is manifested in sudden falls by the patient without loss of consciousness, in which the patient remains absolutely motionless for periods of time ranging from a few seconds to a minute or two. During this cataleptic attack, the individual cannot move a muscle despite his efforts; such a state of anxiety follows the first attack that the patient thinks that death is near. In other cases, the attack is not a total paralysis of the body, but is confined to one particular section, such as limbs, eyelids, hand, or legs. Sometimes the attack is so fleeting that the patient presents only a slight motion of collapsing, such as a curtsey or a nod. A tingling sensation, the feeling of choking, painful cramps, or other phenomena of a subjective nature may precede the attack.

Other forms of narcoleptic attacks are: *waking cataplexy*, or a painful paralysis of the body, usually during the brief period of transition between sleeping and wakefulness; *sleeping cataplexy*, the same symptoms, which appear in the transition from wakefulness to sleep; *active narcoleptic oneirism*, more like some type of dreamy hallucination, which may be called nightmares, hypnagogic hallucinations, or narcoleptic somnambulism. Although these forms of narcolepsy are less frequent phenomena, they are considered forms of narcolepsy insofar as they are disturbances of a hypnic nature, which appear in persons with other typical narcoleptic conditions.

ETIOPATHOGENESIS. On the basis of vast therapeutic experience, the previous idea that narcolepsy was etiopathogenically identified with epilepsy has been discarded. Today the theory of a constitutional cause prevails, at least in the sense that some particular constitutional basis exists for a peculiar mesodiencephalic predisposition, which favors the sudden appearance of narcoleptic manifestations. This seems particularly true in the so-called idiopathic forms and certain symptomatic forms, caused by organic alterations (encephalitic, traumatic, luetic, tumoral) in the mesodiencephalic region, that is, that important part of the cerebral base comprising the hypophyseal region, the posterior diencephalon, and the contiguous anterior mesencephalon, which constitutes the center of the sleep-regulating apparatus.

A morbid syndrome with fleeting interruptions of thought, speech or movement is observed in children. The patient maintains a fixed look, with eyeballs upward and eyelids blinking, while the limbs become limp. Sudden recurrences many times a day are usually without effect on the health or normal psychological development of the patient, who will ordinarily show a strong nervous or neuropathic tendency. After some years, the disease, which is particularly resistant to diverse sedatives and drugs, will disappear. Debate continues on the question of the disease and its relationship to epilepsy, spasmophilia, hysteria, and narcolepsy. Many prefer to refer to it as a morbid condition of its own, called *pyknolepsy*. Today, pyknolepsy is most frequently linked to cataplexic attacks.

To understand how manifestations apparently different, such as paroxysms of sleep and cataplexic loss of muscular control, can appear in the same narcoleptic syndrome, it is helpful to note that sleep is a physiological act characterized by loss of consciousness and marked hypotony of the muscles. Broadly speaking, sleep consists in a psychological element and a motor element; it is apparent that in a disease affecting the hypno-regulatory apparatus, there may occur both seizures of total or of partial sleep, in which psychic activities are maintained while motor and muscular activities are temporarily suspended. Partial, psychic sleep, as in narcoleptic somnambulism, is an inactivation of the psyche while the motor activity and apparatus function perfectly.

Narcolepsy, though rare, is not exceptional; it begins at early age, generally puberty; it is a chronic disease, which is continual and practically incurable. Of late, due to the systematic use of medicines such as sympamine and ephedrine, the morbid symptoms regress to a marked degree, so that the patient may resume his activities. The therapeutic effect of this medicine is not a radical one, but transitory and symptomatic.

MORAL AND JURIDICAL CONSIDERATIONS. In medical literature definite cases of presumed crimes have turned out to be the effect of narcoleptic attacks. Obviously a jury has the responsibility to exempt imputability from an individual who commits crimes or offenses as a result of narcoleptic seizures; the same is true of moral imputability. There is a question whether the narcoleptic is to be considered normal when not under the effects of a seizure. Intellectual powers do not seem altered to any extent by the morbid condition in which the mesodiencephalon finds itself. Emotional and volitive powers, however, seem to be, in theory, at least, considerably impaired. The diencephalon is indispensable for emotional life, and disturbances suffered are reflected in the activities of that life.

The emotional system is the real, propulsive organ of the will, so that volitive efficiency is impared by any diencephalitic alterations. Since narcolepsy is a manifestation of mesodiencephalitic affliction, a narcoleptic is believed to manifest definite weaknesses in the emotional and volitive life. A moderate and limited disorder, because of localized damage to the hypnic sphere, causes intermittent attacks which generally revert to narcoleptic symptoms. This is a factor accounting for the lack of severe emotional or volitional disturbances in the narcoleptic. With regard to relapses into sin and other weaknesses of conscience and moral conduct, it may be helpful in confession to bear in mind the possibility of such a volitive-effective deficiency in the narcoleptic. *Riz.*

NARCOSUGGESTION. *See* Truth serum.

NARCOTHERAPY. Experts in the history of medicine detected in ancient therapeutic practices of some of the primitive and uncivilized peoples the first traces of the modern method of prolonged sleep used in the treatment of certain types of psychoses and neuroses. The Samoyeds seem to cure madness by having the patient inhale smoke from burning special feathers which produce a beneficial sleep lasting a day or even longer.

The first scientific experiments in prolonged sleep by Epifanio showed definite results in the treatment of a variety of mental illnesses. The sleep was prolonged for a period of approximately one hundred hours; by subcutaneous injections of overlapping doses of sodic luminal (two gr. per day), by artificial feeding, or, during the periods of semi-sleep, natural feeding.

Other scientists tried and improved the same method, by other narcotics and methods of administration, nearly always ignoring Epifanio's pioneering work. Among these, Klaesi (1922), to whom the discovery of narcotherapy is ordinarily but erroneously attributed, became particularly famous.

The technique of narcotherapy consists essentially in the following procedure: the patient put to bed in a quiet place and kept under close observation, receives intermittent doses, orally, by enema, or by injection, of a quantity of narcotic drug sufficient to make him sleep from four to eight days or longer—an almost natural sleep, from which, in fact, the patient can be awakened either by noise or tactile stimuli. He is able to nourish himself during the periods of semi-sleep between the effects of dosages; he can also be kept in perfect hygienic conditions. In the last few years, narcotherapy has been employed extensively in Russia, where, according to a recent publication of the Muscovite Feldman, treatment

continues ten to fifteen days with four to eight hours of wakefulness a day for nourishment, etc. In this way smaller doses of narcotic can be employed (0.25 gr. per day). These are generally given orally and can be further reduced by a reflex-conditioning process. In Italy and other countries, "ganglioplegics" have been used with satisfactory results in place of narcotics (*see* below).

This method of prolonged sleep has broad applications in psychiatry for the treatment of some neuroses and psychoneuroses, particularly of the obsessive type, which have been particularly resistant to other forms of shock therapy. It is also used in the treatment of essential hypertension, gastro-duodenal ulcers, artophantasm pains of amputees, and various allergies. Narcotherapy spares the fatigued cortical cells of external stimulations, thus strengthening and restoring normal activity, and, perhaps electively, supplying equilibrium to the vegetative nervous system by a direct tone restoration on the diencephalic centers.

ELECTRONARCOSIS. In 1898 Leduc published the first experiments in electronarcosis, that is, in the narcotic action exercised by an electric current applied to a dog in gradually increasing intensity. Other attempts along the same order, with varying degrees of success, preceded the brilliant results reported by the electroshock therapy (*see* Shock therapies). Frostig Van Harrenveld and collaborators initiated a new type of transcerebral electrotherapy for the treatment of the mentally ill, in which low voltage electricity was used which permitted longer applications. This was called electronarcosis, a method midway between narcolepsy and electroshock. According to the English researchers, Paterson and Milligan, E. B. Tietz, the New Zealander Medicott, and the Italians Cabitto and Riboli, the results obtained by this method are not less effective than other shock therapies, and should be tried before any radical psychosurgical intervention.

ARTIFICIAL HIBERNATION. This method, first studied in France (Laborit,

1951) and in America for surgical purposes, is based on the principle that the lowering of body temperature reduces the quantity of oxygen needed by the tissues and causes a minimum cardiovascular activity; this, in turn, allows extremely delicate surgical operations such as are performed on the heart. Artificial hibernation is obtained by inhibiting the neuro-vegetative system through the use of appropriate medicines, which produce a gradual decline in the metabolic process and, therefore, body temperature and cardio-respiratory activity—a condition described by some as a "state of slowed-down life." The cooling of the body can be increased or accelerated by additional physical means.

More recently, it has been observed that medications used for the neuro-vegetative system can be used also in neuropsychiatry, since they cause a temporary relaxation of the nervous structures. For an effective inhibition of the neuro-vegetative system, nowadays a "ganglioplegics cocktail" is also used. Consisting of a mixture of drugs (largactil, serpasil, antihistamines, barbiturates) in carefully prepared dosages, it acts on the different levels of the neuro-vegetative system and breaks up the processes of reaction which are at the base of neuropsychological dysfunctions.

Artifical hibernation, or *controlled hypothermy*, has also been found useful in the treatment of some serious child toxic-infections. Research appears to be on the way to wider beneficial developments.

MORAL CONCLUSIONS. There are no ethical restrictions against narcolepsy as a treatment. The use of ordinary narcotics, accompanied by active psychotherapy (questioning the patient while under the influence of the drug, and making certain suggestions to him during the periods of semi-sleep), involves moral norms already indicated for narco-analysis. *See also* Truth Serum. The same applies concerning artificial hibernation. The ethical observations made in the article on shock-therapy, are valid also in electronarcosis.

NARCOTICS. Strictly speaking, narcotics cannot be considered medicine, because their effect is not a cure of the individual but only insensibility to pain, which nevertheless remains along with the illness or disorder that causes it. Narcotics do not even cause a partial regression of the illness; actually, they have no particular effect on the illness except for an anomalous effect on the nervous system of the patient. The effect of narcotics is an inhibiting of normal reaction by the nerves in order that the patient may feel no pain. Some narcotics cause not only unconsciousness but complete insensibility as well (ether and chloroform); the patient falls into a deep sleep, during which he feels no pain. Other narcotics do not produce a general anesthesia, but dull to a considerable degree the sensibility of the nerves (opium, cocaine, morphine).

General anesthesia by ether or chloroform is permitted only when necessary or helpful in an important surgical operation. Anesthesia permits the surgeon to operate calmly and, at the same time, it spares the patient severe pain. General anesthesia, however, is not immune from risks. A physician, therefore, may not resort to the use of general anesthesia without proportionately grave reasons; he shall take into consideration the condition of each individual patient, to reduce to the minimum the danger of possible complications. Other narcotics, such as morphine, are used principally for relieving pain; but they are also taken for sensual pleasure. One of the disadvantages of narcotics is that they are habit-forming, leading inevitably to more frequent use and larger doses whether for pleasure or sedative. If small doses relieve pain caused by acute illness, morphine is not dangerous to a patient's health and, therefore, it is not forbidden by the law. The use of large doses, however, is dangerous and may cause death; hence, the prescription and administration of large doses of morphine are sinful. Carrying out the doctor's order is no excuse for a nurse, because no one can lawfully carry out orders which are openly contrary to God's commandments. The administration of narcotics in frequent but not lethal doses can cause considerable damage to a patient's physical and psychological condition, and even death. The frequent use of narcotics by persons who are physically well is sinful and entails a twofold danger: the ruin of one's health, and addiction (*see* Drugs).

The habitual use of narcotics is, therefore, forbidden by the moral law unless under the supervision of a prudent and conscientious doctor. The moral law demands that a physician use great caution in prescribing or administering narcotics such as morphine; nor may he prescribe it simply to satisfy the patient or to avoid annoyance. In general, morphine should not be used for long illnesses. The practice of teaching a patient self-administration by injections or supplying narcotics or the necessary implements is to be strongly reproved. The habitual use of morphine is a widespread evil, which, if not well supervised, leads to addiction and ruination of one's health. Experience has demonstrated that the cure of drug addicts is very difficult. *Ben.*

NATION. *Nation* (Latin, *nasci*—to be born) conveys the notion of birth. The Romans used the term *natiónes* to indicate foreign nations, inferior in culture. During the Middle Ages the same term was used to indicate the different races of civilized peoples. In the universities, foreign students were grouped according to their different *natiónes*. In the Council of Constance the *universalitas christiana* was conceived (1414–1418) on the basis of the community of nations. England is the first example of a modern nation and State with common language and common traditions. France followed, and gradually the whole of the civilized world. During the last century, the concept of nation became a very powerful one. In view of its long evolution, it is rather difficult to establish the fundamental elements that make up a nation.

In its first aspect, a nation appears as a society founded on the following natural elements: (a) *unity of origin and* race; (b) *geographical elements;* (c) *language;* (d) *religion;* (e) *State.*

(a) *Unity of origin and race.* Race, whether understood as a type of human species with determined physical or cultural structure (Gobineau), or as a complete grouping adjusted to given surroundings (Darwin, Lamarck), is a natural but not exclusive element of nation. Almost all nations consist of a mixture of different types of peoples.

(b) *Geographical elements.* Anthropography maintains that a nation is the product of its climate and location. Certainly the law of adaptation to surroundings affects the body and mind of man, but to make this partial element as if it were the only general element, would be erroneous if applied to the explanation of races. Territory is, indeed, necessary to a nation but does not, of itself, form a nation. There are territories on which more than one nation lives.

(c) *Language.* This is, of course, an important, but partial, element: Danes, Swedes, and Norwegians speak the same language; yet they are three distinct nations. The same can be said of North America and the English, or of the use of Spanish among many nations. Conversely, the Swiss nation speaks three different languages, perhaps four.

(d) *Religion.* The influence of religion is varied: a national religion constitutes a strong bond for the nation; but if the political boundaries do not coincide with the religious boundaries and religion causes deep conflicts, it does not inevitably break the national bond. The influence of religion is particularly strong in the East as a predominant factor in the formation of nations, States, and cultures.

(e) *State.* State (*q.v.*) and nation are not the same. The absolute State does not coincide with the nation; in fact, they are often at odds. In some countries, as in England, France and Italy, nation and State coincide perfectly, and it was under their influence that the *Societé des Nations* (Society of Nations) was organized in Geneva. In many, the State does not represent the nation, but rather several nations bound together by historical events or economic and political interests. Thus, is it possible to have a nation in the sense of State, and a nation in a cultural sense; both elements are essential. That these natural elements may produce a nation they must be aided by spiritual elements, that is, the recollection of past common life and belief in a common destiny. This national sentiment must then produce the will to create a concrete order of government. In other words, it is necessary that these elements be translated into a will to live together; implicit unity becomes an explicit unity. Although these elements are important, they do not represent the essence of a nation nor cause a nation to be founded; they are rather effects which presuppose certain facts from which to arise.

MORAL EVALUATION. Man is not an isolated being, but a member of society. From this arises a twofold tendency: one, toward individual interests; the other, toward common interests. Since a nation is a collection of individuals, these two tendencies are also found in a nation. Exaggeration of the first tendency leads to nationalism; exaggeration of the second element leads to *cosmopolitanism* and *internationalism*. A nation is an ethical good, a benefit to humanity, representing an ingeniously articulate social structure in which forces are working toward the betterment of its members.

To scatter or to destroy a nation is to commit a sin against humanity; nature itself created the nation, for all nature tends to unity. Thus, too, the nations into which humanity is divided must tend to unity for their reciprocal improvement, for only by collaboration can the human goals of social, economic, and cultural progress be attained. Therefore, nations cannot be the last phase of human history. We are witnessing today efforts made by nations for wider collaboration through the United Nations Organization (UN), on the principle that the individual nation does not lose its own identity any more than a man in his family; the individual finds therein

perfection and greater meaning and value. *Per.*

NATIONALISM. *See* Imperialism, Nation.

NATIONALIZATION. *See* Socialization.

NATIONAL-SOCIALISM. *See* Racism.

NATURALISM (ECONOMIC). *See* Liberalism.

NATURAL LAW. *See* Law, natural.

NECESSITY (NEED). Moral theologians speak of necessity in a general and in a specific sense. Concerning necessity in general, *see* Excusing Cause. In a specific sense, necessity is the need of my neighbor, which, according to moral theologians, may be spiritual or material. Susceptible of many degrees, necessity is generally classified as extreme, grave, and ordinary. Material or spiritual need is extreme if a person, without receiving the needed help, would certainly lose his temporal or eternal life; the need is grave if, without the help of another, one is in danger of losing a temporal good of great importance other than his life, or in serious danger of eternal damnation; the need is ordinary (common, light) if one is in economic straits or faced with dangers and difficulties which every sinner experiences in a spiritual way.

Irrespective of the nature of the goods, the obligation of assistance is judged by the personal inconvenience entailed, the degree of relationship with the needy, the foreseeable effectiveness of assistance, and the extent of the need by the neighbor.

The following generally accepted rules concern those in need. *Spiritual necessity.* (a) We must give proper spiritual help to anyone in *extreme* spiritual necessity (if there is hope for effective results), even if it entails great inconvenience to us, possibly the risk of our life; thus, one is required to risk one's life to warn one who, without knowing it, is in danger of losing his life while in the state of mortal sin. (b) We must give help to one who is in *grave* necessity even if it should cause us great inconvenience, but not at the risk of our life, except in public need or special obligations of office or duty binding us to assist. (c) We must help anyone who is in *ordinary* necessity; this is done according to the rules laid down for fraternal correction (*q.v.*).

Material necessity. Concerning material necessity, a distinction must be made depending on the need for oneself or another. (a) The duty of helping others who are in material need often is discharged by almsgiving (*q.v.*). (b) If help is given in other ways (for example, warning one's neighbor of an impending danger), it will be sufficient to apply to the individual cases the criteria indicated above in spiritual matters.

In the case of one's personal material need, moral theologians agree on the following rules. (a) One who finds himself in extreme personal need may use or even take from another the amount of goods necessary to alleviate his extreme need, unless the proprietor has need of the goods for the same reason. These, of course, must be things of ordinary use. Moreover, if the need no longer exists, and the things taken are still existent, they must be restored to their rightful owner. (b) In cases of grave and ordinary necessity, one is not permitted to take things belonging to another, not even for use, unless it is a thing of little value with respect to the gravity of the need. For necessity in the sense of superior force, *see* Accident, and Violence. *Gra.*

NECESSITY (OF MEANS AND OF PRECEPT). Concerning things necessary for the attainment of eternal salvation, moral theologians make a distinction between necessity of means and necessity of precept. That is called necessary by *necessity of means* which is absolutely indispensable for salvation, so that the lack of it, even involuntary or due to ignorance, renders it impossible for one to enter the kingdom of heaven: such is, for example, the state of grace. That is called necessary by *necessity of*

precept which is commanded in such a way that its omission or lack of it, if voluntary and culpable, would exclude one from eternal life, but would not, if involuntary or not culpable: such is the observance of any law obliging under pain of mortal sin. Usually, whatever is necessary by necessity of means, of its own nature is indispensable for eternal life; in these cases the necessity is called intrinsic. Moral theologians speak also of extrinsic necessity of means: means that are such by free, divine institution, so that their lack (inculpable) can sometimes be supplied, by God's permission, by others; thus, for instance, baptism of water is necessary by extrinsic necessity of means, but this requirement can be supplied by the baptism of blood or desire. *Gra.*

NECROMANCY. *See* Divination.

NECROPHILIA. *See* Perversion, Sexual.

NECROSCOPY. *See* Autopsy, Medicine, Legal.

NECROSPERMY. *See* Sterility.

NEGATIVISM. *See* Schizophrenia.

NEGLIGENCE. In a general sense, negligence is the lack of proper diligence in carrying out one's duties. Thus, it is not a special sin, vice, or defect; its malice depends on the nature and gravity of the duty neglected. Moral theologians are usually concerned with the culpability and the effects of negligence in some special cases, such as neglect to acquire the knowledge necessary for one's profession, or the failure to seek the owner of a thing found or possessed in bad or dubious faith, as well as passive forms of co-operation in which a damage was caused to another.

In a particular or more specific sense, negligence is sometimes taken as the lack of promptness of the will, or excessive sloth in the interior struggle to a voluntary decision. Considered as such, it differs from laziness, which is sloth or failure in the execution of voluntary determinations (*see also* Guilt, Prudence). *Gra.*

NEIGHBOR. A man's neighbor is one who shares human nature. No other creatures, whether animals or angels, are man's neighbor. *Neighbor* is a universal term; that is, one which extends to every human being without any exception—all mankind, including the most remote, unknown, and diverse peoples from the point of view of race, color, nation, religion; or enemies, whether national or personal (*see* Enemy); and deceased persons.

This is the gamut of the command, which Jesus gave to His followers, to love their neighbor (*see* Charity). By reason of their elevation to supernatural life, in which all participate either by actual possession (sanctifying grace), or because they are called by God to possess it, all men are truly sons of God and brothers of Jesus Christ. Man's Redemption made it possible for all men to be neighbors to each other in a stronger and stricter sense. A Christian who bears in mind the fact of the common bond of supernatural life with others, does not hesitate to call all men his brothers (*see* Charity). *Ben.*

NEO-MALTHUSIANISM (BIRTH CONTROL). In a general sense Neo-Malthusianism is the deliberate frustration of the human sexual act for the purpose of preventing the act from achieving its natural end, namely, conception. The sexual act is frustrated either by a deliberate interruption of the act itself or by the use of contraceptives. The latter is properly referred to as Neo-Malthusianism, while the former is called onanism. Here we shall deal with Neo-Malthusianism as a contraceptive method. Concerning onanism, *see* Birth control. Thomas Malthus (1766–1834), an Englishman, taught that the increase of the world's population was excessive in proportion to the increase of its means of sustenance. He compared a geometrical increase in the world's population (2, 4, 8, 32, etc.) as against arithmetical increase in the food production (2, 4, 6, 8, 10, etc.); hence, the fatal consequence

of over-population, accompanied by a growing impoverishment of the poorer social classes. The only remedy against such evil was, according to Malthus, a limitation of the birth rate, to be obtained by: (a) delaying the time of matrimony, which would also allow man to attain a more stable economic position for the support of his family; (b) voluntary control of procreation by rigid chastity, not only in the pre-marital period but also in marriage by limiting the number of children according to one's financial means. This was called Malthusianism.

This doctrine, which had staunch followers and formidable adversaries, was not immoral. But Francis Places, a disciple of Malthus, deserted his master, proposing, instead, methods which imposed no restraint concerning sexual relations but frustrated procreation. Places was soon followed by others who continued to promote the doctrine of a necessary limitation of births, for the reasons given by Malthus and more personal and egoistical motives, which led to the invention and the use of contraceptives as a method to guarantee the pleasures of sexual life without the natural consequences of offspring and the responsibilities connected with them. Malthusianism has wrongly been associated with the latter practice, which is entirely different from the method proposed by Malthus.

Neo-Malthusianism, the doctrine of Francis Places, is carried out today by the Malthusian League (England), the Niew-Malthusiaanche Bond (Holland), the International Neo-Malthusian Federation, and the Birth-Control Federation. The latter has a central organization in the United States of America and spreads its perverse ideas in many parts of the world.

The malice and sinfulness of Neo-Malthusianism lies in the deliberate frustration of the sexual act. The sexual act is a natural act ordained by God, Creator of nature, for the specific purpose of the procreation of children in lawful marriage. Man may or may not perform this act; but, if he does, he must do it in the proper manner. To frustrate this act is a sin; if the act is frustrated in its essence, the sin is in itself grievous, that is, mortal. The practice of Neo-Malthusianism is an essential frustration of a natural act, for the purpose of the act, conception, is thus made impossible— a violation of a grave precept of the law of nature which no motive or intent can justify. Although many religious leaders have made grave concessions in defiance of the natural moral law on this point (*see* the Lambeth Conference of the Anglican clergy), in numberless ecclesiastical documents the Catholic Church has repeatedly condemned the practice of Neo-Malthusianism as a grievous sin (cf. S.C.S. Off., May 20, 1851; April 19, 1853; March 26, 1897; Nov. 23, 1922; S. Penit., a dozen answers and decisions from Nov. 15, 1816, to June 3, 1916). In a more solemn manner, the encyclical *Casti Connubii* (Dec. 31, 1930), which, according to some authors, contains an infallible *ex cathedra* declaration, stated "that any use whatsoever of marriage, in which through human malice the act is frustrated of its natural virtue of procreation, is against the law of God and nature, and that those who dare commit such actions are guilty of grievous sin." The reason is given by the same encyclical: "Since the matrimonial act is, of its very nature, directed to the generation of offspring, those who, in using it, willfully frustrate its purpose commit actions against nature, which are vile and intrinsically immoral."

Concerning the cooperation by the other party to the practice of Neo-Malthusianism in marriage, *see* Onanism. *Ben.*

NERVOUSNESS. *See* Cerebral Functions, Impulse, Inhibition.

NE TEMERE. *See* Matrimony, form of.

NEURALGIA. *See* Analgesics.

NEURASTHENIA (SEXUAL). *See* Impotence.

NEURASTHENIA (PSYCHASTHENIA, NEUROPSYCHASTHENIA).
Neurasthenia is a functional psychoneurosis in which neurological symptoms are more notably prevalent than psychological, while the opposite is true in psychasthenia. In view of the great number of symptoms common to both, many scholars consider such division unnecessary, even absurd, and speak only of neuropsychasthenia. According to a definition which has become classic, neurasthenia consists of *an irritable weakness* of the nervous centers; it is observed in *constitutional neurasthenia*. This is usually a psychogenic process observed in abnormal individuals, affected by a morbid hereditary condition, with similar symptoms, who from their infancy have shown anomalies of character and vegetative disequilibriums. It is found in *acquired* or *symptomatic neurasthenia*. These are pseudo-neurasthenic forms, linked, that is, to other morbid processes, which immediately disappear when the basic disease is cured.

Real or constitutional neurasthenia, more frequent in males, usually appears between the age of twenty-five and forty. This fact has given support to the false notion that a *nervous breakdown* is the root of psychoneurosis, with which it is ordinarily confused. The duration of neurasthenia and its resistance to treatments is longer, the deeper the heredo-constitutional ground in which it developed. Occasional causes of this disorder can be fatigue, particularly mental, sexual disorders, toxic-infections, etc. These pathogenic elements are also the cause of relapses, frequently observed after periods of improvement.

The fundamental symptom of neurasthenia is a deep and paradoxical sense of muscular and mental tiredness to which no noticeable relief comes from rest; as a matter of fact, it appears worse in the morning, although it does improve in the evening. There are headaches (usually described like a helmet weighing on the head, or an iron band around it) and other more annoying painful sensations, either localized or moving into any part of the body, which are felt and described by the patient as tickling, prickling, burning, or icy sensations, etc. Trembling of fingers and cardiac erethism (tachycardia, palpitations of an anxious nature, anginal attacks, etc.) are frequently present; also, gastro-intestinal disturbances (white tongue, loss of appetite, heaviness after meals, attacks of diarrhea, etc.); disorders of the genital regions (see Psychoneurosis, Sexual); insomnia or, even more frequently, disturbed sleep. A variety of psychological disturbances, mostly of a neuro-vegetative type with hyper-orthosympathetic background, accompanies constantly this variety of phenomena. These disturbances are generally accompanied by a moody disposition, a constant and worrisome analysis of the various somatic disorders, a morbid and pavid hypochondria, or even attacks of anxious oppression that cause the infirmity closely to resemble psychasthenia. This becomes more so when, after years of ineffective treatments, during which the patient loses all hope of regaining his health and his hypochondrial anxieties are greatly increased, these phenomena assume the stubbornness and the disturbing elements proper to real obsessions, characteristic of psychasthenia (q.v.).

The treatment of neurasthenia, more than other types of psychoneuroses, aims at re-adjusting and strengthening the altered somatic functions; hence, large use is made of medications for the nerves, accompanied by hydrotherapies and physiotherapies for the purpose of strengthening the organism and re-invigorating its tonicity. But prudent and patient psychotherapeutic treatments must never be neglected (see Psychoneurosis and Psychotherapy), in order to check the patient's anxious introspection, restore his hope for recovery, and give faith in the future. Without this, treatment is doomed to failure and often aggravates the morbid state of the patient, who, after fleeting improvements, becomes quite disappointed with the special medicines, relentlessly sought after from clinics, from medical books, or the medical page of daily newspapers.

MORAL PROBLEMS. Concerning neurasthenics, these are important moral problems: (1) a method of dealing with these persons, (2) the possibility of suicide.

(1) Too frequently, when the patient maintains his good humor, the neurasthenic is considered a *malade imaginaire* by the members of his family, more an object of ridicule than of sympathy. It is well to know that *imaginary ill people do not exist;* persons such as neurasthenics, who do not show easily noticeable infirmities, are nonetheless suffering individuals; their suffering becomes more acute when they are not believed or, still worse, when they are ridiculed. One, therefore, must never make fun of these unhappy individuals or consider them fakers. On the other hand, too much sympathy can be harmful, as it often increases their natural tendency to consider themselves seriously and incurably ill. Prudence suggests patience with their oft-repeated complaints, comforting words of hope and encouragement against despair. In this way we collaborate effectively with the work of the physician. These patients are, at times, more receptive to the words of a priest than those suffering from other psychoneuroses (hysterics and psychasthenics); thus, it would be well for the relatives to take such patients to an experienced priest, who is often able to restore them to a considerable degree of tranquillity and a more serene Christian outlook.

(2) It must not be forgotten, with regard to the second moral question, that because of his obstinate sufferings, the neurasthenic may, though rarely, attempt to take his own life. Such deplorable acts, not imputable to the unfortunate individual because of his mentally disturbed condition, are at times the result of neglect on the part of the patient's relatives, who failed to deal with him prudently and charitably and delayed treatments which would have alleviated the sufferings of the patient and prevented him from crossing the border of despair. *Riz.*

NEUROCRINIA. See Hypophysis.

NEUROLOGY. *See* Medicine.

NEUROSIS. See Psychosis.

NEUROPSYCHASTHENIA. See Neurasthenia; Reflexes, conditional.

NEUROPSYCHIATRY. Aspects of this modern and flourishing branch of neuropsychiatric disciplines are dealt with in other articles (see Cerebropathies, Phrenasthenia, Paralysis), particularly the clinical treatment of more serious morbid conditions. Here we shall confine ourselves to illustrating recent progress made with the relative repercussions in the fields of psychology, pedagogy, and morals.

During the impressive and successful sessions of the First World Congress of Psychiatry held in Paris, in 1950, members interested in neuropsychiatry of the child endeavored to establish a uniform modern classification of character-behavior disorders in children. They proposed the adoption of the following terminology as certainly necessary for a proper understanding of this important subject. Disorders of behavior, with the exception of those caused by intellectual deficiency or phrenasthenia (*q.v.*), undoubtedly constitute the most important chapter of child neuropsychiatry, both for the large number of individuals involved and the notable number of cures achieved through the timely use of appropriate treatments. These disorders are called "disorders of behavior," which, according to their degree of gravity, imply that the individual is maladjusted to family, school, or social life. They are divided into four categories: (a) *Symptomatic disorders of organic processes:* encephalopathies, traumas, dysendocriniases, etc. (b) *psychopathic disorders:* serious disorders of a dissociative, cyclothymic, anti-social, or obsessive type; (c) *neurotic disorders:* less serious manifestations comprising certain phobias, anxieties, impulsiveness, instabilities, etc.; (d) *simple reactive conditions:* unorganized and principally exogenous emotional crimes, aggressive behavior, etc.

ETIOPATHOGENESIS. The genesis of disorders of behavior, whether organic or functional, and the importance of heredi-

tary or acquired causes, that are linked to degenerative, toxic, traumatic factors and poor domestic or environmental influences, are varied in each case. The morbid value of these different causes is important in each case; often, more than one cause contributes to the maintenance and increase in gravity of a given morbid syndrome. Omitting the enumeration and treatment of various causes of mental and nervous diseases in children, we shall summarize some recent general views bearing on this matter.

The etiology of these morbid forms at one time stressed syphilis; nowadays, the pathogenic value of the *treponema pallidum* is on the decline, due, perhaps, to a better "hygienic consciousness" by the parents or to progress in biological research. On the other hand, illnesses caused by filterable viruses, whether they attacked the child in the first days after birth, or the mother during pregnancy, are receiving an increasingly greater attention. Thus, it has been demonstrated that a simple attack of chickenpox suffered by a woman during her first months of pregnancy can cause not only serious meningoencephalitic conditions in the fetus (with deaf-mutism, microcephalism, etc.) but also malformations and all kinds of monstrosities. Also, the study of the "RH factor" (see Blood types) and traumatic lesions suffered during delivery are increasingly important, as, more frequently than suspected, causes of cerebral lesions, which, in turn, give rise to various forms of epilepsy, phrenasthenia, and other serious neuropsychological disorders.

Psychopathological heredity, in a broad sense, is an important element in these cases, but environment is no less important. According to Benvenuti, "At birth psychological heredity is only a probability, not at all a certainty . . . What appears to be transmitted is not the disease but simply a predisposition to it. This hereditary predisposition often consists only in a lesser capacity of resistance in the nervous system to disease, which develops only when, besides a favorable ground, particular influences are added." These influences are constituted primarily by environment. "If the hereditary factor," according to Benvenuti, "is a possibility, environment offers conditions in which these manifestations are realized." E. W. Jaensch goes so far as to state that when these manifestations arise from the superior strata of our psychological personality, environment is more important than genetic factors, because, as strata of a later acquisition, they are more liable to disease. Hence, the great moral responsibility of parents in seeing that their children grow up psychologically sound; hence, also, the ethico-social importance of child-welfare and efforts directed at preventing the harm which may result from congenital defects, and attempts to provide favorable environmental conditions.

Psychiatrists and psychologists agree in attributing to an unhealthy or improper family environment the cause of many disorders of behavior in children. The so-called "nervous child" (a euphemistic term of common use, which comprises nearly all the morbid states in the third and fourth (c, d) groups of disorders of behavior (*see* above), is more often than not the product of unsuitable domestic environment. Recent and numerous statistical findings clearly show that these environmental failings consist principally of disagreements between parents (quarrelsomeness, divorce, desertion by the father or, worse, by the mother, etc.) and defective rearing of the children (excessive concessions or severity, and, more harmful, unjustifiable change from one excess to the other). These are often caused by psychopathological defects (hysterico-neurotic type) in the parents, especially the mother. One must add the condition in which the child, by a mistaken sense of protection on the part of the parents, is surrounded with excessive care and attention; he is obliged to live constantly in a restricted family circle, participating in all the phases and happenings of a disordered and agitated life of adults; often, out of fear of illness and other dangers, he is prevented from associating with children his own age; sometimes he is even made to sleep in the same room with his parents.

Because of these extremes the children are deprived of those natural stimuli necessary for the formation of their character, as a result of which they will fail to receive, in the words of Nasso, "the integrating influence that living with other children would bring to their psychological faculties. In other words, they will be missing the opportunity of becoming adjusted to others, of learning to respect the rights of others, of recognizing an ultimate authority. Many of them, as adults, will suffer from an inferiority complex, and will be incapable of facing life's struggle."

THE PROBLEM OF THE ONLY CHILD. A deplorable sense of hedonism, a mistaken sense of protection for one's offspring, the undeniable restrictions of urban life are responsible for an ever-increasing number of families with one child. Aside from harmful political and social consequencs of this deplorable custom, in the field of child neuropsychiatry, we shall point out the biological error of many parents who, having begotten a defective child, are afraid lest they bring into the world other afflicted children. The fact of the matter is that in families where the first child was born sick and defective, often no other child shows the same liabilities. Furthermore, it is a known fact that environmental and educational defects, such as mentioned above, are found above all in the case of families with only one child, who, because of greater intrinsic vulnerability proper to them, contribute the largest number of cases of neuropsychological morbidity in children. With regard to this subject, Van Krevelen's recent report on the only child and psychiatry, attributes as a cause the *"defective upbringing"* of these children, based on too many concessions, excessive preoccupation and affection for them, the root of a large part of their disorders of behavior, their retarded and distorted development of personality, their disharmony in developing an emotional or intellectual life, anxieties, neuroses, negativistic reactions, unconscious "refusal to grow up," etc.

Apart from the more serious nervous

and mental diseases which can be helped by surgical interventions and electro-shock therapy, *"minor"* child neuro-psychiatric conditions, comprising those annoying disorders of behavior which assume great social importance because of their frequency, are nearly always susceptible of helpful treatment, which shall be all the more effective as it is more promptly given. In no other field, perhaps, as in this one, is the principle of *case by case* more valid: each morbid form depends, in a varying degree, on two or more pathogenic factors (constitutional, endocrinal, neuro-vegetative, traumatic, environmental, etc.); each child becomes sick in a determined way, with a certain sequence of symptoms due to a different chain of causes and reactions to the causes generating the disease. For these reasons, treatment must always be preceded by diligent clinical, psychological (individual and environmental), electro-encephalographic study, which helps in discovering the causes of the specific disturbance and evaluating its presence. Basically, the treatment consists in the administration, from time to time, of vitamins, hormones, and glutamic acid; in individual and group psychotherapy; hygienic and educational assistance to the families; and, in special cases, in the removal of the young patients from harmful environment to special institutions, where they are placed under a suitable work therapy directed at bringing about their social readjustment.

MORAL CONCLUSIONS. As demonstrated above, character-behavior disorders, which have such a widespread influence on the mental health of children, are based on a variety of pathogenic factors. Some of these are exclusively of a medical nature; others, certainly no less important, are outside the medico-surgical field, and they can be suitably corrected by a greater degree of moral discipline in the home. These last factors are caused essentially by a dissociative process in the family and by a faulty education of offspring. These are due to discord between parents or, worse, the disruption of the family unit by legal separation, or divorce or else to the mistaken idea that the children's life must be made as easy as possible, by keeping them away from any kind of competition with others their own age, and by the modern tendency of generally satisfying all their whims, sparing them all difficulties and efforts. These elements are all too favorable to the development of all types of child psycho-neuroses; what is more important, they hinder the child's natural development, harm the harmonious formation of his character and make him less spiritually fit to face the inevitable difficulties of life.

In a recent book, *The Way To Security*, the American psychologist H. C. Link has competently illustrated these concepts. He has come to the conclusion that the first and constant duty of parents is to teach their children to do the things which they must do, even if they do not feel like doing them, and not to do the things which they must not do. On the other hand, since the child naturally imitates his parents, it is clear that if the parents live the right kind of life, the child will spontaneously follow them on the same road; he will acquire a sense of serene self-confidence and balanced self-control which are the best defense against psychoneuroses.

The lesson Catholics must learn from the study of child neuropsychiatry is principally this: the structure of a *Christian* family must be defended and protected also for the sake of the mental health of the children; their family must be one in which the parents collaborate, in different ways but with joint understanding and love, for the spiritual well-being and the true and long-lasting happiness of all the children which a provident Creator has disposed them to have. *Riz.*

NEUROSURGERY. Neurosurgery is surgery of the nerves and nerve structure. Although neurosurgery has been practiced since ancient times, as proved, among other things, by the skulls of prehistoric man, which bear the signs of therapeutic trepanation, only in the last few decades has it become a separate branch of surgery. In fact, it requires such a large variety of special studies and particular operative and post-operative techniques that, of necessity, it can only be practiced by surgeons who have specialized in it.

For practical reasons we shall limit our remarks to two questions with particular relationship with ethics: (1) surgery for alleviation of pain; (2) cerebral surgery.

SURGERY FOR ALLEVIATION OF PAIN is one of the greatest achievements of modern neurosurgery. Pain is effectively mastered, sometimes with immediate and definitive results, by the removal of certain portions of the sympathetic system or its branches, or by cutting certain posterior roots or nerve trunks, or parts of the spinal cord. These and other less radical interventions are always morally proper because they restore to the patient the joy of living, or the hope of recovery, or patience to bear the principal infirmity. Often, more stubborn and severe physical pain is caused by inoperable carcinomas. Furthermore, if it does not require a serious intervention that increases the probability of death, which is not allowed and should be replaced with the use of analgesic medicines, surgery for pain alleviation does not harm consciousness but, on the contrary, it removes disturbances which long and serious suffering can, at times, render intolerable. It also eliminates the danger of suicide and the heinous crime of euthanasia (*q.v.*).

CEREBRAL SURGERY. Great progress has been made with neurosurgery of the brain in comparison with past work, confined to timid probings and the conservative elimination of extra-cerebral tumors. Today, large sections of the brain are removed, or even, after the example of the American surgeon Dandy, an entire cerebral hemisphere, as in cases of infantile spastic hemiplegy joined with serious epilepsy and mental disorders. These and other surgical interventions of a destructive nature are morally permitted, provided that they do not cause a considerable shortening of life and are required by widespread neo-plasms, or other serious infirmities affecting an important region of the brain (*see* Cerebral Function). On the other hand, any destruction required by the existence of organic defects is, insofar as its neuropsychological function is concerned, less harmful and debilitating than the defects themselves. This fact increases the lawfulness of surgical intervention, because it is usually a case involving a seriously diseased organism, in which the danger of death is imminent. Some reservation of a moral nature, however, must be expressed with regard to modern cerebral operations, such as leucotomy, lobotomy, topectomy, etc., which will be treated at length under Psychosurgery. *Riz.*

NEUTRALITY. Neutrality is the state of refraining by a nation from taking part directly or indirectly in a war between other nations or groups of nations, and consequent a condition of immunity from invasion or use by the belligerents. It can be considered a simple fact or a juridical condition. Neutrality as a fact is simply non-participation in a war; as a juridical condition, it indicates a juridical relationship which, because of war, arises between belligerent and non-belligerent or neutral nations. As soon as the state of war is established between two nations or groups of nations, special rights and obligations arise between belligerent and non-belligerent nations.

NEUTRALITY AS A RIGHT. Whether there is a right of neutrality or not, that is, whether a nation has the right to remain neutral in the case of an international armed conflict, it must be noted that for many centuries jurists and nations have given a negative answer. There have always been neutral nations or States. The Romans called neutral peoples *pacati*, because they kept the peace, or *medi*, because they remained in between the belligerents, not helping either one side or the other, or both sides in the same measure. But neutrality was not recognized as a right. The nations that did not take part in the war were considered either friends (*socii et amici*) or enemies (*hostes*). During the

Middle Ages neutrality was not recognized as a real right, although, in practice, more States kept neutrality than in later periods.

There have been jurists, as Grotius, who believed that nations are bound to help a belligerent nation wage a just war; that only when it is doubtful which belligerent is fighting for a just cause can one remain neutral. In more recent times, especially in the seventeenth century, many jurists and nations admitted a real right to neutrality, based on the sovereignty or independence which each nation possesses. This right was clearly recognized by the nations at the International Congress in Paris, in 1856, and at the International Congress for Peace, in 1907. At the fifth session of this latter Congress, juridical rules were established concerning reciprocal rights and obligations of neutral and belligerent nations in times of war on land; and at the thirteenth session, the rights and duties were applied to naval warfare.

Nevertheless, nowadays some politicians and jurists believe that, by virtue of the necessary bond of mutual dependence between nations and the consequences which wars inevitably bring to all nations, there is no real right to remain neutral. Much less, they say, can a right to neutrality be admitted, when the nations are members of a large international organization such as the existing United Nations Organization. As a principle, the right of neutrality in war cannot be denied to individual nations who are not members of a common international organization. In individual concrete cases, however, should it be evident that some nations are waging a defensive war against aggression in the interest of the whole international community, a grave moral obligation arises for other nations to help, within the limits of their capabilities, those who are fighting a just war for the common good.

RIGHTS AND OBLIGATIONS. There are many rights and reciprocal obligations between belligerent and neutral nations. Neutral nations may not send their citizens to fight on either side of the belligerents, not even in the guise of volunteers. Individual citizens, however, except when there is a particular prohibition by the State, are permitted to enlist as volunteers in the armies of a belligerent foreign nation. Neutral nations may not permit armies or war material of belligerent nations to cross their territories. It is not, however, contrary to the obligations of neutrality, if their subjects trade, even in arms, with belligerent nations. Belligerent nations can, in naval warfare, exercise the right of inspection of ships belonging to neutrals and confiscate all goods which constitute the so-called *contraband of war*. The right of inspection may only be exercised on the open sea or in the territorial waters of the enemy nation. *Pas.*

NEUTRALITY (SCHOLASTIC). *See* School, Lay.

NEWS AGENCIES. News agencies are public or private business concerns engaged in gathering political, financial, commercial, maritime, and other types of news from all parts of the world for the purpose of transmitting them to the public or to the press by phone, wire, or special weekly or monthly bulletins or letters.

The first such agency orginated in Paris under the First Empire and was called *Havas*, after the name of its founder; it underwent great development, especially between 1835 and 1858, and, during this period, it perfected its means of communication. There soon arose other news agencies patterned after *Havas*: in Germany, the Agency *Wolf*; in England, *Reuter*; in Switzerland, *Orell-Fussli*; in Italy, *Stefani*, replaced by ANSA (National Agency of Associated Press) at the end of the Second World War; *ARI*; *Centro Informazioni Stampa*; *Corrispondenza*; *Diplomazia*; *ORBIS* (News Organization of Press Bulletins); *Societa Anonima Mediterranea*; *Roma*; in Russia, Tass; in the U.S.A., A.P., I.N.S., U.P.I., etc.

Fides is a religious international news agency concerned with missionary news. It was established by the Superior Council of the Pontifical Society for the Propagation of the Faith in 1927, for the purpose of gathering news from all the Catholic missions, and transmitting it to the press, especially the Catholic press. It is highly organized into a well-knit worldwide network of local correspondents appointed by Bishops, Vicars and Prefects Apostolic, and regional correspondents, who handle articles and news of wider interest. All local and regional branches of the network are connected with the central office in Rome by which a weekly news report is released to the world press in the principal languages. It also has a special news-photo service, *Fides-Photo.* The official Catholic news agency in the U.S.A. is the N.C.W.C. News Service, Washington, D.C.

MORAL ASPECT. News agencies have the same moral obligations as the press (*q.v.*), since whatever news is gathered by them is released to the public through the press. Wherefore, (a) means employed to gather news and information must be lawful and moral. (b) Release and publication of news, in whatever manner obtained, must not be detrimental either to public or private welfare. It is not, therefore, lawful to obtain State secrets, or any other kind of classified material, by bribing persons having access to such material. Much less is it lawful to obtain such material by deceptive practices, theft, or forceful entry into government, commercial or business offices. Nor is it lawful to resort to measures that infringe upon human freedom, such as alchohol (*see* Intoxication), hypnotism (*see* Hypnotism), drugs (*see* Narcotics), or any other means capable of weakening man's will or confusing his mind for the purpose of extracting information which he would never divulge if he had the full use of his faculties. All such practices constitute a veritable crime against the dignity of the human person. (c) Care must be exercised that the release and publication of news, though true, cause no public or private harm. Never, therefore, is it permitted, for any private motive whatsoever, to divulge news that might endanger international security or the relations between nations, or the internal security of a State, or

news that might cause scandal or lead to public revolt. Likewise, no motive, either of public or private interest, can justify the publication of news obtained through betrayal of professional secrets or one's office or trust, for such public or private interest, no matter how important, has but a transitory value, whereas public confidence is a permanent good that must prevail over eventual private damage or transitory public damage. (d) Finally, news agencies have the obligation of releasing the news in its entirety—that is, they may not mutilate the material by withholding or suppressing circumstances that help to bring out the news in its true and full light, except in the case of public harm. News agencies must not use the news they supply as an instrument for partisan politics. *M.d.G.*

NEWSPAPER. *See* Journalism, Press.

NEW TESTAMENT. The New Testament, a complement and fulfillment of the Old (*q.v.*), comprises the following books: the Gospels of Matthew, Mark, Luke and John, which hold the prominent place among the books of the Bible; one historical book: the Acts of the Apostles; fourteen letters of St. Paul: one to the Romans, two to the Corinthians, one to the Galatians, two to the Thessalonians, two to Timothy, one to Titus, one to Philemon and one to the Hebrews; also, seven letters called Catholic or Canonical: one of James, two of Peter, three of John, one of Jude; and a prophetical book, the Apocalypse.

The principles given by the Redeemer as a Christian norm of conduct are found in the Gospels; the other parts of the New Testament, particularly the Pauline letters, are a faithful echo, as it were, of Christ's teachings, sometimes in the form of commentary, at other times as a practical application. These principles stand above the moral Law of Moses, which Jesus completed and perfected, (Matt. 5:17) and above any other moral code devised by man. Jesus offered the Heavenly Father (Matt. 5:48) and Himself (John 13:15) as the models of virtue and holiness, inviting everyone, without distinction, to follow His teachings (Matt. 2:29 f.); He also freed morality from all types of formalism (cf. Matt. 5:20; Mark 5:7 ff.; John 4:23 f). To those who wish to aim beyond these principles Jesus offers the evangelical counsels.

The first, and substantially only, general precept is to love God above all things (Matt. 6:33) and one's neighbor as one's self (Matt. 5:23–44; 10:37; Gal. 5:14; I Cor. 13; Rom. 13:8 ff.; 15:1–6); the unification of the two precepts is something completely new (Mark 12:28–34, and parallel passages); new also is Christ's definition of *neighbor*. Love of God demands obedience to His Will (Matt. 7:21; 12:50); full confidence in His Providence (Matt. 6:25–32); prayer from the depth of one's heart (Matt. 6:7 ff.; 7:7–12); faith in Jesus (John 7:38; I John 5:1–4).

The duties towards one's neighbor are a part of our filial relation toward God, and a principal part at that (John 4:19–21). In fact, St. James (1:27) says that true religion in the eyes of God consists in taking care of orphans and widows (precept of charity) and in keeping oneself undefiled in this world. Love of neighbor has as its natural consequence, tolerance (Luke 9:49 f.), kindliness (Phil. 4:4, "I *say rejoice . . . Let your modesty be known to all men*"). From these all other virtues flow (Phil. 4:8–9; Rom. 12:9–21), the forgiveness of offenses (Matt. 18:21–35), almsgiving (Matt. 6:2 f.; Luke 11:41). From charity toward oneself, the obligation to seek one's own salvation, arise voluntary poverty (Matt. 16:24 ff.; Luke 14:25–35), penance (Matt. 4:17; Gal. 5:24), vigilance, prayer (Luke 12:35–53; Mark 9:28), humility (Matt. 18:2–5; 20:26 ff.).

The Incarnate Word is not only our brother; He declared that whatever we do to the least of His brethren we do it to Him (Matt. 25:34–45; 10:40 ff.; Mark 9:37). He who *lays down His life for His friends* (John 15:13; Rom. 5:6 ff.) spurs us towards this height of love,

where, by charity, we serve one another (Gal. 5:13 ff.).

The two dogmas, the divine fatherhood of God and man's brotherhood in Jesus, transform our relations with our fellow man. For a Jew, his neighbor was either a born Israelite or one who had become such. For Jesus (Luke 10:25–37, parable of the Good Samaritan) even an enemy is our neighbor: the law of love is unrestricted. Love is not essentially gratuitous (Luke 6:32–35; Matt. 5:46 ff.). The moral law of Judaism and natural ethics was based on strict right and rigorous commutative justice: an individualistic and rigorous conception. In formulating the precept of charity, Jesus proclaims a doctrine by which one man sees in the other another self; this sovereign kingdom of love does not, in any way, infringe upon justice, which is *the lowest step of love*. Judaism says: "*See thou never do to another what thou wouldst hate to have done to thee by another*" (Tob. 4:15). Jesus, instead, prescribes: "*Therefore all things whatever you would that men should do to you, even so do you also to them; for this is the Law and the Prophets*" (Matt. 7, 12; Luke 6, 31). The Jewish formula is based on the protection of right; the Christian formula, instead, full of love, opens an infinite field to generosity.

Jesus also gives principles of domestic and social morality. He places the family back on a divine basis; he insures its stability; he restores the dignity of womanhood by prohibiting absolutely any real divorce (J. BONSIRVEN, *Le divorce dans le N.T.*, Paris, 1948). He praises voluntary virginity embraced for the sake of the kingdom of God (Matt. 19:10 ff.; I Cor. 7), and states that any lustful desire for a woman amounts to committing adultery (Matt. 5:28). St. Paul (Eph. 5:22; 6:9) picks up these principles and gives them a practical application. The family of Nazareth is a radiant example for the Christian family. Properly speaking, the Gospels do not contain a systematic code of social morality, but national and international peace and happiness cannot flourish unless society conforms to Christian principles.

Christian charity has transformed the customs of the peoples and has caused its influence to be felt in almost every field, in the evolution of law, legislation, social progress and economic life (Matt. 22:21; Mark 12:17; Rom. 13:1–7; I Peter 2:13–17 on relations between Church and State). Christianity does not separate morality from religion: God Himself prescribes practical works. As a matter of fact, in the kingdom of God which is the Church, laws are not simply proposed from the outside, for the Church is an organism of supernatural life; the faithful who allows himself to be led by grace will feel in the depth of his conscience a double inclination (Rom. 6–7): an awareness of the conduct he must follow, and an interior impulse and heavenly aid that gives him the ability to pursue that conduct (Rom. 8:12–18).

In conclusion, all this can be summed up in a state of surrender to the flow of love which originates from God and returns to Him (John 4:13 f.; 7:38). We are not under a moral law dictated only externally, much less a rationalistic or natural morality. True Christian behavior means following in the footsteps of the heavenly Father, who gives of His gifts and of Himself in every way and disinterestedly (J. Bonsirven). *Spa.*

NEW WORK, DENUNCIATION OF.
See Denunciation.

NON-CATHOLICS. The term *non-Catholic* comprises those not members of the Catholic Church. The Encyclical Letter *Mystici Corporis Christi* (Pius XII, June 29, 1943) states: "Actually, only those are to be considered as members of the Church who have been baptized and profess the true faith and have not been so unfortunate as to separate themselves from the unity of the Body or were separated from it by a lawful authority by reason of very grave faults."

Specifically, then, non-Catholics are: (a) non-baptized persons, though catechumens (under instruction); (b) heretics, because they do not profess the true faith; (c) schismatics, because they separated themselves from the Church; so also apostates. Excommunicated persons, though excluded by lawful authority from the communion of the Church, are not properly speaking non-Catholics, since their exclusion is intended to be only temporary, and they still maintain the faith and remain subject to the discipline of the Church.

Error, of itself, has no right to exist; other religions, of course, are acknowledged on the basis of the good faith of their members. The Church has the right to apply disciplinary measures only to her own subjects, insofar as their profession of faith is concerned (Syllabus, 77–79; Leo XIII, Encycl. *Immortale Dei*, Nov. 1, 1885; *Libertas*, June 20, 1888). Regarding baptism, it is unlawful to baptize a child of non-Catholic parents (outside the danger of death), without the consent of at least one of the parents or the child's guardian (Can. 750–751). All non-Catholics have the obligation to profess the religion which in good faith they believe to be the true one; if they are in doubt, they are bound to investigate until they reach a reasonable degree of certainty.

RELATIONS WITH THE CATHOLIC CHURCH. Baptized non-Catholics are, by reason of their baptism, subject to the Church (Can. 87), and, as such, owe obedience to her laws, except those from which the Church has either explicitly (e.g., Can. 1099, par. 2) or implicitly exempted them. And though they have no right to it, the Church does not deny them a certain participation in the means of grace in her possession, but in different degrees, depending on whether they are baptized or not (*see* Apostasy, Catecumen, Heresy, Infidels, Schism). The Church has always prayed for non-Catholics; from the very beginning of her existence, with increased interest in the last few centuries, she has sought to bring about their conversion. Although non-Catholics do not belong to the visible body of the Catholic Church, they are said to have a certain relationship with the Mystical Body of Christ "by an unconscious desire and longing." In view of this, the possibility of salvation for them, particularly those who are in good faith, is by no means to be discounted (*see also* Baptism, Faith). *Dam.*

NOOPSYCHE. *See* Psyche, pathology of.

NORM (Juridical). *See* Norm, Moral.

NORM (Moral). Human actions are subject to various norms; some (artistic and technical rules) give rise to no obligation, while others do. Among those of a binding nature, the moral norm stands out. Its characteristics are usually defined primarily in contrast with juridical norm. Moral theologians are not all in accord on this subject, but we shall outline the points on which they generally agree.

The moral norm bears directly on the interior aspect of our actions, while the juridical norm tends to regulate our actions in their exterior manifestation. The moral norm carries an obligation in conscience, and therefore before God; the juridical norm, instead, implies obligation toward a human being (individual or group) who can demand its fulfilment. The moral norm requires voluntary execution; the juridical norm admits compulsory execution. Exteriority, bi-lateralness, coercibility may be summed up into social order, which is an essential characteristic of the juridical norm, not of the moral. One must not think, however, that the two norms are always separable and deal with different things. The moral law governs all human actions, including those of a juridical nature; it is true that the field of law occupies a special area of ethics, but it is not outside the field of ethics. The very exercise of coercion, which usually supposes a moral failing in the one to whom it is applied, is subject in its use to the moral law.

Alongside the moral and juridical norms, often one also finds mentioned a religious norm, although variously conceived; sometimes as an entirely separate norm, at other times as a special form of the moral or the juridical norms; sometimes as the source of norms which can be either juridical or moral. Irrespective of its various aspects, the religious norm always implies a refinement of the moral norms; it considers the obligation in a direct and explicit relation to God; its specific object consists of acts of divine worship, to whose end it may direct all moral acts.

Law, ethics and religion are three parallel norms; thus, it is erroneous to consider ethics and religion as imperfect norms achieving their perfection only in the juridical form.

There are other norms which may be considered only as halfway laws, or on the way of becoming or of ceasing to be laws. Those norms constitute a rather confused field in which different authors distinguish various groups: usages, customs, traditions (insofar as these do not as yet, or else no longer, constitute a traditional law). It is difficult to give a definition of each of these groups, because their limits are not well defined; one can only say that they lack either one or several of the characteristics attributed to juridical norm; and that which is more frequently lacking is coercibility, at least in a socially organized form, a characteristic proper to law. *Gra.*

NORM (Religious). *See* Norm (Moral).

NORMAL-LINED, NORMO-TYPE. *See* Constitution, Biotypographical.

NOTARY. The notary is a public officer who attests to or certifies deeds and documents to make them authentic, and takes affidavits, depositions, and protests of negotiable papers. In some countries, the notary exercises the variety of functions as they existed in the Roman Law: *notarii, tabelliones, tabellarii, exceptores* (Nov. 44; 73); in other countries, he covers only one or the other of such offices. Generally, he is called notary public.

NOTARY IN CANON LAW. In the Church discipline, the notary, inherited from Roman Law, was always used. Pope Innocent II, at the Lateran Council, prescribed that a notary be used also in canonical trials, but forbade ecclesiastics from practicing the notarial profession. This prohibition is still maintained in Canon Law insofar as its exercise as a civil profession is concerned (Can. 139, par. 2). Pope Boniface VIII abolished the notary in trials of heretics; from the thirteenth century onward, the custom prevailed whereby the judge was to be accompanied by an ecclesiastical notary for placing any document into a canonical trial. Under the present discipline a notary is absolutely necessary for canonical trials; unless the acts are drawn up or at least signed by a notary, they shall be considered void (Can. 1585, par. 1). The office of notary is incompatible with that of promoter of justice, defender of the bond, advocate or procurator for the parties. A notary is appointed by the local Ordinary for all acts or for one act only; his office is always strictly territorial (Can. 374, par. 2).

In canonical trials the notary draws up the acts and judicial proceedings; he reads them verbatim to the parties, witnesses and signs them (Can. 1643); he also signs all acts of the judge, decrees, and sentences (Can. 1874, par. 5); he files them in archives, and makes authentic copies of them (Can. 374; 1645, par. 3). The notary holds an important place also in the disciplinary system of the Church; according to dispositions of the general law (Can. 373-374, 503), every diocesan and religious Curia must have a notary.

NOTARY IN CIVIL LAW. The office and function of a civil notary are in many ways different from those prescribed in Canon Law. In countries which follow Roman Law, the office of notary is an extremely important and responsible one; it is a public, often irremovable office, endowed with executive power. Its functions extend to the most diversified types of juridical, civil, commercial, and hereditary acts. A notary is bound by professional secrecy except in cases of damage to himself, to the State, to an innocent party, or in cases of fraud and bad faith. In countries where the English Law is followed, the office of notary is a rather minor office with a function limited to the certification of signatures affixed to legal, commercial, or hereditary acts and the like.

MORAL OBLIGATIONS. The notary, whose office it is to certify to the truth, must be, above all, a man of truth and a reputable citizen of the community. Ecclesiastical notaries, clerics or laymen (except in criminal cases of the clergy, in which the notary must be a priest), must be men of unblemished reputation and above all suspicion.

NOTARIES' FEES. *See* Notary, Honorarium.

NOTICE. *See* Publicity, Press.

NOTORIOUS. *Notorious* is generally said of a fact or an act which is unequivocally public, manifest, and evident. Canon Law speaks of *notoriety of law* and *notoriety of fact*. *Notoriety of law* is a condition which arises after a sentence of a competent judge has become irrevocable or after a judicial confession by the criminal; *notoriety of fact* is a condition which arises from a widespread knowledge of a fact which cannot be denied, concealed, nor condoned by any excuse admitted in the law (Can. 2197, n. 2). Both forms add something to the notion of public crime in the sense that notoriety of law produces a certainty, controlled by the law, which would cease if the control ceased, as by *restitutio in integrum* or by the indefensibility of a sentence that is void; notoriety of fact reflects upon the perspicacity and the ordinary knowledge of the people. And while a public crime or fact must be proved in court, a notorious crime or fact, once established, exempts from the necessity of proof (Can. 1747, n. 1). In fact, a notorious crime may, by its very nature, make the process unnecessary, according to the principle of Canon Law, *notoria non egent probatione* (notorous things need no proof) (Can. 1747, n. 1). This principle, however, is not accepted in civil law; in fact, the procedure followed in the secular courts in the examination of witnesses differs entirely from the Canon Law procedure.

NOVATION. *See* Obligation.

NOVICE, NOVITIATE. A novice (Latin, *novitius*—new, inexperienced, recent) is an untried, inexperienced, or new person to a state or type of life. The term applies particularly to aspirants to the religious life within a particular order. The period of training and acquaintance with such a religious order takes place in a house set aside for those purposes and called the novitiate. This period of trial in the religious life is under the guidance and direction of a director who is called the master (mistress) of novices. (*See* Religious, Congregation, Order).

The use of a period of trial before the final aggregation to religious life dates back to the early beginning of religious life. St. Jerome testifies to this about Hilarion (PL. 22, 30); St. Pachomius, in Chapter IV of his Rule, says that those aspiring to life in a monastery shall "remain some days outside the door . . . and diligently test themselves . . . After this, having laid down their civilian clothes, they shall put on the monastic habit." In the following centuries monachism emphasized and determined more exactly the requirement of this period of trial. St. Benedict, in his *Regula Monasteriorum*, gives precise rules. In Chapter 58, in fact, he recommends that he who wishes to enter a monastery be subjected to a triple gradual trial: (1) Scrutinized as to his right intention, (2) he shall be admitted as a guest, (3) and finally as an accepted person who wishes to enter God's service. St. Benedict also determines the duration of the trial as one year, during which the aspirant shall wear layman's clothes. From monastic legislation, the novitiate passed, first as custom and then as obligation, to other religious institutions. Alexander IV (1254–1261) imposed it on the Dominican Fathers; Boniface VIII (1294–1303) extended the obligation to the mendicant Orders; from these it passed to other institutions. The Council of Trent (1545–1547 [Sess. XXI, ch. 15, *De relig.*]) made it a necessary requirement for the validity of profession. The length of the period of trial was left to the discretion of the individual institution.

CONDITIONS FOR A VALID AND LAWFUL NOVITIATE. In the present law, a year of novitiate is absolutely necessary for the validity of profession (Can. 572); it must be made in a house thus approved by the Holy See for institutes of pontifical right, or by the Ordinary, for those of diocesan right (Can. 554); it must last a full, uninterrupted year (Can. 555). It usually starts with the investiture or taking of the habit and lasts for a whole year (Can. 553). For *valid* admission to the novitiate, the Code of Canon Law prescribes the following conditions: (a) the candidate must not have been a member of a non-Catholic sect; (b) he must have completed his fifteenth year of age; (c) he must not be compelled by grave fear, deception, or force; (d) he must be single; (e) he must not be bound by religious profession in another institute; (f) he must not be subject to imminent penalty for crimes committed; (g) he must not be either a residential or titular Bishop; (h) he must not be bound by oath to serve a diocese or the missions. For a *lawful* admission, the following conditions have to be met: (a) if the candidate is a cleric in sacred orders, he must have the permission of the local Ordinary, lest the faithful committed to his care suffer spiritual harm; (b) the candidate must be free from debts which he is unable to pay; (c) he must be free from administrative or business responsibilities from which litigation might ensue; (d) he must be free from the obligation of supporting his parents, grandparents, or children; (e) if he is to enter the priesthood, he must be free from all irregularities; (f) candidates of an Eastern Rite, wishing to enter a religious group of the Latin Rite, must have the permission of the Sacred Congregation for the Eastern Church (Can. 542).

The superior who admits new candidates must make certain by diligent investigation that the above conditions are properly fulfilled, and that any impediment be absent; this he must do through his own investigation, and above all by testimonial letters, when candidates are men (Can. 544, 545). Women candidates must also be examined by the local Ordinary or his delegate, two months before their admission to the novitiate, concerning their free will and pious intention (*exploratio voluntatis*) (Can. 552).

The novitiate must be made under the guidance of the master of novices, whose exclusive task is to form and direct the novices in their religious life (Can. 561). The master must be at least thirty-five years old, must be ten years professed (perpetual profession) and must possess the virtues of prudence, charity, piety, religious observance, and greater than ordinary ability (Can. 559, 560, 561, 562).

The essential purpose of the novitiate is to enable the novices to learn the obligations of religious life in general, especially those of the order they wish to enter; they must examine themselves on their capacity to assume the burdens and duties relative to their religious profession. On the part of the religious order, the novitiate is a year of trial concerning the aptitudes of the candidate and the probability that he will carry out the tasks which shall be given to him (Can. 565).

A novice has no strict obligation to observe the Constitution and Rules of the institute as do those already professed; nonetheless, he is morally bound to do so. This duty flows from obedience to the master of novices and his legitimate superiors, to whose care he has committed himself.

As in the previous legislation, the Code of Canon Law imposes on religious novices with simple vows, the renunciation of the administration of his possessions and the assignment of their fruits; before taking temporal vows, he must draw up a will concerning his present and future worldly goods (Can. 569). *Mand.*

NOVI OPERIS NUNCIATIO. *See* Denunciation.

NUDISM. Nudism, a movement which began a few decades ago in Germany, insists on the uselessness and even the harmfulness of clothing; hence, it proposes and promotes its total, or almost total, abolition. For propaganda and experimental purposes, parks and clubs were instituted wherein the members of this movement met for athletic exercises, bathing, games, work, dances, etc. Needless to say, such activities gave rise to serious abuses and scandals.

Nudism is based on the following reasons: (a) *hygiene*; clothes are alleged to be the cause of many infirmities and bodily weaknesses, while the heat and light from the sun are said to be the best cure for and preventives of many illnesses; (b) *aesthetics*; the body is more beautiful when nude than when covered with clothes; (c) *morals and pedagogical ethics*; the tendency to use clothing to hide the body, and the sense of mystery in which natural parts of the body and life are hidden, promote morbid curiosity and exaggerated sensibility. As proof of this, the example is offered of savage tribes among whom complete nudity is coupled with a high sense of sexual morality. Modesty, according to nudism, is the result of a long, unhappy habit; it would be a great benefit to morality if it were abolished.

MORALITY. Nudism must be absolutely rejected. The reasons given in its defense are extremely weak. Insofar as hygiene is concerned, it is very doubtful that all climates would permit abolition of all clothing, especially in view of the fact that our bodies have developed in these conditions for generations and for centuries. The heat and light of the sun are certainly beneficial to the human body, but these effects can be generally obtained without complete nudity and certainly without nudistic exhibitions. The aesthetic reasons are, for the most part, false. Complete nudity may offer aesthetic pleasure in figurative art, but rarely in real life. The most serious errors are, however, on moral grounds. Modesty (*q.v.*) is not at all an artifical sentiment, for it is deeply rooted in the human soul. By attributing all curiosity and excitability to the mystery in which sexual life is clothed, nudism denies completely the existence and the disastrous effects of original sin; experience shows that nudity as a habit does not eliminate temptations (*see* Education, Sexual). The validity of alleged morality among savage tribes despite the practice of complete nudity does not hold; first, because it is very rare; secondly, because generally it is a sign of moral decadence rather than of purity; finally, the differences of conditions and circumstances are such as to eliminate any basis for comparison (*see also* Nudity). *Dam.*

NUDITY. Nudity is not in itself immoral. After forming the human body, God declared it to be very good (Gen. 1:31). The cause of the inordinate desires provoked by the sight of nudes is not in the human body as such, but in our perverted nature as a result of original sin. Consequently, man generally is unable to look at a naked body without feeling the effects of concupiscence. It is true that education has emphasized too much the negative side of nudity and that the habit can noticeably diminish its stimulating effects (*ab assuetis non fit passio*), but the habit cannot uproot inordinate passions (*see also* Modesty). For these reasons limitations and precautions are necessary in exposing or viewing a naked body; neglect of these measures constitutes a sin by reason of the scandal given and to the extent to which it is given, or to the extent of the danger to which one exposes himself.

Exhibiting or looking at a naked body is, in itself, indifferent, but it can become a sin by reason of the improper motive or the inordinate effects it may cause, such as scandal (*q.v.*), lustful feelings, etc., unless justified by a proportionately grave reason: medical, care of the body, duty in life, etc. See Immodesty. The nude in art constitutes a special problem. First, the thesis, held by individualism, that art is outside the range of morality, is clearly false (*art for art's sake*). Like all other manifestations of life, art is subject to God's law. Nudity in art, of course, does not, in itself, offend against this law. In fact, in religious art nudes have been employed to a considerable extent. The Church has never shown an exaggerated opposition to nudes. Art (*see* Art, morality of) cannot function without nudes; first, because the human body is the most perfect perceptible beauty in God's creative work; secondly, because many concepts and ideas can be only imperfectly expressed by clothed forms. But in this more or less necessary use of nudes there are limits which cannot be trespassed without violating moral law; in a case of conflict with the moral law, even the greatest works of genius must be sacrificed. Consequently, (a) it is forbidden to exhibit or create images that are objectively obscene (*see* Image, Obscene); (b) furthermore, images not objectively obscene are not necessarily suitable for anyone to see; some individuals, especially the young, lack artistic perceptibility necessary to appreciate properly the artistic value of the great masterpieces, and can easily be led to baser sentiments. In art the public welfare comes first. In general, regarding art and morality, youth should be trained to have a positive appreciation of true works of art and to be able to see the ideological side in artistic nudes. *Dam.*

NULLITY OF MARRIAGE. A marriage may be null because of defective consent, a diriment impediment, or a substantial defect of form. However, to establish the nullity of a marriage, except in the case mentioned in Can. 1990 ff. (regarding some impediments that can be positively proved by certain and authentic documents), a judicial process is required, and, although matrimonial causes never become irrevocably adjudged, yet a quasi-judgment may be obtained after two sentences in favor of the nullity. Consequently, if no legitimate appeal is made by the defender of the bond after ten days following publication of the second sentence, the parties have the right to contract a new marriage (Can. 1987).

NULLITY AND ANNULMENT. A declaration of nullity of a marriage must be clearly distinguished from the annulment of the same, which occurs when the bond is dissolved by the power of the Supreme Pontiff, as in the case of a marriage *ratum non consummatum* (*see* Marriage *ratum*), by the application of the Pauline Privilege (*q.v.*). Concerning the marriage of those who are not subject to the laws of the Church, its nullity is decided by the legitimate competent authorities in accordance with just positive laws. *Fel.*

NUMBER (GOLDEN). *See* Liturgical Year.

NUMBER (Of Sins). The question concerning the number of sins is made difficult and complicated by the diverse criteria of enumeration usually used. We shall begin with the following observations: (a) sins are as many as are the complete sinful acts with distinct objects: he who kills Tom with one rifle shot and Harry with another shot commits two sins of homicide; (b) the sins are as many as are the moral species, though they are contained in one object and violated by only one act: one who, through calumny, harms his neighbor economically, commit three sins: one against veracity, another against the good name of his neighbor, and a third against the financial status of his victim. In such cases, ordinarily, it is also said that there is one sin but threefold malice.

Norms for the Various Possibilities. Less clear and certain are the rules usually given regarding two possible cases: (1) a plurality of acts with one object; (2) a plurality of objects with only one act. In the first case, singleness of object can give a certain unity also to the acts; however, if the acts achieve their own clear distinctiveness and completeness, they cannot be absorbed into the singleness of the object, and constitute as many distinct sins as acts; this happens when the series of acts is interrupted by voluntary retraction or by a long interval. It must be noted that this interruption is more frequently present with acts which are independent of one another; less common, in those which are connected as means to a specific end. Shorter interruptions are sufficient to multiply the sins of simple pleasure in a crime, more than in planning and preparing for a crime.

In the second case, singleness of act has also a certain unifying effect upon the plurality of the objects. To avoid confusion, it must be kept in mind that here we speak of moral rather than physical objects. Therefore, the criterion of their multiplication is also moral. Thus there are as many objects of sin as there are violations of the moral law. The number of stolen objects in the theft of cattle, for example, is not given by the heads of cattle stolen, but by the number of proprietors robbed; the animals are simple quantity, but each proprietor places his own right on the scale of justice, the violation of which constitutes a sin. Moral theologians differ in many ways nor can their opinions be easily merged into one, although it must be noted that in actual fact their differences are more often nominal than real. Does a flier who throws a bomb on an inhabited center commit one or many sins? Between those who see only one sin because the action is one and those who reckon the number of sins by the number of victims, there seems to be the same difference which exists when one says a hundred pounds or a hundredweight. All these distinctions are made for the purpose of clarifying the manner in which the more complex sins are to be mentioned in confession. It is worth noting that moral theologians who see only one sin in the cases of one act with a multiplicity of objects teach that in confession one must indicate the multiple object, at least vaguely if it is only vaguely known, as in the case of the flier dropping the bomb on an inhabited area. This ought to be sufficient and helpful for a good Christian who seeks to make a good confession. *Gra.*

NUNC DIMITTIS. *Nunc dimittis,* a nostalgic canticle expressing a farewell to life and a longing for the light of heaven, is recited at Compline of the Divine Office. It was proclaimed for the first time by the prophet Simeon, whom scholars identify, but without solid proof, with the famous Rabbi Simeon, son of Hillel and father of Gamaliel, teacher of St. Paul. Simeon had the joy of holding the future Messiah in his arms, when Jesus was presented in the temple by His parents (Luke 2:29–32). Inspired by the Holy Ghost, Simeon recognized in that Child the expected Messiah. God promised him that he would see the Messiah; he was given not only to see Him but to touch and embrace Him. According to an apocryphal writer, Simeon was a priest, but this has not been proved; much less has it been proved that he was a high priest.

For vividness of expression, conciseness of style, and lyrical phrasing, this canticle recalls to mind the best compositions of David. It may be divided into two stanzas: in the first, Simeon expresses his joy at seeing the Messiah (20–30); in the second, he speaks of the beneficial effects of the coming of the Messiah for all men (31–32). The Messiah is the light that will dispel the ignorance in which the pagan world is entangled; the Messiah will also set aside a special glory for the people of Israel, since salvation shall come from among the Jews. The plea to God to dismiss His servant was the reason for inclusion in the vesper liturgy (*Const. Apostol.* VII, 48). As a psalmodic chant, it is frequently used in religious functions. *Pal.*

NUNCIO, APOSTOLIC. The Apostolic Nuncio is the pontifical legate (*q.v.*) who, in the territory of his jurisdiction, has the ordinary vicarial office of maintaining, in accordance with the directives of the Holy See, diplomatic relations with a civil government and vigilance over the condition of the Church, concerning which he reports to the Supreme Pontiff. If he presides over a province of minor importance, he is more properly called Internuncio. Both the Nuncio and the Internuncio have a right to the title of Excellency, and are considered Deans of the Diplomatic Corps. Today they are usually titular Archbishops. If they are made Cardinals, they receive the title Pro-nuncios.

A Nuncio, as well as an Apostolic Delegate (*q.v.*), has, besides his ordinary jurisdiction, certain delegated powers. He takes precedence over all Ordinaries, except Cardinals; if he is a Bishop, he can, without the permission of the Ordinary, bless the people in all the churches, except the Cathedral, and pontificate at the throne and under the canopy (Can. 269). Concerning cessation of the office, *see* Pontifical Legate. *Fel.*

NUPTIAL. See Matrimony.

NUPTIAL BLESSING. See Matrimony, form of.

NUPTIALS, FORBIDDEN TIMES OF. The present discipline in the Church in Canon Law (Can. 1108) states that marriage can be contracted at any time of the year (par. 1); the solemn celebration of marriage is forbidden from the first Sunday of Advent to the feast of the Nativity of our Lord inclusively, and from Ash Wednesday to Easter Sunday inclusively (par. 2); local Ordinaries, however, if the liturgical rubrics allow, may permit the celebration of marriage in these stated times if there exists a just cause, with an admonition to the bridal couple to abstain from excessive pomp (par. 3).

The older discipline of the Church which rigorously forbade the celebration of nuptials for noticeable periods is little more than a memory at present times. The Council of Trent reserved the following periods of times during which "the blessing of the nuptials, the taking of the bride to the bridegroom's house, and nuptial feasts were forbidden"; these periods were from the first Sunday of Advent to the Epiphany and from Ash Wednesday to the Octave of Easter. In some places, these former customs are still more or less rigorously adhered to, but the Code of Canon Law mitigated the ancient norm despite ancient origins, for it deemed it more proper to give couples a wider choice of time for the celebration of the marriage. *Bar.*

NUPTIALS (SECOND). Canon 1142 of the Code of Canon Law states: "Although chaste widowhood is most honorable, second and other nuptials are valid and lawful, provided that the solution of the prior marriage was lawfully obtained according to the norm of Can. 1069, par. 2." This doctrine, which goes back to St. Paul (Cor. 7:8 ff.), after much debate during the course of the centuries, has become generally accepted.

A second (valid) marriage, technically termed by Canon Law improper bigamy, makes a person irregular, that is, ineligible for Sacred Orders (Can. 984, n. 4). In the ancient Church a penance was imposed on those who married a second time, and in some lands popular disapproval of second nuptials is still strong today. The Church ignores the waiting period of ten months or three hundred days, required by some civil legislations before a widow or widower (*see* Widowhood) is permitted to remarry. *Bar.*

NURSES, TRAINED. A nurse is a man or woman professionally dedicated to the care of the sick. By nature a woman is particularly suited for this very delicate occupation. Consequently, women by far outnumber men, who are invariably restricted to caring for their own sex. The nurse's work is generally of two types: (a) general care, exercised in a clinic, hospital, sanatorium and the like; (b) private care of one patient in the home or hospital. The function of a visiting nurse, a specialist, into the homes of the poor who are sick, or on other special missions of care, is an extension of the work of the hospital nurse.

It is not at all uncommon to see a member of a female religious community carry on the duties of a nurse in clinics or hospitals under their care. The Church has always considered the care of the sick an exquisite work of Christian charity and one through which the principles of Christian and supernatural life are implemented. For this reason, many religious orders, especially of women, engage in the care of the sick as their exclusive mission or as one of the activities of their religious life.

MORAL OBLIGATION. The duties of a nurse call for complete dedication and the possession of many Christian virtues, especially a great charity, sweetness, patience, and compassion for the sufferings of the sick. By virtue of a contract, expressed or implied, the nurse is at the service of the patient and the attending doctor. A nurse has many moral obligations in common with the doctor, particularly concerning the life, the physical integrity and the health of the people entrusted to her care. Therefore, it is a crime for her to put to death by euthanasia (*q.v.*), abortion (*q.v.*), or embriotomy (*q.v.*), or to mutilate, cause sterility, or experiment on the human body (*see* Doctor).

The nurse is not a doctor but a doctor's helpmate. Thus, she must carry out the doctor's instructions and leave to him any decision or responsibility concerning medications and the treatment of the patient. She must refrain from doing anything of importance without the consent of the doctor, irrespective of the pressure placed upon her either by the patient or the latter's relatives. In certain circumstances, by virtue of existing practices between doctor and nurse, the latter is allowed to do certain things without the expressed consent of the doctor, or to presuppose his *tacit* consent. It is, however, clear that in the relationship between nurse and doctor, the fundamental moral rule applies in which one must obey God rather than man. Thus, at no time shall she carry out orders which she knows to be contrary to the moral law. In a case of doubt, of course, she may obey.

It is unlawful for her to assist a physician or surgeon by helping, preparing, or partaking in an act which is evil in itself, such as giving a deadly injection, or puncturing the membrane of a fetus unable to live outside the maternal womb. If it is a question of collaborating in an act that is not evil in itself, such as giving anesthesia to a patient who is going to undergo an unlawful operation, this collaboration is not sinful if there is a justifying reason, such as avoiding a serious harm or other serious consequences for herself or others. The graver the unlawful action, the more serious must be the reason justifying her co-operation.

A nurse must have great charity and patience toward the patient, especially when he is suffering great pain, but she also must be firm in resisting the unreasonable and sometimes harmful wishes of a patient or the patient's relatives. When a full disclosure of a patient's true condition appears to serve a useful purpose or to be necessary for the welfare, especially spiritual, of the patient, the nurse must speak with all sincerity and frankness. She is not caring for an illness, but for an ill person, that is, an individual who not only has a body but also an immortal soul. As a good Christian, the nurse should be solicitous for the spiritual well-being of the patient, and use all her diligence in seeing to it that the patient receives the sacraments, e.g., extreme unction, in due time. The nurse is the collaborator of the doctor and of the priest: two helpmates of the sick. *Ben.*

NUTRITION. Normally, man nourishes himself by eating and drinking. Man has a moral obligation to preserve his life and health; hence, he is morally bound to nourish himself. To abstain totally from all nourishment is a sin of suicide (*see* Hunger strike). Moreover, man has the moral obligation to take sufficient nourishment to keep himself healthy and strong enough to carry out efficiently the duties of his state of life.

Against this obligation one can sin either by taking too much nourishment or too little (*see* Fasting, Gluttony, Temperance). The obligation to nourish oneself is suspended when God miraculously sustains one's life and health. Some of the saints have lived for a long time in this state. Such cases are, indeed, very rare and presuppose a special inspiration of the Holy Ghost. *Ben.*

NYMPHOMANIA. *See* Perversion, Sexual.

O

OATH. An oath is calling God to witness the truth of a statement or the sincerity of a promise. The invocation of God's name may be *direct*, as "God is my witness," "I call upon God to be my witness," or *indirect*, through some creatures who bear a relation to God, such as the blessed in heaven, the sacraments, the Cross, or the Gospel. An oath may be *assertory* or *promissory* depending on whether one calls on God to witness the the truth of what he affirms or denies, or the sincerity of a promise. Assertory oaths include the past and the present; promissory oaths, directed to the future, have the force of an assertory oath. By a promissory oath one calls God as witness to the truth of his present intention to oblige himself to fulfilling a promise. Concerning the future, he interposes God so that the person to whom the promise is made may know for certain that the promise made to him will be kept in due time.

An oath is lawful and praiseworthy, as it clearly appears from the propositions condemned by the Church. But, as St. Thomas warns (*Summa Theol.* II–II, q. 89, a. 5), oaths are to be considered necessary in life, similar to medicine, not to be used habitually, but seldom and cautiously.

The validity of an oath is based on two conditions: (1) intent to swear and (2) an unequivocal formula. The intention must be at least virtual, because without such an intention the invocation of God as a witness is no longer a human act. A human act is such if at least words or signs are used which indicate that it is an oath. An unequivocal form is also required, by which expressly or tacitly God is invoked as witness. In other words, the oath must be externally expressed by words or signs indicating that God is called upon as witness to the truth of an assertion or to the honesty and fidelity of a promise. These words or signs are indicated by laws, customs, or formulas, usually employed in the locality where the oath is taken and accepted as such.

In the internal forum, in general, the value of the oath is judged by the intention. In the external forum, instead, the formula or formulas generally used are important only. In fact, an oath may be taken which, because of the words or signs used, must in itself or by reason of the circumstances be held as an oath in the external forum, even though it may not be such before God by reason of a lack of intention. Canon 1321 of the Code of Canon Law is quite explicit in this regard: "An oath must be interpreted strictly according to law and the intention of the swearer; but if the latter acts deceitfully, it must be interpreted according to the intention of the one in whose favor the oath is made."

An oath is lawful if: (1) the swearer is convinced of the truth of his assertion or if he has a firm purpose to keep his promise; (2) if the assertion is morally lawful; (3) if there is a sufficient reason for oaths. *Jusiurandum . . . praestari nequit, nisi in veritate, in judicio et in justitia* (Can. 1316, par. 1).

An oath may be taken only about the truth, in an assertory oath; in a promissory oath, justice must be observed. Concerning the person taking the oath, in both types of oath, prudence and good judgment are required. Truth is harmony between the words used and the knowledge and the intention of the swearer. Thus, truth excludes in the assertory and the promissory oath, lying and deceit. A false oath or perjury (*q.v.*) is in itself mortal sin (*ex toto genere suo*), because it is an act of grave irreverence to God, who is called upon to witness a falsehood (Proposition 24, condemned by Innocent XI: *Denz.* n. 1174).

A feigned oath is not without guilt (Proposition 25, condemned by Innocent XI: *Denz.* n. 1175), but the sin committed by a feigned oath may be mortal or venial depending on each individual case.

An oath may be taken for a good reason and with prudence. Lack of this condition makes it a venial sin, as long as there is no danger of swearing falsely. This danger very often is present with those who are in the habit of swearing.

In an assertory oath justice is required, in the sense that the act of the person affirming or denying a thing under oath must be morally lawful and not contrary to an obligation to secrecy. This condition is required in a promissory oath, in the sense that one may not make a promise concerning an illicit thing. Lack of this condition, if one considers only the violation of the virtue of religion, is of itself a slight sin in the assertory oath, unless the oath be a guarantee for a gravely sinful act, such as calumny. It is a grave sin in a promissory oath, if the thing promised is seriously evil; if the evil is slight, the gravity of the disrespectfulness toward God and, therefore, of the sin, is questionable in view of the diverse opinions in this regard (Cf. St. Alph., *Theol. Mor.,* III, 146; I. D'Annibale, *Summula theol. mor.,* II, Rome, 1908, n. 26).

The obligation to keep an oath may cease for intrinsic or extrinsic reasons. Cessation for intrinsic reasons means that an oath ceases if the object promised by oath has changed substantially, or new circumstances have made the oath either sinful, indifferent, or contrary to a higher good (Can. 1319, n. 2). Likewise, if the *ultimate purpose* or the condition attached to it ceases or is not attained (Can. 1319, n. 3).

An oath ceases for extrinsic reason by condonation of the person in whose favor the oath was made (Can. 1319, n. 1), by direct or indirect invalidation by one who has dominative power on the will of the swearer or the object of the oath, and by dispensation or commutation by legitimate authority (Can. 1319, n. 4).

Those who have the power to annul, commute, or dispense from a vow, have the same power concerning promissory oaths. But if the dispensation from an oath involves an injury to the rights of another and he refuses to condone the obligation, then, the Holy See alone can dispense from the oath by reason of necessity or benefit for the Church (Can. 1320).

A promissory oath must be interpreted strictly according to law and the intention of the person taking the oath; but if the swearer acts deceitfully, it must be interpreted according to the intention of the person in whose favor the oath was made (Can. 1321).

To assure the proper fulfillment of certain offices or the carrying out of certain responsibilities, ecclesiastical law often requires the taking of an oath. The profession of faith is made under oath (Cans. 1406–1408). The following are obliged to take an oath: cardinals (Cans. 234, 2394) and bishops (Can. 332, par. 2); clerics who wish to be incardinated into a diocese other than their own (Can. 117, n. 3); candidates for sacred orders (Cans. 956, 994, par. 2); diocesan consultors (Can. 425, par. 2), officials of the Curia (Can. 364, par. 2, n. 1); chapter censors, who check the forfeits or *fallentiae*; delegates to the chapter of a religious institute during elections (Can. 506, par. 1).

An oath is frequently used in the judicial process of canonization (Can. 2037, par. 1, and Can. 2047, par. 2). Ordinarily, with the exception of the Bishop, all the members of the Tribunal must take an oath (Cans. 1621; 1941, par. 2; 2037; 2144), including witnesses and experts (Cans. 1758; 1767; 1797; 1944; 2145). For these the oath may be about the truth relative to the evidence to be submitted (*de veritate dicenda*) or already given (*de veritate dictorum*), or the secrecy to be kept (*de secreto servando*) (Can. 1623, par. 3; 1625, par. 2–3; 1769; 1944, par. 1). An oath may also be used as proof in certain specified cases; the parties may be requested to take an oath not only *de veritate dicenda* (Cans. 1744; 1746; 1824, par. 3) but also a *supplementary oath* to strengthen an incomplete proof (Cans. 1829–1831) and an *estimatory oath*, to assess a damage that cannot be otherwise estimated (Cans. 1832–1833). A decisive oath administered by one party to the other may decide a controversy (Cans. 1834; 1846; 1662).

Extra-judicial perjury in a cleric may be punished with penalties to be evaluated by the superior (Can. 2323). In a case of judicial perjury, a layman is punishable with personal interdict and a cleric with suspension (Cans. 1755, par. 3; 1743, par. 3).

In concordat agreements, often provisions are made for the oath of bishops by which the latter promise to respect the head of the State, have others respect him, and not take part in actions harmful to the State or to public order. Resident archbishops, bishops, and coadjutors with the right of succession are sworn into office by the head of the State by virtue of concordat agreements.

In the laws of many nations the oath is no longer considered an act of religion but simply as a promise or solemn assertion. *Pal.*

OATH OF HIPPOCRATES. Hippocrates (460–365 B.C.), a physician of a family of physicians, is considered the founder of scientific medicine. The myth surrounding Hippocrates and the extraordinary veneration accorded to his work by posterity render a true evaluation and distinction of the historical person from the traditional one most difficult.

The *Corpus Hippocraticum*, a large collection of works attributed to Hippocrates by antiquity, contains writings by other authors. Among those writings, most assuredly Hippocratic, are the following: *Concerning Dieting, Concerning Prognosis, Concerning Aphorisms* (this latter volume, a widespread book on medicine, was considered for two millenia as the fundamental medical textbook), *Concerning the Physician's Labo-ratory, Concerning Wounds and Ulcers, Concerning Epidemics, Concerning Airs, Concerning Water and Places*.

The Hippocratic Oath. In the writings of the *Corpus Hippocraticum*, a remarkable importance is attributed to the so-called Oath of Hippocrates; this belongs to an earlier period, but is firmly linked with the school of Hippocrates.

The Oath: "I swear by Apollo, Physician, by Asclepius, by Health, by Panacea, and by all the gods and goddesses, making them my witnesses, that I will carry out, according to my ability and judgment, this oath and indenture. To hold my teacher in this art equal to my own parents; to make him partner in my livelihood; when he is in need of money, to share mine with him; to consider his family as my own brothers, and to teach them this art, if they want to learn it, without fee or indenture.

"To impart precept, oral instruction, and all other instruction to my own sons, the sons of my teacher, and to indentured pupils who have taken the physician's oath, but to nobody else.

"I will use treatment to help the sick according to my ability and judgment, but never with a view to injury and wrongdoing. Neither will I administer a poison to anybody when asked to do so, nor will I suggest such a course. Similarly, I will not give to a woman a pessary to cause abortion. But I will keep pure and holy both my life and my art.

"I will not use the knife, not even, verily, on sufferers from stone, but I will give place to such as are craftsmen therein. Into whatsoever houses I enter, I will enter to help the sick, and I will abstain from all intentional wrongdoing and harm, especially from abusing the bodies of man or woman, bond or free.

"And whatsoever I shall see or hear in the course of my profession, as well as outside my profession in my intercourse with men, if it be what should not be published abroad, I will never divulge, holding such things to be holy secrets.

"Now, if I carry out this oath, and break it not, may I gain forever reputation among all men for my life and for my art; but if I transgress it and forswear myself, may the opposite befall me."

The physicians of the School pronounced this oath as they began the practice of their profession; by it they solemnly promised Apollo and all their gods to fulfill scrupulously their duty, to respect always their master, to use the most honest and skillful way of curing patients, to abstain from practicing abortion, poisoning and any other act harmful to the patient; they swore, finally, to keep professional secrecy and consider their art as sacred.

This oath, from which even now the work of the physicians draws its inspiration, shows the heights attained at the time of the medical profession at the time of the School of Coo. From the fact that no priestly rites or divine help are hinted at, it must be inferred that those who took the oath were laymen, freely practicing medicine.

A beautiful copy of the Oath of Hippocrates from the thirteenth century reproduced in the form of a Latin Cross is kept in the Vatican Library.

The Hippocratic Oath contains rules of high medical ethics; later, Christianity adopted this oath as its own, ennobling it further with the aura of supernatural charity. *Riz.*

OBDURACY, IN CENSURES.

Obduracy in censures is a persistent continuation in a state of serious lawlessness, which has led to the infliction of excommunication or suspension, without any sign of repentance. "One who for a year will obstinately remain under the censure of excommunication becomes suspect of heresy" (Can. 2340, par. 1). (Cf. *Conc. Trid.*, Sess. XXV, c. 3, *De ref.*) Though this suspicion cannot be considered a penalty, yet it is the source of other penalties: the suspension of the privilege of performing legitimate acts after due admonition; a suspension *a divinis* for a cleric, after a second unheeded admonition; the incurring of all penalties to which heretics are liable, unless he shall have amended within six months (Can. 2315).

It is a disputed question whether or not obduracy is a new violation in the juridical sense. In any case, the effects are the same as those of a penalty.

Obduracy was instituted for a twofold purpose: one, primarily in the interest of the guilty individual, to induce him to relinquish his state of sin, at least externally and as quickly as possible; the other, primarily social, is intended to protect the penalty and the authority by which it was imposed by attaching serious consequences.

One may speak of obduracy only if excommunication was nominally pronounced, has become notorious by notoriety of fact, and the guilty party did nothing to obtain absolution for the period of an entire year.

The state of obduracy may also be added to suspension. "The cleric who for six months remains under a suspension censure must be seriously admonished, and if after the lapse of a month from such admonition he fails to abandon his obstinacy, he shall be deprived of any ecclesiastical benefice or office that he may hold in the Church" (Can. 2340, par. 2). *Pal.*

OBEDIENCE.

Obedience is the execution of an order received, either expressly or tacitly, from a superior. To comply with the mere wish of a superior is not obedience in the strict sense of the word; the action, however, actually may be inspired with the spirit of obedience.

Obedience may be *material* or *formal*. *Material* obedience is the execution of an order received without any explicit intention of conforming to the will of the superior; *formal* obedience is the execution of an order with the formal intention of conforming to the will of the superior or simply because it was ordered.

Our duty is to obey God and those to whom God has delegated a part of His authority. The motive for our obedience must be upright (*see* Intention, Right); formal obedience is not necessary, though certainly praiseworthy. Since the authority of human superiors is limited, the obligation to obey them has definite limits. For instance, it is not lawful to obey a superior who commands something contrary to divine or ecclesiastical laws: "We must obey God rather than men" (Acts 5:29). Strictly speaking, one is not bound to obey a superior who orders something outside the bounds of his sphere of power or authority, although obedience would certainly be a praiseworthy thing in such cases. In fact, to avoid scandal or harm to the community, one is obliged at times to obedience. Because of the possibility of error in such questions, in case of a doubtful obligation to obedience, it must be presumed that the command is within the sphere of the superior's authority and, hence, must be obeyed.

The practice of true obedience admits of various degrees of perfection: the first is the faithful execution of an order received, with an observation of all the particulars of time and manner indicated by the superior; the second is the prompt execution without internal opposition to the will of the superior; the third is a conformity of judgment to the superior in the execution of a command. This is not a judgment upon a command as prudent or opportune, which it may not be in reality, but the abstention from any judgment of the propriety or motive for the lawful command, out of a conviction that nothing is more profitable nor pleasing to God than to obey.

One may sin against obedience by excess, if one obeys commands contrary to a higher law or precept; this is servility. This is a mortal sin if it involves a grave transgression of a law or precept, or the end to be obtained is in serious conflict with the moral law. One may sin against obedience by defect, if one fails to obey an order within the competent authority of a superior; in other words, a legitimate injunction. This is disobedience.

Disobedience may be of two types: *material* disobedience is the transgression of a superior's legitimate order without the explicit intention of not conforming to the will of the superior; *formal* disobedience is the failure to obey the order of a superior explicitly as legitimately commanded because one does not wish to submit to the superior's will. The rea-

son for this disobedience may be contempt for a superior, or contempt for a specific precept of a superior, which one does not wish to submit to in a specific case. Every sin is, at least, a material disobedience. Formal disobedience is a sin of a special nature.

Material disobedience is a grave sin, if it hinders the attainment of an important end intended by the command. It is also grievous if a lawful precept is obeyed, but with the intention in the act to conflict with the moral law. Formal disobedience is a serious sin, if contempt for authority or for a specific precept of authority is implied; if contempt is merely for the precept, the sin is generally not mortal.

Obedience to a human superior in lawful commands, if not motivated by selfish reasons but honest motives, does not degrade but ennoble man, for it is submission to God Himself, from whom all power proceeds. Also obedience provides certainty of freedom from error: a superior may err in commanding, but a subject never errs in obeying a lawful injunction. Obedience strengthens the will as the noblest sacrifice man can make to God, which Holy Scripture, speaking of obedience, calls greater in value than sacrifice (I Kings 15:22). *Man.*

OBEDIENCE (Vow of). See Vow, Religious.

OBJECT, LEGAL. See Law, Ecclesiastical.

OBJECTOR, CONSCIENTIOUS. In a broad sense, a conscientious objector may be anyone who on moral grounds resists an injunction by the public authority. In this sense a martyr is a conscientious objector. In a strict sense, however, a conscientious objector is a citizen who refuses, by offering passive resistance, to serve in the military service of his country for personal reasons of conscience. These motives of a humanitarian, moral, or religious nature bring him to the conclusion that the use of arms is absolutely condemned.

This phenomenon, of a fairly recent

origin, has nothing to do with the passive resistance which existed in many countries at the beginning of the last century and consisted of an opposition to the establishment of compulsory military service on the ground that it was unjust.

The conscientious objectors' movement was enhanced by pseudo-religious motives of some Protestant sects (Mennonites, Quakers, Witnesses of Jehovah, etc.), who misinterpreted passages of Holy Scripture. The phenomenon is, in its origin, proper to such countries as England, Canada, the United States, etc. On legal grounds, they have succeeded in obtaining a special statute by which conscientious objectors are assigned to auxiliary services or ordinary work. This is done in Australia, Canada, Denmark, Finland, England, Norway, New Zealand, the United States and Sweden; there is a difference in the extent to which recognition is given to the motives alleged. Some States require religious motives. Later the movement spread to Latin countries through the aid of pacifist and humanitarian currents and fostered by the vision of the horrors of two world wars. The impression produced by the World War I was so great that, during its final two years, the movement of conscientious objectors slowly developed into a crusade against war. It was not limited to countries already at war, but took on the character, particularly after the United States of America entered the conflict, of a real crusade of the civilized world against the powers of the old system, as a system of violence and barbarity. The hope was to establish a new order which would make war impossible for all times.

But as the war ended, the new order did not come into being, and the terror of another world war again hovered over the world. World War I had appeared so disastrous a plague that everyone was expected to be ready and willing to do anything to avoid a repetition of it; but a great difference of opinions ensued as to the means to achieve this end. Some, afraid of attack, armed themselves more than before; others, exasperated over the inability of the rulers of nations to re-establish the peace desired by the whole world, organized a people's revolt against war to avoid taking part in it. This attitude gave rise to the "League of Those Opposed to War." In every country it fostered opposition to military service. War was not avoided. The conscientious objectors' movement remained a sporadic phenomenon which did not prevent totalitarian nations from unleashing war wherever and whenever they wished.

Following World War II, the conscientious objectors' movement became more active in Latin countries. But the net effect of it all seems to have been one of harm, for it weakened the democratic countries in favor of totalitarian nations. This fact must be kept in mind also when making a moral evaluation of this phenomenon.

Among Catholics, some uphold the lawfulness of conscience objection against war, provided that it is not fraud nor an act of sabotage against a nation. The most specious reasons in favor of this thesis allege the right to follow the dictates of a subjective conscience; the objective immorality of war, because of a disproportion between the rights to be defended, as oppressed nationalities, territories to annex or defend, and the immense losses to be borne; the injustice of compulsory conscription; a Christian repugnance to the use of force; and the divine command: "Thou shalt not kill." These advocates are more the unwitting promoters of a pacifist humanitarianism than followers of Catholic thinking and Catholic tradition. Generally, Catholics reject the thesis of conscientious objectors, and this passive resistance is considered, at least, as a violation of civic duties and legal justice.

The common good, in fact, requires that the citizens share both in the advantages and disadvantages of collective life, among which are compulsory military service, unless abolished by law, and the necessary armed defense of country (see Country, Patriotism).

Personal advantages must be sacrificed to the superior demands of society. Furthermore, the use of arms is, in itself, indifferent. If the motive of national defense is just, the instrument used for that defense, that is, the use of force, is also justified and lawful, as it is in legitimate self-defense for an individual. The use of modern arms is so absolutely disastrous that rulers must ponder and weigh the issues before assuming responsibility for war. It may be necessary to omit a vindication of rights, particularly in view of the great disproportion between these limited gains and the enormous destruction apparent in modern war. All this, however, does not make illegal the use of force for the defense of one's rights. This maximum social good of a moral nature is superior to all other material goods. "Thou shalt not kill" does not exclude the right of self-defense, either for an individual or a nation (see Self-defense).

The two fundamental principles, namely, the requirements of the common good and the instrumentality of war, refute the motives alleged by conscientious objectors to avoid military service. Because of their speciousness some of these motives deserve a closer examination. The conscientious objector maintains that if we could persuade a certain number of soldiers in all countries to refuse to be drafted for military service, war would become materially impossible. The argument must be considered from a twofold aspect: law and fact. In law, if a just war is possible, the duty of rulers is to prepare their country to wage war, if it becomes inevitable. If conscription is necessary for this end, laws promulgated for conscription are just and citizens must obey them. The action of a conscientious objector is rebellion and disobedience against lawful authority. In matters of fact, a conscientious objector causes a social disruption, which is hardly conducive to insuring peace. They exasperate, by reaction, nationalistic passions, and become the instrument of social disorganization in the hands of individuals whose motives are not to guarantee peace. Genuine conscientious objectors, who advocate the elimination of war, are generous idealists, whom everyone should respect for their sincerity, even if their attitude must be deplored;

but they lend themselves to a dangerous game and actually work for quite another end than that in which they believe. In fact, since war is but the consequence of ideas and a state of mind, it is precisely this to which all attention must be directed. The psychosis of war will certainly not be destroyed by fighting against war, but by substituting for the present state of mind a spirit of collaboration among nations; this is the only way by which international order can be surely established. Conscientious objectors also suffer from a psychosis of war, except that they react in the opposite direction of extreme nationalists.

Thus, if they declare nationality of secondary importance, they equivocate, because that is true only in a purely theoretical sense. In fact, in real and concrete circumstances, as history bears out, nationality holds great importance. An case must also be considered of an aggressor State guided by political motives of expansion and annexation. This would mean not only destruction of prosperity and well-being, but the destruction of the entire moral order, which is by far more important than all material goods.

In any case, a nation has a sacred duty to defend itself to the extreme limits of its ability, rather than permit extinction or domination. It is the duty of any nation unjustly attacked to defend itself to the extreme limit of its resources, even death. Christian charity requires that other nations do their duty and come to the aid of such a nation. *Pal.*

OBLATION, OFFERING. An oblation or offering is an object presented to God in a ceremonial action. Such an oblation or offering is synonymous with sacrifice. In a more specific sense, an offering is a gift, particularly money, given to a Church for maintenance and activities. This latter sense is the subject of this article.

Although an offering is a free and spontaneous act, yet, in a certain sense, it implies an element of definite obligation derived at least in part from the natural law, insofar as it is impossible to maintain a fitting worship due to God without churches, sacred vessels, and ministers. Insofar as it concerns the sustenance of the priest, this obligation is of divine-positive law.

Offerings and oblations as acts of cult toward the divinity are of ancient origin, for the practice is found in all religions. In the history of the Church one finds this obligation has been discharged in various ways. In the early Christian times there were two types of offerings: *oblationes communes* during the Eucharistic Sacrifice and limited at one time to offerings of bread and wine, and *oblationes peculiares* or all other types of offerings (Cf. *Canones Apostolorum*, Cans. 3–4; *Constitutiones Apostolicae*, 8, c. 31; PL 1128, c. 3, x, 5, 40; c. 42, x, 5, 3).

In the beginning, both special and common offerings were intended for the bishops and the clergy. Early in the history of the Church, however, offerings were to be divided into four parts: one for the bishop, another for the clergy, the third for the poor, and the fourth for the church (c. 23, xii, 9, 2). Later, bishops and councils enacted various regulations for the distribution of offerings. In the beginning, these offerings were spontaneous and voluntary, but as early as the fifth century, a tendency arose to regard these as obligatory, for with a decline of piety and fervor in the faithful, the offerings gradually diminished. The Council of Mainz (585) was the first to impose an obligation to make offerings.

In some widespread areas, customs have been preserved of making offerings according to the tithes system, the offerings of first fruits (*primitiae*—Can. 1504). In some areas the faithful are required to make an offering for the administration of the sacraments, the proclamation of the banns of marriage, dispensations, burials, in an amount fixed by custom or synodal regulations. *Pal.*

OBLIGATION, CONTRACTUAL. A contractual obligation is a juridical relationship in which one or more creditors have the right to exact a definite payment from one or more debtors under an obligation to satisfy these payments even by the use of their own patrimony if necessary.

Obligations may arise from agreements, unlawful acts (crimes), or actions or facts which are apt to produce these obligations as contracts. There has been much discussion concerning the origin of obligations. According to Bonfante, an obligation arising from a contract is derived from the obligation determined by a criminal act. Others hold that crime may have given rise to contract by reason of a pecuniary arrangement between the parties. If the object of an obligation is a payment, this must be *possible, lawful, determined* or *clearly determinable*, and must include *interest* for the creditor. Its impossibility may be *original* or *successive, absolute* or *relative, physical* or *juridical*.

Obligations may be optional, i.e., a choice of forms of payment, *partial, cumulative, reciprocal, divisible*, and *indivisible*.

The guarantees given for an obligation may be *personal*, i.e., the moral or juridical value of the promise made by the debtor, or *real*, i.e., an object which the creditor can either keep or sell if the obligation is not satisfied. There are many forms of guarantees, the principal ones are privilege for movable and immovable goods, pawn, and mortgage (*see* Guaranty).

An obligation may become extinct by *innovation of object*, i.e., the original obligation is exchanged for a new obligation with a different object or title; by *innovation of subject*, i.e., the substitution of a new debtor in place of the original one; by *remission*, i.e., the creditor remits the debt and returns the debenture to the debtor; by *compensation*, i.e., two persons with reciprocal obligations exchange two pecuniary debts in proportion to the amounts owed; or by *fusion*, i.e., the debtor and the creditor are one and the same person.

MORAL ASPECTS. The moral principles of obligation apply principally to fulfillment. In fulfilling an obligation a debtor must employ the diligence of a responsible head of the family. In discharging obligations inherent to a professional activity, diligence depends on the nature of the activity exercised. The debtor who fails to pay promptly what he owes must compensate for damage caused, unless he can prove that his failure or delay in carrying out his obligation was due to an impossibility caused by conditions which are not imputable to him. These rules flow from principles of the natural law and are, therefore, binding in conscience.

Obligations arising from a contract are binding in conscience from the first moment of stipulation, except if clauses included by the parties stipulate otherwise; the same may not be said concerning obligations arising from other sources. *Bau.*

OBLIGATION, LEGAL. *See* Law.

OBLIGATIONS OF STATE IN LIFE. *See* Duties; Ethics, Professional.

OBREPITITIOUS DISPENSATION, OR DECREE. *See* Dispensation, Rescript.

OBSCENITY. Obscenity is defined as *nudus allectans*, that is, a nude to which is connected an allurement to an active and, at least, implicitly willful evil act. The real danger is not in nudity as such. Nudity, of course, is offensive to modesty, but it becomes lustful if presented with reference to acts which have a connection with obscene objects, or acts which are unnecessarily ambiguous.

Illustrations or writings with a distant connection to sex may cause a moderate excitation, but not necessarily become obscene. In order to be obscene, the allurement caused by them must be active and intentional, at least implicitly.

For passive enticement, moral theologians classify the parts of the body according to the varying degree of influence which they exercise in exciting sexual pleasure: decent (face, hands and feet), moderately decent (chest, back, arms and thighs) and indecent (genitals and adjacent areas).

With respect to the above classification, it should be pointed out that modesty, as a psychical restraint toward sex, must be protected by avoiding any, even indirect, inordinate reference to sex as in illustrations or narratives, which, though not actually obscene, have nevertheless a stimulating effect toward an improper use of the sexual instinct.

Thus, the sight of the more private parts of a person's body is of itself capable of greatly exciting sexual concupiscence. It follows that printed reproductions of indecent nudes should be absolutely banned as detrimental to the moral sense.

Obscenity is not so much in the objectivity of a common reaction, as in the open violation of a right which is congenital and natural to every individual. Any act or object capable of arousing sexual concupiscence outside its proper limits and scope must be considered obscene.

Thus, publications of themselves capable of stimulating a vivid memory of libidinous actions or sexual relations, which arouse excitement and emotion in persons who lack a healthy sense of purity or produce psychical reactions in those who have a lively moral sense, are obscene. The obscenity is due, not to a conflict with normal sensibility of the masses, but to the fact that despite a limited radius of harmful effects, even in one lone individual, the offense constitutes a violation against the dignity of the human person, with respect to the natural degree of modesty related to sex.

As an offense against modesty, obscenity does violence to not merely a sentiment, as the result of externally imposed conditions of and effect of environment, domestic or social education, but to the sentiments engendered by the law of nature itself. Modesty can be violated by any medium or instrument, any type or form of typographical presentation or means of promotion. Obscenity, more or less cleverly disguised, contains criminal or sinful intent.

Writings and drawings, various forms and types of printed matter, on the market of pornography and sex exploitation, unsolicited private mail, foreign magazines, pictures of movie stars, theatrical and revue artists, beauty contest candidates, post-cards apparently of an artistic nature or supposedly promoting movies, novels and love stories, immoral jokes and the like, are especially and openly obscene in their contents. In modern jurisprudence and criminal codes, obscenity is a difficult legal matter. The variety of opinions and definitions of obscenity are extremely uncertain, broad, and fluctuating. Modern opinions are generally based on a fluctuating popular sentiment with particular reference to opinions prevaling in a school, city, or certain environment. These, often called the sentiment of the community on moral issues, actually are the result of vested interests or personal views.

The theory of popular sentiment or judgment by a community amounts to a criterion based on the opinion of the average man or woman of the community. These represent compromise between exaggerated, refined attitudes on modesty and inferior, debased sentiments.

According to this theory, obscenity is not determined by a definite criterion or an absolute, exclusive moral criterion, but by a relative, average, and comparative criterion based on the average and ordinary sentiment prevailing at the moment in the community. According to this precarious criterion of the sentiment of the community, morality assumes a meaning completely severed from any natural foundation. Such opinions reduce morality to a product of the moment, so that what may have been considered obscene at one time cannot be considered obscene now because of a changed public conscience or a changed public judgment, and vice versa.

Against this fluctuating conception of obscenity, the unchangeable, natural, moral law binds all men, irrespective of religious affiliation or social position.

Another field in which the concept of the obscene varies is the field of art.

Absolute independence is claimed for this field, and unrestrained freedom is invoked by art amateurs, admirers, and those upon whom art exercises great fascination. Against this attitude, art itself sets specific limits within which obscenity must always be contained. Above all, the character of the exposure must be profound and elevating, in form and content, so that any sensual trait, detail, or content, negligible from the standpoint of its obscene character, remains elevated by the splendor of artistic intent expressed by the artist and by the serious nature of the work. Reproductions dictated by reasons of gain, commercial speculation, impure delight, and sensual pleasure, of nudes taken from actual works of art, without an educational purpose but with evident intent to exploit the exhibition of nudes as an incentive to increase of sales is a grave offense against modesty which should be severely checked because of their potential of greatly exciting sexual concupiscence. Concerning the relation between art and morals, *see* Art, morality of; Speech, Obscene; Vulgar, Evil. *Pal.*

OBSERVANCES, SUPERSTITIOUS. Superstitious observances are practices employed to obtain through the aid of occult forces an effect outside the known power of the method or natural means used. Sometimes these practices are called simply *superstition*. In this sense superstitious observances embrace a large variety of practices which belong more to the realm of folklore and the history of religion than to moral theology. Moral theologians, however, have traditionally dealt with them.

Superstitious practices, when connected with religion, may become meaningless or ridiculous distortions of true devotions or practices. Superstitious practices may seek to obtain knowledge of occult facts or future events; such practices are referred to as divination (*q.v.*). Superstitious practices may also center on expressions of a false belief in objects supposedly having special powers of protection, as amulets, talismans, fetishes, numbers, etc.

Superstitious practices must be judged according to the moral category to which they belong. *Vain worship* is generally a venial sin, unless scandal or contempt for God or ecclesiastical laws result. *Divi-*

nation is a grave sin, as are other superstitious practices which from the moral standpoint belong to the same species as divination (*see* Divination). *Magic* with the explicit invocation of the devil is always and without exception a very grave sin. *Superstition*, as observances or divinations employed by the populace, in ignorance of the true significance of these practices, may not involve the formal sin of divination, although these practices must be prudently uprooted.

The approved use of medals, holy water, religious exercises for a specified number of days, as in novenas, are not superstitious practices, for no power is attributed to these in themselves, nor does the desire and request for divine aid depend on these conventional procedures. These are the expressions of trust in the prayers of the Church, whose authority sanctions these objects and blesses them, or in the protection of the saint invoked by these practices. To none is attributed a certain efficacy beyond that of prayer in general, the dispositions of the one who offers the prayer, and the relation of the requested favors to eternal salvation. *Pal.*

OBSESSION (Infirmity). Obsession (Latin, *obsidere*—to block, hinder, occupy), as an illness, must be clearly distinguished from diabolical obsession or possession, which is domination by a wicked spirit who controls to his own wishes and desires the actions or speech of the individual (*see* Exorcism, Spiritualism).

Individuals in diabolical obsession show two different states: one of crisis, the other of calm. Crisis begins with a violent, psycho-motor agitation, with alternating contortions and rigidity, serious vasomotor disturbances, a state of paralysis of the sensory apparatus, blasphemous and impious cries, rolling of eyeballs, and frothing at the mouth. After the crisis, the patient has no recollection of any such disturbances. During the periods of calm, the individual acts in a perfectly normal way without any indication of possession by an evil spirit, although signs

of mutism, blindness, or other pathological disturbances may occur.

There is an analogy between the symptoms in diabolical possession and in neuropathic convulsions. To detect with certainty the cases of obsession, one must look for the principal symptoms listed under Energumen. If these symptoms are absent, it is probably a simple case of neurosis, not to be confused with rare diabolical obsession. The symptoms of a crisis of agitation may easily be due to neuropathic illnesses, such as epilepsy or hysteria, and have nothing to do with diabolical possession.

True obsession in a psychiatric sense is different both from diabolical obsession and the pseudo-convulsive obsessions mentioned above. Such obsession, with its own causes, symptoms, and effects, is a form of obsessive psychosis or psychasthenia (*q.v.*). It is called *obsessive* because there prevails in the patient mental representations which are in contrast with his personality and beliefs. Such representations are not necessarily of a pathological nature but act in a pathological way, insomuch as they dominate the patient's thinking (they *occupy* it) and distort its natural development. *Riz.*

OBSESSION, DEMONIACAL. See Exorcism; Medium, Spiritualism.

OBSESSION, IMPULSIVE. See Psychasthenia.

OBSTACLE. See Extreme Unction; Grace; Sacraments, Reviviscence of.

OBSTETRICS. Obstetrics, as a branch of medical science, deals with the scientific treatment of mother and child during pregnancy, childbirth, and the postnatal period. The term is derived from the practice of having women present at childbirth, although not necessarily midwives. In the United States most obstetricians are male physicians with specialized training.

As in all branches of medicine and specialized training, obstetrics requires more than ordinary spiritual and technical qualifications in those who practice it, such as serenity and calmness of spirit, an ability to make quick decisions, notable skill, and a sound moral conscience. The obstetrician must always be capable of important decisions and carrying them out promptly, for often the well-being of the mother and child depends completely on such decisions. Many important ethical problems connected with obstetrics are dealt with under Abortion, Therapeutic abortion, Feticide, Twins, Pregnancy, etc. In the following paragraphs we shall dwell on similarly important moral questions related to pregnancy.

SPONTANEOUS ABORTION. To the lues and other causes of spontaneous abortion known *ab antiquo* (*see* Abortion), recently there has been added a new one, which is caused by a special fetal disease from a particular agglutinin, called a *Rhesus factor*, or *RH factor* (*see* Blood types).

This may not be the place for a description of the importance of various means tried from time to time to prevent spontaneous abortion (anti-luetic drugs, rest, B and E vitamins, progesterone, estrogens, auto-blood, plasma transfusions, etc.). We shall underscore, instead, the obligation on the part of the obstetrician to use every technical and moral means to prevent spontaneous abortion, although the parents favor leaving things *to a natural course*, or might welcome a spontaneous interruption of pregnancy. The safety of the child and the health of the mother make this protective action by the doctor imperative.

PREMATURE BIRTH. Premature birth is the birth of a child between the 180th and 265th day after conception. Its course does not differ greatly from natural birth occurring at the end of a completed pregnancy. The prognosis in a premature childbirth, as far as the mother is concerned, is no more alarming than in normal cases. Insofar as the child is concerned, the prognosis is a reserved one, since the fetus, born alive, often dies because of frailness, difficulty in feeding, or disease in the mother (nephropathies, syphilis, tuberculosis, etc.). These usually are responsible for the spontaneous and premature interruption of pregnancy.

Thus, whenever a *spontaneous premature birth*, habitual in certain women, is feared and the fetus is known to be alive, the obstetrician must, as in a case of spontaneous abortion, use every possible prophylactic method to delay the birth of the child.

When grave reasons demand it, it is lawful to *provoke a premature childbirth* provided the life and further development of the newborn child by the use of incubators, etc., is properly safeguarded. Furthermore, it is always advisable to delay obstetrical intervention as long as possible, because the nearer a woman comes to the 270th day of pregnancy, the more certainty for the life of a fetus is present. It is understood that the greater the danger for the mother, the more prematurely must she be delivered. It is not lawful to deliver a premature child before the 180th day of pregnancy or the sixth month.

OBSTETRIC OPERATIONS. Obstetric interventions are intrinsically lawful; the decision in each case rests upon the surgeon, who must be guided by his experience and by the nature of the *emergency*. In making the decision, however, the obstetrician shall keep in mind his moral obligation to save both mother and child, and to avoid those interventions which do not offer at least the possibility of saving both lives entrusted to him. Furthermore, the operation shall be as conservative as possible, i.e., avoiding mutilation which is not deemed indispensable.

DISEASES AND PREGNANCY. Diseases accompanying pregnancy can be distinguished, rather didactically, into *diseases caused by pregnancy* and *diseases during pregnancy*, which accidentally complicate the pregnancy. The latter may consist of diseases existing before, or developed during, pregnancy.

These diseases, whether acute or chronic, somatic or psychological, infectious or traumatic, occasion from a moral point of view important and delicate questions concerning possible harm to the fetus and possible treatments which must safeguard, as far as possible, regular development of the fetus.

With regard to treatments, we limit ourselves to mentioning that, between two helpful treatments in combating a given disease, the obstetrician has the moral obligation to choose the one which will cause less harm to the unborn child. If in order to save the mother, it becomes necessary to use a treatment which presumably might harm or prove fatal to the fetus, such a presumption must not prevent the obstetrician from using that medicine or therapeutic method, for such conduct, similar to the principles applied to indirect abortion (*see* Abortion, Therapeutic), is not motivated by an intentional suppression of the unborn child and is, therefore, lawful.

Lastly, mention must be made of psychoses caused by pregnancy or in the post-natal period. Both pregnancy and childbirth are liable to cause psychotic conditions or mental deteriorations to such a serious degree that a complete mental derangement may follow. In these cases a twofold etiopathogenesis must be admitted: on one side, external causes linked to the pregnancy, as toxicosis, or to the delivery, as loss of blood, intense pain; on the other hand, a constitutional predisposition in the patient, as serious as the relevancy and persistence of the psychotic state. These diseases usually present no particular characteristics, for they appear with similar frequency apart from pregnancy or childbirth. Induced abortion and frequently induced premature birth must be excluded from the therapy of these psychoses, which are of a mixed nature, both obstetric and psychotic. *Riz.*

OBSTINACY. Obstinacy is a firm and unreasonable adherence to one's own opinion, which refuses to abandon an enterprise or particular attitude when it is clear that one should do so.

Obstinacy in itself is a venial sin. It is, however, a mortal sin if one would rather commit a grievous sin than yield to reason or arguments, or if because of an excessive attachment to one's own views, one fails to fulfill a grave obligation or runs the risk of committing a mortal sin (*see* Sins aginst the Holy Ghost).

OCCASION. *See* Occasionist.

OCCASIONIST. An occasionist is a person who is in habitual danger of sinning because of a particular person, place or thing (occasion of sin). This occasion of sin may be either *proximate* or *remote*. It is called *proximate* if it gives rise to an immediate danger of sin; *remote*, if the danger of sin is not immediate. According to a common opinion, a proximate occasion of sin makes the sin very probable, even though sin may not be committed every time, or almost every time that the occasionist finds himself in the occasion. From past experience, usual contingencies, and individual dispositions, it is possible to know whether an occasion is proximate or remote. For greater precaution, one should abide by the judgment of his confessor.

Occasions are also *absolute* or *relative*. An *absolute* occasion of sin creates a danger of sin for all men; a *relative* occasion of sin creates a danger of sin for some men because of subjective dispositions. Occasions of sin may also be permanent, temporary, or intermittent.

All are obliged to avoid the occasions of sin. This obligation is serious if the occasion of sinning mortally is proximate; but this obligation ceases if it is impossible to remove the occasion. It also ceases if a failure to remove or avoid an occasion of sin is not in itself sinful, but produces, independently of the danger of sin, a good effect which cannot be obtained in any other way. This good effect compensates for the danger of sin connected with it. In such cases one is obliged to use the proper means to render the occasion of sin as remote as possible. If, however, there is no hope of avoiding sin, the aforesaid conditions are no longer valid and one must avoid the occasion altogether at all cost; this is true, provided that the occasion can be avoided.

To fail without sufficient reason to avoid an occasion of sin is to become guilty of the same sin as that which is risked by the dangerous occasion. To remain in an occasion of sin is a mortal sin, if there is serious danger of committing a mortal sin; the sin is multiplied each time the occasion is desired or permitted with renewed willfulness.

One must diligently avoid occasions of sin, and not seek to find too readily excuses or sufficient reasons for not removing the occasion of a sin.

The most useful means in avoiding sin or the occasions of sin are: prayer, frequent Holy Communion, the thought of the presence of God and the Last Things, devotion to the Blessed Virgin Mary, mortification of the senses, sincerity and frankness in confession, especially in questions of doubtful sins or occasions. *Man.*

OCCULT. *Occult* (Latin, *occultare*—to hide) is a term opposed to *public*; it represents a quality which may apply to a crime, impediment, document, fact, etc.

OCCULT CRIME. In the Code of Canon Law a crime is called occult if it cannot be proved in an open court, since it is not sufficiently known by a large number of people in a place and is not in danger of proximate divulgation as a material fact or imputable to an individual (Can. 2197, n. 4). An occult crime must not be susceptible of becoming publicly known, at least as far as the subjective element is concerned, though a few persons may know of the crime, yet will not divulge it.

An occult crime cannot be prosecuted by judicial trial (Can. 1933, 1); it may be liable to exceptional sanctions, such as suspension *ex informata conscientia* or others which do not require ordinary judicial procedure (Can. 2186 ff.).

A denuntiation and a special, secret inquiry, which always must precede a canonical trial in the public forum, are directed precisely to discovering a crime for the public or external forum with the intention that, for judiciary reasons, the crime become public (Can. 1939).

OCCULT IMPEDIMENT. In the Code of Canon Law an occult impediment is a matrimonial impediment which is not susceptible of proof in the external forum, even if the impediment is of its very nature public (Can. 1037). *See* Impediments, Matrimonial. *Pub.*

OCCULTATION. *See* Cooperation.

OCCULTISM. *See* Magic, Metapsychology.

OCCUPANCY. Occupancy is the exercise of the right of possession by material and physical control over an article or place; the very act of taking possession of something which has no juridical relation to another person may occasion a right of occupancy. Thus occupancy, resulting from acquisition of property, may become a right in things belonging to no one (*res nullius*); such articles by right become the property of the first occupant.

For a right of occupancy, certain conditions must prevail: (a) the article or place must be capable of occupancy as private property; areas for public use are not susceptible to occupancy; (b) on the part of the occupant, there must be an intention of taking possession of the object at the moment in which he finds it; (c) there must be no legal, just, or valid prohibition against such occupancy.

Susceptible of occupancy are movable objects which do not belong to any one. In modern codes, abandoned objects and animals which may be hunted or caught fall under this category. The particular legislation of the country in question establishes the limits and formalities within which possession may be established. (*See* Fishing, Hunting, Treasure). *M.d.G.*

OCTAVE. An octave is the celebration or commemoration of a feast day for a period of eight successive days. It indicates the degree of solemnity of a particular feast day.

Octaves can be traced back to the fourth century, when, by the example of an Old Testament custom, the dedication of the Constantine basilicas in Jerusalem and Tyre was commemorated by a celebration lasting eight successive days. At the same time the octaves of Easter and Whitsunday were being celebrated. As baptismal feasts, these were followed by eight days of additional explanation of the sacrament of Christian initiation to the newly baptized. In the seventh century the octave of feastdays of the saints were first celebrated. At the reform of the Missal and Breviary, Pope St. Pius V reduced a large number of such octaves. St. Pius X and recently Pius XII further reduced these (Decree of the Sacred Congregation of Rites on the simplification of rubrics, March 23, 1955: AAS, 47 [1955], 218–224). Today the octaves of Christmas, Easter, and Whitsunday alone are celebrated; all others, whether feasts of the Universal Church or a particular area or order, have been suppressed. *Cig.*

OFFENSE. *See* Contumely, Insult, Abuse.

OFFICE, DIOCESAN (For Catechetical Instruction). Since the institution by Pope Pius XI of a particular department within the Sacred Congregation of the Council (Motu Proprio *Orbem Catholicum,* June 29, 1923) for the direction and promotion of catechetical instruction in all parts of the world, in every diocese an office must be established within the curia under the responsibility of the Ordinary for the promotion of catechetical instruction in each diocese. The tasks of the diocesan office for catechetical instruction include organizational and directive work in a vast area of education, from kindergarten to university, from the farm to the industrial plant, from cultural to artistic professions.

Its work entails an accurate census of those who should be receiving catechetical instruction as well as those who are able to give such instruction. A foremost task of the catechetical office is the promotion of courses in religion and catechetical pedagogy for the preparation of teachers of religion. These courses end with regular examinations and the conferral of appropriate certificates to those qualified to teach religion in parochial and public schools which permit this instruction.

Such courses must be established particularly in Catholic schools by selecting from among the senior classes those who show greater aptitude for such work,

keener intelligence, and outstanding moral qualities.

It is also a particular task of the office of catechetical instruction to promote conventions and study weeks to exchange new ideas and experiences in the religious and secular scholastic fields, so that the teaching of religion becomes more attractive and successful.

The office of catechetical instruction includes men and women from Catholic colleges or other schools, from Catholic Action groups and other organizations engaged in religious and moral education. A well organized group of teachers can be effective in bringing great moral benefits to the family and society, through coordinated methods of teaching religion.

Men and women from all walks of life, professions, and social conditions are invited to dedicate themselves to that which is the fundamental work of the Church.

OFFICE, DIVINE. *See* Breviary, Choir.

OFFICE, HOLY. *See* Congregations, Roman.

OFFICE OF THE BLESSED VIRGIN. The early Middle Ages witnessed a tendency, in monasteries especially, not to be content with the recitation of the ordinary canonical hours, but to add other prayers to these. The principal ones became a short office, composed of a psalm or two, in honor of the saint or particular feast of the day. This custom, prevailing in the monasteries, initiated the practice of a recitation of a little office in honor of the Blessed Virgin Mary, which was said in addition to the office of the day. St. Ulrich, Bishop of Augsburg (d. 973), is the author of one such office. This custom was later adopted by the secular clergy, until it became quite common in the twelfth century; the Little Office was recited on days when the nine-lesson office was not prescribed. Pope St. Pius V did away with this general obligation but allowed some religious orders to retain it as a particular obligation. Saint

Pius X abolished this obligation at a later date.

The Little Office of the Blessed Virgin has a greater significance in modern times, for a considerable number of congregations of women have made the recitation of the Little Office their daily prayer, as a devotion in honor of Mary, the model of Christian virginity, and as a means of placing themselves under the protection of the Blessed Virgin, Mother of God. *Pal.*

OFFICERS, MILITARY. Governmental authority encompasses a variety of functions, including those involving the administration of the military. Those who preside over the various departments of military administration are called officers or officials. They hold jurisdiction in the preparation of military personnel for the defense of the country. The status of officials, then, consists of a series of duties and rights connected with a specific position or rank.

DUTIES. According to the principles of Christian morality, besides duties common to all citizens, a military officer assumes two types of special obligations: one toward the State, the other toward the military personnel under his command. Toward the State, a grave obligation in justice and fidelity exists by virtue of his oath of office; toward the military personnel, he is obliged to protect their moral as well as their spiritual welfare and life. Thus, to order military exercises or training on a Sunday without necessity, would be a serious sin; likewise, it would be sinful if a commander failed to remove from his subordinate subjects, insofar as it is within his power, all serious occasions of sin or to expose his subordinates to physical danger without a justifying reason.

CRIMES. The classification of military crimes and respective penalties is not the same in every country; hence, the reader must consult the military codes of each respective country. However, it is assumed that the following classification applies to a considerable number of countries to some extent. Generally, the crimes which a military officer may commit are of excess or of defect. Crimes of excess are: (1) to undertake hostile actions neither ordered nor necessary nor authorized by his government; (2) by such actions to expose his subjects to reprisals; (3) apart from necessity to attack an enemy against an order of his superior officers; (4) to protract unduly hostilities. Crimes of defect are: (1) to surrender a post or fortress without necessity; (2) to be guilty of negligence in the defense of a post or military position under attack; (3) to surrender in the open field without necessity; (4) to relinquish his command without necessity; (5) to provide for his own protection but not for his troops under his command; (6) to fail to carry out a definite command.

This list of crimes indirectly classifies the duties of an officer, especially during times of military conflict or action in war. An officer is also usually forbidden to hold civilian office as mayor, governor, etc., in time of war.

Authors on international law hold that belligerents must respect all enemy possessions; a war does not change the law of private right. Any unnecessary damage to enemy property is considered a violation of their rights which calls for reparation of damage. Victory is not a title to immunity from punishment for acts of violence; it merely guarantees the possibility of obtaining reparation for just juridical claims already existing. It would be a crime against justice if an officer permitted his soldiers to ransack enemy territory and damage and destroy everything on their path, like bands of criminals. A Christian officer may not duel, even under the title of defending one's honor; a duel is an offense against the supreme right of God, the arbiter of life and death, and the honor of a military officer must not be vindicated by an act which goes beyond human and reasonable limits (*see* Duel, Suicide). *Tar.*

OFFICIAL, CIVIL. *See* Official, Public.

OFFICIAL, PUBLIC. The State is a moral person, which must fulfill its functions through necessary physical persons, duly invested with appropriate authority in the fulfillment of the obligations of society and the protection of its right. The various functions of public officials are carried out on the basis of provisions of law or other regulations which vary from State to State. Ordinarily, definite requirements are demanded in a person who seeks a public office. These are: citizenship, possession of civil and political rights, and an age proportionate to the importance of the office. In the strictly juridical field, a public official is not himself the subject of rights, for these belong to the State. Nevertheless, one often hears of the rights of a public official. What is actually meant are rights which the individual official exercises by reason of office. The rights vary according to the functions exercised in or for the government.

RIGHTS. Once elected, public officials have a right before the State to exercise their office according to divine and human laws without interference; the right to receive, except office accepted without pay, adequate compensation in proportion to the service rendered; a right to remain in office for the stipulated time, provided that they remain loyal to their duties; the right to a suitable vacation or other benefits.

DUTIES. Besides the duty common to all citizens to promote the common good, a public official assumes a specific obligation in strict justice toward the government for a proper fulfillment of duties committed to him. With regard to individual citizens, besides legal obligations in justice, and the duty to distribute honors and burdens with equity, a public official may contract further obligations in strict commutative justice. This occurs, for example, in contractural obligations assumed by the government as a private person, or in obligations of strict justice with respect to individual citizens, as in the assignment of various positions of employment by competitive examinations.

(a) In assuming any office, a public official must have adequate preparation to fulfill properly the duties involved. To accept an office with a knowledge of one's own personal inadequacy is an act of fraud which violates the tacit agreement of the possession of a minimum capability, implied in seeking or accepting any office. In case of doubtful capability to fulfill an office, one must not accept the office, for no one may make himself the probable cause of damage to another.

(b) Once a person has accepted an office, he must perform it diligently; grave negligence is a grave sin against justice, which carries an obligation to restitution for damage caused. No inconvenience inherent in the fulfillment of duties excuses one from rendering faithful service, because individual welfare must give way to the public welfare and because this is an implicit and tacit promise in the acceptance of the office itself.

(c) The obligations of a public official in the exercise of his functions are manifold. He must take care that all respect in him the authority of the State, and make himself useful to the State and to individual citizens. As a lawmaker, or member of the executive branch, or custodian of law and order, he must not abuse the mandate received, but endeavor to promote the public welfare with justice, absolute disinterestedness and diligence. If, by reason of office, a public official comes into contact with the public, he must show a spirit of charity and understanding for all. An official of subordinate rank has a grave obligation to maintain a hierarchical subordination toward his superiors in all those things related to his office. Hence, he is obliged to fidelity in his work and to professional secrecy. Subordination, however, must not be confused with servility, which implies the toleration of injustices by his superiors for the purpose of gaining their friendship or promotion.

(d) Moreover, a public office is not a throne from which to dominate others or acquire wealth. Hence, he who has received the trust of a public office may not extort money or gifts by acts pertaining to his office, unless this is permitted by law or approved custom. Such behavior is always dangerous because it promotes favoritism and dishonesty. In direct extortion, there exists an obligation to restitution; in acceptance of gifts freely given, restitution is conditional until judicial sentence. These obligations and evasions or violations acquire a specific character according to the various positions of public officials.

THE PUBLIC OFFICIAL IN HIS LEGISLATIVE FUNCTION. In modern constitutional States, legislative functions are performed by two legislative branches: senators and representatives. The legislator is required by legal justice to honest cooperation in making good laws. An obligation of commutative justice flows from his acceptance of office. Hence, a public official may not cooperate in making a law openly unjust, or a law whose purpose is intrinsically evil; for injustice, whether detrimental to religion, morals, the family or each individual citizen, cannot be implemented by executive law.

PUBLIC OFFICIALS IN THEIR ADMINISTRATIVE FUNCTION. They have obligations of legal and commutative justice toward the State, by reason of office. Since the State is a public person, greater diligence is expected in its behalf than toward private citizens, who possess separate means of protecting rights. More common forms of corruption in this field are improper favoritism (*q.v.*) and the selling of exemptions from laws.

For *public officials in their juridical function, See* Judge, Magistrate. *Pal.*

OFFSPRING. *See* Children, Marriage, Piety, Duty.

OILS, HOLY. The holy oils include the following: (1) *oleum infirmorum*, used for the anointing of the sick (*see* Extreme Unction); (2) *oleum catechumenorum*, used in exorcism in ancient times for anointing cathecumens or candidates for baptism, during the period of immediate catechetical preparation for baptism, but used at present in the baptismal rite; (3) *sacrum chrisma*, an oil mixed with other rare and perfumed substances, used in the administration of the sacrament of confirmation (*q.v.*).

These oils are called *holy* not only because of the use that is made of them, but also because of the special *blessing* or *consecration* given to them in a solemn form by the Bishop on Holy Thursday. This function is forbidden during the time of interdict (Can. 2271, n. 2). In the consecration of the holy oils the Bishop is assisted by twelve priests, seven deacons, and seven subdeacons. The Bishop and the priests, each in turn, breathe on the oils to communicate to them the Holy Spirit. They chant the salutation *Ave, Sanctum Oleum; Ave, Sanctum Chrisma*, and kiss the oils. Formularies for the blessing of the oils are found in the earliest periods of Christianity, especially in the *Euchologium Serapionis* of the fourth century and in the *Traditio Apostolica* of Hyppolitus of Rome in the third century.

The holy oils are kept in special vials in every church in a special chest called *ambry* generally attached to the wall of the sanctuary (Can. 735, 946). The Bishop is required to inspect them when making his canonical visitation in parish churches (*see* Visitation, Diocesan; Vessels, Sacred).

The holy oils may be used as the matter of a sacrament, or in the rites of the sacraments. These must be blessed by the Bishop on the previous Holy Thursday. Holy oils blessed in former years may not be used, except in case of necessity (Can. 734, par. 1). Concerning the oil for the lamp of the Blessed Sacrament, *see* Holy Eucharist, Custody of the Blessed Sacrament. *Cig.*

OLIGOPHRENIA. *See* Phrenasthenia.

OLYMPICS. *See* Sports.

OMISSION (Sins of). *See* Sin.

ONANISM. Among theologians, *onanism* is commonly used to indicate the marriage act performed with positive frustration of conception. It is called thus from the sin of Onan referred to in Sacred Scripture (Gen. 38:8–10). Generally, it is also called Neo-Malthusianism (*q.v.*), from the name of the English sociologist, Malthus. By *onanism* some persons, particularly doctors, mean direct voluntary pollution.

Conjugal onanism may be practiced in a natural way, that is, by interrupting the conjugal act, or by the use of contraceptives, which prevent the semen from reaching its proper destination or destroy its fertility (*see* Birth Control). Unnatural onanism is a sterilization of man or woman for the purpose of preventing procreation (*see* Sterilization). Whichever method is used, conjugal onanism is gravely sinful because such practice is contrary to the laws of nature governing the marriage act. For this reason, it is strongly condemned by the Church (*see* Neo-Malthusianism).

As a result of the practice of onanism there arises in the intimate life of married people a problem of cooperation in sin for which the following principles are valid: (1) If a married person intends to engage in the practice of onanism, the other spouse is under no obligation to consent to the marital relation. In fact, strictly speaking, he or she is not allowed to take part in such an action. (2) However, in view of the impossibility of refusing all cooperation, Catholic moralists have endeavored to indicate the degree of cooperation a Catholic may be permitted to give (*see* Cooperation). Cooperation is justified only if participation in the formal malice of the evil act is excluded. It all depends, therefore, at what point the act becomes so vitiated as to render the cooperation that follows formal. It is universally accepted that natural onanism does not vitiate the act until the moment of its interruption; therefore, cooperation up to that point is lawful if warranted by proportionately serious reasons, as a danger of serious quarrels, adultery, difficulty of abstaining over long periods, etc., on the condition that there be no intention of consenting to the other's sin and with an obligation, in charity, to admonish the sinning party (*see* Declaration of the S. Penitentiary, Nov. 16th, 1816; April 23rd, 1822; Feb. 1st, 1823; June 8th, 1842; April 3rd, 1916; *Casti Connubii*,

Dec. 31st, 1930). With regard to artificial onanism, it is certain that the use by the husband of means which prevent the transmission of the semen into the proper place vitiates substantially the act from the very beginning. In this case, the wife must resist any kind of cooperation in the same way as a woman who is violently attacked (*see* Rape). (*See* Declaration of the S. Penitentiary) April 16th, 1853; June 3rd, 1916; S. C. of the Holy Office, May 21st, 1851; April 19th, 1853.) The use of contraceptives by the wife, including those means which prevent the passage of the semen after ejection, probably does not take away the husband's right to ask for the marital right, even if, despite all dutiful admonishments, the wife refuses to discontinue the use of these means at the time of marital intercourse.

MASTURBATION. Masturbation is the production of orgasm by excitation of the genital organs, as by manipulation or friction, without heterosexual intercourse. In a moral sense it stimulates complete sexual satisfaction outside of copulation; thus, it comprises not only the emission of the semen but a complete sexual satisfaction, whether it be in man or woman, adolescents or children, eunuchs, etc., if they are capable of it. The pollution may be directly voluntary, if intentionally provoked, or indirectly voluntary, if caused by some other voluntary action, without voluntary pleasure in the pollution itself. Direct voluntary pollution is properly called masturbation.

Direct voluntary pollution, as a means or an end, is always a mortal sin. In the Holy Scriptures it is condemned as a sin which excludes a person from the Kingdom of Heaven (I Cor. 6:10; Gal. 5:19; Eph. 5:4). In fact, pollution, as the execution of a generative act implying the frustration of its principal purpose, is directly opposed to a social good of great importance, namely, potential human life. Pollution is a form of lust against nature. The decrees issued by the ecclesiastical authorities confirm the grave intrinsic malice of this sin. (*See* Proposition 49a, condemned by Innocent XI, March 4, 1697, Denz. 1199; the decrees of the S. C. of the Holy Office, March 24, 1890, and August 2, 1929, in which pollution artificially provoked for artificial fecundation or for the discovery or treatment of a disease was declared unlawful.) Indirect voluntary pollution is a grave or venial sin, depending on the extent of the influence by the unlawfully posited action. A proportionately honest cause removes moral guilt. So-called nocturnal pollution, which usually occurs in sleep, is a purely physiological phenomenon by which nature spontaneously rids itself of superfluous semen. This is outside the field of moral imputability. It would be gravely sinful to consent to accompanying pleasure, since such pleasure is only lawful if directed at the act of generation, properly performed in marriage.

Examination of the seminal fluid, connected with the preceding question, at times may be deemed useful for juridical reasons, as validity or invalidity in a marriage, or for medical diagnostic or therapeutic reasons. An honest motive cannot justify an unlawful means. The only licit way is the collection of fluid after a lawful, voluntary and natural emission, or by an exploratory puncture.

ONANOFF, REFLEX OF. *See* Impotency.

ONEIRISM. *See* Narcolepsy.

ONEIROMANCY. *See* Divination, Dream.

OPENING LETTERS. *See* Secret.

OPERATION, OBSTETRICAL. From the moral standpoint, an obstetrical operation is a special type of surgical operation in which two human lives are involved: the life of the mother and the fetus. For this reason obstetrical operations are governed by special moral rules. (a) A surgeon who performs an obstetrical operation must do everything possible to save both the life of the mother and that of the fetus. (b) He must bear in mind a grave obligation to save the soul of the fetus; therefore, he

must see to it that the latter is baptized as soon as possible. (c) He must never perform an act which would result in a direct murder either of the mother or of the fetus; therefore, he must never perform an *embryotomy* or cause a *direct abortion*. (d) If both lives cannot be saved, he may save the life of the mother only if the death of the fetus would result *indirectly* (*see* Effect, Double, Feticide, Gynecology, Obstetrics. *Ben.*

OPERATION, SURGICAL. A major surgical operation is considered by moral theologians an *extraordinary* means of cure; hence, a surgical operation is not obligatory, strictly speaking, unless a person is extremely important for social or domestic reasons.

A surgeon is permitted to perform an operation only if it is necessary or useful for the physical welfare of the patient. Experimental operations, performed for the benefit of medical science, are contrary to the moral law. Furthermore, a just proportion between the good which one hopes to obtain through the operation and the dangers connected with it must exist.

A doctor or surgeon may not perform operations outside his competence, except in cases of extreme necessity. He must, instead, refer the patient to a specialist in the field. Surgeons who proceed quickly without real necessity to perform serious operations may violate the moral law. For unnecessary operations, *see* Surgery, Psychosurgery. *Ben.*

OPINION. The concept of *opinion* is intimately connected with the so-called moral systems (*q.v.*), and has been widely discussed by moralists in the past three centuries. To avoid confusion, a distinction must be made between the objective and subjective meaning of the term *opinion*. Objective opinion is a proposition by which a doctrine is expressed; subjective opinion is a state of mind. These states of mind appear in four ways: (1) full adherence; (2) adherence with a fear of error; (3) a suspension of judgment, which is deliberate and intentional; (4) complete ignorance (*q.v.*).

Opinion is found under the second category, in which a judgment is made with a fear of possible error. If this fear were absent, there would be a full adherence or certainty in the judgment; if adherence is lacking altogether in the judgment, one has a state of doubt.

Such a mental state seems to be a psychological absurdity; in fact, it would be if judgments were derived from the cognitive faculty alone. The difficulty is solved by the observation that the appetitive faculties, of which the will is supreme, intervene each time that the object of one's knowledge fails to release sufficient light on a subject to compel an assent by the intellect. In moral issues this light is not always present, but frequently is absent in theoretical morality and much more frequently in applied moral cases, in which a multiplicity of concrete circumstances contribute to an obscurity of truths, already doctrinally understood in theory. The field of morality, particularly practical applied morality, is favorable to *opinion*; that is, to persuasion obtained through the intervention of the will, which overcomes the uncertainties of the intellect and orders adherence, despite the recognized and anticipated possibility of error.

To accept this concept of opinion in a *subjective* sense involves two consequences: (a) it is impossible for a person to hold two opinions on a specific question; if he adheres to one term of a dilemma, he cannot at the same time adhere to the other; (b) our opinions reveal the general dispositions of our mind, because they depend on the will, which is subject to the influence of our entire mental predisposition and formation.

In its *objective* sense, one can speak of many co-existing opinions in regard to one problem, a so-called diversity of opinions. Comparisons can be made for the varying degrees of probability by weighing the reasons in favor of one or the other; thus one may also speak of improbable, solidly probable, and most probable opinions.

A distinction is usually made also between intrinsic and extrinsic probability; the former is based on arguments deducted from the nature of the action with objective considerations; the latter is based only on the authority of the scholars holding to this or that opinion. *Gra.*

OPINION, PUBLIC. A general state of mind at a specific time in a regional, national, or world community of people, especially concerning social and political events, is called public opinion.

Public opinion has gained great importance, especially in modern times, because of a great development of the press and the advent of democratic forms of government. Public opinion is termed a fourth and the most important power of a State, since all others should draw inspiration and impetus from it. The more traditional democratic nations are extremely sensitive to its fluctuations.

Public opinion, in reality, raises problems whose solution is difficult. The origin, real extent, reliability, value, and efficiency of public opinion can be determined only by a wide approximation.

Public opinion usually is concerned with contingent interests and difficult aspects of social living. Leaders, especially in communities with a democratic system, have a duty and a right to consider it a national indicator; however, they may not use it to justify any violation of the moral order. Public opinion may be followed only in the realm of the good. *Pav.*

OPIUM. *See* Drugs.

OPPOSITION, CONSTITUTIONAL. *See* Political Party.

OPPRESSION. The imposition of undue moral, legal, material, or economic burdens, which exceed the limits established by either natural or positive law, is called oppression. Oppression may be practiced by a branch of the government, a group or an individual.

No human power is unlimited. A legislator, for instance, may only direct and control persons and materials insofar as the requirements of the common good and the security of the State demand. Accordingly, fiscal laws which exceed the limits of the needs of the public treasury, even if the taxpayer is able to afford them, are to be considered oppressive. Considered oppressive also are laws which restrict the liberty of citizens in the pursuit of their normal activities, unless they are motivated by a higher common good. This applies to both intellectual and material activities, as freedom of the press, commerce, association, election to public office, etc.

Decrees of the executive power which either ignore existing laws or apply them carelessly to cases not foreseen by the legislator, and decrees which subject the citizens to controls and police investigations not justified by the requirements of public order, are likewise oppressive.

Demands by the rich upon the poor beyond the bound of charity may be a form of oppression; nor should the rich subject the poor to inhuman sequestration, foreclosure, attachments, or other legal devices, if they are unable to meet their debts, rent, or other obligations for reasons that justify their failure.

Employers who fail to pay employees a just wage or demand labor beyond the normal strength of their employees or not in conformity with their sex, age or health are guilty of oppression despite the silent submission by employees, due to their need for employment and the opportunity to earn a living, as well as the avoidance of further mental, moral, or physical difficulties. Of course, oppression exists toward the employer if servants, employees, or wage-earners under pressure of unions or other groups, by means of strikes or other forceful intimidations, compel the employer to pay a higher wage than deserved.

Finally, it is oppression for leaders of parties to compel their members to a cumulative action harmful to their own good or the common good, or inspired solely by personal gains or motives contrary to the material, moral, or religious interests of the members. Such abusive methods often compel authority to employ total suppression of freedom.

It is oppression also if the dominant parties in a nation through their political action deny to minority parties full liberty of action and speech, suppressing by unjust means the right of legitimate opposition to government action. The abuse of power, like the abuse of freedom, is immoral. Both could be fatal to the life of a nation. *M.d.G.*

OPTION. *See* Chapter, Cardinal.

ORACLES. *See* Divination.

ORATORY, SACRED PLACE. An oratory is a place set aside for private divine worship, and not for the public worship by the faithful at large (Can. 1188, par. 1). This is proper to a church. An oratory is a small chapel or special place with an altar or shrine, called in ancient times *aedicula, asceterium, sacellum sacrum,* but later called *oratorium.* The term *oratorium* was first applied to small chapels near monasteries, where monks used to say their prayers before entering the church. The same term was also applied to altars or public chapels built in rural areas, independent of parish churches; then, for reasons of convenience, oratories were built in private homes. In the sixth and seventh centuries, chapels built in cemeteries and other places were called oratories, but they had no baptistry nor could they be used for public services.

Today the Church has a public legislation concerning oratories (Can. 1188–1196). Three kinds are properly recognized: (a) *public oratory,* erected principally for the benefit of a community, or, if for private individuals, in such a way that all the faithful have a legitimately established right to attend while public divine services are being held in it; (b) *semipublic oratory,* built for the benefit of a religious community or a religious association of faithful but not open to anyone at all, such as seminary chapels, chapels of religious communities, orphanages, prisons, etc. (Can. 1188, par. 2, n. 2); (c) *private* or *domestic oratory,* built in a private home to be used only by a certain family or a particular person (Can. 1188, par. 2, n. 3).

According to Canon Law, public oratories are governed by the same laws as churches (see Church). Insofar as the rubrics permit, all sacred functions may be conducted in them.

For the canonical erection of a public oratory the explicit permission, in writing, of the local Ordinary is necessary. Permission of the Vicar General is not sufficient without a special mandate. The Ordinary or major superior, if the oratory belongs to an exempt religious order, or a delegate of either has the right to bless and lay the cornerstone of a public oratory (Cans. 1162–1163, 1191). In its construction, traditional rules must be followed: the priest must face the East when he celebrates Mass; the oratory may not lead to the living quarters of lay people; no secular use may be made of the basement or the space over the apse (Cans. 1162–1163). Public oratories may be used for public worship only after consecration or blessing (Can. 1191).

A semipublic oratory requires the authorization of the local Ordinary, who must inspect the area first in order to check the conditions under which divine worship will be conducted (Can. 1192). After authorization has been obtained, the oratory may no longer be converted to secular uses but be reserved exclusively for divine worship. It is not permitted to build a dormitory above an oratory, unless the two are separated by a double ceiling (Decr. 2812, S. C. Rit.). If a double ceiling is impossible, an indult must be obtained from the Holy See, which requires the erection of a canopy above the altar if the Blessed Sacrament is to be preserved in the oratory (Decr. 4213, 3; 3525, 2, S. C. Rit.). The Ordinary may authorize the erection of more than one oratory in educational institutions, hospitals, etc., if they are deemed necessary or useful (Can. 1192, par. 4). It is not required that semipublic oratories be blessed or consecrated; all sacred functions may be conducted in them, except those excluded by the rubrics or forbidden by the Ordinary. Concerning sacred functions conducted in public and semipublic oratories, the calendar and the missal of the diocese must be followed, unless a special privilege is obtained. It is forbidden to use the oratory as a school, theater, or storage room.

No authorization of the Ordinary is required for the erection of a private oratory. No solemn benediction is used, and it has no patron titular. It may be blessed with the formula used for the blessing of a new house (novae domus) found in the Roman Ritual (Can. 1196; Rit. Rom.: De benedictionibus, n. 16). An apostolic indult as well as inspection and approval of the Ordinary (Can. 1195, par. 1) is required if the Holy Sacrifice is to be celebrated in these oratories. The Sacred Congregation of the Sacraments usually requires that the following rules be observed for the establishment of private oratories: (a) only one Mass may be said each day, which must be a low Mass (Decr. 3896, S. C. Rit.); (b) the presence at Mass is required of at least one of the main beneficiaries of the Indult; (c) Mass may not be said on the following days: Easter, Pentecost, Christmas, Epiphany, Ascension, Corpus Christi, Immaculate Conception, Assumption, St. Joseph, Sts. Peter and Paul, and All Saints Day (see also Can. 1195). If a holy day of obligation is transferred to the following Sunday, the prohibition applies to the Sunday (Decr. 3890, I, 1 S. C. Rit.). All functions of parochial right are forbidden in these oratories. However, Holy Communion may be distributed to all those present, except for matters of parochial rights (Decr. 4201, S. C. Rit.).

The Ordinary may from time to time (per modum actus) permit Mass to be celebrated in private oratories even on the most solemn days, provided that just and reasonable motives are present, which must be different from those for which the Indult was originally granted (Can. 1195, par. 2). It is the exclusive right of the Holy See to authorize the preservation of the Blessed Sacrament in a private oratory (Can. 1265, 2); the authorization of the Ordinary suffices for keeping relics of saints or blessed (Can. 1282, par. 2). In private oratories the calendar of the celebrating priest must be used (*Decr.* 4248, S. C. Rit.).

Concerning the fulfillment of the obligation to hear Holy Mass on Sunday, Canon 1249 declares that this may be done in churches, public oratories, and cemetery chapels, but not in domestic or private oratories, unless the Indult of the Holy See permits. In general, the tenor of Indult is as follows: "That the privilege of fulfilling the obligation to hear Mass on Sunday (in a private oratory) is valid only for the master of the house, his children, and close relatives, such as in-laws and other relatives living with him, for his servants in his employ at the time, and for guests of note (*nobilibusque hospitibus*)." Hence, those who do not belong to the family, except servants, do not satisfy their Sunday obligation by hearing Mass in a private oratory (Vermeersch-Creusen, *Epitome Juris Canon.*, III, n. 502).

Private oratories of cardinals, bishops, vicars, and prefects apostolic enjoy the privileges of semipublic oratories (Can. 1189).

Cemetery chapels are considered private oratories (Can. 1190); the Ordinary may allow several Masses to be said there each day (Can. 1194); those who hear Mass there on a holy day of obligation fulfill their Sunday obligations.

In order that Holy Mass may be said in oratories or cemetery chapels, it is necessary that they be built in such a way that the bodies of the dead are not buried less than one meter away from the altar or underneath the altar (Can. 1201, par. 2). In cemetery chapels the Requiem Mass may always be said provided that it does not fall on a first or second class feast day, Sunday, a holy day of obligation, or a privileged vigil or octave (*Decr.* 3903 S. C. Rit.).

Regulations concerning the desecration or profanation of a church (*q.v.*) also apply to oratories in general. Since private oratories are not solemnly blessed, they do not incur the effects of desecration or profanation. Nevertheless, good sense, aesthetic taste, love of cleanliness and decency, respect for the majesty of God, devotion, and Christian piety should prompt everyone, priests and faithful alike, to see to it that any irreverent act be avoided in sacred oratories as well as acts unworthy of the house of God, such as secular meetings, charitable benefits, moving pictures, etc., (Can. 1178). *Tar.*

ORDERS, HOLY. Order means primarily a relation among things by reason of origin, position in space, priority in the succession of events, superiority or inferiority under any aspect. By extension, it means any pre-eminence or a relationship of superiority. Thus, the special power used in the celebration of the unbloody sacrifice of the New Law and in the administration of the sacraments is called holy orders; it is also the outward rite by which such power is conferred.

The *power of order* consists of various minor or major grades. All those who belong to these ranks constitute the *hierarchy of order.*

In the Latin Church there are seven orders. Four are minor orders: ostiariate, exorcist, lectorate, and acoylte; three are major orders: subdiaconate, diaconate, and priesthood. Tonsure, which precedes orders, does not confer power but prepares a candidate for the reception of orders, by separating him from the world and preparing him for the work of divine worship. In the Greek Church there are now four orders: two minor, lectorate and subdiaconate (which includes ostiariate and acolyte); two major, diaconate (which includes exorcistship) and priesthood. The highest rank of the hierarchy of orders, the priesthood, includes the priesthood and the episcopate.

The episcopate, priesthood, and diaconate, of which mention is made immediately after the first Pentecost, are certainly of divine institution. The other orders appear as distinct ranks only from the third century. The offices to which the candidates are assigned by virtue of these orders have always been in existence in the Church. It is, however, a disputed question among theologians whether these orders are of divine or ecclesiastical institution. There is no decisive reason for believing that the minor orders were not instituted by Jesus Christ at the same time that subdiaconate and diaconate were instituted but were made separate when particular needs in the Church required this.

The rite in use to confer the episcopate, priesthood, and diaconate is undoubtedly a sacrament. Theologians do not agree that the rites for conferring minor orders are part of the sacrament of holy orders or merely sacramentals. To admit the divine institution of minor orders implies a sacramental nature in the rite by which they are conferred.

However, there is only one sacrament of holy orders; the various orders below the priesthood are degrees of power at the service of the priesthood. The episcopate is the fullness of the priesthood.

The essential requirement for ordination to major orders is the imposition of a bishop's hands with recitation of a special prayer; for the other orders, it is the handing over of the instruments which signify the power conferred and the recitation of a corresponding formula. A validly consecrated bishop is the ordinary minister of the sacrament of holy orders; the extraordinary minister is a priest who has received the power to confer minor orders, either by law (Can. 951) or by a special, personal indult of the Apostolic See. Thus, tonsure and the minor orders can be validly conferred by cardinals (Can. 239, par. 1, n. 22), vicars and prefects apostolic, abbots and prelates *nullius* (Can. 957, par. 2). Regular abbots *de regimine*, if they are priests and have received the abbatial blessing, may confer the minor orders to their own subjects (Can. 264, n. 1).

The episcopal consecration may lawfully be performed only by a bishop who has received the apostolic mandate (Can. 955). For the other orders, diocesan clerics shall be ordained by their own Ordinary, or by another bishop after he has received dimissorial letters from their own bishop (Can. 955). The candidates' own bishop is the bishop of the territory in which the candidate for orders has a domicile; however, if he is not a native of the place in which he now resides, he must state under oath his intention of remaining permanently in a diocese which accepts him (Can. 956).

Non-exempt religious are governed by the common law concerning diocesan clerics (Can. 964, n. 4). Exempt religious cannot be ordained by any bishop without dimissorial letters from their own superior (Can. 964, n. 2). These dimissorials must be sent to the bishop of the diocese in which the house to which the candidate belongs is located (Can. 965). However, only if a see is vacant, or the bishop is absent or belongs to a different rite, if no ordination is held at that particular time or the bishop gives his consent, may an exempt religious superior direct the dimissorial letters to another bishop (Can. 966, 967, 1006, par. 2).

For valid ordination it is required that the candidate be a baptized male and have an explicit intention, at least habitual, or receiving the orders. Fear, even grave, does not affect the validity of ordination; upon proof, fear could constitute a canonical reason to free the individual from obligations connected with the reception of orders (Can. 214). For a lawful ordination the following are required: (a) *Divine calling* or a vocation (*q.v.*). (b) *Intention* on the part of the ordinandi to receive all orders up to and including the priesthood (Can. 973, par. 1); however, the bishop cannot oblige a candidate to receive major orders (Can. 973, par. 2). (c) The *state of grace:* to receive an order which is certainly part of the sacrament in the state of sin would be a sacrilege (*q.v.*). (d) The candidate must have received the *sacrament of confirmation.* (e) *Moral character* in conformity to the order which is to be received (Can. 974). (f) *Canonical age:* twenty-one years of age is minimum requirement for subdiaconate; twenty-two years for diaconate; twenty-four years for the priesthood; thirty years for the episcopacy; for the minor orders, no specific age is required of a candidate, except that theological studies must have been begun. (g) *Adequate knowledge:* for example, candidates may be promoted to tonsure and the minor orders at the beginning of their theological studies; to the subdiaconate, at the end of the third year of theology; to the diaconate, at the beginning of the fourth year of theology; to the priesthood after the first semester of the fourth year of theology. (h) Orders must be received in *proper succession* (Can. 977). (i) *Observance of the prescribed interstices or intervals (see* Interstices). A minimum period of time between orders is determined by the Ordinary between tonsure and the minor orders and between individual minor orders, unless the latter are given all at the same time; one year between acolyte and subdiaconate; three months between subdiaconate and diaconate; a similar period of time between diaconate and priesthood (Can. 978). (j) *Canonical title (see* Title of sacred ordination). For irregularities and simple impediments, *see* Irregularities and impediments.

Besides the afore-mentioned requirements, there are others asked of those to be admitted to holy orders. (a) The *suitable moral conduct and adequate scholastic preparation* required for ordination demand that definite control be exercised over the candidates; this is done by living in a seminary, which is mandatory during the period of their theological studies (Can. 972). (b) Furthermore, if the candidate is a secular cleric or a religious, he must present the following documents: (1) a *certificate of a previous order;* for the tonsure, baptismal and confirmation certificates; (2) a *certificate* attesting to the completion of the *required studies* (Can. 976); (3) a *certificate* of good moral conduct; (4) a *testimonial letter* from the bishop of the territory in which the candidate lived for a time sufficient to contract a canonical impediment (Can. 994, par. 1); (5) *testimonial letters* from his major superior, if the candidate is a religious; an exempt religious must present the dimissorial letters from his

major superior containing all these elements (Can. 964, n. 2; 955). (c) The candidate must take an examination on several treatises of theology (Can. 996, par. 1–3; 997, par. 2). (d) The publication of the names of those to be ordained is to be made in the home parish church before each of the major orders, except in the case of religious with perpetual vows (Can. 998, 999). (e) A retreat of three days must precede tonsure and minor orders; of six days for the major orders (Can. 1001). (f) Furthermore, a profession of faith must be made before receiving the subdiaconate (Can. 1406, n. 7).

The Mass of ordination and of episcopal consecration must always be celebrated by the ordaining minister or bishop (Can. 1003). The candidates must receive Holy Communion at the ordination Mass (Can. 1005). All other prescriptions, rites, and ceremonials prescribed for each respective ordination in the *Roman Pontifical* and other approved liturgical books must be accurately observed by the ordaining minister.

The episcopal consecration may not be conferred except during Holy Mass on Sundays or on the feasts of the Apostles. Major orders, strictly speaking, are to be conferred during Mass on Ember Saturdays, the Saturday before Passion Sunday, or Holy Saturday; for a grave reason the bishop may confer them on any Sunday or holyday of obligation. Minor orders must be conferred on Sunday or feasts of double class. Tonsure may be conferred on any day and at any hour (Can. 1006).

Concerning the place of ordination, general ordinations are to be held at the cathedral church in the presence of the canons of the cathedral chapter if this exists. If the ordinations are held in another place of the diocese, they should be held in the principal church, if possible, with the local clergy in attendance.

Particular ordinations may take place in other churches, even in the chapel of the bishop's residence, a monastery, or a seminary. Tonsure and minor orders may be conferred in a private oratory (Can. 1009).

After ordination, the name of each candidate ordained, the name of the ordaining minister, the date and place of ordination must be recorded in a special book (*Liber ordinatorum*) which is to be carefully kept in the archives of the diocese in which the ordination took place. The parish priest must also record it in the baptismal register. Concerning the conduct of the physician on problems pertaining to the capacity of the subject for the sacrament of holy orders, *see* Sacraments.

The sacrament of holy orders produces an indelible character in the soul; the priesthood moulds the ordained to the likeness of Christ, the High Priest, and makes him a minister of Christ in offering the unbloody sacrifice of the New Testament and dispensing the graces of the sacraments. The minor orders give a participation in this character and relative power. The sacrament of holy orders increases sanctifying grace, the infused virtues, and the gifts of the Holy Spirit. It provides a constant right to receiving, at the proper time, special actual graces to carry out in a worthy manner the power received. According to a well-founded opinion, the sacrament of holy orders also produces a special and permanent strength against obstacles and difficulties.

INDIVIDUAL ORDERS. The *ostiariate*, or office of porter, gives authority to open the church and sacristy, to ring the bells, to expel from the church unworthy persons and to look after the sacred vessels, vestments, etc.

The *lectorate* gives authority to read the Holy Scriptures in church; in ancient times the lector also blessed the bread and the first fruits.

The *exorcistship* gives authority to expel devils from obsessed persons, whether baptized or cathecumens, by the imposition of hands and the recitation of special prayers. The solemn exercise of this power is now reserved to the priest.

The *acolythate* gives the authority to carry candlesticks and torches, to light the lamps in the church, and to serve water and wine at the Eucharistic sacrifice.

The *subdiaconate* gives the authority to chant the epistle at solemn Mass, to assist the deacon at the altar, to handle the paten and the chalice, to pour the water into the chalice, and to wash the corporal and other sacred linens.

The *diaconate* gives the authority to chant the Gospel at solemn Mass, to assist the priest at the altar, to baptize, and to administer the sacrament of the Holy Eucharist in extraordinary circumstances.

The *priesthood* confers the authority to offer the unbloody sacrifice of the New Testament, to administer the Holy Eucharist, to forgive sins, and to bless.

The *episcopate* is the fullness of the priesthood and confers the power of confirming and ordaining. *Man.*

ORDERS, MINOR. *See* Orders, Holy.

ORDERS, RELIGIOUS. The term *order*, joined with the word *religious*, has had various meanings in canonical history: a *certain mode of living* arranged by various founders and approved by the Church for those who wished to live a more perfect Christian life; a *rule of a particular state* professed by members of an association of the faithful under the jurisdiction of duly approved superiors; a *society of men or women pursuing a life of Christian perfection* by the profession of certain vows, voluntarily made, and by the observance of certain rules to which they voluntarily submit. According to current canonical legislative concept, a *religious order* is a religious association of men or women bound to the observance of definite rules approved by the Holy See in community life and to the *perpetual* and *solemn* vows of chastity, poverty, and obedience (Can. 487; 488, n. 2; *see* Religious vows, Religious person).

Religious orders, as the *religious state* itself, may be said to have been instituted and directly handed down in substance by the Divine Saviour Himself, for He spoke repeatedly of the beauty and perfection of the three religious vows. Suarez calls the religious state an institution "of divine right," not as a precept but as a counsel (*De statu relig.*, tr. 7, book 3, ch. 2). The later religious orders with special aims certainly did not come directly from Jesus Christ, but from holy men who, inspired by divine grace, undertook to live a specific form of regular life under the supervision of bishops or lawful superiors. By letters of commendation, favors and privileges to certain religious or monastic associations, and by actual papal Bulls of approval, among the monastic rules expressly approved by the Holy See are those of St. Basil, St. Augustine, St. Benedict, and St. Francis.

The Fourth Lateran Council (1215) forbade the introduction of a new rule without papal authorization; it ordered, instead, that each new religious group or association adopt one of the four rules already approved. This has been done by founders of new religious communities, who, after choosing a rule already approved, added special features to adapt it to the special aim of their new organization. The rule chosen by most of the new foundations is that of St. Augustine. In the juridical language of the Church, only the orders properly so-called have a *rule*, and only their members are called *regular* (Can. 488 n. 7); religious congregations, instead, have *constitutions*.

The Church's approval does not extend to the essence of the religious state, but to the particular form or way of life; as a result, those who follow it are considered religious juridically with all the rights and privileges proper to religious.

The various types of religious life differ in purpose. The primary or essential aim is the same for all religious, namely, Christian perfection and the practice of the evangelical counsels; but they differ in the secondary aims which each religious family proposes as its own special objectives. Thus, we have *contemplative*, *active*, and *mixed* orders, depending on the objective of their rules, the personal sanctification of their members, or the sanctification of others through the work of the apostolate. (The classification of *contemplatives* is not accepted by many canonists and moralists.) These orders differ in the particular apostolates of the religious life; thus the designations of *clerical, lay,* or *military* orders dedicated to *hospital work, schools,* and *education*. They vary in the manner of pursuing a life of perfection; accordingly, religious are classified as *monks, mendicants,* and *non-mendicants*. They differ in *the nature of the vows they take*; whence, they are called religious of *solemn* or *simple* vows. They vary in *juridical position* with regard to the local Ordinary; hence, they are called *exempt* or *non-exempt* (*see* Can. 488).

The rules of later institutes are based on the four main monastic rules approved by the Holy See. The *Rule of St. Basil* (fourth century) is professed by almost all Greek and Eastern monks; the *Rule of St. Augustine* (fourth century) is followed by Augustinians, Premonstratensians, Dominicans, Trinitarians, Mercedarians, Servants of Mary, etc.; the *Rule of St. Benedict* (sixth century), is followed by Benedictines, Camaldolese, Cistercians, etc.; the *Rule of St. Francis* (thirteenth century) is followed by the Friars Minor, Conventuals and the Capuchins.

Other orders which do not follow these ancient rules have special constitutions approved by the Holy See. These are Carthusians, Carmelites, Jesuits, etc. There have risen in the Church parallel orders of women living in community life; a third rule of life may be adapted for the faithful in the world (*see* Third Order).

The primary, immediate end of religious orders is the personal sanctification of their members; the supreme, ultimate aim is the honor, glory, and service of God.

The religious orders and institutes represent the complete fulfillment of the Gospel, through the observance of the evangelical counsels. The practice of the evangelical counsels requires a religious formation and a life of piety and prayer which is difficult to achieve in the outside world.

In addition to guidance in the pursuit of perfection by the practice of the three evangelical counsels, religious orders attend to the moral, religious, and material needs and welfare of their neighbor, through manifold works of charity, and an apostolate conducted within the Church by the religious orders in preaching, missions, schools, hospitals, etc. It would be difficult to find in the outside world many generous souls capable of performing with such dedication real miracles of charity as do the members of the religious orders and institutes. Religious men and women are truly the most noble members of the Mystical Body of Christ.

The internal government of religious orders and institutes is regulated by their respective constitutions, statutes, and rules. Common canonical features are: a superior general assisted by consultors or assistants, who in some orders limit his power; a procurator general, who oversees the interests of the institute or order in matters concerning the Holy See; superiors in charge of each province (major superiors), each with assistants or consultors; superiors for each individual house or convent, called local superiors (Can. 499).

The general, the provincials and their vicars are called major superiors; those in charge of individual convents or houses are minor superiors, except superiors of monasteries of the ancient orders, like Benedictines, who enjoy greater autonomy.

Each order has a cardinal protector, whose sole function is to promote, by counsel and patronage, the welfare of the particular religious order (See Cardinal protector).

A general, provincial, or other equally important official can be elected only from members, professed for at least ten years, born in legitimate wedlock, and at least forty years of age in orders of men or monasteries of nuns; in other institutes the minimum age is thirty years (Can. 504). All superiors of both sexes and chapters, required by disposition of the constitutions, have so-called *domestic* power over their subjects: the duty to foster observance of the constitutions, to give precepts with regard to religious life, administer the property of the order, and, if necessary, command and inflict punishment. Only superiors and chapters of exempt clerical orders possess ecclesiastical *jurisdiction* (*q.v.*) in the internal and the external forums (Can. 501). Major superiors are ordinaries with respect to their subjects (Can. 198).

One becomes a member of a religious order upon pronouncing the vows; this must be preceded by a period of suitable preparation (*See* Novitiate, Religious, Vows, religious.)

Civil authority, as such, has no jurisdiction over religious orders and institutes. Thus, no government has the right to hinder their work or to dissolve religious orders and congregations.

Suppression and confiscation of property of religious orders must be considered a despotic act contrary to divine and human justice, as well as ecclesiastical and civil laws.

ORDERS, SACRED (Impediments). The Code of Canon Law decrees that clerics in major orders cannot contract valid matrimony (Can. 1072). The major orders which impose the obligation of chastity are: episcopate, priesthood, diaconate and subdiaconate; hence, a marriage contracted after reception of any of these orders is null and void (Council of Trent, Sess. XXIV, ch. 9). Clerics of the Eastern Rites are permitted to marry before ordination to major orders.

A cleric who has received the tonsure or minor orders (ostiariate, lectorate, exorcistship, and acolyte) contracts a valid and lawful marriage, but automatically loses his clerical status (Can. 132, par. 2).

This impediment of a purely ecclesiastical nature is based on the example of Jesus Christ and the great dignity of chastity. Moreover, it provides greater facility and liberty for the celibate cleric to exercise his pastoral ministry. It is a disputed matter whether the obligation of chastity flows only from ecclesiastical law or from the solemn vow of the cleric.

In the Latin Church the impediment was made definite in the fifth century; its observance was a cause of unceasing struggles against Nicolaitism in the early Middle Ages and against the Protestants in the sixteenth century. In general, civil legislations do not recognize this impediment.

At present, the Supreme Pontiff is more likely to dispense from the obligation of celibacy assumed with subdiaconate and diaconate, but rarely in the case of the priesthood, and never in the case of the episcopate. In the past, general dispensations were granted at one time or another, as at the time of the Napoleonic restoration.

Clerics in major orders who attempt marriage by a mere civil ceremony not only lose their rank and benefice (Can. 188, n. 5) but become irregular (Can. 985, n. 3), and incur *ipso facto* excommunication reserved *simpliciter* to the Holy See. They are also liable to degradation.

Similar penalties are incurred by religious of solemn vows (Can. 1073). They may obtain a dispensation from the Holy See without too much difficulty, if they are not priests. *Bar.*

ORDINANCE. *See* Government, Sentence.

ORDINARY. *See* Jurisdiction, Ecclesiastical; Superior, Religious; Bishop, Vicar-Capitular, Vicar-General.

ORDINES. *See* Liturgical Books.

ORGANS (Transplantation of). *See* Transplantation of organs.

ORIENTAL (Congregation). *See* Congregation, Roman.

ORIENTATION, PROFESSIONAL. Professional orientation is a process by which a person is prepared to enter a field of work which best corresponds to his natural aptitudes, acquired abilities, and the requirements of the common

good. Thus properly understood, professional orientation has a twofold aim: the good of the individual and the welfare of society. An individual who concentrates upon one aim alone risks falling into an unhealthy individualism or an oppressive sociologism.

In professional orientation, which is beneficial and effective, are found difficulties which many believe insuperable. To prepare an individual for a profession or trade requires exact knowledge of the individual's aptitudes and the requirements of the trade; this may be impossible due to a constant flux in both. Nevertheless, definite elements remain which should suffice to establish criteria for professional orientation.

Further difficulties arise in determining the age for orientation to a profession. At an early age, a lack of sufficient data may hinder a wise decision; at a later age, it may be useless. Furthermore, an individual undergoes constant changes in periods of development, some of which are profound and radical. For this reason, risk is involved in counseling one towards a profession or trade. In reply, it might be noted that an individual acquires marked characteristics in adolescence, which furnish a reliable criterion for orientation, without excluding adjustments and radical changes whenever new and unforeseen difficulties or developments arise.

A third source of difficulty is the attitude of the administrators of professional orientation services. A more reasonable segment of them recognizes the necessity of making their task a combined effort with teachers, doctors and psychotherapists, priests and parents. The teacher, dealing with the pupil during his long period of development, should be able to offer a judgment upon his fundamental attitude and aptitude for a specific profession; the doctor should manifest his opinion on contrary inclinations in the subject for or against a profession; the psychotherapist, in the light of the views of the teacher and doctor and a knowledge of the actual conditions and difficulties involved in the particular profession, should probe in his observations and interviews the particular mental reactions of the candidate, to decide if he has the required dispositions to undertake this vocation.

One of the most delicate moral problems is to establish the moral force in each individual case: whether the proffered professional orientation advice is of obligation or counsel. If the State takes upon itself the work of professional orientation of its citizens, an undesirable practice, it must never adopt coercive measures; this would mean an oppression of the human person and give rise to thousands of abuses and intolerable conditions. Professional orientation in some countries has already assumed the aspect of a social service practice, for the most part, based on the personal initiative of each individual under the control of public authority. This must be administered by suggestion or counsel. This should seek to dispose the individual and his family in the best possible manner toward a proper choice of vocation with regard to the future. Nor must the supernatural element or the efficacy of God's grace be neglected with regard to this very important matter. *Pav.*

ORIGINAL SIN. *See* Baptism, Grace, Sin.

ORNAMENTS, FEMININE. The tendency for every human being, especially women, to embellish their body is entirely natural, and, within certain limits, to be approved. In fact, nature, contrary to the animals, has given the human intellect the faculty to further improve one's physical appearance. It is true that one finds innumerable admonitions against various kinds of feminine ornaments in the Holy Scriptures (Isaiah 3; I Tim. 2:9–10; I Peter 3:3), and in the writings of the Fathers (Clement of Alexandria, *Paedagogus*; Tertullian, *De cultu foeminarum*, *De virginibus velandis*, St. Cyprian, *De habitu virginum*, and numerous other sermons and letters). This attitude of the Fathers was continued down through the centuries by preachers and pastors of souls. The reason for their negative attitude must be sought, not in a deliberate disdain for human beauty or reasonable ornament, but in the excesses which feminine ornaments too frequently reach. No one has emphasized the dignity of the human body more than Christian religion, which proclaims it as the temple of the Holy Ghost, which bears God in its members (I Cor. 6:19–20). Precisely in view of this dignity, only those ornaments are permitted which give emphasis to the beauty of the human body as the seat of a spiritual soul. Feminine embellishments, therefore, constitute a sin if they exceed proper limits, either by reason of an evil intention (seduction, vanity), or disorderly effects (scandal, waste of time, waste of money, etc.). The intention to seduce makes the act gravely sinful. Vanity is generally a venial sin; its effects may have varying degrees of gravity. The rule for determining if in reality an ornament is excessive depends on factors of time and place and the personal condition of the individual (*see also* Modesty).

Special attention has always been accorded to feminine embellishments such as rouge, lipstick, and other beautifying devices, which give women an appearance other than the one which nature has really bestowed upon them. These items contain a certain degree of deception. However, according to common doctrine, it is a sin to use feminine devices which would deceive others in a positive manner with regard to the real beauty of a person. It is not sinful to make a moderate use of ornaments generally used in certain regions, because they, in reality, do not deceive any longer; nor is it wrong to use ornamental devices for the purpose of hiding physical defects from accidents, illnesses, or other causes (*See also* Equivocation, Modesty). *Dam.*

ORNITHOMANCY. *See* Divination.

ORPHANAGE. *See* Foundation, pious; Welfare.

ORTHOSYMPATHETIC. *See* Endocrinology.

O SALUTARIS. *See* Lauda Sion.

OSCILLATIONS, ECONOMIC. *See* Cycles, economic.

OSTENTATION. *See* Pride.

OSTEOLOGY. *See* Anthropology.

OUR FATHER. The Our Father is the prayer taught and recommended by Jesus Christ Himself; for this reason it is called The Lord's Prayer. We read in the Gospels: "In this manner therefore shall you pray: Our Father . . ." (Math. 6:9, ff.; Luke 11:1, ff.). The Lord's Prayer consists of an introduction and seven requests, and ends with Amen. "It is the most excellent of all prayers because it came out of the mind and heart of Jesus and encloses in seven short requests all that we should ask of God as His children and as one another's brothers" (Saint Pius X, *Catechism*, n. 425). It is also the most *efficacious* prayer: (a) because it is most acceptable to God; we pray to Him with the very words of His Divine Son; (b) because it arouses easily in the mind of those who say it, sentiments of humility, veneration, loving and persevering trust, and conformity to the will of God; these are the conditions for proper prayer (*see also* Prayer). It is also the guide and pattern of all other prayers. "To pray rightly and properly, we can say nothing that is not contained in the Lord's prayer" (St. Augustine, *Ep. ad Probam*, c. 12: PL 33, 502).

INTRODUCTION. Though composed of few words, the beginning is important, full of wonder in its content, and most suited to dispose God to bestow His gifts upon us. In addressing petitions to ordinary men in power, an effective beginning disposes them to listen; in our petition to God, the suppliant, on the contrary, must be the one who must be well disposed. We must, before all, open our heart to trust: the word *Father* serves this purpose well. We must banish selfishness if we are to make ourselves worthy of a Father "who makes his sun to rise on the good and on the evil, and sends rain on the just and the unjust" (Matt. 5:43); that is why we use the word *our*, and not *my*. Finally, the words "*Who art in heaven*" increase trust and inspire sentiments of humility and veneration, in teaching us to esteem heavenly goods above all (Matt. 6:33), and to seek earthly goods only in order to gain heavenly goods.

FIRST THREE PETITIONS. In the first three petitions, as good children of God, we ask: (a) that His name be known and honored in the whole world; (b) that His kingdom may come; (c) that men on earth may fulfill His holy will as the angels and the blessed fulfill it in heaven. We ask primarily that *God's name be glorified* because the glory of God must be dearer to our heart than all material goods or blessings. By *kingdom of God* is commonly understood a three-fold spiritual kingdom: (a) God's kingdom in us by means of His grace; (b) His kingdom on earth in His Holy Church; (c) God's heavenly kingdom, of which we are potential citizens. In the third petition, "*Thy Will be done on earth as it is in heaven*," we ask for the grace to do in everything and under all circumstances the will of God, by obeying His holy commandments as readily and fervently as the angels and the blessed obey in heaven; we also ask for the grace to respond to divine inspirations and to conform to the will of God if tribulation visits us.

LAST FOUR PETITIONS. In the last four petitions, we ask for everyone: (a) spiritual and corporal nourishment; (b) forgiveness of sins; (c) aid against temptations; (d) deliverance from evil.

Each word of the fourth petition, "*Give us this day our daily bread*," is full of profound teachings. Note the trustful tone of *Give us*, in which one can almost hear the echo of the first words, *Our Father*. The sense of trustful detachment contained in the words *this day* banish, as it were, all undue preoccupation for the morrow (cf. Matt. 6:25), and make petition to God a daily task (cf. Luke 18:1; I Thess. 5:17).

The *trespasses* referred to in the fifth

petition are our sins, which are called debts, because of our obligation to satisfy divine justice either in this life or in the next. As a necessary condition for obtaining God's forgiveness we must forgive our brethren: "For if you forgive men their offenses, your heavenly Father will also forgive you your offenses. But if you do not forgive men, neither will your Father forgive you your offenses" (Matt. 6:14ff; cf. the parable of the unmerciful servant Matt. 18:35ff.).

In the sixth petition, *"And lead us not into temptation,"* we ask God to free us from temptations or, at least, to give us the grace to overcome them (*see* Temptation).

With the last petition, *"But deliver us from evil,"* we ask God to free us from the greatest evil, sin, and eternal damnation, the penalty for sin. We also seek deliverance from evil which may offer an occasion of sin, for we cannot expect to be exempted from every suffering in this life or every evil, but merely from that which God considers evil for us. Indeed, the sufferings of this life help us to do penance for our sins, to exercise virtue, and, above all, to imitate Jesus Christ, our Head, whom we must imitate in His sufferings if we wish to share in His glory (cf. Matt. 16:24; Rom. 8:17; I Pet. 4:13).

The word *Amen* at the end of the last petition means "So be it." As we have asked, so shall we expect; this confirms our trust in the divine promises: *"Therefore I say to you, all things whatever you ask for in prayer, believe that you shall receive, and they shall come to you"* (Mark 11:24).

ITS USE IN THE LITURGY. The Our Father is most frequent in the liturgy. From the earliest times the Our Father was recited at Holy Mass in preparation for Communion. The Our Father is recited at baptism, at the end of confirmation, at extreme unction, in the prayers for the soul of a dying person, at funeral services, and in all blessings. Often, in liturgical acts, the Our Father is recited in an undertone. This ought to move us to a deeper recollection and to renew in us the true spirit of prayer by conforming our supplications to the model prayer taught by Jesus Christ Himself. *Ses.*

OUTRAGE. *See* Insult.

OWNERSHIP, IMMATERIAL. *See* Author, rights of.

P

PACIFISM. *See* Militarism.

PARALYSIS. Voluntary movement is due to the synergic activity of two systems of neurons or nerve cells. One, the central pyramidal or cortico-spinal system, includes the pyramidal cells of the cerebral motor cortex coursing through the brain and spinal medulla; this terminates in the anterior gray horn of the spinal cord, near the motor cells of the opposite side. The other, the peripheral system, consists of cellular groups or motor cells of the encephalic trunk, spinal medulla, and respective fibers whose function is to reach the muscles of the same half of the body.

Paralysis is the loss of the power of motion caused either by interruption, destruction, or compression of the paths of motion at any point in their extension. The characteristics of paralysis differ appreciably; the realization of this diversity permits the doctor to diagnose the exact point in the neuropathy which makes it easier to treat a lesion involving either the peripheral or central neurons. In peripheral or flaccid paralysis, there is a loss of muscular tone and complete atrophy, together with muscular paralysis or loss of movement. In central or spastic paralysis, the only loss is in the power of voluntary motion; muscular movement is preserved; the tone and reflex movements are increased at times.

TYPES OF PARALYSIS. From the viewpoint of pathogenesis, *paralysis* or *paresis* (incomplete paralysis) is organic or functional, depending on the presence or absence of anatomical lesions. The most typical forms of functional paralysis are found in hysteria (*q.v.*).

From the aspect of distribution of the paralysis, there are many types. *Tetraplegia* is the loss of the power of motion in all four limbs; *cervical* (upper) *paraplegia* affects only the upper limbs; *crural* (femoral) *paraplegia* affects only the lower limbs; *monoplegia* involves one limb; *prosoplegia* is a paralysis of the face; *ophthalmoplegia* is paralysis of the muscles of the eyes.

MORAL NOTES. Paralysis, in itself, does not reduce imputability; but this may be excluded or reduced, at times, if mental disturbances accompany the paralysis at the same time. *Riz.*

PARALYSIS, PROGRESSIVE. Progressive paralysis is a serious ailment caused by syphilis. Anatomically, it consists of a special type of inflammation that usually strikes the cerebral cortex and adjacent meninges. Its clinical picture is made up of two groups of symptoms, neurological and psychic; it usually appears about ten years after venereal disease has been contracted. In some rare cases, progressive paralysis is due to hereditary syphilis.

STUDY OF SYMPTOMS. The most typical and constant neurological symptoms of progressive paralysis are: disturbances in speech (disartria) or in the pupils (pupils are small, irregular, rigid to light); trembling (more noticeable in lips and fingers); disturbances in writing or in reflexes. Sometimes there is an epileptic crisis or attacks of apoplexy, followed by temporary paralysis.

Psychic symptoms are varied. According to the predominant form, one may speak of: *neurasthenic* symptoms of vague worries, discomforts, etc.; *expansive* symptoms of euphoria, excitement, extravagant delusions of grandeur; *depressive* symptoms of despair, fantastic delusions of hypochondria or of ruin. As the illness progresses, the mental decay and the demented state continues to grow worse, and, at the terminal stage, the paralytic is reduced to a purely vegetative existence.

TREATMENT. Until a few decades ago, progressive paralysis inevitably led to death within two or three years from the time of appearance. Modern therapeutic methods often check the illness and bring about improvements that are sometimes so complete that the sick person is able to fully resume a normal life and occupation. These methods were first used by the Viennese doctor Wagner von Juaregg, who treated paralytics with injections of malarial blood.

Other methods involve injections of vaccine, sulphur, drugs, and the use of electric waves and shock treatments. In recent years, great importance has been attached to penicillin in large doses.

From the moral viewpoint, an individual suffering from progressive paralysis may be considered not morally responsible from the beginning of the disease, since it primarily is an attack upon the cerebral cortex. This prescinds from any responsibility in cause.

In these cases, early diagnosis is necessary to prevent the afflicted person from committing serious wrong, neglecting duties, or wasting money, which might cause great harm to himself and his family. It is also important to initiate as soon as possible one of the therapies mentioned, for it is well-known that the sooner these are adopted, the more effective are the results.

PARANOIA. Paranoia is not a sickness in the proper sense of the word, but a constitutional defect, more or less latent in early life but later developing by a slow process into a systematic and lucid delusion, strongly supported by an unshakeable faith and noticeable capacity for criticism, which is very acute but always unilateral.

Before the onset of delusion, the psychopathic constitution of the future paranoiac, which modern French psychiatry refers to as a constitution of a defensive type, generally reveals itself as a tendency to bickering, sophistry, exaggerated pride, vanity and lack of trust.

These temperamental characteristics are found at the basis of every delusion, once the illness has become fully established.

It should be noted that a number of youthful paranoiacs are self-taught, particularly antisocial, and inadaptable.

DELUSIONS. The delusions of the paranoiac are lucid, never border on the absurd or fantastic, and pervade the whole conduct of the sick person. They are generally not accompanied by hallucinations, nor do they lead to a true and lasting case of madness. This distinguishes them from the delusions of a paranoid dementia praecox (*see* Schizophrenia), progressive paralysis (*q.v.*), and from other psychoses. These delusions are reducible to two main types: delusions of *grandeur* or delusions of *persecution*. Delusions of *grandeur* are thought to be due to an excessively proud notion which the subject has of his own personality or some particular aspect of his personality. Hence, some center on ancestral grandeur, in which the ill person believes himself to be the long-lost descendant of a royal dynasty; some concern pseudo-scientific or inventive grandeur, in which discoveries of perpetual motion or the formula for squaring a circle are claimed; some treat of political, religious, or erotic grandeur.

Delusions of *persecution* come from a feeling of distrust toward others, which receives its initial spark from an injustice or a failure which paranoiacs refuse to attribute to themselves or circumstances. Instead, they are anxious to blame a person, group, or nationality for their wrongs. Since the paranoiac is alert, careful, suspicious, and distrustful, suffering from delusions, he sees various plots and maneuvers aimed at harming him. He gives meaning to the most banal gestures, talk, or events, all of which he refers to himself in some way. Finally, when he has become short-tempered and unwilling to endure these any longer, he is seized by the urge to defend himself; thus the persecuted becomes the persecutor in his reactions. He then becomes a clever, inflexible, cruel persecutor; thus it is not rare that a paranoiac seriously wound or murder harmless or innocent individuals who, he believes, are out to persecute him.

Closely related to this delusion of persecution are: delusions of *litigation*, which lead to involvement in a whole series of court cases, whose outcome is often to reduce him to poverty and convince him more and more that the judges are treating him unfairly because of favoritism or corruption; delusions of *jealousy*, in which the object of the persecution is the spouse of the sick person, who suffers a constant subjection to outrages and vexations by the sick person.

Since paranoia is more a constitutional defect than a true psychosis, it is, in general, incurable and worsens with the passage of years. Often it renders the person unfit or dangerous to society. Hence the wisdom of commitment to a psychiatric hospital when a suspicion arises of his danger to society, before waiting for the actual deed which may be serious criminal activity.

In the early stages, when the person is somewhat doubtful of his delusions, prudent psychotherapeutic treatment may be of help; a great deal of wisdom must be exercised because of the suspiciousness and tenacious vindictiveness of the people of this type. The tendency to blame others for disappointment and failure is a hindrance to proper medical care and confinement, since this type is convinced that he is not sick; quite clever in hiding his delusions, he is prepared to make charges and protests against alleged abuses inflicted on him by relatives or doctors, who wish to commit him. He will not hesitate to turn to acquaintances, relatives, newspapermen, and courts in resisting these attempts to commit him.

Crimes committed by paranoiacs as a result of delusion are beyond the realm of imputability, because a true paranoiac lacks the ability to properly understand and will these actions. Moral questions are more delicate and difficult in paranoiacs who boast of mystical experiences. Since people with this type of delusion generally are guided by the content of their delusions, it is not easy to spot the disease from the beginning, without a good psychiatric examination. But it helps if we keep in mind that these paranoiacs, who are always convinced that they are destined to carry out a supernatural mission to save mankind in danger, never limit themselves to personal works of religious asceticism, but quickly take on the attitude and conduct of reformers and apostles, fanatically critical of lawful authority. They reveal in a short time their mental derangement, despite the enthusiastic acclaim of their followers—generally simple souls or partially sick themselves. *Riz.*

PARAPHRENIA. Between pure paranoia (*q.v.*) and the paranoid type of schizophrenia (*q.v.*) is a chronic hallucinatory psychosis called *chronic hallucinatory delusion*, or, to use the term coined by Kraepelin, *paraphrenia* (*dementia praecox*, according to Freud). This psychosis is characterized essentially by these four elements: (a) a systematically constructed delusion that develops gradually and usually takes the form of delusions of persecution; (b) the presence of hallucinations that support and feed the delusion; (c) failure of all logical persuasion to remove the delusion or weaken the person's conviction in this regard; (d) retention of full intellectual power, aside from the delusion, and absence of any sign of deterioration of the personality.

As one can see, *paraphrenia* is clearly distinguished from pure paranoia by the presence of hallucinations; it differs from paranoid schizophrenia in that the delusion is more coherently organized, the intellect retains its full functional ability, and there are no dissociative symptoms.

COURSE OF THE DISEASE. The development of *paraphrenia* is usually slow and deceptive; it usually begins with a vague sense of discomfort, a certain feeling of depression, vague ideas of mistrust. Later, these begin to affect the general demeanor of the sick person; he becomes suspicious, tends to remain apart, and then becomes more and more explicit in declaring that he is the victim of persecution on the part of relatives, friends, or strangers, who are suspected of using strange and mysterious means (waves, rays, telepathic influence, etc.).

Once it reaches this point, the *syndrome* of delusion grows stronger. Fed by any external or internal occurrence, it makes ineffective all logical attempts at dissuading him; the sick person will live with his mind completely and totally absorbed in his delusion.

The paraphrenic is generally as incurable and untreatable as the paranoic; he is not responsible for his actions, even less for the crimes or violations that he eventually commits under the impulse of his delusions, or as a reaction to such attacks. For other moral corollaries, *see* Paranoia *and* Schizophrenia. *Riz.*

PARDON OF ENEMIES. *See* Enemy.

PARENT. A *parent* is one who begets or brings forth offspring, whether as mother or father.

The duties of parents are to love their children; to provide for the life, physical health and mental welfare of their children; and to educate them according to their condition in life, as the natural law dictates (Can. 1113).

Parents have a right to be loved and respected by their children in words and deeds; to be obeyed in all lawful things concerning their education and the domestic order; and, finally, to receive whatever assistance their children can provide.

The virtue governing the relations between parents and children is the virtue of piety, against which it is possible to sin gravely by neglect of serious duties. *Pal.*

PARENTS, AUTHORITY OF. *Parental authority* is a combination of powers and duties that parents have with regard to their children, who are minors and still under their protection and control. These powers and duties are based on the natural law, the bond of blood and mutual relationship arising between a parent and his children.

Positive law deals with parental authority principally in the matter of inheritance and other interests pertaining to the children.

Canon Law, following the principles of the natural law, states that minors are subject to parental authority, and, if the parents are missing, to the authority of their lawful guardians (Canons 89; 93, par. 1).

For inheritances and other merely civil acts, the Church has no particular laws concerning parental authority, but entrusts the matter entirely to the civil law.

Certain acts belong to the sphere of canonical legislation; some particular norms exempt minors who have reached a certain age from parental authority, as laws pertaining to the choice of a church or particular place of burial (Can. 1223–1224), and in court cases involving spiritual matters or matters connected to spiritual things (Can. 1648, par. 3).

For the moral duties of children to parents, *see* Children. *Cip.*

PARISH. The term *parish* may refer to all of the faithful under the jurisdiction of a pastor, or to the church where the latter exercises his office, or more properly to the territory and the faithful entrusted to the care of a pastor (*plebs christiana coadunata pastori*).

During the Church's first three centuries, there was strict unity and centralization of ecclesiastical government in the diocese: the bishop was the monarchical head of the local community and took care of all functions, spiritual and temporal.

In the fourth century, parishes began to be founded in country districts to care for the spiritual needs of many converts to the Christian faith. In episcopal cities, until the year one thousand, the care of souls continued to be carried on as in the past by the bishop himself directly, or through cathedral priests and deacons; there was only one city parish and one pastor. Even though there might be other churches in the episcopal city, these latter were never parochial, nor independent in the true sense of the word, except in the cases of Rome and Alexandria. The development of canonical life made the members of the chapter (*q.v.*) the natural auxiliaries to the bishop; they took his place at parochial functions in the city and in suburbs. They strongly defended this privilege in the face of attempts made in the tenth century, and later, to put monks in place of the secular clergy in caring for souls.

City parishes probably arose first in France (cf. Council of Limoges: Mansi XIX, 543-44). This system was introduced in Italy at a later date (12-13 century) because the canons had opposed the claims of the priests of minor churches and the monks (cfr. Ughelli, *Italia sacra*, Venice 1716 ff.; I, 819; II, 495, 538; III, 88, 395, 555; IV, p. 454). The division into city parishes became customary, except where a cathedral chapter might retain control by delegating a vicar to carry on the ordinary parochial functions. The Council of Trent prescribed a clearer division of territory and duties in the exercise of parochial activities and functions (*Sess.* VII, c. 7; XXIV, c. 13, *De reform.*).

Subsequently, the Sacred Congregation of the Council exerted every effort to do away with vicars and removable pastors, by affirming that one placed in charge of the care of souls in the parish should be irremovable.

CURRENT LAW. The parish as an institution is a legal person, frequently distinct from the parish church or a benefice itself. At times, however, it is considered one with a benefice; its erection, re-establishment, and suppression are governed by the laws dealing with benefices (*see* Benefice).

A parish may be completely independent, joined *in temporalibus et spiritualibus*, or *in temporalibus* to some other office or ecclesiastical institution. *Pleno jure*, the legal person to which it is joined retains the habitual care of souls, but the actual care of souls is entrusted to a vicar.

A parish is *irremovable* if the pastor enjoys full stability; it is *removable* if the pastor enjoys less stability; it is *ad nutum* if the pastor can be removed at the pleasure of the Ordinary or superior. The Code favors stable parishes.

A parish is *secular* or *regular*, depend-ing on whether it is entrusted to the diocesan or the religious clergy. If it is joined to a religious community *in temporalibus*, then the actual care of souls is entrusted to a pastor of the diocesan clergy; otherwise it must be entrusted to a vicar of this particular religious community. A parish is *territorial* if it covers a certain definite territory—the general rule; it is *personal* if it is made up of certain particular classes of people (e.g., soldiers); it is *memorial* if it takes in some particular family. Personal parishes also have certain territorial boundaries, if, for example, there are a number of parishes in the same territory for people of different nationalities.

Finally, parishes are divided into mother churches and daughter churches. Since the latter historically originated with the former, they may be held by law to certain signs of honor toward the mother church.

Quasi-Parishes. A *quasi-parish* is akin to a parish; it is established in a place where the Church hierarchy is not yet fully established, i.e., only vicariates and prefectures-apostolic (*q.v.*). Quasi-pastors are always removable.

The parish is the center of religious life. The faithful must look to it for the administration of the sacraments, at least baptism, confirmation and matrimony. It is a good thing to attend to the other practices of religious life in one's own parish.

The parish is also the main center where religious instruction in the family is integrated by catechism for children and adults, missions for the people, ordinary preaching.

The parish is also a center for Catholic Action and charitable welfare activities. The success of these groups and their activities depends on the cooperation displayed by individuals, on the means at the disposal of the parish church, and on the parish societies. Parents should direct their children to look upon the parish as a center where spiritual life is nourished and developed and where they receive the proper guidance for their own apostolic work. *Fel.*

PARKINSON'S DISEASE. *See* Paralysis.

PARSEEISM. The religion of a restricted number of Persian followers of Zarathustra (Zoroaster) is called *Parseeism*. Its followers fled Persia, during the Arab invasion in 641 A.D., and they finally settled in Bombay, India (circa 700 A.D.). Today, approximately 100,000 have remained faithful to their religious traditions, except for some modifications brought about by contact with the English and Hindus. Some tiny centers of this religion, which remained in Anatolia, have taken the name of *Ghebri*.

Zarathustra or Zoroaster, probably a native of Medea, reformed the ancient religion of the Persians, which was based on the deification of the heavens and natural phenomena along monotheistic lines. Zarathustra (660–583 B.C.) replaced the ancient naturalistic religion with the worship of the one God, whom he called *Ahura Mazda* or *Ormazd* (wise lord), the creator and conserver of all the goodness which he previously created from nothing by his all-powerful word.

His throne is surrounded by six holy spirits (*Amesha Spenta*); these are also vindicators of justice, lovers of truth and purity, brilliant, in perfect harmony of thought, word, and action. Their names are: *Asha Vahista* (justice); *Vohu-Manah* (good thoughts); *Khshathra Vairya* (God's rule over men); *Armaiti* (humility); *Haurvatat* (perfection); *Ameretat* (immortality).

The doctrine of Zarathustra is contained in the *Avesta*, which was originally divided into twenty-one books, but now into five sections. Zoroastrianism became the national religion of Persia in 226 A.D., when the Sassanides, in the person of Ardashir I, gained control and maintained rule until the time of the Mohammedan invasion in 636.

The moral teaching of Zoroastrianism contains abstractions that fundamentally express God's providence in governing the world; to this, individuals must respond with a sincere, interior adherence, which might be summed up in a triple command: *think well, speak well, act well.* He who is faithful to right (*Asha*) according to the norms of truth and justice; he who pays heed to good thought (*Vohu-Manah*); he who observes social laws from the authority of *Khshathra* with docile obedience (*Armaiti*)—he will be rewarded with integrity of life (*Haurvatat*) and finally with blessed immortality (*Ameretat*).

Beneath this supreme court, a lower host of *yazata* (venerable) is headed by *Sraosha* (obedience), the god and priest, who offers the first sacrifice, guides souls in their voyage beyond the grave, protects men against evil spirits, as conquerors of *Aeshma Daeva* or *Asmodeus*. Other in this group are *Mithra* (faithful one), a solar divinity, who is the guardian of oaths; *Vayu* (god of the winds); *Anahita* (goddess of fertility); the *Fravashi* (protectors of men), who were originally the spirits of ancestors.

Zarathustra's original concept, clearly monotheistic, contained a lucid and bright picture of future life and excluded bloody sacrifices of polytheistic rites in favor of prayer and good works. After his lifetime, this was replaced by a dualistic concept based on two opposing principles of good and evil, called *Ahura Mazda* and *Angra Manyu*. Each was at the head of his own legions and committed to the great struggle between good and evil.

The Mazdean conceives all life as a battle of good against evil. *Angra Manyu* (*Ahriman*), the tormenting spirit, seeks to destroy the good creation of *Ahura*. To accomplish his wicked ends he uses every means opposed to the good things that have been created by his adversary: sterility, darkness, natural disasters, sickness, death. He has a legion of greater and lesser spirits to aid in his destructive work; these are called *Daevi* or liars. Their special abode is in the cold and sterile places of the north, but they go everywhere, appear in a thousand forms, and afflict men, especially those faithful to Zarathustra. All the evil in the world is due to them; this evil will go on unabated until good finally triumphs, at the end of the world. The best way to escape their traps is the practice of worship, which purifies and trains man to withstand the blows of the evil spirits.

From the social point of view, Zarathustra protected the lower classes from the oppression of the nobles, priests, and magicians; he praised an active life and farm-labor as productive of moral and material goods. (The man who sows grain sows holiness.) In this way he gave meaning to human life and equipped it to fight against external enemies or the lazy resignation to one's state in life, a characteristic of the inhabitants of Iran. On the other hand, he did not stress introspection, which is so dear to Indian thought.

Today, as, in the temple of fire, sandalwood feeds the fire that the parsees venerate as the noblest manifestation of *Ahura Mazda.* Five times a day the priest pronounces, along with words of benediction, the three words that sum up the Mazdean code: *humata,* good thoughts; *hukhta,* good words; *hvarahta,* good actions. A proof of sound moral Zoroastrian principles is the belief in the individual judgment awaiting the soul after death, and in a general judgment that will come at the end of the world, when the reign of evil will be shattered once and for all, after a great battle in which the demons will be conquered and *Ahura Mazda* will annihilate *Angra Manyu. Tur.*

Radical dualism places Parseeism with polytheistic religions, although the colossal duel between good and the prince of evil will terminate at the end of the world with victory for good.

If fire-worship involves merely veneration and not adoration, it still seems to be a carry-over from primitive forms of Parseeism that were tainted with fetishism.

Though the position of women in Parseeism is much more elevated than in Mohammedanism or Hinduism, it is still clearly an inferior one.

Care for the dead, sacred in all religions, to some extent is expressed in ways that are extremely repugnant to the common feelings of mankind. Bodies are exposed in special round buildings called *towers of silence,* where they eventually become food for vultures.

And so one finds here little resemblance to the more noble elements of Christian moral teaching, such as mortification, interior mortification in particular, or the practice of charity, as a positive element. *Pal.*

PARTHENOGENESIS. Parthenogenesis is reproduction without fertilization of the ovum by a male, or conception by a female by purely artificial means, without the use of spermatozoa but by physical or chemical stimuli intended to bring about and continue the segmentation of the ovum.

Morality. Even if it should one day prove possible in human conception, parthenogenesis would not be licit, as it appears from official teaching of the Church on artificial insemination (*q.v.*). Cf. Pius XII, Address of September 29, 1949; May 19, 1956; the Sacred Congregation of the Holy Office, March 24, 1897.)

It is true that this practice would entail no sin of masturbation, as in the case of artificial insemination in the strict sense, but all other objectons raised against artificial insemination (*q.v.*) apply here.

The procreation of children is lawful only in marriage and by marriage. Marriage alone protects the dignity of spouses and guarantees the best conditions for rearing children.

Not the production of germ-cells, but the generative act, i.e., the human and natural act, occasions the relationship of paternity with moral and juridical consequences so important both for the new individual and society. A child who came into existence through parthenogenesis would be deprived of a father on the human and the biological level. Actually, he would be deprived of a right to a very important benefit that nature and the Creator intended him to have in his own personal interest and in the interest of society.

Furthermore, it would mean the end of the family, the foundation of society. *See also* Reproduction. *Pal.*

PARTICIPATION IN PRODUCTION.

A proposed solution to a main problem between capital and labor, this is a middle of the road arrangement between the ordinary labor contract and a cooperative system of production. In the latter, members share in the success or failure of the firm completely. In various forms of participation, as members of the corporation, the workers stand to gain benefits over and above a regular salary and a greater degree of security in their employment.

Participation in production may be one of the three following methods: (a) participation of workers in discussions of technical and administrative problems of the firm; (b) profit-sharing; (c) ownership of stock by the workers.

In the first case, the collaboration usually does not extend beyond establishing mixed groups engaged in formulating general plans that are not strictly binding on the head of the corporation, or offering suggestions to help increase the firm's efficient operation and to improve the working and living conditions of the employees. The second type involves sharing part of the company's divisible profits with employees beyond a regular salary and on the basis of length of service and merit. In the third type, the employees are given stock in the company. Often the stock is distributed on the basis of profits set aside for distribution among the employees by the purchase of stocks for them. This ownership of stock on the part of the employees makes them co-owners *pro quota*.

The three forms of participation pointed out above are the more common ones. They are intended to tone down the exaggerated individualism of an economico-social system based on private property, private initiative, and right of ownership. There is a growing belief in the world today that historical trends indicate substantial modifications and possibly complete elimination of labor contracts based on salaries, in favor of one form or another of participation in the fruits of production.

The practical realization of more perfect social justice for every man can be attained if the system of participation is pursued with moderation, with eyes fixed on the spiritual goals that man wants to reach, without losing sight of the hard, cold realities and laws that govern the economic life.

Christian social doctrine looks with favor on participation in the fruits of production.

In *Quadragesimo anno*, Pius XI considered salaries an inadequate form of recompense and hoped that "workers might gain an interest in the ownership or in the administration of the means of production, and share in profits to some extent," and he felt that it was necessary "in the future for the rich to accumulate only a just proportion of capital with a generous share to be distributed to the workers." Pius XII shared this concern and became the standard-bearer of a social order that "will make it possible for all groups of society to have some property, even though modest, which they could call their own" and "a new social order built on a democratic basis even as far as economic life is concerned."

Since it is not the proper function of spiritual power to propose the juridico-organizational methods of participation in the fruits of production, the Church does not attempt to anticipate technical solutions to problems of this kind, but rather confines itself to preparing the way for them, by encouraging them, measuring them against the principles of justice and equity, and pointing out the proper limits and conditions for their application. *Pal.*

PASSION. In the traditional language of Scholasticism, the term *passion*, sometimes called *concupiscence*, had a broad meaning; it referred to sentiments, emotions, and passions. The word *passion* is disappearing from modern scientific usage; those who still use it attribute to it a disparaging connotation, which involves sentiments and emotions, often immoral, that have become habitual in an individual.

Allowing the term its former meaning, a passion is any human tendency or inclination in which the senses participate.

Thus understood, there are in man eleven passions. Six are concupiscible: love and hatred, desire and aversion, pleasure and sorrow; five are irascible: hope and despair, daring and fear, and anger. This classification is somewhat empirical; as a matter of fact, from school to school, one may find considerable variation in the number of passions. Without discussing the merits of such variety, we note that some reduce the passions to two, pleasure and sorrow; they consider the whole series generally mentioned forms of these two. Others accept the classification above but reduce them all to one, love; the other ten are mere modifications of love.

The moral value of the passions has been the object of different and even contradictory evaluations. From the songs of Homer, where the passions hold a place of honor, down to the Stoics, who despised them, there is a whole gamut of evaluations bordering on the incredible or arising in part from different ways of understanding them. Catholic moral doctrine neither glorifies nor condemns them *en masse*; it sees in them an indestructible element and a precious aid, but also a constant danger for man's higher life. Stoic passivity is obviously unattainable; even if it were attained, it would entail a harmful mutilation, inasmuch as it would deprive man of the help and perfection he has a right to expect from his senses. Thus, passions must be considered a factor of human life, but one to be subordinated to man's higher faculties, which they must serve and obey. This criterion is important in the educational field. It is a grave mistake to concentrate on the training of man's intellectual faculties while neglecting his passions. For these must be trained, by directing them toward objects that are morally good, or placing them under the control of reason. Gra.

PASSIONS AND HUMAN ACTS. Passions are usually divided into *antecedent* and *consequent*.

Antecedent passion is a tendency of the sensitive appetite, independent of any free act of the will. A passion of this kind cannot be sinful. Because of its vehemence, it may diminish or, in exceptional cases, even completely exclude all responsibility for acts committed under its impulse. Antecedent passion, however, is not always necessarily of such a nature as to inhibit completely the full exercise of freedom and, therefore, exclude serious guilt. The physical makeup of each individual is such that one or another passion may rise more quickly and strongly for some than others. This is called a man's *predominant* passion.

Consequent passion is a tendency of the sensitive appetite that depends on a free act of the will. It includes the passions that arise naturally by reason of a free and strong affection existing in the will, those that are deliberately stirred up by the will, and those that have preceded the free exercise of the will, but which the will fails to repress or restrain as effectively as it should. Consequent passions in no way diminish responsibility for acts committed under their impulse, but rather increase it; they share in the morality of the act of the will of which they are the result.

Whether regulated and controlled or directed toward an object which one may not legitimately enjoy, man's passions are vivid forces capable of generating effective help toward good. If they are uncontrolled and impetuous, passions blind man's intellect and lead to sin.

Unruly passions easily give rise to moral defects. The predominant passion, in particular, can, if controlled, be of great help to good, but, uncontrolled, it gives rise to a predominant defect (*see* Defect, Predominant).

As soon as one becomes aware of an inordinate passionate tendency, he is obliged to do all that he can to check and remove it; one who fails to resist an inordinate antecedent passion commits a sin. The sin may be mortal if he does nothing or is particularly negligent in removing a passion that places him in a serious danger of committing mortal sin.

The means of controlling passions are: to avoid external acts or gestures that can stimulate the passions; to forget the object of the passion, by diverting the mind and imagination to something good; to turn the mind to moral thoughts and prayer; to perform acts contrary to the passion itself. Concerning the psychological process and influence of passions on the action of the will, *see* Human Act. Man.

PASTOR. A pastor is a priest or legal person to whom a parish has been canonically entrusted, with responsibility for the care of souls, which is exercised under the jurisdiction of the local Ordinary.

The pastor is a true shepherd of the faithful; he exercises ordinary authority in the internal forum as well as domestic authority; he has charge of the administration of the parish property and benefices. He may be aided by the *consilium fabricae* if such a council exists for a benefice.

Per se, the pastor is irremovable; ordinarily he may govern only one parish. The Ordinary cannot arbitrarily remove jurisdiction from him, but can limit it for just and serious reasons. The Ordinary, who always remains the supreme Shepherd of the diocese, can designate others to perform individual acts of the parochial ministry. According to Can. 451, par. 2, quasi-pastors, in charge of quasi-parishes, and parochial vicars or administrators (*q.v.*) who have full parochial authority, are to be regarded as pastors to all effects and purposes.

APPOINTMENT. It is the right of the Ordinary to appoint pastors; the vicar general has no power in this regard; the vicar capitular or administrator has only the right to confirm the election or accept the presentation of the new pastor to a vacant parish and install him in office. The vicar capitular can generally name pastors to parishes if the see has been vacant for at least a year. The vicar general has all of these rights if the see is impeded (Can. 429, par. 1).

If appointments to parishes are customarily made by competitive examination (*concursus*), this practice must be observed; otherwise, the Ordinary shall make the appointments, bearing in mind that he is under obligation to choose the man who, in his judgment, is best qualified for the post. In the United States, all secular pastors are freely appointed by the bishop, the only manner of appointment of pastors.

A pastor has the care of souls from the moment he takes possession of his benefice; he must make the profession of faith at that time.

RIGHTS AND OBLIGATIONS. The pastor's principal rights are: to confer baptism solemnly; to bring the Blessed Sacrament to the sick of the parish publicly, according to the custom of the place; to administer Viaticum and extreme unction to the dying, with the exception of the cases where the law itself makes exceptions; to publish the banns for marriage and holy orders; to assist at marriages and impart the nuptial blessing; to conduct funeral rites for parishioners and those not of his parish who have chosen his church for the funeral service; to bless the baptismal font on Holy Saturday; to hold public processions and solemn benediction outside the parish church. But in capitular churches the chapter may reserve these functions to itself, and, with respect to processions, all rights acquired by others remain in force (*see* Functions, Pastoral).

The pastor has a right to the special offerings made to enable divine worship to be carried on, as well as those made on the occasion of the administration of certain sacraments and sacramentals. The minimum amount for these offerings is generally established by the diocesan curia or by the provincial council; such offerings belong to the pastor, even if someone else carries out these functions with his consent, unless diocesan regulations or customs dispose differently, so that such offerings are shared in by the assistant priests.

The pastor is also administrator of any parish property and juridically represents the parish, the benefice and the parish church, the last two of which comprise a distinct entity from that of the parish. The law gives to a pastor the right to dispense from the observance of fast and abstinence and of feast days in individual cases.

The principal obligations of the pastor, apart from those consequent upon his office, which bind in justice, are residence in the parish house, application of Mass for the people on the days prescribed, diligent preservation of the parish records.

As father and pastor of souls, he must employ all possible means for the instruction and religious formation of the faithful, and promote the practice of Christian virtues and charitable works which will be beneficial to his people. He should organize groups and associations of Catholic Action and provide spiritual assistance for the young, the poor, the weak, the orphans, and all those who are most in need.

An irremovable pastor can be removed by a judicial process for a crime that renders him unworthy of his office or by administrative process in cases indicated and in the manner prescribed by the Code (Can. 2147 ff.). *Fel.*

PATERNALISM. *Paternalism* expresses a principle according to which the relationship between one governing and his subjects is similar to the relationship between a father and the members of his family. Those entrusted with the power of government have both juridical and moral duties with respect to subjects; the latter are to consider the head of government as a father whose business it is to look after their welfare, to whom they are expected to show gratitude, trust, and obedience.

The paternal system is the only workable one in civilizing barbaric or semibarbaric peoples. It was prevalent among peoples who, though civilized, were not ready for a regime of political liberty; this was true of the European nations until the time of the French Revolution. The ruling House of Austria, especially under Maria Teresa, was the most famous form of this system until the nineteenth century. *The paternal government of Her Majesty* was the phrase that constantly recurred in the official documents of that monarchy. The so-called *reform* princes of the eighteenth century stressed this note of paternalism in their undertakings.

Absolutism (*q.v.*) generally tried to justify itself by this system, especially in the eyes of Christian nations. And, of course, it succeeded in doing so whenever and wherever the historical situation and psychological conditions of the people did not demand a regime of liberty, that is, the concrete realization of the natural capacity of every citizen to participate, through legitimate representatives or in some other way, in government, and, hence, to act as the lawful opposition to the government itself.

Paternalism ceases in the same way as a father's paternal authority over his children; that is, when his dependents have reached full maturity, an awareness of autonomy, and sense of independence. It is a moral duty for those who govern to recognize when this maturity has been reached by their people and to favor and promote it as a proof of recognition of the natural rights of man and also to prevent dangerous reactions. *Boz.*

PATERNITY (Tests). Maternity is an established fact, but paternity is merely a presumption that must be proven by indirect methods. Two legal presumptions *favor legitimitatis* (in favor of legitimacy) exist in law: one presupposes the paternity by the husband; the other involves a legal period of conception, from the maximum to the minimum period of pregnancy (300th to the 180th day before birth). In this latter case, cohabitation with a husband presupposes paternity by the husband, unless proof exists to the contrary.

Two forms of investigation are usually employed. (a) *Morphological studies.* The physical characteristics of the child and of the supposed father are studied; these investigations are based on accurate anthropometric observations by experts. It sometimes is possible to establish peculiar resemblances between the two indicated subjects. These may furnish, with good approximation, a moral certainty of paternity. This approximation increases, if the investigation is centered on two probable fathers; in this case, the anthropometric method, generally carried out through a polysymptomatic diagnosis, often provides a solution to the problem, since morphological characteristics are hereditary.

(b) *Study of blood groups.* For basic notions on this subject and *agglutination reactions* used to determine the various groups, *see* Blood Groups. Here we shall point out that since blood groupings are hereditary, according to the well-defined laws of Mendel, their study is a help in recognizing or, more precisely, excluding paternity. For, if the blood group of the child is different from that of the mother and from that of the supposed father, then the latter is *certainly* not the father of the child. This delicate reaction can sometimes be an absolutely certain proof of paternity. *Riz.*

The biological methods used to establish paternity are based on studies that identify laws governing the transmission of hereditary characteristics; the practical value of these studies is greater in the negative sense by the exclusion of paternity than in the positive sense of an establishment of paternity.

From the ethical point of view, there is nothing wrong with these methods of investigation nor with the goal they pursue. As a matter of fact, it is commonly believed that paternity tests have been kept alive by ecclesiastical legislation, especially with respect to the essential obligations of parents in supporting children and giving them a name. The Napoleonic code sanctioned the prohibition of paternity tests, in an effort to contain the evil brought on by the French Revolution in this regard; but this prohibition was gradually clarified and modified. It should be noted that the function of paternity tests is to help to meet a moral obligation whereby men as well as women are held accountable for their conduct. The only test that should be excluded is that which would cause harm to a legitimate family, for this is condemned by morality and public decency (*See* Legitimation). *Pal.*

PATHOLOGY. Pathology, the study of the nature and causes of diseases which involve changes in structure and function, is divided into several branches. The principal ones are *general pathology,* which studies the general facts and laws according to which the aforementioned changes take place; *special medical pathology* and *special surgical pathology,* which study, respectively, ailments requiring physical, medical, or surgical treatment and describe causes, development, symptomatology and results; *veterinary pathology,* which studies the diseases of domestic animals; *vegetable pathology,* which deals with diseases of useful plants and agricultural products.

Until the middle of the nineteenth century, sickness was regarded as a thing in itself, an extraneous element that invaded the human body in the form of a parasite. On the pathogenesis of morbid processes, Hippocrates held that every sickness came from an abnormal mixture of four *humors* existing in the organism; blood from the heart; mucous (or *phlegm*) from the brain; *yellow bile,* representing the dry element secreted by the liver; and the *black bile* that goes from the spleen to the stomach and corresponds to the wet element. This strange humoral pathology of dyscrasies considered it fundamental to define the *temperament* as well. According to the ancients, temperaments were sanguine, phlegmatic, choleric or melancholic. This approach prevailed, practically without opposition, in medical sciences until a hundred year ago.

Through the efforts of R. Virchow, the founder of *cellular pathology,* the study of ailments was placed on a solid experimental basis, thanks to tireless microscopic research and keen observations on all sorts of healthy and sick tissues from the human organism. A few years later, the studies of Pasteur and of Koch gave impetus to bacteriological research and, later, to complicated *immunization phenomena* that take place in organisms attacked by pathogenic germs.

Quite recently, through the work of De Giovanni, Viola, Pende and other outstanding scientists, studies on the constitution, endocrinology (or internal secretion glands) and vitamins have assumed enormous importance as a useful corrective to the exaggerated histological and mechanistic orientation of the school of Virchow. This has produced a kind of *Neo-Hippocraticism* in the field of medical practice.

Today, the tendency of pathology is to maintain a proper balance between the various tendencies just mentioned, with continued investigation of morphological pathology and bacteriology, humors and constitutions, biochemistry and physiopathology and the like. In short, a study is made not only of the pathogenic agents but also of organic *soil* in which they exert their harmful influence, for the purpose of acquiring a more exact knowledge about the complicated processes entailed in all diseases, in order to combat them more effectively.

It would be too long and hard a task to recall all the progress that has been made in pathology in recent times. But we feel that a passing mention should be made of at least some of the more important advances, particularly for therapeutic purposes.

First of all, the studies of H. Selye on the pathogenesis of morbid processes, despite certain obscure or disputed points, represent the most fruitful working hypothesis in the field of modern pathology. Today, as a result of the work of the Polish-Canadian endocrinologist, everyone recognizes the importance of *stress* (state of suffering caused to the organism by any environmental morbid stimulus), and the *state of alarm* that follows upon it, and of the *general syndrome of adaptation* constituting the reaction promoted by the diencephalon and affecting, through the hypophysis, the surrenal glands and other organs which try to reestablish the balance disturbed by the stress-causing agent.

Secondly, we shall mention the research conducted on *nuclear pathology* immediately following the bombings of Hiroshima and Nagasaki, with respect to the pathogenic effects of atomic bombs on the organism, the various means of protection, and the application of care-fully measured nuclear radiation in the treatment of certain diseases.

The pathology of *antibiotics, virus infections* (assuming an ever wider importance) and especially *poliomyelitis* (which ended in the discovery of anti-poliomyelitis vaccine by Doctor Salk) constitute other important achievements of contemporary pathology. *Riz.*

Insofar as Christian doctrine is interested in the harmony of the human composite, it cannot remain indifferent to modern advances in pathology, since it is not simply a question of restoring health to the physical part of man but also of restoring his capacity for intellectual pursuits and higher accomplishments through which man may be expected, by the grace of God, to attain a higher perfection and greater effectiveness for good (cf. Pius XII, Allocution to the delegates to the Congress of National Societies of Gastro-Enterology, April 26, 1952, in *Pio XII, Discorsi agli intellettuali*, Rome, 1955, p. 323-325). *Pal.*

PATIENCE. Patience is the virtue of enduring physical and moral sufferings with a calm spirit. Christian patience is not the result of pride or insensibility, but of self-mastery, inspired by supernatural motives.

There are different degrees of patience: in the beginning, one bears suffering without complaint or spirit of rebellion; then, without any either internal or external regret; and, finally, with joyfulness.

Patience is necessary; hence it is a matter of obligation. One may sin against it by excess, that is, allowing himself to become insensible to all evil, either affecting himself or others. One may sin against patience by defect, becoming internally upset in the face of adversities. This is impatience, which generally is expressed externally in words, gestures, actions, and easily leads to a variety of other faults.

In general, sins against patience are venial. But one may also sin mortally, especially if he fails to control himself in small things and in the face of little difficulties.

The principal means that facilitates the practice of patience is meditation on the example of Christ and the saints, and on the benefits and blessings derived from patience. Meditation can easily help us turn our sufferings into satisfaction for sins. Patience makes sufferings less burdensome; it is called the root and guardian of all virtues. *Man.*

PATRIARCH. A prelate endowed with episcopal dignity who presides over a patriarchate is termed a *patriarch*. In the Eastern rites, patriarchs enjoy special powers over their subjects. There are at present six Eastern patriarchates.

In the Latin rite, there are at the present time four patriarchal sees: Venice, Lisbon, the East Indies and the West Indies. In the Latin rite, this is merely an honorary title, which entails the right of precedence before primates (Cans. 271, 289), with further due consideration for the rights of the episcopal Ordinary, as presented in Canon 347. *Fel.*

PATRIMONY. A *patrimony* consists of a whole series of rights and obligations, active and passive juridical relationships pertaining to an individual, family, or organization, which admit of financial value.

Patrimony, in this sense, applies to cases in which the totality of the assets is lower than the totality of the obligations; as a result, these are not to be considered wealth in the proper sense.

TITLE OF ORDINATION. In Canon Law, patrimony is a title of ordination, which is the totality of goods intended to provide a decent support for the cleric (*see* Cleric, goods of; Title of sacred ordination).

CLERICAL PATRIMONY. The goods of a cleric are considered patrimonial, if they are derived from any secular source whatsoever, such as inheritance, gift, or income from secular endeavors. Those derived from the exercise of the sacred ministry are termed *quasi-patrimonial* goods; among these are Mass offerings

and donations for religious services or ecclesiastical functions. *Ecclesiastical* goods are income or revenue derived from an ecclesiastical benefice or the fruits of a benefice. *M.d.G.*

PATRONAGE. *Patronage* is the sum total of privileges and obligations granted by the Church to Catholic founders of a church, chapel or benefice, and to their successors (Can. 1448). It is also called *right of patronage*. The right of patronage does not exist in the United States. In fact, since such rights and privileges interfered with the free management of ecclesiastical affairs by those who are divinely appointed superiors of the Church, the Code of Canon Law, in Canon 1450, abolished henceforth the right of patronage, although it is honored wherever it was acquired before the promulgation of the Code (1918).

THE PRINCIPAL PRIVILEGES OF PATRONS ARE:

(a) *The right of presentation.* If a benefice becomes vacant, the patron has the right to present within four months, if a shorter time is not stipulated by the law of the foundation or by custom, a cleric for the vacant church or benefice (Can. 1457). If found to possess the qualifications required by common and particular laws, the bishop must accept him (Can. 1455).

(b) *The right to obtain in equity sufficient revenues from the church or benefice if without his fault he is reduced to great poverty,* although he had previously renounced his right of patronage in favor of the church, or if the pension reserved to him at the time of the foundation has become inadequate to relieve his indigence (Can. 1455).

(c) *The right to display the family coat of arms in the church of the patronage, the right of precedence over all other laymen in processions and similar functions,* to have a special seat in the church, but outside the sanctuary and without a canopy. These rights exist if legitimate local customs sanction them (Can. 1455).

THE TYPES OF PATRONAGE ARE AS FOLLOWS:

(a) *Real,* if the patronage is inherent to some object, so that its possession automatically confers the right of patronage; *personal,* if the right is vested directly in the person.

(b) *Ecclesiastical,* if it belongs to an ecclesiastical person by reason of his sacred office, or to a religious body, or to an entity of ecclesiastical nature; otherwise, it is *laical,* even if possessed by a cleric as a private person. However, it is called *mixed,* if joined to the ecclesiastical there is also a lay element, as in the case of the pastor and a family.

(c) *Hereditary,* if it is transmitted by law or testamentary succession, so that it may go to outsiders; otherwise, if it is to remain in the testator's family, it is called *family* patronage. If it can be passed to remote ancestors or descendants, it is called *tribal;* if the same person is concurrently heir and member of the family or tribe, it is called *mixed* patronage.

The sad experience of struggles among numerous patrons, simoniacal bargaining, the presentation of unworthy persons, the meddling by patrons in sacred functions, led the Church, after the promulgation of the Code, to forbid all patronages in the future and to restrict those already existing. Thus: (a) No new patronage can be validly constituted (Can. 1450). Titles by which it could be acquired in the past cease to produce such an effect. The bishop is given the faculty to grant temporarily, or even perpetually, spiritual benefits in exchange. At most, a bishop may permit the founder to attach to the benefice a condition that the first conferral be made to him or to a cleric of his choice (Can. 1450). (b) Ordinaries shall endeavor to bring about a gradual elimination of existing patronages, or at least of the right of presentation, by offering in return to patrons and their relatives spiritual suffrages, even *in perpetuum* (Can. 1451). (c) If the right of presentation belongs by election to the people of a city or a parish, the choice shall be limited to one of three clerics designated by the Ordinary (Can. 1452).

TITLES. The titles of transmission of patronage are *original* or *non-original.*

(a) *Original titles* give rise to a patronage that did not exist before. Endowment, building a church or chapel, land for such constructions are *ordinary* titles; the privilege and the acquisitive prescription of a non-bound church or benefice are called *extraordinary.*

(b) *Non-original* titles presuppose an existing title that is transmitted to others. These are: (1) prescription against a preceding patron; before the Code it required forty years if the patron was a monastery, pious institute, or a church; ten years if *inter praesentes;* twenty years if *inter absentes* with a colored title (*see* Prescription) or thirty years *inter absentes* without a colored title if a private person is involved; (2) succession within the circle of the family, or tribal group, or by testamentary disposition: non-Catholics, or persons belonging to secret societies condemned by the Church, are always excluded; (3) alienation, which may take place either by an *inter vivos* donation of the personal patronage, or by assignment to other patrons of one's own share of the personal right.

Any form of alienation, to be valid, needs the Ordinary's approval (Can. 1453).

EXTINCTION AND SUSPENSION OF THE RIGHT OF PATRONAGE. The right of patronage may either cease or its exercise may be suspended.

It may cease, (a) if the patron has renounced his right partially or totally; his renunciation, however, must not be damaging to other patrons, if there are others, and, if particular obligations are attached to it, it cannot be done without the superior's consent; (b) by revocation of the right by the Holy See, or by suppression of the church or the benefice; (c) by lawful prescription against the right; (d) by failure to re-build or repair the church or to refurbish its endowment within the time appointed by the Ordinary; (e) by the extinction of the family or line to which the personal patronage was reserved (Can. 1470); (f) by attempted simoniacal transfer of the patronage; (g) by the lapse of a patron into apostasy, heresy, or schism; (h) by usurpation or unjust detention of church property or a benefice; (i) by murder or mutilation of the rector or any other cleric assigned to the service of the church or of the beneficiary, committed by the patron personally or through others; in the latter case, the right is lost also to the heirs, while in cases f, g and h, it is lost to the patron only.

The exercise of the right of patronage may be *suspended*, (a) if the church collapsed or fell into a condition of disrepair, or the revenues fell short, until the patron has remedied such conditions (Can. 1469); (b) if the right passes to a non-believer, a public apostate from the faith, a heretic or schismatic person or one belonging to condemned secret societies, or to a person excommunicated by a declaratory or condemnatory sentence (Can. 1453); (c) if the patrons are minors and the parents or tutors are non-Catholic (Can. 1456); (d) if a censure or *infamia iuris* was applied against the patron, for as long as the condemnation lasts; (e) if the patron committed a crime entailing disqualification from performing lawful ecclesiastical acts (Canons 2294, 2353, 2363, 2375, 2385). M.d.G.

PAYMENT. In a strict sense, *payment* means the return of something owed or the discharge of a debt (*q.v.*). Indebtedness of its very nature tends to an end, as a bond that is destined to cease; the natural way of eliminating a debt is by payment of the debt by the debtor. But there are also other ways of satisfying a creditor's right, either by forced payment or equivalent compensation, including any loss suffered by the creditor.

The payment of a debt may also be made by a third party; in this case, the debtor's obligation is considered fulfilled, despite the indirect method.

Finally, among other ways of extinguishing a debt, some involve compensation, others condonation.

Payment, as a juridical act, does not require a special attitude or intention on the part of the debtor. Nor is any particular disposition of the will necessary on the part of the creditor in accepting payment. It is a question of strict justice; more attention is to be paid to equality between the debt and its payment than to the spirit in which the obligation is fulfilled.

A debtor must employ the care and diligence of a responsible person in fulfilling his obligation with exactness.

The debtor or a third party can pay a debt even against the will of the creditor (*solvere pro ignorante et invito cuique licet*), as long as it is not a case involving intangible service, which in the interest of the creditor must be performed personally by the debtor.

A creditor may legitimately refuse to accept payment by a third party if the debtor expresses opposition to such payment; however, he may ignore the debtor's opposition and accept payment.

Payment must be made to the creditor, his legitimate representative, or another person named by the creditor, or authorized by the law or a judge to receive payment; such a person is simply a collector for the creditor.

Payment presupposes a corresponding debt. It must extend to the entire indebtedness and must consist of the same thing received in loan, unless a special agreement was made to the contrary. Furthermore, in order that the debt may be extinguished, it is necessary that the debtor be the owner of the thing he uses to extinguish the debt and that he be capable of disposing of it.

The dispositions of civil law with respect to payment usually bind in conscience as well, since their purpose is to spell out the equality that must exist between what is borrowed and what is owed, and to protect credit in general. Besides strict justice, the creditor must also observe the requirements of charity in his dealings with his debtor; this also applies to the debtor in his dealings with a creditor. In the matter of payment, the Code of Canon Law (Can. 1529) follows civil law.

With respect to the buying-power of money and to whether or not one can use the nominalistic principle, in which financial loans are to be paid on the basis of the face-value of the money involved at the time of agreement, *see* Loans. *Pal.*

PEACE, INTERIOR. *Interior peace* is a tranquillity of soul flowing from the consciousness of being in the grace of God, and from mastery of the spirit over the senses or all other things capable of disturbing the mind. This tranquillity, whose possession and preservation was the object of Christ's wish to His disciples and of the prayer "Peace be with you" of the early Christians, and which was termed by our Lord as His "true peace," is opposed to the apparent peace of those who seek happiness in the possession of earthly goods and live apart from God (John 14:27).

Man, as he is on this earth, will never be able to acquire a total control over his senses; hence, he will always experience difficulties. But his soul is capable of achieving such a degree of submissiveness and union with God that nothing will disturb it interiorly. *Man.*

PEACE, SOCIAL. *See* Security, Social.

PENANCE, CANONICAL. A burden imposed upon an offender, who accepts it freely in order to redeem himself, in order to avoid a legal penalty deserved for his offense or to obtain absolution or dispensation from a penalty he has already contracted (Can. 2312, par. 1) is a *canonical penalty.*

Thus, it is not the practice of mortification that a Christian may impose upon himself, nor the sacramental penance imposed by a confessor as satisfaction for sin (*q.v.*), but a penance imposed in the external forum.

The specific aim of a canonical penance is to lead the offender to do penance. The superior uses these penances, not as a substitute for canonical penalties in cases where there is a lesser degree of guilt on the part of the offender, but rather as a corrective medium which the offender accepts as a form of expiation that has a perfecting value. At the same time, the superior sees that the requirements of justice are met when he inflicts a canonical penance, for the example of a guilty person working out his own redemption through penance is a great boon to the spiritual welfare of the members of the Church.

Hence, in imposing specific penances, the superior should take into consideration not so much the gravity of the offense (Can. 2312, par. 3) as the disposition of the offender, the status of the person involved, and the concrete circumstances of the offense. No public penance may be imposed for an occult offense (Can. 2312, par. 2).

No definite rules are indicated in the Code, in order that the superior may be free to apply this or that penance according to the case and his judgment.

Thus, Canon 2313, par. 2, permits him, in case of necessity, to add a penance to the penal remedies of admonition (*q.v.*) and correction. This procedure, aside from the main advantage of gaining the cooperation of the offender toward his own correction, exempts him from a censure and gives the superior an opportunity to practice the virtue of meekness, which ought to prompt the entire exercise of his coercive power.

The principal canonical penances are listed in Canon 2313: (a) recitation of certain specified prayers; (b) a pilgrimage or other works of devotion; (c) special fasts; (d) alms to charitable causes; (e) a retreat for a few days in a religious house. The Ordinary may follow these or even impose others, if he sees fit. *Pal.*

PENANCE (Sacrament). The sacrament of penance is a visible rite of a judicial nature in ·which a priest, acting in the name of God, grants forgiveness to one who, sincerely sorry, confesses his sins and agrees to do suitable penance for them.

Matter and Form. The elements which make up the sacrament are the absolution of the priest, called *form,* and the three acts of the penitent: contrition, an intention to make satisfaction, and the confession of sins (*proximate matter*). Contrition and the intention of doing penance comprise part of the sacrament, insofar as they are manifested in a sensible manner. For details concerning these acts of the penitent, *see* Confession, Contrition, Purpose of Amendment, Satisfaction. These acts presuppose the *remote matter,* which consists of sins committed after baptism. Mortal sins which have been committed after baptism and have not yet been directly forgiven by the power of the keys (Can. 901) comprise the *necessary* remote matter of the sacrament; all venial sins committed after baptism, whether already confessed or not, as well as mortal sins which have already been properly confessed and directly forgiven, are *free* and *sufficient* remote matter (Can. 902). Sins committed before baptism and imperfections which do not involve any guilt are *insufficient* matter; doubtful sins are *doubtful* matter; with this matter alone, the sacrament is invalid or doubtfully valid.

Sins are called remote matter (matter *circa quam*) inasmuch as the acts of the penitent mentioned above, which constitute the proximate matter, and the sentence of absolution are referred to these.

SUBJECT. All those who have committed any sins, mortal or venial, after baptism, can validly receive the sacrament of penance, even if these sins have already been forgiven in the sacramental rite of penance.

By divine command all mortal sins committed after baptism must be confessed (*see* Confession). Catholics are bound to confess once a year, or more often if confession is necessary to avoid new serious faults, or if they are in danger of death. Confession is also required of anyone who is aware of being in the state of mortal sin and wishes to receive Holy Communion. Everyone is urged to receive the sacrament of penance often, even every week, as a helpful practice.

There are difficulties concerning the administration of this sacrament, especially in the case of a dying individual, who is unconscious, and in the case of heretics. With regard to the dying, if

the unconscious person has previously given signs of repentance to a priest or has asked for a priest, he should be absolved absolutely; if he could not give signs of repentance, he should be absolved conditionally, even if he has not led a model Christian life, so long as he did not reject the ministrations of the priest right to the end. In the latter case, although some maintain that conditional absolution may be given on the supposition of a change in his will, there is no obligation to do so. Since we cannot exclude the possibility that life may continue for a short time after breathing has ceased, it is permitted to give absolution conditionally to one who is apparently dead—up to one hour later, if death was the result of a prolonged illness, and four or five hours later, if death was sudden. Absolution may be given in these cases, even where there may be some doubt that the dying person is really a Catholic.

Apart from the danger of death, heretics and schismatics may not be absolved unless they are first reconciled with the Church (Can. 731, par. 2); in the danger of death, there may be some cases in which they may be absolved conditionally, if formal reconciliation with the Church is impossible.

DISPOSITIONS. A valid reception of the sacrament of penance requires on the part of the penitent confession, contrition with a purpose of amendment, and the intention to make satisfaction.

In order that the sacrament may effect grace and the forgiveness of sin, contrition must extend at least to all mortal sins not yet forgiven, and it must be of such a nature that sin is detested more than any other evil so that any intention of sinning again is excluded.

It is an unsettled question whether the sacrament of penance can be valid and yet unfruitful, i.e., fail to produce remission of guilt and grace. Some theologians hold that this is possible, if the penitent's contrition is supernatural in its motive, and yet, through no fault or without realizing it, his contrition lacks some of the other qualities necessary for the sacrament to produce grace and remission of guilt.

One who approached the tribunal of penance aware that he did not have the dispositions required for the sacrament to remit sins, or with a serious doubt about the presence of these dispositions because of grave carelessness on his part, would commit a grave sacrilege. This is also true of one who failed to make as complete a confession as required, or was aware of guilty negligence in his examination of conscience which involved a serious danger of omitting a grave sin.

EFFECTS. In those who are properly disposed, the sacrament of penance produces sanctifying grace accompanied by the infused virtues and the gifts of the Holy Spirit, i.e., an increase of grace and good habits that accompany it. The grace of the sacrament of penance comes from an act of pardon on God's part for the offense of sins; hence, it deletes the guilt or stain of sin, which the sinful act produced on the soul, unless it was erased previously. In the latter case, there can always be a new pardon or a repeated renunciation on the part of God of the right to hold the sinner away from His grace. Divine pardon is the deletion of guilt on the soul of the sinner even for sins forgotten, but not necessarily to venial sins, or to all venial sins.

The sacrament of penance effects a constant right to receive special actual graces at the proper moment, so as not to fall back into sins that have been forgiven; it also produces in the soul, according to a well-founded theory, a special permanent vigor that heals the wounds caused by the sins already forgiven.

Besides producing grace in the soul that had no grace, the sacrament of penance also effects a revival of merits and restores to meritorious works performed before sin an efficacy for eternal life which was lost.

Theologians do not agree that the sinner always regains grace in an equal or greater degree than before his fall. The denial of this view rests on serious motives and fits in perfectly with the teaching of the Council of Trent (*Denz.* n. 799). The more perfect the dispositions of the penitent, the more abundant the fruits produced by the sacrament.

If the sacrament of penance is received with defective dispositions, it produces simply a fundamental title to forgiveness and grace which will be granted as soon as the conditions that are lacking become present.

According to a well-founded opinion, the first effect of the sacrament of penance is always to produce such a title.

MINISTER. The minister of the sacrament of penance is the priest with jurisdictional power in the internal and sacramental forum over the penitent (Council of Trent: *Denz.* nn. 902, 903; Canons 871, 872). This power is distinct from the power of orders, conferred in ordination to the priesthood. Jurisdiction may be *ordinary*, if it is connected with an office; or delegated, if it is granted by one with ordinary jurisdiction. The sacred canons determine ordinary and delegated jurisdiction. But in danger of death, every priest is granted jurisdiction for the dying person. Absolution from certain specific censures and particularly serious sins is reserved to the bishop or to the Holy See; in danger of death, however, there is no restriction on jurisdiction (Can. 882).

Ordinary jurisdiction is possessed by all who have the care of souls as their office, e.g., residential bishops, pastors and those who enjoy the same rights as pastors, the canon penitentiary of the cathedral church and collegiate churches, the superiors of exempt clerical religious in accordance with their constitutions. For the latter, jurisdiction is limited to their subjects; for the others, it can be exercised over subjects and non-subjects; apart from their respective territories, they can absolve only their own subjects (Can. 991, par. 1). In the jurisdiction necessary for exempt clerical religious, jurisdiction includes the confessions of the religious professed and novices, as well as servants, students and their guests, if they are living in the religious house (Can. 514, par. 1, and Can. 875).

The power of ordinary jurisdiction for

confession ceases with the loss of office, excommunication, interdict, or suspension from office after a declaratory or condemnatory sentence (Can. 873, par. 3).

Jurisdiction may be delegated either by a person with the faculty of delegation (*ab homine*), or by law itself (*a jure*). Persons who may delegate jurisdiction are: local Ordinaries (Can. 874) and superiors of an exempt clerical religious order, designated by the constitutions (Can. 875). Neither canons (Can. 401) nor pastors may delegate others, though they themselves possess ordinary jurisdiction. Special jurisdiction is required for a priest who hears the confessions of religious women, professed and novices. This may be conferred only by the Ordinary of the place in which the religious house is located (Can. 876).

Cardinals may hear confessions of religious women anywhere (Can. 2391, n. 1). Confessors of religious (Can. 239, n. 1) who need this special faculty are the ordinary (Cans. 520, par. 1; 524, par. 2), the extraordinary (Cans. 521; 524, par. 2), supplementary (Can. 521, par. 2), special (Can. 520, par. 2), but not so-called occasional confessors (*see below*).

Delegation for hearing confessions must be transmitted directly, either orally or in writing (Can. 879, par. 1); delegation cannot be presumed nor is it to be conferred on one who does not possess the required prudence and learning, proof of which must be obtained by examination (Can. 877).

Delegated jurisdiction may be limited to definite, specified places or groups of people for a limited time (Can. 199, par. 1); in any case, it does not extend beyond the diocesan territory, if it is given by the local Ordinary, nor beyond the particular community, if it should be conceded by the religious superior. Jurisdiction ceases upon revocation by the authority which delegated it, or by expiration of the time for which it was granted, or by cessation of the reason for which it was given; jurisdiction may cease by renunciation of the one who received this delegation, if this renunci-

ation is accepted by the one who delegated authority. Jurisdiction does not ordinarily cease if the one who delegated it leaves office, unless this is expressly indicated in the original delegation of jurisdiction (Can. 207).

The law itself gives delegation directly in certain circumstances: (a) in danger of death (*q.v.*); (b) in a case of common error, unawareness that the faculties have expired, or positive and probable doubt (*see* Jurisdiction, supplied); in these cases, jurisdiction is extended to all priests and all penitents, provided that the conditions demanded by the law are fulfilled; (c) priests on sea voyages can always absolve their fellow-passengers, as long as they have been approved for confessions by their own Ordinary, or by the Ordinary of the port of embarkation or some intermediate port. They can also absolve any of the faithful who come to them on board, or whom they meet on land during any of the stops lasting for a period of three days; after this length of time, they must secure proper jurisdiction from the local Ordinary, if it can easily be done. This faculty begins at the start of the voyage and ends at its completion (Can. 883).

The same faculties are also valid for air travel (Motu proprio of Pius XII, Dec. 16, 1947: AAS 40 [1948], 17).

This is more an extension of a faculty than a new one. The same thing may be said of the following cases: Although, as we have seen, a special jurisdiction (*ad hoc*) is required for the confessions of religious women, nevertheless, in case of serious illness, any religious woman may summon any priest approved for hearing the confessions of women, to hear her confession (Can. 523). Apart from the case of grave illness, whenever a religious woman deems it useful or necessary for the tranquillity of her conscience, she may confess to any confessor approved for women, in a church, public or semi-public oratory, or in any place designated for the confessions of women, and, in case of sickness or other true necessity, even in another place (Can. 522; Comm. for the Interpretation of the Code, Nov. 24, 1920; Feb. 12, 1935; see Occasional confessor).

Both ordinary and delegated jurisdiction may be restricted by so-called *reservations* (see Reservations of sins, Reservation of censures). With respect to the tasks and the qualities required in the minister, see Confessor *and* Absolution. Concerning possible abuses on the part of the minister while hearing confessions, see Confession, Solicitation. With respect to confessions of habitual sinners, occasionists and recidivists, see Sinner, Habitual; Occasionist, Recidivist. On the obligation of the sacramental seal, see Seal, Sacramental.

Practical Advice. It is very advantageous to one's spiritual life to approach the sacrament of penance often, even every week, taking great care to be properly disposed. It is also useful to repeat accusations of one or another sin of one's past life, though already forgiven. With respect to a doctor's duty about advising a sick person to receive the sacrament of penance, see Sacraments (Conduct of the physician with regard to the). *Man.*

PENANCE (Virtue of). Penance, as a virtue, is a habit which disposes one to atone for the offenses deliberately committed against God through sin. In perfecting the will, penance resembles the virtue of justice, because it implies the payment of a strict debt, as it were; but it differs from justice, insofar as it cannot offer adequate reparation to God for mortal sin.

A distinction must be made between penance as an infused virtue and as an acquired one. The *infused* virtue of penance is a supernatural habit; it exists in all who live in grace, enabling them, with the help of actual grace, to perform supernatural acts of penance. The *acquired* virtue of penance is a firm inclination to perform acts of penance; this results from the frequent repetition of these acts and bestows a particular facility for them.

The *formal* object of the virtue of penance is the consonance between reparation, due to God for offenses committed by sin, and a special exigency of our nature, either as it is in itself or elevated by grace. Its *material* object consists of all the acts that tend to give worthy recompense to the Lord offended by sins. A distinction must be made between the *elicited* act of the virtue of penance, i.e., the will to make reparation to God for sins committed, and the *necessary* acts, such as contrition, the purpose of amendment, confession, and satisfaction, which consists in the privation of self in pleasant joys or the acceptance of unpleasant burdens. To perform those acts, which are necessary, the virtue of penance relies on other virtues, whose acts can be directed toward the end of penance. The virtue of penance is stimulated by the theological virtues, especially the infused virtue of charity.

The virtue of penance, toward which man has a natural inclination and which is enjoined by the natural law, is the object of a special commandment. The infinite satisfaction which was offered by Jesus Christ on the cross does not remove man's need for penance, but places him in a position to offer reparation acceptable to God and beneficial to man himself. The institution of the sacrament of penance does not dispense man from doing personal works of penance. *Man.*

PENITENTIARY, APOSTOLIC. The Sacred Apostolic Penitentiary is the primary tribunal of the Roman Curia.

It is a tribunal of mercy, pardon, redemption—a kind of appendage to the sacrament of penance for cases reserved to the Holy See.

Its jurisdiction is most extensive. The Code of Canon Law says in this regard: "This Sacred Tribunal, acting only in the internal forum, grants favors, absolutions, dispensations, commutations, sanations, condonations; it examines and solves cases of conscience" (Can. 258, par. 2). It says "only in the internal forum," because the other Offices of the Holy See take care of matters in the external forum. Only in exceptional instances do the decisions of this sacred Tribunal have force in the external forum (Can. 1047, Can. 2251; Apostolic Constitution *Quae divinitus*, March 25, 1935: AAS, 27 [1935], 97–113).

Since the pontificate of Pope Benedict XV (April 25, 1917), the Office of Indulgences has been attached to the Tribunal of the Sacred Apostolic Penitentiary; "it has the task of passing judgement on everything that has to do with the use and granting of indulgences, without infringing on the rights of the Holy Office with regard to the doctrinal part of indulgences and the discipline concerning new devotions" (Can. 2251, par. 2).

Recently, Pope Pius XII reorganized the Sacred Apostolic Penitentiary through the aforementioned Apostolic Constitution *Quae divinitus*.

Before this, it had been governed for almost two centuries by the Apostolic Constitution *In Apostolicae* of Pope Benedict XIV (April 13, 1744). This states and the Constitution *Quae divinitus* repeats that the Supreme Pontiffs "have from most ancient times wanted the Roman Curia to have the Office of the Apostolic Penitentiary as a kind of fountain open to the faithful for cleansing away sins, to which all the faithful from every part of the Catholic world can turn with confidence—either personally or through a sealed letter with name withheld—to find a suitable, free, and prompt remedy for their spiritual ills."

Now, the Sacred Apostolic Penitentiary consists of two sections: (1) Tribunal, and (2) Indulgences (Can. 258).

It is governed by the Cardinal Major Penitentiary (*q.v.*), assisted by a prelate who is regent.

The office of the Secretariat comprises besides the regent, a secretary, two substitutes (one for the Tribunal and the other for Indulgences) and ten other officials (*Quae divinitus*, nn. 1–2; *Annuario Pontificio*, Vatican City, 1956, p. 932 ff.).

The Sacred Apostolic Penitentiary also includes a board of prelates who meet periodically, with the Cardinal Major Penitentiary presiding; they constitute his council, the so-called *Signatura Sacrae Paenitentiariae Apostolicae*, and treat of the more complicated and serious questions (*loc. cit.* nn. 5–6b).

All other cases are dealt with, in *sessions* for the Tribunal or Indulgences, by the regent and the secretary, with the substitute of each respective section attending. The three officials participating are responsible *in solido* to the Cardinal Major Penitentiary for the decisions made in these sessions; the Cardinal can, if he chooses, reserve to himself final approval of all decisions made in these sessions (*loc. cit.*, n. 6a).

More important cases of the *Signatura* and sessions are then referred to the Holy Father by the Cardinal Major Penitentiary in his routine audiences (*loc. cit.*, n. 6c).

Recourse may be made to the Sacred Apostolic Penitentiary directly by the person concerned, or, with his explicit permission, by his confessor (Cans. 2252, 2254, and 2290). In practice, it is better for the confessor to do this.

The case is to be proposed without names or with fictitious names (Titius, Titia, Caius, Caia, and the like), briefly, with all of the circumstances necessary or helpful toward a more precise judgment of the case.

The explanation may be given in the vernacular, although it is better if done in Latin, as long as clarity and precision do not suffer.

The place and date should always be included; at the end of the letter, the full address to which the reply is to be sent should be clearly indicated.

The envelope should bear the name of: *The Most Eminent Cardinal Major Penitentiary*, or: *The Sacred Apostolic Penitentiary*, and be sent to: *Vatican City* or *Via della Conciliazione, n. 34, Rome. Ses.*

PENITENTIARY, CANON. A *canon penitentiary* is the canon of the chapter (*q.v.*), specially assigned to the ministry of hearing confessions.

According to the Code of Canon Law, every cathedral church must have a canon penitentiary (Can. 398, par. 1). One may be appointed in collegiate churches (Can. 398, par. 2).

This office requires special gifts of learning and prudence. The one chosen should be at least thirty years of age; he may not accept or exercise any office in the diocese that involves jurisdiction in the external forum (Can. 399).

Canon Law gives the canon penitentiary of a cathedral or collegiate church ordinary faculties (which cannot be subdelegated) to absolve from sins or censures reserved to the bishop. He may use these faculties outside the diocese in behalf of the faithful of his own diocese, or within his own diocese, in behalf of those from outside the diocese (Can. 400, par. 1).

Apart from the ordinary faculties just mentioned, canon penitentiaries frequently have delegated faculties to absolve from certain censures reserved to the Holy See. They may obtain such faculty from the Holy See on the recommendation of their Ordinaries or from their own Ordinary in the case of faculties which he can subdelegate and which he has either from the law itself or, by a special privilege, from the Holy See.

The canon penitentiary must be at the disposal of the faithful, in the confessional assigned to him in the cathedral or collegiate church, on the days and hours which the bishop shall judge most opportune; he may remain in the confessional, if need be, even during the time of choir (Can. 401, par. 2). *Ses.*

PENITENTIARY, MAJOR. The *Major Penitentiary* is the Cardinal who presides over the Sacred Apostolic Penitentiary (*q.v.*). His official title is: SS. DD. Nostri Papae et S. Sedis Apostolicae Major Paenitentiarius (Major Penitentiary of our most holy Lord, the Pope, and of the Holy Apostolic See). He is the Major Penitentiary of the Pope above all: it is his task to assist the Holy Father at the moment of death. He is also the Major Penitentiary of the Apostolic See; as such, he governs the Sacred Apostolic Penitentiary with full powers over all the faithful in cases of conscience and granting indulgences (Apost. Const. *Quae divinitus*, March 25, 1935: AAS, 27 [1935], 97–113).

He has full power of jurisdiction for hearing confessions in the four patriarchal basilicas of Rome, St. John Lateran, St. Peter in the Vatican, St. Mary Major, St. Paul outside the Walls, and the basilicas of Italy which are indirectly subject to the Pope, such as that of St. Francis at Assisi or St. Anthony in Padua. He names the minor penitentiaries (*q.v.*) whose duty it is to hear confessions in these places. He also grants certain special faculties to absolve from censures and to dispense from vows, irregularities, and impediments. He can grant similar faculties to other confessors throughout the world.

The office of the Major Penitentiary is so important that he keeps all his powers during the vacancy of the Holy See and, in grave and urgent cases, he can perform acts usually reserved personally to the pope (Apost. Const. *Quae divinitus*, n. 12; Apost. Const. *Vacantis Apostolicae Sedis*, n. 17: AAS, 38 [1946], 72).

During the papal conclave, the Major Penitentiary is permitted to remain in communication with the Office of the Sacred Penitentiary; letters bearing the seal of this office are not subject to inspection prescribed for all other correspondence (Apost. Const. *Quae divinitus*, n. 12; Apost. Const. *Vacantis Apostolicae Sedis*, n. 17).

If the Major Penitentiary dies while the Holy See is vacant, the cardinals must come together at the first opportunity and name a cardinal to fill the office of Major Penitentiary during the vacancy (*Vacantis Apostolicae Sedis*, n. 14).

The Major Penitentiary in Certain Sacred Ceremonies. Every year during Holy Week, the Major Penitentiary, accompanied by the prelates of the Sacred Apostolic Penitentiary, proceeds to the four patriarchal basilicas for the ceremony of the *penitential rod.* On Palm Sunday, he attends St. John Lateran; on Wednesday, St. Mary Major; on Holy Thursday, St. Peter in the Vatican; on Good Friday, St. Paul outside the Walls for the special ceremonies of each day.

At St. John Lateran, he is received by a delegation from the Lateran chapter and the college of minor penitentiaries of the Lateran. After visiting the Blessed Sacrament, the Major Penitentiary proceeds to the throne at the left side of the nave; there, he receives the *penitential rod* from the regent of the Sacred Penitentiary, and touches it to the head of the regent and the other prelates, the minor penitentiaries (*q.v.*) and the faithful who come. This act of humility has been endowed with an indulgence of 7 years (AAS, 24 [1942], 239). This ceremony is carried out in the same way in the other three patriarchal basilicas.

During a Holy Year, the Major Penitentiary plays an important role, not only in the preparation of the Apostolic Constitutions and respective Instructions, but also in the ceremonies of the opening and closing of the Holy Door. At the opening of the Holy Door, the Major Penitentiary presents to the Holy Father the silver hammer with which the latter strikes the door three times (*Ritus servandus in aperitione Portae Sanctae*, Typis Polyglottis Vaticanis, 1949, p. 4 ff.). For the closing of the Holy Door, the Major Penitentiary presents to the Holy Father the silver trowel with which the latter thrice lays the cement in the middle of the threshold of the Door. Taking back the trowel, the Major Penitentiary offers the Holy Father, one at a time, three golden bricks. The pope takes the silver trowel and cements the right and left of the three golden bricks; he places two bricks to the right and one brick to the left in line with the first three. The rest are then put in place by the four minor penitentiaries and the masons (cfr. *Ritus servandus in clausura Portae Sanctae*, Typis Polyglottis Vaticanis, 1950, pp. 6–8).

Cardinal Penitentiaries in History. The earliest mention of the office and title of Cardinal Penitentiary dates back to the end of the twelfth century. In earlier times mention is made of penitentiaries (*presbyteri paenitentium*), but not of a Cardinal Penitentiary.

Some of the Cardinal Penitentiaries who deserve special mention are: (1) St. Raymond of Peñafort, the Dominican author of the *Decretals* and the Penitentiary of Pope Gregory IX from 1230 to 1234; (2) Blessed Peter of Tarentaise, a Dominican, who became Pope Innocent V in 1276; (3) Blessed Nicolo Albergati, a Carthusian, who died in 1443; (4) Domenico Capranica, the founder of the Capranica College, who died in 1458; (5) Giuliano della Rovere, elected Pope Julius II in 1503; (6) St. Charles Borromeo, who was the first to name a vice-penitentiary because of the press of other duties; (7) Ippolito Aldobrandini, who became Pope Clement VIII in 1572; (8) Francesco Saverio Castiglioni, later Pope Pius VIII (1829). *Ses.*

PENITENTIARY, MINOR. Minor penitentiaries are religious appointed to hear confessions in the four patriarchical basilicas: St. John Lateran, St. Peter in the Vatican, St. Mary Major, and St. Paul outside the Walls.

Minor penitentiaries are dependent on the Major Penitentiary for necessary jurisdiction and special faculties, but they do not belong to the Tribunal of the Sacred Apostolic Penitentiary. Besides hearing confessions, they apply the *penitential staff* to the heads of penitents seeking to gain the indulgences attached to that particular action (AAS: 24 [1942], 239).

By custom, minor penitentiaries for each basilica are members of a particular religious order: Friars Minor at St. John Lateran; Friars Minor Conventuals at St. Peter; Dominicans at St. Mary Major; Benedictines at St. Paul outside the Walls.

At the special ceremonies of a Holy Year, minor penitentiaries are entrusted with special tasks: at the beginning of the Holy Year, they wash the entrance to the Holy Door; at the closing of the Holy Year, they complete the task of laying the bricks which seal the door. During the Holy Year they are also granted special faculties, which are determined by the Apostolic Constitution proclaiming the Holy Year. *Ses.*

PENSION, ECCLESIASTICAL. An *ecclesiastical pension* is a right granted to a cleric by competent ecclesiastical authority for a just cause to receive a portion of the fruits of a benefice. Title to the benefice is retained by the possessor of the benefice. Payment is either annual or at specified times. The just cause is usually the exercise of an ecclesiastical office without a benefice or one that is insufficient. More frequently, the pensioner is incapacitated, in need, or has been removed from another benefice (Cans. 2154, par. 1; 2161, par. 2).

A pension is not a benefice, since it does not meet the requirements of a title attached, objective perpetuity, nor of an office essentially connected to it (Can. 1412, par. 4). The pension or right to an income may be attached to an office on a perpetual basis, as, for example, the permanent parochial vicariate, which is set up in a parish with a pension from the income of the parish. According to the nature of the pension, competent ecclesiastical authority may dispose that (a) the pension coincide with the life of the pensionary; (b) with the life of the beneficiary; (c) or be established permanently (Can. 1429).

In the first case, the right of the pensionary is, in fact, a personal obligation of the beneficiary; hence, if the latter dies, it ceases. In the second case, the obligation is real, rather than personal, since it is imposed upon the benefice and passes on to all who hold the benefice for the lifetime of the pensionary (relative perpetuity). In the third case, not only is this a real obligation but it does not cease with the death of the pensionary; this right is passed on to succeeding pensionaries (absolute perpetuity).

The pension can be abolished or suspended by virtue of a penal provision (Cans. 2291, par. 7; 2298, par. 6; 2299, par. 3; 2336, par. 1), or *post sententiam declaratoriam*, if the pensionary has committed a crime involving degradation or deposition (Cans. 2303–2305). Except for cases mentioned in Canons 2303–2305, a cleric cannot receive a pension if he has incurred infamy of law (Can. 2294), is excommunicated, suspended or interdicted by virtue of a declaratory sentence (Canons 2265, par. 1; 2275, par. 3; 2283).

Power of the Ordinary. The supreme pontiff has the power to establish any pension whatsoever, either temporary or perpetual (Canons 1429, par. 3; 1518; 1499, par. 2). Pensions are not favored by law, since they lend themselves to abuses condemned by the Council of Trent (Sess. XXIV, c. 13; cf. C. 21, X, III, 5; C. 3, X, III, 6). Hence, the power of Ordinaries in their own territories is limited by the prescription of Canon 1440; the direct result of these laws forbids a benefice which results in a diminution of income. Therefore, any power which they possess must come from the express disposition of the legislator, if it is contrary to that principle.

The powers of the Ordinary are as follows: (1) In filling non-parochial benefices, local Ordinaries can, for just reasons, to be enumerated in the document conferring the benefice, impose temporary pension to perdure throughout the lifetime of the beneficiary, as long as a suitable portion of the income is left for the benefice (Can. 1429, par. 1). (2) In a parish benefice, Ordinaries can impose pension only in favor of the pastor or vicar of the parish who has relinquished that office, but only for the lifetime of the individual; it must not exceed one-third of the net income of the benefice (Can. 1429, par. 2).

These provisions were recently explained indirectly by special regulations from the Sacred Congregation of the Council (*see* Ecclesiastical goods, Ecclesiastical benefices). Ordinaries are thus permitted to provide for worthy priests who fulfilled important work in the ministry for which they were not sufficiently remunerated at the time, as in the field of education or seminary teaching. V*io.*

PENTECOST. The date of Pentecost, as the fiftieth day after Easter, is of Jewish origin, but the meaning of the feast is strictly Christian. The fiftieth day after the Jewish Pasch, the celebration of deliverance from Egypt, was the feast of the harvest and first fruits (Exod. 23:16), the feast of Weeks (Exod.

36:22; Deut. 16:10), and the feast of the Law which God promulgated on Mount Sinai. For these reasons, it was the second of three great Jewish feasts. Pentecost acquired a primary position among Christian feasts, together with Easter. The Apostles and the first Christian converts from Judaism celebrated Pentecost according to the customs of their ancestors. At the same time they began to commemorate the descent of the Holy Spirit, which occurred on that day, and, as the power of the Spirit was more and more evident in the works of the Apostles, the meaning of the Christian Pentecost grew more important to the early Christians and easily transplanted older notions of the Old Testament.

Meaning. The *new* Passover marked the beginning of the gospel harvest and its first fruits. Under the inspiration of the Holy Spirit, St. Peter promulgated a new Law, fifty days after the Easter of redemption, the true liberation of the people of God. The Fathers of the Church easily found many analogies in explaining the meaning of Pentecost to the faithful. Tertullian speaks of it as a great feast commemorated with many ceremonies (*De Corona Milit.*, 3; *De Bapt.*, 19); Origen treats of it (*Contra Celsum*, 8:23). The Council of Elvira (c. 300) recalls the duty of celebrating this feast, which was celebrated in the most solemn form in the second half of the third century. The *Apostolic Constitutions* (5:20) ordain that its celebration be prolonged for an octave; the *Peregrinatio Aetheriae* (*Silviae*) gives a minute description of its celebration at Jerusalem toward the end of the fourth century. In the West, it was greeted with fervor and gradually linked with Easter, as the second baptismal feast, with the same rite of Easter. The administration of baptism is shown in Tertullian (*De Bapt.*, 19) to have taken place, not only on the eve of Easter and Pentecost, but throughout the entire period of fifty days. At the end of the fourth century, as is evident in Jerome (*In Zach.*, 14:8), the last day of this period, the eve of Pentecost, and the eve

of Easter were established for the baptism of catechumens.

The liturgies for the two vigils are similar. The catechumens would gather on the eve of Pentecost, as they did on the eve of Easter, to receive their last catechetical instructions and for readings from the Bible, prayers, the blessing at the baptismal font, baptism, confirmation and Holy Mass.

In many churches, an attempt to imitate Holy Saturday, with a blessing and exposition of the paschal candle and chanting of a modified *Exultet*, became a custom on the eve of Pentecost. Later, in the Middle Ages, in a desire to portray, in a sensible manner, the miracle of the Cenacle, both the blowing of the wind and the tongues of fire were imitated through the sounds of trumpets and showers of roses. Thus, because of the latter symbol, Pentecost became known in many countries as the *Easter of the Roses*. In other places, a dove was released as a symbol of the Holy Spirit; seven priests, representing the seven gifts of the Holy Spirit, incensed the altar during this ceremony of the Mass for Pentecost.

The teaching of Pius XII (Enc. *Mediator Dei*) stresses the exhortation by the Church at Pentecost that all Christians submit to the action of the Holy Spirit, by enkindling divine charity in their hearts, so that each day they may grow in virtue and dedication, to become holy imitators of the holiness of Christ the Lord and His heavenly Father. *Opp.*

PERCEPTION. *Perception* is an act of the mind by which one becomes aware of an object of the sensitive world as actually present. It is, therefore, a psychological process, reflective and integrative, which utilizes one or more sensations to furnish meaning, through the process of a formation of images and mental representations of the world. Thus, for example, the sensations of light and color are supplied by the sense of sight, but awareness of the form of objects and their significance depends on a process of perception.

Awareness of the object of our senses

is implicit in the phenomenon of perception. In other words, perception is not merely a simple sensitive-sensorial phenomenon, but the product of a psychological process of a complexity of sensations, checked against the preexisting mnemonic traces of one's experience. Some scientists identify perception with *sensation*, but psychological analysis has demonstrated that, besides the sensitive and sensorial factor, there is in perception also an activity of the mind; hence, the two terms are to be considered two distinct things. We can hear without perceiving, as when we are distracted or in pathological cases of *psychological deafness or blindness*, in which one has the sensation of sound or color, but the object from which that sound originates or to which that color belongs is not recognized. *Riz.*

Modern psychologists believe that there is a more profound difference between sensation and perception. If a piece of cloth looks black in ordinary artificial light, it may well appear purple in the sunlight. A similar principle may also be applied to philosophical terms. In fact, there are unconscious sensations, but there are no unconscious perceptions; thus, too, in perception, there is not only an actual fact, but there is always an intellectual element also.

According to Rosmini, "The intellectual perception of bodily things is a judgment by means of which the mind holds as existing something perceived by the senses" (*Nuovo Saggio*, n. 337). Elsewhere (*Psicologia*, p. I, p. 3, c. 2, 4) he clarifies this further: "In order to explain the union of soul and body, it is proper to admit that the rational soul has *a primitive, natural, continuous perception of the basic animal feeling* because, being rational, it cannot be connected with such feeling except by a rational act; and of all rational acts the first, namely, that which communicates immediately with the reality of the being, is perception."

SCHOLASTIC PHILOSOPHY. Those who explain the union between soul and body by the application of the theory of matter and form, cannot accept completely the idea of Rosmini. However, we must agree with him that perception is a judgment. It is not rare to find, in books of philosophy, perception defined as a judgment by which the intellect affirms the existence and qualities of external objects. Sensation has as its object a tangible, concrete quality. I see a colored thing or I smell a scent in such and such a way. Perception, instead, has as its object a thing of which I affirm existence and certain qualities; this thing is white, tasteful, with definite extension, etc. Hence, it is clear that sensation is to perception what simple apprehension is to judgment. As truth is not properly found in simple apprehension but only in judgment, so, too, truth is not properly found in sensation but in perception. What the normal man sees as red, a Daltonist sees as green, an icteric individual sees as yellow. A cane partially immersed in water appears broken. Tom judges as warm what Dick thinks cold. There is no falsehood here. To be sure, it is a matter of experience. It would be falsehood if man, as a reasonable being, were to endeavor to attribute to the object the mere fact of sensation. Errors in perception may originate from insufficient attention, illusions, hallucinations, and improper position.

However, this is a field where many controversies still exist.

PERCEPTION IN MORAL THEOLOGY. The question of perception assumes great importance in moral theology in the formation of a positive and true conscience. One must follow a certain conscience, even if the certainty is erroneous. In order to attain norms of conscience, that is, ultimate-practical judgments concerning the goodness or evil of an act, a syllogism is needed, in which the major premise expresses a law, and the minor a specified action with a determined object. This object must be well known in order that one may judge whether and to what extent it falls under the law. In all of this, perception, that is, the knowledge of the actual objects of the sensible world, is not absent; this knowledge will be used immediately or at a later time, if the occasion demands. *Ver.*

PEREGRINATION, ROMAN. *See* Indulgence; Pilgrimage.

PERFECTION, CHRISTIAN. Perfection in general is a full actualization of potential qualities. In an absolute sense, a being is perfect if it is complete in its nature—that is, lacks nothing fitting or becoming to its nature (*Summa Theol.,* II-II, q. 184, a. 1). However, there is a relative perfection of any being, which consists in a proximate approach to its complete perfection in the highest degree possible.

Man's absolute perfection is in the future life: it consists in the perpetual possession of God and His beatific vision. Man's relative perfection, on this earth, consists in approaching as close as possible to the state of the blessed in paradise—that is, in achieving full development of the life of grace, a beginning of the heavenly life. This is called *Christian perfection.*

This perfection, together with a great love of God, includes not only the observance of that which is a matter of precept, but also supererogatory works of virtue and the practice of the gifts of the Holy Ghost. Perfection can exist without the effective exercise of the evangelical counsels, but not without living according to the spirit of these counsels. It is evident that all this includes the virtue of mortification (*q.v.*).

A hierarchical order exists among the actions that constitute Christian perfection. Primarily, perfection on this earth consists in loving God as much as possible; this can be deduced from Holy Scripture (Matt. 22:39 ff.; Luke 10:25 ff.; John 14:23; Rom. 13:10; I John 4:10), and from the very nature of the love of God, which, among all good acts, is that which more strictly unites man with the Lord, on earth. After love of God, the love of neighbor for the sake of God and the effective practice of fraternal charity are next in this hierarchical order.

There are limits beyond which one cannot go: in this life, contemplation and love of God cannot remain uninterrupted, nor is it possible always to act in such a way as to prescind completely from one's own well-being (Innocent XII, *Condemnation of Semi-Quietism, Denz.* n. 1327). Furthermore, under present conditions, it is impossible, without a thoroughly extraordinary aid of God, to avoid all venial sins of pure frailty (Council of Vienna, *Denz.* n. 471; Council of Trent, *Denz.* n. 833). The lives of the saints, however, demonstrate the heights to which man can rise if generous cooperation with the grace of God is given.

Christian perfection requires that man love God in such a manner as to avoid any fully deliberate venial sin; this does not exclude rare venial faults due to frailty, immediately and thoroughly detested, and fully deliberate imperfections. One must strive to glorify God under any circumstance, and to the highest possible degree. A profound habitual uprightness of the will must necessarily be joined to this love of God, out of respect for the Supreme Being and all created goods. Hence, the absence of any disorderly attachment even to the smallest created thing demands a thorough control of the will over the sensitive faculties. He is perfect who is so habitually disposed that he might pass from earth to heaven without the need of suffering in purgatory. Such a state cannot be but the effect of long and hard struggles against oneself and painful purifications, borne with great generosity. Christian perfection, however, does not exclude the desire and hope for one's own beatitude, for they are part of man's perfection on this earth.

OBLIGATION TO PERFECTION. Everyone is obliged to strive for perfection, each according to his own condition. The Holy Scriptures stress sanctity greatly and preach clearly the necessity of great renunciation and deep charity so that an impartial man should be fully convinced of the fact that perfection is not only a matter of counsel, but of precept as well (Matt. 5:48; 10:37 ff.; Luke 14:26 ff.; Eph. 1:4; 4:13; I Pet. 1:15; Apoc.

22:11). The Fathers insisted on the necessity of progress on the way of salvation, and, consequently, of striving for perfection. Pius XI, in his encyclical on the occasion of the centenary of the death of St. Francis de Sales, re-emphasized the traditional teaching that all Christians, without exception, must tend to sanctity (AAS: 15 [1923], 50).

In any form of life, as soon as the process of growth comes to a halt, decay sets in, because in every living being disintegrating forces, if not checked, bring sickness and death. The same occurs in the spiritual life: together with tendencies to good, other tendencies impel us to evil; if we cease to strive toward progress, our defects take the upper hand and temptations become more frequent and strong. If we do not arouse ourselves from our lethargy, the moment comes when, from a state of gradual weakness, we shall fall into mortal sin.

It is of the greatest importance to have from the beginning a firm intention to reach perfection. In fact, it is a psychological law that we shall not advance for long on an arduous road without the lively desire of reaching the goal to which it leads; the search for perfection is a difficult thing indeed. *Man.*

PERIODICAL. *See* Press.

PERJURY. *Perjury,* in a broad sense, is an unlawful oath, that is, an oath lacking in one of the three conditions required for a valid oath: truth, judgment and justice (*see* Oath). In a strict sense, *perjury* is a false statement supported by an oath.

The doctrine concerning perjury was already known to Roman law. A *perjurus* was punished with infamy (D. 3, 2, 1; C. 2, 4, 41), and if his act caused the death of an innocent person, he was condemned to death (D. 48, 8, 1). This was developed more fully by moralists, incorporated into Canon Law and, finally, modern civil legislation.

The doctrine of the moralists is summed up by St. Thomas in II-II, q. 98, of his *Summa Theologica.* In four articles he demonstrated that a false oath

is an essential part of perjury (art. 1); that perjury, since it implies contempt of God, is always a mortal sin (art. 2–3); that an individual who demands an oath from another individual does not sin if he is unaware that the latter will swear falsely, but, if aware, he commits a sin; an official, however, who requests from an individual an oath by order of the law commits no sin, whether the individual swears truthfully or falsely.

The intrinsic reason why perjury in a strict sense is always a mortal sin is that it contains the specific malice of contempt of God.

In the *Decretals,* as in the Roman law, perjury involved the consequences of infamy (X, III, q. 5, c. 9; X, II, 20, 34). Ecclesiastics guilty of perjury were deprived of all offices and benefices (X, III, 22, 9); in the case of laymen, forty days of fasting and seven years of public penance were imposed (C. 81, q. 1, c. 8). The Code of Canon Law deals with perjury in connection with a deposition, judicial testimony, and penal law.

One found guilty of lying in giving a deposition is to be punished with exclusion from legal ecclesiastical acts for a period established by the judge, in accordance with the circumstances. If, prior to his judicial deposition, he has taken an oath to tell the truth (*de veritate dicenda*), he incurs personal interdict if he is a lay person, or suspension if he is a cleric (Can. 1743, par. 3). The same rules are applied to the false depositions of witnesses (Can. 1755, par. 3). One guilty of perjury is considered an unreliable witness (Can. 1757, par. 2, n. 1). In such a case, he shall be excluded as soon as he shall have been so declared in court, without any special declaration of disability. He is also excluded from functioning as an expert (Can. 1795, par. 2). The crime of extrajudicial perjury is dealt with in Canon 2323. The penalty for such a crime is left to the prudent judgment of the Ordinary, who is to give the matter more serious consideration if a cleric is involved; this applies in both assertory or promissory perjury. *Vio.*

PERPLEXITY. *See* Conscience.

PERQUISITES. Contributions made for the proper maintenance of the clergy on the occasion of the celebration of sacred functions, in the issuance of certificates, dispensations, or other documents are called *perquisites*. They are considered *quasi-patrimonial* assets of the cleric.

In the Code of Canon Law, perquisites are offerings (Can. 736), or remunerations (Can. 463, par. 1). In view of the reference of both Canons to Canon 1507, par. 1, where the general term *tax* or *fee* is used, offerings and donations seem to mean the same. Can. 1410, instead, refers separately to remunerations, offerings, and stole fees (remunerations due to parish priests), which leads to the supposition that the legislator intended to make a distinction between these various terms.

A difference must be admitted between *offerings* and *remunerations* (stole fees resemble the latter). This difference is based principally on the purpose for which they are given. Offerings are entirely spontaneous, whereas remunerations are related to a specific function, performed in the interest of the faithful, and are in a sense protected by law. Therefore remunerations differ from offerings with respect to their binding force and the title of right. These include not only remunerations from generosity, but also those from quasi-contracts. Perquisites, strictly speaking, are remunerations and stolar fees.

Perquisites may be classified as follows: (a) *Chancery and records fees* for copies of records of parochial registers (Can. 470); documents concerning marriage by proxy (Can. 1089, par. 1); certificates of publications or banns announced (Canon 1029, par. 1). The Code prescribes the same formalities as in diocesan taxes: proposal and discussion in provincial councils and diocesan conferences, and approval of the Holy See (Canons 463, par. 1; 736 and 1057). (b) *Black stole fees* (so called because on these occasions the priest wears a black stole) are funeral fees for funeral services, according to diocesan regulations. Only the portion of the remuneration that goes to the parish priest (funeral fee) comes under the name of perquisites. The schedule of funeral fees must be drawn up by the Ordinary, according to a moderate scale (Canons 1234–1237). (c) *White stole fees* include remunerations ordinarily given or exacted for the administration of certain sacraments and sacramentals. The provincial council or diocesan conference shall determine such fees, with the approval of the Holy See (Canons 463, par. 1; 736, 1507).

Stole fees usually belong to the parish priest (pastor), although another priest may have performed the particular service (Can. 463, par. 3), unless otherwise stipulated by common or particular law. The parish priest is forbidden to exact more than the diocesan schedule allows; otherwise, he is bound to restitution (Canons 463, par. 2; 1235); he is also liable to canonical penalties (Can. 463, par. 3). Anything above and beyond the established fee may be accepted only if it is freely offered.

The parish priest shall administer sacraments and sacramentals gratuitously for those unable to pay for services (Canons 463, par. 4; 1235, par. 2). *Pal.*

PERSECUTION. There is no need to demonstrate that persecution is an evil. It is important to consider the behavior of a Christian in time of persecution and, above all, whether it is lawful for him to flee in face of persecution.

LAWFULNESS OF FLIGHT. By virtue of the precept to practice the faith, a Christian is forbidden to renounce the true faith in time of persecution, even by external simulation, whether explicit or implicit, if by words or actions in given circumstances this would practically amount to abjuration. In itself, however, the precept does not oblige a Christian simply to accept the dangers of persecution, offering himself to the persecutors, or passively awaiting his own fate. Contrary to the exaggerated views of Tertullian (*De fuga in persecutione*), the early Fathers, such as St. Athanasius (*Apologia de fuga sua*) taught the lawfulness of flight by pointing out the words and example of Jesus Christ Himself and of the Apostles (Matt. 10:23; 24:15–18; Luke 4:29; John 8:59; 11:54). But a distinction has always been made in this doctrine between the ordinary faithful and a pastor of souls. The former are free to flee from death or other impending dangers from persecution, even by *dissimulating* their faith, except if they are interrogated about their faith by lawful authority. The pastor of souls has the grave obligation to remain with his flock, if his presence is essential for the salvation of the souls committed to him, despite the necessity of exercising his office secretly, or if his flight would cause serious scandal: *"The good shepherd lays down his life for his sheep"* (John 10: 11–12). However, if such a need or scandal does not exist, a pastor of souls is free to flee, especially if his presence were to be useful in another place for his flock, the common welfare, or at the cessation of the persecution.

NECESSITY OF FLIGHT. It is an act of highest virtue, an heroic act, to face death or other torments for religious convictions. The obligation to protect one's own life, to avoid the danger of renouncing the faith, or to prevent the crimes of others, forbids, as a rash act, the spontaneous offering of self to the persecutors, except under the inspiration of the Holy Spirit for love of God and neighbor. One is not obliged to flee by positive efforts the dangers of persecution. Such an obligation would seem to exist only in cases of grave danger to one's perseverance in the faith or in the absolute necessity of saving a particular person for the welfare of the community. In actual practice, however, both cases allow room for serious doubts, because the grace of God can strengthen a Christian in facing persecution generously and without pride, and can also raise up other capable men who, confirmed by the example of others who have given their lives for the faith (*sanguis martyrum semen christianorum*), can produce an equal good for the Church. *See also* Faith; Profession of Faith. *Dam.*

PERSEVERANCE. *Perseverance*, in a broad sense, is the pursuit of an under-taking or endeavor until its completion. In a strict sense, it is the pursuit of a good despite annoyances which originate in some factors usually extraneous to the endeavor. St. Thomas, in his *Summa Theologica*, speaks of perseverance as the continued pursuit of a good until its completion, without permitting ourselves to be disturbed by the particular annoyances which arise from necessary, repetitious activity over a long period of time (II-II, q. 137, a. 3). This steadfastness, akin to fortitude, is of the greatest importance in the spiritual life.

One may sin against perseverance either by excess or by defect. One sins by defect in a faint-hearted failure to pursue a proper good or duty because of special annoyances or burdens. One sins by excess in pertinacity or stubbornness in pursuing an activity or desire that is unwise, harmful or unlawful.

Weakness of spirit and pertinacity are, of themselves, venial sins; but they can be grave sins if that which is omitted or pursued is grave, or because of other circumstances.

MEANS. In order not to yield to tiredness or discouragement in good, one should consider the shortness of life and the endless eternity of the reward that will crown our endeavors. Legitimate rest and moderate recreation are also useful in sustaining perseverance. Faced with apparent failure of our efforts, we must remember that God does not always demand that we be successful in our undertakings; often He is satisfied with our honest efforts.

FINAL PERSEVERANCE. Final perseverance is continuance in the state of grace until the end of life; this is a condition for one's eternal salvation. The Council of Trent calls this a great gift (*magnum donum*) and asserts that even a person living in grace must always have a salutary fear lest he lose this gift (Council of Trent, *Sess.* VI, c. 16, can. 2). Final perseverance is not an object of true merit (*de condigno*). The just, however, can deserve this great gift by congruous merit (*de congruo*): under this aspect, it may be said that final perseverance is an infallible object of the *prayer of peti-*

tion (q.v.). Finally, final perseverance is merited, not by one or more specific acts during a certain time, but by a series of good acts spread over one's entire life (F. Suarez, *De Gratia*, 12, 38, 14). *Man.*

PERSEVERANCE, FINAL. *See* Perseverance.

PERSON, HUMAN. The word *person* has many meanings. In Christian philosophical tradition it is defined as an individual substance of rational nature, or, more briefly, a rational individual.

It has great importance and value in the ethical order because free will is necessarily united to the rationality of the individual subject; hence the person is the only cause from which moral acts proceed and the center to which they are attributed and imputed.

The value of the human person also stems from its destiny, since man alone is destined to a transcendent and eternal end.

These considerations serve to clarify the relations between the individual person and society, for they demonstrate that in the ethical order, and especially from the standpoint of final end, the person has a definite priority or transcendence over society; thus, the conclusion that society is a means to the attainment of personal ends.

VIOLATIONS. Violations against the human person are violations of the moral law. These can be committed in many ways; the gravest are forced ignorance and slavery. The former, in oneself or in others, is a very grave sin because it attacks the very foundations of human personality and human life lived according to human principles. The latter is also grave, because a slave is prevented from exercising the very faculties that make him a person and is placed in the hands of a master as a beast of burden or as a material *thing*.

Other lesser violations are committed through exaggerated pressures of society upon the individual.

The tendency to suppress personal values under the pretext of social exigencies is favored today by pseudo-philosophical and pseudo-scientific theories included under the somewhat vague name of *sociologism*. These currents unite in agreement that the function of the human individual is purely social, and therefore inconceivable and non-existent apart from society. From society man gets his value, and in society he is completely absorbed. Christian philosophy stresses the substantial fundamental value of the human person and strongly opposes these enslaving doctrines.

JURIDICAL PERSON. The term *person* is used in the juridical field with a slightly different meaning. Jurists call *persons* those who are the subjects of rights, as such. Accordingly, a human individual, deprived of certain rights, is not a juridical person. The same term *person* is applied to societies, associations, and foundations, in the sense that certain rights are recognized for such groups of men or things as moral and legal persons or entities. *Gra.*

PERSON, JURIDICAL. *See* Person, Human.

PERSONALITY. In a broad biological sense, *personality* is a complex of somatic and psychological characteristics of the person. The somatic and psychological constitution of the individual, in turn, consists of *temperament*, a psychological gift strictly bound to somatic factors, and *character*, the synthesis of the psychic and moral acquired traits of the subject. These distinctions, useful for understanding, study and evaluation of an individual, have a scholastic foundation. Personality, a harmonious whole, is in reality indivisible; character itself is linked intimately to temperament and somatic constitution, which comprise its foundation and, in turn, distinguish character.

We might concern ourselves at this point with the psychological constitution that corresponds to the psychological personality with all its components. Somatic constitution of the individual is treated in the article "Constitution, Biotypical."

TEMPERAMENT. Temperament is a

complex of instinctive-impulsive tendencies, more or less unconscious, and endowed with elevated affective drives, which determine our spontaneous manner of being and acting, that is, our *nature*. These are the basis of habitual conduct and stem from a combination of hormones and the nervous system, the so-called dynamic elements of the organism. This combination is subject to heredity and to the influence of disease-generating factors which may have been particularly active in the course of the development of the individual.

Since the combinations of organic elements from which the temperamental tendencies stem admit of almost an infinite variety, temperaments, each one in its manifold shades, are typical of each individual. Furthermore, individual temperament undergoes very noticeable variations because of age and various physiological conditions, modifying the morphological, metabolic, and neuro-endocrine substratum from which the temperament develops.

CHARACTER. Character is definitely a psychic or, more properly, a moral property, which is gradually acquired through judgment, training, education, and experience. It equals the deliberate and active adaptation of the temperament to the requirements of social living and specific individual aims.

In other words, character stems from a harmonious function between hereditary-constitutional tendencies, consisting of organic factors prevalently of a neuro-hormonic nature, and the results of experience and education. Under certain aspects, character resembles habit.

CLASSIFICATION. Personality, in its current and precise meaning as a *psychic* or, better, a *moral* entity, is the resultant of congenital temperament and acquired character. Personality is synonymous with acquired character. The study of personality and the classification of its multiple subdivisions is called *characterology*.

Each individual has his own personality, which can be distinguished by habitual disposition and passions. These predominant sentiments, fostered by bio-logical causes or higher ideals, characterize lasting conduct and give significance and distinction to the individual personalities. Personalities have been classified in a variety of ways, generally on the basis of their fundamental psychological characteristics. For brevity's sake, we restrict ourselves to recalling the classification, given by Jung, of extrovert and introvert personalities.

INDISCRIMINATE TERMINOLOGY. In psychiatric language, the terms *constitution, temperament, character* and *personality* are used indiscriminately and indifferently to indicate the complexity of tendencies, sentiments, dispositions, and intellectual peculiarities which distinguish the mentality of various categories of psychopaths and constitute a typical background. From these areas individual morbid episodes will arise; from them a nosological individualization is obtained. Thus, we speak of an hysterical constitution and of an hysterical temperament; of a degenerate personality and of a degenerate character; of a psychasthenic character and of a psychasthenic temperament, and so on. Such indiscriminate terminology is, strictly speaking, inaccurate, but common to many authors.

Subject to broad variations, as ordinary observation indicates, a personality is considered normal if it appears sufficiently stable and harmonious. If, however, a personality manifests conspicuous anomalies and alterations, we are in the area of insanity, the aberration of personality in the psychic order.

Character, temperament, and personality have a noticeable influence on morality and, consequently, on the imputability of actions. In normal cases, one cannot speak accurately of a determining influence. Prescinding from the fact that character admits of correction and improvement by training and, therefore, from any question of responsibility *in causa* if these are neglected, impulses in normal individuals come under the control of the will antecedently or consequently. In judging the value of acts, in education, spiritual direction, pastoral practice, and daily living, one must always consider the habitual dispositions of character and temperament (*Summa Theol.*, I–II, q. 63, a. 1).

Various dispositions of character and temperament explain how the practice of one virtue is easily acquired and maintained by some individuals, but in others is very difficult. *See also* Person, Human. *Riz.*

PERSONALITY, PSYCHOPATHIC. *See* Psychopathy.

PERSUASION. *See* Hypnotism; Psychotherapy.

PERTINACITY. *See* Fortitude (virtues connected with), Perseverance.

PERVERSION, INSTINCTIVE. *See* Immorality, Constitutional.

PERVERSION, SEXUAL. With the exception of the symptomatic cases of mental illnesses, such as schizophrenia, profound deviations of the procreative instinct belong to an extensive group of psychoneuroses, hysteria, and psychasthenia. According to other scholars, such disturbances constitute a chapter of so-called constitutional moral imbecility (*see* Immorality, Constitutional). It is probable, without excluding the will as a factor, that at least the more serious and detestable forms of perversion stem from a pathological basis, perhaps of a phrenasthenic nature. Otherwise it is difficult to understand why sex perverts are more or less frequent offenders, or why an offense is neither preceded by any painful internal struggle nor followed by remorse, as in the obsessive impulses of true psychasthenics. Some scholars, particularly modern ones, have pointed to hormonic disorders as the basic causes of the predisposition to sexual perversions.

CLASSIFICATION AND CHARACTERISTICS. The types of sexual perversion are numerous, but are usually distinguished into two categories that are determined by the purpose of the object of the perversion.

The first category includes perversions which seek the normal object of sexual life, but in a way that is not the ordinary physiological or psychological relation. Among these types are numbered *scopophilia*, in which the individual experiences an abnormal sexual stimulation in the presence of nudity in the opposite sex; *exhibitionism*, in which nude exposure of one's own body stimulates sexual excitement from the fact that others are watching; *sadism*, in which satisfaction is attained through violence reaching, in extreme cases, murder by disembowelment or suffocation; *vampirism*, or cannibalism; *masochism*, in which the individual attains sexual satisfaction by being abused or treated violently.

Other forms of perversion are based on an abnormal relationship to various objects of the sexual sphere. Among these perversions, which are directed to objects that are abnormal, are: (a) *homosexuality*, in which one makes an individual of his own sex the object of eroticism (*sodomy*, between males; *pederastry*, between an adult and a child; *Lesbianism* or *Sapphism*, between females). Furthermore, homosexuals are considered to be either *active* or *passive* partners in eroticism; the degree of perversion is greater in passive males and in active females who are homosexuals. In these cases, an insufficient psycho-sexual differentiation of the subjects or hermaphrodite structures seem to be at the root of the disturbance. In its milder form, homosexuality is expressed by *tranvestitism* or *eronism*, that is, sexual pleasure in wearing clothes of the opposite sex. (b) *Fetishism*, consisting of sexual satisfaction through contact with the body or ornaments of a person of the opposite sex (the desire for the possession of a fetish object is generally of an obsessive nature, which can unloose unrestrainable impulses to steal that particular object). (c) *Bestiality*, in which the individual finds satisfaction in sexual relations with animals. (d) *Necrophilia*, in which sexual satisfaction is attained with corpses, which is the worst type of perversion and bears a certain relation to sadism.

SEXUAL HYPERESTHESIA. A group of psychosexual anomalies ought to be considered separately, despite the fact that they have some points in common with sexual perversion. These include *satyriasis* in man and *nymphomania* in woman. With the exception of the frequent symptomatic forms of a neurological or psychiatric nature, they are psychodegenerative conditions, which in the more advanced stages can cause excesses and frenzies, harmful to the sphere of conjugal life and dangerous to public morality.

MASTURBATION. Masturbation is a misuse rather than a perversion of the sexual instinct. If indulged in during the prepubescent and pubescent periods, this may become a possible cause of neuroses and impotency. It is a form of psychoneurosis, or even of mental derangement, as in phrenasthenics, schizophrenics, etc.). It may extend to normal marriage relations either by substituting or associating them to the latter. Sometimes masturbation is practiced by adults unable to have normal marriage relations (e.g., in jail or prison); in such cases, its psychopathological significance is non-existent. Under similar accidental circumstances, homosexuality and bestiality have a relatively minor morbid character.

TREATMENT. Concerning the psychological or religious treatment of all these diseases, including minor and socially less dangerous forms of psychoneurosis, the reader may consult the article on *chastity*. We may add here that, if psychotherapy alone does not prove successful, especially in deeply rooted disorders, this is due to the fact that their cure is difficult and unpredictable even from their medical aspect.

Despite this, surgical corrections and intensive therapeutic treatments often furnish good results and must be tried, provided that they do not conflict with the moral law. They should be tried also because of their suggestive influence and the possibility of associating with them psychotherapeutic treatments which could prove to be of even permanent benefit. In the field of opotherapy we should like to point out, in particular, *extracts of epiphysis*, since its anti-sexual effectiveness has been widely proved. In fact, these extracts are believed to exercise a conspicuous restraining action on the libido and psychosexuality, by decreasing the sexual hyperesthesias. But it is necessary to have recourse above all to spiritual remedies, such as prayer, frequent reception of the sacraments, mortification, and flight from the occasions of sin.

As a remedy against masturbation many suggest marriage. In some cases, it will be necessary to help certain individuals to conquer their aversion to marriage, for they wrongly consider themselves incapable.

At any rate, the physician shall not counsel sexual relations apart from marriage as a therapeutic means against sexual deviations; moreover, he must dissuade from marriage anyone whom he certainly knows to be homosexual.

It is morally wrong to advise masturbation, either directly or indirectly, regardless of the motive.

Contrary to the beliefs of the past, current opinions deem masturbation less harmful to health. However, it will be proper to insist on the necessity of preserving, and intensifying, the sense of moral guilt for mortal sin, rather than morbid incurable consequences. The same must be done with regard to other forms of sexual perversion which involve degrees of greater gravity and culpability.

MEDICO-LEGAL OBSERVATIONS. From the medico-legal point of view, perversion of the erotic instinct requires investigation in order to single out the symptomatic cases of real and proper (irresponsible) psychoses from mere expressions of sexual depravity, which are more or less punishable, according to the degree of obsessive impulsiveness that may have provoked the criminal action (exhibitionism, rape, pederasty, and the like). Instead of jail, these psycho-degenerates should be sent to psychiatric hospitals or other places to receive appropriate treatment and possible cure. By means of therapy, work, clean and honest habits of living, sustained by spiritual aids, they may improve to such an extent as to be no longer dangers to society. *Riz.*

PHARMACIST. The pharmaceutical profession is a handmaid of the medical profession. The pharmacist is the physician's collaborator in the preparation of medicines which are important to medical science and art. In ancient times, the pharmaceutical art was practiced by physicians or monks. In modern times, the work of the pharmacist is no less important, but performed mainly by chemists employed by large pharmaceutical houses, producers of patented medicines for pharmaceutical use.

A pharmacist must be well versed in his field so that he may competently prepare medicines. He must use care and diligence so as to avoid any error that could cause grave damage. He may not sell medicines which he knows are harmful to certain persons, nor give medicines other than those prescribed by the physician, unless he is certain that the substitute medicine is equally effective and equivalent in cost. He may not sell or suggest useless medicines, the only effect of which would be the seller's profit. He may not sell dangerous medicines without a doctor's prescription, nor medicines or other devices generally used for sinful purposes. He must keep professional secrecy in the same manner as doctors do. (See Deontology, pharmaceutical. *Ben*.

PHILANTHROPY. See Assistance (public and private).

PHOBIA. A *phobia* (Greek, *phobos*—fear) designates, in psychiatry, a form of illness or attitude of fixed or obsessive idea which represents a fear of some danger or a damage to be suffered, which is exaggerated in the mind of the sick person. The sick individual would like to be rid of these abnormal representations or unfounded, excessive fears, but is unable to do so. This failure irritates and depresses, as the tormenting idea assumes an ever-increasing proportion, which causes him to experience a state of painful anguish.

Phobias are almost innumerable, for they concern any aspect or event of daily life. The more common and important ones are dealt with under Psychasthenia (*q.v.*), a psychoneurosis in which these disturbances are often present. The moral aspects of this subject are also dealt with under the same entry. *Riz.*

PHOTOGRAPHER. A *photographer* is one who practices the art of photography, particularly for commercial purposes. Civil law considers photography one of the arts and grants to the photographer the protection of copyright. In some countries, a license from competent authority is required to practice photography as a trade.

The photographer may not publish or sell a person's picture without the express or tacit consent of the person and, after his death, of the person's heirs. The person who assents to publishing his picture may revoke this, although there remains a duty to indemnify all damages caused to the photographer. The photographer is allowed to publish a picture if it possesses scientific, didactic, or general cultural value, or concerns a fact or event of public interest. The scientific, didactic or cultural value of the portrait must be objective and not merely in the photographer's opinion.

MORALITY. It is improper to photograph, print, or exhibit pictures which offend modesty or morality. To do so is to be guilty of co-operation in evil and an incitement to corruption. For grave reasons, extremely rare, it may be permissible to photograph nudes. The publication or general distribution of such photographs is never permissible. The Catholic photographer must value the principles of morality and foster true nobleness and human dignity. *Tar.*

PHRENASTHENIA. The term, coined by Verga from two Greek words (*phren*—mind, and *astheneia*—feebleness), indicates an arrest or retardation of psychic development in an individual, caused by varied pathological disturbances in an infant's brain, before birth, during delivery, or at a later time.

Phrenasthenia is synonymous with *oligophrenia* (mental deficiency).

According to some authors, phrenasthenic or oligophrenic persons are divided into *idiots* and *imbeciles*. Idiots are individuals whose brain shows real and proper anatomical lesions; imbeciles, instead, are individuals who show no appreciable cerebral alterations, but an evolutive, congenital mental defect produced by causes escaping observation, usually of a hereditary-degenerative nature. According to the well-known De Sanctis classification, idiots may be affected by *cerebropathic phrenasthenia* or by a *biopathic phrenasthenia*.

Many scholars do not accept these distinctions based on anatomical-pathological grounds; these differentiate idiots from imbeciles only according to the seriousness of the symptoms of their psychic deficiency.

IDIOCY, IMBECILITY, MENTAL DEBILITY. *Idiocy* or cerebropathic phrenasthenia embraces the more severe morbid forms. It is generally found in persons with an advanced state of mental deficiency, who are unable to speak or learn, or who show conspicuous neuropathological symptoms, such as microcephaly, various types of paralysis, and the like. Clinically these indicate the existence of a serious cerebral infirmity. To the category of cerebropathic phrenasthetic individuals can be added those in whom the psychic development has been arrested, not because of an anatomical alteration of the brain, but because of a serious endocrine insufficiency, usually of a thyroidal origin; in this case, one may speak more properly of cretinism (*q.v.*).

Imbecility, usually identified with biopathic phrenasthenia, consists of a lesser psychic deficiency in individuals capable of learning and susceptible of education. Neurological alterations are few or altogether absent. Psychic anomalies in imbeciles concern the character and moral sense more than intelligence. A milder form of imbecility is *mental debility*. Individuals so affected, called simpletons or weak-minded, are defective in superior intellectual activities; they are rather silly, monotonous, credulous, and incapable of deep sentiments. In these, the elementary psychic activities are fully developed, and neither the ethical sphere nor their instincts present aberrations or notable deficiencies.

Mongolism belongs, in some respects, to phrenasthenia. It is a rather uncommon somato-psychic congenital anomaly characterized by a peculiar look, reminiscent of the Mongolian race, by a retarded development of the skeleton, and by an oligophrenic condition ranging from idiocy to imbecility. The disturbance is believed to originate in hypoplasia of the cerebral crust and in the endocrine glands.

RETARDED AND UNSTABLE PERSONS. In idiots, imbeciles, and feeble-minded people, the characteristics of an arrest of psychic development are visible in adult age; in others, a retardation of their mental evolution may sooner or later reach normalcy. These so-called retarded *persons* are ordinarily distinguished from the unstable, in whom retardation is found in the volitive-affective sphere. Thus, *unstable persons* are characterized by restlessness, variable temperament, lack of affectivity, hypobulia, selfishness; the *mentally retarded* are shallow, easily distracted, without logic, ideas, or imagination.

Scholastic achievement in children so disturbed is poor. In retarded children this is due to difficulty in learning, while in the unstable it is due to a great difficulty in adjusting to discipline.

MORAL AND PEDAGOGICAL CONSIDERATIONS. In the field of phrenasthenia, the most important moral problems concern the education of the patients, their social usefulness, and their penal responsibility.

The education of phrenasthenic persons is all the more important as one considers that it is, generally, the only method of cure for such patients. In fact, with the exception of cretins, who are not truly phrenasthenic patients, or those with hereditary lues, for which a specific treatment is still possible, all other cases—by far the greater number—can benefit from pedagogical treatments. These treatments, which require a minimum of active collaboration from the patient, are not applicable to patients with more pronounced idiocy; in so-called curable cases, the educational treatment, which is of necessity constant, long, and systematic, will aim at discovering first a few intellectual capacities in the deficient child on which to build. To have them participate in games, to fix their attenion on some particular things, to train their memory, to stimulate their imagination—all these activities increase their general psychic level. An intelligent mother could be an excellent instructor for a phrenasthenic child; but if shortage of time or lack of skill in the patient's relatives make such educational programs impossible, it is advisable to convince the family to entrust the patient to some appropriate institute, in which astonishing results are achieved. This occurs even with phrenasthenic patients who, because of ignorance in their own relatives, were neglected and left to themselves. Both social ability and penal responsibility are always diminished in phrenasthenic persons, or completely absent according to the degree of psychic deficiency. This must be carefully evaluated in each individual case by appropriate professional examination.

Concerning also the many and delicate questions that may arise in the field of Canon Law, with particular reference to the ability to contract marriage and cases of nullity due to force and fear, the judgment of the cases must always be based on a careful medical and legal examination of each individual patient.

In conclusion, it should be mentioned that the minor *phrenasthenic patients* (imbeciles, weak-minded and inconstant persons) contribute extensively to criminality, chiefly to juvenile delinquency. The imbecile's antisocial qualities, aggravated by a perverse environmental influence and the concurring action of alcohol and other toxic elements, often make him a docile and servile instrument of criminality. Hence, the importance of a religious and social education for these patients, otherwise destined to increase the ranks of thieves and prostitutes. *Riz.*

PHYSICIAN. The duty of a physician, noble and important, is directed to the attainment of a primary good in life,

namely, health and life. This activity is shared by every man insofar as he is responsible for the proper preservation and care of his own health; thus the work of a physician is an ordinary human necessity, human activity raised to the level of art and science through study and application. The work of a physician, like every human activity, is subject to the supreme law governing human life—that is, the moral law. A good physician, whether general practitioner or specialist, must observe the moral law, the commandments of God. A physician who understands the nature of his important office knows that the transgression of the moral law, whether by acts or counsel, is opposed to his duty. He knows that he acts as a good physician only if he strictly adheres to the norms of the moral law. A well-instructed Christian physician will not only observe the moral law but set an example by upright conduct to his colleagues. The words of Cicero apply to him as to every one else: "That which is not upright is not at all useful," or those of St. Thomas: "Nothing is forbidden by the law of God except that which is in conflict with our own good."

Every physician must be at the service of his patients, for every sick person has the right and duty to take good care of himself, which he does by seeking the knowledge and skill of a physician. For this reason, a physician has the consent of the patient for everything that he may do to him, in the ordinary treatment of a given illness, but not in the case of dangerous or costly treatments. Therefore, it is unlawful for a physician to use such treatments without the express consent of the patient or his parents, if the patient is a child, a minor, or mentally incompetent. He must explain the case in the best way possible. If it is impossible for the physician to obtain the proper consent because the patient is unconscious and the case is urgent, he may presume consent and do whatever he deems necessary to save or cure the patient. If an operation or other treatment is useful or necessary for the welfare of the patient which he refuses to agree to, the physician must desist from any action. It is the patient's right to take care of his own body. A physician's only concern is to help him with his science and skill but he has no right to force his patient to submit to his treatments.

OBLIGATIONS OF A PHYSICIAN. A physician has "the obligation not only to acquire a solid scientific culture but also to continue always to develop and integrate his professional knowledge and aptitude; it is a matter of strict moral duty, of an obligation that binds in conscience before God because it concerns an activity which is closely connected with the essential welfare of the individual and the community" (Pius XII, Address to Physicians, November 12, 1944).

A physician has the duty to cure entirely or at least partially, according to his ability. To this duty and, therefore, to the nature and dignity of the office of physician are opposed killing (see Abortion; Embryotomy; Euthanasia), abandonment of a patient to death (see Euthanasia, Negative), sterilization, or other mutilations not required for the general welfare of the individual. Neither the permission nor the command of the supreme authority of the State can make killing or mutilation by a physician lawful at any time. The sacred axiom *"It is necessary to obey God rather than men"* applies to the physician. A physician treats the man, not the sickness. He must have high regard for human life and values, especially supernatural values. "For this reason, it can never be lawful to sacrifice eternal welfare to any temporal goods, even the most precious ones" (Pius XII, *loc. cit.*).

Thus, a good physician will never give counsels contrary to the sixth commandment, which binds every man to be chaste and pure of heart and body. "Thus, the eighth commandment has equally its place in medical deontology. A falsehood is never permitted to anyone. Yet there are some cases in which a physician, even if queried, without saying a positively false thing, may withhold part of the truth, especially if he knows that

the sick person would not have the strength to bear it. But there are other cases in which he undoubtedly has the duty to speak clearly; a duty before which any other medical or humanitarian consideration must yield. It is unlawful to feed a sick person or his relatives vain hope, or an illusory security, thus endangering his eternal salvation or the fulfillment of obligations of justice and charity" (Pius XII, *loc. cit.*).

A serious duty of a physician is *professional secrecy (q.v.)*. This obligation involves the common good, and, therefore, is a strict one. But it is not in natural or Christian ethics *an absolute obligation. In fact, it would not be suitable to the common good, if that secret were to be put at the service of crime or fraud* (Pius XII, *loc. cit.*).

The profession of physician demands so much from a man who chooses it that it is often referred to as a vocation. In order to practice it well, many moral qualities are needed besides the general talents of knowledge and experience. These include: great charity and compassion, a lively Christian faith, and a deep respect for the Creator and for man, a favored creature of God. Holy Scripture, the Church, and mankind have words of blessing for a good physician, for he is held in high esteem. The Church also respects him as an honored collaborator of the priest. The true well-being of mankind cannot be furthered unless physicians of bodies and souls understand one another and collaborate together. Only a deeply religious physician can rise to the heights of his noble office. *Also see* Deontology, Medical. Ben.

PHYSIOGNOMY. See Graphology.

PHYSIOTECHNIQUE. *See* Psychotechnique.

PICKETING. *See* Sabotage; Strike.

PIETY. *Piety* is understood here as duty, respect, and loyalty towards family and country. In this specific sense, it is the moral virtue by which we render our parents and country the respect and love which is their due.

Piety is an essential part of justice. The *material* object of the virtue of piety consists of devotion and respect (*obsequium et cultus*). Devotion is centered upon the duties to be performed toward parents, relatives, and country in times of need; respect is the manifestation of esteem, gratitude, honor, and the like.

The *formal* object or motive of the virtue of piety is a recognition of the ties or links binding us to parents and country as principles of our existence. In fact, God, the supreme principle and conserver of life, uses creatures as secondary principles through which He communicates life to others and directs them to their own destiny. Now, as we render to God, the supreme principle of life, the honor due to Him through the virtue of religion (*q.v.*), so, through the virtue of piety, we render our parents and country the honor due to these areas of life.

The foundation of the virtue of piety, therefore, is the strict bond existing between those who are united by the same blood and live in the same country.

The object to which piety is directed, or the terminal object of the virtue of piety, are parents, country, and relatives. The act of piety (*obsequium et reverentia*) applies principally to parents as the proximate principle of our existence, but indirectly to other relatives. Parents, too, are required to practice the virtue of piety toward their children and, therefore, to perform acts of the same virtue (*obsequium et reverentia*), by providing worthy training, adequate support, suitable social position, and treatment as sons and not as servants.

Apart from the relations between parents and children, the bond of the virtue of piety is as strong as the relations of dependency. In fact, the basis of the virtue of piety is the common proximate origin or ancestry. The intimate union which exists between the subject and the virtue's object is a union, which assuredly admits of various degrees, but which does not exist except between individuals of the same family circle.

Piety toward kinsmen is different from *charity* towards one's neighbor. Piety honors parents as the sources of life and education, and others as participants in the same proximate bond of blood. Charity (*q.v.*) concerns a common bond of humanity, one of blood, but more remote. Piety toward country differs from *legal justice*, because the principal motive of justice is to provide for the welfare of the community by the observance of law, but the chief motive of piety is the good bestowed by country in human development and education.

The virtue of piety is enjoined by the fourth commandment (Exod. 20:12; Deut. 5:16; Eph. 6:2–3): "*Honor thy father and thy mother so that thou mayest be long in the land which the Lord thy God giveth thee.*" This commandment sets down the bases of the life of the family and society.

Family life is wholly an exchange or relation of rights and duties. Neither has the father only rights nor the children only duties. Fathers and children are subject to the most sacred laws of God, different according to diverse relationships but certainly interrelated.

(a) The first duty of parents is *to love their children*; the duties of supporting, protecting, and educating them flow from this. This love must be sound and prudent, not blind. It must look to the true and lasting welfare of the children, rather than to their immediate satisfaction. Consequently, it must seek first the welfare of their soul, subordinating or, if necessary, sacrificing all for this. Hence it is a grave sin for parents to hate their children or curse them by wishing grave evils upon them. To drive them from their homes without a grave reason or to love their children with extravagant affection, by granting them every request, or to yield to an unjustified bias or preference for some above others—these are frequent sins committed by parent toward children.

(b) The second duty of parents is *to provide for the physical welfare* of their children; this implies supervision, provision for their maintenance, advice and direction in the selection of their state in life. Supervision over the lives of the children seeks to prevent any injury to their health from the very first moment of conception. Thus, it is a grave sin for pregnant women to engage in activities which may be injurious to the child; it is a grave sin for husbands to demand that their wives engage in such activities, or to physically abuse them while in state of pregnancy. It is a grave sin for mothers to habitually ignore dangers to their children.

The obligation to provide for their children's maintenance includes not only feeding but clothing and lodging. Thus, it is a grave sin for parents to deny their children the necessities of life as long as they are unable to provide for themselves; to squander income in gambling, drinking, and the like; to compel their children to go begging or to live a hard life without necessity; to abandon them without a good reason in orphanages.

Direction and counsel of offspring in the election of a suitable state of life, which fits their talents, implies creating conditions favorable to the attainment of that end. Thus, it is gravely sinful if parents fail to use at least ordinary diligence in saving part of their income for their children. To neglect to help their children in learning a trade or occupation or to fail to assist them in marriage or entrance into the religious life would be sinful, depending on the circumstances. To force upon their children a certain state of life as a choice is a grave violation of parental duties, since this is a right which belongs to the free decision of the children.

(c) The third duty of parents is *to provide for a sound spiritual training* for their children. This grave duty, therefore, implies: (1) instructions for their children, particularly in religion, which must be given by the parents, or by suitable teachers, priests, religious, or other organizations. On this point, parents must see that their children are baptized and receive First Communion at an early age. They must send them to classes in Christian Doctrine, instruct them personally, or send them to schools suitably guided by Christian principles. (2) Good example is a doubly grave duty for par-

ents; to blaspheme or to perform indecent acts before their children or to fail to observe the precepts of the Church may be serious sins. Correction and punishment are also necessary duties for parents.

With due proportion, the same obligations are incumbent upon tutors with regard to their charges or any other person who acts in the place of the parents.

Brothers and sisters are bound by duties of fraternal love, to be expressed by extending help to one another, at least in cases of extreme or grave necessity.

A husband and wife are bound by the virtue of piety; certain duties of piety are common to both, and others belong to each individually. Their common duties are: *love,* which is of obligation and holy, since it is primarily a true union of souls; *cohabitation,* which implies a common table and bed under ordinary circumstances; *marital fidelity* in conjugal acts, which are the exclusive rights of each; a *reasonably good manner of living,* suited to their state in life; this is the primary duty of the husband but may be subordinately proper to the wife.

The obligations proper to the husband are: sound domestic *administration,* but not possession, because this is subject to different arrangements; upright financial and fair household *government.*

Obligations proper to the wife are: *respect* toward her husband; *obedience* to him in the management of the home; and proper *care* of the home.

The obligations which children have toward their parents are based on the fact that they cannot repay adequately the various benefits which they received from their parents. In view of the absence of perfect equality between them and the permanent state of dependency by children upon their parents, the virtue of piety differs from the virtue of justice.

Thus, children must have toward their parents: (a) *internal and external love;* for this reason, it is a grave sin for children to hate or show hatred toward their parents, privately or publicly, or to fail to assist them in their spiritual and material needs. (b) A *holy respect,* to be shown by words, and deeds; the gravity of failure in such a matter depends both on the act itself and on the circumstances. (c) *Obedience* in all lawful things, as long as they are subject to their authority (minor age); in practice, as long as they remain in the paternal home and receive their maintenance from their parents.

Concerning *the choice of their state in life*, the children *per se* are not obliged, except in extraordinary cases, to obey their parents under the virtue of piety toward them. They are expected to consult their parents concerning the person they wish to marry, but they are not bound to obey them. If it is a question of choice of the religious or the priestly state, they are not obliged to ask their parents' counsel; in fact, at times it may be advisable not to (Can. 542; *Summa Theol.*, II–II, q. 101, a. 4). With respect to the *choice of a profession*, the parents cannot impose their preference on the children, no matter how beneficial it may be for the latter to follow their parents' advice. Concerning the matter of hereditary relations between children and parents, *see* Children, Education, Food, Family, Father, Paternal Authority. On duties of piety toward country, *see* Country.

Since piety is a special virtue, its violation constitutes a special sin; however, the special malice is probably present only if the violation occurs between persons more closely related by blood ties (consanguinity in the direct line or in the first degree of the collateral line) and only for violations regarding persons and personal goods, not real goods (theft). Concerning other kinsmen and in-laws, the violation of the virtue of piety probably constitutes only an aggravating circumstance of the specific sin. *Pal.*

PIETY (Devotion). Piety, as devotion, involves the worship due to God, and comprises a recognition and a submission to Almighty God as the supreme source of all good and as our Father in Heaven. This worship must be interior and exterior; it involves praise, thanksgiving, petition, adoration of God, with

expressions of sincere sorrow for violations against His Will and the humble petition for pardon for sins. There is a duty to render to God private worship and to participate in activities of public worship by the Church.

This participation is accomplished by attendance at Holy Mass and other liturgical services, and by joining in the singing of hymns and the public recitation of prayers. Piety extends also to acts of veneration rendered to the saints. Concerning the gift of piety, *see* Gifts of the Holy Ghost.

We must be faithful to our practices of piety or devotion and endeavor to perform them with the greatest care and recollection, which their nature requires. Much care must also be used not to confuse genuine piety with a vague sentimentalism or a distracted recitation of a great number of long prayers. Among the more important acts of piety are: assistance at Holy Mass and reception of the sacraments, morning and evening prayers, visits to the Blessed Sacrament, frequent ejaculatory prayers, grace before and after meals, recitation of the rosary, devout practice of the Stations of the Cross, recitation of the Angelus, and, of course, mental prayer (*see* Meditation) and examination of conscience (*q.v.*).

The people's Missal (*see* Missal) and the Psalter (*see* Breviary) hold first place among devotional books; for mental prayer, the Holy Gospel and the *Imitation of Christ* are recommended. *Man.*

PILOT. *See* Medicine, Aviation.

PIRACY. Piracy (Greek, *peirates*—a pirate) is either an act or continued activity in robbing vessels at sea. A *corsair* engages in robbery of enemy ships with permission of the authority on which he depends, whereas the pirate robs all vessels. Piracy may be applied in a figurative sense to plundering or theft on land.

Piracy is very ancient (Thucydides, I, 4 ff.). Both the Greeks and the Romans fought hard battles against pirates. The barbarian invasions of the Roman Empire were preceded by many acts of piracy consummated on the boundaries of the Empire. Often the invaders were pirates rather than conquerors, e.g., the Normans. With the spreading of Islamism, the Arabs often gave themselves to piracy, particularly in the Mediterranean. Today, organized piracy has disappeared, except on the great rivers of China.

The principles applied to theft and robbery (*q.v.*) are valid for piracy. Piracy is in itself a grave sin; the matter may be absolutely or relatively grave, depending on the nature of goods plundered, the circumstances, and the victim. If an act of piracy were venial in itself, it could, by reason of circumstances, become grave matter, since it hinders a nation's trade, which increases prices of imported goods and indirectly affects a nation's exports. *Sir.*

PITUITARY GLAND. *See* Hypophysis.

PLACENTA. *See* Endocrinology.

PLACE, SACRED. In ancient times an area removed from common use and reserved for worship to God was called a *sacred place.* This is the etymological meaning of the Latin term *sacer;* thus, a place where religious rites were performed was called *Deo sacrum,* that is, set aside for or reserved to the divinity. Objects, persons, and places were consecrated to the various divinities, so that not only were the temples of the gods considered sacred, but also the forests, tombs, statues of heroes, and persons of kings, etc.

In Canon Law, the juridical term *sacred places* embraces areas set aside for divine worship or for the burial of the faithful; these places are dedicated by a special consecration or blessing (Can. 1154). In the above definition the four types of sacred places mentioned in the Code of Canon Law are: churches (*q.v.*), oratories (*q.v.*), altars (*q.v.*), and cemeteries (*q.v.*). In order that these places may be called essentially sacred and properly be dedicated to worship, authentic designation by ecclesiastical authority alone is competent and required. Furthermore, churches, oratories, cemeteries, and the like, no matter by

whom they were erected, are not sacred unless the Church authorities permit or recognize the consecration or blessing according to the liturgical rubrics (Can. 1154).

According to the canonical concept, a place is called *sacred* only by reason of a blessing or consecration. Sacred places are classified: (a) according to their use as places for divine worship, churches and oratories, or places for ecclesiastical burial; (b) according to the manner of their deputation, that is, consecrated places or simply blessed. Thus, altars are consecrated; churches and oratories are consecrated or blessed; cemeteries are blessed with a solemn or simple blessing. Sacred places are distinguished by their end (worship) and their constitution (consecration or blessing). Pious places are generally joined to ecclesiastical institutes, collegiate or non-collegiate. Pious places, instituted for the benefit of charity, education, welfare, and the like, such as monasteries, orphanages, seminaries, hospitals, etc., must be erected by ecclesiastical authority or with ecclesiastical approval.

The local Ordinary is the only minister in the *consecration* of sacred places, even if the place to be consecrated belongs to exempt religious (Can. 1155, par. 1), provided that the Ordinary has the episcopal rank. A vicar-general cannot consecrate places except by special mandate. A local Ordinary who is not a bishop can give permission for consecration to any bishop (Can. 1155, par. 2); without this permission the consecration by a bishop is valid but illicit (Cans. 1147, par. 3; 1157). Any priest may *bless* a sacred place, if he is delegated by the Ordinary of the territory in which the sacred place is located, if the place belongs to the secular clergy or to non-exempt religious, or by the major superior if the place belongs to exempt religious (Canon 1156). An authentic document shall attest to the fact of the consecration or blessing of a place, and a copy of the document shall be kept in the episcopal curia and in the archives of the respective church (Can. 1158). Nor is it permitted to repeat the blessing or consecration of a place if there is proof that it was done (one witness is sufficient; in case of doubt, it must be repeated *ad cautelam*) (Can. 1159).

JURIDICAL EFFECTS. Sacred places are exempt from the jurisdiction of the civil authority; only the legitimate ecclesiastical authority lawfully exercises jurisdiction over them (Can. 1160), not only by divine right, but also by the nature of the power of the Church, which alone has the right to legislate with regard to sacred things. This is true in certain countries where the churches are recognized as juridical persons. This, however, is not done in the U.S.A., because no official recognition endows a religious denomination with powers of its own, despite the climate of great freedom in which the Church carries on its mission, and the many privileges it enjoys.

Canon Law no longer speaks of the non-negotiability of sacred places, but, generally, they are considered to be non-negotiable in the sense that they cannot be disposed of except in special cases. They are not to be used for a different use than that for which they were established. Although they can be the object of private rights, that is, privately owned, they must always be used exclusively for worship, unless their sacred character is taken away from them because of desecration or profanation (*see* Churches, Cemeteries).

If sacred places are sold or exchanged, the fact that they are consecrated or blessed is of no consideration in estimating their value (Can. 1539, par. 1); this would constitute a crime of simony (Can. 728). In other words, not the place or object but its sacred character is absolutely unmarketable.

Sacred places must be held in high respect and veneration as befits divine worship; any indecorous behaviour in such places is forbidden. *Tar.*

PLAGIARISM. *Plagiarism* is a partial or total appropriation of another's literary, musical, artistic, cinematographic, or theatrical works. It is plagiarism to publish the manuscripts of another under one's own name against the author's will,

or to steal an inventor's secret and publicize it as one's own. It is also plagiarism to translate a book of another and publish this as one's own original work, or to appropriate definitions, or passages of a book and publish these as one's own material.

Plagiarism is theft; as such, it is a grave sin. If plagiarism is insignificant in extent or in scientific value, objectively speaking, it is not sinful or, at most, a venial sin. Subjectively one must consider the plagiarizer's intent and conscience.

Concerning the matter of authors' right over their own works (books, works of art, etc.), one must abide by local and international laws, which, generally, are not only based on the natural law but often interpret it by determining when plagiarism is committed. *See* Author (rights of). *Sir.*

PLAINTIFF (Petitioner). A person who institutes court action by entering a bill of complaint or legal claim to seek recognition of a right or redress for an injury is a *plaintiff*. The person against whom action is brought is the *defendant*.

Plaintiff and defendant in a trial come under the general heading of parties or litigants. While always retaining their initial and principal positions, plaintiff and defendant each assume the role of the other during the course of the trial. Thus, in raising exceptions, the defendant assumes the role of plaintiff, inasmuch as he is obliged to furnish proof in support of his exceptions. Moreover, if the defendant asks compensation or if, for other reasons, he advances a true and proper claim of his own (counter-claim) to reduce or nullify the plaintiff's claim, he then becomes plaintiff by counter-suit, while the plaintiff becomes defendant.

Among ancient jurists there was a tendency to proceed immediately to the examination of the positions of the plaintiff and the defendant and of their specific characteristics, without seeking to discover the elements common to both or proper to each, or the relations concerning a controverted substantial right.

But here and there one encounters jurists who note, perhaps deliberately, that the basic element in the concept of plaintiff is the fact of bringing action in one's own name. And today the science of judicial procedure has, through a slow elaboration, succeeded in giving that concept its own autonomy. The terms *plaintiff* and *defendant*, therefore, are not based on the nature of the matter in dispute, but on procedural relations; they are correlative terms, whose basic concepts mutually refer to each other (Can. 1646).

The factor that designates the plaintiff is a judicial claim after the bill of complaint has been accepted by the judge. The same bill defines the defendant, who is necessarily a passive subject, in a judicial relationship established by the litigants and the judge. It is not necessary that the action, brought by the plaintiff as set forth in the judicial petition have a concrete basis, or even that it relate directly to the plaintiff himself. This is evident in the sentence handed down. But the plaintiff and the defendant remain such even if the plaintiff is condemned or loses. The only requirement for determining the plaintiff in a case is that his bill of complaint be not rejected at the very outset (*in limine litis*). The substance of the matter taken up in the trial does not enter as a factor in the designation of the plaintiff.

PERSONAL REQUISITES. Though Canon Law recognizes for all a right to refer complaints to court, to formulate and present a judicial petition to a competent judge, and to defend it in the course of the trial, nevertheless a person must possess certain essential requisites before he can qualify as plaintiff in an ecclesiastical court. If these requisites are lacking, the person is disqualified (*non habet personam standi in judicio*); consequently, his petition is summarily dismissed or rejected. First of all, one must be a subject juridically competent to defend his petition before the tribunal; only a baptized person can be such a subject (Can. 87). Secondly, one must have the right to institute a court action; this right is not enjoyed by a non-Catho-

lic, an excommunicated person or, in cases of nullity of marriage, by the party who was the cause of the impediment. Thirdly, it is required that one be able to perform freely and expeditiously all the procedural acts required by a normal development of the trial, i.e., to set forth and defend his own rights and judicial claims in court. Some persons, because of age, impediment, or other circumstance, may be unable to defend their rights in court. Finally, the plaintiff must possess the right to execute personally the acts required.

In order to safeguard the proper administration of justice, Canon Law provides adequate and suitable measures in cases where persons are incapacitated or disqualified from acting as plaintiffs.

Obviously, civil law is much broader than canon law in its consideration of the roles of plaintiff and defendant, although certain restrictions and conditions obtain even in secular courts, e.g., the citizens of a foreign country may not act as plaintiffs at certain times and in certain circumstances.

In criminal cases, instead, the plaintiff is predetermined by law as the person of the *prosecuting attorney*. In ecclesiastical courts this role is fulfilled by the *promoter of justice*. But the legal mechanism of instituting and conducting the trial is analogous. In fact, a criminal trial may not begin until the promoter of justice (prosecutor) presents his allegations against the defendant or submits the charges to the judge. The promoter of justice, as a public agent assuming the position of party to a controversy, is at the same time committed to defend all public interests. It is his duty, for instance, to contest a marriage if the parties in it are unable to stand trial or in certain cases may not wish to avail themselves of their proper rights. And though the promoter of justice is a public official serving no private interest, he cannot be denied the right of being a party—that is, plaintiff—in a trial. *Pug.*

LICITNESS OF JUDICIAL ACTION. The exercise of Christian charity in its genuine sense implies that the essential rights and goods of human nature, such as life, a good name, property, etc., be fully respected and preserved. The function of the law established to safeguard the moral order cannot be different. Moreover, charity is *preservative* not only of the neighbor's essential rights, but also of the normal and ordinary goods inherent in the life of every free man. Wherefore, charity, even before justice, forbids all deception, fraud, violence, and the like and, at the same time, prescribes that one keep his word, satisfy his obligations, and so on.

As a natural reaction to the many possible infractions of the moral order, there exists in man a particular inclination to defend himself against all possible harm (*jus praeventionis*), against all actual harm (*jus defensionis*) and against all actual injury (*jus urgendae satisfactionis*). This defensive inclination in man is controlled by a special virtue, considered a potential element of justice, namely, vindicative punishment (*Summa Theol.*, II–II, q. 108). This virtue is proper not only to superiors, but also to subjects, although the latter, except on rare occasions (*see* Self-defense), may not exercise it except through the channels of competent authority.

RECOURSE TO AUTHORITY. In cases, therefore, of a controverted right, of compensation for damages sustained, or of reparation for a serious injury received, it is generally licit and sometimes necessary to turn to public authority. The Apostle Paul appealed to Caesar in order to free himself of the insidious charges of the Jews (Acts 25:11). Public tribunals are not only useful institutions, but necessary for a decisive settlement of disputes, for curbing criminals, and for the prevention of vengeance in the defense of particular rights. Wherefore, St. Paul in his letter to the Romans aptly and justly states that magistrates are an object of fear only to evil-doers, for magistrates, as ministers of God, do not carry the sword without reason (Rom. 13:3–4).

MODERATION OF DEFENSE. A true Christian, in protecting and defending his rights or in suing for recovery of damages, must absolutely refrain from all misrepresentation, calumny, willful deceit, and the like, and he must follow the dictates of Catholic morality, which prescribe that every defense be conducted in a charitable manner (*ut omnia in caritate fiant*). Wherefore, (a) recourse to public authority must not be made with vengeance, spite, or malice but in a spirit of justice and for a good reason. In despising and punishing the sinful act, love of neighbor must always prevail (*puniatur peccatum, diligatur proximus*—Eccl. 7:10; James 1:20; Ephes. 26); while seeking to remove error, the errant themselves are always to be loved (*interficite errores, diligite errantes*), as the Fathers were wont to say in their struggle against heretics. (b) Neither during nor following the trial should one nurse a spirit of malevolence, anger, or hatred against his adversary; but let enemies in court be friends outside (*quamvis inimici causae, amici tamen personae simus*).

Rules of Moderation. Human nature, by itself, finds it extremely difficult and arduous to moderate the sentiment of rebellion and revenge in the face of injury or wrong. Hence, reason, illumined by faith, steps in and states: Forgive and you shall be forgiven (*dimittite et dimittemini*—Luke 6:37; Matt. 5:44; Eccl. 28:3).

All this does not mean that one may not vindicate his own rights; on the contrary, sometimes there is an obligation to do so. But vindication of rights is to be carried out with prudence and moderation; the purpose must be always to pursue one's rights, not to attack a person. Consequently, if the disputed matter concerns something of small value, rather than expose oneself to the danger of offending against charity and mercy (Luke 23:34) and incur unreasonable expenses, one should be ready to forego his right to sue or prosecute. If for grave reasons one is compelled to defend his rights, one should guard against harboring hatred in his heart toward the adversary and against allowing passion to rule in the litigation. One should always be disposed to conclude a friendly settlement, if possible, and always be ready to forgive and forget. *Tar.*

PLANNED ECONOMY. *Planned economy* is an intermediate position between economic free trade (*q.v.*) and collectivistic or communistic economy. It is closer to free trade than to collectivism; it is intended to bring about gradually, but inevitably, a State-controlled economy.

Planned economy inevitably harms the freedom of work and the autonomy of the individual and leads to total socialization (*q.v.*).

It seems that a real medium between the two typical forms of economic life should be sought in a system other than free trade, where mistakes are corrected and deficiencies squared short of excessive interference by the State, which might destroy basic freedoms. *Pal.*

PLEASURE, DELIBERATE. Generically speaking, *deliberate pleasure* or *complacentia* is the feeling of pleasure or joy experienced in attaining and possessing a desired object. Moralists, however, usually restrict the term to delectation that accompanies the possession in the imagination or thought of a pleasurable object which is, in reality, absent.

A deliberate pleasure is morally good or evil, depending on the moral nature of its object. A deliberate evil pleasure is a sin of thought, whose specific malice depends on its object. A sin of thought may conceivably involve added malice in the circumstances surrounding the object. But this seldom happens, because rarely does the mind reproduce the concrete circumstances attending upon the object as it is in reality.

To avoid confusion in this matter, it is necessary to bear in mind that one may think of an object with widely different mental attitudes, each with a different degree of morality. Especially important is the distinction between a theoretical (scientific) and practical attitude. It is a theoretical consideration for a judge to dwell on the minute and gory details of a homicide, for a doctor to analyze the biological concomitant fac-

tors of the act, for a psychiatrist to study the psychic elements that occasioned it, for a moralist to consider the ethical nature of a specific form of pleasure. It is a practical attitude, instead, to reflect upon murdering an enemy, to experience the joy of revenge, or to reflect upon lewd thoughts and representations for the purpose of procuring a sexual excitation. In the scientific attitude, thinking of an evil object may be lawful and good; in the practical attitude, it is something immoral in itself and constitutes deliberate pleasure in evil. The gravity of the sinful pleasure or sinful thought is measured not only by the object, but also by the usual subjective factors of advertence and consent. *See* Thought, sins of. *Gra.*

PLUTOCRACY. *See* Capitalism.

POISON. *Poison* is any substance introduced into the organism to produce illness and eventually even death by a chemical or biochemical process.

The biological action exerted by the poisonous substance can be the result of particular conditions which may cause a substance to assume poisonous properties. Such conditions may be caused by the substance itself, in its chemical composition, dosage, physical properties, methods of administration, etc., or by the organism to which it is administered due to age, sex, race, physiological or pathological state, reaction to administration, idiosyncrasies, habits, responses, etc. The behavior of the substance in the organism, through absorption, diffusion and elimination, and the presence of other substances with synergistic or antagonistic properties, as well as climatological and environmental factors may affect the person. The distinctions between poison and drugs cannot be shown with exactness; nor can a distinction also be drawn between poisons and food. This is of extreme importance in the field of forensic toxicology.

Poisons are classified according to various criteria. We shall point out the more important classifications:

(a) *Chemical classification.* According

to their chemical constitution, poisons are *inorganic* (metals and metalloids) and *organic* (hydrocarbons, alcohols, ethers, aldehyde, keton, phenol, acid, alkaloid, etc.).

(b) *Biochemical classification.* Based on the chemical action that the poison exerts on the whole organism or on individual organs, we have *general* poisons (oxidizers, reducers, catalytics, substituents, etc.) and *specific* poisons (organic bases, glucosides, vegetable proteins, and animal proteins).

(c) *Physiological classification.* According to the organ on which they exert their action and in conformity with their manifestation, poisons may be *irritant* and *corrosive* if they destroy more or less deeply the teguments by simple contact, even before they are absorbed (strong acids, poison gas, etc.); *hematic* if they act on the blood, subdivided on a basis of the blood elements affected and the different methods of attack; thus, snake poison causes the emission of hemoglobin from the red globules, or carbon oxide chemically changes the hemoglobin itself, etc.; *cardiac* (phosphor, nicotine, etc.); *blood poisons* (atropine or adrenalines); *nervous poisons* (chloroform, morphine and barbiturates that affect the brain; lead, cocaine and curare that act on the peripheral nervous system); *muscular* (quinine, veratrine, etc.); *gastrointestinal* (ipecacuanha, cobalt and nickel salts, etc.); *hepatic* (arsenic, alcohol, etc.); *broncho-pulmonary* (chloric acid, iodines, etc.).

More than the pharmacological study of poisons, the biological methods of poisoning, and the medical means of combating these, we deem it proper to review in this article, in a quick and cursory way, poisons frequently used in cases of murder and suicide. First of all, we shall note that "the nature of such poisons varies in different countries and times, according to the natural potential of raw materials, industrial development, and collective suggestions which cause psychic contagions comparable to fashion" (Mameli).

In Europe, after the year 1850, poisonous substances more commonly employed were: copper and lead salts, poisonous herbs, strong acids, especially arsenic, which in France is first among poisonous agents. With the development of the match industry and the use of white phosphor, poisonings were carried out with this new substance for the next fifty years. Toward the end of the nineteenth century, poisonings by phosphor ceased almost entirely, due to legislative provisions which forbade use of this in industry. Meanwhile, with the increased use of gas light in the home, the number of poisonings by carbon oxide (present in the composition of gas at the rate of five to ten percent) also increased. This form of poisoning was in previous vogue because of its easy preparation by incomplete combustion of carbon or other organic material. Carbon oxide has almost always been used for suicidal purposes; in fact, at the end of the last century, poisonings by this means represented about twenty-five per cent of all cases of suicide. This kind of poisoning is still quite common. Corrosive sublimates appeared in the statistics in the second half of the nineteenth century, as one of the more frequently used poisons. Their use has decreased consistently, since they are no longer, as at one time, within the reach of all. In the late decades of the nineteenth century, the employment for suicidal purposes of phenol, potassium permanganate, tincture of iodine and other antiseptics became widespread. After the First World War, with the great increase of narcotic intoxications (*see* Narcotics), poisonings by hypnotic drugs, especially barbiturates, also increased. This form of poisoning still prevails.

Of the two means frequently used for suicidal purposes, men prefer firearms, women, poison; this preference is also found in committing murders. Presumably, a woman chooses poison because of an instinctive horror of firearms and the difficulty of obtaining and learning to use these. Psychological characteristics in the female sex seem to eliminate violence as a means of committing murder or suicide.

FORENSIC TOXICOLOGY. Medical and

legal verification of poisonings are required every time that the judicial authority suspects that a death may have been caused either accidentally or intentionally by poison. These are based on the following *criteria of judgment*: (a) *clinical*, concerning the symptomatology shown by the individual; (b) *necroscopic*, based on the reports following autopsy; (c) *chemical*, involving an appraisal of the quantitative and qualitative results of toxicological analysis made on the viscera; (d) *physiotoxic*, based on the effect produced by the substance in question, by visceral extracts or suspected liquids, by experiment on animals particularly and characteristically sensitive to the poisonous substance in question.

Verification of the poisoning, ticklish and difficult for the reasons indicated at the beginning of the article, must be based not so much on one or the other of the above-mentioned criteria but on all of them, also taking into account all contingent specific information relative to the circumstances in the case. This represents an additional criterion, or an *anthropologico-environmental* criterion.

The means used to carry out suicide or homicide has no great significance in the ethical field; it can be, at most, an aggravating circumstance. But it does have great relevance in the criminal field. In crimes of murder or injuries, modern penal codes consider the use of poisonous substances as an aggravating circumstance from the standpoint of the malice of the means employed. The provision is fair and perfectly understandable if one considers the moral difference between a crime perpetrated suddenly, as a result of anger, and poisoning, which is almost always the result of evil plans, plotted undercover, with astuteness, perseverance, and malicious intent.

Usually, in crimes committed by the use of poisons, there are also other aggravating circumstances that must be considered, such as "committing the crime with abuse . . . of domestic relations." These include not only poisoning in a family, but even the killing of priests by injecting arsenic or other poisons into the bread and wine used for the Eucharistic Sacrifice. In the latter case, from the canonical point of view, the crime of sacrilege exists in the abuse of the matter of the Eucharistic Sacrifice, and, if the poisonous substance surpasses one third of the bread and wine, in the invalidity of the Eucharistic Sacrifice. In addition, one may also incur the specific penalties provided against sacrileges. (*See* Sacrilege.)

MORAL NOTES. To poison an animal is not sinful, if one observes the general rules concerning the treatment of animals (*see* Maltreatment of Animals, Vivisection). To take or give to another a poison for purposes other than treatment is a grave sin against the fifth commandment (*see* Narcotics). This may be venial if, because of a slight dosage, the damage to the person is slight. Those who produce, sell, or distribute poisons must use extreme diligence in retaining these in their custody, that no mistaken use or mishap might result in serious harm to another. It must be easily identifiable by clear and distinct labelling, and kept out of the reach of young children. Pharmacists or others must use circumspection, diligence, and responsibility in observing rigorously the laws aimed at lessening the dangers connected with poison. *Riz.*

POLARITY, AFFECTIVE. *See* Affectivity.

POLEMICS. *Polemics* (Greek, *polemikon*—warlike) refers to an oral or written disputation or debate in the defense of a specific opinion. In a stricter, historical meaning, *polemics* is a scientific disputation (*q.v.*) about a religious truth; later, it was called *controversy*. In fact, the term *polemicist* was applied first of all to the Fathers and theologians of the Church; only later was it extended to scientists, literary men, and politicians in their respective fields. Following Christianity's triumph over paganism, the Church Fathers relinquished the apologetic tone and engaged in polemics against unbelievers and heretics, seeking the most suitable method of defending

Christianity, while opposing its adversaries at the same time. For this reason polemics became a science, foremost among theological sciences.

Polemics is a difficult art, for a polemicist must use weapons that could be dangerous to his own cause and unwittingly aid the cause of his adversary. Polemics may readily degenerate into *diatribe*, if the debater goes beyond proper limits in defending truth or revealing falsehood, or if he employs a violent and vulgar tone. One wishing to engage in polemics must have the following requisites: (a) a true and profound scientific knowledge of the subject; (b) a sustained eloquence, certainly lively and keen, but without useless flattery or cajoling; (c) elevated sentiments and serenity of mind; (d) care not to offend against charity, mindful that one may condemn error but not the errant. Truth, facts, and conciseness are the best rules for polemics, when joined with a charity that conquers all hearts.

Catholics are forbidden to engage in public disputations or polemics with non-Catholics without permission of the Holy See or, in urgent cases, of the local Ordinary (Can. 1325). *Tar.*

POLICE. *See* Officer; Officer, Military.

POLICY. *See* Insurance, Private.

POLIOMYELITIS. *See* Paralysis, Infantile.

POLITICAL PARTY. Political parties were known in ancient Athens and Rome; the Middle Ages had Guelphs and Ghibellines, Whites and Blacks; Dante immortalized the image of a *party man* in the person of Farinata degli Uberti.

What is of greater interest today is the new notion of *party* as the driving force and basis for the organic development of political life. It goes beyond the traditional notion of a force serving particular interests, with a veneer of idealism. According to an older concept, a party works to bring about the triumph of its own interests through the destruction of the opposition party. The result is an assertion of power that is harmful to the common good (*q.v.*), since it favors only one group of citizens. This in turn leads to a justifiable reaction on the part of the others and to a continual state of veiled or open civil war. History shows this tendency of parties to forget the obligation to place the *common good* above their own particular interests. The new notion of political party, instead, is based on the recognition of a higher good and the party's readiness to sacrifice its own lust for power for the good of the nation. The welfare of the nation alone is the goal of political activity in all its citizens; in respect to the nation, parties are simply instruments to be employed only if and when useful for promoting the welfare of the greater number of citizens in accordance with the times and circumstances.

This new concept developed gradually from the constitutional and parliamentary life of England. Here, from ancient times, political liberties were conceived as a system of checks and balances in the observance of agreements entered into, and in the exercise of power by those who were considered its depositaries. This gave rise to the *Magna Charta*, which regulated the relationships between the King, the large land-owners (Lords), and the cities with their small land-owners (Commons). In the Houses convened by the King, there was free discussion and free voting; one of their principal aims was to defend their right not be to taxed without consent. With the passage of time, the importance of these Houses, especially Commons, grew. As their meetings became more regular, their functions and discussions extended to a larger variety of fields; parties began to form as groups representing different currents of interests. But even then, relations between the parties were governed by the traditional principle of checks and balances, as a basis for their self-preservation. This control was exercised in the name of a higher good that all parties recognized, i.e., the good of the State, represented physically in the person of the King. The party that gained ascendancy accepted the criticism of another party in all public discussions as a kind of stimulus and a contribution. The minority group came to be called *His Majesty's opposition.* In this way, the opposition became an integral part of the whole system of government, not simply by virtue of parliamentary custom, but, more recently, as a *real* right, enjoying the legal benefit of electing an official head of the opposition with a salary equal to that of a minister.

The history of political parties in the democracies of the continent from the time of the French Revolution is not as edifying. It witnessed parties of the right and of the left; dictatorial parties, intolerant of opposition and ruthless in the elimination of all other parties; and finally, the rise, on the ruins of the dictatorships, of a host of parties representing nearly every shade of political ideas and beliefs, and hindering rather than promoting the common good.

A basic element in any party ought to be not only an ideal program, but a disposition to cooperate with the party in power or other parties in the normal juridical functions of government, and a willingness to subordinate its own advantages to the common good of the nation. The so-called political opposition should not deflect from the principle of a basic cooperation with the party in power, despite any difference about the means to be used in the attainment of the common good. Criticism can be sharp and opposition pointed, but never to the point that the normal functioning of government and the regular activity of the executive branch are totally crippled. A party or member of a party who opposes a just law that is helpful to the community, simply because of fear that the party in power will also benefit in popularity and prestige, acts as an enemy of the common good. This contradicts the very reason for the existence of a plurality of parties, which is the contribution which they can make to the common good through criticism and public discussion. The *concordia discors* of an assembly that is truly free can bring great benefits to society; but this can only come about if each party has as keen a sense of respect and esteem for the liberty of others as it has for its own.

A sincere love for the common good as the supreme end and a sincere love for liberty as the means to attain this end are indispensable for the coexistence of parties in a free society and for their effective cooperation in promoting the common good of all citizens. *Boz.*

POLITICS. The term *politics* has a long history and evolution. The Greeks applied it to the city-state. When more complex political bodies were established, consisting of several cities and provinces, the term *politics* was used to indicate this higher body, although it retained its primary relation to the public affairs of an individual city. Subsequently, politics went beyond the limits of the State and came to indicate mutual collaboration between States, i.e., international politics. This evolution was natural and logical, because, with the expansion by the citizens, the welfare of a State came to depend largely on interstate relations. Today, the project of a world federation, or at least of a federated Europe (*see* UN), is fostered in many quarters.

Politics may be *local, national,* and *international.* From the standpoint of its subject matter, politics may be *internal, foreign, cultural, economic, social,* etc. All are interlaced, subdivided, and interdependent; thus, economic politics may be *financial, commercial, industrial, agricultural,* etc.

Politics may be generally defined as *activity revolving around public affairs concerning all the citizens of a community;* it is the *res publica* seeking the achievement of its aims. In this sense one can also speak of Church politics or ecclesiastical organs handling the public affairs of the Church.

Finally, *politics,* referred to daily life, indicates a certain method of behavior, a method of acting with discretion, shrewdness, with a view to the attainment of a specific end.

Politics may be divided into *political action* or practical politics, i.e., the art of government, and the *science of govern-*

ment. That which is personal in political art becomes objective in political science, although this distinction is not accepted by all. Political art does not necessarily presuppose politics as a science, but it is rather a gift of nature, which is all the more effective if accompanied by political science.

POLITICS AS SCIENCE. This includes primarily everything connected with the State. The scientific limits of politics in a strict sense are not the same for all authors. Political science must supply the norms of political activity; but even these rules are subject to morality, because morality extends beyond politics. Different solutions to political problems may be equally acceptable from the standpoint of the moral law.

The law of the State contains the juridical norms by which duties, obligations, and privileges are established for all members of the State, in their mutual relations. International law comprises the norms that regulate the relations between the States, whether these norms are derived from general ethical and juridical principles or acquire their value on the basis of expressed or silent mutual agreements between States. The difference is obvious. The science of both national and international law, however, is always bound to principles and truths recognized by reason and positive regulations. Its task is to draw, in a logical and systematic way, consequences from principles. Politics, on the contrary, does not deal with a permanently established fact but with changeable ends and means based on certain conditions. The ends vary in a double sense; first, because the content of the tasks changes as a result of historical evolution and cultural progress; secondly, because the circumstances vary. Therefore, *politics* could be defined as the science in which full and systematic consideration is given to the various points of view in the choice of the means by which, at a given moment, the ends of the State can be realized in the best possible way (Seipel).

PRACTICAL POLITICS. Politics in its practical application, the art of government, consists in the selection of the methods for the concrete realization of the ends of the State. It includes the task of maintaining the independence of the nation, and preserving certain institutions created by the historical evolution of the nation itself. Methods vary according to the forms of government: monarchy, republic, democracy, dictatorship, etc. The essential end of the State, however, is the common welfare (*q.v.*). In fact, society is a unit of order, and the common good is the aim of the order. Thus, the end of society is the lasting fulfillment of the common good (Pius XII).

The means to the end vary according to the progress of the people in their social, economic, and cultural life, and according to the degree of development of the juridical order. At one time, it may be necessary to strengthen authority; at another, the freedom of the individual may need greater protection; at another, it may be necessary to aid the needy, etc.

Contrary to the theories advocated at the time when liberalism ruled supreme, politics today must pay close attention to the welfare of society. The State cannot exhaust its role in the *juridical State*, but, if necessary, it must pursue a social, agricultural, financial, and democratic program, directed to greater social security for its citizens, aid to education, and, wherever needed, land distribution.

POLITICS AND MORALS. The State is the defender of law and promoter of order; but law and order have their roots in the moral law. Thus, the State is based on the moral order. Political actions are concrete human actions and, as such, cannot be morally indifferent.

The State is to perfect the human person, not vice versa. First comes man's virtue, then the power of the State. Unfortunately, compromise between politics and morals is often found in practice. Politics is constantly endeavoring to be a law unto itself, readily disclaiming all ties with ethics and religion, although quick to resort to these whenever it is found expedient for the attainment of its ends (*see* Machiavellism). Anything is permitted if it is to strengthen the power of the State, despite the fact that the power of the State is only a condition for the attainment of the ends of the State. This destructive concept looks at everyone and everything from the political aspect, excludes every consideration of ethics. However, it is the function of ethics to define what social justice is, leaving to politics the determination and realization of concrete forms of justice. In State constitutions, no form of government is of itself unjust if it is based on the principles of justice and the common good. But it is a violation of justice to seek to introduce or preserve a bad constitution, for such policy is contrary to the end of the State.

Efforts made by political parties to acquire a more dominating influence for the sake of correcting or radically eliminating existing conditions, that are controversial by nature, are permitted only if the aim is not to promote exclusively the interests of the party itself and immoral methods are not used. Objectives in government cannot be opposed to the moral law, for a double standard of morality must not exist, one for private life and another for public life. No State can justify crime. Certain conditions, however, must be considered from a different point of view: the interest of the community and the private citizen. A private citizen may condone the violation of one of his rights, but the head of a State must not. *Per.*

POLLUTION. See Onanism.

POLYANDRY. *Polyandry* is a social and civil relationship in which a woman possesses more than one husband at the same time. Polyandry is absolutely contrary to the divine positive law on marital unity and to the natural law itself, since it frustrates the primary end of marriage: the procreation and education of offspring. It also is opposed to the secondary ends of marriage: mutual assistance and peaceful cohabitation of a couple.

Polyandry was never permitted nor tolerated either throughout the period of the Old Testament or among the pagan peoples of ancient times, even among those who widely condoned prostitution.

SUCCESSIVE POLYANDRY. Polyandry properly so-called implies two or more husbands at the same time. Some writers speak of successive polyandry, which amounts to the second marriage of a woman after the death of the first husband. The lawfulness of second marriage is expressly recognized by the Holy Scriptures (I Cor. 7:39; Rom. 7:2–3) and by the doctrine and tradition of the Church (*see* Marriage). But attempted marriage of a woman after civil divorce can rightfully be considered as a form of polyandry. *Bar.*

POLYGAMY. *Polygamy* is a social and civil relationship in which a man retains more than one wife at the same time. It is contrary to divine positive law governing the marriage union (Gen. 2:24; Eph. 5:31; Can. 1013, par. 2). It is not in an absolute sense contrary to the natural law, for it does not hinder the procreation of offspring, although it impedes the attainment of the secondary ends of marriage, especially mutual aid between the married couple, by lowering the dignity of woman.

In the Old Testament, God tolerated polygamy for a certain time, as it appears from the examples of Abraham, Jacob, David, and other eminent men of the Old Law whom Holy Scripture does not reproach. Frequently, the Mosaic Law presupposed a plurality of women, as in the prescription concerning the distribution of inheritance among the children of two wives (Deut. 21:15). Nor does the fact that sometimes in the Holy Scriptures the second wife is called a concubine constitute a real difficulty, for at other times she is called wife (Gen. 16:3).

It is a disputed question among exegetes and theologians as to when this dispensation was given by God. Evidence seems to favor the period after the Flood (Gen. 16:2), when mankind became so reduced in number by the punishment that it required rapid propagation. (The words of Gen. 21:12 could be construed as implying a concession by God.)

It seems probable that this concession by God was extended to other peoples outside the Hebrew race. But with the proclamation of the New Law, the concession, almost wrested from God by reason of the moral obtuseness of man, was revoked, and marriage was restored to its original unity. The language of Christ in this sense is very explicit (Matt. 19:3–9; Mark 10:1–12; Luke 16:18). Tradition and the practice of the Church agree with it, especially against deviations of Protestants (Council of Trent, *Sess.* XXIV, *Can.* 2).

POLYGAMY AND MODERN CIVIL CODES. Monogamy is an accepted principle in the civil codes of the more progressive nations, although the liberality with which divorce is granted in several of those countries amounts to a form of successive polygamy. *Bar.*

PONTIFF, SUPREME. The government of the Church is monarchical and absolute. The will of the monarch is limited by the divine natural or positive law and, in a certain sense, is moderated by the presence of bishops who, as successors of the Apostles, are of divine institution. The bishops, of course, are dependent on the Roman pontiff, from whom, according to present organization, they also receive the personal and territorial extent of their powers.

According to Catholic doctrine, the pope is the supreme head of the Church, a sovereign in the spiritual, political, and temporal sense. In the positive aspect, his sovereignty implies the right of authority over his subjects; from a negative aspect, it implies absolute independence from other human powers in the same order. A territorial criterion is not necessarily included in the concept of sovereignty, and it is rather a limitation of its exercise. The pope, personally, as head, prince, representative, and organ of the activities of the Catholic Church, possesses a spiritual and political sovereignty, apart from his qualification as head of the State of Vatican City. His spiritual primacy is not simply a primacy of honor, as a requirement for the unity of the Church or a concession from the bishops, much less from the Catholic States, but it is an active and factual primacy of real jurisdiction, directly derived from God, according to the definition of the First Vatican Council (Can. 218). Naturally, it participates in the nature of the society over which he presides; therefore, the pope is first of all, and in a proper sense, spiritual sovereign of the Church.

From his spiritual sovereignty there flows, of necessity, a political (governing) sovereignty, based on the fact that, since the Church is a juridically perfect society and, therefore, a member of the international society, its head must also be a sovereign in the international and political sense. Finally, as head of the Vatican City State, the pope is also a sovereign in a temporal sense.

ATTRIBUTES OF PAPAL SOVEREIGNTY. The Roman pontiff exercises the prerogatives proper to sovereignty by internal government, in which, through the bishops, papal legates, metropolitans, ordinaries of mission territories, and direct contacts, he is in constant touch with the faithful, and by external relations and contacts with the political and international world through the rights of active and passive membership through envoys. This does not imply a strict obligation of reciprocity; if a State sends diplomatic representatives to another State, it does not necessarily follow that the latter must, in turn, send a diplomatic representative to the former with corresponding rank. In the ecclesiastical organization, internal legates are distinguished from external ones. Nobody has the right to impede the pope from sending his own representative or apostolic delegate (*q.v.*) to the bishops and faithful within the Church. The apostolic delegate has no diplomatic or political character. In missions to courts or governments, the papal envoys follow the usual norms of political envoys.

As a prerogative of sovereignty, the pope has the right of personal immunity by which he is responsible only to God for his own acts of government. He can be held accountable neither to the Church nor to any State. In religious and political matters, the pope is the judge and ultimate defender of public morality.

Another prerogative of the pope's sovereignty is his dominion over ecclesiastical property: an eminent domain of jurisdiction flowing from public right, by which he can, for reasons of public benefit, make appropriate laws, fix taxes and duties, expropriate and confiscate ecclesiastical property and determine the methods and norms of administration. Finally, the pope is entitled to the honorary rights of sovereignty, a flag, external signs of honor and reverence, precedence, and the like.

IMPEDIMENTS TO THE EXERCISE OF PAPAL SOVEREIGNTY. Of course, the theories of the so-called *regio exsequatur*, among others, are in irreducible opposition to papal freedom and sovereign rights. Based on an exaggerated jurisdictionalism, they restrict the free communication of the pope with the bishops and the Christian people and reduce to nought his sovereignty and independence. The theory of appeal *ab abusu*, with the absurd pretention of checking papal activity for the protection of its subjects, is an evidently unjust intrusion by the civil State. It is a juridical absurdity, for it goes from the lower to the higher order, ignoring the diversity of realms in which the two authorities move and act.

The effective temporal sovereignty of the pope prompts us to make a brief reference to the now settled Roman Question. This question arose on September 20, 1870, with an attack upon the small Papal State and an ensuing occupation of Rome by Italian troops. The sectarianism of the time pretended to have settled the dispute by means of the plebiscite of October 2, 1870, and the *Legge delle Guarentigie* (Law of Guarantees). Evidently a one-sided solution could not settle the question; in fact, the Holy See continued to protest that only an independent territory could offer a sufficient guarantee to its effective independence and freedom. The pope continued to exercise in a restricted measure his sovereign powers in the piece of territory that had not been occupied. He always maintained a small nucleus of armed men and exercised from time to time sovereign judiciary powers even in non-ecclesiastical things. He legislated as a sovereign and maintained diplomatic relations with other nations outside and beyond any control. Through much discussion of the subject, the notion developed according to which the temporal State was no longer considered an essential element of papal sovereignty, although it was regarded as one of the means established by Providence for the protection of an effective, personal, visible, tangible sovereignty of the pope. Thus, on February 11, 1929, the question was solved by the conclusion of the Lateran Pact and the establishment of the Vatican City State.

PAPAL PRIMACY AND ITS EXERCISE. The spiritual sovereignty of the pope is a logical and natural consequence of his primacy in the spiritual order, a primacy not only of honor but of supreme and full jurisdiction over all the Church, in matters concerning faith and morals, discipline, and the government of the Church. As vicar of Christ on earth and successor of St. Peter, the pope is the high priest, the supreme doctor, whose duty it is to direct all the work of world evangelization, the legislator and judge of all Christians, and the supreme defender of their rights. He reserves to himself the affairs of greater importance, termed *causae maiores* (Can. 220). His power is episcopal, ordinary, and direct over each individual church and over each individual bishop and the faithful (Canons 218, par. 2; 1556). As supreme head of the Universal Church, he is also, by right, patriarch of the West, primate of Italy, metropolitan of the ecclesiastical Roman province, and bishop of Rome.

The universal primacy of the pope historically has not been exercised in the same way through the centuries. Historical development did not parallel dogmatic development, which intrinsically admits of no change, but has paralleled the external development of its practical manifestation. Sovereignty is exercised through the power of order as well as jurisdiction; but the power of order of the pope is not substantially different from the power of order possessed by each individual bishop. His power of jurisdiction has no other limits on earth except those assigned to it by divine right and the divine constitution of the Church. Its highest manifestation, known as the divine mandate of an *ecclesiastical magisterium*, is attained by *papal infallibility*. Defined by the First Vatican Council, on July 14, 1870, this was always inherent in the person of the pope, by which declarations and solemn definitions in matters of faith and morals bind the whole Church. Infallibility, however, is not to be confused with impeccability.

The power of jurisdiction includes legislative, judiciary, and coercive powers. By virtue of the legislative power, the pope alone, or in union with the ecumenical council, makes general laws for the whole Church, and particular laws for a specific class of the faithful. For certain individuals, he dispenses from such laws, regulates the administration of the universal Church, appoints bishops, etc. In the judiciary field he reserves to himself certain causes, either by reason of the persons or of matters involved. In addition, he reserves to himself the remission of certain ecclesiastical penalties (Canons 1557, 1558).

The organs through which the pope exercises this complex activity in the government of the Church comprise the Holy See, which consists of all the ecclesiastical departments, known as congregations, tribunals, and offices (*see* Can. 107).

THE ELECTION OF THE POPE. In ancient times the election of the pope did not differ from the election of other ecclesiastical prelates. It was conducted by the clergy and people of Rome, with some participation by the suburbicarian bishops. At one time or another, papal election did suffer from outside lay influence. In order to assure a maximum of independence in the papal election, it was later reserved to cardinals alone. Today, it is substantially governed by the Constitution of St. Pius X, *Vacante Sede Apostolica*, December 24, 1904; in

its particular details, by the Constitutions of Leo XIII, *Praedecessores Nostri*, May 24, 1882; St. Pius X, *Commissum Nobis*, January 20, 1904; Pius XI, *Cum proxime*, March 1, 1922; Pius XII, *Vacantis Sedis Apostolicae*, December 8, 1948.

The form of election is either by inspiration, compromise, or ballot. If the elected accepts, he immediately is invested with full authority; if he is not a bishop, he will be consecrated as soon as possible by the Dean of the College of Cardinals, who is also the suburbicarian bishop of Ostia (*see* Conclave).

The office of Supreme Pontiff ceases at the death of the reigning pope; it can also terminate by resignation of the pope.

After the pope's death and until his successor is elected, the ordinary government of the Church is conducted collectively by the cardinals. Resignation from the papacy is a matter of history. It is not necessary that it be made known to the whole Church in order that the election of a successor may be arranged. *Pug.*

POPULATION. *Population* is a term expressing the total number of inhabitants of a region, city, or country. The composition and size of the population continually change in a natural process of births and deaths or in the social phenomenon of migration and movement in the radius of a given area.

The study of the laws that regulate the movement of peoples and changes occurring between various sectors of social life is the object of demography (*q.v.*). In this article we deal directly with the moral problems that accompany the natural and social movements of populations.

But in order to do justice to this study, it is necessary to set aside certain prejudices prevalent today among many sociologists, politicians, and economists, and to follow the doctrine of the Church on this subject.

One of the most common prejudices is that population growth is an evil, at least in some nations, when, in fact, it is one of the greatest endowments, and that the health of the race is an absolute good to be sought for by any means.

On the contrary, Church doctrine is based on the principle that every man has an inalienable right to the attainment of his end, consisting of an earthly life and protection of that life, regardless of age or social condition, and against any unjust aggressor. Consequently, any problem, whether economic, demographic, or social, must be solved on the basis of these principles.

The main lines of the Church doctrine are laid down in a letter of September 15, 1953, sent by the Pro-secretary of State to the President of the Permanent Committee of Social Weeks of Italian Catholics: "No solution of demographic problems can ever be considered as conforming to justice and truth if it fails to take into account the sacred and intangible value of human life, or if it fails in any way to observe the norms that govern its orderly transmission."

"The absolute necessity that the goods created by God for all men be distributed equitably among all, according to the principles of justice and charity . . . is fundamental in the examination of the difficult population problem. . . . It follows, then, that an adequate study of the relations between density of population and means of sustenance must be conducted on a world-wide basis, with the operative solidarity of all the peoples, in order that, having removed the artificial barriers that divide them, a more orderly circulation of people, capital, and material goods may follow." (Twenty-sixth *Social Week of Italian Catholics*, Palermo, September 27 to October 3, 1953. *The Problems of Population*, Rome, 1954, p. 13.)

Moving from the general to the particular, population problems can be examined from various aspects. This we shall do on the basis of Catholic doctrine.

DEMOGRAPHIC-STATISTICAL ASPECT. The importance of monogamy and a general agreement among all the peoples in their respect for freedom and justice deserve to be well emphasized: ". . .

The best population structure is that in which a monogamous marriage is observed in fact and in spirit by all married persons; one in which the members of each family and of all families are bound by ties of assistance and solidarity; or one in which entirely free and spontaneous choices of each individual reconcile the fulfilment of the individual's aspirations with those of others, according to the principles of the moral law" (L. Livi: "*La struttura ottima della popolazione*" in *op. cit.*, p. 43).

MEDICAL-BIOLOGICAL ASPECT. While the progress of medical science, on the one hand, is instrumental for a decrease in the number of deaths, it is highly regrettable and censurable, indeed, that the iniquity of man, on the other hand, is instrumental in a decrease in the number of births.

Since physical life is not the supreme good among human values, the systematic sterilization of individuals with hereditary diseases must be opposed, along with Malthusianism and its pernicious and immoral practices. Catholic eugenics must be promoted as the result of genetic laws harmoniously developed and fully observed. Catholic moral doctrine insists on the high value of human life.

It is unlawful to turn eugenics into an instrument whereby man will seek from life the satisfaction of his passions yet shirk his responsibilities. Economic or similar difficulties, if present, must all be solved in the light of the law of God, not against it.

ECONOMIC-SOCIAL ASPECT. The demographic problem of economic capacities is too often presented in alarmist fashion as an emergency problem.

"The problem of economic resources required for the increase of population is more a problem of the moral than the technical order, in the sense that, if it is bound to a progress of the productive methods, it is also bound to the conditions of application of human labor and to the operative acceptance of the principle of the universal community of interests in time and space" (Golzio, "*Movimento demografico e risorse economiche*" in *op. cit.*, p. 131). For a solution to the problem of the number of citizens and their employment in the State and in the entire world, and for a solution to the economic increase consequent upon this demographic problem, there is needed ". . . a realistic awareness concerning human solidarity: a solidarity among all the citizens of the same country as well as among various peoples in the world. This is an absolute condition if the economy is to be truly placed at the service of man" (F. Vito, *"Movimento demografico e sviluppo economico"* in *op. cit.*, p. 167). On the question of emigration, historical, economic, social, and moral aspects are only a part of the whole problem, which must be considered, above all, with a deep sense of humanity and understanding.

POLITICAL-MORAL ASPECT. This aspect was illustrated clearly and authoritatively by Pope Pius XII, who pointed to the Christian social spirit as the leaven that must feed the entire mass of human beings: "Guard the noble flame of *fraternal social spirit* which, half a century ago, was rekindled in the hearts of the fathers by the luminous and illuminating words of Leo XIII; do not allow nor permit it to grow dim . . . nourish it, revive it, lift it up and expand this flame; carry it wherever there comes to you a groan of suffering, a lament of misery, a cry of pain; revive and strengthen it constantly with the burning love drawn from the Heart of the Redeemer" (Address commemorating *Rerum Novarum*, June 1, 1941).

METAPHYSICAL-MORAL ASPECT. The only lawful means for the transmission of life is monogamous marriage; the primary and essential end of marriage itself is the procreation and rearing of offspring. This is the position of the Church's perennial doctrine, and the "heritage of Christian tradition" (Pope Pius XII) against all the theories directed at perverting the hierarchy of ends, endeavoring to put the perfection of the spouses, their mutual aid, etc., first and foremost. The crimes against the primary end of marriage are onanism, Neo-Malthusianism, and artificial insemination,

because these destroy the end assigned by God to the marital institution.

The formation of a clear, upright, public moral conscience concerning the human reproductive functions and marriage institution, must emphasize that every act which is directed at the destruction of human life is immoral. This is necessary for the education of every Christian by the natural law.

The chief enemy against the preservation of life is hedonistic egoism, which is also opposed to transmission of life. He who does not love is at least a potential annihilator of life; "everyone who hates his brother is a murderer" (John 3:15).

Finally, education must extend to all aspects of life; it must prevent the hypertrophy of man's animal life, the hypotrophy of human life strictly taken, and the atrophy of the divine life in him. "The great misery of the modern social order is that it is not profoundly Christian, nor really human, but solely technical and economic. It no longer rests on what should be the basis and solid foundation of its unity, that is to say, a character, common to all by reason of their human nature, and a character as children of God, by reason of the grace of their divine adoption. . ." "A common evil binds all classes of society, that is, weakness of soul, devoid of all spiritual and religious life. . ." (Pius XII). *Pal. G.*

PORNOGRAPHY. *See* Images, Obscene; Nudism; Press.

PORTER. *See* Holy Orders.

PORTION, LAWFUL. *See* Will.

PORTIUNCULA. *See* Indulgence.

POSITIVISM. *Positivism* is a philosophical system which denies that human thought has the faculty of transcending the results of experience; this system excludes everything but natural phenomena or the properties of knowable things, together with their relations of coexistence and succession.

This philosophical attitude, carried into the ethical order, undermines ethics in its very roots, because ethics rests on the transcendent and the absolute. Moral precepts are not the product of experience, but are intended to be applied to the world of experience; they are superior requirements, which the historical world must observe, and which would be valid even if, in fact, men never observed them.

Positivism denies all this; it denies to ethics every normative or preceptive value and tries to substitute for it a science of custom built on the pattern of natural sciences, whose task it is, not to dictate preceptive norms, but to record the facts. In this light, the new science would no longer teach us what we must do but it would relate and explain to us the things that we do.

This doctrine is ill at ease in the face of an awareness of duty and the persuasion of an inevitable validity for certain moral and juridical principles beyond all transgressions and human negations. To explain that awareness and persuasion, two facts historically and positively established, the positivists turn to different methods, according to the school to which they belong. We shall recall the evolutionist solution, which seeks the root of these two facts in the history and prehistory of man, affirming that his habits, repeated for many centuries, have become so strong that they assume the aspect of categoric duties. The structure of our ethics would, thus, be the result of transforming or sublimating heredity.

Besides this now obsolete theory, a more recent one, which is called *sociologism*, states that the historical, evolutionary illusion is replaced by an actual, daily illusion, in which the individual attributes to mysterious and ultramundane causes things which he learns from the society in which he lives. Hence, he believes all social exigencies are absolute, transcendent, and binding; among these, first place must be given to those requirements which come under the name of ethics.

To the objections against positivism in general we add one against ethical positivism: none of its solutions to the problem of duty is satisfactory. Human conscience knows how to distinguish duty from habit, however deeply rooted and atavistic it may be; and human individuals sometimes accept the duty to rebel openly against social pressure. Gra.

POSSESSION. *Possession* is a condition of fact, according to which a person has such a relation to a thing that he can dispose of it at will, prescinding from all circumstances whether or not he is the owner of the article.

In ordinary language the term *possession* is generally used as synonymous with *ownership* (*q.v.*), but juridically they are two different concepts. (For this reason, the Roman sources state: *Nihil commune habet proprietas cum possessione:* D. 41, 2, 12, 1.) An *owner* is one who has the full right to enjoy and to dispose of a thing regardless of whether or not he actually has the corresponding exercise of such right (*see* Ownership). Instead, a *possessor* is one who *actually* enjoys possession and the right to dispose of a thing, prescinding from the circumstance of whether or not he has also *full right* to it.

Ownership indicates a condition of right; possession, instead, indicates a condition *of fact*, which may be protected by law and, as such, productive of juridical effects.

With this premise it becomes easier to understand the teaching of the Roman jurists who stated that one might be owner and still not be possessor, have the possession and still not be owner, or be both owner and possessor (*Separata esse debet possessio a proprietate. Fieri etenim potest, ut alter possessor sit, dominus non sit; alter dominus quidem sit, possessor vero non sit: fieri potest, ut et possessor idem et dominus sit:* D. 43, 17, 1, 2). The *lessee* or *tenant* have the possession of the land but they are not its owners; on the contrary, the *owner* and *lessor* are its proprietors but not its possessors. Only he who has purchased the land and directly cultivates it, is both its owner and possessor.

CONSTITUTIVE ELEMENTS. Two elements necessarily concur in the formation of possession: (1) *material*, corresponding to the fact that a thing is disposable (*corpus possessionis*); (2) *intentional* or *psychological*, a will to keep the thing at one's own disposal to the exclusion of others (*animus possidendi*). The meeting of these two elements gives rise to possession.

Anything juridically suitable for commerce can be the object of possession. By provision of law, possession of noncommercial things (*extra commercium*) for which no ownership can be acquired, remains inoperative. According to Canon Law, these are: spiritual things, i.e., sacraments, ecclesiastical jurisdiction, indulgences, etc., and temporal things so connected with spiritual things that they cannot exist independently of them, e.g., an ecclesiastical benefice (Can. 727). Although, strictly speaking, possession can neither be declared nor effected except on a material thing, it is admitted that certain rights can also be the object of possession, which in such case are termed *quasi-possessions* or *iuris possessio*.

KINDS OF POSSESSION. In the possessor the intentional element of possession (*animus*) admits of various degrees: (a) *animus detinendi*, the simple generic will to retain an item, which one can in a material sense dispose of; (b) *animus domini seu rem sibi habendi*, or the intention of keeping the article as one's own or of acting as the real owner of the right corresponding to the condition of fact; (c) finally, it may be *animus domini* accompanied by the *opinio domini*, the conviction that the thing is really one's own.

To the three degrees of the *animus*, there correspond three kinds of possession:

In the first case, *natural* or *general possession* (called *simple possession* or *simple retention*) is proper to anyone who can materially dispose of a thing. *Natural possession* is termed *precarious possession* or *possession in the name of another*, if he who has the thing holds it, not in his own name, but in the name and interest of another, as in the case of a depositary, manager, and salesman.

In the second case, *lawful possession* is natural possession, qualified by the intention of keeping the thing as one's own and according to the conditions required by the law. In order to be lawful and have corresponding legal protection and effectiveness, it is necessary that the possession be *continuous, uninterrupted, peaceful* (at least at the initial moment), *public, unambiguous,* and that there be the *intention of keeping the thing as one's own.*

In the third case, *possession in good faith* is lawful possession to which is joined a conviction of the existence of a just claim, the falsity of which is unknown. This belief that one is exercising his right makes one unaware of the fact that one may be injuring the right of another.

Good faith is presumed by civil law, so that it is always the duty of the plaintiff to prove bad faith; it is sufficient that it may have existed in the beginning, at the time of the acquisition of the thing. A supervening bad faith does no harm (*mala fides superveniens non nocet*); however, good faith is of no avail if ignorance is the result of grave guilt.

For theologians, this is *juridical* good faith. It must be distinguished from *theological* good faith, an invincible ignorance of the fact that the right of another is being violated. It excludes all guilt; it is not presumed, but either exists or does not exist; contrary to the principle *mala fides superveniens non nocet*, it must exist for the time required for prescription.

On the contrary, *possession in bad faith* is the retention of a thing by one having the intent to injure, by possession, the right of another, or by deliberately ignoring this right. The state of subjective uncertainty concerning the lawfulness of the title on which possession rests, creates, in turn, a *possession in doubtful faith.*

According to law, simple retention does not constitute possession, although possession is presumed in one who actually exercises this right, unless it is proved that he began to exercise this right simply by retention.

One whose possession began by retention cannot acquire possession unless title is changed by a cause originating with a third party or as result of opposition to the possessor. Thus, he who has possession, corresponding to the exercise of a real right on an object of another, cannot acquire possession of the thing itself until the title is changed in the manner indicated above. This change is called *interversion* of possession.

ACQUISITION AND LOSS OF POSSESSION. Possession is acquired by the simultaneous combination of the two elements which constitute it: the actual disposable nature of the thing (*corpus*), and the will to keep it (*animus*). (*Adipiscimur possessionem corpore et animo, neque per se animo, aut per se corpore*: D. 41, 2, 3, 1; D. 50, 17, 153.)

The element *corpus* becomes concrete in the physical apprehension (*adprehensio*) of the fungible property or in the material insistence on the thing itself in the case of non-fungible property. This is determined either directly, by the sole fact of *adprehensio* and the insistence, if it is an original acquisition, or by the giving (*traditio*) of a personal property or *immissio in possessionem* of a real property, if it is a derived acquisition. The traditional forms are: *traditio symbolica* or *ficta* (by exchanging a symbol of the thing); *traditio longa manu* (the thing simply is marked); *traditio brevi manu* (the thing is already retained by reason of another title); *constitutum possessorium* (an owner transfers a thing to another person, who agrees to retain it as if he were the owner, as, for example, in a lease).

The element of intent (*animus*) is determined either by explicit declaration or by exterior acts that unequivocally manifest this; among these are *adprehensio*, which follows *traditio* or taking possession after the *immissio in possessionem*. Possession is lost if one or both of these constitutive elements are lacking.

PROTECTION OF POSSESSION. For the defense of possession, both canonical and civil laws speak of and make use of the so-called possessory actions; among these actions are the action of reintegration (*actio recuperandae* or *redintegrandae possessionis*), sometimes termed *actio de spolio*, and the action of maintenance (*actio retinendae or manutendae possessionis*) carried out according to the nature of possession in the terms intended by the law.

Natural possession is protected against violent and clandestine dispossession, by the action of reintegration effected within a year from dispossession, unless the thing be retained for reasons of service or hospitality (Canons 1694, 1698).

A *lawful* possession is protected not only by the action of reintegration to be effected within a year, but also by the action, within the same period of time, of maintenance against any molestation or disturbance of the possession of a real property, provided that the possession has existed for a year, continuous, uninterrupted, and has not been acquired in a violent or clandestine manner (Can. 1695).

A possession in good faith is protected by both actions of reintegration and maintenance according to the terms indicated above.

In addition, Canon Law contains the action of acquisition of possession (*action adipiscendae possessionis*) in defense of the right of possession of a specific property or the exercise of a specific right (Can. 1693).

The reasons why the law grants a real protection of possession, a situation sometimes objectively unjust, are to be found principally in the need for every legal system to eliminate to the maximum extent uncertain juridical situations, especially in the field of inheritance, and thus to guarantee the indispensable conditions for the maintenance of public order and to prevent citizens from taking the law into their own hands with consequent violent conflicts (*ne cives ad arma veniant*).

In the moral and partly in the juridical field, the position of the possessor with respect to rights and duties, particularly the obligation of restitution of a thing to its owner, varies, depending on whether the possession was acquired in good faith, bad faith, or doubtful faith.

Their respective treatments are found under the following headings: Prescription (q.v.), Restitution (q.v.), Possession in good faith (q.v.), Possession in bad faith (q.v.), and Possession in doubtful faith (q.v.).

Here, we shall limit ourselves to only a few fundamental principles:

(a) Civil laws concerning possession in good faith, insofar as they are considered just and not opposed to the natural law, are binding in conscience and authorize the possessor in good faith, at the least by a probable opinion, to avail himself with safe conscience of the above-indicated benefits which the law grants to him. The same cannot be said of simple lawful possession, not acquired in good faith.

(b) Consequently, the possessor in good faith, if the time has elasped for prescription as established by the law, can become the owner of the thing and consider himself as such also in conscience. This is also valid, according to a probable opinion, for the acquisition of ownership over individual personal goods, provided that they were not stolen or found, in which possession amounts to ownership.

(c) If good faith is found lacking before the time required for prescription, there ensues the definite obligation to restore the thing to its owner, though the possessor retains the right to the fruits and other benefits granted by the law, according to the terms indicated above.

(d) If there is a doubt about the lawfulness of title or the right to benefits, a possessor in good faith can in conscience retain the thing until the judge has decided on the claim by a third party. In this case, the important presumption of right in favor of the possessor (*in dubio, melior est conditio possidentis*) is validly applied.

(e) In doubtful cases, the following well-known principles may be fundamentally used as guiding principles: *Res clamat ad dominum* (a thing claims its rightful owner); *Res fructificat domino*

(the fruits of a thing go to its owner); *Res perit domino* (a thing perishes at the expense of the owner), *Nemo cum alterius iniuria locupletari debet* (no one may grow rich at the expense of another).

(f) A possessor in bad faith is bound to restore the thing with all separate or accrued benefits at the time of restitution and to redress the damage (*damnum emergens* and the *lucrum cessans*) insofar as it was foreseen or foreseeable. He cannot enjoy in conscience the benefit of acquisitive prescription, as recognized by law to a lawful possessor.

(g) A possessor of doubtful faith is required to make diligent inquiry about the actual facts. If the doubt continues even after investigation, he may keep the thing, if he was in good faith at the beginning; according to some, even if he was in doubt from the beginning. *Zac.*

POSSESSION, DIABOLICAL. See Hallucination; Medium; Exorcism; Obsession.

POSSESSION IN BAD FAITH. A *possessor in bad faith* intentionally and willingly retains the property of another.

Obligations of a possessor in bad faith concerning the property possessed:

(a) A possessor in bad faith, as the unjust possessor of the property of another, must restore the property to its owner, as soon as possible, unless a sufficient reason exists that justifies delay. It must be the actual property (*res individualis*) that is restored and not another, even if of the same kind or equivalent to it, because the object of the owner's right is that specific property. There are, of course, exceptions to this rule, as in the case of a thief who restores things of equivalent value in order to protect his honor, or in the case of the loss of a property, whether it perished or not. But at least the equivalent must be restored, because the injured owner must be indemnified.

(b) The property must be restored to its lawful owner, even if one received it from a thief. However, if the one who intentionally acquired stolen goods no longer can recover his money, he may licitly give back the property to the thief in order that he may attend to his duty.

There seems to be nothing improper in this, for the property is returned to the status in which it was previously, thus avoiding further damage to the owner. In case of eviction, that is, if the owner requests the property from the actual holder, the latter cannot demand his money from the thief, if at the time of his purchase he was aware of the stolen nature of the property, unless the contrary was agreed upon in the contract of sale. If the person who possesses in bad faith undergoes eviction—this is an essential point—he has no right of redress or recompense. He is not the victim of injustice; for, since he knew at the time of the purchase that the property belonged to another, he has no right to benefit by the condition implied in the sale: that the property does not belong to another and is not demanded by its owner lawfully.

(c) The property may not be an object of prescription; this comprises another essential difference, for the lack of good faith is an essential condition demanded by prescription.

(d) If the property underwent a change of value during the time of its unjust possession, it may be well to distinguish a double change in value, exterior or interior, since this change may be either the effect of a condition intrinsic to the property or of external circumstances, independent of the property. For interior or *intrinsic* change, two hypotheses include all possible cases: (1) If the property, held by the possessor in bad faith, improved of itself, it must be restored to its owner with the acquired improvement, because the increase belongs to the owner, even if it would not have improved under its lawful owner. The unlawful possessor, however, may deduct the cost of his personal labors. (2) If the property has undergone a deterioration with consequent decrease in value, it is necessary to investigate whether these changes would have occurred had the property remained with the lawful owner.

In the first case, it is sufficient to restore the property in the condition in which it was, for the possessor in bad faith is not responsible for any specific damage. In the second case, if the deterioration would not have occurred under a lawful owner, the possessor in bad faith is required to restore the property and to make compensation for the deterioration; otherwise, the owner would suffer unjust damage.

In exterior or *extrinsic* change, a double hypothesis applies to such a change: (1) If the owner sold the property during a time of rise in prices or had to buy one in such a time, the possessor in bad faith must restore the higher value of the property in question. Otherwise, the owner would suffer an unjust damage. This applies whether or not the possessor in bad faith still possesses the property, and whether he consumed it during the time of a rise or fall in prices. (2) If the owner sold the thing at a time of decline in prices, it will be necessary to formulate various hypotheses, for it is not possible to offer one general solution for all cases.

Thus, if the owner sold the property when its value was in decline and the possessor in bad faith consumed it when its value was high, the sounder opinion is that the possessor in bad faith, who consumes the thing at the time when it is worth more, removes it from the possession of the owner at that moment, causing him damage to be estimated according to the price at the moment. This is the damage that he is required to restore.

If the owner sold the property during the time of falling prices and the possessor in bad faith consumed it during the same period (or had it stolen regardless of the price condition), according to an apparently more equitable opinion, it is sufficient to make restitution according to the lower price, which represents the actual damage to the owner's interests.

It is clear that the hypotheses above do not include all cases. Yet they offer principles for solution. In view of the fact that restitution is ordinarily based on the price prevailing at the moment of theft, it is impossible to determine with exact certitude all circumstances included in such events.

Fruits may be derived directly from the property itself or may be exclusively the result of human ingenuity. In the first case, it is obvious that since they belong to the property and constitute, as it were, a unity with the property itself, they belong to its proprietor. In the second case, they belong to the one who produced them by his own ability and labor. Accordingly, a possessor in bad faith shall be permitted to retain the fruits of his industry but he must restore natural or civil fruits.

Concerning these latter fruits, he must restore those that he has actually obtained, even if the owner would have never gotten them, for he must make restitution to the owner for the entire damage. The possessor in bad faith must also restore the fruits obtained by others, unless they themselves made restitution, since he is also the cause of this damage by cooperation.

It is obvious that the possessor in bad faith can deduct the expenses incurred for the production and collection of the fruits.

The possessor in bad faith can deduct the money spent for necessary and useful expenditures which the owner himself would have incurred in preserving or expanding the property. Otherwise, the owner, besides restoration of damages, would receive a surplus which is not by right his.

A possessor in bad faith does not enjoy the same right in respect to luxury expenses, which are not useful but merely ornamental to the property. These are arbitrary expenditures which the owner is not required to make good.

These rules of natural equity are recognized by many modern civil codes. Thus, the Italian code states: "The possessor, although in bad faith, is entitled to a reimbursement of expenditures incurred for extraordinary repairs. He is also entitled to an indemnity for improvements made on the property, provided that they exist at the time of the restitution."

On the contrary, according to the civil laws of other countries, such as England and the United States, the owner is not in any way required to make allowance for expenditures sustained by the possessor in bad faith. Yet, since such provisions are only penal, the possessor in bad faith is allowed to deduct the expenses mentioned above, if he can. In fact, it is a generally accepted principle of the natural law that expenses made in behalf of the property and, consequently, of the owner demand compensation for the benefits attained from such property.

In addition, it should be noted that these benefits should be real and notable, since the owner could not be expected to refund the expenditures unless he were to receive a real and proper benefit from them.

Often even luxury expenses are beneficial, since they increase the property value; hence, they too must be refunded. And even if expenditures are made for things of little benefit, the possessor in bad faith can deduct the amount of such expenditures, if they are separable from the thing itself without damage to the property or to its owner.

The possessor in bad faith is required to make restitution for all unjust damages at least vaguely foreseen. He is a responsible cause of them. Those damages are foreseen if considered ordinary, but one is not required to make restitution for extraordinary damages which could not normally be foreseen. The possessor in bad faith must make reparation both for *lucrum cessans* (lack of gain) and *damnum emergens* (actual damage), so that the owner can recover all that he would have had if the property had not been taken from him.

The measure of the lack of gain and the damage to be restored must be determined by the degree of certainty on the part of the owner to reap gain or avoid damage, apart from all circumstances which might have hindered such realization.

The possessor in bad faith is certainly obliged to pay interest, if the owner would have collected interest on his money. If the owner would not have profitably invested his money, the obligation to restitution still exists, since today interest is considered ordinary fruit of money.

If stolen property perished, there are two main hypotheses which apply:

(a) *The property perished while in the possession of the possessor in bad faith and this would not have happened with the lawful owner.* The possessor, as the cause of the loss, is bound to restore the property and all damages according to the principles explained above.

(b) *The property perished while in possession of the possessor in bad faith and this would have happened even if it had been in the possession of the owner.* The possessor in bad faith is not bound to make restitution: (1) if the property would have perished, had it been in the possession of the owner, for the same cause and within the same time; (2) if it would have perished while in the possession of the owner within the same period of time but for a different cause, since the possessor in bad faith is not an efficient cause of the damage, nor did the condition of the owner become worse. As a matter of fact, some authors apply the same principle, even if the property would have perished at a different time while in the possession of the owner, in which case the possessor in bad faith would be bound only to make restitution of any profit made.

However, the latter rule could not be applied (and therefore the possessor in bad faith must make restitution) if the property perished while in the possession of the owner, and he would have received indemnity for the damage from an insurance company. Nor does it apply in the case where the property perished while in the possession of the owner due to injustice of a third party, for the latter would be obliged to indemnify the owner, according to the civil law of many nations.

Yet, these decisions, as adjuncts to the natural law, may be considered binding penal obligations after a decision of the judge.

(c) *The property taken by a possessor in bad faith would have perished while in the possession of the lawful owner.*

In this case, the property must be re-stored to the owner, whether the possessor in bad faith saved it from danger, or the property remained safe because taken and held for a long time. In fact, the property does not cease to belong to the owner nor does his right to it cease to exist, simply because it was protected from danger by another.

However, one is not bound to make restitution if the thing was consumed at the place and time of the danger because it could not be saved; the reason is that, if a thing would have been lost anyway, it is considered devoid of every value for the owner.

Yet, much caution is needed in judging the circumstances of these cases to avoid running the risk of false judgments. *Pal.*

POSSESSION IN DOUBTFUL FAITH. A possessor in doubtful faith is uncertain about the lawful possession of a property or a thing.

A possessor in doubtful faith, whether he doubts at the beginning or only in the course of possession, is bound to make every effort to remove doubt; otherwise, he would expose himself to the danger of retaining the property of another as his own by culpable negligence.

There are the various hypotheses and obligations in the case of persistent doubt.

(a) If a possessor held the property in good faith until the doubt set in and the doubt remains after a diligent inquiry, he may retain the property with greater tranquillity. The lawfulness of this is in the fact that, in the case of equally probable rights or of persistent doubt, the condition of the possessor (*melior est conditio possidentis*) is favored. The possession, begun in good faith, gives rise to a greater presumption of lawfulness and gives the possessor a right which must prevail both before his own conscience and before society (*in the external forum*), unless it is superseded by other motives or stronger presumptions. This is the more reliable opinion held by moralists, although an opinion holding to a division of the object between the parties, according to the degree of probability, is not to be entirely disregarded.

(b) In the case where *doubt precedes possession*, one must distinguish:

(1) If possession of a thing began with a doubt and another was deprived of the possession he had of the thing, the one depriving is obliged to restore the thing to its former owner, unless it is evident that he likewise had begun his possession in bad faith.

(2) If one acquired the property by another title, such as purchase, and after a diligent inquiry doubts still remain whether or not the one from whom he acquired the property was really its owner, he must, according to the degree of doubt, restore it to its probable owner or give it to the poor, if the owner is unknown. The reason for this is that the possession of a thing begun in doubtful faith is not wholly justified; consequently, he who acquired it cannot retain everything; on the other hand, there are reasons to maintain that he is bound to restore the entire thing.

The possessor in doubtful faith, however, may retain the entire property, if by purchase-sale, donation, etc., he succeeded one who possessed the thing in good faith, or if he acquired possession by title of occupation until such a time as the real owner may appear. It is probable that a possessor may not be obliged to make restitution in doubt, if he was able to form a sure conscience concerning the lawfulness of his possession by means of reflex principles, arguing, for instance, from the principle that an obligation should not be imposed unless proven with certainty (*non est imponenda obligatio, nisi de ea certo constet*) and the like.

(3) In the hypothesis that one initially possessed the property of another in good faith, and then, after the start of doubt, he failed to find its true owner despite diligent inquiry, and consumed the property on the basis of his possession, the possessor in doubtful faith is bound to make restitution only in proportion to his real enrichment.

(4) If none of the doubtful owners of an object possess the property in fact,

and doubt is equally founded, the object must be divided among the claimants according to the degree of doubt. If the property cannot be divided, it must be sold and the money obtained shall be divided according to the same principle; with the consent of the others, one of them could be permitted to buy shares belonging to the others; by common consent, lots may be drawn and the thing assigned to the winner.

(5) If an heir doubts whether the testator possessed his goods by a lawful right, he can, after serious consideration, in the face of a remaining doubt accept or keep his inheritance, if it is certain that the preceding testator possessed his goods in good faith. For, if the axiom *In doubt, the right of the possessor is to be favored* is applicable to the former owner, it also applies to his successor, especially if the two constitute one legal person.

(6) Finally, in a doubt whether one began possession in good or bad faith, the presumption is in favor of the one who possesses, because crimes are not presumed but must be proven. Yet, if someone is actually in bad faith and doubts whether he began to possess in the same bad faith, the presumption is that he was also in bad faith at the beginning. *Pal.*

POSSESSION IN GOOD FAITH. A *possessor in good faith* is one who retains the thing of another in the belief that it is his own, and, therefore, is unaware that the right of another is being violated. This good faith, however, must not have been caused by grave negligence. Good faith is always presumed in external relations, until the contrary is proved.

The retention of a thing of another, though in good faith, does not cease to be objectively unjust, and the obligation to make restitution (*q.v.*) holds even in such a case.

Restitution is an act by which restoration is made to the rightful owner of a thing (or its equivalent), which was lost as a result of a violation of commutative justice (*q.v.*); by this restoration the normal relations required by justice itself are fully re-established.

Thus, to unjust possession, even if in good faith, the principle applies whereby everything claims its proper owner (*res clamat domino*); for no one may be unjustly deprived against his will of what is *his,* and if one has something that does not belong to him, he must give it to him who lost it (*Summa Theol.,* II–II, q. 62, a. 6). He who retains the thing of another is either in good faith, bad faith, or in doubt whether the thing is his or not (doubtful faith).

The obligations of a possessor vary according to whether he is a possessor in good, bad, or doubtful faith; hence, we shall consider them separately. These obligations are manifold, as they may concern the thing possessed, the income derived from it, expenditures, or damages.

OBLIGATIONS. (a) He who retains a thing of another in good faith, except in prescription (*q.v.*), must either restore to its owner the thing itself if it still exists (*res clamat domino*), or its equivalent value and whatever benefits he obtained from it (*in quantum ipse ditior factus est*) if the thing no longer exists. For it is contrary to the natural law that one become rich at the expense of another (*locupletari non potest aliquis cum alterius iniuria aut iactura: Regulae iuris in VI,* 47).

(b) Restitution must be made *as soon as possible,* i.e., as soon as the possessor in good faith becomes aware of the fact that he has a thing belonging to another; he who neglects to fulfill this obligation through his own negligence, becomes a possessor in bad faith, who is required to repair the damages caused by delayed restitution.

If one in good faith purchased a thing from a person who is not its owner, and later discovers this, he is required to look for the owner; if he finds him, he must simply restore the thing to him because, by the fundamental norm of the natural law and general positive provisions, he has the right to the whole thing and can, therefore, claim it as his own, without

giving compensation for it. A purchaser, however, can sue the seller, who is obliged to repay for the object sold. According to moral theologians, provisions of civil law can also be followed in conscience. Yet, it must be noted that the rule according to which former moralists made it a strict obligation for the buyer in good faith to restore the thing in every case, must be carefully weighed today. In fact, in our modern life, almost all things are fungible, since many things of the same kind can, without grave inconvenience, be purchased with money. Thus, the obligation to restitution weighs, not on the purchaser, but rather on the thief who retains the thing itself or its value. At times, however, if the stolen thing is not fungible (e.g., an antique picture), the owner can reasonably remain unsatisfied until the thing itself is restored to him. In such a case, the strict obligation of restitution applies to the purchaser in good faith. However, moral theologians in general affirm that he who bought an article in good faith, which in fact belongs to another, can rescind the contract as soon as he becomes aware that the object acquired belongs to another; he can return the article to the thief so that he can recover the price paid to him for the article.

(c) If the property no longer exists, neither in itself nor in an equivalent value, but merely in some form of profit derived from the thing itself, and if the retainer was always in good faith, he now is not obliged to restitution. He is not bound to restore it by reason of his acceptance of the property (*ex titulo rei acceptae*) because the property or its equivalent no longer exists. His act was done without formal injury, but by a compelling motive for a lawful use of the property.

In the latter case, if the possessor in good faith gave the property away, he may be required by reason of charity, if he can do it without damage to himself, to admonish the recipient to restore the property to its owner, or to inform the owner so that he may recover his own property.

(d) If the possessor in good faith sold the property to a third party: (1) if the owner got it back from the purchaser, he must restore the money to the buyer, provided he was in good faith; (2) if the owner will no longer be able to recover it, because the retainer cannot be located, according to the more common opinion he is under no obligation, provided he derived no profit from the purchase except the fruits of his own industry.

In this case, he is considered to have never bought the property, and no injustice was done to the owner because the property innocently went through the hands of the purchaser, who then became the seller. On the other hand, the owner still has the right to recover his property and may claim it anywhere.

(e) If the property of another no longer exists, either in itself or in its equivalent, and the possessor in good faith has benefitted by its use, even though through his own industry, he is required to restore the equivalent of his gains to the owner.

The possessor in good faith may probably retain the profit made, if he sold the property to a third party and it then perished. The property was lost naturally without injustice to the owner, and the purchaser was not subject to eviction.

Modern codes of civil law recognize for the possessor in good faith the right to retain the fruits attained during the period in which he was in good faith until the day of legal suit.

Natural fruits are said to be collected if they are separated from the soil or from the plants, branches, or roots. On the contrary, the civil revenues are collected by law from day to day, so that they belong to the possessor in good faith for the period of time during which he possessed the property of another in good faith.

Many modern authors state that this provision of the civil law, under the required conditions, is valid for the realm of conscience, since this is a case in which the legislator makes laws in his own field to promote the common welfare, to favor thrift and diligence by owners, and to protect the gains made in good faith by avoiding legal disputes.

Thus, the *conditions* required for the application of such civil provisions are as follows: (1) a right must not extend beyond the duration of the good faith; (2) such good faith must not only be theological, but also juridical; the possessor must possess the object as owner by virtue of a title in itself capable of producing the transfer of the property.

However, if it lacks only one of the established conditions, the question of the fruits must be solved according to the natural law, which requires that all the fruits remaining but not produced by one's own industry, as well as those which no longer exist, be restored to the owner, because the possessor has become richer from them.

In restoring the property of another, the possessor in good faith may retain: (a) the necessary expenses incurred for the preservation of the same property in the cases in which he is held to restitution of revenues or fruits;

(b) the expense incurred to obtain revenues not yet obtained; in addition, he may even retain the property itself until he recovers these expenses or is compensated for them;

(c) the expenditures incurred for the improvement of the property, in proportion to the increased value acquired by the property itself, as the result of the improvements;

(d) luxury expenses in proportion to the increase of the value of the property itself; or else he is allowed to remove the luxury items if, by so doing, the property itself is not damaged; otherwise, an accessory improvement must remain with the main object of the improvement.

In restoring a property, the possessor in good faith may not deduct expenses incurred to obtain the fruits which he derived from the mere possession of the property. *Pal.*

POSSESSION (of a benefice). Taking possession of a benefice is occupying a benefice with the intention of exercising the office and enjoying the benefits attached thereto.

The conferral of the title is not sufficient for one to collect the revenue from the benefice and make it his own; it must be accompanied by what is usually called *institutio corporalis* (investiture or installation), that is, the superior's act by which the beneficiary is put in actual possession of the benefice.

As a general rule, he who has the right of conferring the benefice has also the right of installing the beneficiary in the possession of the benefice, either personally or by delegating another. At one time, the archdeacon had the right to institute both benefices and dignities; but under the existing law, in non-consistorial benefices the installation of a beneficiary to the possession of a benefice rests with the Ordinary, who can delegate another (Can. 1443, par. 2).

CONDITIONS. The installation of a beneficiary in a consistorial benefice, e.g., the episcopate, is normally carried out by presentation, before a competent board, of the apostolic letters conferring the benefice; the benefice of an abbot, by the conferral of the abbatial see; that of a canon by the assignment of the stall in the choir and chapter; that of a parish priest by the conferral of the parochial insignia and the handing over of the keys, etc.

(a) The installation by which the beneficiary takes possession of his benefice must be made in the manner prescribed by the particular law or by lawful custom, unless the Ordinary for a just and reasonable cause explicitly and in writing dispenses with that manner or rite; in this case, the dispensation takes the place of the formal taking of possession (Can. 1444, par. 1).

(b) The local Ordinary shall specify the time within which possession of the benefice must be taken; and if this is allowed to elapse without a just reason, the Ordinary must, under Canon 138, n. 2, declare the benefice vacant (Can. 1445).

The effects of a lawful possession are: possessory interdiction (Can. 1447); the right to the revenue as one's own; the claim to the title; and the possibility of prescription (Can. 1446). *Pal.*

POSTULANCY. *Postulancy* (Latin, *postulare*—to demand) is a time of probation during which one desirous of entering a religious order or institute is juridically considered an aspirant to that life and submits to a preliminary test preparatory to the novitiate (*q.v.*), a first scrutiny of his vocation and aptitudes. Postulancy takes different names in the various religious orders, *postulancy, candidacy*, etc.

As an obligatory, juridical institution, postulancy is rather recent, although in the generic sense its beginnings can be traced back to the very origin of religious life. Pope Clement VIII first requested a probationary period for lay brothers of mendicant orders in 1603. The practice was extended to other religious groups but was imposed as a law only in 1901 by a decree of the Sacred Congregation of Religious. For the first traces of real canonical postulancy for religious women, one must look at the constitutions of the congregations of simple vows of the eighteenth century which, revised and corrected by the Sacred Congregation, created in a short time the true and proper juridical institution, first incorporated in the norms of 1901 and, later, in the legislation of 1917. By a decree of August 15, 1912, the Sacred Congregation of Religious made postulancy obligatory for nuns.

Presently, the Code of Canon Law requires postulancy for religious organizations of women and for lay brothers of the communities of men of papal and diocesan right (Can. 539). However, it does not seem that postulancy is required for the validity of the novitiate and subsequent professions. Canonical postulancy must last six whole months, unless the constitutions of the respective religious group direct otherwise.

Since postulancy has the definite aim of preparing a candidate for the religious life, the Code requires superiors to see that postulants are assigned to houses in which the religious discipline is diligently observed (Can. 540). Postulants have no formal obligation to observe the constitutions and rules of the religious organization, yet they have the duty to conform to them by reason of their voluntary submission to superiors and the religious discipline of the institute. Postulants may be given a special habit to wear, which must be different from that of novices and professed religious (Can. 540). *Mand.*

POSTULATOR. According to Canon 2003 of the Code of Canon Law, all the faithful or groups of the faithful have the right to introduce a cause of beatification before a competent ecclesiastical tribunal. If the petition is accepted, they have the right to promote and pursue the cause to the end; in other words, they may become plaintiffs in the cause, either personally if priests, or, as is the rule, through a lawfully appointed procurator (Can. 2004).

Thus, he who promotes and deals with a cause of beatification, personally as plaintiff or proxy in the name of others, is called a *postulator* (Can. 2004, par. 2).

The postulator exercises the function of (1) plaintiff in a cause of beatification or canonization, similar to the plaintiff in a civil process; (2) in the liturgical rite of beatification, he requests publication of the relative decree, and in the rite of canonization, through a consistorial lawyer, he requests the enrollment of the blessed in the canon of the saints.

The postulator must be a priest, either secular or religious, with residence in Rome (Can. 2005). If he acts as procurator, he must exhibit the lawful mandate to the tribunal, i.e., a mandate executed according to canonical rules (Can. 1659) and approved by the Sacred Congregation of Rites (Can. 2006). There can be only one procurator for each cause; but since the procurator often cannot personally promote the cause outside of Rome, he can be represented, by lawful mandate, by others called *vice-postulators* (Can. 2005). If the postulator has received the mandate only for a specific cause, he is called simply a *postulator;* if he is appointed for all the causes of a religious order, he is called *procurator general*. The mandate of a procurator terminates for the same reasons

that the mandate of other canonical procurators is terminated (Can. 2008).

DUTIES. (a) The postulator and vice-postulators must take an oath, called *iusiurandum calumniae,* which means that they will proceed during the whole cause according to truth, and that they will not employ any fraud (Can. 2037, par. 4). (b) They shall attend the proceedings leading to the proclamation of a blessed or a saint; in particular, they shall promote the cause at the diocesan level, by means of a search of all the writings of the servant of God for the so-called trial of the writings (*processus scriptorum:* Can. 2047, par. 1); by the introduction of witnesses in the informative process, by writing articles on the life, reputation, virtues, miracles, and doctrines of the servant of God, submitted to the promoter of the faith (*q.v.*) and used in the questioning of witnesses; by introducing the cause before the Sacred Congregation of Rites; by paying all the expenses of the process, from money collected for this purpose from the faithful and according to the instructions of the Holy See. *Led.*

POVERTY. One of the three great evils of fallen nature is the unquenchable thirst for material goods, which, once acquired, easily become the object of anguished worries and, often, take hold of the human heart to the point of turning it from God. This slavery is the opposite of what was willed by God, who had made man king of creation. In order to restore the order overturned by sin, the Lord counselled the renunciation of the goods of the earth (Matt. 19:21; Mark 10:21; Luke 12:33; 18:22). Effective poverty is neither a matter of precept nor an essential condition for perfection; it is, however, necessary for man to be detached, at least internally, from earthly goods. This detachment constitutes spiritual poverty extolled by the Lord in the Sermon on the Mount (Matt. 5:8), without which even effective poverty would not benefit the soul.

The internal detachment from material goods consists in desiring goods only in the measure in which they are really necessary or useful to reach one's true end, which is God, and in being ready, if it is God's will, to accept the loss of these without grumbling or rebellion against the dispositions of Divine Providence. To love material goods more than that is an excessive and, therefore, sinful attachment. The sin is mortal if one's love of material goods is such that he is disposed to sin gravely by reason of them.

The means by which one must attain internal detachment from material goods are: the thought of man's ultimate end and the fleeting value of earthly things, the desire for eternal goods, and a great trust in the Lord (Matt. 6:25 ff.).

There is also an interior poverty involving higher goods, that is, friendship, talents received from the Lord, esteem and affection of others, joys resulting from one's good works. One who desires to attain perfection must be also internally detached from these goods. For the vow of poverty, see Vows, Religious. For poverty in the sense of lack of the necessities of life, see Need. *Man.*

POWER (Abuse of). *See* Abuse of Power.

POWER, DOMINATIVE. *See* Superior; Superior, Religious.

POWER, PATERNAL. *See* Father, Parents.

PRAISE OF GOD. A worship that emphasizes and extolls the beneficent greatness of God, as revealed through His works, is called *praise of God.* According to Holy Scripture (Psalms 18:2; 99:3), all the works of creation extoll the greatness of God, but the notes of this hymn of praise echoing in the visible world can only be picked up by man, God's most perfect work of creation, whom all inferior creatures must serve (Rom. 2:36; 14:7–8; I Cor. 6:20).

Praise calls for further praise, and all human creatures, hearing God's praises sung by nature, are invited, as it were, to join their chorus.

The praise of God may be expressed in many ways and included in every act of worship. The Church has found it suitable to express praise in songs (*see* Sacred songs) and music, through which the artistic rendering of the most profound human and religious sentiments is realized. *Pal.*

PRAYER. In a broad sense, *prayer* is the elevation of the mind to God; in a restricted sense, it is a petition to God for a good, necessary, or suitable need. These two classic definitions date back to St. John Damascene (d. 754). The first definition includes all forms of prayer; the second, prayer of petition. In Holy Scripture, the word *prayer* almost always has the meaning of *petition to God* for something suitable.

(a) Prayer may be mental or internal, and vocal or external.

Mental prayer is that in which one employs the mind and the heart; examples of this are *meditation* (*q.v.*) on Christian truth, and *contemplation* (*see* Contemplation, and the catechism of St. Pius X, No. 416).

Contemplation, the highest form of mental prayer, was defined thus by Pseudo-Augustine (PL, 40, 802): *perspicuae veritatis iucunda admiratio* (a joyful admiration of a clear truth).

Meditation, instead, may be defined as the holy and reasoned consideration of religious truths, tending to arouse sentiments of love of God and holy things, with the determination to lead a perfectly Christian life.

Between the two forms of mental prayer there exists a substantial difference: contemplation is *intuitive;* meditation is *discursive.*

Meditation is easier than contemplation; both are accessible, at least in simpler form, even to the unlettered.

Some simple souls without great intelligence may not be able to meditate because they are incapable of a reasoned consideration, but nevertheless, full of faith and wisdom, these can rise without effort to the heights of contemplation (Matt. 11:25; Luc. 10:21).

Vocal prayer, also called simply *prayer,* is prayer that is expressed in words, in which the mind and heart join (Catechism of Pius X, n. 417).

(b) Prayer may be *public* or *private*. *Public* prayer is said in the name of the Church, by a priest or other minister, according to a formula prescribed by the Church. Public prayer is always vocal. *Private* prayer is said on one's own initiative, in one's own name and authority. Private prayer may be *mental* or *vocal*.

(c) Prayer may be of *adoration* (latreutic), *thanksgiving* (eucharistic) or *petition* (impetratory). The meaning of these types of prayer is clear in itself. The prayer of petition includes *propitiatory* prayer, in which one requests the remission of sins and punishment, and the prayer of *intercession*, in which one seeks graces for others.

PRAYER OF PETITION. Prayer in a strict sense, that is, as a *petition to God* for things that are necessary or suitable, involves the following points: (a) the *purpose*; (b) the *object* of the petition; (c) *to whom, for whom,* and *how* our petition is to be directed; (d) its *necessity*; (e) the *results* of prayer.

(a) The *purpose* of the prayer of petition is the worship of God and a request for His grace. By our petitions, however, we do not claim to make our needs in any way manifest to God, because God, who is omniscient, already knows these needs fully (Matt. 6:7, 32). Nor do we claim to alter the divine decrees, since God is immutable. But by prayers offered in the proper manner, we intend to fulfill the *condition* which God imposes and requests, in order that we might receive His graces (Matt. 7:7 ff.; Mark 11:24; Luke 11:9 ff.; John 14:13; 15:16). For, ordinarily, God grants favors and graces only to those who ask for them (Catechism of Pius X, n. 419). God wants us to engage in prayer because, by burning with the desire to obtain what we wish, we advance in virtue by an equally fervent effort, and thus become worthy of receiving those benefits which in our limited weakness we are unable to obtain of ourselves (*Catechismus ad parochos*, p. 4, n. 360).

By prayer, we exercise and increase not only the virtue of *religion* but *humility*, by professing to be God's poor; *faith*, by believing in His omnipotence and goodness; *hope*, by being confident in His aid; *charity*, by striving for an intimate union with Him.

(b) *It is proper to ask for those things which may be properly desired* (St. Augustine, *Ep. ad Probam*, c. 6 ff.: PL 33, 498 ff.). Therefore, one may pray not only for his spiritual but also his temporal welfare, with a priority on the spiritual ("But seek first the kingdom of God and his justice, and all these things shall be given you besides": Matt. 6:33). There is no limitation or condition, although temporal goods must take second place (Prov. 30:8 ff.), with an implicit condition, that they contribute to the salvation of one's soul: "that we may so pass through the good things of this life as not to lose those which are eternal" (prayer of the Third Sunday after Pentecost).

In reply to the question: "What things may we ask of God?" (Catechism of St. Pius X, no. 423), the answer is: "We must ask God for His glory, and eternal life and temporal graces for ourselves as well, as Jesus Christ taught in the Lord's Prayer." The Our Father (*q.v.*) is, under this aspect, a model of prayer.

Other admirable models of prayer of petition, and especially of the manner in which one asks for temporal benefits, are the prayers of the *Missal* and the *Ritual*. A typical example is the prayer for rain as reported in the *Ritual*: "O God, *in whom we live, move and are, give us a suitable rain, so that, having been aided sufficiently in our present needs, we may seek with greater faith the eternal goods.*"

(c) *To whom should one pray?* A petition may be directed to someone for two reasons: (1) in order that he may *grant* that which is asked; or (2) that he may *recommend* that it be granted. In the first way we direct our supplications to God; in the second way we direct our prayers to the Blessed Virgin and the saints. Thus, for example, in the Litany of the Saints, we ask God that He have mercy on us, that He grant our prayers, that He be favorably disposed to us, that He may forgive us, that He may spare us from evil, that He vouchsafe to hear us. We ask the Blessed Virgin, the angels, and saints to pray and to intercede for us.

For whom should one pray? We are to pray for those who can be helped by our prayers: (1) all those who are pilgrims in this life (I Tim. 2:1; Matt. 5:44; liturgy of Good Friday); (2) the souls in purgatory. In fact, one of the works of spiritual mercy enjoins us "*to pray to God for the living and the dead.*"

How to pray. In order to pray well, one must pray: (1) *with reverence and humility* (Luke 18:9 ff.; James 4:6); (2) *with faith* (Matt. 7:7 ff.; Luke 11:9 ff.; John 16:23; James 1:6 ff.); (3) *with perseverance* (Luke 11:5 ff.).

Trust, if it concerns temporal benefits or material difficulties, is filial abandon to the beneficent will of God, from whom we expect, with a spirit of humility and resignation to His will, to receive that which is most useful for our soul.

Prayer will be more acceptable: (1) if offered in the name of Jesus (John 16:23); (2) if sustained by the intercession of the Blessed Virgin and the saints; (3) if said by a person in the state of grace (Psalm 33:16; John 15:7 and 16:26 ff.; James 1:6 ff.; 5:16).

(d) *Necessity of prayer of petition.*

(1) *Necessity of precept and of means.* In the Catechism of St. Pius X (no. 419), in reply to the question: "Is it necessary to pray?" the answer is: "It is necessary to pray and to pray often because God commands it; ordinarily, only if one prays, does God give him spiritual and temporal graces."

Prayer is, therefore, of necessity of precept (because God commands it), and, in the case of adults, ordinarily of necessity of means, that is, as a means to obtain grace and, through grace, eternal life.

(2) *The command and example of Christ.* Our Saviour, Jesus Christ, said: "*Ask and it shall be given you; seek and you shall find; knock and it shall be opened to you. For everyone who asks receives; and he who seeks finds; and to him who knocks it shall be opened*" (Matt. 7:7 f.). "*Amen, Amen, I say to you, if you ask the Father anything in my name, he will give it to you.*" (John 16:23). "*Pray that you may not enter into temptation*" (Luke 22:40).

And St. Luke, in his Gospel, reminds us that Jesus proposed a parable in order to teach that one "*must always pray and not lose heart*" (Luke 18:1).

To His teaching, as always, Jesus added example. The Gospel reports several prayers of Jesus: "*And rising up long before daybreak, he went out and departed into a desert place and there he prayed*" (Mark 1:35). "*And when it was late he was there alone*" (Matt. 14:23). Here we have an example of *morning* and *evening* prayer.

The Apostles echo the Master's teaching, "Pray without ceasing" (I Thess. 5:17; Rom. 12:12; Col. 4:2 ff.; I Pet. 4:7). They speak of His example (Acts 1:14; 2:42; 3:15; 6:1 ff.).

(3) *An indispensable means of salvation.* St. Alphonsus summarizes in a noted expression the Christian doctrine regarding the need for prayer for an adult under ordinary circumstances: "He who prays will certainly be saved; and he who does not pray will not be saved." This is the meaning of those words: In order to be saved, one must possess habitual or sanctifying grace—namely, that supernatural, permanent gift of God which transforms our soul and makes it partake of the divine nature (II Peter 1:4). As adopted children of God (John 1:12; I John 3:1; Rom. 8:14 ff.), we become co-heirs with Christ of the eternal kingdom (Rom. 8:17).

The principal sources of this habitual grace are the sacraments, if properly received. Inclined as we are to sin, we cannot preserve for long time habitual or sanctifying grace unless God sustains us with His actual grace. This is also a gift of God, supernatural but transient, whose function is to illumine man's mind and to move his will to know and to do good, in order that he may save his soul.

Prayer is the main and most abundant

source of actual grace. As a source of actual grace, prayer surpasses all other means of salvation, including the sacraments, because it alone assures us of those efficacious actual graces. These obtain, without infringing upon our freedom, an efficacious response by which we overcome temptation and live in the grace of God until death.

If the sacraments can be said to be the food and medicine of our soul, prayer is its breath (Commentary on the Rule of St. Benedict: PL 66, 329). For the preservation of life, food alone is not sufficient, but one must also breathe; so, too, for the life of the soul, reception of the sacraments is not enough: one needs frequent prayer. It may be added that in order to receive a sacrament well, prayer is a necessary requirement in an adult person.

When is prayer necessary? Prayer may be considered (1) as an act of worship of God or (2) as a petition for aid.

As an act of worship, it is necessary many times in life; as a petition for aid, it is necessary whenever we are in danger of offending God (Matt. 26:41; Mark 14:38; Luke 22:40), or in times of grave, public calamity (Matt. 24:28; Mark 13:18; Luke 21:36).

The obligation of rendering worship to God, in practice, is fulfilled by participating in acts of worship, especially by hearing Holy Mass and receiving the sacraments.

The obligation of praying for aid, at least for an adult person, should be fulfilled each day, because each day one is exposed to the danger of losing grace.

Morning and *evening* prayers, considered as an act of worship, are not obligatory under pain of sin, because there is no law which requires that one pray at specific hours of the day. But if they are considered as a petition for aid, he who neglects them frequently and does not pray during other times of the day commits at least a venial sin, because he exposes himself to the danger of yielding to temptation. Charity toward oneself demands that this danger be avoided.

Thus, if one wishes to obtain greater assurance of the possession of the grace of God, he will make it his duty to say some prayers every day, in the morning and in the evening. Furthermore, during the day, if tempted, he will use ejaculatory invocations to direct his thoughts and affections to God. Also recommended is prayer before and after meals.

(e) *The fruits of prayer.* Prayer produces three main fruits and many secondary ones.

The three principal fruits are: *merit, satisfaction, impetration.* These are, in fact, common to all good works performed in the grace of God; but prayer has, on its own account, an especially efficacious impetratory power.

God, in fact, by virtue of His goodness, is expressly and solemnly committed to grant, under certain conditions, that which one asks of Him (John 16:23). If the necessary conditions are fulfilled, God definitely grants the favor requested.

Among the secondary fruits are the following: illumination of the intellect, strengthening of the will, increase of faith, hope, and charity, humility and all other moral virtues; consolation, and spiritual joy.

The promise of the Lord testifies to this: "*Ask and you shall receive, that your joy be full*" (John 16:24). Fitting too are the words of St. Augustine (PL 39, 1949): "*He who has learned to pray well has truly learned to live well.*" Ses.

PREACHING. Preaching, in a broad sense, means the perennial and constant oral teaching or transmission of the Divine Revelation, through the medium of the Church; the apostolic, doctrinal message is propagated by the Church. In a particular sense, preaching is the explanation in the name of the Church of the Christian truths to a community of adult faithful assembled for religious services. More exactly, it is the oral transmission of the revealed word by a lawfully authorized preacher. The constitutive elements and characteristic notes of preaching are contained in this definition: (a) oral transmission; (b) God's word; (c) a community of adult faithful, assembled in the name of the Church; (d) the mission of the Church (Can. 1328).

Preaching by a particular speaker cannot be considered an isolated, free, independent, and merely personal act of the speaker, although it is attributed to him as a free moral act. It is an act intimately connected by a causal *relationship to the teaching authority of the Church from which it derives its life,* and cannot be separated, for it is a function and manifestation of the life of the Church. Consequently, the ecclesiastical magisterium constitutes the fountain-head of all sermons (Canons 1322, 1327); through it, the particular functions of the preaching ministry are in a living relation with one another and with the fountain-head itself.

For humanity to be saved, *truth* was a primary and indispensable *good.* Teaching was a vital action of the Redeemer, who began his work by preaching (Matt. 4:17), with the proclamation: "*I am the light of the world . . . I am the truth.*" The essential Word of God, the Way, the Light of men, appeared in Christ; in Him every grace and truth became personalized (I John 4:17). The fulfillment of the revealing action of Jesus came about through the preaching of the Apostles (Acts 1:1 f.).

Preaching has always conformed to this grand mission. The Church, universal heir of the Savior from the day of her foundation, is the depository of the *apostolic magisterium,* the possessor and infallible teacher of supernatural truths; her word is a power and command instituted by God as the instrument in the development of the work of redemption.

Preaching is an absolutely necessary, vital *function of the Church* and one of its inalienable sovereign rights (Matt. 28:9; Mark 16:15). The Church is essentially not only a *praying* organism, but a *teacher,* just as her Head and Founder is *a Teacher,* in the truest sense of the word. To preach, therefore, is a function of the Church, a work of *God and men,* a united synthesis of the human and the divine, the natural and the supernatural. This is the supreme law and a vital condition for real and true preaching; in fact, on the determination

of this principle depends the essence and efficacy of preaching. The essence and basis of preaching cannot be fixed by an *a priori* philosophical method nor even from the idea of religion, but it must be deduced from Divine Revelation. The cry of grace and victory, "*And the Word was made flesh*" (*Et Verbum caro factum est*), proclaims the humanization of the word of God.

Thus, preaching is not the result of a natural, civil evolution but must be considered a *free creative act* of God. Neither Christianity nor its propagation are simply the effect of natural evolution. Christ is the first *preacher* and the very substance of preaching. Without positive Revelation, there would be no preaching; without Revelation in Christ and through Christ, there would be no Christian preaching. This rests on the foundation laid by God Himself and, like the apostolic preaching, it proclaims, even today, *Jesus* alone. In truth and by virtue of a divine authority (I Peter 4:11), the content is always the Gospel, according to the Lord's command (Mark 16:15; Matt. 24:14; II Cor. 4:5; I Cor. 1:23).

DIVINE INSTITUTION. This essential interior relation between preaching and supernatural Revelation is sufficient to establish its specific character; hence, *it cannot* be considered a species of general, rhetorical art, as if it were a counterpart of secular eloquence.

Preaching is neither *delivering speeches* nor giving religious lectures, in general. Preaching means showing mankind the *facts* and the *doctrine* of salvation, particularly all that the Divine Savior did and taught, by making Him known and bearing witness to Him (Acts 20:20). If preaching rejects this causal relation to Revelation, then sacred eloquence is not different from secular eloquence. The term *God's word* characterizes preaching as a specific creation and a divine institution, by removing it from the sphere of simply natural and human acts. This accounts for the heights and depths that should be found in a sacred speaker. This explains also the grave warning of St. Augustine concerning the necessity that the preacher pray for himself and others ("*Orando pro se ac pro illis quos allocuturus sit antequam dictor*": *De doctr. Christi*, 4, 15).

The sacred speaker cannot and must not allow the human element to prevail over the supernatural element; the word of salvation must not ignore what Christ Himself stated about His own preaching, "*My doctrine is not mine but his who sent me*" (John 7:16).

The very enticing slogan "To modern man one must preach in a modern way" must be taken with a grain of salt. The truths of faith are unchangeable, nor can we *rationalize over them* in order to accomodate ourselves to a particular spirit of the time. If the Gospel must be for man a *doctrine of salvation*, he must bow to its sanctity and objectivity, and accept it as real energy of soul and as God's voice (Dante, *Paradiso* 29, 103 ff.).

Preaching always loses effectiveness if it is too human or mundane. The priest in the pulpit is a sacred speaker, not a philosopher, sociologist, journalist, or man of letters; he may also be all or a little of all these, but he must remember that the purpose of preaching is not winning praise and compliments from the audience, but the salvation of souls. If the preacher lacks this purpose, he not only commits a sin, but deprives his word of that divine efficacy promised by Christ to His disciples and followers. *Tar.*

PREBEND. *See* Benefice, Ecclesiastical; Chapter.

PRECARIUM AND COMMODATUM. (Loan). A *precarium* is a free contract by which the use of a thing is granted until the grantor revokes the concession. *Precarium* for the Romans was a concession (*precibus*) common to ancient Roman society. It was not considered a contract, although it should be listed among unnamed contracts, because it did not create any binding relationship; the grantor could at any time bring a real action before the court in order to recover the object from any possessor.

By virtue of a protection of possession, the subject of *precarium* was considered a possessor; if he was disturbed in or deprived of his possession, he was protected by possessory interdicts. Such interdicts were not effective against the grantor (*rogatus* or *precario dans*) who would oppose the *exceptio precariae possessionis*. Afterwards, the grantor also obtained an *interdictum quod precario* (a more easy form of real action). In the Justinian law, *precarium* meant simple detention of an object (*precario possidere, esse in possessione*, i.e., *pro alieno possidere*).

COMMODATUM PRECARIUM. Present-day canonical law for contracts concerning ecclesiastical goods adopts the civil law of the different countries (Can. 1529).

The thing loaned must be returned if the termination of the loan comes due, if the lessee has used the thing according to the purpose for which it was given him, or if an urgent and unforeseen need occurs requiring the lender to use the thing himself.

The holder of the thing must exercise the same care that a good father would employ about his own property; he is responsible for damages resulting from fraud or grave neglect. Finally, he must return the thing in due time. Ordinary expenses must be paid by the borrower. *Sir.*

PRECEDENCE. As a technical canonical term, *precedence* means an external honor and a special reverence due to a physical or juridical person. This right consists chiefly in holding a more honored place in meetings, processions, councils, etc. It can be said that precedence is a natural requirement in every hierarchically constituted society, and, thus, also in the Church.

Precedence in Canon Law is governed by general and special rules. Special rules apply to cardinals (Canons 233, 236, 237, 239), papal legates (Can. 269), patriarchs, primates and archbishops (Can. 280), bishops (Can. 347), vicars general (Can. 370), chapters (Can. 408), vicars forain (Can. 450), parish priests and parish vicars (Can. 478), religious (Can. 491) and ecclesiastical associations (Can. 701).

Aside from these special rules, the following general rules are to be noted (Can. 106):

(a) The representative of a person, generally, takes the position of precedence belonging to the person he represents, with few exceptions in councils and similar assemblies.

(b) One who has any authority over other persons has precedence over them, e.g., the metropolitan over all the bishops of his province; the religious superiors of both sexes over their subjects, even if these have a higher order.

(c) Among several persons none of whom has authority over the others, the right of precedence belongs to the one who has a higher rank, i.e., a higher dignity or other preeminence. Thus, cardinals hold first place, then papal legates, patriarchs, primates, metropolitans and archbishops in their own provinces, bishops in their own dioceses, and so on. If various persons have the same rank, the one who has a higher order takes precedence over others; if they are of the same order, precedence is decided by seniority in rank, then in the order and, finally, by age.

(d) When proceeding collectively, the secular clergy precedes the religious clergy, and the religious precedes the laity (Can. 491).

(e) The above-mentioned rules are similarly applied even to juridical persons. The rite (Latin or Eastern) has no effect on precedence.

(f) The local Ordinary can in an urgent case decide controversies regarding precedence. In this case, his decision is binding even on exempt religious when they proceed collectively with others; and no recourse with a suspensive effect is allowed against it, although a recourse with devolutive effect to the Holy See is permitted. *Led.*

PRECEPT. An order or command by a lawful superior by virtue of dominative or jurisdictional power is termed a *precept*. As an act of jurisdictional power,

it is to be restricted either to one person, or to the community as such for a limited time. If it is given to a community for the common good, it lacks permanent character, for it does not extend beyond a definite time, or the lifetime of the superior who gave it. Generally, properly speaking, a precept is an order given to one individual or a number of individuals separately.

A precept differs from a law, because a precept stems from the power of either jurisdiction or domination or domestic power, such as that possessed by a father, husband, master, or religious superior without jurisdictional power. Since it chiefly and directly aims at the private welfare, it is not limited to a territory, but applies to the individual wherever he may be or go (*ossibus haeret*).

In reality, this type of precept is given either in the *internal forum*, for the purpose of protecting only the spiritual welfare of an individual, or in the *external forum*, for the purpose of keeping order in society by avoiding scandals, preventing crimes, and maintaining ecclesiastical discipline. The former ceases with the termination of the authority of the one who gave it; all its effectiveness is exercised in the realm of conscience. Hence, it falls entirely in the field of pure morals. The latter, instead, can be enjoined judicially, and it ceases upon termination of the order of the superior, unless it was imposed by a written document or in the presence of two witnesses (Can. 24). If the superior omitted this formality, it is presumed that he intended to follow the ordinary rule, according to which precepts are limited to one's time in office, unless there is provision for a forced execution in the external forum.

Until recent times, doctrine concerning a precept was lacking in exactness, and was made even more obscure by controversies. The Code of Canon Law has removed various doubts. Two questions in particular have been solved: (a) a precept binds outside the territory, except when the precept stemmed from an authority not limited to a particular territory, or arose from an agreement, or was confirmed by a pact; (b) it does not necessarily cease with the termination of the jurisdiction of the one who gave it; this, too, was denied by the majority.

Furthermore, a necessary condition was added, which demanded a written document and the presence of two witnesses.

Besides the distinction between a precept given by a superior with domestic or jurisdictional power, and the precept with binding force in the external forum or simply in the internal forum, a precept may also be: (a) *Territorial* or *personal*. In itself, a precept is presumed to be personal, but there can also be a territorial precept binding only in the territory in which it was given. (b) *Temporary*, which ceases by its very nature at the appointed time; or *perpetual*, which does not cease except by dispensation, revocation, etc., or because of impossibility of observance, a cessation of the purpose intended by the precept or of the authority of the superior (there are possible exceptions in this regard). (c) Given to a *physical person* or to a *community*, as such. It is to be observed that, even if it is given individually to all the members of a community, it may not for this be given to the whole community, as such. (d) *Carrying* a penal sanction or without such sanction. The latter is one of the so-called penal remedies.

A precept, as a penal remedy, is an order which is given with a threat of penalty. A precept should indicate to the subject exactly what he should do or avoid doing. In reality, it is a more serious penal remedy than a warning or a correction; it has, in a sense, the value of a condemnatory sentence with an attached condition.

As a general rule, the superior must first warn and correct before resorting to a precept, because the Code permits recourse to the latter only if warnings and corrections have failed, or their ineffectiveness is foreseen. Their ineffectiveness, however, ought not to be easily presumed; besides, the superior, before he resorts to a precept must have gathered sufficient evidence to establish the seriousness of the scandal given, the proximate occasion of the violation, or the existence of a grave social disorder.

With regard to procedure, the precept shall be valid in court if given in writing before two witnesses. Finally, a distinction must be made between a penal precept, by which an act is imposed or its omission ordered under threat of penalty, and a penalty inflicted by precept (*per modum praecepti*); on this point *see* Penalty. *Pal.*

PRECEPT, HOLY DAY. *See* Sanctification of Holy Days.

PRECEPTS OF THE CHURCH. Ecclesiastical or divine laws, imposed by the Church for the spiritual good of the faithful and binding in conscience, are called *precepts of the Church*. (Concerning the juridical significance of the term *precept*, see article on Precept.) The Catechism lists six such precepts, but their number could be larger or smaller: (1) to hear Mass on Sundays and holy days of obligation; (2) to fast and abstain on the days appointed; (3) to go to confession at least once a year; (4) to receive Holy Communion at least during Easter time; (5) to contribute to the support of the pastor; (6) to observe the laws of the Church concerning marriage.

With respect to the matter of the first precept, *see* Sanctification of Holy days; for the second, *see* Abstinence and Fasting; for the third, *see* Confession; for the fourth, *see* Communion and Easter Duty; for the fifth, *see* Clergy (goods of the), Ecclesiastical Benefice, Tithes, Mass offering and Ecclesiastical Tax; for the sixth, *see* Marriage (Form of).

The precepts of the Church are treated in that part of moral theology termed *special*. Those authors who emphasize the vitalistic, psychological aspect of special moral theology arrange the subject matter according to various virtues; the Church precepts are thus distributed under the various virtues. Others, instead, concentrate more on the deontological and preceptive aspects of moral theology, and treat the subject matter along the lines of the ten commandments and the precepts of the Church. *Pal.*

PRE-EMPTION. *See* Insolvency, Bankruptcy.

PREFECT, APOSTOLIC. The *prefect apostolic* is a prelate who, in the name of the Sovereign Pontiff, rules, with ordinary authority, over a part of a mission territory in which the faith has been established for a short time with, therefore, a rather small number of faithful and missionaries. The part of the missionary territory under his jurisdiction is called *prefecture apostolic.* Often, the prefect apostolic is not a bishop but enjoys in his own territory the same authority as a local Ordinary, unless the Holy See has made some restrictions in a particular case. In addition he has many delegated faculties. While in office, within the limits of his territory, he enjoys the privileges of honor accorded to participating prothonotaries apostolic and may give all blessings reserved to the bishops, except the pontifical blessing. He may consecrate chalices, patens, and portable altars; he may grant an indulgence of fifty days or administer confirmation (*q.v.*), first tonsure (*q.v.*) and minor orders (Can. 294, par. 2).

PROPREFECT. After his arrival in a territory, the prefect apostolic must designate, as soon as possible, a suitable priest, unless he has already a coadjutor with the right of succession. This priest has the title of *proprefect;* to this proprefect he confers appropriate delegated powers. The proprefect succeeds by right (*ipso iure*) the prefect apostolic if he dies or is unable to fulfill his duties. In this case, the proprefect has all ordinary and delegated powers of the deceased or incapacitated prefect, but he must notify the Holy See in order that a new prefect may be appointed as soon as possible. In the meantime, he will appoint a priest as his deputy. If no proprefect or deputy have been appointed, the missionary who has the oldest letters of introduction, or from several missionaries of the same rank the senior in the priesthood (Can. 309), succeeds by right to the direction

of the prefecture, unless the Holy See decrees otherwise.

APPOINTMENT AND FACULTIES. The prefect apostolic is appointed by the Holy See by letter from the Sacred Congregation for the Propagation of the Faith. He takes charge as soon as the letter of appointment is presented to the one who in the meantime governed the prefecture; his office terminates in the same manner as other Ordinaries, from whom he differs in this: he may be removed *ad nutum S. Sedis.*

The prefect apostolic has the right and duty to govern the mission, both in spiritual and temporal things, and to this end possesses legislative, judiciary, and executive powers.

Since he has no cathedral chapter, the prefect shall appoint a council of at least three older and more experienced missionaries, whom he shall consult, at least by letter, concerning the more serious and difficult affairs. The diocesan synod, which the prefect cannot convoke, is replaced by the congregation, which shall be assembled at least once a year, with both religious and secular clergy.

Concerning the relations between the prefect and the missionaries and religious, *see* Cans. 295–298.

Though the prefect is not required to make the *ad limina* visit, every five years he must send a report to the Sacred Congregation for the Propagation of the Faith concerning the condition of the Church under his jurisdiction. He is also required to reside in his territory, and visit the prefecture whenever necessary. He must apply the Mass *pro populo* on eleven of the more solemn feasts and establish both the ordinary and secret archives (*q.v.*). Finally, he must take particular care of the training of the native clergy (Cans. 293–305). *Fel.*

PREGNANCY. *Pregnancy* is the particular state of a woman carrying in her womb a fecundated ovum in the process of development and growth. Pregnancy is called *simple* if the product of conception is one, or *multiple* if the product of conception is *twin* or bigeminal, *triple* or trigeminal, etc. Pregnancy may be *phys-*

iological (normal or natural), or *patho-logical* if it proceeds in an abnormal way due to complications caused by local or general disease. Pregnancy may be also *uterine* or *topical* (ordinary) or *extra-uterine* or *ectopic* (outside the uterus). We speak, finally, of *false* or imaginary pregnancy, called *pseudocyesis*, in women who, in abnormal conditions, show subjective symptoms of pregnancy, without pregnancy existing in reality. This is a syndrome pertaining distinctly to psychosomatic medicine (*q.v.*), in which a psychic factor (fear of pregnancy, keen desire for a child, family dissensions, and the like) is generally responsible for endocrinal and neuro-vegetative alterations giving rise to symptoms of seeming pregnancy.

The duration of pregnancy in humans is normally 280 days, counting from the beginning of the last menstrual period, or 270 days if it is possible to know exactly the beginning. In any case, the computation is approximate; hence, the physiological minimum and maximum usually given are of 255 and 300 days respectively; this is due to the fact that neither the exact moment nor the location of the meeting between the ovum and the sperm are known, nor the way followed by the ovum before it becomes fecundated and before adhering to the wall of the uterus.

At any rate, the probable date of delivery may be computed by counting nine months from the beginning of the last period and adding 6 or 7 days.

SYMPTOMS OF PREGNANCY. They are usually grouped into three categories:

(a) *presumptive symptoms:* certain general, subjective and objective modifications common to a pregnant woman, as sympathetic phenomena due to neuro-vegetative disturbances, lack of appetite, nausea, alteration in the sense of taste, and the like;

(b) *probable symptoms:* these consist of certain modifications in the genital regions of the woman, such as absence of menstrual flow, enlargement of the uterus, and the like;

(c) *certain symptoms:* these are phenomena which indicate the presence of the fetus; one such sign is sufficient to ascertain the fact of pregnancy (observation of small fetal parts, dual cardiac beat).

Since a clinical diagnosis of pregnancy is very difficult in the first weeks of gestation, *biological tests* have proven to be of considerable diagnostic value, particularly the reaction discovered by S. Ascheim and B. Zondek, which is almost 100% accurate.

The state of pregnancy not only carries with it deep modifications of the pregnant woman's genital organs, but also more or less conspicuous changes in the entire female body, and an increase of toxic substances produced by both the woman and the fetus, hence overtaxing the kidneys or liver of the mother, which are charged with eliminating and neutralizing these toxic substances respectively, with the aid of hypophysis and cortical surrenal hormones.

MORAL DUTIES OF THE PHYSICIAN. The physician must take particular care of a woman in gestation, both in protecting the fetus against possible diseases of pregnancy and in eliminating conditions which may place the woman in the danger or temptation of committing abortion. He must give his patients timely norms for diet, clothing, daily habits, personal cleanliness, and the like. A diligent physician must treat carefully and promptly any infection and be solicitous in preventing the recurrence of abortion in the case of women subject to habitual spontaneous abortion.

A solicitous physician must be concerned about the woman's health as well as that of the fetus.

Biological diagnosis of pregnancy is lawful only with approval of the interested party, or, if the woman is incompetent, when the physician deems it necessary for the protection of the fetus.

We shall mention here that a physician may give a woman in gestation specific treatments or perform surgery even if a probable abortion were to follow, provided that those treatments or operations be not the direct cause of the abortion, that they be deemed necessary for serious reasons of health, that the mother be aware of the possible consequence of abortion, and that she give her consent. If an injury to the fetus is foreseen to occur from such treatments, e.g., radium, these may not be given. A physician, on the other hand, may subject a woman to particular physical treatments if absolutely necessary, although damage is foreseen in future pregnancies.

If conditions warrant it, the physician is under an obligation to draw a viable fetus from a dead mother's womb; a practical certainty, not a mere assumption, of death of the fetus may discharge the physician from such an obligation. For the purpose of baptizing the fetus, the physician must draw it out even if non-viable (*see* Section, Caesarean).

The use of anesthesia in a normal delivery is lawful, provided that its administration is such that no injury is anticipated either for the mother or the fetus. Anesthesia may be suggested to those women who are particularly fearful of the pains of childbirth.

In the imminence of a pathological delivery, if both mother and child can be saved only by a serious surgical operation, the physician has the obligation to propose it, and the mother is under obligation to accept it, despite a certain risk for her, particularly because of the eternal salvation of the fetus. Embryotomy (*q.v.*) or any other type of surgical operation directed at the killing of the unborn child may *never* be resorted to. The obligation on the part of the mother, however, ceases if the operation appears to be very dangerous. Nevertheless, the physician may try it with the mother's consent, provided that there is at least the probability of saving the child and that the operation is not conducive to the direct killing of the mother.

Painless delivery by the use of anesthetics is subject to certain restrictions and reservations, but painless delivery by the use of the psycho-prophylactic method may be used without reservations or restrictions.

This method, originated by G. Read, a London physician in 1933, and perfected by Nicolaiev about ten years later, uses the principles and techniques of conditioned reflexes (*q.v.*); it is rapidly spreading all over the civilized world, through the efforts of the French obstetrician Lamaze, who adopted it in Paris, about 1950, and who has become an enthusiastic promoter.

The method consists in explaining to a woman in gestation how delivery takes place, in teaching her certain specific exercises of respiration, relaxation and the like, in helping her by persuasion and examples to overcome fears, nervousness, anxiety, and other conditions.

It is a fact that by this method, called *fearless delivery*, extraordinary results are attained, not only with respect to the woman, who after the experience of the benefits of this method will meet future pregnancies with a more serene mind, but with respect to conjugal relations and even children born under better conditions. The delivery is more rapid and less dangerous for the child.

This method, which eliminates all pain in half of the cases and makes it quite bearable in the rest, deserves the greatest diffusion. The lawfulness of this method was explicitly acknowledged by the late Pope Pius XII in an admirable speech on the subject, delivered on January 8, 1956 (AAS: 48 (1956), 82–93).

MORAL DUTIES OF THE WOMAN IN GESTATION. A pregnant mother has grave duties toward God, who called her to participate with Him in the work of creation of a new life which she carries within herself. She has moral duties toward the unborn child, whose development is directly entrusted to her. She also has duties toward her husband and toward the society into which the coming child will be born. In order to protect the new life, she must avoid those exercises, habits, and other activities that might cause injury to the fetus. Thus she shall avoid excessive toil, strenuous sports, narcotic intoxication, and excessive smoking. Failing in these duties, she could be held accountable for many difficulties arising in connection with the birth and the health of the child. *Riz.*

PREGNANCY (ECTOPIC). The word *ectopic* means *out of place*. In reference to pregnancy, it means gestation which is out of the normal place (uterus); hence ectopic gestation is also called extra-uterine pregnancy, because the fertilized ovum develops outside the uterus. Depending on the site of implantation of the ovum, extra-uterine pregnancies are classified as tubal, ovarian, and abdominal. With extremely few exceptions, extra-uterine pregnancies are of the tubal type. It is a rare case in which an ectopic fetus reaches viability, although a timely laparotomy may permit extraction of a living fetus. Ordinarily, however, an ectopic pregnancy terminates at an early phase of gestation, due to hemorrhagic or suppurative factors which require immediate surgical intervention to save the mother.

CONDUCT OF THE PHYSICIAN. In all extra-uterine pregnancies, the proper norm of conduct for a physician is to maintain a vigilant and diligent surveillance over the pregnant woman and be ready to intervene with timely surgical action as soon as hemorrhagic or other pathological factors demand it. If the hemorrhage is due to the rupture of the tube and the fetus is living, though not viable, a surgical intervention is permissible. The surgery is imperative, and the consequent death of the fetus is simply an indirect effect of surgical action, whose therapeutic purpose is to check the hemorrhage. (*See also* Abortion, Therapeutic.)

According to most theologians, in the case of a tubal pregnancy, the ligation of the maternal blood vessels and removal of the tube is morally permissible *even before the rupture of the tube* or *before hemorrhage*, which creates an *imminent* danger of death for the mother. The reason is that a gradual disintegration of blood vessels constitutes a pathological condition in the mother, distinct from the mere fact of the presence of the fetus.

PRELATE. Properly speaking, *prelates* are those who have ordinary jurisdiction in the external forum (Can. 110). Thus, bishops and those who possess episcopal or quasi-episcopal authority are called

prelates: those who in the Sacred Congregations come immediately after the cardinals, the auditors of the Sacred Roman Rota, and a few other officials of the Roman Curia. The superiors general and provincials of exempt clerical religious are called *prelates regular.*

All others who have the title of prelate, either in the Curia or outside, such as prothonotaries apostolic and *domestic* prelates, are honorary prelates. Among these are the four so-called tassel prelates: vice-chamberlain of the Holy Roman Church; the auditor and the treasurer of the Reverend Apostolic Chamber, and the majordomo of His Holiness; there are four *palatine* prelates: the majordomo of His Holiness, the chamber master, the auditor of His Holiness, whose duties are now given to the secretary of the Apostolic Signature, and the master of the Sacred Apostolic Palace (*q.v.*).

COLLEGES OF PRELATES. Some prelates constitute colleges or groups, with special rules, offices and privileges; such colleges are: *prothonotaries apostolic de numero, auditors of the Sacred Roman Rota, clerics of chamber, voters of signature* (to the latter are joined also: the *referendarii* of signature, who do not constitute a college).

All prelates have special insignia and honors. Tassel prelates, patriarchs, bishops, deputy prelates (assessors), secretaries of Sacred Congregations, the Secretary of the Apostolic Signature, the Dean of the Sacred Roman Rota and the substitute of the Secretary of State all enjoy the title of *Excellency.*

PRELATES NULLIUS. A title which is entirely unique is that of *prelate nullius;* it refers to a prelate, bishop or non-bishop, who rules with quasi-episcopal authority over a territory that is exempt from the jurisdiction of all other bishops. The territory itself is termed a *prelature nullius (dioeceseos).* The prelate *nullius* resembles an abbot *nullius* in his powers of authority (Can. 319). *Fel.*

PREMEDITATION. A deliberate criminal act, based on a singularly malicious intent, which is tenaciously and continually considered and carried out to the point of consummation, is called *premeditation*. Premeditation does not arise with the first consideration of a criminal action but after one begins to formulate the actual intent to commit the crime. The traditional circumstances of a calm and collected mind (*frigido pacatoque animo*) or the contrived plan of a crime are not the essential elements of premeditation; rather, the unchanged and constant persistence in the motive, direction and determination of the will comprise the essence of premeditated crime. The element of time between the initial intent and final consummation of the premeditated crime or between the initial stirrings of criminal intent and the determined decision to act is of secondary importance. Furthermore, an abnormal will and premeditation are antithetical terms, for one cannot tenaciously will an act, if he is not endowed with a normal capacity of will. A rigid criminal intent has already rejected the influence of judgment and ordinary inhibitory motives; it thus hinders conscience, which is already involved in the criminal notion, from permitting even a superficial reappearance of any critical or inhibitory elements. Even the motive must stem from a particularly evil cause, since an ordinary motive is evidently not sufficient nor does a motive not particularly directed toward the particular crime suffice.

Premeditation is considered an aggravating circumstance, since it spells calculation, coldness, a firm, reflective determination and, therefore, greater stubbornness and dangerousness in the criminal. Doctrine and jurisprudence admit the impossibility of premeditation in a mentally ill person in whom the idea of evil normally assumes the form of impulse; the irresistibility of an impulse is incompatible with a free capacity to will, or with a responsible, continued decision to commit a crime. Incompatibility between premeditation and provocation (*q.v.*) is also admitted, inasmuch as provocation leads one to act by virtue of an almost unrestrainable impulse in a reaction which obviously does not go with a meditated decision.

Canon Law, following Roman tradition, does not consider premeditation a special aggravating cause of crime but rather a way of measuring a fraud, in which the first step is represented by impulse, the second by deliberation, and the last by premeditation, by which one evaluates pros and cons of a crime and prepares the means suitable for its execution, not in a climate confused by impulse or reaction, but in an atmosphere of perfectly conscious determination. There are, in the canonical code, traces of premeditation, inasmuch as Canon 2206 considers imputability arising from a voluntarily aroused passion (*passio voluntarie et deliberate excitata vel nutrita*) as an aggravating element if the will directly moves the feelings, by exciting them, to an increase of hate and arousing a conscious and firm resolution to commit the crime. In itself, one who ponders and plans a crime while in a state of passion has no less capacity for meditating and willing than one acting and planning a crime in a calm state of mind. Passion is but exasperation of desire; it would be an absurdity to think that the threat of punishment, established precisely to serve as a counterstimulus against certain desires, were to have no effect in those very cases in which it is more particularly needed.

In moral theology, premeditation is synonymous with deliberate intention (*q.v.*), and an aggravating circumstance. *Pug.*

PREMONITION. *Premonition*, in metapsychology (*q.v.*), indicates a paranormal phenomenon of anticipation of the future; such phenomena are also called *precognition, clairvoyance,* and the like.

Manifestations of premonition in normal individuals occur by way of exception, and almost always only in a state of diminished consciousness (sleep, hypnosis); however, they are believed to be present with particular frequency in some *mediums*.

Numerous investigators have conducted extensive inquiries in premonitory phenomena, e.g., a notable study conducted by the *Society for Psychical Research* of London on about a thousand certified cases. They have concluded that the hypothesis of fortuitous coincidence is to be excluded before the mass of facts investigated.

Many and diverse interpretative hypotheses are formulated of premonition; however, none of the interpretations brought forth, whether of a psychological, philosophical or physico-mathematical nature, is such as to satisfy the requirements of scientific proof.

Concerning the hypotheses that can be accepted by Catholic scholars, *see* Metapsychology. At this point, we shall endeavor to clarify a question ordinarily raised on the subject of premonition. Some seem inclined to place the premonitory manifestations on the same level as prophecies; but this alleged identity cannot be accepted, because *prophecy* is always the revelation of something of a supernatural nature by God for the salvation of man.

This is proved by the entire history of the Old Testament, which attains its full realization in the New Testament. Thus, it is not a question of an isolated phenomenon or a series of separate phenomena, but of the entire history of the Jewish people, foreseen and predicted in full details by major and minor prophets. The prophecies, therefore, have nothing in common with the para-normal phenomena of premonition. *Riz.*

PRESBYTERATE. *See* Holy Orders.

PRESCIENCE. *See* Premonition.

PRESCRIPTION (Usucapio). *Prescription* (Latin, *praescriptio*—title, disposition) is a title or disposition by way of exception in behalf of a plaintiff in a trial. In modern civil and ecclesiastical legislation, prescription is a means by which a person acquires a right, is released from an obligation, or obtains a dismissal of an action on the grounds of a lapse of time or the intervention of specific circumstances or conditions.

Prescription may be *acquisitive* or *extinctive*. *Acquisitive* prescription confers a new right (*in re*), which the Romans termed *usucapio*; *extinctive* prescription releases a person from an obligation, and is called liberating. Another form of prescription, called *presumptive*, was introduced in the Middle Ages and remains in the law today. It is based on the expiration of a period of time within which the law presumes the extinction of certain debts. This form, maintained in modern codes of law, is improperly termed *prescription*, since it is more a presumption.

The proximate, direct source of prescription is the positive law, although the remote, indirect source is found in the natural law. Gaius proves that this custom and institution conforms to the natural law (Fr. 1, D. 41, 3).

With an appeal to the common good, the Roman lawyer demonstrates the need for prescription for the following reasons: (a) to avoid a situation in which the rights of ownership are left for a long period or indefinitely in a condition of uncertainty; (b) to end disputes; (c) to spare the possessors of property worries and fears that would prevent further improvements of their property; (d) to punish the laziness and negligence of those who failed to adequately protect their own rights.

For all these reasons, which in the final analysis amount to a requirement of the public good, we hold that prescription is rooted in the natural law. Since it is the right of the civil laws to spell out in matters of justice the range of the natural law, moral theologians are unanimous in teaching that the conditions prescribed by the civil law for prescription are generally, with due restrictions, valid not only in the external forum but also in conscience.

It must be added that Church legislation considers prescription a lawful means of acquiring ownership. This appears from the canons of the Fourth Lateran Council (c. 41: *Denz.* 439), the *Decretals* (c. 3, X, 2, 26), and the Code of Canon Law, which recognizes prescription for ecclesiastical property, as in various civil legislations (Can. 1508), with the exception of conflicts with the natural (Can. 1512) and the canonical (Can. 1510–1511) laws. This reservation, of course, is always to be made with respect to civil laws. For this reason, the moral judgment on the laws governing prescription may differ from one country to another; hence, we refer the reader to the legislation of each respective region or State. In the treatment of this subject, we follow the provisions of Canon Law and of modern civil legislation patterned generally after the Roman law.

As stated above, prescription implies acquisition or liberation from an obligation, with the lapse of a certain period of time and in determined conditions. Of these conditions, some concern *acquisitive*, others *extinctive*, others both types of prescription.

(A) *The conditions for acquisitive prescription or usucapio* are: (1) possession, (2) good faith, and (3) a title.

(1) *Possession*. Possession must be lawful. Possession is understood here as retention of a thing or the enjoyment of a right to be obtained by prescription exercised by us or by others who may hold the thing or who may be exercising the right in our own name. Possession is lawful if it is continuous, uninterrupted, peaceful, public, unequivocal, and the possessor deliberately holds the thing as his own. The thing must be retained as one's own (*animo domini*) because prescription must be first of all dominative. Furthermore, possession must be public, not clandestine, in order that the individual against whom the prescription is invoked may be able to vindicate his own right. It must be certain, not doubtful, for otherwise the second condition, good faith, would be lacking; finally, it must be uninterrupted and peaceful, that is, continuous without interruption, either natural or civil.

(2) *Good faith*. *Bona fides* is a firm persuasion by which one prudently judges himself possessor of the thing he retains as his own. Good faith, ordinarily, is *theological* or *juridical*: the former concerns subjective persuasion; the latter concerns a persuasion based on a certain external title, without any defect of form. Theological good faith may be taken

in a strict sense, as a belief that excludes ownership by another, or in a broad sense, as the belief that excludes an obligation to restore to the owner a thing which is known to belong to another.

In order that prescription may be binding in conscience, according to the more common opinion, it must be based on theological good faith, not only at the beginning, but during the entire period of prescription.

(a) This is the sense of the Church definitions. Alexander III and Innocent III (the latter in the Lateran Council, IV, Chap. 21) solemnly proclaimed, "It is necessary that he who invokes prescription must, at no time, have been conscious of holding someone else's property" (X, 2, 26, 5 and 20). And the Code of Canon Law (Can. 1512) requires this good faith in cases of prescription of ecclesiastical goods.

(b) Reason tells us that no one must draw a benefit from fraud or from his own bad faith, for this would be contrary to a good social order. It is against the very concept of justice that one who culpably possesses the property of another, can make that property his own if he is supposed to restore it to its owner. Nor can civil law favor iniquity or injustice.

(c) Furthermore, the civil legislator, who in certain cases does not require good faith, is presumed to do this, not to protect iniquity but to clarify certain situations, particularly in view of the impossibility for the legislator to enter the internal forum of conscience.

Besides theological good faith, *juridical good faith*, i.e., based on a title, is also required, at least in the beginning.

Three things are particularly opposed to good faith in acquisitive prescription: bad faith, doubtful faith, and gravely culpable ignorance. Bad faith always prevents prescription; initial doubtful faith makes an investigation mandatory; but in an insoluble doubt, a solution on the basis of an accepted principle (*In dubio melior est conditio possidentis*: in doubt, the right of the possession prevails) may be permitted. This is valid, even if the doubt occurs after the start of the prescription. Prescription is interrupted only if, following an investigation, it can be ascertained that the thing belongs to another. Gravely culpable ignorance, whether of law or of fact, nullifies good faith. Invincible or non-imputable ignorance or slightly culpable or imputable ignorance, if of *fact*, does not nullify good faith; if of *law*, it certainly does not nullify theological good faith, and, according to some modern civil codes, not even juridical faith.

Concerning a transmission of good faith with transmission of possession, note the following:

(a) If successor and predecessor are in good faith, the time of the possession of both, required for prescription, is computed together. The reason is that the predecessor is considered as transmitting to his successor all the right inherent in the thing itself.

(b) If the predecessor was in bad faith, then the successor in good faith must follow, even in conscience, the laws of the country or region. According to ancient Roman law, a direct universal successor could not invoke prescription because, from an ideal point of view (*per fictionem iuris*), he was considered as being one with the deceased predecessor; this, however, was not so in the case of a particular or indirect successor. The civil codes of different countries view this matter with certain variations.

(3) *Title. Title* is a cause suitable for transmission of ownership. A title may be *real, colored, precarious, putative,* or *presumed.* According to the natural law, no *real* title is required for prescription, for it would be useless to invoke prescription, as the title could, of itself, effect transmission of ownership. However, a title is required, even if civil law does not require it, for no good faith is possible without a title on which it might be based. Thus, a title is required suitable to occasion good faith. Certainly a colored and a putative title is such, but not a vitiated or precarious title, because the latter carries a note indicating the purpose for which possession is given, which is not that of transfer of property. Nor is a title presumed by law, if in fact the title does not exist and no inquiry is made to ascertain the truth.

(B) *Conditions for liberative prescription.* Ordinarily, the conditions required for acquisitive prescription are also valid in a liberating prescription. However, since possession with respect to liberative prescription is simply non-recognition of the obligation on one side, with no-claim on the other, and since the title is identified with the lawful non-recognition of a debt, it is evident that, practically, possession and title do not differ from good faith. Similar to liberative prescription, although essentially different, is lapsed prescription, which is present if, after the time set by the parties, judge, or law has elapsed, no action may be entered. At times, if the expiration time is established by law, it is difficult to distinguish whether it is a case of liberating or lapsed prescription. At any rate, the same rules apply with regard to the obligation in conscience. The question may be raised here as to what constitutes good faith in a liberating prescription. In answer to this question the following distinction must be made:

(1) If the obligation is, not to lend something, but a question of being acted against, does good faith consist simply in not unjustly inhibiting another from using his right or in the belief that the other person does not have the right that he alleges? It is the case of the so-called stewardship.

(2) The same thing must be said if the obligation is to do something, not only to bear it, but in such a way that the debtor is not bound to act except if he is requested to do so, as in the case of paying off a legacy. The reason in both cases is quite evident, for it would be unjust to force the debtor to urge the creditor to use his right in his own behalf. Each individual is defender of his own rights.

(3) On the contrary, if the obligation is to lend something, it is not fair to lend it only at the time of the request. Good faith, then, is present only when one is ignorant of his obligation. There is no prescription in conscience. This is

a common opinion among moral theologians.

Extinctive prescription, it must be observed, is not limited only to financial obligations, but it extends to any kind of obligation. In the field of procedural law, Canon 1701 deals with such matters by admitting extinction of the action by prescription in civil suits. In this case, no prescription may be invoked without good faith (Canons 1701; 1508–1512). Concerning criminal actions, the law admits of extinction (Can. 1702); in fact, good faith is not required, and the guilty party is not bound in conscience to pay the penalty before a condemnatory sentence.

(C) *Conditions for both types of prescription.* These are *prescriptibility of the thing*, and *sufficient time* to bring about prescription.

(1) Prescriptibility of a thing is a capacity to be subject to prescription both by nature and by law. All those things or rights which by their very nature stem from the natural or divine-positive law are not subject to acquisitive prescription, and all obligations stemming from the same source as above are likewise not subject to liberative prescription. Thus, for instance, obedience to one's superior and the Church's independence of the State are not subject to prescription. Not subject to prescription because of their free use are those things which cannot be privately owned, such as public roads, rivers, and the like. Further determinations in this regard are made by the law. For objects or rights not subject to prescription by law, the reader must consult the civil codes of each country.

According to Canon Law, the following are absolutely *not* subject to prescription: rights and obligations which can be obtained only by apostolic privilege; the certain and undisputed boundary lines of ecclesiastical provinces, dioceses, parishes, vicariates and prefectures apostolic, abbeys, and prelatures *nullius;* Mass stipends and obligations; ecclesiastical benefices without title; the exemption from the right of visitation and obedience on the part of any ecclesiasti-

cal authority; payment of the *cathedraticum* (Can. 1509, par. 2, 4–5, 7–8). Other entities, rights, and obligations are not free from prescription without definite conditions; among these, sacred objects, consecrated or blessed, may not be possessed by private persons; spiritual rights which lay persons are incapable of acquiring cannot be claimed by prescription, nor can ecclesiastical benefices without title be prescribed (Cans. 1510, par. 2; 1509, par. 6).

(2) Time. Both acquisitive and liberative prescription require that a period of time must elapse before prescription may be validly invoked; before this period, prescription is not admissible. The length of time is determined by the competent authority. Thus, there are short (within ten years), long (twenty, thirty, or forty years) and very long prescriptions (one hundred years).

Canon Law accepts, in this respect, even for ecclesiastical property, the determinations of civil codes (Can. 1508), with some exceptions (Can. 1511, par. 1–2): immovable goods, movable precious goods, rights and claims, both personal and real, of the Holy See (100 years), and for goods belonging to legal ecclesiastical persons (30 years).

(D) *Prescription in the United States.* Prescription in the United States applies chiefly to rights over real estate property, adverse possession of the real estate itself, and the so-called statute of limitation, which does not recognize claims for payment of debts after a certain length of time. If one, by mere negligence, allows another to use his real estate property, or to exercise a certain right over it for a statutory time, the latter acquires a vested right to use the property or to exercise that right over it. The adverse possession of the land of another develops into a title to the land if its occupation is effected openly and remains undisturbed for a period of twenty years or less, which is the statutory time. The statute of limitation has the effect of making certain debts not enforceable by the creditor beyond the statutory period of time.

The statutory period varies in different states even with respect to the same type of debts. The law, however, admits that the debt itself is not cancelled by the statute of limitation; what happens is that the creditor is unable to enforce it by law.

Canon Law does not admit any prescription without good faith, so that no lapse of time will free a debtor from the obligation of paying the debt which he knows he still owes. Good faith is also required in prescription affecting real estate property, whether it concerns the title to land, the acquisition of rights over it, or the liberation from a burden weighing on one's real estate. The lapse of statutory time specified by the civil law confers no rights in conscience, unless good faith is present. *Pal.*

PRESENCE OF GOD. There is a general presence of God in all things, called presence of *immensity*; in fact, God works directly in every creature, preserving and moving it to action. But there is also a *special presence*, which is the indwelling of God in the soul living in grace (Wis. 1:4; John 14:23; Rom. 5:5; I Cor. 3:16; 6:19; I John 4:9 ff.). God not only operates in the soul living in grace, but at times He gives Himself to that soul in such a manner that the soul can almost experimentally know and enjoy Him.

It is exceedingly helpful to keep oneself in the presence of God. The thought of the presence of God enables one to refrain from sin and move toward perfection. It increases trust in God and may produce a sweet joy, helpful to the soul. It leads to a great respect for oneself and others; it inclines one to treat persons and things with meekness. The thought of the indwelling of the Divine Persons in the soul is also an incentive to entreat frequently and intimately the Divine Guest; in this manner, the practice of the presence of God prepares a soul for a life of strict union with Him. *Man.*

PRESS. As a powerful means of communication of ideas, whether in the form of books, booklets, newspapers, magazines, pamphlets, posters, or the like, the press is one of the most effective means for spreading religious information, as well as irreligion and immorality. The press, particularly newspapers and magazines, exercises enormous power in the forming of public opinion, by producing decisive effects in almost all areas of social life. This is the basis for its extraordinary importance and great responsibility.

Freedom of the Press. Freedom of speech and, hence, of the press, is a fundamental natural right of the human person, but this right has certain limitations that depend on the content of the printed work and the circumstances surrounding its publication. With regard to the content, it enjoys liberty only with regard to truth or, at least, debatable opinion. Whatever is false and immoral has no right to exist, much less to be diffused. As a matter of fact, such ought to be positively suppressed, for a great number of readers lack the judgment necessary to distinguish truth from sophistry, and the moral strength to resist the temptations caused by evil writings (*Syllabus*, n. 79; Leo XIII, Enc. *Libertas*, June 20, 1888). The printing of false and immoral ideas can be tolerated only to avoid greater evils. In practice, freedom of the press often amounts to a form of tolerance, a permission for something in itself evil, but which is given in view of a greater good. The greater good would be the avoidance of despotism on the part of a human authority, like the State.

With respect to the circumstances surrounding publication, freedom of the press may be limited legitimately for sound reasons of prudence or timeliness. These reasons would seem to make it proper and often even desirable to have a type of censorship (*see* Censorship) before resorting to prohibition by civil or ecclesiastical authority. The Church practices a form of preventive censorship, which democratic governments shrink from, except in times of emergency, because of an often exaggerated and artificially produced concern to prevent the danger of despotism at the cost of the protection of good morals.

Immoral books, booklets, and magazines are one of the main sources of moral corruption. The apostolate for a good press, to combat the wicked and promote what is economically and culturally good, must be one of the main activities of Catholics in our days. Catholic publications must place themselves at the service of truth and morality and subordinate all considerations of economic gain to this duty. Authors and publishers of immoral writings are guilty of the sin of scandal and share in all of the sins that are committed as a result of these books, insofar as they have to some extent foreseen them. Writing for newspapers and magazines that usually attack religion and good morals amounts to cooperation in sin; this may be justified only by grave and proportionate reasons. The Code of Canon Law expressly forbids this form of cooperation, but allows the judgment of the Ordinary to permit it under certain circumstances (Can. 1386, par. 2). See also Libraries, Cooperation, Reading, Scandal, News Agencies. Dam.

PRESUMPTION. The word *presumption* has various meanings. In procedural law it indicates a conjecture based on appearances or evidence that is none too clear. Generally, it means an act of arrogance, a transgression that exceeds the ordinary way of sinning, an undertaking superior to one's own powers or the aid that one may expect from others, even a hope that goes beyond the proper limits.

A distinction must be made between presumption as directly opposed to hope in God (*q.v.*), and presumption not opposed, at least directly, to this hope.

The former consists in the expectation of the means necessary for attaining salvation in a way that is opposed to the motives of theological hope, either by substituting one's own powers for the omnipotence of God in the attainment of eternal life (*Pelagian presumption*), or by substituting one's own will to divine dispositions, hoping to obtain remission of sin without repenting and eternal life without good works or without observing the commandments (*Lutheran presumption*). A sin against faith is often connected with this type of presumption.

Presumption not directly opposed to hope in God is the expectation of receiving from God unseemly things, such as aid to perform an evil act or acts outside the ordinary order of Divine Providence which were not promised by God, such as the possibility of repenting at the end of life, meanwhile neglecting the observance of the commandments, or expecting to be preserved from sin without avoiding the occasions of sin; also, by taking advantage of the mercy of God in sinning or in postponing repentence, or by presuming to obtain with equal facility the remission of many sins as well as fewer sins. One who sins mortally by presuming on the mercy of God in receiving pardon, must clearly declare this circumstance in confession, because it changes the species of the sin.

If one sins with the intention of repenting afterwards or with a genuine hope of obtaining God's pardon, he has not yet become guilty of presumption.

Presumption, directly opposed to hope in God, is always a grave sin and causes the loss of the infused virtue of hope. A subjectively grave sin, however, requires a completely deliberate act. Even presumption that is not directly opposed to theological hope is generally a grave sin. The sin of presumption is venial if one expects to obtain a special grace, with a will fully submitted to God's, or if, neglecting prayer and the avoidance of sinful occasions, one only expects ordinary and slight help from God, or if one sins venially with the expectation of forgiveness.

The causes of presumption are: vainglory, pride, and a lack of consideration. The remedies against presumption are: humility, a consideration of God's justice and the gratuitousness of supernatural gifts. Man.

PREVENTATIVES. See Pharmacist; Neo-Malthusianism.

PREVENTION (of forum). *See* Forum; Trial.

PREY, MARITIME. *See* Booty (Right of).

PREY (Right of). *See* Booty (Right of).

PRICE. In general, *price* is the condition on the basis of which goods are exchanged. It represents the relation between the quantity of one item, usually money, exchanged or demanded in barter or sale for another. Specifically, price is the amount at which transactions take place in the market.

Market prices are determined on the basis of conditions that are responsible for equilibrium in the market: cost of production, preferences of merchants, amount of services or goods supplied and demanded, and the economic position of merchants. These elements give rise to a supply and demand for merchandise. In an ideal market, under so-called conditions of free competition (*q.v.*), a single price is established for a specific merchandise; thus the quantities of merchandise bought and sold at that price are equalized. The different conditions of the market, such as unfair competition, monopoly (*q.v.*), and oligopoly, give rise to different types of stabilization or equilibrium.

Modern economic doctrine has given fullest development to these principles as well as to the formation and dynamics of prices which depend on the relation of competition to subsidiarity existing between exchanged merchandise.

It is a widespread opinion that to impose a price different from the stabilized price in a perfectly free competitive market would result in damage to the social organism. But this theory fails to take adequate account of the antagonism between the commercial agents and the respective positions of strength always present with varied intensity in an actual market. An evident case of these positions of strength concerns wages (*q.v.*). The concept of fair price is a corrective of the more serious consequences of excessive variations in strength between contracting parties. Fair price (*q.v.*) implies an external intervention in the market; it is, therefore, a controlled price, although every controlled price must be presumed to be a fair price in the meaning indicated above.

Other widely employed qualifications of the concept of price are: (a) *current price*, opposed to estimated price, which does not result from exchanges on the market, but is a nominal price; (b) *average price*, deduced from the average of current prices (*also see* Purchase, Sale).

Interest, discount, salary, rent, etc., indicate particular forms of prices. *Gol.*

PRICE CONTROLS. Price controls are devices by which the government sets a limit on the selling price of an article, thus eliminating the activity of a free market on prices. Controlled prices are prompted usually, not by economic motives, but by the exigencies of the political and social orders. There exists a long history of such increasing interventions on the part of government in the economic life of nations, since profound changes have been wrought on the free market by exceptional circumstances, such as wars, depressions, and revolts.

Usually price controls are employed for periods of greater scarcity in certain items, during a period of rigid demand, when supply enjoys a privileged position with regard to the demand for an item.

Higher prices than those formed by a free market can be at times employed for protection of specific categories of production. Government intervention tends to guarantee an adequate remuneration for social reasons.

In principle, such interventions are legitimate, if they are necessary. The application of such price controls, at a lower level than that of a free market, implies an expansion of demand and a restriction of supply, with an opposite reaction for prices controlled at a higher level than the free market. This requires further intervention by government to control the variations in supply and demand, usually by ration tickets, compulsory distribution, etc.

Abuses and inconveniences, arising from a condition of unstable equilibrium, and the cost of administration of these controls are such as to suggest extreme caution in the use of price controls. These should be confined to exceptionally grave circumstances. Widespread and permanent employment of price controls presupposes a controlled economy, which ought to be avoided, except in serious circumstances of grave crises. *Gol.*

PRICE, JUST. A just price corresponds to the value of the item to be bought. This may be fixed by law, by common or natural bidding, or by a conventional price for objects outside of commerce, as famous paintings, antique objects, etc.

If the legal price is in use, it must be observed in conscience, except in times of emergency or if the price is fixed by an authority in such a way that it is obviously and enormously damaging to the individual, despite the fact that, in general, it is sufficiently remunerative.

If the legal price is neither observed nor enforced by effective provisions, or if changed circumstances render it evidently unjust, as a depreciation of the value of the currency or a sudden increase in the cost of production, in which the seller would not receive fair profits (ten or fifteen per cent of net), then one might follow the common price. The seller may not demand more than is commonly considered the maximum price, and the buyer may not pay less than is commonly considered the minimum price.

Common price is called by some the *current* price. One must beware of possible equivocation; for, frequently, the common current price of an item in a free market is not necessarily a just current price. This would be to approve of a black market, which every sensible person condemns, or to favor those who become rich at the expense of needy buyers. Thus, a distinction must be made between a just current price, even if not existent in actual marketing, but based on the ordinary estimation of buyers, and an unjust current price, which may be forcibly and generally ac-cepted by buyers. The fact that such things are done does not make them lawful, for crime does not become lawful when it is commonly committed.

Common price or current price, in the sense of ordinary and natural, presupposes not only the common estimation or evaluation of sellers and buyers, but also a freedom of expression by buyers without compulsion or necessity, and, finally, a fair estimate by a capable, equitable, and disinterested person. *Pal.*

PRIDE. Pride is an inordinate esteem of self; it is inordinate because it is contrary to reality or truth. Pride is essentially an act or disposition of the will which is based on an exaggerated or exalted opinion of one's own self.

Pride may be expressed in four different ways: (a) by taking credit for talents, as if they had not been received from God, or by glorying in good deeds, as if they were not primarily the result of divine grace; (b) by regarding as due to one's own ability something which in reality is a gift of God; (c) by minimizing defects and attributing to oneself qualities not actually possessed, or by exaggerating those possessed; (d) by holding oneself above others, or disdaining others, in whom one sees nothing except faults, greatly magnified.

If pride is carried to a point where one loaths to acknowledge that everything is a gift of God, or fails to submit to God or His representatives, it is a grave sin. This was the sin of Lucifer and of Adam and Eve; it is also the sin of those who refuse obedience to the authority of the Church, or refuse to accept the traditional interpretation of her dogmas. If not carried to this extent, pride, of itself, is a venial sin. Pride is a mortal sin if one is disposed to commit a grave sin to extoll oneself, and if pride leads to judgments, actions, or words that are grievously sinful.

Not all sins are sins of pride, but pride can lead to all sorts of sins; for this reason, it is called the root of all sins. The following are sins which almost necessarily flow from pride: (a) presumption, (b) ambition, and (c) vain-glory.

Presumption is the attempt to accomplish by one's own ability things which are beyond one's powers. Of itself, it is a venial sin. It becomes a grave sin if it is the result of a culpable error in a matter of faith; if it causes a notable damage to another; if it implies a danger that such damage could be caused, as when one accepts or undertakes an important office without the necessary qualifications; or if, because of it, a person is exposed to a serious danger of committing a grave sin.

Ambition consists in an immoderate coveting and search for dignities and honors, which are not deserved, but sought for honor's sake out of vainglory. Dignities and honors are mere aids or means for the sanctification of one's soul or for doing good to others; hence, they must not be loved and sought for, except for such purposes. Of itself, ambition is a venial sin, but it may become a grave sin if one is disposed to commit a grave sin in order to win a coveted honor or dignity, or if one gains the coveted honor or dignity through grave harm done to others, or by gravely illicit means.

Vainglory is an immoderate desire to manifest one's excellence and to receive praise from others. One may be guilty of vainglory by seeking glory for glory's sake; by seeking to win praise for non-existing reasons or for things deserving little or no praise; by seeking glory from those whose judgment has little or no value; by seeking to be esteemed and praised for a quality or deed as if one were its principal author, forgetting that every good gift is from God. Of itself, vainglory is a venial sin, but it may become a grave sin if one is disposed to sin gravely in order to win praise, if one seeks his own glory with grave harm to his neighbor, or if one seeks to be honored and esteemed for something which is gravely sinful. There is, however, a desire for esteem and praise that is not morally wrong; it is the quest for acknowledgment of qualities in order that God may be glorified and the possibili-

ties of doing good may be enhanced. Though such desire is not in itself sinful, it can, however, become for one a danger of falling into the sin of vainglory.

There are also other defects that may be considered manifestations of vainglory, such as *boasting*, talking about oneself, one's family, one's own accomplishments for the purpose of winning praise; *ostentation*, seeking to draw attention by certain ways of acting, by prodigality and singularity; *hypocrisy*, feigning a particular virtue without endeavoring to acquire it. Pride leads easily to hardness of heart and intolerance of others, who easily become an object of severe criticism on the part of the proud person. *Man.*

PRIEST. *See* Holy Orders.

PRIMACY OF THE ROMAN PONTIFF. *See* Pontiff, Sovereign.

PRIMATE. The title of *primate* was in the beginning similar to that of patriarch (*q.v.*) or metropolitan. It was given to metropolitans with certain prerogatives of jurisdiction and honor, granted by privilege or custom. Such were the bishops of Carthage, Bordeaux, Lyon, Canterbury, Mainz, Trier, Salzburg, and others.

In present-day law the title of *primate* is only an honorary title (Can. 271); it is given to the bishop of the most important see in every nation, which is thus called the *primatial see*.

The primate, who is always a metropolitan, takes precedence over all other bishops and archbishops (Can. 280), except the local Ordinary (Can. 347) in his own diocese. The sovereign pontiff, as bishop of Rome, is the primate of Italy; the archbishop of Toledo, since the time of Urban II (1088), is the primate of Spain; the archbishop of Malines is the primate of Belgium; the archbishop of Strigonia is the primate of Hungary; and the archbishop of Salzburg is the primate of Austria. The primatial sees in France were suppressed in 1801, but the archbishop of Lyon still maintains the title. *Fel.*

PRINCIPLES, REFLEX. Generic principles to which recourse is made in order to give a solution to unsolved or difficult problems are called, in moral theology, *reflex principles*. If a problem cannot be solved by intrinsic, direct, clear evidence, one may seek to solve it with generic, indirect, extrinsic (reflex) reasons. It is evident that the solution thus obtained is not an exact solution to the problems because it is not deduced from considerations intrinsic to the problem itself, but is the solution of another problem applied to the problem on hand by the use of the so-called reflex principle.

Some of the more common reflex principles are:

A *doubtful law is not binding.* By this principle, we are not bound to observe provisions of a law whose existence is affirmed by some jurists but denied by others. Nor can the judge condemn us as transgressors of such a law.

In doubt, the possessor's condition takes precedence. If two persons in dispute over a property are without decisive reasons in favor of either of the contestants, the one who actually possesses the property in question is favored.

In doubt, presumption favors the validity of an act (*In dubio standum est pro valore actus*). In a dispute concerning the validity of a contract or a will, the act is considered valid unless its invalidity is proved by definite and positive reasons.

In doubt, the accused is favored, or *No one is presumed wicked unless his wickedness is proved* (*Nemo malus nisi probetur*); in other words, if the plaintiff in a trial fails fully to prove his charge, the accused or defendant is exonerated of the accusation.

INTERPRETATION. By a simple formulation, these principles reveal a marked judiciary or procedural flavor. For this reason one must be very cautious in using them in the field of morality. However, not all applications of these principles are to be excluded. Thus, for instance, in a question dealing with a purely ecclesiastical law that is doctrinally doubtful, we are certain that no sin is committed if we fail to observe it, because the principle that a doubtful law (whether the *doubt* concerns the doctrine or the law) does not bind, is expressly accepted by Canon Law (Can. 15). *Gra.*

PRISON. A prison is an establishment set apart for the custody of criminals or persons held for questioning or investigation; in other words, a prison is an enclosed place in which an individual's personal freedom is restricted.

In juridical language, this definition is specified by an added note or circumstance: the detention or restriction of freedom is executed by virtue of law and order through civil authority. This specifically juridical meaning is recent in the historical evolution of law and penal jurisprudence, for originally incarceration was considered confinement or custody and not punishment (*Carcer non est poena, sed custodia debet esse*).

The notion of a prison handed down by the ancient writers is most appalling (Cf. Cicero, *Oratio pro Milone*, 22; Seneca, *Controversiae*, IV, c. 27; T. Livius, *Historia*, I; Lucretius, *De rerum natura*, III). The prisons of the times were shocking both from a material and a moral standpoint.

Through the beneficent influence of Christianity, the extremely miserable and wretched conditions of prison life were somewhat mitigated. The divine counsel urging visitation of prisoners was highly instrumental in giving rise to an attitude of compassion, mercy, and assistance toward prisoners (Matt. 11:13; 25:34–36; Hebr. 13:3).

Directly inspired by the teaching and example of Christ Our Lord, the Church from the beginning manifested great concern and solicitude both for the spiritual and the material welfare of prisoners. At an early period bishops established associations or confraternities especially dedicated to the task of assisting the incarcerated, the exiled and the prisoners of war. Special prayers for the imprisoned were frequently prescribed. The redemption of captives was declared obligatory at the Council of Orléans in 511, and in a subsequent synod, also at Orléans (519), the archdeacon was enjoined to visit prisoners on Sundays to minister to their needs. In the Carolingian era, Charlemagne ordained in a capitulary session that it was obligatory to visit the imprisoned. Lenten and Paschal seasons usually brought a measure of comfort and relief to prisoners. In fact, Valentinian I in 367 granted the so-called *indulgentia paschalis*: an edict authorizing the release of all the prisoners for the Easter festival. Similar efforts by the papacy were constantly directed toward mitigating the lot of prisoners. In this connection, it suffices to mention *jus asyli* and *jus intercessionis episcoporum.*

In 1488 Innocent VIII instituted the *Compagnia della Misericordia* (Society of Mercy), placing it under the patronage of Saint John the Baptist. He entrusted to this society the express mission of rendering assistance to the prisoners condemned to death, beginning from the period of detention to the moment of execution and burial. A similar organization (*Pietà dei carcerati*) was established by Gregory XIII in 1575. Other popes, e.g., Eugene IV (1435), and Paul III (1548), issued new ordinances designed to improve the physical and moral lot of prisoners. Clement XI (1703) erected the famous penitentiary of St. Michael and introduced radical reforms in the application of penalties.

The civil authorities of certain regions endeavored at various times to bolster the efforts of Christian charity with provisions of their own. Thus, Louis XII, in 1619, appointed St. Vincent de Paul chaplain of convicts condemned to forced labor. But the combined efforts of the civil authorities and Christian charity could only place a limited check on enormous abuses, by bringing a measure of physical and religious comfort to inmates. The unwholesome atmosphere of prisons, the lack of regulatory legislation, the cruelty and insolence of prison authorities—all these factors greatly limited the Christian mission of mercy.

In the middle of the seventeenth century, a movement began to substitute certain forms of corporal punishment with hard labor on public projects, such as road construction, fortifications, mines, and the like.

Scanarola (1635), Howard (1790), and Beccaria (1794) succeeded in arousing the social conscience by exposing the horrible prison conditions as one of the greatest infamies of humanity. This led to the establishment of somewhat more suitable penal institutes. And while, of course, the detention of criminals with consequent restriction of freedom was considered a necessary penalty, the idea began to take shape that incarceration should aim at reformation rather than punishment of the culprit; work was to be regarded as an instrument of re-education.

Imprisonment as a Penalty. A prison sentence has a twofold purpose: (a) As a vindictive penalty, imprisonment is designed to render satisfaction to divine and human authority and to society for the violation of justice. One who disturbs the moral, social, and juridical order undoubtedly deserves to be punished, because such an individual has committed a crime (*quia peccavit*). Crime demands satisfaction or expiation. This vindictive aspect of prison views the crime committed in retrospect. (b) However, expiation or satisfaction cannot and must not be the sole objective of a prison penalty; this must be directed to another purpose: the rehabilitation of a delinquent through a disciplinary program designed to check his evil instincts and sinful inclinations. Such a program has an eye to the future and the prevention of further crime (*ne peccetur*). This is the remedial or medicinal aspect of imprisonment as a penalty. Viewed in this light, jail or prison is not simply a place of punishment or expiation, but also of re-education and rehabilitation. In 1703, Clement XI had the following inscription written on the walls of St. Michael's Penitentiary in Rome: *Parum est coercere improbos, nisi probos efficias disciplina* (It avails little to punish the wicked, unless you reform them by training).

The aim of modern penology is not merely to punish a criminal or to imprison him for the sole purpose of liberating society of a dangerous individual, but also to re-educate the criminal so that he may become a useful member of society. Modern prison laws, preserving an austere and rigorous character, inculcate training and work programs, as well as courses in religion and other subjects for inmates. Modern prisoners receive hygienic and medical care. Male and female prisoners are detained in separate places; juvenile delinquents are isolated from older groups. Moreover, in almost every country an attempt is made to offer assistance and guidance to parolees and former convicts.

Escape from Prison. Moralists posit the question whether it is licit to escape from prison while serving a legally imposed sentence. As a rule, any attempt at jailbreak is punished by public authorities. In Roman law, prison escapees were frequently punished by the death sentence (cf. C. 9, 4, 4); in later legislation the penalty was less severe.

Several moralists (cf. Aertnys-Damen, *Theol. Mor.*, I [Aosta-Turin; 1947], n. 1244), on the premise that escape from prison is actually punishable at law, argue that one is morally bound to serve a legally inflicted prison sentence. The whole purpose of the law forbidding and punishing jailbreak, they add, is to safeguard the public interest. Hence, all persons lawfully arrested and detained on a criminal charge are morally bound not to free themselves from the scope of this law.

Numerous other authors, perhaps with greater cogency, argue that a prison inmate is morally free to work out his escape, because he has no obligation to remain in prison, i.e., he is not bound to apply the penalty to himself. It is the duty of others to guard a captive and keep him in jail (cf. Ballerini-Palmieri, *Opus morale*, IV, 632; G. D'Annibale, *Summula*, II, 601; A. Tanquerey, *Theol. moral.*, II, n. 1001, etc.). Hence, from a moral standpoint, an inmate who is lawfully and rightfully detained, has the right to try to escape from prison. Nor should he be punished simply for having escaped, unless the escapee committed violence, fraud, or another unjust violation; if no violence or injustice is committed, there is no crime and, therefore, no punishment. Moreover, an escape is not held to restitution for damage incurred by the guards as a result of his jailbreak, provided that no violence or injustice was committed. In point of fact, the prisoner exercises a right, and the damage to the guards is only indirectly caused. *Tar.*

Penal Medicine. As previously noted, the problem of physical and mental hygiene in prisons and other penal institutes is highly important for the rehabilitation of inmates. Admittedly, this is not an easy problem, and yet too important to be passed up lightly.

The problem of moral rehabilitation of prisoners is even more complex and difficult. But we cannot escape the fact that prisoners are the ones who stand in need of an intensive religious and moral training. In Italy, the Sacred Congregation of the Council, with the approval of the proper civil authorities, has recently instituted a Commission of Chaplains who are to supervise and carry out the program of moral re-education of prisoners. *Riz.*

PRIVILEGE. *Privilege*, in a strict sense, is a favorable private law. It differs from indult (*q.v.*) by virtue of a rather long duration.

A privilege may be *contra legem* or *praeter legem*, depending on whether it is granted as something against the law or beyond the law. A privilege is *affirmative*, if it grants the faculty of doing something; *negative*, if it gives the faculty of omitting something. It is *odious* or *favorable* according to whether the favor granted is injurious to a third party or not. Furthermore, a privilege may be *gracious, remunerative, conventional* or *onerous*, depending on whether it is granted through mere liberality or gratitude, a free or an onerous contract. Finally, a privilege may be *personal* or *real*, depending on whether its immediate subject is a person or a thing.

Privileges are acquired by direct grant, communication, legitimate custom, or by prescription. A privilege is acquired by *direct grant*, if the sovereign directly grants it, either in writing or orally (*vivae vocis oraculo*); in the latter case, however, the privilege may not be used in the external forum unless it can be so proven. The pope has the right to grant privileges beyond or against even the universal ecclesiastical law; the Ordinary may grant only privileges beyond (*praeter legem*) or against (*contra legem*) a particular law.

Privileges by *communications* are acquired when a privilege granted to one person is extended in the same manner and to the same extent to others. The communication is in a principal form (*aeque principalis*) if, once the communication is made, each privilege stands by itself, as if it has been directly granted. Otherwise, it is accessory, if the communicated privilege remains dependent on the principal privilege, which it follows. The Code of Canon Law establishes (Can. 64) the conditions for the communication of privileges; it is henceforth forbidden by the present legislation among the various religious organizations (Can. 613).

Since *custom* (*q.v.*) is a source of privileges, it is necessary that it be lawful. Finally, lawful *prescription* (*q.v.*) is a source of privileges; unlike custom, it applies both to the community and the individual. The Code of Canon Law (Can. 63, par. 2) establishes that the only such lawful prescription is one of one hundred years or from time immemorial.

In view of its special nature, a privilege does not need promulgation, despite the fact that it is a law. But a privilege, taken in a strict sense, requires acceptance by the recipient because a benefice is not given to one who is opposed (*invito beneficium non datur*: D. 50, 17, 69).

A privilege must be interpreted according to its scope, nor may anyone extend it or restrict it. In case of doubt, the rules given for doubtful rescripts are to be followed: privileges beyond the law and favorable privileges are to be interpreted broadly (*see* Rescript); those

against the law and odious privileges are to be strictly interpreted. Yet, the restriction must not be so rigorous as to deprive the recipient of any benefice, for this is clearly contrary to the intention of the grantor (Can. 67, 68).

No one is obliged to make use of a privilege granted for his private benefit, unless the obligation arises from another source (Can. 69). But if the privilege was also granted for the public good, the recipient may be obliged to use it. In case of two concurrent privileges, the rules given for rescripts are to be followed.

Privileges contained in the Code cease by law or general customs to the contrary. Others terminate by special revocation (Can. 72); by cessation of the right of the grantor, if the privilege was granted with the clause *ad beneplacitum nostrum* (or equivalent phrase); by the death or extinction of the recipient of the privilege (Can. 102), by its suppression by the lawful authority, or by cessation for a period of one hundred years (Can. 74); by lawful prescription in cases of odious privileges (Can. 76); by cessation of the contrary cause; finally, by expiration of the period of time, or exhaustion of the number of cases for which the privilege was granted (Can. 77). (Also cf. Canon 207, par. 2, for faculty in the internal forum.) A privilege does not terminate by abuse. *Fel.*

PRIVILEGE, CANONICAL (*privilegium canonis*). See Clergy, privileges of.

PRIVILEGE OF CLERICS. See Clergy, privileges of.

PRIVILEGE OF FORUM (*privilegium fori*). See Clergy, privileges of.

PRIVILEGE OF IMMUNITY (*privilegium immunitatis*). See Clergy, privileges of.

PRIVILEGE OF JURISDICTION (*privilegium competentiae*). See Clergy, privileges of.

PRIVILEGE, PAULINE. The so-called *Pauline privilege* is contained in the First

Epistle to the Corinthians (7:12 ff.). The canonical discipline concerning this matter is found in Canons 1120 to 1127. However, since the norms contained in these Canons are rather general, there arises a varied and wide casuistry. The only authority empowered to deal with this is the Sacred Congregation of the Holy Office.

Only the bond of a *legitimate marriage*, even consummated, can be dissolved by the application of the Pauline privilege; that is, the bond of a marriage contracted by two unbaptized persons, one of whom is converted to the Christian religion. The Pauline privilege is not applicable to a marriage contracted between a baptized and an unbaptized person with a dispensation from the impediment of disparity of worship (Can. 1120).

CONDITIONS. If one of the parties to a *legitimate marriage* is converted and baptized (even into a Protestant sect), he may avail himself of the Pauline privilege under the following conditions: (a) He must interpellate the unbaptized party and ask whether he also will convert and receive baptism or, at least, whether he is disposed to live peacefully, without offense to God (Can. 1121) and without hindering the baptized party from practicing freely his or her religion, from rearing the children in the Christian faith, and without inducing him or her to sin. (b) These inquiries on the future conduct of the unbaptized party are called *interpellations*. In some cases, with permission of the Holy See, the interpellations can be omitted, especially if they are considered useless or too irksome.

These interpellations must be made by ecclesiastical authority, that is, by the authority of the Ordinary; the unbaptized party must be given a certain time for the reply. If this does not come within the fixed time, it is presumed negative. In exceptional cases private interpellations are permitted (Can. 1121).

If the result of the interpellations is negative, the baptized party has the right to contract a new marriage with a Catholic person, provided that he did not give the unbaptized party a just reason for leaving. This applies to conduct after conversion.

The converted party does not lose the right to contract a new marriage, even if he continues to live with the unbaptized person.

The bond of a legitimate marriage is dissolved only if the converted party contracts a new marriage (Can. 1126).

In a conflict between a legitimate bond of marriage and the gift of faith, the latter prevails.

SPECIAL FACULTIES. Further concessions, based on the Pauline privilege, are granted by three famous papal Constitutions: *Altitudo*, of Paul III (June, 1537); *Romani Pontificis*, of St. Pius V (Aug. 2, 1571); and *Populis*, of Gregory XIII (Jan. 25, 1585). The Constitutions are incorporated in the Code of Canon Law, under documents VI, VII and VIII. The special faculties therein contained are extended to all places in the world where the same circumstances prevail. The Constitution *Altitudo* allowed converts in the West Indies, who as pagans had several wives, to keep the wife they preferred, if they could no longer remember which one they had married first. *Romani Pontificis* allowed a convert in India to retain the wife who consented to being baptized with him. *Populis* made still further concessions with regard to the marriage of negroes carried off to America, in which the converted party found it impossible to make the necessary interpellations, or if the interpellation remained unheeded within the time allotted. In such cases, a new marriage may be entered into with any member of the faith and is valid even if, later, it becomes known that the other party was unable to answer the interpellations or had been baptized. *Bar.*

PRIVILEGE, SABBATINE. More than a privilege in a technical sense, the Saturday privilege is a form of promise, made by the Blessed Virgin in a private revelation to St. Simon Stock, to free from purgatory the souls of the members of the Carmelite Order on the Saturday after their death.

In this connection, a decree of the Holy Office, February 11, 1613, permits the Carmelites to preach "that the Blessed Virgin will aid the souls of the Carmelite Friars and their confreres after their death . . . by her continuous intercession . . . especially on Saturday, dedicated by the Church to the Blessed Virgin."

The devotion of the Sabbatine privilege—or, rather, this pious belief—is found fully developed in the second half of the fifteenth century. It is impossible to search earlier records or documentary evidence. Furthermore, the authenticity of the Sabbatine Bull *Sacratissimo uti culmine* (1322) attributed to Pope John XXII is strongly contested. The Bull is only preserved in a digest form contained in the confirming Bull of Alexander V (1409), reproduced by Clement VII (1530) in the Bull *Ex clementi*, in which the apparition to St. Simon Stock and the promise of the Blessed Virgin of a liberation from purgatory on the Saturday following death are related with great details. "In this form [the Bull] is now judged to be certainly spurious."

CONDITIONS FOR THE SABBATINE PRIVILEGE. In order to be eligible for the Sabbatine privilege, (a) the associates of the Carmelite family are required to wear the brown scapular; (b) they must observe chastity in conformity with their own state in life; (c) those who can read must recite daily the Little Office of the Blessed Virgin (cf. reply of the Sacred Congregation of Indulgences, December 3, 1892); those who are illiterate are to abstain from meat on Wednesdays and Saturdays. In connection with the latter conditions, one may benefit by the diocesan indult in which authorized confessors can commute abstinence from meat to a recitation of seven Paters, Aves and Glorias (Declaration of January 14, 1901).

More recent popes have frequently made references to the Sabbatine privilege; the latest was made by Pius XII, in a letter commemorating the seven-hundredth anniversary of the apparition of the Blessed Virgin to St. Simon Stock (February 11, 1951). *Pal.*

PROBABILIORISM. *See* System, Moral.

PROBABILISM. *See* System, Moral.

PROCEDURE. *See* Trial.

PROCESSION, RELIGIOUS. A *procession* is a group of persons moving in an orderly fashion. A procession may be spontaneous, or be diligently organized for religious, political, social, or other purposes.

Religious processions are groups of the faithful marching in an orderly fashion under the leadership of the clergy, from one place to another, for the sake of fostering devotion, recalling God's blessings, or imploring divine aid.

Symbolically, a religious procession indicates the marching of the Church militant toward her heavenly goal. In the early times of the Church, owing to persecution, Christians could not hold religious processions, except in the case of burial, which was considered, however, a civil act. After the Peace of Constantine, processions became more frequent. From the fourth to the seventh century, processions were held for the same purpose as today: a translation of relics, an installation of a bishop or king, in thanksgiving, on Rogation Days, and in a general emergency, epidemic, unusual rainy weather, and the like. Of more recent date are the processions in honor of the Blessed Sacrament. They became frequent in the fourteenth century, after the introduction of the feast of Corpus Christi.

Medieval symbolism (Durandus, *Rationale Div. Off.*, 4, 6, 14) saw in processions an antitype of the exodus of the people of Israel from Egypt, a symbol of the Church's pilgrimage toward the celestial homeland. For this reason, the *Roman Ritual* (X, 1, 1ff.) prescribes processions not already ordered by the *Roman Missal*, as on Candlemas Day, Palm Sunday, Corpus Christi, and others. It states that a procession revolves around great and divine mysteries, and that those who devoutly participate therein gain priceless benefits.

Processions may be *ordinary* and *extraordinary*. *Ordinary* processions are those which take place on fixed days of the year, according to liturgical prescriptions, or customs of the Churches; *extraordinary* processions are held on other days for other public causes (Can. 1290, par. 2).

Canon Law attaches great importance to the Corpus Christi procession. In this connection, it prescribes that, except for lawful customs to the contrary, only one solemn procession may be held on the feast of Corpus Christi, which must originate from a church of higher dignity, with all the secular clergy, religious communities of men, even exempt religious, and lay confraternities participating in it; cloistered regulars and those living three miles away from the city are not required to take part in the procession (Can. 1291, par. 1).

Other parishes and churches, secular and regular, may conduct their own processions outside their churches, during the octave of Corpus Christi; but if there are several churches, the Ordinary shall fix the day, the hour, and the course of each procession (Can. 1291, par. 2).

The local Ordinary, after consultation with the cathedral chapter, may institute extraordinary processions for a public cause, in which all those who are required to participate in ordinary processions shall participate (Can. 1292).

Religious, both exempt and non-exempt, may not hold processions outside their churches and convents without the Ordinary's permission, except the procession on the octave of Corpus Christi (Can. 1293).

The clergy assigned to a church must participate in its processions (Can. 1294, par. 2). Neither a parish priest nor any other priest is allowed to establish new processions, transfer, or abolish the usual ones without permission of the local Ordinary (Can. 1294, par. 1). *Pal.*

PROCESS OF ASSOCIATION. *See* Psyche, Pathology of.

PROCESS OF INTEGRATION. *See* Psyche.

PROCURATOR. *See* Superior, Religious.

PROCURATOR, PROCURATORIAL MANDATE. In the Imperial Age numerous categories of Roman public and fiscal agents, or administrators, were called *procurators*. More frequently, however, procurators were and are, even today, individuals commissioned to tend the business of another (Ulpian, D. 3, 3, 1). This mandate may be *expressed* or *silent; general* or *specific;* for *legal* or *business matters.* The act of conferring a procuratorial mandate is called *power of attorney*, and it must specify in a clear and unequivocal manner the nature of the mandate, namely, the duties of the procurator.

POWER OF ATTORNEY. The *power of attorney in matters of litigation* authorizes a person to perform all those acts ordinarily regarded as necessary for the institution and prosecution of a trial. Exceptional acts are normally excluded, and a special mandate is required for each case. The power of attorney must be given in writing, certified and sworn to under oath at the chancery of the court before it may be accepted.

Among the *powers of attorney in business matters*, proxy to contract marriage has a special relevance; in this, one who is unable to be present at his wedding ceremony appoints another to represent him at such a ceremony (*see* Marriage, Proxy).

A procurator in litigations represents the party in a trial. He is absolutely necessary when the party possesses no legal capacity or, by reason of his dignity or state of life, cannot or prefers not to appear in court. In other cases the appointment of a procurator is left to the discretion of the parties. However, if the judge demands it, the parties must appear in person.

A procurator must possess those moral and intellectual qualities that enable him to fulfill his mandate. According to Canon Law, he must be a Catholic, of legal age, and well versed in canonical laws (Canons 1649; 1655, par. 3; 1656, par. 1–2; 1657, par. 1, 3; 1658; 1660; 1662; 1665; 1757, par. 2, n. 1).

Moral obligations of a procurator are, fundamentally, reduced to the observance of the procuratorial mandate, which implies ordinary diligence in fulfilling the assignment effectively. Of course, the proxy shall act invalidly and is bound to restitution for damage if he goes beyond the extent of the mandate. *Pug.*

PROCURATOR OF THE SACRED APOSTOLIC PALACES. The procurators of the Sacred Palaces appeared as a definite institution for the first time under the pontificate of Innocent III (1130–1143). Organized into a college by Benedict XII, in 1340, they were granted numerous privileges from later popes. In the beginning, they were entrusted with defending causes before the *Auditorium Sacri Palatii*; when this was transformed into the Sacred Roman Rota, they were given the right, not exclusively however, to defend canonization causes before the Rota as well as the consistory. Later the college lost its importance, although it was preserved generally for ceremonial duties.

St. Pius X and Benedict XV revitalized the college. Pius XI restored to it the right to defend causes before the Sacred Roman Rota and fixed at twelve the number of procurators of the Sacred Apostolic Palaces (Pius XI, Const. *Ad incrementum*, August 15, 1934, n. 85). *Pug.*

PRODIGALITY. *Prodigality,* the opposite of avarice and contrary to just and fair management of goods, consists in an *irrational excess of spending and donating.* A prodigal has no other guide than fancy. He forgets that God made him the administrator, not owner, of his wealth, and that his prodigality can be harmful to himself and others. Generally, a prodigal individual sacrifices the future to the present. By waste and extravagant expenditures, he deprives himself of the benefits that riches provide or may properly provide. Prodigality is, of course,

preferable to avarice (*q.v.*), because, in general, it is coupled with many social qualities. It is more easily condoned, since the prodigal shares his pleasures with others. But it is damaging to family and society more than avarice, because a prodigal squanders capital that is needed for maintaining the family or for improving the lot of society.

Prodigality is, in itself, a venial sin. "It is a sin," St. Thomas states (*S. Theol.,* II–II, q. 119, a. 1), "not because of the amount irrationally squandered but because of the disorder it implies." A prodigal may become guilty of mortal sin, if his waste gives rise to grave scandal by leading him to violate certain precepts, fail to pay just debts or give alms, ruin the financial standing of his family, lead others to evil. By a strange contrast, the prodigal frequently is sparing in things in which he should be generous; often those who spend extravagantly on futile and superfluous things, such as clothes, banquets, clubs, etc., are stingy with the poor and unfair with employees. A prodigal's lust for spending and his vanity lead him to almost any device, including cheating, gambling, and defrauding, in order to satisfy his ever-increasing thirst for pleasure. *Tar.*

PRODUCTION. *Production,* in a broad, scientific sense, is the creation of economic goods. Formerly economists were inclined to restrict the term to certain particular activities. Thus, for merchants, production meant foreign commerce; for others, it was agriculture and mining. In reality, nothing is produced or destroyed under heaven; but the activity of man, aided by savings turned to productive aims and applied to products (either raw natural forces or already transformed), is able to make them capable of satisfying human needs or increasing a capacity they already possess. In other words, it is capable of increasing its usefulness. Understood in this broad sense, production includes commerce, transportation, and agricultural or industrial activities.

In a strict sense, production has a less extensive scope in agricultural and industrial activities. As such, it may be defined as a human activity turned to the creation of goods. The organs of production are the enterprises which unite and organize the factors in production (work, natural materials and capital) and direct them to the fulfillment of their aim.

Depending on the type of participation with nature, production is agricultural (biological) or industrial (non-biological). Non-biological activity is directed to the extraction of raw materials (*q.v.*) contained in the depths of the earth. Industrial activity is concerned with transformation of products obtained from agricultural and mining activities and natural resources. This is further distinguished according to the types of merchandise produced. These are the more important industrial activities: basic or heavy production; production of instrumental goods for further productions, such as metallurgy, chemistry, or mechanics; production of durable consumers' goods, such as home appliances, motor vehicles, etc.; and production of non-durable consumers' goods, such as foods and textiles. The building industry is classified separately.

Those charged with the responsibility for promoting the common welfare have, above all, the duty of fostering production in accord with all needs and factors. Among the circumstances to be taken into consideration, is that of not debasing human dignity for the sole purpose of greater production and not overvaluing production itself.

The goods of nature are for man's use; they are used in accord with the purpose for which they were created when they are utilized by man. Man, however, must not be so excessively preoccupied with the production of such goods as to neglect more serious duties. Anxious concern for food, clothing, and the future is equivalent to a return to a pagan philosophy of life, based on ignorance of God and His Providence (Matt. 6:25). An equitable distribution of the fruits of production is one of the factors of production which should not be neglected at any time. *Mai.*

PROFESSION. Strictly speaking, a *profession* is an occupation other than commercial, mechanical, agricultural or the like, to which one devotes himself. Thus, taken in the sense of liberal profession, its main characteristics seem to be competence, independence, and humaneness.

(a) *Competence.* To be a professional teacher, physician, magistrate, engineer, and the like, one must acquire an adequate degree of formal education, usually attained through a rather long scholastic curriculum.

(b) *Independence.* A professional individual for the most part develops his own specific activity freely, by his own personal initiative. This, however, is not an absolute criterion, because many professional individuals are subject to fixed time-tables, definite programs or directives of others, as in the case of teachers, magistrates, physicians, and engineers. The fact remains, however, that since the nature of their activity is mainly intellectual, they are responsible for the quality and value of their work, besides the mere execution of it.

(c) *Humaneness.* This means that *man* constitutes the direct sphere of this work. These tasks develop man's mind and spirit, cure his body, organize his productive energies, regulate his relations with society according to principles of justice and equity, and so forth. Obviously, even this element must not be pursued with excessive rigidity; an industrial director, for example, has not only the task of organizing workmen in an industrial plant, but also the no less delicate task of establishing the productive process. He may have other duties, but in carrying out these other tasks, he must deal with other men who are to assist him in his decisions and actions.

Professional activity is essentially social, which by its very nature is exercised on and in behalf of others. *For this reason, it is described and practiced as a service.* Certainly, one has the right to expect from his work an economic benefit. However, his guiding norm must be to keep his profession in harmony with the moral law. Thus, for a teacher it will be the teaching of truth; for an engineer, progress in the technical field, and so on. The practice of a profession exclusively for selfish gains is an inversion of values and a cause of disintegrating effects on human society. *Pav.*

PROFESSION OF FAITH. The obligation to faith binds man not only to an internal assent to revealed truths but also to an external profession of the faith. Jesus Christ willed that the life of faith be manifested in a visible body, an external communion, the Catholic Church (Matt. 10:32; Luke 12:8; Rom. 10:9–10). This obligation implies negative duties, which are binding at every moment of one's life, and positive duties, which become effective only in particular circumstances.

NEGATIVE OBLIGATIONS. The obligation to profess the faith forbids rejection of the true faith or profession of a false faith for any reason whatever under any circumstances, even in a matter of life and death (Matt. 10:33; Luke 11:26; 12:9; II Tim. 2:12; *see also* Blasphemy, Persecution). Such rejection could be *direct*, that is, with the explicit intention of rejecting the faith, at least externally; or *indirect*, that is, acts or words which, in themselves or by reason of circumstances, indicate an implicit rejection of the faith or the profession of a false faith. An example of indirect disavowal is *communicatio in sacris activa*, that is, an active participation in rites or religious services of non-Catholic religions or sects, which, besides the danger of scandal or loss of one's faith, would constitute an objective rejection of the Catholic faith, even if such intention did not exist internally. A merely passive or civil attendance, that is, a material presence without participation in services and without demonstrating solidarity with their beliefs, though generally illicit, may be tolerated under circumstances requiring such presence for proportionately grave reasons of charity (friendship, or other civil duties) or to avoid notable harm, provided that all danger of scandal or loss of faith be avoided (Cans. 1258, 2316).

POSITIVE OBLIGATIONS. The obligation to profess the faith in a positive manner is binding only in circumstances in which silence or evasion would imply an implicit rejection or contempt of the faith, or would be detrimental to God's honor and to the salvation of one's neighbor (Can. 1324, par. 1). In other circumstances, such as indiscreet queries, useless vexations, and the like, despite the virtue of the act of faith, to remain silent or conceal one's faith by ambiguous words may be licit for a just cause, and, at times, advisable. In general, secret conversions to Catholicism are not permitted, because ordinarily advantage from publicity is greater than any personal disadvantage. In an exceptional case, serious reasons may justify concealment for a brief period of time. A positive obligation of making a profession of faith is sometimes required by ecclesiastical legislation, by canonical laws (baptism, orders), or by disciplinary laws, especially on the occasion of promotion to ecclesiastical offices or dignities (Can. 1406). *Dam.*

PROFESSION, RELIGIOUS. *Profession* (Latin, *profiteri*—to declare before a magistrate) is a public form of life by which one manifests his will to tend to the attainment of evangelical perfection. In this sense, one speaks, e.g., of religious profession in secular third orders, where the candidate, without religious vows, binds himself to live in his own state a more religious life than other Christians, according to the spirit of a religious order of his own choice.

In a strict sense, however, *religious profession* means a public profession of the vows of poverty, chastity, and obedience in a religious order or society approved by the Church, by which one assumes the obligation to tend to evangelical perfection and to submit to the authority of the lawful superiors of the community.

Religious profession, as a juridical act, became gradually a spontaneous self-dedication to God. Many Christians from the early days of the Church promised to observe the evangelical counsels. The concept of religious order (*see*

Order; Congregation, Religious) developed from this.

In present-day law, religious profession may be *temporary* or *perpetual, solemn* or *simple.* These depend upon the nature of the vows: simple or solemn, perpetual or temporary (*see* Vow, Religious).

Religious profession is a juridical act whose effect is the introduction of the professed into the religious state, by incorporation into a religious order. Under this aspect, religious profession may be considered a special bilateral contract between the religious order and the candidate. The latter offers himself publicly and binds himself to live according to the rules and the spirit of the community, under the authority of the religious superiors. The religious order, in turn, accepts the professed as a member and binds itself to provide him with all necessary means for the attainment of the goal of the religious state and to provide for his maintenance. Yet, the analogy between profession and a contract is wanting under many aspects, especially because, as in marriage, many obligations and juridical effects of the profession are not dependent upon the will of the professed but, in a certain sense, that of the Church itself. Consequently, religious profession may be more properly termed a divine-ecclesiastical, public institution, productive of definite effects in the law of the Church, despite the fact that it is freely made.

The profession of religious vows and its acceptance by superiors in the name of the Church is a second, yet essential, aspect of the juridical act of religious profession. By virtue of this, religious profession not only acquires a high moral value as a consecration of the soul to God, with the promise to live a life of perfection, but it also has an external juridical value, since the candidate professing promises publicly before the Church's representatives to live in that state of dedication and perfection proper to those who live according to the evangelical counsels.

The Church accepts, in the name of God, the expression of such a will and grants the professed membership in the religious state with all rights, privileges, and duties proper to a canonical religious state, as defined in the Code of Canon Law.

The right of admission to religious profession belongs to the major superior, who must make certain of the absence of any impediment, and of the fact that the candidate has the qualifications required by Canon Law and the constitutions of the respective religious order, both for the validity and lawfulness of the profession (Can. 572, 575).

For a valid profession, the Code of Canon Law requires that the candidate be at least sixteen years old for first temporary profession, and at least twenty-one for perpetual profession; he must have made a valid novitiate of one year, and must be admitted to profession by the lawful major superior, with the vote of his council; the profession must not be based on duress, fear, or deception; it must be expressed outwardly and received by the major superior or his delegate. For validity, perpetual vows must be preceded by a three-year period of temporary vows (Can. 572).

For a lawful profession, the following are required: (a) observance of a definite rite; (b) signing of an appropriate document by the candidate; (c) a retreat of several days. For solemn profession, the candidate is also required to renounce the right of ownership of his property (Can. 581, 576).

The juridical or moral effects mentioned above are common to all professions, but the Code of Canon Law enumerates some specific effects proper to each individual profession. Thus, a religious of temporary vows enjoys all spiritual privileges of the religious order he joined and is bound to observe all its rules and constitutions but has no active or passive voice, unless the constitutions explicitly so state (Can. 578). A solemn profession invalidates all contrary acts (Can. 579); consequently, a marriage attempted by a religious of solemn vows is invalid (Can. 1073). Profession renders a solemnly professed religious incapable of possessing any property (Can.

582). It grants candidates for sacred orders with solemn vows the faculty to be ordained by the *title of poverty* (Can. 982, par. 1; *see* Title of Sacred Ordination). It removes any irregularity from illegitimacy (Can. 984, n. 1). It imposes the obligation of choir on clerics and nuns (Can. 610, par. 3). It dissolves a ratified non-consummated marriage of baptized persons, if one of the parties enters a religious order by apostolic indult (Can. 1119).

A simply professed religious retains the fundamental right of ownership to his property, and unless holy orders are added, he contracts marriage validly although illicitly (Canons 579; 569; 580, par. 1). *Mand.*

PROFESSOR. Any individual habitually engaged in the teaching of a science or an art as his primary occupation is called a *professor.* In a more strictly juridical concept, a professor is one who offers his scientific or artistic professional service upon payment of a salary.

Obviously, there are different kinds of professors, according to the various sciences and arts.

QUALIFICATIONS. The main moral qualifications for a fruitful exercise of the office and mission of professor are a true vocation or natural inclination to science or art, ability and continued study leading to his improvement, uprightness, and unselfishness (*see* Teacher). Reducing his high calling to the level of just another occupation is a degradation of science and art and an injustice to youth, their families, and country.

The ordinary technical requirement for teaching is a college degree, which, of course, testifies to the academic qualifications of an individual.

A professor's authority in the classroom is, in a certain sense, absolute; he is responsible within the limits of his institution and the laws governing it. While he has much freedom with respect to the method of teaching, he must conform to the decisions of his own school superiors and to established programs. Specifically, a professor is gravely

bound in conscience: (a) to devote to his teaching as many weekly hours as the nature and extent of his teaching require, and, therefore, may not misuse the class hours in rambling or losing time, without being guilty of injustice with respect to education and the terms of his contract; (b) he is required to observe the appointed schedule; (c) he must supervise laboratories, studies, and other activities connected with his work; (d) he is responsible for any lack of discipline which may occur in his class through his own fault.

A professor must be able to combine clearness of method with genuine knowledge and love of truth. A professor of higher education has even greater responsibility, for, while he is permitted greater freedom in his scientific inquiries, he must make sure that he shall impart to his students only genuine scientific truths capable of opening to his students new horizons to true scientific knowledge. *Tar.*

PROFIT. See Price, Just; Exchange; Company, Stock.

PROFIT-SHARING. *See* Participation.

PROHIBITION. *See* Alcoholism, Drunkenness.

PROLACTIN. *See* Hypophysis.

PROLAN A. *See* Gonads; Hypophysis.

PROLAN B. *See* Gonads; Hypophysis.

PROLETARIAT. *Proletarius* for the Romans (Cicero, *De Republica II*, 24, 40) was *capite census,* that is, one listed as capable of serving the State by his work and ability to procreate children; it was in opposition to *adsiduus,* listed as one who could help the State by his position as a landowner. Today, by *proletariat* is understood the mass of working people engaged in heavy physical work, paid for the most part according to a system of wages, under economic conditions which exclude possession of capital. There is a strict connection between the real and the etymological meaning of the term. Even in modern times the working class has often been considered a productive force capable of preserving its efficiency by the procreation of children.

The proletariat, in its chief aspects indicated above, is a product of the rise of great industry and the success of economic utilitarianism. The use of complex machineries required the investment of extensive capital which only a few could afford; hence, the totality of the workers could not contribute to production (*q.v.*) except in physical toil, compensated by a system of wages.

The ever-increasing employment of machines caused such a constant reduction in the number of workers that it resulted in an over-abundant supply of manpower and a depreciation of labor.

The increased number of ordinary laborers, compelled to live on a meager wage, and the promotion of new social economic theories gave rise in the working class to an attitude of rebellion against other social classes and the political structure of society. With this profound cleavage there developed social agitations and bitter disturbances. The elimination of the proletariat and the many social difficulties arising from it remain the most serious problem of our times. The solution consistently indicated by recent popes, Leo XIII, Pius XII, and John XXIII (*see Mater et Magistra*), lies in giving the workers the opportunity to assume greater responsibilities in business and production and a proportionate share in the ownership of the means of production and in the benefits of all the sectors of public life. *Pav.*

PROMISCUITY. *See* Coeducation; School, Lay; Sexuality.

PROMISE. A *promise* is a pledge in the form of a gratuitous contract, by which one binds himself to do or give something to another who accepts it. It concerns a gratuitous and useful thing, accepted by the one to whom it is promised. The thing promised may be a personal or real consideration. In order

that the promise may produce binding legal effects, it must be admitted by the law in the individual matter. If the promise has a time limit, it may be revoked before the expiration of the time. If the condition foreseen in the promise has been fulfilled, or the action itself has already taken place, the revocation of the promise is not valid.

A promise is invalid from the beginning, if it is based on prodigality (*q.v.*), because the matter is unlawful. Yet, if the matter is divisible, the promise remains for that part which is lawful. The promise terminates if the promise is useless to the promisee or impossible; if the principal cause which motivated it no longer exists, or the circumstances surrounding the promise or the condition of the persons have so changed as to lead to the belief that they would have hindered or prevented making such a promise; finally, through the death of the promiser or promisee in promises binding by fidelity. Some believe that a promise binds in justice and under pain of grave sin (*sub gravi*); others, by fidelity and not gravely (*sub levi*). It seems more reasonable to admit that the obligation depends on the intention of the promiser, to be ascertained by all possible concrete evidence; and that, in case of doubt, the obligation binds only under venial sin. *Sir.*

PROMOTER OF THE FAITH. The *promoter of the faith* is a prelate for the processes of beatification and canonization, who protects the rights and public interest of the Church (*ad ius tuendum*) by opposing the recognition of a blessed or a saint until the practice of heroic virtues and miracles is proven beyond doubt (Can. 2010). Thus, the promoter of the faith is the postulator's opponent; he is popularly called *the devil's advocate*. There are promoters of the faith in the Sacred Congregation of Rites and in diocesan tribunals. The promoter of the faith in the Sacred Congregation of Rites is called *general promoter of the faith*; he is assisted by an assessor of the same Congregation, called *general* *vice-promoter of the faith.* Both are appointed by the supreme pontiff.

In diocesan tribunals there are two types of promoters: (1) promoters of the faith for apostolic processes or trials, chosen by the general promoter of the faith and called *sub-promoters* of the faith; (2) promoters of the faith for ordinary trials, appointed by the local Ordinary, called simply promoters (Cans. 2010–2011).

The promoter of the faith has the right and duty to take part in all phases of a trial; hence, he must always be summoned (Can. 1587). It is his duty to see to it that objective truth be established in a trial. For this reason, he shall propose, through judges, suitable questions for the witnesses on points formulated by the postulator, which he must deliver sealed to the judges, who are under obligation to maintain complete secrecy about them. In addition, the promoter has the right to have *ex officio* witnesses summoned and to raise all necessary objections, even against the witnesses introduced by the postulator. The judges also may summon official witnesses even if the promoter of the faith does not request them, but he must be notified of this (Canons 2012, 2024, 2059, 2070, 2072, 2078, 2079, 2086, par. 2; 2090, 2100, 2110, par. 2). *Led.*

PROMOTER OF JUSTICE AND DEFENDER OF THE BOND.

These two offices in the ecclesiastical forum are the equivalent of the office of prosecutor (*q.v.*) in civil law trials. Both offices may be exercised by one and the same person. To the *promoter of justice* are reserved all accusations in criminal trials (Can. 1934) and the right, with or without the cooperation of the interested parties, to attack the validity of a marriage (Can. 1970, par. 2) or of sacred ordination. He is also bound to take part in all civil trials in which the Ordinary believes that the public welfare is involved (Can. 1586). The *defender of the bond* has the right and duty to defend the bond in all causes of marriage or sacred ordination, and those in which

his intervention is tacitly prescribed, not only for the defense of the bond, but also for reasons of public order connected with the observance of the laws and the regular administration of justice.

The principal and substantial difference between the promoter of justice and the defender of the bond is this: the promoter of justice is free in his conclusions because *certat pro rei veritate;* a defender of the bond must always *ex officio* defend and uphold the validity of the marriage bond and ordination when attacked. Both are public officials and represent in a trial the general interest of the faithful to safeguard the law and the bond. The final word is reserved to them in the ordering and prosecution of canonical proceedings.

The promoter of justice and the defender of the bond in canonical trials do not properly represent any authority, because public power is indivisible; yet they are custodians of the law. Although, strictly speaking, they are not parties to the dispute (*see* Plaintiff), they defend the interests of the public welfare in a trial and must act as substitutes for the party that may be absent. Their office is ecclesiastical in a broad sense (Can. 145) and, though in theory it is disputed whether they have jurisdiction, in practice they are considered not to have jurisdiction.

Despite the notable differences, particularly from the point of view of procedure, between the promoter of justice and the defender of the bond on one side, and the promoter of the faith (*q.v.*) in causes of canonization on the other, all have in common the general characteristic of a defender of the faith and the public welfare of the Church. *Pug.*

PROMULGATION OF LAW.

Promulgation of a law is an act by which the law is made known and imposed on the community by the lawgiver. From the standpoint of the moral and natural laws, there is no specific method of promulgation of a law. It suffices that the promulgation reveals the will of the legislator and is suited to making the community aware of the law. There is more than one method of promulgating laws.

The natural law and natural rights become known to an individual through the use of reason; divine-positive law was promulgated in the Mosaic legislation and the preaching of the Gospel; positive human laws are promulgated by different methods according to the different forms of society. These methods are generally indicated in the fundamental, constitutional laws of the societies. In the Church, the laws established by the Holy See are promulgated in *Acta Apostolicae Sedis* (*q.v.*); each Ordinary may establish his own method of promulgating laws in his own diocese. Promulgation of a law is distinguished from divulging the same; to divulge a law is to publish a law in a way that all the subjects are made aware of it. This, of course, requires a more or less lengthy period of time, depending on circumstances. In order to avoid the inconvenience of having a law that is binding on subjects who are unaware of its official promulgation, a definite period of time is generally allotted between promulgation and the actual effect of a law so that largest possible number of subjects may learn of the promulgation of the law in question.

CANON LAW. In principle, the laws of the Holy See do not go into effect and, therefore, are not binding, until three months have elapsed from the date of publication in *Acta Apostolicae Sedis* (Can. 9).

The period of time intervening between enactment and the effect of a law is called *suspension of the law*. During suspension, no one is bound to observe the law, even though he is aware of it; but when the suspension is over, all are bound to observe the law, even if they are not aware of it. One who is ignorant of it can be morally excused for its non-observance, provided that his ignorance is inculpable; however, he is liable in particular circumstances for the juridical consequences arising from transgressions of that law. *Gra.*

PROOF, DERMATOGRAPHIC. *See* Inhibition.

PROPAGANDA FIDE. (Sacred Congregation). *See* Congregation, Roman.

PROPAGATION OF THE FAITH. *See* Missions.

PROPERTY, PRIVATE (Right of). The concept of ownership is one that is not deduced from other notions. It is a notion which man's mind immediately perceives from things themselves. It is original and primary, not an artificial, juridical synthesis, such as mortgage, exchange, banknotes, and the like. To be sure, juridical science can and must deal with these notions, but as notions derived from a primary one. Therefore, in order to avoid ambiguities on the subject of ownership, the distinction must always be kept in mind between the primary notion of ownership, which is valid for all times and all mankind, and a conventional notion that includes other aspects which either broaden the concept of ownership or restrict it. Thus, if a precise definition of property cannot be had, in a broad sense this is possible. One can proceed by two methods: enumerate the functions of property, or define its limits. The first method leads us to perfect dominion, to the broadest powers and the absolute faculty to dispose of property; the second makes us aware of the fact that ownership may cease either (a) by its physical limitation or (b) when the right of another begins. Despite this, certain difficulties are not avoided, in practice, but these revolve around material discipline more than a question of principle. In a very broad sense, property could be defined as anything related to a physical or juridical person, whether individual or collective, which, by reason of a full dominion conferred to a definite person, is not connected with any other person and, consequently, is opposed to what is common by the principle of opposition.

In view of man's selfish inclinations and a lack of clarity in the natural law, the State must determine and reduce to a juridical form the social functions of ownership. Leo XIII and Pius XI warned against either exaggerated individualism or exaggerated collectivism, by urging the constant preservation of balance between the two extremes. Nor must this balance be static, but must be regulated by positive juridical provisions dictated by the actual circumstances of the times.

Above all, owners must be mindful of their duties toward God. Those who deny the supreme dominion of God over all things and any consequent ethical responsibility on the human possessor, destroy the moral basis of his right of ownership. In addition, ownership has certain obligations toward the community by reason of the social nature of man. Owners must not use their right of ownership against the common good, but must render the work productive and provide opportunities for non-owners to earn fair wages, so that they may not only earn their living, but also rise to a condition of ownership. This is particularly necessary in a free enterprise system. Nor must one forget that, besides juridical obligations, man has other obligations, particularly of charity.

RIGHT AND USE OF PROPERTY. Failure to distinguish between *right* and *use* of property gives rise to many confusions and errors. It is the function of the *right* of ownership to draw a line between what is mine and what is yours. Any trespassing of this right will result in an unlawful attack on the right of another. Even if one remains within the limits of one's own right, moral disorders may still occur in the use of such right. In order to avoid any abuse against the right of ownership, man must possess and practice the virtue of *commutative* justice; all other virtues will help him to use property. It is not true that property and its honest use are restricted by the same limitations, nor is it true that the right of ownership is lost by its abuse or nonuse of it (*Quadragesimo anno*). *Per.*

RIGHT OF OWNERSHIP. (a) *Natural Right*. All visible goods are given to man as instruments of work and as means for the attainment of his proper end. Man tends instinctively to ownership. It is quite natural for man to dispose not only of his energies and faculties, but also of his possessions, which are simply an extension of himself. Thus, man tends instinctively to occupation of items which belong to nobody. Nor has he ever thought that this right is given him by society.

Furthermore, in view of his rational nature, which impels him not to depend on chance for his own future and that of his family, but to provide for his needs in due time, man aspires not only to the possession of the fruits of the land but to the land itself, as a stable element of future security. The same is true for the inventor of a new machine or for the author of a book.

The experience of recent times offers new arguments in favor of ownership as a natural right. The right of ownership is a guarantee of the right of individual freedom against the intrusions of a totalitarian State in the area of personal freedoms. In those places where the right of private ownership has been destroyed, even civil, cultural, and religious life has been enslaved. Since every man has duties to fulfill, he must have a right to the possession of temporal goods. In order that this potential right may become an effective reality, it requires an act of individual will. Temporal goods are not given by nature and the Creator to certain persons only, but are placed at the disposal of all men as individual possessors of them.

(b) *Moral Reasons*. Against the doctrine of communism we shall underscore not only the licitness but also the moral necessity of private ownership. Man is a spiritual being whom all creatures must serve; he in turn must serve God. In the order of creation, the imperfect is at the service of the perfect. The supreme dominion over all creatures belongs to God; temporal dominion belongs to man. The foundation of every right and juridical relation is the interior inclination to juridical good by a person; the right of ownership is natural to man. In view of the responsibilities which man must fulfill, this right surpasses in its premises and consequences the strict economic sphere, extending even to the problem of man's personal freedom with respect to his end. With this in view, it is clear that the right of ownership has also a theological and moral aspect. Furthermore, since man has the capacity and the natural forces for self-determination and dominion over nature's goods, whereas the State and society must depend on the individual as their agents, it is clear that neither the State nor society is the primary, much less the sole, possessor of the right of ownership.

SOCIAL FUNCTION OF OWNERSHIP. The doctrine sustaining and justifying the lawfulness of the right of private ownership of the means of production also maintains that private ownership has an inherently social function, in the sense that its subjects must use it to satisfy their own interests in harmony with those of society. For this very reason, the right itself, in its concrete reality, must conform to historical conditions in the various human communities and adapt itself to their evolution.

It is apparent that, normally, man cannot fully develop his personality without possessing property; consequently, man's nature demands that he either be or become an owner. Recognition of the right of ownership implies the possibility of widest expansion. Greed, of course, is restrained by the limits imposed on the right of ownership by the positive law.

PROPHYLAXIS. See Medicine, Psychosomatic.

PROPOSITIONS, CONDEMNED. In the exercise of its teaching or magisterial authority, the Church may follow two methods: one, *positive*, more frequently used, is a direct teaching on some point of truth or doctrine; the other, *negative*, is a condemnation of an unacceptable and false doctrine. These doctrines are usually summarized into short formulas, which then become the condemned propositions. This method is less frequently employed.

The more commonly known of the propositions condemned by the Church are: (a) five propositions containing the doctrine of Jansenius (1653); (b) eighty propositions contained in the *Syllabus of Errors* by Pope Pius IX; (c) forty propo-

sitions in which the more offensive doctrines of Rosmini were condemned and rejected (1887).

Less known were the forty-one propositions of the doctrines of Luther, rejected in 1520. Still less known but very important for moralists are the forty-five propositions condemned by Alexander VII (1665–1666), and the sixty-five propositions condemned by Innocent XI (1679); all of these refer to moral errors stemming for the most part from probabilist opinions.

In condemning certain propositions the Church generally attaches to them a qualification (*theological note*) which indicates the degree of opposition to Catholic doctrine. These are the more frequent notes: (a) *heretical*, that is, opposed to a dogma in a direct and immediate manner; (b) *erroneous*, that is, only indirectly opposed to a particular dogma, but directly opposed to some truth deduced from dogmas; (c) *approaching heresy*, if a proposition contradicts doctrines generally believed in the Church but not yet defined as dogmas; (d) *suspicious, or tending to heresy*, if a proposition is at variance with doctrines generally believed by the faithful but in a lesser degree than the preceding ones; (e) *rash*, if it is an unfounded statement, even in matters having no strict relation with faith; (f) *offensive to the Christian sense, scandalous, unreliable* . . . and other similar formulas with evident meaning, which indicate an objectionable aspect, simply on the basis of their timeliness.

A condemnation may be issued on a purely *doctrinal* point by dogmatic or moral theologians; in such a case, the value of the condemnation is as serious as the scientific authority of those who pronounced it. Today an official and authoritative condemnation is issued only by the pope or by organs of the Holy See (Roman Congregations, Biblical Commission, etc.). Councils and bishops could also pronounce condemnations of errors.

From the moral point of view it may be important to know the duty of the faithful with respect to such condemnations. In other words, is external acquiescence on the part of the faithful sufficient or must they submit with internal adherence?

(a) Internal assent *ex professo* includes condemnations pronounced in an official and authoritative manner; for those pronounced in a simply doctrinal way, the ordinary rules of prudence and scientific dependability are sufficient.

(b) External acquiescence is always a matter of duty, and it amounts to the elementary duty of obedience to the lawful authority. This obligation is considered in Canon 2317, which contains penalties incurred by those who obstinately teach or defend doctrines condemned by the Holy See or a general council. It is to be noted, however, that this Canon concerns propositions not condemned by the note of heresy; if a proposition has simply been declared heretical, then whoever teaches it incurs the sanctions stipulated for heretics or supporters of heresy, as indicated in other Canons (2314, 2315, 2316, 2318, 2319).

(c) External acquiescence includes the duty of adapting our external conduct to the prohibition contained in the condemnation, by refraining from professing in practice the proscribed doctrine.

(d) On the other hand, it is clear that internal adherence is never required to go beyond the terms of the condemnation. Thus, if a proposition is condemned as *not certain*, we are not bound to consider it as false; it is sufficient that we say that it is *not certain*.

(e) Internal adherence is always required if the condemnation is pronounced by an infallible authority (pope or general council) as such.

(f) Though it is a debated question among moralists whether the faithful must give internal adherence to condemnations pronounced by non-infallible authorities, such as the Roman Congregations, this adherence, nevertheless, is commonly regarded as an obligation. However, it is not necessary that this adherence be absolute, as in the case of dogmatic definitions, or that the possibility of any doubt to the contrary be excluded. It suffices for one to have a so-called *prudential* adherence, inasmuch as it rests, not on an infallible authority, but simply on a solid presumption that the condemnation is the result of a correct judgment. Consequently, scholars are not forbidden, after giving external adherence, to continue to look into the reasons to the contrary, provided that this be done without scandal and with full respect for the decisions of the competent authority. *Gra.*

PRO-PREFECT APOSTOLIC. *See* Prefect Apostolic.

PROSTITUTION. *Prostitution*, or harlotry, is a common and venal lewdness among a class of women. It is commonly considered by moralists as a form of fornication (*q.v.*), but, in fact, prostitutes lend themselves to all kinds of lust, according to or against nature. Prostitution implies continuity and recidivity, and often seduction, as aggravating circumstances.

Whether prostitution should be suppressed or tolerated by the public authority is an ancient question. Several moralists, including St. Thomas (*De regimine principum*, 1, c. 14), were of the opinion that harlotry could be tolerated in order to avoid greater sins and greater harm from adultery, rape, unnatural sins, etc., or as a means of keeping within certain limits an evil which is quite difficult to extirpate. However, they laid down certain conditions and precautions: that it be permitted only in large cities, in the least respectable quarters, and that full opportunity be given to prostitutes to return to a better way of living. This was, generally, the practice in the Middle Ages.

Other theologians (including St. Alphonsus) were opposed to this opinion; their view has become the prevailing one today. The reasons are: (a) sins and excesses do not diminish at all if tolerated, but in fact increase; (b) tolerance gives rise to other serious evils, such as easier occasions of sinning, lower public morals, debasement of the dignity of woman, increased seduction (*q.v.*), traffic of women (*q.v.*), etc. Various modern States tolerate prostitution in practice. Some of these States prohibit brothels, others (few today) allow them under restrictive conditions because it helps check the hygienic condition of prostitutes and prevents, to some degree, the spread of venereal diseases. A few countries permit prostitution as a matter of fact, without requiring registration of prostitutes (*See also* Evil, Lesser). *Dam.*

PROTECTIONISM. *See* Free Trade; Exchange; Commerce.

PROTECTOR (Cardinal). *See* Cardinal Protector.

PROTECTOR (Saint). *See* Saints.

PROTESTANTISM (moral theology of). Catholic moral theology treats of free human acts as acts to be avoided (sins) and acts to be performed (virtues). For these are means (meritorious acts) to the attainment of man's supernatural end, eternal life. Moral theology, therefore, presupposes free will.

Assuredly, Protestants do speak of free human acts, but present points difficult to understand. (a) How can such acts be called free by those who deny free will (Lutherans)? (b) How can sinful acts be avoided and virtuous acts performed by those who believe that, before attaining justifying faith (trust), all of man's acts are sinful (Lutherans and others)? (c) How can virtuous acts performed by man after justification (in the Protestant sense) be a means to the attainment of his supernatural end, if they are not meritorious (nearly all Protestants)? (d) How can some be predestined by God to eternal punishment (Calvinists)?

By definition, Catholic moral theology is distinguished from other branches of theology: (a) from *dogmatic theology*, which concerns dogmas; (b) from *ascetic theology*, which treats of the ordinary means required for the attainment of perfection; (c) from *mystical theology*, which treats of the extraordinary means to be added to the ordinary ones; (d)

from *pastoral theology*, which deals with the duties of pastors of souls; (e) from *Canon Law*, which deals only with matters of the external forum; (f) from *polemics*, which is used to defend the Catholic doctrine, and to attack opposing doctrine; (g) from *exegesis*, which interprets and explains the Bible.

According to J. F. Buddeus, Protestant moral theology includes every one of these branches of theology, as well as Canon Law. However, so he declares, moral theology includes only what he calls *divine law*.

Perhaps it would be more exact to say that Protestants group the various branches of theology under the name of *Christian theology*, or simply *theology*. In their books of theology one finds dogmatic questions (mysteries of the Holy Trinity and the Incarnation), moral questions (the ten commandments), points of asceticism mixed with mysticism, pastoral questions (offices of the ministers), polemics, exegesis, and Canon Law.

Protestant theological publications in which one finds parts of moral theology are numerous. It may be sufficient to mention the seventy or more volumes of *Anglo-Catholic Theology*, containing almost all the works of the more famous Anglican theologians.

Buddeus in his History of Moral Theology offers a list of the leading Protestant moral theologians.

Protestants do not consider confession as a sacrament. When they broke away from the Catholic Church in the sixteenth century, the leading sects preserved confession as a requirement to be fulfilled before receiving Communion, but gradually they reduced it to a kind of *confiteor*, repeated by all the faithful and followed by an absolution of the minister. This method is still practiced in many denominations, except the Anglo-Catholics. Thus, it was not necessary for them to examine their conscience on the number, gravity, circumstances of sins; still less did they make private confession to the minister. Yet, in their books of moral theology, the ten commandments and other moral points are treated to provide guidance to those who must give advice or preach.

On examining the doctrines treated in their moral theology, it is easy to see that several are unacceptable from the Catholic viewpoint.

Thus, for example, all sins are mortal and worthy of hell. Limborg teaches that even the slightest sin makes us guilty of disobedience to God, who, if He should wish to proceed according to the severity of His justice, should punish it with eternal death.

Faith is not the theological virtue taught by Catholic theologians but a trust in God, which suffices for justification; according to some, once such justification is attained, it can no longer be lost, for the justified is certain of final perseverance.

Although it can be generally stated that, in the explanation of the ten commandments, Protestants follow the doctrine of the Catholic Church, yet, in the revival of an ancient heresy of the Iconoclasts, they consider as idolotrous the veneration that Catholics give to the Blessed Mother of God and to the saints. Certain positions, which were not dealt with in the sixteenth century, but in more recent times, advocate the lawfulness of certain practices condemned by the Catholic Church, such as birth control and euthanasia. Many Protestants regard them as lawful. On divorce and remarriage of divorced persons, even some of the older sects, which for some time had preserved traditional Catholic doctrine, are now steadily departing from it.

In their teaching on the sacraments they have departed almost completely from the doctrine of the Catholic Church. They reject five sacraments, and in the two which they maintain, baptism and the Eucharist, they employ a different matter and form. The Baptists and many others deny the validity of infant baptism. Concerning the Eucharist, or the Lord's Supper, all reject the Real Presence as understood by Catholics; hence they regard the adoration of the Blessed Sacrament as an act of idolatry.

For ecclesiastical law, Protestants who follow Christian doctrine (Anglicans and Lutherans, where their denominations are national Churches) recognize the State as the supreme ecclesiastical authority. In the case of other groups, e.g., Calvinists, their presbytery claims to hold the scepter of Christ, as the pope holds the keys of Peter. By the scepter of Christ is meant particular assemblies and the government which they have fashioned. It would, then, be a matter of ecclesiastical laws established by an authority that is believed ecclesiastical, but which in fact is purely civil or lay.

In summarizing, (1) it is apparent that Protestant moral theology treats assuredly of the ten commandments; but since Protestants do not admit an infallible interpretation of the law of God, but believe in a free interpretation of Holy Scripture, they have interpreted many points of the Bible in a manner that is unacceptable to the Catholic Church. (2) They accept two sacraments, but treat them from the point of view of dogmatic theology and polemics, which gives the individual writers an opportunity to expound a sacramental doctrine for their own denomination and to attack that of others. (3) They accept virtues and contrary vices, but rather in the sphere of ascetical theology. In this, if they are not influenced by anti-Catholic prejudices, they argue correctly, by following Catholic doctrine, but, unfortunately, without the means which the Catholic Church offers for the attainment of perfection, such as the sacraments, devotion to Our Lady, the saints, and so on. (4) Their ecclesiastical laws are derived from different sources.

The wrong opinion which Protestants have had of Catholic moral theology may be seen in the parallelism which they draw from the *Supplementa ad secundum tomum theol. Lutheri* by John Henry Majo, Frankfurt on the Main, 1710.

Protestant Doctrine. Christ is the High Priest. The law of Christ is the grace of life. Sacrifice is the living Body. Good works are to serve one's neighbor. Sins are transgressions. Punishment is eternal death. Reward is eternal glory.

Ministers are preachers of the Gospel. The result is a cheerful cross.

Catholic Doctrine (according to the Protestant notion). The pope is the High Priest. The law of Christ is the tradition of Canon Law. Sacrifice is Eucharist and money. Good works are the ceremonies. Sins are transgressions. Punishment is false excommunication. Rewards are the riches of the world. Ministers are the mouthpieces of the papal Bulls. The results are bad consciences.

Following the Oxford Movement, so-called Anglo-Catholics have endeavored to introduce confession; therefore, they have developed a moral theology from Catholic writers, including even casuistry, once so greatly maligned by Protestants. Since they do not recognize the authority of the pope, they pay no attention to the doctrine or moral norms indicated by the Holy See on such subjects as birth control, strikes, artificial insemination, and the like, in which they have often taken erroneous positions. *Cri.*

PROTHONOTARY APOSTOLIC. *See* Prelate.

PROTODULIA. *See* Worship.

PROVIDA MATER ECCLESIA. *See* Orders, Religious.

PROVIDENCE. *Providence,* properly speaking, is the plan according to which God directs all created things to their proper end. It resides in the divine intellect but it presupposes a volition of the end. The execution of the plan conceived in God's mind, which in the ultimate analysis is the government of creatures, follows the volition of the end. Since plan and execution are intimately connected, in practice providence is understood as the combination of both.

As a plan, divine providence extends directly to all things, even the least. Execution also extends to all things, but not always directly, because God often uses His creatures as secondary causes, through which He produces the desired effect.

Divine providence, without fail, reaches its end in everything and in every part of the preconceived plan. Therefore, it excludes *chance,* if understood as that which happens outside the causality of God. What we call chance is an existing thing; but this, too, is caused and foreseen by God, as part of the *governing plan* conceived and executed by Him. The double truth—that God directs everything to a good end according to that plan which is in accord with His infinite wisdom and omniscience, and that our activity, free, though a mystery, has its place in the execution—is the basis of the doctrine whereby we believe that the right attitude toward divine providence is a full, tranquil, and serene trust, without neglect of the good that we are able to perform and which we know is pleasing to God. If we seek to do what God has made known to us through His commandments and counsels, through the circumstances of life and inspirations, and especially through the commands of those who have the right to command, everything will go well and end well. We are like babies carried by a powerful and infinitely good Father who directs everything in such a manner that no creature can make any movement of resistance that will disturb the execution of His will. This will is none other than love, benevolence, and goodness without bounds. In such circumstances no one should be afraid. Yet, it is necessary to bear in mind that this does not mean exclusion of hardships, trials, pains, sickness, poverty, etc., just as the goodness of a father would not exclude necessary punishment of a child to train him properly, or a painful operation to save a child from death or life-long paralysis. Thus, suffering is not left out of the plans of providence, but is directed to man's benefit. This is a sufficient motive for bearing it, if it cannot be avoided by just and lawful means. This gives full serenity and resignation or even a joyful heart (*see* Sorrow).

The providence of God is seen and admired, not only in the relations between the individual and God, but also in the relations between nations and the Divine Mind, the Ruler of human events.

St. Augustine, among the Fathers of the Church, emphasized more than all others the dogma of providence. In his *City of God* he writes "Two loves have established two cities: love of self, driven to the point of contempt of God, has created the city of Babylon [the city of sin]; love of God, driven to the point of contempt of self, has created the city of God. The two cities, always and everywhere confused in this world, are in continuous dissension between them" (Chapter XVI, 28). In this picture St. Augustine sketches his plan and explains his doctrine of the action of God in the world, by showing that in Christianity, despite obstacles created by man's enemy, God leads a part of humanity, which, out of love for Him, gathers in His *City*, toward its eternal destiny and final triumph in heaven. With a stroke of genius Augustine provides the first synthesis of a philosophy of history, embracing in a single glance the destinies of a world grouped around the religion of the Gospel. If understood, it reaches back to the origin of things and leads humanity to its ultimate ends.

This grandiose vision of human history explaining and illustrating the action of God on earth, was pursued by other Fathers and writers up to the time of the great Bossuet. Concerning human prudence, *see* Prudence (virtues connected with). *Ben.*

PROVINCIAL. *See* Superior, Religious.

PROVISION, CANONICAL. *See* Benefice; Possession of benefice.

PROVOCATION. The legal concept of *provocation,* in modern jurisprudence, was unknown to the Romans, although it must be admitted that they had an indirect notion, since they increased the penalty for the criminal who had committed a premeditated crime. The concept of provocation was developed in Canon Law, in which a crime committed in an outburst of anger caused by a just reason was considered less grave. With the progress of modern psychology and criminology, provocation has been ac-

cepted and perfected in modern codes of law.

In Canon Law, provocation is a cause that lessens imputability in all crimes (Can. 2205, par. 4). It can also be invoked, if the crime did not immediately follow the provocation, but was committed during the state of excitement produced by it (Can. 2218, par. 1). In fact, while it is true that one who acts in a state of provoked anger shows even greater determination, yet anger cannot but lessen a person's capacity in the use of inhibitive faculties and lead his will into error. Concerning provocation to duel, *see* Duel. *Pug.*

PROXY MARRIAGE. *See* Marriage, Proxy.

PRUDENCE. Taken in a broad sense, *prudence* consists in devising, choosing, and preparing appropriate means for the attainment of any purpose or for avoiding any evil. In this sense, one speaks of a prudent industrialist or businessman; in the same sense, the Lord stated that the children of the world are wiser than the children of light.

If the end in view is neither particular nor intermediate, but ultimate, one has prudence in its eminent sense: the intellectual and moral virtue by which one judges and does that which he must properly do or omit doing in each particular case.

As a virtuous act, prudence consists in judging, without unnecessary hesitation or delay, a being as simply good at the moment (*simpliciter bonum, hic et nunc*), which one should desire in order that he might attain his ultimate end, namely, God. Such judgment occurs particularly if one refrains from carrying out an action that is opposed to the moral law or commandments. This judgment, however, is, under a certain aspect, dependent on the will. Since the will desires that which is presented to it as genuinely good, the choice depends, under another aspect, on a simultaneous prudential judgment. These two mutually dependent acts form a complete whole in their moral aspect.

Within the range of prudence is diligence proportionate to the gravity of the thing under consideration and to subjective conditions in forming a conscience before action. Thus one becomes sure before taking a definite action that it conforms to the objective norms of morality. In order to be able to form a good conscience in all cases, one must consult his own experience, analyze carefully the general norms of morality and all the details of the situation at hand. He must be able to foresee the difficulties and obstacles which may arise in the future so that he may not be surprised and beset by unforeseen circumstances. He must think of possible consequences which a specific act may produce for ourselves and for others. He must be intelligent and humble enough to consult wise and experienced men, without neglecting the best of all counselors, the Holy Spirit. In forming a conscience, it is very helpful to follow the rules which one's spiritual director offers.

Since we are ordained to a supernatural end, our prudence will be genuine if it seeks light from the revealed truths and the truths of logic.

The intellect can fail in prudence in any number of ways. Defects in this virtue might assume the following forms: (a) *rashness* and a lack of consideration, which judges an action good without having used all the necessary means to form a conscience or without sufficient consideration of necessary actions to be done; (b) *hesitation* or a lack of promptness in making decisions about what appears to be one's duty in a particular circumstance; (c) *negligence* in not deciding at all what must be done in a particular case; (d) *inconstancy* or withdrawal from a previous decision made. All of these forms of imprudence are necessarily dependent upon a simultaneous defective self-determination of the will. Determination, in turn, depends on a simultaneous imprudent judgment. These two acts form a whole moral unit. Culpability, presupposing freedom, can exist primarily only in the act of the will. The acts of the other faculties, including the intellect, are not sinful except by par-

ticipation, that is, insofar as they are dependent upon an inordinate act of the will. An imprudent judgment partakes of the imputability of the act of the will on which it depends.

Rashness and impetuosity are mortal sins if they cause a serious danger of transgressing the moral law in grave matter or are the result of contempt for the rules of prudence or a grave precept. Hesitation, in itself, is a venial sin; it is, however, a mortal sin if the will fails to use the intellect in deliberating seriously about the advisability of fulfilling a grave duty. The degree of guilt of negligence depends on the nature of the thing omitted.

There are also sins caused by excessive prudence. Among these sins are: (a) Contrivance, selection, and use of means apt to gratify the immoderate desire for material goods, honors, and pleasures (*prudence of the flesh*). The degree of guilt depends on the intention and the nature of the means used. (b) Contrivance and selection of subtle means to attain either a good or a bad end, particularly those which appear to be honest and show no evil intention of injuring one's neighbor (*astuteness*), and the use, by word or deeds, of subtle deceit or fraud. The guilt is slight or grave depending on the intention and the extent of the injury caused. (c) *Excessive solicitude* in acquiring and preserving temporal goods for the future. The guilt is grave, if one makes these things his ultimate end or if his anxiousness is such as to cause him to neglect a grave duty. A moderate concern for temporal things is not sinful, but prudent. *Man.*

VIRTUES DEPENDENT ON PRUDENCE. Each cardinal virtue is surrounded, like a nucleus, by lesser virtues. These are generally termed subdivisions of that virtue. They may be subjective, integral, or potential parts of it.

The subjective or lesser subdivisions of the virtue of prudence are: *personal*, if they concern the individual; and *collective*, if they concern the government of a community. The collective virtue of prudence may in its own right be subdivided into *domestic*, if it applies to the family or lesser community; or *political*, if it applies to a perfect society, civil or ecclesiastical. Administrative, military, international prudence are parts of political prudence.

The integral parts of prudence are attitudes which perfect it. Some of them perfect the cognoscitive element by the memory of the past, understanding of the present, docility, diligence, and reasonableness; others perfect the perceptive aspect, by thrift, circumspection, and caution.

The *memory* of the past is a treasure of experiences which supply norms for handling present situations. *Understanding* is the proper knowledge and practical evaluation of the circumstances in which one actually finds himself. *Docility* (*q.v.*) disposes a person to accept and appreciate lessons of the past.

Diligence, or wisdom, prompts, quickens, and sustains a person in the vigilant exploration of what he must do. *Reasonableness* ponders and evaluates logically all the elements involved. *Thrift* prompts a person to think ahead as if to foresee the future, which is the result of the past and the present, and to prepare for this. *Circumspection* leads a person to guard against surprises and disillusions. *Caution*, or vigilance, leads a person to attentively consider the danger or damages which may occur, and to predispose effectively preventive means.

The potential parts of prudence are lesser virtues which arise from it and are in turn of service to it. They have the same relationship to prudence as man's faculties to his soul. These virtues are good counsel, good sense, and the sense of exception.

Good counsel (*eubolia*) is the habit of searching diligently and finding at the proper time and place the proper means for the end in view. *Good sense* (*synesis*) is the habit of sound judgment and appraisal, according to ordinary rules. The *sense of exception* (*gnome*) is the habit of recognizing cases that exceed more or less the ordinary norms, to take these into account according to the demands of higher principles. This habit directs and controls the proper application of a rule and the proper use of equity and *epicheia* (*q.v.*). *Pal.*

PRUDENCE (moral system). *See* System, Moral.

PSALTERY. *See* Liturgical Books.

PSEUDO - HALLUCINATION. *See* Hallucination.

PSEUDO-HERMAPHRODITISM. *See* Hermaphroditism; Impediments, invalidating.

PSEUDOLOGY, PHANTASMAL. *See* Memory, Pathology of.

PSEUDOMENTIA. As a rare morbid syndrome which simulates, under various aspects, genuine dementias, *pseudomentia* was first described by Wernicke from observations among prisoners. This *prison psychosis* is similar to Ganser's syndrome, so called after the scholar who observed it among individuals in a reformatory.

The symptoms characterizing the two diseases are so similar that several writers consider them one and the same psychosis. Fundamentally they consist of a strange contrast between the manifestations of thought, which the individual seems to have lost in the most elementary forms, while he retains the ability to make the most complex calculations. He may not be able to multiply two times two or make other simple calculations or actions, such as fitting a key into a lock or lighting a match, but he may show extreme propriety in his dress, habitual normal conduct, and clear notions on his own illness and interests, which are not at all demented. Yet he may have forgotten the most obvious notions or say or do things systematically in reverse; he reveals at the same time a great variety of deficiencies. Such forms are *pseudomentias*. This name is justified by the fact that pseudomentia deals with completely reversible manifestations and afflictions; yet he has a favorable prognosis, whereas dementia is incurable and progressively fatal.

Although pseudodemented individuals behave as if demented, there are also patients who behave as infants when they are really adults. Such individuals are also afflicted by what is called *hysteric puerilism* (Bleuler), which should be mentioned here as a psychosis, because it has several affinities with the preceding disturbances. It is a prison psychosis and afflicts men awaiting trial. Fortunately a favorable prognosis offers cure in a few months. Those affected by hysteric puerilism usually call themselves pet and endearing names, speak by using verbs in the infinitive form, have no sense of the value of money, play all day like little children and engage in other extravagant foolishness.

The three pseudo-demential syndromes described above, together with hysteria, psychasthenia and similar disturbances, belong to the group of so-called *reactive psychoses* or *psychogenic reactions* consisting of episodical mental disturbances "which are observed in predisposed individuals under the impact of intense and prolonged emotional stress, internal conflicts, or under exceptional difficulties. Such disturbances develop according to a purely psychogenic mechanism" (Gozzano).

The environmental conditions giving rise to the three syndromes under discussion are almost always provided by prison and reformatory life. Evidently, the abnormal situation in which the individual lives and, still more, the expectation of a sentence, prompt the prisoner to seek refuge in mental illness, as an evasion from a sad reality. This *escape to sickness* is not the result of a calculated simulation, but an unconscious one common among hysterics, which makes it very difficult, in practice, to distinguish it from that of ordinary simulators.

Further complication arises from the fact that those syndromes are often caused by a desire, perhaps unconscious, of avoiding deserved punishment, since, as Bostroem noted, such prison psychoses lead one to the belief that the individual is guilty; the innocent do not seek refuge in illness.

Pseudodementia, however, is not exclusive to prisoners. Sometimes it is observed as an effect of a traumatic condition, particularly resulting from an accident which led to a legal controversy. Moglie maintains that in similar cases it is always "a form of conscious and vulgar simulation." This opinion is supported by the fact that the pseudodementia disappears "as a fog in the wind as soon as liquidation of the indemnity has taken place." Most of the scholars concerned with this question are of the opinion that, even in the case of accident and legal dispute, pseudodementia is the expression of an unconscious simulation. Our opinion is that in the matter of post-traumatic pseudodementia, besides genuine and honest cases, it is possible to have others prompted by fraudulent aims. The difficult task of the expert will be that of singling out one case from the other.

Pseudodemential syndromes are judged on the basis of ordinary hysterical psychoses and, if they occur after a trauma, on the basis of psychoneurotic post-traumatic conditions. Concerning the ethical inferences derived from them, *see* Hysteria, Psychoneuroses of War, Psychoneurosis, Traumatic. *Riz.*

PSYCHASTHENIA. *Psychasthenia* is a common psychoneurosis, consisting of fixed ideas whose morbid character, generally, does not stem from content but from a stubborn persistence, which dominates the patient's entire attention and influences his conduct against his will. Hence, a continuous feeling of malaise, worry and anxiety, with episodic phobic, obsessional exaltation. The affliction is also called *obsessional psychosis* by some scholars, or *anxiety neurosis* by others, depending on the greater emphasis placed on obsessional ideas or anxiety.

At the root of the phobic-obsessive episodes, there is almost always a peculiar psycho-emotional inclination. The patients, intelligent, honest, judicious, a bit too reflective, are generally timid, scrupulous, irresolute individuals, desirous of protection and guidance, inclined to depression and pessimism, hypobulic, hypersensitive and excessively introverted, often more superstitious than religious, preoccupied and more or less distrustful of their neighbor and their own power and capacity. Fundamentally conscious of their own intellectual ability, they have a high opinion of themselves that makes them exacting and tyrannical in their family circles.

This *psychasthenic temperament* is generally accompanied by a micro-splanchnic habit and a neuro-functional hyperactivity of the orthosympathetic system due to hereditary causes, faulty upbringing, and perhaps slow toxinfec-tive processes, among which tuberculosis seems to prevail. True morbid symptoms appear only in adulthood—often be-tween the twentieth and the fortieth year of age—at times spontaneously; in such cases, the psychoneurosis has slow development and a less favorable prog-nosis. Frequently, because of debilitating illnesses, traumas, especially the so-called psychotraumas, exhaust the already low vitality of the individual, curtail his weakened *vital impulse* (Janet), aggra-vate *psychic hypertension* (Janet), and thus usher in a phobic, obsessional syn-drome. This condition becomes even more aggravated because of a type of conditioned reflexes (*q.v.*) to excessive introspection, that characterizes the tem-perament of the individual; these occa-sion anxieties which of themselves favor the reappearance and persistence of the obsession. This is particularly so if the obsession is the result of an emotional sensitivity to a particular, painful, or-ganic condition.

The nature of obsessional ideas (*fixed, compulsory, invincible*) is most varied. Often they are linked with absurd and anxious fears, which, for this reason, are called *phobias: rupophobia*, an abnormal dislike for dirt or filth, which inclines the patient to a perpetual struggle against any contact; *pathophobia*, or fear of par-ticular diseases, such as syphilis, tuber-culosis, and the like; *taphophobia*, ab-normal fear of being buried alive, etc.; *agoraphobia*, dread of crowds of people; *claustrophobia*, fear of being confined in a space; *monophobia*, abnormal fear of being alone; *acrophobia*, morbid fear of high places. In these phobias, elements of a subjective insufficiency seem to be prevalent. In these cases, if the patient finds himself in the dreaded area of his pathological anxiety, there ensues a series of disturbances of a functional nature: a sense of pressure on the epigastrium, nausea, perspiration, tachycardia, sudden general asthenia and the like; these are accompanied by a painful emotional up-set, capable of paralyzing his intellect. Some obsessions affect the vegetative functions: one such condition is *eruto-phobia*, fear of blushing before others, that goes back to adolescence; or psychic *impotency* with an obsessive basis, which may even become *gynephobia*, abnormal aversion to the company of women.

Other obsessions affect the psychic functions of the individual: the fear of loss of memory; dread of responsibility; tormenting mental examinations and ideational sophistications of every kind; *arithmomania*, insane interest in numbers and unnecessary counting; or *meta-physical* delirium, seeking the why and how of everything. In some individuals every sense of certainty seems annihi-lated and all ideas appear to the mind only in a doubtful form (*folly of doubt*). This is distinguished from real deliriums in that the doubts and suspicions are not supported by subjective convictions; as a matter of fact, in all obsessions of psy-chasthenics, they are energetically repudi-ated by the individuals. Finally, other obsessions consist in the representation of acts that are now futile, now un-seemly, now altogether criminal, called *impulsive obsessions*. They are particu-larly horrowing to the patient because the idea of the act, in itself hateful and repugnant, is accompanied by distrust in one's inhibiting power so that execution appears inevitable and imminent. In reality, while the resistance that the sick person opposes to the actuation of the futile obsessive ideas is minimal, which is due to the fact that execution of the act produces a momentary relief and satisfaction for the impulse created by the obsessive idea, it becomes practically insurmountable when the character of the obsessive idea is criminal. Thus crimes, especially crimes of an obsessive origin (suicide), are not altogether rare. This depends on the strenuousness with which the moral, joined to the critical sense, opposes the criminal impulse, despite an extenuating struggle.

Frequently, the content of obsessive ideas finds its explanation in psychic factors which should aways be sought out for psychotherapeutic reasons also. Thus, for example, remorse for a fault committed and, therefore, the need for spiritual cleansing may be satisfied in a symbolic manner by fomenting an obsessive need for continual washing of the hands; this is observed in individuals affected by rupophobia. The psychogenesis of many obsessional ideas is, indeed, admitted by almost all experts on the subject.

Various phobias and obsessions seldom remain isolated. For the most part, they merge or follow one another with alternating periods of respite. Any aberration is generally and evidently related to debilitating somatic forms, with psychic causes responsible not only for the sudden oncoming of the first crisis, as already stated, but also for relapses, worsenings, or improvements.

Thus, misunderstanding and domestic dissension exert an unfavorable influence, while a serene and friendly atmosphere tends to lessen the obsessions. These also may subside if the sick person confides his suffering to a trusting and experienced person. Sometimes very unpleasant and grave events may so distract the individual from his fixations as to bring about his cure.

Medicinal treatments are of little value, except if the obsessive episode is caused by a debilitating sickness. Among other things, a moderate use of alcoholic drinks may contribute to raising the tone of cenesthesis. Physiotherapy, associated with an intelligent and discreet psychotherapy, is more effective, provided that discussions and persuasive efforts are avoided. The patient, in fact, has no need of them, and by proceeding with categorical affirmations the doctor will condition the patient's emotions and lead him to face the causes of his disturbances. By such treatments the prob-

abilities of improvement shall be greatly enhanced. Professional or occupational activities, sports that engage his attention and stimulate courage, a circumspect, coherent, and friendly re-education to altruism, sociability and optimism, rational changes in habits and environment, all improve the psychasthenic temperament of the patient. Furthermore, the patient will doubtless derive benefit from religion, even in conversation with learned and discreet priests who, by their wise and intelligent words, try to strengthen the faith of these individuals, by directing their lives towards works of charity and fortifying their character by a keen discipline of mind and action. It goes without saying that to many psychasthenics religion offers comfort, protection, a sense of security, and an effective aid in enduring suffering and, ultimately, lessening it.

In the more severe cases, it will be necessary to try narcotherapy (*q.v.*), and, if the organic and social life of these patients is deeply disturbed, it may be necessary to resort to lobotomy (*see* Psychosurgery).

The psychasthenic, a basically upright and honest individual, may commit a crime only if he yields to an impulsive criminal obsession. This may occur only after long and atrocious interior struggles, in which he will have sought in vain for protection and supervision from the members of his family to help him avoid the execution of his compulsive idea. This background, the remorse and horror that follow the execution after a fleeting phase of euphoric liberation, the whole painful history of the tormented, fearful, and agitated life of the patient always makes diagnosis of the case simple and easy. Generally, a crime committed under these circumstances is rarely imputable, if at all, since it is committed at a time of greatly reduced or totally lacking responsibility.

The anxieties, sufferings, agitations, and anguish of a scrupulous and doubtful conscience are well-known to confessors of psychasthenics. They know what to do in directing and comforting these unfortunate individuals. It may be well to underscore, however, the advisability that the priest direct the sick person to a competent psychiatrist with whom he shall work for a more effective treatment and eventual cure of the patient. *Riz.*

PSYCHE (pathology of). The etymology of the word *psyche* is directly from Greek (*psyche*—breath, wind) and is similar to the meaning of the word for *soul* (*anemos*). In modern scientific terminology, the term *psyche* is used to indicate the manifold volitive, intellectual, and emotional activities of the individual. These constitute the object of psycho-pathology and psychiatry. The term *soul*, as a spiritual reality, independent of the material of the body, is the area belonging to philosophy and theology. There is no question of distinct and separate entities, but of various aspects of the same reality, for by the term *psyche*, psychiatrists mean the totality of actions which come from the soul as from a principle; this is the meaning applied to the term *soul* by philosophers and theologians.

The psychologist, but more frequently the psychiatrist, considers the psychic world and phenomena as the totality of processes bound to somatic life, in an interrelationship and interdependence that far exceeds abstract concepts or distinctions. Numerous psychic activities are linked to each other by processes of *association*, a reciprocal influence which modifies their action, or by processes of *integration*, in which various activities form a single whole, the *psyche*. These activities may be further subdivided into two groups: strictly intellectual and volitive activities, the so-called processes of *thought*, which are believed by modern scholars to constitute the *noopsyche* (*sophropsyche*); and processes which are considered to refer to the instinctive-affective life or feeling, bound in a particular way to organic functions. These are believed to constitute the *tymopsyche*; this distinction, however, is theoretical.

In practice, *noopsyche* and *tymopsyche* are intimately interrelated. Our affective world influences the will and directs the course of reason, while behavior, though essentially emotional, is the result of logical consideration or intellectual activities in part.

Concerning the methods whereby thought processes are elaborated, it may be briefly stated that the physical world supplies stimuli transformed into sensations and perceptions; these are the basic, raw material; attention selects and utilizes the material; memory and association preserve and expand it; reason leads to a formation of comparison, a comprehension of logical consequences and relations, and the final formulation of judgments.

Organic somatic conditions, such as toxic infections and psychic states of emotional disturbances, as well as constitutional deficiencies, are factors which frequently produce mental illnesses. These belong to the study of psychiatry.

These may afflict either the *noopsyche* or *tymopsyche*, as in progressive paralysis, schizophrenia, etc. They may cause an alteration of the intellectual sphere in forms of oligophrenia or senile dementia; they may afflict the emotional life as in cyclothymia. In other cases, the morbid derangement afflicts, in a somewhat more limited way, this or that single mental faculty. This is observed, for example, in early stages of *senile dementia* with an isolated *deficiency* of memory, or in certain young individuals stricken by *encephalitis* who may present a deep perversion of the moral sense.

PSYCHOPATHOLOGY OF CONSCIOUSNESS. *Consciousness* is psychological consciousness, namely, a psychic state which permits us to utilize the impressions received from the external world and the products of our internal activity (Gozzano).

In a state of *unconsciousness*, verified in a coma, narcosis, and perhaps deep sleep, all contacts with the environment and psychic activities are suspended. But between the wakeful consciousness of a normal individual and absolute unconsciousness there is a whole series of gradations. Consciousness grows dim in drowsiness, in lethargy produced by noticeable cerebral pressures, and in many toxic and infectious conditions. Sensations are perceived with delay and imperfectly; alertness is lethargic and poor; and the memory is defective. The higher psychic processes of ideation, association and critique require enormous effort.

A particular debility of consciousness is present in the *crepuscular state*, which is a systematic falsification of the relations with the external world, as in dreams. Ideation (*q.v.*) is still sufficiently coherent, but, without contact with environment, it feeds on false perceptions. Crepuscular states are observed in *amentia* (*q.v.*), in certain psychic equivalents of *epilepsy* (*q.v.*), and in *hysteria* (*q.v.*). In the latter morbid form, the alteration generally consists of a clear separation of part of the psychic activity from the rest of the personality: hence, episodes of *sleep-walking, dual personality*, and other deviations of consciousness. Concerning the relations between conscious and subconscious, *see* Unconscious.

MORAL CONSIDERATIONS. Grave quantitative and qualitative alterations of the psychic faculties nullify, wholly or in part, penal imputability and civic responsibility; but moral imputability, the diminution of responsibility and semi-imputability of the sick individuals can obviously be formulated only after a diligent psychic examination of the individual.

Legal responsibility and imputability in contingent lapses remain in the lighter forms of illnesses; these basic deviations in many respects are still in the realm of normalcy and constitute only variations of a character nature, partly the result of natural tendencies, partly of educational-environmental factors. The same may be said with respect to certain forms of minor mental debility (*see* Phrenasthenia) and, above all, to certain forms of egocentricity and egoism which the individual recognizes and deliberately maintains either out of self-interest or pride, with a conscious contempt for feelings of altruism and charity.

On the subject of penal imputability and civil responsibility, the advice of a psychologist, as consultant to judges, would seem to be most useful in determining the psychological traits of the individual, the degree of capacity for intention and will; this would be a consequent benefit to the triumph of justice and truth. *Riz.*

PSYCHIATRY. *See* Psyche, pathology of; Psychoses.

PSYCHIC PHENOMENA. *See* Psyche, pathology of.

PSYCHOANALYSIS. Psychoanalysis is both a theory and a practical therapy; founded by the Viennese physician Sigmund Freud, it has met with incredible favor in almost all European and American countries.

This theory of psychoanalysis may be said to claim an understanding and explanation for all of man's activities, whether psychic, moral, pathological, or normal, though unconscious, primigenial and rudimentary sexual drives that are innate in man. As a *therapy*, psychoanalysis claims to cure certain morbid syndromes by the disclosure of an unconscious complex which is supposed to have caused such syndromes. In fact, according to Freud, the whole human psychic life may be divided into two areas, which the Viennese scholar represented as two connecting rooms: the *unconscious* area (*das Unbewüsst, das Es*) and the *conscious* area (*das Ich*). The unconscious area swarms with rudimentary instincts of a sexual and perverse nature, such as are found in those who have not yet experienced the effects of a civil or moral training. These instincts constitute a vivid and dynamic part of psychic elements called *complexes* which represent the experience, particularly ancestral, of the individual: for this reason, it is possible to speak of a Narcissus complex (autoeroticism), of an Oedipus complex (incestuous instinct), and the like.

Freud includes unconscious instincts under the term *libido*, as the principle of pleasure (*Lustprinzip*). As the educational and moral work of formation of the individual begins, the conscious element, *das Ich*, rises in opposition to libido. As mediator between *das Es* and the external world, *das Ich* is endowed with particular organs, namely *consciousness*, which may be termed the discretional sense of the psychic faculties, and *volitive mobility*, by which it can act in the external world. *Das Ich* possesses faculties of judgment and critique, by which it preserves its coherence and thus enjoys or rejects pleasure. Finally, it has particular methods of expressing itself, for the most part conventional, such as language. Consciousness, therefore, is always at the service of the *Ego*. Inasmuch as it attends to the task of manifesting the moral exigencies of the external world, it can be termed *moral consciousness*.

Das Es and *das Ich* are in constant struggle; on the one hand, the *unconscious* is the primary mover, though shameful and perverse, of human activity; on the other, *das Ich* is the protector of order and the moral exigencies of the external world; for this reason it exerts a ferocious censorship on *das Es*. The escape routes from this struggle (Freud speaks of psychodynamism) are three: (a) the two elements attempt a compromise, and the sexual instincts, remaining essentially such, become externally *sublimated* (e.g., the Oedipus complex in the religious sentiment, or in true and filial love of children towards their parents, and so on); (b) due to weak censorship through lack of training or a poor moral sense, the perverse instincts triumph and occasion sexual perversions and inversions; (c) finally, because of strong repression exerted by censorship, the instincts take refuge under a morbid syndrome, giving rise to nervous illnesses and morbid symptoms which, basically, are but symbolic representations of repressed instinctive tendencies.

Furthermore, the unconscious instincts find their satisfaction not only in sublimation but also in *sleep*, whose pattern consists entirely of a sexual symbolism which enables psychoanalysts by symbolic explanations to understand the obscure depth of the unconscious, and in *Fehlleistungen* or misdirected efforts or blunders in daily life, due to an almost automatic and oppressive prevalence of strongly repressed unconscious instincts.

Doubtless, the most controversial part of Freud's doctrine is *sublimation*, as an explanation of all of man's moral activities. According to him, the religious sentiment is an instinct, charity is an instinct, Christian mortification is an instinct, and so are all the noblest sentiments. Only the external appearance is noble and sublime; the substance remains shameful and perverse. In a similar way Freudian psychoanalysts explain art and the artistic phenomenon: fundamentally, the artist is simply an introvert who satisfies his strongly repressed and unsatisfied instinct by the symbolism of his artistic productions.

These theories aroused exaggerated and passionate enthusiasm and reactions. In 1912, two of Freud's disciples (Alfred Adler and Carl Gustav Jung) broke away from Freud. Jung became altogether the *bête-noire* of Freud (cf. Jung, *The Problem of the Unconscious*); later, Bleuler and Stekel joined them. Numerous psychoanalytic theories are found today in contrast with Freud's psychoanalysis. Important developments have taken place in the United States, spearheaded by Karen Horney, F. Alexander, Carl Rogers and others.

Jung gave Freud's *libido* a broader meaning by including in it all vital instincts. On the contrary, Adler substituted *libido* with the lust for power, as the propelling center. Clearly, the theories of the master underwent such transformations that it would be difficult to classify them in an exhaustive manner.

But to avoid confusion, we limit our explanation and criticism to Freud's doctrine, since it is the only one well-defined and followed today in theory and practice.

CRITICISM. The moral conclusions indicated above demonstrate quite clearly the absurdities to which Freudian psychoanalysis leads. Furthermore, Freud's entire edifice, undoubtedly original and imaginative, was built on his own limited experience and experiments with psychically retarded individuals. Freud based his conclusions on facts obtained from hysterics primarily or from secondary and banal facts in man's individual and social life (dreams—*Fehlleistungen*). Moreover, it is impossible to explain his so-called sexuality in infants, in the sense intended by Freud, or its permanence in sublimation, when it occurs, for the sexual aim is absolutely missing. Finally, it is absurd to confuse man's spiritual activity with his sexual material activity, or, worse still, to make the latter the primary and essential cause of the former. Obviously, it is a case of naked materialism, though colored with Hegelian dialectic. The *super-Ego* (an ideal *Ego*), which the individual supposedly would achieve as a synthesis of a thesis (*das Es*) and an antithesis (*das Ich*), is but idle, superficial oversimplification.

Finally, the allegation that exaggerated repression of the instincts is a normal cause of illnesses of the nervous system can be denied as a gratuitous assertion of psychoanalysts, who by such beliefs betray, among other things, a poor medical preparation.

PSYCHOANALYTIC THERAPY. *Psychoanalytic therapy* is based on psychoanalytic doctrine. Its fundamental principle is this: the unconscious complex, in a violent repressed state, causes the morbid syndrome; this must be brought into the area of consciousness, through the methods of free association, experimental association, and psycho-electric reactions.

The first method induces the patient to state without restraint whatever may come to his mind until a *catharsis*, or purification, is effected in him by the confession of all the things which have remained concealed in the unconscious.

The method of experimental association requires more direct work by the physician inasmuch as he must propose to the patient sample words, stimulus words, and inductive words, to which the patient will reply by *reaction* words. A clock checks the time that intervened between the stimulus word and the reaction word.

Finally, the method of psycho-electric reactions is a measurement of psychic disturbances experienced by the patient while the stimulus word is pronounced.

A manometer, with which the patient is connected gauges these reactions.

The alleged effectiveness of these and other methods of psychoanalytic therapy is strongly questioned by serious physicians who, though inclined to accept some conclusions of Sigmund Freud, are opposed to a full employment of psychotherapy.

From the moral point of view, we shall quote the opinion of an eminent physician-psychologist, Father Gemelli, who thus concludes his article on "Psychoanalysis and Catholicism": "For all these reasons, a Catholic cannot accept [Freudian] psychoanalytic doctrines; he cannot submit to [Freudian] psychoanalytic treatments; no Catholic should entrust his ill relatives to the treatments of [Freudian] psychoanalysts. [Freudian] psychoanalysis is a danger since it is the morbid result of the gross materialism of S. Freud" (A. Gemilli in *Vita and Pensiero*, May, 1950, 254).

Father Gemelli scored, among other things, attempts made in the Catholic field at combining Freud's theory with Catholic doctrine (cf., e.g., M. Choisy, *Psychoanalysis and Catholicism*).

To express Father Gemelli's conclusions in terms more familiar to moral theologians, we stated that, in view of the limited efficacy and the dangers connected with psychoanalysis, one who willfully and freely uses or submits to it commits a mortal sin (cf. Father Felici, "*La psichoanalisi*," in *Boll. del Clero Romano*, April, 1952, 114). This statement became the object of controversy especially in France and America, despite the fact that in a press release to the American Catholic Press we specified what had already been clearly stated in the introduction to the article, that our opinion referred exclusively to Freud's materialistic and pansexual psychoanalysis. It is evident that so severe a judgment would not apply to other psychotherapies which, though improperly called psychoanalytic, are nevertheless far removed from the doctrine of S. Freud.

In a speech delivered to the participants in the First International Congress of Hystopathology of the Nervous System, on September 17, 1952, Pius XII, referring to the "pansexual method of a certain school of psychoanalysis" (an obvious reference to the Freudian school in the strict sense), reproved it as contrary to the rules of Christian and human morality, whose limits cannot be violated, not even under the pretext of scientific inquiries or treatment (see address of Pius XII to the participants in the Fifth International Congress of Psychotherapy and Clinical Psychology, April 15, 1953).

PEDANALYSIS. *Pedanalysis* is a teaching method based on doctrinal and therapeutic standards of psychoanalysis. It aims at *channelling* in the child the unconscious instincts uncovered through free confessions, dreams, etc. Pedanalysis includes an extensive sexual education given to groups, such as schools, and the like. In view of the obviously pernicious effects produced in practice, it is to be rejected and disapproved. *Fel.*

PSYCHODEGENERATION. *See* Apathy.

PSYCHOLOGY. *Psychology* is the science which treats of the mind in any of its aspects. The term, as such, is of rather recent usage. Aristotle called his treatise *Peri psyche* (*De anima*—About the Soul). Melanthon (b. at Brethon in 1497, d. at Wittenberg in 1560) is believed to have been the first to use the term *psychology*. Yet it is certain that Goclenius Rudolf (b. at Corbach in 1547, d. at Marburg in 1628) published a book in 1590, at Marburg (*Psychologia, hoc est, de hominis perfectione animi*), in which he collected various opinions on the origin of the soul and on other psycho-theological questions. Otto Casman, published a book (Hanover, 1594, Frankfurt, 1604, *Psychologia anthropologica, sive animae humanae doctrina*), in which he termed anthropology (*q.v.*) the science that studies man; he divided it into *psychology* and *somatology*. Then he subdivided somatology into anatomy and physiology. After Wolff, the use of the term gained ground, and, after Kant, became common usage, although in the

English language *mental science, mental philosophy, intellectual philosophy* and *philosophy of the human mind* are employed.

The mind may be the object of a variety of studies. One may study the nature of psychical phenomena, such as sensations, feelings, thoughts, and volition, for the purpose of identifying their cause. This is called *rational psychology.* The various phenomena may also be studied in their proximate causes for the purpose of formulating certain laws according to which such phenomena occur. This study is called *experimental* or applied psychology. The latter is, at least in part, presupposed by the former, because, if philosophy is to be truly such and not simply philosophical pretense, it must be based on data acquired on age, place, environment, education, and physical conditions.

PSYCHOLOGY AND MORALITY. The study of morality requires a perfect knowledge of man. A machine, however simple and inexpensive, operates according to the mind of the one who designed and constructed it, not according to the whim or desire of the operator. Thus, man, though a free agent, is above all the product of his Maker, who is God (*Ipse fecit nos et non ipsi nos:* Psalm 99:3). The Author of nature has certainly assigned to man an end, suited to his intelligent and free nature, to which he must tend. If he tends to this end, he fulfills his nature. If he seeks his own invented ends, he pursues either secondary, useful ends or those contrary to the primary end intended by his Maker. In pursuing these ends, he may attain them physically by physical freedom; unless, however, they are subordinated to his ultimate end, they will be morally harmful. Erroneous moral theories fail to recognize man as he really is; some defy God by making man an absolute arbiter of his own actions; others debase man to the level of brutes, for they deny those qualities by which man is essentially distinct from animals (see Morality, Independent). Nor is morality based on the customs of some or even many individuals, because, as psychology teaches, with free beings, an obligation is not the same as an action or custom. Man must be considered from the standpoint of his psychological makeup, since he does not always exercise his intelligence and freedom perfectly, despite the fact that his intelligence and freedom truly exist.

Psychological states can render man judicious or rash and negligent; they can obscure the mind or permit full use of freedom; they can influence decisions contrary to the judgment of the mind or cause reactions or other impediments, which may, even though indirectly, block or impede the use of free will. These facts give rise to moral theology, which is the study of human acts and of conditions that increase, lessen, or nullify man's free will. *Ver.*

Man has a body with physical and chemical functions. There are three functions in man common to all vegetative life: nutrition, growth by intussusception, and reproduction; three functions are common to all animal, sensitive life: feeling, appetite, and locomotion. Some scientists would stop here as if this were the whole man. But further study discloses that man has two higher faculties, absolutely unique: intelligence and will, which are, by nature, distinct from his senses and sensitive appetite. Consequently, these require not only a principle which is distinct from that of anorganic and vegetable substances, but from that of brute animals. One must not be deceived by those things which man has in common with animals and things. Man is distinguished from all others by what is proper to him. Thus, we notice that man understands non-material things and that he wills freely. We must conclude that he is endowed with a spiritual faculty (soul) by which he tends, not to this or that happiness, but to absolute happiness, which alone is capable of satisfying all his longings.

Moreover, the term *psychology* is applied to special modes of feeling, judging, and acting, both by human groups and individuals, as well as to a state of mind prevailing at a particular moment according to which one feels, judges, and acts. And here we should distinguish between those who are psychologically sound and those who are ill (*see* Psychoneurosis, Psychosis.)

PSYCHOLOGY, APPLIED. *See* Psychotechique.

PSYCHONEUROSIS. The diseases of the central nervous system which are not based on anatomical alterations but on a defective development of neuropsychic functions, because of a strange change in energy of the organism, are called *psychoneuroses*. They are functional diseases characterized principally by psycho-affective disturbances. They do not attack the individual's intelligence, except if the mind is hindered and disturbed as a result of an emotional crisis. Purely neurological factors (like physical tiredness, definite motorial disturbances and neuro-vegetative imbalance) contribute in varying degrees to the onset of each individual morbid condition.

Psychoneuroses are primarily of a nervous (neurasthenia, traumatic neurosis, etc.) and a psychic nature (hysteria, reactive impulsions, pseudodementia, psychasthenia, etc.). In practice, mixed forms are more frequent (neuropsychasthenia, hysteroneurasthenia, etc.).

ETIOPATHOGENESIS. The constitutionalist school sees in psychoneuroses the consequence of evolutional deficiencies and biochemical imbalance of the nervous centers. Others hold to a purely physical origin of such conditions, which, according to the psychoanalytic school, are caused by intrapsychical conflicts between an enormously developed *libido* and the censures of the *ego*: hence, regressions toward parental sexuality are common in hysteria, and autoeroticism, especially in psychasthenia. For a criticism and refutation of these extreme theories, *see* Psychoanalysis.

Perhaps both groups of factors, the biochemical-humoral-neurological and the psychological, concur in psychoneuroses. This would apparently give rise, presumably through the vegetative nervous system, to a process of reciprocal influences and morbid symptoms. This explains, among other things, how each psychoneurotic is more or less receptive both to medicinal treatments and psychotherapy.

Physical, and especially moral, traumas, exhaustion, infections and forms of intoxications are the immediate cause of each morbid episode, while the disease has its first beginnings in the anomalous somatopsychic constitution of the individal or perhaps is associated with some slow form of toxicosis. Because of these factors, a temporary obstacle develops against the normal functioning of the psychic system of the individual; he then becomes incapable of reacting correctly to psycho-affective conscious or unconscious events of importance and loses his own autonomy.

In the constitutional, psychoneurotic makeup of the individual, slightly or not even apparently ill, the traumatic or toxic agent upsets the normal neuropsychical balance and a sharp crisis ensues. In the course of this disturbance, the psychoneurosis appears in its full extent, extending at times even to the sphere of the intellect. Subsequently, the balance is gradually restored and the crisis leaves, though not always, a greater weakness against future, morbid attacks. Only with the passing of years, toward old age, does a psychoneurotic become completely calm; perhaps due to a weakening of the power of self-criticism or of the functions and reactions of his higher psychic faculties.

A clinical description of the leading psychoneuroses is given in the articles concerning each individual disease. The reader will also find moral observations. For the purpose of avoiding repetitions, we shall, instead, deal briefly with the general treatment of psychoneuroses, quite similar for each of the individual morbid forms and primarily based, but not exclusively, on psychotherapy. Psychotherapy is used for prophylactic or preventive purposes in a psychoneurotic predisposition or for curative purpose in the cases of established clinical forms.

PROPHYLAXIS. The prophylaxis of psychoneurotics is particularly directed to so-called nervous children, and to those, apparently well, who are born of neuropathic, hysterical, or psychasthenic parents. It consists in the removal of the child from his family to a serene but firm upbringing, without excessive rigorism but also without effeminacy. It avoids beginning school too soon and, then, in alternating study with work and games or sports, diligently bans idleness and day-dreaming. An intelligent and methodical training of the will is necessary for the *obstacles* against habits of renunciation and perseverance. It combats patiently selfishness in excessive solicitude for the body and personal advantages. Air, light, bathing, open air activity, sports, exercises, even those that are not exempt from risks (riding, canoeing, mountain climbing), and a suitable spiritual training will contribute effectively to forming an upright, stable, positive, and serene conscience. These young potential candidates for doubts, obsessions, phobias, and other disorders and incongruities of a psychoneurotic conscience should receive a particularly diligent and wise religious upbringing in which God's mercy rather than His justice, and His love and recompense more than His punishment, a simple and confident filial respect for God as a Father, more than fear of Him is properly inculcated.

PSYCHONEUROSIS, SEXUAL. *Psychoneuroses* include all disorders of the sexual sphere not based on important organic alterations but, to a large extent, on psychogenic factors. Thus, the following are automatically excluded from the treatment: (1) serious malformations, atrophies, and mutilations capable of appreciably hindering or obstructing the generative activity; (2) alterations of a degenerative, inflammatory or cicatricial nature which, by affecting the innervation of the genitals, may considerably alter their structure or function; (3) disorders caused by endocrine diseases or particular dyscrasic or toxinfective conditions; (4) generative disorders, of a strictly psychoneurotic nature, but symptomatic of more serious and general psychic illnesses (phrenasthenia, schizophrenia, mania, senile dementia, progressive paralysis, epilepsy, alcoholism, etc.). These may in a variety of ways have disturbed the generative instinct.

On the basis of these premises and exclusions, there remain the generative disorders appearing as an isolated or almost isolated condition, largely independent of somatic alterations and psychotic or psychoneurotic-functional conditions.

Psychoneuroses affect the sexual behavior by determining quantitative or qualitative deviations, with a concomitant disorder of the generative appetite. If that appetite is non-existent, weak, excessive, or perverted, we will speak respectively of *anesthesia, hypoesthesia, hyperesthesia* or *parasthesia*. The latter may arise if the appetite is stimulated by thoughts or things which usually do not stimulate other individuals, or if it does not become aroused in situations which would arouse other individuals.

This occasions a conspicuous series of morbid conditions, caused by emotions or without appreciable reasons in persons predisposed to such morbid conditions. Psychoanalysts undervalue or reject altogether the importance of the constitutional *basis* and attribute the greatest value to so-called infantile psychotraumas; the persistence of erotic phases in early life, the separation of primitive instincts and other similar motives are believed to be the basis of every deviation or deformation of sexual life or of psychoneuroses in general. According to such a theory, they are the result of a repression of anomalous erotic tendencies. The exaggerations of this school are evident. For their refutation, *see* Psychoanalysis.

EDUCATIONAL PROPHYLAXIS. Concerning sexual education of young persons, it must be stated that neither complete ignorance nor excessive or public instruction in such matter is the right approach. In the first case, the child is prompted to satisfy his natural curiosity, seeking information from individuals who may give it in a manner that may be disturbing or improperly imparted. In the second case, since he is immature, a complete understanding of the generative processes may lead to misuse of sexual faculties; so-called group sexual education can easily become a source of incitement to vice (*see* Education, Sexual), unless it is given with a great sense of decorum, genuine responsibility and restraint.

Very significant for the prevention of the disturbances under discussion is a proper sexual behavior of the older members of the family in the presence of children. Parents must not only avoid any immodest and scandalous words, or deeds, but must use great discretion in discussing matters of sex. Furthermore, parents shall abstain both from severe quarrels and from manifesting excessive tenderness to each other in the presence of children. This is important in order to spare the latter emotional shocks at an age when they are likely to have a damaging impact on young lives. Concerning proper therapy, *see* Perversions, Sexual; Psychotherapy.

In view of the fundamental value of the sexual instinct in the dynamism of life, its manifold relations to man's activity in society (continuity and integrity of the species), and the practice of Christian living, the study of sexual psychoneuroses is extremely important also from the ethical point of view. *Riz.*

PSYCHONEUROSIS, TRAUMATIC. *Traumatic psychoneurosis* is a polyform psychogenic reaction in constitutionally predisposed individuals caused by a morbific process. Its main phases are: (a) accidental trauma; (b) emotional shock from accident; (c) anxiety about a feared irreparable injury from accident; (d) anxious desire that adequate reparation for the injury be made by the one responsible for it. The individual will react to these different factors, more or less unconsciously, by psychoneurotic attitudes of a protective-defensive nature that tend to deepen hypochondriacal convictions, or to gain sympathy, adequate compensation, etc. This explains why the development of a disease requires a psychically suitable predisposition; hence, the fact that in a group accident only a few individuals develop a case of psychoneurosis which assumes a peculiar and generally hysterical, psychasthenic, or neurasthenic character, determined by the constitutional predisposition in which the trauma has developed. An anatomical integrity of the ideo-affective processes accounts for the fact that psychoneurotic symptomatology appears and becomes stabilized a considerable period of time after the traumatic episode, i.e., a period of *meditation* or *rumination*, in which the individual becomes increasingly more convinced by an auto-suggestive process of having suffered irreparable injuries to his health. And at the same time neurofunctional disorders unite with the psychic condition. Finally, the morbid picture tends to be consolidated and to become aggravated with time, especially if indemnification is denied or has to be bargained for through bureaucratic procedures, for in such a case the psychogenic reaction of the individual increases; on the contrary, the condition tends to become cured after an equitable compensation.

The location and gravity of the physical trauma are not relevant in a determination of the disturbance which usually ensues from physically slight traumas. Beginning with a morbid self-introspection, it becomes more serious as small disorders are magnified and exploited with further aggravation for the psychoneurosis, while the appearance of a conspicuous, organic form will distract the patient from his morbid fixations, and the psychoneurosis will subside to the point of total disappearance.

PROGNOSIS. Traumatic psychoneuroses, even those which, like the *pseudodementia* of Wernicke, assume a more alarming aspect, have generally a favorable prognosis. However, there are cases in which the cure is impossible, either because of dystrophic conditions, anchylosis, or other irreversible organic disorders which no psychic treatment or other method affects, or because, in time, a serious neuro-functional disturbance may develop, which will affect the general trophism of the injured person and aggravate the psychoneurosis itself by weakening the power of defense in the entire organism.

At this point, it does not seem superfluous to add that, notwithstanding therapy and indemnification, some individuals are not cured but continue to show those disorders: cephalea, vertigo, lapses of memory and behavior, noticed after the incident. In these cases, as an accurate clinical examination would show, it is not a matter of psychoneurotic functional disorders but an organic meningocerebral condition of traumatic origin, whose treatment is chiefly radiological and surgical.

Concerning morality, traumatic psychoneuroses present material for observation from various aspects.

(a) Clearly immoral, as a violation against the seventh commandment, is any conscious attempt to invent illness for gain; and by reason of their greater mental ability and social standing, more reprehensible are lawyers and physicians who might advise such dishonest tactics and defend their clients in a court of law.

Fraud is a sin and a grave sin, even if it is the government or a wealthy corporation that is defrauded, provided that the conditions for a grave sin are present.

(b) A preconceived distrust on the part of physicians who examine the victims in behalf of an insurance company or other agency is likewise immoral. Diligence must never be separated from good faith. Difficulty in establishing whether a given symptom is alleged or genuine is no reason for a doctor to be superficial in his examination, or to presume simulation. The possibility or frequency of simulation does not give a physician the right to consider every unfortunate person a simulator, even if this or that symptom may actually be a result of simulation, as a defensive-protective device; and one should always remember, before issuing a judgment, that a deliberate (fraudulent) simulation is clearly distinct from indeliberate (psychoneurotic) simulation.

(c) Finally, the excessively involved bureaucratic procedure used with respect to post-traumatic psychoneurotics is objectionable. Although simulators may grow weary, yet genuine psychoneuroses certainly become aggravated. Modern German scholars have coined for traumatic psychoneuroses the appropriate term *Rechtsneurosen* or *neuroses by right,* that is, the right of being compensated for an unforeseen damage. Any delay in the settlement of traumatic psychoneuroses results in a damage both for the sick individual and society, since the latter loses for a long period of time the useful services of a worker, who becomes an invalid.

(d) A physician will act honestly and wisely in the capacity of arbiter, if, after a definite diagnosis of the traumatic psychosis, he can convince the injured party that it is expedient for him to limit his claims in order to avoid a very long litigation with uncertain results, and can also convince the party responsible for the accident that it is a case in which the sick individual is susceptible of early improvement if an early conclusion and definition of the question can be arranged. *Riz.*

PSYCHONEUROSIS OF WAR. The causes of mental diseases are of three kinds: organic (somatic), psychic, and constitutional. A mental illness is seldom based on only one of these three factors; almost always on two of them; very often on all three. The same occurs in mental illnesses caused by war, whether they depend, at least in appearance, on craniocerebral traumas, starvation, or fright. In the first two cases, besides the more obvious and immediate somatic cause, a constitutional factor must play its part; otherwise, it could not be explained why only a slight number of the injured from cerebral or nutritional causes would have shown psychotic disturbances. The same is true of disturbances from fear, whose genesis may be merely psychogenic or even organic, due to a concomitant endocrine-functional disorder, but which is increased somewhat by a natural predisposition.

To achieve better understanding of these wartime or war-caused psychoneuroses, as far as one can observe, these are basically brought about by three different elements: cerebral lesions, privation of nutritional or somatic necessities, and psychotraumas.

In *cerebral lesions* the psychotic condition may be either the result of serious injuries to large portions of the nervous parenchyma, of particular types of hemorrhages, or other microderangements, produced by violent agents, apparently of modest entity (such as the *displacement of air* by the fall of bombs or of other explosive devices in the vicinity of the individual). The symptoms of these psychoses (also called *encephaloses*) consist for the most part in confusional, delirious and hallucinatory states similar to those encountered in dementia (*q.v.*); these are curable in a few weeks or a month.

A *traumatic dementia* (Kraepelin) of a chronic nature occurs much more rarely. Sometimes the psychosis arises slowly and indirectly, e.g., the cerebral injury gives rise to epilepsy, and the latter, after a long period of time, develops into *epileptic dementia.* It is well understood that in a case of large cerebral injuries, or demential phenomena, it is no longer a question of war psychosis but of real and proper organic psychosis.

Privations, if serious and protracted, may cause psychoses of various kinds. In exhaustion or starvation, which were observed during the last war in concentration camps of prisoners and deportees, or among civilian populations of zones most exposed to starvation, delirious conditions were not rare. In a lack of vitamin B, more or less grave psychotic disturbances may join the polyneurotic disorders proper to beri-beri; in a lack of vitamin C, depressive or demential syndromes sometimes appear together with scurvy; in a lack of vitamin PP, one may be faced with a neurological condition, pellagra, often accompanied by a type of feeblemindedness.

So-called *psychotraumas* (strong or protracted emotions, worries, etc.) produce a variety of *reactive psychoses* (*see* Pseudodementia), stuporous states, dysthymia, reactive depression and excitement, hypochondria, psychasthenic syndromes and, above all, hysteric psychoses. When the psychic trauma occurs in a particularly violent manner, as in bombardments or serious and extensive war action, a sudden inhibition of the higher processes of the will and self-control may occur. At that point, the lower psycho-reflexive mechanisms produce *explosive reactions* (Kretschmer), which find their most expressive characteristics in irra-tional *motorial rages*, strange motions, howls of terror, mad racing in every direction, and other known, contagious manifestations of panic. The explosive reactions generally vanish within a few hours; at other times they give rise to more lasting psychoses, as those men-tioned above, which can also occur with-out being preceded by a motorial rage.

PATHOGENESIS. In psychoses arising from organic cerebral injuries, one is faced with more or less grave alterations of cortical cells and other phenomena of reaction on diencephalic centers near the third ventricle. If the traumatic effects on the cerebral parenchyma are reversi-ble, the mental disturbances disappear completely; at times, more or less modest psychotic and psychoneurotic syndromes remain, although it is also possible that the demential conditions mentioned above may develop. The latter conditions may occur more readily in aged indi-viduals, particularly if arteriosclerotic; on the other hand, it seems that the same cranial trauma may give rise to a process of cerebral arteriosclerosis.

In psychoses resulting from serious lack of food and vitamins, true and proper toxic phenomena affecting the cerebral substance may occur, which, after a long period of time, may give rise to degenerative processes. In mental syn-dromes arising from lack of vitamin C (scurvy), it is not improbable that patho-genesis is related to small encephalitic hemorrhages (Nardini). In certain cases the aforesaid intoxication is liable to cause an endocrine, functional disorder which, in turn, leads to the onset of a psychosis.

In reactive psychoses, more numerous among war psychoses, morbid conditions rise and develop in a simple psychogenic process: war traumas (violent or con-tinued emotions, crises of panic, states of anxious expectation, etc.) act on natu-rally predisposed individuals as a causa-tive factor of the psychoneurosis, which, presumably, would not have arisen if the emotive-traumatic condition had not oc-curred. Often the psychoneurosis, espe-cially of a hysteric type, is unconsciously determined by a desire of the individual to avoid a dangerous situation "by taking refuge in the illness" (Bonhoffer). How-ever, not all cases of war psychoses are interpreted in a utilitarian sense, so to speak; a strong fright is always able to produce, at least in predisposed indi-viduals, conspicuous changes in their psy-chic equilibrium, or even sudden death.

OTHER NOSOLOGICAL OBSERVATIONS. Psychoses and psychoneuroses are not peculiar to war, because mental condi-tions may also occur in peace-time as a result of cranio-cerebral traumas, lack of vitamins, or a strong emotion. The fact remains, however, that these various pathogenic crises occur with greater fre-quency and gravity in time of war. For this reason, it was deemed proper to treat of the various morbid conditions in a single article, devoted precisely to war psychoses.

Although wars favor the rise of psycho-neuroses, military service, even in war, is not of itself a morbific factor; for some *minor neuropaths*, it may offer a better opportunity for treatment and cure, in view of the particular conditions in which they find themselves, and the greater facilities available to them.

An attack of war psychoneurosis re-quires the combination of two causes, one external (bomb explosion, starvation, terror, etc.) and one internal (predis-position). Each of the two causes con-tributes to the attack of the psychosis in a quantitatively different way; in a nor-mal predisposition, the psychosis arises in proportion to the gravity and violence of the exogenous cause; a normal exogenous cause may create a most serious psy-chosis in one who is particularly predis-posed as an individual. In this as in many other sections of pathology, the principle applies: the firmer and more valid the internal individual resistance, the less does the exogenous cause pro-duce a psychosis; conversely, the weaker the internal resistance, the easier it is for a psychoneurosis to result from even the least serious of causes. The predisposition factor is always greater than any traumatic factors.

All war psychoses generally have a favorable prognosis, especially if treated with modern therapies that are capable of preventing the development of permanent morbid convictions. By consolidating the emotional sphere, they restore moral serenity, confidence, and optimism. The chronic illness, particularly if cerebro-anatomical injuries cannot be held responsible for irreparable mental derangement or other psychoneurotic syndromes of a neurasthenic type, leaves room, according to the circumstances of development and clinical condition, for a well-founded suspicion that *psychoneurosis of appetence* or *revindication* supplanted the original psychogenic war reaction, as in ordinary *traumatic psychoneurosis (q.v.)*, or that it is not a matter of war psychoses but of schizophrenia *(q.v.)*, progressive paralysis *(q.v.)*, or other serious mental disturbance not caused by war.

MEDICO-LEGAL OBSERVATIONS. On the basis of the above considerations, a medico-legal evaluation of war psychoses might seem easy. Since practically all such conditions attain a rapid and complete cure, and cases which are not cured after some months are to be numbered largely among simulations and psychoses not of a war nature, the task of a medico-legal expert would appear extremely simple and clear. In reality, however, cases are complicated.

(a) *Delayed consequences of cranio-cerebral war traumas.* Although the greater number of cranio-cerebral injuries become cured and leave no chronic psychotic residue or essentially demential syndrome, many do create a number of neuropsychic disturbances which are basically developed into serious problems at a later date by the subject; these comprise a variety of illnesses, chief among which are: cephalalgic, vertiginous disturbances, changes of temperament, mood, and cenesthesis, lethargy of ideation, loss of memory, and the like.

"The interpretation of this so-called delayed post-traumatic neuropsychic syndrome," Vercelli writes, "particularly when it appears at a considerable length of time from the traumatic accident in which the trauma has had an acute consequence, is clearly a very delicate matter. In these cases, in which the subjective symptomatology is not confirmed by an objective one, the tendency is to deny any connection with a trauma or the organic nature of the syndrome. Thus it is classified immediately as an accidental condition, with the suspicion of total or partial simulation."

Modern means of research separate the banal and purely functional traumatic psychoneuroses from forms caused by profound encephalitic injuries. These naturally deserve a larger compensation in view of the notable effect on the working capacity of the patient.

(b) *Cranial lesions and chronic alcoholism.* If cranial-cerebral traumas are followed by mental weakness, they give rise to important and manifold alterations of mood, temperament, and feelings. In similar cases the individual is driven to intemperate drinking (*see* Dypsomania).

The occurrence of such a possibility must be taken into account in pensions of disability, because the psychosis and other ailments produced by alcohol may be the indirect result of war injuries; therefore, the individual must be adequately indemnified for his war-connected disability.

(c) *Persistent psychoneurotic war disturbances.* The persistence of functional psychoneuroses many years after the occurrence of lesions is considered of accidental nature, generally temporary, and, if they do recur, the cause must be sought for in a new pathogenic condition, independent of the war. It is a new psychogenic reaction due to a natural tendency of the individual to such conditions. In a case of accidental occurrence, the patient, due to a more or less conscious process of simulation, is inclined to connect the neuropsychic disturbances to those experienced at the time of the accident, but, in reality, the new condition is a new situation which does not affect in any appreciable manner the general condition or the working capacity of the individual.

In similar cases, there would seem to be no cause for indemnification because of a lack of war-connected disability.

(d) *Progressive paralysis and war*. The theory that progressive paralysis may be caused by war service is indefensible, because it is a known fact that it is produced by syphilis. Yet, in certain cases, one may not exclude war service as an occasion for the illness, or an aggravation of its development. We refer to cases in which, precisely because of war, a syphilitic infection could not be properly or promptly treated or to those cases in which discomfort, suffering or fatigue, proper to wartime or prison life, fostered the appearance of the psychosis either by shortening its period of customary incubation, or by making its symptomatology and development more serious.

In such cases a certain connection to war service is generally recognized, and, therefore, a title to pension or indemnification.

(e) *War schizophrenia*. Although research on heredity and medical statistics have shown that the great majority of schizophrenics become sick by reason of hereditary predisposition, and that neither among the troops nor the civilian population was there any increase in the number of such disturbed individuals during the war (Bonhöffer, Bleuler, and others), yet the competent authorities of many countries usually recognize the right to compensation for victims of these grave psychoses if one of the following conditions is verified: (1) the rise of schizophrenia after a cranial-cerebral trauma, or other grave encephalitic damage suffered because of the war; (2) the rise of psychosis during or after a long and truly abnormal period in war service or in prison.

In recent times, the *criteria of indemnification* for war psychoses have been considerably broadened in many countries, irrespective of the scientific point of view.

MORAL PROBLEMS. The ethico-juridical problems which may develop from war psychoses, insofar as moral and penal responsibility are concerned, are not substantially different from those which arise from other psychoses and psychoneuroses. Thus, we refer the reader to the articles concerning the individual mental ailments, limiting ourselves here to noting that no general rules can be established applying to all cases, for each case must be studied and solved on the basis of the extent of the particular morbid condition under examination.

In general, the seriousness of many war situations (total devastating bombardments, or prolonged gun firing, enemy hoards thirsty for slaughter, guerrilla warfare, protracted and extensive discomforts, deprivations and fatigue caused by detention in concentration camps and the like) explain and partly justify, even apart from the cases of genuine war psychoses, abnormal behavior and reactions which in some cases may have led to suicide (*q.v.*) or other criminal acts. These may be caused by *explosive reactions*, mentioned above, unforeseen breakdowns due to general exhaustion, or, more frequently, to the wearing down process of anxious, obsessive disturbances.

Finally, concerning the aftermaths of war psychoses and relative compensation, the criterion indicated with respect to traumatic psychoneurosis (*q.v.*) applies here: neither shall the pensioner simulate or exaggerate his morbid condition for which he requests indemnification, nor shall the physicians be guided too stringently by considerations of a fiscal nature or by suspicion, but shall perform their difficult task with a spirit of humanitarian understanding. *Riz.*

PSYCHOPATHOLOGY. *See* Psyche, pathology of; Medicine, Legal.

PSYCHOPATHY. As it appears from its etymology (Greek *psyche*—mind, spirit; *pathos*—affliction), *psychopathy*, frequently termed *psychosis* (*q.v.*), is synonymous with *mental illness*.

In the light of modern psychiatric achievements, it is well to maintain the distinction between psychopathies and psychoses. *Psychoses* are true and proper mental illness with an anatomico-pathological basis and serious results. *Psychopathies* are not diseases, but rather stable anomalies with a congenital background, of the instinctive-affective sphere, which may be found even in individuals with a normal or above-normal intelligence. Though psychopathies are generally congenito-hereditary disturbances, sometimes they may be the result of light encephalic disorders of the past. Kraepelin supposed that they were due to a limited arrest of development in the brain, as opposed to phrenasthenia (*q.v.*), i.e., a general arrest of development; but his hypothesis does not explain all the disturbances in question.

The classification of psychopathies or *psychopathic personalities* is extremely difficult, because the whole group of psychopathies is differentiated from the mass of psychoses more by the exclusion than by the presence of characteristic symptoms. Basically, there is nothing really characteristic in the so-called *minor psychiatry*, which includes many anti-social temperaments, so-called psycho-degenerates, moral weakness, sexual perversions, hyperexcitability, instability, eccentricity, and several types of light or latent psychoses.

Every psychopath is different, though he has in common with the other members of this unfortunately large family an ethical debility and an emotional imbalance which render nosographic characterization difficult, so that it is useless to try to construct *typical* morbid or entirely *pure* forms. It is not so much a matter of psychopathological conditions, as of tendencies, reactions, and developments of abnormal and varied psychopathic personalities.

One of the most complete classifications of psychopathic personalities is that proposed by K. Schneider. According to this author, psychopaths are hyperthemic, depressive, of bad disposition, insecure, asthenic, histrionic, fanatical, voluble, cruel, inclined to criminality, bizarre, hypo-evolutive, suspicious, impulsive, unstable. These make the largest contribution to the various forms of criminality.

The more common psychopathic development of these abnormal personalities and the more frequent manifestations of psychopathological symptoms evolving in an endogenous disposition as a result of exterior incidents and environmental solicitations are sensitive (or delirious-sensitive), paranoic, hypochondriacal and obsessive developments.

The psychopath usually turns to the aid of the physician, not with respect to his abnormal physical make-up, but to the reactive phenomena caused by it, which often assume the appearances of a banal neurosis or disorders of an entirely different nature.

Therapy is particularly difficult because a psychopathic personality cannot be changed.

One can only hope to obtain an improvement that will permit the sick person to have a better moral and social life, checking all excesses, restraining more dangerous instincts, mitigating hyperexcitability, strengthening moral tone, and so on.

There can be no fixed rules; each individual must be dealt with after a patient, wise, and comprehensive study of his living and environmental conditions, and of his intellectual and ethical level.

More than sedatives, hypnotic and narcotherapeutic practices of dubious and transitory efficacy, pedagogic psychotherapy aimed at inhibiting pathological instinctive tendencies, outdoor life, moderate sports activities, and occupational therapy will be of considerable aid to psychopaths.

Sick persons with antisocial and criminal tendencies can be helped more by instilling in their minds the persuasion that they themselves, with God's help, must endeavor to control their own abnormal tendencies.

If one succeeds in convincing them that it is to their great advantage to follow the moral law, they may, though incapable of fully understanding the value of such laws, perhaps adopt themselves to those laws, and thus obtain improvements which they could not obtain from ordinary therapies mentioned above. *Riz.*

PSYCHOSIS. *Psychosis* denotes a mental disease; it is used interchangeably with *psychopathy*, which embraces psychic derangements with a physiological basis.

Psychiatry, the science concerned with psychoses (psychopathies), investigates causes, symptoms, development, anatomical and pathological changes, prophylaxis, therapy and the like.

At one time among primitive peoples, mental diseases were believed to be the result of influences of the evil spirits or a punishment from the divinity. But as early as the time of Hippocrates we find the modern concept: *Hac parte* (the brain) *sapimus et intelligimus et hac ipsa insanimus.*

Psychoses, considered as cerebral disturbances, may involve hereditary, constitutional, congenital, morbid anomalies and predispositions, or may be the result of traumas, toxinfections, debilitating disorders, strong emotional impacts, and the like. The seat of lesions or anomalies is prevalently in the cortex.

Moreover, according to modern theories, the causes of psychoses include a long series of etiopathogenic factors or a *chain* of causes, consisting of: (1) an exterior determining factor (infectious agent, trauma, and the like); (2) an immediate or intermediate cerebral factor in direct relation with the exogenous agent; (3) a distant factor (organic background, hereditary or acquired predispositions). The latter, the psychosomatic element, is undoubtedly the most important factor. The psychosis must be understood as an alteration of the entire psychic personality, affecting variably the volitive, affective, and intellectual spheres. Such an alteration may be caused by an exogenous factor with deep roots in the physic make-up of the individual. This seems confirmed by studies on heredity, by the fact that the same morbid agent can unloose the most diverse forms of psychoses, and the fact that different causes can give rise to one and the same mental disorder. The classification of psychoses is a subject that has wearied psychiatrists uselessly, since each is lacking in one respect or another.

This is due to the considerations pointed out in the preceding paragraph and to the fact that, contrary to events in surgical and medical pathology, none of the psychic symptoms permits tracking to a single cause or definite morbid process, not even in a typical morbid condition. The same syndrome (depressions, excitement, delirium, confusion) can be encountered in the most diverse mental disorders, and every psychosis may, in various states, present the most dissimilar syndromes.

For the sake of orientation, we shall outline, not a classification, but various groups of mental ailments, according to a prevalent clinical criterion:

(1) *Acquired psychoses, of an essentially exogenous nature, as the effect of an external cause on the brain:* (a) psychoses resulting from alcohol and other intoxicants (morphine, cocaine, and the like); (b) psychoses of an infectious origin (syphilitic psychoses, rabies, dementia, etc.); (c) arteriosclerotic and senile psychoses; (d) psychoses from infantile or adult cerebropathies; (e) psychoses from thyroid disturbances.

(2) *Endogenous psychoses originating mainly from congenital physical anomalies:* (a) melancholic or manic-depressive psychosis; (b) paranoia or paraphrenia; (c) psychopathic personalities (*see* Psychopathy); (d) biopathic phrenasthenias, and the like.

(3) *Mixed psychoses originating from congenital anomalies and from acquired illnesses:* (a) schizophrenia; (b) reactive psychoses (traumatic neuroses, hysteria and other psychoneuroses).

From the anatomical, pathological point of view, alterations found in the brain of the sick person may develop into psychoses of the following nature: (1) organic, accompanied by cerebral lesions or malformations; (2) or functional, without any appreciable hystological alterations, but due to more or less hypothetical biochemical disorders. Although the functional forms, including almost all mental illnesses indicated under the first two of the three groups above, outnumber the organic, yet with the advances made in research, the number of the latter tends to increase, while the former are decreasing.

A recent classification, based on psychological motives, groups the mental disorders into four classes: reactions, developments, phases, and processes. *Riz.*

PSYCHOSIS, AFFECTIVE. *See* Cyclothymia.

PSYCHOSIS, ALCOHOLIC. *See* Alcoholism.

PSYCHOSIS, CHRONIC HALLUCINATORY. *See* Paraphrenia.

PSYCHOSIS, CIRCULAR. *See* Dysthymia.

PSYCHOSIS, COLLECTIVE. *See* Contagion, Psychical.

PSYCHOSIS OF THE EVOLUTIONAL AGE. *See* Dysthymia.

PSYCHOSIS, MANIC-DEPRESSIVE. *See* Cyclothymia; Dysthymia.

PSYCHOSIS, OBSESSIVE. *See* Obsession; Psychasthenia.

PSYCHOSIS, PRISON. *See* Pseudodementia.

PSYCHOSIS, PUERPERAL. *See* Obstetrics.

PSYCHOSIS, REACTIVE. *See* Dysthymia.

PSYCHOSURGERY. By this term are understood all those modern surgical operations performed directly on the brain, such as lobotomy, leucotomy, lobectomy, topectomy, thalamotomy, and other operations of lesser importance.

The school of E. Moniz (originator of the first operation of this kind in 1935) includes all *psychosurgical operations* under the term *pre-frontal leucotomy.* Others call *leucotomy* the technique, originated by Moniz, consisting of the introduction through a small frontal gap of a special instrument called leucotome for the severance of certain nerve con-

nections of the pre-frontal cortex (*see* Cerebral Function). H. M. Fiamberti has proposed the severance of these connections in a trans-orbital operation.

Pre-frontal lobotomy refers to the dissection (effected by Freeman and Watts of the U. S. A.) of the greater part of the white substance of the pre-frontal lobe.

A still more radical surgical operation is *pre-frontal lobectomy* which entails the complete removal of the pre-frontal lobe (Ody, Peyton, and others).

Topectomy, performed more recently by Pool and Heath, consists in the removal of a more or less ample portion of the pre-frontal cortex.

Finally, *thalamotomy* (originated by Spiegel and Wycis) consists in the dissection of the optic thalamus, along its dorso-medial nucleus.

Other recently proposed psychosurgical operations, such as *gyrectomy* (Penfield), removal of certain frontal circumvolutions, *temporal lobotomy* (Obradon-Algade), *parietal lobotomy* (Yahn and his collaborators), have not given satisfactory results. In 1948, Gutierrez-Mahony developed the excision of the *post-central revolution* (ascending parietal circumvolution) for the treatment of painful limb-phantasm (*see* Cerebral Function), but this actually belongs to neurosurgery (*q.v.*).

Obviously, this is not the place to go into technical details nor to discuss the pros and cons of psychosurgery.

We shall limit ourselves to stating that all these operations, leucotomy, lobotomy, lobectomy or topectomy on pre-frontal lobes, and thalamotomy aim at severing the thalamus-pre-frontal projection system. This system is one in which, according to the latest anatomical, physiopathological, and clinical studies, the higher emotional processes merge. The suppression of those connections, either by the destruction of the thalamic centers or by dissecting the nerve threads which link them to the pre-frontal centers, or by complete removal of the latter, eliminates emotional tension. This effects a reduction of the emotional resonance produced by persisting grave pains; the disappearance of anxiety, psychic tension, restlessness, worry, dysphoria, depression, hypochondriacal ideas; a reduction of obsessions and deliriums; decrease of subjective participation by the individual in psychic and physical pain; a reduction of the condition of anticipation of pain (Elithorn); a diminution of interest of the sick person in himself and a change from diffident, cross, worried, and unadaptable introversion to a yielding and optimistic extroversion.

In addition to these important benefits attained from the operation, the patients, generally, show to a more or less evident degree a lesser amount of introspection, a certain decrease in interior life, scruples, remorse, tendencies to intellectual-spiritual perfection; a weakening of the powers of creative activities and command: in short, a certain degree of banality and impoverishment of their personality. Even the religious feelings become weak and act with lesser effectiveness on the individual's conduct.

In other words, psychosurgery renders the patients more adaptable to environment, less emotional and worrisome, but interiorly inclined either to apathy or to a sort of infantile euphoria.

The therapeutic action of leucotomy and analogous operations is not specific; it relieves various symptoms and diseases (schizophrenia, dysthymia, psychasthenia, etc.) by modifying the anatomical, biological roots of emotional reactions of the personality.

According to rather optimistic statistics of Freeman, psychosurgery fails in twenty per cent of the cases by the death of the patients, or because of failure to bring about any improvement in the morbid condition; it brings a limited benefit in thirty per cent of the cases; in the remaining fifty per cent of the cases it produces magnificent results from the point of view of social adaptation. Undoubtedly, the latter percentage will improve when the patients are better selected, operated on at an earlier date and with improved techniques.

Recently (1954), Dr. Lindstrom has proposed, instead of lobotomy, *a pre-frontal irradiation by ultrasonic waves.* This system would have the advantage of being more susceptible to control than surgical operations.

As a rule, there is no objection from the moral point of view to psychosurgery as an extreme means of helping individuals, deeply and irreparably tormented by pain, anxieties, obsessions and deliriums with wide emotional repercussions. Yet, every honest surgeon will agree that these techniques are not yet perfected and, since they could definitely transform the patient into an abulic automaton or an agitated person without any moral sense, one ought to turn to psychosurgery only if other curative methods (psychotherapy, narcolepsy, and shock therapy) fail. Furthermore, operable cases should be carefully selected, rejecting, in general, those by nature inclined to superficiality, lack of scruples, egocentricity, instability and lack of moral sense, who would be worse from the ethical standpoint.

It also must be pointed out that not even the flattering successes of psychosurgery have shed any light on the question concerning the pathogenesis of psychoses and the so-called localization of psychic processes. In fact, as A. Meyer also points out, the recurrence of the symptoms of psychoneurosis, dysthymia, and schizophrenia after a pre-frontal lobotomy, and the persistence of dissociative symptoms after a bilateral frontal lobectomy, render at least doubtful the theories that localize in the frontal lobe the morbid process from which these psychoses stem. *Riz.*

PSYCHOTECHNIQUE. *Psychotechnique* is the practical applications of psychology (*q.v.*). H. Münsterberg defined it as follows: "Psychotechnique is a science concerned with the practical applications of psychology for socially useful cultural aims." However, the term lends itself to misunderstanding inasmuch as it leads to the supposition that psychotechnique requires suitable instrumental techniques, whereas these are only accessory, though helpful, to general psychological study. "In fact," M. Ponzo writes in this respect, "psychotechnique simply teaches a method (technique) of employing the psychic means for socially useful practical aims; for this reason, no study or psychotechnical application can, in any case, abstract from the knowledge of general psychology, from which it derives and on which it rests."

Many maintain that psychotechnique is synonymous with *applied psychology*, but that is not exact, as it appears also from Münsterberg's definition.

The modern trend of psychotechnique and almost all its many applications are due to Münsterberg. It actually goes back to earlier times, when the basis of *physiotechnique* was first laid down. *Physiotechnique* is an indispensable premise to psychotechnical inquiries; in fact, psychotechnique presupposes and includes the applications of physiology.

Attempts in this field are found in the writings of Leonardo da Vinci and, even more, of Galileo Galilei, who endeavored to apply to human energy the principles of mechanics for the study of physical work. In the seventeenth century, the first mention of aptitudes for each type of work or of biological foundations for professional orientation (*q.v.*) is found in the works of Fr. Facchia, Pascal, and principally of Bernardine Ramazzini. In the following century, Bernouilli, Schultze, and Coulomb made a study of physical activity in the various occupations and emphasized the importance of speed in the rhythm of work and the efficacy of rest with respect to efficiency. In the second half of the nineteenth century, numerous investigations, conducted by A. Mosso and his school, on labor and on physical and psychic professional work make an important contribution to present-day psychotechnique.

Psychotechnique is increasingly being applied to the protection of the individual's health, the social order, jurisprudence with particular respect to the evaluation of depositions, to pedagogy and especially to industrial work. New and useful fields of application of psychotechnique are art, science, trade, the armed forces, problems of urbanization, traffic, and the like. These fields are bound to increase, for wherever there is man's activity, there will be material for useful psychotechnical studies.

These investigations, if correctly understood, must not be limited to a group of organs or functions, but must extend to the whole organism.

In fact, for a complete appraisal of an individual it is necessary to study all the intellectual and moral aptitudes from the natural and supernatural standpoint. These exercise great influence on the human person. In view of the importance and widespread applications of psychotechnique to the problems of work, called *Taylorism*, a separate treatment appears necessary.

Taylorism, from the name of F. W. Taylor (1856–1915), at first a worker, then a chief mechanic, and later an engineer, sought a rationalization and standardization of factory work for the threefold purpose of greater production, better production, and lesser fatigue.

Prior to Taylor's studies, it was a common opinion that the professional training of the worker, whether in schools or laboratories where he completed his apprenticeship, was sufficient to teach him the most rational method of work. With time and actual practice, the worker would complete, almost spontaneously, his technical training for an efficient, speedy, and rational fulfillment of his tasks. On the contrary, Taylor proved easily that, except for a few rare cases, the worker is unable to attain by himself the most rational method of work, since it is practically impossible to work and at the same time to analyze the methods of work. In order to reach such a goal, someone must accurately study the worker during his working activity, for the purpose of establishing a *normal minimum time* that a skillful worker may theoretically continue for years in the performance of his work, without damaging his health. The basis for remuneration was established on the time factor. Taylor proposed to increase or diminish this basis according to the degree of skill of the individual worker.

However, soon it was clear that Taylorism gave excessive importance to manual technique and completely disregarded the worker's personality with his individual and spiritual characteristics. Furthermore, it was observed that the organization of labor exclusively based on time produced a nervous tension in the workers, causing dangerous repercussions on the psychic and physical condition of the individual. This led to further studies in order to avoid excessive labor by the worker, by seeking to adapt the work and the machine to the worker, and by a greater study of the problems concerning the professional selection and orientation of workers for the purpose of choosing each type of individual possessing the best physical and psychic aptitudes.

These inquiries, which extend to the most varied fields, from hygiene to biotypology, from physiology to experimental psychology, constitute the fundamental task of modern psychotechnique for a rational and moral organization of human labor.

Psychotechnique, in its more recent applications, is a biological discipline that has many contacts with morality, which ought to permeate and integrate its entire field. In fact, it studies every activity of man and teaches the best psychophysiological methods of making man's work most productive with the least effort for the worker.

No one can fail to realize the importance of these studies, which have had the effect of increasing man's individual productivity in all fields of endeavor, in factories as in schools, in the military services as in public life. They have contributed to man's freedom of choice, and to the development of personality. Psychotechnique may be considered as one of the most valuable accomplishments of Western civilization.

According to Gartew, the Director of the Moscow Labor Institute, Soviet Russia pursues an entirely different method with respect to labor techniques. As the Director explained a little before the Second World War, it is not necessary in Russia to orient and select the individuals in accordance with their psychosomatic characteristics, since every worker must adapt himself to any kind of activity whatever. It will be sufficient to stimulate work by rewarding the more capable while punishing those who are inefficient. Furthermore, the criterion by which workers are assigned to this or that manual or intellectual labor is based on the condition of the labor market, the social need of this or that category of workers. Only one selection is made, namely, that of supervisors, instructors, and directors.

It is evident that, from the standpoint of respect for the human person, man in Russia is hardly different from a machine, as he must obey the mechanical regime, adjusting his psycho-physical traits for force, now for speed, now for accuracy, and so forth, exclusively on a basis of the need of the collectivity, or on the basis of the decisions of the leaders. This biological communism, void as it is of every logical, ethical, and scientific basis, is unnatural and certainly in direct contrast with the characteristics of the human person. *Riz.*

PSYCHOTHERAPY. This is the treatment of the sick by psychic means. It may be empirical or systematic. *Empirical psychotherapy*, dictated by common sense and by a natural desire to aid in some manner those who suffer, consists in comforting the sick with encouraging and understanding words and suitable counselling.

Systematic psychotherapy is perhaps linked with uncivilized peoples who, in order to free the sick from their suffering, had recourse to magic practices and other devices of wizards or persons particularly dedicated to the cure of the sick (Weiss). Its modern methods are based principally on the *animal* magnetism of Mesmer (*see* Metapsychology); they present numerous and varied practices according to the fancies of their promoters, with one common denominator for them all, i.e., suggestion.

SUGGESTION AND PERSUASION. Suggestion may be used in three forms: hypnotism, wakefulness, or autosuggestion.

The psychotherapist imposes his own ideas and will on the patient by appealing to his imagination and emotions. This imposition is direct in heterosuggestion; indirect in autosuggestion, in which the operator limits himself to suggesting to the patient, verbally or in writing, various states of mind and formulae to be repeated by the patient to obtain the desired effect.

In the past, great therapeutic value was attributed to hypnotic suggestion for the functional illnesses, particularly hysteria. But this is not so today, because such suggestion can rapidly suppress obstinate, tormenting symptoms. Hypnotic practices increase and emphasize psychic dissociation, which is the root of psychoneurosis, by aggravating the fundamental conditions in which these symptoms thrive.

Suggestion in a state of wakefulness aims at skillfully strengthening the patient's confidence in the possibility of cure. Of course, the field of action of this method is rather limited, but more reliable.

The advocates of autosuggestion, especially Coué and Baudouin, are enthusiastic and regard it as the panacea of every evil. Several authoritative scholars have underscored the deceptiveness of its results and its danger, particularly in psychoneurotic individuals. Since autosuggestion acts on these in a manner similar to that of hypnotic heterosuggestion, it tends to exalt a morbid sensitivity, restrict the field of consciousness, focus attention on the disturbance to be cured, which might ultimately worsen and make the morbid syndrome chronic.

P. Janet, after a study of the various psychotherapies based on suggestion, advised decidedly against any form of autosuggestion, adding that in the rare cases in which suggestion is really indicated, it must be heterosuggestion, practiced with caution and discretion by truly competent and honest physicians.

Quite different and with much wider application in psychotherapy is *persuasion*, directed not only to the imagination and the emotions of the patient but, above all, to his reason. In fact, this psychotherapeutic method, whose most strenuous and fortunate supporter was Dubois, seeks to influence the patient by reasoning to persuade him of the groundlessness of ideas which apparently constitute the nucleus of his psychoneurotic disorder.

Unfortunately, it should be added, neuropsychic illnesses, even more typically *functional*, are not always and only the product of faulty reasoning, but stem from more profound causes, linked to organic conditions, distortions of the instinctive-affective sphere, neuro-vegetative alterations, hormonic deficiencies or imbalance. These are at times aggravated by faulty reasoning. Therefore, persuasion, of itself, can have but a limited and transitory effect; Dubois' numerous successes were chiefly the result of a disguised suggestion, emanating from the personality of the renowned professor, who exercised a powerful influence on the emotional sphere of the patients who flocked to him with a preconceived and blind confidence that they would be cured. In fact, suggestion may be exercised by any means, whether direct or indirect, even unknown to the therapeutist himself.

PSYCHOANALYTIC THERAPY. Freudian psychoanalysis claims to discover the real and distant causes of psychic diseases (neuroses, psychopathies, or psychoses) and to suppress them by a unique method based on the supposition that such disturbances stem always and only from abnormalities of unconscious psychic processes. Such abnormalities are generally caused by recollections of past sexual experiences that have been thrust into the subconscious, from which they cannot escape because they are held back by *censorship*, which is a result of training. They give rise to *conflicts* that easily produce psychoneurosis (*q.v.*).

By means of detailed confessions, extracted through interrogations, of dreams skillfully interpreted, of *lapsus*, etc., psychoanalysis claims to draw from the subconscious, the depository of one's past, all sexual recollections, including the most remote and difficult to confess. The emergence of such recollections is supposed to cause pathogenic unconscious processes to become conscious processes and, consequently, to lose their morbific power, once they are in the higher zone subject to the critical and reasoning control of the *Ego*. By this process psychoneurosis is supposed to be cured.

Concerning the origin, theoretical principles, practice, and value of this doctrine, *see* Psychoanalysis.

It may suffice to observe here that, although an honest and discreet analysis of the psyche can contribute to the diagnosis and cure of psychoneurosis, Freudian psychoanalytic method is morally objectionable. To relate all psychoneurotic manifestations to sexual factors, as the more rabid psychoanalysts maintain, is absolutely unjustified. Furthermore, to excite or to suggest sexual images, is something that could be truly dangerous, since it amounts to instilling in the suggestible mind of the patient ideas and images which perhaps he never had, and which can be the cause of extensive moral suffering to him, and the real cause of psychoneurosis.

The method of modern psychotherapy is an eclectic one, probably because of our increased knowledge of the many causes of psychoneurosis.

Frequently, persuasion is sufficient; in fact, it is always advisable to begin with persuasion, because it is an absolutely innocuous method. This is what Frankl refers to by his *logotherapy*, which rests on the recuperative spiritual capacities of the patient. In certain cases, by a calm, serene, cordial conversation with a psychoneurotic, a psychotherapist is able to convince him that his disturbances are caused by an emotional condition; are maintained only by the recollection of the same emotional condition or by unfounded fear of incurability of the illness; that his sickness is a passing condition; that his disturbances are the effect of a bad habit, etc. This could be sufficient to obtain a cure or a rapid improvement that could also lead to a complete cure, if integrated with persuasive work and rational sports, hydrotherapeutic and ergotherapeutic activities.

Often, simple persuasion is insufficient; it will be necessary to add to it specific medication to restore neuro-vegetative balance, to repair endocrine deficiencies, or to restore normal functioning to certain internal organs.

At other times, particularly in individuals with pronounced hysterical symptoms, one could try a stimulating action directed to more visible morbid symptoms (electric stimulations on muscles which the patient believes paralyzed, etc.) or, with due caution, narcoanalysis (*see* Hypnotism) or narcotherapy (*q.v.*).

In other words, in psychotherapeutic treatments the physician is not required to follow rigid preconceived schemes, but to adopt variable criteria and directions according to the diagnosis of the ailment, and the phase of the morbid process.

It is a known fact that, in order to be effective in the practice of his profession, a physician must possess not only intelligence, technical skill, and uprightness, but understanding, tact and compassion. These qualities are more important in a psychotherapeutist. The patience, stability, and psychological intuition of a therapeutist are often subjected to hard tests before the patient will open his mind to him with confidence, and before his apprehensive hope or desperation can be changed into a feeling of trust.

Every act, gesture and word of the physician is carefully studied by the patient, who draws reasons for discomfort or confidence in the desired recovery. This imposes a very circumspect discretion upon the psychotherapeutist. Finally, considering the easy impressionableness of the sick, who waver between the comforting benefits of religious belief and a bitter pessimism, the encouraging words of a believing physician, intended to calm and strengthen a doubtful, uncertain, and disturbed mind, will always be a happy contribution to the spiritual readjustment of the patient, whose ultimate recovery may greatly depend upon him.

Every Catholic psychotherapist has certainly noticed in the practice of his profession the favorable effects of a simple, casual phrase directed to assuring an uncertain religious conscience, or to encouraging a person's trust in God, or to interesting him in some charitable work. This, of course, is genuine psychotherapy, because the psychoneurotic is an egocentric or egoist; if a psychotherapeutist is successful in fostering higher, generous, and humanitarian thoughts in the patient's mind, he will have gone a long way to the cure of his psychoneurotic patient. *Riz.*

PUBLIC. *Public* means that which relates to, belongs to, affects, or concerns a nation, state, or community in general.

In Canon Law, the term *public* assumes a different meaning, depending on whether it is used as opposed to *private* (public and private right) or as opposed to *occult* (public or occult matrimonial impediments and crimes).

As it applies to a matrimonial impediment, *public* affects the quality of the impediment in such a way that it can be proved in the external forum. This element has no reference to any particular property inherent in the nature of the impediment, but simply to the external circumstance that the existence of the impediment can be proved in the external forum by documents, witnesses, and the like. According to this concept, an impediment is public if proof can be given of the fact giving rise to the impediment (Can. 1037; Pont. Comm. for Interpr. of CIC, June 25, 1932).

Canon 1971, however, admits a further distinction with respect to matrimonial impediments: impediments by their very nature (*natura sua*) public are distinct from impediments which are *de facto* (actually) public. This distinction concerns the manner by which the public aspect of the impediment can be proved.

Canonists, however, hold that this distinction has no relevance in the dispensations from matrimonial impediments. Thus, the distinction of impediments *natura sua* or *de facto* public and impediments *natura sua* or *de facto* occult remains simply a theoretical distinction.

The concept of *public* and *occult*, if referred to crimes, affects above all the publicity or non-publicity of the crime (Can. 2197). A crime is public if it has already been divulged, or if it is such that it will be easily divulged to a large number of people.

The notion of divulgation embraces three factors: divulgation already effected, circumstances under which the offense was committed, and actual circumstances surrounding the offense on discovery.

An offense is also materially public as a fact, and formally public as an offense.

This notion has relevance in canonical procedure, inasmuch as only public offenses are subject to criminal procedure (Can. 1933, par. 1). *See also* Notorious, Occult. *Pug.*

PUBLICITY. *Publicity* consists of various means and devices designed to promote the particular interests of a definite person, place, cause, or the sale of a product. Publicity may be had in various ways, but generally it is either oral or written in the form of printed advertisements. Oral publicity, by far the more ancient form of advertising, was carried on by professional criers or heralds in ancient times; it continues in use in small communities or by street vendors. Today, however, publicity in print is a more essential and extensive form of advertising, whether it be by billboards, classified columns, or other media. Perhaps more widespread is the combination of oral and written publicity which is found in modern television.

In the Middle Ages professional criers and heralds were organized into a guild. In a certain sense, this was the first organization of publicity technicians.

The first newspaper advertisement appeared in 1630, in the *Gazette de France*. The first newspaper devoted entirely to commercial advertising was the *Petite affiche*, which appeared in France in 1715. The first illustrated billboards, black and white and of small size, appeared around 1830, when lithography came into use. A few years later, with the introduction of chromolithography, multicolor billboards began to appear everywhere.

Today, publicity is a true and proper science, with schools of specialization, where new forms of publicity are studied constantly, from magazines and brochures to flyers and post cards mailed to home owners, from announcements by radio, movie and television, to publicity by blimps and planes.

Publicity is not an easy art. The technicians in this field have so developed the laws of psychology and psychophysiology that they are able to determine the degree of receptiveness of sense organs, particularly vision and hearing, and the intensity of external action on such organs to produce the particular effect desired.

Unfortunately, there is also a tendency to exploit, through immoral publicity, man's lower instincts. This is particularly so in the case of publicity for moving pictures and other theatrical performances.

It is, of course, the duty of the public authority to protect by diligent vigilance the moral life of the people. But it is also the duty of right-minded and decent citizens to protest by appropriate means any attack made upon the moral life of men, women, and children of the community by unscrupulous advertisers, who are guided simply by prospects of gain, irrespective of the moral harm involved. *Pav.*

PUERPERAL PERIOD. The *puerperal period* follows childbirth immediately and, except for complications, usually does not last beyond forty days. The end of the period is generally indicated by the reappearance of the regular menses.

The use of the marriage rights during the puerperal period is forbidden by the physiological condition of the woman. If the new mother is nursing her child, she is dispensed from the obligation of fasting and abstention, for she has the duty to take special care of herself, lest her neglect cause harm to her infant child. For the same reasons, a new mother is dispensed from the obligation of going to Mass until she is able to do

so without grave inconvenience or the danger of incurring grave inconvenience. According to an ancient custom, introduced into the Church from an ancient Jewish practice, when, after the puerperal period, the new mother is able to go to church, she is received at the church door by a priest in surplice and stole. Then she is led into the church with special prayers and ceremonies (*Rit. Rom., Tit. VIII, c. 6*). Following the example of the Jewish custom, which prescribed the offering of a lamb and a dove by a rich mother, or two doves by a poor one (Lev. 12:6–8), the new mother offers a candle to the church. This ceremony or sacramental is called the *Churching of Women. M.d.G.*

PUNISHMENT, CAPITAL. The Christian religion developed in a world in which capital punishment was a juridical institution. Lactantius was one of the few Christian writers of the early centuries who opposed capital punishment as contrary to the commandment "Thou shalt not kill." The Church never approved this extreme view, but condemned this error, which was espoused by the Waldenses, Anabaptists, Quakers, etc. Calvinists and other Protestants went to the other extreme, for they taught that capital punishment should be incorporated into the laws of every State, and that its suppression is against God's commandment as proclaimed in the Scriptures (Gen. 6:9; Rom. 14:4).

The traditional doctrine of the Church is that capital punishment is not opposed to the divine law, nor is it required by this law as a necessary thing; its necessity depends on circumstances. A Catholic may accept or reject the doctrine of capital punishment on the basis of circumstances and his evaluation, but he may not state that the application of this penalty is a violation of the natural law. The reasons in support of this position are as follows:

(a) *Revelation.* The Holy Scriptures attribute to civil authority the right to take the life of a criminal, as a right belonging to its natural and ordinary jurisdiction (Gen. 9:6; Ex. 21:22 ff.; Lev.

24:17; Deut. 19:11; Rom. 13:4. (b) In all stages of civilization and under all forms of government humanity has considered capital punishment as in keeping with the *moral law*. It is inconceivable that such a large part of humanity could be so seriously mistaken about a leading precept of the natural law. (c) *Intrinsic reason:* To punish is to deprive a man of a benefit as retribution for an evil committed. Even life is a benefit. To exclude capital punishment would mean a reason why privation of life is not a just retribution for the crime. Nor is it enough to say that life is too great a good to be deprived of, because there are also enormous crimes that are committed; nor that man has a natural right to life because man also has a natural right to bodily integrity, liberty, and safety. If every good to which man has a natural right were to be excluded, the number of just penalties would be so reduced that the power of punishing crime would be almost totally eliminated. The allegation that capital punishment is an irreparable damage is true of any penalty. Even the damage of ten years in prison cannot be made up. The gravity of capital punishment, however, binds all responsible persons to do all that is humanly possible to void erroneous condemnations. Infallibility, of course, cannot be achieved in human things, but the prudence required for acts of very grave importance shall suffice. One must not lose sight of the fact that by omitting the imposition of the required punishment for the maintenance of public order in society, the lives of good citizens may be exposed to grave dangers. There is every good reason to doubt that abolition of capital punishment would result in a benefit to society, for, according to St. Thomas, what has been considered useful for a long time must not be abolished (*Summa Theol.,* I–II, q. 97, a. 2).

From the practical standpoint, the expediency of capital punishment appears to be a great deterrent against crimes for which no other intimidation seems to be adequate.

It is a matter of fact that capital punishment was maintained in the various legislations until the middle of the eighteenth century.

Many States have maintained the death penalty: the United States, England, France, Spain, Russia, and Vatican City.

Today capital punishment is carried out by hanging, beheading, the electric chair, the gas chamber, and the firing squad, depending on the criteria by which the various States are guided.

DEATH PENALTY AND MILITARY CODES. Capital punishment as the most severe form of punishment is found in use in the armed forces and wartime administrations from the remotest times and with almost all peoples, even as it is maintained today in all military codes. This penalty is justified by the necessity of maintaining military discipline and preventing the commission of very serious crimes, such as treason and desertion.

It is indeed, "a disagreeable necessity, but one that cannot be disregarded, if a firm discipline in the military forces is to be maintained, without which the latter would become more a cause of damage than a means of security." *Ben.* and *Pub.*

PURGATORY. *See* Last Things.

PURIFICATOR. *See* Chalice.

PURITY. The term *purity* has a variety of meanings. In a very generic sense, it is the virtue that moderates man's behavior with respect to his sexual life and all things related to that life. Thus, it includes both chastity (*q.v.*) and modesty (*q.v.*). In a very specific sense, often it is identified with chastity (*see* Chastity, Modesty).

PURITY OF INTENTION. *See* Intention, Right.

PUSILLANIMITY. *See* Fortitude (virtues connected with).

PYROMANCY. *See* Divination.

PYROMANIA. *See* Dipsomania.

PYX. *See* Custody of the Blessed Sacrament; Vessels, Sacred.

Q

QUASI-CONTRACT. According to Roman Law and other legislations influenced by Roman Law, *quasi-contract* is an obligation arising from certain voluntary and lawful facts other than contracts, such as the conduct of another's business and the payment of an indebtedness. According to theologians, a quasi-contract indicates an obligation or obligations arising from the tenure of an office.

Ancient theologians, taking the conduct of another's business as the basis, taught that all obligations of justice flowing from an accepted office arose from an implicit contract (quasi-contract). Thus, the duties of judges, lawyers, doctors, tutors, etc., came within the sphere of an implicit contract.

Apart from the two primary sources of obligation, namely contract and crime, Roman legalists listed other sources, completely distinct from these, under the title *"ex variis causarum figuris"*; however, since the diversity of norms affecting this mixed source of obligations did not conform entirely to the norms affecting the sources of contract and crime, it became convenient in the Justinian period, for scholastic and practical reasons, to distinguish a further source of obligation in different terms as *quasi-contract* and *quasi-crime*.

In modern civil codes, jurists have substituted for *quasi-contract* other forms. Since, however, the *quasi-contract* has been maintained in theological language, *quasi-contract* is here understood as an obligation voluntarily assumed by a lawful and free act placed by one of the parties without the consent, even tacit, of the other party, although this consent is legitimately presumed. To this kind of quasi-contracts belong all obligations arising from an accepted office, inasmuch as they arise, according to the majority of theologians, from a form of implicit contract in a broad sense, or, according to others (Serafino da Loiano), from a quasi-contract in a strict sense in which a consent or agreement is obtained by the concourse of will of many persons.

Those who are under obligations arising from a quasi-contract or *ex officio*, as such, are responsible only for infractions due to a juridical guilt (*q.v.*) to which a theological guilt (*q.v.*) is linked. According to the general opinion of God-fearing people, one who assumes an office does not intend normally to bind himself more strictly. If juridical guilt alone were sufficient to occasion moral responsibility, no conscientious person would dare assume an office.

Therefore, a superior, judge, lawyer, physician, surgeon, pastor, confessor, etc., are not held responsible for a damage caused in the fulfillment of their duty unless they have at the same time committed a grave theological sin. In view of the fact that these offices require a great degree of diligence, an apparently minor negligence may easily become grave. Furthermore, a specialist who has claim to greater competence and diligence in the discharge of a specific duty, for which he obtains a larger compensation or fee, could be held liable to reparation for a lesser juridical guilt insofar as he implicitly obligated himself to do more than others could or would do. For this reason, a negligence on his part, though in itself light, could, in his case, be considered at times a grave sin. *Pal.*

QUASI-DOMICILE. See Domicile.

QUASI-PARISH. See Parish.

QUESTION, RURAL. In a restricted sense, the rural question concerns the regulation of labor and economic relations in form contracts between farm-hands and farmers. In a broader sense, the farm question embraces all the problems connected with a vast, almost world-wide movement or process of reorganization aimed at bringing about broad changes in the field of agriculture: land reclamation and transformation, adoption of modern and progressive agricultural methods, taxation, introduction, modification, and extension of existing business and agricultural organizations, development of cooperative agriculture, extension of agricultural loans and credits, professional agricultural training, industrial processing of farm products and social improvement of the farmer and migrant worker.

In its widest implications, the rural question has become quite acute in the last few decades, due to three main factors: (a) the enormous progress achieved in the field of agriculture; (b) invasion of the rural areas by urban people, and the opposite phenomenon of urbanization of farmers in areas of the world; (c) the growth and rapid development of a sense of dignity among farmers and farm-workers, which makes them intolerant of the status of inferiority, formerly bestowed on them in comparison with other classes in other industries.

Because the complexity and wide diversity of conditions in various areas renders the rural question difficult to solve uniformly, two things must be well protected: (a) the fundamental rights of the human person; (b) the right of the family to maintain and develop its structure and fulfill its mission in society. *Pav.*

QUESTION, SOCIAL. By *social question* is meant that complexity of problems revolving around the socio-economic betterment of the working class. Such problems have become more acute in the last century due to the advent and development of large corporations. Formerly many considered the social question as merely the problem of distribution of wealth in a society living under a wage system. Today, however, its scope generally is much wider, embracing all aspects of the socio-economic condition of the working man in a capitalistic system: hence it involves technical-professional training, social education, union organization, the inclusion of labor relations in the juridical systems, urbanization, the strengthening of the domestic institution, the family, and so forth. These problems are indeed particularly complex and urgent and characterize the dynamic way of life prevalent in the past century and even more so in the present.

The fundamental positions adopted in the social question are three. A conservative school, with the theory that the economic world evolves according to laws and to set deterministic principles, and any direct intervention, private or public, would have merely a disruptive effect. Today, this theory is no longer followed, not even by conservatists themselves, who now teach that the difficulties of the capitalistic system can and must be eliminated or reduced by appropriate and wise action of the public authorities.

The followers of a socialist doctrine maintained that the only possible solution to social problems was a radical transfer of ownership of the means of production from private hands to the State. One socialistic school, Communism, insists that this can only be attained by means of revolution; another school of democratic reformists maintained that this must be done by the spontaneous and voluntary evolution of society.

The advocates of Christian socialism stress that the social question admits of a sane solution without recourse to the complete collectivization of the means of production. They insist that the capitalistic system can be profoundly transformed in its structure and operations with the retention of private initiative and the principle of private property as its foundation.

The social question, contrary to the theory held by the conservative school, is not merely an economic and social question; primarily it is a moral one. The various basic solutions overlook the fact that the workingman must be considered not merely as a means of production but as a human person. Hence the economic system, which ignores the dignity of the human person, must be modified with the consideration of man's integral personality, which is clearly not an economic but a moral problem.

Since the social question is a moral question, intervention by the Church is more than lawful. The jurisdiction of the Church in temporal and social matters was asserted by Pope Pius IX in his condemnation of the proposition that the Church had no right to establish any obligation in conscience for the faithful in matters of the temporal order (Denz. 1727).

Among various documents of the Church magisterium, *Rerum Novarum* (Leo XIII) and *Quadragesimo Anno* (Pius XI) deserve particular mention. These state the essential reasons justifying intervention by the Church in social questions:

"We approach the subject [the social question] with confidence, and in an exercise of rights belonging to us. For no practical solution of this question will ever be found without the assistance of religion and the Church. It is We who are the chief guardian of religion and primary executor of functions proper to the Church; We must not by silence neglect the duty incumbent upon Us.

"It is the Church that proclaims from the Gospel those teachings by which the conflict can be brought to an end, or at least made far less bitter. The Church uses her efforts not only to enlighten the mind, but to direct by her precepts the life and conduct of men" (Leo XIII, *Rerum Novarum*).

". . . We lay down the principle long since clearly established by Leo XIII that it is Our right and Our duty to deal authoritatively with social and economic problems. It is not, of course, the function of the Church to lead men to transient and perishable happiness only, but to that which is eternal. Indeed, the Church believes that it would be wrong for her to interfere without just cause in such earthly concerns; but she never can relinquish her God-given task of interposing her authority, not indeed in technical matters, for which she has neither the

equipment nor the mission, but in all those that have a bearing on moral conduct. For the deposit of truth entrusted to Us by God, and Our weighty office of declaring, interpreting and urging in season and out of season the entire moral law, demand that both social and economic questions be brought within Our supreme jurisdiction, insofar as they refer to moral issues. Although economic and moral sciences are guided each by its own principles in its own sphere, it is false that the two orders are completely distinct or that the former in no way depends on the latter" (Pope Pius XI, *Quadragesimo Anno*).

"Always moved by religious motives, the Church had condemned the various forms of Marxist Socialism; and she condemns them today, because it is her permanent right and duty to safeguard men from currents of thought and influences that jeopardize their eternal salvation" (Pope Pius XII, Christmas Radio Message, December 24, 1942).

"The Church has been and is always fully conscious of her responsibility. Without the Church, the social question is insoluble" (Pope Pius XII, Radio Message to the Workers of Spain, March 11, 1951). *Pal.*

QUIETISM. Quietism, a doctrine developed by the Spanish priest Michael Molinos (1640–1698), taught that perfection consists in a total passivity of the soul completely surrendered to God so that He may act on it without its cooperation according to His own pleasure. Thus by neutralizing its own faculties, the soul achieves a true union with God, who then lives and reigns in it. In such a state, the soul need not make acts of faith, hope, mortification, or other virtues, nor ask of God any specific thing nor confess its sins. It need not apply itself to vocal prayer and may reduce mental prayer to a vague state of quiet, called acquired contemplation. In this state, the soul, which no longer has any distinct idea of God and His perfections, of Christ's humanity or of any other thing, abstains from every act whatsoever. In this contemplation it must remain for its entire life, unless God elevates it to infused contemplation. It must not dwell on its own defects, reward, or punishment. It must maintain a state of pure indifference to its own perfection and salvation. It must not even resist temptation, but must maintain itself in an entirely passive state and reject all fears and scruples.

Precursors of this doctrine were the Euchites, Beghards, Fraticelli and Spanish Illuminates. Following the footsteps of Lacombe and Guyon, Fénelon (1651–1715) established a mitigated form of quietism called semi-quietism.

According to Fénelon, at the attainment of a perfect love of God, man neither wishes nor does anything out of self-interest or a desire of reward, but solely for God and His glory. He neither desires nor hopes to gain eternal salvation as his supreme good, but only insofar as this is willed by God and directed to God's glory.

In extreme trials of the interior life, a soul might, upon reflection, become invincibly convinced of just damnation by God and thus in this state offer the absolute sacrifice of his eternal salvation.

The doctrine of quietism, in substance, was nothing more than a practical, naturalistic passivity, which eliminated Christian asceticism, falsified the principles of genuine mystical theology, and was reminiscent of Buddhistic *Nirvana*. Since it falsely and flagrantly contradicted the Gospel, its practice led inevitably to most damaging consequences, not long in coming. Sixty-eight propositions from the unpublished works of Molinos, consisting of letters and testimonies of penitents, were condemned by Pope Innocent XI (Denz. 1221–1228).

Semi-quietism did not produce the same destructive effects, yet it was not free from errors. It is true that man can and must love God with a complete, disinterested love and that other infused virtues are influenced by the virtue of charity, but this does not alter the motive for these virtues nor eliminate the necessity of their practice. Pure love of God, though intense, does require that, in the hope and desire of eternal salvation, man does not prescind from the fact that God is the Supreme Good. Indifference regarding one's salvation is incompatible with love, and unreasonably incompatible with the absolute sacrifice of eternal salvation. Twenty-three propositions of Fénelon were condemned by Pope Innocent XII (Denz. 1327–1349). *Man.*

R

RACE. A race is a group of individuals, homogeneous by reason of their exterior traits and the hereditary qualities of their germinal plasma, which transmit psychosomatic characteristics practically unchanged from one generation to another. Race is a biological entity, subordinate to species and comprised therein. The union of two races of the same species will produce fertile hybrids (*mestizos*) in whom distinctive traits are transmitted in accordance with the laws of Mendel.

Variety is change due to external causes or environment. This change is due to disappear, both in the individual and in the species, if the cause that produced it ceases to exist.

HUMAN RACES. To better understand the meaning of the term *human race*, it is well to distinguish it from the terms *nation* and *people* (*q.v.*) with which it is often erroneously confused.

Race is an anthropological, naturalistic entity, akin to animal and vegetative species, with its own anatomical, physiological, and psychic characteristics which distinguish it from other human races.

People is a sociological entity which may be described as a group of individuals who speak the same language and have the same cultural background. One and the same people may consist of various races.

Nation is a political entity made up not only of diverse races but of diverse peoples and inhabitants of different territories who are nevertheless united to some degree by the same cultural ties.

J. F. Blumenback (1752–1840) classified the races of mankind on the basis of various morphological peculiarities and not merely on the basis of the color of the skin. He distinguished 5 fundamental races: Caucasian (light skin); Mongolian (yellow skin); Ethiopian (black skin); American (copper skin); Malayan (dark brown skin). According to this classification—still in use among nonspecialists in anthropology—the Caucasian race is considered as the fundamental type, and the other races are mere deviations from this type.

The most recent division of the races of mankind is that of Eickstedt (1933). He is the author of the most complete treatise on the subject to date. He places the origin of mankind in Central Asia. From there human groups (respectively whites, blacks and yellow-skinned) spread out in successive anthropogenetic waves toward the West, South, and East; with the passing of thousands of years, they became increasingly more refined to the point where they developed into thirty-six races today, twelve Europoid, ten Negroid and fourteen Mongoloid.

This, as well as earlier classifications, is far from perfect. Undoubtedly it is no easy task—we might even say it is impossible—to classify the races in a system that will take into account every single biological fact or scrutinize all the morphological peculiarities of mankind and order them in a universally acceptable hierarchical scale.

In any event, the study of the diversity of races continues. Moral theology, as indicated in the article on Anthropology, follows this study with keen interest.

RACES AND PSYCHE. Undoubtedly there are psychic as well as morphological differences between races. Positive and rigorously proven study of these latter differences is yet scanty, due in part to the intrinsic difficulty of the subject and in part to the accumulation of pseudo-religious, philosophical, and, above all, political prejudices which ham-

1015

per an impartial study of the subject. Furthermore, it should not be forgotten that the numerous and constant cross-breedings among races, as well as influences of environment, have undoubtedly modified somewhat the original psychic qualities of races.

It is, therefore, beyond one's power of comprehension how, on the basis of the known datum of psychic differences among races, one could possibly arrive at a classification of a whole hierarchy of differences, much less, the conclusion that one race is superior to all others. Indeed, individual dispositions, qualities, and characteristics do differ more or less markedly from one race to another. But neither studies of applied psychology nor the history of inventions and civilization back up claims of achievements as proper to one race or another. Claims of racial supremacy are essentially based on hypotheses, if not on outright errors, for the sole purpose of defending at any cost a preconceived thesis.

Concerning the myth of the *Nordic race* and the Church's viewpoint on the moral corollaries, *see* Racism. *Riz.*

RACISM. Racism is a doctrine which asserts that race is the essential and initial factor in man's refinement and in the historical and cultural evolution of all peoples. There are psychic and morphological differences between races. But no one may legitimately conclude that a hierarchy of races exists, much less that one race is absolutely superior to the others. In Hitler's Germany *National Socialism* taught that blood, transmitted from generation to generation, was the principle of all vegetative, animal, cognitive, and volitive life. It propounded that all perfections—physical, intellectual, and moral—in the individuals of a race as a homogeneous whole were the foundation of morality and law. From this it concluded that whatever helped to insure the purity of blood and the vigor of a race was just, honest, and lawful. Furthermore, it taught the doctrine of absolute superiority of the Nordic Aryan race over all other races, and consequently anti-Semitism arose. Nazi racism,

devised for the sake of placing on a pseudo-scientific basis the doctrine of Pan-Germanism, the superiority of the German people and its right to rule the world, did not have many followers outside Germany.

SCIENTIFIC EVALUATION. As a scientific theory, racism lacks a positive basis. Race theories for the time being, among the more serious thinkers, are in a state of uncertain flux and can lead to diametrically opposed conclusions (G. Schmidt, *Race and Nation*). Differences between races do exist, but science has not been able to determine the psychic differences capable of transmission by heredity, nor are races immutable. Race, far from a static entity, is subject to change. Racial peculiarities, at first believed constant, have been proven to be variable. Then, too, one cannot speak of a superior, pure race destined to dominate other, naturally inferior races; it is absolutely arbitrary to attribute this title to the Nordic Aryan race. There are ethnical groups possessing somatic, psychological, and cultural qualities superior to other groups, but these are accidental, rather than permanent, differences, dependent on environment and historical and hereditary factors. Nor is there any scientific proof whatsoever that differential characteristics, qualities, virtues, or weaknesses of a race stem from the blood.

Particularly in the case of Europe, no scientist would dare assert that there are pure races, since beyond the shadow of a doubt all European nations are made up of an admixture of races fused together by a variety of causes.

CATHOLIC DOCTRINE AND RACISM. It is the task of science to establish the truth or the error, the degree of probability or certitude of various hypotheses concerning the human races, the laws of hereditary transmission of organic and psychic peculiarities of each individual racial group, and the like. Nazi racism, however, departing as it did from the field of free scientific research, set down principles and adopted legislative norms openly opposed to the fundamental dogmas and the moral laws of Catholic doctrine. Catholic doctrine teaches the unity of mankind, existing from the very beginning of a direct creation by God; it maintains that the whole of mankind was redeemed by Jesus Christ and is destined to the same supernatural end. Brothers in the natural and the supernatural order, men enjoy the same human rights, regardless of the race to which they belong; hence, no particular race can boast of an essential superiority over others and none can claim to be the only chosen one. Furthermore, Catholic doctrine teaches that the soul is created by God; that it is essentially the same in all men, not dependent on matter or blood, although accidental differences due to bodily organism favor the activities of the spirit in various degrees. All these truths were denied by Nazi racism in its attempt to reduce morality and law to pure racial hygiene. This aberration went so far as to impose compulsory sterilization on individuals who were sick or considered inept for the production of healthy and useful offspring, capable of preserving the purity and vigor of the blood. *Man.*

RADIESTHESIA. *See* Rhabdomancy.

RADIO. Radiophony, commonly called radio, was developed from radiotelephony in the United States of America in 1919. Radio broadcasts have spread rapidly throughout the world. At the present time the system used by broadcasting stations is either competitive or commercial, as in America, or monopolistic, as in Europe, under government control.

Radio broadcasting may be considered as a *public service*, an *information medium*, and as a *form of art*, a medium for specific kinds of broadcasts, radio-theatre, radio-revues, documentaries, etc.

With millions of listeners, greater than the number of spectators at theatres, movies and other public events put together, radio is practically available to all at all hours of the day. While it is an instrument of recreation par excellence, it is also a formidable medium for the diffusion of news, ideas, sentiments, and customs.

Moral aspect. Programs, generally, are under the control of radio stations and, in certain places, under censure commissions; yet at times, programs present questionable moral value. Obviously, an ethical code for all radio programs would be highly desirable, especially if a self-imposed censorship, such as it exists in many places, fails to uphold the principles of a sound moral doctrine, particularly insofar as the moral character of family and religion, honesty and decency are concerned.

A Catholic does not satisfy the Church precept by hearing Mass over the radio, because physical presence at Mass is required for the fulfillment of the law (*see* Sanctification of holy days). However, a Papal Blessing, if given *urbi et orbi*, is validly received over the radio (*see* Decree of S. Penitentiary, June 15, 1939, AAS, 31 [1939], 277).

The Archangel Gabriel is the patron of communications. *Gal.*

RADIOMANCY. *See* Therapy.

RADIOPHONY. *See* Radio.

RADIOTHERAPY. *See* Therapy.

RANCOR. *See* Hatred.

RAPE. In the terminology of modern theologians *rape* is a violent sexual relation either with a virgin (rape in a strict sense) or with any other woman (rape in a broad sense). Violence is understood not only as a physical but moral force (serious threats, deception). This includes excessive insistence and abuse of persons who do not possess full use of their mental faculties.

Rape adds to the sin of fornication (*q.v.*) a grave sin of injustice, because it implies violation of the right of the woman to the use of her generative faculty according to her own choice. If the victim of rape is a virgin, the sin of injustice is twofold, because virginity is a good of greatest value, distinct from the right she has to the use of her own body according to her free choice. The free consent of the woman eliminates all injustice insofar as she is concerned; according to modern moral theologians, this applies also in the defloration of a virgin against the will of her parents because the virgin, even a minor, can validly but illicitly decide the use of her own body independently of the will of her parents.

In a case of violence, the woman is obliged to use all the means at her command to avoid the sexual act, short of exposing herself to the danger of death, or to other grave harm, such as grave infamy. In such extreme circumstances a mere passive attitude is permissible, provided that there be no grave danger of willfully consenting to the act. If in trying to avoid the coitus, the act is completed in a manner that frustrates conception, this indirect effect is imputable only to the aggressor; it does not take away from the woman the right of self-defense. It is a disputed question whether, immediately following intercourse, the woman may use positive means to prevent conception or must let nature take its course.

The unjust aggressor is obliged to make reparation of all damages due to his crime. In particular, he must enable the woman to contract marriage in the same manner as if she had never been violated, even by marrying her himself, provided that all other conditions are favorable. If he deceived her with a false promise of a future marriage, he is obliged to marry her, not simply to make good on his promise, but also in reparation for the damage done. If, as a result of rape, a child was born, the man is obliged to provide for the proper rearing of the child and all the expenses incurred by the mother. Often the best form of reparation is marriage, if it can be properly arranged and offers a reasonable prospect of success. *Dam.*

RAPTUS MELANCHOLICUS. *See* Anxiety, Dysthymia, Melancholy.

RASHNESS. *See* Prudence.

RATE. A table or schedule of prices, established particularly for public utilities and services like transportation, communication, or certain professions, is called a rate. Sometimes it refers to prices of certain monopolies, commodities, or other articles of consumption, particularly if the price is fixed by the public authority.

Rates may be: (a) *Proportional,* if the rate varies in proportion to the service or the quantity of goods received; such are rates relating to gas, light, telephone, etc. (b) *Differential,* if the basis of the rate decreases with the increase of the service. For example, in many European countries one pays a fixed amount for the first sixty miles of railroad transportation and a lower rate for the second sixty miles. Therefore, the railroad rate is called *differential* because a decreasing, variable basis is applied to successive spans of a journey. (c) *Single,* if it has a fixed basis, despite variation in the service rendered, such as postal rates. Thus, for letters which do not weigh over half an ounce, one pays the same postage, regardless of the distance.

Public services, today, are supplied by public or semi-public enterprises. The latter, managed by private franchises, are required to conform to specified conditions, especially in prices. The criterion by which the public authorities are generally guided in the gradual formulation of rates is that of distributive justice; to cover the cost of the service, prices are set in a way that the service be rendered in the best manner to the advantage of the greatest number of users. Take, for example, the railroad service. If a single average price were established for every unit of distance—the most advantageous to a monopolistic group—many would be prevented from availing themselves of the railroad services, while others would be in a position to benefit from such service if the prices were higher than the average. Thus a scale of rates corresponding to various economic levels of the citizens is established by the government or authorized agency, and expenses are met with the total amount of receipts, and the service is accessible to the greater number of citizens. City administrations follow the same criterion in setting rates for their various services.

A moral problem arises in the field of professional services and payment as to whether or not the interested parties are obliged to conform to rates fixed by authority. The rates are generally established to protect the customers. Consequently, since they are established, as it is presumed, according to a criterion of equity, they must also be rendered in conscience. On the other hand, professional people may not demand a higher price for their services than normal; they may accept higher fees if freely offered or due to them for extraordinary, essential services, provided these prices are kept within the limits of justice. May extraordinary services be rendered at a lower price? It would seem so, except when done for the purpose of unfair competition.

RATE OF DISCOUNT. *See* Interest.

RATE OF INTEREST. *See* Interest.

RATIONALISM. Rationalism is a philosophical system which believes human reason is the only means to acquire knowledge of truth. It excludes all elements either inferior to reason, as the senses, or superior to reason, as divine revelation.

In the field of ethics, rationalism attacks, and rightly so, sensism, sentimentalism, or similar doctrines which make man's lower faculties a basis and measure of his moral duties. But it errs in the extreme rejection of the notion that such faculties are at least simple secondary factors moving man to ethical action.

Rationalism cannot be reconciled with Catholic doctrine because it rejects any norm imposed by God through revelation and teaches a morality independent of God, which is dictated purely by reason raised to the dignity of a autonomous lawgiver.

This isolation from all below or above reason historically tended to isolate the individual by separating him from the burden of social and traditional ties. It is, therefore, individualistic, inasmuch as it does not admit the validity of social ties unless based on the consent of the single individuals (*contractualism*). It is revolutionary in tendency, inasmuch as it does not recognize the value of tradition.

These notes explain how rationalism has exaggerated the importance and oftentimes falsified the concepts of natural law and natural religion by advancing forms of autonomous morality and by endeavoring to draw ethics away from the influence of historical tradition and revelation (*see* Morality, Independent). *Gra.*

READING. The reading of books is a morally indifferent act, which may become good or bad, depending on the content of the reading, the manner of reading, or the particular age and maturity of the reader. In general, reading done with evil intention or as the cause of an inordinate desire or effect, as a danger of sin against faith or morals or a danger to one's physical, psychical, or moral life is illicit. Only a proportionate necessity or utility (study, etc.) can justify running the risks of such dangers (*see* Immodesty, Occasionist, Impurity, Faith). Not only the real and true damage caused by reading evil books is considered here but also the fact that frequent reading of sensual or sexual books can have serious, disturbing effects on the health, mental balance, and desire for serious work of the reader, especially a young person. Frequently such reading can lead to an unreal or false notion of the basic realities of life.

The Church, the teacher of truth and guardian of morals, by positive law forbids reading books and writings which are the source of serious danger to one's faith or morals (*see* Index of Forbidden Books). *Dam.*

REASON, AUTONOMY OF. *See* Rationalism.

REASONABLENESS. *See* Prudence.

REASONING. Reasoning is a process by which one passes from one truth already known to another truth not yet known. It is, therefore, opposed to intuition, which is the direct vision of a truth without the mediation of another truth. Through intuition we have certitude of axiomatic principles underlying many sciences; through reasoning we arrive at the consequences of such principles. Such consequences, disposed in well ordered series, constitute the whole structure of science.

The most simple and fundamental form of reasoning is the *syllogism*. It consists of three propositions: the first is a universal principle and is called the major premise; the second states a fact and is called minor premise; the third applies this universal principle to the statement of fact and is called a conclusion.

In the ethical sphere every judgment of conscience can be considered the conclusion of a syllogism. Thus, if a person finds himself in a position to commit theft and does not, he bases his conduct on this syllogism: Theft is unlawful; if I were to take this object I would be committing a theft; therefore, I would be committing an unlawful act; I shall not do it. In the majority of cases this reasoning is not so explicit; the universal principle is so deeply rooted in man's conscience that it exercises its influence even without formal expression. Generally it is clear that an underlying principle applies to the fact confronting us; hence, the only proposition that the individual enunciates explicitly to himself is the conclusion of an implied syllogism. This conclusion is the judgment of conscience. From the ethical standpoint it is very important to note how the rational process of reasoning, implicit and subconscious as it may be, can be easily hampered and distorted by subjective tendencies. These tendencies usually exert a disturbing influence on the statement of fact (minor premise of syllogism), although in the more serious cases they can also affect the universal principle. For example, frequently a person contemplating theft is satisfied

with perverting a fact by rationalizing that his condition of want and the wealth of the other person are sufficient to justify the actual theft. But it is also possible that one might becloud the major premise by saying, for example, that the respect for another's property is but a misconception since in reality all property is the result of theft to begin with. With this radical reversal of logic the thief attempts to free himself once and for all from the censuring voice of his conscience.

This perversion of reasoning is due to the influence of the will, desire, and passions on judgments of conduct. In such cases the rational process is affected by the chaotic action of emotional tendencies to the point that one will construct syllogisms which are correct in form but erroneous in content. *Gra.*

REASON OF STATE. *See* Machiavellism, Machiavellianism.

RECESS. *See* Contract.

RECIDIVIST. A recidivist is one who has confessed a sin several times and then has lapsed back into the same fault without even temporary amendment; that is, the relapse occurred soon after confession, almost in the same way, with the same facility, and without any serious effort to avoid new lapses. Such a state of affairs gives rise to the presumption that in preceding confessions there was no truly firm purpose of amendment.

A recidivist must be sincerely sorry for his sins, have a firm purpose not to commit the same sin and take the necessary means to accomplish this. Before absolution the confessor should have some assurance that the penitent does have such sorrow and purpose of amendment, for without them the recidivist would not have the proper dispositions for absolution. With deep humility and willingness, a recidivist should accept the advice and counsel of the confessor and try energetically to put them into practice. He should also make use of suitable means not to relapse into the same sin, such as prayer, frequent reception of the sacraments, the presence of God and the Four Last Things, devotion to the Blessed Mother, mortfication of the senses and the like. *Man.*

RECLAMATION (of land). Reclamation is a program of rendering marsh, swamp, or waste lands suitable for cultivation or habitation. Reclamation service generally consists in improving arid sections through irrigation projects, construction of dams and reservoirs, canals and aqueducts, roads and tunnels, power plants, transmission and communication lines, etc. A complete reclamation program would also include provision of lots for home-building, construction of churches, schools, hospitals, and the like.

The social and moral value of such an undertaking is of paramount importance. A reclamation program almost always requires government action, particularly for financial reasons, since an undertaking of this nature involves an outlay of enormous capital, which can only be made available through government intervention. It goes without saying that such governmental intervention is indeed welcome, especially if private capital is unequal or unwilling to undertake such projects because of a generally low profit yield in this type of investment.

In the course of the centuries many achievements have been recorded in land reclamation. Worthy of note in this regard is the work of the Benedictine monks during the Middle Ages. In modern times, due to an increased density of population, reclamation programs have become considerably intensified, although much still remains to be done to improve the lot of many people not only in the new nations but in otherwise rich and progressive countries. *Pav.*

RECOLLECTION. Taken in a strict sense, recollection is a fixing of attention on God and spiritual things, without allowing the other faculties to become interested in anything extraneous to these considerations.

It is important for one's spiritual progress to live as recollected as possible. In fact, certain actions demand recollection.

For instance, it would be culpably irreverent to speak to God and at the same time deliberately apply onself to other activities. A certain habitual recollection is also necessary to avoid distractions in prayers and many dangers of sin. *Man.*

RECOMMENDATION. *Recommendation* means to entrust or give charge; it implies an act of beseeching by word or writing another to protect, favor, or take into consideration a definite thing or person. In itself a good deed as a manifestation of charity and goodness, it implies appreciation of the internal and external qualities of a person. It is quite proper to *recommend* someone if by such act a deserving person can regain an unjustly lost reputation, or economic and social status. In order that recommendation may be morally right and just, it is necessary that it be made: (a) with prudence; (b) with a right intention, without deception, and with *truth and justice* (I Peter 2:1; Matt. 5:37, and 10:16), especially if it involves delicate tasks such as the education of youth or positions of responsibility, as an administrative position; (c) and that mere favoritism be excluded as something reproved by God (cf. Deut. 16:19; Prov. 24:32; Luke, 20:21; Acts 6:34), especially in positions granted by competitive examination (*see Summa Theol.*, II–II, q. 63, a. 1; Canons 153; 232; 267; 459).

One would sin, even grievously, if for unworthy motives, such as monetary remuneration or personal interest, one were to employ authority, prestige or name to recommend persons who are unworthy, unfit, and inept. There would arise in such a case the obligation to make reparation for any damage caused by such practice.

By recommending a person, of course, one vouches for the actual physical and moral conditions, the virtues and capabilities of the person he recommends and not for what this person may do at a later date, unless the recommendation itself was a fraud. In this case the one giving the recommendation becomes a cooperator in the evil done by his protege and must bear responsibility for it (*see* Cooperation).

REDUCTION OF CLERIC TO LAY STATE.

This consists in depriving a cleric of his clerical state and of all rights, privileges and the external juridical condition proper to him. In other words, a cleric is returned to the condition of an ordinary member of the laity. Obviously, this reduction must be understood in a juridical sense, insofar as the laicized cleric may not lawfully exercise the power of orders and is forbidden to exercise validly the power of jurisdiction, with the exception of administration of the sacraments in a case of extreme necessity (Cans. 2261, 2281, 2303, 2304). By virtue of the reception of the sacrament of holy orders, a laicized cleric possesses a sacramental character which is indelible even for orders of ecclesiastical institution. Reduction of a cleric to the state of the laity is, generally, the result of the application of penal discipline, although cases may occur apart from penal discipline. The procedure for the reduction of a cleric to the state of the laity differs for a cleric in major or minor orders (Can. 949).

A cleric in major orders may be reduced to the state of the laity, (a) by a *rescript of the Holy See*, as a subdeacon dispensed from the obligations assumed through the ordination, including celibacy; (b) by *decree or sentence* of an ecclesiastical court according to the dispositions of Canon 214 either by an administrative decree or by trial; (c) by the penalty of *degradation* (Can. 2305), inflicted for specific crimes (Cans. 2314, par. 1; 2354, par. 2; 2368, par. 1; 2388, par. 1), or a cleric already deposed (Can. 2303) and deprived of the right to wear the ecclesiastical garb (Can. 2304), who continues for a year to give grave scandal (Can. 2305, par. 2). Since degradation is a most severe penalty, the law prescribes that the tribunal appointed for the trial be composed of five judges (Can. 1576, par. 1, n. 2); if the sentence is final, it produces juridical effects immediately (Can. 2305, par.

3), without the solemnities of degradation, as prescribed by the *Roman Pontifical* (pars III, *Prima degradationis forma*). A degraded cleric in major orders is reduced to the state of the laity without the obligation to recite the Divine Office, although he remains bound by the obligation of celibacy (Cans. 135, 213). (d) By *disposition* of the law (*ipso iure*), if a subdeacon or other cleric is given permission to contract marriage; in such a case, though no mention is made in the rescript, the cleric is understood by reasons stipulated in the law (*ipso iure*) to be reduced to the state of the laity (Cans. 1043, 1044).

A cleric in minor orders is returned to the state of the laity (a) *ipso iure* (Cans. 132, par. 2; 141, par. 1 and 2; 669, par. 2); (b) *at his own request* (Can. 136, par. 2); (c) *by decree of the ordinary*, if he is judged unsuited for clerical life; (d) *by a sentence* (Can. 2305, par. 3), which, of course, happens rarely.

As a result of his reduction to the state of the laity, the juridical condition of a cleric is as follows: (a) he is stripped of any office, benefice, privilege and right proper to a cleric, and forbidden to wear the clerical garb (Can. 213, par. 1); (b) a cleric in major orders is relieved of all obligations proper to a cleric in major orders, with the exception of celibacy, unless he received holy orders through grave and unjust fear (Cans. 214; 213, par. 2). Vio.

REFERENDARIUS. *See* Prelate.

REFLEXES, CONDITIONED.

A conditioned reflex is the establishment of a new relationship, acquired accidentally or experimentally, between a given stimulus and a response which previously had no connection with the stimulus. Conditioned reflexes are clearly distinct from common reflexes (absolute or unconditioned reflexes). Conditioned reflexes are reactions to a given stimulus and are necessarily produced as the result of a process of determinism which becomes constant. To give an example: the tapping of the patella ligament (absolute stimulus) produces the well-known patellar reflex (absolute reflex); but if at the same time we ring a bell when we tap, or light a lamp, or employ some other means of exposing the subject to a conditioned stimulus, which by itself would not cause a reflex movement in the leg, then, after a certain number of times, an association is formed and the auditory, visual, or tactile stimulus alone will be sufficient to produce the patellar reflex movement, without the need of tapping the tendon. This is termed the conditioned patellar reflex. Another example: the presentation of food produces salivation (absolute reflex); repeated presentation of food in an association with a certain sound or other stimulus, in itself irrelevant, will produce eventually a conditioned salivary reflex with the mere reproduction of the artificial stimulus of sound.

The importance of conditioned reflexes from the biological point of view is well-known. In fact, the newborn animal has a small number of absolute reflexes, whose number, in turn, depends on the degree of development of the nervous system at the time of birth. Its subsequent, gradual adjustment to the environment is the product of new and ever more complex and organized absolute reflexes, and an enormous quantity of conditioned reflexes which regulate or direct the total behavior of the animal in the various stages of its life.

Conditioned reflexes are not as constant and invariable as absolute reflexes; their variableness and relatively labile nature are not defects, but the principal element in fundamental biological importance, since only in this manner is the animal able to struggle and react successfully to constantly changing environmental conditions. Only the *conditioning process* would permit the animal to modify his behavior reactions; hence, conditioned reflexes principally form the basis of American schools of *behaviorism*, a modern psychological doctrine which seeks to study organisms objectively. The behavior of organisms is determined to a degree by innate reactions to outside stimuli and to a much

greater degree by reactions acquired through the process of conditioned reflexes.

HISTORICAL NOTES. The theory, practice and the name of conditioned reflexes are linked to the name of the Russian physiologist Ivan Petrovic Pavlov, whose polemics at the start of this century with the Russian neurologist W. Bechterev on the priority of formation of these reflexes, on the best way to form them and their name are forgotten issues. Here we need only recall that Bechterev started experimental research on conditioned reflexology about 1885 and used the term *associative reflex* or *associated reflex* to define the reaction he discovered. About 1899 Pavlov, on the basis of ancient and exact studies of cerebral activity by I. Sechenov, the father of Russian physiology, started research on conditioned salivary reflexes into which he delved deeply for about forty years and with which he managed with the aid of numerous pupils to build the modern theory of conditioned reflexes. These are also called *acquired reflexes, acquisition reflexes, individual reflexes,* and, the more generic name, *psychic reflexes.*

FUNDAMENTAL PROPERTIES, DYNAMICS, AND THE LAW OF CONDITIONED REFLEXES. A conditioned reflex may be acquired through varied stimuli: visual, auditory, tactile, and so forth. However, it is indispensable that it be developed on the basis of a pre-existing reflex, absolute or conditional. A conditioned reflex never takes place spontaneously. The most diverse organs (heart, vasomotor system, pupils, muscles, glands, etc.) may become an *organ to execute conditioned reflexes.* From Pavlov's time, the salivary glands have been used principally for technical convenience and uniformity; the quality and intensity of the responses are determined by measuring the drops of saliva flowing out through a particular fistula.

Under equal conditions, the more intensive the absolute reflex and the greater the *optimum* of intensity, duration and frequency of the conditioning stimuli, the more easily is the conditioned reflex established.

The principal characteristics of conditioned reflexes are as follows: (a) *Specificity*. A conditioned reflex produced by a given sound cannot be caused by tactile, olfactory or other stimuli, nor by a sound of different pitch or timbre than that which determined the conditioning. (b) *Addition*. If two conditioned reflexes have been produced by diverse sense effects, as sound and color, upon the same organ, the simultaneous application of both stimuli will produce a stronger response, representing the sum total of the two individual reflexes. (c) *Stability*. Any conditioned reflex becomes with time enfeebled and finally disappears. However, by new associations between the conditioned and the absolute stimulus, it reappears with particular rapidity, as if the preceding production of the conditioned reflex had traced in the nervous system an indelible path. (d) *Extinction*. Numerous repetitions of a particular conditioned stimulus, without being accompanied at any time by absolute stimulus, result in the exhaustion of the conditioned reflex. The extinction also is specific and involves only one specific conditioned reflex.

The following phenomena constitute the principal processes which occur in the dynamics of the conditioned reflexes:

(a) *Stimulation*. This is the first and indispensable factor in any biological activity. (b) *Inhibition*. This is a temporary weakening or annulment of all conditioned reflexes or of one merely. This is an active process brought about by adding a new stimulus to the habitual, conditioned stimulus (external inhibition) or caused by the excessive brevity of intervals between successive applications of the conditioned stimulus, or other peculiarities of technique (internal inhibition). (c) *Differentiation*. An important form of internal inhibition, this corresponds to the *specificity* already mentioned. If, for example, one tries to produce a conditioned reflex to a sound with 800 vibrations per minute, at first this reflex will appear even for other sounds; it later fixes itself on the sound

selected, while the others lose their effectiveness. In this manner we can appreciate the great sensitivity with which an organism perceives environmental phenomena, and distinguishes one from the other or, as we say, analyzes them. (d) *Disinhibition*. This is the inhibition of the inhibition, also called *counterinhibition* or *liberation*. (e) *Irradiation*. (f) *Concentration*. Both the stimulation and the inhibition, regardless of the stimulus used, at first irradiate over the entire surface of the cerebral cortex; hence, a *generalization* and the *differentiation* of the conditioned reflex. (g) *Reciprocal induction*. The effect of an exciting or inhibiting conditioned stimulus is increased if applied immediately after an inhibiting or exciting conditioned stimulus. This phenomenon is of great importance in the functioning of the cortex, since it prevents the progress of irradiation.

Concerning the so-called *chains of conditioned reflexes*, it is known that, whereas in dogs it is possible to produce a *second rate*, conditioned reflex (that is, a conditioned reflex obtained from a conditioned reflex already established), or even a *third rate one* (only occasionally and in exceptional cases), in man these *super-reflexes* or conditioned reflexes of a higher order can multiply almost to an indefinite number (Bechterev). This helps to understand how a true *structure of reflexes* can be established; hence, the deduction, indeed arbitrary, by certain authors who assert that all apparently spontaneous activities of man are nothing more than an inescapable chain of conditioned reflexes.

NEUROPHYSIOLOGICAL AND PSYCHOLOGICAL PROBLEMS. The foundation of the reflexological theory cannot be considered definitely established; among other things, the afferent path of the conditioned reflex is still uncertain. The very difference, established by Pavlov and other eminent students of reflexology, between absolute and conditioned reflex, is not as yet truly proven.

Furthermore, experience has taught that conclusions justified by research conducted on a particular animal species are never wholly applicable to other species. Even less can we apply to man, indistinctly, reflexological conclusions obtained from research on animals. For, in addition to the long series of factors influencing the formation of experimental conditioned reflexes which account for a variableness at times disconcerting, such as environmental conditions, fatigue, proximity to mealtime, etc., many additional factors are more properly peculiar to man, such as mental fatigue, suggestibility, emotional charge, the interest felt by the subjects of the experiment, and the like. These and other less tangible elements concerning the internal conditions of various individuals justify the perplexity of many students in the study of human reflexes. Many rightfully doubt that a relationship between intelligence and conditioned reflexes can be established.

On the other hand, conditioned reflexes are important to the study of the functioning of the human cortex and represent a delicate and priceless value in neurophysiology and clinical neuropsychiatry. It suffices to mention the progress made by the conditioned reflex method not only in comparative physiology of the nervous system but also in the fields of neurophysiology and human psychology. This is particularly useful in the development of infant sensitive-sensory activity and infant perception, the formation process of language, the training of a child, mnemonic laws, compartmental problems, and the like.

Here we are going to limit ourselves to examining in the light of the science of conditioned reflexes, learning, sleep, and neuroses. These subjects are important in themselves and in relation to morality.

CONDITIONED REFLEXES AND LEARNING. As mentioned earlier, to students of reflexology and behaviorism, conditioned reflexology, learning, behavior, and conduct are, basically, one and the same thing, in the sense that conditioned reflexes are the foundation of all human activities. It is necessary, however, to add, with respect to learning, that such a concept is wholly inadequate to explain the complicated learning process.

This process is not merely passive; in it active elements are present as *the will to learn*, which transcend the conditioning process. The conditioned reflex, as Hilgard stated, is one of the causes but not the sole cause of learning. However, the use of conditioned reflexes in psychotechnique, professional selection, and orientation and in pedogogy may be helpful. The results may already be seen in the tentative applications made.

CONDITIONED REFLEXES, SLEEP AND HYPNOSIS. To Pavlov and his followers, sleep and internal inhibition are one and the same phenomenon. It has been demonstrated (Krasnogorsky) that a tendency to inhibition increases towards evening, and that this increase concerns preferably the sight and the hearing. Therefore, a stable irradiation of inhibition, sleep, would seem to start from the optic and acoustic centers, perhaps because these are more fatigued. It should be noted however, that presently, following the research by eminent scholars on the diancephalo-mesencephalic hypnagogic functions, sleep cannot be conceived as a phenomenon limited to the functions of the cortex. Important endocrine-vegetative mechanisms also participate in sleep.

When a low-tension inhibitory process spreads over the entire cortex, it often happens that an *awake point* persists: a focus of excitement through which the experimenter keeps contact with the animal and can easily awaken him by stimulating the nerve endings that originate from that particular point. This very interesting phenomenon bears an evident relationship to those special states which occur spontaneously or artifically in man, which are called, respectively, *partial sleep* and *hypnosis*. In partial sleep, a reawakening is obtained more frequently by a particular stimulus (for example, the whimpering of a baby for his mother), while a more intensive stimulus of another nature will not succeed in interrupting sleep. In the case of hypnosis the subject is awakened only in connection with certain specific signals by the hypnotizer.

CONDITIONED REFLEXES AND NEU-

ROSES. During the course of his researches Pavlov had the opportunity to study *experimental neurosis*. He noticed, and this phenomenon has been widely confirmed, that frequently during the process of establishing a conditioned reflex, the dog—who up to that time had been calm and docile—became restless with signs of anxiety, or, vice versa, torpid and sleepy, so that he could no longer be utilized in reflex experiments, frequently for several months. These experiments either were improperly conducted or the animal's particular make-up possessed an imbalance of higher nervous activity. Pavlov was able to demonstrate that in those dogs, excitable by nature (which would correspond to the *choleric temperament* of Hippocrates), the inhibition was greatly reduced and the animal easily became uncontrolled and nervous during the experiments, whereas in the weak type of dogs (corresponding to the *melancholic temperament* of Hippocrates), the neurosis caused by the prevalence of the inhibitory process usually showed depressive characteristics. The first form, which Pavlov called *hyperesthenia*, was of brief duration and could be completely cured with rest and large doses of bromide. The second form, which he called *neurasthenia*, had a long duration, uncertain recovery and the cure could be achieved only with small doses of bromide and caffein.

It is easy to see the symptomatic relationships between these two types of experimental neuroses and *neurasthenic erethism* and *neurospsychasthenia* in man. Among the causes of human neurosis pathogenic environmental factors may have partly disturbed the cerebral functions through the improper mechanism of conditioned reflexes (abnormal stimulation, excessive inhibition, and the like).

CRITICAL CONSIDERATIONS. In the course of the present article we have made certain reservations and criticisms of the theory of conditioned reflexes, particularly with regard to certain extreme conclusions which do not appear justifiable. Let us now take up again this extremely important subject from the ethical and practical standpoint. In fact, reflexology involves such important, serious and far reaching moral problems (for example, free will) that it would do the subject no justice if we were to limit our treatment to a few brief comments.

A century ago Sechenov wrote: "All acts of the conscious and unconscious life are *reflexes* from the point of view of their mechanism." This position has been rigidly adhered to by Pavlov and almost all students of the science of reflexes. The behaviorist Watson further asserted: "Our most complicated adult conduct can be explained in terms of chains of simple conditioned responses." It is, therefore, understandable how a large number of scholars, under the influence of these teachers, came to consider the solution to the problem of human psychic activity in a purely mechanistic sense, since it consists, according to them, simply of conditioned reflexes, usually of a higher order. Individual conduct, even in its social aspects, allegedly is conditioned exclusively by a complicated series of reflexes; our whole psychic world of thoughts, judgments, scientific elaborations, the imaginativeness of art, etc., is merely a *chain of reflexes, a structure of reflexes* which can be completely explained through reflexological studies.

Numerous scholars, however, have risen against such a completely materialistic concept of psychic activity, by pointing out the limitations and extreme one-sidedness of this view. Those who have followed scientific trends in the last few years cannot help but notice how the ranks of these critics keep constantly growing. We limit ourselves to merely mentioning Buytendjk from Holland and Gemelli from Italy, who, though using different words, both maintain that the idea of the reflex as the fundamental phenomenon in every nervous function is untenable. There are no *reactions*, but *actions*, they write, and intelligence is not a series of isolated reflexes; it consists of the faculty of producing spontaneous actions with a differentiated configuration, that is, of rational activity and adaptation to changing environmental conditions, and of activity directed to an end. The biological structure of the individual is far more complicated than any conceivable mechanical chain of reflexes.

With respect to Pavlov's conditioned reflexes, Kuppers notes correctly that, between salivation and the psychic state of the appetite, the same relationship exists as between the secretion of tears and sadness. This observation shakes deeply the structure of conclusions built by Pavlov on his important experiences. Conditioned reflexes are too artful and, as Lenz has demonstrated by his experiments on men whom he requested to indicate their impressions as the experiments were being performed, are much more torpid and stereotyped than the conscious responses. Therefore, they are absolutely inadequate for an integral study of the human psyche.

This, of course, is not a denial of the importance of conditioned reflexes with respect to psychic activities in general, but of its exclusiveness. "It is certain," Molhant writes, "that the higher order of conditioned reflexes have considerable importance in our psychic life and constitute the basis of our psychic activity insofar as it is dominated by habit. But besides this, there is in man another form of psychic activity in which the cerebral associative function is no longer governed by the more or less fatal conditioned responses, but by conscience and free will. It is a *superior psychic activity*, that is, a conscious and voluntary adaptation with an inherent character of infinite perfectibility for the present and for the future."

In conclusion, if on the one hand the ingenious and truly physiological method of conditioned reflexes holds great importance in the analysis and interpretation of many processes involving cerebral activity, on the other hand the really superior psychic functions transcend the laws and the process of conditioning.

We are dealing with man's exclusive birthright, constituted by conscience, reasoning, and will. If some extreme supporters of the so-called *objective psychology* reach the point of denying the existence of a moral conscience, of pure spiritual speculation and of a free will, this denial is not rational. For, by so doing, the most important characteristics of the human personality would remain unexplained; hence, any conclusion arrived at, after making these exclusions, must of necessity be erroneous. *Riz.*

REFORM. *See* Protestantism, Moral theology, Protestant.

REFORMISM. Reformism, particularly fashionable at the end of the nineteenth century in the socialist camp, is a tendency to abandon revolutionary aims and adopt the use of legal means to achieve the transformation of a bourgeois state into a socialist state, by influencing public opinion, obtaining a parliamentary majority, initiating and developing a system of social laws and gradually achieving a new regime.

Reformism, as a method, can be adopted by any political party or group, independently of the content of its program. It is, therefore, opposed to the concept of *revolution* (*q.v.*) which implies a violent break with the party in power and the use of violence. It is obvious that the method of successive reforms, intended to realize those changes that the common good requires as necessary to the life of a people, is reasonable, more suitable to mankind, and more useful to the community. It is desirable that this method were always practiced, as a sign of civil and political maturity. Opposition, based on prejudice or selfish attachment to the *status quo*, to reforms considered desirable by an impartial and enlightened study, as well as a wish to return always and at any cost to petty *restoration*, is a grave fault. It is an affront to social justice, capable of driving to violent reactions due to exasperation. On the other hand, it could be equally wrong to preach violent methods, systematically denigrating reformism as hypocrisy, fraud, or sign of ineptitude. *Boz.*

REGINA COELI. *See* Angelus Domini.

REGULARS. *See* Orders, Religious; Religious.

REJUVENATION. Rejuvenation is a process used to repair the effects of reduced internal secretions (*see* Endocrinology). This reduction of hormone secretions produced by the sex glands is due to aging.

The methods used for this purpose are: (a) transplantation of sexual glands from a young person or animal; (b) ligatures of the deferent ducts of these glands; (c) injections of extracts of animal sex glands. These methods generally are effective only if it is a *premature* aging caused by a disease of the sexual glands.

If the sole purpose of the operation is to prevent the normal phenomenon of aging or simply to regain and prolong the enjoyment of sexual pleasure, without a real, honest usefulness, it seems unworthy of a Christian. Regarding the methods used, it should be noted: (a) the transplantation of organs, outside exceptional cases, is generally unlawful because it normally implies a mutilation of the person from whom the organ is taken (*see* Transplantation); (b) ligatures of the deferent ducts is against natural morality because it implies a mutilation of the individual; (c) the injection of extracts of animal glands is not in itself wrong; it is lawful if in the particular case the individual's health is not endangered and the motive is good and honest. *Ben.*

RELAPSE, CENSURE. *See* Censure, Urgent case.

RELATIONSHIP, LEGAL. In questions of legal relationship, the Church follows the actual civil laws of individual countries. Hence, if the particular legislation of a country considers legal relationship a marriage impediment (diriment or impeding), the Church recognizes it as such to the same extent.

Legal relationship arises from the act of adoption (*q.v.*), whereby a person takes the child of another into his family as his own. Adoption gives rise to the relationship of consanguinity and of affinity in the same way that natural blood relation does.

LEGAL ADOPTION AS AN IMPEDIMENT OF CIVIL LAW. In some countries, legal adoption is regarded as a diriment impediment to marriage; in others, as an impeding impediment only; and in still other countries, as no impediment at all.

Despite this diversity in civil legislation and notwithstanding the Church's accommodation to established civil norms, the following may be stated: wherever the impediment of legal adoption exists, for contracting a religious marriage the dispensation granted by the Church suffices.

Legal adoption is a typical case of the Church's attempt to simplify matters by adopting, whenever possible, the laws of the respective countries, a policy pursued long before the promulgation of the Code of Canon Law (*see* Canonization of Laws). *Bar.*

RELATIONSHIP, SPIRITUAL. Spiritual relationship is a kinship that arises from baptism or confirmation. In the case of baptism, a relationship arises between the baptized person and the person baptizing, and between the baptized and sponsors; in the case of confirmation, it arises between the person confirmed and the sponsor (*see* Baptism, Sponsor).

IMPEDIMENT. According to Canons 1079 and 768, marriage is prohibited between the minister of baptism and the baptized person, and also between the baptized person and the sponsor. Spiritual relationship arising from baptism constitutes a diriment impediment of lesser degree in regard to marriage; a dispensation is easily obtained. The impediment arises only from a valid baptism, solemn or private. Before the Code, the relationship and the impediment were more extensive. No impediment of spiritual relationship arises from confirmation (*q.v.*). *Bar.*

RELICS, VENERATION OF. In a religion, as spiritually centered as Christianity, the remains of certain dead are surrounded with special care and veneration. This is because the mortal remains of the deceased are associated in some manner with the holiness of their souls which await reunion with their bodies in the resurrection.

The word *relic* (Latin, *relinquo*: I leave, abandon) generally means a part, sometimes of considerable size, of the remains of a martyr or a saint. Such a part of a human body, either a minute fragment or one entire limb, with the approval of ecclesiastical authority, can be the object of public and solemn veneration manifested by solemn services such as processions.

In Christian antiquity the remembrance of the champions of the faith was not limited to reading their respective *Acta* or to liturgical commemorations in the diptychs, i.e., in tablets which registered the names of the saints, of bishops, of benefactors of the Church, both living and dead for citation in the Mementos of the Mass. This remembrance included also the preservation and veneration of their relics.

Many chapels and basilicas rose where the bodies of martyrs and saints were kept. Clothing and other personal belongings of a saint came to be considered relics. This was because of the widespread belief, beyond measure in the centuries of the early Middle Ages, that the wonderworking power of the saint was to be found not only in the entire body but also in every part of it and in objects that had been in contact with his person.

Relics were placed in a *capsa* if the whole body was concerned; in a *capsella* or relic case in the event of bones or ashes. To these containers is connected the history of the most celebrated shrines in the different countries. In this regard not a few incidents of theft and gross impostures indicate the popular desire to possess relics sometimes exceeding the bounds of reason.

From the first centuries of Christianity, especially after the Constantinian epoch, cases of wood, ivory and various metals containing relics were deposited in altars at the time of their dedication or buried near the tombs of the dead or even worn around the neck. The most ancient example is the reliquary (*Lipsanoteca*) of Brescia of the first half of the fourth century; those of the fifth and sixth centuries are numerous. Naturally, these cases followed various artistic styles of Romanesque and Gothic.

DISCIPLINE AND VENERATION. Relics are distinguished into *insignes* and *non-insignes*. *Insignes* of the saints and of the blessed are the body, head, hand, knee or that part of the body in which a martyr suffered, provided it be entire and not small in size. The rest, *non-insignes*, may be preserved with due honor, even in private houses or carried by the faithful (Can. 1282, par. 2). The *insignes* may not be left in private houses or private oratories without express permission of the Ordinary (Can. 1282, par. 1); and may not be given away or transferred to another church without an apostolic indult. The same should be done with relics that are highly honored, though not *insignes* (Can. 1281, par. 1).

Relics, before exposition to public veneration, must first be authenticated either by a cardinal or by the local Ordinary (excluding the Vicar General unless by special mandate) or by another ecclesiastic who has such a faculty by apostolic indult (Can. 1283, par. 1–2).

Relics for which the authentication has been lost may not be exposed for veneration, unless upon the prudent judgment of the local Ordinary (excluding the Vicar General except by special mandate, Can. 1285, par. 1). The Ordinary shall remove from veneration the relics which he knows not to be certainly authentic (Can. 1284); however, he may permit the veneration of ancient relics, though not authenticated, unless there is found certainty of falsity or counterfeit (Can. 1282, par. 2). The Church, although permitting the discussions of the learned on the authenticity of various relics, does not desire exaggerated and untimely criticisms (Can. 1286). On the other hand, the Church punishes with excommunication reserved to the Ordinary anyone who exposes, manufactures, distributes or sells false relics (Can. 2326); it recommends caution so that in cases of inheritance relics be not sold (Can. 1289, par. 1) and that they be well protected (Can. 1289, par. 2).

For exposition to veneration, relics must be closed in reliquaries or sealed cases (Can. 1287, par. 1). A relic of the True Cross, on account of the respect owed to our Lord Jesus Christ, may not be placed in a reliquary together with other relics of saints but must be kept apart (Can. 1282, par. 2). The relic of the Cross in the possession of a bishop goes to the cathedral on his death; if the bishop had several dioceses, it goes to the cathedral where he died, or that one which he last left if he died outside his diocese (Can. 1288).

Relics may not be placed above the tabernacle in which the Blessed Sacrament is kept, nor on an altar where it is exposed and not even in front of the tabernacle doors. Transfers of bodies or *insignes* from one part to another of the same church can be made with permission of the bishop. Transfer from one church to another requires permission of the Holy See (Can. 1281, par. 1). Relics of the *beati* may not be carried in procession or exposed, except in a place where, by permission of the Holy See, Mass and office in their honor may be celebrated (Can. 1287, par. 3).

For the use of holy relics in the consecration of an altar, *see* Altar. *Cig.*

RELIGION. In a broad sense, *religion* means the whole series of relations between man and God: moral relations of a natural or rational nature (natural religion) and of a supernatural nature (revealed religion). As a science, religion is the study of these theoretical and practical relations. In a less broad sense, religion implies all acts of worship which man renders to God, and thus the moral habit which inclines him to perform such acts in the natural and the supernatural order.

St. Thomas places the metaphysical root of religion in man's fundamental deficiency, and in this he agrees with the conclusions of ethnology and psychology.

The awareness of this deficiency makes man feel the need to be guided and helped by God, the Supreme Being.

Psychologically speaking, natural religion arises in the following manner: Man, by his reasoning power, from the observation of things around him reaches a knowledge of God as the first cause, and recognizes that only God can be the first beginning and last end of all things and of man himself. He considers God's excellence and infinite perfections, His omnipresent, universal, and indefectible goodness. He recognizes how he himself is the object of this effusion of divine goodness and, consequently, rises from admiration to love. He loves God and seeks Him in himself and in other creatures. Man's sincere love gives rise to a reverential fear whereby he fears to displease the person he loves. If this person happens to be almighty, omniscient, omnipresent and just, he fears to incur His just punishment. Hence, there arises a compound sense of knowledge, gratefulness, love, fear, respect, and veneration which is the very foundation of the virtue of religion.

The necessity of religion is based on the natural law; human nature itself and the end to which this nature is ordained demand religion. Since everything created depends on God for its existence, it is only just that rational man should give recognition to this fact. If the end of man is to give glory to God, and if on this depends his own human happiness, it is necessary that man direct his efforts to render that glory to God.

If religion is necessary, it is also useful. This can be clearly seen *a posteriori* if one considers the equilibrium it bestows on man, permeating all the other moral virtues, between the extremes of an exaggerated pride and a discouragement which leads to despair. This equilibrium grows with an increased knowledge of God and a more intense practice of religion.

As a supernatural moral habit, religion is that virtue which regulates the relationship between the creature as such and God the Creator. Scholastics considered this virtue to be related to justice, since it has as its object giving God what is due to Him. Since every creature, especially an intelligent creature, in its totality belongs to God, its Creator, Sanctifier and Last End—consequently absolute Lord and Master—it follows that religion inclines man to return to God the full service of body and soul and all that he possesses. This return is essentially carried out by the practical recognition of the dominion of God over all intelligent creatures and of one's personal, complete dependence on God. The recognition of a creature's nothingness is not in a negative sense as if a creature did not exist, but in a positive sense by recognizing that all that a creature has or is depends on divine omnipotence. This practical recognition, in all its diverse manifestations, is called worship (*see* Worship). Thus, the classic definition of religion as the virtue that inclines man to give God the worship due Him.

Every intelligent creature is capable of this virtue, even our Lord Jesus Christ in His Sacred Humanity; in fact, He is the religious man par excellence, in whose religion we participate, for in union with Him alone we can fulfill our religious duty toward God.

Religion as a grave obligation flows clearly from the fact of our absolute dependence on God and from His absolute dominion over us, both in the order of nature and of grace. After the three theological virtues, it becomes our first, most important obligation in the realm of moral virtues.

Furthermore, the virtue of religion with all its acts is positively enjoined by the first three commandments of God (Is. 20:2–11; Deut. 5:6–15; Matt. 4: 10). In addition, ecclesiastical legislation has further determined the public exercise of this virtue (Cans. 729–910; 937–1109; 1133–1249; 1255–1321). A wide range for its free exercise is given to various forms of private devotions (*see* Devotions).

Vices Contrary to the Virtue of Religion. Man can fail in the virtue of religion by excess, i.e., by rendering reli-

gious honors in a manner that is not fitting or by directing them to persons to whom they are not due; or by defect, i.e., by positively dishonoring God. Scholastics label the first form *superstition* in the generic sense of the word. This may consist of undue worship or idolatry (*q.v.*), divination (*q.v.*), superstitious practices (*q.v.*), particularly magic (*q.v.*). The second type may include irreligion (*q.v.*) with its various aspects, such as tempting God, blasphemy, perjury, sacrilege, simony, which are treated individually in this volume. *Pal.*

RELIGION, FALSE. Judged entirely as a system of teaching and cult, every non-Christian religion is a false one, since it is not the religion which God revealed and which He wishes to be followed. Furthermore, every Christian sect which is not Catholic is also false, since it does not accept and practice the whole content of Revelation. On the other hand, considered in its single elements, every non-Christian religion and every non-Catholic sect may contain truth mingled with error.

From the moral standpoint the question of the objective truth or falsity of a religion in its component elements is connected with the responsibility involved in adherence by an individual to a false religion and the practice of its rites.

One who practices a false religion in good faith is evidently free from the sin of one who practices it in bad faith. From this it does not follow that a false religion practiced in good faith will bring to a person the spiritual effects brought by the true religion. Nevertheless, if the follower of a false religion practices rites which do not express falsehood and are not immoral, one need not deny that he can obtain some spiritual good from it.

The question "Who is in good faith?" is still more subtle and delicate. The answer is bound up with the conscience of each single individual. It is reasonable to suppose that a person living in surroundings where the true faith is unknown is in good faith. It is generally regarded as impossible for a Catholic to deny his religion and embrace another in good faith. *Gra.*

RELIGION, FREEDOM OF. *See* Freedom of thought, of conscience, of religion.

RELIGIOUS. The word *religious* is a generic term signifying one who takes vows in a religious community (*see* Religion). In its evolution, the word has had various meanings: (a) a rule, discipline or definite way of life practiced by certain of the faithful in their activities; (b) a condition of those who assimilate their own life to a way of life different and distinct from the condition of seculars and the ordinary faithful; (c) a community or association of adherents of the faith constituting one moral entity and subject of law.

Ordinarily we call *religious* those Christians, the faithful of both sexes, consecrated to God in an Order approved by the Church and professing the three evangelical vows. In Canon Law a religious is one who freely undertakes, over and above the commandments common to all the faithful, the observation of the evangelical counsels through the vows of poverty, chastity, and obedience (Can. 487). Specifically, the Code of Canon Law terms *regular*, one who professes vows in an *Order*; *religious*, one who professes simple vows in a *Congregation*; *nun*, a woman dedicated by solemn vows; *sister*, a member of a *Congregation*.

NATURAL AND JURIDICAL REQUISITES. For the proper notion of the word *religious* there are five essentials: one in natural divine law and four required by the Church. Every Christian is of course bound to make the effort to be perfect (Matt. 5:48); however, not all are bound to strive for perfection in the same way, but each according to the virtues characteristic of his own condition. If religious are bound to tend towards perfection by the exact observance of the three evangelical counsels, there is required in them a special, divine vocation (Matt. 19:11). This special vocation we call an essential by natural, divine law,

as the true foundation for becoming a religious and assuming the particular obligations of a state of perfection different from that common to the rest of the faithful.

There are four signs of a true vocation to the religious life: two external and two internal. The internal are: (a) a steady inclination in the natural order, and still more in the supernatural, to the religious state; (b) a right intention, which is to say that the religious life should be embraced, not for temporal, but supernatural benefits. The good sought in the religious life must be a greater certainty of eternal salvation, zeal for bringing about the welfare of neighbor by the apostolate, etc.

The external signs of a religious vocation are: (a) the absence of canonical impediments; (b) physical and moral suitability for the obligations of the religious life (Can. 538). Physical weakness, poor intelligence, wavering will, insincerity, etc., are all negative signs that show that one is not called to the religious life. Since the religious vocation is an invitation and not a command, no one is obliged to follow it. A counsel (religious vow) remains a counsel. The *appropriateness*, however, of following a clearly recognized vocation must be kept in mind, lest one be deprived of many efficacious graces, without which perhaps one might commit many grave sins and place one's eternal salvation in danger.

The four requisites demanded by the Church for a religious are: (a) a stable form of life—that is, a way of life in which one steadily perseveres; (b) life in common, if not absolutely required by the essence of religious life, is nevertheless prescribed by the Church for a valid recognition of religious life (Can. 487); (c) the observance of the evangelical counsels by the vows of poverty, chastity and obedience; (d) the approval of the Church. Only the Church has the competence and right to judge whether a form of life is or is not in conformity with evangelical perfection.

Hence, the essence of the religious state consists in the fact that religious bind themselves to strive according to their vocation in a community towards a more elevated grade of perfection than is necessary for all by means of the observation of the three evangelical counsels and an established rule. Thus, we can say that, from the point of view of the vows, all religious are equal and are distinguished only by the various rules and particular constitutions.

ADMISSION AND NOVITIATE. One becomes a member of a religious community by pronouncing vows, which must be preceded by a preparatory stage called postulancy (q.v.). In the case of orders or congregations with perpetual vows, it is necessary for women and lay brothers to pass a period of at least six months as postulants (Cans. 539–541); in other congregations the stage of postulancy (q.v.) can exist for various durations according to the respective constitutions. The postulancy is a period of trial, in which the candidates explore their conscience, study the arrangements of the religious community, and give proof of their constancy.

In all religious communities the period of novitiate (q.v.) is necessary as a sequel to the postulancy. This is carried out in a novitiate under the exclusive direction of a master of novices. Novices have no communication with the professed religious. The novitiate is invalid unless carried out for a year without interruption and after the novice has completed his fifteenth year. At the end of the novitiate, if the superior considers the aspirant suitable for the religious life, he admits him to the temporary vows, which ordinarily are for three years, but can be extended for a second period of three years. At the close of the temporary vows the religious, provided he has completed his twenty-first year, can take the perpetual or solemn vows (Cans. 542–575).

Those cannot be validly accepted as religious: (a) who belonged to a non-Catholic sect (Can. 542); (b) who have not reached the required age of fifteen years (Can. 555); (c) who enter the religious life under grave fear or deception (Cans. 103–104); (d) who are married and the marriage bond still

exists (Can. 542); (e) who were professed in another religious community; (f) who are condemned for a grave crime or can be accused of one; (g) who have had the bishopric conferred on them or have been simply named to it (Can. 542); (h) who, as clerics, are bound by oath to the service of a diocese or mission, as long as their oath continues to bind.

Only in communities of women in which solemn vows are taken does Canon Law prescribe the *dowry* (Can. 547), that is, a determined sum of money that the postulant must bring in entering the convent, and which she must leave to the convent and religious community as a contribution to her maintenance during her natural life in the religious community. In congregations of sisters with simple vows the dowry is necessary only in the measure prescribed by the particular constitutions (Can. 547, par. 3).

OBLIGATIONS. Religious are held to all the general obligations of clerics (Cans. 124–142) insofar as nothing explicitly or implicitly incompatible is concerned (Can. 592). Religious are obliged to lead an exemplary life and to participate actively in acts of worship, penance, and piety. They have *voluntarily* undertaken the duty of using specific means which are only of counsel in order to attain a special perfection. Hence they are no longer free in the choice of the means by which to arrive at perfection, but are obliged to tend towards it by maintaining the vows and observing the practices of piety and the exercises of virtue prescribed by the rules of their own institute (Can. 593). The Church prescribes the means most suited to religious perfection: life in community (Can. 594); money and goods in a common stock (Can. 594, par. 2); annual spiritual exercises; daily assistance at mass; weekly reception of the sacrament of penance and frequent Holy Communion (Can. 595); wearing of the religious habit inside and outside the religious house (Can. 596).

Special dispositions are established for the observance of the vow of poverty

(Can. 594, par. 2) by holding goods in common; of chastity by the cloister (Can. 597–607). In conformity with the rules and constitutions, religious owe special obedience to their superiors (Can. 499). By virtue of the specific duty of their state, all religious are bound to tend constantly toward perfection. A religious would sin gravely against this obligation if he had contempt for or were positively negligent in the attainment of perfection.

PRIVILEGES. All religious enjoy the ecclesiastical privileges spoken of in Canons 119 to 123 and Canon 614: (a) the privilege of personal immunity; (b) that of immunity from the civil forum; (c) that of retaining what is needed for a maintenance suitable to their proper state; (d) immunity from military service. These privileges of state may not be renounced by the religious; on the contrary, he is bound to lay claim to them and to put them in practice, if it is permitted by the civil legislations of the various civil states.

As for special favors, indulgences, and privileges directly granted by the Holy See to each religious order, these privileges are enjoyed by: (a) all the professed of temporary or perpetual, solemn or simple vows; (b) by novices and lay brothers (Can. 614). The exclaustrated enjoy only those that are purely spiritual (Can. 639); the secularized and those dismissed from the order or congregation lose every privilege of their religious community (Cans. 640, 2385); religious of both sexes, without vows but living in community, enjoy the said privileges but not those peculiar to religious strictly so called, unless they have obtained a special right to them (Can. 580).

A special privilege reserved to regulars is that of exemption (*q.v.*) from the jurisdiction of the local Ordinary. In general, the privilege of exemption is extended: (a) to rules and constitutions already approved by the Holy See (Can. 618, par. 2, n. 1); (b) to internal regime and discipline, except in the cases expressly named in the Code (nevertheless, the Ordinary can and should see that discipline is observed in lay reli-

gious communities according to the constitutions, Can. 618, par. 2, n. 2); (c) to the administration of a religious community. Hence the local Ordinary cannot demand an account or inspection of the respective administration registers (Can. 618, par. 2, n. 1) except in cases contemplated by the Code (cf. Can. 533, par. 1, n. 1, and Can. 549). The privilege of exemption ends for religious illegally outside the religious house (Can. 616), or for a small house (*domus non-formata*, Can. 617).

By a general indult, legitimately granted by the bishop, the obligation of a general law (*e.g.*, that of fasting) terminates for all the religious living in the diocese, except for the vows and constitutions peculiar to each community (Can. 620).

DISMISSAL. The religious ceases to be part of the religious community: (a) by passing into other religious communities, which can be done only by virtue of a pontifical indult (Can. 632–636); (b) by leaving the religious community, with a pontifical indult; (c) by dismissal (*see* Dismissal).

In the case of temporary vows, at the termination of the vows, the religious is free not to renew them. The religious community can for just reasons not grant to the religious a renewal of perpetual or solemn vows (Can. 637).

The Holy See can always grant to a religious the indult of exclaustration (*q.v.*), that is, permission to live for a specified time outside the convent. This indult does not separate the religious from his community. He remains bound to the observance of the duties imposed by his vows. He may not, however, wear the religious habit; he is deprived of active and passive voice in elections; he becomes subject to the bishop of the diocese in which he resides (Can. 639). The Holy See can also grant the indult of secularization (*q.v.*), which permanently separates the religious from his community and puts an end to all the rights and duties derived from the profession (Can. 640).

Discharge or dismissal takes place *ipso facto* for all religious who are guilty of these three things: (a) public apostasy from the Catholic faith; (b) flight with a person of the opposite sex; (c) attempt to contract marriage, ecclesiastical or civil. In these cases the major superior, with his chapter or council, needs only to pronounce a declaration of the fact (Can. 647). If, however, it is a question of male members of a community who have taken perpetual or solemn vows, their dismissal can take place only after three grave offenses against the common law of the Church or against the particular obligations of the community, and after they have received two admonitions and incorrigibility has been ascertained. If it is a question of women religious, grave exterior causes are sufficient, that is, such as are known within the community, if at the same time the subject is found incorrigible (Cans. 649–668).

The religious who has been dismissed ceases to belong to the community if he has made only temporary vows. But if he has made solemn or perpetual vows, despite the loss of all rights in the community, including that of wearing the religious habit, he remains bound by his vows, except in special cases involving an indult from the Holy See (Cans. 669–672). *Tar.*

RELIGIOUS ORDER (Congregation). In Canon Law a religious order (congregation) is a society approved by the Church, the members of which strive for evangelical perfection by the public vows of poverty, chastity, and obedience, according to the laws proper to their society (Canon 488).

The pursuit for evangelical perfection by living a more perfect life than ordinary Christians, began spontaneously among the faithful, moved as they were by the words and example of Jesus. Jesus Christ lived as a poor man (Matt. 8:20; Luke 9:58); He practiced perfect chastity; He was obedient to His Father (John 4:34; 8:29) and He invited others to follow Him on the same path (Matt. 19:16). It was only natural that many, from the very beginning, should accept His invitation. Among them were many ascetics and holy virgins, of whom the

Fathers speak, men and women who practiced the virtue of chastity for the purpose of close union with God (Tertullian, *De Virginibus velandis:* PL 2, 957). These persons lived in cities, close to churches or episcopal residences. With the start of persecutions, however, and from a desire for greater solitude, many of the faithful, between the third and fifth century, withdrew to caves, deserts, or mountains. Thus arose the hermits, such as St. Paul, St. Anthony, etc. The Church, of course, could not fail to take an interest in such a movement of perfection among her children. So it was that she soon intervened and, by her legislation, gave the movement juridical recognition. It is due to the hermits and monks that juridical elements are clearly required of associations in order that their members may be considered religious in the ecclesiastical sense of the law. The *Decretals* (1234) contained ecclesiastical legislation which considered as a religious institute only those societies in which solemn vows were professed.

Solemn vows deprive the professed religious of the capacity to possess goods and render any attempted marriage null and void. The professed religious remains irrevocably bound to the religious institute (*see* Vows, Religious). The obligation to choir, papal cloister, and papal exemption are necessary aspects of every religious institute.

Historical circumstances severed this juridical structure by depriving those faithful, who lived the common life praised by the Church, of the title to be called *religious*. These faithful took simple vows, in which they retained the capacity to possess goods but were forbidden the exercise, use, and free administration of these goods; attempted marriage, furthermore, for these religious was not invalid, although a serious sin. These members also were not irrevocably bound to the religious society, which had the right to dismiss them. They had no obligation to choir, papal cloister, and were dependent on the local Ordinary, except for matters pertaining to internal government of the society. The first societies that were called religious institutes, though they did not have the structure required by the *Decretals*, were the Clerics Regular, Jesuits, Barnabites, Theatines, etc.

The juridical principle which widened the concept of religious institutes and religious societies was formulated in 1583 and 1584 by the Bulls of Pope Gregory XIII, *Quam Fructuosus* and *Ascendente Domino*, in which scholastics of the Society of Jesus were termed true religious, despite the fact that they did not profess solemn vows.

The practical application of this new juridical principle was hampered by the prescriptions of the Bulls of Pius V *Lubricum Vitae Genus* (1568) and *Circa Pastoralis*, which were directed against the rise of non-traditional forms of religious institutes. Notwithstanding this opposition, new associations of men, called congregations, prospered, first with the approval of local Ordinaries and later of the Holy See.

The approval of congregations of women with simple vows was more strenuously opposed; only in the nineteenth century are clear signs of papal approval found. The main issue involved a clear definition of the authority of a superior-general; a nun travelling from diocese to diocese to visit various houses of the institute seemed a very novel notion. In the constitution *Quamvis Iusto* (1749), issued on the occasion of the foundation of the English Madames of Mary Ward, Benedict XIV paved the way for pontifical approval. In the following century, because of the insistent requests on the part of bishops and in view of the excellent fruits of the labors of the new congregations, the Holy See finally granted the title of true *religious* institutes to these congregations.

For the purpose of protecting and controlling congregations located in various dioceses and to limit the authority of the local Ordinaries over such groups, the Holy See enacted a fundamental distinction between pontifical institutes with the approbation of the Holy See and diocesan institutes with merely the approbation of the local Ordinary. Be-

sides orders and congregations, religious institutes in the canonical sense, other forms of societies developed, which eventually were granted juridical recognition. These were called secular institutes; they lived a common life but without vows. These were approved by Pope Pius XII in 1947 by the Constitution *Provida Mater Ecclesia* (*see* Secular Institutes).

Religious societies are variously classified: (a) *Orders* are institutes in which solemn vows are professed; *congregations* are institutes with simple vows. (b) Clerical institutes have a majority and ruling body represented by clerics; lay religious institutes have a majority of non-clerics. (c) Exempt religious institutes have been withdrawn from the jurisdiction of the local Ordinaries; non-exempt are dependent on the jurisdiction of the local Ordinaries. (d) Diocesan institutes are approved by the local Ordinary; pontifical institutes are approved by the Holy See. (e) Mendicant institutes are founded with the purpose of not possessing goods as such in their own name, or have received this title by privilege; non-mendicant institutes can possess goods as a legal, moral person. (f) Institutes may have a centralized form of government or a local government. (g) Contemplative institutes have a main dedication to prayer and divine worship; active institutes are primarily dedicated to external, apostolic works and works of charity; mixed institutes combine an external, active apostolate with the contemplative life of prayer.

Local Ordinaries have the power to erect new institutes; however, previous permission of the Holy See must be obtained with respect to requirements concerning the founder, constitutions, purpose, economic means, members, and the like (Can. 492). The suppression of a religious institute is reserved exclusively to the Holy See (Can. 493).

A diocesan institute that has spread to many dioceses may ask the Holy Father for pontifical approbation, if it enjoys moral, religious, and economic stability. This approbation is granted in stages: first, a temporary approbation of the constitutions of the institute; next, a decree of praise; last of all, a final and a definite approval. *Mand.*

RELIGIOUS, SACRED CONGREGATION OF. *See* Congregations, Roman.

RELIQUARIES. *See* Relics; Vessels, sacred.

REMEDIES, PENAL. One of the main consequences of an evil act is the disturbance of order in society (Can. 2210, par. 1, n. 1); this evil offends all of society by violating its laws; it causes scandal, diminishes general security, and incites to evil. The Church stated as much in the days of the Roman law, when crimes were classified as public and private (Paulus, *Sent.* V, 1, 6). Consequently, the primary purpose of punishment is the re-establishment of order in society, disturbed by the commission of an offense. Although punishment is the final, unavoidable means which the authority can use against the author of a crime, this should be considered in its potential aspect with respect to elements of danger.

When we speak of danger we state a concept outside the field of penal law, for one cannot speak of crime except if there is a violation of the penal law. Neither can one speak of punishment except with respect to the author of a crime. Nevertheless, civil authority, whose duty it is to maintain public order, not only has the duty to restore public order after it has been violated, but also has the responsibility of preventing crime by taking care of those conditions which, if not checked, will probably lead a delinquent to the commission of crime. All laws, insofar as they serve the general social order and the common good, must be considered remote means of prevention; penal laws, in particular, have a specific preventive purpose implied in the threat of punishment for violations. For certain individuals, remote preventive means are ineffective because these individuals find themselves in a situation of immediate danger of committing an offense or of engaging in a damaging form of behavior even though no actual offense will be committed. Hence, the need of means or remedies directed to preventing this danger. In Canon Law these remedies, called *penal remedies* (*remedia poenalia*), are: *admonition, rebuke, precept,* and *surveillance* (Can. 2306).

Admonition (*q.v.*) is a warning given by the Ordinary to one who is in a proximate occasion of committing an offense or who is suspected of having committed an offense. The warning includes the determination of what is to be done or to be avoided (Can. 2307, 2310). *Rebuke* is an injunction by the Ordinary on one who by his behavior is causing scandal (Can. 2308). Both admonition and rebuke may be administered privately or publicly (Can. 2309). *Precept* is a more serious preventive measure because it enjoins a norm of behavior with the threat of punishment for nonobservance (Can. 2310). *Surveillance* is a more serious remedy, applied particularly if a person is in danger of relapsing into the same offense and for the purpose of increasing the penalty (Can. 2311).

From the aforesaid it is clear that penal remedies *are not forms of punishment.* Punishment is a reaction to a criminal act; a penal remedy concerns a situation of danger or suspicion. A penalty can only be directed against elements which constitute a crime; penal remedy, instead, is applicable even if the danger does not lead to an offense (cf. Can. 2308). Penalty restores a disturbed social order; a penal remedy is based on the need to protect society. Penalty is a repressive measure inflicted by the judge; a penal remedy is a preventive measure, by its very nature administrative, although it can also be administered by a court (Cans. 1947–1953). Since this danger may manifest itself in a criminal or non-criminal, penal remedies may be of two kinds: attempts to combat danger before a crime (Can. 2307) or suitable to a condition of danger after a crime (Can. 2311).

Much importance is given in the Code of Canon Law to penal remedies. It may suffice to consider, on the one hand, the large number of superiors and authorities in the external forum who have the obligation to see to it that the law is duly observed, as well as the importance of the precept as a legal measure against crime (Can. 2195, par. 2).

To conclude, it may be said that penal remedies in Canon Law correspond to preventive measures in modern codes of law which are called administrative security measures. *Vio.*

REMORSE. Remorse is anguish of conscience for an evil committed.

Conscience, intended as an application of the ethical norm to a particular case, is distinguished by the theologians into *antecedent, concomitant,* and *consequent* conscience. *Antecedent* conscience judges the moral value of the act before it is performed: *concomitant* conscience accompanies an act with its judgment.

This triple stage, in which the activities of conscience are centered, as a rule acquires its tone from the first practical moral judgment which precedes an act. The act must be judged—during and after its accomplishment—in conformity with the judgment formulated before acting. In fact, only this has a normative value, whereas the judgment of an act already completed can only have the value of testimony or of verdict.

Remorse is an aspect of consequent conscience. The verdict of condemnation of a wrong deed in a conscience that is not completely inured to evil, is followed by a motion of repentance which we call remorse. Since the conscience is not a constitutive norm of the order in society but a manifestation of it, it is not absolute and autonomous, but subordinate and relative, essentially dependent on the supreme and absolute norm (the eternal law of God); hence it is the voice of God, *praeco Dei.* Thus, remorse is, in a way, a rebuke that God directs to the sinner and an illuminating grace whose absence is, in itself, a terrible punishment for so-called obdurate consciences.

This rebuke on the part of God through remorse is both tragic and merciful, as it reflects two attributes of God:

justice and mercy. These tragic and merciful aspects of remorse are vividly illustrated in certain episodes of the Bible: in the story of Cain after he killed Abel (Gen. 4:3–16), or in the narration of the betrayal of Judas (Matt. 27: 3–10), in the parable of the prodigal son (Luke 15:11–32).

It is interesting to note the different reactions and the course which remorse takes in the consciences of those who are moved by it. For some, remorse is the first step in the process of repentance leading to conversion (*q.v.*); for others it is a cause of despair often leading to suicide as the only escape from that voice of conscience. These are the two directions that man may follow in the agitated expectancy, before this first grace of illumination granted to the sinner by the merciful bounty of God.

Sin is an act of rebellion against God; it is pride for a sinner to refuse to recognize his sin. Remorse invites him to do so and to repent.

Remorse that is not accompanied by humility fixes the mind of the sinner on sin. But for the humble who accepts his responsibility, remorse is the first step to contrition.

Materialistic psychoanalysis is obviously incapable of understanding this feeling of guilt; if it encounters guilt in clinical work, it considers it as an obstacle to the emotional equilibrium and social adjustment of the patient. We may grant that such may be the case with neurotic individuals, and that sometimes it takes on obsessive forms. For normal people the explanation of this psychological mystery is simply our necessary dependence on God by nature and grace and the need we have of Him. If sin deprives us of or dims our vision of Him, the soul feels its equilibrium shaken by reason of the preference given to a false good, a creature, instead of true good, God.

If sin consists in a degradation of an irrational creature torn away from its axis and subjected to vanity, St. Paul speaks of a kind of cosmic remorse; the whole of creation "groaneth" and anxiously longs "for the adoption of the sons of God," so that it, too, might participate in "the liberty of the glory of the children of God" (Rom. 8:22). *Pal.*

REMOVAL. In Canon Law *removal* (*remotio, amotio*) in a strict sense means dismissal from ecclesiastical office for reasons other than crime; in other words, removal is non-penal or administrative (Can. 2147). Penal removal, instead, is ordinarily called deprivation of office (*privatio* or *privatio poenalis*); this is a vindicative penalty (Can. 2298, n. 6). The Code of Canon Law distinguishes between privation and removal, as in Canons 183, 195, 2401. However, in other Canons the Code includes under the word *privatio* non-penal actions of administrative removal in Canons 192, 193, 1923.

This distinction between administrative removal (non-penal) and deprivation (penal) is of practical interest in the application of a penalty. Whereas penal deprivation may be applied to offices whose incumbents are removable or irremovable, an administrative removal may be applied only to offices that are removable (Cans. 192, 2299; *see also* Irremovability, Benefice). An exception to this rule is an administrative removal from pastoral office according to special rules to be explained.

PROCEDURE. (1) Any reasonable motive, according to the prudent judgment of the Ordinary, is sufficient for administrative removal, even if the incumbent has committed no offense. (2) No particular procedural details are set up by the Code; everything is left to the judgment of the superior, who is carrying out the removal process, but one point is firmly upheld: natural and canonical equity must always be observed. The sole competent individual to effect removal is the legitimate ecclesiastical superior over that particular office; the chapter which elected, postulated, or presented the incumbent to an office cannot remove the elected person (Can. 195). (3) A removal is only effected by a legitimate ecclesiastical superior. (4) The office-holder, who has been re-

moved, can appeal to the Holy See against the decree of the Ordinary.

REMOVAL FROM PASTORAL OFFICE. The administrative removal from pastoral office differs from the general rule of Canon 192, concerning administrative removal from ecclesiastical office, on two points: (1) administrative removal may be applied to irremovable pastoral offices, despite the general rule prohibiting its application to irremovable offices; (2) a particular procedure is prescribed for removal from a pastoral office, even in the case of an irremovable pastor, although such a procedure is usually not prescribed for removal in general. This procedure for removal from an irremovable pastoral office is to be applied to secular priests, since the removal of an incumbent belonging to a religious order requires no special procedure. Such parish priests belonging to religious orders may be removed by the Ordinary or the competent religious superior, provided that there exists a legitimate reason (Can. 454, par. 5). The procedure for administrative removal of parish priests belonging to the secular clergy is governed by Canons 2147–61 of the Code of Canon Law. The causes for which they may be removed are the same for removable or irremovable incumbents; that is, causes rendering their ministry ineffectual or harmful, even without fault on the part of the priest. Among these causes are: infirmity, ineptitude, dislike by parishioners, loss of good name, etc. (Can. 2147). The procedure employed in the removal of an irremovable pastor differs from that of a removable pastor. The juridical status of the irremovable incumbent to a parish office is more stable than that of the removable incumbent.

Canon Law also recognizes removal from the exercise of legal ecclesiastical acts (*ab actibus ecclesiasticis, legitimis exercendis*) as a vindicative penalty (Can. 2291, n. 8). This involves exclusion from specific offices or specific rights. These are enumerated in Canon 2256, n. 2; they are the offices of judge, defender of the bond, promoter of justice, notary or promoter of the faith. *Led.*

REMOVAL, OFFICIAL. The Code of Canon Law speaks of removability regarding ecclesiastical *offices* and *benefices*. It distinguishes between removable and irremovable offices or benefices (Cans. 192, par. 2–3; 1411, n. 4). They are also called temporary and permanent (*temporaria* et *perpetua*). The difference between these two categories consists in the greater or lesser stability of the persons enjoying title to such benefices or offices. From a juridical point of view, the titulars of removable offices and benefices may be separated from their office or benefice by competent ecclesiastical authority more easily than the holders of irremovable offices and benefices. The difference between removability and irremovability is brought out by the Code in dealing with the concept of privation of office and the manner of deprivation. The local ordinary may not deprive an ecclesiastic of an irremovable office, except by a process conducted according to the norms of Canon Law (Can. 192, par. 2). On the contrary, a true and proper process is not required for deprivation (*privatio*) of a removable office, but such deprivation may be decreed by the Ordinary for any reasonable motive, according to his prudent judgment (*prudenti ejus arbitrio*), even though the cleric may have committed no offense. The deprivation of a removable pastorate is an exception; particular norms apply to such a case, as will be indicated later. But in other cases of privation of office the Ordinary is bound to observe natural equity; anyone who has been deprived of an office may have recourse against the decree of the Ordinary to the Apostolic See, i.e., to a competent court of the Roman Curia. The recourse is granted *in devolutivo* only, i.e., pending the appeal, the decree of the Ordinary stands (Can. 192, par. 3). In the case of certain offices, as a vicar general, vicar forane, officialis, vice-officialis, removability is left to the will of the Bishop (Cans. 366, par. 2; 446, par. 2; 1573, par. 5).

In benefices, the difference between removability and irremovability is indicated by the Code in dealing with the manner of conferring such benefices. The benefice is said to be removable or irremovable, insofar as it has been conferred revocably or permanently (Can. 1411, n. 4). In effect, the difference is the same as for offices. The punitive deprivation of an irremovable benefice may be enforced only in the cases expressly stated by the law, while the privation of a removable benefice may be decreed also for other reasonable causes (Can. 2299, par. 1).

REMOVABILITY AND IRREMOVABILITY OF PARISHES AND PASTORS. The concept of removability and irremovability have a particular application with respect to pastors. According to Canon 454, those who administer a parish should enjoy stability *per se*: that is, they should govern the parish permanently. On the other hand, the same Canon provides that all pastors may be removed for specific reasons from office. Hence, the stability of pastors in their office is relative, not absolute. The difference in stability in office may be due to the status of the parish: whether it too is considered an irremovable or movable parish. This particular concerns secular priests. Religious priests who are pastors (*parochi ad religiosam familiam pertinentes*), due to their particular position of submission to their religious superiors and rule, are to a greater degree movable at will; and this is independent of the fact that they may be administering a parish which is either movable or irremovable (Can. 454, par. 2 and 5).

The movability or irremovability of a parish depends upon the manner in which it was founded. According to the spirit of the Code, parishes, as a rule, ought to be irremovable, i.e., removable only by way of exception. This is so at least for ordinary parishes; quasi-parishes are all movable. Parishes that were founded as irremovable cannot be made movable without the consent of the Holy See. Movable parishes, on the other hand, can be declared irremovable by the local Ordinary (not, however, by the vicar general or vicar-capitular), after consultation with the cathedral chapter (Can. 454, par. 3–4) or diocesan consultors.

The difference between removable and irremovable pastors is also brought out by the manner of removal from office. Concerning removable pastors, a distinction is to be made between religious and secular pastors.

As already noted, religious pastors are always movable at will (*ad nutum*). No special procedure is necessary for their removal from office; they may be removed through a simple administrative process, either by the local Ordinary or by the competent religious superior. Neither needs the consent of the other, and neither is bound to manifest the reasons for the removal, but each is obliged to notify the other of the recall. But, although no special procedure is prescribed for the removal of a religious pastor, nevertheless a legitimate reason is required. In case of disagreement over the removal, recourse to the Holy See is permitted but *in devolutivo* (Can. 454, par. 5).

For the removal of a secular pastor, whether movable or irremovable, a special procedure is prescribed. The method, however, differs, according to a movable or irremovable pastor. This difference of procedure is indicated in various canons. Canon 2299, par. 1, treats in a general way of the deprivation of a benefice as a penalty (*in poenam*), which applies to pastors. Canons 2173 and 2174 treat of the deprivation of a parish for infraction of the law of residence. Canon 2180 deals with punishments for an infraction of the law of celibacy. Canon 2184 deals with proceedings for infraction of the general duties of a pastor. Canons 2147 ff. and 2157 ff., deal with the removal of a pastor for reasons which render his further administration harmful and useless, even though by no fault of his own. In all these cases the juridical position of an irremovable pastor is seen to be more stable than that of a removable one. The same is true in the transfer of a pastor, not as a penalty but for the good of souls (*ob bonum animarum*),

even though he may be administering his parish well. The bishop may propose a transfer to an irremovable pastor, but he cannot transfer him against his will, unless special faculties from the Holy See have been obtained (Can. 2163, par. 1). A removable pastor, however, may be transferred even against his will, provided that the new parish is at least equally important and the norms prescribed by the Code are duly observed (Can. 2163, par. 2). *Led.*

REMOVAL OF UTERUS. *See* Obstetrics, Sterilization.

REMUNERATION. *See* Work, Honorarium, Wage.

RENT. *See* Lease.

REPARATION. *See* Injury, Damage.

REPARATION FOR SCANDAL. *See* Scandal.

REPRISAL. A reprisal is a coercive act by an individual or nation against another individual or nation because of a violation of a legitimate right. The aim of a reprisal is to exact reparation for material damage suffered, to punish a wrongdoer, or to remove an actual violation. All three aims may be present simultaneously.

A public reprisal is exercised by one country against another country; a private reprisal is by one individual against another of the same or different country. Reprisals may occur either in peacetime or in time of war.

Reprisal differs from *retortion*. In retortion one places the same act as placed by another individual or country; reprisal presupposes the violation of a right but retortion presupposes a fact which causes damage but is not a violation of rights.

According to some jurists, reprisal originates from the German *faihida* or private vengeance perpetrated between individuals of the same country. The matter of reprisal was first left to private initiative but then, to eliminate grave abuses, the practice was gradually controlled through appropriate statutes enacted by various municipalities. A so-called Magistrate of Reprisals was created for this purpose. In the sixteenth century reprisals almost entirely disappeared because the authority of the State had grown increasingly stronger; the State eventually abrogated to itself the prerogative of defending the injured rights of its citizens.

Reprisals also involved citizens of different countries. An offense perpetrated by a citizen of one country against a citizen of another country would give rise to a reprisal, not only against the foreign offender personally, but against any other citizen of that country. This form of reprisal gradually disappeared, so that eventually the governments themselves began to intervene in the defense of their own citizens by demands for satisfaction suited to the wrong suffered. Consequently, reprisal became a juridical institution which concerned the State alone.

MORALITY. A government may licitly take reprisal for the violation and satisfaction of the violation of a right, (a) if a real right was violated; (b) if the reprisal is exercised, not by private citizens on their own initiative and authority, but by the government itself through individuals authorized by the government; (c) if it is exerted against a guilty government and not against innocent private individuals.

The liceity of reprisal, directly taken against the subjects of a guilty state, is based on the principle of solidarity and co-responsibility between a state and its subjects, especially if reparation cannot be obtained directly from the offending state.

Reprisal must never be contrary to the principles of humanity and morality. For instance, no country may, even in time of war, put prisoners to death or allow its soldiers to commit immoral acts against the subjects of another belligerent nation or in an enemy occupied territory, as a form of reprisal. See War.

REPRODUCTION. Reproduction includes those processes of great complexity by which living beings conserve their species by producing other individuals similar to themselves. At times the terms *generation* and *procreation* are used.

These processes consist physiologically of portions of nucleated plasma (the offspring), separating from an adult organism (the parent); they bear different names, according to the manner in which the offspring are formed.

In simpler organisms, as protozoa, filiation takes place by the separation of any of its parts from the body of the parent. This form of reproduction is called *agamic*, *asexual*, or *monogenetic*; it is subdivided, in turn, into *scission* or *hemitomy*, a characteristic of amoeba and annelidas, where it takes place by the division of the parent into two halves; *gemmation*, by sponges and coelenterates, where one or more small fragments or gemma separate and become new beings by undergoing a transformation, as the parent continues life with its individuality; *sporulation* or *conidiatomy* by sporozoans which takes place by the fragmentation of the mother cell into many small daughter cells or spores.

In the metazoa, *gamic*, *sexual* or *amphigonous* reproduction prevails; it is characterized by the formation of a new being from special germinal cells or *gametes*, highly differentiated, which are called *ova* and *spermatozoa*. One single germinal cell cannot create a new organism, except in exceptional cases (*parthenogenesis*); in all other cases the participation is required of another germinal cell which at times comes from the same organism, called *monoecious* or *hermaphroditic*, but usually from another organism with different morphological characteristics. In the latter case, the organism that produces the sperm is the male and the one that produces the ovum is the female. Germ cells are produced by special organs called *gonads* (*q.v.*), i.e., spermaries or testicles in the male, ovaries in the female.

FERTILIZATION. The union of the two gametes (the female ovum and the male sperm) gives rise to a *fertilization* process which can take place outside, as in a water environment with fishes, or inside the female's body; in the latter case, the male and the female possess special organs capable of insuring the union of the two gametes and the protection and nourishment of the fertilized egg. In mammals the protective receptacle is called *uterus*; here, the embryo, in order to nourish itself and grow, establishes a very close relationship with the maternal organism through a complex organ, mostly vascular, called *placenta*.

Those animals that lay their eggs outside their bodies (even if fertilization occurs internally, as in the case of birds) are called *ovipara*; their eggs are provided with a special protective cover. In other animals, called *vivipara*, the development of the fertilized egg takes place in the mother's body from which, at birth, a developed embryo is born, as in mammals.

The laying of the eggs by oviparous animals, and the birth of already developed young in viviparous animals involves particular instincts and biological adjustments, a so-called parental care, capable of providing the best conditions for the development and growth of the young. These adjustments are even found in vertebrates, both the species in which the young at birth are already capable of obtaining their own nourishment, and those with inept young, where parental care involves a true rearing of the offspring which lasts until they are capable of leading an independent life.

FREQUENCY OF THE REPRODUCTIVE PHENOMENA. When an organism has reached sexual maturity, reproduction generally assumes a periodic character, whereby phases of inertness of the gonads alternate with phases of great functional activity (the reproductive season). This alternating is attributed principally to seasonal variations of environment, which has as its purpose providing more favorable conditions for the development of the offspring. During the reproductive season, in one or both sexes of many animals, there occur marked morphological, metabolic, and other changes.

MORAL NOTES. It is a well-known fact that in higher vertebrates and in man, nature has provided a particular pleasure to be associated with the union of the two sexes. This is a compensatory factor, for gestation, birth, and the raising of offspring are sources of suffering and concern, which parents would be inclined to avoid without this incentive. Therefore, the practices suggested by the advocates of artificial birth control (*q.v.*) which seek to avoid a fruitful union violate the moral law, because the physical pleasure connected with the use of the marital right is a means and not an end; hence, it is contrary to the law of nature to seek this pleasure but exclude the principal purpose of the union of the sexes.

For other moral considerations concerning reproduction, *see* Impotency; Marriage; Perversion, sexual. *Riz.*

REPUTATION (Good). Reputation is a general esteem of a person's excellence. It is a good of great *moral* value and, of course, important also to the goods and advantages of the *material* order. Every man has a right to protect his general esteem or reputation even if his behavior does not really conform to it. A person who enjoys a good reputation has also the duty to protect it, first as a personal good, then as a good belonging to others, his children, relatives, colleagues, and so forth. To damage or destroy the reputation of one's neighbor is a sin of defamation. Defamation consists of two distinct sins, calumny and detraction; both violate the virtue of justice (*see* Defamation).

RESCRIPT. A rescript is a written reply by the Holy See or Ordinary to a request made or an interrogation directed to it. The reply, if given to settle a dispute, is termed a rescript of justice (*rescriptum justitiae*); if the reply implies granting a favor, it is termed a rescript of favor (*rescriptum gratiae*). The rescript of favor is not to be confused with a rescript *granted in a favorable form*. More than the object of the dispensation, the rescript *granted in favorable form* concerns the manner in which the concession is granted; in this type of rescript the reply is given directly to the applicant; whereas in the committed type of rescript the reply is directed to the applicant through a third person: a confessor, pastor, or local Ordinary, etc. Finally, in current law, a rescript may be granted *according to, outside of,* or *against* the law (*secundum legem, praeter legem, contra legem*). Although every rescript presupposes a petition, sometimes this petition is presumed; in this case, the rescript is said to be granted *motu proprio*; that is, it is due to the spontaneous will of the superior without prior petition.

ACTIVE AND PASSIVE SUBJECT OF RESCRIPT. Those who grant rescripts in the Church are the Supreme Pontiff and Ordinaries within the sphere of their proper competence. Any of the faithful may petition a rescript, even if under censure, unless he is either expressly forbidden, as *excommunicati vitandi* and those under censure by a condemnatory or declaratory sentence, or silently interdicted, as heretics and schismatics, even in good faith, if they are notorious or have joined a non-Catholic sect (Can. 361).

A rescript may be obtained for a third person even without his consent. If the rescript implies granting a favor, it contains a clause to the effect that the favor may be enjoyed despite contrary custom, statute, law, or rights of third persons (Can. 46).

FORMAT AND CONDITIONS OF A RESCRIPT. Every rescript consists of three parts: (1) presentation, (2) petition, (3) signature. The first and second parts are prepared by the petitioner and contain in brief the reasons of fact and law which motivate the request. The first and second parts constitute the *expositive* part of the rescript; the third part, called *dispositive*, contains the superior's decision. In current procedure the expositive part of the rescript is prepared by an official of the Curia who draws it from the request of the petitioner (*supplice libello*) to whom the truth or falsity of the reasons is charged.

Often certain conditional clauses are appended to a rescript; their observance may affect either the lawfulness of the rescript, in which case they are more properly called *admonitions,* or its validity (*essential conditions*). Essential conditions are in the clauses expressed by the particles: *If, provided (si, dummodo)* or a similar expression (Can. 39). An interesting question was raised by canonists with respect to the value of the clauses expressed in an ablative absolute. Jurisprudence, before the Code was not opposed to attributing an essential value to some clauses expressed in the ablative absolute; but after the Code, canonical jurisprudence generally opposed attributing essential value to such clauses.

SUBREPTION & OBREPTION IN RESCRIPTS. All rescripts are considered granted on condition that the petition is based on truth (*Si preces veritate nitantur*). A rescript, however, may be vitiated either by the concealment of truth (*subreption*) or by an actual false statement (*obreption*). A rescript may be substantially vitiated only if it failed to mention particulars required by the custom and practice of the Roman Curia as necessary for validity (Can. 42, par. 1). Some cases of subreption are mentioned in Canons 43–46. Obreption may concern either the fact or the causes for which the favor is asked. Now, the causes are called *motive* if, of themselves, they are such as to induce the superior to grant the petition. If only one cause is given in the rescript, it is understood to be a motive cause. They are called *impulsive,* if they make conferral of the concession easier, although, in themselves, they would not be sufficient to induce the superior to grant the favor in question. If several causes are mentioned in a rescript, their nature may be established by bearing in mind not only the dispositions of the law and the juridical importance of the thing expressed, but also procedure and common doctrine. At any rate, if the favor is granted on the basis of reasons considered impulsive, all of these reasons together form one motivating cause. The obreption does not invalidate the rescript, if at least one of the motivating causes be true (Can. 42, par. 2). If the suppression of the truth or the false statement is found only in one part of the petition, then this error does not necessarily invalidate other parts of the rescript (Can. 42, par. 3). Nor does concealment of the truth or a false statement invalidate a dispensation from an impediment of minor degree, even if the only motive reason advanced in the petition is false (Can. 1054). In rescripts given in a favorable form, the petition must be true at the moment of the signature; for rescripts committed to another, it is sufficient that the petition be true at the moment of execution (Can. 47).

CONCURRENCE AND INTERPRETATION OF RESCRIPTS. Two or more rescripts are said to be concurrent if they are obtained for the same matter. If two rescripts are mutually contradictory, the particular rescript prevails over the general in the points that are specifically detailed (Can. 48, par. 1). If both rescripts are equally particular or general, then the rescript issued first in order of time prevails (Can. 48, par. 2), unless the second rescript makes mention of the first or the petitioner did not use the earlier either through guile or grave negligence. If both rescripts were granted on the same day and it is not clear which of the two was issued first, then both rescripts are invalid and, if the occasion warrants, recourse is to be made again to the superior (Can. 48, par. 2).

Rescripts must be interpreted according to the criteria of juridical logic; nor is it lawful to extend the concession of the superior to other cases besides those indicated in the rescript. In doubtful cases one can follow a more liberal interpretation, except in rescripts which refer to litigations, infringe upon acquired rights of third parties, grant favors against the law (contra legem), or those which involve the acquisition of an ecclesiastical benefice (Can. 50).

EXECUTION OF RESCRIPTS. Rescripts granted in a favorable form do not require a third person for juridical validity; rescripts committed to another, in order

to be valid, must be executed or applied by a third person, indicated by the one who grants the rescript. Generally this is the Ordinary, pastor, superior, confessor, etc. If, as it generally happens, no time is indicated for execution, a rescript may be presented any time provided that there be no fraud or deception in the delay (Can. 52). The executor is called necessary (necessarius) if he is ordered by the rescript to give it to the petitioner, provided that all the conditions required are properly fulfilled; he is called voluntary (voluntarius) if it is left to his judgment to execute the rescript. The executor, whether necessary or voluntary, cannot fulfill his mission unless he has received and verified for the letter of commission, authenticity and integrity. To this an exception is made if the superior who issued the rescript notifies the executor in advance of the content of the rescript (Can. 53).

As stated, the necessary executor cannot refuse to carry out the rescript unless it is clear that the rescript is invalid by reason of a suppression of facts, a false statement, conditions in the rescript which the executor knows have not been fulfilled, or the executor judges the recipient of the rescript to be so unworthy of the favor that its concession would be a cause of scandal to others. In this latter case, however, suspending the execution, he shall immediately inform the superior who granted the favor (Can. 54, par. 1). A voluntary executor may or may not grant the execution of the rescript according to his prudence (Can. 54, par. 2).

Unless delegation be expressly prohibited by the rescript or the executor was personally selected (industria personae), another person may execute the rescript. If the substitute is specifically named in the rescript, the execution may not be entrusted to another (Can. 57, par. 2). A successor in office can always execute a rescript unless the predecessor was personally appointed (industria personae).

The execution of the rescript must be made according to the terms of the mandate; it becomes invalid unless it conforms to the essential conditions and the substantial form of procedure (Can. 55). The execution of rescripts concerning matters of the external forum should be done in writing (Can. 56). If the executor makes a mistake, he has the right to repeat the execution of the rescript (Can. 59, par. 1). The tax for the execution shall be determined in the provincial council and approved by the Sacred Congregation of the Council (Can. 1507).

REVOCATION AND CESSATION OF RESCRIPTS. A rescript may be revoked: (a) by a special act of the superior, but effective only from the time at which the one who obtained the rescript is notified of the revocation (Can. 60, par. 1); (b) by a contrary law issued by an authority superior to the one that issued the rescript or by a law issued by the same superior in which he expressly revokes the rescript (Can. 60, par. 2).

A rescript ceases due to an intrinsic reason (*ex natura rei*), by a resolutive condition, the death of the petitioner in a purely personal favor, or renuntiation of the petitioner if the favor was granted only for his own personal benefit. Finally, the Code states (Can. 61) that rescripts do not cease by a vacancy of the Holy See or diocese, unless it is so stated in a particular clause of the rescript. One such clause might be *ad beneplacitum nostrum*, which, of course, is understood to cease upon the death of the grantor. It ceases if a rescript confers on a certain individual the authority to grant a favor to other individuals mentioned in the rescript itself, and the one who has received such authority has not yet begun to make use of it when the see becomes vacant (*res sit adhuc integra*). However, if a rescript contains not merely a favor but a privilege or a dispensation, then the Canons of the Code on privileges and dispensations shall be properly observed (Can. 62). *See* Dispensation, Privileges. *Feld.*

RESERVATION OF CENSURES.
Reservation is an act of an ecclesiastical superior, who reserves to himself the examination of a case, thereby depriving inferiors of jurisdiction and power to judge such a case, as Canon 893, par. 1, points out in dealing with the reservation of sins. The characteristic element of reservations consists precisely in this: a case is reserved to a higher tribunal. Not every restriction of jurisdiction implies a reservation, but reservation implies necessarily a limitation of jurisdiction; this, however, is not the principal effect of reservation. The primary effect is formally the action of the superior by which he reserves a case to himself alone. Hence, it may be concluded that, if the superior does not reserve a case to himself, there is no reservation. Such is the case of the priest accomplice who is deprived by the Code of all jurisdiction over a sin in which he was the accomplice; the jurisdiction of such a priest is restricted but the sin is not reserved.

RESERVATION IS NOT A PENALTY. As indicated in Canon 893, in the genuine notion of reservation, it is clear that reservation is not primarily a penalty. In the matter of confession, for instance, the reservation directly affects the confessor and not the penitent. The penitent is indirectly affected through the confessor, whose jurisdiction is restricted by the limitations of the reservation. Accordingly, the reservation must be judged in time and place with respect to the confessor priest. If the priest at the time and place of absolution has jurisdiction, he can absolve from sins, at one time reserved or committed in places where they are reserved; if, instead, the priest at the particular time and place is subject to the reservation, he cannot absolve from sins, even at one time not reserved or committed in places where they were not reserved (Pontifical Commission for the Interpretation of the Code of Canon Law, Nov. 24, 1920).

RATIONE SUI AND RATIONE CENSURAE. The reservation may have as its object either the *sin* or the *censure*. The reservation may be affected directly upon the sin or indirectly through something with which the sin is connected. In the first instance we have the sin reserved *ratione sui*: the superior reserves to himself the absolution of the sin as such. In such a case the ordinary confessor, lacking special faculty, would illicitly and invalidly absolve from such a sin (*see* Reservation of Sin).

But the superior may reserve to himself a sin indirectly reserved, that is, through something connected with the sin. The reservation falls thus upon the sin indirectly and secondarily, through something connected with the sin, on which the reservation principally falls. The censure is usually that which is linked to the sin. The censure is the object of reservation. Thus, one has a sin reserved because of censure (*ratione censurae*). In this case the principal object of the reservation is the censure of excommunication, interdict, suspension, etc. The reservation falls upon it directly and on the sin indirectly; the sin is reserved only on account of the censure. The censure is reserved; the sin is not reserved. Since the sin is bound to the censure, it cannot be absolved as long as the censure is not absolved. If the censure is no longer in force, for some reason such as an absolution from the censure in the external forum, ignorance, grave fear, or doubt, in this case the sin is not considered reserved and any confessor may absolve from it.

Reserved censures as such are either *ab homine* or *a jure*. Ab homine censure is applied to an individual by a particular precept or condemnation by sentence; it is always reserved to the superior who issues the condemnatory sentence, or his successor, or his delegate. Censure *a jure* may be reserved to the ordinary or to the Holy See. Those reserved to the Holy See are of three kinds, reserved to the Holy See *simply*, in a *special manner*, and in a *very special manner* (*simpliciter, speciali modo, specialissimo modo*). The third part of book five of the Code of Canon Law, *De poenis in singula delicta*, contains the various censures reserved *a jure*, enumerated and divided according to the subject matter.

The reservation of censures implies the following considerations: (a) Reservation must be required by the particular gravity of the crime, by the need to provide more conveniently for ecclesiastical discipline or by the need to assist more effectively the conscience of the faithful. (b) No reserved censure may be added to a crime that already has a censure reserved to the Holy See. As a matter of fact, most authors affirm that a censure established by the Ordinary is nullified by an intervening censure reserved to the Holy See, and justly so. A lower tribunal must give way to a higher tribunal if this begins to adjudicate a case. (c) Reservation, like any other law, is considered territorial. It is effective, therefore, only in the territory in which it is established; outside the limits of that territory it loses its force, even if the individual goes out of the territory for the purpose of avoiding the reservation (*in fraudem legis*). In fact, the reservation is not a penalty for the penitent, but concerns directly the subordinate authority, namely, the confessor. Only indirectly does it affect the penitent. It is clear that since it deals with odious matter, a reservation is given a strict interpretation.

Any censure, no matter how incurred, is removed only through absolution. This, unlike the dispensation in the case of vindicative penalties, is an act of justice; it cannot be denied to the individual who complies with the requirements for absolution. The superior has the right to judge such requirements. To absolve from private censures, the following rules must be kept in mind: (a) When a confessor, ignoring the reservation, absolves from the censure and from the sin, the validity of such an absolution extends to censures reserved *speciali modo* to the Holy See, but not to those reserved *specialissimo modo* or *ab homine*. (b) A general absolution from censures includes even cases withheld in good faith, with the exception of the censures reserved *specialissimo modo*; it does not extend to cases withheld in bad faith. These provisions are based on the concession by the legislator. (c) From stricter conditions for absolution required in ordinary cases (Can. 2253), one moves to greater facilities in urgent cases (Can. 2254) and in cases of impending death (Can. 2252). Concerning the reservation of benefices, *see* Benefice. *See also* Urgency, Urgent case. *Pug.*

RESERVATION OF SIN. Reservation of a sin is the withholding by an ecclesiastical superior of jurisdiction to absolve from a sin or censure which the superior, generally a bishop, reserves to himself. It is a restriction of jurisdiction (Can. 893).

That the Church has the power to reserve certain sins is beyond doubt; in fact it is a matter of faith, found in the Council of Trent (Sess. XIV, *De poenitent.*, c. 11). This restriction of jurisdiction is proper not only to Canon Law but also to modern civil codes.

The primary and formal aim of reservation of sin is a restoration of discipline for the protection of the general welfare of Christians by censuring serious sins, as abortion, sterilization, etc. An ecclesiastical superior, particularly a bishop, is more capable of protecting the common welfare than the parish priest, by applying penalties to particular cases and the imposition of salutary remedies (Cf. Council of Trent, Sess. XIV, c. 7, and Canon 897).

The secondary aim of the reservation of a sin, consequent upon the primary, involves a medicinal purpose, for it concerns the private welfare of the faithful themselves, through the amendment of the sinner who would tend to avoid a sin more effectively with a knowledge of a penalty attached to the sin. Hence, the wise provision of Canon 899, par. 1, requesting the Ordinaries to inform the faithful concerning reserved sins.

The reservation, at times, may be penal; in such an event it is established to be applied as a particular penalty for a particular sin, in which recourse to a higher, appropriate superior for forgiveness by absolution becomes necessary.

KINDS OF RESERVATION. From the standpoint of the one who reserves the sin, the reservation may be *papal, episcopal,* or *religious,* depending on whether they are enacted by the pontiff, a bishop or religious superior-general.

From the standpoint of the reservation in itself, the sin may be reserved *ratione sui,* if the sin is directly reserved, simply as a sin, whether a penalty is attached or not; a sin may be reserved *ratione censurae* (by reason of a censure attached), if the reservation concerns directly the penalty attached to the sinful act, and the sin only indirectly. Only because of the censure is the sin indirectly reserved; the reservation of a sin ceases at the same time that the censure is removed by absolution in the sacrament of penance (Can. 2246 and 2247).

Generally, cases reserved to the pope are reserved by reason of the censure; in other cases only the sin is reserved, without a consideration of a censure. In Canon Law one sin alone is reserved to the pope *ratione sui:* false denunciation of an innocent priest accused of the crime of solicitation (Can. 894). This sin is reserved independently of the excommunication that the false accuser may incur (Can. 2363).

The following persons can reserve sins or special cases by censures (Can. 893): (a) The Roman Pontiff for the entire Church; (b) the local Ordinary (Can. 198), except a vicar-capitular and a vicar-general, unless they possess a special mandate; (c) superior-generals, not provincials or local superiors, of exempt clerical religious orders; abbots *sui juris* in the monasteries under their dominion (Cans. 893, 896, 518, 519).

In order that the reservation may achieve its end (Council of Trent, Sess. XIV, c. 7), it is necessary that the utility and necessity of the reservation be ascertained by the local Ordinary after discussing the matter in a diocesan synod, with the Cathedral Chapter, or with more prudent and experienced pastors of souls (Can. 895). Such a reservation does not remain in force beyond the time deemed necessary (Can. 897). The reason is clear: instead of being a source of edification and spiritual welfare, a reservation could become a cause of harm because many of the faithful would remain in sin and probably stay away from the sacraments. By a general prescription of the Church (Can. 897), reserved cases must be few in number and involve more serious, external crimes. Venial and internal sins, therefore, may not be reserved; nor sins which are due more to human frailty than to perverse will, provided that there is no particular malice connected with them (*Instructio S. Officii*, July 13, 1916). No sin may be reserved which is already reserved to the Holy See (Can. 898).

Five conditions are required for a sin to be reserved. The sin must be: (a) *serious*, that is, *mortal*, objectively and subjectively; in other words, committed with full knowledge and full consent; (b) *external*, that is, committed by an external act, even if unknown by others; (c) *specific*, not merely indicated in a general way; in other words, the elements of the case or sin—which are, after all, the reason for the reservation—must be specified; (d) *complete in its species*, that is, it must be consummated, not a mere attempt; (e) *certain*: it must be so certain as to exclude any doubt of law or of fact, regarding the sin or the reservation; in other words, it must be *certainly reserved, certainly committed, certainly mortal*. Therefore, if there should be any doubt as to whether a definite reserving law covers a certain case, or whether a certain sin was truly committed, or whether it is a serious sin, subjectively and objectively, the reservation does not apply. The law about reservation, as an odious thing, must be understood in a strict sense; if in doubt, the confessor is free to absolve the penitent (Cans. 19; 209; 2246, par. 2). These conditions are commonly required, according to all authors, and are furthermore recognized by common usage. With respect to particular conditions or special exceptions, one must consult the rules of each diocese and exempt religious congregation or order.

Sins reserved to the Ordinary (Can. 899, par. 3) cease to be reserved (Cans. 882; 900): (a) *In danger of death*; any priest, even if not authorized to hear confessions, may validly and lawfully absolve any penitent from sins or censures (Cans. 882; 2252). (b) *In the case of ill persons who cannot leave their home*. These may be absolved from reserved sins by a priest authorized to hear confessions. Absolute impossibility is not required; moral impossibility, i.e., a grave difficulty is sufficient. Thus, the aged, paralytics, prisoners (Can. 900) are included in the category of sick persons. (c) *For persons who are about to contract marriage*. (d) *If the request is made of the legitimate superior for the faculty to absolve a particular individual and the faculty is denied*. Then an ordinary confessor may absolve him. It is necessary however, that the faculty requested be not a general but a specific case. (e) *If a confessor believes that he cannot ask for the faculty to absolve without causing serious inconvenience to the penitent or without danger of violating the seal of confession*. The judgment of these circumstances is left *solely* to the confessor and to no one else, not even the penitent. The inconvenience to the penitent must be considered morally serious, with the particular circumstances of the case under consideration, such as the age, sex, moral and physical conditions of the penitent, etc. Furthermore, it is not required that the inconvenience be either certain or very probable; it is sufficient if a probable moral, spiritual, material or economic inconvenience exists. For example, if the penitent could not return to the same confessor, if it were burdensome to remain in sin until the priest obtained the faculty from a superior, if it were feared that the penitent would not return to confession, or if there were danger of public disgrace if the penitent would have to abstain from receiving Holy Communion. (f) *In places outside the territory of the superior who reserved the sin or case*. The reservation ceases to be in force if the penitent were to leave the territory deliberately to obtain absolution (Can. 900, par. 3); the reservation is territorial.

Those who have ordinary power to absolve from reserved sins are: (a) the superior who reserved the sin or case; (b) the vicar-general and the respective vicar-capitular; (c) all those confessors who have been so authorized may absolve from reserved sins or cases. By general dispositions of the Code of Canon Law (Can. 899), the following have the power to absolve from reserved sins: (a) the canon penitentiary; (b) the rural deans empowered by the Ordinary; (c) the parish priests, using the term broadly, during the time of the Easter duty; (d) individual preachers, during the time of a mission, spiritual exercises, and the like.

Whenever a penitent accuses himself of having committed a reserved sin, the confessor immediately shall examine whether or not the conditions required for the reservation are present. If it appears that the sin is truly reserved and that the confessor lacks the power, he must advise the penitent to apply to the reserving superior or a confessor who can absolve him, or to return within a few days when he shall have obtained the faculty to absolve. If the case is urgent, then the reservation ceases (Cans. 900; 2254).

If the penitent is unaware of the reservation, he must be warned and instructed in order that he may have a greater abhorrence of the sin committed, but he cannot be absolved, unless it is an urgent case. *Tar.*

RESERVE, FINANCIAL. A financial reserve is income not consumed or distributed, but set aside to meet possible future losses. The reserve fund, consisting of profits not divided, may be considered as capital or net capital.

Reserves are of two kinds: *disclosed* or declared, and *hidden*, tacit or secret. Declared reserves, in turn, may be *general* or *specific*. Reserves may be demanded by law (legal reserve fund), by charter, or voted on by stockholders (optional and extraordinary reserves), as reserves from fluctuations in the market value of stock, reserves for uncollectable credits, reserves for the deterioration of merchandise, etc. Other special reserves, sometimes required by law for particular types of firms, are *amortization funds* for installations and machinery, *depreciation funds*, *coverage against risks*, and *employees' retirement funds*.

The amortization of installations and machinery before the time foreseen, that is, while they still have value and are being utilized industrially, constitutes a tacit or hidden reserve which increases the value of the capital. The same may be said of the overvaluation of stocks or merchandise. The good-will value of a firm may be considered a tacit reserve.

Secret or *illicitly concealed* reserves are deliberately established by devaluating assets, concealing them entirely or, worse, by showing fictitious losses. These reserves are created for illicit purposes and constitute real frauds (*see* Finance, Fraud).

Bank reserves (monetary) have their own particular characteristics. These consist of cash assets or other easily convertible securities which private banks, credit institutions, or central banks keep on hand to meet sudden demands or for cashing checks. *Bank reserves* or gold reserves in a more restricted sense are established with gold and foreign currency by certain banking institutes to cover or guarantee money placed into circulation.

As stated above, secret reserves become real and proper frauds. An honestly constituted reserve fund, however, is one of the most elementary measures of prudence and a guarantee owed to the stockholders and others. For this reason the observance of civil laws which regulate bank reserves are normally binding in conscience. *Bau.*

RESIDENCE. Residence is the provision of Canon Law under which a parish priest or other cleric holding an office or a benefice is required to live habitually in or near the place where he performs the duties of his office. This law requires not only a material or passive residence but a legal and active one; it is not so strict that it forbids any absence except as indicated in the law itself. For good and just reasons a cleric may be absent intermittently. These reasons must be grave, and, if time permits, must be approved by the local Ordinary. According to the common doctrine, Christian charity, impelling necessity, obedience due to superiors or an obvious benefit to the Church or State are generally considered good reasons for a cleric to be absent from the place of his benefice.

The Code of Canon Law prescribes grave penalties for clerics who violate the law of residence. Such penalties consist of privation of the *fruits* of an office for the duration of the unauthorized absence, the privation of the office, benefice, or dignity (Cans. 2168–2175; 2381; 188, n. 8). From the historical point of view it may be noted that many ancient synods insisted on the observance of the law of residence. Alexander III enacted a universal law at the III Lateran Council by which all the holders of a benefice were required to observe the law of residence.

To correct an abuse which resulted from a strict interpretation of the law of Alexander III involving only curates and canons, the Council of Trent decreed that the law extended also to the Ordinaries. The present Code has substantially retained the discipline established by the Council of Trent.

The following are held to the law of residence: (a) Clerics, including those who have no benefice or office requiring residence, are forbidden to be absent from their diocese for a notable length of time without at least the presumed permission of their Ordinary (Can. 143); (b) Cardinals of the Roman Curia are obliged to reside in Rome and are not allowed to leave the city of Rome without permission of the Roman Pontiff (Can. 238, par. 1); (c) The Ordinary is bound to reside personally in the diocese, even though he may have a coadjutor bishop. The Ordinary is allowed to be absent for three months a year, either continuous or interrupted (Can. 338). Vicars and prefects apostolic (Can. 301, par. 1), canons and holders of benefices, excepting a three-month vacation each year, or in alternate choir service, on the days on which they are not obliged to be in choir (Cans. 418–419), and diocesan consultors must live either in the episcopal city or in surrounding localities (Can. 425, par. 1). The vicar capitular has the same obligation as the local Ordinary (Can. 440). The vicar forane or dean, who, if not a pastor, must reside in the territory of the deanary or in a surrounding place according to the dispositions of the Ordinary (Can. 448, par. 2). The parish priest must live in the parish house near his church. The Ordinary may allow a parish priest to live elsewhere provided that this will not interfere with his parochial duties. He is permitted an absence of two months a year for vacation purpose (Can. 465, par. 1). The acting vicar, vicar econome, vicar substitute, and auxiliary vicar (*adiutor*) are bound to the law of residence, with some restriction for the last two (Cans. 471, par. 4; 473, par. 1; 474; 475, par. 2–3). Religious superiors are bound to reside in their religious house (Can. 508).

The law of residence is binding in conscience gravely not only by virtue of the law of the Church, which, of course, is very clear and explicit in this regard, but also because otherwise those who are held to it would find it very difficult to attend to their responsibilities. *Feld.*

RESIGNATION. Resignation is an act by which a person renounces an object or a right which he presently has (*in re*) or which is due to him in the future (*in spe*). One can renounce an office, inheritance, a right of prescription or the like.

CANON LAW. Resignation in Canon Law is the spontaneous renunciation of an office made to a higher superior with the right to accept this resignation. It may be an implicit or explicit renunciation; implicit, if the law recognizes it as inherent in a particular act. A resignation may be accepted if it is motivated by a legitimate reason, i.e., reasons of conscience, health, environment, and the like (Can. 184, 189). The validity of a resignation demands that the one resigning be fully aware of the action he is performing and, furthermore, that it not be brought about by unjust intimidation (Can. 185); this does not exclude an invitation or request by a legitimate superior for the resignation of an official. In such a case the resignation is free, even if made under threat of removal, as long as there are good reasons for such a demand.

The resignation has no effect until it is submitted in writing or orally to a superior with the right to accept it, and it is thus accepted (Can. 187). The acceptance by a superior is necessary for resignation of a free appointment, a confirmation of an election, and the approval of a presentation or postulate (Can. 187, par. 2). Thus the College of Cardinals has no control concerning the resignation of a Roman Pontiff (Can. 221), nor does the Cathedral Chapter in the resignation of the Vicar Capitular (Can. 443), nor does the chapter of a religious order over the resignation of a superior elected by it, unless this occurs during the time of the election itself.

The incumbent to an office, who abandons it before he is notified of the acceptance of his resignation by his superior or who makes his resignation to strangers, must be punished by law, in addition to penalties which he incurs immediately *ipso facto* (Can. 2399, 2400).

Canon 188 mentions specific cases of implied resignation, in which the office becomes vacant *ipso facto*. These are: (a) if a cleric makes a religious profession, one year later, his parochial office becomes vacant, and all other offices become vacant after three years (Can. 584); (b) if a cleric fails to assume an office within the period of time fixed by law or, in default of this, the period of time fixed by the local Ordinary; (c) if a cleric accepts another office, incompatible with the first; (d) if a cleric contracts marriage, or attempts to contract marriage in a civil ceremony; (f) if a cleric enlists without permission in the military service; (g) if a cleric puts aside the ecclesiastical garb without a just cause and refuses to resume the garb within a month after admonition by the local Ordinary; (h) if a cleric unlawfully deserts the residence to which he is bound with the failure to return, respond, or heed the admonition of the Ordinary, and this desertion of his resi-

dence takes place without a sufficient legitimate reason or cause. *See also* Beneficiary; Property, Ecclesiastical; Election, Ecclesiastical; Patronage; Parish Pastor; Privilege. *M.d.G.*

RESIGNATION, CHRISTIAN. Christian resignation is a virtue whereby one endures some physical or moral suffering without mumuring or rebellion against the will of God.

The Lord, as Ruler of the universe, considers each single event from a view that is different from that which may be in the mind of man; hence no obligation demands that a man accept and will by a positive act of the will whatever appears to be willed by God. Man, however, can never contradict the will of God and rebel against it; to do this with full deliberation would be a grave sin. It is, however, a matter of higher perfection and more meritorious for man, not only to refrain from murmuring and rebellion, but also to will in a positive spirit of soul that which is in accordance with the dispositions of Divine Providence, and for the reasons willed by God.

Man's resignation should consist in his complete abandonment into the hands of God, so that he desires and wills only whatever God wants as the best thing for his soul. *Man.*

RESISTANCE TO TEMPTATION. *See* Temptation.

RESISTANCE TO UNJUST POWER. One of the clearest duties of every citizen is to respect authority and obey just laws. If, however, there is no right to command or the command is opposed to reason, eternal law or divine command, then disobedience to man in order to obey God becomes a duty (Leo XIII, Enc. *Libertas*, June 20, 1888).

Resistance to unlawful power or the abuse of public power may be passive or active. *Passive* resistance consists in nonobedience. The lawfulness of this position is very clear among moralists. The law is a prescription intended according to the requirements of reason, for the welfare of the community; the unjust power of an unjust law does not deny this principle of authority insofar as it concerns subordination to legitimate authority. As a matter of fact, disobedience to unjust laws becomes a duty every time a law prescribes acts against the natural law, positive-divine, or ecclesiastical law; for, one must obey God first, then man, as the Apostle teaches (Acts 5:29). If passive resistance to unjust laws were practiced by an entire people, it would serve as a strong deterrent against abuse of public power.

ACTIVE RESISTANCE. Abuse of authority may also be opposed by *active* resistance. Active resistance, however, may be lawful or unlawful. One may deny the lawfulness of resistance exercised within the limits of the law. But if lawful means alone do not suffice, a resistance beyond the scope of civil law may be justified; in other words, resistance may be carried on by means neither sanctioned nor approved by the legislation of a State. Civil law is not the sole norm of morality, nor do the moral and the legal always coincide. It is necessary, therefore, to distinguish what is lawful and unlawful from the licit and illicit. Resistance, even by the use of force, against unjust laws is lawful if there are no other means of defense. Abuses of public power imply violations of rights, injustices, injuries, acts of force, aggressions against which it is lawful to oppose, not an aggressive, but a defensive, resistance. And if, for example, the sole effective resistance against aggression is recourse to force, its use is lawful if all other means have been exhausted. The rights of the individual, family, and society have a priority in time and importance over those of the civil authority.

POLITICAL REVOLT. A power that habitually enacts serious, unjust laws is a tyrannical government. Is a revolt directed to its elimination lawful? The question presents grave difficulties more in the practical than theoretical order. First of all, it is difficult to establish whether a power is completely and patently opposed to the common good and, therefore, loses its legitimacy. This,

of course, occasions the right and duty of defending the public welfare. It is obvious that if we admit the right of direct action, even armed, it would mean that every time the citizens disapprove of the actions of public authority there would be civil war and, therefore, endless wars. In the Middle Ages, when Europe was solidly Christian, a moral power superior to the States existed in the person of the Pope, who did not depose the sovereigns, as it is often erroneously asserted, but maintained and declared that a sovereign had lost his legitimate right to rule because of his tyranny and that he had no longer any right to obedience from his subjects. Today, since this supreme judge of morality is not recognized and accepted by everyone, it is extremely difficult to judge clearly when a regime loses the right to rule by reason of its abuse of power. Furthermore, the danger to the public welfare must be really grave and urgent and there must be no other way of effective resistance. Truly democratic societies have several means both effective and relatively swift by which to liberate themselves from an evil government, primarily in the electoral vote. Finally, there must be a well-founded hope of success and a judgment that the advantages will compensate the damages. Revolt is a serious disturbance of the social order capable of leading to excesses and of creating even worse conditions than the ones that a revolt is intended to correct; therefore, it must be used as a last means for the protection of society, and only if it is absolutely necessary for the public welfare. *Man.*

RESISTANCE TO VIOLENCE. *See* Rape, Violence.

RESOLUTION. With respect to the sacrament or virtue of penance, resolution is a firm act of the will to sin no more. A resolution is more than a simple desire or inclination to amend one's ways; yet it is not a true promise made to God or to the confessor. A resolution does not necessarily exclude a certain fear of relapse, based on inconstancy of the will or difficulties foreseen for the future.

A resolution may be explicit or implicit. An *explicit* or *formal* resolution is an act distinct from contrition (*q.v.*), by which one expresses a determination not to repeat the sin. An *implicit* or *virtual* resolution is the act of contrition, insofar as it contains a determination to sin no more and is capable of directing the will to an explicit resolution concerning the future.

Furthermore, a resolution may be *absolute* or *relative*. An *absolute* or firm resolution extends to all possible cases and excludes every intention to repeat the sin; the penitent is determined to undergo the loss of any good rather than repeat the sin. This firmness is *virtually* contained in contrition if the sin is detested more than any other evil. An absolute resolution implies that the penitent is disposed to use the necessary means not to fall again into sin: under this aspect the resolution is called *efficacious*. A *relative* resolution does include an intention of not repeating the sin in a definite way although sin is not yet detested more than any other evil.

No sin, venial or mortal, is forgiven even in the sacrament of penance without a resolution to avoid sin in the future. According to common doctrine, an implicit resolution is sufficient; however, to be certain of adequate contrition and to derive greater fruits from the reception of the sacrament of penance, an explicit resolution is required. In fact, one should consider contrition inadequate if he did not make an explicit resolution with respect to avoiding future sins.

Resolution must be *absolute* and *efficacious*. If a penitent is burdened with mortal sin or confesses mortal sins not already directly absolved in confession, his resolution must extend to all of these sins, but not necessarily to venial sins, unless he confessed these venial sins. One who has only venial sins to confess, shall make a resolution not to commit venial sins similar to one of the sins confessed, or to a particular kind of sin

confessed, or to the more fully deliberate ones, or he shall resolve to diminish the number of venial sins. It is evident that no remission of venial sins is obtained unless a resolution is made to avoid them in the future.

In receiving the sacrament of penance a penitent must pay particular attention to contrition and resolution, and take care that this extends to all venial sins mentioned in confession. It shall be helpful to him to be mindful in a particular way, though not exclusively, of a particular kind of venial sins. Concerning lack of resolution to avoid future sins, *see* Sins against the Holy Ghost. *Man.*

RESPECT. In theological language, respect is the virtue by which due honor is rendered to persons who are outstanding for virtue and dignity. Respect is the complement of the virtue of piety; hence, in due proportion, the rules governing the virtue of piety apply also to respect. Respect has many points of similarity to the virtue of obedience (*q.v.*). Respect and obedience are two distinct virtues; the same relation exists between them as between obedience and piety (*q.v.*). *Pal.*

RESPONSIBILITY. Responsibility is a condition in which a subject is required because of a special obligation or reason to account for an action or deed. As such, responsibility is added to imputability, which, in itself, is the simple attribution of an act to a particular individual. Responsibility may be *moral* or *legal*. Moral responsibility is based on the psychological imputability (morality) of an act; *legal* responsibility is based on a disposition of law.

To be reasonable a law must endeavor to conform its norms to psychological and moral reality; yet, at times, due to definite requirements of the social order, it might omit doing so. This is particularly the case in violations punished by law insofar as they imply a definite danger of abuse; these prescind from any moral responsibility in a violator. In matters of penal law, therefore, or in questions of reparation of damages, moralists and jurists are in general agreement usually, as in cases of fraud or the deliberate will and intent to deceive or damage. Frequently disagreement arises in cases involving guilt due to negligence, since a jurist tends to emphasize responsibility in the negligent individual, while the moralist tends to diminish this responsibility.

In natural events or misfortunes, it is clear that no one is responsible for actions of another, unless one causes such an act by way of participation or negligence, either real, as in moral responsibility, or presumed, as in legal responsibility.

At times one speaks of other forms of responsibility, such as political, historical, etc. Political responsibility is the duty to account for certain actions before a legislative or political body; historical responsibility is more vague and intangible.

Responsibility, which is real in the proper sense of the term, puts us before conscience as it were, and through conscience, before the judgment of God. *Gra.*

REST (HOLY DAYS). *See* Sanctification of Holy Days.

RESTITUTION. The term *restitution* means the restoration of an article of any type whatsoever to its rightful owner. In the moral field, restitution means the return to an individual of possession or dominion over an article, rightfully owned by him (*Summa Theol.* II–II, q. 62, art. 1). Since dominion over certain things cannot be restored, as life or limb, moralists and civil authorities mean by restitution the restoration by reparation of a wrong done, whether the reparation is made by restoring the same article or another form of compensation. Therefore, restitution is the restoration of a violated right or material loss of another person.

In this moral sense, restitution is an act of commutative justice by which one restores to the rightful owner a thing unjustly taken or repairs damage un-

justly caused. Restitution is an external act of commutative justice, inasmuch as the end of that virtue is to restore equality between the damage and the compensation, which is effected by means of restitution.

NECESSITY OF RESTITUTION. Some heretics and Protestant theologians asserted that restitution was not necessary in order to attain eternal life and that alms were sufficient to remove the sin of theft.

Opposed to such erroneous theories is the doctrine of the Catholic Church. According to this teaching, restitution is absolutely necessary *in re vel in voto*, that is, in fact or promise, for those who have seriously violated a strict right of another person. This moral principle has a foundation in Sacred Scripture, as Ezech. 33:15; Exod. 22:1–5; II Kings 16; Tob. 2:20; Luke 19:8; John 5:4, etc. It is also summed up by Saint Augustine: "If the sinner does not restore something which he can restore, he does not have repentance but a facsimile merely. The sin is not removed if he does not restore what he took away; but, as I said, he must restore it if he can." (*Epist.* 153 *ad Maced.*, n. 20; PL 33, 662). This expression was inserted by Gratian in his Decree (C. 14, q. 6, c. 1).

That restitution is binding in conscience is proven by reason itself, for it is based on the nature of a perfect right. We can use force to defend our strict right; but this would be futile and immoral if, after being violated, it were not restored. Furthermore, he who does not make restitution, though able to do so, in fact continues the theft or the injury by depriving his neighbor of a good that belongs to him. Restitution is required by the concept of the common good of society which would become a den of thieves if the obligation of restitution were not upheld. Lastly, no sin can be pardoned without sincere contrition and the firm intention of sinning no more. But he who unjustly keeps the articles of another and does not restore them to him, though able to do so, appears to have neither true contrition nor a firm purpose of sinning no more.

DEGREES OF NECESSITY OF RESTITUTION. Restitution is not necessary by "necessity of means," because one may also be saved without it if he cannot make restitution and provided that he intends to as soon as he shall be able. Restitution is necessary by "necessity of precept," that is, by law, since to retain what belongs to another is a violation of justice, the first precept of the natural law, by which we are to give to each his own and not to do to another that which we would not want to be done to us.

The precept of restitution, affirmative in its enunciation, is really negative, for it is united to the precept which forbids the undue appropriation of a thing belonging to another. The omission of restitution is an unjust, continued retention of the thing of another. From this follows the obligation to restitution at once by reason of the injury or damage caused to another.

ROOTS OF RESTITUTION. The causes from which the obligation of restitution arises are called by theologians the roots of restitution. They consist in a fact or a deliberate action of an individual, in which damage resulted to a neighbor. There are as many roots to restitution as there are species of actions causing unjust damage to a neighbor. Moralists, in general, list four such roots: (a) unjust acceptance of the thing of another; (b) unjust retention of the same; (c) a damage unjustly caused; and (d) a contract or quasi-contract entered into by two or more people.

In the first case one would have theft (*q.v.*) under all its forms and species in an undue appropriation of another's goods, carried out in opposition to the will of its rightful owner.

The second consists in the actual and unjust retention of a thing belonging to another. Stealing, therefore, and the unjust retention of the goods of another are not substantially different as far as guilt is involved, although one must consider the variety of ways that one retains unjustly the goods of another. For example, one who finds a lost thing does not necessarily become owner; the thing always belongs to its rightful owner. One is said to unjustly retain the thing of another if, though able to do so, he fails to satisfy a debt on time, by employing absurd or egotistical pretexts. Again, one is said to unjustly retain the goods of another if he does not pay a worker his just salary or does not pay him on time. One who has borrowed things, whatever they may be, must return them at the proper time; he must return them even if they are not asked for or the owner has forgotten or does not need them.

The third root of restitution consists in the damage caused to a neighbor's material interests. In this sense, one is responsible for an unjust damage he causes to a neighbor's possessions, or the loss of a thing to which he has a just right; this can happen in innumerable ways (*see* Damage). However, in order that he be bound to restitution, it is required not only that the damage to one's neighbor be the result of a voluntary cause but also of injustice, for only in this case does one violate justice. It is possible voluntarily to cause a damage to a neighbor without violating justice, as when one opens a store close to that of a neighbor and competes with the prices of his merchandise.

WHO IS BOUND TO MAKE RESTITUTION? One who stole, caused an unjust damage, or retains goods not his own is bound to restitution. It is necessary to take into consideration the manner in which one came into possession of these goods. If he inherited them from one who acquired them unjustly, he must restore them to their rightful owner, and if he sold or consumed such, he must restore an equivalent value. If, instead, he bought them rightfully from an unjust possessor, he must restore them to the rightful owner but he has the right to be indemnified for the price he paid. If the goods were bought unlawfully or at a suspicious price, they must be returned to the rightful owner without reimbursement.

Furthermore, if persons concurred in causing a damage but their action did not imply equal participation in the damage, each one is held responsible in proportion to his individual participation. If, instead, they planned a deed together and their participation was equally necessary or effective, all are equally bound to make restitution in *solido*, i.e., for the entire damage.

To WHOM MUST ONE MAKE RESTITUTION? Restitution must be made to the one who suffered the damage or was robbed. If he is dead, it is due to his heirs. Therefore, one does not satisfy such an obligation simply by giving alms to the poor; the poor have no right to that which in justice belongs to another. If one does not know the person who suffered the damage and it is impossible to find him, the equivalent of the damage can be given in alms to the poor or other charitable works. If the one to whom restitution must be made is dead, the right which he held does not die with him but passes on to his legitimate heirs, to whom, therefore, restitution shall be made.

WHAT MUST BE RESTORED? One must restore the thing, itself; if it is lost or consumed, its equivalent value. If the thing was retained in bad faith from the beginning by a deliberately unjust manner, it must be restored with all its fruits. If it was retained in good faith from the beginning but later one discovered the error, the fruits accrued from the time of this discovery must be restored (*see* Possession).

TIME OF RESTITUTION. Restitution, as an obligation of commutative justice, must be made as soon as possible for several grave reasons. Until one shall have made restitution, and one is able to do so, he persists in the sin; in fact, the situation worsens each day, because it is unjust to hold goods belonging to another and the damage to the lawful owner increases with time, since he cannot put his goods to fruitful use. The intention to make restitution does not suffice; justice must be satisfied.

THE GRAVITY OF THE OBLIGATION OF RESTITUTION. Although the obligation of restitution is serious in itself as a means of restoring a violation of commutative justice, there are conditions which allow the suspension and even the cancellation of such an obligation. The obligation is suspended in a physical or moral incapability on the part of the one who caused the damage to another as long as this condition of poverty endures. But one who is able to repay gradually is held to the obligation to the extent to which he is able to make restitution both with respect to the amount and to the time. The reasons which may cancel the obligation altogether are as follows: free and valid condonation on the part of the one who has the right to dispose of his own goods; mutual compensation; lawful prescription, that is, a prescription that meets all the conditions demanded by law and good faith (*see* Prescription). There is also a settlement or remission of debt obtained from the Pope for a just cause; this, of course, normally concerns ecclesiastical goods or goods of doubtful ownership.

RESTITUTION IN CIVIL LAW. Civil codes, in general, admit the ethical principles of restitution, but they often are based on the concept of crime. Therefore they enforce a compensation for damages. For specific applications, confer the respective civil legislations.

Since the civil law cannot scrutinize the interior motives, it is understandable that it should exact juridical proof, exterior declarations, testimony, and the like. Divine justice does not need such proofs. The pretexts used in an attempt to ally one's conscience with respect to the obligation of restitution have no value in the light of a law that is felt in every honest mind and heart. *Tar.*

RESTORATION. *See* Legitimacy.

RESTRICTION, MENTAL. Mental restriction is an act of the mind by which the speaker restricts the meaning of the words to a sense which is not their obvious sense. Mental restriction may be *mere mentalis* or *late mentalis*. A mere mental restriction expresses a truth in a way that makes it impossible for the hearer to perceive a truth; a broad mental restriction makes it possible for a hearer to understand the truth expressed by the words of the speaker.

Purely mental restriction (*mere mentalis*) is sinful because it equals a lie (*q.v.*). The broad mental restriction (*late mentalis*) is lawful in certain cases. Its intrinsic purpose is, not to lead into error or to deceive, but to withhold a truth or part of a truth which may not be disclosed. In order that this may be lawful, however, it is necessary that the speaker be obliged to withhold a truth and that there be no other ways of doing so except by a mental restriction (*late mentalis*). *Ben.*

RETARDED. *See* Phrenasthenia.

RETORTION. *See* Retaliation.

RETREAT, SPIRITUAL. A spiritual retreat is a period of prayer, instructions, spiritual readings, examination of one's life, special practices of devotion and meditation, for one or more days in an atmosphere apart from ordinary affairs.

A spiritual retreat contributes much to the strengthening of convictions; it tends to give a more intimate knowledge of the state of soul; it increases in it detestation for sin and its causes; it leads to generous resolutions and to desire greater perfection. A spiritual retreat is also a period of more abundant graces.

A monthly day of recollection and an annual retreat of several days is highly commendable, especially if made in a quiet and solitary place (closed retreat), under the guidance of an experienced spiritual director. *Man.*

LEGISLATION. The Code of Canon Law indicates a minimum time the clergy, religious men and women are required to give to spiritual retreat. Seminary students must make a retreat every year, but no set number of days is indicated (Can. 1367, n. 4). Candidates for the first tonsure and minor orders must make a retreat of three full days. Before receiving major orders, however, they must make a retreat of at least six days. If candidates are to receive more than one major order within a period of six months, the retreat before the diaconate

can be reduced to three days (Can. 1001, par. 1). If the ordination is deferred beyond the period of six months, it is left to the judgment of the Ordinary whether or not the retreat should be repeated (Can. 1001, par. 2). Canon Law indicates also the place where the candidates should make their retreat and the manner in which the Ordinary is to be informed of it (Can. 1001, par. 3–4).

Candidates for religious orders and congregations, are required to make a retreat of eight days before the novitiate (Can. 541) or the religious profession (Can. 571, par. 3). All religious must make an annual retreat (Can. 595, par. 1, n. 1); secular priests are required to make a retreat at least every three years (Can. 126), but it is a general practice, enforced by diocesan dispositions, for all priests to make a yearly retreat. St. Ignatius Loyola is the patron of spiritual retreats (Const. *Summorum Pontificum*, July 25, 1922).

The more recent Supreme Pontiffs have strongly recommended to all the faithful and to priests the frequent and faithful practice of spiritual retreats (Cf. Pius XII, *Menti nostrae*, September 23, 1950). *Pal.*

REVENUE. In general, revenue is income gathered without impairment of pre-existing wealth, and provided by the application of labor to this wealth which thereby creates new wealth.

The concept of revenue applies mainly to national income, as a central basis of a modern economy. National income is the annual flow of goods and commercial services produced for and by a national economy after the deduction of that part required for technical and economic amortization, maintenance of pre-existing wealth, and the amount necessary for the repair of damages ordinarily insured. To equate the goods and services which constitute the national income and to express it in summary form, one must equate the monetary value of various elements.

Revenue ordinarily constitutes the basis for the taxation of wealth; this gives rise to moral questions about the honest reporting of revenue earned, fair distribution of taxes, etc. (*see* Custom, Tax). That part of revenue not put to immediate use is called savings, and its honest, functional value both for the individual and society is unquestionable (*see* Reserve). The distribution of revenue among various elements contributing to its increase is one of the gravest moral and social problems of our times (*see* Distribution, Economic; Social question). *Mai.*

REVIVISCENCE OF SACRAMENTS.

Reviviscence in general indicates a property in an object by which certain beings are capable of resuming vital activity after manifesting the symptoms of death. The term is applied analogically to the sacraments; it is used to designate the return of the supernatural life to the soul, after the soul has been wrapped in the supreme death, the loss of grace. Thus one speaks of a reviviscence of grace, virtue, or merit. The application of the term *reviviscence* to the sacraments is not altogether satisfactory, because the sacrament, which is said to revive, in reality previously exercised no vital action. In modern theology, a sacrament is said to revive if it was validly received, yet did not produce grace because of a certain moral obstacle (*obex*); then, subsequently, when the moral obstacle has been removed by the performance of required acts or rites, the sacrament confers grace by virtue of the rite previously administered.

Thus, on the basis of the above principle, it is clear that various conditions are required for sacramental reviviscence: *on the part of the subject*, the *obex* or absence of the moral disposition of soul must be removed; *on the part of the sacrament*, the external rite must be completed previously in a *valid but fruitless administration of the sacrament*, i.e., supernatural grace is not received in the reception of the sacrament because of a moral obstacle in the subject. The matter and form of the sacrament must have been performed already, because if the sacramental sign is still acting, e.g., if one repents of mortal sins before the

rite of confirmation is completed, then one cannot speak of reviviscence but of the ordinary conferral of grace. The external rite must have terminated with a *definite effect* on the penitent or recipient. Since reviviscence implies a true and proper efficiency in the external rite, this would be inconceivable if at the time of its administration the rite left no imprint or ontological vestige; only an actually existing reality can produce an effect. Finally, *on the part of God*, it is required that He confer grace in this extraordinary manner.

From these facts one can deduce that those sacraments revive in which these conditions are verified. Three conditions must be verified in all sacraments, with the exception of penance: the removal of an *obex*, a valid but formless sacrament, the external rite fully terminated. The only thing that remains to be seen is whether the other conditions are present, namely, the permanence of an effect and the will of God to grant grace by an extraordinary means.

The permanence of a real effect, i.e., a *character*, is verified in baptism, confirmation and holy orders; so, too, the positive will of God is presumed from the fact that, otherwise, original sin could not be remitted in an individual who received baptism unworthily. In this manner spoke St. Augustine and S. Fulgentius (*see* Rouet de Journel, *Enchiridion Patristicum*, n. 1621, 2269; St. Gregorius Magnus, Denz. 249). In confirmation and holy orders the faithful would be deprived of graces extremely helpful to the fulfillment of the duties of their state as soldiers and ministers of Christ. In extreme unction and matrimony, the permanence of an interior unction (*interior unctio*) or of a conjugal bond (*vinculum conjugale*) is clear; it is imprinted in the soul, for, in fact, every act, voluntarily performed, causes an ontological modification in the soul. The disposition of divine will is inferred, since in the hypothesis of a lack of reviviscence, the faithful would be deprived of those aids which are very efficacious in enabling them to overcome temptations at the end of life or in facing successfully difficulties of conjugal life. Thus, it seems that only penance and the Holy Eucharist do not revive; the former because, according to the more probable opinion, it cannot be a valid and formless sacrament at the same time; the latter because it would be contrary to the norm of divine operation. In fact, the hypothesis of a reviviscence of the Holy Eucharist would amount to this: if the faithful received Communion sacrilegiously throughout life, at the end, by a simple act of contrition in the sacrament of penance, he would receive as many increases of grace, as were the sacrileges committed. Obiously, it is unthinkable that God would reward sin.

EFFECTS OF REVIVISCENCE. The sacrament that revives produces grace *ex opere operato*. It is disputed whether this happens through a physical or a moral causality. Thomistic doctrine of physical efficiency seems more probable (*see* Sacrament) because, in the five sacraments which revive, an ontological element, a character or modification of the soul, can become a physical instrument in the hands of God as principal cause of grace.

In 1925, Marin-Sola sought to give a deeper theological explanation to the reviviscence of the sacraments on the basis of the Thomistic principle of the baptismal character as a *receptive power* with respect to the other sacraments. Every sacramental administration, if validly performed, implies, according to the above principle, an actualization of this receptive power, which becomes ontologically modified. Such modification follows the nature of the sacrament received. Therefore, it will be *permanent* in the sacraments that cannot be repeated, like baptism, confirmation, holy orders; it will be *temporary* in extreme unction and matrimony; *momentary* in penance and the Holy Eucharist. This would explain why three sacraments that imprint a character always revive; why extreme unction revives only for the same illness and matrimony only during the same conjugal bond; why penance and the Holy Eucharist never revive. Despite some weak points, this theory is followed by many theologians. *Pio.*

REVOLUTION. A revolution is a radical and often violent attempt to overthrow a government or constitution. The degree of violence may vary in a revolution; bloodshed, intrigue, popular demonstrations, military action are frequently involved and, at times, may reach serious proportions. An essential element of a revolt is that the change of regime is not effected by peaceful evolution or reciprocal agreement between the power that withdraws and the new government which takes over. A revolution may be caused by an act of high officials or a revolt by the masses. The first type is more properly called a *coup d' état*.

LEGITIMACY OF REVOLUTION. John of Salisbury in the twelfth century, followed by John the Little in the fifteenth century, held the belief that the murder of a tyrannical ruler, even by a private citizen, was lawful. They based their theories on the rights of a community and its power to uphold these rights against those who would unjustly violate them. The thesis of John of Salisbury was condemned in general terms by the Council of Constance in 1415 (Denz. 690). These decrees, however, were not approved by the Pope.

Yesterday's question on tyrannicide has become today's issue on the lawfulness of revolution. It is evident that revolution is not desirable in itself, due to the grave harm likely to follow for those who participate and those who see themselves violently deprived of authority legitimately obtained. Danger of further violence usually accompanies the first outbursts with subsequent public disturbances and disorder.

The question remains whether a revolution is ever lawful. It is certain that the use of force does not and cannot create a right; judging from external factors, it appears that in a revolution there is a clash between a legal right in the existing juridical position of a duly constituted government and a new interest which prevails by force and which claims, through this means, legality in gaining control of the government. Actually those who do not recognize the natural law accept revolutions as the physical development, as it were, of political life and as necessary to mankind. In this development the emergence of new forces gives rise to changes. The violence created is compared by the new leaders to the violence of natural phenomena, like a tidal wave or a storm; on these grounds it is fully justified by them. In this manner, the *fact* is made equal to *law* by those who hold that the only law is positive law and that the State is the source of law.

The question remains unanswered: How under these conditions can the concept of a *legally constituted state*, which is such not only in name but in essence, be defended? The question is easily disposed of when one accepts the natural law as a law of itself superior to the State, from which the State receives its fundamental reason to be a legally constituted entity as well as the general principles on which to build its own positive laws. In accordance with the principles of the natural law, the State exists only to guarantee and promote the *common good* (*q.v.*) of its citizens. This is its end, though the historical circumstances for its beginning may have been different. Different also may be the way in which the essential powers (legislative, judiciary and executive) are distributed. Times, of course, change in accordance with a providential law, which for a Christian is an expression of Divine Wisdom and Will. For such changes, often new needs arise which are likely to affect the ruling power as well as the form of government itself. The growing importance of a social class, its awareness of its own worth and strength, its growing consciousness of the need to have a voice in government, will, of necessity, have repercussions on the public life of a nation. Hence, wisdom demands that this new force be taken into proper account. The common good demands that these forces be brought into the administration, broadly speaking, of the State, thus avoiding disturbances which would inevitably develop if such forces were to be denied a legitimate field of operation.

The ideal solution, then, is to achieve a reasonable understanding between the forces in power and the new forces. But, often, this is not done, either because of excessive demands and inordinate activities by the new forces or because of narrow-mindedness and excessive attachment to power on the part of those in authority. But the question arises whether, having honestly exhausted all peaceful means of winning recognition, which is extremely important, including threats and passive resistance, it may be lawful as *ultima ratio* to turn to active resistance and, therefore, to revolution.

Many of the Scholastics, among them St. Thomas, and many of the great theologians of the sixteenth century, like St. Robert Bellarmine, Molina, Suarez, Lessius, have distinguished, with slight variations between one and the other, the case of a usurper and that of one who abuses his power (*tyrannus usurpationis* and *regiminis*). With regard to the usurper, on the basis of the principle of the legitimacy of active resistance against an unjust aggressor, they have maintained that both the people as a whole and each private citizen has the right to kill, for by so doing society would be exercising the right of legitimate self-defense. In fighting him it would not be violating any right of sovereignty. This of course is always an extreme remedy. They deny the lawfulness of killing such a sovereign who abuses his power, if done on the initiative of a private individual; but they affirm, if there is no higher authority to whom an appeal can be made, the entire nation, represented by its most worthy citizens, can rise against him and decide on capital punishment for him if it be deemed necessary for the common good. The subsequent Catholic tradition, including St. Alphonsus M. de Liguori, has shown itself more rigid. This position is reflected in Proposition 63, condemned in the *Syllabus*: "It is lawful to deny obedience to the legitimate rulers and to rise against them" (Denz. 1763).

Today, under the influence of the sad

experience of governments that disregard the respect due to the human person, there is a return to the Scholastic view, presumably prompted by changed historical circumstances. Excluding arbitrary judgment on the part of an individual, the people, as a whole, have the right to defend themselves against a government which has become despotic, thereby placing itself outside the law; in extreme cases, citizens have the right to active resistance.

A way of action based on these principles may appear an act of violence, but it is actually the exercise of a natural right, which authorizes the use of force if another unjustly opposes it. Naturally, the judgment as to whether or not the conditions of unlawfulness exist is not left to anyone indiscriminately but to a considerable number of prudent and God-fearing men. The limits which the moral doctrine imposes on revolutionary acts may be summed up in this formula: *cum moderamine inculpatae tutelae*—the same formula applied to lawful self-defense and to a just war. A revolution is thus considered an *ultima ratio*, but *ratio*. And if it does succeed, it is not justified on the basis of the *accomplished fact* but by reasons of law and right that inspired it. These reasons may not be accepted by all, but they are not, therefore, less true. Allowance must be made for those who hold another view in total good faith. The matter is different, of course, for those who seek a change of regime only as an occasion for satisfying their violent instincts or ambitions, or who oppose a revolution simply on the basis of culpable, selfish motives. *Boz.*

RHABDOMANCY. *Rhabdomancy* (Greek, *rhabdos*, rod; *mantia*, divination) indicates divination carried out by the use of a divining rod. Of ancient origin, the modern use of the term comprises a search and discovery of articles such as water or mineral concealed in the earth. This is carried out by a person who, employed for this purpose, makes use of articles such as special rods or the equivalent articles of divination, and a particular talent for using them.

Rhabdomancy, as understood in this second, more precise sense, is as early as the sixteenth century. In this period the divining rod was employed to locate veins of metal or coal in German mines. Later the method was employed for the search of water.

Abbé L. de Vallemont, in his classic work *La physique occulte ou traité de la baguette divinatoire* (Paris, 1693), was a leader in early studies of this phenomenon. He opposed the theory advanced by some in his time that rhabdomancy was the effect of the influence of the devil, by maintaining that the causes were purely natural. He described the various types of natural causes.

The rhabdomancer usually operates as follows: with a forked rod, held in both hands at the extreme ends of a branch, he walks over the terrain to be explored, with the central section of the branch extended before him. When he comes into proximity with the water or vein of ore which he is searching for, the wand is guided by automatic muscular movements, moving in a variety of ways to indicate the spot where excavations are to be made. He usually can estimate where the excavations are to be made and to what depths, by the motion of the wand over the water or the ore. Some rhabdomancers make use of a pendulum or other gadgets; others do not employ any instruments at all.

INTERPRETATION. Scholars of rhabdomancy, subsequent to de Vallemont, have given two diverse interpretations. Some have continued to consider it a physical phenomenon, in the sense that certain radiations emanate from water, metals, or other objects concealed in the underground, that are capable of sensitizing the particularly receptive neuro-muscular apparatus of rhabdomancers. Others tend to view rhabdomancy as a particular aspect of that branch of extrasensory knowledge defined as cryptesthesia (*see* Telepathy). The hypothesis of these latter scholars seems to be corroborated by the fact that some rhabdomancers can operate without physical presence at a scene but merely by making use of maps and topographical charts of the region where water or some metallic vein is being sought. In any event, research in the field of rhabdomancy is still in progress today.

Catholic scholars make a distinction, first of all, between true rhabdomancy, which consists in searching, with or without a divining wand, for metals, etc., concealed in the underground, and other activities which only retain the name and the intent of rhabdomancy. For the so-called rhabdomancer furnishes the desired indications solely through the use of topographical charts. It is, therefore, a question of two distinct phenomena. If the first can be explained by energies and radiations which are more or less occult, but nevertheless of a natural order, the second, going beyond all laws of nature, must be considered as a preternatural phenomenon, comparable to other phenomena pertaining to the realm of metapsychic investigations. Genuine rhabdomantic activity would, therefore, seem to be lawful; for the other type, moral reservations are obviously in order, until the facts are established.

RADIESTHESIA. A few years ago, for a short time, the fad of the pendulum returned to vogue, not for the purpose of detecting objects buried underground, but rather as a means of establishing the state of health of the writer of a given letter or searching into the illness of a particular organ.

These practices, known now for quite some time and more properly called radiesthesia, were severely criticized by Father Agostino Gemelli. He defined radiesthesia as *"a caricature of the preternatural,"* adding, "If rhabdomancy was to be considered harmless and irrelevant as far as religion was concerned, as long as it was confined to the search for water, petroleum and minerals, it can no longer be so if it assumes the form of radiesthesia . . . particularly when it seeks to take the place of positive sciences, such as medical sciences; for in such cases we may well be confronted with something which, to say the least, is very close to superstition . . ." And he warns that

neuropathic persons, in particular, could very easily fall prey to such conditions.

The Church has shown some concern with respect to practices of radiesthesia and has cautioned Catholics against the moral dangers possible and has forbidden clerics and religious to engage in its practice (Degree of Holy Office, March 26, 1942: AAS, 34 [1942], 148).

Here again we are dealing with phenomena of a metapsychic nature about which science has not pronounced as yet with any degree of certainty. We are excluding here, of course, the tricks of the so-called radiesthesists and those futile society games indulged in merely for purposes of amusement.

Other scholars, besides the aforementioned Gemelli, are of the opinion that rhabdomancy and radiesthesia are none other than manifestations of the subconcious producing imperceptible voluntary movements which are then amplified and transmitted to the pendulum or other instruments in the hands of the operators.

As for the application of radiesthesia to medicine, which at one time aroused special interest, we must add that this is not objectively illicit as long as it has not been proven that natural forces are insufficient to explain the above-mentioned phenomena.

In eventual recourse to radiesthesia the doctor should, however, be careful to conduct his research on patients who are in no way aware of the problematic semeiological properties of the instrument, or in any event on patients with a clearly balanced nervous system, in order to avoid producing or aggravating in the neurotic individual manifestations for which the experimenter would be morally responsible. *Riz.*

RIGHT. This word is used in several different senses. Sometimes it is used to mean the entire juridical (legal) system of a society. At other times, it indicates only the laws of this system. Taken in these two senses, it interests the jurist directly, and only indirectly the moral theologian, insofar as the juridical order implies an obligation of conscience. For the ancient moralists the term *right* had an objective meaning which indicated the right thing, due in justice, the object of the moral virtue of justice. For modern moralists, right has a rather subjective meaning, that indicates the faculty to exact or to do something.

Understood as such, right can assume diverse forms according to the diversity of the sources from which it stems. These can be reduced to two: positive and natural laws. The first is a strictly juridical (legal) faculty and, as such, is the concern of the jurist; the second, not necessarily detached from the first, but accompanying it, is, properly speaking, a moral faculty that is the concern of the moralist.

Right, according to modern moralists, is, therefore, a moral faculty. This qualification distinguishes right from a mere legal faculty and excludes it from a physical power or physical force.

However, moralists also teach that a certain force goes with right, but they speak rather of an ethical force which they call *inviolability*. This possesses two aspects: a negative one in which it is not licit to act against the right of another, and a positive one in which the possessor of a right can apply the use of force against anyone who might attempt to impede the exercise of right. This second aspect is called *coercibility of a right*.

Right is generally distinguished into right *in re*, and right *ad rem*. A right *in re*, called real, has as its object a specific thing belonging to a possessor of a right so that he may claim it from any person who might be retaining it. A right *ad rem* implies a personal obligation, and is directed, not to a thing, but to a person from whom alone the holder of the right can claim the thing. The owner of a thing has a real right (*in re*) upon the object belonging to him; the creditor has a right which may be called personal (*ad rem*) to have the thing returned by the debtor. Moralists speak also of a strict or perfect right and of a broad or imperfect right. The interpretation of this distinction is not always uniform. In general, strict right is the right of

which we have spoken. An imperfect right is that in which some of the elements described above are lacking, particularly the aspect of inviolability; but in such case the term *right* is improperly used. *Gra.*

RIGHTS, HUMAN. *Human rights*, as a formula, gained great recognition following the French Revolution, which had made it one of its battle cries. The term had been incorporated in the Constitutions of several states of the United States of America; some see traces of it in the famous English Magna Charta of the thirteenth century. From a study of its content one can detect its origin in the philosophy of history and in Christian doctrine, for the latter's proclamation of the dignity and value of the human person affirmed the rights of man unequivocally. In the twentieth century, two great wars gave rise to an increased interest in the formula and its content by scholars and political bodies, such as the United Nations Organization. (Cf. Declaration of Human Rights, Dec. 10, 1948).

The general content of the formula *human rights* is quite clear. It means that every man, by the very fact that he is a human being, regardless of his national origin, race, religion, or other distinctions, possesses certain fundamental rights that are inalienable.

At various political conventions, men have endeavored to reach a basic understanding with regard to the following rights: (a) physical life, that is, bodily and psychic life; hence, it is forbidden not only to kill but also to mutilate or render a human person incapacitated; (b) personal liberty, which excludes slavery, forced deportation, and the like; (c) freedom from want, guaranteeing to every human person the means indispensable to life; (d) equality before the law of every individual; (e) political freedom for every citizen to participate in the government of his country.

The technical difficulties encountered in the juridical application of these rights arise from two sources, one intrinsic to the rights themselves, the other extrinsic, which relates to the appropriate organ by which those rights are to be protected. The intrinsic difficulty consists of an indefiniteness inherent in those rights and duties, insofar as the previous points are concerned. It is rather easy to determine a right to life and one's corporal integrity; it may be difficult to determine the range of one's right to political liberty and, even more difficult, his rights and duties regarding freedom from want. Since the juridical order demands a considerable degree of certitude, it is easy to see that a hard road lies ahead of the jurist. Often, the difficulty is aggravated by the fact that the jurist is faced with two diverse subjects whose mutual relations are difficult, an individual on one hand and society on the other. The extrinsic difficulty, as said above, consists in determining the proper organ to guarantee the rights of man. The State appears to be inadequate, because it is against abuses by the State that the individual is compelled to appeal for respect of his human rights. It, then, appears necessary to establish specific organs, international or supranational, charged with the precise obligation to protect rights. This solution seems to disconcert certain jurists, who, though not conscious of their positivistic attitude, fear lest the juridical dogma of State supremacy be dealt a severe blow. On the other hand, admitting the establishment of superior courts of human rights, who could guarantee their impartiality and effectiveness?

In view of the above considerations, some observations concerning the *ethical value* of the rights of man appear to be in order. First of all, it can be properly said that the rights of man represent conditions useful to man's moral growth. This formula sets limits to their value. They are conditions, not the achievement, of ethical perfection. Life, liberty, and rights can be utilized or wasted with obvious damage. These are useful conditions. Obviously, one's ethical perfection is easier to attain in an atmosphere of liberty than under the yoke of slavery, although it must not be forgotten that man is capable of brutalities in any situation; a slave may be ethically superior to his own master.

OBLIGATION TO PROTECT HUMAN RIGHTS. The obligation to protect human rights and the extent of this obligation flow from the ethical value of the rights themselves. Here it must be observed that the situation varies depending on whether the obligation concerns oneself or others. In the first case, the obligation goes from the end to the conditions; in the second case, it goes from the conditions to the end. The reason for the inversion is evident. Every individual is the master of his own ethical perfection, of which he bears direct responsibility. Hence, he will keep his eyes on it, measuring the degree of necessity of the external conditions. With respect to other individuals, we can only give them external aid, and our attention will be directed to that in the hope that each individual will use it to his best advantage. Hence, there will arise situations in which an individual could decline certain rights on the ground that they are not indispensable for his perfection; but as long as he has not renounced them, others have the obligation to respect them. Now, society, with its juridical organization, is related to the individual, as individuals are related to each other. Society's immediate obligation is to insure the external conditions capable of leading to perfection until it becomes evident that certain persons are going to abuse their rights with apparent detriment to society.

It will be helpful to observe that no juridical order can guarantee that the proper objective of the rights of man is going to be attained. It can be obtained if, while safeguarding the rights of man, each individual endeavors to improve himself, by making proper use of his rights and freedom. This, of course, shows patently the radical insufficiency of the juridical organs in regulating human life. More important than the proclamation of the rights of man, is the work performed to improve the ethical standards of individuals and peoples. *Gra.*

RIGHT TO LIFE. The right to life is a natural right which every man possesses simply because he is a human being. Hence, a fetus in its maternal womb has a right to life; so does a child or other individuals who do not possess the use of reason, such as the insane, idiots, and the like. The criminal and the aggressor all human beings have the right to life. The source of their right is their rational nature, that is, their human nature. Man possesses this right in relation to any other man, society, the State and public authority.

The right to life is inalienable. Since the object of the right is a human act or omission rather than a thing, it follows that the right to life is none other than the right not to be killed or hindered from living. The right to life is absolutely inviolable. It has, however, certain natural and intrinsic limitations. Right in general is subject to limitations expressed in the rules of coercibility of the right. Hence, my right to live does not mean that another has no right to defend himself legitimately against me, if I become an unjust aggressor, or that society has no right to punish me with capital punishment, if I become guilty of a serious crime. In these two cases, therefore, the killing of a man, under the necessary conditions is not a violation of his right to life. From this clear-cut concept of the right to life flows the moral doctrine concerning the killing of a man under the two distinct headings of lawful self-defense and capital punishment. *Ben.*

RIGORISM. *See* Moral Systems.

RING. The ring, as part of pontifical and episcopal insignia, is mentioned in the liturgy as early as the twelfth century. However, its use as a distinguishing mark of authority dates back to the seventh century, originating from the practice of sealing letters and documents with a signet ring. For this reason, the liturgical ring of a prelate is always set with a precious stone. Later, the ring became emblematic of the bishop's betrothal to the Church; thus it acquired a mystical significance. Today the bishop has two rings: an *ordinary* ring, always worn, and a ring to be worn at Pontifical Mass.

The supreme pontiff has three rings: an *ordinary* ring, a *pontifical* ring, as every other bishop, has, and the *Fisherman's ring* of Saint Peter, which is used to seal papal briefs; its origin is historically connected with those briefs themselves. Cardinals also receive a ring in the secret consistory, as a distinguishing mark of their great dignity. Abbots, prelates *nullius,* and prothonotary apostolic participants (*de numero participantium*) are privileged as well to wear a ring with a single diamond (Can. 325). Among other prelates, only prothonotaries apostolic supernumeraries and those *ad instar participantium* are allowed to wear the ring, but only in pontifical functions. All other clerics are forbidden to wear a ring (Can. 136, par. 2, and Can. 811, par. 2) during the celebration of Mass, unless permission was granted by apostolic indult or privilege.

The faithful who devoutly kiss the ring of the Holy Father gain an indulgence of 300 days; the ring of a cardinal, 100 days; and the ring of a patriarch, archbishop, bishop, vicar-apostolic and prefect-apostolic, 50 days (Holy Office, April 18, 1909; Sacred Penitentiary, November 21, 1945).

The liturgy makes provision for a ring in the marriage ceremony, which is blessed before placement on the bride's hand. In many places a mutual exchange of rings between bride and groom (double-ring ceremony) occurs; in this both rings are blessed. The liturgical use of the ring at a wedding dates back to the Romans, with the bestowal on the part of the man of marriage gifts and tokens to the woman.

Those who have legitimately acquired a doctoral degree may also wear a ring signifying this (Can. 1378). *Cig.*

RISK (Financial). An effect of a continuous economic activity, over a period of time and of the consequent need to make continuous predictions on future market conditions, *risk,* as a technical term, is a mathematical probability that predictions will be realized. If the activities or events in question are regular, the risk can be determined with sufficient approximation. If conditions are fluctuating, the risk becomes unpredictable.

Risk is a source of remuneration for the entrepreneur, the capitalist, and also certain categories of workers. This form of remuneration is a result of a temporary semi-monopolistic condition in which those who succeed in business temporarily find themselves. In any case, this remuneration within proportionate limits is morally justified. *Mai.*

RITE. *See* Rubric.

RITES, CONGREGATION OF. *See* Congregations, Roman.

RITES ON THE SACRAMENTS. *See* Sacrament.

RITUALE. The *Rituale* is a book containing formulas to be recited and the norms or rubrics to be observed in the administration of all the sacraments except holy orders (cf. *Pontificale*), in exorcism, blessings, etc. The prayers and rubrics for conferring holy orders are contained in the *Pontificale* (*q.v.*).

The *Roman Ritual* (*Rituale Romanum*) in its present form was compiled by order of Paul V, who gave the entire Latin Church a precise and uniform rule for the administration of the sacraments and sacramentals. The *Ritual* of Paul V was amplified by Benedict XIV. Pius XI authorized the publication of the edition which was revised according to the provisions of Canon Law, the rubrics of the *Roman Missal*, and more recent decrees of the Holy See; this edition was brought up to date by Pius XII (1952). The Psalms used in this latest edition are the new translation approved by a *motu proprio* of Pius XII in 1945.

CONTENTS. The Church, by virtue of the power received from its Divine Founder, has surrounded the elements of divine origin in the sacraments with a series of accessory ceremonies, to emphasize the meaning and the effects of the sacraments and to increase the reverence and the devotion of the faithful.

The custom of the imposition of the hands and the recitation of prayers for the purpose of driving away from the faithful, as well as from objects used by them, the influence of the devil (exorcism (*q.v.*), has existed in the Church from the earliest times. Similarly, there has always been the custom of blessing people and things. There are three kinds of blessings: dedicatory, imploratory, and both dedicatory and imploratory.

Dedicatory blessings are used in the dedication of a person or a thing to God and His worship, and confers a new state of being, as in the benediction of virgins, oratory, bell, altar linens, vestments, etc.

Purely *imploratory* blessings are used to obtain God's favor. These may be imparted to individuals, imploring particular benefits on their behalf, such as the blessing of the sick, of mothers after childbirth, etc., or may be bestowed on irrational creatures in order that they may not be harmful to man, as the blessing of an animal, house, the sea. They may ask God to grant fertility to the fields or that the use of particular things may benefit spiritually and corporally those who use them, as the blessing of food, drink, work tools, vehicles.

The *dedicatory* and *imploratory* blessing confers a new state of being on particular things and asks the Lord at the same time to remove from the places, where these things shall be placed, anything which may be harmful to man and preserve from evil those who will use them with devotion or will carry them on their person. The blessing of water, palms, candles, *Agnus Dei*, scapulars, medals, rosaries, and the like are examples of this type. Ecclesiastical authority has attached indulgences to the use of certain blessed objects. A thing blessed with a dedicatory blessing keeps its sacred character, unless some intervening circumstance by virtue of a special disposition of the Church makes it lose its sacred character. (For a more detailed account, *see* Benediction and Consecration.)

The custom of processions with singing and lights, and the observance of special ceremonies for the burial of the faithful deceased have come down to us from the earliest days of the Church (*see* Procession).

We must have a high esteem for the ceremonies and blessings of the Church and try to understand their profound significance; we must also have great respect for people and things dedicated to God. It is, indeed, a commendable practice to have frequent recourse to the blessings of the Church. Even the frequent and devout use of blessed objects is of great usefulness; in fact, it is an act of faith and trust; by virtue of the intercession of the Church, which is always heeded by the Lord, it is another means of obtaining graces to live righteously and to be protected against the nefarious influence of the devil.

Different from the above-mentioned blessings are other blessings that are not given officially in the name of the Church. These blessings may, nevertheless, be very beneficial, especially if bestowed by one who has authority over the person or thing blessed—for example, the blessing of children by their parents. *Man.*

RIVER. See Accession.

ROBBERY. Robbery is a form of theft in which the injustice, inherent in the seizure of the property of another, involves a further injustice in the use of violence upon another. Armed robbery is a special form of robbery, punished by law with particularly severe penalties.

Morally speaking, a robber becomes guilty of two specifically distinct sins of injustice: theft and violence. Besides the penalties inflicted by law, a layman, as a robber, is punished by Canon Law; this punishment involves exclusion from all legal ecclesiastical acts and any office that he might hold in the Church. If the robber is a cleric, he shall be punished by an ecclesiastical tribunal with penalties of penance, censure, privation of office, benefice and dignity, or finally deposition; these penalties depend on the gravity of the crime (Can. 2354, par. 1–2). *See also* Extortion. *Fel.*

ROCHET. *See* Sacred Vestments.

ROD, DIVINING. *See* Rhabdomancy.

ROGATIONS. Rogations are penitential processions (*q.v.*), composed of the singing of the Litany of the Saints and appropriate ceremonies in petition for a good harvest. Major rogations (*litaniae maiores*) fall on the feast of Saint Mark (April 25) and were instituted for the purpose of replacing similar pagan customs (the so-called *Robigalia* in honor of the god or goddess *Robigo*). Minor rogations (*litaniae minores*) occur during the three days before the Ascension feast and are of Roman-Gallic origin.

The substitution for the *Robigalia* or urban, pagan, Roman processions dates back to the fourth century and Pope Liberius (352–366). This substitution of the Litanies and a procession was called *Maior* (the term is encountered in an invitation of the year 598), to distinguish the procession from other similar but less ancient solemn processions in Rome.

Minor rogations date back to St. Mamertus, Bishop of Vienna (d. *circa* 470), who began them on the occasion of great calamities in his diocese. They actually came from Gaul, and were related to other pagan processions which they replaced: the *Ambarvalia*, which took place in rural areas at the initiative of the landowners during the days between May 17 and May 30. These minor rogation days were celebrated first in Gaul and later introduced into Italy.

With the exception of the Station Churches, the major and minor rogations have the same liturgy. The procession is highlighted by the singing of the Litany of the Saints, which in the ninth century replaced the Psalms. Despite the loss of their ancient, severe, penitential character, which prevailed in Gaul, they have retained the penitential color (purple) of the sacred vestments (cope and tunic) for the procession and the Mass. In rural areas the procession goes through the country roads along cultivated fields; in some countries it commences with the blessing and distribution of ashes and the celebration of Mass in black vestments. *Pal.*

ROMAN PILGRIMAGES. *See* Indulgence.

ROSARY. In a material sense, the rosary is a string or chain of beads used to count certain vocal prayers occurring in frequent repetition. In a wider sense, the term indicates particular forms of prayer, such as the *rosary* of the Blessed Virgin, in which the beads are used to keep count of the *Aves* and *Paters* recited in frequent repetition and according to a set pattern and number.

HISTORICAL BACKGROUND. The practice of counting repeated prayers with pebbles, berries, etc., is very ancient and was found both among pagans and Christians. In the fourth century, a certain monk named Paul was known to count with pebbles the *Pater nosters* as he recited them. The rosary beads came into common use in the fifteenth century following a wide diffusion of the devotion of the rosary. The origin of this form of prayer is rather obscure. It was not until the close of the medieval period that authorship of the rosary was attributed to St. Dominic by Alan de la Roche (*Alanus de Rupe*, d. 1475), who fervently recommended in his preaching this devotional practice. After the devotion became widespread, the popes added their stamp of approval by applying indulgences to the recitation of the rosary and earnestly recommending its practice, especially in times of grave calamity. Noted is the Brief *Consueverunt* (Sept. 14, 1569) of St. Pius V, who saw in the rosary an omen of victory at Lepanto (Oct. 4, 1571). With nine admirable encyclicals on the rosary, Pope Leo XIII gave great impetus to the work of Ven. Bartolo Longo (d. 1926), noted promoter of the devotion of the rosary and founder of the renowned Shrine at Pompei, a center of Marian devotion. An appeal for the daily recitation of the rosary is also contained in

the encyclical *Ingruentium malorum* of Pius XII (Sept. 15, 1951).

The devotion of the rosary, also called *Our Lady's Psalter*, consists in the norally uninterrupted recitation of 150 (the number of psalms) Hail Marys, divided into fifteen decades, each beginning with the Our Father. The recitation is accompanied by a brief meditation on the principal mysteries of the life, death, and resurrection of Christ and on the life of Christ's mother.

According to the *Roman Breviary* (Lesson IV of 2nd Nocturn of the Feast of the Holy Rosary), the rosary is a form of prayer wherein we say fifteen decades of Hail Marys with an Our Father between each decade, accompanied by meditation on one of the mysteries of our redemption.

Pius XII, in the above-cited encyclical enumerates the following characteristics as proper to this form of prayer: (1) the rosary is a prayer both *vocal* and mental; it provides recitation and meditation. (2) It is a brief devotional practice which may be broken into small units, capable of being fitted into spare moments. (3) It is a prayer compatible with manual or material occupations. (4) It is suitable to everyone's mental ability. (5) Through the mysteries, it leads to the contemplation of important personages and events. (6) It is an easy prayer to resort to. (7) It is a natural prayer to turn to in the vicissitudes of life. (8) It affords inspiration for great undertakings. (9) It is a defensive and offensive weapon against the infernal powers. (10) It is social in character, lending itself to collective and public recitation. (11) It is an easy prayer to learn and retain. (12) As noted, it bears an analogy with the Psalter.

In due course of time, a particular form and blessing were required for the rosary. At present the prescribed form is that of a chaplet, not a band, bracelet, and the like. (Incidentally, the requirements set forth in this paragraph apply also to other types of rosaries.) The beads must be linked together in sets of ten (seven and three in other rosaries); they may not be substituted with carved or etched ringlets, whether golden or silver. The beads must be of solid material such as wood, glass, mother-of-pearl, marble, alabaster, or even tin and lead; but these last two types of beads cannot be indulgenced. The chain may be of metal, leather, silver, hemp, or similar material. In order to be indulgenced, rosary beads must be blessed. Except for special faculties, rosaries and chaplets of the Seven Dolors must be blessed according to the long or short form contained in the *Roman Ritual* (*q.v.*); for other beads, the form of blessing is optional; a sign of the Cross is generally sufficient.

INDULGENCES ATTACHED TO THE RECITATION OF THE ROSARY. The practice of reciting the rosary has been enriched with numerous indulgences, which may be gained even by those not belonging to the Confraternity of the Holy Rosary (*see* Confraternity). Some of these indulgences are as follows: (1) an indulgence of ten years may be gained each day the rosary is recited; (2) a plenary indulgence may be gained on the last Sunday of the month, if one has recited the rosary for at least three weeks, and provided that one goes to confession, receives Holy Communion and visits a church or public oratory; (3) those who recite five decades of the rosary before the Blessed Sacrament publicly exposed or reserved in the tabernacle may gain, each time, a plenary indulgence, provided that they go to confession and receive Holy Communion (Pius XI, Brief of Sept. 4, 1927).

To gain the ordinary indulgences for reciting the rosary, the following conditions are required: (1) that one recite at least five decades, not necessarily without interruption but on the same day, and that one meditate on the mystery assigned to each decade (St. Pius X, July 8, 1908); (2) that the meditation on the mysteries of the life, death and resurrection of the Lord be made, at least mentally, during the recitation of the *Aves* or *Paters* (Decree of July 1, 1839). It is not, however, necessary that the mysteries be announced before the recitation of the individual decades (Decree of July 1, 1839). The meditation on the mysteries is thus arranged: Joyful Mysteries on Monday and Thursday; Sorrowful Mysteries, on Tuesday and Friday, Glorious Mysteries on Wednesday, Saturday and Sunday; however, one is free to meditate on any mystery, regardless of the day of the week (Decree of July 1, 1839).

A Dominican priest, or other priest having special faculties, may attach particular indulgences to rosaries. (The latest indulgence of 500 days was granted to those who carry on their person and kiss blessed rosary beads, March 30, 1953; AAS 45 [1953] 311.) Rosary beads blessed by the pope are enriched with apostolic indulgences.

CHAPLET OF OUR LORD. This was instituted in 1516 by Blessed Michael of Florence (d. Jan. 11, 1522), a Camaldolese monk. The chaplet consists of thirty-three Our Fathers, in memory and veneration of Our Lord's thirty-three years on earth. To the Our Fathers are added five Hail Marys (one before each decade) in commemoration of the five wounds of Christ, and at the end the *Credo* is recited in honor of the Apostles. This chaplet is proper to the Order of Camaldolese monks and was enriched with special indulgences by Leo X and successively by other popes.

FRANCISCAN ROSARY OF THE SEVEN JOYS OF THE BLESSED VIRGIN. The Franciscan rosary according to the tradition preserved in the Seraphic Order dates back to the year 1422. It consists of seventy Hail Marys and seven Our Fathers, with a *Pater* and *Ave* added for the intention of the pope. To the original seventy Hail Marys two more have been added, in order to complete the probable number of seventy-two years that Our Lady is believed to have lived on earth. St. Pius X (Dec. 4, 1906) attached several indulgences to this rosary, the blessing of which is reserved to a priest of one of the three Franciscan families.

ROSARY OF THE SEVEN DOLORS OF THE BLESSED VIRGIN MARY. This chaplet originated in the Order of the Servants of Mary. It consists of seven parts, in memory of the seven sorrows of Our

Lady, each part consisting of a *Pater* and seven *Aves;* at the end, three more Hail Marys are added in commemoration of the tears of the Blessed Virgin. It has been enriched with indulgences (July 18, 1877). The faculty of blessing this chaplet is generally reserved to the priests of the Order of the Servants of Mary, although other priests also have such faculty.

THE BRIGITTINE ROSARY. Originated and propagated by St. Bridget of Sweden (d. 1373), this rosary is recited in honor of Our Lady and in commemoration of the sixty-three years which, according to another opinion, the Blessed Virgin is said to have lived on earth. It consists of six decades, each consisting of one Our Father, ten Hail Marys and a Credo; a *Pater noster* is added at the end to attain the number of seven in memory of Our Lady's seven sorrows and joys, and this is followed by three *Aves* to complete the number of the Virgin's sixty-three years. The chaplet is indulgenced (Sac. Congregation of Indulgences: Jan. 6, 1886, and Dec. 8, 1887). The blessing of this chaplet was reserved upon extinction of the Brigittines to the Order of Canons Regular of the Most Holy Redeemer but the faculty is also enjoyed by other priests.

ROSARY OF THE CRUCIFERS. To those devoutly reciting the rosary of the Blessed Virgin, blessed by the Master General *pro tempore* of the Canons Regular of St. Augustine of the Order of the Holy Cross (commonly known as Crucifers), Leo X granted an indulgence of 500 days for every *Pater* and *Ave* (Brief *Regularem vitam,* August 20, 1516). The faculty of blessing this rosary is reserved to this Order but it may also be granted to other priests. It is enjoyed as a privilege by priests belonging to the Pious Union of Clergy for the Missions.

ROSARY IN HONOR OF ST. MICHAEL THE ARCHANGEL AND THE ANGELIC CHOIRS. This is made up of nine large beads, each followed by three small ones; on the large beads are recited the *Paters,* on the small ones the *Aves.* Four other large beads follow for the recitation of four more *Paters.* To gain the indulgences granted by Pius IX (Aug. 8, 1851), it is required that special invocations be directed to the individual angelic choirs. The faculty of blessing and indulgencing this rosary is extended to all priests empowered to bless sacred objects. *Pal.*

ROTA, SACRED ROMAN. The Sacred Roman Rota is the ordinary tribunal of the Holy See for the reception of appeals. It originated in the apostolic chancery which was in existence at the time of Pope Lucius III (1181–1185). This chancery was the office in which judiciary acts were recorded and rescripts prepared. It also assigned judges; hence, it was also called *audientia,* just as the place where the Pope deliberated was called *auditorium.* This chancery was headed by a chancellor. Afterwards this title was reserved to the Pope, and the chancery was headed by a vice-chancellor. The first official after the vice-chancellor was the auditor-contradictarum; chaplains came next.

The Pope reserved to himself the *contestatio litis* and the issuance of the sentence, but the interrogation was conducted by cardinals or chaplains. At the beginning of his pontificate, Innocent III (1198–1216) would hear the reports of the chaplains (*auditori*) and the advice of the cardinals; then he would issue the sentences personally. Later he assigned to the chaplains the duty of issuing the sentences, after consultation with the cardinals, and reserved to himself the approval of the sentences. Eventually, the cardinals withdrew from the hearings and the office of judging cases rested entirely with the chaplains or auditors.

The interrogation was conducted by the chaplains as cases were introduced, but as the cases increased in number the magisterial function of the chaplains became permanent and they became known as *auditores causarum curiae domini papae.*

After Gregory X (d. 1276), the chaplains formed a permanent tribunal within the pontifical consistory; however, it was

John XXII who gave them their own seat where they could adjudicate cases even in the absence of the Pope, whose intervention in the trials, after Clement IV (1265–1268), had become even rarer.

In 1331, John XXII, by the constitution *Ratio iuris*, organized the tribunal in a definitive manner with its own special regulations and convenient seat at Avignon. It seems that the name *Rota* originated from a revolving wooden stand containing the documents of each cause. According to another explanation, the tribunal takes its name from the rotating system of the judges in trying cases. Sixtus IV (1472) brought to twelve the number of chaplains or auditors.

The election of the auditors of the Rota always has been reserved to the Pope, but certain rulers were granted the privilege of nominating auditors. The king of Spain could nominate two, one for Aragon and one for Castile; the king of France and the king of Germany could each nominate one. The same privilege was granted to Bologna, Milan, Venice, Ferrara, and Perugia.

The auditors were selected from among the most renowned jurists (*doctoris juris famosi*), who were distinguished for honesty and rectitude. After John XXII, the auditors were divided into three categories: the first consisted of the youngest, who judged cases in the first appeal; the last was made up of the oldest, who judged cases in the third appeal. Later on, the groups consisted of a relator (*ponens*) and one-third of the auditors of the entire college, that is, four auditors, who sat at the left of the relator.

The Rota always was considered a delegated tribunal, even after Gregory XVI (1834) made it the ordinary civil tribunal for cases in the Papal States. Its jurisdiction was never clearly defined until Benedict XIV, in his constitution *Justitiae et pacis* (1747), assigned to the Rota, as a tribunal of second and final appeal, the more important cases dealt with in the first appeal by the Roman Curia, the Tribunal of the Cardinal Vicar of Rome, and the Auditor of the Apostolic Chamber, and causes referred to the Roman Curia for adjudication in the third instance. Pius VIII (1821) also made the Rota a supreme tribunal for commercial causes of the Papal States. In 1870 the activities of the Rota tribunal were suspended, but St. Pius X re-established it by his constitution *Sapienti Consilio* (1908), assigning to it all questions to be handled in a judiciary manner by the Roman Curia.

PRESENT REGULATIONS. The new regulations of the Rota were established by the *Lex Propria Sacrae Romanae Rotae et Signaturae Apostolicae*, published with the above-mentioned constitution, *Sapienti consilio* (1908). These were followed by the *Regulae servandae apud Sacrae Romanae Rotae Tribunal* (1910), which contained the rules of procedure. When the Code of Canon Law was published, the regulations of the historical tribunal were brought into conformity with the Code by *Normae Sacrae Romanae Rotae tribunalis*, published September 1st, 1934, which are still in force.

The Rota is composed of a certain number of auditor-prelates or judges, appointed personally by the Pope; at the present time there are sixteen auditors, one French, one English, one German, one Polish, two Spanish (Concordat with Spain, Aug. 27, 1953, art. 25, no. 21), two North American, and the rest Italian. The senior judge presides over the Rota as *primus inter pares*. In case of vacancy, the next judge in line of seniority becomes the president (Norms, art. 3, par. 2).

Priests, born in wedlock, with a degree *in utroque jure*, of mature age, outstanding for honesty, rectitude, learning, and prudence may be appointed auditors. They cease to hold office either by promotion to another office or by reaching the age of seventy-five years (Norms, art. 2).

The function of public prosecutor is exercised by a promoter of justice and a defender of the bond. Both must be priests of mature age, with a degree *in utroque jure*, outstanding for personal integrity, prudence, and juridical learning. They are proposed by the Rotal college and appointed by the Pope (Norms, art. 4). The same qualifications are required in their substitutes (Norms, art. 5).

Other officials are notaries, scribes, distributors, accountants, cursors and apparitors. The notaries must be lawyers. The recorders must be priests with a degree in Canon Law, selected through competitive examination by the Rotal college and confirmed by the Pope.

The counsels for the defense are the consistorial advocates and the Rota advocates, clergymen or laymen, with at least a degree in Canon Law, who have obtained a related diploma.

The Sacred Roman Rota is today an ordinary collegiate tribunal (Norms, art. 1); it tries cases either in separate groups of three auditors constituting one court or in joint sessions (*videntibus omnibus*). The rotating courts consist of a dean and two others in descending order, down to the last auditors; the first group consists of the dean, sub-dean and third auditor; the second of the sub-dean, third auditor and fourth auditor, and so forth (Norms, art. 15, par. 1). Each rotating group is not only a section of the tribunal but also a court of appeal of the preceding court. In each case the appellate court consists of the auditors who immediately precede the auditors of the court against which an appeal is made (Norms, art. 15, par. 2).

The cases referred to the Rota are assigned to the various courts by the dean (Norms, art. 14) through a decree designating also the *ponens;* the rule requires that the *ponens* be the oldest of the three judges (Norms, art. 18), and that he also act as president of the court (Norms, art. 19). The dean may for a good reason appoint another auditor as *ponens,* after consultation with the other members of the court (Norms, art. 19, par. 3).

The tribunal sits in joint session on cases referred by the *Signatura Apostolica* to the Rota, in a case involving *restitutio ad integrum* and other cases which the

Pope may commit to it. The Pope at times sets the number of auditors at five or seven. The present jurisdiction of the Rota extends to all ecclesiastical cases, civil and criminal, except those personally reserved to the Pontiff (Can. 1557, par. 1) or to the Holy Office (Can. 1555, par. 1).

The Rota is essentially a court of appeals, but in some cases it tries cases at first instance. As a court of appeals, the Rota tries cases heard in lower tribunals (diocesan) or in a preceding court of the Rota. Therefore: (a) it is similar to lower tribunals of second appeal when it hears appeals from diocesan tribunals of first instance (Can. 1599, par. 1), with the exception of matrimonial cases tried in the Italian regional tribunals, which cannot be heard by the Rota except on third appeal (Rescript of the Secretariat of State, Oct. 16, 1954); (b) it hears appeals from sentences pronounced by tribunals of second appeal if these are not *res judicata* (Can. 1599, par. 1, n. 2). Regarding sentences given by lower tribunals, the Rota also tries cases of nullity (Can. 1906), and hears appeals for a new trial after two uniform sentences in cases concerning the state of life of persons (Can. 1603).

The Rota, on the other hand, cannot agree to review cases on appeal if the appeal is against a sentence issued by a preceding court of the Rota; this right is reserved to the *Apostolica Signatura* (Can. 1608, par. 1, nn. 3 and 4).

Since the establishment of the State of Vatican City, the Rota is also a court of appeals for cases tried by the Vatican tribunal in first instance. In such cases, however, jurisdiction must be exercised within the territory of the State (*Fundamental Law of the Vatican State,* June 7, 1930, art. 10, 14).

As a tribunal of first instance, the Rota tries cases which by law are reserved to the tribunals of the Holy See (Can. 1557, par. 2), and, as a rule, also those which the Pope has reserved to himself (Can. 1599, par. 2). In such cases all instances are within the jurisdiction of the Rota tribunal. *Rob.*

ROTARY CLUB. The Rotary movement, so-called from its emblem, a toothed wheel, was founded in Chicago, in 1905, by a lawyer called Paul Harris. It spread so rapidly throughout the United States and other countries that in 1912 the *Rotary International* was established. In 1933, it already had 147,000 members in 3,600 clubs. The members, generally middle-class professional men, meet regularly at their clubs where a spirit of fellowship is fostered. The Rotary Club's purpose is to promote in its members feelings of rational ethics, and especially, the ideals of honesty and service to society, which contribute to a happier social life. Its ethics do not pretend to be founded on supernatural or religious dogma since the movement seeks to enlist members of all religions, but solely on natural reason.

This principle of non-dogmatic ethics gives the Rotary a character of religious indifference and, in the last analysis, is based on mere utilitarianism. He who serves best gains the most. Furthermore, due to a similarity of ethical principles and a close relationship, the Rotary Club has shown, in the course of its history, signs of kinship with masonry (*see* Secret Societies).

The character of religious indifference creates serious dangers to the faith of its members, and for this reason the Catholic Church has, on repeated occasions, shown a disapproval of this movement insofar as Catholics are concerned. The Sacred Consistorial Congregation, on February 4, 1929, declared that bishops cannot permit their priests and clerics to belong to the Rotary Clubs or to attend their meetings. There is no general prohibition for laymen, but in some countries (Spain, France and Holland) the episcopate has thought it wise to warn the faithful against the dangers arising from membership in such clubs, and forbade in some cases contact with them, according to the rules of the Code of Canon Law (Can. 684). On December 20, 1950, the Sacred Congregation of the Holy Office extended these rules, restated the prohibition to the clergy against membership in the Rotary, and exhorted laymen to observe the prescription of Can. 684, which forbade membership in associations which reject or are suspected of rejecting vigilance on the part of the Church. *Dam.*

RUBRICS. Rubrics are guides or rules for actions to be observed in the performance of liturgical services. As the name implies (*ruber*—red), they were printed in red on the margin of liturgical books. At first the term was used in a much broader sense; in the sixteenth century it became a technical term for notes which explained the ceremonies and the manner of performing them.

The first systematic collections of rubrics was the *Ordines Romani* (*see* Liturgical Books). Today, the sole valid rubrics are contained in the official liturgical books; explanations are given by competent bodies such as the Sacred Congregation of Rites, which are charged with their interpretation.

Rubrics has become a separate science among ecclesiastical sciences. The complete knowledge and understanding of the liturgy is left to them, so that through such knowledge and history one can achieve a true understanding of the rubrics.

Since the sacraments are sacred things, the Church included in the *Ritual* many instructions and prescriptions for their proper administration. Therefore, except in the case of grave necessity, it is not permissible to administer the sacraments by neglecting the rubrics prescribed in the *Ritual* (Council of Trent, Sess. 7, Can. 13, *De sacramentis in genere*, Denz. 856; *also* Can. 733).

Ordinarily, all are required to use the *Roman Ritual*, but certain churches are allowed to use their own ritual. The rubrics of the *Ritual* are not all binding in the same manner; they are distinguished into *essential* rubrics linked to the essence of the sacraments and the application of *matter* to *form*, or *accidental* rubrics concerning the proper rather than the valid administration of the sacraments. Rubrics are also distinguished into *preceptive* rubrics, which are binding in conscience, or *directive* rubrics, which contain counsels and guiding norms. In practice, however, it is difficult to say which rubrics are preceptive and which are directive. As a general rule it may be said that, since the rubrics have the force of positive ecclesiastical law, they produce an obligation in conscience, which may be slight or serious according to the importance of the subject. But as positive laws, the rubrics, if they are accidental, are not binding in the face of grave inconvenience. If, however, a rubric allows the manner of performance of an act to the judgment of the priest or minister of the sacrament, the rubric has simply directive value.

The same questions, raised with regard to the rubrics prescribed for the administration of the sacraments, are also raised with regard to the rubrics prescribed for the celebration of the Mass. Despite divergency of opinion, the following conclusions may be considered as practically certain: (a) The prayers of *preparation* before and of *thanksgiving* after the Mass do not oblige under penalty of sin. (b) A priest who, because of illness, must omit or modify certain prescriptions does not need authorization, if it is a matter of small importance; if, however, it concerns important matters, he must obtain permission of the competent authority. (c) With respect to the color of the vestments, a change, in itself, is not a serious offense; the same may be said about substituting one Mass for another, contrary to the prescription of the Calendar (*q.v.*); it may, however, be a serious offense if the change were to be a cause of scandal. (d) The omission from the *Ordinarium Missae* of an invariable part may more easily be a serious offense than the omission of one of the variable parts. A deliberate omission of a considerable part of the Mass is, in itself, always a serious offense. A part omitted may be said at a different place, provided that this does not give rise to wonder on the part of those present; on the contrary, it is better to omit this altogether, unless it is an essential part.

The so-called *Preces post Missam*, or prayers after the Holy Mass, prescribed by Leo XIII may be legitimately omitted, in a conventual Mass, or if the Mass is celebrated with extraordinary solemnity, or if a liturgical function follows immediately after the Holy Mass. (By a recent disposition, if a sermon was preached during the Mass, these prayers may be omitted.)

The unauthorized addition of new ceremonies to the Mass or other sacred functions constitutes useless or vain worship. Usually a venial sin, it may become grave if it is a cause of scandal. For recent changes made in some rubrics of the Breviary and the Missal, *see* Breviary and Missal. *Cig.*

RUGBY. *See* Sports, Dangerous.

RULES AND CONSTITUTIONS. The complete set of laws that govern a religious institute and the life of its members are its rules and constitutions.

Rule, in its proper sense, means an instrument used to draw straight lines; in a figurative sense, it came to signify a universal statement, the foundation of other notions or deductions. In its juridical sense, it indicates a precept or norm to be followed in the proper government of persons. This latter meaning was introduced in the legislations for religious, wherein it came to indicate a set of precepts directing religious life in the attainment of evangelical perfection. Up to the sixteenth century, *rule* meant the fundamental legislation, characteristic of each individual religious institute, as established by its founder. In this sense one spoke of the great rules of St. Basil, St. Augustine, St. Benedict, and St. Francis, which served as basic law for religious institutes. However, since such rules contained only ascetical and moral precepts on many points, they necessarily had to be complemented by juridical elements called *constitutions.* These, of course, contained determinations of secondary importance with respect to the *rule* itself.

From the sixteenth century on, *constitutions* came to designate indiscriminately legislation proper to the new orders and congregations. Later, the two words assumed different meanings; *constitutions* came to signify fundamental laws generally approved by the Holy See, and *rules* meant a series of particular determinations of secondary importance with respect to the constitutions.

The Code of Canon Law has sanctioned the meaning of the two words in such a manner that *constitutions* mean the fundamental laws of every religious institute, while *rules* mean the particular dispositions concerning the government and mode of life of the respective institutes. These do not necessarily require approbation of the Holy See. These naturally reflect the spirit of the constitutions.

Before granting local Ordinaries permission to erect a religious institute, the Holy See wishes knowledge of the constitutions and demands a copy of the same from the Ordinary, to ascertain that they are compiled in the proper manner and do not contain strange, bizarre, or unusual practices not in conformity with the sacred canons.

No one will doubt the moral value of the constitutions as far as their binding force is concerned, since the religious solemnly binds himself to observe them from the moment of his religious profession (Can. 593). It is not an easy task, however, to determine precisely the moral nature and the gravity of an action or omission on the part of a religious, contrary to the dispositions of the constitutions and the rules.

Without going into various opinions concerning this question, the following principles may be set forth: (1) The religious constitutions, in accordance with the present practice of the Church, are not binding under pain of sin generally. They are considered penal laws and, as such, are binding in conscience only to the extent that one must satisfy the penalty imposed for transgression. (2.) By way of exception, constitutions bind in conscience under pain of sin in the following cases: (a) If they enforce norms of the law of God or of the Church. Because the constitutions regarding the government, formation, profession, and enclosure are laws imposed by the Code of Canon Law, these general laws bind all religious. (b) If they determine fundamental norms concerning the government of the institute, or its purpose, apart from any dispensation from the Holy See. (c) If they concern the religious vows, so that an infraction is a sin against the vows. (d) If they are legitimately imposed by superiors by virtue of the vow of obedience. In fact, additional sin is committed if one violates them out of formal contempt. (e) If the omission or violation of prescriptions of the constitutions, not binding under sin, is accompanied by bad motives, such as sloth, scandal, and the like, the violation of the constitutions incurs the malice of the motive that induced the violation.

Since the strength of a religious institute depends on the observance of the constitutions, superiors can and must impose suitable penances on transgressors of the constitutions in order to enforce observance of same.

Finally, it cannot be denied that, though a particular transgression may not constitute a sin, it nevertheless carries within itself a positive imperfection since it entails the violation of a juridical disposition which the rules and constitutions impose on a particular group of persons obliged to their observance. *Mand.*

S

SABOTAGE. The word *sabotage* is of French derivation (*sabot*—wooden shoe, *saboter*—to tread with a wooden shoe). In a wide sense, *sabotage* is the willful and malicious disturbance or disruption of another person's activity or work. Strictly speaking, it is the premeditated and insidious damage or destruction of the property or labor of another as an act of reprisal.

Originally, the term meant to perform an assigned work poorly or carelessly. Gradually it came to signify various tactics and devices employed in obstructing the regular process of production, i.e., in paralyzing or destroying the means of production (machinery, equipment, instruments, tools, etc.). Thus sabotage developed into a weapon of labor groups or other forces seeking to obtain a social or political revolution. By 1843 it became highly developed in France, where special courses were conducted to turn it into a real science.

Sabotage is practiced in a variety of ways. It may take on the form of passive resistance or feigned loyalty, slothful work, occupation of a plant or factory, picketing to prevent others from working, rendering the means of transportation unsafe. It may aim at reducing production, wasting material, damaging the quality or value of manufactured goods, etc.

The preferred tactics or methods of sabotage are: slowing down the railways, cutting steel wires, pouring sand into the gears of machinery, loosening bolts, etc. Everything possible is done to irritate and embarrass the employer and at the same time to diminish or cripple production. Generally, sabotage is practiced secretly; this, of course, makes detection of responsibility difficult.

Sabotage is not limited to the field of industry and labor. It may be practiced in almost any sphere. During the last war, sabotage became an almost universal practice, with both sides resorting to the systematic destruction of bridges, railways, aqueducts, electric power plants, not to mention the frequent acts of reprisal and revenge, the burning of entire villages, wholesale massacres, etc.

Many condemn the practice of sabotage for various reasons. Thus, Sorel states that labor unions must not seek to destroy machinery and equipment, because some day labor will gain possession and control of these means of production. The German labor unions, generally, oppose sabotage as a form of extortion. In recent years, sabotage has become an ordinary communist weapon for the advancement of dictatorial aims. This kind of sabotage is obviously immoral.

As a weapon of war against the enemy, sabotage must be considered lawful if practiced in a just war with due consideration for the innocent civilian population.

As a weapon in the hands of labor groups, sabotage, unlike a strike, is clearly unlawful, inasmuch as it involves damage or destruction of the property of another. *Per.*

SACRAMENT. A sacrament is "a visible sign of invisible grace instituted for our justification" (Council of Trent), or "an outward sign instituted by Christ to give grace" (Baltimore Catechism). The causality of a sacrament is immediate; that is, the sacramental rite itself effects what it symbolizes, not by virtue of a moral value arising from the dignity or dispositions of the person administering or receiving the sacrament, but *ex opere operato*, i.e., by virtue of an efficacy communicated to it by Christ, the author of the sacraments (Council of Trent, Denz. n. 851).

In each sacrament two elements are distinguished: the *matter* and the *form*. In those sacraments which involve the use of a visible thing, as in baptism, confirmation and extreme unction, a distinction is made between remote (the thing used) and proximate matter (the actual use).

The divine institution of the sacraments does not imply that Jesus Christ Himself determined the matter and form of each sacrament, even to the smallest details (*usque ad infirmam speciem*), although He did this for baptism and the Holy Eucharist. According to a well-founded opinion, Christ determined in a general manner the matter and form of certain sacraments (baptism, Holy Eucharist), leaving to the Apostles and the Church to determine further the elements of the other sacraments.

As conditions of time and place demanded, prayers and ceremonies were added to the essential rite, by competent ecclesiastical authority either to emphasize their efficacy, urge a greater reverence, or better dispose the faithful to a more fruitful reception of the sacraments (Council of Trent, Denz. nn. 856, 931).

The sacraments are seven in number: baptism, confirmation, Holy Eucharist, penance, extreme unction, holy orders, and matrimony (Council of Trent, Denz. n. 844).

The principal minister of the sacraments is Jesus Christ; secondary ministers are those to whom Jesus Christ granted His sacerdotal power; through them, Jesus Christ Himself acts as principal cause.

For the validity of the sacraments, neither faith nor the state of grace is required in the visible minister; accordingly, the Church has always held valid, sacraments duly administered by heretics and sinners. Nevertheless, the intention (will) to act as ministers of Jesus Christ, i.e., to do what Jesus Christ intended or what the Church intends by such a rite, is necessary. This intention, however, need not be actual and explicit; a virtual and implicit intention is sufficient.

With the exception of baptism, which can be validly administered by anyone, and matrimony, which the baptized spouses themselves confer on each other, a valid administration of the sacraments requires that the minister have the priestly power. For holy orders (*q.v.*), and *ordinarily* for confirmation (*q.v.*), the episcopal power is required (cf. Apostolic Indult concerning the administration of confirmation to persons who are in danger of death from grave illness, by qualified priests, AAS, January 1, 1947). Concerning penance, the priestly power and ecclesiastical jurisdiction are required. Thus, the minister of the sacraments could be an ordained or a non-ordained person, depending on the particular sacrament.

Furthermore, for lawful administration of a sacrament the minister must be in the state of grace, free from censures, except in a case of necessity, and, ordinarily, must have been commissioned by the lawful ecclesiastical authority.

A sacrament that imprints a character may be validly received only once. Reception of a valid baptism is an indispensable condition (*sine qua non*) for the valid reception of all other sacraments. Additional conditions are required for a valid reception of penance, extreme unction, holy orders and matrimony (*see* each sacrament in particular). Those endowed with the use of reason must also have the intention of receiving a sacrament as a means of sanctification. This intention, however, need not be always actual or virtual; a habitual intention suffices. Neither is it necessary that it be explicit; an implicit intention suffices.

In order that a sacrament may produce its effect, which is grace, other dispositions are required in the subject. Thus, for the reception of a sacrament of the dead by one who is not in the state of grace, a supernatural and universal contrition for all mortal sins, which demands faith and hope and a firm determination not to sin any more, at least mortally, is required; for a sacrament of the living, ordinarily, the state of grace is required.

One who receives a sacrament without the proper intention, or with the knowledge of being ineligible or not duly disposed to reception, commits a grave sin of sacrilege. The same applies in the case of one who, with a reasonable doubt of his dispositions, receives a sacrament without doing his best to properly dispose himself.

The main benefit accruing from the reception of the sacraments is sanctifying grace, accompanied by the infused virtues and the gifts of the Holy Spirit. Baptism and penance are intended to confer grace to those who have not grace; for this reason, they are called sacraments of the dead. For the seriously ill who are not able to make their confession, extreme unction has the value of a sacrament of the dead. However, if one receives such a sacrament while in the state of grace, he will receive an increase of grace and of the virtues and gifts connected with it. The other sacraments were instituted to increase grace in those already possessing it; thus, they are called sacraments of the living. By way of exception, however, they may produce grace in those who have not grace, as in one who receives a sacrament of the living without being aware of the fact that he lacks the necessary dispositions but has supernatural contrition for his mortal sins with the firm will to sin no more, at least mortally. When the necessary conditions are wanting, which alone could enable an individual to receive grace, the sacrament will not be productive for the time being of sanctifying grace or the other benefits connected with it. Such benefits, however, shall be forthcoming (except in the Holy Eucharist and, according to many theologians, penance) as soon as the impediment is removed, provided that the individual still has a title to the grace through the sacrament. The title remains as long as the spiritual need remains for which the sacrament was provided. If the reception of the sacrament was not sacrilegious, that is, if the obstacle to grace was only a negative one, and no mortal sin was subsequently committed, the individual will receive the benefits the moment he will have elicited an act of contrition (imperfect); if the reception of the sacrament was sacrilegious, i.e., if there was a positive obstacle to grace, or a grave sin was committed after reception of the sacrament with a negative obstacle, grace is produced in the soul the moment in which remission of mortal sins is attained either through perfect contrition or by the reception of a sacrament with the proper dispositions.

Sanctifying grace produced by the reception of a sacrament is accompanied by a special blessing called *sacramental grace*. This is a constant title to the reception, at the proper time, of special actual graces enabling the individual to perform those acts by which the end proper to the sacrament is attained. According to a sound opinion, sanctifying grace also gives an internal strength in addition to ordinary grace and the infused virtues. If the necessary dispositions are wanting in an individual who has the proper intention of receiving a sacrament other than the Holy Eucharist (and, according to many, also penance), the sacrament creates in the soul a title to sanctifying grace, called *res et sacramentum*. Certain theologians, with good reason, hold that all the sacraments, except the Holy Eucharist, always first produce such a title to grace. For the sacraments that imprint an indelible character, the title to grace is the character itself; in the other sacraments, this title is a real mark produced in the soul of one receiving the sacrament, but it is not indelible. In fact, it vanishes when the special need which the sacrament was to supply ceases.

Three sacraments, baptism, confirmation, and holy orders, imprint an indelible *character* (*q.v.*) on the soul of the recipient. The efficacy of the sacraments, in itself, is not limited to a particular degree; the sacraments, however, do not produce their effects with equal measure, but according to the Divine Will and the dispositions of the recipient (Council of Trent, *Denz.*, n. 199). Concerning reviviscence of the sacraments, *see* Reviviscence of Sacraments; for repetition of a sacrament, *see* Repetition of Sacraments. *Man.*

SACRAMENTAL GRACE. *See* Grace, Sacrament.

SACRAMENTALS. Sacramentals are rites or sacred objects employed by the Church for the purpose of obtaining from God, through her intercession, temporal and spiritual favors (Can. 1144). Sacramentals are of ecclesiastical institution. Nevertheless, Christ authorized and commissioned the Apostles to bestow blessings and perform exorcisms against the power of the devil. And the Church, from the very beginning, has always observed the practice of blessing persons and objects and of imposing hands upon the people for the purpose of removing from them or objects used by them the influence of the evil spirits. The Holy See alone has the power to establish new sacramentals and to change or abolish those already in use (Can. 1145).

The sacramentals produce their effect, not *ex opere operato*, but *ex opere operantis Ecclesiae*, i.e., not by virtue of their own efficacy or action, but by the prayer and intercession of the Church. Since the prayers of the Church are always acceptable to God, it follows that God always hears such prayers. It is clear, however, that the Church implores favors only for those who use the sacramentals with proper faith and devotion and in a manner not contrary to higher spiritual benefits, provided that the favors requested are not opposed to the dispositions of Divine Providence. Whenever these conditions are verified, the sacramentals produce the effect for which they were instituted. Sacramentals are temporary or permanent. *Temporary* sacramentals comprise exorcisms and blessings.

Exorcisms (*q.v.*) consist in delivering persons and things from diabolical influence through the imposition of hands, prayers to God, and injunctions to the devil. Exorcisms are either *solemn* or *simple*. Solemn exorcisms are employed to drive out evil spirits in cases of demoniacal possession; *simple* exorcisms are designed to restrain the power of the devil, i.e., to prevent him from causing harm to persons or things.

Blessings (*q.v.*) consist in implorations or dedications. They may be purely invocative, constitutive, or invocative and constitutive at the same time.

Purely *invocative* blessings do not impart any sacred character to the person or thing receiving the blessing, but are mere supplications for some favor from God. Some of these blessings are imparted to persons, e.g., the nuptial blessing, the blessing of a sick person, the blessing of St. Blaise, the blessing of a woman after childbirth, etc. Other invocative blessings are bestowed on things for man's safety and protection, such as the blessing of a house, vehicle, sea, etc.; for man's temporal and spiritual benefit, such as the blessing of food, drink, instruments of work, etc.; for the purpose of fruitful production, such as the blessing of animals, fields, crops, etc.

Constitutive blessings are those in which persons or things are dedicated to God and His divine service, acquiring thereby a new mode of being, i.e., a new spiritual character or relationship. Such blessings are verbal or real. Merely *verbal* blessings are imparted without the use of holy oils, such as the blessings of virgins, oratories, altar cloths, vestments, etc. *Real* blessings are those which entail the use of holy oils, e.g., the blessing of the baptismal font, the consecration of a chalice, paten, altar, church, bell, etc.

Invocative-constitutive blessings are those which impart a new spiritual character to certain articles intended for man's use as protection against evil or aids to salvation, e.g., the blessing of water, palms, candles, *Agnus Dei's*, scapulars, medals, rosaries. Ecclesiastical authority has attached indulgences to certain blessed articles.

Permanent sacramentals are persons or things dedicated to God and His divine service, e.g., a blessed oratory, a consecrated chalice, holy water, etc. A thing that has once acquired a constitutive blessing, unless totally destroyed or sold, preserves its sacred character.

EFFECTS. As an immediate effect, sacramentals produce neither sanctifying grace nor the title to receive such grace, but actual graces to carry out properly Christian duties or obligations in a new state of life, to resist more readily the assaults of the devil, to arouse detestation for past sins. Also, they are means of restraining demoniacal influence, of repelling evil and of attaining temporal benefits. Indirectly, sacramentals may also produce the remission of venial sins or partial remission of the temporal punishment due to sins already forgiven. The measure in which the sacramentals produce their effects will largely depend on the degree of fervor and the dispositions of the individual receiving or using them.

MINISTER. The power of exorcising diabolically possessed persons, whether baptized or catechumens, is conferred by the third of the minor orders, that is, the order of exorcist. In the present discipline of the Church, however, this function is reserved to priests, who are the lawful ministers of the sacred rites in which the exorcisms occur, e.g., in solemn baptism. Solemn exorcism may be conducted only by express authorization of the Ordinary (Can. 1151) and with great circumspection; simple exorcisms may be performed by an ordinary priest, with all due regard, however, for the rights of the pastor, e.g., in the solemn administration of baptism.

Blessings, except those reserved to the pope, bishops or others, may be imparted by any priest. Blessings reserved to the pope include: the blessing of the *Agnus Dei* (*q.v.*) and the *pallia*; those reserved to bishops and those authorized by Canon Law or the Holy See include: consecrations of sacred objects, places and other blessings in the *Pontificale, Rituale* or *Missale*. Blessings may be reserved to specific religious orders; among these are special blessings attached to rosary beads for privileged indulgences. Blessings reserved to a pastor include: the nuptial blessing, the blessing of a home on Holy Saturday, and the blessing of the baptismal font. The faculty for imparting many reserved blessings may be delegated to another priest. Otherwise, reserved blessings, imparted by a priest without the necessary faculties, are valid but illicit, unless the contrary is stated by the Holy See (Can. 1147, par. 3).

Deacons and those in the order of lector may validly and licitly impart only those blessings expressly indicated by law (Can. 1147, par. 4).

SUBJECTS OF BLESSINGS. Blessings are imparted primarily to the faithful; if there is no prohibition of the Church, non-Catholics may receive blessings in order that they might receive the light of faith or physical health (Can. 1149). The following persons are excluded from the reception of sacramentals and blessings:

(a) excommunicated Catholics after a declaratory or condemnatory sentence (Can. 2260, par. 1); (b) those under a personal interdict (Can. 2275, par. 2; (c) Catholics who have contracted a mixed marriage validly but without having requested or received the required dispensation, until they shall have obtained a dispensation from the Ordinary (Can. 2375). Exorcisms may be performed not only over the faithful and catechumens but also over non-Catholics and excommunicates (Can. 1152).

The faithful are urged to have a high regard for sacramentals and a great respect for persons and things dedicated to God and His divine service. The frequent reception of blessings instituted and approved by the Church is highly recommended. Also, the frequent and devotional use of blessed articles is of great value. In fact, the use of blessed articles is properly considered an act of faith and trust, for such sacred objects are the means of receiving, through the power of the Church, actual graces for leading a good life, as well as temporal and spiritual benefits which may well contribute to eternal salvation. They are also capable of removing or nullifying the influence and power of the evil one.

OTHER BLESSINGS. To be distinguished from those described and enumerated above, certain blessings not given in the name of the Church may, nonetheless, have a salutary effect, especially if imparted by one with authority over the person or thing receiving the blessing, e.g., the parental blessing imparted to one's child. *Man.*

SACRAMENTARIES. *See* Liturgical Books.

SACRAMENTS AND PHYSICIANS.

BAPTISM. The physician is morally obligated to administer baptism to an infant in danger of death, in the absence of a priest. This obligation exists for an attendant nurse as well.

In a case of impelling necessity, baptism is to be administered to the embryo or fetus before being expelled or drawn out of the womb. If another part of the body other than the head shows, the water is to be poured on that part with the following phrase of condition: *If this baptism is valid, I baptize you in the name of the Father and of the Son and of the Holy Spirit.* If the child is born alive, the baptism shall be repeated with this form: *If you are not baptized, I baptize you,* etc. In a serious danger of death, baptism shall be administered through an appropriate small tube inserted in the mother's womb, possibly through broken membranes, with the conditional form or intention: *If this baptism is valid,* etc. The baptism shall be repeated with the form: *If you are not baptized, I baptize you,* etc., in a successful delivery. Baptism is not valid if the water is poured only upon the mother's body; it is doubtfully valid if poured only on the membranes surrounding the fetus. Thus, in the case of an aborted fetus with some signs of life, it will be proper to use the ordinary form while cautiously breaking the membranes in a basin of lukewarm water; the same procedure shall be followed with an aborted fetus showing no signs of life, saying the words: *If you are alive, I baptize you in the name of the Father,* etc.

The repetition of conditional baptism in danger of death should be done, preferably by a priest, after the danger of death has ceased.

Baptism of Monsters. The birth of monstrous individuals is caused by deviations in the embryonic development of the generative elements, by traumas, or by a variety of physicochemical actions on the embryo.

Psychic causes, such as disturbed imaginations, shock, unsatisfied desires for particular foods, or other popular myths have no value at all. Likewise unfounded are those notions of the ancients and of the Middle Ages, which considered monstrosities the result of the whims, revenge, or anger of evil spirits, the intervention of the devil, or the result of bestiality.

On the basis of these premises, it is apparently certain that monsters are to be baptized.

In cases of double, symmetrically joined monsters, two baptisms are to be administered; this procedure is to be followed in double, non-symmetrically

joined monstrosities, but the baptism is to be conferred conditionally on the parasite. Baptism must be conditionally administered if the monstrosity is in reality a shapeless mass. The same rule applies in the case of a vesicular mole or cystic deformation on the fetal part of the placenta. Since newborn monsters are usually destined to an early death, it is advisable to baptize them without delay; this may be done by the physician, unless a priest or sister is present.

PENANCE, HOLY EUCHARIST, EXTREME UNCTION. To a Catholic patient, even if remiss in the observance of his religious duties, the physician must suggest a priest, for the latter's work can do much to restore serenity to a patient's disturbed, restless, or depressed spirit. Often, it will prove of great help toward total recovery. In many cases of psychasthenia (*q.v.*), the intervention of a prudent confessor can bring wonderful benefits even to the physical well-being of a patient.

In a case of grave illness, the physician has the duty to suggest to the patient, directly or through another, the advisability of receiving the sacraments of penance, Holy Eucharist, and extreme unction. With respect to extreme unction, it should be noted that one must not wait until the patient is in a dying condition or in a state of unconsciousness to suggest the administration of a sacrament that is more beneficial if received in a state of consciousness. A Catholic physician shall always, personally or through another, caution a non-Catholic patient concerning the gravity of his illness.

HOLY ORDERS. Neither eunuchs, hermaphrodites, or pseudo-hermaphrodites (*see* Hermaphroditism) with notable morphological anomalies can be admitted to the priesthood. Nor would a Voronov operation be of much help (*see* Endocrinology), because, as experience shows, it would be a matter of temporary modification and the ordination would, in such a case, be at least doubtful.

Candidates for the clerical or religious life with a tendency to sexual perversion (*q.v.*) must be handled with much prudence. After examining these individuals, the physician shall give his objective judgment concerning the advisability of sending them home. Since these conditions have a psychoneurotic basis, which compulsory chastity would be likely to aggravate, a physician should discourage from the very beginning these individuals from studying for the priesthood, which would probably be for them a source of serious anguish and perhaps deplorable scandals.

Masturbation, if not accompanied by particular neuropsychic anomalies, is not exactly a perversion but rather a deviation of the sexual instinct, liable to radical recovery in cases of young men who are spiritually healthy and capable of self-control. Nevertheless, the physician shall bear in mind that traditional canonistic and theological doctrines prescribe, for those who are capable of self-control, a period of trial long enough to give a moral certainty of amendment.

If an aspirant to the priesthood is troubled by excessive doubts, obsessions, phobias, or other morbid forms, the superiors shall have him examined by a good psychiatrist who alone can determine whether it is a matter of transitory anomaly or a real and proper psychosis. In such a case, if the treatments fail to bring about a cure, he must be resolutely barred from the priesthood, which, among other qualities, requires also a vigorous and serene spirit.

A doctor shall at no time suggest to an unmarried person, especially if bound by vows, in matters of sexual perversion (*q.v.*), any relaxation of the vow of chastity.

MATRIMONY. A physician's opinion is often required either with respect to a person's fitness for marriage, or to correcting imperfections and infirmities affecting an individual's marital capacity, or with respect to the nullity of certain marriages. These questions are dealt with under Diriment impediments to marriage, Impotency, Matrimony (use of), Sexual psychoneurosis, Pre-nuptial examination, etc.

The physician often receives confidential accounts of domestic difficulties, anomalies of character or behavior of one or both parties to a marriage, which foreshadow eventual trouble. In such cases, the physician ought to suggest that they discuss their problems with a prudent priest, marriage counsellor, or other professional person capable of restoring a certain degree of serenity to their minds and their home. Nor shall the doctor fail to impress upon them the necessity of mutual understanding and generous forbearance of their respective faults, particularly in view of the moral and material welfare of their children. *Riz.*

SACRAMENTS, REPETITION OF. A second administration to the same individual of a sacrament ordinarily administered only once, is called a repetition of the sacrament. It is lawful to repeat any sacrament, conditionally, if there is a doubt concerning its validity. Moralists distinguish between doubt of fact and doubt of law. Doubt of fact refers to actual circumstances: whether as sacrament was conferred at all, or whether it was conferred in the proper manner with the proper matter, form, and intention. A doubt of law is a doubt about the validity of a sacrament, based on a disagreement concerning the validity of matter or form. If the sacrament whose validity is doubted is necessary to salvation or if the validity of another sacrament depends on it, it must be repeated as long as a moral certainty of its validity is lacking. Thus, the salvation of man requires that baptism, penance, and extreme unction of an unconscious dying person be repeated if there is a reasonable doubt about their validity. To avoid the danger of idolatry, doubtfully consecrated hosts must be consecrated again conditionally; thus, too, to avoid an invalid administration of other sacraments, the sacrament of holy orders must be repeated (Can. 1007), if there is doubt about its validity. In the case of doubtful administration, the sacraments which imprint a character must be repeated (Can. 732, par. 2). *Pal.*

SACRAMENTS (Sacred Congregation of the). *See* Roman Congregations.

SACRED HEART OF JESUS (devotion to). ORIGIN. The Gospel narrates that, after Christ expired on the Cross, one of the soldiers pierced His side with a lance, causing an immediate flow of blood and water (John 19:34). In the first centuries of the Church's existence, the pierced side of Christ became the object of tender considerations. The Fathers of the Church referred to it as the mysterious fount of all grace. In the Middle Ages, the divine Heart itself, wounded by a spear, was the object of a particular devotion among contemplatives of both sexes. Yet only in comparatively recent times did the Church formally approve explicit worship of the Sacred Heart. In 1765, about one hundred years after our Lord's apparitions and revelations to St. Margaret Mary Alacoque, Clement XIII approved the Office and Mass in honor of the Sacred Heart. Pius X extended the feast of the Sacred Heart to the universal Church; Leo XIII raised it to a feast of greater solemnity and consecrated the whole human race to the Sacred Heart. Finally, Pius XI enriched the feast with a privileged octave and also revised the formulary of the Office and Mass.

NATURE. Absolute worship is due to the humanity of Christ by reason of the hypostatic union with the Second Person of the Blessed Trinity. Moreover, because the Sacred Heart was perforated by a lance, and because of the intimate connection between the soul's sentiments, especially love, and the heart, as the organ which manifests the symbol of sensible affections, it is only natural that the Sacred Heart of Jesus should be honored in a particular manner.

The material object of the devotion to the Sacred Heart is the physical, living Heart of Jesus, and at the same time the Person of the Word, to which it subsists. This devotion consists of three elements: *adoration*, as indicated above; *love*, expressed by the consecration of our being and possessions to the Sacred Heart; and *reparation* or atonement for the indifference, ingratitude and indignities committed by so many individuals (Pius XI, Encyclical *Miserentissimus Redemptor*, in AAS (1928), 165–178.

The devotion to the Sacred Heart of Jesus is an excellent form of worship, productive of very salutary effects within us. Indeed, since the Sacred Heart of Jesus is the most perfect Model of love of God and neighbor, as well as the Source

and Model of all virtue, it is not possible to have sincere devotion to the Sacred Heart, without at the same time striving to imitate this divine Exemplar.

PRACTICE. Besides the Nine First Fridays, the following practices are highly recommended: Communions of reparation on each First Friday of the month; attendance at public services in honor of the Sacred Heart; observance of the feast of the Sacred Heart with fervor and devotion; daily performance of some pious exercise during the month of June; frequent and pious recitation of the litany of the Sacred Heart; display and veneration of the image or picture of the Sacred Heart, which should be in every Christian home; consecration of one's person, intentions, and works, as well as one's own family, to the Sacred Heart. *Man.*

SACRED SCRIPTURE. *See* New Testament, Old Testament.

SACRED VESTMENTS. This term includes all vestments and liturgical insignia worn by various officials and assistants at divine services.

VESTMENTS. The present liturgical vestments are derived, after numerous modifications, from the form of dress in vogue among the ancient Romans. Under the influence of the invaders, the flowing and majestic garments of the Romans were gradually discarded as civilian wear, but remained in use for liturgical functions. At first, there were no set rules governing the form and color of vestments; these matters were determined by tradition and custom. But in the tenth and eleventh centuries, norms were established, requiring vestments in accord with a mystical interpretation of each color. Thus, black indicates mourning (funerals); purple signifies penance (Lent, Advent); red denotes fortitude and blood (Holy Spirit and feasts of martyrs); white symbolizes glory and purity (feasts of our Lord, our Lady, holy virgins, and saints who are not martyrs); green, a color without special significance, is used on Sundays which commemorate no special feastday. In due course of time, clearly distinct from secular attire, liturgical vestments, like all other objects of worship, were naturally blessed; probably this began in the ninth century.

The liturgical vestments include the following: the *amice*, an oblong piece of white linen, worn around the neck, and originally placed on the head and extending about the neck and shoulders; the *alb*, a full-length, white linen tunic with sleeves, the lower part of which frequently is made of lacework or embroidery; the *cincture*, which serves the practical purpose of binding the alb around the waist; the *surplice*, a sort of loose, abbreviated alb with very broad sleeves, introduced in the northern countries and worn over winter robes (*superpelliceum*); the *rochet* (from the German *rock*, meaning coat), a knee-length, narrow-sleeved white linen vestment, the lower part of which is richly trimmed with lace; this is worn by bishops and prelates today as a mark of authority.

Other sacred vestments are: the *chasuble*, originally a long, sleeveless mantle or cloak closed all around and covering the whole body, with a narrow opening for the head. Rendered excessively heavy and stiff by materials of brocade and damask, the chasuble was gradually trimmed at the sides, first to elbow length, then to its present form. It is the distinctive outer vestment of the celebrant at Mass, worn by bishop and priest alike. The material of the chasuble must be silk (natural or artificial) and its color is determined by the liturgy of the day.

The *cope* is a cloak worn by bishops, priests, and lesser ministers in liturgical functions apart from Mass. Originally, the cope was a hooded cloak worn to protect the individual from rain during processions. The *dalmatic*, today the distinctive vestment of the deacon, was at one time worn only by the pope and the Roman deacons; gradually the privilege of wearing the dalmatic was extended to bishops and prelates outside Rome and, finally, to all deacons. The dalmatic, a knee-length, loose-fitting robe with wide sleeves, is closed in front and open at the sides as far as the shoulders. The distinctive ornamentation of this vestment consists of two vertical stripes of red and gold running from the shoulder

to the hem. The *tunic* is a robe, similar to a dalmatic, but with long, narrow sleeves; today it is the distinctive vestment of the sub-deacon. According to present usage, the tunic and dalmatic are alike both in form and ornamentation.

The sacred apparel of the bishop includes a *pectoral cross* with chain or cord; a *mitre*, worn as a headdress; *sandals and stockings* or buskins (*caligae*), corresponding to the color of the vestments; the *gremial* or apron to cover the knees, a sign of jurisdiction, if jurisdiction is possessed; the *crosier* or pastoral staff, made of precious metal and rounded at the top.

These vestments, together with the ring, pallium (*q.v.*), tunic and dalmatic, worn by the bishop under a chasuble, are called *pontifical* vestments and insignia.

INSIGNIA. In ancient times the *maniple* was an ornamental handkerchief carried by Roman officials as a symbol of authority and used, when presiding at gatherings or games, to signal the start and end of a game or function. Today, the maniple is a narrow band of silk cloth, of the same color as the chasuble, worn by bishops, priests, and other ministers at Mass. Originally, it was a distinctive apparel of the bishop, used to signal the chanters to begin or stop singing. Later, its use was extended to all ministers at the altar. The *stole* (its ancient Latin name was *orarium*) was from the beginning and is still today a distinctive mark of authority. It is worn only by deacons, priests, and bishops. Deacons wear it on the left shoulder, crossing at the breast back to the right side. The stole of the priest extends from the back of the neck across the shoulders to the breast, where the two halves cross each other. If worn over a surplice, however, the two halves fall straight down. The bishop wears a stole in the same manner as the priest, except that it is never crossed at the breast, where he wears his pectoral cross. The stole is of the same color and material as the chasuble. The *pallium* (*q.v.*) is the liturgical insignia of archbishops, bestowed on them as a privilege. To each archbishop the pope, upon petition, sends the pallium, after he first places it on the tomb of St. Peter. It is a circular band of white wool, worn about the neck, breast and shoulders, with two pendants, one hanging down in front, the other in the back. It is set with six black crosses and held together by three large gold pins. The pallia are made from the wool of two lambs blessed each year in Rome on the feast of St. Agnes.

JURIDICAL NORMS. It is first to be noted that all sacred vestments and insignia must be in conformity with the liturgical laws, ecclesiastical tradition, and the laws of sacred art (Can. 1296). They are to be carefully preserved in a decent place, and inventory is to be taken regularly (Can. 1296, par. 1–2; 1302). The obligation of providing sacred vestments and furnishings rests upon those who are to attend to the maintenance of a church edifice (Cans. 1297; 1186). The cathedral church shall furnish the bishop gratuitously with the use of sacred vestments (Can. 1303, par. 1). Normally, the use of sacred vestments is to be offered gratuitously to all clerics in all churches, unless a church is particularly poor, and the Ordinary has permitted that a moderate fee be charged for the use of sacred furnishings and vestments for the celebration of Holy Mass (Can. 1303, par. 2–4).

Certain vestments and articles require a blessing before they may be used. Blessing is required for the following: corporal, pall, amice, alb, maniple, stole, chasuble, cincture, and altar cloths. The blessing is not required but may be bestowed on the following: cope, dalmatic and tunic. The chalice veil, humeral veil, burse and purificator require no blessing.

When required, the following have the power to bless sacred apparel: cardinals and bishops without exception; local Ordinaries who are not bishops for churches and oratories within the limits of their territory; the pastor within the limits of his parish; religious superiors for their own churches and oratories and for those belonging to nuns subject to the regular superior; rectors of churches for their own churches; priests delegated by the Ordinary (Can. 1304).

Sacred vestments and furnishings that have been blessed lose their blessing: (a) if they have suffered such damage or change that they have lost their original shape and are no longer suited for their purpose; (b) if they have been used for unbecoming purposes or have been exposed for public sale (Can. 1305, par. 1). They are at all times to be preserved from any indecorous or sacrilegious contact (Can. 1306, par. 1–2).

The sacred vestments and all other sacred articles of cardinals may be freely donated or bequeathed by them to religious places or persons; otherwise, they become the property of the pontifical sacristy, with the exception of the ring and pectoral cross (Can. 1298). With a few reservations indicated in the Code, the sacred vestments and furnishings of residential bishops go to the cathedral church, except the ring and pectoral cross under certain conditions (Can. 1299, par. 1–2). In the case of other clerics, sacred vestments and other furnishings go to their proper church (Cans. 1300, 1301). Concerning sacred linens used in connection with the chalice, *see* Chalice. *Cig.*

SACRIFICE. Of all the various acts of internal and external cult by which man endeavors to express his religion and devotion, the total offering of oneself is, indeed, a comprehensive and an all-embracing one. Since man is not allowed to carry this act to the point of immolation or killing of self to do homage to God, civilized man replaces it with the offering of things which God puts under his dominion, such as animals, fruits, precious objects, as a symbol of a total offering of self to God. Such an act of religion is called sacrifice; it is a typical act of religion.

Sacrifice, as an act of cult, is found in all religions. In revealed religion, after the Old Testament, Jesus Christ as mystical Head of mankind gave us a new sacrifice which He offered Himself to the Father by His death on the Cross (*q.v.*); He satisfied Divine Justice offended by man and won for man re-instatement in God's grace and hope for heavenly glory. This is the sacrifice of the Mass (*q.v.*), a mystical representation and renewal of the sacrifice of Calvary, in which Christian worship finds its highest expression. In fact, nothing can give God more glory and better express our submission to Him than the renewal of the sacrifice which Christ made of Himself on the Cross, as a representative of mankind. The Mass is the one means by which society can satisfy its natural duty of giving God the highest proof of its submission. *Pal.*

SACRIFICE OF LIFE. In theologico-moral language, one is said to sacrifice his life if he kills himself rather than disclose important secrets to the enemy. Some consider such an act as real suicide; others consider it heroism, particularly if done to avoid a great damage. The common moral opinion stands opposed to the condonation of such an act on the principle that no one is free to take his own life for any reason whatsoever. Obviously, this is not to be confused with the case of one who, from a supernatural motive, accepts natural death rather than seek to have his life prolonged by exceptional means (*see also* Martyrdom). *Pal.*

SACRILEGE. A sacrilege is the violation or abuse of a sacred person, place, or object. It falls into one of three types: (a) *personal*, (b) *local*, (c) *real*.

A *personal* sacrilege is directed against one who is sacred by reason of the clerical or religious state. This may be committed by acts of *physical violence* against the person, such as killing or detention in prison; by summoning the person before a civil court in opposition to the laws of the Church; by prescribing military service for sacred persons; by sins against the sixth commandment with a person bound by public vow of chastity.

A *local* sacrilege is a violation against a sacred place, such as a church, public oratory, or a cemetery that has been duly blessed. This sacrilege may be committed by murder or grave bloodshed; by burial of an unbeliever or excommunicated individual after judicial sentence; by using a sacred place for evil or improper purposes; by grave sins committed by shameful actions, theft, serious fighting, etc.; by violating the right of asylum or the privilege of immunity; finally, by destroy-

ing or plundering the sacred place in whole or in part.

Things are considered sacred if intended for the service of God, either in divine worship or of their own nature. Among these are sacraments, relics of the saints, the words of Holy Scripture. By disposition of ecclesiastical authority, consecrated object or objects blessed for special reasons are considered sacred.

A *real* sacrilege consists in the unworthy use of sacred things or in the theft and unjust appropriation of ecclesiastical property. Cases of real sacrilege are: (a) unworthy administration or reception of the sacraments; (b) casting away relics for some reason; (c) misuse of the words of Scripture for indecent, unbecoming, or ludicrous purposes; (d) profanation of images, statues and paintings, or similar acts. The destruction of blessed articles, such as a rosary, religious statue, medal, or painting, is not in itself forbidden, if it is done out of necessity without irreverence.

Sacrilege is a grave sin against the virtue of religion, which inclines man to treat all sacred things with respect. Sacrilege is a special sin, distinct from the sin involved in a particular action; thus, homicide committed in a church is a sin of murder and sacrilege. There may be different species in a single act; to kill a priest in a church is both a personal and local sacrilege and a sin of murder. *Ben.*

SADNESS. Sadness is a state of depression, caused in the will by an evil that is present and abhorred (*spiritual* sadness). This disposition of the will is always accompanied by an affliction of the sensitive appetite, which can be termed *sensitive* sadness. These sensitive feelings may arise independently of the free act of the will and exist without a corresponding spiritual sadness.

The causes of sadness may be external evils, such as a wrong done to us, a disaster to a beloved person; or internal, as a sinful act or the loss of a pleasant good. Sadness does not necessarily require the physical presence of a cause; its imaginary presence is sufficient. Thus the object of sadness can be a reality of the past preserved by the memory or foreseen for the future. By its nature, sadness burdens the soul and hinders the incentive to work; it may at times hinder all activity entirely.

Sadness may at times be lawful, if the cause is due to a legitimate desire or detestation of an object. Many forms of sadness are beneficial, such as grief over sins committed; other types of sadness are unlawful by reason of their cause, as grief over the absence of an unlawful pleasure or desire, or the presence of detestation of a good or duty which we are obliged to perform.

A good deed, not of obligation and voluntarily performed at some time in the past, may be made an object of sadness or regret if the regret stems from an honest motive and does not give rise to the danger of omitting the fulfillment of a duty.

Since sadness is a natural complement to other acts, no guilt is ever found primarily or exclusively in spiritual or sensitive sadness. Sadness cannot be considered sinful, unless a free and inordinate will participates in the sadness, with which it constitutes a unity in its moral aspects. Such an act may be an act of aversion from that which causes sadness; it may also be an implicit or explicit refusal to remove an excessive impulse to sadness that has preceded the free exercise of the will. In the first case the degree of guilt depends on the nature of the object. In the second case the guilt is, of itself, venial; yet, it could also be mortal if the undismissed sadness were to constitute a grave danger of committing mortal sin. A sadness, of itself inordinate, which precedes the free exercise of the will, cannot be formally sinful; but as soon as one becomes aware of its presence, he is bound to do everything possible to overcome it.

If the object is not inordinate, sadness must be kept under control, not be allowed to obscure the mind or hinder one's activities. Failure to restrain an excessive sadness, that is not reprehensible, is of itself a venial sin; yet, the sin could become grave, if the excess of sadness were to cause serious scandal or prevent the fulfillment of an important duty.

A careful control of the feelings of sadness is of great importance for all, but particularly for those who are temperamentally inclined to melancholia. To succeed in this, it is necessary to consider everything in the light of faith and eternity and to have great trust in the Lord. We should endeavor at all times to generate and spread some degree of joy and serenity. *Man.*

SAINTS. In a general sense, saints are all those (angels and men) who enjoy the vision of God in heaven. In a particular sense, saints are special persons who, according to the judgment of the Church, have practiced the virtues in an heroic degree. This fact is officially declared by a canonization decree or other equivalent document of the Church. Saints are distinguished into various categories: apostles, martyrs, pontiffs, confessors, virgins, and holy women.

CULT. The exalted dignity of the saints and their close union with God make them worthy of veneration (*q.v.*). This is called *dulia*, to distinguish it from the cult due only to God, called *latria* or adoration. Veneration consists in an internal and external acknowledgment of the supernatural excellence of certain men and women as friends of God and deserving of admiration and imitation. The cult of the saints is not prejudicial to the cult due to God, because by venerating the saints we honor God Himself.

From the most ancient documents of Christian literature, we learn that, from the very beginning of the Church, veneration was accorded to the martyrs and their relics (*q.v.*). In the fourth century the same veneration was extended to bishops who had excelled in holiness of life, and soon also to anchorites and other faithful who, by a life of austerity, had become in some way similar to the martyrs. The veneration of images of the saints similarly goes back to the earliest times of the Church, as the catacombs demonstrate.

Against the position of Protestants, the Council of Trent solemnly asserted the lawfulness and usefulness of the veneration of the saints, their images and relics

(Denz. 984–988). The veneration of the images and relics, however, is not an absolute, but a relative, cult.

We venerate the saints in many ways: by celebrating their feast days, by displaying and adorning with flowers and lights their statues or images, by doing works of charity or mortification in their honor, by venerating their relics. Saints may also be venerated by promises made to them or by making them witnesses or patrons of a vow made to God.

Imitation of the saints is another way of venerating them; imitating their example amounts, after all, to imitating Christ Himself (1 Cor. 4:16).

The saints are also venerated by prayers to them. The Council of Trent defined the lawfulness and usefulness of turning to the saints for aid (Denz. n. 984); in the liturgy, the Church makes explicit the appeal to their mediation (*see* Intercession). There is no strict obligation to invoke the saints. It is, nevertheless, greatly beneficial to do so frequently; to omit it altogether could be culpable, especially if it implied neglect of one's own salvation. Guilt could also be grave if based on contempt, either of one's own salvation or the intercession of the saints. We may also turn our pleas to the saints to obtain from the Lord spiritual or material benefits for ourselves or others, as necessary or useful for the salvation of souls.

Catholics are urged to have a particular devotion to the saints assigned as patrons at the time of their baptism, whose names they bear, and also to the saints who shared the same state in life or who in a particular way practiced the virtues of which one is more particularly in need.

Privately one may invoke the aid of those who died as saints or martyrs, even though they have not been beatified or canonized (*see* Beatification). Private veneration of their images and relics is also permitted. Baptized children who died before attaining the use of reason, though they are not an object of veneration in the Church, may nevertheless be privately honored, as they certainly are enjoying God's vision. Concerning the souls in purgatory, the Church directs no public veneration to them, although pri-vate veneration is permitted. According to some theologians, including St. Thomas, these souls would seem rather to be in need of help themselves. Today, however, the opposite opinion prevails, based on the view that, once set free from their place of purgation, they will undoubtedly help their benefactors in gratitude for the aid they themselves received from them. *Man.*

SALE. See Buying and Selling.

SALVE, REGINA (HAIL, HOLY QUEEN). The *Salve, Regina* is a prayer or hymn in honor of the Blessed Virgin. In use as a prayer or hymn since the eleventh century at the time of the First Crusade it was sung daily by pilgrims and soldiers.

It has been attributed to Ademarus, Bishop of Puy (d. 1098), and to Peter, Bishop of Santiago de Compostella (d. 1003); but Hermann Contractus, a monk at Reichenau (d. 1054), is considered by many as the true author of both text and melody.

The *Salve, Regina* is a devout invocation, directed to Mary as the heavenly Mother of those living in this valley of tears, that she may reward them, after their exile, with the joy of contemplating the fruit of her womb, Jesus. According to Dante, the souls of princes sing it in the valley of flowers in Ante-Purgatory (*Purg.* VII, 82–84).

Its liturgical use must be ascribed to the Dominican Friars at first, and the Franciscans later. The *Salve* is recited as a closing antiphon at the end of the breviary, from the first Vespers of the feast of the Holy Trinity until None of the Saturday before Advent. Since 1884, its recitation is generally obligatory after the private celebration of Holy Mass, unless another function immediately follows or a sermon was preached during the Mass. *Pal.*

SANATION (SANATIO IN RADICE). A *sanation*, technically termed *sanatio in radice*, of a marriage is an act which entails, besides a dispensation from or a cessation of a diriment impediment, a validation of a marriage with a further dispensation from the law of renewal of consent; thereby it has retroactive force, by a fiction of law, which gives to a marriage the same canonical effects which would have occurred if the marriage had been valid from the beginning (Can. 1138, par. 1). The *radix* or root healed is in the consent of the parties, since in a marriage forbidden by an invalidating law, such as a diriment impediment or a defect of form, the consent which naturally would be efficacious remains juridically inefficacious from the beginning; thus the consent produces no juridical effect, and the contract is invalid. If the impediment which caused the nullity of the marriage is of an ecclesiastical law, the Church can dispense from it and render the marriage valid, because, after the impediment or obstacle has been removed, the consent, which still endures, becomes immediately efficacious nor does it demand renewal from either natural or positive law.

The marriage becomes valid from the moment of the bestowal of grace (*ex nunc*), but, insofar as the canonical effects are concerned, it is considered valid, unless something different is expressly said, from the moment of its celebration (*ex tunc*). By a fiction of law, the Church removes retroactively all the effects of the invalidating law, considers the marriage as validly contracted from the beginning, and acknowledges the children as legitimate. If the impediment which rendered the marriage null has already ceased (for example, the impediment of age), the Church grants only the dispensation from the law of renewal of consent and the legitimation of children, and makes both retroactive, by a fiction of law, to the moment at which the parties expressed their consent. This validates the marriage from the moment of the bestowal of the grace. The sanation is perfect and total if it includes the double dispensation from an impediment and the law of renewal of consent, with the dating of canonical effects to the moment of the celebration. It is imperfect or partial if all these effects do not concur, i.e., only the canonical effects are made retroactive because the parties or one of them is dead, or one of

the spouses only is required to renew consent, or the dispensation is made effective, not from the beginning of the marriage, but some intermediate time.

PREREQUISITES. (a) The marriage must be invalid by reason of an impediment of ecclesiastical law or for lack of form, because the Church cannot dispense from divine law, either positive or natural (such as impediments of bond or impotency). If a marriage was attempted with an impediment of positive or natural divine law, according to Canon 1138, par. 2, the Church does not heal this, not even when the impediment itself ceases to be. Such would be the case of a husband who, after a civil divorce from his wife, civilly marries another woman and upon his first wife's death asks for the *sanatio in radice* of his civil marriage. Another case would be a woman who, despite her antecedent and perpetual impotency, marries and afterwards, with the impediment removed by a surgical operation, asks for a *sanatio in radice* of her marriage. In the aforementioned cases, notwithstanding paragraph 2 of Can. 1139, the sanation is allowed for very serious motives; in such cases, of course, it is granted only from the moment the impediment ceased, since the Church, even by a fiction of law, cannot make a marriage valid retroactively to the beginning, if it involved an impediment of positive or natural divine law. From these the Church cannot dispense.

(b) The consent of both parties must have been naturally sufficient, though juridically inefficacious, from the beginning. Without a true conjugal consent, the root to be healed, a sanation of the marriage is not even conceivable. If in the beginning a true consent was wanting but supplied afterwards, the *sanatio in radice* is only possible from the moment in which the true consent was given. If one party had given his true consent while the other had not, the latter must renew true consent. According to the old law, the consent was presumed to be true only if the contracting parties were in good faith and had contracted marriage according to the prescribed form. According to present practice, the possibility of a true consent is not excluded; thus the *sanatio* is permitted, even if the parties were aware of the impediment or attempted civil marriage.

(c) The consent must endure. Once given, it is presumed to endure as long as it is not revoked. Nor is it considered revoked if the parties do not get along or would be disposed to separate if they knew about the nullity of their marriage, or are already living apart, or a trial for nullity is pending. In these cases, however, the *sanatio* is not given. Nor is the consent to be considered revoked if one or even both parties refuse to renew it, for it is one thing to revoke and another to be unwilling to renew a consent.

(d) Concerning mixed marriages, the Holy Office requires a moral certainty that the non-Catholic party will not hinder the Catholic education of the children. In the absence of this certainty, the Holy office requires that the Catholic party promise to do his utmost to have the children baptized and educated in the Catholic religion.

(e) For granting a *sanatio in radice* a grave reason is required, which is present, for instance, if one of the parties refuses to renew the consent in the prescribed manner, while both are aware of the nullity of their marriage; or if both parties are unaware of the nullity of their marriage and subsequent awareness would create a danger of separation; or if the Ordinary, pastor, or confessor is responsible for the nullity. It is always a grave reason if the spiritual welfare of the parties and the legitimation of offspring are involved.

The granting of the *sanatio in radice* is reserved to the Holy See (Can. 1141). Delegated power, however, is given at times to Ordinaries, particularly in the mission fields. The bishops of the United States have power to grant the *sanatio in radice* for marriages attempted before a civil official or a non-Catholic minister, if one of the parties is a non-Catholic (baptized or unbaptized) and the ordinary validation ceremony is not possible, because either the non-Catholic party cannot be told of the invalidity without the risk of great harm or disturbance to the Catholic party or because the non-Catholic would not agree to observe the

caonical form of marriage and sign the prescribed promises. The Ordinary may subdelegate pastors to grant the *sanatio*, but only in individual cases.

The Sacred Congregation of the Sacraments grants to the bishops of the United States the faculty to grant the *sanatio in radice* for marriages invalid by reason of a diriment impediment of lesser degree (Can. 1042), if it would give rise to great inconvenience to require a renewal of consent from a party unaware of the impediment. The *sanatio* may be requested by both parties, one of them, or by a third person, carefully giving a circumstantial account of the case, and noting in particular whether the consent existed from the beginning and still endures, and the parties are in good faith, as well as a reason for sanation instead of a simple validation of the marriage. In making known the favorable concession of the grace to the interested parties, the executor of the rescript must comply with the clauses added to the same rescript, unless it be granted in a manner whereby no execution is needed, as ordinarily happens if the parties are not aware of the nullity of their marriage and cannot be warned without inviting a danger of separation. A *sanatio* granted for the external forum is to be entered in the matrimonial register; one granted in the non-sacramental internal forum is to be recorded in the diocesan secret archives (Can. 1047); a *sanatio* granted in the sacramental internal forum is not to be recorded, lest the sacramental seal of confession be violated. *Pal.*

SANCTIFICATION OF SUNDAYS (Holy Days).

The commandment to keep holy the Sabbath is a positive obligation to assist at Mass on Sundays and holy days and includes the negative duty to abstain from servile occupations.

Almost all people have had fixed days for honoring their gods in the performance of sacred religious rites. The Jewish people, besides the Sabbath, dedicated other special days to recalling the particular benefits that were received from God (Exod. 26:8).

Christian holy days were appointed as early as apostolic times. The observance of Sunday, instead of the Sabbath (Col. 2:16; I Cor. 16:2; Apoc. 1:10), in memory of the Lord's Resurrection, stands out by reason of its antiquity, for it was ordered by the Apostles themselves. The Councils of Elvira (306) and Sardis (343) speak of the obligation to attend Mass.

Afterwards the number of holy days was considerably increased. The Synod of Szaboles, Hungary, in 1092 (Can. 38), lists 38 besides Sundays; Toulouse, France, in 1229 (Can. 26) enumerates 26; Oxford, in 1222 (Can. 8) numbers 53. When complaints were made about real or alleged damages resulting to the economy, the number of holy days was reduced at the Council of Tarragona, held in the year 1239 (Can. 5); the same was done by Simon, Archbishop of Canterbury, in 1332. Gerson and Pierre d'Ailly urged the Council of Constance in this direction but their pleas were not heard. Following abusive interventions of lay princes, the problem was fully faced by St. Pius X, who, by a *motu proprio* of July 2, 1911, reduced the number of days of obligation so that by general law only eight days besides Sundays were to be observed: the Nativity, Circumcision, Epiphany, and Ascension of our Lord, the Immaculate Conception and the Assumption of the Blessed Virgin, the feast of the holy Apostles Peter and Paul, and the feast of All Saints.

By the same *motu proprio*, St. Pius X decreed that no changes were to be made with respect to lawfully abrogated days of obligation without consulting the Holy See. The list of St. Pius X was incorporated in the Code of Canon Law with the addition of two other days: Corpus Christi and St. Joseph's (Can. 1247).

SUNDAY REST. Tertullian (*De oratione*, n. 23) speaks of the observance of Sunday rest. A written law, however, is not found before Constantine. He first decreed that no judicial acts and public works be conducted on Sunday (*Cod. Theod.*, VIII, 8, 1, 3); the same prohibition applied to exhibitions and other public amusements (*Cod. Theod.*, XV, 5, 2): Theodosius II extended the prohibition to major holy days, Eastertime, and Pentecost (*Cod. Theod.*, XV, 5, 5).

The work of plowing the field was exempted by Constantine, but, as time went on, even plowing was prohibited by various synods. The Council of Laodicea (381) interpreted the law in a much broader way; that is, the law binds only if it can be observed. The Council of Arles (538) was among the first councils that enumerated the prohibited works.

NATURE OF THE PRECEPT. Sanctification of Sundays and holy days is a precept that flows from the natural law, which requires that there be a stated time in which public cult be given to God. It is a precept of the positive divine law, which prescribes participation in the sacrifice of the New Law. It is a precept of ecclesiastical law, which determines the time and the manner in which these are carried out. The determination of days of rest from servile works is of ecclesiastical law. Catholic States should acknowledge the holy days of obligation determined by the Church. It is debated whether rest from work on Sundays is of divine positive law or of ecclesiastical law. Noldin, Schmidt, Tanquerey, Prümmer hold that it is of divine law; Vermeersch holds to the contrary, since the Old Law was abrogated by our Lord.

The seriousness and extension of the precept may be summed up as follows: (a) On holy days of obligation one must hear Mass and abstain from so-called servile works under penalty of mortal sin (Prop. 52, condemned by Innocent XI: Denz., n. 1202) unless lawful custom or a special indult allows exceptions. Judicial acts and fairs are also forbidden (Can. 1248). This law binds all those who are seven years old and have attained the use of reason. (b) The holy days of obligation for the whole Church, except when particular exception have been granted, are: Christmas, the Octave of Christmas (New Year's Day), Epiphany, Ascension, Corpus Christi, Immaculate Conception, Assumption, St. Joseph's, the feast of the holy Apostles Peter and Paul, and the feast of All Saints (Can. 1247, par. 1). All other holy days have been abrogated. Also, patron feasts are no longer days of obligation, and the local Ordinary may transfer the external solemnity to the following Sunday (Can.

1247, par. 2). In the U.S.A., the holy days of obligation were reduced to six by the Holy See at the request of the Third Plenary Council of Baltimore: Christmas, the Circumcision (Octave of Christmas), Ascension, Immaculate Conception, Assumption, and All Saints' Day.

OBLIGATION OF MASS. This obligation arises from the fact that in the New Law the holy Sacrifice of the Mass is a public act of worship to God by the whole Christian community. By reason of solidarity with this community, the faithful are required: (a) *To attend the whole Mass*, from the beginning to the final blessing. Smallness of matter in the omission of some parts of the Mass is admitted. The gravity of the omission is to be judged according to the importance of the part of the Mass omitted, and the extent of the omission. One is allowed to attend two half Masses in succession, provided that the Consecration and Communion be parts of the same Mass. (b) To attend Mass *as offered by a Catholic priest*, irrespective of the rite. (c) To attend Mass *in any church, public or semi-public oratory, and private cemetery chapels*. The obligation is satisfied also by attending Mass celebrated outdoors or, with approval of the local Ordinary, in any fitting place other than church or oratory (Can. 822, par. 4; Pont. Comm. Interpr. Cod., March 26, 1952: AAS, 44 [1952], 497). Only those who have a privilege (Can. 1249) fulfill the obligation by attending Mass in a private oratory. (d) *The faithful must be physically present* in a moral union with the celebrant. They must have the implied intention of offering an act of worship, and at least an external attention (*see* Mass).

Causes which may excuse from the observance of the precept are those arising from illness, great distance, necessity of assisting a sick person, the danger of incurring a serious material or moral harm and the like.

REST FROM SERVILE WORK. Canon 1248 prescribes that on holy days of obligation one must abstain from servile work, from judicial proceedings and, unless lawful customs or special indults allow exceptions, from public markets, or public buying and selling.

Servile work, as an occupation, primarily implies the use of physical power for material purposes, such as sowing, plowing, printing, cobbling, and the like. *Liberal works* are performed rather by the employment of mental powers, such as in reading, teaching, playing music, and the like. *Common works* are performed by all, such as playing games, eating, etc. The two latter categories of works are not forbidden on feast days. According to modern concepts (*Rev. Apol.* 62, 1936, 290, 462: *Nouv. Rev. Théol.*, 63, 1936, 32, etc.), the distinction into service, liberal, mixed and common works, upon which the lawfulness or unlawfulness of their practice on holy days is based, appears rather obsolete. This terminology arose under a different social and economic order in a society divided into slaves and free men. Modern economic systems, life, and industrial development have created such an interrupted rhythm of activities as to make a Sabbath rest or Sunday rest after the Jewish fashion impossible. But it may be well to point out that the positive side of the law outweighs the negative; in other words, the main thing is to attend to one's spiritual interests in a positive way, by attending Mass. Rest from work is but a means to better attain the end of a sanctification of the day of the Lord.

With this in view, work which makes the observance of the positive aspect of the law impossible is of itself prohibited. Of course, if the work is necessary and indispensable, it may constitute an excusing cause from the fulfillment of the precept; but, in that case, the law is merely suspended and not annulled.

Obviously, the precept is not to be looked upon with a pharisaical spirit, but according to the spirit of Christ, who proclaimed the Sabbath to be made for man, not man for the Sabbath.

The principle of at least twenty-four hours' weekly rest, coinciding with Sunday insofar as possible, is now incorporated in the principles of the International Labor Organization. (See International Labor Charter).

Judicial acts also are forbidden, insofar

as they require juridical procedures or interfere with public rest.

For the same reason, all commercial occupations, such as marketing, buying and selling, or public auctions, are forbidden. Local customs, however, permit some of these activities. Generally, it is not forbidden for private individuals to discuss or agree on the purchase or sale of land, house, cattle, and the like.

When is the violation of the negative part of the precept a grave sin? Engaging in servile work for a period notably longer than two hours constitutes grave matter. Concerning judicial acts, grave matter is judged rather from the quality of the act than from other considerations. Engaging in marketing, conducting fairs, public buying and selling is grave matter because a greater number of people consider such activities a grave violation.

Causes excusing from the obligation of Sunday rest are: custom, work of religion, and necessity.

The Supreme Pontiff can dispense for the whole Church from both the negative and positive aspects of the precept. Local Ordinaries in their own diocesan territories and pastors in their parishes can dispense single individuals or single families (Can. 1245, par. 1) from the observance of such obligations if there is a good reason.

In clerical exempt organizations, the superiors enjoy the same faculties as pastors with respect to all persons subject to them, in accordance with Can. 514, par. 1, and Can. 1245, par. 3. *Pal.*

SANDALS. *See* Sacred Vestments.

SAPPHIC LOVE. *See* Sodomy.

SATISFACTION. In a wide sense, *satisfaction* refers to any compensation for an injury caused to another; in a strict sense, it is reparation to God for offenses and sins against His Divine Majesty. Thus satisfaction includes all penitential acts, but mainly the mortification of self by sacrifices of legitimate pleasures or the endurance of sufferings in a spirit of reparation for outrages committed against God by sins. Only matters of a penal nature have satisfactory value in the strict sense; but in the state of fallen nature, every good work is in some sense penal.

Satisfaction is *sacramental*, i.e., as the penance which the confessor enjoins upon a penitent, or *non-sacramental*, ie., a satisfaction undertaken on one's own initiative.

Among satisfactory works the following may be included: the sacrifice of legitimate pleasures, endurance of unpleasant tasks, bearing annoyances and afflictions in a spirit of reparation, prayers, fasts, alms, or other pious works, as are mentioned by the Council of Trent (Denz. 906, 923).

Satisfaction may be offered to God for one's own sins or for the sins of others; in fact, good deeds performed in the state of grace may serve as satisfaction for the sins of those who are united with us by the bonds of charity (Gal. 6:2), particularly the souls in purgatory.

NECESSITY. One of the effects of any sin is an obligation to undergo punishment. The vicarious satisfaction of infinite value offered by Jesus Christ through His passion and death does not remove the possibility and obligation of the sinner to offer his own satisfaction. Instead, it enables him to perform satisfactory works that will be acceptable to God. These works draw their value from the merits of the passion and death of our Lord Jesus Christ, and, far from reducing the universal effectiveness of the sacrifice of Jesus Christ Himself, they emphasize it more and more.

In forgiving a fault, the Lord could also wipe away the punishment for all times and completely. This He does in the case of baptism. But with regard to sins committed after baptism, God has disposed that a temporal punishment should remain after sin is forgiven. This punishment will be wiped out either here on earth or in purgatory, through satisfactory works or indulgences (Matt. 16: 24; Luke 3:8; Rom. 8:17; Coloss. 1:24; I Peter 2:21; Council of Trent: Denz., nn. 807, 840, 904, 922, 925).

The intention to make satisfaction is one of the elements in the sacrament of penance; in fact, it is necessary in order that the sin may be forgiven. This need not necessarily be explicit, for it is contained in contrition or attrition, if they have the proper qualities. It is obviously lacking if the penitent refuses to accept a penance imposed by the confessor. The actual performing of sacramental satisfaction is not an essential but an integral part of the sacrament; the penance enjoined has a special satisfactory value.

It is sinful deliberately to omit the penance enjoined by the priest in confession. The sin is grave if the penance omitted is a serious one imposed for a mortal sin, not previously remitted in the sacrament of penance. If a considerable part of the penance or an important circumstance connected with the penance is omitted, or if the penance omitted is a serious one imposed for a venial sin that readily leads to mortal sin, it is also gravely wrong deliberately to omit its performance.

Prayers given as a penance are to be recited orally. If the prayers are such as are usually recited in a responsorial way, such as psalms or the rosary, they may be recited in this manner.

Sacramental penance must be carried out by the penitent himself with an intention of doing penance. If someone should have a doubt as to his intention after he has performed the good work imposed upon him, he may presume to have had the necessary intention, provided that the work performed was not the object of another precept nor directed to another intention. One who performs his sacramental penance in the state of mortal sin is not obliged to repeat this, unless the particular work enjoined was one which of its very nature called for the state of grace, e.g., the reception of Holy Communion. Such a penance will not bring about the remission of any part of the temporal punishment still due for sins already forgiven.

The penitent may not take it upon himself to change the penance imposed upon him by the priest. If the performance of the penance presents serious difficulties, the penitent should explain this in confession and ask for a commutation. If the confessor sets a time-limit, then the penance must be performed within the time set; if no time is specified, the penance should be performed as soon as it can be done without incurring serious inconvenience. It is not necessary to complete the penance before going to Holy Communion. However, to delay the performance of sacramental penance without a good reason is a sin which could also be mortal, if the medicinal effect of the penance is hindered to such an extent that it results in a serious danger of relapse into mortal sin, or if the delay would result in a considerable reduction of the satisfaction enjoined. A person who has failed to carry out his sacramental penance at the proper time is still bound to do so as soon as possible.

Since, in many cases, sacramental satisfaction is not enough to wipe out the temporal punishment due to sins already forgiven, it is worthwhile to add other penances, such as offering the trials of life to God. According to some theologians, the prayer *Passio Domini*, recited by the priest at the end of the absolution, raises all of the penitent's good works to the level of sacramental satisfaction.

Satisfaction performed on earth in the state of grace is also meritorious; this is proof of the great mercy of God. In purgatory, however, satisfaction is no longer meritorious because the time for meriting is to end at death. *Man.*

SATURNISM. *See* Diseases, Professional.

SATYRIASIS. *See* Perversion, sexual.

SCANDAL. Of Greek origin, *scandal* means a stumbling block. It is "any word or deed not fully upright which is the occasion of sin to another" (St. Thomas). Scandal may be *active* or *passive*, depending on whether it is given or suffered. Generally, scandal is active and passive. Scandal is active only, if one commits an act in itself capable of causing spiritual harm to another, but the latter resists the bad influence and commits no sin. Scandal may be only passive, if one takes occasion for scandal from conduct which is good under every respect. This was the case of the Pharisees, who were scandalized over the doctrine and the beneficent activity of Jesus. Indignation or astonishment over evil or unusual behavior of another is improperly called scandal. In fact, indignation at unseemly conduct may be a good act.

Active scandal is unbecoming conduct in act, word, or omission which is the occasion of spiritual harm to another. Sometimes actions, not evil in themselves, have nevertheless the appearance of evil and as such may lead another to sin, as St. Paul's instruction to the faithful of Corinth concerning the buying and eating of animals sacrificed to idols. St. Paul points out that, though such a thing, in itself, is not a sin because idols do not really exist, yet, if others think that this action is illicit, there is the danger that they may do it because they see other Christians do it. One must refrain from buying and eating such meat, because it is illicit to perform an action that will be an occasion of sin to others.

Scandal may be *direct* or *indirect*. *Direct* scandal is an act which of its very nature causes another to sin. Direct scandal may be given in a twofold manner: by directly intending to cause another's spiritual ruin, which is called diabolical because it follows the pattern of the evil spirit, or by satisfying one's own passion for reason of gain. Scandal is *indirect* if an evil act is committed which in itself does not require or involve another's sin, though the circumstances in actual fact will certainly or probably cause another to sin.

If the scandal consists in imitating what one sees other people do, it coincides with bad example. There are also other forms of scandal. A woman who dresses in an indecent manner gives scandal not only because of the bad example she gives other women but also because she is likely or certain to arouse lust in men.

Scandal is a mortal or venial sin depending on whether it is the occasion of grave or light sin to another. One who gives scandal sins against the virtue of charity toward one's neighbor, because this virtue obliges one not to cause harm, material or spiritual, to one's neighbor. Moreover, by giving scandal one becomes a cooperator in the sin of another. While it is always sinful to give active scandal,

in instances of passive scandal no sin is committed, if scandal proceeds from ill will, which sees an occasion of sin in conduct otherwise correct; or if this scandal comes, due to the ignorance, lack of education, or moral formation of another, from an act, either not sinful in itself or necessary for the attainment of a good whose importance justifies our behavior. In such cases, there is no sin of scandal whatever.

Scandal is exceedingly detestable in the eyes of God. "*Woe to the world because of scandals! Woe to the man through whom scandal does come! Whoever causes one of these little ones who believe in me to sin, it were better for him to have a great millstone hung around his neck and to be drowned in the depths of the sea*" (Mt. 18: 5–7). It is not enough to avoid doing what is in itself sinful, but one must also avoid anything which, though not a sin, might offer the occasion of sin to another.

The same duty of charity toward neighbor that obliges one to avoid scandal also obliges to reparation for the spiritual harm caused to another insofar as conditions permit. Generally, a public scandal will require a public act of reparation. In many cases, good example publicly and bravely given seems to be a valid and often adequate reparation for scandals given by a sinful life. *Ben.*

SCAPULAR. For St. Benedict and his monks, as historians relate, the scapular originally was a dresslike garment which the monks wore over their habit while engaged in manual labor. Such a garment was in no way different from the one used by the farmers working in the fields (PL: 66, 771).

Later on, the scapular became complementary to the habit of the religious orders. When these began to unite to their orders lay groups, they gave them a part of their own habit to signify unity. For some, it was a cord or cincture; for others, the greater number, it was the scapular in a reduced form, which today consists of two small pieces of woolen cloth worn across the shoulders and the chest.

There are two main types of scapulars:

(a) scapulars as *essential* insignia proper to contraternities (such as the Carmelite scapular), these are a part of the reception ceremony; (b) scapulars, neither essential nor distinctive of any association, that give the faithful wearing them the right to gain indulgences, like the Blue Scapular. Besides these, there are sixteen other small scapulars now used among Catholics.

Scapulars must be made of woolen cloth, neither knitted nor embroidered (*Decr. Auth.*, n. 423, ad 2: AAS, 27, 692). The wool must be of the color proper to the respective scapulars; embellishments are allowed, provided that the prescribed color is predominant (*Decr. Auth.*, n. 423, ad 3–4). The two parts of the scapular are joined by two strings which are not an essential part of the scapular; they are not required to be of wool or any particular color, except the scapulars of the Passion and of St. Joseph, whose strings must be respectively red and white.

The shape of the scapular must be either rectangular or square; no other form is permitted (*Decr. Auth.*, n. 423, ad 5).

Scapulars must be blessed by a priest with the faculty to conduct the investiture. The mere sign of the Cross is not sufficient for the blessing, but a formula, proper to each scapular, contained in the *Roman Ritual*, must be used (AAS, 19 [1927], 558, ad 1–2). Various scapulars may be blessed at the same time with a single formula, provided that the investing priest has a special indult, usually granted by the Sacred Congregation of Rites. The same priest who blesses the scapular must also conduct the ceremony of investiture.

In the case of scapulars which carry affiliation to a particular confraternity, the name of those so invested must be entered in the register of the respective organization. However, in the case of a large number of people, the Sacred Congregation of the Council usually dispenses with the inscription and allows each candidate to invest himself with the scapular.

In the case of soldiers, the Holy See has given permission for each one of them, at any time and place, to invest himself with any scapular without any particular ceremony or blessing (Secretariat of State, March 22, 1912).

The scapular must be worn at all times and in such a manner that one part will rest on the shoulders and the other on the chest. It may, however, be removed at certain times, during bathing or certain types of work. For a good reason, a scapular may also be pinned to one's clothing, but it may not be sewn to it.

To foster the spiritual welfare of the faithful, the Holy See has permitted a scapular medal to be worn in place of a cloth scapular. The medal must have on one side the image of our Lord Jesus Christ showing His Heart, and the image of the Blessed Virgin on the other (AAS [1910], 22).

Among the many scapulars approved by the Holy See, granting many spiritual favors, the principal ones are: (a) the scapular of the Holy Trinity, proper to the Order of the Most Holy Trinity; (b) the red scapular of the Passion, proper to the Congregation of the Mission; (c) the scapular of the Seven Sorrows, of the Order of the Servants of Mary, or Servites; (d) the scapular of Mt. Carmel of the Carmelite Order; (e) the blue scapular, proper to the Theatines.

The Code of Canon Law does not directly speak of scapulars but simply of distinctive habits which may be worn by those faithful who are enrolled in one of the many Catholic associations (Cans. 694, 704, 706). The Code leaves all details concerning scapulars to the statutes and rules of each organization, duly approved by competent authority. *de A.*

SCHISM. *Schism* (Greek, *schizo*—I cut, separate) is a technical theological term to indicate a separation of a group or of an individual from the unity of the universal Church, with the retention of belief in the true faith. On this latter point a schism differs from a heresy or apostasy. This unity of the Church has a twofold aspect: a union of the faithful among themselves in the bonds of charity; and a union of the members with the Head in the bond of obedience. To lack either of these aspects constitutes a sin of schism (Can. 1325, par. 2). In practice, however, after an initial break, these two elements will coincide in their effects. In itself, schism could exist without heresy, i.e., as a mere *de facto* separation or rebellion without a theoretical denial of the authority of the pope, as occurred in the Great Western Schism of 1378-1418 A.D. In practice, however, heresy usually creeps into a schism, since eventually it becomes necessary to deny the dogma of papal infallibility and all other dogmas declared after the schism or break. This occurred in the schism of the Eastern dissident Churches. It must be noted that individual members of the flock as well as groups may become schismatic.

A schism may be *material*, i.e., in good faith (as many Eastern schismatics); or formal, in bad faith. The sin that arises from a schism is serious in its matter as a grave sin of disobedience. Obedience is due to the Supreme Head of the Church. Theologians, following St. Thomas, list schism with the sins against charity because it is a breach of peace among the faithful. Schism is less grave than heresy and irreligion, because these are offenses against the revelation of God, the Supreme Head of all men and Infinite Truth.

The juridical relationship of schismatics to the Catholic Church is similar to that of heretics and the Church: they live outside of communion with the Church and are under excommunication, although they may participate in a limited manner in the spiritual benefits of the Church.

It is debated whether Eastern schismatics exercise jurisdiction validly in view of their separation from the Church, but the Church accepts the validity of their jurisdiction, insofar as it is the wish of the Church to provide jurisdiction in the external and internal forum in common error (Can. 209). *Dam.*

SCHIZOPHRENIA. One of the most serious and widespread mental diseases, schizophrenia is a profound disturbance of the psychic function which generally begins at the time of the puberal crisis or in the following period of ten years;

it has a chronic course, which usually leads to decay that often assumes the aspect of dementia.

Overemphasizing this aspect, E. Kraepelin, in 1860, coined the term, still in use today, of *dementia precox*, to indicate that the sick individuals became in a short time precociously demented. Under that term he included three distinct psychoses: hebephrenic, catatonic, and paranoid; all of them presented demential characteristics and it was possible to find hebephrenic, catatonic, and paranoid elements alternating or associated in the same individual (*see* Hebephrenia).

Kraepelin and several other scholars searched for a single, fundamental, psycho-pathological process that might explain all the different symptoms of the psychosis. Such a process was isolated by E. Bleuler as a grave defect of articulation or "association" existing not only among the spheres of thought, feelings, and action, but also among the very elements of thought. This associative disturbance was called *schizophrenic dissociation* and the term *schizophrenia* (Greek, *schizo*, I divide, cut, disassociate; and *phren*, intellect) has, in the last thirty years replaced the term *dementia precox* coined by Kraepelin.

SYMPTOMATOLOGY. Schizophrenia may start and develop in an insidious, ambiguous way or suddenly explode into a *delirious outburst* or some other conspicuous psychopathic episode. In clear contrast with the former mental balance of the individual, who is often endowed with outstanding mental ability, the disease often develops in predisposed individuals who have a *schizothemic* or *schizoid temperament*, usually accompanied by a longitype or leptosomatic morphological constitution (*see* Constitution, Biotypological; Cyclothymia). Schizophrenia, fully developed, is characterized by a changing multitude of disturbances like the following. Ideation may suffer an *associative ataxy* or lack of coordination in speech, at times profoundly disconnected, chaotic, or revealing a sharp contrast between formal logic and an exaggerated exactness of terms, on the one hand, and an extraordinary incongruity of content, on the other. The same can be said about his writing. Hallucinations and illusions, seemingly paradoxical and absurd, are frequent. *Emotional life* is deeply disturbed, mostly in a kind of *freezing of feelings,* a marked *sentimental inanity* which causes the patient to become detached from all family affections. Cerletti goes as far as to hold that the central psychopathological nucleus of schizophrenia consists in a weakening and total extinction of the activity of the thymo-psyche (the instinctive-affective sphere). This, of course, necessarily gives rise to *intrapsychic ataxy* (illustrated by Stransky), which is a disturbance of the volitive processes no longer upheld and moved by emotional impulses.

Disturbances of the will and behavior are usually more noticeable and common in all patients. At times, the disease appears in the form of a profound indolence; at other times, the patient reaches such a state of inactivity as to lapse in extreme cases into *catalepsy,* during which he fails to react even to painful stimuli; at times, he imitates automatically all gestures he may see other people make (*echopraxy*); at other times, he opposes a strenuous resistance to every attempt to change the position of his body or he may react in exactly the opposite way to all suggestions (*negativism*). Apparently unmotivated and unexpected impulses may develop into criminal acts. Phases of prolonged excitation are likely to be experienced by the patient, who much more frequently may make strange and unusual *mannerisms* or gestures repeated again and again with monotonous uniformity and for a long time (*stereotype.*)

VARIETY AND COURSE. Schizophrenia may be *hebephrenic, catatonic, paronoiac,* or *simple,* depending on whether the prevailing factors are: (a) dissociative disturbances of the mind among thoughts, affections, and conduct; (b) the fettering or other serious disturbances of the will; (c) persistent delusional build-ups, at times, accompanied by hallucinations; (d) affective obtuseness and inertia of the will. The distinction of one from the other is not always easy, but, irrespective of its clinical form, schizophrenia always has a chronic course. At times, the patient, almost unnoticeably, runs all the steps of a scale which may reach so deep an intellectual decay as to be comparable, at least in appearance, to the most serious forms of true dementia. At other times, the sick person remains indefinitely suspended, as it were, in a state of affective-volitive obtuseness which makes him look like a stolid and bizarre, foolish and whimsical child, absolutely incapable of self-control and self-restraint. In some cases, the disease may become arrested for long periods of time; it may show considerable improvement, but at other times it plunges into a sudden crisis. It is also possible to have alternate episodes of serious dissociation and brief periods of seemingly almost complete normality.

At any rate, irrespective of the course of the psychosis and the actual phase of the morbid process, one must never forget that such patients are potentially dangerous and may at any moment explode in the gravest, most absurd, and unexpected acts.

TREATMENT. Until some years back, medical science was almost completely helpless in the face of schizophrenia. Today this disease can be treated effectively by the use of a variety of *shock* therapies, such as insulin comas, convulsive fits provoked by cardiozol, electric-current treatment, acetilcoline, and the like. The best results are obtained by the use of electroshock in catatonic forms of schizophrenia; insulin shocks in hebephrenic and simple forms; in paranoid forms, which strongly withstand curative action, insulin shocks must be associated with cardiozol or electric convulsions. In any case, the earlier the treatment, the better the chances for effective results. In recent years, the use of the so-called ganglioplegic therapy (a treatment consisting of chloropromazine, largactil, reserpine, or serpasil, etc.) has gained considerable ground in the psychiatric field and is helpfully employed in the treatment of schizophrenia.

MORAL OBSERVATIONS. A schizophrenic must always be considered a dangerous, irresponsible individual, regardless of the course of the psychosis and the actual stage of the disease. From this, spring forth two important corollaries: a schizophrenic must be considered legally incapable from the clinical beginning of the disease, though he may still show a sufficient psycho-intellective activity. Athymia, egocentrism, estrangement from environmental reality (*autism*), intrapsychic ataxy and other phenomena characterizing the schizophrenic mentality from the very beginning make it extremely unlikely that the patient, despite eventual appearances to the contrary, could be considered juridically capable.

The same, if not more emphatically, must be said concerning penal responsibility. In this connection, it must be added that often the commission of crime discloses the psychosis, in the sense that it becomes apparent through a crime whose absurdity, uselessness and oddity, to gether with subsequent abnormal behavior of the culprit, reveal its pathological origin.

From the purely moral aspect, the imputability of these sick individuals is doubtful. It would be necessary to establish to what point and to what degree the individual may have been free and not compelled by the impact of the disease; but this judgment is often humanly impossible. Generally, however, these sick individuals cannot be held capable of grave moral responsibility.

The ever-present danger, at times even grave, of the possible harm that a schizophrenic might cause to himself or others, makes early admittance to a psychiatric hospital or other establishment for the treatment of the mentally ill all the more urgent, because the sooner the treatments are initiated, the better the chances of recovery. *Riz.*

SCHIZOTHYMIA. See Cyclothymia.

SCHOOL. More than the technical aspect of the school, we shall treat here the rights and duties of the family, the Church, and the State concerning the problem of education (*q.v.*).

FAMILY AND EDUCATION. The Church has always strongly defended the natural right of parents to educate their children. This right stems directly from the natural life which they gave their children. "By nature, parents have a right to train their children, but with this an added duty that the education and instruction of the child be in accord with the purpose for which, by God's blessing, he was begotten. Therefore, it is the duty of parents to make every effort to prevent any invasion of their right in this matter; to make absolutely sure that the education of their children remains under their own control in keeping with their Christian duty; above all, to refuse to send them to those schools in which there is danger of imbibing the deadly poison of impiety". (Leo XIII, *Sapientiae Christianae*, January 10, 1890). And the same Pontiff later declared: "Paternal authority can neither be abolished nor absorbed by the State, for it has the same source as human life itself" (Leo XIII, *Rerum novarum*, May 15, 1891).

Therefore, "parents are bound by a most grave obligation to provide, to the best of their ability, for the religious and moral as well as the physical and secular education of their children, and to care for their temporal well-being" (Can. 1113).

It would be ideal if the father brought his child to his complete physical, intellectual and moral development and then turned him over to society as a man, but this does not occur. The family takes care of the education of the children for the first years only; then it is not able to do so because of the lack of means and time. The school becomes thereby the next social factor. But does this, therefore, necessarily mean that the family loses its rights over the children and these become the property of the State? "On this point," says Pius XI, "the common sense of mankind is in such complete accord that they would be in open contradiction with it who dared to maintain that the children belong to the State before they belong to the family, and that the State has an absolute right over their education. Untenable is the reason they propose, namely, that man is born a citizen and, hence, belongs primarily to the State; they do not bear in mind that, before becoming a citizen, man must exist, and existence does not come from the State, but from the parents" (Pius

XI, *Divini illius Magistri*, Dec. 31, 1929).

The State has no right to destroy the natural rights of the family; it must recognize and protect them. The State does not beget the children; but parents do. Hence, they belong to the parents, to whom belongs also the right to educate them as they think best.

But the concept of liberty must be properly understood by parents. It must not be a despotic freedom, by which they impose ideas and feelings upon their children without rational restraint. Family relations, though intimate, are always relations between human beings, and children also have a personality of their own, which must be respected. They have their own mind and a will that is naturally free. In short, even in this area, freedom must be understood with the limitations that freedom itself demands. "Do unto others as you would have others do unto you" remains the fundamental norm of every social relation. My freedom ends where the right of another begins.

In practice, the rights of parents with respect to the school may be reduced to the following: (a) The right to conduct schools under their direct control and responsibility. (b) The right to decide on the type of religious and moral education (without prejudice to God's rights) for all public and private schools. It is an act of tyranny on the part of the State to impose a type of education which parents condemn as contrary to the exigencies of their conscience. (c) The right to inspect and to intervene, within certain limitations but efficaciously, in the school which their children attend. (d) The right to demand from the State the type of school that meets the actual exigencies and educational aims of the population, if private initiative is unable to do so.

All these rights flow clearly and strictly from the fact that children belong to their parents, and from the freedom of conscience which no State can disregard without violating the most fundamental and indisputable obligations of the State towards its citizens.

CHURCH AND SCHOOL. The source of all the rights of the Church as a visible and spiritual society, is the unequivocal command of Christ: "All power in heaven and on earth has been given to me. Go, therefore, and make disciples of all nations, baptizing them in the name of the Father and of the Son and of the Holy Spirit, teaching them to observe all that I have commanded you; and, behold, I am with you all days, even unto the consummation of the world" (Matt. 28:18–20). The Church was constituted by her Founder as the universal teacher and sole guide able to lead men to the end for which they were created, namely, to God. Of course, those who do not believe in man's supernatural destiny will reject the right and authority of the Church. But the Church cannot, without betraying her mission, neglect the right of vigilance over the education of all the faithful, particularly children. And where the Church's rights concerning education are not recognized, she still has the duty to point out to Catholic parents the dangers related to a secular school (*q.v.*), where religion is ignored.

The rights of the Church over the faithful are similar to the rights of parents over children. They are rights of parenthood. In giving a child the life of the body, the parents acquire all the duties and rights necessary for bringing this natural life to full development. So, too, the Church, by giving her faithful the supernatural life of grace through baptism, assumes all the duties and claims all the rights necessary for the development of divine grace in her members. These rights are superior to the rights of the parents, for spiritual matters are superior to material ones. Of course, here, too, the Church will always respect a just concept of freedom of conscience.

In view of the above, the Church has the right to be unopposed in the exercise of her mission to teach religion in all the schools attended by Catholic pupils, with a similar power to approve the teachers, books, and curricula.

But the Church cannot be content with this. Religion, unlike other school subjects, is a science of practical living; it must, therefore, extend to all aspects of education. The Church is independent of all earthly power in the origin as well as the exercise of her formative mission, not only with regard to her proper end and object, but also with respect to the means necessary and suitable for attaining that end. The Church, therefore, has the right to supervise the whole school organization concerning religion and morality, and to remove whatever may be contrary to it. In the words of Pius XI: "Nor may even physical culture, as it is called, be considered outside the range of her maternal supervision, for the reason that it also is a means which may help or harm Christian education" (Pius XI, *Divini illius Magistri*). The Church deems the matter of maternal supervision of education to be of such paramount importance as to incorporate it in her Code: "The religious teaching of youth in all schools is subject to the authority and supervision of the Church" (Can. 1381).

And finally: "The Church has the right to establish schools of every type, elementary, secondary, and of higher education as well" (Can. 1375).

These are clear and unavoidable consequences of the Church's mission to lead all men to salvation; and whoever opposes these rights of the Church opposes the very rights of God. Conscious of this, the Church has, at the cost of immense sacrifices, always attended to the education of youth. "When it is a question of the good education of youth, we have no right to fix a limit to the pains and labor that result, however great these may be" (Leo XIII, *Sapientiae Christianae*, Jan. 10, 1890).

THE STATE AND EDUCATION. The State, taken as a whole and with all the complexities of its functions, is a perfect society, insofar as it has all the means necessary for the attainment of its end. But it is an institution which undoubtedly presupposes both the individual and the family for which it came into being.

Applying these general principles to the particular case of the State, since the parents have, from the law of nature, the right to educate their children, the State may intervene only when those who are primarily responsible for it fail or are, for any reason, unable to carry out their obligations.

To presume to substitute the work of the parents with that of anonymous State employees is clearly absurd. This is amply confirmed by statements of religious men and women of all ages and conditions who have devoted themselves for many centuries to the education of children, and who have always held that there is no real substitute for the parents' care of their children.

The State cannot claim absolute competency in the field of education, also, by reason of the inadequate nature of its end. In fact, the end of the State is concerned with the welfare of the community; in other words, it is social, whereas education is eminently personal and directed to the individual. "Public authority has no right in the normal state of society to take over private education. It is, of course, a different thing for the State to offer to parents appropriate aid for an adequate education of their children, without compelling them to use it; giving such help is a sign of great social progress." In other words, the State may have its own schools, but only if private initiative is lacking or inadequate to the need. It shall be a motive of pride for the State to procure an environment favorable to the development of the mental faculties of all its citizens, and to see to it that truth and obvious error are not accorded the same right in all fields.

ABUSES BY THE STATE. The greatest abuse, at least from the Catholic standpoint, is the so-called State monopoly on education. Aside from the consideration that any monopoly, especially that on culture, is contrary to sound progress, the fact remains that it is a grave injustice for the State to compel citizens to send their children to "lay" State schools because no private schools are permitted, as it is also to deny private schools much-needed aid out of the taxpayers' money simply because they are religion-oriented schools (*see* School, Lay).

SCHOOL, LAY. According to Can. 1381, local Ordinaries have the right and duty to see that nothing is taught or done contrary to faith or good morals in any of the schools of their respective territories, to approve the teachers and textbooks and to demand that, in the interest of religion and morals, objectionable teachers and books be replaced. A school that shuns these provisions is called a *lay school*.

There are various types of lay schools. A religious lay school, though not under ecclesiastical control, has nevertheless Catholic teachers, gives religious instruction and follows a scholastic program, oriented wholly to the principles of Christian doctrine and morals. Another type of lay school has no connection with any religious denomination, although it is oriented toward the principles of natural religion (*non-denominational school*). A third type consists of schools which teach no religion at all, but maintain a respectful silence towards all denominations (*neutral school*). Finally, another type of school maintains a hostile attitude towards religion and fights the Catholic religion systematically or intermittently or indirectly, attacking either her doctrines, basic laws or institutions (*anti-religious school*).

Among Catholic nations—for example, in Italy—the State school system is lay in its administrative organization, in the appointment of teachers and curricula, but it allows the teaching of religion in primary and secondary schools.

"For the mere fact that a school gives some religious instruction (often extremely stinted) does not bring it into accord with the rights of the Church and of the Christian family, or make it a fit place for Catholic students. To be this, it is necessary that all the teaching and the whole organization of the school, and its teachers, programs and textbooks in every branch be regulated by the Christian spirit, under the direction and maternal supervision of the Church; so that religion may be in very truth the foundation and crown of the youth's entire training and this in every grade of school, not only in the elementary, but the intermediate and the higher institutions of learning as well" (Pius XI, *On Christian Education*, December 31, 1929).

At different times during the past century the Church has felt the necessity of reminding Catholic parents of their obligation in this regard.

Canon 1374 of the Code of Canon Law states: "Catholic children shall not attend non-Catholic or non-denominational schools, nor schools called mixed, that is, open also to non-Catholics. It is the right of the local Ordinaries alone to judge, in accordance with the instructions of the Holy See, under what circumstances and with what safeguards against the danger of perversion, attendance at such schools may be tolerated."

An anti-Christian education constitutes a grave, proximate intellectual and moral danger for the pupils. A neutral education is practically unworkable, as long experience has demonstrated in all countries. "A school from which religion is excluded is contrary to the fundamental principles of education" (Pius XI). Education without religion leads the pupil to religious indifferentism and scepticism; at best, it does not give him an integral Christian training. Finally, a school outside the supervision of the ecclesiastical authority as indicated in Can. 1374, does not give the Catholic pupil sufficient safeguards and guarantees.

Catholics are duty-bound to attend a Catholic school as the best guarantee for the safety of their faith and their moral life. *Man.*

SCIENCE, NECESSARY. By necessary science is meant the degree of knowledge an individual is required to acquire by reason of his state in life. Everyone by the fact that he is a human being, is obliged to know the basic principles of religion and natural morality, i.e., the existence of God as Judge of men, and the ten commandments. If he is not able to do so on his own, he is bound to attend some form of religious instruction.

As Christians, we are bound to learn the principal truths of our faith, that is, the existence of a One, Triune God; the Incarnation, the substance of the articles of faith contained in the Apostles' Creed; prayer, including some substantial notions of the *Lord's Prayer*; the sacraments, particularly baptism, the Holy Eucharist, and penance; the fundamental teachings of the Gospel and the general precepts of the Church besides the ten commandments. This knowledge must be in proportion to the capacity and degree of general education of the individual. In accordance with our position in life, we must learn the duties attending upon our particular state. Thus, children, parents, servants, masters, judges, physicians, and priests are obliged to know their own specific duties.

Not everyone is required to acquire the greatest degree of knowledge for a profession or a trade; this, of course, depends on the position which one holds. But everyone is bound to acquire an average degree of knowledge which will enable him to handle ordinary and rare cases, at least to lead him to the possible solutions from study, consultation, or reflection.

As the responsible subject on one's own activities, each individual has the duty to ascertain the licitness of every act he is about to perform.

One who lacks necessary knowledge in his profession is responsible for all errors committed and their consequences, according to the principles indicated in the articles on ignorance and causal responsibility (*voluntary in causa*). *Gra.*

SCRUPLE. An exaggerated, groundless, unreasonable fear of sin in the past or present is called a *scruple*. This may occur in a single instance or act, as a momentary outcome of ignorance, error or inadvertency, in which case the morality of the action is judged according to those norms usually applied to an erroneous or doubtful conscience (*q.v.*). An habitual state of scruples, however, may occur, in which there is a constant tendency to an exaggerated fear of sinning. This is of interest to the moralist, for this state is a true spiritual disease which ultimately leads to a morbid obsession (*see* Psychasthenia).

The scrupulous individual sees sin where there is no sin; he is seized by a subtle, futile and constant fear lest he sin. He is characterized by an extreme condition of concern about scarcely possible or impossible circumstances, stubborn attachment to his own opinion,

fickleness of mind, and extreme reluctance to accept the judgment of another, such as his confessor.

The doubts and false opinions of the scrupulous individual usually revolve around a fact, not principles. Often his scruples only extend to certain matters, such as integrity of confession, Eucharistic fast, rash judgments, fraternal correction.

Since it is a disease, scrupulosity is to be treated at times with the application of rules which seem to depart somewhat from the ordinary ones.

A sure remedy would be absolute obedience to a wise spiritual director; but this cannot be easily obtained, precisely because the scrupulous person is morbidly attached to his own opinion. Thus, he must combat this exaggerated attachment; he must learn to accept his director's judgment and instructions; nor should he always change directors in the hope of finding one who agrees with him. A scrupulous person must be directed to a consideration of the fatherly goodness of God more than to a consideration of His justice; he must avoid idleness, melancholy and a prolonged or deep self-examination. In more severe cases, he should be urged to see a psychiatrist. *Gra.*

SCULPTOR. A sculptor is one who exercises the art of shaping any type of figure, by a chisel or other cutting or carving instrument, from a solid material, such as stone, marble, wood, ivory, etc.

The origins of this art are lost in the obscurity of time, when man made use of it to adorn his house as well as his temples. By his art a sculptor glorifies God and communicates with other men in a language that tends to raise their hearts and minds to the beautiful and the good. Unfortunately, however, even sculpture in the hands of men forgetful of the true notion of art, has contributed in the past and does contribute in modern times to the corruption of morals by impudent nudity of seductive images and lustful exhibitions, contrary to art itself and to modesty (*see* Art, morality of).

A sculptor is bound to follow the true norms of art and not to use the latter as an instrument of evil. A Catholic may not make or carve idols to be used for worship. He is permitted, however, to assist in such work by a purely material cooperation, if it is required by truly grave reasons (*see* Excusing Cause). *Tar.*

SEAL OF CONFESSION. The seal of confession is the obligation of the priest to maintain absolute secrecy concerning knowledge gained in the administration of the sacrament of penance. Imposed by Christ in instituting the sacrament, this obligation has repeatedly been inculcated by ecclesiastical authority (Council of Trent, Sess. IV, Denz. 438; Canon 889). No advantage or disadvantage permits violation of the seal of confession. If a confession was not completed, if the penitent was not absolved because of a lack of proper dispositions, if the confession was made in good faith to one who was not a priest or did not have the power to absolve, the seal of confession is binding nevertheless.

The obligation of the seal of confession applies to confessors and those who have direct or indirect knowledge of things which come under the sacramental seal (Can. 899, par. 2). Among these are: interpreters used for confession; those who accidentally or on purpose have heard part of another's confession; those to whom things were referred that are matter of the sacramental seal; superiors who are asked for faculties to absolve from a reserved case; theologians consulted by a confessor with the consent of the penitent; those who accidentally read a list of another person's sins, if the list represented the person's confession or was used as an aid to confession.

The seal of confession extends to all sins confessed as well as to the person who has confessed them. It is absolutely forbidden to say that a certain penitent accused himself of many venial sins or of a mortal sin. The seal also covers particular details that the penitent mentioned to help explain his sins, e.g., the purpose he had in mind, the occasion, his accomplices. The seal includes anything that would give rise to a suspicion that a certain person had confessed a certain sin, or anything that would cause embarrassment for a penitent or someone else, such as the fact that absolution was refused or a heavy penance imposed, practical advice given to the penitent, or even the fact of confession if it can lead to a suspicion that the penitent was guilty of some specific mortal or venial sin or hidden defects (e.g., scrupulosity, weakness of will, irresoluteness), which the confessor has learned as a result of having heard the confession.

Qualities, virtues, special graces and good works made known in confession do not in themselves fall under the sacramental seal; but they do if they were revealed to help explain a sin (e.g., ingratitude to God), or if revealing them might give rise to a suspicion of any sin. In any case, they come under the heading of natural secret.

If a person is in doubt whether or not something falls under the sacramental seal, he has an obligation to keep it secret. If, on the other hand, the confessor already knows from another source something that was mentioned to him in confession, this knowledge, which he had independently, does not fall under the seal. But he must be careful lest he give scandal in making mention of it. The same thing is true whenever a penitent gives another person express permission to reveal something that he has revealed in confession.

VIOLATION. A distinction must be made between direct and indirect violation of the seal of confession. *Direct* violation of the seal consists in revealing a sin that was learned through confession, along with the identity of the person who confessed it, either by naming him explicitly or supplying details which amount to an express designation. The violation is direct even if hearers are unaware that the information came from confession. Direct violation of the seal is a very serious sin. A confessor who commits a direct violation of the seal of confession would, by that very fact, incur an excommunication which is reserved in a most special way to the Holy See (Can. 2369, par. 1). Salutary penalties are to be inflicted on any other person who dares to commit a direct violation of the seal, even excommunication (Can. 2369, par. 2). We might observe that in certain circumstances, though a person remains silent, his external manner of action might constitute a violation, even direct, of the seal of confession.

Indirect violations of the sacramental seal are words, actions or omissions which create a danger that others may come to know or suspect something pertaining to the seal. This type of violation is in itself a serious sin; but it may be only a venial sin if the danger is slight under all aspects. The penalties mentioned in Can. 2368, par. 1, can be inflicted upon a confessor who breaks the sacramental seal indirectly; others guilty of this type of violation may be punished by penalties in proportion to the seriousness of their offense, even to the point of excommunication.

PRACTICAL COROLLARIES. Along with the obligation of the sacramental seal, there is an obligation to make no use whatever of information gained through confession that might be harmful to the penitent or others, or that may be legitimate in itself, but would bring contempt on the sacrament of penance. This obligation exists even if this use involves no danger of revealing matter under the sacramental seal (Innocent XI, Denz. n. 1220; Can. 890, par. 1). Such use is a serious sin, unless the damage caused is completely negligible. Not even the pretext of edifying an audience excuses from this obligation (Congregation of the Holy Office, June 9, 1915).

It is obvious that the knowledge acquired in confession does not remove obligations that the confessor may have independently of confession, e.g., the obligation to watch over his subjects; but a superior may not use knowledge gained in hearing confession for government in the external forum (Can. 890). To prevent unfortunate situations and misunderstandings in this relationship between the internal and external forum, the Church normally forbids the superiors of colleges, seminaries, etc., to hear the confessions of their subjects (Cans. 891; 138, par. 3). *Man.*

SEA-SICKNESS. See Cynetosis.

SECRET, DISCLOSURE OF. A secret, from the standpoint of the moral law, is a truth or fact, known to one or few persons, that must be kept concealed from others.

A secret may be *natural, promised,* or *committed.* A *natural secret* is one which must be kept by reason of the natural law or the very nature of the thing itself, disclosure of which would cause a grave damage or displeasure to another. A *promised secret* is that which one has promised to keep after having received the information. A *committed secret,* also called rigorous secret, is one which is communicated to another simply on condition that he will not divulge it. The promise may be explicit or implicit. If the implicit promise is connected with the exercise of an office, the secret is called *official* or *professional.* It is possible to have a secret which is at the same time natural and committed.

A *purely promised secret,* if it is not a natural secret, generally occasions a light obligation, so that its violation is a venial sin. The obligation is grave if the promise had the character of an important contract or if, in the positive circumstances, its violation is likely to cause grave damage. The violation of a *natural secret* is a mortal or venial sin according to the seriousness of the matter. The gravest obligation is found in a *committed secret.* Its violation is in itself a mortal sin, although levity of matter, considered in its effects, is admitted. Violation of a *professional secret* (*q.v.*) is a particularly grave sin and a sin against society. The common good demands that men should feel free to entrust their affairs to physicians, lawyers, priests, counsellors, etc., without fear of violations of that trust.

A special type of professional secret is the *sacramental seal* of confession (*see* Seal of Confession). It obliges the most absolute kind of secrecy, at all times and under all circumstances, except the case in which the priest is specifically released from it by the individual confessing it. Other secrets are not so absolute that they cannot be disclosed under certain circumstances. The greater the obligation to keep a secret, the graver must be the reason for its disclosure. The common good or the private good of the person knowing the secret or the welfare of other individuals could be sufficient reason for the disclosure of a secret, which must be done with much prudence. If the damage resulting from keeping a secret is greater than its benefits, one may and often must reveal it. Caution must be used not to disclose more than necessary, or to persons who have no right whatsoever to it. Sometimes, an individual may want a secret to be kept especially from certain persons to whom disclosure would cause graver harm or more serious displeasure than to others.

Thus, too, there are times when a professional secret may be disclosed for grave and exceptional reasons; in fact, such disclosures may be obligatory, as in the case of one who uses the secret to cheat or harm another person, especially if simple and unlearned in a very grave manner. A committed or professional secret is a form of contract, binding to the extent that the general consensus allows and human exigencies demand.

No secret may be disclosed to superiors or other authorities except by the norms indicated above, or if a person has a perfect right to know, as in the case of a judge who lawfully requests pertinent information of a witness. *Ben.*

SECRET, PROFESSIONAL. As a form of committed secret, a professional secret consists of information obtained by reason of office or profession. From a moral point of view, a committed secret must be evaluated from the fact that it is committed after explicit or implicit promise, and according to the nature of the communication itself. In a committed secret, the promise is explicit if one explicitly requests that secrecy be maintained and the other party promises to do so; it is implicit if by its very nature the information is given under secrecy and accepted as such. Such is a professional secret.

Lawyers, physicians, druggists, theologians, spiritual directors consulted outside of confession, and other professional men are bound by professional secrecy by reason of office; they implicitly promise secrecy upon assumption of their office. Professional secrecy must be maintained with respect to anything connected with the exercise of office. Professional secrecy is based on the virtue of commutative justice; its violation involves an obligation to make reparation for the damage caused.

In some countries, the matter of professional secrecy is enforced by positive law, which exempts from the obligation of testifying those bound by professional secrecy. However, there is no definite agreement between law and jurisprudence with respect to the offices involved or the basis for keeping secrets.

Jurists, today, generally hold that the obligation to keep professional secrets of a moral nature is absolute; secrets of physicians and jurists are generally held as absolute; other secrets are considered absolute or relative depending on the extent of the damage their disclosure is liable to cause. *Pal.*

SECRET SOCIETY. Secret societies of a religious nature have existed among primitive and civilized peoples, particularly in times of great religious decline. Examples of such societies are the mystery-cults of Dionysus, Mithra and Isis at the beginning of the Christian era, and many alchemist societies at the time of the Reformation. In the last few centuries, secret societies have generally taken on a political or cultural nature. The political societies have been distinguished frequently by their hostility toward the Catholic Church or existing forms of civil society.

Generally, a good society need not be hidden. Thus, secrecy imposed on the members of a group concerning its by-laws or its activities cannot but lead to justifiable doubt and suspicion of the honesty of its aims. Experience has shown that almost all secret societies, religious, cultural or political in nature, have become seed-beds for plots against the Church or State and have led their members to religious indifferentism.

Catholics are forbidden, under pain of mortal sin, to join any society which requires an oath of secrecy (Instruction of the Sacred Congregation of the Holy Office, May 10, 1884). The Church has adopted sterner measures with regard to secret societies that are a positive threat to the life of the Church or State. From the beginning of Freemasonry, the Church forbade any participation by the faithful in Freemasonry or any group closely allied to it, and inflicted ecclesiastical censures on those who disobeyed (Clement XII, *In Eminenti*, April 20, 1738; Benedict XIV, *Providas*, March 18, 1751; Pius IX, *Apostolicae Sedis*, October 12, 1869).

Current ecclesiastical legislation in the Code of Canon Law has retained excommunication, reserved simply (*simpliciter*) to the Holy See, for Catholics who enroll in Masonic or other organizations opposed to the Church or lawful civil authority and government (Can. 2335). Membership in certain secret societies, such as the Odd Fellows, Sons of Temperance, etc., is forbidden, but not under the penalty of excommunication. *Dam.*

SECRET (Stealing of). The moral law condemns not only the unwarranted disclosure of a secret but also the effort to steal a secret of another, particularly by unjust and dishonest means, such as threats, indiscretions, eavesdropping, opening letters, etc. One who does so simply to learn a secret but intends to preserve secrecy, commits a sin of curiosity which is generally not grave. However, if the stolen secret is very important, the sin might become mortal. To deliberately open and read letters without the sender's or the receiver's permission is in itself a grave sin against justice. The sin may be venial if one is certain that the letter contains matters of little import. It is lawful for religious superiors and parents to read the letters of their subjects and children, especially if done to avert a grave damage to the common or private welfare.

Religious superiors may not open letters received or sent by members of the religious group to the Holy See, the Apostolic Delegate, the Cardinal Protector, major superiors or the local superior, if he is absent (Can. 611).

METHODS OF DISCOVERY. The search for methods to uncover secrets or probe for truth, especially from suspected criminals, dates far back into ancient eras. So many methods have been tried from time to time, that it seems no system has been left untried to penetrate the minds of fellow men, to gain important secrets or to induce the confession of a crime. At one time, an effective method was torture; now it is the third degree interrogation. Primitive peoples used narcotic potions; civilized nations use intravenous injections of barbiturates. But the intent is the same.

In 1925, P. R. Vissie stated that individuals treated with *scopolamine* become incapable of lying. Six years later, House made the same statement of his *truth serum*, a mixture of *morphine* and *scopolamine* which, if injected into an individual, produced a twilight sleep in which he would readily confess crimes he had committed. This dramatic term of the American scholar is still in use despite the fact that it is not, strictly speaking, a serum, nor always effective in discovering the truth. House's serum did not show the expected results when tested by other researchers; it has since been abandoned. Divry and Bobon have maintained recently that, in the infamous Camp at Dachau, confessions were obtained through the use of *mescaline*. At the present time, the fashionable truth serum is a group of narcotic barbiturates used especially in *narcoanalysis*, the psychological study of the mentally ill.

In this regard, it should be noted that the use of narcosis, produced in a variety of ways, to facilitate questioning of psychiatric patients for the purposes of diagnosis and cure, has always interested psychiatrists. Prescinding from the empirical methods of historical medicine, Long (1842), Griesinger (1845), Morton (1846), Sedillot (1847), Baron (1896), Basque (1907), Claude (1924), Deshaies (1938), and others used ether for this purpose; Lacassagne (1867), Spencer (1878), Marchand (1906) used chloroform narcosis.

In 1921, Laignel-Lavastine was probably the first to use a barbiturate preparation (*nembutal*) intravenously; its narcotic effects were followed by "an exteriorization of feelings" in the sick person and by a "revelation of their subconscious." In 1930, the Americans Bleckwen and Lorenz and the Dutchman Meerloo used other barbiturate derivatives to arrest serious *catatonic* conditions. In 1932, Lindemann and Gullotta obtained the same results, and in the same year D. McMillan used nembutal for psychological investigation of individuals afflicted with various mental illnesses. The use of barbiturate narcosis was resumed in 1937 by Horsley, who coined the term *narcoanalysis*. Thereafter, it was used more and more, especially in North America, where narcoanalytic procedure was adopted for the treatment of psychoneuroses and the slow and painstaking rehabilitation of individuals suffering from serious emotional disturbances from the war.

TECHNIQUE. Truth serum is identified with barbiturates in the sense that the narcoanalytic procedure we have mentioned seems to be the most common method of using drugs to obtain confessions from accused persons. It will be well to devote some attention to the methods and various effects of narcoanalysis, in order to complete what has been mentioned in a previous article, under Hypnotism.

Of all the many barbiturate derivatives that can be injected intravenously, the principal ones are *sodium pentothal* and *narcovene serum*. Recently an *amytalsimpamina* combination has begun to be used; it avoids putting a subject completely to sleep but results, instead, in a long period of sub-narcosis which is useful for psychotherapy and general questioning.

The narcoanalytic procedure is always more or less the same. The patient is put to bed in a quiet room with soft lighting and the barbiturate is then injected. As the narcotic is slowly administered, the subject is asked to recite numbers aloud; this induces sleep and indicates that the patient is in sleep. Doctors make use of the pre-narcotic phase to being questioning; this is also resumed and filled out by suitable suggestions and psychotherapeutic advice for the post-narcotic passage from sleep to reawakening. During these twilight pre- and post-narcotic periods, spontaneous statements reveal complexes and feelings usually locked up in the subconscious; whatever is said, along with the gestures or mimicking expressions that sometimes accompany the recall of a painful event, is carefully noted down, since this usually represents material for further questioning, interpretation, suggestions, on which the psychotherapeutic action of the doctor will be based.

This is, in brief, the narcoanalytic technique as used in psychiatry, particularly in the field of psychoneurosis (hysteria, neurasthenia, psychasthenia, etc.), where it may be a very effective factor because of its diagnostic value. It should be used in the study of a recent psychosis. It has been observed that narcoanalysis, by lifting the veil from seemingly normal conduct, can lay bare the defects in the psychical edifice which might reveal an initial case of schizophrenia in one that has seemed to involve an ordinary psychoneurosis. This is of great benefit to the sick person, for he can be subjected to shock-therapy treatments in time. Or it may happen that seeming schizophrenia will reveal itself to be a psychasthenia of a pseudo-schizophrenic nature. We might add that barbiturate narcosis, if properly and prudently used, is practically harmless both to life and any hypothetical aggravation of the psychosis under study.

Narcoanalysis has found wide application in psychiatry to check or complete information, to penetrate into the depths of a personality, to unmask latent forms of neurosis, to check the effects of shock-therapy (*q.v.*) and to help treat many psychoneuroses. The results obtained by narcoanalysis, in about half the cases, are nil, in the sense that questioning during pre- or post-narcotic phases reveals nothing helpful to the diagnosis, neither changes of the emotions, nor appreciable results in the treatment.

NARCOANALYSIS AS TRUTH SERUM. Apart from clinical use, narcoanalysis is sometimes employed in legal medicine. In clinical work, the narcoanalyst is dealing with a person willing to cooperate in hopes of regaining his health. In the field of judicial investigations, studies are often made on individuals who, by faking or feigning, are interested in keeping their real psychological or psychopathological status concealed. Experience teaches that this often hinders the acquisition of the truth through narcoanalysis. An hysterical young woman under narcoanalysis gave full details of a crime committed in her presence by her lover. Fuller investigation showed clearly that the crime had never taken place. The so-called truth serum could become a lie serum; so it ought to be used with a great deal of prudence. Casati tells of a patient who, when asked under narcoanalysis about a certain episode that she had always kept hidden, replied that even if truth serum were injected into her, it would be a mistake to think that she could be induced to say what she had made up her mind not to say; and with this, she shut herself up in an impenetrable silence. This would seem to prove, as other researchers discovered, that, if someone has a special reason for not wanting to reveal certain facts, he succeeds in keeping quiet about them despite the use of barbiturate narcosis.

Cortesi and others, on the other hand, maintain that confessions received during a narcoanalytic investigation represent the truth. They favor such investigations, especially if it is necessary to make a psychiatric diagnosis of an individual. Although the psychological examination shows no definite facts, yet with respect to certain *anamnestic* elements, it is logical to suppose that there is some particular kind of abnormality that may at times prove to be serious enough to envelop the whole psychic personality of the individual. And they conclude: "If narcoanalytic investigation is reserved to competent psychiatrists, it should be considered as simply one more means of psychological investigation among many . . . tending to facilitate the external manifestation of morbid elements that may have affected the individual's ability to understand and to will, and that may be very valuable in establishing the eventual danger the individual may pose to society."

Edward is also in favor of the use of narcoanalysis in psychiatric studies, as long as professional secrecy is respected.

Our conclusion that narcoanalytic treatments are often ineffective and sometimes unreliable is no reason for discarding them completely in judicial investigations, provided that the personality and liberty of the individual are protected and investigations are carried out in accordance with moral law. It is wise to limit their use to cases where usual psychiatric methods fail to provide a diagnosis and to accept the results with great caution and reserve.

This reservation is not necessary if narcoanalysis or any procedure based on narcosis is used in the strictly neurological field, i.e., to uncover the organic or functional nature of a paralysis or something similar. In cases of this kind, this type of procedure usually supplies important data and, from a scientific point of view, there are no basic objections to a proper and prudent use.

Lastly, in the area of police and judicial investigations, the use of barbiturate narcosis would seem to be more precisely a truth serum; the use of narcoanalysis is not scientifically justified, because, over and above the fact that narcoanalysis is often ineffective, those who are definitely faking are able to make a stout defense, even in subnarcosis, of points they have reason to conceal or inhibit. The opposite also can be true: an innocent person, weakened from long imprisonment and crushed by the steady hammering of questioning by officials and in a sleepy state caused by barbiturates, may suffer a spiritual collapse; under the suggestive influence of interrogators, he may confess crimes he never committed. This understandable surrender of the will, for which the way was paved by earlier material and moral suffering and which was finally effected by abnormal pressures exerted in the course of narcoanalysis by the police, may explain the fantastic *confessions* of Cardinal Mindszenty, Clementis, or other political victims, unless these are outright fabrications on the part of those who performed the judicial investigation.

Even if such procedure were effective, it still would be an unlawful violation of basic, inalienable rights of the human person. A guilty person has a right, as a human being, to physical and spiritual inviolability; hence, he has a right to absolute freedom regarding any confession, for no one can be forced to incriminate himself and bring about his own doom. To expect a guilty person to confess a crime goes beyond the limits of the ordinary powers of human nature. It borders the area of heroism, which can be suggested but not imposed. Furthermore, a criminal has a right to protect his own reputation.

The common good is endangered less by setting free a criminal who is objectively guilty than by condemning an innocent man forced to make self-incriminating revelations during a twilight state.

Some hold that the use of narcoanalysis is lawful and similar to clinical use, if the accused freely consents to submit out of a legitimate desire to prove his innocence. Others feel that not even this would be lawful, since it sets a dangerous precedent for other criminals, who might refuse to submit to narcoanalysis in similar circumstances. Even if this were lawful, the value of the proof would not go beyond that of any other psychological investigation.

The scientific and moral criticism or reservation mentioned for the value and use of narcoanalysis applies to lie-detectors and other methods, based on the unpredictable effects of stimulants, narcotics, inebriating substances, such as ether, alcohol, and scopolamine.

In various countries behind the Iron Curtain, or nations where judicial processes are both frequently mysterious in their developments and absurd in their conclusions, insofar as the accused usually hasten to admit guilt and accept joyfully the punishments inflicted on them, it seems likely that some new methods of drugs or truth serums have been developed, which might be in the long run more effective; among Western scientists this is not yet known. The whole thing seems doubtful on the basis of what we know about the different effects of drugs and the various ways men behave in the face of torture, persuasion, and force. None of the physical or chemical means known to us can force individuals to admit a crime committed, for other individuals, under the influence of the same means, will confess crimes actually never committed.

Other methods of uncovering lies have been employed from time to time but with little practical utility, either because of technical difficulties or uncertain results. Some of these methods consist in recording changes in pulse rate or the electrical conductivity of the skin. These are then recorded by special instruments during the questioning; the variations indicate psychological or emotional reactions. Other methods are based on an evaluation of the reaction-time of the answers to questions or to a series of word stimuli that are either indifferent or linked to the crime under investigation. Supposedly, the guilt of a person is revealed by the reaction-time of the responses. More recently, use has been made of electroencephalographic tests (*see* Waves, Brain); in these the emotional reactions are registered during the process of debates over the punishment to be inflicted on the offenders.

These and other methods of subtle inquiry in the psycho-physiological order are scientifically worthy of attention; but they lend themselves to frequent errors in interpretation, because of the resistance of the persons tested. They are not really useful for uncovering lies unless, as Raper remarks ironically, one uses another lie-detector to discover whether the lie-detector is telling the truth.

From the technical or scientific point of view, the use of narcoanalysis and related methods often has been ineffective and has provided erroneous results. One must accept its findings with great prudence, from the moral point of view. The liceity of this modern method will vary according to its use.

(a) In the clinical field, it is morally licit to use narcoanalysis and other methods of sounding the depths of personality, as long as the person involved fully consents to the treatment, after he is informed that in the course of the treatment he may reveal thoughts and memories that he would rather keep secret. It seems licit to employ one of these methods for serious reasons on those individuals who are not in a position to give their consent because of illness. A large number of these cases, which demand narcoanalysis and treatment, are precisely due to a psychosis which prevents a spontaneous contact with a doctor or their environment in general. In such a case, consent of the legal guardian of the sick individual must be obtained.

A doctor who proceeds with narcoanalysis without gaining the consent of the person involved, or his legal guardian, would be blameworthy morally and also, in some countries, subject to the sanctions of the civil penal codes.

Great prudence must be used in each case, especially in individuals who are not mature, stable or spiritually well-formed, or if there is a danger of a violation of the moral or religious law, as the virtue of chastity.

(b) In the medical-judicial investigative area, narcoanalysis or other methods are not left to the free choice of the interested parties completely nor to the individual expert. The judge must specify in detail the conditions and guarantees for safeguarding the rights and liberty of the individual involved.

(c) In the penal-judicial field, the use of truth serum to obtain a confession for a crime of which the accused is suspected, or to uncover a secret, is morally wrong, because it violates the basic rights of the individual not to become his own accuser and to jealously preserve secrets confided. *Riz.*

SECRETARIAT OF STATE. The Secretariat of State is an office of the Roman Curia, which, together with the Apostolic Chancery (*q.v.*), the Apostolic Datary (*q.v.*), and the Apostolic Camera (*q.v.*), constitutes the third class of Vatican departments (Congregations, Tribunals, and Offices).

The origin of the Secretariat of State must be traced to the *Secretariatus Papae,* existing in rudimentary form as early as the thirteenth century as a curial body. This body was a distinct group, whose members later composed the *Camera secreta,* which until the fourteenth century was closely linked to the Apostolic Camera (*q.v.*).

For this reason the *Secretarii Papae* were personal secretaries to the pontiffs, engaged in drawing up documents and handling religious and political affairs. The oath of fidelity was required in matters which concerned the Apostolic Camera. This was required at the time of Martin V; the choice of secretaries was made from among the most renowned humanists of the time. Until the reign of Calixtus III, the number of *Secretarii Papae* varied greatly; he restricted them to six (*de numero*) and left undetermined the number of *super-numerarii.* Under Innocent VIII, the *Secretariatus Papae* became *Secretariatus Apostolicus,* and the new college of twenty-four apostolic secretaries became a part of the Curia. The *Secretariatus Papae* was reserved to the Pope's personal appointment by the example of Eugene IV, who named a *Secretarius secretus,* and Sixtus IV, who named *Secretarii domestici et palatini.* At the time of the reorganization of the Apostolic Secretariat by Sixtus V (1586), the secretaries, trustworthy persons chosen by the Pope to remain after the reform, were three in number, and constituted a new nucleus for the formation of the present notion of Secretariat of State.

From the time of Innocent X (1644–1655), the Secretary of State has generally been a cardinal. With the suppression by Innocent XI of the College of Apostolic Secretaries (1678), the last tie between the office of private secretary and the past was eliminated. By the Constitution *Romanum decet Pontificem* (June 22, 1692), by which nepotism was suppressed once and for all, Innocent XII made this new condition permanent. After that, the Secretariat of State took on its present form, similar to a civil minister of Home and Foreign Affairs. Some changes were made in the pontificate of Gregory XVI (1833), which were later revised by Pius X. Other changes, caused by the decline of the temporal power of the popes (1870), restricted the field of activities of the Secretariat of State exclusively to matters of ecclesiastical government.

Today, the Secretariat of State consists of a number of functionaries who assist the Cardinal Secretary of State in handling matters under his control.

Since 1908, after the reorganization of the Roman Curia by St. Pius X (a reorganization which was retained by the Code), the Secretariat of State consists of three divisions under the direction of a Cardinal Secretary of State who is also the Prefect of the Congregation for Extraordinary Ecclesiastical Affairs.

(a) The first division (*Extraordinary Affairs*) is directed by the Secretary of the Sacred Congregation for Extraordinary Affairs, who, assisted by an undersecretary, attends to matters concerning relations between the Holy See and various nations.

(b) The second division (*Ordinary Affairs*), directed by the *Substitutus* of the Secretary of State, attends to matters concerning the ordinary government of the Church, which are regularly entrusted to it by the Supreme Pontiff or Cardinal Secretary of State; at times, it assigns matters, sent directly to the Pope, to competent departments.

(c) The third division (*Apostolic Briefs*), under the direction of the Chancellor of Apostolic Briefs, is charged with drafting, mailing and filing papal briefs. To the Secretariat of State are attached the Secretariat of *Briefs to Princes* and the Secretariat of *Latin Letters*, entrusted with composing in Latin the Acts of the Supreme Pontiff (Can. 243). *Cip.*

SECT. See Heresy, Schism, Societies, Secret.

SECTION, CAESAREAN. The extraction or delivery of a fetus by an incision into the maternal uterus, usually through the abdominal wall, is termed a *Caesarean section*. This operation is performed if abnormal conditions make a delivery dangerous or impossible through normal methods. The purpose of this operation is to preserve the life of the mother and fetus, or the life of either, if one is already dead. This incision may be made at times to administer the sacrament of baptism to the fetus, following the death of the mother. A disputed historical point is the fact that the origin of the term is due to the name of Julius Caesar, who was sup-posedly delivered at birth through this method.

(a) The Caesarean section performed after the death of the mother concerns moral theology only with regard to the fetus. The section is performed to save the life of the fetus or to baptize a dying fetus (*see* Baptism, Fetus). A Caesarean section is lawful even if the fetus would not survive outside the maternal uterus; leaving it in the uterus of the deceased mother would be of no help toward keeping it alive. The operation must be performed, under grave obligation, if (1) it is probable that the fetus is still alive, although no probability exists in the first three months of pregnancy; (2) there is a person who can perform the operation and extract the fetus alive. The obligation is binding on a physician, midwife, or any other person capable of performing the operation.

Relatives have the obligation to request this of the physician or other capable person; it is wrong to oppose the operation if a competent individual is willing to perform it. There should be no question of a lack of reverence for the deceased mother by such an operation; on the contrary, great supernatural benefits may result from it, and it is not unusual that there might be a natural benefit for the fetus concerned.

(b) A Caesarean section performed on a *living* mother. First of all, this operation is lawful if the physician is certain that the fetus can live outside the maternal uterus. Otherwise it is direct abortion (*see* Abortion). Secondly, it is lawful if it is not expected to be fatal to the mother. If these conditions are present, the operation is not an intrinsically evil act. It is certain, however, that the operation is always a difficult, serious, and dangerous one for the mother and fetus. Therefore, a Caesarean section is lawful only if there are no other less dangerous means, which are not forbidden by the moral law. See *also* Embryotomy and Feticide. *Ben.*

SECULARIZATION. Secularization (Latin, *saeculum*—world) is an indult granted to a religious by lawful ecclesiastical authority, to live permanently outside his religious community. A religious who has obtained such an indult is completely separated from his organization and released from his religious vows.

Formerly, there were three kinds of secularization: *ad tempus*, i.e., temporary or equivalent to present-day exclaustration (*q.v.*); *ad nutum S. Sedis*, that is, according to the judgment of the Holy See, which consisted in a permission given to the religious to live outside the religious society for a year or more until he found a benevolent order which would provide, for his sustenance; and *perpetual secularization* (permanent), by which the religious was reduced to the lay state. The second type was abolished in the nineteenth century, and the third frequently was accompanied by the *suspensio a divinis*. Furthermore, a difference existed between a religious of solemn vows and one of simple vows, namely, that the latter was dispensed from the vows at the time of secularization, while the former was not, except by a specific apostolic dispensation.

PRESENT LAW. In the law, presently, there is only one type of secularization for all types of religious, which has the juridical effect of separating the religious totally and permanently from his religious institution and relieving him of the vows and other obligations arising from the rule and constitutions. Naturally, a religious in major orders remains bound by the obligations attached to the clerical state, unless the Holy See disposes otherwise (Can. 640).

The secularized religious cannot wear the religious habit and, if in major orders, he may not without dispensation from the Holy See hold any benefice in a major or minor basilica; he may not be appointed to a teaching position in seminaries, nor may he hold an office in diocesan curias or religious houses (Can. 642). If the secularized religious wishes to return to a religious organization, besides the apostolic indult (Can. 542, n. 1), he must make a new novitiate and profession as if he were a new candidate, unless the Holy See shall grant him a specific apostolic dispensation (Can. 640, par. 2).

The Holy See grants an indult of secularization for members of congregations of papal right; the local Ordinary, for those of diocesan right (Can. 638). As for exclaustration (*q.v.*), so too for secularization, the Holy See requires, besides the written petition to the Holy Father, the recommendation of the Superior General and the Procurator General of the religious society. Moreover, it is generally required that an Ordinary be found who is willing to accept in his diocese a secularized religious in major orders (Can. 641, par. 1). *Mand.*

SECULARIZATION (of Cemeteries). *See* Cemeteries.

SECULARIZATION OF ECCLESIASTICAL PROPERTY. *See* Confiscation.

SECURITY, SOCIAL. Social security embraces the total complexity of provisions dealing with the numerous aspects of assistance to individuals or groups of individuals in particular needy circumstances, such as accidents, old age, illness, unemployment, etc.

Social security has made great progress in modern times, especially in countries based on the free-enterprise system of wages and salaries. Insecurity for the working class is inherent in such circumstances as free-enterprise; hence, the urge to protect the workers against such eventualities as unemployment, sickness, old age, accidents, etc.

In its progressive development, social security has moved through three main phases: a private, mutual form of security; a social, public insurance with increasingly larger participation by the State; its present form of wide social security in which benefits are received by the citizens, based not so much on the basis of a contractual bond but by the very fact that they are citizens. This system is in force in Great Britain, where every citizen, from the cradle to the grave, is assured of a minimum amount of income when he is faced with certain particularly grave problems.

The three phases indicated above are not necessarily exclusive, for in many of the more developed nations mutual forms of insurance of a private nature coexist with social security provisions of a public nature.

Social security is a definite sign of progress in the development of social relations as long as certain fundamental socio-economic rights are safeguarded, such as freedom to work, freedom to save, and freedom of consumption; freedom to choose and exercise one's own profession; the right of private ownership; the responsibility of parents in the government of a family. Such freedoms and responsibilities must not be restricted to the point that they are reduced to a mere illusion. See Assistance, Public and Private; Prudence. *Pav.*

SEDE VACANTE. *See* Conclave.

SEDITION. *See* Revolution.

SEDUCTION. Seduction is one of the most serious forms of transgression against good morals and sexual decency. It consists in forcing or persuading a person to lend himself to another's lustful intents. This crime is consummated at the very moment in which the passive subject really commits the act. It does not seem essential to the criminal act that it be done for monetary gain or that it become a habit. These circumstances may give rise to specific types of crime or may increase the gravity of the crime.

The Code of Canon Law considers seduction, especially in relation to its punishment, under a triple aspect: whether the active subject is a lay person, a cleric in minor orders, or a cleric in major orders.

In the case of a layman, after a sentence of guilt, the seducer is punished (*ipso facto*) by infamy (*infamia iuris*), a penalty which is incurred automatically without sentence of a judge (*penalty latae sententiae:* Can. 2357, par. 1). The judge, however, can add other punishments, if the case warrants it. In the case of a cleric in minor orders, in addition to the punishment indicated in the previous case, the culprit, according to the gravity of the crime, must be punished with other penalties to be imposed by the judge (*ferendae senten-*

tiae). These penalties may even include his dismissal from the clerical state (Can. 2358). In the case of a cleric in major orders, the punishment is suspension, *infamia iuris,* privation of office, benefice, pension, assignment, and even deposition in more serious cases. These are to be inflicted by the judge *ferendae sententiae* (Can. 2359, par. 2). *Vio.*

SEE, HOLY. Strictly speaking, the *Holy See* or *Apostolic See,* an older term preferred until this century, meant only the office of Supreme Pontiff in the function of his primacy (*see* Pontiff, Supreme). This meaning, in fact, has been retained by official documents.

In the broader sense, the Holy See is generally not only the Supreme Pontiff, but all the ecclesiastical departments which assist in the government of the Universal Church and constitute the Roman Curia (*see* Curia).

It, therefore, includes the Sacred College of Cardinals, independently of the tasks assigned to each one of them outside the Roman Curia (*see* Cardinals), the Roman or Sacred Congregations (*q.v.*), the Tribunals (*see* Sacred Penitentiary, Sacred Roman Rota, Apostolic Signature), the Offices strictly so-called, and Papal Commissions.

The Code of Canon Law (Can. 7) has clearly fixed this twofold meaning of *Holy See,* already officially used as far back as 1892.

The Holy See is a true juridical person (Can. 100, par. 1); as a matter of fact, it is a pre-eminently public juridical person. This personality is based on divine right. It is debated, however, whether such right belongs to the Holy See in its broader or in its strict meaning. It is certain, nevertheless, that the Roman Curia (Congregations, Tribunals, Offices) has a true juridical personality and that such a personality extends to each individual department.

Concerning the jurisdiction of the Roman Pontiff over the whole Church, his prerogatives as universal, infallible teacher, his rights as supreme legislator, universal administrator of ecclesiastical property and supreme judge, *see* Pontiff, Supreme, and Magisterium.

Concerning independence and freedom of the Holy See in the international sphere, *see* Pontiff, Supreme, and Vatican City. *Cip.*

SELECTION, NATURAL. *Selection* is a process, originally empirical, to which man has turned since ancient times, for improving the breeding of domestic animals and the production of fruit and produce. Such a process consists in selecting only the better specimens for reproductive purpose.

To *artificial selection*, which exercises a positive influence over the species and the race, Charles Darwin added *natural selection*, or a process in nature which furthers the evolution of organisms. Such a process exercises merely a negative action, in the sense that adverse environmental circumstances and the struggle for life eliminate less able individuals of every species, and ultimately keep the species in a more stable condition.

Empirical attempts at human selection and the improvement of individual or mass biological status were initiated about a century ago by Galton's and Mendel's studies and findings, which gave rise to two new disciplines, *eugenics* and *eugenism.*

Eugenics deals with the physical, moral and intellectual improvement of the human race by careful and judicious mating. It is, in other words, a hygiene of the genotype.

Eugenism (or *euthenics*) deals with the circumstances of environment and heredity which tend to bring about happy and healthy existence.

MORAL COROLLARIES. Studies concerned with human selection are in no way opposed to Catholic moral doctrine. On the contrary, Catholic moral teaching favors all research that tends to improve humanity, whether through environmental reclamations, spreading hygienic norms, or strengthening children, and the like. The same moral doctrine, on the other hand, opposes any deviation and exaggeration of eugenistic studies that treat man as no different than a domestic animal and, in open disregard of justice and charity, propose violent and coercive means for the betterment of the race. *Riz.*

HUMAN SELECTION, MARRIAGE AND THEOLOGY. Human selection for marriage may be practiced by public authority through laws, by private counselors, or by individuals. In the former case, human selection would chiefly consist in the exclusion from marriage of physically and psychically defective individuals. This, of course, is in contrast with the law of nature, by which every man has the right to establish his own family and beget children.

Human selection through counsels and instructions or by a diligent choice of one's own consort is not in itself morally objectionable, although such methods could come into conflict with the natural moral law and Catholic moral doctrine. In fact, many speak, write, counsel and act as if the health of the body were man's only *main* good, disregarding man's moral and supernatural interests. The Catholic Church teaches that man's ultimate end is everlasting happiness in heaven, and his earthly end is moral and supernatural perfection. This may be attained by a physically defective human being. Man's purpose in life is not to generate children simply that they may improve the human race, but that they may glorify God, their creator, and become citizens of heaven. However, since the Church considers physical health and, even more, mental health as a good of great value with respect to the moral and supernatural life, it follows that a human selection based on the choice of a healthy mate capable of procreating healthy children is of itself morally acceptable. *Ben.*

SELF-DEFENSE, LEGITIMATE. Right is coercible. Thus, it is lawful to use force in order to prevent the violation of one's right. In general, private individuals are not allowed to use force. They have the right to seek the intervention of public authority. However, a legitimate defense of one's right against an actual unjust aggressor is proper, for the protection of the right itself demands it.

CONDITIONS. A legitimate use of violence against an aggressor is not sinful, provided that the damage done to the aggressor is not greater than the legitimate defense requires. In other words, if one can defend himself against an unjust aggressor by wounding him, he sins if he kills him instead. Of course, if the threat is impending, it is permissible for the attacked to do whatever he deems necessary at that particular moment.

An aggressor is unjust if his action is contrary to the divine law or human laws which determine the right of self-defense. It is not required that he be morally guilty. I am permitted to defend myself against a maniac or one who erroneously believes he has a right to kill me. He who carries out a just action is not an unjust aggressor, even if it caused another a grave damage. At times, just acts can cause damage to others: the detention of a condemned criminal is an act which is damaging to the criminal himself, but it is not unjust. Hence it is not lawful for a condemned criminal to use violence against the guards or wardens, by killing or injuring them in any manner. Violence is lawful only if directed at preventing violence about to take place. Danger, the knowledge or suspicion of a future aggression is not sufficient to justify violence. If the aggression has been consummated and it is only a matter of having a damage restored, it cannot be called self-defense. The victim must follow another procedure and seek the intervention of public authority (police, court, etc.). There must be a just proportion between a violent self-defense with its probable consequences for the aggressor and the good which is defended. A right which one possesses with regard to his cat, for instance, is coercible and can be defended by the use of a violent repulsion of the attacker. However, killing or gravely injuring the aggressor of one's cat could never be justified, for there is no proportion between the means and the end, although the end is to prevent the killing of one's cat. Thus, killing an aggressor is permitted only for the defense of one's life, one's bodily integrity against grave mutilations or grave injuries, and in the case of a woman to protect her corporal virginity. Taking another's life is not permissible, if it is to defend one's material goods or riches, except if the goods are so important that the owner cannot lose

them without plunging into absolute or even relative poverty (a notable and humiliating diminution of one's social standing), and the circumstances leave little hope that such goods could ever be regained by legitimate means. *Ben.*

SELF-LOVE. Not all love of self is reprehensible; our nature is indeed worthy of love, and the Lord Himself has proposed love of self as the pattern of love due to one's neighbor (Matt. 22:39). Moreover, since man is created to the image of God and through grace participates in the divine nature, the same precept that obligates us to love God implicitly obliges us to love ourselves also. We are required to love not only our soul, but also our body, insofar as it assists the soul in its quest for God, and will, one day, participate in the soul's happiness. We must desire and seek our own true good, that is, the sanctification of our soul, and everything else that is necessary or truly useful for the attainment of this end. In loving ourselves, however, a certain measure is to be observed: love of self must, in fact, be such as to be reconcilable with loving God more than ourselves and loving our neighbor as much as ourselves.

Whenever this prescribed measure is transgressed, love of self becomes sinful and is more properly called self-love. An immoderate love of self tends to turn everything and everyone to one's own utility and satisfaction, with no regard for God's glory and the welfare of others. The inclination to self-love is a great wound inflicted upon our nature by original sin, and, in the final analysis, every sin stems from an erroneous love of self. Self-love may also infiltrate our good works, radically destroying our religious exercises and charitable works. One who loves himself to the point where he would be ready to transgress a grave precept rather than give up any self-advantage obviously commits a mortal sin.

REMEDIES. To root out inordinate self-love from our souls, several things are necessary: internal and external mortification, a generous acceptance of suffering, careful scrutiny of our intentions in their subtle and deceptive forms of egoism, a sincere disclosure of one's conscience to one's spiritual director, earnest prayer for divine enlightenment and, finally, a fervent love of God, which, as in the case of the saints, would lead to despising self and inordinate affections within one's soul. *Man.*

SEMINARIES AND UNIVERSITIES (Congregation of). *See* Congregations, Roman.

SEMINARISTICUM. *See* Seminary; Taxes, Ecclesiastical.

SEMINARY. A *seminary* is an institution dedicated to the training of young men for the priesthood or sacred ministry in the clerical state. The *diocesan* seminary is intended to train men of a particular diocese under the bishop's jurisdiction; an *interdiocesan* seminary is intended to train men from several dioceses or ecclesiastical provinces.

The direction and administration of a diocesan seminary are directly under the jurisdiction of the bishop; the provincial or interdiocesan seminary is administered in accordance with special provisions enacted by the Holy See for such seminaries (Can. 1357, par. 3 and 4).

The Code of Canon Law (Can. 1354) urges bishops to erect in their own dioceses a minor seminary for the training of young boys which is separate from the major seminary for the study of philosophy and theology. If a diocese is unable to have its own major seminary, the bishop shall send his students either to the seminary of another diocese or to an interdiocesan or regional seminary.

In every seminary there must be a *rector* for discipline, teachers, an *econome*, distinct from the rector, for administration, at least two ordinary *confessors* and a *spiritual director*. Each seminary must have two *boards of deputies*, one for the discipline, the other for the administration. The members of each board, appointed for six years, are to be consulted by the bishop in matters of greater importance.

The Code of Canon Law prescribes that, besides ordinary confessors, there must be extraordinary confessors whom the seminarians should be free to consult, without, of course, disrupting the discipline of the seminary.

ADMISSION AND TRAINING. The admission of young men to the seminary and their religious, moral, and scientific training (Cans. 1363–1370) are conducted according to appropriate regulations which are the fruit of prudent judgment and long experience. In his apostolic exhortation *Menti nostrae* (September 23, 1950), Pius XII, of happy memory, offered wise practical suggestions to the effect that, without neglecting in any way the sound principles of priestly ascetics, seminarians should be made aware of the many exigencies of modern social life, and that, in their training, particular attention should be given to developing in them a true sense of responsibility. The institution and organization of present-day seminaries date back to the Council of Trent and the tenacious work of St. Charles Borromeo. We are also greatly indebted to St. Pius X for the enhancement of discipline and spiritual formation in the seminaries, and to Pius XI for the reorganization of the curricula. *Fel.*

SEMITISM. *See* Judaism.

SENILISM. *See* Gonads.

SENSATION. Sensation is a cognitive activity, which refers to the immediate stimulation of a bodily organism, such as sight, hearing, smell, etc. It is specifically the direct result of a present, immediate stimulation of sense organs.

The external object produces not only a material impression (physiological change) in the bodily organ, but also a mutation in the sensitive cognitive faculty. This mutation consists in receiving a likeness (*species*) of the external object, which is necessary for actuation of the cognitive operation of the sensitive faculty.

Sensation has, therefore, two aspects: one passive and one active. It is both a condition (*passio*) resulting from the object's active impression on the sense, and a cognitive and organic operation, such as sight, hearing, etc., by which the sensitive faculty, united with the organ, attains an external object.

The cognitive organic operation is proper to an individual composed of soul and body. Its proximate origin is the material organ endowed with a cognitive power in the soul, which corresponds to this degree of cognition (sensitive power or faculty). It is, in fact, our own experience that tells us that our eye is seeing and our ear is hearing, and it is exactly this condition of materiality in our senses that places sensation among the lowest cognitive operations. Thereupon, if it is a cognitive act, our act of hearing cannot have as its intrinsic cause only a corporeal organ, but the latter also must be endowed with a cognitive power. A clear distinction must be made between the psychical cognitive act and the physiological act of the organ.

The psychologist describes sensation as the simple content of consciousness, which comes forth when a sensorial organ is stimulated by physical stimuli, such as light, sound, and heat.

Sensations originating from different sensorial organs are clearly distinguished from one another according to their quality. But the qualities and intensities of each sensorial field are on a continuous level.

It has been debated whether the so-called *affective* tone is a property of sensation or a particular psychic factor. We incline to the belief that it is a distinct psychic process (feelings), but it may be remarked that many sensations, particularly in certain favorable circumstances, may arouse feelings of pleasure and displeasure. Particularly, the sensorial complexes constituting the material content of our perceptions are apt to arouse in us at times deep and complicated feelings and emotions. So, a melody may seem to us *allegro, maestoso* or *triste* or may occasion a depressing effect. To the production of this affective tone our past experiences and intellectual activity contribute.

The *five senses* classified by Aristotle are contested by modern psychologists, but the description of the sense organs on the basis of histological studies has simply introduced subdivisions of the traditional classification without adding anything substantially new. These subdivisions concern chiefly the sense of *touch*, in which they usually distinguish pressure, heat, cold, and pain (not to be confused with sorrow). Furthermore, studies have been made of tactile sensations from sensorial organs in the muscles, tendons, articulations (sensations of motion), entrails (organic sensations), and the sense of balance in the ampullas and semicircular canals of the labyrinth located in the internal ear.

The study of sensations is not given today all the attention which it seems to deserve, chiefly because new and wide fields of research have opened in the area of applied psychology.

Physiology is also concerned with the study of sensations. The results attained in the study of nervous conditions are very notable indeed, but they are far from being decisive.

Moral theology is keenly interested in the study of sensations. According to St. Thomas, morality is simply the road of man's return to God. Man comes from God by creation but he goes back to God through his moral life. St. Thomas, dealing with passions or impulses of the sensitive appetite, speaks of the impulse which moves man to overcome obstacles in the attainment of a good that is difficult to attain; this impulse he calls hope. The last end, a difficult good, needs the agency of hope. Unfortunately, among sensations, depressing and asthenic ones undermine hope, and thus many become disheartened and yield to difficulties.

Sensations also serve to form ideas; therefore, the clearer and the more perfect the sensations, the clearer the ideas will be.

Much vigilance must be exercised over sensations by reason of the appetites and inclinations that follow from them, which often may lead one from the path of good onto the path of evil, frequently very attractive. *See also* Affectivity. V*er.*

SENSITIVITY. *See* Affectivity; Cerebral Functions.

SENSUALITY. In its ordinary meaning *sensuality* means lust. In theological language, sensuality (*sensualitas*) is distinguished both from *sensibilitas* and from *sessualitas*, and conveys the notion of willful indulgence in the pleasures of the senses, from objects capable of exciting venereal commotions, as the sensitive pleasure felt by touching impure things, by kissing a person of the opposite sex, etc. Thus, sensual pleasure is not purely sensitive pleasure or the satisfaction caused by conformity of a sensible object, outside the sexual field, with its respective sense (for example, the satisfaction of eyesight or of touch caused by seeing or touching pleasant things). Nor is it venereal pleasure proceeding from the use of the sexual faculties. Sensual pleasure is also called *carnal*; this term can cause misunderstanding inasmuch as former theologians meant by this term an incomplete venereal pleasure (*see* the 40th proposition condemned by Alexander VII, Decr. May 18, 1666, Denz. 1140).

Theoretically, the morality of sensual pleasure is the same as that of any other sensitive pleasure. If it is caused by an honest act and enjoyed as such, it is licit; if it is sought solely for the pleasure itself, it is a venial sin. In view of the close relation between sensual and venereal pleasures, caused by an association of ideas and sensations, it is very easy to pass from one to the other with the consequent danger of consent. An act performed out of sensuality, therefore, will generally be a venial or mortal sin according to the gravity of the danger of venereal commotion and consent. In fact, in such actions, hidden and, consequently, direct voluntary lust is not rare. *Dam.*

SENTENCE. In general, a sentence, considered from a procedural standpoint, in civil affairs is a legitimate pronouncement by a judge concerning a controverted issue of fact or of law (Can. 1868, par. 1); in criminal or penal matters, it takes the form of a pronouncement by a judge concerning the culpability of an individual relating to a specific offense or crime, with the further application of a penalty, if the defendant is found guilty.

In civil matters, ecclesiastical and lay, a sentence is the result of a controversy between two or more parties; in penal matters, the controversy technically is between the accused and society, represented by the public prosecutor or State's attorney, whose duty it is to see that crimes be not unpunished. A sentence generally results from two elements supplied by the judge, who, after he seeks to discover the objective truth of the facts in order to separate right from wrong, by a positive act of his will imposes upon the parties a solution to the controversy.

A sentence is called *interlocutory* if it decides an incidental question during a trial; it is called *definitive* if it settles the principal question at issue. Other pronouncements, left to the discretion of the judge, are called decrees (Can. 1868). In penal matters, sentences are also *condemnatory* or *absolutory* and *declaratory*; the latter confirms and strengthens the law and does not call for execution (Cans. 2223, par. 4; 2232, par. 2; 1948, n. 2).

A sentence may be rendered by a single judge or a group of judges (Cans. 1870–1872, 1572, 1596, etc.). In all cases the judge must possess moral certainty with respect to the objective truth of the controverted matter. This, of course, does not exclude the possibility of error, in view of the human limitations which exclude knowledge of hidden motives of the parties (Can. 1869).

In a case, considerable value is afforded so-called *presumptions*, except in marriage cases, which enjoy the favor of law (*favor iuris*), and those of the Pauline privilege, liberty, etc. (Cans. 1825–1828, 1904, 1972, 1014, 1127, etc.). In a collegiate tribunal, moral certainty resides in the collective will of the judges found in an absolute majority vote (Can. 1577, par. 1). Each distinct controverted point must be taken up separately, and each of them shall be given its own separate decision. The area of difference among the judges may be eliminated or reduced by a discussion of the case. Every sentence must in its opening words contain an invocation of the Divine Name.

Furthermore, it must state the name of the judge or judges, the names and respective domiciles of the defendant, plaintiff, procurator or procurators of the parties, defender of the bond and/or the promoter of justice if both or either took part in the trial. Then follows a brief statement of the case with all claims made by the parties, and, finally, the definitive part of the sentence is given with the reasons supporting it (Can. 1874, par. 1–4).

The sentence must settle the controversy with reasons of fact and of law on which the definitive part of the sentence is based; it must indicate the cost of the trial and who is to bear it (Cans. 1873–1874). The sentence closes with the date and place where it was rendered; it must be signed by the judge or judges and the court notary (Can. 1874, par. 3). The sentence is published either by summoning the parties to hear its solemn reading by the presiding judge or by notifying the parties that the sentence is at the court, where they may go and read it, or where such custom exists, by sending a copy to the parties' domicile (Can. 1877). From the actual date of publication of the sentence in one of the three ways indicated begins the period of ten days within which the appeal may or must be made (Can. 1881). Failure to make the appeal within the stipulated time precludes the possibility of further prosection by ordinary methods; the sentence becomes *res iudicata*, i.e., passes into a definitive judgment and must be executed (Cans. 1888; 1902, n. 2). Sentences concerning the status of individuals are not *res iudicata* (irrevocably adjudged) even though they become executory (Cans. 1903; 1989; 1998, par. 2).

From the moral aspect, a sentence must be respected inasmuch as it has the value of law in a particular case. Naturally, if the law is not clear, the presumption is in favor of the judges, and the sentence shall be respected once it has become executory, to avoid greater difficulties. If the sentence is evidently iniquitous or unjust, it does not bind in conscience and no one may be compelled to respect it; insofar as the external forum is concerned, it can be contested according to the provisions of the law. If it is not contested within the time allotted, it must be borne in the external forum, at least as a penalty for one's own negligence. *Pug.*

SENTIMENT. *See* Affectivity.

SEPARATION (OF HUSBAND AND WIFE). Canonical discipline with respect to separation is expounded in Canons 1128–1132 of the Code of Canon Law. Married persons are bound to preserve the community of conjugal life, unless a just motive excuses them from this obligation. Separation may be effected by mutual agreement or by one of the parties without the consent of the other. Separation may be temporary or permanent.

Reasons for Permanent Separation. Permanent separation by mutual agreement may be had in two cases: (a) if one or both spouses enter a religious institute; (b) if the man is admitted to holy orders. Today, it is not possible to enter any religious society or be admitted to holy orders without the permission and consent of the other party (Cans. 542, 987). If one party is guilty of adultery, the other has the right to interrupt cohabitation even permanently, although the marriage bond remains. This right is forfeited, however, if the other party approved of, was the cause of, or expressly or tacitly forgave the unfaithful party, or became guilty of the same crime. There is tacit condonation if the innocent party, with knowledge of the consort's adultery, has maintained normal conjugal relations with the unfaithful partner. Condonation is presumed if within six months the innocent consort neither expelled nor left nor brought appropriate action against the adulterous spouse. Suspicion of adultery, however, is not sufficient; there must be certainty.

The innocent party, who legitimately leaves the unfaithful partner either on his own initiative or upon sentence of the judge, is not obliged to readmit the guilty party to cohabitation; he may do so, however, unless the adulterer, with the consent of the innocent party, has embraced a state of life inconsistent with marriage (Can. 1130).

REASONS FOR TEMPORARY SEPARATION. If one party joins a non-Catholic sect, raises the children in heresy and irreligion, leads a criminal and despicable life, threatens grave corporal or spiritual harm to the other party, or makes common life too difficult to bear, the other party may lawfully leave the guilty party. This, however, must be done with permission of the local Ordinary, unless there would be danger in delay. In all these cases cohabitation must be resumed if the reason for separation no longer exists. However, if the separation was permitted by the Ordinary for an indefinite period of time, the innocent party is not obliged to resume cohabitation.

After the separation, the children must be placed in the custody of the innocent party; if one of the parties is a non-Catholic, the Catholic party shall have custody of the children, unless in either case the Ordinary decides otherwise for the good of the children, with full protection for their Catholic education.

Separation is an extreme remedy fraught with many dangers to continence; hence, it should be resorted to only if all other remedies have proved ineffective.

The Church has competency in this matter for all Catholics, but sometimes tolerates, in concordat agreements, that the causes of separation be dealt with by the civil judge. *Bar.*

SEQUESTRATION. *Sequestration* is the removal of property from a person in possession of it, pending further proceedings. Thus, if an individual has shown that he has a certain right over a thing retained by another and he is about to suffer a damage unless the thing is placed in the custody of a third party, he has a right to obtain from the judge a so-called sequestration of the object involved.

In similar conditions it is possible for one to obtain from the court an injunction *against the exercise of a right* against another, if a damage might come to the other party while awaiting the conclusion of a trial (Cans. 1672–1675; 1697 par. 3; 1699 par. 3).

Sequestration and injunction are licit and honest provided that the motive is just. The custody of the property must be entrusted to a reliable person, called a sequester, who shall be appointed *ex officio* by the judge if the parties fail to agree on a sequester. The receiver must use the same diligence in preserving the property as he would in the case of his own goods, and keep the property at the disposal of the judge and of the party to whom the property has been awarded. He must return it with any other fruit or increase which may have come to it during custody. The judge may, at the request of the sequester, establish an equitable remuneration for the service rendered by the sequester. *Pug.*

SERVANT. A person employed by another for menial offices or other labor is called a servant. This word is from the Latin *servus*, meaning *slave*.

In Roman law servitude appears as a true *locatio hominis* (hiring of a slave), not a *locatio operis* (hiring of services), as in the concept of modern law. The concept of the spiritual and moral dignity of work was unknown to the Romans. The condition of servants was not much different in the late Middle Ages. Much credit goes to the Church and her teaching concerning the spirituality of the soul and equality among men, created by the same God and redeemed by the same Savior, Jesus Christ, for having caused slavery to be gradually stricken out of many legislations.

Today, the concept of servant, with a few exceptions, is based on *locatio operis* (service).

Servants are bound by justice to do their work conscientiously and not to leave their employment before the termination of their contract, unless there exists a good reason for doing so.

They are obliged to restitution if they neglect their master's property, assuming that they were hired to guard and protect his possessions. They may not resort to occult compensation on the pretext of excessive work or small pay.

Naturally, to obligations on the part of the servant there correspond obligations on the part of the employer (*q.v.*).

A Catholic servant is permitted to work for a heretic or unbelieving employer if the latter does not demand from the servant any service contrary to the teaching of the Catholic religion, permits the fulfillment of religious duties, and no spiritual danger exists for the servant. The servant must not obey his or her employer if the latter were to demand that which is against the moral law, or in any way opposed to the law of God or the Church. *Tar.*

SERVICE, MILITARY. Nations are not yet so secure or firmly united as to feel safe from any attack or abuse. A nation may be threatened by internal or foreign enemies; hence, the necessity for nations to have armed forces capable of defending themselves from any unjust aggressor. The *end*, however, of the force must also determine its size, for military power is not to be made an end in itself, but a *means for adequate protection of the nation.*

On the other hand, since the arms burden is a grave and dangerous one for all the citizens, it follows that armaments must be kept within moderate limits. Thus, *standing armies* are justified only insofar as they are a painful necessity. Only a grave collective necessity can justify the separation of young men from their families and their actual or prospective conscription in the armed forces.

COMPULSORY CONSCRIPTION. In ancient Rome, military service was first of all a right of every citizen who was willing to participate in the defense of his country, the sum total of their personal, material, and moral possessions. In later periods, armies consisted of hired troops or *soldiers* (so-called from *solidum*, which was the pay they drew) who placed themselves under a prince's orders or the leadership of a mercenary commander. The establishment of compulsory conscription, or military service, as it is today, dates back to the French Revolution (January 1, 1794).

The French principle of a general and personal obligation to serve in the military forces was accepted by all the States with few exceptions.

Some nations adopted a basic system of voluntary service; but a marked tendency toward compulsory conscription followed because voluntary service does not yield expected results.

Militarism, however, understood as a separate class or autonomous profession and force within the State, is contrary to Catholic moral principles (cf. Benedict XV, *Pacem Dei munum pulcherrimum,* May 23, 1920; Pius XI, *Nova impedent,* October 2, 1931).

LICITNESS OF MILITARY SERVICE. Military service is, in itself, neither a sin nor an occasion of sin, for, according to St. Augustine, *Non enim militare delictum est, sed propter praedam militare peccatum est* (Sermo 82, n. 1 *in Mont.*). The military career contains nothing intrinsically illicit. Even St. John the Baptist did not condemn the "militia," nor did he tell the soldiers inquiring from him what they might do to earn eternal life to quit the army or the military service; but he told them to become citizens of the kingdom of God and *"to abstain from all vexations and from all calumnies and be satisfied with your pay"* (Luke 3: 14; cf. St. Bonaventure, *In Evang. Lucae:* c. 3, v. 14, n. 21: Opera omnia, VIII [Quaracchi, 1895], p. 77). Soldiers must neither exploit their uniform nor the authority that they may have.

A serviceman's fundamental duty is the performance of works of justice and courage; therefore, he is bound to guard and defend the common good with greater care than his own body. His work may also be a meritorious one, inasmuch as it is meant to be the work of peace, justice, and order.

When military service is established by law, it becomes a personal duty in legal justice and obedience to the law of the nation for all fit citizens to undergo a training that will enable them to defend, when necessary, the public and social good. Military service is unjust and immoral if it violates the natural laws, that is, if it is made binding on disabled persons or those strictly needed for the support of a family, or if it disregards the privilege of immunity for clerics (Can. 121). Military service may also be unjust if it becomes harmful to the material and spiritual welfare of the soldiers themselves, or if the practice of religion and morality is not sufficiently promoted and protected. When selective service laws remain within just bounds, they give rise to an obligation of legal and social justice if there is compulsory conscription, and to an obligation of commutative justice if the selective system is based on voluntary service. In other words, those who join by voluntary enlistment are bound by commutative justice to serve the time agreed upon. Those, instead, who are subject to compulsory conscription commit no grave sin if in time of peace they evade the draft by means which are not intrinsically unlawful. It may, on the contrary, be a grave sin if illicit means are used, such as corrupting the draft board or the examining physician. This shall be all the more serious if it happens in time of war or other grave need for the country. *Tar.*

SEXOLOGY. The sum total of facts and theories pertaining to sexual phenomena considered anatomically, physiologically, pathologically, psychologically, ethnologically, etc., is termed *sexology*.

Sexuality is a biological phenomenon, which, in man and in the greater part of animals, is characterized by *gonochorism* (separate sexes) and *anisogamy* (sexually differentiated organisms for male and female). The best and most comprehensive definition, not of sex (which is an abstract term), but of the sexes, is found at the beginning of Aristotle's treatise on generation: "Male is the animal that generates in another being; female, the one that generates in itself."

DETERMINATION OF SEX AND SECONDARY CHARACTERISTICS. From a biological point of view, it would be of great interest to know the factors that concur in the determination of sex, that is to say, the causes that make an individual belong to one or the other sex. But the problem, certain aspects of which have also a decidedly ethical importance, is as obscure as ever, despite numerous and profound studies made on the subject. Here we shall limit ourselves to summarizing, with Hartmann, the more important conclusions obtainable from the sum total of facts as known up to the present time:

(a) every sexually differentiated individual has within himself the potentialities of the opposite sex;

(b) the determination of sex consists in an inhibitory process whereby the opposite sex is prevented from being realized, without, however, losing its potentialities;

(c) the determination of sex may result from non-hereditary causes (generally, a different nutrition) or, as happens in all higher organisms, from hereditary or *genotypic* factors.

Regarding the determination of secondary sex characteristics, that is, the determining causes of the morphological, physiological, and physical differentiation of the sexes, it is known that in lower animals the determinants of secondary sex characteristics operate independently of gonadal hormones, whereas in vertebrates they depend on gonadal hormones, variously influenced by the secretions of other endocrine glands (*q.v.*), particularly the pituitary gland (*q.v.*).

DEVELOPMENT OF HUMAN SEXUAL ACTIVITY. According to the majority of modern sexologists, sex activity (which does not necessarily imply the concourse of an individual of a different sex nor a genital activity) begins at birth, not at puberty. If we are to lend credence to the assertions of psychoanalysts, who especially insist on these views, the sex activity of the child goes through three stages of development: oral, ano-urethral, and phallic. Psychologically, during these pregenital phases of his sexual life, the child is alleged to undergo various experiences. To say the least, these views of psychoanalysts, based as they are on crude materialism, are grossly exaggerated.

HOMOSEXUALITY. Studies on the sexual development of the child and the existence in each sex of limited anatomical characteristics of the opposite sex, have led to the supposition that in each individual there is an original bisexuality, which is successively oriented or channelled into either the male or female sex, depending on the original disposition and external influences and factors.

In the homosexual, however, this orientation has followed a defective and devious course, perhaps due to obscure hormonal substrata, perhaps also to psychological influences that must be minutely studied. These are at times exaggerated by psychoanalysts, who insist on the pathogenic importance of certain factors, inspired by the usual pansexualistic theory.

Not all students accept these views; many, following Ombrédanne, maintain that in somatically normal individuals homosexuality is a vice, an acquired deviation of tendencies, and not a disease.

Whatever the physician's personal views in this matter, he must not regard homosexuality or any other sexual aberration as incurable, but as curable by remedies and measures that are intrinsically licit, as indicated in the article on Sexual Perversions.

Concerning other perversions, the pathology and general psychopathology of sex, *see* Gonads; Perversions, Sexual; Psychoneurosis, Sexual. *Riz.*

SEXUALITY. *Sexuality*, as a term, includes everything pertaining to sex; from a moral point of view, it refers particularly to *sensuality* (*q.v.*), which is the disposition to consider sexual satisfaction as the only or the main source of contentment. This, in turn, is the main element in *sensualism*, the hedonistic philosophical theory which considers sense pleasure to be the supreme purpose of all activities.

In practice, sexuality usually becomes a form of aberration of the sexual instinct, because it subordinates the natural purpose of procreation to unbridled pursuit of sense pleasures. This satisfaction is sought in ways condemned by Catholic moral teaching (*see* Prostitution, Birth Control (Neo-Malthusianism), Sexual Perversions).

In the last thirty years, a number of experts in the field of sexology, under the leadership of M. Hirschfeld, director of the *Institut für Sexualwissenschaft*, in particular, have created a movement aimed at bringing about sexual reform. They hold that formal chastity is impossible and that, therefore, any kind of sexual behavior should be permissible. The promoters of this *science of sex* look upon the teaching of the Bible and of the Church as bonds that might have been useful in primitive times among semibarbaric populations, but which now have not only been outgrown but also have become unattainable and, therefore, a useless burden. If the human race is to achieve happiness, so they hold, then hedonism, along with unrestricted satisfaction of the senses, must regain the ascendancy it enjoyed in the golden age of paganism. Obviously, no Catholic may subscribe in any way to the above principles, which are not only heretical, but are an authentic prescription for fostering animal-like selfishness, crime, and debauchery.

Unfortunately, modern society, especially in countries that have veered away from the spiritual influence of the Catholic Church, has been according more and more acceptance to many of the principles proposed by Hirschfeld and his followers, with the result that homosexuality, especially in intellectual circles, free love, birth control, divorces, and many other serious moral, social and pathological evils have increased.

MORAL CONCLUSIONS. Catholic moral teaching, which regards purity as one of mankind's most precious possessions, decidedly condemns sensuality in any form, and appeals at the same time to responsible leaders to make all possible efforts to encourage women to return to their natural responsibilities of the home for which they were created, thus enabling men to earn enough to maintain a decent home and mode of living. Furthermore, parents are strongly reminded to keep a respectful and intelligent vigilance over their children's friendships and recreations lest they be led down the road to moral and social disaster. Young people themselves must bear in mind that, although a proper relationship with those their own age of the opposite sex is not in itself wrong, it can easily become so if they relax proper restraints and the sense of respect for the person of another, which religious teaching inculcates and which ought to be the natural result of a well-balanced character and lofty ethical standards. *Riz.*

SHINTOISM. The national religion of Japan is called *Kami-no-miki* (the way of the *Kami,* the gods), or Shinto, which distinguishes it from *Butsu-do* (the way of Buddha). *Kami,* signifying high or superior, applies to anything materially high, such as hair, or to anyone having a superior power or quality, such as a tribal chieftain or ancestral spirits. In the course of time and through the influence of China, these were made the objects of true and proper cult, beginning with the emperor Mikado. The powerful spirits personifying the phenomena and forces of nature are worshipped. The sun, *Amaterasu,* was conceived as a female deity, governess of the heavens, ancestress of the imperial family, whose sovereign ruler was believed invested with divine prerogatives, until the end of the Second World War. Shintoism, therefore, a strictly nationalistic paganism, has remained in Japan, even after Chinese influence and Buddhism elevated the cultural and religious level of the country.

The native culture, unable to form a philosophical system out of the data of its traditional mythology, was compelled to give way to the loftier moral vision of Buddhism,which came into Japan from China by way of Korea, in 552 A.D. At first, Buddhism was widely and favorably received by the educated classes, to whom it seemed vastly superior than the sheer naturalism of Shinto. Later, it was also accepted by the people, particularly when two monks, Denghio and Kobo, in the ninth century succeeded in fusing Buddhism and Shintoism, thus giving rise to one system called *Riobushinto.* In other words, Shinto became twofold; the deities were considered as two manifestations, Shintoistic and Buddhistic, of one and the same divine figure. Riobushinto prevailed for over one thousand years, until it was abolished, following the revolution of 1868.

SHINTOISM STATE. This revolution, nationalistic in spirit, sought to bring about a restoration of pure Shinto, but without success. Buddhism, deeply rooted in the Japanese soul after thirteen centuries, organized itself into sects (*Tendai, Sin-gon, Zen, Jodo, Shin, Nichiren*), all designed to offer the people refuge in Buddha, in the face of constant agita-

tions caused by civil wars. Wherefore, in order to preserve national solidarity, the government, after struggle and the impossibility of imposing Shintoism as a national religion, finally recognized, in 1877, the autonomy of the Buddhistic organizations. And in 1926 it declared the Shinto temples (*Jinja*) national monuments, with the priests as officials of the State. The functions carried out in the Shinto temples were to be civil ceremonies, designed to keep alive in the people the ancient rites and traditions of the country and to foster devotion to the sovereign. Basing itself precisely on this formal declaration of the Japanese government that State Shinto is merely a civil rite, the Catholic Church, in 1939, declared it permissible for Catholics to participate in the civil ceremonies of State Shinto, and in the private functions of Japanese religious life on such occasions as marriages, funerals, and the like.

This laicized form of Shintoism, perpetuated for the sake of maintaining national solidarity (*koku-tai*), numbers about 111,000 *Jinja* or temples, all dependent upon the Office of Shintoist Temples, connected to the Ministry of the Interior. The most important sacred temple is that of Ise, wherein the goddess *Amaterasu,* ancestress of the imperial family, is venerated.

SECTARIAN SHINTOISM. Besides the State Shinto, there is also a sectarian or religious Shinto. This comprises thirteen sects, all juridically recognized and almost all originating in the nineteenth century. These are controlled by the Office of Religions, in the Ministry of Public Instruction, as are all other Christian or Buddhistic religious organizations. The dogmas and worship of these sects are, with some modifications and adaptations, similar to traditional Shintoism. Their shrines are not to be called *Jinja,* but *Kiokai* (churches), like those of other religions. Sectarian Shinto, which collectively numbers about sixteen million believers, represents a popular religion, not devoid of superstitious practices.

MORALITY. Shintoist morality is of an aristocratic type, for it is an emanation of the chivalrous classes (*Samurai*). Its code, not written but handed down by tradition, is called *Bushido,* a term signifying the way that the perfect knight must follow. Its ethical principles, purely civil in character, are borrowed from Confucianism. They extoll recititude, by which one is prompted to judge according to justice; this is the basis of moral life, as the skeleton is to the body. They extoll courage, which is a combination of audacity and tolerance; benevolence that renders a person sympathetic to the suffering of others; courtesy, when accompanied by sincerity, the sentiment of honor and self-control.

Pure and original Shinto is in no way concerned with the inner life of the individual. To judge from furnishings contained in ancient tombs, Shinto admits belief in the survival of the soul, which is also demonstrated by the widespread practice of ancestral worship. Concerning the destiny of the soul, its reward or punishment in the hereafter, Shinto is silent. The negative or silent attitude regarding the soul's destiny is necessarily reflected in Shintoist morality, which is concerned with ritualistic and physical purity more than with internal purity. It regards as impure all contacts with corpses or with blood, infirmities such as albinism and leprosy, in a word, all that is distressing, disgusting, and repugnant to the senses. All of these are eliminated by a ritualistic purification. Naturally, this is a description of pure and original Shinto, not of the later forms whose moral doctrine was developed with the assistance of Confucianism and Buddhism. *Tur.*

Sectarian Shintoism is pure paganism, of which the chief point, until recently, was the worship of a living being, the Mikado. Today it continues in the practice of ancestral worship. Hence, its cult is filled with superstitious practices.

State Shintoism, which can no longer be regarded as a religion, is but an external manifestation of a renewed nationalism, with the tendency to justify every form of excess, including suicide, from patriotic motives.

Shintoist morality, as already noted, is not based on interior perfection but on external rectitude and ritualistic purity. In its later forms, because of its contacts with Buddhism and Confucianism, it accepted with the positive part also the negative aspects of those religions. *Pal.*

SHIPWRECK. The loss of a ship or vessel at sea because of an accident, fire, storm, or the like is called a *shipwreck.* This occasions moral problems.

In ancient times, shipwrecked persons had no legal protection, because shipwreck was considered a punishment of the gods. The Romans were the first to protect *res fractae* or *res in naufragio amissae;* as a matter of fact, they sanctioned deportation as the punishment for plunderers of shipwreck, a punishment confirmed in the *Basilici* (LIII, c. 22). Common law has always condemned plundering wrecked vessels; in fact, it was customary to offer special rewards to divers who recovered objects from vessels wrecked at sea. This custom degenerated in the Middle Ages.

In Venice a special office was instituted, called the *Soprastanti* (standing above), for the recovery and sale of shipwrecked objects in behalf of the lawful owners. However, until the eighteenth century, civil authority in many countries retained the *right of shipwreck,* that is, all claims to shipwrecked things and persons. Modern legislations do not follow a uniform criterion. In some countries, things lost by shipwreck are considered as lost objects, and special laws exist for their recovery and sale.

State laws, wherever they exist, concerning objects recovered from shipwreck are generally binding in conscience; they are not merely penal laws but moral and penal, unless the law specifically states the contrary. The old custom of *shipwreck rights* is certainly against nature, at least insofar as persons are concerned. It is quite proper for the State to have special legislation regarding articles lost by shipwreck, giving a right to compensation for their recovery and for the public or private custody of shipwrecked objects.

For details concerning the various legislations in the matter, the reader must consult the particular legislation involved, bearing in mind that, in general, such laws are binding in conscience. *Sir.*

SHOCK THERAPY. Shock therapy represents an important chapter in modern psychiatry, but this therapeutic method is linked to the methods of ancient times, employed in the treatment of mental illnesses.

Passages of the most ancient Sanskrit literature tell of the efforts to cure the insane by frightening them with the threat of death from a serpent, wild beast or execution by royal guards. Roman physicians treated the mentally ill with torments, chains, etc., as well as strong emotional shocks. Scribonius Largus, the physician of Emperor Claudius, may be considered the forerunner of the modern use of electric shock treatments of Cerletti and others. He employed the torpedo fish in the treatment of prolonged and frequent headaches because of a form of electrical discharge given off by the fish. In the Middle Ages, striking, whirling, or subjecting a patient to terrifying experiences were among the most popular means used for curing the mentally disturbed. "It seems in a way to be the destiny of the mentally ill to be treated with violent means," Buscaino wrote some time back, "for in early times they received real blows; today, it is still blows, not physical, of course, but chemical . . . or biochemical."

Since Wagner von Jauregg used malaria therapy to fight progressive paralysis in 1917, there has been an intense revival and development throughout the scientific world of research into cures for mental illnesses, which once seemed beyond the reach of therapeutic methods. The greatest contribution made by the Viennese doctor is to have rekindled hope in the hearts of psychiatrists and suffering humanity.

We shall not list all the methods of shock therapy that have been proposed and tried; we shall mention only those that have attained greater use: (a) *Pyretotherapy.* Directly derived from malaria therapy, this was designed to produce the beneficial effects of malarial fever without the risks of malaria itself. Used in the beginning only for the cure of progressive paralysis, it was later applied to mental illnesses, especially schizophrenia. It is a treatment in which the patient's temperature is artificially raised by an injection of vaccine or radiation repeated over a period of time.

(b) *Insulin therapy.* This was first proposed for the treatment of schizophrenia in 1933 by M. Sakel. It consists in a series of intravenous injections of insulin, administered in steadily increasing doses until the sick person reaches a coma and remains in it for a definite time. Complete cure may require as many as eighty or more lapses into coma, with an average of six a week.

(c) *Cardiazol convulsive therapy.* This was suggested by the Hungarian V. Neduna, in 1934. He accepted the notion, not completely correct, of an antagonism between epilepsy and schizophrenia. He sought to cure the latter by artificially producing epileptic attacks. The means he used to produce the epilepsy was a rapid injection of five or more cubic centimeters of *cardiazol* (ten percent) intravenously.

(d) *Electric convulsive therapy.* This treatment, developed in 1938 by Hugh Cerletti, produces convulsive attacks by running a quantity of electric current through the brain. The method, which has come to be called electric shock, is simple, practical, economical, and harmless; it can be used at the home of the sick person or in a doctor's office. Because of these advantages, it has been widely adopted throughout the civilized world.

Although the kinds of shock therapy differ in methods, many experts in this difficult problem think that the basic action is the same. Basically all produce helpful changes in the biochemistry of a brain disturbed by mental illness. Since, as all biological studies on the emotions show, emotions influence, even if in a superficial and accidental manner, not only the thought processes but the entire neuro-vegetative function, we can no longer exclude the possibility that the very ancient types of psychotherapy, based on physical and emotional shock, may have had a certain scientific basis akin to modern shock therapies. However, the latter have been tested on the basis of precise biological concepts with favorable clinical results. On the other hand, those ancient treatments in use for thousands of years may justify the hypothesis, since statistical data are lacking, that they must have produced some cures or appreciable improvement. Otherwise, they would have ceased.

Hence, shock therapies must be considered, at least at the present stage of our knowledge, as a rational treatment, whose effectiveness had already been perceived by the ancients to some extent, even if their applications remained crude.

INDICATIONS. On the basis of a vast international experience, the following indications of shock therapies appear as definitely established. Insulin therapy is effective principally in the *hebephrenic*, paranoid, and simple types of schizophrenia (*q.v.*). Convulsive therapy, principally electroshock, is especially recommended in cases of catatonic schizophrenia, manic-depressives, especially in the melancholic phase, involutional and confusional psychoses, epileptic psychoses and the accelerated withdrawal by morphine addicts from the use of the drug (*see* Drugs, Narcotic). At times, if one method of shock therapy fails, another may prove helpful or a combination of methods may be the answer.

MORAL COROLLARIES. Despite agreement by experts on the value of shock therapy, a few voices have been raised in disagreement; it is only right to mention them and discuss their positions objectively.

Some condemn shock therapy as *too aggressive* a method. Others, like Baruk, condemn it for violating the moral personality of the sick person. Boss maintains, on the basis of psychoanalytical inferences, that the originators and proponents of these treatments are individuals driven by aggressive impulses. The exaggerations of these opponents are obvious; and yet, as even Lopez-Ibor admits, their protests are of some value since they tend to place in proper perspective a problem that deserves the greatest attention—namely, moral limits to this type of treatment.

Treatment that is very aggressive in itself is no reason for condemning it, for it is no more aggressive than an operation, and no one would dream of charg-

ing a surgeon with being aggressive. Again, the use of shock therapy without the consent of the patient does not automatically make it immoral, for the lack of consent does not result from the nature of the treatment, but from the fact that the condition of the patient makes it impossible for him to make a free decision. The use of electroshock therapy, as Lopez-Ibor stresses on this point, involves the same type of moral violence that is used in giving an injection to a patient to quiet him. It employs, however, much less violence than was originally necessary for confining him in a psychiatric hospital. Yet no one disapproves of quieting persons who are mentally disturbed, nor do they object to their admittance to mental institutions. The dangers involved in shock therapy are practically insignificant and far less serious than those dangers involved in the mental illness itself.

Thus, any moral condemnation of shock therapies as such must be rejected. Obviously, a physician must proceed with prudence and intelligence, particularly if he deals with persons who, because of their mental illness, are not mentally competent. For this reason, the doctor who makes decisions must have the support of a conscience that is calm, sure of itself, and possessed of high ideals. One ethical principle a psychiatrist must use as the basis for decisions and the use of shock therapy: he must determine, on the basis of his own knowledge, experience, and good conscience, apart from any thought of financial gain, the treatment he ought to use, beginning with milder types of treatments.

Often, in practice, the choice is anything but easy. In a case of slight melancholy, for example, it might seem better to use medicines as a less expensive and less painful method; but experience shows that even apparently mild cases can, at times, become very serious.

At any rate, in all cases of the mentally ill the selection of the treatment to be used in each case must be made after thoughtful consideration and with an upright conscience, having uppermost in one's mind the best interest of the patient and his return to a useful social, moral, and spiritual life. *Riz.*

SICK. *See* Infirm.

SIGNATURA, APOSTOLIC. The supreme tribunal of the Holy See as well as the supreme tribunal of the State of Vatican City is called the *Apostolic Signatura.*

The origin of the Signatura coincides with the institution of *referees.* From ancient times, there were two branches of the Signatura—one called *Signatura gratiae;* the other, *Signatura justitiae*— each with its own field of competency. The two departments date back to the sixteenth century, when the Roman Pontiff charged certain referees with the task of accepting and deciding judicial matters, leaving to all other referees the handling of privileges, dispensations, exemptions and the like.

The apostolic referees were officials of the Curia who received the petitions and claims of the faithful, referred them to the Supreme Pontiff, and submitted to the same Supreme Pontiff the rescripts for his signature. For this reason they were called *Referees of Signatura,* whence also the name *Signatura.*

These referees first appear around the end of the thirteenth century. In the beginning, the same Pontiff signed with his *fiat* the concession of a petition; at other times the vice-chancellor stamped it *"concessum."* Eugene IV (1431–1437) authorized the referees to sign certain dispensations. The number of referees, rather small at the beginning, gradually increased to 75 under Martin V and then to over 100. Sixtus V fixed the number at 100.

The competency of the former *Signatura Justitiae* was similar to that of a Supreme Court, and it judged, not the merits of the case, but the procedure.

Its competency embraced spiritual cases in the whole Church and secular controversies involving the temporal patrimony of the Church.

Under Gregory XVI its organization and competency were patterned to some extent after the French Supreme Court. The tribunal was inactive from 1870 till

it was suppressed by St. Pius X, who also abolished the *Signatura Gratiae.* He established a new supreme tribunal, the *Apostolic Signatura,* which is more or less similar to the former *Signatura Justitiae.* The competency of this tribunal was more accurately fixed and enlarged by Benedict XV, June 28, 1915 (AAS: 7 [1915], 320 ff.).

ORGANIZATION OF THE TRIBUNAL. The supreme tribunal of the *Signatura Apostolica* is a collegiate tribunal, composed of several cardinals, one of whom holds the office of prefect (Can. 1602).

In deciding certain issues, they are helped by a group of *voting prelates,* seven in number, and by a group of *prelate referees,* whose number is not fixed. The prefect presides over and signs the acts in the name of the Roman Pontiff.

The prefect, secretary, under-secretary and the voting prelates compose the *Congress,* which handles minor affairs; all other cases are referred to the full tribunal (*Plena Signatura*).

COMPETENCY. By virtue of Canons 1603 and 1604, the Apostolic Signatura has ordinary and delegated power.

(1) By ordinary power the Signatura tries the following cases: (a) Violations of secrecy by a judge of the S. R. Rota or damages caused by the judges of the S. R. Rota by reason of invalid or unjust acts, in trials in appeal. (b) Pleas of suspicion against one of the auditors or judges of the Sacred Rota; in this case, after a ruling is made, if necessary the case is referred to the S. R. Rota for the prosecution of the trial. (c) Pleas of nullity against a sentence of the Sacred Rota. (d) Petitions for *restitutio in integrum,* against a sentence of the Rota which has become a *res iudicata,* and recourse against sentences of the Sacred Rota in marriage cases which the Sacred Rota refused to accept for new trial. Ordinarily, in these cases the Signatura does not decide with respect to their intrinsic justice, but only concerning form and external justice, that is, whether the sentence of the Sacred Rota is invalid or not or whether *restitutio in integrum* and recourse should be granted; but once the sentence is declared invalid, *restitutio in integrum* granted, or recourse admitted,

the case is sent for trial to the S. R. Rota. It is not excluded that the Signatura may reserve to itself the right to try the case with the participation of the entire tribunal (*Plena Signatura*). Recently, the Congress of the Signatura, by delegated power of the Roman Pontiff, has tried causes involving the petition of a new trial rejected by the S. R. Rota. (e) Dispute over competency which may arise between inferior tribunals (Can. 1612, par. 1).

(2) The *Signatura Apostolica* passes on written petitions to the Roman Pontiff which request that a case be committed to the Sacred Rota.

(3) On the basis of some concordats (cf. Concordats with Italy (1929), art. 34; Austria (1934), art. 7, par. 4; Portugal (1940), art. 25), the Signatura Apostolica has the right to conduct a formal examination of the sentences of nullity and rescripts of dispensations *super rato*, before they may be submitted to civil tribunals for civil effect.

(4) According to the Code for the Eastern Church, *de processibus* (Cans. 81–84), the *Signatura Apostolica* is the Supreme Tribunal for Eastern rite Catholics.

The duties, faculties and privileges of voting prelates and referees are decreed in the Constitution Ad *incrementum*, August 15, 1934 (*see* Prelate).

PROCEDURE. The procedure followed by this tribunal is fixed by *Lex propria S. Romanae Rotae et Signaturae Apostolicae* (tit. II, ch. 1, Canons 38–43); *Regulae servandae* in trials by the Supreme Tribunal of the Signatura Apostolica, March 6, 1912 (AAS: 1 [1909], 30–31; 4 [1912], 187) and *Appendix ad regulas servandas*, November 3, 1915. But since these rules were not fully incorporated in the Code, in case of conflict the norms contained in the Code prevail (Cans. 1602–1605).

Although other tribunals must, under penalty of invalidity, offer reasons of law and of fact on which their sentences are based, the decisions of the *Signatura Apostolica* are effective if the reasons of fact and of law are lacking. Nevertheless, at the request of either party to a trial or *ex officio*, the supreme tribunal of the *Signatura Apostolica* may permit that the motives on which the sentence is based be published according to the proper law of the tribunal (Can. 1605). *Pal.*

SIGN OF THE CROSS. *See* Cross, sign of.

SIKHISM. As a religious movement, started by Nanak (1469–1538), Sikhism combines Hinduism and the rigid monotheism of Mohammedanism. It contains elements of the polytheism of the *Veda* and the religious philosophy of Brahmanism. The term comes from Sikh (disciple); its religious doctrines are presented in the *Granth* (Book) or *Adi Granth* (First Book), which distinguishes it from later compilations.

BELIEFS. Sikhism rejected the Brahman priesthood, the worship of images, both of which were dear to Hindus but contrary to Mohammedanism. In lieu of image worship, they divinized the sacred book. They believe in the transmigration of souls (*samsara*) and respect for the sacred cow, although they are permitted to eat the meat of animals. They are forbidden to use tobacco. Other theological speculations of the Sikhs are too confused to reconcile all its religious currents, beyond that of a pronounced pantheistic element.

At one time, the Sikhs offered armed opposition to the Mongols and attained a strong military power under their *gurus* (teachers). The independent State which they founded lasted until the annexation by the British in 1849.

At present, the religious center of Sikhism is at Amritsar with its golden temple of Harimandar; there are more than 4,500,000 members of the sect, as well as many cultural centers, schools, orphanages, and even a bank. *Tur.*

COMMENTS. Theological speculation of the Sikhs leads to pantheism of a very low form that tends to idolatry and fetishism, in the divinization of the sacred book. It is an odd mixture of Hinduism and Mohammedanism that has not resulted in a blend which is harmonious, but suffers from the excesses of both, in the moral sphere at least. *Pal.*

SIMONY. The word *simony* originated with the Gospel story of Simon Magus, who attempted to purchase from Saint Peter spiritual power derived from the imposition of the hands and the convocation of the Holy Spirit (Acts 8:18).

Simony is a special form of sacrilege, which consists of an illicit bargaining or trading in spiritual goods or benefits by the use of money.

Simony includes both agreements that are illicit by divine law and also those which the law of the Church prohibits in order to provide greater protection and reverence for spiritual goods.

Simony of divine law consists in an illicit exchange of temporal goods for spiritual goods (as sacraments, indulgences) or for temporal goods that are inseparably connected with spiritual goods (as church benefices). It also occurs if the spiritual value enters even partially into the object of a contract (Can. 727, par. 1).

It should be noted that, though the consecration or blessing does not preclude sale of an object (Cans. 1532, par. 1, and 730), nevertheless, the object loses its blessing if it is exposed for public sale. If the sale involves rosary beads, these lose all indulgences attached to them even in the case of a private sale (Cans. 1305, 924, par. 2).

The malice of simony comes not merely from the harmful exchange of spiritual goods for those of a lower order, but from the fact that by such actions the ministers of these goods wrongfully arrogate to themselves a dominion over them and thus use these for their own temporal advantage. This malice is always implicit in such a contract, despite any stipulation or intention to exclude any equating of the spiritual or supernatural and the material.

Simony of ecclesiastical law is an illicit exchange of temporal goods connected with spiritual goods for other similar goods; of spiritual goods for other spiritual goods; of temporal goods, if prohibited by the Church because of the danger of scandal or irreverence, for other temporal goods (Can. 727, par. 2). This does not involve the malice of the former type, but there is a danger of committing this evil as well.

In current Canon Law, a number of cases involve simony of ecclesiastical law: a prohibition against payments by a cleric for benefices to the person who confers the benefice, to a patron, or others at the time of the conferral of the benefice (Can. 1441); exchanges of benefices by private renunciation in favor of a third party, especially in exchange for some good (Can. 1486). In a question of litigation, all transactions (*q.v.*) are forbidden. In the matter of Mass stipends, the mere appearance of trafficking or trading is prohibited (Can. 1827).

Simony of divine law admits of no parvity of matter; any unlawful exchange is a serious sin (*ex toto genere suo*). There can be parvity of matter for simony of ecclesiastical law.

The Church has always condemned simony. From the earliest centuries, those guilty of simony were threatened with the most serious punishments, such as excommunication and deposition (*Canones Apostolorum*, 28).

In the first centuries, simony must have been limited since the Church was poor and persecuted. The only recorded case is that of Paul of Samosita, Bishop of Antioch, who made venal use of ecclesiastical jurisdiction (Eusebius, *Historia eccles.*, VII, 30).

In the fourth and fifth centuries, simony frequently became a problem, for the Church began to possess wealth and to accept as catechumens many who were not fervent. Furthermore, Arianism had adversely affected discipline in the Church.

In the following centuries, simony invaded the monasteries, which were, at times, quite wealthy; even the higher levels of the hierarchy did not escape the tarnish of this unholy business.

But the spread of the evil marked the beginning of reform under the energetic action of the pontiffs. This was a successful reform movement until the crisis of the Renaissance and the strong abuses which led to the Reformation and the legislation of the Council of Trent.

Sanctions. Present legislation lists the

following sanctions against simoniacal practices:

(a) Simoniacal contracts are invalid. If it is made for the sake of a benefice, office or dignity, a simoniacal provision renders the contract null and void. If simony occurs on the part of an intermediary, even though it was done maliciously against the will of the one receiving the benefice, the contract is invalid (Cans. 729; 1470, par. 1).

(b) On the penal side, those guilty of simony incur automatic excommunication (*simpliciter S. Sedi reservata*), privation of the right of presenting, nominating or electing; and, if clerics, they must be suspended (Cans. 2392, 2327). Such penalties are incurred whether the simony is of divine or of ecclesiastical law.

(c) In a case of simoniacal ordination or simoniacal administration of the sacraments, both the minister and the subject of the sacrament are suspect of heresy (Can. 2371). *Pal.*

SIMPLICITY. In a very general sense, *simplicity* means the absence of composition or complication. Its theological use and meaning vary.

Simplicity as a virtue is a consistency between one's words and his inner feelings; it is the opposite of duplicity. It is also used to indicate the absence of complexity in one's attitudes; the opposite of this would be affectation in words, gestures, apparel, or other things. By *simplicity* one might mean the attitude of soul which judges everything in the supernatural light of faith and seeks nothing except God and His glory. In this sense, sin is contrary to simplicity.

Genuine simplicity provides man with a special likeness to God, who is essentially simple; it is a sign of loftiness of mind and spirit, an essential requirement for sanctity. Jesus highly praised and recommended the virtue of simplicity (Matt. 10:16).

SIMULATION. Simulation consists of a form of pretense, in conduct or attitude, at times habitual or longstanding, whose purpose is to mislead others to form a false judgment of one's internal state. As an act akin to lying, simulation may strive to make one appear morally better or worse than he is; it may also be practiced in intellectual, physical, or other matters to present a false impression.

When simulation is intended to win consideration, honor, praise or reward, because of an apparently virtuous or holy life, it is termed *hypocrisy*. As a sin, it belongs to the same category as lying, for it is more or less a lie expressed in conduct or actions. This is a slight sin, if intended in a joking or light matter or to avoid a harm; it may be gravely sinful, if a serious harm is the consequence. The gravity of the sin depends on the gravity of the harm created. *Sen.*

SIMULATION, JURIDICAL. Canon and civil law recognize the existence of simulation in juridical affairs. In Canon Law this may occur in simulation of a Mass, the sacraments or a profession of the faith. In contracts Canon Law yields to civil law.

Sacramental simulation consists in positing a sacramental sign without the intention of administering the sacrament, so that others believe it is being administered. Simulation differs from dissimulation: dissimulation is the positing of a *non-sacramental* sign in circumstances which would make others believe that a sacrament is being administered. Simulation makes use of the proper sacramental external signs, without the intention of administering the sacrament; it is never permitted, but is intrinsically wrong. Dissimulation is permitted for serious reasons. To simulate the celebration of Mass and the hearing of a confession are sins and crimes punished with excommunication, which is reserved in a special manner to the Holy See (Can. 2322, par. 1). The simulated absolution of a partner in a sexual sin is also a crime (Can. 2367).

Canonical doctrine on simulation finds its widest application in simulation of consent in matrimony. In the matrimonial contract, partial, absolute, or relative simulation occurs if one of the contracting parties makes a positive act of the will, whether known to the other party or not, concerning the substance of the contract or an essential property of the contract which excludes the necessary consent for a valid marriage (Can. 1086, par. 2). The party concerned intends one thing, but says another. Thus the effectiveness of the consent expressed is nullified by a positive act of the will which contradicts or restricts the marriage by conditions or provisions which render consent ineffective in producing its juridical effects because of the inherent contradiction. Canonical matrimonial jurisprudence makes a clear distinction between the intention or conditions that are opposed to or exclude marital obligations and those intentions or conditions which violate obligations assumed by the law (*see* Consent, Matrimonial). *Pug.*

SIN (ACTUAL). Actual sin is a human act in violation of the law of God. It may consist of a *thought, word, action* or *omission.* All sins are classified on the basis of this division.

Since it is a human act, sin always supposes knowledge and free will in the subject, and, as a result, some degree of malice. Hence, the distinction into sins of ignorance, weakness, and malice is not to be understood to mean that in the first two cases there is a complete lack of knowledge in the act or of all possibility of resisting temptation, for there would be no sin at all. It means that ignorance or weakness in the subject was sufficiently grave to *partially* excuse his sin. If they were of such nature as to excuse him completely, then moralists call this a *material* rather than a *formal* sin; in other words, this would be an objective violation of the moral law, but not imputable to the subject.

The transgressed *divine law* may be natural or positive. Human laws may oblige in conscience so that a violation of them would constitute a sin, but they have this binding force only insofar as, based on divine law, they command obedience to authorities in legitimate matters. Transgressions of human laws are sinful insofar as they involve divine law. There is no sin except insofar as it relates to God.

SPECIES OF SINS. Opposition to divine law may be of two kinds—thus the basis for the distinction of sins into *mortal*

and *venial.* This distinction is also referred to as the *theological species of sin.* A mortal sin is one which deprives the soul of sanctifying grace and makes it deserving of hell; a venial sin is one which does not produce these serious effects, although it weakens the action of grace in man and makes him deserving of temporal punishment (purgatory). Theologians, discussing the nature of these two species of sin, state that mortal sin opposes man's ultimate end, insofar as it destroys the order to that end, whereas venial sin does not overthrow this order, since it opposes means that are not absolutely indispensable for the attainment of the end. Mortal sin is a complete loss of direction; venial sin is only a delay along the way to the attainment of one's end.

MORTAL SIN. Three elements or conditions are required for a mortal sin: *serious matter, sufficient awareness, full consent of the will.*

(a) *Matter.* It is difficult to lay down a universal norm for determining its seriousness. Moralists limit themselves to formulating it for individual commandments or sins. It may be noted, however, that certain violations always imply serious matter, but in others the matter may be serious or light, depending on the greater or lesser quantity of the matter involved.

(b) *Awareness.* It might be pointed out that awareness may be complete, in the sense intended here, without involving any reflex action or long meditation. All that is required is the degree of attention that a normal individual, who is not distracted, employs in carrying out matters of ordinary importance. It does not call for explicit intention to offend God; this awareness is always implicit in the conscience of anyone who adverts to the immorality of his action.

(c) *Consent.* Consent is full if given with that ordinary degree of liberty that we have when we are still exercising control over our decisions, though we may be under the impulse of some passion. This third element is often the most difficult one to establish, especially in the case of internal sins or sins involving a passion. The habitual dispositions of the individual, along with the circumstances surrounding the situation, will help us to arrive at a judgment that has the greatest probability of being close to the truth.

The effects of sin consist in a combination of consequences which sin bestows on the soul of the sinner. They are generally referred to as habitual guilt, that is, the privation of sanctifying grace in mortal sin, and the diminution of fervor in venial sin; the punishment of hell for mortal sin or purgatory for venial sin; and eventual suffering on earth.

All the above refers to personal sin, which theologians distinguish from *original* sin. See *also* Guilt, Theological; Number of sins (numerical distinction of sins); Remission of sins; Sin, species of. *Gra.*

SIN (CAPITAL). The term *capital* is applied to sins to which man's fallen nature is more inclined and which are the source of other faults. The name does not mean that each of these is necessarily a mortal sin. Sometimes the term *capital sins* is applied to tendencies toward sins; in this case, it would be better to speak of capital defects or vices.

Number. The Fathers and ancient writers spoke of capital sins and gave a different number to them until, on the authority of St. Gregory the Great, the number seven was generally accepted. These are: *pride, avarice, lust, envy, gluttony, anger, sloth.*

St. Thomas (*S. Theol.,* I–II, q. 84, a. 3 and 4) justifies this number by pointing to the goods toward which fallen man tends and the evils that he seeks to avoid. There are three created goods to which human nature is mainly inclined: its own excellence, hence pride; pleasures of the senses, hence gluttony and lust; wealth, hence avarice. There are, on the other hand, two evils from which fallen nature flees in particular: lessening of one's own excellence, hence envy; loss of one's peace and quiet, or pain, hence sloth and anger.

Sacred Scripture (Eccles. 9:15) calls pride the principle of all the other sins; it was, in fact, the sin of the fallen angels and of Adam, and, of its very nature, it can lead man to any sin.

In order to make spiritual progress and to save his soul, man must, of necessity, avoid the capital sins and battle against his inclinations toward them. This struggle has the effect of re-establishing within man an order disrupted by sin. *Man.*

SIN (CAUSES OF). *Internal Causes.* An inordinate love of self is the principal cause of every sin and constitutes its very soul; this love is at the same time ignorance, concupiscence, and malice. Insofar as one of these elements may prevail on the others and exercise a particular influence in determining the commission of a sin, we can have sins of ignorance, concupiscence, or malice.

In sins of ignorance, the error which causes the sinful act concerns not only the practical judgment on the opportuneness of the action, but also the speculative judgment or knowledge and information that should be possessed.

Sins of concupiscence, on the other hand, have their source in the passions; the sins of malice are rooted in the perversity of the will. The latter type are more serious and more dangerous sins than the former, because they are more deliberate and persist more stubbornly in the soul.

External or Remote Causes. Along with the internal causes, we have to consider external and indirect causes, such as the devil, scandal, cooperation; or remote causes, such as habits, loss of grace, etc.

The causality of the capital sins (pride, avarice, lust, gluttony, anger, envy, sloth) is remote; they derive their name not from being more serious than other sins, but from the fact that they are more likely to stimulate the appetites and, thus, more easily dispose and induce the will to committing other sins. *Pal.*

SIN (SPECIES OF). Sins are not all of the same kind. They are distinguished into various species, i.e., moral or theological classifications. The *theological species* of a sin is a distinction of sin into mortal or venial; it is called theological because it follows directly from the sin's relationship to God. The *moral species*, on the other hand, is based on the particular ethical structure of the sinful act; that is, it stems from the particular malice contained in that particular act. Since this malice is fundamentally tied up with the object of the sinful act, it is usually said that the moral species of a sin flows from its object. Some moralists prefer to say that it stems from the virtue to which the sin is opposed, or from the law that is transgressed by the sin. But this variation in formula is more a question of doctrinal subtlety than a real difference in the matter; for both the laws and the virtues are specified by their objects.

NORMS. A difficulty may arise with regard to the first formula, the fundamental distinctive criterion, from the fact that in ordinary language one speaks of circumstances that change the species of a sin, that is, give it a new moral species of its own. But this difficulty is readily disposed of by recalling that, strictly speaking, from a moral point of view, these circumstances are not circumstances at all but part of the object (*see* Circumstances).

From the general rule to the particular rules used to determine the species of sins, moralists usually use the criterion of virtues because it is easier to grasp. They maintain that acts constitute sins of a different moral species if they are opposed: (a) to different virtues, or to the same virtue but in a way that is (b) contrary, (c) or simply different. Thus, theft and fornication are sins of different species: theft is opposed to justice; fornication, to chastity. Despair and presumption concerning salvation are sins opposed to the same virtue of hope; but they are of different species, for they are opposed to hope in contrary ways: the first by defect, the second by excess. Blasphemy and non-observance of a vow are both sins against religion, but they have a different moral species, because they offend this virtue in terms of two different aspects.

Some moralists add another rule by saying that sins have a different moral species if they transgress commandments that are formally different. But this does not seem to add anything new, for the formal difference in the commandments arises from the virtue that lies at their basis.

It should be noted that there may be specifically different malices in one and the same act; this always happens whenever a single act is commanded or forbidden by virtues or commandments that are formally different. Thus in adultery there is a double malice, of lust and injustice; to lead someone into blasphemy entails two sinful moral species: scandal and irreligion. *Gra.*

SIN, VENIAL. *See* Sin.

SINNER, HABITUAL. The habitual sinner, also called consuetudinarian, is one who, by frequent repetition of a gravely sinful act, acquires a strong tendency to that act. Man may become a consuetudinarian with respect to any sin. However, a sinful habit is more easily acquired in certain matters, such as gluttony, lust, cursing and blasphemy, than in others. A perverse tendency is acquired much more easily if an individual has an hereditary predisposition to it. A sinful habit renders the practice of virtue more difficult; in fact, the habit can grow until it reaches a point of nearly irresistible power. Because of this fact, a habit at times lessens the culpability of acts committed under its influence, without, however, necessarily removing even grave guilt. This is particularly true if there is an underlying responsibility in cause.

PRACTICAL NORMS. Any vice whatsoever may be reduced or eliminated provided that adequate means are employed. The consuetudinarian is bound to detest his acquired perverse tendency, to have a firm will to rid himself of the habit and to employ the proper means to achieve this end. Anyone who is not so disposed is lacking the necessary dispositions for receiving absolution.

Adequate means are: an awareness of the divine presence; prayer; frequent reception of the sacraments; meditation on

Christ's passion, the brevity of this life or the last things; finally, the practice of acts contrary to this perverse tendency.

One who neglects to employ the necessary means to rid himself of a bad habit by this very fact implicitly consents, even if confusedly, to the inordinate acts resulting from an unresisted vice. These acts, though committed unknowingly, are imputable to a greater or lesser extent, depending on the degree of negligence in resisting the vice.

On the contrary, if an individual has a hatred against a vice and uses the necessary means to uproot it, then indeliberate acts committed under the influence of such a habit are not imputable to him.

The will of the consuetudinarian, who sincerely converts and recovers grace, turns away from the particular vice; nevertheless, there still remain within him the physical propensity to the sin. Hence it is that, even after his conversion, the individual may still feel a strong attraction toward the sin. This explains why the individual is confronted with the danger of relapse immediately following his return to God, and why it is necessary, therefore, to exercise constant vigilance and take special precautionary measures.

An individual who, through frequent repetition of a venially sinful act, has contracted a strong inclination towards such an act, is not called a consuetudinarian. He has, however, the obligation to combat even such a habit. This obligation is grave if the proclivity to this venial habit and the frequent repetition of it were to constitute a serious danger of falling into mortal sin. *Mand.*

SINNER, PUBLIC. Public sinners are those whose continuation in a state of serious sin has been made known through a condemnatory sentence or is actually known by a large part of the inhabitants of a place or members of a community. Individuals are also classified as public sinners if their serious offense is not yet publicly known, but will be shortly; or if they are obviously in the state of mortal sin, e.g., those who are completely drunk or dressed in a fashion that is gravely scandalous.

Public sinners include, among others, those who have given serious scandal through repeated drunkenness or blasphemy; those excommunicated or placed under interdict by name; those who have clearly incurred infamy; those living in concubinage; prostitutes known by many people to be such; those who are widely known to be carrying on an illegal profession or who freely and publicly belong to forbidden associations, e.g., the Masons, the communist party, and similar organizations.

OBLIGATIONS. It is obvious that in order to be absolved, a public sinner must sincerely repent of his sins and be firmly resolved to do all that he can as soon as he can to repair the scandal he has given.

A person may not be given Holy Communion (or Viaticum and extreme unction) publicly in a place where he is publicly known as a sinner until the fact of his reform has become publicly known and reparation has been made for the scandal given (Can. 855; *Rituale Romanum, tit.* 4, c. 1, n. 9). In certain cases, it is enough for the man to publicly approach the tribunal of penance and receive Holy Communion devoutly. But wherever there was a permanent, external cause of scandal, this must first be removed, e.g., by separating from a partner in sin, stopping visits to a place of ill-repute, retracting false doctrines that have been spread, abandoning an illegal profession, cutting off all relationship and ties with a forbidden society. This must be done in a way that can readily become public; in danger of death, it should be done in the presence of two trustworthy witnesses who will make the retraction or the separation known.

In the case of a public sinner who has reformed but finds it impossible to make up immediately for the scandal that he has given, Holy Communion (and in particular Viaticum) may be administered to him secretly or even publicly in a place where he was not known as a sinner. Public sinners who have given no sign of repentance before their death must be denied ecclesiastical burial (Can. 1240, n. 6). *Man.*

SINS AGAINST THE HOLY SPIRIT.
This expression is drawn from Scriptural texts (Matt. 12:31; Mark 3:29; Luke 12: 10). In Scripture, by the expression "to speak against or to blaspheme the Holy Spirit" is meant the systematic opposition of the Pharisees to any influence of grace, when, out of malice, they attributed to the devil the miracles that Christ had performed to prove His divine mission and to save men.

The Fathers of the Church and the Scholastics extended the term to all sins implying contempt for or rejection, through bad will, of the means that divine goodness has provided for man to stay away from sin and attain salvation. A rejection of this kind is a very special offense against the Holy Spirit, to whom the divine works of sanctification are attributed. A sin against the Holy Spirit always presumes the absence of any circumstances that might mitigate the seriousness of the guilt.

NUMBER. Since the time of Peter Lombard, the sins against the Holy Spirit have been listed as six in number: *despair of one's own salvation; a presumption of attaining eternal life without merits or repentance; attacks against or denial of Christian truth*, if it is known to be revealed by God; *envy of someone else's supernatural good; obstinacy in evil*, or the determination to keep on sinning; the *resolution not to repent*, or to resist the influences of grace until death.

Each of these sins involves a rejection of the means of salvation. A person who despairs refuses to trust in the divine mercy, which is the cause of salvation. One who is presumptuous pays no attention to divine justice, which leads to fear and the avoidance of sin. A person who fights against truth, which he knows has been made known by God, rejects the gift of revelation. One who is envious of the spiritual good of another opposes the work of grace in souls. One who is hardened in sin does not wish to think about the things that would lead him to detest it. Finally, the man who is impenitent pays no attention to the disorder and wickedness of sin, which might lead him to repentance.

There are still other sins that might be called sins against the Holy Spirit, e.g., blasphemy against the Most Holy Trinity or against the person of the Holy Spirit, and mortal sins committed out of pure malice.

IRREMISSIBILITY. The Lord declared that he who speaks against the Holy Spirit will be forgiven neither in this world nor in the next (Matt. 12:32). In this statement, our Lord was not referring to all the sins that are now called sins against the Holy Spirit, but only to the sin that had been committed by the Pharisees. Our Lord put it this way, not because God could not or would not pardon the Pharisees' blasphemy against the Holy Spirit, but because He foresaw their stubborn resistance to truth and to grace, even unto death. One who commits a sin against the Holy Spirit puts the salvation of his soul in the greatest possible danger, for he opposes the very goodness that bestows conversion and repentance. Yet the truth that God does not want the death of the sinner but his conversion applies also to him. He can turn back to God, with the help of grace, which is offered in sufficient measure to everyone. *Man.*

SINS OF THOUGHT. *Thought* is used here in the common, broad sense that takes in all internal acts. The fact that someone can sin by thought alone is easy enough to understand, if we think of the interior nature of the moral law and the divine omniscience. Progress in ethical practice and knowledge implies a recognition of the ever-greater importance of the inner aspect of an evaluation of good and evil.

Limiting ourselves to the consideration of sin, we find that the internal element may stand in four different relations to the external: the internal may accompany, precede, follow, or be independent of the external; that is, it may be concomitant, antecedent, consequent, or independent of the act.

Concomitant refers to the internal element of awareness or consent, without which there is, on the part of the subject, no truly sinful act. Taken in this first aspect, the interior element does not constitute a sin of thought distinct from the act; instead, it is absorbed as a constitutive element by the single sin, which will have two aspects, internal and external.

Antecedent applies to an internal act with reference to an external act yet to be performed. In this second hypothesis, it constitutes a sin by itself, which is called a sin of desire (*q.v.*).

Consequent refers to an internal act which has for its object an external act already completed. In this third case also, the internal act constitutes a sin by itelf, which is called a sin of delight (*see* Delight).

It should be pointed out that the concomitance, antecedence or consequence is understood morally, not with material chronological exactness. The internal act usually precedes the external and continues beyond it in such a way that it envelops it completely. But as long as all of this takes place with the usual psychological continuity, moralists do not see any break in concomitance. For antecedence or consequence, they require that there be a notable lapse of time between the internal and external act, or that there be mental activity of such a nature as to break the continuity of the process in the will, such as repentance, retraction, etc.

Independence refers to internal acts that in no way refer to external acts either yet to be performed or already completed. In this sense, one may commit sins of pride, hatred, rash judgment. The sin of thought which is called voluntary complacency (*q.v.*) is of this fourth type, if the object is purely imaginary, never realized nor to be realized by the subject. This may also be of the second or third type, if it is accompanied by a remembrance or sinful delight or deliberation to act in desire. *Gra.*

SINS THAT CRY TO HEAVEN FOR VENGEANCE. Since the sixteenth century, it has been the custom to apply the term "sins that cry to heaven for vengeance" to certain faults that gravely violate the social order, and which Sacred Scripture expressly says cry to heaven for vengeance, i.e., call down God's punishment on those who commit them.

There are four such sins: homicide (Gen. 4:10); sodomy (Gen. 19:13); oppression of widows and orphans (Ex. 22:22 ff.); depriving workers of their just wage (Deut. 24:14 ff.; James 5:4). *Man.*

SLAVERY. In its fundamental notion slavery is an absolute and unconditional dependency of a human being on another's will. The conditions of slaves were different according to the peoples and the times. In the Arian patriarchal family, a slave obeyed his master in the same manner as his wife and children obeyed him; but the former had no right to leave his master, to whom he belonged like a thing or an animal. Among other peoples, a slave was considered more or less a thing or an animal which the master could sell or kill with impunity; by law, the slave had no right, not even to practice religion.

In ancient Rome the condition of slaves was still harsher; and it became worse as domestic religion lost ground and wars and conquests increased. Slaves were considered, at least from the legal standpoint, in the same manner as animals and things. In the era of Humanism, slavery was revived in the lands of the New World by so-called *black slave trade.* There are other modern forms of slavery, such as compulsory labor camps, in use in many a Communist country.

Conceived and practiced as complete subjection of one man to another, a negation of man's juridical personality, or the deprivation of the essential rights of liberty and autonomy of the human person, slavery is against the natural law. For an ethical evaluation of slavery in the different forms in which it has been and still is, however illegally, practiced by some peoples, it is necessary to take into consideration all the circumstances accompanying such practices. A distinction must be made between law and fact; within the scope of the law itself, one must study norms as a whole and try to understand the contradictions which often exist between one norm and the other. Thus, while the slave was denied legal rights in some places and times, not only did he enjoy the right to marry but also the fundamental right of ransom. If, in addition to this, one takes into account certain benefits which the slave had from the very fact of his condition, such as the right to be supported by the master all through life and to relative economic security connected with such support, it may be possible to understand how, in a Christian climate, slavery could survive as long as it did.

For a clear understanding of the Christian doctrine and spirit concerning this subject, the reader owes it to himself to read the Epistle of St. Paul to Philemon. *Pal.*

SLEEP. In its widest biological meaning, *sleep* may be defined as the normal form of rest following activity of an organism, which restores the organism to normal functioning. It usually takes the form of a loss of consciousness among men and animals, yet this periodic rest can be observed in some form in the most simple of organisms, including plants. Man sleeps to avoid or prevent poisoning of his system; during the wakeful and active state, an accumulation of toxins from metabolic processes increases in proportion to the activity of the organism. The state of sleep provides favorable conditions for the elimination of these waste products. In the hypnic state, all rhythmic processes of vegetative life are considerably reduced, with a resultant benefit to the organism.

Generally speaking, sleep reaches maximum intensity during the first or second hour, if one measures by the strength of stimulus necessary to arouse a response; after this point, intensity decreases suddenly by a half or three-quarters until a spontaneous awakening, prior to which a slight increase in intensity is again noted. In a small number of individuals, however, maximum intensity is reached during the second half or phase of sleep. The deeper the sleep, the more restorative are its effects, for in profound slumber organic activities are reduced to such a level as to afford the greatest oppor-

tunity for replenishing one's normal powers.

During sleep, various vital functions undergo more or less profound modifications. In neuro-vegetative or nutritional functions, the following changes are noted in the hypnic phase: the rate of respiration and circulation is lowered (by approximately one-fifth); arterial blood pressure drops; the basal metabolic rate is reduced; sweat secretion is increased and other secretions are decreased; gastro-intestinal contractions diminish somewhat in intensity; on the whole, a relative parasympatheticotonia. All cerebro-spinal functions, correlation or coordination, such as muscle tone, mobility, reflex irritability, and sensitivity diminish. Finally, as sleep becomes deeper, all intellectual or psychic functions are progressively suppressed, until there is complete absence of attention, perception, will, judgment, affectivity, and consciousness, except in the imagination, the seat of man's dream life. The imaginative faculty continues to function in light and moderately deep sleep; it is suspended in profound or heavy slumber, during which dream activity seems to be completely lacking. Sleep disturbed by dreams may be said to be partial or incomplete sleep. Some authors maintain, with Bichat, that all sleep is partial, since the lower *psyche*, consisting of automatic movements, always remains more or less active, giving rise among other things to dream activity. Hence, for such authors, all sleep is accompanied by dream events; the fact that some people seem to dream frequently and others rarely or never is explained, according to these authors, as the result of affective and mnemonic factors. In other words, dreams affect and impress people differently; impressionable individuals are inclined to remember their dreams; non-impressionable persons are unable to recall dream events, even after awakening.

ORIGIN OF SLEEP. In a sleeping person cerebral cortical activity is considerably reduced. According to the school of Pavlov, the hypnic phenomenon is an inhibitory process explained in terms of conditioned reflexes. Through repeated monotonous stimulation, an inhibitory conditioned reflex is set up in a part of the cerebral cortex. This inhibitory process then becomes generalized by spreading to the rest of the cortex and eventually to the entire brain. Inhibition of activity in one part of the brain tends to inhibit the activity of the whole brain.

According to scientific research in clinical experiments, the sleep-controlling center is said to be located in the posterior portion of the hypothalamus and in the adjacent anterior portion of the mesencephalon, at the base of the caudal part of the third ventricle, near the opening of the aqueduct of Sylvius. Most probably (as Salmon maintains), the sleep-controlling center is subject to the influence of particular hormones secreted by the adjacent pituitary gland (*see* Hypophysis).

In the final analysis, it would seem that the phenomenon of sleep consists in a partial, easily reversible inhibition of consciousness and centrifugal and centripetal stimuli, which results from cortical inhibition set up by the sleep-controlling center in the diencephalon-mesencephalon area. This center, stimulated by various, complex chemical products (endocrine, toxic, metabolic), initiates a sleep-inducing action to prevent excessive fatigue and assist the restoration of the organism.

INSOMNIA. Insomnia is a total or partial lack of sleep, a tormenting condition affecting a considerable number of people. Complete insomnia, in which the individual is literally unable to close an eye, is rare and cannot last more than a few nights without causing serious damage to one's health. Ordinarily, insomniacs, though unaware of it, manage a few cat naps between long periods of wakefulness; these partially fulfill the need for rest and sleep. The usual victims of insomnia are neurasthenics, but it also occurs in manic-depressive individuals, or those afflicted with toxic and toxinfective diseases, in persons undergoing moral or physical crises, or suffering from extreme fatigue or over-exhaustion.

The treatment for insomnia naturally varies according to the nature of the cause of the condition. In all events, the elimination of the cause must be the basis of any cure. In the so-called cases of insomnia *sine materia* of neuropathics, before resorting to sedatives or, worse still, hypnotic drugs (opiates, aldehydes, barbiturates, etc.), diligent hygienic treatment should first be tried in conjunction with physical therapy, under the guidance of a capable and conscientious neurologist.

HYPERSOMNIA. Hypersomnia or excessive sleep is distinguished, according to its intensity, into *somnolence* or *lethargy*. The causes of hypersomnia are: organic diseases of the encephalon area, such as epidemic encephalitis, cerebral tumor, meningitis, sleeping-sickness, cerebral anemia, etc.; toxins, either exogenous (due to excessive use of drugs) or endogenous (as in diabetes or uremia); hormonal insufficiencies and the like. Sometimes, as in the aged, diurnal somnolence is accompanied by nocturnal insomnia.

The treatment for hypersomnia will likewise vary according to the different causes that gave rise to the condition.

DYSSOMNIA. Other anomalies of the hypnic function, apart from insomnia and hypersomnia, are included under the generic term *dyssomnia* or *parasomnia*. These qualitative anomalies of the sleep function are: terrifying dreams or nightmares; crises of nocturnal fear or *pavor nocturnus*, characteristic of certain nervous children; *somnambulism*, which, in its widest sense, includes *somniloquy* or the practice of talking in one's sleep; *oneiric delirium*, a confusional state, accompanied by hallucinations, occurring in semi-vigilance; *abnormal movements executed during sleep*, not to be confused with the physiological spasms occurring in sleep, such as described by De Lisi and other authors; *narcolepsy, cataplexy, catalepsy*, and the like.

Such anomalies (*see* Narcolepsy, Somnambulism) are, basically, variations or manifestations of *partial* sleep. In other words, because of certain acquired morbid conditions, such as overeating, slight poisoning, excitability or extreme nervousness, or other pathogenic factors that escape our notice, a dissociation of sleep takes place, whereby the generalized physiological inhibition of the brain of normal sleep is replaced by partial inhibition; i.e., a portion of the cortical area remains active and awake. As a result, the motor functions are dormant and inactive, but the psyche remains awake, as is verified in various forms of cataplexy (*see* Narcolepsy). In other cases, the inhibiting action of sleep is limited to the substratum of consciousness, so that the individual is capable of executing complex motor actions or movements, as in somnambulism (*q.v.*). In still other cases, cortical inhibition is more or less complete, with one sole activity remaining awake or excitable, such as the grinding of teeth and other anomalous movements observed in the state of sleep.

MORAL CONSIDERATIONS. Two phenomena, both occurring in sleep, may be the subject of moral discussion: dreams with sinful content and nocturnal pollutions.

Dreams with sinful content, largely erotic in nature, in themselves lack all moral relevance. Such dreams may be indirectly brought about by insufficient custody of the senses during the day or carelessness in actions and thoughts. In such instances, erotic dreams may serve as useful alarm signals to the practice of modesty of the eyes and control of thoughts. Sometimes, on awakening, an individual will dwell upon the unchaste content of his dream, a practice which obviously is morally imputable.

Apart from this, an erotic dream has no moral value or imputability; this ought to reassure and calm those individuals who fear that impure dreams are incompatible with their firm resolve to practice continence and their desire for total purity.

Nocturnal pollutions are in themselves purely physiological phenomena, natural occurrences, devoid of all moral meaning. The preceding observations apply here also.

It may be useful to add that sleeping in a dorsal recumbent position and the filling of the bladder are both conducive to a congestion of the genital organs and,

hence, to excitation of erotic dreams and pollutions. It is advisable, therefore, to eat and to drink moderately, and to sleep on one or the other side. Sedatives or sleeping pills should be unnecessary except in most exceptional circumstances.

In penal courts, no one is considered responsible for occurrences or deeds committed during sleep; however, in Canon Law (X, 5, 10, 3), imputability for crimes occurring during sleep is sometimes admitted, but only as a responsibility in cause, insofar as the agent, having foreseen a certain effect, did not use the proper means to prevent it. *Riz.*

SLOTH. Sloth is deliberate boredom or disgust with spiritual works, particularly in the performance of duty, because of the sacrifice and effort involved. *Sloth* may also signify a repugnance to grace or the friendship of God, due to the sacrifice and labor necessary to maintain this. Sloth, then, is not to be confused with mere sadness over the inconvenience or effort involved in a virtuous act or with the indeliberate feelings of repugnance toward spiritual things.

The causes or origin of sloth may be due to a variety of factors, which more or less lead to this vice. The proximate cause, however, is most generally self-love, inclining a person to avoid any sacrifice and effort and to seek comfort in sluggishness and indolence.

Sloth not only leads to lack of fervor in one's actions and the minimizing of imperfections and venial sins, but also to the neglect of grave duties. It may also lead to despair of salvation. A slothful person has an aversion toward individuals who, by word or example, seek to promote good; at times he reaches a point where he wishes that spiritual values did not exist or that he had no knowledge thereof. He comes to detest all things spiritual and to deny his very baptismal vows. Finally, sloth inclines one to seek consolation in forbidden pleasures.

General sloth is sinful. If it causes the neglect of a grave duty or constitutes a grave danger of neglecting a serious duty, it becomes gravely sinful. Culpable transgressions occasioned by sloth do not, however, constitute as many sins numerically distinct from sloth as there are transgressions, but, from a moral standpoint, they form one sin with sloth. As a specific vice, sloth is a mortal sin by its very nature, since it is opposed to divine charity; subjectively, however, the sin may be venial, due to lack of full consent on the part of the will.

Sloth can be conquered by thinking frequently about the real purpose of life and the examples of Christ and the saints; by laying bare one's conscience to one's confessor and humbly accepting his counsels; by frequently making an accurate examination of one's conduct; by practicing mortification in those very things in which one is more slothful. *Man.*

SOBRIETY. Sobriety refers to the maintenance of a proper degree of moderation in pleasurable matters; it refers, in the strict sense, to moderation in the use of alcoholic beverages. This form of moderation is a special safeguard of the dignity of man as a human being and a Christian, and is an aspect of the virtue of temperance. The use of alcoholic beverages is not evil in itself, but it demands moderation, for such drinks in excess deprive man of the use of reason. Saint Paul speaks of its proper use in writing to his disciple Timothy: "Stop drinking water only, but use a little wine for thy stomach's sake and thy frequent infirmities" (I Tim. 5:23).

In some cases, complete voluntary abstinence from alcoholic beverages is praiseworthy, if done in a spirit of mortification or good example, for it is sometimes necessary to avoid excesses if one has inherited a strong inclination to drinking or contracted a habit by excessive drinking.

A person may sin against sobriety by excess, that is, going beyond the proper limits in the use of alcohol (*see* Gluttony), or by defect, in an unreasonable opposition to any use of alcohol.

Connected Questions. There is an analogy between the use of alcoholic beverages and narcotic drugs (*q.v.*), such as morphine, cocaine, or opium. Their use is not absolutely evil in itself, but it may easily become wrong, because of the danger of contracting an irresistible habit, of serious harm to health, and of rendering oneself unfit for useful or productive work. The use of drugs for medical purposes is licit as long as necessary precautions are taken.

The consequences of immoderate use of alcoholic beverages are serious for the drinker and his family (*see* Alcoholism). The improper use of drugs produces more fearful consequences, for it can quickly create a need so strong that the addict may not hesitate to commit crimes in order to obtain drugs. A gradual withdrawal through reduction of the amount of drugs taken by a narcotic addict is practically the only treatment that can lead to a cure. *Man.*

SOCIALIZATION. Originally, socialization meant striving for a socialist economic system. Socialists are distinguished into *revisionists* or *reformers*, who advocate a natural evolution of the economy over a long period of time, and *revolutionaries*, who advocate a change in the economic system by the use of force. The latter advocate suppression of private property and capitalistic exploitation, and the adoption of a general supply center in place of a market for the needs of the nation. They seek to place the entire economy in the hands of government agencies charged with the distribution of the products according to needs. There is no essential difference between the two schools; both tend toward the same end: the abolition of private property and the realization of a socialist economy. The difference lies in the manner of bringing this about.

On the basis of various theoretical structures, there is a variety of socializations. One would not do away with private property but would transfer it from present owners to the workers. This form of socialism has now lost all support. Another would make business the property of the local community, which represents the unit of socialized economy. Still another, nationalization or State ownership, makes firms the property of the State, which will then operate them. It should be observed that the word *nationalization* recurs frequently and is applied to various types of socialization. Finally, *socialization*, a broader concept than nationalization, is distinguished into partial or total socialization, according to whether the aim is to suppress private property and private initiative altogether or to remove certain enterprises from the private domain in order to protect the interests of the individual.

On the basis of the manner in which socialized enterprises are administered, one can distinguish: (1) *cooperative socialization*, which is achieved through cooperative emancipation from capital; (2) *economic democratization*, which regards production leaders as indispensable but, in the interest of the workers, makes their activities subject to higher organs of the national economy.

Expropriation and Compensation. The State and the community, which were once rich, were deprived of their possessions in the era of economic liberalism. The State became poor, a debtor, dependent on taxes. The tendency by the State to reacquire the economic position it once had is an anti-liberal reaction but not necessarily socialism. The assertion that only private ownership is justified is just as wrong as that which states that only collective or State ownership is justified. The State has a right to ownership, but this does not mean that it can do away with private ownership in unjustified expropriation (*hot socialization*) or weight it down with such heavy taxes that it cannot survive (*cold socialization*). There is also a kind of *veiled socialization* that takes place, e.g., when the State or a community takes over housing and freely disposes of it.

With respect to the form of socialization called nationalization, it should be noted that a reasonable expropriation, especially if demanded by the actual social and economic conditions of a nation, is justified from the standpoint of Christian social doctrine, whose firm guiding principle is the common good with due respect for private ownership and its social function.

Socialist Socialization. Socialists, on the other hand, proceeding from an *a priori* principle laid down a century ago, proclaim that expropriation and socialization are the objectives of a socialist economic order, without respect for the actual conditions or requirements of the common good. A total socialization, proclaimed by the socialists a century ago, began to gain ground following the First World War when the socialists came to share political authority in the various democratic countries and began to push socialization of railroads, mines, and other things. More moderate from that time on, they seem satisfied with a gradual socialization which does not threaten the economic life of a country, though they still retain their objective of total socialization. Socialization is enhanced by the evolution of an economy of concentration and monopoly in recent times and by the ever-increasing intervention of the State in economic life, especially during the last great depression and in the pre- and post-war periods. The general tendency has been in the direction of restriction of private ownership; hence, it is no surprise if, within the limits of needed reforms, on the question of ownership the economic reforms advocated by the Catholic social school are in agreement in some practical points with the reforms advocated by the socialist school. Despite this, the differences between the two are basic. For Catholics, private ownership stands as the basis of the social order and gives way to socialization only if the common good requires it. The socialists, on the other hand, do not admit any social function in private ownership; in fact, they strive to do away with it. They do not ask if they have any right to expropriate or abolish private property, but only whether certain enterprises are ripe for socialization and it is wise to do so. For them total socialization must necessarily follow upon partial socialization. The same is true of *cold socialization*, the favorite method for dealing with recalcitrants.

Socialists claim that socialization makes *society* the owner of the means of production. The phrase has a double meaning, because the fact of the matter is that a socialized economy will eventually be organized and directed by a single individual or economic czar in whose hands will be concentrated vast power, so that everything and everyone will, to some degree or other, be dependent on him.

Furthermore, if private property is suppressed, the strongest guarantee of personal, social, and cultural liberties disappears with it.

SOCIALIZATION AND THE ECONOMY. The immediate task of providing for the well-being of the individual does not belong to society but to the individual himself. The State must guarantee the common good so that every citizen may live in freedom by the fruit of his work. Through the juridical system, especially dealing with ownership, the State must direct, protect, and watch over the common good and put down disorders and abuses. It must see to it that at least the basic needs of food, lodging, and clothing are not lacking, and in case of extreme need, it must provide what is needed. The State may participate in the economic life, but it is an injustice to inject itself into every aspect of the economic life of a country. Socialization is justified only if it is demanded by the common good, as an exceptional and extreme measure ultimately intended to put new life and vigor back into healthy private initiative. The socialization of a particular sector of the economy can be accepted: (a) if production fails to meet the interests and needs of the people; (b) if the financial condition of the State is such that it must be transferred to the State; (c) if, in general, the common good requires it.

In conclusion, total socialization and totalitarian State economy, as advocated and practiced by communists and left-wing socialists, must be rejected as a denial of man's natural rights which occasions a new and more powerful kind of bureaucracy and an aristocracy of the proletariat. At the same time, one also must reject the doctrine and practice of economic conservatism that sees un-bridled competition as a necessary cause of the formation of private capitalistic monopolies. Socialization, dictated by reasons of economic necessity, bent on protecting small property owners, increasing healthy ownership, and making man economically, politically and socially free, is certainly a sound doctrine both from the economic and the moral point of view (*See* Economy, Planned). *Per.*

SOCIAL WEEKS. These are conventions or seminars at which topics of a social nature are discussed. They represent the greatest expression of social studies by Catholics, principally in Italy, Belgium and France. The procedure employed at these conventions is to select a basic topic—labor, profession, freedom, school, business enterprise—and to develop it systematically in a series of discussions. The aim is to examine historical situations and actual problems in the light of Christian principles, with a view to offering solutions and outlining orientations in the various fields of social endeavor.

In the last fifty years these social weeks have exercised a notable orientative influence on organized groups of militant Catholics. *Pav.*

SOCIAL WORK. *See* Social Worker.

SOCIAL WORKER. Organized social work has undergone rapid development in recent years, especially in English-speaking countries. Individuals engaged in the field of social service, called social workers, strive to promote social welfare by offering guidance, direction, and service to persons in need of assistance. In England and, even more so, in the United States, the particular aim of social service is to find direct and immediate solutions for specific and ordinary problems of life, to teach methods of self-control and to help people to help themselves, a highly endorsed formula among the British and Americans.

The activities of social workers are usually divided into three general categories: *case work* (to solve the individual problems of social maladjustment); *group work* (to solve the particular problems of special groups); and *community organization* (to promote cultural and recreational programs and other types of activity on a community level). With the gradual extension of social service to such different fields as labor, school, mental hygiene, child guidance, domestic adjustments, vocational rehabilitation, etc., the number of social workers has steadily increased. In the United States alone there are today more than forty schools offering college courses in social work to members of both sexes.

It is clear that organized social service, as exercised in the widely different spheres of modern social life, is a highly important moral activity. Along with doctors and nurses, teachers and judges, employers and business leaders, social workers are in a position to make positive and worthwhile contributions to the material and spiritual welfare of mankind.

In its higher and nobler phases, social service may be considered a form of apostolate closely allied to the charitable activities of the Church, for by counseling the weak and the doubtful, instructing the ignorant, consoling the afflicted, visiting the sick, and the like, they carry out the principal *works of mercy*. In view of the above, it would seem that social work requires a special vocation. Some of the requisites of a social worker are the ability to cope with problems of a wide variety, an understanding of particular situations and environments, psychological insight into human nature, the readiness and facility for communication, an ability to win the confidence of others. Moreover, a social worker is required to be kind, sympathetic, understanding, tolerant, and self-sacrificing. Only such Christian qualities and virtues can raise the activities of a social worker to the high level of a moral apostolate. Without such qualities, social work becomes purely naturalistic and materialistic, solely concerned with bodily welfare and temporal happiness.

Furthermore, a social worker should look upon religion as a valuable aid to social service, not merely in the sense that it provides a subjective and psychological uplift in the face of problems and suffering, but in the sense that it is the most important objective factor in shaping character. By giving religion the proper place in social service, human life acquires a higher meaning and the human person takes on a higher dignity and worth. At the same time, the social worker should supernaturalize the practice of his or her charitable and benevolent activities. *Riz.*

SOCIETY. Catholic authors do not agree completely on the nature of society, but are unanimous in its essential points. They deny that society exists of itself and for itself, as something completely transcendent with respect to the individuals. But they admit that society is not simply the sum total of these individuals who are its members.

This double affirmation is of capital importance. This separates the Catholic position from individualist or totalitarian systems. Individualists deprive society of its proper reality. Totalitarians, instead, make society an absolute. Catholic teaching, midway between these extremes, states that society is a new reality with respect to individuals; it is ontologically distinct, with its own unity of order. At the same time, society in its form of being is essentially relative, for it exists only in the persons who comprise it.

Since the function of society is the common good, it necessarily carries with it prerogatives inherent to the common good. By virtue of its purpose, it aims at a transcendent good, and can demand sacrifices of personal advantages from particular individuals. Since individuals are members of a social body, the good of the whole precedes the good of its parts.

On the other hand, if the destiny of man requires a good that is strictly individual, with an absolute value demanding full personal freedom, then society must respect and favor, as far as possible and without restrictions, the rights of the individual in seeking the attainment of this good. For if he should be prevented from attaining it, he would no longer serve the good of human nature. Society must maintain this attitude with respect to the eternal and supernatural destiny of the individual. The transcendent value of the human person must be strictly sustained in this respect; the power of society, therefore, is limited.

On the level of temporal activities and goals, the situation is different: the hierarchy of values in this order is reversed. It remains true, however, in this area as well that society must be governed in its attitudes by the strictly personal rights and aims of individuals. Thus the destiny of the human person involves, besides the pursuit of strictly individual goods, the search for an essentially personal social and common good for all men; this common good demands service of the whole community of individuals and of the individual person for the common welfare of the community.

Purpose. The goal of society is the happiness of the community and each individual member of society, insofar as they are members of this community. Certain particular goals, necessary for the full development of the individual, can be obtained only by the cooperation of all in society.

The actual producers of the common good are the members of the community, joined together in a union of wills and purposes toward one and the same goal. This purpose sets in motion the physical and spiritual energies of the members of the community, who contribute to the common welfare.

The incentive toward solidarity is brought about by the compelling needs of human life, which each seeks to satisfy by creating conditions favorable to this. The resultant good is a collective benefit which belongs to each and every individual member; he possesses an inalienable and personal right to enjoy this to the extent that he assisted in creating it.

On the basis of these principles, it is clear that society is an orderly collection of individuals striving for definite common goals to be attained by the use of common means. Four elements comprise

a society: (1) a common end; (2) plurality of individuals; (3) the necessary means to the end; (4) unity under authority. Of these elements, the common end is most important, for it determines the nature of the society, as temporal or spiritual, private or public, etc.; its power or right to means in a hierarchy of values; and the relationship of the society to other societies.

The juridical status of a society depends on its purpose. It may be *free* or *necessary*; in a free society its subjects are free to join or not; a necessary society is one which the members are obliged to join either by natural necessity or by the positive will of God. A society is *perfect*, if it pursues a perfect end with full rights in its own order. An *imperfect* society pursues an imperfect end, which is incomplete and limited in its rights and obligations, as is any human goal.

The special obligations of society to its members consist mainly in that of distributive justice or commutative justice: to render to each member his due, according to equitable proportion. The rights of society are summarized as the obligations which each member has in legal justice to the society. *Pal.*

SOCIETY OF ST. VINCENT DE PAUL. HISTORICAL BACKGROUND. This group was founded in 1833 by a group of young Catholic students at the Sorbonne in Paris, under the leadership of Frédéric Ozanam, a citizen of Lyons, who was born in Milan, in 1813. He died at Marseilles in 1853, at the age of forty. Endowed with a keen intellect and ardent spirit, Ozanam was a professor at the Sorbonne who won recognition for his writings on Medieval Christianity, Dante, the Franciscan poets, etc. A group of students sought, by their participation in conferences and discussions on history, to defend the value of Christianity and the healthy influence of the Church against those who believed that the Church had outlived its usefulness. Ozanam and his companions organized a society to visit poor families and minister to their needs. Thus originated the first *Conference of Charity*, later called

Society of St. Vincent de Paul, which is spread over the Christian world, with 20,000 Conferences today.

The rule of the Society, published in 1836 and still in force, defines the religious character of the organization, whose primary end is the sanctification of the members through charitable service. The fundamental, primary object remains that of visiting poor and needy families weekly and assisting them by every possible means. The rule states that "no work of mercy should be regarded as foreign to the spirit of the Society." This clause gives the widest latitude to the selection of works in which members may engage; in fact, the organization has from the beginning dedicated itself to a wide variety of charitable activities. Religious and social patronage of young workers, care of the sick, visitation of prisoners, custody of paroled youths, care of homeless boys, clubs for boys are some of these works.

So rapid was the growth of the Society that in 1852 Ozanam was able to report the existence of more than 800 Conferences throughout France and other European countries. The formula of Vincentian charity has demonstrated adaptability to all conditions, times, and places.

The Society also has a feminine counterpart. The first group was established in 1856 at Bologna, where general headquarters are still maintained. This group, though distinct from the men's association, has the same rule with the specific purpose of practicing charitable works among needy girls and women. The group maintains close collaboration with the General Council of the men's association, and in recent years both men and women have joined efforts in promoting charitable activities.

Although the Conferences of St. Vincent de Paul have never sought nor received formal canonical erection in accordance with the norms of Canon 686, par. 1, they are not lay associations. Their purpose is the exercise of charity according to the spirit of the Church. The Church praises and recommends the organization, granting special indulgences to all active members and assigns a Car-

dinal Protector for the Society. Moreover, the individual Conferences are each assigned a chaplain. All this clearly implies ecclesiastical approbation.

STRUCTURE. The Society of St. Vincent de Paul is a union of charitable associations called Conferences; each Conference has a president and exercises autonomy regarding its internal activity. Each Conference takes its name from the particular place where it is established; if several Conferences exist in the same locality, each assumes the name of a different saint or blessed, thereby distinguishing it from the other units. All the Conferences of the same territory are united into a particular council, subordinate to a central or superior council, usually on a diocesan level and, in some instances, on a national level. Finally, the general direction of the entire society is exercised by the General Council, with headquarters in Paris, which possesses the right to approve the aggregation of individual Conferences, upon recommendation of the respective superior council, if there be one. Aggregation is necessary in order to share the spiritual indulgences granted to the Society. Anyone wishing to join the Society need simply contact the president of a local Conference.

The Conferences hold weekly meetings, in which an account is given of the poor families visited, the conditions found therein and the reasons for recommending aid, followed by a discussion of ways and means to provide actual relief for these indigent families on future visits. The meetings are opened and closed with prayer, and in the course of the meeting a short selection is read from some spiritual treatise. Before the closing prayer, a secret collection is taken up among the members present, with the proceeds going into the treasury. While the traditional method of relief remains that of providing the necessities of life, the general council recognizes that modern conditions require more specialized forms of aid; hence, it recommends the integration of *charitable relief* with *personal service.*

Besides active members, the Society

has corresponding and honorary members. Corresponding members are those who changed residence and are unable to find a local Conference in a new neighborhood. They remain united with their original Conference by means of correspondence, prayer, contributions or personal service to the cause of charity. Honorary members do not take part in ordinary meetings but may be invited to extraordinary sessions. They are required to make an annual contribution to the local Conference. Honorary members become affiliated to the Society in the same manner as ordinary members. A Conference may also have simple subscribers or benefactors, who help to promote the charitable work of the organization through prayer and contributions. Strictly speaking, these latter do not form part of the Society but share in some of its spiritual benefits. *Baro.*

SODOMY. Sodomy, a sin committed by the inhabitants of Sodom (Gen. 19), in the proper sense, is copulation between persons of the same sex. Sexual acts that do not involve intercourse are reducible to this type of sin, unless they are committed simply for the purpose of stirring up sexual pleasure, because they involve affection for the wrong sex. In an improper sense, *sodomy* is applied to intercourse between persons of different sexes if performed in an unnatural manner.

Sodomy, in the proper sense, is called *Lesbianism* or *Sapphic love* if it occurs between women; if children are involved (in which case, the element of violence often enters), it is called *pederasty*. Homosexuals have an almost innate tendency to this sin, for, by reason of a perversion of their natural instincts, they have no interest in the opposite sex and find sexual pleasure only with persons of the same sex (*see* Perversion, sexual).

Sodomy is an abominable sin (Gen. 13:13; Lev. 18:22; 20:13; Rom. 1:26–27; I Cor. 6:9; I Tim. 1:10). It is intrinsically opposed to the nature and primary end of the sexual act. As lust contrary to nature, it is a specifically different sin from pollution (Prop. 24, condemned by Alexander VII, Decree of Sept. 24, 1665). *Dam.*

SOLICITATION. Solicitation, a form of seduction, in a strict sense means a tempting or inducement of another to improper or sinful acts against the virtue of purity. Described as a form of art to lead another to sinful acts, solicitation may occur by means of explicit words, counsel, promises, signs or any other method that reveals the evil intention of the solicitor. In a broad sense, it applies to any attempt to lead another into evil; in this article it is synonymous with seduction.

THE CRIME OF SOLICITATION. In order to safeguard the sanctity of the sacrament of penance, the Church has attached very severe penalties to the crime of solicitation (Cans. 894, 904, 2363, 2368). This crime refers to any act by which a confessor in the sacrament of penance either induces a penitent to sin seriously against chastity or accepts the inducements of a penitent against chastity (Can. 904). Thus, solicitation is twofold: active or passive.

The penalties for the commission of solicitation in confession range from suspension of the right to celebrate Mass and hear confessions to the loss of all benefices, offices, and rights; from the loss of active and passive voice to deposition and degradation.

OBLIGATION OF DENUNCIATION. The Church, the jealous guardian of souls and the holy sacraments, imposes a serious obligation upon a penitent who has been a victim of solicitation in confession to denounce to the proper ecclesiastical authority, either the Holy Office or the local Ordinary, any confessor who is guilty of solicitation in confession. This denunciation must take place within one month of the time of the actual solicitation. The reason for this is not merely to correct the offender but to prevent repeated offenses, thereby safeguarding the proper administration of the sacraments and the salvation of souls. A penitent who has been solicited in confession incurs the penalty of excommunication if he fails to denounce the guilty priest within one month; this excommunication cannot be absolved until he fulfills his obligation of denunciation.

FALSE DENUNCIATION. The Church is severe with a confessor who has been guilty of solicitation in confession; it is no less severe with a penitent who, because of jealousy, bitterness, idle gossip, or twisted interpretations, dares to accuse a priest falsely of solicitation in confession. One guilty of false denunciation of solicitation in confession incurs excommunication especially reserved to the Holy See. Such a person cannot be absolved, even at the moment of death, without a previous formal retraction of the false denunciation (Can. 2363). In addition, a false denunciation of this kind is the only sin in itself (*ratione sui*) reserved to the Holy See (Can. 894). *Tar.*

SOMNAMBULISM. Considering its etymological derivation (Latin *somnus*—sleep; *ambulo*—walk), *somnambulism* should, strictly speaking, signify that particular condition of dyssomnia in which a subject walks while in sleep. In its wider acceptance, however, it refers to the episodic unfolding, during sleep, of automatic activities, to such an extent that the subject performs functions similar to those performed during the waking state, such as rising from bed, talking, taking steps, reading, writing, and the like. Often the somnambulist, despite obfuscation of consciousness, demonstrates remarkable motor coordination and an unusual acuity of specific senses.

CAUSES. Somnambulistic episodes seem to occur when oneiric mental representations attain such a degree of intensity as to act upon the motor centers of speech, walking, etc., thereby calling these centers into action.

Somnambulism is usually observed in hysterical or neuropathic individuals endowed with a vivid imagination. It occurs more frequently in the infancy-childhood stage, more often in the female than in the male. It is sparked by some vivid daytime emotional experience. At times, it is observed in epileptics (*q.v.*), in whom it constitutes an epileptic equivalent, characterized by the violence of its manifestations, by a lack of response to questions asked during the course of the crisis, and by a sudden awakening. At other times, it is a symptom of narcolepsy (*q.v.*). Finally, somnambulism may occur in states of induced hypnosis (*q.v.*), where its cessation is brought about by the same stimuli (breathing on the face, and the like) that interrupt the hypnotic state.

A somnambulist performs his automatic movements with eyes wide open and staring fixedly, with the pupils generally contracted. While walking, he is careful enough to avoid obstacles, but proceeds with a rigidity that resembles that of an automaton. He is frequently capable of answering questions from bystanders, is highly suggestible, as if in a state of artificial hypnosis. Upon awakening, he has no recollection of anything that he may have done in his sleep.

THERAPEUTIC COROLLARIES. During an actual crisis, it is better to refrain from any attempt to awaken a somnambulist. If he must be awakened because of the perilous situation in which he is involved, this should be done cautiously and tenderly and, if possible, in such a way that the subject, upon awakening, will not be aware of the danger which existed. In the treatment of somnambulism, a physician must strive to remove the habitual morbid condition (hysteria, neurasthenia, epilepsy, etc.) rather than concentrate on the symptoms.

MORAL EVALUATION. From a moral standpoint, an individual is absolutely irresponsible for anything committed during a somnambulistic crisis. However, there may be indirect imputability, insofar as the agent may have been responsible in cause. The same applies in the field of Canon Law (Can. 2201, par. 1, 3). Moreover, considering the high susceptibility and suggestibility of somnambulists, onlookers or bystanders must avoid suggesting improper, injurious, or dangerous actions, for it is never permissible to take advantage of unconscious patients in any way at all, especially since suggestions and commands only serve to worsen the somnambulistic crises and to increase the suggestibility of the individual, thus aggravating the disease of which somnambulism is but a manifestation. *Riz.*

SOUL. *See* Body and soul; Psyche, Pathology of; Psychology.

SOURCES OF MORALITY. *See* Human Act.

SOURCES OF MORAL THEOLOGY. REVELATION AND REASON. Moral theology, as a practical science of human behavior in the supernatural order, rests fundamentally on divine *Revelation*, which theology considers its object (*obiectum formale quo*).

The doctrinal sources of moral theology are Holy Scripture and Tradition (primary source), of which the Church is guardian and interpreter. In this, moral theology does not differ from dogmatic theology; like the latter, it is a true science, though not autonomous, insofar as it is subordinated to the science of God, from which it derives indirect evidence of its principles.

Thus, for the proper understanding of theology, it is necessary to bear in mind that its task is not only to demonstrate the content of Revelation, but also to increase its understanding through theological speculation, and to draw from it all that the human mind is capable of deriving from it. This, of course, does not mean a rationalizing of theology, because, even if man's reason deduces from Revelation what is virtually contained in it, it operates always under the light of Revelation. As a matter of fact, commencing from its own principles but always moving under the leadership and control of the magisterial authority of the Church, reason can also complete the analysis and scientific exposition of the data of Revelation, when reason defends the data of Revelation against difficulties.

What is true of theology in general applies in a particular manner and to a greater degree to moral theology, for, as a science governing human actions in the supernatural order, it necessarily contains all those norms that are to be observed, including the entire natural law, at least implicitly confirmed by Revelation itself.

It is disputed among theologians whether it is sufficient for one to consider all natural laws as implicitly revealed. But, in view of the task that human reason is expected to exercise in demonstrating and examining such laws, its principles may, also on this ground, be considered as a subordinate and secondary source of moral theology.

THE TEACHING AUTHORITY OF THE CHURCH. It may be asked whether the teaching authority of the Church is to be held as only a criterion and guide for the interpretation of sources or as one of the very sources of moral theology. In this respect, one must bear in mind the specific nature of moral theology as a practical science concerning human actions and the equally practical mission of the Church, which is to guide and to help man reach his supernatural end, by pointing out to him with certainty the path to follow. The teaching authority of the Church, insofar as it declares in an authentic and authoritative manner all that is contained in the law (the natural law included) and that which by virtue of the same law one must necessarily do, must be considered as a positive source of morality, and not a mere negative criterion of a knowledge of truth. *Pal.*

SPIRITUALISM. *Spiritualism* is a particular interpretation of certain parapsychic phenomena allegedly produced by the souls of the dead (*see* Metapsychology); it also refers to the doctrine and practice of summoning the souls of the dead.

The historical origins of spiritualism go back to 1847, when an 11-year-old girl named Kate Fox, who lived with her family in a house near New York, heard a strange *rapping* on the wall and observed other unusual phenomena. She began to think that this might be the work of a *disembodied spirit* of some dead person, and thought of asking the invisible source of the raps to rap a definite number of times to confirm her notion. Her wish was granted. This was the beginning of a series of conversations between the girl and some of her acquaintances and the *spirit*, who answered, using the conventional alphabet, by raps on the wall, and later on by striking the floor with the foot of a table. A few years later, the Fox family moved to England, but the use of *talking* or *self-moving tables* had already spread very quickly in America.

The widespread and enduring vogue of spiritualism is best explained on the basis of sentimental reasons. In most cases, the people involved are indifferent or negligent about religion, and yet are eager to have a material proof of the immortality of the soul, or to get in touch in a tangible way with their dead loved ones without having to meet the demands and obligations of a religion based on dogma.

A. Kardeck, who drew up the main lines that have guided spiritualism since 1857, maintained, in imitation of Hellenistic Neo-Platonism, that man is made up of a physical *body* that dissolves at death, an indestructible *spirit* capable of further perfection, and a *perispirit* (or fluid body) that binds the spirit to the body during life and remains attached to the spirit after death. This *perispirit* makes possible displays of paranormal activities on the part of living people, the phenomena of a physical nature produced by mediums and communication between the living and the dead. From that time on, an enormous pseudo-scientific literature based on these communications of mediums has supplied ample, detailed, and completely unproven information on the disembodiment of spirits, and on their existence in the world beyond, their gradual perfection in various *spheres* of the suprasensible universe, and the reasons that prompt spirits to come back to the living to help or protect them.

INTERPRETATIONS. Although the spiritualistic theory has been losing ground steadily among students of *metapsychology* and is replaced more and more by naturalistic psychological theories, it still has strong supporters who defend their position. They stress the fact that,

thus far, there is no satisfactory scientific explanation of these phenomena, which fit very easily, as they claim, into the spiritualist theory.

Naturalists reply that, since metapsychological experimental research is still lacking scientific certainty, it would be harmful to depend on unsubstantiated suppositions which might cause an abandonment of scientific work of research. Since some types of paranormal phenomena, at one time explained only on the basis of a spiritualistic notion, are now explained, as even spiritualists admit, on a naturalistic basis, it would seem logical to infer that other phenomena could be explained in the same way.

In short, the controversy involving the spiritualistic theory of parapsychological phenomena still continues.

ETHICAL PROBLEMS. As pointed out at greater length in the article on Metapsychology, Catholics are fully agreed that the paranormal phenomena that the spiritualists believe to be the work of disembodied spirits are due to interventions of the devil, whenever one can exclude fraud and deception or no clear explanation in the scientific order can be found for each individual phenomenon. There have been a few Catholics who have admitted the possibility of the intervention of other beings, of whose existence we would not otherwise be aware, but these are isolated voices and their theory has no solid foundation.

The Church has repeatedly spoken against spiritualistic practices and warned the faithful against them by denouncing the danger they pose for the health of soul and mind. In this latter regard, we can state that spiritualistic sessions, even those carried on just for pleasure, as a form of game, are harmful to mental health, especially if some of those taking part in them are lacking in mental balance.

Finally, spiritualism is never lawful, not even as a means of therapy. Worcester and other psychiatrists, whom Scremin cites, are supposed to have cured various cases of mental illness in this way. This is understandable if one considers the intense emotional shocks in spiritualistic and pseudo-spiritualistic seances and the further possible beneficial effects of these on psychoneurotic individuals. Nevertheless, this system is to be condemned, even if the doctor is merely pretending and stages a fake seance, which excludes diabolical intervention.

It is never proper nor justifiable to recur to deceit and trickery to achieve a result that is good and useful in itself, for psychiatry now possesses other shock therapeutic methods that are quite effective, lawful and advisable. It is absolutely objectionable to recur to spiritualism, that is, to summon a departed soul, even to effect a cure, because the souls of the departed cannot enter into communication with the living on this earth simply by being called by a *medium*, but only by special divine permission which may not be sought in this way. It is quite possible that diabolical spirits rather than souls may respond to spiritualistic evocations.

On the negative side of spiritualism, one may add the disastrous effects that this practice is liable to produce on the religious and moral sentiments of those who take part in it.

All of this fully explains and justifies the stand that the Church has taken in this matter. As late as 1917, a decree was issued by ecclesiastical authorities forbidding this: "It is not lawful . . . to take part in spiritualistic seances, whether through a *medium* or without one" (AAS: 9 [1917], 268). *Riz.*

SPIRITUALITY, SCHOOLS OF. The term *schools of spirituality*, of rather recent coinage, is applied to the various training procedures in Christian perfection.

The ultimate goal of each school is identical, and so are the basic means for its attainment. In fact, the call to perfection and its attainment depend on God's giving Himself to man, directly or through His divine Son, and on man's generous and constant cooperation with grace and his consequent growth in charity.

But though the attainment of perfection is basically the same, yet numerous forms vary in their accidental aspects. Proof of this is the large number of religious families or congregations, from contemplative orders to groups engaged in active apostolic and charitable works.

Aside from external differences, really superficial, each of these various religious groups has a different way of employing the means for attaining interior perfection. The relative importance assigned to each means or the preference for one or other of the many ways determines which means may be used more profitably. Various schools lay stress on the various attitudes of the soul in its relationship with God and in its imitation of this or that saint as a model of spiritual life.

The origin of the various schools of spirituality may be considered from these three points of view: *historical*, i.e., the existence and development of the various types of schools; *theoretical*, i.e., the cause of diversity in schools; *practical*, i.e., one's personal attitude with respect to the origin, development, and variety of such schools.

Leaving the last question aside, since it is a practical question involving the direction of souls, the existence of various schools from an historical and doctrinal point of view is not due to various schools of speculative theology, as one might think, but to the fact that God has raised up various champions of holiness at different times, each with a distinct spiritual individuality, corresponding to the times, places, and purposes intended by Divine Providence. Thus, to the rise of these schools, which under the action of God and at a particular moment come to face new tasks and to answer new needs, a major contribution is made both by a founder's personal experience of the interior life and by the results attained in the spiritual formation of the first followers, who set a pattern to be imitated by many other individuals in their quest for spiritual perfection.

Subsequently, the theologians came with analyses and inquiries to furnish a doctrinal basis to the characteristics particular to each school. Mutual contacts between the various schools, new experiences registered, and new champions of holiness add new effectiveness to the vitality of the various schools while still remaining loyal to the original pattern of holiness.

Thus there arose, in a more or less chronological order, the *Augustinian, Benedictine, Dominican, Franciscan, Jesuit, Carmelite, Berullian* schools, the school of *St. Alphonsus Liguori,* and, finally, the school of present-day secular institutes (*q.v.*).

The variety of schools of spirituality is thus explained on the basis of the differences found in human beings, in their inclinations, and in the fact that Christian perfection is so lofty an ideal that it permits various degrees of participation.

In general, it is a mistake to try to reduce the characteristics of each school to an over-simplified outline. Since each is Catholic, each implicitly contains all that Jesus taught as necessary or useful to Christian perfection. For this reason, even though one school may stress this or that particular truth or virtue, e.g., Franciscans stress poverty, still no school will exclude the other truths and virtues.

This variety emphasizes the wondrous richness of the Gospel and the divine life of the Church shining forth in unlimited possibilities of good and of grace, all admirable, indeed. This explains also the union and the mutual esteem existing between the various spiritual families, for, despite their differences, they glorify harmony in unity (John 17:22 ff.).

Obviously, if one belongs to a religious family that has its own school of spirituality, he should follow that school, patterning his life on the principles it recommends.

In directing others, it is wise, if they have shown no particular preference, to guide them according to the general principles of ascetical and mystical theology, contained in the ordinary teaching of the Church. But if one inclines to a particular school, he should be directed in the footsteps of the safest and most authoritative masters of the particular school to which he inclines. *Pal.*

SPIRITUAL READING. Spiritual reading is reading directed to knowledge of the supernatural life. If done in the proper manner, spiritual reading is an effective means of sanctification. Every Christian should do some spiritual reading each day, such as a page of Holy Scripture or a chapter of *The Imitation of Christ.* Spiritual reading is ordinarily prescribed by rule for all religious.

Among the books used for spiritual reading, Holy Scripture is the best, especially the Holy Gospels, the Acts of the Apostles, and the Epistles. The books of the Old Testament make useful reading if preceded by a certain preparation, especially in the matter of the historical books. Initiates will find in these books pages of marvelous beauty; and if the weakness of God's servants is often related together with their good works, it is to remind us of human weakness and to show forth divine mercy.

Besides Holy Scripture, the spiritual works of the saints make useful reading, for example the works of St. Augustine, St. Jerome, St. Leo, St. Gregory the Great, St. Basil, St. John Chrysostom, St. Anselm, St. Bernard, St. Albert the Great, St. Thomas, St. Bonaventure, St. Catherine of Siena and many others, such as *The Imitation of Christ.* Among the ascetical works of the more modern saints must be mentioned those of St. Ignatius, St. Teresa of Avila, St. John of the Cross, the Ven. Blosius, St. Francis de Sales (*Introduction to the Devout Life, Treatise on the Love of God*), St. Grignion de Montfort (*Treatise on True Devotion to the Blessed Virgin, The Secret of Mary, Circular Letters to the Friends of the Cross*), St. Alphonsus Liguori (ascetical works), St. John Eudes (*The Life and Reign of Jesus in the Christian Soul, The Admirable Heart of the Mother of God*), St. Thérèse of the Child Jesus (*The Story of a Soul, Letters* and *Poems*).

Side by side with the spiritual works of those who have been canonized or beatified by the Church, there are many others that can be read with great spiritual profit.

To the reading of books on spiritual

doctrine it is useful to add the lives of the saints. In these lives we see how men and women, in the midst of difficulties similar to ours and often much greater, rose to a high degree of perfection. The actual examples of the saints generally move to the practice of virtue more than the exposition of high spiritual doctrine.

METHOD. In order to profit by spiritual reading, one must read, not with a critical spirit, for curiosity or vanity or conversation on spiritual subjects, but with a profound spirit of faith and the sincere desire to improve one's spiritual life. It is also necessary to read slowly, to understand fully the meaning of the words, to pause on the more striking considerations, and to stimulate in one's will sentiments and resolutions. In this manner, spiritual reading gradually becomes a prayer. After a certain lapse of time, it is good for one to read again certain books which were found helpful in the past. It is better to delve more deeply into the doctrine expounded in a very good book, such as *The Imitation of Christ*, than to read superficially many books of lesser value. Finally, one must make a serious effort to practice something of what he reads (Rom. 2:13). It is suggested that a prayer be said before and after spiritual reading, asking the help of the Holy Spirit for a fruitful reading and thanking Him for inspiration given to us. *Man.*

SPONSORS.

A sponsor is a person who at baptism or confirmation stands up or vouches for the one who is baptized or confirmed. By so acting he becomes a spiritual father or mother to the baptized or confirmed individual.

NECESSITY. No one shall be solemnly baptized unless he has a sponsor; it is, however, lawful to have two sponsors, a man and a woman (Canon 764). If baptism is administered privately, even by a lay person, a sponsor should be secured, if this can be done without too great difficulty (Canon 762, par. 2). If baptism is repeated conditionally, the same sponsor should be employed as at the first baptism if possible; if this cannot be done, a different sponsor may be secured. In a conditional baptism, however, no spiritual relationship (*q.v.*) ensues unless the same sponsor is used on both occasions (Canon 736, par. 2).

At confirmation the candidates should have, if possible, a male or female sponsor (Canon 793). For just reasons, it is allowed to have one man as sponsor for a group of men and one woman as sponsor for a group of women.

For *valid* sponsorship, a sponsor at baptism (1) must be a baptized person; (2) who has attained the use of reason and has the intention of being a sponsor; (3) he must not belong to any heretical or schismatic sect; (4) he must not have incurred any declaratory or condemnatory sentence of excommunication or labor under infamy of law (*infamia iuris*) or be barred from performing ecclesiastical acts; (5) he must not be the father or mother or spouse of the person to be baptized; (6) he must have been designated by the person to be baptized, his parents or guardians, or the minister of baptism; (7) furthermore, the sponsor must, either in person or by proxy, physically touch or hold the person being baptized, or receive him immediately after baptism from the sacred font or from the hands of the minister of baptism (Canon 765).

The requirements for a *licit* sponsor at baptism are as follows: (1) the sponsor must be fourteen years of age, unless for a just reason the minister deems it proper to admit younger persons; (2) the sponsor must not be under excommunication by reason of a notorious crime, or barred from performing legal ecclesiastical acts, or under interdict, or be a public criminal, or be disgraced by infamy of law or fact (*infamia juris aut facti*), such as Freemasons, Communists, or those living in concubinage; (3) the sponsor must know the first rudiments of the faith; (4) he must not be a novice or a professed member of a religious order or congregation, unless it is a case of necessity and the permission of the superior was duly obtained; (5) the sponsor must not be a cleric in sacred orders unless he has the Ordinary's permission.

Requirements for sponsorship at confirmation: Besides the requirements indicated for sponsorship at baptism, a sponsor at confirmation must be a confirmed person, and must touch either personally or by proxy the person to be confirmed, during the administration of the sacrament. The sponsor at confirmation must be a different person from the one at baptism, unless for a just reason the minister of the sacrament deems it proper or necessary or confirmation is administered immediately after baptism; the sponsor must be of the same sex as the person confirmed unless the minister of the sacrament, for a just reason and in a special case, would permit otherwise. It is a sin, generally grave, for one to propose as sponsor a person he knows to be unfit or one who is not qualified to act as sponsor; it is also a sin for one laboring under such circumstances to accept the office of sponsor.

A Catholic is never allowed to act as sponsor at a baptism administered by a heretic or schismatic; he may assist as a simple witness, for grave reasons, and on condition that his presence is not construed as approval of the sect.

DUTIES OF SPONSORS. By reason of office, sponsors are bound to take a lasting interest in their spiritual children, insofar as their religious education and the practice of Christian living is concerned, particularly if the parents neglect to attend to it (Canons 769 and 797). These obligations are grave.

The sponsors and the minister at baptism contract a spiritual relationship with the person baptized. This relationship constitutes an impediment to marriage (Canon 1079) and any carnal sin committed between them is of an incestuous character. The bond of spiritual relationship which arises between the sponsor of confirmation and the person confirmed does not constitute an impediment to marriage. *Man.*

SPORTS (Dangerous). The primary purpose of all sports is the integrated formation of man through the exercise of one's psycho-physico-moral faculties. Thus, sports activities are generally healthful.

Concerning reasonable and just limits within which the care and culture of the body may be fostered, *see* Culture, Physical. Concerning promiscuous intermingling of the sexes at games, *see* Education, Nudism, Sex. For degenerative forms of sports, *see* Acrobatics. Here we shall consider the morality of sports involving danger or risk.

Sports yielding the greater number of casualties and victims are boxing, wrestling, football and so-called motor sports.

BOXING. All medical men are agreed in extolling the art of boxing as a healthy and virile form of exercise contributing much to the harmonious development of the whole body. At the same time, they do not hesitate to point out many dangers and risks involved in prize fighting, especially professional boxing. This negative and undesirable aspect of pugilism is in the very nature of the sport as a contest of brute force.

Present rules are wholly inadequate in eliminating the dangerous and undesirable aspects of the game. Then, too, the deplorable fact is that the rules, especially concerning medical examination before and during the encounter, are not observed everywhere strictly enough.

Victory in boxing is attainable in any of three ways: by knocking down one's opponent for at least ten seconds (knockout); by battering him until he is forced to quit (technical knockout); by outboxing him on points (decision). The type of victory generally preferred is the knockout, by delivering a well-aimed blow to a particularly sensitive area (chin, lower jaw, lower region of the heart) of the opponent's body. This is capable of causing nervous shock and complete unconsciousness.

The more common injuries sustained by fighters are: fractures of the metacarpals, nasal bones, and jawbones; auricular injuries (cauliflower ears); dislocations of bones and joints, etc. Frequently, boxers suffer more or less serious cerebral concussions with consequent psychical disturbances. Of 2,500 registered professional boxers in America, half are reputed to be afflicted with punch drunkenness (traumatic encephalitis), resulting from successive blows over the years, a condition from which fighters never recover, for cerebral injuries never heal.

As a cause of contusions and excoriations (skin abrasions), fighting, according to experts, ranks first in percentage among the so-called dangerous sports; for wounds and fractures, it places third after football and other heavy contact sports.

WRESTLING. As a contest of strength or skill, wrestling dates back to ancient times and is practiced among all peoples, although in widely different forms or styles. Generally, it may be described as a hand-to-hand combat between two unarmed contestants, who seek to throw each other by a method of body holds and interlocking limbs.

Closely approximating the description given and one of the best-regulated and disciplined games is the Greco-Roman style of wrestling. In this type of contest one is forbidden to gain a fall through violent tactics; also twisting fingers, strangle holds, striking, scratching and tripping are all barred.

In free-style wrestling, tripping is permitted, as well as the use of any sportsmanly hold. In practice, all holds are permitted with few exceptions. In this type of wrestling, any hold dangerous to life or limb or designed to make the opponent suffer is considered unsportsmanlike.

Despite all such restrictions, however, participants frequently sustain lesions of the vertebral column, thorax, joints, eyes, and particularly muscular distortions and distentions. In most cases, the victims experience serious disturbances as a result of such injuries. In *jujitsu* (Judo) no holds are barred; any method whatever is permissible to gain a fall over the opponent. In fact, in this particular style of wrestling, painful holds and violent blows are the most common method of gaining a fall. However, it is to be noted that most tactics employed in wrestling, while appearing to be very painful, are actually innocuous.

FOOTBALL. Less dangerous than contests involving only two contestants are the so-called *collective* or team sports, with the notable exception of football, which must be considered as one of the roughest of team sports.

Without going into the intricate aspects and rules of the game, the main object is to carry the ball through the enemy line to the opposite end-zone, which involves hard blocking and tackling on almost every single play. The principal target of attack, of course, is the ball-carrier, whom the opposition must always seek to bring down in whatever way possible.

Even in its practice phase, football is very rough and strenuous. Ironically, aside from some of its undesirable aspects, the game itself represents one of the highest forms of team play.

MOTOR SPORTS. Under this heading are included such activities as motorcycle, automobile, motorboat racing, etc. These are improperly designated as sports, for their main objective is not the exercise of man's psycho-physico-moral faculties, but the testing and development of technical and mechanical instruments. Needless to say, such sports, particularly if necessary precautions are not observed, can become highly dangerous to self and others and cause numerous serious injuries or deaths.

MORAL EVALUATION. The principles governing the morality of participation in dangerous sports are very simple:

(a) Only for a proportionately grave reason is it permissible for one to expose himself to the danger of death. Hence, (b) a more or less grave reason is likewise required for one to engage in activities or professions involving danger to life or health. Both these principles flow from the more general principle which states that man is not absolute master and arbiter of his life.

In applying these principles to sports, it always must be kept in mind that a danger is not proximate in the same manner for all persons. The factors of experience, practice, and personal ability must of necessity be taken into account, for such factors can easily convert a proximate danger into a remote one. From this it also follows that the first requisite for one to engage in dangerous sports is prudence in its most simple form—that is, to evaluate properly one's own powers and qualities.

Inflicting injuries on an opponent in the course of a contest may be the ordinary means and necessary condition for attaining victory or simply an accidental effect of an otherwise good purpose. In the first case, the sport is intrinsically evil, immoral, hence, inadmissible. Thus, if boxing were based only on achieving victory by serious bodily injuries inflicted on the opponent or by *knockout*, it would have to be condemned outright. In the second possibility, accidental injuries would be tolerated by reason of the principle of the double effect, which makes participation in dangerous sports lawful provided that it is justified for a proportionately serious reason.

It is to be noted that participation in the so-called aggressive sports always and necessarily requires a justifying cause, for the danger of injury in such games is always proximate. On the other hand, to engage in sports in which the danger of injury is only remote, a justifying cause is not required under penalty of serious sin.

The question now arises as to what constitutes a sufficient and justifying reason for participation in sports involving a proximate danger of injury. Certainly excluded is the most commonly given reason or excuse that such strenuous sports contribute to physical health and growth. It is wholly absurd for anyone to seek physical development in games that can cause serious injury and death. Those doctors who advise boxing and wrestling as excellent means of physical education recommend these sports for private exercise in friendly sparring bouts, and not for professional exhibition and competition.

Mere entertainment, monetary gain, and reward are not sufficient motives in themselves for engaging in sports involving a proximate danger of injury. These motives are undoubtedly sufficient if the danger is simply remote, as, e.g., in basketball, soccer, and the like.

Character training may, in certain instances, as in military academies, constitute sufficient reason for justifying and permitting the exercise of dangerous sports activities. These activities, however, must be kept within the scope of a justifying motive, namely, the good of the individual and society. If a sport is intrinsically evil, to intend the cause is to intend the effects, and, therefore, all the effects, both good and evil, are imputable. If, however, a dangerous sport is justified for specific reasons under certain conditions, a problem arises concerning the imputability of the injuries and ensuing damage. In this case, as already noted, the double effect must be considered: a good effect, victory over the opponent, which is sought through the contest, and a bad effect, such as a possible injury, which is not directly intended. Furthermore, no wrong or injury is done to an opponent who, at least in practice, willingly accepts the act of aggression with all its effects or consequences.

But if the aggression is in itself unsportsmanly, then, it becomes immediately unlawful and there is an obligation on the part of the aggressor to make reparation for the damages inflicted, since the unsportsmanlike tactics constitute an obvious violation of another's right. This is so even independently of any civil legislation. In other words, to deprive a man of his senses, even if for only a few seconds, by a blow unleashed for that purpose is never lawful.

Dangerous sports, particularly so-called aggressive sports, aside from their more undesirable aspects, are contrary to the Christian concept of man and his dignity. *Pal.*

STABAT MATER. A liturgical hymn extolling the sorrows of the Blessed Virgin Mary at the foot of the Cross, the *Stabat Mater* recalls Calvary, with a recourse to her mediation on our behalf. The author ardently longs to share in the Passion of the Incarnate Word and in the compassion of His Mother. He concludes with a petition for the salvation of his own soul.

ORIGIN. There are many ancient editions of the hymn. The oldest dates to the beginning of the fourteenth century.

The fact that this version has come down to us from missals and liturgical books indicates that the Church adopted the hymn for official use quite early and introduced it into its liturgical tradition. Because of the various editions, the problem of a critical reconstruction of the original text is so difficult as to be practically impossible, since the length of the hymn varies from forty to a hundred lines. The version found in the *Roman Missal* was approved by a decree of Benedict XIII, in 1727; it consists of sixty lines.

The author is not known with certainty. The names of St. Bernard, St. Bonaventure, Innocent III, John XXII and Gregory IX have been mentioned. According to a widely accepted opinion, the hymn is attributed to Jacopone da Todi, although the arguments in his favor are not conclusive. As a matter of fact, the internal arguments drawn from a stylistic comparison with other poetry of Jacopone are quite uncertain.

The external arguments favoring Jacopone are from the manuscript tradition, which is not decisive either. Two of the more ancient codices of the fourteenth century and the Brescia edition of 1495 favor it, but there are others opposed to it.

Today the *Stabat Mater* is one of five sequences found in the Roman Missal, the others are: *Veni, Creator* (q.v.), *Lauda Sion* (q.v.), *Victimae Paschali* (q.v.), and *Dies irae* (q.v.). Content places the *Stabat Mater* among the hundred or more hymns dealing with the *Compassio Mariae* (cf. collections of sacred medieval hymns, by Blume, Chevalier, etc.). Although written in Latin, this sequence follows the newer rules on rhythm.

It is a composition of great lyric value. At the present time, its recitation is prescribed for the Mass of the feastday of the Sorrowful Mother (Sept. 15). *Pal.*

STAMP OF MANUFACTURER. See Copyright.

STANDARD. See Insignia.

STANDARD OF LIVING. The *standard of living* is the level of economic and social well-being attained by a people, a family, or an individual. The standard of living may be considered from the point of view of a nation, a family, or an individual. The extent and variety of consumption is the most reliable index of the standard of living.

Another index is the relation between nominal salary and the average level of prices.

Statistical surveys show in every country a notable increase in the standard of living during the last hundred years. However, for many individuals and families, the standard of living is lower than the minimum required for the normal maintenance of life.

The standard of living is estimated by a study of expenditures for food, clothing, housing, recreation and pleasurable articles (amusements, liquors, tobacco, luxury objects, etc.) against the general income.

The part allocated for *food* is in inverse proportion to the income: more than one-half of a small-size income (low standard of living); one-third of a medium-size income (middle standard of living); and a rather small percentage of a high income (high standard of living).

The part allocated for *clothing* increases with a rise in income, for a person's needs increase as his income increases.

The proportion for *housing*, under normal conditions of the housing industry, is nearly equal for various income changes.

To decide if a standard of living is high or low, one must examine the percentage of the total of these three main expenditures against the general income.

Often the standard of living varies from one area to another in the same country, depending on the degree of industrialization of the respective zone, the rate of unemployment, and the size of the families. The standard of living, however, depends not only on the prosperity of the people but also on the way that they employ their wealth. For instance, there are those who possess considerable financial means and yet live according to a very low standard of living. On the other hand, there are people who possess very limited financial means and yet manage to live according to a decent standard of living.

It is the duty of all peoples to live within their means.

With respect to individuals, sections of a country, or entire countries with a low standard of living, it is the duty of the wealthy and government to help them attain a decent and satisfactory standard of living in order that all peoples may enjoy the benefits of civilization. *Pav.*

STATE (Civil Society). The concept of *State*, as civil society, is not clearly and definitely established, for every school of political, social, or juridical thought has its own theory. The majority, however, agree on a definition, which makes the State the highest form of a juridical and political organization of society thus far. This definition would seem to be valid even if the people of the world were to succeed in bringing about a complete juridical and political federation of world States in the future.

Morality and the State. The Hegelian school makes the State the creator of moral norms and considers it the historical realization of ethical perfection. Catholic doctrine holds not only individuals, but also the State, subject to the moral law. This subordination is twofold, *passive* and *active*. By virtue of its passive subordination, the State is not above morality; it is not beyond good and evil; it cannot do or command things that are evil; it cannot neglect real obligations or forbid their fulfillment; its power is not unlimited; political crimes are against the moral law; a citizen has the right and duty to disobey the State whenever it commands an immoral action.

By virtue of its *active* subordination, the State, as an organization of ethical beings, must be mindful of the essentially ethical nature of its citizens and promote ethical standards within the limits of its own authority. Among

Christian peoples, the State is not expected to teach morality, but it must protect morality by all the means at its disposal, especially through its legal code and ordinances. For these are the organs best fitted to bring about and maintain the external and social conditions which are indispensable requirements for internal morality.

The ethical nature or mission of the State is clearly emphasized in Christian tradition. This is true not only of the optimistic view, which looks even upon civil society as the fruit of the expansive force of a fundamentally good human nature, but also among the pessimistic theories, which look upon the State as a necessary evil, a means of common defense against an all too common wickedness.

Even in the latter view, the State would have an ethical mission, for, even though it took its origin from evil, it would oppose evil by necessity, even if not quite effectively. *Gra.*

STATE (and Economics). Substantially, three theories have been proposed with regard to the State's role in the economic field.

The first theory, *conservative*, excludes the State altogether from this field. It is based on the fact that economic life is directed by deterministic laws and has in itself all the strength and resources it needs to regain its equilibrium whenever it has been disturbed.

The second theory, *socialist*, holds that all means of production should first be collectivized and the State should plan the whole economic life.

The third theory, an *intermediate* position, holds that the State should intervene to supply what is lacking in the economy; in other words, the economy should be run principally through personal initiative based on private ownership of the means of production. The State has the duty of coordinating individual undertakings, directing them to the attainment of the common good, revitalizing them if depressed, and replacing them if they fail.

It is the duty of the State to safeguard

and promote the common good. Of course, a sufficiency of economic means is an essential element for the common good, for if the citizens have to struggle for the bare necessities of life, they would not have sufficient time to dedicate themselves to the pursuit of spiritual values and to the development of their whole personality.

Thus, the State cannot remain indifferent to whether or not its citizens are assured sufficient means; it must see to this by intervention in matters of production or distribution of wealth whenever necessity should require it and to the extent to which such an intervention is deemed necessary. This is the position of those who support the third theory. But there is no way of fixing once and for all the modalities of State intervention since this depends on the historical circumstances of the moment, which vary a great deal in time and place. But the principle of non-intervention by the State in the functions that private persons can fulfill either individually or in groups must be firmly maintained, and any State intervention must always aim, not at supplanting private initiative, but rather at making up for their defects, initiating, guiding, and coordinating their efforts.

Today it can be said that many of those who are seriously concerned with problems affecting the life of society are busily at work in search of a socio-economic formula that will satisfy the demands of justice without smothering the natural exercise of freedom. At the present time, the State has entered economic life everywhere. In the West, the tendency is toward a greater intervention, but fear has been expressed that this may involve a suppression of the human person. In the Slavic world, on the other hand, where State intervention reached its peak, there seem to appear signs of relaxation toward liberty (savings, small holdings, inheritance, currency, internal commerce, foreign loans). In any case, the conviction is growing that a reconciliation of liberty with the demands of justice on the practical level will be obtained only if men learn to reconcile their own interests with the common good. *Pav.*

STATISTICS, APPLIED. *Statistics* is understood principally as the technique and appropriate method of investigating collective phenomena measured by repeated observations (*methodological* statistics). *Statistics* also refers to the application of this method of investigation to various types of collective phenomena (*applied* statistics).

The application of the statistical method gives rise to a number of separate disciplines, depending on the particular category of phenomena under study. Hence we have anthropometry, biometry (the application of statistical calculations to biological phenomena), economic statistics, social statistics, demographic statistics. The last two are of particular interest to the moralist.

Social Statistics. Social statistics are concerned with various categories of activities related to social life. These activities may be intellectual, moral, religious, ecclesiastical, judicial and the like. Those that are of greater interest to the moralist are: (a) *moral statistics*, concerned with activities and morality in general; (b) *religious statistics*, concerned with the quantitative study of religious factors, whether directly or indirectly; (c) *ecclesiastical statistics* or the extended study of Church activities, acts of worship, and persons and things of worship. Thus, they may study the number of the secular and religious clergy, congregations of sisters, missionaries, average age of missionaries, attendance at the sacraments or catechism, etc.

Demographic Statistics. Students of morality are interested in the application of statistical methods to the study of population figures, called *demography*. The relations, rhythm and laws that govern these factors would remain unknown if one confined himself to individual observations or the consideration of only a few cases.

The principal subjects treated under demographic statistics are: the dynamics of population, statistics on the causes of death, sickness, social diseases, migrations. Demography also studies the social, political, economic, and moral circumstances that aid or retard the demographic rhythm. Statistics are also used to gain a knowledge of certain aspects in the social and domestic life of a country or of a period with a close relation to moral problems.

Statistics of this type must be gathered on a large scale and correlated with studies and interpretations of experts, such as priests and doctors, who are better able to make up for the deficiencies of dry statistical data by contributing priceless experience. Today, the statistical study of a people from the standpoint of morality is focused on an analysis of factors underlying the current serious decline in birth rate, since it is generally true that the morality of a family or of a people is quite effectively reflected in its demographic development.

Some of the factors responsible for increase in population are: the marriage rate, in direct relationship with the economic prosperity and the social structure of a country; birth rate, usually in inverse proportion to the economic conditions; mortality rate, related not only to the scientifico-biological progress but also to hygienic and moral conditions; the environment, for farm areas are notably more prolific than industrial areas; epidemics and contagious diseases, and the like.

Aside from disasters, wars, pestilence and emigration, the major factors responsible for decrease in population are the movements of people from rural areas to large cities, industrialization, greater prosperity and conversely greater demands of modern living, breakdown in family life, divorce and the like.

All these factors should be studied with a view to improving the moral well-being of the people, on which also largely depend their social, economic, and domestic well-being. *Riz.*

STATUTE. The term *statute* admits of a variety of meanings which have one common point: a law, ordinance, or the like. Historically the word has come to be used to express a solemn, formal act declaring the fundamental rules of the juridical procedures of a particular association, organization, or institute.

Every legal institute, public or private, has statutes of its own, either imposed upon it by a higher authority or freely approved by its members. In the first case, we are obviously dealing with necessary societies, such as the Church and the State; in the second case, it is a question of free association, either in Church or State, in which the members freely establish their own statutes, just as they freely joined the society. Observance of such statutes usually is not binding, but is a condition for the existence of the association, membership in it, or the enjoyment of its rights and privileges.

STATUTES AND CANON LAW. In canonical legislation, statutes may be *public* or *private*. They are usually intended to complete or modify the general legislation of the organization to cope with particular situations or problems for which the general laws are inadequate. With this in mind, Canon 22 keeps in force those particular statutes that contradict the Code, as long as there is no clause explicitly voiding them.

The following organizations and groups must have special statutes: (a) Cathedral and collegiate chapters; all dignitaries, canons, and holders of benefices must observe them faithfully. Once they have been drawn up by the chapter and approved by the bishop, they cannot be abrogated or modified without the latter's consent. If the chapter fails to establish statutes within six months from the time of their appointment, the bishop shall compose them and present them to the chapter (Can. 410). (b) An association of the faithful must submit statutes to be examined and approved either by the Holy See or the local Ordinary, who can modify or correct them (Cans. 689; 715, par. 1). (c) Diocesan seminaries in administrative, disciplinary, and teaching functions must be based on and governed by statutes (Can. 1357, par. 1, 3); the rector must inculcate the exact observance of these statutes (Can. 1369, par. 1). Pontifical institutes and faculties are provided appropriate statutes by the Holy See, even if these universities or institutes are under the direction of religious congregations (Can. 1376, par. 2).

In many cases, legitimately existing statutes modify general provisions of the Code; *motu proprio* concessions do not have force against a particular statute, unless they contain a clause expressly indicating this (Can. 46).

Statutes complete the general norms regarding the following: the method of procedure and performance of juridical acts of non-collegiate legal persons (Can. 101, par. 2); elections to special offices (Can. 160); rights to levy tithes (Can. 1502); funeral fees for persons buried outside their own parish (Can. 1230, par. 7); division of income of a benefice between a predecessor and his successor (Can. 1480); the right to baptize in places where there are no parishes or quasi-parishes (Can. 740); enrollment (Cans. 694, 696, 723, par. 4) or dismissal from a society (Can. 696, par. 1–2); liturgical functions for associations (Can. 717); conditions for enjoying rights, privileges and spiritual favors (Can. 692); the manner of collecting offerings for societies (Can. 691, par. 2); lawful representation of ecclesiastical legal persons, such as chapters, sodalities, collegiate groups, before the courts (Can. 1653, par. 3); duties of censors assigned to record absence from choir (Can. 395, par. 4); summoning of extraordinary chapter meetings (Can. 411, par. 2); the rights and obligations of the parochial vicar in a parish joined to a religious house, chapter or other legal person (Can. 471, par. 4); the obligation of residence for the office of curate (Can. 476, par. 5–6); precedence within chapters (Can. 408, par. 1); appointment of proxies for contracting marriage (Can. 1089, par. 1); rights and duties of a chapter (Can. 397); selection of members of a chapter for celebrant, deacon and subdeacon (Can. 416).

Statutes replace ordinary provisions of the Code in the following matters: vacations of members of a chapter, since statutes can require a longer choral service (Can. 418, par. 1); replacement of a

sick canon by a chapter member in the application of the conventual Mass (Can. 417, par. 2); distributions *inter praesentes* for a jubliarian canon (Can. 422, par. 2); the right of associations to collect alms and offerings (Can. 691, par. 3); the annates on benefices (*media annata*), which the bishops can reserve to themselves (Can. 1482); the designation of tellers in canonical elections (Can. 171, par. 1); vicars and prefects apostolic for the assignment of religious missionaries (Can. 296, par. 2; 297).

EVALUATION. Statutes are particular laws. Their observance, generally, is not binding in conscience, but is a condition for the existence of the association or membership and enjoyment in its rights and privileges. *M.d.G.*

STATUTE OF LIMITATION. *See* Prescription, Usucapio.

STEP-SON. *See* Affinity.

STERILITY. Sterility is the inability to procreate or beget children; as a physiological condition, it is not necessarily permanent in the male or female.

Sterility may be *natural* or *violent*. *Natural* sterility results as the effect of a normal, natural process, which occurs in the female after the approximate age of forty-five, or a defect or malfunctioning of the organs of generation because of sickness, deformity, etc. *Violent* sterility is caused by some form of external activity, such as a wound, deliberate human action, surgical operation or otherwise (*see* Sterilization).

Sterility may be *permanent* or *temporary*. Temporary sterility admits of cure or surgical operation to remedy the defect.

To cause sterility directly is a grave sin against the fifth commandment; also, indirectly to cause or fail to prevent sterility is, in itself, a grave sin, if it is possible to avoid the danger. Serious and proportionate reasons may exist for exposing oneself to sterility.

CAUSES. *Male* sterility may be due to a variety of causes: the absence of gonads; an inability to produce seminal fluid or spermatozoa (*azoospermia*); the production of dead spermatozoa (*necro-spermia*); production of spermatozoa without vital activity sufficient to propel themselves the required distance (*asthe-nospermia*); a sealing off of the deferent ducts (*atresin*); the impossibility of emitting seed in the vagina, due to a serious *epispadia* or *hypospadia* or *ejaculatio praecocissima* (premature ejaculation); a hypopituitary condition or more serious constitutional complications. More than one-third of sterile marriages are thought to be due to the male.

Female sterility is usually the result of one of the following causes: a congenital or acquired *dysendocriniasis*; the absence or complete atrophy of the gonads; a defect in transmission and communication with the uterus and vagina; an absence of or deformity in the uterus which impedes passage of seminal fluids; a uterus which is markedly infantile; ova incapable of fertilization; excessive acidity of the utero-vaginal secretions or similar anomalies which kill the spermatozoa; serious inflammations or tumors in the genital organs or openings; age of the married couple.

A biological disaffinity between the germ cells of a healthy man and woman may exist, so that this biological incompatibility of the sexual elements in combination may result in sterilization in one marriage partnership but not necessarily in a more suitable or different partnership.

A sterile marriage may result from a condition of reduced fertility on the part of both partners, each of whom would be fertile presumably if he or she had married a very fertile individual. In sterile unions, a study of probable deficiencies may eliminate many of the factors that cause sterility.

THERAPY. Growing concern about sterility in marriage has had the effect of increasing the work of research conducted in every country to provide better knowledge of its causes and help repair the increasingly serious harm it produces.

Much discussion on the various aspects of the question took place at the Second World Congress on Fertility and Sterility, held in Italy, in May 1956. The importance of the subject was emphasized by Pope Pius XII in an address to the delegates to the Congress.

In the field of therapy, various surgical operations, such as *epididymodeferential anastomosis* for male sterility, and *salpingostomy* for female sterility, have been perfected in recent years. Confirmation has been obtained for the need of eventual local *treatments* as well as the usefulness of hormone preparations, *liver* extracts, vitamins A and E, etc. A change of climate and environment or rest from the usual occupations has proved helpful in many cases.

STERILITY AND MATRIMONIAL LAW. Current juridical norms governing marriage make a clear distinction between impotency, which constitutes ground for nullity, and sterility, which, as the Code of Canon Law clearly states, neither invalidates nor impedes a marriage (Can. 1068, par. 3). Since, for canonists, impotency applies to a person not only unable to exercise the conjugal act, but also unable to complete it in a manner suitable for procreation, one might be misled into thinking that sterility is just grounds for nullity of marriage, because it, too, makes procreation impossible. The teaching and decisions of the canonists equate some forms of male sterility with true impotency in the strict sense; but they are unyielding in all cases in which sterility depends on the age of the spouses or on anomalies, even very serious ones, affecting the female *genital* sphere, as long as they do not prevent union. This difference of judgment on conditions that equally impede conception and generation might seem, at first, to be unreasonable or perhaps the result of scientific notions exploded centuries ago.

Careful consideration of the strictness of canonists on this point indicates a sound logical basis; Canon Law has shown great prudence by its provisions to avoid breaking up marriages. Since it is known that approximately ten percent of marriages are unfruitful, all marriages might become liable to separation or attack for dissolution after one or both parties has become too old for procreation. It further eliminates the possibility of fraud, since an apparently harmless X-ray might produce more or less lasting lesions which were capable of affecting *spermatogenesis* or *ovogenesis*. It also eliminates the possibility that a prognosis of permanent sterility might be disproved by facts. Furthermore, precisely because of the indissolubility of a sterile marriage, many sterile married persons undergo prolonged treatments to cure the condition.

In the final analysis, the Church follows the law of nature for procreation, which is concerned principally with conserving the species, although this may at times impose sacrifices on the individual. The Church knows that the marriage bond is occasionally a heavy burden for married people, but she defends the indissolubility of that bond in order to safeguard offspring and future generations. On the other hand, she is maternally lavish with aiding those who are less fortunate, never failing to point out to them that a submissive acceptance of the sacrifice required is a source of consolation and a guarantee of future happiness. *Riz.*

STERILIZATION. A surgical operation which aims at rendering a person incapable of procreating or begetting children is termed *sterilization.*

The act may consist of total or partial amputation of the genital organs, or a lesion that makes the organs incapable of operating properly. The lesion may result from the use of biological or biochemical elements, by infusion or extraction of chemical elements from the body, or from X-rays, radium, etc.

It is important to distinguish between castration and sterilization. Castration is a removal of the glands (gonads) which produce generative material or seed. Sterilization leaves the glands intact but removes or renders inoperative other organs necessary to generation. In their effects, there is no significant difference between these operations as far as the power of generation is concerned. But since the sexual organs produce not only procreative seed or material, but also hormones which are of significant importance to the health of the whole person, their removal by castration produces particularly harmful effects on the physical well-being of the person.

MORALITY. Sterilization is a serious mutilation, even if the surgical operation involves a very small material part of an organ without any harmful or unpleasant effects on the physical health of the patient. The criterion for judging the seriousness of a mutilation is the loss of an important vital function; in the case of sterilization, it is the loss of the faculty of generation.

The fact that a person does not intend to exercise this generative power or is bound not to use it for life does not remove the serious guilt of sterilization.

The moral doctrine on sterilization is that concerning mutilation, but applied to a special case. The doctrine may be summed up in the following points:

(a) Sterilization is permitted if failure to amputate a diseased reproductive organ or part of it would result in serious harm to the whole body. It would seem that this rule does not in itself exclude castration, if abnormal functioning of these glands were responsible for a *real mental illness* for which there is no other remedy. Sterilization is never permitted if its purpose is to enable a person to live a sinful life, to avoid a new pregnancy even if it would endanger the life of a woman because of an abnormal condition in her organs. (In this case, the proper and natural means to avoid conception is to forego the act that makes conception possible.)

(b) The sterilization of an innocent person is an intrinsically evil act and, hence, a serious sin. This applies to sterilization of oneself or another, whether at one's own initiative or ordered by law. Whether it is resorted to for social or eugenic reasons (*see* Eugenics), or to prevent the natural result of the conjugal act (that is, procreation), sterilization is immoral. Consequently, laws that impose sterilization on any persons to avoid defective offspring are immoral, even if such children are a burden to society.

The State has no right to deprive innocent subjects of bodily integrity, to which they have a sacred and inviolable natural right, even against the State. Sterilization is an immoral means. Its use will do more harm than good, on the basis of the concept of morality and usefulness as explained by Cicero: "One rule holds for all: what is immoral can never be regarded as useful" (*Ethic.*, c. 20). No one can claim that he is promoting the good of the people by violating laws which God, as Creator of the people, has laid down for man's welfare.

In the Encyclical *Casti Connubii*, Pius XI condemned sterilization, whether motivated by social or eugenic reasons, and even if imposed by law (AAS: 22 [1930], 364–565). The condemnation was repeated by the Holy Office in a Decree of February 22, 1940 (AAS: 32 [1940], 73). Recalling these condemnations, Pius XII raised his voice strongly against this form of violation of the natural law: "*Direct sterilization—that is, that which aims, as means and as end, at making procreation impossible—is a serious violation of the moral law, and hence forbidden. Even public authority has no right to permit it on any grounds, much less to prescribe it or to have it performed on innocent people*" (Address to Midwives, October 20, 1951).

(c) Sterilization as punishment is not explicitly condemned by the Church; however, this does not mean that it is lawful. Two things are required to justify a punishment: (1) That it be imposed on an individual who is subjectively guilty of a serious crime. Sick people who exercise their natural right to procreate children are not guilty, not even if the results of the exercise of such a right be burdensome to society. The insane, demented, idiots and the like, who are not fully responsible for their acts, cannot in justice be punished by sterilization. If they are so punished, it is not really a punishment but a preventive measure under the pretext of punishment. (2) That the punishment be productive of good. Since sterilization does not destroy the capacity for sexual pleasures but, in fact, increases in certain respects greater indulgence, it is not a fitting punishment. *Ben.*

CASTRATION. This form of sterilization consists of a removal of the sexual glands; such an operation is performed principally in the treatment of cases of cancer of the reproductive organs.

VAS LIGATIO. Vas ligatio is a form of castration, which does not imply complete mutilation or severance of the reproductive gonads; it ties and seals off the two deferent ducts to prevent the flow of spermatozoa to their natural outlet. It is supposed to stimulate the endocrine functions of the testicles and result in a rejuvenation of the individual by a reactivation of the *potentia coeundi*.

This operation is morally wrong if it can be presumed that the individual intends to use his reacquired sexual vigor outside marriage, unless the primary purpose intended is the cure or improvement of a diseased condition that cannot be cured in any other way. L. Scremin holds that vas ligatio is proper if used to correct impotency; but our opinion is that the matter is at the very least doubtful, since the operation, even if aimed at correcting marital impotency, results in sterility and constitutes a mutilation of the person, slight as it may be. *Riz.*

STOCK MARKET. The term *stock market* may mean: (a) a building, room or other place designated for trading or dealing in securities (stocks, bonds, shares and other similar titles); (b) the actual buying and selling of such securities; (c) the sum total of security transactions concluded in the course of a day (e.g., today's market registered a slight rise in comparison to yesterday's market); (d) also a juridico-economic institution or agency, regulated by the government in certain countries.

The stock market may deal in all values, movable and immovable commodities, private and public securities; preferably, however, it deals in public and private securities and in market values or prices.

OPERATIONS. Stock market transactions may be conducted for the purpose of investment or speculation. In the former case, securities are actually bought and paid for in full and are turned over by the buyer to the seller, who keeps them for the income they are expected to yield. In the latter case, transactions are determined by the turn of the market or by the rise and fall of the price of stocks. Speculative methods are varied and involved: securities are traded *on margin, on buyer's option, in a bullish market, in a bear market,* etc. The main idea behind these speculative operations is to buy at one time and sell at another, taking advantage of changes in prices in the interval, and thus hoping to realize a profit or avoid a loss.

Every stock market issues a daily report of stock transactions by listing price quotations, which include opening and closing prices as well as high and low for the day. The greater stock exchanges serve to record the pulsations of all economic life throughout a country.

Stock. The stock of a company is a title to a specific gain for money given as a loan to a company, of which one becomes a creditor. The debt is satisfied by payment of what is owed, remission of debt, compensation, fusion of debtor and creditor, by rescission of contract, settlement, or prescription.

Shares. Similar to stock, the share is a title arising from a sum of money given to a company for which a benefit is obtained which varies in proportion to the total profits of the company.

It is lawful to buy and trade in stocks and shares, provided that there is nothing illicit in the product of a company and that the administrators of the shares abide by stipulations, without fraud, and manifest the diligence of a family head.

In the case of clerics, special rulings apply. Clerics are forbidden to engage in trading either personally or through others (Can. 142). They are not forbidden, however, to buy stocks or shares, provided that they do not engage in any stock trading or have an active part in the administration or business of the companies (*S. Officio,* April 15, 1885), under penalty of excommunication reserved in a special way to the Holy See (AAS: 42 [1950], 330–331) and other

ecclesiastical penalties, according to the prudent judgment of the Ordinary (Cans. 2380, 2324). *Sir.*

STOLE FEE. Stole fees are customary offerings made to the parish priest by the faithful on the occasion of the administration of certain sacraments or sacramentals. They are called *stole fees* because the priest wears a stole in administering such rites. They are not to be considered payment or compensation for the sacred things or for the spiritual ministration, for this would be simony (*q.v.*), but a contribution toward the maintenance of the clergy for work only externally connected with and separable from the sacred ministration (I Cor. 9:13).

HISTORY. Since the early centuries of Christianity, in the fourth and perhaps the third century, a custom existed by which the faithful gave the clergy goodwill offerings on the occasion of the administration of the sacraments and of other sacred functions. Except for some sacraments, the Church tolerated this custom, but strictly forbade exacting fees either before or after the administration of the sacred rites (*pactiones et exactiones*). More severely did she prohibit any administration of sacred rites dependent on the payment of such fees (Cans. 99–104; C. I, q. 1; C. XIII, q. 2, C. 12). However, despite severe canonical prohibitions, fees were exacted. The principal cause of this abuse must be sought, according to present-day opinions, in the precarious economic condition of many priests who officiated at the so-called *Eigenkirchen* or owned churches —that is, privately owned by lay or clerical persons or by clerical institutions. As a remedy against such conditions, in the eleventh century, the Church began to exact the so-called *portio congrua* (equitable compensation), which was to be given to the priests by the owners of private churches or chapels. This *portio congrua* was later prescribed by the Fourth Lateran Council as a general practice (Ch. 30, x, 3, 5; *cf. also* Ch. 12, x, 3, 5). This came about as the result of attacks by heretics upon the free-will offerings given by the people to the priest on the occasion of the administration of sacred rites. The Church found herself compelled to come to the defense of the practice of free-will offerings and approved a practice somewhat different from that followed before the Council. Hence, in the Fourth Lateran Council (1215) it was decreed: "The priest must, as in the past, administer sacraments and sacramentals even when no offering is received; but the custom of giving a certain offering on such occasions is to be considered a praiseworthy and pious custom to be maintained by the faithful. The priest, therefore, has a right to the customary offerings following the administration, and the bishop can and must see to it that the same be done by those who out of heretical perversion maliciously refuse to observe such laudable customs introduced by the devotion of the faithful" (Ch. 42, x, 5, 3).

The principles established by the Lateran Council have remained essentially unchanged in modern canonical legislation.

PRESENT-DAY LEGISLATION. (a) According to Can. 463, the pastor has the right to stole fees established by long custom or by appropriate legislation, but only to these and no others (Can. 736). There exists no general norm determining these stole fees, because it depends on particular legislations, which may vary according to nations and territories. The *Codex Iuris Canonici* states only that they can be imposed in connection with the administration of the sacraments and sacramentals (Cans. 736; 1507, par. 1). The priest has no right to impose them, but a provincial council or assembly of the bishops of an ecclesiastical province can, with the approval of the Holy See, do so. Stole fees for funerals and burials (*black stole fees*), which may be established only by the local Ordinary with the consent of his cathedral chapter, are exceptions (Can. 1234). Besides stole fees for funerals and burials, the Code maintains stole fees (*emolumenta stolae*) for marriages (Can. 1097, par. 3). An almost common doctrine speaks

of stole fees for baptisms (*white stole fees*). But, as stated above, stole fees for particular ministrations are established by particular legislations in each region.

(b) Ordinarily the pastor has the right to the revenues, even if another priest discharges the ministration (Can. 463, par. 3), unless common law or a particular legislation directs otherwise, as in the case of Can. 463, par. 3: the part over and above the established fee may be given to the priest who administers the rite if it is certain that those making the offering so intended it (cf. Canons 1216, 1223, 1236, 1237).

(c) If the pastor exacts more than he is entitled to, he is bound to make restitution (Cans. 463, par. 2; 1235, par. 1). If he is recidivous, he is subject to canonical penalties, including removal from office (Can. 2408). The pastor may not refuse to administer gratuitously to those who are not able to pay for the services (Cans. 463, par. 4; 1235, par. 2), nor may he refuse the administration of sacraments or sacramentals to those who refuse to make the legitimate contributions, as stated by the Fourth Lateran Council. The local Ordinary, however, can, if he deems it prudent, compel the recalcitrants to pay the legitimate fees (Can. 2349), even by the application of canonical penalties.

In many countries stole fees are also regulated by civil law and sometimes include the lay servers as well. In other countries stole fees are replaced by other revenues from taxation for worship. *Led.*

STUDENT. A student is a person who devotes himself to mastering a particular science or branch of learning in a systematic and disciplined way.

A Christian has an obligation to study because he cannot, without knowledge and training, fulfill his obligations as a faithful child of God. Hence, a Christian owes it to himself to attend to his intellectual development.

This duty is basically personal; hence, it may vary from one person to another, depending on two principal circumstances: (a) the individual's position in society; (b) the general cultural level of the society in which the individual lives in terms of his occupation or profession.

Hence, every young student must look upon studying as a strict duty and acquire the amount of knowledge, training and technical ability necessary to his occupation or profession, and as a useful member of the community. A person who takes up a profession without the necessary preparation is not only guilty of sin by reason of his inability to carry out his duties in a proper manner, but he is also responsible for any damage that might result from lack of preparation. And it is his responsibility if his profession fails to give the satisfaction that one has a right to expect and which is necessary for effective and profitable work.

Besides the personal obligation for all students as members of society to study, every student also has particular obligations to others: (a) To *parents or guardians*, who have the responsibility to provide for the proper education of their children in a personal and natural obligation, the student owes a debt of gratitude and an obligation of justice with respect to the expenses they incur for him. So he would be at fault if he wasted these expenditures and frustrated the care and efforts that his parents bear by reason of his education.

(b) *Teachers*, by accepting the responsibility to parents and country for the education of the young, have a right to *respect*, which should be displayed by the student in speech, internal attitude, and external deportment. Hence, a student must refrain from ridiculing his teachers, lying about them or provoking them to anger. Violations could constitute serious sins, unless it should be clearly a case of insignificant matter, a thoughtless or foolish act. The teacher should be shown *love* and *obedience* in all things that are not against the law of God and the dictates of Christian conscience.

(c) *Companions* must not be led into disorderly conduct in school, or by reading books or publications offensive to good morals and the like.

Every student should bear these two things in mind. (a) Schoolwork and study are not intended to benefit the parents or the teachers but the student himself. (b) Knowledge is not a gift, but is acquired through hard work. In itself, study does not excuse a person from fasting or from the obligation of hearing Mass on Sundays and holydays of obligation. It does not give anyone the right to read forbidden books without obtaining the proper permission (*see* Books, forbidden); and even if permission is obtained, natural and divine law demand that everyone avoid or make remote any occasion of sin (Can. 1405).

Every school is and should be like a family where all are united as in one soul, one spirit, one heart. Among other virtues, a student should possess the virtue of sociability and docility to profit by the teaching of the instructor and, thus, prepare himself in the proper manner for a useful position in society. *Tar.*

SUAREZ, FRANCIS. Francis Suarez, a Jesuit, was the first theologian of modern times, a model of scientific and scholarly moral thinking. Pope Paul V bestowed upon him the title *Doctor Eximius.*

He was born at Granada, Spain, January 5, 1548. He entered the Society of Jesus on June 16, 1564. After the completion of his training, he taught philosophy at Salamanca and Segovia (1571–1574); theology at Valladolid, Segovia, and Avila (1574–1580); theology at the Roman College (1580–1585) and at Alcala (1585–1593) when the great controversies on grace were taking place. He received his doctorate at Evora and continued to teach at Coimbra, from 1597 to 1615. During this period, he was summoned to Rome to defend his opinion on the treatise *De poenitentia,* in which confession from a distance and absolution *in absentia* are advocated—both of which were condemned by the Holy Office. Suarez died at Coimbra, June 16, 1564.

WORKS. With the exception of the special treatises on justice, Suarez wrote of all the subjects as they were treated in the *Summa Theologica* by St. Thomas Aquinas. They follow in part the

Summa, but reflect in general the personality of Suarez, especially his renowned treatise *De legibus.* The works of Suarez are usually arranged in the same order followed by the *Summa,* although the composition and publication of these articles were different.

In the second edition of Paris, the works of Suarez are distributed as follows: *De Deo uno et trino* (1606); *De angelis* (1620); *De anima* (1621); *De fine ultimo, actibus, et peccatis* (1628); *De legibus* (1612); *De gratia* (1619, 1651, 1655); two series of theological opuscules appeared in 1599 and 1859; *De Incarnatione* (1590); *De vita Christi* (1592); *De sacramentis, baptismo, confirmatione, extrema unctione* (1620); *De censuris* (1603); *Defensio Fidei* (1613); *Disputationes metaphysicae* (1597).

One of the oustanding Jesuits in the early years of the Society, his work for the most part is dedicated to the field of theology, but his philosophical writings accentuate the originality and disengagement of his thought from the influences of Saint Thomas; he is noted for his theories on modalism, the identity of essence and existence in a creature, a more pronounced distinction between substance and accidents. These theories gave rise to opinions on theological questions which show originality more than they make lasting contributions to theological development. Clear contributions to theology are his expositions on the salvific will of God and Mariological studies.

Singular aspects of his theology are: the character of divine relations; an explanation of the intuitive vision of God; an explanation of causality of the sacraments; an explanation of the essence of the Holy Sacrifice of the Altar; an explanation of the Eucharistic presence; a thesis concerning subsistence, especially in relation to the Incarnation; the concept of congruity in questions of grace; and, in general, his eclecticism.

In his practical theology, more so than in his speculative, Suarez follows directly and immediately St. Thomas. The *De legibus,* which is his greatest work in this field, is an ample commentary on the nineteen questions of the *Summa Theologica* of St. Thomas relating to practical theology, one of the most extensive and profound works on this subject.

In a number of moral and political questions Suarez endeavored to complement Thomistic intellectualism with a more concrete consideration of human psychology by assigning a greater role to the will (voluntarism) and liberty, particularly in his writings on right and law, in his analysis of a doubtful conscience, beatitude, and the origin of civil society.

This voluntarism is, however, complementary; in other words, it is not an absolute and exclusive voluntarism which results from his intensely searching analyses. Other questions in which the Suarezian viewpoint brought greater precision to the common doctrine are: the constitutive element of morality; the notion of penal law; positive imperfection, presented as different from venial sin. Suarez is regarded as one of the most eminent jurists, a theorist of general and political law.

It is undoubtedly in political matters that Suarez appears more original. This is all the more remarkable in view of the fact that this field had been scarcely explored by St. Thomas; in fact, only in later centuries did political science attain a new and truly flourishing development.

Also to be noted is the contribution of Suarez to the formulation of the theory of the indirect power of the Church over the State. International law had in Suarez one of its greatest elaborators. Notable are his contributions to the delimitation of the concept of *jus gentium* and to the idea of a natural community of nations.

Suarez was also associated with initial efforts of the great casuistic movement at the end of the sixteenth and the beginning of the seventeenth centuries.

Although he did not disdain casuistry, it is clear that he refused to be a pure casuist. In fact, casuists have never looked upon him as one of the masters in casuistry. On the contrary, he found himself playing a principal role in the formulation of moral systems (*q.v.*).

Against an exaggerated probabilism, which he attributes to Medina and Lopez, and probabiliorism, which he attributes to St. Antoninus, Soto, and others, he gave the principle: *Tene certum et omitte incertum.* This comprises an exaggerated tutiorism, for which he cites no sponsor of the doctrine.

Suarez sustains the legitimacy of following a truly probable opinion in doubts of law. In support of this position he lists human fragility, the intolerable burden that would be placed on all men for comparative investigations, the insufficiency of promulgation of a law that remains seriously doubtful. There are, however, cases, he adds, in which a truly probable opinion may not be followed. These are: doubts of fact, in which, either because of justice or charity, one is obliged to avoid an actual harm or inconvenience; doubts relating to the necessity of a means probably indispensable for the attainment of a definite end, particularly the necessary end of eternal salvation. What is particularly to be noted in this analysis is the fact that the limits of probabilism are already strongly delineated, especially in matters regarding a doubt of fact.

The main lines of moderate probabilism are clearly traced. Had his successors adhered more closely to his doctrine, many discussions might have been averted and the opposition against probabilism undoubtedly would have met with less success.

A comprehensive study of his practical theology shows that, although his criticism of, and efforts to complement, Thomism may have been insufficient to make of Suarez the leader of his own school, they do give him a great stature and personality. His influence was notable.

St. Alphonsus Liguori considered Suarez one of the most important theologians of the past and made frequent reference to him in his *Theologia Moralis.* In the first editions of his work, in his list of important authors, whose decisions are of particular weight, he includes Suarez. And it is interesting to observe how Suarez, who in the fourth edition of St. Alphonsus' work (1760) is placed second among twenty-two authors listed, in the fifth edition is given first place among thirty-five authors. In subsequent editions, however, he follows Card. De Lugo, who holds first place (l. III, n. 572).

In the nineteenth century and in our own day, moralists accord Suarez respect and consideration, particularly for his *De legibus, De religione* and *De sacramentis.* These are regarded as classical works. In the listing of authors given by certain moral theologians, e.g., D'Annibale, Lehmkuhl, Bouquillon, Genicot, Prümmer, etc., Suarez is given first place. *Pal.*

SUBCONSCIOUSNESS. Problems of the subconscious, unfortunately, have not yet been solved to complete satisfaction. Difficulties are due to the nature of the matter itself and to the different mentality of those attempting a solution.

According to Freud (1856–1939), a disciple of Charcot at Paris and professor of neuropathology at the University of Vienna, the subconscious takes in all the phenomena previously present in consciousness, which at a given moment one is not aware of, but which can easily be recalled. Asked why it is that some forgotten facts are more or less easily recalled to memory while others are not, Freud answered that this depends on a greater or lesser opposition between such phenomena and certain fundamental exigencies of the individual. When incompatibility develops, the facts lapse into the unconscious, from which they no longer emerge.

However, it is necessary to distinguish clearly between consciousness and subconsciousness. Consciousness, even in its multiple stages, always remains consciousness, because *the more and the less* do not change the species of a thing (*plus et minus non mutant speciem*). We may indeed speak of diminished consciousness or of semi-consciousness, but in all cases it will always be consciousness. Subconsciousness, then, must embrace another sphere, namely, of phenomena previously belonging to consciousness but at a given moment forgotten, as Freud would stress. However, one must disagree with this, for that which causes certain phenomena to lapse into the unconscious is not the act of recall (incidentally, the act of recall is a fact of the future, not of the present), but rather their impossibility of recall. Between the conscious and the subconscious there appears, it would seem, the mythological Cerberean inhibitor. The images upon which concept and thought depend (Scholasticism proves that the intellect is extrinsically dependent on the senses) are impressed in the phantasy, an organic power, and are aroused according to certain laws, operating under certain specific conditions, i.e., if certain facts are verified. These facts shall have to be all the more forceful as the image is less deeply fixed in the imagination. Hence, an extrinsic and future fact cannot cause a phenomenon to lapse from the subconscious into the unconscious, thereby changing its species.

There are, to be sure, instances in which images can no longer be aroused, not because of a vague incompatibility with the fundamental requirements of the individual, but because a portion of the organ of phantasy, wherein a definite image is impressed, has been removed, injured or diseased, so that it can no longer function properly. In such a case, it may be conceded that, since the image is no longer preserved, or since it is no longer of any service, the psychic fact itself has also lapsed into the unconscious.

One must not think that the subconscious is something sterile, for it is capable of exerting considerable influence on conscious facts or at least on the activities of an individual. We might, by way of example, compare the subconscious to a subterranean spring which keeps the ground above it humid and fertile, or to the sea, which, despite the fact that light penetrates only to a certain depth, conceals a great stirring of life even in its lower depths. An event, though long forgotten, leaves behind a trace of contentment or gloom, as the case may be. A

fact no longer adverted to keeps alive a ray of hope. A decision taken, even if followed by a momentary distraction, tends to the performance of certain acts that are necessary for the attainment of a desired end. Sometimes an impression alters, even definitively, the psychological state of an individual. An example will often exercise its influence secretly. A habit inadvertently impels one to action.

THE VOLUNTARY AND PERCEPTION. The perennial philosophy, from medieval times called Scholasticism, admits a threefold voluntary: virtual, habitual and causal.

(a) *Virtual voluntary* is present if a person, having made a decision with full advertence and deliberation, proceeds under the influence of this decision to perform acts necessary for its realization, though the decision itself may not be adverted to at every moment, due to distraction or other reasons. Thus, Titius decides to steal something in the home of Caius. Then, no longer paying any actual heed to the decision taken, he proceeds to the task of preparing counterfeit keys and putting into execution the necessary means for the successful theft.

(b) *Habitual voluntary* consists in an individual's state of mind resulting from the performance of an action, which lasts until the will retracts it, repents and effects certain acts necessary for sanctification. This state, even if not adverted to, always leads an individual toward a certain laxity and takes merit away from good acts already performed.

(c) *Voluntary in cause:* these are habits voluntarily contracted; they are natural habits, subsequently adverted to but allowed to go unchecked because of lack of effort and the drive of passion, which permits them to become stronger. Habits become a second nature and impel one to perform acts inadvertently, but with the voluntary in cause enduring until it is retracted and until one does everything possible to amend.

The applications of the voluntary in cause could be multiplied indefinitely.

From all this, one can easily understand that, although the study of the subconscious as such, is but of recent origin, its notion was clearly, though not scientifically, known to older Scholastics, who made use of it in various cases. *Ver.*

SUBDEACON. *See* Holy Orders, Celibacy.

SUBJECT. In the context of this article the term is used as a noun, meaning one who is under legitimately constituted authority. In the feudal system, subjects were called *vassals*. Since there are several forms of legitimate authority, there are likewise several kinds of *subjects*: the faithful, subjects of the Church; citizens, subjects of the State; religious men or women, subjects of a religious institute, etc.

The juridical foundation on which the rights and duties of subjects are based is society as a disposition of the natural law. It derives from positive human dispositions, insofar as they conform to the nature of various societies and to the natural and divine laws.

Juridical systems governing the status of subjects may be said to be threefold: (a) the Code of Canon Law for the Church; (b) civil codes for civil society; (c) the free will of each individual. By this, of course, we do not exclude the divine positive law, specifically determined by the ten commandments.

With respect to Canon Law, one becomes a subject of the Church through baptism (Can. 88), in which he is recognized as a juridical person with particular rights and duties. Infidels and catechumens are obviously excluded, but not heretics and schismatics. In the concept of ecclesiastical legislation there prevails the character of *territoriality*, which means that a law is effective mainly on the basis of a specific area or territory; but it is also possible to have *personal* laws (Can. 14, par. 1, n. 1). Generally, however, one becomes the subject of a special ecclesiastical law, unless it is a general law for the entire Church, by residence in a certain territory (Can. 8, par. 2, nn. 13–14). Since the Church's concern is the welfare of souls, she exempts from its laws habitually demented

persons, idiots, and those who have not as yet attained the age of discretion (7 years of age: Can. 12). Sufficient use of reason is based on the ability to commit a mortal sin. The Church does not exempt anyone from invalidating or debilitative laws, or from laws based on avoiding common danger, which are established to safeguard the spiritual and moral welfare of the faithful (Cans. 16 and 21).

Civil codes speak of *citizen* and *citizenship*, rather than of subjects, by which membership is indicated in the organic political collectivity of the State. According to civil law, one becomes a citizen and, therefore, the subject of the State in various ways: (1) by birth in that State, i.e., the bond of blood (*jure sanguinis*); (2) by marriage (*jure matrimonii*); (3) by choice (*jure electionis*) or the process of naturalization. In the civil forum the criterion of territoriality of law prevails, in the sense that, generally speaking, one becomes subject to the local law. Penal laws and laws concerning public order, right conduct, and contracts are applied to all persons residing within a certain particular territory.

One may also become a subject by submitting freely to the particular laws of societies, associations, religious institutes, etc., which in general are personal bonds.

RIGHTS. As a subject, man has first of all the right to a certain degree of free and safe movement, so that he may freely fulfill his duties toward God and himself and his obligations toward his neighbor. For the fulfillment of such duties, every subject has the right to safety of person and life against personal abuses as well as the right to material and moral means necessary for the attainment of his ultimate end and all intermediate ends. Since good reputation is indispensable to man, he has also the right not be be hindered by illicit means from acquiring a good reputation, nor to have it destroyed by his fellow men. Every subject also has the right to a total or partial enjoyment of material and nonmaterial goods, the right to employ or to be employed, the right to engage in activity more suitable to his faculties and ability as a human person.

MORAL OBLIGATIONS. The moral obligations of every subject in general are: (a) *Respect* for legitimate authority, in the persuasion that such authority derives power from God. It is, therefore, the duty of a Christian to honor persons who are not worthy to hold office, since it is not personal morality that renders authority legitimate. Violations against the honor due to lawful authority, whether by word, writing, or deed, are generally considered *grave*. (b) *Obedience* to the laws of the State or community to which one belongs, not out of fear, but a sense of duty. Interior respect for the law and a will to carry out its prescriptions to the best of one's ability are the main duties of subjects. Respect and obedience to the law are the basis of civil virtue, a fundamental requirement for the prosperity, harmony, and peace of every society. Positive law as such, even civil, if it is not in conflict with the natural or divine law, is sacred; a deliberate transgression is in general sinful. (c) *Loyalty*, a ready disposition of inner respect by which one considers as sacred both the written and the unwritten law. Loyalty renders a Christian actively interested in the welfare of the nation, community, association or other society. This gives rise to the duty to participate in the activities of the community, association, etc., and to promote their interests through the exercise of social, civil, and political rights, of which the most important one with respect to one's country is the right to vote. Every individual has his own share of responsibility to the life and prosperity of his country. He must not, therefore, be indifferent to the type of leaders his country shall have, but is obliged, through the exercise of his vote, to see to it that his nation, state, or local community be governed by individuals who are honest and capable of working for the common good, and that those who would do harm to the common good be kept out of office (*see* Elections, Civil).

Participation in actions or movements designed to subvert the political and social order, to imperil the very existence of government, to disturb peace and internal security are crimes against loyalty to one's country. A subject is further obliged to pay levies and taxes to the State (*see* Tax); fiscal agents are spoken of by St. Paul as agents of God Himself (Rom. 13:1 ff.). *Tar.*

SUBLIMATION. *See* Psychoanalysis.

SUBORNATION. *See* Witness.

SUBREPTION. *See* Rescript.

SUFFERING. In the physical order, suffering has an important function, which may be considered useful or even indispensable. In fact, in a great number of cases, pain is the only symptom of disturbance in the body, as a disease, infection, or other hurt. Warned by pain, man turns to appropriate measures aimed at avoiding serious consequences. Since pain is, in itself, difficult to bear, it makes man sensitive to possible damage and danger. Without pain, the function of the physician would be greatly impaired and man might suffer grave harm or death.

In the supernatural order, in the more limited sense of physical pain or its wider meaning of trials, anguish, and crosses, suffering has the role of atonement. Suffering is the penalty by which satisfaction is made to God's justice offended by sin. Both Revelation and faith teach that in man's present state, that is, in his fallen and redeemed nature, by divine disposition, suffering is the means by which the penalty due to original and actual sin is paid. For this reason, Jesus Christ, the Son of God, became man and, though completely free from even the slightest personal sin, accepted the most cruel sufferings in His most holy soul and in His most innocent body and assumed the entire burden of man's sins. To be a Christian means to follow in the footsteps of the Master, bearing the cross, and accepting all sufferings in atonement for the sins of man. Man's suffering, united to the suffering of Jesus Christ, has an atoning function. Atonement of sin, in fact, is the very purpose of suffering. In the supernatural order in which we live, by God's mercy suffering is useful in atoning for sin.

In assigning to suffering such a function in man's weakened nature, God shows in an admirable way both His infinite justice and mercy. He forgives sin but not without exacting satisfaction of an infinite value, possible only by virtue of His mercy, in which He gave mankind His own Divine Son as victim for man's sins. Thus, man's life, just as it is, with its sufferings and trials, is ordained to a universal end, whereof the manifestation of God's infinite majesty is a part. Sorrow and suffering do not disturb the harmony of the divine plan, which consists in all things being ordained to their proper end. On the contrary, these contribute to this harmony, for by their proper function they make creation a more perfect manifestation of God's greatness, while they extoll God's infinite justice and mercy. This, in brief, is the answer to the often repeated query, "Why does God permit that man should suffer?" This, in other words, is the theological reason for suffering. Often, man approaches the problem of suffering in an entirely alien manner; in other words, instead of asking why it is that, despite the presence of sorrow and suffering, the universe, as we see it, is still good and worthy of God's infinite wisdom, man often asks, "Why didn't God create a world free from suffering?" God, of course, could certainly have done this. Why did He not do it? There is no real answer, except that God willed to create the world as it is. This is clear from the fact that such a world does exist. Why God elected to create this kind of world and not another is not given to man to know. This knowledge is not necessary to him. It is sufficient for him to know the purpose which all the elements in the world, including suffering, are to serve.

MORAL DUTY. It is not forbidden to avoid or shirk suffering if this can be done by proper means, that is, without violating one's obligations or the moral law (*see* Therapy). A good Christian at least accepts with resignation the trials and sufferings which God imposes on him, often through a set of circumstances, sometimes permitting certain defects and evil deeds by other men. It is more perfect to accept them with supernatural joy, by following the example of the Apostles, who, after being scourged, "went . . . rejoicing that they were accounted worthy to suffer reproach for the name of Jesus" (Acts 5:41).

A good Christian accepts suffering with resignation and even joy for love of God, to make reparation to God for his own sins and those of others, to exercise the important Christian virtues of patience and mortification, and to imitate as closely as he can the suffering Christ, the Ideal for every Christian to imitate on this earth, sustained by the hope of gaining admission into heaven in imitation of the triumphant Christ. To accept gladly or even to seek suffering for these supernatural motives, if he could avoid it without committing sin, is for man a much higher degree of perfection. Trials and sufferings, which God sends to man to purify him and unite him to Himself, can become an occasion of man's turning away from God. The reason for this is often due to a grave misunderstanding, in the sense that man feels that he is made to suffer because God does not love him. Setting aside all the theological reasons, whose evaluation requires a certain maturity, it will be sufficient to think that no one suffered as much as did Jesus, the Son of God made man. And, after Jesus, there is no other person in the whole world who suffered as much as Mary did, despite the fact that she was the most favored and blessed among all women. If, then, it were true that trials and sufferings are an indication of lack of God's interest or love for man, it would be accurate to say that God did not love anyone less than His own Son or Mary, whom he chose to be His Son's Mother. This is plainly absurd.

Hence, the trials and sufferings that man is called to bear are in no way whatsoever a sign that God does not love him or that God loves him less than others. Everything, including suffering, is an effect of God's infinite love for man, which man is expected to repay by his own measure of love, even though he may be loaded down with suffering and great trials. Christ expects this much of us; He, Himself, and His Blessed Mother set the example and merited for man the graces that are to enable him to bear the difficult task. (For sorrow for sin, *see* Contrition.) *Ben.*

SUFFRAGAN. *See* Bishop.

SUFFRAGE. *See* Elections, Ecclesiastical, Political.

SUGGESTIBILITY. *See* Hypnotism.

SUGGESTION. Suggestion is influence exercised by one person over another by means of ideas, convictions, sentiments, proposals, and actions.

Many convictions which later become the guide for our actions do not stem from personal experience, but from the verbal or written suggestions of another. The process of education and instruction is largely based on the suggestive influences of the words or examples of another.

As personal experience becomes organized, the emotional tendencies consolidated and character strengthened, increasing resistance to suggestions is the result, so that suggestions are less and less acceptable as they pass through the sieve of an ever-increasingly subtle criticism. Hence, psychic immaturity and ignorance lend themselves to the passive acceptance of suggestions; these are more easily and readily assimilated as they harmonize with the experience and preconceptions, the mood and moral credo of the individual under suggestion. For this reason, there is a maximum susceptibility to suggestion at the time of intense emotional outbursts, for then the critical sense becomes submerged and every ethical restraint loosened. This explains those outbursts of collective madness called *psychic contagion.*

We are susceptible to suggestions each day of our lives, although it might be but to a slight degree. There is, however, a specific form of suggestion found among neurotic individuals who passively execute the orders given by the suggesting person. This suggestion is distinguished into *hypnotic suggestion* and *suggestion in the waking state.*

The hypnotic state is the effect of suggestive acts and is, in its own turn, a most favorable state for suggestion. In general, the personality of the hypnotist is only of secondary importance; what matters most of all is the degree of suggestibility on the part of the subject. This is found to the greatest degree in individuals, usually psychoneurotic or neuropathic, whose psychic mechanism has not attained or is unable to preserve the equilibrium proper to a normal adult. The inhibition of higher faculties and the automatism connected with the psychic disassociation induced by hypnosis cause the subject unknowingly to carry out certain actions commanded by the hypnotist, temporarily to experience mental states suggested to him, to undergo, always temporarily, modifications in his kinesthetic powers, etc. From all this, one can see the advantages and harm that ensue from hypnotic suggestion if applied therapeutically (*see* Psychotherapy). For, while hypnotic suggestion may succeed in suppressing hysterical symptoms, at the same time it aggravates, by increasing dissociation, the pathological dissociative tendencies of the patient.

Suggestion in the waking state is closer to generic suggestion. Although it does not offer the amazing results of hypnosis, neither does it show its major drawbacks.

AUTOSUGGESTION. A particular form of suggestion, by the subject upon himself, is *autosuggestion,* in which the individual believes something that does not really exist, or perhaps believes that a given object or event is presented in forms and under circumstances which do not acually correspond to reality. To such illusionary belief, which is impulsive, unreasonable, and uncritical, there is added, in the more serious cases, a disengagement of consciousness, to such a point that in the individual deprived of complete psychic activity (the basis of every true voluntary act) only the lower, simple, instinctive, and automatic activities are exercised. Hence, the various automatisms and restrictions in the sphere of consciousness.

Autosuggestion, also called *immediate credence*, is commonly encountered in primitive people, children, women, and phrenasthenics. Occasionally, it also occurs as the result of nervous depression, distraction, fatigue, emotion, and the like.

SUGGESTION AND MIRACLES. Some authors have resorted to hetero- or autosuggestion in an effort to explain miracles. According to such authors, miracles are the product of suggestive practices exercised on functionally disturbed and generally hysterical patients by individuals who, by virtue of their deep faith and renowned works of piety, succeed in attaining a dominant control over the masses. Miracles are the product of an autosuggestive process, induced in the same category of infirm individuals by a blind belief in the thaumaturgical effects of a relic, a sacred image and the like, and strengthened as a result of collective suggestion or psychic contagion, by the additional circumstance that such sick people find themselves in places (shrines) that have acquired a reputation for being particularly favorable to miraculous cures.

There is no denying the fact that in certain cases suggestion or autosuggestion may produce extraordinary effects on predisposed subjects suffering from functional disturbances. But this proves the necessity of a severe critique to discern whether these are the effects of suggestion or genuine miracles. Certainly, suggestion can in no way explain the cure of organic infirmities. It is a fact that, though suggestion may cause functional or neuropathic symptoms to disappear, it cannot cure organic or anatomical diseases. Since an organopathic affliction is frequently accompanied by functional superstructures, which may aggravate and complicate the fundamental disease, suggestive practices may suc-

ceed in reducing, modifying, or doing away with those superstructures, but the pathological organic nucleus will remain and continue its fatal course, despite all suggestive efforts.

Concerning diminution of moral imputability, *see* Hypnotism. *Riz.*

SUICIDE. Suicide is an act by which one takes his own life voluntarily and intentionally. It is also described as the direct killing of oneself. The word *direct* serves to distinguish suicide from indirect, accidental, or unintentional killing of oneself.

Deliberate and willful suicide is an intrinsically evil act and, therefore, it is never lawful. No motive can justify suicide, neither a good to be derived nor an evil to be averted.

This doctrine is based on the teaching of the Church, rooted in Sacred Scripture and Tradition and on sound reason. God is the author of life; hence, life is a gift of God given to man in order that he may give glory to his Maker by good deeds, performed in life, until he returns to his Maker to receive the reward for his good deeds or the punishment for the evil he did on earth. Suicide is contrary to man's strongest natural inclination of self-preservation. The moral consensus of mankind, which looks upon life as a thing of greatest value, has always disapproved of suicide. Suicide is primarily a sin against oneself because one deprives oneself of the greatest material good; it is an offense against God, because He alone has the right to dispose of man's life. It is inconceivable how anyone could possibly extol suicide, as is sometimes done in books and newspapers.

Canon Law considers suicide a crime. Furthermore, those who have attempted suicide are considered irregular (Can. 985, n. 5); they are to be punished with other penalties (Can. 2350, par. 2). In civil law suicide is not considered a crime. However, anyone inducing or aiding another to commit suicide is punishable by law, even if the suicidal attempt was unsuccessful.

PATHOLOGICAL SUICIDE. Some maintain that suicide is a pathological accident, symptomatic of mental aberration. This hypothesis is based on the reasoning that life is a good of such high value that anyone renouncing it voluntarily must be mentally ill. Despite the fact that self-preservation is the strongest and deepest instinct rooted in the essence of man's life, the fact remains that individuals, because of economic, philosophical, emotional or other reasons, at a certain moment arrive at the judgment, with perfect mental lucidity, that life is no longer worth living. After they stifle the instinct of self-preservation, with full knowledge of what they are doing, they commit suicide. These instances, of course, are less frequent than pathological suicides; nevertheless, they do occur. Ecclesiastical legislation, which denies religious burial to one who in his full senses committed suicide, is based on this experience.

The question may be posited: When can a suicide be called pathological? According to Levy-Valensi, a suicide may be considered to be caused by pathological reasons if no apparent motive seems to have been present or if it is known that the person was suffering from mental disturbance.

Before proceeding to examine pathological suicides, we shall attempt to review the causes, damage, and the prophylaxis of non-pathological cases of suicide.

There are those who believe that climate or meteorological factors exert a certain influence toward suicide, though to a lesser degree than psychological, religious, political, and social factors. In support of this theory, they refer to statistics which indicate that during the second quarter of the year (April–July) the rate of suicides is 40% higher than at any other time; this would make the spring and summer months the time of the year when suicides are much more frequent. Furthermore, it is known that dragging morning hours are more conducive to suicide, that suicide is preferably committed in the second and fourth lunar phase, and that it is of more frequent occurrence in cold countries, es-

specially in Scandinavia. Also, men are much more prone to suicide than women. Statistical data indicate that at one time the ratio was 4 to 1; today it is 3 to 2, obviously a result of increased participation by women in industrial and social life, increased masculinization in habits and attitudes, and complicated modern living. The greater percentage of male suicides is due to man's lesser tolerance of suffering and a weaker religious faith. Certainly lack of faith is among the principal causes of suicide.

According to statistics based on differences in religion, the following figures are said to obtain: for 100,000 persons there are about 10 suicides in Protestant countries, 6 in Catholic countries, and slightly less than 5 among Jews. These figures confirm, among other things, that suicide is not always the result of mental aberration; otherwise, the Jews, who, in proportion to other races, record a higher number of psychopaths, would not have such a low percentage of suicides.

Furthermore, political, economic and social conditions influence the rate of suicides, for it is higher in cities and industrial centers than in rural areas. The reason is that civilization brings not only progress, but also anxieties, unattainable wants, intoxication, religious indifference, boredom with life: all factors favorable to suicide. Culture and training contribute little toward combating the evil of suicide; as a matter of fact, they unwittingly contribute to the tendency by unnecessarily crude and detailed descriptions of suicides in the daily newspapers, novels, theatrical and cinematographic presentations.

However, the more important causes leading to suicide are rooted in the spirit of the individual himself. As Sermizzi points out, it is a question of spiritual causes stemming, not from mental aberration, but from a particular sensibility characterized by the following causes: (a) lower neuropsychic resistance to the excessive output of energy demanded by modern social living, exacting professions, or burdensome responsibilities (this lower resistance becomes further weakened by syphilis, alcoholism, and other toxinfective factors); (b) increased impressionability, further heightened by excessive mental strain, which stresses anxieties, preoccupations, and distress.

To these must be added a lack of high ideals, aims, and aspirations, for, if man no longer has an objective in view, he ceases to appreciate the beneficial force of imperatives, duties, and missions. Life loses its attractiveness; the future becomes dark and bleak; the idea of suicide begins to take root in his depressed and tired spirit.

The causes of non-pathological suicides are most variable. The more frequent ones are: impoverishment from financial setbacks, gambling losses, etc.; disappointment in love; the death of a loved one among elderly couples; nostalgia or brooding reminiscence.

SUICIDES AMONG CHILDREN. Extremely sad and deserving of diligent and solicitous study is the phenomenon of suicide among children and adolescents, which shows an alarming increase. The causes differ from those which influence adults to self-destruction.

It would seem that a child should be the last one to think of suicide since the incentives for suicidal action are generally absent from a child's young life. Instead, due to a precocious and excessive degree of sensibility, partly from hereditary factors, partly from unhappy or poor environmental conditions, too many youthful lives are caught in the maelstrom of suffering, disappointment, frustration and neglect.

The causes that are more likely to drive a young boy or girl to suicide are: fear of cruel or humiliating punishment; severe castigation, administered either by overly severe, sick, or degenerate parents; continuous physical and moral maltreatment, humiliation, derision and the like; physical illness and pain; constant domestic quarreling; finally, in adolescents, a driving passion of love with all its delusions.

A serious error contributing to the suicides of children, into which too many parents and teachers fall, is to consider infantile disappointments as infinitesimally trifling or insignificant in comparison with the suffering of an adult. This may be true in an absolute sense, but we must admit that, if the passions and sufferings of the young are less violent than those of adults, so, too, their capacity of control is less pronounced, and more tender and sensitive are their emotions. Defective training or unhealthy environment may also create in the life of a child conditions of grave injustice or suffering, from which he finds it difficult to escape.

Also to be kept in mind is the fact that, because of pressing economic necessities, our hustling and feverish pace of living seems to have a tendency to cause children to age prematurely. Such a premature exposure to a complicated life places an untimely burden of studies on his mind, robs him too soon of his precious simplicity, throws him into the tense existence of adult living, and subjects him to the contagion of emotions that are too big for his age: all of which easily leads to various forms of instability that may culminate in irreparable tragedies.

Humanity, as the result of hereditary factors, disillusionment, disturbances, and customs accompanying modern *civilization*, becomes ever more susceptible to neurosis. This is passed on to children, who are more impressionable, hypersensitive, neuropathic: all of which creates a morbid terrain, particularly favorable to the development of suicidal ideas and tendencies.

PROPHYLAXIS. The increasing rate of suicides demands that positive action be adopted to stem the tide of this grave moral and material calamity.

Unfortunately, suicide exerts a strange power of allurement and imitation over certain weak characters. In view of this, every effort should be made to strip suicidal accounts of any exhibitionist and sensational element and to restrain by appropriate methods the press and the movie industry from portraying suicide as a central theme or extolling it as a gallant and heroic thing. Efforts must be made to increase and deepen in man the fear of the Lord, to instill greater confidence in the goodness of God and hope and resignation in adversity.

Efforts must be intensified to provide moral and economic assistance to the poor, the needy, the orphans; to form a healthier attitude toward marriage and the family; to combat the distribution of narcotics, to increase sobriety, good manners, and employment; to encourage participation in wholesome sports, which can be a great source of health and optimism.

Efforts must be made to increase the availability of consultors or practitioners of mental hygiene. Dedicated to the study of neuropsychopathic children, environment and remedial therapy against disease, these may provide information designed to raise the material and spiritual health of family life, and to contribute effectively to a holy anti-suicide crusade.

SUICIDE AND PSYCHIATRY. Although suicide is not rare among persons apparently healthy or with a slight abnormality, it does occur with frequency among psychotic and psychopathic individuals. In such individuals, suicide, truly pathological, may present itself under one of the following forms:

(a) *Involuntary suicide.* This is a question not so much of suicide as of involuntary accident befalling phrenasthenics or demented individuals. The individual who drinks poison, but believes that he is drinking plain liquor, and the individual who drowns in a desperate attempt to escape from some frightening hallucination are examples of this accidental form.

(b) *Obediential suicide.* This is brought about by voices heard by the hallucinated individual, urging him to kill himself.

(c) *Suicide of escape.* This is the most important and frequent form of suicide; it comprises the suicide of melancholics, carried out because the sick individual feels very despondent or believes that life is not worth living. This type of suicide, preceded by an elaborate and logical conviction, reached after lengthy reflection by a lucid mind but one weighed down with suffering or remorse, is the result of careful and astute preparation. The individual resorts to all kinds of strange devices to carry out his plan. The suicide of neurasthenic hypochondriacs, psychasthenics and manic-depressive individuals is similar to the type just described. In certain melancholics suicide is not a planned affair, but is carried out on the spur of the moment, under seizure of an irresistible impulse. Many hallucinated individuals, in the state of feverish delirium, amentia, delirium tremens, etc., kill themselves to escape from frightening hallucinations. Some patients suffering from obsession kill themselves under a severe stress of anxiety brought on by a crisis of some sort. There are cases where obsessive fear of suicide will drive a patient to a suicidal action: a comparable case is the action of psychoneurotic soldiers who become severely distressed at the thought of possible death because of an imminent attack, and hence turn to suicide as a way out.

(d) *Suicide of the unbalanced.* This type of suicide is carried out by mild melancholics, who become bored with life without due motive. At one time, they were referred to as *spleen*-sick individuals. They may be overcome by a feeling of nostalgia for the old family homestead in a distant land or, especially in the case of youths, become visibly shaken by an undeserved reprimand. It also typifies the suicide attempted by hysterical persons in a theatrical manner without going through with the act, or of vainglorious individuals who seek publicity by wild gestures of attempted suicide.

(e) *Suicide of the demented.* This type of suicide is characterized by the fact that it involves elements of dementia, a lack of coordination, incoherence, absurdity, futility, lack of motivation.

(f) *Suicidal pacts.* Suicidal pacts ending in the extermination of an entire family are usually engineered by some melancholic member of the family, whose obsession and fear of ruination drive him to destroy the very persons he loves, in order to save them from inescapable disaster. Suicidal pacts consummated by couples are indicative of psychopatic, unstable, and restless lovers, who seek in death a peace and a union which society refuses them. Frequently it is a case of homicide followed by suicide, as the pathologically jealous lover slays his beloved, only to follow her shortly to the grave.

(g) *Indirect suicide.* Usually this type of suicide is resorted to by a melancholic who wants to do away with himself but, because of lack of courage or religious principles, refrains from accomplishing the act himself. Instead, he seeks out death by exposing himself to lethal danger, e.g., by throwing himself into the thick of battle or, in countries where capital punishment still exists, by committing a certain crime with the hope that justice will mete out to him the death penalty. *Riz.*

SUMMAS FOR CONFESSORS (Summae confessorum).

Summas for Confessors or *Summae casuum et de casibus conscientiae* is a name given to a series of writings listing the norms of law to be applied in the internal forum of penance. Some follow a logical order; others are arranged alphabetically.

Summas followed upon the penitential books (*q.v.*). Previously, a series of manuals of a pastoral nature taught how the sacrament of penance was to be administered: the *Manualia parochialium sacerdotum, Parochialia curatorum, Confessionalia,* and especially the famous *Poenitentiale* of Robert of Flamesbury, written in the years 1208–1215. Interest in these grew when the Fourth Lateran Council (1215) imposed the obligation to confess at least once a year for all the faithful of both sexes. As a matter of fact, shortly after this Council, a *Summa de poenitentia,* which came to be known as the *Innocentiana,* was written by Thomas Chabham, an Englishman. Others were written by Master Paul, of Hungary, and Frater Conradus.

In the thirteenth century, three *summas* attracted special interest:

(a) The *Summa Raymundiana,* composed by St. Raymond of Peñafort, O.P. (d. 1275), is undoubtedly the most famous and important for its intrinsic worth and the great influence it exer-

cised. The first three parts of the work seem to have been written at Barcelona between the years 1222–1228 or 1229; in any case, these were not finished before the year 1227, and were finally put into circulation in 1234. The fourth part, *De matrimonio,* prepared around the years 1235–1236, is a reworking of the *Summa de matrimonio* of Tancredi. A summary of this *summa* in verse, composed in the middle of the thirteenth or fourteenth century by Adam the Teuton, was called the *Summa pauperum* or the *Summula de summa.*

(b) The *Summa Monaldina* or *Summa de jure tractans,* was composed in an alphabetical order by Monaldus, O.F.M., some time before 1274.

(c) The *Summa Johannina,* an amplification of the *summa* by St. Raymond of Peñafort. John of Fribourg, O.P. (d. 1314), wrote this between the years 1280–1298 and added to it the juridical part contained in the Fourth Book of the *Decretals.*

There are two other *summas* that have not yet been edited and published which should be listed with these: the *Summa confessorum* of John of Erfurt or Saxony, O.F.M., written toward the end of the thirteenth century in a logical order, contains a collection of many canonical norms; the *Summa de officio sacerdotis,* composed by Albert of Brescia, O.P. (d. 1314), at the end of the thirteenth or the beginning of the fourteenth century, propounds the doctrine of St. Thomas Aquinas.

Special mention must be made of the *Summa Astesana,* finished in 1317 by Astesanus or Astaxasus, O.F.M., a native of the city of Asti (d. *circa* 1330).

The *Summa rudium,* intended for the use of less intelligent priests without extensive training, was the anonymous work of a religious of the Order of Preachers. Composed after the death of Pope John XXII, between the years 1334–1338, it is a summary of the *Summa Johannina.*

The *Summa Pisana* or *Magistrutia* or *Pisanella,* was written at Pisa by Bartolomeo of San Concordio, O.P. (d. 1347), some time before Dec. 7, 1338. Nicholas of Osimo, O.G.M., added a supplement, which is mostly of a juridical nature.

Worthy of note are the following works of the fifteenth and the beginning of the sixteenth centuries: (a) The *Summa Angelica* or *Summa casuum conscientiae*, arranged by Angelo Carleto of Chivasso in the year 1486. It is based on the *Summa Pisana*. (b) The *Summa Baptistiniana* or *Rosella*, arranged in alphabetical order by Battista della Sale (also called Trovamala), O.F.M. (d. *circa* 1494). (c) The *Summa Tabiena* of John Cagnozzo of Tabia (the *Tabiense*), was finished in the year 1515.

Finally, the *Summa Silvestrina* or *Summa summarum*, written in alphabetical order at the beginning of the sixteenth century by Silvester Prierias (Mazolino Sabaudo), O.P., who served as Master of the Sacred Palace (d. 1523). *Pal.*

SUPERIOR. The word *superior* may be considered under a variety of aspects. (a) Etymologically, it means one who is placed or stands above another (Latin, *superior*). (b) In the common meaning, a superior is one who has the principal authority in a community or group, religious or civil. (c) In a broad juridical sense, a superior is one who, by reason of his office, exercises over his subjects at least a dominative power. In the strict sense, the superior is one who may command by the vow of obedience; such an exclusively monastic concept is sanctioned by Canon Law (Cans. 488, par. 8; 402–517).

In the Church, the natural root or foundation of the juridical term *superior* is found in the very concept of a hierarchical authority, which signifies sacred rank or order and is realized in the various gradations of superiors exercising authority in a legitimately approved institute. Such authority is twofold: *dominative* and *jurisdictional*. Dominative power is from the natural law: submission freely promised to superiors, that these may direct subjects to the attainment of the end for which the institute was founded. Jurisdictional power is given by the Church for religious societies, i.e.,

from the supreme power of the Keys, which the Church received from Jesus Christ for the eternal salvation of the faithful. Dominative power is private, conditional, and not necessary; jurisdictional power is absolute and necessary.

In civil society, political authority stems from nature along with the public society over which it presides. Civil authority is the right to govern civil society that it may attain its proper end. Contemporary juridical doctrine is unanimous in holding that sovereignty is an original faculty of which the State is the subject and immediate title-holder. The body politic (the people) possesses this power as a natural endowment; the rulers of a State possess it as a derived title, inasmuch as the possession and legitimate exercise of such power presupposes a conferral on the part of the people. The obligation to obedience on the part of individuals is strictly commensurate to the end.

Since there are two supreme and independent societies, there are two main kinds of superiors to whom man must render obedience: ecclesiastical and civil superiors.

Moral Obligations. Every legitimate superior, whoever he may be, and in whatever manner he may have been elected or appointed to office, represents God, from whom all authority proceeds. Thus, no superior enjoys unlimited and absolute power, but a power limited by natural and divine law, and by the human law of particular codes or constitutions. The first and fundamental duty of every superior is to promote the common good of the community or society over which he presides; in no way may he use power to personal advantage or for relatives and friends. He must, therefore, endeavor to study and understand what is the common good of the community he governs and what are the means best suited to attain that good, which is different for civil or religious society.

In the case of the civil authority, a superior must diligently attend: (a) to the administration of commutative, distributive or vindicative justice, without favoritism; (b) to the security of the individual citizen, as well as of the community; (c) to promoting and safeguarding public morals, not permitting false and libertine freedoms; (d) to protecting the poor and assisting the needy. Since religion is the highest spiritual good of the people, it must be properly safeguarded and defended; dissemination of pernicious ideas or the exercise of destructive freedom is not to be unrestrainedly permitted.

Concerning religious superiors, *see* Superior, religious. *Tar.*

SUPERIOR, RELIGIOUS. A *religious superior* is one who exercises authority over the members of a religious society by virtue of lawful election or appointment. For the ancient monks, especially St. Benedict, the concept of *monastery* was that of the true family of God (*Dei familia*). In fact, the monks were guided to monastic perfection by a *spiritual father* (*Abbas*), who was father of the monastery itself. This meant that he was their father for life or in perpetuity. Such perpetuity of office, however, was not adopted by mendicant orders because of a different concept of authority, which gave rise to the legal and juridical notion of a person presiding over religious communities with the title of *praepositus, praefectus, praeses, superior*.

In Canon Law superiors are distinguished into *major* and *minor* or local. Major superiors are invested with domestic and jurisdictional authority; minor superiors possess merely public domestic authority. *Major superiors* are: the abbot primate of confederated Benedictine Congregations; the abbot superior of a monastic congregation; the abbot and abbess of a monastery or house *sui juris*, even though federated (*see* Abbot); the highest superior of a religious institute (praepositus general, master general, etc.); the provincial, or superior, who, possessing the same power over an autonomous religious institute, is known by other names, such as inspector, visitator, and the like; finally, all vicars of the above-mentioned major superiors,

when actually invested with ordinary powers (Can. 488, n. 8).

Minor or local superiors are those who direct a house of an order or congregation (Can. 505). They are variously called guardian, prior, president, and the like.

AUTHORITY. In general, the authority of superiors must be said to possess a public character, insofar as it is derived from the Church, which recognizes the religious institute itself as a legal person (Can. 501). In this sense, the power of superiors is essentially the same in all the religious institutes. This does admit of different degrees of extension, depending on the nature of each religious organization inasmuch as the Church recognizes a certain autonomy in a general ecclesiastical, governmental framework. Thus, although in all religious institutes there is a public domestic authority, in exempt clerical religious institutes there is also a power of jurisdiction, because these institutes are considered, in typically canonical language, quasi-perfect or self-sufficient societies, almost entirely detached from a diocese. Non-exempt religious institutes maintain greater ties with the diocese, from which they are free only in matters pertaining to the strictly internal government of the religious organization (Cans. 501, 618).

Within the sphere of public domestic authority itself, there are degrees of participation in or relative independence from a diocese, inasmuch as other characteristics proper to the authority of religious superiors besides that of self-sufficiency are attributed to religious institutes by the Church. Some such characteristics are: the priestly character, the distinctive quality of religious of pontifical or diocesan right, the nature of solemn or simple vows, etc. (*see* Exemption).

ELECTION. The election of proper superiors is one of the typical rights belonging to religious institutes from their very inception (Can. 504). The Roman Pontiff is the internal superior of every religious organization and, as such, has authority over all religious. He may exercise this either through the Sacred Roman Congregations, by appointing special visitors, or even by appointing superiors of his own choice (Can. 499).

The methods and juridical requirements for the election of superiors are stated in Canon Law and the constitutions of each religious institute. General conditions for electing the supreme head of a religious institute in the Code demand that the individual elected be at least forty years of age, that he be professed 10 years, that he be of legitimate birth, and that he possess all the qualities required for holding an ecclesiastical office (Can. 504). The duration of the office of superior is likewise determined by the constitutions, on the basis of Canon Law for temporary tenure in office for all superiors, major and minor, with few exceptions (Can. 505). As a matter of fact, in the case of minor superiors, it is prescribed that, after a second three-year term, they may not be appointed superiors in the same house, except by permission of the Holy See, to be sought in each case (Can. 505).

RIGHTS AND POWERS. The extent of authority enjoyed by the various elected superiors is subject to a variety of factors, such as the nature of the religious institute, its system of government, its division into provinces, regions, etc. Generally speaking, the superior general enjoys full power over all persons, things, and places of the religious institute (Can. 502); the provincial enjoys certain powers given to him by the Code, such as the acceptance of candidates, matters concerning their formative training, their admission to the novitiate, the dismissal of professed members with temporary vows, etc.; other powers may be delegated to him by the superior general. If the institute is not divided into provinces or similar organizations with a degree of autonomy, the superior general directly retains all powers, which, however, he may delegate to various superiors of quasi-provinces, quasi-regions, quasi-delegations, etc.

Minor superiors have authority over the members of the house which they govern, according to the norms of the constitutions. The local superiors of *sui juris* houses or of *sui juris* monasteries are also major superiors; hence they enjoy wider authority than minor superiors. During their terms of office, clerical superiors with jurisdictional powers are called prelates, according to canonical terminology (Can. 110); if major superiors, they are called religious ordinaries (Can. 198).

DUTIES. It is a fundamental obligation of every religious superior to endeavor, by every means possible, to guide all the members toward the attainment of the proper end of the institute, which is their individual and collective sanctification, in accordance with the rules of the institute. Another fundamental obligation is to seek the attainment of the specific end of the religious institute, as proposed by the founder and approved by the Church, whether it be mission work, education, works of charity, preaching, writing, or other activities. In fulfilling his duties, the superior must exercise prudence, piety, charity, kindness, firmness. Major superiors must observe the obligation of residence (Can. 508); they must see to observance by their subjects of the dispositions of the Holy See (Can. 509); they must make regular visitation of the houses and persons of the religious institute (Can. 511), a quinquennial report to the Holy See (Can. 510), and see to it that the proper religious and moral training be given to the members of the community (Can. 509, par. 2), according to their respective status.

By disposition of the Code, each religious institute must have not only a general council, but a provincial and local one to assist the superior in accord with the norms of the Code and the constitutions, by consultative or deliberative vote (Can. 516). Moreover, for the administration of temporal affairs, an oeconomus (procurator general), provincial and local, shall be appointed, except if particular reasons suggest that the office of oeconomus be combined with that of the superior (Can. 516, par. 2). All religious institutes of pontifical right shall also have a procurator general to transact affairs of his institute with the Holy See (Can. 517). *Mand.*

SUPERSTITION. A term admitting of many interpretations, *superstition* may signify a belief in the sum total of occult practices or one single practice in particular. In theological language, superstition is a vice contrary to the virtue of religion, as an excess. The sin of superstition may consist of unseemly, irreverent worship of God, or divine worship of a finite person or thing. In this last generic sense, superstition is here treated.

Rendering unbecoming worship to God may stem from false devotion, but also from a mentality akin to that which prompts occultist practices; namely, the idea of control over a divine being by the compelling power of certain formulas or rituals. Examples of false devotion would be kissing a chalice after consecration, fasting on Christmas Day. Examples of superstition due to a mentality of seeking magic are: chain prayers; certain pious practices at some popular shrine or pilgrimage, contrary to approved customs or against an express prohibition of the Church; certain types of prayer carrying the promise of infallible success in temporal favors. Both types of superstition constitute what theologians call vain or futile worship. But one may also practice superstition by rendering to God a worship that is false. The symbolism of the rites employed may be evil, as employing the cult of the Old Testament in the period of the New Testament; for the Old Testament was essentially meant to prefigure the New. False actions may be employed to propagate as true what are really false miracles, prophecies, revelations, or rites. These may be performed by an unqualified person, such as the celebration of Holy Mass by a person who has not received the priestly orders.

Divine worship given to a creature (*cultus falsi numinis*) is either idolatry (*q.v.*), divination (*q.v.*), or superstitious practice (*q.v.*). The subject is amply treated under each of these respective headings.

MORALITY. Superstition in the generic sense is always sinful, since it is a lack of due respect to God. But a judgment of gravity will depend on its different species. Generally speaking, vain or futile worship is considered a venial sin, except in cases of scandal, contempt, or immoral ceremonies. Scandal would be present if the vain practice were to cause a notable loss of respect for religion among non-believers. To render false worship is ordinarily a grave sin, because it constitutes a misrepresentation in a matter of grave importance and is frequently prejudicial to religion, since it bases religion on falsity. The so-called pious frauds (*pia fraus*) are to be condemned despite the intention to edify. Truth has no need of being sustained by deception. The worship of a false god is always and without exception a grave sin (*see* Divination, Idolatry). No believer should ever resort to false religious practices, which, as the Council of Trent defines them, are a false imitation of true religion (*Sess.* XXII, *Decretum de observandis et evitandis in celebratione Missae*). The Code of Canon Law (Can. 1216, par. 1) admonishes local Ordinaries to be vigilant against the introduction of any superstitious practice in the matter of divine worship, public or private, or in the daily lives of the faithful (*cf. also* Can. 1295). *Pal.*

SUPERVISION. *See* Remedies, Penal.

SUPPLICATION. Supplication is an earnest petition, through the use of God's name, directed to a person in order that he might perform or omit an action in our behalf. The act of the virtue of religion by which the suppliant expresses his submission to God and the acknowledged preeminence of His Divinity may be termed *supplication*.

Supplication is an act of *latria*, if made by direct use of the name of God or of things in which the Majesty of God particularly is evident, such as the passion and death of Christ. It is *hyperdulia* or *dulia*, if it is made in the name of the Blessed Virgin or the saints.

Supplication may be in plain form, in private, or in a solemn manner, that is, in the name of the Church by her ministers in the prescribed manner.

It may also take the form of prayers, as the litany of the saints, or the form of command, which is only addressed to an inferior being, such as the devil. Supplications conducted by the priest, who is expressly appointed by the Church, may be directed in the name of God in this authoritative manner against the devil, either to induce him to leave a possessed individual or to desist from troubling people or inanimate things. These are called exorcisms. *Pal.*

SUPRARENALS. Suprarenals, also called suprarenal glands or, less appropriately, suprarenal capsules, derive their name from the fact that they are two endocrine glands (*see* Endocrinology), each weighing from six to seven grams, and situated, like a tiny cap or Phrygian tam, at the upper end of each kidney. About three cm. in height, four cm. in length, each suprarenal body, like the hypophysis (*q.v.*), consists of two parts genetically, morphologically and functionally different: the cortex and the medulla.

The *cortical substance* (or *suprarenal cortex*), of mesodermic origin, secretes into the blood androgenous and estrogenous hormones, glyco-regulatory hormones and desoxycorticosterone (or cortin), which is the most important. The medullary substance, representing one-fifth of the interior of each suprarenal, contains an abundance of vessels and nerves, and the cells composing it (called chromaffin cells because deeply stained with chromium salts) are of ectodermic origin, originating in primitive cell bodies of the sympathetic nervous system. Accessory masses of chromaffin cells are found throughout the entire organism, wherever ganglia and orthosympathetic nerves are found.

The suprarenals play a fundamental role in the development, nutrition, tone and normal excitability of the nervous system, both in its effector and vegetative processes. The cortical substance contributes to the proper tonality of the cerebral cortex, with respect to both the

intellective and the psychomotor processes. It also serves to reinforce the parasympathetic and anabolic functions. The medullary substance contributes specifically to the tonicity of the orthosympathetic system.

The suprarenal hormones, because of their intimate correlation with the liver, kidneys, the reticulendothelial system and the lymphatic glands, perform fundamental protective and antitoxic functions, which are absolutely indispensable for our biological defense against all sorts of toxinfective attacks. Hyperfunction of the suprarenals is characterized by splanchnomegaly, hypertrichosis, notable muscular development, great endurance to mental and physical fatigue, hypertensive tendencies. At times, largely as a result of adenomas or other suprarenal tumors, pathological hyperfunction of the suprarenals is noted, which brings on a precocious puberty in children and hirsutism, diabetes, strong hypertension, obesity, amenorrhea and other grave anomalies in adults.

Hypofunction of the suprarenals presents characteristics which are the opposite of those shown by hyperfunction: hypoplasic asthenia, weakness of muscular activity, hypotension, depressive attacks, etc. It is on such terrain that infections, especially tuberculosis, take root. These infections in many cases alter or destroy, by a more or less gradual process, the suprarenal bodies and eventually lead to Addison's disease or so-called "brown disease" (because of the discoloration of the skin which is present). This is characterized, in addition to the meanodermic condition mentioned, by painful and progressive asthenia, hypotension, violent and painful epigastric or solar crises, loss of appetite, persistent vomiting, spells, impotency, and amenorrhea.

The prognosis of Addison's disease, at one time absolutely hopeless, today has greatly improved, thanks to an early adoption of adequate remedial measures: injections of total extracts of suprarenal cortex, subcutaneous implantation of tablets of desoxycorticosterone, a rich diet of carbohydrates and sodium chloride, vitamin C, etc. In serious cases of supra-renal hyperfunction, successful results are obtained by resorting to enervation of the suprarenals or, in the case of neo-plasms, to suprarenalectomy.

A profound alteration in biological, psychic, and behavior patterns may oc-cur which, because of a slight excess or deficiency in the secretion of these very minute glands, which can be de-tected by diligent histological and bio-chemical analysis, is sufficient to make a person, vigorous, courageous, optimistic or, on the contrary, weak, timid, tired and depressed. While the anomalies pre-sented in these two different types of human personality are not such as to destroy the volitive powers of the indi-vidual, still they are capable of turning the individual's thoughts, norms of life, aspirations, and behavior in opposite di-rections. This must be kept in mind by educators, who should resort to the coun-sels and prescriptions of constitutional medicine to correct the more or less delicate character anomalies and devi-ations in young persons.

For deviations of a more serious ethi-cal character, such as are encountered in certain individuals of hyper-suprarenal condition, inclined to crimes of violence, *confer* Thyroid.

Concerning the relation of the present discussion to problems of impotency and nullity of marriage, one must keep in mind all that has been said regarding suprarenal hyperfunction due to tumors, in which serious defects of the sexual processes may be hidden under a false appearance of exuberant virility. Such conditions are always to be taken into ac-count and adequately evaluated by the medical expert and magistrate in the interests of justice, although it is unlikely that purely functional deficiencies are such as to constitute sufficient cause for nullity of marriage. *Riz.*

SUPRARENAL CAPSULE. *See* Supra-renals.

SURGEON. *See* Surgery, Doctor, Oper-ation, Surgical.

SURGERY. The term *surgery* (Greek, *cheir*—hand; *ergon*—work) is used to indicate the treatment of lesions by manual or operative procedures. Today it denotes that branch of the art of medi-cine which makes use of the hands and instruments in the treatment of definite diseases, illnesses, and injuries.

Once considered a lowly and crude art, surgery has slowly and steadily climbed to a position of major importance. With the discovery in the last century of he-mostasis, anesthesia (*q.v.*), antisepsis and asepsis, the modern surgeon, along with the diagnostician and pathologist, plays an important and significant role in the practice of medicine.

RESPONSIBILITY OF SURGEONS. Practi-cally all moral questions relating to surgery reflect the tremendous respon-sibility that rests on the shoulders of the surgeon. This theme was brilliantly de-veloped by Pius XII in an allocution to the members of the Sixth International Congress of Surgeons (*see Osservatore Romano*, May 23, 1948).

A surgeon's responsibility, as noted by the Pope, derives from the fact that on his efforts and work depend the integrity of the human body, liberation from suf-fering, and the life of patients. A sur-geon's responsibility begins long before actual performance of the operation, for he determines the advisability, time, and method of operation. This responsibility is further increased whenever the par-ticular case at hand suggests the adop-tion of new techniques.

New techniques involving an element of risk are permissible on the following conditions: (a) that the patient be in real danger of death; (b) that there be some probability of saving the patient's life through their adoption; (c) that the patient and his family be duly advised of the risk involved.

A surgeon's responsibility reaches its apex during the actual operation. The surgeon is expected to operate with the greatest degree of sensibility and calm-ness. Sensibility helps him to visualize the image of the suffering Christ in the person of his patient, while calmness enables him to perform his delicate and difficult task with courage and diligence. In the words of Pius XII, "lacking sensibility, the surgeon would be merely plying a trade; lacking calmness, his hand would be rendered unsteady, thereby jeopardizing the success of the operation and perhaps the very life of the patient. Such an intimate drama places a heavy strain on a man endowed with conscience and heart, but it imparts a sacred character to the medical profession" (*loc. cit.*).

Nor does a surgeon's responsibility end with the completion of the operation, but it continues during the entire period of convalescence and sometimes beyond because of possible unexpected developments or complications.

At all events, irrespective of the outcome of the operation, if the surgeon performed it with all the technical skill at his disposal and with charity, he can feel peace before God and his conscience.

BODILY MUTILATIONS. Regarding the performance of mutilating operations, the moral principle involved is twofold: (a) the bodily parts are subordinate to the welfare of the whole organism; (b) man does not possess full dominion over his body or limbs. Hence it follows that: (a) bodily mutilations directed to the welfare of the whole organism are morally permissible; (b) any bodily mutilation designed to remove or suppress a natural function is morally illicit.

In the light of the above principle, it is morally justifiable and even laudable for an individual to sacrifice or surrender one of his twin organs (an eye, a thyroid lobe, etc.) to remedy a pathological condition in another person, because such surrender does not destroy the specific function (visual, metabolic, etc.) of the organ removed; this is carried on by the remaining organ. The intention of the donor, in such a case, is not to deprive himself of a natural function, but to render possible a similar function in a less fortunate fellow man. If the donation is made disinterestedly, it becomes all the more meritorious.

Also morally justifiable are so-called *organ-banks* (eye, blood, bone, etc.) in many hospitals. The purpose of such

banks is to preserve organs, tissue, blood, etc., donated by individuals for the laudable purpose of remedying pathological conditions in others.

Surgery designed to correct the sex of hermaphrodites is morally permissible if it is performed with prudence and skill and for the sole purpose of harmonizing psychosomatic structures with their relative functions. On the contrary, all operations designed to induce sterility are never permissible. All operations or mutilations that are requested in order to avoid either military service or pregnancy are illicit; operations designed to kill or accelerate the death of individuals born with deformities or malformations, such as monsters, are also illicit and immoral.

In the case of *symmetrical, twin, joined monsters* (i.e., two individuals, more or less equally developed, attached to each other), the suppression of one in favor of the other is illicit. It is equally unlawful to amputate one of the heads of a dicephalous monster with a single trunk.

In the case of *asymmetrical, twin, joined monsters* (i.e., a well-developed *autosite*, upon which lives an incomplete *parasitic* twin), removal of the parasitic twin is permissible only (a) if it is certainly dead; (b) if it is solely an amorphous mass of flesh; (c) if it is merely a limb. Otherwise, the parasitic twin, even though prejudicial to the life of the autosite, may not be removed. Apropos of asymmetrical twin monsters, teratological treatises relate the case of the autosite Lazarus Colaredo (born in 1617), to whose thorax was attached a parasitic twin, named John Baptist, with malformed head and rudimentary limbs and with autonomous, though greatly reduced, psychosomatic functions. The twins lived for a period of twenty-eight years.

PLASTIC SURGERY. The recent and important branch of surgery whose main object is the elimination of functional disorders or the repair of external defects by grafting of bone or tissue is referred to as plastic surgery. In the words of Manna, "the main purpose of plastic surgery is to restore, within the limits of human possibility, the original features given to an individual by the Creator, features made to the image and likeness of God."

When the main purpose of plastic surgery is to repair damaged noses, deformed lips, or remove old-age lines, improve looks, etc., it is called *esthetic surgery*, which presents a few problems of particular interest to moral theology. In general, it may be stated that to undergo featural changes for frivolous motives is morally reprehensible for two reasons: (a) such changes represent a deception; (b) frequently the element of risk involved in such surgery far exceeds the results attained. If external appearances are of great importance and value in one's chosen career, as in the case of actors and actresses, extenuating circumstances are admissible. Of course, if one's main purpose is to correct a grave defect, plastic or esthetic surgery is morally justifiable and even commendable.

OTHER MORAL AND JURIDICAL QUESTIONS. Surgical mistakes and accidents, unless clearly due to willful negligence or culpable lack of knowledge (extremely rare in practice), are not liable to prosecution. As a rule, surgical mistakes and accidents are the result of errors in diagnosis or technique, which, in view of the imperfections of human nature, are bound to occur occasionally (Fraure). If surgical mistakes and accidents were actionable at law, none except the safest and simplest operations would be performed, with grave consequent harm to suffering humanity.

In this connection, it is well to note that certain operations are extremely dangerous and unpredictable, either because of their very nature or because of the patient's grave condition. And it is precisely in such circumstances that the sterling courage and selflessness of a good surgeon stand out. Fully aware that he might be jeopardizing his reputation in such a grave situation, a good surgeon will proceed with the operation, solely concerned with saving the patient's life, if possible. It might here be added that refusal to perform an operation for selfish reasons is always morally reprehensible. Also morally censurable are all useless or unnecessary operations, performed for the sole purpose of material gain. Apropos of this theme, it might be well to quote the words of T. Billroth, eminent and outspoken surgeon of the past century, "The most glorious surgical feats, unless necessary or truly useful, are crimes." *Riz.*

SURPLUS. In the meaning of this article, *surplus* refers to an excess of goods; as an excess, it is a relative term, for temporal goods may be considered necessary to satisfy the basic needs of living in a way of life that is in conformity with one's position in life.

Thus surplus is simply that which remains over and above the needs of one's own proper state. The term *state* or *position in life* includes all the temporal goods necessary to lead a life in accordance with one's proper social conditions. Man is both an individual and a member of society; he is united with others in bonds of solidarity for the welfare of society itself. These bonds of solidarity must extend to the necessities of life and be in proportion to each one's need, as is suggested by reason itself and confirmed by divine precept (Eccl. 4:1; Luke 11:41; Matt. 25:41–42).

The distribution of surplus goods is based on legal justice, in the case of common or grave necessity, and on commutative justice, in the case of extreme necessity.

In cases of extreme or very grave necessity, those who have must give out of their surplus and, if need be, even of the necessities of life, as much as the needy person requires to overcome his dire necessity. This applies to cases of grave, but not extreme, necessity; there is an obligation to give from one's surplus goods, but not from one's own necessities in life. Common necessity makes variable demands on the amount of surplus goods to be distributed from one's resources. According to moralists, persons of ordinary circumstances ought to give to charity about two percent of surplus goods; more prosperous persons ought to give from two to five percent. In cases of extreme necessity, the precept is gravely binding, but not in common necessity and perhaps not in grave necessity.

The observance of this important precept has often been called to the attention of the faithful by the popes, particularly by Leo XIII in *Rerum Novarum* (May 15, 1891), and Pius XI in *Quadragesimo Anno* (May 15, 1931). *Ben.*

SUSPENSION (Ecclesiastical penalty). Suspension, as a canonical or vindicative penalty, has gradually been developed as a mitigation of more serious penalties since the third century. The *Decretals* mention suspension *ex informata conscientia*; the Council of Trent extended suspension as a penalty for regular and secular clerics (Council of Trent, *Sess.* XIV, c. 1, *De ref.*).

Suspension is a penalty by which a cleric is deprived of the exercise of the rights of his office, benefice, or both. The latter is a *general* suspension; the former two are called *special* (Can. 2278). Suspension may be inflicted on a cleric by regular sentence or special precept (Can. 1933, par. 4).

If a penalty is inflicted by judicial sentence, the reason for the suspension is indicated in the process itself; if it is inflicted by a special precept, usually in notorious crimes, the ordinary rules for precepts must be observed. The reasons for suspension should be provided unless it is a suspension *ex informata conscientia*. This does not require that the bishop give reasons for inflicting the penalty (Can. 2186, par. 2).

EFFECTS. The effects of suspension are considered separately for each individual application of the penalty. A general suspension forbids the exercise of the powers of orders, jurisdiction, simple administration, or actions connected with an office (Can. 2279, par. 1).

Suspension from jurisdiction, in general, forbids any exercise of the power of jurisdiction in either forum, whether ordinary or delegated jurisdiction (Can. 2279, par. 2). A suspension *a divinis* forbids any act exercising the power of orders, such as celebrating Holy Mass,

hearing confessions, administering the sacraments, etc. (Can. 2279, par. 1); it does not prohibit the reception of the sacraments of confession or of the Holy Eucharist as a layman.

Suspension *from orders* forbids the exercise of the power of orders received in ordination; suspension *from sacred orders* forbids the exercise of the power of orders received by ordination to sacred orders (Can. 2279, par. 1). There also may be suspensions from the exercise of a particular order, from the power of conferring a particular order, or from the exercise of a particular act of the ministry. Suspension *a pontificiis* forbids the exercise of pontifical acts or the exercise of episcopal powers (Can. 2279, par. 1). Suspension from a benefice does not suspend or deprive the cleric of the power of administering a benefice, but of spending the income for his own use; income must be used for charity or divine worship, as the sacred Canons indicate or the will of the one inflicting the suspension declares. Administration can be expressly removed (Can. 2280, par. 1). If the possessor of a benefice continues to receive the income of a benefice, he is bound to restitution and may be compelled to do so by canonical penalties, if he neglects to fulfill this obligation of a suspension (Can. 2280, par. 2). If a suspension is inflicted on a legal body or moral person, it affects either the individual offenders or the community as a whole (Can. 2285).

CESSATION. To violate a suspension inflicted as a remedial or medicinal penalty results in an irregularity (*see* Irregularity, Impediment). Obstinacy in a violation for six months furnishes a right to the superior to take more serious action.

Suspension, as a medicinal penalty, ceases with absolution (*q.v.*); as a vindicative penalty, it may cease through expiation, dispensation, pardon, and the like.

SUSPENSIO EX INFORMATA CONSCIENTIA. This is an extraordinary remedy (Can. 2186, par. 2), in which a cleric is suspended from office because of a crime that is certain (Can. 2190) but physically or morally impossible to prove in the external forum. Suspension from a benefice is not employed. Ordinarily a vindicative penalty, the reasons for the suspension are to be made known or kept secret from the cleric according to the prudent judgment of the Ordinary (Can. 2193). The cleric, however, has the right of recourse to the Roman Congregations which have competence in these matters. He must do so through administrative procedures and the Ordinary must make known the reasons for the suspension to the Congregation (Can. 2194).

This penalty may be inflicted only for occult crimes (Can. 2191, par. 1), which are not notorious or generally public. This penalty is intended to protect both justice and the personal reputation of the offender. A public crime can be punished by suspension *ex informata conscientia,* if trial is impossible or impeded by the cleric himself (Can. 2191, par. 2).

The penalty of suspension, considered under all its aspects, is an effort to temper the demands of strict justice with consideration for the individual personality, common good, and ethical or social reasons proper to Church law and the interest of souls. *Pug.*

SUSPENSION (OF SENTENCE). Suspension of a sentence means that the infliction of a penalty is suspended. This may occur either as a favor granted or if execution of the penalty would be inhuman because of the poor health or the disturbed mental condition of the culprit (Can. 2223, par. 3, n. 4; *cf. also* Can. 2288).

Suspension of a sentence is occasionally demanded by both the natural and the juridical order. It responds to one of the aims of punishment, which is to help the culprit amend his ways. *Pug.*

SUSTENANCE. Sustenance indicates supplying or being supplied with the necessities of life, food, clothing and shelter.

Parents are obliged to provide the proper support for their offspring, whether legitimate or illegitimate. This obligation arises from the fact that parents transmit life, whether within a valid or reputedly valid marriage or within an illegitimate union. In the latter instance,

of course, certain exceptions are admitted if the support of offspring is assumed by a public institution or a private person (*See* Adoption, Affiliation).

Parents are obliged to support their children until such a time as they are able to provide for themselves. That is to say, they are certainly obliged to provide for children to the age of puberty, and even beyond that period. This obligation exists beyond majority age if the children are unable to provide for themselves or find themselves in difficult circumstances. The quantity and quality of sustenance are to be determined by the socio-economic status of the parents. On the other hand, children are obliged to provide for the support of their needy parents. The same obligation, but to a lesser degree, obtains between brothers.

Frequently the matter of support is regulated by positive laws. Such laws are to be regarded as binding in conscience; they are to be considered as a determination of the natural law in an area that is very broad. *Pav.*

SUSURRUS. Similar to detraction and defamation, *susurrus* means speaking evil of one's neighbor with the intention of causing discord between good friends or of disturbing good relations among individuals.

Susurrus is a detestable, disgusting, petty sin. In itself, it is a graver sin than defamation or detraction, because a good friend may be of more value than honor, or love may be of greater worth than honor or fame. It is not the sin of susurrus if one attempts to break a wicked friendship by lawful or licit moral means. *Ben.*

SYLLABUS. The *Syllabus* designates a series of propositions dealing with the principal errors condemned by Pope Pius IX. The condemnation of these errors was contained in the encyclical *Quanta cura* (December 8, 1864).

The pastoral instruction of the Bishop of Perpignan, which condemned the errors of the era in eighty-five propositions, was used as the basis of the later condemnation by the Pontiff. He set up a commission to study the document; sixty-one propositions were retained and each was provided with a theological censure attached. These propositions and censures were submitted to the judgment of 300 bishops who had gathered at Rome for the canonization of the Japanese Martyrs. The bishops concurred in the condemnations attached to these. But they were not published, because a journalistic indiscretion of the *Mediatore* of Turin stirred up a public furore about the propositions and occasioned violent attacks on the Holy See. As a result, the Pope first postponed and then abandoned the idea of a condemnation in the form of a papal bull.

Since, however, he had already pointed out and condemned in various public documents (allocutions, encyclicals, apostolic letters) the errors contained in the propositions, the Pope instructed the Commission to formulate them in the form of propositions, indicating the source of each so as to point out its dogmatic value. The promulgation was made in two distinct but simultaneous documents: the encyclical *Quanta cura* and the *Syllabus* (Dec. 8, 1864), which were sent in different forms to the bishops. The encyclical carried the usual heading *Venerabilibus Fratribus*, etc.; the *Syllabus* was accompanied by a simple letter from Card. Antonelli, Secretary of State. The promulgation met with unanimous acceptance and support from the whole Catholic episcopate.

The errors condemned in the *Syllabus* have reference to: naturalistic pantheism and absolute rationalism (prop. 1–7); moderate rationalism (8–14); indifferentism and *habitudinarianism* (15–18); the Church and its rights (19–37); civil society and its relationship with the Church (39–55); natural and Christian ethics (56–64); Christian marriage (65–74); papal temporal power (75–76); and liberalism (78–80).

Concerning the juridico-theological value of the *Syllabus*, we should note the following: (a) Its preparation was an act of pontifical authority, since the Pope made it his own and assumed all responsibility for it, although it was edited by a commission. Nor does the form of promulgation affect its value. Other pontifical acts were promulgated by attaching them *ad valvas*, that is, to the doors of the Roman basilicas. In this case, an alternate method of direct communication to the bishops was chosen. The manner or form of promulgation is always a matter of free choice for the legislator. (b) It has a value of its own, distinct from that of the individual documents from which the propositions were drawn. The relationship between the *Syllabus* and the documents that preceded it and the common opinion of the bishops following the promulgation, make it clear that this was the intention of the Pontiff. (c) It is a doctrinal act: the Pope labels the propositions as erroneous and puts the faithful on guard against the dangers arising from such doctrines.

With regard to its theological value, the situation is different. Some of the propositions contain real and proper heresies, especially pantheism, naturalism, and absolute rationalism; others have to do with matters of religious policy and are not so opposed to the faith that they might not be able to exist without harm to the faith under different circumstances. Others are not heretical, but historically false; as such, they cannot be material for dogma, e.g., that the vow of chastity of candidates for ordination, which nullifies matrimony, dates back to Boniface VIII. Consequently, no new censure is attached to the errors contained in the *Syllabus* over and above the ones established by the documents from which they were drawn. M.d.G.

SYMPATHY. *Sympathy* has a variety of meanings. In this article it means an instinctive attraction toward another person. In itself, it is not sinful; but every individual must carefully control his feelings of sympathy lest he be led to dangerous occasions. Sympathy toward a person of the opposite sex may lead to the love that prepares for and accompanies marriage, but also to an inordinate passion and vice. In the same way, attraction toward those of the same sex may lead to true friendship or to the so-called sensual friendship, which is a fertile ground for unnatural vices.

Failure to repress a dangerous attraction to another person becomes a mortal sin if it becomes a serious danger of mortal sin. *Man.*

SYNOD, DIOCESAN. A diocesan synod is the lawful assembly of the clergy of a diocese and others, required to attend, which is convoked by the bishop to deal with problems affecting the particular needs of the clergy and faithful of the diocese (Can. 356, par. 1). The bishop is the only legislator in a synod; he alone signs all laws enacted (Can. 362). Yet it is important and useful for a bishop to hear the opinions and suggestions of others on the laws suggested. In certain nominations, such as synodal examiners, judges, and parochial consultors, the vote of the fathers of the synod has a deliberative force (Can. 385, par. 1).

The bishop is obliged to hold a synod every ten years; the following are to be invited and take part: vicar general, canons of the cathedral church, diocesan consultors, rectors of the major seminary, vicars forane, representatives of each collegiate chapter, pastors of the city in which the synod is held, a representative of each deanery, abbots *de regimine*, representatives of clerical congregations, chosen by the provincials, and those, finally, whom the bishop invites.

The synod should be held in the cathedral church, but it is permitted to hold the non-solemn sessions elsewhere (Can. 357, par. 1). The synod is legitimately convoked if a sufficient number of representatives is present, and no one is excluded who has a right to be present. It is presided over by the bishop or a priest delegated by the bishop (Can. 357, par. 1). The officials of the synod to be chosen by the bishop are: the promoter, whose duty it is to see that all is done in accordance with the law; a secretary; a notary for official publication of the acts; and, finally, a master of ceremonies.

The sole recourse against synodal de-crees is *in devolutivo*; that is, the laws retain their force in the meantime. *Fel.*

SYPHILIS. Syphilis was so named in 1530 by Girolamo Fracastore, doctor and humanist, who, in his famous poem *Syphilis, seu de morbo gallico*, told of an American shepherd, Syphilis, who had offended the gods and was stricken with a serious disease that quickly spread through the population. But we are not certain about its true origin. On the basis of passages in *Leviticus* (13–15) and evidence found in the bone-structure of ancient skeletons, some scholars hold the opinion that syphilis has been a sad heritage of man from most ancient times. Others maintain that syphilis was an infection unknown in the civilized world until the sailors of Christopher Columbus contracted it in America and carried it back to Europe. It spread all over the European Continent in an epidemic of exceptional seriousness at the end of the fifteenth century. Scillazio refers to it in a letter, sent from Barcelona on June 18, 1495, as a disease that had spread rapidly from France (*qui nuper Gallia defluxit in alias nationes*).

CHARACTERISTICS. Syphilis is an infectious disease caused by a particular *spirochete* discovered by Schaudinn in 1905. About a fiftieth of a millimeter long, it is called *treponema pallidum* or, less properly, *spirochaeta pallida*. The germ enters the organism by contact, through the tiniest openings in the skin; and, following a period of *incubation* of two to four weeks, a characteristic node or tumor, called *syphiloma initialis*, becomes ulcerated (*primitive syphilitic ulcer, hard ulcer*), and is accompanied by pain in the lymph glands.

Sexual contact is the more common form of contamination. There are also other forms, such as contact with articles, infection resulting from contact by doctors, midwives, nurses, breast feeding and so forth. The infection takes place without the usual early symptoms in cases where the *treponema* has directly entered the bloodstream. Infections, indeed very rare, may result from blood transfusion or in a congenital infection of a fetus.

After one or two months, the general symptoms that characterize the so-called *second stage* of the infection appear: syphilitic roseola, swelling of all the lymph glands, more or less serious abdominal pains, slight fever, and a feeling of weakness (asthenia), and discomfort, headaches, etc. With the passage of time, the symptoms decrease to a point of disappearance.

After three or four years, the *tertiary period* begins. These symptoms attack individual internal organs (liver, kidneys, pancreas, etc.) with profound changes.

Approximately ten to twenty years later, the so-called *quaternary period* takes place. It is characterized by symptoms of a constantly progressive type that do not respond to specific treatment. These symptoms affect the heart, especially the aorta, and the nervous system in progressive paralysis (*q.v.*) and *tabes dorsalis*.

Syphilis is easily transmitted to offspring. At one time it was thought that the transmission took place through germinal elements, but today most hold that it takes place, after conception, through the mother's bloodstream. Hence it is more accurate to speak of *congenital syphilis* than *hereditary syphilis*.

From a social point of view, congenital syphilis is worse than acquired syphilis, for it reduces the power of fertility in the spouses, causes abortions, premature births, and infant mortality.

An increased proneness to disease and death are frequent results. Syphilis is one of the main causes of brain diseases in infants and of so-called mental degeneration, which is so largely responsible for mental illnesses and crimes.

TREATMENT. Syphilis can be diagnosed easily and with certainty at any stage of the disease through the use of blood tests. The most important test was devised by Wassermann in 1906. Today syphilis is the easiest of serious diseases to treat and one that admits of complete cure since the discovery of penicillin.

Of course, the treatment will be all the more effective, the earlier it is given and the more frequently it is repeated at intervals over a three-year period. The patient must remain under clinical and seriological observation for the rest of his life, to counter any new attack of this extremely chronic disease at the beginning.

PROPHYLAXIS. The best method is continence.

ETHICO-SANITARY CONSIDERATIONS. The first and most obvious obligation for every diseased person is to avoid transmitting his illness to others. This means that proper precautions must be taken, especially in the case of members of the family.

Recent statistics show that syphilis is diminishing both as to the seriousness of its symptoms and its extent. It seems that this favorable course of events is not the result of any provision made for prophylaxis or treatment, but is rather tied to the natural evolution of the disease. Like any other contagious disease, syphilis, too, is supposedly wearing itself out.

This consideration, which could be disproved by new outbreaks of syphilis, does not detract from the value of prophylaxis and treatment.

A serious hindrance in the fight against the spread of syphilis arises from professional secrecy (*q.v.*), which must be maintained. A doctor is strictly bound not to reveal such a disease without the explicit consent of the sick person. It is true that civil law sometimes attaches penalties to someone knowingly transmitting venereal diseases, but these sanctions are for the most part theoretical and can rarely be carried out effectively.

An effective fight against syphilis is possible if appropriate widespread education, periodic check-up, and suitable treatment are provided for those afflicted by this disease. Sweden is one country that has undertaken suitable measures in this field since 1918, with notable results. This is the road that should be followed by all other nations that wish to attain worthy biological and economic improvement for their peoples. A good step forward along this road would be the one suggested by Tommasi, consisting of a test for all citizens at various key points in life (entrance into school, enrollment in military service, discharge, employment, marriage). Tests of this kind would have the effect of bringing to light latent and unknown cases, which could then be treated with relative promptness and effective results. *Riz.*

SYSTEM, CANONICO-JUDICIAL.

Besides legislative branches charged with the responsibility of issuing regulations to be observed by subjects, every organization must have branches charged with the administration of justice or with settling in a definitive way controversies which arise in the application of law to particular cases.

In societies such as the Church, which are organized hierarchically, the sovereign has absolute powers (the Supreme Pontiff for the Church). Without limitations except from divine law, justice could, in theory, be administered personally by the sovereign himself. But it is quite proper and often necessary that there should be groups especially appointed for that purpose, due to the enormous amount of work which would weigh upon the head of a government and the obvious advantages which would result from the administration of justice by specialized groups. These bodies are the tribunals.

If it is impossible for justice to be administered by a single tribunal in civil States, this is more true of the Church, whose field of action extends to all parts of the world, although the number of cases is less than in many modern civil States.

ECCLESIASTICAL TRIBUNALS AND JURISDICTION. In the Church, in addition to central tribunals, located in Rome, which have jurisdiction over cases from all parts of the world (Cans. 1597–1605), there are local tribunals, whose jurisdiction extends to a definite territory or groups of persons.

Since a diocese is the basic territorial boundary of the Church, there is in every diocese a tribunal to judge in first instance all cases within that territory, with few exceptions (Can. 1572 ff.). Furthermore, in each ecclesiastical province, the tribunal of the primary diocese or metropolitan see is the tribunal of first instance for the diocese itself and a tribunal of appeals for cases tried in first instance in another diocese or a suffragan diocese of the province (Can. 1594). It may be noted here that an individual has the right to request that a decision in second instance be given by the tribunal of the Sacred Roman Rota (*q.v.*) rather than by the ordinary appeals tribunal (Can. 1599, par. 1, n. 1).

This is a basic outline of the judicial organization of the Church. Tribunals are organized in a different manner to adjudicate cases concerning certain religious orders (Can. 654 ff.), cases in mission territories, cases concerning the faithful of the Eastern rites (*see* Curia, Roman), sacred ordination (Can. 1993), beatification (*q.v.*), and canonization.

In certain cases due to lack of personnel, or difficulties due to distance, it is difficult to follow the various jurisdictional steps. The Holy See sets up regional tribunals by grouping together the tribunals of first instance in a certain territory with appeals tribunals (regional tribunals), or by creating local tribunals of third instance. *Cip.*

SYSTEM, MORAL. A moral system is a method of handling a concrete, practical situation or solving a practical doubt in the moral order; this comprises the application of general principles to a difficulty of conscience in which uncertainty or doubt exists as to whether an act which one is about to perform is lawful.

Problems of uncertainty or doubt in moral questions arise when a proposition asserting the lawfulness of an act and another denying this are more or less probable opinions in the objective sense (*see* Opinion).

A judgment of conscience which wavers between two opposite opinions cannot be an ethical norm of conduct; conduct must be based on certainty. Certainty is attained either by reconsidering the whole question more carefully or, if this is impossible or yields no results, by using reflex principles of morality (*see* Principles, Reflex).

However, it is still possible that this certainty may not be attainable because of some fear, arising from error or ignorance about principles or facts, that one will violate the law no matter which course one might choose. In such a perplexed conscience, it is not possible to put off action altogether until a more careful examination of the ethical values involved in the decision is made; prudence suggests that the solution which seems less involved should be adopted, preferring, for example, the common good to individual good, natural law to positive law, etc.

ORIGIN AND CONTENT OF MORAL SYSTEMS. The principles referred to above are called *reflex*, because, though extraneous to the moral content of the particular act about which one is doubtful, they are, nevertheless, indirectly connected with its ethical value, which may be basically the same as that of the doubt disturbing the conscience.

These reflex principles, not unknown to the Fathers and Scholastics, were developed systematically in the sixteenth century. The early Fathers were generally inclined to a rigoristic attitude, although examples of decisions favoring liberty are not wanting. Thus, in a case of doubt whether a war is just or not, St. Augustine does not forbid a soldier to fight in it. In a similar way, St. Gregory Nazianzen defends liberty against the rigorism of Novatian.

Under the influence of juridical principles and the exaggerated objectivism of Aristotle, the Middle Ages were wont to solve doubt by a tutiorist solution, which was moderate. Statements that could be considered the basis for a well-understood probabilism are also present. St. Thomas himself gives a tutiorist solution in treating the question of doubt *ex professo*; but in dealing with the knowledge required before a law becomes binding, he lays down the basis for a broader and more humane solution. There is a more humane tendency in the fourteenth century on the part of certain authors who are satisfied with a moral certitude in the broad sense (Gerson) or

with greater probability (Nider, St. Antoninus).

An even broader approach is that of the school of Salamanca, due to the work of Francisco de Vittoria and, above all, Bartolomeo Medina, who was the first to propose and defend the rights of liberty explicitly, despite stronger reasons in favor of the law (probabilism).

Medina's thesis attracted wide support and stirred up criticism as well. This became increasingly bitter because of the excessive leniency with which some interpreted and used it, by reducing the concept of probability to a mere enumeration of names and authorities (laxism). Some critics limited themselves to condemning excesses of this kind; others attacked more moderate authors as well and thus adopted an extreme position of absolute tutiorism, which the Church had to reject just as it had rejected the laxist approach.

This is the origin of the various systems that have developed between tutiorism on one extreme and laxism on the other.

Absolute *tutiorism* maintains that one must always follow the safest path, even if the reasons denying the existence of some particular precept enjoy maximum probability (Sinnich). This doctrine was condemned by Alexander VIII (cf. F. Claeys-Bouüaert, "*Autour de deux décrets du Saint-Office*" . . . 2 mars, 1679 . . . 7 décembre, 1690, in *Ephemerides Theologicae Lovanienses*, 29 [1953], 419–444). To escape condemnation, a *mitigated tutiorism* (Opstraet, Steyaert, Gerdil), though still based on the same concern to avoid the danger of any infraction of the law whatsoever, even a material one, permitted the freer course in a case of doubt if the reasons in favor of liberty were really *most* probable.

A more moderate and humane position is *probabiliorism*, which demands that the motives in favor of liberty be simply more probable. It also demands this greater probability because the ethical norm must correspond to the logical norm in the sense that, if certitude is lacking, the intellect cannot reasonably adhere to a proposition that seems less probable (Gonet, Bossuet, Tirso Gonzalez and the greater number of modern Dominicans).

Equiprobabilism agrees with the preceding system in holding as morally certain any opinion sustained by more probable reasons. But in a case where there are two opinions of equal force, one favoring liberty and the other favoring enforcement of law, it applies the juridical principle of possession (Gousset, D'Annibale, Tanquerey, and, in general, Redemptorists).

A new *system of compensation* or *of Christian prudence*, as it is called, proceeds on a completely different basis (Laloux, Manier, Potton, Prümmer). This measures the degree of obligation in the law against the degree of knowledge that the person has of the law; it then requires that the danger of a possible infraction of the law be compensated and justified by proportionate reasons.

Pure *probabilism*, instead, rejects all calculation and prescinds from any comparison; it stands for liberty at all times, as long as there are serious reasons for questioning the existence or the extension of a moral bond that is not necessarily linked to the achievement of a specific end (Medina, Reiffenstuel, Goepfert, Bouquillon and almost all theologians of the Society of Jesus).

Laxism was never professed as a system by anyone; it is simply the practical degeneration of probabilism, if the latter is interpreted and applied with too much leniency in the attempt to minimize all moral bonds as much as possible, by preferring a convenient ignorance to careful study and trying to clothe the most absurd and ridiculous opinions with the colors of probability (Caramuel, Juan Sanchez, Moya, etc.).

CRITICAL REMARKS. Tutiorism implies an exaggerated esteem of man's reasoning capacity and presupposes an erroneous notion of the ethical order. The very complexity of the ethical elements proper to man's acts and their profound psychological diversity often prevent man, in his search for morality, from attaining an absolute certitude that would exclude all possibility of error. As a result, if error occurs, man is not morally responsible for it; it remains outside the ethical order, as does a material infraction of the law that depends on it. This consideration is directly opposed not only to absolute *tutiorism* but to its mitigated form as well and to any other system based on the same suppositions.

Nor is it true, as the supporters of *probabiliorism* hold, that in a case of doubt one must follow the opinion that appears to be more likely, just as it is not necessary to be theoretically certain of a less probable opinion favoring liberty in order to be able to follow it. Greater probability is not a criterion of greater truth nor does it destroy the value of opposite motives which make the obligation doubtful and, hence, practically non-existent.

The principle of possession is a transfer of a juridical norm into the ethical field; this norm is valid only in the case of a certain possession opposed to a doubtful right; whereas, if the doubt revolves around the existence of a law, one can at no time speak of certain possession on the part of the law, not even in a case where it was previously binding.

Nor is it clear how the principle of compensation can be transferred into this field and be applied only to those cases where the evil is foreseen as an accidental result of one's actions. In a case of doubt, instead, the hypothetical infraction of a law is ontologically linked to the activity carried on, in which it inheres, so that it is not simply tolerated but actively accepted by the agent and imputed to him as long as it is thought that such an infraction is subject to real moral imputability.

To avoid this serious difficulty, it is absolutely necessary to make a distinction between the ontological and the moral orders. The only way to avoid this thesis, that a violation of the ontological order necessarily entails a violation of the moral order in a doubt concerning the existence or extension of a law, is to accept this distinction between the moral order and the ontological order. To admit this principle is to accept probabilism.

The Principles of Probabilism. (a) In a positive and prudent doubt about the existence or extent of a particular precept, it is not wrong to follow an opinion favoring liberty, even if the opposing opinion, a more rigid one, is based on weightier reasons, as long as the former still retains a probability with respect to the latter. As long as doubt exists, the existence of the law is not sufficiently revealed, so that, even if the law really does exist, it remains extraneous to the subject and does not bind in conscience. Nor is conscience bound by reflex principles of more rigid systems, since these, too, appear by no means certain. Thus, short of falling into tutiorism, there can be no objection to standing for liberty.

(b) The case is different, however, if the doubt revolves around a means which appears as probably indispensable for the attainment of a particular end which is also necessary. In such a case, prudence dictates that one follow the safer course.

In these cases, it is not just a question of the rightness or wrongness of an action; that depends proximately upon reason and conscience. Rather, it is a question of the value of the action itself, or of a *conditio sine qua non* (indispensable) for attaining an end. These things do not depend upon us, for our evaluation cannot change the nature of things. Thus, in the face of a doubt whether or not explicit belief in the mysteries of the Trinity and the Incarnation is a necessary means for eternal salvation, one may not neglect instructing a person in these mysteries before conferring baptism or administering penance to him.

In the same way, an unbeliever or a heretic who begins to doubt the truth of his own religious position may not give up his search by relying on a supposed probability for his views and nothing more. Thus, it is a sin for one who has the true faith to suspend judgment on a truth proposed for belief, since such a suspension goes against his obligation to make an act of faith; and if the doubt persists, he becomes a heretic (Can. (1325).

(c) The same may be said if a positive doubt exists concerning a fact that is a condition for the fulfillment of a certain law. For the fact that we are sure of the precept implies an obligation to choose the surest means. A doubt concerning the existence of a law affects the obligation itself, which cannot become a moral obligation unless the individual is aware of it. Nevertheless, a doubt concerning a fact does not affect the nature of the fact and, hence, it does not make us certain that we are fulfilling the law.

Thus, the law of charity demands that one receive a certainly valid baptism for himself and others. A religious law (an obligation of charity or justice may be involved as well) forbids us, as a general rule, to expose the sacraments to the danger of nullity, in the same way that justice requires that we make sure that we are respecting the rights of others.

(d) But if the fact is a condition for the obligation itself, the doubt of fact resolves itself into a doubt of law; thus there is no certainty that a moral bond exists.

(e) Finally, a negative doubt of fact cannot reasonably weaken a moral certitude that was previously acquired. This certitude, in regard to human acts, sometimes arises from a presumption. For this reason, generally in case of doubt, one must judge on the basis of ordinary contingencies (*in dubio judicandum est ex ordinarie contingentibus*). In a negative doubt concerning the existence of a specific fact, the fact cannot be presumed (*factum non praesumitur, sed probandum est*). If there is certainty of the fact, one can presume that the act was performed validly (*in dubio, standum est pro valore actus*).

If, in a particular case, no principle offers certainty in resolving a doubt or if the doubt is completely negative, the solution will vary according to the different functions that the fact fulfills with respect to the law: a fact which in reality is a condition in a prohibition does not hold in a prohibition. Thus, a doubt about the fact of breaking the fast before receiving the Holy Eucharist does not prohibit the reception of the sacrament. If, however, the law makes a certain action obligatory and a determined con-dition for granting a faculty or perform-ing a valid act, any negative doubt con-cerning the fulfillment of the precept or verification of the condition must be solved in the tutiorist sense. *Pal.*

T

TABAGISM. *See* Diseases, professional.

TABERNACLE. *See* Custody of the Most Holy Eucharist.

TABES, DORSAL. *See* Syphilis.

TACHYPSYCHOLOGY. *See* Constitution, Biotypological.

TALENT. *See* Intelligence.

TALK, OBSCENE. Obscene talk is a conversation about sexual matters conducted in a libidinous manner. Conversation about sex is not obscene if motivated by an honest reason like medical consultation, sexual instruction properly imparted, etc. However, in such cases, the norms of prudence must be followed. In moral theology the subject of obscene language is dealt with in connection with acts of impurity, because obscene language is wont to stimulate one's sexual instincts through the imagination (*see* Impurity). The malice of obscene language stems from evil intention, such as seduction, perverse sexual initiation, intent to arouse sexual reactions, frivolous conversations, and jokes which, though generally not a grave sin, are nevertheless highly censurable among Christians. Malice may be due to inordinate passion, venereal disturbance, scandal, etc. Listening willingly to an obscene conversation is a sin, either because of cooperation in an illicit matter by approval or encouragement, either implicit or explicit, or because of danger of committing an impure act or experiencing sexual excitation. Every individual is bound by charity to defend public morality and to discourage obscene conversation to the extent that conditions of the moment warrant it. Those with a position of authority have a special duty in this regard. *Dam.*

TAMETSI. *See* Marriage, Form of.

TANTUM ERGO. *Tantum ergo* are the opening words of the next to the last stanza of the hymn *Pange Lingua* (*q.v.*). The last two stanzas of the *Pange Lingua* are the official hymn for Benediction of the Most Holy Sacrament.

The *Tantum Ergo* summarizes the entire meaning of the hymn. The author first invites the faithful to praise and glorify the mysteries of Christ's Body and Blood shed for the salvation of the world; then, he recalls the institution of the Holy Eucharist, and, after he notes the effects of the most salient aspects of the mystery of the Real Presence, he urges all to venerate Jesus in the Most Holy Sacrament of the Altar. *Cig.*

TAOISM. Taoism, the doctrine of *Tao* (Way), derives its name from the book entitled *Tao Te King* (*Book of the Way and of Virtue*). Its fundamental doctrine is attributed to the philosophers Laotse (Laotzu), Chuang Tzu, and Lieh Tzu, but its compilation does not precede the fourth-third centuries B.C.

Laotse, a contemporary of Confucius, is more unknown than Confucius regarding details of his life and thought, as well as the relation that his personality had with the religion bearing his name. He was born about 604 B.C. Of his life nothing is known. Tradition connects him with countries to the west of China where he is alleged to have gone in his declining years on a journey from which he never returned.

Before leaving, he is alleged to have left as a spiritual testament his *Book of the Way and of Virtue*. This book contains a moral system which is linked in a confused, mystical way to his religion. The order in the universe, which Confucius had also taken as a basis for his system, is condensed by Laotze into the word *Tao* (way), that is, the norm according to which the universe is disposed and the government of man, the earth, and the heavens are coordinated. "Man is governed according to the standard of the earth, the earth according to that of the heavens, the heavens according to the standard of *Tao* and *Tao* according to his own standard." Taoist cosmogony can be briefly traced thus: a first single principle (*Tao*), initially concentrated and inactive, erupted into emanation and production. As a result of this emanation, this principle produced the heavens, the earth, and the air, interposed between the other two elements. All other beings derived from heaven and earth, since the air is simply the matter of the heavens and the earth. The principle lives and works in everything; it does not think but is the source of thought; it does not will but it is the law. The destiny of every being emanates from it. The sole duty of man is to unite himself with the primordial principle, by willing that which it wills and doing that which it does (Wieger). In conclusion, *Tao* is the omnipotent, omnipresent, and extraordinary principle of the universe. The principle of virtue is found in the knowledge of such a principle. Therefore, the minute science of ritual is useless, and the feverish engagement in the material affairs of the State is futile. One must limit his needs to strict necessities and reduce his desires; he must keep away from excitements and disturbances which cause him to lose tranquility or distract him from the meditation of *Tao*. This is the precept (*Wu Wei*) of Taoism. Virtue, for Laotze, is not in action but in piety, thrift, and humility; under this aspect it is opposed to the moral-political activism of Confucius.

How this system of mystical rationalism could have risen to, and been connected with, Taoism, a religion of an inferior order, full of popular and magi-

cal elements, is not easy to understand. Many scholars are wont to see the influence of Indian thinking, confirmed by the legend of the journey of Laotze to the West. It may suffice to say with De Groot that the origin of Taoism as a religion is lost in the shadows of time but that it is a collection of all the animistic beliefs, magical practices, and coarse superstitions which form the basis of popular religion in China and elsewhere.

Its moral doctrine, primarily a search for egoistical preservation of life by the removal of the dangerous or harmful, prescribes: (a) reduction of desires and cultural pursuits which render the mind childish; (b) preparation by physical exercises (breathing exercises, gymnastics, diet, etc.) and spiritual practices (pure life, meditation, etc.) aimed at achieving immortality of the body. This immortality at one time was sought by means of alchemistic and talismanic practices.

Its organization as a Church, with temples, a priestly and monastic hierarchy, and a supreme head (elected by casting lots) who resided at Lunghu in Kiang-si under the title of Tien-se, i.e., Celestial Teacher or divine master, goes back, according to De Groot, to the first century A.D. It must be attributed to Chang-tao-ling (34–156 A.D.), the famous miracle worker, skillful manipulator of the elixir of life, and successful exorcist. Undoubtedly, he personifies the passage of Taoist doctrine from a philosophical state to a religion.

The Chinese republic of Sun-yat-sen (1911) would not bestow any special privilege upon the Celestial Teacher, but, in 1927, ordered the seizure of property owned by Taoism in Kiang-si, and converted its shrines in the various cities into schools or barracks. The Communist government has since confiscated the land properties still remaining in continental China.

Exact statistics of the followers of Taoism are not possible, due to a process of osmosis among the three great religions of China—Buddhism, Taoism, and Confucianism. The *abbé* E. d'Espierres, whose figures are accepted by the *Guide of the Catholic Missions* (Rome, 1934), gives the figure at 393,000,000 under the aggregate entry "Religions of China."

Taoism, as a religion, combines animistic beliefs, magical practices and forms of superstition proper to the coarsest forms of religions. Its positive moral doctrine, which is quite inferior to the superior teachings of Confucius, is oriented toward mortification of the ego and a pessimistic outlook. When it preaches that life has no meaning, that it is better to await quietly the rest beyond the grave, it is logical to conclude that for them work and effort are useless. From the social aspect, its moral doctrine, which teaches rulers to attend only to keeping the people well fed and ignorant, is anti-educational and retrograde. Entirely opposed to these teachings are Christian social ethics and the moral doctrine of Confucius, who aimed at bettering government by the princes who ruled over the nation (*see* Confucianism). *Pal.*

TAPHOPHOBIA. *See* Psychasthenia.

TAVERN-KEEPER. A tavern-keeper is one who runs or manages a tavern, that is, a place where food and drinks are served, and at times lodging provided. A tavern-keeper is, in a certain sense, the equivalent of the old time hospitaller or hospice-keeper (Latin, *hospes*—one who provides lodging for strangers). Hospitality was regarded among all peoples as a natural sentiment of man; any action contrary to it was judged generally as criminal. Thus arose out of Christian duty, or for reasons of trade, special places for strangers or travelers.

Besides these places, the Romans also had places of refuge for vagrants, where idlers indulged in all kinds of vices, plots against the state, and all types of crimes. Such places were called *taberna, popina, caupona,* etc. With a few variations, such places still exist, wherein food and drink are served, and sometimes lodging, generally to persons of low social standing, without fixed domicile or family ties.

The trade of tavern-keeper was considered by some of the older moral theologians as morally objectionable, because, in general, taverns were attended by individuals of low social standing and unscrupulous nature, and were places where certain individuals spent many hours of the holy days in revelries, drinking and gambling, with complete neglect of religious and domestic obligations. However, today a number of moral theologians hold the tavern-keeper no longer directly responsible for such negligences by his patrons, nor do they consider the trade of tavern-keeper, in itself and of itself, immoral or improper unless the tavern operator is guilty of improper activities or objectionable allurements. Generally, a Christian-minded tavern-keeper, who observes the prescriptions of the law, may legitimately feel that he is engaged in an honest and moral trade. For other moral obligations, *see* Innkeeper. *Tar.*

TAX, TAXATION. A tax is revenue which the State or other authority or governing body collects from individuals and corporations for the support and the maintenance of certain public services.

Taxes for public services involve services absolutely necessary for community living, enjoyed by all citizens in general, and *indivisible.* Such are national defense, a maintenance of order, and the administration of justice. To maintain these services, the State or other public body needs adequate financial means which citizens would not contribute in sufficient measure on a voluntary basis.

Taxes are *direct* if they are assessed on actual possessions, such as taxes on real estate or personal income; *indirect* taxes are concealed in the purchase price of consumer goods; *real*, if applied to a property irrespective of the economico-social circumstances of the person who owns it or develops it (taxation of farmland); *personal*, if applied to an individual's overall income; *proportional*, if the tax scale is the same for each taxable unit; *progressive*, if the scale increases by degrees for each subsequent taxable unit.

The payment of taxes entails serious moral problems. The very nature of taxation constitutes an expression of social responsibility. Taxes are levied for the purpose of enabling public authority to maintain services for the benefit of all citizens, though not all contribute in equal measure. Those who govern a country cannot arbitrarily establish taxes. These must be estimated according to positive public needs of the collectivity at a specific historical period or on the basis of the actual contributing ability of the citizens. This evaluation is clearly a complex, delicate, and difficult task indivisibly linked with the concept of political and social life. Thirdly, a duty exists for legislative bodies to choose the least burdensome system of taxation with the best public services possible (see Contribution, Finance, Justice, Taxation, Tax). *Pav.*

TAX, ECCLESIASTICAL. An ecclesiastical tax is a legitimate assessment imposed by the competent ecclesiastical authority, either in behalf of some particular ecclesiastical institution (seminary tax), or for acts of so-called voluntary jurisdiction, or for dispensations or other favors and rescripts from the Holy See, or on the occasion of the administration of sacraments and sacramentals.

It is *a lawful* assessment because it is established according to canonical laws (Can. 1507, par. 1–2; Can. 1234, par. 1) or lawful customs, and because any simoniacal pact is excluded. In other words, any barter between spiritual and material things is forbidden. A distinction must be made between a tax, which is obligatory, and donation, which is a free offering. Taxes are due to acts involving the exercise of the sacred ministry, rescripts of the Holy See, and assessments necessary for the government of the Church or common good. Ecclesiastical tax applies equally and uniformly to all the faithful and is governed by the sacred canons (1507, 1566, 1224, 1909).

Besides taxes and fees imposed on all the faithful (see Stole Fees, Ecclesiastical Burial), there are other taxes imposed only on the clergy or ecclesiastical property, such as *censum, seminaristicum, cathedraticum,* and *maintenance.*

Censum, in a strict sense, is an annual tax levied on ecclesiastical property, paid to a superior or an ecclesiastical legal person for a just reason, approved by the Church, as a token of submission. In a broader sense, *censum* is an extraordinary collection levied by the pope or bishop on ecclesiastical revenue for a just reason. The supreme pontiff has the power to levy temporary or perpetual tax on ecclesiastical property.

A form of *censum* was the so-called Peter's Pence, which in earlier times was mandatory in some regions. It was paid to the pope as acknowledgement of the supreme rule of the Holy See or as protection and exemption from ordinary taxes. Types of *censum* are also certain extraordinary papal levies, such as the *right of spoils (jus spolii),* levied on certain possessions upon the death of clerics; *the right of recreation,* levied on the revenues of vacant benefices; *the right of the annate,* levied on ordinary and small services; *the taxes* imposed on the occasion of the conferral of the pallium, or for dispensations or other benefits.

According to the present discipline, the bishop cannot impose either a perpetual or temporary pension lasting for the entire life of the pensionary (see Pension). An exception is made in the case of a parish priest or parish vicar (administrator) who relinquishes his parochial benefice. Only for a just reason, to be indicated in the act of conferring the benefice, may he impose a temporary pension lasting for the whole life of the person on whom the benefice is conferred. This pension, however, must be such as to leave the possessor of the benefice sufficient revenue for adequate maintenance (Can. 1429). The bishop has the right to impose the following taxes: (a) *seminaristicum,* (b) *cathedraticum (synodaticum),* (c) *subsidium caritatum* established at the time of erection, and (d) a *maintenance* tax.

The *seminaristicum* (seminary tax) is a general and proportional tax levied by the Ordinary on ecclesiastical property

(Can. 1356, par. 1) in behalf of the seminary, if this lacks its own special funds. The tax must not exceed five per cent of the net income and must be reduced if the income of the seminary increases. In many places, there are foundations, scholarships, and donations given for the maintenance of the seminary in place of the *seminaristicum* (seminary tax).

Concerning *cathedraticum,* see article on *Cathedraticum.* The *subsidium caritatum* is an extraordinary and moderate tax which the bishop may impose on all benefices (Can. 1515) for a special and urgent need of the diocese. This tax was permitted by the Third Lateran Council (1179 A.D.). Strictly speaking, approval of the chapter was required for such tax; as a matter of fact, Pope Innocent XI ordered that a bishop could levy such tax upon assuming the government of his diocese but only according to the amount levied in the forty years prior to his installation. The Code removed these restrictions and, today, frequent recourse is made to it in order to provide for the needs of the diocese. The general policy, however, is based on the extent of the benefice. On this basis, special faculties were given to all the bishops by the Sacred Congregation of Council. A particular tax may be levied for the benefit of the diocese or the patron at the time of the foundation of a benefice or the consecration of an ecclesiastical institute.

The *procuratio* is the payment of board and lodging for the bishop or his delegate and his attendants during apostolic visitation.

The Provincial Council, with approval of the Holy See, for apostolic dispensations, such as matrimonial dispensations, etc., and the Ordinary have the right to determine ecclesiastical taxes. Bishops who raise ecclesiastical taxes or exact higher taxes than those established are subject to heavy pecuniary fines (Can. 1408). Recidivists are subject to suspension or removal from office, and have an obligation to restitution of all that was unjustly extorted.

Taxes are lawful and binding in conscience if they are levied according to the spirit of the ecclesiastical law. Whoever exacts unlawful taxes may become guilty of the sin and crime of simony and is bound to restitution *sub gravi* or *sub levi,* depending on whether the matter of their crime was grave or light. *Sir.*

TAYLORISM. *See* Psychotechnique.

TEACHER (Master). *Teacher* or *school master* (Latin, *magister, magis, magnus*—higher or above ordinary individuals) indicates a learned man, trained in some science or art. Hence, it was applied to one who taught an art or science; later, to any man skilled in some profession. Some scholars believe that *teacher (master)* was orginally a title of authority, power, or office, rather than an indication of learning. Hence, the terminology *master of the house, courts, palace, ceremonies,* etc. Later, rectors or prefects of public schools, lawyers, physicians, and magistrates were called masters. The term *master* was also used as equivalent of *doctor* in an academic degree giving one the authority to teach philosophy, theology, or arts. *Master,* without specification, has in our times a variety of meanings. The most common of them is that of *teacher* or *schoolmaster,* who guides and instructs children or youths.

A teacher's mission is a difficult and responsible one. To be successful, a teacher must be endowed with particular qualities: (a) *A vocation.* He should not devote his life to teaching without a calling, lest his become just another job. (b) *A healthy body.* Teaching is an energy-consuming task, which requires the teacher to be in constant personal contact with the pupils. (c) *Practical ability, alertness and skill* in presenting subject matter clearly. A teacher's aim must reach the soul of his pupils, striving very earnestly to mold the whole man.

Lust for money should never be his primary motive. A teacher who seeks material gain alone shall fail in his mission. Of course, he must earn his living, but he must always remember that he is much more than a common wage-earner; he is a teacher.

A teacher with little knowledge fails to inspire his pupils; hence, he has a grave obligation to acquire proper knowledge, for knowledge gives him the prestige necessary to effective teaching.

It is a teacher's duty to mold the minds of his pupils by imparting well-grounded knowledge, exactness of judgment by thoughtful and fair observations, and a power of reasoning based on sound logic. To impart knowledge constitutes only one half of a teacher's obligation, for he must educate the whole man, his intellect and will, his heart and soul. A teacher who confines his efforts simply to instructing the mind and leaves to others the work of educating the whole man, errs gravely. No greater evil can be done to a pupil than to corrupt his mind; for it is the mind that governs man. The heart follows an enlightened and well trained spirit. For this reason a teacher cannot ignore religion. He must personally live and teach it to his pupils by the example of a just and moral life.

In practice, a "neutral" or lay school is inconceivable and a source of absurdities. A school is either Christian or godless. There is no middle way. *If the school is not a temple, it will be a den* (*see* School).

A teacher must integrate the mother's and father's mission. He must cultivate in his pupils affection and gratitude toward their parents, a spirit of obedience, laboriousness and thrift, and a sound religious and moral character. A teacher must instill in his pupils (a) honesty of mind and heart, words and actions; (b) a right conscience, pointing out the true internal and external enemies of man; (c) a firm will, through fortitude and self-denial; (d) integrity in all its aspects. He must be vigilant in upholding morality, for a distorted conscience has no regard for anything. (e) He must promote politeness in which charity flourishes, teaching the young the necessity of acquiring gracious manners and respect for their fellowmen. (f) Lastly, a teacher must prevent, or correct with

impartiality, justice, and tact, all errors; he has the authority of a father and the chrism of knowledge. An ancient sage stated that a teacher holds in his hands peace and war, the welfare and prosperity as well as the ruin of a nation, depending on the measure of loyalty and responsibility with which he performs his mission. A bad teacher can destroy in a short time the good seed a Christian mother planted in the heart of her child. Therefore, an evil or negligent teacher is morally responsible for any damage caused as well as for any erroneous ideas allowed to grow among his pupils. A teacher could sin gravely before God, if he violated the parents' rights with regards to the moral and intellectual education of those entrusted to him through a failure to correct error, or to promote study and discipline, by bad example or by harmful doctrines.

A teacher sins against justice, and is bound to repair the damage done, if he showed unjust preferences in prizes and diplomas to unworthy pupils. A teacher sins against justice and is, therefore, bound to make restitution, if he wasted time or failed to develop school programs as he should.

TEACHERS, RELIGIOUS. *See* School, Lay.

TECHNOPATHIES. *See* Diseases, professional.

TE DEUM. *Te Deum* are the opening words of a hymn of the Church, renowned as a beautiful, ancient *doxology*.

In keeping with the consistent form proper to doxologies, the hymn is composed of one part directed to extolling the glory of the Father, ending with a small, Trinitarian doxology (verses 10–13). This is followed by the glorification of Christ and His redemptive work, and a plea for help for those whom Christ has redeemed with His Precious Blood. The final verse is a selection from the Psalms, chosen by the monks who used the hymn as a concluding prayer of morning *laudes,* as the reference to the beginning of the day seems to indicate (monastic rules of St. Caesarius, St. Aurelian of Arles, and St. Benedict).

This hymn has been erroneously attributed to St. Ambrose and St. Augustine, but more accurately the author seems to have been Niceta, bishop of Remesiana or Romaziana (Rumania). Bishop Niceta, who lived in the fifth century, enjoyed renown as a sacred composer. The oldest manuscript in which the hymn appears is the *Antiphonary of Bangor* (monastery of Ireland) belonging to the seventh century.

The *Te Deum* is constantly used as a hymn of thanksgiving in the joyful events in the life and history of an individual or a city, and is prescribed by the *Roman Pontifical* as a closing hymn at consecrations of bishops, abbots, kings, and queens. In ancient times it had a specific Eucharistic character as a prayer of thanksgiving after Communion. Today it is suggested to priests as a prayer of thanksgiving after Mass. *Cig.*

TEDIUM (Boredom). In theology, tedium is a state of willful aversion for salutary works, particularly the fulfillment of duties, because of the sacrifice and exertion demanded (*see* Sloth, Idleness). Tedium must not be confused with annoyance or sadness caused by the effort or work connected with virtue, nor with indeliberate feelings of disgust for that which is burdensome.

The factors which more or less directly lead to tedium are numerous; the proximate cause of this evil is always an inordinate love of self, which, more than any other element, prompts an individual to shun exertion.

Tedium not only leads a person to act without enthusiasm and to belittle imperfections and venial sins, but also to neglect important duties. Tedium tends to a repugnance or lack of desire for spiritual concerns; spiritual matters or despair of salvation are detested as tedium seeks for consolation in unlawful things.

Tedium is sinful. It is a mortal sin if it involves the neglect of a grave duty or if it constitutes a grave danger to neglect such a duty. However, culpable transgressions caused by tedium are not numerically distinct from tedium itself, of which they are a result, but form, from the moral standpoint, a complete whole with it.

Tedium can be checked and uprooted by remembering the purpose of life and the examples of Jesus Christ and the saints, and by a great esteem for small acts of mortification each day, in those things in which tedium is felt more strongly. *Man.*

TELEPATHY. According to Osty's definition, telepathy (Greek, *tele*, far; *patheia*, sensibility) is a paranormal faculty of knowledge by which an individual perceives at some distance events or thoughts in another person or place without the normal help of the senses or intellect. Thus, telepathy could be considered an extrasensorial relation between two psychic agents.

The phenomenon takes place either in the course of a spiritistic session or in any experimental or metapsychical apparatus. In the first case, one speaks of *spontaneous* telepathy, in the second, of *experimental* telepathy. These are distinguished by reason of other important characteristics. Thus, a high level of emotional tone usually assumes fundamental importance in actual verification of *spontaneous* telepathic events, such as in the death or mortal danger involving beloved persons. *Experimental* telepathy selects objects or thoughts that are emotionally indifferent. Furthermore, spontaneous telepathic communication is usually quite unconscious, for in many cases it occurs in sleep; in experimental telepathy the agent usually assigns great importance to the inquiry.

TELEPATHY AND CLAIRVOYANCE. At one time, telepathy was distinct from *clairvoyance*, which is the paranormal knowledge exercised upon an event extrinsic to the perceiving subject. In time, it was discovered that the distinction was merely empirical, for telepathy is only a particular phase of clairvoyance.

The more reliable among modern scholars of metapsychology hold this latter opinion; they attach no great value to the supposed distinction but include the two phenomena under the single term of *cryptesthesia* (hidden sensibility) suggested by Richet.

VARIOUS OPINIONS. Several hypotheses have been advanced in explaining the intimate workings of telepathy. Many think that telepathic communications, similar to radio communications, involve brain waves between two minds, one transmitting, the other receiving. However, the independence of the phenomenon from a distance factor and the essential differences, at times conspicuous, between the thoughts or emotional occurrences and their paranormal perception conflict with this hypothesis, which has not been in any way scientifically proven. According to another hypothesis, to which H. Bergson and S. Freud lean, telepathy arises from a dynamic *unconscious*. An unknown event, independent of categories of space and time in favorable circumstances, is aided by an intensive emotional charge to facilitate the immediate perception of the psychical processes of the subconscious, and assume momentarily a mastery over the more philogenetically developed means of communication (rational language). But this hypothesis also lacks an essentially scientific basis. According to spiritualists (*see* Spiritualism), one must see in telepathy the intervention of disincarnate entities.

Following in the footsteps of most trustworthy modern metapsychologists, we can safely conclude that no hypothesis concerning the nature of telepathic processes has yet reached the status of scientific theory.

With respect to Catholic thinking on this subject, *see* Metapsychology. *Riz.*

TELEPHONE. The telephone is an electrical apparatus used for reproducing sound, especially articulate speech, across a distance. Today the use of the telephone is widespread and unites men across great distances, by rendering direct communication possible from the most distant places.

The use of the telephone occasions several moral and canonical problems.

(a) To steal secrets by listening into telephone conversations, wire-tapping, eavesdropping, etc., is unlawful unless there exists a reason or obligation to do so, as in the case of parents and children's conversations with questionable friends. Such a violation is a sin against the virtue of justice (*see* Secret). Wire-tapping of a telephone conversation for the sake of the public welfare, for example, to uncover a suspected criminal, may be lawful for the public authority, as long as the period of emergency or the need of a search continues, provided that such emergency need is not transformed into an oppressive device. Wire-tapping is unlawful if practiced by private individuals, regardless of the reason. (b) To employ the telephone to disturb the domestic peace of others is morally illicit and, in some nations, a crime; this practice is an offense against the virtue of charity. (c) In granting faculties and dispensations, the use of the telephone is, of itself, not forbidden, provided that no danger of fraud exists and the law does not require a written permission for licitness. It is permitted to grant over the telephone the faculty to hear confession, to permit a deacon to baptize, to allow a priest to confirm within his jurisdiction, to binate or to hear confessions. Moreover it is permissible to grant by telephone the faculty to officiate at a wedding, unless such practice is forbidden by a particular law. At any rate, the telephone, radio, or telegraph is for the most part an extraordinary means; in an urgent case, even if it were possible to apply to the Holy See or the Ordinary for faculties by means of the telephone, such recourse is considered an extraordinary inconvenience; in such matters extraordinary powers are granted in dispensations to the Ordinary, parish priest, or the confessor (Can. 81, 1043, 1045). Consequently, the Sacred Congregations do not grant dispensations or faculties by telephone. If requested to do so by telephone, the clerk assigned to that work may and does convey the information that the dispensation was granted. Of course, it is only the relative rescript that testifies to the fact that the petition was granted.

(d) Telephone and confession. Almost immediately after the invention of the telephone, it was asked if confession was valid and licit if made over the telephone. The authorities unanimously replied in the negative with respect to lawfulness, except in cases of extreme necessity, i.e., when there is no other way of going to confession but by telephone. In fact, it seems to entail many problems, such as the danger of fraud, possible jest with a consequent profanation of the sacrament, the danger of a violation of the seal of confession, etc.

With respect to validity, most authors reply in the negative, for various reasons: the voice through the telephone is modified and is no longer a human voice but a mechanical one; the moral presence required for the reception of the sacrament is lacking.

The reasons given, however, are not entirely convincing. Moral presence seems to be sufficiently established by the oral-auricular communication that would intervene between confessor and penitent. Questioned on the subject, the Sacred Penitentiary took no position, declaring that there was no reply to be given. This could also be interpreted to mean that the solution of the doubt was not within its competency but rather within the competency of the Sacred Congregation of the Holy Office.

In practice, one may have recourse to the telephone if there is no other way of going to confession. The value of such a confession, of course, would seem to be doubtful. For greater safety one would need to repeat the confession at a later date, and make in the meantime an act of perfect contrition. The use of the telephone or earphone in the confessional, of course, is permitted for those who are hard of hearing.

Similar questions could be raised with respect to radio, but here the difficulties increase. Absolution by radio is permitted, but only in emergency, as in the case of the chaplain of a ship who absolves conditionally the crew of the ship in danger of sinking, without any possible way to assemble the personnel for collective absolution. Even here, it is evident that for greater safety one must make an act of perfect contrition.

(e) *Absolution from censure.* In the case of absolution from censure, the use of the telephone is admitted without any condition, because in this case the physical presence of the penitent is not required as in confession. *Pal.*

TELEVISION. Television sums up in one single performance what the theater, cinema, and radio offer, and creates great interest and a notable influence on the public. Hence, its exceptional importance from the social point of view. In fact, television is bound to affect more and more the recreational, domestic, cultural, intellectual, and moral habits of the public as time goes on, and its availability increases among all classes of people.

The most disturbing aspect of television is the danger which it creates especially for its young viewers. A widespread alarm is voiced especially in America, where an unrestrained competition between broadcasting companies on one side and a lack of sufficient and practical control of programs on the other, make television an abiding danger for the moral health of millions of viewers. Two of the most unfortunate aspects of television programs are represented by the erotic and suggestive behavior of actors and actresses and the excessive use of emotional plots, such as detective dramas, murders, crimes, violence, glorification of criminals, etc. These aspects are analogous to movies, yet television reaches a larger number of viewers, who, by reason of particular conditions of time and place, are more extensively and easily exposed to the suggestiveness of such programs.

If television is the most fascinating and effective means of communication of news, knowledge, ideas, cultural and educational programs (positive aspect), it is also a medium which offers serious moral dangers (negative aspect). According to inquiries, studies, and statistics of educators, priests, psychologists, artists, physicians and sociologists, these are negative aspects of television: (a) an unconscious, materialistic outlook with great detriment to the spiritual and intellectual welfare of the individual; (b) distraction from study and nobler work by continuous performances; (c) a danger to physical development of children who prefer the television screen not only to study but also healthful athletic activities in the open air. In the face of this serious problem, a timely and energetic program and control is necessary for the types of shows and the habits which television seems to foster in its audiences.

JURIDICO-THEOLOGICAL OBSERVATIONS. The obligation to hear Mass on Sundays and holy days is not fulfilled by viewing it on television, for the law requires physical presence for the fulfillment of the precept (*see* Sanctification of Holy Days). The viewing of the Holy Sacrifice on television is intended for the sick or other lawfully hindered persons simply as a means of quickening devotion and an aid to maintaining a patient and spiritual attitude in their more difficult moments.

However, the Papal Blessing is validly received by television, just as it is validly received by radio (cf. Decree of Sacred Penitentiary, June 15, 1939: AAS, 31 [1939], 277). Pope Pius XII instituted a Pontifical Commission for Motion Pictures, Radio and Television in order to study the problems related to faith and morals because of such media (Audience of December 16, 1954; AAS, 46 [1954], 783-784). *Gal.*

TEMERITY. *See* Prudence; Judgment, Rash.

TEMPERAMENT. *See* Pathology; Personality.

TEMPERAMENT, APATHETIC. *See* Apathy.

TEMPERAMENT, CHOLERIC. *See* Reflex, Conditioned.

TEMPERAMENT, CYCLOTHYMIC. *See* Cyclothymia.

TEMPERAMENT, EPILEPTIC. *See* Epilepsy.

TEMPERAMENT, MELANCHOLIC. *See* Reflex, Conditioned.

TEMPERAMENT, NERVOUS. *See* Metereopathy.

TEMPERAMENT, PSYCHASTHEN-IC. *See* Psychasthenia.

TEMPERAMENT, SCHIZOID OR SCHIZOPHRENIC. *See* Cyclothymia, Schizophrenia.

TEMPERANCE. Temperance, in a broad sense, consists in maintaining a moderation in activities. In a strict sense, temperance is an habitual moderation in all activities, but especially pleasures connected with eating, drinking, and the use of the sexual faculty. The pleasures of taste and touch are the primary object of temperance; all acts connected with these pleasures are the secondary objects of temperance.

Man's faculties and acts have a final end to which they are primarily directed by their very nature. This direction is an expression of God's will, which obliges man; no act is ever lawful if, in its performance or other circumstance, it ceases to be directed to the primary end of the faculty exercised or of the act itself; that is, if it hinders the attainment of this end. Nor is it lawful for one to exclude, even by one's intention, the primary end of the faculty used or of its act. The primary end of food and drink is to maintain a good physical and spiritual state of being in our activities, which tend to God, our ultimate supernatural end. The end of the sexual act is the propagation of the human species. Therefore, it is never lawful in eating or in drinking to go beyond whatever is healthy physically or spiritually; nor is it lawful to perform the sexual act in a manner detrimental to the propagation of the human species nor to exclude such ends in our intentions. All have the obligation to nourish themselves sufficiently, and spouses have the mutual obligation not to deny the exercise of legitimate conjugal rights in conjugal life.

As an incentive designed to facilitate and render more certain the attainment of these ends, God Himself added a special gratification to those acts directed to the preservation of the individual and the species. Therefore, it is lawful to enjoy the pleasure connected with a moderate use of food, drink, or the marital act performed in the proper manner.

In these acts, as in all other actions, man seeks an object which is desired and loved; he intends to acquire an end or specific good for himself. A right intention does not necessarily aim formally and explicitly at the attainment of the primary end of the faculty and its act. It is licit to intend the attainment of an end for which, in fact, the act is, of itself, secondarily ordained. To take food or drink to please the person who offers it, to participate in a banquet, to encourage mutual, friendly contacts, or to increase social good-will are legitimate intentions; to perform the marital act as an honest remedy against concupiscence, as an aid to mutual affection, provided that the primary end of the act is never excluded, even mentally, are licit intentions.

It is unlawful to take food or drink even in moderate quantity or to perform the sexual act for the sole enjoyment of the sense of taste or touch (Innocent XI, Denz. 1158, 1159). All moral theologians agree that it is an inordinate act to pursue pleasure by excluding in a positive manner, even if merely by an intention, the primary end of the act. Some theologians, however, consider it equally unlawful for a person to pursue a pleasure without at least an implicit intention to subordinate the act to a higher and more honest end, so that the action is governed by reason.

The moderate use of food and drink and the fulfillment of the marital act in the proper manner are capable of motivation ordained to ends higher than these specific aims. To intend such a higher purpose increases the value of the act from a moral standpoint; it also gains merit if the act is performed in the state of grace. Thus, it is a greater perfection to take food and drink to obey the Lord or to give glory to God than simply to satisfy a need.

One may sin against temperance by excess, by seeking more than a proper amount of pleasure connected with taste or touch; this is called intemperance. Intemperance is a debasement of the human dignity of an individual; hence it is more revolting than many more serious sins. One may sin against temperance also by defect, by fleeing the enjoyment of taste or touch, although reason may recognize its legitimate necessity and the light of faith may counsel it.

Among the suitable means for strengthening the virtue of temperance and in particular conjugal chastity and the perfect continence obligatory for the unmarried, are the following: remembrance of the presence of God, recollection of one's dignity, the frequent reception of the sacraments, fervent love of God, filial love toward the Blessed Mother of God, and mental prayer.

The principles governing the use of other pleasurable objects, such as the use of tobacco, perfumes, and similar items, are governed by the virtue of temperance.

Some moral theologians consider the use of these items lawful if not employed in excess, despite the fact that pleasure is the sole purpose intended. Other theologians affirm with good reason that, since these pleasures are by nature simply means for relief of body and mind, they are lawful if intended, not merely for pleasure itself, but as an antidote against tiredness of body and mind due to work or other factors. Nor does this subordination imply difficulty or demand any effort as long as it is intended according to the requirements of reason. To direct these acts to an end more intimately united with God increases the value of an act from the moral standpoint. *Man.*

TEMPLE. *See* Church.

TEMPORA SACRA. *See* Liturgical Year.

TEMPTATION. Temptation, in a moral sense, is testing the virtue of a person, either out of curiosity, for pedagogical reasons, or to bring out virtue. God may tempt man, but only in the latter sense (Gen. 22:1; Deut. 13:3; Prov. 17:3). In the latter specific sense, which is the sense of this article, temptation is any solicitation of the will to perform an act contrary to virtue. Man's life is filled with temptations (Job. 7:1; Matt. 10:34; Rom. 7:19–25). Although these constantly challenge man's virtue, yet they provide an opportunity to prove virtue. They also have the effect of increasing man's capacity and fervor, and, therefore, merit (Eccl. 2:5; 34:9; 34:11; II Cor. 12:9; I Pet. 1:6, 7). This explains why God permits them. Temptations are of themselves always an evil; they are good only accidentally (*Summa Theol.*, I, q. 48, a. 5 ad 3; III, q. 41, a. 2 ad 2).

Temptation proceeds through three phases: (a) representation of a pleasurable thing through the imagination, accompanied by an instinctive pleasure of the sensitive appetite (*see* Impulse); (b) advertence of the intellect, to which the thing appears first as desirable, then as contrary to the moral law; from this dual knowledge, an internal struggle develops between pleasure and duty; (c) a decision of the will; only in this last phase is sin committed or a virtuous act performed (*Summa Theol.*, I–II, q. 74 a. 4).

To temptation man must oppose a double resistance: (a) a *preventive* effort, against occasions of sin, implied in the words of Jesus Christ: "*Watch and pray*" (Matt. 26:41); (b) *actual* resistance, whether a positive or merely a negative opposition, in neither consenting nor rejecting. Against every temptation man must oppose at least a negative resistance. However, if temptation is strong, as in temptations against faith and purity, negative resistance is not sufficient because it is not adequate to remove the danger of sin. In this case, positive opposition is necessarily required; to omit this would constitute a grave sin (cf. Error of Quietism condemned by the decree of the Sacred Congregation of the Holy Office, August 28, 1687, Prop. 17 and 37). Such opposition may be direct, an act of will, or indirect, the removal of the seducive image by occupying oneself in other things, like praying, etc. Omission of positive removal of the representation of the fantasy constitutes in itself a venial sin, because it is always an inordinate thing which constitutes a danger; yet a legitimate reason often justifies a negative attitude toward it, if, for example, the representation is accompanied by a necessary or useful action, or if the active effort made to expel the representation would rather increase the temptation or the disturbance of the mind, or if temptations are very frequent. *Dam.*

TEMPTING GOD. To tempt God is to urge God to manifest one or more of His perfections in order to verify His existence or His attributes experimentally. In the proper sense, it is a lack of faith or a culpable doubt concerning the existence of God or His attributes. It also arises from a presumptuous confidence in God, or vain curiosity about a relative attribute of God, that is, His relationship with creatures, such as divine providence or mercy. This is tempting God in a less proper sense. An example of tempting God, in a proper sense, is to beg God for a miracle or a catastrophe as proof of His existence. Tempting God, in a less proper sense, is to expose one's life to danger trusting God to save him. Of course, both temptations can be expressed by words, prayer, defiance, or stipulation. If these are carried out with the expressed intent of investigating God and His attributes experimentally, it is called formal or expressed temptation of God; it is called virtual or interpretative temptation of God if the facts and words are not implemented by an expressed demand or challenge; as such, these acts are no more than an invitation to God to manifest Himself.

A formal tempting of God is always and in every instance a mortal sin. As clearly indicated in Holy Scripture (Matt. 4:7; Deut. 6:16; Ex. 17:7; Ps. 67:18), it is a sin against the virtue of religion; in fact, to ask God to submit to our experiments is a grave irreverence against Him, our Supreme Lord and Father. In addition, a formal tempting of God is an expression of a doubtful faith or rash confidence in God, or, in minor cases, of vain curiosity. Thus, it is a sin of heresy (*q.v.*), of rashness (*see* Hope), or of disrespect against God by making Him an object of our curiosity. Frequently, in cases of defiance, a formal tempting of God is connected with blasphemy (*q.v.*).

Virtual or interpretative tempting of God is also a mortal sin in more serious cases. However, this less strict form of tempting God admits the possibility of venial sin, for, outside of the direct intent to subject God to our experiments, the gravity of the offense against God depends on the extent to which facts or words contain a rash demand of a divine intervention as well as the type of intervention requested. *Pal.*

TENDENCY. *See* Affectivity.

TENSION. *See* Anxiety.

TERRORISM. The word was coined as a result of the so-called period of *Terror* of the French Revolution. The *law of suspects*, enacted by the National Assembly to guard the newly proclaimed Republic (1793) from enemies of the new government, suppressed the most elementary guarantees of security and individual liberty. Denunciation of the most harmless citizens suspected of opposition to the new regime was sufficient to put them in imminent danger of death. Immediate arrest and a summary judgment before special courts of justice, controlled by the so-called *Committee for Public Security*, followed. The guillotine operated without interruption until the fall of Robespierre. The victims of French terrorism were numerous, and terror was universal due to the uncertain fate hanging over everyone.

Subsequent to the French Revolution, any system that aimed at spreading a general sense of fear to discourage the people from activities or a defense of their ideas and rights by new revolutions was called terrorism. The methods vary: by law, as the afore-mentioned law *of suspects;* by sporadic acts of violence and shocking cruelty; by ominous threats to heads of families; by a well organized spy system which causes a general distrust among the citizens; by new methods of inquiry and torture, particularly by the so-called political police charged with the task of persecuting the lawful opposition to the government and hindering all political activities.

As a denial of human rights, any form of terrorism is detestable and contrary to divine and human laws. *Boz.*

TERTIARY. *See* Third Order, Secular.

TESTAMENT, LAST WILL. The last will or testament is an act of the will (*mortis causa*), essentially unilateral and revocable, by which a person determines the disposition of his property, in whole or part, to be carried out after his death. In dealing with this subject modern laws differ a great deal not only with respect to the various forms of a last will or testament but also in the extension of its effects. For all such variations and details the reader must consult the code of the respective country.

For a general criterion concerning the obligations of conscience of those who are included in a testamentary inheritance as active or passive subjects (testator, appointed heir, legatees, substitute heirs or legatees, testamentary executor, administrator of unassigned inheritance, etc.), the basic consideration involves primarily the moral value of the respective civil legislation.

In the matter of inheritance, civil laws must be considered, in principle, just and necessary specifications of the law of nature, which in this regard is limited to a few fundamental but general principles. Such civil laws are binding in conscience unless they are in some way contrary to divine law or to specific dispositions of canonical law (Can. 1529).

The only area of possible conflict with canonical laws concerns testamentary dispositions *ad causas pias*. In such a delicate matter, which involves the relation of the soul with God, the canonical legislator intervenes: (a) to declare valid the disposition on the basis of the natural and ecclesiastical laws, i.e., a natural right not canonically restricted, and to demand that the heirs be admonished of the obligation incumbent upon them to carry out a pious will even if civilly invalid because of a defect of form (Can. 1513); (b) to declare that the executor of a pious will is, *ex officio*, the Ordinary of the place, and that any clause in the will that might be contrary to this law must be considered non-existent (Can. 1515).

Therefore, civil laws concerning the nullity and invalidity of wills that are defective in form, trust funds and fideicommissary substitutions, are not binding in conscience if they involve pious causes; hence, the obligation in conscience to carry them out remains in force even though a will lacks proper legal form.

In positive law there is no obligation to make a will. In the natural law there is no direct and specific obligation. On the basis of the natural law, however, certainly there is an indirect obligation in the following cases: (a) if the last will and testament represents the only means by which grave obligations of justice and piety incumbent upon the testator can be satisfied; (b) if it is foreseen that inheritance *ab intestato* would cause in due time injustices, grave violations of charity, or litigations.

The possibility of such occurrences is neither unfounded nor infrequent, since the law, though quite specific and detailed, cannot foresee every possible occurrence. What, for instance, of the case of a son who sacrificed years of life and an independent career to manage his father's business, while his brothers instead went their ways into independent and lucrative professions or positions?

In the absence of equitable dispositions in the father's last will and testament, an unjust situation might occur for the generous son if matters were settled according to the dispositions of law. In such circumstances, if foreseen, there exists a real obligation in conscience, of itself grave, to make a will. In all cases, a timely disposition of one's possessions is not only a wonderful norm of wise administration but it is always an act of piety and Christian charity. *Zac.*

TESTAMENT, NEW. *See* New Testament.

TESTAMENT, OLD. Moral theology shall preserve its value as long as it remains in a definite way the science of God (T. Deman, *Aux origines de la théologie morale*, Montreal–Paris, 1951). In other words, all moral acts must be based on fundamentally theocentric perspectives. This element precisely differentiates moral theology from ethics; ethics is based on human reason, moral theology on revelation, which contains the history of man's relations with God. Revelation involves two distinct, yet closely connected, phases: one, imperfect, multifaceted and preparatory, which stretches from the beginning to the coming of Christ; the other, final, starts with the Incarnation of the Word and projects itself beyond time. The latter revelation not only presupposes the former but it contains many of its precepts; in fact, besides the precepts of the natural law, it contains and sanctions positive precepts, enunciated in the former. The early phase is contained in the Sacred Books of the Old Testament (covenant between God and Abraham, Israel and David, directed to the salvation of mankind through the redemption wrought by Jesus Christ); the second is contained in the Books of the New Testament (definitive covenant sealed by the blood of Christ, as the end result and realization of the preceding one). Both covenants revolve around Jesus Christ as their object: the first, preparatory to His coming; the second, the actual reality.

The Books of the Old Testament. The Old Testament consists of the following books, grouped in four categories: (a) Pentateuch (the five books of Moses): *Genesis, Exodus, Leviticus, Numbers, Deuteronomy;* (b) historical books: *Josue, Judges, Ruth, Samuel* (Books I and II of Kings, according to the Vulgate), *Kings* (Books I, II, III, and IV, according to the Vulgate), *Paralipomenon* (I and II) or *Chronicles* (I and II), *Esdras and Nehemias, Tobias, Judith, Esther, Machabees* (I and II); (c) didactic or poetical books: *Job, Psalms, Proverbs, Ecclesiastes, Canticle of Canticles, Wisdom, Ecclesiasticus;* (d) prophetical books: *Isaias, Jeremias, Lamentations, Baruch, Epistle of Jeremias, Ezechiel, Daniel,* and twelve minor prophets, *Osee, Joel, Amos, Jonas, Michaeas, Nahum, Habacuc, Sophonias, Aggeus, Zacharias, Malachias.* In all these books, depending on the literary style and scope proper to each group or environmental circumstances and characteristics of each book (author, period, etc.), the rules governing man's relations with God, himself, and his neighbor, i.e., moral conduct, are inculcated and taught.

Moral and General Content. (a) Sacred Scripture presupposes, first of all, a creating God, who gives orders to His creatures and expects to be obeyed by them (Gen. 1–3; Ex. 20:2). He who denies the existence of God is foolish and shall be doomed to corruption (Sap. 13–15). (b) God created man intelligent and free *to His own image and likeness* in order that he may work out his own salvation (Gen. 1:26 f.). After the violation of God's command (Gen. 3), man did not lose this power. *"If thou do well, shalt thou not receive? But if ill, shall not sin forthwith be present at the door? But the lust thereof shall be under thee, and thou shalt have dominion over it"* (Gen. 4:7; *see also* Eccl. 31:10). God is always ready to come to his aid in his struggle against evil (Ps. 141:1–4), provided that man turns to God. (c) Every moral act will receive its sanction, particularly after the present life (Gen. 2:17; 3:16–24; 4:11 f.; Ex. 20:5 f.; Ps.

73:49; Ez. 18; Eccl. 7:40; Wis. 2:23 f.; cf. *Divus Thomas,* 55 (1952), 435 ff.). Retribution may be collective or individual, of a material nature, tangible, as it were, according to the mentality which the Israelites had in common with other Semites. (d) Moral laws originate from the sovereign will of God. From the essential will come norms which reflect necessary relations between the nature of God and that of man. These are the immutable laws of natural morality. According to St. Paul (Rom. 1:18–23; 2:14–16), these laws were written in man's heart. Later, God formulated them explicitly in the Decalogue (Ex. 20:2–17). The Decalogue is the statute, the essence of the covenant; the rest of the Old Testament is the history of this covenant; we find the Decalogue with its precepts in all the events in the Old Testament. The worship of one, true God, closely allied to the moral precepts, is inseparable in the Testament, for duties of fidelity toward God and duties of justice toward neighbor constitute the entire and constitutive element of devotion in its full meaning.

The Decalogue. At the center of the prophetic teachings, from Isaias to Malachy, we find the Decalogue substantially, if not formally, inculcated. The practice of the natural virtues, justice, goodness toward neighbor, and similar precepts are placed above the precepts of positive morality (Is. 58:3–7; Os. 6:6, etc.). In the Decalogue, the external cult to God, implicit in the first commandment, remains a complementary element; the essential element is the true sentiment of grateful devotion toward God, of piety more than religion. (Cf. the precept of love of God in Deut. 5:10; 6:5; 10:12; 11:1–13; 30:15–20) and pure moral conduct (I Sam. 15:22; Mich. 6:6 ff.; Is. 1:10–17; 43:23 ff.) The sapiential or didactic books recall these precepts in a particular manner: duties toward neighbor and oneself; chastity; justice, charity, truthfulness (Job. 13:1–34); these unite teachings from Revelation with those from experience or sound reason. The Book of Psalms, like a flower garden containing the best of all other books, adds the flavor of poetry and teachings of its own. It has in common with the books of the Law an enthusiastic devotion to the Divine Law (Ps. 1, 19, 119); with the sapiential books, its moral teachings (Ps. 15, 37, 82, *etc.*) and reflexions on man's destiny (Ps. 39, 49, 73, etc.); with the prophetical books, an ardent spirit, interior worship (Ps. 40, 50, 51), zeal for justice and protection of the weak (Ps. 10, 12, 58, 82, 94).

ECCLESIASTICUS. *Ecclesiasticus,* named from its use in worship and the preparation of catechumens as an official catechism, can be considered a sufficiently complete moral treatise suited to all states and circumstance of life. For this reason, St. Jerome and Cassiodorus called it a *collection of all virtues.* In fact, it contains a compendium of duties toward God, parents, and neighbor. In it are taught humility, meekness, and compassion for the unfortunate (Eccles. 1:4–10); Sin comes from man's free will, not from God; sin never goes unpunished (Eccles. 14:20–16:23). Generosity and foresight are necessary virtues, as well as restraint of passions, proper use of the tongue, continence of the mind and discipline of the tongue (Eccles. 16:24–25, 27).

MOSAIC LEGISLATION. In the beginning, the Old Testament presents primitive legislation: the precept of work (Gen. 2:15), prohibition of eating human flesh (Gen. 9:1–4), and, in the covenant with Abraham, the command to circumcize all males (Gen. 17:11–14).

Next came the Mosaic Legislation (Exod.–Deut.), given to the nation as such, to regulate in Israel the national, tribal, and domestic life. It had also the task of separating the Israelites from all idolatrous peoples in order to preserve their worship and morals from all contamination; in other words, it contained aspects limited to the period preparatory to the coming of Christ.

The Mosaic Law codified usages and customs, although imperfect, which were deeply rooted in the people and could not be easily eradicated. Such customs, however, involved only secondary precepts of the natural law from which a dispensation from God was possible, such as polygamy, divorce, vengeance, retaliation; this dispensation was for a people too hard-hearted to be immediately elevated to an absolute moral purity (Matt. 19:8).

But the same law contained moral and religious principles of a permanent value, which exceeded by far those of all other Semitic peoples. In comparison with a Christian ideal, one may properly discover the imperfection of these standards, but realism indicated that no unattainable standards should be imposed because of the severity of the times and the hard-hearted spirit of the people. This hard-heartedness is found in the historical books, with narrations of various crimes, jealousies, and moral brutalities of every kind during the dark period of Judges, especially under the wicked kingdoms of Samaria and Judea until the time of exile, from the ninth century to the year 587 B.C.

THE PROPHETS. Besides Samuel and David, the prophets promoted a true, progressive movement of moral ideas, which resulted in a renewed spirit in Israel after the exile and was manifested in the later sapiential literature (*Ecclesiastes, Ecclesiasticus,* and *Wisdom*).

In His teaching against the Pharasaical intrigues, Christ renewed the high moral impetus of the great prophets, and abrogated those positive moral precepts, now no longer adequate or compatible with the universality and *new wine* of the new covenant founded on love. *Spa.*

TESTIMONY. *See* Witness.

THANATOLOGY. Thanatology (Greek, *thanatos,* death; *logos,* study), a branch of legal medicine, is the science of organic and physical changes in a human body and its organs due to death. Thanatology prescinds from any investigation concerning the cause of the fatal event, but concerns itself primarily with verification of the fact of death and the establishment of the exact time at which the death occurred (Gerin).

From a strictly ethical point of view,

verification of the fact of death is of primary concern for, despite regulations of judicial authority and scientific progress in this field, which seem to have reduced to the minimum the danger of burying persons merely apparently dead, the mere possibility of such an occurrence constitutes sufficient ground for justifiable concern.

In apparent death, although the three fundamental functions for the preservation of life, i.e., the nervous, respiratory and circulatory function, are always seriously impaired, the fact remains that nervous and respiratory functions can be suppressed for a relatively long time and yet the person may still be alive. "Only methods directed to ascertaining the definite arrest of the circulatory system as the only function which not even in apparent death can be permanently interrupted have any real value" (Gerin).

Methods employed are almost free from error. (a) Intravenous injection of a sodium solution of fluorescein, which is highly diffusive. By this method circulation is preserved, and thus life itself; the fluid travels with the blood and at death turns the cornea green and the teguments yellow (Icard method). (b) Subcutaneous injection of ether; this fluid backs up through the hole of the needle if the person is already dead, but in apparent death, it remains under the skin (Rebouillat method). (c) For an absolutely accurate diagnosis, it is necessary to employ methods which will check directly the functional condition of the heart. This can be done by an introcardiac injection of a radio-opaque substance, followed by a series of X-rays which permit not only study of the condition of each section of the heart but also reveal the presence of coagulation in the heart cavities, which furnishes further conclusive proof of real death. (d) A similarly sure method is the electrocardiogram, which, as an additional advantage, can be used in the patient's home. The electrocardiac examination of a body (electrothanatology), carried out for a length of time by cardiocinetic action, offers confirmation of a real and definite arrest of the heart if the indi-

cator shows an unbroken horizontal line (Frache).

Perhaps it is superfluous to add that, aside from the methods indicated above, the *signs of death* commonly known and observable are in sequence: a cessation of breathing; a cessation of circulation; general muscular limpness for about an hour; progressive temperature loss; hypostasis, in which blood, no longer accelerated by cardiac activity, flows into sloping parts of the body, where red, blue, and purple specks, gradually more diffuse and intense, appear within two or three hours after death; the *rigor mortis*, which follows the limpness and begins in the muscles of the jaws and neck; finally, putrefaction, which appears in the form of a greenish stain on the right inferior quadrant of the abdomen, twenty-four hours or more after death and presents the natural sign of absolute certainty of death.

THERAPEUTIC-DIAGNOSTIC METHODS. In some cases, such as asphyxia, electrocution, sudden arrest of the heart, etc., between cessation of circulation and real, definite, and irrevocable death, a brief period exists when it is possible to revive a patient by quick, adroit manipulations. For the most part these consist of artificial respiration, injections of adrenaline or other stimulants, and direct massage of the heart. These manipulations, an extreme therapeutic remedy, often succeed in snatching the individual from death; their failure, however, amounts to positive irreversibility of the phenomenon, which indicates certain proof of death.

Such methods are also useful in *premature diagnosis of real death*, required in cases of amputation of parts of the corpse for therapeutic purposes, such as corneal, cutaneous, vascular, meningeal transplantations, etc. For such uses, early verification of death must be made by the use of the latest methods of forensic thanatology, among which is electrothanatology.

In an address delivered on May 14, 1956, Pope Pius XII illustrated the Church's thought concerning various problems of thanatology. The illustrious

Pontiff recognized the lawfulness of amputations of parts of a corpse for therapeutic purposes. He also praised the spirit of charity of the donor, but recalled the illicitness of such amputations if they are carried out in opposition to existing laws or without the authorization of the relatives of the deceased. In this connection the Holy Father added that the public at large must be made aware of the advantages of yielding the corpses of their dear ones to the interest of science and in behalf of others who would benefit by it. However, referring to one of his allocutions delivered two years before, Pius XII restated that in the amputation of organs or parts of organs "the norms of the natural moral law must be respected, which forbid the treating of a human corpse simply as a thing, or as an animal."

Therefore, no physician may conduct, even for scientific reasons, an autopsy before the lawful period has expired. We maintain that departure from this can be permitted only if he has been able to diagnose with certainty the presence of real death and provided important motives of study or cure are involved.

If explicitly requested by a dying person or members of his family, a physician may promise to perform an operation that will ascertain the fact of death; his action will be within the bounds of the moral law provided that he avoid any means which might eventually kill a person not already dead. Accordingly, he may use an introcardiac injection of cardiocinetics for a series of electrocardiograms. If the heart fails to indicate any functional revival, the physician will be able to assure the relatives of the fact of death; at the same time, he shall have interpreted the will of the deceased in the best possible way. *Riz.*

THEATER. The theater, of very ancient origin, reached its height of perfection in the Greek and Roman classic dramas and comedies. After the fall of classical culture, a popular, religious theater developed in the Middle Ages under the auspices of the Church. In the beginning, the religious theater was a part of the religious functions performed in the Church. Later, it moved outside the Church and dealt with a variety of religious subjects, such as the Redemption, the Holy Eucharist, legends of saints, and moral topics. The Reformation and, later, Humanism inflicted severe blows on the popular, religious theater, for, along with this religious theater, there developed secular theater during the Middle Ages, which flourished in the Renaissance, as the entertainment of the upper class. In subsequent centuries it continued to develop in art and literature.

The popular, religious theater, which had never entirely disappeared (*e.g.,* the mysteries of the Passion in Oberammergau, revived in the last decades), not only made remarkable progress as a mass form of theater but an effective means of propaganda and religious education. The secular theater, as entertainment and an artistic literary medium, is also a carrier of ideas and convictions, and, due to the tremendous progress achieved by the cinematographic art, its influence has waned among less educated people, although its importance in more cultured circles is still noteworthy.

The theater is in itself morally indifferent (*Summa Theol.,* II–II, q. 168, art. 3, ad 3), but it can be used to a good end; hence, the great interest of the Church in the religious theater. The strong condemnations of the Fathers of the first centuries of Christianity (Tertullian, St. Cyprian and St. John Chrysostom) are explained by the perverse and anti-Christian nature of the theater of that time. Even in our days, the theater is certainly not devoid of grave dangers to faith and morals from the standpoint of the subject matter of many dramas and comedies as well as the indecent manner of words, actions, and costumes in which they are executed. Concerning more specific rules, *see* Cinema. Special dangers come from certain dances, like ballets, which, with the exception of the truly artistic, often must be labelled simply perverse in view of the sensual motions and scanty and suggestive costuming used by ballerinas. *Also see* Artist, Amusements, Varieties. *Dam.*

THECA. *See* Relics, Veneration of; Vessels, Sacred.

THEFT. Theft was defined by Roman law as a fraudulent taking, use, or possession of a thing for reasons of gain, and contrary to natural law (*contrectatio fraudolosa, lucri faciendi causa, vel ipsius rei vel etiam usus eius possessionis, vel quod lege naturali prohibitum est admittere:* Inst., I, 4, 1). Today, theologians speak more particularly of theft as the secret taking of an object against the legitimate owner's will for the purpose of gain. If secrecy is absent, the act is properly called robbery (*q.v.*). If the lawful owner is not reasonably opposed to the act, no theft is committed. Finally, if the purpose of gain is absent, the taking of an object is rather a matter of damage (*q.v.*). Thus, it is not theft if the owner consents, expressly or tacitly, or if an object is taken for reasons of extreme necessity (*q.v.*), as occult compensation (*q.v.*). If a wife takes from her husband, either absent or unreasonably opposed as an avaricious man, something necessary for herself, for the support and decorum of her children, for almsgiving in keeping with the family's financial condition or for aid to parents in need, it is not theft.

The fraudulent use or possession of an object, in Roman law characterized as theft, is no longer considered as theft by modern jurists. If theft implies the violation of another virtue beside justice, or of justice in a specifically different field, this is called *qualified* theft. Robbery and sacrilegious theft (*see* Sacrilege) are considered *qualified* theft. The former represents a violation of justice in two specifically distinct areas: the right of ownership and the right to personal safety. The latter represents violation of the virtues of justice and religion.

Generally speaking, theft is a serious sin. In his Epistle to the Corinthians, St. Paul writes, ". . . nor *thieves* . . . nor *extortioners shall possess the kingdom of God*" (I Cor. 6:10). Theft violates commutative justice. Robbery violates justice; sacrilegious theft violates the virtues of justice and religion.

As an owner may be opposed in many ways to the loss of property belonging to him, so too the sin of theft admits of degrees, even to the point of constituting only a slight sin. Accordingly, the owner of a property may be less opposed to theft committed by his wife than by his children, less to theft by his children than by his servants, less to theft by his servants than by total strangers. Since theft could be more serious in one case than another, the determination of its gravity is to be prudently made in each individual case, after all circumstances have been taken into consideration.

Furthermore, opposition to a loss may be based on the entity or quantity of the stolen goods. Accordingly, theologians distinguish between grave and light matter. The matter is absolutely grave, if the stolen property is such that, while it may not cause grave damage to a rich owner, it gives the community reason for serious concern in view of the potential effects upon society if such deeds were to be tolerated without grave moral sanction. Thus, whether the owner is a physical or a legal person, rich or poor, the matter is always considered grave. On the contrary, if the loss is not such as to disturb the present or future social order, though it causes damage to the owner, the matter is considered relatively grave. It is not easy to determine the extent of grave matter. Renowned theologians teach that a sum of fifty to one hundred dollars is grave matter in an absolute sense; relatively grave matter may be the sum representing the average daily wages of the person against whom theft is committed. It is also relatively grave matter if a thing or money is stolen from a person to whom it is absolutely necessary for his livelihood. If small theft is repeated frequently for a certain period of time, it may coalesce to constitute a grave sin.

Finally, theft is more or less grave according to the manner in which it is committed. A person may be more opposed to a large theft committed at one time than to a small theft repeated with a certain frequency. Repeated petty thefts, venial sins if taken separately, may become a mortal sin either because of the intention motivating them if, for instance, one commits small thefts successively against one or more persons, with the intention of taking a sum that would constitute a grave matter; or because of the conspiracy with which they are perpetrated, if, for instance, two or more persons acting in accord steal small sums which together would constitute grave matter; or, finally, because of the large number of small thefts committed so frequently that a moral unity exists among small thefts. However, small thefts become grave matter only if the last small theft is added to the others so that together the amount is grave—absolute grave matter, if the damage is caused to more than one person; relative, and twice the normal amount, if the damage is caused to a private person. But if, after reaching the proportion of grave matter, one continues with the same bad will to commit petty thefts, morally linked with the previous ones, no new venial sins are committed, though the sin becomes increasingly graver.

It is clear that if restitution is made of some stolen goods in the meantime, the moral unity of the petty thefts is interrupted.

RESTITUTION. Since theft violates commutative justice, the thief is bound to make restitution (*q.v.*) in proportion to the damage caused. Let it be noted that the sin of theft is not forgiven unless there is a positive good will to return to the owner that which was unjustly taken from him.

The Code of Canon Law punishes with interdiction from all lawful ecclesiastical acts and deprivation of office a lay person convicted of notable theft. The punishment of a cleric convicted of the same crime (Can. 2334, par. 1–2) is a matter within the competency of the ecclesiastical tribunal.

In all civil legislations theft is considered a crime and is severely punished. *See also* Appropriation, Restitution. *Fel.*

THEFT OF THE THOUGHT. *See* Hallucination.

THEOLOGY, MORAL. The part of theology which deals with human actions and studies the rules of human conduct in their relationship to the principles of revelation is called moral theology. Christian ethics does not eliminate, but embraces and perfects, natural ethics. For this reason, moral theologians include in their treatises the norms of the natural law. The field of moral theology embraces natural and supernatural ethics. It is the function of moral theology to dictate norms for all human activities in order that they may conform to the principles of reason and Christian revelation. Since human activities as human, i.e., free, are dominated by the concept of the end of man (*q.v.*), the first treatise of moral theology deals with that subject. This is followed by a study of the human acts from the standpoint of their psychological structure, that is, of what is proper to man as man (voluntareity), or of that which is in man as an animal (passions). Moral theology goes into the examination of man's habits, first, from the general or prevalently psychological aspect, and, secondly, from the exclusively moral aspect as virtues and vices (sin). This is followed by a study of the concept of law and the different kinds of laws (natural and positive; divine and human; ecclesiastical and civil) and by a treatise on grace as the means God gives to man in order that he may be able to observe his moral duties. The special treatises which follow the study of law deal with the immense variety of human actions grouped around the three theological virtues and the four cardinal virtues. This arrangement gives rise to treatises on faith, hope, charity, prudence, justice, fortitude, and temperance.

The picture presented here may be termed the classical picture as it is drawn from the *Summa Theologica* of St. Thomas. Modern theologians have revised it more or less extensively. All have separated from moral theology the treatise on grace, which they join to dogmatic or theoretical theology. Many have reduced the general treatises, although they have added one on conscience, largely concerned with the question of so-called moral systems (*see* Systems, Moral). Concerning special moral theology, many prefer to treat this according to the commandments of God and the Church, rather than the virtues.

There is also a difference of method between the school of St. Thomas and modern theologians in this part of theology. The Angelic Doctor gave greater importance to philosophical and theological principles, to positive (virtue) and supernatural elements. Among modern theologians, some tend to expand casuistry to the neglect of principles. They give greater importance to the negative side by speaking more of sin than of virtue, under-emphasizing the supernatural and perfection, limiting themselves to teaching methods of avoiding sin. If to these negative and minimizing tendencies one adds the widespread aversion against profound and original studies, with consequent tendencies to transcriptions and synopses of school manuals, one will readily recognize that the causes which made Cardinal D'Annibale, and, more recently, Father Vermeersch, deplore the modern decline of moral theological science, have not been eliminated.

The negative and minimizing attitude just recalled has given rise to the consciousness of a need for a complement to moral theology; this, of course, is found in ascetical theology, which teaches a way of perfection. *Gra.*

THEOLOGY, MORAL, PROFESSIONAL. Professional moral theology deals with the moral obligations of professional people. It may be defined as the science, founded on faith, reason, and experience, which deals principally with external human acts as the means by which man may in his occupation foster the temporal glorification of God and his own eternal salvation, which is the ultimate supernatural end of man. By *professions* are understood not only the liberal professions but all other occupations, services, offices, etc.; in other words, the various ways by which man exercises his working potential. In a broader sense, one finds under *professions* those permanent states of life which involve the assumption of certain obligations toward others, as the married, religious, and clerical states. But in such instances one speaks more properly of *obligations of one's state in life* than of professional morality.

The moral norms, including relevant technical and juridical norms which govern professional life, differ in no way from the norms of morality governing man's activities in other areas. There is no moral code or moral theology for the professional man distinct from the general moral law which applies to all the people. The same divine law sets the norms to be followed in all cases and moments of life, professional or not. Man's conduct at every hour and minute of his life, professional or otherwise, will be judged according to the same law.

However, moral theology, which studies human acts in the framework of the end to which they are to be directed, consists of two parts: (1) *fundamental* or *general theology*, which deals with the ultimate and obligatory end of the human acts, namely, the glorification of God through knowledge and love, and the general means by which one shall tend to this ultimate end; (2) *special moral theology*, which deals with the particular means for tending to this same end: particular virtues, rights, and duties of man. Special moral theology, however, may apply to all or to some particular groups.

Of course, man is both a private individual and a member of a society in which he normally exercises an occupation. Consequently, he has rights and duties corresponding to these two functions. As a private person, he is bound to promote the glory of God in himself and others. As a man engaged in a professional occupation, he is bound to work for the glorification of God through the productive activity which he exercises. The duties of a private individual belong to individual moral theology; the duties of a professional man form the object of professional moral theology.

The nature of the work which one does produces a variety of technical and moral problems with particular needs and special exigencies. Besides the general duties which everyone, as an individual, has toward God, himself, and his neighbor, other duties of charity, justice, religion, and gratitude arise from his profession or occupation. These duties stem from more general principles common to all, yet professional moral theology looks upon them from the standpoint of a particular trade or profession.

One must not think that professional moral theology excludes casuistry completely. It has its own casuistry as it has its own moral norms, its own ascetical and mystical aspects, because it cannot be content simply with what is strictly a matter of duty, but it must also indicate that which is a matter of counsel, leading to greater perfection. In this respect, professional casuistry, ascetical and mystical theology may be considered integrating parts of professional moral theology.

From this viewpoint, pastoral theology can be looked upon as a part of professional moral theology, inasmuch as it deals with the exercise of the rights and duties of the pastors of souls. However, in view of its own special, practical importance, pastoral theology is treated separately from professional moral theology.

HISTORICAL NOTES. Although professional morality is currently of great importance in modern writings, professional moral theology is not new. The first Christian writers, faced with problems caused by the assimilation of Christians into the society of their times, discussed the trades and professions which Christians could lawfully enter. The exaggerations of Tertullian give us an idea of the seriousness of the problem.

The majority disagreed with him when he took the position that Christians could not serve as soldiers, merchants, teachers, or public officials (*De Idolatria*, 24: PL 1, 633 ff.). They agreed with him when he forbade Christians to manufacture idols and statues as an occupation directly connected with the promotion of idolatry. At any rate, the problem was raised.

In a subsequent period one finds an occasional moralist who is particularly interested in these specific problems and duties. The moral doctrine of St. John Chrysostom sought to integrate the whole man within the scope of Christian ethics; for this reason he deals with the subjects of slave and master (A. Puech, *Un réformateur*, Paris, 1891, p. 38 ff.), professional funeral mourners, and circus clowns (*ibid.*, p. 37 ff.).

In the early Middle Ages, when Christian writers were scarce, moralists handled the specific problems of the various professions. Raterius of Verona (d. 974) in his *Praeloquia* (PL, 136, 145–344) lays down a norm of conduct for various states of life and various offices, including bishops and kings.

Later, St. Antoninus of Florence (*q.v.*), the originator of a separate treatise of moral theology, discussed professional moral theology; his followers are found in every century. Among the propositions condemned by Alexander VII and Innocent XI, several involved professional moral theology.

The rapid development of industrialism in the nineteenth century, the increase of social problems and variety of professions, the progress in modern technology—all enhanced the importance of professional moral theology; unfortunately, however, modern treatises of moral theology do not devote to it the attention it really deserves.

Despite this neglect, the problems of professional moral theology are discussed not only by theologians but also by Catholic professional groups in many countries.

One of the problems which prevents greater progress in this branch of moral theology is the failure of moralists to become thoroughly familiar with professional techniques which undergo a constant state of change and improvement. This difficulty can be effectively overcome only if a greater understanding and collaboration is established and maintained between moral theologians and professional specialists. It would be impossible to give even a brief summary of the norms of morality for each individual profession; but general principles can be summarized as a basis of professional moral theology. (a) The professions, assigned to each by God as a form of vocation, are not privileges but sources of responsibility. They are the talents of which the Gospel speaks (Matt. 25:15), for which we must render an account. (b) Every profession, necessary and useful for the common good, is morally good and in conformity with human dignity. Through any of them one can find salvation. This does not exclude a certain hierarchy among them by reason of origin, perfection, need, and difficulties of each profession. (c) Divine Providence gives to each one different talents, natural and supernatural gifts; it places each one in different conditions of life, financial opportunities, and assigns to each one, at least in a general fashion, a possible way to follow. The choice of a specific profession is left to the free will of the individual, nor can the State even indirectly force this free choice. However, it can, together with the family, school, and professional associations, encourage a choice (Pius XII, Christmas radio message, 1942). A double area of duties springs from this: one, preliminary, is related to the selection of a profession; the other stems from the profession previously chosen.

Besides petition to God for the necessary illumination, a selection implies a realistic evaluation of the talents, capacities, and preferences of the individual, with the possibility of fulfilling such plans; due consideration for social exigencies and the moral and spiritual advantages or disadvantages must be employed.

Counsels of parents, superiors, and spiritual directors are certainly an aid for making such an important choice. The responsibility connected to the choice is in proportion to the unfavorable spiritual and material consequences which one foresees for himself and for others. The use of illicit means to attain an office or a profession implies a violation of the virtues of justice and charity. Furthermore, the selection of a profession obliges one to prepare himself adequately for the fulfillment of the tasks connected with it. A lack of adequate preparation may burden the conscience due to imputability *in cause* for harmful effects which follow in the practice of his profession.

Regarding duties in a state already embraced, one must bear in mind that these specific duties do not diminish the binding nature of general, common duties. A fundamental obligation common to all professions is that duties be carried out with the diligence that the private welfare requires. Theoretical and practical ability must accompany this diligence; at least ordinary ability equal to the abilities of the individual and the responsibilities of the office is required. The moral norms which regulate the activities of a professional man in relation to his capability and responsibility constitute the deontology of his respective profession.

One who made a mistake in the selection of a profession to which he is irrevocably committed must repent of any possible guilt and fulfill his duties to the best of his ability with reliance on divine aid.

The particular duties of each individual profession are dealt with in their respective articles: Lawyer, Pharmacist, Judge, Teacher, Physician, etc. *Pal.*

THEOLOGY, PROTESTANT (Moral). *See* Protestantism; Protestant Moral Theology.

THEORY, CIRCULAR. *See* Affectivity.

THEOSOPHY. Theosophy (Greek, *theos*, god; *sophia*, wisdom) is the knowledge of God obtained through an experiential intuition of reality rather than a discursive process of the intellect.

In concrete, theosophy refers to doctrines professed by the Theosophic Society, founded in 1873 by Helen Petrovna Blavatsky (1831–1891). The leaders of this philosophy were Eliphas Levy, Fabre d'Olivant, Annie Besant, Edward Schure, etc. Pantheism, based on a concept of man as a spiritual being, essentially one with the universal spirit and reincarnation, the metempsychosis of the ancients, are cornerstones of theosophy, to which obscure and unintelligible occultistic doctrine is added.

In this occultism a complete series or progressive scale of error makes use of simple illusions or fantasies, combined with deceit, fraud, and swindle to produce superstition, irreverence, and open obscenities.

The theory of reincarnation or metempsychosis of the ancients is a chief tenet of theosophy, perhaps the only belief common to all its followers. Amid great variety of doctrines most believe that the human soul is not a pure spirit, but an association of many elements, separated from the body at the moment of death, which enter upon a new existence by becoming incarnate in another body so that the soul might remedy mistakes committed or endure a new period of trial until it reaches perfection and is reabsorbed in the Great One.

Is theosophy a religion? The answer is No, because it lacks inspiration and nobility of sentiment indispensable to religion, and because it is not based on an act of faith in the revelation of a divine, superior being. Is it a philosophy? Not at all, because, dogmatic and aprioristic, it asserts without proof a long series of undemonstrable propositions.

Much less is it a code of morality. Perhaps the contrary is true, for often it is used as a pretext to make immorality lawful by idealists, dismayed at the variety and contradiction in religions, attracted by the prospect of transcendent, occult doctrines, or allured by a kind of mysticism which theosophy seems to spread generously among restless spirits, eager for novelty. *Pal.*

THERAPY. Therapy is a branch of medicine dealing with prevention and cure of diseases. The purpose of therapy may be prophylactic, etiologic, or symptomatic. The means employed are surgical and medical therapy, which involves pharmacotherapy, immunotherapy, dietetic therapy, physiotherapy, and psychotherapy.

The disappearance of a diagnostic curative concept, based on clinical anatomical observations, came at the end of the last century. Our era can be called the era of pathology and *functional* therapy, since modern clinical study, in the form of *neo-Hippocratism* (*see* Pathology), is essentially based, not on a morphological study of individual organs, but a total functional evaluation of the sick organism. Of course, the examination of various organic apparatuses is by no means neglected; as a matter of fact, it is integrated with general biochemical, biotypological, and neuropsychological studies as the best method enabling the physician to make a proper diagnosis and thus prescribe treatment best suited to the patient from the standpoint of his individual exigencies, particular reactions to morbid causes, particular constitution of various organs, body and mind, temperament and character.

Prof. Pende, eminent scholar of constitutional medicine, holds that "today one may not quite deserve the almost sacred name of physician, if he believes to have understood and definitely cured a patient with medicines and surgical instruments applied only to one single organ, one little wheel of a marvelous complexity of parts and functions which involves the patient's organism."

To enumerate the numerous therapeutic media used by medicine in recent years is not necessary; we merely recall the great progress achieved by surgical therapy in the field of heart and lung diseases through artificial hibernation (*see* Narcotherapy). In the physiotherapeutic field, we shall recall the use of ultrasonics, useful above all in the therapy of pain, and the increase of radiation therapy, due to radioisotopes and a so-called radiotherapy of movement. Finally, we shall mention the use of the gamma-globulin therapy in the prophylaxis and treatment of viruses; the discovery of new antibiotics with broader and better application; the introduction of ganglioplegics (*see* Narcotherapy) in neuropsychiatric therapy; and the use of preventive medicines.

The relationships between therapy and morals are close and numerous. First, the physician has, always and above all, the duty of treating with the greatest diligence and the intention of gaining the best results through the most harmless and, under equal conditions, the least expensive means. Various corollaries flow from this: in common cases, remedies of known effectiveness and harmlessness are to be employed; in cases in which the customary medications are ineffective, the physician may have recourse to special remedies; if confronted with dangerous or particularly serious illnesses, dangerous curative methods may be employed, provided that the patient consents or, if unable, relatives of the patient do so. Between two remedies with identical chemical composition or equal effectiveness, the physician must prescribe the less expensive one, even if such a choice were to require of the physician a longer time in the preparation of the prescription than would be required in a patented medicine.

Between special and ordinary, but equally effective, medicine, the physician ordinarily prescribes the former, due to pressure of business or mental laziness. He may do so in good conscience only if he knows for certain that the speciality is definitely superior to any other product which the pharmacist could furnish, or if the physician has to deal with a patient who has lost faith in the ordinary products used for some time without apparent benefit. In such a case, the choice of a *new*, little-known speciality, skillfully presented and more costly than the ordinary product, could be a more effective weapon in the hands of the physician, for it would also have a psychotherapeutic effect on the patient, enabling him to overcome more easily a

morbid condition (usually functional or nervous) which resisted customary treatments.

Generally, it is not lawful for a patient or his family, particularly in grave illnesses, to expect a cure by a direct intervention of God, and thus refuse ordinary therapeutic aids. Such an attitude, far from pious resignation, could amount to tempting God. All theologians, in the footsteps of St. Alphonsus, warn that in the presence of danger of death, it is never lawful to refuse medical or surgical treatments. However, if the illness is such that often it can be cured without medication, then one can, without committing a sin, refuse such remedies.

The opposite extreme, the abuse of medicines, seems to be equally unlawful, particularly if done without medical prescriptions. Such abuse is injurious to health, since almost all medicines, if taken for too long a period or indiscriminately, may produce serious effects. In countries with a more dynamic civilization (Northern Europe and North America) an increasing percentage of sickness and death is caused by cardio-circulatory, neoplastic conditions. In these countries there is an abuse of antibiotics, sulfamides, sedatives, antineuralgies, etc. (In 1953–54, Denmark reported an annual consumption of thirty-eight aspirin tablets per inhabitant.) It is not improbable that a connection might exist between the two facts.

In the practice of his profession, a physician must be mindful not to prescribe remedies or give advice that could have injurious moral repercussions, such as prescription of untimely or excessive hormones, careless prescription of narcotic drugs, plastic surgery, if legitimately presumed that the patient requested this for reprehensible reasons. Much less may a physician counsel birth control practices, sterilization, or other sinful methods.

Finally, the physician should not disregard the curative value of counsel, wisely employed in the solution of psychological conflicts that are of importance in the origin and persistence of psychoneuroses and other illnesses. Let the physician keep in mind that such conflicts are often the result of a more or less conscious and persistent violation of Catholic moral principles: in other words, they stem from dishonesty, lust, and excessive egotism, the sources of worries, anxieties, and serious psycho-affective and neuro-vegetative disturbances. Often, a timely word and prudent counsel can be effective in opening the patient's eyes and in bringing about an improvement not only in his spiritual but in his physical condition.

Besides the *duty of treating* a patient, a physician also has a *right to treat* him with remedies which he considers more appropriate for the particular case on hand. A deliberate refusal on the part of the patient to comply with the treatment prescribed authorizes the physician to abandon the case (*see* Withdrawal from a case).

Furthermore, often a physician has the duty of non-treatment, or, as Mozer recently wrote, "the duty of not intervening." We have in mind cases in which the urgent summoning of a physician is caused more by an understandable anxiety of the sick person or his family than by a real need for immediate attention. In such cases, a physician, who resorts to sedation for mere psychological purposes, and other appropriate assistance, has a duty to examine the patient as required for an exact diagnosis. He may postpone to a later time active intervention with greater probability of success. In other words, treatment must never be motiviated by the "necessity of doing something" but be the result of mature reflection. The right to treat a patient does not of itself justify the adoption by a physician of extraordinary therapeutic methods, either pharmaceutical or surgical. In an extraordinary or a particularly acute case, it is always lawful for a physician to have recourse, with authorization from the sick person or his family, to new and possibly dangerous therapies, concerning which the attending physician remains sole judge before his conscience. In cases of a definite unfavorable prognosis, remedies, more probably harmful, may

be used, if there is a probability of cure, with the consent of the sick person or his family.

Finally, the physician who may have discovered a new treatment, remedy, or surgical operation can test it on a man if this person is in danger of death and provided that it holds a good probability of success. The probability must be drawn from adequate theoretical studies, experiments on animals, etc. Neither the certainty, frequently false, that a case is absolutely desperate, that the patient is an incurably deranged person (even deranged persons can improve), especially if the individual is incapable of refusing and has no relatives to protect his human rights, justifies certainly dangerous remedies for the simple purpose of experimentation. Such an act is morally abominable, because it degrades suffering humanity to the level of guinea pigs or other laboratory animals, and ignores the rights of the human person and the norms of charity.

Has the physician the duty to restore to life one affected by an incurable and painful disease who suffers an attack that would be fatal if the patient were left to himself? The answer is in the affirmative, for to remain inactive would be a form of euthanasia (*q.v.*), so-called "euthanasia by omission" (Palmieri). The supreme task of a physician is to battle against death to the end in order to snatch from its power any sick person who turns to him for help. This is particularly so in view of the fact that truly incurable infirmities are increasingly on the decline and that the struggle against suffering is daily enriched with newer weapons.

"Cure your patients," Augustus Murri exhorted his pupils: "If you cannot cure them, relieve their suffering; if you cannot relieve them, console them and, in every case, adhere to the strict observance of the silent and solemn agreement which has always existed between physician and sufferer, that you shall do everything possible to snatch him from death to the very last instant of his life."

At times, a problem may arise in the physician's mind whether he should save the life of a patient incapable of expressing his own will, at the cost of a grave, mutilating surgical operation. In this case, the physician is required to do everything he can to save the patient's life, even if that entails a grave mutilation.

Concerning surgery, particularly to a destructive degree, there must be good probability of recovery before a patient may be subjected to the risk of operation. It is not lawful to subject a sick person to useless risks, not even if the individual were to voluntarily offer himself.

Finally, a few words concerning *vaccinations*. In spite of generally moderate inconveniences and sporadic serious harm (cases of encephalitis may occasionally result from an anti-smallpox vaccination), their usefulness has been widely demonstrated by medical statistics. Thus, those physicians are in error who profess disbelief in the usefulness of vaccinations. Such an attitude is a cause of great harm because it encourages evasion which may well favor forming dangerous epidemic nests. *See also* Deontology, Pharmaceutical. *Riz.*

THERAPY, PSYCHOANALYTIC. *See* Psychotherapy.

THERAPY, SHOCK. *See* Shock-Therapy.

THIRD ORDER, SECULAR. The origin of secular third orders is as ancient as monastic life itself. Before the eleventh century, laymen joined the Benedictine Order but still remained in the world. Since they followed parts of the Benedictine rule, they were called oblates of St. Benedict. The Emperor St. Henry (d. 1024) was one of the first oblates.

The third orders, properly so-called, appeared in the twelfth century, chiefly at the initiative of St. Norbert, founder of the Premonstratensians (d. 1134). He gave Theobald, count of Champaigne, and other persons a white scapular and a rule of life in the world. St. Francis of Assisi likewise in 1221 gave a

norm of life to various persons, already living a life of penitence according to direction from Francis. These persons constituted the first Franciscan Third Order. Other third orders were soon established by the Dominicans, Augustinians, Carmelites, etc.

A secular third order consists of a group of people living in the world, who endeavor to attain Christian perfection in a way consistent with secular life, by following rules approved for them by the Holy See, under guidance of a religious order, and according to the spirit of the same order (Can. 702, par. 1). A secular third order is a real order because it tends to Christian perfection, yet it differs from *religious orders*, because its members do not bind themselves with vows proper to religious nor do they live in community life. Furthermore, secular third orders differ from *third orders regular*, which are professed religious with solemn or simple vows, as well as from associations of the faithful, in constitutional structure, in their diverse purposes and by the fact that the secular third orders are not subject to the jurisdiction of the Sacred Congregation of the Council like other associations of the faithful, but are dependent on the Sacred Congregation of Religious (Can. 251, par. 1).

A third order, divided into several associations, legitimately established, is called a *sodality of tertiaries* (Can. 702, par. 2). Such sodalities are established by a formal decree of erection, which is read at the ceremony of erection, preserved in the archives.

The secular third orders are subject to the following general rules: (a) Though subject to the superiors of their respective order, all tertiaries remain under the supervision of the local Ordinary. (b) The tertiaries may, but are not obliged to, participate collectively in public processions, funerals, and other ecclesiastical functions, where they must march under their own insignia and standard (Can. 706). The faculty granted to tertiaries by a decree of the Sacred Congregation of Rites, on June 30, 1905, to walk in a procession with the first order and under the same standard is believed to have been repealed. However, if they wear not only the scapular but the entire habit, they may march under the standard of the first order. (c) The law of separation (Can. 711, par. 1) does not apply to sodalities of the third order (AAS, 25 [1933], 506). On the contrary, several sodalities of the same third order may exist, not only in the same church but in the same oratory, divided according to sex, age, and language. (d) The third orders are exclusively intended for the faithful who live in the world, not for members of a religious institute or religious congregation, approved by the Supreme Pontiff or by the bishop, with perpetual or temporary vows. Consequently, religious may not be admitted into third orders (Can. 704, par. 1). (e) Those who belong to one third order cannot belong to another third order without an apostolic indult from the Sacred Congregation of Religious (Can. 705).

The following particular rules apply to social work: (a) Sodalities of third orders, as such, are forbidden to mix in civil or purely financial affairs. The same may be said for so-called *mixed* social works, which, bound to a work of religion or charity, may, however, run the risk of deviating from the religious end of the third order because of financial factors connected with them. To these mixed social works belong the various associations of laborers, farmers, and women who, in addition to moral and spiritual welfare, strive for an honest improvement in their lives according to their own constitutions (Letter of St. Pius X, September 8, 1912: AAS, 4 [1912], 585). However, groups established within the sodality for the temporal welfare of its members, such as credit unions, mutual aid groups, are not forbidden. As a matter of fact, it is quite proper for tertiaries to maintain, according to their capabilities, special funds for the aid of the sick, large families, etc. (b) Tertiaries are not forbidden to belong, individually, to Catholic financial associations whose aim is to acquire temporal benefits or increase their holdings by totally honest means.

(c) All tertiaries are urged to promote works of religion. Thus, they will not only read religious writings, but they will endeavor to circulate these among the people, and thus cooperate in the Christian education of less fortunate children and uneducated people. (d) All tertiaries are obliged to visit the sick and aid the needy: therefore, they cannot fail to practice all the works of mercy (Apostolic letter *Prope diem*, February 6, 1921: AAS, 13 [1921], 33). Pope Pius XI, in a letter addressed to the Prior General of the Carmelites of the Ancient Observance, on October 28, 1922, highly commended the Carmelite Third Order in Brazil, which in charity, at its own expense, erected a large number of hospitals for the sick and playgrounds for athletic activities of the young (AAS, 14 [1922], 639).

The following religious orders enjoy the privilege of third orders: Premonstratensians, Dominicans, Franciscans, Carmelites, Augustinians, Minims, Servants of Mary, Trinitarians, Mercedarians, and Benedictines.

The work of the tertiaries in the history of the Church has been effective in the development of religious charitable works. Today the third orders can be a great spiritual help. When Canon 684 states that those faithful members of associations established or approved by the Church are worthy of commendation, this applies even more to third orders. As the various associations undertake a specific work of charity or of public worship, the third orders tend to perfect the whole Christian life, which includes the practice of all the virtues. For this reason the Supreme Pontiffs have never ceased to exhort the faithful to join the third orders, lavishing highest praises on them and making available to them many privileges and abundant spiritual benefits. *de A.*

THOMAS AQUINAS (St.). St. Thomas, the greatest teacher of scholastic theology, was born at Roccasecca (Frosinone), Italy, early in 1225, to the count of Aquin. Thomas received his primary education at the Benedictine monastery of Monte Cassino. From 1239 to 1244 it seems that he attended the School of Arts at the University of Naples, where he studied under Martin and Peter of Ireland. After he joined the Order of Preachers, probably in April, 1244, in an attempt to deter him from his vocation, his brothers apprehended him and kept him in prison for several months until 1245, when he was able to regain liberty. It is not known where he made the novitiate nor when he began his studies in the Order. He was a pupil of St. Albert the Great, perhaps at Paris before 1248, but certainly at Cologne (1248–1252). In 1252 he went to Paris to teach theology. He taught for twenty-two years (1252–1274) which may be divided into four periods: (1) his first teaching in Paris (1252–1259); (2) his first teaching in Italy (1259–1269); (3) his second teaching in Paris (1269–1272); (4) his second teaching in Italy (1272–1274).

During the summer of 1272, Thomas was sent to Naples to establish a new general house of studies for the Order in the form of a university. There he directed the teaching of theology until December 6, 1273. After some days of rest at his sister's home, he started a journey to the Ecumenical Council of Lyons, in the month of January, 1274.

In February he was taken ill at the home of his niece at the castle of Mainz. He was taken to the Cisternian Abbey at Fossanova (between Rome and Naples) and died there on March 7, 1274, at forty-nine years of age. His body was later translated to France, where it rests at Toulouse in the Abbey of St. Denis.

The scholarly work of the Angelic Doctor, as he was called, is immense. It comprises almost thirty-four volumes in the *Vives* edition. There are: (a) *Philosophical Commentaries*. These extended to the essential part of the works of Aristotle and to the *Liber de causis*. (b) *Scriptural Commentaries*. Thomas left numerous commentaries on various books of the Bible: Job, Psalms, the Canticle of Canticles, Isaias, Lamentations of Jeremias, the Gospels of St. Matthew and St. John, and the Epistles

of St. Paul. *The Golden Chain* is a collection of Patristic passages relative to the text of the four Gospels. (c) *Theological Commentaries*. Under this heading the following works may be included: Commentaries on Boethius (*De Trinitate, De hebdomadis*), on pseudo-Dionysius (*De divinis nominibus*) and on Peter Lombard (*In libros Sententiarum*). In size, his *Commentary on the Sentences* excels by far all the other works of this group; indeed, it is often placed among the great works of theological synthesis left by St. Thomas because its vast commentary gives us the first overall view of theological problems. (d) *Works of Theological Synthesis*. His confrere, Raymond of Peñafort, requested him to write a work that could be used as a vade mecum by the Dominican missionaries working for the conversion of Moslems and which would present Catholic doctrine in a way to suit their spiritual and cultural needs. Thomas conceived the plan of a great work, known as *Summa contra Gentiles*, or at times wrongly called *Summa Philosophica*. The first part (Books 1–3) deals with the Christian truths accessible to reason; the second part (Book 4) contains a study of the mysteries taught by revelation alone, which pagans cannot accept without first assenting to Faith. He began the *Summa contra Gentiles* in Paris in 1258, but completed it in Italy during the pontificate of Urban IV (1261–1264). Thomas had reached full maturity. At this time he started to work on the *Summa Theologiae*, which was to be his masterpiece. The first part was finished about 1269. This remains a masterpiece fully attuned to the human spirit. In the *Summa Theologiae*, divided into three parts, St. Thomas summarized all of theological knowledge with unsurpassed clearness and insuperable depth. We shall outline a synthesis of the part dealing with moral theology, as that which concerns us more directly. Thomas left his masterpiece incomplete; the *Supplementum* to the third part was written by Reginald of Piperno, his inseparable companion, according to the method of the *Com-*

mentary on the Sentences. (e) *Scholastic Disputes.* St. Thomas left a rich collection of *Quaestiones disputatae ordinariae* and *Quaestiones quodlibetales.* (f) *Philosophical Pamphlets: De principiis naturae; De ente et essentia; De aeternitate mundi; De unitate intellectus; De substantiis separatis.* (g) *Theological Pamphlets: De articulis fidei et Ecclesiae sacramentis; De regimine principis* (or *De regno*); *De regimine Judaeorum.* (h) *Apologetic Pamphlets: De rationibus fidei contra Saracenos, Graecos et Armenos; Contra errores Graecorum.* (i) *Pamphlets for the Defense of the Mendicant Friars: Contra impugnantes Dei cultum; De perfectione vitae spiritualis; Contra retrahentes a religioso cultu.* (j) *Pamphlets on Spirituality: Expositio orationis dominicae; Expositio symboli Apostolorum; Expositio de Ave Maria.* To complete the enumeration of the various categories of Thomas' writings we mention the *Office of the Most Blessed Sacrament,* writings on canonical law, letters, and speeches.

THE MORAL THEOLOGIAN. Theology reaches full maturity with St. Thomas' architectural elaboration of its parts and his logical fusion of the positive and rational elements proper to this science. Moral theology is dealt with in the *Commentary on the Sentences of Peter Lombard* and in *Questiones disputate;* it is treated in a complete, harmonious, and systematic way in the second part of the *Summa Theologica.*

The moral theology of St. Thomas, which differs from that of Peter Lombard and Alexander of Hales, is theocentric (*De motu creaturae rationalis in Deum*) with a psychological and dynamic foundation. The movement of a rational creature toward God is accurately studied in its finality (*S. T.,* I–II, q. 1–6); its internal and external resources—human acts (q. 7–48), habits (q. 48–89), law and grace (q. 90–114)—and its vital development in the theological (*S. T.,* II–II, q. 1–47) and moral virtues (II–II, q. 48–171). Consideration for the personal conditions in which each person may find himself, as

in an active or contemplative life or various offices, also is thoroughly explained.

Notice must be taken of the intellectualism of St. Thomas as opposed to the voluntarism of Duns Scotus. In the acute analysis of the human act, which theologians as a whole have integrally accepted, Thomas carefully demonstrated that each act of the will is preceded by a respective act of the intellect which prepares the will and renders the act possible.

To acts properly human, St. Thomas adds acts common to men and animals (passions) which influence human acts and increase or diminish imputability. Imputability, an essential property of human acts, arises mainly from the moral intent, the object of the act and the circumstances. The human acts that are morally good become meritorious if performed by a person in the state of grace.

Faculties and habits, either good (virtues) or bad (vices), are the principal sources of human acts.

The virtues are arranged into three classes: intellectual, moral, and theological, with many ramifications. Vice is studied under the aspect of habit and as an act (sin).

The doctrine of sin is most elaborate in St. Thomas. The devil can direct man toward evil, but God, above all, can act on the soul by His law and grace.

In giving ample development to general principles, St. Thomas asserts the necessity of bringing these into the practical order so that moral formation may be complete. Thomas does not indulge in casuistry; on the contrary, he classifies the objects with an ethical character by grouping them around the theological virtues of faith, hope and charity and the cardinal virtues of prudence, justice, fortitude and temperance.

These are the main structural lines of Saint Thomas' moral theology, which he applies to the states of life in a special way at the close of his treatise (*Summa Theol.,* II–II, q. 171–189). To complete this general survey of Thomistic theology, mention should be made of his doctrine of grace, so necessary to fallen man and his mystical theology, i.e., man's intimate communion with God; of ascetical theology, and the doctrine concerning the sacraments.

Moral theology is treated by St. Thomas, together with dogmatic theology, in a measure that far exceeds previous writers and with a completeness hitherto ignored. The second part of the *Summa*, the most original part of the whole work, is exclusively dedicated to moral and ascetical questions.

Thomas used a method of composition, similar to that of Alexander of Hales, but it was more rigorous and invariable as a system. First, he proposes a question; then he subdivides it into articles, in which he presents the opposing arguments, states a proposition that supports and proves the question, and concludes with an answer to the objections raised. The use of positive proofs from Sacred Scripture, the authority of the Church and that of the Fathers, though succinct, is found in almost every article.

In the *Summa Theologiae*, Saint Thomas used the scholastic, positive, and casuistic method of theology, but the scholastic method was emphasized because of the purpose of his writing in general. The harmonious fusion of all three methods provides greater completeness and effectiveness, for the practical utility and guidance value of moral theology. *Pal.*

THURIBLE. *See* Vessels, Sacred.

THYMUS. *See* Endocrinology.

THYROID. The thyroid (Greek, *thyreos*, a large, oblong shield; *eidos*, form) is a large endocrine gland (*see* Endocrinology), of semi-circular form, consisting of two lobes joined by a connecting band or isthmus. It is located in the neck in front of the trachea and has an average weight of about 20 grams, although it varies notably in individuals. It has a lobular construction; each lobule shows under microscopic examination numerous closed spaces or follicles containing a homogeneous substance filled with iodine, called *thyroid colloid*, and

secreted by epithelial cells which form the walls of the follicles. Of the thyroid hormones (*q.v.*), partly mingled with colloid, but in larger quantity emptying directly into a rich vascular network surrounding the gland, the most important of all is thyroxine.

The thyroid exercises strong stimulating action primarily on the morphogenesis of the organism, i.e., the morphological evolution and normal development of life, affectivity, and intelligence.

In exercising its numerous activities the thyroid acts by stimulating the orthosympathetic nervous system; it further functions in combination with medullary and suprarenal action, prehypophysis, testicles, and parathyroids. It exercises an opposite action with respect to the endocrine pancreas, posthypophysis, thymus, suprarenal cortex and, partly, the ovaries.

THYROID SYNDROMES are usually divided into two large groups: hyperthyroid (*hyperthyroidism*) and hypothyroid (*hypothyroidism*) depending on whether the disease results from an excess or a defect of thyroid secretion. With regard to hyperthyroid syndromes, mention should be made of *dysthyroidism*, since, apart from over-secretion of thyroid hormones, sometimes a qualitative alteration occurs to which, generally, are attributed the most serious cases of hyperthyroidism, called *Basedow's disease*.

(a) Forms of *Hyperthyroidism*. In simple *hyperthyroidism* one observes an increase in internal respiration in all tissues, definite oxidizations of basal metabolism, and, hence, an increase of appetite despite a loss of weight; frequent rises in temperature, moist skin leading to perspiration, intolerance of heat, increase of diuresis, increased excitation of the orthosympathetic with particular, emotive tachycardia. Additional symptoms are: hypocalcemia with neuromuscular hyperexcitability; an increase of systolic and a decrease of dystolic pressure, and therefore an increase of differential pressure, tachykinesia with motorial agility but also with easy exhaustion. Morphological traits are: graceful nimbleness with charming facial features, large eyes, plentiful and shining hair, very good teeth, etc. Mentally, there is rapidity in the processes of thought with a tendency to fantastic creativity, hypermotivity, and great humoral change.

Basedow's disease or *Flajani-Graves-Basedow disease.* This name comes from the three physicians who at different periods individualized and described it with greater accuracy. An irregular, toxic or metaplastic hyperthyroidism—the so-called *dysthyroidism*—chiefly is caused by the circulation of too much thyroid secretion, insufficiently processed. Basedow's disease appears usually in constitutional hyperthyroidism as a result of intensive or repeated emotional traumas, or as the aftermath of infections which act on the thyroid, and determine the metaplastic hypersecretion mentioned above. Goiter, tremor, intense tachycardia, anxiety, and a progressive loss of weight with a pronounced thymopsychical weakness and sudden emotive-impulsive discharges are the leading phenomena clinically characterizing this serious disease.

Much more frequent are the cases of the so-called *oligosymptomatic hyperthyroidism,* in which it is possible to observe separately: cardiac disorders such as emotive cardioerethism, extrasystoles, pseudo-anginal crisis, etc.; gastro-intestinal disorders like spasmodic dyspepsia, vomiting crises, diarrhea, etc.; nervous disorders such as hyperexcitability, unmotivated alternations of moods, abnormal emotivity, etc.; metabolic disorders such as progressive loss of weight.

(b) Forms of *Hypothyroidism.* The clinical symptomatology resulting from thyroid insufficiency is described in the article on cretinism, wherein, because of the importance of their moral reflections, special emphasis was laid on symptoms of psycho-deficiency which characterize such illnesses.

Here, we shall add that these forms of hypothyroidism, appearing in adults, usually have a constitutional basis in which a clear mixedematose picture can more easily be uncovered because of various infective diseases and serious hyponutri-

tion. During or after the menopause of pluriparous women, this occasions a suspected pathogenesis of pluriglandular thyroid and hypophyseal insufficiency due to the interdependence of these two endocrine glands, since repeated pregnancies can produce a usury, excessive consumption of thyroid and prehypophyseal hormones.

For types of hyperthyroidism apparently favored by the agitated and psychotraumatic way of living of our times, the following treatments are indicated according to the gravity of the syndrome: partial surgical resection of the gland, roentgen-therapy, and, for the lightest cases, treatment with diodothyrosine, tartar of ergotamine and ovary preparations for women. Sedatives, rest at high altitude, and food, rich in fats and carbohydrates but lacking in animal proteins, will effectively integrate the treatment.

In hypothyroid syndromes thyrodine, iodine and a protein-rich diet are especially beneficial.

Clinical experience shows that many difficult, unstable, restless persons, prone to excitement and depression, are not such because of a *bad character* or inadequate education but are afflicted with hyperthyroidism in one of the various forms of oligosymptomatic hyperthyroidism which attacks primarily the nervous system. The phenomenon is predominant among women; hence, one must consider this in rectifying their slight but not always harmless faults through effective antithyroid preparations.

Furthermore, it may be helpful to know that due to statistical studies of criminal anthropology it appears that megalosplanchnic individuals with hyperpituitary or, especially, hypersuprarenal deficiencies are prevalent in those guilty of personal crimes, such as murder, etc., whereas a microsplanchnic hyperthyroid deficiency prevails in thieves and swindlers. The illness appears in occasional, impulsive, delinquents, evidently because of psychopathological symptoms of imbalance, instability, emotionalism, reactive impulsiveness, etc., which characterize hyperthyroid individual persons. To this one may add that, in the female sex, beauty of features, hypo-ovarianism, and hyperthyroidism may partly be responsible for turning a woman against maternity and, therefore, against the wholesome chores of domestic life.

Concerning constitution and criminality we note that "a person's constitution does not represent an irreparable fatality but merely a potential condition very favorable to the rise of the phenomenon called criminality." *Riz.*

TIME (Reckoning of). The reckoning of time has great importance for the validity of juridical affairs. This matter is regulated by Canons 32–35 of the Code of Canon Law on the basis of the following premises: (a) *Natural* time is that which runs from one moment to another; *civil* time is that which runs from one day to another; *continuous* time is that which does not undergo interruption; *useful* time is that in which one can exercise or use a right. (b) If it is not clearly stated that time is to be taken as indicated in a calendar, a year consists of 365 days; a month, 30 days; a week, 7 days; and a day, 24 hours. (c) The hours are to be reckoned according to the custom of an area. A certain freedom is allowed in reckoning the time concerning the private celebration of Holy Mass, the private recitation of the Breviary, the reception of Holy Communion and the law of fast and abstinence. (d) In the stipulation of contracts, one must conform to the prescription of civil law. Upon these premises the Code of Canon Law establishes the following rules: (1) If the time is specified (for instance, in the month of March, or next year), one must follow the calendar. (2) If the time is not specified, a distinction must be made: (a) if the time *a quo* is not determined in some manner, one must distinguish various cases; if the time *a quo* coincides with the beginning of a day, this is reckoned as the first day and the period expires at the beginning of the day after the last day; if, instead, the time *a quo* does not coincide with the beginning of a day, the first day is not computed but the final day is; (b) if the month does not have a 30th or 31st day, the period expires at the beginning or end of the last day of the month; (c) finally, if acts are to be renewed at a fixed period, the time expires on the recurrence of the day on which it began, but the new act may be renewed at any time in that day. *Fel.*

TIME (Use of). By the proper use of time is meant that, apart from the time allowed for rest and recreation necessary to the body, one must neither be idle nor engaged in futile things. Man's life in this world is brief; he has only this life in which to prepare for eternity; hence, it is a matter of greatest importance to make the best use of his time in such a way that each moment of his life may be written in the book of life and be productive of rich fruits for eternity. Wasting time is always a harmful thing and practically always sinful, at least venially.

In order to use one's time in the best possible way, a rule of life is of greatest use, that is, a fixed rule according to which one's time is arranged; in fact, it protects an individual from many hesitations which cause him to waste time, and it removes the danger of yielding to one's own pleasures, whims or laziness. Moreover, faithfulness to a rule of life strengthens one's will. In order that a rule of life may really serve its purpose, it must be arranged with great discretion, with consideration of one's own strength, the environment in which one lives, and the importance of the various activities undertaken. This rule must include hours of rising and retiring, a time and method for performing spiritual exercises and the activities required by one's own state in life; the time and duration of meals and recreations, which allows for a certain latitude in substituting one practice with an equivalent or more suitable activity, as well as for postponing or shortening one activity if charity or other serious reasons should require. The first and the last moments of the day should be consecrated to prayer and to an examination of the day's activities. It is also helpful to set aside certain times of the day for prayer, e.g., for the recitation of a part of the rosary. Prudence suggests that the rule of life be arranged with one's own spiritual director. A rule of life should be observed without exaggerations but diligently and with the intention of pleasing God. *Man.*

TIMIDITY. Timidity or timidness is an excessive fear which is not proper to circumstances. If one omits a duty by reason of excessive fear, it is no longer timidity but *cowardice.*

A timid person sins by defect against fortitude. Timidity is a mortal sin if out of timidity one omits a grave duty or creates a grave danger of omission of such a duty.

Fear of unfavorable comment or derision, called human respect, must never cause one to neglect his duty. The fear of displeasing friends or of becoming a victim of injury or other injustice should not deter any one from doing his duty. Man must fear the judgment of God, nor that of men, which is very often erroneous. *Man.*

TIMOPSYCHE. *See* Psyche, pathology of.

TITHES. Tithes are the tenth part of the fruits or income, due to someone by reason of a definite title. In a stricter sense, tithes are the tenth part of the fruits of one's revenue or income, which are due to ministers of the Church for divine worship and the sacred ministry. Much importance was attached to tithes in the Old Testament. Renowned is, indeed, the decree of Charlemagne published at the mixed Council of Paderborn (785 A.D.), which prescribed the payment of tithes to the Church and priests. Wise dispositions were enacted by the Third Lateran Council (1179 A.D.) to check abuses by lay authorities. At the time of the French Revolution all tithes were abolished by civil power, first in France and, then, in other countries; although at times, a partial compensation was made with goods which came to be part of a benefice. Today, as a result of changed social and economic conditions, the Church accepts other forms of contributions for the needs connected with divine worship. Notwithstanding, the disposition of Can. 1502 of the Code of Canon Law is fully valid which prescribes that *tithes* and *primitias* (first fruits of fields, orchards, etc.) be paid according to particular laws and laudable customs of each country. *Fel.*

TITLE AND HONOR. A *title* (*titulus honorarius, dignitas*) as a general term means a dignity, rank, or office. An *honor* is an external mark of distinction as a title to recognition, for which usually there corresponds a *decoration*, as a material sign indicative of personal distinction by reason of merit, bravery, virtue, or an historical commemoration of a particular event.

Passion for titles and honors is as old as humanity, and rulers have often availed themselves of this means to gain followers. In ancient Greece certain honorary expressions related to a physical or moral quality of a person were attached as proper names. In Rome, where the family name was accurately transmitted, titles and honors were awarded to outstanding citizens as a prize for heroic or beneficial deeds performed in behalf of the country. Thus, various crowns, *triumphalis, civica, muralis, navalis,* etc., were joined to specific titles, as *Scipio Africanus,* etc.

In the late period of the Empire and at the time of feudalism, titles of every description, such as duke, marquis, count, baron, etc., were very common. Afterwards, as the power of the subjects diminished and royal absolutism increased, the desire for vain honorary titles on the part of the nobility and aspirants to nobility also increased.

Today, titles and honors are considered *social ornaments* bestowing a right to bedeck oneself exteriorly with necklaces, crosses, bands, ribbons, and similar insignia in a connotation of *sociability* and *seriousness.* The extent of seriousness is dependent on the nature of the title or honor.

Ordinarily, the prerogative of granting honors belongs to the head of the State. The decorations of the equestrian orders presuppose a title or equestrian rank in one of the orders recognized by the State. In this case, the titular is allowed to use the corresponding personal titles together with the insignia. Decorations granted for bravery or merit are in the nature of a prize or recompense, such as a medal, or merit cross; these do not carry any particular formal title or symbol of honor.

The honors of a private order, though publicly recognized, consist of academic titles granted by universities, such as the titles of *bachelor, master, doctor*; or professional diplomas, such as *industrial expert, qualified workman*, etc. These titles, earned through personal study or work, give the subject a certain right, e.g., to clerical, mechanical, or professional competitions; many times they are a necessary requirement for the attainment of a definite position.

Titles, honors, and decorations are intended as certification of meritorious distinction for deeds of a social or public nature. The legitimate acquisition of these titles bestows on a person a right to wear the decoration corresponding to the title, nor can such right be hindered or restricted by anyone except the authority that granted it.

There are papal honors which include special distinctions and honorary titles. With the exception of the Order of the Holy Sepulcher, the orders of knighthood are for the laity. Of other papal honors, some are only for members of the clergy, others for lay persons, others for clergy and laity. Since the honorary distinctions for the laity do not affect the heraldic laws of the civil State, the right of the Church on this point is exercised with absolute independence of the laws of the State.

The equestrian papal orders are as follows: (1) *Supreme Order of Christ*; (2) *Golden Spur*; (3) *Plain Order*; (4) *Order of St. Gregory*; and (5) *Order of St. Sylvester*.

As a rule the Church does not grant such titles and honors to non-Catholics or members of dissident Christian Churches. The honorary distinctions granted to lay persons, aside from those properly termed honors (*equestrian orders*) consist of lay offices at the papal court, as the numerous titles of secret chamberlains, honorary chamberlains of cape and spur, numerarii, and supranumerarii. These are honorary offices to which are attached special titles and privileges, such as precedence, etc. Ecclesiastics cannot belong to equestrian papal orders. Honorary distinctions may be attached to the office or to the person and permit the use of insignia (prelate robes, rings, coat of arms, etc.) or specific titles. Titles, purely ecclesiastical, include the title of *Eminence* for cardinals; mixed civil and ecclesiastical include the title of *Excellency* and *Monsignor* (*see* Cardinal, Prelate, Bishop).

The medal *Pro Ecclesia et Pontifice*, instituted by Pope Leo XIII, July 17, 1888, for special merits, is not connected with an equestrian title and may be granted to women and members of the clergy.

Dignities among the clergy were instituted to promote discipline. The general prerogative for the bestowal of dignities is formulated for the first time as common law in the Code (Can. 396, par. 1). The following appointments are reserved to the Holy Father: (a) cardinals (Can. 232); (b) pontifical legates (Can. 265); (c) abbots and prelates *nullius* (Can. 320); (d) bishops (Can. 329); (e) episcopal coadjutors (Can. 350).

Canon Law recognizes academic titles and the canonical effects which academic degrees have in the Church. These effects are: (a) preference in the conferral of benefices or offices to those who have obtained the doctorate or licentiate in some sacred science, such as bishops (Can. 331, par. 1, n. 5), vicars general (Can. 367, par. 1), canon theologian or penitentiary (Can. 339, par. 1), teachers in seminaries (Can. 1366, par. 1), promoter of justice and defender of the bond (Cans. 1589, par. 1, 1508, 2017–2018); (b) the right to wear apart from sacred functions a particular insignia, such as a *ring* with stone or a *doctor's biretta* (Can. 1378).

Mere honorary titles or dignities are forbidden to religious by reason of their particular profession of a life of humility and detachment from everything vain and human. But if the constitutions allow, titles of major offices actually held in the religious organization are tolerated (Can. 515). Titles of *doctor*, *master*, or *lector* are not considered titles of honor.

Titles and honors as a mark of distinction or reward to well-deserving persons must be worthily worn by the recipients. If they become unworthy of them by improper deeds or behavior, they disqualify themselves from bearing such titles and honors. In fact, the privilege becomes void by defect of personal dignity upon which it is supposed to rest. However, one may continue to carry it as long as his reputation remains good outwardly, for he is not expected to bring disgrace upon himself by divesting himself of it openly. Decorations and titles are added reasons why the recipients should set good example, through which, in a spirit of true humility, they ought to gain higher esteem among the people. Titles do not render men illustrious, but recipients must add luster to the titles by their mode of living and acting. *Tar.*

TITLE OF SACRED ORDINATION.

Title of sacred ordination is understood in Canon Law as a form of economic security for the maintenance of a cleric so that he may not be required to engage in unbecoming occupations or begging. Therefore, the title must be secure for the whole life of the cleric and sufficient for a suitable maintenance (Can. 979). The title is required for ordination to major orders; without the title no one can be lawfully ordained (Can. 974, par. 1, n. 7). If the bishop has knowingly ordained a candidate without an apostolic indult, he automatically incurs suspension from the faculty of conferring orders for one year, which is reserved to the Apostolic See (Can. 2373, n. 3). Moreover, he must assume for himself and his successors the obligation

of providing the needy cleric with suitable maintenance until the cleric finds a suitable source of support (Can. 980, par. 2-3). If a cleric in major orders loses his title, he must secure for himself another, unless his bishop believes that his sustenance is provided for in another manner (Can. 980, par. 1).

The norms of Canon Law on canonical title are the result of a long historic evolution. In the early centuries of the Church, many clerics were ordained, for they were essential for the service of the individual churches. The church to which the newly ordained was attached provided for his sustenance out of its own revenue (so-called relative ordinations). As the churches were then called titles (*titulus*), it was said that the cleric was ordained for this or that title, e.g., *ad titulum Clementis*, that is, for the church title of St. Clement. This explains how the word *titulus* was used in ordination more properly for a specified office in the church in which the ordained cleric served and received his sustenance. Sustenance, later, was called *beneficium*, i.e., a benefice (*q.v.*). The *beneficium* became an ordinary and necessary title for ordination (*titulus ordinationis ordinarius et necessarius*). To protect the dignity of the clerical state, only those who had a canonical title, i.e., an ecclesiastical benefice, could be ordained, and ordinations without title, called absolute ordinations, were strictly forbidden (Council of Chalcedon, 45; cf. c. 1, D. 70). The prohibition was not strictly observed, and in the tenth century many clerics were not attached to any church but wandered from place to place. The Third Lateran Council (1179) renewed the prohibition and in addition prescribed that no deacon or priest (Innocent III extended this to subdeacons, cf. X, 3, 5, 16) could be ordained without a canonical title or benefice, and that a bishop who ordained anyone in default of a benefice was to provide out of his own revenue for the support of the cleric ordained, unless the latter could support himself by his own possessions or paternal inheritance (X, 3, 5, 4). This exception, however, gave rise to a new title, *titulus patrimonii* (the title of patrimony [X, 3, 5, 23]), to which later was added a *titulus pensionis* (the title of pension). Both were approved with certain restrictions by the Council of Trent (Sess. XXI, *De ref., cap.* 2). Following the Council of Trent, the *titulus missionis* (the title of the mission) and, recently, the *titulus servitii diocesis* (the title of service of the diocese) were added. Regulars were ordained, since the Council of Calcedon (451), *ad titulum monasterii, professionis, paupertatis,* i.e., under the title of the monastery, religious profession, or poverty, whereas, according to the Constitution *Romanus Pontifex* of St. Pius V (October 14, 1568), the rules for the secular clergy applied also to religious.

Canon Law recognizes the following titles of ordination: (A) *For the secular clergy:* (1) The ordinary canonical title is today the title of a benefice (*titulus beneficii*); actually, however, it is seldom used because the number of suitable ecclesiastical benefices is not sufficient. (2) In the absence of the title of a benefice, the patrimonial title (*titulus patrimonii*) consisting of a private patrimony, and the title of pension (*titulus pensionis*) consisting of the right to credits with third parties (physical or juridical person, either ecclesiastical or civil) are permitted. It is the right of the Ordinary to establish, according to the needs of the times and places, the amount of a patrimony or a pension, as well as necessary guarantees that the title provide adequate income for life, for a suitable maintenance of the cleric (Can. 979, par. 2). (3) If the cleric has neither a title of a benefice, patrimony, nor pension, two subsidiary titles are admitted by Canon Law: the title of service of the diocese (*titulus servitii diocesis*), or, in territories subject to the Sacred Congregation of the Propagation of Faith, the title of the mission (*titulus missionis*). The cleric must bind himself by oath to dedicate himself for life to this service under the authority of a legitimate Ordinary. The Ordinary is bound to provide for the maintenance of the priest by conferring on him a

benefice, office or salary (Can. 981). (4) In Germany the title of board (*titulus mensae*), in practice from the fifteenth century, is admitted by particular law. This is a juridical obligation of a physical or juridical person (often the ruler of the State) to take care of the maintenance of the cleric if he cannot provide for himself. To compensate for inadequacies connected with this other title, special emergency welfare organizations for priests have recently been organized in some countries. In return for payment of a specified yearly premium they will receive an allowance in case of necessity. (B) *For the regular clergy:* (1) The religious community must provide for the maintenance of those professed with perpetual vows. The title of a religious with solemn vows is called a title of *poverty* or *religious profession* (*titulus paupertatis seu professionis religiosae*); of religious with simple vows, *title of common board, or of the Congregation* (*titulus mensae communis, Congregationis*). (2) All other religious are governed by the law for the secular clergy with respect to the title of ordination (Can. 982). *Led.*

TITULAR (Bishop). *See* Bishop.

TITULAR (Saint). *See* Altar, Church, Worship, Saints.

TOBACCO. *See* Food; Drugs, Pleasurable.

TOLERANCE. Tolerance (Latin, *tolerare*—to support, to bear) indicates a reaction of mind that permits, for some proportionate good reason, an evil or improper situation or person. In the practical order the evil is generally a vice; in the intellectual order it is an error (*q.v.*) which is allowed to exist without positive approval.

Tolerance is usually related to specific moral and religious principles; of this form of tolerance we speak here.

To refrain from opposing any doctrine on the principle that all doctrines are equally good is called *dogmatic tolerance*. A passive attitude concerning an erroneous opinion, without approval of the error, is called *practical tolerance*.

Dogmatic tolerance is not lawful, because it is an attitude that flows from dogmatic or moral relativity; practical tolerance may be permitted for proportionately good reasons. In the face of a real fact or evident truth, one cannot be tolerant to the point of approval of the attitude that considers these non-existent or false truths. This attitude implies non-belief of a truth, non-conviction in our beliefs, absolute indifference to an apparently banal matter, or a moral relativism concerning truth and error. The acceptance of moral and religious relativity leads to absolute dogmatic tolerance with respect to religious and moral ideas. History confirms this.

Rationalists, considering man endowed with total autonomy and confining God to the realm of the suprasensible and unknowable, proclaim human reason as the absolute criterion of truth and the individual will as the autonomous source of morality. This produces a tolerance of moral and religious ideas, which must be absolute. These liberal principles were incorporated into the *Declaration of the Rights of Man and of the Citizen* (September, 1791); through this declaration they became part of the legislation of many nations. Error could be not only publicly defended but also propagated and taught. The precious heritage, treasured by civilized humanity, including paganism, for thousands of years, was considered *obscurantism* or dogmatic tolerance. The practical conclusion was that no moral idea must be considered a norm to which individuals and society are obliged to conform. Thus many States, convinced of the need for absolute intolerance, permitted any religious, moral, or philosophical idealogy to be defended and propagated. These nations allowed political movements of every tenor, even with political ideas opposed to the liberal postulates of liberty and equality.

This was the origin of the secular State, concerned neither with God, revealed religion, Church, divine or ecclesiastical laws. Secularism prescinds completely from all that and recognizes no authority or source of rights apart from itself. The reasons advanced to justify this are the diversity of religious beliefs among the people which the State cannot judge; thus, to avoid favoring a section of the people, it tolerates all opinions without paying heed to any.

In reply to these rationalizations we note that people are divided in every field and that the government, though not expected to solve any doctrinal questions, must follow a practical policy. The State cannot ignore the religion of its citizens on the ground of liberty; it is the duty of the government to see to it that no law be made nor any governmental action enacted against the religious conscience of its people.

Freedom of worship has its limitations, in the sense that the State may not tolerate rites contrary to natural morality. (Cf. Pius IX, *Quanta cura*; Syllabus, December 8, 1864; Leo XIII, *Immortale Dei*, November 1, 1885; *Libertas*, June 20, 1888; T. Meyer, *Institutiones iuris naturalis*, I, Friburgi i. B., 1885.)

It would be inaccurate to hold that the State must always eliminate, if possible, all moral and religious errors on the grounds that their tolerance is itself immoral. The duty to restrain moral and religious error is not in itself an ultimate end of action. This duty is subordinate to higher and more general ends which, in certain circumstances, allow or even convey the notion that tolerance of error is perhaps the best way to promote a general good.

This clarifies the two principles which answer concrete cases with respect to the attitude of a jurist, politician, or a Catholic head of government for a formula of moral and religious toleration. These principles are: (1) that which is not true or moral has no objective right to existence, promotion, or practice (*dogmatic intolerance*); (2) failure to impede error by law and coercive provisions can be justified in the interest of a higher and greater good (*practical tolerance*). In a specific case, i.e., as a question of fact, the Catholic statesman shall be directed by his own conscience (Pope Pius XII, Address to Italian Catholic Jurists, December 6, 1953; AAS [1953], 794–802). *Pal.*

TONE, AFFECTIVE. See Dysthymia.

TONE. See Constitution, Biotypological.

TONSURE. Tonsure is a sacred rite, instituted by the Church, in which a baptized man is consecrated to God in a particular way and is numbered among the clergy in order that he may be admitted to the sacred orders. Tonsure, therefore, is so called from the cutting of hair, which is an admonition and symbol of renunciation of the vanities of the world. Tonsure is not one of the orders but a preparation to them. Through it a person becomes a cleric (*q.v.*), acquires the privileges and rights of the clerical state, and becomes subject to ecclesiastical jurisdiction and a candidate for ecclesiastical benefices.

By law, a tonsured man has a right and obligation to wear an ecclesiastical habit (*q.v.*) in a visible way, unless there is a custom to the contrary, as in the United States. The clergy belonging to an order or religious congregation follow the particular prescriptions of the order or congregation with respect to the tonsure.

It is difficult to state how long a cleric may fail to visibly display tonsure without sinning gravely; yet the common opinion is that, apart from parvity of matter, it is a grave sin not to wear the ecclesiastical habit and the tonsure after the explicit admonition of the Bishop.

Concerning penalties imposed upon clerics who fail to wear the habit, *see* Habit, ecclesiastical. *Fel.*

TORT. Tort is damage suffered by one of the parties to a bilateral juridical agreement (contract, testamentary disposition, etc.) by reason of a notable disproportion between the consideration received by one side and the benefit received by the other, which caused one of the parties to obtain an immoral profit.

Tort, a typical institution of post-classical Roman Law with a Christian flavor, was introduced by Justinian on the basis of principles of equity (*aequitas*). These were aimed at a rescinding action to one who, because of damage suffered but not because of fraud or violence *ab extrinseco*, is unable to use the ordinary legal action of annulment.

In a strict sense, tort is a specific act, not to be confused with damage in general, that arises from an agreement or contract, because of fraud, fundamental error, or defective consent (*see* Damage, Restitution).

The specific issue of tort occurs only if a disproportion between the agreement and counter-agreement becomes a damaging factor, caused by a fact, itself juridically independent of the full consent of the damaged party. It is independent of any condition, and of necessity damages one party; the other party took advantage of this to obtain an undue benefit.

Normally, therefore, the damage resulting from a tort is never such as to vitiate the consent, invalidate the contract, or furnish ordinary reasons for annulment. Since it indicates a violation of the relation of just equality (under natural law, obligatory in bilateral onerous transactions, because of damage caused to one side in an *unfair* benefit obtained by the other), positive provisions must furnish in some way the means by which the damaged party may be compensated. This is made possible by granting the damaged party the right to institute an action for rescinding the contract. It is *simple* tort, if the value of the compensation given or promised is less than one half the value of the counter-compensation; it is *grave* tort or *ultra dimidium*, if compensation is larger than one half; it is *extremely grave* tort if compensation is larger than two-thirds.

In Canon Law the action rescinding a contract is granted if, *ex errore*, one of the parties has suffered a grave damage of more than one half the value of the object (Can. 1683, par. 2).

It is doubtful whether a tort constitutes a violation of a strict relation of commutative justice. The owner of a thing can give it away or sell it for less than its value, according to the Romanistic axiom: *Naturaliter concessum est, quod pluris sit minoris vendere* ("It is not against the natural order to sell for less something that is worth more"). But when the disproportion is manifest and the condition of necessity of the injured is exploited with an undue gain for the other side, and if the obligation of reestablishing the just terms of the transaction is not actually a matter of commutative justice, it certainly falls within the sphere of legal and social justice. Hence, to a grave tort there corresponds a grave obligation in conscience to make restitution or to compensate the injured party for the damage suffered, after a sentence rescinding the relation.

Tort taken in a strict sense, that is, a specifically technical one, does not exclude the freedom of consent on the part of the damaged party nor does it include a fraudulent action on the part of the other party. For tort, in a wider sense, that is, equivalent to damage in general, *see* Damage, Restitution. For personal injury or damage *see* Damage, *and* Mutilation. *Zac.*

TOTALITARIANISM.

Totalitarianism, a word of recent coinage in the years which followed the First World War, is a form of government which supplants parliamentary government by an absolute rule of fact and of law under the external appearances of democracy. For example, an absolute form of government with a democratic mask reigns in Russia in place of the absolute form of government of the Czar. This resembles a Napoleonic government by plebiscite, with additional methods suggested by diverse circumstances. Totalitarianism is carried out in a more or less ruthless manner. Fascism in Italy before its final failure was less severe than Nazism in Germany, but the principle was the same: *Nothing outside the State; everything within the State for the State.*

Direct application of this principle eliminated every concept or action that did not completely and exclusively subordinate man to the State. Modern totalitarianism identified the State with the dictator and a few gregarious confidants. The concentration of all power without limit or control into the hands of one man signified, not a suitable expedient in exceptional circumstances for the duration of an emergency, but the best method of assuring national unity and the most effective and productive development of the resources of the people in an age of complicated technology. Parliaments, elections, and rivalries of parties were considered detrimental to public welfare, productive of disorders, and detrimental to general progress and achievement of goals set by the dictator.

This aspect of totalitarianism is full of dangerous consequences. Continued dictatorship always becomes, as history proves, obnoxious despotism, which ends in catastrophe.

The history of Fascism and Nazism confirms the experience of preceding centuries, which witnessed the sad fate of Napoleon I and Napoleon III. This is merely the external aspect of totalitarianism. Much more serious for human conscience and more apt to offer reasons for wider reflexion is the intimate essence and basic philosophy of totalitarianism, expressed by *Nothing outside the State, everything within the State for the State.* This judgment, if taken literally and unreservedly, constitutes a denial of the fundamental value of the human person. The authors of the doctrine of the modern State during the nineteenth century seem to have been unaware of the contradiction which they propagated with respect to the spirit of the liberal tendency of the age. Born of the *Declaration of the Rights of Man and the Citizen,* termed *immortal principles,* this doctrine made the State the *source of all rights,* so that every right for man, identified as the citizen, depends essentially upon the mind and will of the collectivity which exists in the State and for the State. As a logical consequence, the freedoms of the *Declaration* made sense only insofar as they were determined and defined by the State. Historical liberalism never explicitly and totally accepted these consequences, but it did not solve the contradiction. By canonizing the doctrine of the State, it paved the way for totalitarian revolution. The fundamental error consists in making the State the source of right, and the failure to distinguish in the human person that which has a *relative* value, and therefore makes the individual subject to the social exigencies and juridical power of the State, and that which has an *absolute* value, which is the supreme constitutive element of the human person. This the State does not possess and, therefore, cannot bestow. The human person comes directly from God. Thus, an ability to attain natural and supernatural truth, to follow morality and conscience, to seek a happiness not merely on earth but an eternal one, to choose freely a way of living, to belong to the universal, human family—all are elements to be considered. The State may intervene with respect to the manner in which a capacity is exercised by an individual, but it cannot destroy its essential nature. There are essential rights by which the human person exists and develops; it is the duty of the State to know and recognize these, and to develop the social climate in which those rights may be exercised and developed. The sovereignty of the State with respect to each individual is exercised by regulating the elements and other forces of human nature so that they may not only cause no harm, but actually contribute to the formation and perfection of the environment. A legitimate State which violates those essential rights of the human person with merely one of its citizens or even aliens, is despotic and unjust. Even if the State has the consent of all citizens, it does not possess authority to violate rights. A clear concept of the human *person* according to Christian teaching is the only source for the exact, comprehensive understanding of the respect due to the individual. It is also the only way by which one can determine the value and limits of the sovereignty of the State and thus avoid the danger of obvious or concealed totalitarianism. *Boz.*

TOTIES QUOTIES. *See* Indulgence.

TOURNAMENT. *See* Duel.

TOXICOLOGY. *See* Medicines; Poison.

TOXICOMANIA. *See* Narcotics.

TRACHOMA. *See* Diseases, Social.

TRADE. *See* Commerce.

TRADE, BALANCE OF. *See* Exchange.

TRADE UNIONS. *See* Unions; Association.

TRADITION. *See* Sources of moral theology.

TRANCE. *See* Hypnotism, Medium.

TRANSACTION. *See* Trade.

TRANSACTION. *See* Act, Juridical; Commerce.

TRANSCRIPT, CIVIL, OF MARRIAGE. A transcript of marriage is a record of a canonical marriage for a bureau of vital statistics under civil authority. The marriage bureau must be informed of the celebration of the religious marriage. The marriage so transcribed produces the civil effects from the day of its celebration. The civil official in charge of records must execute the transcript as soon as possible, if free from error. *Bar.*

TRANSFUSION, BLOOD. Blood transfusion, a means of preventing death due to a blood disease or the loss of a large quantity of blood, is a transfer of the blood of one person into the body of another person by an infusion of blood, previously collected and preserved or obtained at the necessary moment from donors. To avoid the harmful effects of blood transfusion to the health of the recipient of the donation, it is necessary that the blood of the donor be the same quality and type as that of the recipient.

As an act involving two persons, the transfusion has a double moral aspect: (a) as a transfusion of the blood of another, transfusion presents no particular moral problem, for it is licit if the results will be for the therapeutic welfare of the patient; (b) as a removal of blood from a person, it is licit if the person consents to the removal of blood from his veins. The question may be reduced to this: Is it lawful to give a part of one's blood for the benefit of another? Moral theologians have never disapproved of such an act. The amount of blood which can be lawfully removed from one's body is not exactly determined. To remove only a moderate quantity is by itself not harmful to a person. It is obviously detrimental and, therefore, immoral to remove too much blood from an individual so that death or other injury to the donor might be a possible result. *Ben.*

TRANSLATION. *See* Pastor; Parish; Bishop.

TRANSMISSION. *See* Heredity.

TRANSPLANTATION OF ORGANS. In general, transplantation consists in the removal of an organ or part of it from the body of a living being (man or animal) and grafting it on the body of another living being so that it may become part of it. Transplantation becomes a special moral problem if the subject of the process is a man, either as donor or beneficiary of the transplanted organ. For corneal, cutaneous, and vascular transplantation from a dead to a living body, *see* Thanotology.

Surgeons have been successful in curing sick persons of physical and mental diseases by grafting on them parts of the organs of another person. At times generative power has been restored by transplantation. Dr. Voronoff has become a promoter of a project involving large-scale transplanting of organs from monkeys to men and women (especially

to individuals eight to ten years old) in order to bring into existence a new kind of human being. These operations have had no effective, favorable results.

Are these transplantings permitted by the moral law? The larger number of moral theologians hold a negative opinion. According to them, the removal of organs or parts of organs from a healthy man is unlawful, because it would involve mutilation (*q.v.*) of a living individual, which is unlawful.

According to others, this altruistic transfer of one's own organs or portions of them (particularly in the case of double organs) is not unlawful, but an heroic act of charity. To refute the grave difficulty raised by those who hold to the first theory that mutilation is unlawful except if required for the health of an individual, they appeal to the moral unity existing among all men in proof of the thesis. In reality, however, moral unity does not prove their theory, for the moral union that binds men together is of an entirely different nature from the union binding the various members into a physical unity (Address of Pius XII to the Italian Association of Donors of the Cornea, May 14, 1956: AAS 48 [1956], 458–467).

If the grafted organ is obtained by lawful surgical amputation and necessary for the recovery of the patient from a serious disease, then, the moral problem affects only the person upon whom the transplanting is carried out. There is no valid reason why it would be unlawful. Antonelli maintained that the grafting itself is contrary to the moral law. His reasons were: (a) The operation is too much at variance with a natural process and, therefore, it does violence to nature. (b) The use of another person's organs is in opposition to the intimate relation between parents and child to which nature tends. (c) The danger of serious harm to the health of the person who submits to the operation and to his offspring is great.

Though these reasons have some value, they do not seem certain and decisive. In any case, they are serious enough to caution the physicians to proceed in this field with the greatest prudence and reservation and with a clear knowledge of the moral principles. Concerning this subject *see also* Grafts. *Ben.*

TRANSPOSITION OF SENSES. *See* Metapsychology.

TRANSUBSTANTIATION. *See* Consecration, Eucharistic.

TRAVELLER (Juridical sense). A traveller or stranger, in the juridical sense, is anyone who is presently located outside the place where he has his domicile (*q.v.*) or quasi-domicile.

A traveller is not bound to observe particular laws of his own territory as long as he is outside of it, unless the transgression of these laws will harm his own territory, or these laws are personal; in the same way, the traveller, since he is not subject to them, is not bound by the particular laws of the place where he resides at the moment, as long as these laws do not concern the maintenance of public order or establish procedure for certain final acts. But he is bound by general laws, even if they are not in force in his own territory; he is dispensed from them if they are not in force in the territory where he is at the moment (Can. 14, par. 1, n. 1–3).

THE TRAVELLER AND THE ADMINISTRATION OF THE SACRAMENTS. With regard to baptism, travellers must as a rule be baptized in their own parishes where they have a domicile or quasi-domicile, if this can be done without difficulty and delay. Otherwise they can be baptized solemnly by any pastor in his own territory (Can. 738, par. 2). A traveller can receive sacramental absolution from any priest approved for confession in the diocese where he is at the moment; and he can also gain indulgences granted by the Bishop in the territory where he is at present.

Can. 1562 provides that a traveller in Rome, even for a very short time, can be cited by the local ecclesiastical tribunal; but he retains the right to be returned home, that is, to be sent back to his own Ordinary. *Fel.*

TREASURE. In legal terms, a treasure is any object of value, which is movable but concealed or interred, and without evident proof of an owner. The definition given by Roman law has the same meaning: *Thesaurus est vestus quaedam depositio pecuniae; cuius non existat memoria, ut iam dominium non habeat* (D. 41, 1, par. 1, n. 1).

Three elements comprise the juridical notion of treasure: an intrinsic or an extrinsic value or preciousness of an object; mobility from an artificial internment or concealment; an owner who cannot be traced or discovered.

It is not necessary that the concealment (*depositio*) be of long standing, provided that the owner, in fact, cannot be proven. However, moral certainty is sufficient; the circumstances of concealment and discovery must be such as to furnish a reasonable motive for retaining the treasure.

Money, jewels, works of art, manuscripts and rare codices, prize vases or, in general, all objects intrinsically valuable or extrinsically esteemed as valuable for artistic, historical, antique, or rare qualities, belong to the notion of treasure.

The acquisition of a treasure is regulated by norms of the positive law of individual nations, and interpretative, practical applications of the principles of the natural law.

From the standpoint of the natural law alone, as a *res nullius* (an object without an owner), the treasure belongs entirely to the one who discovered it by right of his discovery or occupancy. In fact, the natural law assigns ownership of *res nullius* to the first occupant.

Modern codes of civil law limit the natural right of the discoverer, by a concurrent right of the owner of the land. Since such limitations appear just and according to right reason, moralists concur in holding that the laws relating to such restrictions are not merely penal laws; consequently, these laws bind in conscience.

Consequently, juridical discipline concerning acquisition of treasure in modern codes generally represents an equitable compromise between the rights of the finder and those of the owner of the land or movable thing in which the treasure was discovered.

According to almost all modern codes: (a) the treasure belongs entirely to the finder, if he is at the same time the owner of the land or movable thing in which it is found. (b) If the treasure is found in the property of another by chance, it is divided equally between the owner of the ground by right of accession and the finder by right of discovery or occupancy. (c) If the treasure was looked for and discovered, not by chance, but by *data opera*, that is, by actual work, with or without the authorization of the owner of the property, certain civil codes do not recognize the right of discovery and occupancy to the finder but only a right of accession in favor of the owner. (d) If the land is subject to emphiteusis, then half of the treasure belongs to the lessee; if it is rented in tenancy, nothing belongs to the tenant.

Accordingly, the finder of the treasure is one who takes the thing out of concealment by his discovery (*inventio*). This is, of itself, an original title of acquisition of property, equivalent to occupancy. Thus, the acquisition on the part of the finder does not require effective possession of the object; the sole fact of discovery is sufficient.

In certain countries, due to particular local conditions, any discovery of an object of archeological, paleontological, or artistic value is governed by special laws, which differ from the general law of these societies or States in that neither the owner of the land nor the manager of the excavations nor the discoverer is considered to have the right of ownership to the discoveries. They must promptly report the findings to competent officials but they have a right to a reward or to an equitable compensation. *Zac.*

TREATY. *See* Contract.

TREATY, INTERNATIONAL. International treaties are commonly defined as agreements or contracts formed between two or more juridical, international, public organizations, that is, between two independent and perfect societies. Concordats reached between the Holy See and various States must be considered real international treaties, for they are agreements between two societies, each one perfect and independent in its own order (*see* Concordat). Treaties are *general* or *particular*, *principal* or *accessory*, *open* or *closed*, and are entitled by particular names according to the subject with which they deal, such as commercial, cultural, military, peace, friendship, non-aggression treaties or pacts, etc.

For a valid stipulation of a treaty, three elements are required: (1) a qualified subject; (2) a lawful object; (3) free consent. All States as members of international, public law are of themselves qualified subjects to contract international treaties. However, some States, by reason of a particular juridical condition, e.g., so-called semi-sovereignty, cannot validly conclude special treaties.

The object of treaties must be physically, morally, and juridically possible. It is presumed that the contracting parties do not wish to assume obligations which they know they are unable materially to fulfill. The object of a treaty must not be contrary to religion or moral law. An international treaty by which two contracting parties commit themselves to deprive a third State of its territory or political independence, would certainly be an invalid treaty by reason of the unlawful nature of its object.

As in all contracts, in the formation of a treaty, freedom of consent of the contracting parties is required. In this regard, the question is posed concerning the validity of a peace treaty reached after a war between a defeated and a victorious power, in view of the peculiar conditions in which the defeated nation finds itself. If the condition under which the defeated state finds itself has a just cause, that is, if the victor nation has waged a just war, the treaty must be held morally and juridically valid. On the contrary, if the condition of compulsion is unjust because the victor nation did not wage a just war, the peace treaty must be considered invalid by reason of the unlawfulness of its object, that is, the obligations imposed without a just cause by the triumphant power. The observance of specific formalities, established by the internal laws of each contracting party and international law, may also be necessary for a valid conclusion of an international treaty. For example, if the constitutional law of the contracting States requires approval of the legislative chamber for the validity of a treaty, it is clear that a treaty concluded without such approval is invalid.

International treaties may be terminated in different ways. Treaties limited to a definite time cease upon expiration of the time unless renewed. Moreover, they may be terminated by mutual consent of the contracting parties, by an unfulfilled condition, by renunciation of rights if the treaty concerns rights affecting only the party renouncing them. Termination of a treaty may also take place by unilateral renunciation by one of the parties, provided that the treaty allowed contracting parties the privilege of rescinding it. In such case, the denunciation must be made at a time and in the manner previously agreed on. A particular form of termination is through a clause termed *rebus sic stantibus*, namely, if the conditions existing at the time of the stipulation of the treaty remained really and substantially unchanged. Yet, if a State wishes to invoke such a clause, it cannot act unilaterally. It must, first, explain to the other party the reason for such an intent, and offer proofs for the allegations. In case of disagreement whether or not the clause *rebus sic stantibus* is valid, the parties must employ one of the known, peaceful means for resolving international conflicts, namely, the mediation of a friendly state, international tribunals, or the United Nations. *Pas.*

TREATY, LATERAN. *See* Vatican City; Pontiff, Supreme.

TRIAL, CANONICAL. In a general sense, a trial includes all the acts exer-

cised by competent, juridical organs in protecting juridical rights. In other words, it includes not only the formal examination of the matter in question but the execution of the sentence. A trial is also referred to as a process, litigation, cause, or the like. *Trial* indicates, also, any writ, summons, or totality of documents or acts attesting to the documentation used in a juridical proceeding.

CANONICAL CIVIL TRIAL. In Canon Law a trial may be *civil* or *criminal*. *Civil trial* is defined as the totality of actions leading to an examination, legal discussion, and definition of a controversy (Can. 1552); the essence of the controversy pertains to a definition.

Civil litigation is accepted for trial insofar as the indispensable elements are present in it which would prompt the judge to take into consideration the petition of the plaintiff, without concern, for the moment, for a judgment on the merit of the allegations contained in the petition.

The suit begins with a judicial petition or bill of complaint or libel (Can. 1706 ff.) which induces the judge to issue a summons to the other party or defendant (Can. 1711 ff.). The definition of the object of the trial by the *contestatio litis* or joining of the issue (Can. 1726 ff.) is the beginning of the judicial action (Can. 1732). The trial is developed through various sessions covering interrogation of the parties (Can. 1742 ff.) and the collection of proofs (Can. 1747 ff.) for the sake of enabling the judge to evaluate the objective truth of the facts. The judge will endeavor to acquire the fundamental knowledge and responsibility through the judicial confession of the parties (Can. 1750 ff.), testimonies of witnesses (*q.v.*), the report of experts, documents (Can. 1812 ff.), the presumptions (Can. 1825 ff.) and the like. The trial culminates with publication of the acts (Can. 1825 ff.) and this is followed by debate or discussion of the legal and factual reasons expounded (Can. 1862 ff.); the trial is concluded with a decision or sentence.

The characteristic note of a canonical trial is that the writing of the acts prevails over oral discussion; secrecy is maintained, though the acts are published, in the sense that the acts are not ordinarily disclosed to third parties; communication between parties is indirect; a trial follows with preference the principle of preclusion, and deals *ex officio* with causes of public interest or, upon request of the parties, causes of private interest.

The proceedings for execution of a sentence in ecclesiastical trials, as in civil trials, belong to the administrative sphere (Can. 1917 ff.).

Besides classic procedures used in marriage trials (Can. 1960 ff.), in trials involving sacred ordination (Can. 1933 ff.), beatification, and canonization, other procedures are used in non-contentious causes (*see* Arbitration).

CIVIL PROCEEDINGS AND MIXED FORUM. Outside those spheres which belong to the Church by exclusive right (Can. 1553 ff.; *see* Clergy, privileges of; Immunity, ecclesiastical), the civil State has both the right and duty to provide for the administration of justice.

In issues of mixed forum, namely where a civil court has concurrent jurisdiction with an ecclesiastical court, the Church maintains a right of prevention (Can. 1553, par. 2) according to which the court first accepting a complaint or citing an offender, has the right to adjudicate the case. The systems of trial and procedure vary in each individual country, and the collection of laws concerning such cases constitutes in many countries a particular code of laws or code of civil procedure.

CANONICAL CRIMINAL TRIAL. A canonical criminal trial consists of all acts involving ascertainment of an ecclesiastical criminal fact and its imputability, subsequent discussion, and a sentence of absolution or condemnation (Can. 1552, par. 2, n. 2). Its object is any public or notorious ecclesiastical crime, with the exception of crimes generally submitted to administrative proceedings (Can. 2168–2194). The penalty is directed not only for the amendment of the offender but also the restoration of the social order disturbed by the crime.

The accusation is reserved to the promoter of justice (Can. 1934), but can be preceded by a denunciation which every faithful has the right to make in the interest of public welfare, or by a complaint of the injured party in his own private interest (Can. 1935). A special investigation follows, which has an official character, despite the fact that it is conducted privately with great diligence to protect the good name of the accused or denounced person (Can. 1938–1945). If there are not sufficient reasons to warrant the institution of a criminal trial, a declaration to that effect is issued and added to the acts of the inquiry, which are to be kept in the secret archives of the Curia; or a communication is sent to the accused, who may be rebuked and punished with salutary remedies and penances (Can. 1946).

On the other hand, if the accused denies all charges or fails to appear, or if the rebuke proves ineffective and is deemed useless, the prosecutor may be ordered by the bishop to initiate the regular criminal trial with formal accusation by the promoter of justice, an examination of the accused, the collection of documentary proof, debate, and a sentence (Can. 1947–1959). *Pug.*

TRIBUNAL, COURT. In Canon Law, the term *tribunal* has a wider meaning than in civil law; often it is synonymous with *judge* (Can. 1890), but more frequently it indicates a group of individuals comprising a judicial body. In ordinary parlance, at times, it also signifies the place set aside for trials and decrees of sentence. Although in statutory law the term has, in its proper sense, a clearly defined meaning due to the limitations of power in the judiciary body, in Canon Law, such limitations do not affect the fundamental character of the tribunal, which applies not only to the first judiciary phases, but also to the superior tribunals of the Holy See, both ordinary (Sacred Roman Rota and Apostolic Signature) and special (Tribunals of the Holy Office, of the Sacred Congregation of Rites for causes of beatification and canonization). As a matter of fact, *tribunal* is sometimes applied to administrative procedures which in their external forms follow to some extent a judiciary investigation similar to civil trials, with interrogations, deductions, proofs, etc.

In the administration of justice, ecclesiastical legislation has established a hierarchy of tribunals, distinguished by a specific function, such as a diocesan or archdiocesan tribunal, metropolitan tribunal, appeals, tribunals of nuncios, tribunals of third degree, regional tribunals for matrimonial matters, ordinary and special apostolic tribunals (*see* System, Canonico-Judiciary). All these, of course, differ in many respects from the arrangement of civil legislation.

In their internal constitution, ecclesiastical tribunals consist of one judge, with or without councillors (*assessores*), or of a group of three or five judges. Some tribunals, such as the Sacred Roman Rota and the Apostolic Signature, must try cases with all judges participating (*videntibus omnibus*).

Essential to every tribunal are the judge or a college of judges, the notary who records the minutes, the promoter of justice, and, depending on the case, the defender of the bond. In statutory law the latter is procurator general.

The jurisdictional limits of each tribunal are dependent on function, rank, matter, persons, and territory. Other criteria may be connected causes and pendency of a suit. A trial begins with the summons by the tribunal of those who are to appear before it; then a determination of the limits of the dispute, a collection of proofs, moderated discussions, and the decision, which applies the law to the fact. If in the performance of these functions the tribunal must go beyond established territorial limits, it must request the assistance of a competent tribunal by means of *rogatory commissions*.

Conflicts of jurisdiction in Canon Law are ordinarily referred to the Supreme Tribunal of the Apostolic Signature for judgment (Cans. 1601, par. 1, n. 6; 1612, par. 2).

The function of tribunals is among the noblest of all functions and one of the most necessary for the welfare of society. Protection of law and order is almost a divine task. Hence, the grave responsibility of judges and other officials of tribunals to see to it that their function is exercised with noblest intent and greatest objectivity (*See* Magistrate; Prosecution). *Pug.*

TRIBUNAL, ECCLESIASTICAL. *See* Judge; System, Canonico-Judiciary.

TRIBUNAL OF THE HOLY SEE. *See* Penitentiary, Apostolic; Rota, Roman; Signatura, Apostolic.

TRIBUNAL, OF INTERNATIONAL JUSTICE. *See* Arbitration, International.

TRIBUNAL OF SPOIL. *See* Booty.

TRINATION (Holy Mass). *See* Bination (Mass).

TROPISMS. *See* Reflexes.

TRUCE OF GOD. *See* Armistice.

TRUST. According to Can. 1516, a trust denotes a juridical act through which a benefactor secretly confides to a person mentioned in his written dispositions the name of another as the recipient of his goods, as the true heir, legatee or donee. The first mentioned is not a true heir or legatee, but a mere executor or trustee of conveyance. The Code of Canon Law (1513–1517) recognizes this act as a lawful way of transmitting goods to "pious causes," notwithstanding possible civil statutes to the contrary. Today a pious founder may make use of this legal procedure to bequeath his goods to a "pious cause," but he must be prepared to face whatever risks such an act may entail as a result of man's bad faith and possible civil dispositions to the contrary. Since the goods are destined to pious causes, the criterion of competency for the Church, despite contrary dispositions of the civil legislator, is always to be followed. *See also* Foundation, Pious; Legacy.

TRUST. *See* Coalition, Merger, Monopoly.

TRUTH. Truth is a subject of interest to students of logic, metaphysics, and ethics. In logic, truth is a conformity between the idea and the object represented by it. In metaphysics, truth is really one with being, from which it is distinguished only in a formal manner, insofar as truth directly expresses the cognoscibility of being. In ethics, truth is harmony between our conduct and the known law, particularly a harmony between belief and its manifestation. Limiting ourselves to the world of ethics, we find three types of truth: religious, moral, and juridical.

RELIGIOUS TRUTH. Religious truth is generally conceived as a dogma to which we must adhere. This we call faith, which in the Christian concept is the foundation of the religious edifice. However, not all religions attribute to specific religious truths the same value. Thus, the official religions of the Greco-Roman world possessed no dogmas, orthodoxy, or faith; these were content with participation in civic worship, without requirements of interior adherence to doctrinal principles. At first glance this seems a great guarantee of spiritual liberty; yet the way was not closed to trials for irreligion, of which Socrates in Athens and a great number of Christians in Roman territory were glorious victims.

TRUTH AND MORALS. From the purely moral point of view, man has three obligations with regard to truth: acceptance, actuation, and manifestation. Acceptance of truth is to recognize truth as it appears to one's mind, as an act not only of the intellect but also of the will which may require a special effort. This happens when the recognizable truth is at variance with our desires and passions. Integral acceptance of the Ten Commandments may require as much abnegation as adherence to dogmas. Actuation is an expression of truth that in New Testament language summarizes the whole Christian life, as a complete harmony between conduct and ethical, religious doctrine. The distinction between actuating and accepting truth rests upon the rejection of ethical intellectualism, in which the two aspects were confused and virtue became knowledge. Our distinction considers these as separable, in the sense that human malice is such that it can rebel against a recognized truth. *Manifestation* of truth, a recognized duty, is often expressed in negative form: "Thou shalt not bear false witness." This, of course, requires harmony between our persuasion and its manifestation, which is usually verbal. Many questions are raised about this duty, to the point that often they become unnecessarily complicated because of a confusion between positive and negative formulas. The positive demand to manifest the truth must be handled with much diligence, because it may collide with other ethical precepts which limit its field of application. One is not compelled to tell all truth, much less to everyone; in fact, moral theology itself often forbids telling certain truths (*see* Veracity). Think, for instance, of criticism whose chief glory is telling truths which would be much better left unsaid. Think of reporting and spying, by which truths are revealed with great social and individual harm. Think of the great importance attached to keeping professional secrecy (*see* Secret, Professional). The negative formula "Thou shalt not tell untruths" is considered by many a categorical one, that is, without possibility of exceptions. Others hold that even this admits of rare exception if the concealment of truth appears necessary to disguise dangerous or harmful truths.

However, it must be observed that lying is not the same as concealing one's thoughts. In many cases, silence or an evasive phrase will be sufficient to protect a secret, to observe the rules of courtesy, or to defend oneself from a threat. However, if silence or an evasive phrase are not sufficient to guarantee these aims, many upright persons, including some theologians, teach that one may lawfully give a reply which is not according to truth. However, the reasons adduced to justify this reply are not always plausible. First of all, it must be stated that if these expressions are permitted it is not because, under the circumstances, they are not regarded as falsehoods, but rather that those who employ them daily are not conscious of telling lies. Although it is true that in such cases the correspondence between word and thought is lacking, such is not the case between word and reality. This is clearly noticeable in theatrical representations, wherein actors speak in a joking way. Thus, if necessity demands that our thoughts not be disclosed, or a voluntary or involuntary indiscretion of others does not permit us to evade the issue, our reply is no longer a way of disclosing our thoughts, but is, in substance, a way of telling the indiscreet individual, "You are not entitled to know my thoughts."

TRUTH AND LAW. In the juridical field truth appears to be abused. Think of the many precautions often forcefully imposed, yet doomed to failure. Think also of the frequent use of deceptions, which are in themselves falsehoods. Add to these the subterfuges that blight daily forensic practice. However, one must admit that *presumptions*, though subject to error, aim at discovering and consolidating the truth. The *deceptions* act as pure technical artifices used to apply definite rules to certain cases which should reasonably be left outside their sphere. Thus, despite appearances, presumptions and deceptions also tend to actuate a just law which is also a true law. Concerning the frequent subterfuges used in the juridical procedure, it must be observed that the law does not sanction them but allows them because it is incapable of preventing them. At any rate, in justice to the juridical profession, it must be stated that efforts are being made among jurists to find ways of limiting the use of juridical deceptions and of reducing dishonesty in contracts and trials. Besides these real or apparent deviations from the truth, the juridical order is faced with the great difficulty, often amounting to an impossibility, of adjusting its decisions to psychological truth in the examination of the human

acts brought before the courts. In this matter, the deficiencies are practically beyond remedy. However, all this is part of the imperfections which affect institutions of human creation, so that it is little wonder if even the law sometimes fails to guarantee the discovery of the truth which, according to its standards, amounts to perfect justice. *Gra.*

TRUTH OF FAITH. From the authority of God arises a grave obligation to believe, at least implicitly, all truths which God has revealed. The fundamental reason for the necessity of faith must be sought in the content of faith (*q.v.*) itself. However, not all revealed truths have the same relation of necessity for salvation. In other words, one truth must be believed by *necessity of means*, another by *necessity of precept*.

What truths demand explicit belief as necessary to salvation? Whoever walks towards a goal must above all know what the goal is. St. Paul is explicit on this point: ". . . *without faith it is impossible to please God. For he who comes to God must believe that God exists and is a rewarder to those who seek Him*" (Heb. 11:6–7). Consequently, it is impossible to approach God, that is, to receive justification without faith in Him, the Author and End of the supernatural order. Belief in these first articles is of necessity of means.

Can the same be said concerning faith in the mysteries of the Trinity and the Incarnation? Before the discovery of the new world, which gave rise to the difficult problems concerning the destiny of unbelievers, theological inquiry did not probe deeply into that problem, for, after the coming of Christ, the necessity of explicit faith in these truths appeared to be logical. Attention focused more on the following scriptural texts wherein an explicit faith in the mystery of the Incarnation seemed emphasized. "*The justice of God, through faith in Jesus Christ* (Rom. 3:22); *so that He himself is just and makes just him who has faith in Jesus* (Rom. 3:26); *we know that man is not justified by the works of the Law but by the faith of Jesus Christ.*

Hence, we also believe in Christ Jesus, that we may be justified by the faith of Christ, and not by the works of the Law . . . (Gal. 2:16). This [Christ] is the stone. . . . Neither is there salvation in any other. For there is no other name under heaven given to men by which we must be saved" (Acts 4:12; see also John, 17:3).

To these texts, rather explicit, many theologians add the following observations: If no one goes to the Father except through Christ, if man receives justification by becoming a member of Christ, if he must put off the old man in order to put on permanently Christ, he must have faith in Christ. Theologians make similar reflections concerning the mystery of the Blessed Trinity, because of its intimate relation with the mystery of the Incarnation and our intimate association with this mystery in the life of grace, and in the life of glory.

On the contrary, others observe that the obligation to have faith is incumbent upon all believers, but the fulfillment of this duty is conditional upon their subjective opportunities. If before Christ an *implicit faith* in the mysteries of the Trinity and the Incarnation was sufficient for salvation, it is difficult to see why the same faith is not sufficient after the coming of Christ, particularly if one considers that He did not change the means of salvation. The apostle Paul explicitly states that two truths are really necessary: namely, God as existent and remunerating (Heb. 11:6–7).

In practice, one must follow the safer opinion in the interest of eternal salvation. Thus, it is unlawful to administer baptism or penance to one who is capable of receiving further instruction if he has no knowledge of the Trinity and the Incarnation (Proposition 64a, condemned by Innocent XI; Denz. 1214). If, however, a dying person can no longer be instructed, he should be baptized and absolved if he believes that God exists and is a rewarder of good and avenger of evil.

NECESSITY OF PRECEPT. All theologians admit a grave obligation of necessity of precept to know explicitly the mysteries of the Trinity and the Incarnation, and other principal theoretical and practical truths of Christianity, such as are contained in the Apostles' Creed, the nature and necessity of Christian prayer, the Ten Commandments and the precepts of the Church, the sacraments which all must receive. But each individual must not be content with this minimum knowledge of Christ; such knowledge must be proportioned to his capacity and needs, in order that his *charity may more and more abound in knowledge and in all discernment* (Phil. 1:9). For many individuals, lack of balance between secular and religious education creates internal crises and particular disorientations.

Finally, besides the truths revealed by God, we are required to give our assent to those truths which are connected with revealed truths and which the Church has defined and offers to the faithful by her doctrinal decrees. *Pal.*

TRUTH SERUM. *See* Secrets, Truth.

TUBERCULOSIS. *See* Diseases, Social.

TUNIC. *See* Sacred Vestments.

TUTIORISM, ABSOLUTE. *See* System, Moral.

TUTIORISM, MITIGATED. *See* System, Moral.

TWINS. Conception in each human pregnancy is usually single, but it is also possible to have more than one child born from the same pregnancy; these are called twins. There seems to be an element of heredity in pluriparous births.

Twins are either biovular or uniovular. Biovular twins are those born from two independent ova which matured at the same time but were fecundated by two distinct sperms. Uniovular twins are born from a single ovum impregnated by a single sperm. In the early phases of embryonic development, the cellular mass divides into two equal parts, forming two distinct *embryonic nodes*, each endowed with equal evolutive power, from which two fetuses develop.

In a biovular pregnancy, the twins (called biovular, fraternal, or dizygotic twins) may be of the same or different sex; they may resemble each other in the same way as children born of the same parents usually do. Each biovular twin has an independent origin from different ova, and the two organisms do not possess identical hereditary characteristics.

Twins born of uniovular pregnancy always belong to the same sex and resemble each other closely, not only in physiognomy and general habits, but even in minute morphological peculiarities, psychological attitudes, and morbid predispositions. This is true above all in *monochorial* pregnancies, in which the two fetuses are contained in a single bag. Twins belonging to this category, who are termed *uniovular, duplicated, identical, homologous, monozygotic twins*, may have somatic characteristics so that one individual is an exact image of the other, and what in one is on the right side is found on the left side in the other. All these resemblances, however, which depend upon the existence of a unique hereditary chromosomic source, are in no way absolute: in other words, there never exists between the two individuals a true identity.

These and numerous other scientific findings, revolving primarily around the constitutional aspect and obtained through a diligent study of monozygotic twins, belong to a relatively recent time. It may even be affirmed that, at least in some countries, systematic studies about these very interesting individuals are only of late being pursued with much interest.

Numerous and important are the problems concerning twins in which moral theology is deeply interested. We shall limit ourselves to those which appear to be the principal ones.

A first and very grave question appears at the time of delivery: it concerns the behavior of the obstetrician in those cases, fortunately rare, in which the two fetuses are almost simultaneously dispatched into the channel of delivery and hinder one another from complete birth. In such sad circumstances, if danger is near and all attempts suggested by the medical art for disentangling by harmless means the two unborn infants appear to be in vain, some authors of obstetrics suggest the beheading of the more involved fetus in order to successfully deliver the other. Catholic ethics, however, forbids this procedure on the obvious ground that it is immoral directly to kill an individual, even if done to save others. On the contrary, the obstetrician, aware of the fact that he can in no case sacrifice either fetus, shall arrange timely recourse to a Caesarean section (*see* Feticide) or to other actions which may offer the possibility of saving both the mother and the fetuses.

Another important question concerns the matter of free will. If the affective, intellective, and volitive qualities were exclusively dependent upon the nervous structures and their functional activity, monozygotic twins ought to show, together with a close identity in structures, also an almost absolute identity of psychic processes and behavior. On the contrary, experience, acquired by observation of the behavior of such twins, and by a study of their psychopathological deviations (as by Luxenburger concerning schizophrenics, and by Lange and Stample concerning criminals), shows that, while the element of heredity is undoubtedly noteworthy, there is also a strictly individual element, autonomous and independent of the basis, capable of modifying original characteristics. This individual element, which in notable measure is the result of educational and environmental factors, accounts for more or less notable differences in the *histories* of grown-up twins. This confirms the possibility of the existence of a free will, showing once more how science does not contradict philosophical conclusions.

At any rate, experience teaches that between monozygotic twins, raised in the same environment and conditions, usually there is one who is master over the other; that often, as years go on, these roles are repeatedly inverted; that between the two there arise remarkable accords and discords, attractions and repulsions, tender affections and deep rancors, capable of leading to criminal acts. This proves that it is possible to have in such organisms considerable spiritual differences, even though the available means are necessarily almost identical in the two individuals.

Concerning the so-called *joined* or *adherent* twins, also called *joined double monstrosities, see* Surgery, Sacrament. *Riz.*

TYPE, MORPHOLOGICAL. *See* Constitution, biotypological.

TYRANNICIDE. *See* Tyranny.

TYRANNY. A tyrant, among the Greeks, was a person who made use of disturbances among the people to seize and centralize control in a city government of popular assemblies. Similar control was seized in the Middle Ages by individual leaders who controlled the popular regime of the communes. However, these tyrants also exercised a beneficial function insofar as they restored order and checked the action of political parties whose blind, fratricidal struggle at destroying each other often ended in the destruction of a city. The initial, beneficial government was in the hands of one person over whom there was no control. Thus, the word *tyrant* gradually assumed an evil connotation, i.e., a despot, ruling, not for the benefit of the governed, but to satisfy his lust for power.

Any abuse of power which trampled on the natural and civil rights of the citizens was called tyranny. Therefore, a tyrannical act implies two elements: the possession of legal power and the abuse of that power by subverting the main purpose of all power: namely, the common good of the people.

Several theologians, especially medieval, considered lawful and meritorious the act of killing a usurper in order to free his country, provided no higher power was capable of providing justice. Today, a common opinion teaches that passive resistance to the unjust laws of a tyrant is legitimate. Attempts to oppose tyrants even by force is lawful, if there exists a good probability of success and the common welfare does not suffer greater damage from such resistance than from the oppression of the tyrant. Today, some moral theologians teach that in extreme public necessity, if every legal means has been exhausted, it is lawful to depose a tyrant, and therefore to change the form of government by force of revolution. *Boz.*

TYROXIN. *See* Endocrinology.

UNCONSCIOUS. The study of the unconscious belongs to the field of psychoanalysis. This science, which considers Sigmund Freud (1856–1939) its patron saint, could be considered a specialization of experimental psychology, if it were not for misunderstanding and disagreement as yet unresolved between scholars of the two sciences.

The term *conscious* is used to indicate both the subject, conscious of himself, and his own conscious activity. *Conscious* is opposed to *unconscious*. To avoid misunderstanding, we shall use the term *conscious* here purely in its psychological meaning. By excluding all living things which, because of their nature never can be conscious, as well as purely sensitive consciousness as foreign to the field of morals, we shall note that consciousness in man admits of various degrees. Accordingly, we distinguish three fields: a field of "consciousness" in a specific sense, comparable to a circle, at the center of which man's attention is concentrated to its utmost, but which decreases as it moves to the periphery from this maximum point of concentration to a complete disappearance. The field of the "subconscious" (*q.v.*), at one time a part of the conscious order, but at this particular moment no longer remembered. The "unconscious" involves everything which never belonged to the conscious insofar as it was never adverted to.

Freud says: "The unconscious is the psychic itself in its essential reality. Its intimate nature, as that of the outside world, is hidden from us, and the conscious gives us incomplete information about it as all our organs do in regard to the outside world." Thus, Freud conceives three states of the memory: (1) a conscious memory, which recalls known facts; (2) a subconscious memory containing forgotten facts which can be easily recalled; (3) an unconscious memory, a receptacle of all memories in general.

We prefer the distinction given above as more precise. The crux of the problem concerns the question whether psychical facts really can and do escape our consciousness.

Scholars are not altogether in agreement about this because they do not propose the question with sufficient clarity. Some wish to prove a *priori* the impossibility of the existence of the unconscious because it would mean a conscious unconscious, which is a contradiction. But, if one observes well, unless one wants to follow the doctrine of Descartes, it is not the case of a psychical fact which falls and at the same time does not fall under the control of the conscious, but the case of a psychical fact which, although it could have fallen under the control of the conscious, in reality did not.

Others claim to prove, always a *priori*, the existence of the unconscious. They cite, among other things, the example of sound vibrations. If, they say, twelve vibrations are necessary to hear a sound, nothing would be heard in the event that the vibrations were only eleven. Therefore, they conclude, the first eleven vibrations belong to the unconscious. We note here a double error. The sensation is not the effect merely of the twelfth vibration but of all twelve together; besides, if the possibility of a fact can demonstrate *a priori* its existence, that which is proven *a posteriori* can no longer be demonstrated.

Leaving aside facts clearly spiritualistic and others seemingly such, for in this case we would be involved in the supernatural, the preternatural or an unknown element, we shall consider here only phenomena from normal or natural life.

In normal life our senses are continually stimulated by surrounding realities. But because of distraction, habit, or will power, we do not notice them. In conversation with one person, we may be unaware of another calling us. Montaigne says, "My perfumes serve my own nose first, only afterwards the nose of my neighbor." A scholar can become so absorbed in his studies as to be oblivious of physical pain. Unconscious phenomena also exist in the intellect. According to the Thomistic system of knowledge, no one adverts to the abstractive process of the agent intellect. In man's emotional life many inclinations, passions, and instincts escape him, especially in infancy. In an abnormal life, also, there are frequent instances of anesthesia (insensibility), unconscious sensations, and activities. These few instances are sufficient to prove the existence of the unconscious. We take the liberty, in our particular case, to include ignorance in the unconscious, as a kind of unconscious.

If the unconscious excludes deliberation, as such, because without intellective knowledge there is no deliberation, it is still possible to have deliberation *in alio*, that is, in the one who acts as well as in one who takes care of or is responsible for the agent. The unconscious may be the result of bad habits. If one acquired such habits with merely a vague awareness of consequences, he is responsible for them before his own conscience and before God, at least until he has divested himself of his bad habits.

In children the existence of an hereditary burden of the passions, inclinations, and evil instincts may escape notice, because, in a germinal stage, the person is not aware of them. It is necessary that parents or, in their absence, those who have charge of the education of the child, be familiar with family characteristics and weaknesses, in order to stimulate in the child the proper virtues with which they shall check the development of evil tendencies.

St. John Bosco, a great master of psychology and practical pedagogy, is duly recognized as a pioneer of the preventive method of education of the young. This solid and practical principle prompted St. Pius X to admit children to Holy Communion before they became prey to evil influences. Concerning ignorance as part of the unconscious, we shall say that bad examples must be checked by an awareness of one's own duty and a love of virtue. *Ver.*

UNCTION, EXTREME. *See* Extreme Unction.

UNEMPLOYMENT. A condition in which a scarcity of suitable jobs exists for those anxious to work is called unemployment. In economics, based on work-salary systems, chronic unemployment may exist for a variety of reasons: a number of workers changing jobs, recessions normally occurring in an economic system based on competition, the seasonal character of some occupations, economic alterations in the manufacture of various goods, and patterns of expansions and depression. Technological modifications and sudden changeovers to extensive automation in production may give rise to unemployment among skilled workers. Ordinarily this is of limited duration, because much of the manpower is gradually absorbed by the effects of increased production potential, consequent upon this technical progress.

Unemployment becomes serious if it assumes a permanent character (structural unemployment) because of a serious lack of proportion between available manpower, means of production, and adequate capital in general.

Unemployment in its various forms is one of the most severe scourges of modern society, because of its adverse effects on the earnings of workers and the stability of the home and society. It is one of the chief causes of poverty in modern society. In the face of unemployment the State has a definite obligation to intervene with appropriate measures directed to the promotion of safeguards by subsidies for the unemployed and the creation of new jobs. *Gol.*

U.N.E.S.C.O. *See* United Nations.

UNILATERAL. *See* Contract.

UNION. *See* Accession.

UNION, PIOUS. A pious union is an association of the faithful whose objective is the practice of a work of mercy or piety (*see* Associations, pious). Institutes with an exclusively philanthropic purpose, despite the charitable or pious aspects of their works, are not considered pious unions. The distinction rests in the motivation: for pious unions, the motive is Christian charity; for philanthropic associations, the motive is mere benevolence that is devoid of supernatural characteristics.

A pious union with power to enroll other pious unions with the same objectives, title, and methods is called a primary pious union. A sodality is a pious union with its own director, assistants, and consultors who preside over it. If by an indult of the Holy See a sodality has the right to enroll other sodalities with the same title and purpose, it is called an arch-sodality. A confraternity is a sodality whose aim is to foster public worship or devotion. *De. A.*

UNION WITH GOD. Habitual Union. Habitual union with God is the bond between God and His creatures, whom He keeps in existence and moves to action. This type of union exists between God and every created being. Ordinarily, habitual union with God is understood as a more intimate and supernatural union between intelligent creatures and the Divine Persons. Such a union exists, at least habitually, between God and every man in the state of grace, both through sanctifying grace, by which man becomes partaker of the Divine Nature, and through the infused virtue of charity, by which, in some way, man is transformed in God, who is loved above all other things and simply for Himself. The habitual union between God and man in a state of justice is not a purely accidental thing, but in a definite sense a substantial or real union, despite the absence of any physical bond. In fact, God, One in nature and Triune in persons, is present in every soul in the state of sanctifying grace, not only as the principle of the preservation and concurrence in act of every being, but as a Good the soul can enjoy as its own (John 14:16 ff.; 14:4; Rom. 5:5; Gal. 4:6).

Actual Union. The actual union between man and God is attained through acts which have God as their object; above all, through acts of love. This union admits of many degrees. One, however, cannot speak of a life of union with God unless his relations with the Three Divine Persons abiding in his soul have become frequent and intimate, though always respectful. Not only those living in cloistered life are called to an intimate union with God but all Christians. The Blessed Trinity abides in all souls in the state of grace for the precise purpose of communing in a special manner with them. St. John the Evangelist speaks of man's fellowship with God the Father and His Son Jesus Christ (I John 1:3 ff.); St. Cyril of Alexandria, commenting on this passage, says: "*Habemus in nobis Deum, habitantem atque diversantem:* We have God living and lodging in us" (*In I Joan.,* 1, 3; PG 73, 158). The life of union with the Blessed Trinity consists in focusing, as it were, the loving gaze of one's mind upon the Divine Guest as though seen, in loving fervently the Blessed Trinity, in offering to God evident proofs of love and attention, in turning to Him in moments of joy and of suffering, in speaking to God heart to heart, though always with great respect, not occasionally but frequently. On earth, contemplation and love of God cannot continue uninterrupted, but a state is possible in which the desires of the spirit seek to be with the Blessed Trinity, in the sense that one would desire to be always with the Lord, so that, as soon as other duties allow, one turns instinctively to thinking of God and conversing with Him without strenuous effort. The thought of oneself has given way to the thought of God, and the inordinate love of self to a love of God and his creatures, so that one may truly say with St. Paul that his conversation is in heaven (Phil. 3:20).

At certain specific moments the actual union with God may also become enjoyable; that is, there are cases when God allows the soul to have almost an experimental knowledge of His presence and amiableness; the mystics speak of embraces between God and the soul.

As intimate union with God does not consist essentially in manifestations of a sense character, this union is not necessarily productive of sensible consolations. One of the great difficulties encountered in the acquisition of union with the Blessed Trinity is precisely the desire for a sensible enjoyment of God and a consequent discouragement which arises when, following the experience of initial joy, the soul is subsequently deprived of such joys for her own good. An intimate union with God, of course, does not imply peculiar ways of acting, negligence of duties, or freedom from difficulties and suffering. It may, however, occasion a state in which the soul experiences no pain in suffering but rather joy at the ability to suffer. Intimacy with God moves the soul to mortification, which is thus rendered less difficult, and gradually leads a soul to a holy indifference to all created things.

In order to achieve an intimate union with God, the soul needs a lively faith in the dogma of the presence of the Blessed Trinity in the soul in the state of grace, and a generous detachment from self and other creatures. He who wishes to live a life of union with God must also live a life of solitude and silence. Man.

UNITED NATIONS ORGANIZATION. The United Nations Organizations is the international organization created after the Second World War in place of the international organization promoted by President Woodrow Wilson after the First World War and known as the *League of Nations.*

Point eight of the Atlantic Charter of August 14, 1941, later incorporated into the common declaration of all the members of the United Nations Alliance (Jan. 1, 1942), indicated that the great powers who were fighting side by side against Germany, Italy, and Japan already had planned the creation of a supranational body with the precise task of preventing the use of force by individual States. This plan was further clarified in a *Common Declaration on Security by the Four Powers* (United States, Great Britain, Russia and China), signed on the occasion of the Moscow Conference, Oct. 30, 1943. It was clear that a restoration of the League of Nations was unthinkable, since the expulsion of the Soviet Union for its aggression against Finland made that organization practically inactive.

Experts of the four above-mentioned nations met at Dumbarton Oaks (Washington, D. C.) in October, 1944, to work out a statute; this was completed at the Yalta Conference, Feb. 11, 1945, where the voting procedure to be followed in the future Security Council was established by the United States, the Soviet Union, and Great Britain. It was on this occasion that Stalin succeeded in convincing Roosevelt of the necessity of establishing the right of veto by the Great Powers (now five, with the addition of France and China). The statute in its final form was signed by forty-nine nations on June 26, 1945, at the San Francisco Conference, and became effective on October 24 of the same year.

The principal organs entrusted with activities outlined in the U. N. Constitution are as follows: (1) a General Assembly composed of all the member States; (2) a Security Council composed of eleven members, five permanent, (China, France, United States, Great Britain, and Soviet Union), the other six elected for a period of two years by the Assembly; (3) an Economic and Social Council, consisting of eighteen members of the United Nations elected by the Assembly for a period of two years; (4) a Trusteeship Council composed of members of the United Nations entrusted with the administration of territories, and elected by the General Assembly for a period of two years; (5) a Secretary General, elected by the Assembly on proposal by the Security Council. Moreover, the Statute comprises also, among the principal organs of the U. N., the International Court of Justice governed by a statute attached to the charter of the United Nations. Since non-member States of the United Nations can appeal to the jurisdiction of the Court, it does not seem that the qualification of the Court as given in the Statute corresponds exactly to the nature of the institution.

Despite the fact that the Charter declared that *the organization is founded on the principle of absolute equality among all its members*, in reality, the member nations of the U. N. do not find themselves with the same equality in the various organs of the institution. The central organ or Security Council, whose duty it is to make important political decisions, shows two aspects in which the *status* of the various members is differentiated in a crude manner: discrimination between permanent and temporary members; the other, more serious, we shall speak of more in detail.

In the Security Council, the decisions on questions regarding procedure are made by a majority of seven members out of eleven; but on all other questions they are made by a favorable majority of seven members, *"including the concordant votes of the permanent members"* (art. 27). It is evident that the aforementioned paragraph gives to the five great powers authority to subordinate to their assent any political action taken by the U. N. This formal adoption of the principle of majority vote, which amounts to acceptance in substance of the principle of unanimity, is not found in the government of the General Assembly where the rule of a two-thirds qualified majority of voting nations is employed for deliberations of greater importance, and the rule of simple majority for deliberations of lesser importance. But, in view of the limited power allotted by the Charter to the General Assembly, it is fair to state that the Statute itself sanctions also, on the juridical plan, the various relationships of strength existing on the political plan.

A decision of the International Court of Justice on April 11, 1949, recognized the international juridical personality of the U. N. also with regard to non-member States. But is the United Nations capable of attaining the objectives of the Charter? These objectives are much wider than those entrusted to the League of Nations, for they include the economic, social and cultural fields. Its principal objective, however, in which its effectiveness is gauged, is always that of maintaining international security and peace. For this reason vast powers of intervention are given to the Security Council, which, in sanctioning the general and absolute prohibition imposed on all States to have recourse to force, except in a case of legitimate self-defense (Art. 51), may use any and all kinds of coercive measures; after all, the obligation of the Council to non-interference in questions of essentially internal competency, as domestic jurisdiction of a member State, constitutes a very relative limitation, since the Council possesses the right of so-called *"competency over competency."* But the existence of the veto power shows that the U. N. can only act if the five great powers agree; so that world peace, today, is more a postulate of the working effectiveness, even if to a limited degree, of the organization born in San Francisco, than the result achieved through its activity.

To these notes on the principal activity of the U. N. must be added its tasks of coordination in various specialized institutions, constituted by particular agreements, for the development on the international plan of cultural activities embracing a variety of fields. Thus, the F.A.O. (*Food and Agriculture Organization*), with its headquarters in Rome, has the task of developing better food products everywhere in the world, better agriculture, and a more efficient distribution of its products; the I.L.O. (*International Labor Office*) is directed to the achievement of greater unity of all the workers in the social movement; the U.N.E.S.C.O. (*United Nations Education, Scientific and Cultural Organization*), for the promotion of education, science and culture; the U.N.R.R.A.

(United Nations Relief and Rehabilitation Administration) for emergency aid and reconstruction.

"The Catholic doctrine on the State and civil society has always been based on the principle that, in keeping with the will of God, nations together form a community having a common aim and common duties. Even when the proclamation of this principle and its practical consequences gave rise to violent reactions, the Church denied her assent to the erroneous conception of an absolutely autonomous sovereignty divested of all social obligations.

"The Catholic Christian, persuaded that his neighbor, and that every nation is a member with equal rights in the family of nations, cooperates wholeheartedly in these generous efforts, whose beginnings might be meager and frequently encounter strong opposition and obstacles, but which aim at saving individual nations from the narrowness of a self-centered mentality; this latter attitude of mind has been largely responsible for the conflicts of the past, and unless finally overcome or at least held in check, could lead to new conflagrations that might mean death to human civilization" (Christmas radio message by His Holiness Pius XII, 1948). *Bog.*

UNITY OF MARRIAGE. *See* Matrimony, Polyandry, Polygamy.

UNIVERSALITY OF LAWS. *See* Law, Natural.

UNIVERSITY. *See* School, Lay.

U.N.R.R.A. *See* United Nations.

UNWORTHINESS. In general, unworthiness is the lack of necessary moral or juridical qualities to perform lawfully useful acts. We are concerned principally with moral unworthiness, because no physical defect may prevent a person from receiving the gifts of God. Moral unworthiness is a public detriment because of possible scandal and increases the moral responsibility of the individual before God and the Church, because of

the new sin which he presumably commits.

In the Church, unworthiness is particularly significant for the administration or reception of the sacraments. The basis of this unworthiness is sin, that is, the absence of the state of grace necessary for the reception of the sacraments of the living, which require this as a condition; in the reception of the sacraments of the dead, this unworthiness consists in the absence of the necessary and proper dispositions for the reception of the sacraments which confer sanctifying grace. Unworthiness presupposes ineligibility to administer or to receive a sacrament; this unworthiness may be merely external if the absolution of the sin is not known to others.

With reference to the sacrament of the Holy Eucharist, penance, and extreme unction, the principle that "no one is to be considered bad without being proven such" (*nemo malus nisi probetur*) holds true. Therefore, one who is not obviously unworthy is considered worthy to receive the above sacraments and not required to prove his moral qualifications. Instead, in the case of those sacraments which are not merely a transitory act but place the individual in a particular state in the Church, such as baptism, confirmation, holy orders, and matrimony, it is not sufficient to demonstrate that there are no motives of unworthiness (negative demonstration), but it is necessary to prove the presence of certain qualifications and attitudes which guarantee a future satisfactory fulfillment of the duties inherent to the new state (positive demonstration).

Unworthiness is *public* if it is the result of a publicly committed crime, a known crime, or public bad conduct. Such are perpetrators of grave crimes, whether condemned or not, prostitutes, public concubines (Catholics who are living only in civil marriage are considered thus), or those who have incurred ecclesiastical penalties following a public sentence. Instead, unworthiness is *occult* if the licentious life or crime is unknown in certain places or is known only to a small number of people.

Since it is a duty of charity not to co-operate in the sin of another and to avoid scandalizing the faithful, the priest must refuse the sacraments to public sinners whether they request them publicly or privately (Can. 855, par. 1). On the other hand, the sacraments cannot be denied to an *occult* sinner who requests them publicly, as his reputation must be protected; but they can and must be denied him if he asks for them privately (Can. 855, par. 2).

A priest who administers the sacraments while not in the state of grace administers them validly; it is a truth of faith that the efficacy of the sacraments does not depend on the worthiness of the minister. However, under such circumstances, he administers them illicitly and commits a sin of sacrilege, unless he is faced with a case of urgent necessity and cannot first recover the state of grace, in the sacrament of penance or by an act of perfect contrition. Confession, however, is prescribed only before celebrating Mass. If a priest is aware of being in a state of sin, he must recover the state of grace by sacramental confession. Perfect contrition suffices only in a case in which there is no opportunity to approach a confessor and necessity demands that he celebrate Mass. He must go to confession as soon as possible (Can. 856, 807).

Anyone who has come under a censure, excommunication (Can. 2260, par. 1), or personal interdict (Can. 2275), is not permitted to receive the sacraments on the assumption that he is in mortal sin (*see also* Interdict, Penalty, Ecclesiastical).

For the same reason the Church severely disapproves of marriage with apostates, persons under censure (excommunicated), and public sinners (Can. 1065–1066). (*See also* Marriage.)

In some modern civil codes, unworthiness enjoys broad application in all forms of inheritance, in the form of disqualification or penalty. The following are some provisions of a general nature. He who is found guilty of unworthiness is excluded from an inheritance and obliged to make restitution for any benefit he

may have obtained from it. Unworthiness as a penalty applies personally to the author of some specified criminal acts (*see* individual civil codes). It does not apply to his children or descendants, who may inherit either in person or by proxy.

In any case, the person declared unworthy can be rehabilitated. This may be accomplished by a public act or by the last will of the person whose property is involved. If not expressly rehabilitated in a will but included in a will by a testator aware of his unworthiness, the unworthy person may inherit within the limits of the provisions of the will. (Obviously, the provisions of civil law are not uniform in all countries. For details the reader must consult the civil code of each individual country or State.—Editor's note.) *Mog.*

URBANITY. Urbanity is a conformity in social behavior to the rules of conduct generally followed among well-bred persons, such as politeness and courtesy in one's relations with others.

There is a positive duty to observe proper manners, generally practiced by other civilized persons.

One may sin against urbanity by defect, that is by a neglect of the rules of good manners; or by excess, that is, by an exaggerated observance of social customs, by the adoption of external behaviour due to vainglory or some other inordinate motive. In themselves such defects are venial sins. *Man.*

URBANIZATION. Urbanization is the mass movement of individuals and families from rural districts into urban centers or cities. Urbanization is a direct result of the development of large industries. As a phenomenon typical of the modern era, its causes are found in the poverty of the rural population and in the better wages paid to industrial workers, although such gains are frequently more imaginary than real.

Urbanization, with its consequent population increases in urban areas, creates a complexity of social and moral problems which can be solved only with great difficulty in some countries. Among these problems are: housing, hygiene, morality, domestic life, and public order. Urbanization creates one of the most disturbing aspects in the life of modern cities, which at present is being solved by the tendency to arrest such movements or to contain them within the normal limits of assimilation into urban populations.

In the United States, another similar problem has developed since the Second World War, which might be termed suburbanization. This movement of large numbers to suburban areas creates identical problems.

It is an obligation, possibly grave, for Catholics to be active in community efforts and legislative actions which initiate and stimulate activities for the welfare of a community, such as sound moral conditions, proper housing, traffic regulations, safety, and recreational or educational facilities for the young of a community. *Pav.*

URGENCY (Urgent case). An urgent case is a particular circumstance in which an individual requires immediate aid or prompt practical solution. Man, at times, finds himself in circumstances neither foreseen by the individual nor by a human lawmaker, in which he must act or decide. Generally, in the field of moral activities, man must act according to a law of nature, a divine or a human positive law. Now, an individual may be obliged in a situation to the observance of a definite positive law and meet at the same time an obstacle to that observance, which may require that a dispensation from the observance of the law be obtained promptly.

Canon Law, whose principal aim is to promote the salvation of souls as well as public order in the Church, contains particular provisions intended to assist conscience in such contingencies, by means of dispensations, absolutions, etc. (Cf. Can. 81; 106, no. 6; 990, par. 2; 1043; 1176, par. 3; 1402; 2254).

In earlier times theologians and canonists treated the matter of urgent cases so extensively that an intricate casuistry resulted (Cf. Sanchez, *Opus moral.*, Lug-

duni, 1637, Vol. II, c. 13, 35–37). Today, moral theologians and canonists generally concentrate more directly on three circumstances listed under Canon 2254: (a) a danger of scandal or infamy resulting from the observance in a particular case of a specific law or penalty; (b) a difficulty arising from the fact that the observance of a certain law is hard and difficult, or from a condition whereby one would be compelled to remain in a state of grave sin; (c) an impelling necessity to perform certain acts requiring freedom of conscience and action.

In any of the above circumstances, a superior may use the faculties granted by the Code for all such cases in the external and internal forums; a confessor may use extraordinary faculties with regard to sacramental absolution within specific limits and under specific conditions (Can. 1045, 2254, etc.). A certainty with regard to scandal or infamy is not required; a probable danger is sufficient to constitute an urgent case. Thus, too, with regard to remaining in a state of sin, an absolute judgment is not required but the actual disposition of the penitent must be considered.

Regarding absolution from sin or censures (ecclesiastical penalties), *see* Censure, Reservation of censures, Reservation of sins. For dispensations from matrimonial impediments, *see* Impediments, Matrimonial (dispensation from). *Tar.*

USE. Use is a real right to an article belonging to another *(ius in re aliena)*, which gives to the user the faculty of making use of an object without impairing its substance and of benefiting by its fruits in a measure proportionate to the needs of the user and his family. It implies the enjoyment of property; this consists in the employment, occupation, exercise or practice of that article.

Use is a limiting modification of usufruct or, in a certain sense, one of the essential aspects of usufruct *(q.v.)*. Of the two rights conferred, namely the use of an article and the enjoyment of the fruits or profit, use is primary. In classical

Roman legal definitions, use did not give to the user the right to derive profits from the article used; this was a later addition introduced by laws of an intermediate period. For this reason Roman texts speak of *nudus usus, id est, sine fructus* (bare usage, without profit) or *Uti potest, frui non potest* (use is permissible, profit is not).

Use is distinguished from usufruct by a limitation in the enjoyment of the article involved. In usufruct, enjoyment is complete and extends to all the fruits or profits; but in use, the enjoyment is limited to merely the fruits necessary for the sustenance of the user and his family. This gives the user a right that is proportionate to his needs, without depriving an owner of other benefits or profits derived from the article itself.

If use is applied to a house, it is called the right of occupancy (*q.v.*); it grants to the user the right to use a house according to his needs (cf. specific civil legislations). As in usufruct, an object that is commercial or negotiable, real or not real, also can be the object of use. The right of use is established by a contract (conventional use) or by a will (testamentary use) or by prescription under the same conditions as usufruct. Since the obligations of a user are regulated by specific civil legislations in various countries, the reader must consult these codes of law. The obligation in conscience to repair or pay for damage is surely common to all, for it prescinds in fact from any civil or local legislations. For norms concerning the extinction of or secession from the right of use as well as the application of these to usufruct, the reader must consult specific local legislations. *Zac.*

USE AND OCCUPANCY. *See* Occupancy, Usufruct.

USE OF REASON. *See* Age; Law, Natural.

USUCAPIO. *See* Prescription.

USUFRUCT. Usufruct is the right to use and enjoy the fruit or profits of an estate or property without impairing the substance which belongs to another. The usufructuary has no right whatsoever to the article itself as ownership, but merely to the use of the article and the profits derived from that use. The usufructuary can neither dispose of the property nor act as an owner in any way.

In this, usufruct differs from emphyteusis; the usufructuary may use and profit from the property of another; emphyteusis confers possession, use, and profit of an owner without actual transfer of ownership. Emphyteusis permits the mortgaging of property. (Use and usufruct differ in the quality of acts permitted: as long as the substance of the property is unimpaired, the faculty of the usufructuary is unlimited to the use and enjoyment of property, whereas use is restricted to the enjoyment of property for the necessities of life for the user and his family.)

The acquisition and constitution of usufruct, the rights and obligations of the usufructuary, the extinction and transfer of usufruct are governed by various specific legislations in various countries, which the reader must consult for particular problems. Since these matters are apart from the rights of ownership, the particular norms of the natural law are not applicable in all cases, and, therefore, one must abide by the dispositions of civil law concerning obligations of a contract. After judicial sentence, this obligation binds in conscience. Usufruct, acquired by a disposition of law or prescription, entitles the beneficiary to use of the property within the limits of law. A victim of loss or damage is not held to such obligations until judicial decision. If the usufruct is acquired by contract or will, one is obliged in conscience to the observance of the regulations governing a title, at least until court decision definitely decides the case. *Pal.*

USURPATION OF GOODS. *See* Confiscation.

USURY. The distinction between usury and interest was officially introduced for the first time in the French Constitution.

Since then all countries have determined a legal interest rate in order to check usury. Usury is the acceptance of a premium for the use of a thing given in loan; usury, objectively, is the premium paid for loaned money or goods. Hence, the essence of usury consists in accepting a premium for a pure loan. However, usury, in a broader sense, indicates taking advantage of another who is in need. In this sense, one hears of usurious price, fees, etc. The only obligation with regard to a loan (*q.v.*) is a return of the same amount of money borrowed. Thus, a loan implies the bestowal in loan of a thing with all its properties; hence it involves the transfer of ownership and gratuity of use. A violation of this constitutes usury.

Usury is called *open* if requested expressly for the loan; *hidd*en, if it is concealed in another contract which also includes the loan, for which a premium is demanded. Usury is properly a sin against commutative justice and, as such, carries the obligation of restitution (*q.v.*). This sin is similar to theft; the quantity of restitution is judged in the same manner as in theft. Those given to usury, therefore, are bound in justice to make restitution of the gains obtained by usury to the debtors or their heirs. If the heirs are unknown or are no longer living, such profits are to be donated to the poor or charity. The same obligation falls upon heirs of usurers in proportion to the value of their inheritance.

Usury is directly forbidden by the natural law, because it is contrary to commutative justice. It always is a sin against justice, whether the loan was made to poor or rich. In the case of the poor, an additional sin against charity is committed.

According to the Sacred Scriptures, the practice of usury among the Jews was forbidden (Es. 22:25; Lev. 25:35–37), but usury was permitted in dealing with Gentiles; however, it was simply tolerated, not considered as lawful. Jesus Christ, explaining the precept of charity, made no distinction between Hebrew and Gentile and stated that loans be gratuitous (Luke 6:30; Matthew 5:42).

In the Councils of the Church, the tendency to prohibit usury grew with the demands to change laws that permitted moderate usury. In the time of the empire, prohibitions by ecumenical councils applied only to clerics. At the time of Gratian, usury was completely forbidden by the Church. Thus, canonists and moral theologians generally accepted the doctrine of St. Thomas, who held that a loan must be essentially gratuitous and all usury was a sin against justice. In the Middle Ages the councils and Roman Pontiffs repeatedly prohibited any form of usury. The Council of Vienna (1315) declared that anyone who obstinately held that usury was not sinful should be punished as a heretic (Denz. 479).

Benedict XIV, in his encyclical letter *Vix pervenit*, confirmed the above-mentioned laws. Any practical mitigation of this discipline is due to economic conditions and the multiplicity of extrinsic reasons. The traditional doctrine, however, remains unchanged.

Canon Law accepts and sanctions this principle in the first part of Canon 1543: "If a fungible thing is given to another in such a manner that it becomes his own and is to be later on returned in kind only, no profit may be made by reason of the contract itself (*ratione ipsius contracti*)." In practice, however, the loan is not consummated simply in the abstract form of its constitutive elements, since concrete circumstances relative to the economical position of the lender and the borrower may be involved and change its effects. Four external circumstances—actual damage, loss of profit, risk to the thing itself, danger arising from delay in returning the good—have an economical value and may, under actual circumstances, constitute titles to a proportionate compensation over and above the restitution of the thing itself. Only titles extrinsic to the loan, when truly present, may justify the right to claim and the duty to pay a just rate of interest.

This is the basis for the concept of interest (*q.v.*) or the premium for the service rendered by lending the capital sum. The interest rate or ratio is the premium paid by the borrower, estimated according to a conventional unit of capital (one hundred dollars) per unit of time (one year). Loss of profit has become today an ordinary effect of loaned money, in view of the fact that, under the present economic system, property as well as money is definitely productive. This justifies the presumption that any loan implies a loss of profit to the lender and, therefore, also the charge of a proportionate compensation. The legal rate of 5% is considered a median profit. (In the U.S.A. the maximum interest rate permitted by law is 6%.) Since there may be special reasons and conditions of fact, it is juridically and morally permitted to the parties to make an agreement either on a rate of interest higher than the conventional or to the total exclusion of all interest. In conclusion, resultant damage could also, in particular cases, constitute a new title for charging a higher rate of interest. (Cf. *Collectanea* of the S. Congregation *de Propaganda Fide*, n. 2118, reply a., 1645, "*ad Miss. Senenses*".)

This clarifies the second part of Canon 1543: "However, in lending a fungible thing, it is not *per se* unlawful to make an agreement concerning legal interest, unless it is certainly excessive. Nor is it unlawful to make an agreement for more than the legal interest, if a just and proportionate title justifies such an agreement."

These provisions are accepted by modern civil codes and legislations. Thus, as stated before, the Code of Canon Law (Can. 1543) accepts the possibility of charging interest, if a just and proportionate title demands it. But neither the Code of Canon Law nor civil codes establish a precise norm according to which the interest rate is to be estimated. Generally, that interest rate is lawful which is considered legitimate by the common judgment of prudent men, with due consideration for local industrial and commercial conditions. Beyond this rate, it would be usury. Also, modern civil codes grant to the parties the possibility of setting equitably between themselves a conventional interest rate.

Usury is not only a sin but in Canon Law is considered a crime. "A lay person who has been lawfully declared guilty of the crime of homicide, abduction, or usury shall be deprived of the right to perform legal ecclesiastical acts and of every position which he may hold in the Church; besides the obligation of reparation for the damages inflicted" (Can. 2354, par. 1).

"If a cleric has committed any of the crimes enumerated in paragraph 1 of this Canon, he shall be punished by the ecclesiastical tribunal in proportion to the gravity of the crime, with penances, censures, deprivation of office, benefice, and dignity, and even with deposition, if the circumstances demand it . . ." (Can. 2354, par. 2). *Pal.*

UTENSILS, SACRED. *See* Vessels, Sacred.

UTERUS. *See* Reproduction.

UTILITARIANISM. Philosophical. Utilitarianism is a system of ethical philosophy in which the moral order is based on the *useful* as the source and standard of good, law, and virtue. The concept of utility is, however, vague and broad; consequently, it may be used to signify diverse doctrines and values. From the aspect of the subject to which the useful is directed, utilitarianism may be egoistical (individual) or altruistical (social). This depends on whether benefits of this system are sought for an individual or for the human race in general as standards of good. From the aspect of the type of good which constitutes the useful, a vast array of utilitarian systems corresponds to the diverse scales of human values as they are generally sought for in life. The lowest values are coarse and fleeting pleasures; the utilitarian and the hedonist are identical. At successive steps, more noble and permanent satisfactions are arranged in a gradated order to the point of Catholic ethics, in which the end of man is an eternal life of happiness, toward which his actions are directed.

Strict utilitarianism limits the useful to the present life and economic order. This philosophy is an outgrowth of the confusion of two distinct concepts: the useful and the moral. Apart from this erroneous identification, utilitarianism is impossible to apply practically. This impossibility increases to the extent that utilitarianism departs from revolting forms of hedonistic egoism. The greater the separation from hedonism, and the greater number of individuals partaking of the useful good, and the nobler the goods considered useful, then the more complicated becomes the utilitarianism until only a prophet could evaluate or understand it.

A sound element in utilitarianism is the instinctive and rational need to associate happiness with virtue, not by confusing two ideals or concepts, but by making happiness a reward of virtue in this life and in the future life. *Gra.*

ECONOMIC. A philosophical, ethical system which advocates as the highest level of human activity the useful, can assume a limited and specific application to the economic field. As a concept of economic life, the utilitarian criterion directs and determines economic benefits with a complete divorce from any religious, ethical, or political norm. This concept is expressed by the cliché "*Business is business.*" In this system, egoism is the propelling force and the soul of economic life; its essential philosophical principle is maximum profit with minimum cost; its characteristic objective is profit. Utilitarianism as a concept of the economic world is a part of the broad, atomistic conception of human reality. Accordingly, the relation between the various spheres of activity exercised by the human spirit is a contiguous and not interdependent relationship. Religion, ethics,

science, politics, law, art, economy are all self-centered and independent of each other. Religion tends to an experience of the divine; ethics to an actuation of the good; science to a knowledge of truth; politics to practical success; law to promoting order; art to the beautiful, economy to the useful. Each is a world in itself, separate from the other. To expect that one should influence the other is to seek for the impossible, for if this were to occur, it would constitute disorder.

This concept of the economic world was translated into action primarily in the last century; typical expressions affirm profit as the supreme objective of production, with subsequent determinations of wages and salaries on the principle of supply and demand. A dehumanization of labor relations, the urbanization of large areas, a concentration of human beings without concern for religious, moral, cultural, hygienic, domestic or social exigencies as well as the progressively fearful spiritual improverishment of the working classes follow.

The truth of the matter is that the useful must be subordinated to the ethical. Accordingly, in the economic field, the usefulness of an action is not a sufficient criterion for its performance, for it is necessary that it be not in conflict with the moral order. After all, if it is true that the ethical does not flow from the useful, it is also true that an action cannot be really useful if it is not ethical. The useful, therefore, is attained through the honest. To act differently is to destroy the unity of the human being, opening the way to practical difficulties of an extremely serious import, such as those mentioned above. *Pav.*

V

VACANCY OF THE HOLY SEE. *See* Conclave.

VACATING OF PROPERTY. *See* Property.

VACCINATION. *See* Therapy.

VAGINISM. *See* Gynecology, Impotency.

VAGUS. *See* Domicile, Traveller.

VAINGLORY. *See* Pride.

VAIN OBSERVANCE. *See* Observances, Superstitious.

VALIDATION, MARRIAGE. A marriage that is null and void from the beginning may be validated. The nullity of the marriage is due to one of three obstacles to a valid marriage: (1) a diriment impediment; (2) a lack of consent; (3) a defect of form.

VALIDATION BECAUSE OF A DIRIMENT IMPEDIMENT. A marriage which is invalid because of a diriment impediment that has not been dispensed may be validated by a simple validation, which implies the removal of the impediment, if this is possible, and the renewal of the matrimonial consent.

(a) *Removal of the impediment* may come about with a lapse of time, as in the case of lack of canonical age or conversion in the case of disparity of worship. This may be done as well by dispensation by the legitimate ecclesiastical authority if the impediment of its nature is capable of dispensation. Not all impediments are dispensable. A marriage with the diriment impediment of the natural law (certain and permament impotency), or of the divine law (consan-

guinity in the direct line, previous marital bond), or of ecclesiastical law which is not capable of dispensation (priesthood, public conjugicide) render validation impossible as long as the impediment continues.

(b) *Renewal of consent.* Ecclesistical law requires that, consequent upon the dispensation or cessation of the impediment, matrimonial consent must be renewed by the party or parties aware of the impediment (Can. 1153). This renewal of consent presupposes a knowledge of the impediment to be removed (Can. 1134). The manner in which this renewal of matrimonial consent takes place varies according to circumstances. If the impediment is public, i.e., known to at least two persons other than the parties themselves and, therefore, can be proved in the external forum (cf. Can. 1037), consent must be renewed by both parties in the form prescribed by law (*see* Marriage, Form of). This may be done quietly and without solemnity (Can. 1135). If the impediment is occult and known only to one party, it suffices that this party alone renew consent privately and secretly, provided that the other party's consent continues. If renewal of consent does not require observance of canonical form, the consent may be considered sufficiently renewed by the parties through continuance of their conjugal duties, or by a purely internal act.

VALIDATION OF INVALID MARRIAGE FOR LACK OF CONSENT. The above norms apply also in the validation of a marriage that is invalid because of a lack of initial consent due to coercion, fear, simulation, etc. However, no dispensation is necessary. The only requirement is that a new and valid consent be given by the party whose original consent was defective. If the defect of consent was public, i.e., provable in the external forum, as in a case of force or fear, the consent must be renewed in the form prescribed by law; if the defect was occult, the consent may be renewed in a private and secret manner.

VALIDATION OF INVALID MARRIAGE BECAUSE OF LACK OF FORM. If a marriage is null because of lack of form, due to the absence of qualified witnesses, or the lack of necessary authorization in the officiating priest, the marriage should be validated by a new contract according to the form prescribed by law (Can. 1137), even if this must be done secretly. If this is impossible or inadvisable, the priest may apply for a *sanatio in radice* (*q.v.*).

In pre-code legislation continued and voluntary cohabitation of the parties automatically validated an invalid marriage, particularly in cases of defective consent. This norm is generally applied in current civil codes. *Bar.*

VALIDITY OF MARRIAGE. *See* Matrimony, Nullity of marriage.

VALIDITY OF THE SACRAMENTS. *See* Sacraments.

VALUE. *See* Price.

VALUE OF USE. *See* Marxism, Exchange.

VAMPIRISM. *See* Perversion, Sexual.

VANITY. Vanity (Latin, *vanitas*—emptiness) is a quality of being useless or devoid of value, worth, truth, etc. In a strict sense, vanity refers to extravagant embellishments beyond one's social condition or the customary usages of time and status. It may signify over-attention and care for one's external appearance. Because of a definite similarity between vanity and vainglory, this is at times referred to as vanity.

In itself, vanity is a venial sin; however, it may become a mortal sin because of grave scandal, expenditures seriously endangering the welfare of a family, an accumulation of debts beyond one's ca-

pacity to repay, or an intention seriously opposed to the moral law. *Man.*

VARIETY. A variety show is a series of short, theatrical acts without any particular interrelationship, such as music, singing, dancing, acrobatics, magic, etc. This form of entertainment, enjoying great popularity in recent decades, can be performed on stage, television, screen, or as a part of a larger show.

In itself, as in all entertainment, a variety show is morally indifferent, but in view of its nature, it easily tends to abuses through departures from any fixed plot or script. In our days a variety show is usually characterized by a great amount of moral shallowness if not open immorality. Attendance at such performances, apart from active participation, may be sinless, venially sinful, or gravely sinful, depending on the actual subjective and objective circumstances. For specific rules, consult the articles on Artist, Singing, Impurity, Music, Dancing, Radio, Theatre, Cinema and Television. *Dam.*

VASECTOMY. *See* Surgery, Sterilization.

VASOLIGATURE. *See* Rejuvenation, Sterilization.

VASOPRESSINE. *See* Hypophysis.

VATICAN CITY. The temporal power of the Church was for many centuries more extensive than today, for, as late as the nineteenth century, the pope ruled over 16,000 square miles of papal States, extending to nearly all of central Italy. In 1870, armies of the Kingdom of Italy occupied these papal territories, and, with the exception of small areas surrounding the Vatican and Lateran in Rome and the villa of Castel Gandolfo, annexed these lands by the Italian law of May 13, 1871, enacted unilaterally by the Italian government and entitled the *Law of Guarantee.*

These events and the voluntary confinement by the pope to the Vatican territory gave rise to a *Roman Question,* which was finally settled with the ratification of the Lateran Treaty on June 7, 1929, between the Italian government and the papacy. This treaty restored to a minimum the temporal power to the Holy See and recognized the latter's full and independent sovereignty over a small but clearly defined territory named Vatican City. Moreover, the treaty solemnly affirmed that "the sovereignty of the Holy See in the international sphere" does not depend on the actual exercise of this sovereignty over a determined territory, but is "an attribute inherent in the very nature of the Holy See, in accordance with its tradition and the demands of its mission in the world" (article 2 of Lateran Treaty).

VATICAN CITY, A TRUE STATE. The territory over which the Holy See enjoys acknowledged sovereignty is known as the *State of Vatican City*. The Holy See is a real, sovereign entity or power with a juridical personality of international right for two reasons: it is the supreme power of the Church and the supreme power of the Vatican State.

The State of Vatican City is a true State with three constitutive elements: territory, population, sovereignty. Yet it possesses certain structural and functional characteristics peculiar to it alone. In international affairs, it is a strictly neutral State (article 24 of Treaty).

In view of the Vatican's territorial limitation and the position of supreme spiritual jurisdiction in the pope, extending to the universal Church throughout the world, the territorial sovereignty of Vatican City has been integrated with a number of privileges, which render the juridical position of the Holy See in Italy more favorable than it would have been had the strict principles of common international right been applied.

In the wording of the Treaty, various privileges are not all granted to the Holy See directly. Some are granted indirectly, as privileges extended to persons, places, or objects at the disposal of the Holy See in the explication of its mission. In this connection, especially is the privilege of extra-territoriality or diplomatic immunity extended to thirteen buildings situated within Rome outside Vatican City, but under the jurisdiction of the Holy See (the major basilicas, office buildings of the various Congregations, Villa of Castel Gandolfo; cf. article 15 of Lateran Treaty).

GOVERNMENT OF VATICAN CITY. The government of Vatican City is in the hands of the reigning pope, who possesses absolute executive, legislative, and judicial powers. With certain limitations, equal powers are vested in the Sacred College of Cardinals during the vacancy of the Holy See.

In all diplomatic relations and in the conclusion of agreements with foreign powers, the representation of Vatican State is reserved to the pope, who deals through the Secretariat of State (*q.v.*).

Directly subject to the pope are: the administration of the goods and property of the Holy See, the Vatican Museum, the Vatican Secret Archives, the Vatican Press, and the Vatican Library.

The exercise of executive powers is delegated to the *Governor of the State*, to whom legislative power for specific matters may also be delegated.

The governor, appointed or replaced by the pope, exercises his functions under the direction of the Pontifical Commission for the Administration of Vatican City. He is assisted by a Central Council and governmental offices. He has at his command the Corps of Papal Gendarmes; for security and police measures he may call on the Swiss Guards.

The consulting organ of the State of Vatican City consists of a *Counselor General*. The right to grant privileges, amnesties, indults, and pardons is reserved to the pope. All legislation pertaining to the State of Vatican City is published in a supplement of the *Acta Apostolicae Sedis* (*q.v.*). Among dispositions issued to date, the most important are those of June 7, 1929, and published on the following day. The Vatican flag consists of two fields: one yellow, near the staff; the other white, displaying the papal tiara with the keys.

Vatican City has a judicial system (reorganized in 1946), specifically consisting of the following: (a) a judge with jurisdiction in minor cases; (b) a tribunal of first instance, consisting of three judges who adjudicate in a body (its composition, however, varies according to the nature of the cases under trial: civil or criminal cases, property cases, ecclesiastical competency, or other ecclesiastical cases); (c) the court of appeals, consisting of the Dean and two auditors of the Sacred Roman Rota; (d) the court of cassation, composed of the Cardinal Prefect of the Apostolic Signature (*Signatura Apostolica*) and two other Cardinals of the same Signature. The function of State's Attorney is exercised by the promoter of justice.

Special norms of the Lateran Treaty and internal Vatican State law regulate acquisition and loss of Vatican citizenship. According to these norms, the following are Vatican citizens: (a) all Cardinals residing in Vatican City or in the city of Rome; (b) all persons who, for reasons of dignity, office, or employment, permanently and legitimately reside in Vatican City; (c) certain close relatives of Vatican citizens, if they are legitimately authorized to dwell in Vatican City. *Cip.*

VEGETARIANISM. A vegetarian is a person who lives entirely on vegetable foods. Vegetarianism denotes not only the fact of subsistence on vegetables alone, but also the doctrine, so to speak, partly philosophical, partly hygienic or therapeutic, which advocates such type of nourishment.

Man is an omnivorous organism, as it appears from many aspects of his anatomic structure (denture or dental structure, intestinal system, etc.). In the vast majority of cases, irrespective of latitude, manner of life, or degree of civilization, man derives his own foods as much from the animal as from the vegetable kingdoms.

Furthermore, physiology teaches that a diet (*q.v.*) exclusively based on foods drawn from the vegetable kingdom, as grains, vegetables, fruit, sugar, and oil, is in the long run insufficient, because for normal functioning man's organism requires a wide, varied diet, prevalently based on vegetables, with a minimum of protein substances from animal products, such as, milk, eggs, meat, fish, etc., and equivalent to about a quarter of a gram daily for every two and one-half pounds of the individual's body weight.

Man is omnivorous by nature and unable to withstand over a long period a strictly vegetarian diet without damaging results; this accounts for the reason that in practice pure vegetarianism is not adopted systematically.

Ethnological inquiries have proved that, although the human dietary system is characterized by a great variety of foods and beverages, this variety is everywhere governed by the physiological laws of dieting in the sense that, irrespective of the variety of foods, men living under analogous climatic conditions consume about the same quantity and quality of leading foodstuffs such as fats, carbohydrates, proteins, vitamins, water, and salts. On the subject of diet, differences among the peoples consist mainly in the diverse manner in which foods are prepared (culinary art).

In addition, ethnology has revealed that primitive peoples, living in tropical zones and particularly subject to a diet low in fats and calories similar to a vegetarian's, have a mixed diet of fowl, fish, and vegetables. If we consider those religious societies and religious orders which for penitential reasons follow vegetarianism, we see that it is never absolute vegetarianism but is tempered by the use, in moderate quantity, of foods drawn from the animal kingdom, as milk, eggs, and fish. Thus, to cite the example of a monastic order deservedly famous for its moderation in the use of food, the Trappist monks combine cereals, vegetables, fruit, and oil with a certain quantity of milk for a daily consumption, according to Dujarric de la Rivière, of 68 grams of proteins, 11 of fats, and 470 of carbohydrates: a smaller amount than the minimum generally indicated by physiologists, but sufficient to permit those monks to conduct an intensive life of prayer and work.

It is a well-known fact that a diet with little or no spices at all, consisting mainly of cereals, green vegetables, and fruit is best for preserving good health and working efficiently. This varied but prevalently vegetarian diet naturally arose several thousand years before the rise of the science of dietetics. This is supported by the fact that bread made of wheat has always been the fundamental food of the peoples of the Mediterraneo-European civilization, while the other foods are, even to this day, referred to as *bread adjunct*.

It is also a known fact that a diet consisting basically of flesh-meat favors acidosis, with results well known to physicians, and is believed to stimulate the sexual instincts (Benedict).

These considerations, together with the respect for the life of animals, especially widespread in many Asiatic populations because of theories of metempsychosis, along with a sentiment of mortification and penitence, have brought vegetarianism and fasting into high esteem with many ascetics and made it mandatory in several religious groups under proper mitigation.

Medicine has no reason to oppose virtuous dietary regulations which have met favorably the test of many centuries. It is to be observed, however, that not all organisms can withstand an identical diet in all circumstances and phases of life. This is known by religious superiors, who are ready to grant mitigations and dispensations whenever they may be required.

Since vegetarianism is not of itself contrary to health, to nourish the body by exclusively vegetable foods is an indifferent act. If done for a good end, as an intention of doing penance, it becomes a good action. *Riz.*

VEIL, CHALICE. *See* Chalice.

VEIL, HUMERAL. *See* Sacred Vestments.

VENERATION OF SAINTS. *See* Worship, Saints.

VENEROPATHIES. *See* Diseases, Venereal.

VENGEANCE. In a general sense, the infliction of physical punishment upon someone as retribution for injury caused to another is called vengeance. If done for good and just motives, e.g., love of justice, or preservation of the juridico-social order, or the correction of an evildoer, by a *competent authority*, according to laws, vindication, of itself, is a good act.

However, if punishment for an evil deed is inflicted out of an ill-feeling toward one who has offended, ill-treated or caused suffering to another, or simply to satisfy one's ill feeling toward his enemy, or for the pleasure of payment in kind, vengeance is an evil act, opposed to that precept of charity which prescribes that Christians love their neighbor even if an enemy. The latter form of vindication is properly called vengeance.

Vengeance is a sin, and opposed to the precept of the Divine Master to love everyone, even enemies, and to pardon sincerely any offense or injury. One of the main characteristics of vengeance is punishment of an offender beyond proper limits, with disregard of the laws which prohibit acts of vindictive justice by private individuals.

In certain regions vengeance is a real, social vice which causes great disturbance to peaceful living. The popular notion according to which vengeance is considered a necessary and honorable act to be performed unless one is a coward, is grossly erroneous and disastrous. A good and well-instructed Christian knows that forgiving an enemy is a more difficult act than revenge, which demonstrates greater moral strength and will power. Self-control requires greater courage than controlling an enemy (*q.v.*). *Ben.*

VENGEANCE. *See* Sin that cry to Heaven for Vengeance.

VENI, CREATOR. The *Veni, Creator* is a hymn of the liturgy of Pentecost, which is used at other extra-liturgical occasions as an invocation to the Holy

Spirit to fulfill His mission as Illuminator, Consoler, and Sanctifier. The text now in use is somewhat modified from the text of the original ancient manuscript.

Its recitation is of obligation at Vespers and Tierce of the Divine Office of the Feast and the Octave of Pentecost and at the ordination of priests. It is used in the rite of Confirmation (*q.v.*), in sacred functions at the beginning of the year, in spiritual retreats, and in the novena of Pentecost.

Wilmart attributes the *Veni, Creator* to an unknown poet who lived at the end of the ninth century, during the Carolingian Renaissance. Thus, the attribution to Charlemagne has no foundation in fact; the thesis of those who attribute it to Rabanus the Moor (d. 856) seems to have greater value.

The most ancient known manuscripts belong to the tenth century. Thus, all attributions of more ancient dates, including the one to St. Ambrose or St. Gregory, are groundless.

INDULGENCES. A five years' indulgence may be gained for the recitation of the *Veni, Creator*; and a plenary indulgence under the usual conditions, if it is recited for an entire month (Brief, May 26, 1796; Sacred Congregation of Rites, June 20, 1889; Sacred Apostolic Penitentiary, February 9, 1934).

A plenary indulgence is also granted to those who assist at the chanting of the *Veni, Creator* on the first day of the year, in a church, public or semi-public oratory, and receive the sacraments of confession and Holy Communion, with prayers for the intention of the Roman Pontiff.

The poetry of the hymn is in couplets; the music belongs to the type of chant called *concentus* by the promoters of Gregorian plain chant; the melody is of the fourth authentic tone, with a solemn but lively tempo. *Pal.*

VENI, SANCTE SPIRITUS. The *Veni, Sancte Spiritus* is a sequence prayer and an invocation of the multiform action of the Holy Spirit on the souls. Through this anthem, the Holy Spirit is invoked with the most tender and inspired words that He may fully exercise His purifying and fruitful action through His sevenfold gifts. It concludes with a petition for eternal joys.

Concerning authorship, the *Veni, Sancte Spiritus* has been linked to the names of Robert the Pious (d. 1031), Herman Contractus, and Reichenau (d. 1054), but Wilmart discounts such allegations and assigns authorship to Innocent III (d. 1216) or, with greater probability, to Stephen Langton, archbishop of Canterbury (1228), contemporary and friend of the same Pontiff. The melody is of the first authentic tone included within a seventh, and, therefore, of an imperfect mode.

The *Veni, Sancte Spiritus* has been received as a sequence of the Roman Missal (1570). It is recited or chanted at the Mass of the feast of Pentecost and during its Octave. *Pal.*

VENOM. *See* Poison.

VERACITY, TRUTHFULNESS. *Veracity*, in a broad sense, indicates a correspondence between one's exterior conduct and internal convictions. In a strict sense, it is agreement between a person's words or signs and his inner persuasion.

Truthfulness is an obligation; in fact the faculty of speech is given us by God, not to deceive ourselves or others, but to bring one's thought to the knowledge of others. St. Paul exhorts the faithful to speak truthfully to each other, because they are members of each other (Eph. 4:25). The duty to speak the truth at all times is not to be understood in the sense that one must divulge without discernment to anyone whatsoever information he possesses. In fact, to refrain from speech is not to deny truth. There are cases in which it is proper and a duty to withhold knowledge. The Lord Himself said that we must be "wise as serpents and simple as doves" (Matt. 10:16). Love of neighbor can furnish exquisite tact to discern that which is proper to say and that which is best to withhold and still remain immune from cunning and slyness.

One may sin against veracity by excess or by defect. Excess reveals information not to be divulged, as a professional secret, without grave motives justifying disclosure. Such disclosures could cause grave injustices. Defect expresses by words or signs a thing contrary to one's interior persuasion; this is lying.

Simulation (*q.v.*), akin to lying, consists in exhibiting a behavior towards others that denotes dispositions and intentions actually different from those entertained in the mind. Such conduct is by its nature directed to deceiving others, and is generally employed as a means to a specific end. A classic example of simulation was Judas' kiss in the Garden of Olives. *Hypocrisy* (*q.v.*) is a kind of simulation. The degree of guilt from simulation depends above all on the end intended and on the damage caused to another.

Dissimulation (*q.v.*), instead, is an attitude which can lead others into error but which does not necessarily deceive them. Dissimulation is resorted to in order to hide something which a person has no right to know. Dissimulation is lawful if used for a good and just motive.

VESPERS. *See* Breviary.

VESSELS, Sacred. Sacred vessels are part of the sacred furnishings of a church. Generally of metal, some are obliged to contain precious metal, either gold or silver. The following vessels are used in connection with the Holy Eucharist: (a) *chalice* (*q.v.*); (b) *ciborium*, a sacred vessel which holds communion hosts in the tabernacle. Its present form came into general use in the sixteenth century. A ciborium may be made of any metal, but the interior must be gold-plated (*Caeremoniale episcoporum*, II, c. 30, No. 3). Ciboria made of glass are forbidden (Sacred Congregation of Rites, *Decreta authentica*, No. 3511). A ciborium may be constructed in any style, provided that it has a solid and large base, a notch in the stand, an internally gold-plated and smooth cup, and a movable cover, surmounted by a cross or image of the Blessed Savior. If it con-

tains the Blessed Sacrament, the ciborium must be covered with a white veil, properly ornamented (*Rituale: Ornatus ecclesiae*, c. 27). In taking Holy Communion to the sick, the ciborium may be replaced by a small gold-plated box-like container, called pix. (c) the *monstrance* or *ostensorium* (*q.v.*) is a sacred vessel for exposition of the Blessed Sacrament at Benediction and other Eucharistic devotions. The use of the monstrance began in the eighteenth century (*See* Benediction, Eucharist, Forty Hours). A monstrance may be made of copper, brass, or other metals, but must be gold- or silver-plated. It must have a base and a notch in the middle of the stand holding the *capsula* in which the consecrated host is placed; it must have a crystal in the front and a small door with glass on the back. It must be surmounted by a cross or image of the Risen Lord (*Decreta authentica*, No. 2957). On the altar, when not in actual use, it must be covered with a white veil (*Decret. Auth.* 4268). Two accessories to the monstrance are a *lunette*, consisting of a small circular case used to hold the Blessed Sacrament in an erect position in the center of the monstrance, and a *capsula* or *luna*, or a small metal box, gold-plated in the interior and surmounted by a cross for the safekeeping of the Benediction host. Strictly speaking, no special blessing is required for a lunette or *capsula* (*luna*). (d) A *communion plate*, or metal disc, gold- or silver-plated, is used to gather fragments of host which might fall during the distribution of Holy Communion (cf. Instruction of the Sacred Congregation of the Sacraments, 1929).

HOLY OILS. The holy oils are a liquid substance extracted from ripe olives, consecrated by a bishop and used in the administration of certain sacraments (Cans. 734 ff.; 781; 945 ff.). There are three kinds of holy oils: (a) Oil of the Sick (*oleum infirmorum*), used in the administration of the sacrament of extreme unction and in the ceremony of the blessing of church bells; (b) Oil of Catechumens (*oleum catechumenorum*), used in the sacrament of baptism, in the ordination of a priest, and in the blessing of the baptismal font; (c) Holy Chrism (*sacrum chrisma*) or oil mixed with balm and used in the administration of the sacrament of confirmation (*q.v.*), in all consecrations, the blessing of the baptismal font, the anointing of the head of the newly baptized, and the anointing of the hands in the consecration of a bishop. Each kind of oil requires a specific container, made of silver or other white metal, firmly secured, and identified by an inscription or letter indicating its specific content. Ordinarily, for reasons of cleanness, glass containers are enclosed in the metal containers. The vases containing the Oil of Catechumens and Holy Chrism are kept in the baptistry; the other, containing the oil of the sick, is kept in an appropriate box along with a purple burse, cotton, and a purificator. In some churches an appropriate chest or *ambry* is provided, usually attached to the wall of the sanctuary. The containers for the oils may be blessed if desired, but this is not an obligation.

RELIQUARIES. Relics (*q.v.*) of saints, whatever the size, are kept in appropriate urns, called reliquaries. The interior of the reliquary must be sheeted with precious metal or, at least, gold-plated; the relic itself must be covered with a silken cloth of the liturgical color proper to martyrs, confessors, virgins, etc. Relics of considerable parts of the body or clothing are kept in reliquaries resembling the shape of the particular part of the body. They must be provided with an appropriate crystal protection; the interior must be made of silk and sealed with the official seal of authenticity.

Other relics are kept in small reliquaries, sealed with the seal of authenticity. When exposed for veneration, they are placed in appropriate reliquaries made of a material and shape left to the discretion of the individual (*ibid.*, No. 3697).

HOLY WATER BUCKET. A metal portable bucket is used to hold holy water into which the aspergill, consisting of a sponge enclosed in a perforated small ball and handle, is dipped. It is used at all blessings in which holy water is used.

THURIBLE AND BOAT. The thurible is a vessel, shaped in the form of a bowl, usually suspended on chains, in which incense is burned. The boat is a small vessel in the shape of a boat, containing raw incense. Thurible and boat may be made of silver, brass, bronze, or other metal.

CRUETS. Cruets are small pitchers (*urceoli*), ordinarily resting in a small basin (*pelvicula*) or plate. Cruets must be of glass or, better, of crystal. If made of other material, they must at least carry a distinctive mark for wine and water. The basin or plate may also be of metal. The use of a larger pitcher and basin is permitted only in Pontifical Masses or other episcopal functions, and for other particular prelates.

PURIFICATION VASE. This is a small metal or crystal vase containing water and placed at the side of the tabernacle for the convenience of the priest or deacon when he is not able to purify his fingers in a chalice after touching the Holy Eucharist. *Pal.*

VESTMENTS, LITURGICAL. *See* Sacred Vestments.

VIATICUM. Holy Communion administered to one in danger of death is called Viaticum.

In danger of death, irrespective of the cause, the faithful are bound by precept to receive Holy Communion (Can. 864, par. 1). In danger of death, Holy Communion may and must be given to children even below the age of discretion if they are able to distinguish the Body of the Lord from ordinary bread and reverently adore it (Can. 854, par. 2). Those who receive Holy Communion in the form of Viaticum are not required to observe the Eucharistic fast. One who may have received Holy Communion the same day is not obliged but strongly urged to receive again if in the course of the day he comes into danger of death (Can. 864, par. 2). Theologians maintain that this applies also to those who receive Holy Communion some days previous to the danger.

To receive Holy Viaticum fruitfully, the faithful are required to have the same dispositions as for ordinary reception of Holy Communion, with the exception of the fasting, which for Holy Viaticum is not required (Can. 858, par. 1; *Christus Dominus*, January 6, 1953: AAS 45 [1953], 30; *Sacram Communionem*, March 19, 1957).

He who receives Viaticum in a sacrilegious manner does not fulfill the obligation of receiving Holy Communion in danger of death; thus, strictly speaking, he is still bound to receive the Holy Eucharist. However, if one commits a grave sin after reception of Viaticum with the proper dispositions, he is required to confess the sin but not to receive Viaticum in order to satisfy the obligation to receive the Sacrament in danger of death.

Viaticum may not be administered, at least publicly, to public sinners unless they have made amends for the scandal given (*see* Sinner, Public).

It is of great benefit and solace to the seriously ill to receive Holy Viaticum in due time or even often if the danger of death is protracted; the graces and comfort which the Holy Eucharist gives to the soul are needed more than at any other time. *Man.*

VICAR APOSTOLIC. A vicar apostolic is a prelate who governs in the name of the Sovereign Pontiff, with ordinary power and jurisdiction (Can. 293, par. 1), an area of mission territory where the faith has already been sufficiently established with a notable number of Catholics and missionaries; this territory is called a vicariate apostolic.

The appointment, rights, and obligations of a vicar apostolic are the same as those of a prefect apostolic, with the following special powers and differences: a vicar apostolic has episcopal consecration and the honorary privileges of titular bishops (Can. 294, par. 1; Can. 308); a vicar apostolic is appointed by an apostolic brief (Can. 293, par. 2); a vicar apostolic has the power to convoke a

synod (Can. 304, par. 2), although he must resort to the Roman Congregations for specific rulings as the prefect apostolic does (Can. 303); finally, he is bound to make an *ad limina* visit and to report on the conditions of the territory entrusted to him, every five years, to the Sacred Congregation for the Propagation of the Faith (Cans. 299–300). The vicar apostolic is required to choose as his vicar another priest, after his acceptance of the vicariate; this priest is called the pro-vicar apostolic (Can. 309). *Fel.*

VICAR CAPITULAR. The vicar capitular is a priest elected by the cathedral chapter to govern a diocese during a vacancy of the episcopal see (Can. 429, par. 3). He must be elected within eight days following the notice of vacancy of the episcopal see (Can. 432, par. 1). The vicar capitular becomes the Ordinary of the place with the authority of a bishop, except for restrictions established by law. The principle *Sede vacante, nil innovetur* (Can. 436) applies to him; in other words, since his administration is only temporary, radical changes and unnecessary innovation are to be avoided (Can. 436).

The vicar capitular has the authority to permit a legitimate bishop to hold pontifical functions in his diocese, or if he himself is a bishop, he can hold pontifical functions, but he may not use the throne or the canopy (Can. 435, par. 2).

He takes precedence over all the members of the diocesan clergy, except bishops unless he is a bishop also. During his tenure of office he has the right to use the insignia and privileges granted to a titular prothonotary apostolic (*see* Prelate); he is also entitled to adequate remuneration (Can. 441, par. 1).

Besides the duty of diligent administration of a diocese, he is obliged to reside in a diocese and to offer Mass for the people (*pro populo*) (Can. 440). His office ceases in the same way as that of other ecclesiastical officials upon the installation of a new bishop (Can. 443, par. 2). He may be removed from office only by the Holy See. A resignation must be submitted to the chapter, but acceptance by the chapter is not necessary for validity (Can. 443, par. 2). A vicar capitular must give an account of his administration to the new bishop (Can. 444).

In the United States, diocesan consultors perform the function of a cathedral chapter as the bishop's council. Thus, whatever part the cathedral chapter has in the government of a diocese is also assigned to the board of consultors. *Fel.*

VICAR FORANE (Dean). A vicar forane is a priest who presides over a deanery, that is, a part of the diocese comprising a definite number of parishes (Cans. 445; 217). The office of dean originated from the rural officials (*officiales rurales*) appointed by the bishop in addition to city officials (*officiales urbani*) as substitutes for archdeacons who become too authoritarian in the administration of the diocese.

A vicar forane has faculties granted by common and particular law, and by special mandate of the Ordinary to whom he is subject. Therefore, he has ordinary and delegated authority, which, in the existing discipline, involves the right and duty to supervise and report to the Ordinary, at least once a year, the state of affairs of parishes under his supervision, to summon priests of his district for conferences on liturgical or moral subjects or for other meetings which the ordinary may have prescribed, in accordance with Can. 131 (Cans. 447–449).

The vicar forane shall have a special seal of the deanery; he takes precedence over all pastors and other priests of his district (Can. 450). He may be removed at will by the Bishop (*ad nutum Episcopi:* Can. 446, par. 2). *Fel.*

VICAR GENERAL. The vicar general is a priest legitimately delegated with ordinary authority to assist the Ordinary in the administration of his diocese (Can. 336, par. 1). Generally, such an office is conferred by the bishop on one priest (Can. 336, par. 3), but because of the diversity of rites or the size of the diocese the ordinary may deem it necessary to appoint two or more vicars general, in which case their authority is exercised cumulatively (*in solidum*). The appointment of the vicar general is left to the free choice of the Ordinary, who has the right to revoke the appointment whenever he deems it proper (*ad nutum*), but always with a sense of equity and for a just cause. The Ordinary may also restrict the authority of his vicar general in accordance with the dispositions of the law (Can. 368, par. 1).

The vicar general has ordinary but vicarious jurisdiction (*see* Jurisdiction, Ecclesiastical) inasmuch as it is exercised in the name of the ordinary with whom the vicar general forms a single consistory (Can. 368, par. 1). The vicar general has the right of precedence in the diocese and the privileges and insignia of a titular prothonotary apostolic. If the vicar general is a titular bishop, he acquires the privileges of honor accorded to titular bishops.

VICAR, PAROCHIAL. The parochial vicar is a priest who takes the place of the pastor in the care of souls. The Code distinguishes five types of vicars: parochial, *oeconomus*, deputy, coadjutor (*adiutor*), and associate.

The parochial vicar is a priest who exercises actual and exclusive care of souls in a parish united *pleno iure* to a legal person, such as a capitular church, a monastery, etc. The parochial vicar is called by law *pastor* with all the rights and duties of a pastor (Can. 471).

The administrator (*oeconomus*) is a priest in charge of a parish during a period of vacancy in a parish; he is entitled to a part of its income for sustenance. Before the appointment of an administrator, an assistant or former pastor shall take charge of the parish, unless other provisions are made; if there are several assistants, the first assistant shall have charge; if they are all equal, the senior in office shall assume charge. If there are no assistants, the nearest pastor shall take charge. If the parish belongs to a religious group, the superior of the house shall take charge of the administration. The administrator has the same rights and duties as the pastor in all things concerning the care of souls. He must, however, do nothing that might cause serious detriment to the rights of the future pastor (Can. 473, par. 1).

The vicar substitute is the priest who takes the place of the pastor in a case of appeal against the sentence of privation of the parish, or during the pastor's absence from the parish for more than one week. The vicar substitute is appointed according to the provisions of Can. 465, par. 4–5, and Can. 1923, par. 2. In matters pertaining to the care of souls he takes the place of the pastor except for the limitations established by the Ordinary (Can. 474).

The vicar coadjutor (*adiutor*) is a priest lawfully appointed to take the place of the pastor incapable of discharging his duties properly because of old age, mental inability, blindness, or other permanent impairment. If the vicar coadjutor takes the place of the pastor in all activities of the parish, he is considered a pastor with all the rights and duties of a pastor; if, on the contrary, he takes only a part of the pastor's duties, his rights and duties are those indicated in the letter of appointment. The Ordinary has the right to assign a coadjutor to an unwilling pastor, but he may not grant the right of succession (Can. 475).

If the pastor cannot take care of all the work of his parish because of the large number of parishioners or similar reasons, the Ordinary shall give him one or more priests called *vicarii cooperatores* (Can. 475, par. 1) or assistant priests. The jurisdiction of assistant priests is delegated; its extent consists exclusively of the delegation given them either by the Ordinary or the pastor. The general law makes no mention of the latitude of their jurisdiction. *Fel.*

VICE. The word *vice* in a broad sense means any defect whatever. In a strict sense, however, it indicates a strong tendency to a gravely sinful act through a frequent repetition of the same act. This repetition of the same act strengthens the pattern traced by the preceding action; it increases the state of dynamic readiness for the repetition of the act and weakens one's power of resistance. This, generally, occurs in much greater degree with evil actions. A sin, committed at first with hesitation and anxiety, is gradually repeated with greater ease, to a point of great indifference. The greater the frequency with which a sin is committed, the stronger also will be the vice. A bad habit is acquired more easily in certain sins, such as gluttony and lust, than in others. A sinful habit is acquired even more readily if there is in a subject an hereditary tendency.

A sinful habit makes more difficult the practice of virtue, and in fact may reach the degree of an almost irresistible force. It may, at times, decrease the imputability of acts committed under such impulse, without necessarily eliminating the grave nature of the act. Though the will of one who turns to God and is re-established in grace does not remain attached to evil, yet the physical propensity toward the sinful habit, previously acquired, still lingers and disappears only gradually. Thus, after conversion, the experience of a great tendency to evil explains why the danger of relapse is strongly felt in the period immediately following conversion. Constant watchfulness and the adoption of prudent measures, aimed at conquering temptation successfully, must be stressed.

Any vice whatever can be broken and eliminated by resisting promptly all impulses and by performing acts contrary. Everyone is bound to oppose vice. He who neglects to adopt the proper means for the elimination of a vice, by this very fact consents to the sinful inordinate acts, which are foreseen in a confused manner as possible effects of an unopposed vice. These acts, if committed without full consent of the will, are imputed to the person in greater or lesser degree according to the negligence involved in not opposing the vice. On the contrary, if one is generally opposed to vice and uses suitable means to eradicate it, the acts which he may unconsciously commit under the impulse of such a vice are not imputable to him. *Man.*

VICE, SOLITARY. *See* Onanism.

VICE, UNNATURAL. *See* Perversion, Sexual.

VICTIMAE PASCHALI. *Victimae Paschali* is a sequence prayer, commemorating the mystery of the Resurrection. Its author was Wipo of Burgundy, in the eleventh century, court chaplain of Conrad II and Henry III.

The sequence begins with an invitation to praise the Paschal Victim, the Lamb of God; from this, it recounts the Victim's great achievements: reconciliation of the faithful with the Father, and triumph over death. Then, in a very vivid manner, the author speaks to Mary Magdalene, who responds by relating her vision of the empty tomb and the angels announcing the Resurrection of Christ. The sequence concludes with a firm belief in the fact of the Resurrection of Christ and a plea to His mercy.

Victimae Paschali was kept in the Roman Missal even after the reform of St. Pius V (1570); it is recited or chanted at Holy Mass after the Epistle on Easter Sunday and during the Octave. *Pal.*

VIGIL. *See* Abstinence and Fasting.

VIOLATION OF CEMETERY. An ecclesiastical cemetery, duly consecrated, may also be violated.

Regarding the causes, effects, and reconciliation of cemeteries, the same principles and practices apply as in the violation of a church (*see* Violation of a Church).

In a place where a church and cemetery are adjoining, violation of one is not communicated to the other, because each is a sacred place distinct from the other (Can. 1172, par. 2). *Ben.*

VIOLATION OF A CHURCH. Violation of a church is any act gravely opposed to the sacredness of a holy place. According to the judgment of the ecclesiastical authority, it has the effect of rendering the church no longer suitable for the celebration of divine worship (Can.

1173), although its consecration or blessing is not affected. Not every unworthy deed nor every sacrilege (*q.v.*) committed on the premises gives rise to the crime of violation of a church. It is the right of the ecclesiastical legislator to decide exactly which acts constitute a violation. Provided they are certain and notorious crimes perpetrated in the church itself, these acts are: (1) murder; (2) outrageous and grave shedding of blood; (3) using the church for irreligious or suicidal acts; (4) burial in the church of an unbeliever or one excommunicated by final sentence of a competent court (Can. 1172).

It is strictly forbidden to conduct acts of divine worship, administer the sacraments, or bury the dead in a violated church. If the violation occurred during divine services, these must be discontinued at once. However, if the violation occurs after the *Sanctus* of the Mass, the priest must continue until the Communion is completed.

Violation of a church does not require a new consecration or blessing, but the rite of *reconciliation*, a special, shorter, and simpler rite. This consists of an aspersion of water, specially blessed by a bishop, or ordinary holy water (Can. 1174). If the church is consecrated, the rite of reconciliation must be performed by a bishop who can, however, delegate an ordinary priest; if the church is merely blessed, it can be reconciled by its rector or parish priest (Can. 1176).

Ecclesiastical superiors have established laws concerning the violation and reconciliation of the church to impress all the faithful with the sanctity of Christian edifices (*see* Sacrilege). *Ben.*

VIOLATION OF A CORPSE. Violation of a corpse is an act of violent profanation of a dead human body by abusive removal from the grave, destruction, mutilation, or defacing.

The malice of this act depends on the motive for which it is committed. Obviously, it does not constitute violation of a corpse if such an act is performed with permission of lawful authority for juridical, scientific, or didactic reasons (*see*

Autopsy). The gravity of the sin of violation of a human corpse depends on the degree of abuse of the human body and the displeasure caused to relatives of the deceased. Violation of a corpse is a crime according to canonical (Can. 2329) and civil laws. *Ben.*

VIOLENCE. Violence is an extrinsic force or motion brought to bear upon an individual against his will by an external agent. It is one of the strongest obstacles against freedom of the will.

Violence may be *absolute* or *relative*. Absolute violence demands resistance by all possible means. Absolute violence destroys free will, and all imputability of the act is then attributed to the violator, if he acts with full freedom of the will.

If the subject does not oppose the act with every possible external resistance or, with external resistance, internally adheres to the act brought to bear upon him, violence is called relative; freedom of the will is not destroyed but diminished in proportion to the adhesion or repugnance present in the mind of the subject.

Absolute violence cannot affect the internal act (elicited) of the will; it can only affect the acts of the human faculties to the extent that they are subject to the rule of will. For violence in relation to marriage, *see* Consent, Matrimonial. *Gra.*

VIOLENCE (Crime). To attack another's individual liberty, by unlawfully compelling him to an action or omission of an act or to endure suffering, which constitute neither a special violation of the law nor a more serious crime, is a crime of violence.

In Canon Law violence is considered a crime of mixed jurisdiction for which prevention is invoked (*see* Court). For this reason the legislator does not specify in detail the characteristics of the crime, which may be summed up in these essential elements:

(a) *The violence must be exerted either on the body* (*physical force*) *or on the mind.* Of course, violence must be such that it does not constitute, of itself,

a different and more serious crime. Thus, criminal acts of violence performed with the intent to interfere with or disturb the normal exercise of ecclesiastical power constitute a specific crime against ecclesiastical authorities (Can. 2331–2340). Criminal acts of violence which interfere with the liberty of canonical elections constitute a specific crime (Can. 2390). Violence exerted by a superior against his subject is the crime of abuse of authority (*q.v.*). Violence experienced in undue appropriation of church property is the crime of usurpation of ecclesiastical wealth (*see* Usurpation; Cans. 2345–2347). Violence causing physical injury is the specific crime of mutilation (*q.v.*). Violence exercised against clerics is included in the violation of the privilege of ecclesiastical immunity (*q.v.*); the violent invasion of a sacred place is also violation of the privilege of immunity (*q.v.*). Coercion into the ecclesiastical or religious state is also a specific crime (Can. 2352). The forcible abduction of a woman into an unsafe place for the purpose of forcing her into marriage or for libidinous acts is included in the crime of rape (Can. 2353); libidinous acts forced upon others are involved in the crimes *contra sextum* (Cans. 2357, par. 1; 2358; *see* Lewdness, Lust, Rape). Forcible appropriation of the property of a lawful owner constitutes the crime of robbery (*see* Theft).

(b) *The object of this violence must be the compulsion of another to act, omit, or suffer something* which otherwise he would not do, omit or endure. Since violence often constitutes a crime in the juridical order of civil States and is punished by them, the Church, in order that the guilty may not be punished twice, does not usually prosecute lay culprits. It is civil law which safeguards public welfare in these acts (Can. 1933, par. 3). Generally the Church refrains from inflicting any punishment, if it is foreseen that the culprit will be punished by civil authority (Can. 2223, par. 3, n. 2). After sentencing by civil authority, the Church punishes the individual guilty of crime of violence with exclusion from lawful ecclesiastical acts and every ecclesiastical office, and obliges the victim to restitution for damage caused (Can. 2354, par. 2). Clerics are subject to penalties *ferendae sententiae* (Can. 2354, par. 2). *Pal.*

VIOLENCE (Marriage of). *See* Consent, Marriage.

VIRGINITY. Virginity may be: (a) *purely physical,* a state in which the bodily integrity of a woman (*claustrum virginitatis*) is maintained; (b) *material* or *natural,* a state of immunity from complete sexual pleasure; (c) *formal* or *moral,* a determination to preserve oneself undefiled both for the present and the future. Physical virginity has only an accidental relation to the virtue of virginity; physical virginity is preserved by the latter, but, in itself, the virtue can exist without physical virginity, if this was lost for other reasons than a sexual act, or against one's will. The virtue can be absent despite the fact of physical virginity, which remained intact notwithstanding a voluntary sexual act. Material virginity supplies the matter of the virtue, formal virginity supplies the form; thus, the virtue of virginity may be defined as immunity from every voluntary, complete, sexual pleasure with the determination to preserve this condition forever. It is a matter of dispute whether mere intention is sufficient to constitute the essence of the virtue, or a real vow is required. St. Thomas, in one part of the *Summa Theologiae* (II–II, q. 152, a. 3, ad 4) held to the necessity of a vow. In order that virginity be a real Christian virtue, bodily integrity and the above-mentioned intent must be due to a higher aim than conjugal chastity (Matt. 19:11–12). According to St. Thomas (other theologians differ), virginity is a virtue distinct from simple chastity (*q.v.*) because it has a special excellence: chastity restrains the satisfaction of the sexual appetite, but virginity totally excludes it.

Virginity, good in itself, is not opposed to any moral precept. The law of propagation of the species is incumbent on the community as a whole, but not necessarily on every individual; in fact, the oft-quoted text of Genesis 1:28 is not an explicit precept but contains a blessing. Furthermore, virginity causes no damage to the physical or psychological health of the individual, as experience well demonstrates. Christian virginity is a virtue that surpasses ordinary chastity. Insofar as the individual is concerned, it denotes victory of the spirit over the flesh. Although the sexual act properly performed and directed is not evil, abstention from it is an act of moral force that perfects man, freeing his mind from obstacles connected with sexual satisfaction and with married life: "He that is without a wife is solicitous for the things that belong to the Lord" (I Cor. 7:25–40). This is the doctrine of Sacred Scripture, the uniform and constant tradition of the Fathers and Doctors of the Church, who assigns a special reward (halo) to virginity. It was thus solemnly defined by the ecclesiastical magisterium (Council of Trent, Sess. 24, Can. 10). Concerning society, virginity is a positive factor to its perfection, since it creates the possibility of performing charitable, spiritual, and intellectual works to which a man in the married state is unable to fully dedicate himself. It creates a spiritual paternity and maternity; and it benefits society with the example of a very exalted virtue capable of lending considerable moral support to moral behavior.

The virtue of virginity can be lost: (a) materially, by an involuntary, complete, sexual act; (b) formally, by revocation of the resolution to preserve it, by internal sin, or by an incomplete sexual act; (c) materially and formally, by a complete sexual act directly or indirectly voluntary. Mere material loss of virginity does not destroy the virtue. Mere formal loss destroys it but it can be restored by receiving the sacrament of penance with a renewal of the resolution. Material and formal loss destroys the virtue irreparably, because natural integrity is lost with it. *Dam.*

VIRILITY. *See* Gonads.

VIRTUAL. *See* Intention.

VIRTUE. *Virtue* has various meanings. In a strict sense, virtue is a firm disposition or habit whose object is morally good acts. St. Thomas defines virtue as a good quality of the soul by which one lives in the proper manner, and which no one can use for evil purposes (*Summa Theol.* I–II, q. 65, a. 4). Virtues may be natural or acquired, supernatural or infused.

Natural virtue is a firm inclination to perform a specific morally good act. This inclination is produced in one of man's faculties by the frequent repetition of such an act. The reduction of obstacles, that is, a decreased resistance by fallen nature, is always connected with a strong inclination; the repetition of the acts, of course, gives rise to the acquisition of virtue.

The four principal natural virtues, called *cardinal* virtues (Latin, *cardo*— hinge), are: prudence, justice, fortitude, temperance. *Prudence* directs the intellect to judge as good only those things which are suitable for the attainment of one's true ultimate end, God. The kinds of prudence are individual prudence and social prudence. *Justice* is the virtue which disposes a person to render to each man his due. The types of justice are: commutative justice, which disposes an individual to give another his due; legal or social justice, which disposes the members of society to give the collectivity its due; distributive justice, which prompts rulers to give their subjects their due and inclines subjects to be satisfied with the equitable distribution of benefits and appointments made by the rulers. *Fortitude* is the virtue which disposes a person for the proper acceptance of dangers and serious difficulties, especially the danger of death. *Temperance* is a virtue which prompts a person to maintain proper moderation in the pleasures of taste and touch; the forms of temperance are abstinence, sobriety, and chastity.

Other natural virtues are related to individual cardinal virtues by reason of a definite resemblance to them. Habits inclining the intellect to devise the most suitable means for the attainment of one's true end, to apply the general norms of morality to particular cases, to interpret intelligently the spirit of the law, in an exceptional case to set aside the letter of the law—all are certainly related to the virtue of prudence. Religion, which inclines a person to render to God due worship; virtues which dispose a person to fulfill his duties toward parents, country, and superiors; gratitude, truthfulness, affability, generosity, punitive justice and equity—all are virtues linked to justice. Magnanimity, which inclines a person to perform with God's help great and heroic deeds of every kind of virtue; magnificence, patience, and perseverance—all are related to fortitude. Meekness, forgiveness, humility, virtues, which incline one to a proper use of the mind, clothes, decorations, luxuries, comforts of life, and external conduct— all are related to the virtue of temperance.

Once acquired, natural virtues grow with frequent practice; if they are not practiced at all, or only rarely, they soon grow weak and die out.

Supernatural virtues are principles of action infused into man's faculties by God Himself, which give man a power to perform, with the aid of God's grace, supernatural acts. These principles are infused in the soul along with sanctifying grace (II Pet. 1:3 ff.; Council of Vienna: Denz. n. 483; Council of Trent: Denz. n. 800). Since infused virtues are not the result of good acts frequently performed, it is possible to have strong inclinations to sin co-existing with them in the period immediately following one's conversion to God. This explains why one who has acquired vices before his conversion would, after his conversion, still feel strongly attracted to evil, with little eagerness for the practice of virtue.

The Council of Trent explicitly refers to this possibility with regard to faith, hope, and charity. These virtues, called *theological* because they have God as their formal and primary material object, are the principal infused virtues. *Faith* is the principle of firm and supernatural adherence to the truths revealed by God, on the authority of a revealing God; *hope* is the principle of a supernatural and firm expectation of supreme beatitude and the means to its attainment, based on the benevolent omnipotence of God, who is infinitely good to man and faithful to His promises; *charity* is the principle of supernatural and disinterested love for God above all other things, because of the infinite lovableness of God, without regard to our well-being; it implies love of ourselves and our neighbor for the sake of God. Charity, with God as its proper object and our supreme end, is the final fulfillment and prime mover of all other infused virtues. Faith and hope, which remain in the sinner without charity, are called "informative," and charity is called "formative."

It is common doctrine that, at the moment of justification, other virtues, called moral, are also infused in the soul, which have as their object a moral good, distinct from God. In fact, in order that we may attain our ultimate end, we must also perform supernatural acts with created good as their immediate end. Infused moral virtues render us capable of performing these acts. These virtues, distinguished in the same way as natural virtues, have the same material object as acquired virtues; a different formal object, that is, a superior and supernatural motive, renders moral virtues essentially distinct from natural virtues. However, their presence does not make natural virtues superfluous; natural virtues as the fruit of frequent repetitions of the same good act give the individual a special ability to operate morally in various fields of human endeavor in which the infused moral virtues have effect.

The sacraments produce an increase of sanctifying grace; each of the infused virtues grows with grace. Good deeds performed in the state of grace merit such an increase. Theologians, however, are not in agreement whether this increase is always given immediately, or only when a meritorious act is performed that surpasses in intensity the virtues already existing in the soul. Through sin, the infused virtues are lost with the loss of grace; faith and hope, however, continue to subsist in the soul, unless a grave sin is committed directly against those two virtues. *Man.*

VIRTUES. INTERRELATION. The interrelation existing among the virtues is a property by which one virtue, practiced with earnestness, in an integral, logical, and perfect sense, postulates other virtues. A single virtue, if perfect, is necessarily connected with all other virtues; in view of the unity of the human person, one cannot adequately tend to the supreme end of life by one specific spiritual activity and remain habitually removed from that same end in other sectors of his spirit. For this reason, the growth of one virtue is connected with a proportional growth of the other virtues. For example, justice requires prudence in the choice and use of the means, and fortitude and temperance in face of risks and enticements. The virtue of religion which ignores the four cardinal virtues is a contradiction. On the other hand, it is possible to have generosity without chastity, and humility without magnanimity, because these are not perfect virtues, in the sense that they do not make man perfect.

There is no doubt, therefore, that the perfect moral virtues, which incline man to perform constantly good works even in the midst of great difficulties, are interrelated. The cardinal virtues, though acquired virtues, are mutually related in a particular way. The theological virtues are not interrelated in their essence, for faith and hope can exist without charity, as in the sinner who does not reject faith and hope. However, they are related as virtues. In fact, faith and hope cannot be called perfect, nor do they avail for eternal life unless vitalized or informed by charity; neither can charity be understood without faith and hope.

Infused moral virtues, in the manner of acquired moral virtues, are mutually connected through the virtue of prudence, which is necessary for their practice; furthermore, each of them is connected with charity, for none could be present without charity, and charity could not exist without infused moral virtues. It is true that grace inclines to activity, and such activity demands virtues or supernatural operative habits as a proximate principle.

At this point it could be asked whether this relation is an intrinsic bond proceeding from their nature or something extrinsic.

Some theologians believe that the connection is dependent exclusively on the legislative will of God. The greater number of theologians, however, believe that there is an intrinsic bond, although not all explain this in the same way. Some hold that the connection is necessarily required by the nature of the virtues and not even the omnipotence of God could increase or eliminate one virtue without increasing or eliminating also the others. This, of course, appears an exaggeration. Others more reasonably teach that charity and the infused virtues are mutually linked by their nature, but the interrelation of grace, faith, and hope exists only by a privilege of God. A slightly different opinion teaches that infused virtues are connected among themselves, with one exception: by the will of God, faith and hope can exist without the infused virtues.

Moral Virtues and Grace. Man, elevated by grace, must have faculties to enable him to perform acts that are connatural to his new state, namely, supernatural acts of virtue. Some hold that the moral virtues flow from grace; others hold that they are simply a requirement of grace, since they were inserted in man's natural faculties by God Himself. Since grace and charity are inseparable, the moral virtues are connected with grace in the same way that they are united with charity. Since the moral virtues must be directed by prudence, and prudence cannot exist without charity, which disposes it to its ultimate end, the moral virtues are indirectly linked with charity.

Grace and charity and faith and hope are infused simultaneously at the moment of justification and increase in equal degree; only accidentally can there be a superiority of faith and hope in a justi-fied sinner. But despite a loss of charity and grace, faith and hope can still exist, as stated above. *Pal.*

VIRTUES, HEROIC. *See* Perfection, Christian; Saints.

VISIONS AND APPARITIONS. The meaning of *vision* and *apparition* relies on the concept of mystery. In Catholic theology, visions and apparitions occupy an important role in the history of revelation and the mystery of divine redemption.

In matters pertaining to God and man's eternal salvation, God alone can reveal absolute truth. In the supernatural field it is not man who first seeks God, but God in His benign condescension seeks man, thus making it easy for man to draw near Him. The faith of our forefathers is based on the belief that our ancestors had a friendly relationship with God. In fact, all sacred writers of the Old Testament link the history of the human race to a special direction given by God. God, the Creator of all, conversed in the earthly Paradise with the first man and woman and, after they were driven out of Paradise, manifested His will to a few privileged persons (Revelation). The Patriarchs and Moses enjoyed a personal relationship with God. After this, the Lord spoke to men of God through His Spirit and revealed His mysteries to them (II Sam. 23:2; Dan. 2:28). Later, new apparitions of God are recounted (Mal. 3:1). In the New Testament, the Son of God reveals to man the mysteries of the divine kingdom (Eph. 3:3; Rom. 15:25–26; I Pet. 1:12; II Pet. 1:4). God, a munificent Lover of men, after a public revelation directed to all mankind, according to His incomprehensible counsels, continues to manifest Himself in a visible manner through visions and apparitions, especially to those who, with humility and detachment from earthly things, seek more earnestly to approach Him and to merit His love.

Teachers of mystical theology insist that visions and apparitions are entirely different from contemplation (*q.v.*). Contemplation essentially springs forth from charity and sanctifying grace; visions and apparitions do not demand grace of themselves, but may occur to sinners that they may be converted, even if, in reality, they do not become converted (cf. Acts 9:5). We do not refer to spiritualistic visions and apparitions (*see* Spiritualism), but to extraordinary *divine mystical phenomena* (A. TANQUEREY, *The Spiritual Life*, n. 1489).

Visions are of three kinds: corporeal or perceptible, imaginary, and intellectual.

(a) *Corporeal* or external visions, called apparitions, are events in which one has a physical perception of an external object of the supernatural order whose psychological process necessarily belongs to the field of sensation. The action, direct or indirect, of this sensation reaches the perceiving subject through a modification of peripheral organs or the central organs which govern the sensitive faculty (*Summa Theol.* III, q. 76, a. 8). In such apparitions, a figure before the eyes of the body may represent Jesus Christ, the Blessed Virgin Mary or a saint; in true visions this is thought to occur through the ministry of the angels. However, it must be observed that, although such visions can truly originate from God or the saints, the devil can and often does assume these same forms in order to deceive those of weak faith or lead them into pride and error. Thus, in judging such visions and apparitions, one must use the greatest caution and discretion; in doubtful cases visions are to be presumed rather as a deception (cf. I John 5:1).

(b) Visions are called *imaginary* if the object is not presented to one's external senses but to the fantasy without any bodily figure or other material presence. It appears to the imagination as real. This kind of vision often gives rise to serious doubts and uncertainties because the evil spirit is capable of entering into them. A vivid fantasy can represent something which leads one to believe it to be of supernatural origin.

(c) *Intellectual* visions are such that nothing appears to the external or internal senses but to the intellect illumined by God as in a flash of clearest light. Thus enlightened, the intellect makes known to the soul without specific representations things pleasing to the Lord. Extreme alertness and prudence are needed in evaluating all types of visions to prevent error. The spiritual writers indicate various criteria by which one may discern the true origin of such visions and apparitions; every good Christian is expected to abide by them. The first and principal rule is given by the Apostle Paul (Gal. 1:8). He teaches that anything contrary to revealed truth, or to what the Church teaches as a truth of faith or necessary to be done, is false and to be considered the work of the devil. Secondly, one must see if any such vision or apparition is conducive to virtue and the detachment of the soul from self-love and esteem and from other material goods (Gal. 5:22–23). Thirdly, if these visions and apparitions lead to good, encourage the observance of the law of God, the precepts of the Church, the love of suffering, humility and obedience, and if they inspire holy thoughts, distrust of self joined with the desire that such visions remain undisclosed, they contain a probability of truth (I John 4:1–4). On the contrary, if they arouse in the soul a sense of self-esteem, an *uneasy sweetness*, obstinacy in one's own opinion, or a desire for publicity, one can, with good reason, regard them either the work of the devil or the result of a deranged mind. Any sudden change in the behavior and the humor of the individual—from mild and meek to hasty and melancholic, from gentle and humble to contemptuous and intolerant of opposition and presumptuous, from wise and considerate to impetuous, from obedient to rebellious—is almost a sure indication that the visions and apparitions originate from the devil or a form of neurasthenia (*q.v.*).

Visions and apparitions always imply a certain danger to one's eternal salvation. God ordinarily permits both true and false visions. Man's life on earth is a constant warfare. Now, a particular distrust of self and of one's own strength and capacities, even concerning actions good in themselves, is pleasing to God. To act in this manner is to behave wisely and prudently, following the example of the Blessed Virgin Mary (cf. Luke 1:26 ff.). There is a possibility of self-deception even in visions and revelations which have had great renown in the Church (Paray-le-Monial, Lourdes, and Fatima). These have been submitted to severe scrutiny and proof from contradiction. If a vision or apparition fails to overcome objections and contradictions, it must by this very fact be considered suspect.

It is unwise to request from God visions and apparitions; in one sense, it is desirable that we do not experience them in view of the many dangers to which they give rise. The best thing is to place oneself in God's hands and to will whatever He wills, in a life in which the daily tasks of one's state are performed with serenity, docility, promptness, and perseverance. *See also* Magisterium, Ecclesiastical. *Tar.*

VISITATION, DIOCESAN. Diocesan visitation is the visit which the Ordinary is required to make annually of at least a part of his diocese. It must be made with diligence, and not be prolonged unnecessarily. It must be so arranged that the entire diocese will be visited at least once every five years (Can. 343, par. 1). If the diocese is too large, the Ordinary may request the help of the Vicar General or another suitable priest. If the Ordinary neglects the visitation of his diocese, the Metropolitan shall report the fact to the Holy See, which will see to it that the visitation is made or ask the Metropolitan to do so (Can. 274, nn. 4–5).

The visitation extends to all those things which fall under the supervision of the Ordinary. The Ordinary must act in a paternal manner regarding the object and scope of the visitation. Decrees and precepts concerning the aim and scope of the visit are always executive; that is, they are effective, not *in suspensivo*, but *in devolutivo* (Can. 345).

The visitation of the Ordinary applies to all persons, things, and religious institutions within the boundaries of his diocese. One may be exempted from the visitation only by a special dispensation granted by the Apostolic See (Can. 344, par. 1). The Ordinary may visit exempt religious only in cases explicitly stated by the law (Can. 344, par. 2).

The Ordinary has the right to take two priests as companions on his visitation whom he selects freely (Can. 343, par. 2). Visitors may demand that the visited house take care of all living and travelling expenses for the Ordinary and his companions, unless contrary customs provide otherwise. No donation or other gifts shall be accepted by the Bishop or his companions, and the Bishop must keep all expenses down to the minimum (Can. 346). *Fel.*

VISITATION, RELIGIOUS. *See* Superior, Religious.

VISIT, EUCHARISTIC. *See* Adoration, Eucharistic.

VISITING. To go to see another out of charity, duty, affection, or respect is called visiting. The habit of visiting is so deeply rooted in our customs that it may become an obligation or *social duty*. Beyond these habits, certain other customs, such as exaggerated acts of respect, expressions of sympathy, affection, and gratitude are called *social etiquette*. More often than not, these expressions are more an insincere formalism than acts of charity, which they seem to have replaced.

Generally, visits may be classified as follows: (a) *visits* of duty, such as visits of felicitation, condolence, farewell, etc.; (b) visits *of friendship*, based on affection and gratitude; (c) visits *of charity*, which stem from an evangelical spirit, as visits to the sick, prisoners, etc.

While Catholic moral theology warmly endorses visits of charity, it urges vigilant prudence concerning the other two kinds of visits. A Christian must act in all circumstances of life in such a way that all his activities are governed by sound moral principles. Thus, in making a visit, one should ask himself: *an liceat,* that is, whether it is proper and useful; *an deceat*, that is, whether it will increase moral danger to oneself or constitute a serious scandal to others; *an expediat*, that is, whether it is made for purely natural and human reasons, to maintain a dangerous friendship or to satisfy a certain passion. The answer to these questions will determine whether or not such a visit is proper for a Christian to make.

The most frequent sins committed on the occasion of visits are slander and ridicule of the faults of others. This is certainly a dangerous occasion of sin. If games, amusements, dances and rather immodest or improper garb are added to idle, uncharitable, and slanderous conversation, such visits cannot be justified as a social duty; in fact, they are contrary to other grave obligations and detrimental to faith and morals. If visits become a routine diversion as part of elegant living, unproductive of any thought or deed of charity or goodness, much of man's spiritual treasure can be gradually lost. All visits afford an opportunity for the practice of virtues such as control of the tongue and general conduct, a truthfulness and Christian affability which is always a source of joy and serenity, and agreeableness and modesty in words and action. For visits between betrothed, *see* Engagement. *Tar.*

VISIT, PREMARITAL. *See* Examination, Premarital.

VITANDUS (Excommunicated). Excommunication (*q.v.*), also called anathema, is related to the Jewish concept of *herem*, which, originally, was a declaration in which accursed individuals or people were ordered to be exterminated in honor of God (Lev. 27:29). At times, it referred to those who were thus punished. The Jews substituted for the death penalty, required by the *herem*, loss of property and exclusion from the society of the faithful. This concept of synagogal excommunication first came into use at the time of Esdra (10:8). The Jews of the Dispersion continued to apply it even to the present, against Spinoza.

Canon Law fixed the meaning of excommunication as a separation from the external communion of the faithful and the prayers and indulgences of the Church, and inflicted it as a medicinal punishment.

In medieval public law, when participation in the life of the Church affected the civil and political capacities of an individual, excommunication amounted to a form of exile from ordinary society and expulsion from offices and dignities. An excommunicated individual was equivalent to *friedlos*, or an outlaw.

At the dawn of the modern era, after the confused and agitated period culminating in the Western Schism, when excommunications became frequent, the difficulties caused by the large numbers under this severe penalty suggested mitigations aimed at the elimination of embarrassments to people living in society. Martin V at the Council of Constance initiated the work of conciliation. From that time, the full effect of excommunication, which consisted in severing the punished individual from Christian communion, was in force only if the excommunicated was declared *vitandus* (a person to be shunned). According to the text of the constitution *Ad evitanda* (1418), which prevailed in practice, there was a twofold excommunication: one inflicted on a *notorious attacker* of a cleric, and one applied to a person *expressly identified by his own name* in the sentence issued by the Holy See or the Ordinary. All other excommunicated were to be considered as *tolerated*; all civil relations and, to a certain point, all religious relations were not forbidden with them.

The Code of Canon Law brought important revisions and clarifications to this subject. It still distinguished the "tolerated" from *"vitandi"* but it greatly limited the classification of the latter, which it reserved to the judgment of the Holy See. In other words, no one is now to be regarded *vitandus* unless excommunicated by name by the Holy See and so declared in the decree or sentence of excommunication. The only exception is the crime of violation of the privilege of the canon (see Clerics, Privileges of), committed against the person of the Sovereign Pontiff. In this case, the guilty individual becomes automatically (ipso facto) excommunicatus vitandus (cf. Canon 2258, par. 2; and 2343, par. 1, n. 1).

Even in this case, the offender is not vitandus unless he was aware of the fact that this penalty was attached to his crime. According to the present law, a vitandus is deprived of passive assistance at divine services (Can. 2259, par. 2), of all dignity, office, benefice, pension or ecclesiastical appointment whatever (Can. 2266). Holy Mass may be offered only for his conversion (Can. 2262, par. 2, n. 2). His company must be shunned even in secular relations except for a just and reasonable cause (Can. 2267). Persons who extend any help or assistance to an excommunicatus vitandus in the commission of the crime to which this penalty is attached, and clerics who knowingly and of their own accord participate with him in divine services or admit him to divine services, automatically (ipso facto) incur excommunication reserved simply to the Holy See (Can. 2338, par. 2). An excommunicatus vitandus in danger of death (Can. 882), with the necessary dispositions, may be absolved, although the obligation remains to have recourse to the Holy See in the usual manner if death did not occur (Can. 2252; see Censure).

Before the sentence or decree of excommunication, an excommunicatus vitandus is not deprived of jurisdiction (Can. 2264); ordinarily, however, removal from office accompanies the declaration of excommunication (Can. 2266). He must be deprived of jurisdiction in the internal forum since he is excluded from divine offices (Can. 2259, par. 2). The divine offices are the functions of the power of order related to divine worship (Can. 2256, n. 1). No excommunicatus vitandus has the right to be present at divine services, except preaching (Can. 2259, par. 1). Furthermore, the presence of a vitandus may not even be tolerated. He must be expelled; if he cannot be expelled, the service must be suspended (Can. 2259, par. 2), unless it can be continued without serious difficulty. Quite obviously, the vitandus is hindered from any active participation in divine services (Can. 2259, par. 2).

Concerning the means of sanctification, a vitandus is excluded from the reception of the sacraments and sacramentals; he must be expelled from the church when he is recognized (Cans. 2260, par. 1; 2232, par. 1; 731, par. 2; 850, par. 1). An excommunicatus vitandus does not share in indulgences (Cans. 2262, par. 1; 925, par. 1). He is deprived of any participation in the public prayer of the Church, except the prayer which the Church publicly makes for him on Good Friday, but one may always pray privately for his conversion. Futhermore, he is deprived of ecclesiastical burial (Can. 1240, par. 1, n. 6); if buried in a consecrated cemetery, this is considered violated and cannot be reconciled until his body is removed (Cans. 1172, par. 1, n. 4; 1175). Any person who presumes to force the ecclesiastical burial of a vitandus incurs a non-reserved excommunication (Can. 1240, par. 1); one who of his own accord gives him ecclesiastical burial incurs the penalty of interdict from entering a church reserved to the Ordinary (Can. 2239). After a declaratory sentence, a vitandus remains deprived of any office, dignity, or position he may have held as well as any ecclesiastical pension (Can. 2266); he invalidly appoints or elects (Can. 2265, par. 2); if he is knowingly elected to office, the election itself is invalid (Can. 167, par. 1, n. 3 and par. 2).

He is not deprived of all privileges by excommunication itself, but by the loss of jurisdiction (Can. 2264). He cannot act in court, unless his spiritual welfare is involved. Yet he is permitted to institute a suit but is not admitted to the trial, where he must be represented by a procurator. He can personally institute a court action only to attack the lawfulness of his excommunication (Can. 1654, par. 1).

For his defense, the vitandus must act through his procurator. Excommunicati vitandi must avoid any communication with the faithful, unless there are grave reasons to justify it (Can. 2267).

On the other hand, the faithful, unless legitimately excused, must refrain from communicating in secular affairs with a *vitandus;* from this law are exempted the members of his family, spouse, children, servants, although the status of a *vitandus* is recognized as sufficient reason for conjugal separation and the rescinding of a work contract. However, the relations of dependence between subject and superior are not affected. *Pug.*

VIVISECTION. Vivisection originally indicated surgical experiment in general on the body of a living animal. Today, it is limited to experiment on a living animal for physiological or pathological study. Experiments conducted for other motives are classified as cruelty against animals. Vivisection performed on a living human body is always forbidden by the moral law. It is unlawful to operate on a human body except to save or to cure the body itself.

Today, many condemn vivisection on animals with the allegation that vivisection contributes little to medicine. If this were true, vivisection would be unlawful as a cruel abuse of animals. However, according to many reliable and competent men, vivisection is useful. Others condemn vivisection because it inflicts much suffering upon animals, although they admit that it is for the good of mankind. If vivisection is useful for man, it is not against the moral law, because animals were created for man. The moral law, however, forbids the infliction of more suffering than necessary, that is, without reason. This would be cruelty and, therefore, a sin, even if in itself only slight. For this reason, useless experiments which serve only to satisfy a vain, scientific curiosity should be avoided as well as experiments on living animals which could be conducted with the same result on dead animals. Local or total anesthesia should be used unless this hinders the success of the test; all care must be taken to limit suffering to the greatest possible

extent. Physicians and medical students must be educated to a sensibility and compassion. It is a praiseworthy thing for protectors of animals to oppose abuses committed in the practice of vivisection, but not totally to condemn it. Their action must be employed and praised, if used as restraint against abuses; exaggeration on their part would interfere with the welfare of mankind. *Ben.*

VOCATION (Religious, Ecclesiastical). Vocation, in a restricted sense, is a call by God and the Church to the priestly or religious state as a more perfect state in comparison with marriage. All are called to the pursuit of virtue and Christian perfection, but it is obvious that not all pursue it in the same manner. This concept is clearly expressed by St. Paul when he says that in an organized body there are many organs, each having its reason for existing, for each one has its own well-defined function. God's wisdom provides for all things by his various callings.

The Author of nature gives to his children tendencies and aspirations, aptitudes and propensities which are true vocations. One is inclined to a life of study, another to active life; one prefers arts, another science.

When we speak of religious or ecclesiastical vocations, we do not refer to a human profession in which allurements and propensities of nature are at work. We refer to very high offices concerned with God, Jesus Christ, the Church, and the Christian people. These demand a special vocation, which must come from God.

This special vocation may be *extraordinary* or *ordinary*. An extraordinary vocation is distinguished from an ordinary one by particular, external signs which manifest by their extraordinary and sometimes miraculous characteristics a call from God, as the vocation of St. Paul.

Here we shall consider only the ordinary vocation as it customarily occurs. It is common doctrine that the objective elements by which an individual may be considered called to the more perfect state are: (a) aptitude and (b) right intention. Aptitude may be either negative, the absence of impediments; or positive, the possession of the required qualities and talents. A judgment of the presence of these qualifications is made by the bishop or the religious superior in the external forum.

Two calls are needed: one, by God, in virtue of the grace of Jesus Christ; the other, by the Church upon certification by the superior, directed to prove the good character of the candidate. The first may be called divine; the second, a selection by the bishop or superior, is termed human.

The historical evolution of the doctrine on vocation leads us, first of all, to examine the sources of Revelation.

Strictly dogmatic, Scriptural texts are rare, but numerous facts and the expressions of the fact of this vocation can be proved (Heb. 5:4; 10:4).

While on the banks of the Sea of Tiberias, Jesus called fishermen and boatmen and said to them: "Come, and I will make you fishers of men" (Matt. 4:19). The Gospel insists on this exclusive right of Jesus Christ to the calling (Matt. 3:13; John 12:16; Acts 1:4; 2:15; 24). The Church has always recognized and respected this right of God to choose His own apostles. If God selects His priests, no one should ask for or accept the priesthood without a divine calling. Studying the long period of elaboration of Scriptural texts during the centuries which preceded the Council of Trent, spiritual directors have reached the following conclusions: (a) A distinction must be made between *interior* and *exterior* vocations; (b) interior vocation, understood at first as an upright intention, is understood more as an invitation from God to the priesthood; (c) exterior vocation is a communication by the Church, as it were, of a divine calling to the priesthood.

The first systematic analysis of vocation to prove its divine origin in this period was made by St. Thomas, who treated this subject on the occasion of his dispute with William of Saint

Amour, who conducted a violent campaign against religious orders, especially the mendicant orders. God, according to St. Thomas, speaks to the soul not only exteriorly (*vel verbo vel scripturis*) but also internally. This interior address is of greater importance than the exterior word, whose efficacy depends on the interior word.

The doctrine of St. Thomas was elaborated in a particular manner in the post-Tridentine period by St. Ignatius, St. Alphonsus, and their commentators. Of particular importance in this literature on vocation in recent times are two works by Canon Lahitton which place a greater emphasis on the exterior element of vocation. These works were actually a reaction against those who insisted too much on the interior element of vocation.

Lahitton first taught that the divine calling was only and exclusively the call by the Bishop (*De la vocation sacerdotale*, Paris 1896). In a second book (*La vocation du sacerdoce*, Paris, 1911) he corrected this extreme theory.

Father Hurtaud, among others, reacted against Father Lahitton's thesis by stating that when God chooses a soul for a mission, He prepares it and renders it fit for the duties to which He calls it. The dispositions on which the judgment by lawful authority is based regarding the aptitude of the subject constitute the divine calling. Yet, the existence of these dispositions does not give any right to ordination, because the Bishop is the only judge of these interior callings. In view of the doctrinal content, the controversy drew the attention of Rome. A committee of cardinals was appointed to study the question, which resulted in a commendation of the second book of Canon Lahitton.

RECENT PAPAL TEACHINGS. The following documents by recent Popes have made a great contribution to the question of the nature of vocation: the Apostolic Letter *Maximum Illud*, of Benedict XV, November 30, 1919; the Apostolic Letter *Officiorum Omnium*, of Pius XI, August 10, 1922, addressed to the Cardinal Prefect of the Sacred Congregation of Seminaries and Studies; the Encyclical *Mens Nostra,* of Pius XI, December 20, 1929, concerning the Spiritual Exercises; and the Instruction issued by the Sacred Congregation of the Sacraments on December 20, 1930.

The teachings of Pius XII on this subject are contained in papal documents as well as in his admirable addresses: particularly the address directed to the students of seminaries and institutes of Rome, on June 24, 1939; the letter for the third centenary of the Society of St. Sulpice, February 28, 1942; the letter to the Cardinals and Archbishops of Spain, May 5, 1942; the apostolic exhortation *Menti Nostrae,* September 2, 1950; and the Encyclical *Sacra Virginitas,* March 25, 1954.

Pius XII recalled that the interior vocation is an inspiration or impulse of the Holy Spirit, a secret voice of God which produces the intimate conviction in the soul that one is called by God. It is well to observe that the call by the Bishop without the interior vocation, would make ordination valid but unlawful; on the other hand, without the external call by the Bishop to the priesthood, the interior vocation is neither authentic nor operative.

A vocation in the comprehensive meaning of the term is both interior and exterior (*vocans intus et extra*). Thus, it can be concluded that both exterior and interior callings necessarily belong to the essence of the religious and ecclesiastical vocation.

The most recent ecclesiastical documents permit us to determine the sense in which the book of Canon Lahitton was declared *egregie laudandum* by the cardinals' committee, appointed by St. Pius X. By such declaration the following were excluded: (a) any right to priestly ordination prior to the free acceptance of the candidate by the Bishop; (b) the need of a perceptible inspiration of the Holy Ghost (*attrait*).

OBLIGATORY NATURE. It is disputed whether a rejection of the special and personal grace of vocation implies, of itself, and therefore always, moral guilt. The question, as a whole, is still unset-

tled. There are strong reasons in favor of an affirmative answer, that one cannot reject a clear divine vocation without moral guilt, whose gravity is to be assessed in each individual. Reasons may be found for a negative reply, namely, that there is no obligation to accept and follow a vocation. In practice, in virtue of the authority of those teaching this more liberal thesis, sin is certainly to be excluded, since this position, which makes an obligation at least doubtful, renders that obligation morally and juridically non-existent in practice.

All admit: (a) that the counsel of itself is not binding; (b) that in a particular case this counsel might involve a grave obligation to follow a vocation as practically the sole means of salvation; (c) that it is possible to sin accidentally through contempt or other circumstances by not following a vocation; (d) that no reprobation or certainty of damnation is to be feared in the failure to follow a vocation.

CARE OF VOCATION. The Church endeavors to promote the rise and development of vocations. She imposes a duty on priests, especially parish priests, to promote, select, and cultivate vocations (Can. 1353). Furthermore, she urges all the faithful, according to their own abilities, to exert great effort in fostering vocations to the priesthood.

Although it is the particular concern of priests to foster vocations, the problem ought to interest all the faithful because it is a problem of the Church. In this regard, Pius XII denounced in his Encyclical *Sacra Virginitas,* March 25, 1954, a modern error: "Some keep young men away from seminaries and young women from religious orders under the pretext that the Church needs more the practice of Christian virtues by the faithful, united in marriage and living in the midst of other people, than by priests and virgins who live apart from society by reason of the vow of chastity."

In the Encyclical *Menti Nostrae,* the Pope had exhorted the people to dispel widespread prejudice against the priestly state. Such an attitude, even if inspired by the sincerest good faith, is certainly contrary to the function of the hierarchy willed and constituted by Christ as "salt of the earth and light of the world" (Matt. 5:13); it fails to heed the anxiety shown by Christ Himself (*Messis quidem multa, operarii autem pauci. Rogate ergo dominum messis ut mittat operarios in messem suam.* Matt. 5:37–38), often repeated by the Sovereign Pontiffs through the centuries, including Pius XI and XII ("The number of priests has become inadequate for the ever-increasing needs": *Menti nostrae*, n. 23). This is included in the Code of the Church.

When the cares of the Church increase in the face of the obvious statistics pointing to a continuous decline in the number of vocations, it becomes irrational behavior on the part of those Catholics who endeavor to dissuade or, worse yet, to oppose good candidates from following a vocation to the priesthood or to religious life. *Pal.*

VOICES, INTERNAL. *See* Hallucination.

VOLUBILITY. *See* Psychopathy.

VOLUNTARY ACTS. A voluntary act is an act or the effect of an act which proceeds directly from a free will operating under the light of rational knowledge. In the conceptual order, it differs from the thing *willed*, which is the object of an act of the will. This object of the act does not proceed necessarily from the will.

Since the activity of man's will contains necessary elements (*see* Will), human acts may be distinguished into *necessary* voluntary acts and *free* voluntary acts. To necessary voluntary acts belongs a general, formal tendency to good or happiness, which is the basis of every human volition; to free voluntary acts belong the specific and concrete elements by which the will pursues a definite and particular good. We treat here of free voluntary acts.

Voluntariness admits of certain degrees: it is *perfect* if the subject knows clearly what he seeks and seeks this with full freedom and consent; it is *imperfect*, if the subject lacks either clarity of knowledge, freedom, or fullness of consent.

One must not confuse this imperfection of the will with a reluctance that the will feels and must overcome to reach a decision. Victory over reluctance is generally a sign of great strength of will, despite the fact that one is said to act against his will in such cases. This, in truth, is precisely an indication that the will acts against other tendencies and overcomes their opposition. We consider, for example, the action of a mother who inflicts punishment upon her child although she prefers to spare him all suffering. In this case an entirely voluntary act is joined to an element of reluctance; for this reason, some theologians refer to this as a conditionally involuntary act, because of the ineffective conditioned involuntariness.

One may cause an act in a *positive* or *negative* manner; this depends on whether or not the causality is exerted by an action or by an omission.

A voluntary act may be *actually* or *virtually* voluntary. The act of the will is always an *actually* voluntary act; the distinction, therefore, applies only to what occurs apart from the will but under its command. An *actually* voluntary act is directly accompanied and caused by an act of the will; for example, to wound an enemy with full knowledge of the effect. A *virtually* voluntary act is not accompanied but caused by a preceding act of the will which endures in its effectiveness.

To these a third type is generally added: the *habitually* voluntary act. This consists of an act in conformity with the will but which the will neither accompanies nor causes. Thus, it becomes difficult to bestow moral value upon such an action insofar as voluntary causality is lacking; the act resembles a voluntary-involuntary act which is not imputable to the agent. Moral theologians do not have recourse to this type of voluntary act except in matters concerning the sacraments, which involve, not the morality of an act, but the validity of the rite involved.

The terms *express, silent, presumed,* and *interpretative* voluntary act do not apply to the voluntary act as such, but to its manifestation and social effects. They are more important in the juridical than in the moral order. It suffices to note that a presumed and interpretative voluntary act can be a non-existent act (*see* Voluntary in Cause). *Gra.*

VOLUNTARY IN CAUSE (Indirect voluntary). To a direct voluntary act (*voluntarium in se*) is opposed the indirect voluntary act (*voluntarium in causa*). The direct voluntary act is an act willed in itself; an indirect voluntary act is not willed in itself but performed with knowledge that a certain effect will follow because of an inseparable connection with the act, although one may not will this effect in itself. A direct voluntary act proceeds directly from the subject; an indirect voluntary act proceeds from the subject but through a direct voluntary act.

The indirect voluntary occurs in two ways: by a positive action or by an omission by the subject. In the first case, it is termed *positive;* in the second, *negative.*

An indirect voluntary act is or can be imputed to the subject. The existence and degree of this imputability create a difficult problem concerning sinful matters. The imputability of an act is easily understood if the will explicitly seeks and desires sin; for in such a case, we have a direct voluntary act, even though its effect may be physically remote. In this connection, at times a person may labor under the illusion of not willing a definite effect to follow from his act, when in reality he does. This happens especially in questions relating to impurity or hatred of one's neighbor.

Concerning a real, indirect voluntary act, the rules for the principle of the double effect apply (*see* Effect, Double). Frequent cases of indirect guilt occur in culpable ignorance, a voluntarily acquired habit, under the influence of voluntary passion, in the state of drunkenness, or in any condition in which one loses control over his actions culpably (*see* Subconscious). *Gra.*

VORONOFF (Method of). *See* Endocrinology, Transplantation of Organs.

VOTE, ACTIVE AND PASSIVE. The juridical term *active and passive vote* is a right of the members of a society to cast their vote on subjects concerning the society itself, particularly the right to elect or be elected to office. Such a right belongs, under certain conditions, to members of ecclesiastical legal persons such as chapters, councils, etc. But it has special importance in religious orders and congregations. The general practice of a vote originated with cenobitic life; it was fully developed in Benedictine monasticism, in which the monks were given the right to elect their own Abbot (*Rules of Monasteries,* Chapter LXIV), who then was confirmed by a bishop or the pope.

The exercise of this right was made subject to certain conditions; it could also be taken away as a form of punishment. Accordingly, the right of active and passive vote was adopted by all religious orders, with a gradual, increasing importance and juridical precision until it acquired a character all of its own. In present day legislation the exercise and determination of the general right of active and passive vote in the religious chapters is considered, at least insofar as exempt religious are concerned, as belonging to the Holy See but granted through the provisions of Canon Law and the constitutions. The Code grants the general right of active and passive vote only to professed religious of perpetual vows, unless the constitutions explicitly give it also to temporarily professed religious (Can. 578).

In the general law and constitutions of each religious group, the actual exercise of active and passive right is made subject to numerous other conditions, such as age, priesthood, etc., according to the respective statutes (*see* Superior, Religious). A religious as well as any member of a legal entity can be deprived of the right of active and passive vote as a penalty for a crime or violation committed.

The following must *be deprived* of active and passive vote by judicial sentence: (a) a religious who conspired against the Roman Pontiff, a Pontifical Legate, or his own Ordinary (Can. 233, par. 2); (b) a religious who directly co-operated in the formulation of laws harmful to the rights of the Church, or impeded the exercise of jurisdiction by the Church in having recourse to civil authority (Cans. 2334, n. 2; 2336, par. 1); (c) a religious who becomes a member of a Masonic or similar sect condemned by the Church (Cans. 2335, 2336, par. 1); (d) a religious who introduced women of any age into a papal enclosure of a religious order (Can. 2342, n. 2); (e) a religious who falsified letters, decrees, or rescripts of the Holy See, or served them while aware of their falsity (Can. 2360, par. 2); (f) a religious who committed the crime of solicitation in confession (Can. 2368, par. 1); (g) a religious who violated community life in a serious manner, and failed to make amend after being duly admonished (Can. 2389).

The following *are deprived* automatically (*ipso facto*) of active and passive vote: (a) religious who apostatized from a religious order, although he (she), afterwards, returned (Can. 2384); (b) electors who sought the unlawful intrusion of laymen in elections reserved to religious (Can. 2390); (c) an electoral college of religious who willfully elected an unworthy person (Can. 2391, par. 1); (d) religious who committed a crime of simony in granting offices, benefices, or dignities (Can. 2392, n. 2); (e) religious with the right to vote who did not request confirmation of an elected superior by lawful ecclesiastical authority, if required to do so (Can. 2393); (f) chapters, monasteries, and all religious who received one presented or appointed to some office without waiting for letters of confirmation from competent ecclesiastical authority (Can. 2394, n. 3); (g) a secularized religious (Can. 640, par. 1, n. 1); (h) religious electors who did not file an application of postulation for an elected superior within the prescribed time (Can. 181, par. 2).

The following may not exercise the right of active and passive vote: (a) religious incapable of performing human acts (Can. 167, par. 1, n. 1); (b) religious who incur a censure or infamy of law after a judiciary sentence (*see* Infamy of Law, Fact); (c) religious who are guilty of the following crimes with their penalties: a disqualification from performing lawful ecclesiastical acts with a declaratory sentence to be issued for such crimes as: perjury in trials (Can. 1743, par. 3), suspicion of heresy (Can. 2315), attempted suicide (Can. 2350, par. 2), attempted mixed marriage (Can. 2375). A disqualification from exercising the right of vote may be incurred automatically (*latae sententiae*) for the following crimes: detention of an unwilling female with the intention of forcing marriage or committing a libidinous act; the detention of a minor female, even with her consent, but against the will of parents or relatives (guardian) for the same purposes (Can. 2353); a layman who once was condemned for murder, rape of children, usury, theft, etc. (Can. 2354).

No right of active or passive voice belongs to cardinals or bishops, even titular, who renounce their office and enter a religious community, unless permission to vote has been acquired from the Holy See; religious living in the world through an indult of exclaustration are deprived of the exercise of voice for the duration of the indult (Can. 639–640).

One may be deprived of the right of active and passive vote by particular law of a religious group, provided that this is done because of a grave sin committed and proven as such in a regular or at least administrative process.

It is, furthermore, quite certain that the major superior of a religious group has the right to punish by the privation of voice a religious guilty of any grave violation or sin (Cans. 2291, 2298). *Mand.*

VOTE. See Elections, Administration, Civil, Political.

VOTERS OF SIGNATURE. See Prelate; Signatura, Apostolic.

VOW (Act of Religion). A vow is a promise made to God with sufficient knowledge and freedom, of a thing that is good, possible, and better than its opposite (Can. 1302). The primary element of a vow is a true promise, that is, an act by which a person assumes a real obligation to do or omit something. A mere resolution or other act lacking sincere intent of binding oneself, despite a customary use of the word *vow*, is not a vow. The will or intent to assume an obligation is necessary. However, in itself, the will to fulfill a promise is not the essential element. A vow can exist without a determination to fulfill it. A vow is always made to God. A promise made to God in honor of the Blessed Virgin Mary or other saints is a vow. We sometimes speak of a vow made in honor of our Lady or a saint. This is less precise language. The sense of the word is clear. A promise made exclusively to Mary would not be a vow but a sacred promise of a different type. The object of a vow must consist of a *higher good*, that is, the object must be a good thing better than its opposite, for otherwise the vow would not be pleasing to God. The object of vow could be fasting, prayer, a pilgrimage, an offering, preservation of virginity by abstention from marriage inasmuch as celibacy is a means of greater perfection and, therefore, better than its opposite or conjugal life. The circumstances of a concrete case can make an act more or less suitable for vow. Thus, a long pilgrimage is not a greater good for a mother who has the duty of rearing and taking care of her children.

The primary value of a vow is as an act of religion which honors God. It renders the actions with which it is carried out good and meritorious under a double aspect, for it adds to their intrinsic goodness the value of an act of religion. In addition, the vow to perform a definite act for a long time or for life is most helpful in making the will firm and constant in acts of goodness and virtue. Holy Scripture praises the vow; in Christian Tradition it has always been held in great esteem, for ecclesiastical authority has always defended its moral value against all opponents, e.g., the Council of Trent (1545–1563) in its decrees against Protestantism.

The objection that a vow deprives a person of his freedom does not prove anything against its value and usefulness. A vow does not destroy a person's *physical* freedom, which is the root of merit. The fulfillment of a vow is an act of free will; in other words, man retains his power to violate a vow. A vow takes away a person's *moral* freedom in the same way that an act productive of a moral obligation, as a contract, a command, or a promise removes freedom. It is not a lessening of freedom, because the binding moral force stems from the person's *own will*. It is freedom exercised in a particular manner, not a lack of freedom.

The vow is *public*, if accepted in the name of God by the ecclesiastical superiors, and creates not only moral obligations but also juridical effects in the public and social life of the Church. Public vows are those of religious. Religious vows are variously subdivided (*see* Vow, Religious). A private vow is not public in the sense described above, even if made and recognized publicly.

The following elements are required on the part of the subject who takes a solemn promise as a vow: judgment and reflection on the importance of the vow, certain moderation, the intention to carry it out for a longer period of time than one day. If the obligation is grave or of long duration, e.g., a lifetime, prudence suggests that the counsel of the confessor or of some competent and prudent person be sought.

Concerning the object of the vow, it is unlawful to vow to dispose of an article which one does not freely possess, for this would contradict the rights of another. Frequently a vow requires the permission of a superior in advance, if the act intended cannot lawfully be performed without this permission.

The obligation created by a vow is a *special* obligation. Failure to fulfill a vow is a particular species of sin against the virtue of religion. It can happen that the action by which one breaks a vow is at the same time contrary to other moral obligations. In such a case, two or more sins are committed by the same act, namely, the breach of the vow or a sacrilege and the sin against justice, chastity, or other virtue.

The obligation to fulfill a vow is, of itself, *grave*, but may be slight if it deals with a thing of small importance. Thus, to leave undone a small portion of a thing promised to God is, indeed, a sin, but not mortal, unless it is done with a contempt of the vow itself. Furthermore, if the individual making a vow has the precise intention of assuming only a *light* obligation, which is possible only in a private vow, then, the obligation is in fact slight and binding only under venial sin despite the fact that, perhaps, the object consists of an important thing. In order to determine a grave sin in the transgression of a vow, the same rules usually apply as in the transgression of the moral law.

The obligation arising from a *public* vow may be terminated only by a dispensation which is always reserved to the Holy See. The obligations arising from a *private* vow may cease either by extrinsic or intrinsic causes. *Extrinsic causes* are created by the action of persons who remove the obligation. This may be done in three ways: (a) By *dispensation*. With the exception of the vow of perfect and perpetual chastity, taken unconditionally after the eighteenth year of age, or the vow of entering a religious order, dispensation from either of which is reserved to the Sovereign Pontiff, the Sovereign Pontiff for all the faithful and Ordinaries for their subjects can dispense from any private vow. Some confessors have faculties concerning dispensation and commutation of the vow, both by virtue of general privileges for religious or by personal delegation. (b) By *commutation*, namely, substituting for the thing promised another act or thing. Those with power to dispense can also commute a vow. If commutation involves substitution with an equal or better action, the individual himself who made the vow can commute a vow, except the two vows reserved to the Sovereign Pontiff. (c) By *annulment*, by a person who has authority over or ownership of the object of the vow. Thus a father can annul a vow made by his minor son without paternal consent to undertake an expensive pilgrimage. Dispensation and commutation of a vow are unlawful, unless there is a sufficient motive. The Sovereign Pontiff, as Vicar of Christ, has the authority to dispense from all vows and to grant this faculty of dispensation to others.

The obligation of a vow terminates by *intrinsic causes* if the essential elements have changed so that the fulfillment of the vow is either harmful or morally impossible or interferes with a greater good. In other words, if the situation is so changed that the vow is inadvisable or even unlawful to carry out in these new circumstances. If the difficulties are only temporary, the obligation is not removed but suspended, so that the vow again binds in force, as soon as the impediments have ceased and its fulfillment has become possible once more. *Ben.*

VOW (Prohibitive impediment). A prohibitive impediment renders a marriage unlawful (illicit) but not invalid. The following constitute a prohibitive impediment to marriage: a vow of virginity by a lay person or one in a religious community; the vow of perfect chastity; the vow of celibacy; the vow to receive Holy Orders; the vow to embrace the religious life (Can. 1058).

A vow, freely and knowingly made and subsequently neither annulled nor commuted by a lawful superior or authority, creates the impediment of vow (Cans. 1311, 1312). By way of exception, the vow of perpetual chastity, pronounced after the completion of the novitiate in the Society of Jesus creates an invalidating impediment (Can. 1073; Bull *Ascendente Domino*, May 25, 1584). The Holy See has, furthermore, reserved to itself any dispensation from the vow of perfect and perpetual chastity, and the vow of entering a religious order with solemn vows, if either was made in an absolute manner (without conditions) after the eighteenth year of age (Can. 1309).

The power of granting dispensations

belongs to the Holy See and is exercised through different Congregations according to each particular case or person. If a religious man or woman requests permission to return to the lay state and to contract marriage, the Sacred Congregation of Religious has the right to grant such a dispensation. If a lay person desires a dispensation from vows which occasion an impediment to marriage, the Sacred Congregation of the Sacraments possesses the power of dispensing. In questions concerning the internal, sacramental forum, the dispensation is acquired through the Apostolic Penitentiary. In cases not reserved to the Holy See, dispensation may be bestowed either by one's own Ordinary or a priest who has obtained from the Holy See the faculty to dispense, provided that the interests of a third party are not thereby infringed upon.

Sometimes the vow terminates by itself, if the vow is temporary, conditional, or the motivating cause of the vow actually ceases to exist.

Members of religious orders, recognized as such by the Church, who have pronounced solemn vows cannot contract a valid marriage; likewise, by special law of the Holy See, certain simple vows have the effect of rendering any attempted marriage null and void. The Sacred Congregation of Religious has the right to grant the necessary dispensation for such a marriage, except to a priest who is a member of the religious order. *Ben.*

VOW, RELIGIOUS. All religious vows are deliberate, free, and public promises made to God and accepted by the lawful religious superiors in the name of the Church, by which promises a person binds himself in the virtue of religion to observe perfect chastity, evangelical poverty, and obedience toward superiors according to the constitutions of the religious institute as approved by the Catholic Church (Cans. 1303, 487, 488). The religious vows are a necessary foundation of the religious state, for this state, essentially a constant striving for perfection, is juridically established by the public promises of the evangelical counsels of poverty, chastity, and obedience. The religious vow, as such, becomes not only an interior act of dedication to God but also a juridical act which presupposes and requires the intervention of the Church. By such intervention, the Church accepts in the name of God the promises made and attaches to them certain specific juridical effects. The first is that the one who pronounces the vows enter the religious, canonical state so that the ideal of perfection is no longer a passing act of fervor but a habitual and binding obligation to the observance of the vows made.

Religious vows must be public, i.e., accepted by a lawful superior in the name of the Church. According to present law (Can. 488), religious vows in the proper sense are all public promises accepted by superiors of a religious community whether of papal or diocesan right, an order or a congregation, exempt or non-exempt, with papal cloister or not (*see* Order, Religious).

Today's juridical concept of religious vow is the fruit of a slow process of evolution. From the beginning, the Church intervened in directing the religious efforts of her children toward perfection by the words and example of Jesus Christ. First of all, it distinguished those who obliged themselves in conscience to observe the evangelical counsels from those who publicly professed the same evangelical counsels before God's ministers. The promises of public profession implied specific juridical effects. The Church determined the necessary conditions for this profession. The juridical elements of public vows acquired increasingly greater consistency among cenobites, monks, canons regular and mendicant friars, so that the principle was codified in the *Decretals* according to which only solemn vows were considered as the vows of religious. Henceforth, this was the only type of public vow recognized as capable of admitting a candidate into the canonical religious state (III, 15, I in VI). The vows involved renunciation of the inherent dominion over property and even capacity of ownership; the right to a valid marriage, attempted against the vow of chastity; and the obligation of choir and papal enclosure. Religious institutes, properly so-called, had but one name, *Orders*, because only in these were solemn or religious vows taken. The Society of Jesus (Jesuits) in the sixteenth century brought about a revision of the concept of religious vow, by permitting a religious, in the proper sense of the word, to retain basic dominion over his own property and the capacity of ownership, while binding himself not to use his temporal goods nor to administer them freely; to promise perfect chastity yet not rendering invalid a marriage contracted by a grave sin against the vow; and to promise obedience without the obligation of choir or enclosure. Such an individual, they said, could be termed a religious in the proper sense, because he truly practiced the evangelical counsels. If his promises and vows were, then, accepted by the superiors of an approved religious society in the name of the Church, he could be called a true and proper religious. After endless discussions, especially in the University of Salamanca, Gregory XIII in his constitution *Ascendente Domino*, March 25, 1584, stated that the vows of the scholastics of the Society of Jesus were to be regarded as true religious vows, that they were true religious though with simple vows, in the sense that they retained a basic capacity of ownership, their marriage was not invalid, they had no choir, etc.

The principle was still opposed, but afterwards was accepted and widely practiced in *congregations* of simple vows which arose in the eighteenth and nineteenth centuries. Religious vows are: (a) *Solemn* or *simple*; the difference between the two is in the juridical effects which the Church attaches to solemn vows. The main juridical effects are that the solemn vow of poverty takes away the capacity of ownership; in a simple vow, the free administration and use of goods is inhibited; the solemn vow of chastity renders invalid a marriage attempted in defiance of it, while the simple vow renders it merely an unlawful marriage

unless the obligation of sacred orders is involved in it; the vow of obedience, however, has practically the same effects whether the vow is solemn or simple. (b) *Temporary* or *perpetual* (*see* Profession, Religious). (c) *Juridical* and *non-juridical* or private; juridical vows are received or defended by the Church in the external forum, while non-juridical vows belong strictly to the internal forum of conscience. Thus, vows, promises, or oaths of societies with community life, or of secular institutes, although they are not real religious vows in the canonical sense, must be considered as *juridical* and not *simply private* vows because they are, in fact, protected by the Church as if they were religious vows (*see* Religious).

The matter and extent of moral obligations derived from the vows are well delineated in the Code of Canon Law and the constitutions of the individual religious groups. By the *vow of obedience* the religious is required to obey lawful superiors in everything they command according to the constitutions and specific rules of the religious order (Cans. 593, 501). The proximate matter of this vow, that is, the specific obligation to which the religious publicly obliges himself, is the formal precepts of his superiors. By the *vow of chastity* the religious binds himself by the virtue of religion not to contract marriage and to abstain from any act contrary to perfect chastity, external and internal. There is no distinction in this field between the matter of the vow and that imposed by the sixth and ninth commandments. That which these commandments forbid under penalty of sin, the vow of chastity forbids to the religious also by the virtue of religion, so that any sin against either commandment always implies double malice for him. By the *vow of poverty*, in general, the religious binds himself to refrain from any purchase or sale without permission of his superiors. Thus, no religious is permitted money to spend freely; the proceeds from his work become the property of the religious institute to which he belongs (Can. 594, par.

2); the religious institute is bound to provide for members the necessities of life, but always according to the spirit of poverty. As stated above, the solemn vow of poverty deprives the professed religious also of the right and capacity of ownership, while the simple vow forbids merely free administration and use of one's own property. Individual constitutions, of course, may have stricter provisions, for the Code specifies only the extremes concerning the simple vow (Cans. 569, par. 1; 581; 583).

Although the three religious vows have a juridical limitation, they do not exclude, but, in fact, imply an obligation for the religious to strive for the acquisition of the respective virtues of poverty, chastity, and obedience in an ever-increasing degree.

As public vows, the religious vows cannot be dispensed but by the Holy See (Can. 1308), except in the cases where the Code itself dispenses from them either by *dismissal* or *secularization* (*q.v.*). *Mand.*

WAGE, LIVING. A living wage is the compensation given to a worker; it may be based on family responsibilities. A living wage may be: (a) *Absolute.* According to a criterion, based on an average wage for family living, in which all workers who perform identical tasks receive the same pay, no matter whether they are married with children, married without children, or single. (b) *Relative.* According to a criterion fixed by the concrete family status and responsibilities of each worker, in which pay varies according to marital status and the number of dependents to be supported.

In the last century, when the economic world was ruled by an individualistic concept, the family wage was considered almost an absurdity. The reason was that human labor was considered like any other merchandise, subject to the law of supply and demand. According to this law, two identical economic goods are equally priced on the same market. It was inconceivable that a worker's wage should change according to his changing responsibilities, for, after all, was not a worker's wage the price of labor, and the productive capacity of laborers about the same? Nowadays, however, it is commonly held that a living wage is demanded by the moral law, and that failure to abide by such a principle will inevitably cause serious consequences upon the world's economy. Economic goods, in fact, are by their very nature directed to satisfy the needs of all human beings. The greater number of men, however, have no other means of providing a reasonable sustenance for their families except the earning from their labor; and such earnings must be on the basis of family responsibilities.

This doctrine is confirmed by the fact that if the workers do not receive a living wage the very structure of the family is weakened and its mission greatly hindered. In fact, the children are, then, prematurely compelled to seek work harmful to their health and moral formation; mothers likewise are faced with the necessity of work, with irreparable harm to the well-being of the family, and with harmful results for the economic and social order. The necessity of a living wage is fully justified on the basis of common sense and the common good of society. It is still a debated matter, however, whether it should be computed according to an absolute or relative criterion. Generally speaking, it may be said that the former is followed in highly efficient economies, while it still seems a matter of necessity to adhere to the latter in economies which have not yet achieved a large degree of development. *Pav.*

WAITERS (Stewards). *See* Innkeepers, Servant.

WAR. A premise of war is that every right is coercible; thus a State has a right to use force if necessary to defend just rights or to exact reparation for the violation of rights by another State. Furthermore, since no supranational organization exists with the capacity of enforcing its just decisions, with acceptance by all nations, the right of coercibility can only be exercised directly by the aggrieved State itself.

In itself, war is not against the moral law; it may be an act of justice, as in the defense of law or the punishment of criminal acts. In concrete cases, however, a just war presupposes the presence of definite conditions.

Among theories concerning war, we

shall point out, first, the theory advocated by State totalitarianism, which stresses the necessity of war for the normal development of human life. The error of this theory is obvious, for war may be justified only as a last resort against the violation of a nation's just rights. Just as the violation of the rights of another nation is neither necessary nor unavoidable, so war is neither necessary nor unavoidable.

The theory of exaggerated pacifists, who consider war immoral under all conditions and insist that armies and armaments should be eliminated, is an erroneous belief. Of course, war should be eliminated from the face of the earth, but not before more appropriate and effective ways than the elimination of arms are found for settling disputes between nations. On the basis of the teachings of the Bible, Tradition, and the teaching authority of the Church, a Catholic may not hold that war, as such, is against the law of God and evil in itself. To understand properly the morality of war, one must consider it as an act of an individual or moral person. In this respect, war becomes an object of the moral law. In other words, the prerequisite condition for an act by a moral entity, such as a war against another State, is that the act be morally right.

Catholic doctrine regarding the morality of war is ancient and venerable; first proposed by St. Augustine, it was clearly elaborated by St. Thomas Aquinas. Thus war is morally licit: (a) if declared by a person who lawfully possesses supreme power in the State; (b) if it is not waged out of evil or personal motives, such as revenge, conquest, ambition, etc.; (c) if it is waged to protect one nation's rights against violation or, in the absence of an intention to make reparation, for a violation by another nation. The purpose of a just war is the preservation of justice and, consequently, of peace. Peace is not disturbed by the declaration of war but through the violation of rights in the juridical order, which actually makes a declaration of war necessary. Since war inflicts grave damage on all people involved and frequently on innocent parties, without a grave and extremely serious violation of rights war is not a licit means. The damage consequent on modern nuclear warfare renders the actual reasons for warfare much more serious than previously acceptable causes or motives. Parties engaged in warfare have a grave responsibility and obligation to reparation for damages suffered by their own subjects in a just war: soldiers killed or wounded, prisoners, families, cities and countries destroyed.

Some religious groups advocate the theory that war in itself is against the law of God ("Thou shalt not kill") and against the Gospel; others, including Catholics, declare that modern warfare can no longer be justified, not even as a means of defense against any violation of rights or goods. The Second World War has shown the enormous destruction of modern war; but that same war showed that there are rights and goods, such as liberty or national freedom, which, in the judgment of good and honest persons and according to the common sense of the people, are worth defending at the cost of enduring the horrors and destruction of a modern war.

According to moral law, not every means is legitimate to bring a just war to an early conclusion. Belligerent nations are strictly obliged to avoid unnecessary damage. It is never lawful to kill or mutilate the innocent to punish a crime, or to frighten the inhabitants of an enemy village. Belligerents also have the responsibility of rendering war as harmless and uncruel as possible by the establishment of international treaties and laws concerning the treatment of wounded and captured soldiers or civilian populations, and by a ban on excessive weapons like gas, atomic or hydrogen bombs, etc.

The value and effectiveness of such laws and treaties are predicated on a universal respect for law. Experience teaches that unjust war is not only an immoral but an ineffective means of settling national or international disputes. (*See* Atomic Bomb, Booty). *Ben.*

WAR BOOTY. War booty refers to the sum total of movable enemy goods seized by belligerents in the course of raids, invasions, or long-term occupations of enemy territory. Any movable property belonging to an enemy, such as arms, ships, money, etc., may constitute war booty. Seizure of such spoils is practiced both in land and naval warfare. (Technically, booty applies to enemy property seized on land, prize to enemy goods taken at sea.)

From earliest times, belligerent powers have always favored, in theory and practice, the right to war booty. Thus, Cicero writes that it is not contrary to the natural law to deprive of their goods those whom it is lawful to kill (De officiis, 1. 3, ch. 6). By virtue of international law, goods taken from the enemy immediately pass into possession of the captor. Among theologians and moralists the common opinion has been that the practice of war booty is licit, but only for States engaged in a just war. St. Thomas writes: "If those who despoil the enemy wage a just war, the things that they have seized in war become their own; this does not constitute rapine, hence, there is no obligation to make restitution" (Sum. Theol., II–II, q. 66, art. 8, ad 1).

In more recent times the right to war booty is generally admitted with definite limitations concerning (a) persons who may exercise such a right; (b) the places where this right may be exercised; (c) the objects which constitute legitimate war booty; (d) the persons to whom such booty belongs.

(a) Among civilized nations with organized armies, the right to booty belongs, not to individual combatants, but to the belligerent powers, which act through their military officials and establish laws governing the manner, place, and time for the exercise of the right of booty.

(b) The right of booty may only be exercised on land territory of the enemy, within the latter's territorial waters, and on the high seas.

(c) There is no doubt that all movable enemy goods exclusively or generally of a military nature, such as armaments of all forms, come under the category of legitimate spoils; for in war it is perfectly licit to weaken the enemy's armed forces or to strengthen and increase one's own. Articles and materials exclusively or generally non-military in nature may not be included within the object of legitimate booty, because they are not necessary for the attainment of the ends of a just war.

(d) Belligerent powers exercising their right of waging war are bound to respect, as far as possible, the ownership rights of the legitimate possessors of captured goods. This right of ownership was recognized at the Second Peace Conference at the Hague (1907), at which, in Article 23 of the Fourth Agreement, it was stated: "It is forbidden to destroy or seize enemy property, unless such destruction or seizure be imperatively required by the necessities of war." Article 52 states: "The requisitions in kind shall, as far as possible, be paid for in cash; if not, a receipt shall be given and payment of the amount due shall be made as soon as possible."

War does not take away the right of ownership. Enemies are not to be regarded outside the law (extra legem) or deprived of every right. They preserve their natural rights, which can never be considered extinct though their exercise may be impeded or restricted by the necessities of war.

MARITIME PRIZE. The right of capture in naval warfare merits particular attention. Considered as lawful prize in wartime are not only warships and all arms found on board, but also merchant ships, even though privately owned or belonging to neutral States, if employed for war purposes.

Uniform international legislation concerning the right of seizure at sea is lacking, nor has the custom of various nations always been the same in this regard.

Prior to the International Conference of Paris (1856), some governments pursued a policy based on the following principle: "Vessels do not follow the nature of cargoes, nor cargoes the nature of vessels"; in other words, if a ship was listed as an enemy vessel, its cargo was not to be placed in a similar category. The only objects of legitimate prize were ships and cargoes belonging to an enemy state or subjects thereof.

During the eighteenth century, a so-called Alliance of Neutral States sought to defend the principle: "Free ship, free goods (free ships also make the goods free)"; in other words, all neutral ships and their cargoes, including goods belonging to an enemy nation or to subjects thereof, were to be deemed free and exempt from seizure, except in cases of contraband of war.

In the International Conference of Paris, two fundamental regulations, to which, however, not all the representative powers acceded, were established: (a) enough goods must be covered by the flag of a neutral State, so that such goods, except contraband of war, are not liable to seizure; (b) the goods of neutral States, except contraband of war, are not liable to seizure, even though transported under enemy flag.

In the Declaration of London (1909), laws were established but never ratified concerning naval warfare. Nothing was determined concerning the right of seizure at sea.

In the twelfth convention of the 1907 Peace Conference at the Hague, a statute was approved for the establishment of a permanent International Prize Court; this institution, however, was never actually organized. Controversies over seizure and disposition of vessels or cargoes are submitted to National Prize Courts, established at the outset of war by the belligerent powers in their own territory (see also Piracy). *Pas.*

WAR, COLD. This new expression indicates a systematic series of acts of war or provocation bearing a semblance of legality. Such acts are perpetrated by one State against another when the latter, due to special conditions, is unable, at least for the time being, to wage an open war or does not wish to become involved in war. The obvious effect of this practice is a further aggravation of the precarious moral conditions existing in international society today. Of course, any action which tends to weaken the bond of respect and mutual trust between nations is a social crime. The leaders, to whom authority is given, are primarily responsible, although it becomes the responsibility of those citizens who are aware of the policies of their leaders and freely endorse them, thereby concurring in their decisions.

Obviously, weapons forged in an arms factory of the world are the last to contribute to initiating wars. The psychosis of war, the "cold war," the "economic war," "nationalistic disputes," "intolerance among peoples," "race and class hatred"—all are due to a collapse of moral values in the heart and mind of the man in the office, street, factory, and to distortions of truth by vicious propaganda through radio, television, the press, schools, business, legislative chambers, political struggles, which are inspired by individuals devoid of the principles of justice, truth and morality.

The distortion of values in the international field erupts into tension, collective insecurity and, finally, war.

The solution to the problem of war and peace lies in the creation or re-establishment of a climate of individual and social morality and respect for treaties. Any other solution is bound to fall short of its goal of assuring humanity an enduring peace. *Boz–Pal.*

WAR, ECONOMIC. Economic war is a series of measures of an economic nature by which nations at war try to impair the economy of enemy nations in order to weaken their resistance. Economic war, as old as humanity, follows the pattern of development in the economic life of nations. Today it includes a complexity of measures ranging from breaking all trade relations of hostile countries to pressure on neutrals for preventing trade relations with the enemy; from seizure of enemy property, even that belonging to private citizens, to buying off in neutral markets goods vital to the enemy.

The morality of economic warfare is governed by the same norms applying to a general war, with the additional caution against possible damage to neutral third parties by unwarranted measures against them. *Mai.*

WARNING. *See* Admonition.

WATER. *See* Baptism, Eucharist.

WATER, HOLY. The use of water in a sacred rite is found in all religions, not only for cleansing the body, but as a symbol of internal purity; the very nature of water lends itself to this symbolism. Egyptians considered the water of the Nile sacred and on certain days carried a supply of water in procession to the temple as lustral water (F. J. Doelger, "Nilwasser und Taufwasser," *Antike und Christentum,* 5 [1936], 153–187). According to ancient pagan authors, Egyptians and Greeks used lustral water in religious rites; such water was prepared after the manner of the Jews for expiatory purposes.

The Romans, perhaps, surpassed all other pagan peoples in the extensive use of ablutions, both in religious and civil life. Lustral water was used at marriage and other solemn occasions; the Vestals were charged with the purification of the temples.

The Mosaic ritual prescribed an extensive use of water as a means of purification. The Law indicated in detailed manner numerous objects, such as animals, actions, circumstances, or facts which created legal impurity and excluded Israelites from the temple, from participation in divine services, and from social congress. Such instances were: eating an unclean animal, contact with a leper, touching a corpse—all were regarded as an image or symbol of sin. A singular rite looked upon as a sort of judgment of God was the bitter water, which a woman suspected of adultery was made to drink (Num. 5:11–31). The Jews used water also for the feast of Tabernacles, not as a symbol of purification, but as a simple sacred ceremony.

From its earliest days the Church introduced the use of water as a liturgical element in the administration of baptism, the consecration of altars, and the imparting of blessings, as attested to by the earliest Fathers. The washing of hands before prayer became such a general practice among Christians that fonts were placed for this purpose at the entrance of basilicas (Eusebius, *Hist. eccl.* 10, 4; PG 20, 866; Paulinus of Nola, *Epist.* 13, 13; PL 61, 215). This water, of course, was simply natural water.

"Lustral water" is generally employed in the blessing of people, buildings, fields, and objects; it is kept in homes and placed at church entrances. The ritual for the blessing of this water consists of exorcism and the blessing of salt, exorcism and the blessing of the water, the mixing of water and salt. The use of lustral water is of ancient origin.

In the West, testimonies regarding the use of holy water are of a later date but these writings refer to an earlier period. In Rome blessing water for aspersions was first performed in private homes; then, towards the end of the eighth century, it was performed in a church. (*Liber Pontificalis,* 1, 54, ed. Duchesne; L. A. Muratori, *Liturgia Romana Vetus,* II, Venice, 1748, p. 225).

Leo IV (841–855) prescribed (PL 95, 679) that this water be blessed every Sunday before Mass and used to sprinkle the people ("*Omni die dominico ante Missam aquam benedicite, unde populus aspergatur et ad hoc vas proprium habete*"). (cf. Hincmar of Reims, *Epist. synod.* 5; PL 125, 774). This custom is still observed today before a conventual or parochial Mass.

The Church recommends the use of holy water apart from liturgical functions for protection against the snares of the devil and as a means of invoking heavenly blessings on homes, fields, work, and individuals. The desire of the faithful to make frequent use of this sacramental eventually gave rise to the practice of placing at the church entrance the so-called holy-water font. The extensive use of holy water in every form of blessing dates back to the eighth–ninth century. It was used to bless graves (Heraldus of Tours, *Capit.* 45), in processions around the church which were customary especially in monasteries. The practice of mixing holy water with salt, unknown to Oriental Rites, is of Western origin in the sixth century. It is derived probably from the fourth book of Kings (2:20), wherein the prophet Eliseus cast salt into the waters of Jericho to dispel unwholesomeness and barrenness. Also, an affinity between these two elements played an important part in the introduction of this practice, for, as water purifies, protects, and preserves from illness, so, too, does salt, particularly noted for the power of preserving. This was indicated by Rhabanus Maurus in his *Inst. cleric*, 2, 55 (PL 107–368) concerning holy water: *"In diversos usus fidelium, ad homines infirmos, contra phantasiam inimici, ad pecorum sanitatem, ad morbos auferendos, et cetera."* Such also is the mind of the Church, expressed in the formulas of the *Roman Ritual: "Ad abigendos daemones, morbosque pellendos . . . effugiat atque discedat a loco, in quo aspersum fueris, omnis phantasia et nequitia vel versutia diabolicae fraudis."* As for the sprinkling of corpses and graves, it is common belief that such a pious practice affords a measure of relief to the deceased souls. The daily use of holy water by the faithful indicates more properly a protection against evil and a renewal of the baptismal vows.

In the Latin Church a practice exists, observed on Holy Saturday or on the Saturday of the Vigil of Pentecost, of bringing holy water before its mixture with holy chrism into homes. In the East this was prohibited; but the rite of blessing water for the private use of the faithful was introduced on the feast of the Epiphany.

Oriental rituals have handed down formulas for the blessing of water; all symbolize the same event: the baptism of our Lord. The formulas contain a hymn of praise and thanksgiving to the person of the Word; a hymn of praise to His divine attributes, particularly His creative power; and a hymn of thanksgiving for all the benefits of the Incarnation. At the recollection of Christ's baptism in the Jordan, a petition is offered for a new manifestation of the Holy Spirit. The hymn concludes with an

expression of the benefits derived from this water: a cause of sanctification, the remission of sins, a cleansing of soul and body, a defense against demons and the protection of home and possessions. The practice of blessing water on the feast of the Epiphany was introduced in Italian churches by Greek communities. Thus Lucius, Bishop of Cosenza in Calabria (1205–1224), relates in his *Ordinarium* that he was wont to perform the exorcism of salt and water on the day of the Epiphany in memory of the baptism of Jesus. The ritual of this practice became the subject of much debate; finally, it was suppressed by the Sacred Congregation of Rites, which substituted another ritual with no reference to the baptism of Jesus. The present *Ordo ad faciendam aquam benedictam* in the Missal and Ritual closely resembles the formula contained in the supplement to the Gregorian Sacramentary, compiled by Alcuin (PL 78, 231 f.).

A special water used for the consecration of a church is "Gregorian" water, which is mixed with ashes, salt, and wine, after each has been blessed. Gregorian water was introduced into the liturgical service after the pagan temples were transformed into Christian churches or new church edifices were dedicated. Indications of this practice are found in ancient writers, especially in St. Optatus of Milevum. But it could not have been a universal practice, because Pope Vigilius did not consider it necessary. St. Gregory the Great established the ritual for consecration of a church ("*Aqua benedicta fiat, in eisdem fanis aspergatur*": *Epist*. 9, 71). For that reason, holy water used on such occasions is called Gregorian or episcopal water, since the consecration is reserved to a bishop.

Another kind of holy water is "baptismal" water. Water is the element privileged to receive the sanctifying influence of contact with Christ Himself, when He was baptized by John the Baptist in the river Jordan. Later, water was chosen by Christ as the matter of baptism (cf. John 3:5). Originally such water did not receive a special blessing. From the Acts of the Apostles (16:

13–15), we know that Lydia and her household were baptized in a river; that the eunuch of Queen Candace was baptized in a stream along the road (Acts 8:26–40); later, when the liturgy had been established, we read that in certain regions the faithful, following the example of Jesus, who was baptized in the Jordan, preferred to be regenerated in flowing waters along a seashore, river-banks, or streamlets. Soon, due to the importance of baptism in the ancient discipline of the Church, the water, which was to serve as the matter of this sacrament, was given a solemn blessing to stress the great reverence and meaning of this sacrament. This solemn blessing eventually found its proper place in the liturgy of Holy Saturday. Undeniable traces of this blessing can be found in the second century. After gradual development, formulas made use of in the present day received final revision in the sixth–seventh century, as confirmed by the Gelasian Sacramentary (cf. B. Neun-heuser, "De benedictione aquae bap-tismalis," in *Ephemerides Liturgicae*, 1930). The complete baptismal liturgy of Holy Saturday is attuned to the greatest solemnity; the prayer assumes the most exalted and distinct form: a preface; the typical meanings attached to water in sacred books and the important events of world history are brought out, and the various effects that this water, upon becoming the instrument of re-demption through the work of the Holy Spirit, must produce in the souls of men are enumerated. ("*Sit haec sancta et in-nocens creatura, libera ab omni impug-nationis incursu, et totius nequitiae purgata discessu: sit fons vivus, aqua regenerans, unda purificans, ut omnes hoc lavacro salutifero diluendi, operante in eis Spiritu Sancto, perfectae purga-tionis indulgentiam consequantur . . . Descendat in hanc plenitudinem fontis virtus Spiritus Sancti.*") Accompanying such exalted and profound language are significant gestures expressing and com-menting upon the power and efficacy of baptismal water. The priest extends his hand and divides the water in the form of a cross, with the intention that this fluid element may aid in the salvation of souls by means of the Cross, whose merits are applied to it; the priest breathes on the water three times, in order that it might become a channel of the Holy Ghost and a divine breath similar to that felt in the Cenacle room; three times the Paschal candle, the sym-bol of the Resurrection of Christ, is dipped into the water, to signify the power of baptismal ablution, which takes a soul out of the death of sin unto divine life; water is sprinkled towards the four corners of the earth, so that it may be-come an overflowing torrent, emanating from the Heart of Christ and descending from Calvary and reaching out to all men in order to transform them into sons of God. One last ceremony places upon the water an almost supreme seal of sanctifi-cation and power: the oil of catechumens and the holy chrism twice are mixed into the water. The Church may, there-fore, justly sing out its vivid desire that by this water all stains be cleansed ("*omnium peccatorum maculae delean-tur*") and that the creature, made to the image of God, lose its former squalor ("*ad honorem sui reformata principii cunctis vetustatis squaloribus emunde-tur*"), and that this water become a real re-birth ("*omnis homo sacramentum hoc regenerationis ingressus in verae inno-centiae novam infantiam renascatur*" (Ph. Oppenheim, *Sacramentum Regen-erationis Christianae*, Rome, 1947, pp. 68–71). Opp.

WAX. See Candle.

WAY OF THE CROSS. See Liturgy.

WEEPING. See Affectivity.

WEIGHTS AND MEASURES. Weights or instruments used for the pur-pose of measuring things may be legal or conventional. Legal measurements are fixed by law or custom; conventional measures are chosen by the parties. There are three ways of measuring the physical size of a thing: the direct measure, the indirect measure, and certain other ap-paratuses such as scales, meters, and thermometers. Weights and measures are essential for the purpose of exchange, and modern legislations are very strict in the matter. It is unlawful to defraud a buyer either by the use of false weights and measures or by tampering with them. It is a grave sin, if the matter is grave; but, in some circumstances, it may also be a grave sin by reason of the internal disposition of the individual, or through coalescence of continued small frauds against the same person or several persons until it constitutes the amount necessary for grave matter. Furthermore, merchants who advertise goods at a lower price in order to attract the buyers, but then alter the weight or measure, may be guilty of violating justice with regard to the other sellers also by reason of unfair competition. *Sir.*

WELFARE. *See* Assistance, Public and Private.

WIDOWHOOD. Canon 1142 of the Code of Canon Law states: "Although a chaste widowhood is more honorable, yet second and further marriages are valid and lawful, provided that termination of the prior bond is clearly established by law." This was the teaching of St. Paul (I Cor. 7:8–9, 39–40); such has been the doctrine and the discipline of the Fathers of the Church since earliest times. The institution of a widow's mourning period of ten to twelve months, during which a widow was not allowed to contract marriage, was never recognized by the Church.

Ecclesiastical discipline is not indifferent to respect for the memory of a deceased husband or wife and praiseworthy customs or usages in that regard, especially for the good of offspring conceived by the widow but not yet born at the time of death of the husband. Yet, the Church law does not forbid the lawful second marriage of a widow.

Although licit and valid, the second or other marriages of widows or widowers are less honorable, because they are indicative of intemperance and less perfectly represent the symbol of Christian marriage as the union between Christ and

the Church. For this reason a widower is not permitted, without a dispensation, to receive sacred orders if he successively contracted two or more marriages (Can. 984, par. 4). A widow who contracts a new marriage cannot receive the solemn or nuptial blessing (Can. 1143) if she already received it the first time.

Strange as it may seem, there are dispositions of civil legislations according to which a widow may not contract a new marriage if at least ten months have not elapsed from the termination of the bond. The prohibition ceases, however, if the widow gives birth to an offspring before the tenth month, or if the bond was terminated by a declaration of nullity due to impotency of the husband. *Bar.*

WIFE. *See* Parents; Marriage.

WILL. According to scholastic and ecclesiastical language, the will is the rational appetite, a faculty by which man tends to an object intellectually, i.e., rationally known and valued. As such, the will is clearly distinct from the sensitive appetite, which is a tendency to objects known through the senses. In ordinary speech this distinction is neglected and it is ignored altogether by some modern psychologists who, under the term "will," include the sensitive appetite. Furthermore, in scholastic tradition, necessary acts are attributed to the will, whereas many modern authors favor the theory that the will elicits only free acts.

Following scholastic tradition and language, we recognize in the will two acts: one *free*, one *necessary*. The volition of good in general is a necessary act, while the choice of each individual good desired is a free act. The will cannot seek anything except under its aspect of good, although the will is not compelled to seek any one particular good, except the only Good capable of enchaining man's will to Himself—God, who is absolute Good; but man's knowledge of God in this life is too obscure to produce such an effect. Insofar as the will necessarily seeks good, which, as a subjective possession, may also be called beatitude, or happiness, the will acts according to its *nature;* insofar as it chooses a particular good, it acts according to its *freedom.*

The following observations are especially useful for moral life: (a) In the choice of its object the will conforms to the judgment of reason; hence, it is absolutely necessary that reason be well enlightened concerning moral duties. (b) The will, however, is not compelled to conform passively to the dictates of reason. Except in self-evident judgments, the will is capable of bending reason itself, directing it to express a judgment that justifies, even erroneously, a course preferred by the will, to the point that a corrupt will corrupts man's mind as well. (c) The will exercises its dominion even on man's lower faculties; thus, all human activities come under its control and command; the will is a ruling faculty, a begetting faculty. (d) The will is the seat of freedom and, therefore, the basis of imputability of man's acts; the acts of the will, like those of other faculties, are neither imputable nor capable of (subjective) moral value except insofar as they are voluntary. (e) Consequently, a good training of the will directed to rendering the will obedient to the voice of duty, strong against its own evil tendencies and those of the lower faculties is important for all purposes of moral life; nor is it to be forgotten that the energies of the will are weakened by reason of original sin, but restoration is possible, not only by natural means, such as reflection and practice, but also by supernatural means, such as prayer and the sacraments. *Gra.*

WILL, FREE. Free will is the psychological freedom of choice and of action consequent upon choice; it is the total conscious process involved in effecting a decided act. Free will is the basis or psychological postulate of moral life, in the sense that an act posited by an individual lacking free will has no moral value.

That man is endowed with free will is adverted to by the fact that everyone considers himself to be the author and master of his own actions, ascribing to himself merit or blame for acting or failing to act, for acting in one way rather than another. This testimony of conscience is strengthened by historical proofs, whereby men have always been considered moral beings responsible for their actions; on the basis of such persuasion, nations enact laws and inflict penalties.

Philosophers confirm this general conviction by pointing out the metaphysical origin of free will in man. They note that the object of man's will is always a good; that man necessarily desires that which is apprehended as good or avoids that which appears to be evil. This, however, is a formal necessity which does not bind the will to a particular concrete object, unless that object appear as entirely good or entirely evil. All created goods, including all actions performed by men, are imperfect; no evil is totally evil without some element of good. This mixed nature of good and evil in finite things renders the will capable of accepting these as good or evil. God alone is a Being in whom pure Goodness is actuated; hence, He alone is capable of binding the will of man to Himself by a necessary bond. In this life man knows God so imperfectly that he remains free of this necessary bond. This freedom in man is called free will. *See also* Determinism. *Gra.*

WINE. *See* Alcoholism, Drunkenness.

WISDOM. *See* Gifts of the Holy Spirit.

WITCHCRAFT. Witchcraft is a form of magic, usually distinguished into white (natural) and black magic. White magic is the art of performing unusual tricks through natural forces, for instance, the amazing skill of a magician. Black magic, instead, is the art of performing extraordinary feats through the help or intervention of the devil. When black magic is practiced merely to win the admiration of others or for profit, it is called simply magic (*see* Magic). It may also be used to harm people in sickness, ill fortune, accidents, and reverses of all kinds. In this case it is designated by the special term *witchcraft*. Witchcraft includes the casting of a spell, enchantment, ritual witchery. Hence, witchcraft is evil for two reasons: (a) because it is practiced through the assistance of evil spirits; (b) because it is used for an evil purpose against one's neighbor.

Witchcraft presents several moral problems: (a) Its practice is obviously forbidden and sinful, since, as black magic, it is collaboration with the devil—a violation of the virtue of religion, which commands us to worship God alone and to seek His aid. Furthermore, it is a sin against love of neighbor and, sometimes, against justice. (b) Collaboration with a magician is improper if this amounts to inviting him to use his magic art in our behalf, particularly to harm another person or for some other evil purpose. May one engage the services of a magician for a good purpose, that is, to undo the effects of an antecedent evil act? This, too, is illicit because witchcraft retains, in any case, the moral malice of magic in view of diabolical intervention. However, it would not be improper if one asked a magician to stop evil effects provided that he could do so by the use of honest means. (c) It is unwise to deny the reality of witchcraft on the ground that it is unbecoming for modern man to believe in the devil's influence. (d) On the other hand, it is also imprudent to admit, without sufficient proof, that a person uses or seeks the devil's intervention.

Witchcraft may be combatted by the following means: (a) the use of remedies indicated by medical science; (b) supernatural means, such as prayer, exorcism, and sacramentals; (c) the elimination of signs and other external devices through which magicians and evil spirits exercise their harmful influence. Superstitious, magical, or more or less ludicrous practices are to be avoided (*see* Superstition). *Ben.*

WITHDRAWAL, FROM MEDICAL CASE.

Every deontological code emphasizes the physician's obligation not to withdraw from a medical case if the patient is still in need of treatment, except when impeded by circumstances beyond his control. In this case, he must promptly notify the patient or his family and suggest the name of a substitute physician.

Such an obligation is rooted in the conscience of every doctor. This obligation gives to his work precisely the character, nobility, and hardships of a definite apostolate, as well as increasing his professional prestige and income. Generally, a doctor who abandons a sick patient becomes guilty of grave fault; however, certain things render it quite proper for him to do so.

The following are the more common causes which may prompt a physician to give up the care of a sick patient:

(a) *Refusal by the patient or his family to pay for the doctor's past medical services*. In this case, if the patient's refusal is not explicit but clear from failure and persistent procrastination, a physician may not discontinue his visits if the patient is in danger of death, gravely or seriously ill. The doctor, of course, with the consent of the patient's family, may entrust the case to another physician, whom he shall inform of the patient's delinquency in the payment of bills. He also may refer the case to appropriate agencies for the sake of collecting his due. It is possible, of course, that the patient's failure to pay may be due to actual financial difficulties. In this case a spirit of charity ought to prevail; the doctor should continue his services, satisfied that whatever modest little contributions he may receive from less affluent people of sincerity is often worth more than any sum of money (*see also* Honorarium).

(b) *Incurability*. At times, a physician, realizing that an illness is incurable, may be inclined to discontinue visits to a patient, due to a feeling that continued visits and fees accepted would be wrong. In such cases the doctor ought to discuss the matter with the patient's family and indicate his willingness to continue his services if requested. A. Pensa writes: "To a sense of Christian charity and faith should be united the strength not to allow oneself to be overcome by weariness, annoyance, discouragement, or scepticism. One must try and try again: though discouraged, he must never give in to discouragement, for Divine Providence may well lend assistance to his efforts. Very often the darkest situations suddenly take a better turn. One must carry on confidently and bravely, in order that he may have no remorse for having abandoned the struggle or for not having waged the battle with sufficient energy." It may happen at times that the patient's family, from a false sense of economy, may wish to dispense the physician from further medical services, whereas the patient himself may wish him to continue his visits. In such a case, the doctor may do well to please the patient by continuing visits on the basis of pure charity, for the satisfaction of instilling hope and confidence in his patient.

(c) *The patient refuses medical aid.* If the refusal is explicit or apparent from the patient's failure to carry out medical directions, an attending physician has every right to discontinue his visits, without suggesting a substitute, provided that he expressly inform the family and the medical association of his decision. Sometimes, however, the uncooperative and hostile attitude of the patient is the result of physical disturbance, which is not the attitude of his family. In such a case the physician shall continue to offer his services, provided that the family will make every effort to have the patient follow the treatment prescribed; on the other hand, the doctor may either suggest that another physician be called in, or, if necessary, that the patient be transferred to a hospital or other health institute.

(d) *Fear of contagion.* It has at times happened that in a case of widespread and dangerous epidemic a physician may have deserted not only the stricken patient but the entire epidemic area itself. Such conduct, of course, is always morally reprehensible, if there are no other doctors available or if it is a case to which a physician was specially assigned.

(e) *Serious disagreement with a consulting physician.* It is a well-known fact that the family physician has no right to object to a patient's or family's wish to call in a consulting physician. However, if the latter is selected by the patient's family, the attending physician is free to withdraw, but is obliged for the benefit of the new doctor to write out a clear and precise report concerning his diagnosis of the case. If, after consultation, serious disagreement arises between the two physicians, the former has the right to enlist the opinion of a second consultant. However, if the family objects to this second consultation and prefers to follow the opinion of the first consultant, then the original doctor has the right to withdraw from the case.

(f) *Therapeutic abortion.* In a case in which therapeutic abortion is requested, the physician must refuse to accede to such request and may withdraw from the case without further ado.

CONCLUSIONS. The question whether or not a physician may withdraw from a medical case receives in moral theology a negative reply, but the few examples cited above clearly show the necessity of resorting to frequent and prudent distinctions in a question of this nature. In practice, the norms to follow in certain delicate professional circumstances must be drawn from the physician's own conscience. A conscience imbued with the principles of charity will not fail to suggest equitable and perfectly moral decisions. *Riz.*

WITNESS. A witness is one who testifies in a cause or gives evidence before a judicial tribunal. Proof by witnesses is admitted in all cases and by all judiciary systems, according to the direction of the judge and rules established by laws. (For Canon Law, cf. Can. 1754, ff.) Apart from judicial confession or physical inspection, proof by witnesses is considered the most common means of establishing evidence.

WITNESSES IN CANONICAL LAW. Witnesses must answer truthfully all questions legitimately put to them by the judge. This they must do by virtue of legal justice and the duty of charity; if one is called to give testimony by reason of his office, he must answer truthfully by virtue of commutative justice.

The following are exempt from the obligation to testify: (a) priests and others who learned things through or on the occasion of sacramental confession, even though they may have been freed from the sacramental seal (q.v.); (b) pastors and other priests, concerning matters which were made known to them by reason of the sacred ministry, outside sacramental confession; (c) persons (civil magistrates, physicians, etc.) who are bound by official or professional secrecy or by reason of advice given in matters connected with professional secrecy; (d) persons who fear that their testimony may cause defamation, vexations, or other grave evils for themselves or their blood relatives, or relatives in marriage to any degree of the direct line or in the first degree of the collateral line (Can. 1755, par. 1 and 2). Witnesses who, in replying to legitimate questions of the judge, knowingly conceal the truth or testify falsely will incur penalties stipulated in Can. 1743. The same penalties are incurred by those who presume to induce a witness to testify falsely or to conceal the truth (Can. 1755).

Exemption from the obligation to answer a judge if summoned to testify concerning certain facts is recognized in the laws of the United States under the heading of "privileged communications." In general, the laws of the various States of the Union recognize four classes of privileged communications: (a) professional communications; (b) political communications; (c) judicial communications; (d) social communications. "At the common law, there was only one class of professional communications privileged. This class comprised communications between attorneys and their clients. By statute, however, other classes were added. These include communications between physicians and their patients, and between spiritual advisers and laymen. In reference to attorney and client, Greenleaf says: 'The protection given by the law to such communications does not cease with the termination of the suit, or other litigation or business,

in which they are made; nor is it affected by the party's ceasing to employ the attorney and retaining another; nor by any other change of relations between them; nor by the death of the client. The seal of the law, once fixed upon them, remains forever, unless removed by the party himself, in whose favor it was placed' " (Hughes, *Law of Evidence*, p. 228).

Concerning physicians, it is essential that the purpose of the communication is to alleviate or to cure. Physical defects or degrading marks on the patient may not be disclosed by a physician nor admitted as evidence, nor the nature of the ailment or disease of the patient, nor prescriptions provided for treatment. The statute of certain states (*see* New York) include registered nurses among those whose professional information is considered privileged.

At common law, communications between spiritual advisers and laymen are not privileged, although in many states such communications are privileged by statute (Clevenger, *New York Practice*, Civil Practice Act, 1920). Canon Law goes further in protecting communications between a priest and a person who confided in him as a minister of religion. This protection is similar to that which civil law accords to communications between attorney and client.

Concerning those excused from testifying under the circumstances indicated (Can. 1755, n. 2), Canon Law is more liberal than civil law. Civil law does not exempt blood relatives or relatives by marriage from testifying in trials involving their relatives, even if it entails great hardship for them to testify. The only exemption in the United States regards confidential communications between husband and wife.

All persons may be witnesses, if they are not explicitly excluded by law, in whole or in part, by reason of a lack of knowledge, judgment, or the will to tell the truth, etc. (Can. 1756). Witnesses rejected by law are: (1) unfit; (2) suspect; (3) disqualified persons. (1) Those under the age of puberty and the mentally ill are considered *unfit* to testify.

(2) The following are rejected as *suspect:* (a) the excommunicated, perjurers, or persons branded with infamy by a declaratory or condemnatory sentence; (b) those who are of such low character that they are considered as undeserving of trust; (c) public enemies who are a party to the controversy. (3) The following persons are *disqualified:* (a) those who are parties to a lawsuit or who act as deputies of the parties, the judge or his assistants, attorneys and others assisting the parties in the case; (b) priests with respect to information learned in confession or on the occasion of confession although separated from the seal of confession; the same disqualification applies to those who might have overheard the words of the penitent; (c) husbands in the case of wives and vice versa; blood-relatives and marriage relatives in the case of persons related to them in any degree of the direct line and in the first degree of the collateral line, except in cases dealing with their civil or religious state, if similar knowledge cannot be obtained from any other source or the public welfare requires that the truth be ascertained (Can. 1757).

The disqualified are entirely excluded; the unfit and the suspect can be questioned by a decree of the judge, if he deems it opportune, but usually without oath; their testimony shall have value merely as an indication and assistance toward proof of the case (Can. 1758).

Witnesses, in general, are introduced by the parties. They may also be introduced by the promoter of justice, the defender of the bond, or *ex officio* by the judge in cases of minors or if the common good may require it. Each party must make the names of his witnesses known to the other party in order that each party may exercise the right of excluding a witness or witnesses introduced by the other party (Can. 1759).

The judge must exclude *ex officio* disqualified witnesses from testifying or testifying of their own accord without summons with the evident intent to delay the case or falsify the truth. The judge has also the right and duty to prevent the introduction of an excessive number of witnesses or witnesses useless or detrimental to the trial (Cans. 1760, 1762, 1764, par. 1). A witness may also be excluded at the request of an opponent if a just reason for his exclusion is proved. But a party cannot object to the introduction of a witness introduced or summoned by himself, although he may contest his testimony (Can. 1764, par. 2–3). The summoning of witnesses must be done according to the prescriptions of the law. A duly summoned witness must respond or make known to the judge the reason for his inability to appear; failure to obey the summons or to give reason for absence, may be punished with appropriate penalties and fines in proportion to the damage caused to the party (Can. 1765–1766).

Before testifying, a witness must take an oath (*q.v.*) that he will state the whole truth and nothing but the truth. Upon completion of the examination of a witness, the judge may, if he deems it prudent, demand an oath concerning the truth of the statements made (*de veritate dictorum*) and promising secrecy with reference to the matter until the acts shall have been published, or even for all time (Can. 1767–1769).

Witnesses must be examined in the place where the tribunal sits, excepting persons constituted in the highest offices, or affected by a physical impediment, or living at great distance from the office of the tribunal (Can. 177).

Witnesses must be examined on specific questions by the judge or his delegate, one at the time and not in the presence of the parties to the controversy. Their testimony must be given orally and be committed to writing immediately (Can. 1770–1777) by the notary, who is obliged to be present for the complete examination of the witnesses. Answers given must be reread to the same witness, who has the faculty to add to, correct, delete or change his statements; finally, the deposition must be signed by the witness, the judge, and the notary (Can. 1778–1781).

Publication of depositions is made by communicating them to the opposing party in order that he may defend himself. If the parties or their proxies were not present at the examination of the witnesses, the judge may order the publication of the testimony soon after the deposition of all the witnesses has been taken down, unless he deems it necessary to defer it until all the proofs have been submitted (Can. 1782).

After the publication of the testimony, the right to reject a witness ceases, unless one shall prove or state under oath that he had no knowledge of the defect of a witness prior to the publication (Can. 1764); the right, however, still remains to take exception to the method of examination or the testimony itself. Moreover, after the publication of the depositions, witnesses shall not be questioned again on the same points, nor shall new witnesses be admitted except with much prudence and for serious motives in cases which never become a *res iudicata* or for serious motives in other cases. Thus is avoided all fraud and danger of collusion (Can. 1783–1786).

A witness has the right to request compensation for expenses incurred and a just indemnity to be fixed by the judge for losses sustained in the interruption of his work (Can. 1787–1788).

APPRAISAL OF EVIDENCE. The testimonies must be examined and weighed by the judge, after a consideration of the status of the witness, the direct and indirect sources of his information, the reliability of his affirmations and the number of witnesses (Can. 1789–1790). The deposition of one witness alone does not constitute full proof, unless a so-called qualified witness testifies to things known by reason of his official capacity. If two or three reliable witnesses testify in court under oath concerning some fact known to them by personal knowledge, with concurring agreement, such testimony is sufficient proof; if the judge deems it necessary either because of the serious nature of the case or because of a condition of doubt concerning the real truth of testimony given, he may request further proof (Can. 1791).

WITNESSES "SEPTIMAE MANUS." In trials concerning impotency (*q.v.*) or non-consummation (*see* Marriage, rati-

fied) each of the married parties must present seven witnesses, called *testes septimae manus*, who are to be selected from among blood relatives, in-laws, neighbors and acquaintances, to give additional strength to the depositions of the parties. They differ from the so-called witnesses *de scientia* (Can. 1974–1975).

WITNESSES IN THE PROCESSES OF CANONIZATION. In order to prove the reputation of sanctity or martyrdom (*q.v.*) of a servant of God, recourse must be made to proof by witnesses. In these cases all the faithful, except a confessor, are bound, even though not summoned as witnesses, to bring to the attention of the Church information which might disprove the virtue, miracles, or martyrdom of a servant of God (Can. 2023). In the first place, all who lived or associated with the servant of God must be called as witnesses by the promoter of the faith, (*q.v.*) even though not proposed by the postulator of the cause (Can. 2024). Here, too, the testimony of blood relatives, in-laws, members of the family, and even heretics or unbelievers may be heard by the court (Can. 2027, par. 1).

WITNESSES IN SUMMARY PROCESSES. In summary processes, proof by witnesses is not entirely excluded. Two or three witnesses, summoned *ex officio* or introduced by the party or parties, may be heard if, according to the bishop's judgment, they are necessary to prove the allegations. They may also be introduced by the opponent and heard in behalf of a defendant. They must, however, be dismissed if the ordinary, after consultation with parish consultors or examiners, believes that they were introduced for the purpose of delaying the case (Can. 2145).

CIVIL AND CRIMINAL JUDICIARY SYSTEMS. Proof by witnesses holds much importance in civil and criminal judiciary systems. In many countries, no one may be exempted from the obligation of testifying in criminal trials except nearest relatives, those bound by professional secrecy, and a few others. An oath is always required of the witnesses, and attempts directed at leading witnesses to perjure themselves are punishable by law.

The specific aims of a witness are reticence and alteration of the truth, or perjury. Violations of justice, charity, or religion are frequently committed, and obligations of making restitution are overlooked. For more specific details, consult the articles on individual sins: Lying, Defamation, and Perjury. The eighth commandment (*see* Decalogue) explicitly forbids bearing false witness. For the witnesses at marriage and nuptials, *see* Engagement, Matrimony (Form of). *Pal.*

WOMAN. The absolute identity of nature and final destiny refutes any opinion which assigns to women a role essentially inferior to that of man. The difference between sexes, though profound, does not detract in any way from the value of the human person. God created woman to be man's companion and helpmate, not his servant and slave. Only if the fundamental values of the spirit are ignored does a humiliating position befall woman. Christianity, by restoring the family to its original integrity, bestowed on woman her original destiny. This restoration is enhanced by the doctrines of Revelation and the Redemption: in the mystical union of the human race in Christ, every fundamental difference disappears, and woman not only possesses the right to be called sister but also a collaborator with the Apostles in their work.

But the profound diversity of characteristics which distinguishes one sex from the other, differentiates also their functions and opposes attempts to establish an absolute equality between the two sexes. In the area of domestic society, a hierarchical order existing between man and woman was not abolished by Christianity; on the contrary, woman's function was raised so that her union with man is symbolical of the hierarchical union which exists between Christ and the Church.

In the sphere of the social life of the Church, a woman's mission is subordinate to that of man, as demonstrated by her exclusion from the sacred hierarchy.

Her role is limited to that of a collaborator in apostolic work.

The place of woman is mirrored in the personality of Mary, the participant in the work of Redemption, the co-redemptrix of mankind. Looking at her, a Christian woman sees clearly the value and extent of her own mission in domestic and social life, and discovers just reasons to value the specific characteristics of her femininity without exaggerating or degrading them. *Pal.*

WORK. Man has a right to work, because he has the duty to work, and every duty supplies a right to the fulfillment of that duty. The right *to* work and the right *of* work are not the same thing. The first has a predominantly negative significance: man cannot be prevented from working if he has the capability for work; the time, place, and nature of the work are left to his own discernment and initiative as long as they are not contrary to the common good. The right *of* work has a positive significance: public authority has an obligation to create opportunities of employment for those who, through no fault of their own and against their will, become unemployed.

The citizen of today has the right *of* work, because it is the duty of the State to eliminate or reduce social evils; this is certainly true of unemployment in notable proportion. The State should eliminate unemployment; it must provide or encourage others to provide work for the idle.

The right *of* work is not a right of commutative justice, which would allow an unemployed person to seek or claim indemnity from the State or other employers in the absence of employment. It is a right of social justice, which involves the duty for the State to promote the common good by opening new avenues for employment.

Some theorize that a State cannot effectively avoid unemployment except by a collectivization of all means of production to thus place the economic life of the country on an equal plane. This is an unacceptable solution, for individual initiative and private ownership of production is quite capable of remedying the situation; there is no reason to maintain that this is not adequate if intervention by government occurs whenever the situation demands the reduction of unemployment. *Pav.*

WORKER. *See* Employee, Work, Proletariat, Wage.

WORKS, PIOUS. *See* Foundation, Pious; Legacy, Pious.

WORLD. The world, in a theological sense, is the world which Jesus condemned because of its scandals (Matt. 18:7) and St. John described as steeped in evil (John 5:19). It includes standards and modes of living which are opposed to Christian principles: a denial of, and hostility to, Catholic religion; religious sloth and indifference; the belief and practice of a false religion; the association of religion with love of pleasure, riches, and luxury; a mediocre and tepid mentality which considers religion an unnecessary item without influence or a barrier to the enjoyment of life. The latter views scandalize both non-believers and believers by showing that religion has little effect on moral life.

The world seeks to spread its standards and allurements. To accomplish this, it makes use of press, entertainment media, and fashions, ridicule and threats, if not direct persecution. We cannot avoid all contact with the world (John 17:15); nevertheless, vanity, bad example, inevitable contacts with worldly people, sneers and threats constitute a real danger.

In order to be able to withstand the impact of this dangerous current, one must have faith in the infallible teaching of Christ, without surrendering in any way to the standards of the world, either out of self-interest or of human respect. A Christian must flee all dangerous occasions, living in the world without being of the world. All have the obligation to edify their fellowman by the example of a good life, fully in conformity to the norms of the Gospel.

Those who because of social position are able to exert a greater influence are more obligated to give good example and make their religious convictions effective in public life. By so doing they will inspire courage in the timid not to yield to the tyranny of human respect, fashion, or personal, selfish interests.

The plight of the world, understood in a Christian sense, does not prevent anyone from giving effective collaboration to projects for the common welfare and cultural progress; the philosophy of the world itself is useful for the achievement of these ends. *Man.*

WORLDLINESS. Worldliness can signify either an attitude and way of life entirely at variance with Christian principles or the behavior of those who follow the standards of the world in their manner of dress, adornments, and amusements without entirely abandoning religious practices or the principles of the Gospels.

Worldliness is sinful excess, which may be grave if carried to the point of indulgence in gravely sinful practices, grave scandal or a way of life gravely opposed to the moral law in general. *Man.*

WRITER. *See* Copyright, Forbidden Books.

BIBLIOGRAPHY

I. GENERAL

Treatises

AERTNYS, J.—DAMEN, C. A., *Theologia moralis secundum doctrinam S. Alphonsi de Ligorio doct. Ecclesiae*,[17] Torino, 1956, 2 vol.

ALFONSO M. DE' LIGUORI, *Theologia moralis* (1ª ed. 1748), critical edit., L. Gaudé, Roma, 1905–1912, 4 vol.

ANNIBALE, J. (D') (Card.), *Summula theologiae moralis* (1ª ed. 1871–73), Roma, 1908–1909, 3 vol.

BALLERINI, A.—PALMIERI, D., *Opus theologicum morale in Busembaum Medullam*, edit. D. Palmieri (1ª ed. 1889), Prati, 1898–1901.

BERARDI, A., *Theologia moralis theologico-practica*, Faventiae, 1905, 5 vol.

BUCCERONI, J., *Institutiones theologiae moralis* (1ª ed. 1887),[6] Romae, 1914–1915, 4 vol.

———, *Enchiridion morale*, Romae, 1905.

COLLI-LANZI, C., *Theologia moralis universa*, Torino, 1926, 4 vol.

DAVIS, H., *Moral and pastoral theology*, London.

DUMAS, J., *Theologia moralis thomistica*, Paris, 1930, 6 vol.

FANFANI, L., *Manuale theorico-practicum theologiae moralis ad mentem S. Thomae*, Romae, 1950 ff.

FERRERES, J. B.—MONDRIA, A., *Compendium theologiae moralis ad normam Codicis iuris canonici*, I,[17] Barcinone-Subirana, 1949–1953.

FRASSINETTI, G., *Compendio della teologia morale di S. Alfonso M. de L.* (1ª ed. 1865), Torino, 1947, 2 vol.

GABRIELE DE VARCENO—SERAFINO A LOIANO, *Institutiones theologiae moralis ad normam iuris canonici quas veteri compendio a P. Gabriele de Varceno confecto, P. Serafinus a Loiano. . . suffecit. . .*, Torino, 1934–1942, 5 vol.

GENICOT, E.—SALSMANS, J., *Institutiones theologiae moralis* (1ª ed. 1897),[16] Brussellis, 1946, 2 vol.

GOEPFER, A.—F. STAAB, K., *Moraltheologie* (1ª ed. 1897), Paderborn, 1923, 3 vol.

GOUSSET, T. (Card.), *Théologie morale à l'usage des curés et des confesseurs*,[13] Paris, 1844, 2 vol.; (German) Aachen, 1851 and Schaffhausen, 1851; (Latin) Milano, 1850.

GURY, J. P.—BALLERINI, A.—PALMIERI, D., *Compendium theologiae moralis*, Romae, 1907, 2 vol.

GURY, J. P.—FERRERES, J., *Compendium theologiae moralis. . . dispositionibus iuris hispani ac lusitani. . . accommodatum*,[16] Barcinone, 1940, 2 vol.

HAERING, B., *Das Gesetz Christi. Moraltheologie dargestellt für Priester und Laien*, Friburgi i. B., 1954. Eng. trans., Westminster, Newman, 1961.

HAINE, A., *Principia dogmatico-moralia universae theologiae sacramentalis*, Leuven, 1875.

HAINE, A.—BUND, J., *Theologiae moralis elementa* (1ª ed. 1881),[11] Leuven, 1906.

HILARIUS A SEXTEN, *Compendium theologiae moralis*, Meren, 1889, 2 vol.

JANVIER, M. A., *L'exposition de la morale catholique*, Paris, 1903–1924.

1313

JORIO, T. A., *Compendium theologiae moralis* (1ª ed. Gury, 1850; revised edit., R. Tummolo, A. Jorio),[4] Neapoli, 1953–1954, 2 vol.

KENRICK, P., *Theologia moralis*,[2] Mechelen, 1860.

KOCK, A., *Lehrbuch der Moraltheologie* (1ª ed. 1905),[3] Freiburg, 1910.

KOCK, A.,—PREUSS, A., *Handbook of moral theology*, St. Loius, 1918–1924, 5 vol.

KONINGS, A., *Theologia moralis S. Alphonsi in compendium redacta* (1874),[6] New York, 1886.

LANZA, A.—PALAZZINI, P., *Theologia moralis*. Taurini-Romae, 1949.

LANZA, A.—PALAZZINI, P., *Principi di teologia morale*. I. *Teologia morale generale*, Roma, 1952; II. *Le virtu*, Roma, 1954; III. *Sacramenti e vita sacramentale*, Roma, 1957.

LECLERCQ, J., *Leçons de droit naturel*.

    I. *Le fondement du droit et de la société*, 3ª ed., Namur- Louvain, 1948.

    II. *L'Etat ou la politique*, 3ª ed., Namur-Louvain, 1948.

    III. *La famille*, 3ª ed., Namur-Louvain, 1950.

    IV. *Les droits et devoirs individuels—Vie—Travail—Propriété*, Namur-Louvain, 1955.

LEHMKUHL, A., *Theologia moralis* (1ª ed. 1883),[12] Freiburg, 1914, 2 vol.

LINSENMANN, F., *Lehrbuch der Moraltheologie* (1ª ed. 1878),[3] Freiburg, 1888.

MARC, C.—GESTERMANN, F.—RAUS, J., *Institutiones morales alphonsianae* (1ª ed. 1885),[20] Lyon, 1939, 2 vol.

MAUSBACH, J., *Teologia morale*, Alba, 1956–1957.

MAUSBACH, J.—TISCHLEDER, P., *Katholische Moraltheologie*,[8] Münster i. W., 1937.

MAUSBACH, J.—ERMECKE, G., *Katholische Moraltheologie*, Münster i. W., 1953–1954.

McHUGH, J.—CALLAN, C., *Moral theology*, New York, 1929, 2 vol.

MECHLINIENSIS, *Theologia ad usum Seminarii Mechliniensis*. Mechliniae 1932.

MERKELBACH, B., *Summa theologiae moralis* (1ª ed. 1932–1933),[5] Paris, 1947, 3 vol.

MORAN, J., *Theologia moralis*, Madrid, 1883, 3 vol.

MORINO, J., *Theologia moralis ad mentem S. Alphonsi M. de Ligorio*, Neapoli, 1910, 2 vol.

MUELLER, E.—SEIBEL, J.—UJCIC, J., *Theologia moralis* (1868–1876),[10] Regensburg, 1923.

NOLDIN, H.—SCHMITT, A.—HEINZEL, G., *Summa theologiae moralis* (1ª ed. 1899–1900), Oeniponte, 1952–1954, 3 vol.

PIGHI, J.—GRAZIOLI, A., *Cursus theologiae moralis* (1ª ed. 1900–1912),[6] Verona, 1946–1947, 4 vol.

PISCETTA, L.—GENNARO, A., *Elementa theologiae moralis*, Torino, 1927–1942, 7 vol.

PROBST, F., *Katholische Moraltheologie*, Tubingae, 1877, 2 vol.

PRUEMMER, D.—MUNCH, O., *Manuale theologiae moralis secundum principia S. Thomae* (1ª ed. 1915),[11] Friburgi i. B., 1953, 3 vol.

PRUNER, J., *Moraltheologie* (1875),[3] Freiburg, 1903.

RODRIGO, L., *Praelectiones theologico-morales comillenses*. Series I. *Theologia moralis fundamentalis*. T. IV. *Tractatus de conscientia morali*, Santander, 1956.

SABETTI, A., *Compendium theologiae moralis*, revised edit., T. Barret (1ª ed. 1884),[32] Cincinnati, 1931.

SCAVINI, P., *Theologia moralis universa ad mentem S. Alphonsi de L.* (1ª ed. 1847),[13] Milano, 1882.

SCHILLING, C., *Lehrbuch der Moraltheologie*, München, 1928, 2 vol.

SCHINDLER, F., *Lehrbuch der Moraltheologie* (1ª ed. 1907–1909),[2] Wien, 1912– 1914, 3 vol.

SIMAR, T., *Lehrbuch der Moraltheologie* (1ª ed. 1867),[3] Freiburg, 1893.

SPORER, P., *Theologia moralis decalogalis et sacramentalis*, Paderborn, 1901, 2 vol.

TANQUEREY, A., *Synopsis theologiae moralis et pastoralis* (1ª ed. 1902),[2] Doornik, 1930–1931, 3 vol.

TAUTU, A., *Compendia de theologie moralà*, Oradea, 1931–1932, 2 vol.

TILLMANN, F., *Handbuch der katholischen Sittenlehre*. Gen. edit., T. Steinbückel, Düsseldorf, 1938.

    I. *Die philosophische Grundlegung*, 1938 (T. Steinbückel), 2 vol.; 2nd edit. (M. Reding), München, 1953.

    II. *Die psychologischen Grundlagen*, 1934 (T. Müncker).

    III. *Die Idee der Nachfolge Christi*, 1934 (F. Tillmann).

    IV. *Die Verwirklichung der Nachfolge Christi* (F. Tillmann).

        1. *Die Pflichten gegen Gott*, 1935.

        2. *Die Pflichten gegen sich selbst und gegen den Nächsten*, 1936 (2nd edit., 1939).

TILLMANN, F., *Il maestro chiama. Compendio di morale cristiana* (trans., C. Colombo), Brescia, 1945.

UBACH, J., *Compendium theologiae moralis*, Freiburg, 1926–1927, 2 vol.

VERMEERSCH, A., *Theologiae moralis principia—responsa—consilia* (3ª ed., 1922– 1923),[3] Romae, 1933–1937, 3 vol.

WOUTERS, L., *Manuale theologiae moralis*, Brugis, 1932–1933, 2 vol.

ZANINETTI, J. S., *Theologia moralis Seminariorum usui accommodata*, Novariae, 1908, 2 vol.

Additional Works

AQUINAS, ST. THOMAS, *Summa Theologica*, Trans. by the English Dominican Fathers, New York: Benziger Bros., 1947.

BOUSCAREN, T. L., S.J., and ELLIS, A. C., S.J., *Canon Law. A Text and Commentary*, Milwaukee: Bruce Publishing Company, 1951 (2nd edit.).

FARRELL, W. A., *A Companion to the Summa*, New York: Sheed & Ward.

HAERING, B., *The Law of Christ*, Vol. I, Westminster, Md.: The Newman Press, 1961.

KOCH, A., *A Handbook of Moral Theology*, Edit. by A. Preuss, St. Louis: Herder Book Co., 1921.

McHUGH, J., and CALLAN, C., *A Catechism of the Council of Trent*, New York: Wagner, 1937.

WOYWOOD, S., *A Practical Commentary on the Code of Canon Law*, New York: Wagner, 1925. (Revised edit. by C. Smith, 1957.)

Summaries

ARREGUI, A., *Summarium theologiae moralis*,[18] Roma, 1948.

BIRNGRUEBER, S., *Laienmoral. Aufstieg zum Göttlichen*, Graz-Wien-Köln, 1953.

CATHREIN, V., *La morale cattolica*, Roma, 1913.

CERIANI, G., *La morale di Cristo*,[3] Milano, 1957.

CONNELL, F. J., *Outlines of Moral Theology*, Milwaukee, 1953.

CORNELISSE, E., *Compendium theologiae moralis*, Quaracchi, 1910.

DE LARRAGA, F.—LUMBRERAS, P., *Prontuario de teologia moral*, Madrid-Buenos Aires, 1950.

ELTER, E., *Compendium philosophiae moralis*, Romae, 1950.

FERRERES, J. B., *Epitome de teologia moral* (ed. A. Mondria), Barcelona, 1955.

GIANNI, S., R. P. Cl. *Institutionum moralium alfonsianarum epitome*, Lyon, 1930.

MASSIMI, M. (Card.), *La nostra legge*,[3] Città del Vaticano, 1952.

OLGIATI, F., *Il sillabario della morale cristiana*, Milano, 1943.

PISCETTA, L.—GENNARO, A., *Sommario di teologia morale*,[2] Torino, 1954.

PRUEMMER, D., *Vademecum theologiae moralis in usum examinandorum et confessariorum*,[4] Freiburg, 1923.

RACCA, P., *Theologiae moralis synopsis*, Taurini, 1919.

SCHILLING, O., *Moraltheologie* (Herders Theologische Grundrisse), Freiburg, 1922.

SEBASTIANI, N., *Summarium theologiae moralis*,[8] Torino, 1925.

STELZENBERGHER, J., *Moraltheologie. Die Sittlichkeitslehre der Königshenschaft*, Paderborn, 1953.

TANQUEREY, A.—QUEVASTRE, E., *Brevior synopsis theologiae moralis et pastoralis*,[9] Doornik, 1929.

TELCH, C., *Epitome theologiae moralis universae*,[6] Innsbruck, 1924.

TEODORO DA TORRE DEL GRECO, *Teologia morale*, Alba, 1955.

Additional Works

HEALY, E. F., S.J., and O'MEARA, J. F., S.J., *Moral Guidance*, Chicago: Loyola University Press, 1960.

HORMANN, K., *An Introduction to Moral Theology*, Trans. by E. Quinn, Westminster, Md.: The Newman Press, 1961.

JONE, H., *Moral Theology*, Trans. by U. Adelman, Westminster, Md.: The Newman Press, 1953 (13th edit.).

KELLY, G., S.J., *Man and His Happiness*, The Theological Library, Chicago: Fides, 1956.

MOHR, R., *Moral and Pastoral Theology, A Summary*, New York: Wagner, 1952.

PALAZZINI, P., and LANZA, A., *General Moral Theology*, Vol. I, trans. by W. J. Collins, Boston: St. Paul Editions, 1961.

Cases and Problems

BUCCERONI, J., *Casus conscientiae*,[6] Roma, 1913, 2 vol.

GENICOT, E.—SALSMANS, J., *Casus conscientiae propositi ac soluti*, Louvain, 1948.

GENNARI, C. (Card.), *Consultazioni morali sui casi e materie svariate che specialmente riguardano i tempi nostri*,[3] Roma, 1913–1915, 2 vol.

GURY, J.—FERRERES, J., *Casus conscientiae*,[5] Barcinone, 1926, 2 vol.

LEHMKUHL, A., *Casus conscientiae*,[4] Freiburg, 1913.

PAGANI, F., *Facti species et quaestiones de re morali*,[2] Novariae, 1921.

PALAZZINI, P.—DE JORIO, A., *Casus conscientiae*, Taurini-Romae, 1957–1958, 2 vol.

ROSSI, G., *Cento problemi di coscienza*, Assisi, 1959.

SLATER, T., *Cases of Conscience for English Speaking Countries*, New York, 1911.

STUDI CATTOLICI, *Rivista di teologia pratica*, Roma, 1957.

TER HAAR, F., *Casus conscientiae de praecipuis huius aetatis peccandi occasionibus,*[2] Torino, 1939.

———, *Casus conscientiae de praecipuis huius aetatis vitiis eorumque remediis,*[2] Torino, 1939.

Additional Works

CONNELL, F. J., *Father Connell Answers Moral Questions*, Edit. by E. J. Weitzel, Washington: Catholic University of America, 1959.

CONWAY, W., *Problems in Canon Law*, Westminster, Md.: The Newman Press, 1957.

JORIO, T. A., *Casus Conscientiae*, 2 Vols., Naples: D'Auria, 1958–1960.

MAHONEY, E., *Questions and Answers*, London: Burns & Oates.

MAHONEY, E., *Priests' Problems*, New York: Benziger Bros., 1959.

MONTAGUE, G., *Problems in the Liturgy*, Westminster, Md.: The Newman Press, 1959.

REGATILLO, E., S.J., *Casus Conscientiae*, 3 Vols., Sal Terrae, Santander, 1957.

History of Moral Theology

BARDY, G., *La théologie de l'Eglise de Saint Clément de Rome à Saint Iréne*, Paris, 1946.

———, *La theologie de l'Eglise de Saint Irénée au Concile de Nicée*, Paris, 1947.

BATTAGLIA, F., *Morale e storia nella prospettiva spiritualistica*, Bologna, 1954.

BRAUN, F. M.—DELVILLE, H.—DESCHAMPS, A., etc., *Morale chrétienne et requêtes contemporaines*, Tournai-Paris, 1954.

BUND, I., *Catalogus auctorum qui scripserunt de theologia morali et practica*, Rothomagi, 1900.

CACCIATORE, I., *S. Alfonso de' Liguori e il Giansenismo*, Firenze, 1944.

CREUSEN, J., *Le Père Arthur Vermeersch S. J.: l'homme et l'oeuvre*, Bruxelles, 1947.

D'ALES, A., *La théologie de Tertullien*, Paris, 1905.

———, *La théologie de saint Cyprien*, Paris, 1922.

DE GHELLINCK, J., *Le mouvement théologique au XIIe siècle*, Bruges-Paris, 1948.

DEMANT, T., *Aux origines de la théologie morale*, Montréal-Paris, 1951.

DIEBOLT, J., *La théologie morale catholique en Allemagne au temps du Philosophisme et de la Restauration, 1750–1850*, Strasbourg, 1926.

DITTRICH, O., *Geschichte der Ethik*, Leipzig, 1923–1933.

DOELLINGER, J.—REUSCH, F. H., *Geschichte der Moralstreitigkeiten in der röm.-kath. Kirche*, Noerdlingen, 1889, 2 vol.

ELORDUI, E., *La moral suareciana*, Salamanca, 1944.

GRABMANN, M., *Geschichte der katholischen Theologie seit dem Ausgang der Väterzeit*, Freiburg, 1933.

GUINDON, R., *Béatitude et théologie morale chez S. Thomas d'Aquin*, Ottawa, 1956.

HOCEDEZ, E., *Histoire de la théologie au XIXe siècle*, Bruxelles-Paris, 1947.

HUERTER, H., *Nomenclator litterarius theologiae catholicae,*[3] Innsbruck, 1903–1913, vol. 4, 1926, vol. 6.

LANDGRAF, A. M., *Einführung in die Geschichte der theologischen Literatur der Frühscholastik*, Regensburg, 1948.

LOTTIN, O., *Principes de morale. II. Compléments de doctrine et d'histoire*, Louvain, 1947.

MAUSBACH, J., *Geschichte der katholischen Moral*, in P. HINNEBERG, *Die Kultur der Gegenwart*,[1] Leipzig, 1906.

———, *Die Ethik des Hl. Thomas von Aquino*, München, 1933.

MEULEMEESTER, M. (DE), *Bibliographie générale des écrivains Rédemptoristes*, Nijhoff, 1933.

MOTRY, H. L., *The Concept of Mortal Sin in Early Christianity*, Washington, 1920.

ORCIBAL, J., *Les origines du Jansénisme...*, Paris, 1948, vol. 3.

PETROCCHI, M., *Il problema del lassismo nel secolo XVII*, Roma, 1953.

PRUNET, O., *La morale chrétienne d'après les écrits johanniques*, Paris, 1957.

ROLAND GOSSELIN, B., *La morale de Saint Augustin*, Paris, 1925.

SCHMITT, A., *Zur Geschichte des Probabilismus...*, Innsbruck, 1904.

SOLANA, M., *Los grandes escolásticos españoles de los siglos XVI y XVII*, Madrid, 1928.

TERNUS, P., *Vorgeschichte der Moralsysteme von Victoria bis Medina*, Paderborn, 1930.

THAIMIN, H., *Saint Ambroise et la morale chrétienne au IVe siècle*, Paris, 1895.

VAN HOVE, A., *Prolegomena*, Mechliniae-Romae, 1954.

VERAJA, F., *Le origini della controversia teologica sul contratto di censo nel XIII secolo*, Roma, 1960.

VERMEERSCH, A., *Cinquant'anni di teologia morale*, Milano, 1930.

VOGEL, C., *La discipline pénitentielle en Gaule des origines à la fin du VIIe siècle*, Paris, 1952.

WEBER, L., *Hauptfragen der Moraltheologie Gregors des Grossen, ein Bild altchristlicher Lebensführung*, Freiburg i. d. B., 1947.

Additional Works

ALEXANDER, A., *A College Moral Theology*, Chicago: Henry Regnery Company, 1958.

HARVEY, J. F., *Moral Theology in the Confessions of Saint Augustine*, Washington: Catholic University of America, 1951.

HEARD, G., *Morals since 1900*, New York: Harper, 1951.

MAUSBACH, J., *Catholic Moral Teaching and Its Antagonists*, New York: Wagner, 1914.

SLATER, T., S.J., *A Short History of Moral Theology*, New York: Benziger, 1909.

II. SPECIAL BIBLIOGRAPHY

Introduction—Principles

ABELLAN, G. M., *Posición de Suarez ante el conflicto entre la libertad y la obligación moral*, Barcelona, 1948.

BONOMELLI, G., *La morale senza Dio*,[2] Roma, 1912.

BOUQUILLON, T., *Institutiones theologiae moralis fundamentalis*,[3] Brugis, 1903.

BREZNAY, A., *Clavis theologiae moralis seu introductio in studium ethicae christianae scientificum*, I, Freiburg, 1914.

CALCARA, A., *Il problema morale nei tempi moderni*, Roma, 1943.

CARTECHINI, S., *De valore notarum theologicarum*, Romae, 1951.

CATHREIN, V., *Filosofia morale*, Firenze, 1913.

CENAL, R., *Los fundamentos metafisicos de la moral según Suarez*, Barcelona, 1949.

CHOLLET, J. A., *La morale é una scienza?*, Roma, 1907.

CICALA, F. R., *Il rapporto morale*, Milano, 1956.

COSTELEIN, A., *Morale*, Bruxelles, 1904.

GILLET, P., *La valeur éducative de la morale catholique*, Paris, 1914.

GONZALES MORAL, I., *Philosophia moralis*,³ Santander, 1952.

GUZZETTI, G. B., *Morale generale*, Torino, 1955.

HAERING, B., *La Loi du Christ*, Tournai, 1955.

JANSSENS, M. E., *La morale de l'impératif catégorique et la morale du bonheur*, Liège, 1921.

KIHN, H., *Encyclopädie und Methodologie der Theologie* (Theologische Bibliothek), Freiburg, 1892.

KRAWTZKY, A., *Einleitung in das Studium der katholischen Moraltheologie*,² Breslau, 1893.

LANZA, A., *Theologia moralis fundamentalis*, Taurini-Romae, 1949.

LECLERCQ, J., *La vie en ordre* (Essais de morale catholique, IV), Bruxelles, 1938.

———, *Le retour à Jésus* (Essais de morale catholique, I), Tournai-Paris, 1946.

LE ROHELLEC, J., *Problèmes philosophiques. La connaissance humaine. Les fondements de la morale*, Paris, 1933.

LE SENNE, R., *Traité de morale générale*, Paris, 1942.

LOTTIN, O., *Principes de morale*, Louvain, 1947, 2 vol.

———, *Psychologie et morale. I. Problèmes de psychologie*, Louvain-Gembloux, 1942.

———, *Aux sources de notre grandeur morale*, Louvain, 1946.

———, *Morale fondamentale*, Paris, 1954.

MACALI, L., *Teologia per i laici*, Padova, 1953.

MARITAIN, J., *Neuf leçons sur les notions premières de la philosophie morale*, Paris, 1949.

MERSCH, E., *Morale et corps mystique*,³ Paris, 1949.

MOHR, U., *Die christliche Ethik im Lichte der Ethnologie*, München, 1954.

PADOVANI, U., *Il fondamento e il contenuto della morale*, Milano, 1947.

PALAZZINI, P., *Morale generale*, Brescia, 1961.

PEINADOR, A., *Cursus brevior theologiae moralis. I. Theologia moralis fundamentalis*, Madrid, 1945.

RAMIREZ, L. M., *De hominis beatitudine*, Salmanticae-Matriti, 1942–1947, 2 vol.

RAPHAEL A S. JOSEPH, *Institutiones fundamentales theologiae moralis*, Aalst, 1884.

REDING, M., *Der Aufbau der Christlichen Existenz*, München, 1952.

RENARD, H., *The Philosophy of Morality*, Milwaukee, 1953.

RIDEAU, E., *Consécration. Le christianisme et l'activité humaine*, Paris, 1945.

ROMANI, S., *Theologia moralis. I. Prolegomena. Lib. I. Introductio*, Romae, 1940.

———, *Disegno di morale generale*, Roma, 1936.

SCHILLING, O., *Apologie der katholischen Moral*, Paderborn, 1937.

———, *Grundriss der Moraltheologie*,² Freiburg, 1949.

———, *Theologia moralis fundamentalis*, München, 1937–1940, 2 vol.

SCHNACKENBURG, R., *Messaggio morale del Nuovo Testamento*, Alba, 1959.

SCHOELLGEN, W., *Die soziologischen Grundlagen der katholischen Sittenlehre*, Düsseldorf, 1953.

SEMERIA, G., *La morale e le morali*, Firenze, 1934.

SERTILLANGES, A., *La philosophie morale de Saint Thomas d'Aquin*, Paris, 1922 (2nd edit., Paris, 1954).

SPIAZZI, R., *La civiltà cerca Cristo*, Milano, 1949.

STURZO, L., *Politica e morale*, Bologna, 1955.

SWEENS, A., *Theologia moralis fundamentalis*, München, 1937-1938, 2 vol.

THILS, G., *Tendences actuelles en théologie morale*, Gembloux, 1940.

———, *Théologie des realités terrestres*. I. *Préludes*, Desclée de Brouwer, 1947.

VERZEROLI, B., *Etica generale secondo i principi della filosofia perenne*, Roma, 1948.

Additional Works

GILSON, E., *Moral Values and Moral Life*, St. Louis: Herder Book Company, 1931.

HIGGINS, T. J., *Man as Man*, Milwaukee: Bruce Publishing Company, 1958.

HORMANN, K., *An Introduction to Moral Theology*, Trans. by E. Quinn, Westminster, Md.: The Newman Press, 1961.

HAERING, B., *The Law of Christ*, Trans. by E. Kaiser, Vol. I., Westminster, Md.: The Newman Press, 1961.

KELLY, G., and FORD, J., *Contemporary Moral Theology*, Vol. I., Questions in Fundamental Moral Theology, Westminster, Md.: The Newman Press, 1958.

The Church Teaches. Documents of the Church in English Translation, St. Louis: Herder Book Company, 1955.

The Sources of Catholic Dogma. A Translation of the *Enchiridion Symbolorum* (Denziger) by Roy Deferrari. St. Louis: Herder Book Company, 1957.

MOUROUX, J., *The Meaning of Man*, New York: Sheed and Ward.

Human Act—Conscience

BAUDUIN, C., *De l'instinct à l'esprit*, Paris, 1950.

BEAUDOUIN, R.—GARDEIL, A., *De conscientia*, Doornik, 1911.

BRETON, S., *Conscience et intentionalité*, Lyon, 1956.

CATHREIN, V., *Die Einheit des sittlichen Bewusstseins der Menscheit*, Frieburg, 1914, 3 vol.

CLOSTERMANN, G., *La coscienza della donna*, Roma, 1953.

CRUYSBERGHS, C., *De conscientia*, Mechliniae, 1928.

DELERUE, F., *Le système morale de Saint Alphonse de L.: étude historique et philosophique*, S. Etienne, 1929.

DELHAYE, P., *Le problème de la conscience morale chez S. Bernard*, Louvain, 1957.

DE MENASCE CATTAUI, G., *Saggi di analisi dell'atto morale*, Roma, 1956.

DE MESMAECKER, H., *Tractatus de actibus humanis*,[5] Mechliniae, 1939.

ETUDES CARMELITAINES, *Trouble et lumière*, Paris, 1949.

FORD, J. C., *Depth Psychology, Morality and Alcoholism*, Weston, Mass., 1951.

FRINS, V., *De actibus humanis*, Freiburg, 1897-1911, 3 vol.

GILLET, M. S., *Conscience chrétienne et justice sociale*, Paris, 1922.

JANKELEVITCH, V., *La mauvaise conscience*, Paris, 1933.

LACROIX, J., *Les sentiments et la vie morale*, Paris, 1952.

LEBRET, L. J.—SUAVET, T., *Ringiovanire l'esame di coscienza*, Roma, 1954.

LECLERCQ, E., *La conscience du chrétien: essai de théologie morale*, Paris, 1947.

LEHU, L., *Philosophia moralis et socialis*. I. *Ethica generalis*, Paris, 1914.

————, *La raison règle de moralité d'après Saint Thomas*, Paris, 1930.

LEPP, J., *Luci e tenebre dell'anima*, Roma, 1959.

LIBERTO A ROCSELARE, P., *Le rôle du mot "habitus" dans la théologie Bonaventurienne*, Rome, 1956.

LUMBRERAS, P., *De actibus humanis*, Romae, 1928.

NOBLE, H. (DE), *La conscience*, Paris, 1923.

NOSENGO, G., *L'educazione morale del giovane*, Brescia, 1955.

ODDONE, A., *La teoria degli atti umani*, Milano, 1933.

ODIER, C., *Les deux sources, consciente et inconsciente, de la vie morale*, Neuchatel, 1943.

PAGANI, J. B., *Tractatus de actibus humanis*, Florentiae, 1924.

PALAZZINI, P., *La coscienza*, Roma, 1961.

PENIDO, M. T. L., *La conscience religieuse*, Paris, 1935.

POELL, W., *La suggestione*, Roma, 1958.

RICHARD, T., *Etudes de théologie morale*, Paris, 1933.

ROSMINI, A., *Apologia in servizio della scienza morale*, edit. C. Riva, Milano, 1954.

ROUSSELOT, P., *Quaestiones de conscientia* (Museum Lessianum, 35), Brussellis, 1937.

SEMERIA, G., *La coscienza*, Firenze, 1937.

USAI, G. M., *La norma oggettiva di moralità presso quattro teologi della scuola gesuitica*, Roma, 1954.

VEREECKE, L., *Conscience morale et loi humaine*, Rome, 1957.

WALSH, G., *De actibus humanis*, Dublin, 1880.

ZARNCKE, L., *Enfance et conscience morale*, Paris, 1955.

ZAVALLONI, R., *La libertà personale*, Milano, 1956.

Additional Works

DUBOIS, J., *Human Acts*, The Theological Library, Chicago: Fides, 1956.

GUARDINI, R., *Conscience*, New York: Sheed & Ward, 1932.

————, *Freedom, Grace, and Destiny*, New York: Pantheon, 1960.

KRAMER, H. G., *The Indirect Voluntary or Voluntarium in Cause*, Washington: Catholic University of America, 1935.

LINDWORSKY, J., *The Training of the Will*, Milwaukee: Bruce Publishing Company, 1929.

MENESSIER, A. I., *Habits and Virtues*, The Theological Library, Chicago: Fides, 1956.

PIAGET, J., *The Moral Judgment of the Child*, Chicago: Free Press, 1948.

PIERCE, C. A., *Conscience in the New Testament*, Chicago: Allenson, 1955.

PLE, A., *Passions*, The Theological Library, Chicago: Fides, 1956.

PONTIFEX, M., *Freedom and Providence*, Twentieth Century Encyclopedia of Catholicism, New York: Hawthorn Books, Inc., 1960.

RODRIGO, L., *Tractatus de Conscientia*, 2 Vols., Santander: Sal Terrae, 1954–1956.

Law

BRYS, J., *Tractatus de legibus*, Brugis, 1942.

CERIANI, G., *La morale di Cristo*,[3] Milano, 1957.

CLAEYS BOUUAERT, F., *Tractatus de legibus, de virtutibus in genere et de peccatis in genere*, Gandavi, 1924.

Composta, D., La "moralis facultas" nella filosofia giuridica di F. Suarez, Torino, 1957.

Dabin, J., La philosophie de l'ordre juridique positif, Paris, 1929.

Davitt, T., The Nature of Law, St. Louis, 1951.

Ermecke, G., Die naturlichen Seinsgründlagen der christlichen Ethik, Paderborn, 1941.

Esteban, A., Concepción suareciana de la ley, Siviglia, 1944.

Fuchs, J., Lex naturae, zur Theologie des Naturrechts, Düsseldorf, 1955.

Funk, J., De iure naturali transcendente ius positivum, Kaldenkirchen, 1947.

Furcic, A., Ratio intima originis legis, Romae, 1947.

Gauvin, J., Les fondements des commandements, Louvain, 1938.

Jung, N., Le droit public de l'Eglise, Paris, 1948.

Lachange, H., Le concept de droit selon Aristote et saint Thomas, 2e éd., Ottawa, 1948.

Laversin, M. J., La loi, Paris, 1935.

Lottin, O., Loi morale naturelle et loi positive d'après saint Thomas, Louvain, 1920.

Maritain, J., Les droits de l'homme et la loi naturelle, Paris, 1945.

Michiels, G., Normae generales iuris canonici, Parisiis-Tornaci-Romae, 1954.

Petroncelli, M., Il principio della non retroattività delle leggi in diritto canonico, Milano, 1931.

Plotzke, U., Comandamento e vita. L'uomo d'oggi di fronte alle beatitudini, Roma, 1958.

Renard, G., Le Droit, l'Ordre et la Raison, Paris, 1927.

——, La nature de la loi, Paris, 1928.

——, La théorie de "leges mere poenales", Paris, 1929.

Riquet, M., Sa majesté la loi, Paris, 1924.

Romineu, H., Le droit naturel. Histoire et doctrine, Paris, 1945.

Sertillanges, A. D., La philosophie des lois, Neuchatel-Paris, 1946.

Suarez, F., De legibus, Antverpiae, 1613.

Trombetta, A., Utrum Ecclesia habeat potestatem praecipiendi actus mere internos, Surrenti, 1920.

Van Hove, A., De legibus, Mechliniae-Romae, 1930.

——, Prolegomena, Romae, 1945.

Additional Works

Begin, R. F., Natural Law and Positive Law, Washington: Catholic University of America, 1959.

Bertke, S., The Possibility of Invincible Ignorance of the Natural Law, Washington: Catholic University of America, 1941.

Bouchet, P., Canon Law, The Theological Library, Chicago: Fides, 1958.

Denning, A., Freedom under the Law, London, 1949.

Doolan, A., Order and Law, Westminster, Md.: The Newman Press, 1954.

Gregoire, V., Laws, The Theological Library, Chicago: Fides, 1956.

Herron, M., The Binding Force of Civil Laws, Paterson, N. J.: St. Anthony Guild Press, 1958.

Metz, R., What Is Canon Law?, London: Burns & Oates, 1960.

O'Sullivan, The Inheritance of the Common Law, Westminster, Md.: The Newman Press, 1951.

Passerin-D'Entrèves, A., Natural Law, London, 1951.

PELLAND, L., *Introduction aux sciences juridiques*, Montreal: Edit. Bellarmin, 1960.

PHELAN, G. B., *Law and Morality*, Milwaukee: Marquette University Press, 1955.

POUND, A., *Introduction to the Philosophy of Law*, New Haven: Yale University Press, 1959.

RILEY, L. J., *The History, Nature and Use of EPIKEIA in Moral Theology*, Washington: Catholic University of America, 1948.

RODRIGO, L., *Tractatus de Legibus*, Santander: Sal Terrae, 1944.

ROMMEN, H., *The Natural Law*, St. Louis: Herder Book Company, 1947.

RYAN, G. A., *Principles of Episcopal Jurisdiction*, Washington: Catholic University of America, 1939.

SIMON, YVES R., *Philosophy of Democratic Government*, Chicago: Loyola University Press, 1951.

ST. JOHN-STEVAS, N., *Life, Death, and the Law*, Bloomington, Ind.: Indiana University Press, 1961.

STONE, J., *The Province and Function of Law*, Cambridge, Mass.: Harvard University Press, 1950.

VECCHIO, G. DEL., *Philosophy of Law*, Trans. by T. O. Martin, Washington: Catholic University of America, 1953 (8th edit.).

Virtues and Sin

BEIRNAERT, L., *Sens chrétien du péché et sentiment de culpabilité*, Paris, 1949.

BERNARD, R., *Le péché*, Paris, 1930.

BILLOT, L., *De virtutibus infusis*, Romae, 1921.

————, *De personali et originali peccato*, Romae, 1931.

BOUQUILLON, T., *De virtutibus theologicis*, Brugis, 1875.

CAPECELATRO, A., *Le virtu cristiane*, Roma, 1913.

CARTON DE WIART, E., *De peccatis et vitiis in genere*, Mechliniae, 1932.

DI MONDA, A. M. (p.), *La legge nuova della libertà secondo S. Tommaso*, Napoli, 1954.

GARDEIL, A., *La vrai vie chrétienne*, Paris, 1935.

GILLON, L. B., *La théorie des oppositions et la théologie du péché au XIIIe siècle*, Paris, 1937.

GOUPIL, A. A., *Les vertus*, Paris, 1939.

GUILLAUME, P., *La formation des habitudes*, Paris, 1936.

HAAS, J., *Die Stellung Iesu zur Sünde u. Sünder nach den vier Evangelien*, Fribourg, 1954.

HOFFMANN, R., *Die theorische Tugend*, Münich, 1933.

HUESMAN, W., *The Doctrine of Leonard Lessius on Mortal Sins*, San Francisco, 1947.

JANKELEVITCH, V., *Traité des vertus*, Paris, 1949.

JERPHAGNON, L., *Le mal et l'existence*, Paris, 1955.

KIRCHGAESSNER, A., *Erlösung und Sünde im Neuen Testament*, Freiburg, 1950.

LACOULINE, P., *Imperfection ou péché véniel*, Quebec, 1945.

LANDGRAF, A., *Das Wesen der lässlichen Sünde in der Scholastik bis Thomas von Aquin*, Bamberg, 1923.

LANFRANCO, A., *La necessità delle virtù morali infuse secondo S. Tommaso*, Casale Monferrato, 1942.

LAUMONNIER, J., *La thérapeutique des péchés capitaux*, Paris, 1922.

————, *L'homme et le péché*, Coll. "Présences," Paris, 1938.

LUMBRERAS, L. P., *De habitibus et virtutibus in communi*, Romae, 1950.

MAUGIERI, G., *Il mistero del peccato veniale*, Firenze, 1942.

MEUNESSIER, A. J., *Les "habitus" et les vertus* (Initiation théologique, vol. III), Paris, 1952.

MONTANARI, F., *Il mistero del peccato*, Roma, 1959.

NOBLE, H. D., *L'amitié avec Dieu*, Paris, 1932.

————, *La vie pécheresse*, Paris, 1937.

OREB, M. J., *Notio peccati in Didaché*, Romae, 1946.

PALAZZINI, P., *Il peccato*, Roma, 1959.

PARENT, J. M., *Les vertus morales infuses dans la vie chrétienne*, Ottawa-Montréal, 1944.

PIEPER, J., *Uber das christliche Menschenbild*, Leipzig, 1936.

REGATILLO, E. F.—ZALBA, M., *Theologiae moralis summa*, Matriti, 1952.

REGNIER, J., *Le sens du péché*, Paris, 1954.

————, *Notes sur la théologie du péché*, Paris, 1957.

STOLZ, A., *Théologie de la mystique*, Chétogne, 1947.

————, *Théologie de l'ascèse*, Chétogne, 1948.

UTZ, F. M., *De connexione virtutum moralium inter se secundum doctrinam S. Thomae Aquinatis*, Oldenburg, 1947.

VIGHETTI, O., *Origine e connessione delle virtu cardinali secondo S. Bonaventura*, Roma, 1947.

VOEGTLE, A., *Tugend und Lasterkatolog im N.T.*, Münster, 1936.

WAFFELAERT, J., *De virtutibus cardinalibus*, Brugis, 1889.

ZIERMANN, B., *De peccato actuali secundum mentem Divi Thomae Aquin*, Bonn, 1935.

Additional Works

CANICE, F., *Humility*, Westminster, Md.: The Newman Press, 1951.

CARLSON, S., *The Virtue of Humility*, Dubuque, 1953.

GARRIGOU-LAGRANGE, R., *The Three Ways of the Spiritual Life*, London: Burns & Oates, 1938.

GATTERER, M., *Educating to Purity*, New York: Pustet, 1922.

HILDEBRAND, D. VON, *Transformation in Christ*, New York: Longmans, 1948.

LASANCE, F. X., *Patience*, New York, 1937.

PARENTE, P. P., *The Ascetical Life*, St. Louis: Herder Book Company, 1955.

PIERSE, G., *Virtues and Vices*, Milwaukee: Bruce Publishing Company, 1935.

POURRAT, P., *Christian Spirituality*, Westminster, Md.: The Newman Press, 1955.

RONDET, H., *Theology of Sin*, Chicago: Fides, 1960.

SHEEDY, C., *The Christian Virtues*, Notre Dame, Ind.: Notre Dame University Press, 1949.

SCHOELLGEN, W., *The Basic Problem of Education in Morals*, Dusseldorf: Patmos, 1956.

VAISSIERE, J., DE LA, *Modesty*, St. Louis: Herder Book Company, 1937.

Faith

AUBERT, R., *Le problème de l'acte de foi*, Louvain, 1945.

BIEDA, I., *Fides humanae salutis initium*—*Doctrina Patrum in primis quinque saeculis*, Romae, 1950.

BRUNNER, A., *Glaube und Erkenntnis philosophische-theologische Darlegung*, München, 1951.

CIVERA, A., *L'oggetto materiale della fede*, Rovigo, 1954.

DESPINAY, A., *Le chemin de la foi d'après Saint Augustin*, Vezelay, 1930.

DONDAINE, A., *Foi chrétienne et pensée contemporaine*, Bruges, 1951.

GOUPIL, A. A., *Les vertus théologales*, Paris, 1935.

GUERARD, DES LAURIERS, M. L., *Dimensions de la foi*, Paris, 1952.

LEFEBURE, D. A., *L'acte de foi d'après la doctrine de Saint Thomas d'Aquin*, Paris, 1924.

MARETT, R., *Glaube, Hoffnung u. Liebe in der primitiven Religion. . .* , Stuttgart, 1936.

OLDRA, A., *Fede raggiante*, Roma, 1936.

PEDERZINI, N., *L'atto di fede*, Roma, 1960.

PRETE, B., *La fede*, Alba, 1953.

REDINGTON, A., *The Act of Faith in the Theology of Suarez*, Roma, 1939.

RINALDI, G., *Il problema della fede*, Milano, 1950.

SCHMITT-EUGLIN, P., *Le mécanisme de la déchristianisation*, Paris, 1952.

SOIRON, T., *Glaube, Hoffnung u. Liebe*, Ratisbona, 1934.

THAMARY, E., *Les vertus théologales; leur culte par la prière et la vie liturgique*, Avignon, 1935.

VANGHELUWE, A., *De actu fidei divinae eiusque infallibilitate*, in *Collat. brugenses*, 49 (1953), 57–64.

———, *De irrevocabilitate fidei*, ibid., 49 (1953) 434–444.

VORGULIN, ST., *La fede nel profeta Isaia*, Roma, 1950.

Additional Works

BARS, H., *The Assent of Faith*, London, 1960.

CRISTIANI, L., *Why We Believe*, Twentieth Century Encyclopedia of Catholicism, New York: Hawthorn Books, Inc., 1959.

D'ARCY, M. C., *The Nature of Belief*, St. Louis: Herder Book Company, 1959.

GUARDINI, R., *The Life of Faith*, Westminster, Md.: The Newman Press, 1961.

JOYCE, E., *What Is Faith?*, Twentieth Century Encyclopedia of Catholicism, New York: Hawthorn Books, Inc., 1958.

LIEGE, P. A., *The Sources of Christian Faith*, The Theological Library, Chicago: Fides, 1957.

Hope

AMIOT, F., *L'enseignement de Saint Paul*, Paris, 1938.

BARTMANN, B., *La nostra fede nella Provvidenza*, Brescia, 1932.

CONALON, G. M., *De certitudine spei secundum S. Thomas*—*Fontes et documenta*, Washington, 1947.

DONNA, P. B., *Despair and Hope. A Study in Langland and Augustine*, Washington, 1948.

Espoir humain et espérance chrétienne. Semaine des intellectuels catholiques, Paris, 1951.

GARRIGOU-LAGRANGE, R., *La provvidenza e la confidenza in Dio. Fedeltà e abbandono*, Torino, 1933.

GAY, C., *Vita e virtu cristiane considerate nello stato religioso*, I, Padova, 1937.

GENTILONI SILVERI, F., *Jean-Paul Sartre contro la speranza*, Roma, 1952.

HERIS, C. V., *Il mistero di Dio*, Brescia, 1950.

JURGENSMEIER, F., *Il corpo mistico di Cristo come principio dell'ascetica*, Brescia, 1937.

KRAMER, C., *Fear and Hope according to Saint Alphonsus Liguori*, Washington, 1951.

LECLERCQ, J., *Essais de morale catholique*, Bruxelles, 1931.

LE TILLY, J., *L'espérance*, Paris, 1950.

LUMBRERAS, P., *De spe et caritate*, Madrid, 1954.

MURA, E., *Il corpo mistico di Cristo*, II, Roma, 1949.

OLIVIER, B., *Petit traité de l'espérance chrétienne*, Liège, 1952.

PEGUY, C., *Das Mysterium der Hoffnung*, Darmstadt und Frankfurt a. M., 1952.

PIEPER, J., *Sulla speranza*, Brescia, 1953.

SERTILLANGES, A. D., *Les vertus théologales. II. L'espérance*, Paris, 1913.

SPICQ, C., *La révélation de l'espérance dans le Nouveau Testament*, Paris, 1930.

URS VON BALTHASAR, H., *Le chrétien et l'angoisse*, Bruges-Paris, 1954.

VAN LOOCK, E., *La révélation de l'espérance dans le Nouveau Testament*, Paris, 1930.

ZIMARA, C., *Das Wesen der Hoffnung in Natur und Ubernatur*, Freiburg, 1937.

Additional Works

MARCEL, G., *Homo Viator*, London, 1951.

OLIVIER, B., *Hope*, The Theological Library, Chicago: Fides, 1957.

Charity

BANNEZ, D., *De fide, spe et charitate*, Lugduni, 1588.

BAUDRILLARD, A., *La charité aux premiers siècles du christianisme*, Paris, 1903.

BOUVIER, L., *Le précepte de l'aumône chez S. Thomas d'Aquin*, Montréal, 1935.

BRUCCULERI, A., *Il pensiero sociale di S. Agostino*, Roma, 1932.

FALANGA, A. J., *Charity the Form of the Virtues According to Saint Thomas*, Washington, 1948.

GEIGER, L. B., *Le problème de l'amour chez saint Thomas d'Aquin*, Montréal, 1952.

GILSON, E., *Wisdom and Love in Saint Thomas Aquinas*, Milwaukee, 1952.

GIORDANI, I., *Il messaggio sociale di Gesu. I. Gli evangeli*, Milano, 1946.

———, *Il messaggio sociale degli Apostoli*, Milano, 1938.

———, *Il messaggio sociale di Gesu—Primi Padri della Chiesa*, Milano, 1947.

GRAHAM, A., *The Love of God*, London, 1939.

GRANIER, C., *Essai de bibliographie charitable*, Paris, 1891.

HAUSHERR, *Philanthropie. De la tendresse pour soi à la charité selon S. Maxime le confesseur*, Roma, 1952.

HEINEN, V., *Fehlformen des Liebesstrebens in moralpsychologischer Deutung u. moraltheologischer Würdigung*, Freiburg, 1954.

HENDERSON, C. R., *Modern Methods of Charity*, New York, 1904.

JANVIER, E., *La charité*, Notre Dame, 1914–1916.

KELLEY, C. F., *The Spirit of Love*, New York, 1951.

LALLEMAND, L., *Histoire de la charité*, Paris, 1902–1912, 5 vol.
LIESE, W., *Geschichte der Caritas*, Freiburg i. B., 1922.
LUKAS VOGEL, G., *Psicologia del profondo*, Roma, 1959.
MAEFFERT, J., *Caritas und Volkoepidemien*, Friburgi, 1925.
———, *Caritas und Krankewesen*, Friburgi, 1927.
MARIN, E. A., *S. Gregorio I, papa della carità*, Roma, 1951.
MICHEL, A., *La question sociale et les principes théologiques. Justice légale et charité*, Paris, 1922.
NEYRON, G., *Petite histoire de la charité*, Paris, 1927.
NICOLAS, J. A., *Dio è l'amore*, Brescia, 1953.
PEPIN, A., *La charité envers Dieu*, Paris, 1952.
PETROCCHI, G., *La carità*, Torino, 1948.
PRENTICE, R., *The Psychology of Love according to St. Bonaventure*, St. Bonaventure, N. Y., 1951.
RICHARD, T., *Etudes de théologie morale. I. Le plus parfait*, Paris, 1933.
RULAND, L., *Morality and the Social Order*, St. Louis, 1942.
SPIAZZI, R., *Teologia della carità*, Roma, 1957.
SPICQ, C., *Prolégomènes à une théologie néotestamentaire de l'Agapé*, Louvain, 1955.
TOMMASO, D'AQUINO (S.), *Quaestiones disputatae de charitate*, ed. Marietti, Taurini-Romae, 1927.
UNION DES RELIGIEUSES ENSEIGNANTES, *L'éducation de la charité*, Paris, 1957.
VALUY, B., *Fraternal Charity*, New York, 1948.
VAN ROEY, E., *De virtute charitatis quaestiones selectae*, Malines, 1929.
VIEUJEAN, J., *L'autre toi-même*, Tournai, 1952.
VITO, F., *La riforma sociale secondo la dottrina cattolica*, Milano, 1945.
WARNACH, V., *Agape. Die Liebe als Grundmotiv der neutestamentlichen Theologie*, Düsseldorf, 1951.
WIGGERS, J., *Commentaria de virtutibus theologicis: fide, spe, charitate*, Lugduni, 1666.

Additional Works

ADAM, A., *The Primacy of Love*, Westminster, Md.: The Newman Press, 1958.
BOYLAN, E., *This Tremendous Lover*, Westminster, Md.: The Newman Press, 1947.
COLIN, L., *Love One Another*, Westminster, Md.: The Newman Press, 1958.
———, *Love the Lord Thy God*, Westminster, Md.: The Newman Press, 1956.
D'ARCY, M. C., *The Mind and Heart of Love*, London, 1954.
GARRIGOU-LAGRANGE, R., *The Love of God and the Cross of Jesus*, St. Louis: Herder Book Company, 1947.
GRAHAM, A., *The Love of God*, London, 1939 (Image Books, Doubleday).
GILLEMAN, G., *The Primacy of Charity in Moral Theology*, Westminster, Md.: The Newman Press, 1959.
ST. FRANCIS DE SALES, *Introduction to a Devout Life*, Westminster, Md.: The Newman Press, 1959.

Religion

ALLEVI, L., *Religione e religioni*, Torino, 1948.
ANWANDER, A., *La religione e le religioni*, Alba, 1956.
BALDUCCI, C., *Gli indemoniati*, Roma, 1959.

BOCCASSINO, R., *Etnologia religiosa*, Torino, 1958.
BOULARD, F., *Premiers itinéraires en sociologie religieuse*, Paris, 1954.
BOUQUILLON, T., *De virtute religionis*, Brugis, 1881.
CAMBIAGHI, P., *Il laicismo*, Padova, 1960.
CURRAN, J. W., *The Thomistic Concept of Devotion*, Chicago, 1941.
DESQUEYRAT, A., *La crisi religiosa del nostro tempo*, Bologna, 1958.
DIGNANT-WILLELMS, *Tractatus de virtute religionis*, Brugis, 1940.
DAUJAT, J., *La vita soprannaturale*, Roma, 1958.
GUARDINI, R., *Introduzione alla preghiera*, Brescia.
HAERING, B., *Potenza e impotenza della religione*, Roma, 1958.
HAINE, A. J. J., *De hyperdulia eiusque fundamento*, Louvain, 1864.
HAMMAN, A., *La prière. Le Nouveau Testament*, Tournai, 1959.
JANVIER, A., *La giustizia verso Dio*, Torino, 1938.
LANZA, A.—PALAZZINI, P., *De virtutibus theologicis ac de religione*, Taurini-Romae, 1955.
MASI, R.—ALESSANDRI, M., *Religione, Scienza e Filosofia*, Brescia, 1958.
MENSCHING, G., *Sociologie religieuse*, Paris, 1951.
OLGIATI, F., *La pietà cristiana*, Milano, 1952.
PENNA, A., *La religione di Israele*, Brescia, 1958.
PIEPER, J., *"Otium" e culto*, Brescia, 1956.
SHEEN, FULTON J., *Religion without God*, New York, 1928.
———, *Philosophy of religion*, New York, 1948.
SUAREZ, F., *De religione*, in *Opera omnia* (ed. Parisiis, 1856 ff., vv. XII–XVI).

Additional Works

CONGAR, Y. M. J., *Lay People in the Church*, Westminster, Md.: The Newman Press, 1957.
D'ARCY, M. C., *Christian Morals*, London, 1937.
HILDEBRAND, D. VON, *Liturgy and Personality*, New York: Longmans, 1943.
HEINISCH, P., *Theology of the Old Testament*, Collegeville, Minn.: The Liturgical Press, 1950.
LEBRETON, J., *The Spiritual Teaching of the New Testament*, Westminster, Md.: The Newman Press, 1960.
LEMONNYER, A., *The Theology of the New Testament*, London: Sands, 1950.
MARSHALL, L. H., *The Challenge of New Testament Ethics*, London, 1946.
SPICQ, C., *New Testament Morality*, The Theological Library, Chicago: Fides, 1956.

Justice and Rights

ANTOINE, C.—DU PASSAGE, G., *Cours d'économie sociale*, Paris, 1921.
ANTONINO DA S. ELIA A PIANISI, *La proprietà*, Campobasso, 1958.
AZPIAZU, G., *L'uomo d'affari*, Roma, 1953.
BAUDHUIN, F., *Déontologie des affaires*, Louvain, 1944.
BECKAERT, J., *Les principes d'un ordre social chrétien*, Paris, 1949.
BELORGEY, G., *L'humilité bénédictine*, Paris, 1948.
BONOMELLI, G., *Questioni religiose, morali e sociali*, Roma, 1897, 2 vol.
BURGHARDT, A., *Etica e revisionismo della proprietà*, Alba, 1960.
CALAFATO, S., *La proprietà privata in S. Ambrogio*, Torino, 1958.

CALVEZ, J. Y.—PERRIN, J., *Eglise et société économique. L'enseignement social des Papes de Lion XIII à Pie XII* (1878-1958), Paris, 1959.

CARLSON, S., *The Virtue of Humility*, Dubuque, 1953.

CARNELUTTI, F., *Teoria generale del diritto*, Roma, 1940.

CARRIERE, J., *De iure et iustitia*, Parisiis, 1839.

——, *De contractibus*, Parisiis, 1844.

CATHREIN, V., *Recht, Naturrecht und positives Recht*, Freiburg i. B., 1909.

——, *Philosophia moralis*, Friburgi i. B., 1927.

CAVAGNIS, F. (Card.), *Institutiones iuris publici ecclesiastici*,[4] Romae, 1906.

C. C. I. F., *La conscience chrétienne et les nationalismes*, Paris, 1958.

CHAMBRE, H., *Christianisme et marxisme*, Paris, 1959.

CHRETIEN, P., *De iustitia*, Metis, 1947.

CLEMENS, R., *Personnalité morale et personnalité juridique*, Paris, 1935.

Code de morale internationale (Union internat. d'études sociales), Paris, 1937.

Code de morale politique (Union internat. d'études sociales), Paris, 1957.

Code social. Esquisse d'une synthèse sociale catholique (Union intern. d'études sociales), Paris, 1927.

CROLLY, G., *Disputationes theologicae de iustitia et iure ad normam iuris municipalis britannici et hibernici conformatae*, Dublin, 1870-1877, 3 vol.

DABIN, J., *La philosophie de l'ordre juridique positif*, Paris, 1929.

DAUPHIN-MEUNIER, A., *La Chiesa e il capitalismo*, Roma, 1956.

——, *La doctrine économique de l'Eglise*, Paris, 1953.

DELAYE, E., *Eléments de morale sociale*, Paris.

DELOS, J., *La communauté nationale dans la communauté humaine*, Lyon, 1946.

DELOS, P.—DE SOLAGES, *Essai sur l'ordre politique national et international*, Paris, 1947.

DELP, A., *L'honneur et la liberté du chrétien*, Paris 1958.

DE LUGO, J., *De iustitia et iure...*, Paris, 1868.

DE MONLEON, J., *Les XII degrés de l'humilité*, Paris, 1951.

DEL VECCHIO, G., *La giustizia*,[2] Roma, 1951.

——, *Diritto ed economia*, Roma, 1954.

DEPLOIGE, S., *Le conflit de la morale et de la sociologie*, Paris, 1923.

Dizionario sociale, ed., A. Fappani, Roma, 1960.

DU PASSAGE, H., *Morale et capitalisme*, Paris, 1935.

EGENTER, R., *Von der Einfachkeit*, Ratisbona, 1947.

Enciclopedia sociale, ed., A. Ellena, Roma, 1958.

FAIDHERBE, A. J., *La justice distributive*, Paris, 1938.

FALLON, V., *Principes d'économie sociale*,[6] Namur-Louvain, 1934.

FANFANI, A., *Summula sociale*, Roma, 1953.

FERNANDEZ, J. M., *Justicia social*, Bogatá, 1955.

FOLLIET, J., *Morale internationale*, Paris, 1937.

——, *Morale sociale*, Paris, 1937.

GAUTHIER, R. A., *Magnanimité...*, Paris, 1951.

GENY, F., *Science et technique*, Paris, 1924.

GERBERT, F., *Das Wesen des Eigentums*, Düsseldorf, 1935.

GILLET, M. S., *Conscience chrétienne et justice sociale*, Paris, 1922.

GIOVANNELLI, G., *Lo sciopero secondo la scuola sociale cristiana*, Roma, 1959.

GIRARD, A.—TONNEAU, J.—LACHANCE, L., *La justice*, Paris, 1952.

GRANERIS, G., *Contributi tomistici alla filosofia del diritto*, Torino, 1949.

GUERRY, F., *La dottrina sociale della Chiesa*, Roma, 1958.

GUITTON, H., *Le catholicisme social*, Paris, 1945.

————, *Propriété et nationalisation*, Anvers, 1945.

HAERING, H. M., *De iustitia legali*, Freiburg, 1944.

HEYLEN, V., *Tractatus de iustitia et iure*,[5] Mechliniae, 1950.

HOOVER, E. J., *Maestros del engaño*, Mexico, 1959.

JANSSENS, E., *Cinq leçons sur la justice*, Gand, 1924.

JANSSENS, L., *Personne et société*, Gembloux, 1939.

JOUSSAIN, A., *Les rapports de l'economie et de la morale*, Paris, 1948.

KOTHEN, U., *L'enseignement social de l'Eglise*, Louvain, 1949.

LACHANCE, L., *Le concept de droit selon Aristote et saint Thomas d'Aquin*, Ottawa, 1948.

La conscience chrétienne et les nationalismes. Semaine des intellectuels catholiques 1958, Paris, 1958.

LACOR, J. L., *La philosophie politique de S. Thomas*, Paris, 1949.

La guerre et les chrétiens (Cahiers de la Pierre-qui-Vire), Paris, 1953.

LECLERCQ, J., *Introduction à la sociologie*, Louvain, 1948.

LECORDIER, G., *Morale du travail*, Paris, 1947.

LEFUR, L., *Les grands problémes du droit*, Paris, 1937.

LESSIUS, L., *De iustitia et iure*, Lugduni, 1653.

LORTAL, R., *Morale sociale générale*, Paris, 1935.

LOTTIN, O., *Le droit naturel chez saint Thomas d'Aquin et ses prédécesseurs*, Bruges, 1931.

LUMBRERAS, P., *De iustitia*, Romae, 1938.

MAGNIN, E., *L'état conception païenne et conc. chrét.*, Paris, 1951.

MARRES, P. H., *De iustitia*, Ruremundae, 1879.

MOLINA, L., *De iustitia*, Coloniae Allobrogum 1733, 5 vol.

MORIN, W., *La propriété privée, droit réel, droit limité d'après saint Thomas d'Aquin et les encycliques de Léon XIII et de Pie XI*, Montréal, 1936.

NEWMAN, J., *Foundations of Justice. A Historico-critical Study in Thomism*, Cork, 1954.

OLGIATI, F., *Il concetto di giuridicità e S. Tommaso d'Aquino*, Milano, 1943.

PAVAN, P., *L'ordine sociale*, Torino, 1953.

PELLOUX, R., *Les citoyens devant l'Etat*, Paris, 1955.

POTTIER, A., *De iure et iustitia*, Leodii, 1900.

RABIER, J. B., *La participation ouvrière au produit et à la gestion*, Paris, 1946.

RENARD, G., *Le droit, la justice et la volonté*, Paris, 1924.

————, *Le droit, l'ordre et la raison*, Paris, 1927.

————, *L'Eglise et la question sociale*, Paris, 1937.

RICHAUD, P., *Annexe au Directoire pastoral en matière sociale*, Paris, 1955.

RIPERT, G., *La règle morale dans les obligations civiles*, Paris, 1925.

RUSTANT, M., *L'automation, ses conséquences humaines et sociales*, Paris, 1959.

SAINT-PIERRE, A., *La vertu chrétienne de tempérance dans la vie religieuse*, Montréal, 1941.

SAUVY, A., *Théorie générale de la population*, Paris, 1952–1954.

SCHILLING, O., *Reichtum und Eigentum in der altkirchlichen Literatur*, München, 1908.

————, *Naturrecht und Staat nach der Lehre der alten Kirche*, München, 1914.

——, *Das Völkerrecht nach Thomas v. Aq.*, München, 1919.

——, *Der kirchliche Eigentumsbegriff*, München, 1920.

——, *Die christlichen Soziallehren*, München, 1926.

——, *Christliche Gesellschaftslehre*, München, 1926.

——, *Katholische Wirtschaftsethik nach den Richtlinien der Enc. Q. anno*, München, 1933.

SCHUSTER, J. B., *De iustitia*, Romae, 1938.

SEMAINE SOCIALE DE FRANCE 1954, *Crise du pouvoir et crise du civisme*, Lyon, 1954.

SKODA, F., *Doctrina moralis catholica de poena mortis. . .*, Romae, 1959.

SOLBERG, P. C.—CROS, G. C., *Le droit et la doctrine de la justice*, Paris, 1936.

STEINBUECHEL, T., *Die Ehrfurcht*, Stuttgart, 1947.

STEVEN, P., *Eléments de morale sociale*, Paris, 1955.

SWEENS, A., *Institutiones theologicae de virtute cardinali iustitiae*, Haaren, 1913.

TANQUEREY, A.—STEVEN, P., *De iustitia*, Paris, 1953.

TEDDE, A., *Problemi sociali alla luce del Vangelo*, Sassari, 1954.

TIBERGHIEN, A., *Sens chrétien et vie sociale*, Paris, 1954.

——, *Introduction aux morales professionnelles*, Paris, 1955.

TURCO, N., *La questione sociale*, Milano, 1946.

VALENSIN, A., *Traité de droit naturel*, Paris, 1935.

VAN GESTEL, A., *De iustitia et lege civili*, Groningae, 1896.

VAN ROEY, E. I. (Card.), *De obiectis et actibus ad iustitiam pertinentibus principia generalia*,[4] Mechliniae, 1923.

VERMEERSCH, A., *Quaestiones de iustitia*, Brugis, 1904.

VIALATOUX, J., *Signification humaine du travail*, Paris, 1953.

VILLAIN, J., *L'enseignement social de l'Eglise*, Paris, 1954.

WAFFELAERT, J., *Tractatus de iustitia*, Brugis, 1885, 2 vol.

——, *Etude de théologie morale sur l'obligation en conscience des lois civiles*, Tournai, 1884.

WELTY, E., *Herders Sozial-Katechismus*, Freiburg i. B., 1951–1958, 3 vol.

WILLAERT, L., *Religion et patriotisme*, Tournai, 1947.

ZAMANSKI, J., *L'avenir de l'entreprise*, Paris, 1947.

Additional Works

GIRARD, A. T., and LACHANCE, L., *Justice*, The Theological Library, Chicago: Fides, 1957.

KAVANAGH, J., *Manual of Social Ethics*, Dublin, 1955.

MARITAIN, J., *The Rights of Man and the Natural Law*, New York: Scribners, 1943.

MESSNER, J., *Social Ethics*, St. Louis: Herder Book Company, 1952.

PIEPER, J., *Justice*, New York: Pantheon, 1955.

STARK, W., *Social Theory and Christian Thought*, London, 1959.

WELTY, E., *Handbook of Christian Social Ethics*, London, 1960.

WU, C., *Fountain of Justice*, New York: Sheed and Ward, 1955.

Fortitude—Prudence—Temperance

ALBERTI, J., *De sexto et nono decalogi praecepto et de usu matrimonii*,[2] Romae, 1914.

ALLERS, R., *Sexual-Pädagogik*, Salzburg, 1934.

ARRIGHINI, A., *Siate puri*, Torino, 1924.

Babina, P., *L'amore e il sesso*, Milano, 1939.

Babina, P.—Edwards, R., *Il tormento della carne*, Milano, 1940.

Barre—Biot—De Greeff—Thibon etc., *Médecine et sexualité*, Paris, 1950.

Berge, A., *L'éducation sexuelle et affective*, Paris, 1948.

Bettazzi, R., *Il casto talamo*, Torino, 1949.

Boschi, P. A., *I libri della purezza—guida bibliografica*, Torino, 1948.

Bureau, P., *L'indiscipline des moeurs*, Paris, 1920.

Cavuzzo, G., *Guida per la difesa della moralità*, Roma, 1952.

Chretien, P., *De castitate*, Metis, 1938.

Combaluzier, Ch., *Science biologique et morale sexuelle*, Paris, 1947.

Deman, T., *La prudence*, Paris, 1949.

Doms, H., *Vom Sinn des Zölibats. Historische u. systematische Enwägungen*, Münster, 1954.

Eschbach, A., *Disputationes physiologicae-theologicae*, Romae, 1913.

Etudes Carmelitaines, *Mystique et continence*, Paris, 1952.

Folghera, J. D., *La tempérance*, Paris, 1928.

Fonsegrive, J., *L'éducation de la pureté*, Paris, 1905.

Fuchs, J., *Die Sexualethik des heiligen Thomas von Aquin*, Köln, 1949.

Gemelli, A., *Non moechaberis*, Florentiae, 1912.

Giese, H., *Sexualität des Menschen...*, Stuttgart, 1955.

Guarnero, L., *L'età difficile*, Torino, 1946.

Gubiert, I., *La purezza*, Torino, 1946.

Henry, A. M., *Prudence chrétienne*. Cahiers de la vie spirituelle, Paris, 1948.

Hering, J., *De fecundatione artificiali*, Romae, 1952.

Hildebrand, D. (von), *Reinheit und Jungfräulichkeit*,[2] München, 1933.

Honore, L., *Elle et toi, jeune homme*, Paris, 1946.

———, *Elle et toi, jeune fille*, Paris, 1946.

Husson, L., *Eléments de morale sexuelle à l'usage des maîtres de l'adolescence*, Paris, 1948.

———, *Il corpo umano* (Insegnamenti pontifici,[9]), Roma, 1959.

Jacquennet, G., *Tu resteras chaste*, Paris, 1931.

Janvier, E., *La temperanza*, Torino, 1937, 2 vol.

Lacroix, J., *Personne et amour*, Lyon, 1942.

Lafeteur, P., *La tempérance*, Paris, 1952.

Lanza, A.—Palazzini, P., *De castitate et luxuria* (Theologia moralis, Appendix), Taurini-Romae, 1953.

Lefevre, E., *La morale, amie de l'art*, Sainte-Anne de Beaupré (Québec), 1947.

Lepore, M., *La purezza come forza del corpo*, Torino, 1938.

Lumbreras, P., *De fortitudine et temperantia*, Roma, 1939.

———, *De prudentia*, Madrid-Roma, 1952.

Marcel, G., *Théatre et religion*, Paris, 1959.

Merkelbach, B. H.—Dantinne, G., *De castitate et luxuria*, Bruxelles, 1955.

Mersch, E., *Morale et corps mystique*, I, Paris, 1949.

Messenger, E. C., *Two in One Flesh*, London, 1943, 3 vol.

Mitterer, A., *Elternschaft und Gattenschaft nach dem Weltbild des hl. Thomas von Aquin und dem der Gegenwart*, Wien, 1949.

Niedermeyer, A., *Handbuch der speziellen Pastoralmedizin*, Wien, 1949–1953, 6 vol.

Novello, G., *La verginità nel laicato*, Roma, 1955.

OLGIATI, F., *I nostri giovani e la purezza*, Milano, 1918.

PAGANUZZI, E., *Purezza e pubertà*, Brescia, 1943.

PASQUALI, G., *Cine, stampa, radio nel pensiero di Pio XII*, Alba, 1954.

PIDOUX DE LA MADUERE, S., *La parrocchia*, Milano, 1958.

PIEPER, J., *Sulla fortezza*, Brescia, 1956.

———, *Sulla prudenza*, Brescia, 1956.

———, *Sulla giustizia*, Brescia, 1956.

RAULIN, A., *La prudence*, Paris, 1952.

RIGAUX, M., *La formation à la pureté*, Paris, 1937–1938, 2 vol.

RIVIERE, J., *Sur le devoir d'imprévoyance*, Paris, 1933.

ROUILLE, D., *Catholicisme et sexualité*, Paris, 1953.

RUITZ, A., *Educazione alla castità*, Torino, 1946.

SCHROETELER, P., *Sitte und Sittlichkeit*, Düsseldorf, 1926.

SCHUSTER, I. (Card.), *Il codice della purezza*, Milano, 1940.

SCREMIN, L., *Il vizio solitario*, Milano, 1946.

———, *La continenza sessuale giovanile e l'igiene*, Torino, 1944.

SOLOVIEV, W., *Le sens de l'amour*, Paris, 1946.

TIHAMER, T., *Giovinezza pura*, Venezia, 1928.

VAN ROEY, E. R. D., *Quaestio specialis de sexto decalogi praecepto*, Arimini, 1906.

VERMEERSCH, A., *De castitate et de vitiis contrariis*, Romae-Brugis, 1919.

VIZMANOS, F., *Las virgines christianas en la Iglesia primitiva*, Madrid, 1949.

WAFFELAERT, J., *De prudentia, fortitudine et temperantia*, Brugis, 1899.

WOUTERS, L., *De virtute castitatis et de vitiis oppositis*, Brugis, 1932.

Additional Works

GAUTHIER, A., *Fortitude*, The Theological Library, Chicago: Fides, 1957.

LEFETEUR, P., *Temperance*, The Theological Library, Chicago: Fides, 1957.

PIEPER, J., *Fortitude and Temperance*, New York: Pantheon, 1954.

———, *Prudence*, New York: Pantheon, 1959.

Truth—Fidelity

C.C.I.F., *L'Eglise et les civilisations*, Paris, 1956.

CHARMOT, F., *L'humanisme et l'humain*, Paris, 1934.

DE LUBAC, H., *Sur les chemins de Dieu*, Paris, 1957.

DEL VECCHIO, G., *La verità nella morale e nel diritto*, Roma, 1954.

GUSDORF, G., *Traité de l'existence morale. La fidélité, première vertu*, Paris, 1949.

HEER, F., *Réalité et vérité*, Louvain, 1955.

HOERMANN, K., *Warheit und Lüge*, Wien, 1953.

JANKELEVITCH, V., *Traité des vertus. Le courage et la fidélité. La sincérité*, Paris, 1947.

LACHANGE, L., *La philosophie du langage*, Ottawa, 1943.

LALOUP, J.—NELIS, J., *Hommes et machines: Initiation à l'humanisme technique*, Tournai, 1953.

———, *Communauté des hommes: Initiation à l'humanisme social*, Tournai, 1954.

LAVELLE, L., *La parole et l'écriture*, Paris, 1942.

———, *Traité des valeurs. Les valeurs intellectuelles*, Paris, 1955, p. 237–293.

MEHL, R., *De l'autorité des valeurs, des valeurs intellectuelles*, Paris, 1957.

MOEHLER, C., etc., *Liberté et vérité*, Paris, 1955.

Molitor, A., *Culture et christianisme*, Tournai, 1944.
Parain, B., *Recherches sur la nature et les fonctions du langage*, Paris, 1942.
Pierre, F., *L'Eglise et l'enseignement des disciplines profanes*, Lyon, 1958.
Robin, A., *La fausse parole*, Paris, 1953.
Sauvage, M., *Socrate ou la conscience de l'homme*, Paris, 1957.
Siewerk, G., *Ontologie du langage*, Paris, 1958.
Urs von Balthasar, H., *Phénoménologie de la verité*, Paris, 1955.

Pastoral Moral Theology

Acken, B. (van), *Der Priesterruf. Ein Beitrag zur speziellen Seelsorge*, Trier, 1931.
Aertnys, J., *Theologia pastoralis tradens praticam institutionem confessarii,*[6] Gulpen, 1916.
Alberione, G., *Appunti di teologia pastorale*, 3ª ed., G. Pistoni, Alba, 1960.
Alfonso Maria de' Liguori (S.), *Pratica del confessore*, edit., G. Pistoni, Modena, 1948.
Amberger, J., *Pastoraltheologie,*[4] Regensburg, 1883–1886, 4 vol.
Arnold, F. X., *Comunità di fede* (Studi pastorali, 5), Roma, 1959.
Bandas, R. G., *Contenuto e metodi della catechesi* (Studi pastorali, 3), Roma, 1959.
Barra, G., *Psicologia dei convertiti*, Roma, 1959.
Barth, A., *Enciclopedia catechetica*, Roma, 1959.
Beguiristain, S., *Rinnovamento pastorale* (Studi pastorali, 1), Roma, 1958.
Benger, M.—Klarmann, U., *Pastoraltheologie,*[2] Regensburg, 1890, 3 vol.
Bergmann, W., *Religion und Seelenleiden*, Augsburg, 1929.
Bless, H., *Psychiatrie pastorale*, Brugis, 1936.
Blouet, J., *Teologia pastorale* (Regimen 6), Roma, 1958.
Borgonovo, G., *Manna pastorale* (Brugis 1ª ed., 1926), Milano, 1948.
Camara de Barros, G., *Compendio di teologia pastorale*, Roma, 1953.
Canaletti Gaudenti, A., *La statistica ad uso della Chiesa*, Roma, 1939 ([1]).
Carbo, J. M., *Pastor bonus*, Romae, 1930.
Carbone, C., *La tattica apostolica nel vangelo*, Roma, 1959.
Chavasse, A., etc., *Eglise et apostolat*, Tournai-Paris, 1953.
Eymieu, A., *Le gouvernement de soi-même*, Paris, 1952, 1953, 1955.
Face au monde d'aujourd'hui: les laïcs dans l'Eglise (Actes du 2e Congres mondial de l'apostolat des laïcs), Roma, 1958, 3 vol.
Fischer, M., *Katholische Krankenseelsorge*, Freiburg, 1934.
Frassinetti, G., *Manuale del parroco novello,*[11] Alba, 1928.
Garrone, G., *L'action catholique*, Paris, 1958.
Gregorio Magno, *La regola pastorale*, ed. Paoline, Roma, 1941.
Groeber, C., *Christus pastor*, Brescia, 1932.
Hamman, A., *L'apostolat du chrétien*, Paris, 1956.
Hartmann, A., *Institutions theologiae pastoralis*... (ed. P. Adelhelmi a Stantio), Assisi, 1932.
Hitz, P., *L'annunzio missionario del vangelo* (Studi pastorali, 4), Roma, 1959.
Il laicato (Insegnamenti pontifici, 4), Roma, 1958.
Il problema femminile (Insegnamenti pontifici, 2), Roma, 1958.
Jungmann, J. A., *Catechetica*, Alba, 1956.
L'apostolat (Problèmes de la religieuse d'aujourd'hui), Paris, 1957.
L'educazione (Insegnamenti pontifici, 3), Roma, 1957.

LEONI, A., *Sociologia religiosa e azione pastorale*, Roma, 1955.

LOMBARDI, R., *Rifare il mondo*, Rocca di Papa (Roma), 1959.

MACCARI, C., *Il sacerdote oggi*, Roma, 1956.

MALO A., M., *L'art de gouverner...*, Montréal et Paris, 1956.

MERKELBACH, B., *Quaestiones pastorales*, Liège, 6 vol., 1926–1937.

MICHELETTI, A., *Summula theologiae pastoralis*,[2] Romae, 1925–1929, 2 vol.

NADDEO, E., *Il vero pastore. Norme pratiche di teologia pastorale...*, Roma, 1922, 2 vol.

NOPPEL, C., *Aedificatio Corporis Christi. Aufriss der Pastoral*, Freiburg, 1937.

PARODI, BONAV. D'ARENZANO, *La catechesi di S. Ambrogio*, Genova, 1957.

PERRIN, J. M., *L'ora dei laici*, Roma, 1957.

PFLIEGLER, M., *Esistenza sacerdotale*, Milano, 1959.

POGGIASPALLA, F., *La diocesi e la parrocchia*, Brescia, 1960.

PRUNER, J. (VON)—SEITZ, J.—THURNHOFER, F., *Lehrbuch der Pastoraltheologie*,[4] Paderborn, 1923–1928, 2 vol.

SEUMOIS, A., *L'anima dell'apostolato missionario*, Bologna, 1958.

SIGMOND, R., *Il problema demografico*, Brescia, 1958.

SINETY, R. (DE), *Psicopatologia e direzione spirituale*,[3] Brescia, 1944.

STOCCHIERO, G., *Pratica pastorale*[5] (Manuali cattolici, 26), Vicenza, 1936.

SUENENS, L. J., *L'église en état de mission*, Bruges, 1956.

TER HAAR, F., *De occasionariis et recidivis*,[2] Torino, 1939.

THILS, G., *Teologia e realtà sociale*, Alba, 1957.

TURCO, N., *Il trattamento morale dello scrupolo e dell'ossessione morbosa*,[2] Torino, 1921, 2 vol.

VAUTHIER, E., *Initiation à l'Action catholique*, Langres, 1955.

WENDEL, F. N., *The Formation of a Lay Apostle*, New York, 1954.

Additional Works

BONZELET, H., *The Pastoral Companion*, Chicago: Franciscan Herald Press, 1956.

BRUNO DE JESUS-MARIE, O.C.D., *Conflict and Light*, New York: Sheed and Ward, 1952.

HILDEBRAND, D. VON, *True Morality and Its Counterfeits*, New York: McKay, 1955.

LINDWORSKY, J., *Psychology of Asceticism*, London: H. Edwards, 1936.

MOORE, T. V., *Life of Man with God*, New York: Harcourt, Brace and Co., 1956.

———, *Heroic Sanctity and Insanity*, New York: Grune, 1959.

NUTTIN, J., *Psychoanalysis and Personality*, New York: Sheed and Ward, 1953.

O'BRIEN, V., *Emotions and Morals*, New York: Grune, 1950.

SNOECK, A., *Confession and Pastoral Psychology*, Westminster, Md.: The Newman Press, 1961.

VANDERVELDT, J., and ODENWALD, R., *Psychiatry and Catholicism*, New York: McGraw-Hill, 1957 (2nd edit.).

Professional Ethics

BAUDHUIN, F., *Déontologie des affaires*,[4] Louvain, 1950.

BICCHIERAI, G., *Il mondo degli affari e la morale*, Brescia, 1935.

CANESTRI, A., *Morale professionale per l'avvocato*, Roma, 1939.

CARRARA, G., *Il boicottaggio*, Milano, 1924.

CHANCHARD, P., *Biologie et morale*, Tours, 1959.

COLONNETTI, G., *La tecnica e lo spirito*, Milano, 1945.

COPPIETERS DE GIBSON, P., *La concurrence déloyale*, Bruxelles, 1936.

COULET, P., *La doctrine catholique du travil: salaire*, Paris, 1920.

——, *Crise de la morale dans les affaires*, Gand, 1922.

CREUSEN, J., *Quelques problèmes de morale professionnelle*, Bruxelles-Paris, 1935.

Ethical Standards and Professional Conduct, ed. B. Y. Landis (Annals of the American Academy of Political and Social Science, Philadelphia, 1955).

GUITTON, I., *Arte di vivere e di pensare*, Roma, 1957.

HILDEBRAND, D. (VON), *La morale professionale cattolica*, Roma, 1935.

JANSSENS, E., *La bourse et la conscience*, Louvain, 1929.

LUJAN GARCIA, J., *Deontologia veterinaria*, Lerida, 1953.

MASINO, C., *Deontologia farmaceutica*, Roma, 1950.

MCALLISTER, J. B., *Ethics with Special Application to the Medical and Nursing Profession*, Philadelphia, 1955.

MULLER, A., *La morale et la vie des affaires*, Tournai-Paris, 1951.

NIEBUHR, R., *Christian Realism and Political Problems*, New York, 1953.

NOSENGO, G.—PIACENTINI, T., *La spiritualità professionale*, Roma, 1954.

PASQUARIELLO, G., *Questioni morali nell'avvocatura*, Roma, 1934.

——, *Il notariato*, Roma, 1940.

——, *La magistratura*, Roma, 1942.

——, *Principi di etica nelle professioni giuridiche*, Roma, 1943.

PAYEN, G., *Déontologie médicale d'après le droit naturel*,[2] Zi-ka-wei, 1935.

PROSPERINI, F., *L'ostetrica e la sua missione*, Roma, 1954.

REGATILLO, E. F.—ZALBA, M., *De statibus particularibus tractatus*, Santander, 1954.

RONSIN, F. X., *Psicologia dei capi*, Roma, 1959.

SALSMANS, J., *Droit et morale. Déontologie juridique*, Bruges, 1925.

SCREMIN, L., *Dizionario di morale professionale per i medici*,[5] Roma, 1954.

TIBERGHIEN, P., *Introduction aux morales professionnelles*, Paris, 1955.

TODOLI, G., *Filosofia del lavoro*, Roma, 1957.

VOLPICELLI, L., *L'orientamento professionale*, Torino, 1958.

Additional Works

BONNAR, A., *The Catholic Doctor*, New York: P. J. Kenedy and Sons, 1952.

BOUSCAREN, T. L., *Ethics of Ectopic Operations*, Milwaukee: Bruce Publishing Co., 1944.

CONNELL, F., *Morals in Politics and Professions*, Westminster, Md.: The Newman Press, 1946.

CRANNY, T., *The Moral Obligation of Voting*, Washington: Catholic University of America, 1952.

CRONIN, J. S., *Catholic Social Principles*, Milwaukee: Bruce Publishing Co., 1950.

DAVIS, J. D., *The Moral Obligation of Catholic Civil Judges*, Washington: Catholic University of America, 1953.

FINNEY, P. A., and O'BRIEN, P., *Moral Problems of Hospital Practice*, St. Louis: Herder Book Company, 1956.

FLOOD, DOM P., *New Problems in Medical Ethics*, 4 Vols., Westminster, Md.: The Newman Press, 1956 ff.

GOOD, F. L., and KELLY, O. F., *Marriage, Morals and Medical Ethics*, New York: P. J. Kenedy and Sons, 1951.

HEALY, E. J., *Medical Ethics*, Chicago: Loyola University Press, 1956.

KELLY, G., *Medico-Moral Problems*, St. Louis: The Catholic Hospital Association, 1959.

KING, W., *Moral Aspects of Dishonesty in Public Office*, Washington: Augustinian Press, 1942.

McFADDEN, C. J., *Medical Ethics*, Philadelphia: F. A. Davis, Co., 1949.

MARSHALL, J., *Medicine and Morals*, New York: Hawthorn Books, Inc., 1960.

O'DONNELL, T. J., *Morals in Medicine*, Westminster, Md.: The Newman Press, 1959.

REGAN, R. E., *Professional Secrecy in the Light of Moral Principles*, Washington: Augustinian Press, 1943.

TODD, J. M. (ed.), *Work: A Symposium*, London, 1960.

Pastoral Medicine

ANTONELLI, J., *Medicina pastoralis*,[5] Roma, 1932, 4 vol.

AULETTA, G., *Storia dell'apostolato cristiano. L'evangelizzazione del mondo*, in *Somma del cristianesimo*, II, p. 509–544.

BARBE, C.—BIOT, R., etc., *Médecine et sexualité*, Paris, 1948.

BIOT, R., *Il corpo e l'anima*, Brescia, 1938.

——, *Médecine et sexualité*, Paris, 1950.

BLES, H., *Psychiatrie pastorale*, Bruges, 1936.

BOGANELLI, E., *Corpo e spirito*, Roma, 1951.

BON, H., *Medicina e religione*, Torino, 1950.

BONNAR, A., *Il medico cattolico*, Alba, 1953.

CAPELMANN, K.—BERGMANN, W., *Pastoral-Medizin*, Paderborn, 1923 (trad. franc. *La médecine pastorale*,[2] Paris, 1926).

COLAGIOVANNI, D.—RUOSI, D., *La delinquenza minorile. Fattori psico-sociali*, Bologna, 1959.

COMBALUZIER, C., *Science biologique et morale sexuelle*, Paris, 1957.

COUSSER, F.—BAILO, P.—ALFIERI, P., *Problemi medico-morali*, Bergamo, 1958.

ESCHBACH, A., *Disputationes physiologicae-theologicae*,[3] Romae, 1913.

ETUDES CARMELITAINES, *Direction spirituelle et psychologie*, Paris, 1951.

FISCHER, M., *Katholische Krankenseelsorge*, Freiburg i. B., 1934.

GERIN, G., *La medicina legale nei suoi momenti storici e nel suo sistema*, Roma, 1949.

HUGON, E., *Les maladies de la volonté: études psych., ascét. et myst.*, Paris, 1924.

KENRY, J. P., *Principles of Medical Ethics*, Cork, 1953.

NIEDERMEYER, A., *Handbuch der speziellen Pastoralmedizin*, Wien, 1949–1952, 6 vol.

——, *Compendium der Pastoralmedizin*, Wien, 1953.

PALMIERI, V. M., *Medicina legale canonistica*, Città di Castello-Bari, 1946.

——, *Ginecologia forense*, Napoli, 1955.

PAVANETTI, E., *Educación sexual de tu Hijo*, Montevideo, 1957.

PAYEN, G., *Déontologie médicale d'après le droit naturel*, Schiangai, 1935.

PAZZINI, A., *Il medico di fronte alla morale*, Brescia, 1951.

PENDE, N., *La scienza moderna della persona umana*, Milano, 1947.

——, *Dove vai uomo?*, Roma, 1958.

PICKETT, C. R., *Mental Affliction and Church Law*, Ottawa, 1952.

PROHASKA, L., *Esistenzialismo e pedagogia*, Roma, 1959.
PUJIULA, J., *La medicina pastorale*, Torino, 1948.
ROSSI, M., *Problemi medico-psicologici dell'adolescenza*, Roma, 1957.
RULAND, L., *Grenzfragen der Naturwissenschaften und Theologie*, I, München, 1935.
SALETTI, G., *La preparazione psico-fisica al parto e la sua valutazione*, Roma, 1959.
SCREMIN, L., *Dizionario di morale professionale per i medici*,[5] Roma, 1954.
SURBLED, G., *La morale dans ses rapports avec la médecine et l'hygiène*,[12-13] Paris, 1922, 1931, 4 vol.

Additional Works

CASEY, D., *The Nature and Treatment of Scruples*, Dublin, 1948. Westminster, Md.: The Newman Press, 1949.
CAMMACK, J., *Moral Problems of the Mental Defect*, New York: Benziger Bros., 1939.
CAVANAGH, J., and MCGOLDRICK, J., *Fundamental Psychiatry*, Milwaukee: Bruce Publishing Company, 1953.
DEMAL, W., *Pastoral Psychology in Practice*, New York: P. J. Kenedy and Sons, 1955.
FORD, J., *Depth Psychology, Morality and Alcoholism*, Weston, Mass.: Weston College, 1951.
LINDWORSKY, J., *Experimental Psychology*, New York: Macmillan, 1931.
MOORE, T. V., *The Nature and Treatment of Mental Disorders*, New York: Grune and Stratton, 1953.
O'BRIEN, J., *The Measure of Responsibility in Persons Influenced by Emotions*, Washington: Catholic University of America, 1948.
Proceedings of the Second Institute of the Clergy on Problems in Pastoral Psychology, New York: Fordham University Press, 1957.
SCHULTE, C., *Nervous Mental Diseases: Their Pastoral Treatment*, London: Caldwell, 1939.
SNOECK, A., *Mental Hygiene and Christian Principles*, Cork: Mercier, 1954.
TERRUWE, A., *Psychopathic Personality and Neurosis*, New York: P. J. Kenedy and Sons, 1958.
ZILBOORG, G. F., *The Psychology of the Criminal Act and Punishment*, New York: Harcourt, Brace & Co., 1954.

Sacraments in General

ANGHILERI, G., *Vita sacramentale*, Milano, 1943.
ARCUDIO, P., *De concordia Ecclesiae occid. et orient. in septem sacramentorum administratione*, Parisiis-Cranaaisu, 1621.
ASMUSSEN, H., *Das Sakrament*, Stuttgart, 1949.
BACCARI, R., *La volontà nei sacramenti*, Milano, 1941.
BILLOT, L., *De Ecclesiae Sacramentis*, I,[7] Romae, 1932.
BOUESSE, H., *Le sauveur du monde: l'économie sacramentaire*, Chambery-Leysse, 1951.
CAPPELLO, F. M., *Tractatus canonico-moralis de sacramentis*, Taurini-Romae, 1947.
CEUPPENS, P. F., *De sacramentis*, Torino-Roma, 1959.

CIAPPI, L., *De sacramentis*, Torino, 1956.

CIMETIER, F., *Les sacrements*, Lyon-Paris, 1942.

DE MEESTER, P., *Studi sui sacramenti amministrativi secondo il rito bizantino*, Roma, 1947.

DE SMET, A., *Tractatus dogmaticus moralis de sacramentis in genere, baptismo et confirmatione*, Brugis, 1925.

EVELY, L., *L'Eglise et les sacrements*, Bruxelles-Paris, 1956.

KING, J. J., *The Administration of the Sacraments to Dying Non-Catholics*, Washington, 1924.

LENNERZ, H., *De sacramentis in genere*, Romae, 1939.

LUGO, F. (DE), *Tractatus de sacramentis. Responsa moralia* (ed. J. B. Fournials, vol. VIII), Parisiis, 1868.

MUNOYERRO, L. A., *Moral médica en los sacramentos de la Iglesia*, Madrid, 1951.

MURPHY, G., *Delinquencies and Penalties in the Administration and Reception of the Sacraments*, Washington, 1923.

PIOLANTI, A., *De sacramentis*, Torino-Roma, 1955.

———, *Corpo mistico e sacramenti*, Roma, 1955.

———, *I sacramenti*, Firenze, 1956.

POURRAT, P., *La théologie sacramentaire*, Paris, 1910.

PROBST, F., *Sakramente und Sakramentalien*, Tübingen, 1872.

RAMBALDI, G., *L'oggetto dell'intenzione sacramentale*, Roma, 1944.

REGATILLO, E. F., *Ius sacramentalium*, Santander, 1945–1949.

RIVA, S., *La didattica sacramentale nella catechesi del ragazzo*, Milano, 1952.

ROGUET, A. M., *Les sacrements*, Paris, 1945.

ROMANI, S., *De sacramentis*, Romae, 1944 (Institutiones canonicae).

ROSATI, M., *La teologia sacramentaria nella lotta contro la simonia e l'investitura laica*, Tolentino, 1951.

SASSE, G. B., *Institutiones theologicae de sacramentis Ecclesiae*, Friburgi i. B., 1897.

SCHMAUS, M., *Die Lehre von den Sakramenten*, Münich, 1952.

SCHOELLING, G., *Les sacrements*, Mulhouse-Tournai, 1938.

SIMONIN, H.—MEERSSEMAN, G., *De sacramentorum efficientia apud theologos O.P.*, Romae, 1936.

SULLIVAN, E. H., *Proof of the Reception of the Sacraments*, Washington, 1944.

VAN DEN EYNDE, D., *Les définitions des sacrements pendant la première période de la théologie scholastique*, Roma-Louvain, 1950.

VILLIEN, A., *Les sacrements: histoire et liturgie*, Paris, 1931 ([1]).

Additional Works

GRENTE, G., *The Power of the Sacraments*, New York: P. J. Kenedy and Sons, 1951.

McAULIFFE, C., *Sacramental Theology*, St. Louis: Herder Book Company.

McCARTHY, J., *Sacraments. (Problems in Theology*, Vol. I). Westminster, Md.: The Newman Press, 1958.

PALMER, P., *Sacraments and Worship. (Sources of Christian Theology*, Vol. I). Westminster, Md.: The Newman Press.

———, *Sacraments and Forgiveness. (Sources of Christian Theology*, Vol. II). Westminster, Md.: The Newman Press.

PHILIPON, M., *The Sacraments in the Christian Life*, Westminster, Md.: The Newman Press, 1955.

Pohle, J., *Sacraments*, St. Louis: Herder Book Company.

Roguet, A. M., *The Sacraments in General*, The Theological Library, Chicago: Fides, 1958.

Salve, R. de, *The Dogmatic Theology of the Intention of the Minister in the Confection of the Sacraments*, Washington: Catholic University of America, 1949.

Baptism

Adler, N., *Taufe und Handauflegung*, Münster, 1950.

Benoit, A., *Le baptême chrétien au second siècle. La théologie des Pères*, Paris, 1953.

Bowen, J., *Baptism of the Infant and Fetus; an Outline for the Use of Doctors and Nurses,*[4] Dubuque, 1939.

Conway, W. J., *The Time and Place of Baptism*, Washington, 1954.

Corblet, J., *Histoire dogmatique, liturgique et archéologique du sacrement du baptême*, Paris, 1851–1882.

Crehan, J., *Early Christian Baptism and the Creed*, London, 1950.

Cuttaz, F., *Les effets du baptême*, Paris, 1934.

D'Ales, A., *Baptême et confirmation*, Paris, 1928.

De Smet, A., *Tractatus dogmatico-moralis de sacramentis in genere, baptismo et confirmatione*, 2ª ed., Bruges, 1925.

Echle, H. A., *The Terminology of the Sacrament of Regeneration according to Clement of Alexandria*, Washington, 1949.

Goodwine, J., *The Reception of Converts*, Washington, 1944.

Jacono, V., *Il battesimo nella dottrina di S. Paolo*, Roma, 1935.

Keaney, R. J., *Sponsor of Baptism according to the Code of Canon Law*, Washington, 1925.

Kenrick, F., *Treatise on Baptism*, Baltimore, 1852.

Laucrenou, E., *Petit traité du baptême*, Paris, 1925.

Lennerz, M., *De sacramento baptismi*, Romae, 1942.

McAllister, J., *Emergency Baptism*, Milwaukee, 1945.

Merkelbach, B. H., *Quaestiones de embryologia et de ministratione baptismatis*, Liège, 1928.

Michel, A., *Les enfants morts sans baptême*, Paris, 1954.

O'Rourke, J., *Parish Register*, Washington, 1934.

Plus, R., *Battesimo e cresima*, Torino, 1933.

Risi, F., *De baptismo parvulorum in primitiva Ecclesia*, Romae, 1870.

Schnakenburg, R., *Das Heilsgeschehen bei der Taufe nach dem Apostel Paulus*, München, 1950.

Waldron, J. F., *The Minister of Baptism*, Washington, 1942 (²).

Confirmation

Blunt, *Confirmation, Its History and Meaning*, London, 1889.

Coleman, J. J., *The Minister of Confirmation*, Washington, 1941.

Coppens, J., *L'imposition des mains et les rites connexes dans le N. T. et dans l'Eglise ancienne*, Paris, 1925.

Cuttaz, F., *Notre Pentecôte, la grace du chrétien militant*, Paris, 1925.

DE ISASI ET GONDRA, F., *Theologia moralis. Tractatus . . . de confirmationis sacramento*, Barcinone, 1930.

DENS, F., *Tractatus de sacramentis in genere et de sacramentis baptismatis et confirmationis in specie*, Mechliniae, 1860.

DOELGER, F. X., *Das Sakrament der Firmung historisch-dogmatisch dargestellt*, Wien, 1906.

HALL, A. C., *Confirmation*, London, 1912.

JANSSENS, L., *La confirmation*, Lille, 1888.

KENRICK, F. P., *Baptism: also a Treatise on Confirmation*, Baltimore, 1852.

KOSTER, D., *Die Firmung im Glaubenssin der Kirche*, Ratisbona, 1948.

LARAS, M., *Confirmation in the Modern World*, New York, 1938.

LENNERZ, H., *De sacramento confirmationis*, Roma, 1945.

MORI, G., *Premilizia cristiana e confermazione*, Imola, 1940.

MOSTAZA RODRIGUEZ, A., *El problema del ministro extraordinario de la confirmación*, Salamanca, 1952.

NEUNHEUSER, B., *Taufe und Firmung*, Freiburg, 1956.

O'DOHERTY, KEVIN M., *The Scholastic Teaching in the Sacrament of Confirmation*, Washington, 1949.

O'DWYER, M., *Confirmation. A Study in the Development of Sacramental Theology*, New York, 1915.

PISTONI, I., *De confirmatione a ministro extraordinario*, Città del Vaticano, 1947.

UMBERG, J. B., *Die Schriftlehre vom Sakrament der Firmung*, Freiburg i. B., 1920.

Additional Works

BENNINGTON, C., *The Recipient of Confirmation*, Washington: Catholic University of America, 1952.

CAMELOT, T., *Baptism and Confirmation*, The Theological Library, Chicago: Fides, 1958.

DZIADOSZ, H., *The Provisions of the Decree, "Spiritus Sancti Munera,"* Washington: Catholic University of America, 1958.

MAHONEY, E. J., *The Priest As Minster of Confirmation*, London: Burns & Oates, 1952.

QUINN, J. S., *The Extraordinary Minister of Confirmation According to the Most Recent Decrees of the Sacred Congregations*, Rome: Officium Libri Catholici.

SMIDDY, T. W., *A Manual for the Extraordinary Minister of Confirmation*, Milwaukee: Bruce Publishing Company, 1949.

Holy Eucharist

ANGLIN, F. T., *The Eucharistic Fast*, Washington, 1941.

ANGULO, L., *Legislación de la Iglesia sobre la intención en la aplicación de la Santa Misa*, Washington, 1931.

BARBERO, G., *La dottrina eucaristica negli scritti di papa Innocenzo III*, Roma, 1953.

BATTIFOL, P., *L'Eucaristia,*[7] Parigi, 1927.

BENEDICTUS XIV, *De sacrosancto Missae sacrificio*, in MIGNE, *Cursus theol. compl.*, XXIII, Parisiis, 1863.

———, *De sacrosancto Missae sacrificio* (Opera omnia, VIII), Prati, 1843.

BERNARDI, V., *De sacrificio Missae*, Treviso, 1934.

BETTINELLI, P., *Le sacrifice*, Paris, 1946.

BORDIN, S., *La partecipazione dei fedeli al sacrificio della Messa*, Finalpia, 1948.

BRILLANT, M., *Eucharistie. Encyclopédie populaire sur l'Eucharistie*, Paris, 1947.

BRINKTRINE, J., *Das Opfer der Eucharistie*, Paderborn, 1938.

BUATHIER, F. M., *Le sacrifice dans le dogme cathol. et dans la vie chrétienne*, Paris, 1931.

BUSCH, B., *De initiatione christiana secundum doctrinam S. Augustini*, Romae, 1939.

CAHILL, D. R., *The Custody of the Holy Eucharist*, Washington, 1950.

CHOLLET, J. A., *La doctrine eucharistique chez les scolastiques*, Paris, 1905.

CLINTON, C., *The Paschal Precept*, Washington, 1932.

COGHLAN, D., *De SS. Eucharistia*, Dublini, 1913.

D'ALES, A., *De Eucharistia*, Parisiis, 1929.

DE LA TAILLE, M., *Mysterium fidei*, Parisiis, 1931.

DE LUGO, I., *Tractatus de vener. Eucharistiae sacramento*, in MIGNE, *Cursus theol. compl.*, XXIII, Parisiis, 1863.

DEMAN, T., *La spiritualité da la Messe*, Paris, 1946.

DENIS, N. M.—BOULET, R., *Eucharistie ou la Messe dans ses variétés; son histoire et ses origines*, Paris, 1953.

DE PUNIET, P., *The Mass, Its Origin and History*, London, 1931.

DONNELLAN, T. A., *The Obligation of the Missa pro populo*, Washington, 1946.

DORONZO, E., *De Eucharistia*, Milwaukee, 1947–1948.

DURIEUX, P., *L'Eucharistie. Memento canonique et pratique*, Paris, 1925.

FILOGRASSI, J., *De SS. Eucharistia*, Romae, 1957.

FRANZELIN, J. B. (Card.), *De Eucharistia*, Romae, 1932.

GARRIGOU-LAGRANGE, R., *De Eucharistia*, Augustae Taurinorum, 1943.

GASPARRI, P. (Card.), *De Eucharistia*, Parisiis, 1897, 2 vol.

GELSELMANN, J., *Die Eucharistielehre der Vorscholastik*, Paderborn, 1926.

GERBER, J. B., *La Sainte Eucharistie. Le sacrement et le sacrifice*, Paris, 1925.

GOLLEY, J., *Time and Place for the Celebration of Mass*, Washington, 1948.

GUTBERLET, C., *Das. hl. Sakrament des Altars*, Regensburg, 1919.

HENRY, J. A., *The Mass and Holy Communion: Interritual Law*, Washington, 1946.

HOLBOCK, C., *Die Bination*, Romae, 1941.

KELLER, G. F., *Mass Stipends*, Washington, 1925.

KOSTLER, L., *De custodia sanctissimae Eucharistiae*, Romae, 1940.

LEPICIER, J. (Card.), *De Eucharistia*, Romae, 1932, 2 vol.

LOMBARDI, E., *De pastorum obligatione applicandi Missam pro populo*, Romae, 1940.

MANY, S., *De SS. Eucharistiae Sacramento*, Parisiis, 1904.

———, *Praelectiones de Missa*, Parisiis, 1903.

MILLER, N. T., *Founded Masses according to the Code of Canon Law*, Washington, 1946.

MUELLER, J., *De SS. Eucharistia*, Innsbruck, 1921.

PASCHER, G., *L'Eucaristia e la communità dei fedeli*, Milano, 1959.

PIOLANTI, A., *Il mistero eucaristico*, Firenze, 1955.

PLUS, R., *L'Eucharistie*, Paris, 1933.

RAUSCHEN, G., *L'Eucaristia e la penitenza nei primi secoli*, Firenze, 1909.

RIGHETTI, M., *Storia liturgica: l'Eucaristia*, Milano, 1949.

ROMITA, F., *De Missarum satisfactione et reductione,* Romae, 1952.

SARTORI, G., *Le concezioni sacramentali del Sacrificio della Messa*, Bassano del Grappa, 1947.

SHEEHAN, D. E., *The Minister of Holy Communion*, Washington, 1950.

SPIAZZI, R., *L'Eucaristia nella vita cristiana*, Alba, 1952.

STADLER, J. N., *Frequent Holy Communion*, Washington, 1947.

SUAREZ, F., *Commentarii et disputationes in III S. Theol.*, Venetiis, 1599 (V. III: De Eucharistia).

THOBOLD, A., *La Messa e il sacerdozio dei fedeli*, Milano, 1939.

TOMAS DE MENDIJUR, *La Comunión del Sabado Santo*, Romae, 1947.

TONDELLI, L., *L'Eucaristia vista da un esegeta*, Alba, 1950.

VAN DER MEERSCH, J., *De cooblatione fidelium in sacrificio Missae*, Bruges, 1947.

VAN HOVE, A., *Tractatus de SS. Eucharistia*, Malines, 1941.

VARALTA, Z., *Natura giuridica del rapporto di offerte e accettazione dello "stipendium Missae"*, Roma, 1942.

VITORIA, J., *El pan y el vin eucaristico*, Bilbao, 1944.

VOLPI, I., *Comunione e salvezza in S. Agostino*, Roma, 1954.

VONA, C., *La quarta "petito" dell' "oratio dominica" nell'interpretazione di antichi scrittori cristiani* (Convivium dominicum—Studi sull'Eucaristia nei Padri della Chiesa antica e Miscellanea patristica), Catania, 1959.

WALTER, E., *La Eucaristia sacramento de la comunidad*, Barcelona, 1953 ([1]).

Additional Works

BERNADOT, M. V., *From Holy Communion to the Blessed Trinity*, Westminster, Md.: The Newman Press, 1947.

GRAIL, A., and ROGUET, A. M., *The Eucharist*, The Theological Library, Chicago: Fides, 1958.

MASURE, E., *The Christian Sacrifice*, Trans. by Dom I. Trethowan, New York: Benziger Bros., 1951 (Vol. I), 1955 (Vol. II).

NICOLAS, M. J., *What Is the Eucharist?* London: Burns & Oates, 1960.

RAUSCHEN, G., *Eucharist and Penance in the First Six Centuries of the Church*, St. Louis: Herder, 1913.

RUDDY, J., *The Apostolic Constitution "Christus Dominus,"* Washington: Catholic University of America, 1957.

VONIER, A., *A Key to the Doctrine of the Eucharist*, (Collected Works of), Westminster, Md.: The Newman Press, 1956.

Penance

ALLERS, R., *Autour d'une psychologie de la confession*, Etudes Carmélitaines, 1949.

ANCIAUX, P., *La théologie du sacrement de la pénitence au XIIe siècle*, Louvain, 1949.

BARDY, G., *La conversion au christianisme durant les premiers siècles*, Paris, 1949.

BATTIFOL, P., *Les origines de la pénitence*,[6] Paris, 1920.

BENAGLIO, G., *Dell'attrizione quasi materia e parte del sacramento della penitenza secondo la dottrina del Concilio di Trento*, Milano, 1948.

BLIC, J. (DE), *Sur l'attrition suffisante*, Lille, 1945.

BOUILLARD, H., *Conversion et grace chez Saint Thomas d'Aquin*, Paris, 1944.

BOUTIN, L. N., *La pénitence, le plus humain des sacrements*, Ottawa, 1950.

BOYER, C., *De poenitentia et extrema unctione*, Romae, 1942.

CAMBIER, O. F., *De divina institutione confessionis sacramentalis*, Lovanii, 1884.

CAMILLARI, M., *Confessori educatori*, Catania, 1953.

CAPPELLO, F. M., *De sacramentis*. II. *De poenitentia*, Taurini-Romae, 1944.

CARPINO, F., *Il "reditus peccatorum"*, Roma, 1937.

CHANSON, A., *Per meglio confessare*, 3ª ed., Alba, 1959.

CHARRIERE, F., *Ego te absolvo. Réflexions sur le sacrement de pénitence à l'usage du clergé*, Mulhouse, 1938.

CHRETIEN, P., *Tractatus de poenitentia*,[2] Metis, 1935.

D'ALES, A., *La théologie de Tertullien*, Paris, 1905.

———, *L'édit de Calliste*, Paris, 1914.

———, *De sacramento poenitentiae*, Parisiis, 1936.

DE ANGELIS, S., *De indulgentiis*, 2 ed., Città del Vaticano, 1950.

DE LUGO, I., *Disputationes scholasticae et morales de virtute et sacramento poenitentiae*, Lugduni, 1666.

DE SAN, L., *Tractatus de poenitentia*, Brugis, 1900.

DONDAINE, H., *L'attrition suffisante*, Paris, 1943.

DORONZO, F., *De poenitentia*, Milwaukee, 1949-1953, 4 vol.

FABBI, F., *La confessione dei peccati nel cristianesimo*, Assisi, 1947.

FAZZOLARO, F., *The Place for the Hearing of Confessions*, Washington, 1950.

FLYK, M., *L'attimo della giustificazione secondo S. Tommaso*, Roma, 1947.

GALTIER, P., *Le péché et la pénitence*, Paris, 1929.

———, *De poenitentia*,[3] Roma, 1950.

———, *L'Eglise et la rémission des péchés aux premiers siècles*, Paris, 1932.

———, *Aux origines du sacrement de pénitence*, Roma, 1951.

GARRIGOU-LAGRANGE, R., *La seconde conversion et les trois voies*, Paris, 1951.

GONZALES RIVAS, S., *La penitencia en la primitiva Iglesia española*, Salamanca, 1950.

GOUGNARD, A., *Tractatus de poenitentia*, Mechliniae, 1939.

GRAEF, R., *Das Sakrament der göttliche Bamberzlichkeit*, Ratisbona, 1950.

GRANDCLAUDON, M., *Comes confessarii. Recueil d'avis aux pénitents*, Mulhouse-Tournai, 1935.

GRAZIOLI, A., *La pratica dei confessori*, Colle D. Bosco-Asti, 1946.

HAHN, J., *Das forum internum*, Würzburg, 1941.

HARTMANN, P., *Le sens plénier de la réparation du péché*, Louvain, 1955.

HEUSCHEN, J., *Penthos. La doctrine de la componction dans l'Orient chrétien*, Roma, 1944.

HEYLEN, V., *De poenitentia*,[8] Mechliniae, 1946.

HONORE, L., *Le secret de la confession*, Bruges, 1924.

HORVATH, A. M., *Heiligkeit und Sünde im Lichte der thomistischen Theologie*, Freiburg (Schweiz), 1943.

HUGUENY, E., *La pénitence*, Paris, 1931.

KELLY, J. P., *The Jurisdiction of the Simple Confessor*, Washington, 1927.

KULTEHBACK, V., *The Sacred Penitentiaria and Its Relations to Faculties of Ordinaries...*, Washington, 1918.

LUGO, I., *Disputationes scholasticae et morales de virtute et sacramento poenitentiae*, Lugduni, 1666.

MANNING, E., *La confessione*, Roma, 1944.

MAURIAC, F.—D'ORS, E., *L'homme et le péché*, Paris, 1938.

McCARTNEY, M. A., *Faculties of Regular Confessor*, Washington, 1949.

McCORMICK, R. E., *Confessor of Religious*, Washington, 1926.

McNEIL, J. T.—GAMER, H. M., *Mediaeval Handbooks of Penance* (Record of Civilization, no. xxix), New York, 1938.

MELLET, M., *La pénitence, sacrement d'amitié*, Bruxelles, 1953.

MERKELBACH, B. H., *Quaestiones de variis poenitentium categoriis. Quaestiones de partibus poenitentiae. Quaestiones de variis peccatis in sacramentali confessione medendis*, Liège, 1927–1935.

MEYER, C. R., *The Thomistic Concept of Justifying Contrition*, Mundelein, 1949.

MORIARTY, G. E., *The Extraordinary Absolution from Censures*, Washington, 1938.

O'BRIEN, C., *Perfect Contrition*, Dublin, 1952.

PALMIERI, D., *Tractatus de poenitentia*, Prati, 1896.

PERINELLE, F., *L'attrition d'après le Concile de Trente et d'après Saint Thomas*, Kain, 1927.

POSCHMANN, B., *Die abendländische Kirchenbusse im Ausgang des christlichen Altertums*, München, 1928.

———, *Die abendländische Kirchenbusse im frühen Mittelalter*, Breslau, 1930.

———, *Poenitentia secunda*, Bonn, 1940.

———, *Buss und letze Oelung. Handbuch der Dogmengeschichte*, IV, Freiburg, 1951.

RAHNER, K., *L'Eglise et le pécheur*, Paris, 1948.

RUS, G., *De munere sacramenti poenitentiae in aedificando corpore Christi mystico*, Romae, 1944.

SALVADOR, A., *Iurisdictionis suppletio ab Ecclesia in errori communi*, Manila, 1939.

SISINIO DA ROMALLO, *Il ministero della confessione nei primordi dell'Ordine francescano in relazione ai diritti parrocchiali*, Milano, 1949.

SPITZIG, J. A., *Sacramental Penance in the Twelfth and Thirteenth Centuries*, Washington, 1948.

TAMBURELLI, G., *La pratica della confessione*, Torino, 1945.

TEETAERT, A., *La confession aux laïques dans l'Eglise latine depuis le VIIe jusqu'au XVIe siècle*, Paris, 1926.

THOMAS, AQ. (S.), *De forma absolutionis*, ed. P. Castagnoli, Piacenza, 1933.

TIMON, D., *Traité de la confession des enfants et des jeunes gens*,[15] Marseille, 1954.

TIXERONT, J., *Le sacrement de la pénitence dans l'antiquité chrétienne*, Paris, 1914.

TROMBETTA, A., *Il valore dell'assoluzione sacramentale nei teologi scolastici*, Roma, 1942.

VACANDARD, E., *La confessione sacramentale nella Chiesa primitiva*, Roma, 1929.

VALENTIN-BRETON, P., *La confession fréquente: histoire, valeur pratique*, Paris, 1945.

VAN ACKER, B., *Die Beichte, das Sakrament der vorsöhnung des Friedens*, Paderborn, 1938.

VOGEL, G., *La discipline pénitentielle en Gaule des origines à la fin du VIIe siècle*, Paris, 1952.

VOOGHT, P. (DE), *La théologie de la pénitence*, Bruges, 1949.

WATKIRES, O., *A History of Penance*, London, 1920 (acatt.).

WILCHES, F. A., *De errore communi in iure romano et canonico*, Roma, 1940.

Additional Works

BOUTIN, L., *Penance: The Most Human of the Sacraments*, Ottawa: University of Ottawa Press, 1954.

BURTON, J. M. T., *Penance and Absolution*, Twentieth Century Encyclopedia of Catholicism, New York: Hawthorn Books, Inc., 1961.

GALTIER, P., *Sin and Penance*, London: Sands, 1932.

HEENAN, J., *Priest and Penitent*, New York: Sheed and Ward, 1937.

KELLY, G., *The Good Confessor*, New York: The Sentinel Press, 1951.

MELLET, M., and HENRY, A. M., *Penance*, The Theological Library, Chicago: Fides, 1958.

O'BRIEN, C., *Perfect Contrition*, Dublin, 1952.

O'BRIEN, J. J., *The Remission of Venial Sin*, Washington: Catholic University of America, 1959.

ROSS, J. R., *The Seal of Confession*, Washington: Catholic University of America, 1960.

SNOECK, A., *Confession and Pastoral Psychology*, Westminster, Md.: The Newman Press, 1961.

TENSING, R., *Extra-sacramental Jurisdiction*, Washington: Catholic University of America, 1944.

WILSON, A., *Pardon and Peace*, New York: Sheed and Ward, 1954.

ZIEGLER, J., *The Obligation of the Confessor to Individual Penitents*, Washington: Catholic University of America, 1959.

Extreme Unction

BORD, J. B., *L'extrême onction d'après lépître de Saint Jacques (V, 14–15) examinée dans la Tradition*, Bruges, 1932.

BOYER, C., *Tractatus de sacramento poenitentiae et de extrema unctione*, Roma, 1942.

BRZANA, J. S., *Remains of Sin and Extreme Unction according to Theologians after Trent*, Roma, 1953.

CAPPELLO, F. M., *Tractatus canonico-moralis de sacramentis. III. De extrema unctione*, Taurini-Romae, 1942.

CHAINE, J., *L'épître de Saint Jacques*, Paris, 1927.

CHAVASSE, A., *Etude sur l'onction des infirmes dans l'Eglise latine du IIIe au XIIe siècle*, Lyon, 1942.

CUTTAZ, J., *Remède divin pour les chrétiens malades*, Tournai, 1950.

DE CLERCQ, E., *Ordre, mariage, extrême onction*, Paris, 1938.

GERSTER A ZEIL, T., *Sacramentum extremae unctionis. Tractatus theologicus*, Taurini, 1936.

GOUGNARD, A., *Tractatus de extrema unctione*, Mechliniae, 1938.

HANLEY, P., *Treatise on the Sacrament of Extreme Unction*, New York, 1907.

IORIO, D., *La sacra unzione degli infermi*, Roma, 1935.

KERN, J., *De sacramento extremae unctionis tractatus dogmaticus*, Ratisbonae, 1907.

KILKER, A. J., *Extreme Unction*, Washington, 1926.

KRYGER, H. S., *The Doctrine of the Effects of Extreme Unction...*, Washington, 1949.

LEDENT, G. M., *Le sacrament des malades*, Liège.

NETZER, H., *Extrême onction*, St. Louis, 1927.

QUINN, A., *Some Aspects of the Dogma of Extreme Unction*, Dublin, 1920.

SCHMITZ, J., *De effectibus sacramenti extremae unctionis*, Friburgi, 1893.

SPACIL, T., *Doctrina theologiae Orientis separati de sacra infirmorum unctione*, Romae, 1931.

STATKUS, F. J., *The Minister of the Last Sacraments*, Washington, 1951.

TEOLOGIA MECHLINIENSIS, *Tractatus de sacramento extremae unctionis*, Mechliniae, 1916.

Additional Works

DIDIER, J.-C., *The Last Rites*, Twentieth Century Encyclopedia of Catholicism, New York: Hawthorn Books, Inc., 1961.

GARRIGOU-LAGRANGE, R., *Life Everlasting*, St. Louis: Herder Book Company, 1952.

GUARDINI, R., *The Last Things*, New York: Pantheon, 1954.

HERBIN, P., *We Die Unto the Lord. . .*, London, 1960.

RENATI, C. G., *The Recipient of Extreme Unction*, Washington: Catholic University of America, 1961.

ROBILLIARD, A. J., *Extreme Unction*, The Theological Library, Chicago: Fides, 1958.

Holy Orders

AGATANGELO DA LANGASCO, *De institutione clericorum in disciplinis inferioribus*, Romae, 1936.

ALISEDA C. SÁNCHEZ, *La doctrina de la Iglesia sobre Seminarios del Concilio de Trento hasta nuestros dias*, Granada, 1942.

ANDRIEU, M., *Le Pontifical Romain au moyen age* (vol. 86–87 di Studi e testi), Città del Vaticano, 1938–1940.

BAISI, C., *Il ministro straordinario degli ordini sacri*, Roma, 1953.

BENEDICTUS XIV, *De synodo dioecesana*, Venetiis, 1788 (Opera omnia, XI).

BERTRAMS, W., *Il celibato sacerdotale*, Roma, 1960.

BEVILACQUA, A., *De episcopi seu ordinari ex novo Codice iuribus et obligationibus*, Romae, 1921.

BOTTE, B., etc., *Etudes sur le sacrement de l'ordre*, Paris, 1957.

BRUNINI, J. B., *The Clerical Obligations of Canons 139 and 142*, Washington, 1937.

CAPPELLO, F. M., *De sacramentis. IV. De ordine*, Taurini-Romae, 1947.

COSTELLO, J. M., *Domicile and Quasi-domicile*, Washington, 1930.

DLOUHY, M. J., *The Ordination of Exempt Religious*, Washington, 1948.

DONOVAN, J., *The Clerical Obligation of Canons 138 and 140*, Washington, 1948.

ESCUDERO, G., *El voto solemne de pobreza*, Romae, 1955.

FENTON, J. C., *The Concept of Diocesan Priesthood*, Milwaukee, 1951.

GASPARRI, P. (Card.), *Tractatus canonicus de s. ordinatione*, Parisiis-Lugduni, 1894, 2 vol.

HUARTE, G., *Tractatus de ordine et matrimonio*, Romae, 1931.

IUBANY ARNAU, N., *El voto de castidad en la ordenación sagrada. Estudio histórico-canónico*, Barcelona, 1952.

LANDUCCI, P., *La sacra vocazione*, Roma, 1955.

LENNERZ, H., *De sacramento ordinis*, Romae, 1928.

MANY, S., *De sacra ordinatione*, Parisiis, 1904.

MOEDER, J. M., *The Proper Bishop for Ordination and Dimissorial Letter*, Washington, 1935.

MORINUS, I., *Comm. historicus et dogmaticus de sacris ordinationibus*, Paris, 1655.

MORONI, A., *La volontà nell' "ordo sacer,"* Milano, 1957.

PELLICCIA, G., *La preparazione ed ammissione dei chierici ai sacri ordini nella Roma del sec. XVI*, Roma, 1946.

QUINN, J., *Documents Required for the Reception of Orders*, Washington, 1948.

REISS, J. C., *The Time and Place of Sacred Ordination. . .*, Washington, 1953.

SALLAGHER, T. R., *The Examination of the Qualities of the Ordinand*, Washington, 1944.

SWEENEY, F. P., *The Reduction of Clerics to the Lay State*, Washington, 1945.

TINELLO, F., *Dottrina sul sacerdozio*, Roma, 1955.

TIXERONT, G., *L'ordine e le ordinazioni*, Brescia, 1939.

TOUTON, G., *Les irrégularités et les autres empêchements aux ordres en droit byzantin*, Rome, 1955.

VAN ROSSUM, G. M., *De essentia sacramenti ordinis*, Romae, 1931.

VEUILLOT, P., *Il nostro sacerdozio* (Documenti pontifici, 3), Milano, 1956, 2 vol.

ZAEHRINGER, D., *Das Kirchliche Priestertum nach dem hl. Augustinus*, Paderborn, 1931 (¹).

Matrimony

ABELLAN, P. M., *El fin y la significación sacramental del matrimonio*, Granada, 1939.

ADAM, C., *La dignità sacramentale del matrimonio*, Milano, 1935.

ALFORD, C. B., *Jus matrimoniale comparatum. Jus matr. in Statibus foederatis Am. Sept. cum iure canonico comparatum*, Romae, 1938.

ANGELINI ROTA, A., *I figli adulterini e incestuosi nel diritto comparato*, Romae, 1940.

BACCARI, R., *L'efficacia civile del matrimonio canonico*, Roma, 1947.

BALLERINI, G., *Matrimonio e divorzio*, Milano, 1920.

BALLINI, A. L., *Il valore giuridico della celebrazione nuziale cristiana dal I sec. all'età giustinianea*, Milano, 1939.

BARTOCCETTI, V., *De causis matrimonialibus* (III. Comm. in judicia eccles.), Romae, 1951.

BECK, B., *De cautionibus sincere praestandis in matrimoniis quibus obstat impedimentum mixtae religionis aut disparitatis cultus*, Romae, 1956.

BERTOLA, A., *Il matrimonio religioso*, Torino, 1946.

BERTON, P., *La conception de la nullité de mariage en droit civil français et en droit canonique moderne*, Paris, 1938.

BERUTTI, P. C., *Il matrimonio*, Milano, 1947.

BIGATELLO, S., *L'uomo, la donna e il matrimonio*, Milano, 1958.

BO, G., *Il matrimonio per procura*, Padova, 1934.

BOGGIANO PICO, A., *Il matrimonio nel diritto canonico*, Torino, 1936.

BOISSARD, E., *Questions théologiques sur le mariage*, Paris, 1948.

BOSCHI, A., *Problemi morali del matrimonio*, Torino, 1953.

BOVA, P., *Matrimonio concordatario e sue controversie*, Milano, 1943.

BRANDILEONE, F., *Saggi sulla storia della celebrazione del matrimonio in Italia*, Milano, 1906.

BRUNELLI, G., *Divorzio e nullità di matrimonio negli Stati d'Europa*, Milano, 1937.

BUONACORE, G., *Il sacramento del matrimonio nel diritto canonico*, Roma, 1931.

CAFFAREL, H., *Pensieri sull'amore e la grazia*, Milano, 1958.

CAPPELLO, F., *De sacramentis. V. De matrimonio*, Taurini-Romae, 1950.

CARNELY, P. W., *The Purposes of Christian Marriage*, Washington, 1950.

CAROZZI, G., *La famiglia nel pensiero di Pio XII*, Milano, 1952.

CASORIA, I., *De matrimonio rato et non consummato*, Romae, 1959.

CASTELLI, P., *Il fidanzamento*, Milano, 1955.

————, *I diritti e i doveri della famiglia di fronte al problema scolastico*, Roma, 1955.

CAVIGLIOLI, G., *Guida allo studio canonico-morale del trattato "de matrimonio,"* Torino, 1941.

CERIANI, G., *La teologia della famiglia*, Milano, 1950.

CHATAM, J. G., *Force and Fear As Invalidating Marriage: The Element of Injustice*, Washington, 1950.

CHELODI, J.—CIPROTTI, P., *Jus canonicum de matrimonio*, Vicentiae, 1942.

CHIERICHETTI, G., *Impedimentum criminis*, Torino, 1958.

CHRETIEN, P., *Praelectiones de matrimonio*, Metis, 1937.

CHRISTIAN, A., *Ce sacrement est grand*, Paris, 1946.

COLOMBO, C.—GOLZIO, S.—PALMIERI, V. M.—LAMI, G., *Natalità e famiglia*, Roma, 1953.

DAUVILLIER, J., *Le mariage dans le droit classique de l'Eglise depuis le Décret de Gratien (1140) jusqu'à la mort de Clément V (1314)*, Paris, 1933.

DAUVILLIER, J.—DE CLERCQ, C., *Le mariage en droit canonique oriental*, Paris, 1936.

D'AVACK, P., *La base giuridica del nuovo diritto matrimoniale concordatario vigente in Italia*, Roma, 1932.

————, *Cause di nullità e di divorzio nel diritto matrimoniale canonico*, Roma, 1940.

DE BERNARDIS, L. M., *Il matrimonio di coscienza*, Brescia, 1935.

DE ECHEVERRIA, L., *El matrimonio en el derecho canónico particular posterior al código*, Vitoria, 1955.

DEL GIUDICE, V., *Il matrimonio nel diritto canonico e nel diritto concordatario italiano*, Milano, 1946.

DEL MAZZA, V., *La famiglia nel pensiero di Pio XII*, Alba, 1952.

DELPINI, F., *Divorzio e separazione dei coniugi nel diritto romano e nella dottrina della Chiesa fino al secolo V*, Torino, 1956.

DE MANARICUA, A. E., *El matrimonio de los esclavos. . .*, Romae, 1940.

DE SMET, A., *De sponsalibus et matrimonio,*[2] Brugis, 1927.

DOEDWELL, E. J., *The Time and Place for the Celebration of Marriage*, Washington, 1942.

DOSSETTI, I., *La violenza nel matrimonio in diritto canonico*, Milano, 1943.

DURIEUX, P., *Le mariage en droit canonique*, Paris, 1924.

ESMEIN, A.—GENESTAL, R.—DAUVILLIER, J., *Le mariage en droit canonique*, Paris, 1929–1935, 2 vol.

EYSINK, A. H., *Matrimonium clandestinum et matrimonium putativum*, Romae, 1957.

FAVILLA, P., *La famiglia*, Roma, 1948.

FEYE, J., *De impedimentis et dispensationibus matrimonialibus*, Lovanii, 1885.

FISCHER, J., *Ehe und Jungfraulichkeit im Neuen Testament*, Münster, 1919.

FOURNERET, P., *Le mariage chrétien*, Paris, 1921.

FREISEN, J., *Geschichte des canonischen Eherechts biz zum verfall der Grossenliteratur*, Paderborn, 1893.

GALLAGHER, J. F., *The Matrimonial Impediment of Public Propriety*, Washington, 1952.

GASPARRI, P. (Card.), *Tractatus canonicus de matrimonio,*[2] Romae, 1932, 2 vol.

GEORG, J. E., *Agenesi e fecondità nel matrimonio*, Torino, 1948.

GIACCHI, O., *Il consenso nel matrimonio canonico*, Milano, 1950.

GIBBONS, M. L., *Domicile of Wife Unlawfully Separated from Her Husband*, Washington, 1947.

GILLMAN, F., *Zur christlicher Ehelehre*, Mainz, 1936.

GOFFI, T., *Morale familiare*, Brescia, 1958.

GOMEZ-LUNA, N., *"Quod Deus coniunxit" o los albores de la fidelidad en el amor humano*, Cucuta, 1949.

GOUGNARD, A., *Tractatus de matrimonio,*[8] Mechliniae, 1937.

GREGNANIN, A., *Il matrimonio della Rep. socialista feder. sovietica russa...*, Roma, 1956.

GRONDIN, E., *Les causes de nullité du mariage entre infidéles*, Tabora, 1954.

GRZYMALA, E., *Ratio sacra in matrimonio canonico et civili*, Romae, 1935.

GUARISE, S., *Gioia di vivere. Note psicologiche sul fidanzamento e sul matrimonio*, Brescia, 1958.

GUZZETTI, G. B., *Matrimonio, famiglia, verginità*, Torino, 1957.

HERRERA, A., *La doctrina canónico-legal del contrato esponsalicio en la legislación y jurisprudencia postridentinas*, Roma, 1942.

HEYLEN, V., *Tractatus de matrimonio,*[9] Mechliniae, 1945.

HILDEBRAND, D. (VON), *Il matrimonio*, Brescia, 1959.

HINZ, L. G., *The Celebration of Marriage in Canada*, Ottawa, 1957.

JEMOLO, A. C., *Il matrimonio nel diritto canonico*, Milano, 1941.

JOMBART, E., *Le mariage*, Paris, 1925.

JONG, M. (DE), *De matrimonii essentia, definitione et indissolubilitate intrinseca...*, Romae, 1949.

JOYCE, G. H., *Matrimonio cristiano. Studio storico dottrinale*, Alba, 1954.

KEVANE, R. A., *Matrimonial Procedure in the Law of Church of England and in the Code of Canon Law...*, Rome, 1957.

KIENITZ, E. (VON), *Die christliche Ehe. Eine Darstellung des Eherechts u. Ehemoral der kath. Kirch.*, Frankfurt, 1938.

LANZA, A., *De fine primario matrimonii*, Romae, 1941.

LAVAUD, B., *Le monde moderne et le mariage chrétien*, Paris, 1935.

LECLERCQ, J., *Mariage chrétien*, Paris, 1947.

LEITE, A., *Competencia da Igreja e do Estado sobre o matrimonio*, Porto, 1946.

LE PICARD, R., *Divorce et bien public. Peut-il être permis de demander le divorce? Que faire contre le divorce?*, Paris, 1946.

LIBOIS, L.—ADAM, M., *Le droit familial*, Thuillies, 1937.

LIGGERI, P., *Problemi di vita matrimoniale*, Milano, 1959.

LINDER, D., *Der "Usus Matrimonii,"* München, 1929.

LIONETTI, D., *Questioni di teologia morale anglicana in base alle conferenze di Lambeth ed ai teologi anglicani moderni*, Roma, 1958.

LO MONACO APRILE, A., *La famiglia nella storia della civiltà*, Alba, 1945.

LORTAL, R., *Morale sociale familiale. I. Matrimoniale et conjugale*, Avignon, 1946.

MAGNIN, E., *Le procès en nullité de mariage dans l'Eglise catholique*, Paris, 1929.

MARTIN, A., *Le mariage. Précis théologique et canonique*, Rennes, 1936.

MAUSBACH, J., *Ehe und Kindersegen,*[4] München-Gladbach, 1925.

MAYAUD, J. B. M., *Indissolubilité du mariage...*, Strasbourg-Paris, 1952.

MELATA, B., *De potestate qua matrimonium regitur et de iure matrimoniali civili apud praecipuas nationes*, Romae, 1903.

MICELI, I., *Le dispense matrimoniali*, Roma, 1941.

O'CONNEL, G., *De intima natura assistentiae matrimonialis*, Romae, 1940.

ODDO BAGLIONI, A., *Il matrimonio condizionato*, Padova, 1938.

ORAISON, M., *L'unione coniugale*, Torino, 1958.

————, *Indissolubilità del matrimonio*, Roma, 1952.

PALMIERI, D., *Tractatus de matrimonio christiano*, Romae, 1880.

PAYEN, G., *De matrimonio in missionibus ac potissimum in Sinis: tractatus practicus*,[2] Zi-ka-wei, 1936, 2 vol.

PERRONE, J., *De matrimonio christiano*, Romae, 1858.

PETERMANN, H., *Matrimonio e fecondità*, Bellinzona, 1937.

PIOLA, A., *La competenza giurisdizionale ecclesiastica sul matrimonio e i suoi effetti civili*, Padova, 1938.

PUIGARNAU, M. J. M., *El consentimiento matrimonial*, Barcelona, 1956.

RAAMSDONK, G. A., *De cessatione impedimenti disparitatis cultus...*, Roma, 1955.

REBUTTATI, C., *Del consenso matrimoniale*, Milano, 1933.

RECKERS, C. A., *De favore quo matrimonium gaudet in iure canonico*, Romae, 1951.

REUTER, A., *Native Marriage in South Africa According to Law and Custom*, Romae, 1957.

ROBERTS, J. B., *The Banns of Marriage*, Washington, 1931.

ROCHOLL, N., *Le mariage vie consacrée*, Thuillies, 1937.

ROSSET, M. P., *De sacramento matrimonii*, Parisiis, 1895–1896.

ROUAST, A., *La famille*, Paris, 1926.

RYAN, T. C., *The Juridical Effects of the "sanatio in radice,"* Washington, 1955.

SALMON, G. M., *De matrimonii sacramento tractatus pastoralis*, Liège, 1930.

SANCHEZ, T., *Disputationes de s. matrimonii sacramento*, Antverpiae, 1620, 3 vol.

SANTORO, R., *L'impugnazione del matrimonio dopo la morte dei coniugi nel diritto canonico*, Roma, 1943.

SCHAEFER, T., *Das Eherecht nachdem Codex i. c.*, Munsterii West., 1924.

SCREMIN, L., *Matrimonio, divorzio e biologia umana*, Milano, 1948.

TER HAAR, F., *De matrimoniis mixtis eorumque remediis*, Torino, 1931.

THAMER TOTH, *Matrimonio e famiglia*, Milano, 1959.

TOMIZAWA TAKAHIKO, B., *Jus missionarium de legibus japonicis circa matrimonii impedimenta*, Romae, 1945.

TRABUCCHI, A., *Il matrimonio putativo*, Padova, 1936.

VINCENTI, A., *La giurisdizione ecclesiastica e laica in materia matrimoniale*, Firenze, 1951.

VLAMING, T.—BENDER, L., *Praelectiones iuris matrimonii*, Bussum, 1950.

VROMANT, G., *De matrimonio* (Ius missionarium, V),[2] Parisiis, 1938.

WATERHOUSE, J. M., *The Power of the Local Ordinary to Impose a Matrimonial Ban*, Washington, 1952.

WERNZ, F.—VIDAL, P.—AUGUIRRE, P., *Ius matrimoniale* (Ius canonicum, V),[2] Romae, 1946.

WOUTERS, L., *De forma promissionis et celebrationis matrimonii*, Bussum, 1919.

WRZASZCZAK, C. F., *The Betrothal Contract in the Code of Canon Law...*, Washington, 1954.

ZORAS, G., *Note bibliografiche sul matrimonio*, Roma, 1921 ([1]).

Additional Works

ADAM, A., *The Sixth Commandment*, Chicago: Regnery, 1956.

ALLERS, R., *Sex Psychology in Education*, St. Louis: Herder Book Company, 1937.

AYRINHAC, H. A., and LYDON, P. J., *Marriage Legislation in the New Code of Canon Law*, New York: Benziger Bros., 1938.

BATZILL, J., *Decisiones Sanctae Sedis de usu et abusu matrimonii*, Roma: Marietti, 1944 (2 Vols.).

COHAUSZ, O., *The Pope and Christian Marriage*, New York: Benziger Bros., 1933.

FABREGUES, J., *Christian Marriage*, Twentieth Century Encyclopedia of Catholicism, New York: Hawthorn Books, Inc., 1959.

FUCHS, S. J., *De Castitate et Ordine Sexuali*, Roma: Gregoriana, 1959.

GILBY, T., *Morals and Marriage*, London: Longmans, 1952.

GRIESE, O., *Rhythm in Marriage and Christian Morality*, Westminster, Md.: The Newman Press.

HENRY, A. M., *Marriage*, The Theological Library, Chicago: Fides, 1958.

HILDEBRAND, D. VON, *In Defense of Purity*, New York: Sheed and Ward, 1939.

HUERTH, H., *De Re Matrimonio*, Roma: Gregoriana, 1959.

LECLERCQ, J., *Marriage a Great Sacrament*, Springfield, Ill.: Templegate, 1954.

————, *Marriage and the Family*, New York: Macmillan, 1947.

MIHANOVITCH, C. S., and others. *Marriage and the Family*, Milwaukee: Bruce Publishing Company, 1952.

MESSENGER, E. C., *Two in One Flesh*, Westminster, Md.: The Newman Press, 1955.

MURPHY, J. P., and LAUX, J. D., *The Rhythm Way to Family Happiness*, New York: Hawthorn Books, Inc., 1959.

ORAISON, M., *Man and Wife: the Physical and Spiritual Foundation of Marriage*, Trans. by Andre Humbert, New York: Macmillan, 1958.

O'MAHONY, P. J., *Catholics and Divorce: a Symposium*, London, 1959.

PERRIN, J. M., *Christian Perfection and the Married Life*, Westminster, Md.: The Newman Press, 1958.

————, *Virginity*, Westminster, Md.: The Newman Press, 1955.

PLE, A., *Chastity*, Trans, by L. C. Sheppard, (Religious Life Series, Vol. 5). Westminster, Md.: The Newman Press, 1955.

ST. JOHN-STEVAS, N., *Birth Control and Public Policy*, Santa Barbara, Calif.: Center for the Study of Democratic Institutions, 1960.

SUENENS, L. J., *Love and Control*, Westminster, Md.: The Newman Press, 1961.

THIBON, G., *What God Has Joined Together*, Chicago: Regnery, 1952.

THOMAS, J. L., *Marriage and Rhythm*, Westminster, Md.: The Newman Press, 1957.

————, *American Catholic Family*, New York: Prentice-Hall.

————, *Catholic Viewpoint on Marriage and the Family*, New York: Doubleday, 1958.

————, *Family Clinic*, Westminster, Md.: The Newman Press, 1958.

TREVETT, R. F., *Sex and the Christian*, Twentieth Century, Encyclopedia of Catholicism, New York: Hawthorn Books, Inc., 1960.

WAYNE, T. G., *Morals and Marriage*, New York: Longmans, 1952 (2nd edit.).

WILKIN, V., *The Image of God in Sex*, London, 1955.

A NOTE ON THE TYPE

IN WHICH THIS BOOK WAS SET

This book has been set in Electra, a type face created in 1935 by W. A. Dwiggins, the well-known Boston artist. This type falls within the "modern" family of type styles, but was drawn to avoid the extreme contrast between "thick and thin" elements that marks most "modern" type faces. The design is not based upon any traditional model, and is not an attempt to revive or to reconstruct any historic type. Since its birth, Electra has met with success because of its easy-to-read quality. This book was composed and printed by the York Composition Company, Inc., of York, Pa., and bound by Moore and Company of Baltimore, Md. The design and typography of this book are by Howard N. King.